Microsoft® OFFICE® 2010
ADVANCED

Gary B. Shelly

Misty E. Vermaat

Contributing Authors

Raymond E. Enger

Steven M. Freund

Mary Z. Last

Philip J. Pratt

Jeffrey J. Quasney

Jill E. Romanoski

Susan L. Sebok

COURSE TECHNOLOGY
CENGAGE Learning™

SHELLY CASHMAN SERIES®

Australia • Brazil • Japan • Korea • Mexico • Singapore • Spain • United Kingdom • United States

COURSE TECHNOLOGY
CENGAGE Learning™

Microsoft Office 2010: Advanced
Gary B. Shelly, Misty E. Vermaat

Vice President, Publisher: Nicole Pinard

Executive Editor: Kathleen McMahon

Senior Product Manager: Mali Jones

Associate Product Manager: Aimee Poirier

Editorial Assistant: Lauren Brody

Director of Marketing: Cheryl Costantini

Marketing Manager: Tristen Kendall

Marketing Coordinator: Stacey Leasca

Print Buyer: Julio Esperas

Director of Production: Patty Stephan

Content Project Manager: Matthew Hutchinson

Development Editors: Jill Batistick, Amanda Brodkin, Deb Kaufmann, Lyn Markowicz, Lisa Ruffolo

Copyeditors: Foxxe Editorial and Troy Lilly

Proofreaders: Chris Clark and Karen Annett

Indexer: Rich Carlson

QA Manuscript Reviewers: Chris Scriver, John Freitas, Serge Palladino, Susan Pedicini, Danielle Shaw, Susan Whalen

Art Director: Marissa Falco

Cover Designer: Lisa Kuhn, Curio Press, LLC

Cover Photo: Tom Kates Photography

Text Design: Joel Sadagursky

Compositor: PreMediaGlobal

For product information and technology assistance, contact us at
Cengage Learning Customer & Sales Support, 1-800-354-9706

For permission to use material from this text or product, submit all requests online at **cengage.com/permissions**
Further permissions questions can be emailed to
permissionrequest@cengage.com

Library of Congress Control Number: 2010934156

softcover binding:
ISBN-13: 978-1-4390-7854-9
ISBN-10: 1-4390-7854-8

hardcover spiral binding:
ISBN-13: 978-1-4390-7855-6
ISBN-10: 1-4390-7855-6

Course Technology
20 Channel Center Street
Boston, MA 02210
USA

Cengage Learning is a leading provider of customized learning solutions with office locations around the globe, including Singapore, the United Kingdom, Australia, Mexico, Brazil, and Japan. Locate your local office at:
international.cengage.com/region

Cengage Learning products are represented in Canada by Nelson Education, Ltd.

Visit our website **www.cengage.com/ct/shellycashman** to share and gain ideas on our textbooks!

To learn more about Course Technology,
visit **www.cengage.com/coursetechnology**

Purchase any of our products at your local college store or at our preferred online store **www.CengageBrain.com**

We dedicate this book to the memory of James S. Quasney (1940 – 2009), who for 18 years co-authored numerous books with Tom Cashman and Gary Shelly and provided extraordinary leadership to the Shelly Cashman Series editorial team. As series editor, Jim skillfully coordinated, organized, and managed the many aspects of our editorial development processes and provided unending direction, guidance, inspiration, support, and advice to the Shelly Cashman Series authors and support team members. He was a trusted, dependable, loyal, and well-respected leader, mentor, and friend. We are forever grateful to Jim for his faithful devotion to our team and eternal contributions to our series.

The Shelly Cashman Series Team

Printed in the United States of America
2 3 4 5 6 7 15 14 13 12 11

Contents

Microsoft PowerPoint 2010

Microsoft Excel 2010

Microsoft **Access 2010**

CHAPTER FOUR

Creating Reports and Forms

Microsoft **Outlook 2010**

CHAPTER THREE
Managing Contacts and Personal Contact Information with Outlook

Appendices

Capstone Project

Preface

The Shelly Cashman Series® offers the finest textbooks in computer education. We are proud that since Mircosoft Office 4.3, our series of Microsoft Office textbooks have been the most widely used books in education. With each new edition of our Office books, we make significant improvements based on the software and comments made by instructors and students. For this Microsoft Office 2010 text, the Shelly Cashman Series development team carefully reviewed our pedagogy and analyzed its effectiveness in teaching today's Office student. Students today read less, but need to retain more. They need not only to be able to perform skills, but to retain those skills and know how to apply them to different settings. Today's students need to be continually engaged and challenged to retain what they're learning.

With this Microsoft Office 2010 text, we continue our commitment to focusing on the user and how they learn best.

Objectives of This Textbook

Microsoft Office 2010: Advanced is intended for a second course on Office 2010 applications. This book assumes that students are familiar with the fundamentals of Microsoft Windows 7, Microsoft Word 2010, Microsoft PowerPoint 2010, Microsoft Excel 2010, Microsoft Access 2010, and Microsoft Outlook 2010. These fundamentals are covered in the companion textbook *Microsoft Office 2010: Introductory.* The objectives of this book are:

- To go beyond the fundaments and offer an in-depth presentation to Microsoft Word 2010, Microsoft PowerPoint 2010, Microsoft Excel 2010, Microsoft Access 2010, and Microsoft Outlook 2010.

- To expose students to practical examples of the computer as a useful tool

- To acquaint students with the proper procedures to create and enhance documents, presentations, worksheets, and databases suitable for coursework, professional purposes. and personal use

- To help students discover the underlying functionality of Office 2010 so they can become more productive

- To develop an exercise-oriented approach that allows learning by doing.

New to This Edition

Microsoft Office 2010: Advanced offers a number of new features and approaches, which improve student understanding, retention, transference, and skill in using Office 2010 programs. The following enhancements will enrich the learning experience:

- Office 2010 and Windows 7: Essential Concepts and Skills chapter prevents repetitive coverage of basic skills in the application chapters.

- Streamlined first chapters for each application allow the ability to cover more advanced skills earlier.

- Chapter topic redistribution offers concise chapters that ensure complete skill coverage.

- Expanded coverage of PowerPoint and Outlook gives exposure to the numerous enhancements made to these applications.

- New pedagogical elements enrich material, creating an accessible and user-friendly approach.

  - Break Points, a new boxed element, identify logical stopping points and give students instructions regarding what they should do before taking a break.

  - Within step instructions, Tab | Group Identifiers, such as (Home tab | Bold button), help students more easily locate elements in the groups and on the tabs on the Ribbon.

  - Modified step-by-step instructions tell the student what to do and provide the generic reason why they are completing a specific task, which helps students easily transfer given skills to different settings.

The Shelly Cashman Approach

A Proven Pedagogy with an Emphasis on Project Planning

Each chapter presents a practical problem to be solved, within a project planning framework. The project orientation is strengthened by the use of Plan Ahead boxes, which encourage critical thinking about how to proceed at various points in the project. Step-by-step instructions with supporting screens guide students through the steps. Instructional steps are supported by the Q&A, Experimental Step, and BTW features.

A Visually Engaging Book that Maintains Student Interest

The step-by-step tasks, with supporting figures, provide a rich visual experience for the student. Call-outs on the screens that present both explanatory and navigational information provide students with information they need when they need to know it.

Supporting Reference Materials (Appendices, Capstones, Quick Reference)

The appendices provide additional information about the Application at hand and include such topics as project planning guidelines and certification. With the Quick Reference, students can quickly look up information about a single task, such as keyboard short-cuts, and find page references of where in the book the task is illustrated. The Capstone Projects allow students to demonstrate mastery of skills across the Advanced content for Word, PowerPoint, Excel, Outlook, and Access.

Integration of the World Wide Web

The World Wide Web is integrated into the Office 2010 learning experience by (1) BTW annotations; (2) BTW, Q&A, and Quick Reference Summary Web pages; and (3) the Learn It Online section for each chapter.

End-of-Chapter Student Activities

Extensive end-of-chapter activities provide a variety of reinforcement opportunities for students where they can apply and expand their skills.

Instructor Resources

The Instructor Resources include both teaching and testing aids and can be accessed via CD-ROM or at login.cengage.com

Instructor's Manual Includes lecture notes summarizing the chapter sections, figures and boxed elements found in every chapter, teacher tips, classroom activities, lab activities, and quick quizzes in Microsoft Word files.

Syllabus Easily customizable sample syllabi that cover policies, assignments, exams, and other course information.

Figure Files Illustrations for every figure in the textbook in electronic form.

PowerPoint Presentations A multimedia lecture presentation system that provides slides for each chapter. Presentations are based on chapter objectives.

Solutions to Exercises Includes solutions for all end-of-chapter and chapter reinforcement exercises.

Test Bank & Test Engine Test Banks include 112 questions for every chapter, featuring objective-based and critical thinking question types, and including page number references and figure references, when appropriate. Also included is the test engine, ExamView, the ultimate tool for your objective-based testing needs.

Data Files for Students Includes all the files that are required by students to complete the exercises.

Additional Activities for Students Consists of Chapter Reinforcement Exercises, which are true/false, multiple-choice, and short answer questions that help students gain confidence in the material learned.

Book Resources

🔒 **Additional Faculty Files**
🔒 **Blackboard Testbank**
🔒 **Data Files**
🔒 **Instructor's Manual**
🔒 **Lecture Success System**
🔒 **PowerPoint Presentations**
🔒 **Solutions to Exercises**
🔒 **Syllabus**
🔒 **Test Bank and Test Engine**
🔒 **WebCT Testbank**
Chapter Reinforcement Exercises
Student Downloads

SAM: Skills Assessment Manager

SAM 2010 is designed to help bring students from the classroom to the real world. It allows students to train on and test important computer skills in an active, hands-on environment.

SAM's easy-to-use system includes powerful interactive exams, training, and projects on the most commonly used Microsoft Office applications. SAM simulates the Microsoft Office 2010 application environment, allowing students to demonstrate their knowledge and think through the skills by performing real-world tasks such as bolding word text or setting up slide transitions. Add in live-in-the-application projects, and students are on their way to truly learning and applying skills to business-centric documents.

Designed to be used with the Shelly Cashman Series, SAM includes handy page references so that students can print helpful study guides that match the Shelly Cashman textbooks used in class. For instructors, SAM also includes robust scheduling and reporting features.

Content for Online Learning

Course Technology has partnered with the leading distance learning solution providers and class-management platforms today. To access this material, instructors will visit our password-protected instructor resources available at login.cengage.com. Instructor resources include the following: additional case projects, sample syllabi, PowerPoint presentations per chapter, and more. For additional information or for an instructor user name and password, please contact your sales representative. For students to access this material, they must have purchased a WebTutor PIN-code specific to this title and your campus platform. The resources for students may include (based on instructor preferences), but are not limited to: topic review, review questions, and practice tests.

Workbook for Microsoft Office 2010: Introductory Concepts and Techniques

This highly popular supplement (ISBN 1-4390-7844-0) includes a variety of activities that help students recall, review, and master the concepts presented. The Workbook complements the end-of-chapter material with an outline; a self-test consisting of true/false, multiple-choice, short answer, and matching questions; and activities calculated to help students develop a deeper understanding of the information presented.

CourseNotes

Course Technology's CourseNotes are six-panel quick reference cards that reinforce the most important and widely used features of a software application in a visual and user-friendly format. CourseNotes serve as a great reference tool during and after the student completes the

course. CourseNotes are available for software applications such as Microsoft Office 2010, Word 2010, PowerPoint 2010, Excel 2010, Access 2010, and Windows 7. Topic-based CourseNotes are available for Best Practices in Social Networking, Hot Topics in Technology, and Web 2.0. Visit www.cengagebrain.com to learn more!

A Guided Tour

Add excitement and interactivity to your classroom with "*A Guided Tour*" product line. Play one of the brief mini-movies to spice up your lecture and spark classroom discussion. Or, assign a movie for homework and ask students to complete the correlated assignment that accompanies each topic. "*A Guided Tour*" product line takes the prep work out of providing your students with information about new technologies and applications and helps keep students engaged with content relevant to their lives; all in under an hour!

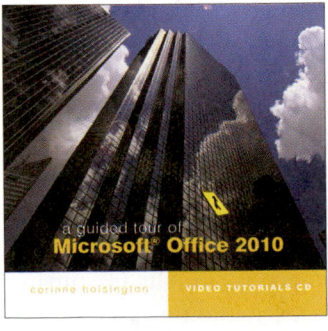
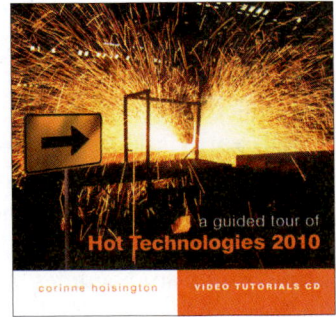
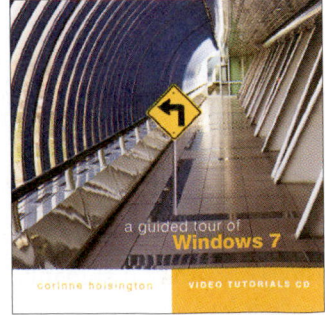

About Our Covers

The Shelly Cashman Series is continually updating our approach and content to reflect the way today's students learn and experience new technology. This focus on student success is reflected on our covers, which feature real students from Bentley University using the Shelly Cashman Series in their courses, and reflect the varied ages and backgrounds of the students learning with our books. When you use the Shelly Cashman Series, you can be assured that you are learning computer skills using the most effective courseware available.

Textbook Walk-Through

The Shelly Cashman Series Pedagogy: Project-Based — Step-by-Step — Variety of Assessments

Plan Ahead boxes prepare students to create successful projects by encouraging them to think strategically about what they are trying to accomplish before they begin working.

Step-by-step instructions now provide a context beyond the point-and-click. Each step provides information on why students are performing each task, or what will occur as a result.

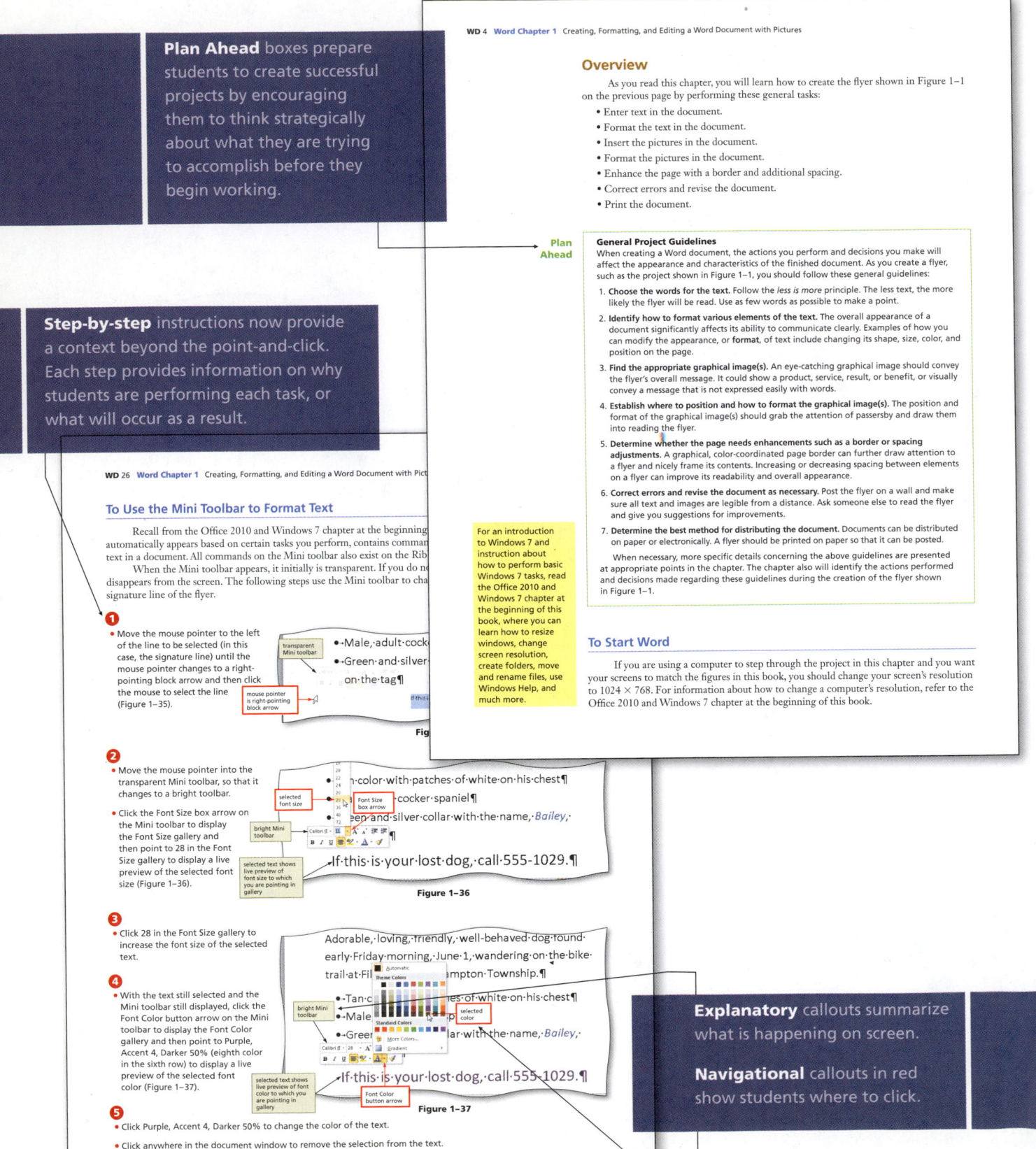

Overview

As you read this chapter, you will learn how to create the flyer shown in Figure 1–1 on the previous page by performing these general tasks:

- Enter text in the document.
- Format the text in the document.
- Insert the pictures in the document.
- Format the pictures in the document.
- Enhance the page with a border and additional spacing.
- Correct errors and revise the document.
- Print the document.

Plan Ahead

General Project Guidelines

When creating a Word document, the actions you perform and decisions you make will affect the appearance and characteristics of the finished document. As you create a flyer, such as the project shown in Figure 1–1, you should follow these general guidelines:

1. **Choose the words for the text.** Follow the *less is more* principle. The less text, the more likely the flyer will be read. Use as few words as possible to make a point.

2. **Identify how to format various elements of the text.** The overall appearance of a document significantly affects its ability to communicate clearly. Examples of how you can modify the appearance, or format, of text include changing its shape, size, color, and position on the page.

3. **Find the appropriate graphical image(s).** An eye-catching graphical image should convey the flyer's overall message. It could show a product, service, result, or benefit, or visually convey a message that is not expressed easily with words.

4. **Establish where to position and how to format the graphical image(s).** The position and format of the graphical image(s) should grab the attention of passersby and draw them into reading the flyer.

5. **Determine whether the page needs enhancements such as a border or spacing adjustments.** A graphical, color-coordinated page border can further draw attention to a flyer and nicely frame its contents. Increasing or decreasing spacing between elements on a flyer can improve its readability and overall appearance.

6. **Correct errors and revise the document as necessary.** Post the flyer on a wall and make sure all text and images are legible from a distance. Ask someone else to read the flyer and give you suggestions for improvements.

7. **Determine the best method for distributing the document.** Documents can be distributed on paper or electronically. A flyer should be printed on paper so that it can be posted.

When necessary, more specific details concerning the above guidelines are presented at appropriate points in the chapter. The chapter also will identify the actions performed and decisions made regarding these guidelines during the creation of the flyer shown in Figure 1–1.

For an introduction to Windows 7 and instruction about how to perform basic Windows 7 tasks, read the Office 2010 and Windows 7 chapter at the beginning of this book, where you can learn how to resize windows, change screen resolution, create folders, move and rename files, use Windows Help, and much more.

To Start Word

If you are using a computer to step through the project in this chapter and you want your screens to match the figures in this book, you should change your screen's resolution to 1024 × 768. For information about how to change a computer's resolution, refer to the Office 2010 and Windows 7 chapter at the beginning of this book.

To Use the Mini Toolbar to Format Text

Recall from the Office 2010 and Windows 7 chapter at the beginning... automatically appears based on certain tasks you perform, contains comman... text in a document. All commands on the Mini toolbar also exist on the Rib...

When the Mini toolbar appears, it initially is transparent. If you do n... disappears from the screen. The following steps use the Mini toolbar to cha... signature line of the flyer.

1
- Move the mouse pointer to the left of the line to be selected (in this case, the signature line) until the mouse pointer changes to a right-pointing block arrow and then click the mouse to select the line (Figure 1–35).

2
- Move the mouse pointer into the transparent Mini toolbar, so that it changes to a bright toolbar.
- Click the Font Size box arrow on the Mini toolbar to display the Font Size gallery and then point to 28 in the Font Size gallery to display a live preview of the selected font size (Figure 1–36).

Figure 1–36

3
- Click 28 in the Font Size gallery to increase the font size of the selected text.

4
- With the text still selected and the Mini toolbar still displayed, click the Font Color button arrow on the Mini toolbar to display the Font Color gallery and then point to Purple, Accent 4, Darker 50% (eighth color in the sixth row) to display a live preview of the selected font color (Figure 1–37).

Figure 1–37

5
- Click Purple, Accent 4, Darker 50% to change the color of the text.
- Click anywhere in the document window to remove the selection from the text.

Explanatory callouts summarize what is happening on screen.

Navigational callouts in red show students where to click.

Q&A boxes offer questions students may have when working through the steps and provide additional information about what they are doing right where they need it.

Experiment Steps within our step-by-step instructions, encourage students to explore, experiment, and take advantage of the features of the Office 2007 user interface. These steps are not necessary to complete the projects, but are designed to increase the confidence with the software and build problem-solving skills.

Break Points identify logical breaks in the chapter if students need to stop before completing the project.

1
• With the shape still selected, click the More button (shown in Figure 3–6) in the Shape Styles gallery (Drawing Tools Format tab | Shape Styles group) to expand the gallery.

Q&A
What if my shape is no longer selected?
Click the shape to select it.

• Point to Intense Effect - Brown, Accent 4 in the Shape Styles gallery to display a live preview of that style applied to the shape in the document (Figure 3–7).

Experiment
• Point to various styles in the Shape Styles gallery and watch the style of the shape change in the document.

2
• Click Intense Effect - Brown, Accent 4 in the Shape Styles gallery to apply the selected style to the shape.

Figure 3–7

Other Ways
1. Click Format Shape Dialog Box Launcher (Drawing Tools Format tab | Shape Styles group), click Picture Color in left pane	(Format Shape dialog box), select desired colors, click Close button 2. Right-click shape, click Format Shape on	shortcut menu, click Picture Color in left pane (Format Shape dialog box), select desired colors, click Close button

---

Selecting Text

In many of the previous steps, you have selected text. Table 1–3 summarizes the techniques used to select various items.

Table 1–3 Techniques for Selecting Text

Item to Select	Mouse	Keyboard (where applicable)
Block of text	Click at beginning of selection, scroll to end of selection, position mouse pointer at end of selection, hold down SHIFT key and then click; or drag through the text.	
Character(s)	Drag through character(s).	SHIFT+RIGHT ARROW or SHIFT+LEFT ARROW
Document	Move mouse to left of text until mouse pointer changes to a right-pointing block arrow and then triple-click.	CTRL+A
Graphic	Click the graphic.	
Line	Move mouse to left of line until mouse pointer changes to a right-pointing block arrow and then click.	HOME, then SHIFT+END or END, then SHIFT+HOME
Lines	Move mouse to left of first line until mouse pointer changes to a right-pointing block arrow and then drag up or down.	HOME, then SHIFT+DOWN ARROW or END, then SHIFT+UP ARROW
Paragraph	Triple-click paragraph; or move mouse to left of paragraph until mouse pointer changes to a right-pointing block arrow and then double-click.	CTRL+SHIFT+DOWN ARROW or CTRL+SHIFT+UP ARROW
Paragraphs	Move mouse to left of paragraph until mouse pointer changes to a right-pointing block arrow, double-click, and then drag up or down.	CTRL+SHIFT+DOWN ARROW or CTRL+SHIFT+UP ARROW repeatedly
Sentence	Press and hold down CTRL key and then click sentence.	
Word	Double-click the word.	CTRL+SHIFT+RIGHT ARROW or CTRL+SHIFT+LEFT ARROW
Words	Drag through words.	CTRL+SHIFT+RIGHT ARROW or CTRL+SHIFT+LEFT ARROW repeatedly

To Save an Existing Document with the Same File Name

You have made several modifications to the document since you last saved it. Thus, you should save it again. The following step saves the document again. For an example of the step listed below, refer to the Office 2010 and Windows 7 chapter at the beginning of this book.

1 Click the Save button on the Quick Access Toolbar to overwrite the previously saved file.

Break Point: If you wish to take a break, this is a good place to do so. You can quit Word now (refer to page WD 44 for instructions). To resume at a later time, start Word (refer to pages WD 4 and WD 5 for instructions), open the file called Found Dog Flyer (refer to page WD 45 for instructions), and continue following the steps from this location forward.

Inserting and Formatting Pictures in a Word Document

With the text formatted in the flyer, the next step is to insert digital pictures in the flyer and format the pictures. Flyers usually contain graphical images, such as a picture, to attract the attention of passersby. In the following pages, you will perform these tasks:

1. Insert the first digital picture into the flyer and then reduce its size.
2. Insert the second digital picture into the flyer and then reduce its size.
3. Change the look of the first picture and then the second picture.

Textbook Walk-Through

Chapter Summary A concluding paragraph, followed by a listing of the tasks completed within a chapter together with the pages on which the step-by-step, screen-by-screen explanations appear.

To Quit Word

The project now is complete. Thus, the following steps quit Word. For an example of the step listed below, refer to the Office 2010 and Windows 7 chapter at the beginning of this book.

1 If you have one Word document open, click the Close button on the right side of the title bar to close the document and quit Word; or if you have multiple Word documents open, click File on the Ribbon to open the Backstage view and then click Exit in the Backstage view to close all open documents and quit Word.

2 If a Microsoft Word dialog box appears, click the Save button to save any changes made to the document since the last save.

BTW

Printed Borders
If one or more of your borders do not print, click the Page Borders button (Page Layout tab | Page Background group), click the Options button (Borders and Shading dialog box), click the Measure from box arrow and click Text, change the four text boxes to 15 pt, and then click the OK button in each dialog box. Try printing the document again. If the borders still do not print, adjust the text boxes in the dialog box to a number smaller than 15 point.

Chapter Summary

In this chapter, you have learned how to enter text in a document, format text, insert a picture, format a picture, add a page border, and print a document. The items listed below include all the new Word skills you have learned in this chapter.

1. Start Word (WD 4)
2. Type Text (WD 6)
3. Display Formatting Marks (WD 7)
4. Insert a Blank Line (WD 7)
5. Wordwrap Text as You Type (WD 8)
6. Check Spelling and Grammar as You Type (WD 9)
7. Save a Document (WD 12)
8. Center a Paragraph (WD 14)
9. Select a Line (WD 15)
10. Change the Font Size of Selected Text (WD 16)
11. Change the Font of Selected Text (WD 17)
12. Change the Case of Selected Text (WD 18)
   (WD 19)

23. Bold Text (WD 28)
24. Change Theme Colors (WD 28)
25. Save an Existing Document with the Same File Name (WD 30)
26. Insert a Picture (WD 31)
27. Zoom the Document (WD 33)
28. Resize a Graphic (WD 34)
29. Resize a Graphic by Entering Exact Measurements (WD 36)
30. Apply a Picture Style (WD 37)
31. Apply Picture Effects (WD 38)
32. View One Page (WD 40)
33. Add a Page Border (WD 41)
34. Change Spacing before and after a Paragraph (WD 44)
35. Quit Word (WD 44)
36. Open a Document from Word (WD 45)
37. Insert Text in an Existing Document (WD 46)
38. Delete Text (WD 47)
39. Move Text (WD 47)
40. Change Document Properties (WD 49)
41. Print a Document (WD 51)

... profile, your instructor may have assigned an autogradable ... f so, log into the SAM 2010 Web site at www.cengage.com/sam2010 ... and start files.

BTW

Quick Reference
For a table that lists how to complete the tasks covered in this book using the mouse, Ribbon, shortcut menu, and keyboard, see the Quick Reference Summary at the back of this book, or visit the Word 2010 Quick Reference Web page (scsite.com/wd2010/qr).

STUDENT ASSIGNMENTS

Learn It Online

Test your knowledge of chapter content and key terms.

Instructions: To complete the Learn It Online exercises, start your browser, click the Address bar, and then enter the Web address **scsite.com/wd2010/learn**. When the Word 2010 Learn It Online page is displayed, click the link for the exercise you want to complete and then read the instructions.

Chapter Reinforcement TF, MC, and SA
A series of true/false, multiple choice, and short answer questions that test your knowledge of the chapter content.

Flash Cards
An interactive learning environment where you identify chapter key terms associated with displayed definitions.

Practice Test
A series of multiple choice questions that test your knowledge of chapter content and key terms.

Who Wants To Be a Computer Genius?
An interactive game that challenges your knowledge of chapter content in the style of a television quiz show.

Wheel of Terms
An interactive game that challenges your knowledge of chapter key terms in the style of the television show *Wheel of Fortune*.

Crossword Puzzle Challenge
A crossword puzzle that challenges your knowledge of key terms presented in the chapter.

Apply Your Knowledge

Reinforce the skills and apply the concepts you learned in this chapter.

Modifying Text and Formatting a Document

Note: To complete this assignment, you will be required to use the Data Files for Students. See the inside back cover of this book for instructions on downloading the Data Files for Students, or contact your instructor for information about accessing the required files.

Instructions: Start Word. Open the document, Apply 1-1 Buffalo Photo Shoot Flyer Unformatted, from the Data Files for Students. The document you open is an unformatted flyer. You are to modify text, format paragraphs and characters, and insert a picture in the flyer.

Perform the following tasks:
1. Delete the word, single, in the sentence of body copy below the headline.
2. Insert the word, Creeks, between the words, Twin Buffalo, in the sentence of body copy below the headline.
3. At the end of the signature line, change the period to an exclamation point.
4. Center the headline and the signature line.
5. Change the theme colors to the Aspect color scheme.
6. Change the font and font size of the headline to 48-point Impact, or a similar font. Change the case of the headline text to all capital letters. Apply the text effect called Gradient Fill – Orange, Accent 1, Outline – White to the headline.
7. Change the font size of body copy between the headline and the signature line to 20 point.
8. Use the Mini toolbar to change the font size of the signature line to 26 point.
9. Select the words, hundreds of buffalo, in the paragraph below the headline and underline them.

Learn It Online Every chapter features a Learn It Online section that is comprised of six exercises. These exercises include True/False, Multiple Choice, Short Answer, Flash Cards, Practice Test, and Learning Games.

Apply Your Knowledge This exercise usually requires students to open and manipulate a file from the Data Files that parallels the activities learned in the chapter. To obtain a copy of the Data Files for Students, follow the instructions on the inside back cover of this text.

Extend Your Knowledge

Extend the skills you learned in this chapter and experiment with new skills. You may need to use Help to complete the assignment.

Modifying Text and Picture Formats and Adding Page Borders

Note: To complete this assignment, you will be required to use the Data Files for Students. See the inside back cover of this book for instructions on downloading the Data Files for Students, or contact your instructor for information about accessing the required files.

Instructions: Start Word. Open the document, Extend 1-1 TVC Cruises Flyer, from the Data Files for Students. You will enhance the look of the flyer shown in Figure 1–76. *Hint:* Remember, if you make a mistake while formatting the picture, you can reset it by clicking the Reset Picture button or Reset Picture button arrow (Picture Tools Format tab | Adjust group).

Perform the following tasks:
1. Use Help to learn about the following formats: remove bullets, grow font, shrink font, art page borders, decorative underline(s), picture bullets, picture border shading, shadow picture effects, and color saturation and tone.
2. Remove the bullet from the paragraph below the picture.

3. Select the text, 10 percent, and use the Grow Font button to increase its font size.
4. Add an art page border to the flyer. If the border is not in color, add color to it.
5. Change the solid underline below the word, cruises, to a decorative underline. Change

add art page border

NEED AN ESCAPE?

change border color and add shadow effect; change color saturation and color tone

remove bullet

• Tango Vacation Club members receive a **10 percent** discount for <u>cruises</u> booked during May. Select from a variety of destinations.

use Grow Font button to increase font size

An experience of a lifetime awaits you.

change to picture bullets

• **Ultimate relaxation**
• **Endless fun and entertainment**
• **Breathtaking scenery**
• **Friendly, attentive staff**
• **Clean facilities**

Interested? Call TVC at 555-1029

Figure 1–76

Make It Right

Analyze a document and correct all errors and/or improve the design.

Correcting Spelling and Grammar Errors

Note: To complete this assignment, you will be required to use the Data Files for Students. See the inside back cover of this book for instructions on downloading the Data Files for Students, or contact your instructor for information about accessing the required files.

Instructions: Start Word. Open the document, Make It Right 1-1 Karate Academy Flyer Unchecked, from the Data Files for Students. The document is a flyer that contains spelling and grammar errors, as shown in Figure 1–77. You are to correct each spelling (red wavy underline) and grammar error (green and blue wavy underlines) by right-clicking the flagged text and then clicking the appropriate correction on the shortcut menu.

If your screen does not display the wavy underlines, click File on the Ribbon and then click Options in the Backstage view. When the Word Options dialog box is displayed, click Proofing in the left pane, be sure the 'Hide spelling errors in this document only' and 'Hide grammar errors in this document only' check boxes do not contain check marks, and then click the OK button. If your screen still does not display the wavy underlines, redisplay the Word Options dialog box, click Proofing, and then click the Recheck Document button.

Change the document properties, including keywords, as specified by your instructor. Save the revised document with the name, Make It Right 1-1 Karate Academy Flyer, and then submit it in the format specified by your instructor.

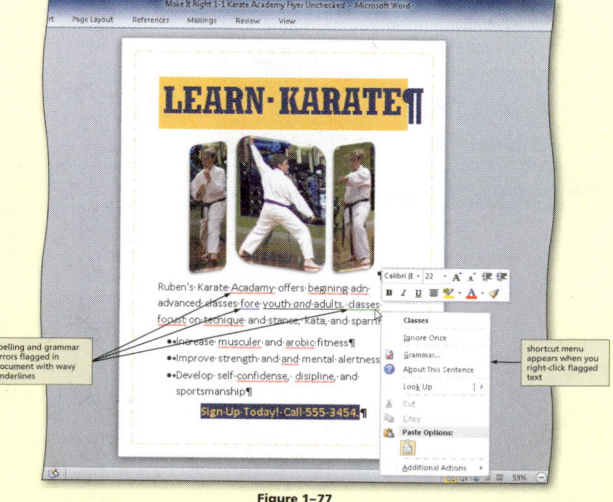

spelling and grammar errors flagged in document with wavy underlines

shortcut menu appears when you right-click flagged text

Figure 1–77

Textbook Walk-Through

WD 58 Word Chapter 1 Creating, Formatting, and Editing a Word Document with Pictures

STUDENT ASSIGNMENTS

In the Lab

Design and/or create a document using the guidelines, concepts, and skills presented in this chapter. Labs are listed in order of increasing difficulty.

Lab 1: Creating a Flyer with a Picture

Problem: As a part-time employee in the Student Services Center at school, you have been asked to prepare a flyer that advertises study habits classes. First, you prepare the unformatted flyer shown in Figure 1–78a, and then you format it so that it looks like Figure 1–78b. *Hint:* Remember, if you make a mistake while formatting the flyer, you can click the Undo button on the Quick Access Toolbar to undo your last action.

Note: To complete this assignment, you will be required to use the Data Files for Students. See the inside back cover of this book for instructions on downloading the Data Files for Students, or contact your instructor for information about accessing the required files.

Instructions: Perform the following tasks:

1. Start Word. Display formatting marks on the screen.
2. Type the flyer text, unformatted, as shown in Figure 1–78a, inserting a blank line between the headline and the body copy. If Word flags any misspelled words as you type, check their spelling and correct them.
3. Save the document using the file name, Lab 1-1 Study Habits Flyer.
4. Center the headline and the signature line.
5. Change the theme colors to Concourse.
6. Change the font size of the headline to 36 point and the font to Ravie, or a similar font. Apply the text effect called Gradient Fill – Dark Red, Accent 6, Inner Shadow.
7. Change the font size of body copy between the headline and the signature line to 20 point.
8. Change the font size of the signature line to 22 point. Bold the text in the signature line.

Studying All Night?

blank line

Let us help you! Our expert instructors teach effective stu
energy-building techniques.

Classes are $15.00 per session

Sessions last four weeks

Classes meet in the Student Services Center twice a week

Call 555-2838 or stop by to sign up today!

Figure 1–78 (a) Unform

In the Lab Three all new in-depth assignments per chapter require students to utilize the chapter concepts and techniques to solve problems on a computer.

Creating a Business Letter with a Letterhead and Table Word Chapter 3 WD 199

Word Chapter 3 STUDENT ASSIGNMENTS

create a building block for Fair Grove Elementary School and insert the building block whenever you have to enter the school name. Resize table columns to fit contents. Check the spelling of the letter. Change the document properties, as specified by your instructor. Save the letter with Lab 3-3 Education Board Letter as the file name.

Cases and Places

Apply your creative thinking and problem solving skills to design and implement a solution.

Note: To complete these assignments, you may be required to use the Data Files for Students. See the inside back cover of this book for instructions on downloading the Data Files for Students, or contact your instructor for information about accessing the required files.

1: Create a Letter to a Potential Employer

Academic

As a student about to graduate, you are actively seeking employment in your field and have located an advertisement for a job in which you are interested. You decide to write a letter to the potential employer: Ms. Janice Tremont at Home Health Associates, 554 Mountain View Lane, Blue Dust, MO 64319.

The draft wording for the letter is as follows: I am responding to your advertisement for the nursing position in the *Blue Dust Press*. I have tailored my activities and education for a career in geriatric medicine. This month, I will graduate with concentrations in Geriatric Medicine (24 hours), Osteopathic Medicine (12 hours), and Holistic Nursing (9 hours). In addition to receiving my bachelor degree in nursing, I have enhanced my education by participating in the following activities: volunteered at Blue Dust's free health care clinic; attended several continuing education and career-specific seminars, including An Aging Populace, Care of the Homebound, and Special Needs of the Elderly; completed one-semester internship at Blue Dust Community Hospital in spring semester of 2012; completed Certified Nursing Assistant (CNA) program at Blue Dust Community College; and worked as nurse's aide for two years during college. I look forward to an interview so that we can discuss the position you offer and my qualifications. With my background and education, I am confident that I will make a positive contribution to Home Health Associates.

The letter should contain a letterhead that uses a shape and clip art, a table (use a table to present the areas of concentration), and a bulleted list (use a bulleted list to present the activities). Insert nonbreaking spaces in the newspaper name. Use the concepts and techniques presented in this chapter to create and format a letter according to the modified block style, creating appropriate paragraph breaks and rewording the draft as necessary. Use your personal information for contact information in the letter. Be sure to check the spelling and grammar of the finished letter. Submit your assignment in the format specified by your instructor.

2: Create a Letter Requesting Donations

Personal

As an alumnus of your historic high school, you are concerned that the building is being considered for demolition. You decide to write a letter to another graduate: Mr. Jim Lemon, 87 Travis Parkway, Vigil, CT 06802.

The draft wording for the letter is as follows: As a member of the class of 1988, you, like many others, probably have many fond memories of our alma mater, Vigil East High School. I recently learned that the building is being considered for demolition because of its age and structural integrity.

Continued >

Cases & Places exercises call on students to create open-ended projects that reflect academic, personal, and business settings.

Microsoft® OFFICE® 2010

ADVANCED

4 Creating a Document with a Title Page, Lists, Tables, and a Watermark

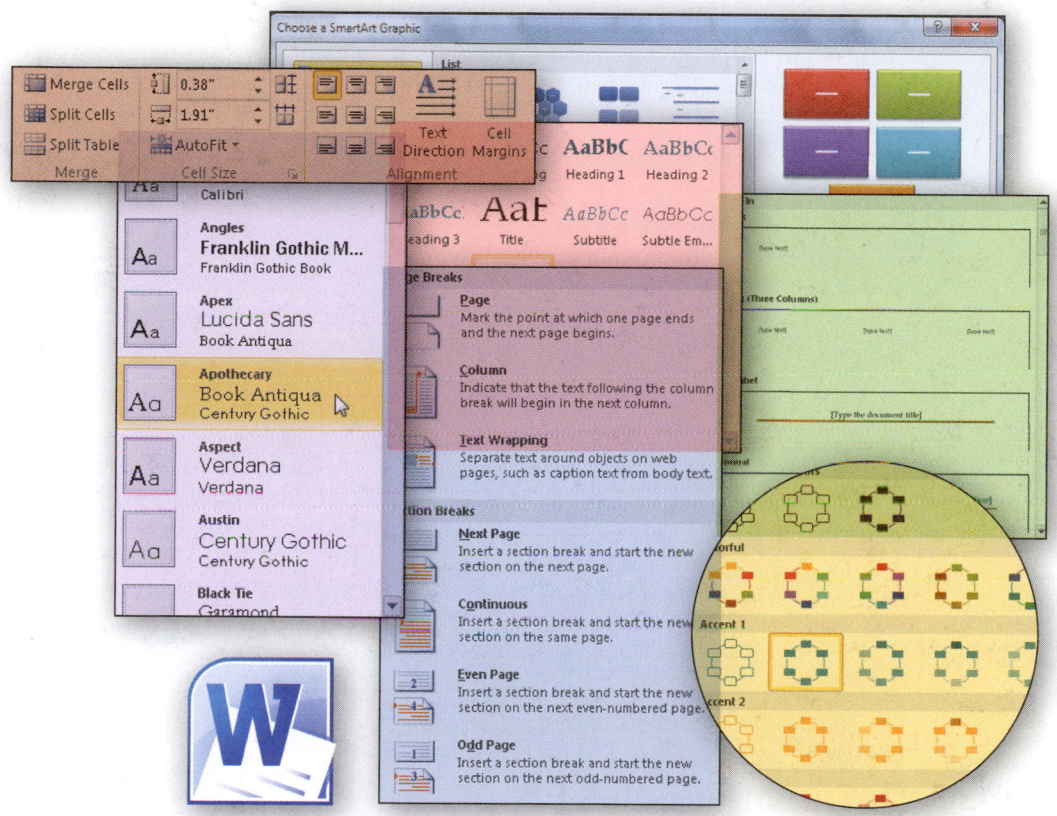

Objectives

You will have mastered the material in this project when you can:

- Border a paragraph
- Change paragraph indentation
- Insert and format a SmartArt graphic
- Apply character effects
- Insert a section break
- Insert a Word document in an open document
- Change theme fonts

- Insert formatted headers and footers
- Sort lists and tables
- Use the format painter
- Add picture bullets to a list
- Create a multilevel list
- Modify and format Word tables
- Sum columns in a table
- Create a watermark

4 | Creating a Document with a Title Page, Lists, Tables, and a Watermark

Introduction

During the course of your business and personal endeavors, you may want or need to provide a recommendation to a person or group of people for their consideration. You might suggest they purchase a product, such as vehicles or books, or contract a service, such as designing their Web page or remodeling their house. Or, you might try to convince an audience to take an action, such as signing a petition, joining a club, or donating to a cause. You may be asked to request funds for a new program or activity or to promote an idea, such as a benefits package to company employees or a budget plan to upper management. To present these types of recommendations, you may find yourself writing a proposal.

A proposal generally is one of three types: sales, research, or planning. A **sales proposal** sells an idea, a product, or a service. A **research proposal** usually requests funding for a research project. A **planning proposal** offers solutions to a problem or improvement to a situation.

Project Planning Guidelines

> The process of developing a document that communicates specific information requires careful analysis and planning. As a starting point, establish why the document is needed. Once the purpose is determined, analyze the intended readers of the document and their unique needs. Then, gather information about the topic and decide what to include in the document. Finally, determine the document design and style that will be most successful at delivering the message. Details of these guidelines are provided in Appendix A. In addition, each project in this book provides practical applications of these planning considerations.

Project — Sales Proposal

Sales proposals describe the features and value of products and services being offered, with the intent of eliciting a positive response from the reader. Desired outcomes include the reader accepting ideas, purchasing products, contracting services, volunteering time, contributing to a cause, or taking an action. A well-written proposal can be the key to obtaining the desired results.

The project in this chapter follows generally accepted guidelines for writing short sales proposals and uses Word to create the sales proposal shown in Figure 4–1. The sales proposal in this chapter is designed to persuade readers to join a health club. The proposal has a colorful title page to attract readers' attention. To add impact, the sales proposal has a watermark consisting of the text, GET FIT!, positioned behind the text and graphics on each page. It also uses lists and tables to summarize and highlight important data.

Figure 4–1 (a) Title Page

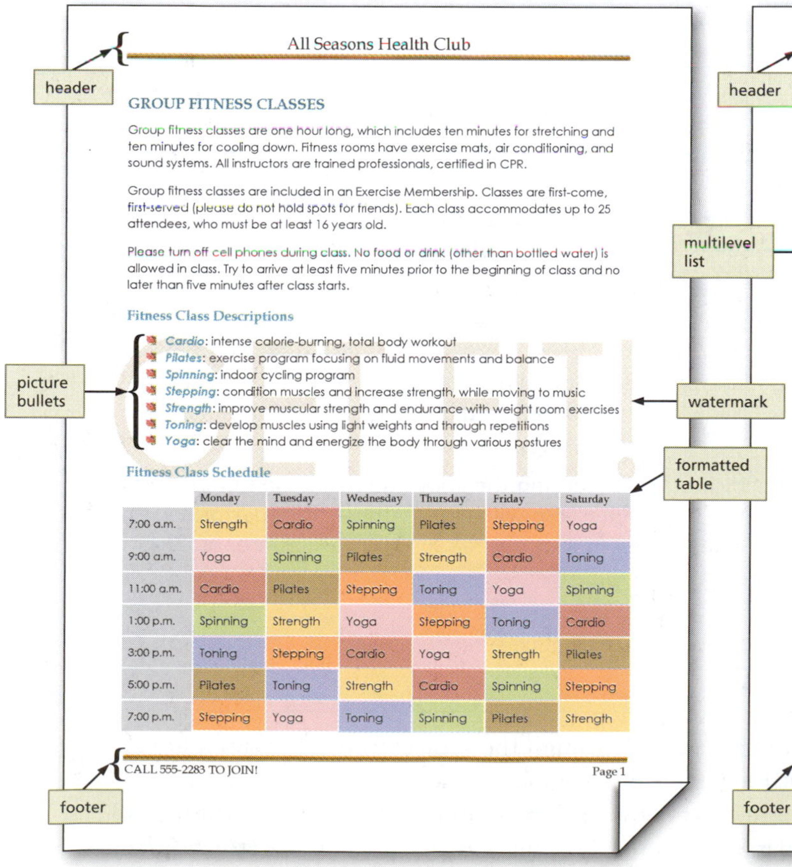

labels: border, border, watermark, Exercise, Gymnasium, Aquatics, SmartArt graphic

All Seasons Health Club

LET US HELP YOU REACH YOUR FITNESS GOALS!

All Seasons Health Club

GROUP FITNESS CLASSES

Group fitness classes are one hour long, which includes ten minutes for stretching and ten minutes for cooling down. Fitness rooms have exercise mats, air conditioning, and sound systems. All instructors are trained professionals, certified in CPR.

Group fitness classes are included in an Exercise Membership. Classes are first-come, first-served (please do not hold spots for friends). Each class accommodates up to 25 attendees, who must be at least 16 years old.

Please turn off cell phones during class. No food or drink (other than bottled water) is allowed in class. Try to arrive at least five minutes prior to the beginning of class and no later than five minutes after class starts.

Fitness Class Descriptions

- **Cardio**: intense calorie-burning, total body workout
- **Pilates**: exercise program focusing on fluid movements and balance
- **Spinning**: indoor cycling program
- **Stepping**: condition muscles and increase strength, while moving to music
- **Strength**: improve muscular strength and endurance with weight room exercises
- **Toning**: develop muscles using light weights and through repetitions
- **Yoga**: clear the mind and energize the body through various postures

Fitness Class Schedule

	Monday	Tuesday	Wednesday	Thursday	Friday	Saturday
7:00 a.m.	Strength	Cardio	Spinning	Pilates	Stepping	Yoga
9:00 a.m.	Yoga	Spinning	Pilates	Strength	Cardio	Toning
11:00 a.m.	Cardio	Pilates	Stepping	Toning	Yoga	Spinning
1:00 p.m.	Spinning	Strength	Yoga	Stepping	Toning	Cardio
3:00 p.m.	Toning	Stepping	Cardio	Yoga	Strength	Pilates
5:00 p.m.	Pilates	Toning	Strength	Cardio	Spinning	Stepping
7:00 p.m.	Stepping	Yoga	Toning	Spinning	Pilates	Strength

labels: header, picture bullets, watermark, formatted table

Figure 4–1 (b) First Page of Body of Proposal

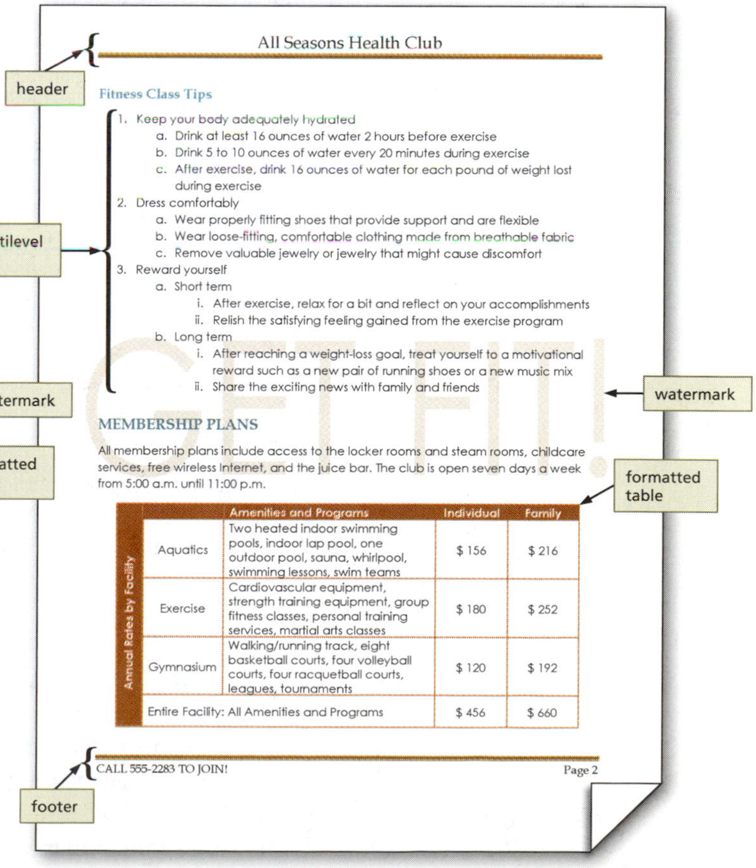

All Seasons Health Club

Fitness Class Tips

1. Keep your body adequately hydrated
   a. Drink at least 16 ounces of water 2 hours before exercise
   b. Drink 5 to 10 ounces of water every 20 minutes during exercise
   c. After exercise, drink 16 ounces of water for each pound of weight lost during exercise
2. Dress comfortably
   a. Wear properly fitting shoes that provide support and are flexible
   b. Wear loose-fitting, comfortable clothing made from breathable fabric
   c. Remove valuable jewelry or jewelry that might cause discomfort
3. Reward yourself
   a. Short term
      i. After exercise, relax for a bit and reflect on your accomplishments
      ii. Relish the satisfying feeling gained from the exercise program
   b. Long term
      i. After reaching a weight-loss goal, treat yourself to a motivational reward such as a new pair of running shoes or a new music mix
      ii. Share the exciting news with family and friends

MEMBERSHIP PLANS

All membership plans include access to the locker rooms and steam rooms, childcare services, free wireless Internet, and the juice bar. The club is open seven days a week from 5:00 a.m. until 11:00 p.m.

Annual Rates by Facility		Amenities and Programs	Individual	Family
	Aquatics	Two heated indoor swimming pools, indoor lap pool, one outdoor pool, sauna, whirlpool, swimming lessons, swim teams	$ 156	$ 216
	Exercise	Cardiovascular equipment, strength training equipment, group fitness classes, personal training services, martial arts classes	$ 180	$ 252
	Gymnasium	Walking/running track, eight basketball courts, four volleyball courts, four racquetball courts, leagues, tournaments	$ 120	$ 192
	Entire Facility: All Amenities and Programs		$ 456	$ 660

labels: header, multilevel list, watermark, formatted table

Figure 4–1 (c) Second Page of Body of Proposal

Overview

As you read through this chapter, you will learn how to create the sales proposal shown in Figure 4–1 on the previous page by performing these general tasks:

- Create a title page.
- Save the title page.
- Insert a draft of the body of the sales proposal below the title page.
- Edit and enhance the draft of the body of the sales proposal.
- Save and print the sales proposal.

Plan Ahead

General Project Guidelines

When creating a Word document, the actions you perform and decisions you make will affect the appearance and characteristics of the finished document. As you create a sales proposal, such as the project shown in Figure 4–1, you should follow these general guidelines:

1. **Identify the nature of the proposal.** A proposal may be solicited or unsolicited. If someone else requests that you develop the proposal, it is solicited. Be sure to include all requested information in a solicited proposal. When you write a proposal because you recognize a need, the proposal is unsolicited. With an unsolicited proposal, you must gather information you believe will be relevant and of interest to the intended audience.

2. **Design an eye-catching title page.** The title page should convey the overall message of the sales proposal. Use text, graphics, formats, and colors that reflect the goals of the sales proposal. Be sure to include a title.

3. **Compose the text of the sales proposal.** Sales proposals vary in length, style, and formality, but all are designed to elicit acceptance from the reader. The sales proposal should have a neat, organized appearance. A successful sales proposal uses succinct wording and includes lists for textual messages. Write text using active voice, instead of passive voice. Assume that readers of unsolicited sales proposals have no previous knowledge about the topic. Be sure the goal of the proposal is clear. Establish a theme and carry it throughout the proposal.

4. **Enhance the sales proposal with appropriate visuals.** Use visuals to add interest, clarify ideas, and illustrate points. Visuals include tables, charts, and graphical images (i.e., photos, clip art).

5. **Proofread and edit the proposal.** Carefully review the sales proposal to be sure it contains no spelling, grammar, mathematical, or other errors. Check that transitions between sentences and paragraphs are smooth. Ensure that the purpose of the proposal is stated clearly. Ask others to review the proposal and give you suggestions for improvements.

When necessary, more specific details concerning the above guidelines are presented at appropriate points in the chapter. The chapter also will identify the actions performed and decisions made regarding these guidelines during the creation of the sales proposal shown in Figure 4–1.

To Start Word

If you are using a computer to step through the project in this chapter and you want your screens to match the figures in this book, you should change your screen's resolution to 1024 × 768. The next steps, which assume Windows 7 is running, start Word based on a typical installation. You may need to ask your instructor how to start Word for your computer.

1 Click the Start button on the Windows 7 taskbar to display the Start menu.

2 Type `Microsoft Word` as the search text in the 'Search programs and files' text box and watch the search results appear on the Start menu.

3 Click Microsoft Word 2010 in the search results on the Start menu to start Word and display a new blank document in the Word window.

4 If the Word window is not maximized, click the Maximize button next to the Close button on its title bar to maximize the window.

5 If the Print Layout button on the status bar is not selected (shown in Figure 4–2 on page WD 207), click it so that your screen is in Print Layout view.

6 If your zoom percent is not 100, click the Zoom Out button or Zoom In button on the status bar as many times as necessary until the Zoom button displays 100% on its face (shown in Figure 4–2).

7 If the rulers are not displayed already, click the View Ruler button on the vertical scroll bar, or place a check mark in the Ruler check box (View tab | Show group), because you will use the rulers for several tasks in the creation of this project.

To Display Formatting Marks

It is helpful to display formatting marks that indicate where in the document you pressed the ENTER key, SPACEBAR, and other keys. The following steps display formatting marks.

1 If necessary, click Home on the Ribbon to display the Home tab.

2 If the Show/Hide ¶ button (Home tab | Paragraph group) is not selected already, click it to display formatting marks on the screen.

To Change Theme Colors

Word provides document themes that contain a variety of color schemes to assist you in selecting complementary colors in a document. You should select a color scheme that reflects the goals of a sales proposal. This proposal uses the Solstice color scheme. The following steps change theme colors.

1 Click the Change Styles button (Home tab | Styles group) to display the Change Styles menu and then point to Colors on the Change Styles menu to display the Colors gallery.

2 If necessary, scroll to and then click Solstice in the Colors gallery to change the document theme colors to the selected color scheme.

Creating a Title Page

A **title page** is a separate cover page that contains, at a minimum, the title of a document. For a sales proposal, the title page usually is the first page of the document. Solicited proposals often have a specific format for the title page. Guidelines for the title page of a solicited proposal may stipulate the margins, spacing, layout, and required contents such as title, sponsor name, author name, date, etc. With an unsolicited proposal, by contrast, you can design the title page in a way that best presents its message.

Plan Ahead

Design an eye-catching title page.

The title page is the first section a reader sees on a sales proposal. Thus, it is important that the title page appropriately reflects the goal of the sales proposal. When designing the title page, consider its text and graphics.

- **Use concise, descriptive text.** The title page should contain a short, descriptive title that accurately reflects the message of the sales proposal. The title page also may include a theme or slogan. Do not place a page number on the title page.

- **Identify appropriate fonts, font sizes, and colors for the text.** Use fonts that are easy to read. Avoid using more than three different fonts because too many fonts can make the title page visually confusing. Use larger font sizes to add impact to the title page. To give the title more emphasis, its font size should be larger than any other text on the title page. Use colors that complement each other and convey the meaning of the proposal.

- **Use graphics to reinforce the goal.** Select simple graphics that clearly communicate the fundamental nature of the proposal. Possible graphics include shapes, pictures, and logos. Use colors that complement text colors. Be aware that too many graphics and colors can be distracting. Arrange graphics with the text so that the title page is attractive and uncluttered.

The title page of the sales proposal in this project (Figure 4–1a on page WD 203) contains a colorful title that is surrounded by a border with some shading, an artistic graphic with text, a colorful slogan, and the faded words, GET FIT!, in the background. The steps on the next several pages create this title page. The faded words, GET FIT!, are added to all pages at the end of the chapter.

To Format Characters

The title in the sales proposal should use a large font size and an easy-to-read font, and should be the focal point on the page. The following steps enter the title, All Seasons Health Club, with the first two words centered on the first line and the second two words centered on the second line.

1 Click the Center button (Home tab | Paragraph group) to center the paragraph that will contain the title.

2 Click the Font box arrow (Home tab | Font group). Scroll to and then click Berlin Sans FB Demi (or a similar font) in the Font gallery, so that the text you type will use the selected font.

3 Click the Font Size box arrow (Home tab | Font group) and then click 72 in the Font Size gallery, so that the text you type will use the selected font size.

4 Type `All Seasons` and then press the ENTER key to enter the first line of the title.

5 Click the Font Color button arrow (Home tab | Font group) and then click Red, Accent 3 (seventh color, first row) in the Font Color gallery, so that the text you type will use the selected font color.

6 Type `Health Club` as the second line of the title (shown in Figure 4–2).

BTW

Normal Style
If your screen settings differ from Figure 4–2, it is possible the default settings in your Normal style have been changed. Normal style settings are saved in a file called normal.dotm. To restore the original Normal style settings, quit Word and use Windows Explorer to locate the normal.dotm file (be sure that hidden files and folders are displayed, and include system and hidden files in your search — you may need to use Help to assist you with these tasks). Rename the normal.dotm file as oldnormal.dotm. After the normal.dotm file is renamed, it no longer will exist as normal.dotm. The next time you start Word, it will recreate a normal.dotm file using the original default settings.

To Border a Paragraph

When you click the Border button (Home tab | Paragraph group), Word applies the most recently defined border, or, if one has not been defined, it applies the default border to the current paragraph. To specify a border different from the most recently defined border, you use the Border button arrow (Home tab | Paragraph group).

In this project, the first line of the title in the sales proposal (All Seasons) has a 6-point red border around it. The following steps add a border to all edges of a paragraph.

1
- Position the insertion point in the paragraph to border, in this case, the first line of the document.

- Click the Border button arrow (Home tab | Paragraph group) to display the Border gallery (Figure 4–2).

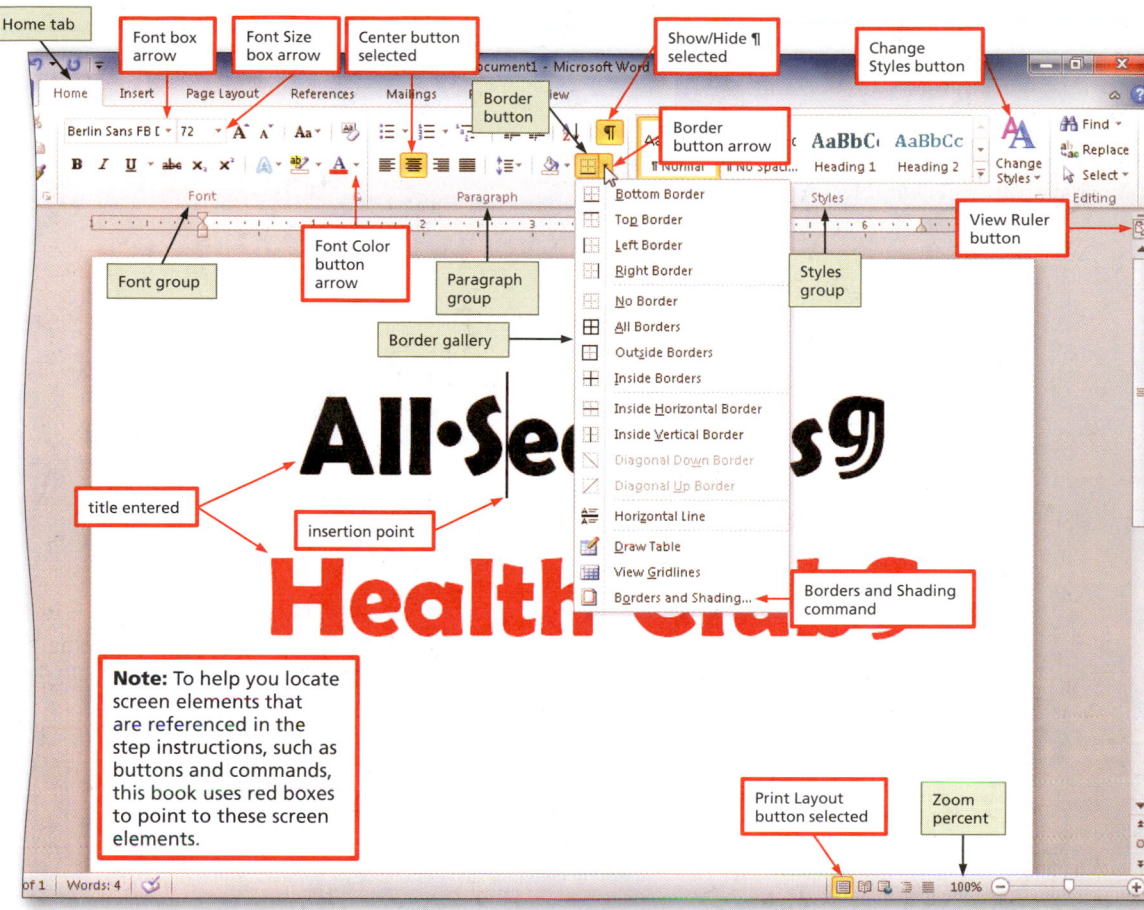

Figure 4–2

2
- Click Borders and Shading in the Border gallery to display the Borders and Shading dialog box.

- Click Box in the Setting area (Borders and Shading dialog box), which will place a border on each edge of the current paragraph.

- Click the Color box arrow and then click Red, Accent 3 (seventh color, first row) in the Color palette to specify the border color.

- Click the Width box arrow and then click 6 pt to specify the thickness of the border (Figure 4–3).

Q&A What is the purpose of the buttons in the Preview area?

They are toggles that display and remove the top, bottom, left, and right borders from the diagram in the Preview area.

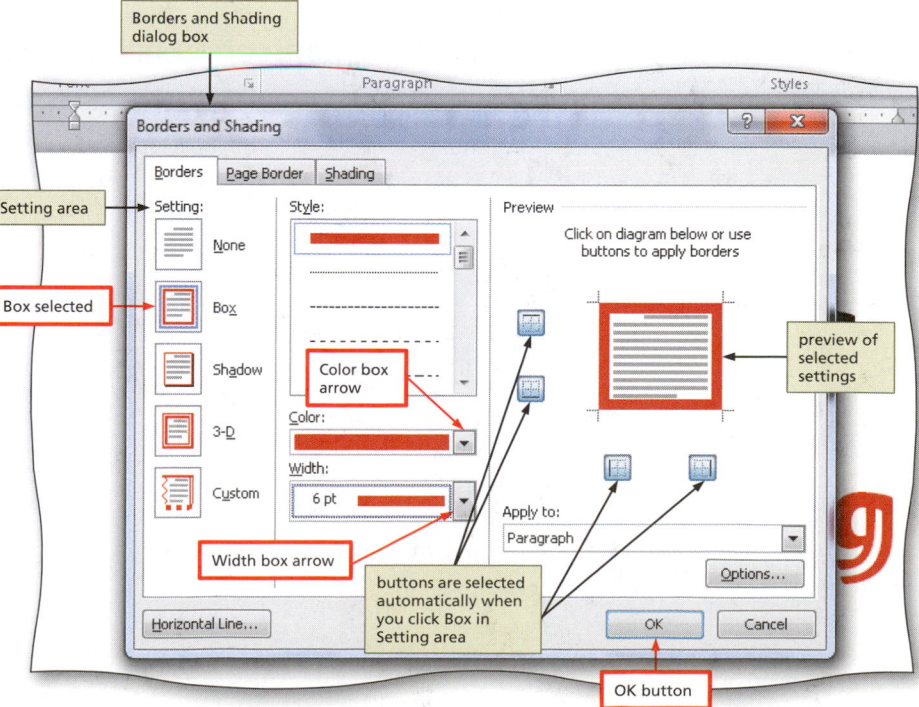

Figure 4–3

● Click the OK button (Borders and Shading dialog box) to place the border shown in the preview area of the dialog box around the current paragraph in the document (Figure 4–4).

Q&A

How would I remove an existing border from a paragraph?

Click the Border button arrow (Home tab | Paragraph group) and then click the border in the Border gallery that identifies the border you wish to remove, or click No Border to remove all borders.

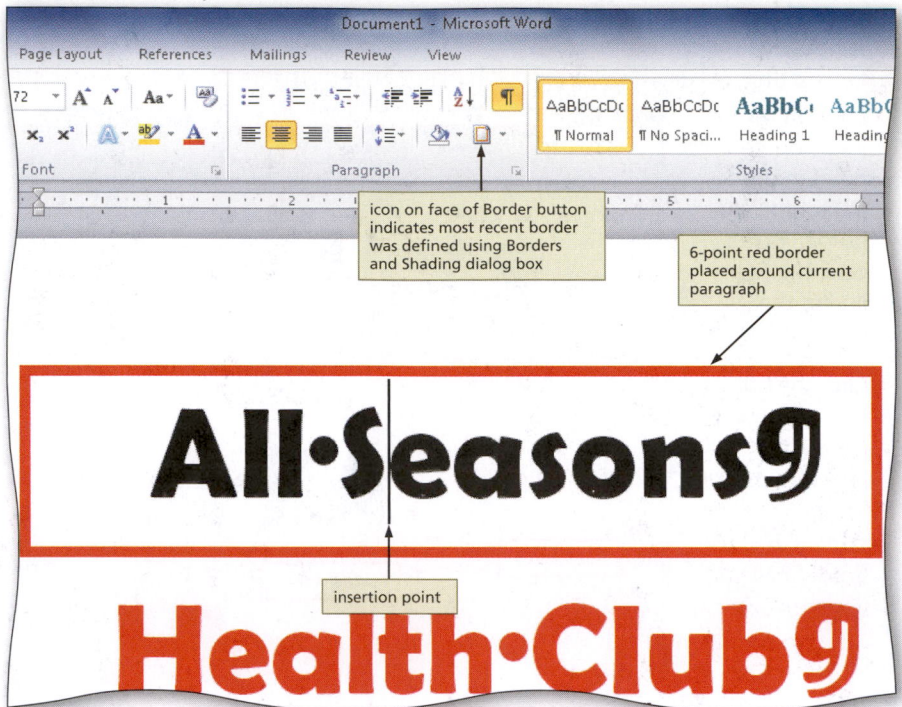

Figure 4–4

Other Ways

1. Click Page Borders button (Page Layout tab | Page Background group), click Borders tab (Borders and Shading dialog box), select desired border, click OK button

To Shade a Paragraph and Change Font Color

To make the first line of the title of the sales proposal more eye-catching, it is shaded in aqua. When you shade a paragraph, Word shades the rectangular area behind any text or graphics in the paragraph from the left margin of the paragraph to the right margin. If the paragraph is surrounded by a border, Word shades inside the border. The following steps shade a paragraph and change font color.

① With the insertion point in the paragraph to shade, the first line in this case (shown in Figure 4–4), click the Shading button arrow (Home tab | Paragraph group) to display the Shading gallery.

② Click Aqua, Accent 1 (fifth color, first row) in the Shading gallery to shade the current paragraph (shown in Figure 4–5).

③ Drag through the words, All Seasons, in the first line of the title to select the text.

④ Click the Font Color button arrow (Home tab | Font group) to display the Font Color gallery and then click White, Background 1 (first color, first row) to change the color of the selected text (shown in Figure 4–5).

To Border Another Paragraph

To make the second line of the title of the sales proposal (Health Club) more eye-catching, it has a 6-point gold border around it. The following steps add a border to all edges of a paragraph.

1 Position the insertion point in the paragraph to border (in this case, the second paragraph containing the text, Health Club).

2 Click the Border button arrow (Home tab | Paragraph group) to display the Border gallery and then click Borders and Shading in the Border gallery to display the Borders and Shading dialog box.

3 Click Box in the Setting area (Borders and Shading dialog box), which will place a border on each edge of the current paragraph.

4 Click the Color box arrow and then click Gold, Accent 2 (sixth color, first row) in the Color palette to specify the border color.

5 If necessary, click the Width box arrow and then click 6 pt to specify the thickness of the border.

6 Click the OK button to place the defined border shown around the current paragraph in the document (Figure 4–5).

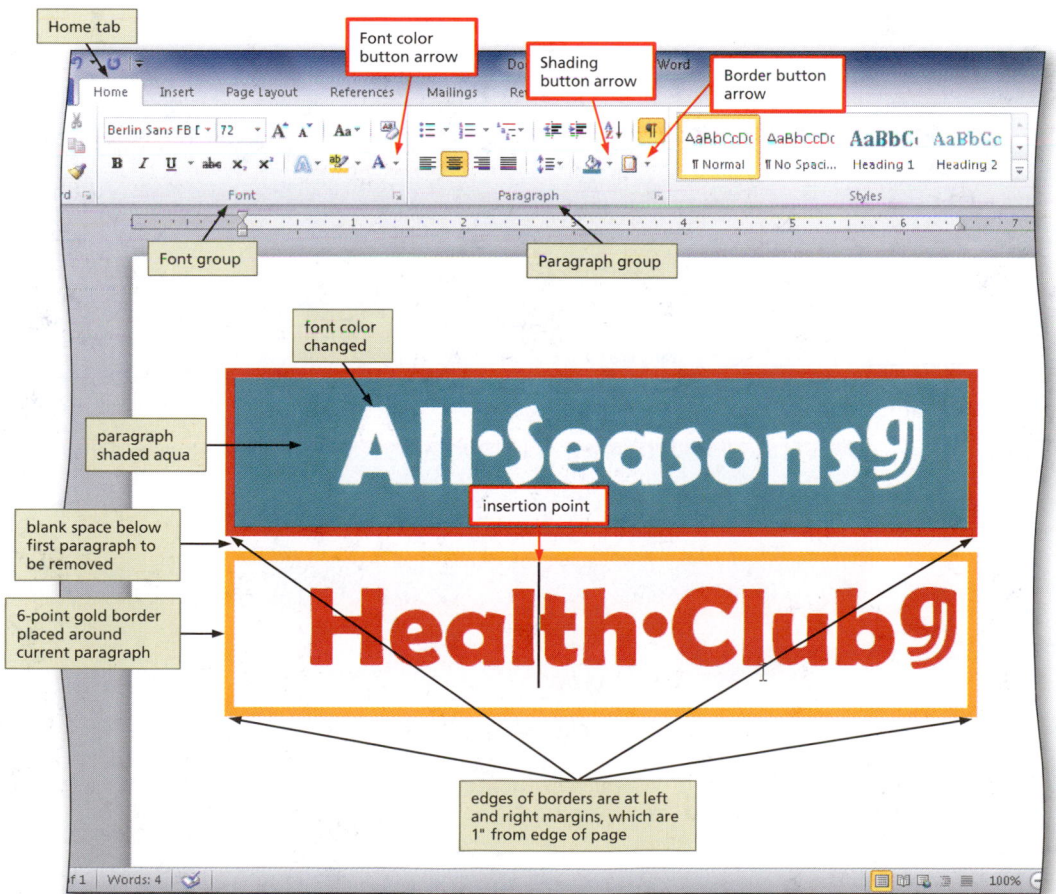

Home tab

Font color button arrow

Shading button arrow

Border button arrow

Font group

Paragraph group

font color changed

insertion point

paragraph shaded aqua

blank space below first paragraph to be removed

6-point gold border placed around current paragraph

edges of borders are at left and right margins, which are 1" from edge of page

Figure 4–5

BTW

The Ribbon and Screen Resolution
Word may change how the groups and buttons within the groups appear on the Ribbon, depending on the computer's screen resolution. Thus, your Ribbon may look different from the ones in this book if you are using a screen resolution other than 1024 x 768.

To Change Spacing after a Paragraph

Currently, a small amount of blank space exists between the two paragraph borders because Word automatically places 10 points of blank space below paragraphs (shown in Figure 4–5 on the previous page). The following steps remove the blank space below the first paragraph.

1 Position the insertion point in the paragraph to be adjusted (in this case, the paragraph containing the text, All Seasons).

2 Display the Page Layout tab. Click the Spacing After box down arrow (Page Layout tab | Paragraph group) as many times as necessary until 0 pt is displayed in the Spacing After box to remove the space below the current paragraph (shown in Figure 4–6).

To Change Left and Right Paragraph Indent

The borders around the first and second paragraphs and the shading in the first paragraph currently extend from the left margin to the right margin (shown in Figure 4–5). In this project, the edges of the border and shading are closer to the text in the title. If you want the border and shading to start and end at a location different from the margin, you change the left and right paragraph indent.

The Increase Indent and Decrease Indent buttons (Home tab | Paragraph group) change the left indent by ½-inch, respectively. In this case, however, you cannot use these buttons because you want to change both the left and right indent. The following steps change the left and right paragraph indent.

1
- With the insertion point in the paragraph to indent (the first paragraph in this case), click the Indent Left box up arrow (Page Layout tab | Paragraph group) five times so that 0.5" is displayed in the Indent Left box because you want to adjust the paragraph left indent by this amount.

- Click the Indent Right box up arrow (Page Layout tab | Paragraph group) five times so that 0.5" is displayed in the Indent Right box because you want to adjust the paragraph right indent by this amount (Figure 4–6).

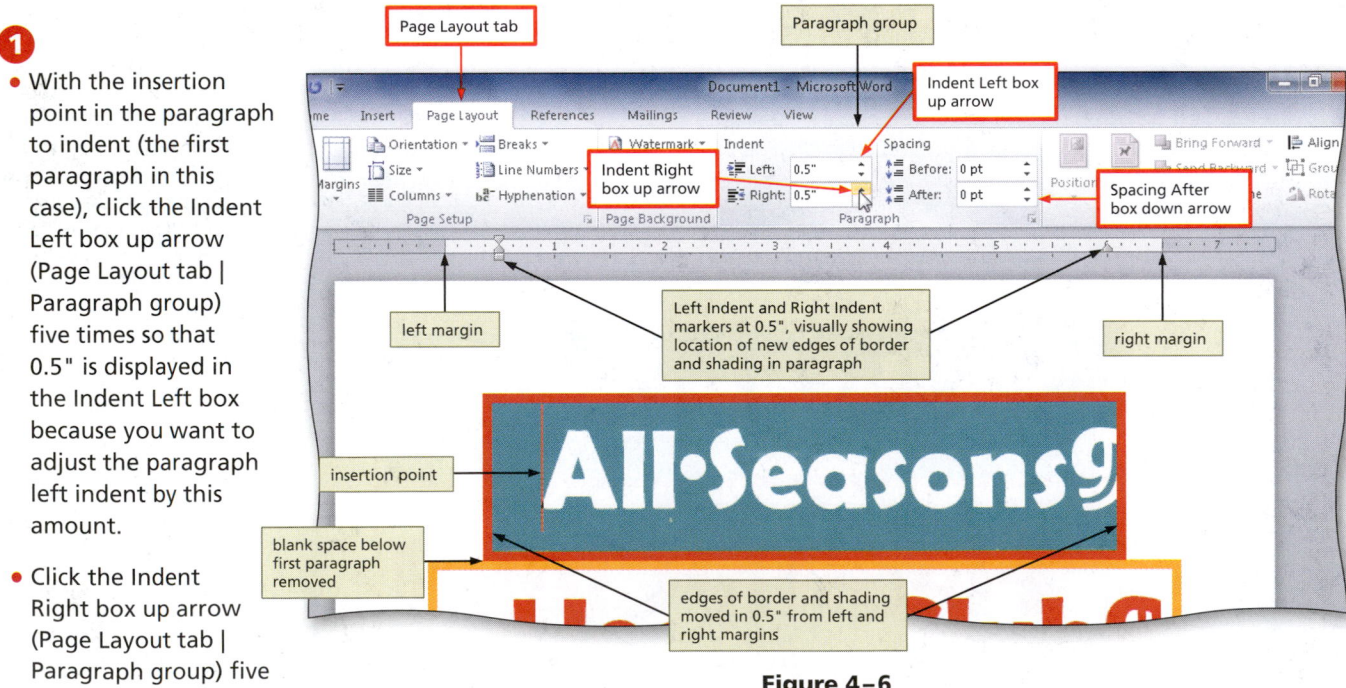

Figure 4–6

🔍 Experiment
- Repeatedly click the Indent Right and Indent Left box up and down scroll arrows (Page Layout tab | Paragraph group) and watch the left and right edges of the current paragraph change in the document window. When you have finished experimenting, set the left and right indent each to 0.5".

2

- Repeat Step 1 for the second paragraph, so that the paragraph containing the words, Health Club, also has a left and right indent of 0.5" (shown in Figure 4–7).

Other Ways		
1. Drag Left Indent and Right Indent markers on ruler	(Paragraph dialog box), set indentation values, click OK button	Indents and Spacing tab (Paragraph dialog box), set indentation values, click OK button
2. Click Paragraph Dialog Box Launcher (Home tab | Paragraph group), click Indents and Spacing tab	3. Right-click paragraph, click Paragraph on shortcut menu, click	

To Clear Formatting

The title is finished. When you press the ENTER key to advance the insertion point from the end of the second line to the beginning of the third line on the title page, the border is carried forward to line 3, and any text you type will be 72-point Berlin Sans FB Demi Red, Accent 3 font. The paragraphs and characters on line 3 should not have the same paragraph and character formatting as line 2. Instead, they should be formatted using the Normal style. The following steps clear formatting, which applies the Normal style formats to the location of the insertion point.

1 If necessary, press the END key to position the insertion point at the end of line 2, that is, after the b in Club.

2 Press the ENTER key.

3 Display the Home tab. Click the Clear Formatting button (Home tab | Font group) to apply the Normal style to the location of the insertion point (Figure 4–7).

Q&A Could I have clicked Normal in the Styles gallery instead of the Clear Formatting button?
Yes.

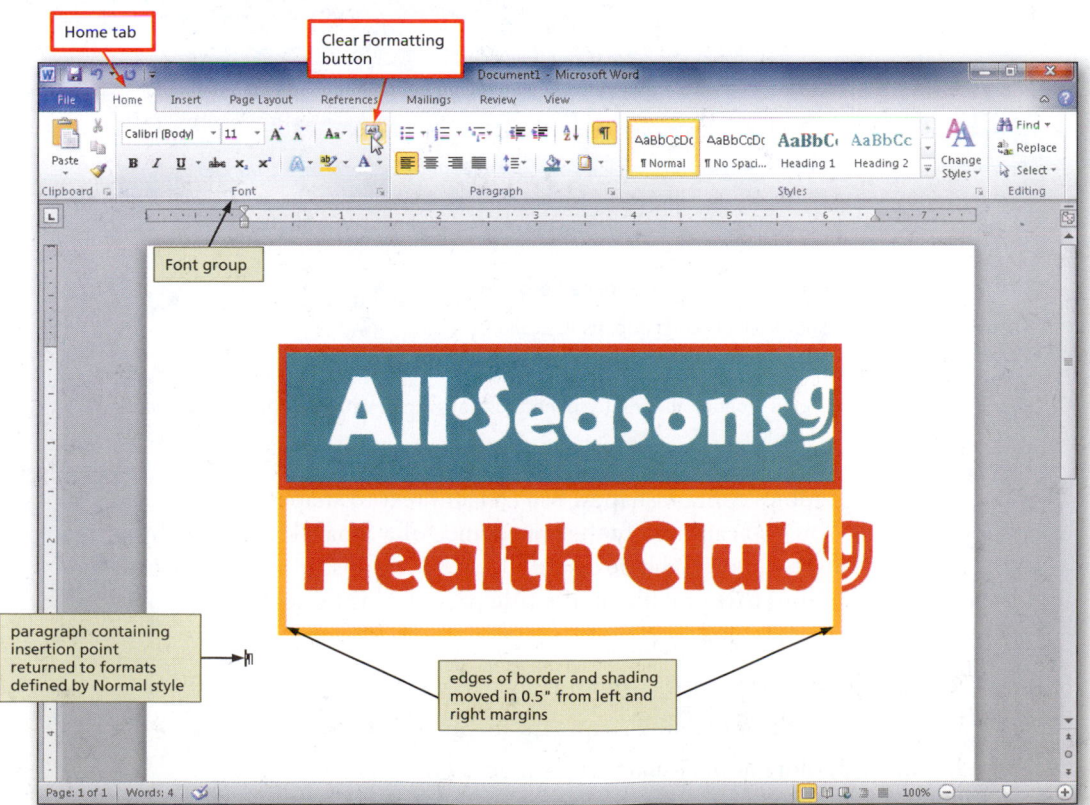

Figure 4–7

To Save a Document

You have performed many tasks while creating this proposal and do not want to risk losing work completed thus far. Accordingly, you should save the document. The following steps assume you already have created folders for storing your files, for example, a CIS 101 folder (for your class) that contains a Word folder (for your assignments). Thus, these steps save the document in the Word folder in the CIS 101 folder on a USB flash drive using the file name, All Seasons Title Page.

1 With a USB flash drive connected to one of the computer's USB ports, click the Save button on the Quick Access Toolbar to display the Save As dialog box.

2 Type `All Seasons Title Page` in the File name text box (Save As dialog box) to change the file name. Do not press the ENTER key after typing the file name because you do not want to close the dialog box at this time.

3 Navigate to the desired save location (in this case, the Word folder in the CIS 101 folder [or your class folder] on the USB flash drive).

4 Click the Save button (Save As dialog box) to save the document in the selected folder on the selected drive with the entered file name.

SmartArt Graphics

Microsoft Office 2010 includes **SmartArt graphics**, which are visual representations of information. Many different types of SmartArt graphics are available, allowing you to choose one that illustrates your message best. Table 4–1 identifies the purpose of some of the more popular types of SmartArt graphics. Within each type, Office provides numerous layouts. For example, you can select from more than 40 different layouts of the list type.

Table 4–1 SmartArt Graphic Types	
Type	**Purpose**
List	Shows nonsequential or grouped blocks of information.
Process	Shows progression, timeline, or sequential steps in a process or workflow.
Cycle	Shows continuous sequence of steps or events.
Hierarchy	Illustrates organization charts, decision trees, and hierarchical relationships.
Relationship	Compares or contrasts connections between concepts.
Matrix	Shows relationships of parts to a whole.
Picture	Uses images to present a message.
Pyramid	Shows proportional or interconnected relationships with the largest component at the top or bottom.

SmartArt graphics contain shapes. You can add text to shapes, add more shapes, or delete shapes. You also can modify the appearance of a SmartArt graphic by applying styles and changing its colors. The next several pages demonstrate the following general tasks to create the SmartArt graphic on the title page in this project:

1. Insert a SmartArt graphic.
2. Delete unneeded shapes from the SmartArt graphic.
3. Add text to the remaining shapes in the SmartArt graphic.
4. Change colors of the SmartArt graphic.
5. Apply a style to the SmartArt graphic.

BTW

BTWs
For a complete list of the BTWs found in the margins of this book, visit the Word 2010 BTW Web page (scsite.com/wd2010/btw).

To Insert a SmartArt Graphic

Below the title on the title page is a cycle SmartArt graphic. The following steps insert a SmartArt graphic centered below the title on the title page.

1

- With the insertion point on the blank paragraph below the title (shown in Figure 4–7 on page WD 211), click the Center button (Home tab | Paragraph group) so that the inserted SmartArt graphic will be centered below the title.

- Display the Insert tab.

- Click the Insert SmartArt Graphic button (Insert tab | Illustrations group) to display the Choose a SmartArt Graphic dialog box (Figure 4–8).

🔑 Experiment

- Click various SmartArt graphic types in the left pane of the dialog box and watch the related layout choices appear in the middle pane.

🔑 Experiment

- Click various layouts in the list of layouts in the middle pane to see the preview and description of the layout appear in the right pane of the dialog box.

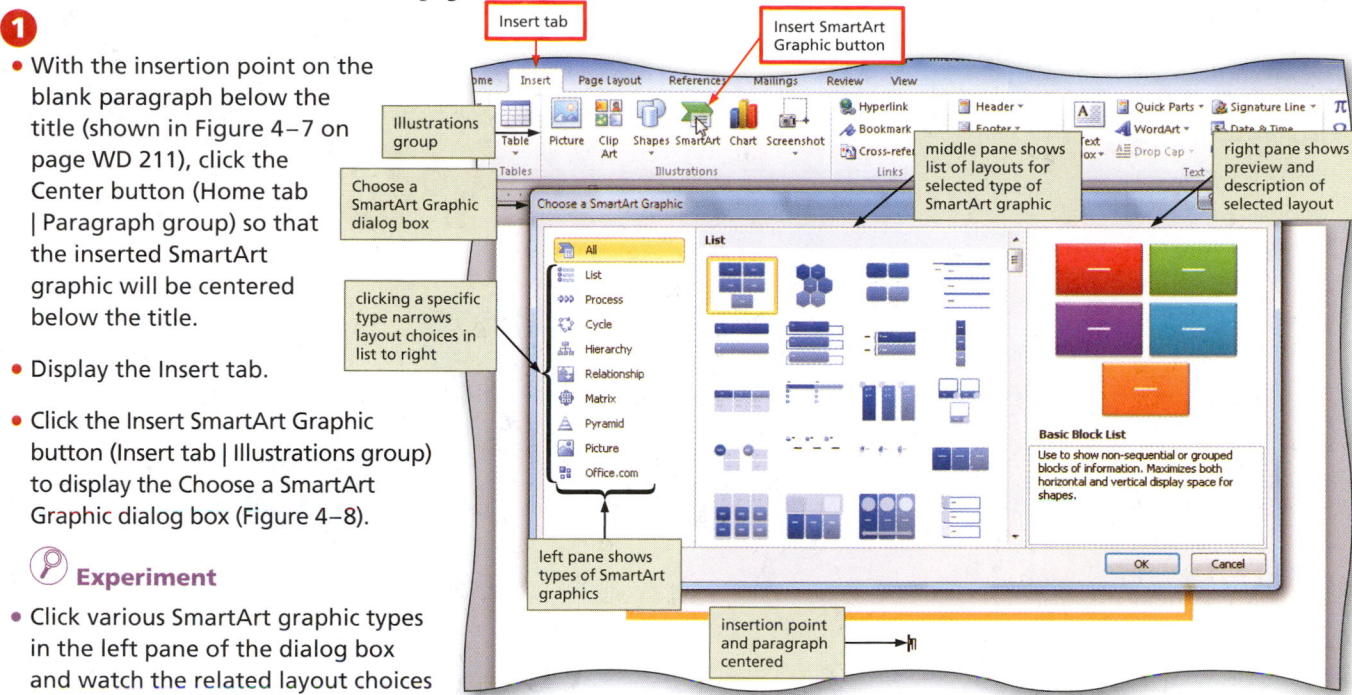

Figure 4–8

2

- Click Cycle in the left pane (Choose a SmartArt Graphic dialog box) to display the layout choices related to a cycle SmartArt graphic.

- Click Nondirectional Cycle in the middle pane, which displays a preview and description of the selected layout in the right pane (Figure 4–9).

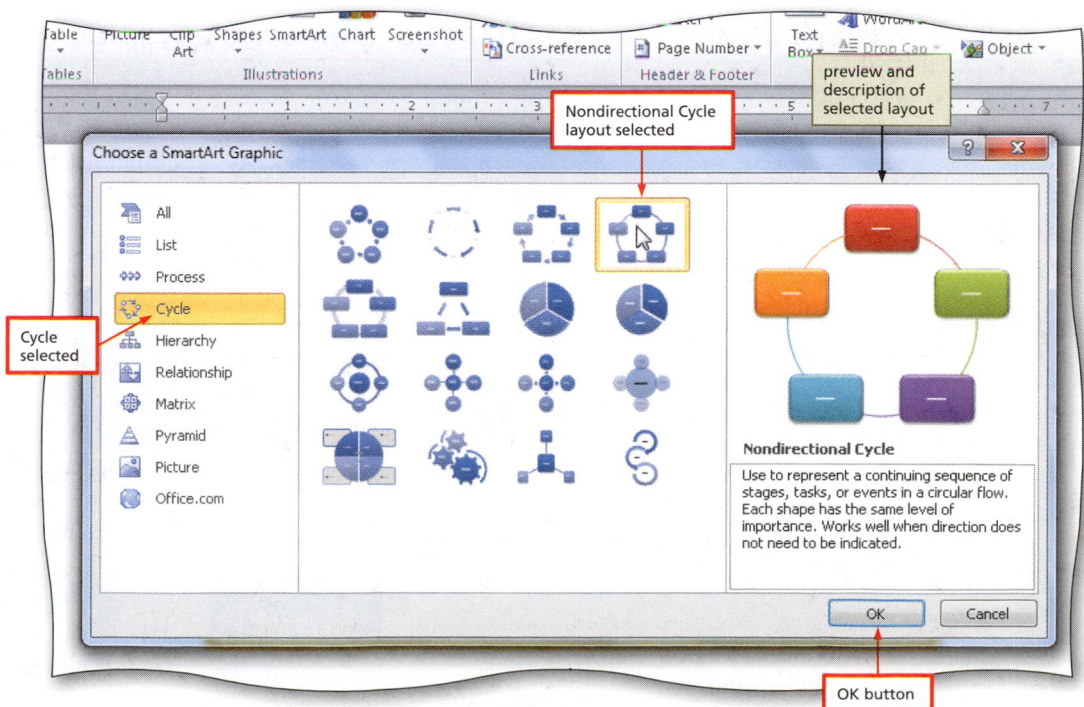

Figure 4–9

3

• Click the OK button to insert the Nondirectional Cycle SmartArt graphic in the document at the location of the insertion point (Figure 4–10).

Q&A What if the Text Pane appears next to the SmartArt graphic?

Close the Text Pane by clicking its Close button or clicking the Text Pane button (SmartArt Tools Design tab | Create Graphic group).

Q&A Can I change the layout of the inserted SmartArt graphic?

Yes. Click the More button in the Layouts gallery (SmartArt Tools Design tab | Layouts group) to display the list of layouts.

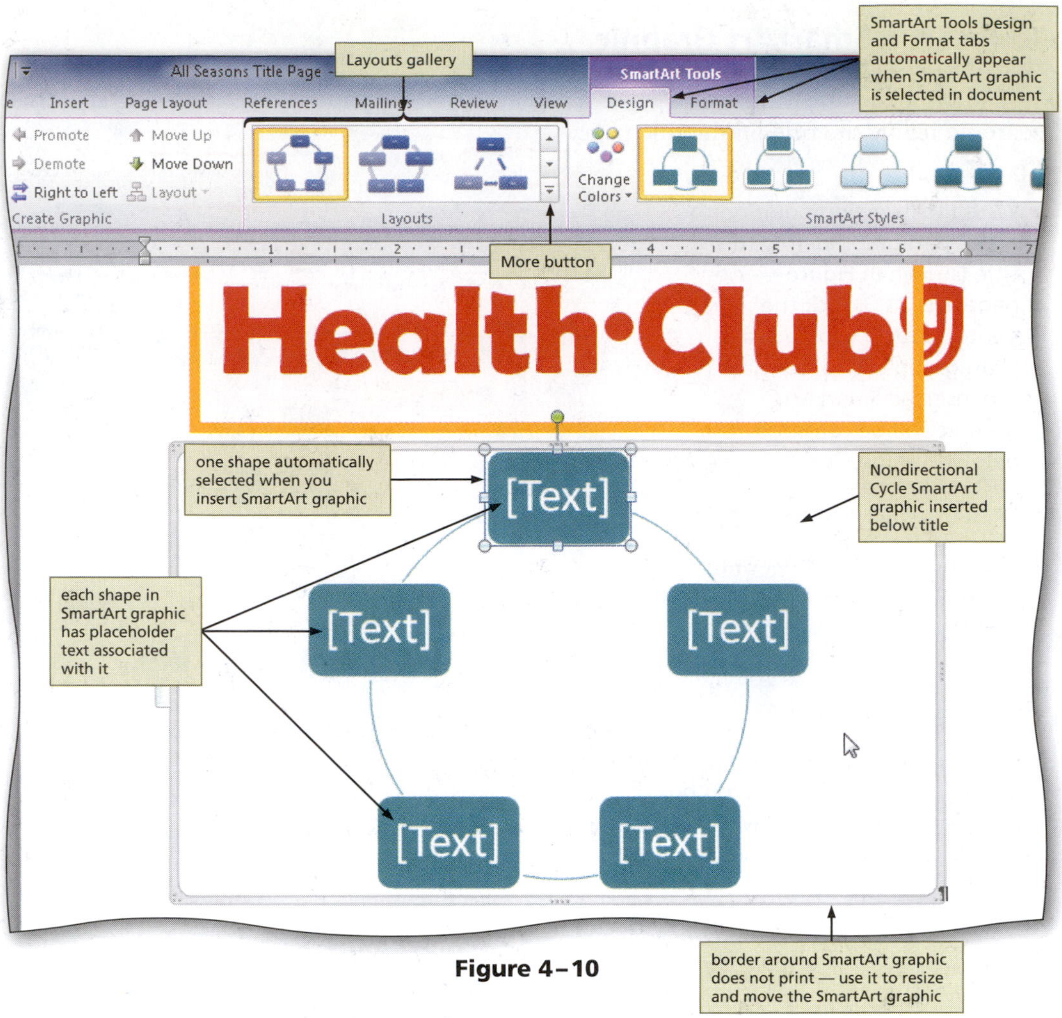

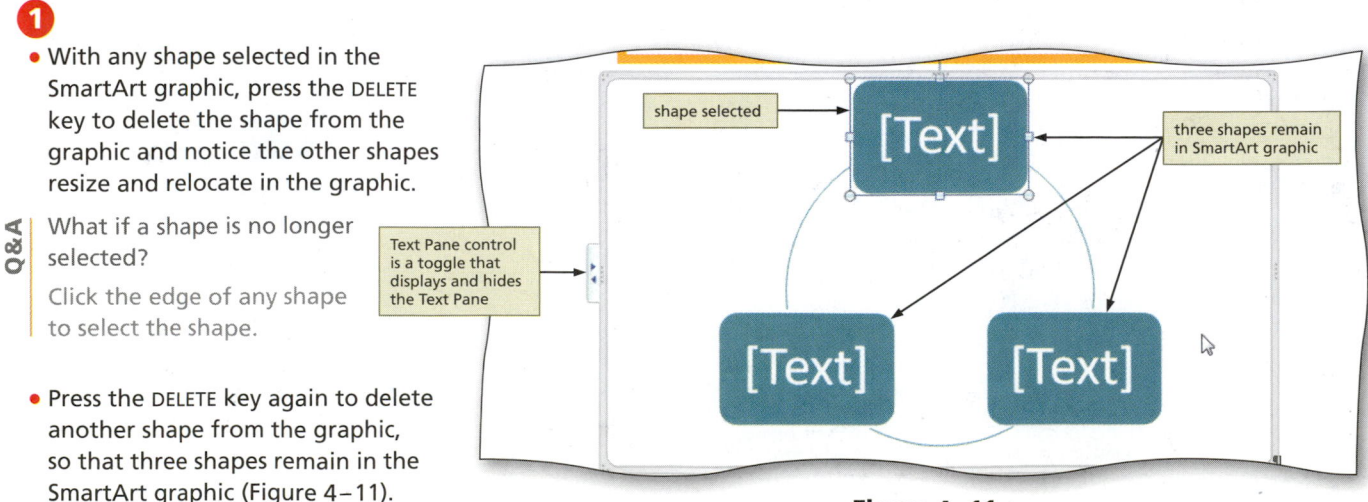

Figure 4–10

To Delete Shapes and Add Text to Shapes in a SmartArt Graphic

The Nondirectional Cycle SmartArt graphic initially has five shapes (shown in Figure 4–10). The SmartArt graphic in this project, however, has only three shapes, each one containing text that describes a type of facility at the health club: exercise, aquatics, and gymnasium. Each shape in the SmartArt graphic initially shows **placeholder text**, which indicates where text can be typed in a shape. The following steps delete two shapes in the SmartArt graphic and then add text to the remaining three shapes via their placeholder text.

1

• With any shape selected in the SmartArt graphic, press the DELETE key to delete the shape from the graphic and notice the other shapes resize and relocate in the graphic.

Q&A What if a shape is no longer selected?

Click the edge of any shape to select the shape.

• Press the DELETE key again to delete another shape from the graphic, so that three shapes remain in the SmartArt graphic (Figure 4–11).

Figure 4–11

2

- With the top shape selected (shown in Figure 4–11), type `Exercise` to replace the placeholder text, [Text], with the entered text.

Q&A How do I edit placeholder text if I make a mistake?

Click the placeholder text to select it and then correct the entry.

Q&A What if my typed text is longer than the shape?

The font size of the text may be adjusted or the text may wordwrap within the shape.

3

- Click the lower-right shape to select it and then type `Aquatics` as the new text.

- Click the lower-left shape to select it and then type `Gymnasium` as the final text in the graphic (Figure 4–12).

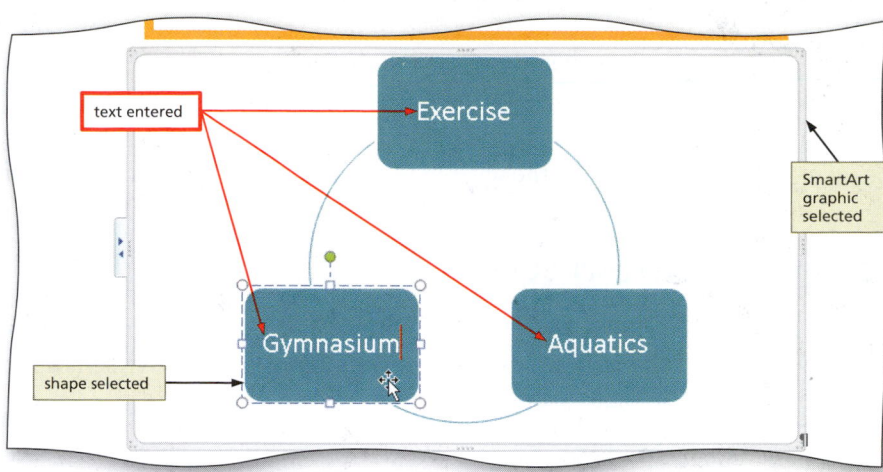

Figure 4–12

Other Ways	
1. Click Text Pane control, enter text in Text Pane, close Text Pane	tab | Create Graphic group), enter text in Text Pane, click Text Pane button again
2. Click Text Pane button (SmartArt Tools Design	

To Change Colors of a SmartArt Graphic

Word provides a variety of colors for a SmartArt graphic and the shapes in the graphic. In this project, the shapes are white inside, instead of blue, and the line connecting the shapes is red. The following steps change the colors of a SmartArt graphic.

1

- With the SmartArt graphic selected (shown in Figure 4–12), click the Change Colors button (SmartArt Tools Design tab | SmartArt Styles group) to display the Change Colors gallery.

Q&A What if the SmartArt graphic is not selected?

Click the SmartArt graphic to select it.

- Point to Colored Outline - Accent 3 in the Change Colors gallery to display a live preview of that color applied to the SmartArt graphic in the document (Figure 4–13).

🔍 **Experiment**

- Point to various colors in the Change Colors gallery and watch the colors of the graphic change in the document window.

2

- Click Colored Outline - Accent 3 in the Change Colors gallery to apply the selected color to the SmartArt graphic.

Figure 4–13

BTW

Resetting Graphics
If you want to remove all formats from a SmartArt graphic and start over, you would click the Reset Graphic button (SmartArt Tools Design tab | Reset group).

TO ADD A SHAPE TO A SMARTART GRAPHIC

If, instead of deleting a shape, you wanted to add a shape to a SmartArt graphic, you would perform the following step.

1. With the SmartArt graphic selected, click the Add Shape button (SmartArt Tools Design tab | Create Graphic group) or click the Add Shape button arrow and then click the desired location for the shape on the Add Shape menu.

To Apply a SmartArt Style

The next step is to apply a SmartArt style to the SmartArt graphic. Word provides a SmartArt Styles gallery, allowing you to change the SmartArt graphic's format to a more visually appealing style. The following steps apply a SmartArt style to a SmartArt graphic.

- With the SmartArt graphic still selected, click the More button in the SmartArt Styles gallery (shown in Figure 4–13 on the previous page) to expand the SmartArt Styles gallery.

- Point to Powder in the 3-D area of the SmartArt Styles gallery to display a live preview of that style applied to the graphic in the document (Figure 4–14).

Experiment

- Point to various SmartArt styles in the SmartArt Styles gallery and watch the style of the graphic change in the document window.

- Click Powder in the SmartArt Styles gallery to apply the selected style to the SmartArt graphic.

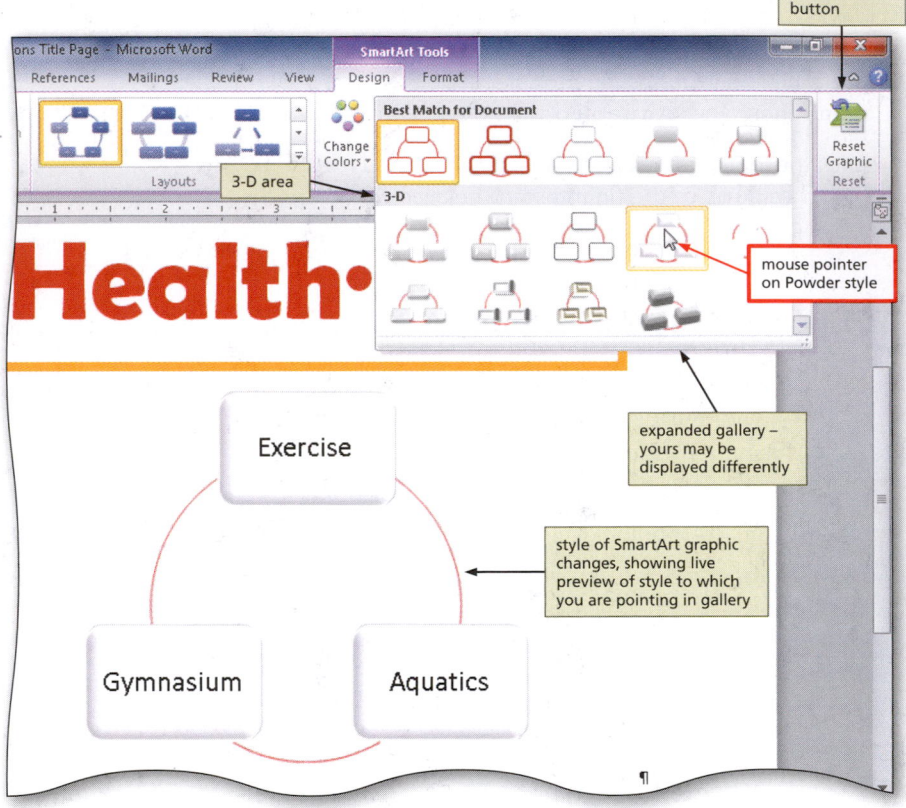

Figure 4–14

To Format Characters and Modify Character Spacing Using the Font Dialog Box

In this project, the next step is to enter and format the text at the bottom of the title page. This text is the theme of the proposal and is formatted so that it is noticeable. Its characters are 36-point bold, italic, aqua Book Antiqua. Each letter in this text is formatted in **small caps**, which are letters that look like capital letters but are not as tall as a typical capital letter. Also, you want extra space between each character so that the text spans the width of the page.

You could use buttons on the Home tab to apply some of these formats. The small caps effect and expanded spacing, however, are applied using the Font dialog box. Thus, the next steps apply all of the above-mentioned formats using the Font dialog box.

- Position the insertion point on the paragraph mark to the right of the SmartArt graphic and then press the ENTER key to position the insertion point centered below the SmartArt graphic.

- Type `Let us help you reach your fitness goals!`

- Select the sentence you just typed and then click the Font Dialog Box Launcher (Home tab | Font group) to display the Font dialog box. If necessary, click the Font tab in the dialog box to display the Font sheet.

- Scroll to and then click Book Antiqua in the Font list (Font dialog box) to change the font of the selected text.

- Click Bold Italic in the Font style list to bold and italicize the selected text.

- Scroll through the Size list and then click 36 to change the font size of the selected text.

- Click the Font color box arrow and then click Aqua, Accent 1 (fifth color, first row) in the Font color palette to change the color of the selected text.

- Click Small caps in the Effects area so that each character is displayed as a small capital letter (Figure 4–15).

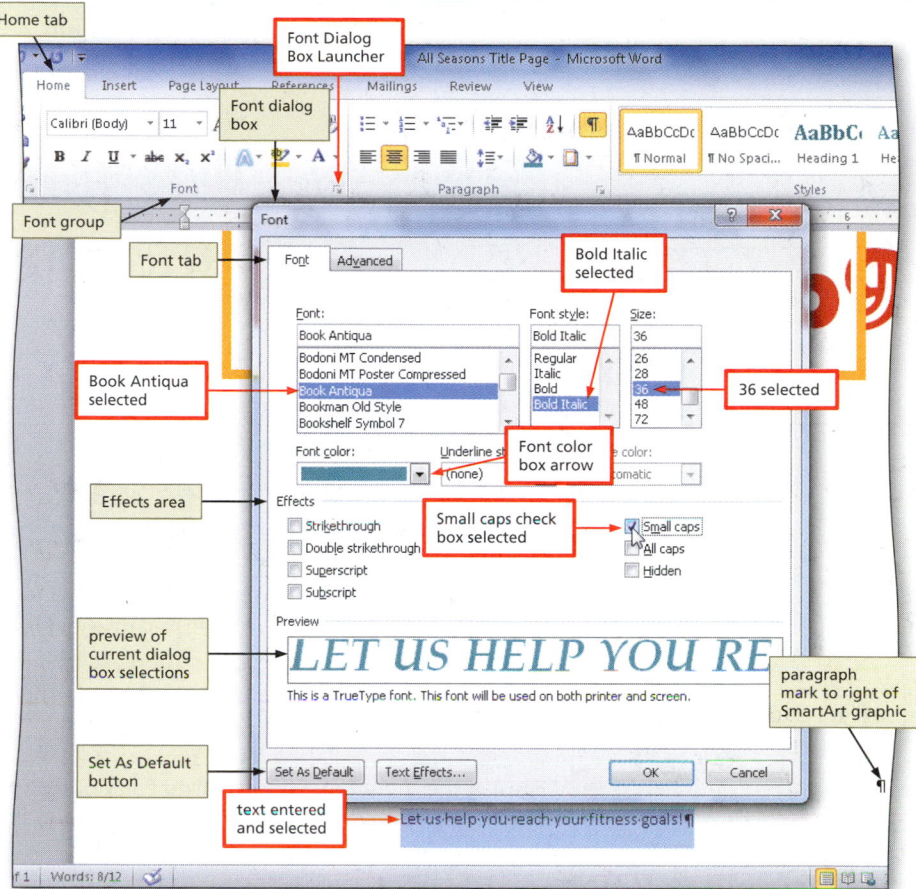

Figure 4–15

- Click the Advanced tab (Font dialog box) to display the Advanced sheet in the dialog box.

- Click the Spacing box arrow and then click Expanded to increase the amount of space between characters by 1 pt, which is the default.

- Click the Spacing By box up arrow until the box displays 4 pt because you want this amount of blank space to be displayed between each character (Figure 4–16).

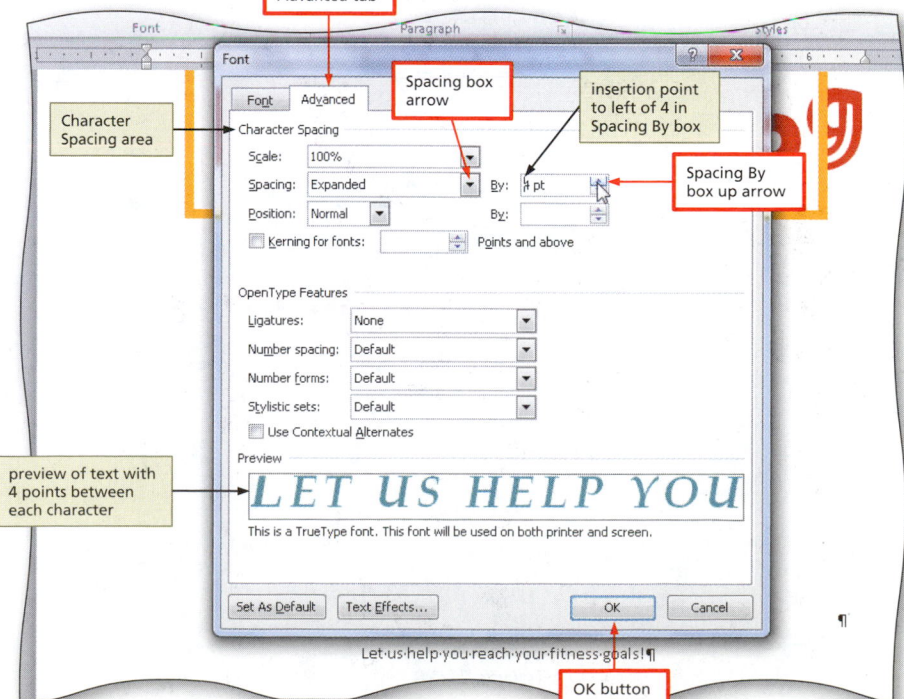

Figure 4–16

3

- Click the OK button to apply font changes to the selected text. If necessary, scroll so that the selected text is displayed completely in the document window.

- Click to remove the selection from the text (Figure 4–17).

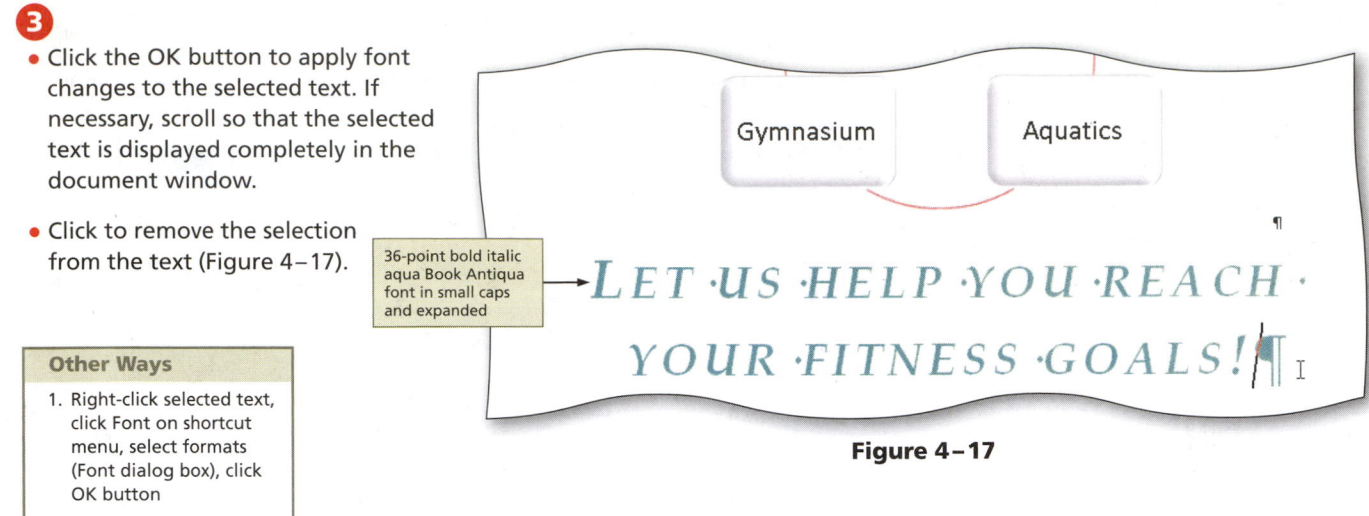

36-point bold italic aqua Book Antiqua font in small caps and expanded

LET·US·HELP·YOU·REACH·

YOUR·FITNESS·GOALS!

Figure 4–17

Other Ways

1. Right-click selected text, click Font on shortcut menu, select formats (Font dialog box), click OK button

To Zoom One Page, Change Spacing before and after a Paragraph, and Set Zoom Level

The next step in creating the title page is to adjust spacing above and below the SmartArt graphic. You want to see the entire page while adjusting the spacing. Thus, the following steps zoom one page, increase spacing before and after the paragraph containing the SmartArt graphic, and then set the zoom level back to 100% because you will be finished with the title page.

1 Display the View tab. Click the One Page button (View tab | Zoom group) to display the entire page as large as possible centered in the document window.

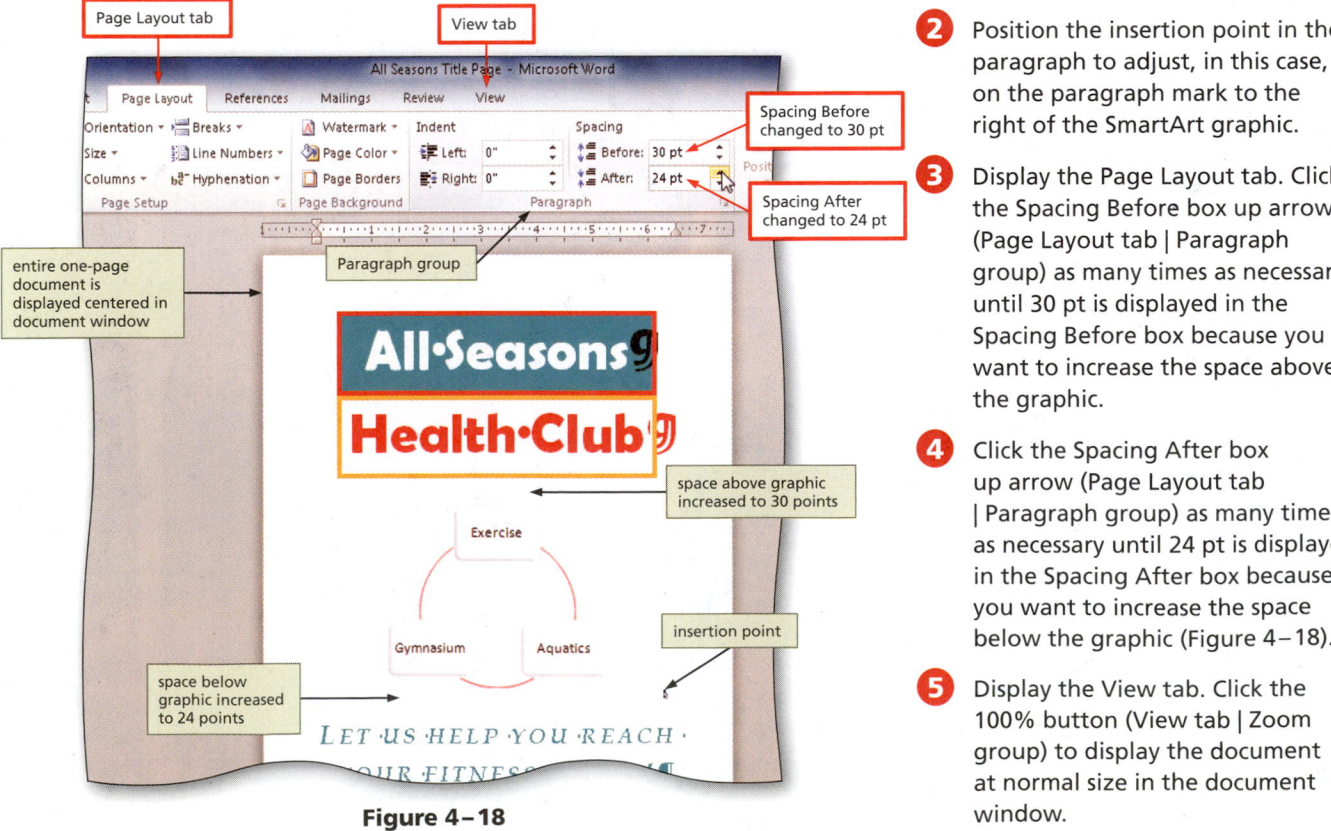

Page Layout tab

View tab

Spacing Before changed to 30 pt

Spacing After changed to 24 pt

entire one-page document is displayed centered in document window

Paragraph group

space above graphic increased to 30 points

insertion point

space below graphic increased to 24 points

Figure 4–18

2 Position the insertion point in the paragraph to adjust, in this case, on the paragraph mark to the right of the SmartArt graphic.

3 Display the Page Layout tab. Click the Spacing Before box up arrow (Page Layout tab | Paragraph group) as many times as necessary until 30 pt is displayed in the Spacing Before box because you want to increase the space above the graphic.

4 Click the Spacing After box up arrow (Page Layout tab | Paragraph group) as many times as necessary until 24 pt is displayed in the Spacing After box because you want to increase the space below the graphic (Figure 4–18).

5 Display the View tab. Click the 100% button (View tab | Zoom group) to display the document at normal size in the document window.

To Save an Existing Document with the Same File Name

The title page for the sales proposal is complete. Thus, you should save it again. The following step saves the document again.

1 Click the Save button on the Quick Access Toolbar to overwrite the previously saved file.

Break Point: If you wish to take a break, this is a good place to do so. You can quit Word now. To resume at a later time, start Word, open the file called All Seasons Title Page, and continue following the steps from this location forward.

Inserting an Existing Document in an Open Document

Assume you already have prepared a draft of the body of the proposal and saved it with the file name, All Seasons Draft. You would like the draft to be displayed on a separate page following the title page.

Compose the sales proposal.
Be sure to include basic elements in your sales proposal:

- **Include an introduction, body, and conclusion.** The introduction could contain the subject, purpose, statement of problem, need, background, or scope. The body may include costs, benefits, supporting documentation, available or required facilities, feasibility, methods, timetable, materials, or equipment. The conclusion summarizes key points or requests an action.

- **Use headers and footers.** Headers and footers help to identify every page. A page number should be in either the header or footer. If the sales proposal ever becomes disassembled, the reader can use the headers and footers to determine the order and pieces of your proposal.

Plan Ahead

BTW

Inserting Documents
When you insert a Word document in another Word document, the entire inserted document is placed at the location of the insertion point. If the insertion point, therefore, is positioned in the middle of the open document when you insert another Word document, the open document continues after the last character of the inserted document.

In the following pages, you will insert the draft of the proposal below the title page and then edit the draft by deleting a page break, changing theme fonts, and applying Quick Styles.

To Save an Active Document with a New File Name

The current file name on the title bar is All Seasons Title Page, yet the document you will work on from this point forward in the chapter will contain both the title page and the body of the sales proposal. To keep the title page as a separate document called All Seasons Title Page, you should save the active document with a new file name. If you save the active document by clicking the Save button on the Quick Access Toolbar, Word will assign it the current file name. You want the active document to have a new file name. The following steps save the active document with a new file name.

1 With a USB flash drive connected to one of the computer's USB ports, click File on the Ribbon to open the Backstage view.

2 Click Save As in the Backstage view to display the Save As dialog box.

3 Type `All Seasons Sales Proposal` in the File name text box (Save As dialog box) to change the file name. Do not press the ENTER key after typing the file name because you do not want to close the dialog box at this time.

4 If necessary, navigate to the desired save location (in this case, the Word folder in the CIS 101 folder [or your class folder] on your USB flash drive).

5 Click the Save button (Save As dialog box) to save the document in the selected folder on the selected drive with the entered file name.

Sections

All Word documents have at least one section. A Word document can be divided into any number of sections. During the course of creating a document, you will create a new **section** if you need to change the top margin, bottom margin, page alignment, paper size, page orientation, page number position, or contents or position of headers, footers, or footnotes in just a portion of the document.

The next two pages of the sales proposal require page formatting different from that of the title page. The title page will not have a header or footer; the next two pages will have a header and footer.

When you want to change page formatting for a portion of a document, you create a new section in the document. Each section then may be formatted differently from the others. Thus, the title page formatted with no header or footer will be in one section, and the next two pages of the proposal that will have a header and footer will be in another section.

To Insert a Next Page Section Break

When you insert a section break, you specify whether the new section should begin on a new page. In this project, the title page is separate from the next two pages. Thus, the section break should contain a page break. The following steps insert a next page section break, which instructs Word to begin the new section on a new page in the document.

1
- Press CTRL+END to position the insertion point at the end of the title page, which is the location where you want to insert the next page section break.

- Display the Page Layout tab. Click the Insert Page and Section Breaks button (Page Layout tab | Page Setup group) to display the Insert Page and Section Breaks gallery (Figure 4–19).

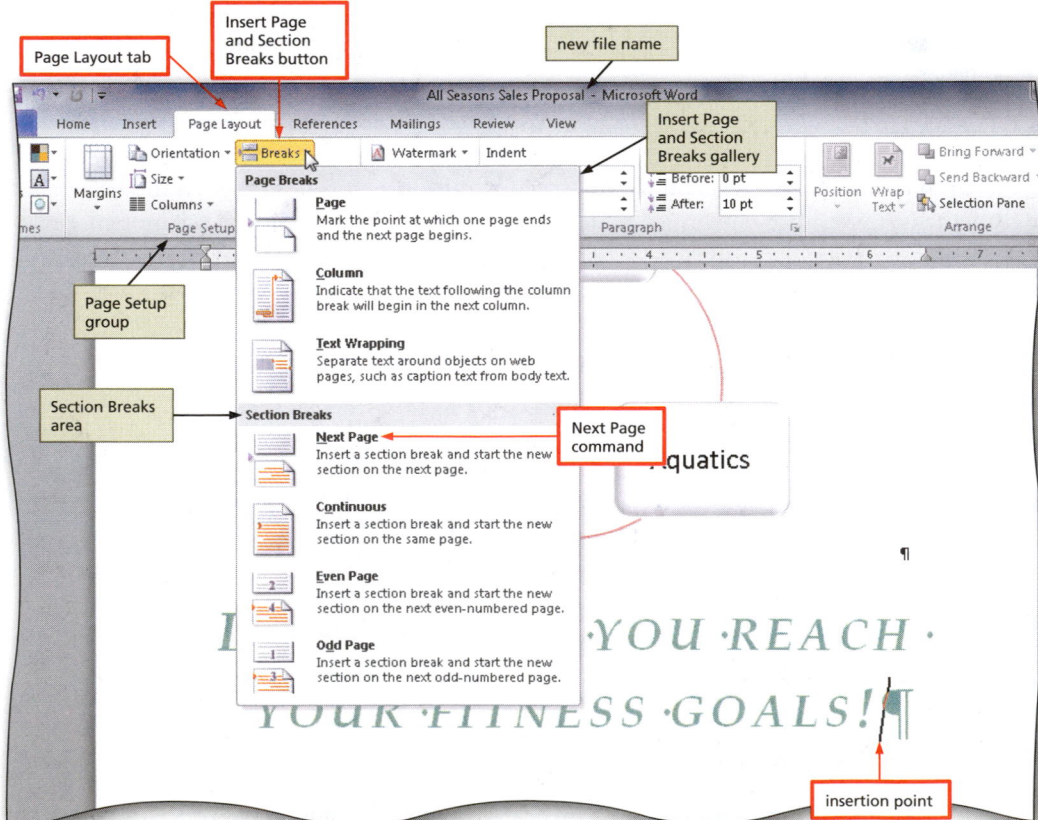

Figure 4–19

• Click Next Page in the Section Breaks area of the Insert Page and Section Breaks gallery to insert a next page section break in the document at the location of the insertion point. If necessary, scroll so that your screen matches Figure 4–20.

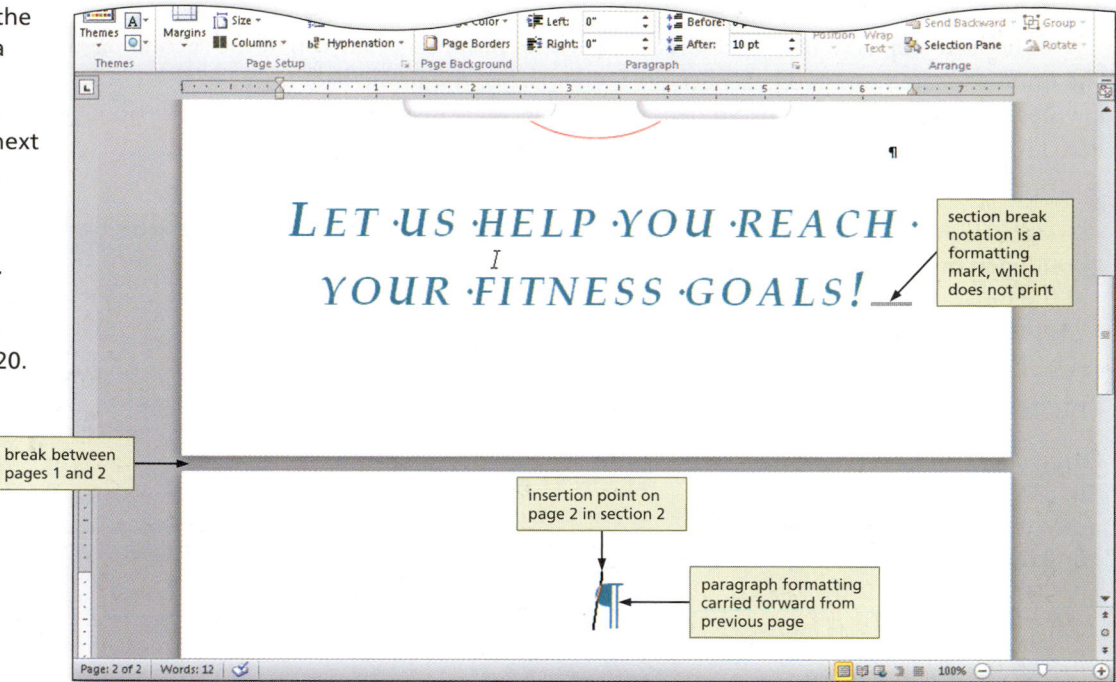

section break notation is a formatting mark, which does not print

break between pages 1 and 2

insertion point on page 2 in section 2

paragraph formatting carried forward from previous page

Figure 4–20

TO DELETE A SECTION BREAK

Word stores all section formatting in the section break. If you wanted to delete a section break and all associated section formatting, you would perform the following tasks.

1. Select the section break notation by dragging through it.

2. Right-click the selection to display a shortcut menu and then click Cut on the shortcut menu to delete the selection.

or

1. Position the insertion point immediately to the left or right of the section break notation.

2. Press the DELETE key to delete a section break to the right of the insertion point or press the BACKSPACE key to delete a section break to the left of the insertion point.

To Clear Formatting

When you create a section break, Word carries forward any formatting at the location of the insertion point to the next section. Thus, the current paragraph is formatted the same as the last line of the title page. In this project, the paragraphs and characters on the second page should return to the Normal style. Thus, the following step clears formatting.

 Display the Home tab. With the insertion point positioned on the paragraph mark on the second page (shown in Figure 4–20), click the Clear Formatting button (Home tab | Font group) to apply the Normal style to the location of the insertion point (shown in Figure 4–21 on the next page).

BTW

Sections
To see the formatting associated with a section, double-click the section break notation or click the Page Setup Dialog Box Launcher (Page Layout tab | Page Setup group) to display the Page Setup dialog box. You can change margin settings and page orientation for a section in the Margins sheet. To change paper sizes for a section, click the Paper tab. The Layout tab allows you to change header and footer specifications and vertical alignment for the section. To add a border to a section, click the Borders button in the Layout sheet.

To Insert a Word Document in an Open Document

The next step is to insert the draft of the sales proposal at the top of the second page of the document. The draft is located on the Data Files for Students. See the inside back cover of this book for instructions on downloading the Data Files for Students, or contact your instructor for information about accessing the required files. The following steps insert an existing Word document in an open document.

 1

- Be sure the insertion point is positioned on the paragraph mark at the top of page 2, which is the location where you want to insert the contents of the Word document.

- Display the Insert tab.

- With your USB flash drive connected to one of the computer's USB ports, click the Insert Object button arrow (Insert tab | Text group) to display the Insert Object menu (Figure 4–21).

Q&A

What if I click the Insert Object button by mistake?

Click the Cancel button (Insert Object dialog box) and then repeat this step.

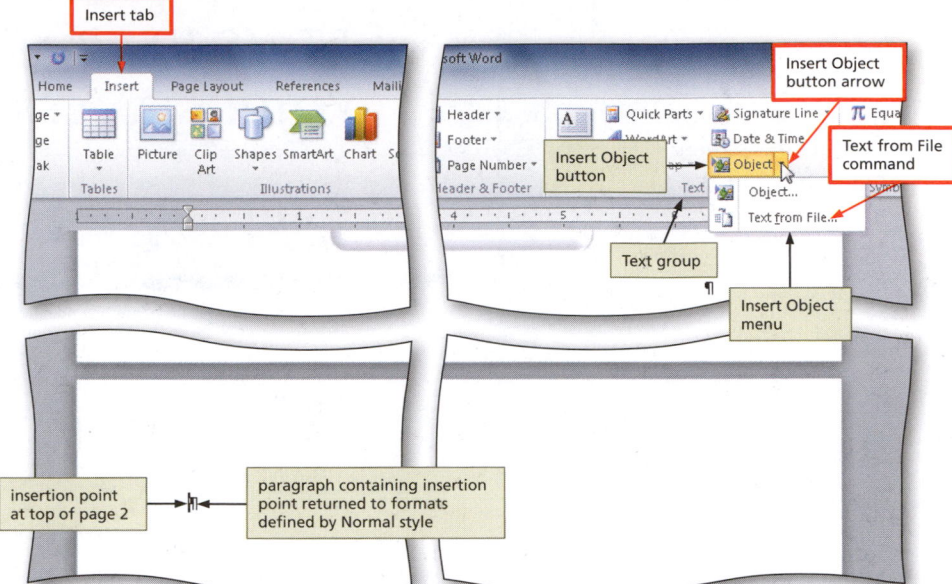

Figure 4–21

2

- Click Text from File on the Insert Object menu to display the Insert File dialog box.

- Navigate to the location of the file to be inserted (in this case, the Chapter 04 folder in the Word folder in the Data Files for Students folder on a USB flash drive).

- Click All Seasons Draft to select the file name (Figure 4–22).

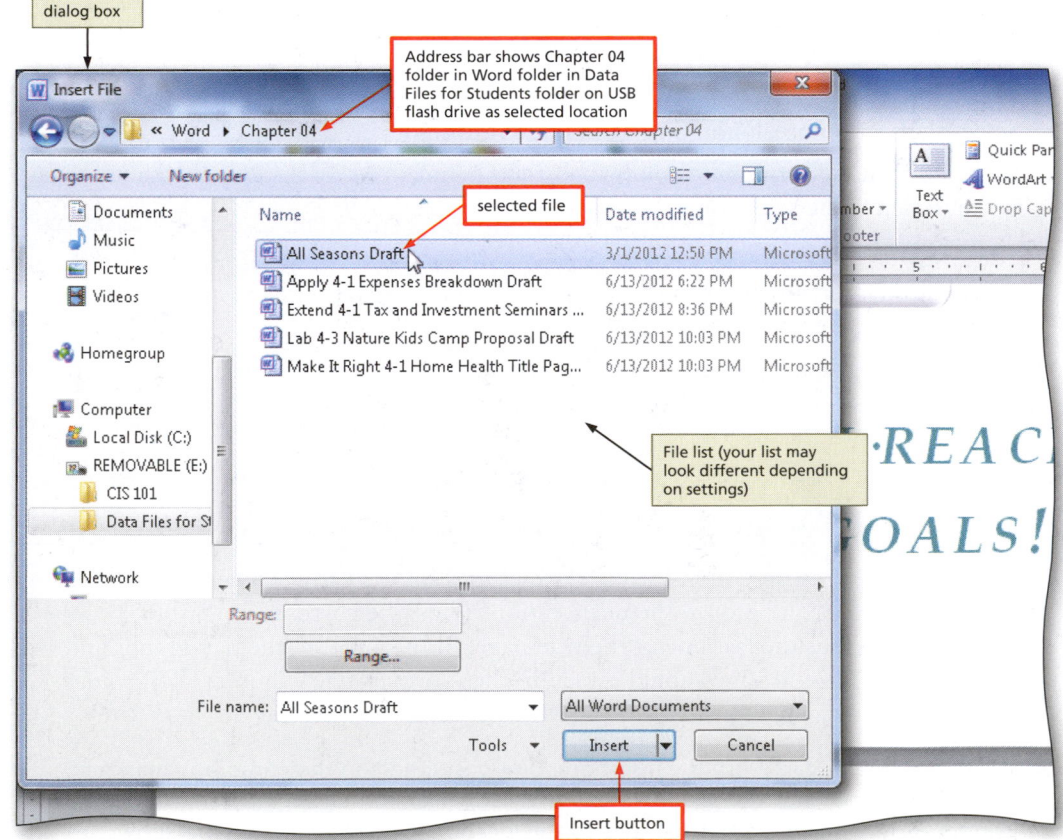

Figure 4–22

3

- Click the Insert button (Insert File dialog box) to insert the file, All Seasons Draft, in the open document at the location of the insertion point.

Q&A Where is the insertion point now?

When you insert a file in an open document, Word positions the insertion point at the end of the inserted document.

- Press SHIFT+F5 to position the insertion point on line 1 of page 2, which was its location prior to inserting the new Word document (Figure 4–23).

Q&A What is the purpose of SHIFT+F5?

The shortcut key, SHIFT+F5, positions the insertion point at your last editing location. Word remembers your last three editing locations, which means you can press this shortcut key repeatedly to return to one of your three most recent editing locations.

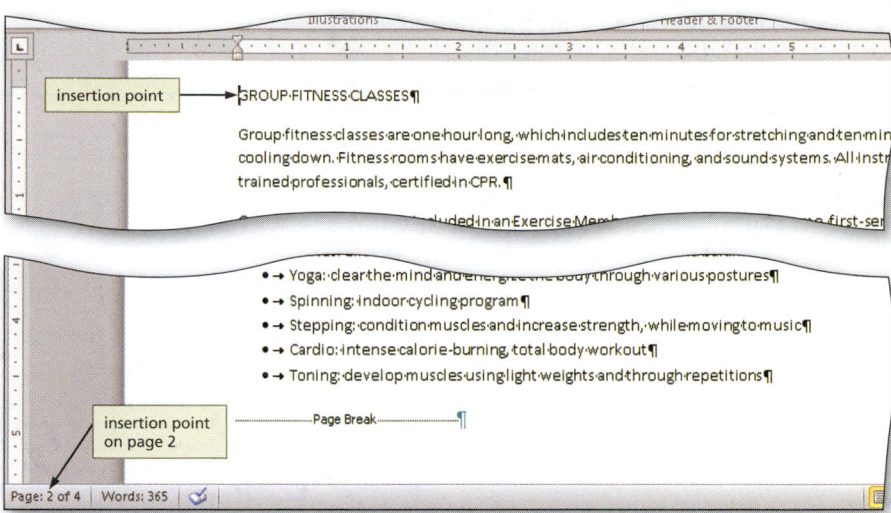

Figure 4–23

Other Ways

1. Click Insert Object button (Insert tab | Text group), click Create from File tab (Object dialog box), click | Browse button, locate file, click Insert button (Browse dialog box), click OK button (Object dialog box)

To Print Specific Pages in a Document

The title page is the first page of the proposal. The body of the proposal spans the second and third pages. The following steps print a hard copy of only the body of the proposal, that is, pages 2 and 3.

1

- Click File on the Ribbon to open the Backstage view and then click the Print tab in the Backstage view to display the Print gallery.

- Verify that the printer name that appears on the Printer Status button will print a hard copy of the document. If necessary, click the Printer Status button to display a list of available printer options and then click the desired printer to change the selected printer.

- Type 2–3 in the Pages text box in the Settings area of the Print gallery (Figure 4–24).

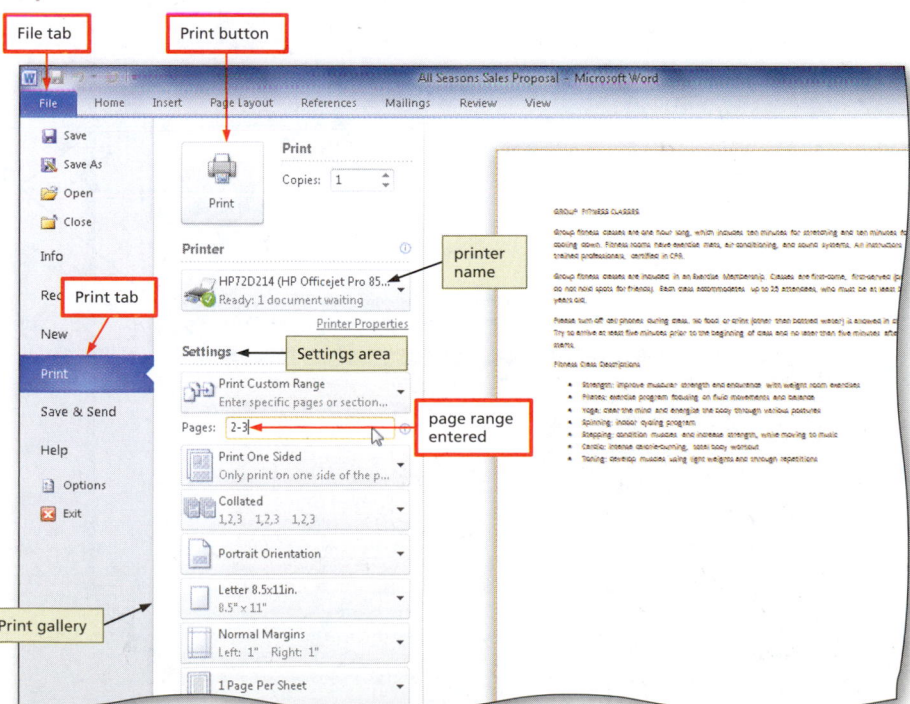

Figure 4–24

2

● Click the Print button to print the inserted draft of the sales proposal (Figure 4–25).

Q&A How would I print pages from a certain point to the end of a document?

You would enter the page number followed by a dash in the Pages text box. For example, 5- will print from page 5 to the end of the document. To print up to a certain page, put the dash first (e.g., -5 will print pages 1 through 5).

Q&A Why does my document wrap on different words than Figure 4–25?

Differences in wordwrap may be related to the printer used by your computer.

Q&A Why does my screen show the document has four pages?

You may have an extra blank page at the end of the document. This blank page will be deleted later in the chapter.

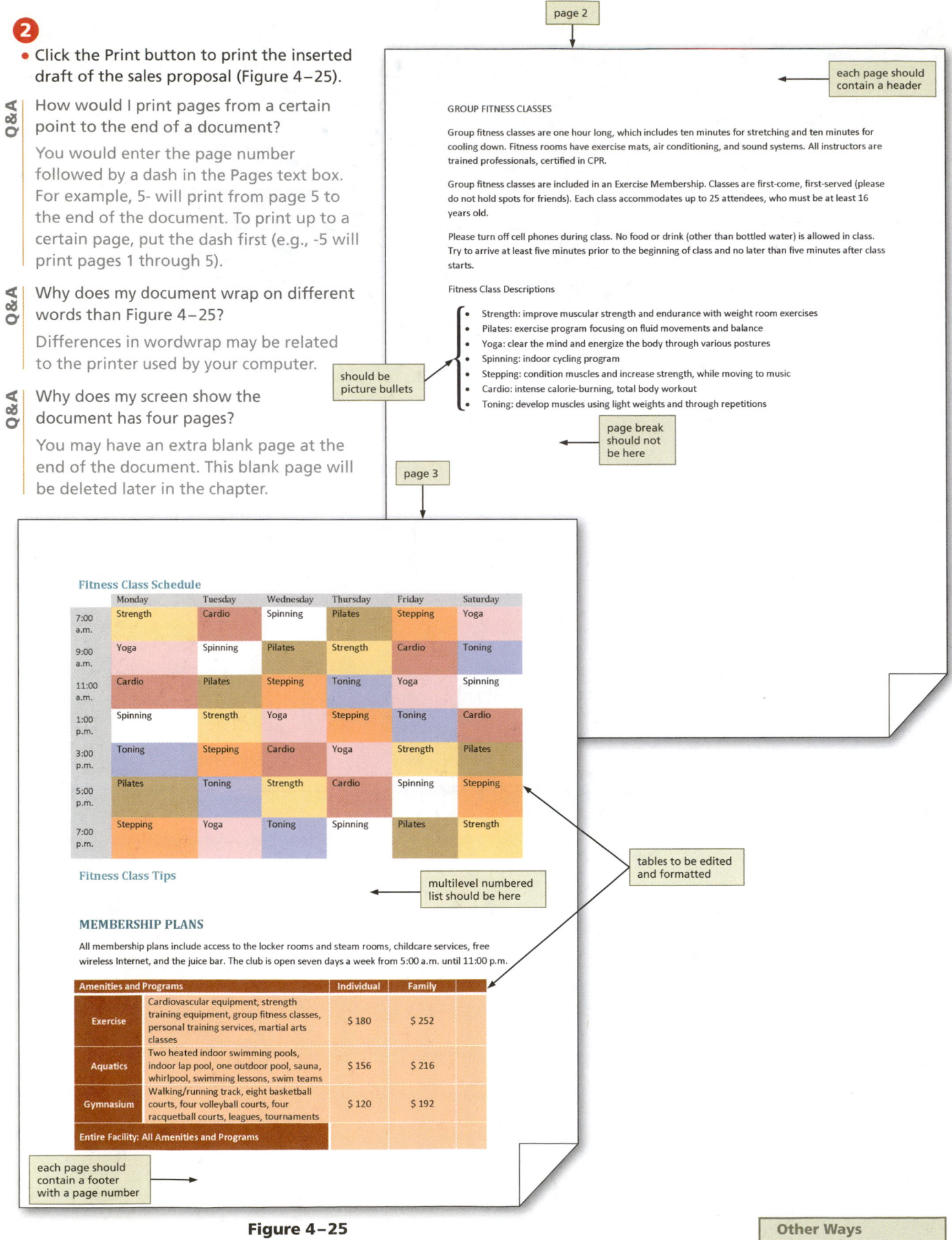

page 2

each page should contain a header

GROUP FITNESS CLASSES

Group fitness classes are one hour long, which includes ten minutes for stretching and ten minutes for cooling down. Fitness rooms have exercise mats, air conditioning, and sound systems. All instructors are trained professionals, certified in CPR.

Group fitness classes are included in an Exercise Membership. Classes are first-come, first-served (please do not hold spots for friends). Each class accommodates up to 25 attendees, who must be at least 16 years old.

Please turn off cell phones during class. No food or drink (other than bottled water) is allowed in class. Try to arrive at least five minutes prior to the beginning of class and no later than five minutes after class starts.

Fitness Class Descriptions

- Strength: improve muscular strength and endurance with weight room exercises
- Pilates: exercise program focusing on fluid movements and balance
- Yoga: clear the mind and energize the body through various postures
- Spinning: indoor cycling program
- Stepping: condition muscles and increase strength, while moving to music
- Cardio: intense calorie-burning, total body workout
- Toning: develop muscles using light weights and through repetitions

should be picture bullets

page break should not be here

page 3

Fitness Class Schedule

	Monday	Tuesday	Wednesday	Thursday	Friday	Saturday
7:00 a.m.	Strength	Cardio	Spinning	Pilates	Stepping	Yoga
9:00 a.m.	Yoga	Spinning	Pilates	Strength	Cardio	Toning
11:00 a.m.	Cardio	Pilates	Stepping	Toning	Yoga	Spinning
1:00 p.m.	Spinning	Strength	Yoga	Stepping	Toning	Cardio
3:00 p.m.	Toning	Stepping	Cardio	Yoga	Strength	Pilates
5:00 p.m.	Pilates	Toning	Strength	Cardio	Spinning	Stepping
7:00 p.m.	Stepping	Yoga	Toning	Spinning	Pilates	Strength

Fitness Class Tips

multilevel numbered list should be here

tables to be edited and formatted

MEMBERSHIP PLANS

All membership plans include access to the locker rooms and steam rooms, childcare services, free wireless Internet, and the juice bar. The club is open seven days a week from 5:00 a.m. until 11:00 p.m.

Amenities and Programs		Individual	Family	
Exercise	Cardiovascular equipment, strength training equipment, group fitness classes, personal training services, martial arts classes	$ 180	$ 252	
Aquatics	Two heated indoor swimming pools, indoor lap pool, one outdoor pool, sauna, whirlpool, swimming lessons, swim teams	$ 156	$ 216	
Gymnasium	Walking/running track, eight basketball courts, four volleyball courts, four racquetball courts, leagues, tournaments	$ 120	$ 192	
Entire Facility: All Amenities and Programs				

each page should contain a footer with a page number

Figure 4–25

To Delete a Page Break

After reviewing the draft in Figure 4–25, you notice it contains a page break below the bulleted list. This page break should not be in the document. The following steps delete a page break.

1
- To select the page break notation, position the mouse pointer to the left of the page break and then click when the mouse pointer changes to a right-pointing arrow (Figure 4–26).

2
- Press the DELETE key to remove the page break from the document (shown in Figure 4–27 on the next page).

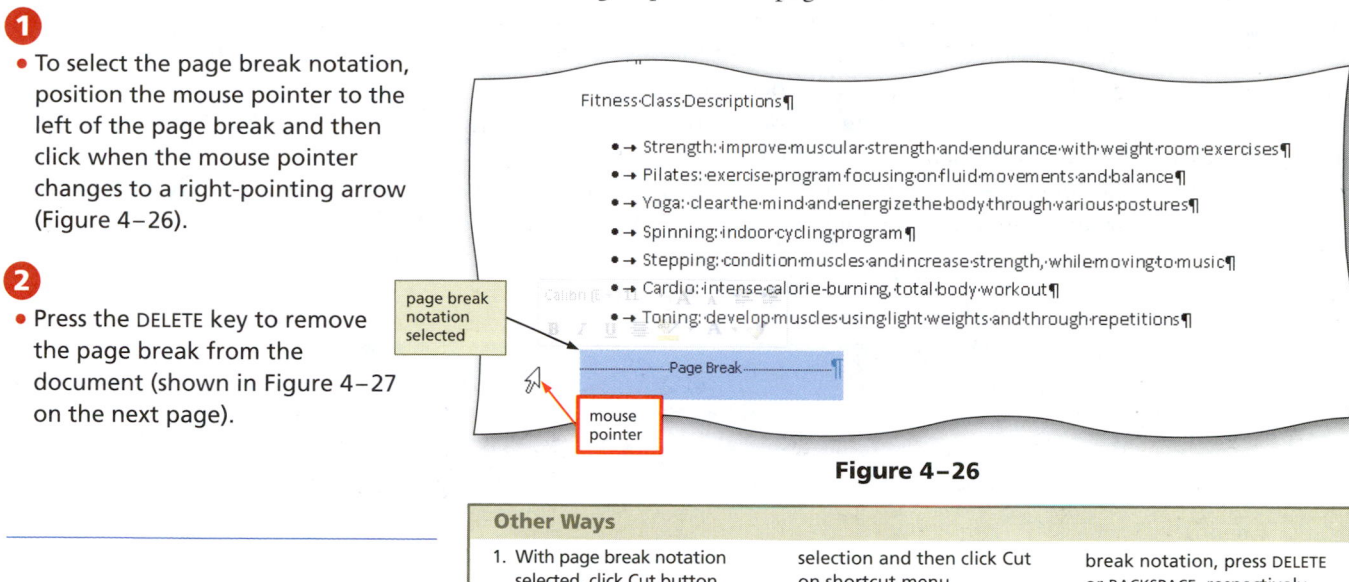

Figure 4–26

Other Ways

1. With page break notation selected, click Cut button (Home tab | Clipboard group)

2. With page break notation selected, right-click

selection and then click Cut on shortcut menu

3. With the insertion point to the left or right of the page

break notation, press DELETE or BACKSPACE, respectively

TO MODIFY THE DEFAULT FONT SETTINGS

You can change the default font so that the current document and all future documents use the new font settings. That is, if you quit Word, restart the computer, and restart Word, documents you create will use the new default font. If you wanted to change the default font from 11-point Calibri to another font, font style, font size, font color, and/or font effects, you would perform the following steps.

1. Display the Font dialog box.

2. Make desired changes to the font settings in the Font dialog box.

3. Click the Set As Default button (shown in Figure 4–15 on page WD 217) to change the default settings to those specified in Step 2.

4. When the Microsoft Word dialog box is displayed, select the desired option button and then click the Yes button.

TO RESET THE DEFAULT FONT SETTINGS

To change the font settings back to the default, you would follow the above steps, using the default font settings when performing Step 2. If you do not remember the default settings, you would perform the following steps to restore the original Normal style settings.

1. Quit Word.

2. Use Windows Explorer to locate the normal.dotm file (be sure that hidden files and folders are displayed and include system and hidden files in your search), which is the file that contains default font and other settings.

3. Rename the normal.dotm file to oldnormal.dotm file so that the normal.dotm file no longer exists.

4. Start Word, which will re-create a normal.dotm file using the original default settings.

BTW

Certification
The Microsoft Office Specialist (MOS) program provides an opportunity for you to obtain a valuable industry credential — proof that you have the Word 2010 skills required by employers. For more information, visit the Word 2010 Certification Web page (scsite.com/wd2010/cert).

To Change Theme Fonts

The next step is to change the font used for the text in the document because you want a different look for the text. If text is entered using the headings and body text fonts, you easily can change the font in the entire document by changing the font set. A **font set** defines one font for headings and another for body text. The Office font set uses the Cambria font for headings and the Calibri font for body text. In Word, you can select from more than 40 predefined, coordinated font sets to give the document's text a new look.

If you previously changed a font using buttons on the Ribbon or Mini toolbar, Word will not alter those when you change the font set because changes to the font set are not applied to individually changed fonts. This means the font of the title on the title page will remain as Berlin Sans FB Demi when you change the font set. The following steps change the font set to Apothecary, which uses the Book Antiqua font for headings and the Century Gothic font for body text.

1
- Display the Home tab.

- Click the Change Styles button (Home tab | Styles group) to display the Change Styles menu.

- Point to Fonts on the Change Styles menu to display the Fonts gallery.

- Scroll through the Fonts gallery until Apothecary is displayed and then point to Apothecary to display a live preview of the selected font set (Figure 4–27).

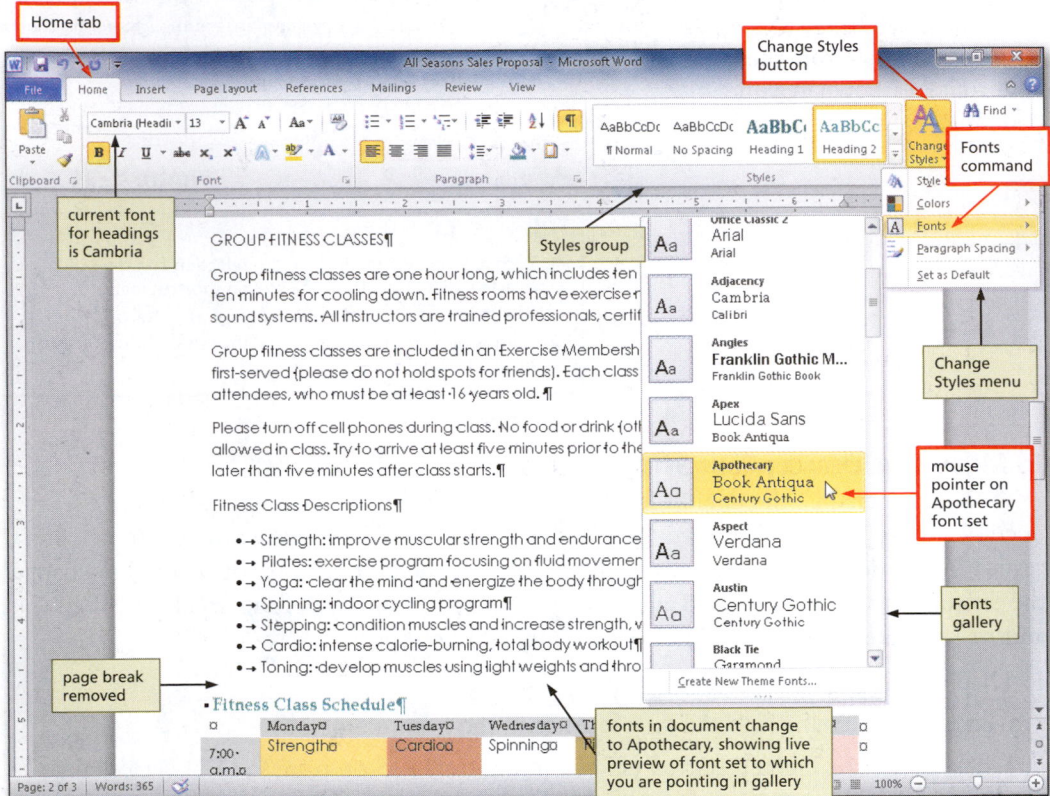

Figure 4–27

 Experiment
- Point to various font sets in the Fonts gallery and watch the fonts of text in the document change.

2
- Click Apothecary in the Fonts gallery to change the document theme fonts.

Q&A What if I want to return to the original font set?

You would click the Change Styles button, click Fonts on the Change Styles menu, and then click Office in the Fonts gallery.

Other Ways

1. Click Theme Fonts button (Page Layout tab | Themes group), select desired font set

To Apply a Heading Quick Style

Word has many built-in, or predefined, styles called Quick Styles that you can use to format text. Three of the Quick Styles are for headings: Heading 1 for the major headings and Heading 2 and Heading 3 for minor headings. In the All Seasons Draft, all headings except for the first two were formatted using heading styles. The following steps apply the Heading 1 style to the paragraph containing the text, GROUP FITNESS CLASSES, and the Heading 2 style to the paragraph containing the text, Fitness Class Descriptions.

1 Position the insertion point in the paragraph to be formatted to the Heading 1 style, in this case, the first line on the second page with the text, GROUP FITNESS CLASSES.

2 Click Heading 1 in the Quick Style gallery (Home tab | Styles group) to apply the selected style to the paragraph containing the insertion point.

Q&A Why did a square appear on the screen near the left edge of the paragraph formatted with the Heading 1 style?

The square is a nonprinting character, like the paragraph mark, that indicates text to its right has a special paragraph format applied to it.

3 Position the insertion point in the paragraph to be formatted to the Heading 2 style, in this case, the line above the bulleted list with the text, Fitness Class Descriptions.

4 Click Heading 2 in the Quick Style gallery (Home tab | Styles group) to apply the selected style to the paragraph containing the insertion point (Figure 4–28).

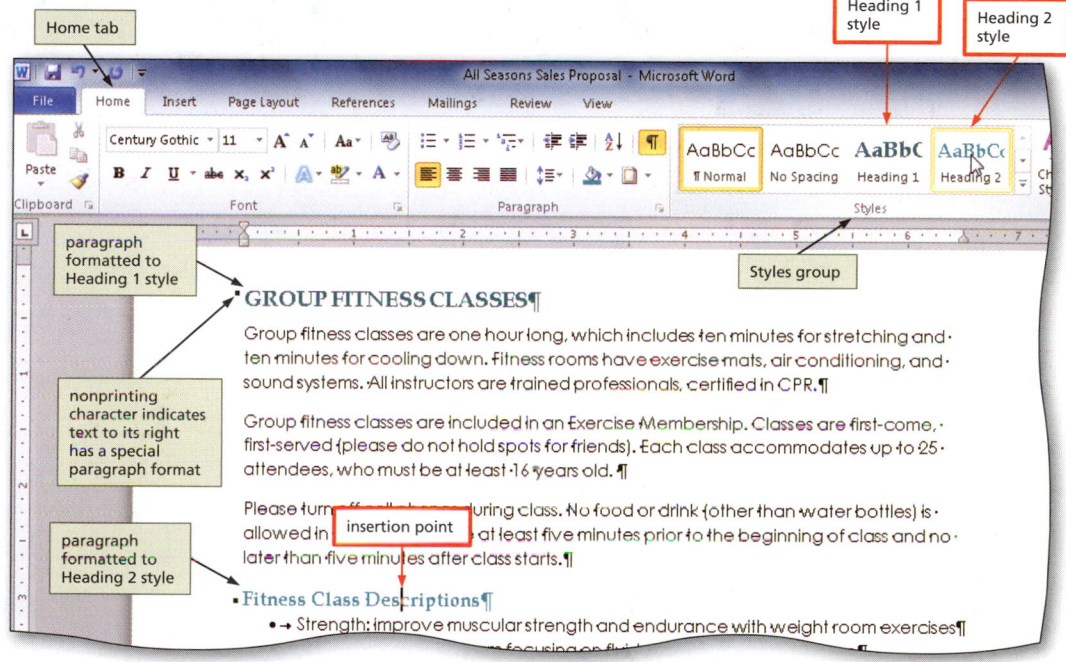

Figure 4–28

To Change Spacing before and after a Paragraph

The next step is to adjust spacing above and below the current paragraph, that is, the heading above the bulleted list. This paragraph is formatted using the Heading 2 style, which places 10 points of space above the paragraph and no space below the paragraph. You would like this paragraph, and all other paragraphs formatted using the Heading 2 style, to have 12 points of space above them and 6 points of space below them. Thus, the following steps adjust the spacing before and after a paragraph.

1 Display the Page Layout tab. Click the Spacing Before box up arrow (Page Layout tab | Paragraph group) so that 12 pt is displayed in the Spacing Before box.

2 Click the Spacing After box up arrow (Page Layout tab | Paragraph group) so that 6 pt is displayed in the Spacing After box.

To Update a Style to Match a Selection

You want all paragraphs formatted in the Heading 2 style in the proposal to use this adjusted spacing. Thus, the following steps update the Heading 2 style so that this adjusted spacing is applied to all Heading 2 paragraphs in the document.

1 If necessary, position the insertion point in the paragraph containing the style to be updated.

2 Display the Home tab. Right-click Heading 2 in the Quick Style gallery (Home tab | Styles group) to display a shortcut menu (Figure 4–29).

3 Click Update Heading 2 to Match Selection on the shortcut menu to update the Heading 2 style to reflect the settings at the location of the insertion point.

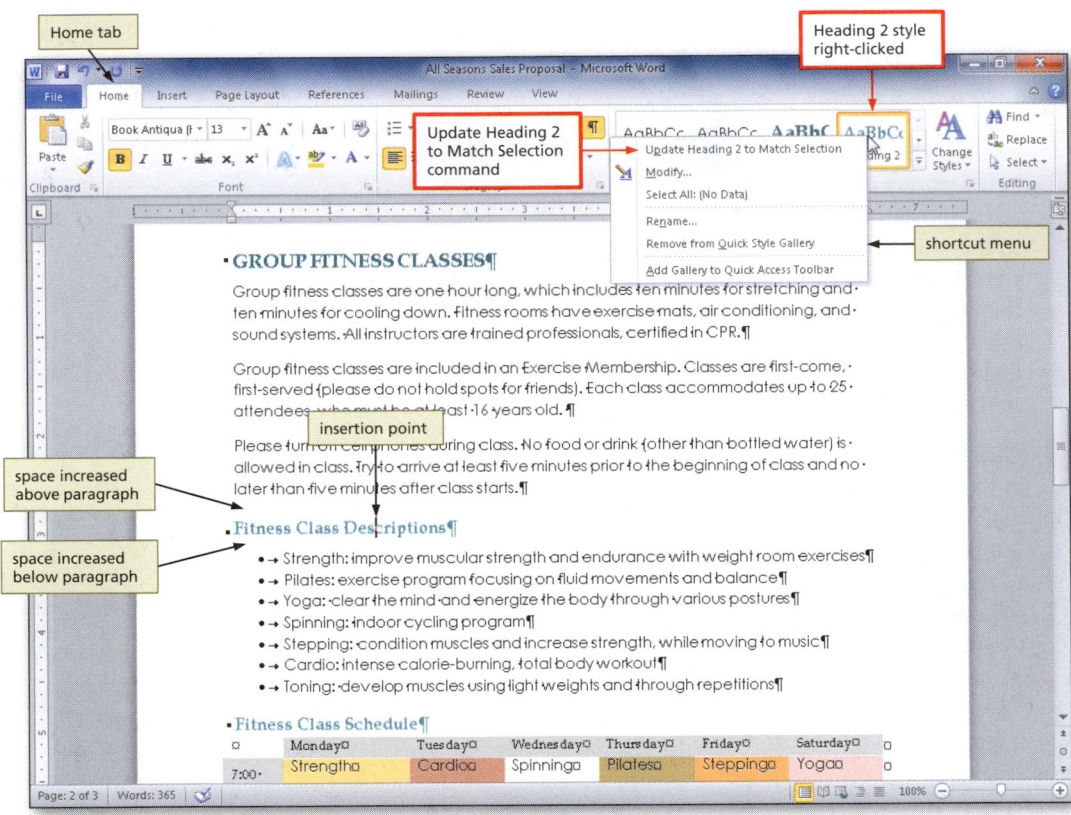

Figure 4–29

BTW

Headers and Footers
If a portion of a header or footer does not print, it may be in a nonprintable area. Check the printer manual to see how close the printer can print to the edge of the paper. Then, click the Page Setup Dialog Box Launcher (Page Layout tab | Page Setup group), click the Layout tab (Page Setup dialog box), adjust the From edge text box to a value that is larger than the printer's minimum margin setting, click the OK button, and then print the document again.

Creating Headers and Footers

A **header** is text that prints at the top of each page in the document. A **footer** is text that prints at the bottom of each page. In this proposal, you want the header and footer to appear on each page after the title page; that is, you do not want the header and footer on the title page. Recall that the title page is in a separate section from the rest of the sales proposal. Thus, the header and footer should not be in section 1, but they should be in section 2. The steps on the following pages explain how to create a header and footer in section 2 only.

To Insert a Formatted Header Different from the Previous Header

Word provides several built-in preformatted header designs for you to insert in documents. The following steps insert a formatted header in section 2 of the sales proposal.

1

- Display the Insert tab. Click the Header button (Insert tab | Header & Footer group) and then click Edit Header in the Header gallery to switch to the header for section 2.

- If the Link to Previous button (Header & Footer Tools Design tab | Navigation group) is selected, click it to deselect the button because you do not want the header in this section to be copied to the previous section (that is, the header should not be on the title page).

- Click the Header button (Header & Footer Tools Design tab | Header & Footer group) to display the Header gallery (Figure 4–30).

 Experiment

- Scroll through the list of built-in headers to see the variety of available formatted header designs.

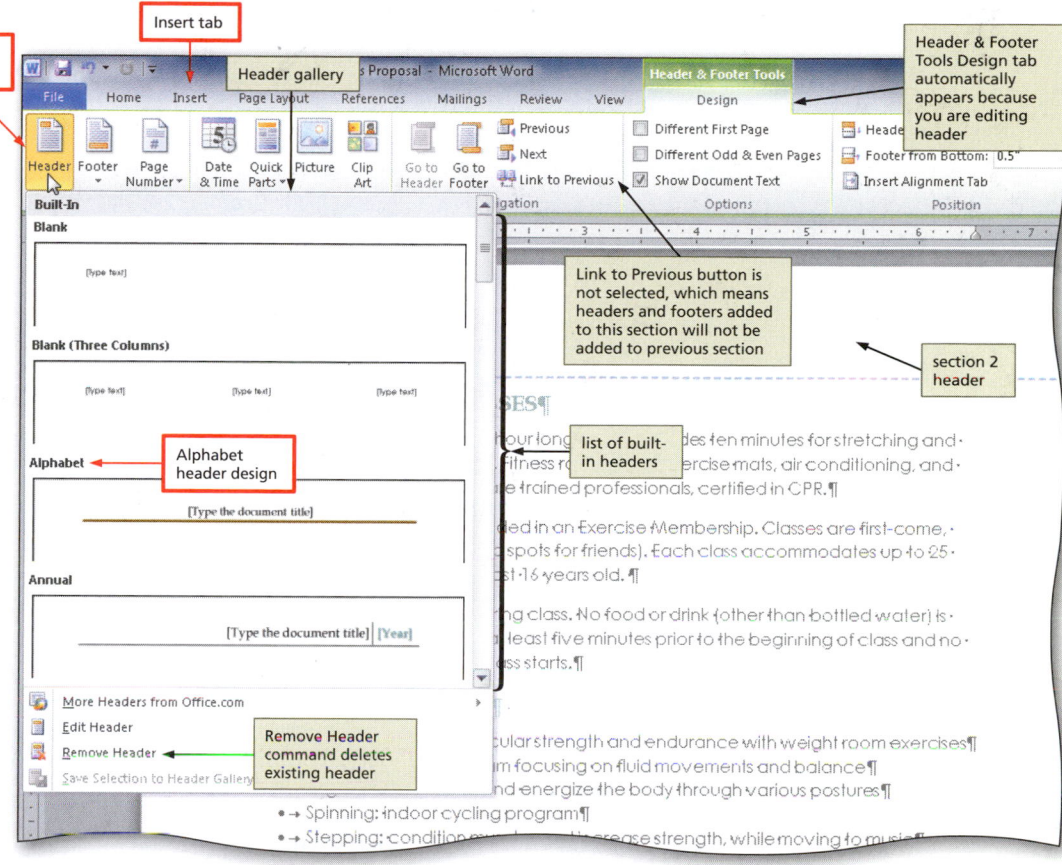

Figure 4–30

2

- Scroll to and then click the Alphabet header design in the Header gallery to insert the formatted header in the header of section 2, which contains a content control (Figure 4–31).

Q&A

What is a content control?

A **content control** is an object that contains instructions for filling in text and graphics.

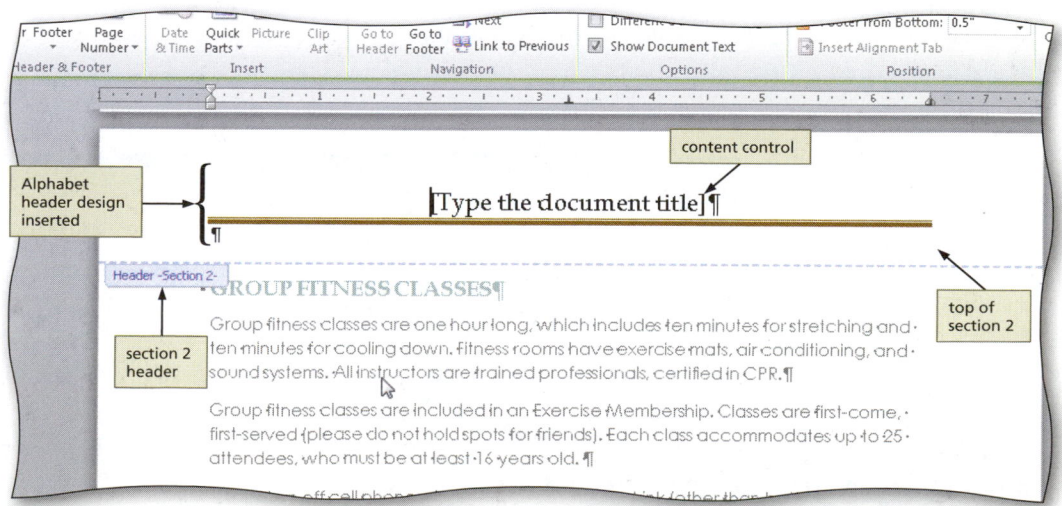

Figure 4–31

3

● Click the content control, Type the document title, to select it and then type **All Seasons Health Club** in the content control (Figure 4–32).

Q&A How would I delete a header?

You would click Remove Header in the Header gallery.

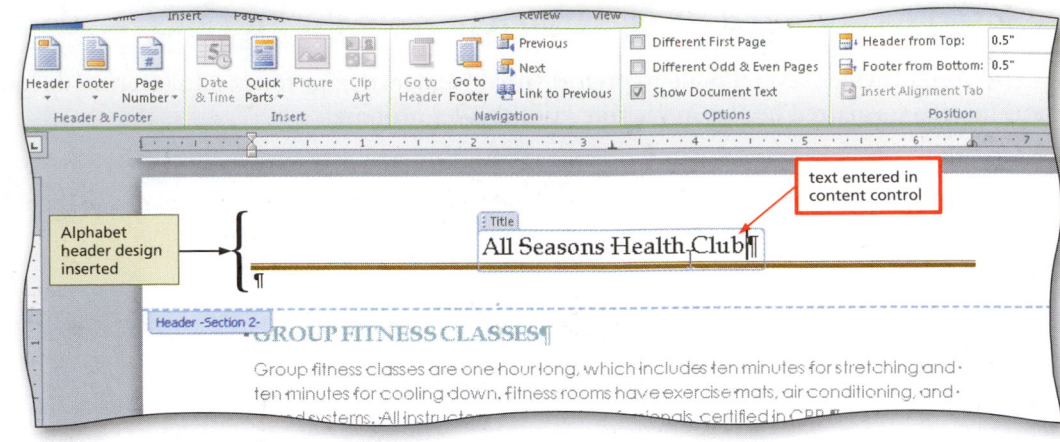

Figure 4–32

Other Ways

1. Click Header button (Insert tab | Header & Footer group), select desired header in list

2. Click Quick Parts button (Insert tab | Text group),

   click Building Blocks Organizer on Quick Parts menu, select desired header (Building Blocks Organizer dialog box), click Insert button

To Insert a Formatted Footer

The next step is to insert the footer. Word provides the same built-in preformatted footer designs as header designs. The footer design that corresponds to the header just inserted contains text at the left margin and a page number at the right margin. The following steps insert a formatted footer in section 2 of the sales proposal that corresponds to the header just inserted.

1 Click the Footer button (Header & Footer Tools Design tab | Header & Footer group) to display the Footer gallery.

2 Click the Alphabet footer design to insert the formatted footer in the footer of section 2.

3 Click the content control, Type text, and then type **CALL 555-2283 TO JOIN!** in the content control (Figure 4–33).

Q&A Why is the page number a 2?

The page number is 2 because, by default, Word begins numbering pages from the beginning of the document.

BTW

Linking Sections
If you wanted the same header or footer to appear in multiple sections, you would select the Link to Previous button (Header & Footer Tools Design tab | Navigation group).

BTW

Page Numbers
If Word displays {PAGE} instead of the actual page number, press ALT+F9 to turn off field codes. If Word prints {PAGE} instead of the page number, open the Backstage view, click Options, click Advanced in the left pane, scroll to the Print area, remove the check mark from the 'Print field codes instead of their values' check box, and then click the OK button.

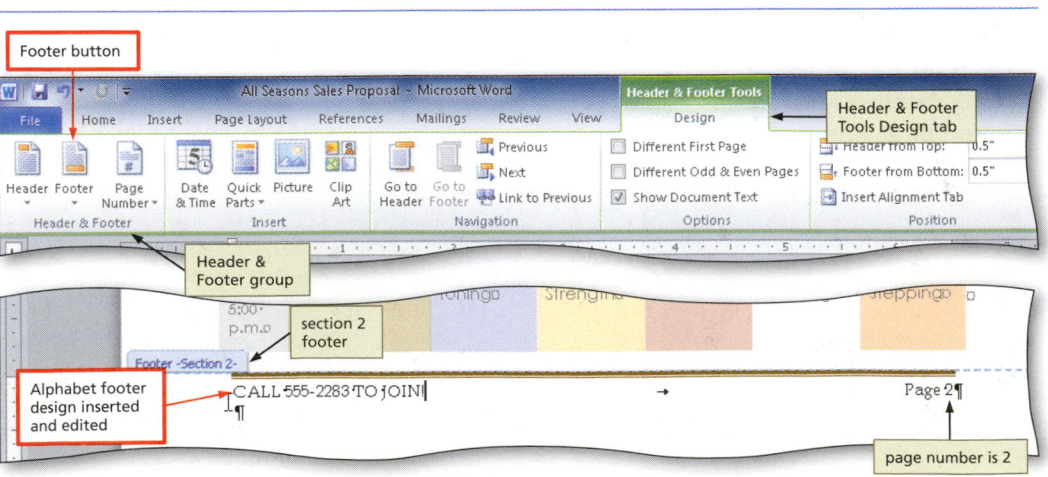

Figure 4–33

To Format Page Numbers to Start at a Different Number

On the page after the title page in the proposal, you want to begin numbering with a number 1, instead of a 2 as shown in Figure 4–33. Thus, you need to instruct Word to begin numbering the pages in section 2 with the number 1. The following steps format the page numbers so that they start at a different number.

● Click the Insert Page Number button (Header & Footer Tools Design tab | Header & Footer group) to display the Insert Page Number menu (Figure 4–34).

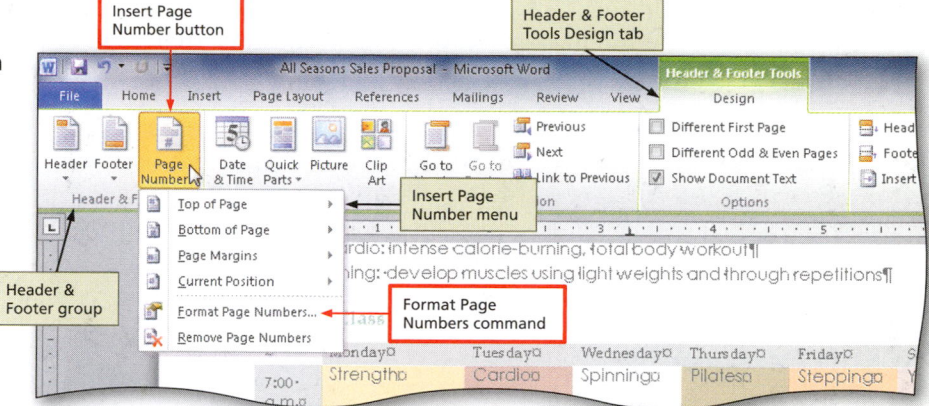

Figure 4–34

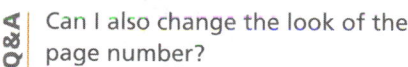

● Click Format Page Numbers on the Insert Page Number menu to display the Page Number Format dialog box.

● Click Start at in the Page numbering area (Page Number Format dialog box), which displays a 1 by default as the starting page number (Figure 4–35).

Q&A Can I also change the look of the page number?

Yes. Click the Number format box arrow (Page Number Format dialog box) for a list of page number variations.

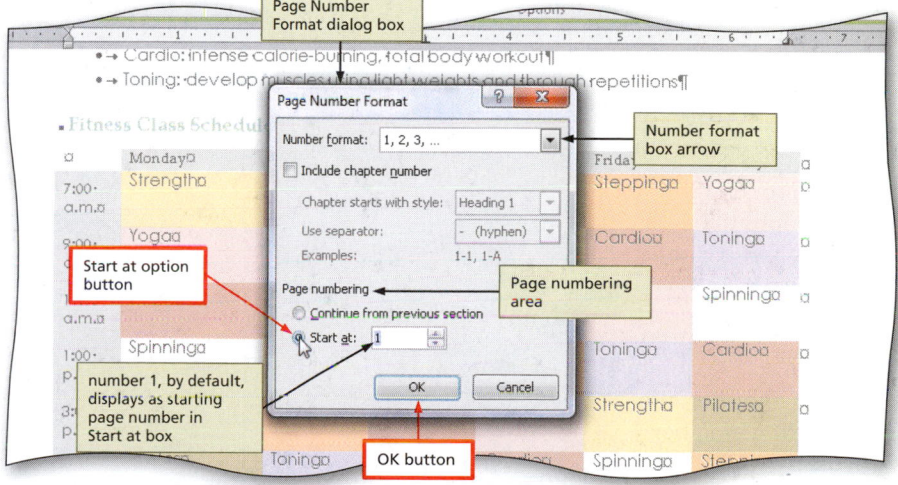

Figure 4–35

● Click the OK button to change the starting page number for section 2 to the number 1 (Figure 4–36).

● Click the Close Header and Footer button (Header & Footer Tools Design tab | Close group) to close the header and footer.

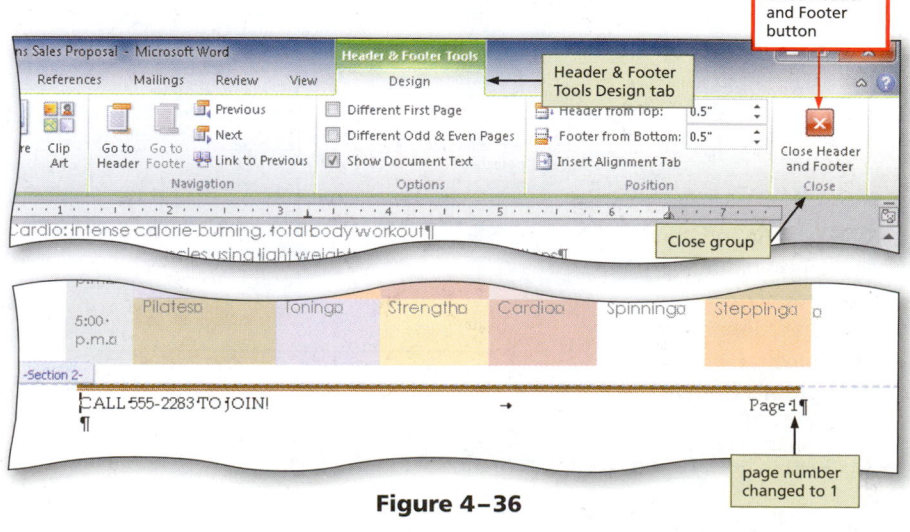

Figure 4–36

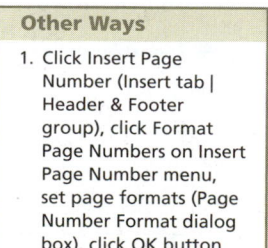

Other Ways

1. Click Insert Page Number (Insert tab | Header & Footer group), click Format Page Numbers on Insert Page Number menu, set page formats (Page Number Format dialog box), click OK button

Editing and Formatting Lists

The finished sales proposal in this chapter has two lists: a bulleted list and a numbered list (shown in Figures 4–1b and 4–1c on page WD 203). The bulleted list is in alphabetical (sorted) order, the first word of each list item is emphasized, and the bullets are graphical instead of simple round dots. The numbered listed has multiple levels for each numbered item. The following pages illustrate steps used to edit and format the lists in the proposal:

1. Sort a list of paragraphs.
2. Format the first word in the first list item and then copy the format to the first word in each of the remaining list items.
3. Customize bullets in a list of paragraphs.
4. Create a multilevel numbered list.

To Sort Paragraphs

The next step is to alphabetize the paragraphs in the bulleted list. In Word, you can arrange paragraphs in alphabetic, numeric, or date order based on the first character in each paragraph. Ordering characters in this manner is called **sorting**. The following steps sort paragraphs.

- If necessary, scroll to display the paragraphs to be sorted.

- Drag through the paragraphs to be sorted, in this case, the bulleted list.

- Click the Sort button (Home tab | Paragraph group) to display the Sort Text dialog box (Figure 4–37).

Q&A

What does ascending mean?

Ascending means to sort in alphabetic, numeric, or earliest-to-latest date order.

- Click the OK button (Sort Text dialog box) to instruct Word to alphabetize the selected paragraphs (shown in Figure 4–38).

- Click anywhere to remove the selection from the text.

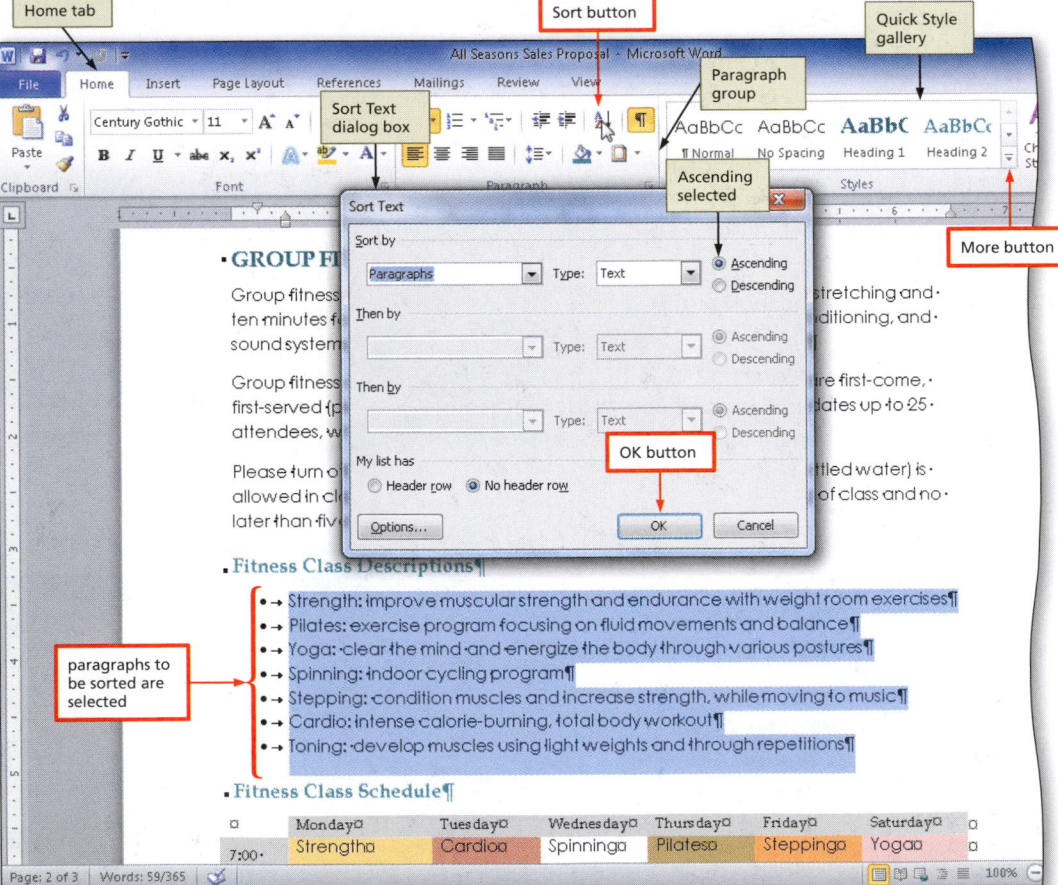

Figure 4–37

To Apply a Quick Style

The first word in each list item is formatted in bold, blue, and italic. Although you could apply formatting using buttons in the Font group on the Ribbon, it is more efficient to use the Intense Emphasis style. If you use a style and decide at a later time that you want to modify the formatting, you simply modify the style and Word will apply the changes to all text formatted with that style. Thus, the following steps format a word using a Quick Style.

1 Position the insertion point in the word to be formatted (in this case, the word, Cardio, in the first list item).

2 Click the More button in the Quick Style gallery (shown in Figure 4–37) to expand the gallery and then point to Intense Emphasis in the Quick Style gallery to see a live preview of the selected format applied to the word containing the insertion point in the document (Figure 4–38).

3 Click Intense Emphasis in the Quick Style gallery to apply the selected style to the word containing the insertion point.

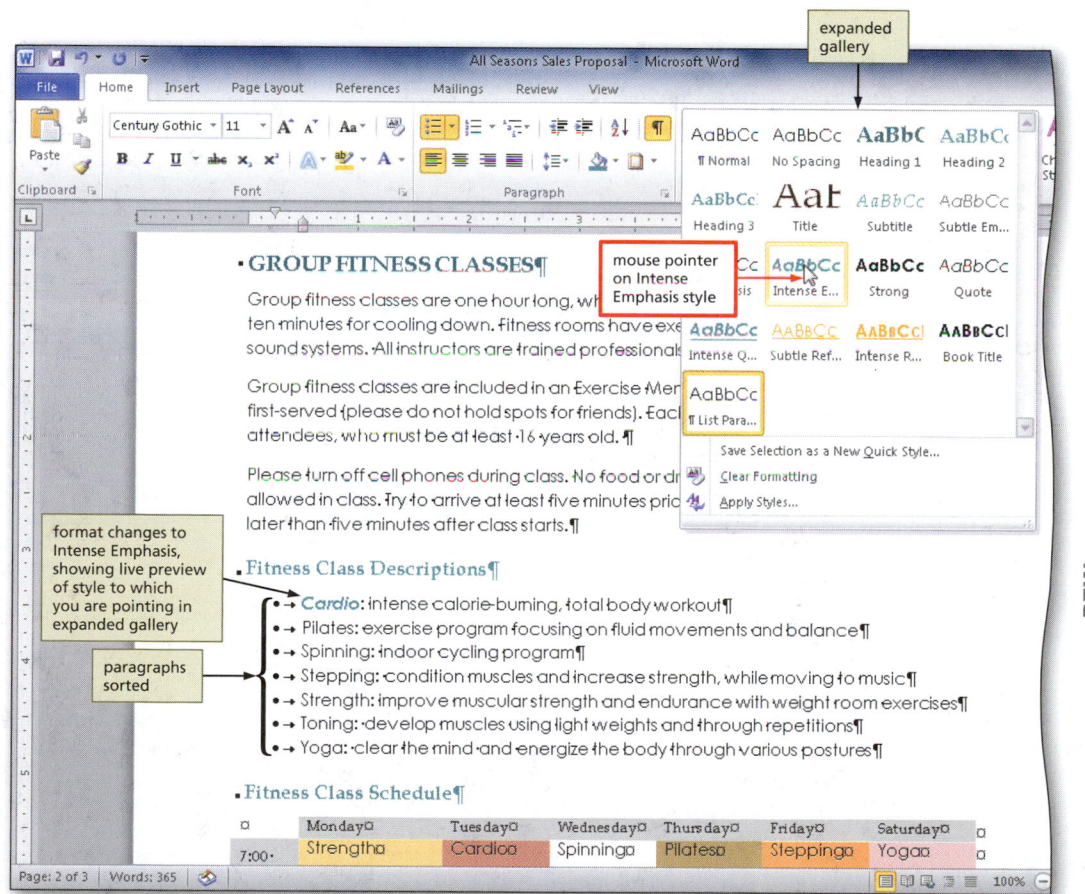

Figure 4–38

BTW

Format Painter
If you also want to copy paragraph formatting, such as alignment and line spacing, select the paragraph mark at the end of the paragraph prior to clicking the Format Painter button. If you want to copy only character formatting, such as fonts and font sizes, do not include the paragraph mark in your selected text.

To Use the Format Painter Button

The first word in each of the remaining list items is to be formatted the same as the first word in the first list item. Instead of selecting each word one at a time and then formatting it, you will copy the format from the first word to the remaining words. The steps on the next page copy formatting.

1

● Position the insertion point in the text that contains the formatting you wish to copy (in this case, the word, Cardio).

● Double-click the Format Painter button (Home tab | Clipboard group) to turn on the format painter.

Why double-click the Format Painter button?

To copy formats to only one other location, click the Format Painter button (Home tab | Clipboard group) once. If you want to copy formatting to multiple locations, however, double-click the Format Painter button so that the format painter remains active until you turn it off.

● Move the mouse pointer to where you want to copy the formatting (the word, Pilates, in this case) and notice that the format painter is active (Figure 4–39).

How can I tell if the format painter is active?

The mouse pointer has a paintbrush attached to it when the format painter is active.

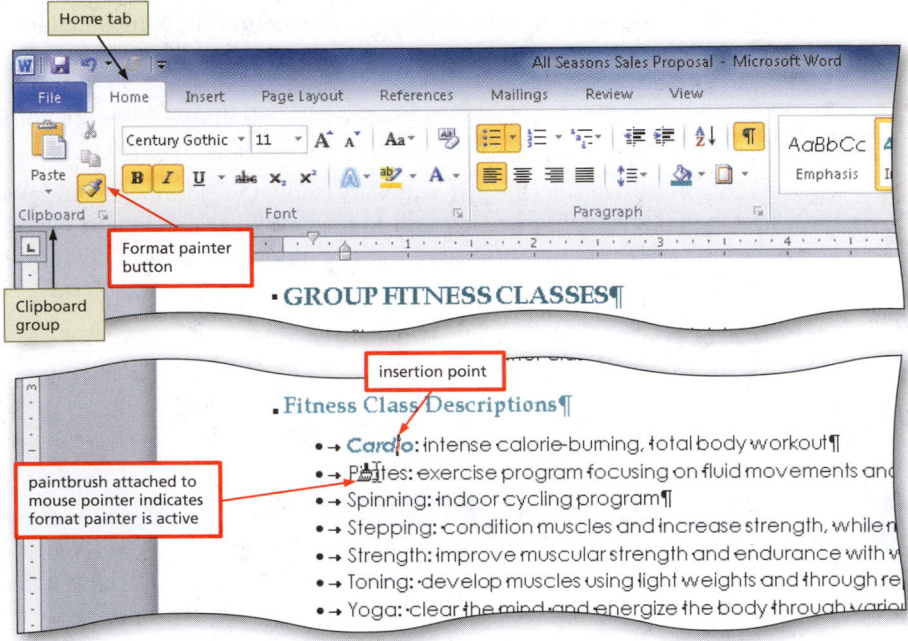

Figure 4–39

2

● Click the first word in the next list item (the word, Pilates, in this case) to paste the copied format to the selected text.

What if the Format Painter button no longer is selected?

Repeat Step 1.

3

● Repeat Step 2 for the remaining first words in the list items: Spinning, Stepping, Strength, Toning, and Yoga.

● Click the Format Painter button (Home tab | Clipboard group) to turn off the format painter (Figure 4–40).

How would I copy formatting to a group of words or paragraphs?

Instead of clicking the text, you would select it.

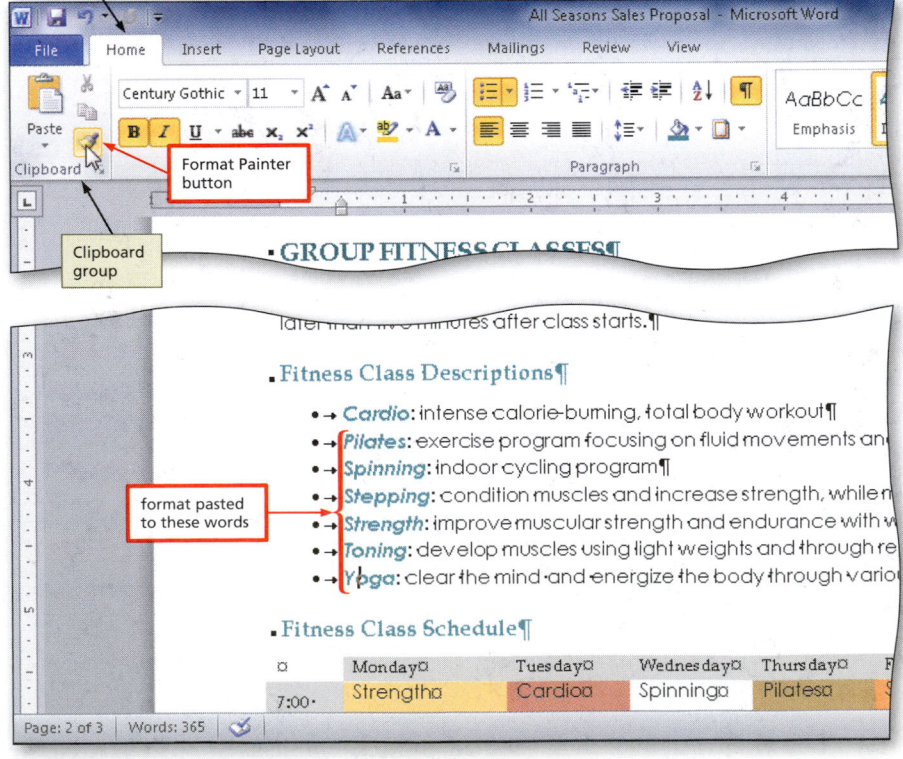

Figure 4–40

To Customize Bullets in a List

The bulleted list in the sales proposal draft uses default bullet characters, that is, the dot symbol. You want to use a more visually appealing picture bullet. The following steps change the bullets in a list from the default to picture bullets.

- Select all the paragraphs in the bulleted list.

- Click the Bullets button arrow (Home tab | Paragraph group) to display the Bullets gallery (Figure 4–41).

Q&A Can I select any of the bullet characters in the Bullet Library area of the Bullets gallery?

Yes, but if you prefer a different bullet character, follow the rest of these steps.

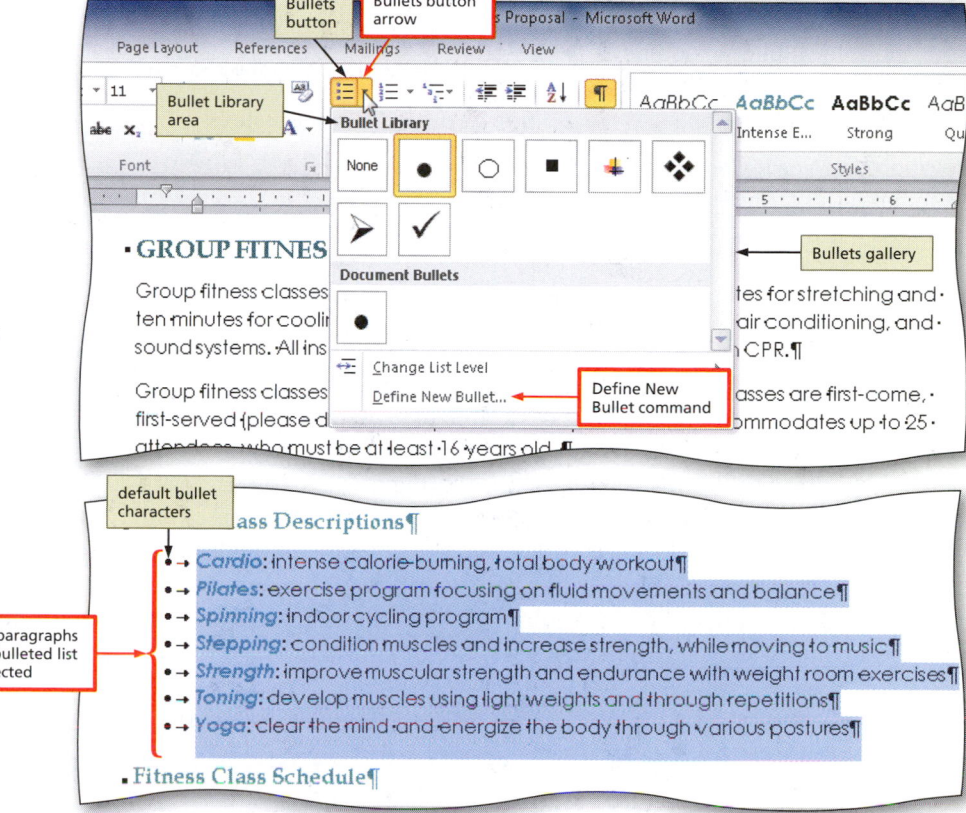

Figure 4–41

❷
- Click Define New Bullet in the Bullets gallery to display the Define New Bullet dialog box.

- Click the Picture button (Define New Bullet dialog box) to display the Picture Bullet dialog box.

🔍 **Experiment**

- Scroll through the list of picture bullets (Picture Bullet dialog box) to see the available bullet characters.

- If necessary, scroll to the top of the list of picture bullets (Picture Bullet dialog box) and then select the picture bullet shown in Figure 4–42 (or a similar picture bullet).

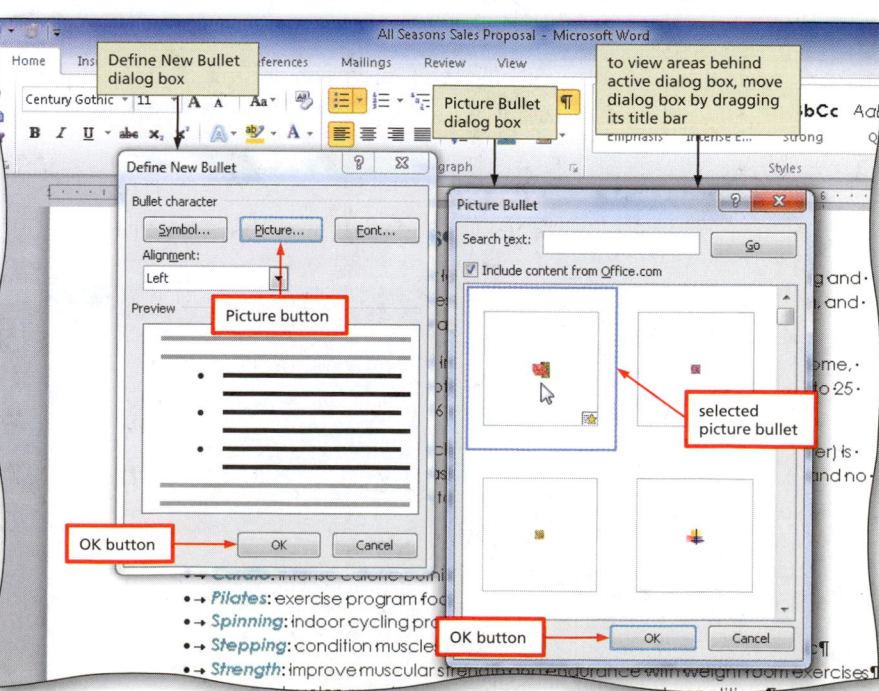

Figure 4–42

3

- Click the OK button (Picture Bullet dialog box) to close the dialog box and show a preview of the selected picture bullet in the Define New Bullet dialog box.

- Click the OK button (Define New Bullet dialog box) to change the bullets in the selected list to picture bullets.

- When the Word window is visible again, click in the selected list to remove the selection (Figure 4–43).

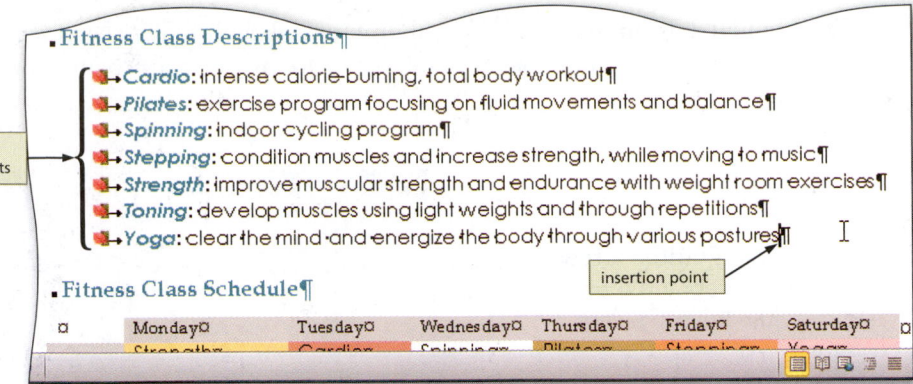

Figure 4–43

To Create a Multilevel Numbered List

The next step is to create a multilevel numbered list below the Fitness Class Tips heading on the last page of the sales proposal in this chapter (shown in Figure 4–1c on page WD 203). A **multilevel list** is a list that contains several levels of list items, with each lower level displaying a different numeric, alphabetic, or bullet character. In a multilevel list, the first level is displayed at the left edge of the list and subsequent levels are indented; that is, the second level is indented below the first, the third level is indented below the second level, and so on. The list is referred to as a numbered list if the first level contains numbers or letters and is referred to as a bulleted list if the first level contains a character other than a number or letter.

For the list in this project, the first level uses numbers (i.e., 1., 2., 3.), the second level uses lowercase letters (a., b., c.), and the third level uses lowercase Roman numerals (i.e., i., ii., iii.). The following steps create a multilevel numbered list.

1

- Position the insertion point at the location for the multilevel numbered list, which in this case is the blank line below the Fitness Class Tips heading on the last page of the sales proposal.

- Click the Numbering button (Home tab | Paragraph group) to format the current paragraph as a list item using the current number format, which in this case is an indented 1 followed by a period.

Q&A What if I wanted a different number format?

You would click the Numbering button arrow (Home tab | Paragraph group) and then select the desired number format in the Numbering gallery, or click the Define New Number Format command in the Numbering gallery to define your own number format.

- Type `Keep your body adequately hydrated` as a first-level list item and then press the ENTER key, which automatically places the next sequential number for the current level at the beginning of the next line (in this case, 2.) (Figure 4–44).

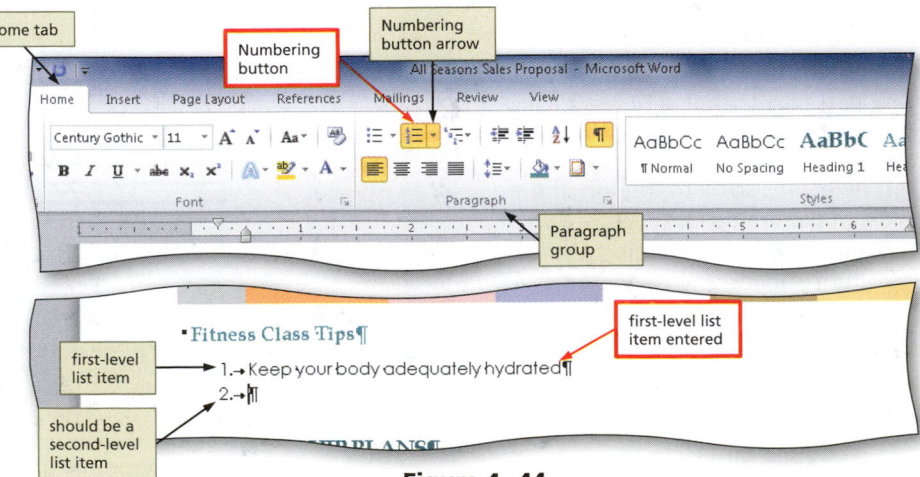

Figure 4–44

2
- Press the TAB key to demote the current list item (the 2.) to the next lower level, which is indented below the higher-level list item (in this case, converting 2. to a.).

Q&A
What if I wanted a different multilevel list format?

You would click the Multilevel List button (Home tab | Paragraph group) and then select the desired list style.

3
- Type the text for list item 1-a as shown in Figure 4–45 and then press the ENTER key, which automatically places the next sequential list item for the current level on the next line (in this case, b.).

- Type the text for list item 1-b as shown in Figure 4–45 and then press the ENTER key, which automatically places the next sequential list item on the next line (in this case, c.).

- Type the text for list item 1-c as shown in Figure 4–45 and then press the ENTER key, which automatically places the next sequential list item on the next line (Figure 4–45).

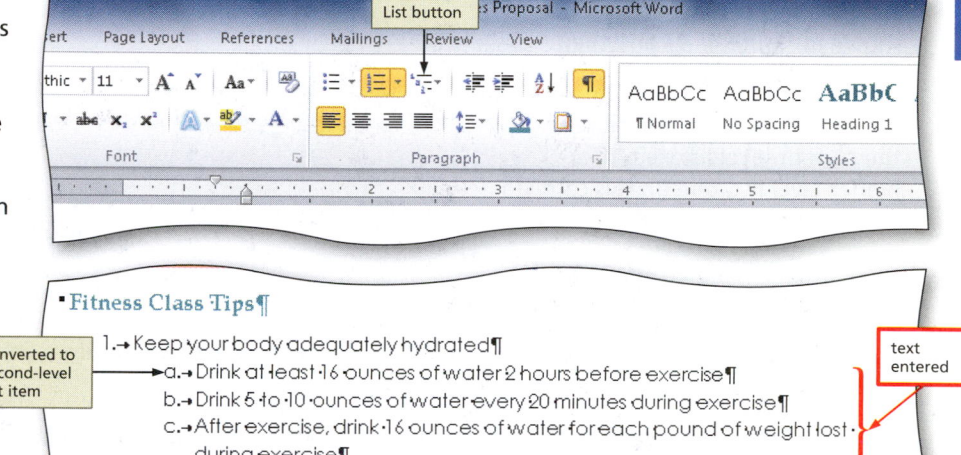

Figure 4–45

4
- Press SHIFT+TAB to promote the current-level list item to a higher-level list item (in this case, converting d. to 2.).

- Type **Dress comfortably** as a first-level list item and then press the ENTER key.

- Press the TAB key to demote the current level list item to a lower-level list item (in this case, converting 3. to a.).

- Type the text for list item 2-a as shown in Figure 4–46 and then press the ENTER key.

Figure 4–46

- Type the text for list item 2-b as shown in Figure 4–46 and then press the ENTER key.

- Type the text for list item 2-c as shown in Figure 4–46 and then press the ENTER key.

- Press SHIFT+TAB to promote the current-level list item to a higher-level list item (in this case, converting d. to 3.).

- Type **Reward yourself** as a first-level list item, press the ENTER key, and then press the TAB key to demote the current-level list item to a lower-level list item (in this case, converting 4. to a.).

- Type **Short term** as a second-level list item and then press the ENTER key (Figure 4–46).

5

- Press the TAB key to demote the current-level list item to a lower-level list item (in this case, converting b. to i.).

- Type the text for list item 3-a-i as shown in Figure 4–47 and then press the ENTER key.

- Type the text for list item 3-a-ii as shown in Figure 4–47 and then press the ENTER key.

- Press SHIFT+TAB to promote the current-level list item to a higher-level list item (in this case, converting iii. to b.).

- Type **Long term** as a second-level list item and then press the ENTER key.

- Press the TAB key to demote the current-level list item to a lower-level list item (in this case, converting c. to i.).

- Type the text for list item 3-b-i as shown in Figure 4–47 and then press the ENTER key.

- Type the text for list item 3-b-ii as shown in Figure 4–47 to complete the multilevel list.

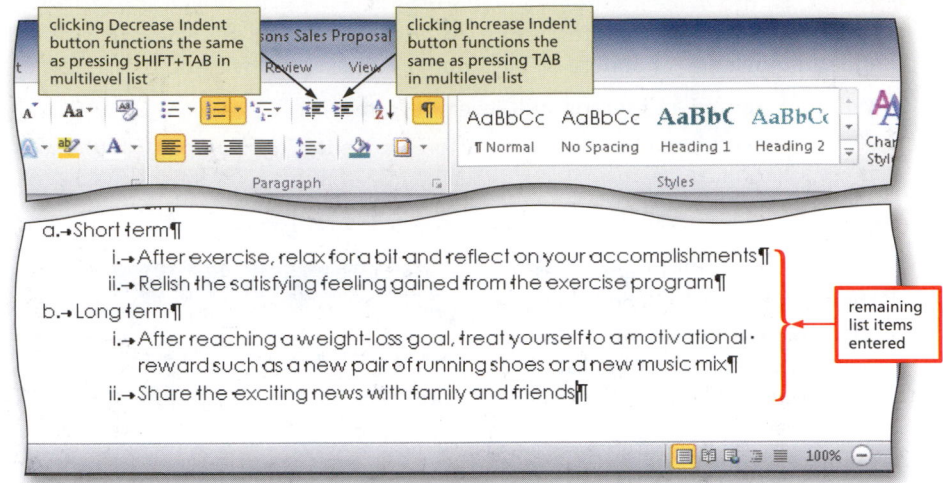

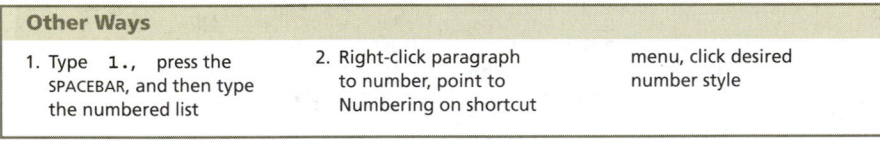

Figure 4–47

Q&A

Can I adjust the level of a list item after it is typed?

Yes. With the insertion point in the item to adjust, click the Increase Indent or Decrease Indent button (Home tab | Paragraph group), press TAB or SHIFT+TAB, right-click the list item, and then click the desired command on the shortcut menu, or point to Change List Level in the Bullets or Numbering gallery and then click the desired list level on the submenu.

Other Ways		
1. Type **1.,** press the SPACEBAR, and then type the numbered list	2. Right-click paragraph to number, point to Numbering on shortcut	menu, click desired number style

To Save an Existing Document with the Same File Name

You have made several modifications to the document since you last saved it. Thus, you should save it again. The following step saves the document again.

1 Click the Save button on the Quick Access Toolbar to overwrite the previously saved file.

Break Point: If you wish to take a break, this is a good place to do so. You can quit Word now. To resume at a later time, start Word, open the file called All Seasons Sales Proposal, and continue following the steps from this location forward.

Editing and Formatting Tables

The sales proposal draft contains two Word tables: the fitness class schedule table and the membership plans table (shown in Figure 4–25 on page WD 224). The fitness class schedule table shows the days and times for various fitness classes, and the membership plans table shows the costs of various membership plans. In this section, you will make several modifications to these two tables so that they appear as shown in Figure 4–1 on page WD 203.

The following pages explain how to modify the tables in the sales proposal draft:

1. Fitness Class Schedule Table
   a. Change the column width for the column containing the class times.
   b. Change row heights so that they are not so tall.
   c. Shade table cells containing Spinning classes.
   d. Change cell spacing.
   e. Change the column width of days of week columns.

2. Membership Plans Table
   a. Delete the extra column on the right edge of the table.
   b. Sort the table contents by facility.
   c. Split table cells so that the heading, Amenities and Programs, is above the second column.
   d. Display text in a cell vertically to the left of the table.
   e. Remove cell shading from the table.
   f. Add borders to the table.
   g. Sum columns in the table.

To Show Gridlines

When a table contains no borders, it sometimes is difficult to see the individual cells in the table. To help identify the location of cells, you can display gridlines, which show cell outlines on the screen. Gridlines are formatting marks, which means the gridlines do not print. The following step shows gridlines.

1
- Display the table to be edited in the document window (in this case, the fitness class schedule table).

- Position the insertion point in any cell in the table.

- Display the Table Tools Layout tab.

- If gridlines are not displayed on the screen, click the View Table Gridlines button (Table Tools Layout tab | Table group) to show gridlines in the table (Figure 4–48).

How do I turn table gridlines off?
Click the View Table Gridlines button again.

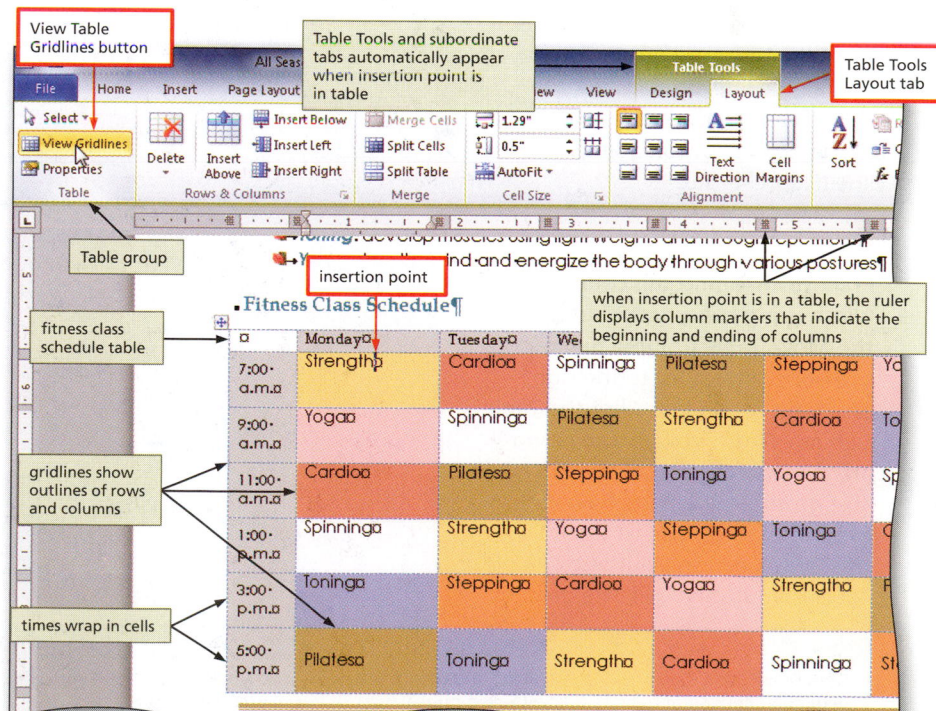

Figure 4–48

To Change Column Width

Notice in Figure 4–48 on the previous page that the leftmost column containing the class start times is not wide enough to fit the contents; that is, the times wrap in the cells. In this proposal, the times should appear on a single line that is just wide enough to accommodate the class start times. Thus, you will change the column width of just this single column. You can change column widths by entering a specific value on the Ribbon or in a dialog box, or by using a marker on the ruler or the column boundary. The following steps change column width by dragging a column's boundary.

- Position the mouse pointer on the column boundary to the right of the column to adjust (in this case, to the right of the first column) so that the mouse pointer changes to a double arrow split by two vertical bars (Figure 4–49).

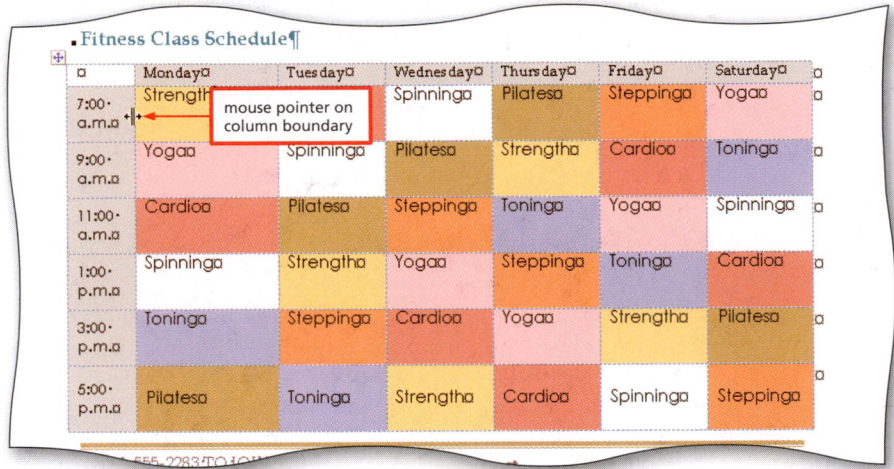

Figure 4–49

- Double-click the column boundary so that Word adjusts the column width according to the column contents. If all of the times still are not displayed on a single line, double-click the column boundary again so that all of the times show on a single line (Figure 4–50).

🔎 Experiment

- Practice changing this column's width using other techniques: drag the Move Table Column marker on the horizontal ruler to the right and then to the left. Click the Table Column Width box up and down arrows (Table Tools Layout tab | Cell Size group). When you have finished experimenting, type `1.29` in the Table Column Width box (Table Tools Layout tab | Cell Size group).

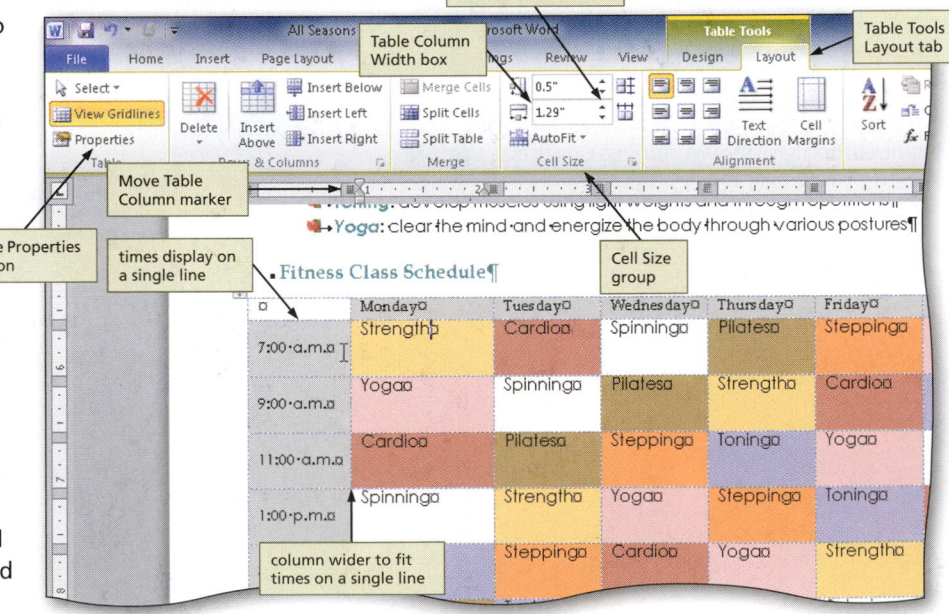

Figure 4–50

Other Ways

1. Drag Move Table Column marker on horizontal ruler to desired width
2. Enter desired value in Table Column Width box

(Table Tools Layout tab | Cell Size group)

3. Click Table Properties button (Table Tools Layout tab | Table group), click

Column tab, enter width, click OK button

To Hide White Space

The fitness class schedule table currently continues on the top of the next page in the document, and the headers and footers make it difficult to see the entire table at once. With the screen in Print Layout view, you can hide white space, which is the space that is displayed in the margins at the top and bottom of pages (including any headers and footers) and also the space between pages. The following steps hide white space, if your screen displays it.

- Position the mouse pointer in the document window in the space between the pages so that the mouse pointer changes to a Hide White Space button (Figure 4–51).

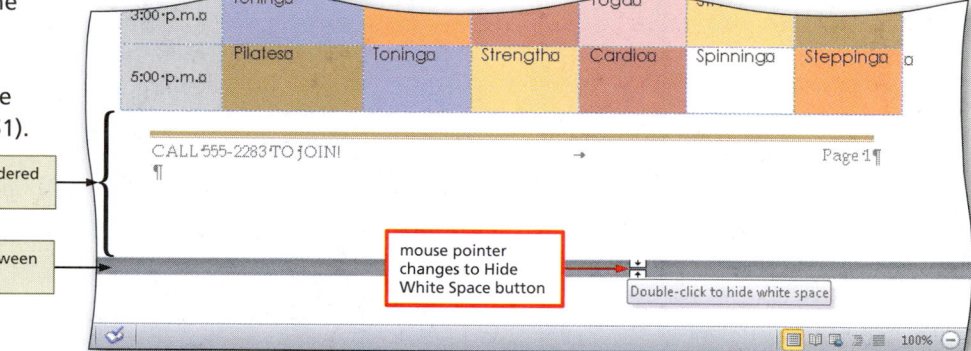

Figure 4–51

- While the mouse pointer is a Hide White Space button, double-click the mouse to hide white space, that is, the top and bottom margins and space between pages (Figure 4–52).

Q&A Does hiding white space have any effect on the printed document?

No.

Q&A How would I show white space again?

You would point to a line between two pages and double-click when the mouse pointer changes to a Show White Space button.

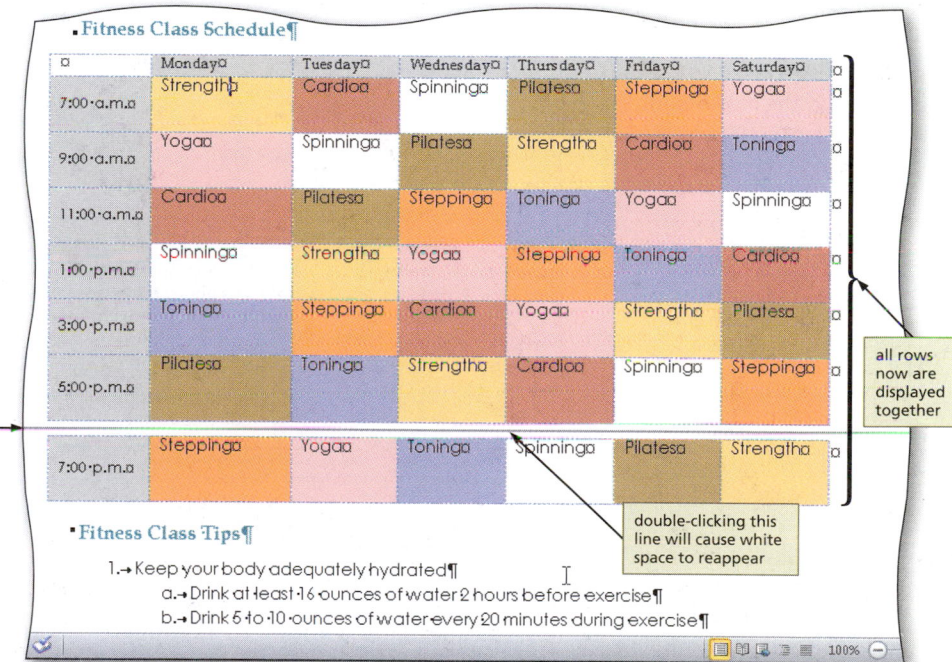

Figure 4–52

Other Ways
1. Click File on Ribbon, click Options in Backstage view, click Display in left pane (Word Options dialog box), remove check mark from Show white space between pages in Print Layout view check box, click OK button

To Change Row Height

The next step in this project is to narrow the height of the rows containing the classes. You change row height in the same ways you change column width. That is, you can change row height by entering a specific value on the Ribbon or in a dialog box, or by using a marker on the ruler or the row boundary. The latter two, however, work only for a single row at a time. The steps on the next page change row height by entering a value on the Ribbon.

1

- Select the rows to change (in this case, all the rows below the first row that contains the days of the week).

Q&A

How do I select rows?

Point to the left of the first row and then drag downward when the mouse pointer changes to a right-pointing arrow.

2

- Click the Table Row Height box up or down arrows (Table Tools Layout tab | Cell Size group) as many times as necessary until the box displays 0.4" to change the row height to this value (Figure 4–53).

- Click anywhere to remove the selection from the table.

Figure 4–53

Other Ways

1. Click Table Properties button (Table Tools Layout tab | Table group), click Row tab (Table Properties dialog box), enter row height, click OK button

2. Right-click selected row, click Table Properties on shortcut menu, click Row tab, enter row height (Table Properties dialog box), click OK button

3. For a single row, drag row boundary (horizontal gridline at bottom of row in table) to desired height

4. Drag Adjust Table Row marker on vertical ruler to desired height

BTW

Page Breaks and Tables
If you do not want a page break to occur in the middle of a table, position the insertion point in the table, click the Table Properties button (Table Tools Layout tab | Table group), click the Row tab (Table Properties dialog box), remove the check mark from the 'Allow row to break across pages' check box, and then click the OK button. To force a table to break across pages at a particular row, click in the row that you want to appear on the next page and then press CTRL+ENTER.

To Align Data in Cells

The next step is to change the alignment of the data in cells that contain the class names. Recall that in addition to aligning text horizontally in a cell (left, center, or right), you can align it vertically within a cell (top, center, or bottom). Currently, the class names have a top left alignment (shown in Figure 4–53). In this project, they should be aligned center left so that they are more centered within the row height. The following steps change the alignment of data in cells.

1 Select the cells containing class names, as shown in Figure 4–54.

Q&A

How do I select a series of cells?

Drag through the cells.

2 Click the Align Center Left button (Table Tools Layout tab | Alignment group) to center and left-align the contents of the selected cells (Figure 4–54).

3 Click anywhere to remove the selection from the table.

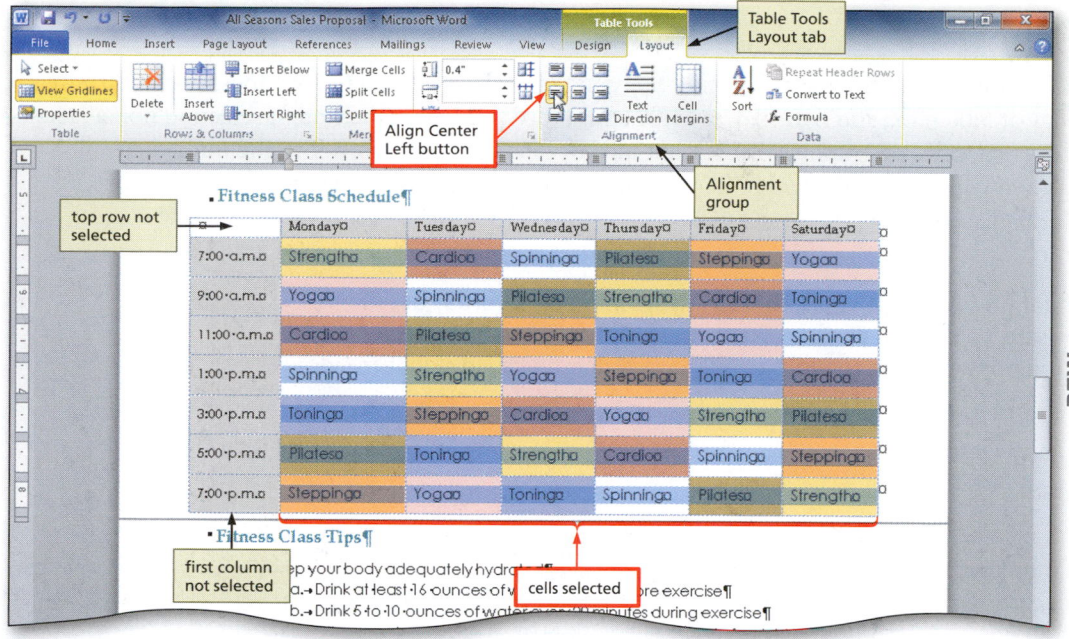

Figure 4–54

BTW

Table Headings
If a table continues on the next page, you can instruct Word to repeat the table headings at the top of the subsequent page(s) containing the table. To do this, select the first row in the table and then click the Repeat Header Rows button (Table Tools Layout tab | Data group).

To Shade a Table Cell

In this table, the cells containing the Spinning label are to be shaded light green. First, you will shade a single cell this color. Then, you will shade the remaining cells. The following steps shade a cell.

1

- Position the insertion point in the cell to shade (in this case, the cell containing Spinning on Monday at 1:00 p.m.).

- Display the Table Tools Design tab.

- Click the Shading button arrow (Table Tools Design tab | Table Styles group) to display the Shading gallery.

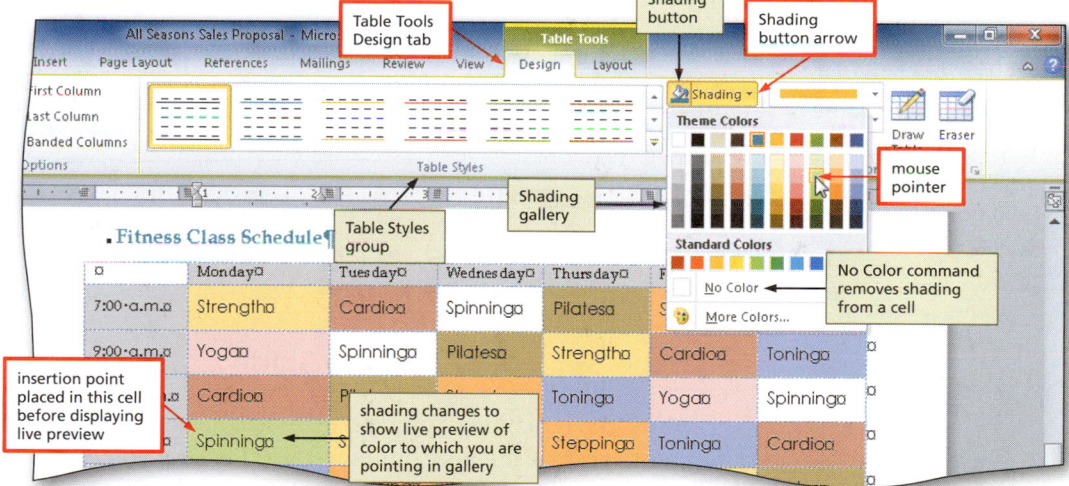

Figure 4–55

- Point to Green, Accent 4, Lighter 60% (eighth color, third row) in the Shading gallery to display a live preview of that shading color applied to the current cell in the table (Figure 4–55).

🔎 Experiment

- Point to various colors in the Shading gallery and watch the shading color of the current cell change.

2

- Click Green, Accent 4, Lighter 60% in the Shading gallery to apply the selected style to the current cell.

Q&A How do I remove shading from a cell?

Click the Shading button arrow and then click No Color in the Shading gallery.

To Select Nonadjacent Items

The next step is to select the rest of the cells containing Spinning: Tuesday at 9:00 a.m., Wednesday at 7:00 a.m., Thursday at 7:00 p.m., Friday at 5:00 p.m., and Saturday at 11:00 a.m. Word provides a method of selecting nonadjacent items, which are items such as text, cells, or graphics that are not next to each other, that is, not to the immediate right, left, top, or bottom. When you select nonadjacent items, you can format all occurrences of the items at once. The following steps select nonadjacent cells.

1
- Select the first cell to format (in this case, the cell containing Spinning on Saturday at 11:00 a.m.). Recall that to select a cell you position the mouse pointer on the left edge of the cell and then click when the pointer shape changes to an upward-pointing solid right arrow.

Q&A   Why start selecting at the right of the table and move to the left?

If you begin selecting from the left, the Mini toolbar may obstruct the view of the next cells you attempt to select.

2
- While holding down the CTRL key, select the next cell (in this case, the cell containing Spinning on Friday at 5:00 p.m.) to select the nonadjacent cell.

- While holding down the CTRL key, select the remaining non-adjacent cells (that is, Spinning on Thursday at 7:00 p.m., Spinning on Wednesday at 7:00 a.m., and Spinning on Tuesday at 9:00 a.m.), as shown in Figure 4–56.

Q&A   Do I follow the same procedure to select any nonadjacent item?

Yes. Select the first item and then hold down the CTRL key while selecting the remaining items.

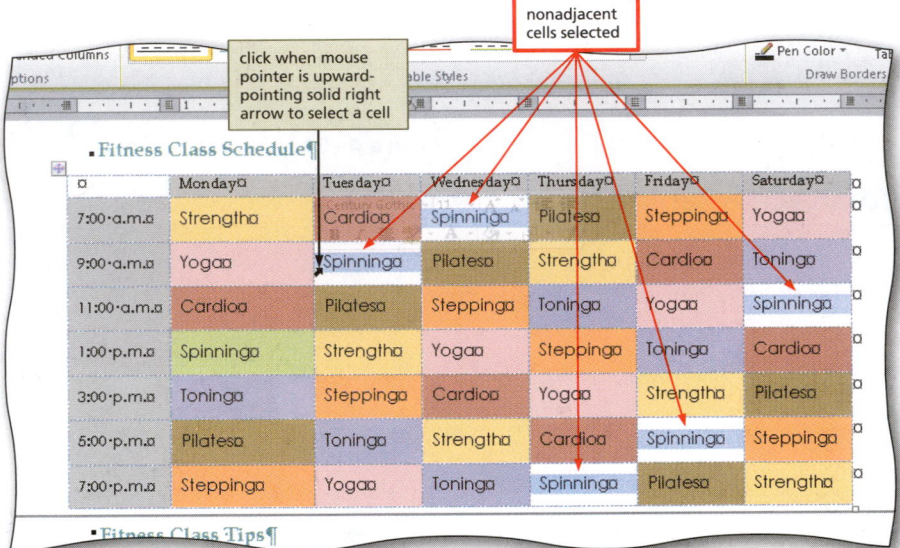

Figure 4–56

To Shade Selected Cells the Same Color

With the remaining Spinning class cells selected, the next step is to shade them the same color green as the first Spinning class. Because you earlier selected this color in the Shading gallery, this color appears on the face of the Shading button. Thus, you simply can click the Shading button to use the same color, which appears on the face of the button. The following steps shade selected cells with the current color.

1   With the cells selected, click the Shading button (Table Tools Design tab | Table Styles group) to shade the selected cells with the current color (in this case, Green, Accent 4, Lighter 60% (Figure 4–57).

Q&A   What if I accidentally click the Shading button arrow?

Press the ESC key to remove the gallery from the screen and then repeat Step 1.

Q&A   What if the current color on the Shading button is not the color I want?

Click the Shading button arrow and then click the desired color.

2   Click anywhere to remove the selection from the table.

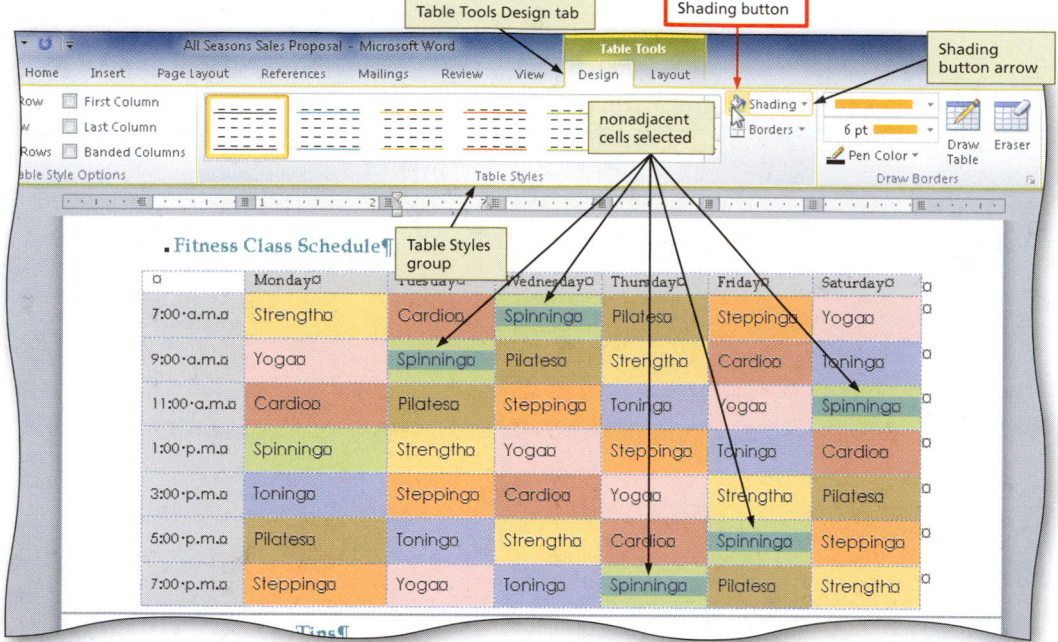

Figure 4–57

To Hide Gridlines

You no longer need to see the gridlines in the table. Thus, you can hide the gridlines. The following steps hide gridlines.

1 If necessary, position the insertion point in a table cell.

2 Display the Table Tools Layout tab.

3 Click the View Table Gridlines button (Table Tools Layout tab | Table group) to hide gridlines in the table on the screen.

To Change Cell Spacing

The next step in formatting the fitness class schedule table is to place a small amount of white space between every cell in the table. The following steps change spacing between cells.

1

- With the insertion point somewhere in the table, click the Cell Margins button (Table Tools Layout tab | Alignment group) to display the Table Options dialog box.

- Place a check mark in the 'Allow spacing between cells' check box and then click the up arrow once so that 0.02" is displayed in this box because you want to increase space between cells by this value (Figure 4–58).

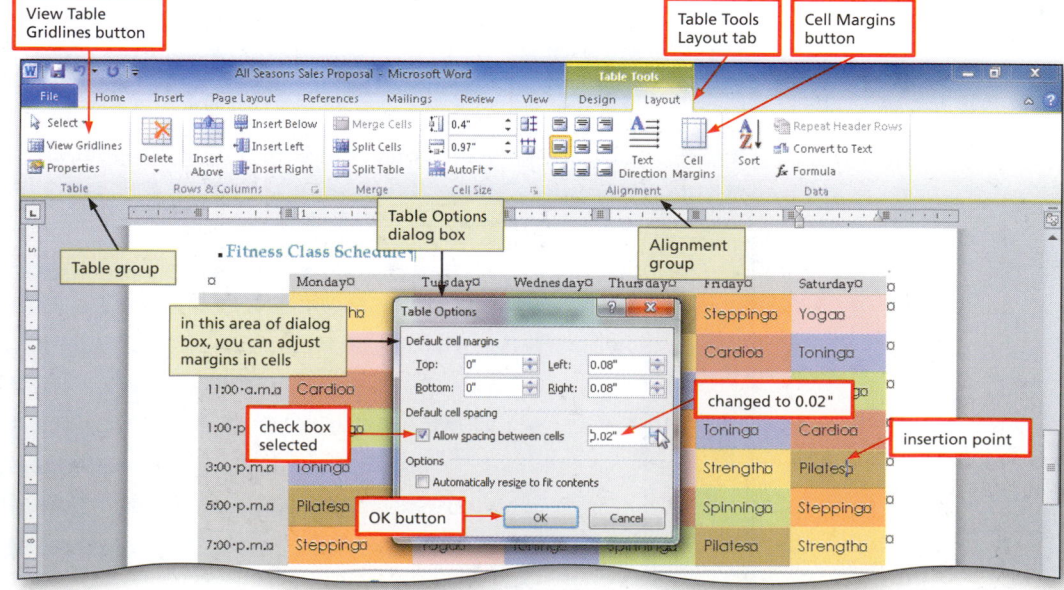

Figure 4–58

2

• Click the OK button (Table Options dialog box) to apply the cell spacing changes to the current table (Figure 4–59).

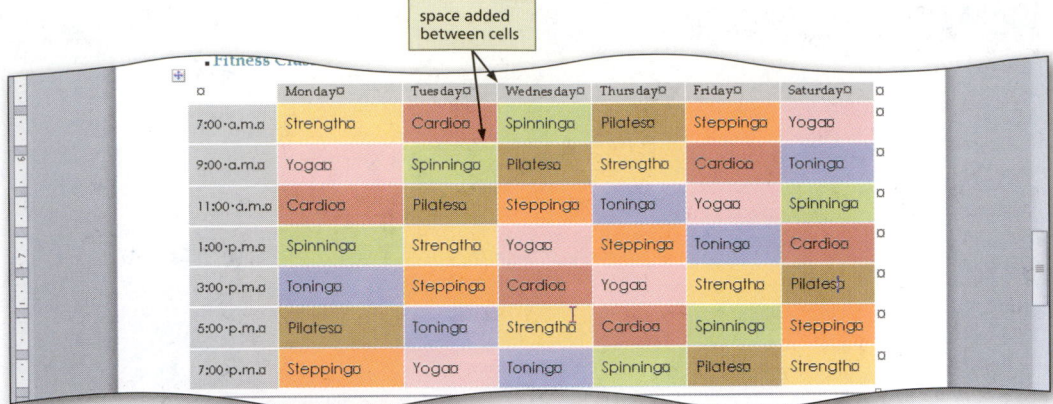

Figure 4–59

Other Ways

1. Click Table Properties button (Table Tools Layout tab | Table group), click Table tab (Table Properties dialog box), click Options button, select desired

   options (Table Options dialog box), click OK button in each dialog box

2. Right-click table, click Table Properties on shortcut menu, click Table

   tab (Table Properties dialog box), click Options button, select desired options (Table Options dialog box), click OK button in each dialog box

---

To Change Column Width

In reviewing the fitness class schedule table, you notice that the days of the week columns are different widths. Thus, the final step in formatting the fitness class schedule table is to change the column widths of the days of the week columns to the same width, specifically .95" so that the table does not extend so far into the margins. The following steps change column widths by specifying a value on the Ribbon.

1 Select the columns to be resized, in this case, all columns except the first.

2 Click the Table Column Width box (Table Tools Layout tab | Cell Size group) to select it.

3 Type **.95** in the Table Column Width box and then press the ENTER key to change the width of the selected table columns (Figure 4–60).

4 Click anywhere to remove the selection from the table.

Table Columns
If you hold down the ALT key while dragging a column marker on the ruler or a column boundary in the table, the width measurements of all columns appear on the ruler as you drag the column marker or boundary.

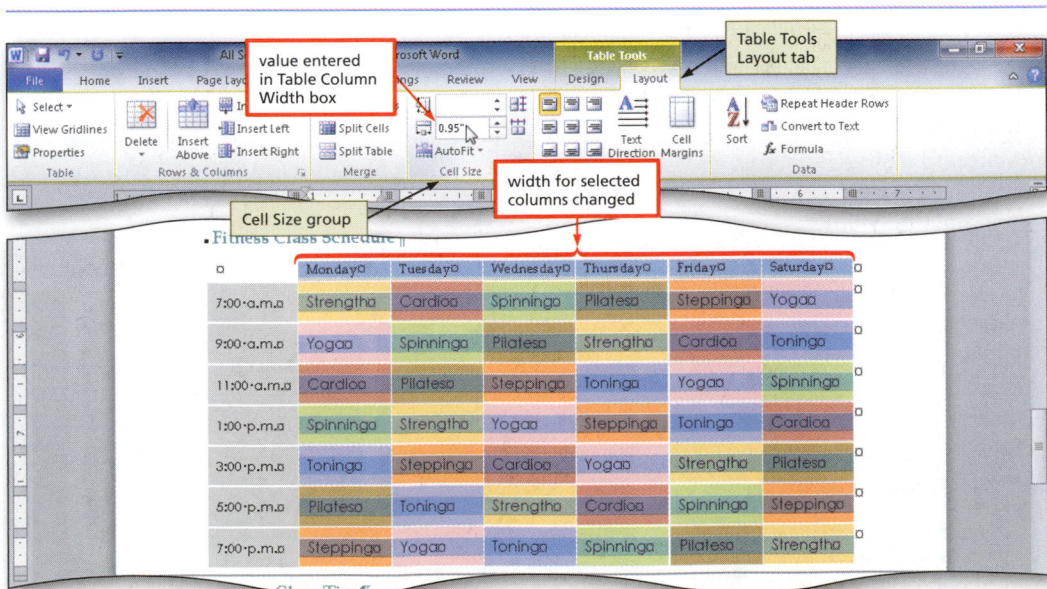

Figure 4–60

To Delete a Column

With the fitness class schedule table finished, the next task is to format the membership plans table. The table in the draft of the proposal contains a blank column that should be deleted. The following steps delete a column from a table.

- Scroll to display the membership plans table in the document window.

- Position the insertion point in the column to be deleted (in this case, the rightmost column).

- Click the Delete button (Table Tools Layout tab | Rows & Columns group) to display the Delete menu (Figure 4–61).

- Click Delete Columns on the Delete menu to delete the column containing the insertion point.

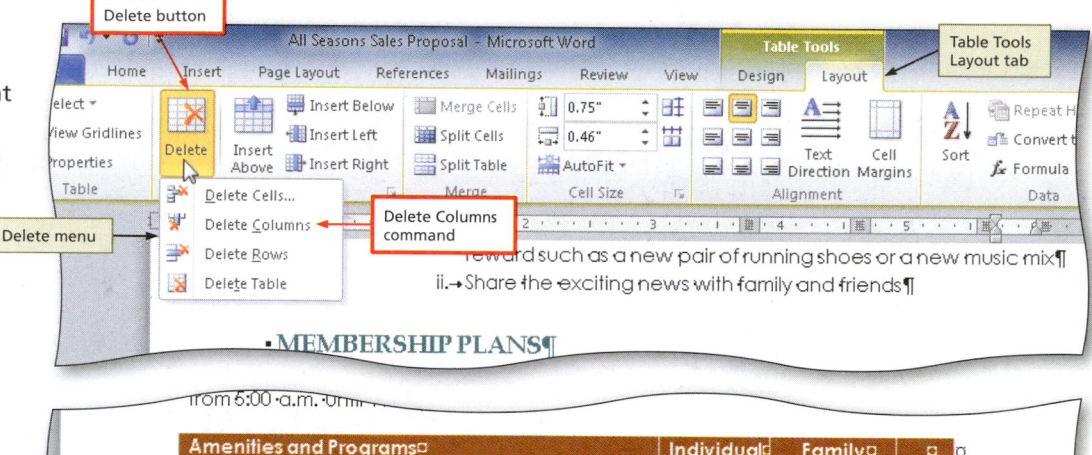

Figure 4–61

Other Ways

1. Right-click column to delete, click Delete Cells on shortcut menu, click 'Delete entire column' (Delete Cells dialog box), click OK button

2. Select column, right-click selection, click Delete Columns on shortcut menu

To Delete a Row

If you wanted to delete a row, you would perform the following tasks.

1. Position the insertion point in the row to be deleted.
2. Click the Delete button (Table Tools Layout tab | Rows & Columns group) and then click Delete Rows on the Delete menu.

or

1. Right-click the row to delete, click Delete Cells on the shortcut menu, click 'Delete entire row' (Delete Cells dialog box), and then click the OK button.

or

1. Select the row to be deleted.
2. Right-click the selected row and then click Delete Rows on the shortcut menu.

BTW

Draw Table
If you want to draw the boundary, rows, and columns of a table, click the Table button on the Insert tab and then click Draw Table in the Table gallery. Use the pencil-shaped mouse pointer to draw the perimeter of the table and the inside rows and columns. Use the Eraser button (Table Tools Design tab | Draw Borders group) to erase lines in the table. To continue drawing, click the Draw Table button (Table Tools Design tab | Draw Borders group).

To Sort a Table

In the draft of this sales proposal, the membership plans are grouped by facility: exercise, aquatics, and gymnasium. These facilities should be listed in alphabetical order: aquatics, exercise, and then gymnasium. Thus, the next step is to sort rows in the table. Sorting tables is similar to sorting paragraphs. The following steps sort rows in a table.

1

- Select the rows to be sorted (in this case, the three middle rows).

Q&A What if I want to sort all rows in the table?

Place the insertion point anywhere in the table instead of selecting the rows.

- Click the Sort button (Table Tools Layout tab | Data group) to display the Sort dialog box (Figure 4–62).

Q&A What is the purpose of the Then by area (Sort dialog box)?

If you have multiple values for a particular column, you can sort by columns within columns. For example, if the table had a city column and a last name column, you could sort by last names within cities.

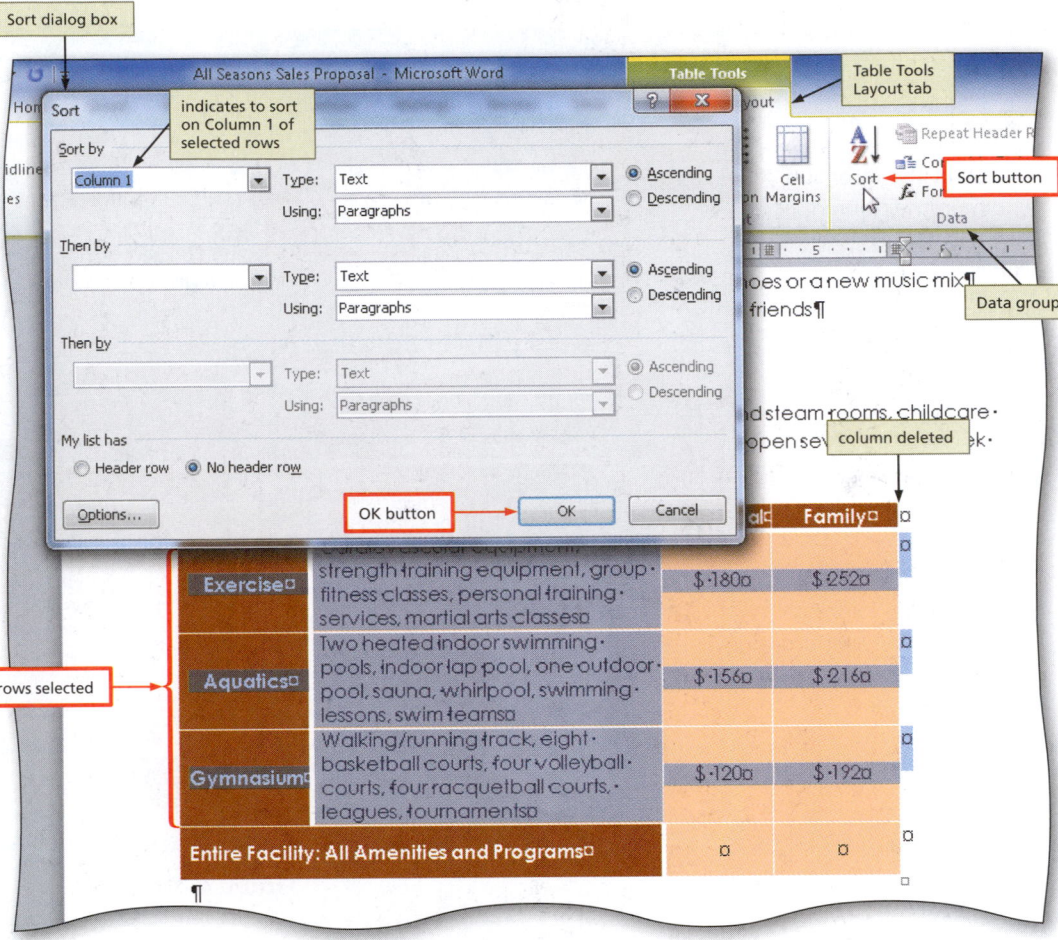

Figure 4–62

2

- Click the OK button (Sort dialog box) to instruct Word to alphabetize the selected rows.

- Click anywhere to remove the selection from the text (Figure 4–63).

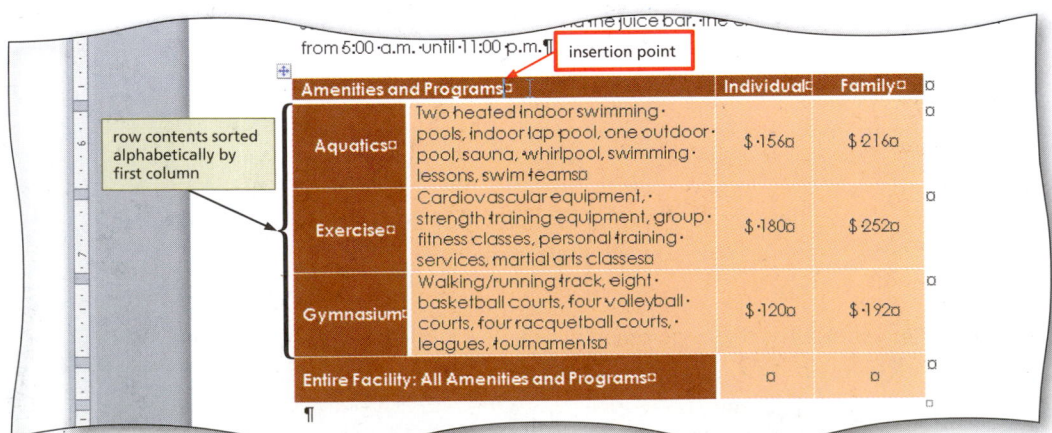

Figure 4–63

To Split Cells

The top, left cell of the table contains the text, Amenities and Programs. In the draft of the sales proposal, this row is above the first two columns in the table (the facilities and the descriptions of the facilities). This heading, Amenities and Programs, should be above the descriptions of the facilities, that is, above the second row. Thus, you will split the cell into two cells. The following steps split a single cell into two separate cells.

1

• Position the insertion point in the cell to split, in this case the top, left cell as shown in Figure 4–63.

• Click the Split Cells button (Table Tools Layout tab | Merge group) to display the Split Cells dialog box (Figure 4–64).

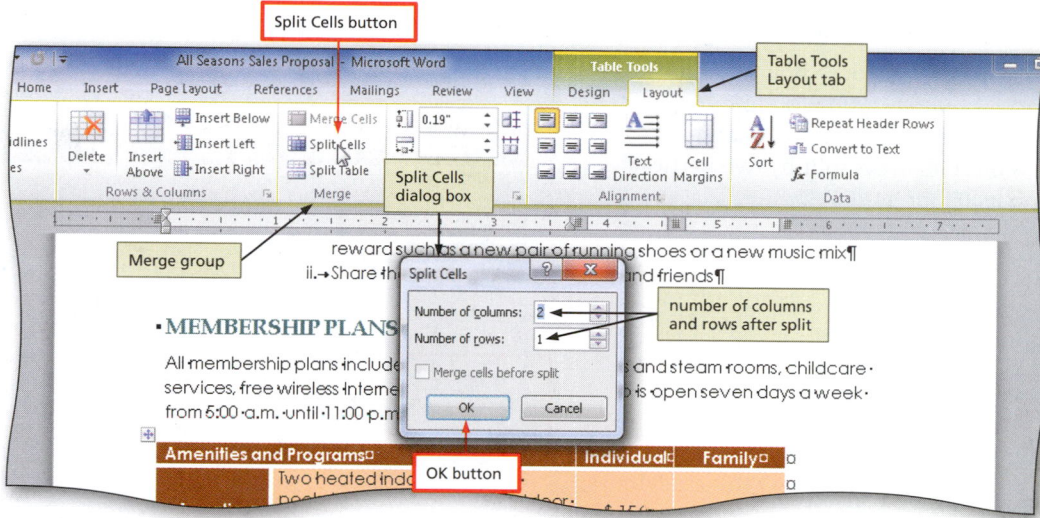

Figure 4–64

2

• Verify the number of columns and rows into which you want the cell split, in this case, 2 columns and 1 row.

• Click the OK button (Split Cells dialog box) to split the one cell into two columns (Figure 4–65).

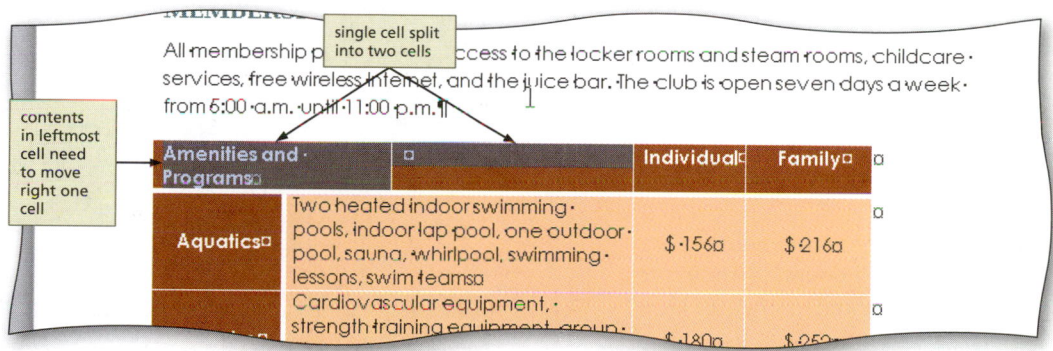

Figure 4–65

Other Ways

1. Right-click cell, click Split Cells on shortcut menu

To Move Cell Contents

When you split a cell into two cells, Word places the contents of the original cell in the leftmost cell after the split. In this case, the contents (Amenities and Programs) should be in the right cell. Thus, the following steps move cell contents.

1 Select the cell contents to be moved (in this case, Amenities and Programs).

2 Drag the cell contents to the desired location (in this case, the second cell in the first row) (shown in Figure 4–66 on the next page).

To Move a Cell Boundary

Notice in Figure 4–66 that the cell boundary to the left of the Amenities and Programs label does not line up with the boundary to the right of the facility types. This is because when you split a cell, Word divides the cell into evenly sized cells. If you want the boundary to line up with other column boundaries, drag it to the desired location. The following steps move a cell boundary.

1
- Position the mouse pointer on the cell boundary you wish to move so that the mouse pointer changes to a double arrow split by two vertical bars (Figure 4–66).

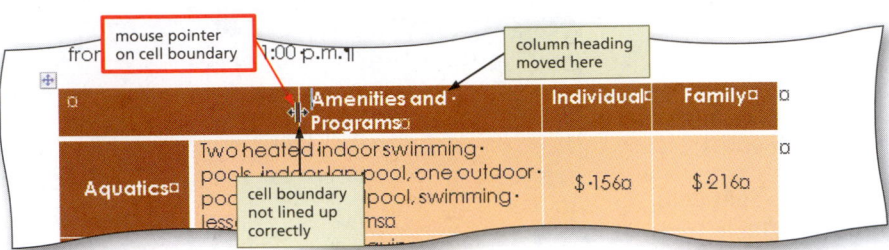

Figure 4–66

2
- Drag the cell boundary to the desired new location, in this case, to line up with the column boundary to its left, as shown in Figure 4–67.

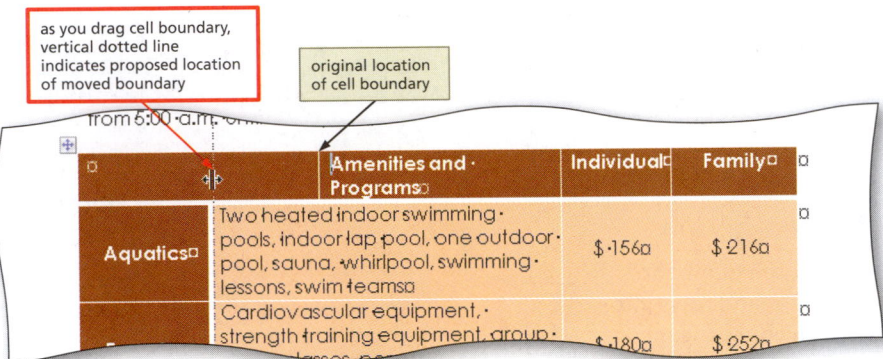

Figure 4–67

3
- When you release the mouse button, the cell boundary moves to the new location (Figure 4–68).

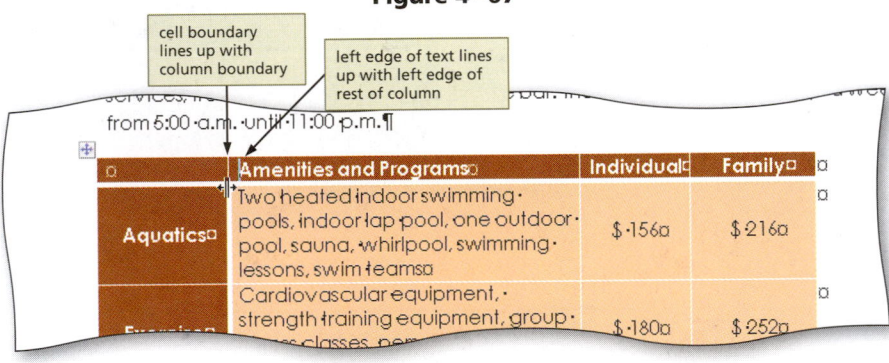

Figure 4–68

Other Ways

1. Drag Move Table Column marker on horizontal ruler to desired width

To Distribute Columns

The final step in formatting the membership plans table is to make the width of the individual and family columns uniform, that is, the same width. Instead of checking and adjusting the width of each column individually, you can make all columns uniform at the same time. The next step distributes selected columns.

1

- Select the columns to format, in this case, the two right columns.

- Click the Distribute Columns button (Table Tools Layout tab | Cell Size group) to make the width of the selected columns uniform (Figure 4–69).

Q&A

How would I make all columns in the table uniform?

Simply place the insertion point somewhere in the table before clicking the Distribute Columns button.

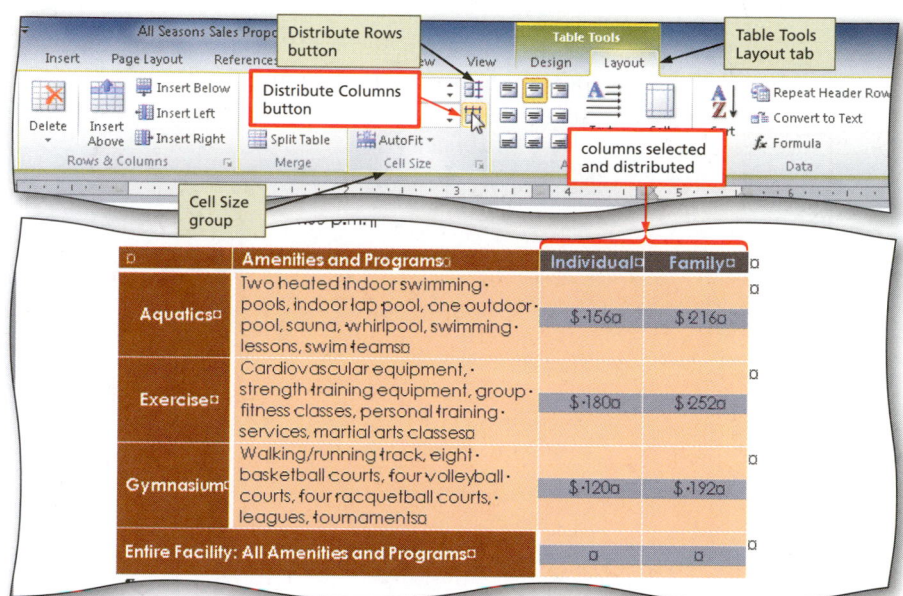

Figure 4–69

To Distribute Rows

If you wanted to make rows the same height, you would perform the following tasks.

1. Select the rows to format.
2. Click the Distribute Rows button (Table Tools Layout tab | Cell Size group) to make the width of the selected rows uniform.

To Insert a Column

In this project, the left edge of the membership plans table has a column that displays the label, Annual Rates by Facility. Thus, the following steps insert a column at the left edge of the table.

1 Position the insertion point somewhere in the first column of the table.

2 Click the Insert Columns to the Left button (Table Tools Layout tab | Rows & Columns group) to insert a column to the left of the column containing the insertion point (Figure 4–70).

3 Click anywhere in the table to remove the selection.

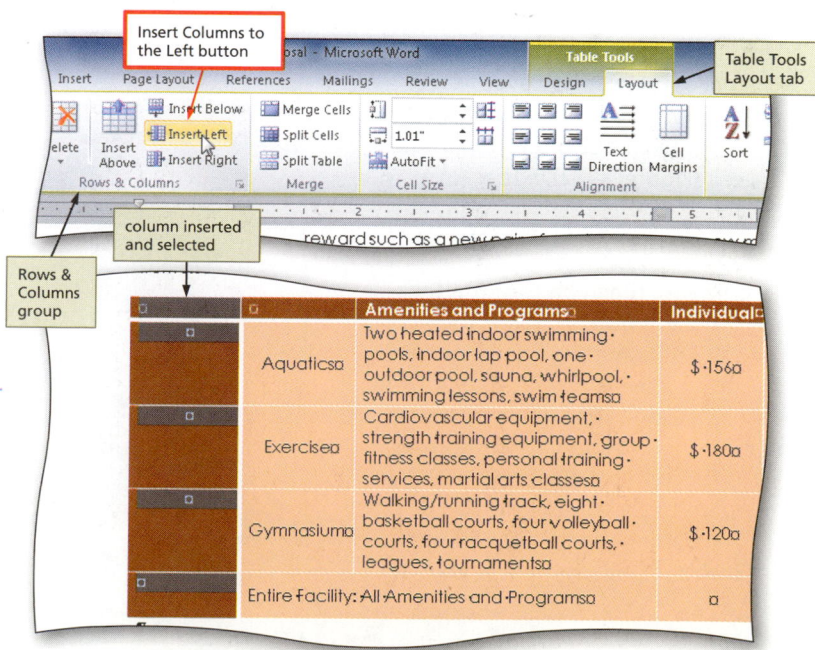

Figure 4–70

To Merge Cells and Enter Text

The label, Annual Rates by Facility, is to be displayed vertically to the left of the bottom four rows in the table. To display this text, the four cells should be merged into a single cell. The following steps merge cells and then enter text in the merged cell.

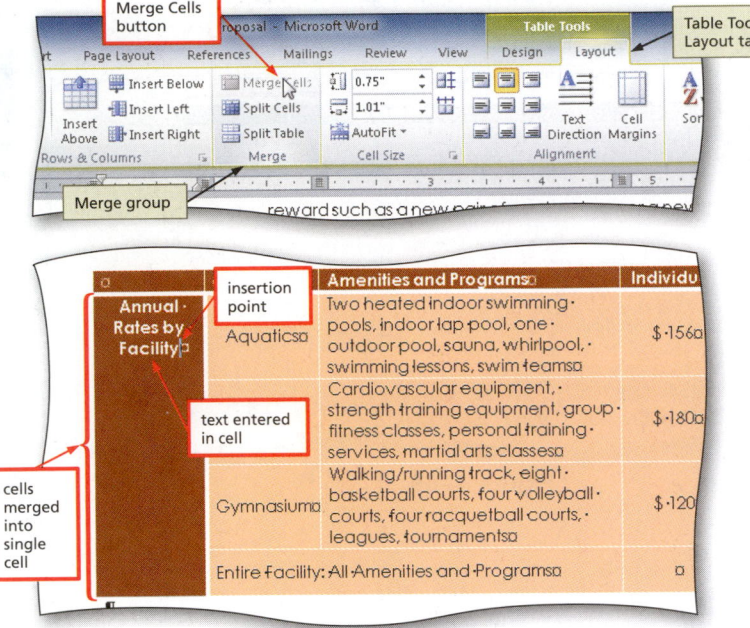

Figure 4–71

1 Select the cells to merge, in this case, the bottom four cells in the first column of the table.

2 Click the Merge Cells button (Table Tools Layout tab | Merge group) to merge the four selected cells into one cell.

3 Type `Annual Rates by Facility` in the merged cell.

4 If necessary, bold and center the entered text (Figure 4–71).

To Display Text in a Cell Vertically

The data you enter in cells is displayed horizontally by default. You can rotate the text so that it is displayed vertically. Changing the direction of text adds variety to your tables. The following step displays text vertically in a cell.

1
- Position the insertion point in the cell that contains the text to rotate (shown in Figure 4–71).

- Click the Text Direction button twice (Table Tools Layout tab | Alignment group) so that the text reads from bottom to top in the cell (Figure 4–72).

Q&A Why click the Text Direction button twice?

The first time you click the Text Direction button (Table Tools Layout tab | Alignment group), the text in the cell reads from top to bottom. The second time you click it, the text is displayed so that it reads from bottom to top (Figure 4–72). If you were to click the button a third time, the text would be displayed horizontally again.

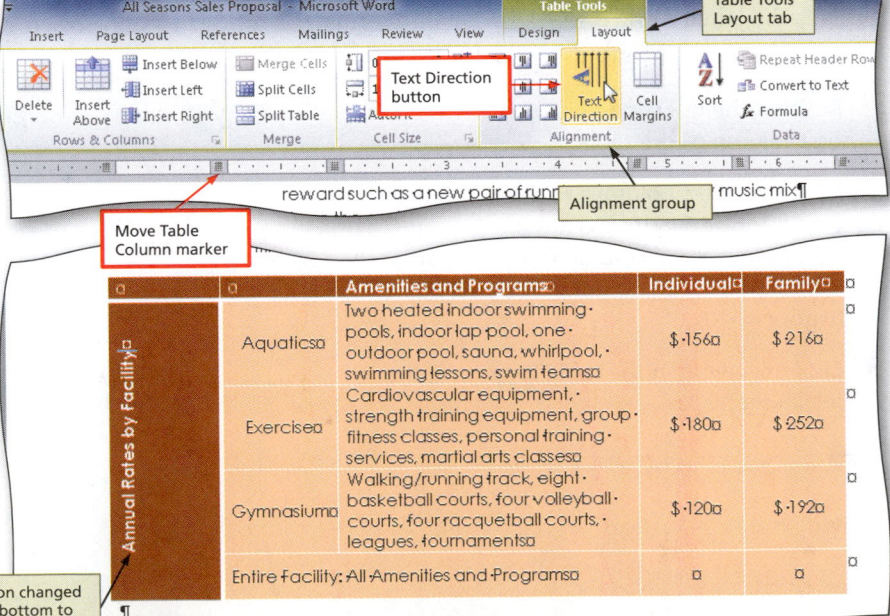

Figure 4–72

To Change Column Width

The cell containing the vertical text is too wide. Thus, the next step is to change the width of that column. If you drag the column boundary as you did earlier in the chapter, it will adjust the width of other columns in the table. If you want the other columns to remain their current widths, drag the Move Table Column marker on the ruler or hold down the CTRL key while dragging the column boundary. The following step changes column width using the ruler.

1 Drag the column's Move Table Column marker on the ruler to the left, as shown in Figure 4–73, to resize the column.

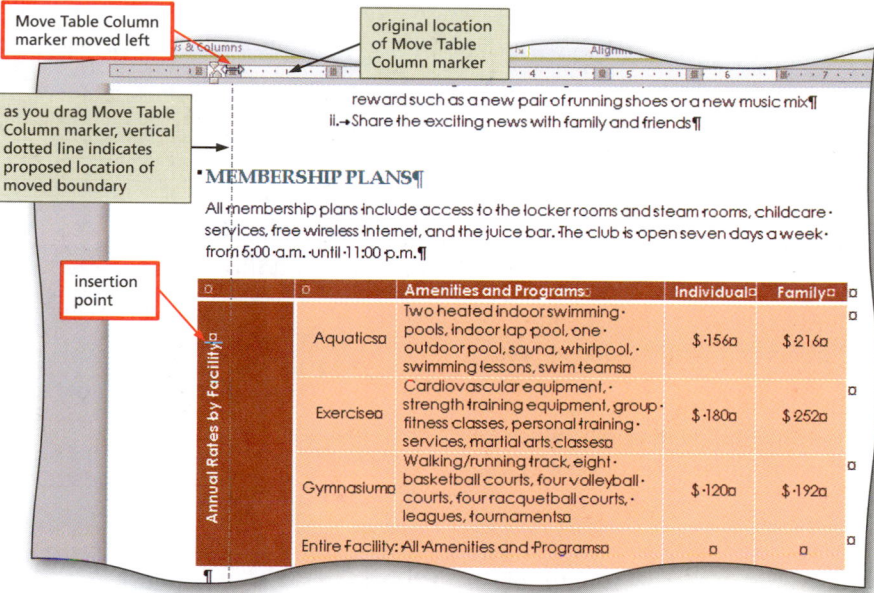

Figure 4–73

To Remove Cell Shading

In this table, only the first row and first column should have shading. Thus, the following steps remove shading from table cells.

1 Select the cells that should not contain shading (in this case, all of the cells below the first row and to the right of the first column).

2 Display the Table Tools Design tab. Click the Shading button arrow (Table Tools Design tab | Table Styles group) to display the Shading gallery (Figure 4–74).

3 Click No Color in the Shading gallery to remove the shading from the selected cells (shown in Figure 4–75 on the next page).

4 Click anywhere in the table to remove the selection.

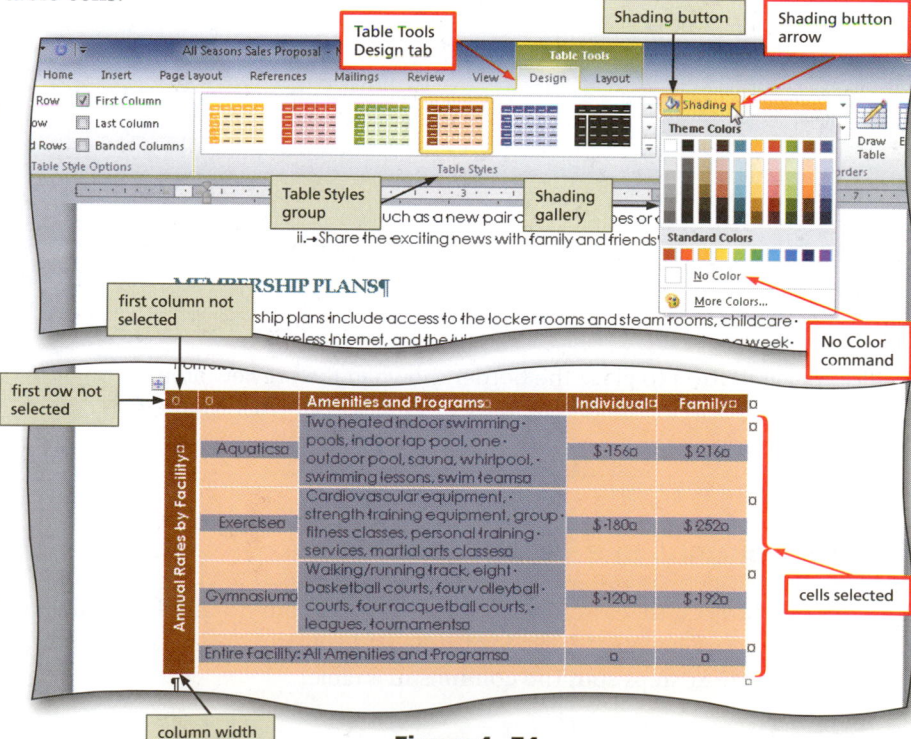

Figure 4–74

To Border a Table

The table in this project has a 1-point, brown border around all cells. Earlier in this chapter when you created the title page, the border line weight was changed to 6 point and the border color changed to gold. Because the table border should be 1 point and the color should be brown, you will use the Borders and Shading dialog box to change the line weight and color before adding the border to the table. The following steps add a border to a table.

- Position the insertion point somewhere in the table.

- Click the Borders button arrow (Table Tools Design tab | Table Styles group) to display the Borders gallery.

- Click Borders and Shading in the Borders gallery to display the Borders and Shading dialog box.

- Click All in the Setting area (Borders and Shading dialog box), which will place a border on every cell in the table.

- Click the Color box arrow and then click Brown, Accent 5 (ninth color, first row) in the Color palette to specify the border color.

- If necessary, click the Width box arrow and then click 1 pt to specify the thickness of the border (Figure 4–75).

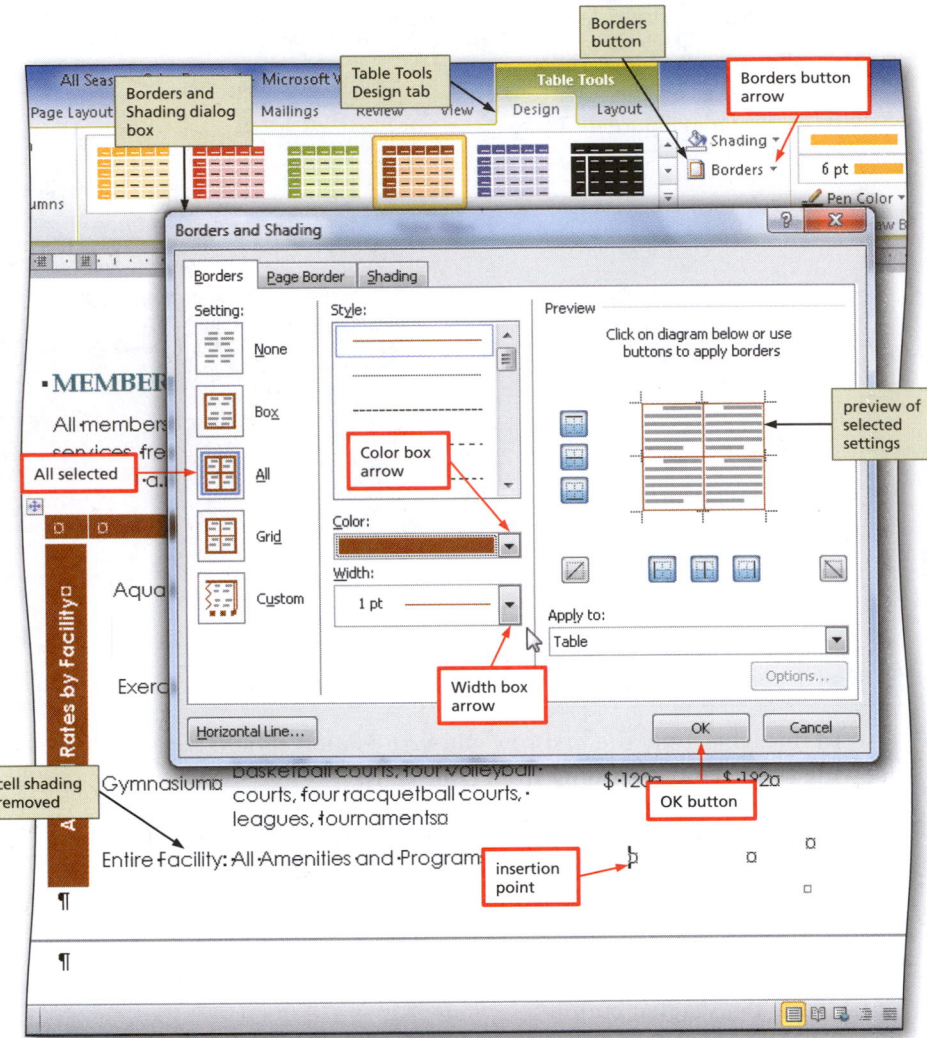

Figure 4–75

- Click the OK button to place the border shown in the preview area of the dialog box around the table cells in the document (shown in Figure 4–76).

To Sum Columns in a Table

In this project, the last row should display the sum (total) of the values in the last two columns: individual and family. Word can calculate the totals of rows and columns. You also can specify the format for how the totals will be displayed. The next steps sum the columns in a table.

1

- Position the insertion point in the cell to contain the sum (last row, second to last column).

2

- Display the Table Tools Layout tab.

- Click the Formula button (Table Tools Layout tab | Data group) to display the Formula dialog box.

Q&A

What is the formula that shows in the Formula box, and can I change it?

Word places a default formula in the Formula box, depending on the location of the numbers in surrounding cells. In this case, because numbers are above the current cell, Word displays a formula that will add the numbers above the current cell. You can change the formula that Word proposes, or type a different formula. For example, instead of summing numbers you can multiply them.

- Click the Number format box arrow (Formula dialog box) and then click the desired format for the result of the computation, in this case, the format with the dollar sign (Figure 4–76).

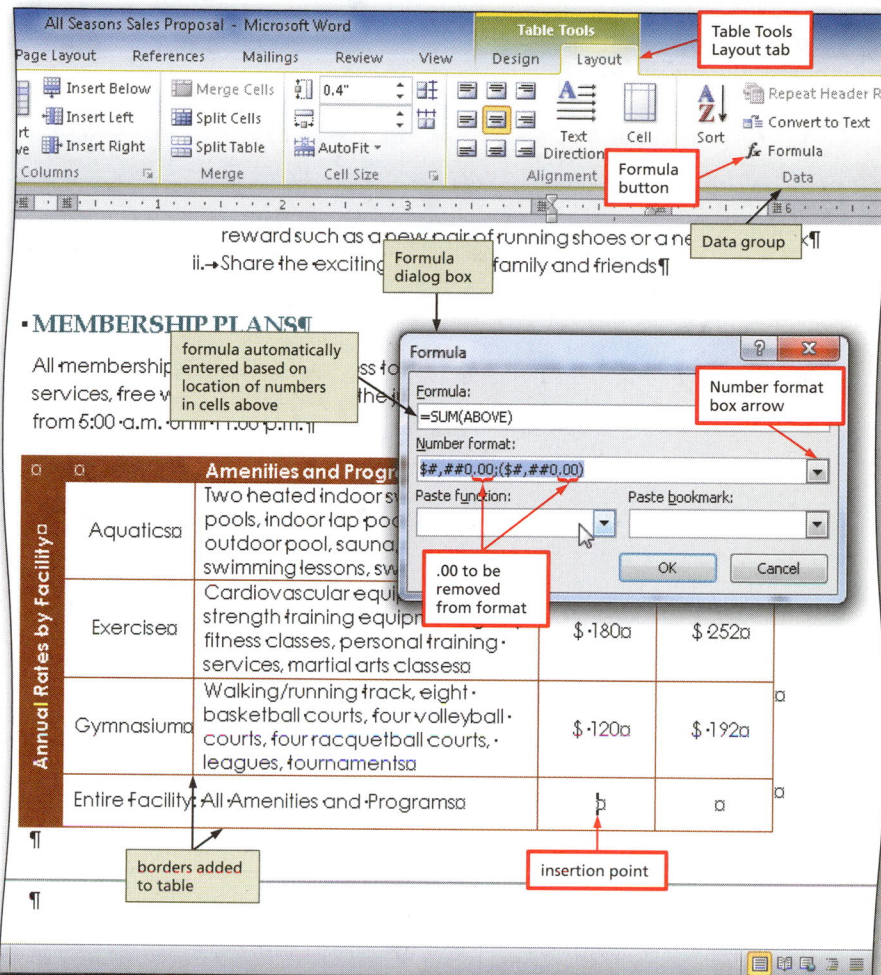

Figure 4–76

3

- Click the Number format box and then remove the two occurrences of .00 in the displayed format because you want the total to be displayed as a whole number, that is, with no cents (Figure 4–77).

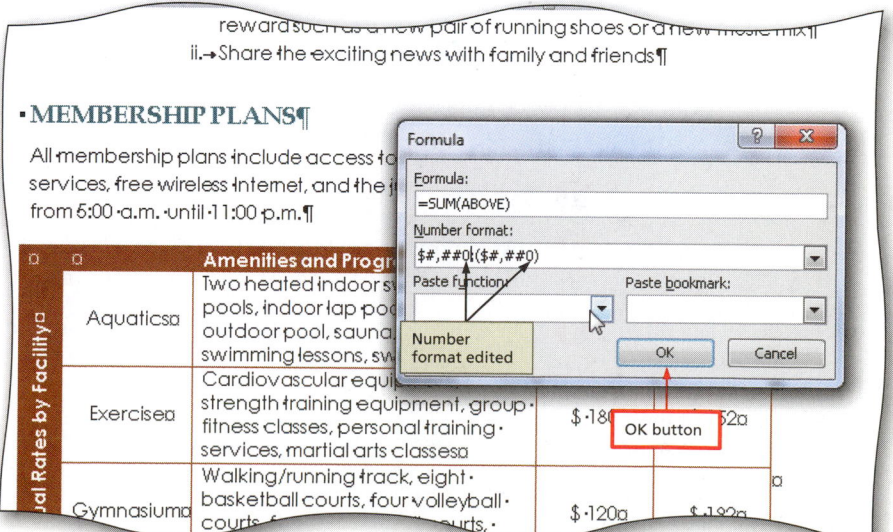

Figure 4–77

4

- Click the OK button (Formula dialog box) to place the sum of the numbers using the specified format in the current cell.

5

- Press the TAB key to move the insertion point to the next cell to sum.

- Repeat Steps 2, 3, and 4 to place the sum of the numbers using the specified format in the current cell (Figure 4–78).

Q&A

Can I sum a row instead of a column?

Yes. You would position the insertion point in an empty cell at the right edge of the row before clicking the Formula button.

Q&A

If I make a change to a number in a table, does Word automatically recompute the sum?

No. You will need to update the field by right-clicking it and then clicking Update Field on the shortcut menu, or selecting the field and then pressing the F9 key.

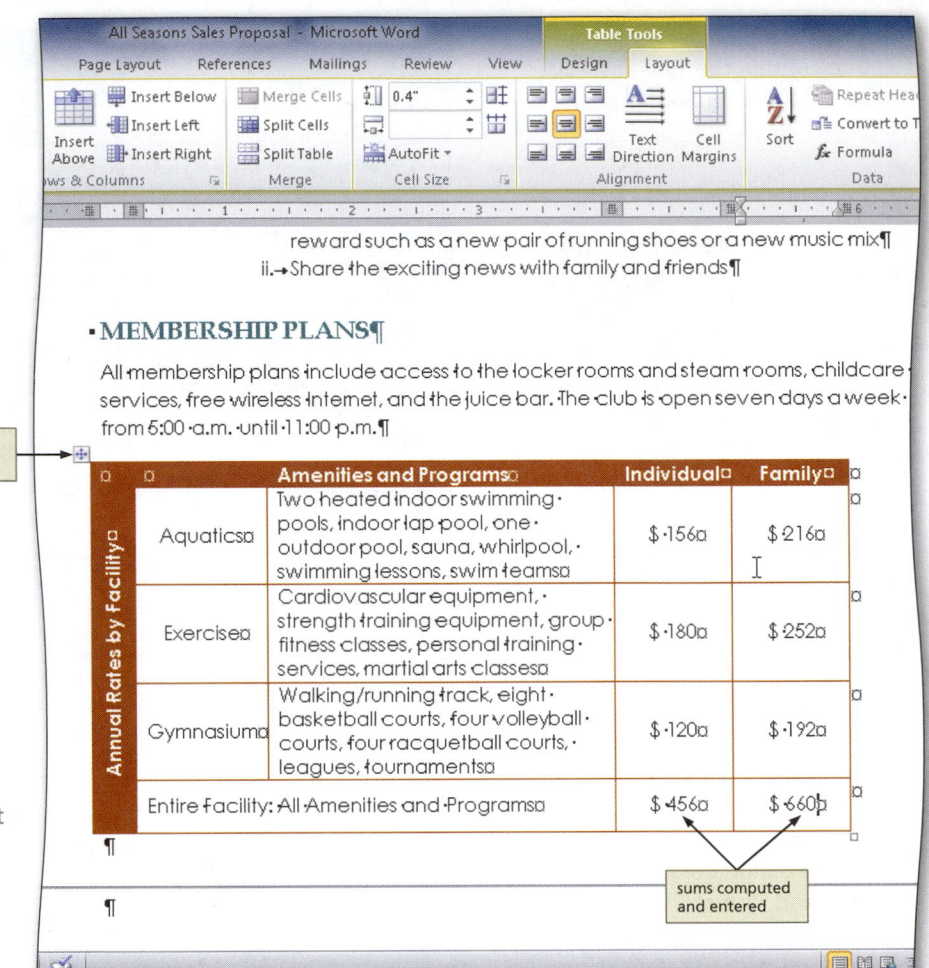

Figure 4–78

To Center a Table

The last step in formatting this table is to center it horizontally between the page margins. The following steps center a table.

1 Select the table.

2 Display the Home tab. Click the Center button (Home tab | Paragraph group) to center the selected table between the left and right margins.

3 Click anywhere to remove the selection from the table.

BTW

Moving Tables
If you wanted to move a table to a new location, you would point to the upper-left corner of the table until the table move handle appears (shown in Figure 4–78), point to the table move handle, and then drag the table move handle to move the entire table to a new location.

To Delete a Blank Paragraph and Show White Space

You notice an extra paragraph mark below the membership plans table that should be deleted because it is causing an extra blank page in the document. You also would like to show white space again, so that the headers and footers are visible in the document window. The following steps delete a blank paragraph and show white space.

1 Press CTRL+END to position the insertion point at the end of the document.

2 Press the BACKSPACE key to remove the extra blank paragraph and delete the blank page. If text spills onto a fourth page, remove space above paragraphs in the sales proposal until the entire proposal fits on three pages, as shown in Figure 4–1 on page WD 203.

3 Position the mouse pointer in the document window in the space below the current page or on the line between two pages so that the mouse pointer changes to a Show White Space button.

4 While the mouse pointer is a Show White Space button, double-click the mouse to show white space, that is, the top and bottom margins and space between pages (Figure 4–79).

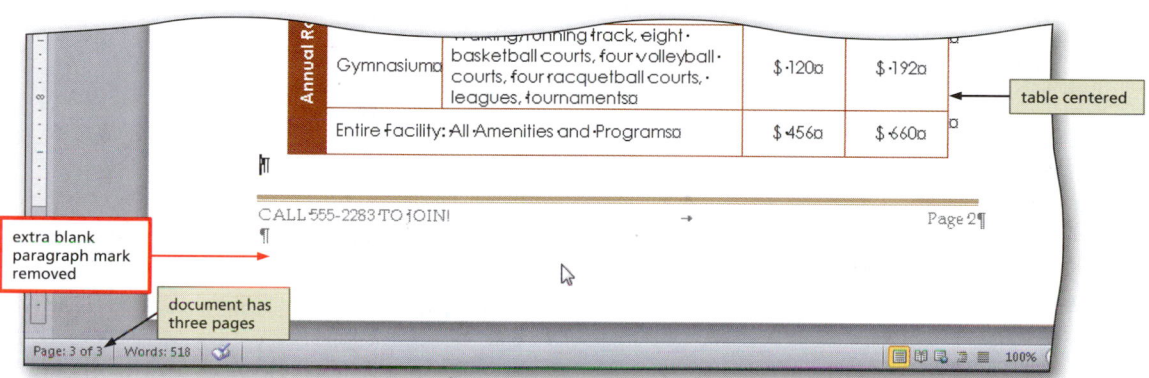

Figure 4–79

Creating a Watermark

The final task in this chapter is to create a watermark for the pages of the sales proposal. A **watermark** is text or a graphic that is displayed on top of or behind the text in a document. For example, a catalog may print the words, Sold Out, on top of sold-out items. The first draft of a five-year-plan may have the word, Draft, printed behind the text of the document. Some companies use their logos or other graphics as watermarks to add visual appeal to their documents.

To Zoom Two Pages

The following steps display two pages (the first two pages) in their entirety in the document window as large as possible, so that you can see the position of the watermark as you create it.

1 Press CTRL+HOME to position the insertion point at the beginning of the document.

2 Display the View tab. Click the Two Pages button (View tab | Zoom group) to display two entire pages in the document window as large as possible.

BTW

Quick Reference
For a table that lists how to complete the tasks covered in this book using the mouse, Ribbon, shortcut menu, and keyboard, see the Quick Reference Summary at the back of this book, or visit the Word 2010 Quick Reference Web page (scsite.com/wd2010/qr).

To Create a Watermark

In this project, the words, GET FIT!, are displayed behind all text and graphics as a watermark. The following steps create a watermark.

1

- Display the Page Layout tab.

- Click the Watermark button (Page Layout tab | Page Background group) to display the Watermark gallery (Figure 4–80).

2

- Click Custom Watermark in the Watermark gallery to display the Printed Watermark dialog box.

- Click Text watermark (Printed Watermark dialog box) so that you can enter the text and formats for the watermark.

- Delete the text, ASAP, and then type **GET FIT!** in the Text box.

- Click the Size box arrow to display a list of available watermark sizes. Scroll to and then click 144 as the watermark size.

- Click the Color box arrow and then click Tan, Background 2 (third color, first row) as the watermark color.

- Click Horizontal, so that the watermark appears horizontally on the page.

- Click the Apply button to show a preview of the watermark on the pages in the document window (Figure 4–81).

3

- Click the Close button (Printed Watermark dialog box) to close the dialog box.

Q&A How do I remove a watermark from a document?

Click the Watermark button (Page Layout tab | Page Background group) and then click Remove Watermark.

Q&A How do I create a picture watermark?

Click Picture watermark in the Printed Watermark dialog box (Figure 4–81), select the picture for the watermark, and then click the OK button.

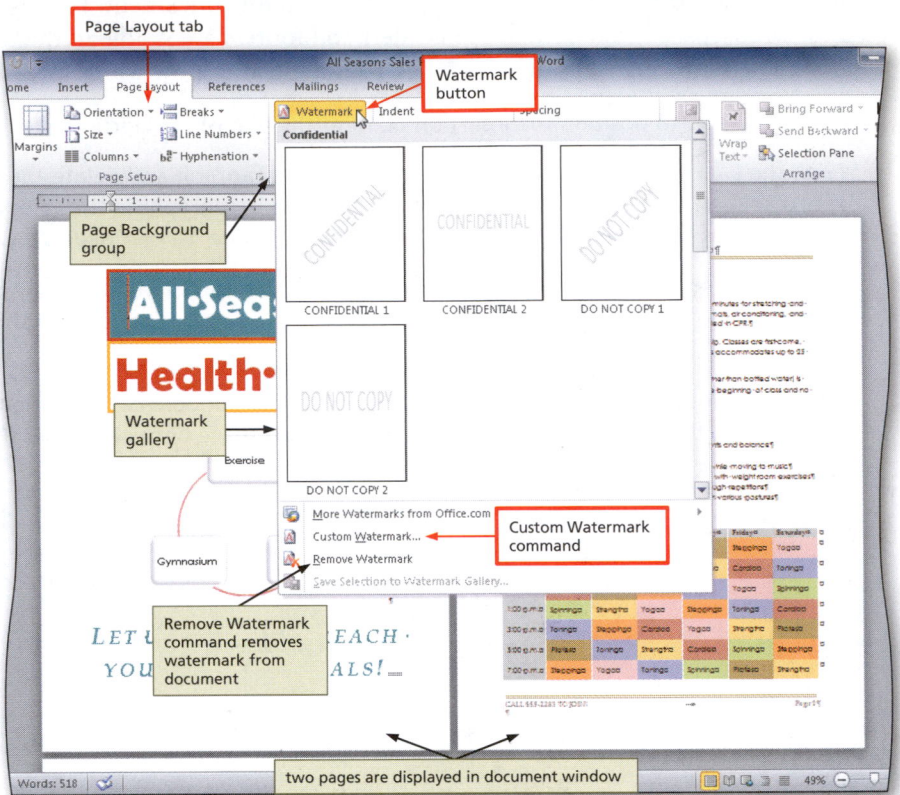

Figure 4–80

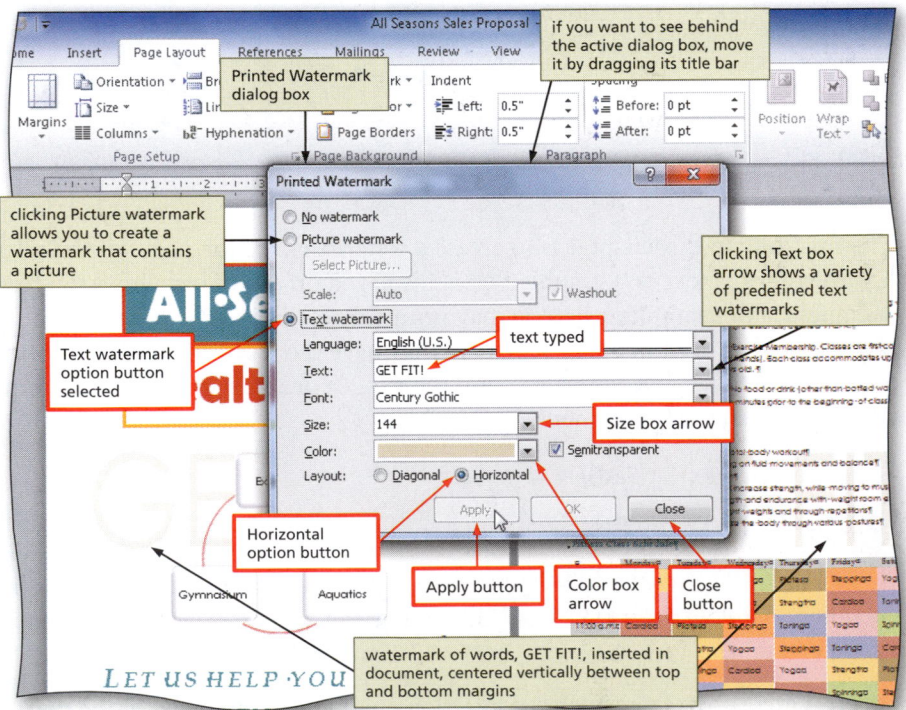

Figure 4–81

Other Ways

1. Click Quick Parts button (Insert tab | Text group), click Building Blocks

   Organizer on Quick Parts menu, select desired watermark (Building Blocks

   Organizer dialog box), click Insert button

To Check Spelling, Save, Print, and Quit Word

The following steps check the spelling of the document, save and print the document, and then quit Word.

1 Display the Review tab. Click the Spelling & Grammar button (Review tab | Proofing group) to begin the spelling and grammar check. Correct any misspelled words.

2 Save the sales proposal again with the same file name.

3 Print the sales proposal (shown in Figure 4–1 on page WD 203).

4 Quit Word.

> **BTW**
>
> **Conserving Ink and Toner**
> If you want to conserve ink or toner, you can instruct Word to print draft quality documents by clicking File on the Ribbon to open the Backstage view, clicking Options in the Backstage view to display the Word Options dialog box, clicking Advanced in the left pane (Word Options dialog box), scrolling to the Print area in the right pane, placing a check mark in the 'Use draft quality' check box, and then clicking the OK button. Then, use the Backstage view to print the document as usual.

Chapter Summary

In this chapter, you learned how to add a border to a paragraph, change paragraph indentation, insert and format a SmartArt graphic, apply character effects, insert a section break, insert a Word document in an open document, change theme fonts, insert formatted headers and footers, sort lists and tables, modify and format existing Word tables, sum columns in a table, and insert a watermark. The items listed below include all the new Word skills you have learned in this chapter.

1. Border a Paragraph (WD 206)
2. Change Left and Right Paragraph Indent (WD 210)
3. Insert a SmartArt Graphic (WD 212)
4. Delete Shapes and Add Text to Shapes in a SmartArt Graphic (WD 214)
5. Change Colors of a SmartArt Graphic (WD 215)
6. Add a Shape to a SmartArt Graphic (WD 216)
7. Apply a SmartArt Style (WD 216)
8. Format Characters and Modify Character Spacing Using the Font Dialog Box (WD 216)
9. Insert a Next Page Section Break (WD 220)
10. Delete a Section Break (WD 221)
11. Insert a Word Document in an Open Document (WD 222)
12. Print Specific Pages in a Document (WD 223)
13. Delete a Page Break (WD 225)
14. Modify the Default Font Settings (WD 225)
15. Reset the Default Font Settings (WD 225)
16. Change Theme Fonts (WD 226)
17. Insert a Formatted Header Different from the Previous Header (WD 229)
18. Insert a Formatted Footer (WD 230)
19. Format Page Numbers to Start at a Different Number (WD 231)
20. Sort Paragraphs (WD 232)
21. Use the Format Painter Button (WD 233)
22. Customize Bullets in a List (WD 235)
23. Create a Multilevel Numbered List (WD 236)
24. Show Gridlines (WD 239)
25. Change Column Width (WD 240)
26. Hide White Space (WD 241)
27. Change Row Height (WD 241)
28. Shade a Table Cell (WD 243)
29. Select Nonadjacent Items (WD 244)
30. Change Cell Spacing (WD 245)
31. Delete a Column (WD 247)
32. Delete a Row (WD 247)
33. Sort a Table (WD 248)
34. Split Cells (WD 249)
35. Move a Cell Boundary (WD 250)
36. Distribute Columns (WD 250)
37. Distribute Rows (WD 251)
38. Display Text in a Cell Vertically (WD 252)
39. Border a Table (WD 254)
40. Sum Columns in a Table (WD 254)
41. Create a Watermark (WD 258)

If you have a SAM 2010 user profile, your instructor may have assigned an autogradable version of this assignment. If so, log into the SAM 2010 Web site at www.cengage.com/sam2010 to download the instruction and start files.

Learn It Online

Test your knowledge of chapter content and key terms.

Instructions: To complete the Learn It Online exercises, start your browser, click the Address bar, and then enter the Web address **scsite.com/wd2010/learn**. When the Word 2010 Learn It Online page is displayed, click the link for the exercise you want to complete and then read the instructions.

Chapter Reinforcement TF, MC, and SA
A series of true/false, multiple choice, and short answer questions that test your knowledge of the chapter content.

Flash Cards
An interactive learning environment where you identify chapter key terms associated with displayed definitions.

Practice Test
A series of multiple choice questions that test your knowledge of chapter content and key terms.

Who Wants To Be a Computer Genius?
An interactive game that challenges your knowledge of chapter content in the style of a television quiz show.

Wheel of Terms
An interactive game that challenges your knowledge of chapter key terms in the style of the television show *Wheel of Fortune*.

Crossword Puzzle Challenge
A crossword puzzle that challenges your knowledge of key terms presented in the chapter.

Apply Your Knowledge

Reinforce the skills and apply the concepts you learned in this chapter.

Working with a Table
Note: To complete this assignment, you will be required to use the Data Files for Students. See the inside back cover of this book for instructions on downloading the Data Files for Students, or contact your instructor for information about accessing the required files.

Instructions: Start Word. Open the document, Apply 4-1 Expenses Breakdown Draft, from the Data Files for Students. The document contains a Word table that you are to modify. The modified table is shown in Figure 4–82.

Whitcomb Services					
Expenses Breakdown					
	1st Quarter	2nd Quarter	3rd Quarter	4th Quarter	Total
Advertising	6,444.22	5,398.99	6,293.49	6,009.29	$24,145.99
Maintenance	1,224.03	982.45	1,029.45	990.32	$4,226.25
Rent	2,200.00	2,200.00	2,200.00	2,200.00	$8,800.00
Salaries	6,954.34	7,300.28	6,887.39	7,102.83	$28,244.84
Supplies	1,932.76	1,727.84	1,623.26	1,887.54	$7,171.40
Total	$18,755.35	$17,609.56	$18,033.59	$18,189.98	$72,588.48

Figure 4–82

Perform the following tasks:

1. Show gridlines.

2. Delete the blank column between the 3rd and 4th Quarter columns.

3. Use the Distribute Rows command to evenly space all the rows in the table.

4. Use the Distribute Columns command to make the 1st, 2nd, 3rd, and 4th Quarter and Total columns evenly spaced.

5. Change the width of the 1st, 2nd, 3rd, and 4th Quarter and Total columns to 1".

6. Use the Formula button (Table Tools Layout tab | Data group) to place totals in the bottom row for the 1st, 2nd, 3rd, and 4th Quarter columns. The totals should be formatted to display dollar signs and cents.

7. Use the Formula button (Table Tools Layout tab | Data group) to place totals in the right column. Start in the bottom-right cell and work your way up the column.

8. Add a row to the top of the table. Merge all cells in the first row into a single cell. Enter the company name, Whitcomb Services, as the table title. Center the title.

9. Split the cell in the first row into two rows (one column). In the new cell below the company name, enter the text, Expenses Breakdown, as the subtitle.

10. Shade the first row Orange, Accent 6, Darker 25%. Shade the second row Orange, Accent 6, Lighter 40%.

11. Add a 1 pt, Orange, Accent 6, Darker 50% border to all cells in the table.

12. Hide gridlines.

13. Change the height of the row containing the quarter headings (row 3) to .01". Change the alignment of these headings to Align Top Center.

14. Change the height of all expense rows and the total row (rows 4 through 9) to 0.3".

15. Change the alignment of the cells in the first column to the left of all the dollar amounts to Align Center Left.

16. Change the alignment of the cells containing dollar amounts to Align Center Right.

17. Center the entire table across the width of the page.

18. Sort the rows containing the expenses.

19. Change the document properties as specified by your instructor.

20. Save the modified file with the file name, Apply 4-1 Expenses Breakdown Modified.

21. Submit the revised table in the format specified by your instructor.

Extend Your Knowledge

Extend the skills you learned in this chapter and experiment with new skills. You may need to use Help to complete the assignment.

Modifying Multilevel List Formats, Drawing Tables, and Creating Picture Watermarks

Note: To complete this assignment, you will be required to use the Data Files for Students. See the inside back cover of this book for instructions on downloading the Data Files for Students, or contact your instructor for information about accessing the required files.

Instructions: Start Word. Open the document, Extend 4-1 Tax and Investment Seminars Draft, from the Data Files for Students. You will define a new number format for the multilevel list, insert a picture watermark, and use Word's Draw Table feature to draw a table.

Continued >

Extend Your Knowledge *continued*

Perform the following tasks:

1. Use Help to learn about defining multilevel list number formats, picture watermarks, and Draw Table.

2. For each level in the multilevel list, define a new number format that is different from the format in the draft file. Be sure to change (at a minimum) the font, font size, and font color of the number format.

3. Insert a picture watermark using the Scales.wmf image on the Data Files for Students.

4. Below the multilevel list, draw the table shown in Figure 4–83. That is, use the Draw Table button to create the blank table.

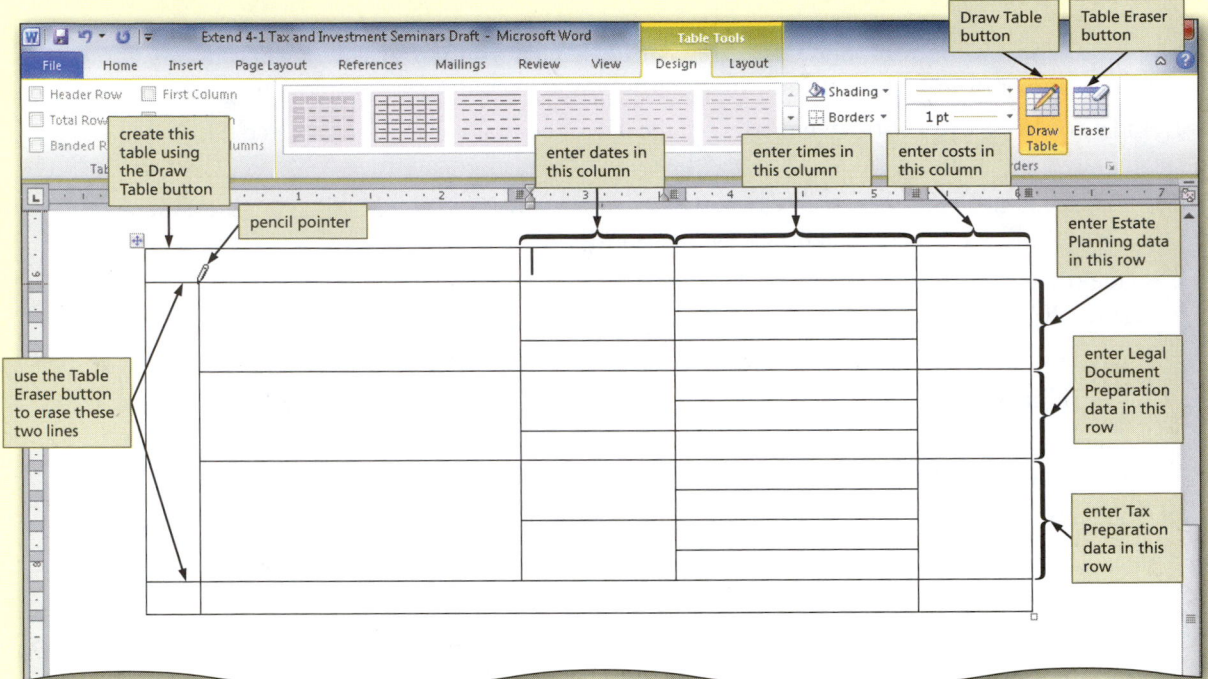

Figure 4–83

5. In the leftmost column of the table, enter the text, Seminar Topic, so that it displays vertically in the cell.

6. In the second column of the table, enter these labels in the second, third, and fourth rows: Estate Planning, Legal Document Preparation, and Tax Preparation.

7. In the top row, enter these headings in the last three columns: Date, Times, and Cost.

8. For Estate Planning, use this data for the table: Cost is $120; January 17 class times are 9:00 – 11:00 a.m. and 7:00 – 9:00 p.m.; January 31 class times are 1:00 – 3:00 p.m.

9. For Legal Document Preparation, use this data for the table: Cost is $140; January 10 class times are 9:00 – 11:30 a.m. and 7:30 – 10:00 p.m.; January 24 class times are 1:00 – 3:30 p.m.

10. For Tax Preparation, use this data for the table: Cost is $125; January 3 class times are 9:00 – 11:15 a.m. and 7:00 – 9:15 p.m.; January 10 class times are 1:00 – 3:15 p.m. and 5:00 – 7:15 p.m.

11. Enter the text, Special Offer: Attend all three seminars, in the bottom row. The cost for the bottom, right cell is $350.

12. Enhance the table as you deem appropriate.

13. Change the document properties, as specified by your instructor. Save the revised document using a new file name and then submit it in the format specified by your instructor.

Make It Right

Analyze a document and correct all errors and/or improve the design.

Formatting a Title Page

Note: To complete this assignment, you will be required to use the Data Files for Students. See the inside back cover of this book for instructions on downloading the Data Files for Students, or contact your instructor for information about accessing the required files.

Instructions: Start Word. Open the document, Make It Right 4-1 Home Health Title Page Draft, from the Data Files for Students. The document is a title page that is missing elements and that is not formatted ideally (Figure 4–84). You are to remove the header and footer, edit the border, change paragraph indents, modify the SmartArt graphic, change character spacing, and adjust font sizes.

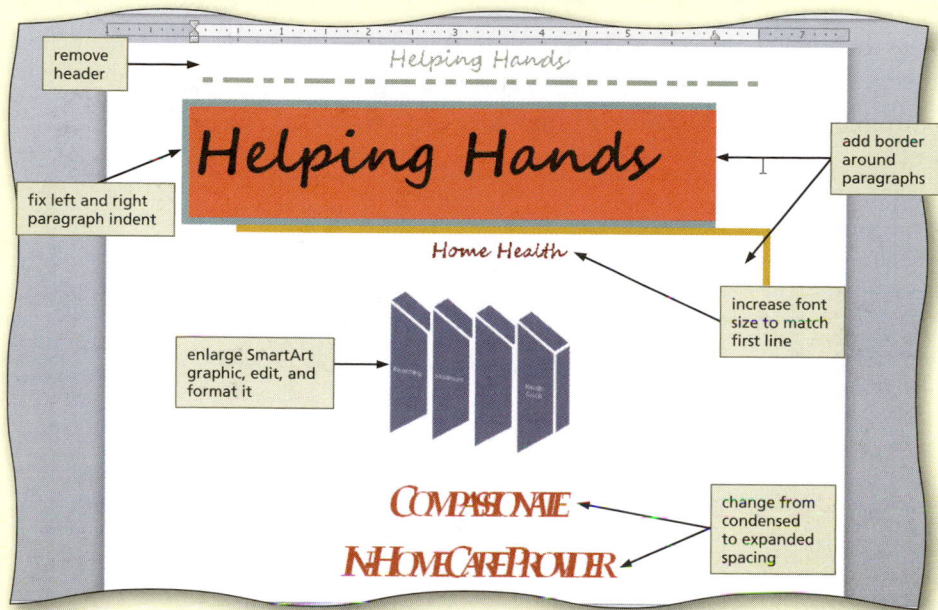

Figure 4–84

Perform the following tasks:

1. Remove the header and footer from the title page.
2. Modify the borders on the first and second lines so that they surround all edges of each paragraph.
3. Change the left and right paragraph indent of the first two lines (paragraphs) so that they have a 0.5" left and right indent.
4. Increase the font size of the text in the second line to match the font size of the text in the first line.
5. Increase the size of the SmartArt graphic on the title page. Delete the shape that has no text in it. Change the word, Maximum, to Optimum in the middle shape. Change the colors of the SmartArt graphic and then change the SmartArt style.
6. Change the zoom to one page.
7. Change the character spacing of the last two lines on the title page from condensed to expanded. The first of the two lines should be expanded more than the second of the two lines.
8. Increase font sizes so that the text is easy to read.
9. Add or remove space above or below paragraphs so that all contents of the title page fit on a single page. Change the zoom back to 100%.
10. Change the document properties, as specified by your instructor. Save the revised document with a new file name and then submit it in the format specified by your instructor.

In the Lab

Design and/or create a document using the guidelines, concepts, and skills presented in this chapter. Labs are listed in order of increasing difficulty.

Lab 1: Creating a Proposal with a SmartArt Graphic, a Bulleted List, and a Table

Problem: The owner of Reflections, a center for employee retreats, has hired you to prepare a sales proposal describing their facilities, which will be mailed to local businesses.

Instructions: Perform the following tasks:
1. Change the theme fonts to the Hardcover font set.
2. Create the title page as shown in Figure 4–85a. Be sure to do the following:
   a. Insert the SmartArt graphic, add text to it, and change its colors and style as specified.
   b. Change the fonts, font sizes, and font colors. Add the paragraph border. Indent the left and right edges of the title paragraph by 0.5 inches.
3. At the bottom of the title page, insert a next page section break. Clear formatting.

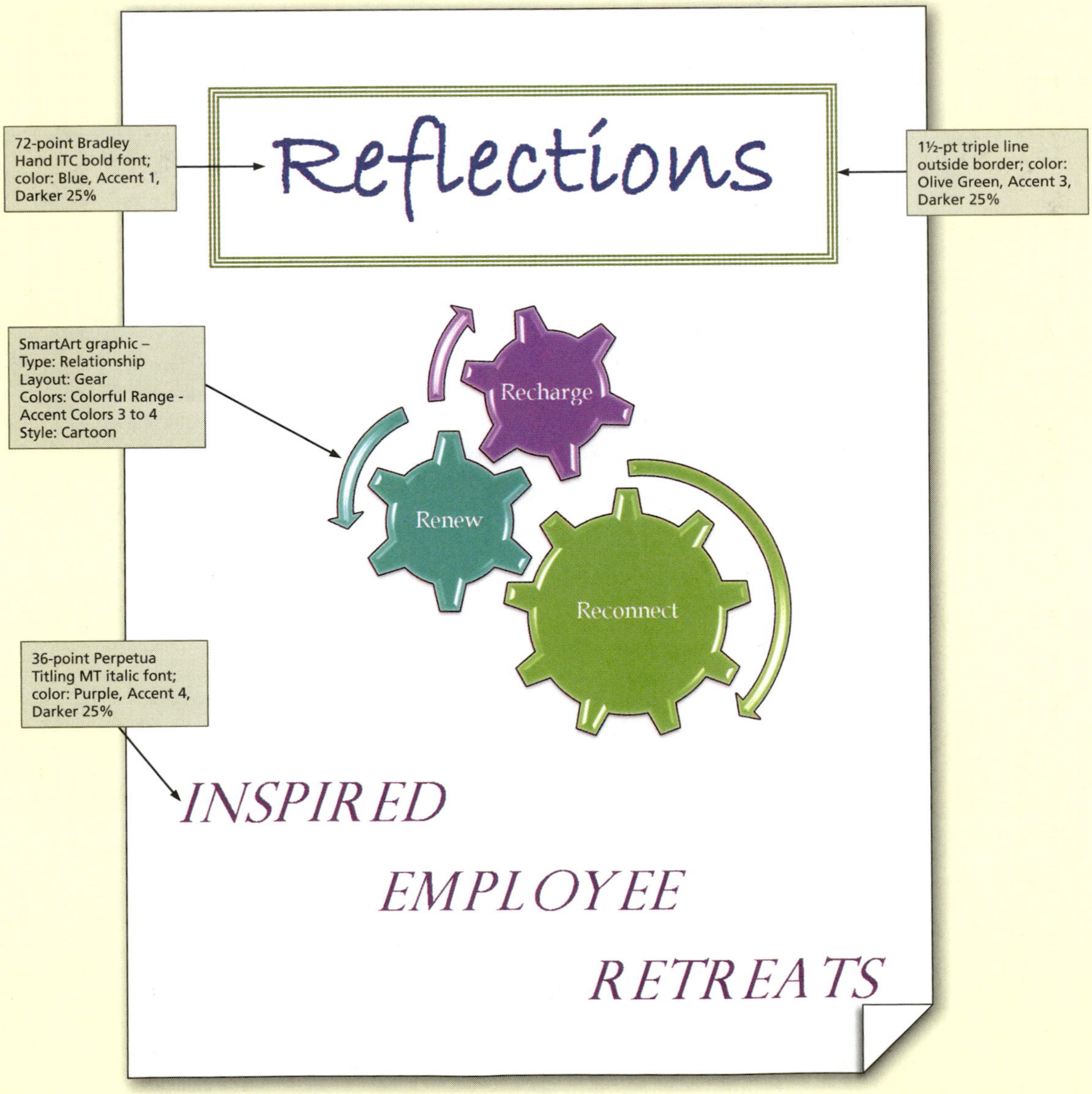

72-point Bradley Hand ITC bold font; color: Blue, Accent 1, Darker 25%

1½-pt triple line outside border; color: Olive Green, Accent 3, Darker 25%

Reflections

SmartArt graphic – Type: Relationship Layout: Gear Colors: Colorful Range - Accent Colors 3 to 4 Style: Cartoon

Recharge

Renew

Reconnect

36-point Perpetua Titling MT italic font; color: Purple, Accent 4, Darker 25%

INSPIRED

EMPLOYEE

RETREATS

Figure 4–85 (a) Title Page

4. Create the second page of the proposal as shown in Figure 4–85b.

   a. Insert the formatted header using the Alphabet design. The header should appear only on the second page (section) of the proposal. Format the header text as shown.
   b. Insert the formatted footer using the Alphabet design. The footer should appear only on the second page (section) of the proposal. Format the footer text as shown. Delete the page number.
   c. Format the headings using the heading styles as specified.
   d. Change the bullets in the bulleted list to purple picture bullets. Format the first word of one bulleted item as shown. Use the format painter to copy the formatting to the remaining initial words in the bulleted list.
   e. Create the table as shown. Border the table as specified. Distribute rows so that they are all the same height. Change the row height to 0.21 inches. Center the table. Left-align text in the first column, and center text in the second and third columns. Shade the table cells as specified.

5. Adjust spacing above and below paragraphs as necessary to fit all content as shown in the figure.

6. Check the spelling. Change the document properties, as specified by your instructor. Save the document with Lab 4-1 Employee Retreat Proposal as the file name.

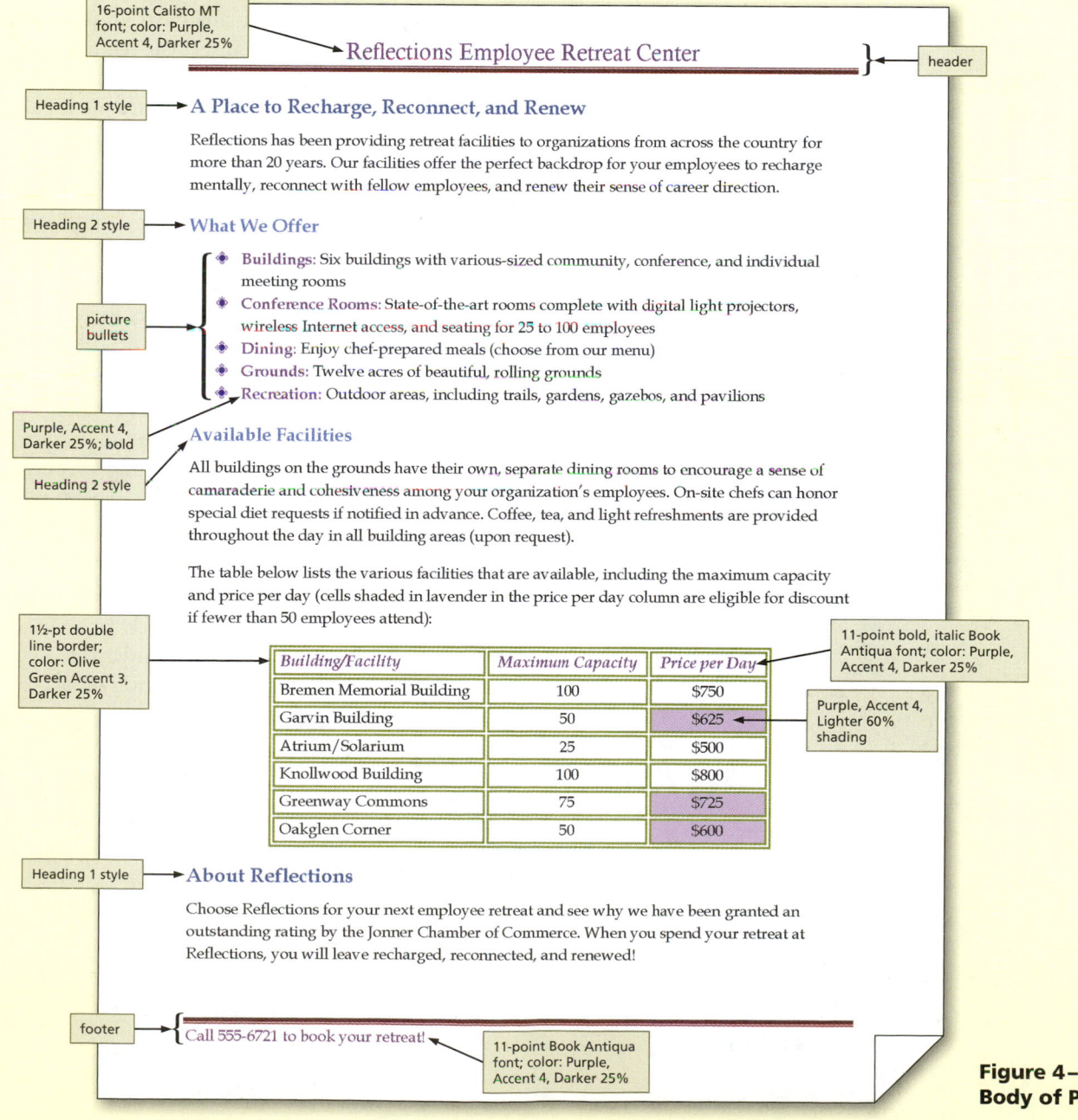

Figure 4–85 (b)
Body of Proposal

In the Lab

Lab 2: Creating a Proposal with a SmartArt Graphic, a Complex Table, and a Numbered List

Problem: The owner of the Wide Eye Java has hired you to prepare a sales proposal describing its monthly service in a first order confirmation.

Note: To complete this assignment, you will be required to use the Data Files for Students. See the inside back cover of this book for instructions on downloading the Data Files for Students, or contact your instructor for information about accessing the required files.

Instructions: Perform the following tasks:

1. Change the theme colors to the Horizon color scheme.
2. Change the theme fonts to the Pushpin font set.
3. Create the title page as shown in Figure 4–86a. Be sure to do the following:

   a. Insert the SmartArt graphic, add text to it, insert the picture, and change its colors and style as specified. The picture file is called Coffee Pot.wmf and is available on the Data Files for Students. (*Hint*: Double-click the middle of the picture placeholder to display the Insert Picture dialog box, locate the picture file, and then click the Insert button (Insert Picture dialog box) to insert a picture.) Resize the picture as necessary.

   b. Change the fonts, font sizes, and font colors. Include the border and paragraph shading around the company name. Expand the characters in the company name, JAVA, by 20 points. Indent the left and right edges of the title paragraph by 0.5 inches.

4. At the bottom of the title page, insert a next page section break. Clear formatting.

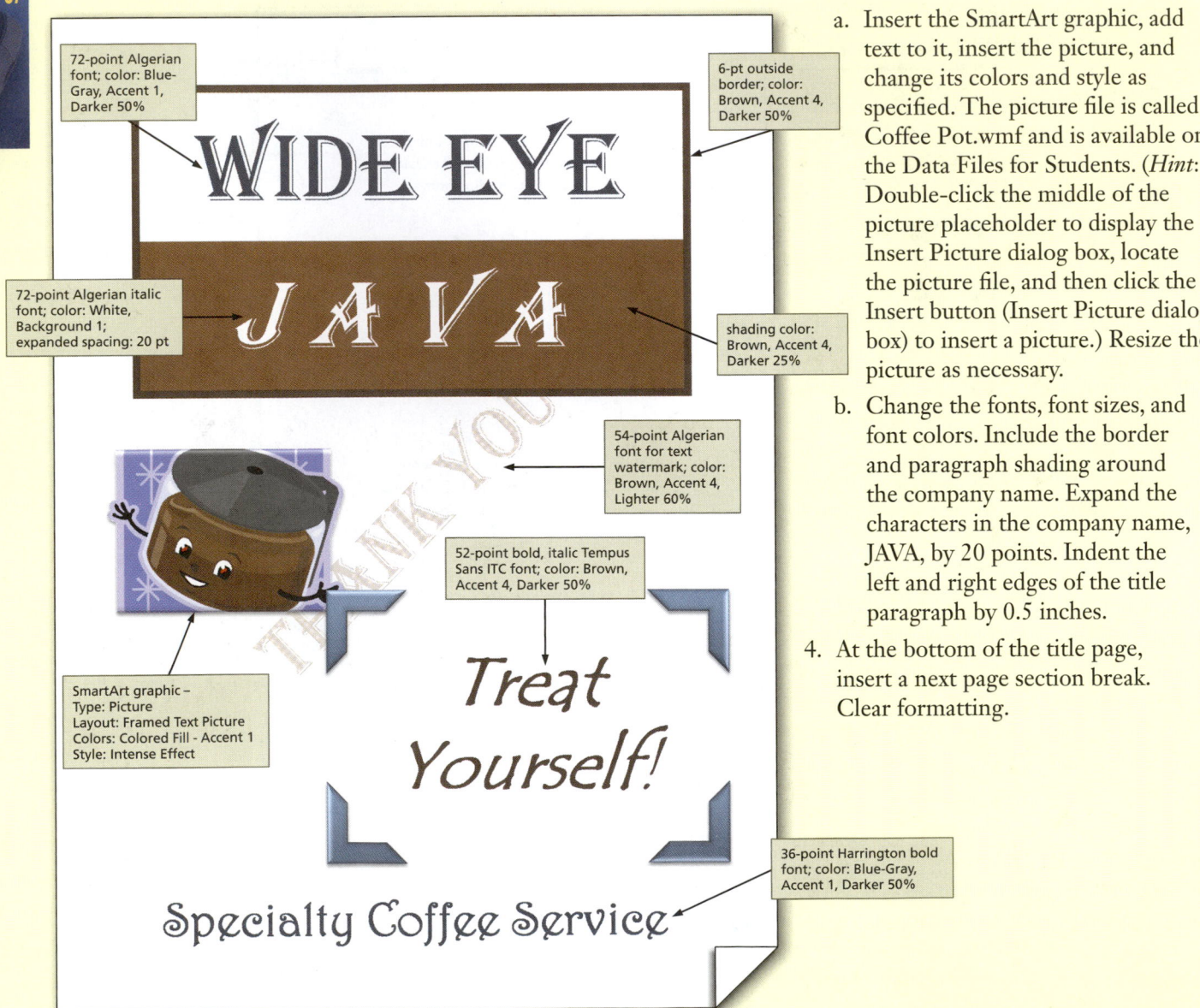

Labels on the figure:
- 72-point Algerian font; color: Blue-Gray, Accent 1, Darker 50%
- 6-pt outside border; color: Brown, Accent 4, Darker 50%
- 72-point Algerian italic font; color: White, Background 1; expanded spacing: 20 pt
- shading color: Brown, Accent 4, Darker 25%
- 54-point Algerian font for text watermark; color: Brown, Accent 4, Lighter 60%
- 52-point bold, italic Tempus Sans ITC font; color: Brown, Accent 4, Darker 50%
- SmartArt graphic – Type: Picture Layout: Framed Text Picture Colors: Colored Fill - Accent 1 Style: Intense Effect
- 36-point Harrington bold font; color: Blue-Gray, Accent 1, Darker 50%

Figure 4–86 (a) Title Page

5. Create the second page of the proposal as shown in Figure 4–86b.

   a. Insert the formatted header using the Alphabet design. The header should appear only on the second page of the proposal. Format the header text as shown.

   b. Format the headings using the heading styles specified. Adjust spacing before the Heading 1 style to 12 point and after to 6 point, and before and after the Heading 2 style to 6 point. Update both heading styles.

   c. Insert the formatted footer using the Alphabet design. The footer should appear only on the second page of the proposal. Delete the page number.

   d. Create the table as shown. Border the table as specified. Distribute rows so that they are all the same height. Change the row height to 0.2 inches. Align center left the text in the Item Description column, align center the text in the Quantity column and the Cost and Total headings, and align center right the dollar amounts in the Cost and Total columns. Center the table. Change the direction of the Food and Nonfood headings. Use a formula to compute the values in the total column (quantity times cost). Use another formula to sum the totals in the order total cell.

   e. Create the numbered list as shown.

6. Create a diagonal watermark with Thank You! as the text. Adjust spacing above and below paragraphs as necessary to fit all content as shown in the figure.

7. Check the spelling. Change the document properties, as specified by your instructor. Save the document with Lab 4-2 Coffee Service Proposal as the file name.

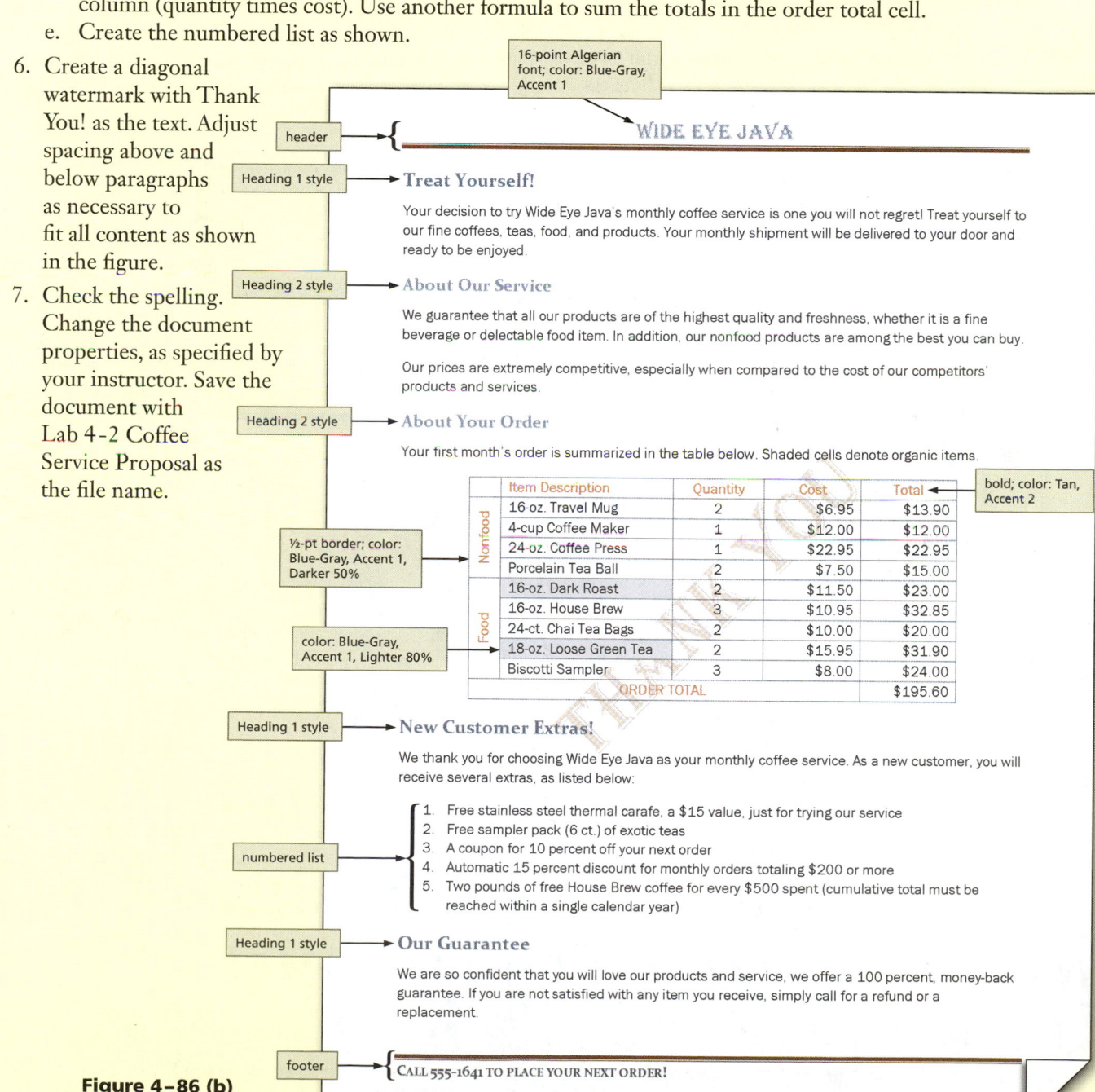

Figure 4–86 (b)
Body of Proposal

In the Lab

Lab 3: Enhancing a Draft of a Sales Proposal with a Title Page, a Bulleted List, Tables, and a Multilevel List

Problem: You work at Nature Kids Summer Camp. Your coworker has prepared a draft of a proposal about the upcoming summer camp. You decide to enhance the proposal by adding picture bullets, a multilevel list, and another table. You also prepare a title page that includes a SmartArt graphic.

Note: To complete this assignment, you will be required to use the Data Files for Students. See the inside back cover of this book for instructions on downloading the Data Files for Students, or contact your instructor for information about accessing the required files.

Instructions: Perform the following tasks:

1. Change the theme colors to the Solstice color scheme. Change the theme fonts to the Aspect font set.
2. Create a title page similar to the one shown in Figure 4–87a.

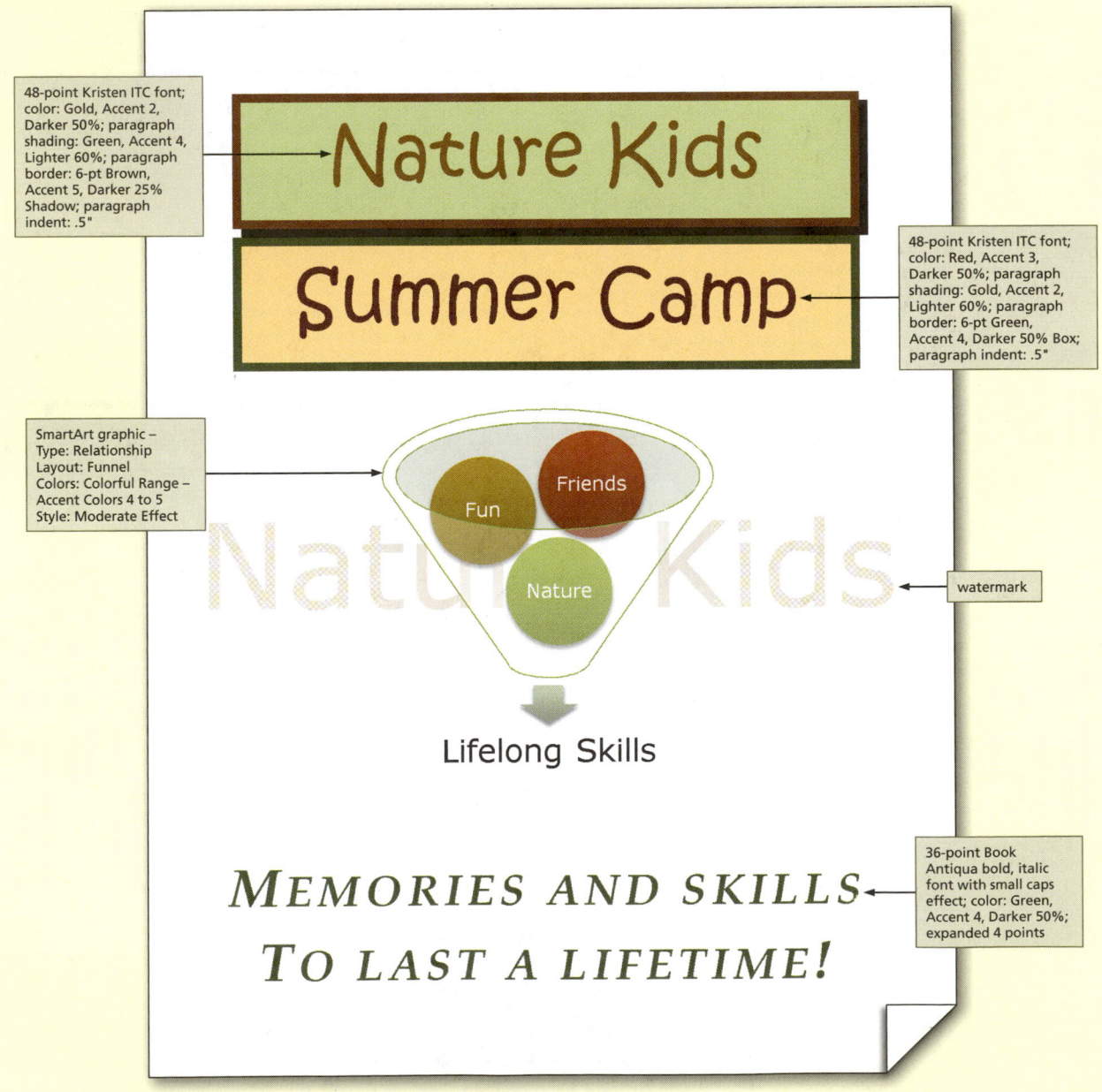

Figure 4–87 (a) Title Page

3. Insert a next page section break. Insert the draft of the body of the proposal below the title page. The draft is called Lab 4-3 Nature Kids Camp Proposal Draft on the Data Files for Students.

4. Modify the first page of the body of the draft so that it looks like Figure 4–87b, by doing the following:

   a. Delete the page break above the Outdoor Activities heading.

   b. Insert a header and footer as shown. The footer should have a page number. Change the starting page number to 1.

   c. Change the style of bullet characters in the list to picture bullets. Format the first words in the bulleted item to the Intense Emphasis Quick Style. Use the format painter to copy the formatting to the remaining words. Sort the bulleted list.

   d. In the table below the bulleted list, shade cells similarly to the figure, adjust alignment of text in cells as shown, and change cell spacing to 0.02 inches between cells.

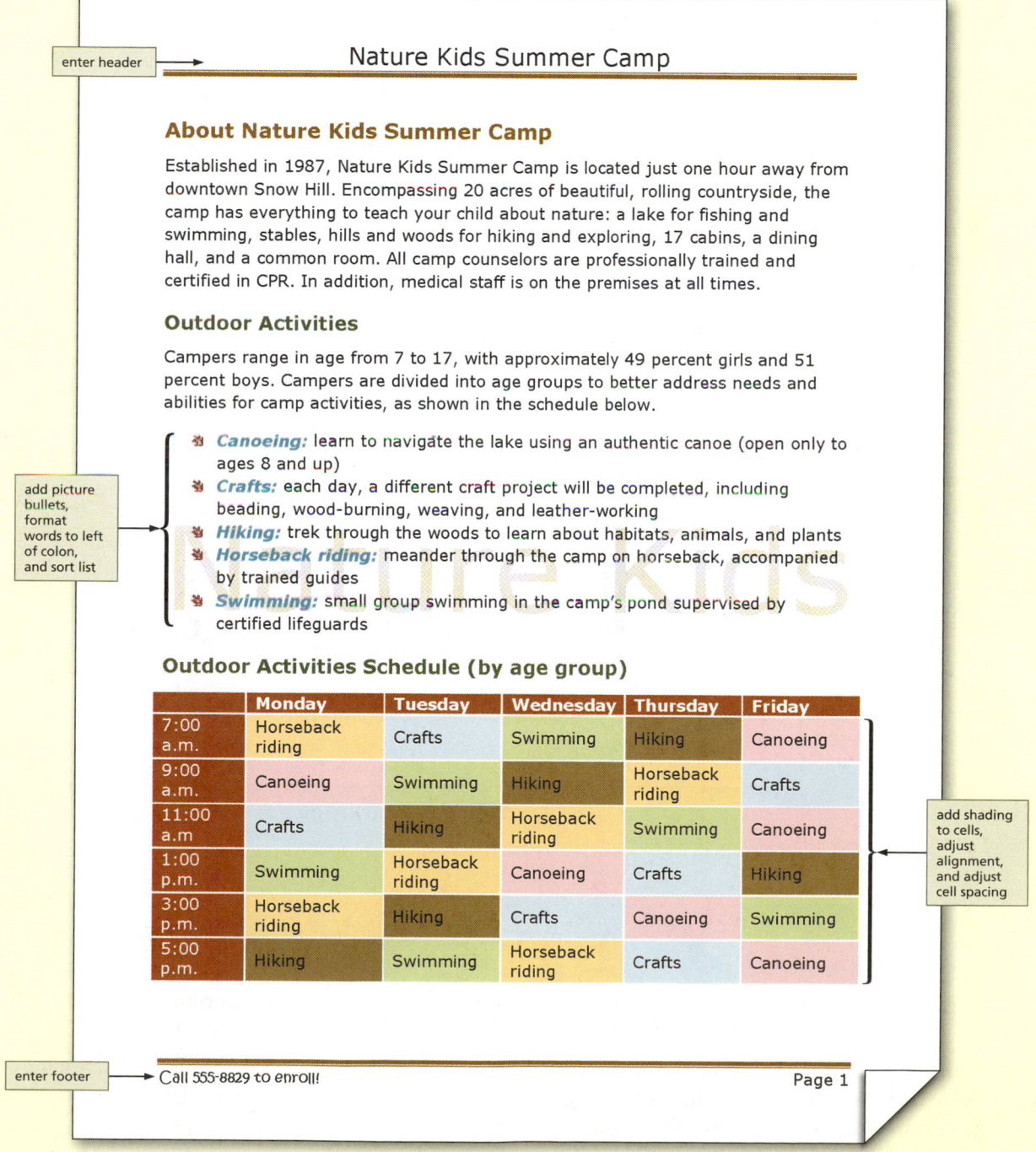

Figure 4–87 (b) Page 1

Continued >

In the Lab continued

5. Modify the second page of the body of the draft so that it looks like Figure 4–87c, by doing the following:

   a. Create the multilevel list below the Camper Tips heading.

   b. Create and format the table as shown below the Camp Fees paragraph.

6. Create the watermark as shown.

7. Check the spelling. Change the document properties, as specified by your instructor. Save the active document with the file name, Lab 4-3 Nature Kids Camp Proposal.

Nature Kids Summer Camp

Camper Tips

1. Bring only the items necessary, as outlined below:
   a. Bedding and linen (sleeping bag or blanket, pillow, and linen)
   b. Hygiene items, such as toothbrush and toothpaste, soap, shampoo, towels, and shower shoes
   c. Personal items, such as portable media players, cell phones, and handheld games, are discouraged strongly
2. Meals are provided, with light snacks available upon request
   a. Campers will be fed at assigned mealtimes, by age and cabin
   b. Healthy, balanced breakfasts, lunches, and dinners (please inform us of any special diet requests/restrictions)
3. Clothing recommendations are as follows:
   a. Footwear
      i. At least one pair each of hiking boots and tennis/running shoes
      ii. Extra socks (at least three extra pairs recommended)
      iii. Plastic or waterproof shoes for shower wear
   b. Clothing
      i. Comfortable clothing suitable for outdoor activity
      ii. Swimwear
      iii. Light jacket or sweatshirts for cool evenings

create this multilevel list

Camp Fees

The costs of attending this camp are outlined in the table below, along with cabin assignments by age group. All meals, lodging, and activities are included in the cost.

create this table

Age Group		Cabin Assignment	Cost
	7	Tadpole Grove Cabins #1, 3, 4, and 6	$425
	8 – 9	Arbor Grove Cabins #2, 5, 7, and 9	$400
	10 – 11	Campfire Hamlet Cabins #8, 10, and 11	$380
	12 – 14	Green Hollow Cabins #12, 13, and 15	$350
	15 – 17	Wilderness Circle Cabins #14, 16, and 17	$325
Additional campers: Each sibling can attend for a flat fee, regardless of age group			$300

Call 555-8829 to enroll!   Page 2

Figure 4–87 (c) Page 2

Cases and Places

Apply your creative thinking and problem solving skills to design and implement a solution.

Note: To complete these assignments, you may be required to use the Data Files for Students. See the inside back cover of this book for instructions on downloading the Data Files for Students, or contact your instructor for information about accessing the required files.

1: Create a Proposal for Tutoring

Academic

As a part-time assistant in the tutoring center at your school, your boss has asked you to design a two-page sales proposal for the center that will be posted on campus. The title page is to contain the name, A+ Tutoring, formatted with a border and shading. Include an appropriate SmartArt graphic that conveys this message: Hard Work and Dedication Lead to Academic Success. Include the slogan, Building Successful Students.

The second page of the proposal should contain the following: heading — Help Is Here!; paragraph — Whether you need help in math, English, or a foreign language, A+ Tutoring is here to help. Conveniently located in the Student Services Building in room S-80, we offer extended hours and specialized tutoring in several different subjects.; heading — Prepare for Success; paragraph — The following are recommended materials and guidelines to help maximize your tutoring experience:; multilevel list — 1) Items to bring: although these items are not completely necessary, they have been found to be helpful during tutoring, 1a) Pens, pencils, highlighters, or other writing implements, 1b) Paper, notebooks, binders, 1c) Textbooks and any supplemental materials for subject (i.e., workbooks, handbooks, lab notes, assigned reading), 1d) Calculator, 2) Be prepared for your tutoring session, 2a) Have a list of questions ready for your tutor, 2b) Provide tutor with background information, 2bi) Is this subject your major?, 2bii) At what point or which topic caused you to fall behind?, 2biii) Do you plan to take additional courses in this subject?, 3) Choose a time slot for your tutoring session that allows you to be alert, punctual, and ready to learn; heading — Tutoring Hours; paragraph — The table below lists the tutoring hours available by subject.; table — row 1 column headings: Subject, Day, Time; row 2: Algebra, Monday – Friday, 9:00 a.m. – 1:00 p.m.; row 3: Calculus, Monday – Wednesday, 2:00 p.m. – 4:30 p.m.; row 4: Geometry, Monday, Tuesday, Friday, 8:00 a.m. – 11:30 a.m.; row 5: Spanish, Wednesday and Friday, 4:00 p.m. – 9:00 p.m.; row 6: German, Wednesday – Friday, 6:00 p.m. – 9:00 p.m.; row 7: French, Tuesday and Thursday, 9:00 a.m. – 2:00 p.m.; row 8: English Composition, Monday – Wednesday, 3:00 p.m. – 7:30 p.m.

Both pages should include the text watermark, Building Successful Students. Use the concepts and techniques presented in this chapter to create and format the sales proposal. Be sure to check the spelling and grammar of the finished document. Submit your assignment in the format specified by your instructor.

2: Create a Proposal for a Family Business

Personal

As a part-time helper with your family business, your sister has asked you to design a two-page sales proposal for the business that will be mailed to local residents. The title page is to contain the name, Steam n Fresh Carpet Cleaning, formatted with a border and shading. Include an appropriate SmartArt graphic with the text: Home, Office, Industrial. Include the slogan, Efficient and Thorough Carpet Cleaning.

The second page of the proposal should contain the following: heading — Why Choose Steam n Fresh?; paragraph — Steam n Fresh Carpet Cleaning is a family-owned business that has been in continuous operation for more than 30 years. We have four facilities in the greater Mitchelltown area, so we are never far from your home or business. And, whether it is your home or your business in need of our services, we have the equipment for the job.; heading — Your Customized Estimate; paragraph — As you requested in your e-mail query, below is an estimate to clean your facility. Note that the prices are discounted at 10 percent, per our online coupon offer.; table — row 1 column headings: Item, Cost; row 2: Air duct cleaning, $70; row 3: 3 offices @ $15 each, $45; row 4: 2 hallways @ $10 each, $20; row 5: Conference room, $25; row 6: 16 chairs @ $3 each, $48; row 7: Lunchroom, $40; row 8: Total, [use the formula command to compute the sum];

Continued >

Cases and Places *continued*

heading — Services Included; paragraph — Our technicians use an eco-friendly, biodegradable solution to clean your items. All furniture pieces (with the exception of large electronic items) are moved and replaced after the carpet beneath them has been cleaned. In addition, we use a patented brush attachment to clean next to the baseboard, which many other cleaners do not.; heading — Optional Services; paragraph — In addition to the standard services included, we offer the following optional services:; multilevel list — 1) Repair, 1a) Deep stain treatment and removal, 1b) Tears, burns, and other damage, 1c) Restretching, 1d) Odor removal, 2) Window coverings, 2a) Draperies of any fabric type or size (priced per panel; cost varies based on width and length of drapery), 2b) Mini and vertical blinds, shades, and other window coverings, 3) 24-hour emergency water damage and flood service.

Both pages should include the text watermark, Steam n Fresh. Use the concepts and techniques presented in this chapter to create and format the sales proposal. Be sure to check the spelling and grammar of the finished document. Submit your assignment in the format specified by your instructor.

3: Create a Proposal for a Construction Company

Professional

As a part-time assistant for Oak Ridge Builders, your boss has asked you to design a two-page sales proposal for the business that will mailed to residents of northwestern Indiana. The title page is to contain the name, Oak Ridge Builders, formatted with a border and shading. Include an appropriate SmartArt graphic that conveys this message: Quality, Design, and Affordability. Include the slogan, Building Better Homes for 50 Years!

The second page of the proposal should contain the following: heading — Select Lots Now Available in Windmere Estates; paragraph — Oak Ridge Builders has just acquired a substantial parcel of lots in the new, prestigious Windmere Estates subdivision. Let us build your new home on the lot of your choice. Windmere Estates offers the following:; bulleted list — Convenient location just 10 minutes from the interstate and approximately 20 minutes from downtown; Wooded lots with mature trees; Community pool, clubhouse, and park; Four-star school district; Reasonable neighborhood association fees provide snow removal, common area maintenance, and street signs; Wide, winding streets complete with sidewalks; heading — Available Lots; paragraph — All lots range from one-third to three-quarters of an acre. Discounts are available to buyers who wish to purchase a double lot. The table below lists the lots available for purchase (shaded lot numbers indicate wooded lot).; table — row 1 column headings: Lot Size, Price, Lot Number; row 2: One-third acre, $37,000, 80; row 3: One-third acre, $35,950, 58; row 4: One-half acre, $40,000, 56 (wooded lot); row 5: One-half acre, $40,000, 74; row 6: One-half acre, $45,000, 47 (wooded lot); row 7: Two-thirds acre, $46,000, 113; row 8: Two-thirds acre, $53,500, 94 (wooded lot); row 9: Three-quarter acre, $50,000, 98; row 10: Three-quarter acre, $57,000, 85 (wooded lot); row 11: Three-quarter acre, $62,000, 87 (wooded lot); heading — About Oak Ridge Builders; paragraph — At Oak Ridge Builders, we have been building affordable, quality housing in this area for more than 50 years. We offer a variety of floor plans, including ranch, bi-level and tri-level, and two-story homes, with or without basements. You can choose from one of our popular designs, or we can build from your plans. We also are happy to customize any floor plan to meet your needs.; paragraph — Take advantage of the various tax credits, discounts, and low interest rates available today. Let us help you build your dream home!

Both pages should include the text watermark, Phase 1 Now Open. Use the concepts and techniques presented in this chapter to create and format the sales proposal. Be sure to check the spelling and grammar of the finished document. Submit your assignment in the format specified by your instructor.

5 Using a Template to Create a Resume and Sharing a Finished Document

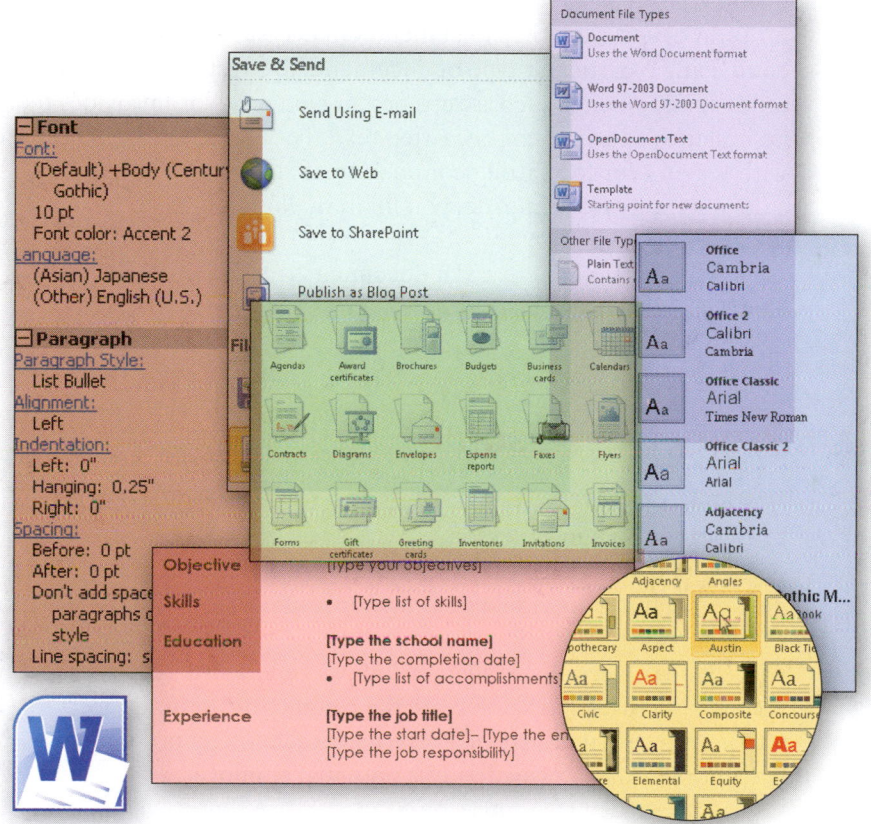

Objectives

You will have mastered the material in this chapter when you can:

- Use a template to create a document
- Change a document theme
- Fill in a document template
- Indent a paragraph
- Insert a building block
- Customize theme fonts
- Create a Quick Style

- Modify a style
- Save a Word document as a PDF or XPS document
- Send a Word document using e-mail
- Save a Word document as a Web page
- Format text as a hyperlink
- Add a background

5 | Using a Template to Create a Resume and Sharing a Finished Document

Introduction

Some people prefer to use their own creative skills to design and compose Word documents. Using Word, for example, you can develop the content and decide on the location of each item in a document. On occasion, however, you may have difficulty composing a particular type of document. To assist with the task of creating certain types of documents, such as resumes and letters, Word provides templates. A **template** is similar to a form with prewritten text; that is, Word prepares the requested document with text and/or formatting common to all documents of this nature. After Word creates a document from a template, you fill in the blanks or replace prewritten words in the document.

Once you have created a document, such as a resume, you often share it with others electronically via e-mail or on the Web.

Project — Resume

At some time, you will prepare a resume to send to prospective employers. In addition to some personal information, a **resume** usually contains the applicant's educational background and job experience. Employers review many resumes for each vacant position. Thus, you should design your resume carefully so that it presents you as the best candidate for the job.

The project in this chapter follows generally accepted guidelines for creating resumes and uses Word to create the resume shown in Figure 5–1. The resume for Riley Clarke, a recent graduate of a veterinary technology program, uses a Word template to present relevant information to a potential employer.

Overview

As you read through this chapter, you will learn how to create the resume shown in Figure 5–1 by performing these general tasks:

• Use a template to create a resume.

• Save and print the resume.

• Save the resume in a variety of formats.

• E-mail the resume.

• Save the resume as a Web page.

• Format the Web page.

Riley Clarke

8982 West Condor Avenue, Donner, OH 44772
804-555-2982 (home); 804-555-0291 (cell)
E-mail: rclarke@worldview.net

Objective	To obtain a full-time veterinary technician position with a veterinary clinic or school in the Midwest.
Education	**A.A.S. Veterinary Technology (Donner Community College)** May 2012 • Dean's List, 3 semesters • Spindle Small Animal Medicine Award, January 2012 • Twin Creek Outstanding Student Scholarship, 2011 – 2012 • *Pet Health Journal*, 1st Place, Client Education Article • Areas of concentration: Anesthesia and surgery Client education Laboratory testing and procedures Patient monitoring and handling Pharmacology Recordkeeping
Experience	**Veterinary Assistant, Donner Animal Hospital** January 2011 – May 2012 Sterilized surgical kits, assisted during routine physical examinations, collected patient histories, walked dogs, communicated with clients, booked appointments, invoiced clients, and performed various administrative duties. **Groomer, Bev's Doggie Care** June 2009 – December 2010 Bathed dogs; brushed, combed, clipped, and shaped dogs' coats; trimmed nails; and cleaned ears.
Memberships	• Ford County Humane Society • National Dog Groomer Association • Society of Veterinary Technicians • Student Government Association, Donner Community College
Community Service	• Answer phones and groom dogs at the Ford County Humane Society, 10 hours per week • Teach pet care basics to local school district students and staff, 8 hours per semester

Figure 5–1

Plan Ahead

General Project Guidelines

When creating a Word document, the actions you perform and decisions you make will affect the appearance and characteristics of the finished document. As you create a resume, such as the project shown in Figure 5–1, you should follow these general guidelines:

1. **Craft a successful resume.** Your resume should present, at a minimum, your contact information, objective, educational background, and work experience to a potential employer. It should honestly present all your positive points. The resume should be error free. Ask someone else to proofread your resume and give you suggestions for improvements.

(continued)

Plan Ahead

(continued)

2. **For electronic distribution, such as e-mail, ensure the document is in the proper format.** Save the resume in a format so that you can share it with others. Be sure that others will be able to open the resume using software on their computers and that the look of the resume will remain intact when recipients open the resume.

3. **Create a resume Web page from your resume Word document.** Save the Word document as a Web page. Improve the usability of the resume Web page by making your e-mail address a link to an e-mail program. Enhance the look of the Web page by adding, for example, a background color. Be sure to test your finished Web page document in at least one browser program to be sure it looks and works as you intended.

4. **Publish your resume Web page.** Once you have created a Web page, you can publish it. **Publishing** is the process of making a Web page available to others on a network, such as the Internet or a company's intranet. Many Internet access providers offer storage space on their Web servers at no cost to their subscribers. The procedures for using Microsoft Office to publish documents are discussed in Appendices B and C.

When necessary, more specific details concerning the above guidelines are presented at appropriate points in the chapter. The chapter also will identify the actions performed and decisions made regarding these guidelines during the creation of the resume shown in Figure 5–1 on the previous page.

To Start Word and Display Formatting Marks

If you are using a computer to step through the project in this chapter and you want your screens to match the figures in this book, you should change your screen's resolution to 1024 × 768. The following steps start Word and display formatting marks.

1 Start Word. If necessary, maximize the Word window.

2 If the Print Layout button on the status bar is not selected (as shown in Figure 5–4 on page WD 278), click it so that your screen is in Print Layout view.

3 Change your zoom to 100%.

4 If the Show/Hide ¶ button (Home tab | Paragraph group) is not selected already, click it to display formatting marks on the screen.

Using a Template to Create a Resume

Although you could compose a resume in a blank document window, this chapter shows how to use a template instead, where Word formats the resume with appropriate headings and spacing. You then customize the resume generated by the template by filling in blanks and by selecting and replacing text.

Plan Ahead

Craft a successful resume.
Two types of resumes are the chronological resume and the functional resume. A chronological resume sequences information by time, with the most recent listed first. This type of resume highlights a job seeker's job continuity and growth. A functional resume groups information by skills and accomplishments. This resume emphasizes a job seeker's experience and qualifications in specialized areas. Some resumes use a combination of the two formats. For an entry-level job search, experts recommend a chronological resume or a combination of the two types of resumes.

(continued)

(continued)

**Plan
Ahead**

When creating a resume, be sure to include necessary information and present it appropriately. Keep descriptions short and concise, using action words and bulleted lists.

- **Include necessary information.** Your resume should include contact information, a clearly written objective, educational background, and experience. Use your legal name and mailing address, along with your phone number and e-mail address, if you have one. Other sections you might consider including are memberships, skills, recognitions and awards, and/or community service. Do not include your Social Security number, marital status, age, height, weight, gender, physical appearance, health, citizenship, previous pay rates, reasons for leaving a prior job, current date, high-school information (if you are a college graduate), and references. Employers assume you will give references, if asked, and this information simply clutters a resume.

- **Present your resume appropriately.** For printed resumes, use a high-quality ink-jet or laser printer to print your resume on standard letter-size white or ivory paper. Consider using paper that contains cotton fibers for a professional look.

To Create a New Document from a Sample Template

Word installs a variety of sample templates for letters, fax cover sheets, reports, and resumes on your computer's hard disk. The sample templates are grouped in ten styles: Adjacency, Apothecary, Black Tie, Equity, Essential, Executive, Median, Oriel, Origin, and Urban. The sample templates in each style use similar formatting, themes, etc., enabling users to create a set of documents that complement one another, if desired. For example, if you create a letter and a resume using the same style, such as Urban, the two documents will have complementary colors, fonts, etc., and a similar look.

In this chapter, you will create a resume using the template with the Urban style. The following steps create a new document based on a sample (installed) template.

1

- Click File on the Ribbon to open the Backstage view.

- Click the New tab in the Backstage view to display the New gallery (Figure 5–2).

Q&A What is the difference between Sample templates and Office.com Templates?

Sample templates are installed on your computer's hard disk, whereas Office.com templates are available on the Web. If you are connected to the Internet when you click the desired template in the Office.com Templates area of the New gallery, Word displays templates from the Web that you can download and use in Word.

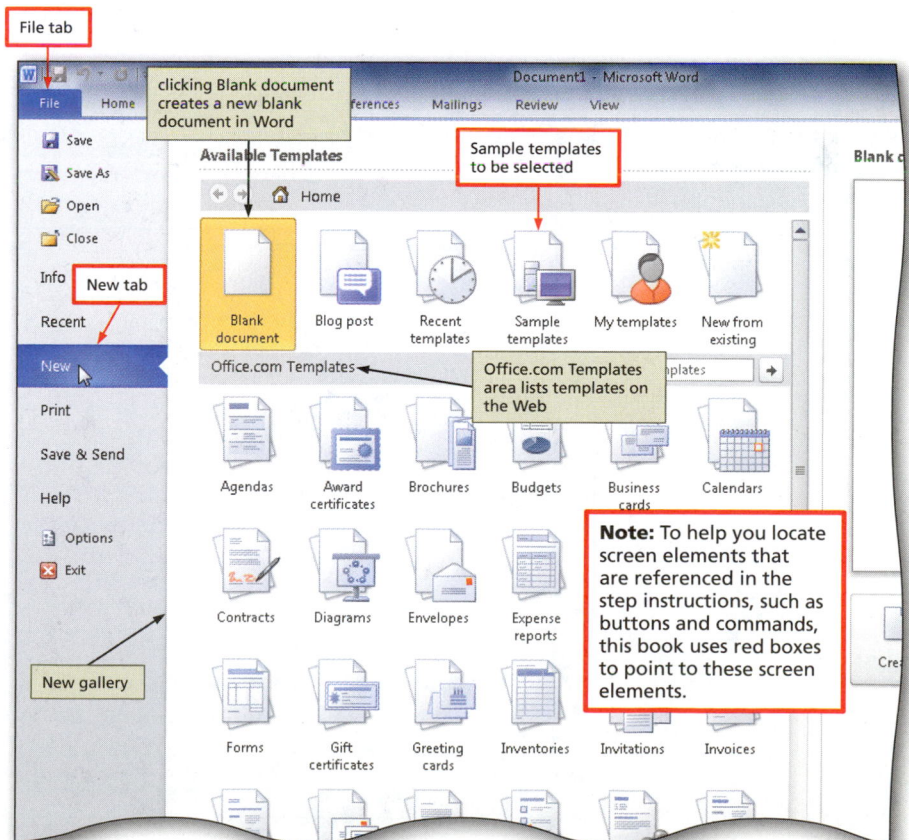

Figure 5–2

2

- Click Sample templates in the New gallery to display a list of templates installed on your computer's hard disk.

 Experiment

- Click various installed templates in the Sample templates list and see a preview of the selected sample template in the right pane of the New gallery.

- Scroll through the Sample templates list and then click Urban Resume to select the template (Figure 5–3).

Q&A

How would I redisplay the original New gallery?

You would click the Back button in the New gallery. To return to the list in Figure 5–3, you would click the Forward button.

3

- Click the Create button to create a new document based on the selected template (Figure 5–4).

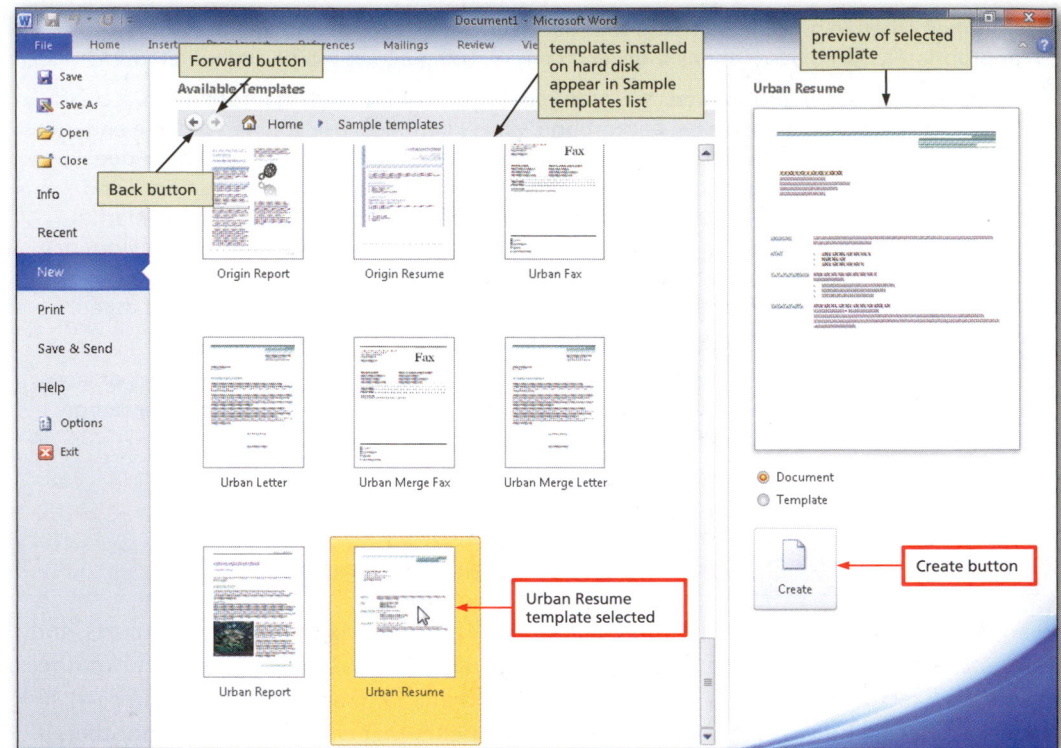

Figure 5–3

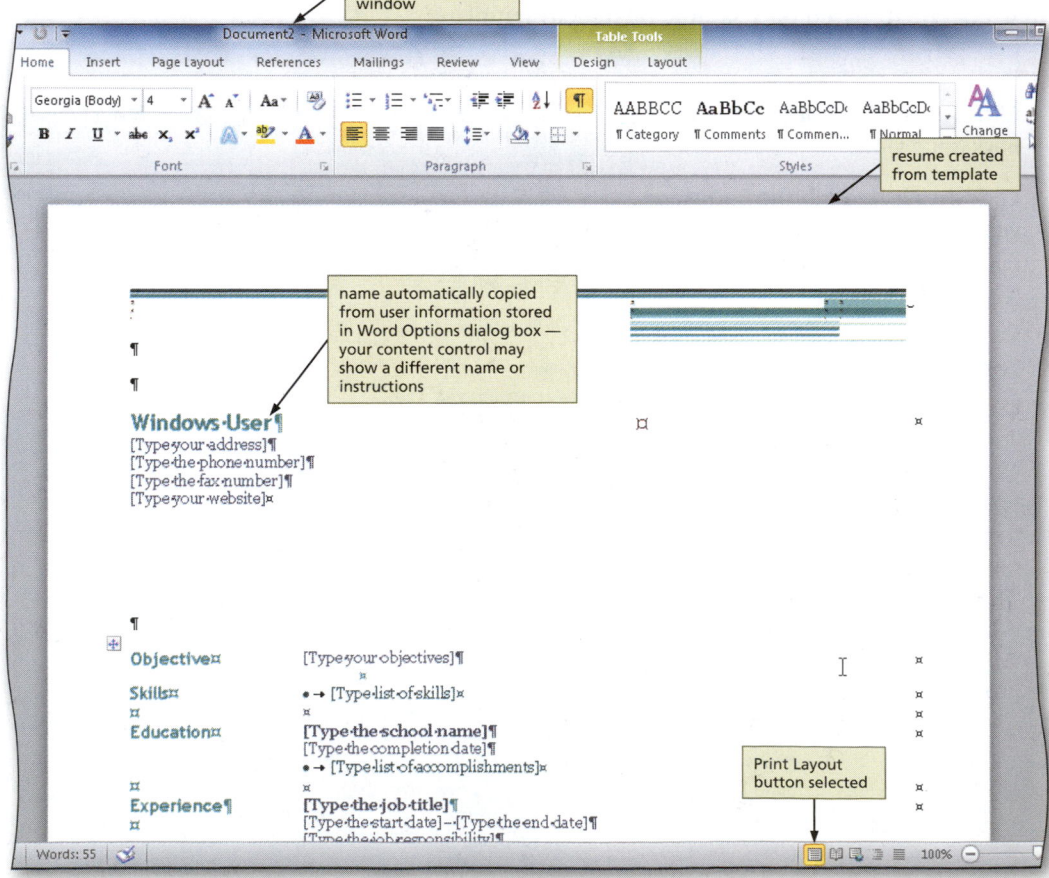

Figure 5–4

TO CREATE A NEW BLANK DOCUMENT

If, instead of a creating a new document from a sample template, you wanted to create a new blank document with the Word window open, you would perform the following steps.

1. Click File on the Ribbon to open the Backstage view.

2. Click the New tab to display the New gallery.

3. If necessary, click Blank document in the middle pane of the New gallery (shown in Figure 5–2 on page WD 277) and then click the Create button in the right pane to open a new blank document window in Word.

   or

1. Press CTRL+N.

BTW

Q&As
For a complete list of the Q&As found in many of the step-by-step sequences in this book, visit the Word 2010 Q&A Web page (scsite.com/wd2010/qa).

To Change the Document Theme

A **document theme** is a coordinated combination of a color scheme, font set, and effects. In previous chapters, you have used a color scheme from one document theme and a font set from another document theme. In this chapter, the resume uses the Austin document theme, which uses the Austin color scheme and Austin font set. Instead of changing the color scheme and font set individually, Word provides a means of changing the entire document theme at once.

The document theme for the current resume is Urban. The following steps change the document theme to Austin.

1

- Display the Page Layout tab.

- Click the Themes button (Page Layout tab | Themes group) to display the Themes gallery.

- Point to Austin in the Themes gallery to display a live preview of that theme applied to the document (Figure 5–5).

🔎 **Experiment**

- Point to various themes in the Themes gallery and watch the color scheme and font set change in the document window.

2

- Click Austin in the Themes gallery to change the document theme.

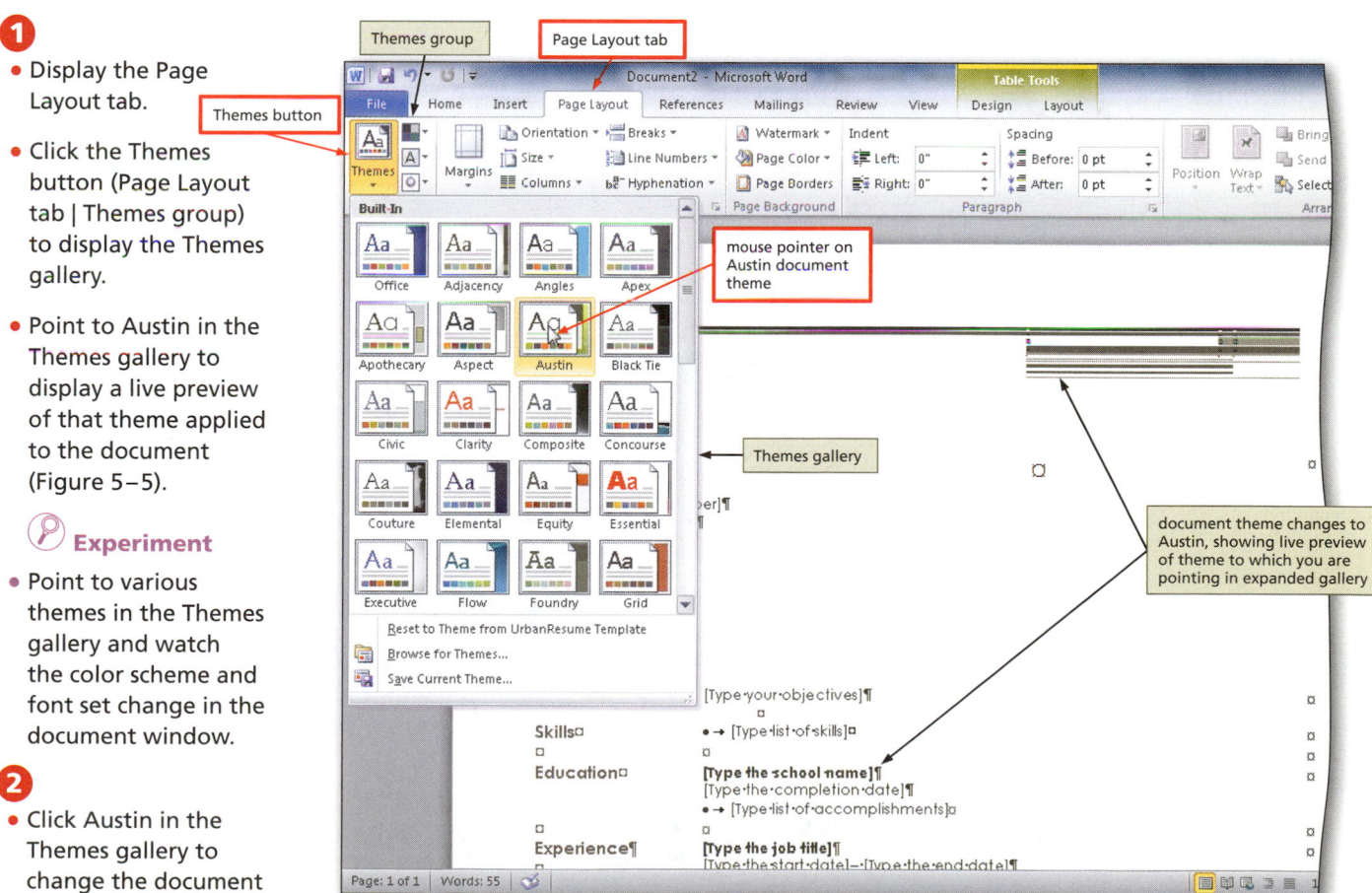

Figure 5–5

To Print the Resume

To see the entire resume created by the resume template using the Austin document theme, print the document shown in the Word window. The following steps print a document.

1 Click File on the Ribbon to open the Backstage view and then click the Print tab in the Backstage view to display the Print gallery.

2 Verify that the printer name on the Printer Status button will print a hard copy of the document. If necessary, change the selected printer.

3 Click the Print button to print the open document using the current document theme (Figure 5–6).

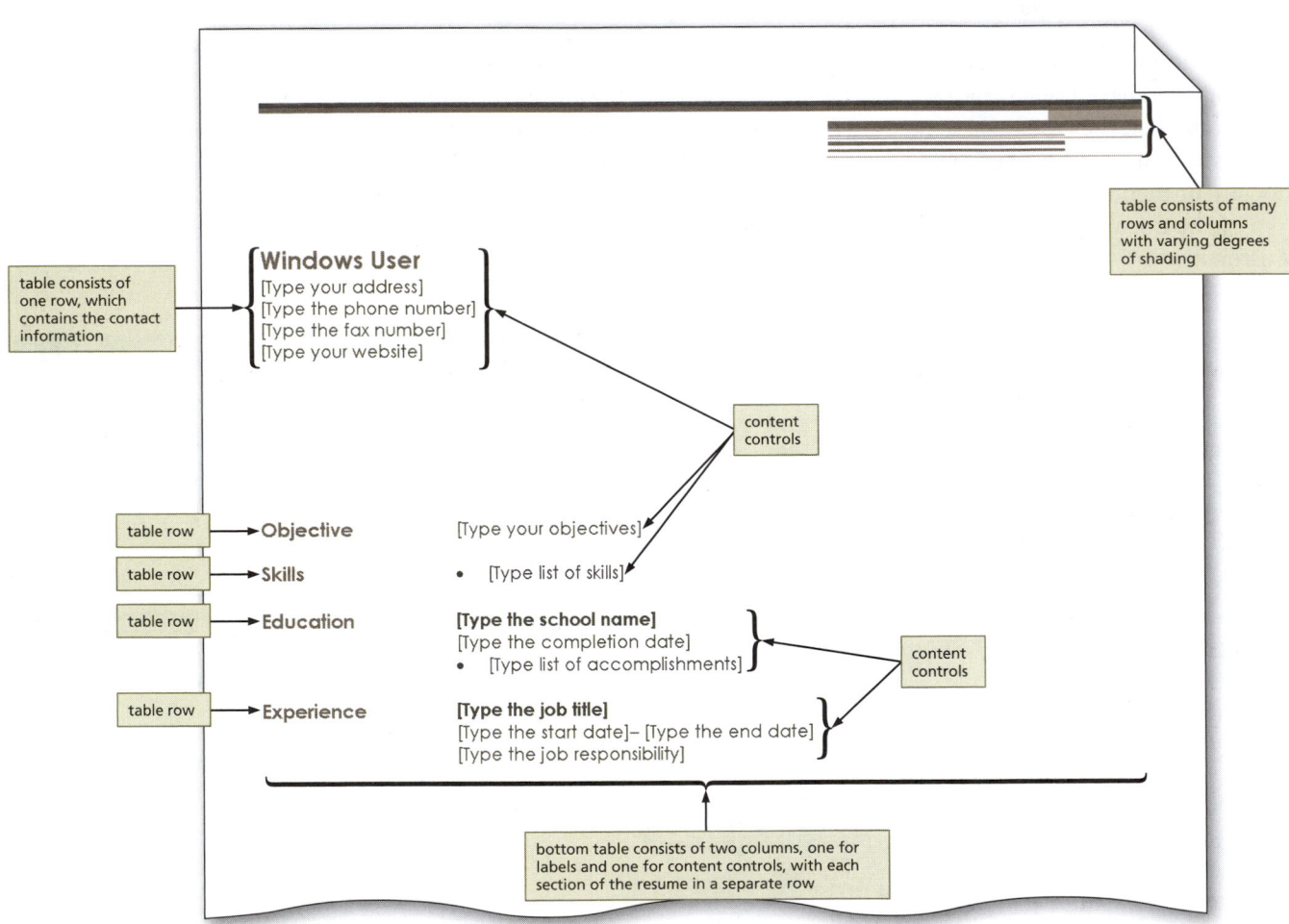

Figure 5–6

Resume Template

The resume created from the template, shown in Figure 5–6, consists of three separate tables. The table at the top of the document consists of many small rows with varying degrees of shading to give a decorative look to the resume. The second table contains content controls for the job seeker's contact information. The third table contains labels and content controls for the Objective, Skills, Education, and Experience sections of the resume.

A **content control** is an object that contains instructions for filling in text and graphics. To select a content control, you click it. As soon as you begin typing in the selected content control, your typing replaces the instructions in the control. Thus, you do not need to delete the selected instructions before you begin typing.

The following pages personalize the resume created by the resume template using these general steps:

1. Change the name at the top of the resume.
2. Fill in the contact information below the name.
3. Fill in the Objective section.
4. Move the Education and Experience sections above the Skills section.
5. Fill in the Education and Experience sections.
6. Add a row for the Community Service section.
7. Change the Skills labels to Membership and Community Service and fill in these sections.

To Change the Margin Settings

The resume template selected in this project uses .75-inch top, bottom, left, and right margins. You prefer a bit wider margin so that the text does not run so close to the edges of the page. Specifically, the resume in this chapter uses 1-inch top, bottom, left, and right margins. The following steps change the margin settings.

1 Click the Margins button (Page Layout tab | Page Setup group) to display the Margins gallery (Figure 5–7).

2 Click Normal in the Margins gallery to change the margins to the selected settings.

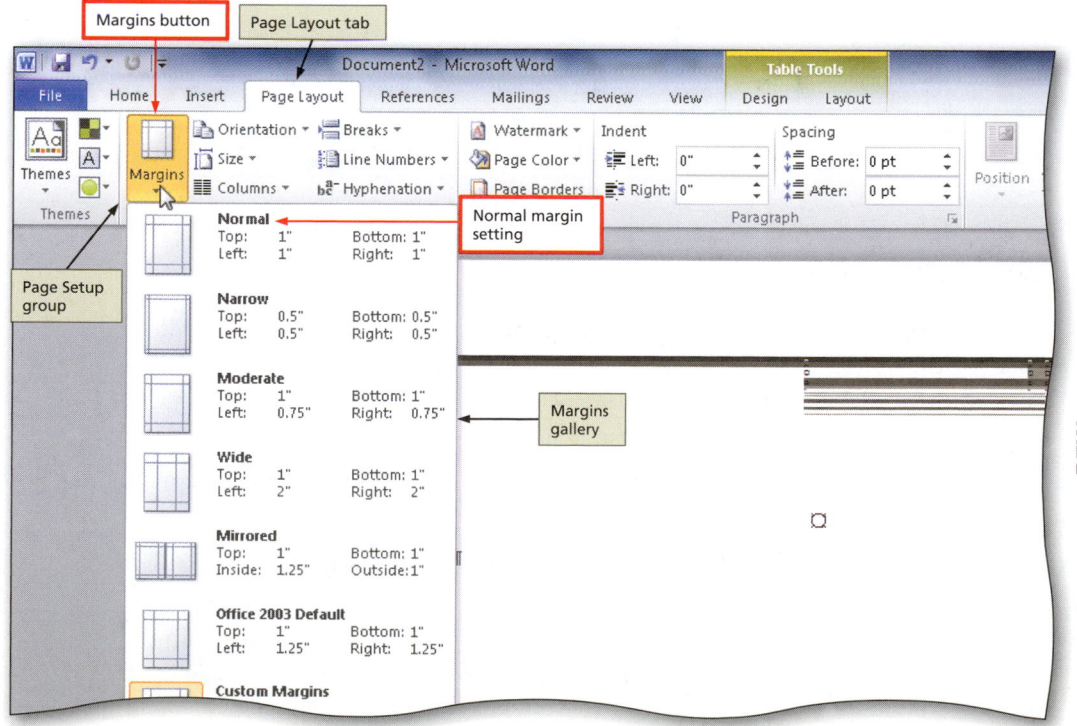

Figure 5–7

To View Gridlines

When tables contain no borders, such as those in this resume, it can be difficult to see the individual cells in the table. To help identify the location of cells, you can display gridlines, which show cell outlines on the screen. The following steps show gridlines.

1 Position the insertion point in any table cell, in this case, the cell containing the Objective label.

2 Display the Table Tools Layout tab.

3 If it is not selected already, click the View Table Gridlines button (Table Tools Layout tab | Table group) to show gridlines in the tables (Figure 5–8).

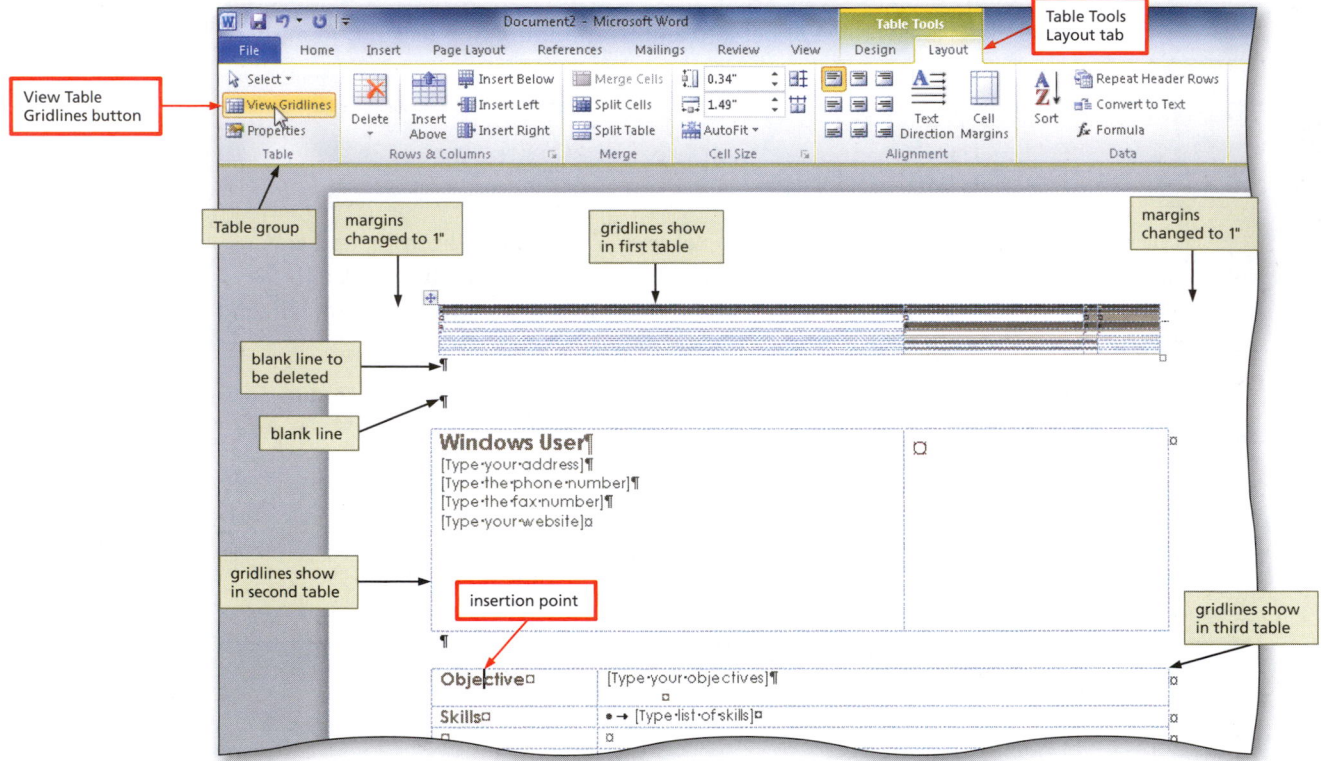

Figure 5–8

To Delete a Line

Two blank lines are above the name in the resume. In this project, to allow more space for the sections in the resume, you delete one of the blank lines above the name. The following steps delete a line.

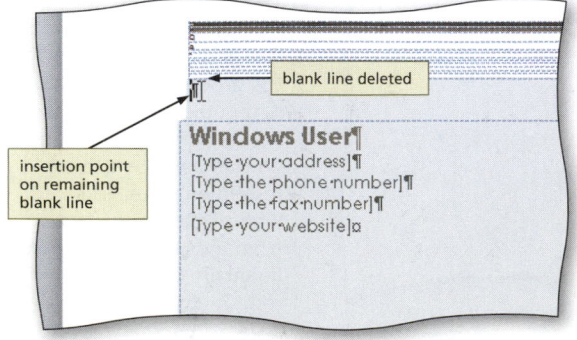

Figure 5–9

1 Position the insertion point on the first blank paragraph at the top of the resume.

2 Press the DELETE key to delete the blank line (Figure 5–9).

Q&A Why is the table containing the contact information shaded gray?

As you move the mouse pointer over the contact information, it may become shaded gray because the entire table is a building block. Recall that building blocks contain named text or graphics that you can reuse in documents.

To Modify Text in a Content Control

The next step is to select the text that the template inserted in the resume and replace it with personal information. The name area on your resume may contain a name, which Word copied from the Word Options dialog box, or it may contain the instruction, Type your name. This content control should contain the job seeker's name.

The following steps modify the text in a content control.

 1

- If the name content control in your resume contains a name, triple-click the name content control to select it. If the name content control in your resume contains the instruction, Type your name, click the content control to select it (Figure 5–10).

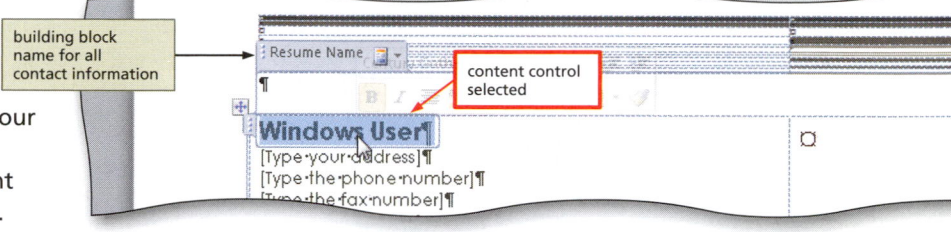

Figure 5–10

2

- Type **Riley Clarke** as the name (Figure 5–11).

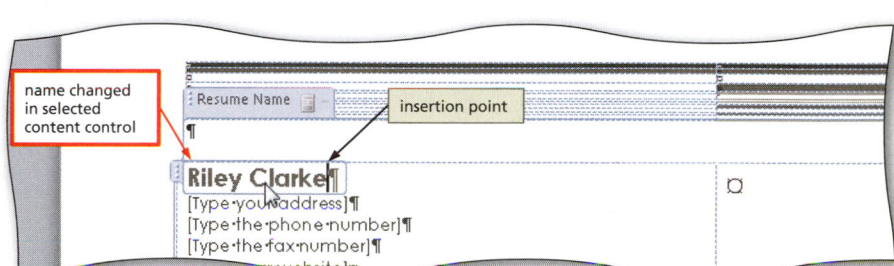

Figure 5–11

To Format a Content Control

The next step is to format the text in the name content control. In this project, the name is changed to a different color with a larger font size to give it more emphasis in the resume.

To modify text in a content control, select the content control and then modify the formats. That is, you do not need to select the text in the content control. The following step formats the name content control.

1

- If the name content control is not selected, click it.

Q&A How can I tell if a content control is selected?

A selected content control is surrounded by a rounded rectangle.

- Click the Font Size box arrow (Home tab | Font group) and then click 22 in the Font Size gallery to increase the font size of the text in the selected content control.

- Click the Font Color button arrow (Home tab | Font group) and then click Brown, Accent 2, Darker 25% (sixth column, fifth row) in the Font Color gallery to change the font color of the text in the selected content control (Figure 5–12).

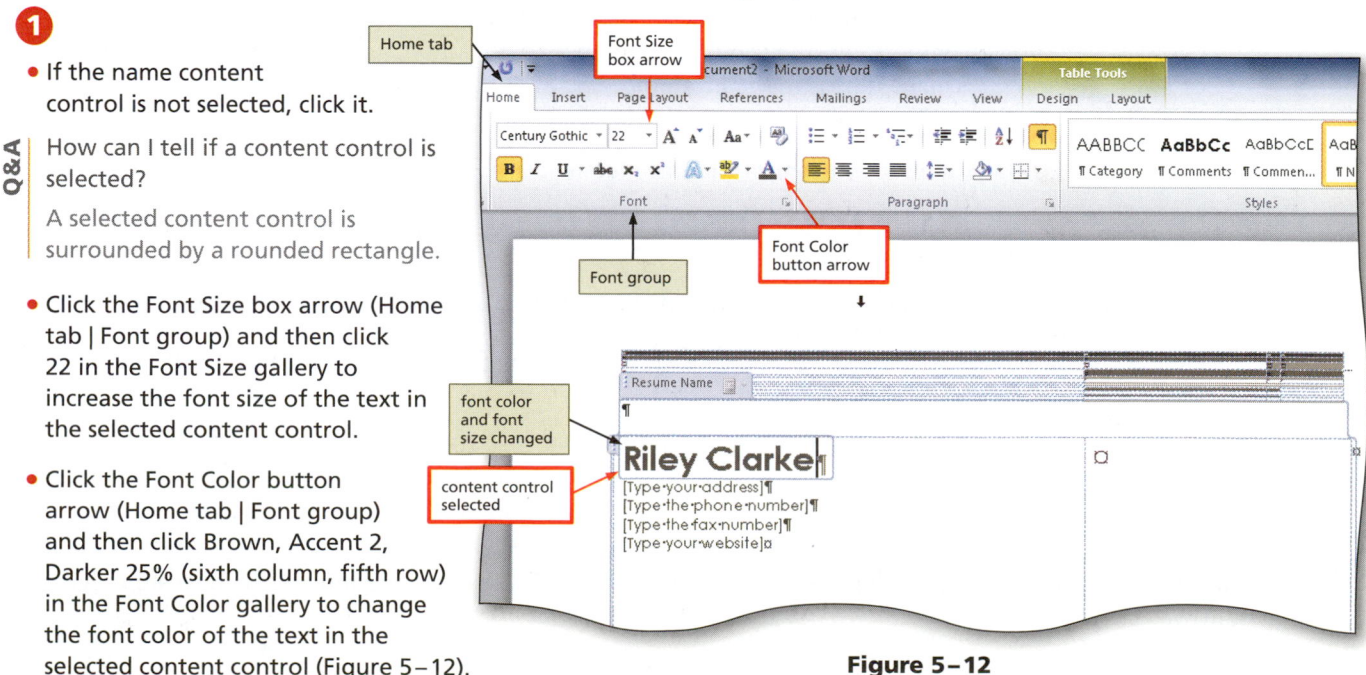

Figure 5–12

To Replace Placeholder Text

The next step is to select the placeholder text, Type your address, and replace it with your address. Word uses **placeholder text** to indicate where text can be typed. To replace placeholder text, you click it to select it and then type. The typed text automatically replaces the selected placeholder text. The following steps replace the placeholder text in the address content control.

• Click the content control with the placeholder text, Type your address, to select it (Figure 5–13).

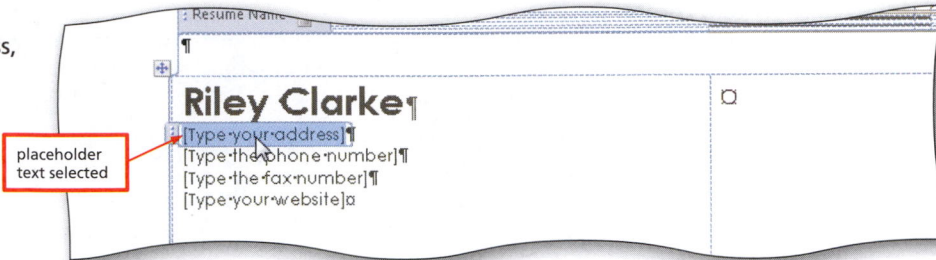

Figure 5–13

2

• Type 8982 West Condor Avenue, Donner, OH 44772 as the address (Figure 5–14).

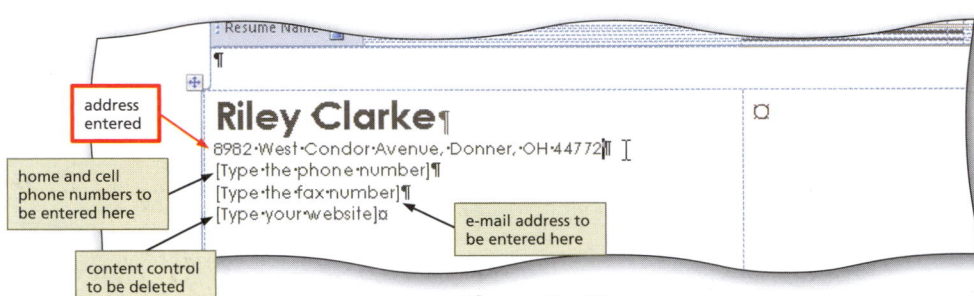

Figure 5–14

To Replace More Placeholder Text in Content Controls

The next step is to select the placeholder text in the phone number and fax number content controls in the resume and replace their instructions with personal information. You will enter home and cell phone numbers in the phone number placeholder text and an e-mail address in the fax number placeholder text (because you do not have a fax number). The following steps replace placeholder text.

1 Click the content control with the placeholder text, Type the phone number, to select it.

2 Type 804-555-2982 (home); 804-555-0291 (cell) as the home and cell phone numbers.

3 Click the content control with the placeholder text, Type the fax number, to select it.

4 Type E-mail: rclarke@worldview.net to enter the e-mail address in place of a fax number.

To Delete a Content Control

You do not have a Web site. Thus, the next step is to delete the website content control. The next steps delete a content control.

1

• Click the content control with the placeholder text, Type your website, to select it.

• Right-click the selected content control to display a shortcut menu (Figure 5–15).

2

• Click Remove Content Control on the shortcut menu to delete the selected content control, which also deletes the placeholder text contained in the content control.

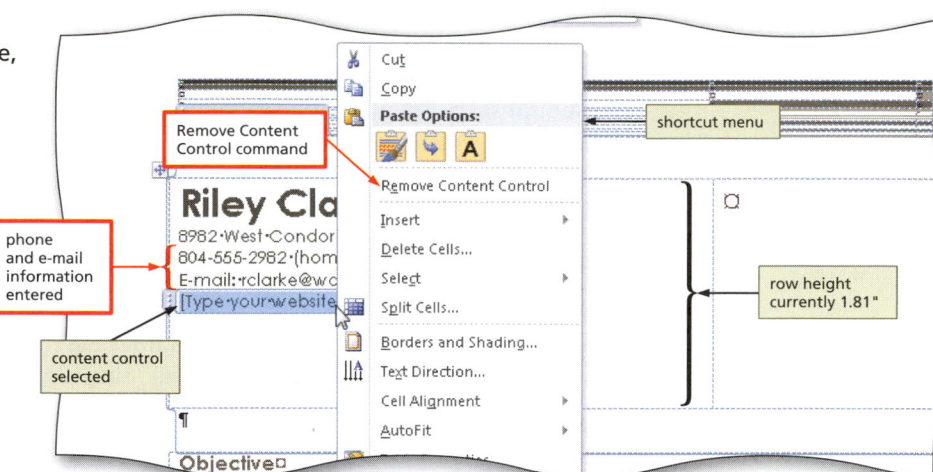

Figure 5–15

Other Ways	
1. With content control selected, click Cut button (Home tab | Clipboard group)	2. With content control selected, press CTRL+X or DELETE or BACKSPACE

To Change Row Height

The row containing the name and contact information currently is 1.81 inches tall (shown in Figure 5–15). This height places an excessively large gap between the e-mail address and Objective section on the resume. Thus, the next step is to reduce this row height to 1 inch. The following steps change row height.

1 With the insertion point in the row to adjust (shown in Figure 5–16), display the Table Tools Layout tab.

2 Click the Table Row Height box down arrow (Table Tools Layout tab | Cell Size group) as many times as necessary until the box displays 1", to change the row height to the entered value (Figure 5–16).

BTW

Remove Content Control
If you discover that Word ignores entries in placeholder text due to certain settings, you can use the Remove Content Control command illustrated in the steps at the top of this page (shown in Figure 5–15) to convert values entered in placeholder text to regular text.

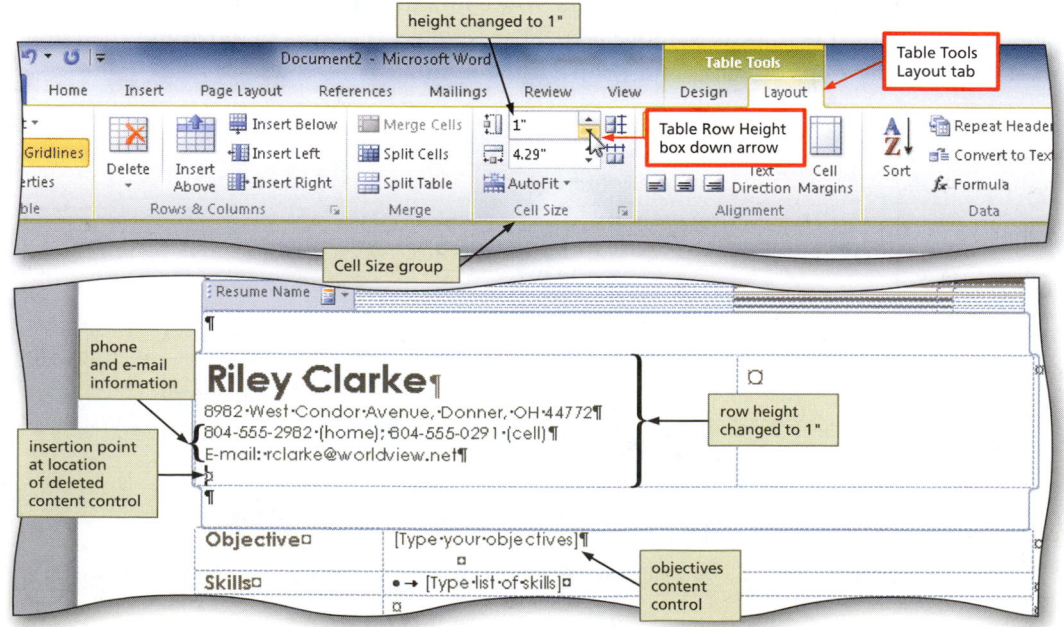

Figure 5–16

To Save the Resume

You have completed several tasks while creating this resume and do not want to risk losing work completed thus far. Accordingly, you should save the document. Thus, you should save it in a file. The following steps assume you already have created folders for storing your files, for example, a CIS 101 folder (for your class) that contains a Word folder (for your assignments). Thus, these steps save the document in the Word folder in the CIS 101 folder on a USB flash drive using the file name, Clarke Resume.

1 With a USB flash drive connected to one of the computer's USB ports, click the Save button on the Quick Access Toolbar to display the Save As dialog box.

2 Save the file in the desired location (in this case, the Word folder in the CIS 101 folder [or your class folder] on the USB flash drive) using the file name, Clarke Resume.

To Replace More Placeholder Text in Content Controls

The next step is to select the placeholder text in the objectives content control in the resume and replace it with personal information. The following steps replace placeholder text.

BTW

Selecting Rows
To move table rows, you must select them first. Recall that to select table rows, you point to the left of the first row to select and then drag downward or upward when the mouse pointer changes to a right-pointing block arrow.

1 In the Objective section of the resume, select the content control with the placeholder text, Type your objectives (shown in Figure 5–16 on the previous page).

2 Type the objective: **To obtain a full-time veterinary technician position with a veterinary clinic or school in the Midwest.**

Q&A Why is a blank line below the typed objective?

The resume template placed blank lines and blank rows throughout to separate sections of the resume.

To Move Table Rows

In the resume, you would like the Education and Experience sections immediately below the Objective sections. Because each section is in a separate row, the next step is to move the bottom three table rows (a blank table row separates the two sections) so that they are immediately below the row containing the Objective section.

You use the same procedure to move table rows as to move text. That is, select the rows to move and then drag them to the desired location. The following steps use drag-and-drop editing to move table rows.

1
- Select the rows to be moved, in this case, the last three rows in the table.

- With the mouse pointer in the selected table items, press and hold down the mouse button, which displays a dotted insertion point and a small dotted box with the mouse pointer.

- Drag the dotted insertion point to the location where the selected rows are to be moved, as shown in Figure 5–17.

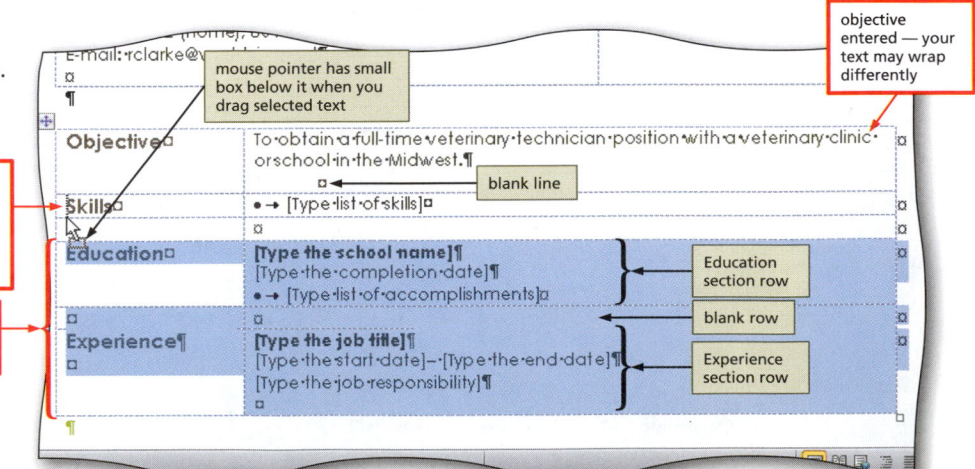

Figure 5–17

2

- Release the mouse button to move the selected rows to the location of the dotted insertion point (Figure 5–18).

Q&A What if I accidentally drag text to the wrong location?

Click the Undo button on the Quick Access Toolbar and try again.

Q&A What is the purpose of the Paste Options button?

If you click the Paste Options button, a menu appears that allows you to change the format of the rows that were moved.

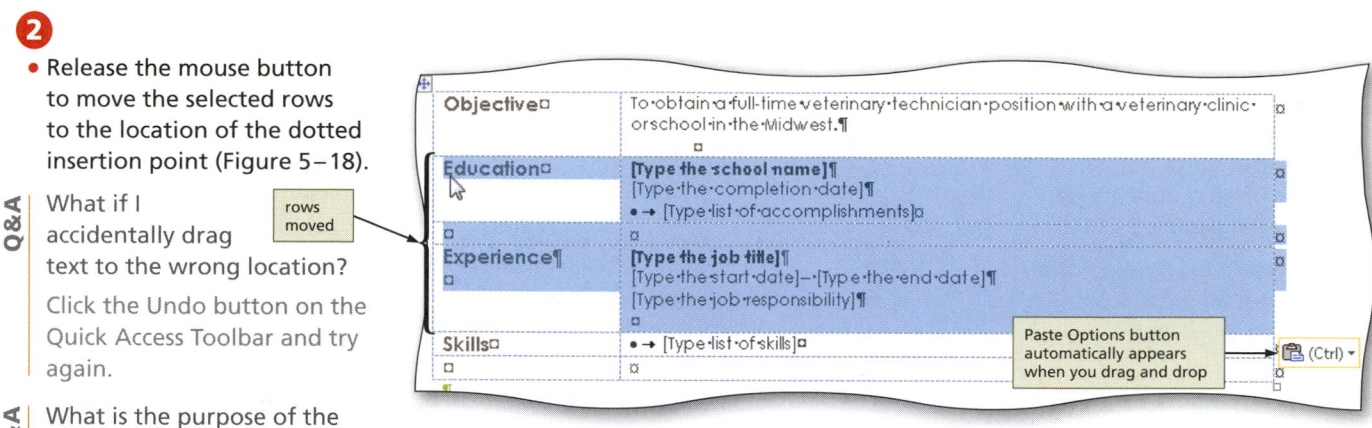

Figure 5–18

3

- Click anywhere to remove the selection from the rows.

Other Ways

1. Click Cut button (Home tab | Clipboard group), click where selected item is to be pasted, click Paste button (Home tab | Clipboard group)

2. Right-click selected text, click Cut on shortcut menu, right-click where selected item is to be pasted, click Keep Source Formatting on shortcut menu

3. Press CTRL+X, position insertion point where selected item is to be pasted, press CTRL+V

To Replace More Placeholder Text in Content Controls

The next step is to begin to enter text in the Education section of the resume. The following steps replace placeholder text.

1 In the Education section of the resume, select the content control with the placeholder text, Type the school name, and then type **A.A.S. Veterinary Technology (Donner Community College)** as the degree and school name.

2 Select the content control with the placeholder text, Type the completion date, and then type **May 2012** as the date.

3 Select the content control with the placeholder text, Type list of accomplishments.

4 Type **Dean's List, 3 semesters** as the first bulleted accomplishment and then press the ENTER key to place a bullet on the next line, ready for the next entry (shown in Figure 5–19 on the next page).

To Use AutoComplete

As you begin typing, Word may display a ScreenTip that presents a suggestion for the rest of the word or phrase you are typing. With its **AutoComplete** feature, Word predicts the word or phrase you are typing and displays its prediction in a ScreenTip. If the AutoComplete prediction is correct, you can instruct Word to finish your typing with its prediction, or you can ignore Word's prediction. Word draws its AutoComplete suggestions from its dictionary and from AutoText entries you create and save in the Normal template.

The steps on the next page use the AutoComplete feature as you type the next bulleted item in the Education section of the resume.

1

• Type `Spindle Small Animal Medicine Award, Janu` and notice the AutoComplete ScreenTip that appears on the screen (Figure 5–19).

Q&A

Why would my screen not display the AutoComplete ScreenTip?

Depending on previous Word entries, you may need to type more characters in order for Word to predict a particular word or phrase accurately. Or, you may need to turn on AutoComplete by clicking File on the Ribbon to open the Backstage view, clicking Options in the Backstage view to display the Word Options dialog box; once this dialog box is displayed, click Advanced in the left pane (Word Options dialog box), place a check mark in the Show AutoComplete suggestions check box, and then click the OK button.

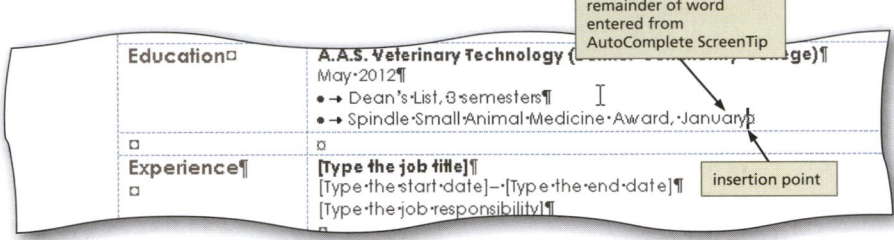

Figure 5–19

2

• Press the ENTER key to instruct Word to finish your typing with the word or phrase that appeared in the AutoComplete ScreenTip (Figure 5–20).

Q&A

What if I do not want to use the text proposed in the AutoComplete ScreenTip?

Simply continue typing and the AutoComplete ScreenTip will disappear from the screen.

Figure 5–20

To Enter More Text

The following steps continue entering text in the Education section of the resume.

1 With the insertion point following the y in January, press the SPACEBAR. Type `2012` and then press the ENTER key.

2 Type `Twin Creek Outstanding Student Scholarship, 2011 - 2012` and then press the ENTER key.

3 Type `Pet Health Journal, 1st Place, Client Education Article` (Figure 5–21).

BTW

AutoFormat
Word automatically formats quotation marks, dashes, lists, fractions, ordinals, and other items depending on your typing and settings. To check if an AutoFormat option is enabled, click File on the Ribbon to open the Backstage view, click Options in the Backstage view, click Proofing in the left pane (Word Options dialog box), click the AutoCorrect Options button, click the AutoFormat As You Type tab, select the appropriate check boxes, and then click the OK button in each open dialog box.

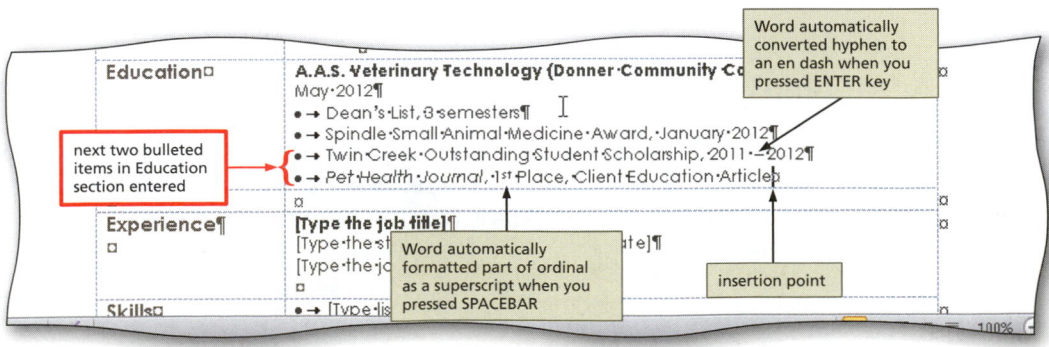

Figure 5–21

To Enter a Line Break

The next step in personalizing the resume is to enter the areas of concentration in the Education section. You want only the first line, which says, Areas of concentration:, to begin with a bullet. If you press the ENTER key on subsequent lines, Word automatically will carry forward the paragraph formatting, which includes the bullet. Thus, you will not press the ENTER key between each line. Instead, you will create a **line break**, which advances the insertion point to the beginning of the next physical line, ignoring any paragraph formatting. The following steps enter the areas of concentration using a line break, instead of a paragraph break, between each line.

- With the insertion point positioned as shown in Figure 5–21, press the ENTER key.

- If necessary, turn off italics. Type **Areas of concentration:** and then press SHIFT+ENTER to insert a line break character and move the insertion point to the beginning of the next physical line (Figure 5–22).

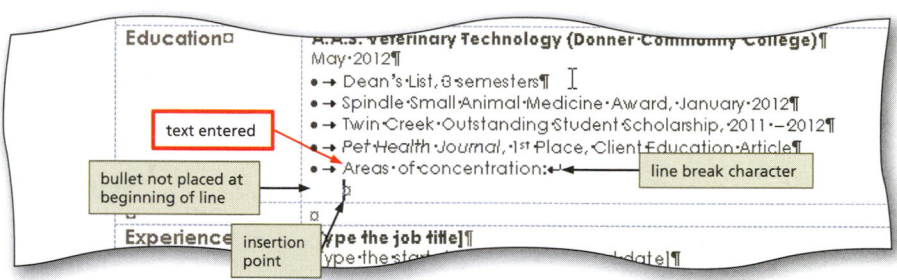

Figure 5–22

❷

- Type **Anesthesia and surgery** and then press SHIFT+ENTER.

- Type **Client education** and then press SHIFT+ENTER.

- Type **Laboratory testing and procedures** and then press SHIFT+ENTER.

- Type **Patient monitoring and handling** and then press SHIFT+ENTER.

- Type **Pharmacology** and then press SHIFT+ENTER.

- Type **Recordkeeping** as the last entry. Do not press SHIFT+ENTER at the end of this line (Figure 5–23).

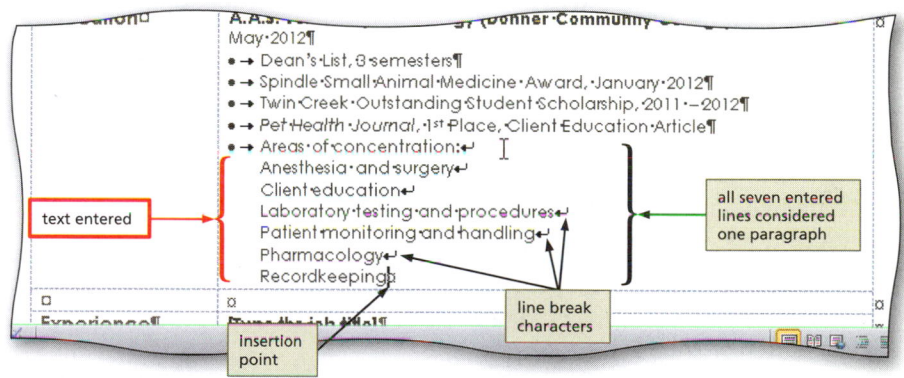

Figure 5–23

To Replace More Placeholder Text in Content Controls

The next step is to begin to enter text in the Experience section of the resume. The following steps replace placeholder text.

❶ Scroll so that the bottom of the resume appears at the top of the document window.

❷ In the Experience section of the resume, select the content control with the placeholder text, Type the job title, and then type **Veterinary Assistant, Donner Animal Hospital** as the job title and place of employment.

❸ Select the content control with the placeholder text, Type the start date, and then type **January 2011** and then press the SPACEBAR.

❹ Select the content control with the placeholder text, Type the end date, and then type **May 2012** as the end date.

5 Select the content control with the placeholder text, Type the job responsibility, and then type this text (Figure 5–24): `Sterilized surgical kits, assisted during routine physical examinations, collected patient histories, walked dogs, communicated with clients, booked appointments, invoiced clients, and performed various administrative duties.`

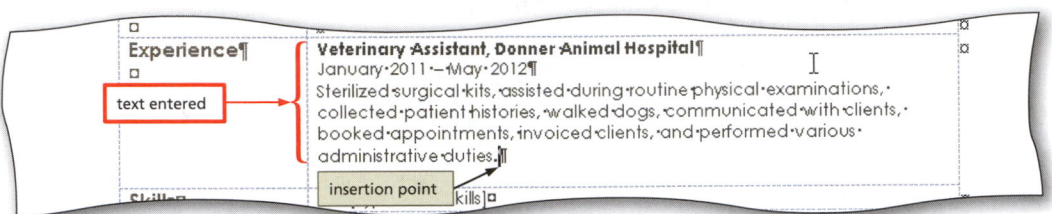

Figure 5–24

To Indent a Paragraph

In the resume, the lines below the job start date and end date that contain the job responsibilities are to be indented, so that the text in the Experience section is easier to read. The following steps indent the left edge of a paragraph.

1
- With the insertion point in the paragraph to indent, click the Increase Indent button (Home tab | Paragraph group) to indent the current paragraph one-half inch.

- To verify the paragraph is indented one-half inch, click the View Ruler button on the vertical ruler to display the rulers (Figure 5–25).

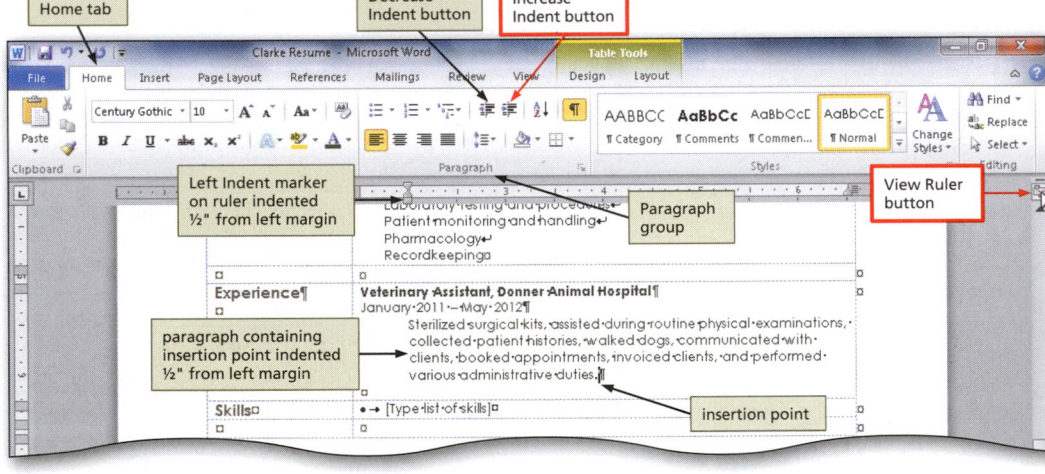

Figure 5–25

Q&A Why was the paragraph indented one-half inch?

Each time you click the Increase Indent button (Home tab | Paragraph group), the current paragraph is indented one-half inch. Similarly, clicking the Decrease Indent button (Home tab | Paragraph group) decreases the paragraph indent by one-half inch.

 Experiment

- Repeatedly click the Increase Indent and Decrease Indent buttons (Home tab | Paragraph group) and watch the left indent of the current paragraph change. When you have finished experimenting, use the Increase Indent and Decrease Indent buttons until the paragraph is indented one-half inch.

2
- Click the View Ruler button on the vertical ruler to hide the rulers.

Other Ways			
1. Drag Left Indent marker on horizontal ruler	3. Click Paragraph Dialog Box Launcher (Home tab | Paragraph group), click Indents and Spacing tab (Paragraph dialog box),	set indentation in Left text box, click OK button	Spacing tab (Paragraph dialog box), set indentation in Left text box, click OK button
2. Enter value in Indent Left text box (Page Layout tab | Paragraph group)		4. Right-click text, click Paragraph on shortcut menu, click Indents and	5. Press CTRL+M

To Insert a Building Block Using the Quick Parts Gallery

The Experience section of the resume in this chapter contains two jobs. The resume template, however, inserted content controls for only one job. Word has defined the sections and subsections of the resume as building blocks, which you can insert in the document. Recall that a building block contains named text or graphics that you can reuse in documents. In this case, the name of the building block you want to insert is called the Experience Subsection building block. The following steps insert a building block.

1

- Position the insertion point on the blank line below the first job entry.

- Display the Insert tab.

- Click the Quick Parts button (Insert tab | Text group) to display the Quick Parts gallery and then scroll through the Quick Parts gallery until Experience Subsection is displayed (Figure 5–26).

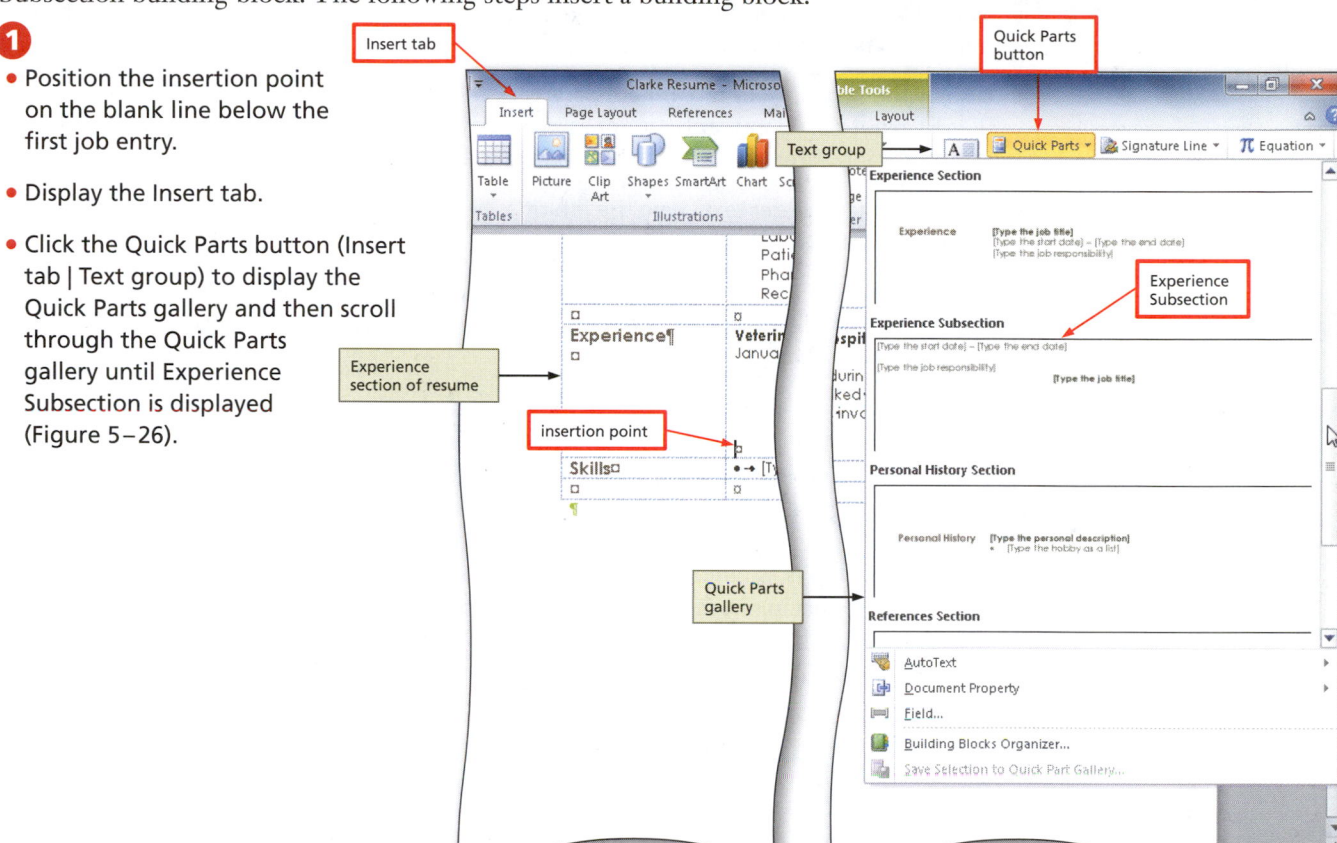

Figure 5–26

2

- Click Experience Subsection in the Quick Parts gallery to insert the building block in the document at the location of the insertion point.

- Press the BACKSPACE key to remove the extra blank space below the inserted building block (Figure 5–27).

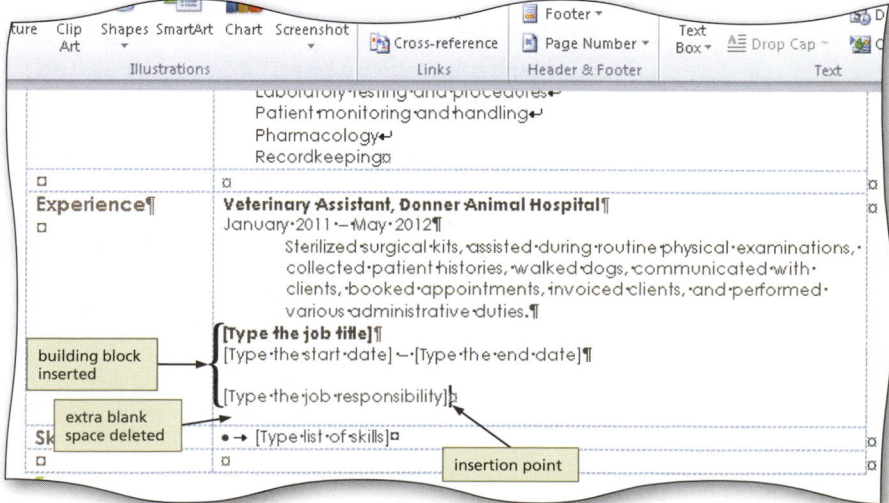

Figure 5–27

To Change Spacing before and after Paragraphs

The inserted Experience Subsection building block does not use the same paragraph spacing as the previous one in the resume. Thus, the next step is to adjust spacing before and after paragraphs in the inserted building block. The following steps change paragraph spacing.

1 Select the placeholder text, Type the end date, because you want to remove the space below this paragraph.

2 Display the Page Layout tab. If necessary, click the Spacing After box down arrow (Page Layout tab | Paragraph group) as many times as necessary until 0 pt is displayed in the Spacing After box because you want to decrease the space below the dates.

3 Select the placeholder text, Type the job title, because you want to increase the space before this paragraph.

4 Click the Spacing Before box up arrow (Page Layout tab | Paragraph group) as many times as necessary until 6 pt is displayed in the Spacing Before box because you want to increase the space above the job title.

To Replace More Placeholder Text in Content Controls and Change Paragraph Spacing

The next step is to enter the remainder of the text in the Experience section of the resume. The line spacing in the job description paragraph currently is 1.15 and should be 1 so that it matches the previous job description. The following steps replace placeholder text and change paragraph spacing.

1 In the Experience subsection of the resume, if necessary, select the content control with the placeholder text, Type the job title, and then type `Groomer, Bev's Doggie Care` as the job title and place of employment.

2 Select the content control with the placeholder text, Type the start date, and then type `June 2009` as the start date.

3 Select the content control with the placeholder text, Type the end date, and then type `December 2010` as the end date.

4 Select the content control with the placeholder text, Type the job responsibility, and then type this text: `Bathed dogs; brushed, combed, clipped, and shaped dogs' coats; trimmed nails; and cleaned ears.`

5 Display the Home tab. With the insertion point in the second job responsibility paragraph, click the Line and Paragraph Spacing button (Home tab | Paragraph group) to display the Line and Paragraph Spacing gallery and then, if necessary, click 1.0 in the gallery to change the line spacing of the current paragraph to single.

6 With the insertion point in the second job responsibility paragraph, click the Increase Indent button (Home tab | Paragraph group) to indent the current paragraph one-half inch (Figure 5–28).

BTW

BTWs
For a complete list of the BTWs found in the margins of this book, visit the Word 2010 BTW Web page (scsite.com/wd2010/btw).

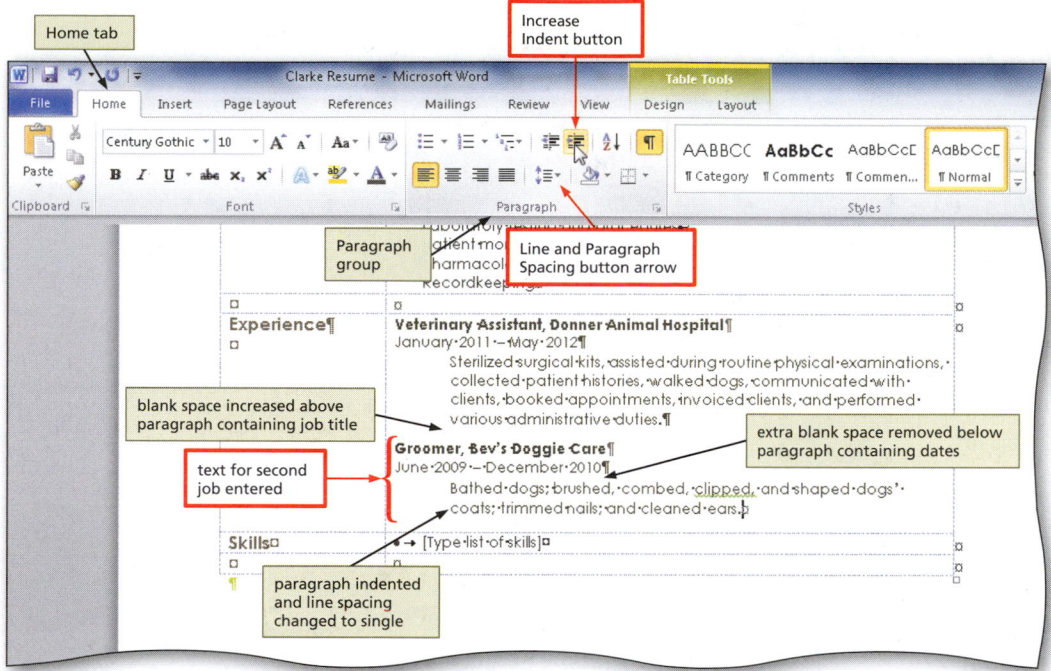

Figure 5–28

To Copy and Paste a Table Item

The last two sections of the resume in this chapter are the Memberships section and the Community Service section. Both of these sections contain a bulleted list. Currently, the resume ends with a Skills section, which contains a bulleted list. Thus, you create a copy of the Skills section so that you can then edit the two Skills sections to finish the resume for this chapter.

The Skills section currently is in one row. Because you want a blank space between the last two sections in the resume, you will copy the row containing the Skills section and then paste it below the blank row at the end of the table. You use the same procedure to copy table rows as to copy text. That is, select the rows to copy and then paste them at the desired location. The following steps copy table rows.

1
• Select the row to be copied, in this case, the row containing the Skills section in the resume.

• Click the Copy button (Home tab | Clipboard group) to copy the selected rows in the document to the Office Clipboard (Figure 5–29).

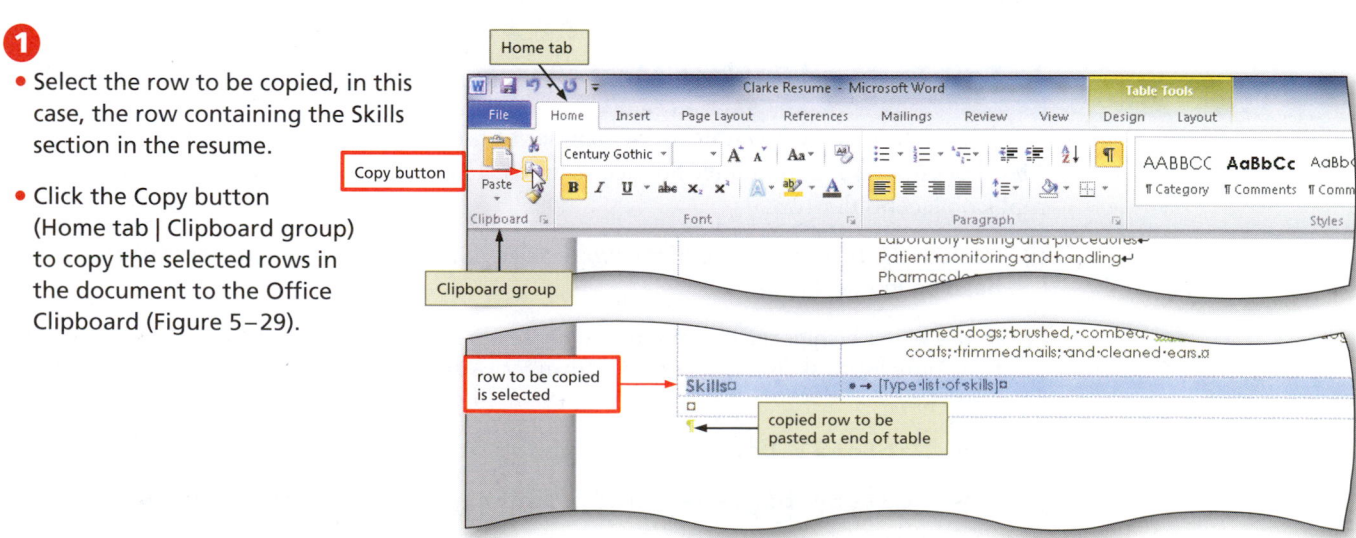

Figure 5–29

2

- Position the insertion point at the location where the copied row should be pasted, in this case, on the paragraph mark below the end of the table.

- Click the Paste button arrow (Home tab | Clipboard group) to display the Paste gallery.

Q&A

What if I click the Paste button by mistake?

Click the Undo button on the Quick Access Toolbar and then try again.

- Point to the Keep Original Table Formatting button in the Paste gallery to display a live preview of that paste option applied to the rows in the table (Figure 5–30).

🔍 **Experiment**

- Point to the three options in the Paste gallery and watch the format of the pasted rows change in the document window.

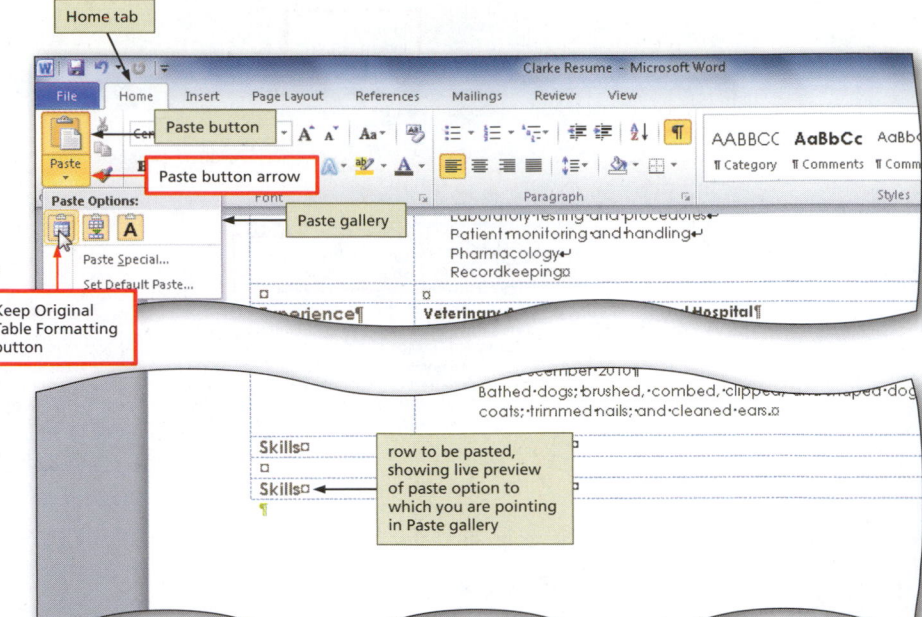

Figure 5–30

3

- Click the Keep Original Table Formatting button in the Paste gallery to apply the selected option to the pasted table rows because you want the pasted rows to use the same formatting as the copied rows.

Other Ways	
1. Right-click selected item, click Copy on shortcut menu, right-click where item is to be pasted, click desired option in Paste	Options area on shortcut menu
	2. Select item, press CTRL+C, position insertion point at paste location, press CTRL+V

To Edit Text and Replace More Placeholder Text in Content Controls

The next step is to enter the remainder of the text in the resume, that is, the Memberships and Community Service sections. The following steps edit text and replace placeholder text.

1 Replace the first occurrence of the word, Skills, with `Memberships` as the new heading in the resume.

2 In the Memberships section of the resume, select the content control with the placeholder text, Type list of skills. Type `Ford County Humane Society` and then press the ENTER key.

3 Type `National Dog Groomer Association` and then press the ENTER key.

4 Type `Society of Veterinary Technicians` and then press the ENTER key.

5 Type `Student Government Association, Donner Community College` as the last membership entry.

6 In the last row of the table, replace the word, Skills, with `Community Service` as the new heading in the resume.

7 In the Community Service section of the resume, select the content control with the placeholder text, Type list of skills, and then type **Answer phones and groom dogs at the Ford County Humane Society,** and then press SHIFT+ENTER to insert a line break.

8 Type **10 hours per week** and then press the ENTER key.

9 Type **Teach pet care basics to local school district students and staff,** and then press SHIFT+ENTER to insert a line break.

10 Type **8 hours per semester** as the last community service entry.

11 Remove the bold format from the bulleted items in the Membership and Community Service sections at the bottom of the resume (Figure 5–31).

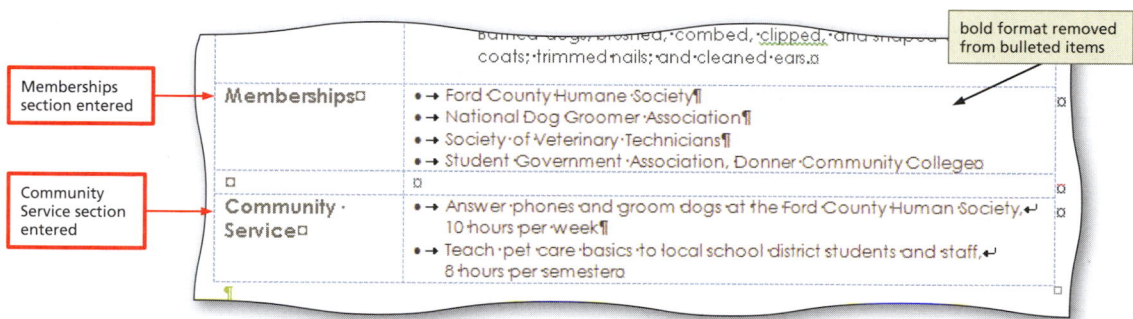

Figure 5–31

To Customize Theme Fonts

Recall that a font set defines one font for headings in a document and another font for body text. This resume currently uses the Austin font set, which specifies the Century Gothic font for both the headings and the body text. To add interest to the resume, the resume in this chapter creates a customized font set (theme font) so that the headings use the Eras Bold ITC font. Thus, the following steps create a customized theme font set with the name Resume Headings for this document.

1

• Click the Change Styles button (Home tab | Styles group) to display the Change Styles menu and then point to Fonts on the Change Styles menu to display the Fonts gallery (Figure 5–32).

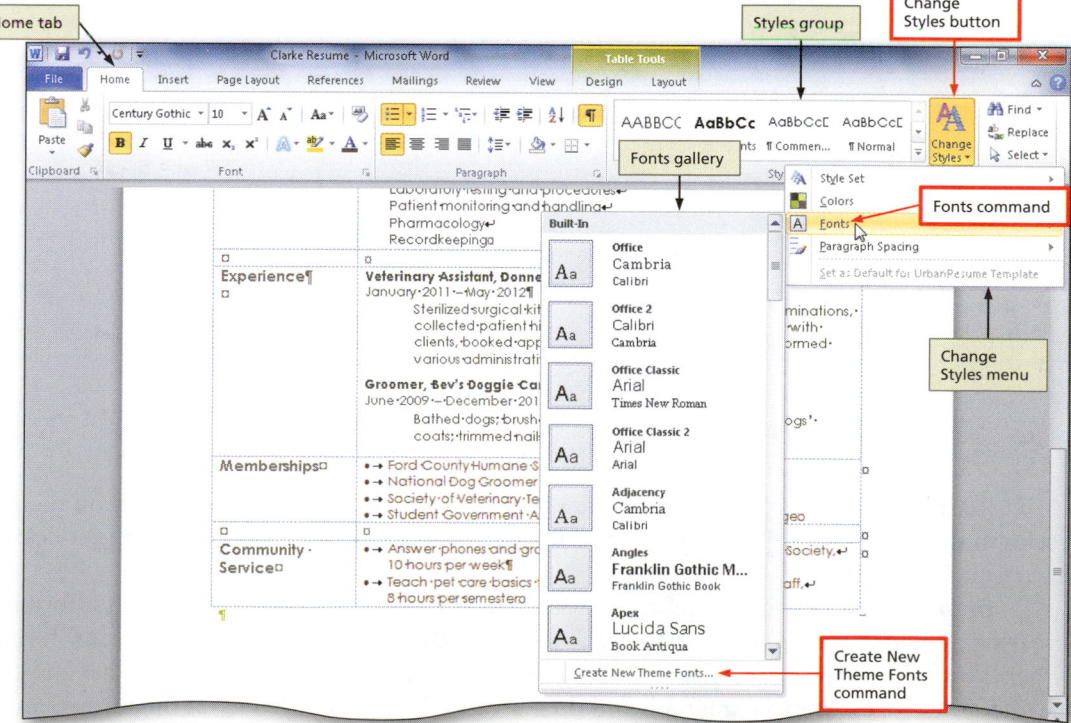

Figure 5–32

2

- Click Create New Theme Fonts in the Fonts gallery to display the Create New Theme Fonts dialog box.

- Click the Heading font box arrow (Create New Theme Fonts dialog box); scroll to and then click Eras Bold ITC (or a similar font).

Q&A

What if I wanted to change the font for body text, rather than or in addition to the font for headings?

You would click the Body font box arrow and then select the desired font for body text.

- Type **Resume Headings** as the name for the new theme font (Figure 5–33).

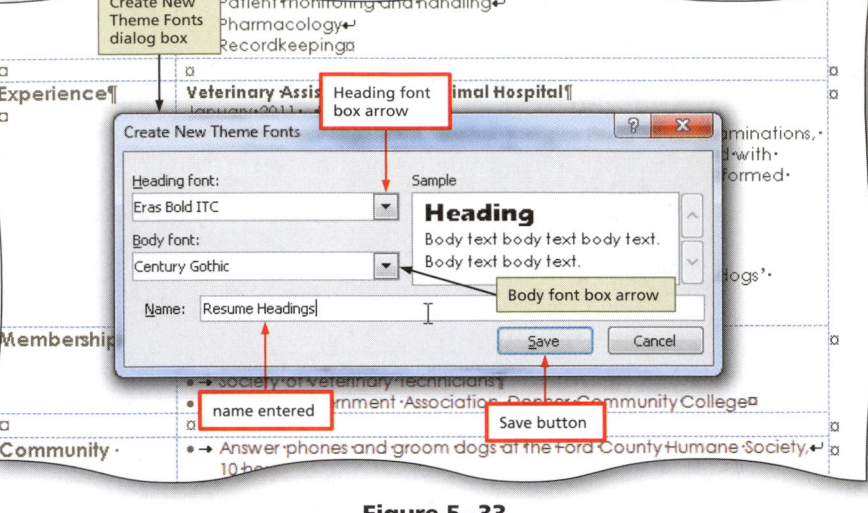

Figure 5–33

3

- Click the Save button (Create New Theme Fonts dialog box) to create the customized theme font with the entered name (Resume Headings, in this case) and apply the new heading fonts to the current document (Figure 5–34).

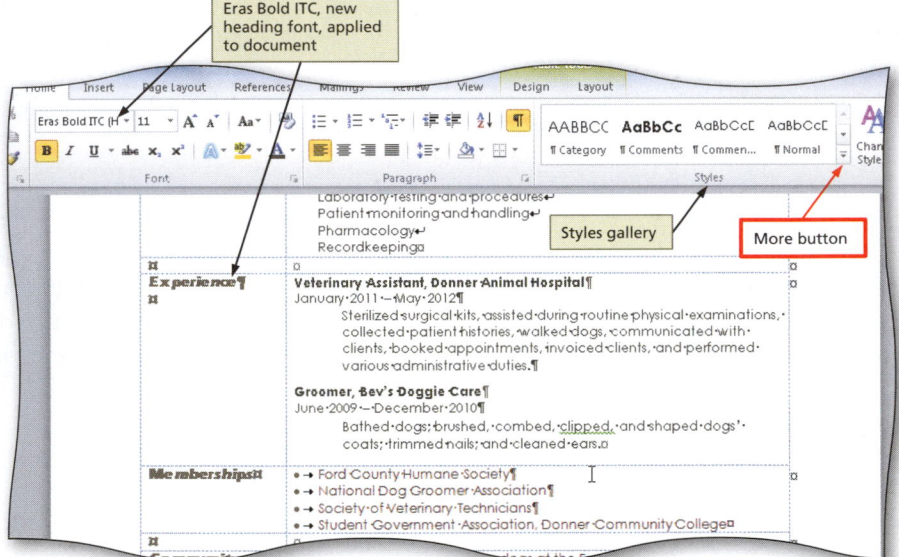

Figure 5–34

Other Ways

1. Click Theme Fonts button arrow (Page Layout tab | Themes group), click Create New Theme Fonts, select
   fonts (Create New Theme Fonts dialog box), click Save button

---

To Create a Quick Style

Recall that a Quick Style is a predefined style that appears in the Styles gallery on the Ribbon. You have used styles in the Styles gallery to apply defined formats to text and have updated existing styles. You also can create your own Quick Styles.

In the resume for this chapter, you want to add more emphasis to the contact information. To illustrate creating a Quick Style, you will change the format of the address line and save the new format as a Quick Style. Then, you will apply the newly defined Quick Style to the lines containing the phone and e-mail information. The next steps format text in a paragraph and then create a Quick Style based on the formats in the selected paragraph.

1

- Scroll up so that the top of the resume is displayed in the document window.

- Select the line of text containing the address information at the top of the resume.

- Change the font of the selected text to Eras Demi ITC and change the font color to Brown, Accent 2, Darker 25% (fifth row, sixth column in the Font Color gallery).

- Click the More button (shown in Figure 5–34) in the Quick Styles gallery (Home tab | Styles group) to expand the gallery (Figure 5–35).

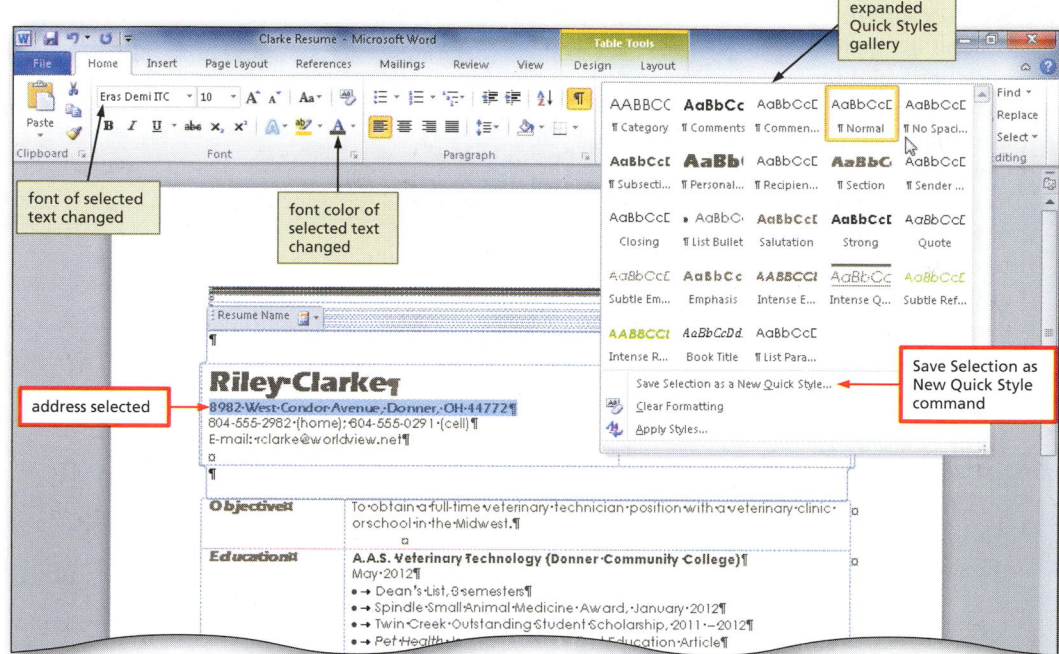

Figure 5–35

2

- Click Save Selection as a New Quick Style in the Quick Styles gallery to display the Create New Style from Formatting dialog box.

- Type **Resume Contact Information** in the Name text box (Create New Style from Formatting dialog box) (Figure 5–36).

3

- Click the OK button to create the new Quick Style and add it to the Styles gallery.

Q&A

How can I see the style just created?

If the style name does not appear in the in-Ribbon Quick Styles gallery, click the More button on the Quick Styles gallery (Home tab | Styles group) to display the expanded Quick Styles gallery.

Figure 5–36

To Apply a Style

The next step is to apply the Quick Style just created to the lines containing the phone and e-mail information in the resume. The following steps apply a Quick Style.

1 Select the text to which you want to apply the style, in this case, the lines of text containing the phone and e-mail information.

Other Ways

1. In some instances, right-click selected paragraph, click Save Selection as a New Quick Style on shortcut menu, enter name of new Quick Style (Create New Style from Formatting), click OK button

2 If the desired style name does not appear in the in-Ribbon Quick Styles gallery (in this case, Resume Contact Information), click the More button on the Quick Styles gallery (Home tab | Styles group) to expand the gallery and then point to Resume Contact Information in the Quick Style gallery to see a live preview of that style applied to the selected text in the document (Figure 5–37).

3 Click Resume Contact Information in the Quick Styles gallery to apply the selected style to the selected text in the document.

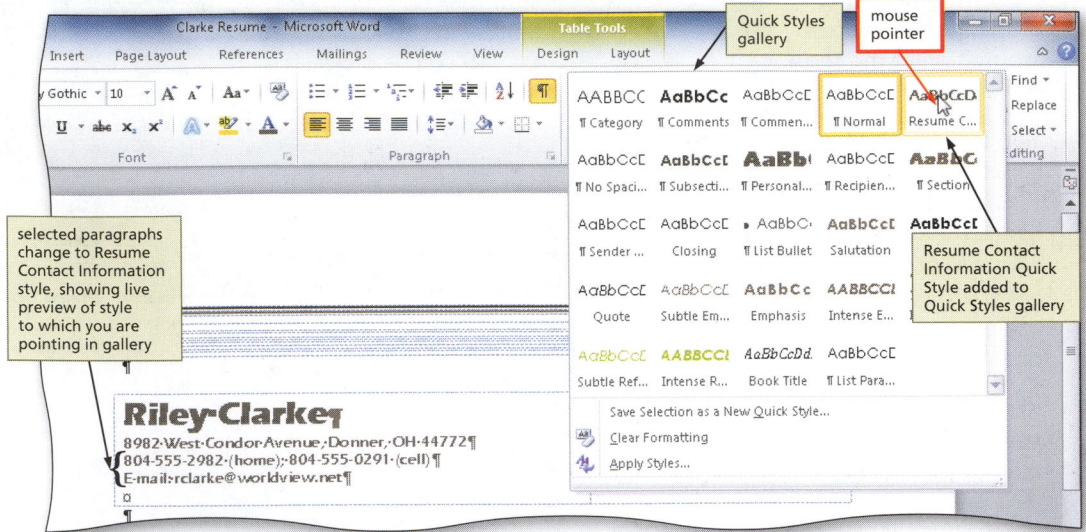

Figure 5–37

To Reveal Formatting

Sometimes, you want to know what formats were applied to certain text items in a document. For example, you may wonder what font, font size, font color, and other effects were applied to the bulleted paragraphs in the resume. To display formatting applied to text, use the Reveal Formatting task pane. The following steps show and then hide the Reveal Formatting task pane.

1

• Position the insertion point in the text for which you want to reveal formatting (in this case, the first bullet in the Education section).

• Press SHIFT+F1 to display the Reveal Formatting task pane, which shows formatting applied to the location of the insertion point in (Figure 5–38).

Experiment

• Click the Font collapse button to hide the Font formats. Click the Font expand button to redisplay the Font formats.

Q&A Why do some of the formats in the Reveal Formatting task pane appear as links?

Clicking a link in the Reveal Formatting task pane displays an associated dialog box, allowing you to change the format of the current text. For example, clicking the Font link in the Reveal Formatting task pane would display the Font dialog box. If you made changes in the Font dialog box and then clicked the OK button, Word would change the format of the current text.

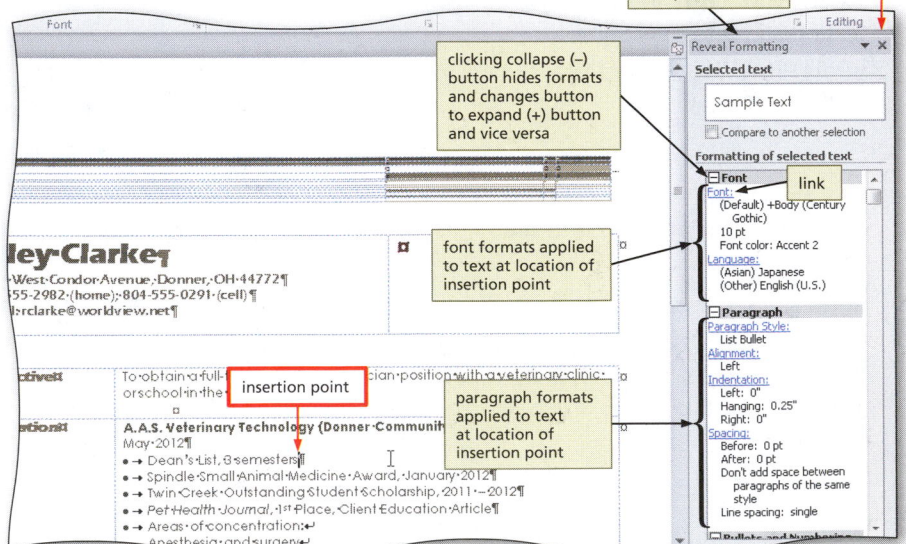

Figure 5–38

2

• Close the Reveal Formatting task pane by clicking its Close button.

To Modify a Style Using the Styles Dialog Box

The bulleted items in the resume currently have a different font color than the other text in the resume. You prefer that all text in the resume use the same font. The bulleted items are formatted according to the List Bullet style. Thus, the following steps modify the font color of the List Bullet style.

1

- Click somewhere in a bulleted list in the resume to position the insertion point in a paragraph formatted with the style to be modified.

- Click the Styles Dialog Box Launcher (Home tab | Styles group) to display the Styles task pane with the current style selected.

- If necessary, click List Bullet in the Styles task pane to select it and then click its box arrow to display the List Bullet menu (Figure 5–39).

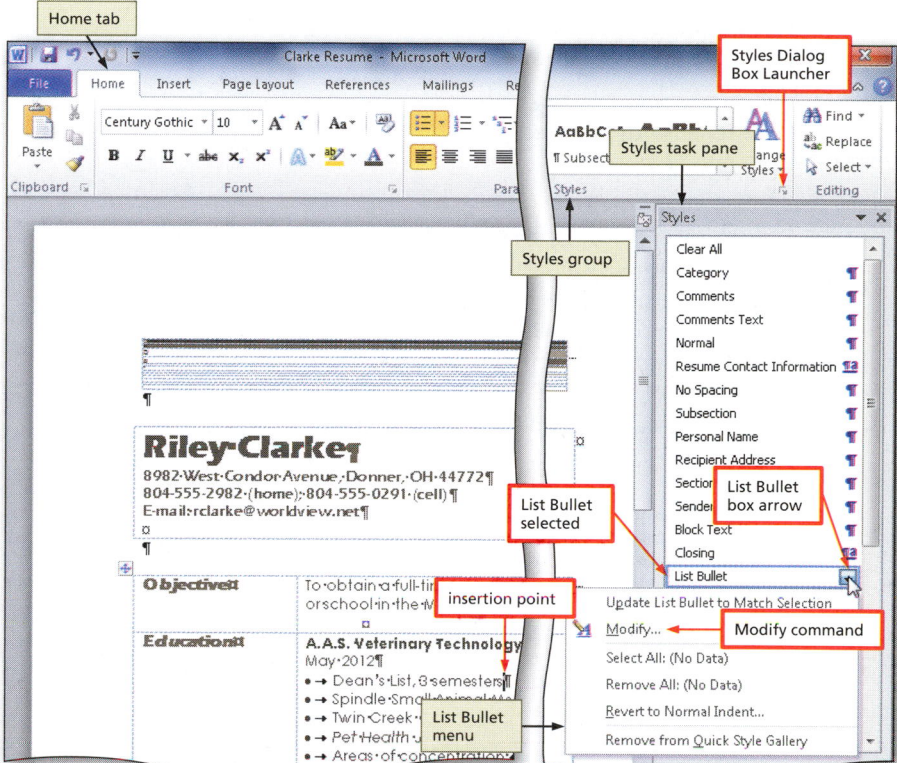

Figure 5–39

2

- Click Modify on the List Bullet menu to display the Modify Style dialog box.

- Click the Font Color button arrow (Modify Style dialog box) and then click Brown, Text 2 (first row, fourth column) in the Font Color gallery to change the font color of the current style.

- Place a check mark in the Automatically update check box so that any future changes you make to the style in the document will update the current style automatically (Figure 5–40).

Q&A

What is the purpose of the Format button in the Modify Style dialog box?

If the formatting you wish to change for the style is not available in the Modify Style dialog box, you can click the Format button and then select the desired command on the Format button menu to display a dialog box that contains additional formatting options.

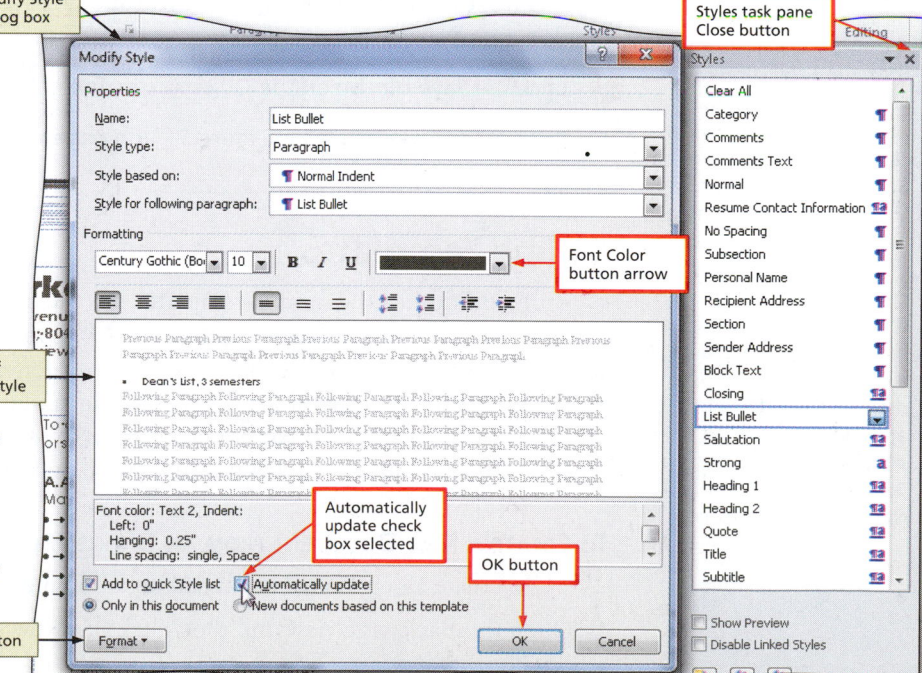

Figure 5–40

3

- Click the OK button to close the dialog box and apply the style changes to the paragraphs in the document.

- Click the Close button on the Styles task pane title bar to close the task pane (Figure 5–41).

Q&A

What if the style is not updated?

Select a bulleted list paragraph in the resume; change the font color of the selected text to Brown, Text 2 using the Font Color button arrow (Home tab | Font group); click the More button in the Styles gallery (Home tab | Styles group); right-click List Bullet in the Styles gallery to display a shortcut menu; and then click Update List Bullet to Match Selection to update all similar styles in the document to the selected styles.

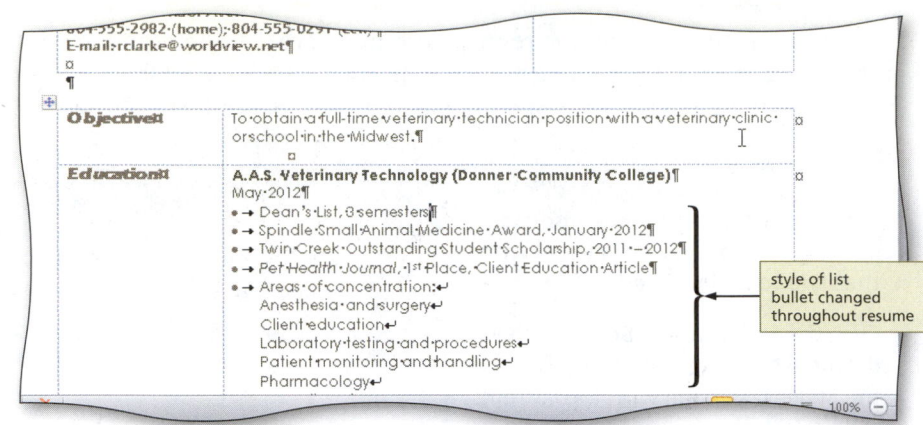

Figure 5–41

Other Ways

1. Right-click style name in Styles gallery (Home tab | Styles group), click Modify on shortcut menu, change settings (Modify Style dialog box), click OK button

2. Click Styles Dialog Box Launcher, click Manage

Styles button, scroll to style and then select it (Manage Styles dialog box), click Modify button, change settings (Modify Style dialog box), click OK button in each dialog box

---

BTW

Conserving Ink and Toner

If you want to conserve ink or toner, you can instruct Word to print draft quality documents by clicking File on the Ribbon to open the Backstage view, clicking Options in the Backstage view to display the Word Options dialog box, clicking Advanced in the left pane (Word Options dialog box), scrolling to the Print area in the right pane, placing a check mark in the 'Use draft quality' check box, and then clicking the OK button. Then, use the Backstage view to print the document as usual.

To Save and Print the Document

The resume is complete. Thus, you should save it again. The following step saves the document again and prints it.

1 Click the Save button on the Quick Access Toolbar to overwrite the previously saved file.

2 Print the resume (shown in Figure 5–1 on page WD 275).

Online Templates

In addition to the sample templates installed on your computer's hard disk, you can access numerous online templates. Available online templates include agendas, award certificates, calendars, expense reports, fax cover letters, greeting cards, invitations, invoices, letters, meeting minutes, memos, and statements. When you select an online template, Word downloads (or copies) it from the Office.com Web site to your computer. Once it is downloaded, you can use the template directly from your computer.

To Create a New Document from an Online Template

To create a new document based on an online template, you would follow these steps.

1. Open the Backstage view and then click the New tab in the Backstage view to display the New gallery.

2. Scroll through the list of templates and folders in the Office.com Templates area in the New gallery.

3. Click the desired folder or template.

4. Repeat Step 3 until you locate the desired template and then click that template.

5. Click the Download button in the New gallery to download the template and create a new document based on the downloaded template.

TO CREATE A NEW DOCUMENT FROM A TEMPLATE DOWNLOADED FROM OFFICE.COM

Word downloads a template from Office.com to the My templates folder on your computer. If you wanted to create another document using the downloaded template, you would do the following:

1. Open the Backstage view and then click the New tab in the Backstage view to display the New gallery.

2. Click My templates in the New gallery to display the New dialog box.

3. Click the desired template (New dialog box) and then click the OK button to create a new document based on the selected template.

> **Break Point:** If you wish to take a break, this is a good place to do so. You can quit Word now. To resume at a later time, start Word, open the file called Clarke Resume, and continue following the steps from this location forward.

Sharing a Document with Others

You may find the need to share Word documents with others electronically, such as via e-mail or via a USB flash drive. To ensure that others can read and/or open the files successfully, Word presents a variety of formats and tools to assist with sharing documents. This section uses the Clarke Resume created in this chapter to present a variety of these formats and tools.

> **For electronic distribution, such as e-mail, ensure the document is in the proper format.**
> When sharing a Word document with others, you cannot be certain that it will look or print the same on their computers as on your computer. For example, the document may wordwrap text differently on their computers. If others do not need to edit the document, that is, just view and/or print the document, you could save the file in a format that allows others to view the document as you see it. Two popular such formats are PDF and XPS.

Plan Ahead

PDF

PDF, which stands for Portable Document Format, is a file format created by Adobe Systems that shows all elements of a printed document as an electronic image. Users can view a PDF document without the software that created the original document. Thus, the PDF format enables users easily to share documents with others. To view, navigate, and print a PDF file, you use a program called **Adobe Reader**, which can be downloaded free from Adobe's Web site.

To Save a Word Document as a PDF Document and View the PDF Document in Adobe Reader

When you save a Word document as a PDF document, the original Word document remains intact; that is, Word creates a copy of the file in the PDF format. The steps on the next page save the Clarke Resume Word document as a PDF document and then open the Clarke Resume PDF document in Adobe Reader.

1

- Open the Backstage view and then click the Save & Send tab in the Backstage view to display the Save & Send gallery.

- Click Create PDF/XPS Document in the Save & Send gallery to display information about PDF/XPS documents in the right pane (Figure 5–42).

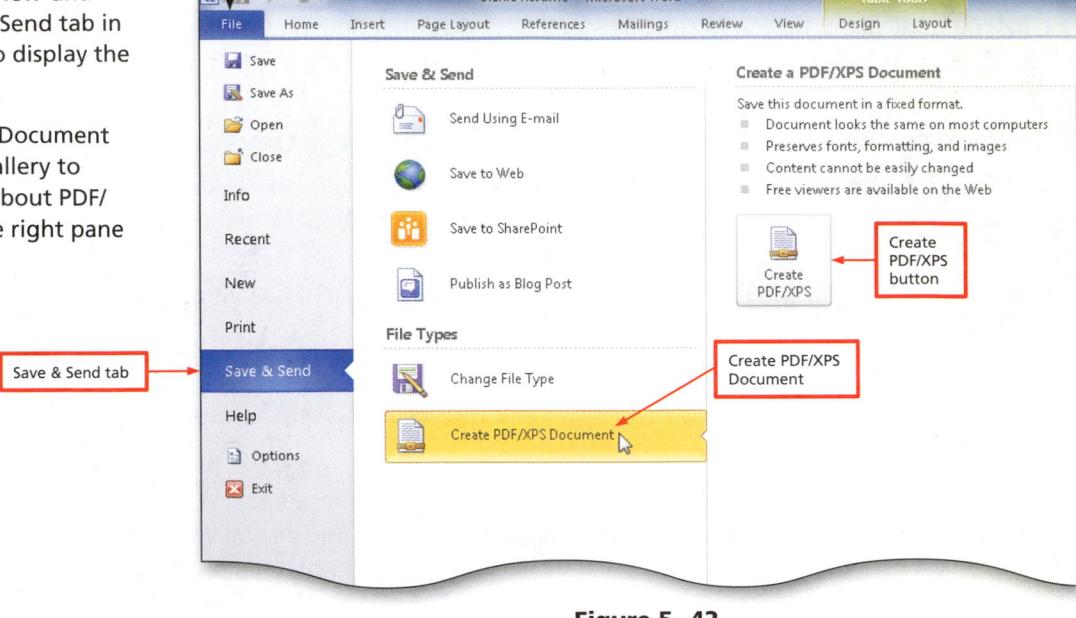

Figure 5–42

2

- Click the Create PDF/XPS button in the right pane to display the Publish as PDF or XPS dialog box.

- Navigate to the desired save location (in this case, the Word folder in the CIS 101 folder [or your class folder] on the USB flash drive) (Publish as PDF or XPS dialog box).

Q&A Can the file name be the same for the Word document and the PDF document?

Yes. The file names can be the same because the file types are different: one is a Word document and the other is a PDF document.

- If necessary, click the 'Save as type' box arrow and then click PDF.

- If necessary, place a check mark in the 'Open file after publishing' check box so that Word will display the resulting PDF document in Adobe Reader (Figure 5–43).

Q&A Why is my 'Open file after publishing' check box dimmed?

You do not have Adobe Reader installed on your computer. After installing Adobe Reader, repeat these steps.

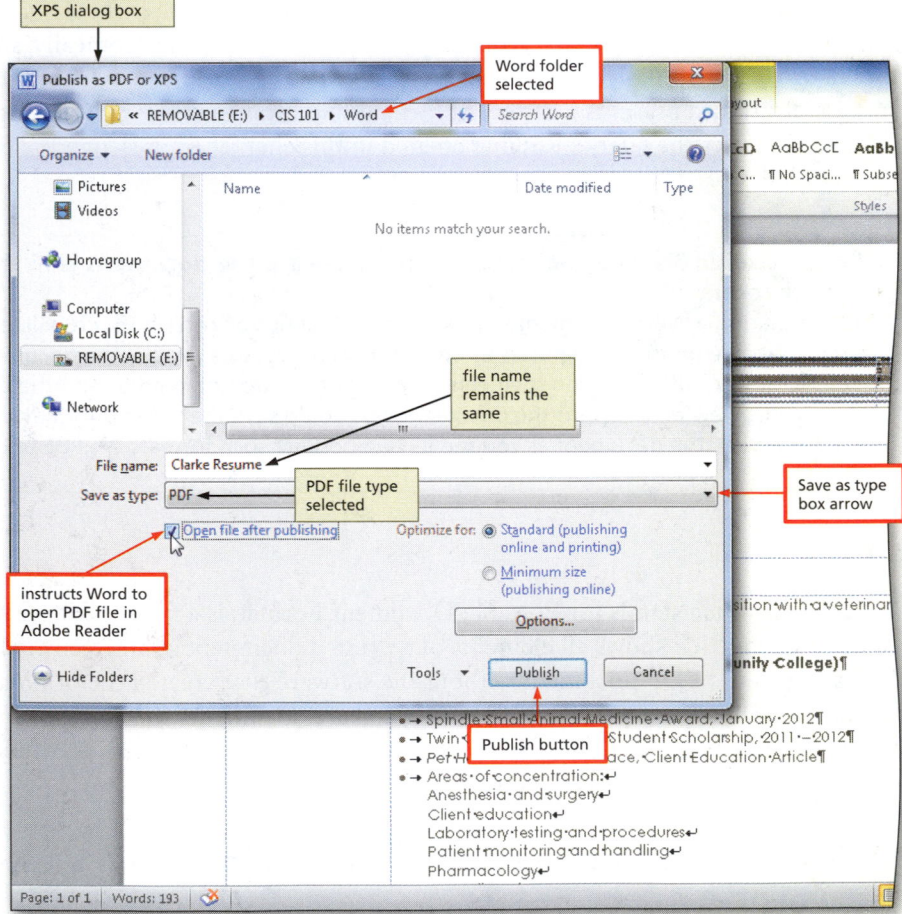

Figure 5–43

3

- Click the Publish button to create the PDF document from the Word document and then, because the check box was selected, open the resulting PDF document in Adobe Reader.

- If necessary, click the Maximize button in the Adobe Reader window to maximize the window (Figure 5–44).

 Do I have to display the resulting PDF document in Adobe Reader?

No. If you do not want to display the document in Adobe Reader, you would not place a check mark in the 'Open file after publishing' check box in the Publish as PDF or XPS dialog box.

 Is the Clarke Resume Word document still open?

Yes. Word still is running with the Clark Resume document opened.

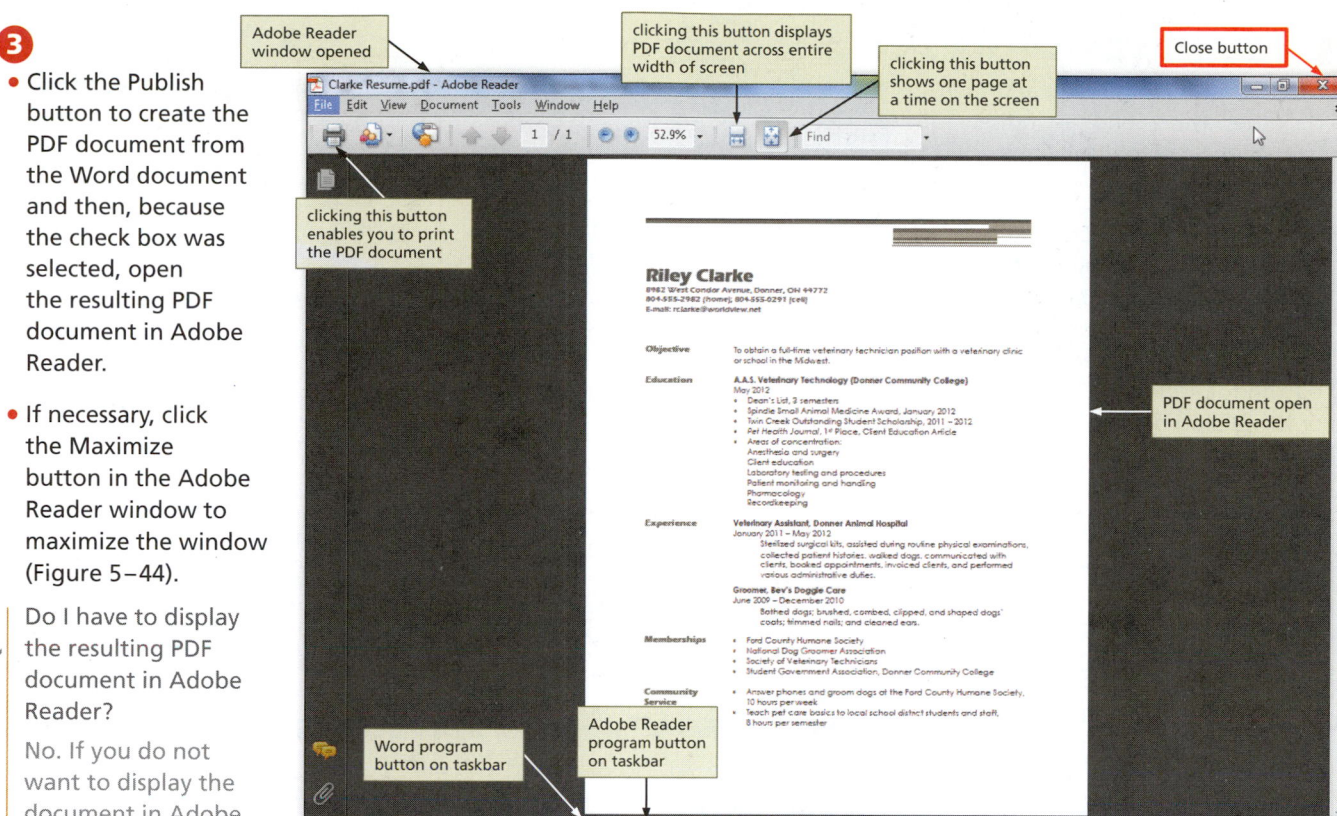

Figure 5–44

4

- Click the Close button on the Adobe Reader title bar to close the Clarke Resume.pdf document and quit Adobe Reader.

Other Ways

1. Press F12, click 'Save as type' box arrow (Save As dialog box), select PDF in list, click Save button

---

XPS

XPS, which stands for XML Paper Specification, is a file format created by Microsoft that shows all elements of a printed document as an electronic image. As with the PDF format, users can view an XPS document without the software that created the original document. Thus, the XPS format also enables users to share documents with others easily. Windows includes an XPS Viewer, which enables you to view, navigate, and print XPS files.

To Save a Word Document as an XPS Document and View the XPS Document in the XPS Viewer

When you save a Word document as an XPS document, the original Word document remains intact; that is, Word creates a copy of the file in the XPS format. The steps on the next page save the Clarke Resume Word document as an XPS document and then open the Clarke Resume XPS document in the XPS Viewer.

1

- Open the Backstage view and then click the Save & Send tab in the Backstage view to display the Save & Send gallery.

- Click Create PDF/XPS Document in the Save & Send gallery to display information about PDF/ XPS documents in the right pane and then click the Create a PDF/XPS button to display the Publish as PDF or XPS dialog box.

- If necessary, navigate to the desired save location (in this case, the Word folder in the CIS 101 folder [or your class folder] on the USB flash drive) (Publish as PDF or XPS dialog box).

- If necessary, click the 'Save as type' box arrow and then click XPS Document.

- If necessary, place a check mark in the 'Open file after publishing' check box so that Word displays the resulting XPS document in the XPS Viewer (Figure 5–45).

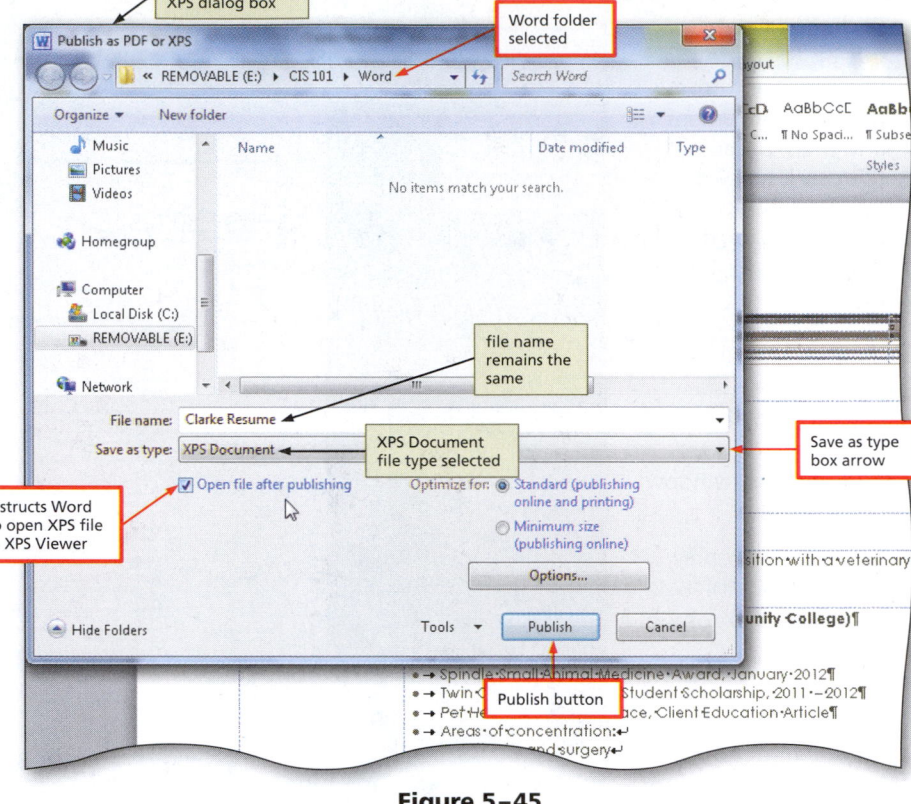

Figure 5–45

2

- Click the Publish button to create the XPS document from the Word document and then, because the check box was selected, open the resulting XPS document in the XPS Viewer.

Q&A What if I do not have an XPS Viewer?

The document will open in a browser window.

- If necessary, click the Maximize button in the XPS Viewer window to maximize the window (Figure 5–46).

Q&A Do I have to display the resulting XPS document in the XPS Viewer?

No. If you did not want to display the document in the XPS Viewer, you would not place a check mark in the 'Open file after publishing' check box in the Publish as PDF or XPS dialog box.

Q&A Is the Clarke Resume Word document still open?

Yes. Word still is running with the Clarke Resume document opened.

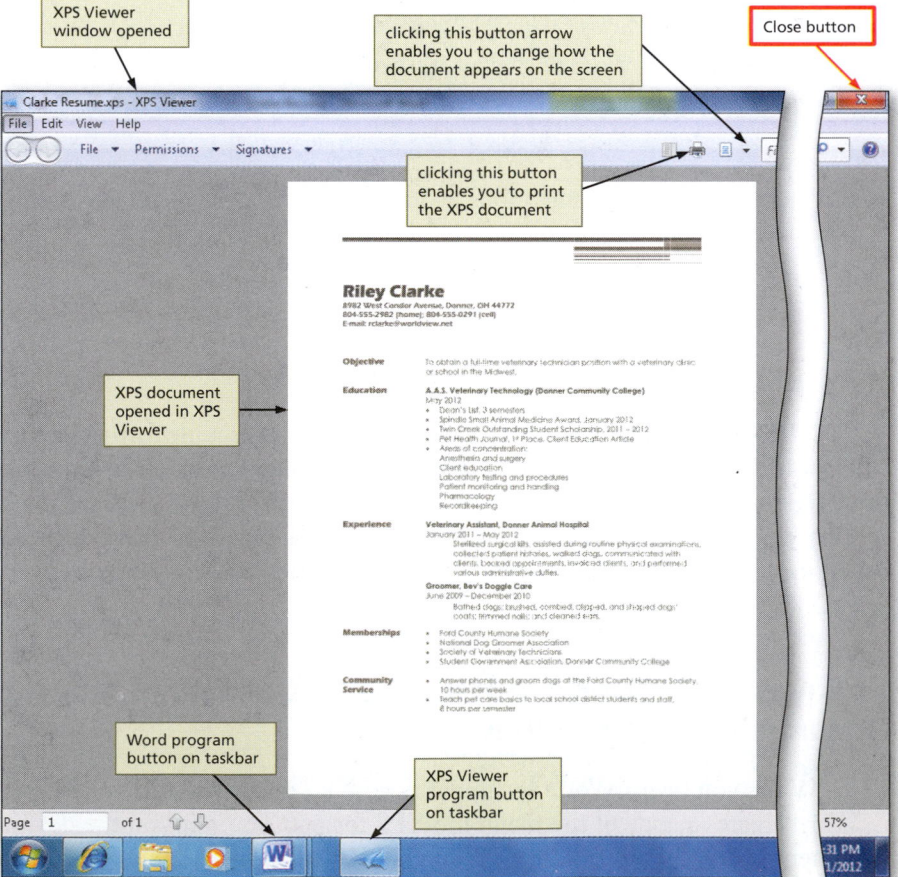

Figure 5–46

- Click the Close button on the XPS Viewer title bar to close the Clarke Resume.xps document and quit the XPS Viewer.

To Run the Compatibility Checker

Assume you have considered saving a document, such as your resume, in the Word 97-2003 format so that it can be opened by users with earlier versions of Microsoft Word. Before saving a document or template in an earlier Word format, however, you want to ensure that all of its elements (such as building blocks, content controls, and graphics) are compatible (will work with) earlier versions of Word. The following steps run the compatibility checker.

1

- Open the Backstage view and then click the Info tab in the Backstage view to display the Info gallery.

- Click the Check for Issues button in the Info gallery to display the Check for Issues menu (Figure 5–47).

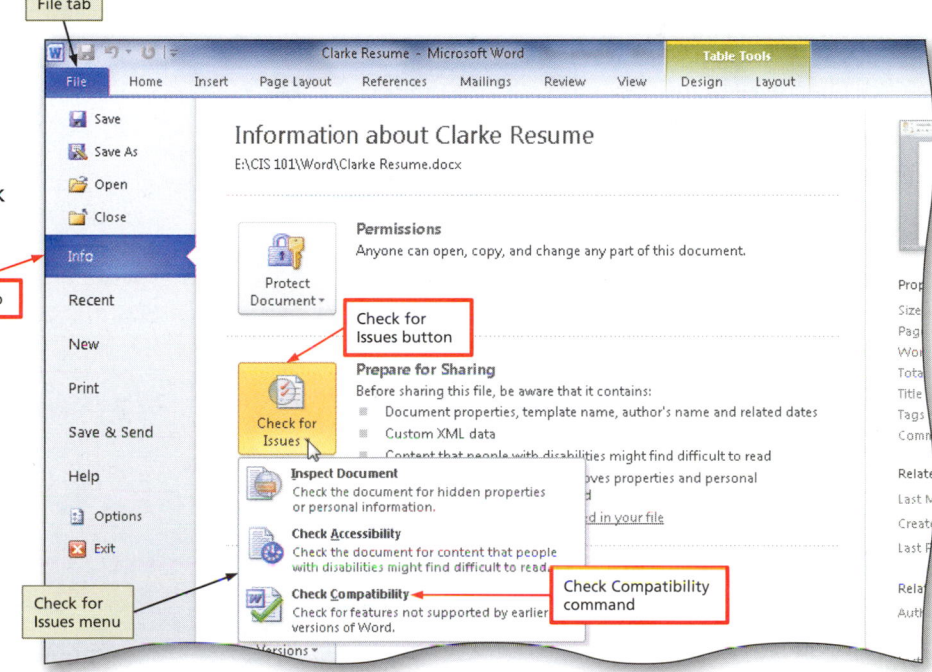

Figure 5–47

2

- Click Check Compatibility on the Check for Issues menu to display the Microsoft Word Compatibility Checker dialog box, which shows any content that may not be supported by earlier versions of Word (Figure 5–48).

3

- Click the OK button (Microsoft Word Compatibility Checker dialog box) to close the dialog box.

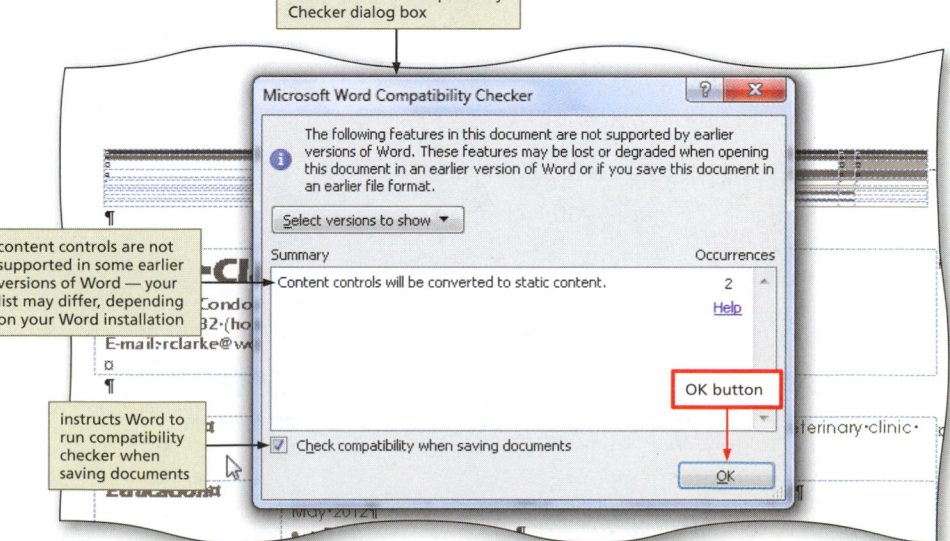

Figure 5–48

To Save a Word 2010 Document in an Earlier Word Format

If you send a document created in Word 2010 to users who have a version of Word earlier than Word 2007, they will not be able to open the Word 2010 document because Word 2010 saves documents in a format that is not backward compatible with versions earlier than Word 2007. Word 2010 documents have a file type of .docx, and versions prior to Word 2007 have a .doc file type. To ensure that all Word users can open your Word 2010 document, you should save the document in a previous version format. The following steps save the Clarke Resume Word 2010 document in the Word 97-2003 format.

1

- Open the Backstage view and then click the Save & Send tab in the Backstage view to display the Save & Send gallery.

- Click Change File Type in the Save & Send gallery to display information in the right pane about various file types that can be opened in Word.

- Click Word 97-2003 in the right pane to specify the new file type (Figure 5–49).

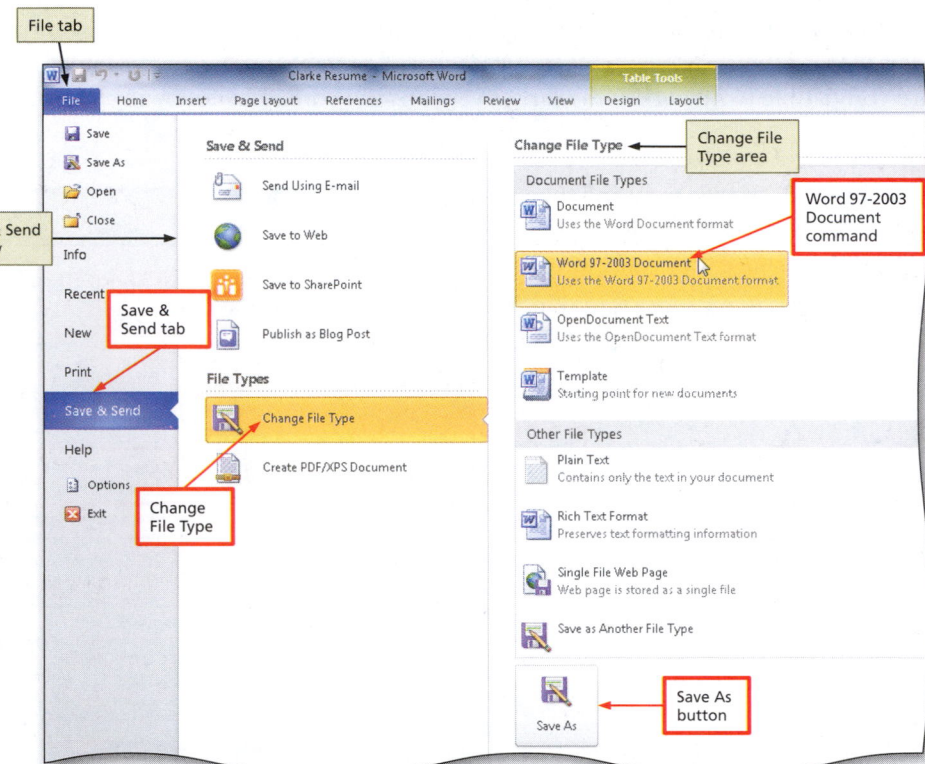

Figure 5–49

2

- Click the Save As button in the right pane to display the Save As dialog box.

- If necessary, navigate to the desired save location (in this case, the Word folder in the CIS 101 folder [or your class folder] on the USB flash drive) (Save As dialog box) (Figure 5–50).

Can the file name be the same for the Word 2010 document and the Word 97-2003 document?

Yes. The file names can be the same because the file types are different: one is a Word document with a .docx extension, and the other is a Word document with a .doc extension. The next section discusses file types and extensions.

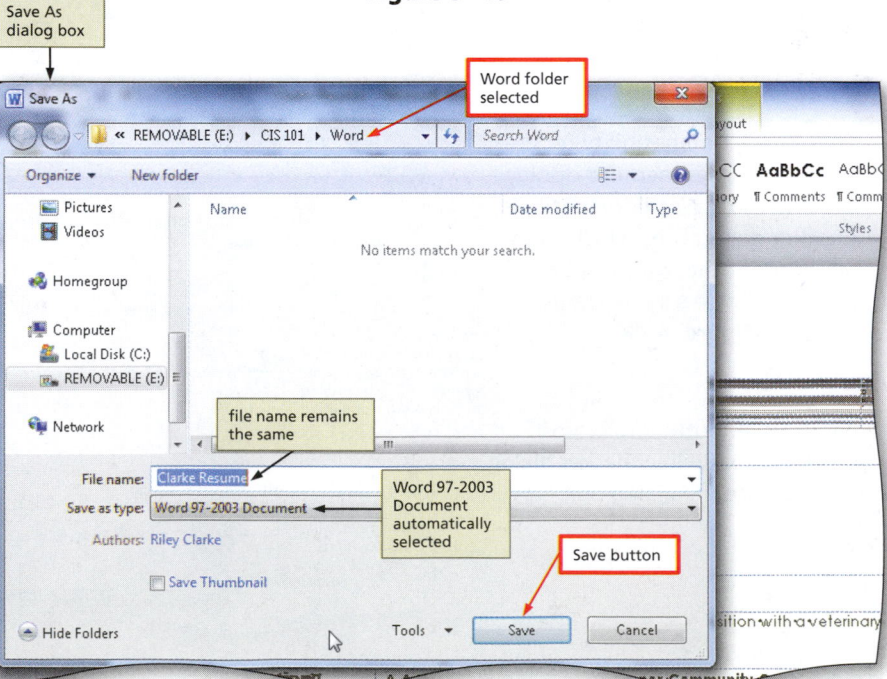

Figure 5–50

3
- Click the Save button, which may display the Microsoft Word Compatibility Checker dialog box before saving the document (Figure 5–51).

Q&A My screen did not display the Microsoft Word Compatibility Checker dialog box. Why not?

If the 'Check compatibility when saving documents' check box is not selected (as shown in Figure 5–48 on page WD 305), Word will not check compatibility when saving a document.

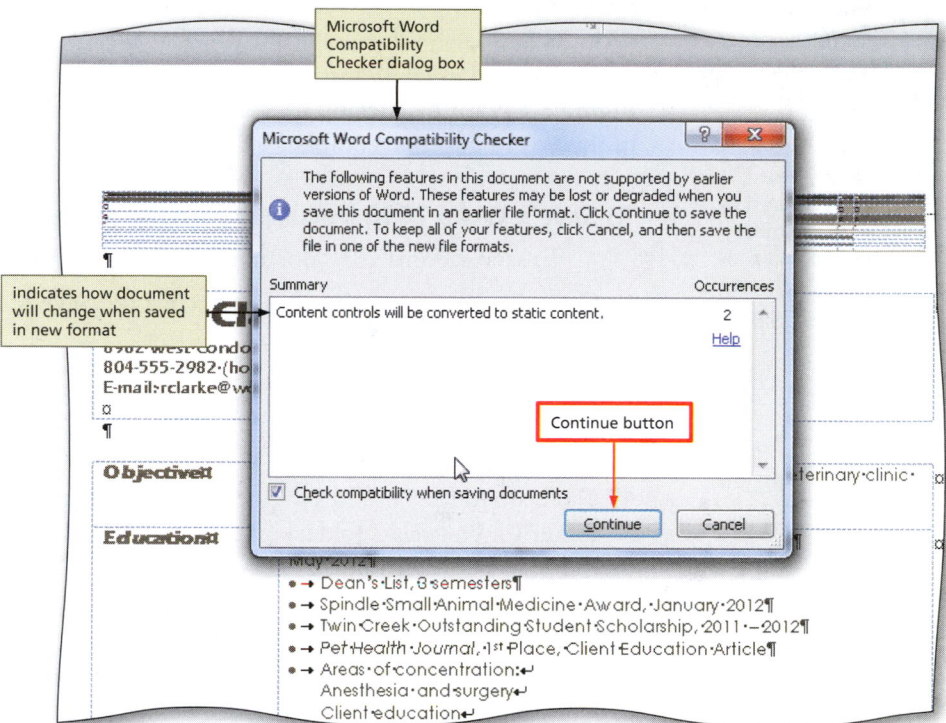

Figure 5–51

4
- If the Microsoft Word Compatibility Checker dialog box is displayed, click its Continue button to save the document on the selected drive with the current file name in the specified format (Figure 5–52).

Q&A Is the Clarke Resume Word 2010 document still open?

No. Word closed the original document (the Word 2010 Clarke Resume).

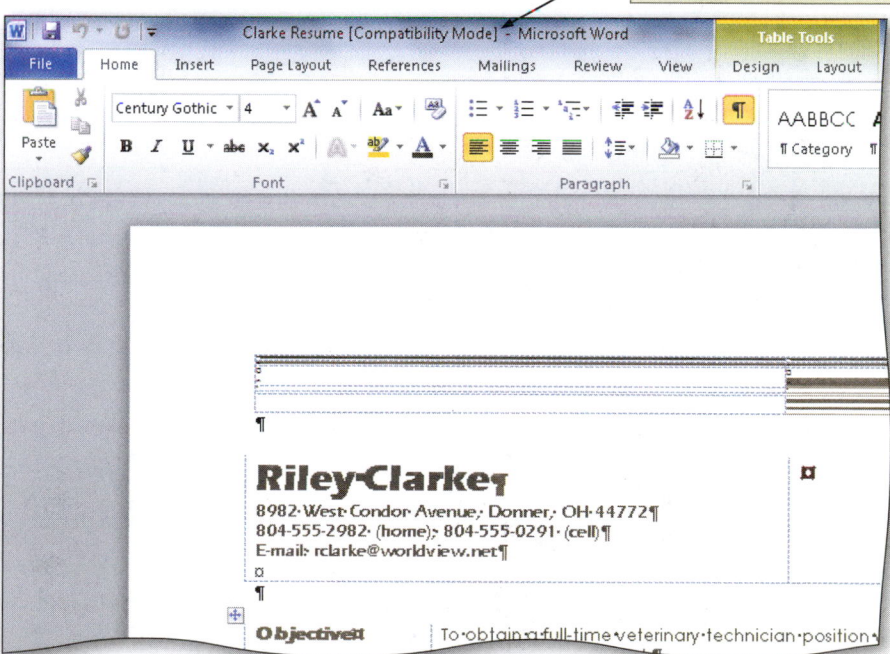

Figure 5–52

Other Ways

1. Press F12, click 'Save as type' box arrow (Save As dialog box), select Word 97-2003 Document in list, click Save button

File Types

When saving documents in Word, you can select from a variety of file types that can be opened in Word using the Save & Send gallery in the Backstage view (shown in Figure 5–49) or by clicking the 'Save as type' box arrow in the Save As dialog box. To save in these varied formats (Table 5–1), you follow the same basic steps as just illustrated.

TO SAVE A WORD 2010 DOCUMENT AS A DIFFERENT FILE TYPE

To save a Word 2010 document as a different file type, you would follow these steps.

1. Open the Backstage view and then click the Save & Send tab in the Backstage view to display the Save & Send gallery.

2. Click Change File Type in the Save & Send gallery to display information in the right pane about various file types that can be opened in Word.

3. Click the desired file type in the right pane to display the Save As dialog box.

4. Navigate to the desired save location (in this case, the Word folder in the CIS 101 folder [or your class folder] on the USB flash drive) (Save As dialog box) and then click the Save button in the dialog box.

5. If the Microsoft Word Compatibility Checker dialog box appears and you agree with the changes that will be made to the document, click the Continue button (Microsoft Word Compatibility Checker dialog box) to save the document on the selected drive with the current file name in the specified format.

Table 5–1 File Types

File Type	File Extension	Windows Explorer Image	Description
Word Document	.docx		Format used for Word 2010 or Word 2007 documents
Word 97-2003 Document	.doc		Format used for documents created in versions of Word from Word 97 to Word 2003
Word Template	.dotx		Format used for Word 2010 or Word 2007 templates
Word 97-2003 Template	.dot		Format used for templates created in versions of Word from Word 97 and Word 2003
PDF	.pdf		Portable Document Format, which can be opened in Adobe Reader
XPS	.xps		XML Paper Specification, which can be opened in the XPS Viewer
Single File Web Page	.mht		HTML (Hypertext Markup Language) format that can be opened in a Web browser; all elements of the Web page are saved in a single file
Web Page	.htm		HTML (Hypertext Markup Language) format that can be opened in a Web browser; various elements of the Web page, such as graphics, saved in separate files and folders
Rich Text Format	.rtf		Format designed to ensure file can be opened and read in many programs; some formatting may be lost to ensure compatibility
Plain Text	.txt		Format where all or most formatting is removed from the document
OpenDocument Text	.odt		Format used by other word processing programs such as Google Docs and OpenOffice.org
Works 6 - 9	.wps		Format used by Microsoft Works

To Close a Document

You are finished with the Word 97-2003 format of the Clarke Resume. Thus, the next step is to close this document. The following steps close a document.

1 Open the Backstage view.

2 Click Close in the Backstage view to close the current open document.

To Open a Recent Document

You would like to reopen the Word 2010 format of the Clarke Resume. Thus, the next step is to open this document. Because it recently was open, the following steps open a document from Recent Documents.

1 Open the Backstage view and then, if necessary, click the Recent tab in the Backstage view to display the list of recent documents in the Recent gallery.

2 To be sure you open the Word 2010 format of the Clarke Resume, point to the file name and verify the file name is Clarke Resume.docx in the ScreenTip (Figure 5–53).

3 Click Clarke Resume (the Word 2010 format) in the Recent gallery to open the document in the Word document window.

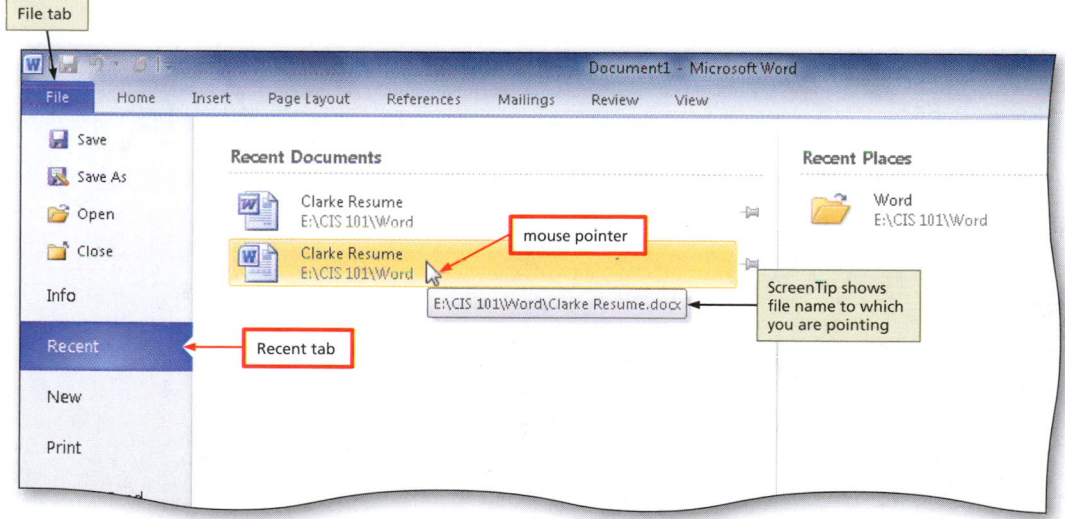

Figure 5–53

For electronic distribution, such as e-mail, ensure the document is in the proper format.
If you e-mail a document, such as your resume, consider that the recipient, such as a potential employer, may not have the same software you used to create the resume and, thus, may not be able to open the file. As an alternative, you could save the file in a format, such as a PDF or XPS, that can be viewed with a reader program. Many job seekers also post their resumes on the Web. Read Appendices B and C for ways to save Word documents on the Web.

Plan Ahead

To Send a Document Using E-Mail

In Word, you can e-mail the current document as an attachment, which is a file included with the e-mail message. The following steps e-mail the Clarke Resume, assuming you use Outlook as your default e-mail program.

- Open the Backstage view and then click the Save & Send tab in the Backstage view to display the Save & Send gallery.

- If necessary, click Send Using E-mail in the Save & Send gallery to display information in the right pane about various ways to e-mail a document from Word (Figure 5–54).

Q&A

What is the purpose of the Send as PDF and Send as XPS buttons?

Depending on which button you click, Word converts the current document either to the PDF or XPS format and then attaches the PDF or XPS document to the e-mail message.

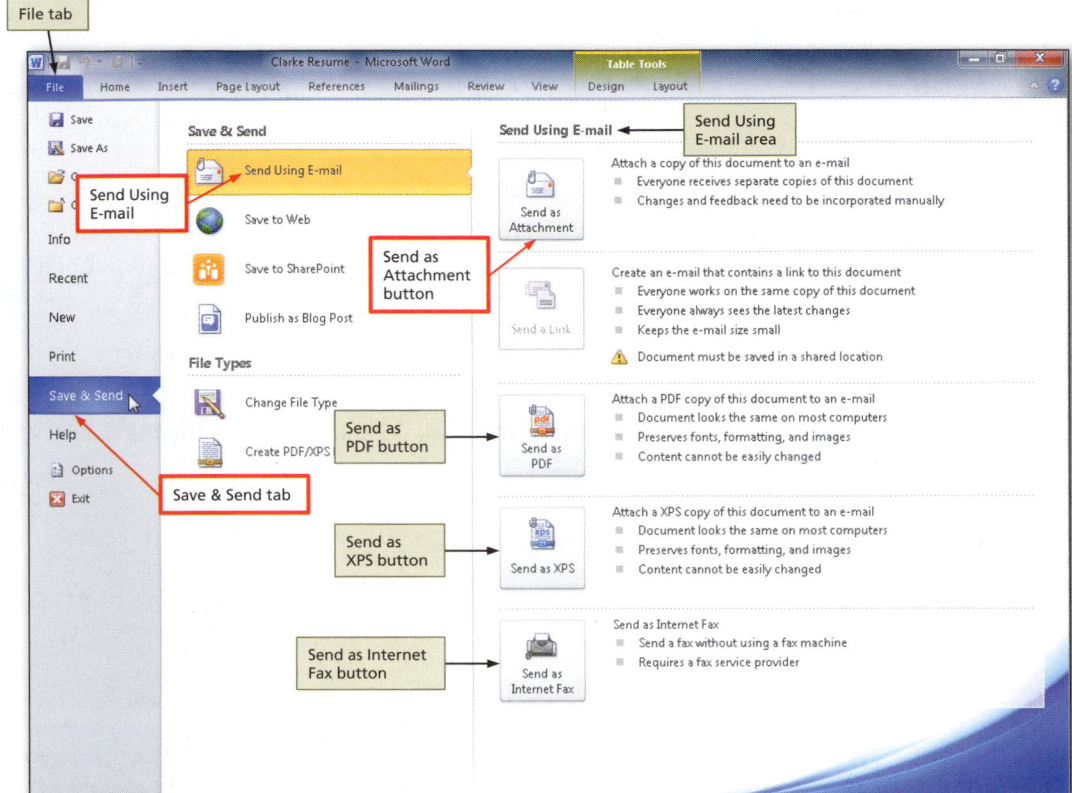

Figure 5–54

- Click the Send as Attachment button to start your default e-mail program (Outlook, in this case), which automatically attaches the active Word document to the e-mail message.

- Fill in the To text box with the recipient's e-mail address.

- Fill in the message text (Figure 5–55).

- Click the Send button to send the e-mail message along with its attachment to the recipient named in the To text box and close the e-mail window.

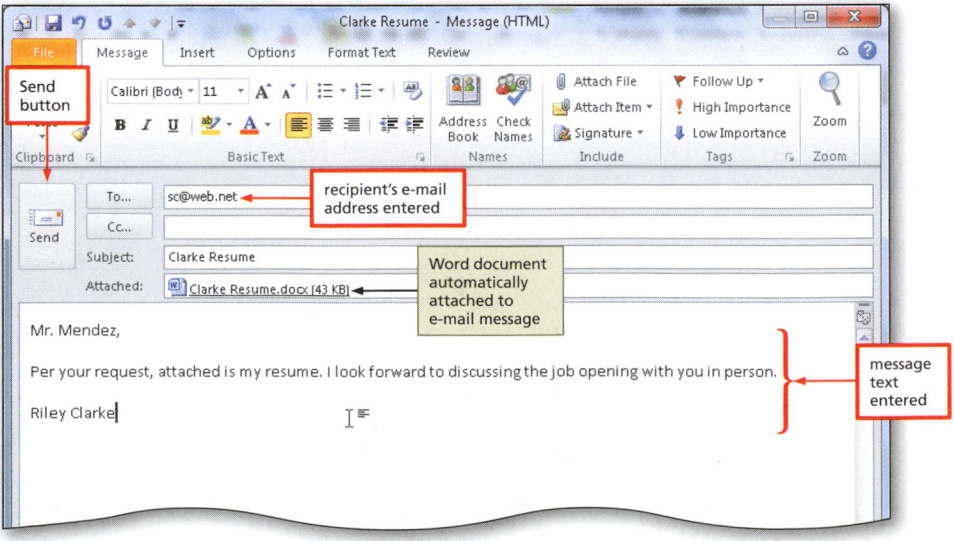

Figure 5–55

TO USE THE DOCUMENT INSPECTOR

Word includes a Document Inspector that checks a document for content you might not want to share with others, such as personal information. Before sharing a document with others, you may want to check for this type of content. If you wanted to use the Document Inspector, you would do the following:

1. Open the Backstage view and then click the Info tab in the Backstage view to display the Info gallery.

2. Click the Check for Issues button in the Info gallery to display the Check for Issues menu.

3. Click Inspect Document on the Check for Issues menu to display the Document Inspector dialog box.

4. Click the Inspect button (Document Inspector dialog box) to instruct Word to inspect the document.

5. Review the results (Document Inspector dialog box) and click the Remove All button(s) for any item that you do not want to be saved with the document.

6. When finished removing information, click the Close button to close the dialog box.

TO CUSTOMIZE HOW WORD OPENS E-MAIL ATTACHMENTS

When a user sends you an e-mail message that contains a Word document as an attachment, Word may display the document in Full Screen Reading view. This view is designed to increase the readability and legibility of an on-screen document. Full Screen Reading view, however, does not represent how the document will look when it is printed. For this reason, many users prefer working in Print Layout view to read documents. To exit Full Screen Reading view, click the Close button in the upper-right corner of the screen.

If you wanted to customize how Word opens e-mail attachments, you would do the following.

1. Open the Backstage view and then click Options in the Backstage view to display the Word Options dialog box.

2. If necessary, click General in the left pane (Word Options dialog box).

3. If you want e-mail attachments to open in Full Screen Reading view, place a check mark in the Open e-mail attachments in Full Screen Reading view check box; otherwise, remove the check mark to open e-mail attachments in Print Layout view.

4. Click the OK button to close the dialog box.

Creating a Web Page from a Word Document

If you have created a document using Word, such as a resume, you can save it in a format that can be opened by a Web browser, such as Internet Explorer. When you save a file as a Web page, Word converts the contents of the document into **HTML** (Hypertext Markup Language), which is a set of codes that browsers can interpret. Some of Word's formatting features are not supported by Web pages. Thus, your Web page may look slightly different from the original Word document.

BTW

Internet Fax
If you do not have a stand-alone fax machine, you can send and receive faxes in Word by clicking the Send as Internet Fax button in the Backstage view (shown in Figure 5–54). To send or receive faxes using Word, you first must sign up with a fax service provider by clicking the OK button in the Microsoft Office dialog box that appears the first time you click the Send as Internet Fax button, which displays an Available Fax Services Web page. You also must ensure that either the Windows Fax printer driver or Windows Fax Services component is installed on your computer. When sending a fax, Word converts the document to an image file and attaches it to an e-mail message where you enter the recipient's fax number, name, subject, and message for the cover sheet, and then click the Send button to deliver the fax.

BTW

Saving as a Web Page
Because you might not have access to SkyDrive or a Web server, the Web page you create in this feature is saved on a USB flash drive rather than to SkyDrive or a Web server.

When saving a document as a Web page, Word provides you with three choices:

- The **single file Web page format** saves all of the components of the Web page in a single file that has a **.mht** extension. This format is particularly useful for e-mailing documents in HTML format.
- The **Web Page format** saves some of the components of the Web page in a folder, separate from the Web page. This format is useful if you need access to the individual components, such as images, that make up the Web page.
- The **filtered Web Page format** saves the file in Web page format and then reduces the size of the file by removing specific Microsoft Office formats. This format is useful if you want to speed up the time it takes to download a Web page that contains many graphics, video, audio, or animations.

The Web page created in this section uses the single file Web page format.

To Save a Word Document as a Web Page

The following steps save the Clarke Resume created earlier in this chapter as a Web page.

1

- With the Word 2010 format of the resume file open in the document window, open the Backstage view and then click the Save & Send tab in the Backstage view to display the Save & Send gallery.

- Click Change File Type in the Save & Send gallery to display information in the right pane about various file types that can be opened in Word.

- Click Single File Web Page in the right pane to specify a new file type (Figure 5–56).

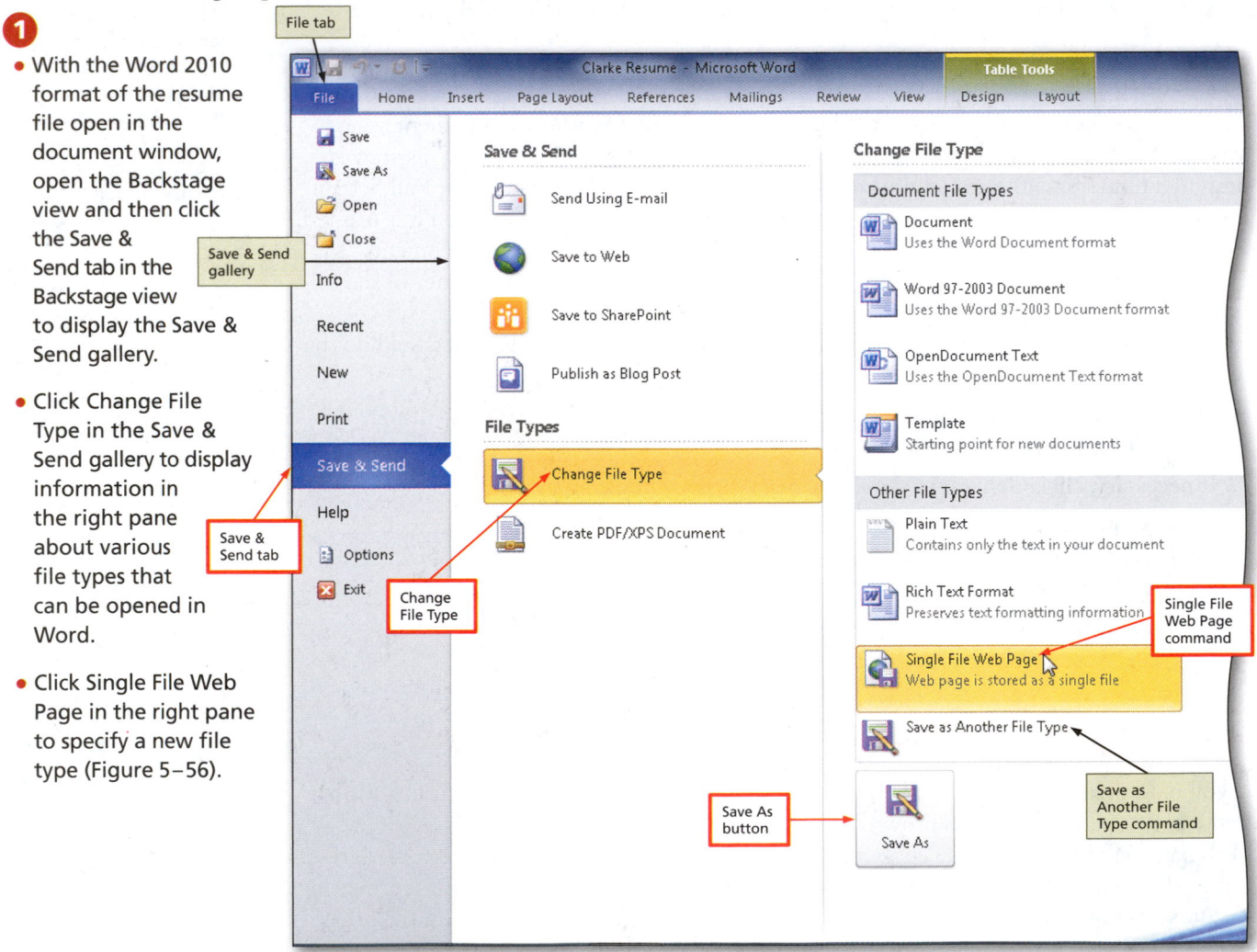

Figure 5–56

Q&A

What if I wanted to save the document as a Web Page instead of a Single File Web Page?

You would click Save as Another File Type in the Change File Type area, click the 'Save as type' box arrow in the Save As dialog box, and then click Web Page in the 'Save as type' list.

2

- Click the Save As button in the right pane to display the Save As dialog box.

- If necessary, navigate to the desired save location (in this case, the Word folder in the CIS 101 folder [or your class folder] on the USB flash drive) (Save As dialog box).

- Type **Clarke Resume Web Page** in the File name text box to change the file name.

- Click the Change Title button to display the Enter Text dialog box.

- Type **Clarke Resume** in the Page title text box (Enter Text dialog box) (Figure 5–57).

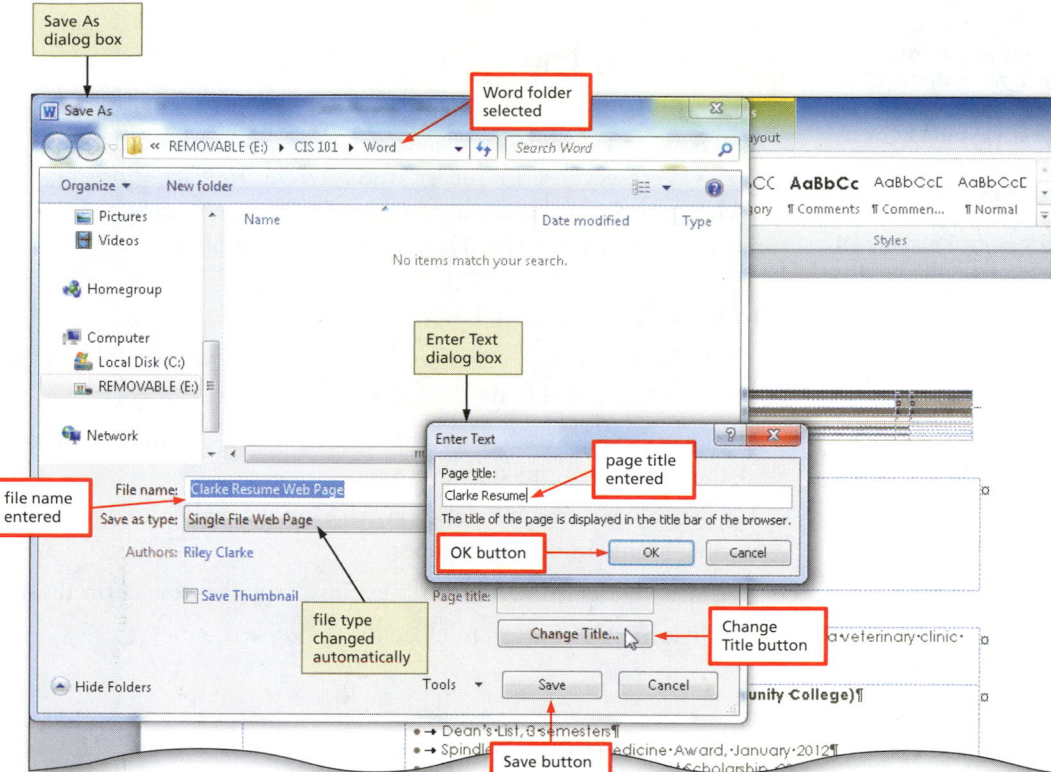

Figure 5–57

3

- Click the OK button (Enter Text dialog box) to close the dialog box.

- Click the Save button (Save As dialog box) to save the resume as a Web page and display it in the document window in Web Layout view (Figure 5–58).

- If the Microsoft Word Compatibility Checker dialog box appears, click its Continue button.

Q&A

Can I switch to Web Layout view at any time by clicking the Web Layout button?
Yes.

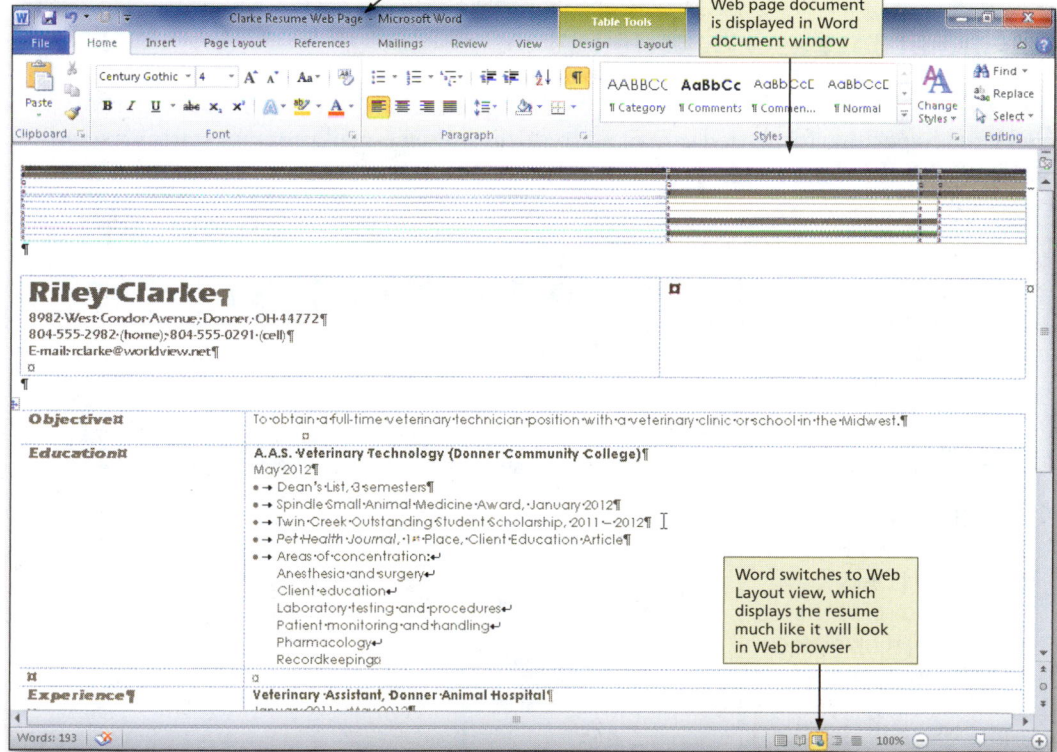

Figure 5–58

Other Ways

1. Press F12, click 'Save as type' box arrow (Save As dialog box), select Single File Web   Page or Web Page in list, click Save button

Saving to the Web

If you have access to and can save files to a Web server or FTP server or have a SkyDrive or Windows Live account, then you can save the Web page from Word directly to the Web server, FTP server, or SkyDrive. To learn more about saving Web pages to a Web server or FTP site using Microsoft Office programs, refer to Appendix B. To learn more about saving to SkyDrive, refer to Appendix C.

TO SET A DEFAULT SAVE LOCATION

If you wanted to change the default location that Word uses when it saves a document, you would do the following.

1. Open the Backstage view and then click the Options in the Backstage view to display the Word Options dialog box.
2. Click Save in the left pane (Word Options dialog box) to display options for saving documents in the right pane.
3. In the 'Default file location' text box, type the new desired save location.
4. Click the OK button to close the dialog box.

Formatting and Testing a Web Page

On the Clarke Resume Web page in this chapter, the e-mail address is formatted as a hyperlink. Also, the background color of the Web page is brown. The following sections modify the Web page to include these enhancements and then test the finished Web page.

To Format Text as a Hyperlink

The e-mail address in the resume Web page should be formatted as a hyperlink. When a Web page visitor clicks the hyperlink-formatted e-mail address, his or her e-mail program starts automatically and opens an e-mail window with the e-mail address already filled in. The following steps format the e-mail address as a hyperlink.

1
- Select the e-mail address in the resume Web page (rclarke@worldview.net, in this case).

- Display the Insert tab.

- Click the Insert Hyperlink button (Insert tab | Links group) to display the Insert Hyperlink dialog box (Figure 5–59).

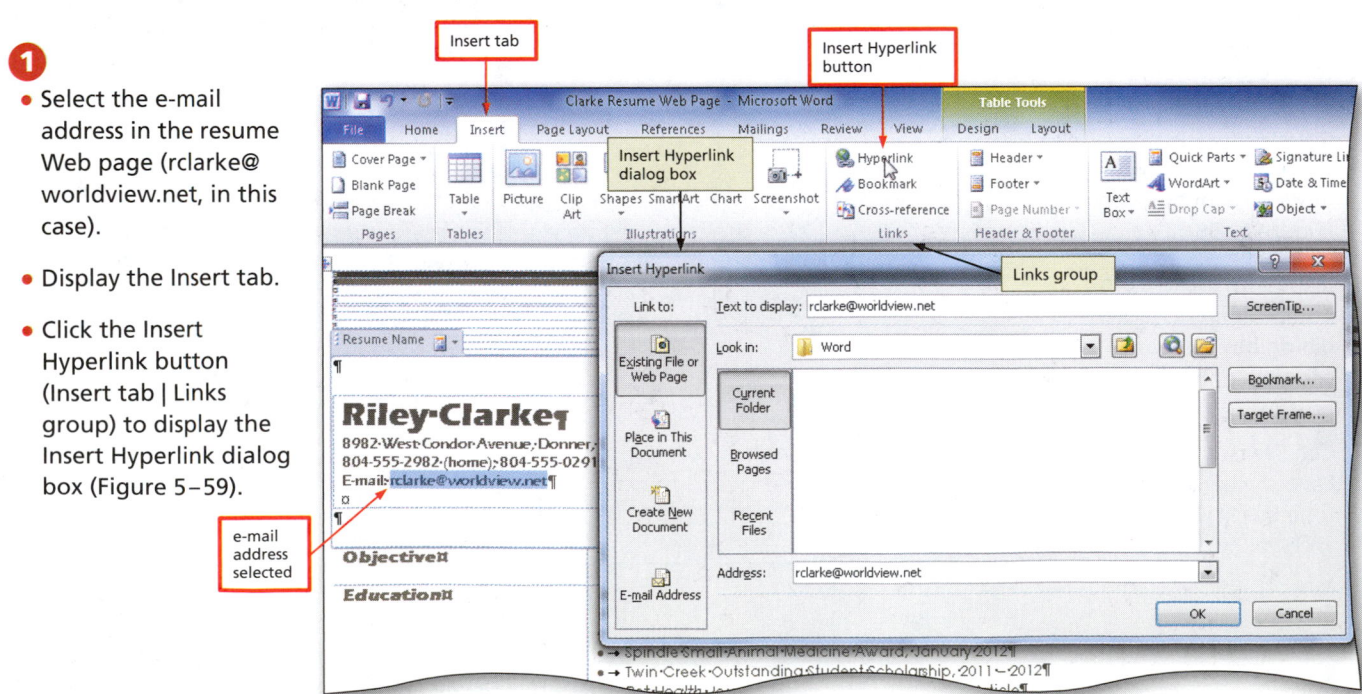

Figure 5–59

- Click E-mail Address in the Link to bar (Insert Hyperlink dialog box) so that the dialog box displays e-mail address settings instead of Web page settings.

- In the E-mail address text box, type `rclarke@worldview.net` to specify the e-mail address that the Web browser uses when a user clicks the hyperlink.

Q&A

Can I change the text that automatically appeared in the 'Text to display' text box?

Yes. Word assumes that the hyperlink text should be the same as the e-mail address, so as soon as you enter the e-mail address, the same text is entered in the 'Text to display' text box.

- If the e-mail address in the 'Text to display' text box is preceded by the text, mailto:, delete this leading text because you want only the e-mail address to appear in the document.

- Click the ScreenTip button to display the Set Hyperlink ScreenTip dialog box.

- In the text box, type **Send e-mail message to Riley Clarke** (Set Hyperlink ScreenTip dialog box) to specify the text that will be displayed when a user points to the hyperlink (Figure 5–60).

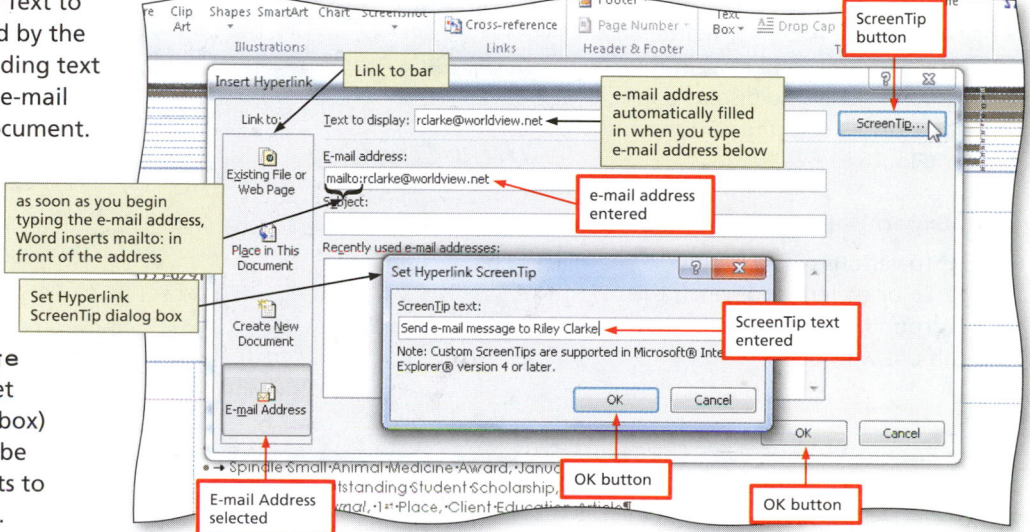

Figure 5–60

- Click the OK button in each dialog box to format the e-mail address as a hyperlink (Figure 5–61).

Q&A

How do I know if the hyperlink works?

In Word, you can test the hyperlink by holding down the CTRL key while clicking the hyperlink. In this case, CTRL+clicking the e-mail address should open an e-mail window.

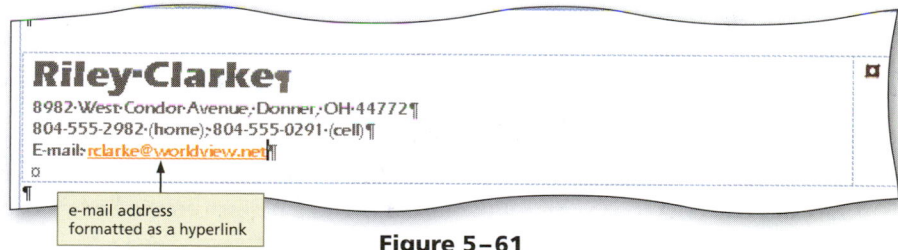

Figure 5–61

Other Ways

1. Right-click selected text, click Hyperlink on shortcut menu
2. Select text, press CTRL+K

To Edit a Hyperlink

If you needed to edit a hyperlink, for example, to change its ScreenTip or its link, you would follow these steps.

1. Position the insertion point in the hyperlink.
2. Click the Insert Hyperlink button (Insert tab | Links group) or press CTRL+K to display the Edit Hyperlink dialog box.

or

1. Right-click the hyperlink to display a shortcut menu.
2. Click Edit Hyperlink on the shortcut menu to display the Edit Hyperlink dialog box.

To Add a Background Color

The next step is to add background color to the resume Web page so that it looks more eye-catching. This Web page uses a light shade of brown. The following steps add a background color.

- Display the Page Layout tab.

- Click the Page Color button (Page Layout tab | Page Background group) to display the Page Color gallery.

- Point to Brown, Accent 5, Lighter 80% (ninth color in second row) in the Page Color gallery to display a live preview of the selected background color (Figure 5–62).

 **Experiment**

- Point to various colors in the Page Color gallery and watch the background color change in the document window.

- Click Brown, Accent 5, Lighter 80% to change the background color to the selected color.

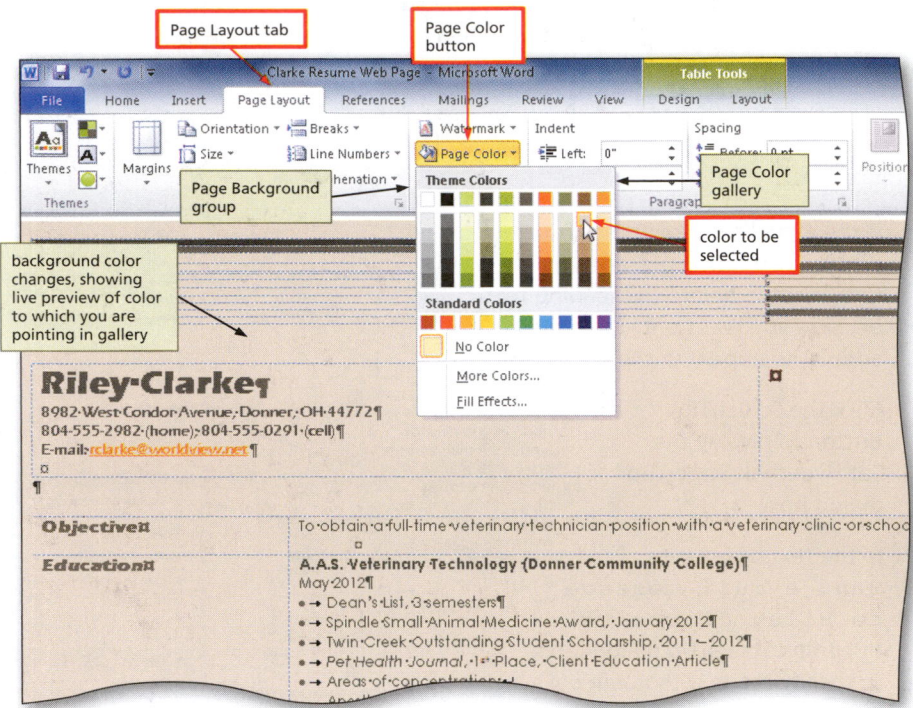

Figure 5–62

To Add a Pattern Fill Effect to a Background

When you changed the background color in the previous steps, Word placed a solid background color on the screen. For this resume Web page, the solid background color is a little too intense. To soften the background color, you can add patterns to it. The following steps add a pattern to the brown background.

- Click the Page Color button (Page Layout tab | Page Background group) to display the Page Color gallery (Figure 5–63).

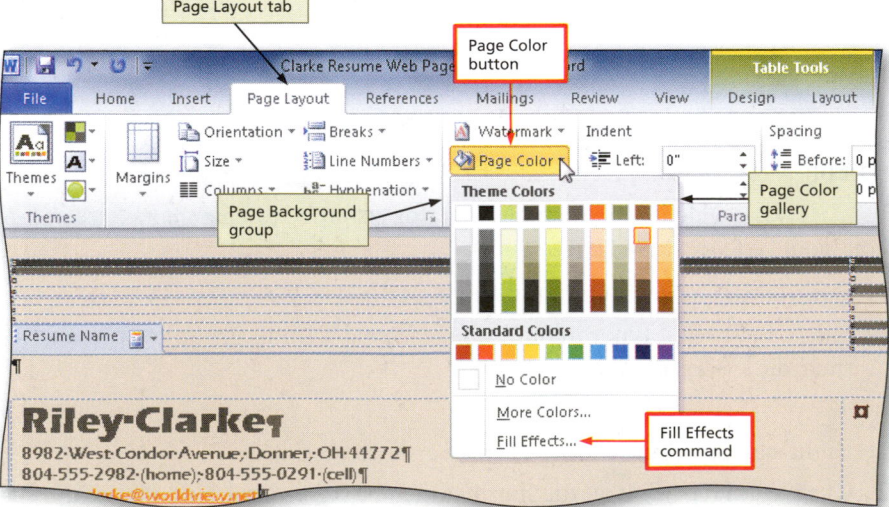

Figure 5–63

2

- Click Fill Effects in the Page Color gallery to display the Fill Effects dialog box.

- Click the Pattern tab (Fill Effects dialog box) to display the Pattern sheet in the dialog box.

- Click the Trellis pattern (seventh pattern in the fifth row) to select it (Figure 5–64).

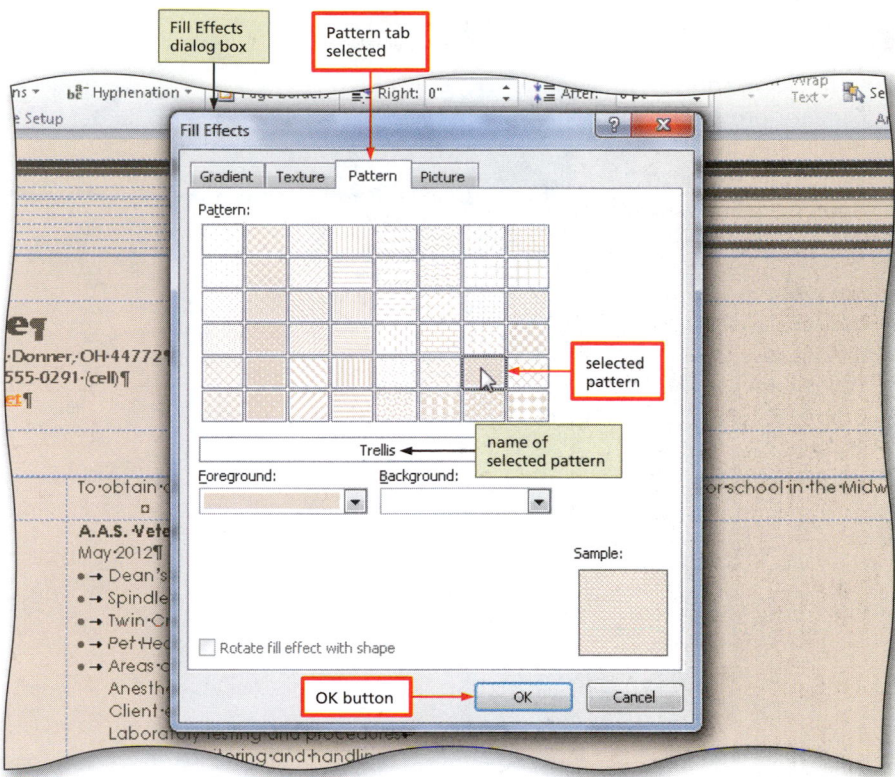

Figure 5–64

3

- Click the OK button to add the selected pattern to the current background color (Figure 5–65).

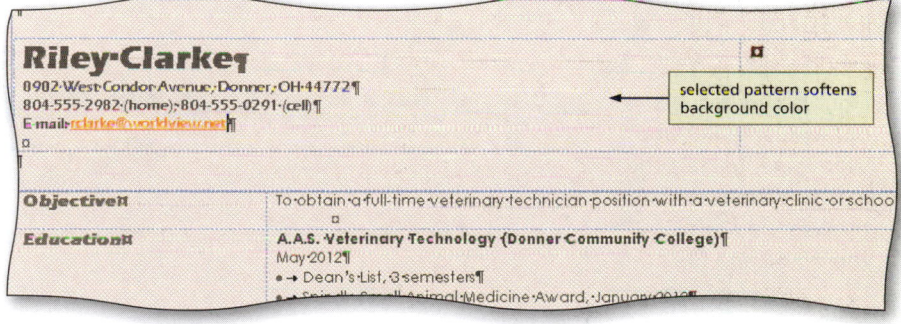

Figure 5–65

To Save an Existing Document and Quit Word

The Web page document now is complete. The following steps save the document again and quit Word.

1 Click the Save button on the Quick Access Toolbar to overwrite the previously saved file.

2 Quit Word.

BTW

Background Colors
When you change the background color, it appears only on the screen and in documents that are viewed online, such as Web pages. Changing the background color has no affect on a printed document.

To Test a Web Page in a Web Browser

After creating and saving a Web page, you will want to test it in at least one browser to be sure it looks and works the way you intended. The steps on the next page use Windows Explorer to display the resume Web page in the Internet Explorer Web browser.

1

- Click the Windows Explorer program button on the Windows taskbar to open the Windows Explorer window.

- Navigate to the desired save location (in this case, the Word folder in the CIS 101 folder [or your class folder] on the USB flash drive) (Figure 5–66).

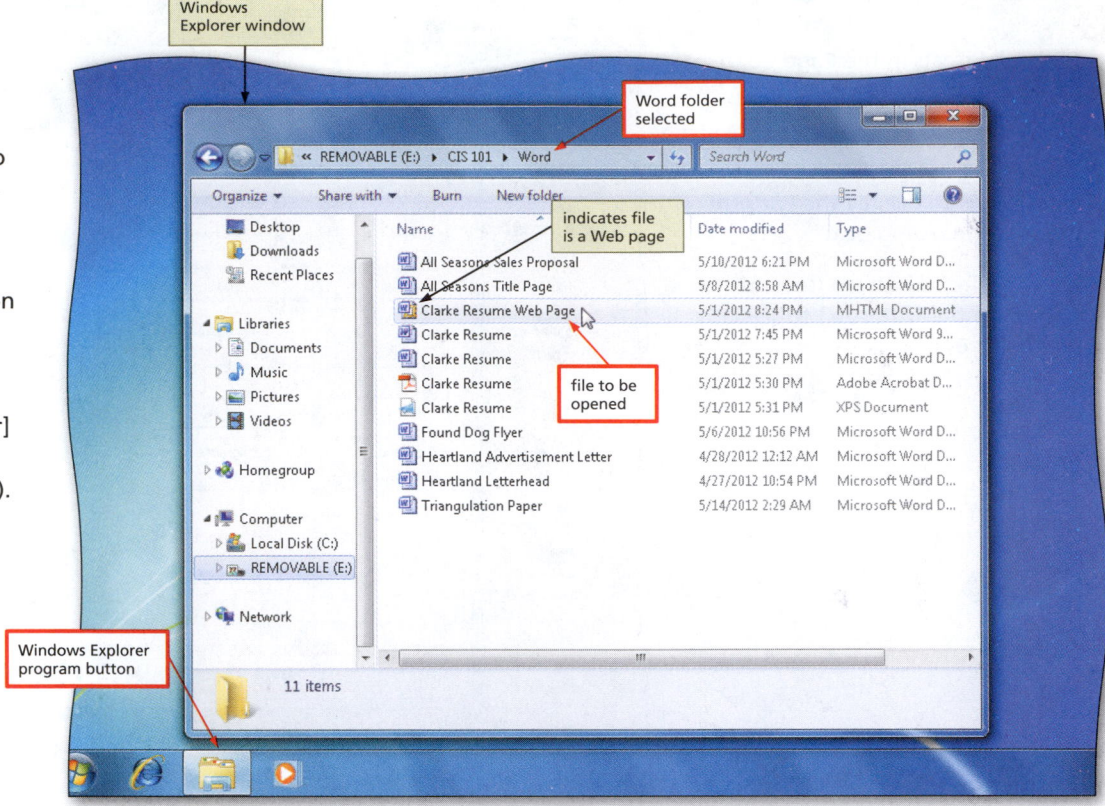

Figure 5–66

2

- Double-click the file name, Clarke Resume Web Page, to start the Internet Explorer Web browser and display the Web page file in the browser window (Figure 5–67).

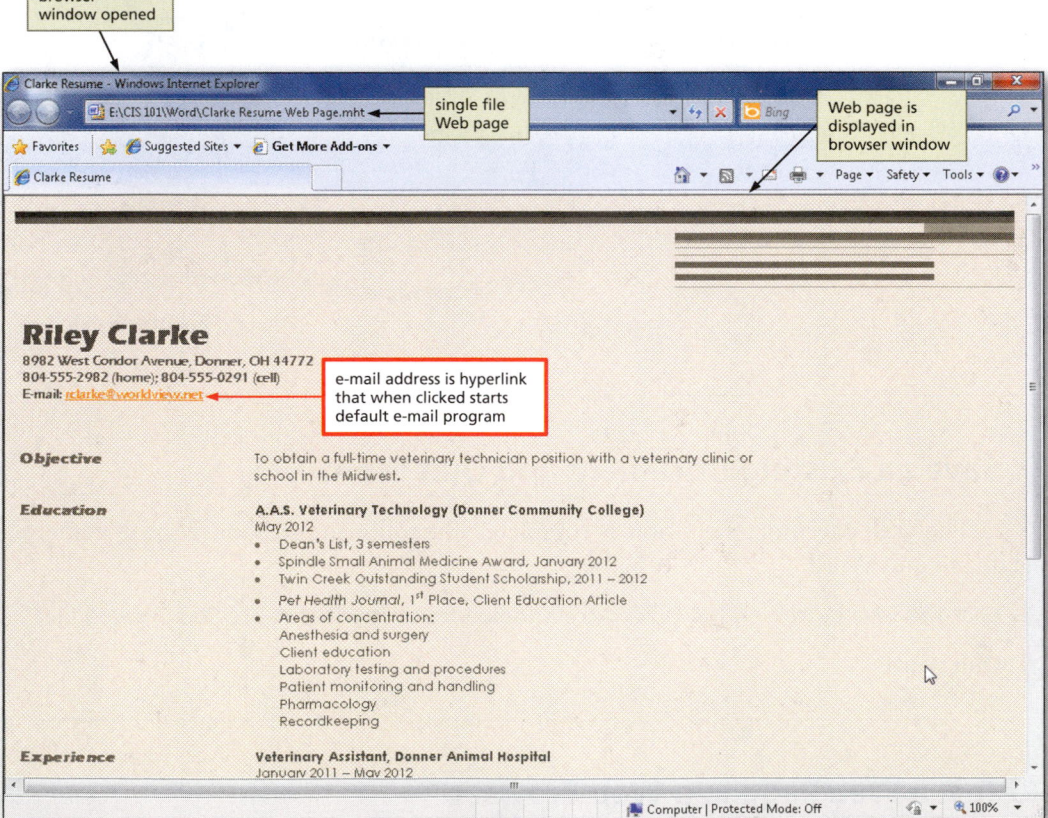

Figure 5–67

- With the Web page document displaying in the Web browser, click the e-mail address link to start the e-mail program with the e-mail address displayed in the e-mail window (Figure 5–68).

- If Internet Explorer displays a security dialog box, click its Allow button.

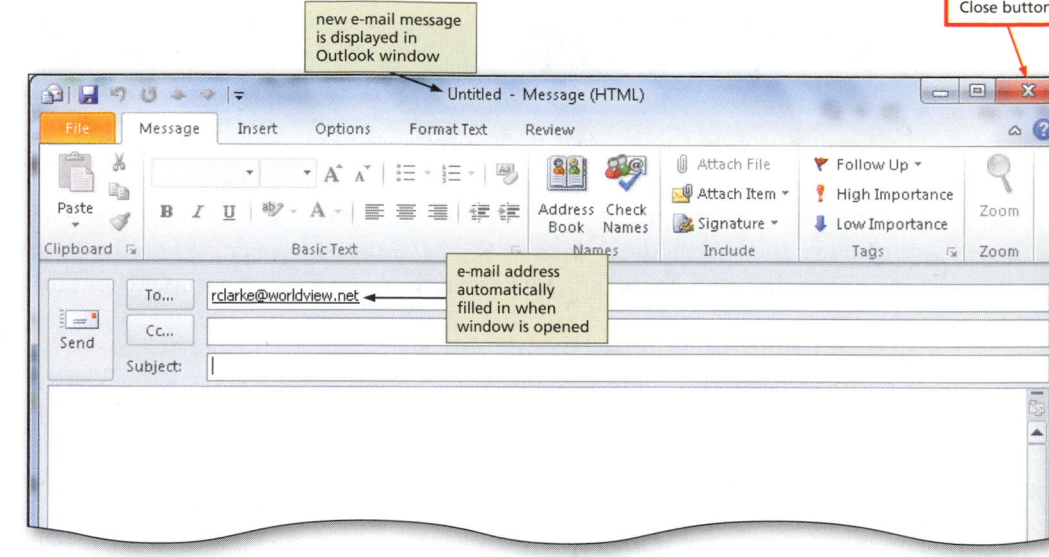

4

- Close all open windows.

Figure 5–68

Chapter Summary

In this chapter, you learned how to use Word to use a template to create a document, change a document theme, fill in a document template, indent a paragraph, insert building blocks, customize theme fonts, create a Quick Style, modify a style, save a Word document in a variety of formats, insert a hyperlink, and add a background color. The items listed below include all the new Word skills you have learned in this chapter.

1. Create a New Document from a Sample Template (WD 277)
2. Create a New Blank Document (WD 279)
3. Change the Document Theme (WD 279)
4. Modify Text in a Content Control (WD 283)
5. Format a Content Control (WD 283)
6. Replace Placeholder Text (WD 284)
7. Delete a Content Control (WD 284)
8. Move Table Rows (WD 286)
9. Use AutoComplete (WD 287)
10. Enter a Line Break (WD 289)
11. Indent a Paragraph (WD 290)
12. Insert a Building Block Using the Quick Parts Gallery (WD 291)
13. Copy and Paste a Table Item (WD 293)
14. Customize Theme Fonts (WD 295)
15. Create a Quick Style (WD 296)
16. Reveal Formatting (WD 298)
17. Modify a Style Using the Styles Dialog Box (WD 299)
18. Create a New Document from an Online Template (WD 300)
19. Create a New Document from a Template Downloaded from Office.com (WD 301)
20. Save a Word Document as a PDF Document and View the PDF Document in Adobe Reader (WD 301)
21. Save a Word Document as an XPS Document and View the XPS Document in the XPS Viewer (WD 303)
22. Run the Compatibility Checker (WD 305)
23. Save a Word 2010 Document in an Earlier Word Format (WD 306)
24. Save a Word 2010 Document as a Different File Type (WD 308)
25. Send a Document Using E-Mail (WD 310)
26. Use the Document Inspector (WD 311)
27. Customize How Word Opens E-Mail Attachments (WD 311)
28. Save a Word Document as a Web Page (WD 312)
29. Set a Default Save Location (WD 314)
30. Format Text as a Hyperlink (WD 314)
31. Edit a Hyperlink (WD 315)
32. Add a Background Color (WD 316)
33. Add a Pattern Fill Effect to a Background (WD 316)
34. Test a Web Page in a Web Browser (WD 317)

Learn It Online

Test your knowledge of chapter content and key terms.

Instructions: To complete the Learn It Online exercises, start your browser, click the Address bar, and then enter the Web address **scsite.com/wd2010/learn**. When the Word 2010 Learn It Online page is displayed, click the link for the exercise you want to complete and then read the instructions.

Chapter Reinforcement TF, MC, and SA
A series of true/false, multiple choice, and short answer questions that test your knowledge of the chapter content.

Flash Cards
An interactive learning environment where you identify chapter key terms associated with displayed definitions.

Practice Test
A series of multiple choice questions that test your knowledge of chapter content and key terms.

Who Wants To Be a Computer Genius?
An interactive game that challenges your knowledge of chapter content in the style of a television quiz show.

Wheel of Terms
An interactive game that challenges your knowledge of chapter key terms in the style of the television show *Wheel of Fortune*.

Crossword Puzzle Challenge
A crossword puzzle that challenges your knowledge of key terms presented in the chapter.

Apply Your Knowledge

Reinforce the skills and apply the concepts you learned in this chapter.

Saving a Word Document as a Web Page and Other Formats
Note: To complete this assignment, you will be required to use the Data Files for Students. See the inside back cover of this book for instructions on downloading the Data Files for Students, or contact your instructor for information about accessing the required files.

Instructions: Start Word. Open the document, Apply 5-1 Computers in Health Care, from the Data Files for Students. You are to save the document as a single file Web Page (Figure 5–69), a PDF document, an XPS document, and in the Word 97-2003 format.

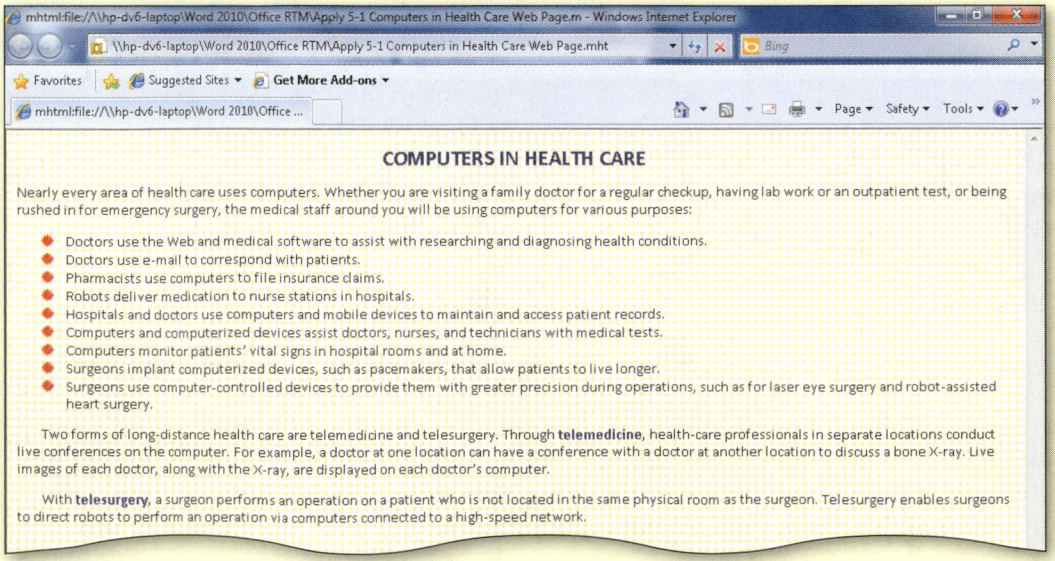

Figure 5–69

Perform the following tasks:

1. Save the document as a single file Web page using the file name, Apply 5-1 Computers in Health Care Web Page.

2. Add the background color Gold, Accent 2, Lighter 80% to the Web page document. Apply the Solid diamond pattern fill effect to the background. Save the file again.

3. Use Internet Explorer to view the Web page (shown in Figure 5–69). Print the Web page. On the printout, identify how this document is different from the original Word document. Quit Internet Explorer and then close the Web page document in Word.

4. Open the original Apply 5-1 Computers in Health Care document. Save it as a PDF document and then view the PDF document in Adobe Reader. Submit the document as specified by your instructor. Quit Adobe Reader.

5. Using the original Apply 5-1 Computers in Health Care document, save the file as an XPS document and then view the XPS document in the XPS Viewer. Submit the document as specified by your instructor. Quit the XPS Viewer.

6. Using the original Apply 5-1 Computers in Health Care document, run the compatibility checker. Save the document in the Word 97-2003 format. Print the document. On the printout, write the issue(s) identified by the compatibility checker.

7. If your instructor allows, e-mail the document saved in #6 to his or her e-mail account.

Extend Your Knowledge

Extend the skills you learned in this chapter and experiment with new skills. You may need to use Help to complete the assignment.

Creating a Multi-File Web Page, Inserting a Screenshot, and Saving to the Web

Note: To complete this assignment, you will be required to use the Data Files for Students. See the inside back cover of this book for instructions on downloading the Data Files for Students, or contact your instructor for information about accessing the required files.

Instructions: Start Word. Open the document, Extend 5-1 Vincent Resume, from the Data Files for Students. You will save a Word document as a multi-file Web page and format it by inserting links, adding a texture fill effect as the background, and applying highlights to text. Then, you will take a screenshot of the Web page in your browser and insert the screenshot in a Word document.

Perform the following tasks:
1. Use Help to learn about saving as a Web page (not a single file Web page), hyperlinks, texture fill effects, text highlight color, screenshots, and saving to the Web.

2. Save the Extend 5-1 Vincent Resume file as a Web page (not as a single file Web page) using the file name, Extend 5-1 Vincent Resume Web Page.

3. Adjust the column widths in the resume table so that the resume fills the window. Convert the e-mail address to a hyperlink.

4. In the leftmost column, below the e-mail address, insert the Web address www.scsite.com and format it as a hyperlink so that when a user clicks the Web address, the associated Web page is displayed in the browser window.

5. Add a texture fill effect of your choice to the resume.

6. Apply a text highlight color of your choice to at least five words in the resume.

7. Change the document properties, as specified by your instructor. Save the document again. Test the Web page in Windows Explorer.

8. Take a screenshot(s) of Windows Explorer that shows all the files and folders created by saving the document as a Web page. Create a new Word document. Insert the screenshot(s) in the Word document. Insert callout shapes with text that points to and identifies the files and folders created by saving the document as a Web page. Change the document properties, as specified by your instructor. Save the document with the file name Extend 5-1 Vincent Resume Windows Explorer Files.

Continued >

Extend Your Knowledge *continued*

9. If you have access to a Web server, FTP site, or SkyDrive (Figure 5–70), save the Web page to the server, site, or online storage location (see Appendix B or C for instructions).

10. Submit the files in the format specified by your instructor.

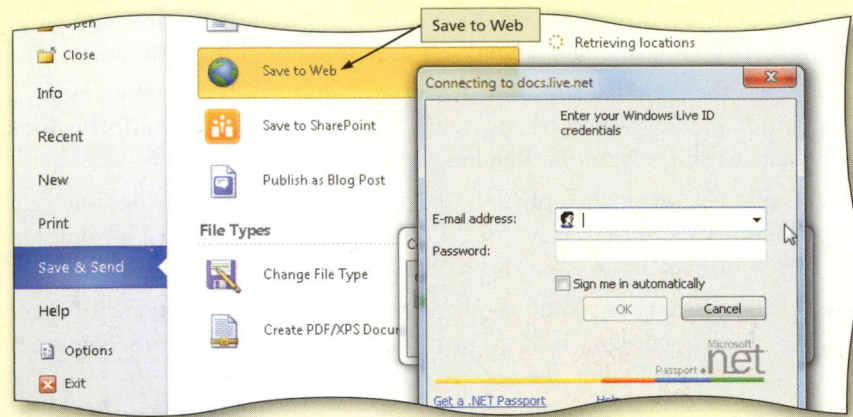

Figure 5–70

Make It Right

Analyze a document and correct all errors and/or improve the design.

Formatting a Resume Created from a Template

Note: To complete this assignment, you will be required to use the Data Files for Students. See the inside back cover of this book for instructions on downloading the Data Files for Students, or contact your instructor for information about accessing the required files.

Instructions: Start Word. Open the document, Make It Right 5-1 Buckman Resume Draft, from the Data Files for Students. The document is a resume created from a template that is formatted incorrectly (Figure 5–71). You are to change the margins, modify styles, adjust paragraph indent, modify a content control, remove a hyperlink format, and change the document theme.

Perform the following tasks:

1. Change the margins, and left and right indent, so that the resume text does not run into the orange borders on the right side of the page and text is balanced on the page.

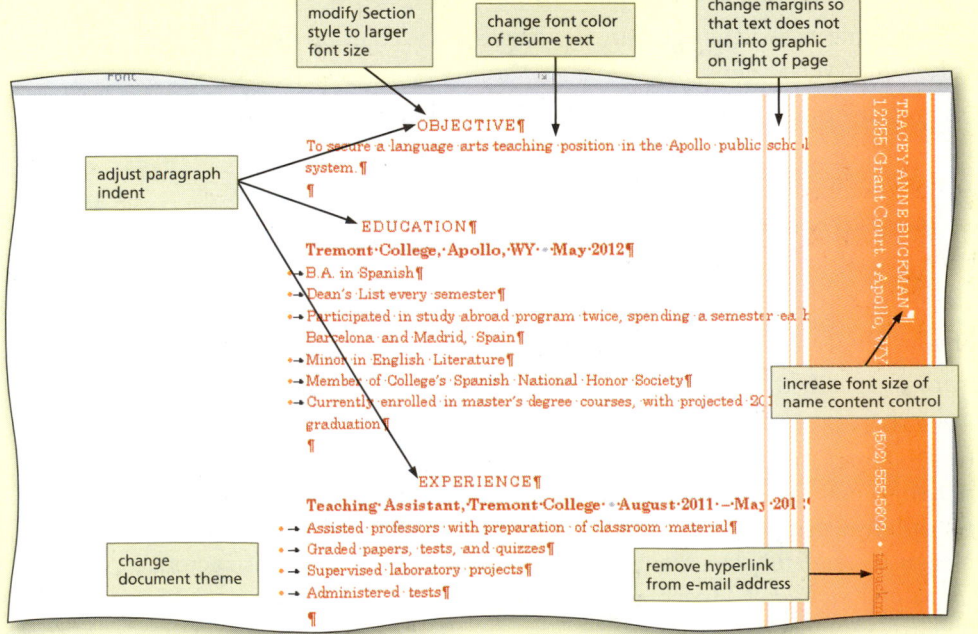

2. Modify the Normal style so that the text is a color other than red.

3. Fix the indent of the first three section headings (OBJECTIVE, EDUCATION, and EXPERIENCE) so that they are aligned with the text on the left, like the SKILLS heading.

4. Use the Reveal Formatting task pane to determine the font size of text in the Subsection style. Modify the Section style so that it uses a font size that is greater than the font size of the Subsection style.

Figure 5–71

5. Increase the font size of the name content control so that it is predominant in the color bar on the right side of the page.

6. Remove the hyperlink format from the e-mail address.

7. Change the document theme to one other than Oriel.

8. Change the document properties, as specified by your instructor. Save the revised document with the file name, Make It Right 5-1 Buckman Resume Modified, and then submit it in the format specified by your instructor.

In the Lab

Design and/or create a document using the guidelines, concepts, and skills presented in this chapter. Labs are listed in order of increasing difficulty.

Lab 1: Creating a Resume from a Template

Problem: You are an engineering student at Western College. As graduation is approaching quickly, you prepare the resume shown in Figure 5–72 using one of Word's resume templates.

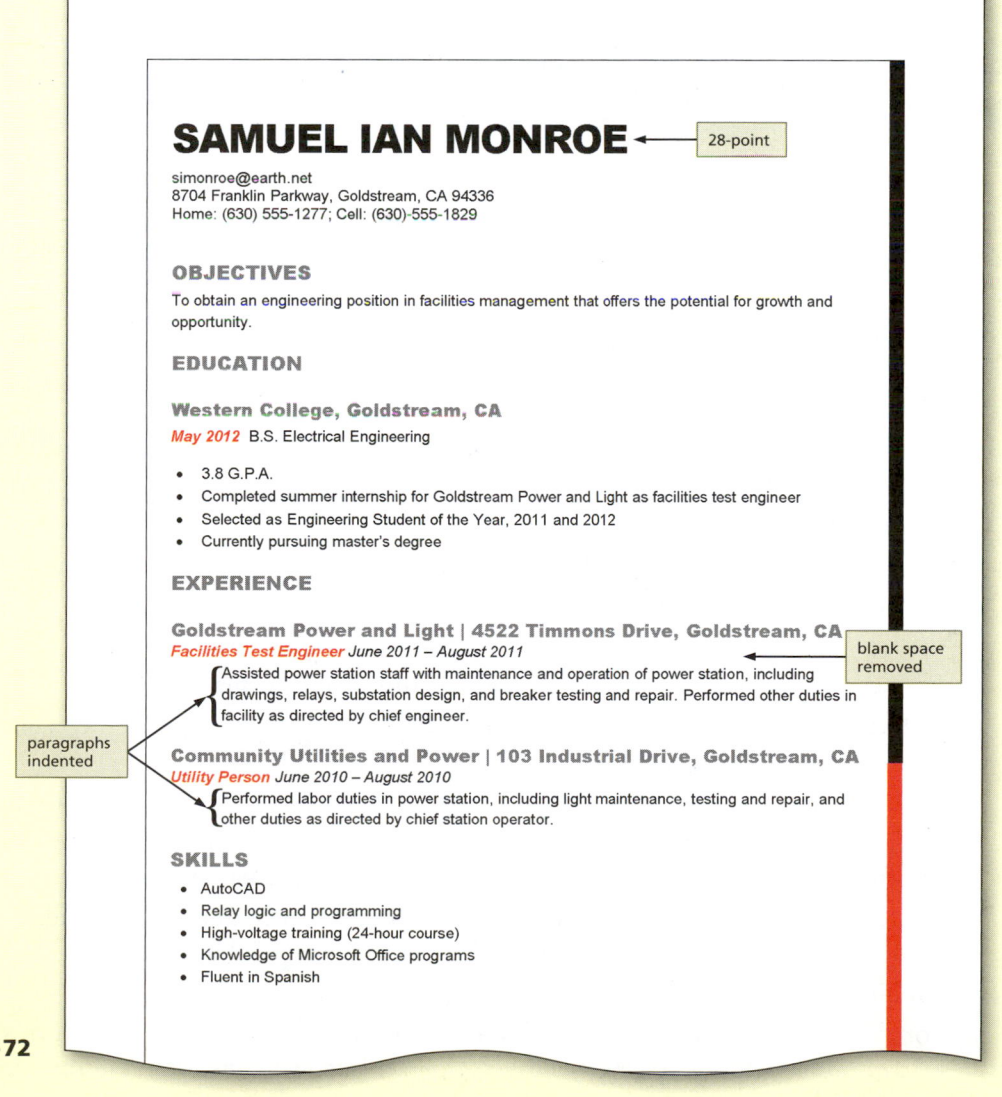

Figure 5–72

Continued >

In the Lab *continued*

Perform the following tasks:

1. Use the Essential Resume template to create a resume.

2. If necessary, change the document theme to Essential.

3. Personalize the resume as shown in Figure 5–72 on the previous page. Following are some guidelines for some sections of the resume:

   a. Use your own name, e-mail address, postal address, and phone numbers, unless your instructor specifies to use the information shown in Figure 5–72. Delete the line containing the website content control.

   b. Insert an Experience Subsection building block so that you can enter the second job information.

   c. In the Experience section, indent the job responsibilities paragraphs one-half inch. Change the space after the job titles to 0 pt.

4. The entire resume should fit on a single page. If it flows to two pages, decrease spacing before and after paragraphs until the entire resume text fits on a single page.

5. Check the spelling of the resume. Change the document properties, as specified by your instructor. Save the resume with Lab 5-1 Monroe Resume as the file name and submit it in the format specified by your instructor.

In the Lab

Lab 2: Creating a Resume from a Template

Problem: You are a physical recreation and education student at Ward College. As graduation is approaching quickly, you prepare the resume shown in Figure 5–73 using one of Word's resume templates.

Perform the following tasks:

1. Use the Urban Resume template to create a resume.

2. Change the document theme to Perspective.

3. Personalize and format the resume as shown in Figure 5–73. Following are some guidelines for some sections of the resume:

   a. Change the Normal style font size to 11 point.

   b. Use your own name, postal address, phone numbers, and e-mail address, unless your instructor specifies to use the information shown in Figure 5–73.

   c. Change margins settings to Normal (1" top, bottom, left, and right).

   d. Reduce the row height of the row containing the name information to 1".

   e. Move rows containing the Education and Experience sections above the row containing the Skills section. Change the name, Skills, to the name, Community Service.

   f. In the Education section, enter line break characters between the areas of concentration.

   g. Insert an Experience Subsection building block so that you can enter the second job information. Indent the job responsibilities paragraphs one-half inch.

   h. Create a customized theme font set that uses Castellar for headings and Lucida Sans for Body text. Save the theme font with the name MacMahon Resume Fonts.

   i. Modify the Section style so that its text is not bold.

   j. Format the address line to 10-point Lucida Sans font with a font color of Brown, Accent 2, Darker 50%. Create a Quick Style called Contact Info using the format in the address line. Apply the Contact Info Quick Style to the phone and e-mail lines.

k. If necessary, format the second bulleted list the same as the first.

l. Adjust the spacing before and after paragraphs so that the resume looks like Figure 5–73.

4. The entire resume should fit on a single page. If it flows to two pages, decrease spacing before and after paragraphs until the entire resume text fits on a single page.

5. Check the spelling of the resume. Change the document properties, as specified by your instructor. Save the resume with Lab 5-2 MacMahon Resume as the file name, and submit it in the format specified by your instructor.

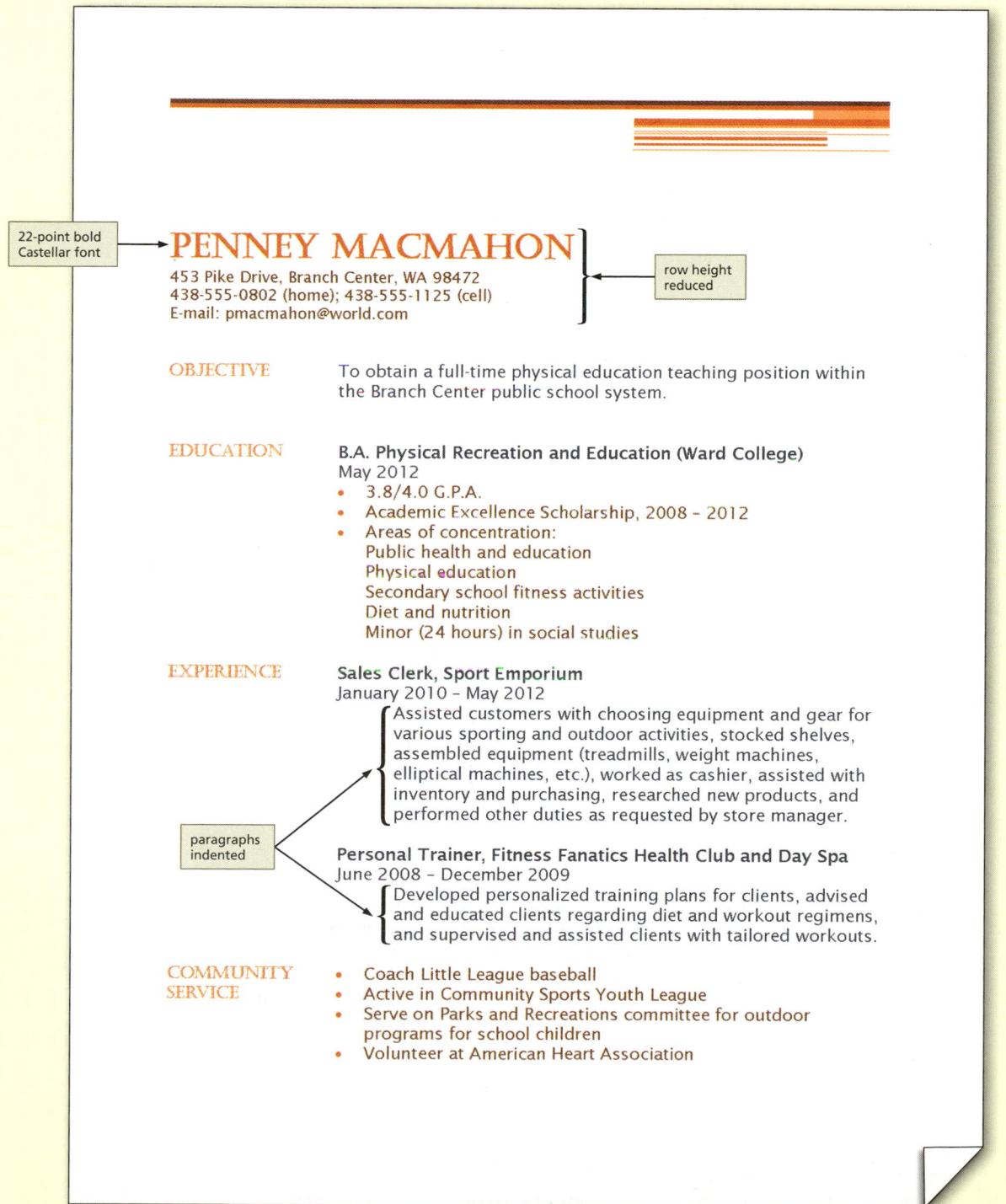

Figure 5–73

In the Lab

Lab 3: Creating a Resume from a Template and a Web Page from the Resume

Problem: You are a library and information science student at Benson College. As graduation is approaching quickly, you prepare the resume shown in Figure 5–74 using one of Word's resume templates.

▶Daniel Austin Ramirez

84 Southland Drive, Jonner, MA 01298
Phone: (787) 555-4611
E-mail: daramirez@global.com

Objectives

To obtain a librarian position in the Jonner County public library system that will offer challenge, experience, and the potential for professional and personal growth.

Education

Master's in Library and Information Science, Benson College (May 2012)
▶ 3.8 G.P.A.
▶ Dean's List, 2011 – 2012
▶ Certified school media specialist

Bachelor of Arts in English Literature, Morgan University (May 2010)
▶ 3.9 G.P.A.
▶ Dean's List, 2007 – 2010
▶ Double minor in information technology (24 hours) and literature (21 hours)
▶ Received Barker Memorial Scholarship, 2007 – 2010

Experience

Shelver (May 2010 –August 2012)
Morgan College (76 Remington Avenue, Jonner, MA 01298)
Alphabetize and shelve books and assist librarians as needed, including arranging displays, collecting fines, working at circulation desk, assisting patrons with book selection, and other duties as directed.

Library Page (December 2008 – May 2010)
Dilton County Public Library (2934 Chelsea Parkway, Dilton, NH 03324)
Assist branch librarians with daily library activities, including shelving books, repair and cleaning of books, and placing protective jackets on new books. Worked with various community stores to attain prizes and incentives for summer reading program; helped librarians with creation and administration of various community programs, including clubs, meetings, visiting and local authors, and speakers.

Figure 5–74

Perform the following tasks:

1. Use the Origin Resume template to create a resume. Personalize and format the resume as shown in Figure 5–74. Change the document theme to Aspect. Use your own name, postal address, phone numbers, and e-mail address, unless your instructor specifies to use the information shown in Figure 5–74. View gridlines so that you can see the four tables in the resume. Delete the top and bottom decorative one-row tables. Adjust the margins, spacing before and after paragraphs, adjust table row sizes, and add or delete blank paragraphs so that the resume looks like Figure 5–74. Check the spelling of the resume. Change the document properties, as specified by your instructor. Save the resume with Lab 5-3 Ramirez Resume as the file name and submit it in the format specified by your instructor.

2. If your instructor permits, e-mail the final resume to his or her e-mail account.

3. Save the resume as a single file Web page using the file name Lab 5-3 Ramirez Resume Web Page. Change the page title to Daniel Austin Ramirez. Convert the e-mail address to a hyperlink. Apply the Orange, Accent 1, Lighter 80% background color to the document. Apply the Dashed downward diagonal pattern fill effect to the background color. Submit the file in the format specified by your instructor.

4. If you have access to a Web server, FTP site, or SkyDrive, save the Web page to the server, site, or online storage location (see Appendix B or C for instructions).

Cases and Places

Apply your creative thinking and problem solving skills to design and implement a solution.

Note: To complete these assignments, you may be required to use the Data Files for Students. See the inside back cover of this book for instructions on downloading the Data Files for Students, or contact your instructor for information about accessing the required files.

1: Create a Meeting Agenda and an Award Certificate

Academic

As a student assistant to the Office of Academic Affairs, you have been asked to create a meeting agenda for the upcoming council meeting, as well as an award certificate for the presentation of the Outstanding Student Award during the meeting. Browse through the Online Templates and download appropriate meeting agenda and award certificate templates and then use the text in the next two paragraphs for content. Use the concepts and techniques presented in this chapter to create and format the agenda and award certificate. Be sure to check the spelling and grammar of the finished documents. Submit your assignment in the format specified by your instructor.

Agenda information: The Excellence in Academics Council is holding a meeting on February 6, 2012, at 7:30 p.m. in the Nutonne College Community Room. Agenda items are as follows: Call to Order, Roll Call, Approval of Previous Meeting Minutes, Chairperson's Report (two items – Volunteer activities and Donor updates), Treasurer's Report (two items – New budgetary restrictions and Dues updates), Outstanding Student Award (two items: – Speech by Alana Sebastian, 2011 recipient, and Presentation of 2012 award to Derrick Jakes), Calendar, and Adjournment.

Award certificate information: The Outstanding Student 2012 is awarded on February 6, 2012, by Julianne Easton, President, Excellence in Academics Council, to Derrick Jakes for his hard work and dedication to his educational goals and for being an exceptional role model for young scholars.

2: Create a Calendar and an Invitation

Personal

To help organize your appointments and important dates, you use a calendar file. While filling in the calendar, you decide to schedule and host a family reunion for which you will need to send out

Continued >

Cases and Places *continued*

invitations. Browse through the Online Templates and download appropriate calendar and invitation templates and then use the information in the next two paragraphs for content. Use the concepts and techniques presented in this chapter to create and format the calendar and invitation. Be sure to check the spelling and grammar of the finished documents. Submit your assignment in the format specified by your instructor.

Calendar information: May 5 – Volleyball tournament at 3:00 p.m., May 8 – Algebra final at 10:00 a.m., May 9 – English final paper due by 11:59 p.m., May 15 – Grandpa's birthday, May 26 – Family reunion from 11:00 a.m. to ?? p.m., June 4 – First day of work!, June 9 – Dentist appointment at 9:00 a.m., June 14 – Lexy's birthday, June 16 – Volunteer Cook at Community Center from 6:00 – 9:00 a.m., and June 20 – Mom and Dad's anniversary (31st). If the template requires, insert an image(s) from the clip art gallery in the calendar.

Invitation information: You and your family are cordially invited to the Brogan Family Reunion, which will be held on May 26, 2012, from 11:00 a.m. to ?? p.m. at the Brogan Farm on 3392 W 2817 North Road, Donner Grove, New Hampshire. Main course and beverages will be provided. Please bring a dish to pass, swimsuits, and lawn chairs. If the template requires, insert an image(s) from the clip art gallery in the invitation.

3: Create a Fax Cover Letter and an Invoice

Professional

As a part-time employee at Milan Office Supplies, your boss has asked to you create a fax cover letter and an invoice for a customer. Browse through the Online Templates and download appropriate fax and invoice templates and then use the information in the next three paragraphs for content. Use the concepts and techniques presented in this chapter to create and format the fax cover letter and invoice. Be sure to check the spelling and grammar of the finished documents. Submit your assignment in the format specified by your instructor.

Milan Office Supplies is located at 808 Boyd Boulevard in Beachcombe, Florida 33115. Phone number is 774-555-6751, fax number is 774-555-6752, e-mail address is milan@earth.net; and slogan is *For the Well Stocked Office*. Customer is Stacy Listernik at Walsh Industries located at 247 Tremaine Industrial Parkway in Beachcombe, Florida 33115. Phone number is 774-555-0123 and fax number is 774-555-0124.

Fax message: Following is the duplicate invoice you requested. Thank you again for your prompt attention to this matter, and thank you for choosing Milan Office Supplies.

Invoice detail: Invoice number is 402 dated March 21, 2012. Salesperson is Samantha Hagen, job number 227-404, payment terms are due on receipt, and due date was March 1, 2012. Items purchased were 20 boxes of hanging folders with tabs at a price of $15.25 per box, 10 ink-jet cartridge refills at a price of $10.49 per cartridge, and 100 reams of 20# paper at a price of $3.19 per ream. All checks should be made payable to Milan Office Supplies.

6 Generating Form Letters, Mailing Labels, and a Directory

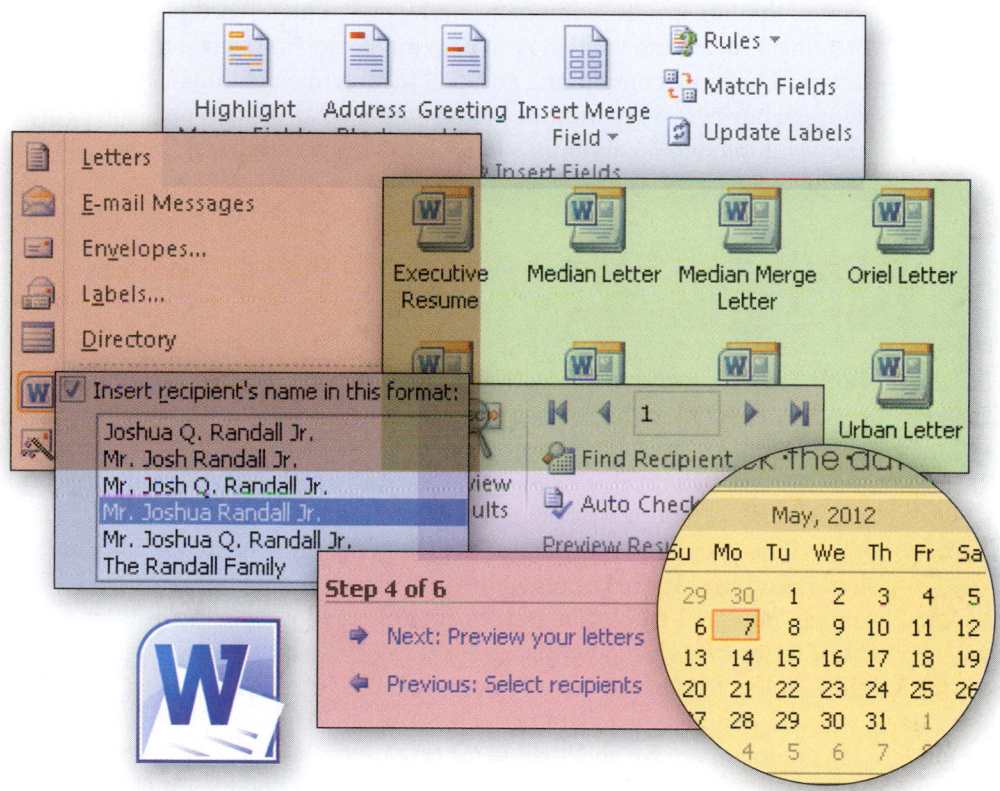

Objectives

You will have mastered the material in this chapter when you can:

- Explain the merge process
- Use the Mail Merge task pane and the Mailings tab on the Ribbon
- Use a letter template as the main document for a mail merge
- Create and edit a data source
- Insert merge fields in a main document
- Use an IF field in a main document

- Merge and print form letters
- Select records to merge
- Sort data records
- Address and print mailing labels and envelopes
- Change page orientation
- Merge all data records to a directory
- Convert text to a table

6 | Generating Form Letters, Mailing Labels, and a Directory

Introduction

People are more likely to open and read a personalized letter than a letter addressed as Dear Sir, Dear Madam, or To Whom It May Concern. Typing individual personalized letters, though, can be a time-consuming task. Thus, Word provides the capability of creating a form letter, which is an easy way to generate mass mailings of personalized letters. The basic content of a group of form letters is similar. Items such as name and address, however, vary from one letter to the next. With Word, you easily can address and print mailing labels or envelopes for the form letters.

Project — Form Letters, Mailing Labels, and a Directory

Both businesses and individuals regularly use form letters to communicate via the postal service or e-mail with groups of people. Types of form letter correspondence include announcements of sales to customers, notices of benefits to employees, invitations to the public to participate in a sweepstakes giveaway, and letters of job application to potential employers.

The project in this chapter follows generally accepted guidelines for writing form letters and uses Word to create the form letters shown in Figure 6–1. The form letters inform potential employers of your interest in a job opening at their organization. Each form letter states the potential employer's name and address, advertised job position, and the employer's type — a practice or a school.

To generate form letters, such as the ones shown in Figure 6–1, you create a main document for the form letter (Figure 6–1a), create or specify a data source (Figure 6–1b), and then merge, or *blend*, the main document with the data source to generate a series of individual letters (Figure 6–1c). In Figure 6–1a, the main document represents the portion of the form letter that repeats from one merged letter to the next. In Figure 6–1b, the data source contains the name, address, advertised job position, and employer type for different potential employers. To personalize each letter, you merge the potential employer data in the data source with the main document for the form letter, which generates or prints an individual letter for each potential employer listed in the data source.

Word provides two methods of merging documents: the Mail Merge task pane and the Mailings tab on the Ribbon. The Mail Merge task pane displays a wizard, which is a step-by-step progression that guides you through the merging process. The Mailings tab provides buttons and boxes you use to merge documents. This chapter illustrates both techniques.

Figure 6–1 (a) Main Document for the Form Letter

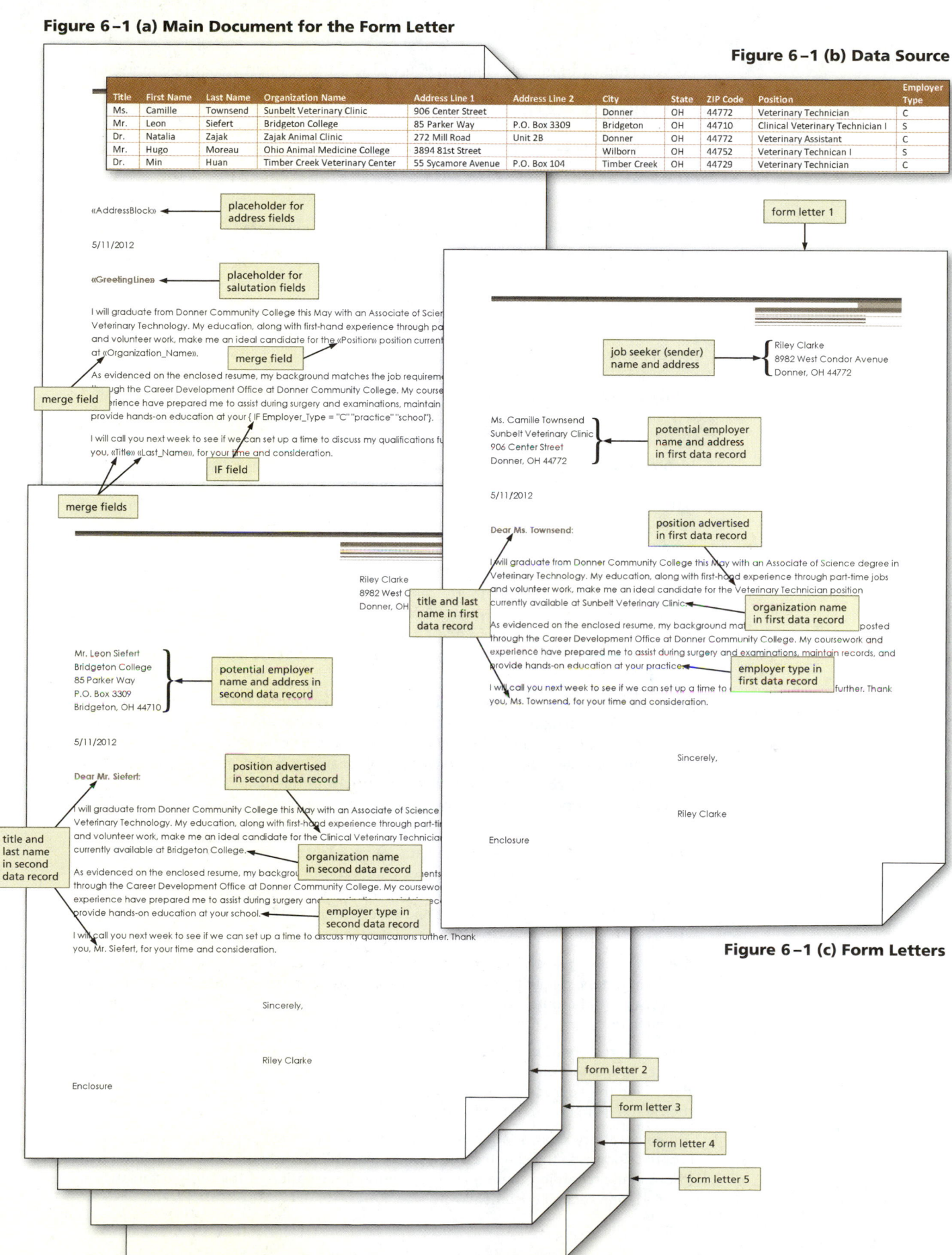

Figure 6–1 (b) Data Source

Title	First Name	Last Name	Organization Name	Address Line 1	Address Line 2	City	State	ZIP Code	Position	Employer Type
Ms.	Camille	Townsend	Sunbelt Veterinary Clinic	906 Center Street		Donner	OH	44772	Veterinary Technician	C
Mr.	Leon	Siefert	Bridgeton College	85 Parker Way	P.O. Box 3309	Bridgeton	OH	44710	Clinical Veterinary Technician I	S
Dr.	Natalia	Zajak	Zajak Animal Clinic	272 Mill Road	Unit 2B	Donner	OH	44772	Veterinary Assistant	C
Mr.	Hugo	Moreau	Ohio Animal Medicine College	3894 81st Street		Wilborn	OH	44752	Veterinary Technican I	S
Dr.	Min	Huan	Timber Creek Veterinary Center	55 Sycamore Avenue	P.O. Box 104	Timber Creek	OH	44729	Veterinary Technician	C

placeholder for address fields

«AddressBlock»

5/11/2012

placeholder for salutation fields

«GreetingLine»

I will graduate from Donner Community College this May with an Associate of Scien
Veterinary Technology. My education, along with first-hand experience through pa
and volunteer work, make me an ideal candidate for the «Position» position current
at «Organization_Name».

merge field

merge field

As evidenced on the enclosed resume, my background matches the job requireme
 through the Career Development Office at Donner Community College. My course
erience have prepared me to assist during surgery and examinations, maintain
provide hands-on education at your { IF Employer_Type = "C" "practice" "school"}.

I will call you next week to see if we can set up a time to discuss my qualifications fu
you, «Title» «Last_Name», for your time and consideration.

IF field

merge fields

form letter 1

job seeker (sender) name and address

Riley Clarke
8982 West Condor Avenue
Donner, OH 44772

Ms. Camille Townsend
Sunbelt Veterinary Clinic
906 Center Street
Donner, OH 44772

potential employer name and address in first data record

5/11/2012

Dear Ms. Townsend:

position advertised in first data record

title and last name in first data record

I will graduate from Donner Community College this May with an Associate of Science degree in
Veterinary Technology. My education, along with first-hand experience through part-time jobs
and volunteer work, make me an ideal candidate for the Veterinary Technician position
currently available at Sunbelt Veterinary Clinic.

organization name in first data record

As evidenced on the enclosed resume, my background mat   posted
through the Career Development Office at Donner Community College. My coursework and
experience have prepared me to assist during surgery and examinations, maintain records, and
provide hands-on education at your practice.

employer type in first data record

I will call you next week to see if we can set up a time to   further. Thank
you, Ms. Townsend, for your time and consideration.

Sincerely,

Riley Clarke

Enclosure

Riley Clarke
8982 West C
Donner, OH

Mr. Leon Siefert
Bridgeton College
85 Parker Way
P.O. Box 3309
Bridgeton, OH 44710

potential employer name and address in second data record

5/11/2012

Dear Mr. Siefert:

position advertised in second data record

title and last name in second data record

I will graduate from Donner Community College this May with an Associate of Science
Veterinary Technology. My education, along with first-hand experience through part-ti
and volunteer work, make me an ideal candidate for the Clinical Veterinary Technicia
currently available at Bridgeton College.

organization name in second data record

As evidenced on the enclosed resume, my backgrou   ents
through the Career Development Office at Donner Community College. My coursewo
experience have prepared me to assist during surgery and examinations, maintain rec
provide hands-on education at your school.

employer type in second data record

I will call you next week to see if we can set up a time to discuss my qualifications further. Thank
you, Mr. Siefert, for your time and consideration.

Sincerely,

Riley Clarke

Enclosure

Figure 6–1 (c) Form Letters

form letter 2

form letter 3

form letter 4

form letter 5

Overview

As you read through this chapter, you will learn how to create and generate the form letters shown in Figure 6–1 on the previous page, along with mailing labels, envelopes, and a directory, by performing these general tasks:

- Identify a template as the main document for the form letter.
- Type the contents of the data source.
- Compose the main document.
- Merge the data source with the main document to generate the form letters.
- Address and print mailing labels and envelopes using the data source.
- Create a directory, which displays the contents of the data source.

Plan Ahead

General Project Guidelines

When creating a Word document, the actions you perform and decisions you make will affect the appearance and characteristics of the finished document. As you create form letters, such as the project shown in Figure 6–1, and related documents, you should follow these general guidelines:

1. **Identify the main document for the form letter.** When creating form letters, you either can type the letter from scratch in a blank document window or use a letter template. A letter template saves time because Word prepares a letter with text and/or formatting common to all letters. Then, you customize the resulting letter by selecting and replacing prewritten text.

2. **Create or specify the data source.** The **data source** contains the variable, or changing, values for each letter. A data source can be an Access database table, an Outlook contacts list, or an Excel worksheet. If the necessary and properly organized data already exists in one of these Office programs, you can instruct Word to use the existing file as the data source for the mail merge. Otherwise, you can create a new data source using one of these programs.

3. **Compose the main document for the form letter.** A **main document** contains the constant, or unchanging, text, punctuation, spaces, and graphics. It should reference the data in the data source properly. The finished main document letter should look like a symmetrically framed picture with evenly spaced margins, all balanced below an attractive letterhead or return address. The content of the main document for the form letter should contain proper grammar, correct spelling, logically constructed sentences, flowing paragraphs, and sound ideas. Be sure to proofread it carefully.

4. **Merge the main document with the data source to create the form letters.** **Merging** is the process of combining the contents of a data source with a main document. You can print the merged letters on the printer or place them in a new document, which you later can edit. You also have the option of merging all data in a data source, or merging just a portion of it.

5. **Generate mailing labels and envelopes.** To generate mailing labels and envelopes for the form letters, follow the same process as for the form letters. That is, determine the appropriate data source, create the label or envelope main document, and then merge the main document with the data source to generate the mailing labels and envelopes.

6. **Create a directory of the data source.** A **directory** is a listing of the contents of the data source. To create a directory, follow the same process as for the form letters. That is, determine the appropriate data source, create the directory main document, and then merge the main document with the data source to create the directory.

When necessary, more specific details concerning the above guidelines are presented at appropriate points in the chapter. The chapter also will identify the actions performed and decisions made regarding these guidelines during the creation of the form letters shown in Figure 6–1, and related documents.

To Start Word

If you are using a computer to step through the project in this chapter and you want your screens to match the figures in this book, you should change your computer's resolution to 1024 × 768. The following steps start Word and verify settings.

1 Start Word. If necessary, maximize the Word window.

2 If the Print Layout button on the status bar is not selected, click it so that your screen is in Print Layout view.

3 Change your zoom level to 100%.

4 If the Show/Hide ¶ button (Home tab | Paragraph group) is not selected already, click it to display formatting marks on the screen.

Identifying the Main Document for Form Letters

The first step in the mail merge process is to identify the type of document you are creating for the main document. Typical installations of Word support five types of main documents: letters, e-mail messages, envelopes, labels, and a directory. In this section of the chapter, you create letters as the main document. Later in this chapter, you will specify labels, envelopes, and a directory as the main document.

> **Identify the main document for the form letter.**
> Be sure the main document for the form letter includes all essential business letter elements. All business letters should contain a date line, inside address, message, and signature block. Many business letters contain additional items such as a special mailing notation(s), an attention line, a salutation, a subject line, a complimentary close, reference initials, and an enclosure notation.

Plan Ahead

To Identify the Main Document for the Form Letter Using the Mail Merge Task Pane

This project uses a letter template as the main document for the form letter. Word provides 10 styles of merge letter templates: Adjacency, Apothecary, Black Tie, Equity, Essential, Executive, Median, Oriel, Origin, and Urban. The letter in this chapter uses the Urban template so that it has a look similar to the accompanying resume created in Chapter 5, which also used an Urban template. The following steps use the Mail Merge task pane to identify the Urban Merge Letter template as the main document for a form letter.

1
• Click Mailings on the Ribbon to display the Mailings tab.

• Click the Start Mail Merge button (Mailings tab | Start Mail Merge group) to display the Start Mail Merge menu (Figure 6–2).

Q&A What is the function of the E-mail Messages option?

Instead of printing individual letters, you can send individual e-mail messages using e-mail addresses in the data source or using a Microsoft Outlook Contacts list.

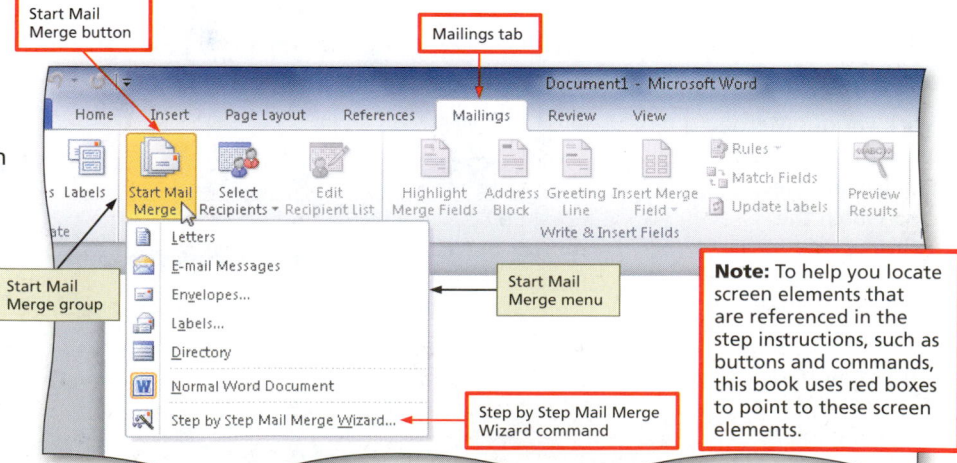

Figure 6–2

2

● Click Step by Step Mail Merge Wizard on the Start Mail Merge menu to display Step 1 of the Mail Merge wizard in the Mail Merge task pane (Figure 6–3).

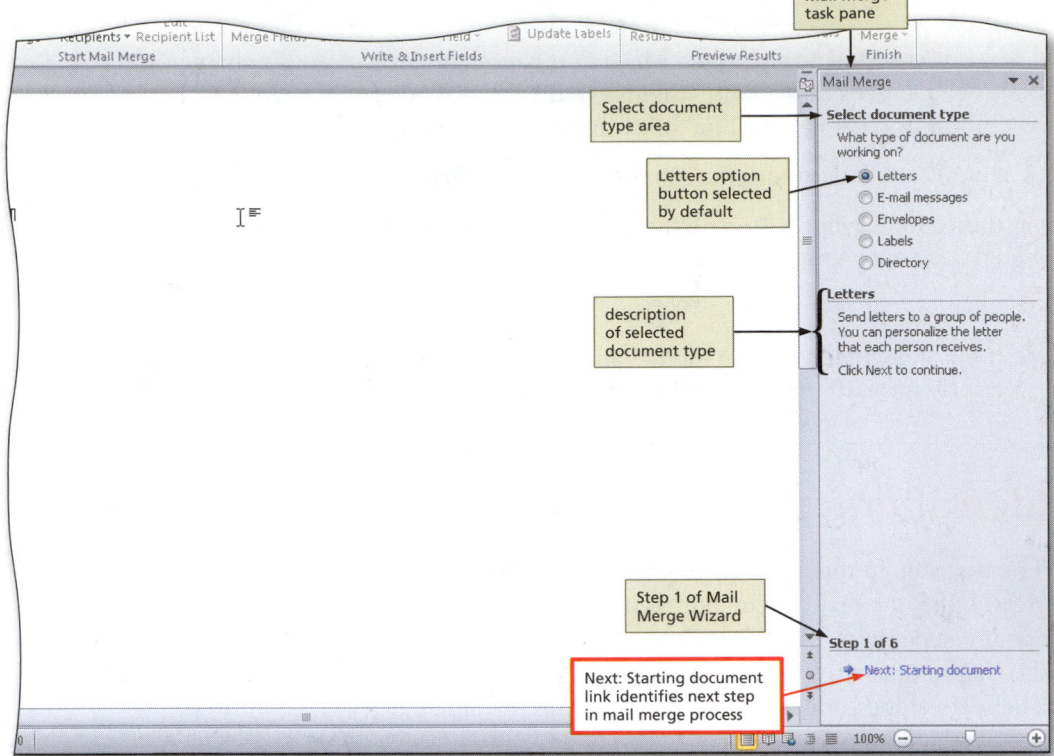

Figure 6–3

3

● Click the Next: Starting document link at the bottom of the Mail Merge task pane to display Step 2 of the Mail Merge wizard, which requests you select a starting document.

● Click 'Start from a template' in the 'Select starting document' area and then click the Select template link to display the Select Template dialog box.

● Click the Letters tab in the dialog box to display the Letters sheet; scroll to and then click Urban Merge Letter, which shows a preview of the selected template in the Preview area (Figure 6–4).

🔍 **Experiment**

● Click various Merge Letter templates in the Letters sheet and watch the preview change at the right edge of the dialog box. When you are finished experimenting, click the Urban Merge Letter template.

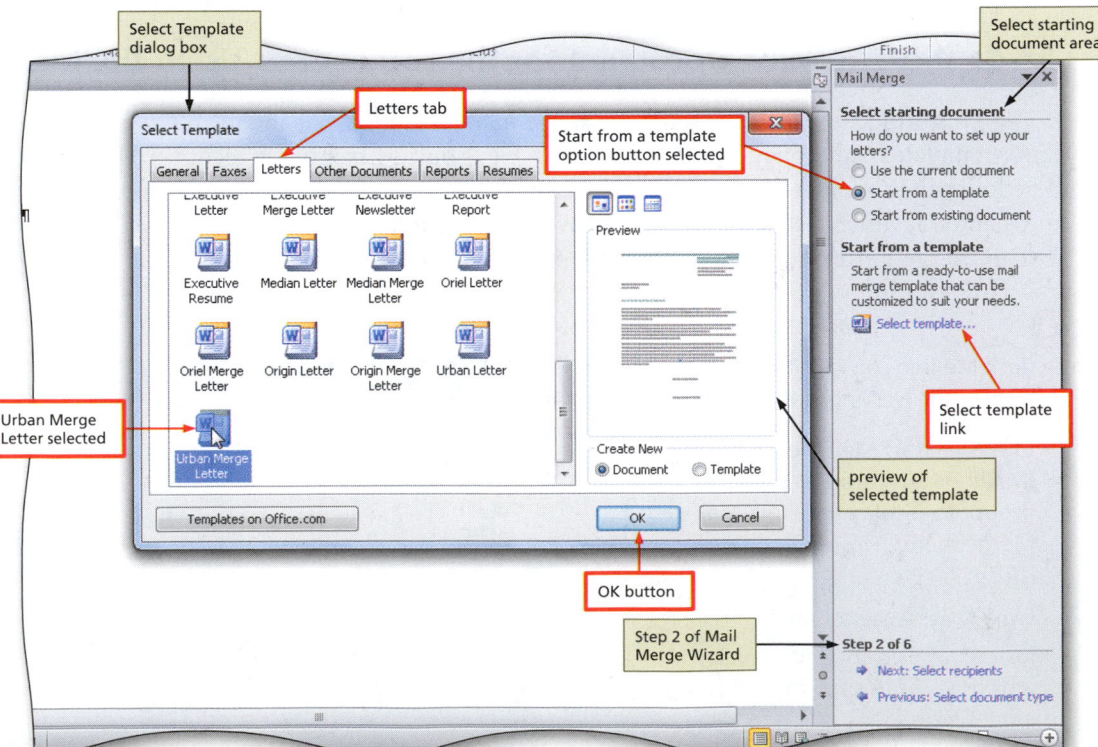

Figure 6–4

4

- Click the OK button to display a letter in the document window that is based on the Urban Merge Letter template (Figure 6–5).

Q&A Can I close the Mail Merge task pane?

Yes, you can close the Mail Merge task pane at any time by clicking its Close button. When you wish to continue with the merge process, you would repeat these steps and Word will resume the merge process at the correct step in the Mail Merge wizard.

Q&A Why does Windows User display as the sender name?

Word places the user name associated with your copy of Microsoft Word as the sender name. Windows User is the user name associated with this copy of Word.

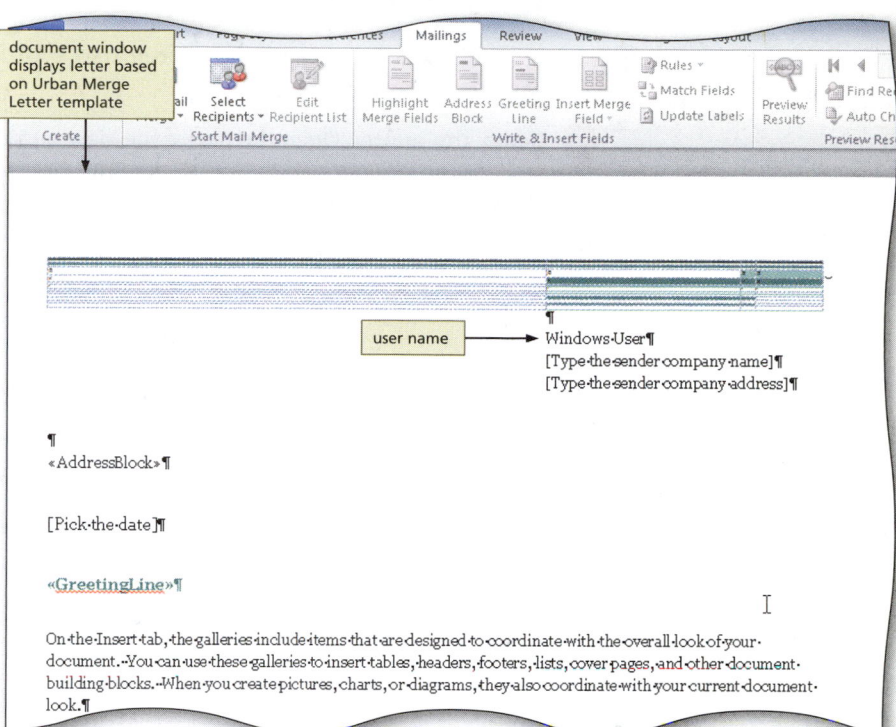

Figure 6–5

Other Ways

1. Open Backstage view, click New, click Sample templates, click desired merge letter template, click Create button.

2. Click Start Mail Merge button (Mailings tab | Start Mail Merge group), click Letters

---

To Change the User Name and Initials

If you wanted to change the user name and initials associated with your copy of Microsoft Word, you would perform the following steps.

1. Open the Backstage view and then click Options to display the Word Options dialog box.

2. If necessary, click General in the left pane.

3. Enter your name in the User name text box.

4. Enter your initials in the Initials text box.

5. Click the OK button.

BTW

The Ribbon and Screen Resolution
Word may change how the groups and buttons within the groups appear on the Ribbon, depending on the computer's screen resolution. Thus, your Ribbon may look different from the ones in this book if you are using a screen resolution other than 1024 × 768.

To Change the Document Theme

The form letter in this project uses the Austin document theme to match the theme used for the resume in Chapter 5. The following steps change the document theme.

1 Display the Page Layout tab.

2 Click the Themes button (Page Layout tab | Themes group) to display the Themes gallery and then click Austin in the Themes gallery to change the document theme.

To Print the Document

The next step is to print the letter that Word generated, which is based on the Urban Merge Letter template.

1 Ready the printer. Open the Backstage view and then click the Print tab, if necessary select the desired printer, and then click the Print button to print the document that is based on the Urban Merge Letter template (Figure 6–6).

Q&A | What are the content controls in the document?

A content control contains instructions for filling in areas of the document. To select a content control, click it. Later in this chapter, you will personalize the content controls.

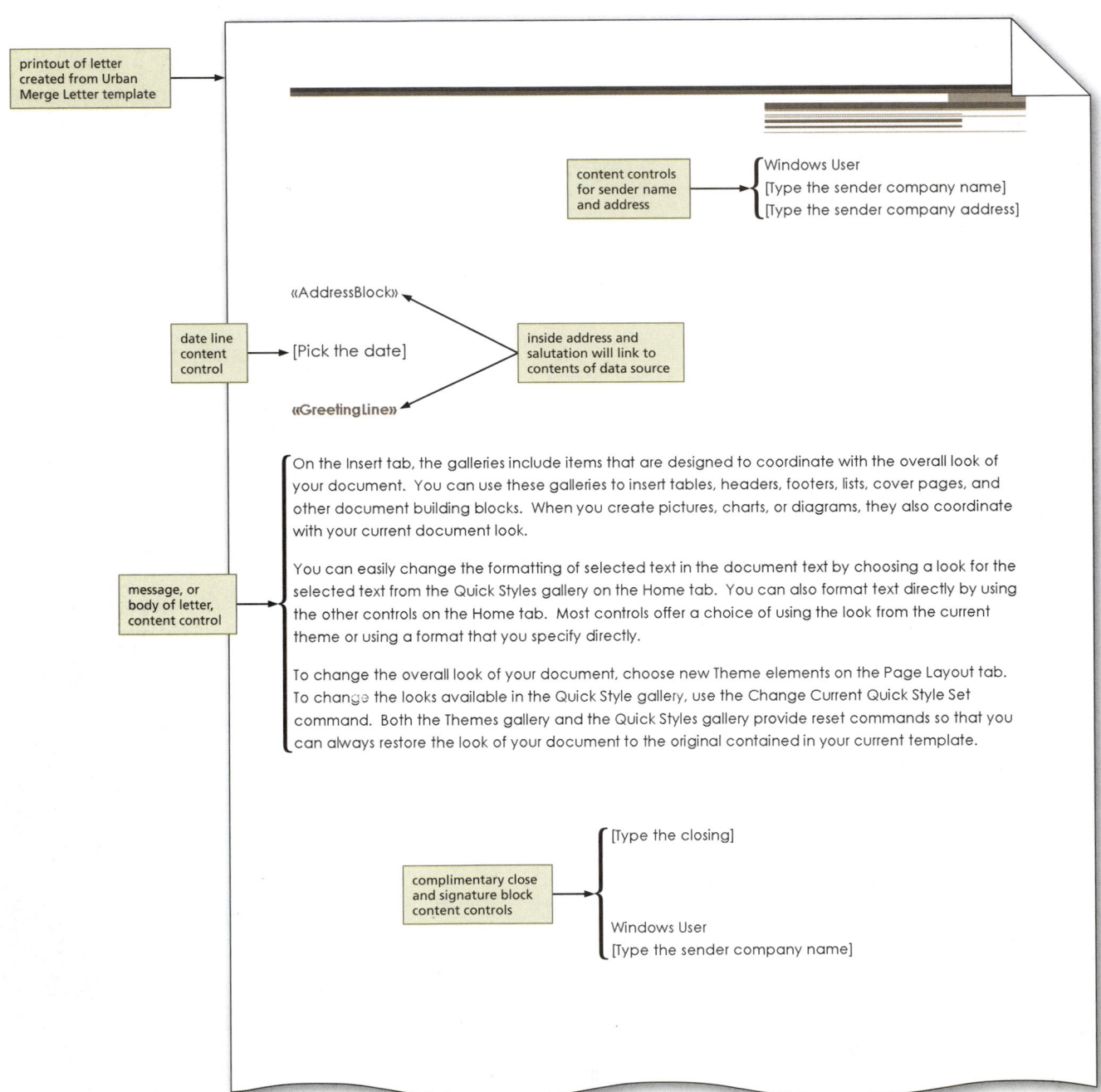

printout of letter created from Urban Merge Letter template

content controls for sender name and address

Windows User
[Type the sender company name]
[Type the sender company address]

«AddressBlock»

date line content control

[Pick the date]

inside address and salutation will link to contents of data source

«GreetingLine»

message, or body of letter, content control

On the Insert tab, the galleries include items that are designed to coordinate with the overall look of your document. You can use these galleries to insert tables, headers, footers, lists, cover pages, and other document building blocks. When you create pictures, charts, or diagrams, they also coordinate with your current document look.

You can easily change the formatting of selected text in the document text by choosing a look for the selected text from the Quick Styles gallery on the Home tab. You can also format text directly by using the other controls on the Home tab. Most controls offer a choice of using the look from the current theme or using a format that you specify directly.

To change the overall look of your document, choose new Theme elements on the Page Layout tab. To change the looks available in the Quick Style gallery, use the Change Current Quick Style Set command. Both the Themes gallery and the Quick Styles gallery provide reset commands so that you can always restore the look of your document to the original contained in your current template.

[Type the closing]

complimentary close and signature block content controls

Windows User
[Type the sender company name]

Figure 6–6

To Enter the Sender Information

The next step is to enter the sender information at the top of the letter. You will replace the name, Windows User, with the sender name. Then, you will delete the content control that contains the company name because the sender is an individual instead of a company. Note that any text you type in this content control also will appear in the signature block. Finally, you will enter the sender's address in the third content control. The following steps enter the sender information.

1 Triple-click the content control at the top of the letter that in this case, contains the name, Windows User, to select it.

2 Type **Riley Clarke** as the sender name.

3 Right-click the content control with the placeholder text, Type the sender company name, to display a shortcut menu and then click Remove Content Control on the shortcut menu to delete the content control.

Q&A

What if my content control already displays a sender company name instead of placeholder text?

Select the text and then delete it.

4 Press the DELETE key to delete the blank line between the name and address content controls.

5 Click the content control with the placeholder text, Type the sender company address, to select it.

6 Type **8982 West Condor Avenue** as the sender street address.

7 Press the ENTER key and then type **Donner, OH 44772** as the sender city, state, and postal code.

To Change the Margin Settings

The Urban Merge Letter template uses .75-inch top, bottom, left, and right margins. You want the form letter to use 1-inch top, bottom, left, and right margins. The following steps change margin settings.

1 Click the Margins button (Page Layout tab | Page Setup group) to display the Margins gallery.

2 Click Normal in the Margins gallery to change the top, bottom, left, and right margins to 1 inch (Figure 6–7).

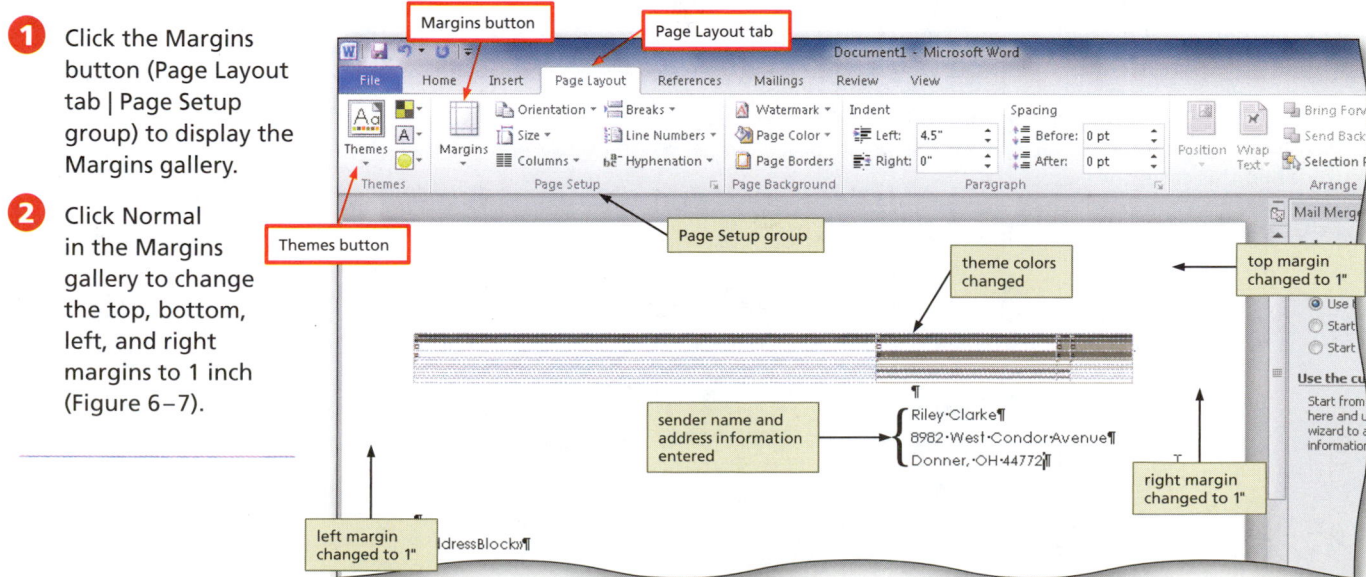

Figure 6–7

To Create a Folder while Saving

You have performed several tasks while creating this project and should save it. The following steps assume you already have created folders for storing files, for example, a CIS 101 folder (for your class) that contains a Word folder. You want to save this and all other documents created in this chapter in a folder called Job Hunting in the Word folder. This folder does not exist, so you must create it. Rather than creating the folder in Windows, you can create folders from Word. The following steps create a folder during the process of saving a document.

1

- With a USB flash drive connected to one of the computer's USB ports, click the Save button on the Quick Access Toolbar to display the Save As dialog box.

- Type **Clarke Cover Letter** in the File name text box (Save As dialog box) to change the file name. Do not press the ENTER key after typing the file name because you do not want to close the dialog box at this time.

- Navigate to the desired location for the new folder (in this case, the Word folder in the CIS 101 folder [or your class folder] on the USB flash drive).

- Click the New folder button (Save As dialog box) to display a new folder icon with the name New folder selected in the dialog box (Figure 6–8).

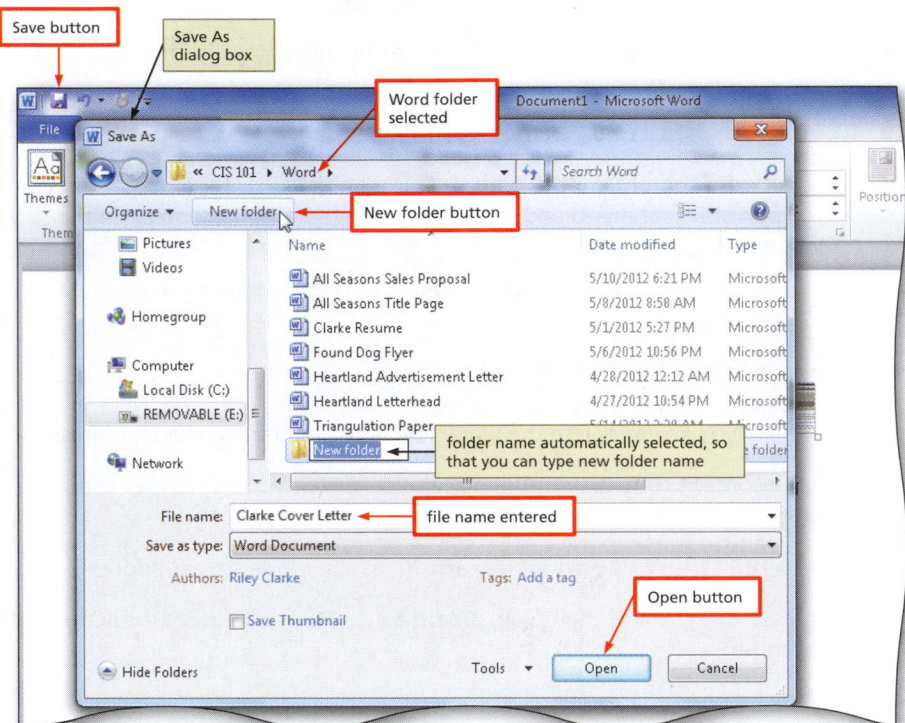

Figure 6–8

2

- Type **Job Hunting** as the new folder name and then press the ENTER key to create the new folder.

- Click the Open button to open the selected folder, in this case, the Job Hunting folder (Figure 6–9).

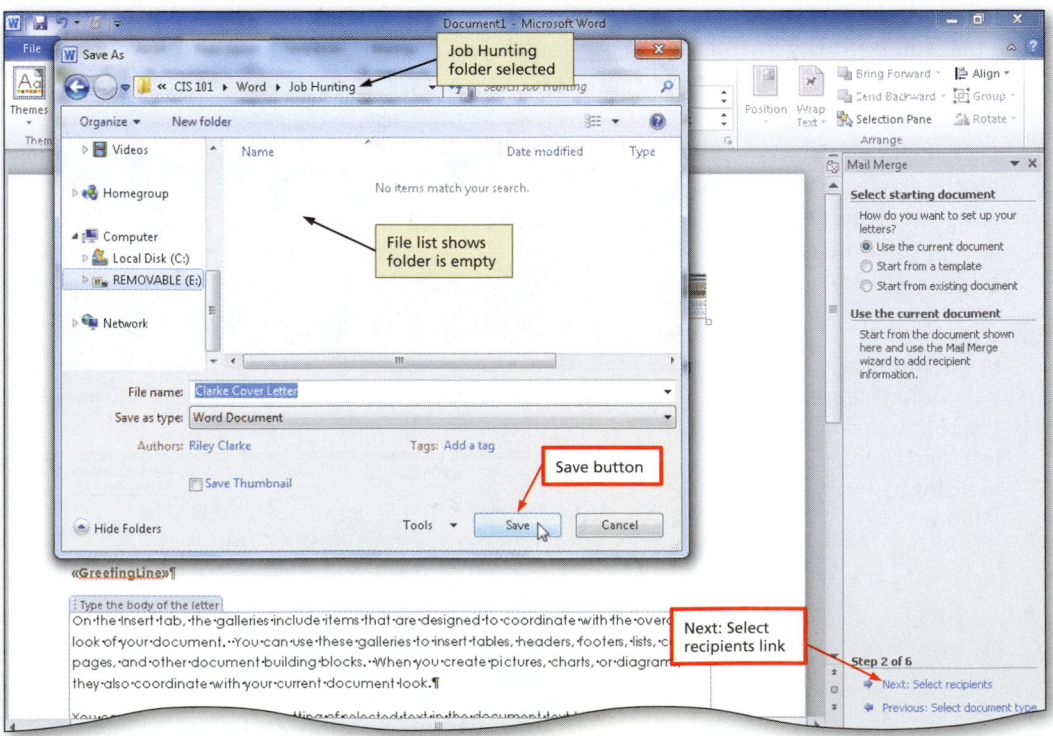

Figure 6–9

- Click the Save button (Save As dialog box) to save the current document in the selected folder on the selected drive.

Can I create a folder in any other dialog box?

Yes. Any dialog box that displays a File list, such as the Open and Insert File dialog boxes, also has the New folder button, allowing you to create a new folder in Word instead of using Windows for this task.

Other Ways
1. Press F12

Creating a Data Source

A data source is a file that contains the data that changes from one merged document to the next. As shown in Figure 6–10, a data source often is shown as a table that consists of a series of rows and columns. Each row is called a **record**. The first row of a data source is called the **header record** because it identifies the name of each column. Each row below the header row is called a **data record**. Data records contain the text that varies in each copy of the merged document. The data source for this project contains five data records. In this project, each data record identifies a different potential employer. Thus, five form letters will be generated from this data source.

Each column in the data source is called a **data field**. A data field represents a group of similar data. Each data field must be identified uniquely with a name, called a **field name**. For example, Position is the name of the data field (column) that contains the advertised job position. In this chapter, the data source contains 11 data fields with the following field names: Title, First Name, Last Name, Organization Name, Address Line 1, Address Line 2, City, State, ZIP Code, Position, and Employer Type.

BTW

Fields and Records
Field and record are terms that originate from the computer programming field. Do not be intimidated by these terms. A field is simply a column in a table, and a record is a row. Instead of as a field, some programmers identify a column of data as a variable or an attribute. All three terms (field, variable, and attribute) have the same meaning.

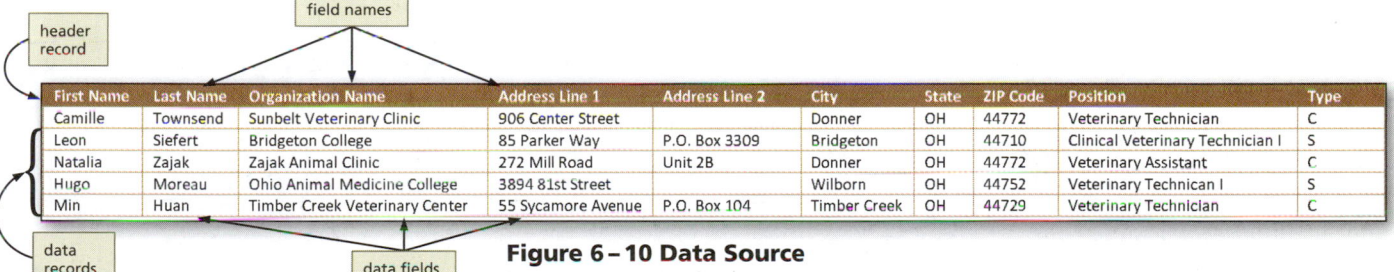

Figure 6–10 Data Source

First Name	Last Name	Organization Name	Address Line 1	Address Line 2	City	State	ZIP Code	Position	Type
Camille	Townsend	Sunbelt Veterinary Clinic	906 Center Street		Donner	OH	44772	Veterinary Technician	C
Leon	Siefert	Bridgeton College	85 Parker Way	P.O. Box 3309	Bridgeton	OH	44710	Clinical Veterinary Technician I	S
Natalia	Zajak	Zajak Animal Clinic	272 Mill Road	Unit 2B	Donner	OH	44772	Veterinary Assistant	C
Hugo	Moreau	Ohio Animal Medicine College	3894 81st Street		Wilborn	OH	44752	Veterinary Technican I	S
Min	Huan	Timber Creek Veterinary Center	55 Sycamore Avenue	P.O. Box 104	Timber Creek	OH	44729	Veterinary Technician	C

Plan Ahead

Create the data source.
When you create a data source, you will need to determine the fields it should contain. That is, you will need to identify the data that will vary from one merged document to the next. Following are a few important points about fields:

- For each field, you may be required to create a field name. Because data sources often contain the same fields, some programs create a list of commonly used field names that you may use.

- Field names must be unique; that is, no two field names may be the same.

- Fields may be listed in any order in the data source. That is, the order of fields has no effect on the order in which they will print in the main document.

- Organize fields so that they are flexible. For example, separate the name into individual fields: title, first name, and last name. This arrangement allows you to print a person's title, first name, and last name (e.g., Ms. Camille Townsend) in the inside address but only the title and last name in the salutation (Dear Ms. Townsend).

BTW

E-Mail Addresses
If you are merging to e-mail messages, you could place an e-mail address field in the data source so that the merge process sends an e-mail message to each e-mail address in the data source, or you could use a Microsoft Outlook Contacts list as the data source, which automatically includes e-mail addresses.

To Create a New Data Source

Word provides a list of 13 commonly used field names. This project uses 9 of the 13 field names supplied by Word: Title, First Name, Last Name, Company Name, Address Line 1, Address Line 2, City, State, and ZIP Code. This project does not use the other four field names supplied by Word: Country or Region, Home Phone, Work Phone, and E-mail Address. Thus, you will delete these four field names. Then, you will change the Company Name field name to Organization Name because organization better describes a school and a clinic (or practice). You also will add two new field names (Position and Employer Type) to the data source. The following steps create a new data source for a mail merge.

1

- Click the Next: Select recipients link at the bottom of the Mail Merge task pane (shown in Figure 6-9 on page WD 338) to display Step 3 of the Mail Merge wizard, which requests you select recipients.

- Click 'Type a new list' in the Select recipients area, which displays the 'Type a new list' area.

- Click the Create link to display the New Address List dialog box (Figure 6-11).

Q&A

When would I use the other two option buttons in the Select recipients area?

If a data source already was created, you would use the first option: Use an existing list. If you wanted to use your Outlook contacts list as the data source, you would choose the second option.

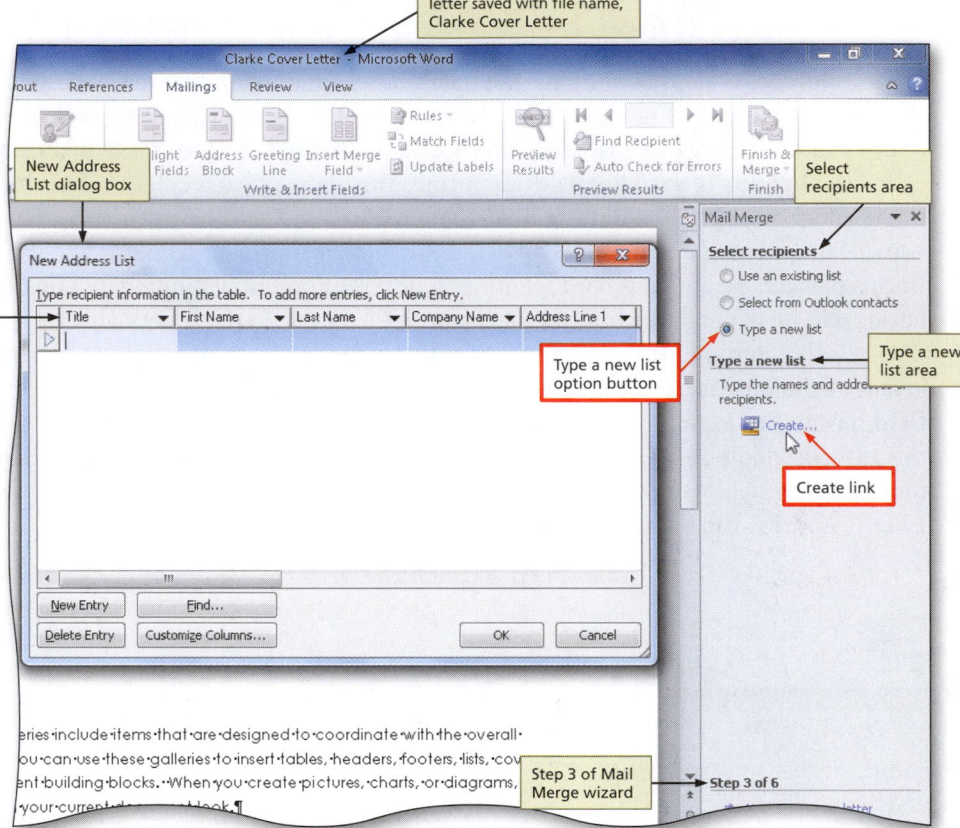

Figure 6-11

2

- Click the Customize Columns button (New Address List dialog box) to display the Customize Address List dialog box (Figure 6-12).

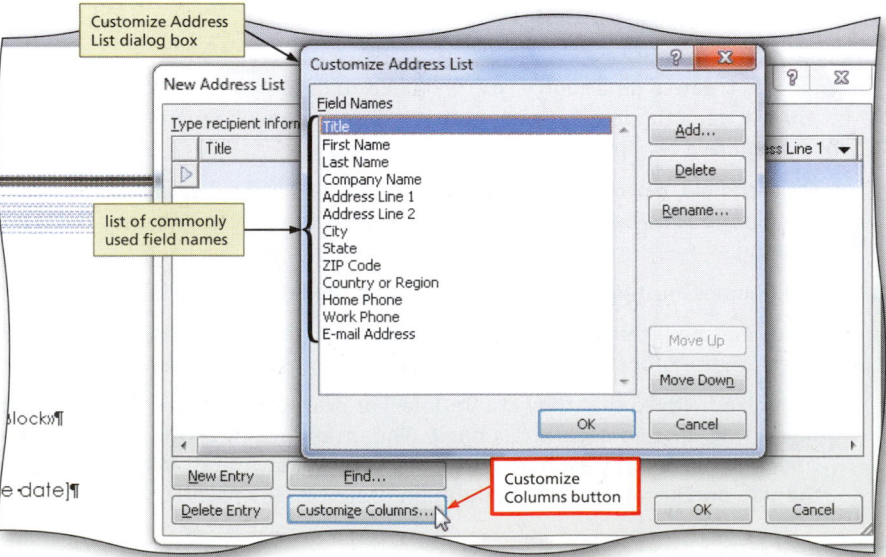

Figure 6-12

- Click Country or Region in the Field Names list to select the field to be deleted and then click the Delete button to display a dialog box asking if you are sure you want to delete the selected field (Figure 6–13).

- Click the Yes button (Microsoft Word dialog box) to delete the field.

- Click Home Phone in the Field Names list to select the field. Click the Delete button (Customize Address List dialog box) and then click the Yes button (Microsoft Word dialog box) to delete the field.

- Use this same procedure to delete the Work Phone and E-mail Address fields.

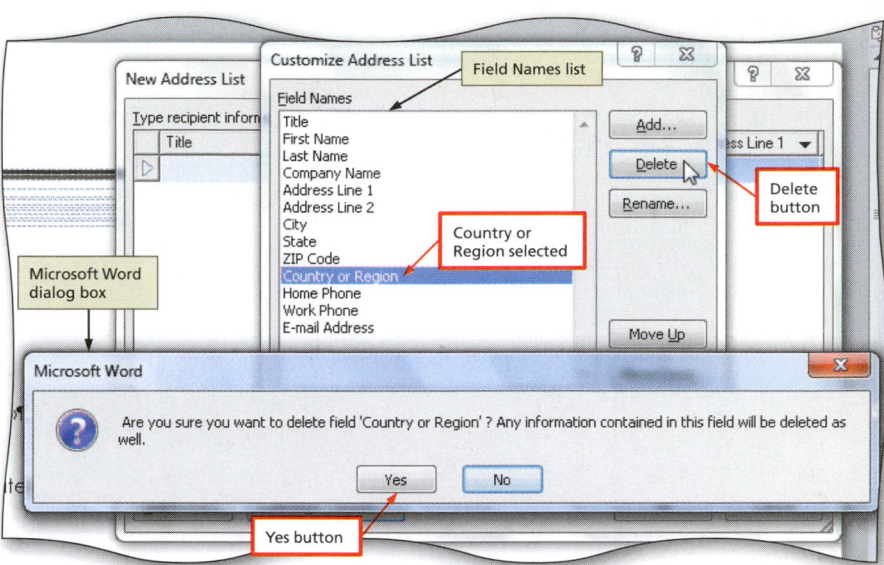

Figure 6–13

- Click Company Name in the Field Names list to select the field to be renamed.

- Click the Rename button to display the Rename Field dialog box.

- Type **Organization Name** (Rename Field dialog box) in the To text box (Figure 6–14).

- Click the OK button to close the Rename Field dialog box and rename the selected field.

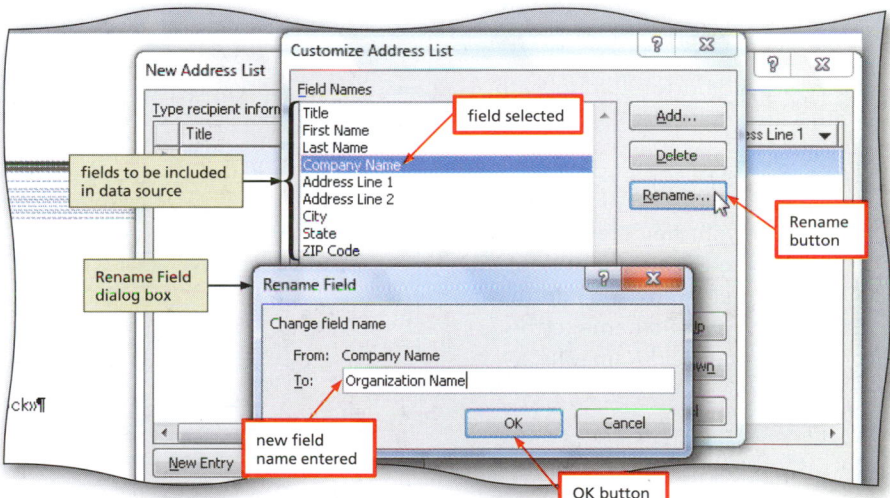

Figure 6–14

- Click the Add button to display the Add Field dialog box.

- Type **Position** in the 'Type a name for your field' text box (Add Field dialog box) (Figure 6–15).

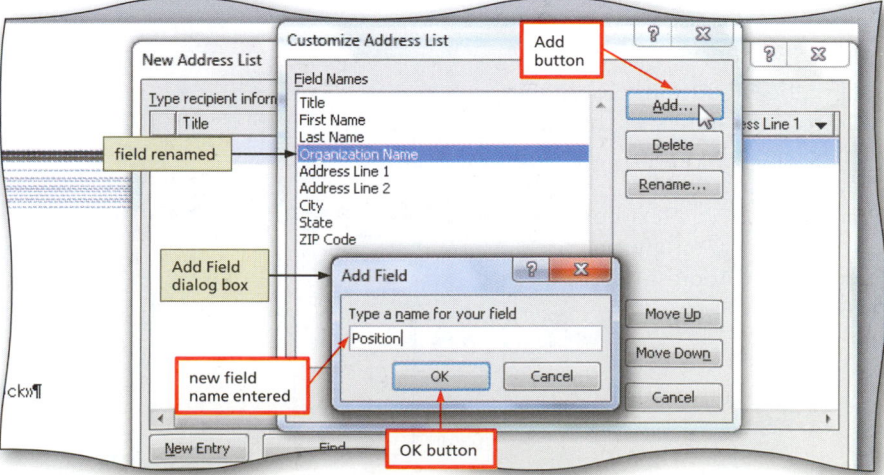

Figure 6–15

• Click the OK button to close the Add Field dialog box and add the Position field name to the Field Names list immediately below the selected field (Figure 6–16).

Q&A

Can I change the order of the field names in the Field Names list?

Yes. Select the field name and then click the Move Up or Move Down button to move the selected field in the direction of the button name.

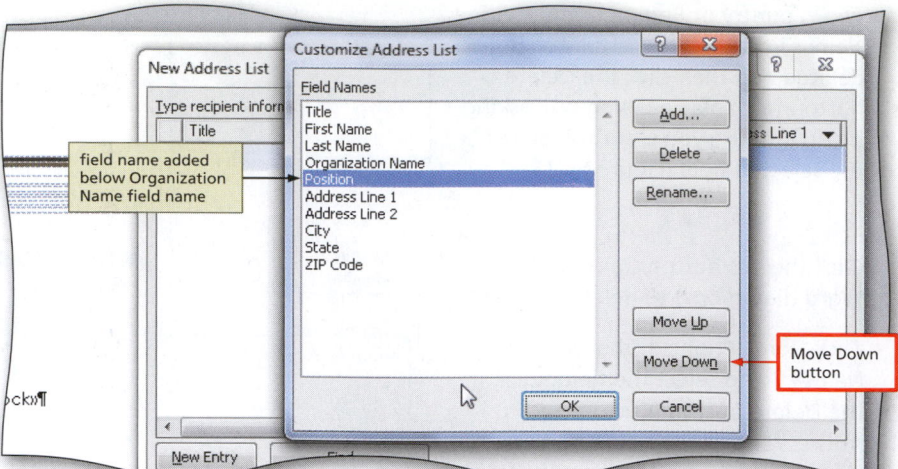

Figure 6–16

• With the Position field selected, click the Move Down button five times to position the selected field at the end of the Field Names list.

• Click the Add button to display the Add Field dialog box.

• Type **Employer Type** (Add Field dialog box) in the 'Type a name for your field' text box and then click the OK button to close the Add Field dialog box and add the Employer Type field name to the bottom of the Field Names list (Figure 6–17).

Q&A

Could I add more field names to the list?

Yes. You would click the Add button for each field name you want to add.

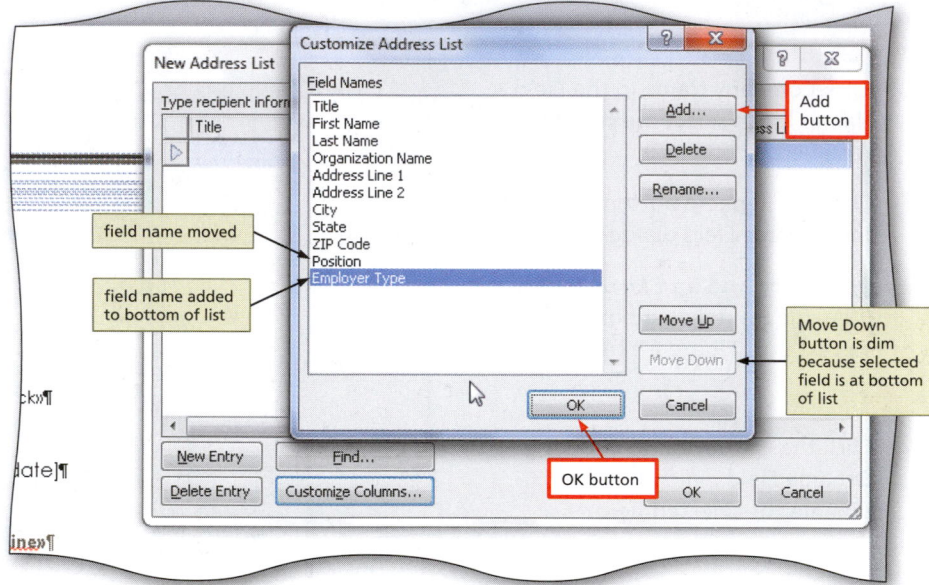

Figure 6–17

• Click the OK button to close the Customize Address List dialog box, which positions the insertion point in the Title text box for the first record (row) in the New Address List dialog box (Figure 6–18).

Figure 6–18

- Type **Ms.** and then press the TAB key to enter the title for the first data record.

- Type **Camille** and then press the TAB key to enter the first name.

- Type **Townsend** and then press the TAB key to enter the last name.

- Type **Sunbelt Veterinary Clinic** and then press the TAB key to enter the organization name.

- Type **906 Center Street** to enter the first address line (Figure 6–19).

Q&A What if I notice an error in an entry?

Click the entry and then correct the error as you would in the document window.

Q&A What happened to the rest of the Organization Name entry?

It is stored in the field, but you cannot see the entire entry because it is longer than the display area.

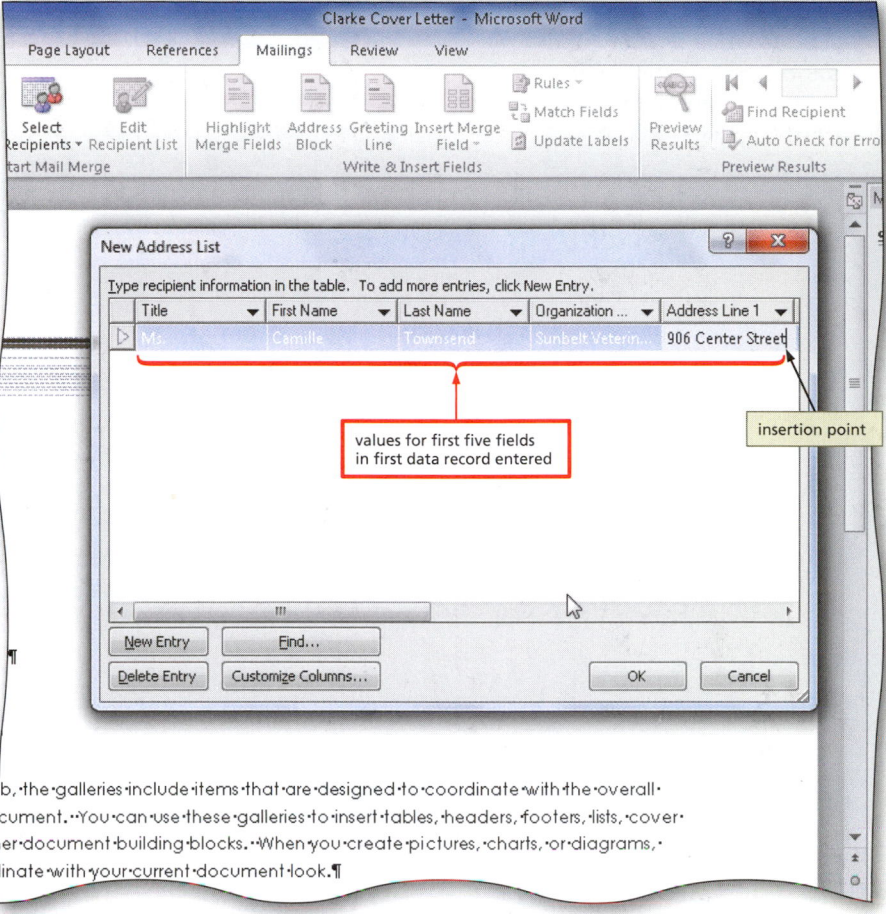

Figure 6–19

- Press the TAB key twice to leave the second address line empty.

- Type **Donner** and then press the TAB key to enter the city.

- Type **OH** and then press the TAB key to enter the state code.

- Type **44772** and then press the TAB key to enter the ZIP code.

- Type **Veterinary Technician** and then press the TAB key to enter the Position.

- Type **C** to enter the employer type (Figure 6–20).

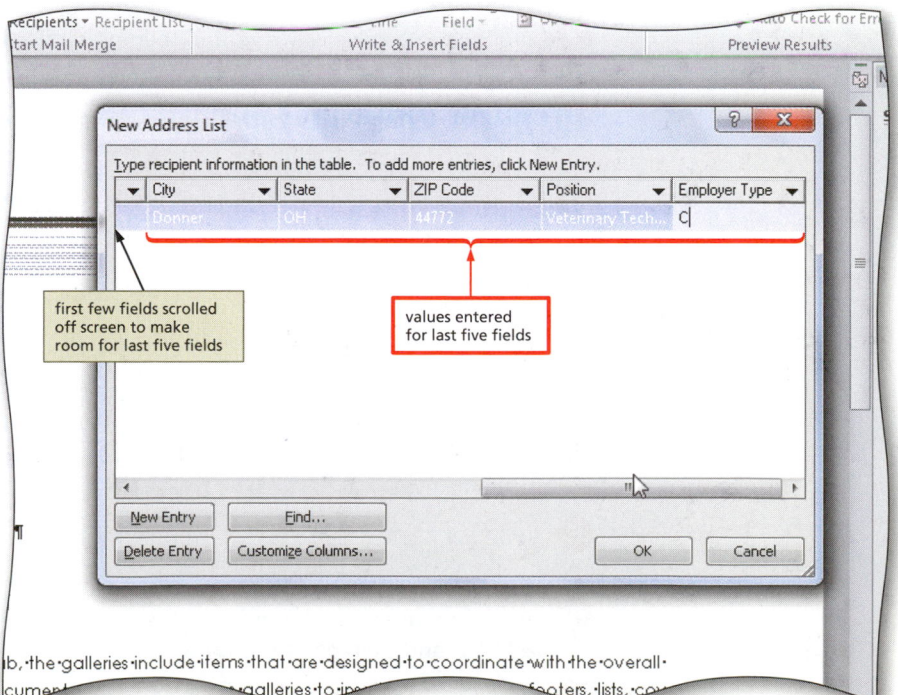

Figure 6–20

13
- Click the New Entry button to add a new blank record and position the insertion point in the Title field of the new record (Figure 6–21).

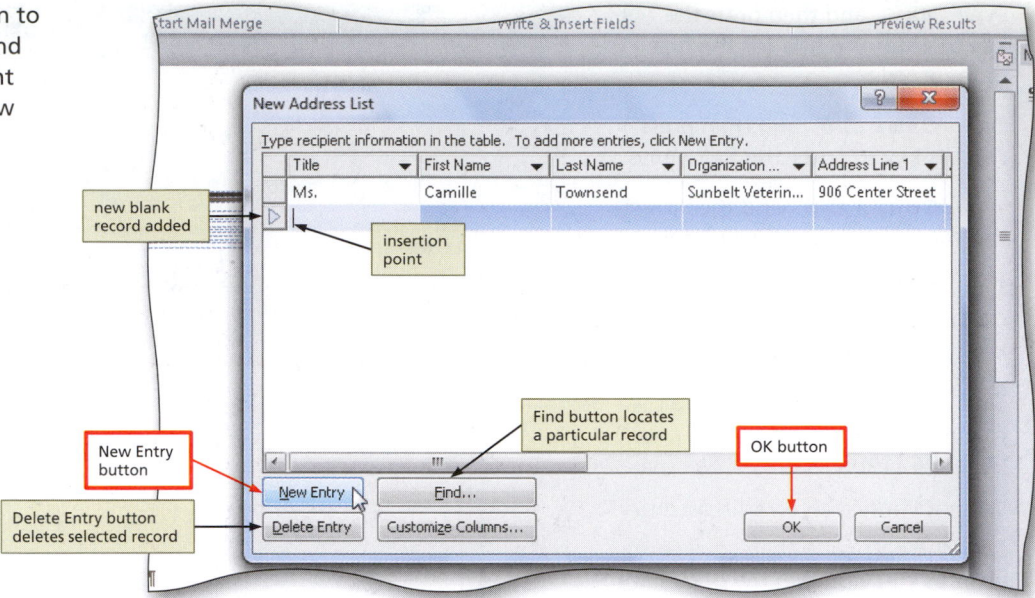

Figure 6–21

To Enter More Records

The following steps enter the remaining four records in the New Address List dialog box.

1 Type **Mr.** and then press the TAB key. Type **Leon** and then press the TAB key. Type **Siefert** and then press the TAB key. Type **Bridgeton College** and then press the TAB key.

2 Type **85 Parker Way** and then press the TAB key. Type **P.O. Box 3309** and then press the TAB key.

3 Type **Bridgeton** and then press the TAB key. Type **OH** and then press the TAB key. Type **44710** and then press the TAB key.

4 Type **Clinical Veterinary Technician** and then press the TAB key. Type **S** and then click the New Entry button.

Q&A

Instead of clicking the New Entry button, can I press the TAB key at the end of one row to add a new blank record?

Yes. Pressing the TAB key at the end of a row has the same function as clicking the New Entry button.

5 Type **Dr.** and then press the TAB key. Type **Natalia** and then press the TAB key. Type **Zajak** and then press the TAB key. Type **Zajak Animal Clinic** and then press the TAB key.

6 Type **272 Mill Road** and then press the TAB key. Type **Unit 2B** and then press the TAB key.

7 Type **Donner** and then press the TAB key. Type **OH** and then press the TAB key. Type **44772** and then press the TAB key.

8 Type **Veterinary Assistant** and then press the TAB key. Type **C** and then click the New Entry button.

9 Type **Mr.** and then press the TAB key. Type **Hugo** and then press the TAB key. Type **Moreau** and then press the TAB key. Type **Ohio Animal Medicine College** and then press the TAB key.

10 Type **3894 81st Street** and then press the TAB key twice.

11 Type **Wilborn** and then press the TAB key. Type **OH** and then press the TAB key. Type **44752** and then press the TAB key.

12 Type **Veterinary Technician I** and then press the TAB key. Type **S** and then click the New Entry button.

13 Type **Dr.** and then press the TAB key. Type **Min** and then press the TAB key. Type **Huan** and then press the TAB key. Type **Timber Creek Veterinary Center** and then press the TAB key.

14 Type **55 Sycamore Avenue** and then press the TAB key. Type **P.O. Box 104** and then press the TAB key.

15 Type **Timber Creek** and then press the TAB key. Type **OH** and then press the TAB key. Type **44729** and then press the TAB key.

16 Type **Veterinary Technician** and then press the TAB key. Type **C** and then click the OK button (shown in Figure 6–21), which displays the Save Address List dialog box (shown in Figure 6–22).

To Save a Data Source when Prompted by Word

When you click the OK button in the New Address List dialog box, Word displays the Save Address List dialog box so that you can save the data source. By default, the save location is the My Data Sources folder on your computer's hard disk. In this chapter, you save the data source to your USB flash drive. The following steps save the data source in the Job Hunting folder created earlier in this project.

1

• Type **Clarke Prospective Employers** in the File name text box (Save Address List dialog box) as the name for the data source. Do not press the ENTER key after typing the file name because you do not want to close the dialog box at this time.

• Navigate to the desired save location for the data source (in this case, the Job Hunting folder in the Word folder in the CIS 101 folder [or your class folder] on the USB flash drive) (Figure 6–22).

Q&A

What is a Microsoft Office Address Lists file type?

It is a Microsoft Access database file. If you are familiar with Microsoft Access, you can open the Clarke Prospective Employers file in Access. You do not have to be familiar with Access or have Access installed on your computer, however, to continue with this mail merge process. Word simply stores a data source as an Access table because it is an efficient method of storing a data source.

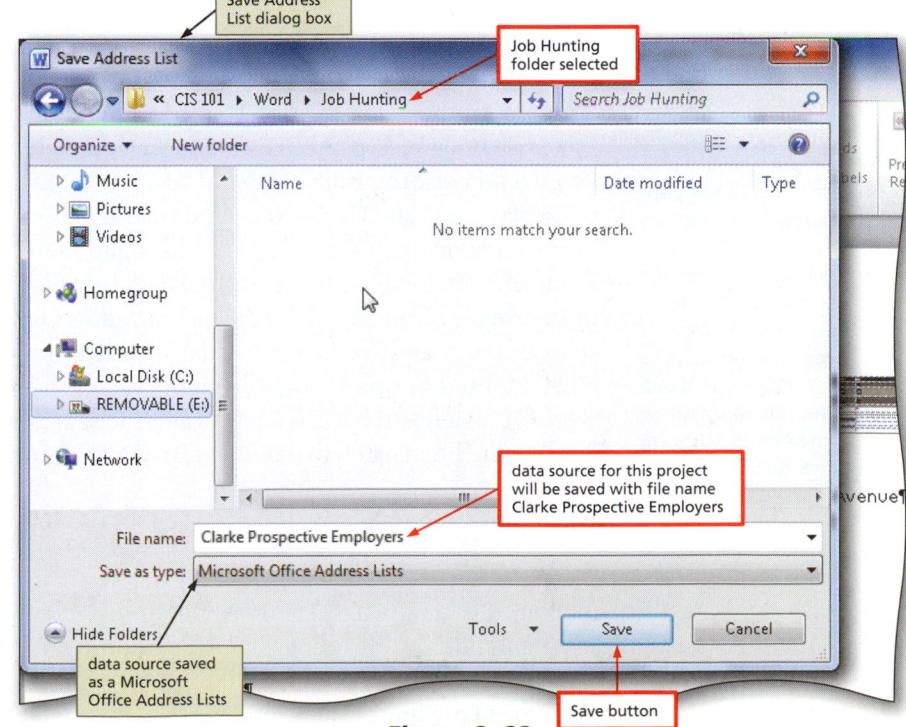

Figure 6–22

2
- Click the Save button (Save Address List dialog box) to save the data source in the selected folder using the entered file name and then display the Mail Merge Recipients dialog box (Figure 6–23).

What if the fields in my Mail Merge Recipients list are in a different order?

The order of fields in the Mail Merge Recipients list has no effect on the mail merge process. If Word rearranges the order, you can leave them in the revised order.

3
- Click the OK button to close the Mail Merge Recipients dialog box.

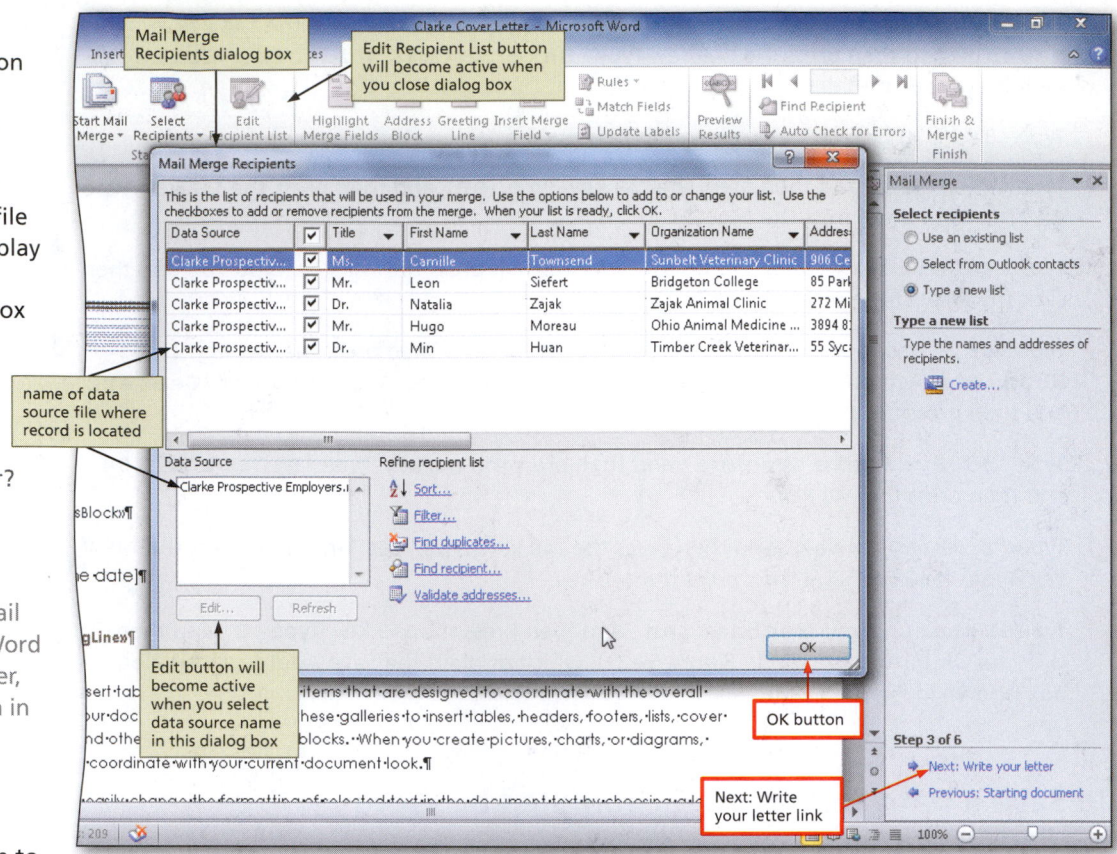

Figure 6–23

Saving Data Sources
Word, by default, saves a data source in the My Data Sources folder on your computer's hard disk. Likewise, when you open a data source, Word initially looks in the My Data Sources folder for the file. Because the data source files you create in Word are saved as Microsoft Access database file types, if you are familiar with Microsoft Access, you can open and view these files in Access.

Editing Records in the Data Source

All of the data records have been entered in the data source and saved with the file name, Clarke Prospective Employers. To add or edit data records in the data source, you would click the Edit Recipient List button (Mailings tab | Start Mail Merge group) to display the Mail Merge Recipients dialog box (shown in Figure 6–23). Click the data source name in the Data Source list and then click the Edit button (Mail Merge Recipients dialog box) to display the data records in a dialog box similar to the one shown in Figure 6–21 on page WD 344. Then, add or edit records as described in the previous steps. If you want to edit a particular record and the list of data records is long, you can click the Find button to locate an item, such as a last name, quickly in the list.

To delete a record, select it using the same procedure described in the previous paragraph. Then, click the Delete Entry button in the dialog box (Figure 6–21).

Using an Existing Data Source

Instead of creating a new data source, you can use an existing Microsoft Outlook Contacts list, an Access database table, an Excel table, or a Word table as a data source in a mail merge. To use an existing data source, select the appropriate option in the Select recipients area in the Mail Merge task pane or click the Select Recipients button (Mailings tab | Start Mail Merge group) and then click the desired option on the Select Recipients menu.

For a Microsoft Outlook Contacts list, click Select from Outlook contacts in the Mail Merge task pane or on the Select Recipients menu to display the Select Contacts dialog box. Next, select the contact folder you wish to import (Select Contacts dialog box) and then click the OK button.

For other existing data source types such as an Access database table, an Excel worksheet, or a Word table, click Use Existing List in the Mail Merge task pane or on the Select Recipients menu to display the Select Data Source dialog box. Next, select the file name of the data source you wish to use and then click the Open button.

With Access, you can use any field in the database in the main document. (Later in this chapter you use an existing Access database table as the data source.) For the merge to work properly with an Excel table or a Word table, you must ensure data is arranged properly and that the table is the only element in the file. The first row of the table should contain unique field names, and the table cannot contain any blank rows.

Composing the Main Document for the Form Letters

The next step in this project is to enter and format the text and fields in the main document for the form letters (shown in Figure 6–1a on page WD 331). You will follow these steps to compose the main document for the form letter.

1. Enter the date.
2. Edit the address block.
3. Edit the greeting line (salutation).
4. Enter text and insert merge fields.
5. Insert an IF field.
6. Merge the letters.

Compose the main document for the form letter.
This chapter uses a template for the main document for the form letter, where you select predefined content controls and replace them with personalized content, adjusting formats as necessary. As an alternative, some users prefer to enter the contents of the main document from scratch so that they can format the letter with business letter spacing while composing it according to the block, modified block, or semi-block letter style.

Plan Ahead

To Display the Next Step in the Mail Merge Wizard

The next step in the Mail Merge wizard is to write the letter. Because you are using a template to write the letter, you do not need to use the task pane for this step. If, however, you were not using a template, you could use this task pane to insert the AddressBlock and GreetingLine fields in the document. The following step displays the next step in the Mail Merge wizard.

1 Click the Next: Write your letter link at the bottom of the Mail Merge task pane (shown in Figure 6–23) to display Step 4 of the Mail Merge wizard in the Mail Merge task pane (shown in Figure 6–24 on the next page).

To Zoom the Document

So that the document is easier to read, you prefer it at 110 percent. Thus, the following step changes the zoom to 110%.

1 If necessary, click the Zoom In button on the status bar as many times as necessary until the Zoom button displays 110% on its face (shown in Figure 6–24).

BTW

BTWs
For a complete list of the BTWs found in the margins of this book, visit the Word 2010 BTW Web page (scsite.com/wd2010/btw).

To Enter the Date

The next step is to enter the date in the letter. You can click the date content control and type the correct date, or you can click the box arrow and select the date from a calendar. The following steps use the calendar to enter the date.

1

- If necessary, scroll to display the letter in the document window.

- Click the date content control to select it and then click its box arrow to display a calendar.

- Scroll through the calendar months until the desired month appears, May, 2012 in this case (Figure 6–24).

2

- Click 11 in the calendar to display 5/11/2012 in the date line of the form letter (shown in Figure 6–25).

- Click outside the content control to deselect it.

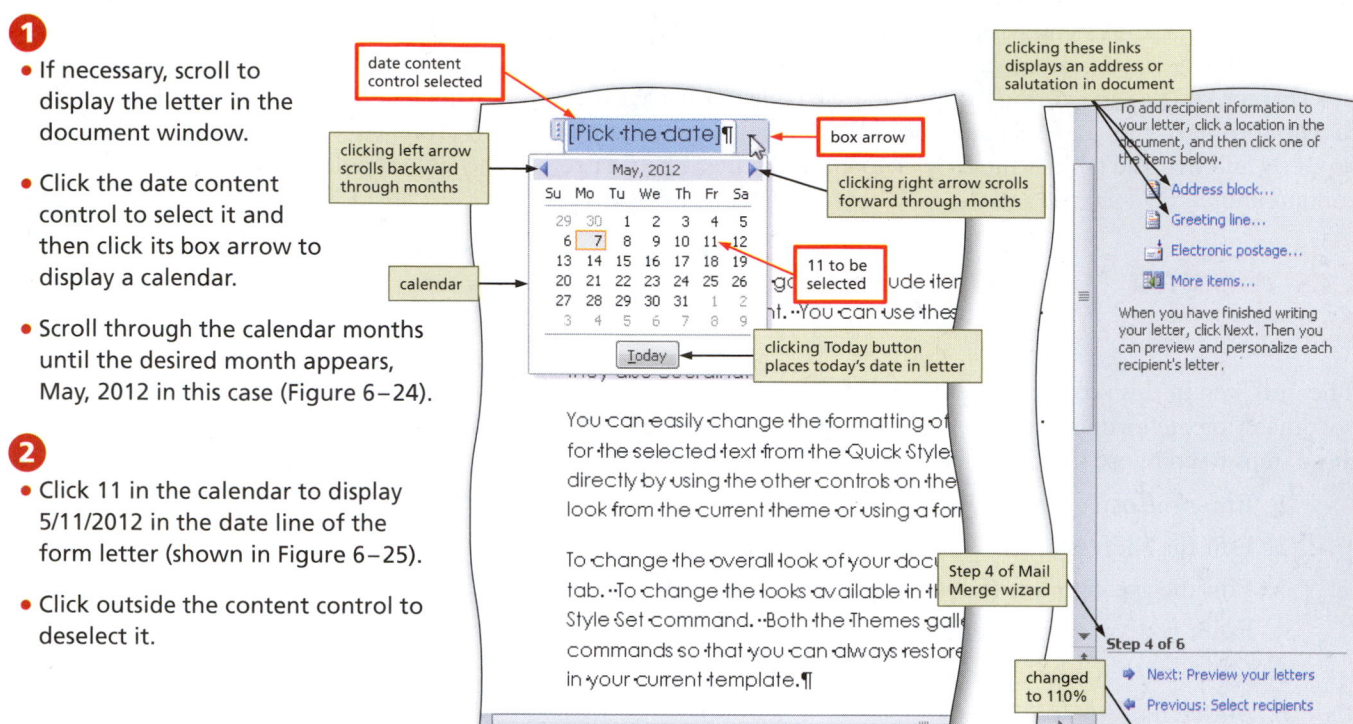

Figure 6–24

Merge Fields

In this form letter, the inside address appears below the date line, and the salutation is placed below the date line. The contents of the inside address and salutation are located in the data source. To link the data source to the main document, you insert the field names from the data source in the main document.

In the main document, field names linked to the data source are called **merge fields** because they merge, or combine, the main document with the contents of the data source. When a merge field is inserted in the main document, Word surrounds the field name with **merge field characters**, which are chevrons that mark the beginning and ending of a merge field. Merge field characters are not on the keyboard; therefore, you cannot type them directly in the document. Word automatically displays them when a merge field is inserted in the main document.

Most letters contain an address and salutation. For this reason, Word provides an AddressBlock merge field and a GreetingLine merge field. The **AddressBlock merge field** contains several fields related to an address: title, first name, middle name, last name, suffix, company, street address 1, street address 2, city, state, and ZIP code. When Word uses the AddressBlock merge field, it automatically looks for any fields in the associated data source that are related to an address and then formats the address block properly when you merge the data source with the main document. For example, if your inside address does not use a middle name, suffix, or company, Word omits these items from the inside address and adjusts the spacing so that the address prints correctly.

The Urban Mail Merge template automatically inserted the AddressBlock and GreetingLine merge fields in the form letter. If you wanted to insert these merge fields in a document, you would click the Address block link or the Greeting line link in the Mail Merge task pane or the associated buttons on the Mailings tab.

To View Merged Data in the Main Document

Instead of displaying merge fields, you can see how fields, such as the AddressBlock or GreetingLine fields, will look in the merged letters. The following step views merged data.

1

- If necessary, display the Mailings tab.

- Click the Preview Results button (Mailings tab | Preview Results group) to display the values in the current data record, instead of the merge fields (Figure 6–25).

Q&A

How can I tell which record is showing?

The current record number is displayed in the Preview Results group.

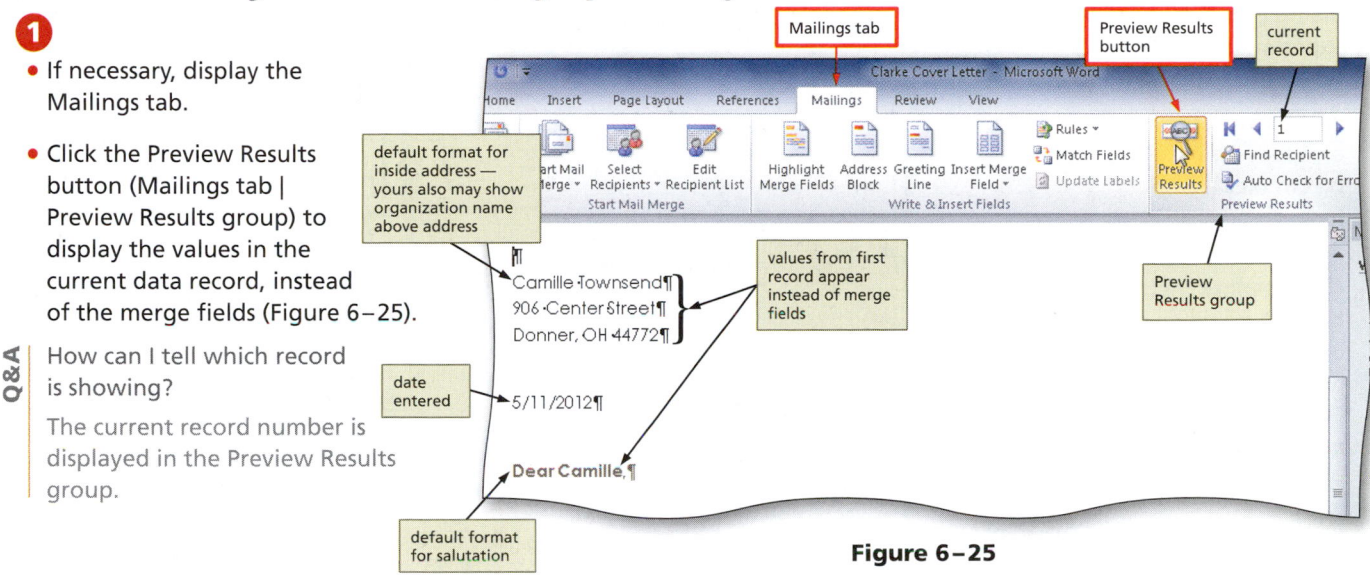

Figure 6–25

To Edit the AddressBlock Merge Field

The **AddressBlock merge field** contains text and fields related to the inside address. The default format for the inside address is the first name and last name on one line, followed by the street address on the next line, and then the city, state, and postal code on the next line. In this letter, you want the potential employer's title (i.e., Ms.) to appear to the left of the first name. You also want the organization name to appear above the street address, if it does not already. The following steps edit the AddressBlock merge field.

1

- Right-click the AddressBlock merge field to select it and display a shortcut menu and the Mini toolbar (Figure 6–26).

Q&A

Why does the AddressBlock merge field turn gray?

Word, by default, shades a field in gray when the field is selected. The shading displays on the screen to help you identify fields; the shading does not print on a hard copy. To select an entire field, double-click it.

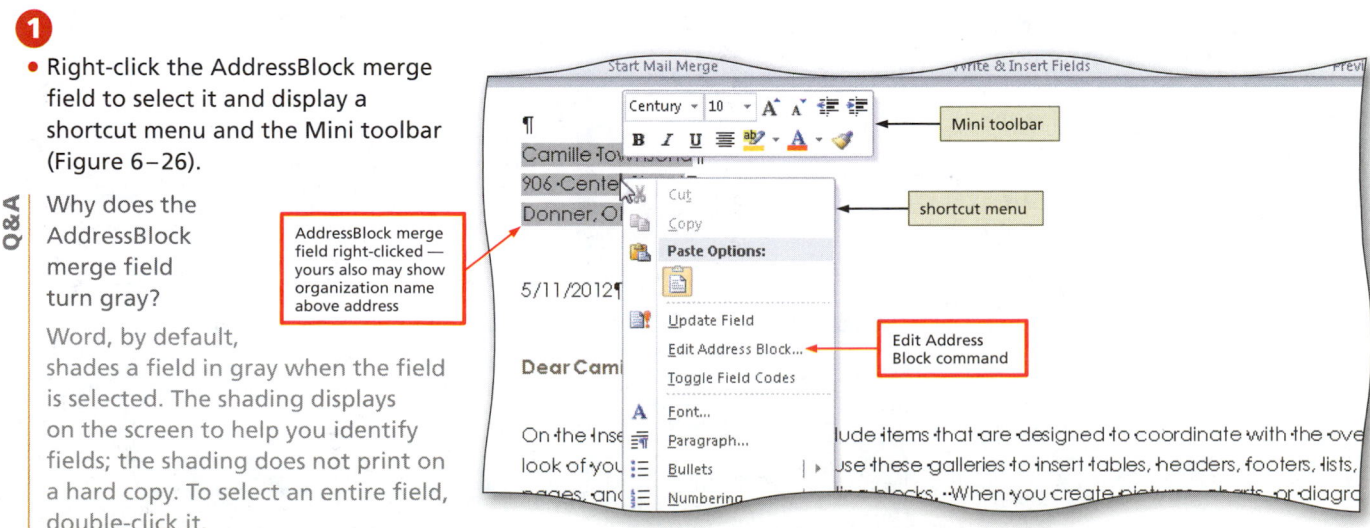

Figure 6–26

2
- Click Edit Address Block on the shortcut menu to display the Modify Address Block dialog box.

- Scroll through the list of recipient name formats (Modify Address Block dialog box) and then click the format, Mr. Joshua Randall Jr., in this list, because that format places the title to the left of the first name and last name.

🔍 **Experiment**
- Click various recipient name formats and watch the preview change in the dialog box. When finished experimenting, click the format: Mr. Joshua Randall Jr.

Q&A

What causes the 'Insert company name' check box to be dimmed?

If your data source does not have a match to the Company Name in the AddressBlock merge field, this check box will be dimmed. Recall that earlier in this project the Company Name field was renamed as Organization Name, which may cause the fields to be unmatched.

- If your AddressBlock merge field does not show the Organization Name above the address, click the Match Fields button (Modify Address Block dialog box) to display the Match Fields dialog box (Figure 6–27); if the Organization Name appears in your AddressBlock merge field, proceed to Step 5.

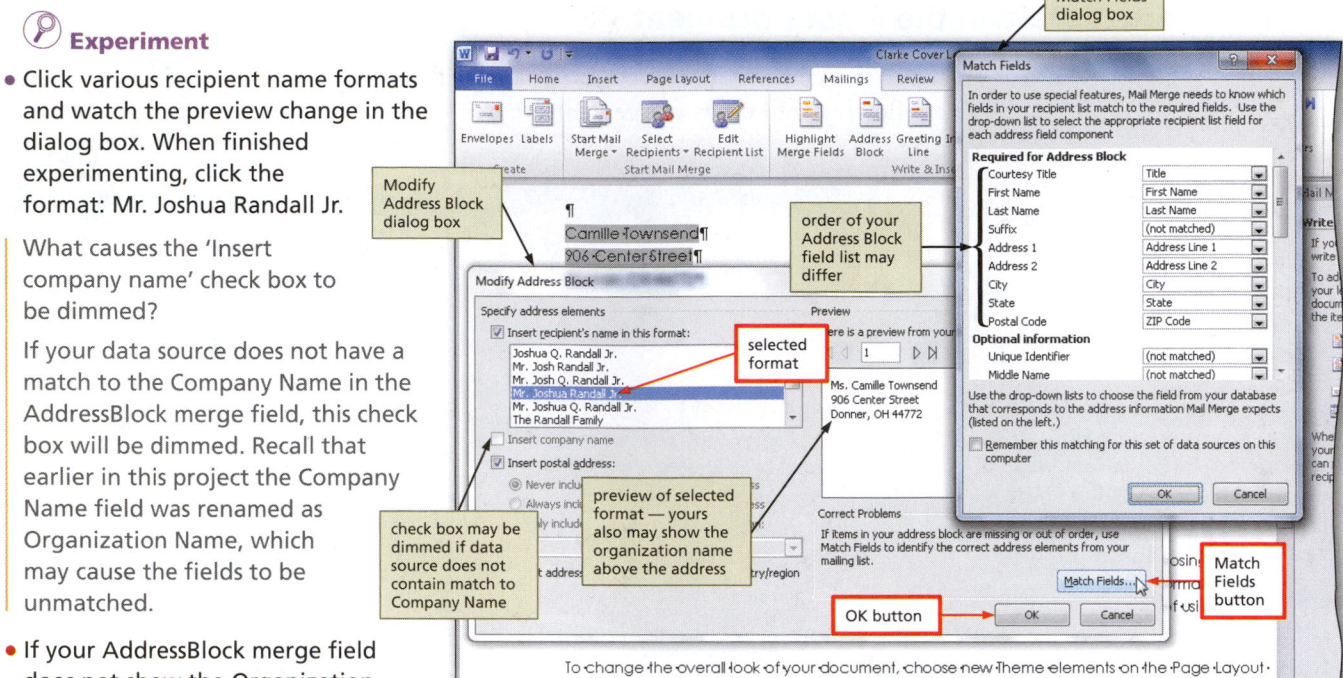

Figure 6–27

3
- If necessary, scroll through the Match Fields dialog box until Company appears.

- Click the Company box arrow (Match Fields dialog box) to display a list of fields in the data source and then click Organization Name to place that selected field as the match field.

- Click 'Remember this matching for this set of data sources on this computer' to place a check mark in the check box (Figure 6–28).

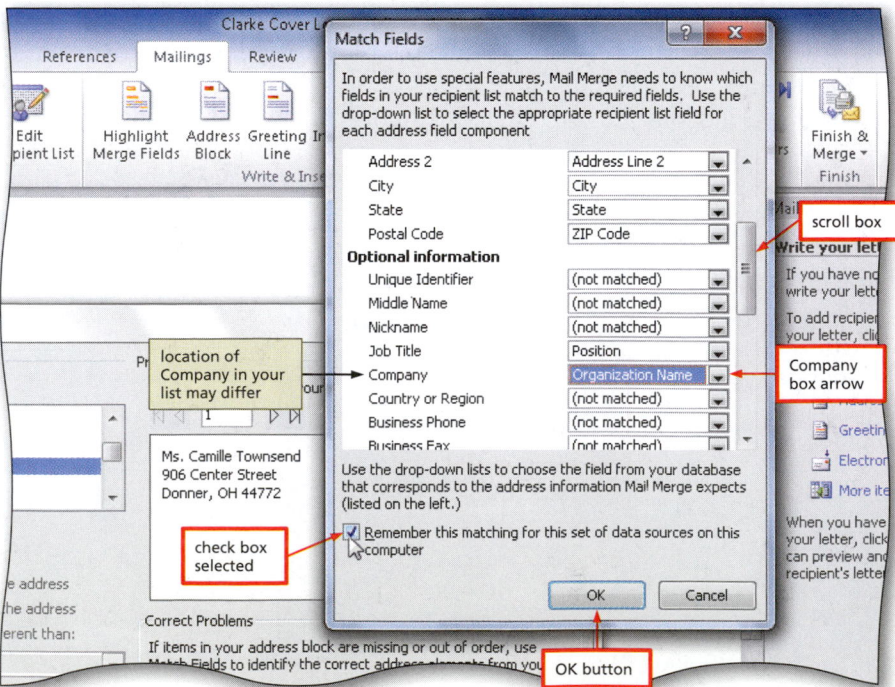

Figure 6–28

4

- Click the OK button (Match Fields dialog box) to close the dialog box, and notice the 'Insert company name' check box no longer is dimmed because the Company field now has a matched field in the data source.

- Click the 'Insert company name' check box to select it, and notice the preview area shows the organization name in the address (Figure 6–29).

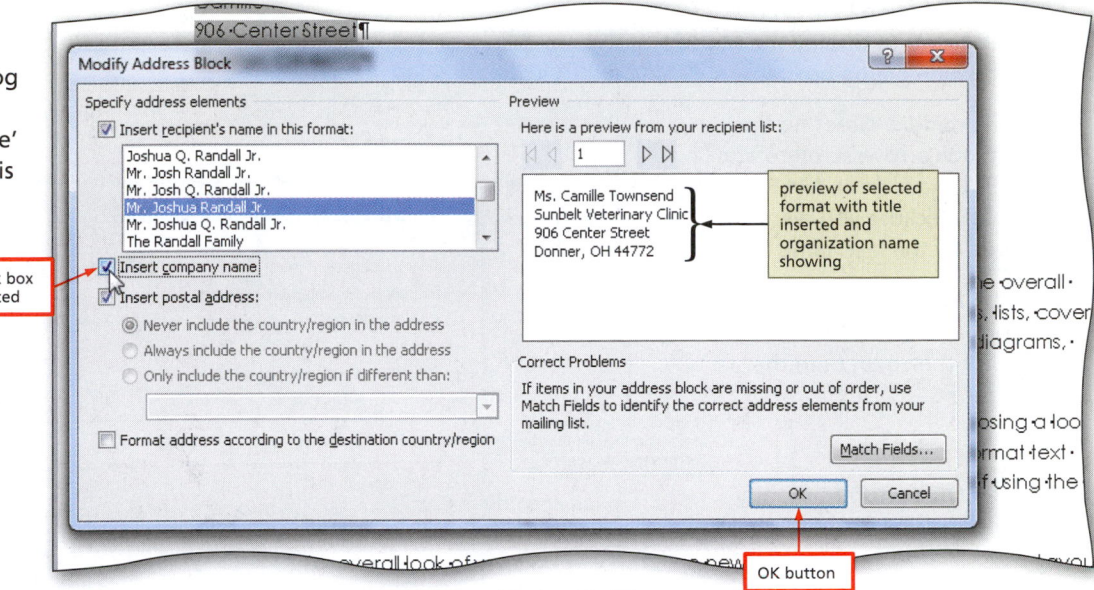

Figure 6–29

5

- Click the OK button (Modify Address Block dialog box) to modify the address block format.

To Edit the GreetingLine Merge Field

The **GreetingLine merge field** contains text and fields related to a salutation. The default greeting for the salutation is in the format, Dear Camille, followed by a comma. In this letter, you want a more formal salutation — Dear Ms. Townsend, followed by a colon. The following steps edit the GreetingLine merge field.

1

- Right-click the GreetingLine merge field to select it and display a shortcut menu and the Mini toolbar (Figure 6–30).

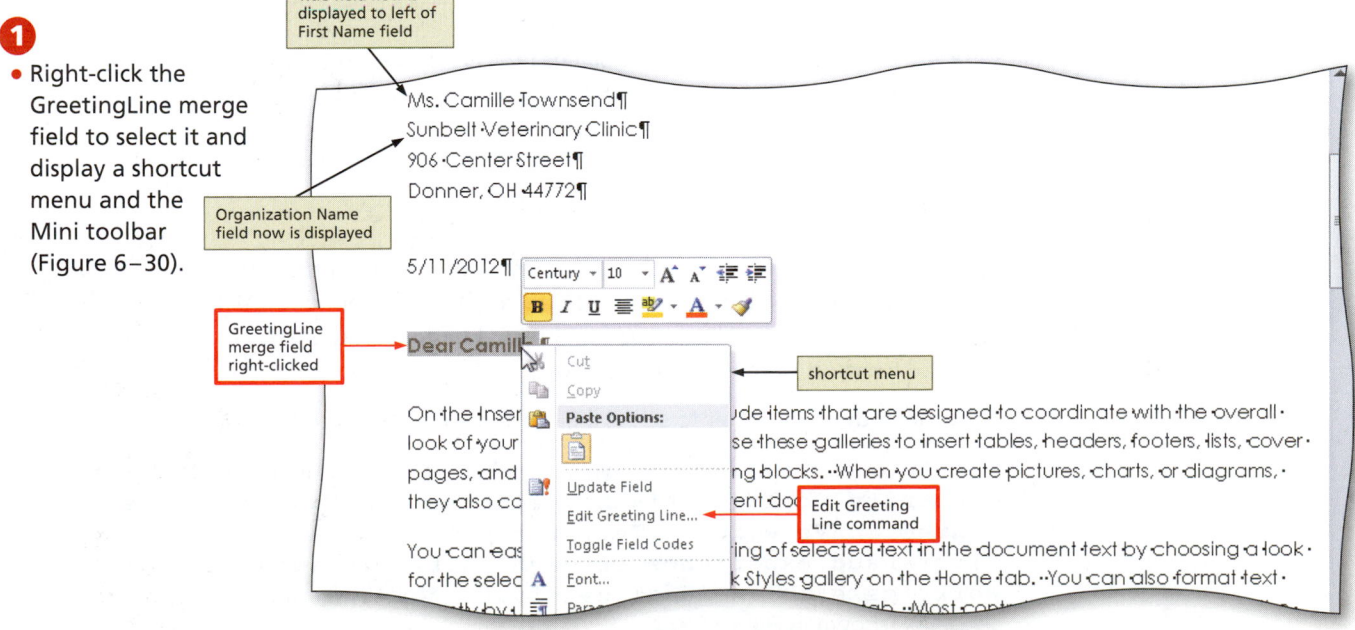

Figure 6–30

2
- Click Edit Greeting Line on the shortcut menu to display the Modify Greeting Line dialog box.

- Click the middle 'Greeting line format' box arrow; scroll to and then click the format, Mr. Randall, in this list because you want the title followed by the last name format.

- Click the rightmost 'Greeting line format' box arrow and then click the colon (:) in the list (Figure 6–31).

3
- Click the OK button to modify the greeting line format.

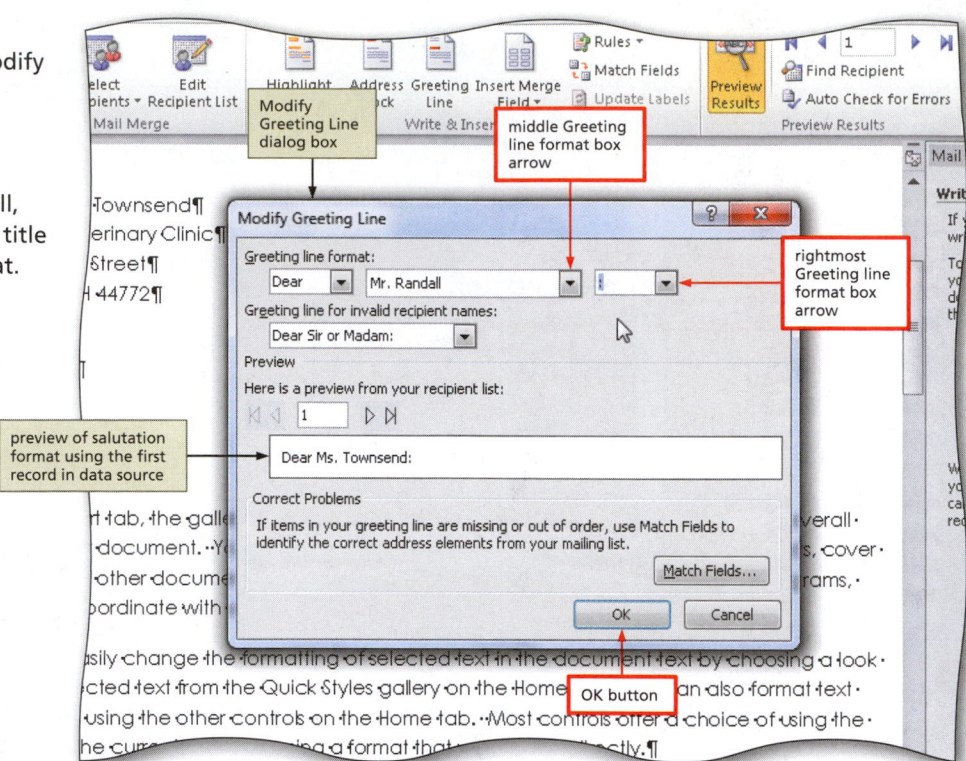

Figure 6–31

To View Merge Fields in the Main Document

Because you will be entering merge fields in the document next, you wish to display the merge fields instead of the merged data. The following step views merge fields instead of merged data.

1 Click the Preview Results button (Mailings tab | Preview Results group) to display the merge fields, instead of the values in the current data record (shown in Figure 6–32).

To Begin Typing the Body of the Form Letter

The next step is to begin typing the message, or body of the letter. This is to be located where Word displays the content control, Type the body of the letter, which contains three paragraphs of informational text. The following steps begin typing the letter in the location of the content control.

1 Click the body of the letter to select the content control (Figure 6–32).

2 With the content control selected, type `I will graduate from Donner Community College this May with an Associate of Science degree in Veterinary Technology. My education, along with first-hand experience through part-time jobs and volunteer work, make me an ideal candidate for the` and then press the SPACEBAR (shown in Figure 6–33).

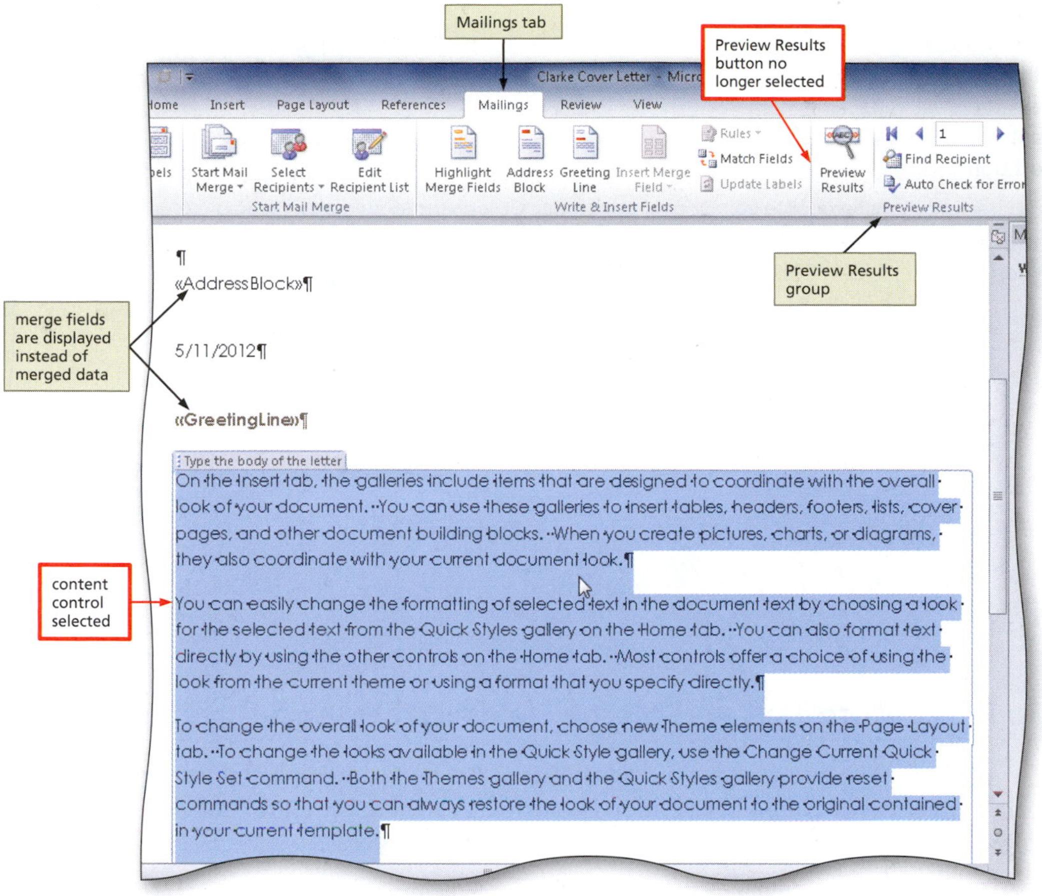

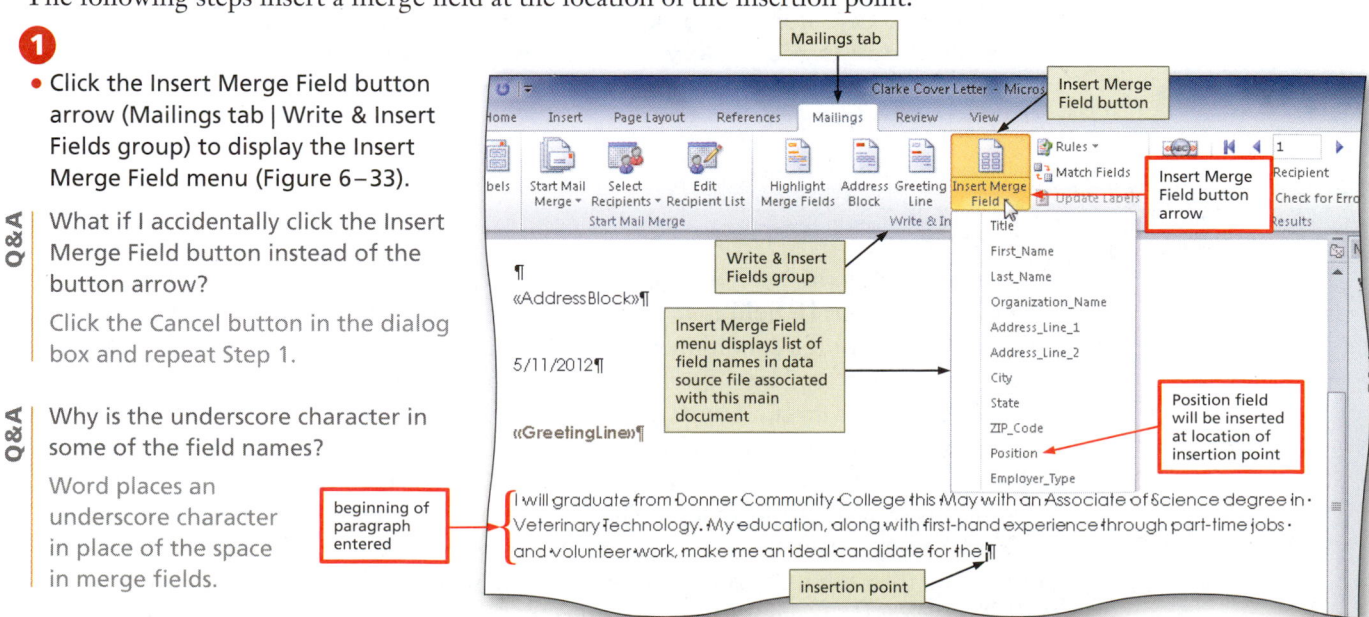

Figure 6–32

BTW

Insert Merge Field Button
If you click the Insert Merge Field button instead of the Insert Merge Field button arrow (Figure 6–33), Word displays the Insert Merge Field dialog box instead of the Insert Merge Field menu. To insert fields from the dialog box, click the field name and then click the Insert button. The dialog box remains open so that you can insert multiple fields, if necessary. When you have finished inserting fields, click the Close button in the dialog box.

To Insert a Merge Field in the Main Document

The second sentence in the first paragraph of the letter identifies the advertised job position. To instruct Word to use data fields from the data source, you insert merge fields in the main document for the form letter. The following steps insert a merge field at the location of the insertion point.

1

● Click the Insert Merge Field button arrow (Mailings tab | Write & Insert Fields group) to display the Insert Merge Field menu (Figure 6–33).

Q&A What if I accidentally click the Insert Merge Field button instead of the button arrow?

Click the Cancel button in the dialog box and repeat Step 1.

Q&A Why is the underscore character in some of the field names?

Word places an underscore character in place of the space in merge fields.

Figure 6–33

2

- Click Position on the Insert Merge Field menu to insert the selected merge field in the document at the location of the insertion point (Figure 6–34).

Q&A

Will the word, Position, and the chevron characters print when I merge the form letters?

No. When you merge the data source with the main document, the value in the Position field (e.g., Veterinary Technician) will print at the location of the merge field, Position.

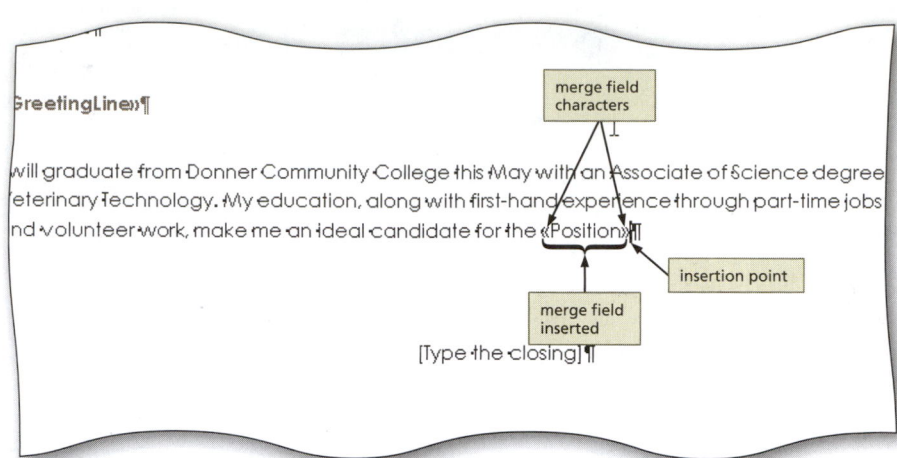

Figure 6–34

BTW

Merge Fields
When you insert fields in a document, the displayed fields may be surrounded by braces instead of chevrons, and extra instructions may appear between the braces. If this occurs, then field codes have been turned on. To turn off field codes so that they are not displayed, press ALT+F9.

To Enter More Text and Merge Fields in the Main Document

The next step is to enter the remainder of the first paragraph and part of the second paragraph, inserting the Organization Name merge field at the end of the first paragraph. The following steps enter more text and merge fields.

1 With the insertion point at the location shown in Figure 6–34, press the SPACEBAR. Type `position currently available at` and then press the SPACEBAR.

2 Click the Insert Merge Field button arrow (Mailings tab | Write & Insert Fields group) and then click Organization_Name on the Insert Merge Field menu to insert the selected merge field in the document.

3 Press the PERIOD key. Press the ENTER key. Type `As evidenced on the enclosed resume, my background matches the job requirements posted through the Career Development Office at Donner Community College. My coursework and experience have prepared me to assist during surgery and examinations, maintain records, and provide hands-on education at your` and then press the SPACEBAR (shown in Figure 6–35).

IF Fields

In addition to merge fields, you can insert Word fields that are designed specifically for a mail merge. An **IF field** is an example of a Word field. One form of the IF field is called an **If...Then:** If a condition is true, then perform an action. For example, If Mary owns a house, then send her information about homeowner's insurance. Another form of the IF field is called an **If...Then...Else:** If a condition is true, then perform an action; else perform a different action. For example, If John has an e-mail address, then send him an e-mail message; else send him the message via the postal service.

In this project, the form letter checks the employer's type. If the employer type is C (for clinic), then the letter should print the word, practice; else if the employer type is S (for school), then the letter should print the word, school. Thus, you will use an If...Then...Else: If the employer type is equal to C, then insert the word practice, else insert the word school.

The phrase that appears after the word If is called a rule or a condition. A **condition** consists of an expression, followed by a comparison operator, followed by a final expression.

Expression   The expression in a condition can be a merge field, a number, a series of characters, or a mathematical formula. Word surrounds a series of characters with quotation marks ("). To indicate an empty, or null, expression, Word places two quotation marks together ("").

Comparison operator   The comparison operator in a condition must be one of six characters: = (equal to or matches the text), <> (not equal to or does not match text), < (less than), <= (less than or equal to), > (greater than), or >= (greater than or equal to).

If the result of a condition is true, then Word evaluates the **true text**. If the result of the condition is false, Word evaluates the **false text** if it exists. In this project, the first expression in the condition is a merge field (Employer_Type); the comparison operator is equal to (=); and the second expression is the text "C". The true text is "practice". The false text is "school". The complete IF field is as follows:

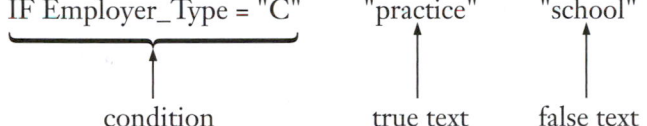

IF Employer_Type = "C"	"practice"	"school"
condition	true text	false text

BTW

IF Fields
The phrase, IF field, originates from computer programming. Do not be intimidated by the terminology. An IF field simply specifies a decision. Some programmers refer to it as an IF statement. Complex IF statements include one or more nested IF fields, which is a second IF field inside the true or false text of the first IF field.

To Insert an IF Field in the Main Document

The following steps insert this IF field in the form letter: If the employer type is C, then insert the text, practice; else insert the text, school.

1

• With the insertion point positioned as shown in Figure 6–35, click the Rules button (Mailings tab | Write & Insert Fields group) to display the Rules menu (Figure 6–35).

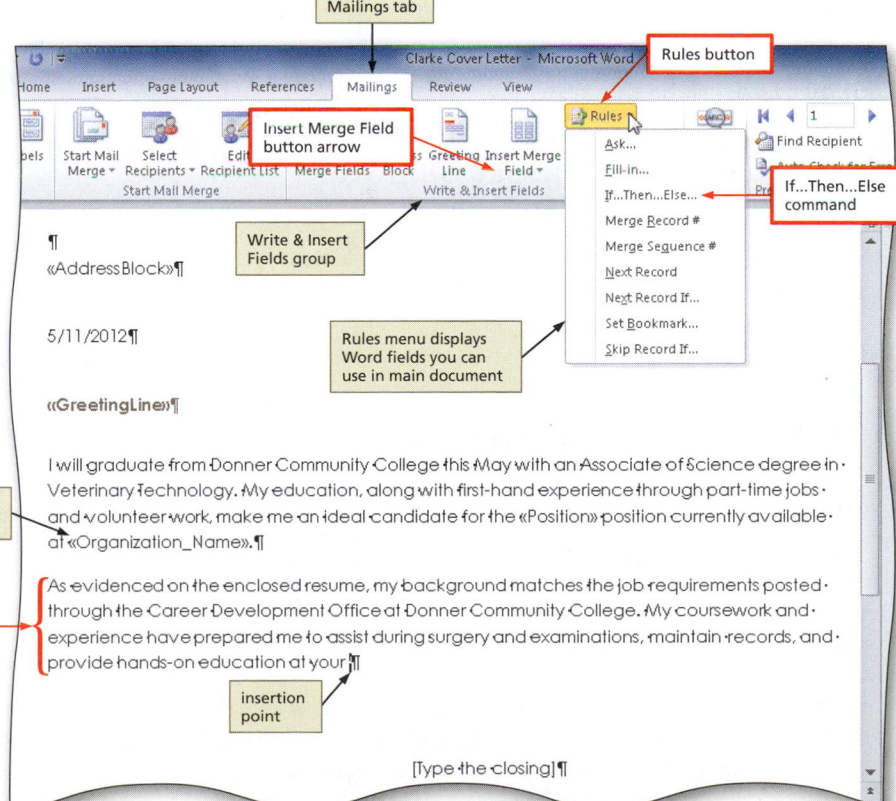

Figure 6–35

2
- Click If...Then...Else on the Rules menu to display the Insert Word Field: IF dialog box (Figure 6–36).

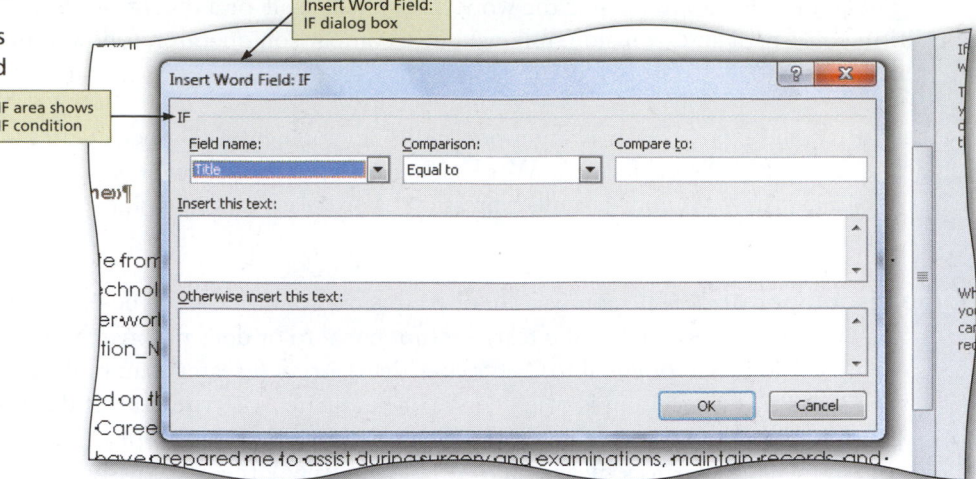

Figure 6–36

3
- Click the Field name box arrow to display the list of fields in the data source.

- Scroll through the list of fields in the Field name list and then click Employer_Type to select the field.

- Position the insertion point in the Compare to text box and then type C as the comparison text.

- Press the TAB key and then type **practice** as the true text.

- Press the TAB key and then type **school** as the false text (Figure 6–37).

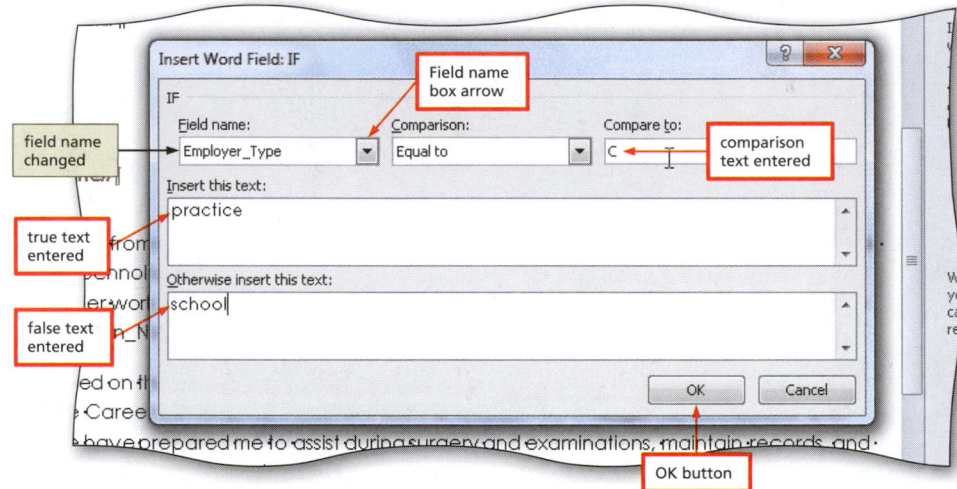

Figure 6–37

Q&A Does the capitalization matter in the comparison text?

Yes. The text, C, is different from the text, c, in a comparison. Be sure to enter the text exactly as you entered it in the data source.

4
- Click the OK button to insert the IF field at the location of the insertion point (Figure 6–38).

Q&A Why does the main document display the word, practice, instead of the IF field instructions?

The word, practice, is displayed because the first record in the data source has a employer type of C.

As evidenced on the enclosed resume, my background matches the job requirements posted through the Career Development Office at Donner Community College. My coursework and experience have prepared me to assist during surgery and examinations, maintain records, and provide hands-on education at your practice¶

field results are displayed for entered IF field, instead of IF field instructions

insertion point

Figure 6–38

Word, by default, evaluates the IF field using the current record and displays the results, called the **field results**, in the main document instead of displaying the IF field instructions. Later in the chapter, you will view the IF field instructions.

To Enter More Text and Merge Fields

BTW

Word Fields
In addition to the IF field, Word provides other fields that may be used in form letters. For example, the ASK and FILLIN fields prompt the user to enter data for each record in the data source. The SKIP RECORD IF field instructs the mail merge not to generate a form letter for a data record if a specific condition is met.

The following steps enter the remainder of the form letter.

1 Press the PERIOD key to finish the sentence.

2 If necessary, scroll to display the bottom of the letter in the document window.

3 Press the ENTER key. Type `I will call you next week to see if we can set up a time to discuss my qualifications further. Thank you,` and then press the SPACEBAR.

4 Click the Insert Merge Field button arrow (Mailings tab | Write & Insert Fields group) and then click Title on the Insert Merge Field menu to insert the selected merge field in the document.

5 Press the SPACEBAR. Click the Insert Merge Field button arrow (Mailings tab | Write & Insert Fields group) and then click Last_Name on the Insert Merge Field menu to insert the selected merge field in the document.

6 Type `, for your time and consideration.`

7 Select the closing content control and then type `Sincerely,` as the closing.

8 Right-click the content control with the placeholder text, Type the sender company name, to display a shortcut menu and then click Remove Content Control on the shortcut menu.

Q&A What if my content control already displays a sender company name instead of placeholder text?

Select the text and then delete it.

9 Press the ENTER key. Display the Home tab and then click the Decrease Indent button (Home tab | Paragraph group) six times to move the paragraph to the left margin. Type `Enclosure` as the last line of text in the letter (Figure 6–39).

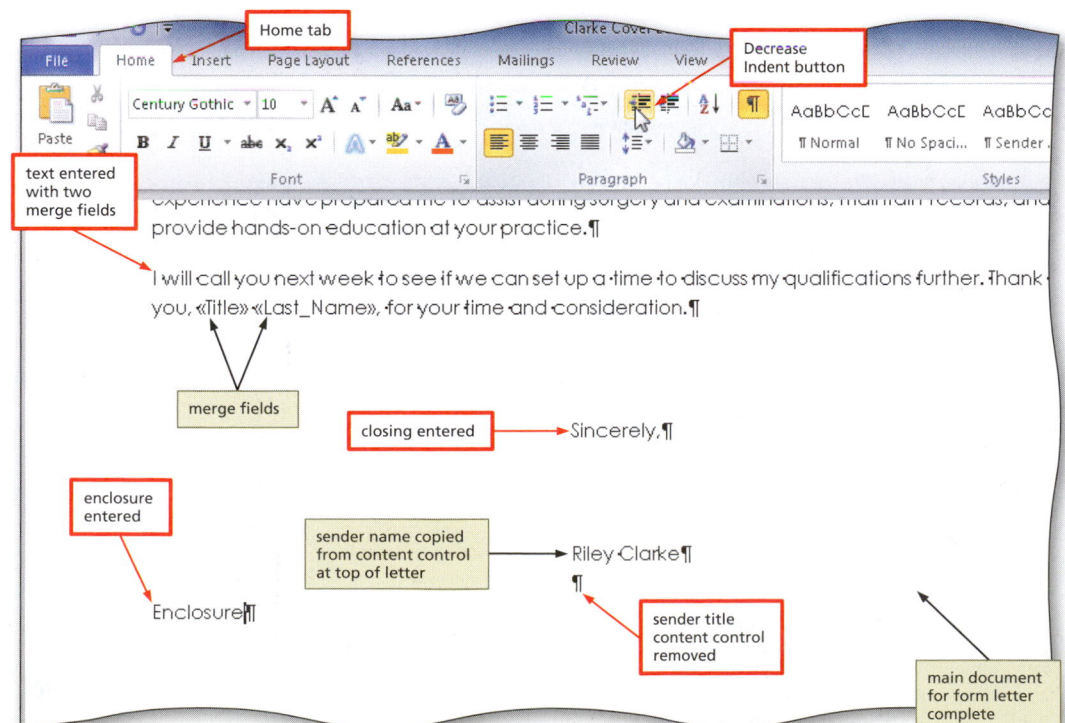

Figure 6–39

To Highlight Merge Fields

If you wanted to highlight all the merge fields in a document so that you could identify them quickly, you would perform the following steps.

1. Click the Highlight Merge Fields button (Mailings tab | Write & Insert Fields group) to highlight the merge fields in the document.

2. When finished viewing merge fields, click the Highlight Merge Fields button (Mailings tab | Write & Insert Fields group) again to remove the highlight from the merge fields in the document.

To Display a Field Code

The instructions in the IF field are not displayed in the document; instead, the field results are displayed for the current record (Figure 6–40). The instructions of an IF field are called **field codes**, and the default for Word is for field codes not to be displayed. Thus, field codes do not print or show on the screen unless you turn them on. You use one procedure to show field codes on the screen and a different procedure to print them on a hard copy.

You might want to turn on a field code to verify its accuracy or to modify it. Field codes tend to clutter the screen. Thus, most Word users turn them off after viewing them. The following steps show a field code on the screen.

- Scroll up to display the letter in the document window.

- Right-click the field results showing the word, practice, to display a shortcut menu (Figure 6–40).

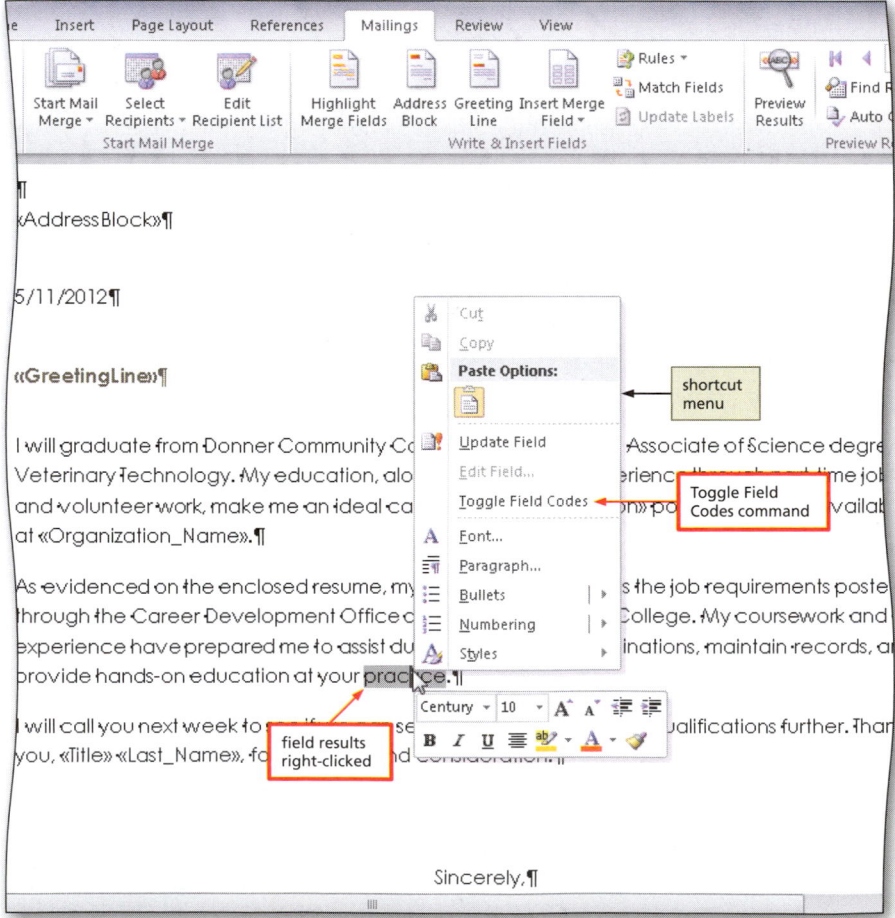

Figure 6–40

2

- Click Toggle Field Codes on the shortcut menu to display the field code instead of the field results for the IF field (Figure 6–41).

Q&A Will displaying field codes affect the merged documents?

No. Displaying field codes has no effect on the merge process.

Q&A What if I wanted to display all field codes in a document?

You would press ALT+F9. Then, to hide all the field codes, press ALT+F9 again.

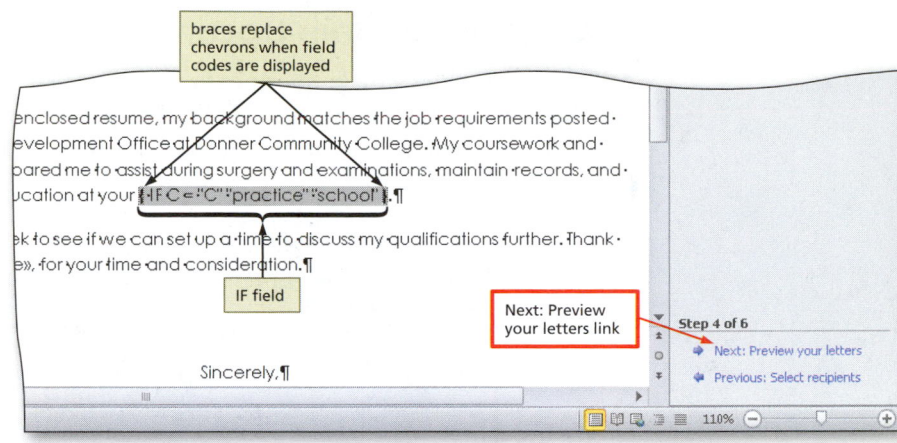

braces replace chevrons when field codes are displayed

enclosed resume, my background matches the job requirements posted · development Office at Donner Community College. My coursework and · pared me to assist during surgery and examinations, maintain records, and · ucation at your { IF C <>"C" "practice" "school" }.¶

ek to see if we can set up a time to discuss my qualifications further. Thank · e», for your time and consideration.¶

IF field

Next: Preview your letters link

Step 4 of 6
→ Next: Preview your letters
← Previous: Select recipients

Sincerely,¶

110%

Figure 6–41

Other Ways
1. With insertion point in field, press SHIFT+F9

TO PRINT FIELD CODES IN THE MAIN DOCUMENT

When you merge or print a document, Word automatically converts field codes that show on the screen to field results. You may want to print the field codes version of the form letter, however, so that you have a hard copy of the field codes for future reference. When you print field codes, you must remember to turn off the field codes option so that merged documents print field results instead of field codes. If you wanted to print the field codes in the main document, you would perform the following steps.

1. Open the Backstage view and then click Options to display the Word Options dialog box.
2. Click Advanced in the left pane to display advanced options in the right pane and then scroll to the Print area in the right pane of the dialog box.
3. Place a check mark in the 'Print field codes instead of their values' check box.
4. Click the OK button to instruct Word to show field codes when the document prints.
5. Open the Backstage view, click the Print tab, and then click the Print button to print the document with all field codes showing.
6. Open the Backstage view and then click Options to display the Word Options dialog box.
7. Click Advanced in the left pane to display advanced options in the right pane and then scroll to the Print area in the right pane of the dialog box.
8. Remove the check mark from the 'Print field codes instead of their values' check box.
9. Click the OK button to instruct Word to show field results the next time you print the document.

To Save a Document Again

The main document for the form letter now is complete. Thus, you should save it again. The following step saves the document again.

1 Save the main document for the form letter again with the same file name, Clarke Cover Letter.

BTW

Converting Main Document Files
If you wanted to convert a mail merge main document to a regular Word document, you would open the main document, click the Start Mail Merge button (Mailings tab | Start Mail Merge group), and then click Normal Word Document on the Start Mail Merge menu.

Opening a Main Document

You open a main document as you open any other Word document (i.e., clicking Open in the Backstage view). If Word displays a dialog box indicating it will run an SQL command, click the Yes button (Figure 6–42).

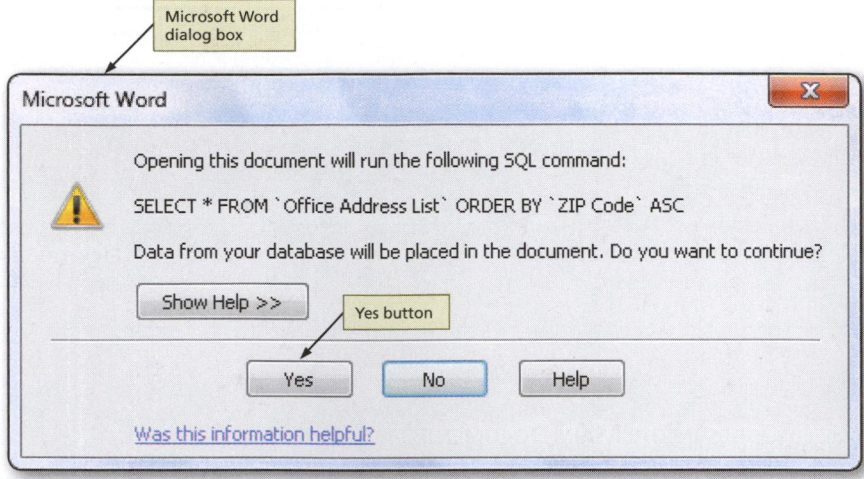

Figure 6–42

Data Source and Main Document Files

When you open a main document, if Word cannot locate the associated data source file or it does not display a dialog box with the Find Data Source button, then the data source may not be associated with the main document. To associate the data source with the main document, click the Select Recipients button (Mailings tab | Start Mail Merge group), click Use Existing List, and then locate the data source file. When you save the main document, Word will associate the data source with the main document.

When you open a main document, Word attempts to open the associated data source file, too. If the data source is not in exactly the same location (i.e., drive and folder) as when it originally was saved, Word displays a dialog box indicating that it could not find the data source (Figure 6–43). When this occurs, click the Find Data Source button to display the Open Data Source dialog box, which allows you to locate the data source file. (Word may display several dialog boxes requiring you to click an OK (or similar) button until the one shown in Figure 6–43 appears.)

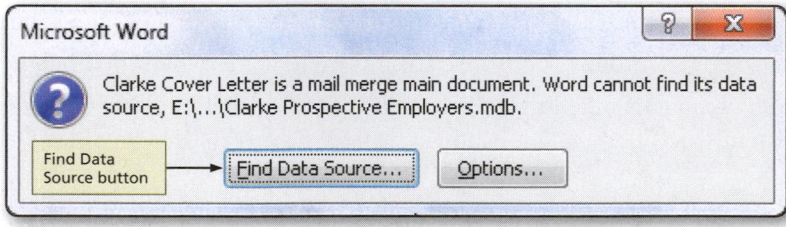

Figure 6–43

Break Point: If you wish to take a break, this is a good place to do so. You can quit Word now. To resume at a later time, start Word, open the file called Clarke Cover Letter, and continue following the steps from this location forward.

Merging the Data Source with the Main Document to Generate Form Letters

The next step in this project is to merge the data source with the main document to generate the form letters (shown in Figure 6–1c on page WD 331). You can generate the form letters to a new document or to a printer. You also can select certain records to merge and sort the records before merging. The following pages discuss these various ways to merge.

To Preview the Merged Letters

The next step in the Mail Merge wizard is to preview the letters. Earlier in this chapter, you previewed the letters using a button on the Ribbon. The following step uses the Mail Merge wizard to preview the letters.

- Click the Next: Preview your letters link at the bottom of the Mail Merge task pane (shown in Figure 6–41 on page WD 359) to display Step 5 of the Mail Merge wizard in the Mail Merge task pane (Figure 6–44).

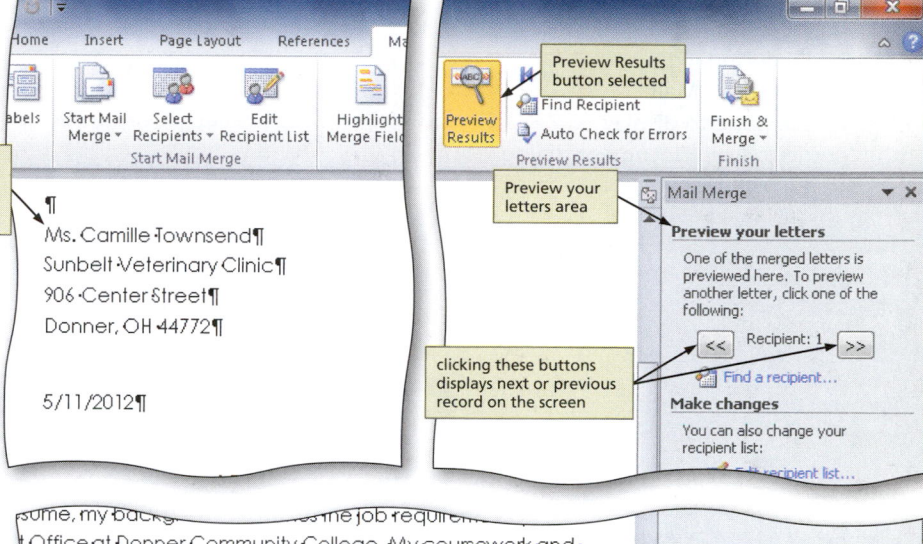

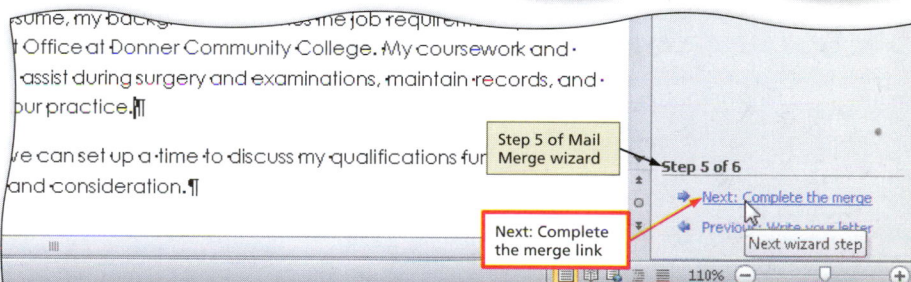

Figure 6–44

Other Ways

1. Click Preview Results button (Mailings tab | Preview Results group)

TO CHECK FOR ERRORS

Before merging documents, you can instruct Word to check for errors that might occur during the merge process. If you wanted to check for errors, you would perform the following steps.

1. Click the Auto Check for Errors button (Mailings tab | Preview Results group) to display the Checking and Reporting Errors dialog box.

2. Select the desired option and then click the OK button.

To Merge the Form Letters to a New Document

With the data source and main document for the form letter complete, the next step is to merge them to generate the individual form letters. You can merge the letters to a new document or to the printer. If you merge the documents to a new document, you can save the merged documents in a file in print them later or you can edit the contents of individual merged letters. Or, you can review the merged documents for accuracy and then close the file without saving it. The steps on the next page merge the form letters, sending the merged letters to a new document and then zoom the document window to display all merged documents at once.

BTW

Locking Fields
If you wanted to lock a field so that its field results cannot be changed, click the field and then press CTRL+F11. To subsequently unlock a field so that it may be updated, click the field and then press CTRL+SHIFT+F11.

- Click the Next: Complete the merge link at the bottom of the Mail Merge task pane (shown in Figure 6–44 on the previous page) to display Step 6 of the Mail Merge wizard in the Mail Merge task pane.

- Click the 'Edit individual letters' link in the Mail Merge task pane to display the Merge to New Document dialog box (Figure 6–45).

Q&A What if I wanted to print the merged letters immediately instead of reviewing them first in a new document window?

You would click the Print link instead of the 'Edit individual letters' link.

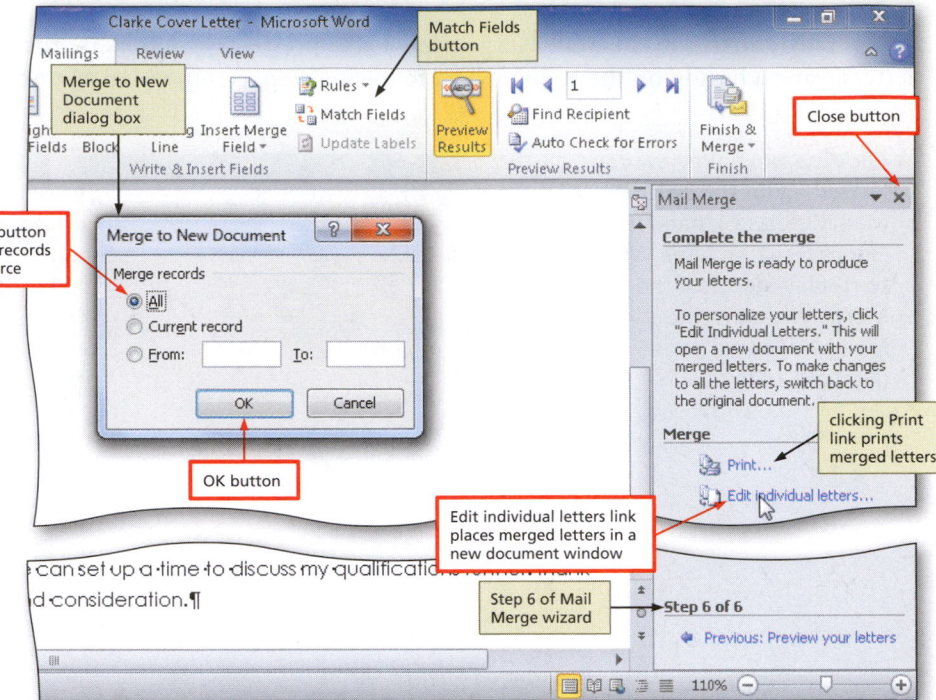

Figure 6–45

- If necessary, click All (Merge to New Document dialog box) so that all records in the data source are merged.

Q&A Do I have to merge all records?

No. Through this dialog box, you can merge the current record or a range of record numbers.

- Click the OK button to merge the letters to a new document, in this case, five individual letters — one for each potential employer in the data source. (If Word displays a dialog box containing a message about locked fields, click its OK button.)

- To see all merged letters at once in the document window, display the View tab and then click the Zoom button (View tab | Zoom group) to display the Zoom dialog box.

- Click the Many pages button (Zoom dialog box) and then point to the third icon in the second row in the grid to specify the number of pages to be displayed in the document window at one time (Figure 6–46).

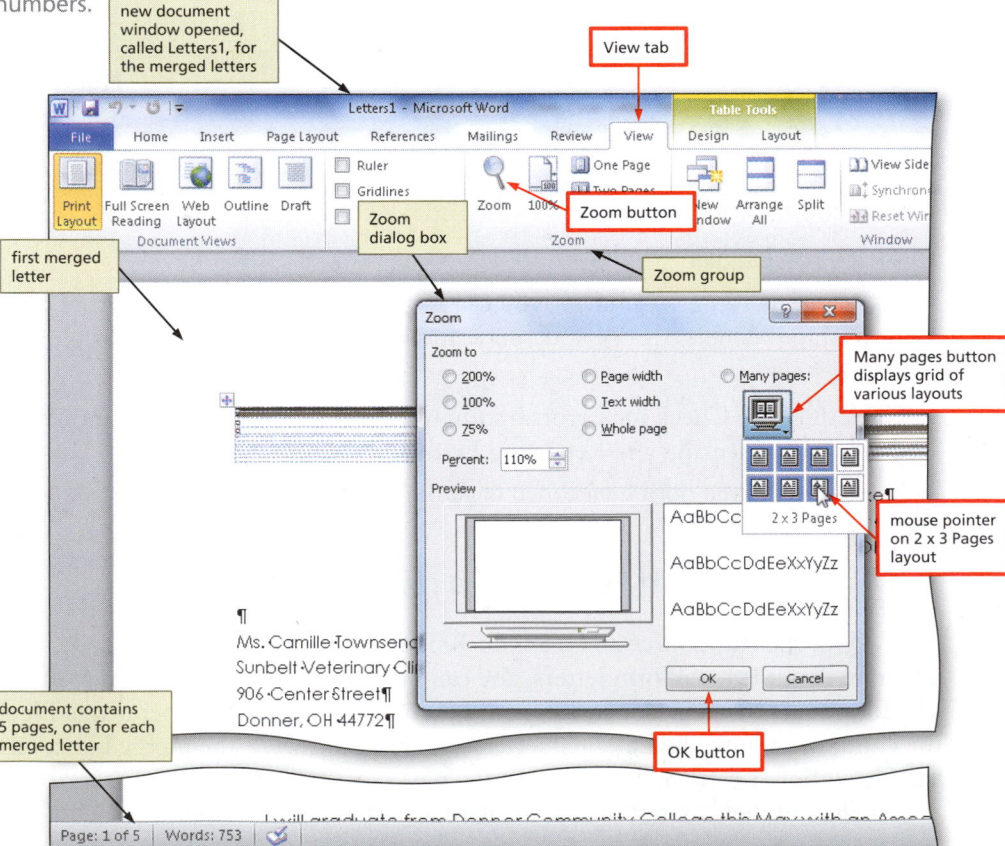

Figure 6–46

4

- Click the 2 × 3 Pages layout in the grid and then click the OK button to display the specified number of pages in the document window at once (Figure 6–47).

Q&A Do I have to display all documents at once in the document window?

No. You can scroll through the documents instead, as you would in any other multipage document.

Q&A Why does my screen show an extra blank page at the end?

You might have a blank record in the data source, or the spacing may cause an overflow to a blank page.

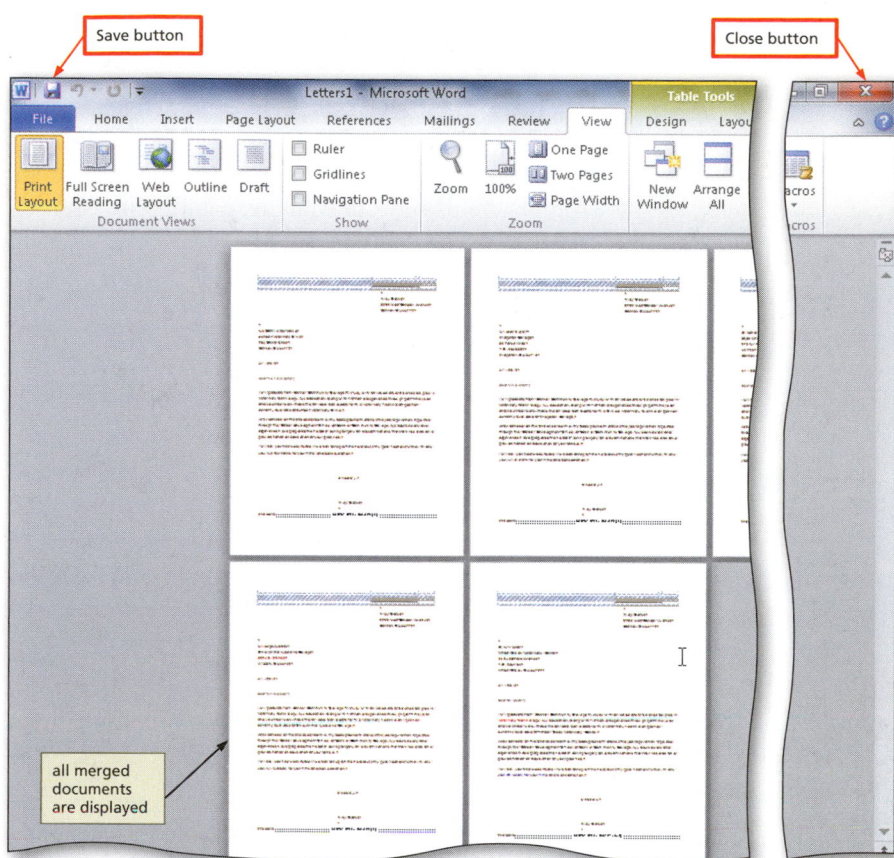

Figure 6–47

Other Ways

1. Click Finish & Merge button (Mailings tab | Finish group), click Edit Individual Documents

To Save the Merged Documents in a File and Close the Document Window

The following steps save the merged letters in a file and then close the document window containing the merged letters.

1 Click the Save button on the Quick Access Toolbar to display the Save As dialog box.

2 Type **Clarke Merged Letters** in the File name text box (Save As dialog box) as the name for the merged documents file. Do not press the ENTER key after typing the file name because you do not want to close the dialog box at this time.

3 If necessary, navigate to the desired save location for the merged documents file (in this case, the Job Hunting folder in the Word folder in the CIS 101 folder [or your class folder] on the USB flash drive).

4 Click the Save button (Save As dialog box) to save the document containing the merged letters in the selected folder using the entered file name.

Q&A Do I have to save the document containing the merged letters?

No. You can scroll through the documents instead, as you would in any other multipage document, and then close the document without saving it.

5 Click the Close button on the right side of the document window to close the document.

6 Click the Close button on the Mail Merge task pane title bar (shown in Figure 6–45) because you are finished with the Mail Merge wizard.

BTW

Merging to E-Mail Messages
If you are merging to e-mail messages, you will click an Electronic Mail link in the Step 6 of 6 Mail Merge task pane to display a Merge to E-mail dialog box. Then, click the To box arrow (Merge to E-mail dialog box) and select the field name that contains e-mail addresses in the data source, enter the subject line for the e-mail messages, select the desired mail format, click All or another option in the Send records area, and then click the OK button to merge the messages to the e-mail addresses.

Correcting Errors in Merged Documents

If you notice errors in the merged form letters, edit the main document the same way you edit any other document. Then, save the changes and merge again. If the wrong field results print, Word may be mapping the fields incorrectly. To view fields, click the Match Fields button (Mailings tab | Write & Insert Fields group) (Figure 6–45 on page WD 362). Then, review the list of fields in the list. For example, Last Name should map to the Last Name field in the data source. If it does not, click the box arrow to change the name of the data source field.

If the fields are mapped correctly, the data in the data source may be incorrect. For a discussion about editing records in the data source, refer to page WD 346.

To Merge the Form Letters to the Printer

To print the merged documents, you could print the document just created that contains the five merged letters, or you can merge the form letters again and send them directly to the printer. The following steps merge the form letters and send them to the printer, using a button on the Ribbon.

1
- If necessary, display the Mailings tab.

- Click the Finish & Merge button (Mailings tab | Finish group) to display the Finish & Merge menu (Figure 6–48).

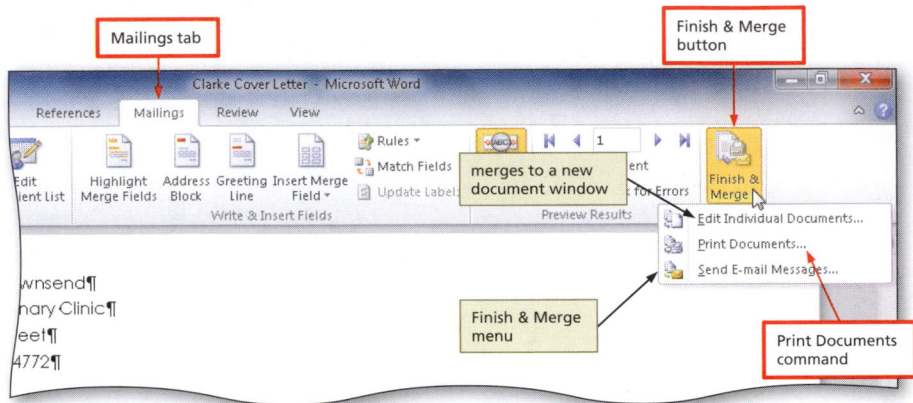

Figure 6–48

2
- Click Print Documents to display the Merge to Printer dialog box (Figure 6–49).

3
- If necessary, click All (Merge to Printer dialog box) and then click the OK button to display the Print dialog box.

- Click the OK button (Print dialog box) to print five separate letters, one for each potential employer in the data source, as shown in Figure 6–1c on page WD 331. (If Word displays a message about locked fields, click its OK button.)

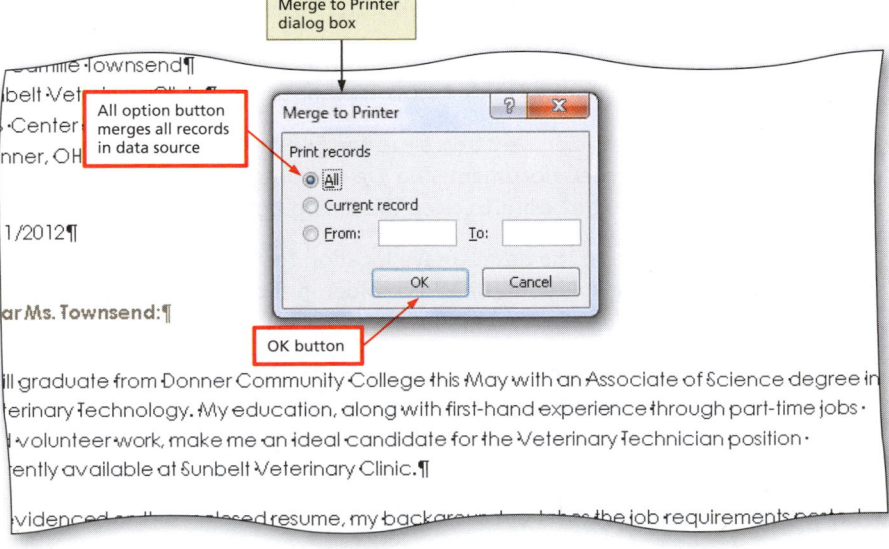

Figure 6–49

Other Ways

1. Print link in Mail Merge task pane

To Select Records to Merge

Instead of merging all of the records in the data source, you can choose which records to merge, based on a condition you specify. The dialog box in Figure 6–49 allows you to specify by record number which records to merge. Often, though, you want to merge based on the contents of a specific field. For example, you may want to merge and print only those employers whose employer type is S (for school). The following steps select records for a merge.

1

• Click the Edit Recipient List button (Mailings tab | Start Mail Merge group) to display the Mail Merge Recipients dialog box (Figure 6–50).

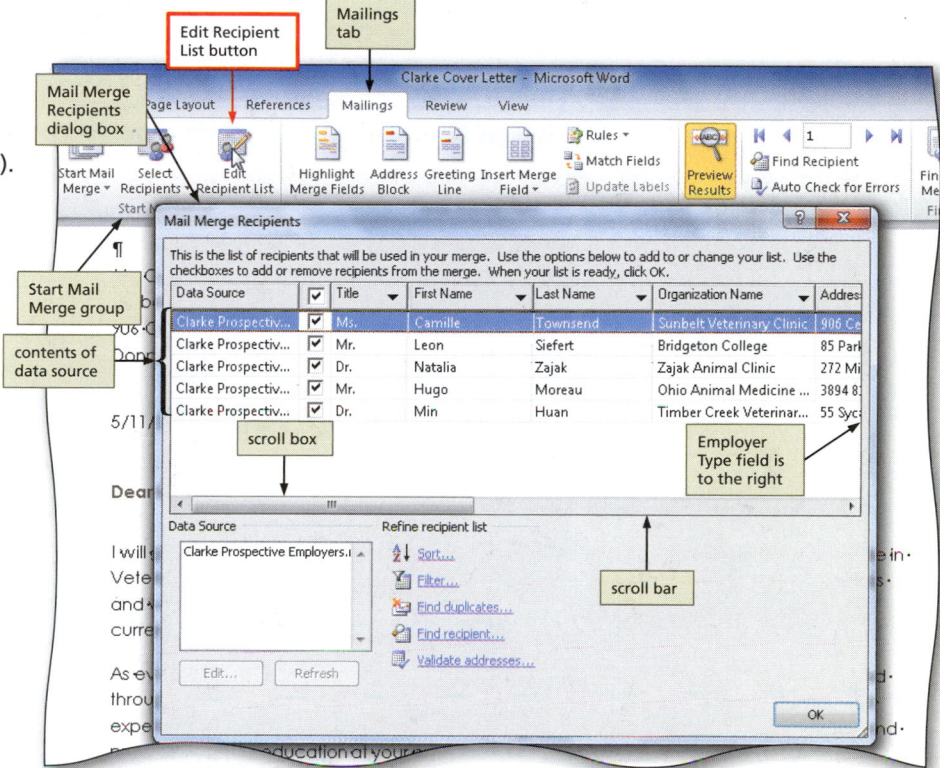

Figure 6–50

2

• Drag the scroll box to the right edge of the scroll bar (Mail Merge Recipients dialog box) so that the Employer Type field appears in the dialog box.

• Click the button arrow to the right of the field name, Employer Type, to display sort and filter criteria for the selected field (Figure 6–51).

Q&A

What are the filter criteria in the parentheses?

The (All) option clears any previously set filter criteria. The (Blanks) option selects records that contain blanks in that field, and the (Nonblanks) option selects records that do not contain blanks in that field. The (Advanced) option displays the Filter and Sort dialog box, which allows you to perform more advanced record selection operations.

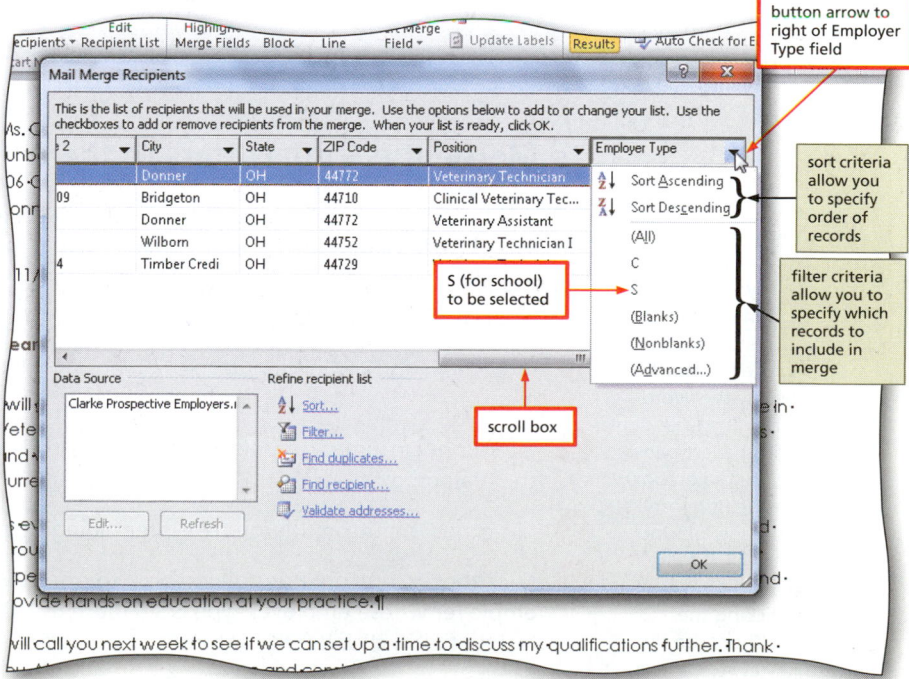

Figure 6–51

3
- Click S to reduce the number of data records displayed (Mail Merge Recipients dialog box) to two, because two potential employers are schools (Figure 6–52).

4
- Click the OK button to close the Mail Merge Recipients dialog box.

Q&A

What happened to the other three records that did not meet the criteria?

They still are part of the data source; they just are not appearing in the Mail Merge Recipients dialog box. When you clear the filter, all records will reappear.

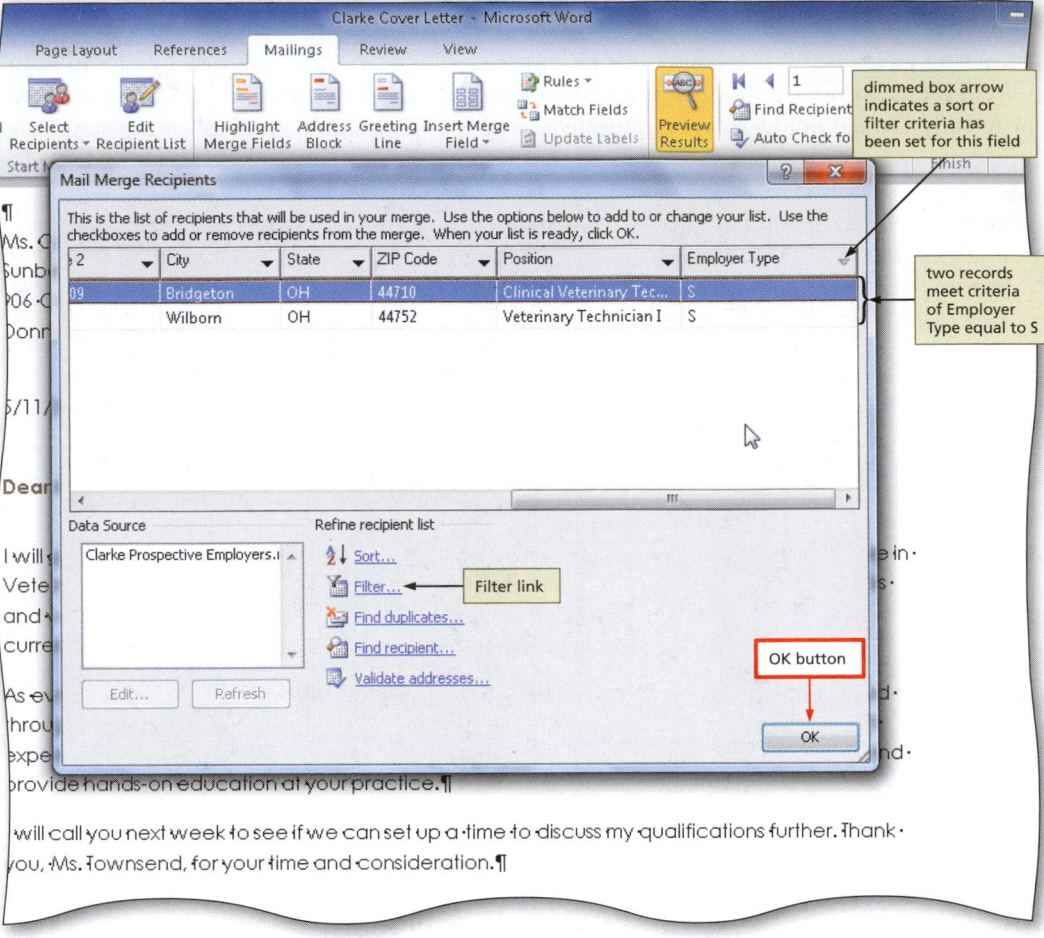

Figure 6–52

Other Ways

1. Click Filter link (Mail Merge Recipients dialog box), click Filter Records tab, enter filter criteria, click OK button

BTW

Conserving Ink and Toner
If you want to conserve ink or toner, you can instruct Word to print draft quality documents by clicking File on the Ribbon to open the Backstage view, clicking Options in the Backstage view to display the Word Options dialog box, clicking Advanced in the left pane (Word Options dialog box), scrolling to the Print area in the right pane, placing a check mark in the 'Use draft quality' check box, and then clicking the OK button. Then, use the Backstage view to print the document as usual.

To Merge the Form Letters to the Printer

The next step is to merge the selected records. To do this, you follow the same steps described earlier. The difference is that Word will merge only those records that meet the criteria specified, that is, just those with an employer type of S. The following steps merge the filtered records to the printer.

1 Click the Finish & Merge button (Mailings tab | Finish group) to display the Finish & Merge menu.

2 Click Print Documents to display the Merge to Printer dialog box. If necessary, click All in the dialog box.

3 Click the OK button (Merge to Printer dialog box) to display the Print dialog box.

4 Click the OK button (Print dialog box) to print two separate letters, one for each potential employer whose employer type is S (Figure 6–53). (If Word displays a message about locked fields, click its OK button.)

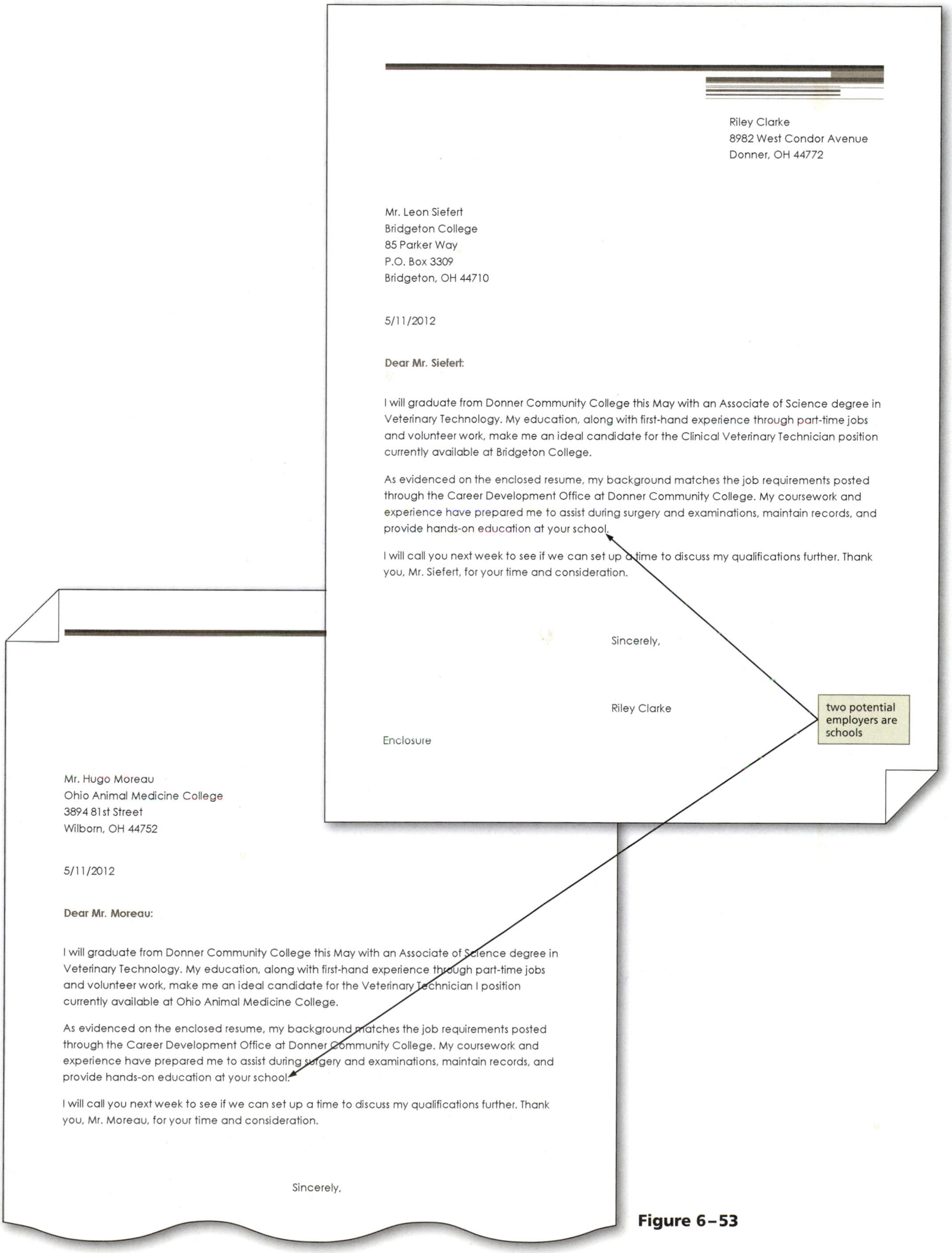

Riley Clarke
8982 West Condor Avenue
Donner, OH 44772

Mr. Leon Siefert
Bridgeton College
85 Parker Way
P.O. Box 3309
Bridgeton, OH 44710

5/11/2012

Dear Mr. Siefert:

I will graduate from Donner Community College this May with an Associate of Science degree in Veterinary Technology. My education, along with first-hand experience through part-time jobs and volunteer work, make me an ideal candidate for the Clinical Veterinary Technician position currently available at Bridgeton College.

As evidenced on the enclosed resume, my background matches the job requirements posted through the Career Development Office at Donner Community College. My coursework and experience have prepared me to assist during surgery and examinations, maintain records, and provide hands-on education at your school.

I will call you next week to see if we can set up a time to discuss my qualifications further. Thank you, Mr. Siefert, for your time and consideration.

Sincerely,

Riley Clarke

Enclosure

two potential employers are schools

Mr. Hugo Moreau
Ohio Animal Medicine College
3894 81st Street
Wilborn, OH 44752

5/11/2012

Dear Mr. Moreau:

I will graduate from Donner Community College this May with an Associate of Science degree in Veterinary Technology. My education, along with first-hand experience through part-time jobs and volunteer work, make me an ideal candidate for the Veterinary Technician I position currently available at Ohio Animal Medicine College.

As evidenced on the enclosed resume, my background matches the job requirements posted through the Career Development Office at Donner Community College. My coursework and experience have prepared me to assist during surgery and examinations, maintain records, and provide hands-on education at your school.

I will call you next week to see if we can set up a time to discuss my qualifications further. Thank you, Mr. Moreau, for your time and consideration.

Sincerely,

Figure 6–53

To Remove a Merge Condition

You should remove the merge condition so that future merges will not be restricted to potential employers with an employer type of S (for school). The following steps remove a merge condition.

1
- Click the Edit Recipient List button (Mailings tab | Start Mail Merge group) to display the Mail Merge Recipients dialog box.

2
- Click the Filter link (Mail Merge Recipients dialog box) to display the Filter and Sort dialog box.

- If necessary, click the Filter Records tab to display the Filter Records sheet (Figure 6–54).

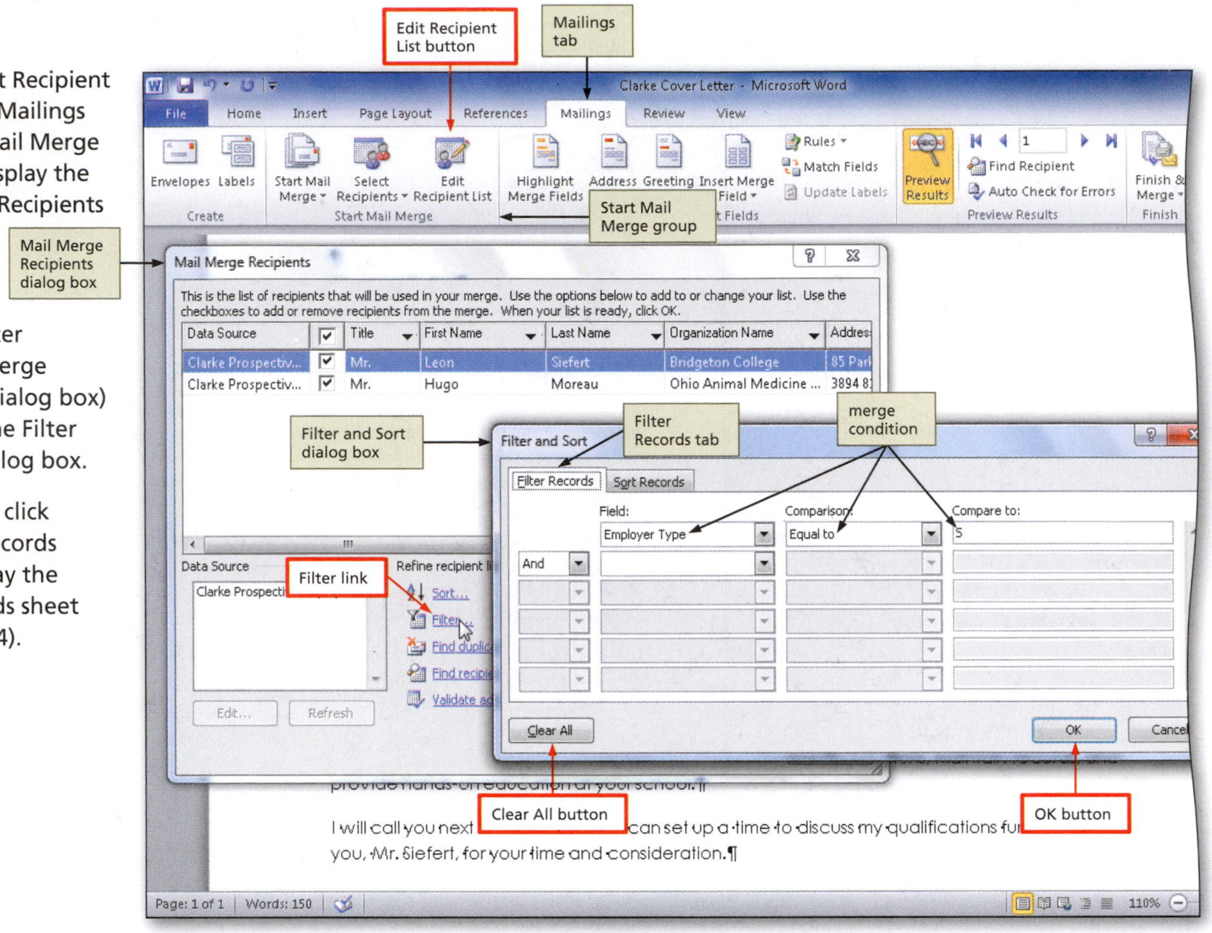

Figure 6–54

Can I specify a merge condition in this dialog box instead of using the box arrow in the Mail Merge Recipients dialog box?

Yes.

3
- Click the Clear All button (Filter and Sort dialog box).

- Click the OK button in each of the two open dialog boxes to remove the merge condition.

To Sort the Data Records in a Data Source

If you mail the form letters using the U.S. Postal Service's bulk rate mailing service, the post office requires that you sort and group the form letters by ZIP code. Thus, the next steps sort the data records by ZIP code.

1

• Click the Edit Recipient List button (Mailings tab | Start Mail Merge group) to display the Mail Merge Recipients dialog box.

• Scroll to the right until the ZIP Code field shows in the dialog box.

• Click the button arrow to the right of the field name, ZIP Code, to display a menu of sort and filter criteria (Figure 6–55).

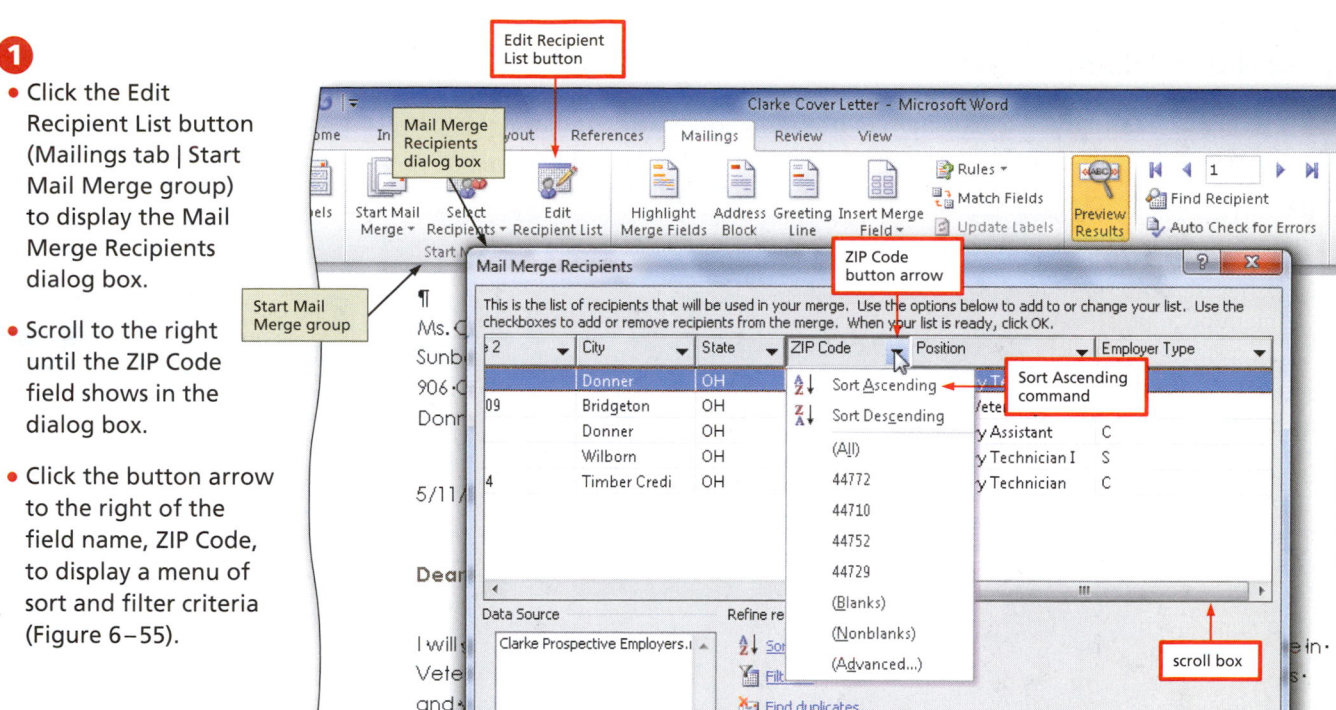

Figure 6–55

2

• Click Sort Ascending on the menu to sort the data source records in ascending (smallest to largest) order by ZIP Code (Figure 6–56).

3

• Click the OK button to close the Mail Merge Recipients dialog box.

Q&A

In what order would the form letters print if I merged them again now?

Word would print them in ZIP code order; that is, the record with ZIP code 44710 would print first, and the records with ZIP code 44772 would print last.

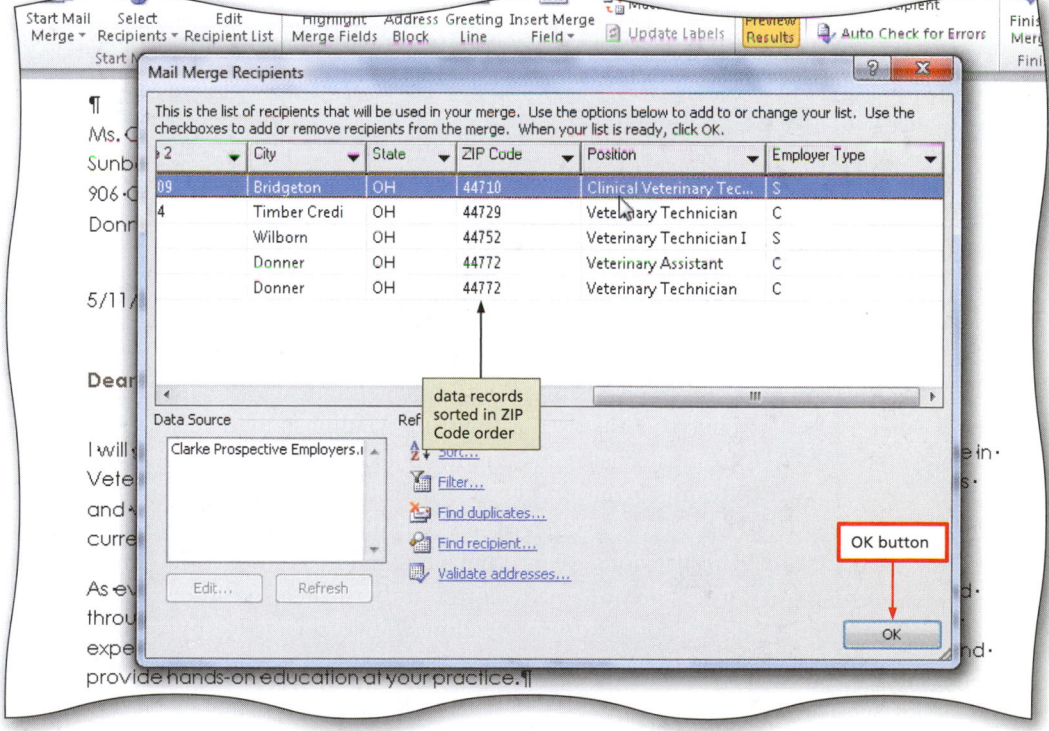

Figure 6–56

Other Ways

1. Click Filter link (Mail Merge Recipients dialog box), click Sort Records tab, enter sort criteria, click OK button

To Find and Display Data

If you wanted to find a particular record in the data source and display that record's data in the main document on the screen, you can search for a field value. The following steps find Zajak, which is a last name in the data source, and display that record's values in the form letter currently displaying on the screen.

1
- Click the Find Recipient button (Mailings tab | Preview Results group) to display the Find Entry dialog box.

- Type `Zajak` in the Find text box (Find Entry dialog box) as the search text.

- Click the Find Next button to display the record containing the entered text (Figure 6–57).

2
- Click the Cancel button (Find Entry dialog box) to close the dialog box.

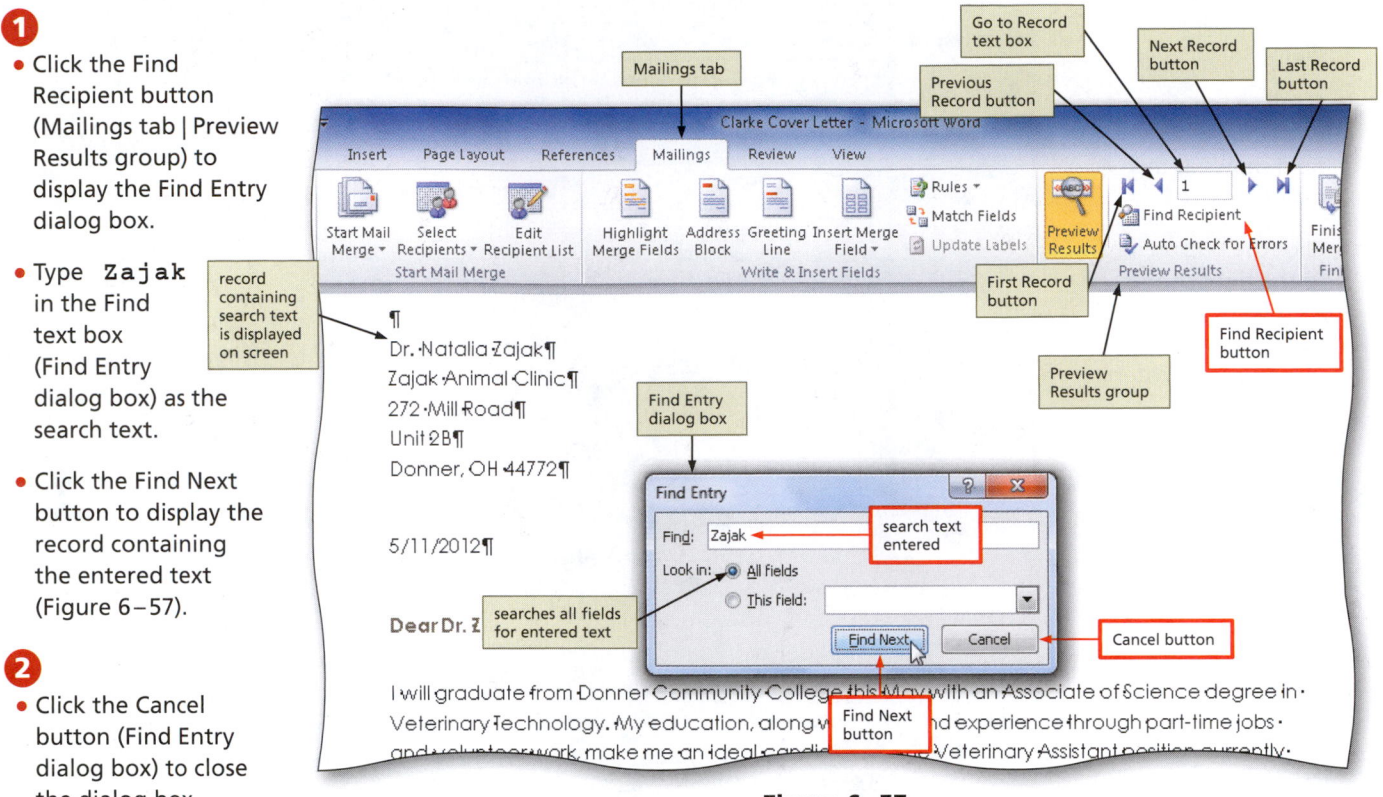

Figure 6–57

Displaying Data Source Records in the Main Document

When you are viewing merged data in the main document (Figure 6–57) — that is, the Preview Results button (Mailings tab | Preview Results group) is selected — you can click the Last Record button (Mailings tab | Preview Results group) to display the values from the last record in the data source, the First Record button (Mailings tab | Preview Results group) to display the values in record one, the Next Record button (Mailings tab | Preview Results group) to display the values in the next consecutive record number, or the Previous Record button (Mailings tab | Preview Results group) to display the values from the previous record number. You also can display a specific record by clicking the Go to Record text box (Mailings tab | Preview Results group), typing the record number you would like to be displayed in the main document, and then pressing the ENTER key.

To Close a Document

The cover letter is complete. Thus, the following steps close the document.

1 Open the Backstage view and then click Close.

2 If a Microsoft Word dialog box is displayed, click the Save button to save the changes.

BTW

Closing Main Document Files
Word always asks if you want to save changes when you close a main document, even if you just saved the document. If you are sure that no additional changes were made to the document, click the Don't Save button; otherwise, click the Save button — just to be safe.

Addressing Mailing Labels and Envelopes

Now that you have merged and printed the form letters, the next step is to print addresses on mailing labels to be affixed to envelopes for the form letters. The mailing labels will use the same data source as the form letter, Clarke Prospective Employers. The format and content of the mailing labels will be exactly the same as the inside address in the main document for the form letter. That is, the first line will contain the title and first name followed by the last name. The second line will contain the organization name, and so on. Thus, you will use the AddressBlock merge field in the mailing labels.

You follow the same basic steps to create the main document for the mailing labels as you did to create the main document for the form letters. The major difference is that the data source already exists because you created it earlier in this project.

BTW

Organizing Data
If you sort data records (pages WD 368 and WD 369) or select records to merge (pages WD 365 and WD 366), the merge process will generate mailing labels or envelopes using the specified criteria.

Generate mailing labels and envelopes.
An envelope should contain the sender's full name and address in the upper-left corner of the envelope. It also should contain the addressee's full name and address, positioned approximately in the vertical and horizontal center of the envelope. The address can be printed directly on the envelope or on a mailing label that is affixed to the envelope.

Plan Ahead

To Address and Print Mailing Labels Using an Existing Data Source

To address mailing labels, you specify the type of labels you intend to use. Word will request the label information, including the label vendor and product number. You can obtain this information from the box of labels. For illustration purposes in addressing these labels, the label vendor is Avery and the product number is J8158. The following steps address and print mailing labels using an existing data source.

Note: If your printer does not have the capability of printing mailing labels, skip these steps and proceed to the section titled, Merging All Data Records to a Directory, on page WD 378. If you are in a laboratory environment, ask your instructor if you should perform these steps or skip them.

- Open the Backstage view. Click the New tab in the Backstage view to display the New gallery. With Blank document selected, click the Create button to open a new blank document window.

- If necessary, change the zoom to 110%.

- Display the Mailings tab. Click the Start Mail Merge button (Mailings tab | Start Mail Merge group) and then click Step by Step Mail Merge Wizard on the Start Mail Merge menu to display Step 1 of the Mail Merge wizard in the Mail Merge task pane.

- Click Labels in the 'Select document type' area to specify labels as the main document type (Figure 6–58).

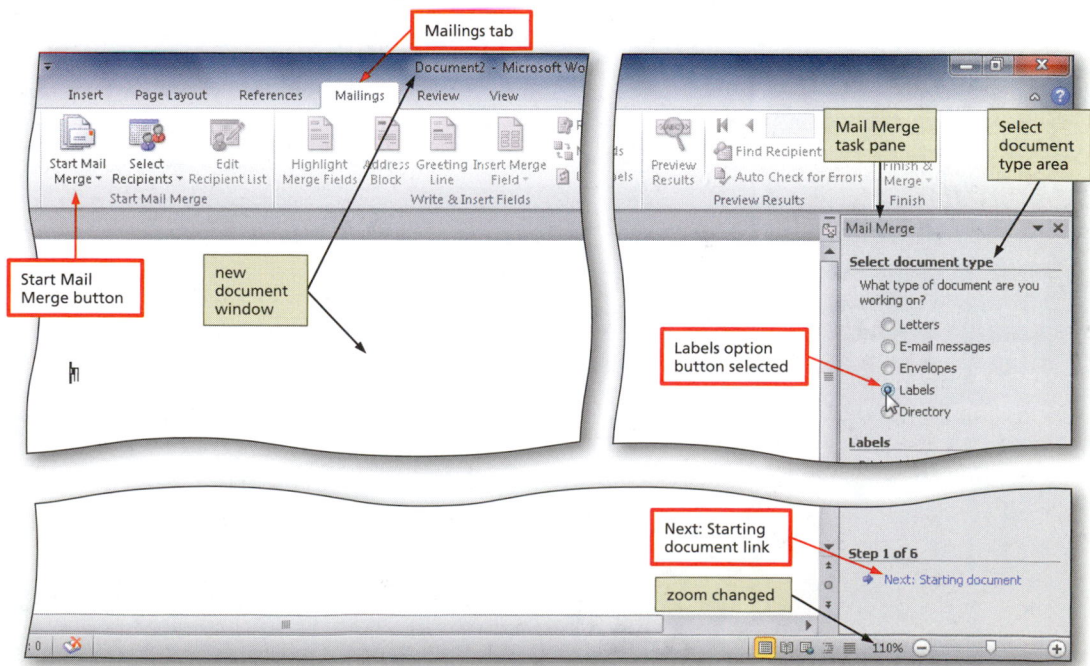

Figure 6–58

2

- Click the Next: Starting document link at the bottom of the Mail Merge task pane to display Step 2 of the Mail Merge wizard.

- In the Mail Merge task pane, click the Label options link to display the Label Options dialog box.

- Select the label vendor and product number (in this case, Avery A4/A5 and J8158), as shown in Figure 6–59.

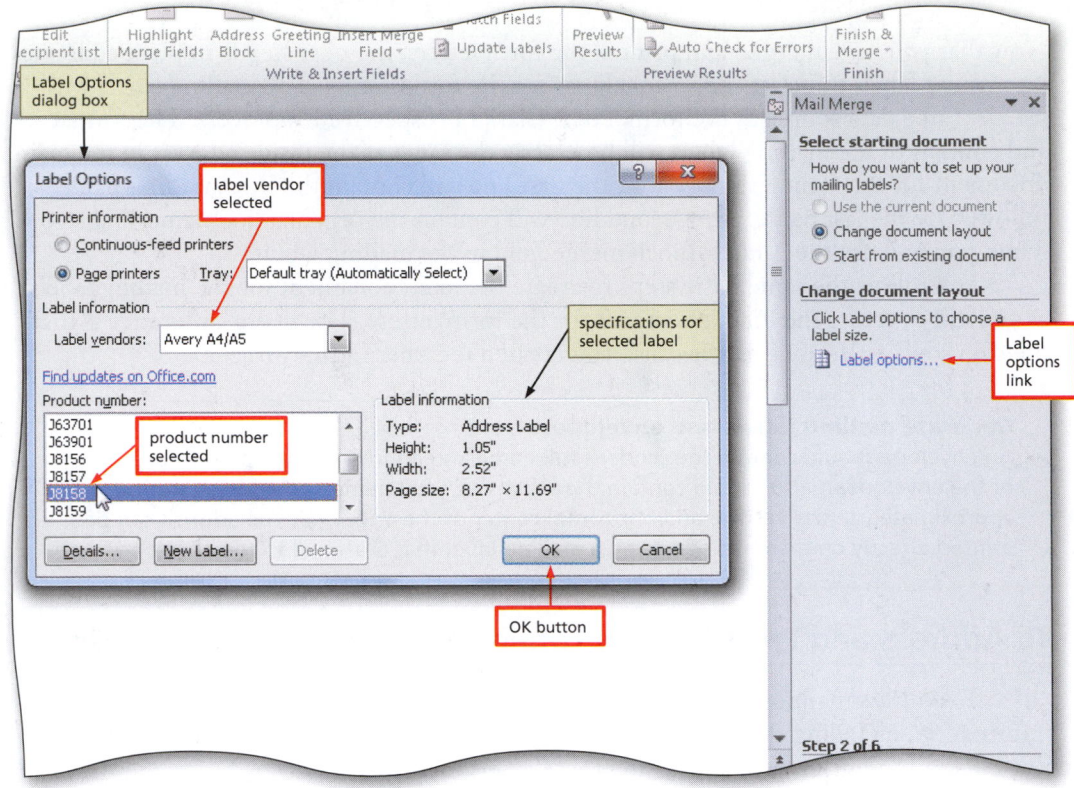

Figure 6–59

3

- Click the OK button (Label Options dialog box) to display the selected label layout as the main document (Figure 6–60).

- If necessary, scroll to display the left edge of the main document in the window.

- If gridlines are not displayed, click the View Table Gridlines button (Table Tools Layout tab | Table group) to show gridlines.

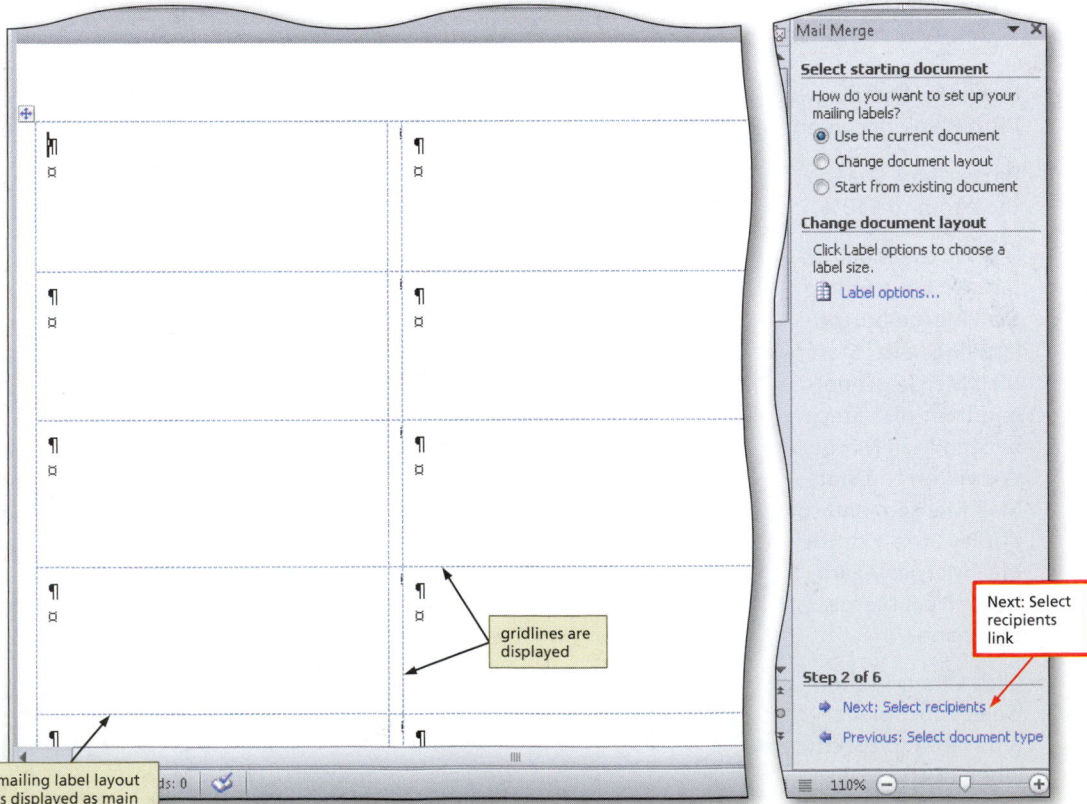

Figure 6–60

- Click the Next: Select recipients link at the bottom of the Mail Merge task pane to display Step 3 of the Mail Merge wizard, which allows you to select the data source.

- If necessary, click 'Use an existing list' in the Select recipients area.

- Click the Browse link to display the Select Data Source dialog box.

- If necessary, navigate to the location of the data source (in this case, the Job Hunting folder in the Word folder in the CIS 101 folder [or your class folder] on the USB flash drive).

- Click the file name, Clarke Prospective Employers, to select the data source you created earlier in the chapter (Figure 6–61).

Q&A

What is the folder initially displayed in the Select Data Source dialog box?

It is the default folder for storing data source files. Word looks in that folder first for an existing data source.

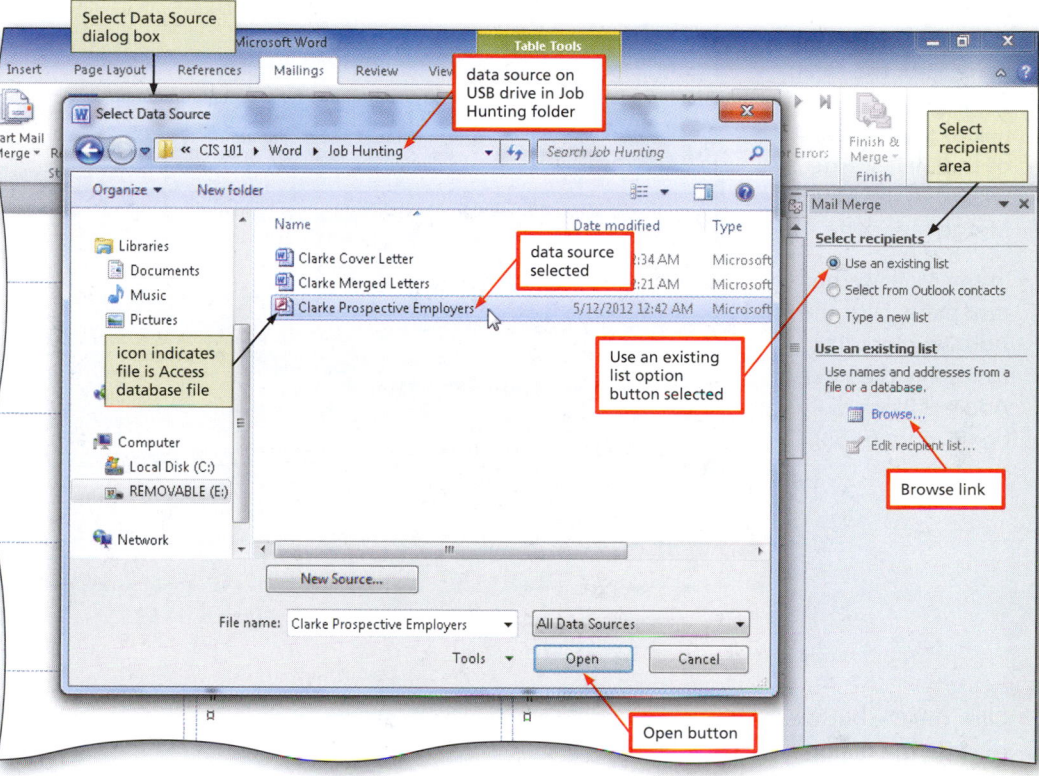

Figure 6–61

- Click the Open button to display the Mail Merge Recipients dialog box (Figure 6–62).

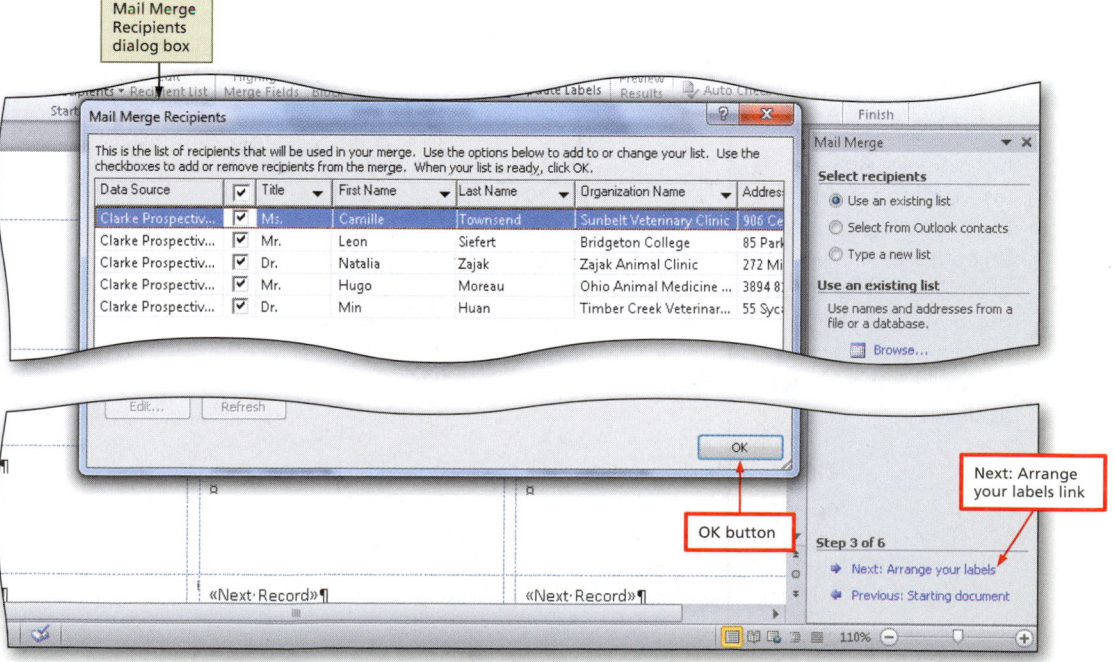

Figure 6–62

6

- Click the OK button (Mail Merge Recipients dialog box) to close the dialog box.

- At the bottom of the Mail Merge task pane, click the Next: Arrange your labels link to display Step 4 of the Mail Merge wizard in the Mail Merge task pane.

- In the Mail Merge task pane, click the Address block link to display the Insert Address Block dialog box (Figure 6–63).

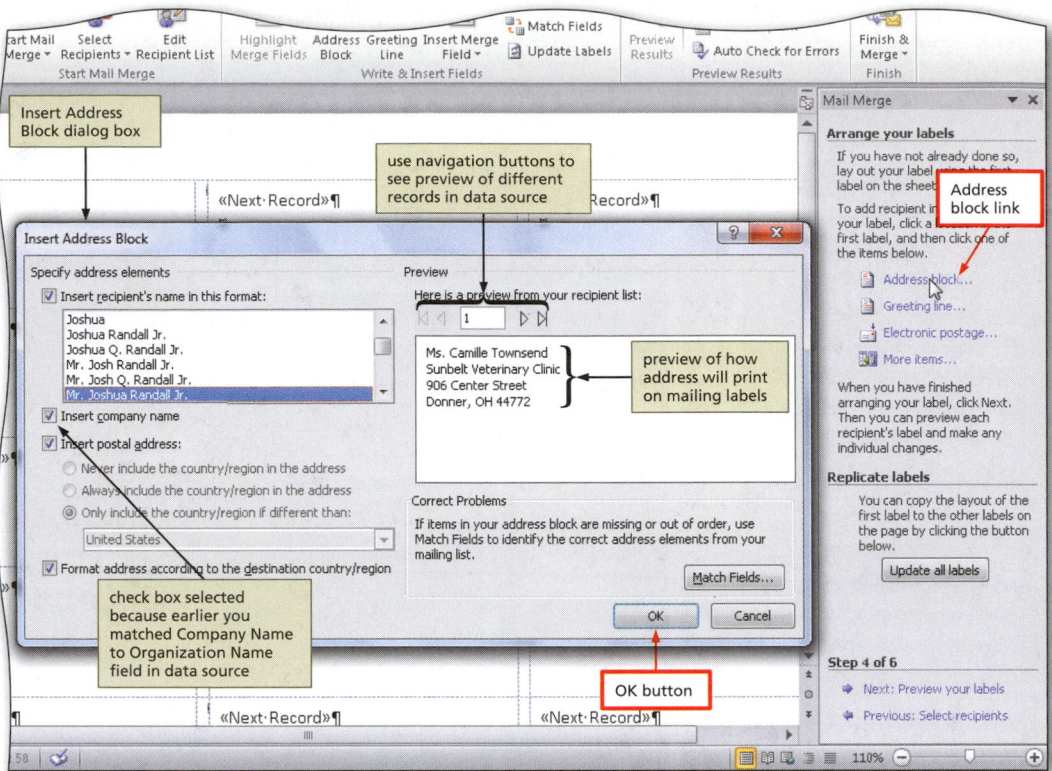

Figure 6–63

7

- Click the OK button to close the dialog box and insert the AddressBlock merge field in the first label of the main document (Figure 6–64).

Q&A

Do I have to use the AddressBlock merge field?

No. You can click the Insert Merge Field button (Mailings tab | Write & Insert Fields group) and then select the preferred fields for the mailing labels, organizing the fields as desired.

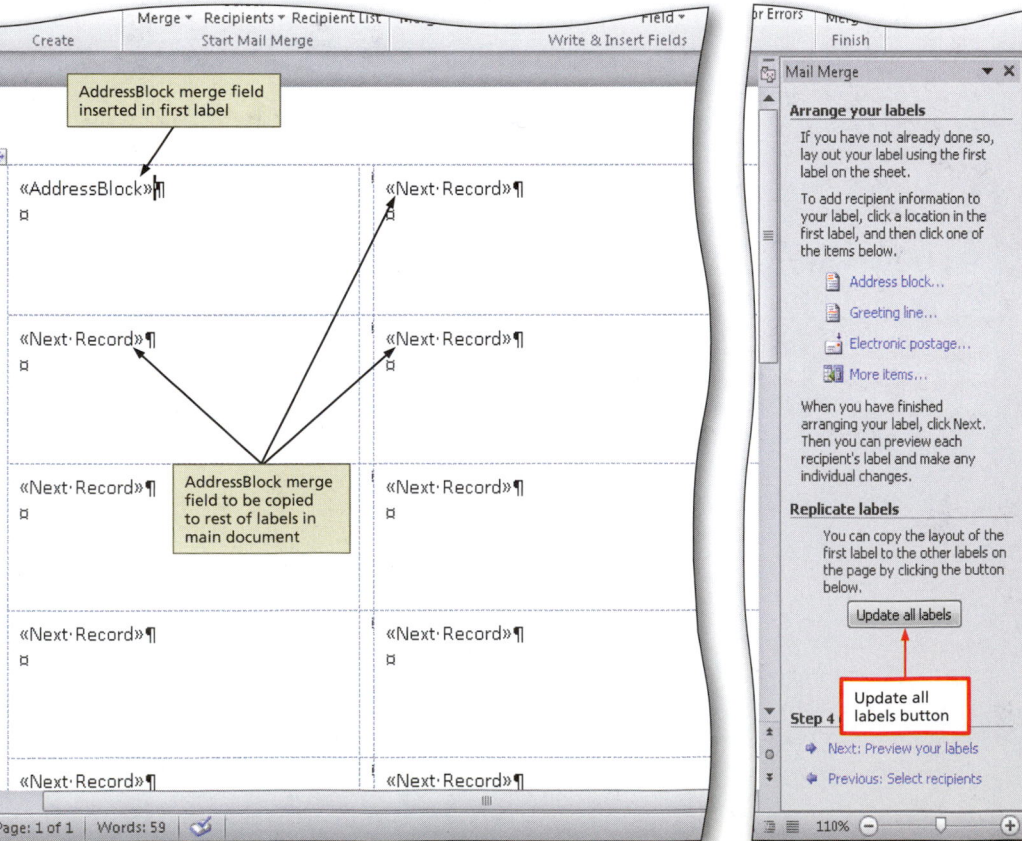

Figure 6–64

8

• Click the 'Update all labels' button in the Mail Merge task pane to copy the layout of the first label to the remaining label layouts in the main document (Figure 6–65).

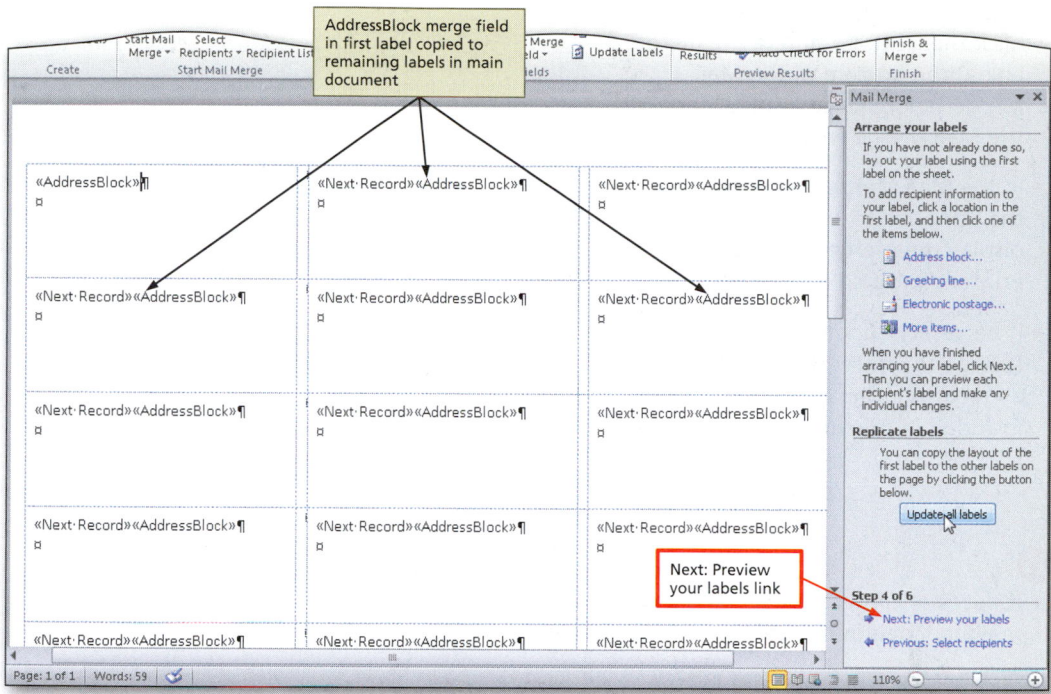

Figure 6–65

9

• Click the Next: Preview your labels link at the bottom of the Mail Merge task pane to display Step 5 of the Mail Merge wizard, which shows a preview of the mailing labels in the document window.

• Because you do not want a blank space between each line in the printed mailing address, select the table containing the label layout (that is, click the table move handle in the upper-left corner of the table), display the Page Layout tab, change the Spacing Before and After boxes to 0 pt, and then click anywhere to remove the selection (Figure 6–66).

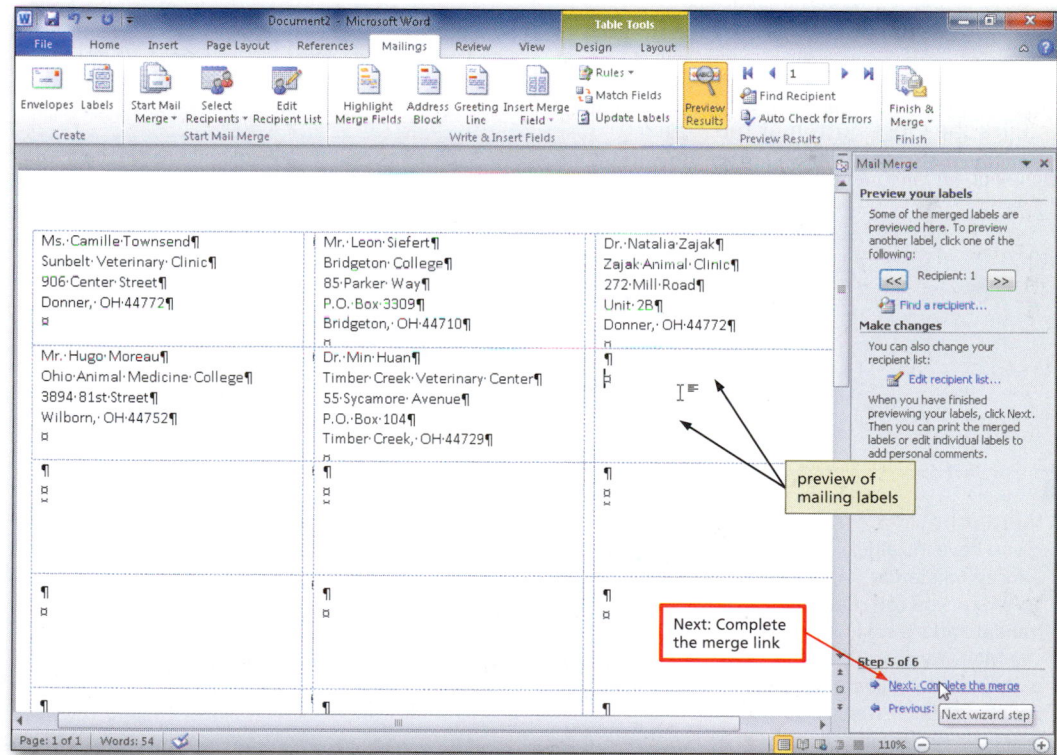

Figure 6–66

Q&A

What if the spacing does not change?

Drag through the labels and try changing the Spacing Before and After boxes to 0 again.

10

- Click the Next: Complete the merge link at the bottom of the Mail Merge task pane to display Step 6 of the Mail Merge wizard.

- In the Mail Merge task pane, click the Print link to display the Merge to Printer dialog box.

- If necessary, click All (Merge to Printer dialog box) so that all records in the data source will be included in the merge (Figure 6–67).

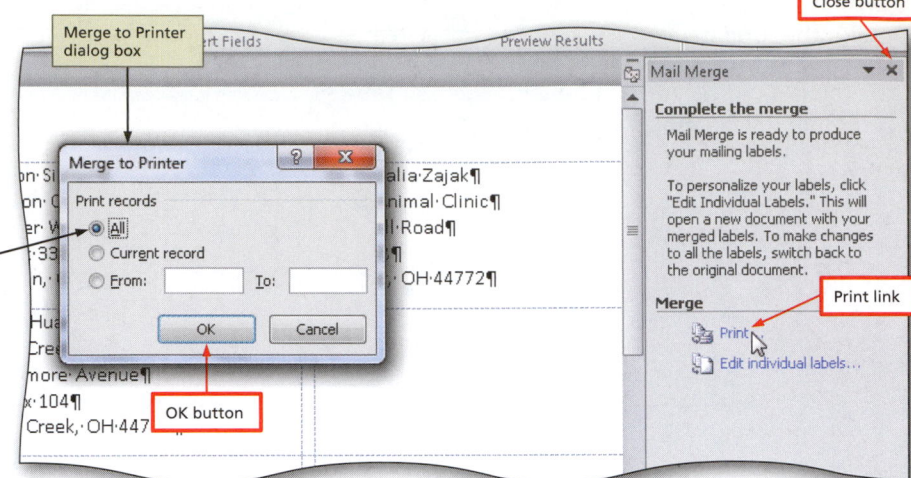

Figure 6–67

11

- If necessary, insert a sheet of blank mailing labels in the printer.

- Click the OK button to display the Print dialog box.

- Click the OK button (Print dialog box) to print the mailing labels (Figure 6–68).

12

- Click the Close button at the right edge of the Mail Merge task pane.

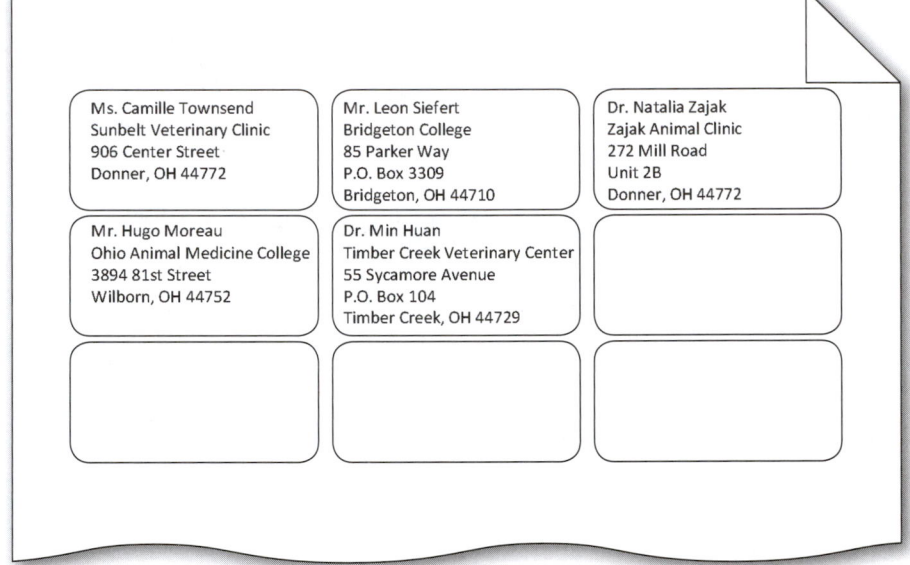

Figure 6–68

Validating Addresses
If you have installed address validation software, you can click the Validate addresses link in the Mail Merge Recipients dialog box to validate your recipients' addresses. If you have not yet installed address validation software and would like information about doing so, click the Validate addresses link in the Mail Merge Recipients dialog box and then click the Yes button in the Microsoft Word dialog box to display a related Microsoft Office Web page.

To Save the Mailing Labels

The following steps save the mailing labels.

1 With a USB flash drive connected to one of the computer's USB ports, click the Save button on the Quick Access Toolbar to display the Save As dialog box.

2 Type `Clarke Mailing Labels` in the File name text box to change the file name.

3 If necessary, navigate to the save location (in this case, the Job Hunting folder in the Word folder in the CIS 101 folder [or your class folder] on the USB flash drive).

4 Click the Save button (Save As dialog box) to save the document in the selected folder on the USB flash drive with the entered file name.

To Address and Print Envelopes Using an Existing Data Source

Instead of addressing mailing labels to affix to envelopes, your printer may have the capability of printing directly on envelopes. To print the address information directly on envelopes, follow the same basic steps as you did to address the mailing labels. The following steps address envelopes using an existing data source.

Note: If your printer does not have the capability of printing envelopes, skip these steps and proceed to the section titled, Merging All Data Records to a Directory, on the next page. If you are in a laboratory environment, ask your instructor if you should perform these steps or skip them.

1 Open the Backstage view. Click the New tab in the Backstage view to display the New gallery. With Blank document selected, click the Create button to open a new blank document window.

2 Display the Mailings tab. Click the Start Mail Merge button (Mailings tab | Start Mail Merge group) and then click Step by Step Mail Merge Wizard on the Start Mail Merge menu to display Step 1 of the Mail Merge wizard in the Mail Merge task pane. Specify envelopes as the main document type by clicking Envelopes in the 'Select document type' area.

3 Click the Next: Starting document link at the bottom of the Mail Merge task pane to display Step 2 of the Mail Merge wizard. In the Mail Merge task pane, click the Envelope options link to display the Envelope Options dialog box.

4 Select the envelope size and then click the OK button (Envelope Options dialog box), which displays the selected envelope layout as the main document.

5 If your envelope does not have a preprinted return address, position the insertion point in the upper-left corner of the envelope layout and then type a return address.

6 Click the Next: Select recipients link at the bottom of the Mail Merge task pane to display Step 3 of the Mail Merge wizard, which allows you to select the data source. If necessary, click 'Use an existing list' in the Select recipients area. Click the Browse link to display the Select Data Source dialog box. If necessary, navigate to the location of the data source (in this case, the Job Hunting folder in the Word folder in the CIS 101 folder [or your class folder] on the USB flash drive). Click the file name, Clarke Prospective Employers, to select the data source you created earlier in the chapter. Click the Open button, which displays the Mail Merge Recipients dialog box, and then click the OK button to close the dialog box. At the bottom of the Mail Merge task pane, click the Next: Arrange your envelope link to display Step 4 of the Mail Merge wizard in the Mail Merge task pane.

7 Position the insertion point in the middle of the envelope. In the Mail Merge task pane, click the Address block link to display the Insert Address Block dialog box. Click the OK button to close the dialog box and insert the AddressBlock merge field in the envelope layout of the main document (Figure 6–69).

BTW

AddressBlock Merge Field
Another way to insert the AddressBlock merge field in a document is to click the Address Block button (Mailings tab | Write & Insert Fields group). Instead of using the AddressBlock merge field, you can click the Insert Merge Field button (Mailings tab | Write & Insert Fields group) and then select the preferred fields for the envelope layout, organizing the fields as desired.

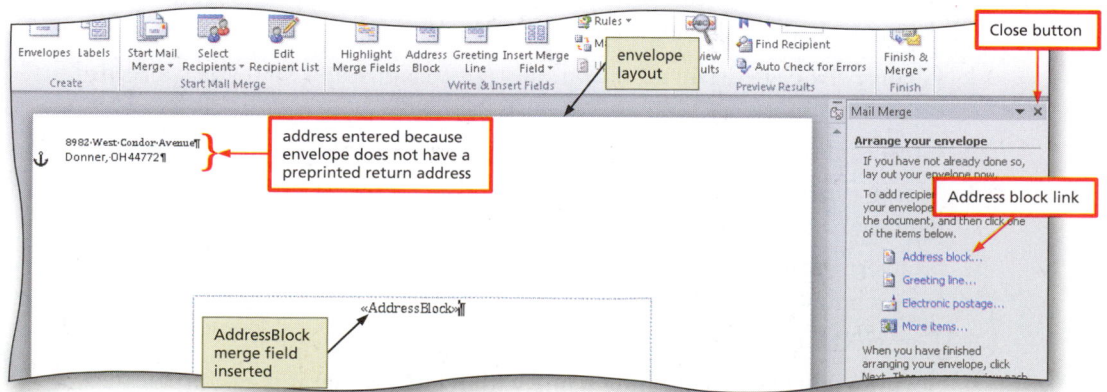

Figure 6–69

8 Click the Next: Preview your envelopes link at the bottom of the Mail Merge task pane to display Step 5 of the Mail Merge wizard, which shows a preview of an envelope in the document window.

9 Click the Next: Complete the merge link at the bottom of the Mail Merge task pane to display Step 6 of the Mail Merge wizard. In the Mail Merge task pane, click the Print link to display the Merge to Printer dialog box. If necessary, click All (Merge to Printer dialog box) so that all records in the data source will be included in the merge.

10 If necessary, insert blank envelopes in the printer. Click the OK button to display the Print dialog box. Click the OK button (Print dialog box) to print the addresses on the envelopes. Click the Close button at the right edge of the Mail Merge task pane.

To Save the Envelopes

The following steps save the envelopes.

1 With a USB flash drive connected to one of the computer's USB ports, click the Save button on the Quick Access Toolbar to display the Save As dialog box.

2 Type `Clarke Envelope Layout` in the File name text box to change the file name.

3 If necessary, navigate to the save location (in this case, the Job Hunting folder in the Word folder in the CIS 101 folder [or your class folder] on the USB flash drive).

4 Click the Save button (Save As dialog box) to save the document in the selected folder on the USB flash drive with the entered file name.

Merging All Data Records to a Directory

You may want to print the data records in the data source. Recall that the data source is saved as a Microsoft Access database table. Thus, you cannot open the data source in Word. To view the data source, you click the Edit Recipient List button (Mailings tab | Start Mail Merge group), which displays the Mail Merge Recipients dialog box. This dialog box, however, does not have a Print button.

One way to print the contents of the data source is to merge all data records in the data source into a single document, called a **directory**. That is, a directory does not merge each data record to a separate document; instead, a directory lists all records together in a single document. When you merge to a directory, the default organization of a directory places each record one after the next, similar to the look of entries in a telephone book.

The directory in this chapter is more organized with the rows and columns divided and field names placed above each column (shown in Figure 6–83 on page WD 385). To accomplish this look, the following steps are required:

1. Change the page orientation from portrait to landscape, so that each record fits on a single row.
2. Create a directory layout, placing a separating character between each merge field.
3. Merge the directory to a new document, which creates a list of all records in the data source.
4. Convert the directory to a table, using the separator character as the identifier for each new column.
5. Format the table containing the directory.
6. Sort the table by organization name within city, so that it is easy to locate a particular record.

To Create a New Blank Document

The following steps create a new blank document.

1 Open the Backstage view.

2 Click the New tab in the Backstage view to display the New gallery.

3 With Blank document selected, click the Create button to open a new blank document window (shown in Figure 6–70).

To Change Page Orientation

When a document is in **portrait orientation**, the short edge of the paper is the top of the document. You can instruct Word to lay out a document in **landscape orientation**, so that the long edge of the paper is the top of the document. The following steps change the orientation of the document from portrait to landscape, so that an entire record will fit on a single line in the directory.

1

• Display the Page Layout tab.

• Click the Page Orientation button (Page Layout tab | Page Setup group) to display the Page Orientation gallery (Figure 6–70).

2

• Click Landscape in the Page Orientation gallery to change the page orientation to landscape.

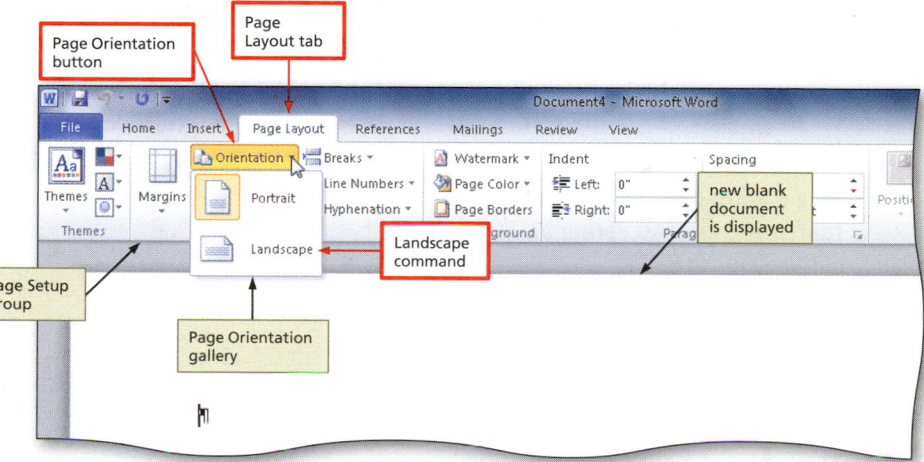

Figure 6–70

To Merge to a Directory

The next steps merge the data records in the data source to a directory. For illustration purposes, the following steps use the buttons on the Mailings tab rather than using the Mail Merge task pane to merge to a directory.

1

• Display the Mailings tab.

• Click the Start Mail Merge button (Mailings tab | Start Mail Merge group) to display the Start Mail Merge menu (Figure 6–71).

2

• Click Directory on the Start Mail Merge menu to select the main document type.

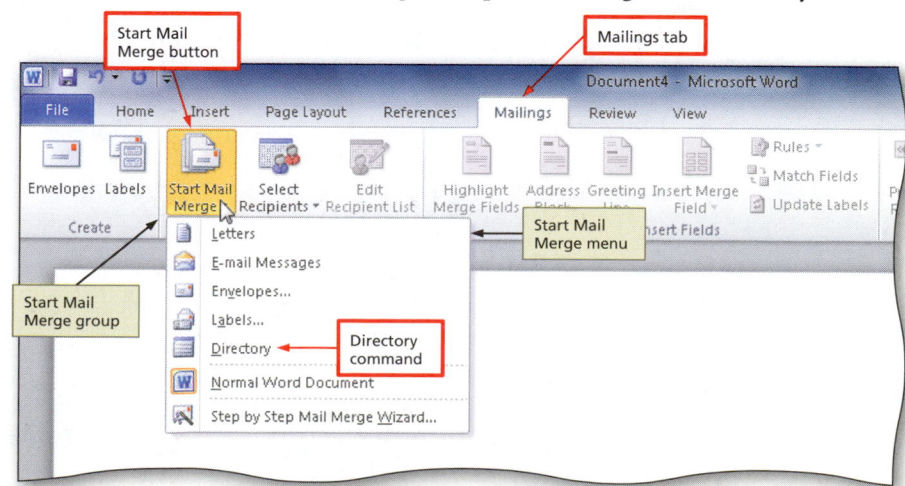

Figure 6–71

3

• Click the Select Recipients button (Mailings tab | Start Mail Merge group) to display the Select Recipients menu (Figure 6–72).

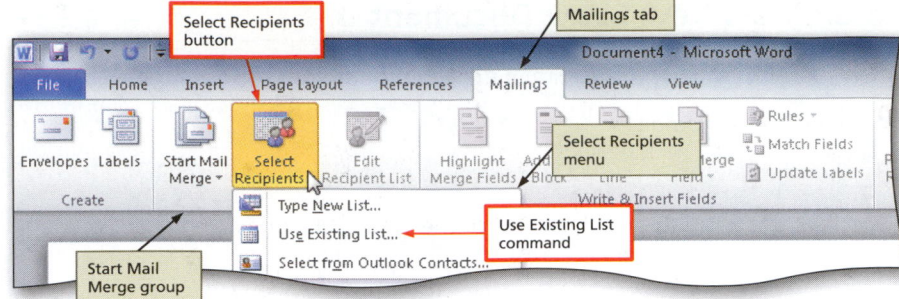

Figure 6–72

4

• Click Use Existing List on the Select Recipients menu to display the Select Data Source dialog box.

• If necessary, navigate to the location of the data source (in this case, the Job Hunting folder in the Word folder in the CIS 101 folder [or your class folder] on the USB flash drive).

• Click the file name, Clarke Prospective Employers, to select the data source you created earlier in the chapter (Figure 6–73).

5

• Click the Open button (Select Data Source dialog box) to associate the selected data source with the current main document.

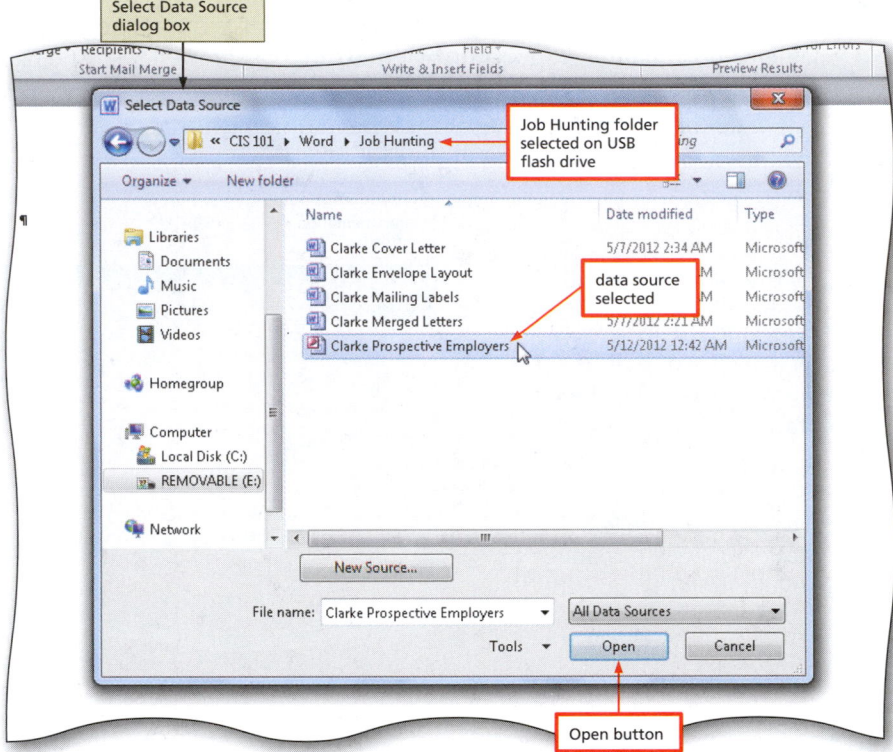

Figure 6–73

6

• Click the Insert Merge Field button arrow (Mailings tab | Write & Insert Fields group) to display the Insert Merge Field menu (Figure 6–74).

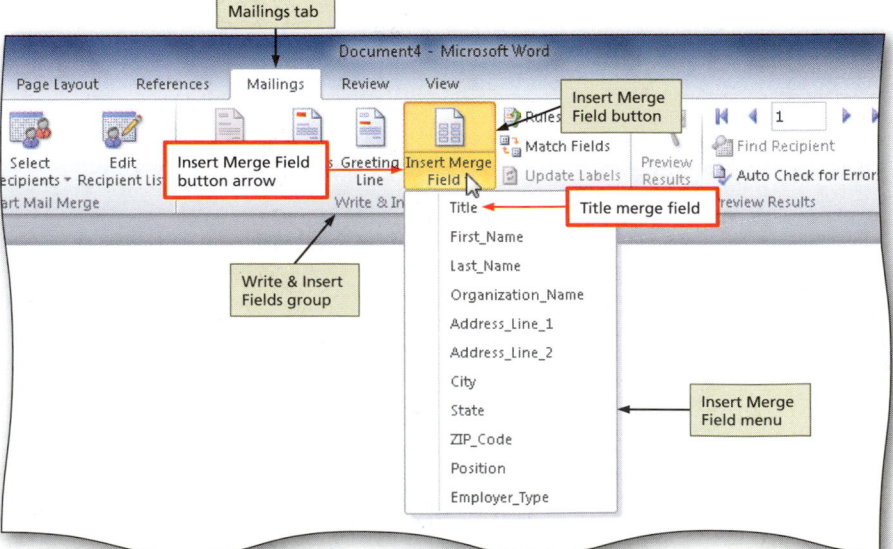

Figure 6–74

- Click Title on the Insert Merge Field menu to insert the merge field in the document.

- Press the COMMA (,) key to place a comma after the inserted merge field (Figure 6–75).

Q&A Why insert a comma after the merge field?

In the next steps, you will convert the entered merge fields to a table format with the records in rows and the fields in columns. To do this, Word divides the columns based on a character separating each field. In this case, you use the comma to separate the merge fields.

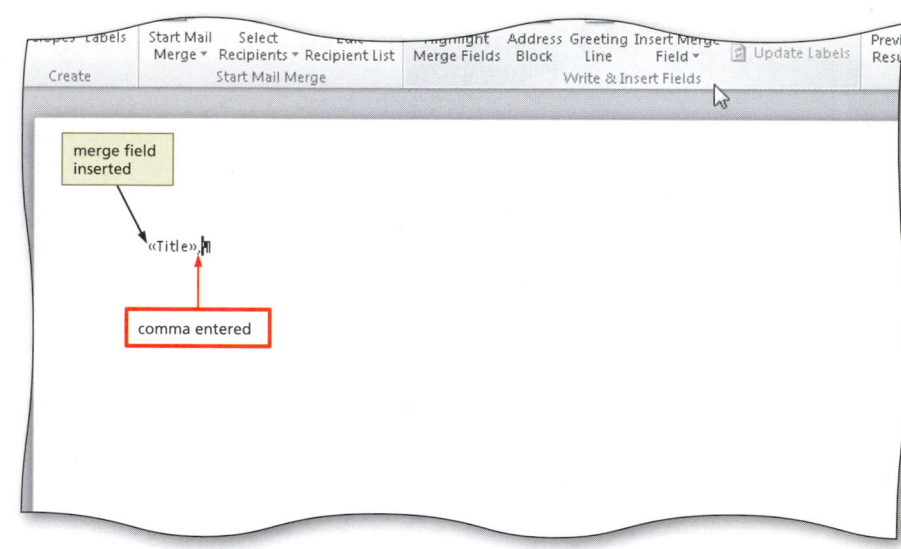

Figure 6–75

- Repeat Steps 6 and 7 for the First_Name, Last_Name, Organization_Name, Address_Line_1, Address_Line_2, City, State, and ZIP_Code fields on the Insert Merge Field menu, so that these fields in the data source appear in the main document separated by a comma, except do not type a comma after the last field: ZIP_Code.

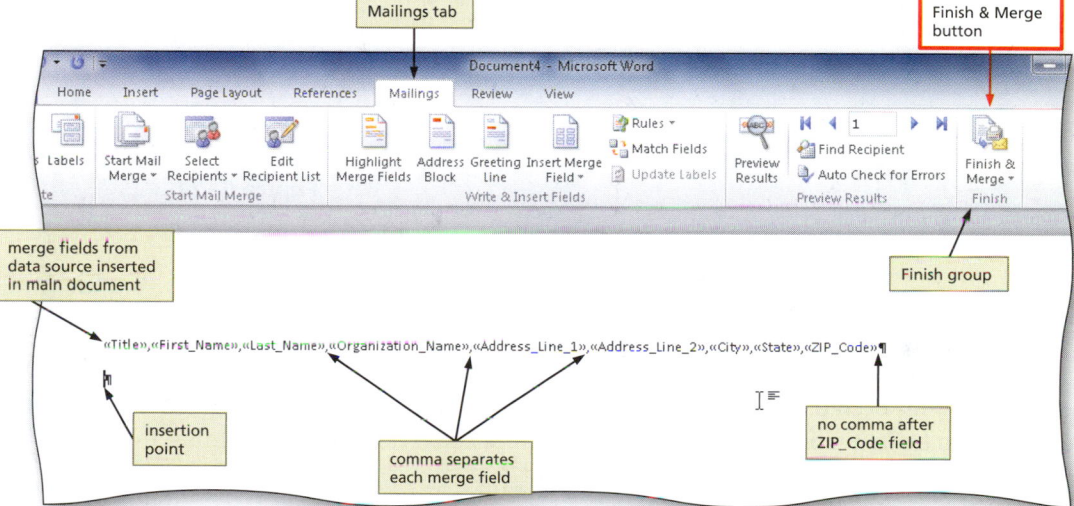

Figure 6–76

- Press the ENTER key (Figure 6–76).

Q&A Why press the ENTER key after entering the merge fields names?

This will place the first field in each record at the beginning of a new line.

To Merge to a New Document

The next step is to merge the data source and the directory main document to a new document, so that you can edit the resulting document. The following steps merge to a new document.

1 Click the Finish & Merge button (Mailings tab | Finish group) to display the Finish & Merge menu.

2 Click Edit Individual Documents on the Finish & Merge menu to display the Merge to New Document dialog box.

3 If necessary, click All (Merge to New Document dialog box).

4 Click the OK button to merge the data records to a directory in a new document window (Figure 6–77).

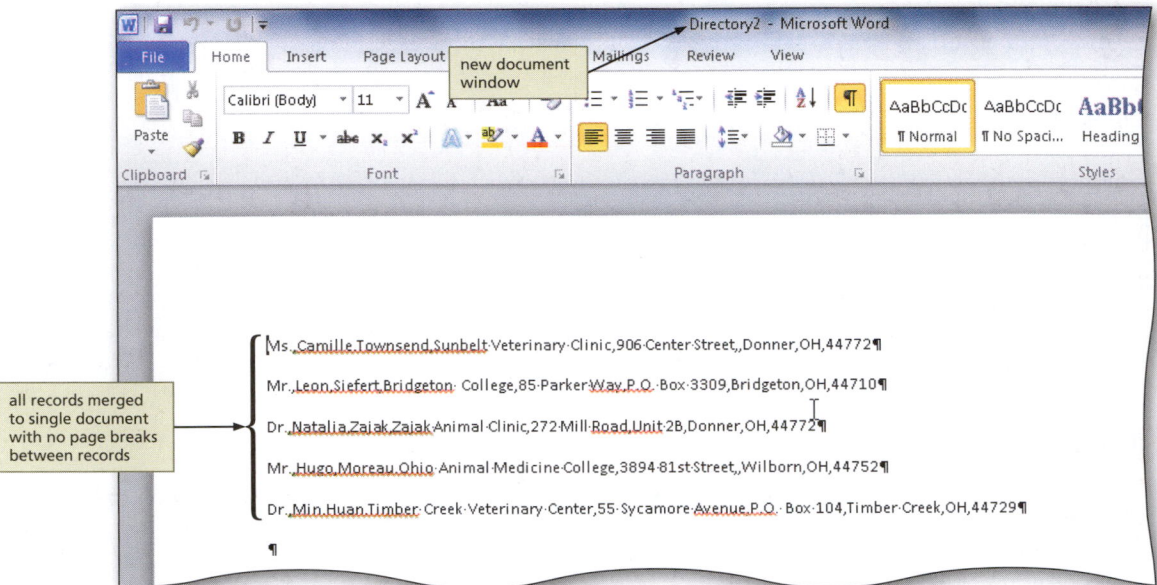

Figure 6–77

To Convert Text to a Table

You want each data record to be in a single row and each merge field to be in a column. That is, you want the directory to be in a table form. The following steps convert the text containing the merge fields to a table.

1

- Press CTRL+A to select the entire document, because you want all document contents to be converted to a table.

- Display the Insert tab.

- Click the Table button (Insert tab | Tables group) to display the Table gallery (Figure 6–78).

Q&A Can I convert a section of a document to a table?

Yes, simply select the characters, lines, or paragraphs to be converted before displaying the Convert Text to Table dialog box.

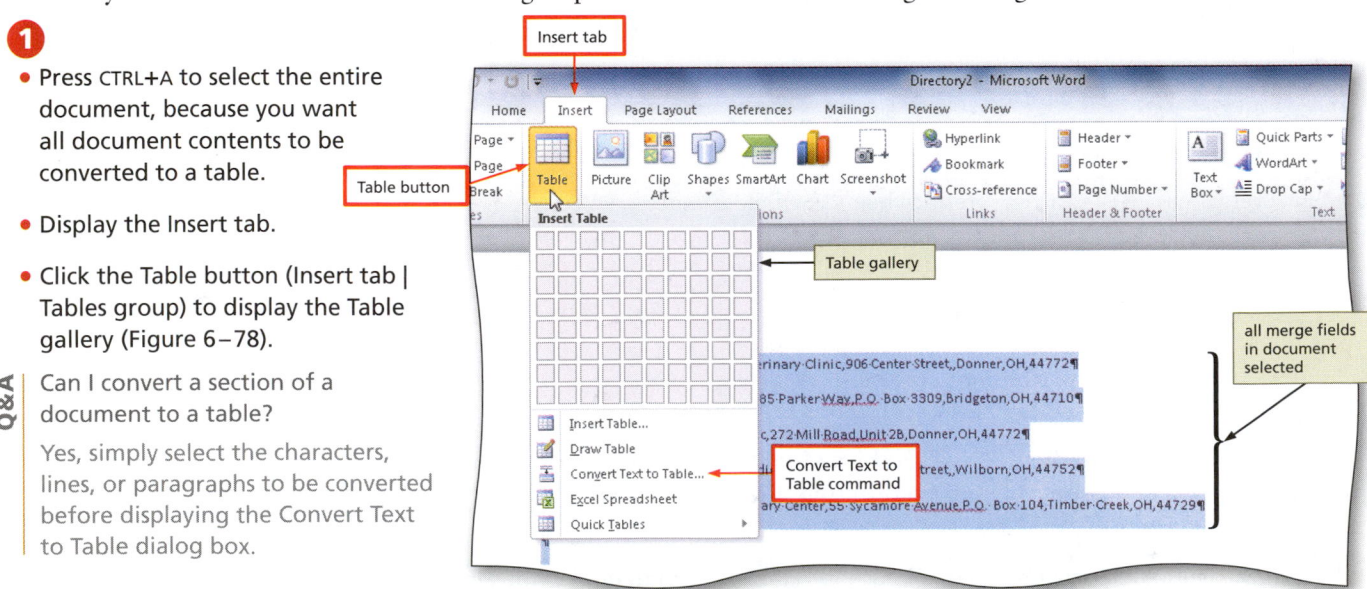

Figure 6–78

2

- Click Convert Text to Table in the Table gallery to display the Convert Text to Table dialog box.

- If necessary, type 9 in the Number of columns box (Convert Text to Table dialog box) to specify the number of columns for the resulting table.

- Click AutoFit to window, which instructs Word to fit the table and its contents to the width of the window.

- If necessary, click Commas to specify the character that separates the merge fields in the document (Figure 6–79).

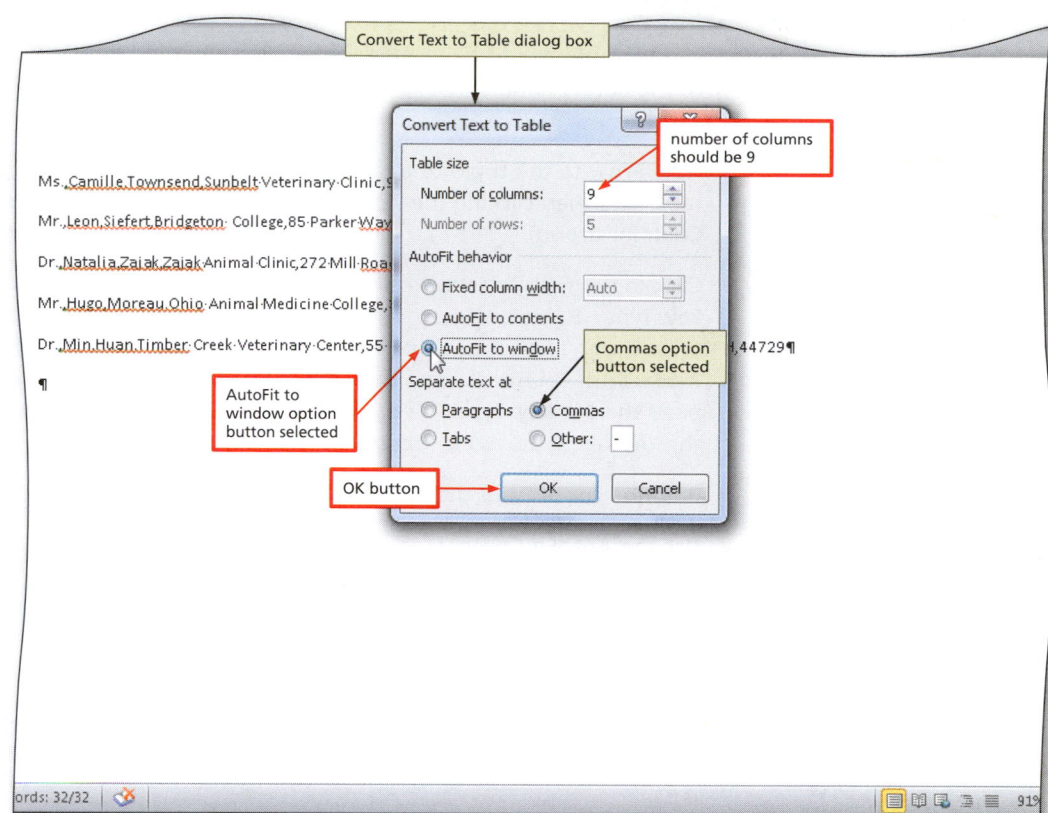

Figure 6–79

3

- Click the OK button to convert the selected text to a table (Figure 6–80).

Q&A

Can I format the table?

Yes. You can use any of the commands on the Table Tools Design and Layout tabs to change the look of the table.

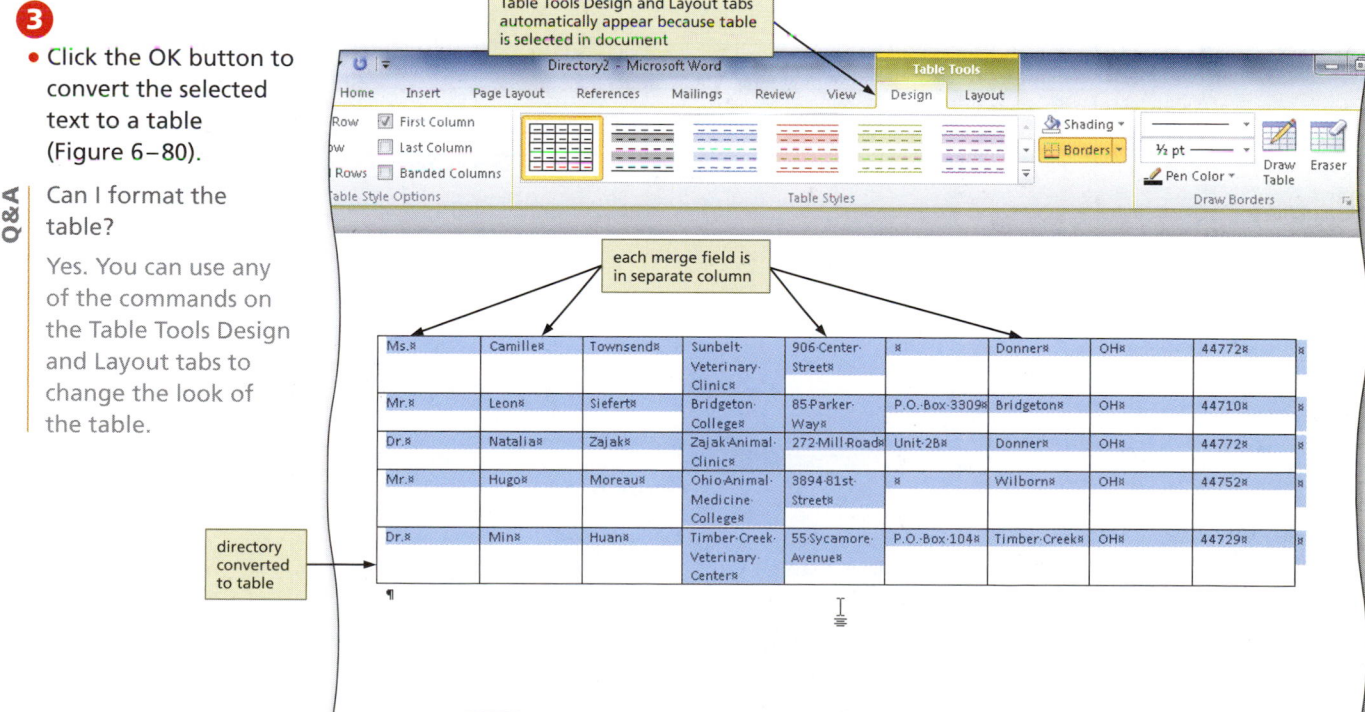

Figure 6–80

To Modify and Format a Table

The table would be more descriptive if the field names were displayed in a row above the actual data. The following steps add a row to the top of a table and format the data in the new row.

1 Add a row to the top of the table by positioning the insertion point in the first row of the table and then clicking the Insert Rows Above button (Table Tools Layout tab | Rows & Columns group).

2 Click in the first (leftmost) cell of the new row. Type **Title** and then press the TAB key. Type **First Name** and then press the TAB key. Type **Last Name** and then press the TAB key. Type **Organization Name** and then press the TAB key. Type **Address Line 1** and then press the TAB key. Type **Address Line 2** and then press the TAB key. Type **City** and then press the TAB key. Type **State** and then press the TAB key. Type **ZIP Code** as the last entry in the row.

3 Bold the contents of the first row.

4 Use the AutoFit Contents command to make all columns as wide as their contents (Figure 6–81).

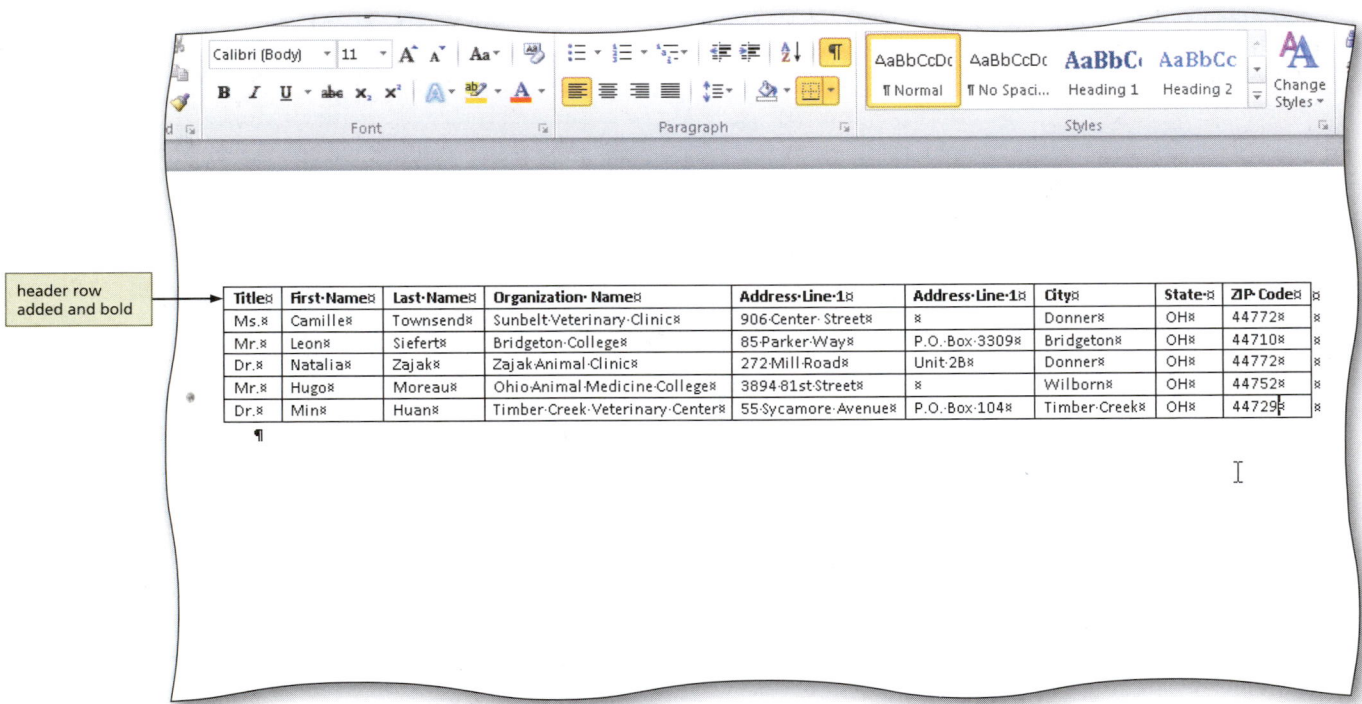

header row added and bold

Title¤	First·Name¤	Last·Name¤	Organization· Name¤	Address·Line·1¤	Address·Line·1¤	City¤	State·¤	ZIP·Code¤	¤
Ms.¤	Camille¤	Townsend¤	Sunbelt·Veterinary·Clinic¤	906·Center· Street¤	¤	Donner¤	OH¤	44772¤	¤
Mr.¤	Leon¤	Siefert¤	Bridgeton·College¤	85·Parker·Way¤	P.O.·Box·3309¤	Bridgeton¤	OH¤	44710¤	¤
Dr.¤	Natalia¤	Zajak¤	Zajak·Animal·Clinic¤	272·Mill·Road¤	Unit·2B¤	Donner¤	OH¤	44772¤	¤
Mr.¤	Hugo¤	Moreau¤	Ohio·Animal·Medicine·College¤	3894·81st·Street¤	¤	Wilborn¤	OH¤	44752¤	¤
Dr.¤	Min¤	Huan¤	Timber·Creek·Veterinary·Center¤	55·Sycamore·Avenue¤	P.O.·Box·104¤	Timber·Creek¤	OH¤	44729¤	¤

Figure 6–81

TO REPEAT HEADER ROWS

If you had a table that exceeded a page in length and you wanted the header row (the first row) to appear at the top of the table on each continued page, you would perform the following steps.

1. Position the insertion point in the header row.

2. Click the Repeat Header Rows button (Table Tools Layout tab | Data group) to repeat the row containing the insertion point at the top of every page on which the table continues.

To Sort a Table by Multiple Columns

The next step is to sort the table. In this project, the table records are displayed in organization name within city. The following steps sort a table by multiple columns.

- Click the Sort button (Table Tools Layout tab | Data group) to display the Sort dialog box.

- Click the Sort by box arrow (Sort dialog box); scroll to and then click City in the list.

- Click the first Then by box arrow and then click Organization Name in the list.

- If necessary, click Header row so that the first row remains in its current location when the table is sorted (Figure 6–82).

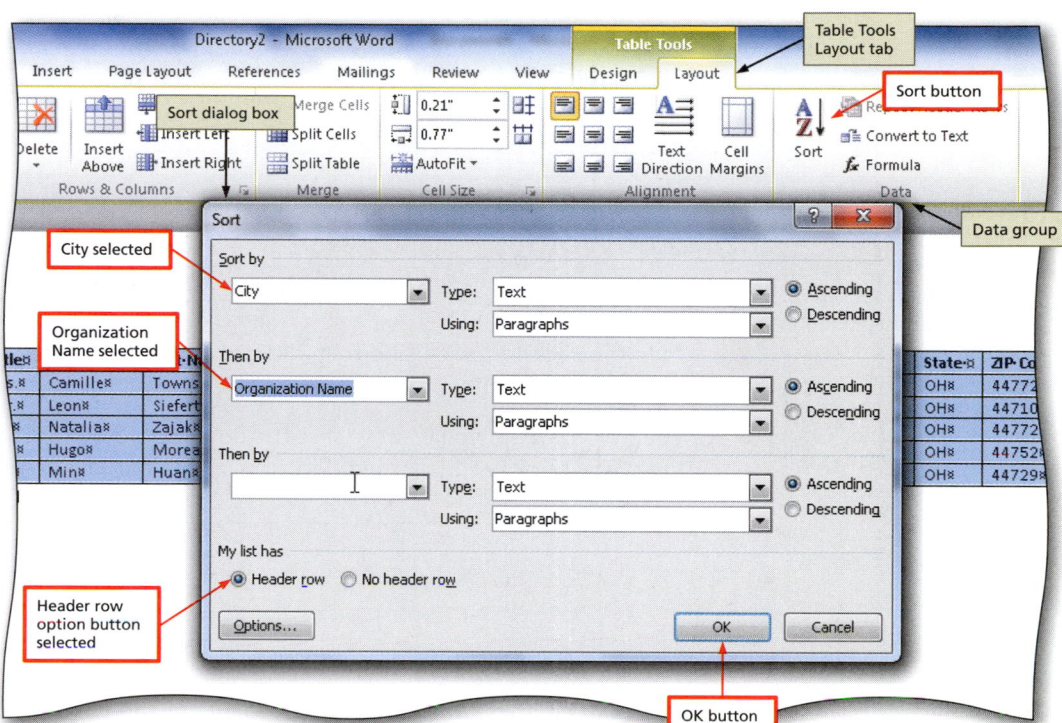

Figure 6–82

- Click the OK button to sort the records in the table in ascending Organization Name order within ascending City order (Figure 6–83).

- Position the insertion point below the table.

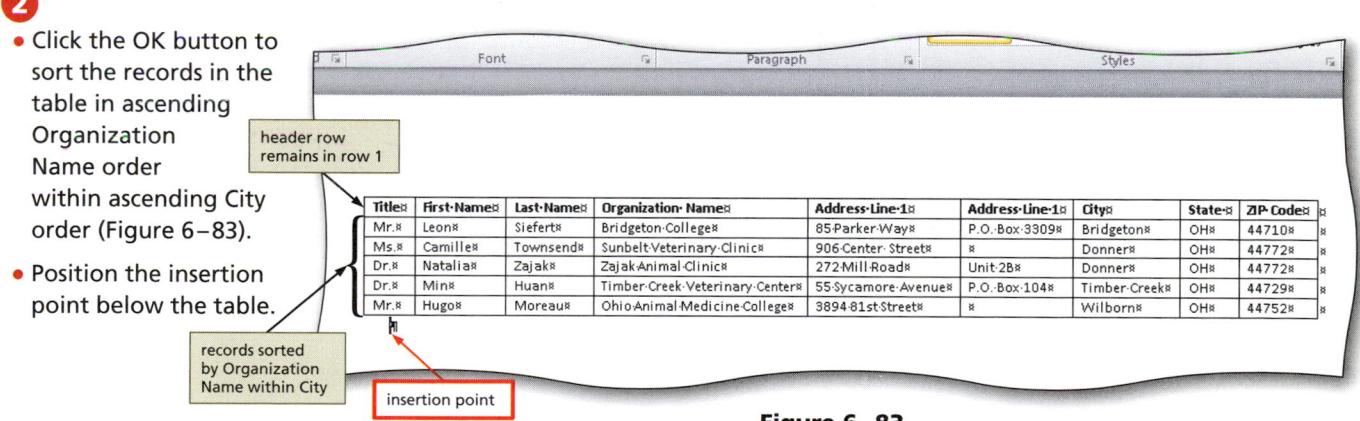

Figure 6–83

To Save and Print the Directory

The following steps save and print the directory.

1 With a USB flash drive connected to one of the computer's USB ports, click the Save button on the Quick Access Toolbar to display the Save As dialog box.

2 Type `Clarke Potential Employer Directory` in the File name text box to change the file name.

3 If necessary, navigate to the save location (in this case, the Job Hunting folder in the Word folder in the CIS 101 folder [or your class folder] on the USB flash drive).

4 Click the Save button (Save As dialog box) to save the document in the selected folder on the USB flash drive with the entered file name.

Q&A

If Microsoft Access is installed on my computer, can I use that to print the data source?

As an alternative to merging to a directory and printing the results, if you are familiar with Microsoft Access and it is installed on your computer, you can open and print the data source in Access.

BTW

Quick Reference
For a table that lists how to complete the tasks covered in this book using the mouse, Ribbon, shortcut menu, and keyboard, see the Quick Reference Summary at the back of this book, or visit the Word 2010 Quick Reference Web page (scsite.com/wd2010/qr).

To Quit Word

The following steps close all open documents and quit Word.

1 Open the Backstage view and then click Exit in the Backstage view to close all open documents and quit Word.

2 When Word asks if you want to save the document used to create the directory, click the Don't Save button. For all other documents, click the Save button to save the changes.

Chapter Summary

In this chapter, you have learned how to create and print form letters, create and edit a data source, address mailing labels and envelopes from a data source, and merge to a directory. The items listed below include all the new Word skills you have learned in this chapter.

1. Identify the Main Document for the Form Letter Using the Mail Merge Task Pane (WD 333)
2. Change the User Name and Initials (WD 335)
3. Create a Folder while Saving (WD 338)
4. Create a New Data Source (WD 340)
5. Save a Data Source when Prompted by Word (WD 345)
6. Enter the Date (WD 348)
7. View Merged Data in the Main Document (WD 349)
8. Edit the AddressBlock Merge Field (WD 349)
9. Edit the GreetingLine Merge Field (WD 351)
10. Insert a Merge Field in the Main Document (WD 353)
11. Insert an IF Field in the Main Document (WD 355)
12. Highlight Merge Fields (WD 358)
13. Display a Field Code (WD 358)
14. Print Field Codes in the Main Document (WD 359)
15. Preview the Merged Letters (WD 361)
16. Check for Errors (WD 361)
17. Merge the Form Letters to a New Document (WD 361)
18. Merge the Form Letters to the Printer (WD 364)
19. Select Records to Merge (WD 365)
20. Remove a Merge Condition (WD 368)
21. Sort the Data Records in a Data Source (WD 368)
22. Find and Display Data (WD 370)
23. Address and Print Mailing Labels Using an Existing Data Source (WD 371)
24. Address and Print Envelopes Using an Existing Data Source (WD 377)
25. Change Page Orientation (WD 379)
26. Merge to a Directory (WD 379)
27. Convert Text to a Table (WD 382)
28. Repeat Header Rows (WD 384)
29. Sort a Table by Multiple Columns (WD 385)

If you have a SAM 2010 user profile, your instructor may have assigned an autogradable version of this assignment. If so, log into the SAM 2010 Web site at www.cengage.com/sam2010 to download the instruction and start files.

Learn It Online

Test your knowledge of chapter content and key terms.

Instructions: To complete the Learn It Online exercises, start your browser, click the Address bar, and then enter the Web address **scsite.com/wd2010/learn**. When the Word 2010 Learn It Online page is displayed, click the link for the exercise you want to complete and then read the instructions.

Chapter Reinforcement TF, MC, and SA
A series of true/false, multiple choice, and short answer questions that test your knowledge of the chapter content.

Flash Cards
An interactive learning environment where you identify chapter key terms associated with displayed definitions.

Practice Test
A series of multiple choice questions that test your knowledge of chapter content and key terms.

Who Wants To Be a Computer Genius?
An interactive game that challenges your knowledge of chapter content in the style of a television quiz show.

Wheel of Terms
An interactive game that challenges your knowledge of chapter key terms in the style of the television show *Wheel of Fortune*.

Crossword Puzzle Challenge
A crossword puzzle that challenges your knowledge of key terms presented in the chapter.

Apply Your Knowledge

Reinforce the skills and apply the concepts you learned in this chapter.

Editing, Printing, and Merging with a Form Letter and Its Data Source
Note: To complete this assignment, you will be required to use the Data Files for Students. See the inside back cover of this book for instructions on downloading the Data Files for Students, or contact your instructor for information about accessing the required files.

Instructions: Start Word. Open the document, Apply 6-1 Fund Drive Letter, from the Data Files for Students. When you open the main document, if Word displays a dialog box about an SQL command, click the Yes button. If Word prompts for the name of the data source, select Apply 6-1 Donor List on the Data Files for Students.

The document is a main document for the Future Leaders Spring Fund Drive form letter. You are to edit the date content control and GreetingLine merge field, print the form letter, add a record to the data source, and merge the form letters to a file.

Perform the following tasks:
1. Edit the date content control so that it contains the date 4/9/2012.

2. Edit the GreetingLine merge field so that the salutation ends with a comma (,).

3. Save the modified main document for the form letter with the name Apply 6-1 Fund Drive Letter Modified.

4. Highlight the merge fields in the document. How many are there? Remove the highlight from the merge fields.

5. View merged data in the document. Use the navigation buttons in the Preview Results group to display merged data from various records in the data source. What is the last name shown in the first record? The third record? The fifth record? View merge fields (that is, turn off the view merged data).

Continued >

Apply Your Knowledge *continued*

6. Print the main document for the form letter by opening the Backstage view, clicking the Print tab, and then clicking the Print button (Figure 6–84).

7. Add a record to the data source that contains your personal information. Type **$25** in the Amount field and **Scholarship** in the Fund field.

8. In the data source, change Shannon Goodman's last name to Milton.

9. Sort the data source by the Last Name field.

10. Save the main document for the form letter again.

11. Merge the form letters to a new document. Save the new document with the name Apply 6-1 Fund Drive Merged Letters.

12. If requested by your instructor, merge the form letters directly to the printer.

13. Submit the saved documents in the format specified by your instructor.

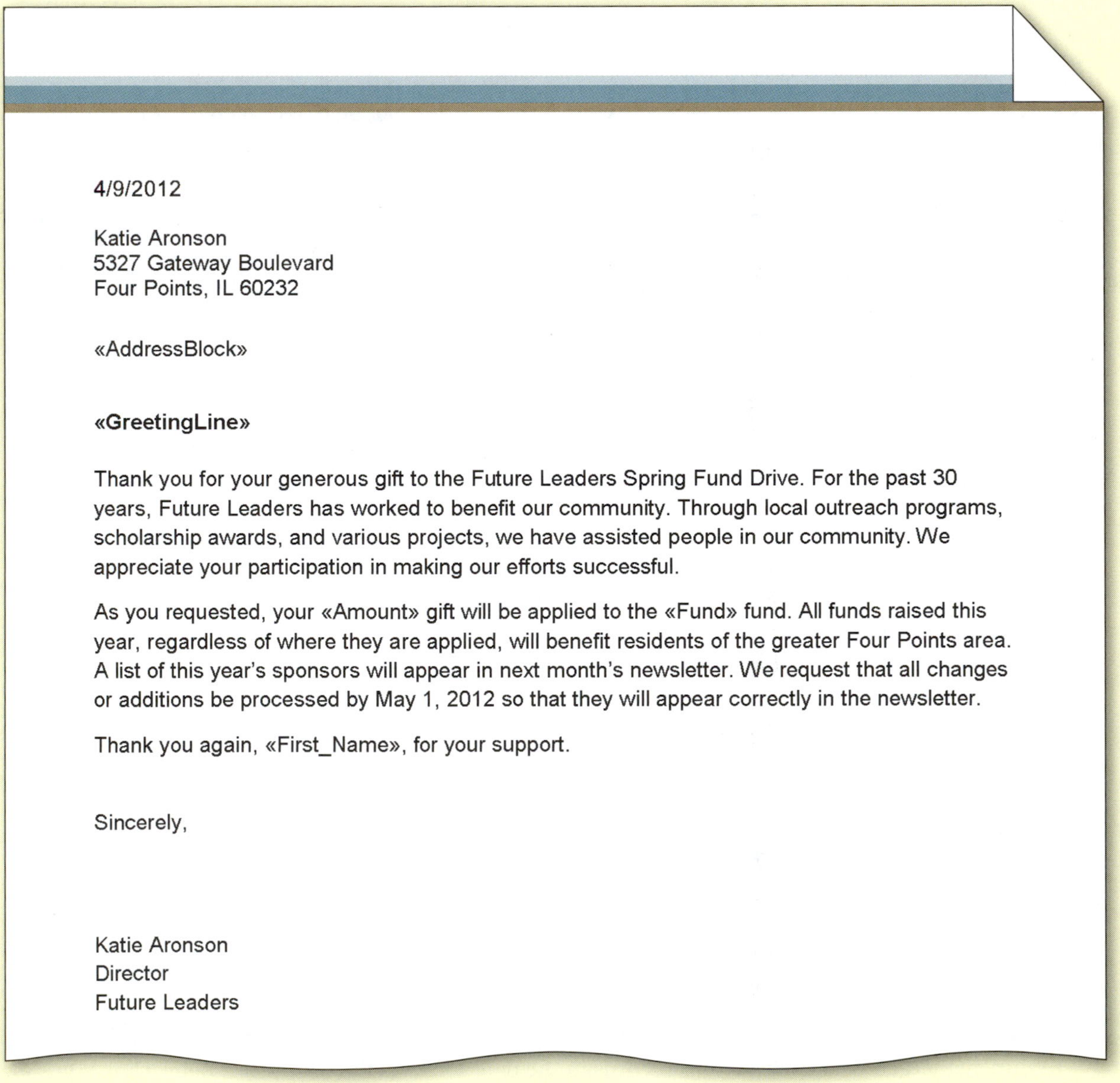

4/9/2012

Katie Aronson
5327 Gateway Boulevard
Four Points, IL 60232

«AddressBlock»

«GreetingLine»

Thank you for your generous gift to the Future Leaders Spring Fund Drive. For the past 30 years, Future Leaders has worked to benefit our community. Through local outreach programs, scholarship awards, and various projects, we have assisted people in our community. We appreciate your participation in making our efforts successful.

As you requested, your «Amount» gift will be applied to the «Fund» fund. All funds raised this year, regardless of where they are applied, will benefit residents of the greater Four Points area. A list of this year's sponsors will appear in next month's newsletter. We request that all changes or additions be processed by May 1, 2012 so that they will appear correctly in the newsletter.

Thank you again, «First_Name», for your support.

Sincerely,

Katie Aronson
Director
Future Leaders

Figure 6–84

Extend Your Knowledge

Extend the skills you learned in this chapter and experiment with new skills. You may need to use Help to complete the assignment.

Modifying a Data Source, Editing an IF Field, Inserting a Fill-In Field, and Formatting a Letter

Note: To complete this assignment, you will be required to use the Data Files for Students. See the inside back cover of this book for instructions on downloading the Data Files for Students, or contact your instructor for information about accessing the required files.

Instructions: Start Word. Open the document, Extend 6-1 Graduation Keepsakes Letter, from the Data Files for Students. When you open the main document, if Word displays a dialog box about an SQL command, click the Yes button. If Word prompts for the name of the data source, select Extend 6-1 Customers on the Data Files for Students.

The document is a main document for a Graduation Keepsakes form letter (Figure 6–85). You will change the margins, change the shape, add a field to the data source, modify an IF field, and add a Fill-in field.

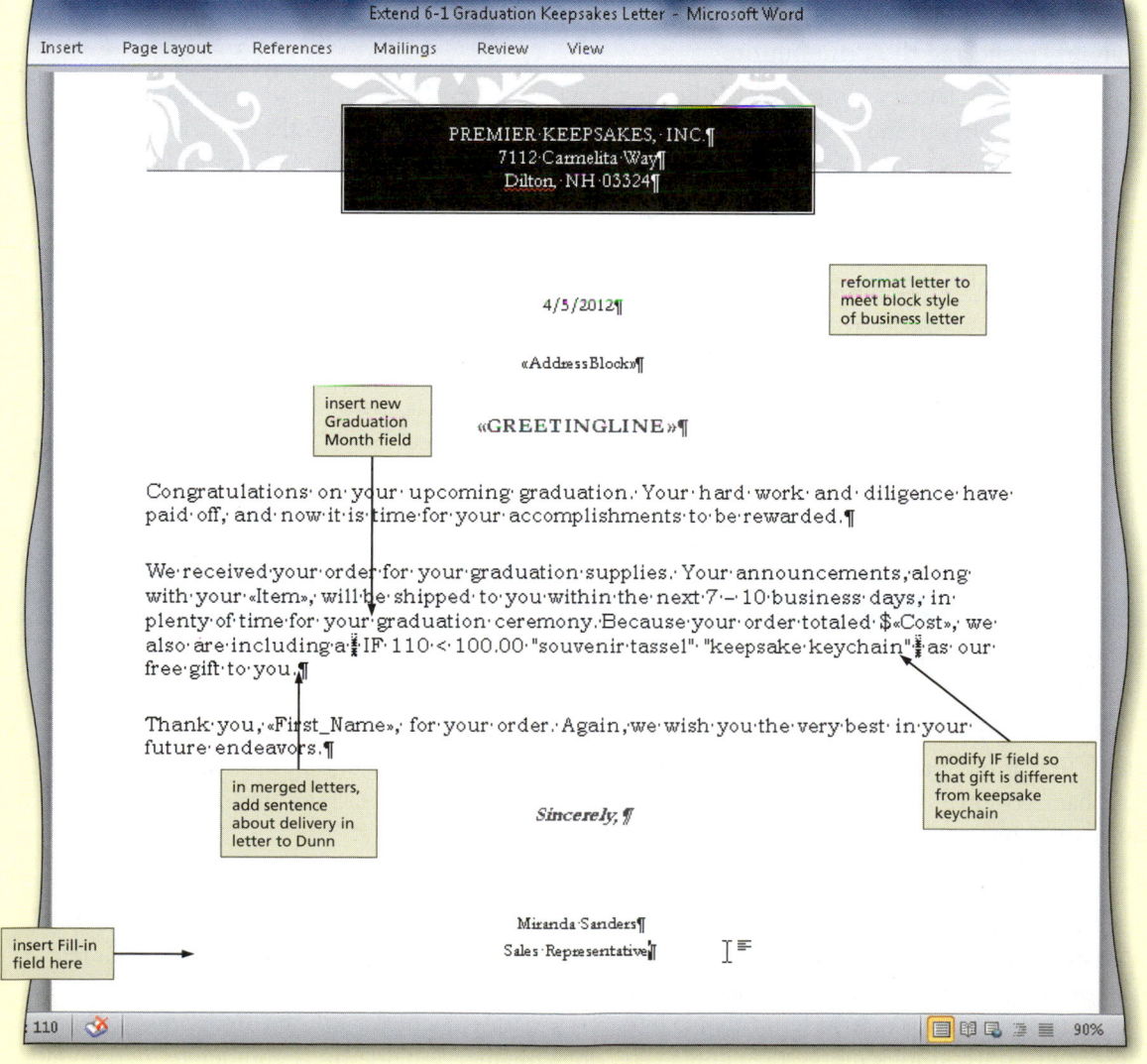

Figure 6–85

Continued >

STUDENT ASSIGNMENTS

Perform the following tasks:

1. Use Help to learn about mail merge, IF fields, and Fill-in fields.

2. Add a field to the data source called Graduation Month. Enter field values for each record: Hernandez – May, Dunn – August, Quint – December, Lee – June, DeSantos – July.

3. Add another field to the data source called Major. Enter field values of your choice for each record.

4. In the second sentence in the second paragraph of the main document, insert the new field called Graduation Month, just before the words, graduation ceremony.

5. Edit the IF field so that the gift for orders greater than or equal to $100 is an item other than a keepsake keychain. *Hint*: Display the IF field code in the document window and edit the IF field directly in the document.

6. At the bottom of the document, insert a Fill-in field, so that you can type a different personalized note to each customer. When you merge the letters, type a note to each customer. The notes should be meaningful to the recipient, related to his or her major.

7. Merge the letters to a new document. Save the merged letters. At the end of the second paragraph in the letter to Dunn, type this sentence: In addition, we are upgrading your delivery method at no charge because of a manufacturer delay.

8. Print the main document for the form letter by opening the Backstage view, clicking the Print tab, and then clicking the Print button.

9. Print the form letter with field codes showing, that is, with the 'Print field codes instead of their values' check box selected in the Word Options dialog box. Be sure to deselect this check box after printing the field codes version of the letter. How does this printout differ from the one printed in Task #8?

10. Change the document properties, as specified by your instructor. Submit the merged letters in the format specified by your instructor.

11. If your instructor requests, create envelopes for each letter in the data source.

12. Reformat the letter so that it is properly spaced and sized according to the block style for business letters.

13. If you know Access and your instructor requests, create the data source in Access and then open the main document with the Access database file as the data source.

Make It Right

Analyze a document and correct all errors and/or improve the design.

Editing Merge Fields, Editing Data Source Records, and Specifying Filter Conditions

Note: To complete this assignment, you will be required to use the Data Files for Students. See the inside back cover of this book for instructions on downloading the Data Files for Students, or contact your instructor for information about accessing the required files.

Instructions: Start Word. Open the document, Make It Right 6-1 Registration Letter, from the Data Files for Students. When you open the main document, if Word displays a dialog box about an SQL command, click the Yes button. If Word prompts for the name of the data source, select Make It Right 6-1 Registrants on the Data Files for Students.

The document is a form letter that is missing fields and requires editing (Figure 6–86). You are to insert an AddressBlock merge field and a GreetingLine merge field, insert and delete merge fields, edit data source records, and filter records.

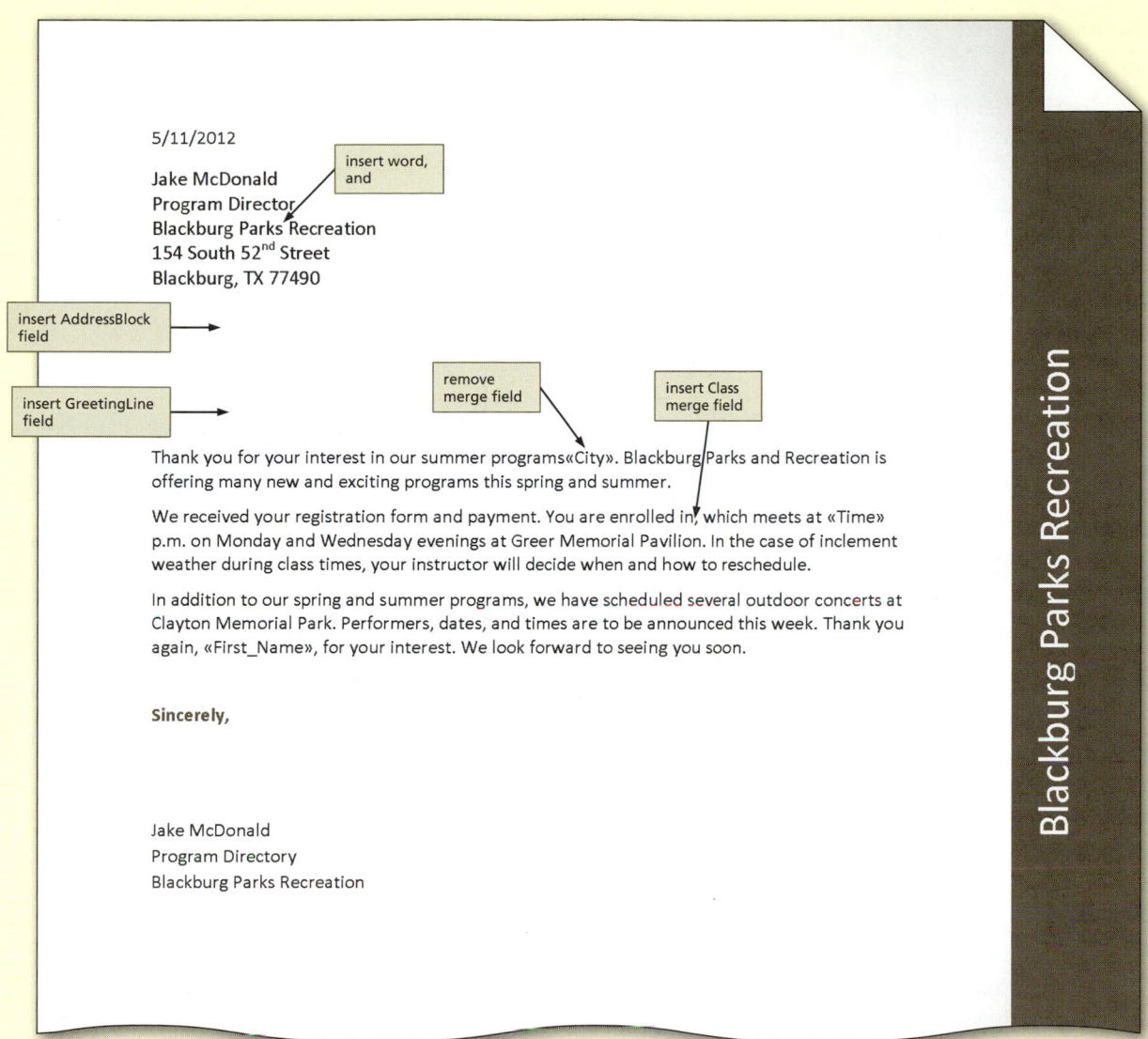

Blackburg Parks Recreation

Figure 6–86

Perform the following tasks:

1. In the return address, change the text, Parks Recreation, to Parks and Recreation (insert the word, and). This update also should be reflected in the signature block.

2. Insert the AddressBlock merge field below the return address.

3. Insert the GreetingLine merge field below the AddressBlock. Use an appropriate salutation and punctuation.

4. In the second sentence in the second paragraph, insert the merge field, Class, before the comma.

5. In the first sentence, remove the City merge field.

6. In the data source, find the record whose last name is Abbott. Fix the State entry so that it reads, TX, and ZIP Code entry so that it reads 79006.

7. In the data source, find the misspelling Drivr and correct its spelling to Drive.

8. Change the document properties, as specified by your instructor. Save the revised document using the name Make It Right 6-1 Registration Letter Modified. Submit the letter in the format specified by your instructor.

Continued >

Make It Right *continued*

9. Specify that only recipients enrolled in Intermediate Tennis should be included in a merge. Merge these form letters to the printer. Clear the filter.

10. Identify another type of filter for this data source and merge those form letters to a new document. In the new document, type the filter you used. Submit the document in the format specified by your instructor.

11. Merge all the records to a new document in last name order. On a page at the end of the merged documents, type the if condition used in the letters. Submit the document in the format specified by your instructor.

In the Lab

Design and/or create a document using the guidelines, concepts, and skills presented in this chapter. Labs are listed in order of increasing difficulty.

Lab 1: Creating a Form Letter Using a Template, a Data Source, Mailing Labels, and a Directory

Problem: You are graduating this May and have prepared your resume (shown in Figure 5–72 on page WD 323 in Chapter 5). You decide to create a cover letter for your resume as a form letter that you will send to potential employers. The main document for the form letter is shown in Figure 6–87a.

Perform the following tasks:

1. Use the Essential Merge Letter template to begin creating the main document for the form letter. If necessary, change the document theme to Essential. Save the main document for the form letter with the file name, Lab 6-1 Monroe Cover Letter.

2. Type a new data source using the data shown in Figure 6–87b. Delete field names not used and add two field names: Position and Publication. Save the data source with the file name, Lab 6-1 Monroe Potential Employers.

3. Save the main document for the form letter again. Edit the AddressBlock and GreetingLine merge fields according to the sample formats shown in the figure. Insert the merge fields as shown in the figure. Delete the blank line at the top of the letter and the sender address in the signature block. Increase the blank space between the sender address and inside address. The entire letter should fit on a single page. *Hint*: The date is part of the footer.

4. Merge the form letters to a new document. Save the merged letters in a file called Lab 6-1 Monroe Merged Letters.

5. In a new document window, address mailing labels using the same data source you used for the form letters. Save the mailing label layout with the name, Lab 6-1 Monroe Mailing Labels. If required by your instructor, merge the mailing labels to the printer.

6. In a new document window, specify the main document type as a directory. Change the page layout to landscape orientation. Insert all merge fields in the document, separating each with a comma. Merge the directory layout to a new document window. Convert the list of fields to a Word table (the table will have 11 columns). Add a row to the top of the table and insert field names in the empty cells. Bold the text in the first row. Change the margins to narrow. Change the font size of all text in the table to 9 point. Apply the Light List - Accent 5 table style. Resize the table columns so that the table looks like Figure 6–87b. Sort the table in the directory by the Last Name field. Save the merged directory with the name, Lab 6-1 Monroe Merged Directory.

7. Submit all documents in the format specified by your instructor.

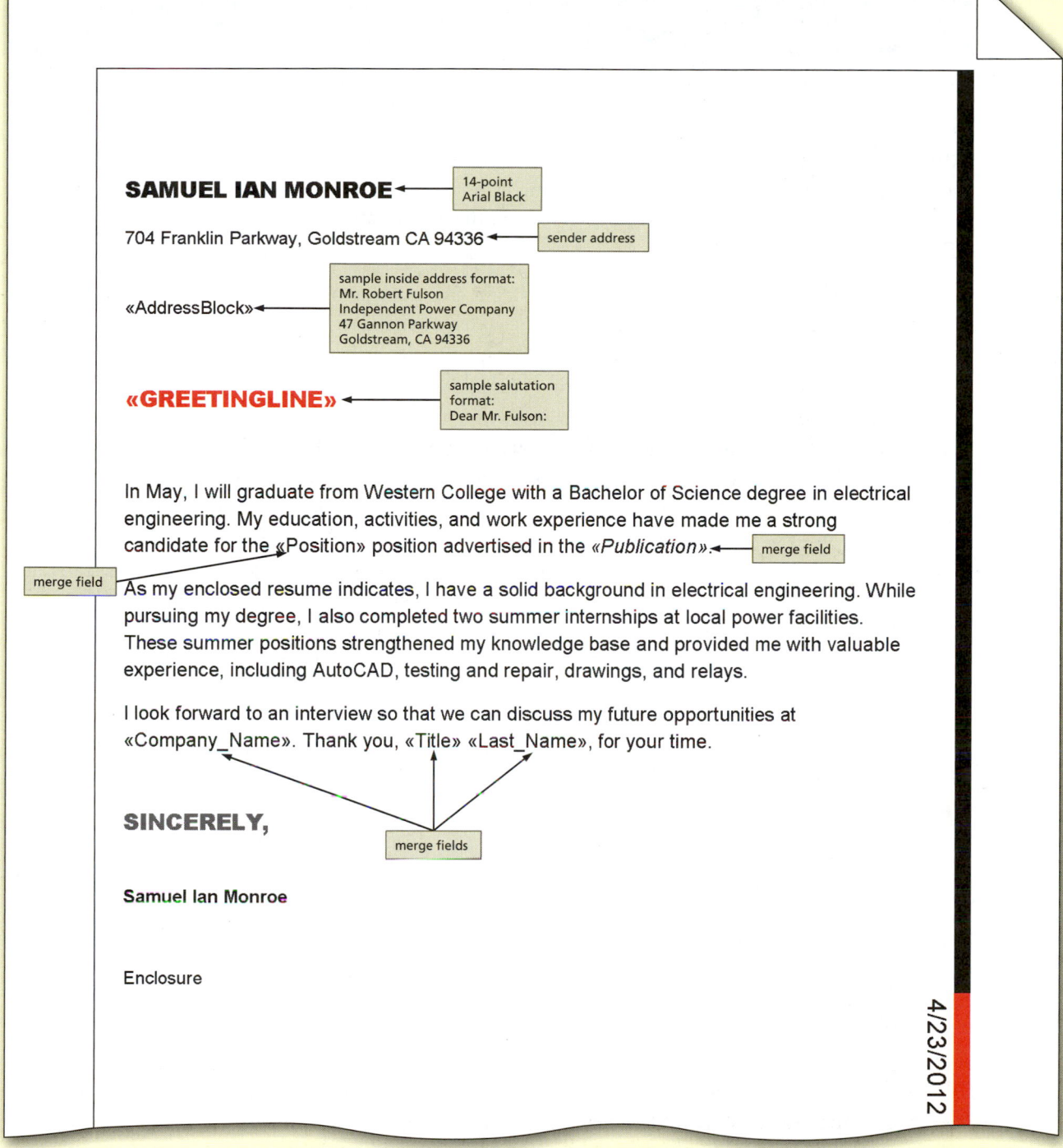

Figure 6–87 (a) Main Document for Form Letter

Title	First Name	Last Name	Company Name	Address Line 1	Address Line 2	City	State	ZIP Code	Position	Publication
Mr.	Robert	Fulson	Independent Power Company	47 Gannon Parkway		Goldstream	CA	94336	facilities engineer	Goldstream Press
Ms.	Nancy	Gross	Green Light Power	700 North 350 East		Goldstream	CA	94336	electrical engineer	Daily Journal
Mr.	Scott	Kazmierek	Frankfort Gas and Electric	7600 Penn Drive		Frankfort	CA	93225	engineering assistant	Frankfort Weekly
Mr.	Juan	Padilla	Arthur Power and Light	99 South Waterway	Building 4	Arthur	CA	94374	assistant facilities manager	Metropolitan News
Ms.	Shari	Warner	Electric Cooperative	322 Iverson Drive		Barrington	CA	94434	test engineer	Barrington Daily

Figure 6–87 (b) Data Source

In the Lab

Lab 2: Creating a Form Letter Using a Template with an IF Field, a Data Source, Mailing Labels, and a Directory

Problem: You are graduating this May and have prepared your resume (shown in Figure 5–73 on page WD 325 in Chapter 5). You decide to create a cover letter for your resume as a form letter that you will send to potential employers. The main document for the form letter is shown in Figure 6–88a. In the letter, the availability date will vary, depending on the job fair attended.

Perform the following tasks:

1. Use the Urban Merge Letter template to begin creating the main document for the form letter. Change the document theme to Perspective. Change the margins to Normal (1-inch top, bottom, left, and right). Save the main document for the form letter with the file name, Lab 6-2 MacMahon Cover Letter, in a folder called Lab 6-2 MacMahon Job Hunting. *Hint*: Create the folder while saving.

2. Type a new data source using the data shown in Figure 6–88b. Delete field names not used, rename the Company Name field as Organization Name, and add two field names: Job Fair and Position. Save the data source with the file name, Lab 6-2 MacMahon Potential Employers, in the Lab 6-2 MacMahon Job Hunting folder.

3. Save the main document for the form letter again. Edit the AddressBlock and GreetingLine merge fields according to the sample formats in the figure. Be sure to match the Organization Name field in the data source to the Company field in the Match Fields dialog box so that the organization name appears in each inside address. Insert the merge fields as shown in the figure. The IF field tests if Job Fair equal to Fairfax; if it is, then print the text, May 21; otherwise print the text, May 14. Delete the sender company name content control. The entire letter should fit on a single page.

4. Merge the form letters to a new document. Save the merged letters in a file called Lab 6-2 MacMahon Merged Letters in the Lab 6-2 MacMahon Job Hunting folder.

5. In a new document window, address mailing labels using the same data source you used for the form letters. Save the mailing label layout with the name, Lab 6-2 MacMahon Mailing Labels, in the Lab 6-2 MacMahon Job Hunting folder. If required by your instructor, merge the mailing labels to the printer.

6. If your printer allows and your instructor requests it, in a new document window, address envelopes using the same data source you used for the form letters. Save the envelopes with the file name, Lab 6-2 MacMahon Envelopes, in the folder named Lab 6-2 MacMahon Job Hunting. If required by your instructor, merge the envelopes to the printer.

7. In a new document window, specify the main document type as a directory. Change the page layout to landscape orientation. Insert all merge fields in the document, separating each with a comma. Merge the directory layout to a new document window. Convert the list of fields to a Word table (the table will have 11 columns). Add a row to the top of the table and insert field names in the empty cells. Bold the text in the first row. Change the margins to narrow. Apply the Light List - Accent 2 table style. Resize the table columns so that the table looks like Figure 6–88b. Center the table between the margins. Sort the directory by the Last Name field within Job Fair field. Save the merged directory with the name, Lab 6-2 MacMahon Merged Directory, in the folder named Lab 6-2 MacMahon Job Hunting.

8. Submit all documents in the format specified by your instructor.

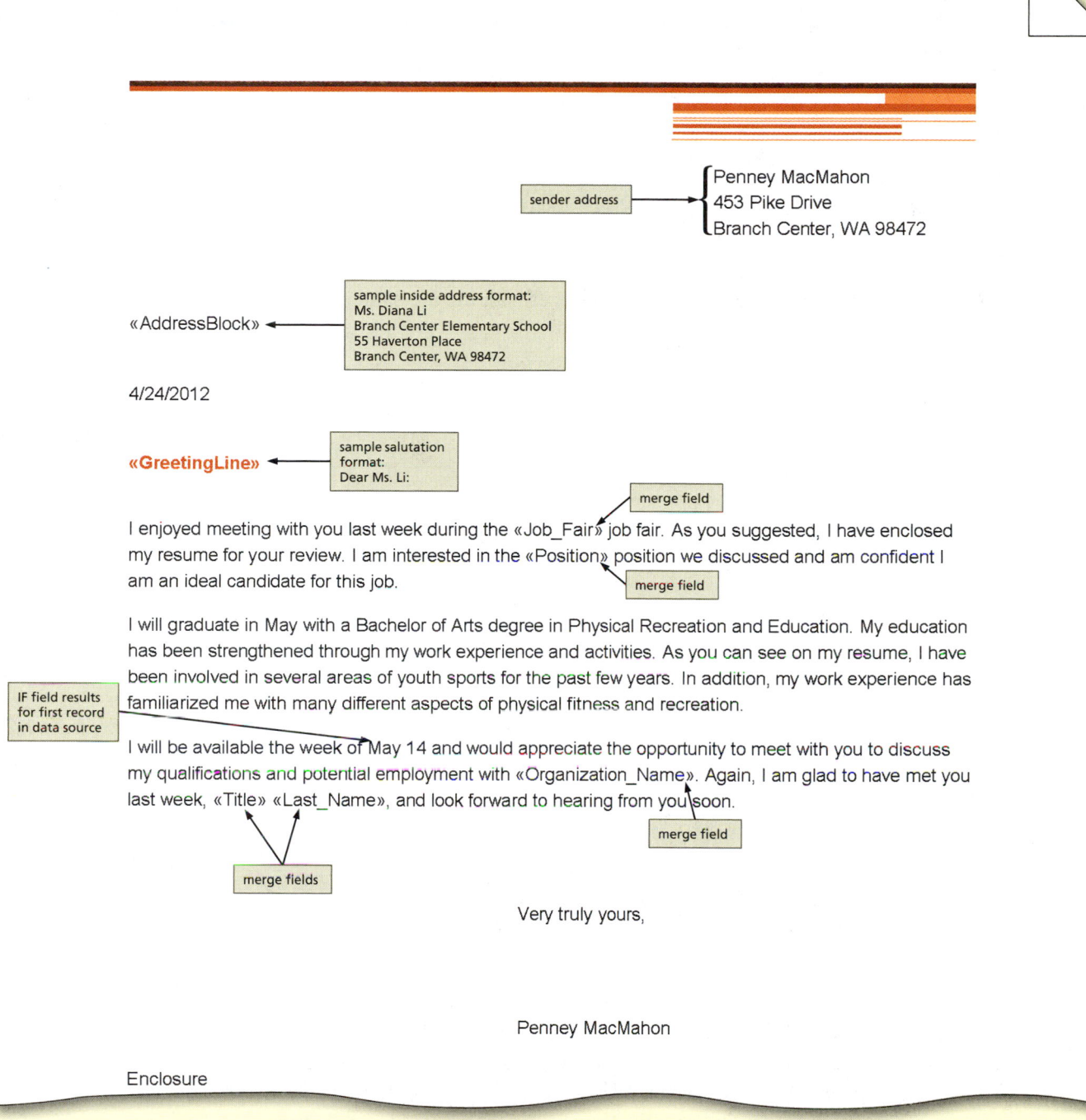

Figure 6–88 (a) Main Document for Form Letter

Title	First Name	Last Name	Organization Name	Address Line 1	Address Line 2	City	State	ZIP Code	Job Fair	Position
Mr.	Seth	Briggs	Branch Center Recreation Center	1274 Washington Avenue	P.O. Box 10	Branch Center	WA	98472	Branch Center	Recreation Director
Mr.	Dwayne	Jackman	Branch Center High School	8290 Morgan Parkway		Branch Center	WA	98472	Branch Center	Physical Education teacher
Ms.	Diana	Li	Branch Center Elementary School	55 Haverton Place		Branch Center	WA	98472	Campus Career Day	Physical Education teacher
Mr.	Stuart	Tan	Fairfax Parks and Recreation	500 Greenway Circle		Fairfax	WA	98446	Fairfax	Assistant Program Director
Ms.	Tammy	Walker	Fairfax Middle School	675 East 175th Street	Suite 15	Fairfax	WA	98446	Fairfax	Physical Education teacher

Figure 6–88 (b) Data Source

In the Lab

Lab 3: Designing a Data Source, Form Letter, and Directory from Sample Letters

Problem: You are graduating this May and have prepared your resume (shown in Figure 5–74 on page WD 326 in Chapter 5). Sample drafted letters for the cover letter are shown in Figure 6–89a and Figure 6–89b.

Perform the following tasks:

1. Review the letters in Figure 6–89 and determine the fields that should be in the data source. Write the field names down on a piece of paper.

2. Do not use a template to create this form letter. In Word, create a main document for the letters. Save the main document for the form letter with the file name, Lab 6-3 Ramirez Cover Letter.

Daniel Austin Ramirez
84 Southland Drive
Jonner, MA 01298

April 16, 2012

Ms. Beth Gupta
Jonner County Public Library
20 Oakton Parkway
North Branch
Jonner, MA 01298

Dear Ms. Gupta:

I have enclosed my resume in response to your advertisement for the Media Specialist position I saw advertised online. I will graduate in May with a Master's in Library and Information Science degree from Benson College.

Throughout my education, I worked in libraries, which has provided me with valuable experience and insight into the running and operation of a library. My coursework and media specialist certification, along with my library experience, make me an ideal candidate for the Media Specialist position.

I look forward to an interview, during which we can further discuss my qualifications for a position with Jonner County Public Library. Thank you, Ms. Gupta, for your consideration.

Sincerely,

Daniel Austin Ramirez

Enclosure

Figure 6–89 (a) Sample Merged Form Letter

3. Create a data source containing five records, consisting of data from the two letters shown in Figure 6–89 and then add three more records with your own data. Save the data source with the file name, Lab 6-3 Ramirez Potential Employers.

4. Merge the form letters to a new document or the printer, as specified by your instructor.

5. Merge the data source to a directory. Convert it to a Word table. Add an attractive border to the table and apply any other formatting you feel necessary. Submit the directory in the format specified by your instructor.

Daniel Austin Ramirez
84 Southland Drive
Jonner, MA 01298

April 16, 2012

Mr. Kirk Green
Jonner County Reference Library
3033 Cameron Boulevard
Jonner, MA 01298

Dear Mr. Green:

I have enclosed my resume in response to your advertisement for the Reference Librarian position I saw advertised in the newspaper. I will graduate in May with a Master's in Library and Information Science degree from Benson College.

Throughout my education, I worked in libraries, which has provided me with valuable experience and insight into the running and operation of a library. My coursework and media specialist certification, along with my library experience, make me an ideal candidate for the Reference Librarian position.

I look forward to an interview, during which we can further discuss my qualifications for a position with Jonner County Reference Library. Thank you, Mr. Green, for your consideration.

Sincerely,

Daniel Austin Ramirez

Enclosure

Figure 6–89 (b) Sample Merged Form Letter

Cases and Places

Apply your creative thinking and problem solving skills to design and implement a solution.

Note: To complete these assignments, you may be required to use the Data Files for Students. See the inside back cover of this book for instructions on downloading the Data Files for Students, or contact your instructor for information about accessing the required files.

1: Create a Form Letter for Dormitory Assignments

Academic

As assistant to the director of housing at Ronson University, you send letters to new students regarding dormitory assignments. Create the data source using the data in Figure 6–90.

Title	First Name	Last Name	Address Line 1	Address Line 2	City	State	ZIP Code	Dorm	Meal Plan	Cost
Ms.	Renee	Shelton	2008 Anderson Avenue	Apt. 12A	Rock Point	WI	42467	Billings Tower	A	$500
Ms.	Adriana	Pi	739 Clifton Place		Fort Benjamin	WI	42240	Goss Hall	B	$750
Mr.	Sam	Steinberg	586 Savannah Court		Rock Point	WI	42467	Court Quad	A	$500
Mr.	Marcus	Darien	3659 Haverston Lane	Unit 5	Darwin	WI	48472	Goss Hall	C	$975
Mr.	Derrick	Riley	65 East Fountain View		Darwin	WI	48472	Pfifer Courts	B	$750

Figure 6–90

Create a form letter using the following information: The school's address is 4541 North 175th Street, Fort Benjamin, WI 42240. After the salutation, the first paragraph in the main document should read: Congratulations again on your admission to Ronson University. We are delighted that you have chosen Ronson to pursue your educational goals. The second paragraph in the main document should read: We received your application for housing and have completed the dormitory assignments. As you requested, you have been assigned to «Dorm». Because you chose Meal Plan «Meal_Plan», a charge of «Cost» has been added to your tuition. A bill reflecting the total amount due will be mailed to you before May 1. The third paragraph in the main document should read: Ours is a vibrant, growing campus, and one on which we hope you will feel at home and welcome. We hope that your experience at Ronson will be enjoyable, memorable, and above all, rewarding. We look forward to seeing you, «First_Name», when classes begin in the fall!

Use your name in the signature block. If required by your instructor, address and print accompanying labels or envelopes for the form letters. Create a directory of the data source records. Use the concepts and techniques presented in this chapter to create and format the form letters, mailing labels or envelopes, and directory. The letter should include all essential elements, use proper spacing and formats for a business letter, and follow the guidelines of the block, modified block, or modified semi-block letter style. (*Hint:* You may need to use outside resources to obtain these guidelines.) Be sure to check the spelling and grammar of the finished documents. Submit your assignment in the format specified by your instructor.

2: Create a Form Letter for Children's Swimming Lessons

Personal

As a volunteer for Lincoln Community Pools, you send confirmation letters to parents regarding swimming lessons for their children. Create the data source using the data in Figure 6–91.

Title	First Name	Last Name	Address Line 1	Address Line 2	City	State	ZIP Code	Child Name	Class Time	Gender
Ms.	Lenore	Simms	500 Morris Street	Apt. 22	Four Points	IL	61922	Sophie	2:00 p.m.	her
Ms.	Tracy	Fenn	388 Chestnut Court		Aaron	IL	61933	Kyle	10:00 a.m.	his
Mr.	Morris	Feldman	709 East 500 South		Four Points	IL	61922	Stefan	2:00 p.m.	his
Ms.	Jane	Tu	430 Cloaken Court	Apt. 8	Aaron	IL	61933	Sarah	10:00 a.m.	her
Mr.	Ben	Skolman	2390 Darien Lane		Aaron	IL	61933	Benny	2:00 p.m.	his

Figure 6–91

Create a form letter using the following information: The center's address is 875 Fifteenth Street, Four Points, IL 61922. After the salutation, the first paragraph in the main document should read: Thank you for enrolling your child, «Child_Name», in our swimming lessons. Teaching your child to swim is both prudent and a priceless investment in your child's future safety. The second paragraph in the main document should read: As you requested, «Child_Name» has been placed in the «Class_Time» class, which meets on Monday, Wednesday, and Friday. The instructor for this time slot is Joe Sanchez. All of our swim instructors are Red Cross certified lifeguards, as well as experienced teachers and/or coaches. The third paragraph in the main document should read: An observation area is available for parents and caregivers who wish to stay during the lesson. Please bring a towel and, if your child requests or is accustomed to wearing them, goggles. All other items will be provided. We look forward to seeing «Child_Name» at «Gender» first lesson!

Use your name in the signature block. If required by your instructor, address and print accompanying labels or envelopes for the form letters. Create a directory of the data source records. Use the concepts and techniques presented in this chapter to create and format the form letters, mailing labels or envelopes, and directory. The letter should include all essential elements, use proper spacing and formats for a business letter, and follow the guidelines of the block, modified block, or modified semi-block letter style. (*Hint:* You may need to use outside resources to obtain these guidelines.) Be sure to check the spelling and grammar of the finished documents. Submit your assignment in the format specified by your instructor.

3: Create a Form Letter Confirming Ticket Sales

Professional

As ticket sales manager of Juniper Theatre Group, you send confirmation letters to customers. Create the data source using the data in Figure 6–92.

Title	First Name	Last Name	Address Line 1	Address Line 2	City	State	ZIP Code	Number of Tickets	Day	Date
Ms.	Alisha	Bright	6914 Leisure Lane		Goldstream	CA	94336	six	Friday	June 10
Mr.	Pete	Stanley	1210 Sunset Court	Apt. 21A	Condor	CA	95702	four	Saturday	June 4
Mr.	Rudy	Tan	5442 West 178th Street		Condor	CA	95702	two	Friday	June 3
Ms.	Carol	Athens	249 Westmore Place	Apt. 4L	Goldstream	CA	94336	two	Saturday	June 11
Ms.	Stacey	Rivera	148 Carver Street		Condor	CA	95702	four	Saturday	June 11

Figure 6–92

Continued >

Cases and Places *continued*

Create a form letter using the following information: The theatre's address is 407 Planters Avenue, Goldstream, CA 94336. After the salutation, the first paragraph in the main document should read: Thank you for your ticket purchase for *Romeo and Juliet*. We are excited about our new facility and are looking forward to our first production here. The second paragraph in the main document should read: Enclosed are the «Number_of_Tickets» tickets you ordered for the «Day», «Date» performance. We recommend that you arrive by 1:30 p.m. to allow ample time for seating. The third paragraph in the main document should read: Light refreshments and beverages will be available for purchase during Intermission. We hope you enjoy our new venue and what promises to be another spectacular production!

Use your name in the signature block. If required by your instructor, address and print accompanying labels or envelopes for the form letters. Create a directory of the data source records. Use the concepts and techniques presented in this chapter to create and format the form letters, mailing labels or envelopes, and directory. The letter should include all essential elements, use proper spacing and formats for a business letter, and follow the guidelines of the block, modified block, or modified semi-block letter style. (*Hint:* You may need to use outside resources to obtain these guidelines.) Be sure to check the spelling and grammar of the finished documents. Submit your assignment in the format specified by your instructor.

7 | Creating a Newsletter with a Pull-Quote and Graphics

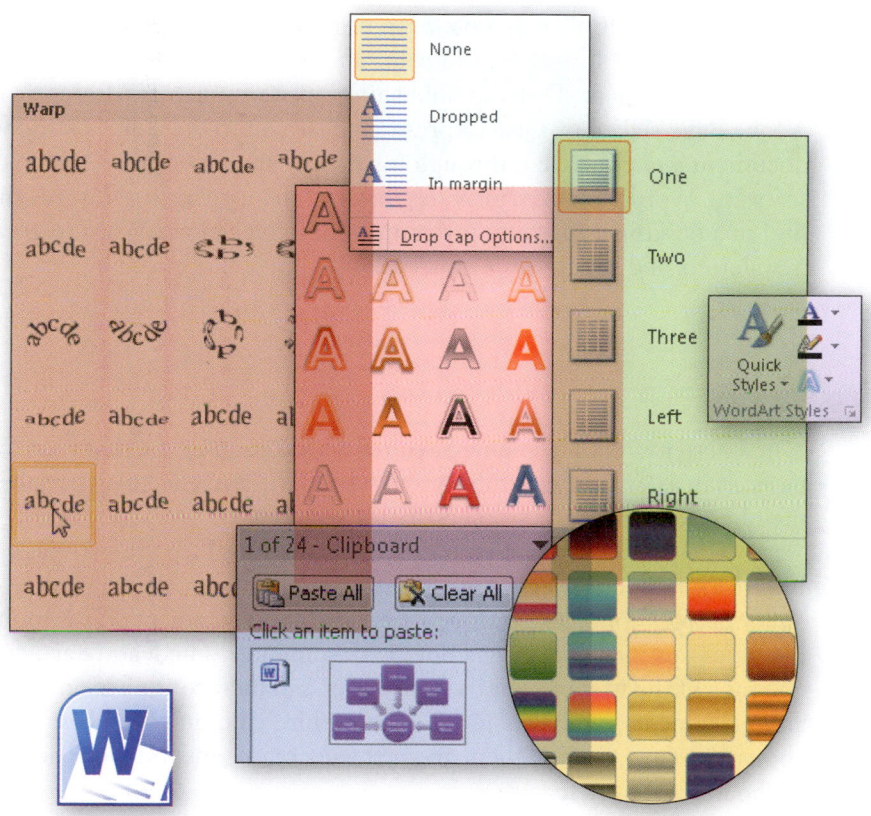

Objectives

You will have mastered the material in this chapter when you can:

- Insert and format WordArt
- Set custom margins
- Set custom tab stops
- Crop a graphic
- Rotate a graphic
- Format a document in multiple columns
- Justify a paragraph
- Hyphenate a document

- Format a character as a drop cap
- Insert a column break
- Insert and format a text box
- Copy and paste using a split window
- Balance columns
- Modify and format a SmartArt graphic
- Copy and paste using the Office Clipboard

7 | Creating a Newsletter with a Pull-Quote and Graphics

Introduction

Professional-looking documents, such as newsletters and brochures, often are created using desktop publishing software. With desktop publishing software, you can divide a document in multiple columns, wrap text around diagrams and other graphical images, change fonts and font sizes, add color and lines, and so on, to create an attention-grabbing document. Desktop publishing software, such as Microsoft Publisher, Adobe PageMaker, or QuarkXpress, enables you to open an existing word processing document and enhance it through formatting tools not provided in your word processing software. Word, however, provides many of the formatting features that you would find in a desktop publishing program. Thus, you can use Word to create eye-catching newsletters and brochures.

Project — Newsletter

A newsletter is a publication geared for a specific audience that is created on a recurring basis, such as weekly, monthly, or quarterly. The audience may be subscribers, club members, employees, customers, patrons, etc.

The project in this chapter uses Word to produce the two-page newsletter shown in Figure 7–1. The newsletter is a monthly publication, called *Savvy Shopper*. Each issue of *Savvy Shopper* contains a feature article and announcements. This month's feature article discusses tips for purchasing a notebook computer. The feature article spans the first two columns of the first page of the newsletter and then continues on the second page. The announcements, which are located in the third column of the first page, inform members about discounts, remind them about the upcoming meeting, and advise them of the topic of the next month's feature article.

The Savvy Shopper newsletter in this chapter incorporates the desktop publishing features of Word. The body of each page of the newsletter is divided in three columns. A variety of fonts, font sizes, and colors add visual appeal to the document. The first page has text wrapped around a pull-quote, and the second page has text wrapped around a graphic. Horizontal and vertical lines separate distinct areas of the newsletter, including a page border around the perimeter of each page.

The project in this chapter involves several steps requiring you to drag the mouse. If you drag to the wrong location, you may want to cancel an action. Remember that you always can click the Undo button on the Quick Access Toolbar to cancel your most recent action.

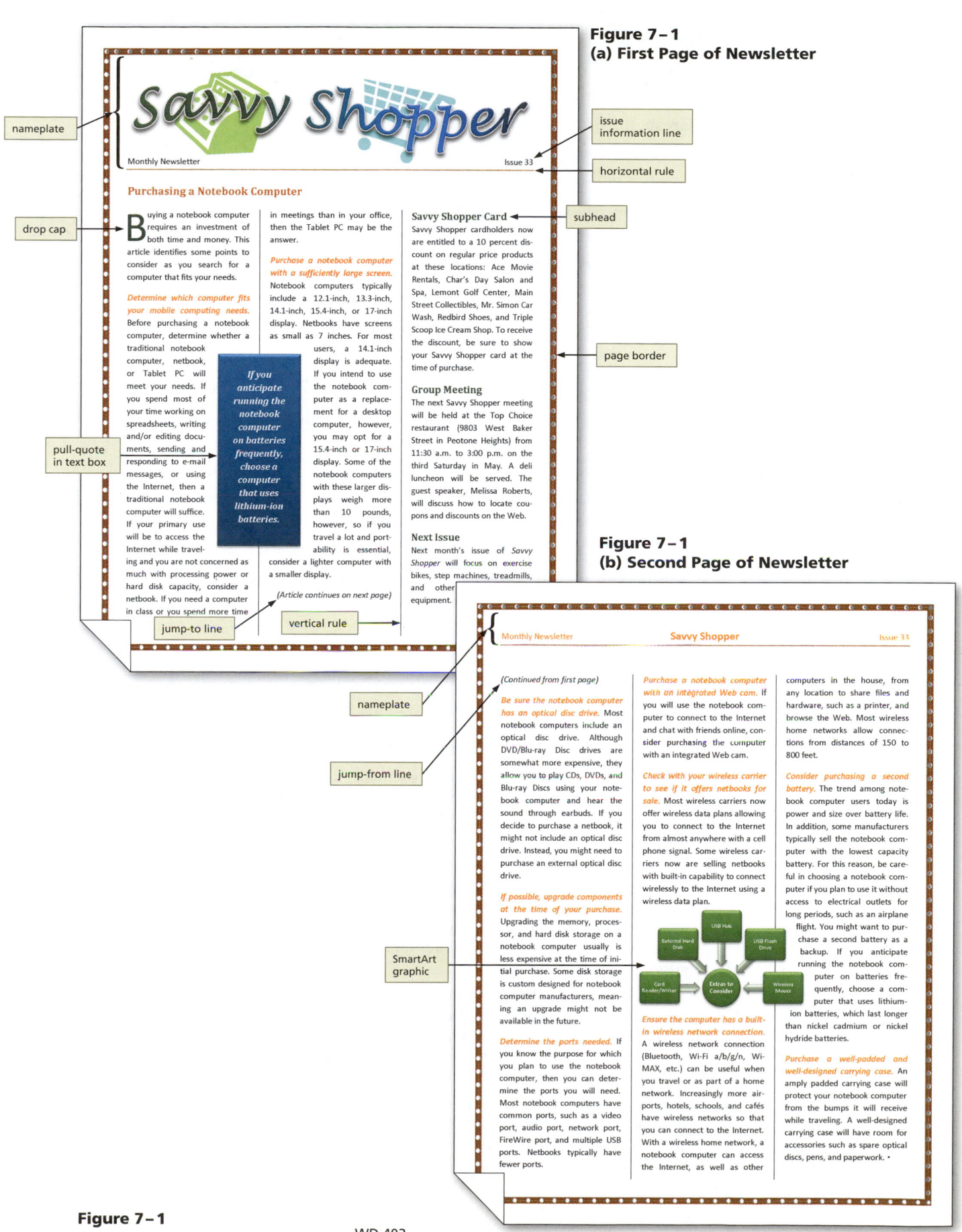

Figure 7–1
(a) First Page of Newsletter

nameplate

issue information line

drop cap

horizontal rule

subhead

pull-quote in text box

page border

jump-to line

vertical rule

Figure 7–1
(b) Second Page of Newsletter

nameplate

jump-from line

SmartArt graphic

Figure 7–1

Overview

As you read through this chapter, you will learn how to create the newsletter shown in Figure 7–1 on the previous page by performing these general tasks:

- Create the nameplate on the first page of the newsletter.
- Format the first page of the body of the newsletter.
- Create a pull-quote on the first page of the newsletter.
- Create the nameplate on the second page of the newsletter.
- Format the second page of the body of the newsletter.
- Print the newsletter.

Desktop Publishing Terminology

As you create professional-looking newsletters and brochures, you should be familiar with several desktop publishing terms. Figure 7–1 identifies these terms:

- A **nameplate**, or **banner**, is the portion of a newsletter that contains the title of the newsletter and usually an issue information line.
- The **issue information line** identifies the specific publication.
- A **ruling line**, usually identified by its direction as a **horizontal rule** or **vertical rule**, is a line that separates areas of the newsletter.
- A **subhead** is a heading within the body of the newsletter.
- A **pull-quote** is text that is *pulled*, or copied, from the text of the document and given graphical emphasis.

Plan Ahead

General Project Guidelines

When creating a Word document, the actions you perform and decisions you make will affect the appearance and characteristics of the finished document. As you create a newsletter, such as the project shown in Figure 7–1, you should follow these general guidelines:

1. **Create the nameplate.** The nameplate visually identifies the newsletter. Usually, the nameplate is positioned horizontally across the top of the newsletter, although some nameplates are vertical. The nameplate typically consists of text, graphics, and ruling lines.

2. **Determine content for the body of the newsletter.** Newsletters typically have one or more articles that begin on the first page. Include articles that are interesting to the audience. Incorporate color, appropriate fonts and font sizes, and alignment to provide visual interest. Use pull-quotes, graphics, and ruling lines to draw the reader's attention to important points. Avoid overusing visual elements — too many visuals can give the newsletter a cluttered look.

3. **Bind and distribute the newsletter.** Many newsletters are printed and mailed to recipients. Some are placed in public locations, free for interested parties. Others are e-mailed or posted on the Web for users to download. Printed newsletters typically are stapled at the top, along the side, or on a fold. For online newsletters, be sure the newsletter is in a format that most computer users will be able to open.

When necessary, more specific details concerning the above guidelines are presented at appropriate points in the chapter. The chapter also will identify the actions performed and decisions made regarding these guidelines during the creation of the newsletter shown in Figure 7–1.

To Start Word

If you are using a computer to step through the project in this chapter and you want your screens to match the figures in this book, you should change your computer's resolution to 1024 × 768. The following steps start Word and verify settings.

1 Start Word. If necessary, maximize the Word window.

2 If the Print Layout button on the status bar is not selected, click it so that your screen is in Print Layout view.

3 Change your zoom level to 100%.

4 If the Show/Hide ¶ button (Home tab | Paragraph group) is not selected already, click it to display formatting marks on the screen.

5 If the rulers are not displayed already, click the View Ruler button on the vertical scroll bar to display the rulers because you will use the rulers to perform tasks in this chapter.

BTW

The Ribbon and Screen Resolution
Word may change how the groups and buttons within the groups appear on the Ribbon, depending on the computer's screen resolution. Thus, your Ribbon may look different from the ones in this book if you are using a screen resolution other than 1024 × 768.

To Set Custom Margins

Recall that Word is preset to use standard 8.5-by-11-inch paper, with 1-inch top, bottom, left, and right margins. In earlier chapters, you changed the margins by selecting predefined settings in the Margins gallery. For the newsletter in this chapter, all margins (left, right, top, and bottom) are .75 inches, which is not a predefined setting in the Margins gallery. Thus, the following steps set custom margins.

1

• Display the Page Layout tab.

• Click the Margins button (Page Layout tab | Page Setup group) to display the Margins gallery (Figure 7–2).

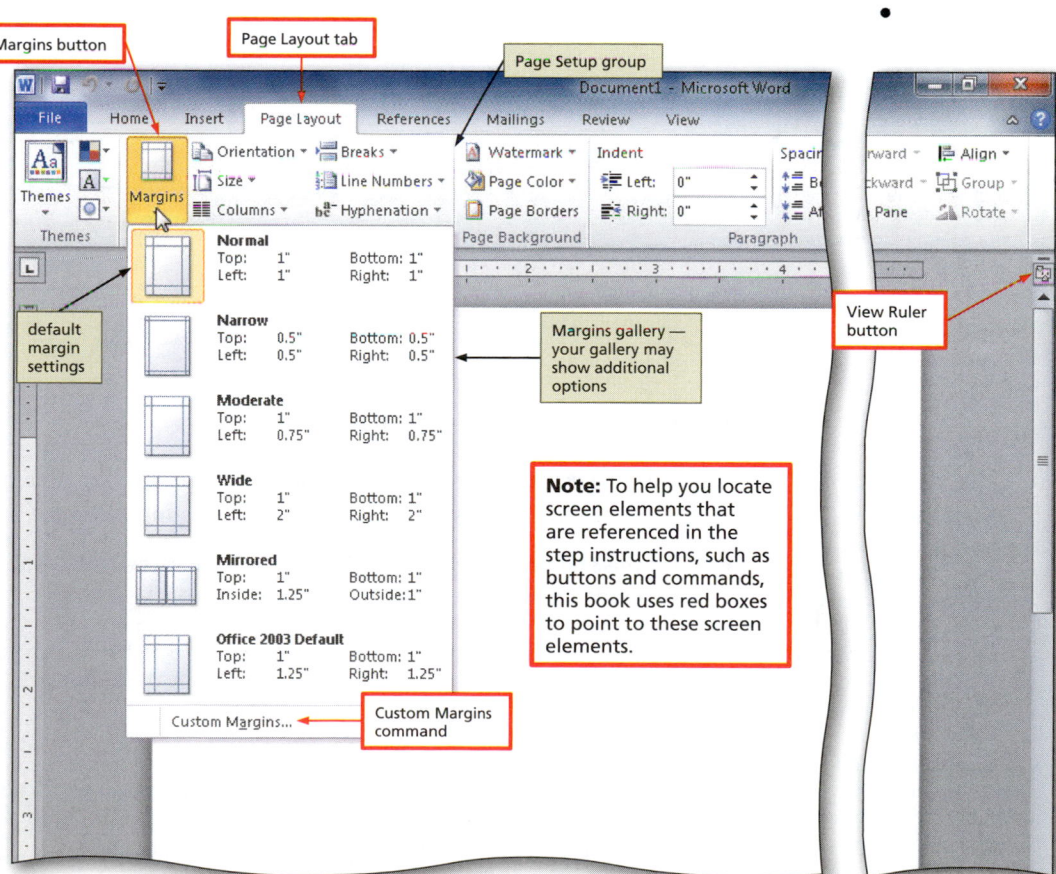

Figure 7–2

- Click Custom Margins in the Margins gallery to display the Page Setup dialog box. If necessary, click the Margins tab (Page Setup dialog box) to display the Margins sheet.

- Type **.75** in the Top box to change the top margin setting and then press the TAB key to position the insertion point in the Bottom box.

- Type **.75** in the Bottom box to change the bottom margin setting and then press the TAB key.

- Type **.75** in the Left box to change the left margin setting and then press the TAB key.

- Type **.75** in the Right box to change the right margin setting (Figure 7–3).

3

- Click the OK button to set the custom margins for this document.

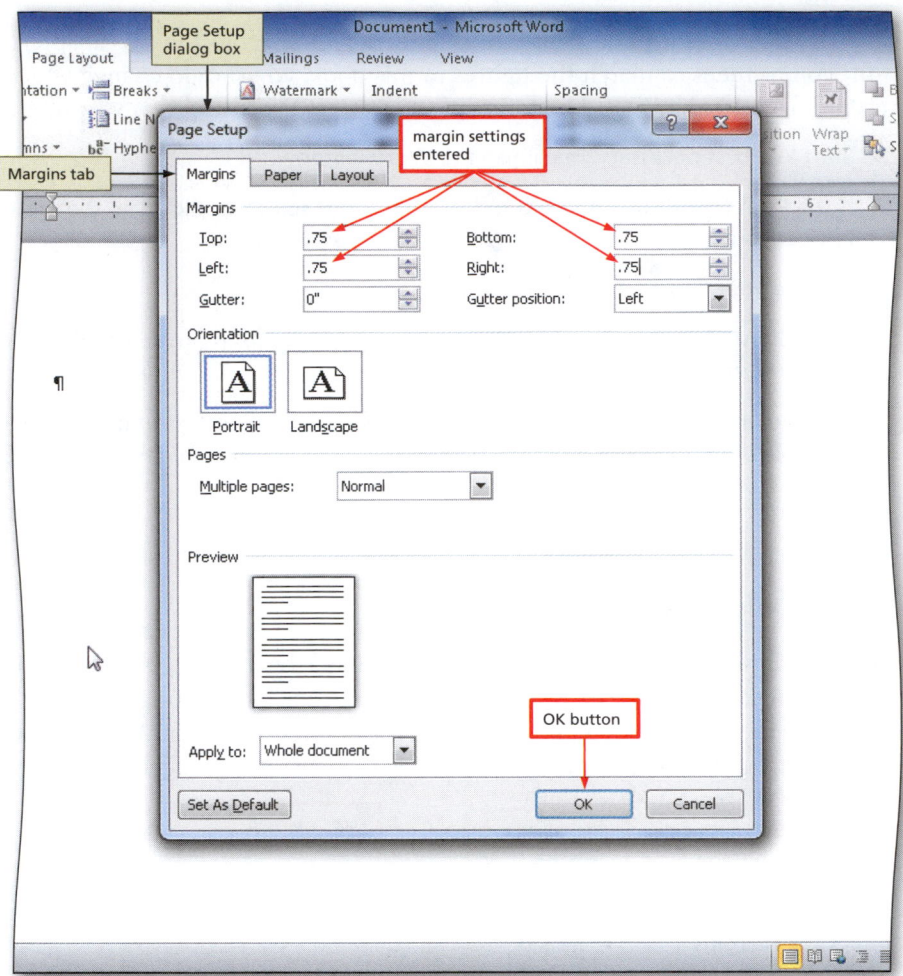

Figure 7–3

Other Ways

1. Position mouse pointer on margin boundary on ruler; when mouse pointer changes to two-headed arrow, drag margin boundaries on ruler

Margin Settings

If you want to see the current margin settings, display the ruler, press and hold the mouse button on the margin boundary (where the blue meets the white on the ruler and the mouse pointer is a two-headed arrow) and then hold down the ALT key while pointing to the margin boundary. To see the numeric margin settings while changing the margins, hold down the ALT key while dragging the margin boundary on the ruler.

To Change Theme Colors

The newsletter in this chapter uses the Aspect color scheme. The following step changes the theme colors to the Aspect color scheme.

1 Click the Theme Colors button (Page Layout tab | Themes group) and then click Aspect in the Theme Colors gallery to change the document theme colors.

Creating the Nameplate

The nameplate on the first page of this newsletter consists of the information above the multiple columns (Figure 7–1a on page WD 403). In this project, the nameplate includes the newsletter title, Savvy Shopper, images of a cash register and a shopping cart, and the issue information line. The steps on the following pages create the nameplate for the first page of the newsletter in this chapter.

Plan
Ahead

Create the nameplate.

The nameplate should catch the attention of readers, enticing them to read the newsletter. The nameplate typically consists of the title of the newsletter and the issue information line. Some also include a subtitle, a slogan, and a graphical image or logo. Guidelines for the newsletter title and other elements in the nameplate are as follows:

- Compose a title that is short, yet conveys the contents of the newsletter. In the newsletter title, eliminate unnecessary words such as these: the, newsletter. Use a decorative font in as large a font size as possible so that the title stands out on the page.

- Other elements on the nameplate should not compete in size with the title. Use colors that complement the title. Select easy-to-read fonts.

- Arrange the elements of the nameplate so that it does not have a cluttered appearance. If necessary, use ruling lines to visually separate areas of the nameplate.

The following pages use the steps outlined below to create the nameplate for the newsletter in this chapter.

1. Enter and format the newsletter title using WordArt.
2. Set custom tab stops for the issue information line.
3. Enter text in the issue information line.
4. Add a horizontal rule below the issue information line.
5. Insert and format the clip art images.

To Insert WordArt

In Chapter 3, you inserted a shape drawing object in a document. Recall that a drawing object is a graphic you create using Word. Another type of drawing object, called **WordArt**, enables you to create text with special effects such as shadowed, rotated, stretched, skewed, and wavy effects.

This project uses WordArt for the newsletter title, Savvy Shopper, to draw the reader's attention to the nameplate. The following steps insert WordArt.

1

- Display the Insert tab.

- Click the WordArt button (Insert tab | Text group) to display the WordArt gallery (Figure 7–4).

Q&A Once I select a WordArt style, can I customize its appearance?

Yes. The next steps customize the WordArt style selected here.

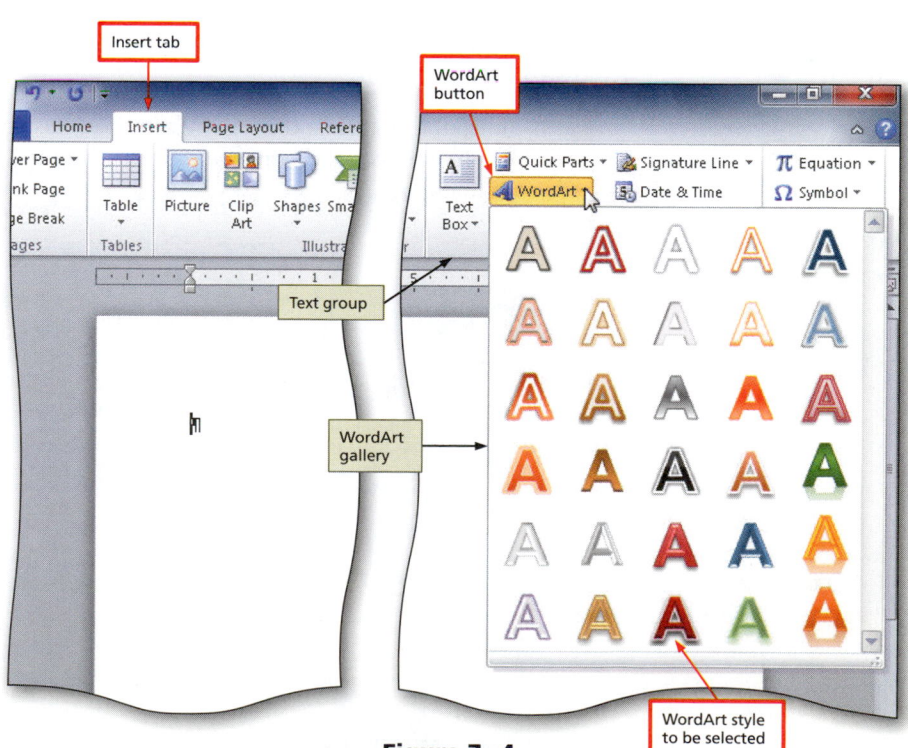

Figure 7–4

2
- Click Fill - Red, Accent 2, Matte Bevel in the WordArt gallery (third WordArt style in last row) to insert a drawing object in the document that is formatted according to the selected WordArt style, which contains the placeholder text, Your text here (Figure 7–5).

3
- Type **Savvy Shopper** to replace the selected placeholder text in the WordArt drawing object (shown in Figure 7–6).

Q&A What if my placeholder text is no longer selected?

Drag through it to select it.

Q&A How do I correct a mistake in the WordArt text?

You correct WordArt text using the same techniques you use to correct document text.

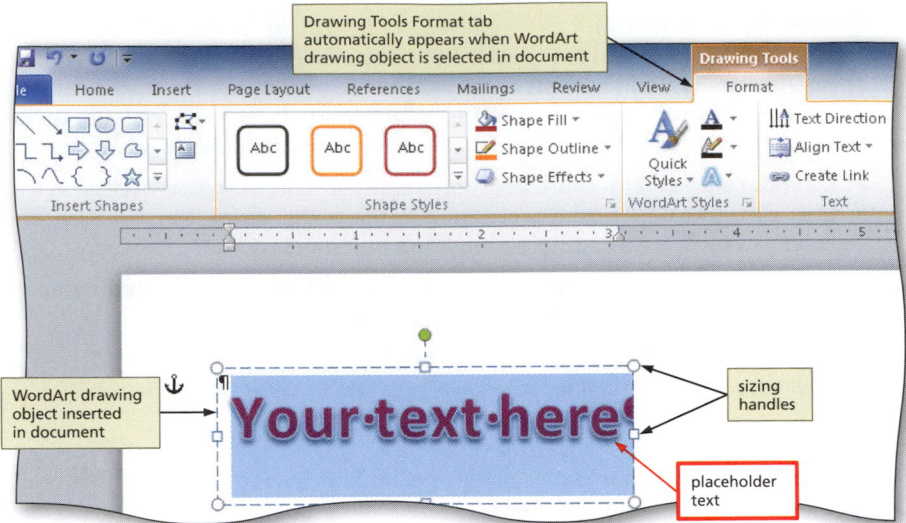

Figure 7–5

To Resize WordArt

You resize WordArt the same way you resize any other graphic. That is, you can drag its sizing handles or enter values in the Shape Height and Shape Width boxes. The next steps resize the WordArt drawing object.

1 With the WordArt drawing object selected, if necessary, display the Drawing Tools Format tab.

2 If necessary, click the Size button (Drawing Tools Format tab | Size group) to display the Shape Height and Shape Width boxes.

3 Change the value in the Shape Height box to 1.44 and the value in the Shape Width box to 7 (Figure 7–6).

4 If the Shape Height and Shape Width boxes display in a pop-up box because they do not fit on the Ribbon, click anywhere to remove the Shape Height and Shape Width boxes from the screen.

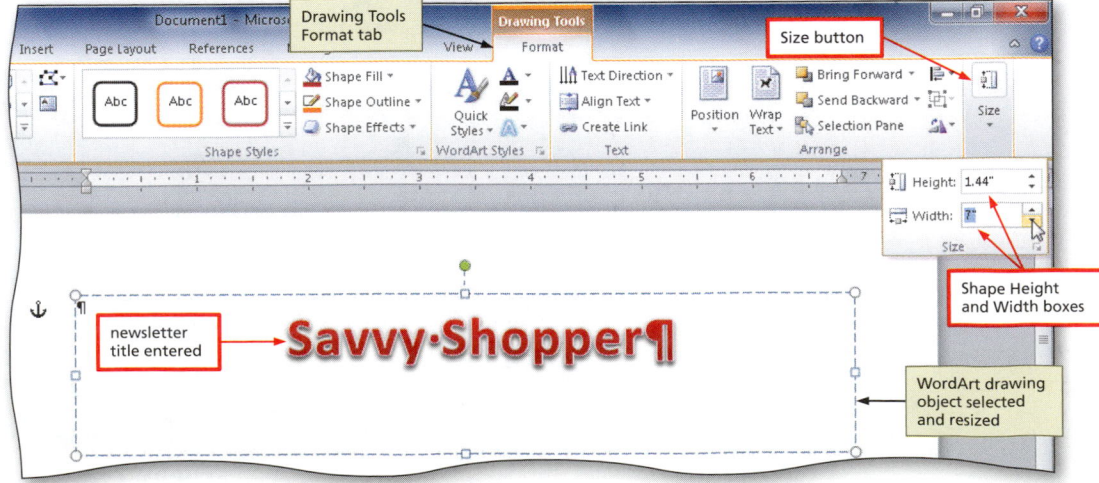

Figure 7–6

To Change the Font and Font Size of WordArt Text

You change the font and font size of WordArt text the same way you change the font and font size of any other text. That is, you select the text and then change its font and font size. The next steps change the font and font size of WordArt text.

1 Select the WordArt text, in this case, Savvy Shopper.

2 Change the font of the selected text to Lucida Handwriting.

3 Change the font size of the selected text to 48 point (shown in Figure 7–7).

To Change an Object's Text Wrapping

When you insert a drawing object in a Word document the default text wrapping is In Front of Text, which means the object will cover any text behind it. Because you want the nameplate above the rest of the newsletter, you change the text wrapping for the drawing object to Top and Bottom. The following steps change a drawing object's text wrapping.

1 If necessary, display the Drawing Tools Format tab.

2 With the WordArt drawing object selected, click the Wrap Text button (Drawing Tools Format tab | Arrange group) to display the Wrap Text gallery.

3 Click Top and Bottom in the Wrap Text gallery so that the WordArt drawing object will not cover the document text; in this case, the paragraph mark moves below the WordArt drawing object (Figure 7–7).

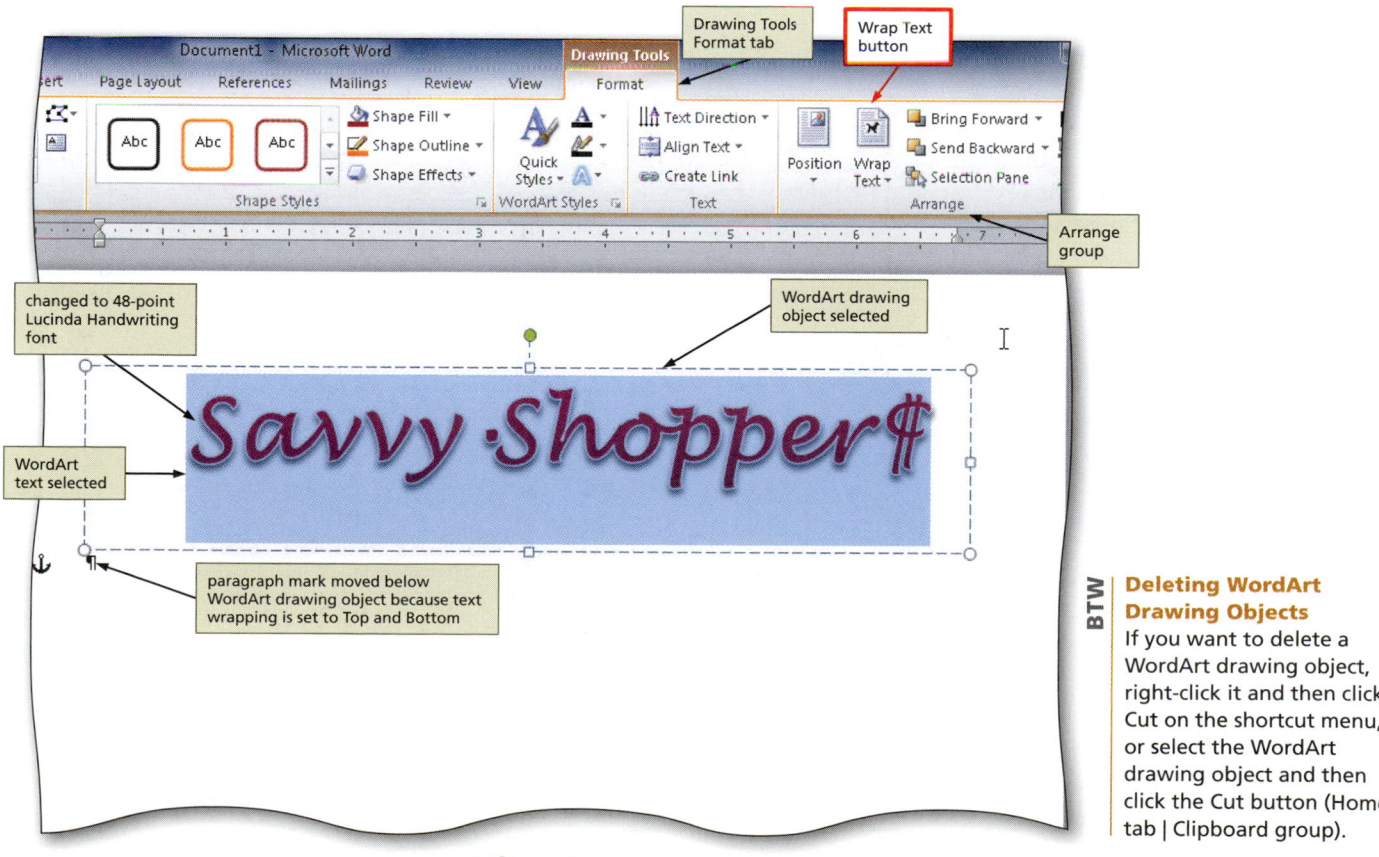

Figure 7–7

BTW

Deleting WordArt Drawing Objects
If you want to delete a WordArt drawing object, right-click it and then click Cut on the shortcut menu, or select the WordArt drawing object and then click the Cut button (Home tab | Clipboard group).

To Change the WordArt Fill Color

The next step is to change the color of the WordArt text so that it displays a green to blue gradient fill color. **Gradient** means the colors blend into one another. Word includes several built-in gradient fill colors, or you can customize one for use in drawing objects. The following steps change the fill color of the WordArt drawing object to a built-in gradient fill color and then customize the selected fill color.

1

- With the WordArt drawing object selected, click the Text Fill button arrow (Drawing Tools Format tab | WordArt Styles group) to display the Text Fill gallery.

Q&A

The Text Fill gallery did not display. Why not?

Be sure you click the Text Fill button arrow, which is to the right of the Text Fill button. If you mistakenly click the Text Fill button, Word places a default fill in the selected WordArt instead of displaying the Text Fill gallery.

2

- Point to Gradient in the Text Fill gallery to display the Gradient gallery (Figure 7–8).

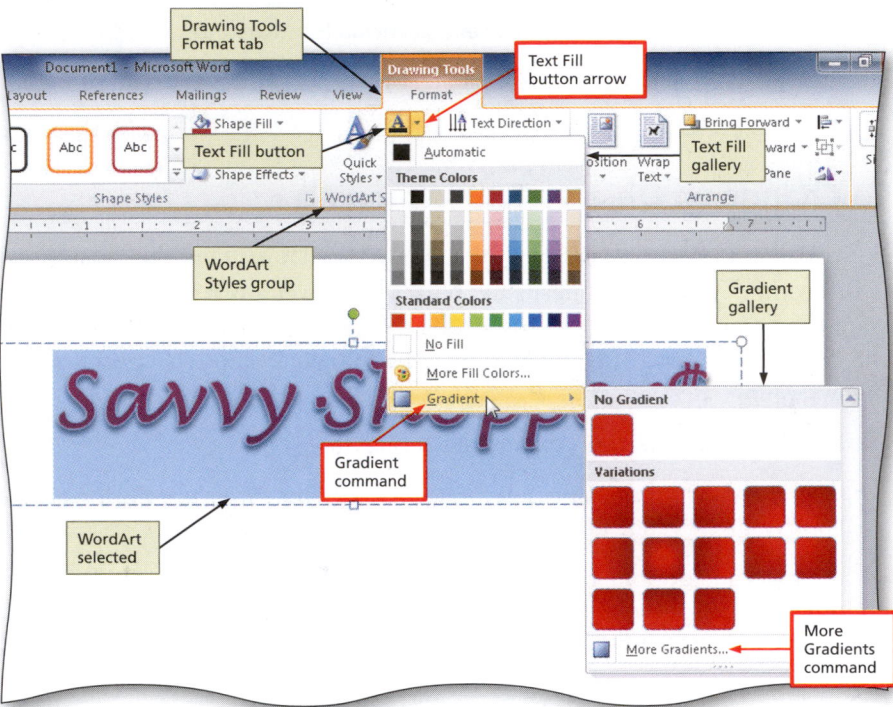

Figure 7–8

3

- Click More Gradients in the Gradient gallery to display the Format Text Effects dialog box. If necessary, click Text Fill in the left pane (Format Text Effects dialog box) and Gradient fill in the right pane (Figure 7–9).

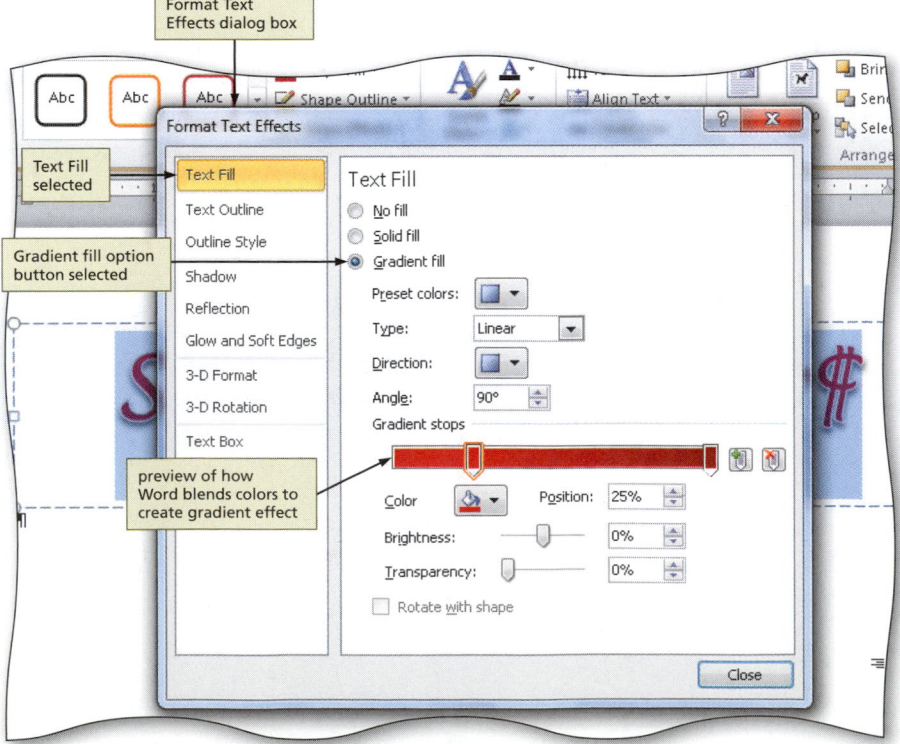

Figure 7–9

4
- In the right pane, click the Preset colors button to display a gallery of built-in gradient fill colors (Figure 7–10).

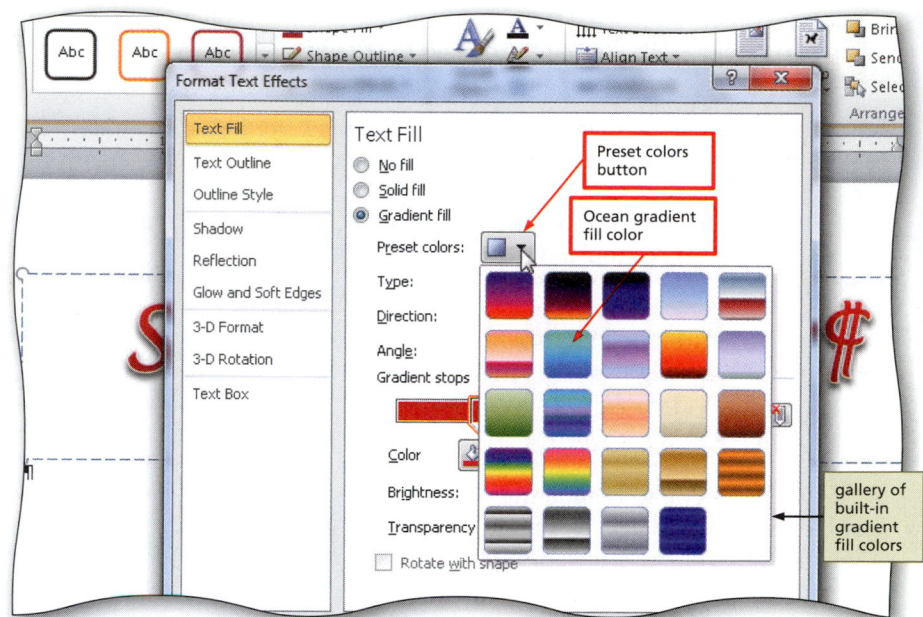

Figure 7–10

5
- Click Ocean (second row, second column) in the Preset colors gallery to select the built-in gradient color, which shows a preview in the Gradient stops area (Figure 7–11).

Q&A

What is a gradient stop?

A gradient stop is the location where two colors blend. You can change the color of a stop so that Word changes the color of the blend. You also can add or delete stops, with a minimum of two stops and a maximum of ten stops per gradient fill color.

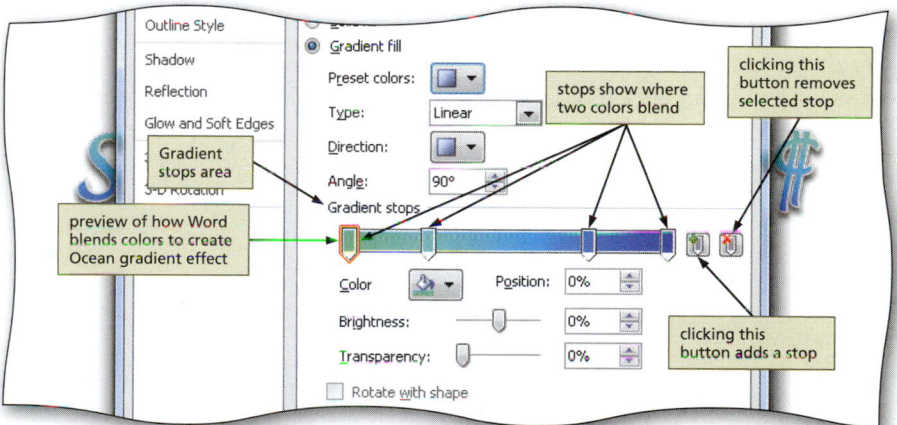

Figure 7–11

6
- If necessary, click the leftmost gradient stop to select it. Click the Color button to display a Color palette, from which you can select a color for the selected stop (Figure 7–12).

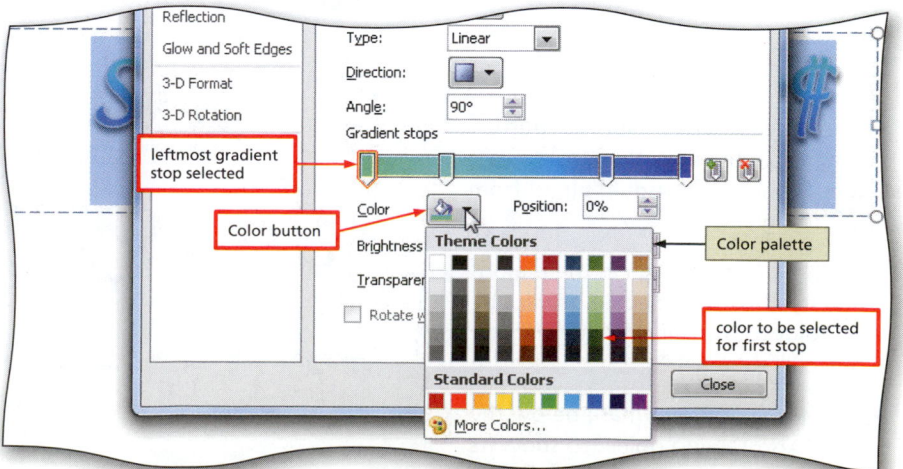

Figure 7–12

7

- Click Dark Green, Accent 4, Darker 25% (fifth row, eighth column) in the Color palette to change the color of the selected stop and the gradient between the selected stop and the next stop.

- Click the second gradient stop to select it. Click the Color box arrow to display a Color palette and then click Dark Green, Accent 4, Darker 50% (sixth row, eighth column) in the Color palette to change the color of the selected stop and the gradient between the selected stop and the next stop.

- Click the rightmost gradient stop to select it. Click the Color box arrow to display a Color palette and then click Dark Blue, Accent 3, Darker 50% (sixth row, seventh column) in the Color palette to change the color of the selected stop and the gradient between the selected stop and the next stop (Figure 7–13).

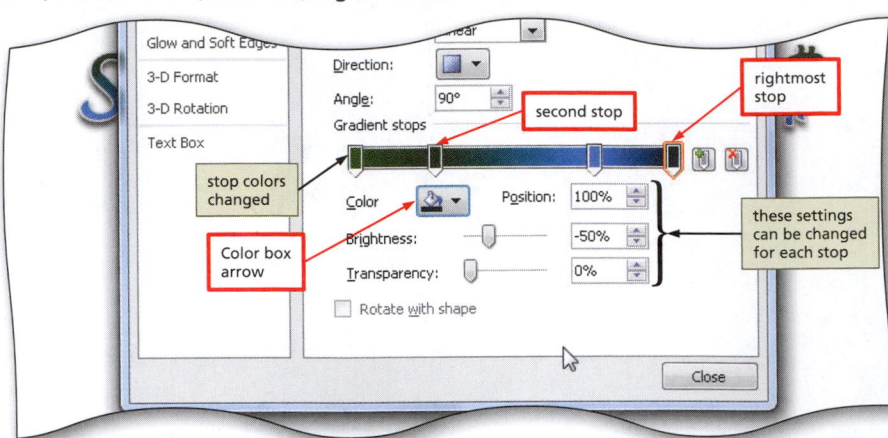

Figure 7–13

 Q&A

Can I move a gradient stop?

Yes. You can drag a stop to any location along the color bar. You also can adjust the position, brightness, and transparency of any selected stop.

8

- In the right pane, click the Direction button to display a gallery that shows a variety of directions for the gradient colors (Figure 7–14).

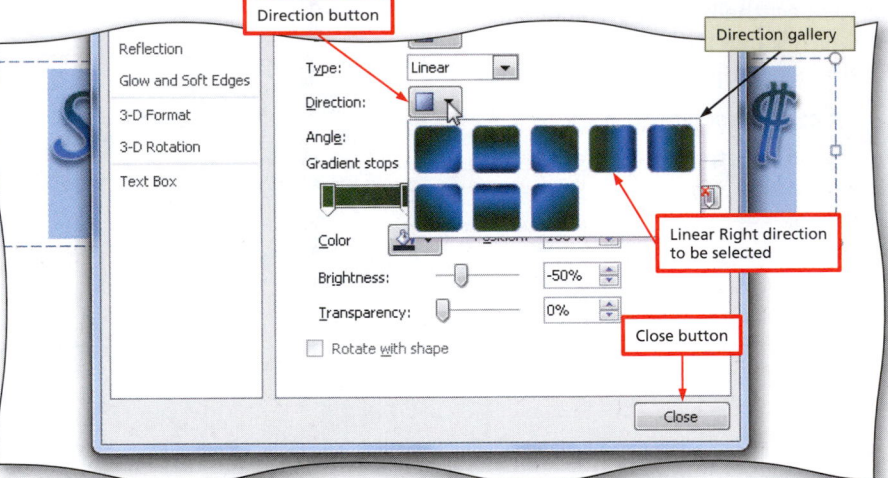

Figure 7–14

9

- Click Linear Right (first row, fourth column) in the Direction gallery to specify the colors should blend from left to right.

- Click the Close button in the dialog box to apply the selected gradient fill color to the selected drawing object.

- Click the paragraph mark below the WordArt drawing object to show its gradient fill colors (Figure 7–15).

Figure 7–15

To Change the WordArt Shape

Word provides a variety of shapes to make your WordArt more interesting. For the newsletter in this chapter, the WordArt has a wavy appearance. The following steps change the WordArt shape.

1
- Click the WordArt drawing object to select it.

- If necessary, display the Drawing Tools Format tab.

- Click the Text Effects button (Drawing Tools Format tab | WordArt Styles group) to display the Text Effects gallery.

- Point to Transform in the Text Effects gallery to display the Transform gallery.

- Point to Wave 1 (first effect, fifth row in Warp area) in the Transform gallery to display a live preview of that transform effect applied to the selected drawing object (Figure 7–16).

Experiment
- Point to various text effects in the Transform gallery and watch the selected drawing object conform to that transform effect.

2
- Click the Wave 1 in the Transform gallery to change the shape of the WordArt drawing object.

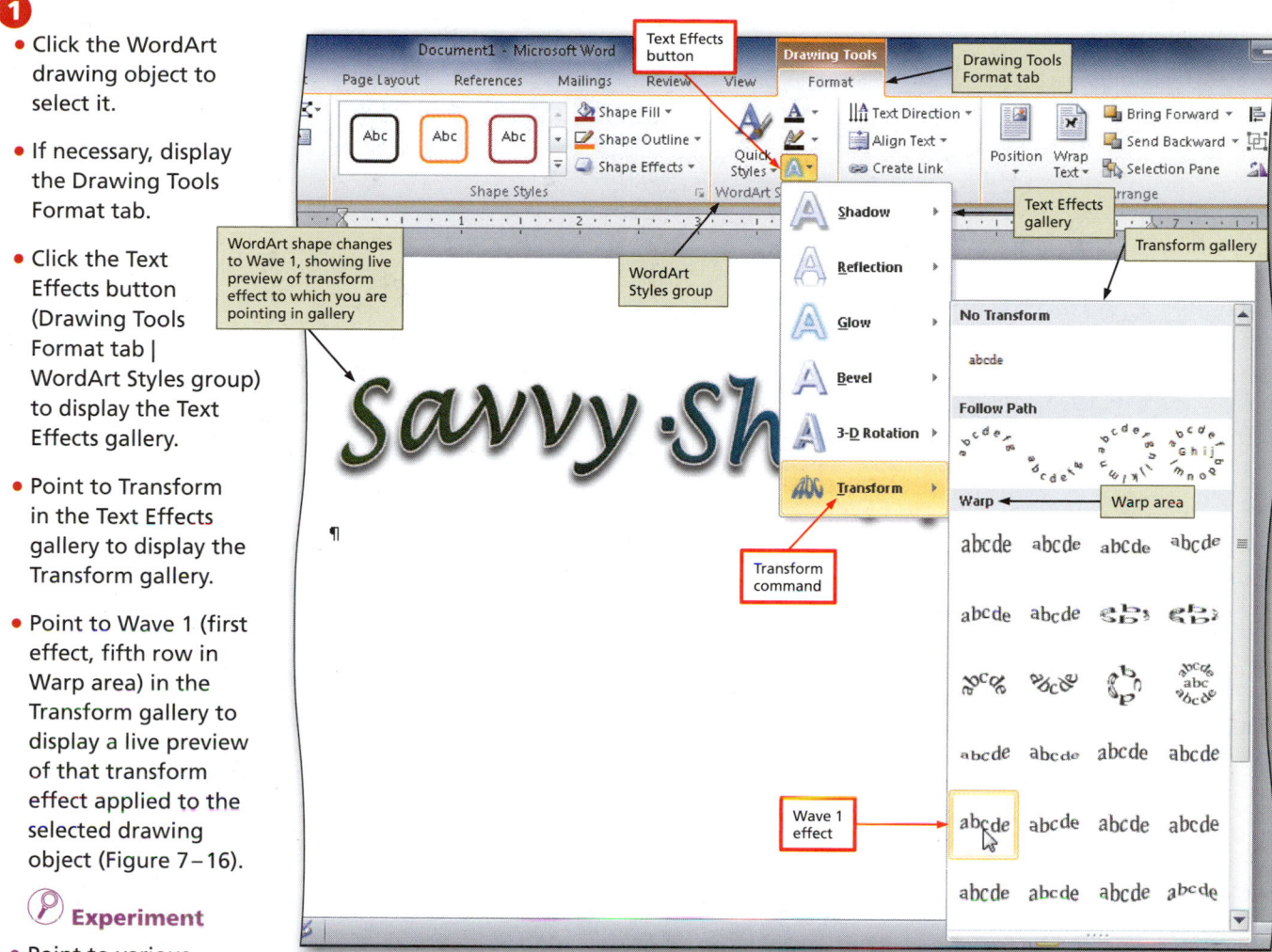

Figure 7–16

To Set Custom Tab Stops Using the Tabs Dialog Box

The issue information line in this newsletter contains the text, Monthly Newsletter, at the left margin and the issue number at the right margin (shown in Figure 7–1a on page WD 403). In Word, a paragraph cannot be both left-aligned and right-aligned. If you click the Align Text Right button (Home tab | Paragraph group), for example, all text will be right-aligned. To place text at the right margin of a left-aligned paragraph, you set a tab stop at the right margin.

One method of setting custom tab stops is to click the ruler at the desired location of the tab stop, which you learned in an earlier chapter. You cannot click, however, at the right margin location. Thus, the steps on the next page use the Tabs dialog box to set a custom tab stop.

- Position the insertion point on the paragraph mark below the WordArt drawing object, which is the paragraph to be formatted with the custom tab stops.

- Click the Paragraph Dialog Box Launcher to display the Paragraph dialog box (Figure 7–17).

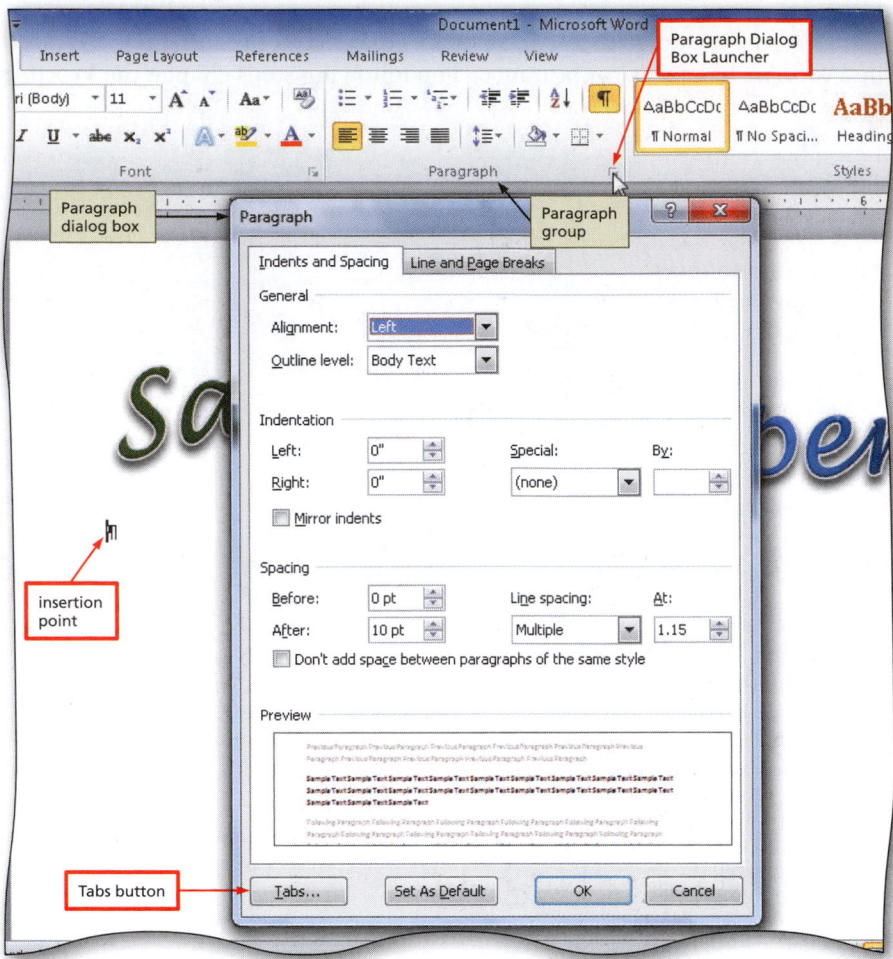

Figure 7–17

- Click the Tabs button (Paragraph dialog box) to display the Tabs dialog box.

- Type 7 in the Tab stop position text box (Tabs dialog box).

- Click Right in the Alignment area to specify alignment for text at the tab stop (Figure 7–18).

3

- Click the Set button (Tabs dialog box) to set a right-aligned custom tab stop.

- Click the OK button to place a right tab marker at the 7" mark on the ruler (shown in Figure 7–19).

Other Ways

1. Right-click paragraph, click Paragraph on shortcut menu, click Tabs button (Paragraph dialog box)

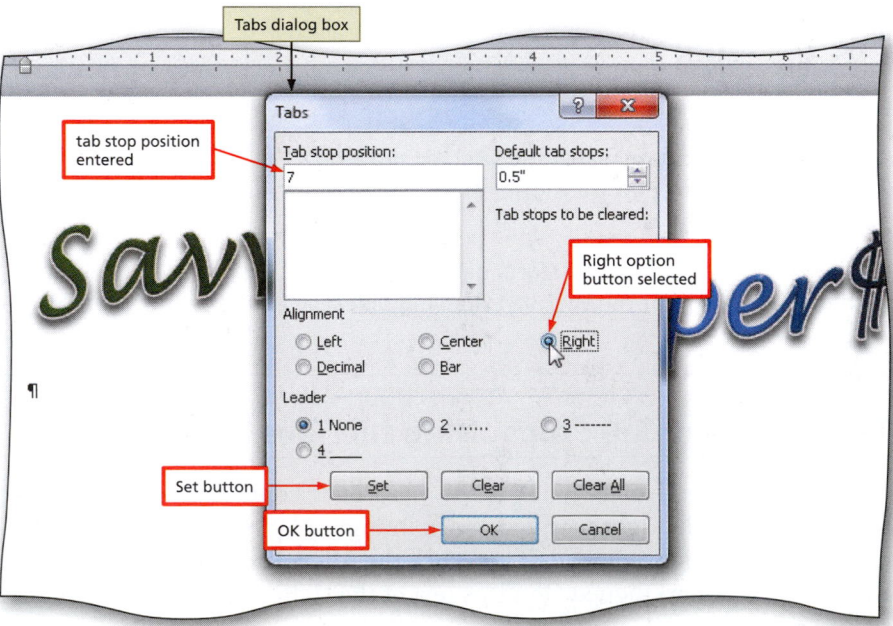

Figure 7–18

To Enter Text

The following steps enter the issue information line text.

1 With the insertion point on the paragraph below the WordArt, type **Monthly Newsletter** on line 2 of the newsletter.

2 Press the TAB key and then type **Issue 33** to complete the issue information line (Figure 7–19).

Figure 7–19

To Border One Edge of a Paragraph

In Word, you use borders to create ruling lines. As discussed in previous projects, Word can place borders on any edge of a paragraph; that is, Word can place a border on the top, bottom, left, and right edges of a paragraph.

One method of bordering paragraphs is by clicking the desired border in the Border gallery, which you learned in an earlier chapter. If you want to specify a particular border, for example, one with color, you use the Borders and Shading dialog box. In this newsletter, the issue information line has a ½-point double-line dark orange border below it. The following steps use the Borders and Shading dialog box to place a border below a paragraph.

1

- Click the Border button arrow (Home tab | Paragraph group) to display the Border gallery (Figure 7–20).

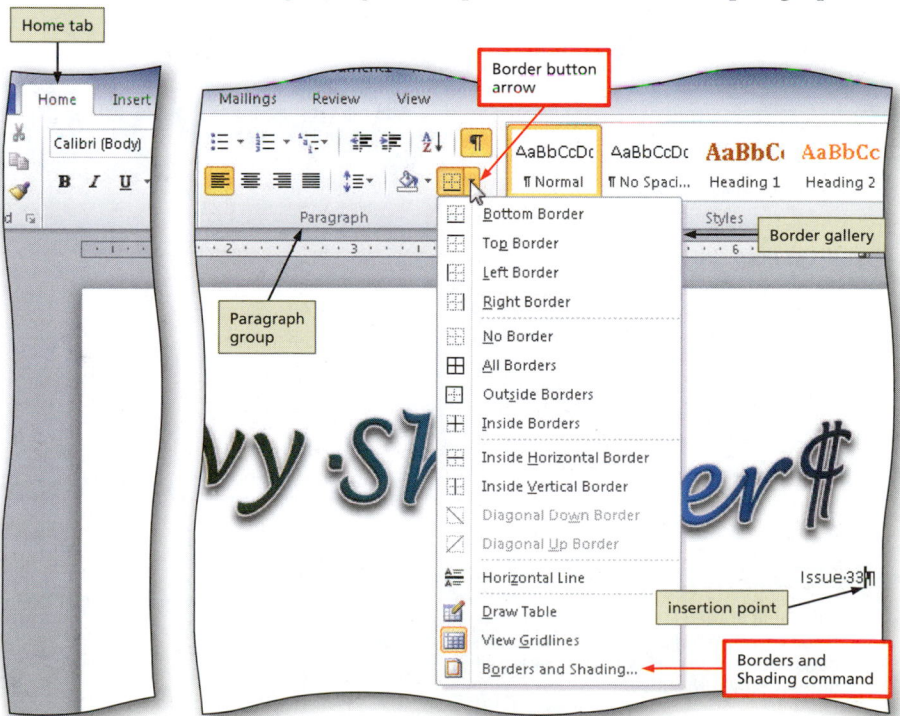

Figure 7–20

2

- Click Borders and Shading in the Border gallery to display the Borders and Shading dialog box.

- Click Custom in the Setting area (Borders and Shading dialog box) because you are setting just a bottom border.

- Scroll through the style list and click the style shown in Figure 7–21, which has two thin lines as the border.

- Click the Color button arrow and then click Orange, Accent 1, Darker 50% (fifth column, sixth row) in the Color gallery.

- Click the Bottom Border button in the Preview area of the dialog box to show a preview of the selected border style (Figure 7–21).

Q&A What is the purpose of the buttons in the Preview area?

They are toggles that display and remove the top, bottom, left, and right borders from the diagram in the Preview area.

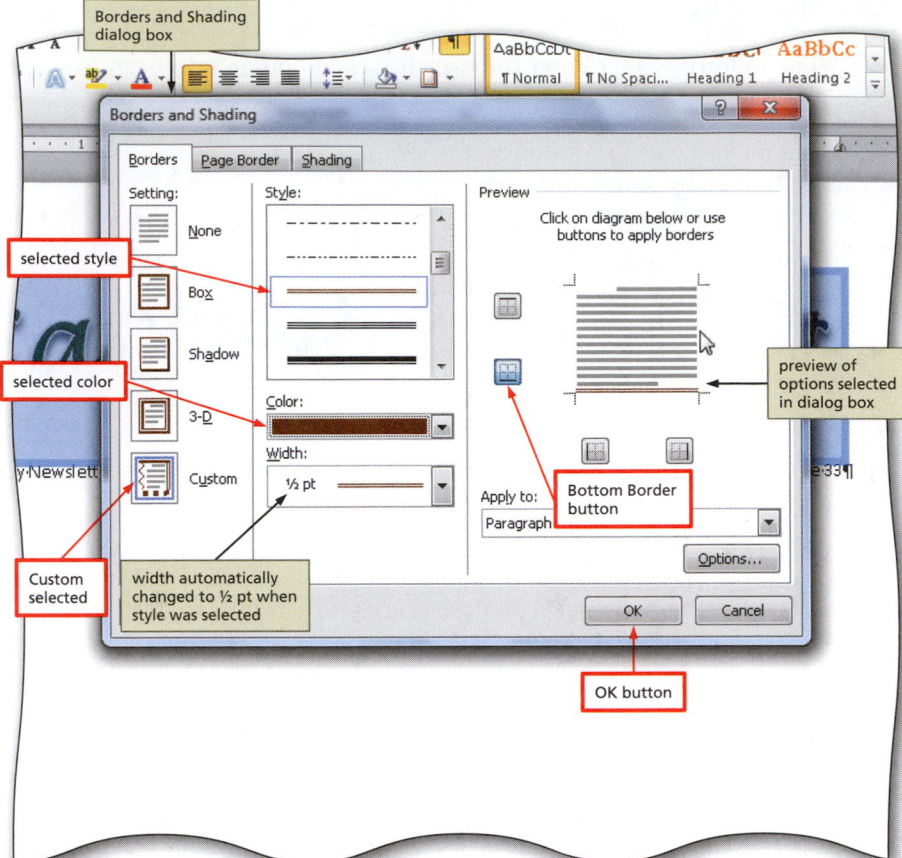

Figure 7–21

3

- Click the OK button to place the defined border on the paragraph containing the insertion point (Figure 7–22).

Q&A How would I change an existing border?

You first remove the existing border by clicking the Border button arrow (Home tab | Paragraph group) and then click the border in the Border gallery that identifies the border you wish to remove. Then, add a new border as described in these steps.

Figure 7–22

Other Ways

1. Click Page Borders (Page Layout tab | Page Background group), click Borders tab (Borders and Shading dialog box), select desired border, click OK button

Note: The following steps assume your computer is connected to the Internet. If it is not, go directly to the shaded steps on the next page that are titled To Insert a Graphic File from the Data Files for Students.

To Insert Clip Art from the Web

The next steps insert an image of a cash register from the Web in the nameplate.

1 Display the Insert tab. Click the Clip Art button (Insert tab | Illustrations group) to display the Clip Art pane.

2 Select any text that is displayed in the Clip Art pane and then type `cash register` in the Search for text box.

3 Be sure the Include Office.com content check box is selected and then click the Go button to display a list of clips that match the entered description.

4 Scroll to and then click the clip art of the cash register that matches the one in Figure 7–23 to insert the selected clip art image in the document at the location of the insertion point. (If the clip art image does not appear in the task pane, click the Close button on the Clip Art pane and then proceed to the shaded steps on the next page.)

5 Click the Close button on the Clip Art task pane title bar to close the task pane.

Q&A

What if my clip art image is not in the same location as in Figure 7–23?

The clip art image may be in a different location, depending on the position of the insertion point when you inserted the image. In a later section, you will move the image to a different location.

BTW

Q&As
For a complete list of the Q&As found in many of the step-by-step sequences in this book, visit the Word 2010 Q&A Web page (scsite.com/wd2010/qa).

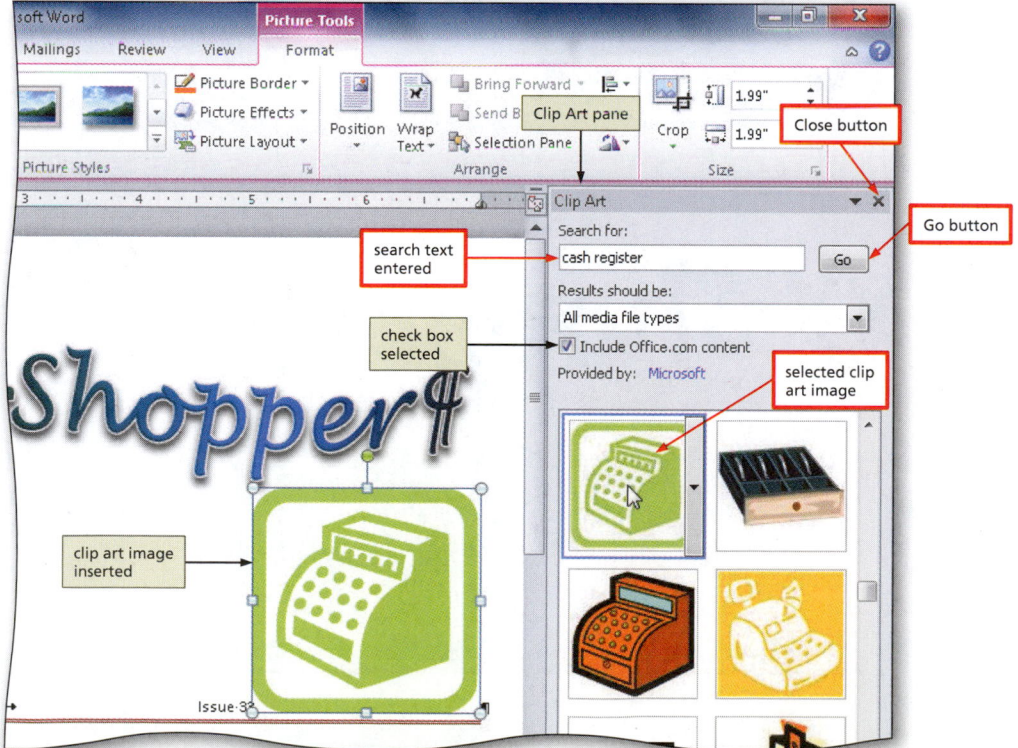

Figure 7–23

To Insert a Graphic File from the Data Files for Students

If you do not have access to the Internet, you can insert the clip art file in the Word document from the Data Files for Students. See the inside back cover of this book for instructions on downloading the Data Files for Students, or contact your instructor for information about accessing the required files. Perform these steps only if you were not able to insert the cash register clip art from the Web in the previous steps.

1 Display the Insert tab. Click the Insert Picture from File button (Insert tab | Illustrations group) to display the Insert Picture dialog box.

2 Navigate to the location of the picture to be inserted (in this case, the Chapter 07 folder in the Word folder in the Data Files for Students folder on a USB flash drive).

3 Click the Cash Register file (Insert Picture dialog box) to select the file.

4 Click the Insert button in the dialog box to insert the picture in the document at the location of the insertion point (shown in Figure 7–23 on the previous page).

To Crop a Graphic

The next step is to format the clip art image just inserted. You would like to remove the green rounded frame from the perimeter of the image. Word allows you to **crop**, or remove edges from, a graphic. The following steps crop a graphic.

- With the graphic selected, click the Crop button (Picture Tools Format tab | Size group), which places cropping handles on the image in the document.

Q&A What if I mistakenly click the Crop button arrow?

Clip the Crop button.

- Position the mouse pointer on the top-middle cropping handle so that it looks like an upside-down letter T (Figure 7–24).

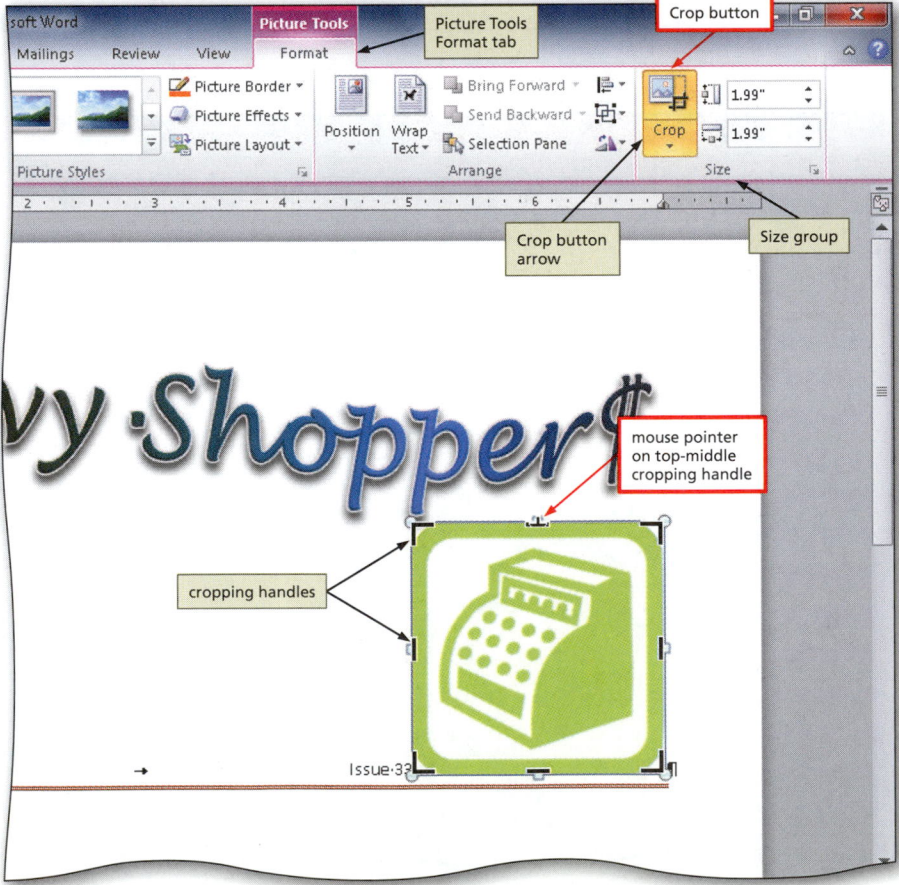

Figure 7–24

● Drag the top-middle cropping handle downward to the location of the mouse pointer shown in Figure 7–25 to remove the frame at the top of the image.

3

● Release the mouse button to crop the graphic to the location shown in Figure 7–25.

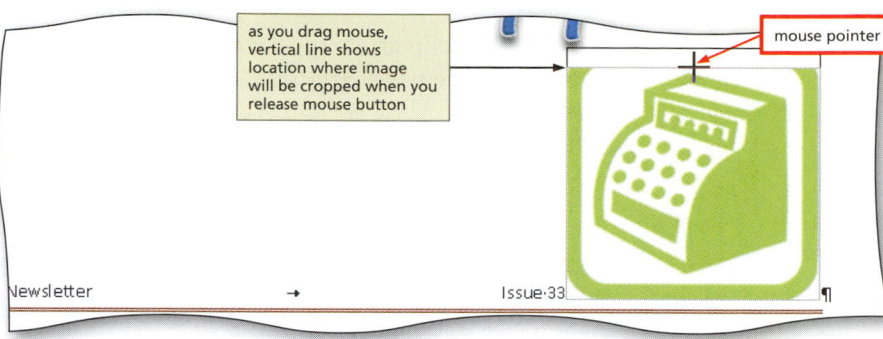

Figure 7–25

● Position the mouse pointer on the left-middle cropping handle so that it looks like a sideways letter T and then drag the cropping handle inward until the frame at the left edge of the image disappears, as shown in Figure 7–26.

● Position the mouse pointer on the right-middle cropping handle so that it looks like a sideways letter T and then drag the cropping handle inward until the frame at the right edge of the image disappears, as shown in Figure 7–26.

● Position the mouse pointer on the bottom-middle cropping handle so that it looks like a letter T and then drag the cropping handle upward until the frame at the bottom edge of the image disappears, as shown in Figure 7–26.

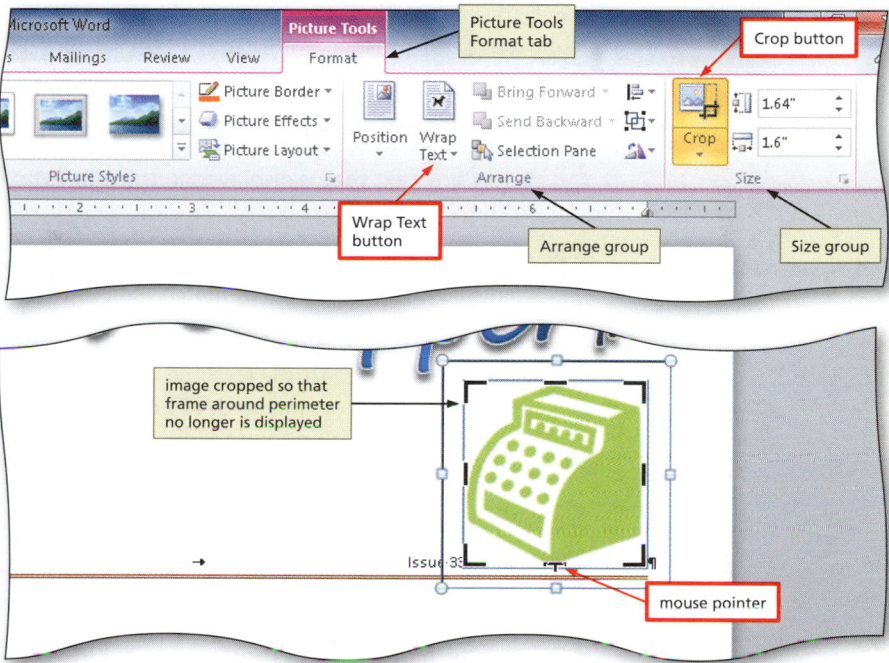

Figure 7–26

5

● Click the Crop button (Picture Tools Format tab | Size group) to deactivate the cropping tool, which removes the cropping handles from the selected image.

Other Ways

1. Right-click graphic, click Format Picture on shortcut menu, click Crop in left pane, enter values in text boxes, click Close button

To Change an Object's Text Wrapping

When you insert clip art in a Word document, the default text wrapping is In Line with Text, which means the object is part of the current paragraph. Because you want the clip art images behind the newsletter title, you change the text wrapping for the clip art image to Behind Text. The following steps change a drawing object's text wrapping.

1 With the clip art image selected, click the Wrap Text button (Picture Tools Format tab | Arrange group) to display the Wrap Text gallery.

2 Click Behind Text in the Wrap Text gallery so that the clip art image is positioned behind text in the document.

To Move a Graphic

The clip art image needs to be moved up so that it is positioned behind the word, Savvy, in the newsletter title. The following step moves the graphic.

1 Point to the middle of the graphic, and when the mouse pointer has a four-headed arrow attached to it, drag the graphic to the location shown in Figure 7–27.

To Insert a Clip Art Image and Then Crop It, Change Its Text Wrapping, and Move It

The next step is to insert a clip art image of a shopping cart, crop it to remove the frame around the perimeter of the image, change its text wrapping to Behind Text, and then move it so that it is positioned behind the word, Shopper, in the nameplate. The following steps insert and format a clip art image.

1 Position the insertion point in the issue information line. Display the Insert tab. Click the Clip Art button (Insert tab | Illustrations group) to display the Clip Art pane.

2 Select any text that is displayed in the Clip Art pane and then type `shopping cart` in the Search for text box.

3 Be sure the Include Office.com content check box is selected and then click the Go button to display a list of clips that match the entered description.

4 Scroll to and then click the clip art of the shopping cart that matches the one in Figure 7–27 to insert the selected clip in the document at the location of the insertion point. (If the clip art image does not appear in the task pane, click the Close button on the Clip Art pane and then follow the shaded steps on page WD 418, inserting the picture called Shopping Cart. Then, proceed to Step 6 below.)

5 Click the Close button on the Clip Art pane title bar to close the pane.

6 With the graphic selected, click the Crop button (Picture Tools Format tab | Size group), which places cropping handles on the image in the document.

7 Drag each of the four cropping handles inward to remove the blue frame from the image, as shown in Figure 7–27.

8 Click the Crop button (Picture Tools Format tab | Size group) to deactive the cropping tool.

9 With the clip art image selected, click the Wrap Text button (Picture Tools Format tab | Arrange group) to display the Wrap Text gallery and then click Behind Text in the Wrap Text gallery so that the clip art image is positioned behind text in the document.

10 Point to the middle of the graphic, and when the mouse pointer has a four-headed arrow attached to it, drag the graphic to the location shown in Figure 7–27.

clip art image moved behind text

clip art image inserted, cropped, and moved behind text

Monthly Newsletter

Issue 33

Figure 7–27

To Use the Selection Pane

The next step is to rotate the clip art images, but because they are positioned behind the text, it may be difficult to select them. The following step displays the Selection and Visibility task pane so that you easily can select items on the screen that are layered behind other objects.

1

- Click the Selection Pane button (Picture Tools Format tab | Arrange group) to display the Selection and Visibility task pane (Figure 7–28).

Experiment

- Click Text Box 1 in the Selection and Visibility task pane to select the WordArt drawing object. Click Picture 3 in the Selection and Visibility task pane to select the shopping cart image. Click Picture 2 in the Selection and Visibility task pane to select the cash register image.

Q&A What are the displayed names in the Selection and Visibility task pane?

Word assigns names to each object in the document. The names displayed on your screen may differ.

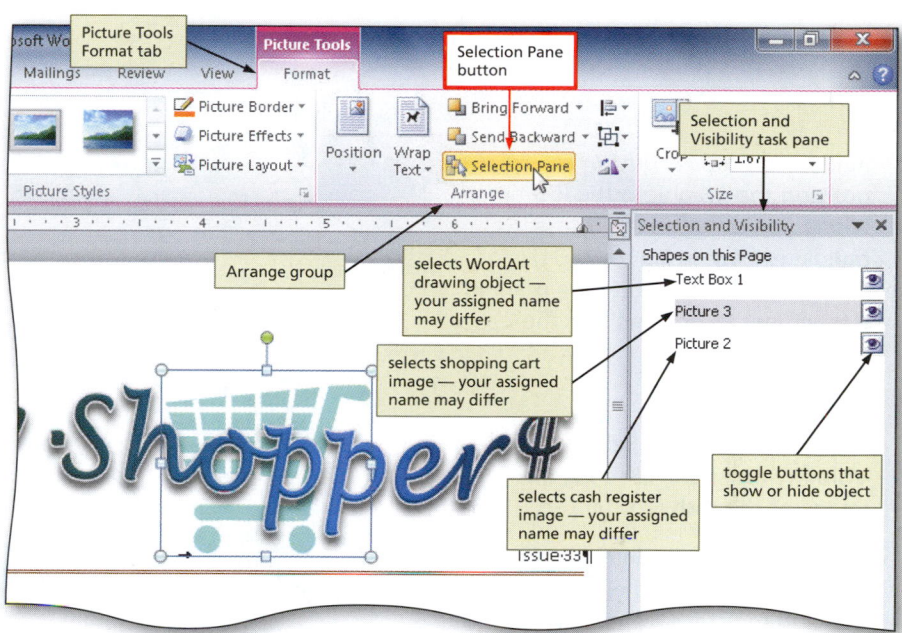

Figure 7–28

To Rotate a Graphic

The images of the cash register and shopping cart in this newsletter are slanted slightly to the right. In Word, you can rotate a graphic. The following steps rotate a graphic.

1

- If necessary, click Picture 3 in the Selection and Visibility task pane to select the image of the shopping cart.

- Position the mouse pointer on the graphic's rotate handle (Figure 7–29).

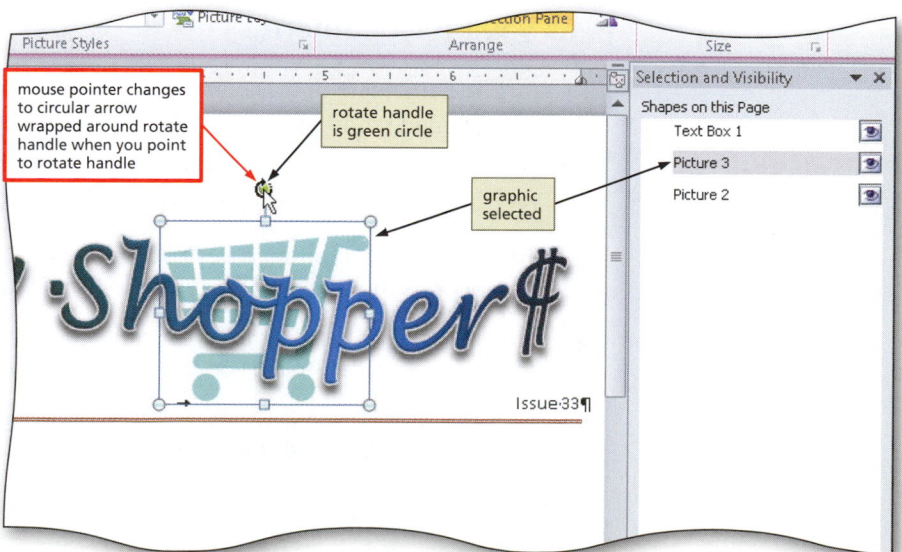

Figure 7–29

2

- Drag the rotate handle rightward and downward to rotate the graphic as shown in Figure 7–30.

Q&A Can I drag the rotate handle in any direction?

You can drag the rotate handle clockwise or counterclockwise.

3

- Release the mouse button to position the graphic in the location where you dragged the rotate handle (shown in Figure 7–31). (You may need to rotate the graphic a few times to position it in the desired location.)

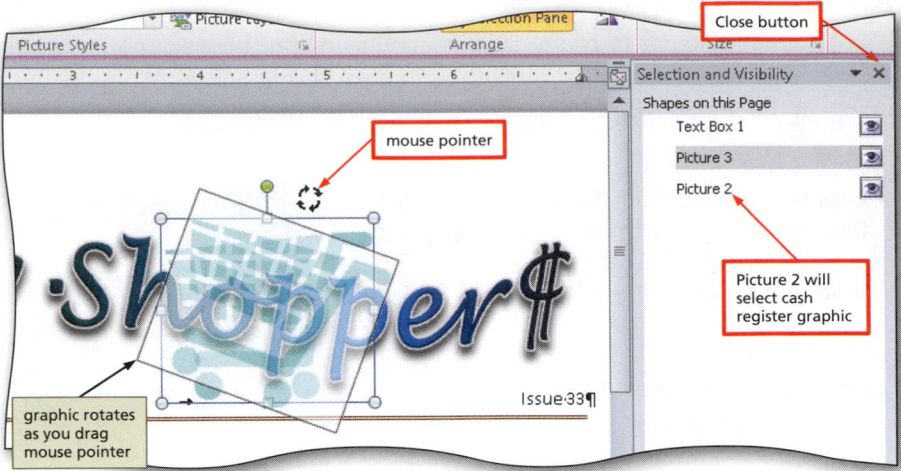

Figure 7–30

4

- Click Picture 2 in the Selection and Visibility task pane to select the image of the cash register.

- Position the mouse pointer on the graphic's rotate handle, in this case, the cash register's rotate handle.

- Drag the rotate handle rightward and downward to rotate the graphic as shown in Figure 7–31.

Figure 7–31

- If necessary, move the images or rotate them again or resize them so that they look the same as those shown in Figure 7–31 and then click the Close button on the Selection and Visibility task pane title bar to close the task pane.

- Click somewhere in the issue information to deselect the graphic (Figure 7–31).

To Save a Document

The nameplate now is complete. The next step is to save the newsletter because you have performed many steps thus far. The following steps save the newsletter.

1 With a USB flash drive connected to one of the computer's USB ports, click the Save button on the Quick Access Toolbar to display the Save As dialog box.

2 Type **Savvy Shopper Newsletter** in the File name text box to change the file name. Do not press the ENTER key because you do not want to close the dialog box at this time.

3 If necessary, navigate to the save location (in this case, the Word folder in the CIS 101 folder [or your class folder] on the USB flash drive).

4 Click the Save button (Save As dialog box) to save the document in the selected folder on the USB flash drive with the entered file name.

Break Point: If you wish to take a break, this is a good place to do so. You can quit Word now. To resume at a later time, start Word, open the file called Savvy Shopper Newsletter, and continue following the steps from this location forward.

Formatting the First Page of the Body of the Newsletter

The next step is to format the first page of the body of the newsletter. The body of the newsletter in this chapter is divided in three columns (Figure 7–1a on page WD 403). The first two columns contain the feature article, and the third column contains announcements. The characters in the paragraphs are aligned on both the right and left edges — similar to newspaper columns. The first letter in the first paragraph is much larger than the rest of the characters in the paragraph. A vertical rule separates the second and third columns. The steps on the following pages format the first page of the body of the newsletter using these desktop publishing features.

Determine the content for the body of the newsletter.

Plan Ahead

While content and subject matter of newsletters may vary, the procedures used to create newsletters are similar:

- **Write the body copy.** Newsletters should contain articles of interest and relevance to readers. Some share information, while others promote a product or service. Use active voice in body copy, which is more engaging than passive voice. Proofread the body copy to be sure it is error free. Check all facts for accuracy.

- **Organize body copy in columns.** Most newsletters arrange body copy in columns. The body copy in columns, often called **snaking columns** or newspaper-style columns, flows from the bottom of one column to the top of the next column.

- **Format the body copy.** Begin the feature article on the first page of the newsletter. If the article spans multiple pages, use a continuation line, called a jump or jump line, to guide the reader to the remainder of the article. The message at the end of the article on the first page of the newsletter is called a **jump-to line**, and a **jump-from line** marks the beginning of the continuation, which is usually on a subsequent page.

- **Maintain consistency.** Be consistent with placement of body copy elements in newsletter editions. If the newsletter contains announcements, for example, position them in the same location in each edition so that readers easily can find them.

- **Maximize white space.** Allow plenty of space between lines, paragraphs, and columns. Tightly packed text is difficult to read. Separate the text adequately from graphics, borders, and headings.

- **Incorporate color.** Use colors that complement those in the nameplate. Be careful not to overuse color. Restrict color below the nameplate to drop caps, subheads, graphics, and ruling lines. If you do not have a color printer, still change the colors because the colors will print in shades of black and gray, which add variety to the newsletter.

- **Select and format subheads.** Develop subheads with as few words as possible. Readers should be able to identify content of the next topic by glancing at a subhead. Subheads should be emphasized in the newsletter but should not compete with text in the nameplate. Use a larger, bold, or otherwise contrasting font for subheads so that they stand apart from the body copy. Use this same format for all subheads for consistency. Leave a space above subheads to visually separate their content from the previous topic. Be consistent with spacing above and below subheads throughout the newsletter.

- **Divide sections with vertical rules.** Use vertical rules to guide the reader through the newsletter.

- **Enhance the document with visuals.** Add energy to the newsletter and emphasis to important points with graphics, pull-quotes, and other visuals such as drop caps to mark beginning of an article. Use these elements sparingly, however, so that the newsletter does not have a crowded appearance. Fewer, large visuals are more effective than several smaller ones. If you use a graphic that you did not create, be sure to obtain permission to use it in the newsletter and give necessary credit to the creator of the graphic.

To Clear Formatting

The next step is enter the title of the feature article below the horizontal rule. To do this, you will position the insertion point at the end of the issue information line (after the 3 in Issue 33) and then press the ENTER key. Recall that the issue information line has a bottom border. When you press the ENTER key in a bordered paragraph, Word carries forward any borders to the next paragraph. Thus, after you press the ENTER key, you should clear formatting to format the new paragraph to the Normal style. The following steps clear formatting.

1 Click at the end of line 2 (the issue information line) so that the insertion point is immediately after the 3 in Issue 33. Press the ENTER key to advance the insertion point to the next line, which also moves the border down one line.

2 If necessary, display the Home tab. Click the Clear Formatting button (Home tab | Font group) to apply the Normal style to the location of the insertion point, which in this case moves the new paragraph below the border on the issue information line.

To Format Text as a Heading Style and Adjust Spacing before and after the Paragraph

Below the bottom border in the nameplate is the title of the feature article, Purchasing a Notebook Computer. The following steps apply the Heading 1 style to a paragraph and adjust the paragraph spacing.

1 With the insertion point on the paragraph mark below the border, click Heading 1 (Home tab | Styles group) to apply the Heading 1 style to the paragraph containing the insertion point.

2 Type **Purchasing a Notebook Computer** as the title of the feature article.

3 Display the Page Layout tab. Change the Spacing Before to 18 pt and the Spacing After to 12 pt (Figure 7–32).

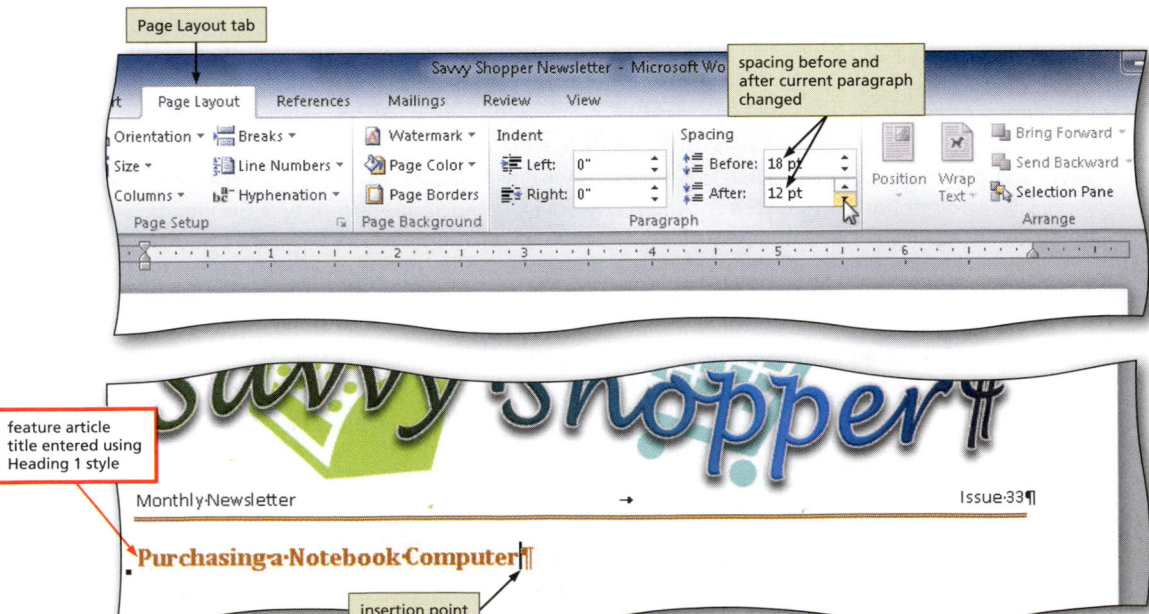

Figure 7–32

Columns

When you begin a document in Word, it has one column. You can divide a portion of a document or the entire document in multiple columns. Within each column, you can type, modify, or format text.

To divide a portion of a document in multiple columns, you use section breaks. Word requires that a new section be created each time you alter the number of columns in a document. Thus, if a document has a nameplate (one column) followed by an article of three columns followed by an article of two columns, the document would be divided in three separate sections.

Organize body copy in columns.
Be consistent from page to page with the number of columns. Narrow columns generally are easier to read than wide ones. Columns, however, can be too narrow. A two- or three-column layout generally is appealing and offers a flexible design. Try to have between five and fifteen words per line. To do this, you may need to adjust the column width, the font size, or the leading (line spacing). Font size of text in columns should be no larger than 12 point but not so small that readers must strain to read the text.

Plan Ahead

To Insert a Continuous Section Break

In this chapter, the nameplate is one column and the body of the newsletter is three columns. Thus, you must insert a continuous section break below the nameplate. The term, continuous, means the new section should be on the same page as the previous section, which, in this case, means that the three columns of body copy will be positioned directly below the nameplate on the first page of the newsletter. The following steps insert a continuous section break.

- With the insertion point at the end of the feature article title (shown in Figure 7–32), press the ENTER key to position the insertion point below the article title.

- Click the Insert Page and Section Breaks button (Page Layout tab | Page Setup group) to display the Insert Page and Section Breaks gallery (Figure 7–33).

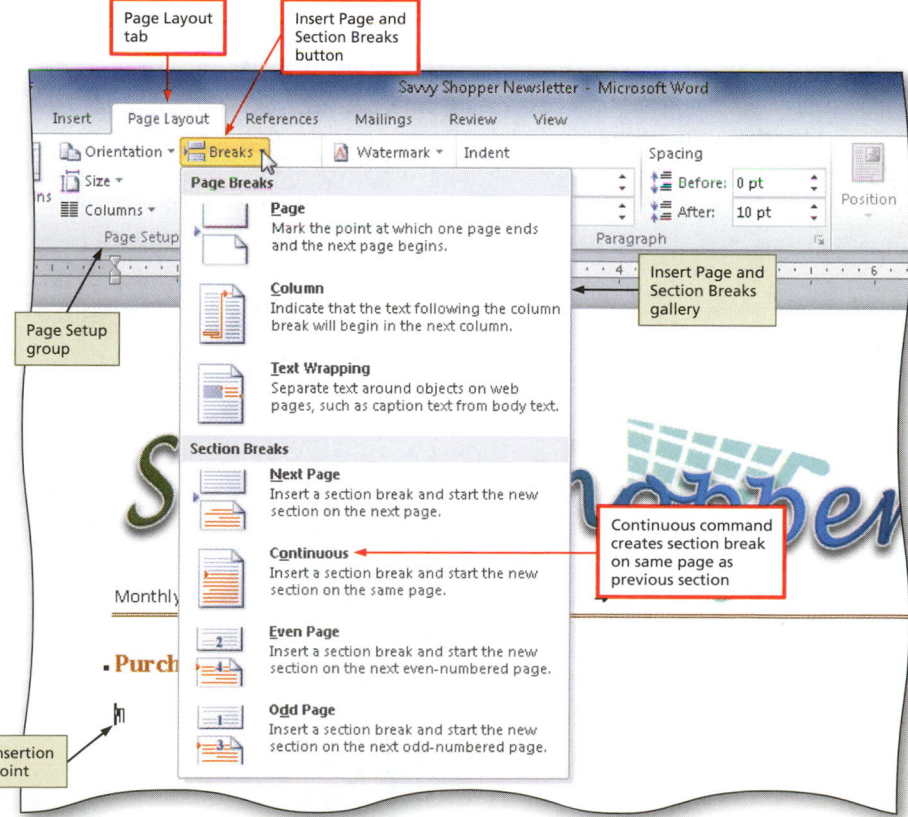

Figure 7–33

- Click Continuous in the Insert Page and Section Breaks gallery to insert a continuous section break above the insertion point (Figure 7–34).

Figure 7–34

To Change the Number of Columns

The document now has two sections. The nameplate is in the first section, and the insertion point is in the second section. The second section should be formatted to three columns. Thus, the following steps format the second section in the document to three columns.

- Click the Columns button (Page Layout tab | Page Setup group) to display the Columns gallery (Figure 7–35).

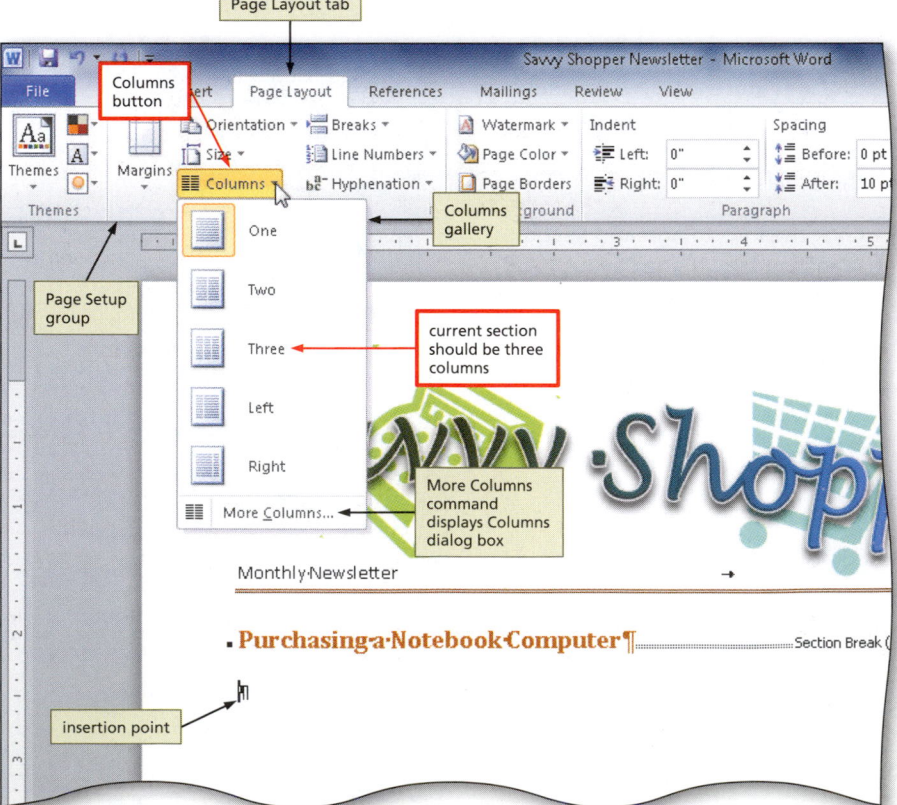

Figure 7–35

- Click Three in the Columns gallery to divide the section containing the insertion point in three evenly sized and spaced columns (Figure 7–36).

Q&A

What if I want columns of different widths?

You would click the More Columns command in the Columns gallery, which displays the Columns dialog box. In this dialog box, you can specify varying column widths and spacing.

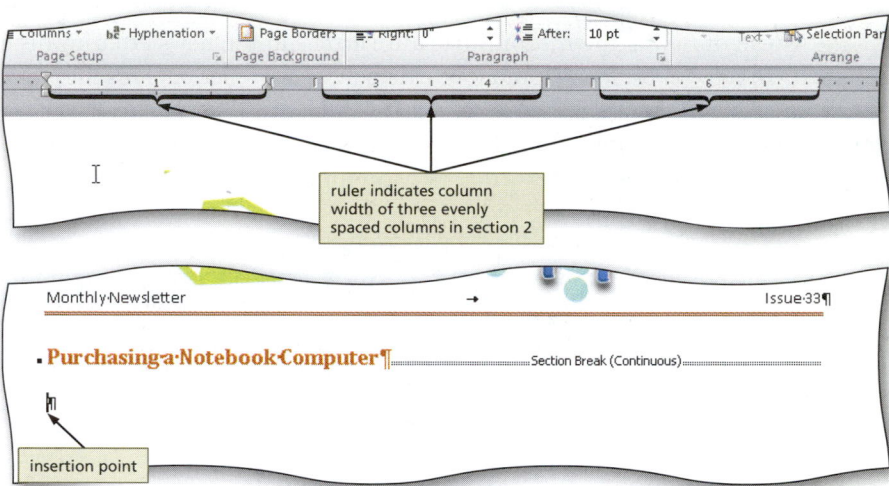

Figure 7–36

To Justify a Paragraph

The text in the paragraphs of the body of the newsletter is **justified**, which means that the left and right margins are aligned, like the edges of newspaper columns. The following step enters the first paragraph of the feature article using justified alignment.

- Display the Home tab.

- Click the Justify button (Home tab | Paragraph group) so that Word aligns both the left and right margins of typed text.

- Type the first paragraph of the feature article (Figure 7–37):
  Buying a notebook computer requires an investment of both time and money. This article identifies some points to consider as you search for a computer that fits your needs.
  and then press the ENTER key.

Q&A

Why do some words have extra space between them?

When a paragraph is formatted to justified alignment, Word places extra space between words so that the left and right edges of the paragraph are aligned. To remedy big gaps, sometimes called rivers, you can add or rearrange words, change the column width, change the font size, and so on.

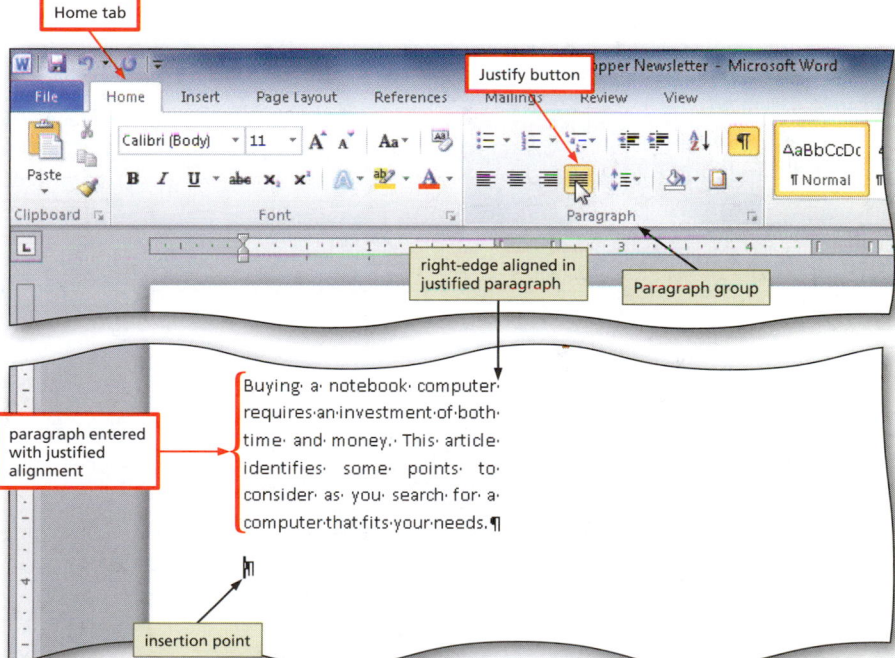

Figure 7–37

Other Ways		
1. Right-click paragraph, click Paragraph on shortcut menu, click Indents and Spacing tab (Paragraph dialog box), click Alignment box	arrow, click Justified, click OK button 2. Click Paragraph Dialog Box Launcher (Home tab or Page Layout tab | Paragraph group), click	Indents and Spacing tab (Paragraph dialog box), click Alignment box arrow, click Justified, click OK button 3. Press CTRL+J

To Insert a File in a Column of the Newsletter

Instead of typing the rest of the feature article in the newsletter in this chapter, the next step is to insert a file named Savvy Shopper Notebook Article in the newsletter. This file, which contains the remainder of the feature article, is located on the Data Files for Students. See the inside back cover of this book for instructions on downloading the Data Files for Students, or contact your instructor for information about accessing the required files.

The following steps insert the Savvy Shopper Notebook Article file in a column of the newsletter.

- Display the Insert tab.

- With the insertion point positioned in the left column as shown in Figure 7–37 on the previous page, click the Insert Object button arrow (Insert tab | Text group) to display the Insert Object menu.

- Click Text from File on the Insert Object menu to display the Insert File dialog box.

- Navigate to the location of the file to be inserted (in this case, the Chapter 07 folder in the Word folder in the Data Files for Students folder on a USB flash drive).

- Click Savvy Shopper Notebook Article to select the file (Figure 7–38).

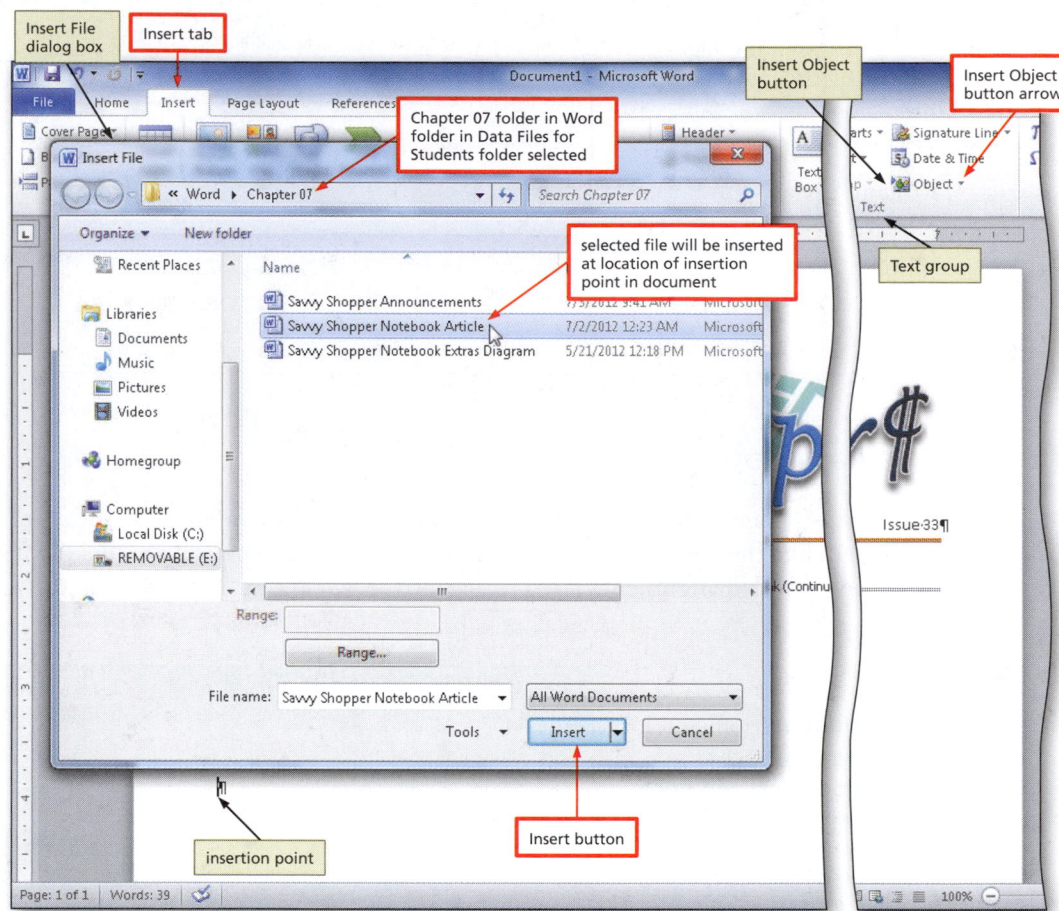

Figure 7–38

- Click the Insert button (Insert File dialog box) to insert the file, Savvy Shopper Notebook Article, in the current document at the location of the insertion point.

- Scroll to display the bottom of the first page in the document window so that you can see how the article fills the three columns on the first and second pages (Figure 7–39).

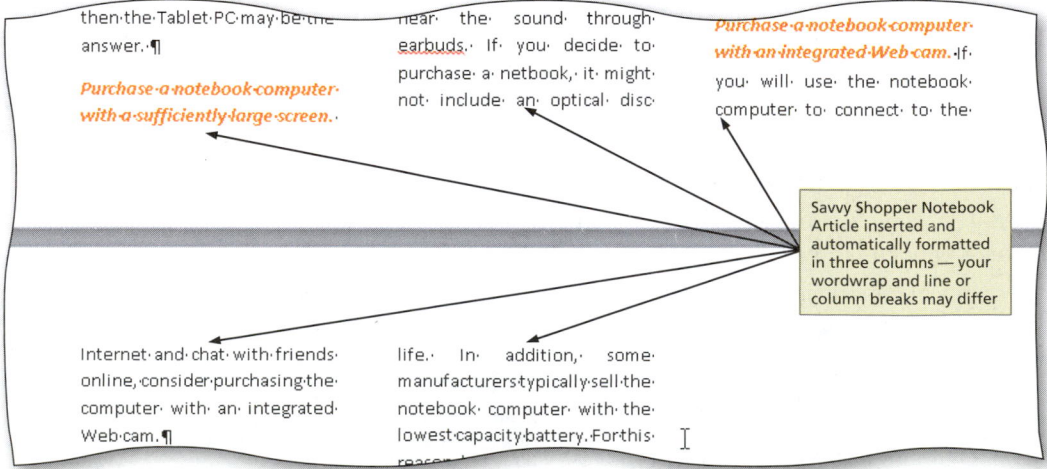

Figure 7–39

To Increase Column Width and Place a Vertical Rule between Columns

The columns in the newsletter currently contain many rivers due to the justified alignment in the narrow column width. To eliminate some of the rivers, you increase the size of the columns slightly in this newsletter. In newsletters, you often see a vertical rule separating columns. Through the Columns dialog box, you can change column width and add vertical rules. The following steps increase column widths and add vertical rules between columns.

1
- Position the insertion point somewhere in the feature article text.
- Display the Page Layout tab.
- Click the Columns button (Page Layout tab | Page Setup group) to display the Columns gallery (Figure 7–40).

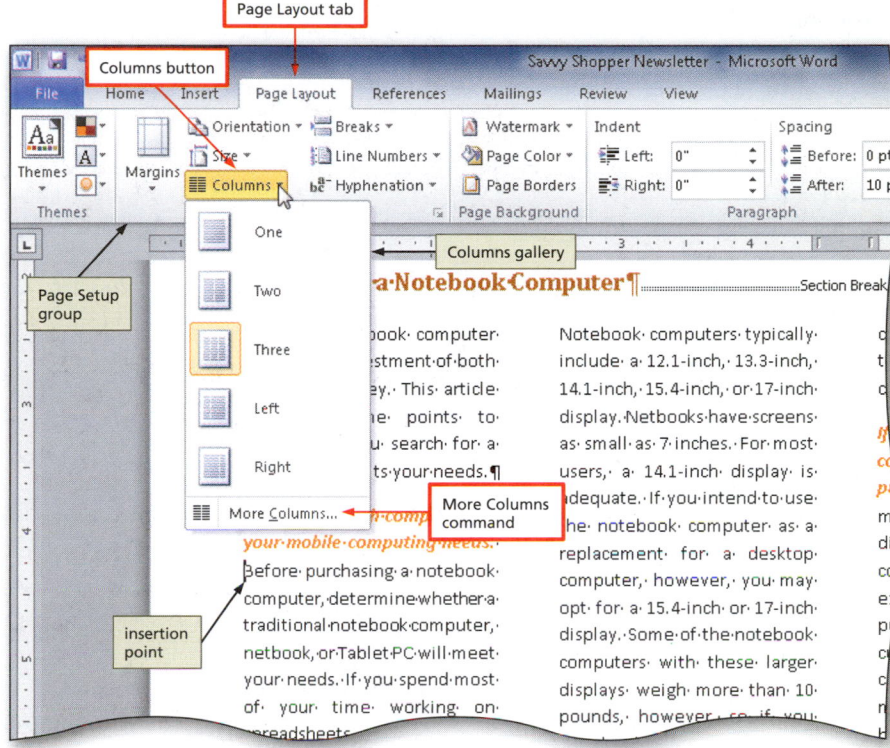

Figure 7–40

2
- Click More Columns in the Columns gallery to display the Columns dialog box.
- In the 'Width and spacing' area (Columns dialog box), click the Width box up arrow as many times as necessary until the Width box reads 2.1".

Q&A

How would I make the columns different widths?

You would remove the check mark from the 'Equal column width' check box and then set the individual column widths in the dialog box.

- Place a check mark in the Line between check box to select the check box (Figure 7–41).

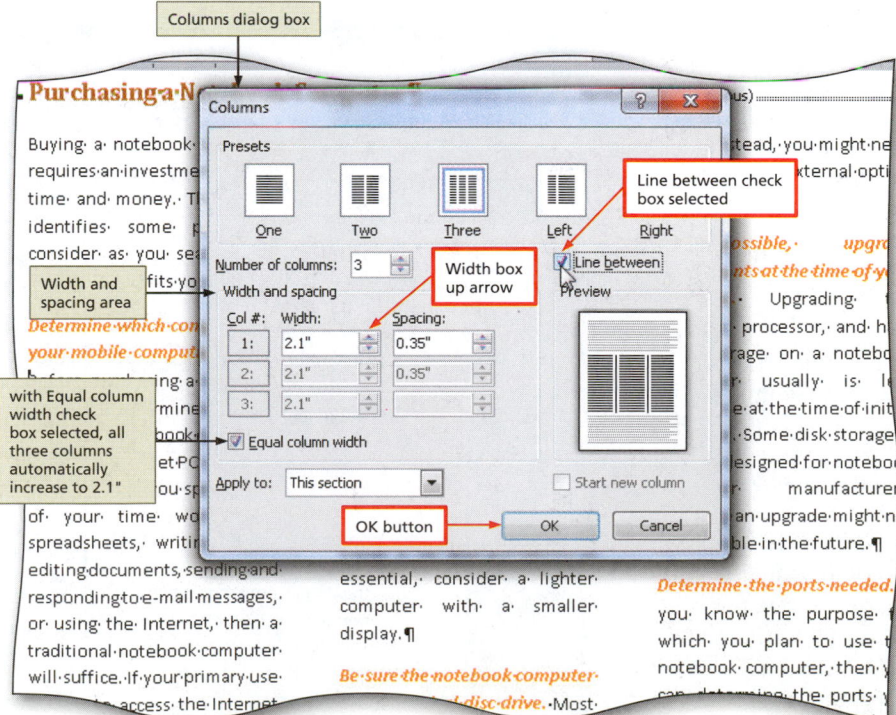

Figure 7–41

3
- Click the OK button to make the columns slightly wider and place a line (vertical rule) between each column in the document (Figure 7–42).

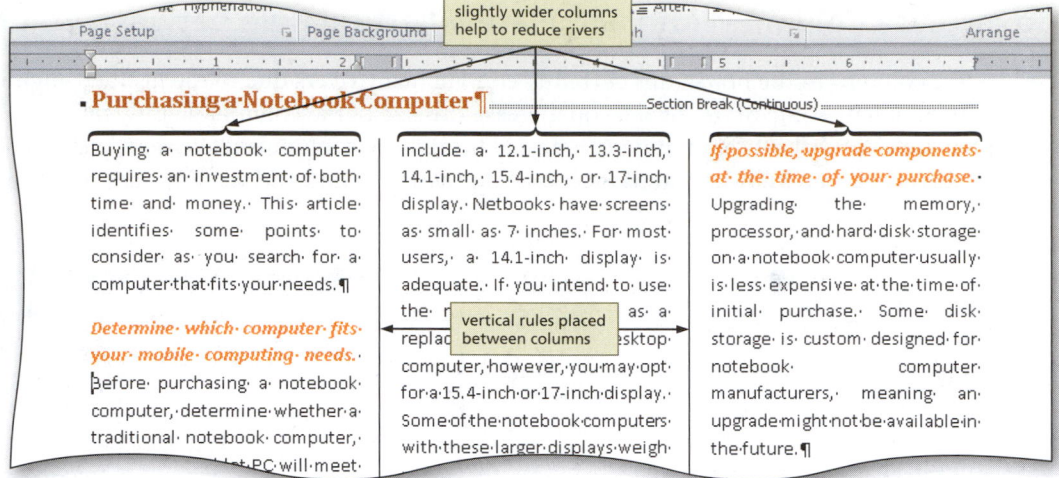

Figure 7–42

Other Ways

1. Double-click space between columns on ruler, enter settings (Columns dialog box), click OK button

2. To adjust column widths, drag column boundaries on ruler

3. To insert line, click Borders button arrow (Home tab | Paragraph group)

To Hyphenate a Document

To further eliminate some of the rivers in the columns of the newsletter, you could turn on Word's hyphenation feature so that words with multiple syllables are hyphenated at the end of lines instead of wrapped in their entirety to the next line. The following steps turn on the hyphenation feature.

1
- Click the Hyphenation button (Page Layout tab | Page Setup group) to display the Hyphenation gallery (Figure 7–43).

Q&A

What is the difference between Automatic and Manual hyphenation?

Automatic hyphenation places hyphens wherever words can break at a syllable in the document. With manual hyphenation, Word displays a dialog box for each word it could hyphenate, enabling you to accept or reject the proposed hyphenation.

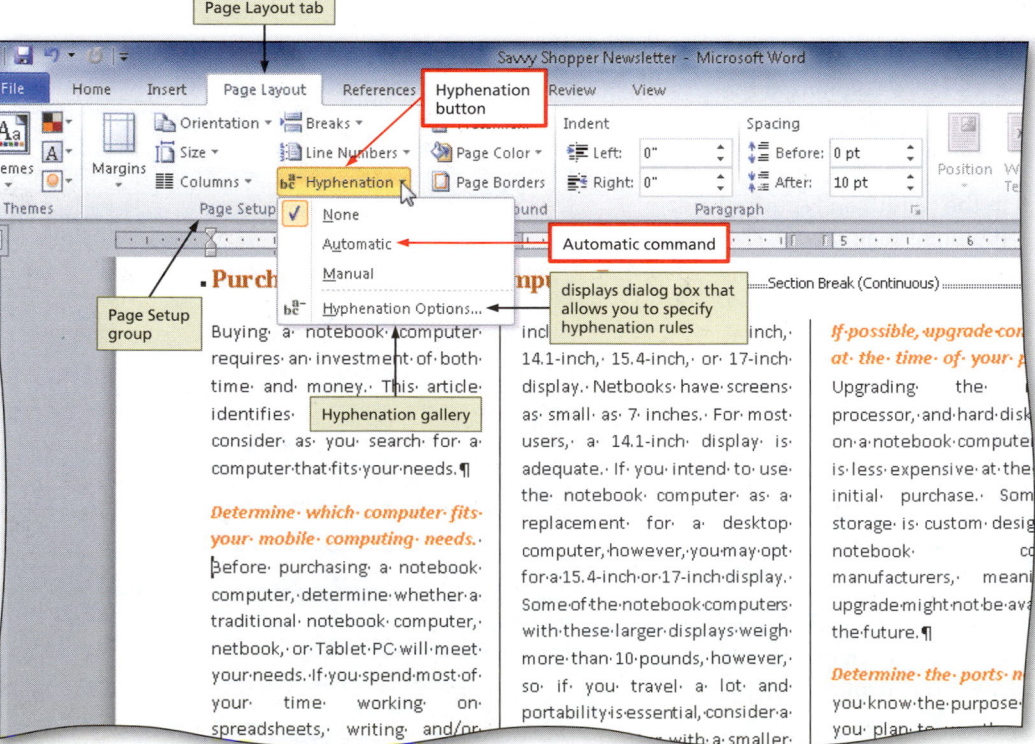

Figure 7–43

2

- Click Automatic in the Hyphenation gallery to hyphenate the document (Figure 7–44).

What if I do not want a particular word hyphenated?

You can reword text and Word will automatically redo the hyphenation.

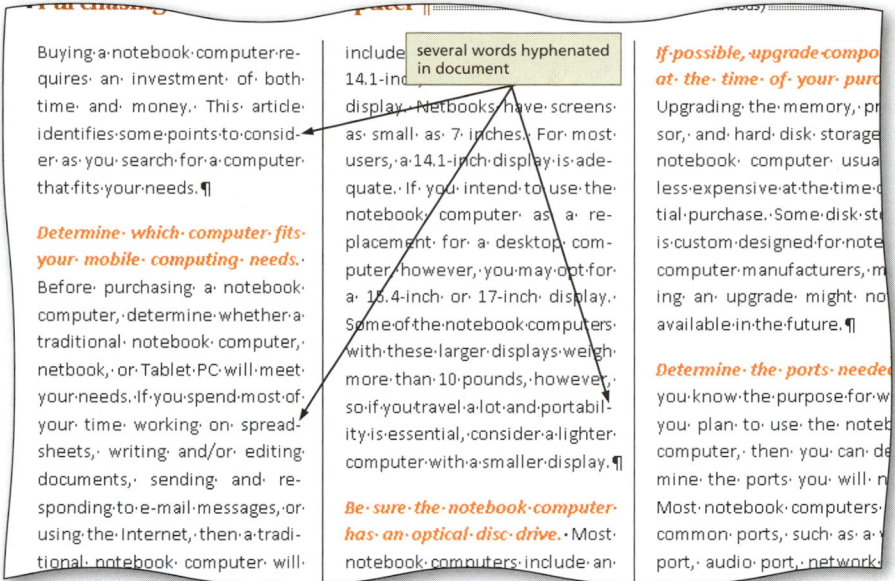

Figure 7–44

To Format a Character as a Drop Cap

The first character in the feature article in this newsletter, that is, the capital letter B, is formatted as a drop cap. A **drop cap** is a capital letter whose font size is larger than the rest of the characters in the paragraph. In Word, the drop cap can sink into the first few lines of text, or it can extend into the left margin, which often is called a stick-up cap. In this newsletter, the paragraph text wraps around the drop cap.

The following steps create a drop cap in the first paragraph of the feature article in the newsletter.

1

- Position the insertion point somewhere in the first paragraph of the feature article.

- Display the Insert tab.

- Click the Drop Cap button (Insert tab | Text group) to display the Drop Cap gallery (Figure 7–45).

Experiment

- Point to various commands in the Drop Cap gallery to see a live preview of the drop cap formats in the document.

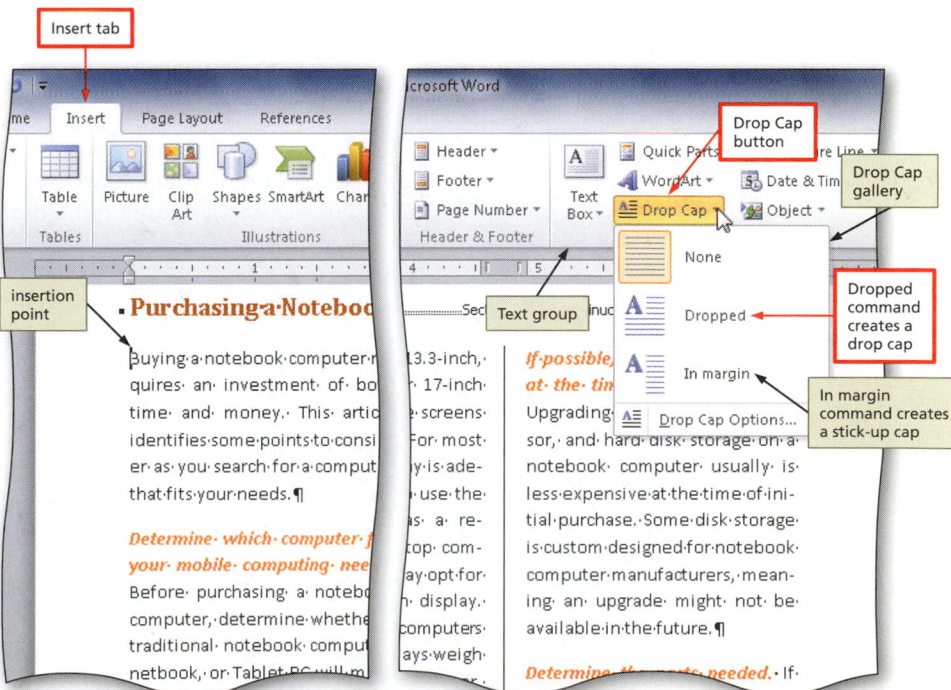

Figure 7–45

2

- Click Dropped in the Drop Cap gallery to format the first letter in the paragraph containing the insertion point (the B in Buying, in this case) as a drop cap and wrap subsequent text in the paragraph around the drop cap (Figure 7–46).

Q&A

What is the outline around the drop cap in the document?

When you format a letter as a drop cap, Word places a frame around it. A **frame** is a container for text that allows you to position the text anywhere on the page. Word formats a frame for the drop cap so that text wraps around it. The frame also contains a paragraph mark nonprinting character to the right of the drop cap, which may or may not be visible on your screen.

letter formatted as drop cap

frame

left edge of drop cap is indented slightly from left edge of paragraph

text wraps tightly around drop cap

Figure 7–46

To Format the Drop Cap

You will change the font color of the drop cap, move it left slightly, and reduce its size a bit. The following steps format the drop cap.

1 With the drop cap selected, display the Home tab, click the Font Color button arrow (Home tab | Font group), and then click Dark Green, Accent 4, Darker 50% (eighth color, sixth row) in the Font Color gallery to change the color of the drop cap.

Q&A

What if my frame no longer is displayed?

Click the drop cap to select it. Then, click the blue selection rectangle to display the frame.

2 Position the mouse pointer on the drop cap frame until the mouse pointer has a four-headed arrow attached to it and then drag the drop cap left slightly so that the left edge of the letter aligns with the left edge of text.

Q&A

What if the drop cap is not in the correct location?

Repeat Step 2.

3 Drag the sizing handles on the frame until the drop cap and the text in the paragraph look like Figure 7–47. If necessary, reposition the drop cap again.

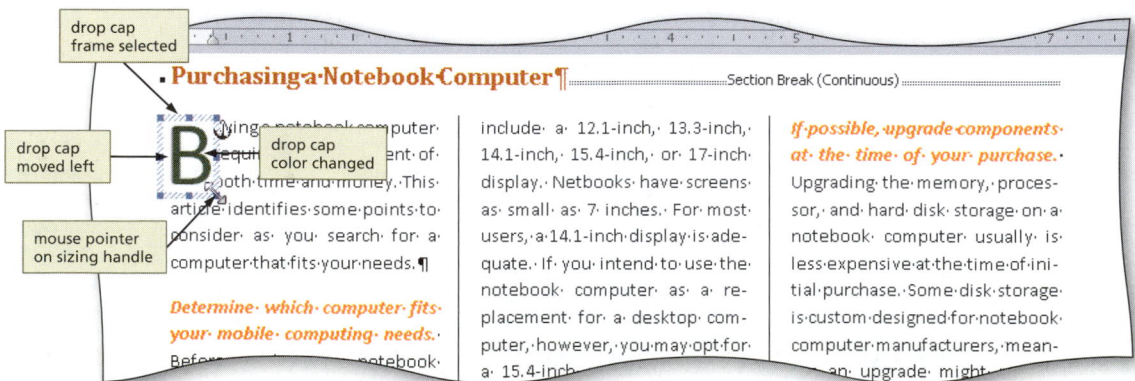

Figure 7–47

To Insert a Next Page Section Break

The third column on the first page of the newsletter is not a continuation of the feature article. The third column, instead, contains several member announcements. The feature article continues on the second page of the newsletter (shown in Figure 7–1b on page WD 403). Thus, you must insert a next page section break, which is a section break that also contains a page break, at the bottom of the second column so that the remainder of the feature article moves to the second page. The following steps insert a next page section break in the second column.

1

• Scroll to display the bottom of the second column of the first page of the newsletter in the document window. Position the insertion point at the location for the section break, in this case, to the left of the B in the paragraph beginning with the words, Be sure.

• Display the Page Layout tab.

• Click the Insert Page and Section Breaks button (Page Layout tab | Page Setup group) to display the Insert Page and Section Breaks gallery (Figure 7–48).

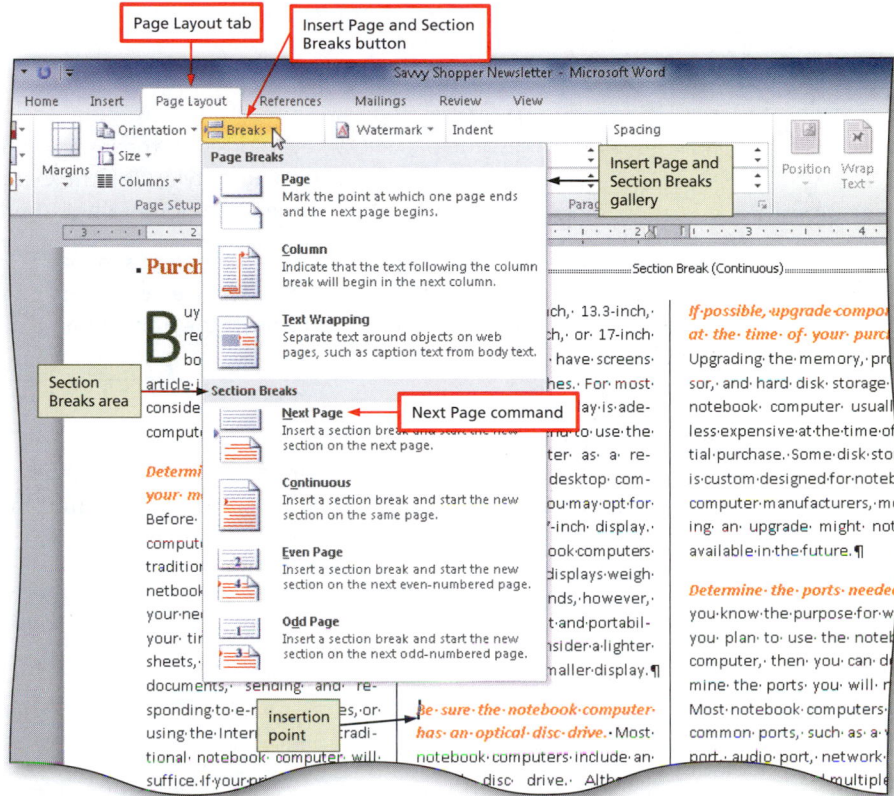

Figure 7–48

2

• In the Section Breaks area in the gallery, click Next Page to insert a next page section break, which positions the insertion point on the next page (Figure 7–49).

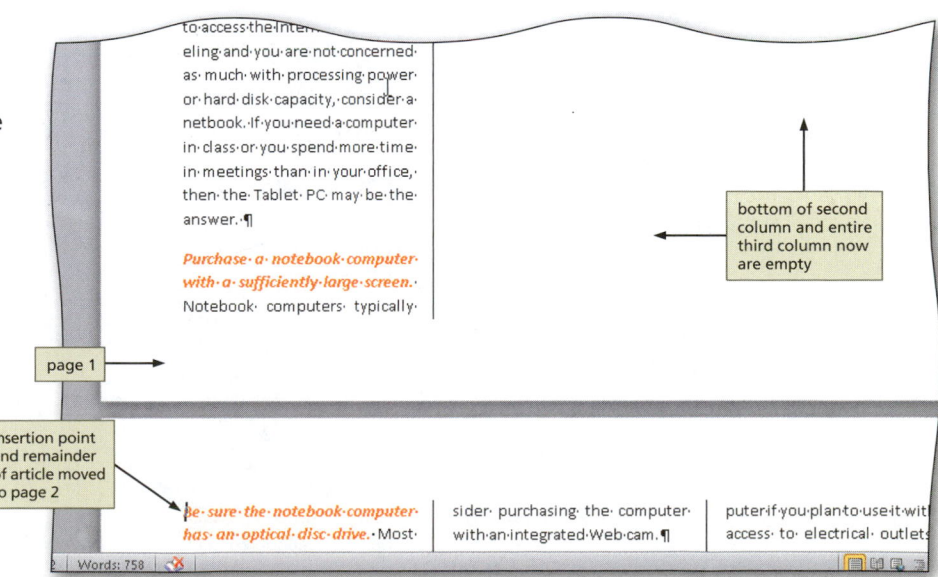

Figure 7–49

To Enter Text

The next step is to insert a jump-to line at the end of the second column, informing the reader where to look for the rest of the feature article. The following steps insert a jump-to line at the end of the text in the second column on the first page of the newsletter.

1 Scroll to display the end of the text in the second column of the first page of the newsletter and then position the insertion point between the paragraph mark and the section break notation.

2 Press the ENTER key twice to insert a blank line for the jump-to text above the section break notation.

3 Press the UP ARROW key to position the insertion point on the blank line. If the blank line is formatted in the Heading 1 style, click the Clear Formatting button (Home tab | Font group) so that the entered text follows the Normal style.

4 Press CTRL+R to right align the paragraph mark. Press CTRL+I to turn on the italic format. Type **(Article continues on next page)** as the jump-to text and then press CTRL+I again to turn off the italic format.

To Insert a Column Break

In the Savvy Shopper newsletters, for consistency, the member announcements always begin at the top of the third column. If you insert the Savvy Shopper Announcements at the current location of the insertion point, however, they will begin at the bottom of the second column.

For the member announcements to be displayed in the third column, you insert a **column break** at the bottom of the second column, which places the insertion point at the top of the next column. Thus, the following steps insert a column break at the bottom of the second column.

1

• Position the insertion point to the left of the paragraph mark on the line containing the next page section break, which is the location where the column break should be inserted.

• Click the Insert Page and Section Breaks button (Page Layout tab | Page Setup group) to display the Insert Page and Section Breaks gallery (Figure 7–50).

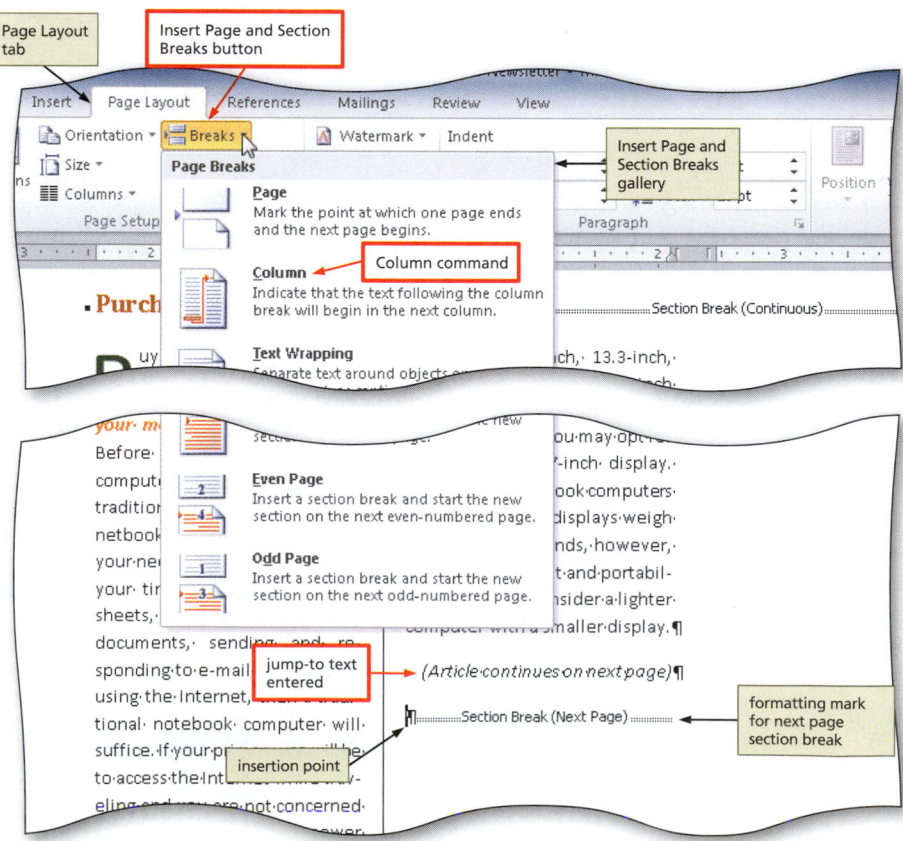

Figure 7–50

2

- Click Column in the Insert Page and Section Breaks gallery to insert a column break at the location of the insertion point and move the insertion point to the top of the next column (Figure 7–51).

Q&A What if I wanted to remove a column break?

You would double-click it to select it and then click the Cut button (Home tab | Clipboard group) or press the DELETE key.

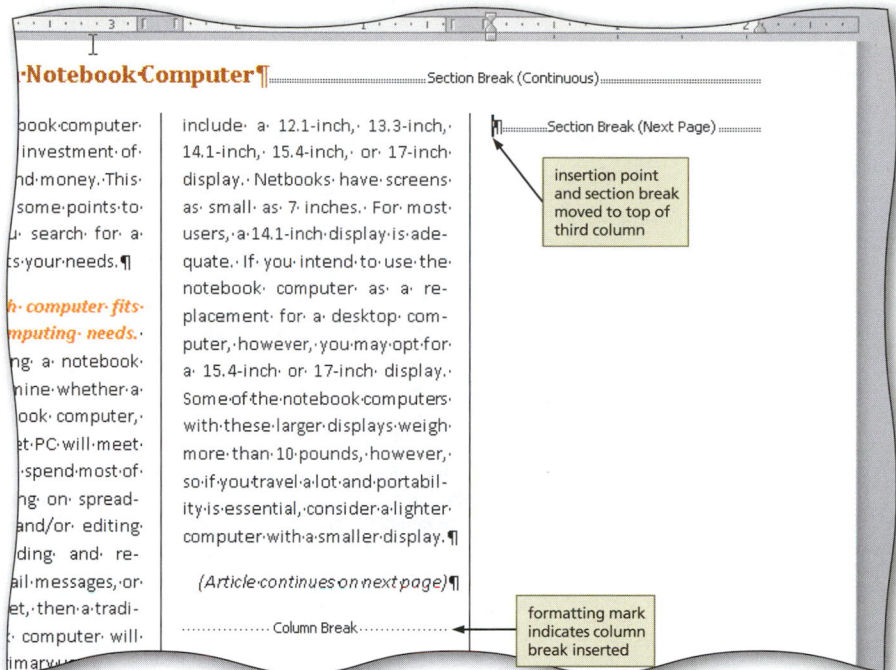

Figure 7–51

To Insert a File in a Column of the Newsletter

So that you do not have to enter the entire third column of announcements in the newsletter, the next step in the project is to insert the file named Savvy Shopper Announcements in the third column of the newsletter. This file contains the three announcements: the first about member discounts, the second about a group meeting, and the third about the topic of the next newsletter issue.

The Savvy Shopper Announcements file is located on the Data Files for Students. See the inside back cover of this book for instructions on downloading the Data Files for Students, or contact your instructor for information about accessing the required files. The following steps insert a file in a column of the newsletter.

1 With the insertion point at the top of the third column, display the Insert tab.

2 Click the Insert Object button arrow (Insert tab | Text group) to display the Insert Object menu and then click Text from File on the Object menu to display the Insert File dialog box.

3 Navigate to the location of the file to be inserted (in this case, the Chapter 07 folder in the Word folder in the Data Files for Students folder on a USB flash drive).

4 Click Savvy Shopper Announcements to select the file.

5 Click the Insert button (Insert File dialog box) to insert the file, Savvy Shopper Announcements, in the document at the location of the insertion point.

Q&A What if text from the announcements column spills onto the second page of the newsletter?

You will format text in the announcements column so that all of its text fits in the third column of the first page.

6 Press SHIFT+F5 to return the insertion point to the last editing location, in this case, the top of the third column on the first page of the newsletter (Figure 7–52).

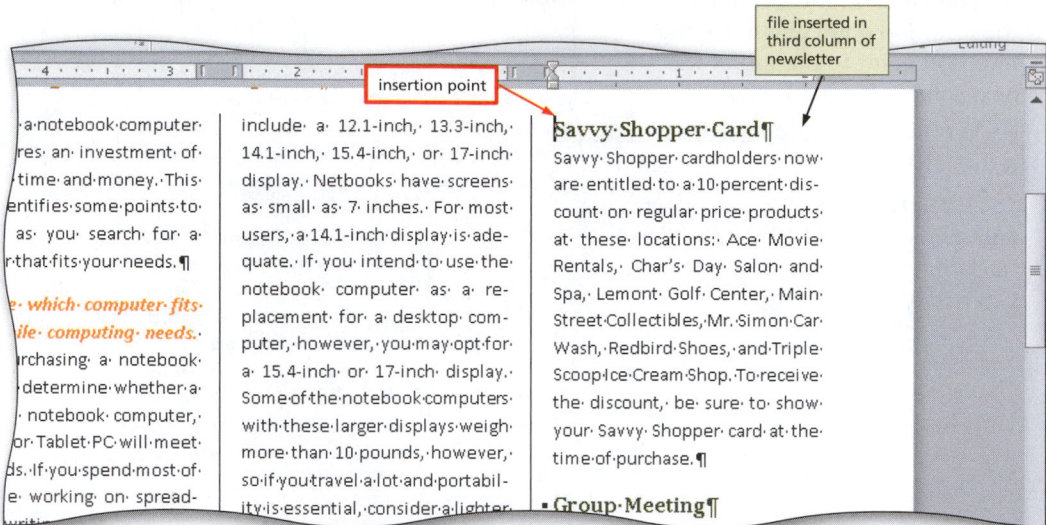

Figure 7–52

To Save a Document Again

You have performed several steps since the last save. Thus, you should save the newsletter again.

1 Save the newsletter again with the same file name, Savvy Shopper Newsletter.

Creating a Pull-Quote

A pull-quote is text pulled, or copied, from the text of the document and given graphical emphasis so that it stands apart and commands the reader's attention. The newsletter in this project copies text from the second page of the newsletter and places it in a pull-quote on the first page between the first and second columns (Figure 7–1a on page WD 403).

Plan Ahead

> **Enhance the document with pull-quotes.**
> Because of their bold emphasis, pull-quotes should be used sparingly in a newsletter. Pull-quotes are useful for breaking the monotony of long columns of text. Typically, quotation marks are used only if you are quoting someone directly. If you use quotation marks, use curly (or smart) quotation marks instead of straight quotation marks.

Quotes Building Block If you wanted to format a quotation in the running text instead of in a text box, Word provides two quote styles: Quote and Intense Quote. To format the current paragraph as a quote, click the More button in the Styles gallery (Home tab | Styles group) and then click Quote or Intense Quote.

To create the pull-quote in this newsletter, follow this general procedure:

1. Create a **text box**, which is a container for text that allows you to position the text anywhere on the page.

2. Copy the text from the existing document to the Office Clipboard and then paste the text from the Office Clipboard to the text box.

3. Resize and format the text box.

4. Move the text box to the desired location.

To Insert a Text Box

The first step in creating the pull-quote is to insert a text box. A text box is like a frame; the difference is that a text box has more graphical formatting options than does a frame. Word provides a variety of built-in text boxes, saving you the time of formatting the text box. The following steps insert a built-in text box.

1
- Scroll to display the top portion of the newsletter in the document window and position the insertion point at an approximate location for the pull-quote (you will position the pull-quote at the exact location in a later step).

- Click the Text Box button (Insert tab | Text group) to display the Text Box gallery.

🔍 **Experiment**

- Scroll through the Text Box gallery to see the variety of available text box styles.

- Scroll to display Puzzle Quote in the Text Box gallery (Figure 7–53).

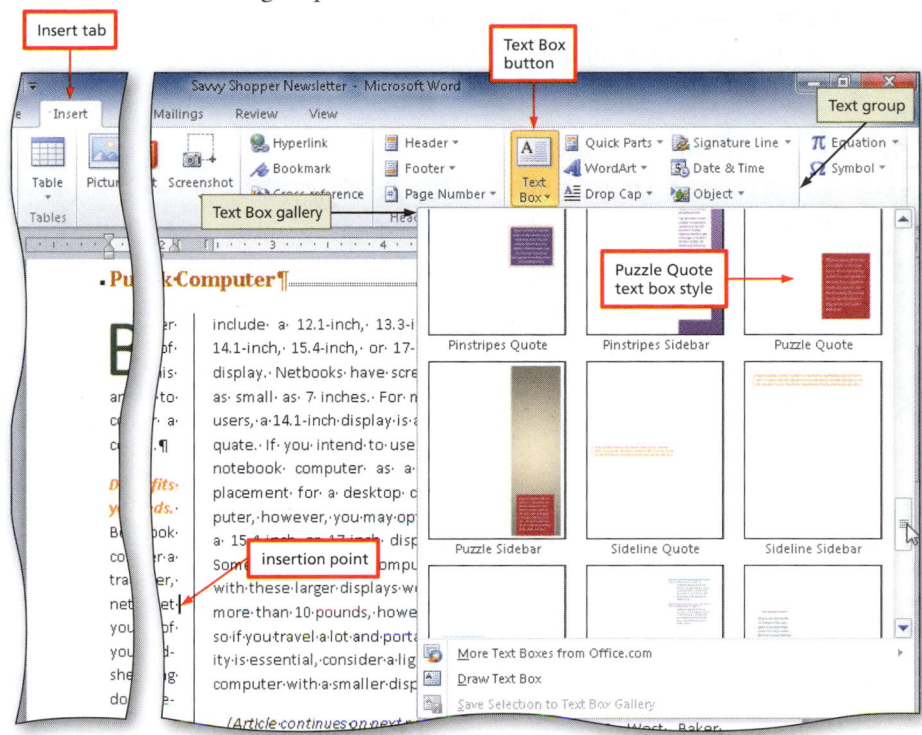

Figure 7–53

2
- Click Puzzle Quote in the Text Box gallery to insert that text box style in the document. If necessary, scroll to display the entire text box in the document window (Figure 7–54).

Q&A Does my text box need to be in the same location as Figure 7–54?

No. You will move the text box later.

Q&A The layout of the first page is not correct because of the text box. What do I do?

You will enter text in the text box and then position it in the correct location. At that time, the layout of the first page will be fixed.

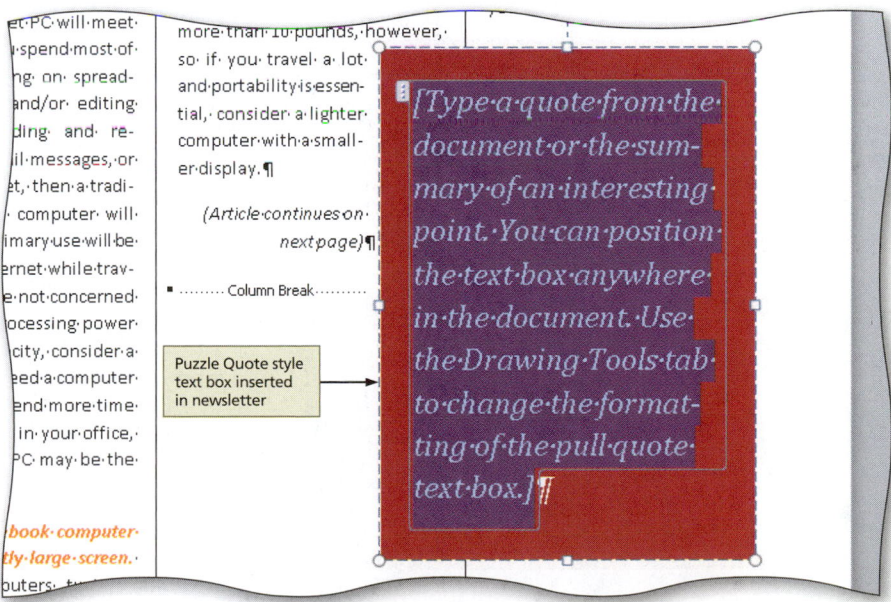

Figure 7–54

Other Ways
1. Click Quick Parts button (Insert tab | Text group), click Building Blocks Organizer on Quick Parts menu, select desired text box name in Building blocks list, click Insert button

To Split the Window

The text that you will copy for the pull-quote is on the second page of the newsletter and the pull-quote (text box) is on the first page of the newsletter. Thus, the next step is to copy the pull-quote text from the second page and then paste it on the first page. To simplify this process, you would like to view the pull-quote on the first page and the text to be copied on the second page on the screen at the same time. Word allows you to split the window in two separate panes, each containing the current document and having its own scroll bar. This enables you to scroll to and view two different portions of the same document at the same time. The following steps split the Word window.

1
- Position the mouse pointer on the split box at the top of the vertical scroll bar, which changes the mouse pointer to a resize pointer (Figure 7–55).

Q&A

What does the resize pointer look like?

The **resize pointer** consists of two small horizontal lines, each with a vertical arrow.

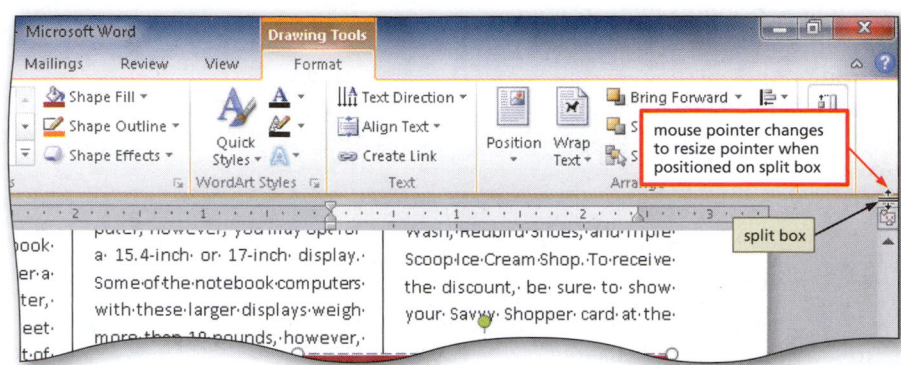

Figure 7–55

2
- Double-click the resize pointer to divide the document window in two separate panes — both the upper and lower panes display the current document (Figure 7–56).

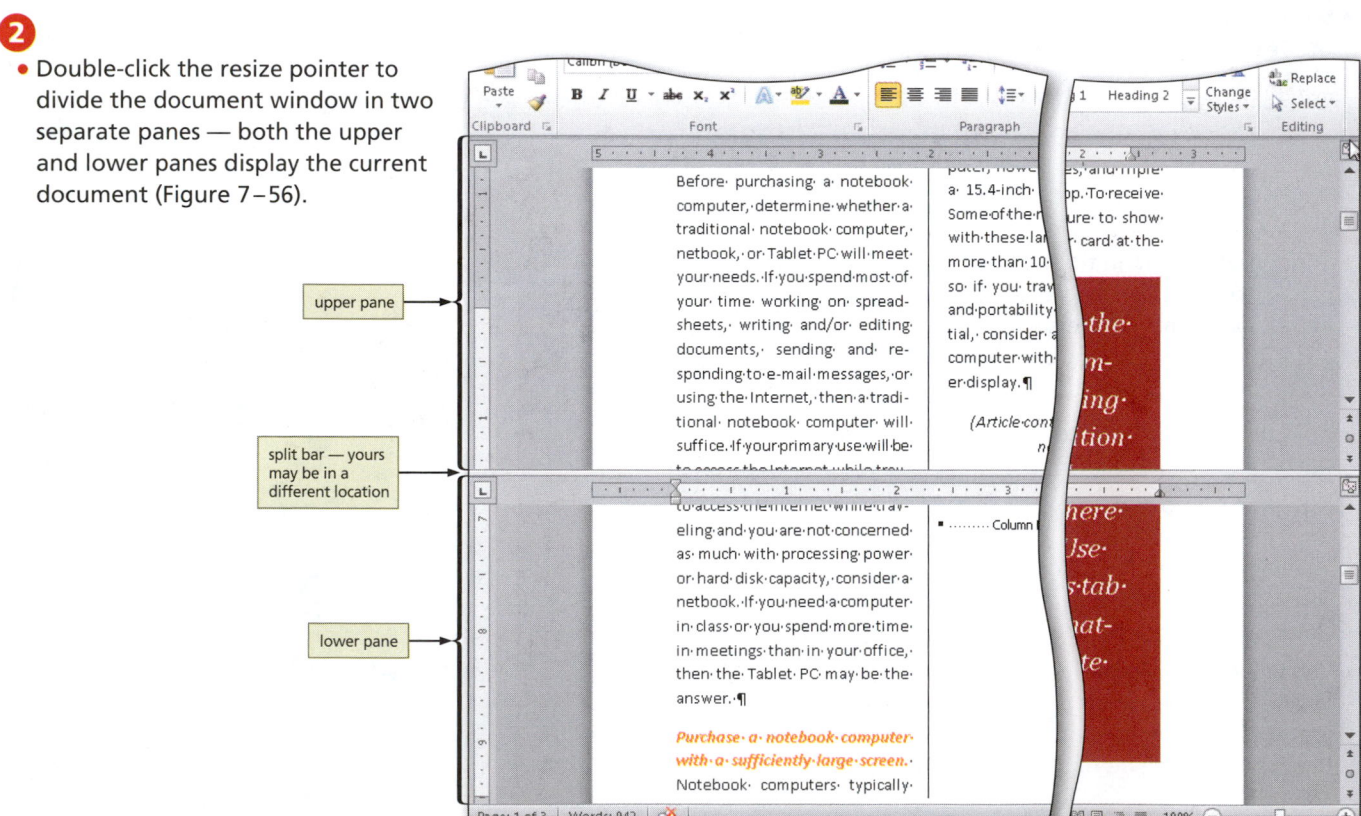

Figure 7–56

Other Ways

1. Click Split button (View tab | Window group), click at desired split location in window

2. Press ALT+CTRL+S, then ENTER

TO ARRANGE ALL OPEN WORD DOCUMENTS ON THE SCREEN

If you have multiple Word documents open and want to view all of them at the same time on the screen, you can instruct Word to arrange all the open documents on the screen from top to bottom. If you wanted to arrange all open Word documents on the same screen, you would perform the following steps.

1. Click the Arrange All button (View tab | Window group) to display each open Word document on the screen.

2. To make one of the arranged documents fill the entire screen again, maximize the window by clicking its Maximize button or double-clicking its title bar.

To Copy and Paste Using Split Windows

The next step in creating the pull-quote is to copy text from the second page of the newsletter to the Clipboard and then paste the text into the text box. The item being copied is called the **source**. The location to which you are pasting is called the **destination**. Thus, the source is text in the body copy of the newsletter, and the destination is the text box. The following steps copy and then paste the text.

1

- In the upper pane, if necessary, scroll to display a portion of the text box.

- In the lower pane, scroll to display text to be copied, as shown in Figure 7–57, and then select the following text: If you anticipate running the notebook computer on batteries frequently, choose a computer that uses lithium-ion batteries

- Click the Copy button (Home tab | Clipboard group) to copy the selected text to the Clipboard (Figure 7–57).

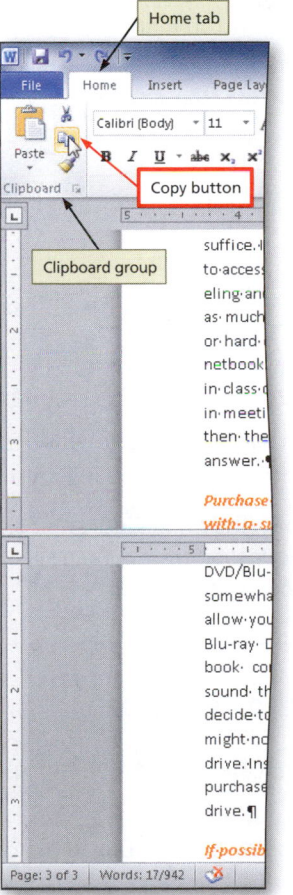
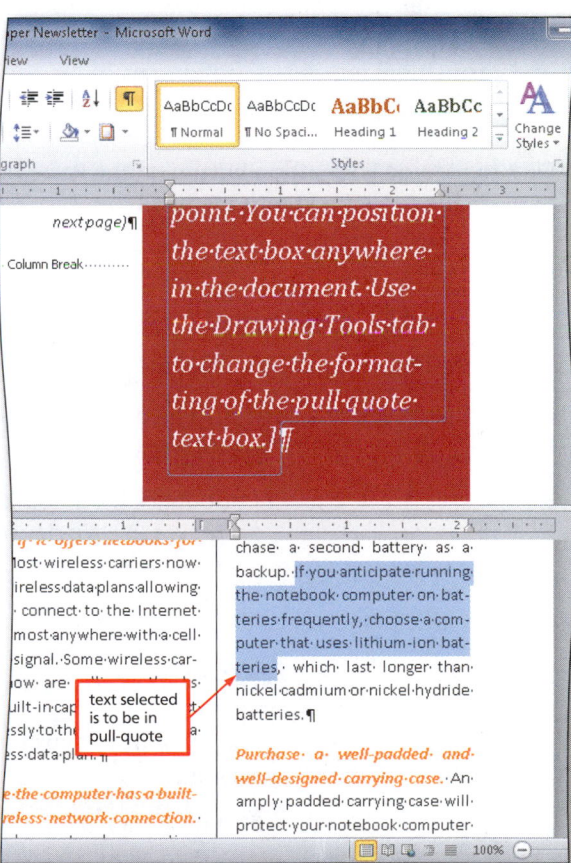

Figure 7–57

- In the upper pane, click the text in the text box to select it.

- Click the Paste button arrow (Home tab | Clipboard group) to display the Paste button menu.

Q&A

What if I click the Paste button by mistake?

Click the Paste Options button to the right of the pasted text in the text box to display the Paste Options menu.

- Point to the Merge Formatting button on the Paste button menu and notice the text box shows a live preview of the selected paste option (Figure 7–58).

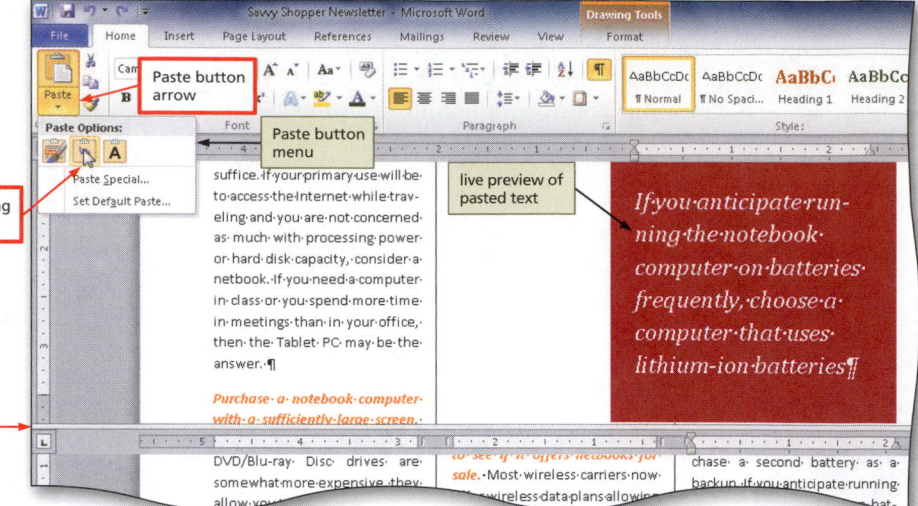

Figure 7–58

Q&A

Why select the Merge Formatting button on the Paste button menu?

You want the pasted text to use the formats that were in the text box (the destination) instead of the formats of the copied text (the source).

3

- Click the Merge Formatting button on the Paste button menu to paste the copied text into the text box.

Other Ways
1. Select text to copy, press CTRL+C; select destination for pasted text, press CTRL+V

To Remove a Split Window

The next step is to remove the split window so that you can continue formatting the second page of the newsletter. The following step removes a split window.

1 Double-click the split bar (shown in Figure 7–58), or click the Remove Split button (View tab | Window group), or press ALT+SHIFT+C, to remove the split window and return to a single Word window on the screen.

To Format Text in the Text Box

The next steps format the text in the pull-quote to color the text and change line spacing to 1.15.

1 If necessary, scroll to display the text box in the document window.

2 Press the PERIOD key to end the sentence in the text box.

BTW

Rotating Text Box Text
To rotate text in a text box, select the text box, click the Text Direction button (Drawing Tools Format tab | Text group), and then click the desired direction on the Text Direction menu.

3 Select the text in the text box.

4 Center the text in the text box.

5 Change the font size to 12 point.

6 Bold the text in the text box.

7 Click in the text box to deselect the text but leave the text box selected.

To Resize a Text Box and Insert a Line Break Character

The next step in formatting the pull-quote is to resize the text box. You resize a text box the same way as any other object. That is, you drag its sizing handles or enter values in the height and width boxes through the Size button (Drawing Tools Format tab | Size group). You do not want any hyphenated words in the text box. Once the text box is resized, you insert a line break character to eliminate any hyphenated words. The following steps resize the text box and insert a line break character.

1 Drag the sizing handles so that the pull-quote looks about the same size as Figure 7–59.

2 Verify the pull-quote dimensions by clicking the Size button (Drawing Tools Format tab | Size group) to display the Shape Height and Shape Width boxes and, if necessary, change the value in the Shape Height box to 3.28 and the Shape Width box to 1.45.

3 If the word, anticipate, is hyphenated in the resized pull-quote, position the insertion point to the left of the a in anticipate and then press SHIFT+ENTER to insert a line break character, which places the word on the next line and removes the hyphen (Figure 7–59).

BTW

Saving to the Text Box Gallery
To save a text box you have created and formatted so that it appears as a selection in the Text Box gallery, do the following: select the text box, click the Text Box button (Insert tab | Text group), click Save Selection to Text Box Gallery, type a name and description (Create New Building Block dialog box), and then click the OK button.

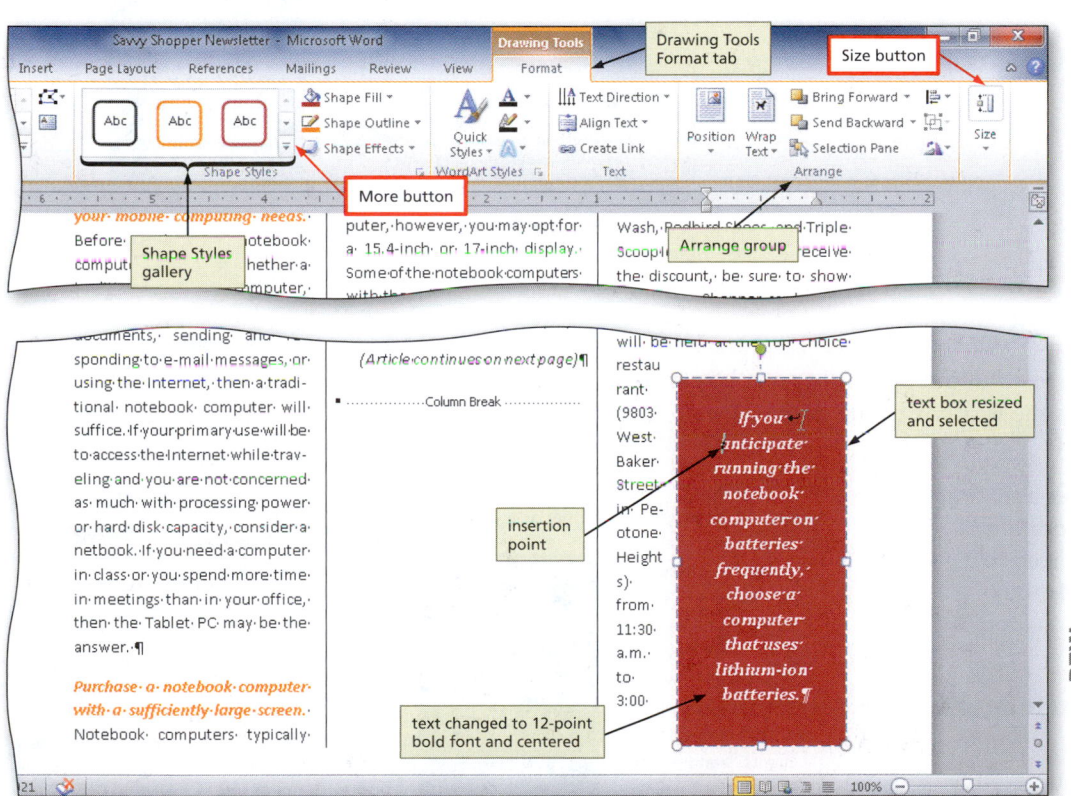

Figure 7–59

BTW

Text Box Styles
Like other drawing objects or pictures, text boxes can be formatted or have styles applied. You can change the fill in a text box by clicking the Shape Fill button (Drawing Tools Format tab | Shape Styles group), add an outline to a text box by clicking the Shape Outline button (Drawing Tools Format tab | Shape Styles group), and apply an effect such as shadow or 3-D effects by clicking the Shape Effects button (Drawing Tools Format tab | Shape Styles group).

To Apply a Shape Style to a Text Box

The next step in formatting the pull-quote is to apply a shape style to the text box to coordinate its colors with the rest of the newsletter. The following steps apply a shape style to a text box.

1 With the text box still selected, click the More button (shown in Figure 7–59) in the Shape Styles gallery (Drawing Tools Format tab | Shape Styles group) to expand the gallery.

2 Point to Intense Effect - Dark Blue, Accent 3 (fourth style, last row) in the Shape Styles gallery to display a live preview of that style applied to the text box (Figure 7–60).

3 Click to Intense Effect - Dark Blue, Accent 3 in the Shape Styles gallery to apply the selected style to the shape.

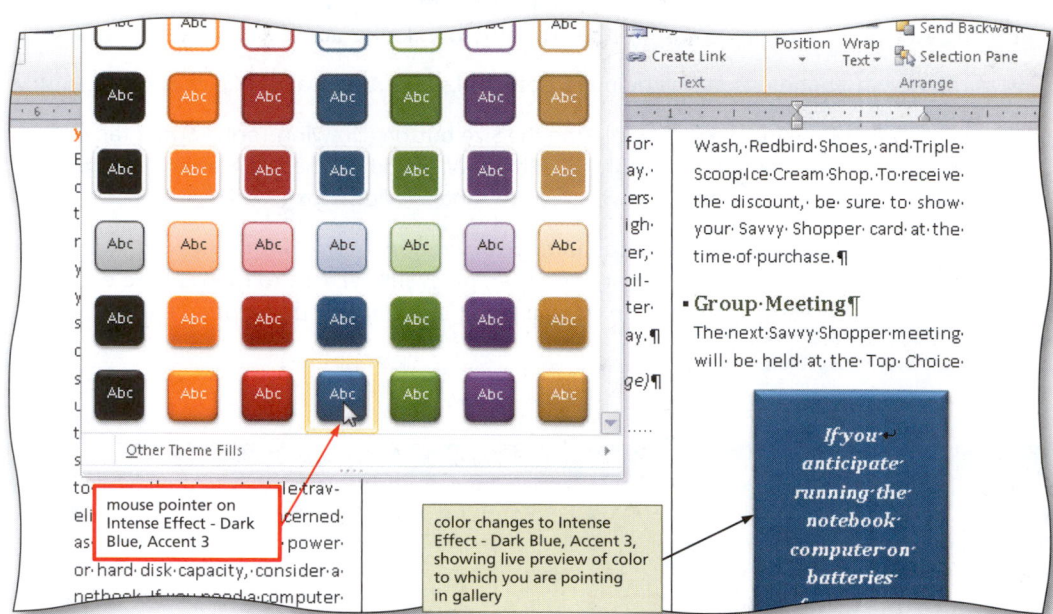

Figure 7–60

To Position a Text Box

The final step is to position the pull-quote text box between the first and second columns of the newsletter. The following step moves the text box to the desired location.

1

- With the text box still selected, drag the text box to its new location (Figure 7–61). You may need to drag and/or resize the text box a couple of times so that it looks similar to this figure.

- Click outside the text box to remove the selection.

Q&A

Why does my text wrap differently around the text box?

Differences in wordwrap often relate to the printer used by your computer. Thus, your document may wordwrap around the text box differently.

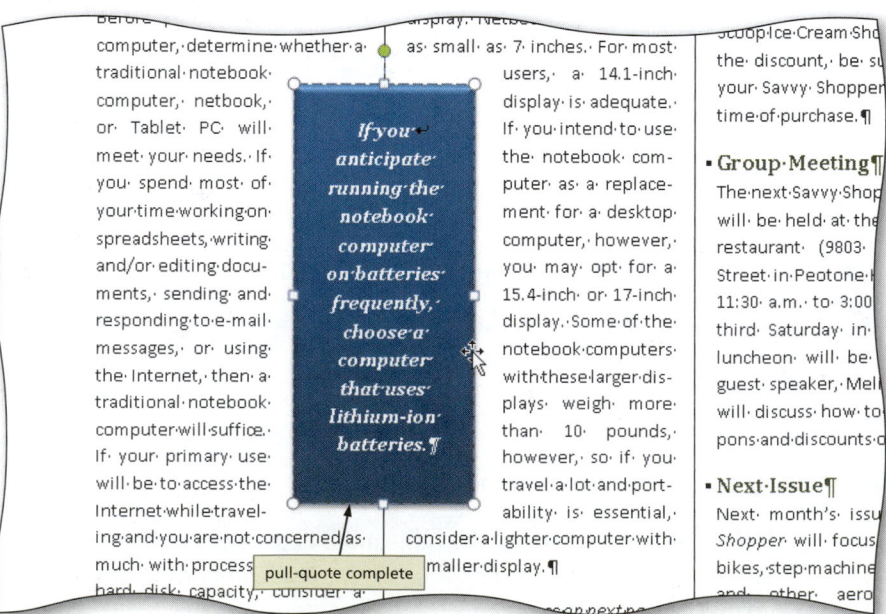

Figure 7–61

To Save a Document Again

You have performed several steps since the last save. You should save the newsletter again.

1 Save the newsletter again with the same file name, Savvy Shopper Newsletter.

Break Point: If you wish to take a break, this is a good place to do so. You can quit Word now. To resume at a later time, start Word, open the file called Savvy Shopper Newsletter, and continue following the steps from this location forward.

Formatting the Second Page of the Newsletter

The second page of the newsletter (Figure 7–1b on page WD 403) continues the feature article that began in the first two columns on the first page. The nameplate on the second page is less elaborate than the one on the first page of the newsletter. In addition to the text in the feature article, page two contains a graphic. The following pages format the second page of the newsletter in this project.

> **Create the nameplate.**
> The top of the inner pages of a newsletter may or may not have a nameplate. If you choose to create one for your inner pages, it should not be the same as, or compete with, the one on the first page. Inner page nameplates usually contain only a portion of the nameplate from the first page of a newsletter.

Plan Ahead

To Change Column Formatting

The document currently is formatted in three columns. The nameplate at the top of the second page, however, should be in a single column. The next step, then, is to change the number of columns at the top of the second page from three to one.

As discussed earlier in this project, Word requires a new section each time you change the number of columns in a document. Thus, you first must insert a continuous section break and then format the section to one column so that the nameplate can be entered on the second page of the newsletter. The following steps insert a continuous section break and then change the column format.

1
- If you have a blank page between the first and second pages of the newsletter, position the insertion point to the left of the paragraph mark at the end of the third column on the first page of the newsletter and then press the DELETE key to delete the blank line causing the overflow.

- Scroll through the document and then position the mouse pointer at the upper-left corner of the second page of the newsletter (to the left of B in Be).

- Display the Page Layout tab.

- Click the Insert Page and Section Breaks button (Page Layout tab | Page Setup group) to display the Insert Page and Section Breaks gallery (Figure 7–62).

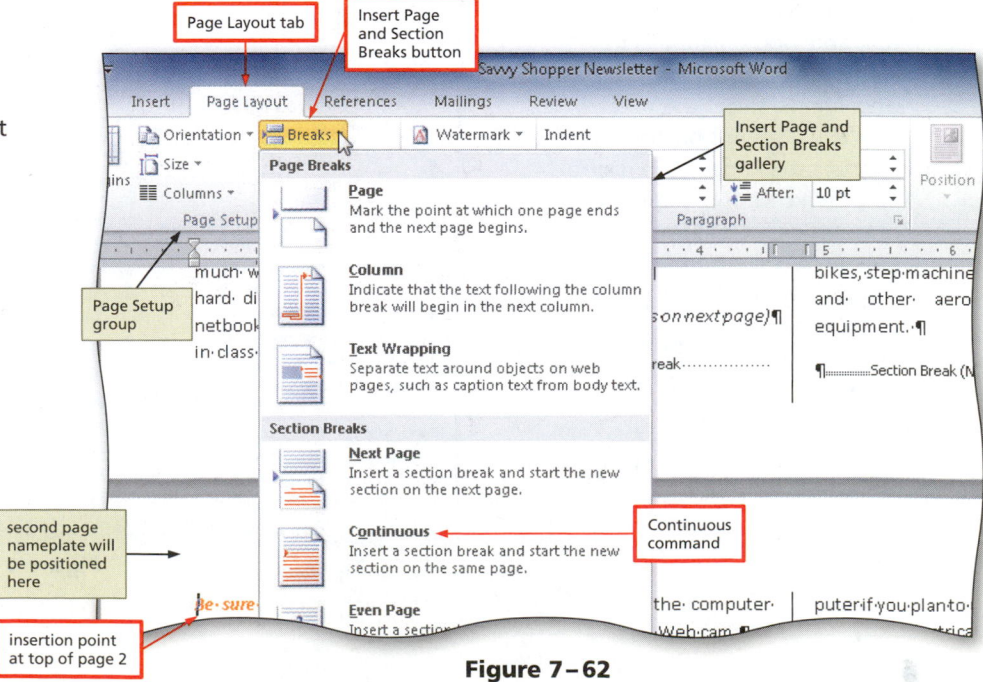

Figure 7–62

2

- Click Continuous in the Insert Page and Section Breaks gallery to insert a continuous section break above the insertion point.

- Press the UP ARROW key to position the insertion point to the left of the continuous section break just inserted.

- Click the Columns button (Page Layout tab | Page Setup group) to display the Columns gallery (Figure 7–63).

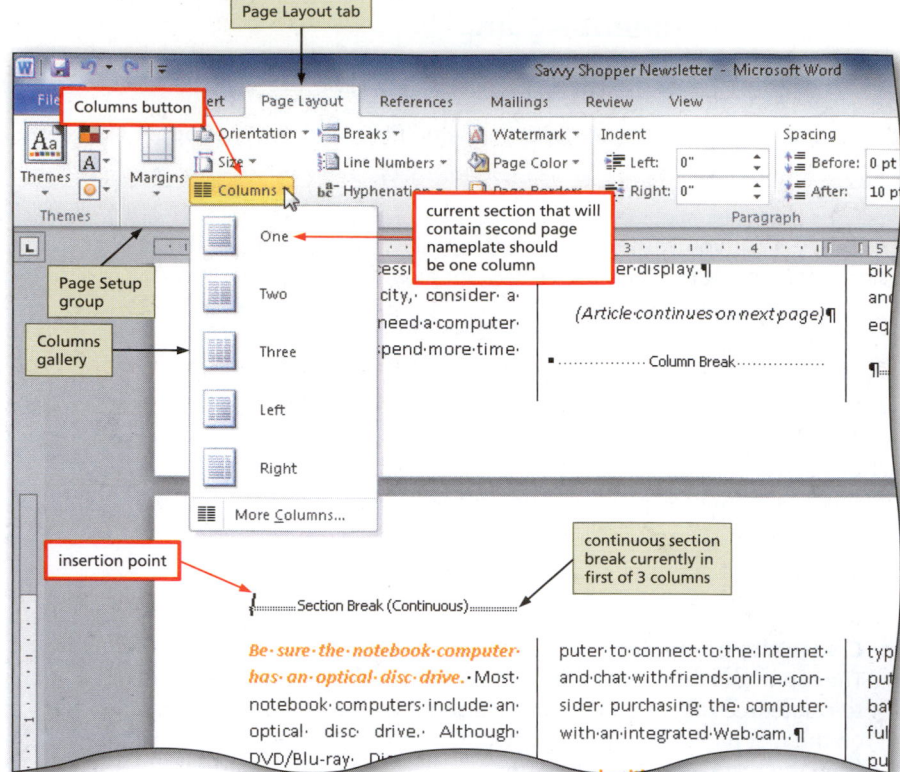

Figure 7–63

3

- Click One in the Columns gallery to format the current section to one column, which now is ready for the second page nameplate (Figure 7–64).

Q&A

Can I change the column format of existing text?

Yes. If you already have typed text and would like it to be formatted in a different number of columns, select the text, click the Columns button (Page Layout tab | Page Setup group), and then click the number of columns desired in the Columns gallery. Word automatically creates a new section for the newly formatted columns.

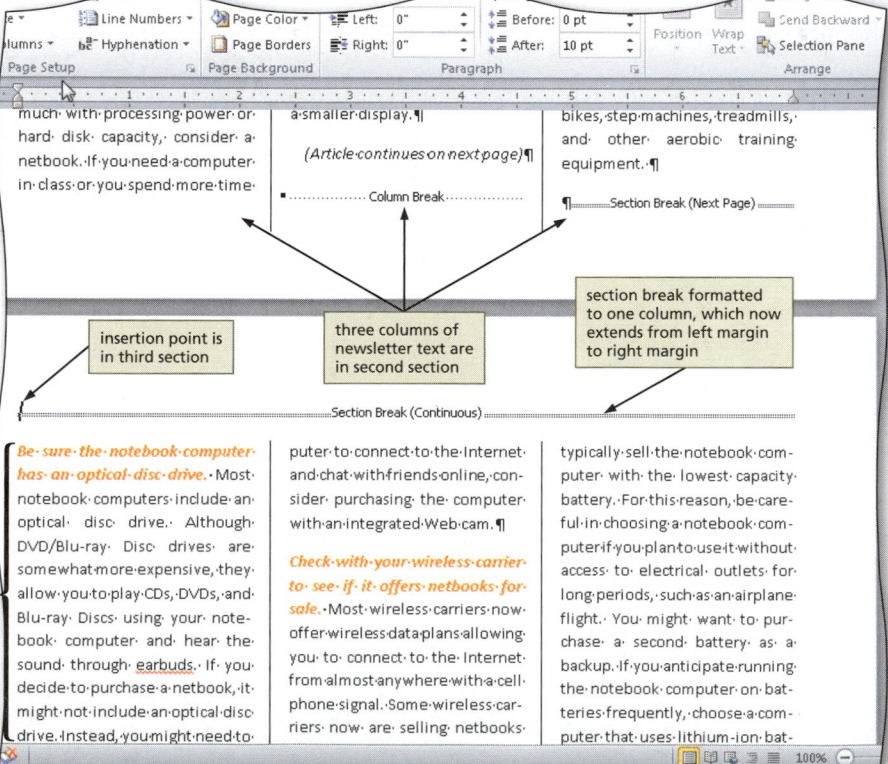

Figure 7–64

To Set Custom Tab Stops Using the Tabs Dialog Box

The nameplate on the second page of the newsletter contains the text, Monthly Newsletter, at the left margin, the newsletter title in the center, and the issue number at the right margin (shown in Figure 7–1a on page WD 403). To properly align the text in the center and at the right margin, you will set custom tab stops at these locations. The following steps set custom tab stops.

1 Press the ENTER key twice and then position the insertion point on the first line of the second page of the newsletter, which is the paragraph to be formatted with the custom tab stops.

2 Click the Paragraph Dialog Box Launcher (Page Layout tab | Paragraph group) to display the Paragraph dialog box and then click the Tabs button (Paragraph dialog box) to display the Tabs dialog box.

3 Type 3.5 in the Tab stop position text box (Tabs dialog box), click Center in the Alignment area to specify the tab stop alignment, and then click the Set button to set the custom tab stop.

4 Type 7 in the Tab stop position text box (Tabs dialog box), click Right in the Alignment area to specify the tab stop alignment, and then click the Set button to set the custom tab stop (Figure 7–65).

5 Click the OK button to place tab markers at the specified locations using the specified alignments.

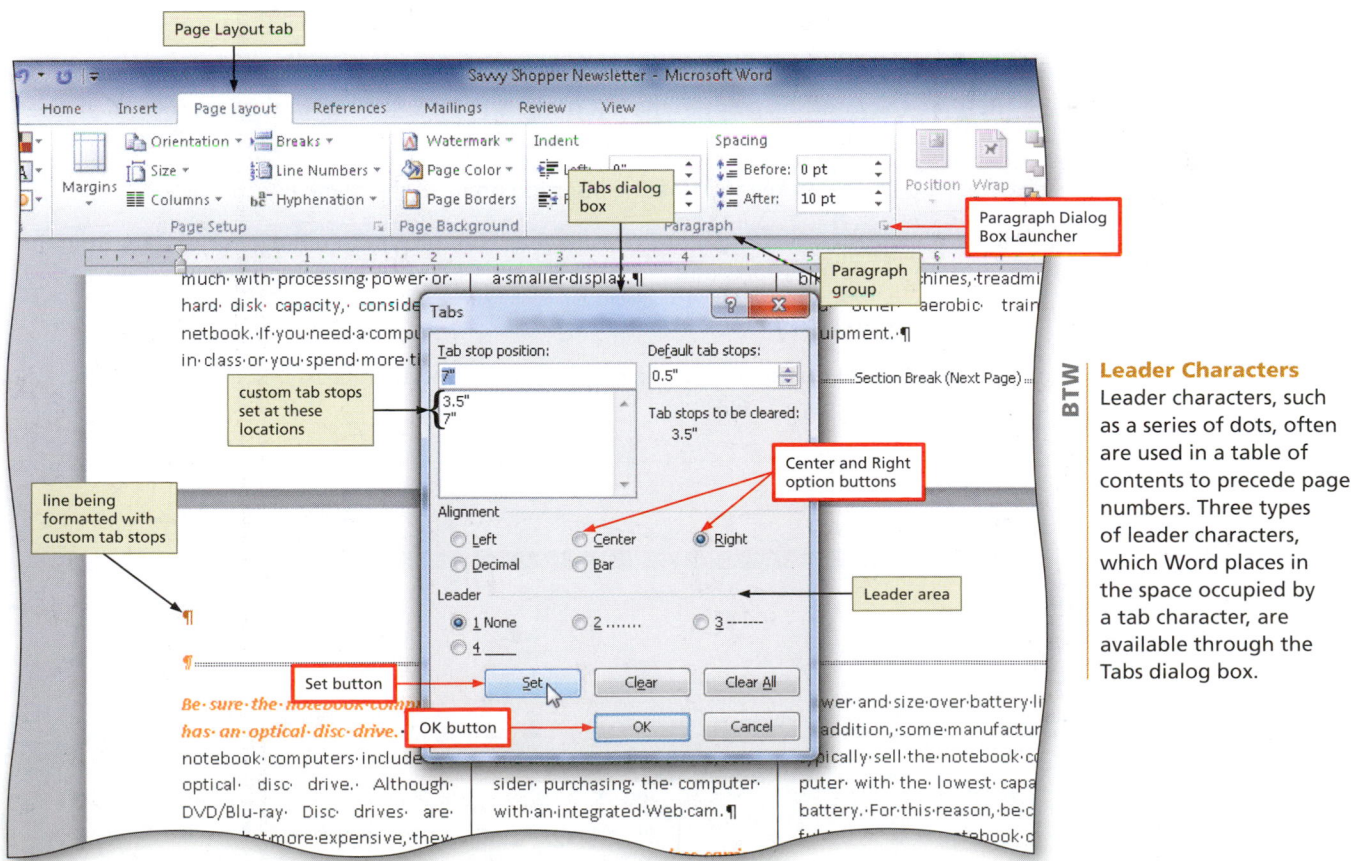

Figure 7–65

BTW

Leader Characters
Leader characters, such as a series of dots, often are used in a table of contents to precede page numbers. Three types of leader characters, which Word places in the space occupied by a tab character, are available through the Tabs dialog box.

To Format and Enter Text and Add a Border

The following steps enter the newsletter title at the top of the second page in the third section.

1 With the insertion point on the first line of the second page of the newsletter, display the Home tab and then, if necessary, click the Bold and Italic buttons (Home tab | Font group) to remove those formats. Type `Monthly Newsletter` at the left margin.

2 Press the TAB key to advance the insertion point to the centered tab stop. Increase the font size to 14 point and then click the Bold button (Home tab | Font group) to bold the text. Type `Savvy Shopper` at the centered tab stop.

3 Press the TAB key to advance the insertion point to the right-aligned tab stop. Reduce the font size to 11 point and then click the Bold button (Home tab | Font group) to turn off the bold format. Type `Issue 33` at the right-aligned tab stop.

4 Click the Borders button arrow (Home tab | Paragraph group) to display the Borders gallery and then click Bottom Border in the list (shown in Figure 7–66).

Q&A Why is the border formatted already?

When you define a custom border, Word uses that custom border the next time you click the Border button in the Border gallery.

To Enter Text

The second page of the feature article on the second page of this newsletter begins with a jump-from line (the continued message) immediately below the nameplate. The following steps enter the jump-from line.

1 Position the insertion point to the left of the B in Be at the top of the first column on the second page and then press the ENTER key.

2 Press the UP ARROW key to move the insertion point to the blank line.

3 Click the Clear Formatting button (Home tab | Font group) to remove formatting from the location of the insertion point.

4 Press CTRL+I to turn on the italic format.

5 Type `(Continued from first page)` and then press CTRL+I to turn off the italic format (Figure 7–66).

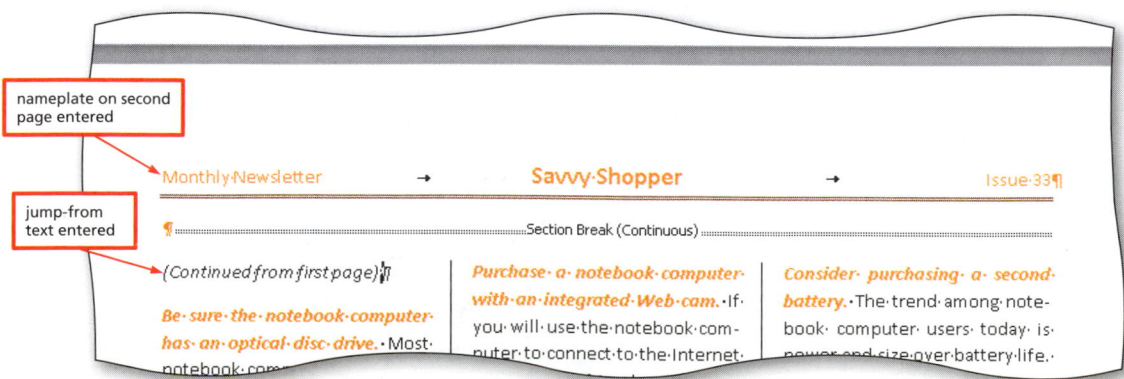

Figure 7–66

To Balance Columns

Currently, the text on the second page of the newsletter completely fills up the first and second columns and almost fills the third column. The text in the three columns should consume the same amount of vertical space. That is, the three columns should be balanced. To balance columns, you insert a continuous section break at the end of the text. The following steps balance columns.

1
- Scroll to the bottom of the text in the third column on the second page of the newsletter and then position the insertion point at the end of the text.

- If an extra paragraph mark is below the last line of text, press the DELETE key to remove the extra paragraph mark.

- Display the Page Layout tab.

- Click the Insert Page and Section Breaks button (Page Layout tab | Page Setup group) to display the Insert Page and Section Breaks gallery (Figure 7–67).

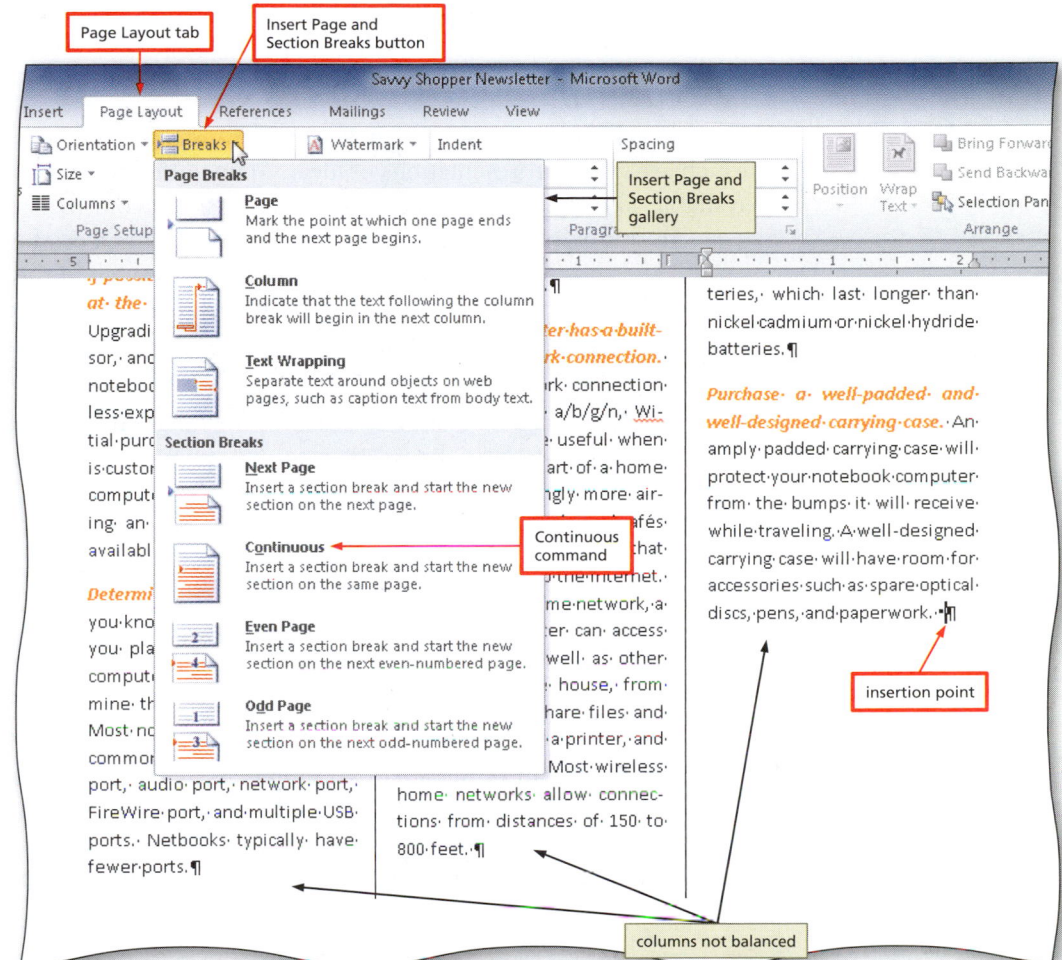

Figure 7–67

2
- Click Continuous in the Insert Page and Section Breaks gallery to insert a continuous section break, which balances the columns on the second page of the newsletter (Figure 7–68).

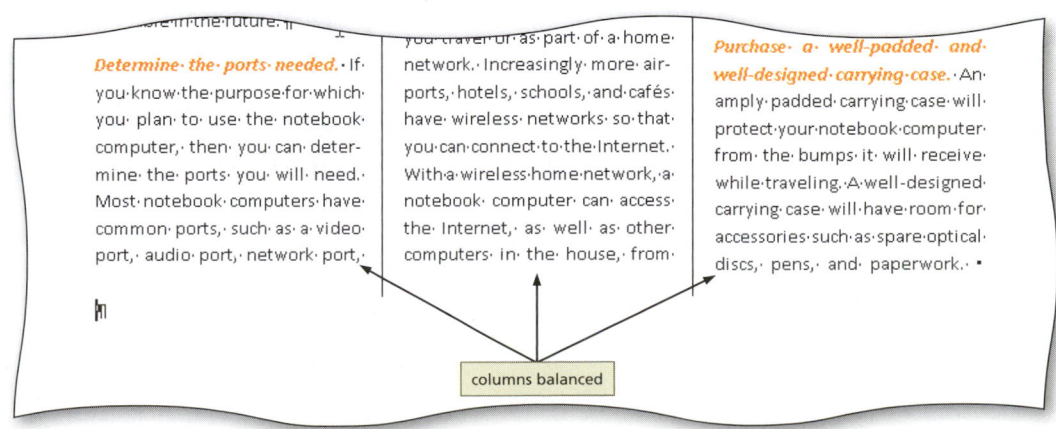

Figure 7–68

To Save a Document Again

You have performed several steps since the last save. Thus, you should save the newsletter again.

1 Save the newsletter again with the same file name, Savvy Shopper Newsletter.

Modifying and Formatting a SmartArt Graphic

Recall from Chapter 4 that Microsoft Office 2010 includes **SmartArt graphics**, which are visual representations of ideas. Many different types of SmartArt graphics are available, allowing you to choose one that illustrates your message best.

In this newsletter, a SmartArt graphic is positioned on the second page, in the second and third columns. Because the columns are small in the newsletter, it is best to work with a SmartArt graphic in a separate document window so that you easily can see all of its components. When finished editing the graphic, you can copy and paste it in the newsletter. You will follow these steps for the SmartArt graphic in this newsletter:

1. Open the document that contains the SmartArt graphic for the newsletter.
2. Modify the layout of the graphic.
3. Add a shape and text to the graphic.
4. Format a shape and the graphic.
5. Copy and paste the graphic in the newsletter.
6. Resize the graphic and position it in the desired location.

To Open a Document from Word

The first draft of the SmartArt graphic is in a file called Savvy Shopper Notebook Extras Diagram on the Data Files for Students. See the inside back cover of this book for instructions on downloading the Data Files for Students, or contact your instructor for information about accessing the required files. The following steps open the Savvy Shopper Notebook Extras Diagram file.

1 With your USB flash drive connected to one of the computer's USB ports, open the Backstage view and then click Open to display the Open dialog box.

2 Navigate to the location of the file to be opened (in this case, the Chapter 07 folder in the Word folder in the Data Files for Students folder on a USB flash drive).

3 Click Savvy Shopper Notebook Extras Diagram to select the file name.

4 Click the Open button (Open dialog box) to open the selected file.

5 Click the graphic to select it and display the SmartArt Tools Design and Format tabs (Figure 7–69).

Q&A Is the Savvy Shopper Newsletter file still open?

Yes. Leave it open because you will copy the modified diagram to the second page of the newsletter.

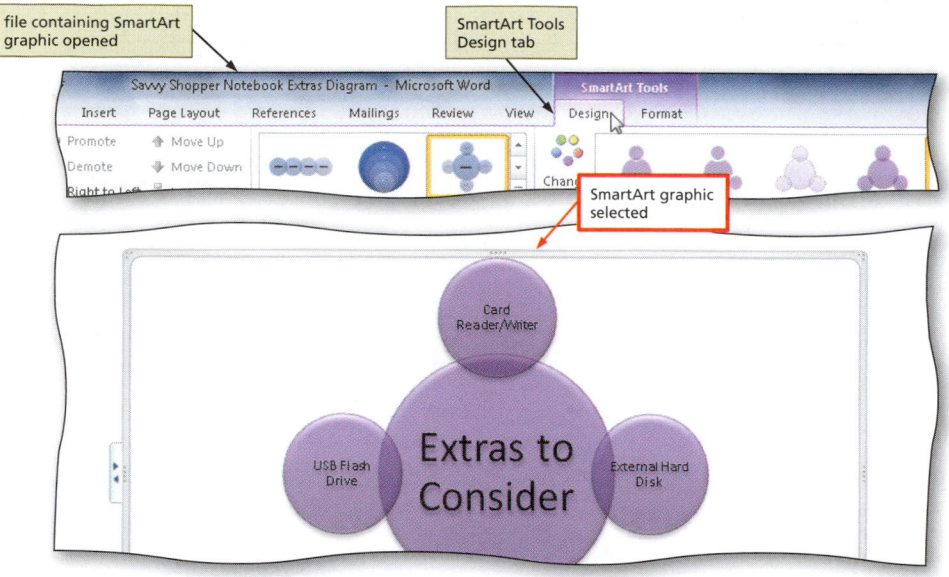

Figure 7–69

To Change the Layout of a SmartArt Graphic

The SmartArt graphic currently uses the Radial Venn layout. This newsletter uses the Converging Radial layout. The following step changes the layout of an existing SmartArt graphic.

1

- If necessary, display the SmartArt Tools Design tab.

- Scroll through the layouts in the Layouts gallery until Converging Radial appears (that is, click the up or down scroll arrows to scroll through the in-Ribbon gallery) and then click Converging Radial to change the layout of the SmartArt graphic (Figure 7–70).

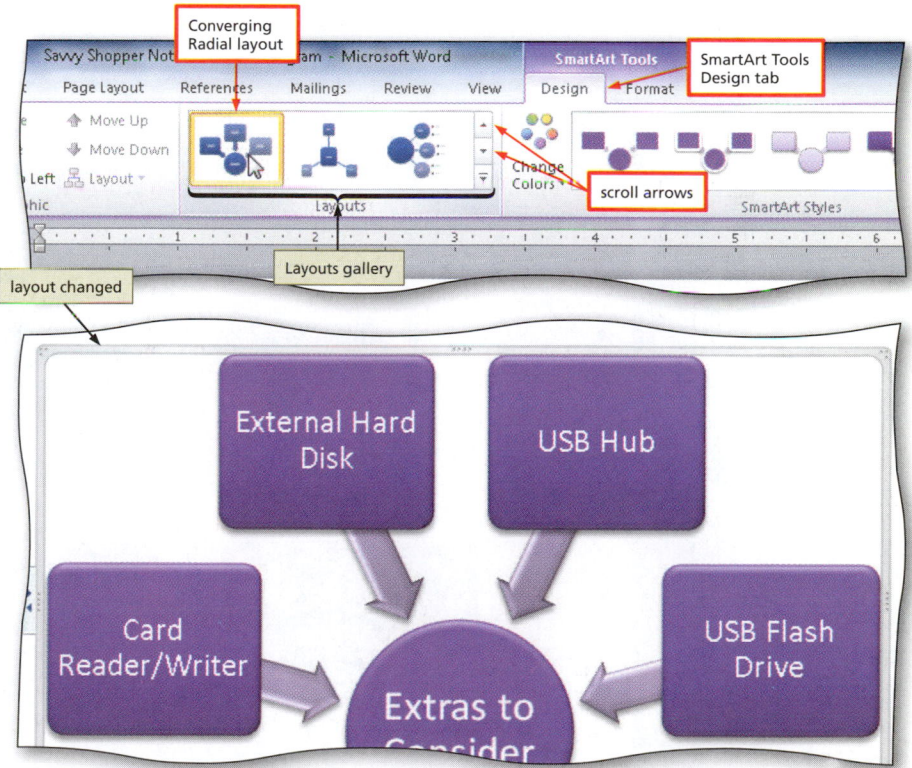

Figure 7–70

Other Ways	
1. Right-click the selected graphic, click Change Layout on shortcut menu, select desired layout	(Choose a SmartArt Graphic dialog box), click OK button

To Add a Shape to a SmartArt Graphic

The current SmartArt graphic has four perimeter shapes. This newsletter has a fifth shape. The following step adds a shape to a SmartArt graphic.

1 With the diagram selected, click the Add Shape button (SmartArt Tools Design tab | Create Graphic group) to add a shape to the SmartArt graphic (Figure 7–71).

Q&A Why did my screen display a menu instead of adding a shape?

You clicked the Add Shape button arrow instead of the Add Shape button. Clicking the Add Shape button adds the shape automatically; clicking the Add Shape button arrow displays a menu allowing you to specify the location of the shape.

Q&A How do I delete a shape?

Select the shape by clicking it and then press the DELETE key, or right-click the shape and then click Cut on the shortcut menu.

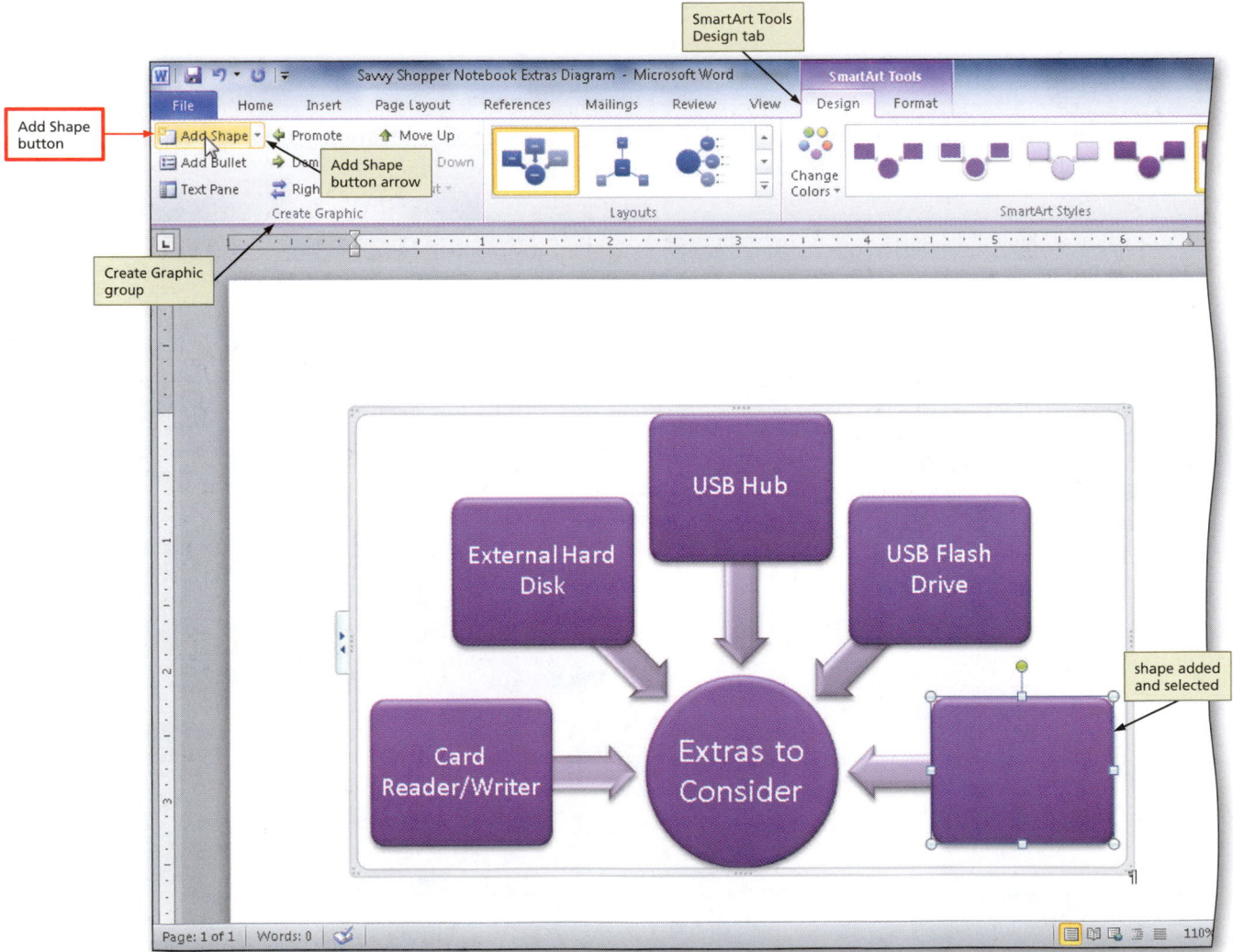

Figure 7–71

To Add Text to a SmartArt Graphic through the Text Pane

In Chapter 4, you added text directly to the shapes in a SmartArt graphic. In this project, you enter the text through the Text Pane. The following steps use the Text Pane to add text to a shape.

1
- Click the Text Pane button (SmartArt Tools Design tab | Create Graphic group) to display the Text Pane to the left of the SmartArt graphic.

2
- In the Text Pane, if necessary, position the insertion point to the right of the bullet that has no text to its right.

- Type **Wireless Mouse** as the text for the shape (Figure 7–72).

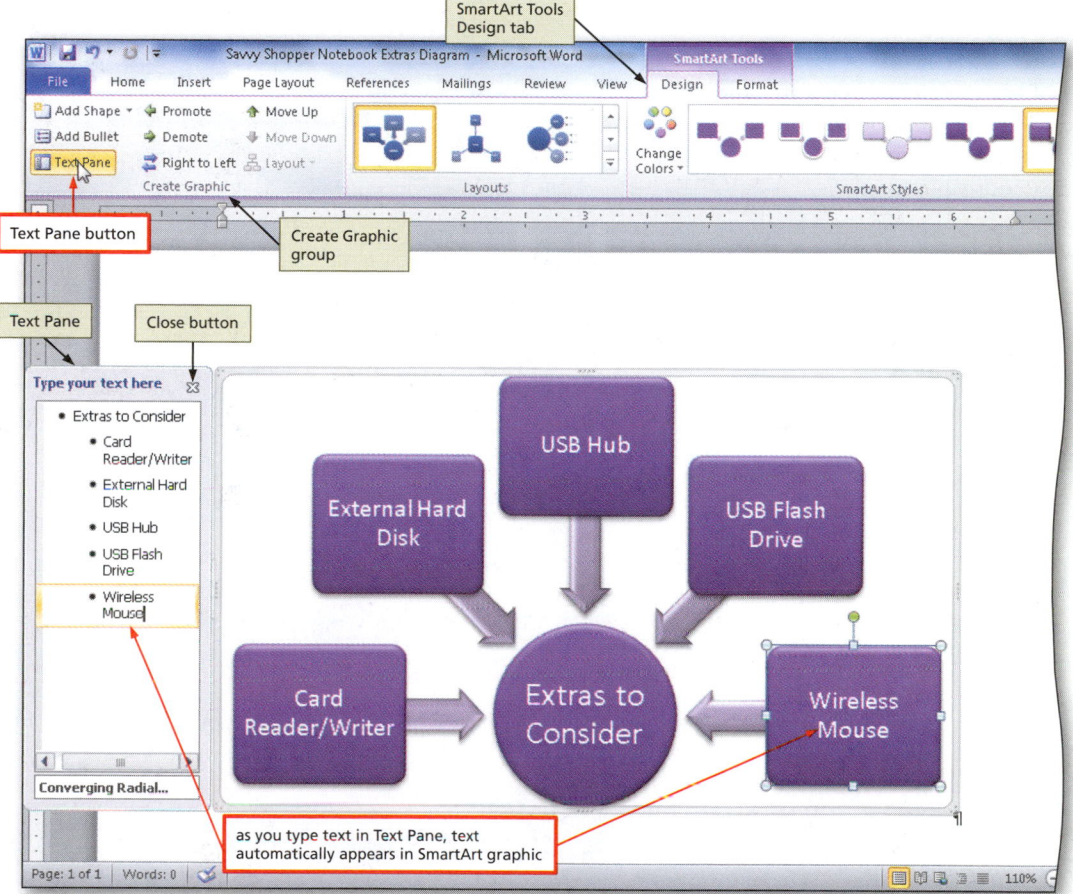

Figure 7–72

3
- Click the Text Pane button (SmartArt Tools Design tab | Create Graphic group) to close the Text Pane.

Can I instead close the Text Pane by clicking the Close button on the Text Pane?

Yes.

BTW

Demoting Text Pane Text
Instead of pressing the TAB key in the Text Pane, you could click the Demote button (SmartArt Tools Design tab | Create Graphic group) to increase (or move to the right) the indent for a bullet. You also can click the Promote button (SmartArt Tools Design tab | Create Graphic group) to decrease (or move to the left) the indent for a bullet.

To Adjust a Shape's Size

You want the circle shape to be slightly smaller in the SmartArt graphic. The following steps reduce the size of a shape in a SmartArt graphic.

1
- Click the circle shape in the middle of the SmartArt graphic to select it.

2
- Display the SmartArt Tools Format tab.

- Click the Smaller button (SmartArt Tools Format tab | Shapes group) to reduce the size of the selected shape (Figure 7–73).

Q&A

Can I increase the size of a shape?

Yes. Select the shape and then click the Larger button (SmartArt Tools Format tab | Shapes group). You also can change a shape by clicking the Change Shape button (SmartArt Tools Format tab | Shapes group).

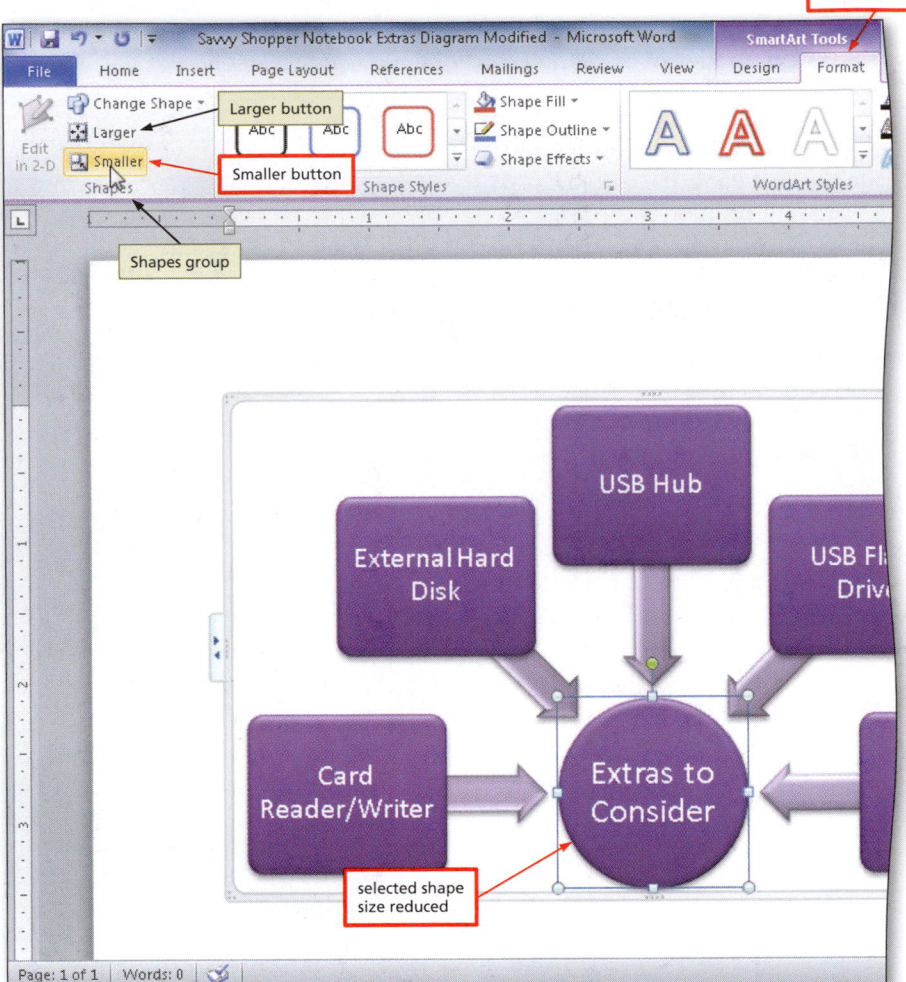

Figure 7–73

To Format SmartArt Graphic Text

To format text in an entire SmartArt graphic, select the graphic and then apply the format. The following steps bold the text in the SmartArt graphic.

1 If necessary, double-click the graphic to select it.

2 Display the Home tab. Click the Bold button (Home tab | Font group) to bold the text in the SmartArt graphic (shown in Figure 7–74 on page WD 454).

TO MODIFY THEME EFFECTS

If you wanted to change the look of graphics such as SmartArt graphics, you could perform the following steps to change the theme effects.

1. Click the Theme Effects button (Page Layout tab | Themes group).
2. Click the desired effect in the Theme Effects gallery.

TO SAVE CUSTOMIZED THEMES

When you modify the theme effects, theme colors, or theme fonts, you can save the modified theme for future use. If you wanted to save a customized theme, you would perform the following steps.

1. Click the Themes button (Page Layout tab | Themes group) to display the Themes gallery.
2. Click Save Current Theme in the Themes gallery.
3. Enter a theme name in the File name text box.
4. Click the Save button to add the saved theme to the Themes gallery.

To Save an Active Document with a New File Name

To preserve the contents of the original Savvy Shopper Notebook Extras Diagram file, you should save the active document with a new file name. The following steps save the active document with a new file name.

1 With the USB flash drive containing the Savvy Shopper Notebook Extras Diagram file connected to one of the computer's USB ports, open the Backstage view and then click Save As to display the Save As dialog box.

2 Navigate to the location of the file to be saved (in this case, the Word folder in the CIS 101 folder [or your class folder] on a USB flash drive).

3 Save the document with the file name, Savvy Shopper Notebook Extras Diagram Modified.

Copying and Pasting

The next step is to copy the SmartArt graphic from this document window and then paste it in the newsletter. To copy from one document and paste into another, you can use the Office Clipboard. Through the Office Clipboard, you can copy multiple items from any Office document and then paste them into the same or another Office document by following these general guidelines:

1. Items are copied *from* a **source document**. If the source document is not the active document, display it in the document window.
2. Display the Office Clipboard task pane and then copy items from the source document to the Office Clipboard.
3. Items are copied *to* a **destination document**. If the destination document is not the active document, display the destination document in the document window.
4. Paste items from the Office Clipboard to the destination document.

BTW

BTWs
For a complete list of the BTWs found in the margins of this book, visit the Word 2010 BTW Web page (scsite.com/wd2010/btw).

To Copy a SmartArt Graphic Using the Office Clipboard

You can copy multiple items to the Office Clipboard through the Clipboard task pane and then paste them later. The following step copies the SmartArt graphic to the Office Clipboard.

- Click the Clipboard Dialog Box Launcher (Home tab | Clipboard group) to display the Clipboard task pane.

- If the Office Clipboard in the Clipboard task pane is not empty, click the Clear All button in the Clipboard task pane.

- With the SmartArt graphic selected in the document window, click the Copy button (Home tab | Clipboard group) to copy the selected text to the Clipboard (Figure 7–74).

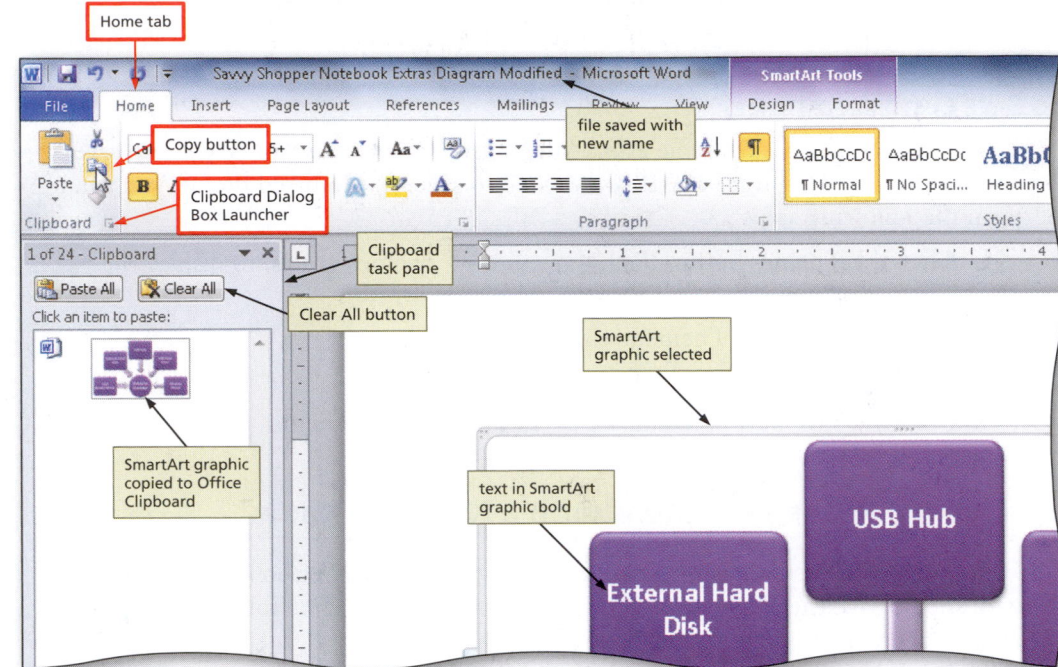

Figure 7–74

To Switch from One Open Document to Another

The steps below switch from the open Savvy Shopper Notebook Extras Diagram Modified document (the source document) to the open Savvy Shopper Newsletter document (the destination document).

- Point to the Word program button on the taskbar to display a live preview of the open documents or window titles of the open documents, depending on your computer's configuration (Figure 7–75).

- Click the live preview of the Savvy Shopper Newsletter on the Windows taskbar to display the selected document in the document window (shown in Figure 7–76).

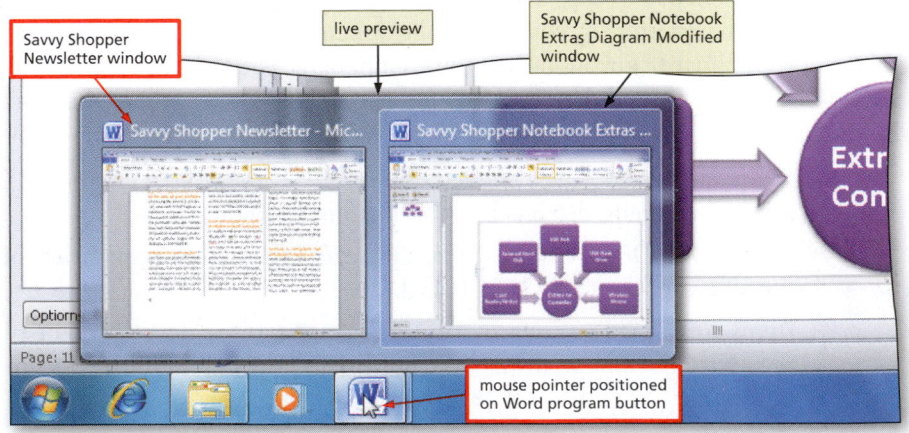

Figure 7–75

To Paste from the Office Clipboard

The next step is to paste the copied SmartArt graphic into the destination document, in this case, the newsletter document. The following steps paste from the Office Clipboard.

- If the Clipboard task pane is not displayed on the screen, display the Home tab and then click the Clipboard Dialog Box Launcher (Home tab | Clipboard group) to display the Clipboard task pane.

- Click the SmartArt graphic entry in the Office Clipboard to paste it in the document at the location of the insertion point (Figure 7–76).

Q&A Does the destination document have to be a different document?

No. The source and destination documents can be the same document.

Q&A What is the function of the Paste All button?

If you have multiple items in the Office Clipboard, it pastes all items in a row, without any characters between them, at the location of the insertion point or selection.

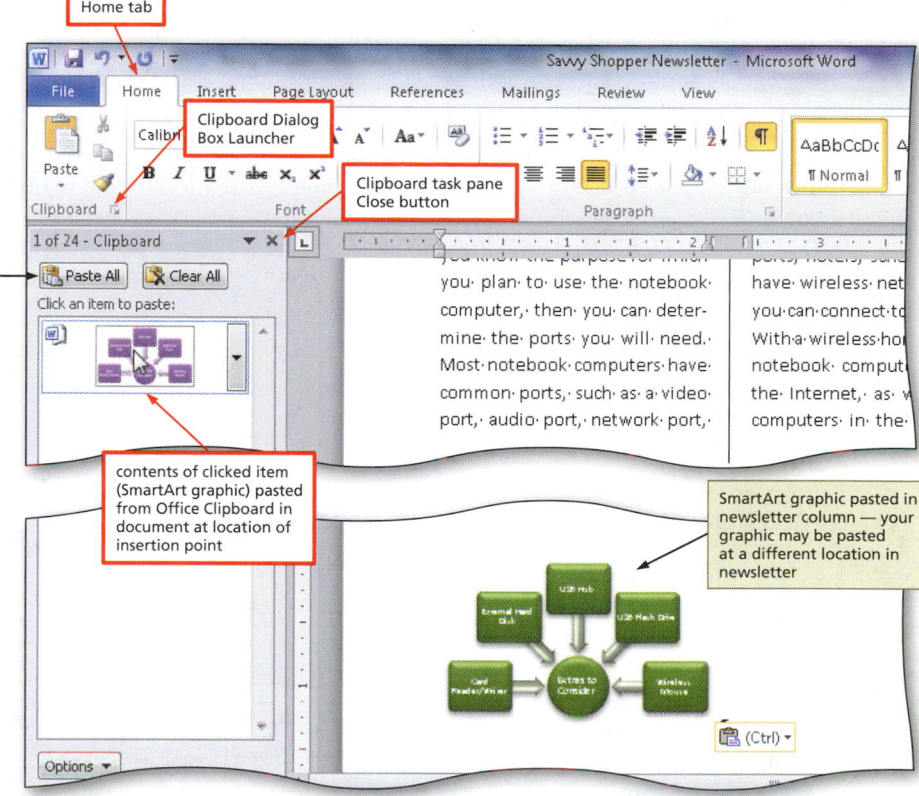

Figure 7–76

- Click the Close button in the Clipboard task pane.

Other Ways
1. With Clipboard task pane displayed, right-click selected item, click Paste on shortcut menu   2. With Clipboard task pane displayed, press CTRL+V

To Format a Graphic as Floating

The text in the newsletter should wrap tightly around the graphic; that is, the text should conform to the graphic's shape. Thus, the next step is to change the graphic from inline to floating with a wrapping style of tight. The following steps format the graphic as floating with tight wrapping.

1 If necessary, double-click the SmartArt graphic to select it.

2 Display the SmartArt Tools Format tab.

3 With the SmartArt graphic selected, click the Arrange button (SmartArt Tools Format tab | Arrange group) and then click the Wrap Text button on the Arrange menu to display the Wrap Text menu.

4 Click Tight on the Wrap Text menu to change the graphic from inline to floating with tight wrapping.

BTW

Clipboard Task Pane and Office Clipboard Icon
You can control when the Clipboard task pane appears on the Word screen and the Office Clipboard icon appears in the notification area on the taskbar. To do this, first display the Clipboard task pane by clicking the Clipboard Dialog Box Launcher. Next, click the Options button at the bottom of the Clipboard task pane and then click the desired option on the menu. For example, if you want to be able to display the Clipboard task pane by clicking the Office Clipboard icon on the Windows taskbar, click the Show Office Clipboard Icon on Taskbar command on the Options menu.

Space around Graphics
The space between a graphic and the text, which sometimes is called the run-around, should be at least 1/8" and should be the same for all graphics in a document. Adjust the run-around of a selected floating graphic by doing the following: click the Arrange button (SmartArt Tools Format tab | Arrange group), click the Object Position button, click More Layout Options on the Object Position menu, click the Text Wrapping tab (Layout dialog box), adjust the values in the 'Distance from text' boxes, and then click the OK button.

To Resize and Position the SmartArt Graphic

The next task is to increase the size of the SmartArt graphic and then position it in the second and third columns on the second page. The following steps resize and then position the graphic.

1 Drag the sizing handles outward until the graphic is approximately the same size as shown in Figure 7–77, which has a height of 2.3" and a width of 2.8".

2 Point to the frame on the graphic and when the mouse has a four-headed arrow attached to it, drag the graphic to the location shown in Figure 7–77. You may have to drag the graphic a couple of times to position it similarly to the figure.

3 If the newsletter spills onto a third page, reduce the size of the SmartArt graphic. You may need to delete an extra paragraph mark at the end of the document, as well.

To Layer the SmartArt Graphic in Front of Text

Notice in Figure 7–77 that the ruling line covers the SmartArt graphic. In Word, you can layer objects on top of or behind other objects. The following steps layer the SmartArt graphic on top of all text.

- If necessary, click the SmartArt graphic to select it. Click the Arrange button (SmartArt Tools Format tab | Arrange group) to display the Arrange menu.
- Click the Bring Forward button arrow to display the Bring Forward menu (Figure 7–77).

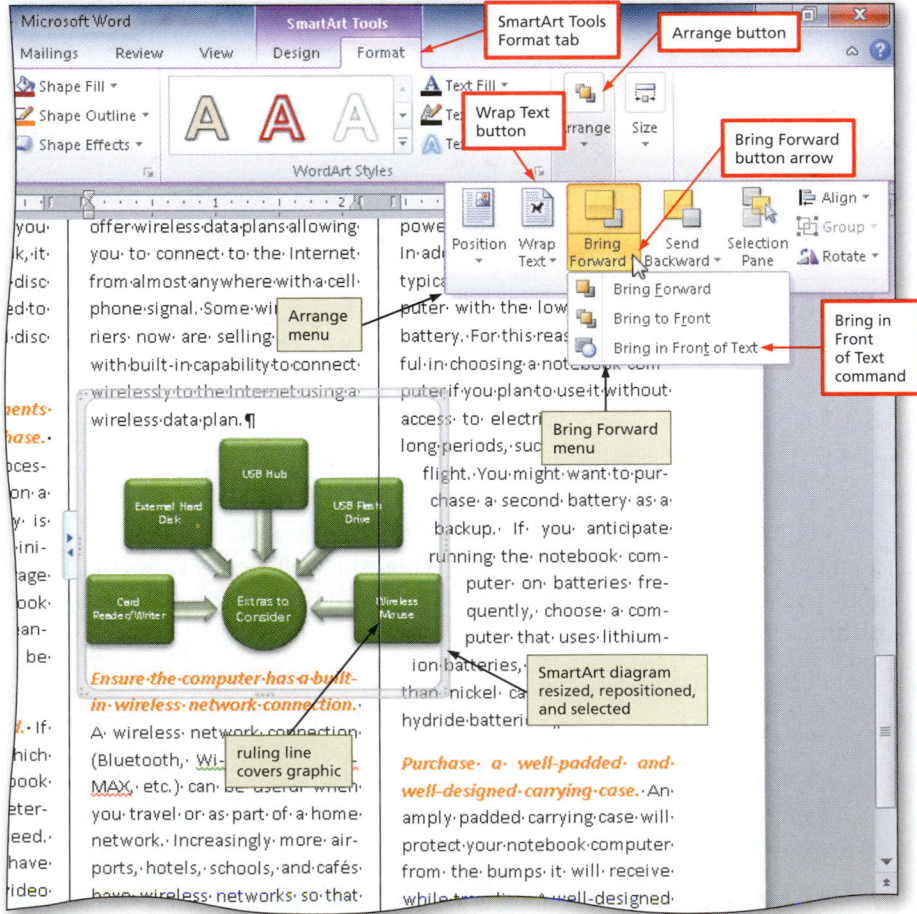

Figure 7–77

2

• Click Bring in Front of Text on the Bring Forward menu to position the selected object on top of all text, which in this case, positions the SmartArt graphic on top of the border (Figure 7–78).

3

• Click outside the graphic so that it no longer is selected.

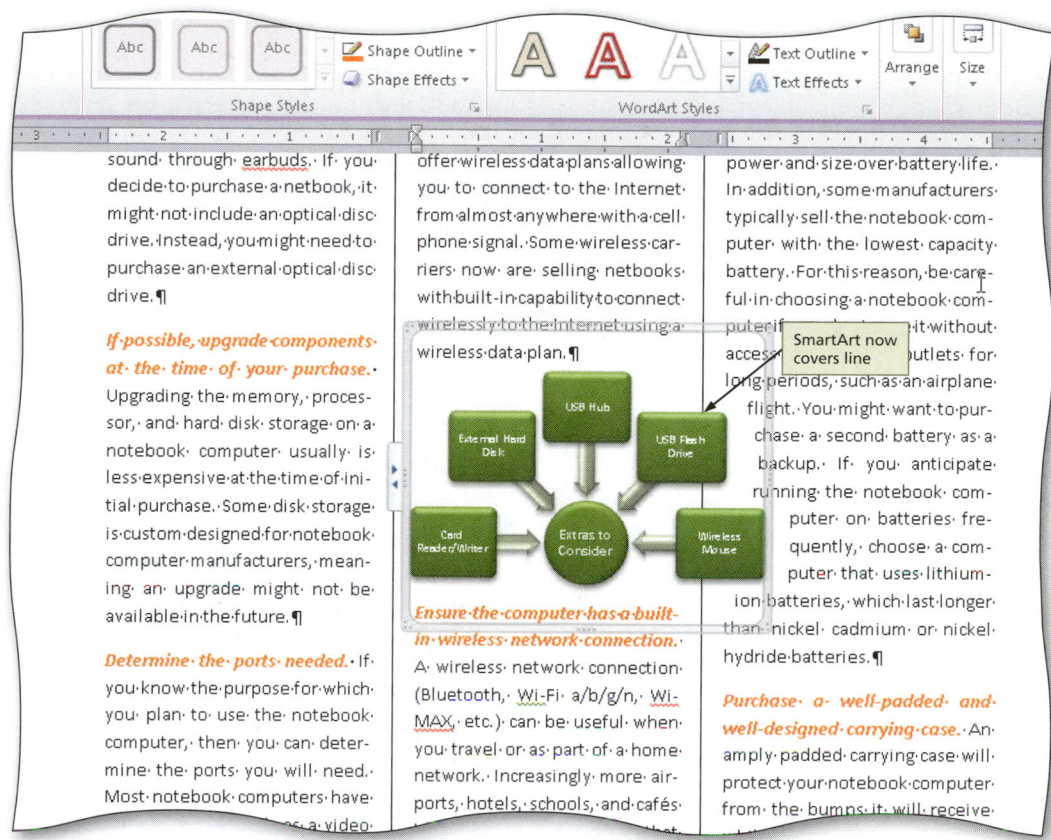

Figure 7–78

Finishing the Newsletter

With the text and graphics in the newsletter entered and formatted, the next step is to view the newsletter as a whole and determine if it looks finished in its current state. To give the newsletter a finished appearance, you will add a border to its edges.

To Zoom Two Pages

The last step in formatting the newsletter is to place a border around its edges. You can place both pages in the document window at once so that you can see all the page borders applied. The following steps zoom two pages.

1 Display the View tab.

2 Click the Two Pages button (View tab | Zoom group) to display both entire pages of the newsletter in the document window (shown in Figure 7–79 on the next page).

BTW

Quick Reference
For a table that lists how to complete the tasks covered in this book using the mouse, Ribbon, shortcut menu, and keyboard, see the Quick Reference Summary at the back of this book, or visit the Word 2010 Quick Reference Web page (scsite.com/wd2010/qr).

To Add an Art Page Border

This newsletter has orange art border around the perimeter of each page. The steps on the next page add a page border around the pages of the newsletter.

- Display the Page Layout tab.

- Click the Page Borders button (Page Layout tab | Page Background group) to display the Borders and Shading dialog box. If necessary, click the Page Border tab.

Q&A

What if I cannot select the Page Borders button because it is dimmed?

Click somewhere in the newsletter to make the newsletter the active document and then repeat Step 1.

- Click Box in the Setting area (Borders and Shading dialog box) to specify a border on all four sides.

- Click the Art box arrow, scroll to and then click the art border shown in Figure 7–79.

- Click the Width box down arrow until the box displays 8 pt.

- Click the Color box arrow and then click Orange, Accent 1, Darker 50% (sixth row, fifth column) on the palette (Figure 7–79).

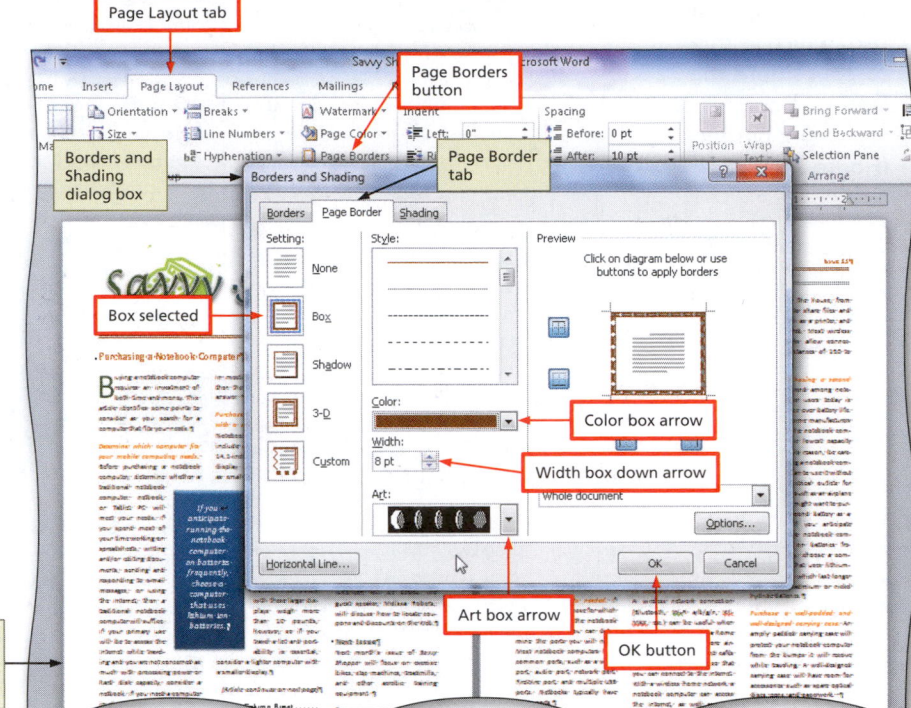

Figure 7–79

- Click the OK button to place the defined border on each page of the newsletter (Figure 7–80).

Figure 7–80

To Save and Print the Document, Then Quit Word

BTW

Conserving Ink and Toner

If you want to conserve ink or toner, you can instruct Word to print draft quality documents by clicking File on the Ribbon to open the Backstage view, clicking Options in the Backstage view to display the Word Options dialog box, clicking Advanced in the left pane (Word Options dialog box), scrolling to the Print area in the right pane, placing a check mark in the 'Use draft quality' check box, and then clicking the OK button. Then, use the Backstage view to print the document as usual.

The newsletter now is complete. You should save the document, print it, and then quit Word.

1 Save the newsletter again with the same file name.

2 Print the newsletter (shown in Figure 7–1 on page WD 403).

Q&A What if an error message appears about margins?

Depending on the printer you are using, you may need to set the margins differently for this project.

Q&A What if one or more of the borders do not print?

Click the Page Borders button (Page Layout tab | Page Background group), click the Options button (Borders and Shading dialog box), click the Measure from box arrow and click Text, change the four text boxes to 15 pt, and then click the OK button in each dialog box. Try printing the document again. If the borders still do not print, adjust the text boxes in the dialog box to a number smaller than 15 point.

3 Quit Word, closing all open documents.

Chapter Summary

In this chapter, you have learned how to create a professional-looking newsletter using Word's desktop publishing features such as WordArt, columns, horizontal and vertical rules, and pull-quotes. The items listed below include all the new Word skills you have learned in this chapter.

1. Set Custom Margins (WD 405)
2. Insert WordArt (WD 407)
3. Change the WordArt Fill Color (WD 410)
4. Change the WordArt Shape (WD 413)
5. Set Custom Tab Stops Using the Tabs Dialog Box (WD 413)
6. Border One Edge of a Paragraph (WD 415)
7. Crop a Graphic (WD 418)
8. Use the Selection Pane (WD 421)
9. Rotate a Graphic (WD 421)
10. Insert a Continuous Section Break (WD 425)
11. Change the Number of Columns (WD 426)
12. Justify a Paragraph (WD 427)
13. Insert a File in a Column of the Newsletter (WD 428)
14. Increase Column Width and Place a Vertical Rule between Columns (WD 429)
15. Hyphenate a Document (WD 430)
16. Format a Character as a Drop Cap (WD 431)
17. Insert a Next Page Section Break (WD 433)
18. Insert a Column Break (WD 434)
19. Insert a Text Box (WD 437)
20. Split the Window (WD 438)
21. Arrange All Open Word Documents on the Screen (WD 439)
22. Copy and Paste Using Split Windows (WD 439)
23. Remove a Split Window (WD 440)
24. Position a Text Box (WD 442)
25. Change Column Formatting (WD 443)
26. Balance Columns (WD 447)
27. Change the Layout of a SmartArt Graphic (WD 449)
28. Modify Theme Effects (WD 453)
29. Save Customized Themes (WD 453)
30. Add Text to a SmartArt Graphic through the Text Pane (WD 451)
31. Adjust a Shape's Size (WD 452)
32. Copy a SmartArt Graphic Using the Office Clipboard (WD 454)
33. Switch from One Open Document to Another (WD 454)
34. Paste from the Office Clipboard (WD 455)
35. Layer the SmartArt Graphic in Front of Text (WD 456)
36. Add an Art Page Border (WD 457)

If you have a SAM 2010 user profile, your instructor may have assigned an autogradable version of this assignment. If so, log into the SAM 2010 Web site at www.cengage.com/sam2010 to download the instruction and start files.

Learn It Online

Test your knowledge of chapter content and key terms.

Instructions: To complete the Learn It Online exercises, start your browser, click the Address bar, and then enter the Web address **scsite.com/wd2010/learn**. When the Word 2010 Learn It Online page is displayed, click the link for the exercise you want to complete and then read the instructions.

Chapter Reinforcement TF, MC, and SA
A series of true/false, multiple choice, and short answer questions that test your knowledge of the chapter content.

Flash Cards
An interactive learning environment where you identify chapter key terms associated with displayed definitions.

Practice Test
A series of multiple choice questions that test your knowledge of chapter content and key terms.

Who Wants To Be a Computer Genius?
An interactive game that challenges your knowledge of chapter content in the style of a television quiz show.

Wheel of Terms
An interactive game that challenges your knowledge of chapter key terms in the style of the television show *Wheel of Fortune*.

Crossword Puzzle Challenge
A crossword puzzle that challenges your knowledge of key terms presented in the chapter.

Apply Your Knowledge

Reinforce the skills and apply the concepts you learned in this chapter.

Working with Desktop Publishing Elements of a Newsletter
Note: To complete this assignment, you will be required to use the Data Files for Students. See the inside back cover of this book for instructions on downloading the Data Files for Students, or contact your instructor for information about accessing the required files.

Instructions: Start Word. Open the document, Apply 7-1 Career Finders Newsletter Draft, from the Data Files for Students. The document contains a newsletter that you are to modify (Figure 7–81).

Perform the following tasks:
1. Change the WordArt shape to Chevron Down.
2. Change the column width of the columns in the body of the newsletter to 2.2".
3. Add a vertical rule (line) between each column.
4. Insert a column break immediately to the left of the R in the Resources heading.
5. Change the style of the pull-quote (text box) to Light 1 Outline, Colored Fill - Tan, Accent 5.
6. Format the first paragraph with a drop cap.
7. Change the alignment of the paragraph containing the drop cap from left-aligned to justified.
8. Change the layout of the SmartArt graphic to Vertical Process.
9. Use the Text Pane to add the text, Continuing Education, to the bottom shape in the SmartArt graphic.
10. If necessary, move the SmartArt graphic and the pull-quote so that they are positioned similarly to the ones in Figure 7–81.
11. Change the document properties as specified by your instructor.
12. Save the modified file with the file name, Apply 7-1 Career Finders Newsletter Modified.
13. Submit the revised newsletter in the format specified by your instructor.

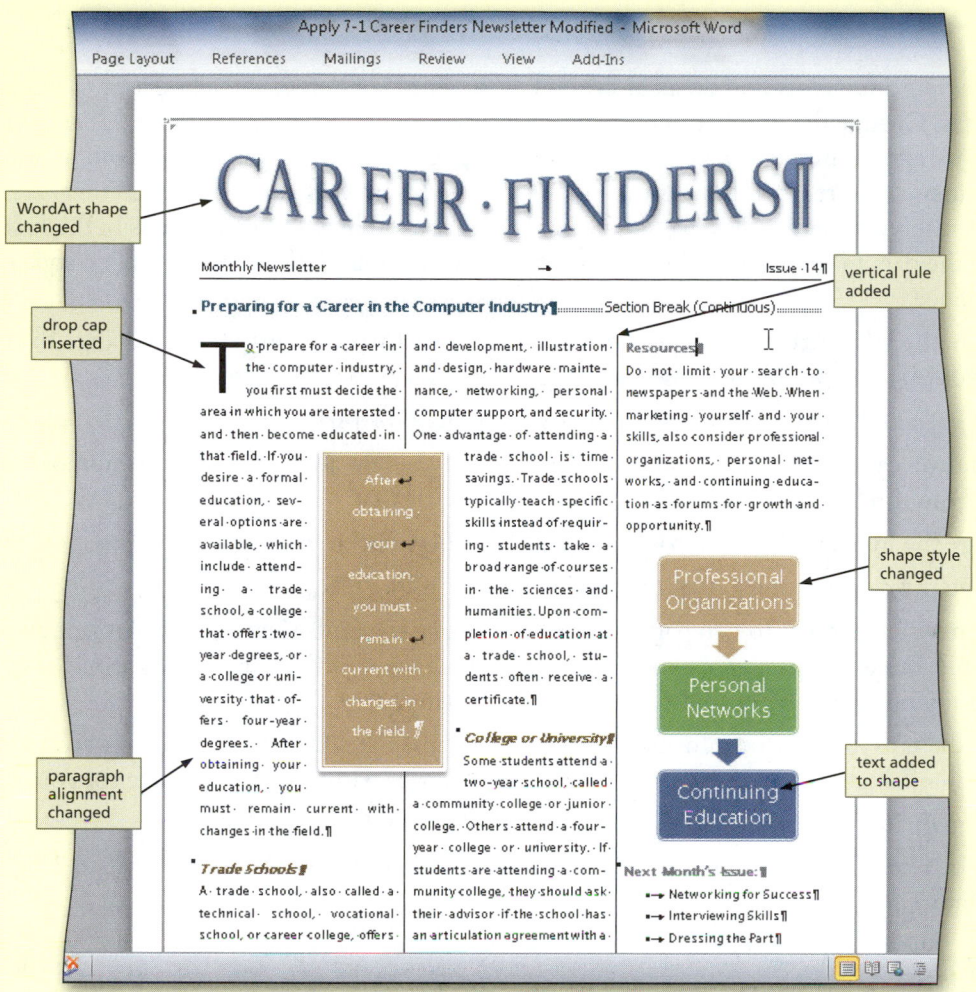

Figure 7–81

Extend Your Knowledge

Extend the skills you learned in this chapter and experiment with new skills. You may need to use Help to complete the assignment.

Adding a Table to a Newsletter and Enhancing a Nameplate

Note: To complete this assignment, you will be required to use the Data Files for Students. See the inside back cover of this book for instructions on downloading the Data Files for Students, or contact your instructor for information about accessing the required files.

Instructions: Start Word. Open the document, Extend 7-1 Classroom Chatter Newsletter Draft, from the Data Files for Students. You will add a table to the bottom of the newsletter, change the format of the WordArt, format the drop cap, adjust the hyphenation rules, move the page border closer to the text, clear tabs, and insert leader characters.

Perform the following tasks:
1. Use Help to review how to create and format a table, if necessary, and to learn about WordArt options, borders, hyphenation, and tabs.

Continued >

STUDENT ASSIGNMENTS

Extend Your Knowledge *continued*

2. Insert a continuous section break at the end of the third column of the newsletter to balance the columns. Change the number of columns in the new section from three to one. Change the style of the paragraph in the new section to No Spacing. Use the Insert Table command on the Insert Table menu (Insert tab | Table group) to display the Insert Table dialog box and then use the dialog box to insert a table that has five rows and four columns. Then, merge the cells in the first row. Enter the data in the table as shown in Figure 7–82. Format the table using a table style of your preference.

3. Change the WordArt to a style to use at least two WordArt style text effects. Change the color of the WordArt text outline. Change the color of the WordArt text fill color.

4. Add a shape fill color to the text box surrounding the WordArt.

5. Add a drop cap to the first paragraph in the body of the newsletter. Change the number of lines to drop from three to two lines.

6. Change the hyphenation rules to limit consecutive hyphens to two and the hyphenation zone to .3".

7. Change the page border so that the border is closer to the text.

8. If the newsletter flows to two pages, reduce the size of elements such as WordArt or pull-quote or the table, or adjust spacing above or below paragraphs so that the newsletter fits on a single page. Make any other necessary adjustments to the newsletter.

9. Clear the tabs in the issue information line in the nameplate. Use the Tabs dialog box to insert a right-aligned tab stop at the 6.5" mark. Fill the tab space with a leader character of your choice.

10. Change the document properties as specified by your instructor.

11. Save the revised document with a new file name and then submit it in the format specified by your instructor.

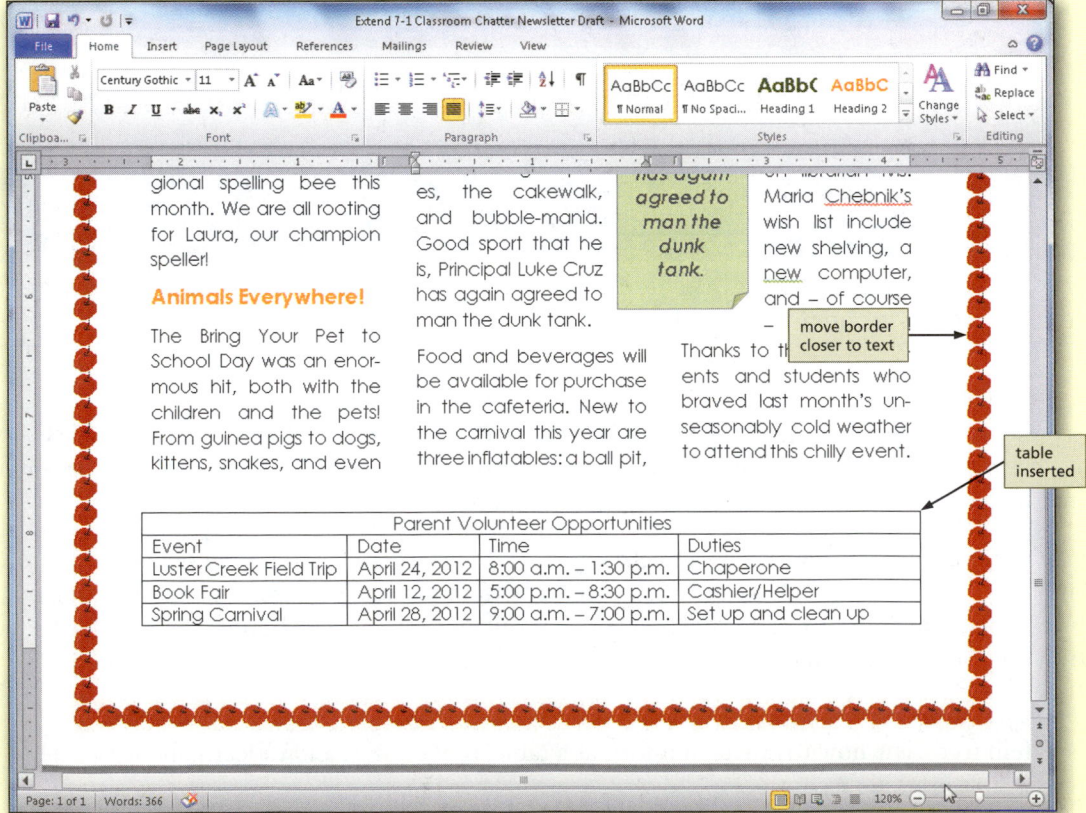

Figure 7–82

Make It Right

Analyze a document and correct all errors and/or improve the design.

Formatting a Newsletter

Note: To complete this assignment, you will be required to use the Data Files for Students. See the inside back cover of this book for instructions on downloading the Data Files for Students, or contact your instructor for information about accessing the required files.

Instructions: Start Word. Open the document, Make It Right 7-1 IT Club Newsletter Draft, from the Data Files for Students. The document is a newsletter whose elements are not formatted properly (Figure 7–83). You are to edit and format the WordArt, format the clip art image and columns, change tab stop alignment, change paragraph alignment, add a drop cap, format the pull-quote (text box), and add a border.

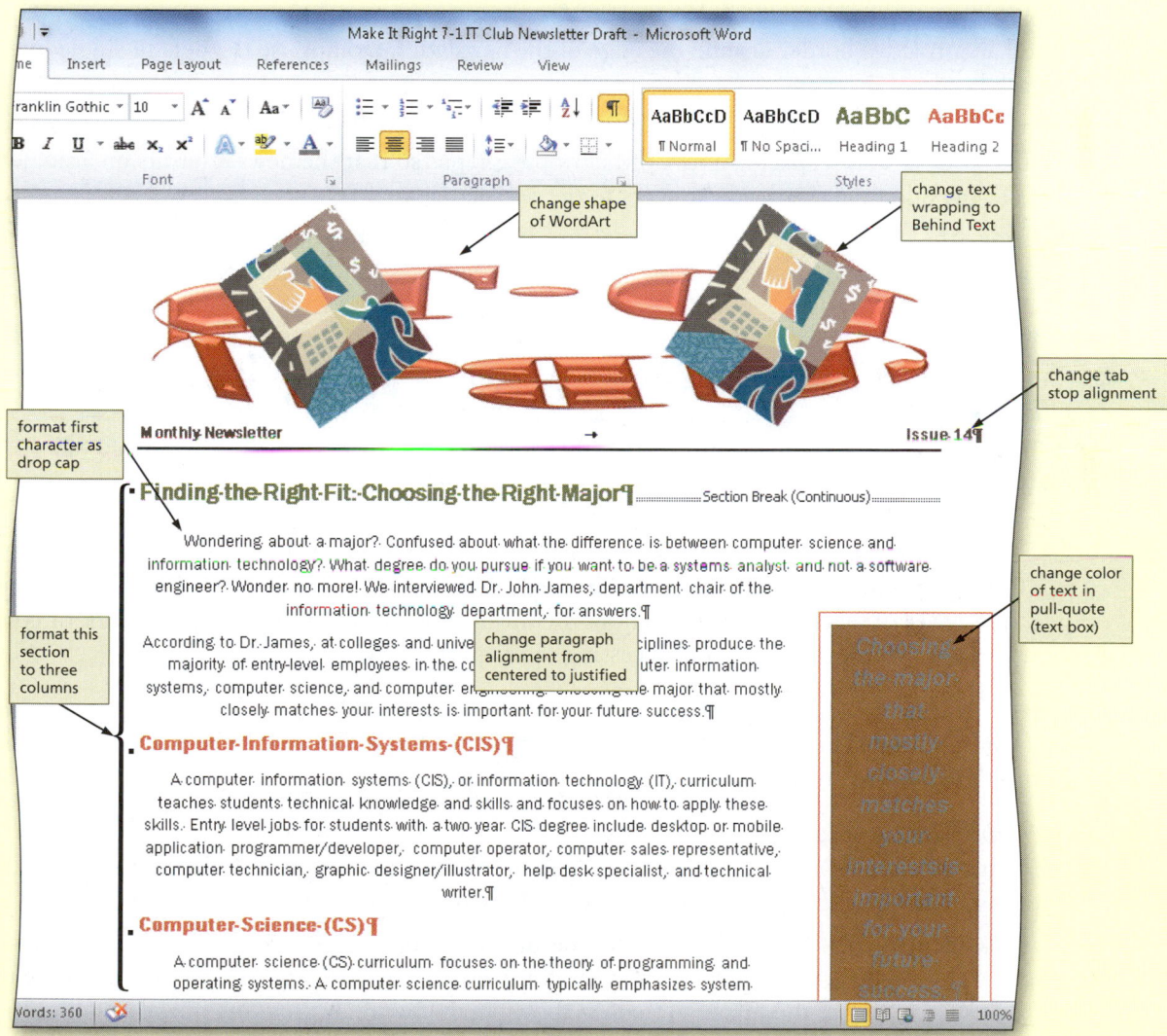

Figure 7–83

Continued >

Make It Right *continued*

Perform the following tasks:

1. Change the shape of the WordArt so that the text is more readable.

2. Format the clip art images in the nameplate to Behind Text. Crop the clip art images so that most of the dollar signs on their right edge are not visible. (*Hint:* Use the Selection and Visibility task pane to select each image.) If necessary, adjust the location and size of the clip art images so that they have a pleasing appearance in the nameplate.

3. Change the alignment of the custom tab stop at the 6.5" mark in the issue information line from centered to right-aligned.

4. Change the number of columns in the body of the newsletter from one to two.

5. Change all paragraphs of text from centered to justified paragraph alignment.

6. Format the first letter in the first paragraph of text as a drop cap. Color the drop cap.

7. Change the color of the text in the pull-quote (text box) so that it is easier to read. Position the pull-quote at the right edge of the newsletter.

8. Add an attractive border around the edge of the newsletter. Do not use the default single line, black border.

9. If the newsletter flows to two pages, reduce the size of elements such as WordArt or clip art or the pull-quote, or adjust spacing above or below paragraphs so that the newsletter fits on a single page. Make any other necessary adjustments to the newsletter.

10. Change the document properties, as specified by your instructor. Save the revised document with a new file name and then submit it in the format specified by your instructor.

In the Lab

Design and/or create a document using the guidelines, concepts, and skills presented in this chapter. Labs are listed in order of increasing difficulty.

Lab 1: Creating a Newsletter with a SmartArt Graphic and an Article on File

Note: To complete this assignment, you will be required to use the Data Files for Students. See the inside back cover of this book for instructions on downloading the Data Files for Students, or contact your instructor for information about accessing the required files.

Problem: You are an editor of the newsletter, *The Common Bond*. The next edition is due out in one week (Figure 7–84). The text for the feature articles in the newsletter is in a file on the Data Files for Students. You need to create the nameplate and the SmartArt graphic.

Perform the following tasks:

1. Change all margins to .75 inches. Depending on your printer, you may need different margin settings. Change the theme colors and theme fonts as specified in the figure.

2. Create the nameplate using the formats identified in Figure 7–84. Create the title using WordArt. Set a right-aligned custom tab stop at the right margin. Use the Clip Art task pane to locate the image shown. Resize the image to the size shown in the figure. Format the image as Behind Text, rotate it, and then position it as shown.

3. Below the nameplate, enter the heading News and Events, as shown in the figure.

4. Create a continuous section break below the heading, News and Events.

5. Format section 2 to three columns.

6. Insert the Lab 7-1 Common Bond Article file, which is located on the Data Files for Students, in section 2 below the nameplate.

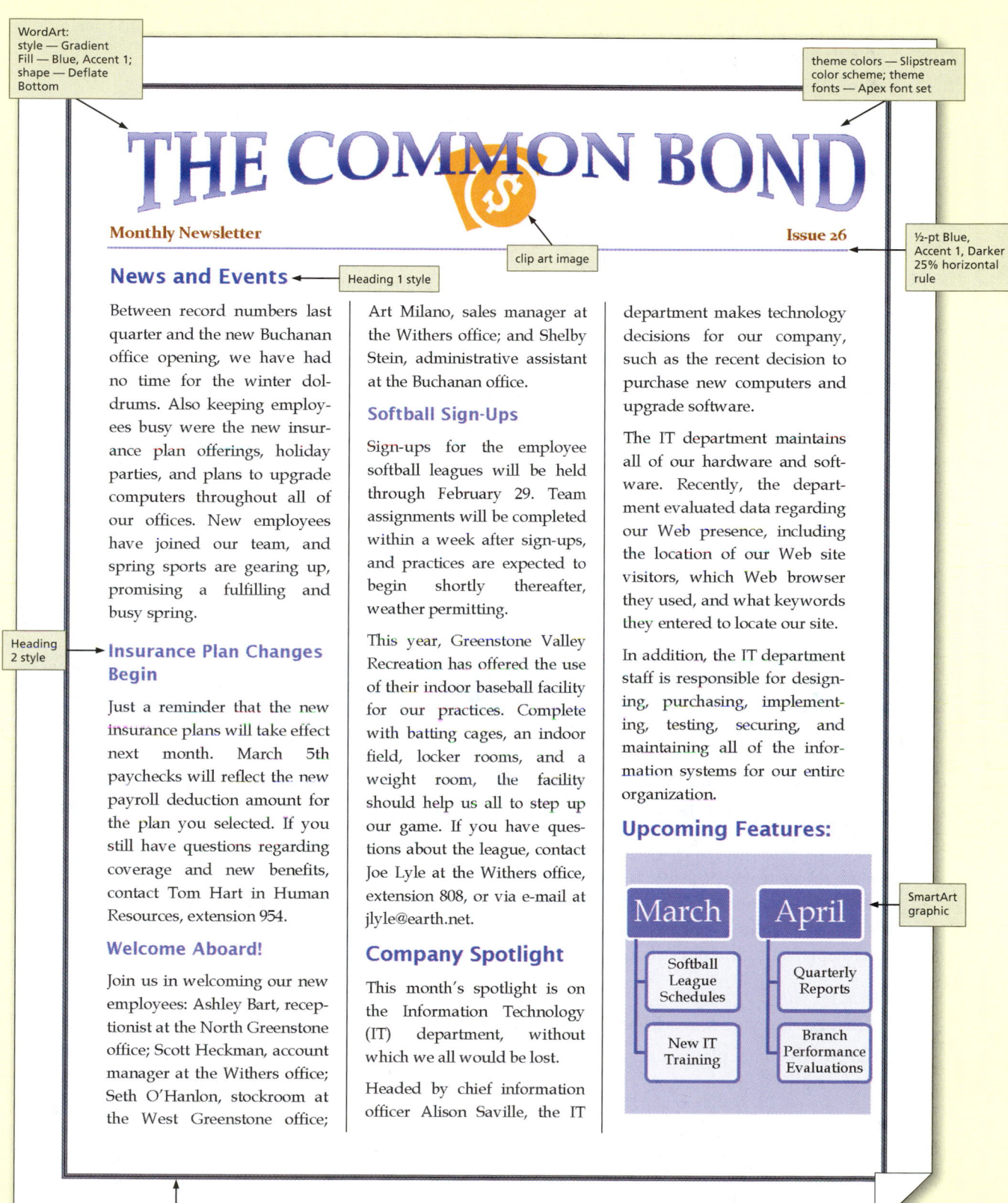

WordArt: style — Gradient Fill — Blue, Accent 1; shape — Deflate Bottom

theme colors — Slipstream color scheme; theme fonts — Apex font set

THE COMMON BOND

Monthly Newsletter   **Issue 26**

clip art image

½-pt Blue, Accent 1, Darker 25% horizontal rule

News and Events

Heading 1 style

Heading 2 style

Between record numbers last quarter and the new Buchanan office opening, we have had no time for the winter doldrums. Also keeping employees busy were the new insurance plan offerings, holiday parties, and plans to upgrade computers throughout all of our offices. New employees have joined our team, and spring sports are gearing up, promising a fulfilling and busy spring.

Insurance Plan Changes Begin

Just a reminder that the new insurance plans will take effect next month. March 5th paychecks will reflect the new payroll deduction amount for the plan you selected. If you still have questions regarding coverage and new benefits, contact Tom Hart in Human Resources, extension 954.

Welcome Aboard!

Join us in welcoming our new employees: Ashley Bart, receptionist at the North Greenstone office; Scott Heckman, account manager at the Withers office; Seth O'Hanlon, stockroom at the West Greenstone office;

Art Milano, sales manager at the Withers office; and Shelby Stein, administrative assistant at the Buchanan office.

Softball Sign-Ups

Sign-ups for the employee softball leagues will be held through February 29. Team assignments will be completed within a week after sign-ups, and practices are expected to begin shortly thereafter, weather permitting.

This year, Greenstone Valley Recreation has offered the use of their indoor baseball facility for our practices. Complete with batting cages, an indoor field, locker rooms, and a weight room, the facility should help us all to step up our game. If you have questions about the league, contact Joe Lyle at the Withers office, extension 808, or via e-mail at jlyle@earth.net.

Company Spotlight

This month's spotlight is on the Information Technology (IT) department, without which we all would be lost.

Headed by chief information officer Alison Saville, the IT

department makes technology decisions for our company, such as the recent decision to purchase new computers and upgrade software.

The IT department maintains all of our hardware and software. Recently, the department evaluated data regarding our Web presence, including the location of our Web site visitors, which Web browser they used, and what keywords they entered to locate our site.

In addition, the IT department staff is responsible for designing, purchasing, implementing, testing, securing, and maintaining all of the information systems for our entire organization.

Upcoming Features:

March	April
Softball League Schedules	Quarterly Reports
New IT Training	Branch Performance Evaluations

SmartArt graphic

½-pt Indigo, Text 2, Darker 25% triple line (thick middle, thin outside) border

Figure 7–84

Continued >

In the Lab *continued*

7. Format the newsletter according to Figure 7–84 on the previous page. Columns should have a width of 2.1" with spacing of 0.35". Place a vertical rule between the columns.

8. Use Word's automatic hyphenation feature to hyphenate the document.

9. Insert a continuous section break at the end of the document to balance the columns.

10. Format the subheads, News and Events, Company Spotlight, and Upcoming Features, using the Heading 1 style, and the remaining headings using the Heading 2 style.

11. Open a new document window and create the SmartArt graphic shown in Figure 7–84. Use the Hierarchy List layout. Add the text shown in the figure. Make the bottom four shapes larger. Save the graphic with the file name, Lab 7-1 Common Bond Features. Use the Office Clipboard to copy and paste the SmartArt graphic in the bottom-right column of the newsletter. (*Hint:* Copy the graphic in the Lab 7-1 Common Bond Features window and then switch to the Lab 7-1 Common Bond Newsletter window, so that you can paste the graphic in the newsletter.) Resize the pasted graphic to fill the column. Apply the Indigo, Text 2, Lighter 80% fill color to the graphic (shape). Note that your graphic may look slightly different from the figure due to variations in the shape size.

12. Add the page border as shown in the figure.

13. If the document does not fit on a single page, adjust spacing above and below paragraphs.

14. Arrange both documents (the graphic and the newsletter) on the screen. Scroll through both open windows. Maximize the newsletter window.

15. Save the document with Lab 7-1 Common Bond Newsletter as the file name and then submit it in the format specified by your instructor.

In the Lab

Lab 2: Creating a Newsletter with a Pull-Quote (Text Box) and an Article on File

Note: To complete this assignment, you will be required to use the Data Files for Students. See the inside back cover of this book for instructions on downloading the Data Files for Students, or contact your instructor for information about accessing the required files.

Problem: You are responsible for the monthly preparation of *The Shutterbug*, a newsletter for photography enthusiasts. The next edition discusses upcoming digital cameras (Figure 7–85). This article already has been prepared and is on the Data Files for Students. You need to create the nameplate and the pull-quote.

Perform the following tasks:

1. Change all margins to .75 inches. Depending on your printer, you may need different margin settings.

2. Create the nameplate using the formats identified in Figure 7–85. Create the title using WordArt. Set a right-aligned custom tab stop at the right margin. Use the Clip Art task pane to locate the images shown, or similar images. Resize the images as shown in the figure. Format the images as Behind Text, rotate the left image, and position the images as shown.

3. Below the nameplate, enter the heading Overview of Digital Cameras, as shown in the figure.

4. Create a continuous section break below the heading.

5. Format section 2 to three columns.

6. Insert the Lab 7-2 The Shutterbug Article file, which is located on the Data Files for Students, in section 2 below the nameplate.

WordArt: style — Gradient Fill — Red, Accent 1, Outline — White, Glow, Accent 2 font — 48-point Berlin Sans FB Demi; shape — Triangle Up

document theme — Civic

The Shutterbug

Monthly Newsletter   Volume 28

Overview of Digital Cameras

Heading 1 style

Digital cameras allow users to take pictures and store the photographed images digitally, as an alternative to traditional film. Because digital cameras with new and improved features regularly are introduced to the marketplace, you should know how to compare the differences among various available cameras. Two important factors to consider are the type of camera you need and its resolution.

Heading 2 style modified to Brown, Accent 4, Darker 50%

Types of Cameras

Three basic types of digital cameras are studio cameras, field cameras, and point-and-shoot cameras. The most expensive and highest quality of the three types of digital cameras is a studio cam-camera, which is a stationery camera used for professional studio work. Used often by photojournalists, the field camera is a portable camera that has many lenses

and other attachments. As with the studio camera, a field camera can be expensive. A point-and-shoot camera is more affordable than its counterparts. It is lightweight, and it provides acceptable quality photographic images for everyday users.

Resolution

Resolution, which is the number of horizontal and vertical pixels, is one factor that affects the quality of digital photos. A pixel, short for picture element, is the smallest element in an electronic image. The more pixels the camera uses to capture a picture, the better the

If you never plan to print any photos larger than 8 x 10", you do not need a camera with a resolution greater than 5 megapixels.

quality of the picture. For a good quality printed photo, you should have a 5 MP (megapixel, or million pixels) camera.

Many consumers mistakenly believe that the digital camera with the highest resolution is the best camera for their needs. A higher resolution increases quality and clarity of the pictures, as well as the size at which you can print the photos before noticing degradation in quality. If you never plan to print any photos larger than 8 x 10", you do not need a camera with a resolution greater than 5 megapixels.

On the Horizon

- Photography exhibit at Frankfort Heritage Museum, March 19 – April 6
- Lecture series by local photographer, Adam Schenkler, Mondays 8:00 – 9:00 p.m. in May
- Matting and Framing workshop, Frame It Right!, Wednesday, May 9, 7:30 – 9:00 p.m.

text box

14-point bold, italic font

8-pt Red, Accent 1, Darker 50% art border

Figure 7–85

Continued >

In the Lab *continued*

7. Format the newsletter according to Figure 7–85 on the previous page. Columns should have a width of 2" with spacing of 0.5". Place a vertical rule between the columns. Modify the Heading 2 style as indicated in the figure.

8. Use Word's automatic hyphenation feature to hyphenate the document.

9. Insert a continuous section break at the end of the document to balance the columns.

10. Add the page border as shown in the figure.

11. Insert a Mod Quote text box for the pull-quote. The text for the pull-quote is in the third column of the article. Split the window. Use the split window to copy the text and then paste it in the text box. Remove the split window. Change the fill color (shape fill) of the text box to Fill - Red, Accent 1. Resize the text box so that it is similar in size to Figure 7–85. Position the text box as shown in Figure 7–85.

12. If the document does not fit on a single page, adjust spacing above and below paragraphs.

13. Save the newsletter using Lab 7-2 The Shutterbug Newsletter as the file name and submit it in the format specified by your instructor.

In the Lab

Lab 3: Creating a Newsletter from Scratch

Problem: You work part-time for the city of Frankfort, which publishes a quarterly newsletter. Figure 7–86 shows the contents of the next issue.

Perform the following tasks:

1. Change all margins to .75 inches. Depending on your printer, you may need different margin settings.

2. Create the nameplate using the formats identified in Figure 7–86. Create the title using WordArt. Set a right-aligned custom tab stop at the right margin. Use the Clip Art task pane to locate the image shown, or a similar image. Resize the image as shown in the figure. Format the image as Behind Text, rotate the image, and position the image as shown.

3. Create a continuous section break below the nameplate. Format section 2 to two columns. Enter the text in section 2 using justified paragraph formatting.

4. Insert a Braces Quote 2 text box for the pull-quote. Copy the text for the pull-quote from the newsletter and then paste it in the text box. Change the fill of the text box to Gold, Background 2, Lighter 40%. Resize and position the text box so that it is similar in size and location to Figure 7–86.

5. Insert the table shown at the bottom of the right column in the newsletter and format it as indicated in the figure.

6. Make any additional formatting required in the newsletter so that it looks like the figure. The entire newsletter should fit on a single page.

7. Save the document with Lab 7-3 Frankfort Heritage Newsletter as the file name and then submit it in the format specified by your instructor.

WordArt: style — Fill — Tan, Accent 2, Warm Matte Bevel font — 36-point Book Antiqua; shape — Square

theme colors — Horizon color scheme; theme fonts — Hardcover font set

FRANKFORT HERITAGE

Quarterly Newsletter   **Volume 32**

3-pt Tan, Accent 2, Darker 25% border

New City Preservation Efforts Underway

Heading 1 style modified to Tan, Accent 2, Darker 25%

This edition of our newsletter outlines the various preservation efforts the Frankfort Heritage Group has undertaken. In addition to the courthouse project, which is in its second year, we have obtained the former Sullivan home on Elm Street and the iconic Pop's Market on Westhaven Lane.

The Sullivan Home

Heading 2 style modified to Blue-Gray, Accent 1, Darker 50%

This beautiful Italianate mansion was once home to the first mayor of Frankfort, Eustace Sullivan. Built in 1845, it is a stunning example of period architecture. It boasts original woodwork, even though much has been damaged. A mahogany staircase in the front entryway is in remarkably good shape. Some upstairs rooms have water damage due to a leaky roof, which has been replaced. Once refurbished, it will house the Frankfort Historical Society. All renovations are underway, and we hope to unveil the home in its former glory by year's end.

pull-quote

> Once refurbished, it will house the Frankfort Historical Society.

During our consultations with previous owners, we spoke with Jessamine Sullivan Ames, great-great-granddaughter of the original owner, who remembers visiting the home as a child. Among her many recollections of the home, she states, "I remember the staircase. My brother, Theodore, loved to slide down the bannister. I also remember Gran making biscuits at the kitchen counter. She'd cut them right on the countertop, claiming the slate made the biscuits better. It was a beautiful, wonderful home, and we always enjoyed visiting during our summer vacations." Frankfort Heritage Group is relying on Jessamine's recollections and many photographs and other clues from residents to direct our restoration efforts. We also extend a heartfelt thanks to Jessamine for her firsthand recollections of the home.

Pop's Market

In its heyday from 1940 to 1962, Pop's Market provided a popular gathering spot for teens and families alike. Located across the street from Orchard Grove Park, it served to quench the thirst of many a hot and weary little leaguer. The original marble countertop remains intact, as do some of the booths. When Pop's Market closed in 1973, it was home to Dante's Grill until 1983 and has remained empty since that time. After renovations, Pop's Market will reopen for business in next spring, in time for thirsty ballplayers to visit.

Volunteers Needed

Light List - Accent 4 table style

Type	Duties
Skilled trades	Carpenters, electricians, roofers, and plumbers
Unskilled laborers	Carry out debris, run errands, buy supplies

10-pt Gold, Background 2, Darker 50% art border

Figure 7–86

Cases and Places

Apply your creative thinking and problem solving skills to design and implement a solution.

Note: To complete these assignments, you may be required to use the Data Files for Students. See the inside back cover of this book for instructions on downloading the Data Files for Students, or contact your instructor for information about accessing the required files.

1: Create a Newsletter about Research and Learning Web Sites

Academic

As a part-time assistant for the English department at your school, you have been assigned the task of creating a newsletter that covers research and learning Web sites, which will be distributed to all enrolled students.

Content to be covered in the newsletter related to research includes the following: A recent Web usability survey conducted by the Nielsen Norman Group found that 88 percent of people who connect to the Internet use a search engine as their first online action. Search engines require users to type words and phrases that characterize the information being sought. Bing, Google, and AltaVista are some of the more popular search engines. The key to effective searching on the Web is composing search queries that narrow the search results and place the more relevant Web sites at the top of the results list. Keep up with the latest computer and related product developments by viewing online dictionaries and encyclopedias that add to their collections on a regular basis. Shopping for a new computer can be a daunting experience, but many online guides can help you select the components that best fit your needs and budget. If you are not confident in your ability to solve a problem alone, turn to online technical support. Web sites often provide streaming how-to video lessons, tutorials, and real-time chats with experienced technicians. Hardware and software reviews, price comparisons, shareware, technical questions and answers, and breaking technology news are found on comprehensive portals. Popular research Web sites include the following: A9.com, AccessMyLibrary, AltaVista, Answers.com, Ask, Bing, ChaCha, CNET, eHow, Google, HotBot, Librarians' Internet Index, PC911, Switchboard, Webopedia, and ZDNet.

Content to be covered in the newsletter related to learning includes the following: While you may believe your education ends when you finally graduate from college, learning is a lifelong process. You can increase your technological knowledge by visiting several Web sites with tutorials about building your own Web sites, the latest news about the Internet, and resources for visually impaired users. The HowStuffWorks Web site has won numerous awards for its clear, comprehensive articles that demystify aspects of our everyday life. It includes ratings and reviews of products written by Consumer Guide editors. A consortium of colleges maintains the Internet Public Library, which includes subject collections, reference materials, and a reading room filled with magazines and books. Volunteer librarians will answer your personal questions asked in its Ask an IPL Librarian form. Popular learning Web sites include the following: AT&T Knowledge Network Explorer, Bartleby: Great Books Online, BBC Learning, CBT Nuggets, HowStuffWorks, Internet Public Library, Learn the Net, ScienceMaster, Search Engine Watch, and Wiredguide.

The newsletter should present the above content as text and graphics. It should contain at least two of these graphical elements: a clip art image from the Web, a SmartArt graphic, a pull-quote, or a table. Enhance the newsletter with a drop cap, WordArt, color, ruling lines, and a page border. Be sure to use appropriate desktop publishing elements including a nameplate, columns of text, balanced columns, and a variety of font sizes, font colors, and shading. Use the concepts and techniques presented in this chapter to create and format the newsletter. Be sure to check spelling and grammar of the finished newsletter. Submit your assignment in the format specified by your instructor.

2: Create a Newsletter about Shopping and Health Web Sites

Personal

As a part-time assistant for the local community center, you have been assigned the task of creating a newsletter that covers shopping and health Web sites, which will be distributed to all center visitors.

Content to be covered in the newsletter related to shopping includes the following: From groceries to clothing to computers, you can buy just about everything you need with just a few clicks of your mouse. More than one-half of Internet users will make at least one online purchase this year. Books, computer software and hardware, and music are the hottest commodities. The two categories of Internet shopping Web sites are those with physical counterparts, such as Walmart and Fry's Electronics, and those with only a Web presence, such as Amazon and Buy. Another method of shopping for the items you need, and maybe some you really do not need, is to visit auction Web sites. Categories include antiques and collectibles, automotive, computers, electronics, music, sports, sports cards and memorabilia, and toys. Online auction Web sites can offer unusual items, including Star Wars memorabilia or a round of golf with Jack Nicklaus. Popular shopping Web sites include the following: Auctions: craigslist, eBay, Sotheby's, uBid, and U.S. Treasury - Seized Property Auctions; Books and Music: Amazon, Barnes & Noble, and BookFinder; Computers and Electronics: BestBuy, Buy, and Fry's Electronics; Miscellaneous: drugstore, Google Product Search, SmashBuys, and Walmart.

Content to be covered in the newsletter related to health includes the following: More than 75 million consumers use the Internet yearly to search for health information, so using the Web to store personal medical data is a natural extension of the Internet's capabilities. Internet health services and portals are available to store your personal health history, including prescriptions, lab test results, doctor visits, allergies, and immunizations. Google Health allows users to create a health profile, import medical records, and locate medical services and doctors. Web sites such as healthfinder.gov provide free wellness information to consumers. Wise consumers, however, verify the online information they read with their personal physician. In minutes, you can register with a health Web site by choosing a user name and password. Then, you create a record to enter your medical history. You also can store data for your emergency contacts, primary care physicians, specialists, blood type, cholesterol levels, blood pressure, and insurance plan. No matter where you are in the world, you and medical personnel can obtain records via the Internet or fax machine. Popular learning Web sites include the following: Medical History: Google Health, Lifestar, Medem, PersonalMD, Practice Solutions, Records for Living, Inc - Personal Health and Living Management, and WebMD; General Health: Consumer and Patient Health Information Section (CAPHIS), Centers for Disease Control and Prevention, family-doctor, healthfinder, KidsHealth, LIVESTRONG.COM, MedlinePlus, and PE Central: Health and Nutrition Web Sites.

The newsletter should present the above content as text and graphics. It should contain at least two of these graphical elements: a clip art image from the Web, a SmartArt graphic, a pull-quote, or a table. Enhance the newsletter with a drop cap, WordArt, color, ruling lines, and a page border. Be sure to use appropriate desktop publishing elements including a nameplate, columns of text, balanced columns, and a variety of font sizes, font colors, and shading. Use the concepts and techniques presented in this chapter to create and format the newsletter. Be sure to check spelling and grammar of the finished newsletter. Submit your assignment in the format specified by your instructor.

3: Create a Newsletter about Career Search and Travel Web Sites

Professional

As a board member of your alumni association, you have been assigned the task of creating a newsletter that covers career search and travel Web sites, which will be distributed to all newly inducted members.

Content to be covered in the newsletter related to career search includes the following: While your teachers give you valuable training to prepare you for a career, they rarely teach you how to begin that career. You can broaden your horizons by searching the Internet for career information and job openings. First, examine some of the job search Web sites. These resources list thousands of openings

Continued >

Cases and Places *continued*

in hundreds of fields, companies, and locations. For example, the USAJOBS Web site allows you to find information for federal jobs. This information may include the training and education required, salary data, working conditions, job descriptions, and more. In addition, many companies advertise careers on their Web sites. When a company contacts you for an interview, learn as much about it and the industry as possible before the interview. Popular career search Web sites include the following: Job Search: BestJobsUSA, CareerBuilder, Careerjet, CareerNET, CAREERXCHANGE, CollegeGrad.com, EmploymentGuide.com, Job.com, Job Bank USA, JobWeb, Monster, USAJOBS, VolunteerMatch, and Yahoo! HotJobs; Company/Industry Information: Careers.org, Forbes, Fortune, Hoover's, and Occupational Outlook Handbook.

Content to be covered in the newsletter related to travel includes the following: When you are ready to arrange your next travel adventure or just want to explore destination possibilities, the Internet provides ample resources to set your plans in motion. To discover exactly where your destination is on this planet, cartography Web sites, including MapQuest and Yahoo! Maps, allow you to pinpoint your destination. View your exact destination using satellite imagery with Google Maps and Bing Maps. Some excellent starting places are general travel Web sites such as Expedia Travel, Cheap Tickets, Orbitz, and Travelocity. Many airline Web sites allow you to reserve hotel rooms, activities, and rental cars while booking a flight. These all-encompassing Web sites have tools to help you find the lowest prices and details about flights, car rentals, cruises, and hotels. Comprehensive online guidebooks can provide useful details about maximizing your vacation time while saving money. Popular learning Web sites include the following: General Travel: CheapTickets, Expedia Travel, Kayak, Orbitz, SideStep, and Travelocity; Cartography: Bing Maps, Google Maps, MapQuest, Maps.com, and Yahoo! Maps; Travel and City Guides: Frommer's Travel Guides, GoPlanit, U.S.-Parks US National Parks Travel Guide, and Virtual Tourist.

The newsletter should present the above content as text and graphics. It should contain at least two of these graphical elements: a clip art image from the Web, a SmartArt graphic, a pull-quote, or a table. Enhance the newsletter with a drop cap, WordArt, color, ruling lines, and a page border. Be sure to use appropriate desktop publishing elements including a nameplate, columns of text, balanced columns, and a variety of font sizes, font colors, and shading. Use the concepts and techniques presented in this chapter to create and format the newsletter. Be sure to check spelling and grammar of the finished newsletter. Submit your assignment in the format specified by your instructor.

4 Working with Information Graphics

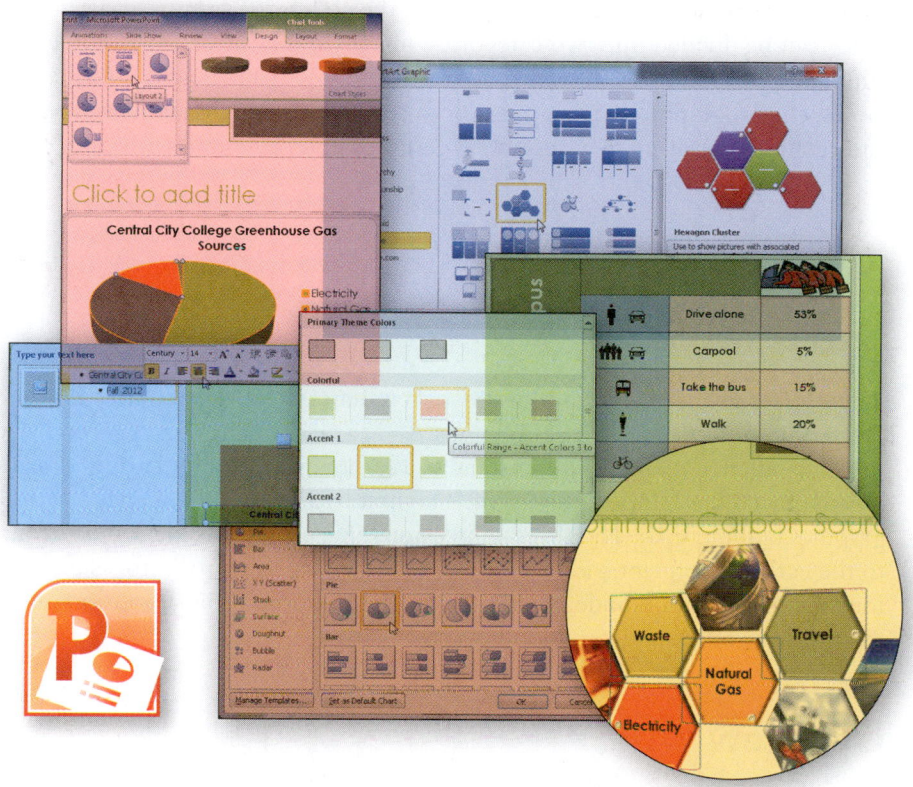

Objectives

You will have mastered the material in this chapter when you can:

- Insert a SmartArt graphic
- Insert images from a file into a SmartArt graphic
- Convert text to a SmartArt graphic
- Format a SmartArt graphic
- Create and format a chart
- Change the chart slice outline weight and color

- Rotate a chart
- Change the chart title and legend
- Create and format a table
- Change table text alignment and orientation
- Add an image to a table
- Insert a symbol

4 | Working with Information Graphics

Introduction

Audiences generally focus first on the visual elements displayed on a slide. Graphical elements increase **visual literacy**, which is the ability to examine and assess these images. They can be divided into two categories: images and information graphics. Images are the clips and photographs you have used in Chapters 1, 2, and 3, and information graphics are tables, charts, graphs, and diagrams. Both sets of visuals help audience members interpret and retain material, so they should be designed and presented with care.

Project — Presentation with SmartArt, a Chart, and a Table

The project in this chapter follows visual content guidelines and uses PowerPoint to create the presentation shown in Figure 4–1. The slide show uses several visual elements to help audience members understand the carbon footprint, or carbon dioxide emissions, created by college students and staff. The first two slides are enhanced with SmartArt graphics and pictures. The three-dimensional pie chart on Slide 3 shows four contributors to the carbon footprint and emphasizes that the largest contributor is electricity. The four-column table on Slide 4 lists the five most common transportation methods students use to arrive on campus.

Overview

As you read through this chapter, you will learn how to create the presentation shown in Figure 4–1 by performing these general tasks:

- Insert and modify a SmartArt graphic.
- Add styles and effects to SmartArt.
- Create a table and a chart.
- Add borders to tables and charts.
- Change table text alignment and orientation.
- Change chart and table styles and colors.

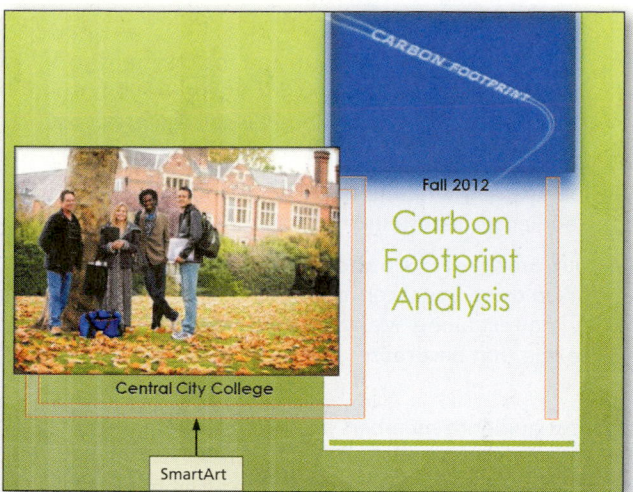

(a) Slide 1 (Title Slide with SmartArt Enhanced with a Picture)

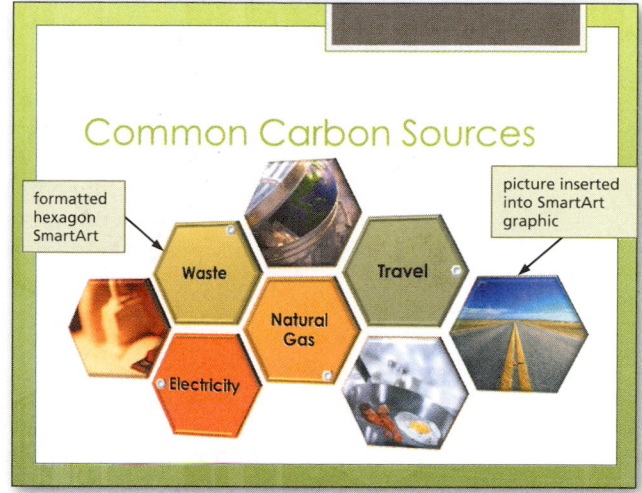

(b) Slide 2 (SmartArt Enhanced with Pictures)

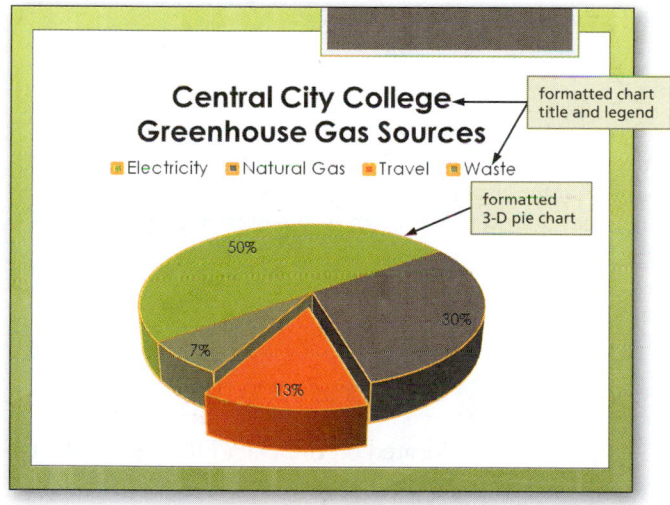

(c) Slide 3 (3-D Chart)

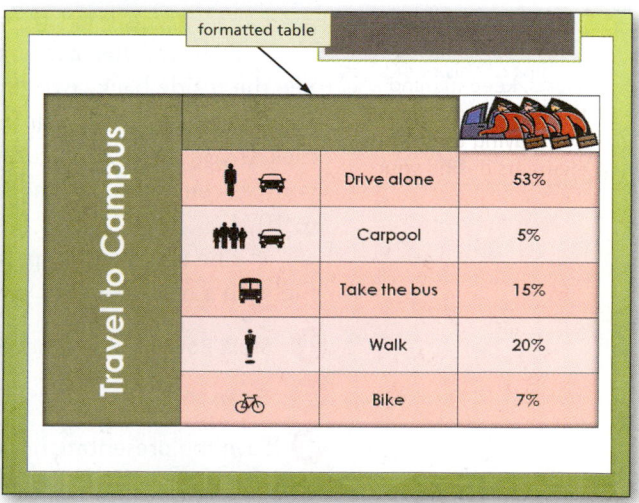

(d) Slide 4 (Four-Column Table)

Figure 4–1

Plan Ahead

General Project Guidelines

When creating a PowerPoint presentation, the actions you perform and the decisions you make will affect the appearance and characteristics of the finished document. As you create a presentation with illustrations, such as the project shown in Figure 4–1 on the previous page, you should follow these general guidelines:

1. **Consider the graphic's function.** Decide precisely what message you want the chart, table, or illustration to convey to the audience. Determine the graphic's purpose.

2. **Choose an appropriate SmartArt layout.** SmartArt illustrations represent ideas and concepts graphically. Audiences can grasp these visual concepts and recall them more quickly and accurately than when viewing text alone. Many SmartArt layouts are available (see Table 4–1), so select the one that best represents the concept you are attempting to present.

3. **Choose an appropriate chart style.** Most audience members like charts to help them understand the relationships between groups of data. Charts express numbers visually, but you must decide which chart type best conveys the points you are attempting to make in your presentation. PowerPoint presents a variety of chart layouts, and you must decide which one is effective in presenting the relationships between numbers and indicating important trends.

4. **Obtain information for the graphic from credible sources.** The text or numbers in the graphics should be current and correct. Verify the sources of the information and be certain you have typed the data correctly. On the slide or during your presentation, acknowledge the source of the information. If necessary, give credit to the person or organization that supplied the information for your graphics.

5. **Test your visual elements.** Show your slides to several friends or colleagues and ask them to interpret what they see. Time the duration they studied each slide. Have them verbally summarize the information they perceived.

When necessary, more specific details concerning the above guidelines are presented at appropriate points in the chapter. The chapter also will identify the actions performed and decisions made regarding these guidelines during the creation of the presentation shown in Figure 4–1.

BTW

BTWs
For a complete list of the BTWs found in the margins of this book, visit the PowerPoint 2010 BTW Web page (scsite.com/ppt2010/btw).

To Start PowerPoint and Open and Save a Presentation

To begin this presentation, you will open a file located on the Data Files for Students. See the inside back cover of this book for instructions on downloading the Data Files for Students, or contact your instructor for more information about accessing the required files. If you are using a computer to step through the project in this chapter and you want your screens to match the figures in this book, you should change your screen's resolution to 1024 × 768.

The following steps start PowerPoint, open the Carbon presentation, and save the file with a new name.

1 Start PowerPoint. If necessary, maximize the PowerPoint window.

2 Open the presentation, Carbon, located on the Data Files for Students.

3 Save the presentation using the file name, Carbon Footprint.

Plan Ahead

Consider the graphic's function.
Determine why you are considering using an information graphic. The SmartArt, chart, or table should introduce meaningful information, support information in your speech, and help you convey details. If you are inserting the graphic simply for the sake of enlivening the presentation, do not use it. Graphics should help your audience understand and retain information and should not merely repeat details they have seen or heard up to this point in the slide show.

Take care in placing a manageable amount of information in your chart or table. Avoid overwhelming your audience with numerous lines in your table or slices or bars in your chart. If your audience is confused or struggling with comprehending the graphic, chances are they simply will abandon the task and wait for you to display the next slide.

Creating and Formatting a SmartArt Graphic

An illustration often can help convey relationships between key points in your presentation. Numerous studies have shown that audience members recall information more readily and accurately when it is presented graphically rather than textually. Microsoft Office 2010 includes **SmartArt graphics**, which are visual representations of your ideas. The SmartArt layouts have a variety of shapes, arrows, and lines to correspond to the major points you want your audience to remember.

You can create a SmartArt graphic in two ways: Select a type and then add text and pictures or convert text or pictures already present on a slide to a graphic. Once the SmartArt graphic is present, you can customize its look by changing colors, adding and deleting shapes, adding fill and effects, adding pictures, and including animation. Table 4–1 lists the SmartArt types and their uses.

Table 4–1 SmartArt Graphic Layout Types and Purposes	
Type	**Purpose**
List	Show non-sequential information
Process	Show steps in a process or timeline
Cycle	Show a continual process
Hierarchy	Create an organizational chart
Relationship	Illustrate connections
Matrix	Show how parts relate to a whole
Pyramid	Show proportional relationships with the largest component at the top or bottom
Picture	Include a placeholder for pictures within the graphic
Office.com	Use SmartArt available on the Office.com Web site

In the following pages, you will follow these general steps to create two SmartArt graphics:

1. Insert a SmartArt graphic.
2. Add text and then format these characters.
3. Insert a picture from a file into the SmartArt graphic.
4. Add a SmartArt Style to the graphics.
5. Change the SmartArt color.
6. Convert text to a SmartArt graphic.
7. Adjust the SmartArt size and location on the slide.

BTW

Improving Audience Retention
Audience members need to use both senses of sight and hearing when they view graphics and listen to a speaker. When they become engaged in the presentation, they tune out distractions, which ultimately increases their retention of the material being presented. Although the exact amount of measured retention varies, one study found that an audience recalled five times more material when it was presented both verbally and visually.

<table>
<tr>
<td>**Plan Ahead**</td>
<td>

Choose an appropriate SmartArt layout.

If a slide contains key points that show a process or relationship, consider using a SmartArt graphic to add visual appeal and enhance audience comprehension. As you select a layout, determine the number of ideas you need to present and then select a graphic that contains the same number of shapes. For example, the Counterbalance Arrows layout in the Relationship area resembles a teeter-totter; it represents the notion that one concept conversely affects another concept, such as the economic principle that supply has an inverse relationship to demand.

</td>
</tr>
</table>

To Insert a SmartArt Graphic

A picture of Central City students and staff would complement the theme of showing the results of the campus's carbon footprint survey. Several SmartArt graphics have placeholders for one or more pictures, and they are grouped in the Picture category. The Snapshot Picture List graphic has one area for a picture and another for text. The following steps insert the Snapshot Picture List SmartArt graphic on Slide 1.

- Display the Insert tab and then click the SmartArt button (Insert tab | Illustrations group) to display the Choose a SmartArt Graphic dialog box.

- Click Picture in the left pane to display the Picture gallery.

- Click the Snapshot Picture List graphic (last graphic in first row) to display a preview of this graphic in the right pane (Figure 4–2).

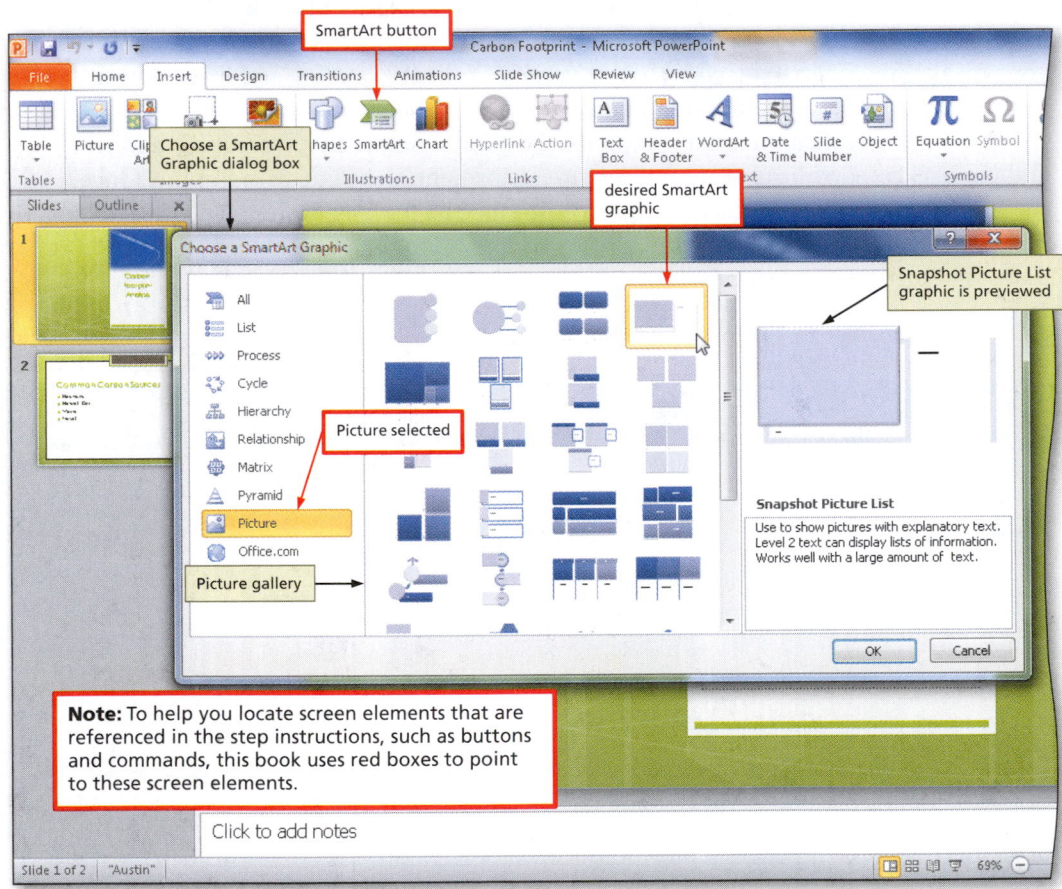

Figure 4–2

2

- Click the OK button to insert this SmartArt graphic on Slide 1 (Figure 4–3).

- If necessary, click the Text Pane button (SmartArt Tools Design tab | Create Graphic group) to open the Text pane if it does not display automatically.

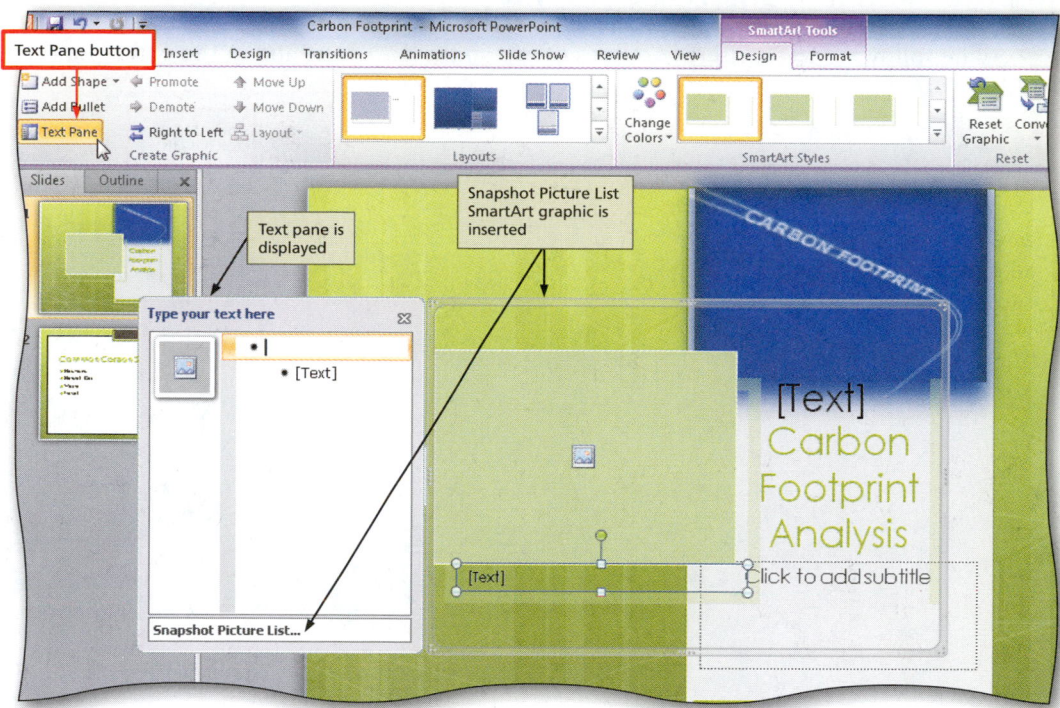

Figure 4–3

Text Pane

The **Text pane** assists you in creating a graphic because you can direct your attention to developing and editing the message without being concerned with the actual graphic. This Text pane consists of two areas: The top portion has the text that will appear in the SmartArt graphic and the bottom portion gives the name of the graphic and suggestions of what type of information is best suited for this type of visual. Each SmartArt graphic has an associated Text pane with bullets that function as an outline and map directly to the image. You can create new lines of bulleted text and then indent and demote these lines. You also can check spelling. Table 4–2 shows the character shortcuts you can use to enter Text pane characters.

BTW

The Ribbon and Screen Resolution
PowerPoint may change how the groups and buttons within the groups appear on the Ribbon, depending on the computer's screen resolution. Thus, your Ribbon may look different from the ones in this book if you are using a screen resolution other than 1024 × 768.

Table 4–2 Text Pane Keyboard Shortcuts	
Activity	**Shortcut**
Indent text	TAB or ALT+SHIFT+RIGHT ARROW
Demote text	SHIFT+TAB or ALT+SHIFT+LEFT ARROW
Add a tab character	CTRL+TAB
Create a new line of text	ENTER
Check spelling	F7
Merge two lines of text	DELETE at the end of the first text line
Display the shortcut menu	SHIFT+F10
Switch between the SmartArt drawing canvas and the Text pane	CTRL+SHIFT+F2
Close the Text pane	ALT+F4
Switch the focus from the Text pane to the SmartArt graphic border	ESC

To Enter Text in a SmartArt Graphic

The following steps insert two lines of text in the Text pane and in the corresponding SmartArt shapes on Slide 1.

- Type **Central City College** in the first bullet line and then press the DOWN ARROW key to move the insertion point to the second bullet line (Figure 4–4).

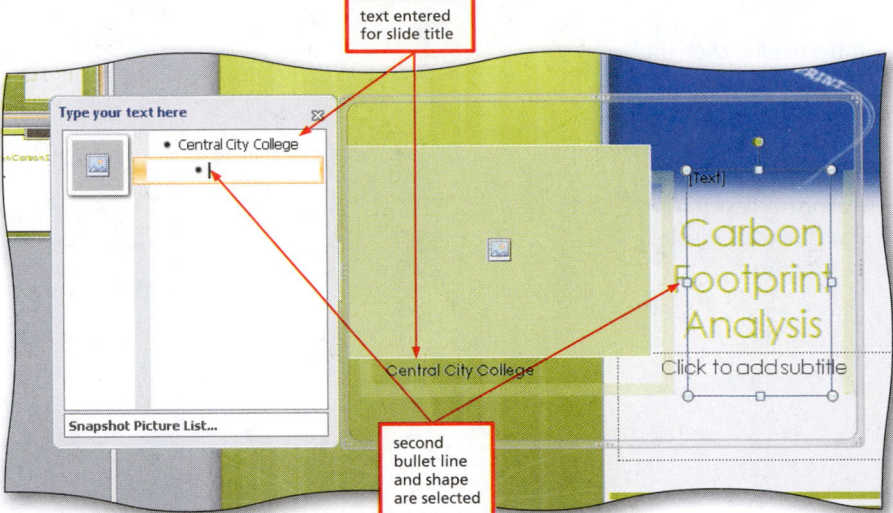

Figure 4–4

- Type **Fall 2012** in the second bullet line. Do not press the ENTER or DOWN ARROW keys (Figure 4–5).

Q&A

I mistakenly pressed the ENTER key. How can I delete the bullet line I just added?

Press the BACKSPACE key twice to delete the line.

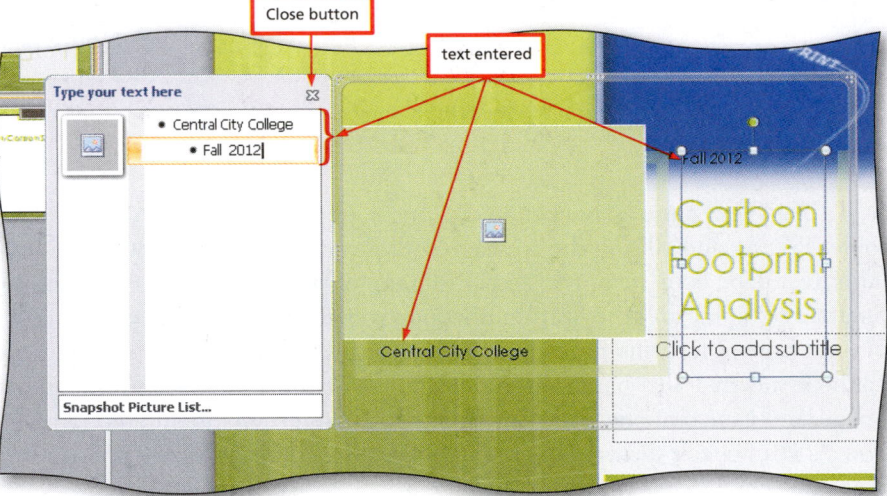

Figure 4–5

To Format Text Pane Characters

Once the desired characters are entered in the Text pane, you can change the font size and apply formatting features, such as bold, italic, and underlined text. The following steps format the text by changing the shape text font color and bolding the letters.

- With the Text pane open, drag through both bulleted lines to select the text and display the Mini toolbar.

Q&A

If my Text pane no longer is displayed, how can I get it to appear?

Click the control, which is the tab with two arrows pointing to the right and left, on the left side of the SmartArt graphic.

2

- Display the Font Color gallery and change the font color to Dark Blue.

- Bold the text.

- Center the text (Figure 4–6).

Q&A
These formatting changes did not appear in the Text pane. Why?

Not all the formatting changes are evident in the Text pane, but they appear in the corresponding shape.

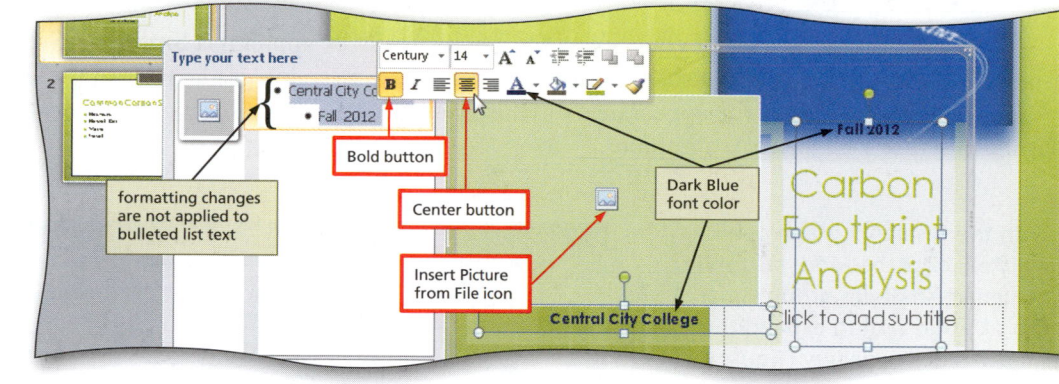

Figure 4–6

3

- Click the Close button in the SmartArt Text pane so that it no longer is displayed.

To Insert a Picture from a File into a SmartArt Graphic

The picture icon in the middle of the Snapshot Picture List SmartArt graphic indicates that the rectangular shape is designed to hold an image. You can select files from the Clip Organizer or from images you have obtained from other sources, such as a photograph taken with your digital camera. The following steps insert an image located on the Data Files for Students into the SmartArt graphic.

1

- With your USB flash drive connected to one of the computer's USB ports, click the Insert Picture from File icon in the rectangle picture placeholder to display the Insert Picture dialog box.

- If the list of files and folders on the selected USB flash drive are not displayed in the Insert Picture dialog box, double-click your USB flash drive to display them.

- Click Students and Staff to select the file name (Figure 4–7).

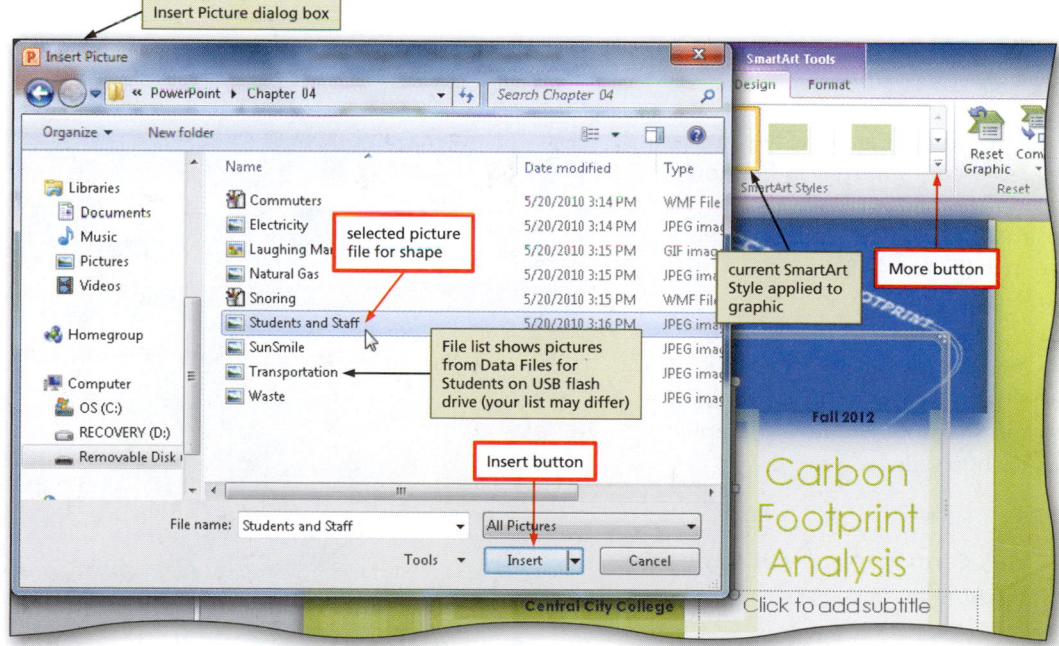

Figure 4–7

Q&A
What if the picture is not on a USB flash drive?

Use the same process, but be certain to select the location containing the picture in the File list.

2

- Click the Insert button (Insert Picture dialog box) to insert the picture into the SmartArt picture placeholder.

To Apply a SmartArt Style

You can change the look of your SmartArt graphic easily by applying a **SmartArt Style**. These professionally designed effects have a variety of shape fills, edges, shadows, line styles, gradients, and three-dimensional styles that allow you to customize the appearance of your presentation. The following steps add the Cartoon Style to the Snapshot Picture List SmartArt graphic.

1

• With the SmartArt graphic still selected, click the More button in the SmartArt Styles group (SmartArt Tools Design tab) to expand the SmartArt Styles gallery (Figure 4–8).

Q&A

How do I select the graphic if it no longer is selected?

Click the graphic anywhere except the picture you just added.

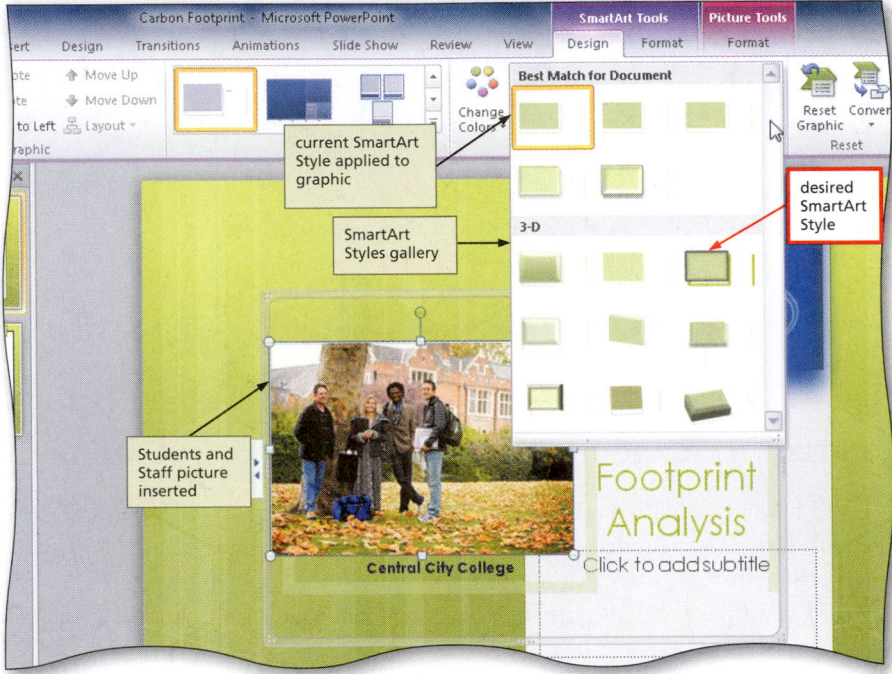

Figure 4–8

2

• Point to the Cartoon Style in the 3-D area (third style in first row) in the SmartArt Styles gallery to display a live preview of this style (Figure 4–9).

 Experiment

• Point to various styles in the SmartArt Styles gallery and watch the Snapshot Picture List graphic change styles.

3

• Click Cartoon to apply this style to the graphic.

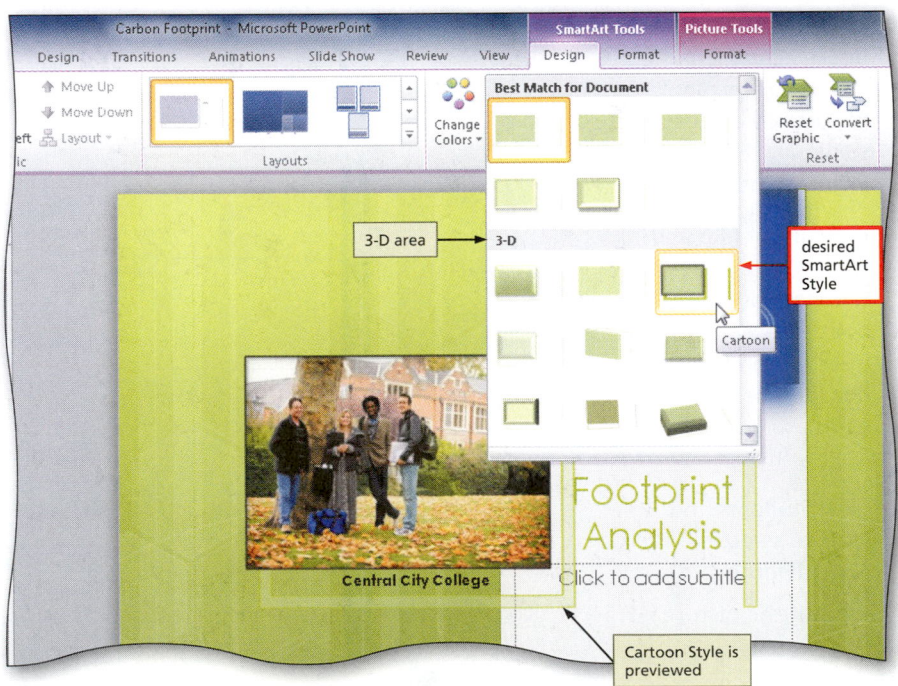

Figure 4–9

To Change SmartArt Color

Another modification you can make to your SmartArt graphic is to change its color. As with the WordArt Style gallery, PowerPoint provides a gallery of color options you can preview and evaluate. The following steps change the SmartArt graphic color to a Colorful range.

1
- With the SmartArt graphic still selected, click the Change Colors button (SmartArt Tools Design tab | SmartArt Styles group) to display the Change Colors gallery (Figure 4–10).

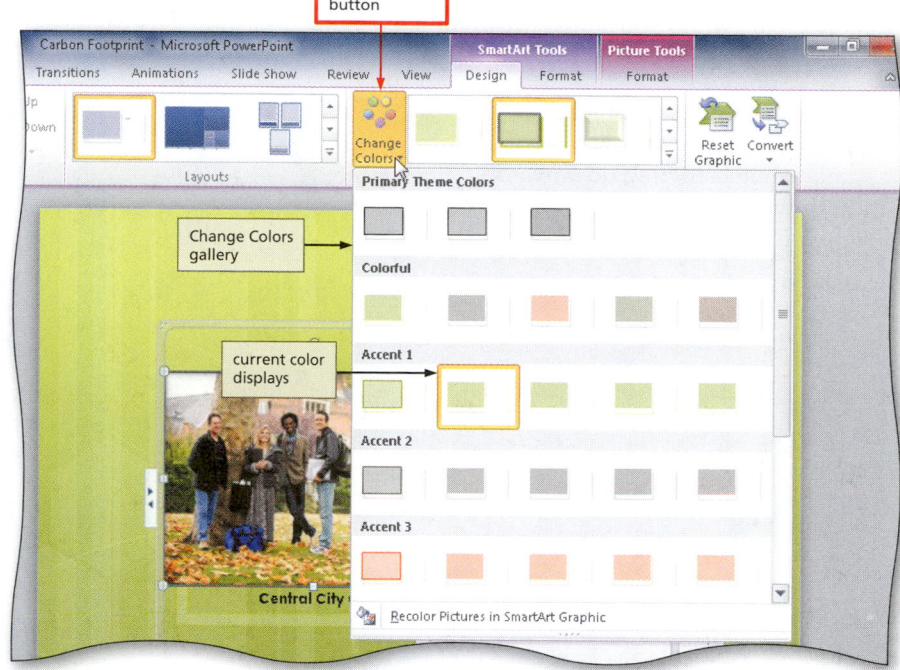

Figure 4–10

2
- Point to Colorful Range – Accent Colors 3 to 4 in the Colorful area (third color) to display a live preview of these colors (Figure 4–11).

Experiment
- Point to various colors in the Change Colors gallery and watch the shapes change colors.

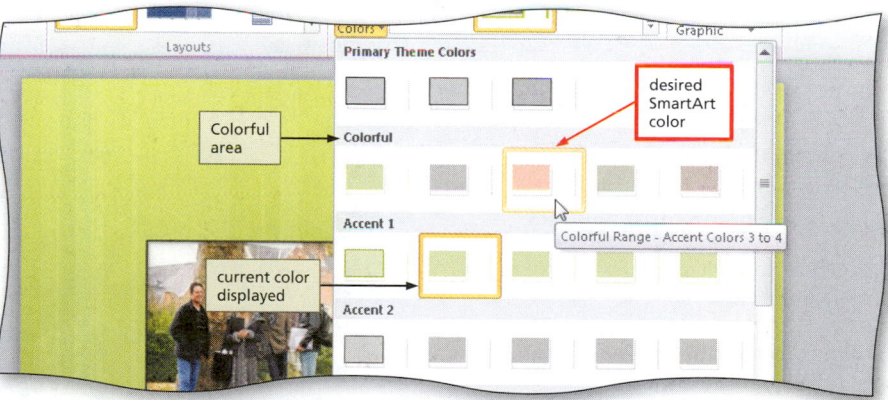

Figure 4–11

3
- Click Colorful Range – Accent Colors 3 to 4 to apply this color variation to the graphic (Figure 4–12).

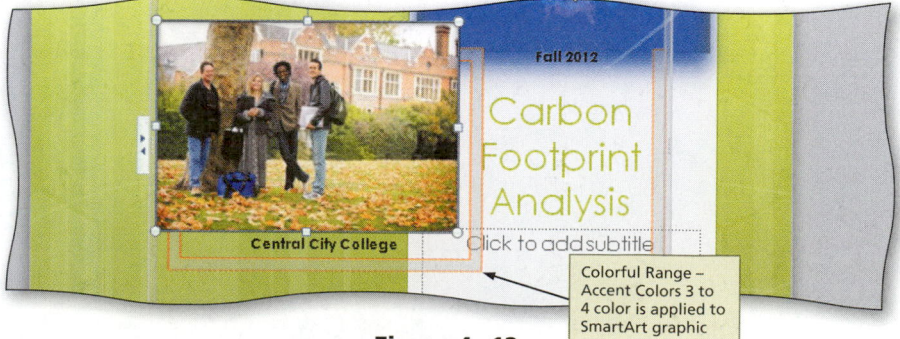

Figure 4–12

To Resize a SmartArt Graphic

When you view the completed graphic, you may decide that individual shapes or the entire piece of art needs to be enlarged or reduced. If you change the size of one shape, the other shapes also may change size to maintain proportions. Likewise, the font size may change in all the shapes if you increase or decrease the font size of one shape. On Slide 1, the SmartArt graphic size can be increased to fill the space and add readability. All the shapes will enlarge proportionally when you adjust the graphic's height and width. The following steps resize the SmartArt graphic.

1

- With the SmartArt graphic still selected, point to the lower-left sizing handle and drag downward and to the left, as shown in Figure 4–13.

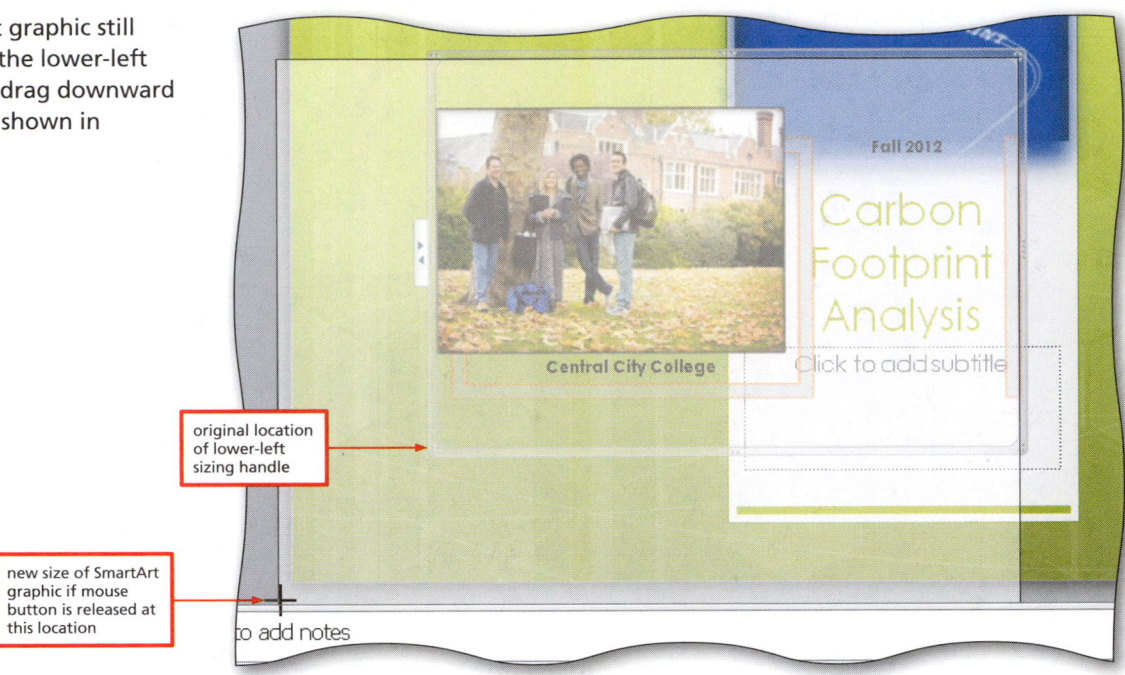

Figure 4–13

2

- Release the mouse button to resize the graphic.

- Press the UP and RIGHT ARROW keys to position the graphic, as shown in Figure 4–14.

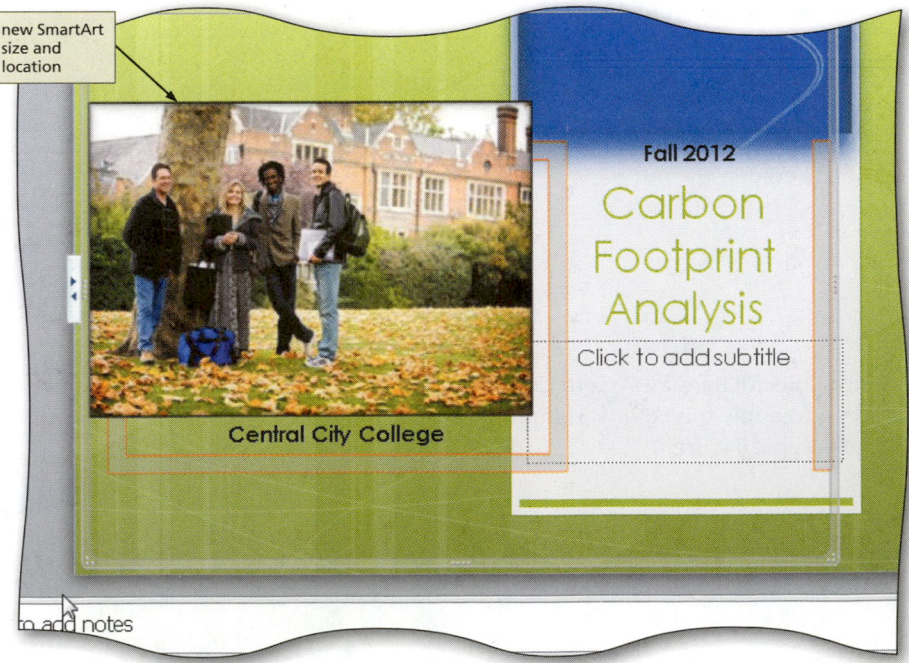

Figure 4–14

To Convert Text to a SmartArt Graphic

You quickly can convert small amounts of slide text and pictures into a SmartArt graphic. Once you determine the type of graphic, such as process or cycle, you then have a wide variety of styles from which to choose in the SmartArt Graphic gallery. As with other galleries, you can point to the samples and view a live preview if you desire. The following steps convert the four bulleted text paragraphs on Slide 2 to the Hexagon Cluster graphic, which is part of the Picture category.

1
- Click the Next Slide button to display Slide 2.

- With the Home tab displayed, select the four bulleted list items and then click the Convert to SmartArt Graphic button (Home tab | Paragraph group) to display the SmartArt Graphics gallery (Figure 4–15).

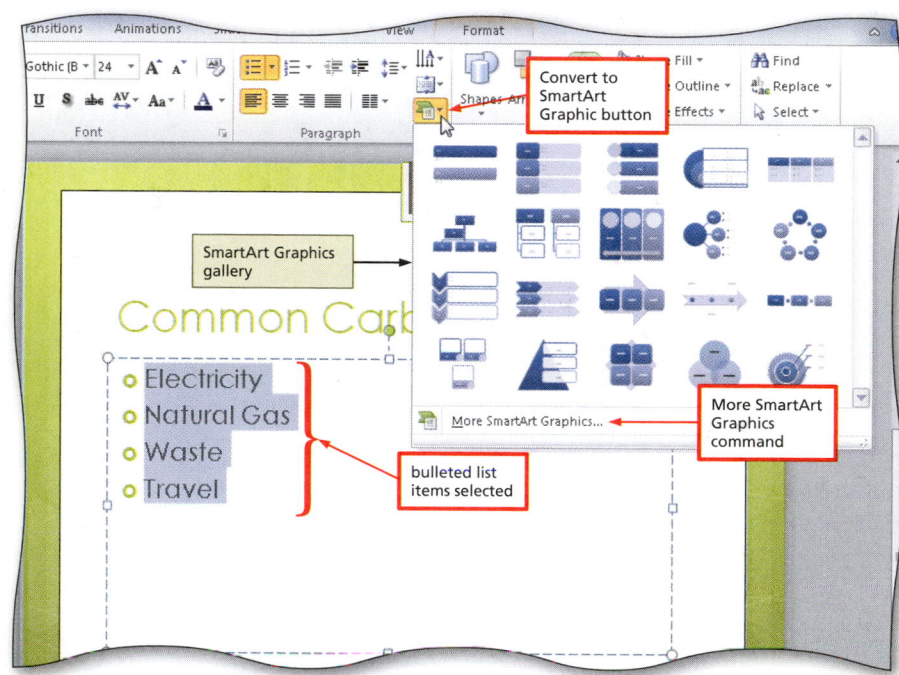

Figure 4–15

2
- Click More SmartArt Graphics in the SmartArt Graphics gallery to display the Choose a SmartArt Graphic dialog box.

- Click Picture in the left pane to display the Picture gallery.

- Scroll down and then click the Hexagon Cluster graphic (second graphic in sixth row) to display a preview of this graphic in the right pane (Figure 4–16).

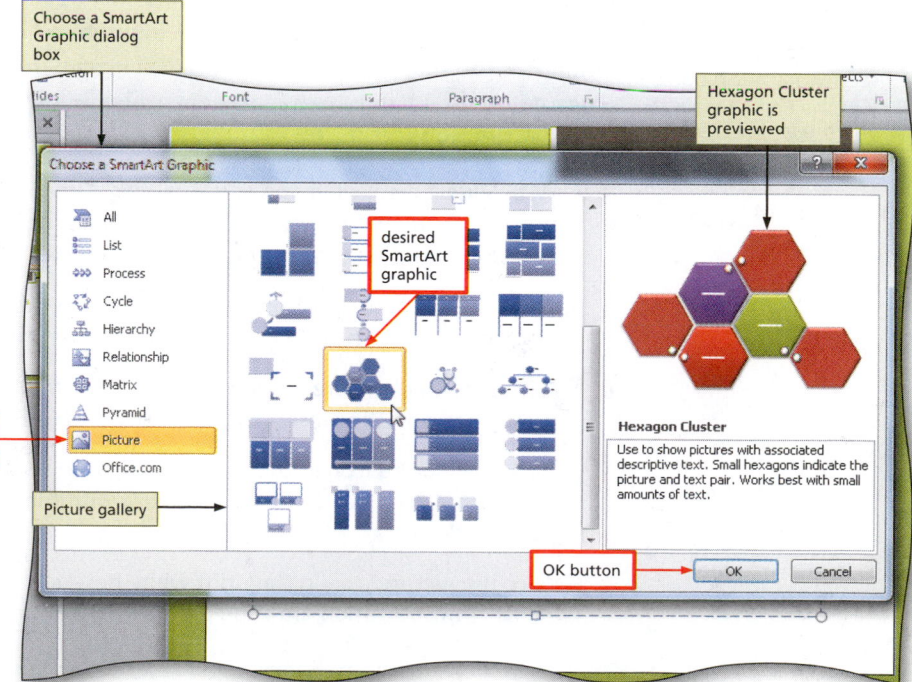

Figure 4–16

3
• Click the OK button (Choose a SmartArt Graphic dialog box) to apply this shape and convert the text (Figure 4–17).

Q&A

How can I edit the text that displays in the four shapes?

You can click the text and then make the desired changes. Also, if you display the Text pane on the left side of the graphic, you can click the text you want to change and make your edits.

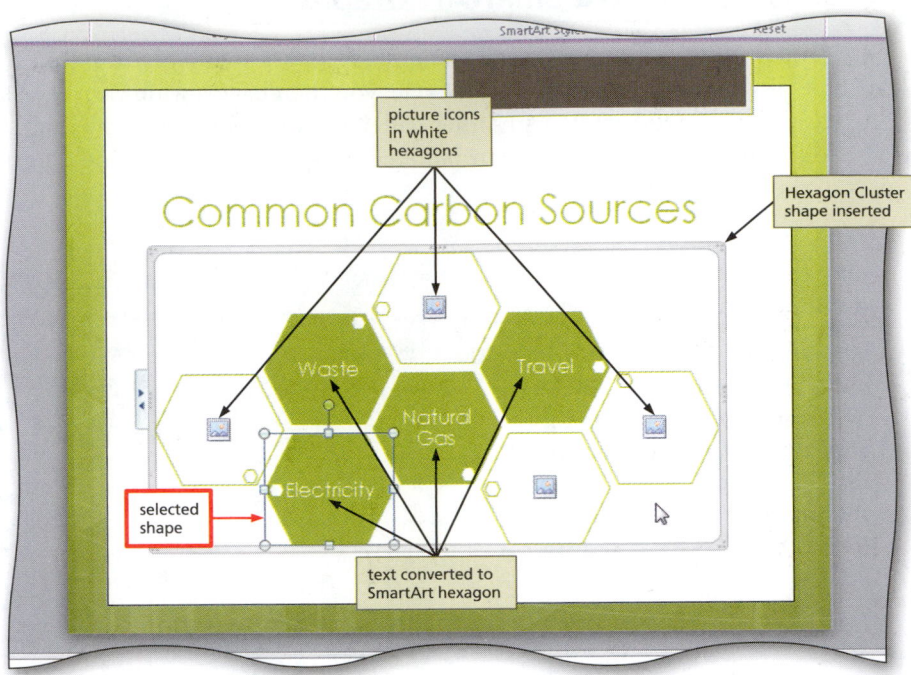

Figure 4–17

Other Ways

1. Click Convert to SmartArt on shortcut menu

BTW

Q&As
For a complete list of the Q&As found in many of the step-by-step sequences in this book, visit the PowerPoint 2010 Q&A Web page (scsite.com/ppt2010/qa).

To Insert Pictures from a File into a SmartArt Graphic

The picture icon in each of the four white hexagons in the SmartArt graphic indicates the shape is designed to hold an image. In this presentation, you will add images located on the Data Files for Students. The following steps insert pictures into the SmartArt graphic.

1 With Slide 2 displaying and your USB flash drive connected to one of the computer's USB ports, click the Insert picture from file icon in the top white hexagon under the word, Carbon, to display the Insert Picture dialog box.

2 Click Waste in the list of picture files and then click the Insert button (Insert Picture dialog box) to insert the picture into the top SmartArt picture placeholder.

3 Click the Insert picture from file icon in the left white hexagon to display the Insert Picture dialog box and then insert the picture with the file name, Electricity, into the placeholder.

4 Click the picture icon in the white hexagon to the right of the word, Natural Gas (below the word, Travel), and insert the picture with the file name, Natural Gas, into the placeholder.

5 Click the picture icon in the right white hexagon and then insert the picture with the file name, Transportation, into the placeholder (Figure 4–18).

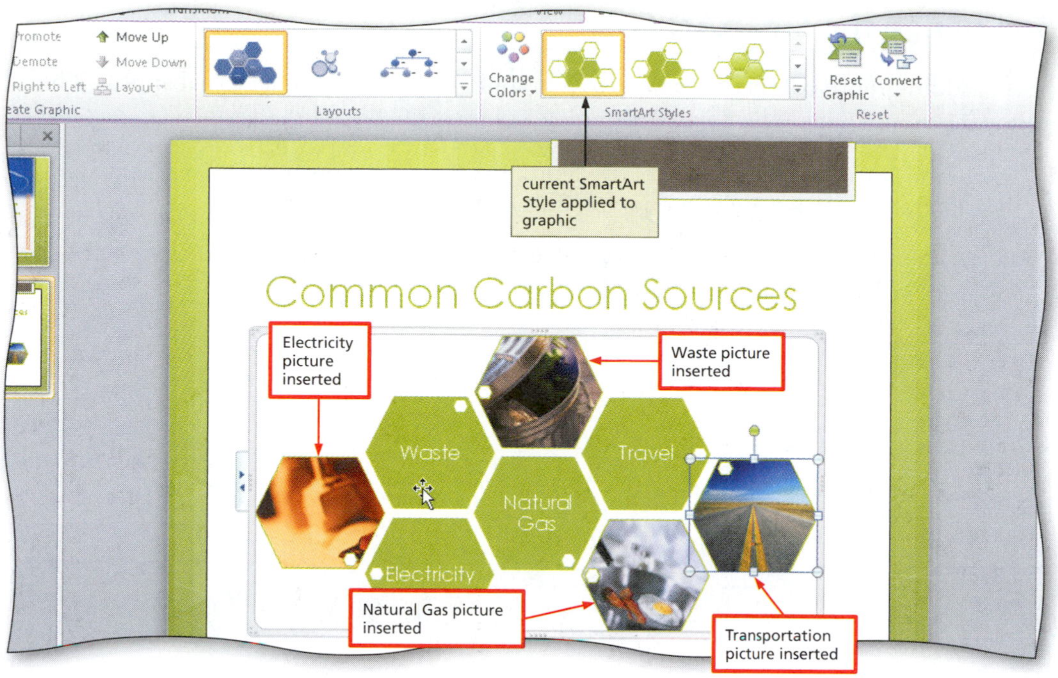

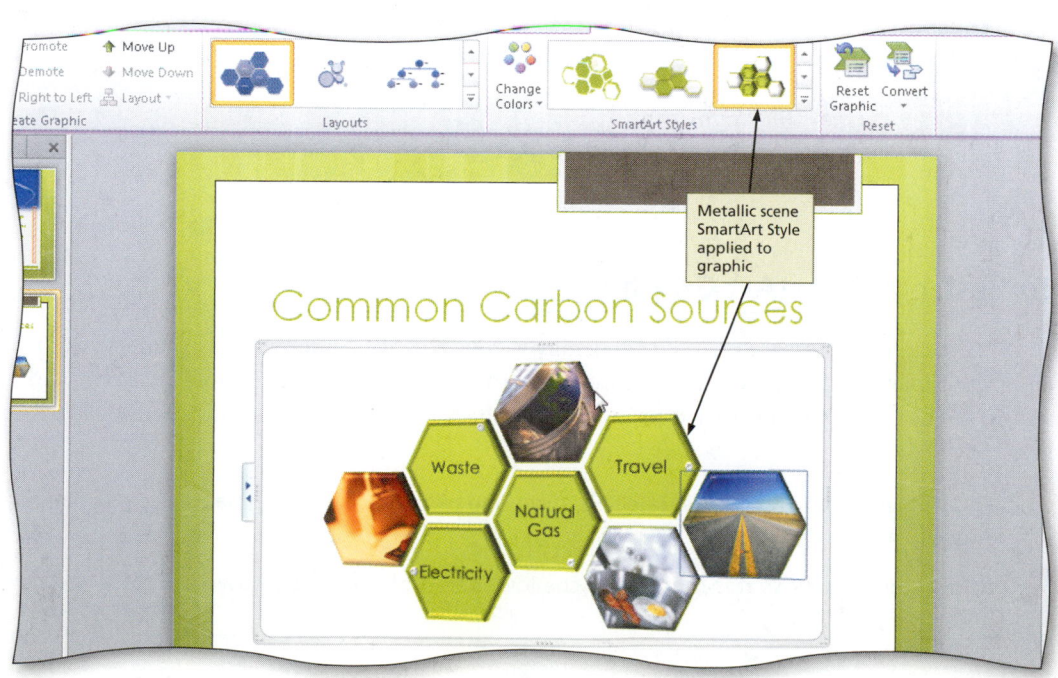

Figure 4–18

To Add a SmartArt Style to the Graphic

To enhance the appearance of the group of hexagons, you can add a three-dimensional style. The following steps add the Metallic Scene Style to the Hexagon Cluster graphic.

1 With the SmartArt graphic still selected, click the More button in the SmartArt Styles group (SmartArt Tools Design tab) to expand the SmartArt Styles gallery.

2 Click Metallic Scene in the 3-D area (first graphic in third row) to apply this style to the graphic (Figure 4–19).

BTW

Addressing Your Audiences
As you show your information graphics, resist the urge to turn to the screen and talk to the graphics instead of talking to your audience. If you turn toward the screen, your audience will get the impression that you are not prepared and must read information displayed on the graphics. Point with your hand nearest the screen and keep eye contact with your audience.

Figure 4–19

To Change the SmartArt Color

Adding more colors to the SmartArt graphic would enhance its visual appeal. The following steps change the SmartArt graphic color to a Colorful range.

1 With the SmartArt graphic still selected, click the Change Colors button (SmartArt Tools Design tab | SmartArt Styles group) to display the Change Colors gallery.

2 Click Colorful Range – Accent Colors 3 to 4 to apply this color variation to the graphic (Figure 4–20).

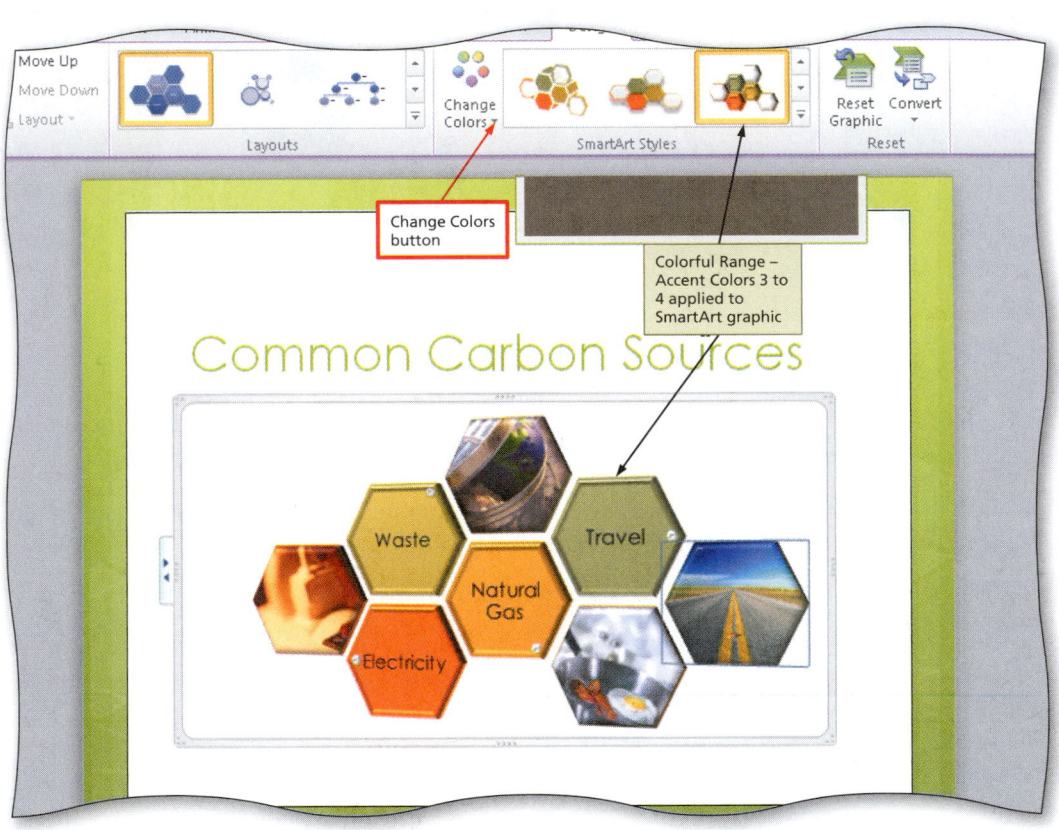

Figure 4–20

To Resize a SmartArt Graphic

Although white space on a slide generally is good to have, Slide 2 has sufficient space to allow the SmartArt graphic size to increase slightly. When you adjust the graphic's height and width, all the hexagons will enlarge proportionally. The following steps resize the SmartArt graphic.

1 With the SmartArt graphic still selected, drag one of the corner sizing handles diagonally outward, as shown in Figure 4–21.

2 Position the graphic so it is centered in the lower area of the slide (shown in Figure 4–22).

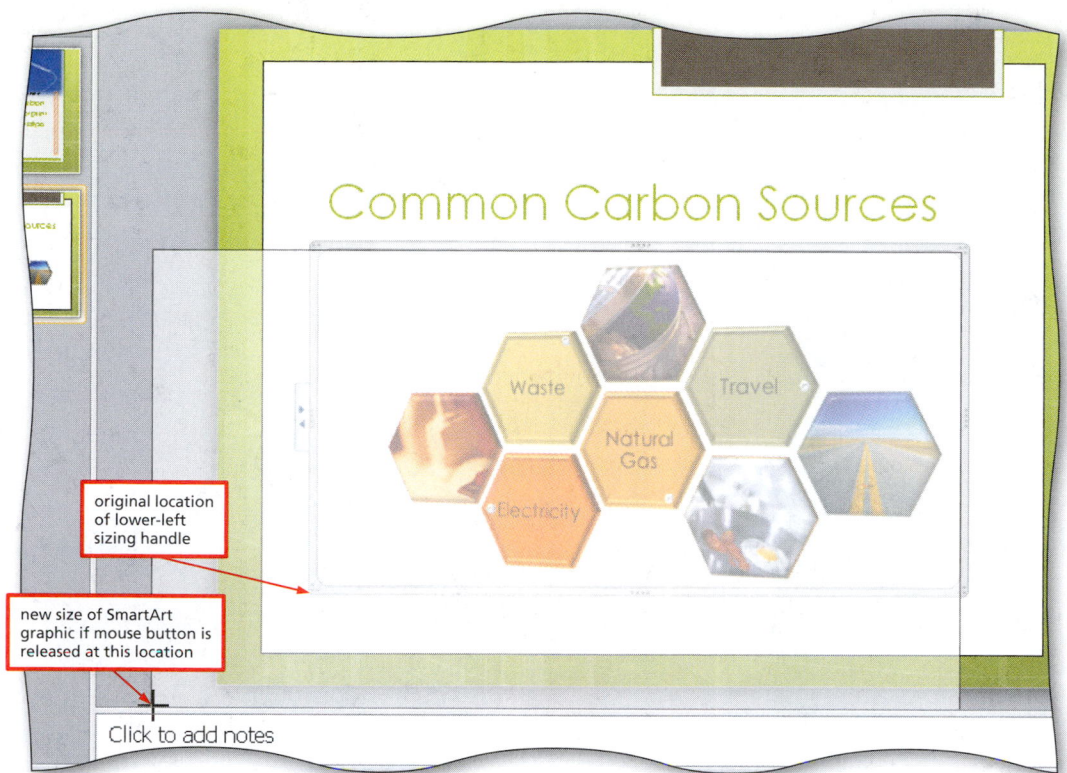

Figure 4–21

To Bold SmartArt Graphic Text

The text in the four hexagons can be bolded for readability. For consistency and efficiency, you can select all four hexagons and then change the text simultaneously. These hexagons are separate items in the SmartArt graphic, so you select these objects by selecting one hexagon, pressing and holding down the CTRL key, and then selecting the second, third, and fourth hexagons. The following steps simultaneously bold the hexagon text.

1
- Click the hexagon labeled Waste to select it. Press and hold down the CTRL key and then click the Electricity, Natural Gas, and Travel hexagons (Figure 4–22).

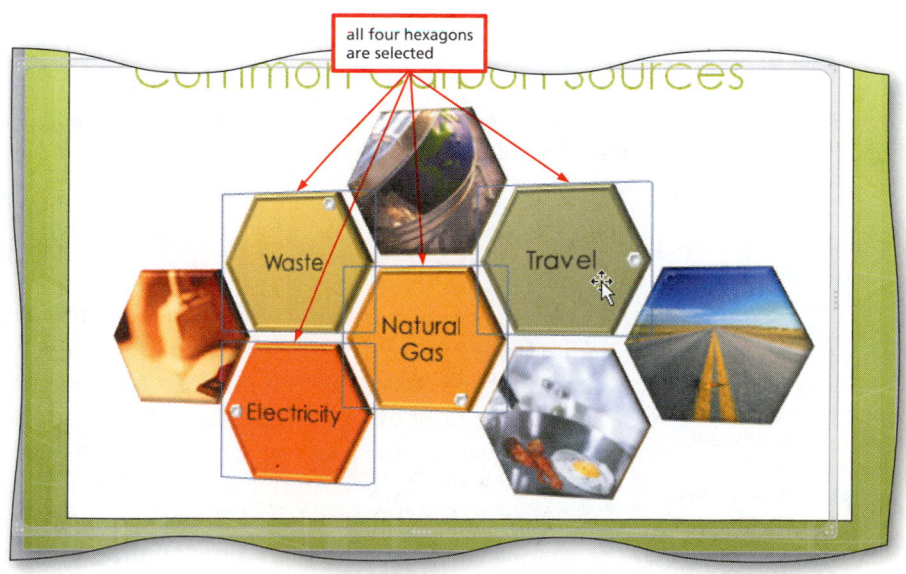

Figure 4–22

2

- Display the Home tab and then click the Bold button (Home tab | Font group) (Figure 4–23).

Q&A

Can I make other formatting changes to the graphics' text?

Yes. You can format the text by making such modifications as increasing the font size, changing the text color, and adding an underline and shadow.

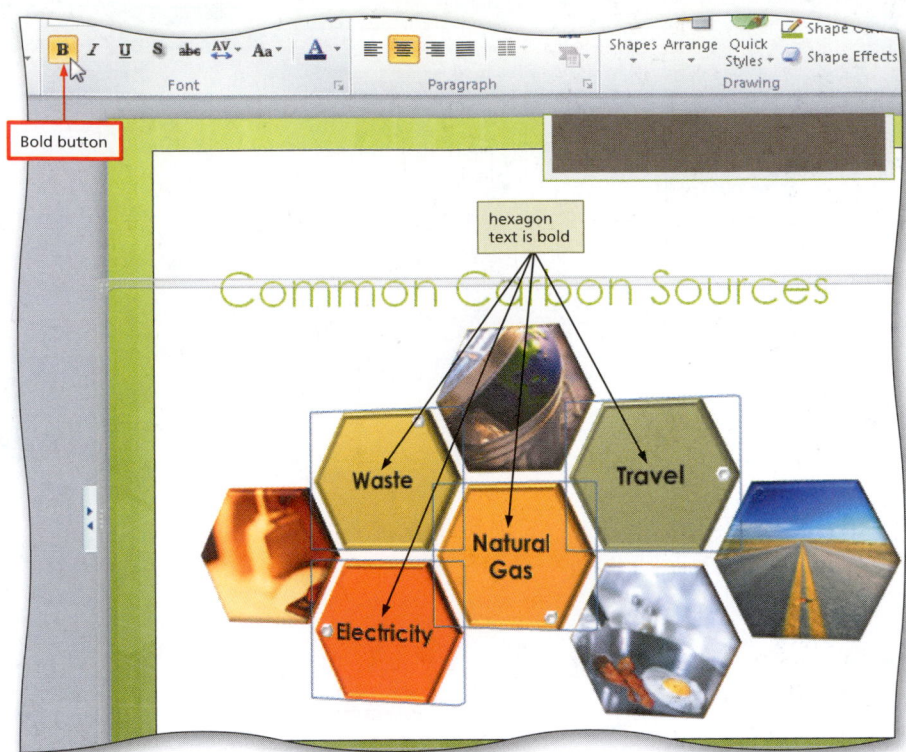

Figure 4–23

To Save an Existing Presentation with the Same File Name

You have made several modifications to the presentation since you last saved it. Thus, you should save it again. The following step saves the presentation again.

1 Click the Save button on the Quick Access Toolbar to overwrite the previously saved file.

Break Point: If you wish to take a break, this is a good place to do so. You can quit PowerPoint now. To resume at a later time, start PowerPoint, open the file called Carbon Footprint, and continue following the steps from this location forward.

BTW

Conducting Research Use reputable sources to obtain data for your charts. Do not assume that something published on the Internet is accurate and reliable. Instead, focus your research on relevant, unbiased sources. The reference librarian at your school can recommend specific databases and Web sites that will provide you with current, accurate data.

Adding a Chart to a Slide and Formatting

Carbon dioxide is a natural by-product of combustion, and administrators at Central City College have determined that four major elements contribute to the campus's carbon ("greenhouse gas") footprint. One-half of the greenhouse gas comes from using electricity, most of which is produced from hydropower dams, coal-burning generators, and nuclear reactors. Another large contributor is natural gas, which is used on campus to heat buildings. Transportation to and from campus adds to carbon dioxide production because most of Central City College's students and staff commute to campus using cars or buses. A fourth carbon footprint contributor is waste; microscopic bacteria eat trash in landfills and convert this garbage into carbon dioxide and methane. The chart on Slide 3, shown in Figure 4–1c on page PPT 203, shows the proportion of these four greenhouse gas sources on campus.

Microsoft Excel and Microsoft Graph

PowerPoint uses one of two programs to develop a chart. It opens Microsoft Excel if that software is installed on your system. If Excel is not installed, PowerPoint opens Microsoft Graph and displays a chart with its associated data in a table called a datasheet. Microsoft Graph does not have the advanced features found in Excel. In this chapter, the assumption is made that Excel has been installed. When you start to create a chart, Excel opens and displays a chart in the PowerPoint slide. The default chart type is a **Clustered Column chart**. The Clustered Column chart is appropriate when comparing two or more items in specified intervals, such as comparing how inflation has risen during the past 10 years. Other popular chart types are line, bar, and pie, the latter of which you will use in Slide 3.

The figures for the chart are entered in a corresponding **Microsoft Excel worksheet**, which is a rectangular grid containing vertical columns and horizontal rows. Column letters display above the grid to identify particular **columns**, and row numbers display on the left side of the grid to identify particular **rows**. **Cells** are the intersections of rows and columns, and they are the locations for the chart data and text labels. For example, cell A1 is the intersection of column A and row 1. Numeric and text data are entered in the **active cell**, which is the one cell surrounded by a heavy border. You will replace the sample data in the worksheet by typing entries in the cells, but you also can import data from a text file, import an Excel worksheet or chart, or paste data obtained from another program. Once you have entered the data, you can modify the appearance of the chart using menus and commands.

In the following pages, you will perform these tasks:

1. Insert a chart and then replace the sample data.
2. Apply a chart style.
3. Change the line and shape outline weights.
4. Change the chart layout.
5. Resize the chart and then change the title and legend font size.
6. Separate a pie slice.
7. Rotate the chart.

BTW

Giving Credit to Your Sources
If you insert a chart that was created by someone else, you must give credit to this person and might need to ask permission to reproduce this graphic. This attribution informs your audience that you did not conduct your own research to construct this chart and that you are relying upon the expertise of another person.

Plan Ahead

Choose an appropriate chart style.
General adult audiences are familiar with bar and pie charts, so those chart types are good choices. Specialized audiences, such as engineers and architects, are comfortable reading scatter and bubble charts.

Common chart types and their purposes are as follows:

- Column — Vertical bars compare values over a period of time.

- Bar — Horizontal bars compare two or more values to show how the proportions relate to each other.

- Line — A line or lines show trends, increases and decreases, levels, and costs during a continuous period of time.

- Pie — A pie chart divides a single total into parts to illustrate how the segments differ from each other and the whole.

- Scatter — A scattterplot displays the effect on one variable when another variable changes.

In general, three-dimensional charts are more difficult to comprehend than two-dimensional charts. The added design elements in a three-dimensional chart add clutter and take up space. Also, legends help keep the chart clean, so use them prominently on the slide.

To Insert a Chart

The next step in developing the presentation is to insert a chart. The following steps insert a chart with sample data into Slide 3.

1

• Click the New Slide button to add Slide 3 to the presentation (Figure 4–24).

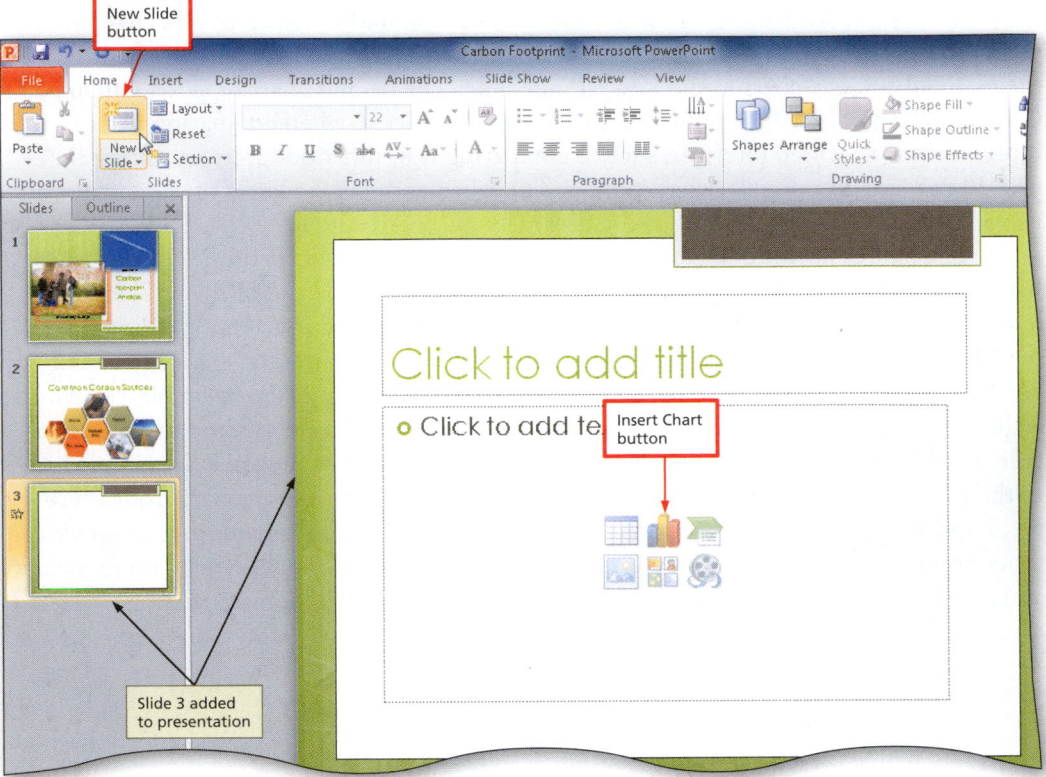

Figure 4–24

2

• Click the Insert Chart button in the content placeholder to display the Insert Chart dialog box.

• Scroll down and then click the Pie in 3-D chart button in the Pie area to select that chart style (Figure 4–25).

 Can I change the chart style after I have inserted a chart?

Yes. Click the Change Chart Type button in the Type group on the SmartArt Tools Design tab to display the Change Chart Type dialog box and then make another selection.

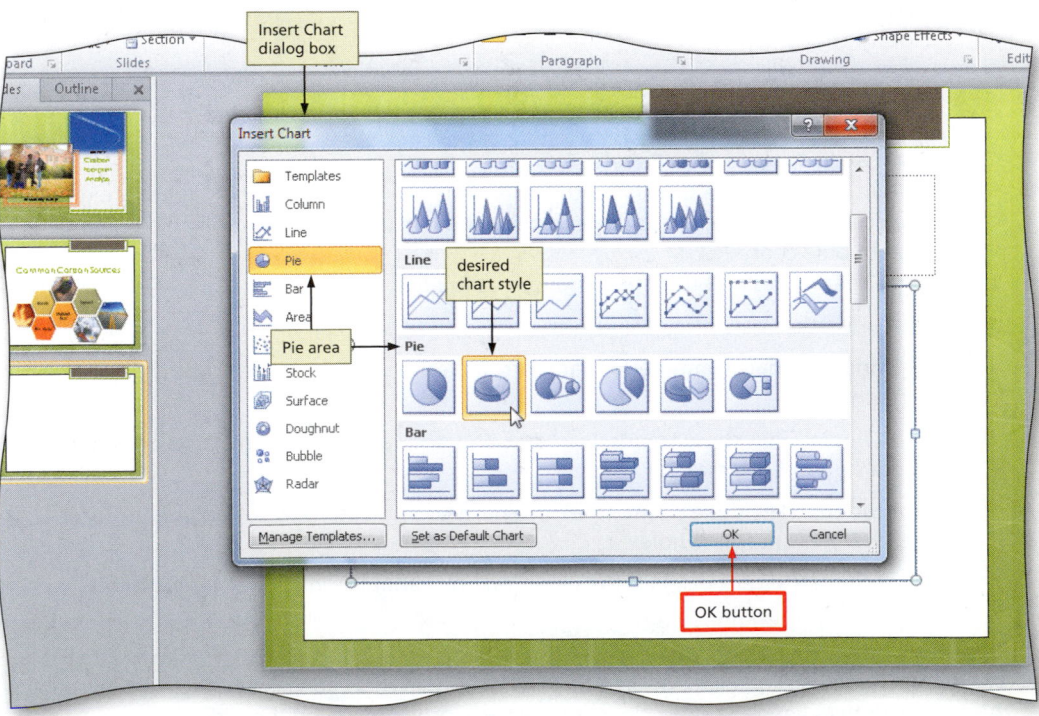

Figure 4–25

3
- Click the OK button (Insert Chart dialog box) to start the Microsoft Excel program and open a worksheet tiled on the right side of your Carbon Footprint presentation (Figure 4–26).

Q&A

What do the numbers in the worksheet and the chart represent?

Excel places sample data in the worksheet and charts the sample data in the default chart type.

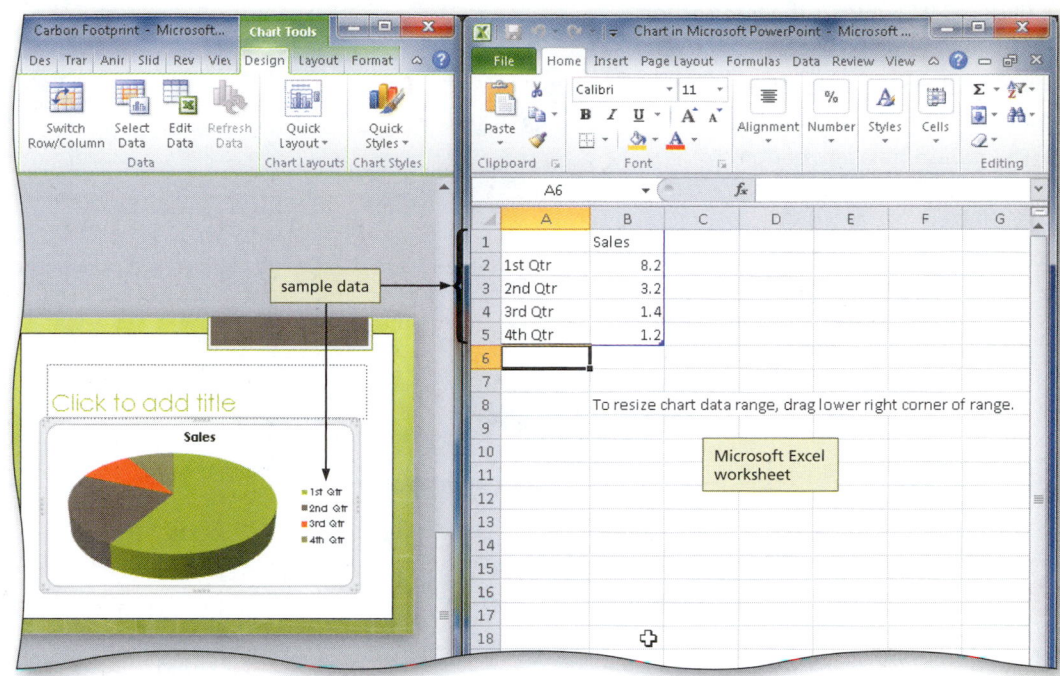

Figure 4–26

<table>
<tr><td colspan="2">**Other Ways**</td></tr>
<tr><td>1.</td><td>Click Pie button (Insert tab | Chart group)</td></tr>
</table>

Obtain information for the graphic from credible sources.

At times, you are familiar with the data for your chart or table because you have conducted in-the-field, or primary, research by interviewing experts or taking measurements. Other times, however, you have gathered the data from secondary sources, such as magazine articles, newspaper articles, or Web sites. General circulation magazines and newspapers, such as *Newsweek* and the *Wall Street Journal*, use experienced journalists and editors to verify their information. Also, online databases, such as EBSCOhost, OCLC FirstSearch, LexisNexis Academic, and NewsBank Info Web contain articles from credible sources.

On the other hand, some sources have particular biases and present information that supports their causes. Political, religious, and social publications and Web sites often are designed for specific audiences who share a common point of view. You should, therefore, recognize that data from these sources can be skewed.

If you did not conduct the research yourself, you should give credit to the source of your information. You are acknowledging that someone else provided the data and giving your audience the opportunity to obtain the same materials you used. Type the source at the bottom of your chart or table, especially if you are distributing handouts of your slides. At the very least, state the source during the body of your speech.

Plan Ahead

To Replace Sample Data

The next step in creating the chart is to replace the sample data, which will redraw the chart. The sample data is displayed in two columns and five rows. The first row and left column contain text labels and will be used to create the chart title and legend. A **legend** is a box that identifies each slice of the pie chart and coordinates with the colors assigned to the slice categories. The other cells contain numbers that are used to determine the size of the pie slices. The following steps replace the sample data in the worksheet.

1

- Click cell B1, which is the intersection of column B and row 1, to select it.

Q&A Why did my mouse pointer change shape?

The mouse pointer changes to a block plus sign to indicate a cell is selected.

- Type `Central City College Greenhouse Gas Sources` in cell B1 to replace the sample chart title (Figure 4–27).

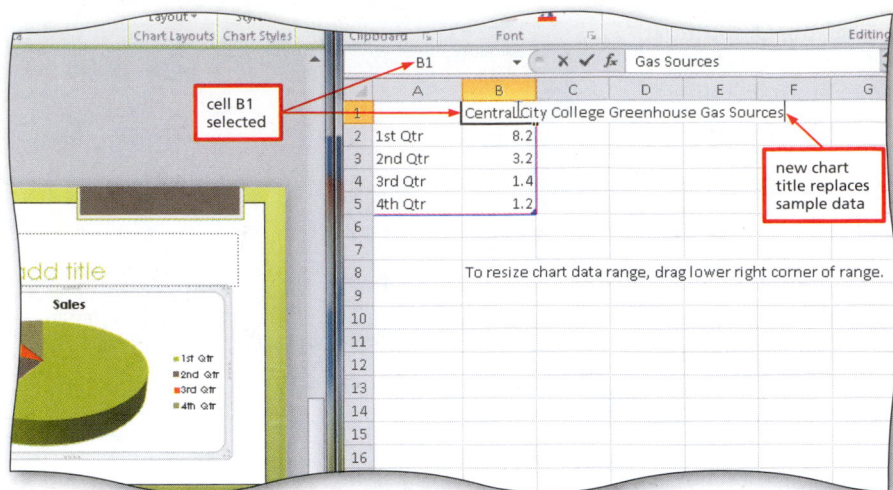

Figure 4–27

2

- Click cell A2 to select that cell.

- Type `Electricity` in cell A2 (Figure 4–28).

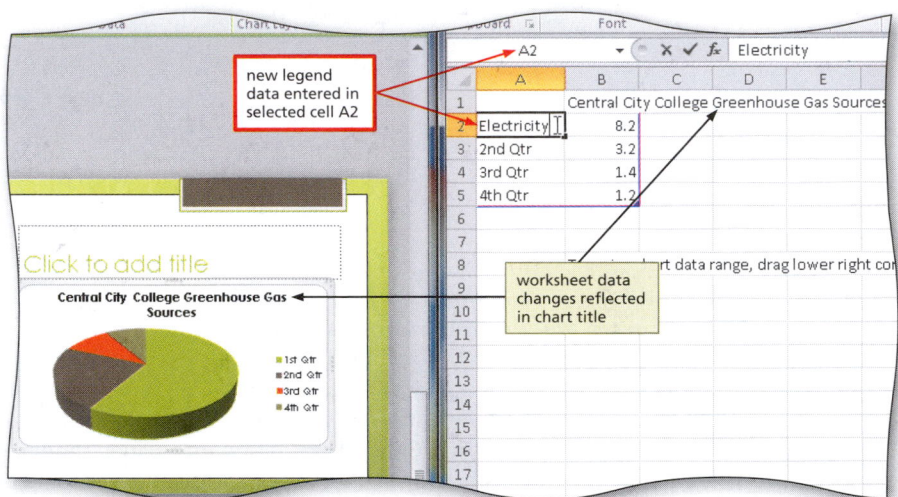

Figure 4–28

3

- Press the DOWN ARROW key to move the mouse pointer to cell A3.

- Type `Natural Gas` in cell A3 and then press the DOWN ARROW key to move the mouse pointer to cell A4.

4

- Type `Travel` in cell A4 and then press the DOWN ARROW key.

- Type `Waste` in cell A5 (Figure 4–29).

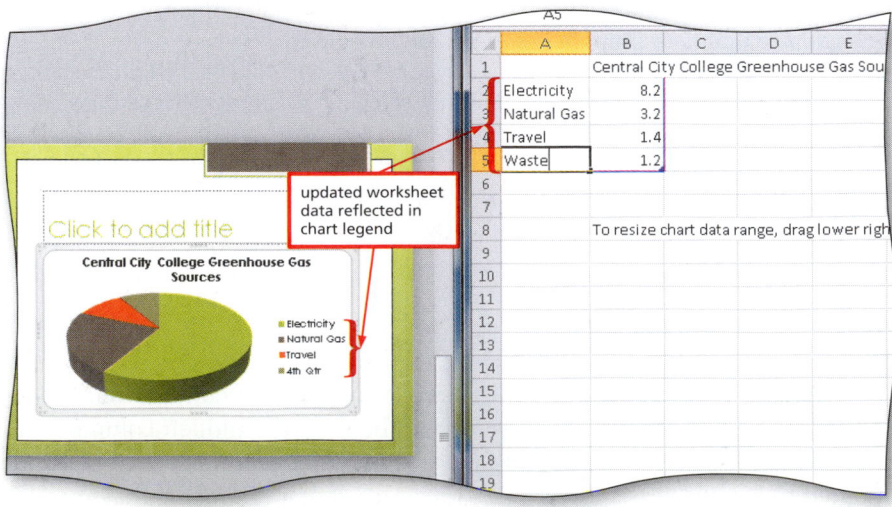

Figure 4–29

5

• Click cell B2, type 50 in that cell, and then press the DOWN ARROW key to move the mouse pointer to cell B3.

• Type 30 in cell B3 and then press the DOWN ARROW key.

• Type 13 in cell B4 and then press the DOWN ARROW key.

• Type 7 in cell B5. Press the ENTER key (Figure 4–30).

Q&A Why do the slices in the PowerPoint pie chart change locations?

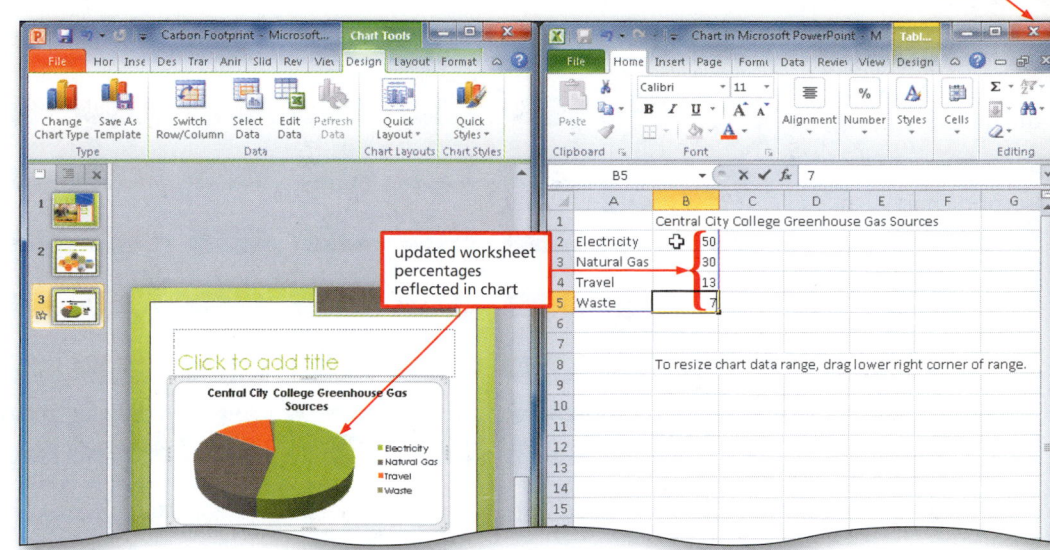

Figure 4–30

As you enter data in the Excel worksheet, the chart slices rotate to reflect these new figures.

6

• Close Excel by clicking its Close button.

Q&A Can I open the Excel spreadsheet once it has been closed?

Yes. Click the chart to select it and then click the Edit Data button (Chart Tools Design tab | Data group).

To Apply a Chart Style

Each chart type has a variety of styles that can change the look of the chart. If desired, you can change the chart from two dimensions to three dimensions, add borders, and vary the colors of the slices, lines, and bars. When you inserted the Pie in 3-D chart, a style was applied automatically. Thumbnails of this style and others are displayed in the Chart Styles gallery. The following steps apply a chart style to the Slide 3 pie chart.

1

• If the entire pie chart area is not selected, click a white space near the pie chart and then click the Chart Tools Design tab to display the Chart Tools Design Ribbon (Figure 4–31).

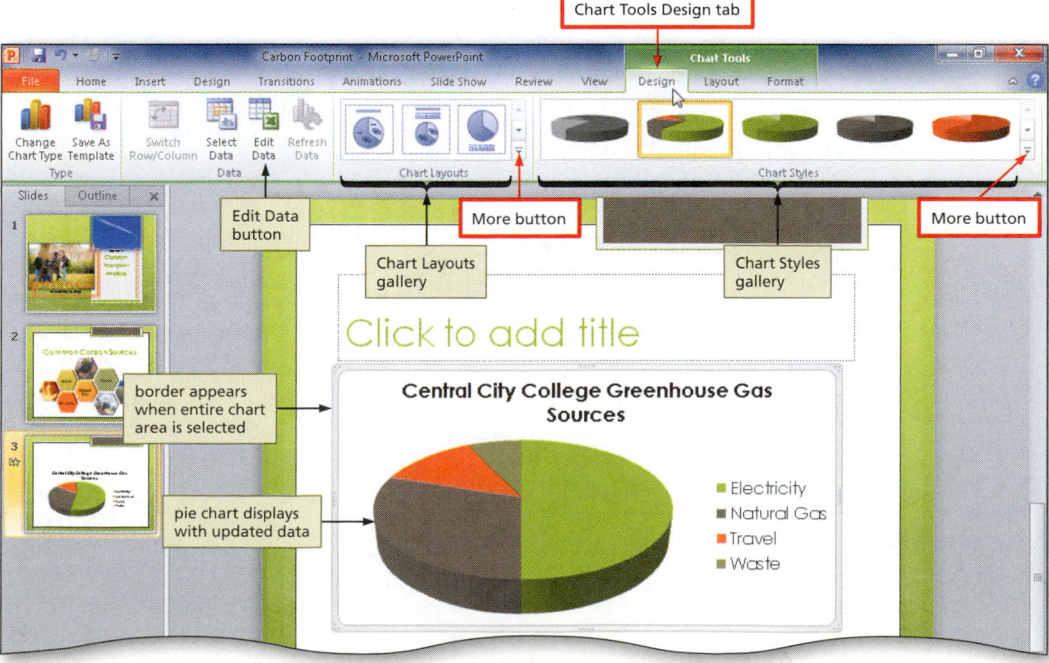

Figure 4–31

• Click the More button in the Chart Styles gallery to expand the gallery.

• Point to Style 10 (second chart in second row) (Figure 4–32).

Q&A Does the Chart Styles gallery have a live preview feature?

This feature is not available.

Figure 4–32

• Click Style 10 in the Chart Styles gallery to apply the selected style to the chart (Figure 4–33).

Q&A Can I change the chart type?

Yes. Click the Change Chart Type button (Chart Tools Design tab | Type group) and then select a different type.

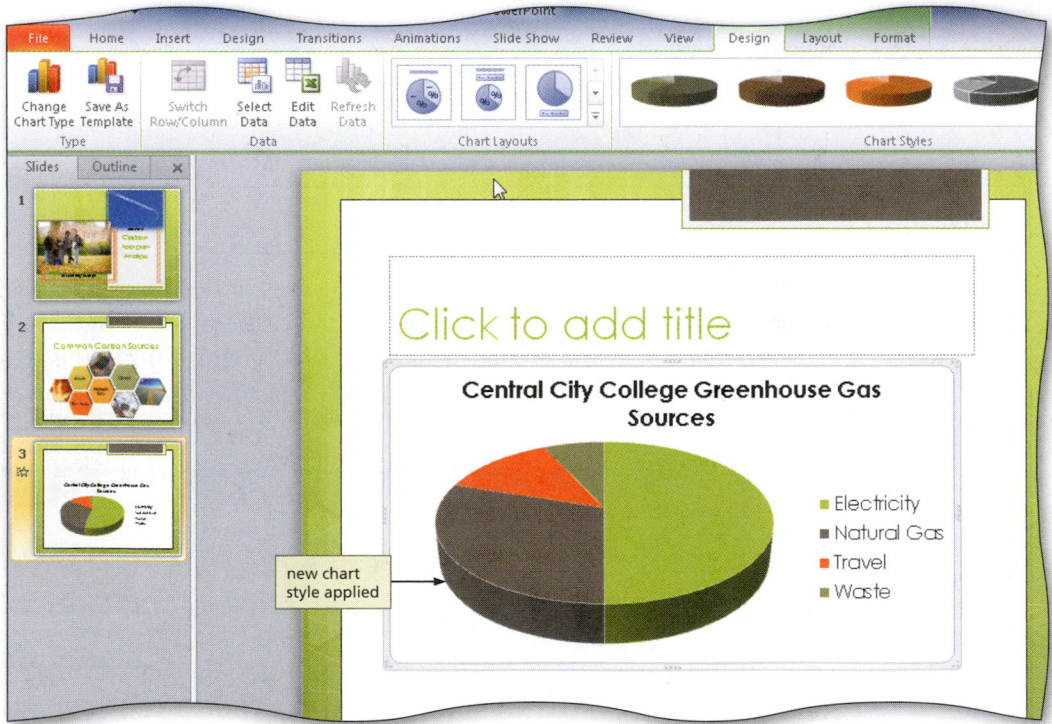

Figure 4–33

To Change the Shape Outline Weight

Chart Style 10 has thin white outlines around each pie slice and around each color square in the legend. You can change the weight of these lines to accentuate each slice. The following steps change the outline weight.

1

- Click the Chart Tools Format tab to display the Chart Tools Format Ribbon.

- Click the center of the pie chart to select it and display the sizing handles around each slice.

- Click the Shape Outline button arrow (Chart Tools Format tab | Shape Styles group) to display the Shape Outline gallery.

- Point to Weight in the Shape Outline gallery to display the Weight list (Figure 4–34).

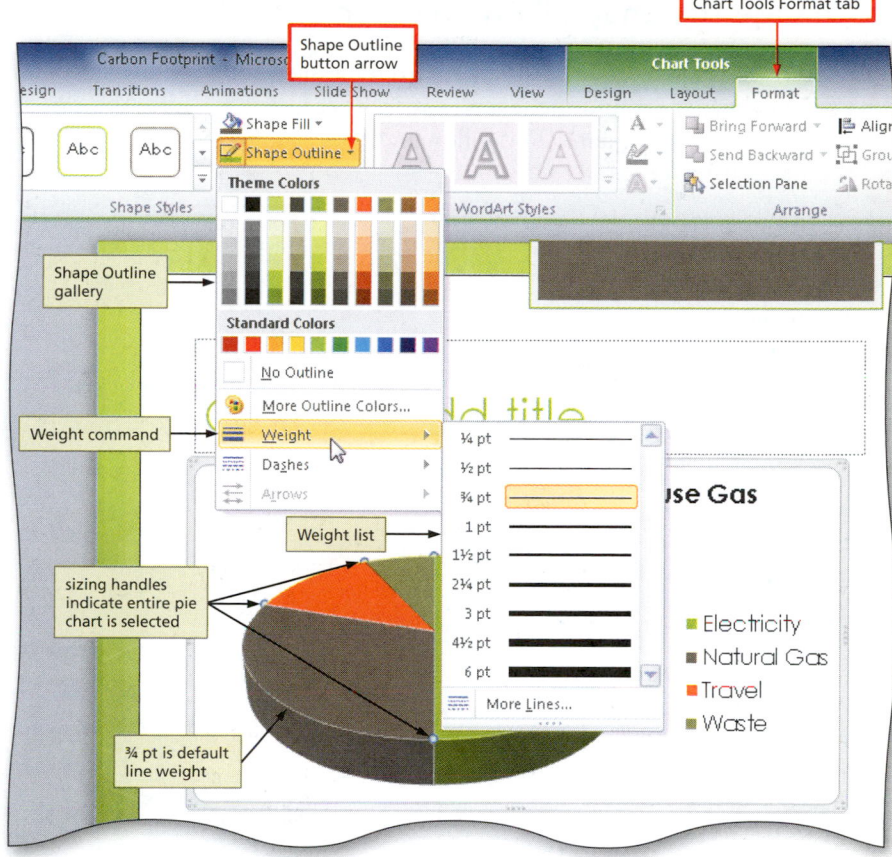

Figure 4–34

2

- Point to 4½ pt to display a live preview of this outline line weight (Figure 4–35).

Experiment

- Point to various weights on the submenu and watch the border weights on the pie slices change.

3

- Click 4½ pt to increase the border around each slice to that width.

Q&A

Can I add a border to other chart elements?

Yes. Select the chart, click the Chart Tools Format tab, and then click the Chart Elements button arrow (Chart Tools Format tab | Current Selection area) to display a list of chart elements that you can format. Click the desired element, click the Format Selection button (Chart Tools Format Tab | Current Selection area), click Border Styles in the dialog box, and then select the formatting changes you desire. You also can change the border color and add effects.

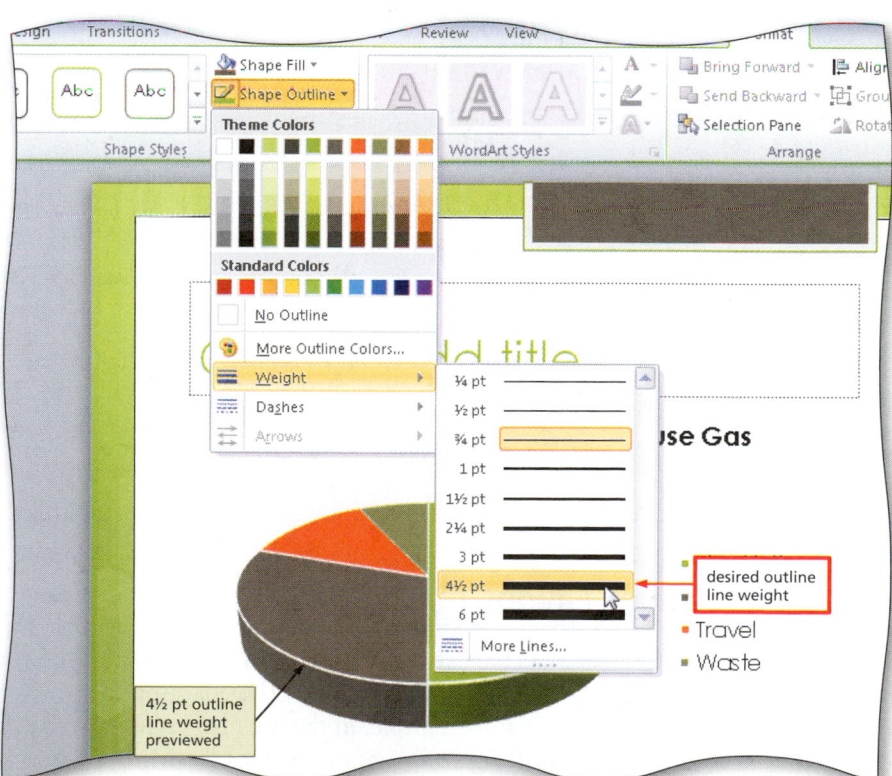

Figure 4–35

To Change the Shape Outline Color

Style 10 has white outlines around each pie slice and around each color square in the legend. At this point, you can't see the border around the legend squares because it is white. You can change this color to add contrast to each slice and legend color square. The following steps change the border color.

- Click the Shape Outline button arrow (Chart Tools Format tab | Shape Styles group) and then point to Orange in the Standard Colors area to display a live preview of that border color on the pie slice shapes and legend squares.

 **Experiment**

- Point to various colors in the Shape Outline gallery and watch the border colors on the pie slices change.

- Click Orange to add orange borders around each slice and also around the color squares in the legend (Figure 4–36).

Q&A

Can I add effects to the borders and other chart elements?

Yes. Each chart element has predetermined types of effects that you can apply, so preset, reflection, and bevel effects may not be available for the element you want to manipulate. Select the desired element, click the Shape Effects button (Chart Tools Format tab | Shape Styles group), click an available effect on the menu, and then click the desired effect in the gallery.

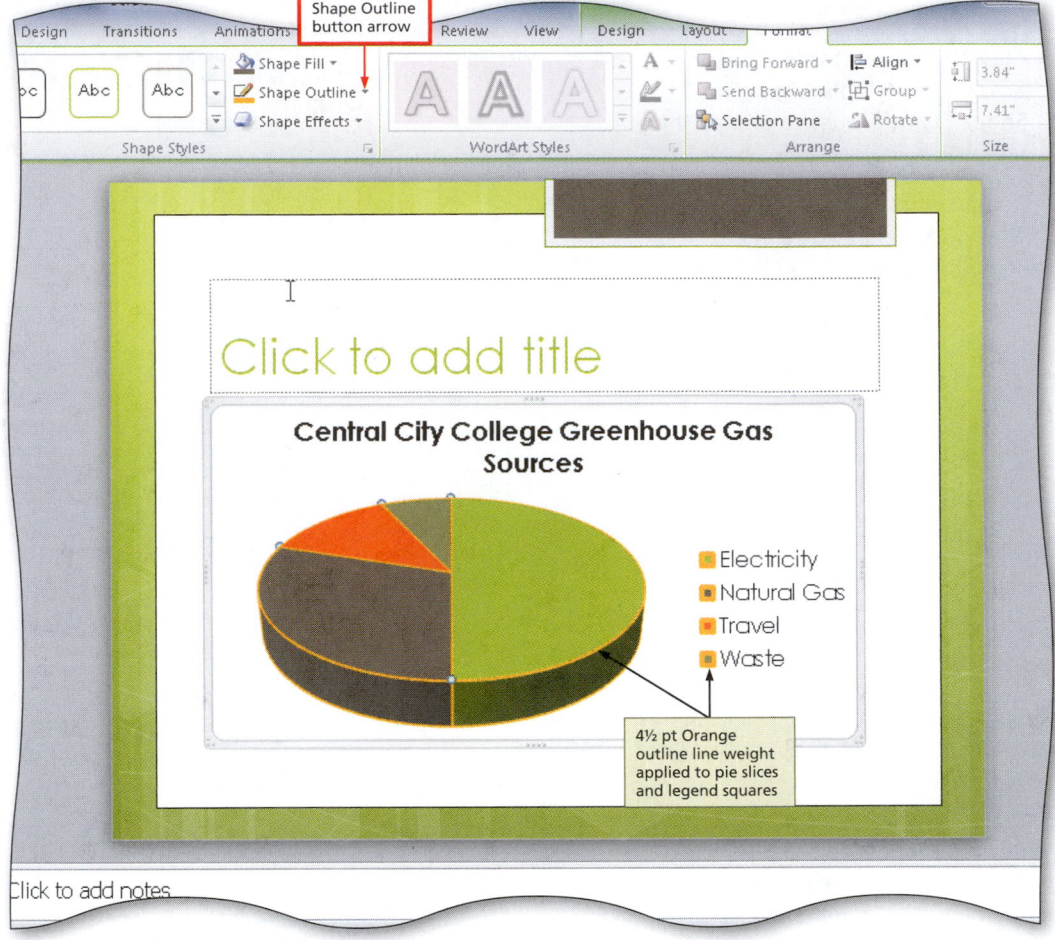

Figure 4–36

To Change a Chart Layout

Once you have selected a chart style, you can modify the look of the chart elements by changing its layout. The various layouts move the legend above or below the chart, or they move some or all of the legend data directly onto the individual chart pieces. For example, in the pie chart type, seven different layouts display only percentages on the pie slices, only the identifying information, such as the word, Electricity, or combinations of this data. If the chart layout displays a title that provides sufficient information to describe the chart's purpose, you may want to delete the slide title text placeholder. The following steps apply a chart layout with a title, legend, and percentages to the Slide 3 pie chart and then delete the title text placeholder.

1

- With the chart still selected, click the Chart Tools Design tab to display the Chart Tools Design Ribbon and then click the More button in the Chart Layouts gallery to expand the gallery.

- Point to Layout 2 (second chart in first row) (Figure 4–37).

Q&A

Does the Chart Layouts gallery have a live preview feature?

This feature is not available.

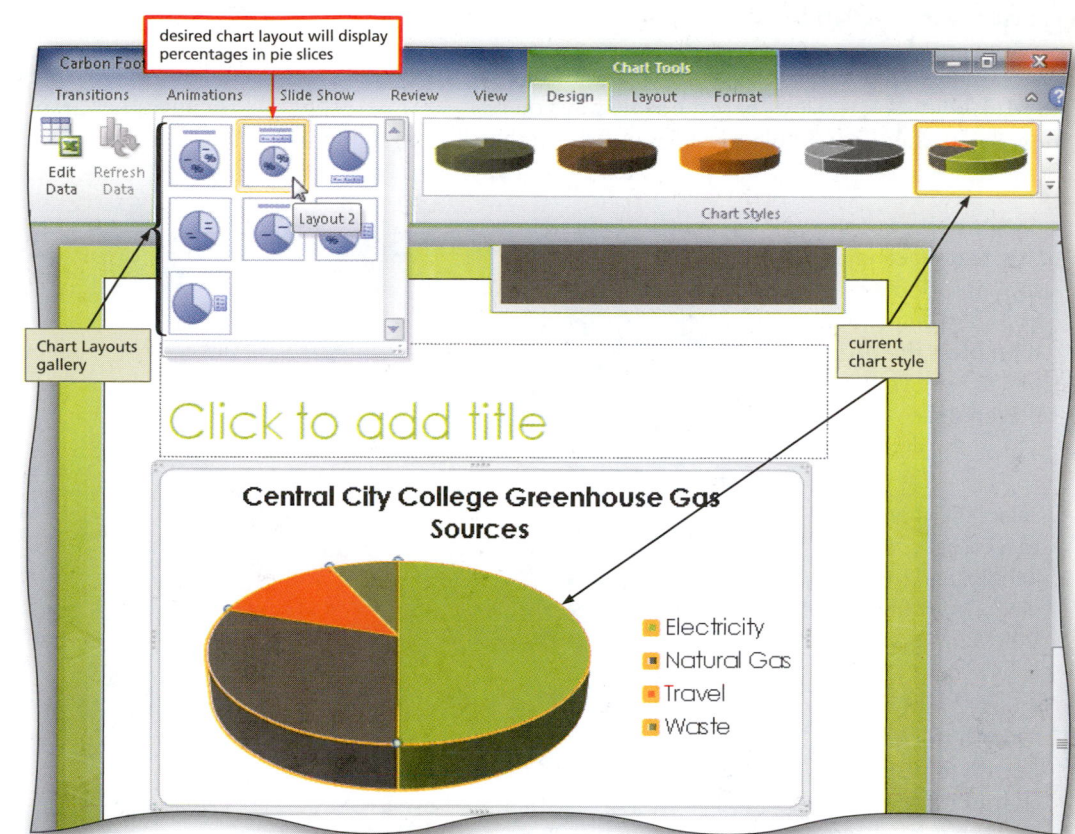

Figure 4–37

2

- Click Layout 2 in the Chart Layouts gallery to apply the selected layout to the chart (Figure 4–38).

Q&A

Can I change the chart layout?

Because a live preview is not available, you may want to sample the various layouts to evaluate their effectiveness. To change these layouts, repeat Steps 1 and 2 with different layouts.

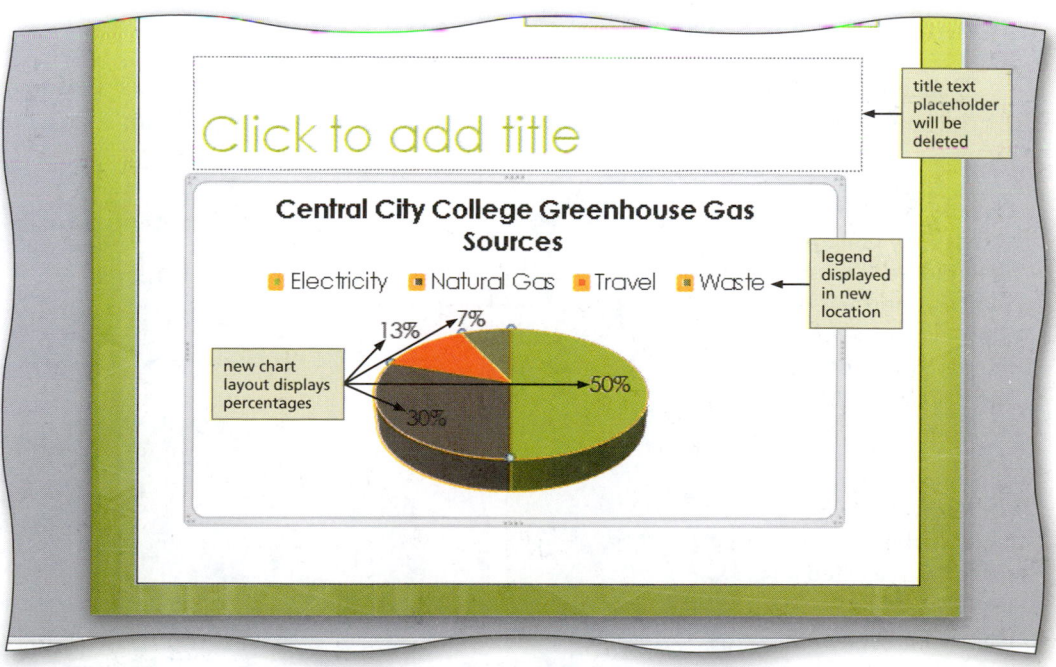

Figure 4–38

To Resize a Chart

Removing the title text placeholder increases the white space on the slide, so you are able to enlarge the chart and aid readability. You resize a chart the same way you resize a SmartArt graphic or any other graphical object. The following steps delete the title text placeholder and resize the chart to fill Slide 3.

1
• Click a border of the title text placeholder so that it displays as a solid line and then press the DELETE key to remove the placeholder.

2
• Select the chart, point to a corner sizing handle, and then drag diagonally outward, as shown in Figure 4–39.

3
• Release the mouse button to resize the chart. Position the chart so it is centered in the slide.

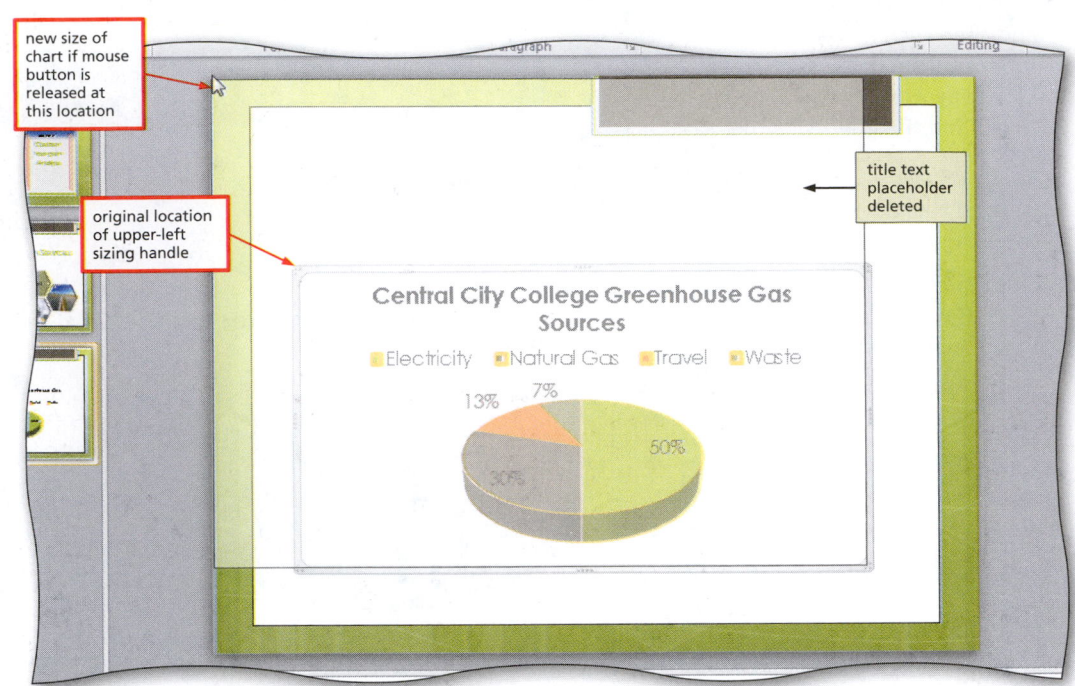

Figure 4–39

To Change the Title and Legend Font Size

Depending upon the complexity of the chart and the overall slide, you may want to increase the font size of the chart title and legend to increase readability. The following steps change the font size of both of these chart elements.

1
• Click the chart title, Central City College Greenhouse Gas Sources, and then triple-click to select the paragraph of text and display the Mini toolbar.

• Click the Increase Font Size button to increase the font size of the selected text to 32 point (Figure 4–40).

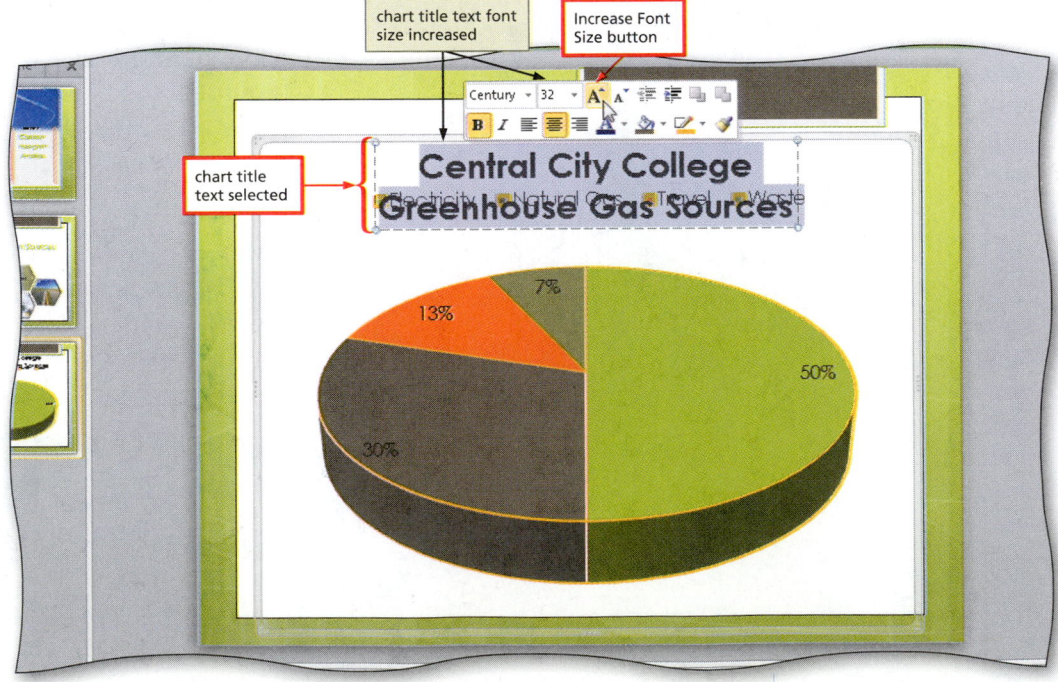

Figure 4–40

2

- Click an area of the chart other than the title to position the new title text.

- Right-click the legend in the chart to display the Mini toolbar and a legends shortcut menu.

- Click the Increase Font Size button on the Mini toolbar to increase the font size of the legend text to 20 point (Figure 4–41).

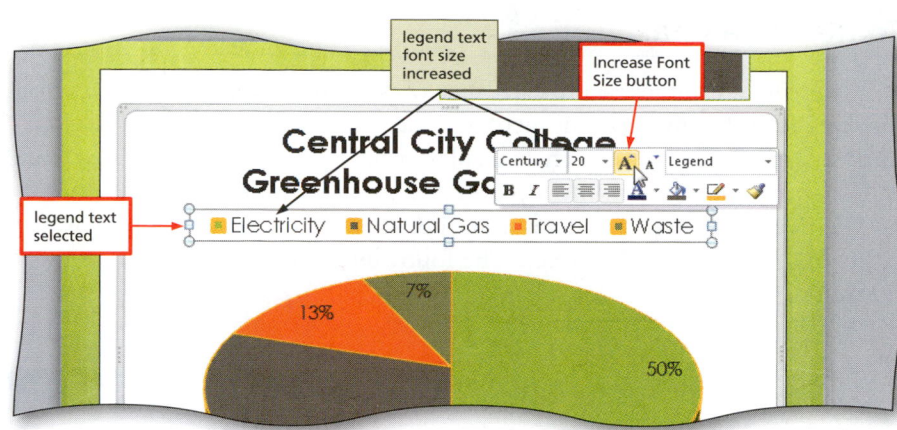

Figure 4–41

To Separate a Pie Slice

At times, you may desire to draw the viewers' attention to a particular area of the pie chart. To add this emphasis, you can separate, or explode, one or more slices. For example, you can separate the orange Travel slice of the chart to stress that Central City College students and staff contribute significantly to greenhouse gas production when traveling to and from campus. The following steps separate a chart slice.

1

- Click the orange Travel slice of the pie chart to select it.

- Click and hold down the mouse button and then drag the Travel slice diagonally toward the word, Electricity (Figure 4–42).

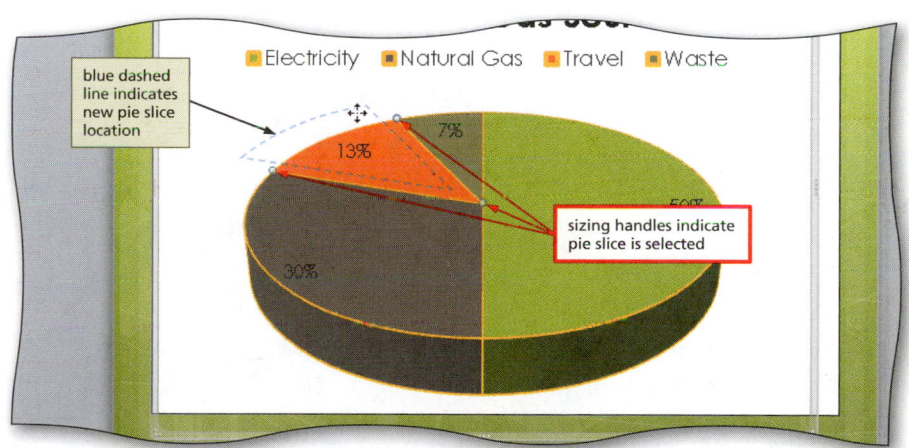

Figure 4–42

2

- Release the mouse button to position the slice in a new location on the slide (Figure 4–43).

Q&A Can I change the size of chart objects?

Charts are composed of several elements, including the horizontal and vertical axes, plot area, chart area, and legend. When you select one of these objects, you then can point to a sizing handle and drag outward or inward to adjust the object's size.

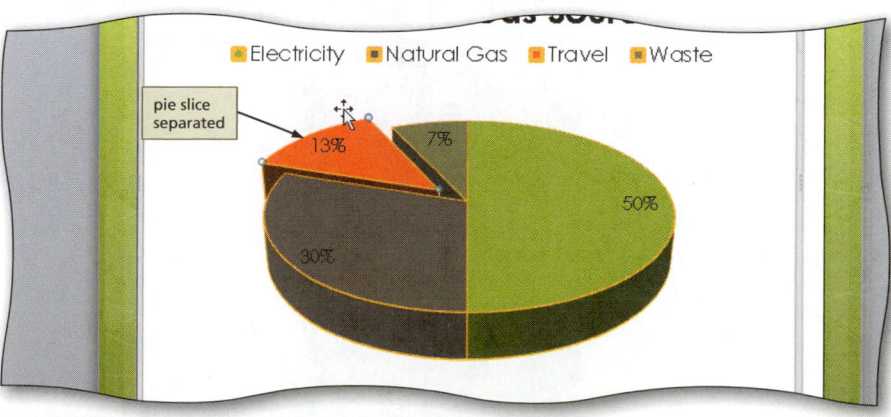

Figure 4–43

To Rotate a Chart

Excel determines where each slice of pie is positioned in the chart. You may desire to have a specific slice display in a different location, such as at the top or bottom of the circle. You can rotate the entire chart clockwise until a particular part of the chart displays where you desire. A circle's circumference is 360 degrees, so if you want to move a slice from the top of the chart to the bottom, you would rotate it halfway around the circle, or 180 degrees. Similarly, if you a want a slice to move one-quarter of the way around the slide, you would rotate it either 90 degrees or 270 degrees. The following steps rotate the chart so that the orange Travel slice displays at the bottom of the chart.

- With the orange Travel slice of the pie chart still selected, click the Chart Tools Format tab to display the Chart Tools Format Ribbon.

- Click the Format Selection button (Chart Tools Format tab | Current Selection group) to display the Format Data Point dialog box (Figure 4–44).

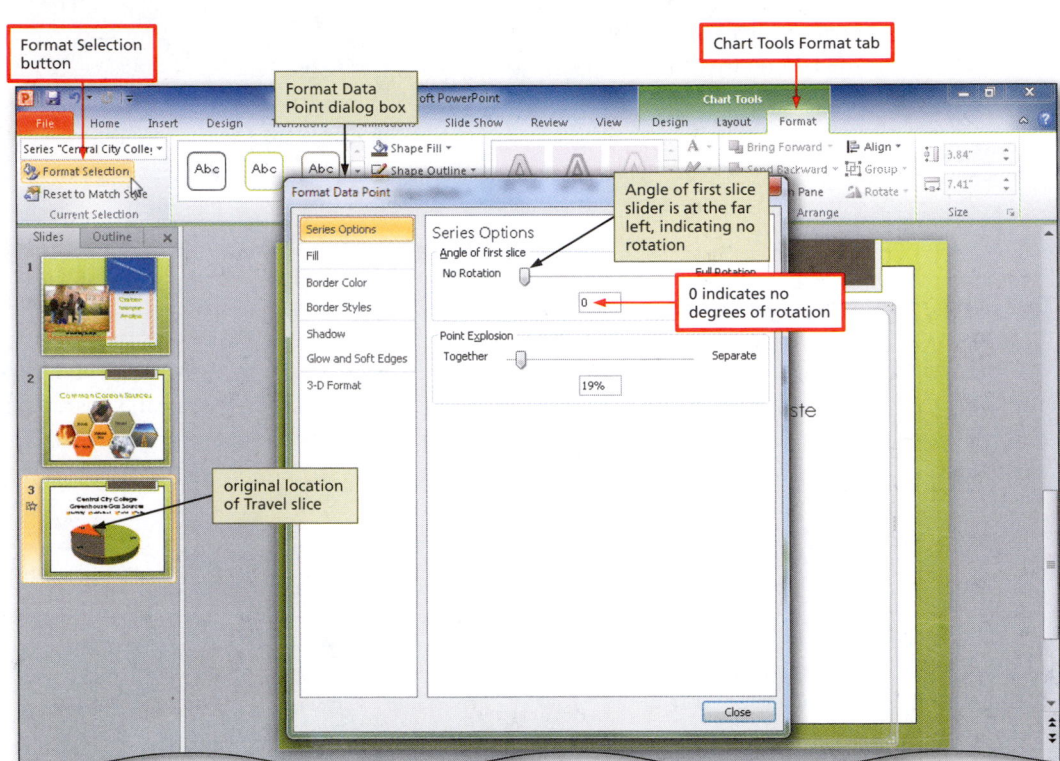

Figure 4–44

- Click the 'Angle of first slice' text box, delete the text, and then type 235 in the box to specify that the Travel slice rotates 235 degrees to the right (Figure 4–45).

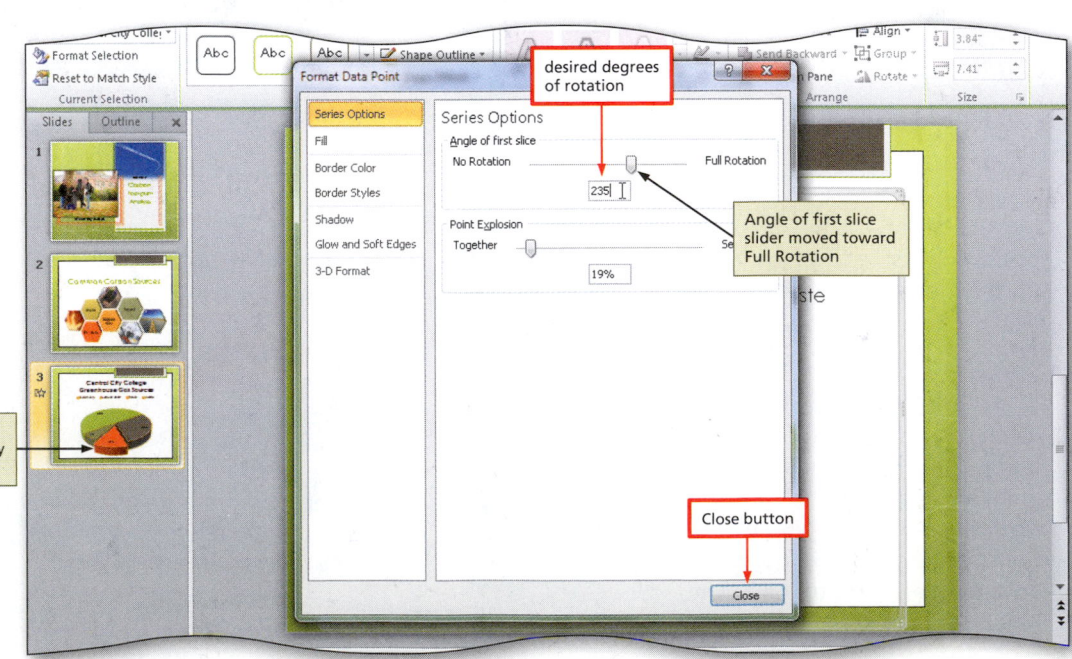

Figure 4–45

3
● Click the Close button to close the dialog box and rotate the chart (Figure 4–46).

Can I specify a precise position where the chart will display on the slide?

Yes. Right-click the edge of the chart, click Format Chart Area on the shortcut menu, click Position in the left pane (Format Chart Area dialog box), and then enter measurements in the Horizontal and Vertical text boxes and specify whether these distances are from the Top Left Corner or the Center of the slide.

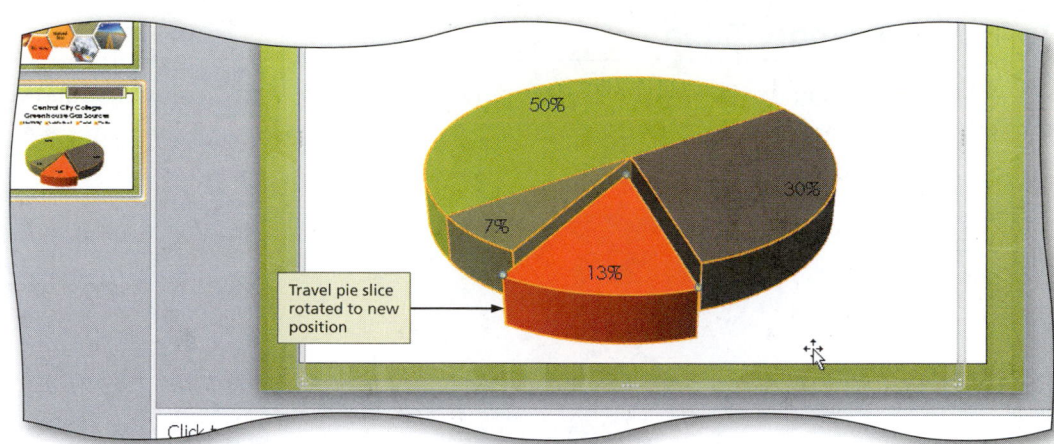

Figure 4–46

Break Point: If you wish to take a break, this is a good place to do so. Be sure to save the Carbon Footprint file again and then you can quit PowerPoint. To resume at a later time, start PowerPoint, open the file called Carbon Footprint, and continue following the steps from this location forward.

Adding a Table to a Slide and Formatting

One effective method of organizing information on a slide is to use a **table**, which is a grid consisting of rows and columns. You can enhance a table with formatting, including adding colors, lines, and backgrounds, and changing fonts.

In the following pages, you will perform these tasks:

1. Insert a table and then enter data and symbols.
2. Apply a table style.
3. Add borders and an effect.
4. Resize the table.
5. Add an image.
6. Merge cells and then display text in the cell vertically.
7. Align text in cells.
8. Format table data.

Tables

The table on Slide 4 (shown in Figure 4–1d on page PPT 203) contains information about the five major methods students and staff use to travel to campus. This data is listed in four columns and six rows. The intersections of these rows and columns are **cells**.

To begin developing this table, you first must create an empty table and insert it into the slide. You must specify the table's **dimension**, which is the total number of rows and columns. This table will have a 4 × 6 dimension; the first number indicates the number of columns, and the second specifies the number of rows. You will fill the cells with data pertaining to transportation to campus. Then you will format the table using a table style.

BTW

Entering Table Data
The table you create on Slide 4 has four columns and six rows. Many times, however, you may need to create much larger tables and then enter data into many cells. In these cases, experienced PowerPoint designers recommend clearing all formatting from the table so that you can concentrate on the numbers and letters and not be distracted by the colors and borders. To clear formatting, click the Clear Table command at the bottom of the Table Styles gallery (Table Tools Design tab | Table Styles group). Then, add a table style once you have verified that all table data is correct.

To Insert an Empty Table

The next step in developing the presentation is to insert an empty table. The following steps insert a table with four columns and six rows into Slide 4.

- Add a new slide to the presentation (Figure 4–47).

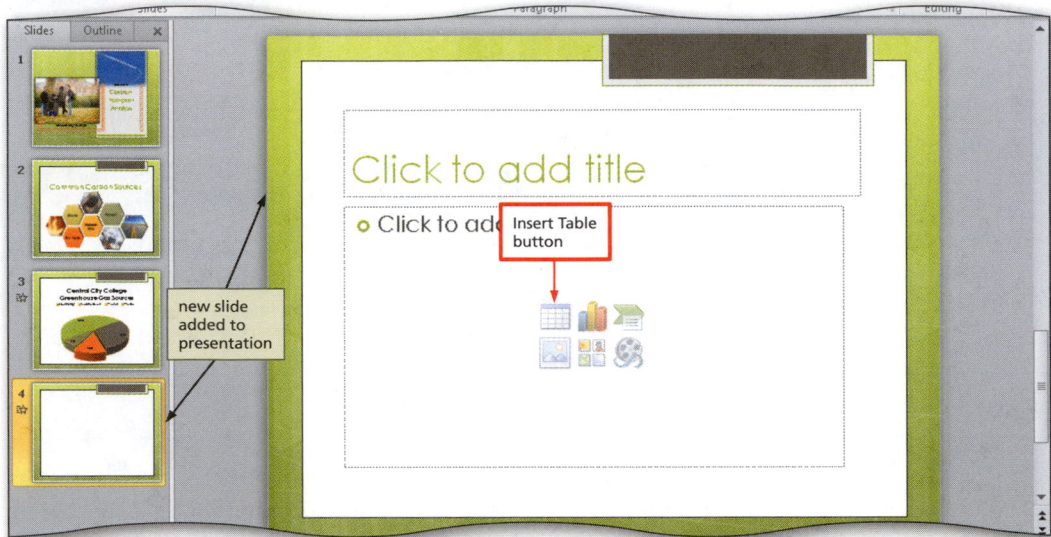

Figure 4–47

- Click the Insert Table button in the content placeholder to display the Insert Table dialog box.

- Click the down arrow to the right of the 'Number of columns' text box one time so that the number 4 appears in the box.

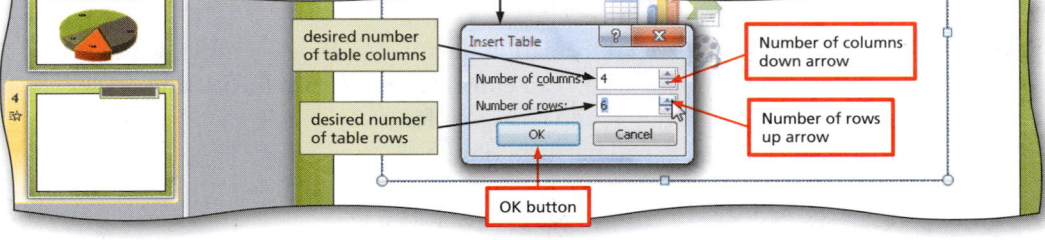

Figure 4–48

- Click the up arrow to the right of the 'Number of rows' text box four times so that the number 6 appears in the box (Figure 4–48).

- Click the OK button (Insert Table dialog box) to insert the table into Slide 4 (Figure 4–49).

Other Ways

1. Click Table on Insert tab, drag to select columns and rows, press ENTER

Figure 4–49

To Enter Data in a Table

The Slide 4 table title will display vertically in the first column. The three columns to the right of this title will contain data with symbols representing the type of travel, words describing this travel, and the percent of students and staff using these modes of travel. The next step is to enter data in the cells of the empty table. To place data in a cell, you click the cell and then type text. The following steps enter the data in the table.

 1

- Click the second cell in the third column to place the insertion point in this cell. Type **Drive alone** and then press the TAB key to advance the insertion point to the adjacent right column cell.

- Type **53%** and then press the TAB key three times to advance to the cell below the words, Drive Alone.

- Type **Carpool** and then press the TAB key.

- Type **5%** and then press the TAB key three times (Figure 4–50).

Q&A How do I correct cell contents if I make a mistake?
Click the cell and then correct the text.

Q&A Can I use the arrow keys to move the insertion point in the table cells?
Yes.

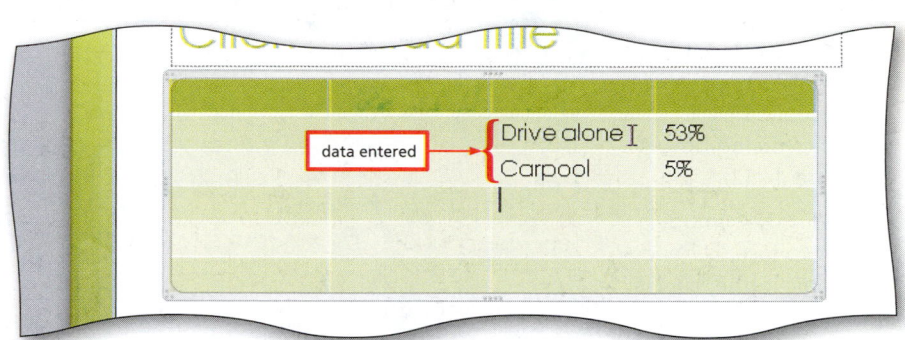

Figure 4–50

 2

- Enter the data for the remaining table cells in the third and fourth columns, using Figure 4–51 as a guide.

Q&A What if I pressed the TAB key after filling in the last cell and added another row?

Right-click the unnecessary row and then click Delete Rows on the shortcut menu.

Q&A How would I add more rows to the table?

When the insertion point is positioned in the bottom-right cell, press the TAB key.

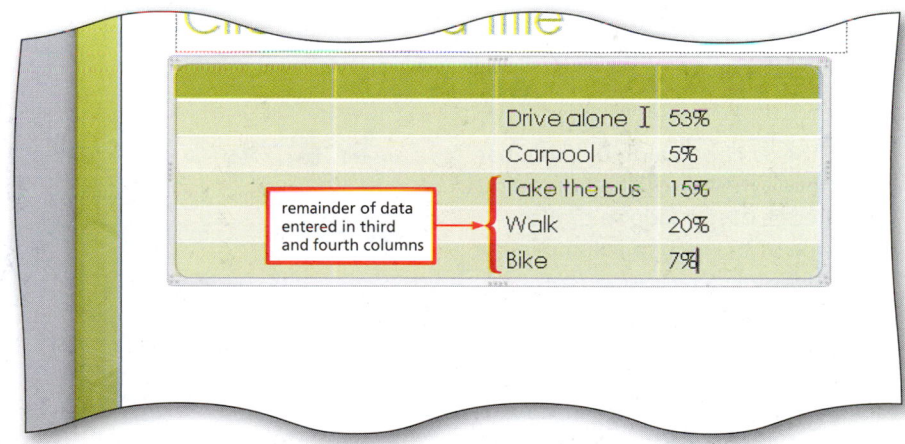

Figure 4–51

To Insert a Symbol

The Slide 4 table title will display vertically in the first column. The three columns to the right of this title will contain symbols and words describing the type of travel and the percent of students and staff using these modes of travel. The second column of the table contains symbols depicting the various modes of transportation. Although you could add clip art or pictures to these table cells, you also can insert special symbols. You insert symbols, such as mathematical characters and dots, using the Symbol dialog box.

The following steps insert symbols in the second table column.

1

- Click the second cell in the second column to place the insertion point in this cell.

- Display the Insert tab.

- Click the Symbol button (Insert tab | Symbols group) to display the Symbol dialog box (Figure 4–52).

Q&A What if the symbol I want to insert already appears in the Symbol dialog box?

You can click any symbol shown in the dialog box to insert it in the slide.

Q&A Why does my 'Recently used symbols' list display different symbols from those shown in Figure 4–52?

As you insert symbols, PowerPoint places them in the 'Recently used symbols' list.

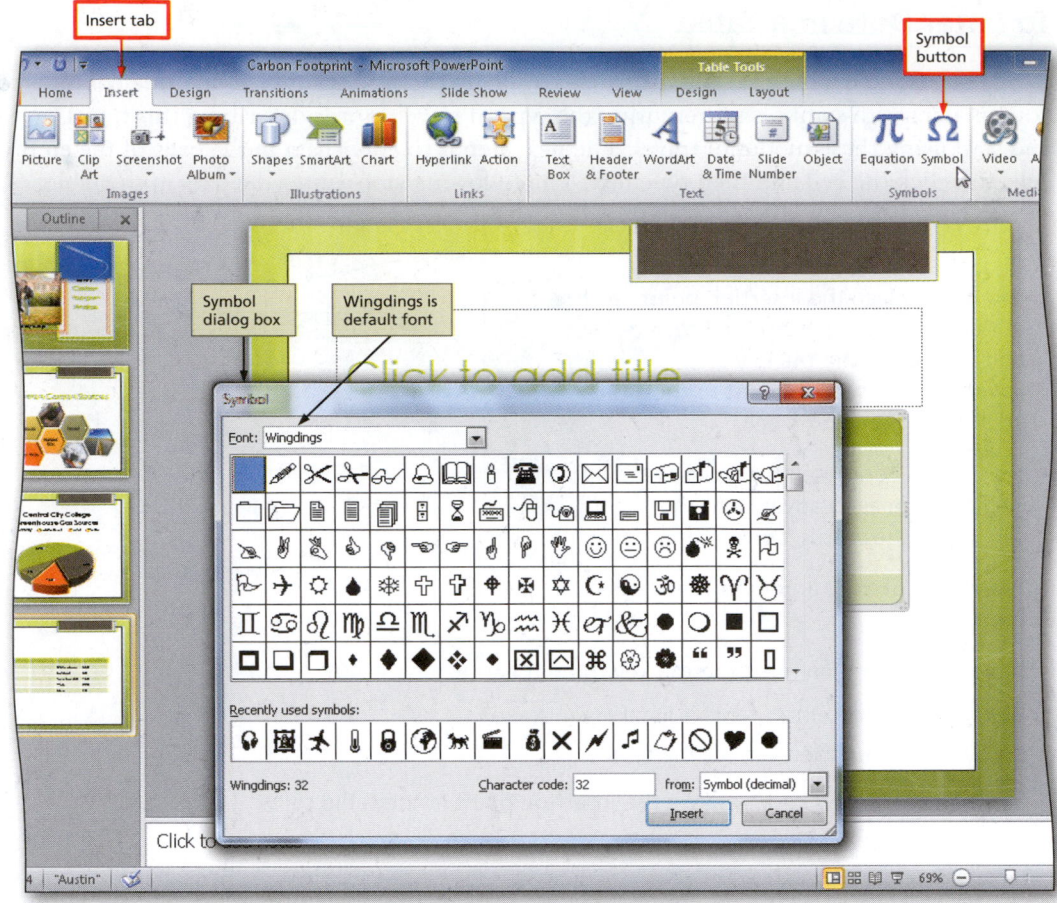

Figure 4–52

2

- Click the Symbol dialog box title bar and then drag the dialog box to the right edge of the slide so that the left side of the second column in the table is visible.

3

- If Webdings is not the font displayed in the Font box, click the Font box arrow (Symbol dialog box) and then scroll to Webdings and click it.

- In the list of symbols, if necessary, scroll to and then click the man symbol shown in Figure 4–53.

- Click the Insert button (Symbol dialog box) to place the man symbol in the selected table cell (Figure 4–53).

Q&A Why is the Symbol dialog box still open?

The Symbol dialog box remains open, allowing you to insert additional symbols.

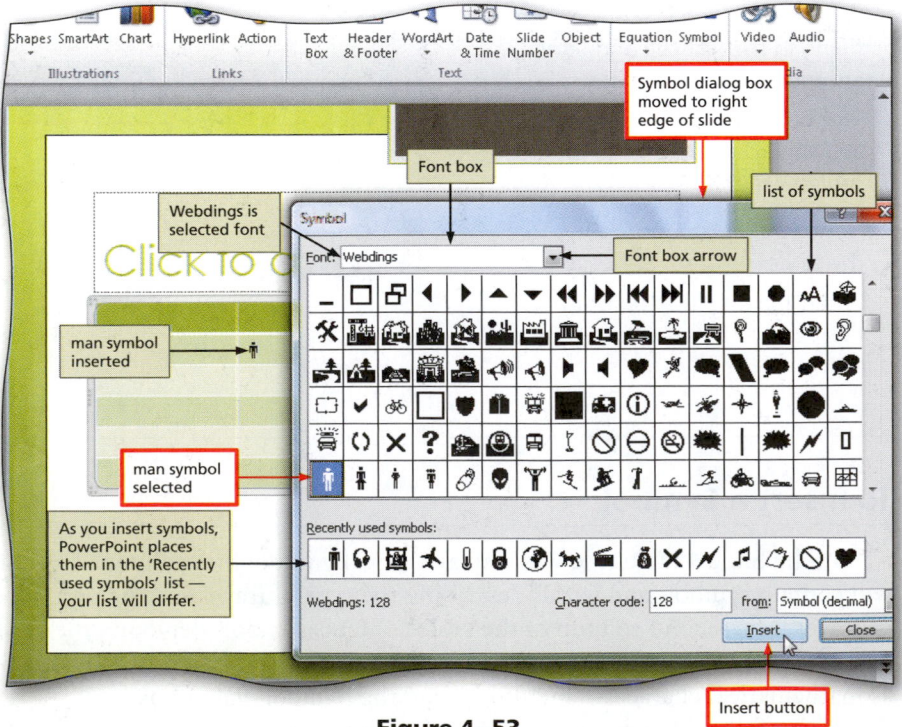

Figure 4–53

4

- In the list of symbols, click the car symbol shown in Figure 4–54.

- Click the Insert button (Symbol dialog box) to place the car symbol beside the man symbol in the selected table cell (Figure 4–54).

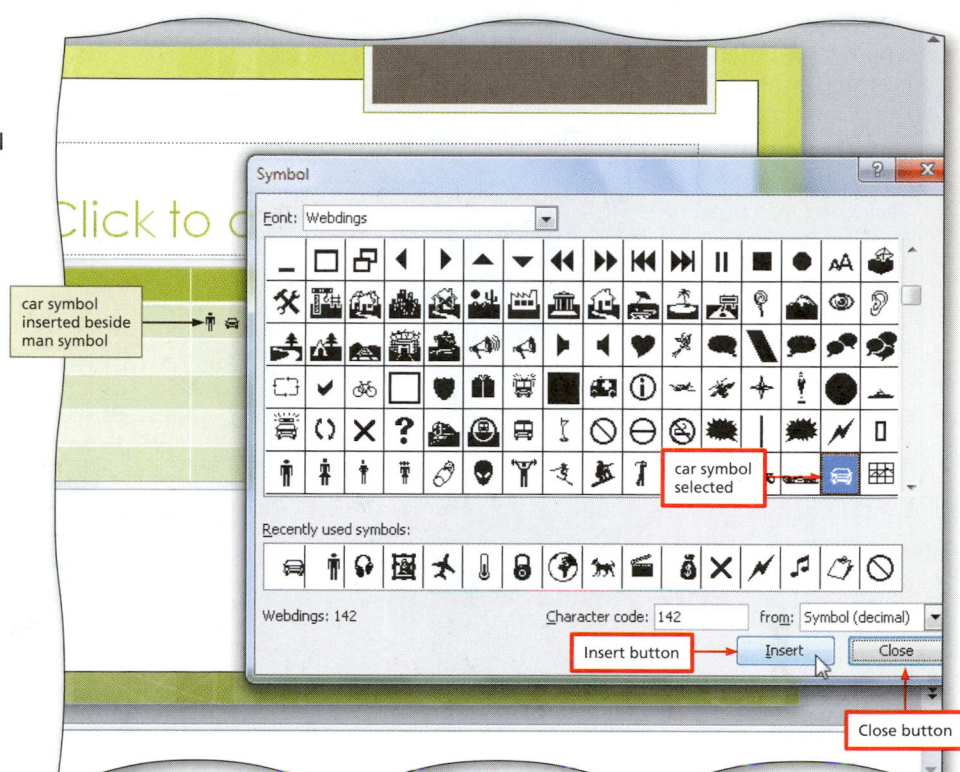

Figure 4–54

5

- Click the Close button (Symbol dialog box).

6

- Press the DOWN ARROW key to move the insertion point to the third cell in the second table column.

- Display the Symbol dialog box and then insert the people and car symbols shown in Figure 4–55.

Q&A

Can I insert the car symbol from the 'Recently used symbols' list?

Yes. PowerPoint designers generally reuse a set of symbols, which conveniently are displayed in this list for this purpose.

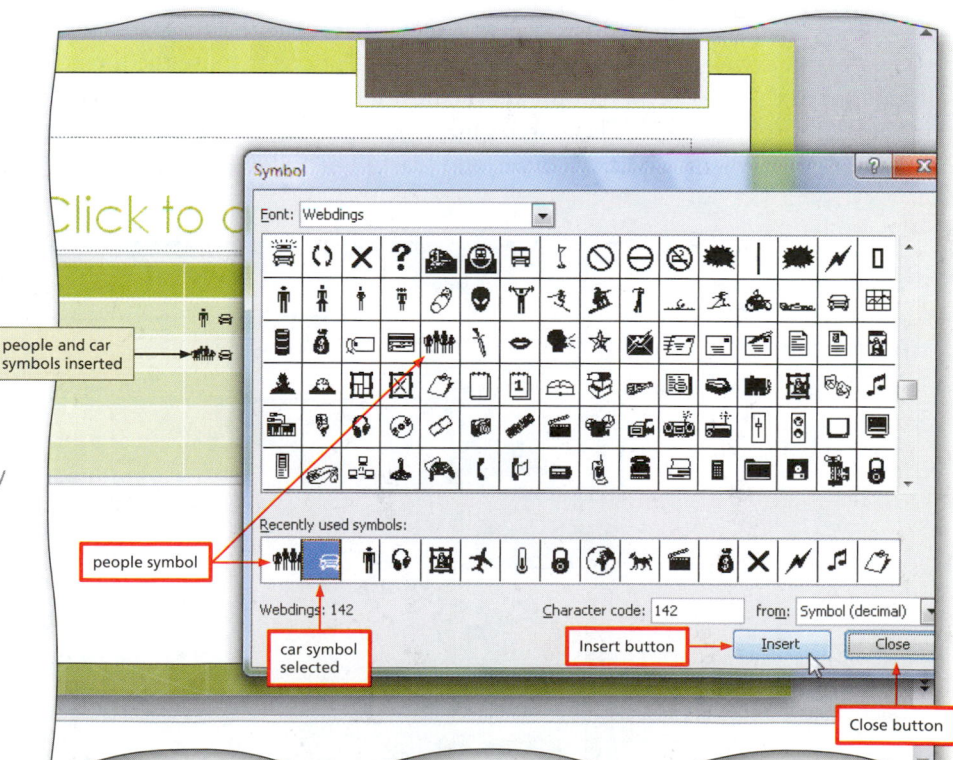

Figure 4–55

7

• Using Figure 4–56 as a guide, continue inserting symbols in the second column.

8

• Click the Close button (Symbol dialog box).

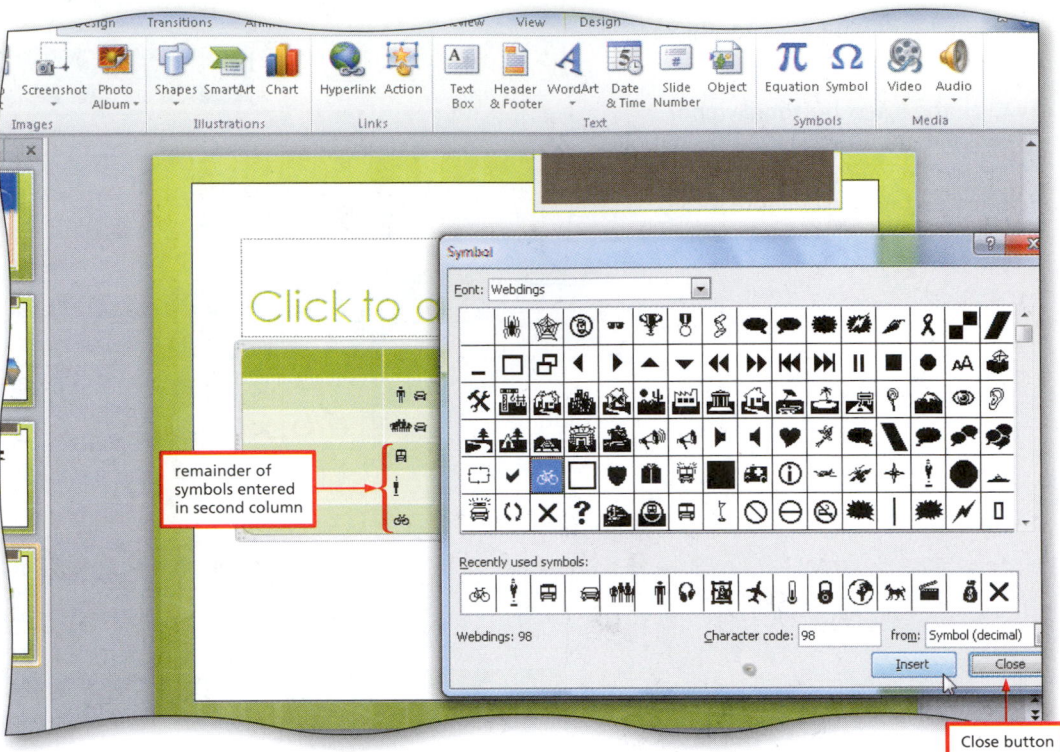

remainder of symbols entered in second column

Close button

Figure 4–56

To Apply a Table Style

A table style is a combination of formatting options that use the theme colors applied to the presentation. When you inserted the table, PowerPoint automatically applied a style. Thumbnails of this style and others are displayed in the Table Styles gallery. These styles use a variety of colors and shading and are grouped in the categories of Best Match for Document, Light, Medium, and Dark. The following steps apply a table style to the Slide 4 table.

1

• With the insertion point in the table, display the Table Tools Design tab (Figure 4–57).

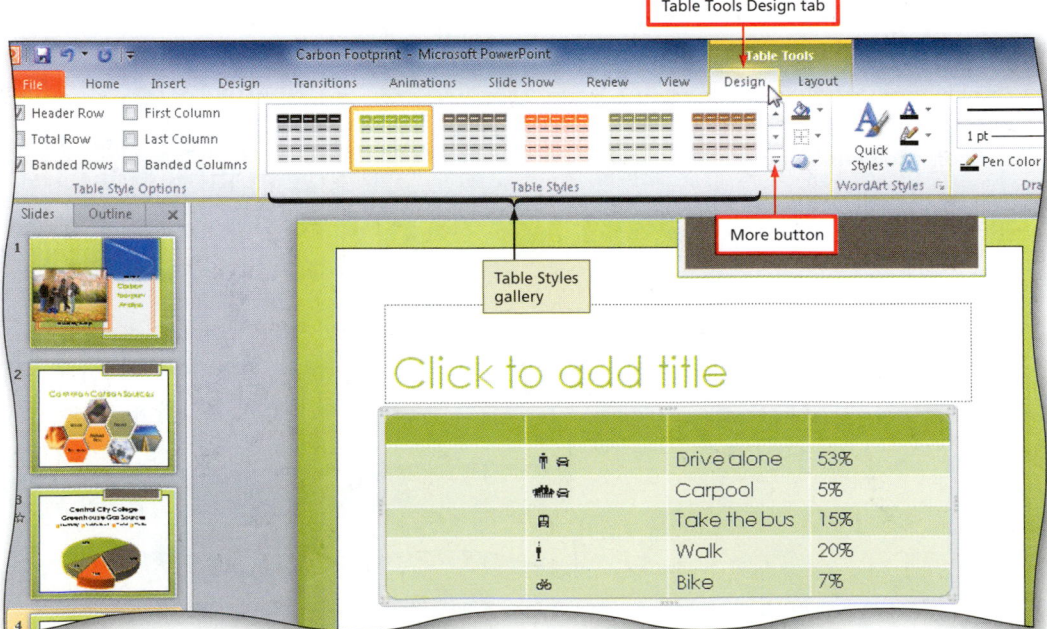

Table Tools Design tab

More button

Table Styles gallery

Figure 4–57

2

- Click the More button in the Table Styles gallery to expand the Table Styles gallery.

- Scroll down and then point to Dark Style 2 - Accent 3/Accent 4 in the Dark area (third table in last row) (Figure 4–58).

Does the Table Styles gallery have a live preview feature?

Yes, but the gallery is covering most of the table, greatly limiting your ability to preview table styles.

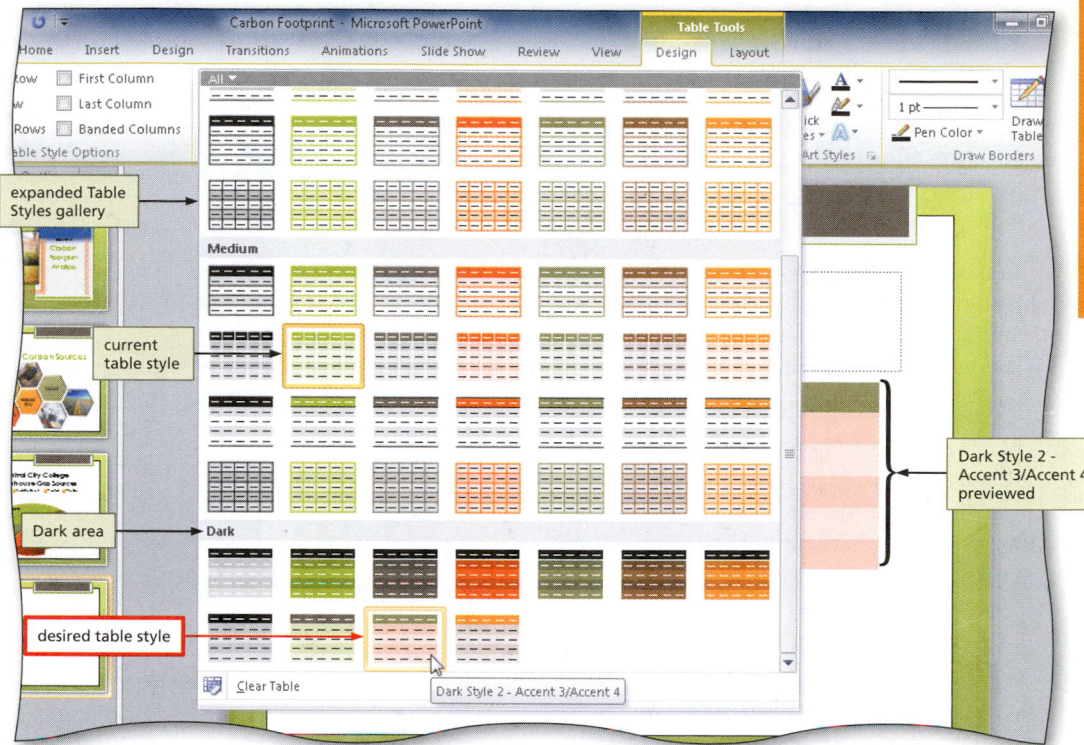

Figure 4–58

3

- Click Dark Style 2 - Accent 3/Accent 4 in the Table Styles gallery to apply the selected style to the table (Figure 4–59).

Can I resize the columns and rows or the entire table?

Yes. To resize columns or rows, drag a **column boundary** (the border to the right of a column) or the **row boundary** (the border at the bottom of a row) until the column or row is the desired width or height. To resize the entire table, drag a **table resize handle**.

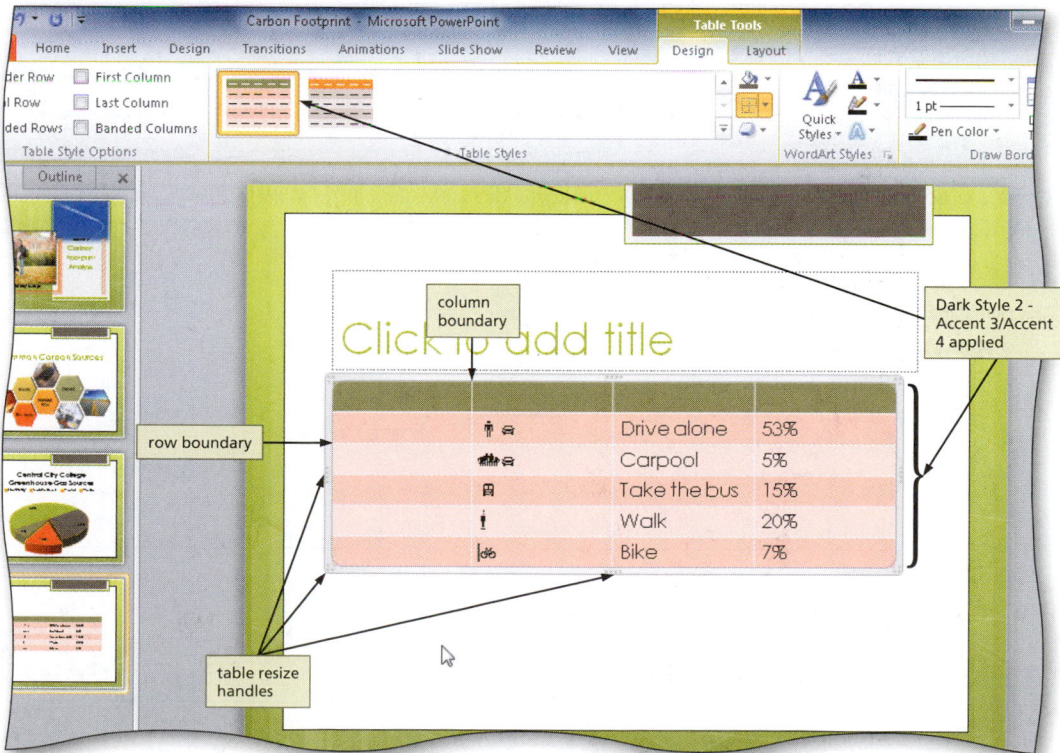

Figure 4–59

To Add Borders to a Table

The Slide 4 table does not have borders around the entire table or between the cells. The following steps add borders to the entire table.

- Click the edge of the table so that the insertion point does not appear in any cell.

- Click the Border button arrow (Table Tools Design tab | Table Styles group) to display the Border gallery (Figure 4–60).

Q&A Why is the button called No Border in the ScreenTip?

The ScreenTip name for the button will change based on the type of border, if any, present in the table. Currently no borders are applied.

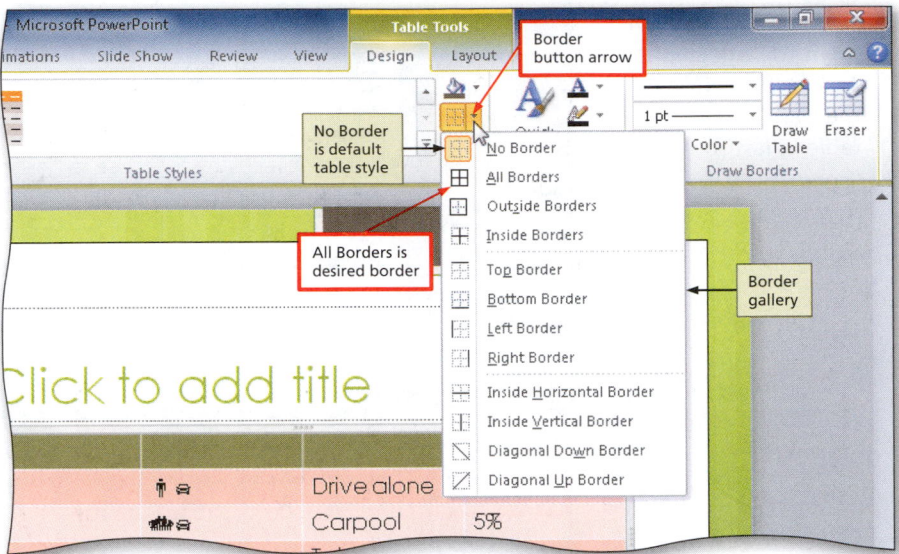

Figure 4–60

- Click All Borders in the Border gallery to add borders around the entire table and to each table cell (Figure 4–61).

Q&A Why is the border color black?

PowerPoint's default border color is black. This color is displayed on the Pen Color button (Table Tools Design tab | Draw Borders group).

Q&A Can I apply any of the border options in the Border gallery?

Yes. You can vary the look of your table by applying borders only to the cells, around the table, to the top, bottom, left or right edges, or a combination of these areas.

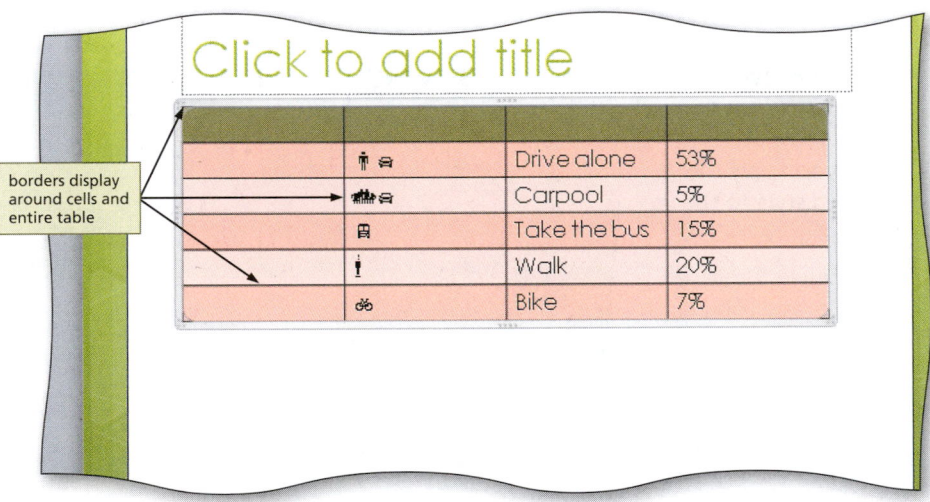

Figure 4–61

To Add an Effect to a Table

To enhance the visual appeal of the table, you can add an effect. PowerPoint gives you the option of applying a bevel to specified cells so they have a three-dimensional appearance. You also can add a shadow or reflection to the entire table. The following steps add a shadow and give a three-dimensional appearance to the entire table.

1

- With the table selected, click the Effects button (Table Tools Design tab | Table Styles group) to display the Effects menu.

Q&A What is the difference between a shadow and a reflection?

A shadow gives the appearance that a light is displayed on the table, which causes a shadow behind the graphic. A reflection gives the appearance that the table is shiny, so a mirror image appears below the actual graphic.

2

- Point to Shadow to display the Shadow gallery (Figure 4–62).

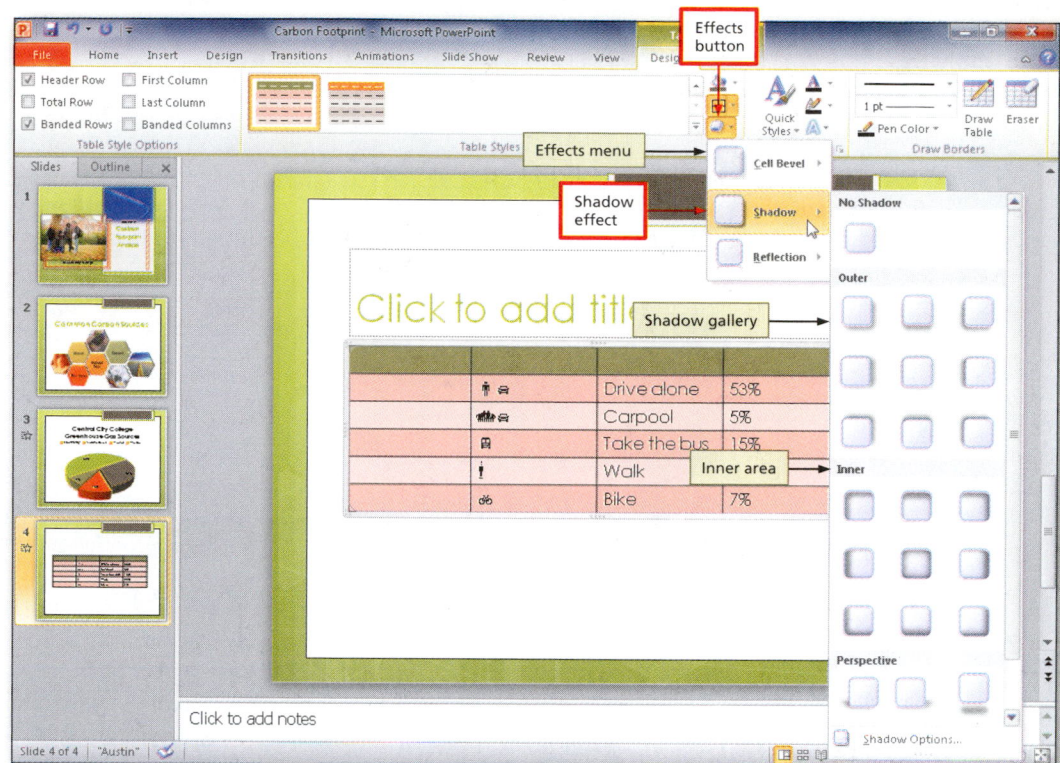

Figure 4–62

Q&A How do the shadows differ in the Outer, Inner, and Perspective categories?

The Outer shadows are displayed on the outside of the table, whereas the Inner shadows are displayed in the interior cells. The Perspective shadows give the illusion that a light is shining from the right or left side of the table or from above, and the table is casting a shadow.

3

- Point to Inside Center in the Inner category (second shadow in second row) to display a live preview of this shadow (Figure 4–63).

🔎 **Experiment**

- Point to the various shadows in the Shadow gallery and watch the shadows change in the table.

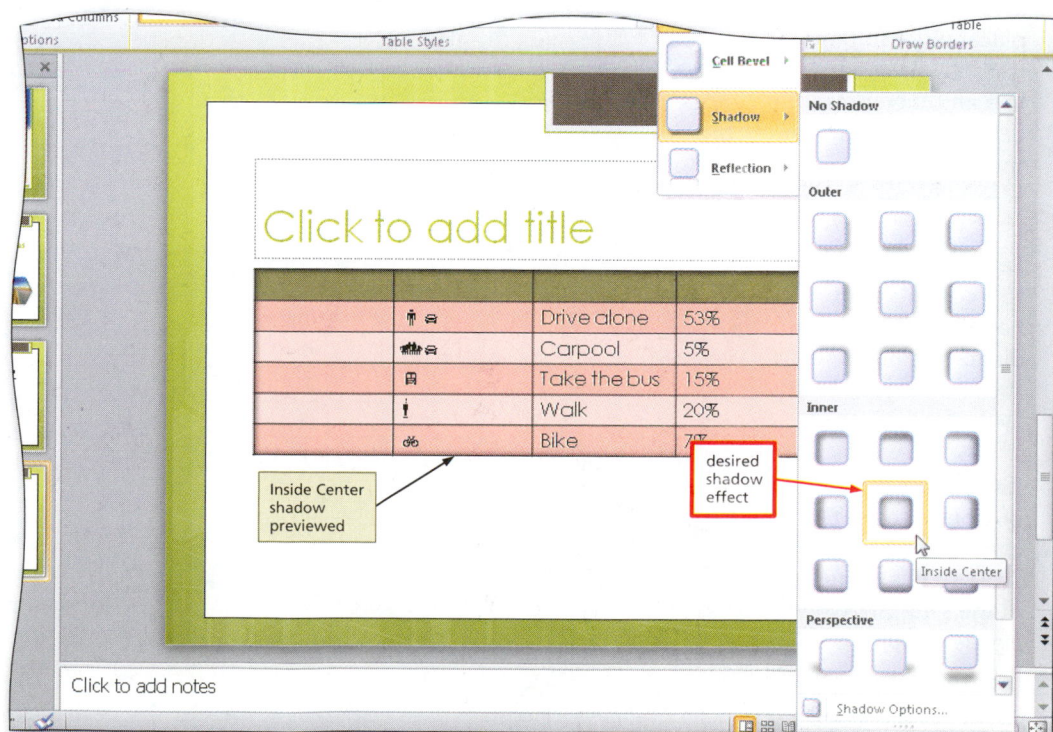

Figure 4–63

4

- Click Inside Center to apply this shadow to the table (Figure 4–64).

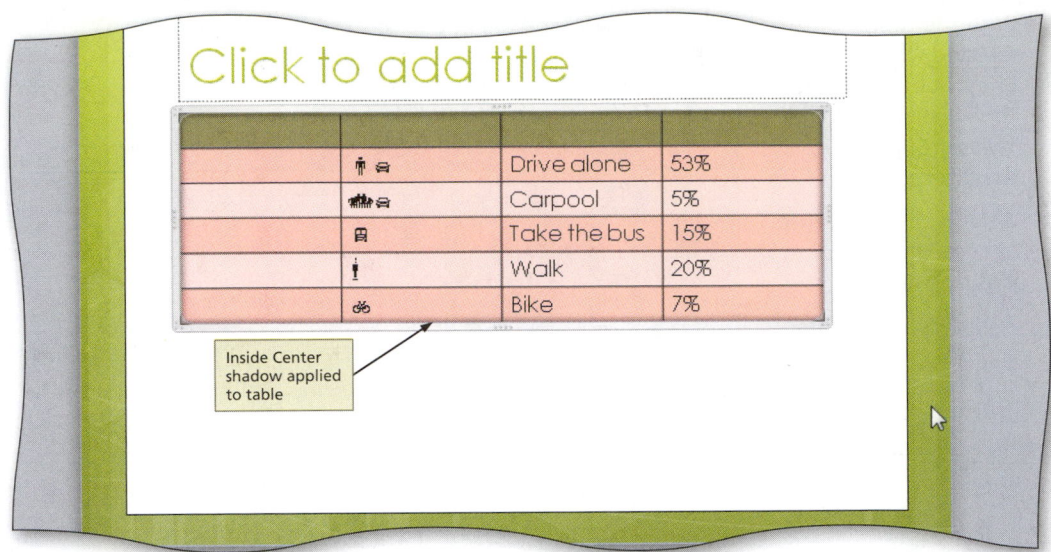

Figure 4–64

To Resize a Table

You resize a table the same way you resize a chart, a SmartArt graphic, or any other graphical object. On Slide 4, you can remove the title text placeholder because the table will have the title, Travel to Campus, in the first column. The following steps resize the table to fill Slide 4.

1

- Click a border of the title text placeholder so that it displays as a solid line and then press the DELETE key to remove the placeholder.

2

- Select the table, point to a corner sizing handle, and then drag diagonally outward, as shown in Figure 4–65.

3

- Release the mouse button to resize the chart. Position the table so it is centered in the slide (shown in Figure 4–66).

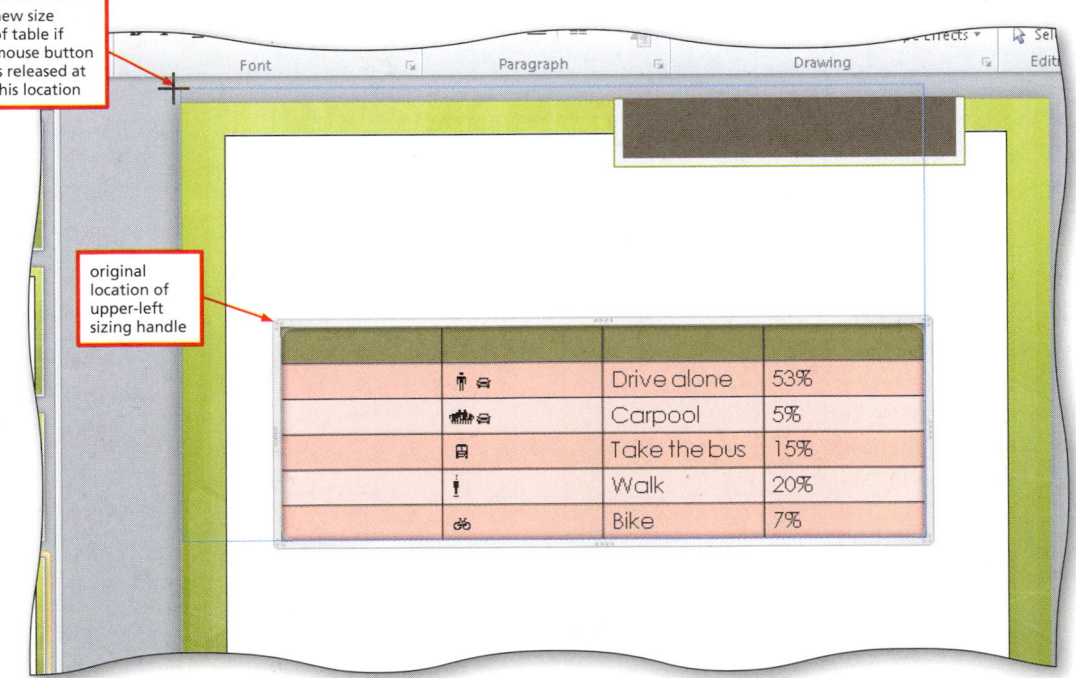

Figure 4–65

To Add an Image to a Table

Another table enhancement you can make is to add a picture or clip to a table cell. The following steps add a commuter picture to the upper-right table cell.

1

- Right-click the upper-right table cell to display the shortcut menu and Mini toolbar (Figure 4–66).

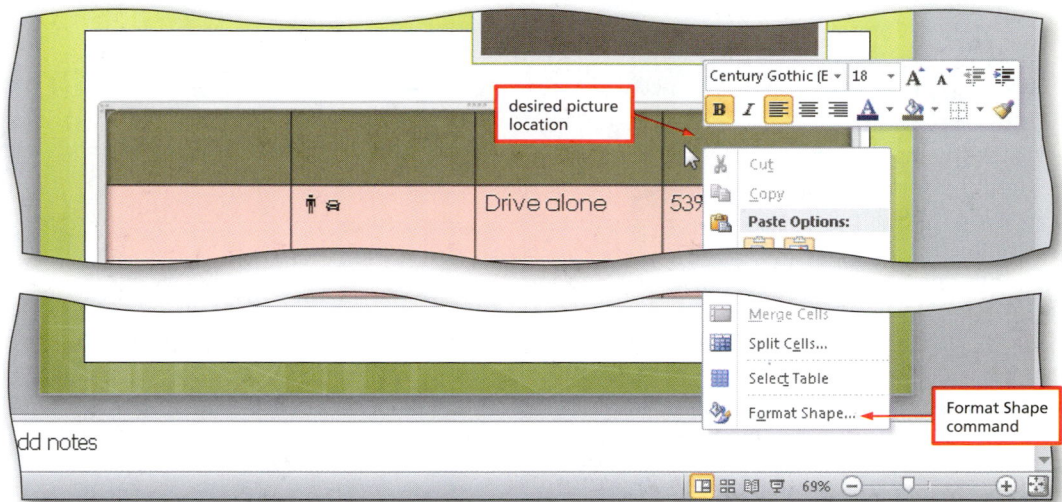

Figure 4–66

2

- Click Format Shape to display the Format Shape dialog box and then click 'Picture or texture fill' (Figure 4–67).

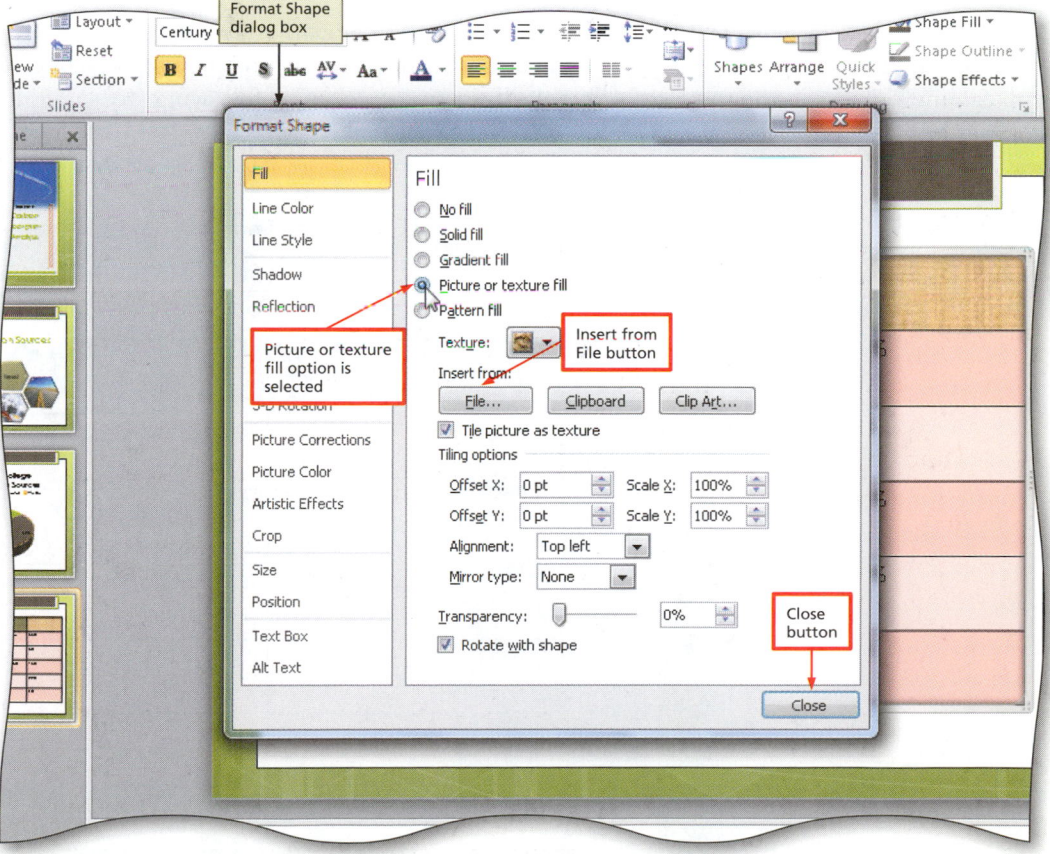

Figure 4–67

- Click the Insert from File button to display the Insert Picture dialog box.

- Select the Commuters picture located on the Data Files for Students and then click the Insert button in the Insert Picture dialog box to insert the picture into the table cell.

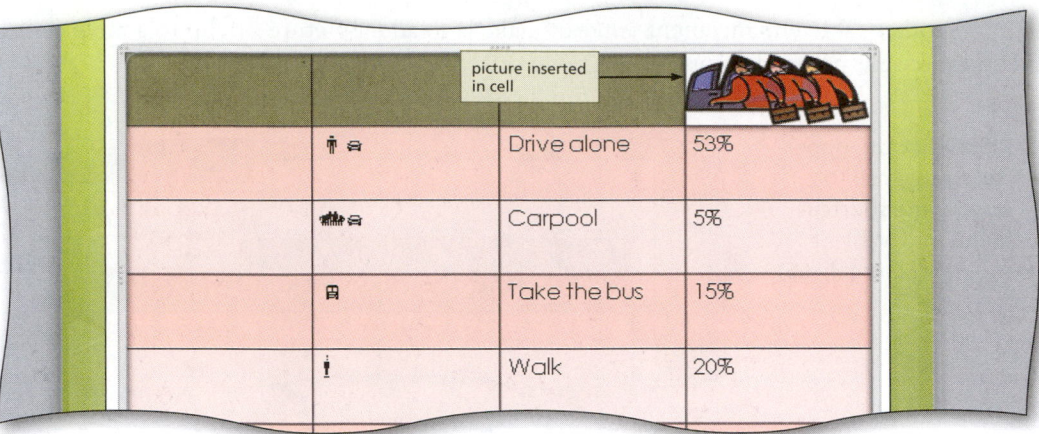

Figure 4–68

- Click the Close button (Format Shape dialog box) (Figure 4–68).

To Merge Cells

To provide space for the table title to stretch across the entire table height, you can merge all the cells in the first column. In addition, the top row of the table will contain only the picture you added to the upper-right cell, so you can merge cells in the top row so it looks like a single cell. The following steps merge the six cells in the first column into a single cell and merge two cells in the first table row.

- Drag through all six cells in the first table column to select these cells (Figure 4–69).

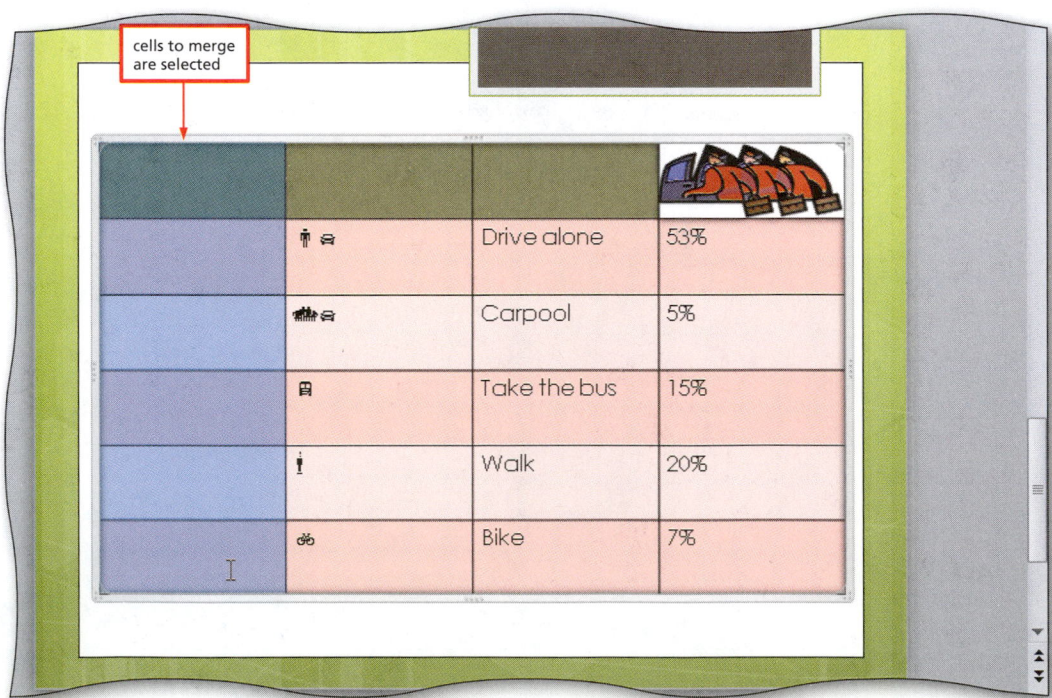

Figure 4–69

● Click the Table Tools Layout tab to display the Table Tools Layout Ribbon.

● Click the Merge Cells button (Table Tools Layout tab | Merge group) to merge the six column cells into one cell (Figure 4–70).

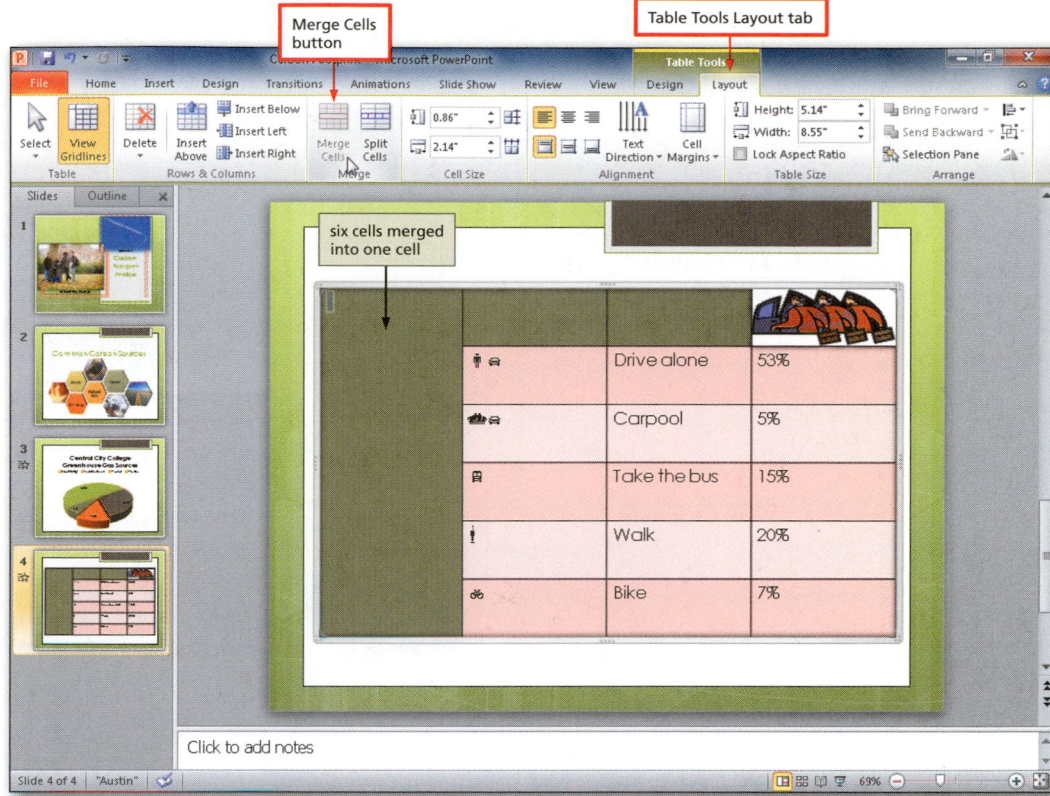

Figure 4–70

● Drag through the second and third column cells in the first table row to select these two cells (Figure 4–71).

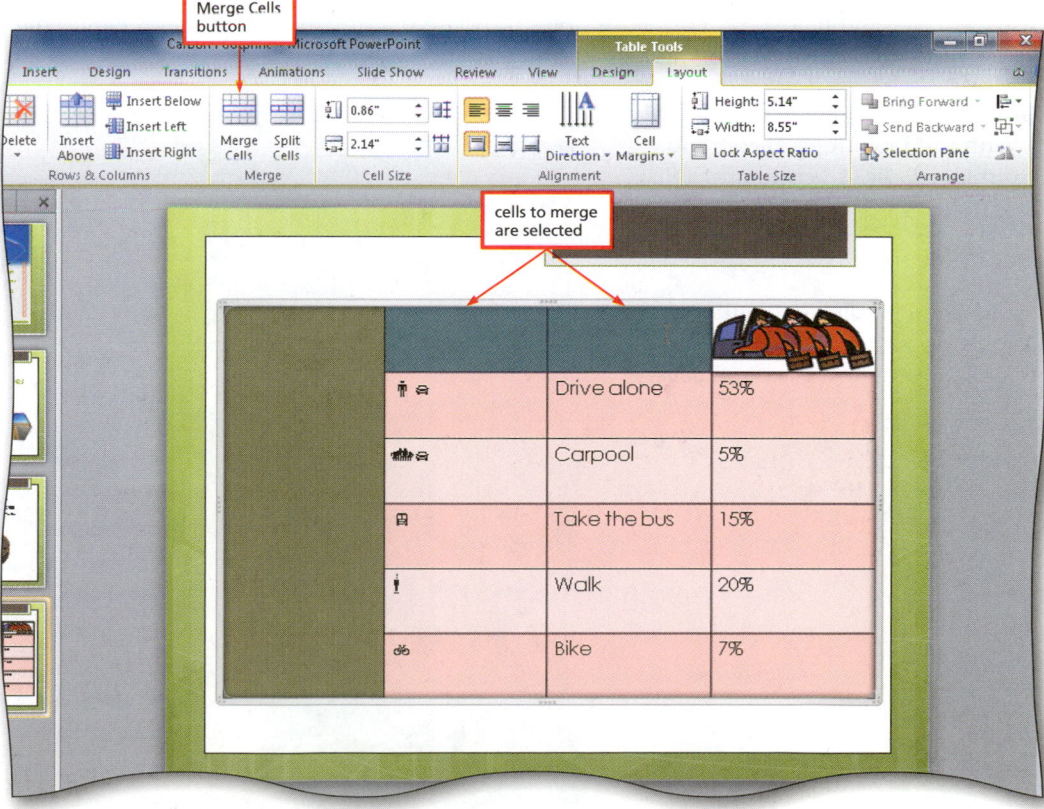

Figure 4–71

- Click the Merge Cells button to merge these cells (Figure 4–72).

Q&A

Could I have merged the cells in the first row before merging the first column cells?

Yes, but you would have achieved different results. If you merge the row one cells, then you would need to merge all first column cells except the first cell.

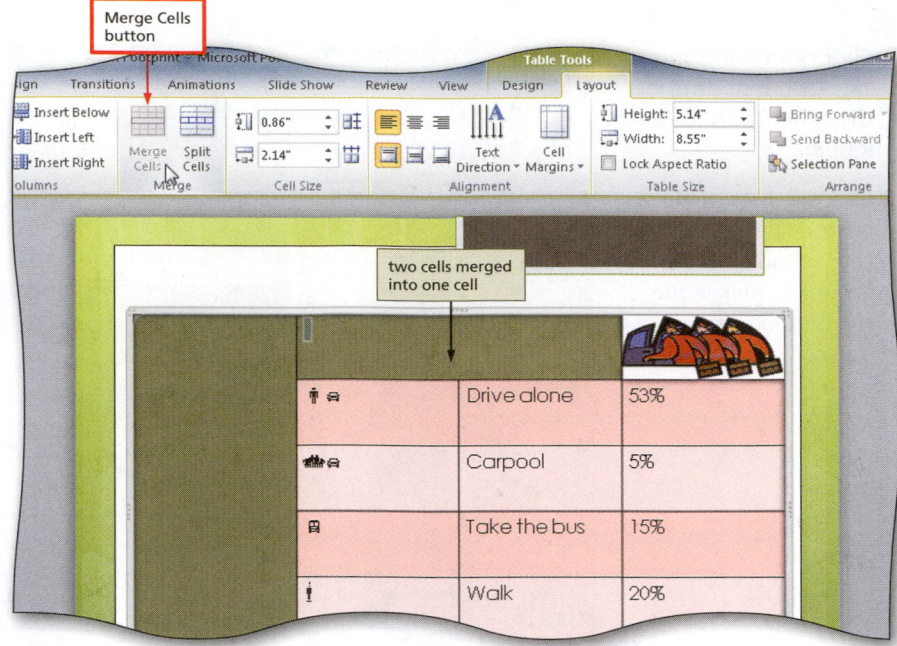

Figure 4–72

Other Ways

1. Right-click selected cells, click Merge Cells on shortcut menu

---

To Display Text in a Cell Vertically

The default orientation of table cell text is horizontal. You can change this direction to stack the letters so they display above and below each other, or you can rotate the direction in 90-degree increments. The following steps rotate the text in the first column cell.

- With the Table Tools Layout tab displayed, click the column 1 cell.

- Type `Travel to Campus` in the table cell.

- Click the Text Direction button (Table Tools Layout tab | Alignment group) to display the Text Direction gallery (Figure 4–73).

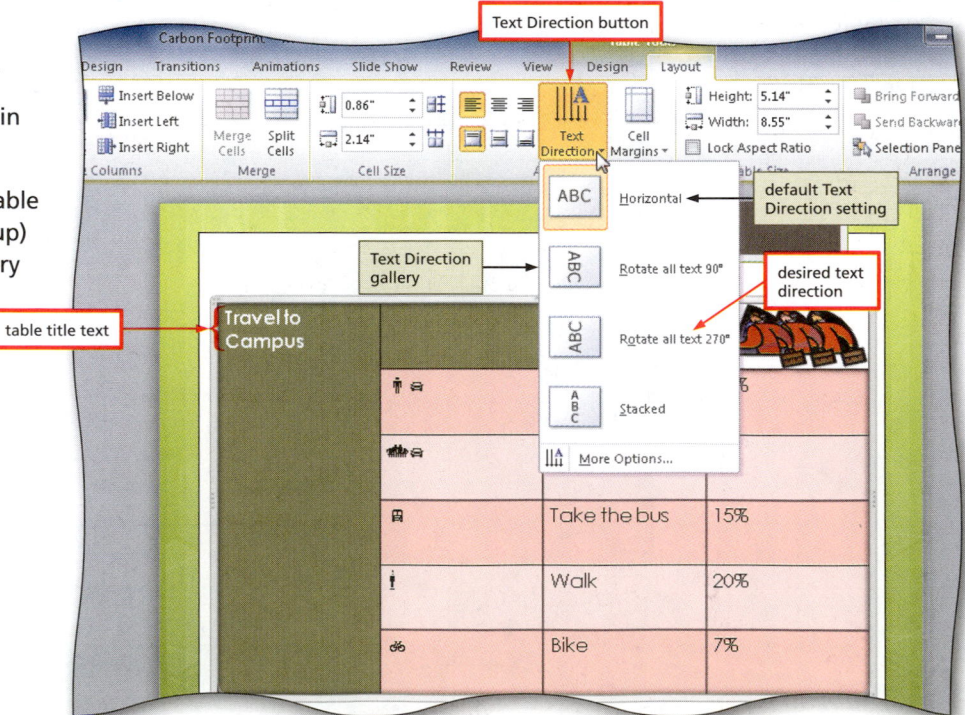

Figure 4–73

2
• Click 'Rotate all text 270°' to rotate
the text in the cell (Figure 4–74).

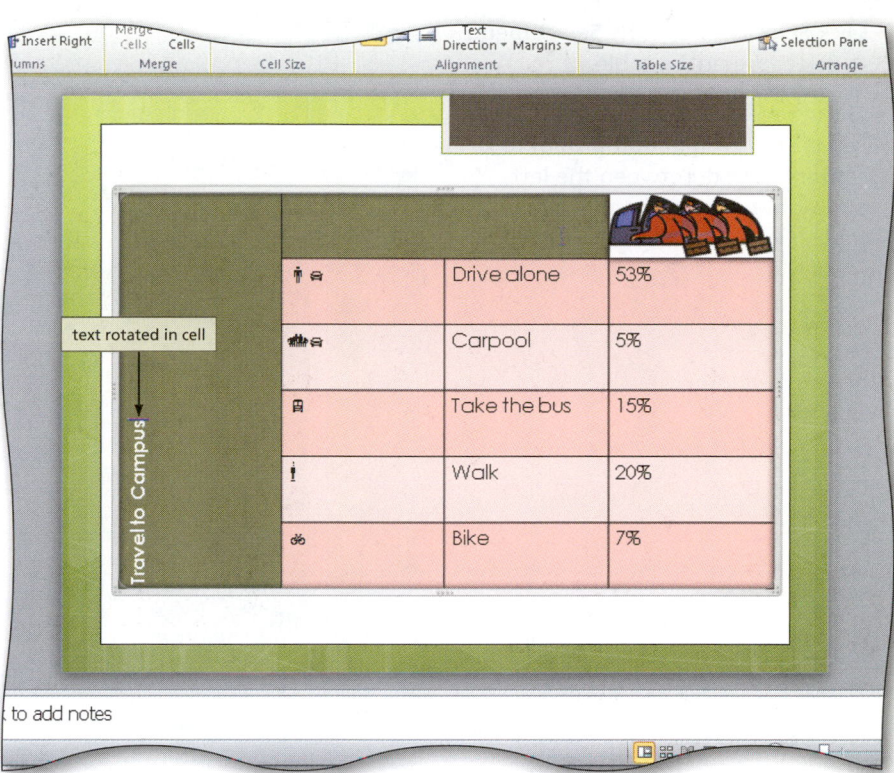

Figure 4–74

Other Ways

1. Right-click selected cells,
   click Format Shape on
   shortcut menu, click
   Text Box, click Text
   direction arrow

To Align Text in Cells

The data in each cell can be aligned horizontally and vertically. You change the horizontal alignment of each cell in a similar manner as you center, left-align, or right-align text in a placeholder. You also can change the vertical alignment so that the data displays at the top, middle, or bottom of each cell. The following steps center the text both horizontally and vertically in each table cell.

1
• With the Table Tools Layout tab
displayed, click the Select button
(Table group) to display the Select
menu (Figure 4–75).

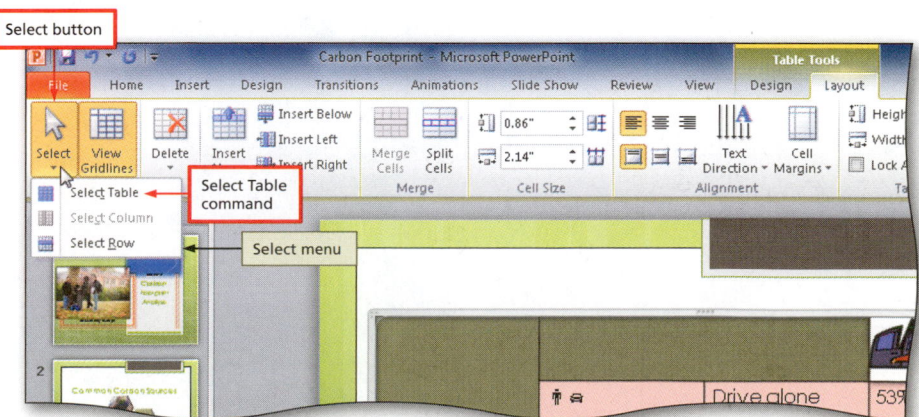

Figure 4–75

2

• Click Select Table in the Select menu to select the entire table.

• Click the Center button (Table Tools Layout tab | Alignment group) to center the text between the left and right borders of each cell in the table (Figure 4–76).

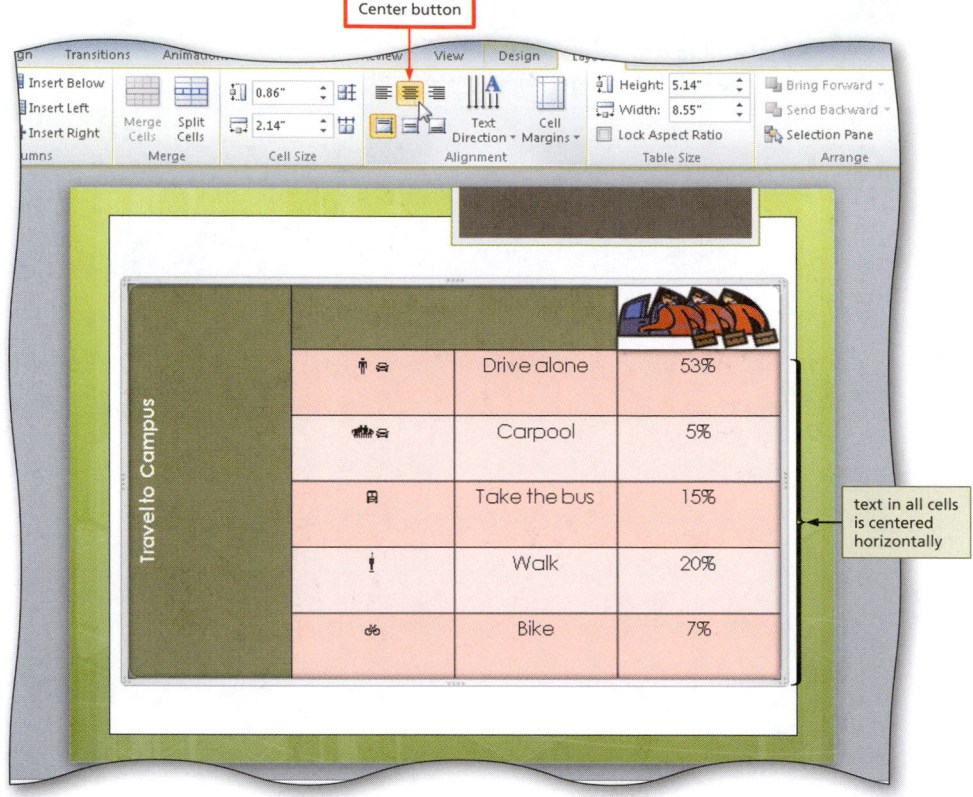

Figure 4–76

3

• Click the Center Vertically button (Table Tools Layout tab | Alignment group) to center the text between the top and bottom borders of each cell in the table (Figure 4–77).

Q&A

Must I center all the table cells, or can I center only specific cells?

You can center as many cells as you desire at one time by selecting one or more cells.

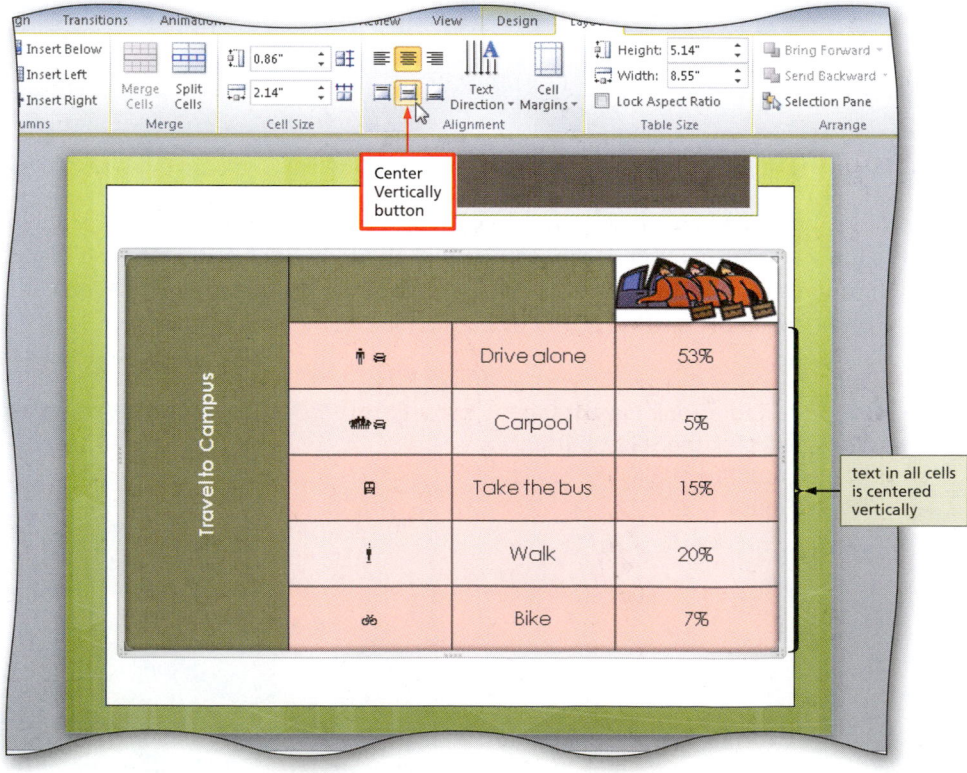

Other Ways

1. Right-click selected cells, click Format Shape on shortcut menu, click Text Box, click Vertical alignment arrow

Figure 4–77

To Format Table Data

The final table enhancement is to bold the text in all cells and increase the font size of the title and the symbols. The entire table is selected, so you can bold all text simultaneously. The title and symbols will have different font sizes. The following steps format the data.

1 Display the Home tab and then click the Bold button (Font group) to bold all text in the table.

2 Select the table title text in the first column and then increase the font size to 36 point.

3 Select the symbols in the second column and then increase the font size to 44 point (Figure 4–78).

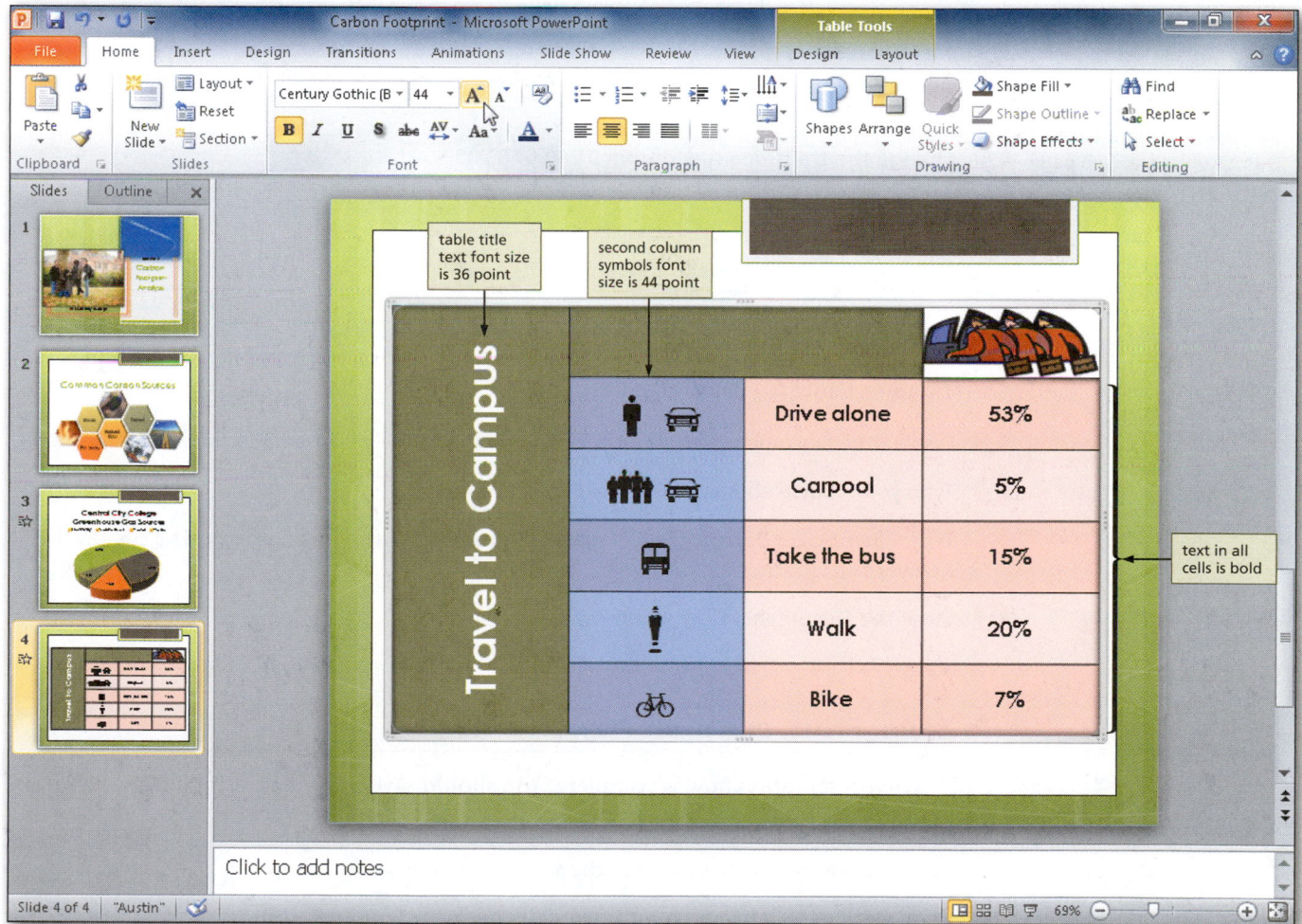

Figure 4–78

Plan Ahead

Test your visual elements.
Proofread your charts and tables carefully using these guidelines:

- Verify that your charts and tables contain the correct data. It is easy to make mistakes when inputting large quantities of numbers or entering many lines of text. Check that numbers are not transposed and that pie chart percentages total 100.

- Be certain that graphics are clearly labeled. The slide title text or the chart title should state the graphic's purpose. Table column headings must indicate the data below them. Chart legends must accompany the graphic if the data is not displayed on the chart itself. Units of measurement, such as degrees, dollars, or inches, should appear for clarity.

- Show your graphic to people unfamiliar with your topic. Ask them to explain verbally what they gather from viewing the material. Determine how long it takes them to state their interpretations. If they pause or look confused, your graphic either has too much or too little information and needs revision.

BTW

Quick Reference
For a table that lists how to complete the tasks covered in this book using the mouse, Ribbon, shortcut menu, and keyboard, see the Quick Reference Summary at the back of this book, or visit the PowerPoint 2010 Quick Reference Web page (scsite.com/ppt2010/qr).

To Add a Transition between Slides

A final enhancement you will make in this presentation is to apply the Orbit transition in the Dynamic Content category to all slides and change the transition speed to 3.00. The following steps apply this transition to the presentation.

1 Apply the Orbit transition in the Dynamic Content category to all four slides in the presentation.

2 Change the transition speed from 01.60 to 03.00.

To Change Document Properties

Before saving the presentation again, you want to add your name, class name, and some keywords as document properties. The following steps use the Document Information Panel to change document properties.

1 Display the Document Information Panel and then type your name as the Author property.

2 Type your course and section in the Subject property.

3 Type `carbon footprint, greenhouse gas, transportation` as the Keywords property.

4 Close the Document Information Panel.

BTW

Certification
The Microsoft Office Specialist (MOS) program provides an opportunity for you to obtain a valuable industry credential — proof that you have the PowerPoint 2010 skills required by employers. For more information, visit the PowerPoint 2010 Certification Web page (scsite.com/ppt2010/cert).

To Save, Print, and Quit PowerPoint

The presentation now is complete. You should save the slides, print a handout, and then quit PowerPoint.

1 Save the presentation again with the same file name.

2 Print the slide as a handout with two slides per page (Figure 4–79).

3 Quit PowerPoint, closing all open documents.

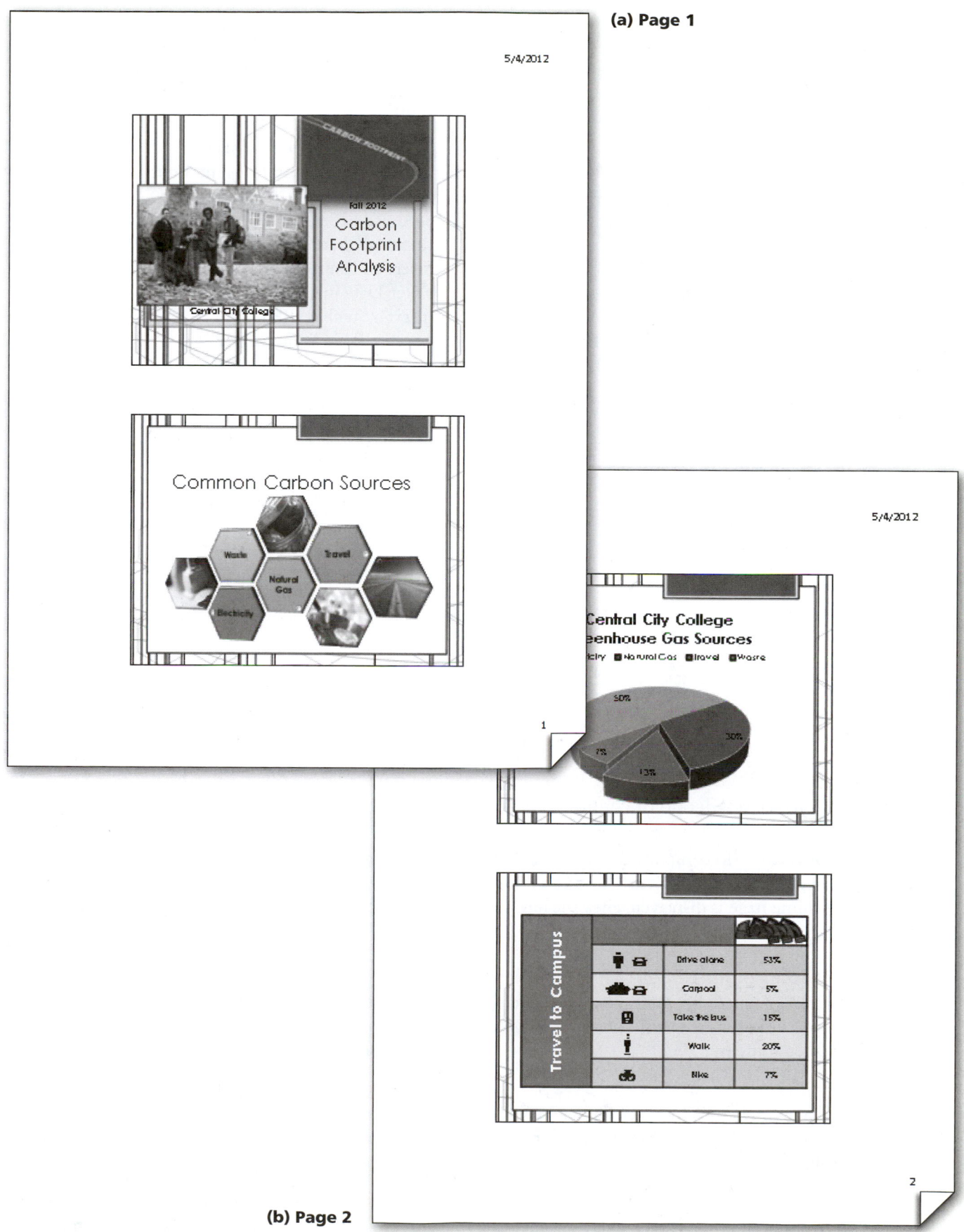

(a) Page 1

(b) Page 2

Figure 4–79

Chapter Summary

In this chapter you have learned how to insert a SmartArt graphic and then add a picture and text, convert pictures to a SmartArt graphic, create and format a chart and a table, change table text alignment and orientation, and insert symbols. The items listed below include all the new PowerPoint skills you have learned in this chapter.

1. Insert a SmartArt Graphic (PPT 206)
2. Enter Text in a SmartArt Graphic (PPT 208)
3. Format Text Pane Characters (PPT 208)
4. Insert a Picture from a File into a SmartArt Graphic (PPT 209)
5. Apply a SmartArt Style (PPT 210)
6. Change SmartArt Color (PPT 211)
7. Resize a SmartArt Graphic (PPT 212)
8. Convert Text to a SmartArt Graphic (PPT 213)
9. Bold SmartArt Graphic Text (PPT 217)
10. Insert a Chart (PPT 220)
11. Replace Sample Data (PPT 221)
12. Apply a Chart Style (PPT 223)
13. Change the Shape Outline Weight (PPT 224)
14. Change the Shape Outline Color (PPT 226)
15. Change a Chart Layout (PPT 226)
16. Resize a Chart (PPT 228)
17. Change the Title and Legend Font Size (PPT 228)
18. Separate a Pie Slice (PPT 229)
19. Rotate a Chart (PPT 230)
20. Insert an Empty Table (PPT 232)
21. Enter Data in a Table (PPT 233)
22. Insert a Symbol (PPT 233)
23. Apply a Table Style (PPT 236)
24. Add Borders to a Table (PPT 238)
25. Add an Effect to a Table (PPT 238)
26. Resize a Table (PPT 240)
27. Add an Image to a Table (PPT 241)
28. Merge Cells (PPT 242)
29. Display Text in a Cell Vertically (PPT 244)
30. Align Text in Cells (PPT 245)

If you have a SAM 2010 user profile, your instructor may have assigned an autogradable version of this assignment. If so, log into the SAM 2010 Web site at www.cengage.com/sam2010 to download the instruction and start files.

Learn It Online

Test your knowledge of chapter content and key terms.

Instructions: To complete the Learn It Online exercises, start your browser, click the Address bar, and then enter the Web address **scsite.com/ppt2010/learn**. When the PowerPoint 2010 Learn It Online page is displayed, click the link for the exercise you want to complete and then read the instructions.

Chapter Reinforcement TF, MC, and SA

A series of true/false, multiple choice, and short answer questions that test your knowledge of the chapter content.

Flash Cards

An interactive learning environment where you identify chapter key terms associated with displayed definitions.

Practice Test

A series of multiple choice questions that test your knowledge of chapter content and key terms.

Who Wants To Be a Computer Genius?

An interactive game that challenges your knowledge of chapter content in the style of a television quiz show.

Wheel of Terms

An interactive game that challenges your knowledge of chapter key terms in the style of the television show *Wheel of Fortune*.

Crossword Puzzle Challenge

A crossword puzzle that challenges your knowledge of key terms presented in the chapter.

Apply Your Knowledge

Reinforce the skills and apply the concepts you learned in this chapter.

Converting Text to a SmartArt Graphic

Note: To complete this assignment, you will be required to use the Data Files for Students. See the inside back cover of this book for instructions on downloading the Data Files for Students, or contact your instructor for information about accessing the required files.

Instructions: Start PowerPoint. Open the presentation, Apply 4-1 Medical, located on the Data Files for Students.

The slide in the presentation presents information about when injured people should seek medical care at a hospital emergency room or an urgent care facility. The document you open is an unformatted presentation. You are to convert the two separate lists to SmartArt and format these graphics so the slide looks like Figure 4–80.

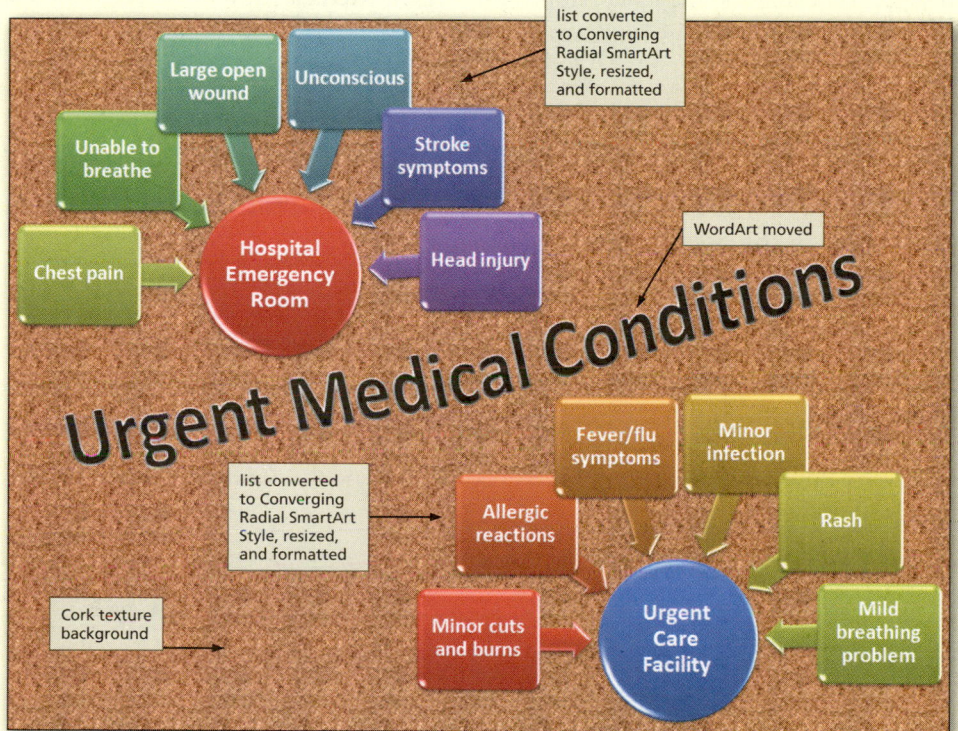

Figure 4–80

Perform the following tasks:

1. Convert the upper-left Hospital Emergency Room list to SmartArt by applying the Converging Radial Style (Relationship area). Change the colors to Colorful Range – Accent Colors 3 to 4.

2. Resize this SmartArt graphic to approximately 4.5" × 5.25". With the Text pane open, select the six Level 2 bulleted lines and then increase the font size to 16 point and bold this text. Select all six SmartArt graphic squares and then click the Larger button (SmartArt Tools Format tab | Shapes group) three times to increase the size of the selected shapes.

3. Select the center Hospital Emergency Room circle, increase the font size to 18 point, and bold this text. Click the Larger button two times to increase the size of the selected shape.

4. Apply the Polished (3-D area) Style and then move this SmartArt graphic to the area shown in Figure 4–80.

5. Convert the lower-right Urgent Care Facility list to SmartArt by applying the Converging Radial Style (Relationship area). Change the colors to Colorful Range – Accent Colors 2 to 3.

Continued >

Apply Your Knowledge *continued*

6. Resize this SmartArt graphic to approximately 4.5" × 5.25". With the Text pane open, select the six Level 2 bulleted lines and then increase the font size to 16 point and bold this text. Select all six SmartArt graphic squares and then click the Larger button (SmartArt Tools Format tab | Shapes group) three times to increase the size of the selected shapes.

7. Select the center Urgent Care Facility circle, decrease the font size to 18 point, and bold this text. Click the Larger button two times to increase the size of the selected shape.

8. Apply the Polished (3-D area) Style to this SmartArt graphic.

9. Move the center WordArt title, Urgent Medical Conditions, to the location shown in Figure 4–80 on the previous page.

10. Insert the Cork texture to format the background.

11. Apply the Clock transition (Exciting area) and then change the duration to 2.00 seconds.

12. Check the spelling and then change the document properties as specified by your instructor. Save the presentation using the file name, Apply 4-1 Urgent Medical. Submit the revised document in the format specified by your instructor.

Extend Your Knowledge

Extend the skills you learned in this chapter and experiment with new skills. You may need to use Help to complete the assignment.

Changing Chart Type and Style and Creating a SmartArt Graphic from Text

Note: To complete this assignment, you will be required to use the Data Files for Students. See the inside back cover of this book for instructions on downloading the Data Files for Students, or contact your instructor for information about accessing the required files.

Instructions: Start PowerPoint. Open the presentation, Extend 4-1 College, located on the Data Files for Students.

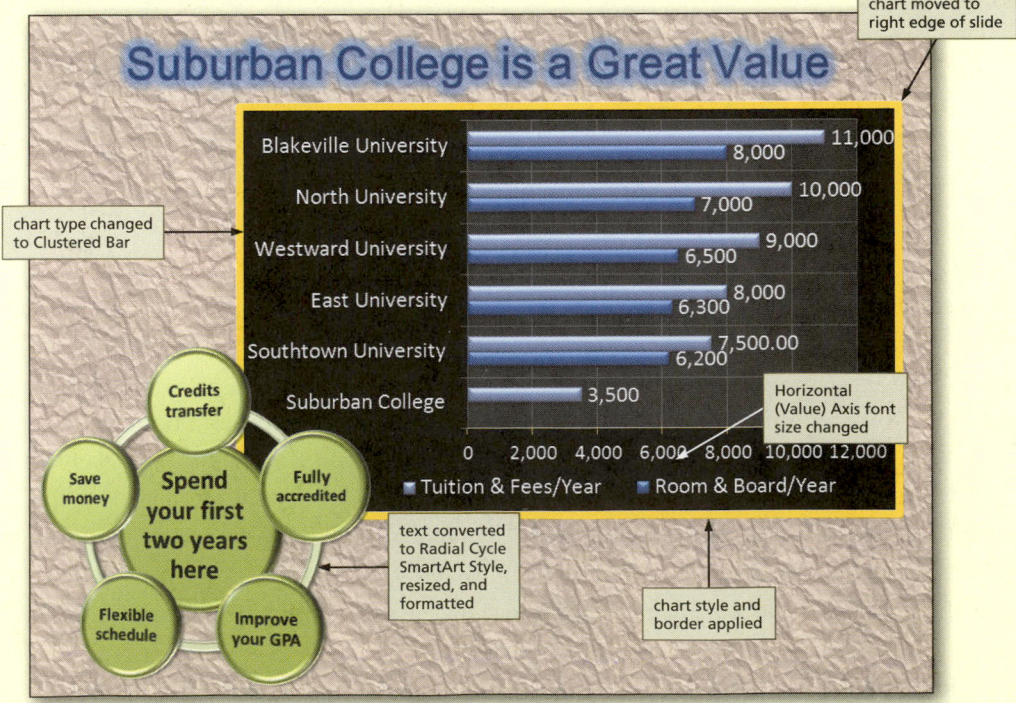

Figure 4–81

You will format a chart by applying a type and style, and then you will create a graphic by converting text to SmartArt.

Perform the following tasks:

1. Change the chart type from Clustered Column to Clustered Bar. *Hint:* Click the chart to select it and then click the Change Chart Type button (Chart Tools Design tab | Type group).

2. Apply chart Style 43 (last style in blue column) and then add a 6 pt. Yellow border to the chart. Move the chart to the right edge of the slide, as shown in Figure 4–81 on the previous page. Right-click the Horizontal (Value) Axis to display the Mini toolbar and then decrease the font size to 16 point.

3. Convert the text in the lower-left corner of the slide to the Radial Cycle layout (first layout in third row in Cycle area) SmartArt graphic. Change the color to Colored Fill – Accent 3 (second color in Accent 3 area). Apply the Metallic Scene design in the 3-D area.

4. Resize this SmartArt graphic to approximately 3.8" × 6.5" and then move the graphic to the location shown in Figure 4–81.

5. Select all six SmartArt graphic circles and then click the Larger button (SmartArt Tools Format tab | Shapes group) three times to increase the size of the selected shapes. Select the center shape and then click the Larger button once to increase the size of this circle. Increase the font size of the center circle text to 24 point and the outer circle text to 16 point. Change the font size of the word, Accredited, to 14 point so it displays on one line. Bold the text in the six circles.

6. Change the document properties, as specified by your instructor. Save the presentation using the file name, Extend 4-1 Suburban College.

7. Submit the revised document in the format specified by your instructor.

Make It Right

Analyze a presentation and correct all errors and/or improve the design.

Modifying a Table

Note: To complete this assignment, you will be required to use the Data Files for Students. See the inside back cover of this book for instructions on downloading the Data Files for Students, or contact your instructor for information about accessing the required files.

Instructions: Start PowerPoint. Open the presentation, Make It Right 4-1 Media World, located on the Data Files for Students.

In your sociology class, you have learned that women tend to have more friends than men do in their personal and online relationships. Table 4–3 lists the more popular social networking Web sites and the percentages of women and men who participate in these groups. This table is displayed partially on the slide in the Media World presentation (Figure 4–82 on the next page). Correct the formatting problems and errors in the presentation while keeping in mind the guidelines presented in this chapter.

Table 4–3 Social Media World		
Males		**Females**
43%	Facebook	57%
45%	Flickr	55%
36%	MySpace	64%
43%	Twitter	57%

Continued >

Make It Right *continued*

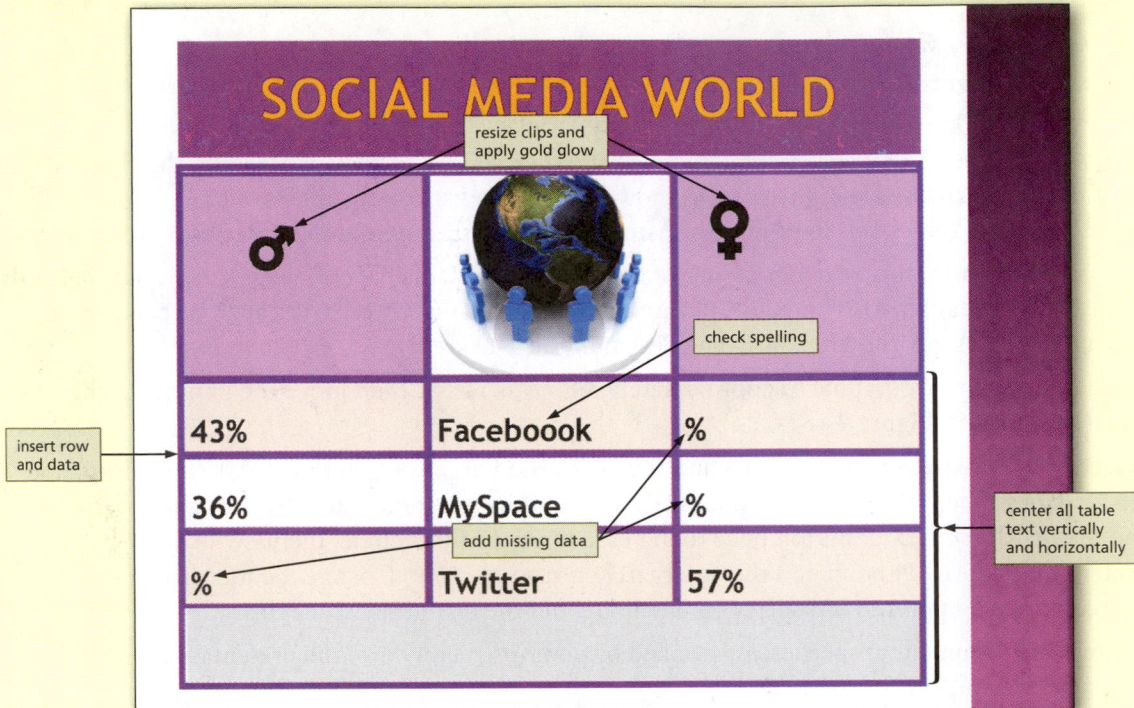

Figure 4–82

Perform the following tasks:

1. Resize the male symbol clip in the cell at the upper-left corner of the table to approximately 1.25" × 1.25". Apply the Gold, 18 pt glow, Accent color 4 (Glow Variations area) picture effect to this clip. Resize the female symbol clip in the cell at the upper-right corner of the table to approximately 1.35" × 0.88". Apply the Pink, 18 pt glow, Accent color 5 (Glow Variations area) picture effect to this clip. Center the male and female clips in the cells.

2. Use Table 4–3 on the previous page to add the missing data in three table cells. Insert a row for the Flickr data by right-clicking any cell in the Facebook row, pointing to Insert on the shortcut menu, and then clicking Insert Rows Below. Using Table 4–3, type the percentages and the word, Flickr, in this new row.

3. Select the table and then apply the Circle effect (Cell Bevel, Bevel area) to the table.

4. Select the four social media rows, center the text horizontally in the cells, and then middle-align this text vertically.

5. Change the slide transition from Shred to Orbit (Dynamic Content area) and then change the duration to 3.00 seconds.

6. Check the slide for spelling errors and then change the document properties, as specified by your instructor. Save the presentation using the file name, Make It Right 4-1 Social Media World.

7. Submit the revised document in the format specified by your instructor.

In the Lab

Design and/or create a presentation using the guidelines, concepts, and skills presented in this chapter. Labs 1, 2, and 3 are listed in order of increasing difficulty.

Lab 1: Inserting and Formatting SmartArt

Note: To complete this assignment, you will be required to use the Data Files for Students. See the inside back cover of this book for instructions on downloading the Data Files for Students, or contact your instructor for information about accessing the required files.

Problem: A pineapple is a type of fruit enjoyed throughout the world. People living in the Caribbean first called this fruit *anana*, meaning excellent fruit. European explorers to the Caribbean then changed the name to pineapple because they thought the outside looked like a pinecone and the inside texture resembled an apple. You visited Hawaii recently and toured a pineapple plantation. Several of the pictures you took are on the slides shown in Figure 4–83 and are on the Data Files for Students. You will convert the four pictures on Slide 1 to SmartArt and add descriptive text. Then you will convert the bulleted list on Slide 2 to a SmartArt graphic, change colors, apply a style, and add a shape fill.

(a) Slide 1

(b) Slide 2

Figure 4–83

Continued >

In the Lab *continued*

Perform the following tasks:

1. Open the presentation, Lab 4-1 Pineapples, located on the Data Files for Students.

2. On Slide 1, change the order of the pictures to match the order shown in Figure 4-83a on the previous page by selecting the picture you want to move and then clicking the Move Up or Move Down buttons (SmartArt Tools Design tab | Create Graphic group).

3. In the SmartArt Text pane, type `Pineapple` as the top Level 1 text that will appear over the central pineapple picture. Type `28,000 plants per acre` as the second Level 1 text that will appear to the right of the first circle, `Needs iron-rich soil` as the text for the middle circle, and `Fruit ready to pick` for the third circle.

4. Change the font for the word, Pineapple, to Forte. Bold this word and then change the font color to Orange. Decrease the size of the placeholder for the word, Pineapple, by dragging the bottom square sizing handle upward being careful not to decrease the size of the word, Pineapple. Move the placeholder toward the top of the slide, as shown in Figure 4–83a on the previous page.

5. Apply the Orange, 18 pt glow, Accent color 6 (Glow Variations area) picture effect to the large pineapple picture.

6. On Slide 2, convert the bulleted list to the Circle Accent Timeline (Process area) SmartArt Graphic. Change the color to Colored Fill – Accent 3 (Accent 3 area). Apply the Subtle Effect (Best Match for Document area) SmartArt Style to the entire graphic.

7. Select all text in the Text pane and then add a shape fill by clicking the Shape Fill button arrow (SmartArt Tools Format tab | Shape Styles group) and then clicking the color, Orange, Accent 6, Lighter 40% (Theme Colors area), as shown in Figure 4–83b on the previous page.

8. For all slides, apply the Reveal transition (Subtle area) and change the duration to 5.00 seconds.

9. Change the document properties, as specified by your instructor. Save the presentation using the file name, Lab 4-1 Growing Pineapples.

10. Submit the revised document in the format specified by your instructor.

In the Lab

Lab 2: Creating a Presentation by Inserting SmartArt and a Chart

Note: To complete this assignment, you will be required to use the Data Files for Students. See the inside back cover of this book for instructions on downloading the Data Files for Students, or contact your instructor for information about accessing the required files.

Problem: Adults generally have four or five sleep cycles every night. Each cycle lasts approximately 90 minutes and is composed of four steps, which are light sleep, intermediate sleep, deep sleep, and rapid eye movement (REM) sleep. Nearly one-fifth of people sleep fewer than six hours each night, and the average hours slept are indicated in Table 4–4. Your speech teacher has assigned an informative speech, and you desire to explain the sleep cycle and the hours slept as part of your talk. You create two slides of a PowerPoint presentation shown in Figure 4–84a and Figure 4–84b. These slides contain clips that are on the Data Files for Students.

Table 4–4 Hours Slept			
Fewer than 6	6 – 6.9	7 – 7.9	More than 8
19%	27%	30%	24%

(a) Slide 1

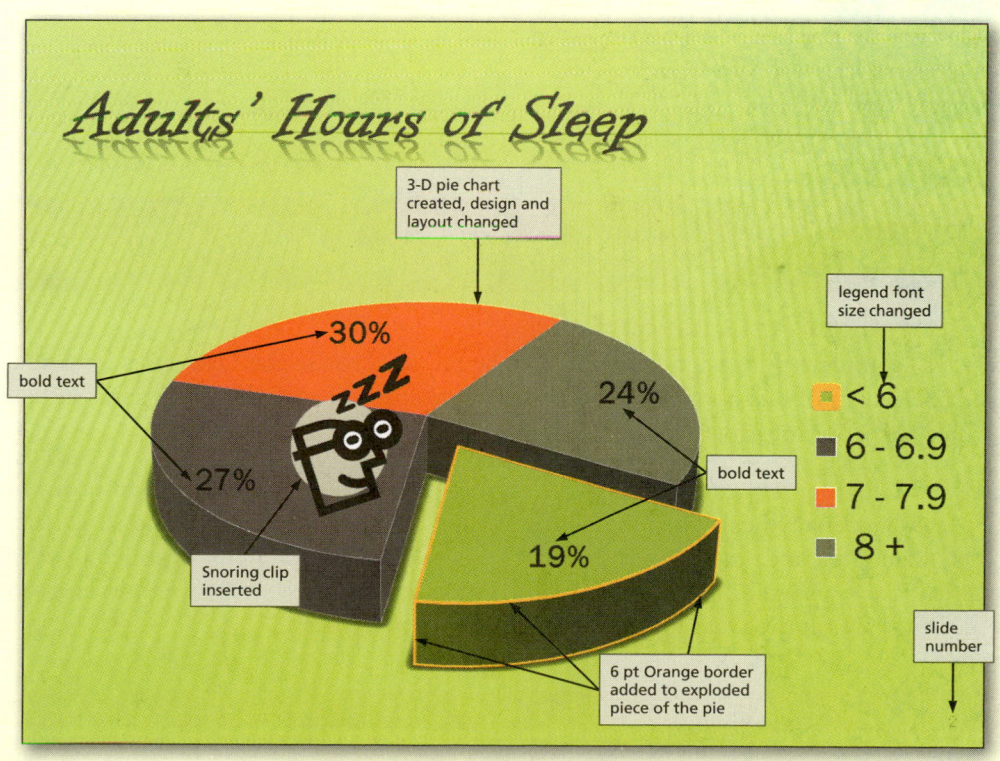

(b) Slide 2

Figure 4–84

Continued >

In the Lab *continued*

Perform the following tasks:

1. Open the presentation, Lab 4-2 Sleep, located on the Data Files for Students.

2. On Slide 1, create the SmartArt graphic shown in Figure 4–84a on the previous page. Replace the sample data with the data in Table 4–4 on the previous page starting with the words, Light Sleep, and moving clockwise. Apply the Segmented Cycle (Cycle area). Change the colors to Colored Fill – Accent 5 (Accent 5 group). Apply the Brick Scene (3-D area) Style. Resize the SmartArt graphic to approximately 5" × 7" and then move this graphic to the upper-right corner of the slide. Bold all words in the graphic.

3. On Slide 2, create the Pie in 3-D chart (second chart in Pie area) shown in Figure 4–84b on the previous page. Apply chart design Style 10 and then change the chart layout to Layout 6. Select the chart title text, Sales, and then press the DELETE key to delete this text.

4. Increase the legend font size to 28 point and the percentages on each pie slice to 24 point bold.

5. Select the chart and rotate it approximately 120 degrees so that the green slice is at the bottom of the pie. Explode the green slice, which represents the percentage of people sleeping fewer than 6 hours, as shown in Figure 4–84. Add a 6 pt border to this slice and then change the border color to Orange.

6. Insert the Man Snore audio clip located on the Data Files for Students into Slide 1, play the clip across slides, hide the sound icon during the show, and loop until stopped.

7. Insert the Snoring clip located on the Data Files for Students into Slide 2 and move it to the location shown in Figure 4–84.

8. Insert the slide number on both slides. Apply the Ripple transition (Exciting area) to all slides. Change the duration to 3.00 seconds. Check the spelling and correct any errors.

9. Change the document properties, as specified by your instructor. Save the presentation using the file name, Lab 4-2 Sleep Cycle.

10. Submit the revised document in the format specified by your instructor.

In the Lab

Lab 3: Creating a Presentation with SmartArt and a Table

Note: To complete this assignment, you will be required to use the Data Files for Students. See the inside back cover of this book for instructions on downloading the Data Files for Students, or contact your instructor for information about accessing the required files.

Problem: Laughter is the best medicine, according to the adage. Sharing a humorous situation with others can have many health benefits, as outlined in Table 4–5. You have read about the positive effects of laughter, and you want to share your knowledge with students enrolled in your health class. You create the presentation in Figure 4–85 that consists of three slides. Pictures and a clip for the presentation are on the Data Files for Students.

Table 4–5 Benefits of Laughter

Benefits of Laughter			
Physical	Lowers blood pressure	Boosts immunity	Decreases pain
Mental	Relieves stress	Eases anxiety	Improves mood
Social	Strengthens relationships	Promotes teamwork	Minimizes conflict

Perform the following tasks:

1. Open the presentation, Lab 4-3 Laughter, located on the Data Files for Students. Change the presentation theme colors to Austin.

2. On Slide 1, insert the Funnel graphic (Process area) SmartArt graphic shown in Figure 4–85a. Type the keywords, Smile, Laugh, Love, in the first three Level 1 bulleted lines in the Text pane, and type the word, HEALTH, in the fourth line. Bold the word, HEALTH.

3. Resize the SmartArt graphic to approximately 5.4" × 7.58". Change the graphic's colors to Colorful Range – Accent Colors 3 to 4. Add the Sunset Scene (3-D area) Style. Move this graphic to the left side of the slide.

(a) Slide 1

Figure 4–85

Continued >

In the Lab *continued*

4. On Slide 2, create a background by inserting the SunSmile picture located on the Data Files for Students and then change the transparency to 80%. Create the SmartArt graphic shown in Figure 4–85b using the Vertical Box List graphic (List area) and the text shown in Figure 4–85b. Change the graphic's colors to Colorful Range – Accent Colors 5 to 6. Apply the Cartoon (3-D area) Style and the Tight Reflection 4 pt offset (Reflection Variations area) shape effect reflection to the graphic.

5. Apply the Shape Outline Green, Accent 1 color to the four blank rectangle shapes in the SmartArt graphic and then change the weight to 4½ pt.

6. Insert the clip of the person laughing, shown in Figure 4–85b, from Office.com. Resize the clip to approximately 2.33" × 1.96" and then move this clip to the lower-left corner of the slide.

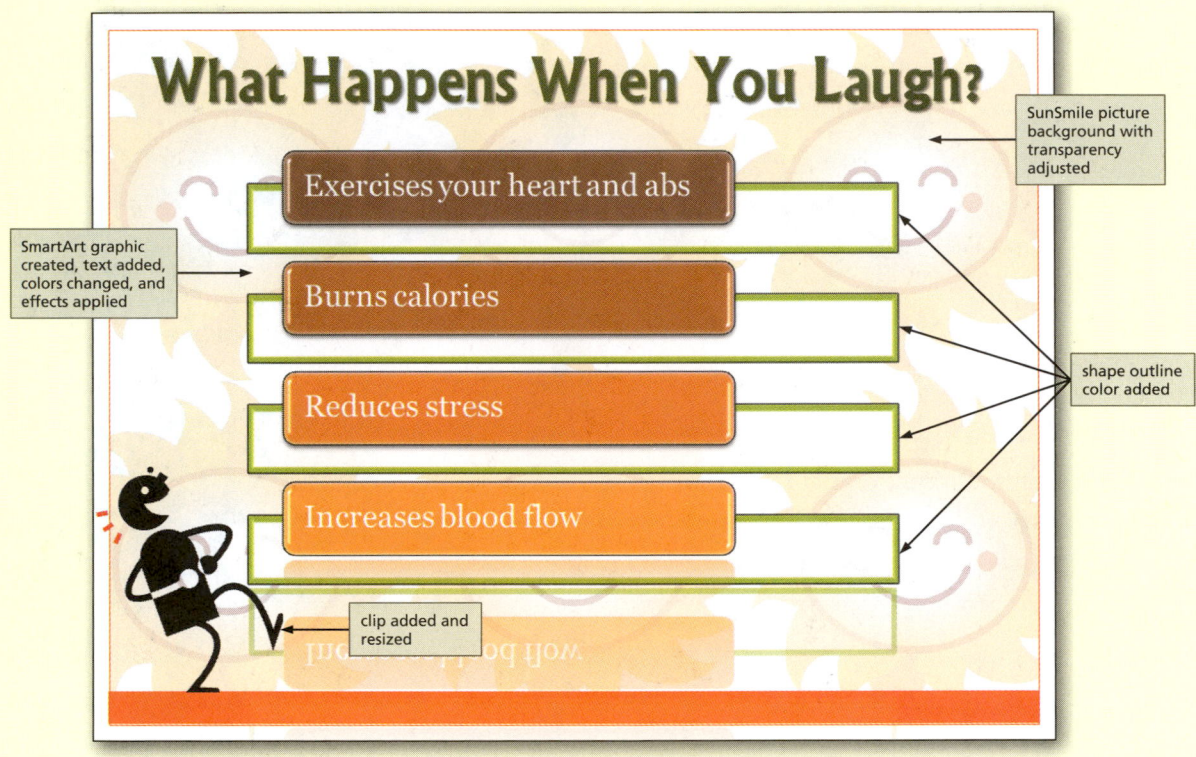

(b) Slide 2

Figure 4–85 (Continued)

7. On Slide 3, insert a table with four columns and four rows, as shown in Figure 4–85c. Merge the second, third, and fourth cells in the Header Row and then change the font size to 48 point.

8. Type the table header and text using the data in Table 4–5 on page PPT 258. Change the font for all cells to Narkisim and then middle-align this text vertically and center this text horizontally.

9. For all cells other than the Header Row, change the font size to 24 point. Bold the text in the first column and rotate the text direction to 270 degrees.

10. Move the table to the location shown in Figure 4–85c and increase the table size. Change the shading of the second, third, and fourth cells in the first column to Green, Accent 1. If the upper-left table cell has a green fill, apply a No Fill format to this cell so that only the cells below it have a green fill.

11. In the first table cell, insert the picture called Laughing Man located on the Data Files for Students. If necessary, increase the size of this clip in the cell, as shown in Figure 4-85c. Then insert the audio clip, Long Laugh, located on the Data Files for Students. Start the audio clip automatically, hide the sound icon during the show, and loop until stopped.

12. Apply the Riblet (Bevel area) Cell Bevel effect to the table.

13. Apply the Doors transition and change the duration to 03.00. Check the spelling and correct any errors.

14. Change the document properties, as specified by your instructor. Save the presentation using the file name, Lab 4-3 Laughter Benefits.

15. Submit the revised document in the format specified by your instructor.

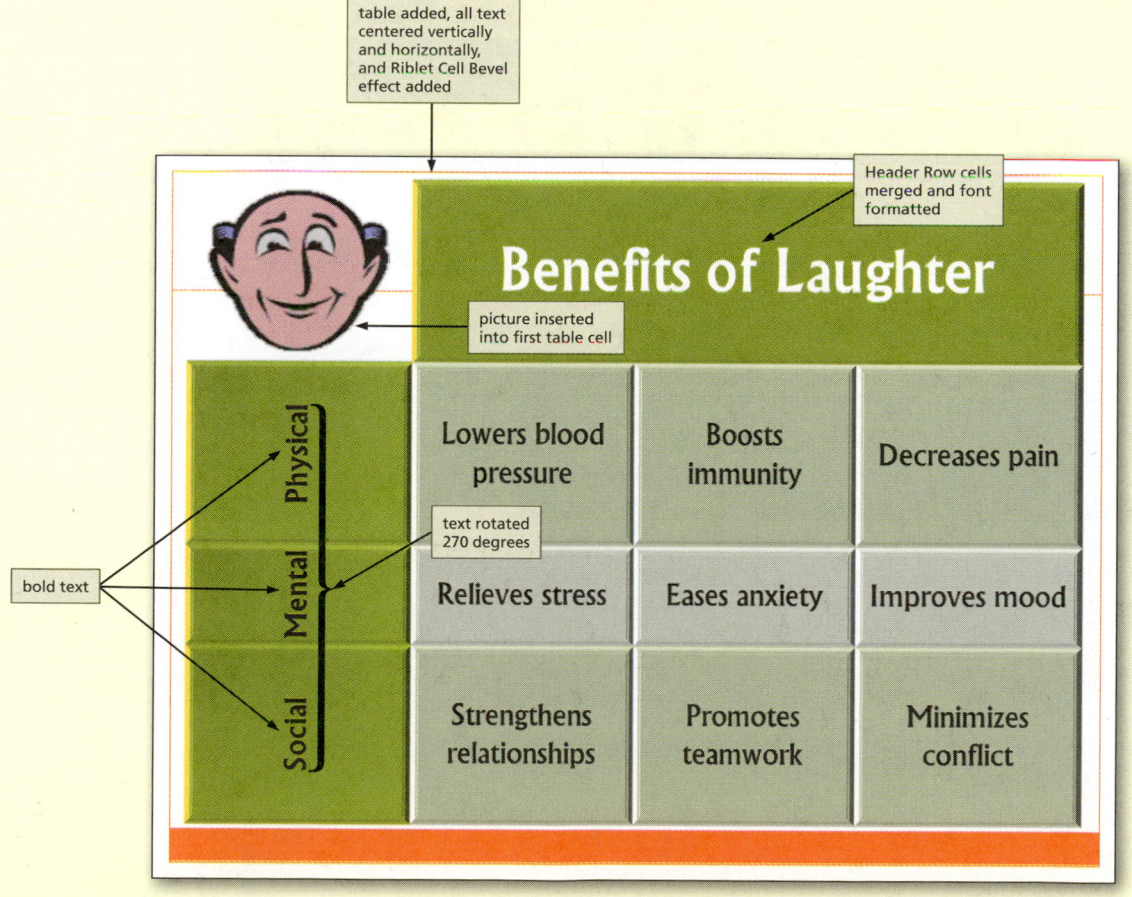

(c) Slide 3

Figure 4–85 (Continued)

Cases and Places

Apply your creative thinking and problem-solving skills to design and implement a solution.

Note: To complete these assignments, you may be required to use the Data Files for Students. See the inside back cover of this book for instructions on downloading the Data Files for Students, or contact your instructor for information about accessing the required files.

As you design the presentations, remember to use the 7×7 rule: a maximum of seven words on a line and a maximum of seven lines on one slide.

1: Designing and Creating a Presentation about Temperature Conversions

Academic

Students in your chemistry class are struggling to convert temperatures from Fahrenheit to Celsius to Kelvin, so you have decided to help them understand the formulas. In addition, you provide some facts to help them see the relationship among the numbers, such as ice melting at 32 degrees Fahrenheit, 0 degrees Celsius, and 273 degrees Kelvin, and water boiling at 212 degrees Fahrenheit, 100 degrees Celsius, and 373 degrees Kelvin. Create a presentation to show the formulas and temperature conversions in two tables. Use the data in Tables 4-6 and 4-7 to create your tables. Apply table styles and add borders and effects, and use at least three objectives found at the beginning of this chapter to develop the presentation. Use pictures from Office.com if they are appropriate for this topic. Be sure to check spelling.

Table 4–6 Temperature Conversion Formulas

Temperature		
From	**To**	**Formula**
Fahrenheit (degrees F)	Celsius (degrees C)	$5 \div 9 \,(F - 32)$
Celsius (degrees C)	Fahrenheit (degrees F)	$9 \div 5 \,C + 32$
Fahrenheit (degrees F)	Kelvin (degrees K)	$(F + 459.67) \times (5/9)$

Table 4–7 Temperature Conversions

Quick Temperature Conversions		
Fahrenheit	**Celsius**	**Kelvin**
212	100	373
86	30	303
68	20	293
50	10	283
32	0	273
14	−10	263
−4	−20	253

2: Designing and Creating a Presentation about Dogs and Cats

Personal

On weekends, you volunteer at an animal shelter, and you notice that fewer dogs and cats are adopted by people living alone than by households having multiple people. You decide to survey the adopting families to see how likely a household is to adopt a dog or a cat if the household has one, two, three, or four members. The data you collect is summarized in Tables 4–8 and 4–9. Share your findings by creating a PowerPoint presentation that contains two pie charts representing survey results. Use at least three objectives found at the beginning of this chapter to develop the presentation. Be sure to check spelling.

Table 4–8 Dogs by Family Size

Dogs by Family Size	
Household Size	Percent
4 or more people	33
3 people	21
2 people	32
1 person	14

Table 4–9 Cats by Family Size

Cats by Family Size	
Household Size	Percent
4 or more people	29
3 people	20
2 people	33
1 person	18

Continued >

Cases and Places *continued*

3: Designing and Creating a Presentation about Light Bulbs

Professional

You are employed at a local hardware store, and many customers desire to change their light bulbs from incandescent to compact fluorescent (CFL). Your manager has asked you to develop a presentation that provides information about equivalent light output, which is measured in lumens. In addition, she wants you to include an explanation that describes the color temperatures recommended for indoor general and task lighting. For example, warm colors (2700–3600 K) are preferred for living spaces because they complement clothing and skin tones; cool colors (3600–5500 K) are best for reading and household tasks because they provide contrast. These temperatures are not related to the heat generated from bulb usage. You decide to create a table using the data in Table 4–10 and a SmartArt graphic using the data in Table 4–11. Insert images in the table and SmartArt graphics from Office.com or your own digital pictures if they are appropriate for this topic. Apply at least one style, border, and effect. Be certain to check spelling.

Table 4–10 Light Bulbs

Incandescent Bulbs vs. CFL Bulbs		
Incandescent	**Minimum Light Output**	**CFL**
40 watts	450 lumens	9–13 watts
60 watts	800 lumens	13–15 watts
75 watts	1,100 lumens	18–25 watts
100 watts	1,600 lumens	23–30 watts
150 watts	2,600 lumens	30–52 watts

Table 4–11 Color Temperatures

Light Sources Warmth and Coolness	
Kelvin (K) Temperature	**Bulb Type**
2600	Incandescent
3000	Warm white
3100	Halogen
4200	Cool white
5000	Daylight

5 | Collaborating on and Delivering a Presentation

Objectives

You will have mastered the material in this chapter when you can:

- Combine slide shows
- Accept and reject a reviewer's proposed changes
- Insert, modify, and delete comments
- Reuse slides from an existing presentation
- Capture part of a slide using screen clipping
- Insert slide footer content

- Set slide and presentation resolution
- Save a file as a PowerPoint show
- Package a presentation for storage on a compact disc
- Save a presentation in a previous PowerPoint format
- Inspect and protect files
- Annotate slide shows with a pen and highlighter

5 | Collaborating on and Delivering a Presentation

BTW

Integrating Differing Perspectives
Audience members often have diverse educational levels, technical skills, and cultural backgrounds. It is important for you to understand how they may interpret material on your slides. Terms and graphics that seem clear to you may raise questions among people viewing your slides. The issues raised and the comments made during the review cycle play an important role in the development of a successful PowerPoint presentation.

Introduction

Often presentations are enhanced when individuals collaborate to fine-tune text, visuals, and design elements on the slides. A **review cycle** occurs when a slide show designer shares a file with reviewers so they can make comments and changes to their copies of the slides and then return the file to the designer. A **comment** is a description that normally does not display as part of the slide show. It can be used to clarify information that may be difficult to understand, to pose questions, or to communicate suggestions. The designer then can display the comments, modify their content, and ask the reviewers to again review the presentation, and continue this process until the slides are satisfactory. Once the presentation is complete, the designer can protect the file so no one can open it without a password or alter comments and other information. The designer also can save the presentation to an optical disc or as a PowerPoint show that will run without opening the PowerPoint application. In addition, a presenter can use PowerPoint's variety of tools to run the show effectively and to emphasize various elements on the screen.

Project — Presentation with Comments, Inserted Slides, and Protection

The six slides in the Windstorms presentation (Figure 5–1) give information on and provide images of two particular types of windstorms: tornadoes and hurricanes. The initial presentation began with three slides, which were sent to a reviewer, Mary Halen. She suggested changes and created a new slide.

When you are developing a presentation, it often is advantageous to ask a variety of people to review your work in progress. These individuals can evaluate the wording, art, and design, and experts in the subject can check the slides for accuracy. They can add comments to the slides in specific areas, such as a paragraph, a graphic, or a table. You then can review their comments and use them to modify and enhance your work. You also can insert slides from other presentations into your file. The Windstorms presentation includes two slides from the file, Hurricanes.pptx.

Once you develop the final set of slides, you can complete the file by removing any comments and personal information, by adding a password so that unauthorized people cannot see or change the file contents without your permission, by saving the file as a PowerPoint show that runs automatically when you open a file, and by saving the file to an optical disc.

When running your presentation, you may decide to show the slides nonsequentially. For example, you may need to review a slide you discussed already, or you may want to skip slides and jump forward. You also may want to emphasize, or **annotate**, material on the slides by highlighting text or writing on the slides. You can save your annotations to review during or after the presentation.

BTW

Documenting Your Thoughts
Your PowerPoint slides are formal documentation of the thoughts you are attempting to present to an audience, so you should seek comments to help ensure that your words and graphic elements are as clear as possible. The words you use on your slides and the handouts you provide are important documents that audience members may reference in the future. Your efforts, consequently, may be visible long after the verbal presentation has concluded.

(a) Slide 1 (Title Slide Enhanced from Reviewer)

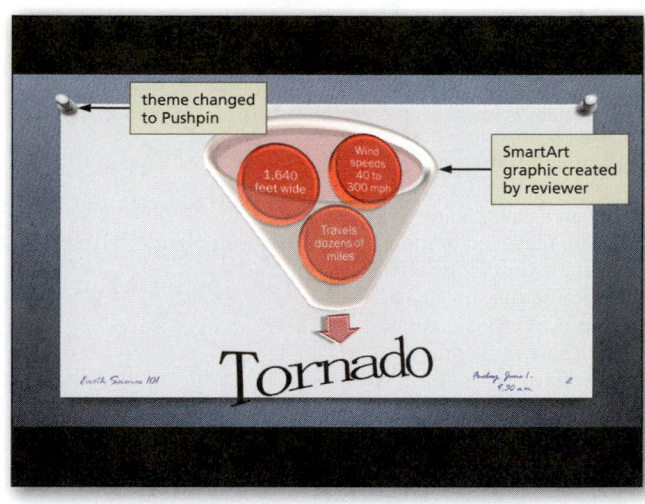

(b) Slide 2 (SmartArt from Reviewer)

(c) Slide 3 (Inserted from Reviewer's Presentation)

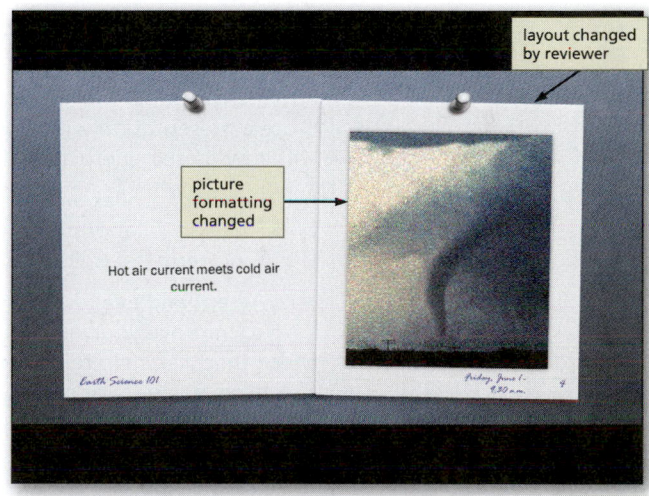

(d) Slide 4 (Enhanced from Reviewer)

(e) Slide 5 (Inserted from Reviewer's Presentation)

(f) Slide 6 (Inserted from Reviewer's Presentation)

Figure 5–1

Overview

As you read through this chapter, you will learn how to create the presentation shown in Figure 5–1 on the previous page by performing these general tasks:

- Review a merged presentation.
- Insert slides and content clipped from slides.
- Secure and share a presentation.
- Use presentation tools.
- Package a presentation for a CD or DVD.
- Save a presentation in a variety of formats.
- Annotate a presentation.

Plan Ahead

General Project Guidelines

When creating a PowerPoint presentation, the actions you perform and the decisions you make will affect the appearance and characteristics of the finished document. As you create a presentation with illustrations, such as the project shown in Figure 5–1, you should follow these general guidelines:

1. **Develop a collaboration plan.** Planning tasks for group members to follow helps ensure success. Collaborators must understand the overall group goal, set short-term and long-term goals, identify subtasks that must be completed, and set a schedule.

2. **Accept and evaluate criticism.** Feedback, both positive and negative, that enables you to improve yourself and your work, is called **criticism**. Written and oral comments from others can help reinforce the positive aspects and also identify flaws. Seek comments from a variety of people who genuinely want to help you develop an effective slide show.

3. **Give constructive criticism.** If you are asked to critique a presentation, begin and end with positive comments. Give specific details about a few key areas that can be improved. Be honest, but be tactful.

4. **Use slide numbers to guide your speech.** A speaker can view the slide numbers to organize the speech, jump to particular slides, and control timing.

5. **Determine the screen show ratio.** Consider where the presentation will be shown and the type of hardware that will be available. Wide-screen displays are prevalent in the home office and corporate world, but their dimensions present design challenges for the PowerPoint developer.

6. **Select an appropriate password.** A **password** is a private combination of characters that allows users to open a file. To prevent unauthorized people from viewing your slides, choose a good password and keep it confidential.

When necessary, more specific details concerning the above guidelines are presented at appropriate points in the chapter. The chapter also will identify the actions performed and decisions made regarding these guidelines during the creation of the presentation shown in Figure 5–1.

To Start PowerPoint and Open and Save a Presentation

To begin this presentation, you will open a file located on the Data Files for Students. See the inside back cover of this book for instructions on downloading the Data Files for Students, or contact your instructor for more information about accessing the required files. If you are using a computer to step through the project in this chapter and you want your screens to match the figures in this book, you should change your screen's resolution to 1024 × 768.

The following steps start PowerPoint, open a file, and then save it with a new file name.

1 Start PowerPoint. If necessary, maximize the PowerPoint window.

2 Open the presentation, Windstorms, located on the Data Files for Students.

3 Save the presentation using the file name, Windstorms Final.

Develop a collaboration plan.

Working with your classmates can yield numerous benefits. Your peers can assist in brainstorming, developing key ideas, revising your project, and keeping you on track so that your presentation meets the assignment goals.

The first step when collaborating with peers is to define success. What, ultimately, is the goal? For example, are you developing a persuasive presentation to school administrators in an effort to fund a new club? Next, you can set short-term and long-term goals that help lead you to completing the project successfully. These goals can be weekly tasks to accomplish, such as interviewing content experts, conducting online research, or compiling an annotated bibliography. After that, you can develop a plan to finish the project by stating subtasks that each member must accomplish. Each collaborator should inform the group members when the task is complete or if problems are delaying progress. When collaborators meet, whether in person or online, they should establish an agenda and have one member keep notes of topics discussed.

Plan Ahead

BTW

Slide Library
In a business environment, PowerPoint presentations may be stored on a centrally located Slide Library that resides on a server. These slide shows may be shared, reused, and accessed by many individuals who then can copy materials into their individual presentations. The Slide Library time stamps when an individual has borrowed a particular slide or presentation and then time stamps the slide or presentation when it is returned. If a particular slide in the Slide Library has been updated, anyone who has borrowed that slide is notified that the content has changed. People creating PowerPoint presentations can track the changes to presentations, locate the latest versions of slides, and check for slide updates.

Collaborating on a Presentation

PowerPoint provides several methods to collaborate with friends or coworkers who can view your slide show and then provide feedback. When you **collaborate**, you work together on a document with other PowerPoint users who are cooperating jointly and assisting willingly with the endeavor. You can distribute your slide show physically to others by exchanging a compact disc or a flash drive. You also can share your presentation through the Internet by sending the file as an e-mail attachment or saving the file to a storage location, such as Windows Live SkyDrive.

In the following pages, you will follow these general steps to collaborate with Mary Halen, who has reviewed your Windstorms presentation:

1. Combine a presentation.
2. Print slides and comments.
3. Review and accept or reject changes.
4. Delete a comment.
5. Modify a comment.
6. Insert a comment.

To Merge a Presentation

Mary Halen reviewed the Windstorms presentation and made several comments about the design. She converted the Slide 1 title text to WordArt and the Slide 2 bulleted list to a SmartArt graphic. She also added a transition to all slides, changed the theme, edited some paragraphs, and added two slides. The following steps merge this reviewer's file with the original Windstorms presentation.

1
• With the Windstorms Final presentation active, display the Review tab (Figure 5–2).

Q&A
Can I track my changes in PowerPoint as I can in other Office 2010 products, such as Word 2010?

No. To detect differences between your presentation and another presentation, you must merge the files.

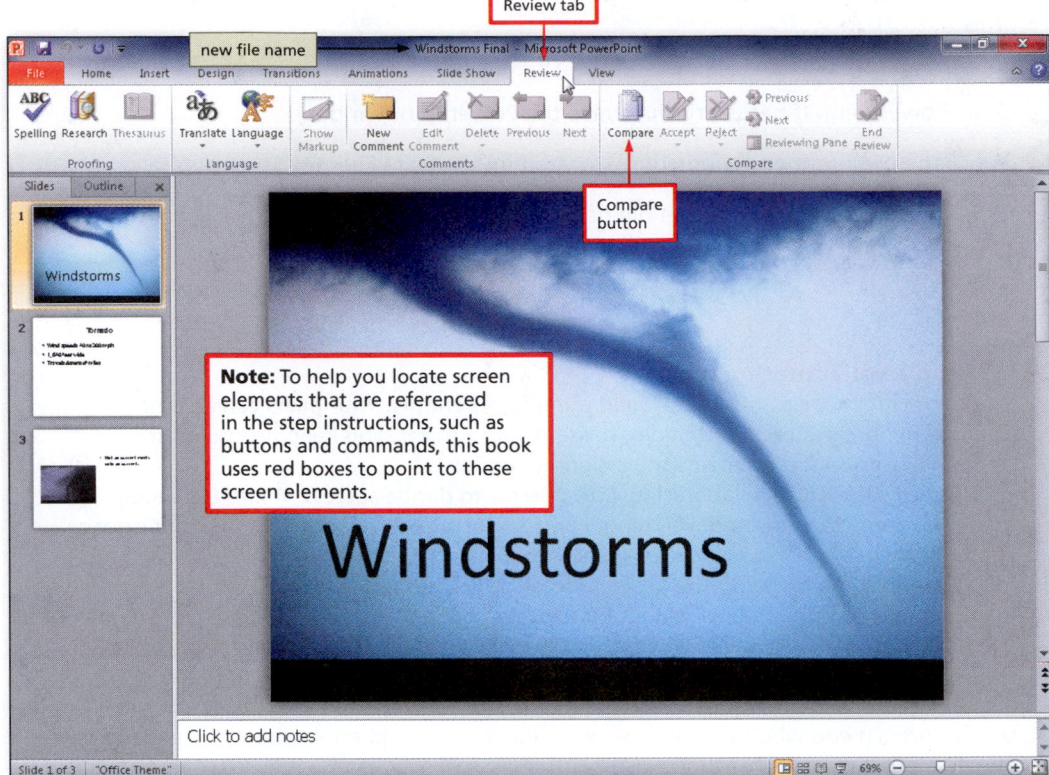

Figure 5–2

2
• Click the Compare button (Review tab | Compare group) to display the Choose File to Merge with Current Presentation dialog box.

• With the list of files and folders on your USB flash drive displaying, click Windstorms – Mary Halen to select the file name (Figure 5–3).

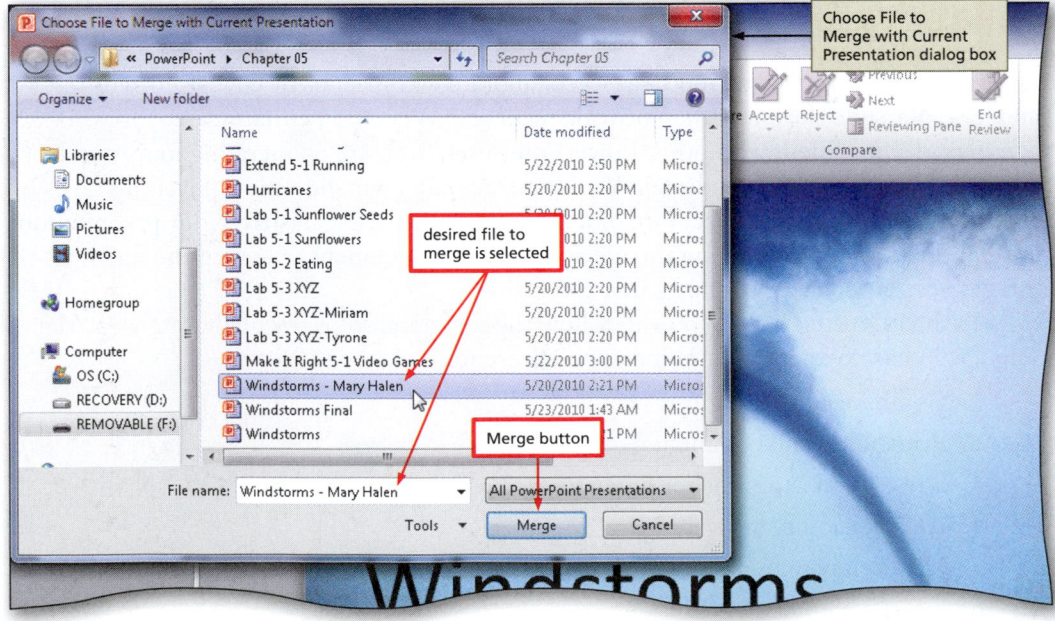

Figure 5–3

3

- Click the Merge button (Choose File to Merge with Current Presentation dialog box) to merge Mary Halen's presentation with the Windstorms presentation and to display the Revisons task pane (Figure 5–4).

 Q&A

If several reviewers have made comments and suggestions, can I merge their files, too?

Yes. Repeat Steps 1 and 2. Each reviewer's initials display in a color-coded comment box.

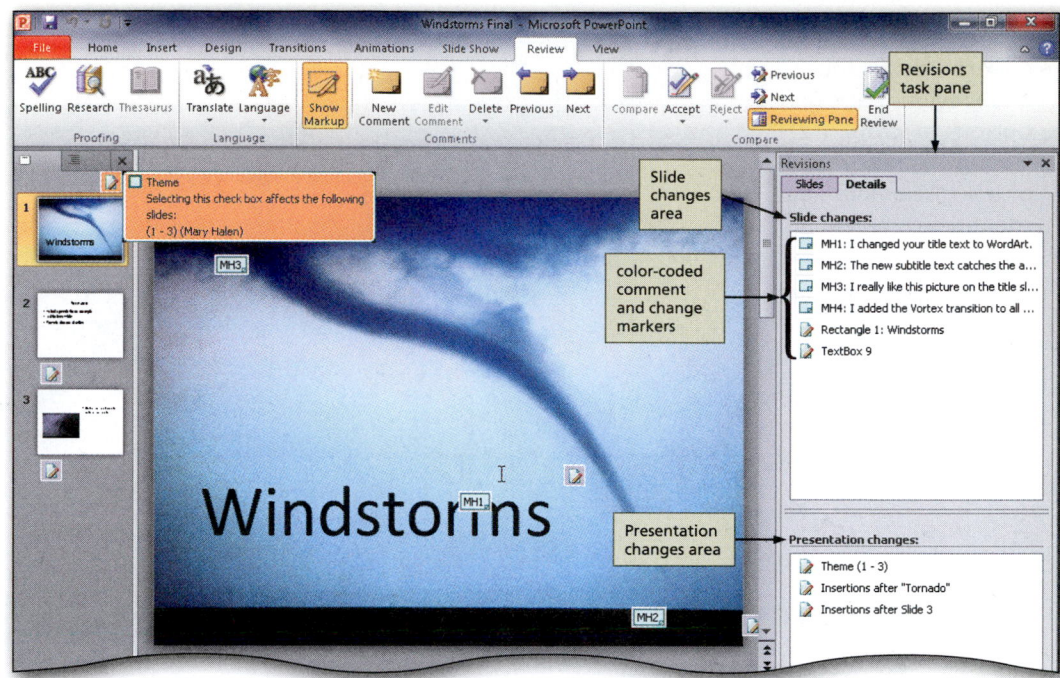

Figure 5–4

To Print Comments

As owner of the original presentation, you want to review the comments and modifications and then make decisions about whether to accept these suggestions. You can print each slide and the comments a reviewer has made before you begin to accept and reject each suggestion. PowerPoint can print these slides and comments on individual pages. The following steps use this slide show to illustrate printing these suggestions.

1

- Open the Backstage view and then click the Print tab to display the Print gallery.

- Click Full Page Slides to display the Print Layout gallery.

- If necessary, click Print Comments and Ink Markup to select this option (Figure 5–5).

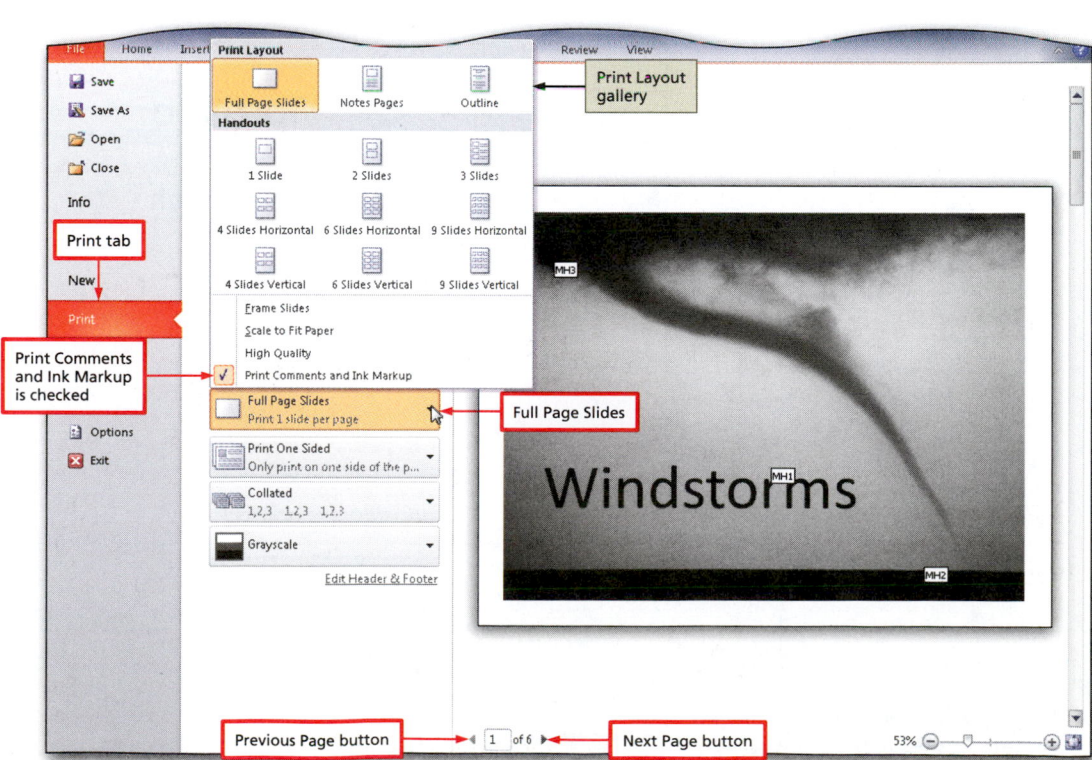

Figure 5–5

2

• Click the Next Page and Previous Page buttons to scroll through the previews of the three slides and the three comment pages.

• Click the Print button to print the six pages (Figure 5–6).

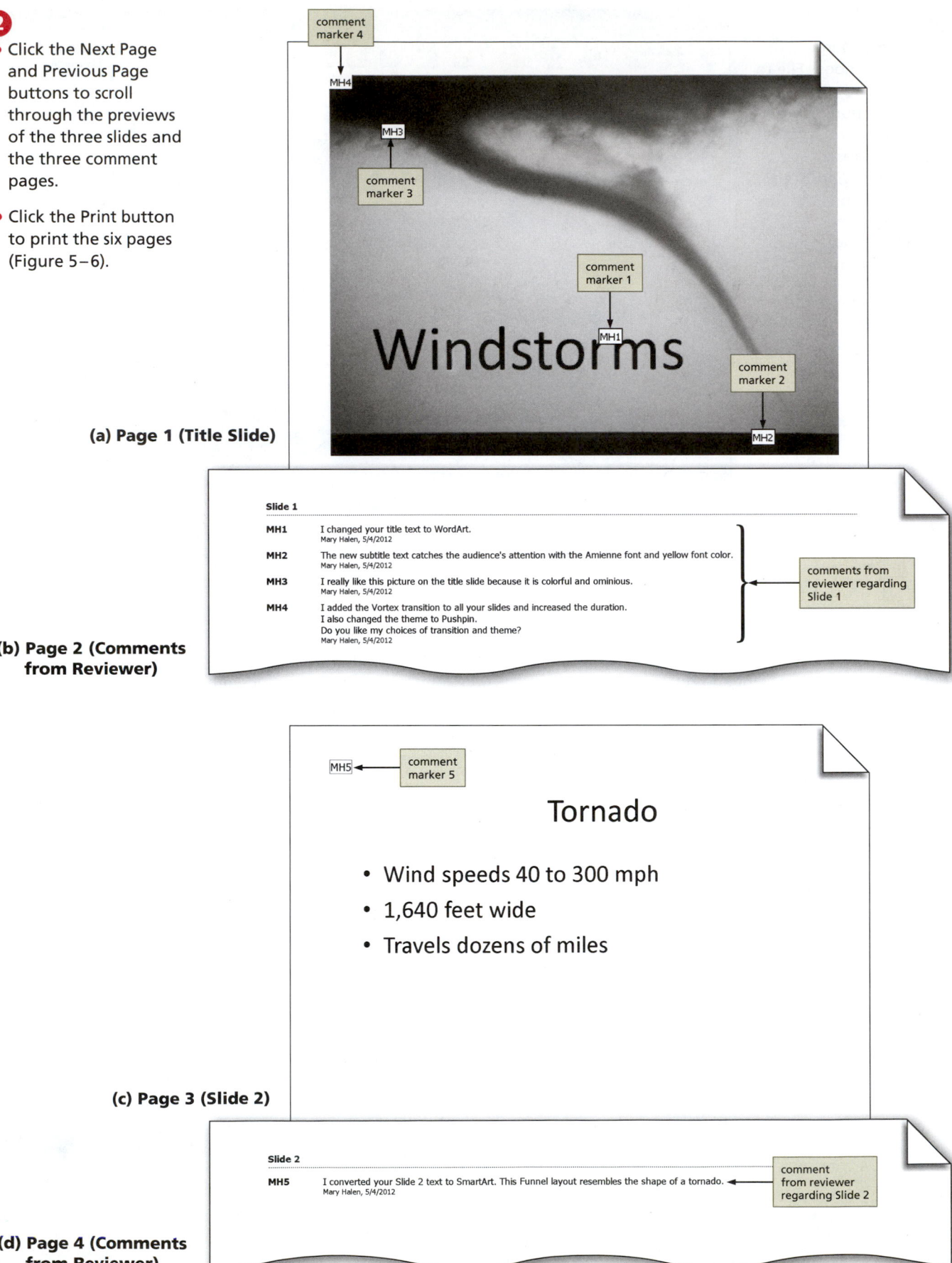

(a) Page 1 (Title Slide)

(b) Page 2 (Comments from Reviewer)

(c) Page 3 (Slide 2)

(d) Page 4 (Comments from Reviewer)

Figure 5–6

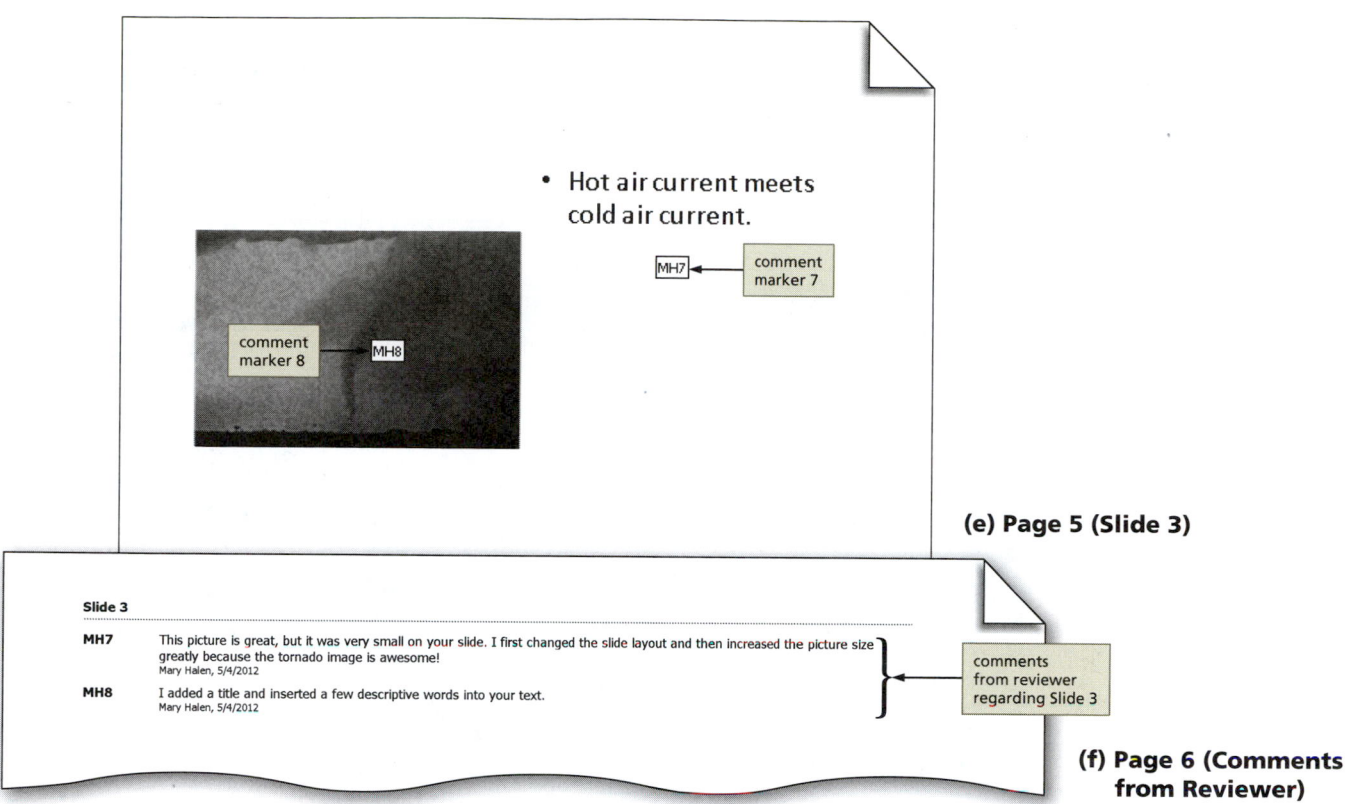

(e) Page 5 (Slide 3)

Slide 3

MH7   This picture is great, but it was very small on your slide. I first changed the slide layout and then increased the picture size greatly because the tornado image is awesome!
Mary Halen, 5/4/2012

MH8   I added a title and inserted a few descriptive words into your text.
Mary Halen, 5/4/2012

comments from reviewer regarding Slide 3

(f) Page 6 (Comments from Reviewer)

Figure 5–6 (Continued)

To Preview Presentation Changes

The reviewer made several changes to the overall presentation and then edited your three slides. You can preview her modifications to obtain an overview of her suggestions. Seeing her edits now can help you decide later whether to accept or reject each change as you step through each revision. The following steps preview the merged presentation.

1

- If necessary, display the Review tab and then click the Reviewing Pane button (Review tab | Compare group) to display the Revisions task pane. With Slide 1 displaying, click the Slides tab in the Revisions task pane to display a thumbnail of merged Slide 1 (Figure 5–7).

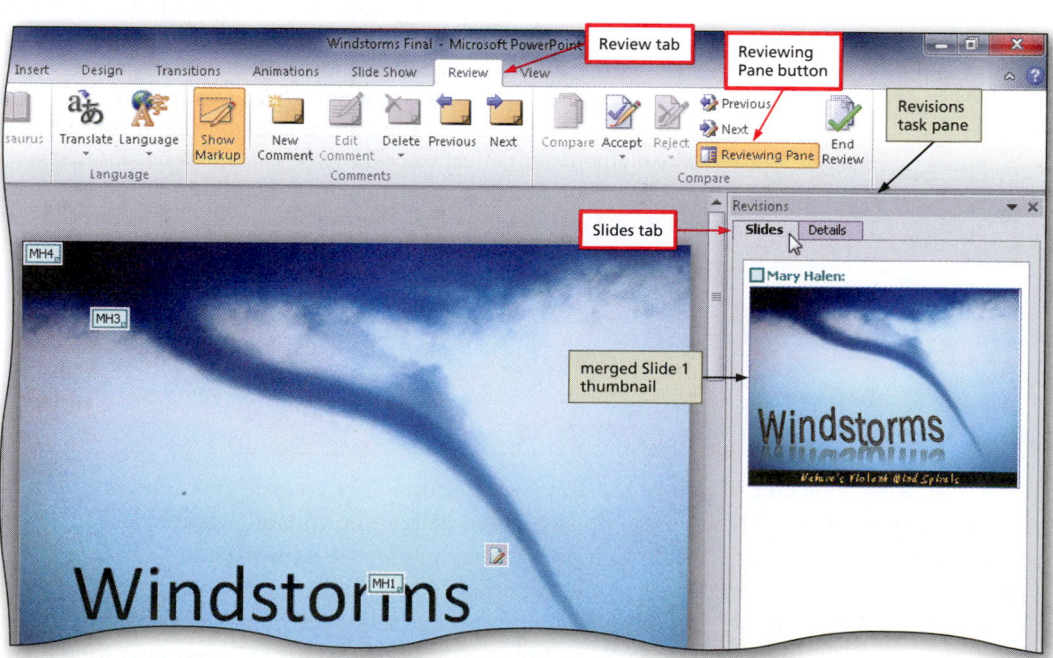

Figure 5–7

2

- Click the Mary Halen check box above the Slide 1 thumbnail to view the proposed changes in the Slide pane (Figure 5–8).

3

- Click the Mary Halen check box again to reject the changes.

Q&A

Can I make some, but not all, of the reviewer's changes on Slide 1?

Yes. PowerPoint allows you to view each proposed change individually and then either accept or reject the modification.

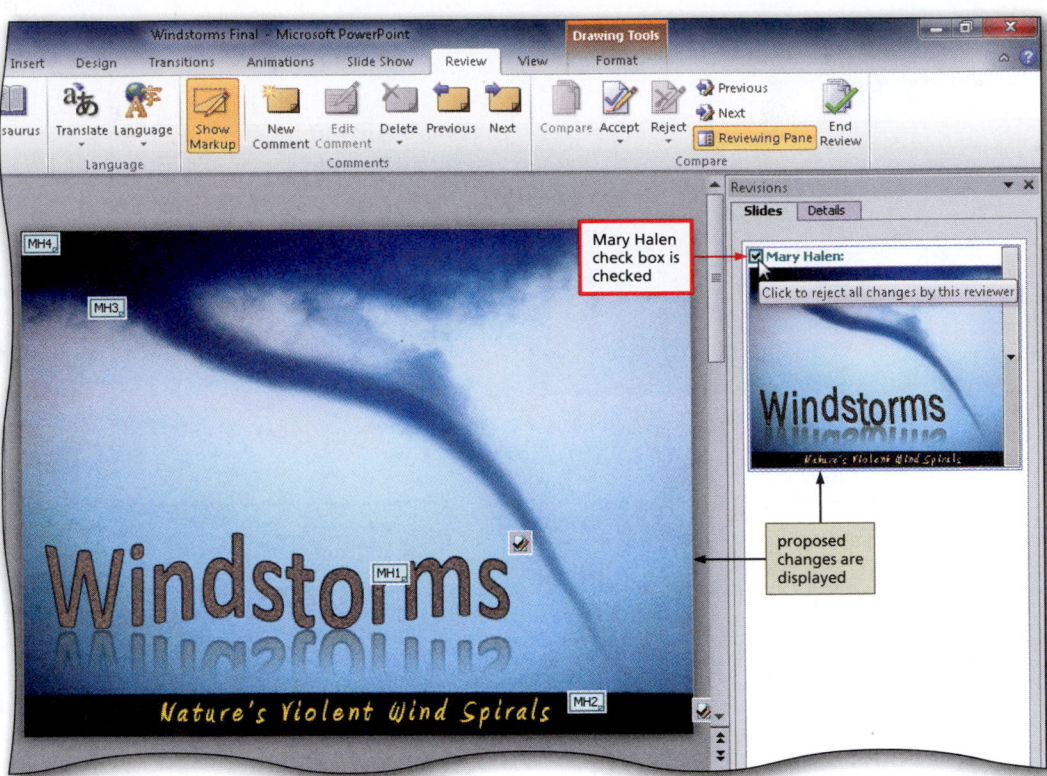

Figure 5–8

Plan Ahead

Accept and evaluate criticism.
Receiving feedback from others ultimately should enhance your presentation. If several of your reviewers make similar comments, such as too much text appears on one slide or that a chart would help present your concept, then you should heed their criticism and modify your slides. Criticism from a variety of people, particularly if they are from different cultures or vary in age, gives a wide range of viewpoints. Some reviewers might focus on the font size, others on color and design choices, while others might single out the overall message. These individuals should make judgments on your work, such as saying that the overall presentation is good or that a particular paragraph is confusing, and then offer reasons why elements are effective or how you can edit a paragraph.

When you receive these comments, do not get defensive. Ask yourself why your reviewers would have made these comments. Perhaps they lack a background in the subject matter, or, on the other hand, they may have a particular interest in this topic and can add their expertise.

To Review and Delete Comments

The Revisions task pane and the Reviewing group help you review each comment. These notes from the reviewer may guide you through the revisions and help you ultimately to decide whether to accept changes or delete the suggestions. Color-coded comment and change markers are displayed in the Revisions task pane. The reviewer's initials display in the rectangular comment marker on the slide and next to the comment marker in the task pane; the initials are followed by a numeral that indicates the sequence by which the reviewer added comments to the presentation. The following steps view and then delete the reviewer's comments for Slide 1.

1
• Click the Details tab in the Revisions task pane to display the comment markers and the change markers in the Slide changes and Presentation changes areas.

Q&A How do I distinguish between the comment markers and the change markers?

The comment markers are horizontal rectangles followed by the reviewer's initials and a number; the change markers are vertical rectangles with a pencil overlay.

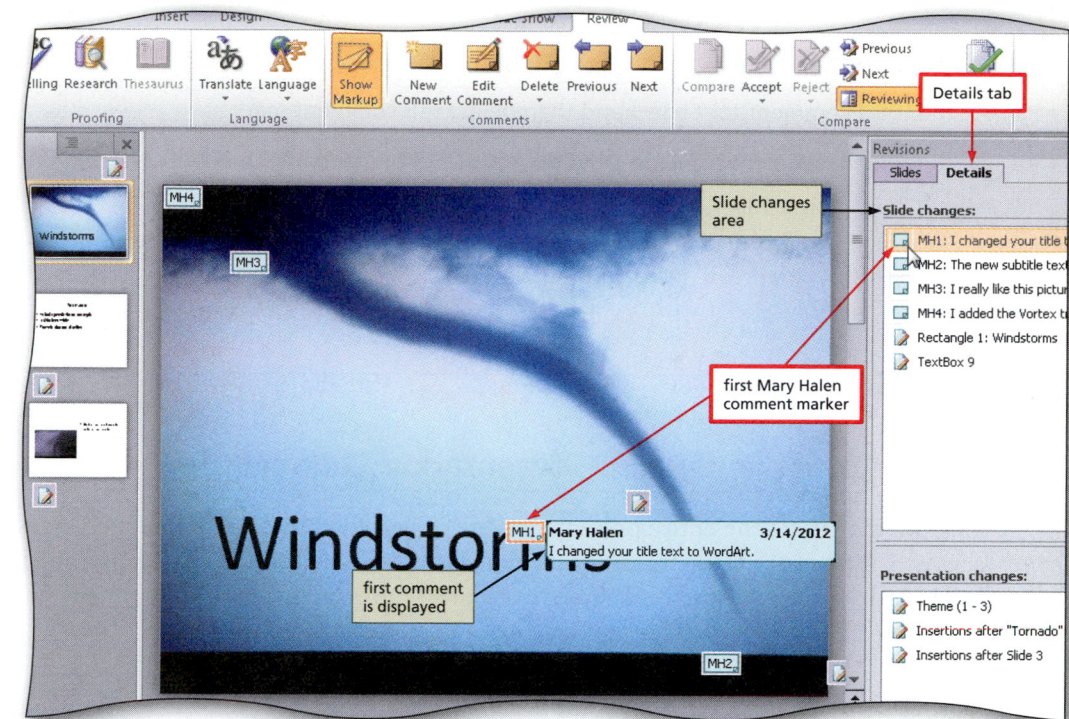

Figure 5–9

• Click the first Mary Halen comment marker, MH1, in the Slides changes area to display the comment (Figure 5–9).

Q&A Why does the number 1 display after the commenter's initials?

The number indicates it is the first comment the reviewer inserted.

Q&A Can I read the comment without clicking the comment marker on the Details tab?

Yes. You can mouse over or click the comment marker on the slide.

2
• Read the comment and then click the **Delete Comment** button (Review tab | Comments group) to delete Mary Halen's first comment.

• Click the Next Comment button (Review tab | Comments group) to view the second comment (Figure 5–10).

Q&A Can I click the comment marker on the Details tab to display the comment instead of clicking the Next button?

Yes. Either method displays the comment.

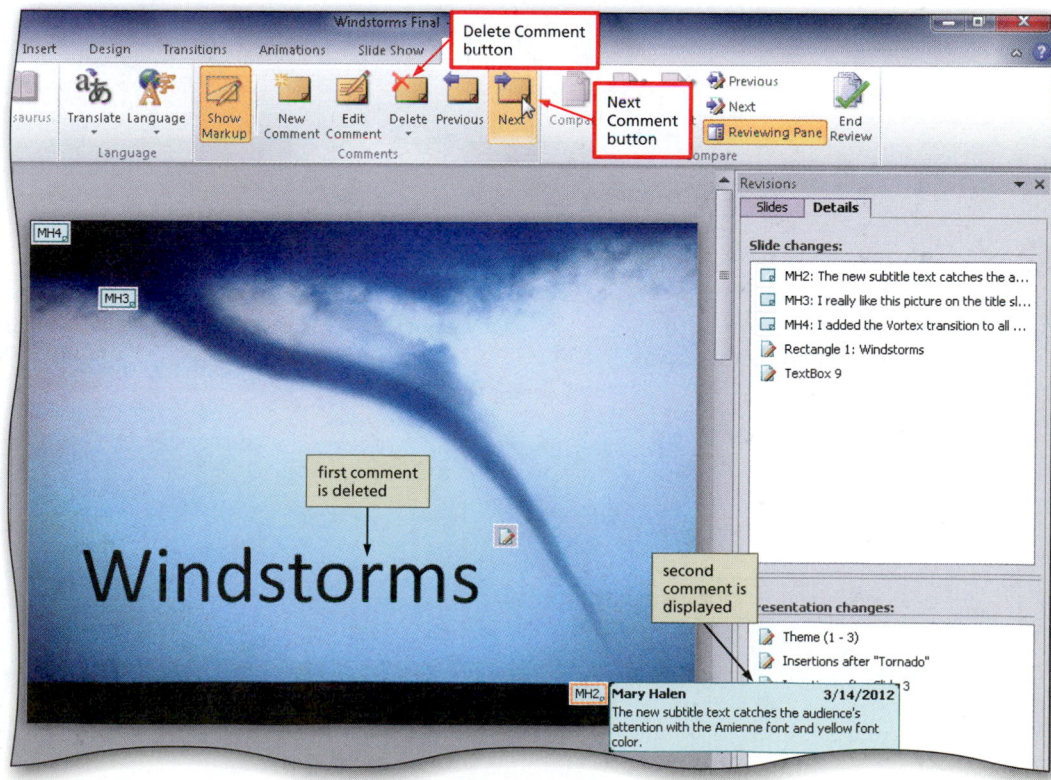

Figure 5–10

• Delete the second comment.

• Review the third comment for Slide 1 and then delete this comment marker.

• Review the fourth comment for Slide 1 but do not delete this comment marker.

Q&A

Why should I not delete Mary Halen's fourth comment?

Mary indicates that she added a transition and changed the presentation theme. You have not accepted her changes yet, so you do not know if you agree with her modifications. You will respond to her question after you have made the changes.

To Review, Accept, and Reject Presentation Changes

Changes that affect the entire presentation are indicated in the Presentation changes area of the Revisions task pane. These changes can include transitions, color schemes, fonts, backgrounds, and slide insertions. The following steps display and accept the reviewer's three revisions in the presentation.

• Click the first presentation change marker, Theme (1 – 3), in the Presentation changes area to display the Theme box with an explanation of the proposed change for all slides in the presentation (Figure 5 – 11).

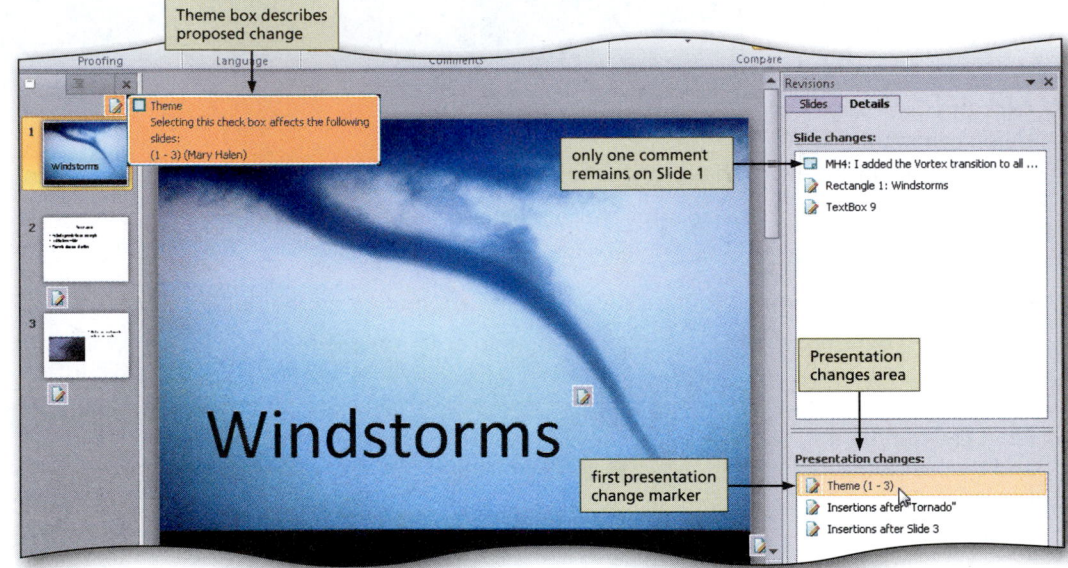

Figure 5 – 11

• Click the Accept Change button (Review tab | Compare group) to view the new Pushpin theme on all slides (Figure 5 – 12).

Q&A

Can I also apply the change by clicking the Theme check box?

Yes. Either method applies the Pushpin theme.

Q&A

If I decide to not apply the new theme, can I reverse this change?

Yes. Click the Reject Change button (Review tab | Compare group) or click the check box to remove the check mark and reject the reviewer's theme modification.

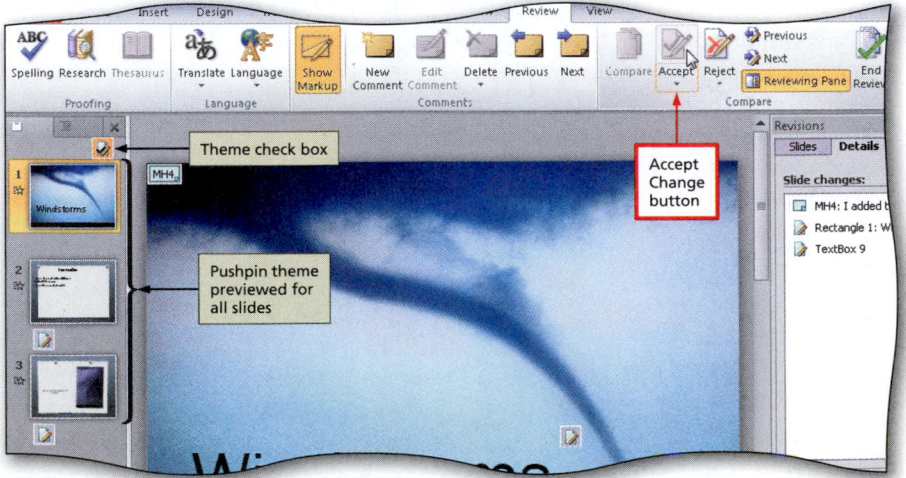

Figure 5 – 12

3

- Click the second presentation change marker, Insertions after "Tornado", in the Presentation changes area to display the review content thumbnail with an explanation of the proposed new slide (Figure 5–13).

Q&A

Why does a check mark appear in the Theme (1 – 3) change marker?

The check mark indicates you have applied the proposed change.

4

- Click the Accept Change button to insert the new slide.

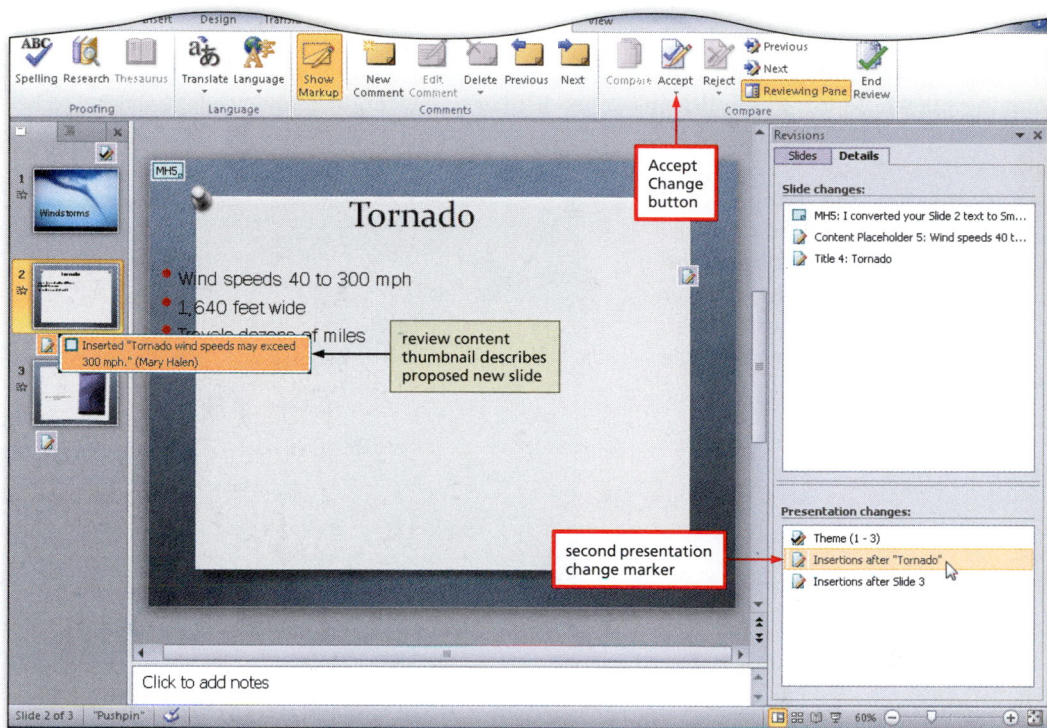

Figure 5–13

5

- Click the third presentation change marker, Insertions after Slide 4, to display the review content thumbnail with a proposed slide to insert in the presentation (Figure 5–14).

6

- Click the Insertions check box to insert the new Slide 5.

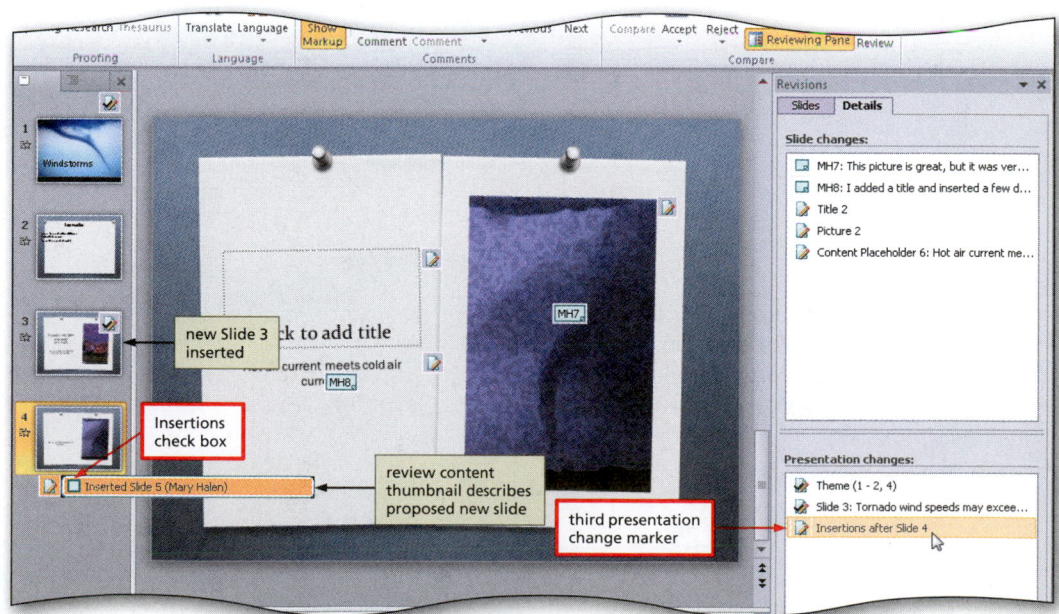

Figure 5–14

To Review, Accept, and Reject Slide Changes

Changes that affect only the displayed slide are indicated in the Slide changes area of the Revisions task pane. A reviewer can modify many aspects of the slide, such as adding and deleting pictures and clips, editing text, and moving placeholders. The following steps display and accept the reviewer's revisions to Slide 1.

• Click the first slide change, Rectangle 1: Windstorms, in the Slide changes area to display the Rectangle 1 box with Mary Halen's three proposed changes for the Windstorms text in the rectangle (Figure 5–15).

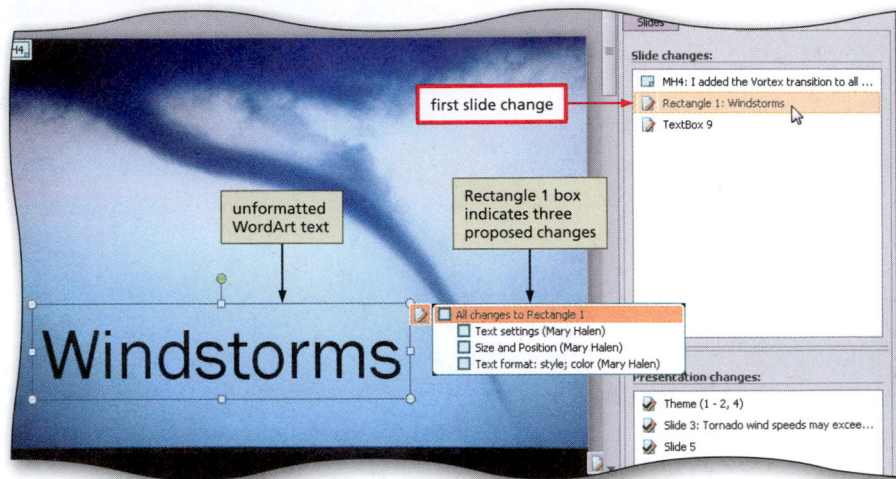

Figure 5–15

• Click the All changes to Rectangle 1 check box to preview the three proposed changes to the Windstorms text (Figure 5–16).

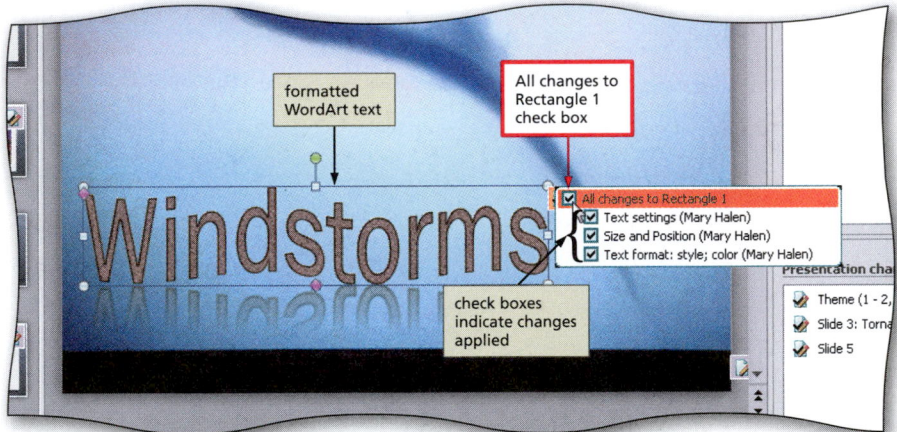

Figure 5–16

• Click the Size and Position check box to preview only the proposed Text settings and the Text format: style, color changes to the Windstorms text (Figure 5–17).

Q&A

Can I select any combination of the check boxes to modify the text in the rectangle?

Yes. Click the individual check boxes to preview the reviewer's modifications.

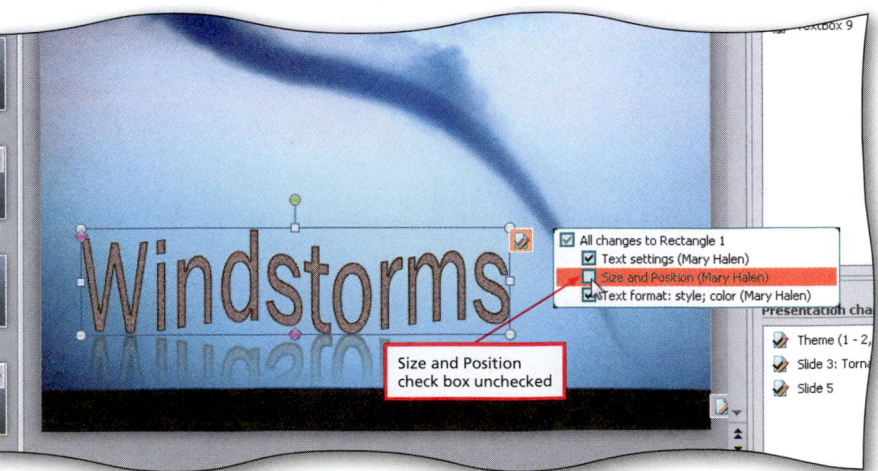

Figure 5–17

4

• Click the second slide change, TextBox, in the Slide changes area to display the Inserted TextBox box.

• Click the Inserted TextBox check box to view the proposed text box (Figure 5–18).

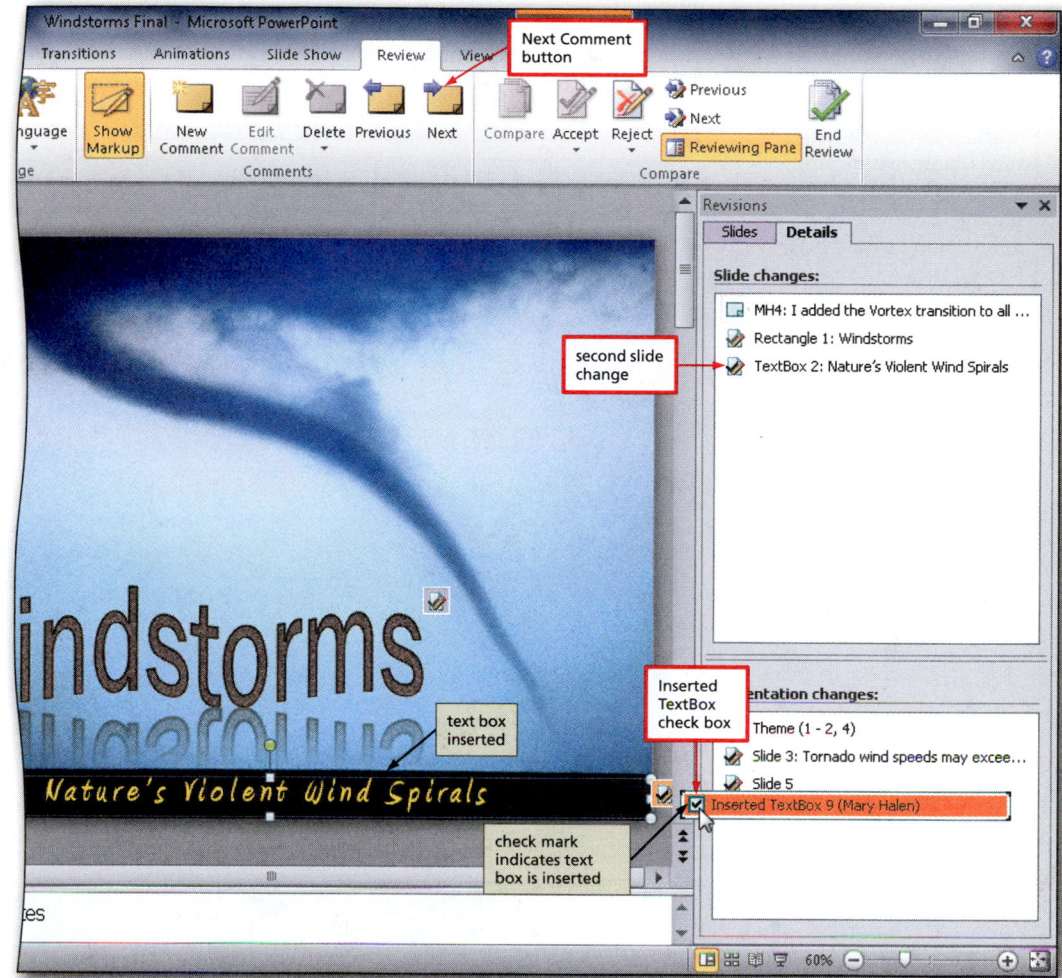

Figure 5–18

To Review and Accept Slide Changes on the Remaining Slides

You have accepted all of Mary Halen's presentation changes and most of her Slide 1 changes. She also inserted comments in and made changes to other slides. The following steps review her comments and accept her modifications.

1 Click the Next Comment button (Review tab | Comments group) to display Slide 2.

2 Read comment 5 and then delete the comment.

3 Click the Content Placeholder 5 slide change and then apply the Canvas contents change.

4 Click the Title 4: Tornado slide change and then accept the change to delete the title text placeholder.

5 Click the Next Comment button to display Slide 3. Read comment 6, but do not delete it.

BTW

Showing or Hiding Markup

You can view the slides without the comments and other annotations by clicking the Show Markup button (Review tab | Comments group). If you then want to see the comments and annotations, click the Show Markup button again.

6 Click the Next Comment button to display Slide 4. Read comments 7 and 8 and then delete them.

7 Click the Next Comment button to display Slide 5. Read comment 9, but do not delete it (Figure 5–19).

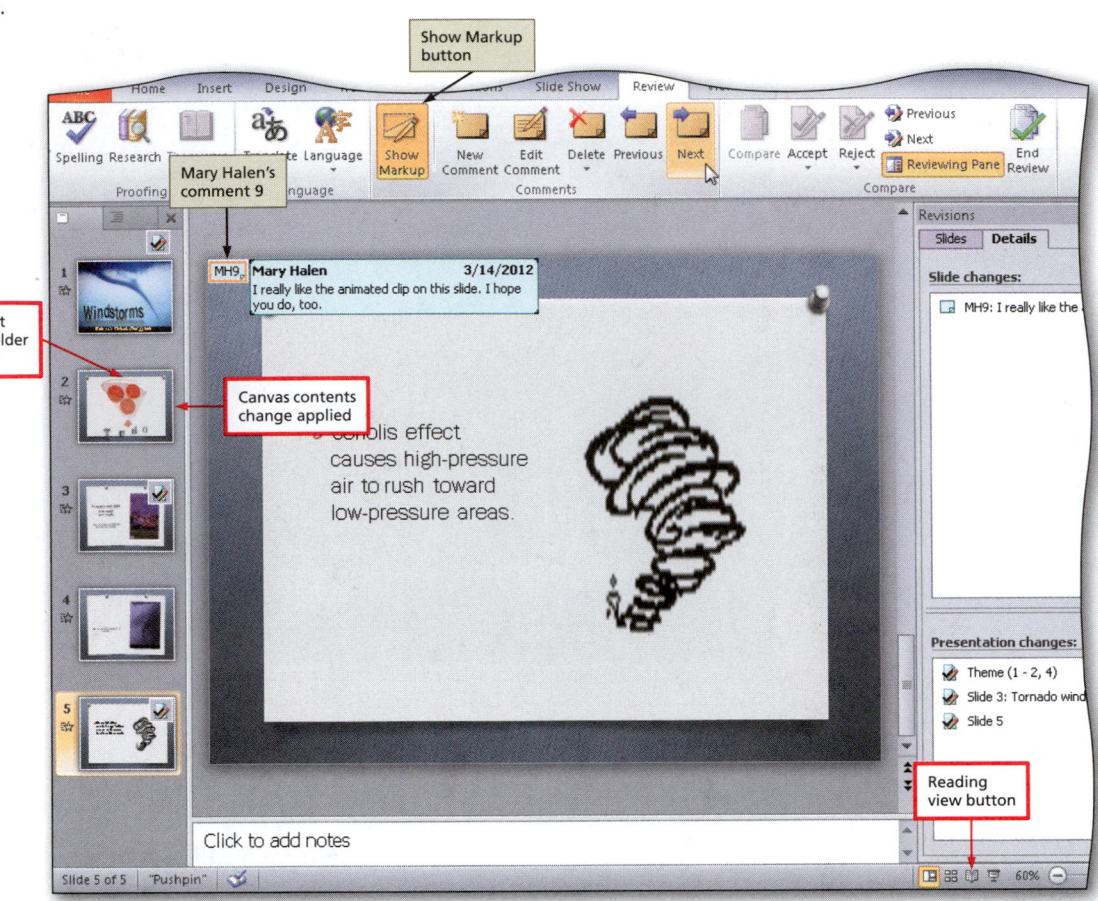

Figure 5–19

BTW

Q&As

For a complete list of the Q&As found in many of the step-by-step sequences in this book, visit the PowerPoint 2010 Q&A Web page (scsite.com/ppt2010/qa).

To Run the Revised Presentation in Reading View

Mary's changes modified the original presentation substantially, so it is a good idea to review the new presentation. The following steps review the revised slides.

1 Display Slide 1 and then click the Reading view button.

2 Click the Next and Previous buttons to review the changes on each slide.

3 After viewing the animated tornado on Slide 5, click the Normal view button.

To Reject a Slide Revision

After running the presentation, you decide that the animation on Slide 5 is distracting and that the text is not part of the material you desire to display in the slide show. Although you initially accepted Mary's change to insert the slide, you decide to reject this modification. The following steps display and reject the reviewer's revision to insert Slide 5.

1
- Click the change marker on the Slide 5 thumbnail in the Slides tab to display the Inserted Slide 5 box (Figure 5–20).

2
- Click the Reject Change button (Review tab | Compare group) to delete Slide 5 from the presentation.

Q&A
Could I have deleted the slide by clicking the Inserted Slide 5 check box to remove the check mark?

Yes.

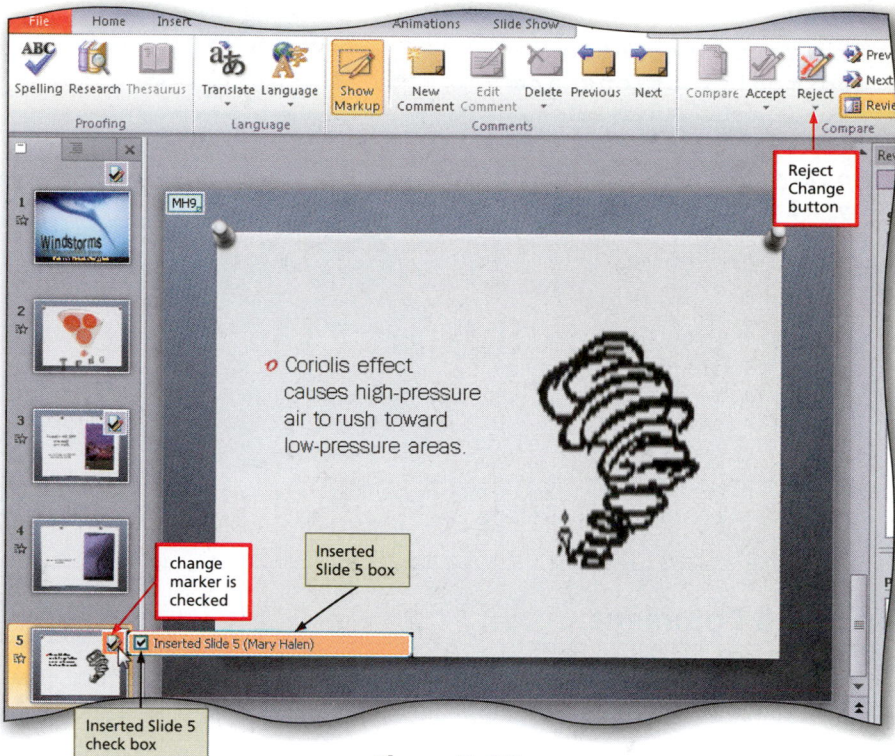

Figure 5–20

Give constructive criticism.
If you are asked to critique a presentation, begin and end with positive comments. Give specific details about a few key areas that can be improved. Be honest, but be tactful. Avoid using the word, you. For example, instead of writing, "You need to give some statistics to support your viewpoint," write "I had difficulty understanding which departments' sales have declined in the past five months. Perhaps a chart with specific losses would help depict how dramatically revenues have fallen."

Plan Ahead

To Insert a Comment

Mary Halen's comments and changes greatly enhanced your slide show, and you would like to send her a copy of the presentation so that she can see what modifications you accepted. You want to insert a comment to her on Slide 1 to thank her for taking the time to review your original slides. The following steps insert a comment on Slide 1.

1
- With Slide 1 displaying, click the Slide pane. Click the Insert Comment button, which displays as New Comment, (Review tab | Comments group) to open a comment box at the top of the slide (Figure 5–21).

Q&A
Why do my initials and name differ from those shown in the figure?

The initials and name reflect the information that was entered when Microsoft Office 2010 was installed on your computer.

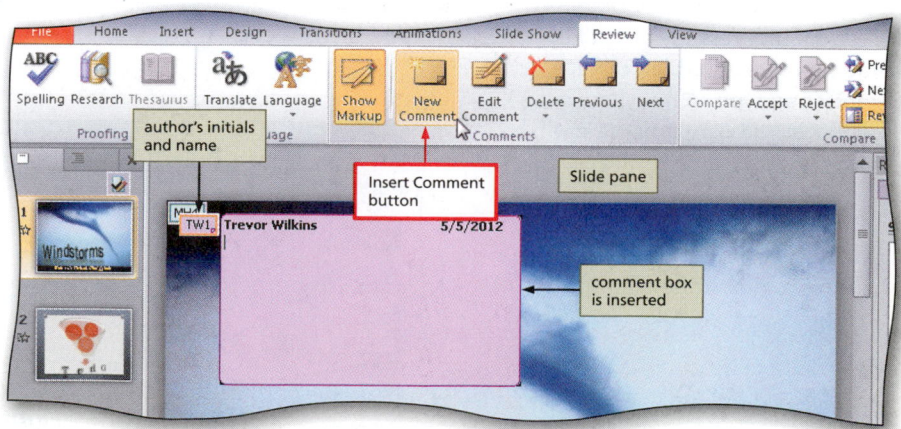

Figure 5–21

2

• Type **Your suggestions and modifications are excellent, Mary. I really appreciate the work you did to enhance my slides.** in the comment box (Figure 5–22).

3

• Click anywhere outside the comment box to hide the text and lock in the comment.

Q&A Can I move the comment on the slide?

Yes. Select the comment and then drag it to another location on the slide.

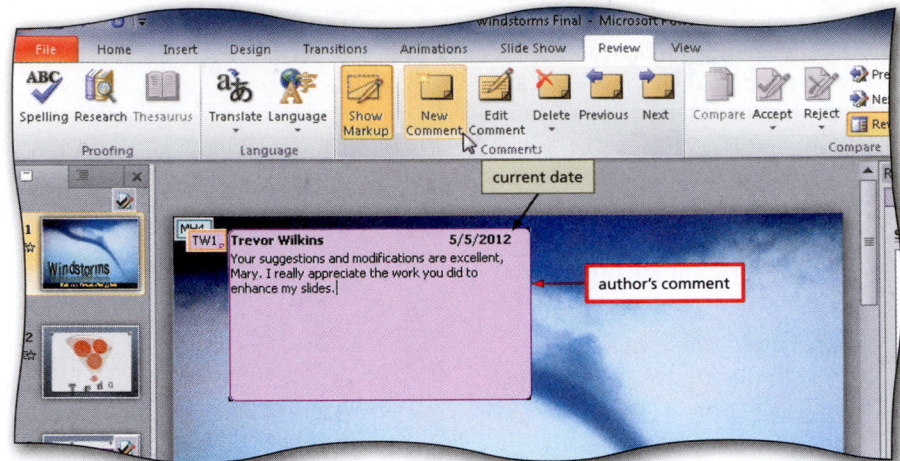

Figure 5–22

To Edit a Comment

Mary asked some questions in the comments she made in her presentation. You want to provide feedback to her by responding to her queries. One method of responding is by editing the comments she made. The following steps edit the comments on Slides 1 and 3.

1

• With Slide 1 displaying, click the MH4 comment marker on the slide to display Mary's fourth comment.

Q&A Can I click the MH4 comment marker in the Revisions task pane to display Mary's comment?

Yes.

• Click the Edit Comment button (Review tab | Comments group) to change the marker comment color and display your initials and name (Figure 5–23).

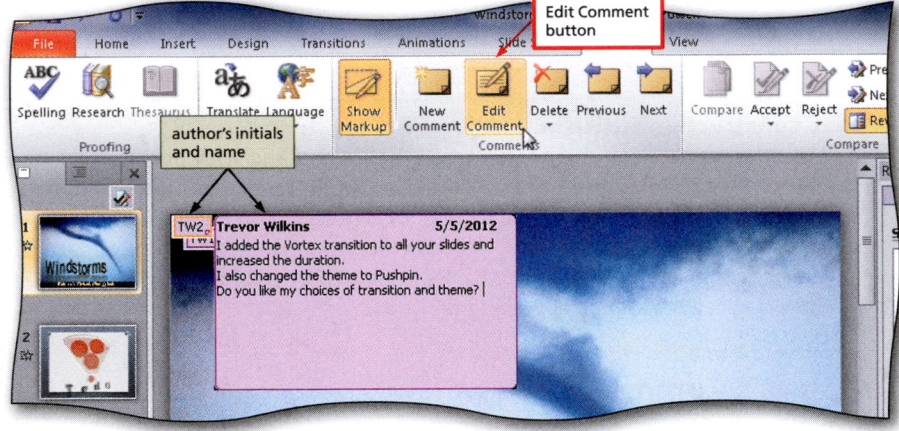

Figure 5–23

2

• Press the ENTER key to move the insertion point below Mary's comment. Press the ENTER key again to insert a blank line and then type **The Vortex transition complements the windstorm topic well. The Pushpin theme is excellent for displaying the photos.** in the comment box (Figure 5–24).

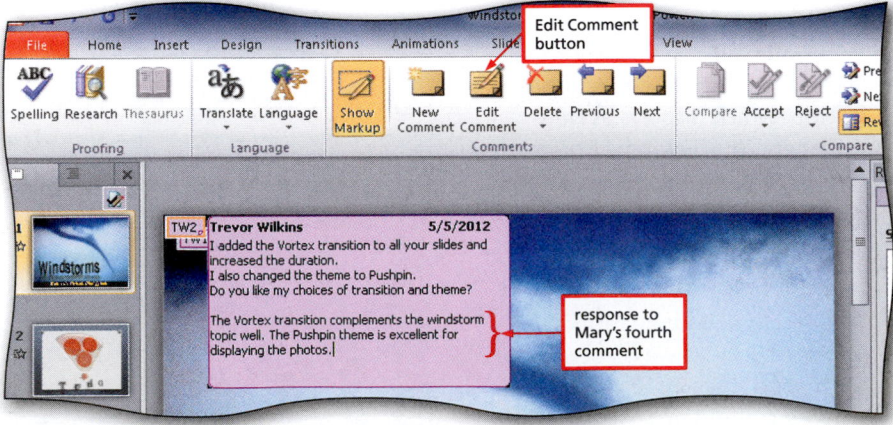

Figure 5–24

- Display Slide 3 and then click the MH6 comment marker on the slide to display Mary's comment.

- Click the Edit Comment button (Review tab | Comments group), press the ENTER key twice, and then type **The devastation from that tornado is amazing! Your slide is outstanding.** in the comment box immediately after Mary's comment (Figure 5–25).

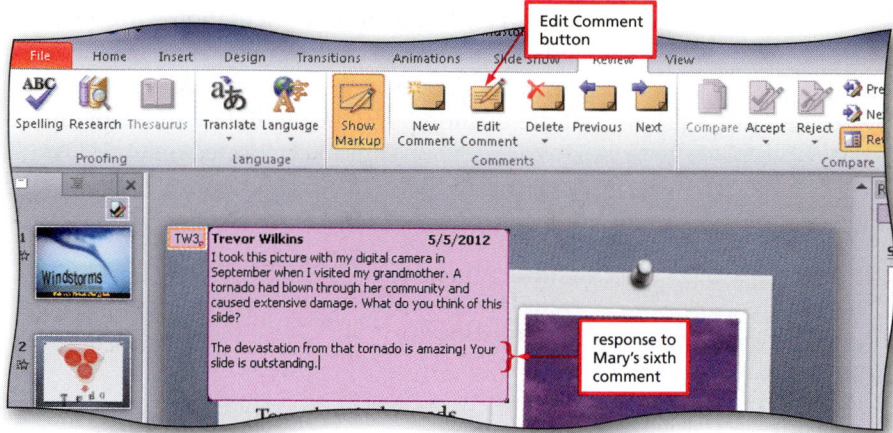

Figure 5–25

To End the Review

You have analyzed all of the reviewer's proposed changes and replied to some of her questions. Your review of the merged presentation is complete, so you can apply all the changes and close the Revisions task pane. Be mindful that you cannot undo these changes after the review has ended. The following steps end the review of the merged slides.

- Click the End Review button (Review tab | Compare group) to display the Microsoft PowerPoint dialog box (Figure 5–26).

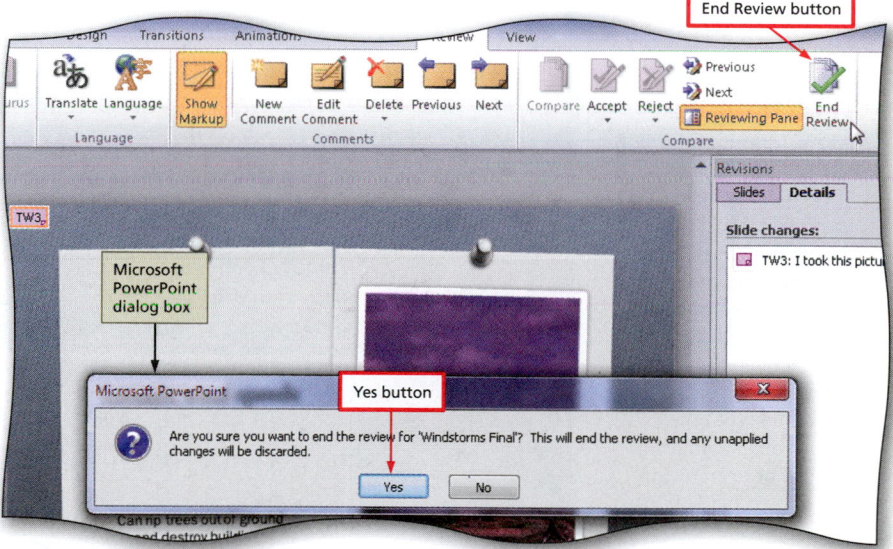

- Click the Yes button (Microsoft PowerPoint dialog box) to apply the changes you accepted and discard the changes you rejected.

Q&A Which changes are discarded?

You did not apply the size and position change to the Windstorms rectangle on Slide 1, and you did not insert Mary's proposed Slide 5.

Figure 5–26

Reusing Slides from an Existing Presentation

Occasionally you may want to insert a slide from another presentation into your presentation. PowerPoint offers two methods of obtaining these slides. One way is to open the second presentation and then copy and paste the desired slides. The second method is to use the Reuse Slides task pane to view and then select the desired slides. The presentation can be stored on a storage medium or in a Slide Library, which is a folder where individual slides are saved.

BTW

BTWs
For a complete list of the BTWs found in the margins of this book, visit the PowerPoint 2010 BTW Web page (scsite.com/ppt2010/btw).

Copying Content from Other Applications

Collaboration can involve combining PowerPoint slides from two or more files, and it also can involve sharing content or objects created using other software. These programs can be other Microsoft Office programs, such as Word and Excel, as well as other programs that support object linking and embedding. A linked object maintains a connection to the program that created it and is updated if the source file is changed. An embedded object, on the other hand, loses its connection to the original software and becomes part of the presentation file. To link or embed content copied from another program, you select and copy the information in that program, position the insertion point at the location on the slide where you want that content to appear, click the Paste button arrow (Home tab | Clipboard group), and then click Paste Special in the Paste Options menu to display the Paste Special dialog box. Click Paste link if you want to link the object to the original software. Or, if you want to embed the object, click Paste (Paste Special dialog box) and then click the entry in the As box that has the word "object" in its name. For example, if you copied part of an Excel worksheet, you would click Microsoft Excel Worksheet Object.

The PowerPoint presentation with the file name, Hurricanes, has colorful pictures and useful text. It contains three slides, and you would like to insert two of these slides, shown in Figure 5–27, into your Windstorms Final presentation. You will capture part of the diamond graphic on Slide 3 and copy this snip to one Windstorms Final slide. The Hurricanes presentation is located on your Data Files for Students. See the inside back cover of this book for instructions on downloading the Data Files for Students, or contact your instructor for more information about accessing the required files.

(a) Slide 1 (Insert and Use Pushpin Formatting)

HURRICANES CAN LAST UP TO 10 DAYS.

Usually form over the sea in tropical areas near the equator.

(b) Slide 2 (Insert and Keep Original Formatting)

HURRICANES LOSE STRENGTH SOON AFTER REACHING LAND.

lower half of diamond clipped and moved to Slide 4

(c) Slide 3 (Snip Part of Graphic)

Figure 5–27

The inserted slides will be placed in the presentation directly after Slide 4. PowerPoint converts inserted slides to the theme and styles of the current presentation, so the first slide will inherit the styles of the current Pushpin theme and Windstorms Final presentation. You will, in contrast, specify that the second slide keep the source formatting of the Hurricanes presentation, which uses the Apothecary theme. You will need to add the Vortex transition to the second slide because you are not applying the Windstorms Final formatting.

To Reuse Slides from an Existing Presentation

The following steps add two slides from the Hurricanes presentation to your presentation.

1

• With your USB flash drive connected to one of the computer's USB ports, display Slide 4 and then display the Home tab.

• Click the New Slide button arrow to display the Pushpin layout gallery (Figure 5–28).

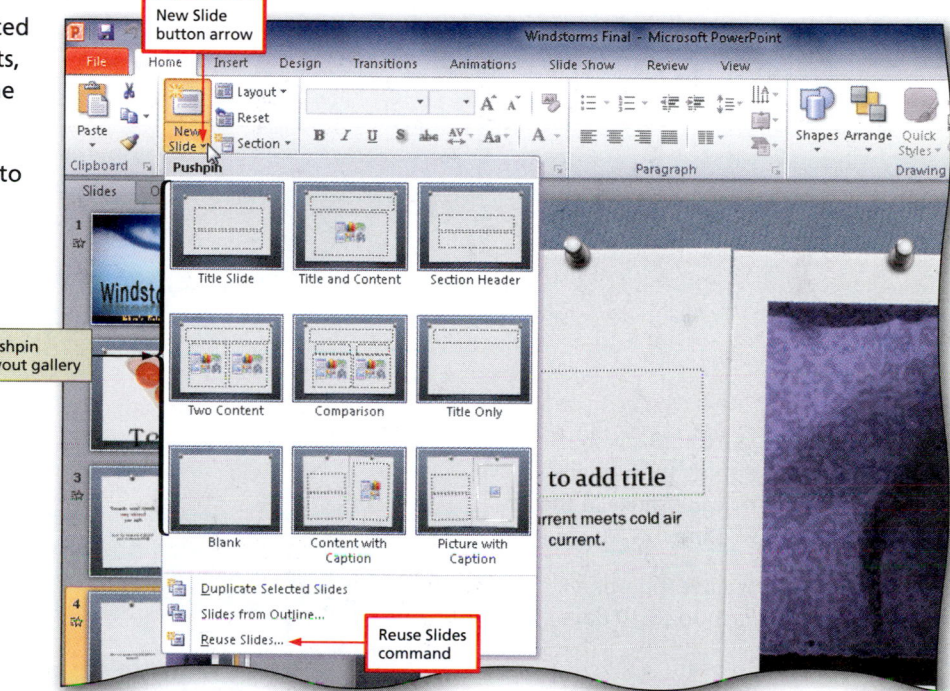

Figure 5–28

2

• Click Reuse Slides in the Pushpin layout gallery to display the Reuse Slides task pane.

• Click the Browse button (Figure 5–29).

Q&A What are the two Browse options shown?

If the desired slides are in a Slide Library, you would click Browse Slide Library to select individual slides that you want to use. The slides you need, however, are on your Data Files for Students, so you need to click Browse File.

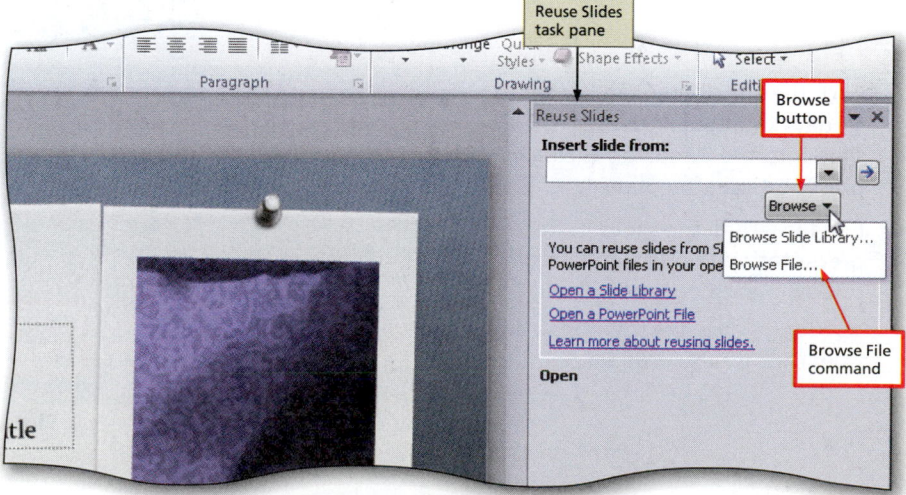

Figure 5–29

- Click Browse File to display the Browse dialog box.

- If necessary, double-click your USB flash drive in the list of available storage devices to display a list of files and folders on the selected USB flash drive.

- Click Hurricanes to select the file (Figure 5–30).

Q&A

What if the file is not on a USB flash drive?

Use the same process, but select the drive containing the file.

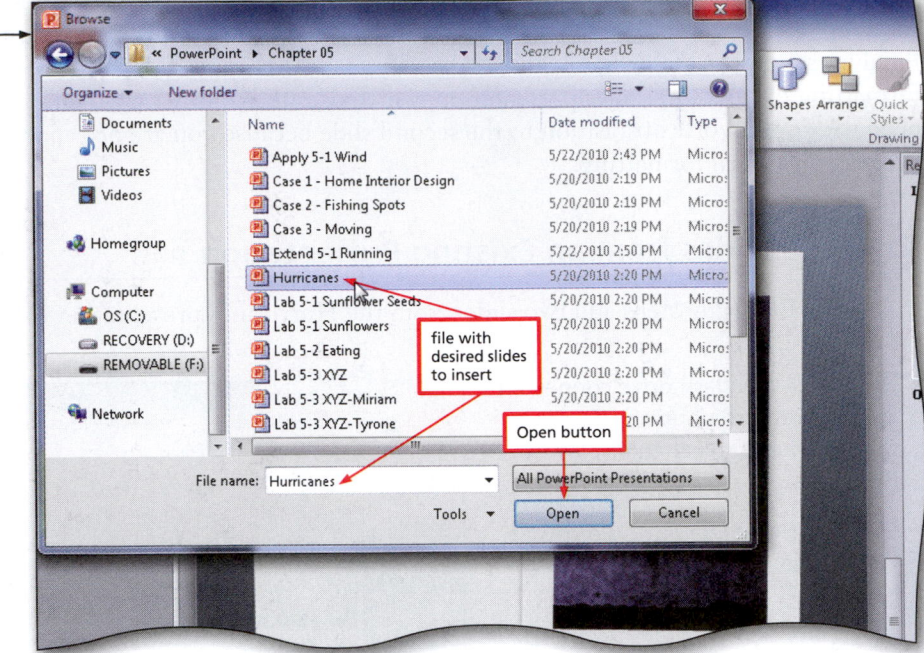

Figure 5–30

- Click the Open button (Browse dialog box) to display thumbnails of the three Hurricane slides in the Reuse Slides task pane.

- Point to the first slide thumbnail, Hurricanes can last up to 10 days (Figure 5–31).

Experiment

- Point to each of the thumbnails in the Reuse Slides task pane to see a larger preview of that slide.

- Click the Hurricanes can last up to 10 days thumbnail to insert this slide into the Windstorms Final presentation after Slide 4.

Q&A

Can I insert all the slides in the presentation in one step instead of selecting each one individually?

Yes. Right-click any thumbnail and then click Insert All Slides.

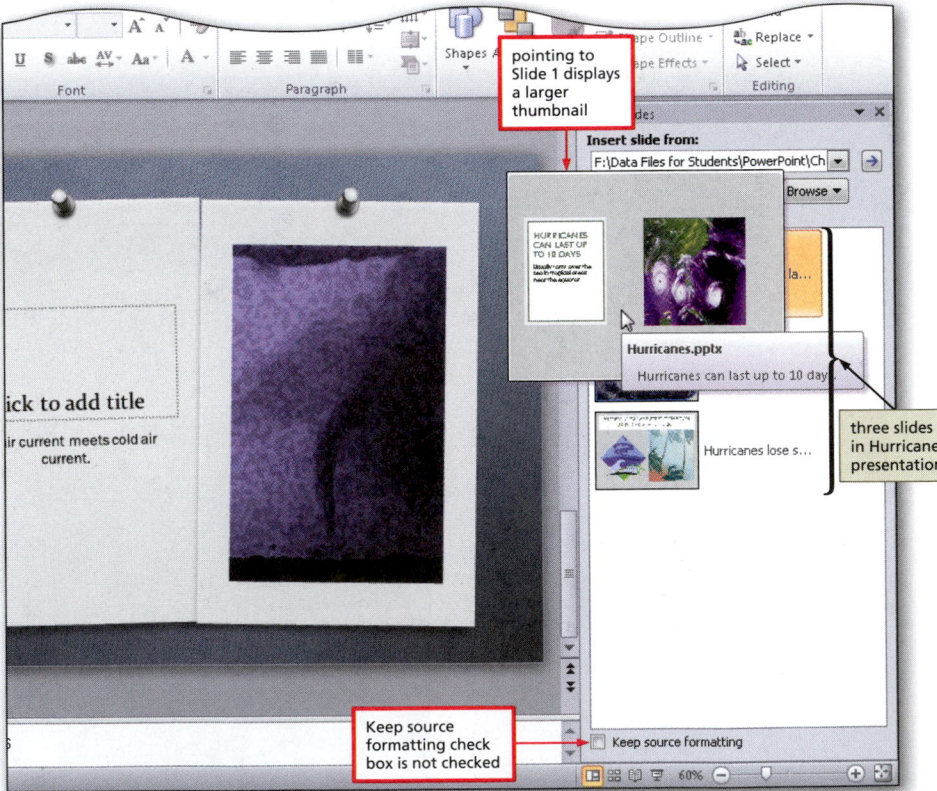

Figure 5–31

6

- Click the 'Keep source formatting' check box at the bottom of the Reuse Slides task pane to preserve the Hurricanes presentation formatting.

Q&A

What would happen if I did not check this box?

PowerPoint would change the formatting to the characteristics found in the Pushpin theme.

- Point to the second slide, which has an aerial picture of a hurricane (Figure 5–32).

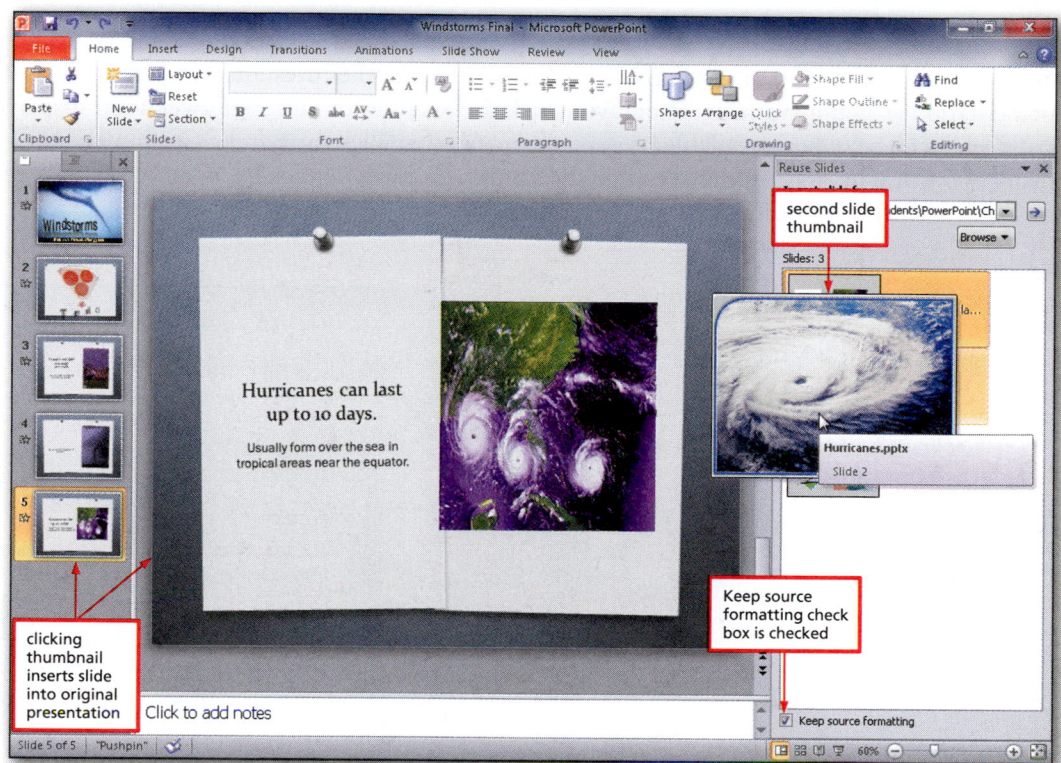

Figure 5–32

7

- Click the second slide thumbnail to insert this slide into the presentation as the last slide in the Windstorms Final presentation (Figure 5–33).

8

- Click the Close button in the Reuse Slides task pane so that it no longer is displayed.

- Apply the Vortex transition to Slide 6.

Figure 5–33

To Capture Part of a Screen Using Screen Clipping

At times you may be developing a presentation and need a portion of a clip or picture in another presentation. You can capture, or **snip**, part of an object on a slide in another presentation that is open. PowerPoint refers to this presentation as being available. When you click the Screenshot button, PowerPoint displays a dialog box and asks you to select a particular available presentation. You then click the Screen Clipping command, and PowerPoint displays a white overlay on the available slide until you capture the snip. The following steps snip part of an image on Slide 3 of the Hurricanes presentation and paste it on Slide 5 in the Windstorms Final presentation.

- Open the Hurricanes presentation from your USB flash drive. Display Slide 3 of the Hurricanes presentation.

- Display Slide 5 of the Windstorms Final presentation.

- Display the Insert tab and then click the Screenshot button (Insert tab | Images group) to display the Available Windows gallery (Figure 5–34).

Figure 5–34

- Click Screen Clipping (Available Windows gallery) to display Slide 3 of the Hurricanes presentation.

- When the white overlay displays on Slide 3, move the mouse pointer near the left point of the diamond until the pointer changes to a cross hair.

- Drag downward and to the right to select the lower half of the diamond (Figure 5–35).

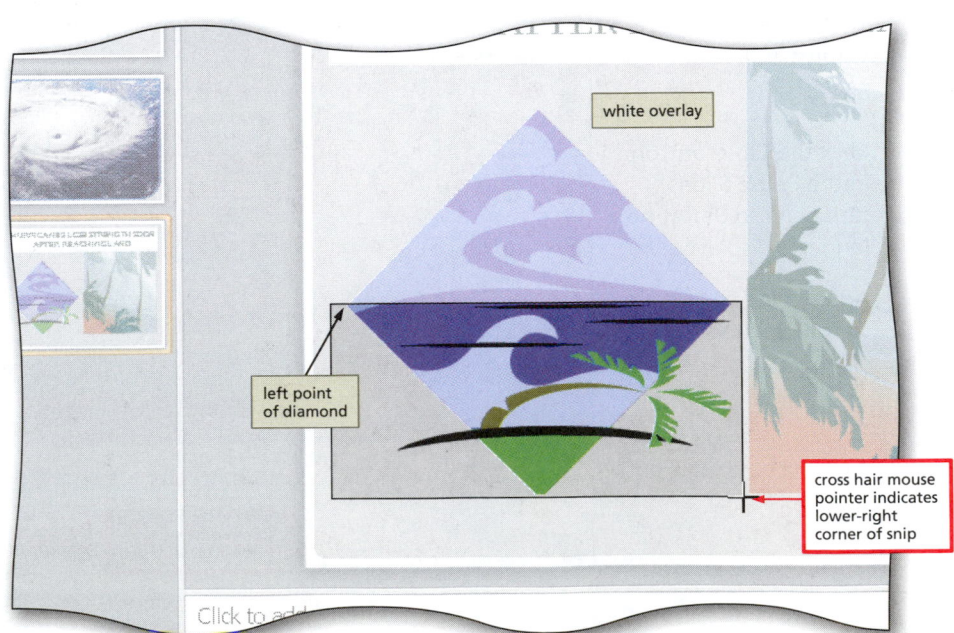

Figure 5–35

3
● Release the mouse button. When the snip displays on Slide 5 of the Windstorms Final presentation, drag the snip above the title text (Figure 5–36).

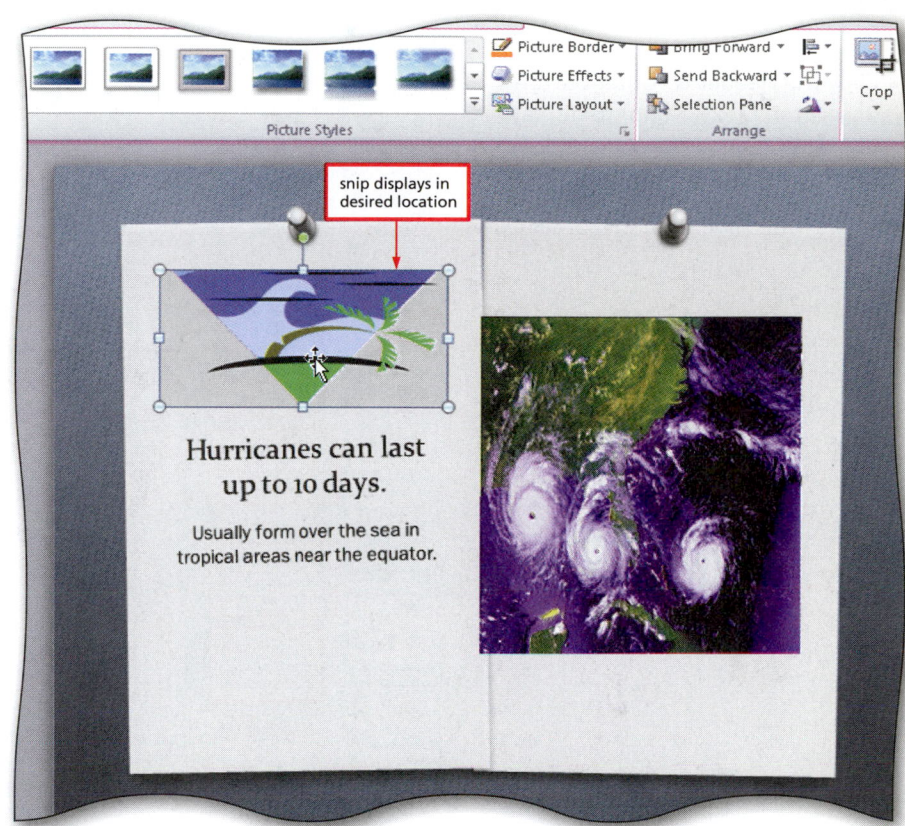

Figure 5–36

Use slide numbers to guide your speech.
Slide numbers help a presenter organize a talk. While few audience members are cognizant of this aspect of a slide, the presenter can glance at the number and know which slide contains particular information. If an audience member asks a question pertaining to information contained on a slide that had been displayed previously or is on a slide that has not been viewed yet, the presenter can jump to that slide in an effort to answer the question. In addition, the slide number helps pace the slide show. For example, a speaker could have the presentation timed so that Slide 4 is displaying three minutes into the talk.

Plan Ahead

To Add a Footer with Fixed Information

Slides can contain information at the top or bottom. The area at the top of a slide is called a **header**, and the area at the bottom is called a **footer**. As a default, no information is displayed in the header or footer. You can choose to apply only a header, only a footer, or both a header and footer. In addition, you can elect to have the header or footer display on single slides, all slides, or all slides except the title slide.

PowerPoint gives the option of displaying the current date and time obtained from the system or a fixed date and time that you specify. In addition, you can add relevant information, such as your name, your school or business name, or the purpose of your presentation in the footer. The following steps add a slide number, a fixed date, and footer text to all slides in the presentation except the title slide.

- Display the Insert tab.

- Click the Header & Footer button (Insert tab | Text group) to display the Header and Footer dialog box.

- If necessary, click the Slide tab to display the Slide sheet (Figure 5–37).

Q&A Can I change the starting slide number?

Yes. The first slide number is 1 by default. To change this number, click the Page Setup button (Design tab | Page Setup group) and then click the 'Number slides from' up button (Page Setup dialog box).

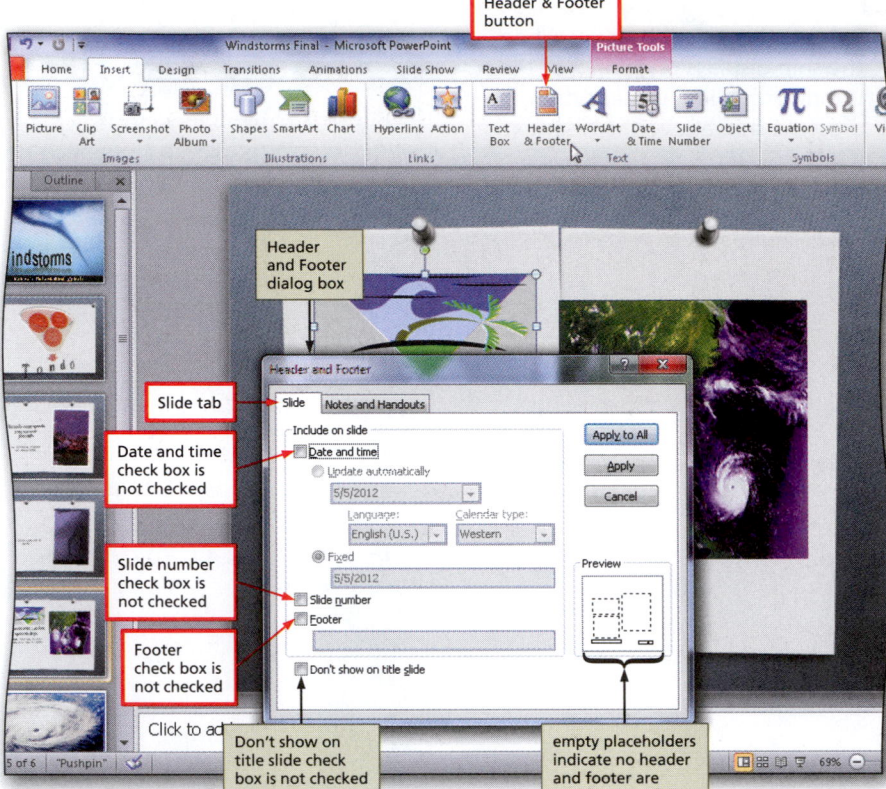

Figure 5–37

- Click 'Date and time' to select this check box.

- If necessary, click Fixed to select this option. Type **Friday, June 1 - 9:30 a.m.** in the Fixed box.

- Click Slide number to select this check box.

- Click Footer to select this check box.

- Type **Earth Science 101** in the Footer box (Figure 5–38).

Q&A What are the black boxes in the Preview area?

The black box in the left footer placeholder indicates where the footer information will appear on the slide; the black box in the right footer placeholder indicates where the date and time information and the page number will appear.

Q&A What if I want the current date and time to appear?

Click the Update automatically option in the 'Date and time' area.

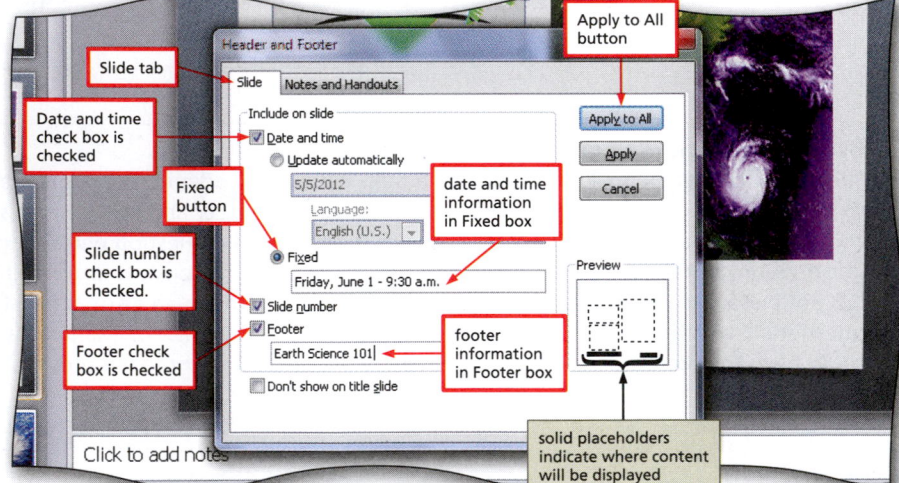

Figure 5–38

- Click the Apply to All button to display the date, time, footer text, and slide number on all slides.

Q&A When would I click the Apply button instead of the Apply to All button?

Click the Apply button when you want the slide number to appear only on the slide currently selected.

To Clear Formatting and Apply an Artistic Effect

PowerPoint provides myriad options to enhance pictures. You can, for example, format the images by recoloring, changing the color saturation and tone, adding artistic effects, and altering the picture style. After adding various effects, you may desire to reset the picture to its original state. The tornado picture on Slide 4 has several formatting adjustments, and now you want to see the original unformatted picture. The following steps remove all formatting applied to the tornado picture on Slide 4 and then apply the Film Grain artistic effect.

1
- Display Slide 4, select the tornado picture, and then display the Picture Tools Format tab (Figure 5–39).

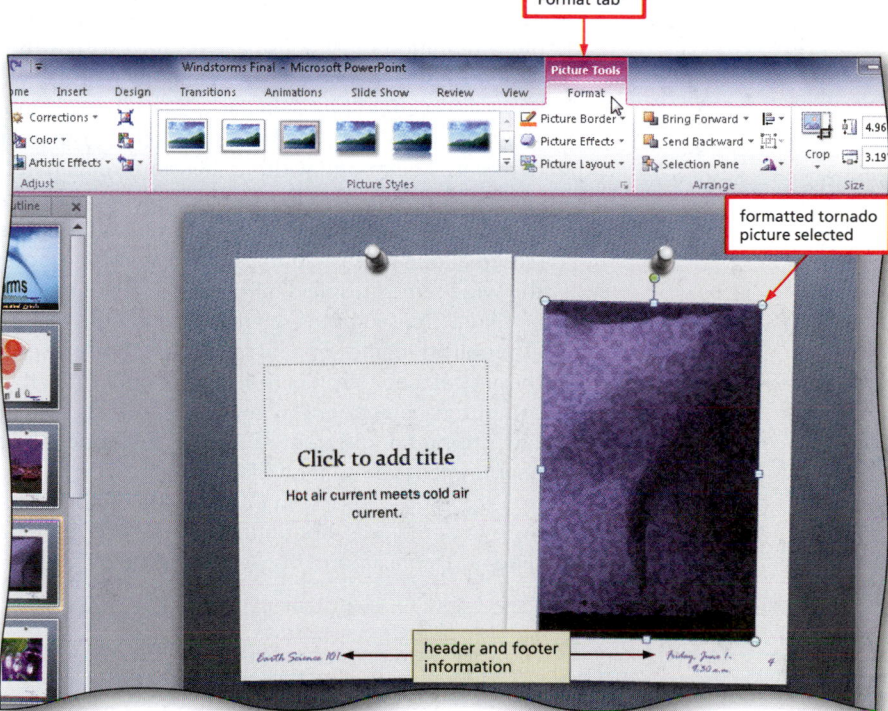

Figure 5–39

2
- Click the Reset Picture button (Picture Tools Format tab | Adjust group) to remove all formatting from the picture.

- Click the Artistic Effects button (Picture Tools Format tab | Adjust group) to display the Artistic Effects gallery (Figure 5–40).

3
- Apply the Film Grain effect (third effect in the third row) to the tornado picture.

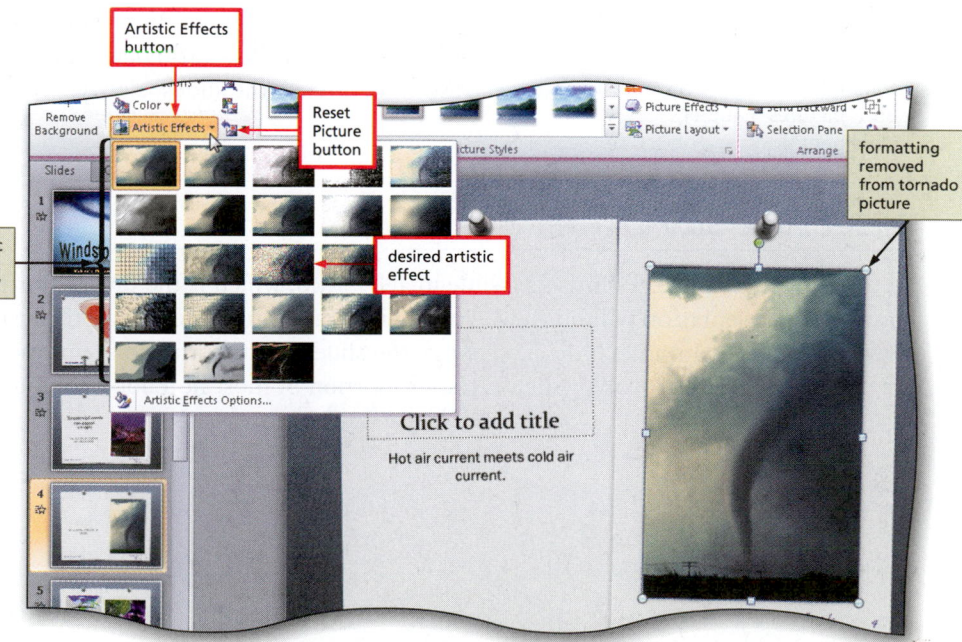

Figure 5–40

Break Point: If you wish to take a break, this is a good place to do so. Be sure to save the Windstorms Final file again and then you can quit PowerPoint. To resume at a later time, start PowerPoint, open the file called Windstorms Final, and continue following the steps from this location forward.

Plan Ahead

Determine the screen show ratio.

Your presentation can be viewed on one of three different screen sizes. A standard monitor has a ratio of 4:3. Many new wide-screen notebook computers have a 16:10 ratio, and high-definition televisions have displays with a 16:9 ratio. These numbers describe the dimensions of the screen. For example, a display with a 4:3 ratio would be four feet wide if it were three feet high. Similarly, a notebook computer screen would be 16 inches wide if it were 10 inches high. While these exact measurements do not fit all displays and screens, the hardware height and width dimensions remain in the same proportion using these ratios.

Changing the default ratio offers many advantages. Audience members perceive a presentation in the wide-screen format as being trendy and new. In addition, the wider screen allows more layout area to display photographs and clips. In rooms with low ceilings, the wide-screen displays mirror the room dimensions and blend with the environment.

Slides created in the 4:3 format and then converted to 16:9 or 16:10 may look distorted, especially if images of people or animals are inserted. You consequently may need to adjust these stretched graphics if they look unnatural. If you present your slide show frequently on computers and screens with varying formats, you may want to save the slide show several times using the different ratios and then open the presentation that best fits the environment where it is being shown.

While the wide screen presents the opportunity to place more text on a slide, resist the urge to add words. Continue to use the 7×7 guideline (a maximum of seven lines on a slide and a maximum of seven words on a line).

BTW

Pixels
Screen resolution specifies the amount of pixels displayed on your screen. The word, pixel, combines the words pix ("pictures") and el ("element").

Setting Slide Size and Slide Show Resolution

Today's technology presents several options you should consider when developing your presentation. The on-screen show ratio determines the height and width proportions. The screen resolution affects the slides' clarity.

To Set Slide Size

By default, PowerPoint sets a slide in a 4:3 ratio, which is the proportion found on a standard monitor. If you know your presentation will be viewed on a wide-screen high-definition television (HDTV) or you are using a wide-screen notebook computer, you can change the slide size to optimize the proportions. The following steps change the default size ratio to 16:9, which is the proportion of most notebook computers.

- Display the Design tab and then click the Page Setup button (Design tab | Page Setup group) to display the Page Setup dialog box.

- Click the 'Slides sized for' box arrow to display the size list (Figure 5–41).

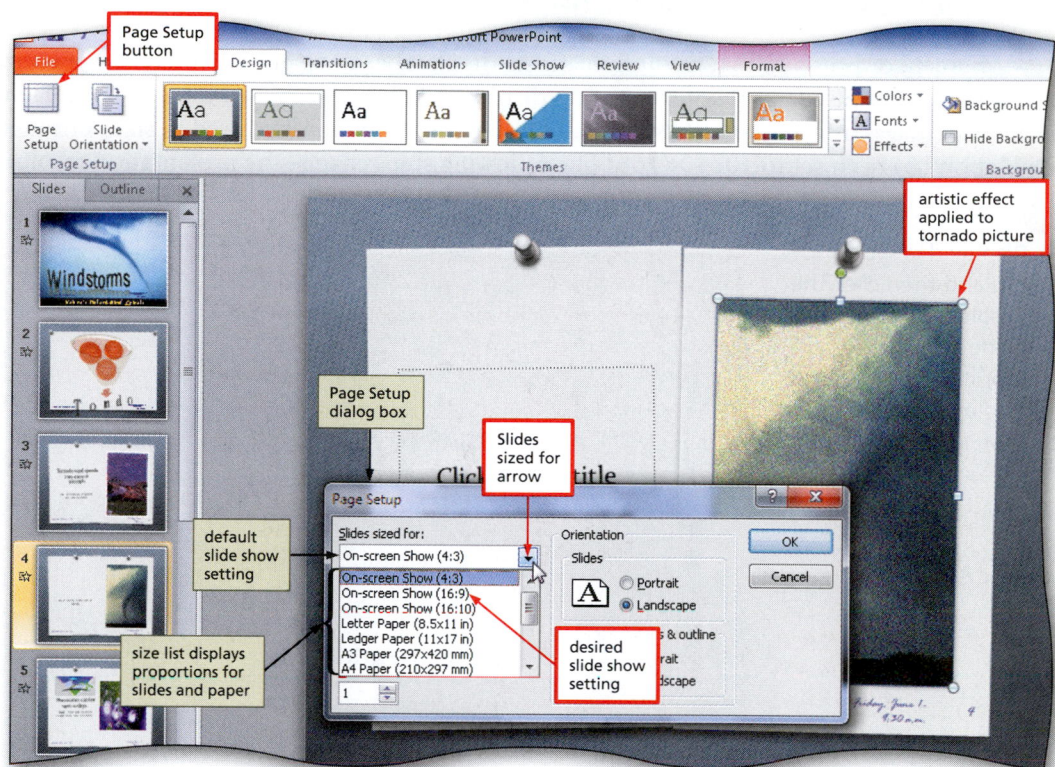

Figure 5–41

- Click On-screen Show (16:9) to change the slide size setting (Figure 5–42).

Q&A

Can I also change the default slide orientation from Landscape to Portrait?

Yes, but all slides in the presentation will change to this orientation. You cannot mix Portrait and Landscape orientations in one presentation. If you need to use both orientations during a speech, you can use a hyperlink to seamlessly jump from one slide show in Landscape orientation to another in Portrait orientation. Hyperlinks are discussed in Chapter 6.

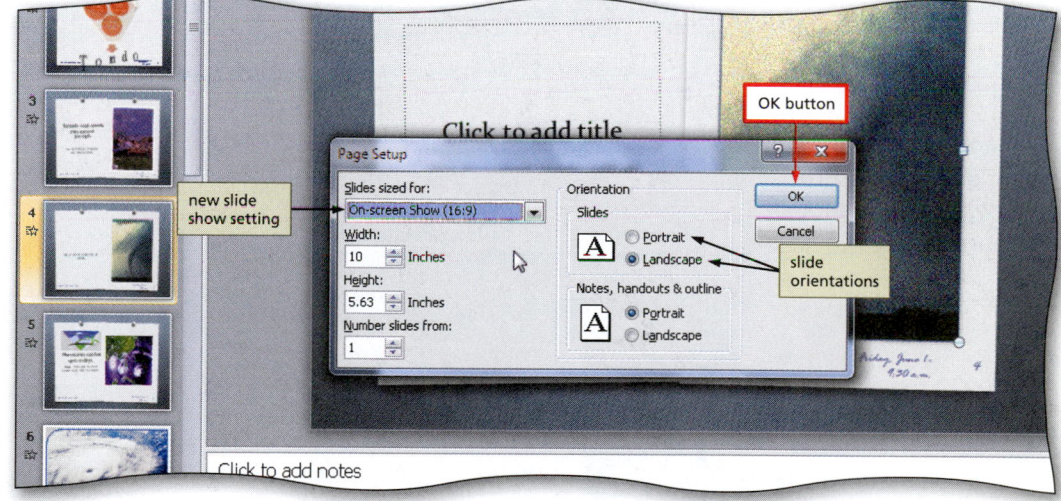

Figure 5–42

- Click the OK button to change the slide size in the presentation.

- Save the Windstorms Final presentation.

To Select Slide Show Resolution

Screen, or presentation, resolution affects the number of pixels that are displayed on your screen. When screen resolution is increased, more information is displayed, but it is decreased in size. Conversely, when screen resolution is decreased, less information is displayed, but that information is increased in size. Throughout this book, the screen resolution has been set to 1024×768. The following steps change the presentation resolution to 800×600.

1

● Display the Slide Show tab and then click the Resolution box arrow (Slide Show tab | Monitors group) to display the Resolution list (Figure 5–43).

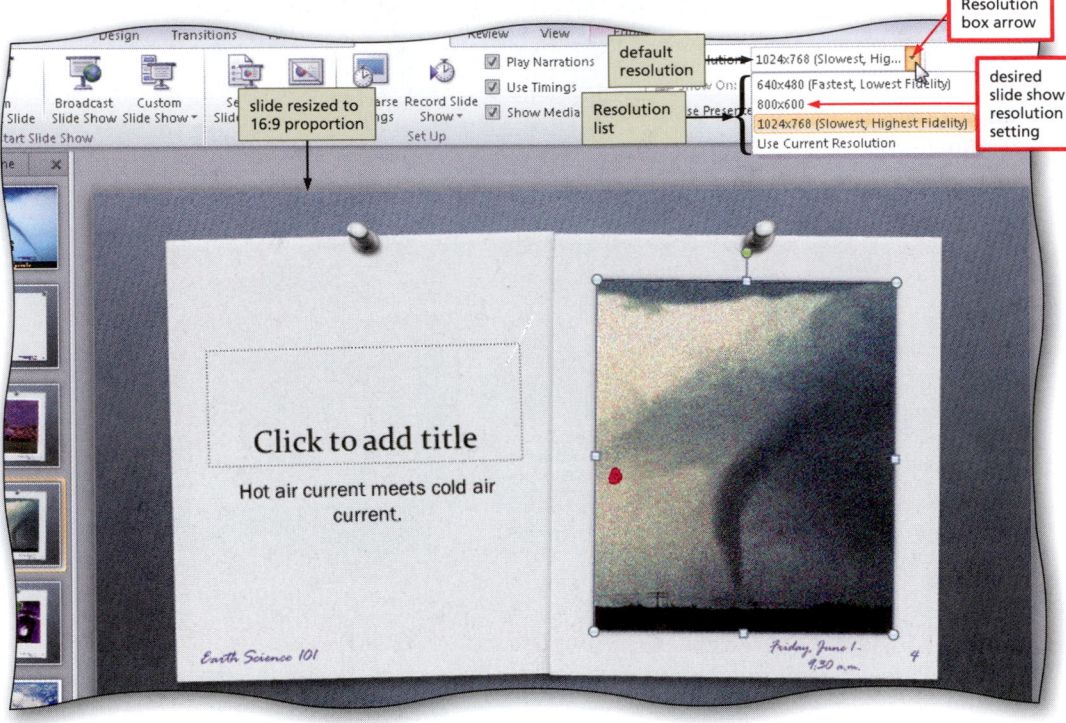

Figure 5–43

2

● Click 800×600 to change the slide show resolution setting (Figure 5–44).

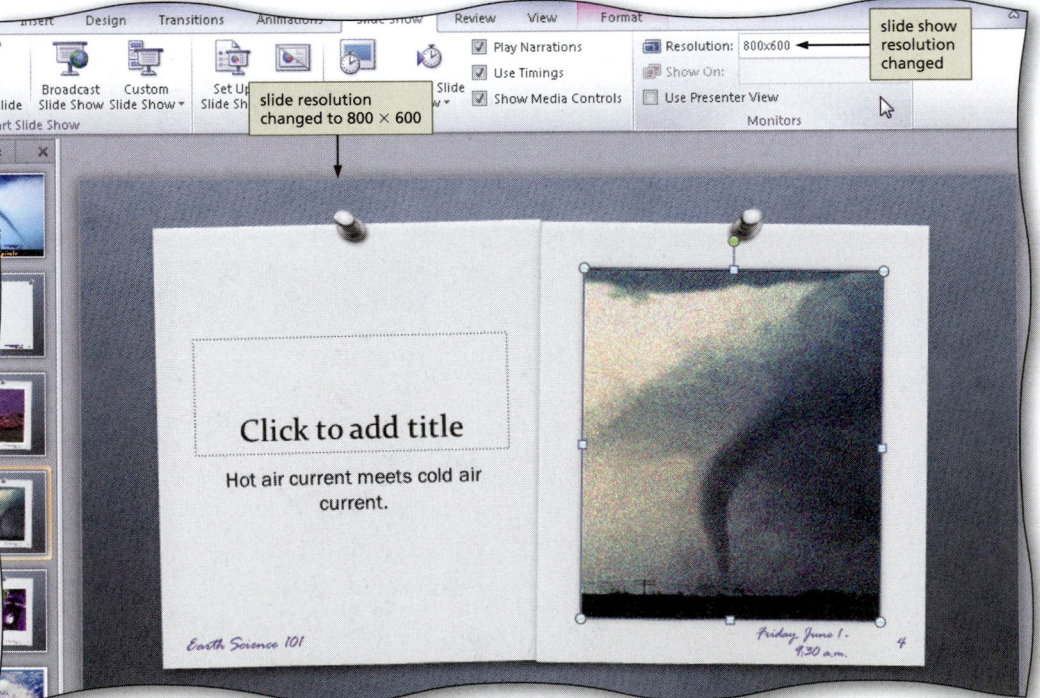

Figure 5–44

Saving and Packaging a Presentation

Both PowerPoint 2010 and PowerPoint 2007 save files, by default, as a PowerPoint Presentation with a .pptx file extension. You can, however, select other file types that allow other computer users to view your slides if they do not have one of the newer PowerPoint versions installed. You also can save the file as a PowerPoint show so that it runs automatically when opened. Another option is to save one slide as an image that can be inserted into another program, such as Microsoft Word, or can be e-mailed.

In the following pages, you will follow these general steps to save the slides in four file types:

1. Save the presentation as a PowerPoint show.
2. Save one slide as an image.
3. Package the presentation for a CD.
4. Save the presentation in the PowerPoint 97–2003 format.

BTW

Saving a Presentation as a PDF or an XPS Document
Electronic images of your slides are identical to the original slides and can be viewed using free viewers, including Acrobat Reader for PDF files and XPS Viewer for XPS files. To save your presentation in one of these formats, open the Backstage view, display the Save & Send tab, click Create PDF/XPS Document in the File Types area, and then click the Create PDF/XPS button in the Create a PDF/XPS Document area. When the Publish as PDF or XPS dialog box is displayed, click the 'Save as type' arrow and then select PDF or XPS in the list. Click 'Standard (publishing online and printing)' if you are going to print high-quality documents or 'Minimum size (publishing online)' if you desire to keep the file size small.

To Save a File as a PowerPoint Show

To simplify giving a presentation in front of an audience, you may want your slide show to start running without having to start PowerPoint, open a file, and then click the Slide Show button. When you save a presentation as a **PowerPoint show (.ppsx)**, it automatically begins running when opened. The following steps save the Windstorms Final file as a PowerPoint show.

1

- Open the Backstage view, display the Save & Send tab, and then click Change File Type in the File Types area.

- Click PowerPoint Show in the Presentation File Types area (Figure 5–45).

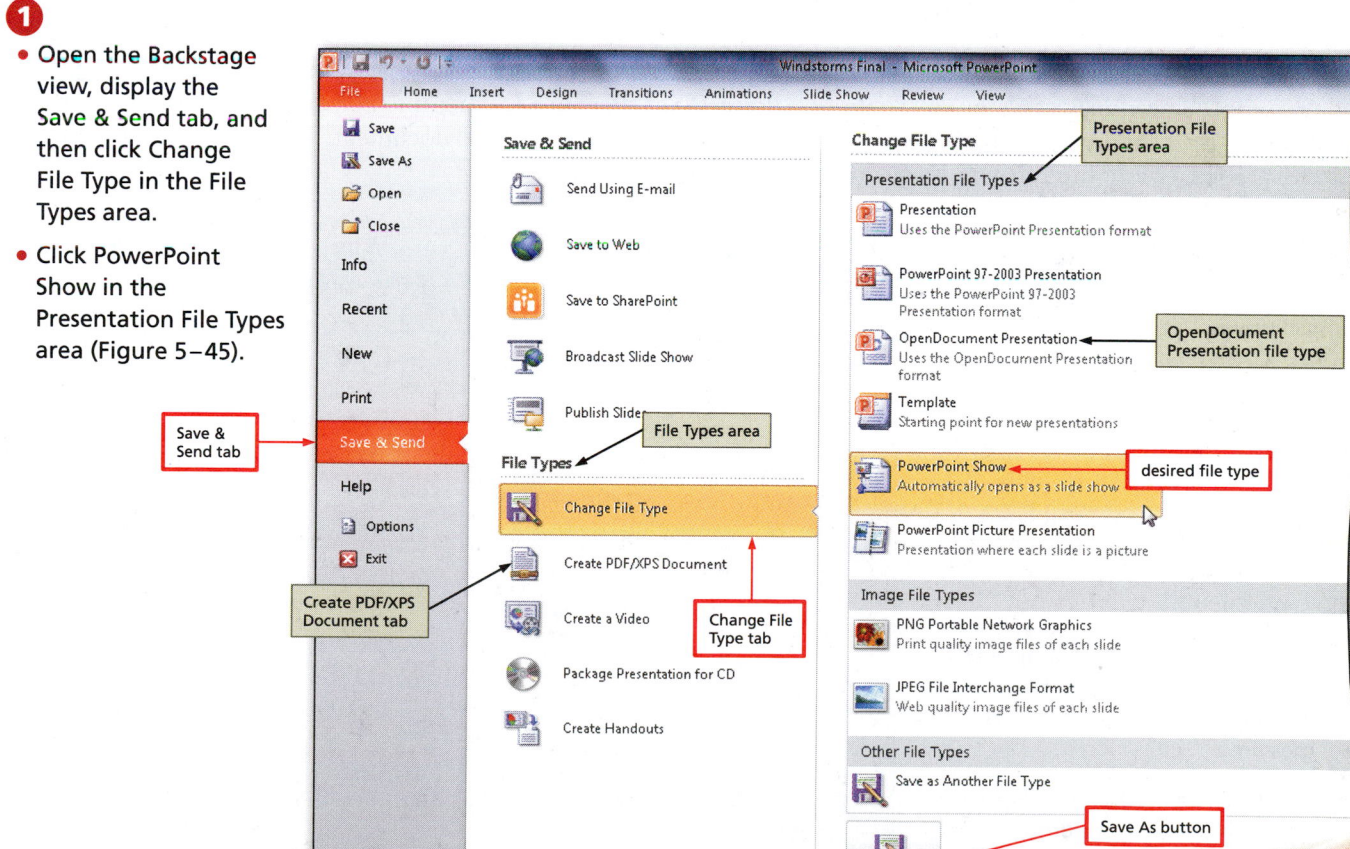

Figure 5–45

2
- Click the Save As button below the Other File Types area to display the Save As dialog box.

- Type **Windstorms Final Show** in the File name text box (Figure 5–46).

3
- Click the Save button (Save As dialog box) to save the Windstorms Final presentation as a PowerPoint show.

4
- Close both the current PowerPoint file and the Hurricanes presentation.

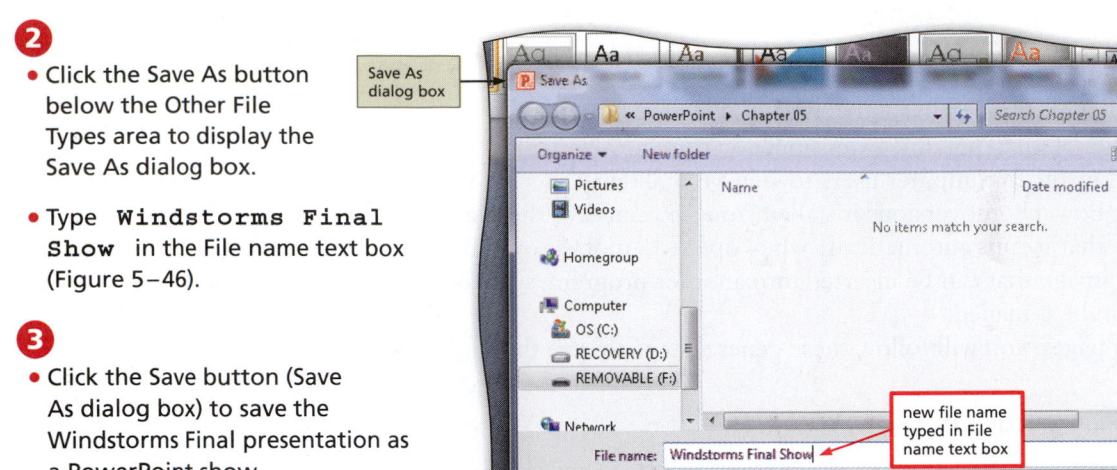

Figure 5–46

Other Ways

1. Click File on Ribbon, click Save As in Backstage view, click 'Save as type' arrow, select PowerPoint Show, click Save button

2. Double-click PowerPoint Show in Presentation File Types area

To Save a Slide as an Image

To create visually interesting slides, you insert pictures, clips, and video files into your presentation. Conversely, the need may arise for you to insert a PowerPoint slide into another file. For example, you can save the information on a slide as an image and insert the image into a Microsoft Word document. The following steps save Slide 2 as a JPEG File Interchange Format image.

1
- Open the Windstorms Final presentation from your USB flash drive.

Q&A

Why do I want to open this presentation?

It is best to use the final .pptx version of the presentation to complete the remaining tasks in this chapter.

- Display Slide 2.

- Open the Backstage view, display the Save & Send tab, and then click Change File Type in the File Types area.

- Click JPEG File Interchange Format in the Image File Types area (Figure 5–47).

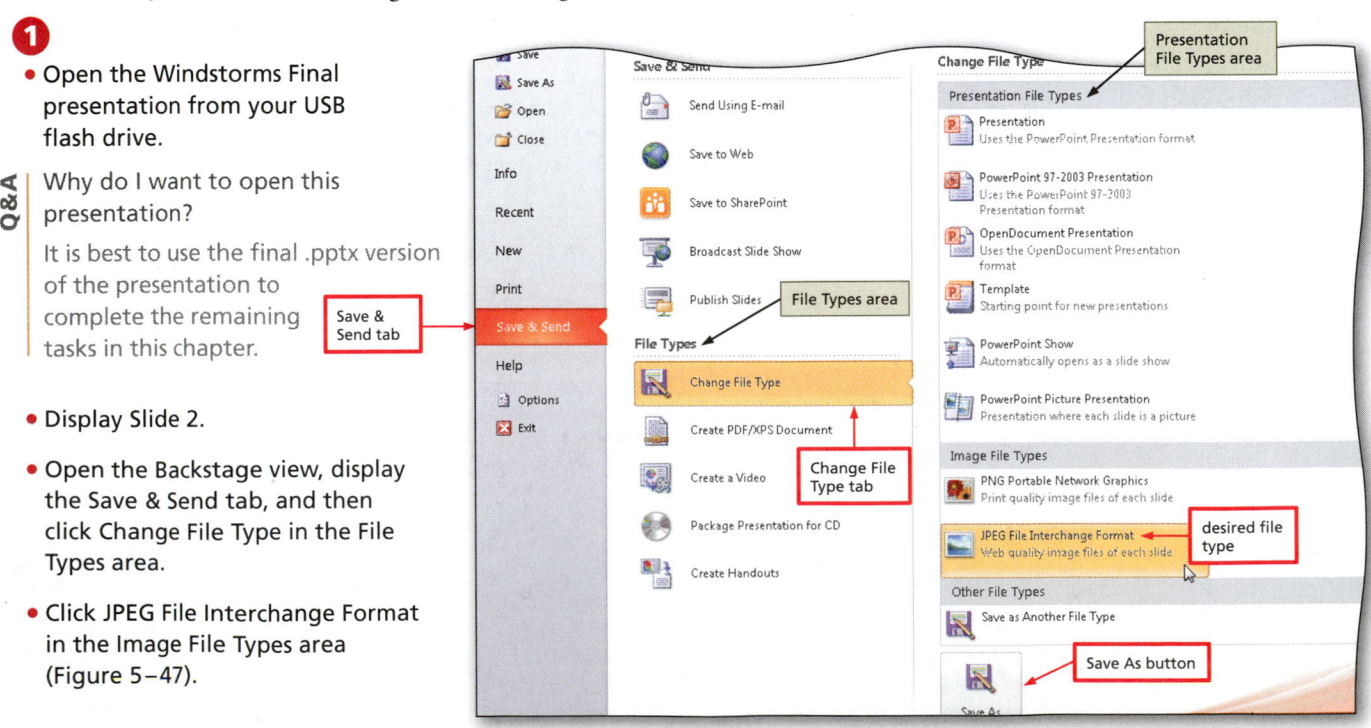

Figure 5–47

2
- Click the Save As button to display the Save As dialog box.

- Type **Tornadoes SmartArt** in the File name text box (Figure 5–48).

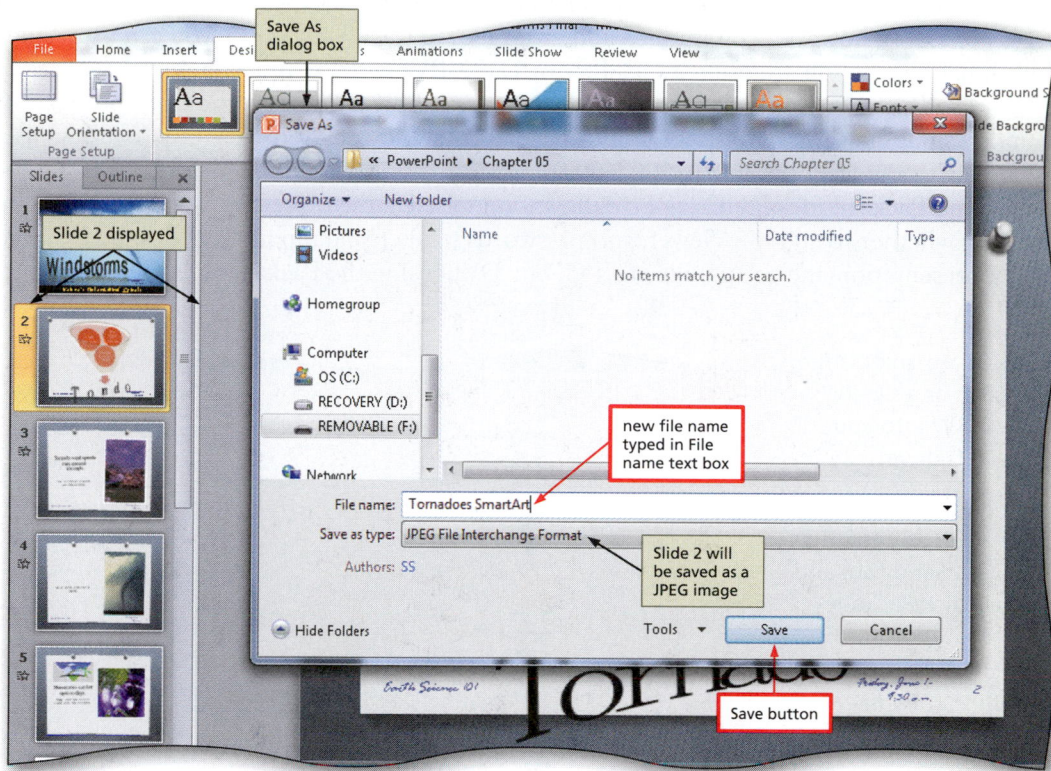

Figure 5–48

3
- Click the Save button (Save As dialog box) to display the Microsoft PowerPoint dialog box (Figure 5–49).

4
- Click the Current Slide Only button (Microsoft PowerPoint dialog box) to save only Slide 2 as a file in JPEG (.jpg) format.

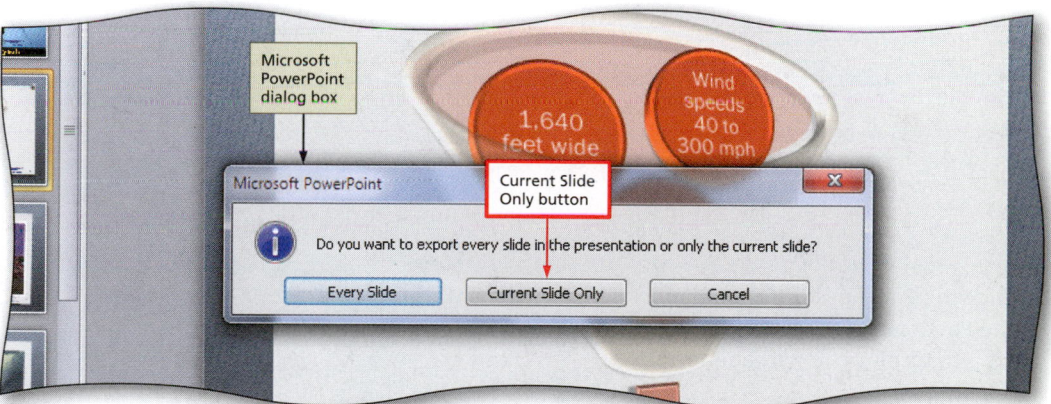

Figure 5–49

Other Ways	
1. Click File on Ribbon, click Save As in Backstage view, click 'Save as type' arrow, select JPEG File Interchange Format, click Save button	2. Double-click JPEG File Interchange Format in Image File Types area

To Package a Presentation for Storage on a CD or DVD

If your computer has compact disc (CD) or digital video disc (DVD) burning hardware, the Package for CD option will copy a PowerPoint presentation and linked files onto a CD or DVD. Two types of CDs or DVDs can be used: recordable (CD-R or DVD-R) and rewritable (CD-RW or DVD-RW). You must copy all the desired files in a single operation if you use PowerPoint for this task because you cannot add any more files after the first set is copied. If, however, you want to add more files to the CD or DVD, you can use Windows Explorer to copy additional files. If you are using a CD-RW or DVD-RW with existing content, these files will be overwritten.

The PowerPoint Viewer is included so you can show the presentation on another computer that has Microsoft Windows but does not have PowerPoint installed. The **PowerPoint Viewer** also allows users to view presentations created with PowerPoint 2003, 2000, and 97.

The Package for CD dialog box allows you to select the presentation files to copy, linking and embedding options, whether to add the Viewer, and passwords to open and modify the files. The following steps show how to save a presentation and related files to a CD or DVD using the Package for CD feature.

1
- Insert a blank CD-R or DVD-R or a CD-RW or DVD-RW into your CD or DVD drive.

- Open the Backstage view, display the Save & Send tab, and then click Package Presentation for CD in the File Types area (Figure 5–50).

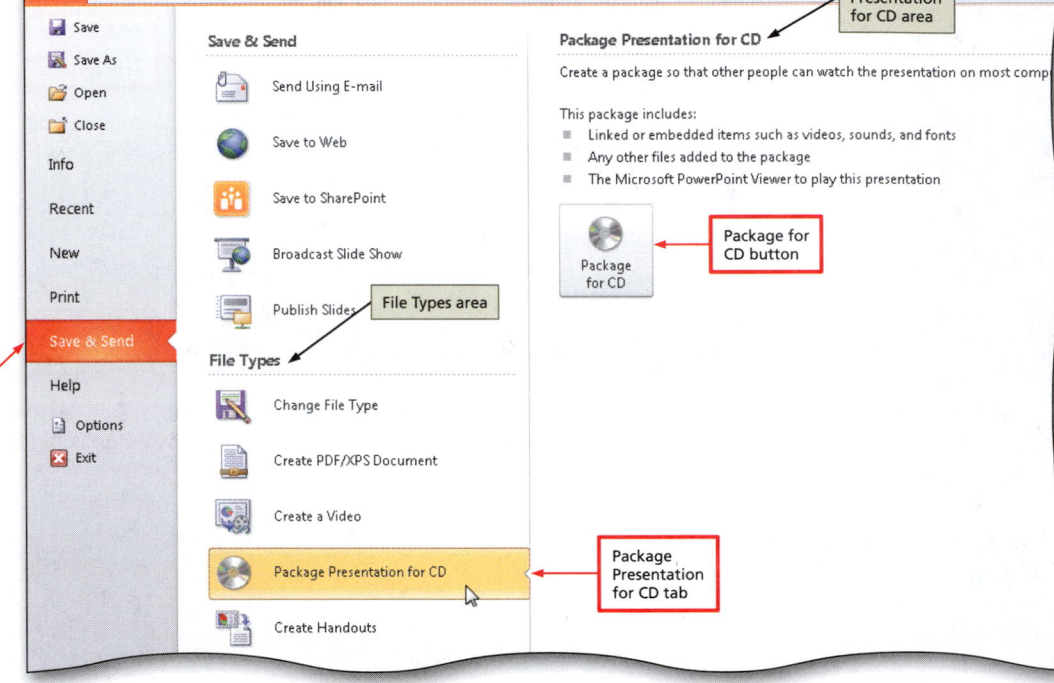

Figure 5–50

2
- Click the Package for CD button in the Package Presentation for CD area to display the Package for CD dialog box.

- Type **Windstorms** in the Name the CD text box (Package for CD dialog box) (Figure 5–51).

Q&A
What if I want to add more files to the CD?

Click the Add button and then locate the files you want to write on the CD.

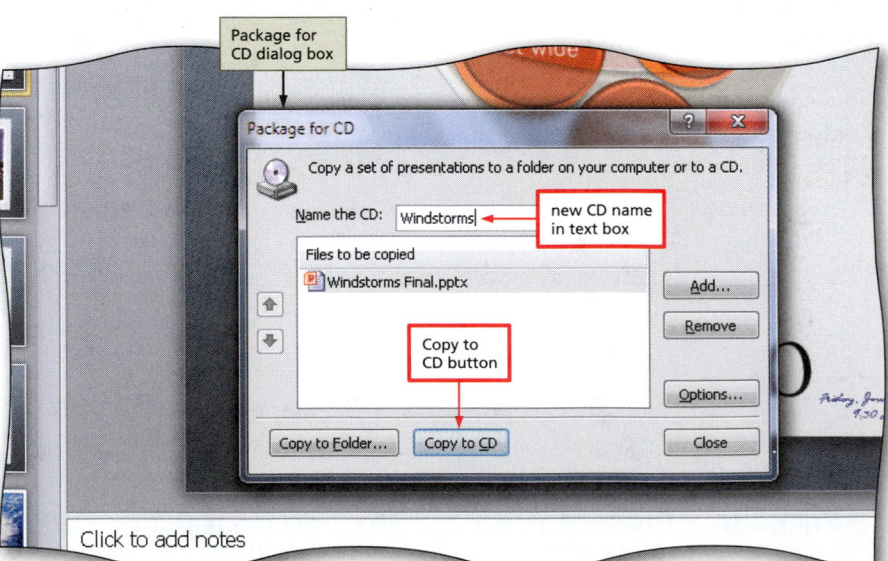

Figure 5–51

3

- Click the Copy to CD button to begin packaging the presentation files and to display the Microsoft PowerPoint dialog box (Figure 5–52).

Q&A What is the purpose of the Copy to Folder button?

If you are copying your presentation to a folder on a network or on your storage device instead of on a CD, you would click this button.

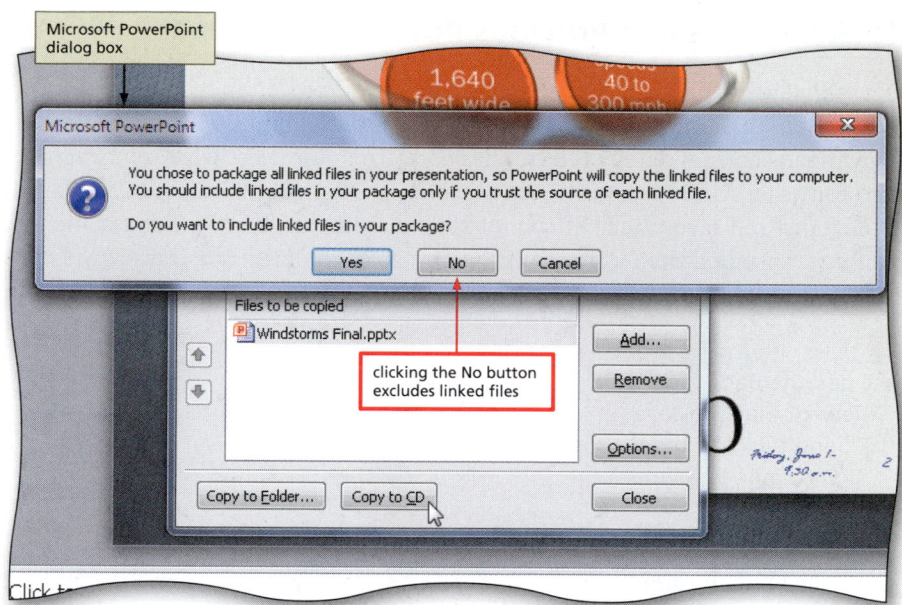

Figure 5–52

4

- Click the No button (Microsoft PowerPoint dialog box) to not include linked files and to display another Microsoft PowerPoint dialog box (Figure 5–53).

5

- Click the Continue button (Microsoft PowerPoint dialog box) to continue copying the presentation to a CD without the comments added to the slides.

6

- When the files have been written, click the No button (Microsoft PowerPoint dialog box) to not copy the files to another CD.

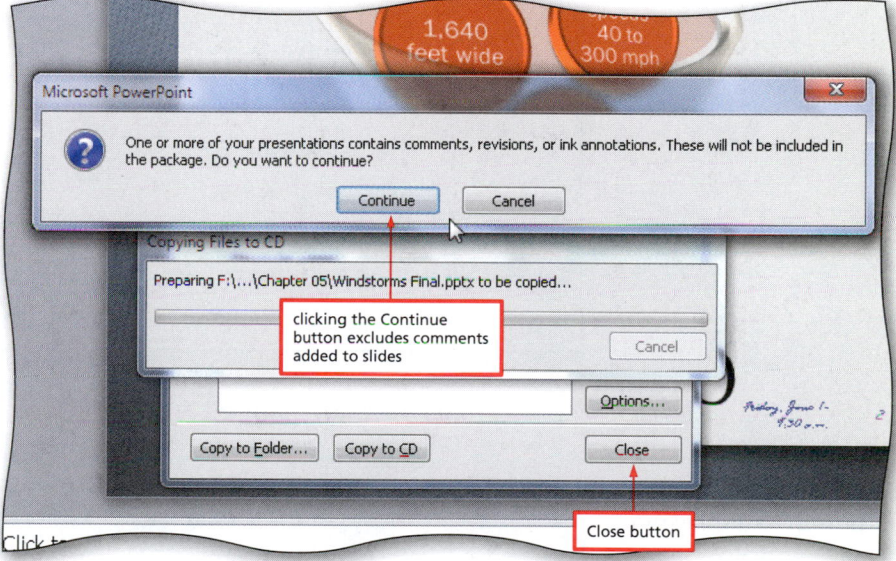

Figure 5–53

7

- Click the Close button (Package for CD dialog box) to finish saving the presentation to a CD.

TO VIEW A POWERPOINT SHOW USING THE POWERPOINT VIEWER

When you arrive at a remote location, you will run the packaged presentation. The following steps explain how you would run the presentation using the PowerPoint Viewer.

1. Insert your CD or DVD into the CD or DVD drive.

2. Accept the licensing agreement for the PowerPoint Viewer to open and run the slide show.

To Save a File in a Previous PowerPoint Format

Prior to Microsoft Office 2007, PowerPoint saved files, by default, as a .ppt type. The earlier versions of PowerPoint cannot open the .pptx type that PowerPoint 2010 and 2007 create by default. The Microsoft Office Downloads and Updates Web site has converters for users who are using these earlier versions of the program and also for other Microsoft Office software. The Microsoft Compatibility Pack for Word, Excel, and PowerPoint will open, edit, and save Office 2010 and 2007 documents. You cannot assume that people who obtain a .pptx file from you have installed the Compatibility Pack, so to diminish frustration and confusion, you can save a presentation as a .ppt type. The following steps save the Windstorms Final file as a PowerPoint 97–2003 Presentation.

1
- Open the Backstage view, display the **Save & Send** tab, and then click Change File Type in the File Types area.

- Click PowerPoint 97–2003 Presentation in the Presentation File Types area (Figure 5–54).

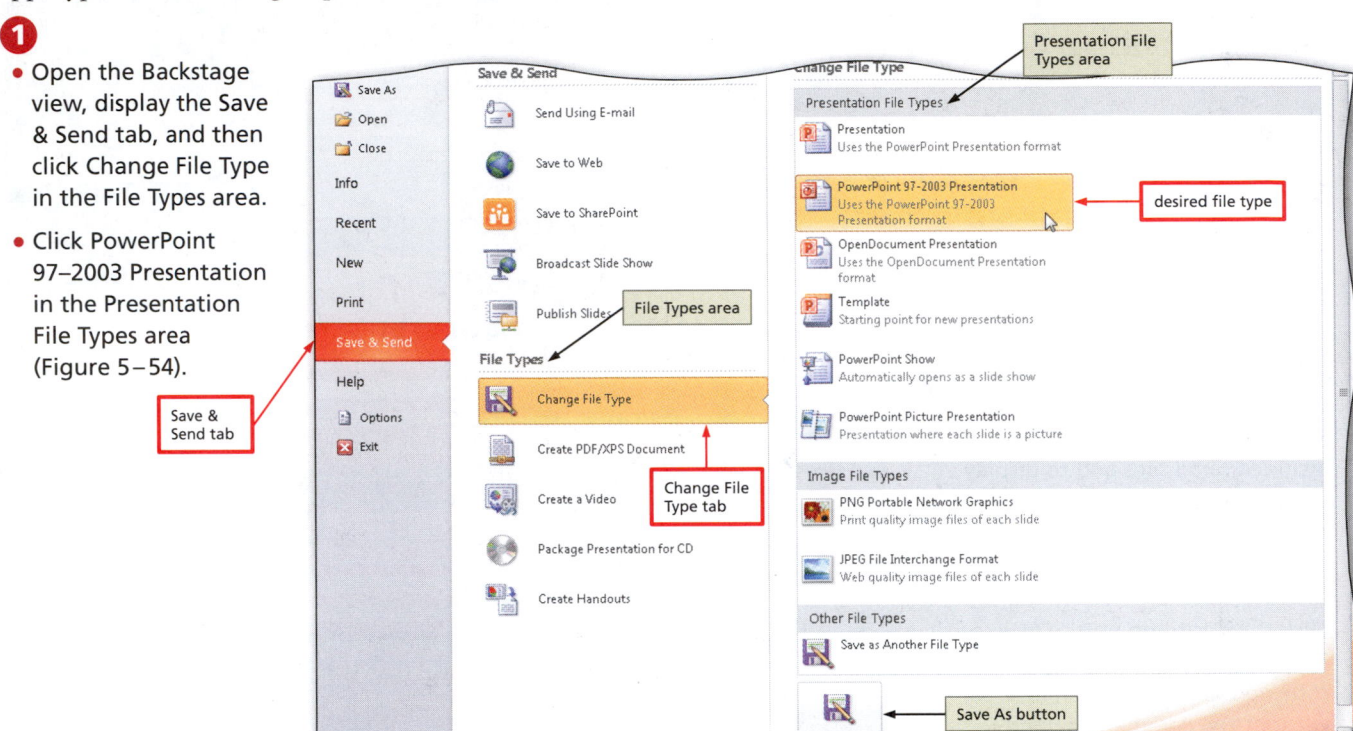

Figure 5–54

2
- Click the Save As button to display the Save As dialog box.

- Type `Windstorms Final Previous Version` in the File name text box (Figure 5–55).

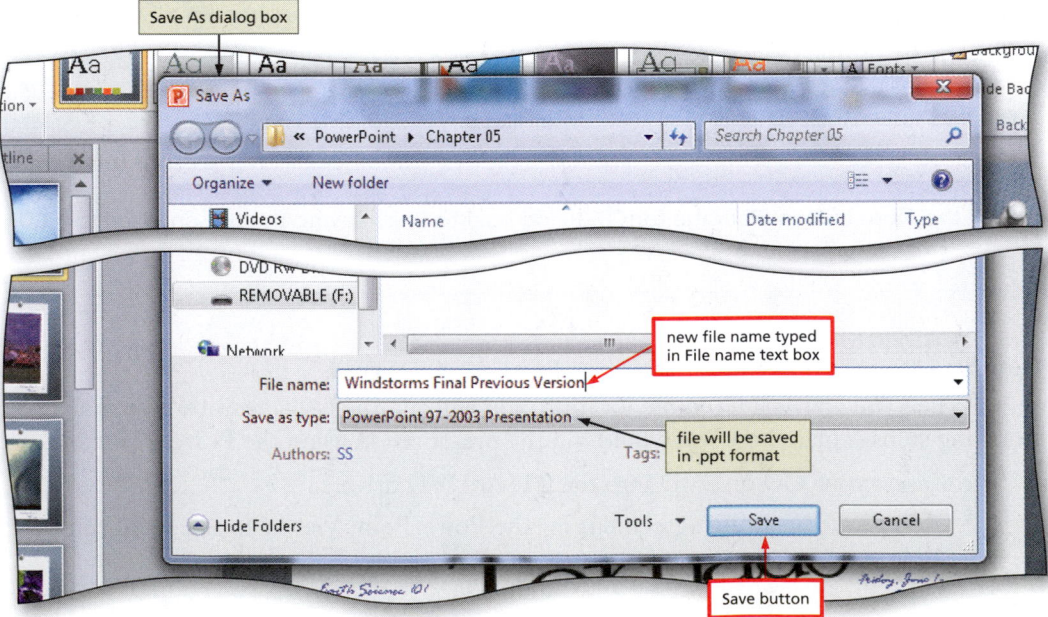

Figure 5–55

3

- Click the Save button (Save As dialog box) to save the Windstorms Final Previous Version presentation as a .ppt type and display the Microsoft PowerPoint Compatibility Checker.

Q&A Why does this Compatibility Checker dialog box display?

PowerPoint is alerting you that the older file version will not keep some of the features used in the presentation. You will learn more about the Compatibility Checker in the next section of this chapter.

4

- Click the Continue button (Microsoft PowerPoint Compatibility Checker) to continue to save the presentation.

5

- Close the current PowerPoint file and then open the Windstorms Final presentation from your USB flash drive.

Q&A Why do I want to open this presentation instead of using the current file?

The current file is saved in a previous version of PowerPoint, so some features are not available when you run the final version of the slide show. It is best to use the more current version of the presentation to complete the remaining tasks in this chapter.

> **Other Ways**
>
> 1. Click File on Ribbon, click Save As in Backstage view, click 'Save as type' arrow, select PowerPoint 97–2003 Presentation, click Save button
> 2. Double-click PowerPoint 97–2003 Presentation in Presentation File Types area

Protecting and Securing a Presentation

When your slides are complete, you can perform additional functions to finalize the file and prepare it for distributing to other users or for running on a computer other than the one used to develop the file. For example, the Compatibility Checker reviews the file for any feature that will not work properly or display on computers running a previous PowerPoint version. In addition, the Document Inspector locates inappropriate information, such as comments, in a file and allows you to delete these slide elements. With passwords and digital signatures, you add security levels to prevent people from distributing, viewing, or modifying your slides. When the review process is complete, you can indicate this file is the final version.

In the following pages, you will follow these general steps to ensure your presentation contains appropriate information and that the contents will not be changed without authorization:

1. Identify features not supported by versions prior to PowerPoint 2007.
2. Remove personal information.
3. Select a password to open the file.
4. Identify the presentation as the final version.
5. Create a digital certificate to state the file contents have not been altered.

BTW

Digital Signatures
A digital signature verifies that the contents of a file have not been altered and that an imposter is not trying to commit forgery by taking ownership of the document. This signature encrypts, or converts, readable data into unreadable characters. To read the file, a user must decrypt, or decipher, the data into a readable form.

To Identify Presentation Features Not Supported by Previous Versions

PowerPoint 2010 has many new features not found in some previous versions of PowerPoint, especially versions older than PowerPoint 2007. For example, WordArt formatted with Quick Styles is an enhancement found only in PowerPoint 2010 and PowerPoint 2007. If you give your file to people who have an earlier PowerPoint version installed on their computers, they will be able to open the file but may not be able to see or edit some special features and effects. You can use the **Compatibility Checker** to see which presentation elements will not function in earlier versions of PowerPoint. The following steps run the Compatibility Checker and display a summary of the elements in your Windstorms Final presentation that will be lost if your file is opened in some earlier PowerPoint versions.

1

- Open the Backstage view and then click the Check for Issues button (Info tab | Prepare for Sharing area) to display the Prepare for Sharing menu (Figure 5–56).

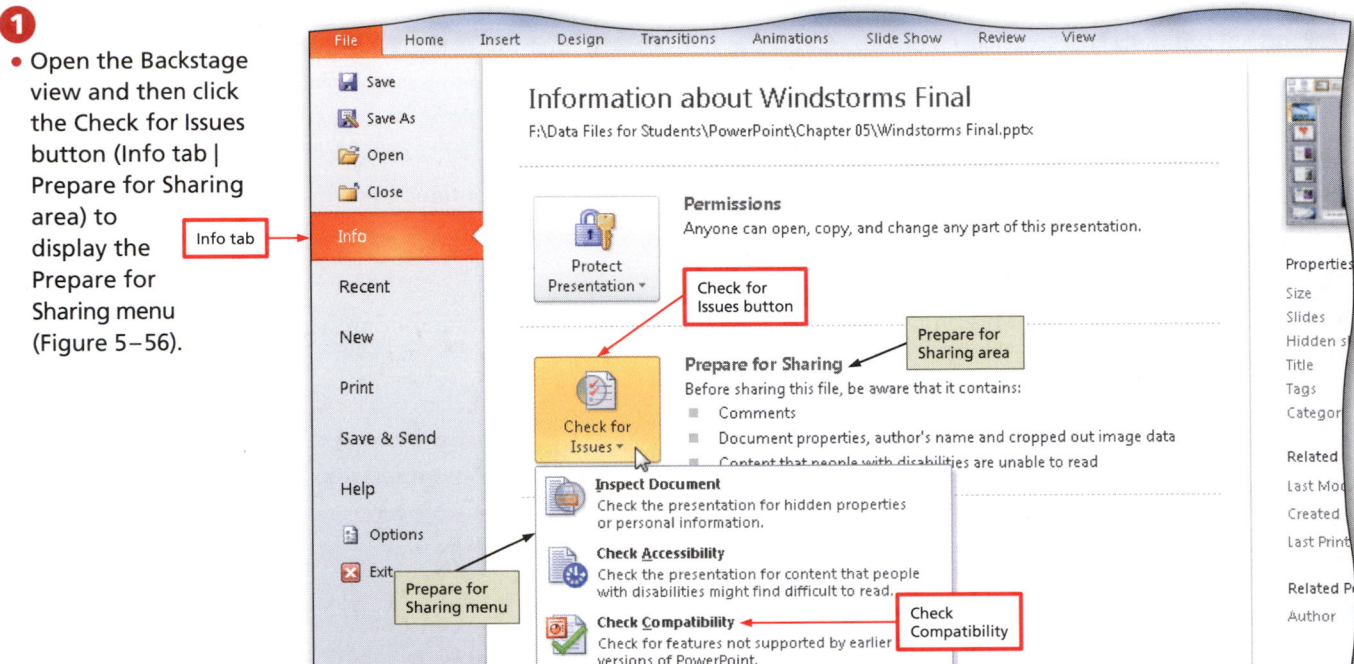

Figure 5–56

2

- Click Check Compatibility to have PowerPoint examine the file and then, after a short period, display the Microsoft PowerPoint Compatibility Checker dialog box.

- In the Summary area, view the comments regarding the three features that are not supported by earlier versions of PowerPoint (Figure 5–57).

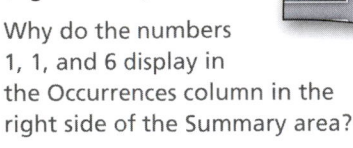

Why do the numbers 1, 1, and 6 display in the Occurrences column in the right side of the Summary area?

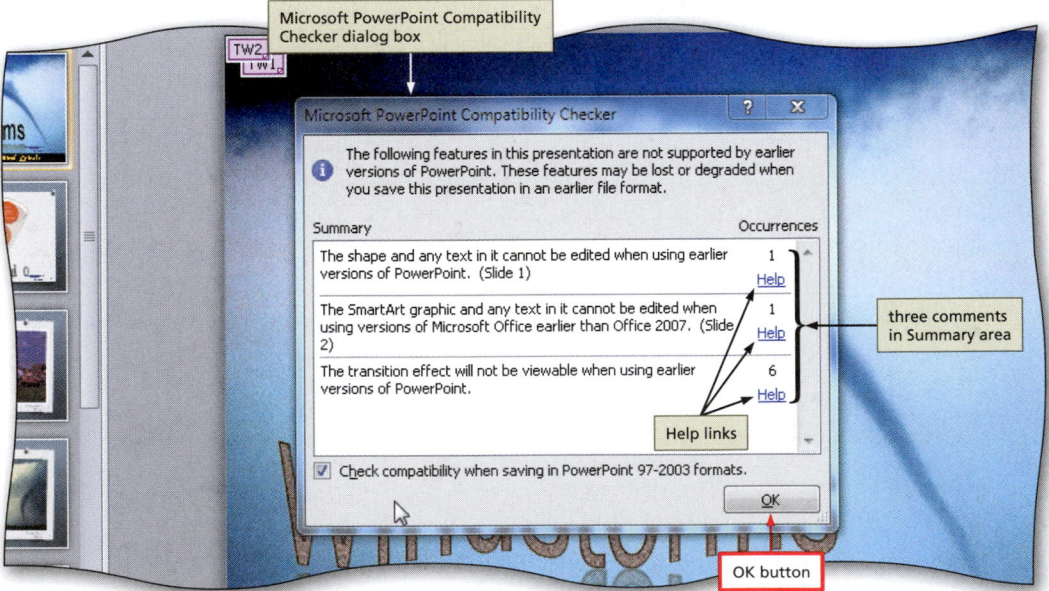

Figure 5–57

The Compatibility Checker found one shape and one SmartArt graphic in your presentation that cannot be edited in previous versions. These graphics will be converted to bitmap images in older versions, so they cannot be ungrouped and modified. In addition, the Vortex transition applied to all six slides will not display if the presentation is opened with any previous version of PowerPoint.

What happens if I click the Help links in the Summary area?

PowerPoint will provide additional information about the particular incompatible slide element.

3
- Click the OK button (Microsoft PowerPoint Compatibility Checker dialog box) to close the dialog box and return to the presentation.

To Remove Inappropriate Information

As you work on your presentation, you might add information meant only for you to see. For example, you might write comments to yourself or put confidential information in the Document Information Panel. You would not want other people to access this information if you give a copy of the presentation file to them. You also added a comment and replied to Mary Halen's questions, and you may not want anyone other than Mary to view this information. The Document Inspector provides a quick and efficient method of searching for and deleting inappropriate or confidential information.

If you tell the Document Inspector to delete content, such as personal information, comments, invisible slide content, or notes, and then decide you need to see those slide elements, quite possibly you will be unable to retrieve the information by using the Undo command. For that reason, it is a good idea to make a duplicate copy of your file and then inspect this new second copy. The following steps save a duplicate copy of your Windstorms Final presentation, run the Document Inspector on this new file, and then delete comments.

1
- Open the Backstage view, click Save As to open the Save As dialog box, and then type **Windstorms Final Duplicate** in the File name text box.

- Click the Save button to change the file name and save another copy of this presentation.

2
- Open the Backstage view and then click the Check for Issues button (Info tab | Prepare for Sharing area) to display the Prepare for Sharing menu (Figure 5–58).

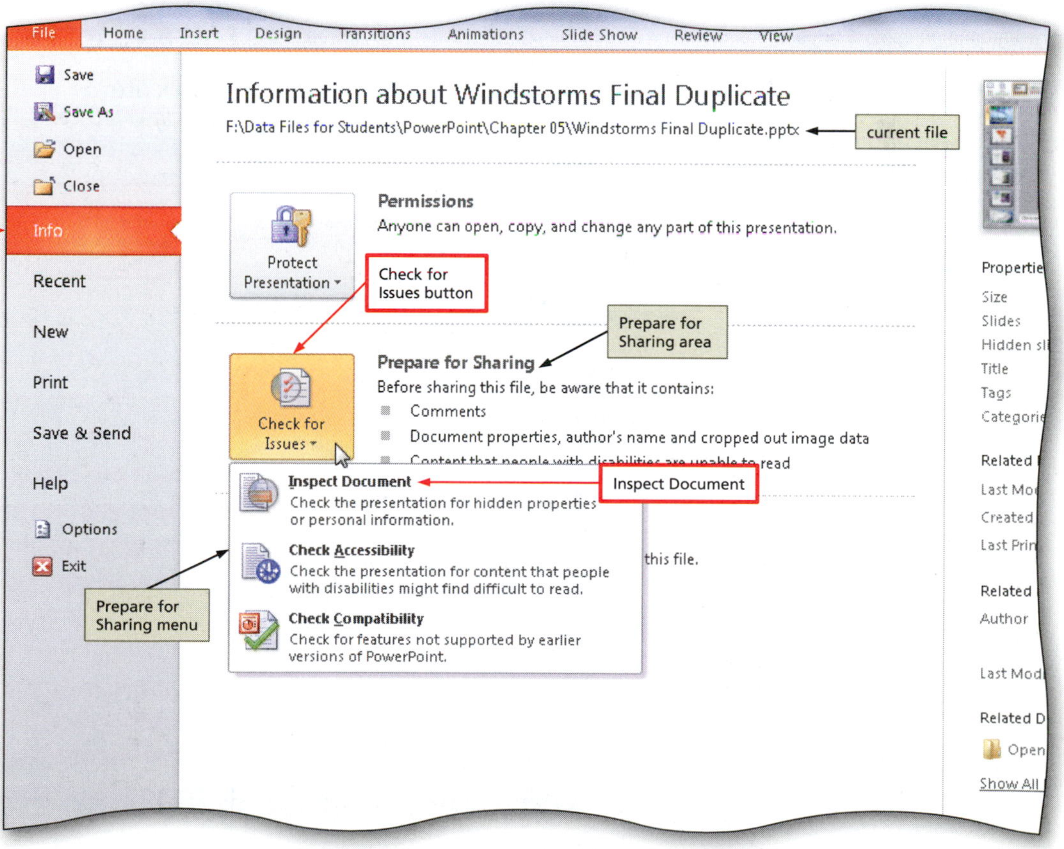

Figure 5–58

3

- Click Inspect Document to display the Document Inspector dialog box (Figure 5–59).

Q&A

What information does the Document Inspector check?

This information includes text in the Document Information Panel, such as your name and company. Other information includes details of when the file was last saved, objects formatted as invisible, graphics and text you dragged off a slide, presentation notes, and e-mail headers.

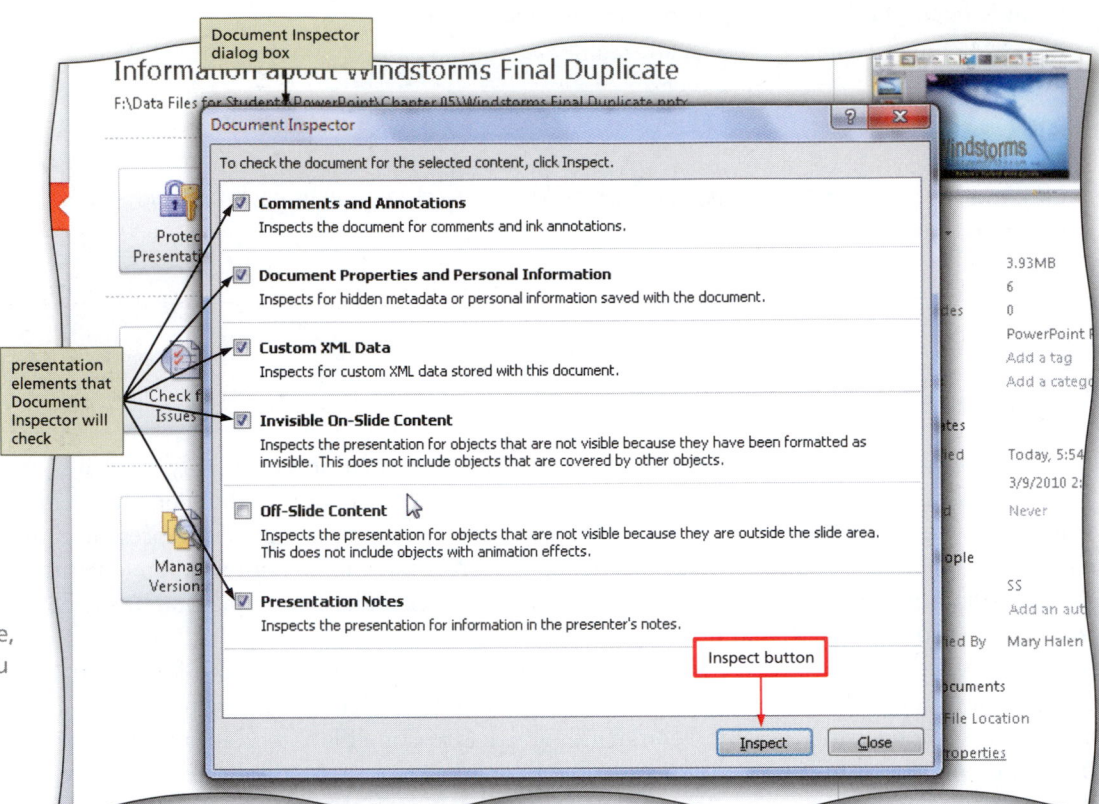

Figure 5–59

4

- Click the Inspect button to check the document and display the inspection results (Figure 5–60).

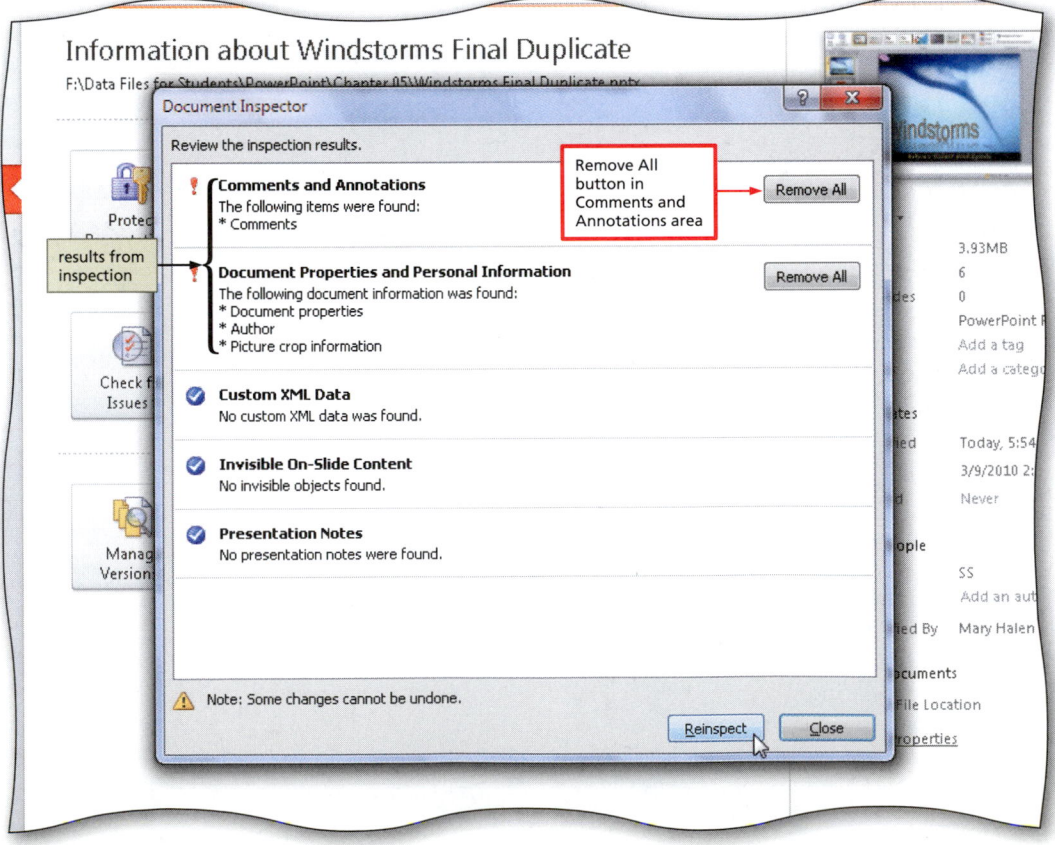

Figure 5–60

5

● Click the Remove
All button in the
Comments and
Annotations area
of the inspection
results to remove
the comments from
the presentation
(Figure 5–61).

Q&A

Should I also remove
the document
properties and
personal information?

You might want to
delete this information
so that no identifying
information is saved.
This information
includes text that
displays in the
Document Information
Panel, such as your
name, course number,
and keywords.

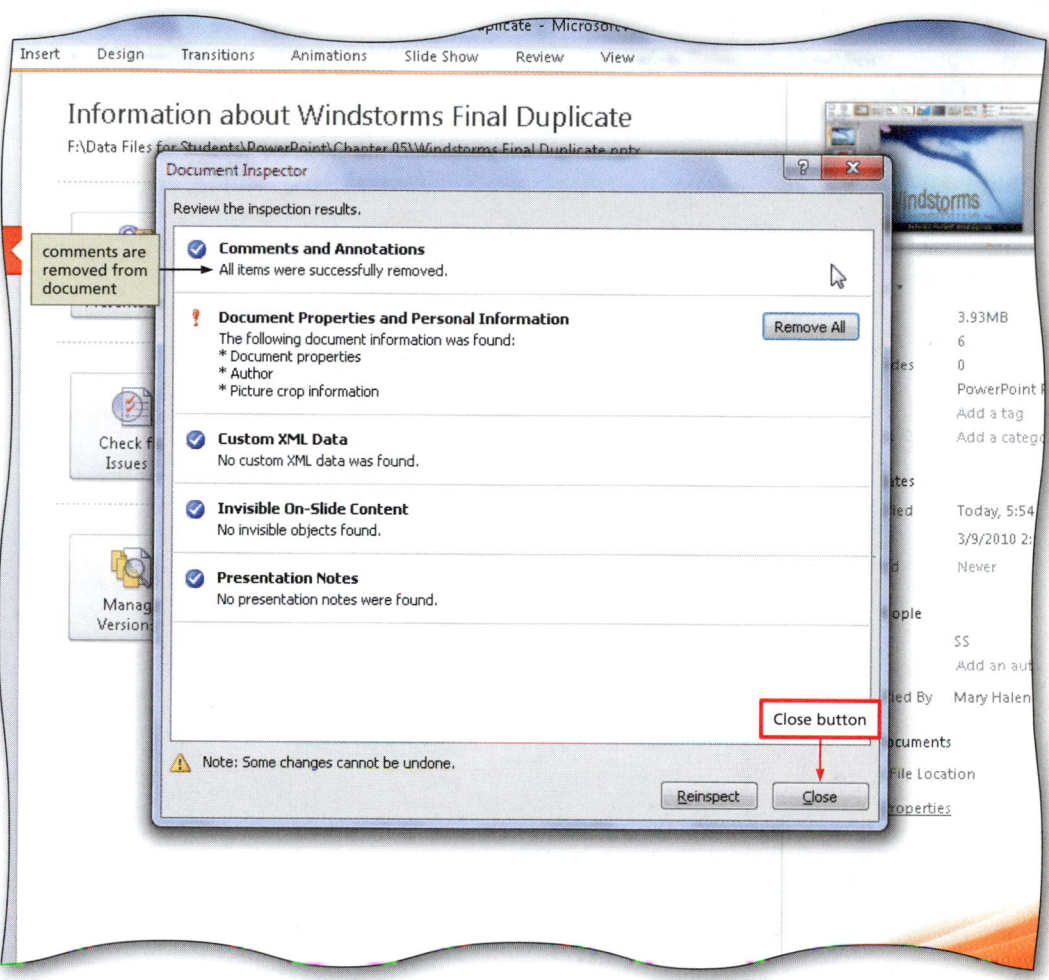

Figure 5–61

6

● Click the Close button (Document Inspector dialog box) to close the dialog box.

Select an appropriate password.
A password should be at least eight characters and contain a combination of letters and
numbers. Using both uppercase and lowercase letters is advised. Do not use a password that
someone could guess, such as your first or last name, spouse's or child's name, telephone
number, birth date, street address, license plate number, or Social Security number.
   Once you develop this password, write it down in a secure place. Underneath your
keyboard is not a secure place, nor is your middle desk drawer.

**Plan
Ahead**

To Set a Password

You can protect your slide content by using passwords. The passwords specify whether a user can look at or
modify a file. The following steps set a password for the Windstorms Final Duplicate file.

- With the Backstage view open and the Info tab displaying, click the Protect Presentation button (Info tab | Permissions area) menu to display the Permissions menu (Figure 5–62).

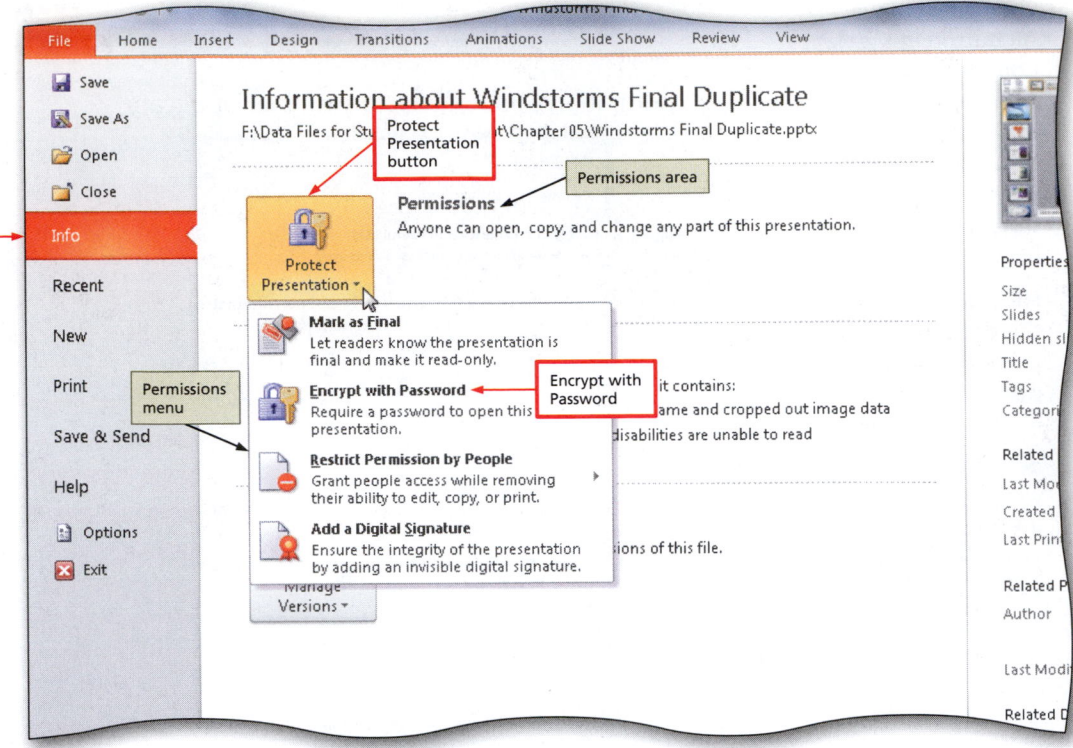

Figure 5–62

- Click Encrypt with Password to display the Encrypt Document dialog box.

- Type **Tornado2Windy** in the Password text box (Figure 5–63).

Q&A

Why do dots appear instead of the characters I typed?

PowerPoint does not display the actual letters and numbers for security reasons. In the next step, you are prompted to reenter the characters to ensure you pressed the desired keys.

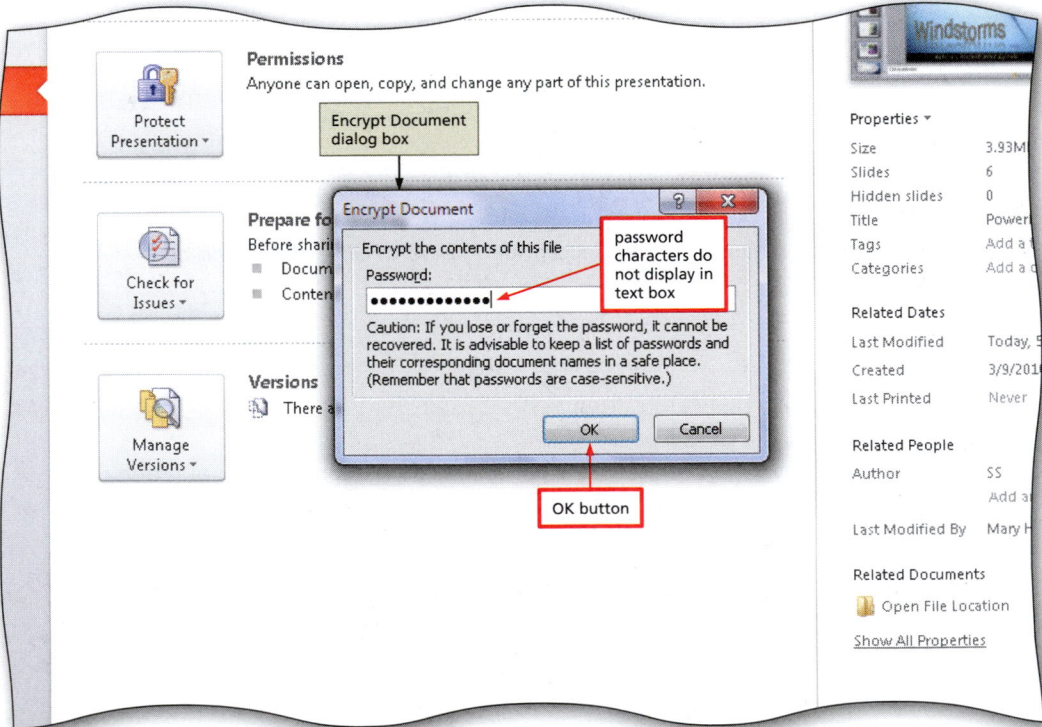

Figure 5–63

3
- Click the OK button to display the Confirm Password dialog box.

- Type **Tornado2Windy** in the Reenter password text box (Figure 5–64).

 Q&A What if I forget my password?

You will not be able to open your file. For security reasons, Microsoft or other companies cannot retrieve a lost password.

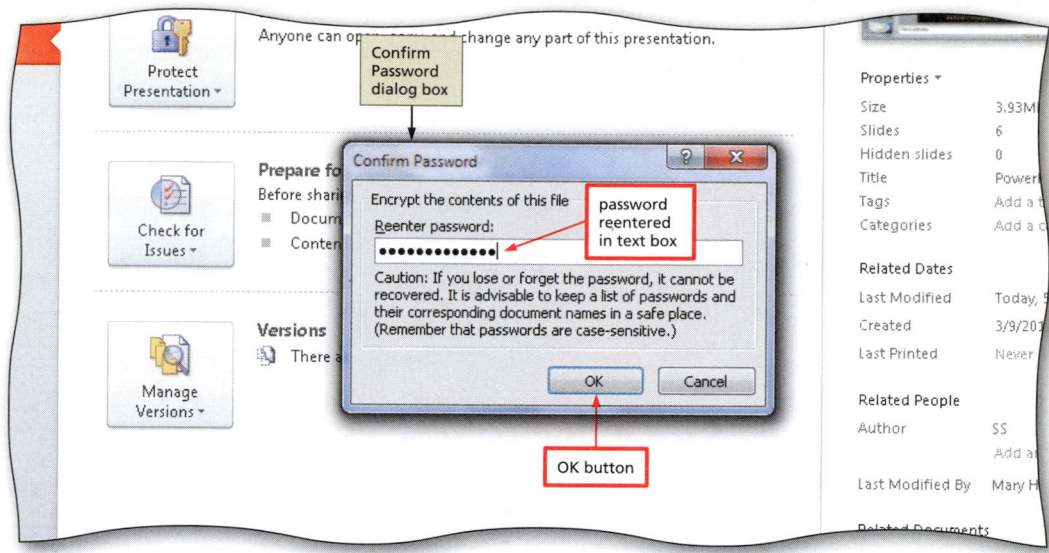

Figure 5–64

4
- Click the OK button in the Confirm Password dialog box.

Q&A When does the password take effect?

You will need to enter your password the next time you open your presentation.

To Open a Presentation with a Password

To open a file that has been protected with a password, you would perform the following steps.

1. Display the Open dialog box, locate the desired file, and then click the Open button to display the Password dialog box.

2. When the Password dialog box appears, type the password in the Password text box and then click the OK button to display the presentation.

To Change the Password or Remove Password Protection

To change a password that you added to a file or to remove all password protection from the file, you would perform the following steps.

1. Display the Open dialog box, locate the desired file, and then click the Open button to display the Password dialog box.

2. When the Password dialog box appears, type the password in the Password text box and then click the OK button to display the presentation.

3. Open the Backstage view and then click Save As to display the Save As dialog box. Click the Tools button and then click General Options in the Tools list.

4. Select the contents of the 'Password to open' text box or the 'Password to modify' text box. To remove the password, delete the password text. To change the password, type the new password and then click the OK button. When prompted, retype your password to reconfirm it, and then click the OK button.

5. Click the OK button, click the Save button, and then click the Yes button to resave the presentation.

BTW

Selecting Passwords
Common passwords are 123456, 12345, 123456789, password, and iloveyou. Security experts recommend using passwords or passphrases that have at least eight characters and are a combination of numbers, letters, and capital letters.

To Mark a Presentation as Final

When your slides are completed, you may want to prevent others or yourself from accidentally changing the slide content or features. If you use the **Mark as Final** command, the presentation becomes a read-only document and cannot be edited. The following steps mark the presentation as a final (read-only) document.

- With the Backstage view open and the Info tab displaying, click Protect Presentation to display the Permissions menu (Figure 5–65).

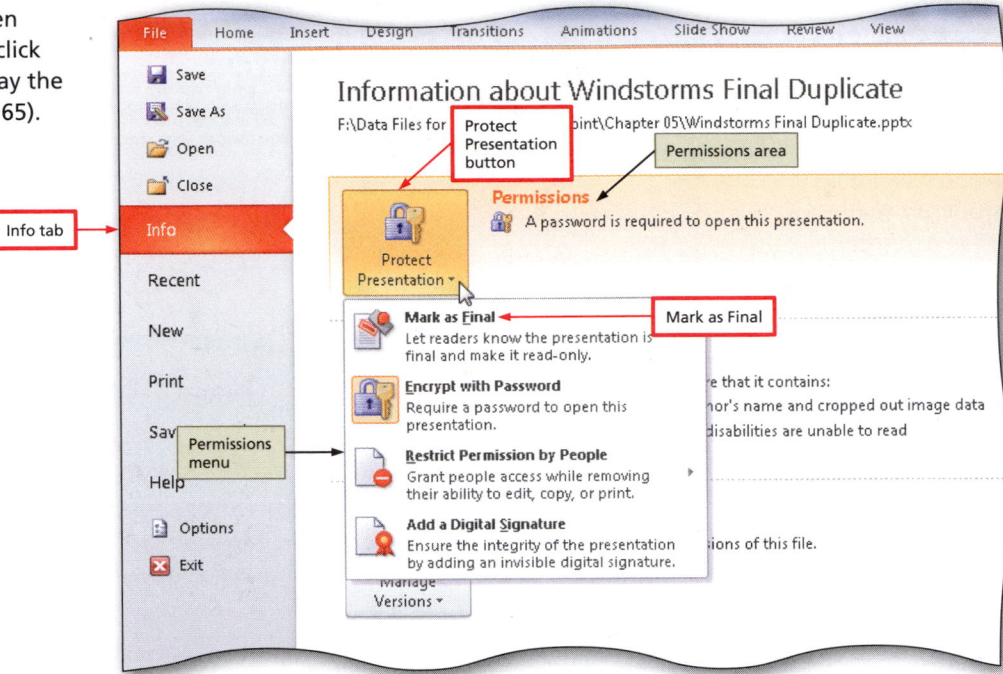

Figure 5–65

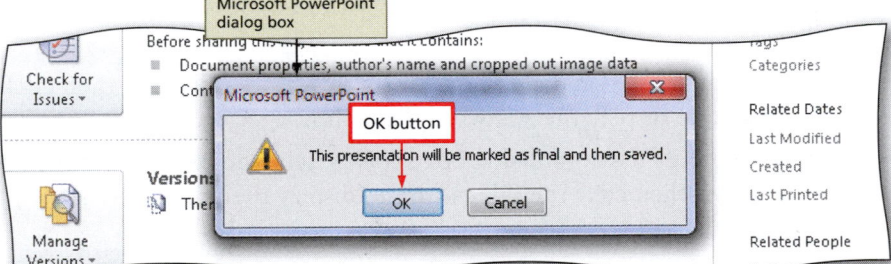

- Click Mark as Final to display the Microsoft PowerPoint dialog box indicating that the presentation will be saved as a final document (Figure 5–66).

Figure 5–66

- Click the OK button (Microsoft PowerPoint dialog box) to save the file and to display another Microsoft PowerPoint dialog box with information about a final version of a document and indicating that the presentation is final (Figure 5–67).

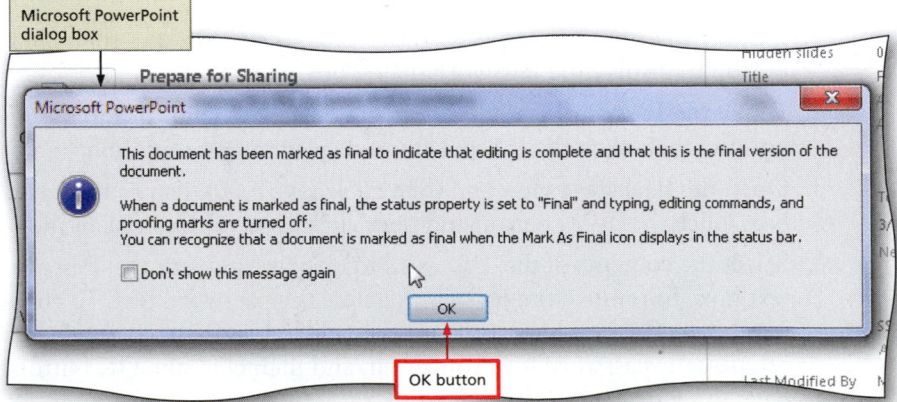

Figure 5–67

Can I turn off this read-only status so that I can edit the file?

Yes. Click Mark as Final in the Permissions menu to toggle off the read-only status.

- Click the OK button (Microsoft PowerPoint dialog box) to return to the Backstage view.

To Create a Digital Signature and Add It to a Document

A digital signature or ID is more commonly known as a **digital certificate**. It verifies that file contents are authentic and valid. Files protected with this certificate cannot be viewed in the PowerPoint Viewer or sent as an e-mail attachment. You can add a digital signature to files that require security, such as a presentation about a company's prototype or a patent application that will be submitted shortly. Only users with Office PowerPoint 2003 or later can view presentations protected by the digital signature. You can obtain an authentic digital certificate from a Microsoft partner, or you can create one yourself. The following steps create a digital signature and add it to the Windstorms Final Duplicate file.

- With the Backstage view open and the Info tab displaying, click the Protect Presentation button (Info tab | Permissions area) to display the Permissions menu (Figure 5–68).

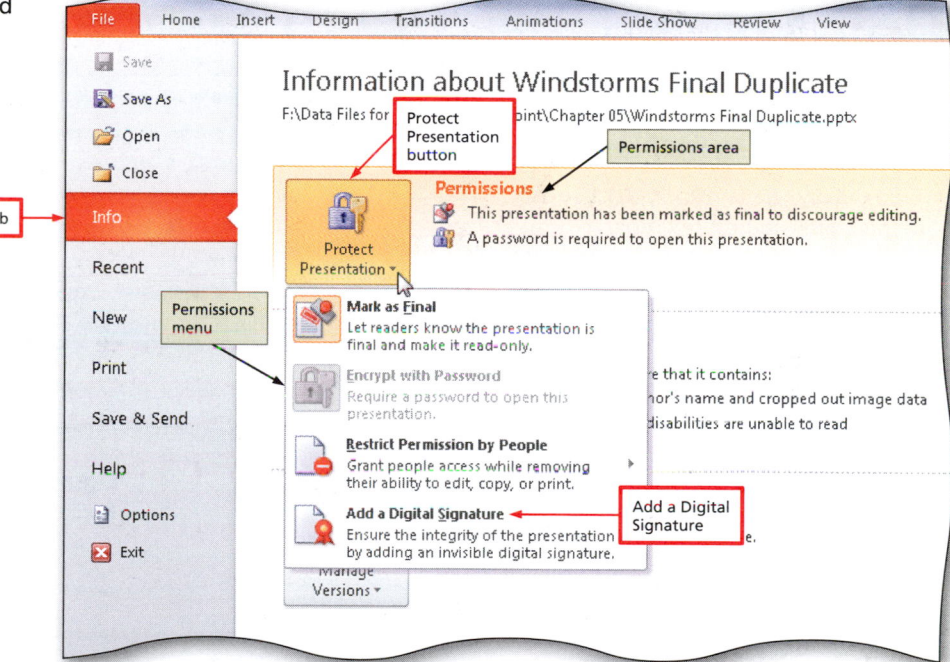

Figure 5–68

- Click Add a Digital Signature to display the Microsoft PowerPoint dialog box (Figure 5–69).

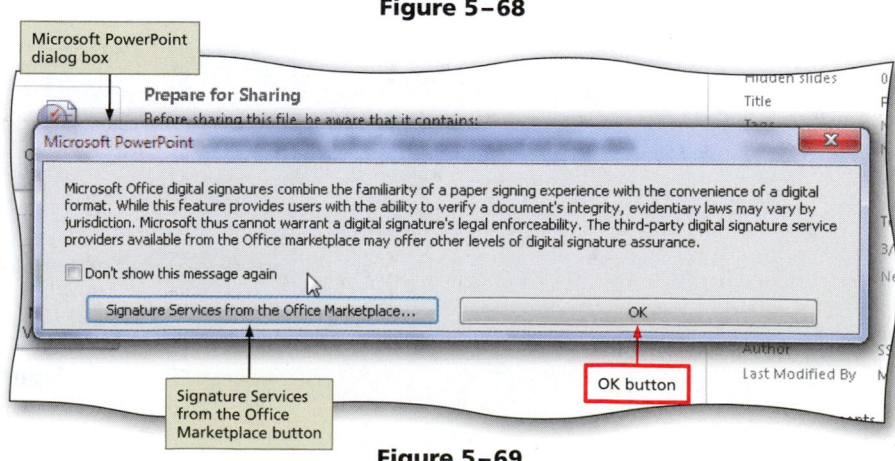

Figure 5–69

3

- Click the OK button to display the Get a Digital ID dialog box.

- Click 'Create your own digital ID' (Get a Digital ID dialog box) (Figure 5–70).

Q&A

What would have happened if I had clicked the Signature Services from the Office Marketplace button instead of the OK button?

You would have been connected to the Microsoft Office Marketplace, which is the same process that will occur if you click the 'Get a digital ID from a Microsoft partner' option button.

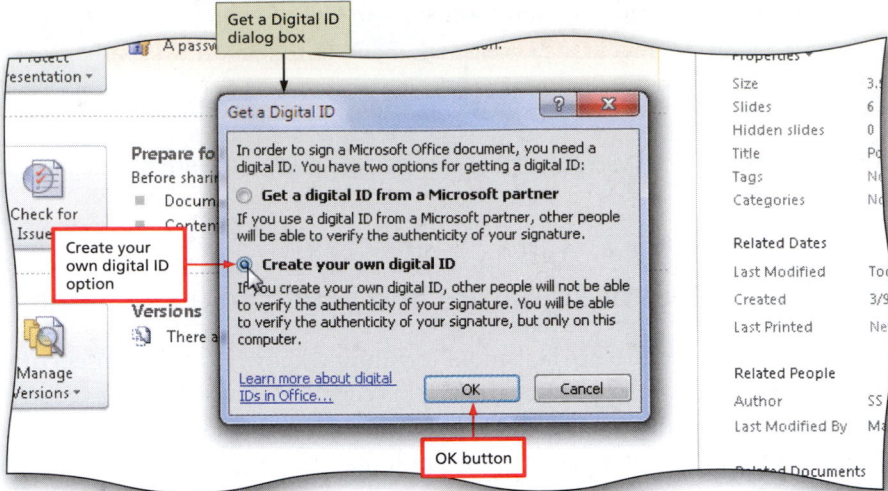

Figure 5–70

4

- Click the OK button to display the Create a Digital ID dialog box.

- If necessary, select the text in the Name text box, and then type **Mary Halen** in this text box.

- Type **mary_halen@hotmail.com** in the E-mail address text box.

- Type **Mary's Weather** in the Organization text box.

- Type **Chicago, IL** in the Location text box (Figure 5–71).

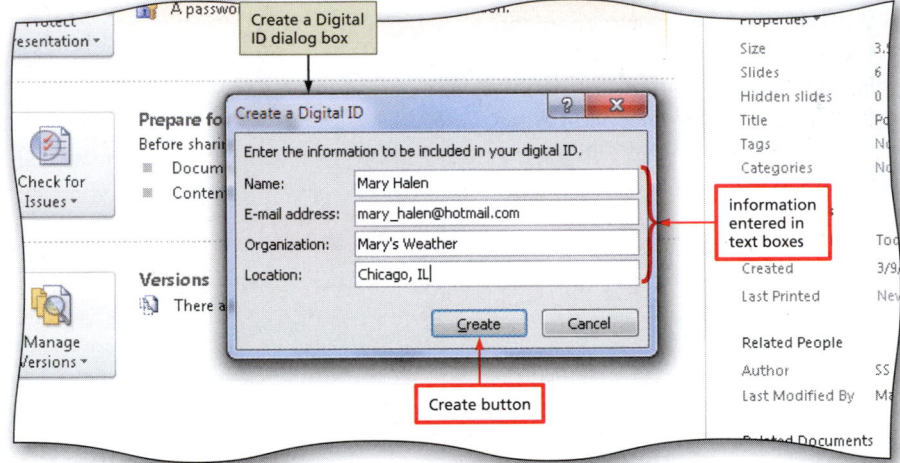

Figure 5–71

5

- Click the Create button to display the Sign dialog box (Figure 5–72).

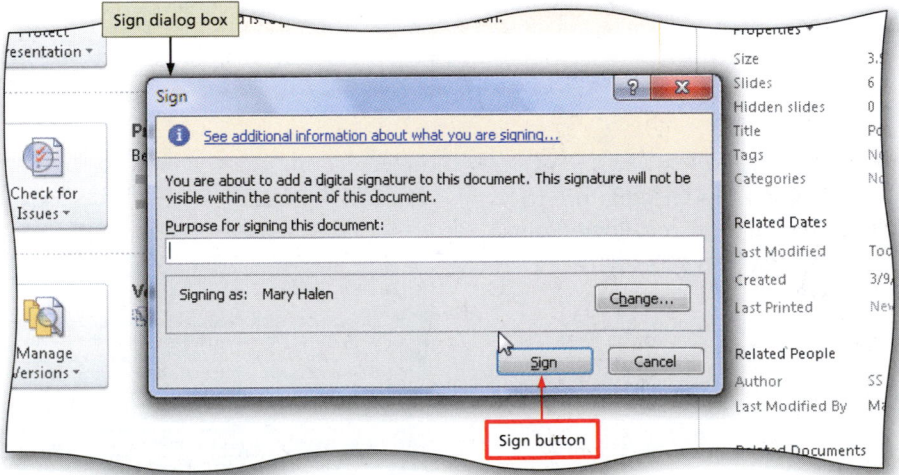

Figure 5–72

6

- Click the Sign button to display the Signature Confirmation dialog box (Figure 5–73).

Q&A   Why would a company want to add a digital signature to a document?

The publisher, who is the signing person or organization, is trusted to ensure the source and integrity of the digital information. A signature confirms that the file contents have not been altered since it was signed.

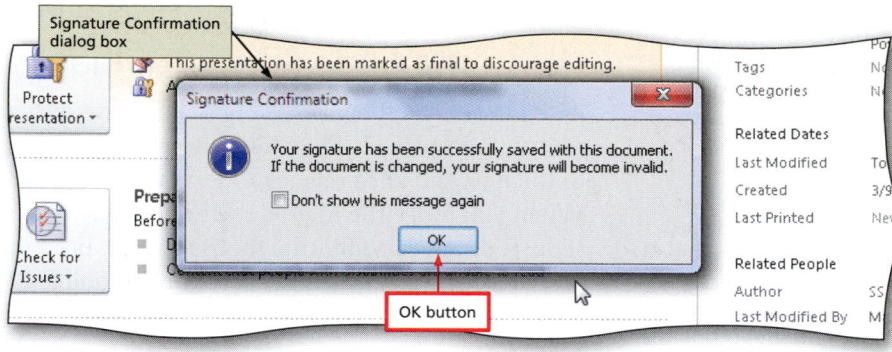

Figure 5–73

Q&A   Can I remove a digital signature that has been applied?

Yes. Point to a signature in the Signatures task pane, click the list arrow, click Remove Signature, click the Yes button, and then, if necessary, click the OK button.

7

- Click the OK button to close the Signature Confirmation dialog box and return to the Backstage view.

Using Presentation Tools to Navigate

When you display a particular slide and view the information, you may want to return to one of the other slides in the presentation. Jumping to particular slides in a presentation is called **navigating**. A set of keyboard shortcuts can help you navigate to various slides during the slide show. When running a slide show, you can press the F1 key to see a list of these keyboard controls. These navigational features are listed in Table 5–1.

BTW

Displaying a Black or White Screen
If an audience member interrupts your planned presentation and asks a question not pertaining to the current slide, you should consider displaying a black or white screen temporarily while you are answering the query.

Table 5–1 Slide Show Navigation Shortcut Keys	
Keyboard Shortcut	**Purpose**
N Click SPACEBAR RIGHT ARROW DOWN ARROW ENTER PAGE DOWN	Advance to the next slide
P BACKSPACE LEFT ARROW UP ARROW PAGE UP	Return to the previous slide
Number followed by ENTER	Go to a specific slide
B PERIOD	Display a black screen Return to slide show from a black screen
W COMMA	Display a white screen Return to slide show from a white screen
ESC CTRL+BREAK HYPHEN	End a slide show

Delivering and Navigating a Presentation Using the Slide Show Toolbar

When you begin running a slide show and move the mouse pointer, the Slide Show toolbar is displayed. The **Slide Show toolbar** contains buttons that allow you to navigate to the next slide or previous slide, mark up the current slide, or change the current display. When you move the mouse, the toolbar displays faintly in the lower-left corner of the slide; it disappears after the mouse has not been moved for three seconds. Table 5–2 describes the buttons on the Slide Show toolbar.

Table 5–2 Slide Show Toolbar Buttons		
Description	**Image**	**Function**
Previous	←	Previous slide or previous animated element on the slide
Pointer	✏	Shortcut menu for arrows, pens, and highlighters
Navigation	▤	Shortcut menu for slide navigation and screen displays
Next	→	Next slide or next animated element on the slide

To Highlight Items on a Slide

You click the arrow buttons on either end of the toolbar to navigate backward or forward through the slide show. The Pointer button has a variety of functions, most often to emphasize, or **highlight**, words or to add **ink** notes or drawings to your presentation in order to emphasize aspects of slides or make handwritten notes. When the presentation ends, PowerPoint will prompt you to keep or discard the ink annotations. The following steps highlight items on a slide in Slide Show view.

- Display the Home tab and then click the Edit Anyway button in the yellow Marked as Final Message Bar near the top of the screen to enable editing the presentation.

- Click the Slide 1 thumbnail in the Slides tab and then run the slide show.

- If the Slide Show toolbar is not visible, move the mouse pointer on the slide.

- Click the Pointer button on the Slide Show toolbar to display the shortcut menu (Figure 5–74).

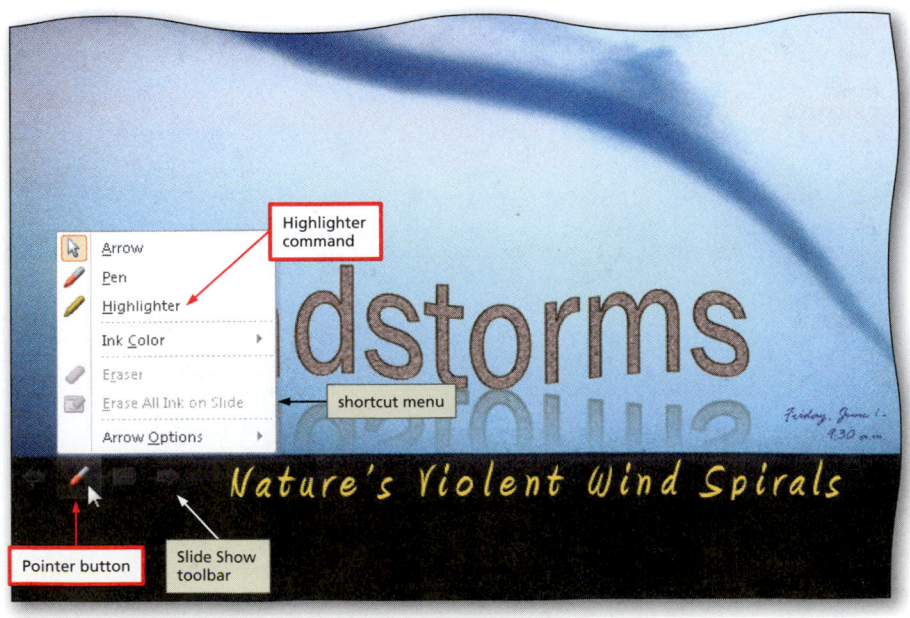

Figure 5–74

2

- Click Highlighter and then drag the mouse over the word, Windstorms. Repeat this action until all the letters are highlighted (Figure 5–75).

Figure 5–75

To Change Ink Color

Instead of the Highlighter, you also can click Pen to draw or write notes on the slides. The following steps change the pointer to a pen and change the color of ink during the presentation.

1

- Display Slide 2. Click the Pointer button on the Slide Show toolbar and then click Pen on the shortcut menu.

- Click the Pointer button on the Slide Show toolbar and then point to Ink Color (Figure 5–76).

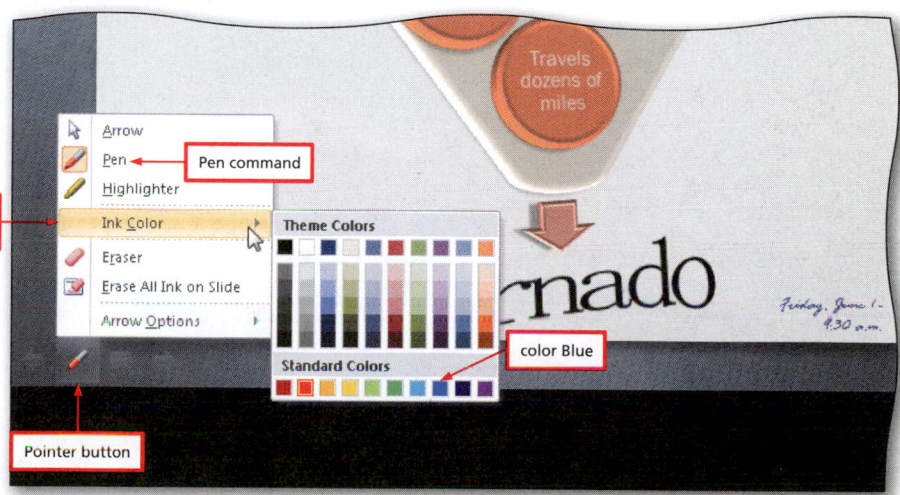

Figure 5–76

2

- Click the color Blue in the Standard Colors row.

- Drag the mouse around the SmartArt graphic to draw a circle around this object (Figure 5–77).

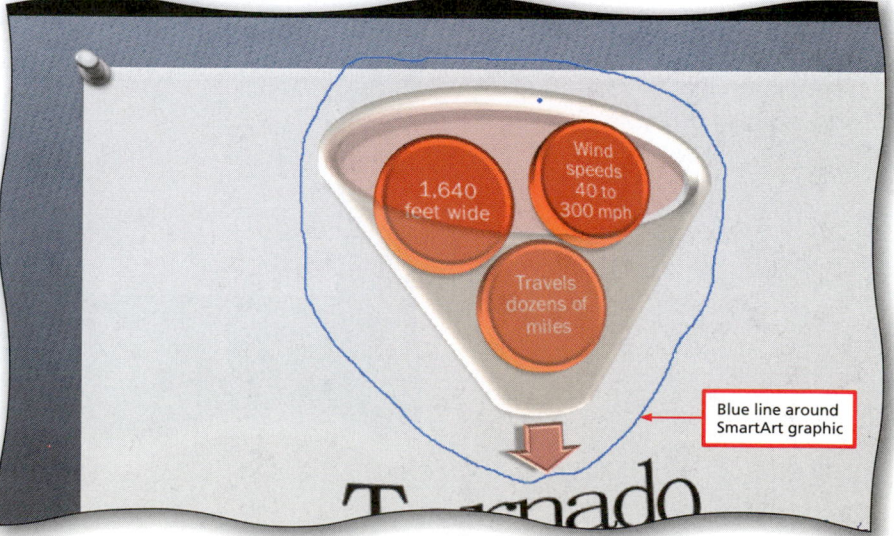

Figure 5–77

3

• Right-click the slide to display the shortcut menu (Figure 5–78).

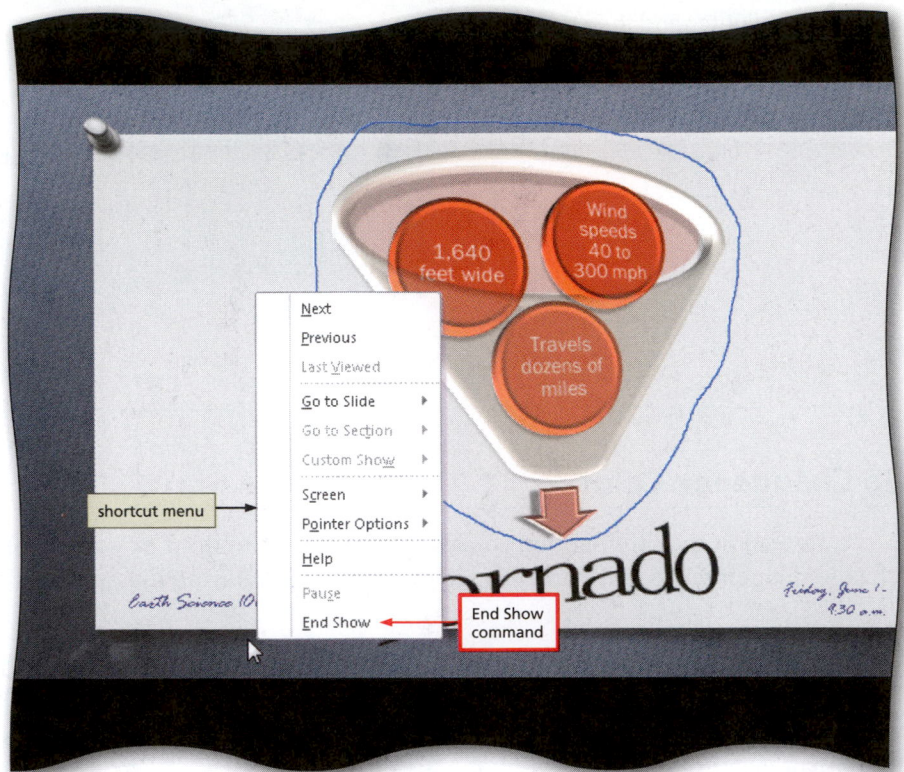

Figure 5–78

4

• Click End Show to display the Microsoft PowerPoint dialog box (Figure 5–79).

5

• Click the Discard button (Microsoft PowerPoint dialog box) to end the presentation without saving the annotations.

Q&A

If I clicked the Keep button in error, can I later discard the annotations?

Yes. Display the slide, click the annotation line to select it, and then press the DELETE key.

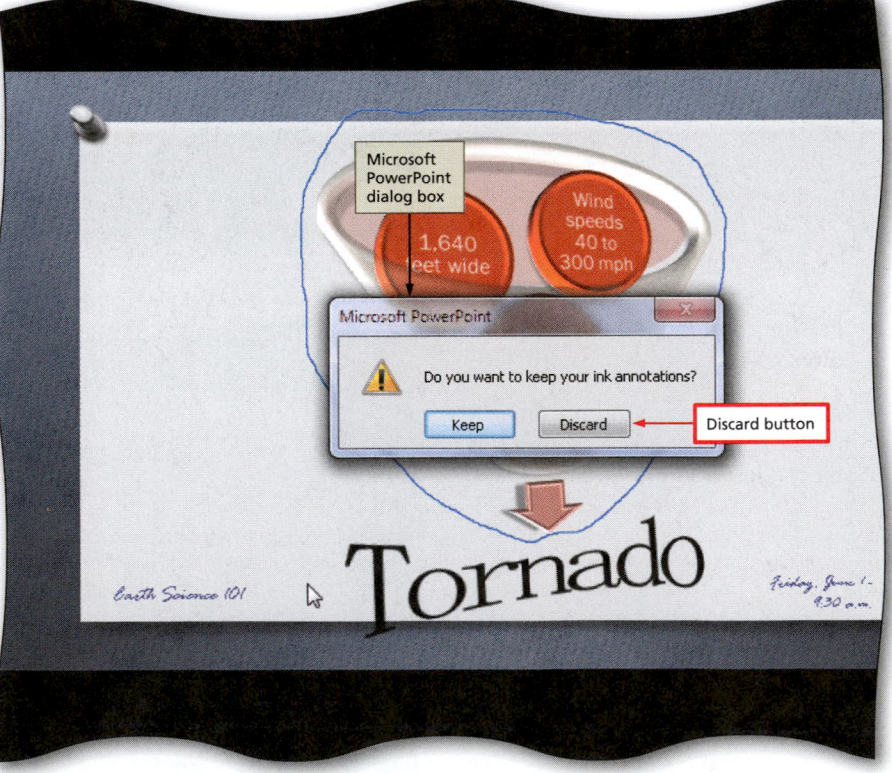

Figure 5–79

TO HIDE THE MOUSE POINTER AND SLIDE SHOW TOOLBAR

To hide the mouse pointer and Slide Show toolbar during the slide show, you would perform the following step.

1. Click the Pointer button on the Slide Show toolbar, point to Arrow Options, and then click Hidden.

TO CONSTANTLY DISPLAY THE MOUSE POINTER AND SLIDE SHOW TOOLBAR

By default, the mouse pointer and toolbar are set at Automatic, which means they are hidden after three seconds of no movement. After you hide the mouse pointer and toolbar, they remain hidden until you choose one of the other commands on the Pointer Options submenu. They are displayed again when you move the mouse.

To keep the mouse pointer and toolbar displayed at all times during a slide show, you would perform the following step.

1. Click the Pointer button on the Slide Show toolbar, point to Arrow Options, and then click Visible.

To Change Document Properties

Before saving the presentation again, you want to add your name, class name, and some keywords as document properties. The following steps use the Document Information Panel to change document properties.

1. Display the Document Information Panel and then type your name as the Author property.

2. Type your course and section in the Subject property.

3. Type `windstorm, hurricane, tornado` as the Keywords property.

4. Close the Document Information Panel.

BTW

Quick Reference
For a table that lists how to complete the tasks covered in this book using the mouse, Ribbon, shortcut menu, and keyboard, see the Quick Reference Summary at the back of this book, or visit the PowerPoint 2010 Quick Reference Web page (scsite.com/ppt2010/qr).

To Save, Print, and Quit PowerPoint

The presentation now is complete. You should save the slides, print a handout, and then quit PowerPoint.

1. Save the Windstorms Final presentation again with the same file name.

2. Print the presentation as a handout with two slides per page. Do not print the comment pages (Figure 5–80 on the following page).

3. Click the Page Setup button (Design tab | Page Setup group) and then change the slide size to On-screen Show (4:3).

4. Click the Resolution box arrow (Slide Show tab | Monitors group) and then change the slide show resolution to 1024 × 768.

5. Quit PowerPoint, closing all open documents.

BTW

Certification
The Microsoft Office Specialist (MOS) program provides an opportunity for you to obtain a valuable industry credential — proof that you have the PowerPoint 2010 skills required by employers. For more information, visit the PowerPoint 2010 Certification Web page (scsite.com/ppt2010/cert).

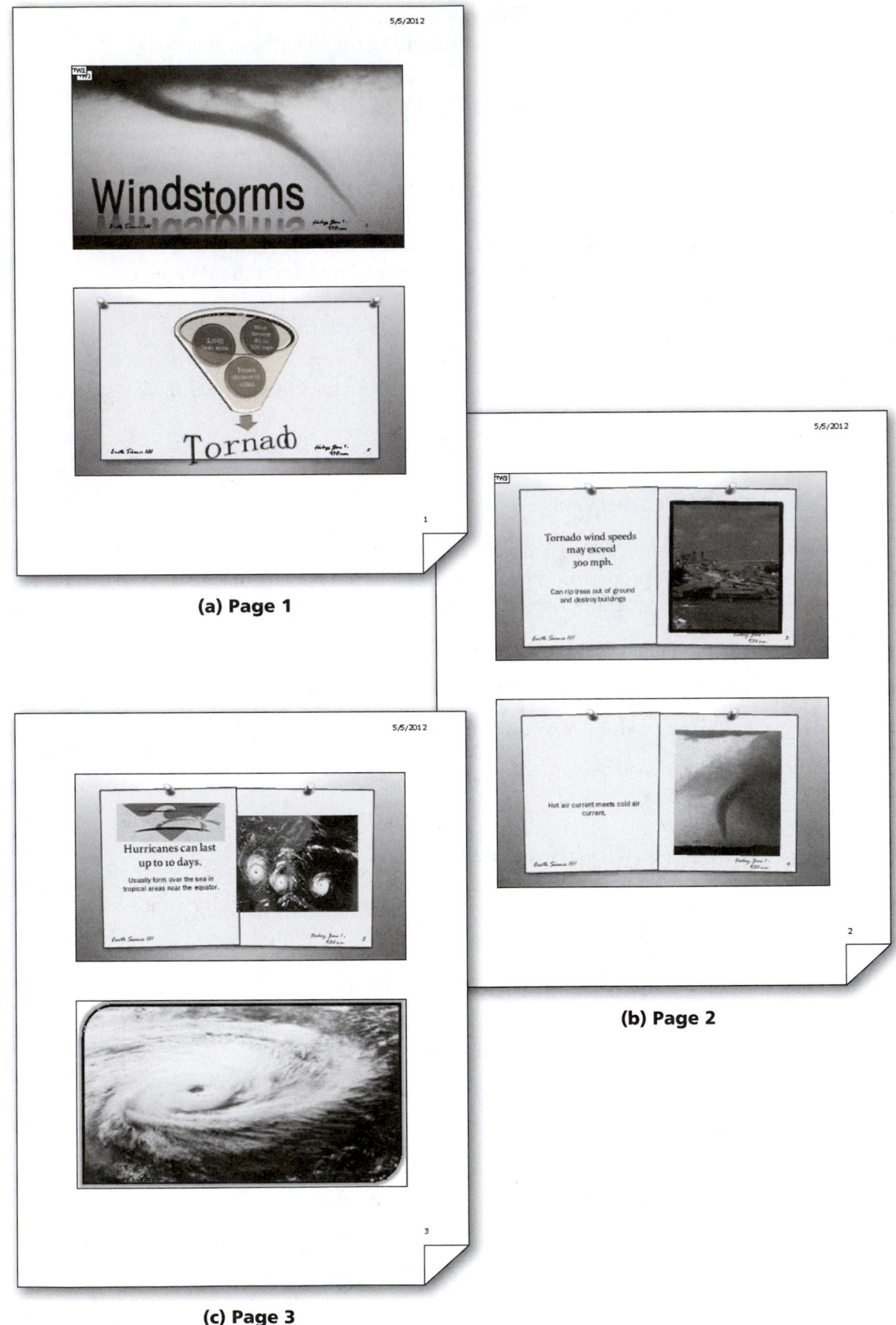

(a) Page 1

(b) Page 2

(c) Page 3

Figure 5–80

Chapter Summary

In this chapter you have learned how to merge presentations, review a reviewer's comments, and then accept or reject proposed changes. You changed the slide size and presentation resolution, protected and secured the file with a password and digital signature, checked compatibility, removed inappropriate information, and then saved the presentation in a variety of formats. Finally, you ran the presentation and annotated the slides with a highlighter and pen. The items listed below include all the new PowerPoint skills you have learned in this chapter.

1. Merge a Presentation (PPT 270)
2. Print Comments (PPT 271)
3. Preview Presentation Changes (PPT 273)
4. Review and Delete Comments (PPT 274)
5. Review, Accept, and Reject Presentation Changes (PPT 276)
6. Review, Accept, and Reject Slide Changes (PPT 278)
7. Reject a Slide Revision (PPT 280)
8. Insert a Comment (PPT 281)
9. Edit a Comment (PPT 282)
10. End the Review (PPT 283)
11. Reuse Slides from an Existing Presentation (PPT 285)
12. Capture Part of a Screen Using Screen Clipping (PPT 288)
13. Add a Footer with Fixed Information (PPT 289)
14. Clear Formatting and Apply an Artistic Effect (PPT 291)
15. Set Slide Size (PPT 292)
16. Select Slide Show Resolution (PPT 294)
17. Save a File as a PowerPoint Show (PPT 295)
18. Save a Slide as an Image (PPT 296)
19. Package a Presentation for Storage on a CD or DVD (PPT 297)
20. Save a File in a Previous PowerPoint Format (PPT 300)
21. Identify Presentation Features Not Supported by Previous Versions (PPT 301)
22. Remove Inappropriate Information (PPT 303)
23. Set a Password (PPT 305)
24. Mark a Presentation as Final (PPT 308)
25. Create a Digital Signature and Add It to a Document (PPT 309)
26. Highlight Items on a Slide (PPT 312)
27. Change Ink Color (PPT 313)

 If you have a SAM 2010 user profile, your instructor may have assigned an autogradable version of this assignment. If so, log into the SAM 2010 Web site at www.cengage.com/sam2010 to download the instruction and start files.

Learn It Online

Test your knowledge of chapter content and key terms.

Instructions: To complete the Learn It Online exercises, start your browser, click the Address bar, and then enter the Web address **scsite.com/ppt2010/learn**. When the PowerPoint 2010 Learn It Online page is displayed, click the link for the exercise you want to complete and then read the instructions.

Chapter Reinforcement TF, MC, and SA

A series of true/false, multiple choice, and short answer questions that test your knowledge of the chapter content.

Flash Cards

An interactive learning environment where you identify chapter key terms associated with displayed definitions.

Practice Test

A series of multiple choice questions that test your knowledge of chapter content and key terms.

Who Wants To Be a Computer Genius?

An interactive game that challenges your knowledge of chapter content in the style of a television quiz show.

Wheel of Terms

An interactive game that challenges your knowledge of chapter key terms in the style of the television show *Wheel of Fortune*.

Crossword Puzzle Challenge

A crossword puzzle that challenges your knowledge of key terms presented in the chapter.

Apply Your Knowledge

Reinforce the skills and apply the concepts you learned in this chapter.

Inserting Comments, Adding a Header and a Footer, Marking as Final, and Saving As a Previous Version

Note: To complete this assignment, you will be required to use the Data Files for Students. See the inside back cover of this book for instructions on downloading the Data Files for Students, or contact your instructor for information about accessing the required files.

Instructions: Start PowerPoint. Open the presentation, Apply 5-1 Wind, located on the Data Files for Students.

The slides in the presentation present information about wind energy. You will insert a comment, add a footer, and then save the file as PowerPoint 2010 (.pptx) document. The slides should look like Figure 5–81a and 5–81b. You then will remove inappropriate information, mark the presentation as final, and save the files as a PowerPoint 97–2003 (.ppt) document. Figure 5–81c shows the new Slide 1.

Perform the following tasks:

1. On Slide 1, add a comment on the picture with the following text: **To be consistent with kilowatts, I suggest you show wind speeds in kilometers per hour instead of miles per hour. I converted them for you: 12 mph = 19.31 Km/H and 14 mph = 22.53 Km/H.**

2. Display the Header and Footer dialog box and add the slide number and the automatic date and time. Type your name as the footer text. Do not show on title slide.

3. Check the spelling and then change the document properties, as specified by your instructor. Save the presentation using the file name, Apply 5-1 Wind Energy.

4. Remove all inappropriate information.

5. Mark the presentation as final.

6. Save the presentation as a PowerPoint 97-2003 (.ppt) document using the file name, Apply 5-1 Wind Energy PPT. Submit the revised documents in the format specified by your instructor.

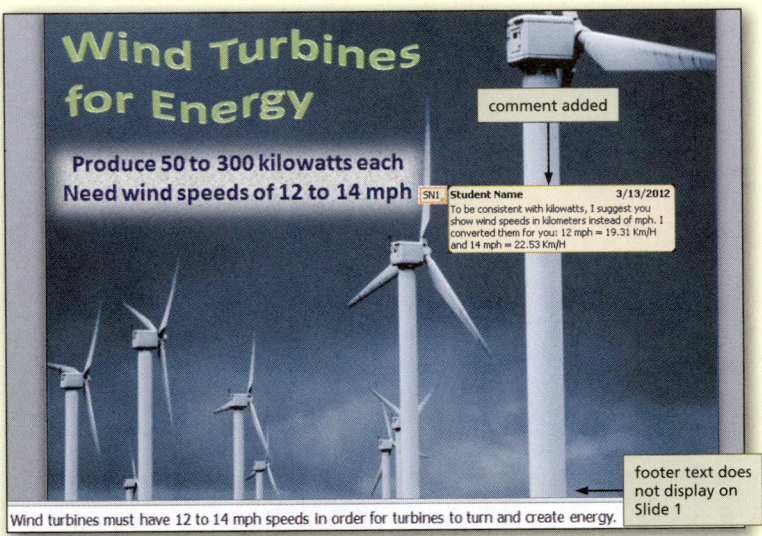

(a) Slide 1

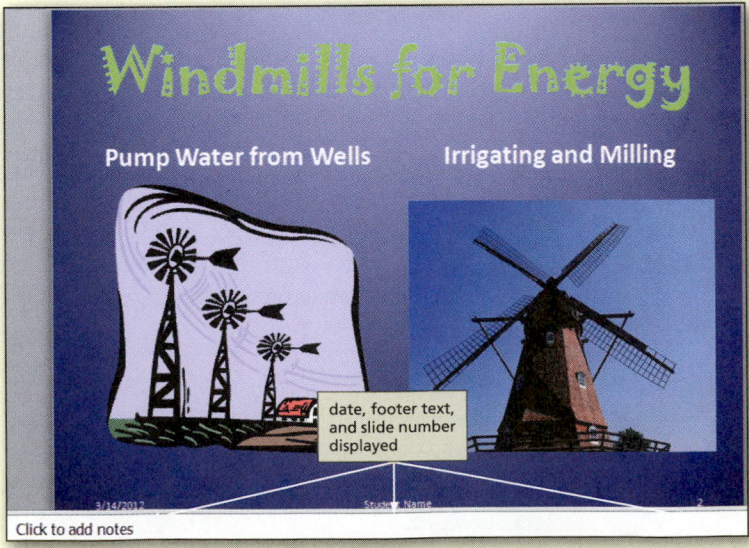

(b) Slide 2

Figure 5–81

(c) Revised Slide 1

Figure 5–81 (Continued)

Extend Your Knowledge

Extend the skills you learned in this chapter and experiment with new skills. You may need to use Help to complete the assignment.

Changing Headers and Footers on Slides and Handouts and Inserting a Screenshot

Note: To complete this assignment, you will be required to use the Data Files for Students. See the inside back cover of this book for instructions on downloading the Data Files for Students, or contact your instructor for information about accessing the required files.

Instructions: Start PowerPoint. Open the presentation, Extend 5-1 Running, located on the Data Files for Students.

You will add a footer and a fixed date to all slides in the presentation (Figure 5–82) and format this text on the title slide. You also will insert a screenshot of marathon information on one slide.

Perform the following tasks:

1. Display the Header and Footer dialog box and then add your next birthday as the fixed date footer text on all slides. Type your school's name as the footer text, followed by the words, Running Club.

2. Display the Notes and Handouts tab (Header and Footer dialog box) and then add the same date and footer text to the notes and handouts.

3. Increase the font size of the Slide 1 footer date to 16 point and change the font color to Red. Italicize this text (Figure 5–82a).

(a) Slide 1

Figure 5–82

Continued >

Extend Your Knowledge *continued*

(b) Slide 2

(c) Slide 3

Figure 5–82 (Continued)

4. Insert a comment on Slide 1 as a reminder to yourself to verify the training dates and times with your school's running club president.

5. Locate information about marathons on the Internet. This information could list previous winners, record times, or routes. Insert a screenshot of one Web page on Slide 3 (Figure 5–82c). You may need to make the screenshot smaller or reduce the size of the two photos at the top of Slide 3.

6. Change the document properties, as specified by your instructor. Save the presentation using the file name, Extend 5–1 Running Club.

7. Submit the revised document in the format specified by your instructor.

Make It Right

Analyze a presentation and correct all errors and/or improve the design.

Clearing Formatting and Correcting Headers and Footers

Note: To complete this assignment, you will be required to use the Data Files for Students. See the inside back cover of this book for instructions on downloading the Data Files for Students, or contact your instructor for information about accessing the required files.

Instructions: Start PowerPoint. Open the presentation, Make It Right 5-1 Video Games, located on the Data Files for Students.

In your psychology class, you are studying the habits of teenagers and if playing video games can have negative effects on their behavior. You contact a local high school and get permission to conduct a survey among the students to find out how they spend their leisure time. Correct the formatting problems and errors in the presentation, shown in Figure 5–83, while keeping in mind the guidelines presented in this chapter.

Perform the following tasks:

1. Change the design from Trek to Slipstream.

2. Set the slide size to On-screen Show (16:9). Change the slide show resolution to 800 × 600.

3. On Slide 1, adjust the chart size so that all text on the chart is visible. Decrease the slide title text font size to 44 point.

4. Adjust the size of the picture and move it to the upper-right corner of the slide so that it is not covering the title text.

5. On Slide 2, decrease the font size of the bulleted text to 20 point and decrease the title text font size to 54 point.

6. Clear the formatting from the picture and adjust the size so that it fits below the bulleted text in the right text placeholder.

7. Display the Header and Footer dialog box, remove the student name from the footer on Slide 2, and do not show the slide number on the title slide.

8. Change the Transition from Fly Through to Cube on all slides.

9. Change the document properties, as specified by your instructor. Save the presentation using the file name, Make It Right 5-1 Teens and Video Games.

10. Submit the revised document in the format specified by your instructor.

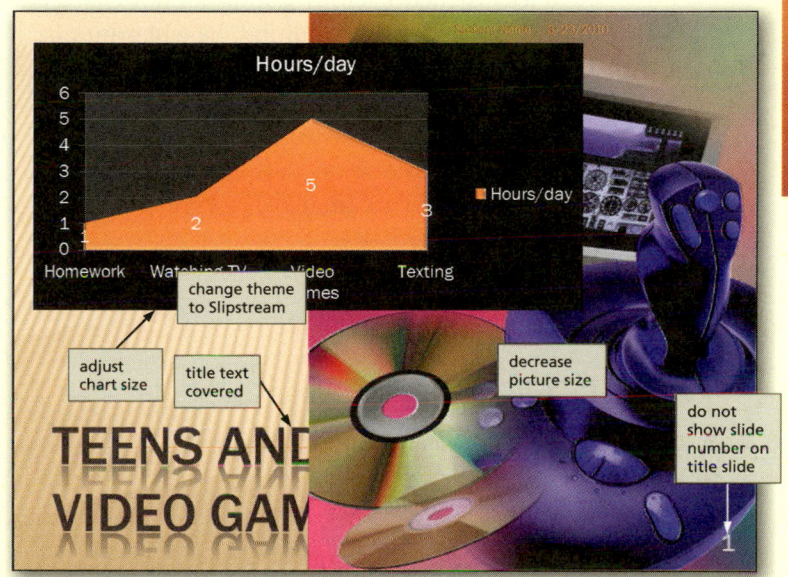

(a) Slide 1

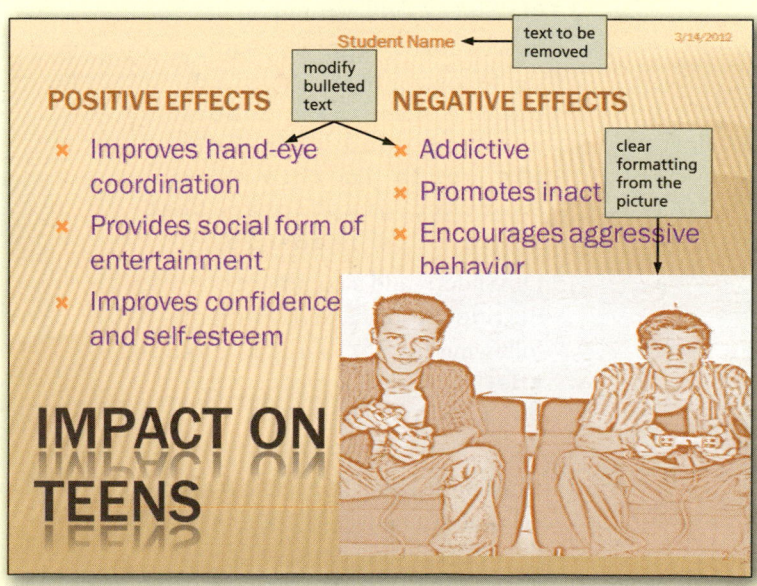

(b) Slide 2

Figure 5–83

In the Lab

Design and/or create a presentation using the guidelines, concepts, and skills presented in this chapter. Labs 1, 2, and 3 are listed in order of increasing difficulty.

Lab 1: Adding Comments to and Protecting a Presentation and Inserting a Slide

Note: To complete this assignment, you will be required to use the Data Files for Students. See the inside back cover of this book for instructions on downloading the Data Files for Students, or contact your instructor for information about accessing the required files.

Problem: The garden center where you work is putting together small gift baskets to hand out to local senior citizens at an upcoming fair. One of the items in the gift basket is a packet of sunflower seeds. Last spring your manager, John Wind, created a PowerPoint presentation about sunflower seeds. He sent you two sets of slides and requested comments. One PowerPoint presentation that he sent to you includes instructions for roasting sunflower seeds, and he would like those instructions to be added to the presentation. In addition, he will print out the instructions to include with the sunflower seeds. You add several comments, insert a slide, check the slides for compatibility with previous PowerPoint versions, and then protect the presentation with a password. When you run the presentation, you add annotations. The annotated slides are shown in Figure 5–84.

Perform the following tasks:

1. Open the presentation, Lab 5-1 Sunflowers, located on the Data Files for Students.

2. On Slide 1, replace Calista Lindy's name with your name. Add a comment on the picture with the following text: **I suggest you enlarge this picture and add a 6 pt Gold border.**

3. On Slide 2, add a comment in the SmartArt graphic with the following text: **I would change the text color and size and then bold the words in this SmartArt graphic so that it is more readable.**

4. On Slide 3, add a comment on the title text placeholder with the following text: **I would change the title text font so it matches the title text font on Slide 2.**

5. After Slide 2, insert Slide 2 (which becomes the new Slide 3, and former Slide 3 becomes Slide 4) from the Lab 5-1 Sunflower Seeds file located on the Data Files for Students. Keep the source formatting.

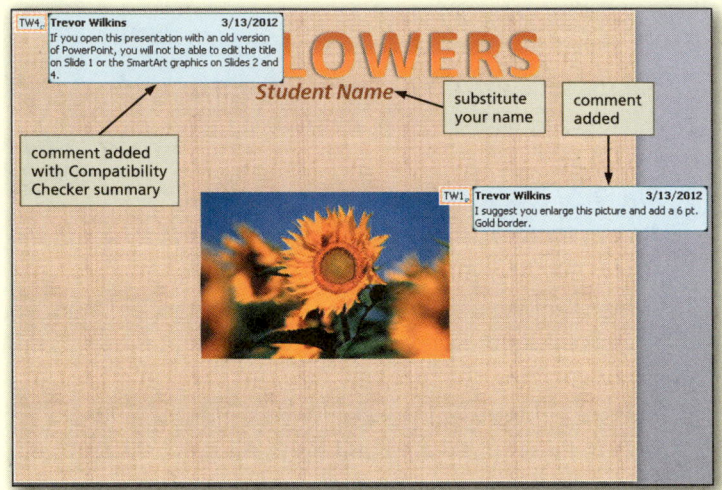

(a) Slide 1

(b) Slide 2

Figure 5–84

6. On the new Slide 3, clear the formatting from the picture.

7. Run the Compatibility Checker to identify the presentation features not supported in previous PowerPoint versions. Summarize these features in a comment placed on Slide 1.

8. Protect the presentation with the password, Sunflowers2Grow.

9. Change the document properties, as specified by your instructor. Save the presentation using the file name, Lab 5-1 Growing Sunflowers.

10. Print the slides. In addition, print Slide 3 again.

11. Run the presentation. On Slide 2, click the Pointer button, point to Ink Color on the shortcut menu, and then click Blue in the Standard Colors row. Click the Pen, draw a circle around the text, Miniature – 2 to 4 feet, in the SmartArt graphic. Click the Next button on the toolbar, click Highlighter, point to Ink Color, and then click Light Green in the Standard Colors row. Highlight the text, Soak seeds overnight in salted water. Save the annotations.

12. Print the slides with annotations.

13. Submit the revised document in the format specified by your instructor.

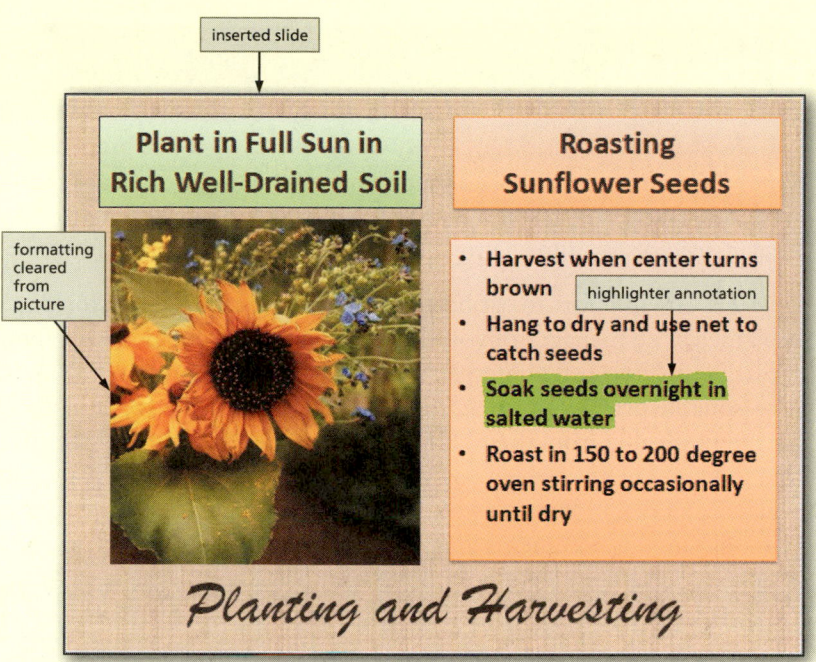

(c) Slide 3 (Inserted Slide)

(d) Slide 4

Figure 5–84 (Continued)

In the Lab

Lab 2: Modifying and Deleting Comments in a Protected Presentation

Note: To complete this assignment, you will be required to use the Data Files for Students. See the inside back cover of this book for instructions on downloading the Data Files for Students, or contact your instructor for information about accessing the required files.

Problem: In an effort to eat healthy and shop economically, stocking up on vegetables and fruits is a good idea. The manager of your local grocery store contacts you about doing a display for the produce department. He is listening to his customers and trying to provide more healthy choices of fresh produce at reasonable prices. Several customers have expressed a concern about handling the fresh produce to get the best value from them. He knows you are studying biology in school and thought you might be able to help. He gives you a password-protected file that he created and asks you to review the slides, which are shown in Figure 5–85. He has inserted comments with questions. You offer some suggestions by modifying his comments and removing inappropriate information.

Perform the following tasks:

1. Open the presentation, Lab 5-2 Eating, located on the Data Files for Students. The password is Produce4Us.

2. Insert the date, time, and your name in the footer on all slides except the title slide. On Slide 1, modify the comment on the title by adding the following text: `Yes, I think the title is a great attention-getter. You really want your customers to eat healthy and make better food choices.`

3. On Slide 2, modify the comment by adding the following text: `You could change the word microbial to bacterial. The statement is good because a lot of people might not know they should not wash produce before storing.`

4. On Slide 3, modify comment 3 by adding the following text: `The presentation will be printed in color and displayed throughout the produce department. These slides will be enlarged, so shoppers should see the pictures easily.` Delete comment 4 on the title text placeholder.

(a) Slide 1

(b) Slide 2

Figure 5–85

5. Mark the presentation as final.

6. Add a digital signature by creating your own digital ID. Enter your name in the Name text box, `mary_halen@hotmail.com` in the E-mail address text box, `John's Supermarket` in the Organization text box, and `Chicago, IL` in the Location text box.

7. Inspect the document and then remove all document properties and personal information.

8. Save the presentation using the file name, Lab 5-2 Healthy Eating. Then save the slides as a PowerPoint 97-2003 Presentation (.ppt) type using the same file name.

9. Print the slides and comments.

10. Submit the revised document in the format specified by your instructor.

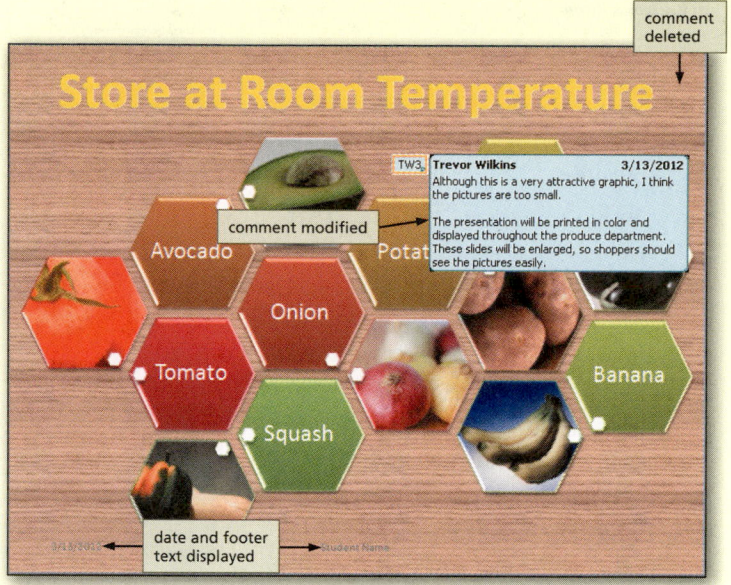

(c) Slide 3

Figure 5–85 (Continued)

In the Lab

Lab 3: Reviewing and Accepting Comments, Using Screen Clipping, and Packaging the Presentation for Storage on a Compact Disc

Note: To complete this assignment, you will be required to use the Data Files for Students. See the inside back cover of this book for instructions on downloading the Data Files for Students, or contact your instructor for information about accessing the required files.

Problem: The XYZ Corporation is promoting its software products. You work in the Marketing department and have developed a PowerPoint presentation, which is shown in Figures 5–86a and 5–86b on the next page, as part of the marketing strategy. You ask your coworker, Miriam Lind, to review the presentation by inserting comments and making revisions on the slides. You use her input to create the final presentation shown in Figures 5–86c through 5–86e on page PPT 327. You also obtain a picture of your department's new director, Sanjai Rukah, from another PowerPoint presentation. In addition, you use the Package for CD feature to distribute the presentation to local businesses.

Perform the following tasks:

1. Open the presentation, Lab 5-3 XYZ, located on the Data Files for Students.

2. Merge Miriam's revised file, Lab 5-3 XYZ-Miriam, located on the Data Files for Students. Accept both presentation changes so that the transition is added and Slide 3 is inserted. Review all of Miriam's comments on Slide 1 and Slide 2. Preview the slides, and then print the slides and the comments.

Continued >

In the Lab *continued*

3. On Slide 1, accept all changes except Miriam's computer clip (Picture 6) at the bottom of the slide.

4. On Slide 2, accept the SmartArt change.

5. On Slide 3, review all of Miriam's comments. Change the layout to Picture with Caption. Type **Meet Our New IT Director** as the title text. Type **Sanjai Rukah** as the caption text below the title text placeholder, as shown in Figure 5–86e. Increase the title text and the caption text font size. Bold and italicize the caption text.

6. Open the presentation, Lab 5-3 XYZ-Tyrone, located on the Data Files for Students. Then display Lab 5-3 XYZ. With Slide 3 still displayed, use screen clipping to capture Sanjai's head shot in Lab 5-3 XYZ-Tyrone. Resize the screen clipping and move it to the location shown in Figure 5–86e.

7. Delete all markup in the presentation.

8. On Slide 1, enhance the building picture by applying the Reflected Bevel, White picture style. Change the color to Tan, Accent color 1 Dark. Resize the picture.

9. Change the document properties, as specified by your instructor. Save the presentation using the file name, Lab 5-3 XYZ Corporation.

10. Save Slide 3 as a .jpg image with the file name, Lab 5-3 XYZ-Sanjai Rukah.

11. Save the presentation using the Package for CD feature. Name the CD XYZ Corporation.

12. Submit the revised PowerPoint file, the Slide 3 .jpg file, and the CD in the format specified by your instructor.

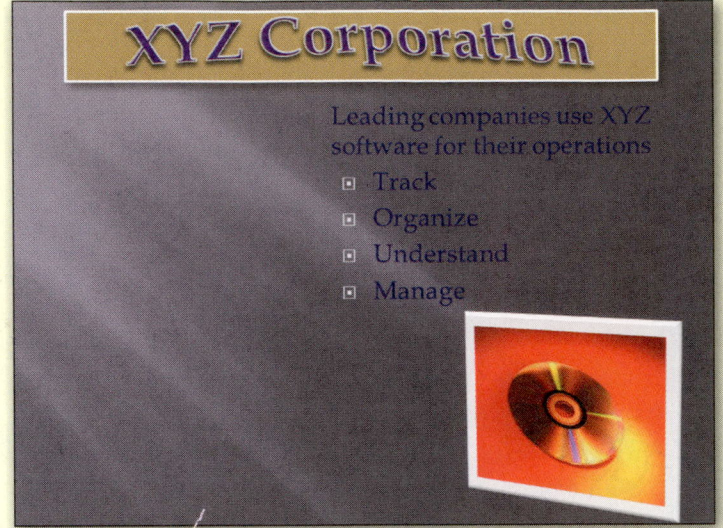

(a) Slide 1

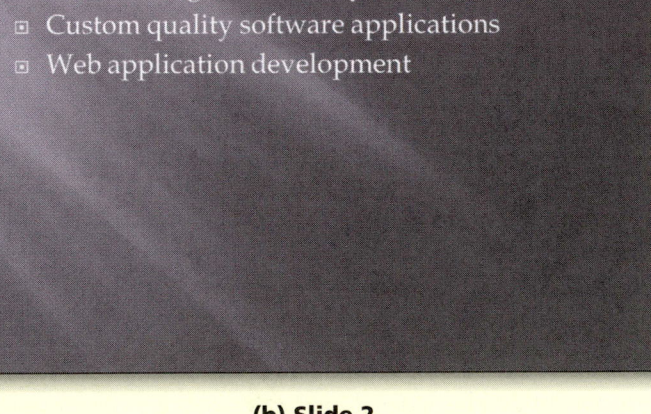

(b) Slide 2

Figure 5–86

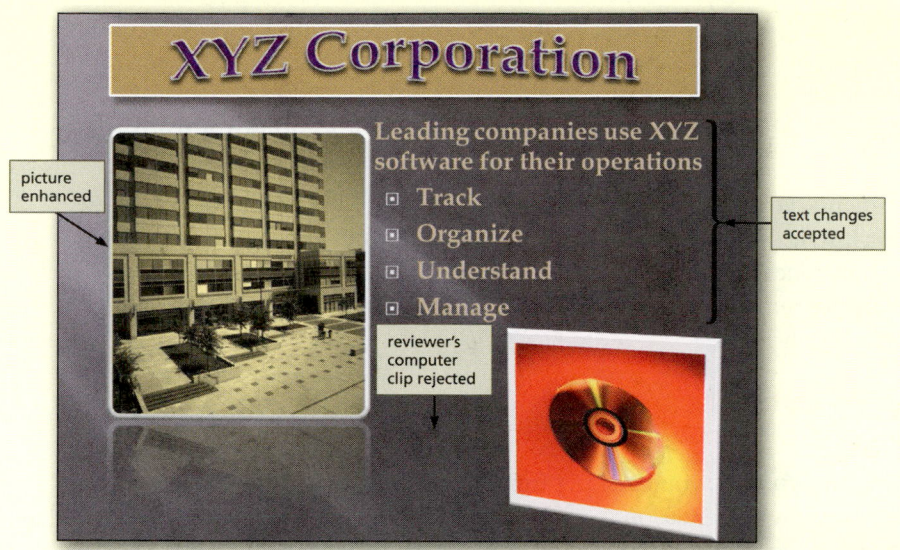

(c) Slide 3 (Revised Slide 1)

(d) Slide 4 (Revised Slide 2)

(e) Slide 5 (Inserted Slide 3)

Figure 5–86 (Continued)

Cases and Places

Apply your creative thinking and problem-solving skills to design and implement a solution.

Note: To complete these assignments, you will be required to use the Data Files for Students. See the inside back cover of this book for instructions on downloading the Data Files for Students, or contact your instructor for information about accessing the required files.

As you design the presentations, remember to use the 7 × 7 rule: a maximum of seven words on a line and a maximum of seven lines on one slide.

1: Designing and Creating a Presentation about Interior Design

Academic

For an assignment in your Interior Design class, you must put together a slide presentation showing a variety of home interior designs. Create a presentation to show at least two examples of living rooms, bedrooms, kitchens, and dining rooms. Apply at least three objectives found at the beginning of this chapter to develop the presentation. Use the file, Home Interior Design, located on the Data Files for Students and insert at least two pictures from each slide. Use pictures from Office.com if they are appropriate for this topic. Insert and modify comments, set slide size, and select a presentation resolution. Add a header and footer with your name included. Be sure to check spelling. Save the presentation in a previous PowerPoint format.

2: Designing and Creating a Presentation about Fishing

Personal

You and your friends have decided to take a summer fishing trip. You volunteered to find the best fishing spots. You have found several destinations, and you want to relay the information to your friends. Use at least three objectives found at the beginning of this chapter to develop the presentation. Using the file, Fishing Spots, located on the Data Files for Students, insert slides into your presentation and capture part of a screen using screen clipping. Add comments to the presentation. Encrypt the presentation with a password and create a digital signature. Be sure to check spelling. Save an individual slide and save the presentation in the PowerPoint 97-2003 format.

3: Designing and Creating a Presentation about Moving

Professional

You are employed at a moving company. Your manager has asked you to develop a presentation to promote the business and show the many services your company provides. He wants you to give customers some hints for making their moving experience a little easier. You create a presentation using at least three of the pictures in the file, Moving, located on the Data Files for Students. Insert comments so you can share your thoughts with your boss. Create two similar presentations and compare and combine the presentations. Be certain to check spelling. Save the file as a slide show so that when your manager opens the file, it displays automatically as a slide show. Package the presentation for storage on a compact disc.

6 Navigating Presentations Using Hyperlinks and Action Buttons

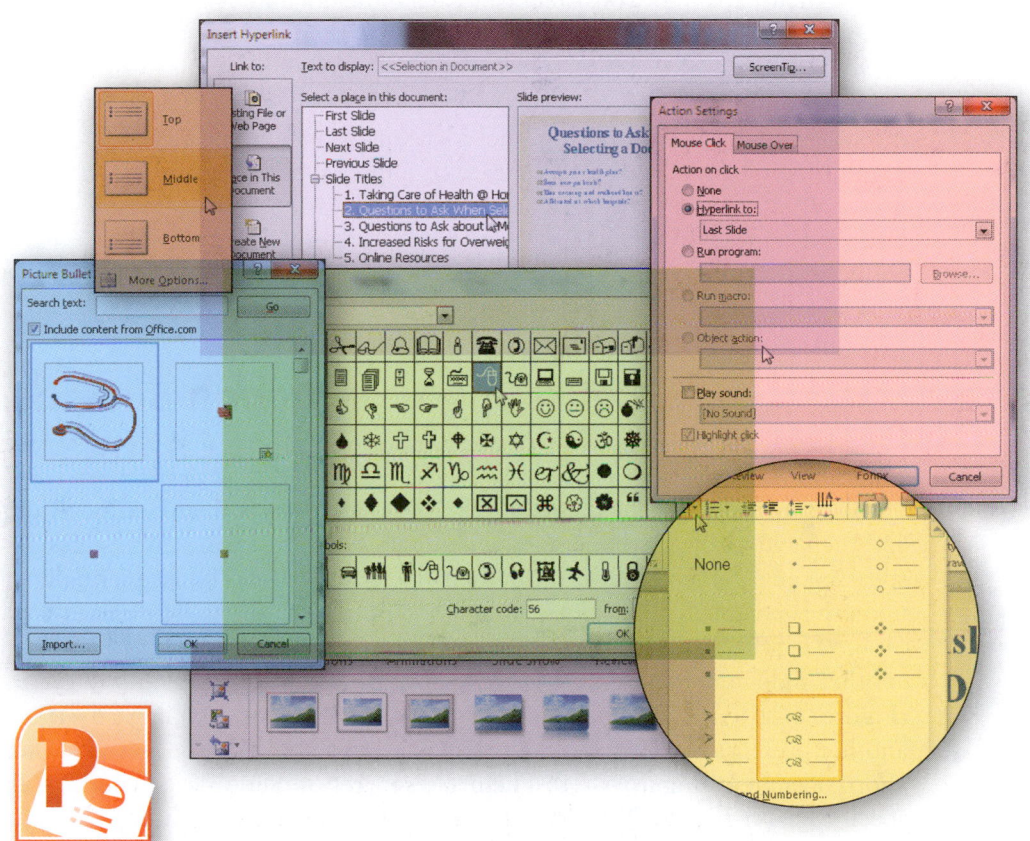

Objectives

You will have mastered the material in this chapter when you can:

- Create a presentation from a Microsoft Word outline
- Add hyperlinks to slides and objects
- Hyperlink to other Microsoft Office documents
- Add action buttons and action settings
- Display guides to position slide elements

- Set placeholder margins
- Create columns in a placeholder
- Change paragraph line spacing
- Format bullet size and color
- Change bullet characters to pictures and numbers
- Hide slides

6 | Navigating Presentations Using Hyperlinks and Action Buttons

BTW

Using Outlines to Organize Thoughts

Two types of outlines can help you get and stay organized. As you plan a speech, a scratch outline is a type of rough sketch of possible major points you would like to make and the order in which they might appear. Once you determine your material and the sequence of topics, you can develop a formal outline to arrange your thoughts in multiple levels of major and supporting details.

Introduction

Many writers begin composing reports and documents by creating an outline. Others review their papers for consistency by saving the document with a new file name, removing all text except the topic headings, and then saving the file again. An outline created in Microsoft Word or another word-processing program works well as a shell for a PowerPoint presentation. Instead of typing text in PowerPoint, as you did in previous projects, you can import this outline, add visual elements such as clip art, photos, and graphical bullets, and ultimately create an impressive slide show. When delivering the presentation, you can navigate forward and backward through the slides using hyperlinks and action buttons to emphasize particular points, to review material, or to address audience concerns.

BTW

Organizing with Sections

One of PowerPoint 2010's new features can help you organize presentations composed of dozens of slides. You can create logical sections, which are groups of related slides, and then customize and give them unique names to help identify their content or purpose. While giving a presentation, you can jump to a particular section. You also can print the slides in a specific section.

Project — Presentation with Action Buttons, Hyperlinks, and Formatted Bullet Characters

Speakers may elect to begin creating their presentations with an outline (Figure 6–1a) and then add formatted bullets and columns. When presenting these slides during a speaking engagement, they can run their PowerPoint slides nonsequentially depending upon the audience's needs and comprehension. Each of the three pictures on the Home Health title slide (Figure 6–1b on page PPT 332) branches, or hyperlinks, to another slide in the presentation. Action buttons and hyperlinks on Slides 2, 3, and 4 (Figures 6–1c – 6–1e) allow the presenter to jump to Slide 5 (Figure 6–1f), slides in another presentation (Figures 6–1g and 6–1h on page PPT 333), or to a Microsoft Word document (Figure 6–1i). The five resources on Slide 5 are hyperlinks that display specific health-related Web sites when clicked during a presentation. The slides in the presentation have a variety of embellishments, including a two-column list on Slide 4 that provides details of the factors associated with obesity, formatted graphical bullets on Slides 2 and 5 in the shape of stethoscopes and computer mice, and a numbered list on Slide 3.

Overview

As you read through this chapter, you will learn how to create the presentation shown in Figure 6–1 by performing these general tasks:

- Open a Microsoft Word outline as a presentation.
- Insert, use, and remove hyperlinks.
- Insert and format action buttons.
- Indent and align text in placeholders.
- Create columns and adjust column spacing.
- Change and format bullet characters.
- Run a slide show with hyperlinks and action buttons.

BTW

Defining Outline Levels
Imported outlines can contain up to nine outline levels, whereas PowerPoint outlines are limited to six levels (one for the title text and five for body paragraph text). When you import an outline, all text in outline levels six through nine is treated as a fifth-level paragraph.

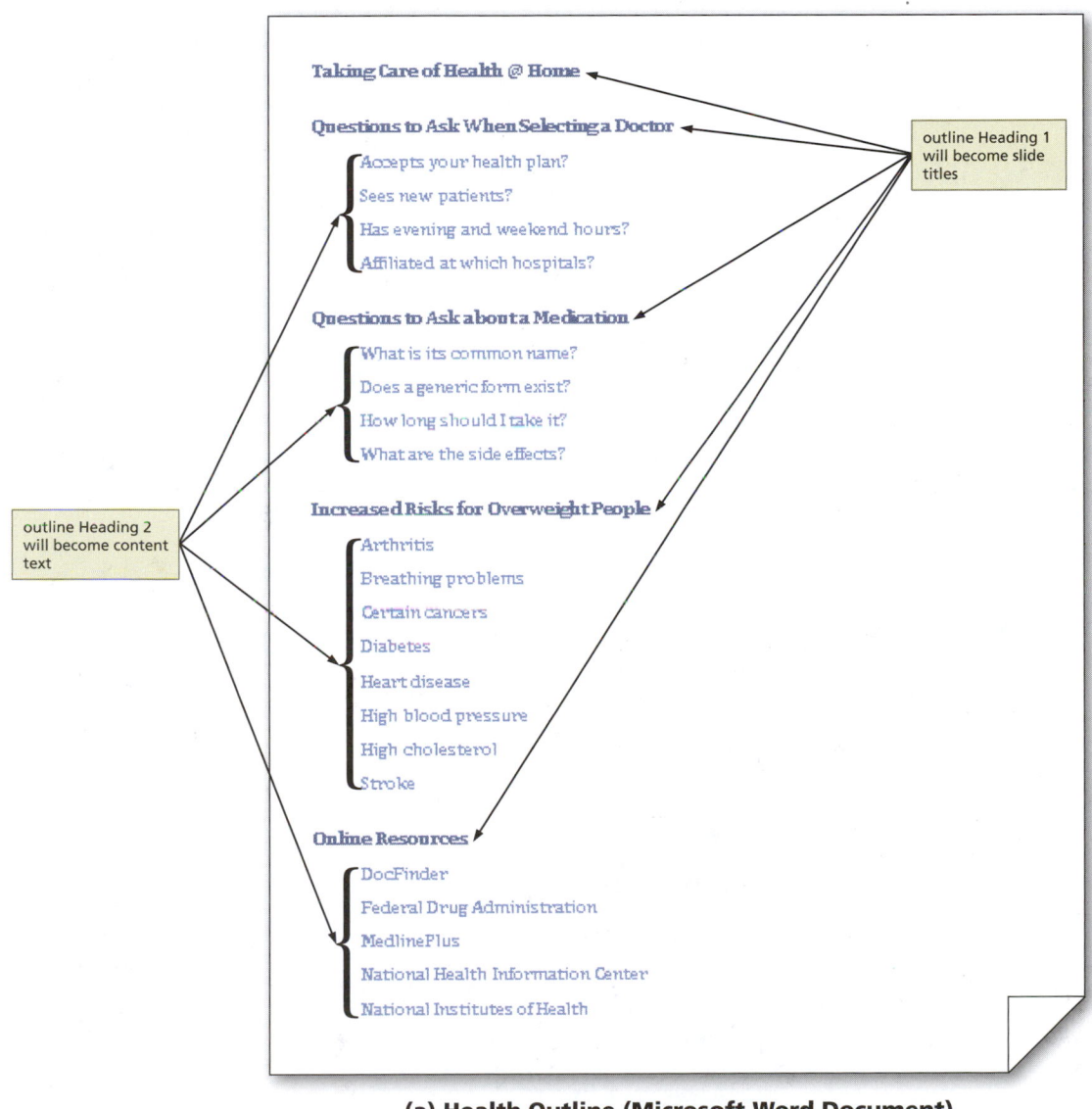

(a) Health Outline (Microsoft Word Document)

Figure 6–1

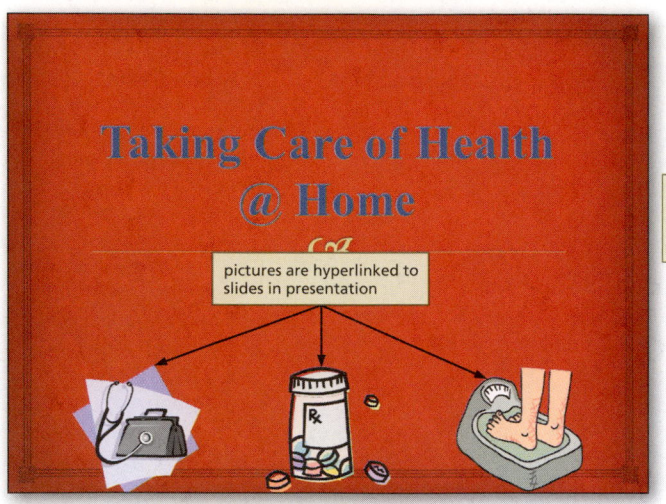

(b) Slide 1 (Title Slide with Picture Hyperlinks)

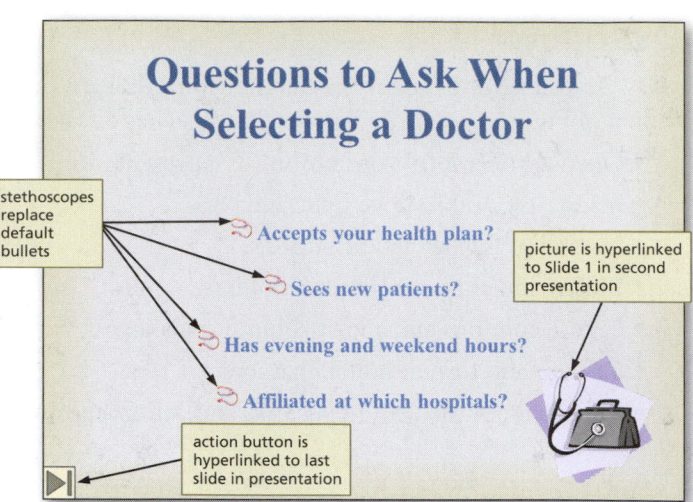

(c) Slide 2 (Centered List with Graphical Bullets)

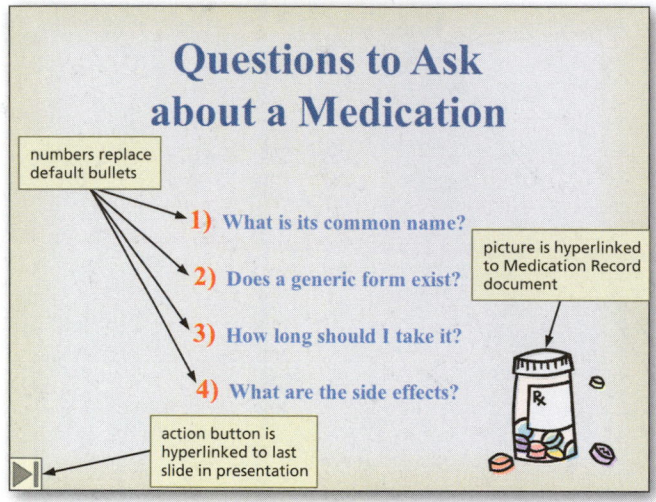

(d) Slide 3 (Numbered List)

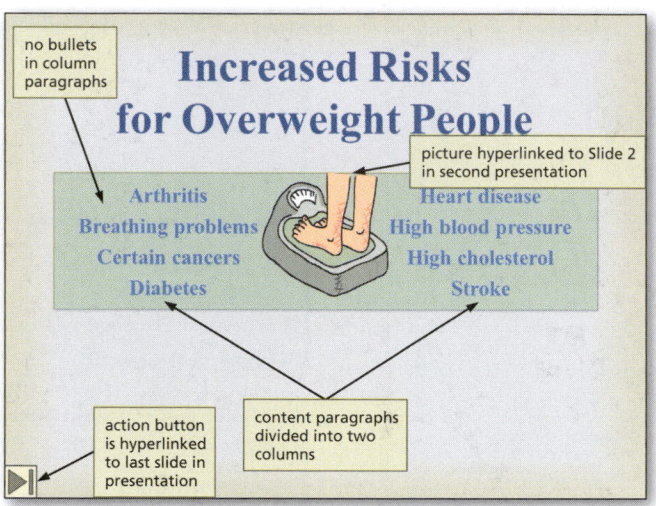

(e) Slide 4 (Two-Column List)

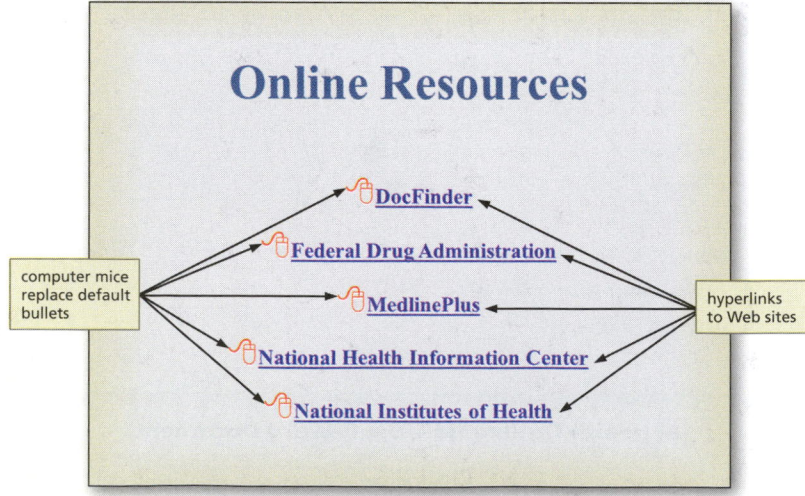

(f) Slide 5 (Hyperlinks to Web Sites)

Figure 6–1 (Continued)

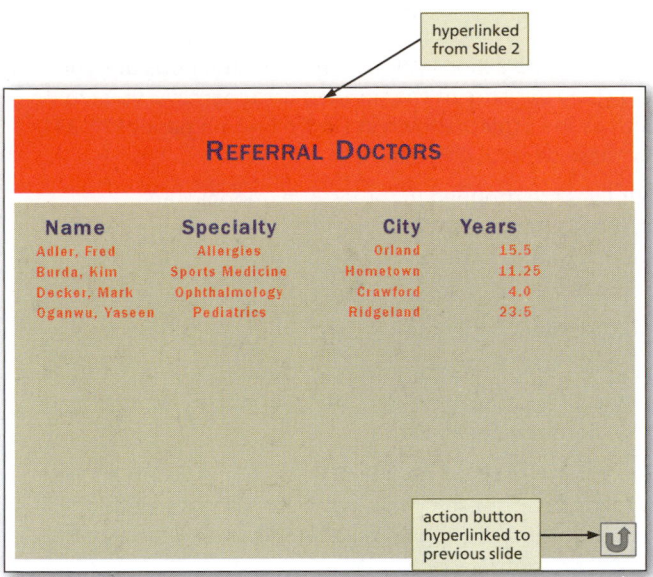

(g) Slide 1 (Hyperlinked from First Presentation)

(h) Slide 2 (Hyperlinked from First Presentation)

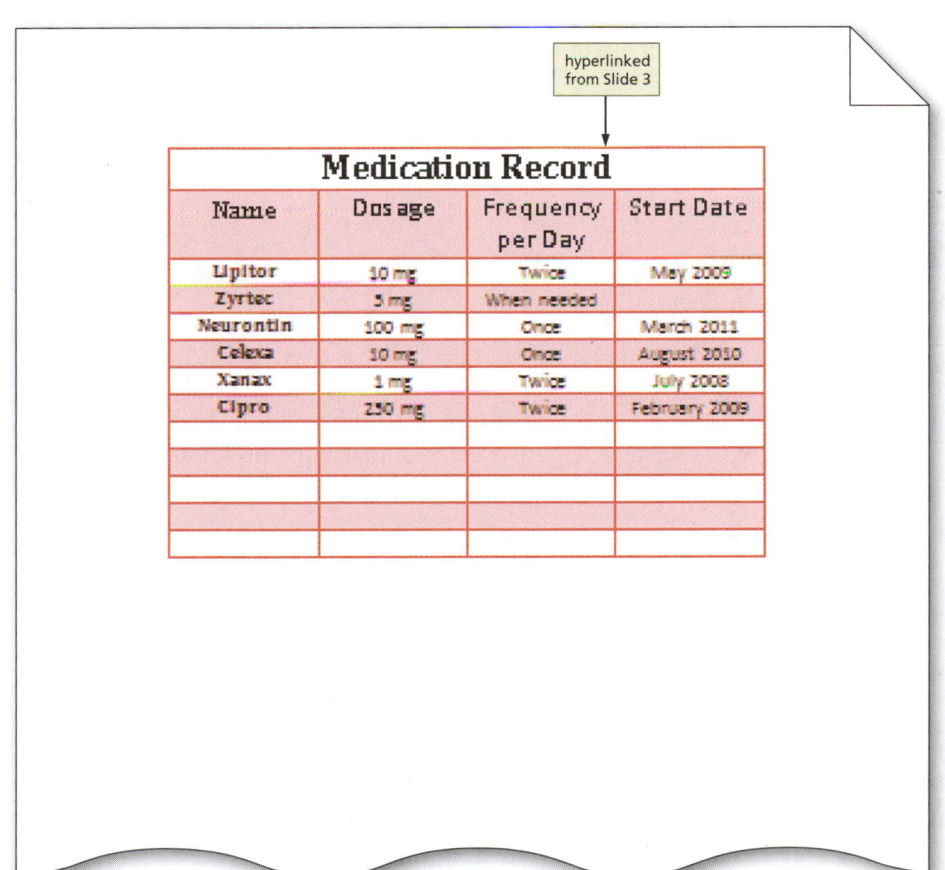

(i) Medication Record (Microsoft Word Document)

Figure 6–1 (Continued)

**Plan
Ahead**

General Project Guidelines

When creating a PowerPoint presentation, the actions you perform and the decisions you make will affect the appearance and characteristics of the finished document. As you create a presentation with illustrations, such as the project shown in Figure 6–1 on pages PPT 331 through PPT 333, you should follow these general guidelines:

1. **Think threes.** Many aspects of our lives are grouped in threes: sun, moon, stars; reduce, reuse, recycle; breakfast, lunch, dinner. Your presentation and accompanying presentation likewise can be grouped in threes: introduction, body, and conclusion.

2. **Choose outstanding hyperlink images or text.** Make the hypertext graphics or letters large so a speaker is prompted to click them easily during a speaking engagement.

3. **Customize action buttons for a unique look.** The icons on the action buttons indicate their functions, but you also can add clip art, pictures, and other graphic elements to add interest or make the button less obvious to your viewers.

4. **Be mindful of prepositional phrases.** A preposition at the end of a title or a bulleted line is disconcerting to audience members. For example, if you say, "This is something I am thinking about," or "Retiring soon is something I dream of," your audience could be waiting for you to continue your thought.

5. **Consider the audience's interests.** Audience members desire to hear speeches and view presentations that benefit them in some way based on their personal needs. A presenter, in turn, must determine the audience's physical and psychological needs and then tailor the presentation to fit each speaking engagement.

When necessary, more specific details concerning the above guidelines are presented at appropriate points in the chapter. The chapter also will identify the actions performed and decisions made regarding these guidelines during the creation of the presentation shown in Figure 6–1.

**Widening the
Tabs Pane**
The Outline and Slides tabs display an icon when the pane becomes narrow. If the Outline tab is hidden, widen the pane by dragging the right border. Work in Outline view when you want to make global edits, get an overview of the presentation, change the sequence of bullets or slides, or apply formatting changes.

Creating a Presentation from a Microsoft Word 2010 Outline

An outline created in Microsoft Word or another word-processing program works well as a shell for a PowerPoint presentation. Instead of typing text in PowerPoint, you can import this outline, add visual elements such as clip art, pictures, and graphical bullets, and ultimately create an impressive slide show.

To Start PowerPoint

To begin this presentation, you will open a file located on the Data Files for Students. See the inside back cover of this book for instructions on downloading the Data Files for Students, or contact your instructor for more information about accessing the required files. If you are using a computer to step through the project in this chapter and you want your screens to match the figures in this book, you should change your screen's resolution to 1024 × 768.

The following step starts PowerPoint.

 Start PowerPoint. If necessary, maximize the PowerPoint window.

Converting Documents for Use in PowerPoint

PowerPoint can produce slides based on an outline created in Microsoft Word, another word-processing program, or a Web page if the text was saved in a format that PowerPoint can recognize. Microsoft Word 2010 and 2007 files use the **.docx** file extension in their file names. Text originating in other word-processing programs for later use with PowerPoint should be saved in Rich Text Format (.rtf) or plain text (.txt). Web page documents that use an HTML extension (.htm or .html) also can be imported.

PowerPoint automatically opens Microsoft Office files, and many other types of files, in the PowerPoint format. The **Rich Text Format (.rtf)** file type is used to transfer formatted documents between applications, even if the programs are running on different platforms, such as Windows and Macintosh. When you insert a Word or Rich Text Format document into a presentation, PowerPoint creates an outline structure based on heading styles in the document. A Heading 1 in a source document becomes a slide title in PowerPoint, a Heading 2 becomes the first level of content text on the slide, a Heading 3 becomes the second level of text on the slide, and so on.

If the original document contains no heading styles, PowerPoint creates an outline based on paragraphs. For example, in a .docx or .rtf file, for several lines of text styled as Normal and broken into paragraphs, PowerPoint turns each paragraph into a slide title.

To Open a Microsoft Word Outline as a Presentation

The text for the Home Health presentation is contained in a Microsoft Word 2010 file. The following steps open this Microsoft Word outline as a presentation located on the Data Files for Students.

1

- With your USB flash drive connected to one of the computer's USB ports, open the Backstage view and then click the Open command in the Backstage view to display the Open dialog box.

- If necessary, navigate to the PowerPoint folder on your USB flash drive (Open dialog box) so that you can open the Health Outline file in that location.

- Click the File Type arrow to display the File Type list (Figure 6–2).

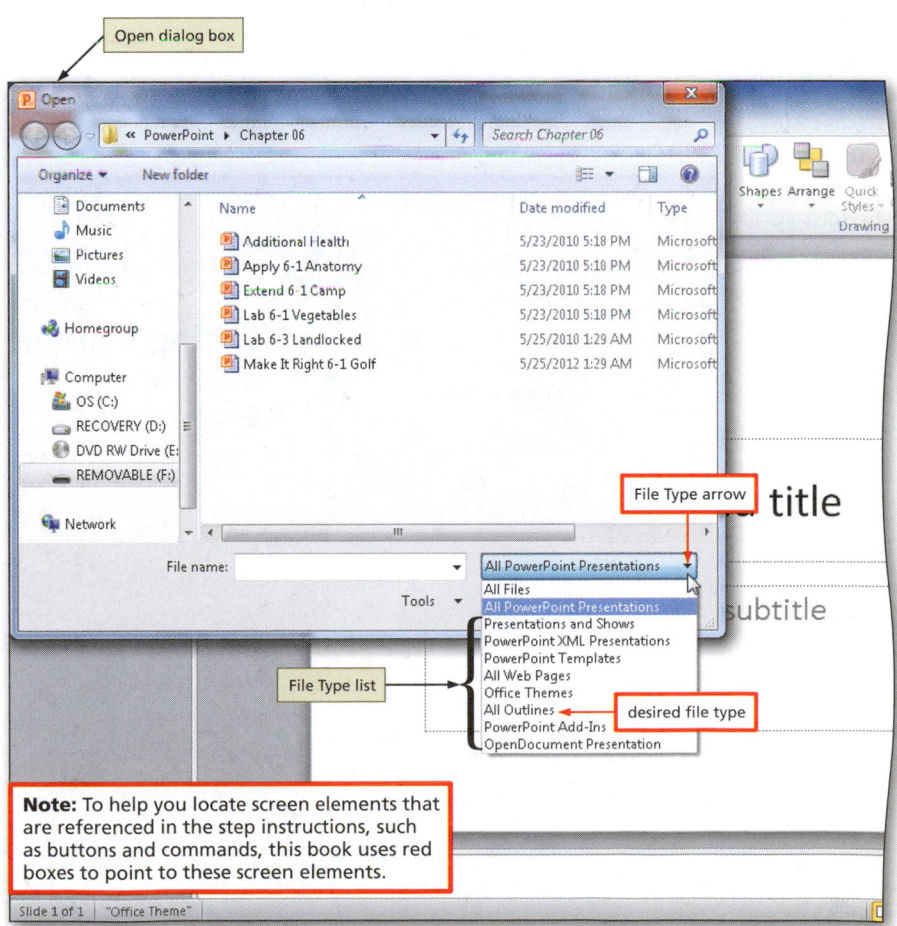

Figure 6–2

2

- Click All Outlines to
  select this
  file type.

- Click Health Outline
  to select the file
  (Figure 6–3).

Q&A

What if the file is not
on a USB flash drive?

Use the same process,
but select the drive
containing the file.

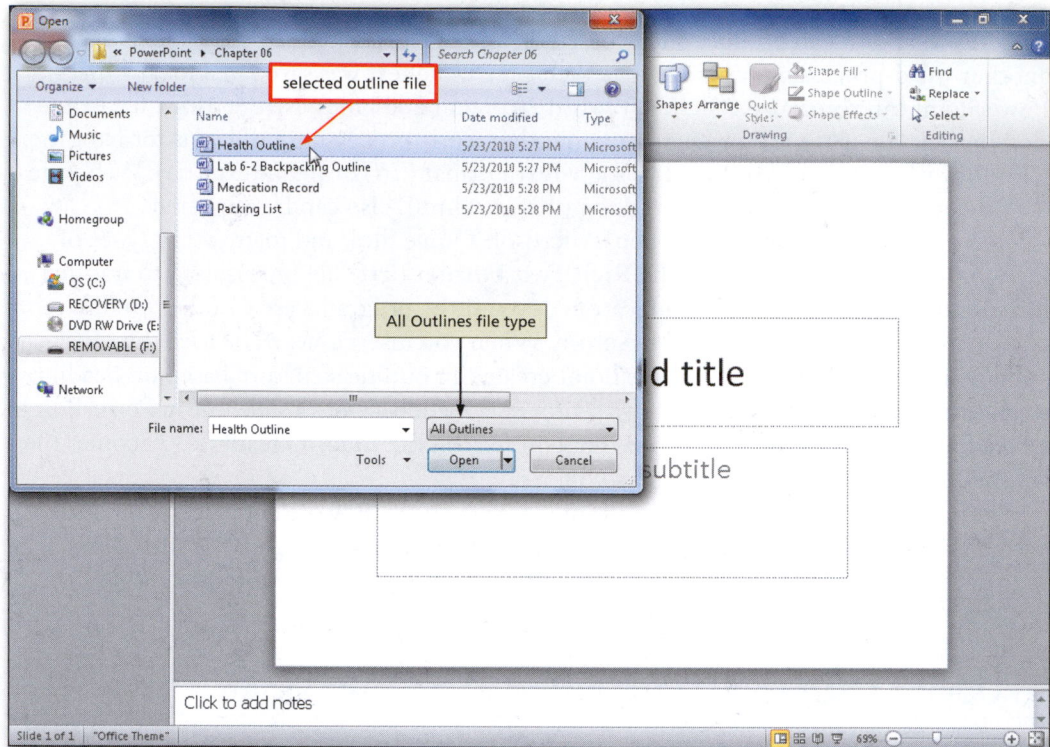

Figure 6–3

3

- Click Open to create
  the five slides in
  your presentation
  (Figure 6–4).

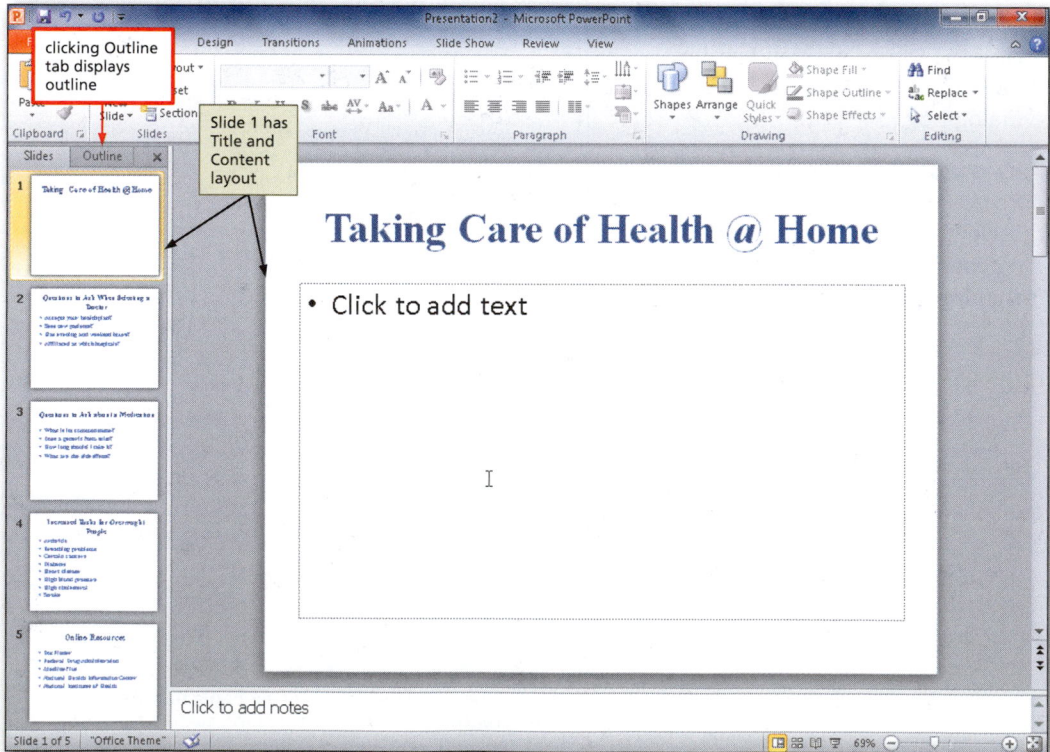

Figure 6–4

4
- Click the Outline tab in the Tabs pane to view the outline (Figure 6–5).

Q&A

Do I need to see the text as an outline in the Outline tab now?

No, but sometimes it is helpful to view the content of your presentation in this view before looking at individual slides.

Q&A

Do I need to change to the Slides tab to navigate between slides?

No, you can click the slide number in Outline view to navigate to slides.

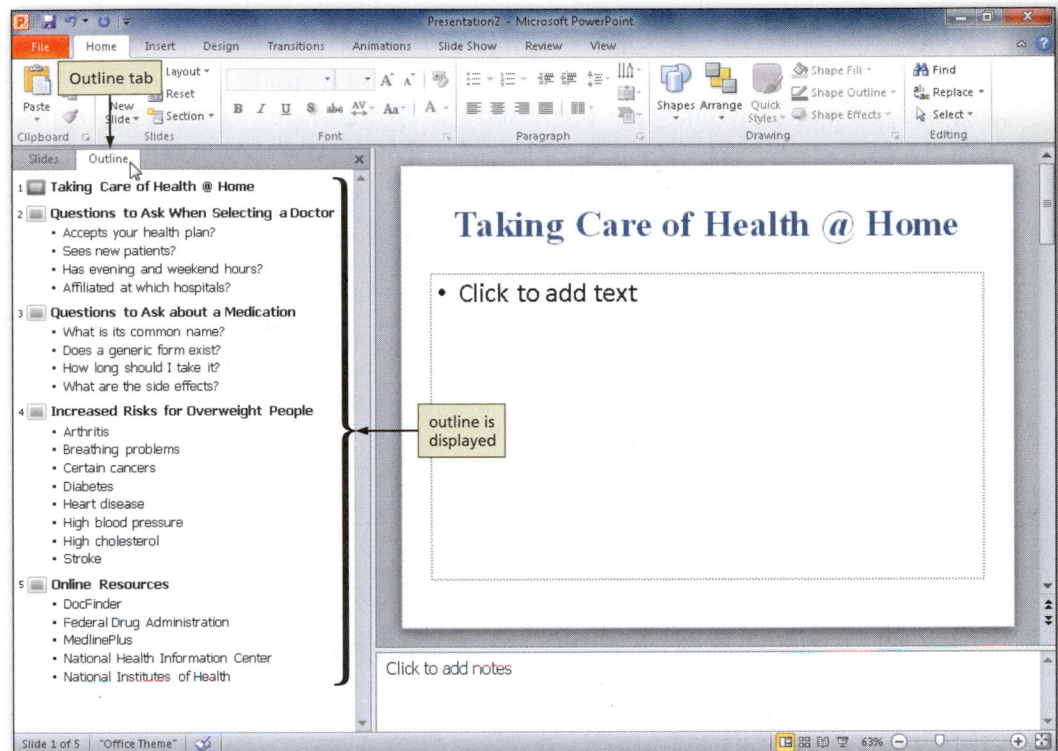

Figure 6–5

Other Ways

1. Click New Slide button arrow (Home tab | Slides group), click Slides from Outline, click File Type arrow, click All Outlines, click Health Outline, click Open button

To Change the Slide 1 Layout, Apply a Document Theme, and Change the Theme Colors

When you created the new slides from the Word outline, PowerPoint applied the Title and Text slide layout to all slides. You want to apply the Title Slide layout to Slide 1 to introduce the presentation. The following steps change the Slide 1 slide layout.

1 With Slide 1 displaying, click the Layout button (Home tab | Slides group) and then click Title Slide to apply that layout to Slide 1.

2 Apply the Hardcover document theme.

3 Change the presentation theme colors to Clarity.

Think threes.
Speechwriters often think of threes as they plan their talks and PowerPoint presentations. The number three is considered a symbol of balance, as in an equilateral triangle that has three 60-degree angles, the three meals we eat daily, or the three parts of our day — morning, noon, and night. A speech generally has an introduction, a body, and a conclusion. Audience members find balance and harmony seeing three objects on a slide, so whenever possible, plan visual components on your slides in groups of three.

Plan Ahead

BTW

The Ribbon and Screen Resolution
PowerPoint may change how the groups and buttons within the groups appear on the Ribbon, depending on the computer's screen resolution. Thus, your Ribbon may look different from the ones in this book if you are using a screen resolution other than 1024 × 768.

To Insert and Size Pictures

Health-related pictures will serve two purposes in this presentation. First, they will add visual interest and cue the viewers to the three topics of doctor visits, medications, and weight-control measures. The three pictures are located on the Data Files for Students. Later in this chapter, you will position the pictures in precise locations. The following steps insert and then size the three pictures on Slides 1, 2, 3, and 4.

1. On the title slide, insert the pictures called Stethoscope, Prescription, and Scale, which are located on the Data Files for Students, in the area below the title text.

2. Display the Picture Tools Format tab and then resize the three pictures so that they are approximately 2" × 2" (Figure 6–6).

3. Copy the stethoscope picture to the lower-right corner of Slide 2, the prescription picture to the lower-right corner of Slide 3, and the scale picture to the lower-right corner of Slide 4.

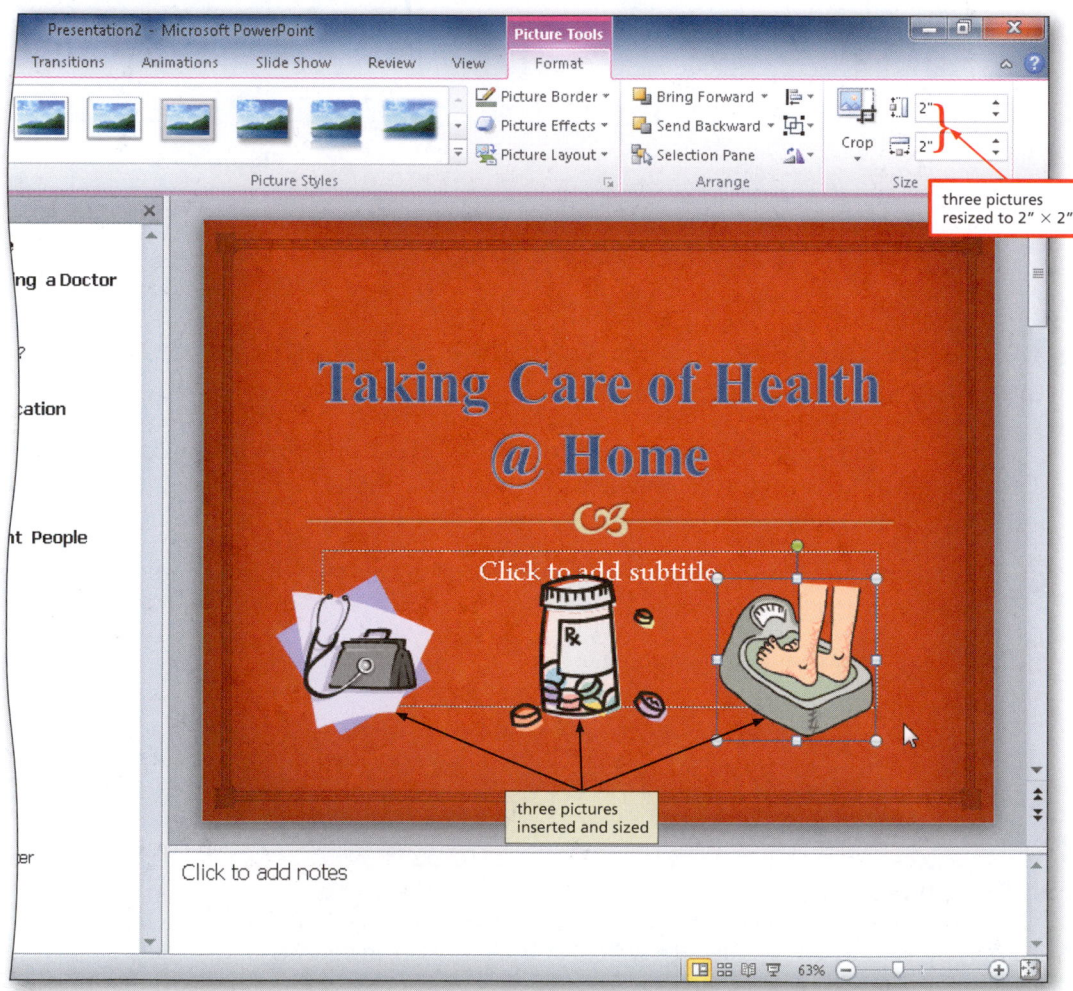

Figure 6–6

To Save the Presentation

With all five slides created, you should save the presentation. The following steps save the slides.

1 Click the Save button on the Quick Access Toolbar to display the Save As dialog box.

2 Save the file on your USB flash drive using `Home Health` as the file name.

Choose outstanding hyperlink images or text.
Good speakers are aware of their audiences and know their speech material well. They have rehearsed their presentations and know where the hypertext is displayed on the slides. During a presentation, however, they sometimes need to divert from their planned material. Audience members may interrupt with questions, the room may not have optimal acoustics or lighting, or the timing may be short or long. It is helpful, therefore, to make the slide hyperlinks as large and noticeable to speakers as possible. The presenters can glance at the slide and receive a visual cue that it contains a hyperlink. They then can decide whether to click the hyperlink to display a Web page.

Plan Ahead

Adding Hyperlinks and Action Buttons

Speakers sometimes skip from one slide to another in a presentation in response to audience needs or timing issues. In addition, if Internet access is available, they may desire to display a Web page during a slide show to add depth to the presented material and to enhance the overall message. When presenting the Home Health slide show and discussing medical information on Slides 1, 2, 3, or 4, a speaker might want to skip to the last slide in the presentation and then access a Web site for further specific health information. Or the presenter may be discussing information on Slide 5 and want to display Slide 1 to begin discussing a new topic.

BTW

BTWs
For a complete list of the BTWs found in the margins of this book, visit the PowerPoint 2010 BTW Web page (scsite.com/ppt2010/btw).

One method of jumping nonsequentially to slides is by clicking a hyperlink or an action button on a slide. A **hyperlink**, also called a **link**, connects one slide to a Web page, another slide, a custom show consisting of specific slides in a presentation, an e-mail address, or a file. A hyperlink can be any element of a slide. This includes a single letter, a word, a paragraph, or any graphical image such as a clip, picture, shape, or graph.

To Add a Hyperlink to a Picture

In the Home Health presentation, each piece of clip art on Slide 1 will hyperlink to another slide in the same presentation. When you point to a hyperlink, the mouse pointer becomes the shape of a hand to indicate the text or object contains a hyperlink. The following steps create the first hyperlink for the stethoscope picture on Slide 1.

1
- Display Slide 1, select the stethoscope picture, and then display the Insert tab.

- Click the Insert Hyperlink button (Insert tab | Links group) to display the Insert Hyperlink dialog box.

- If necessary, click the Place in This Document button in the Link to area.

- Click 2. Questions to Ask When Selecting a Doctor in the 'Select a place in this document' area (Insert Hyperlink dialog box) to select and display a preview of this slide (Figure 6–7).

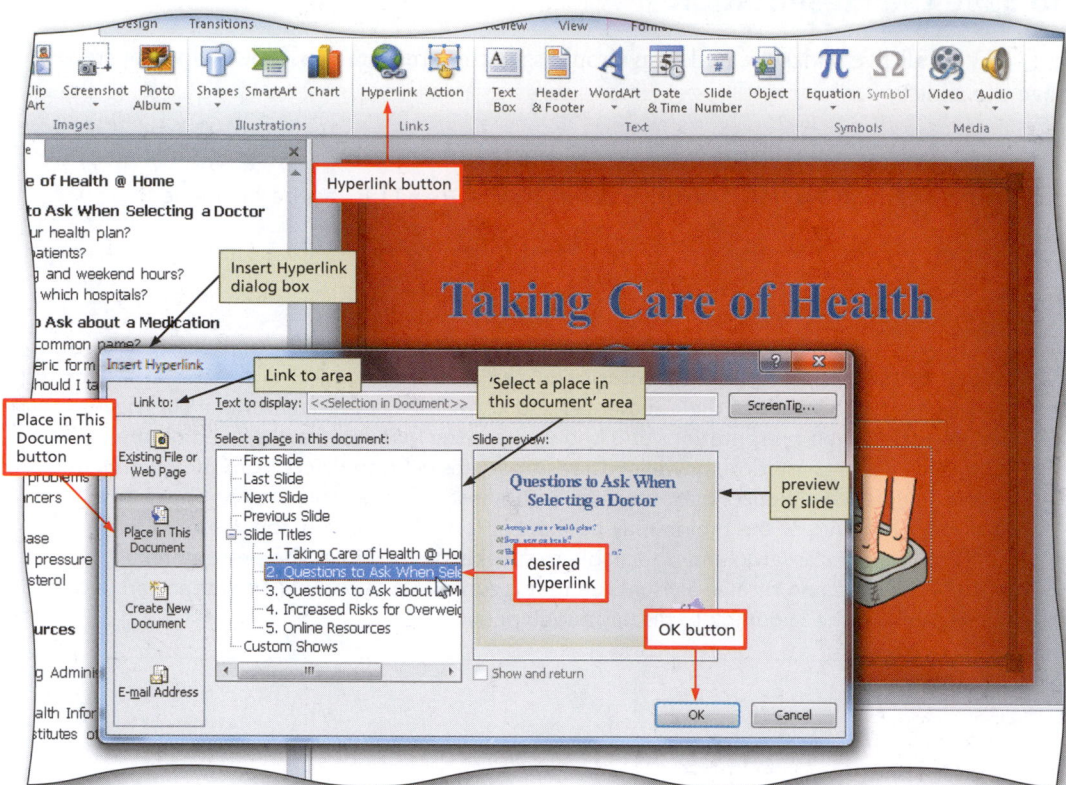

Figure 6–7

Q&A Could I also have selected the Next Slide link in the 'Select a place in this document' area?

Yes. Either action would create the hyperlink to Slide 2.

2
- Click the OK button to insert the hyperlink.

Q&A I clicked the stethoscope picture, but Slide 2 did not display. Why?

Hyperlinks are active only when you run the presentation, not when you are creating it in Normal, Reading, or Slide Sorter view.

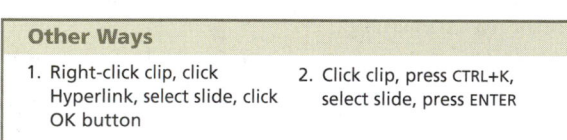

Other Ways

1. Right-click clip, click Hyperlink, select slide, click OK button

2. Click clip, press CTRL+K, select slide, press ENTER

To Add a Hyperlink to the Remaining Slide 1 Pictures

The hyperlink for the stethoscope clip is complete. The next task is to create the hyperlinks for the other two pictures on Slide 1.

1 On Slide 1, click the prescription picture.

2 Click the Insert Hyperlink button and then click 3. Questions to Ask about a Medication to select this slide as the hyperlink. Click the OK button.

3 Click the scale picture, click the Insert Hyperlink button, and then click 4. Increased Risks for Overweight People. Click the OK button.

To Add a Hyperlink to a Paragraph

On Slide 5, each second-level paragraph will be a hyperlink to a health organization's Web page. If you are connected to the Internet when you run the presentation, you can click each of these paragraphs, and your Web browser will open a new window and display the corresponding Web page for each hyperlink. By default, hyperlinked text is displayed with an underline and in a color that is part of the color scheme. The following steps create a hyperlink for the first paragraph.

1

- Display Slide 5 and then double-click the second-level paragraph that appears first, DocFinder, to select the text.

- Display the Insert Hyperlink dialog box and then click the Existing File or Web Page button in the Link to area (Figure 6–8).

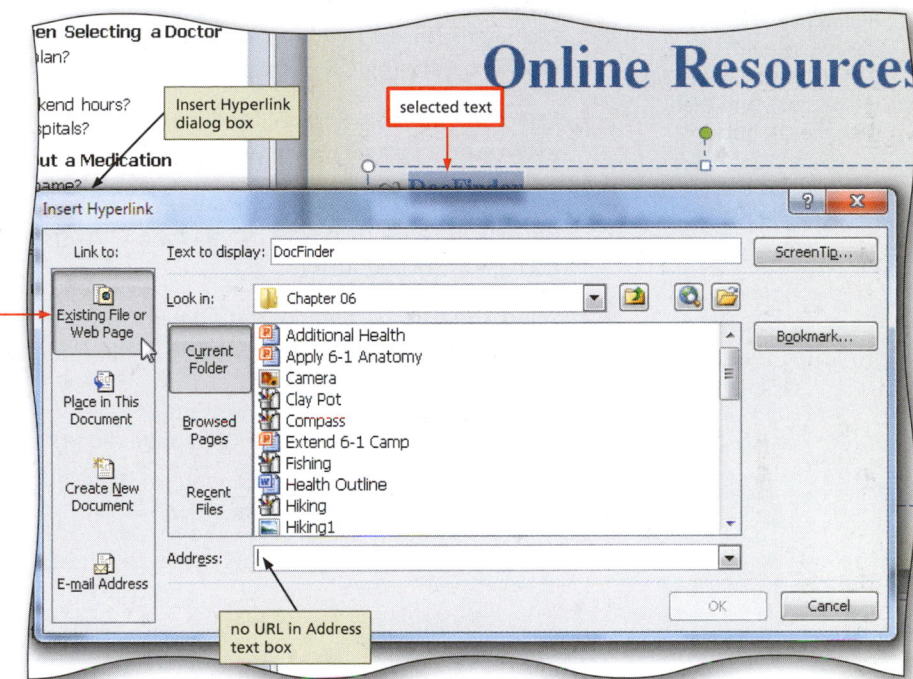

Figure 6–8

2

- Type **www.docboard.org** in the Address text box (Figure 6–9).

3

- Click the OK button to insert the hyperlink.

Q&A Why is this paragraph now underlined and displaying a new font color?

The default style for hyperlinks is underlined text. The Clarity built-in theme hyperlink color is Blue, so PowerPoint formatted the paragraph to that color automatically.

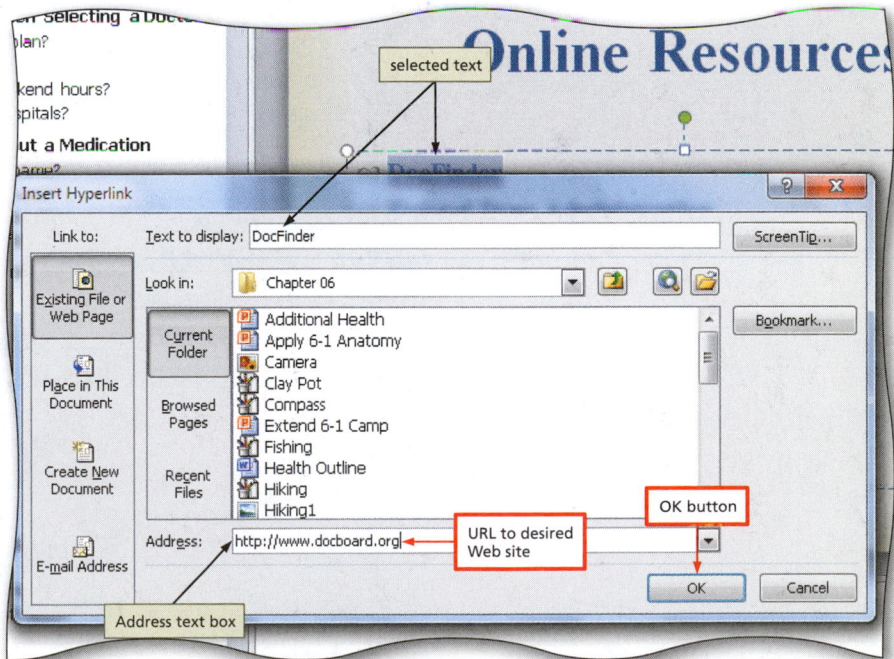

Figure 6–9

Other Ways	
1. Right-click selected text, click Hyperlink, type address, click OK button	2. Select text, press CTRL+K, type address, press ENTER

BTW

Customizing ScreenTips
You can create a custom ScreenTip that displays when you hover your mouse over a hyperlink. Click the ScreenTip button (Insert Hyperlink dialog box), type the desired ScreenTip text (Set Hyperlink ScreenTip dialog box), and then click the OK button.

To Add a Hyperlink to the Remaining Slide 5 Paragraphs

The hyperlink for the second-level paragraph that appears first is complete. The next task is to create the hyperlinks for the other second-level paragraphs on Slide 5.

1 Triple-click the second-level paragraph that appears second, Federal Drug Administration, to select this text.

2 Display the Insert Hyperlink dialog box and then type `www.fda.gov` in the Address text box. Click the OK button.

3 Select the third paragraph, MedlinePlus, display the Insert Hyperlink dialog box, type `www.medlineplus.gov` in the Address text box, and then click the OK button.

4 Select the fourth paragraph, National Health Information Center, display the Insert Hyperlink dialog box, type `www.health.gov/nhic` in the Address text box, and then click the OK button.

5 Select the fifth paragraph, National Institutes of Health, display the Insert Hyperlink dialog box, type `www.nih.gov` in the Address text box, and then click the OK button (Figure 6–10).

Q&A

I clicked the hyperlink, but the Web page did not display. Why?

Hyperlinks are active only when you run the presentation, not when you are creating it in Normal, Reading, or Slide Sorter view.

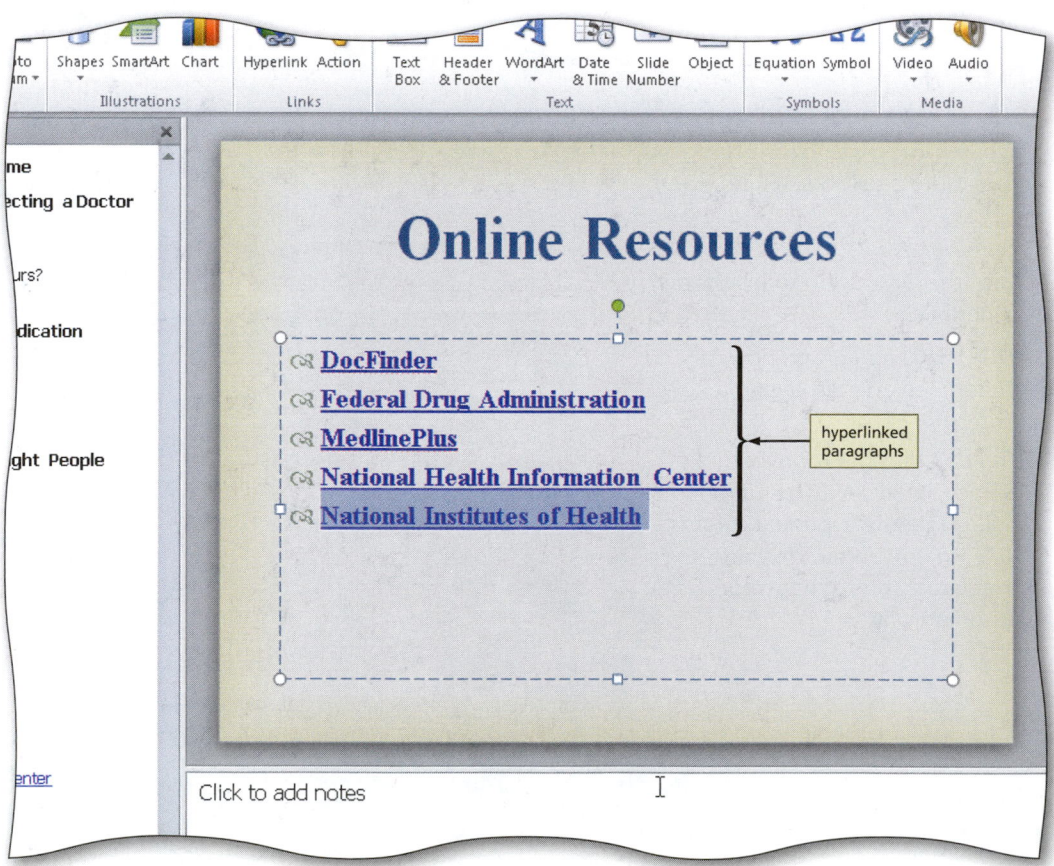

Figure 6–10

> **Customize action buttons for a unique look.**
> PowerPoint's built-in action buttons have icons that give the presenter an indication of their function. Designers frequently customize these buttons with images related to the presentation. For example, in a grocery store presentation, the action buttons may have images of a coupon, dollar sign, and question mark to indicate links to in-store coupons, sale items, and the customer service counter. Be creative when you develop your own presentations and attempt to develop buttons that have specific meanings for your intended audience.

**Plan
Ahead**

Action Buttons

PowerPoint provides 12 built-in action buttons. An **action button** is a particular type of hyperlink that has a built-in function. Each action button performs a specific task, such as displaying the next slide, providing help, giving information, or playing a sound. In addition, the action button can activate a hyperlink that allows users to jump to a specific slide in the presentation. The picture on the action button indicates the type of function it performs. For example, the button with the house icon represents the home slide, or Slide 1. To achieve a personalized look, you can customize an action button with a photograph, piece of clip art, logo, text, or any graphic you desire. Table 6–1 describes each of the built-in action buttons.

BTW

Q&As
For a complete list of the Q&As found in many of the step-by-step sequences in this book, visit the PowerPoint 2010 Q&A Web page (scsite.com/ppt2010/qa).

Table 6–1 Built-In Action Buttons

Button Name	Image	Description
Back or Previous		Returns to the previous slide displayed in the same presentation.
Forward or Next		Jumps to the next slide in the presentation.
Beginning		Jumps to Slide 1. This button performs the same function as the Home button.
End		Jumps to the last slide in the presentation.
Home		Jumps to Slide 1. This button performs the same function as the Beginning button.
Information		Does not have any predefined function. Use it to direct a user to a slide with details or facts.
Return		Returns to the previous slide displayed in any presentation. For example, you can place it on a hidden slide or on a slide in a custom slide show and then return to the previous slide.
Movie		Does not have any predefined function. You generally would use this button to jump to a slide with an inserted video clip.
Document		Opens a program other than PowerPoint. For example, you can open Microsoft Word or Microsoft Excel and display a page or worksheet.
Sound		Does not have any predefined function. You generally would use this button to jump to a slide with an inserted audio clip.
Help		Does not have any predefined function. Use it to direct a user to a slide with instructions or contact information.
Custom		Does not have any predefined function. You can add a clip, picture, graphic, or text and then specify a unique purpose.

To Insert an Action Button

In the Home Health slide show, the action buttons on Slides 2, 3, and 4 hyperlink to the last slide, Slide 5. You will insert and format the action button shape on Slide 2 and copy it to Slides 3 and 4, and then create a link to Slide 5 so that you will be able to display Slide 5 at any point in the presentation by clicking the action button. When you click the action button, a sound will play. This sound will vary depending upon which slide is displayed. The following steps insert an action button on Slide 2 and link it to Slide 5.

1
- Display Slide 2 and then click the Shapes button (Insert tab | Illustrations group) to display the Shapes gallery.

- Point to the Action Button: End shape in the Action Buttons area (fourth image) (Figure 6–11).

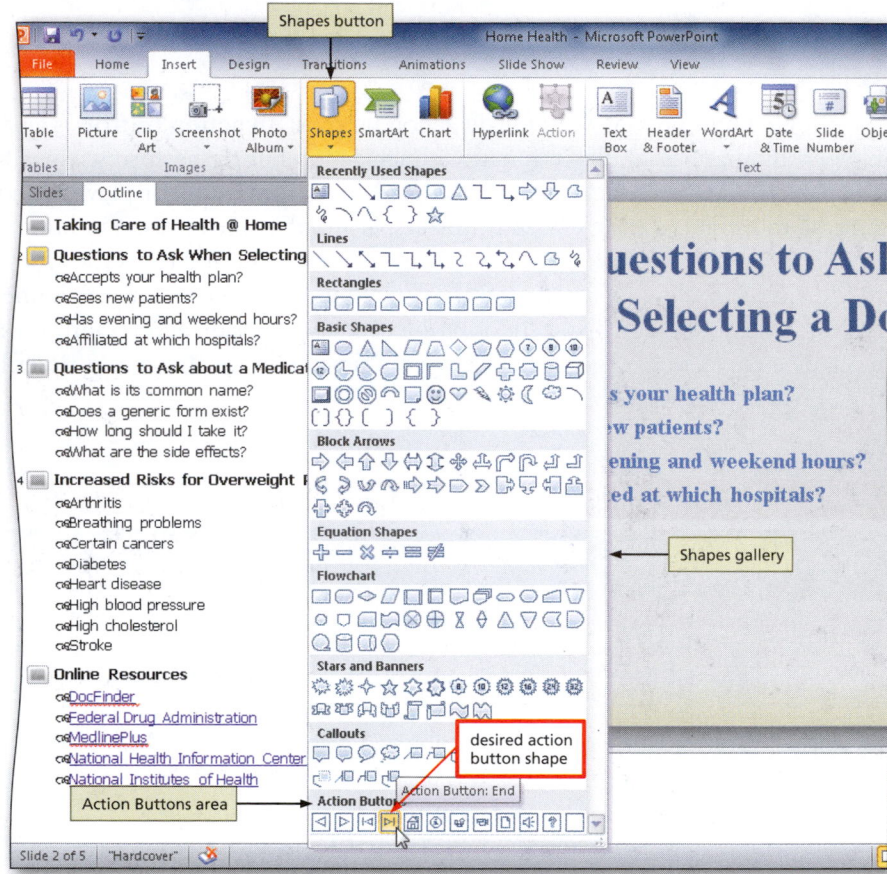

Figure 6–11

2
- Click the Action Button: End shape.

- Click the lower-left corner of the slide to insert the action button and to display the Action Settings dialog box.

- If necessary, click the Mouse Click tab (Action Settings dialog box) (Figure 6–12).

Q&A

Why is the default setting the action to hyperlink to the last slide?

The End shape establishes a hyperlink to the last slide in a presentation.

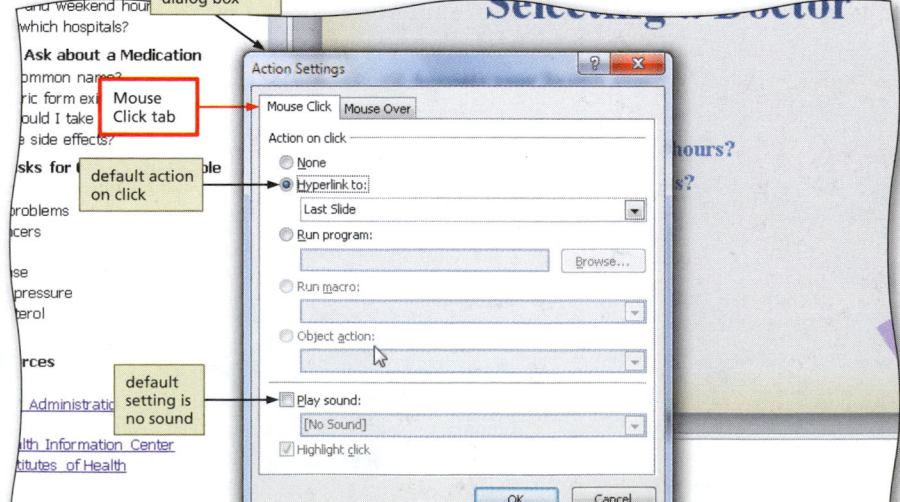

Figure 6–12

3

• Click the Play sound check box and then click the Play sound arrow to display the Play Sound list (Figure 6–13).

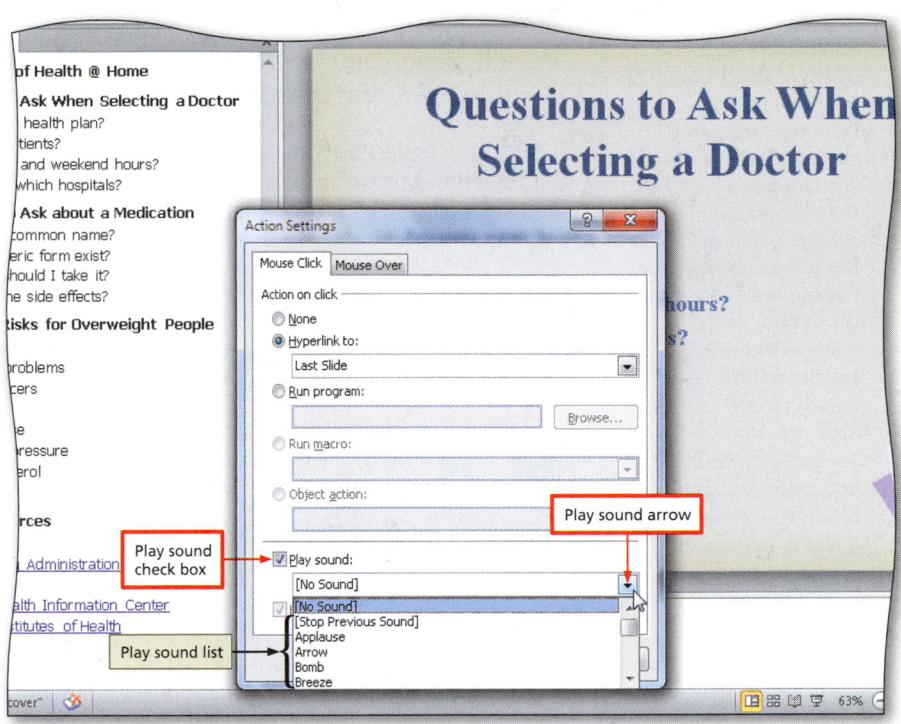

Figure 6–13

4

• Scroll down and then click Push to select that sound (Figure 6–14).

Q&A

I did not hear the sound when I selected it. Why not?

The Push sound will play when you run the slide show and click the action button.

5

• Click the OK button to apply the hyperlink setting and sound to the action button and to close the Action Settings dialog box.

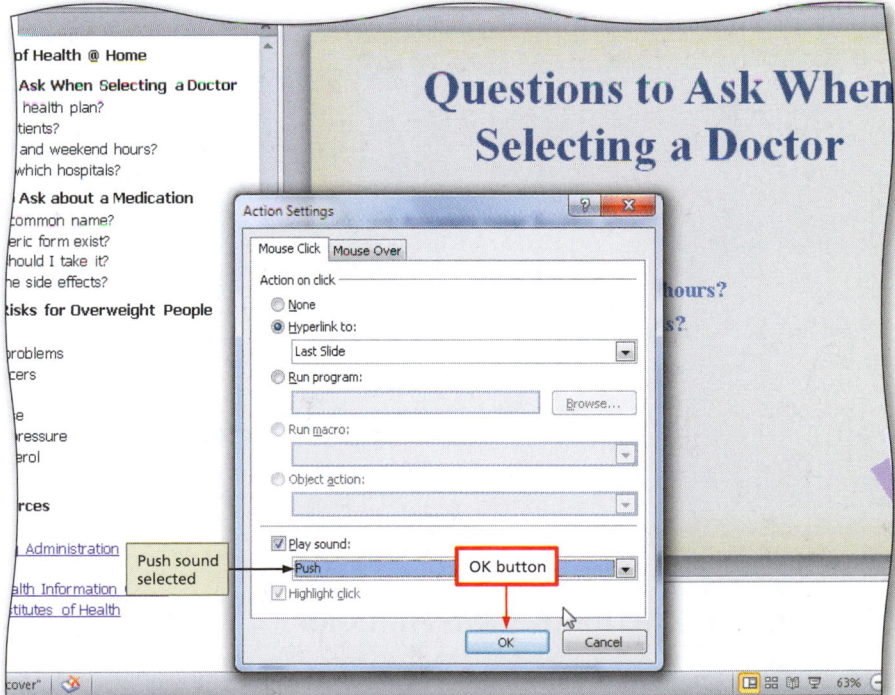

Figure 6–14

BTW

Customizing Action Buttons

This project uses one of PowerPoint's built-in action buttons. Designers frequently customize these buttons with images related to the presentation. For example, in a school the action buttons may have images of a book, silverware, and question mark to indicate links to the library, the cafeteria, and the information desk. Be creative when you develop your own presentations and attempt to develop buttons that have a specific meaning for your intended audience.

To Size an Action Button

The action button size can be decreased to make it less obvious on the slide. The following step resizes the selected action button.

1 With the action button still selected, display the Drawing Tools Format tab and then size the action button so that it is approximately 0.5" × 0.5". If necessary, move the action button to the location shown in Figure 6–15.

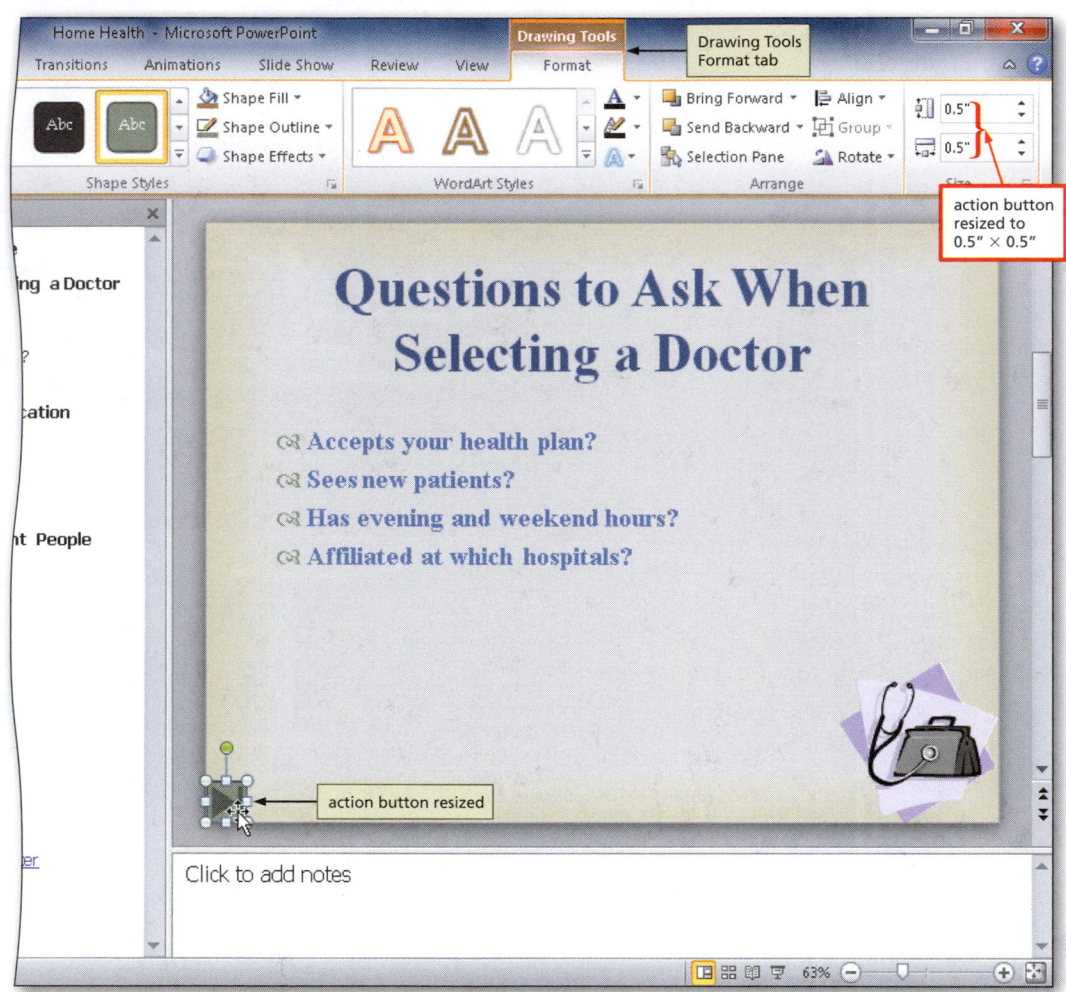

Figure 6–15

To Change an Action Button Fill Color

The action button's Gray interior color does not blend well with the light yellow border on the slide. You can select a new fill color to coordinate with the slide edges. The following steps change the fill color from Gray to Light Yellow.

1

● With the action button still selected, click the Shape Fill button arrow (Drawing Tools Format tab | Shape Styles gallery) to display the Shape Fill gallery (Figure 6–16).

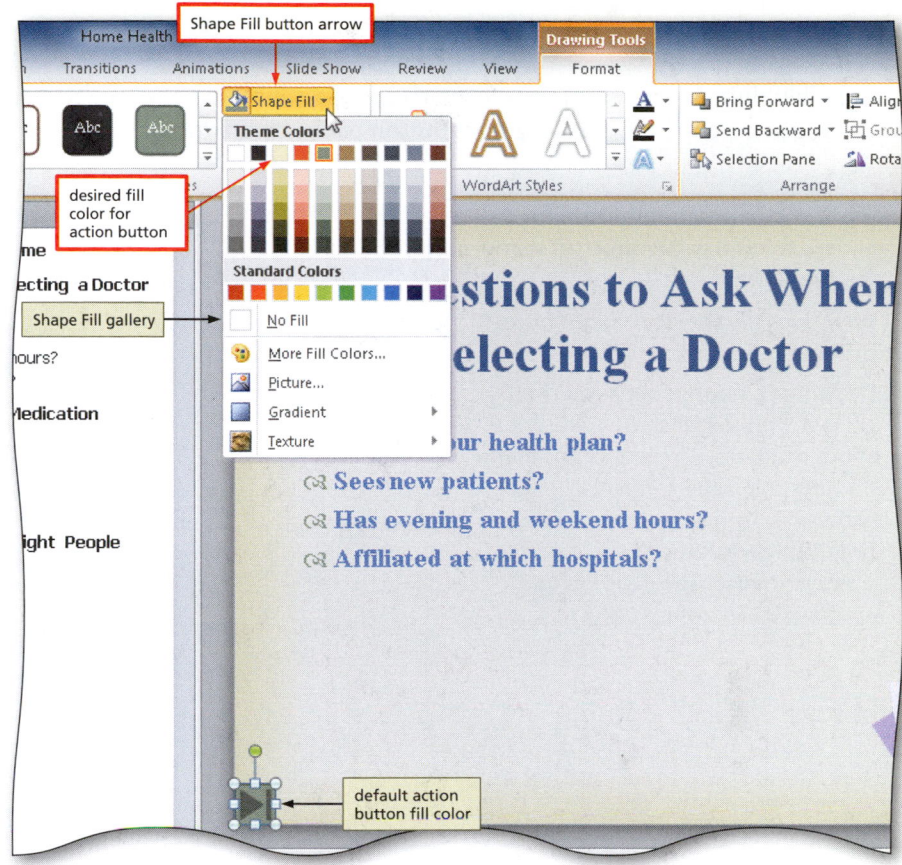

Figure 6–16

2

● Point to Light Yellow, Background 2 (third color from left in first row) to display a live preview of that fill color on the action button (Figure 6–17).

 **Experiment**

● Point to various colors in the Shape Fill gallery and watch the fill color change in the action button.

3

● Click Light Yellow, Background 2 to apply this color to the action button.

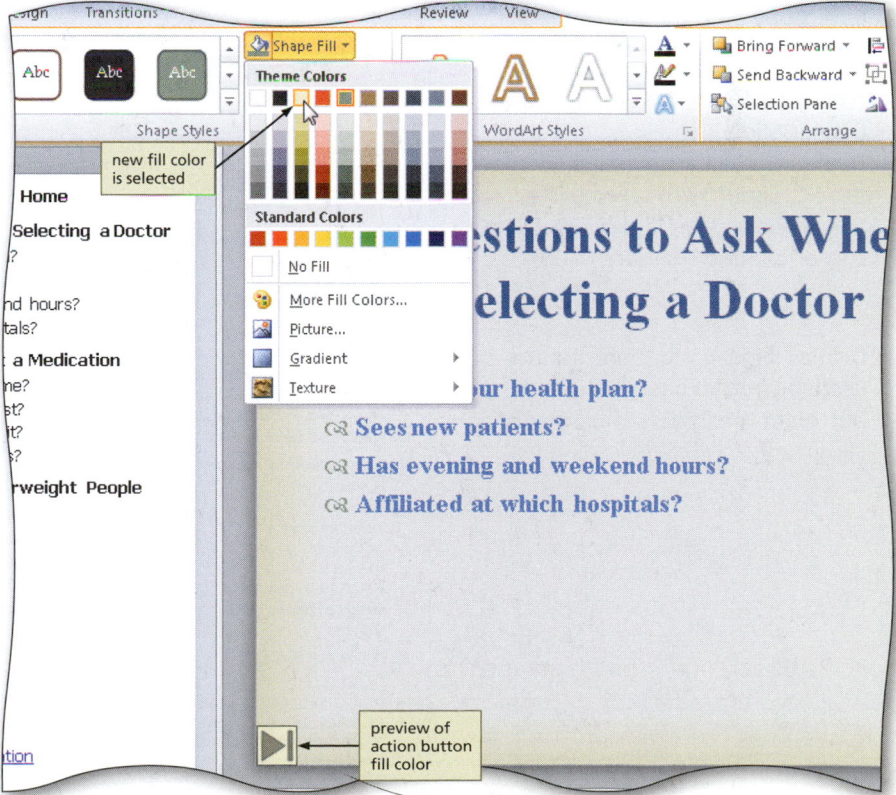

Figure 6–17

To Copy an Action Button

The Slide 2 action button is formatted and positioned correctly. You can copy this shape to Slides 3 and 4. The following steps copy the Slide 2 action button to the next two slides in the presentation.

1

- Right-click the action button on Slide 2 to display the shortcut menu (Figure 6–18).

Q&A

Why does my shortcut menu have different commands?

Depending upon where you right-clicked, you might see a different shortcut menu. As long as this menu displays the Copy command, you can use it. If the Copy command is not visible, click the slide again to display another shortcut menu.

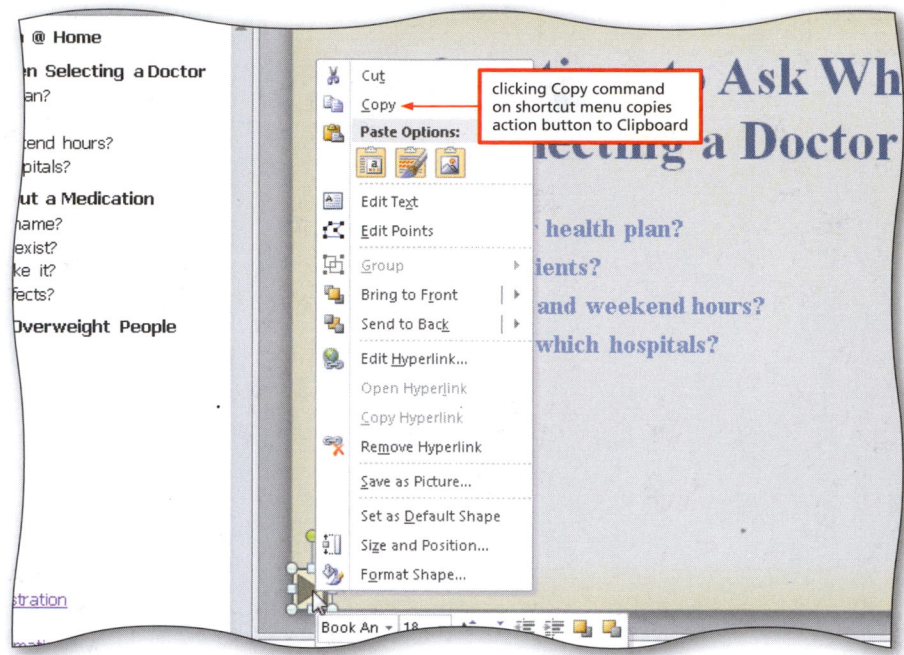

Figure 6–18

2

- Click Copy on the shortcut menu to copy the action button to the Clipboard.

- Display Slide 3 and then click the Paste button (Home tab | Clipboard group) to paste the action button in the lower-left corner of Slide 3 (Figure 6–19).

3

- Display Slide 4 and then click the Paste button to paste the action button in the lower-left corner of Slide 4.

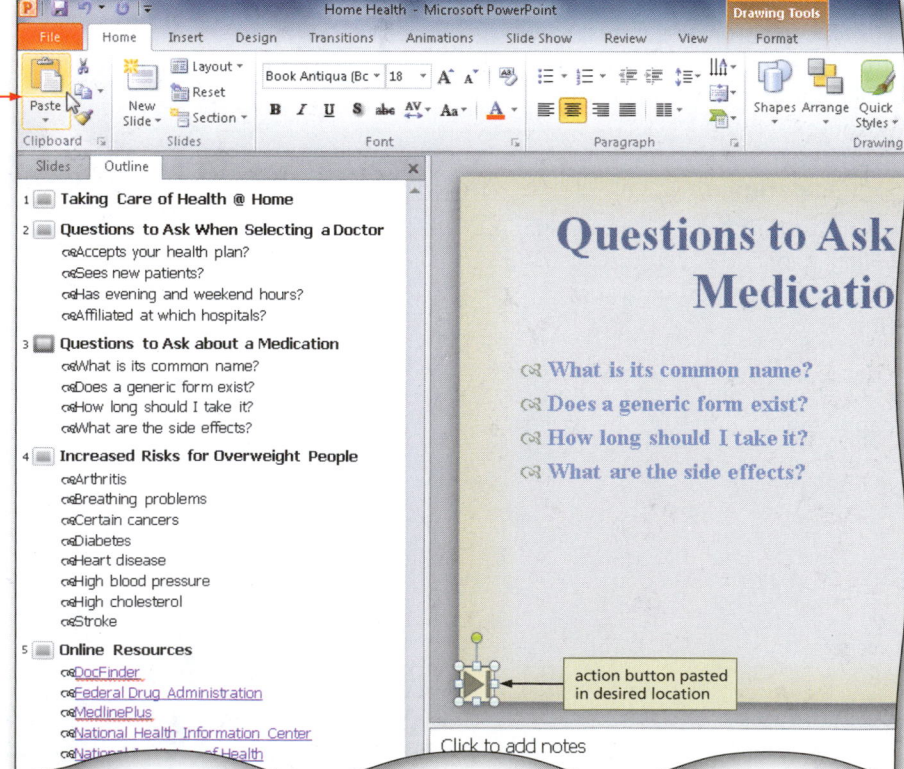

Figure 6–19

To Edit an Action Button Action Setting

When you copied the action button, PowerPoint retained the settings to hyperlink to the last slide and to play the Push sound. For variety, you want to change the sounds that play for the Slide 3 and Slide 4 action buttons. The following steps edit the Slide 3 and Slide 4 hyperlink sound settings.

- With the action button still selected on Slide 4, display the Insert tab and then click the Action button (Insert tab | Links group) to display the Action Settings dialog box.

- Click the Play sound arrow to display the Play sound menu (Figure 6–20).

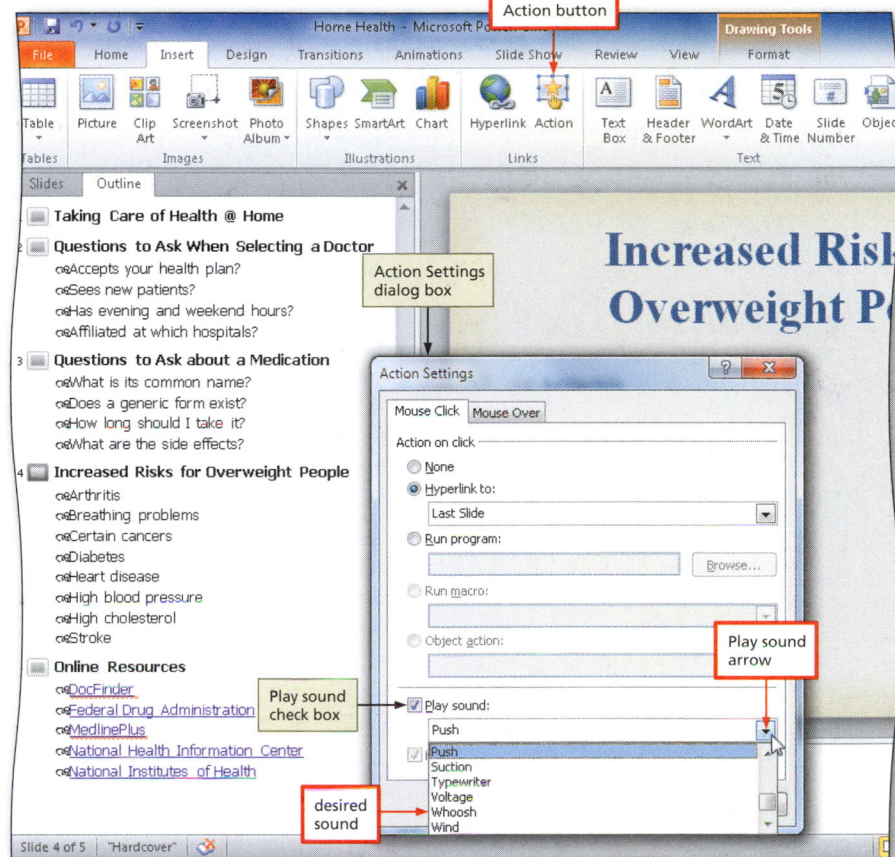

Figure 6–20

- Click Whoosh in the Play sound list to select the Whoosh sound to play when the action button is clicked (Figure 6–21).

- Click the OK button (Action Settings dialog box) to apply the new sound setting to the Slide 4 action button.

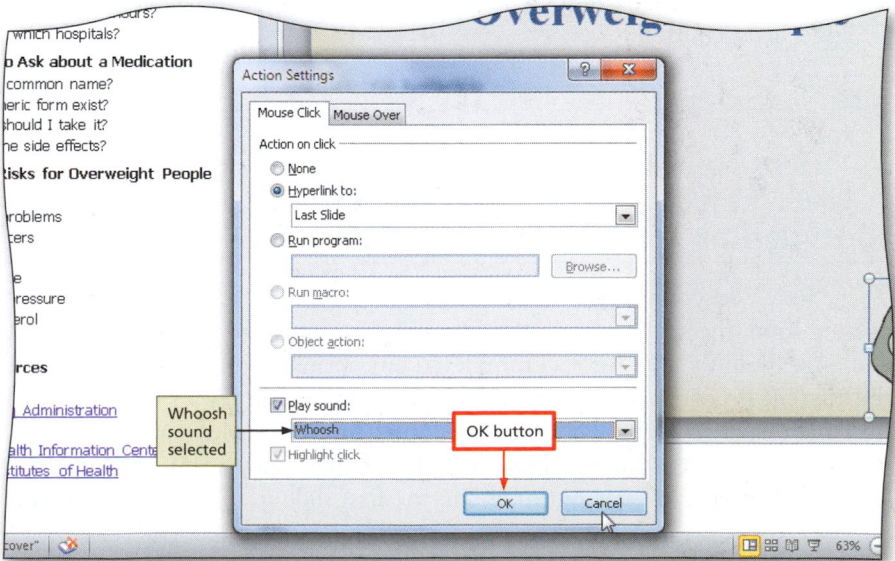

Figure 6–21

4

- Display Slide 3, select the action button, and then click the Action button (Insert tab | Links group) to display the Action Settings dialog box.

- Click the Play sound arrow to display the Play sound menu.

- Scroll up and then click Breeze in the Play sound list (Figure 6–22).

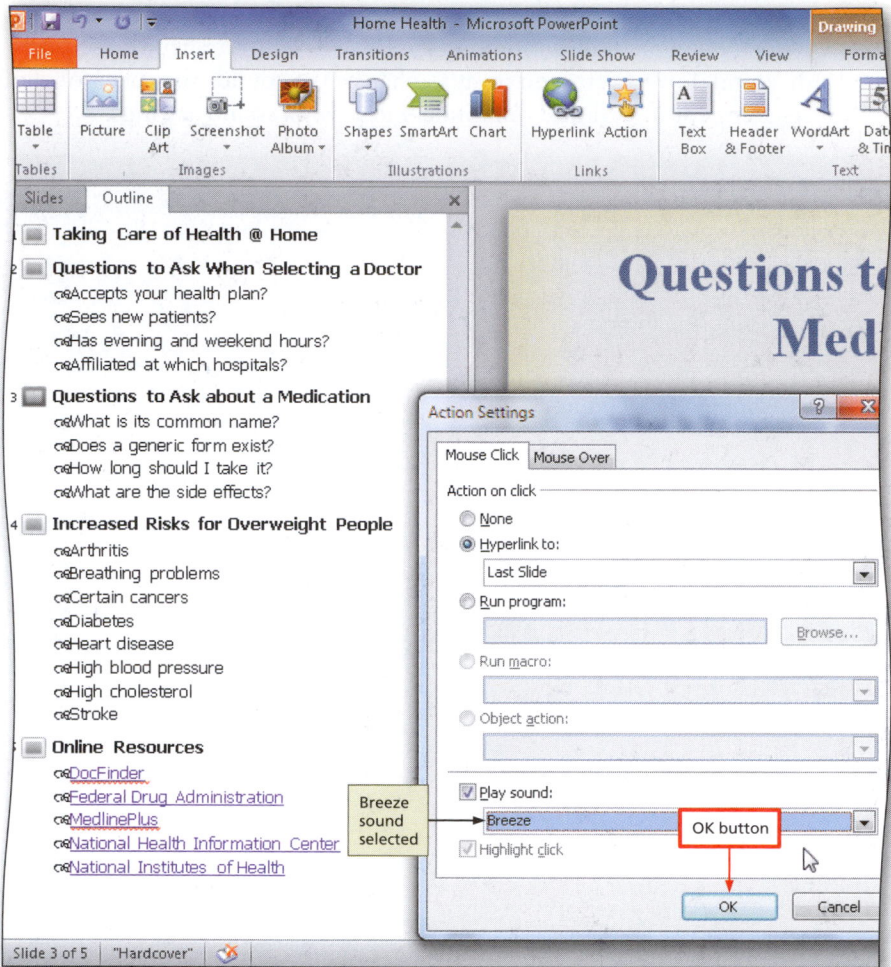

Figure 6–22

5

- Click the OK button (Action Settings dialog box) to apply the new sound setting to the Slide 3 action button.

To Hyperlink to Another PowerPoint File

Slide 2 in your presentation provides information for patients to ask a potential doctor. When running a presentation, the speaker may decide some useful information might be a list of referral doctors, especially if an audience member asks for recommended physicians. While hyperlinks are convenient tools to navigate through the current PowerPoint presentation or to Web pages, they also allow you to open a second PowerPoint presentation and display a particular slide in that file. The first slide in another presentation, Additional Home Health, lists details about several doctors, including their names, specialties, and number of years of practice. The following steps hyperlink the stethoscope on Slide 2 to the first slide in the second presentation.

1

- Display Slide 2 and then select the stethoscope picture.

- If necessary, display the Insert tab and then click the Action button (Insert tab | Links group) to display the Action Settings dialog box.

- Click Hyperlink to in the 'Action on click' area and then click the Hyperlink to arrow to display the Hyperlink to menu (Figure 6–23).

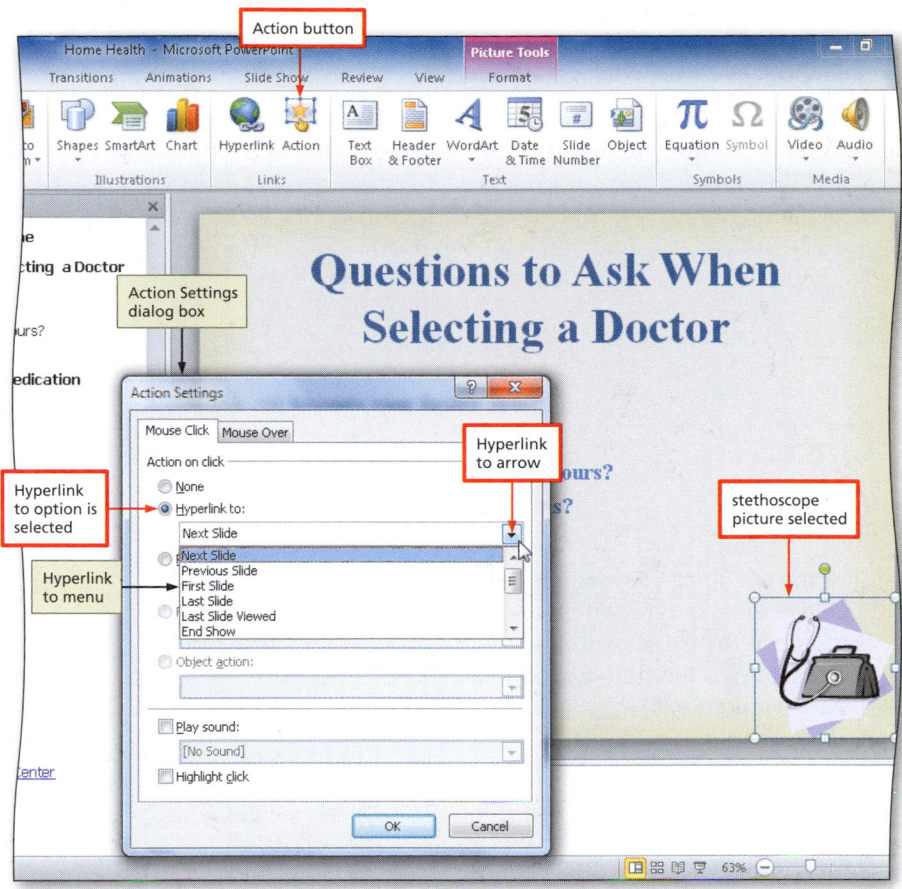

Figure 6–23

2

- Scroll down and then click Other PowerPoint Presentation to display the Hyperlink to Other PowerPoint Presentation dialog box.

- Click Additional Health to select this file as the hyperlinked presentation (Figure 6–24).

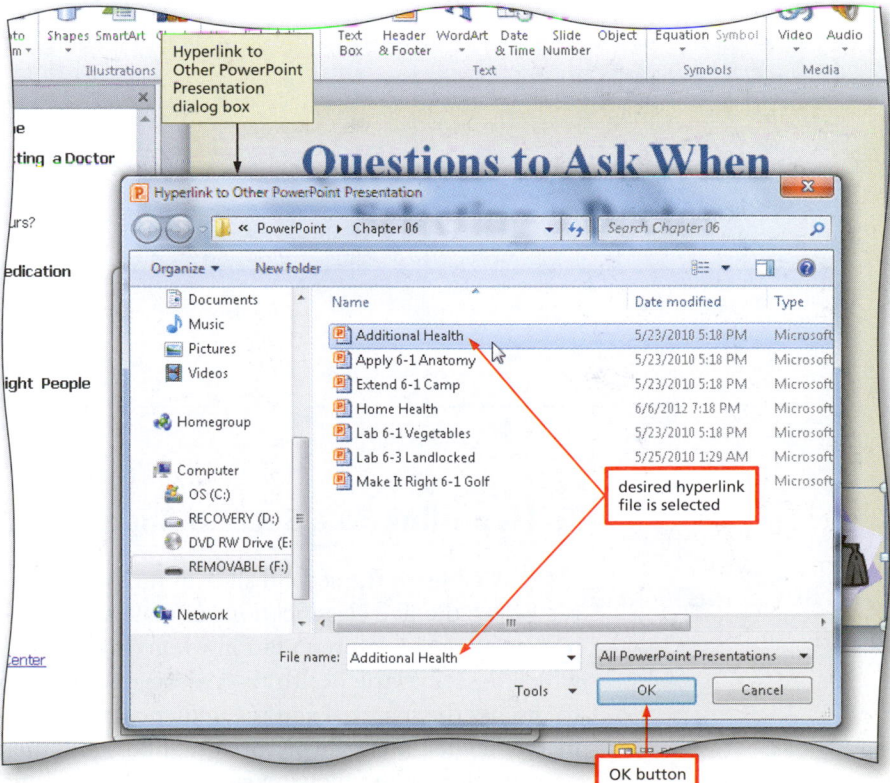

Figure 6–24

3
- Click the OK button to display the Hyperlink to Slide dialog box (Figure 6–25).

What are the two items listed in the Slide title area?

They are the title text of the two slides in the Additional Health file.

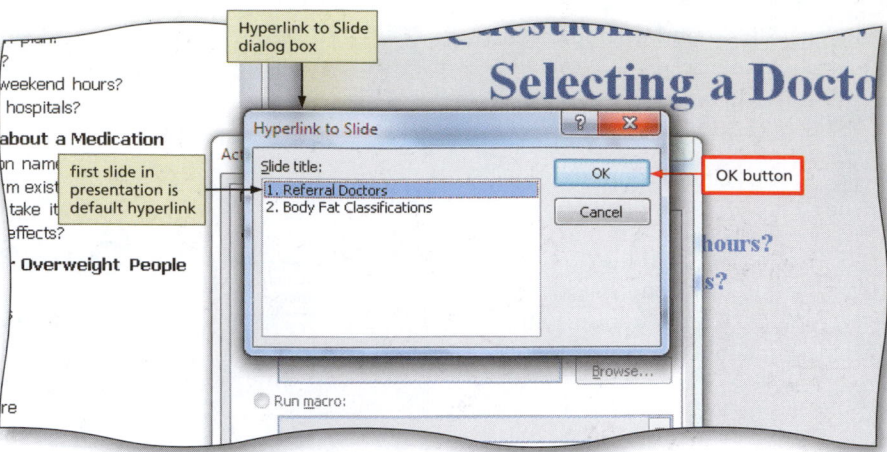

Figure 6–25

4
- Click the OK button (Hyperlink to Slide dialog box) to hyperlink the first slide in the Additional Health presentation to the stethoscope picture (Figure 6–26).

5
- Click the OK button (Action Settings dialog box) to apply the new action setting to the Slide 2 picture.

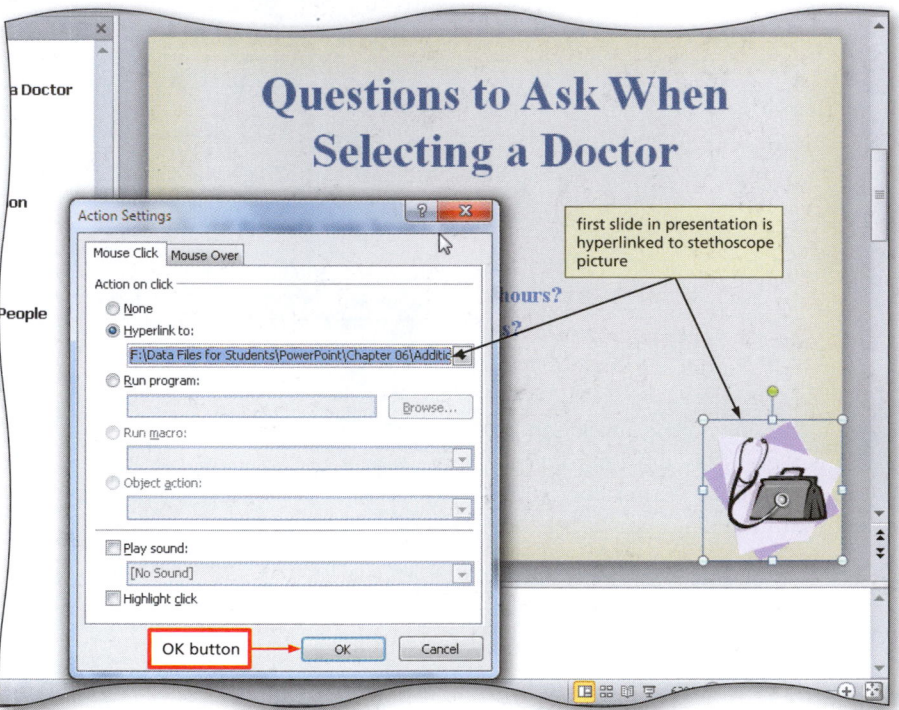

Figure 6–26

To Hyperlink to a Second Slide in Another PowerPoint File

A table on the second slide in the Additional Health presentation has information regarding the five classifications of male and female body fat. This slide might be useful to display during a presentation when a speaker is discussing the information on Slide 4, which describes the health risks associated with being overweight. If the speaker has time to discuss the material and the audience needs to know these specific body fat percentages, he could click the scale picture on Slide 4 and then hyperlink to Slide 2 in the second presentation. The following steps hyperlink Slide 4 to the second slide in the Additional Health presentation.

1 Display Slide 4, select the scale picture, and then click the Action button (Insert tab | Links group) to display the Action Settings dialog box.

2 Click Hyperlink to in the 'Action on click' area, click the Hyperlink to arrow, and then scroll down and click Other PowerPoint Presentation in the Hyperlink to menu.

3 Click Additional Health in the Hyperlink to Other PowerPoint Presentation dialog box to select this file as the hyperlinked presentation and then click the OK button.

4 Click 2. Body Fat Classifications (Hyperlink to Slide dialog box) (Figure 6–27).

5 Click the OK button (Hyperlink to Slide dialog box) to hyperlink the second slide in the Additional Health presentation to the scale picture.

6 Click the OK button (Action Settings dialog box) to apply the new action setting to the Slide 4 picture.

BTW

Verifying Hyperlinks
Always test your hyperlinks prior to giving a presentation. Web addresses change frequently, so if your hyperlinks are to Web sites, be certain your Internet connection is working, the Web sites are active, and that the content on these pages is appropriate for your viewers. If your hyperlinks direct PowerPoint to display specific slides and to open files, click the hyperlinks to verify your desired actions are followed and that the files exist.

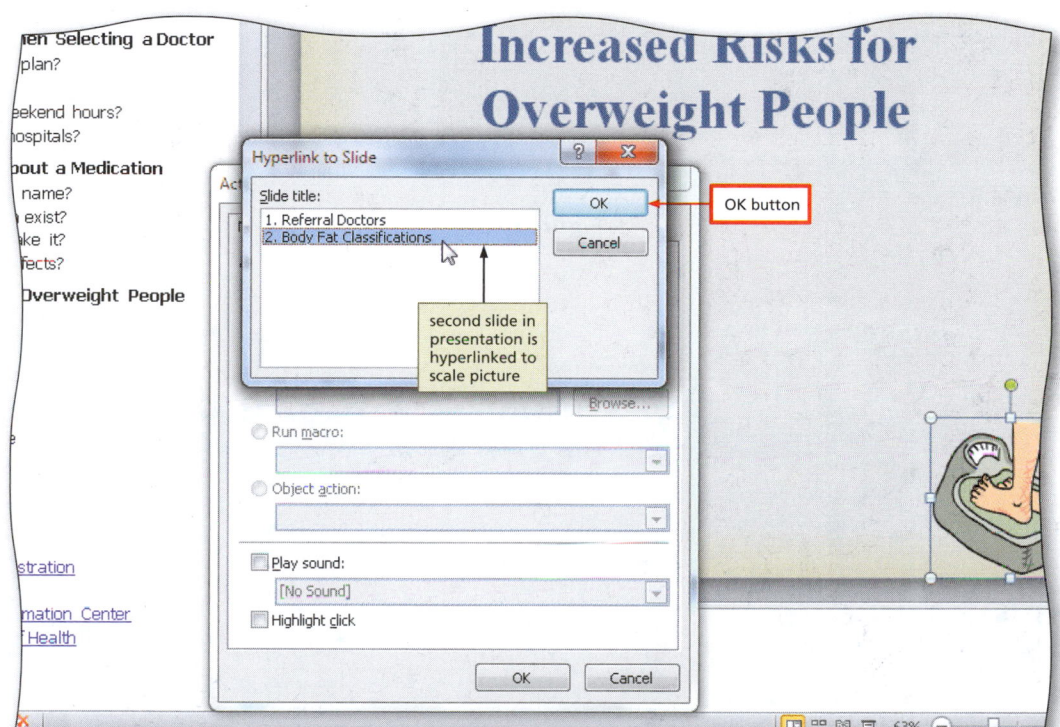

Figure 6–27

To Hyperlink to a Microsoft Word File

Doctors recommend their patients keep a current record of all prescribed and over-the-counter medications. This list should include the name of the drug, the amount taken per day, and the date when the patient started taking this medication. A convenient form for recording these details is located on the Data Files for Students. The file, Medication Record, was created using Microsoft Word, and it would be useful to display this document when discussing the information on Slide 3 of your presentation. PowerPoint allows a speaker to hyperlink to other Microsoft Office documents in a similar manner as linking to another PowerPoint file. The following steps hyperlink the prescription picture on Slide 3 to the Microsoft Word document with the file name, Medication Record.

- Display Slide 3, select the prescription picture, and then click the Action button (Insert tab | Links group) to display the Action Settings dialog box.

- Click Hyperlink to, click the Hyperlink to arrow to display the Hyperlink to menu, and then scroll down to the end of the Hyperlink to list (Figure 6–28).

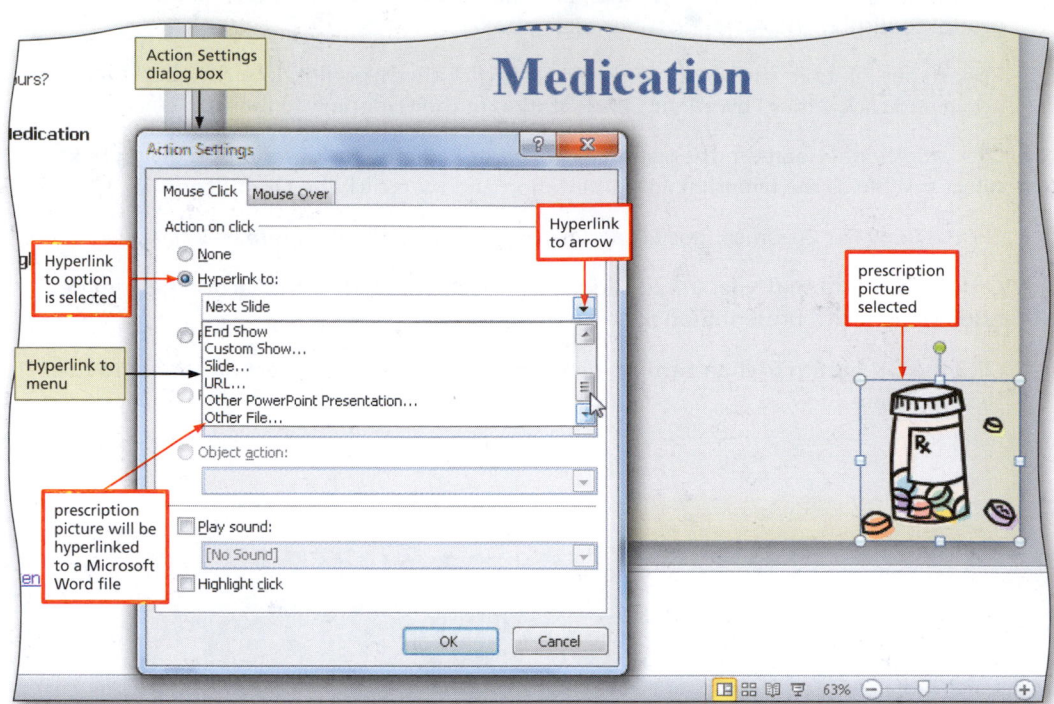

Figure 6–28

- Click Other File to display the Hyperlink to Other File dialog box, scroll down, and then click Medication Record to select this file as the hyperlinked document (Figure 6–29).

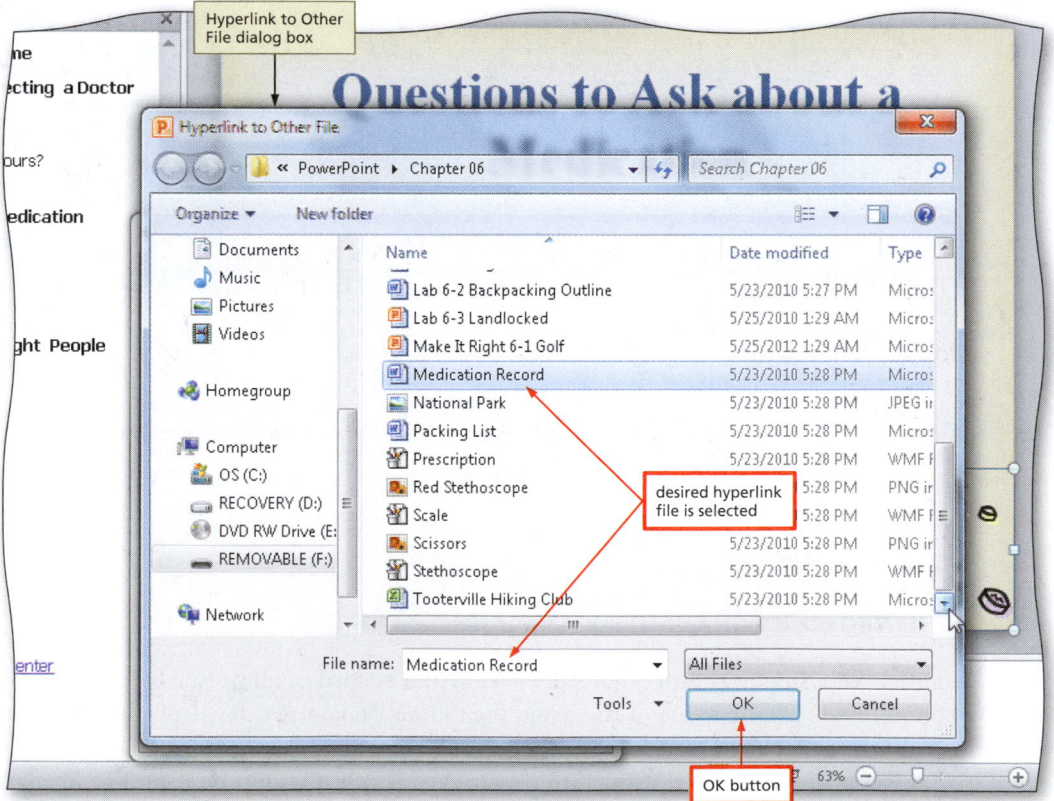

Figure 6–29

3

• Click the OK button (Hyperlink to Other File dialog box) to hyperlink this file to the prescription picture action button (Figure 6−30).

4

• Click the OK button (Action Settings dialog box) to apply the new action setting to the Slide 3 picture.

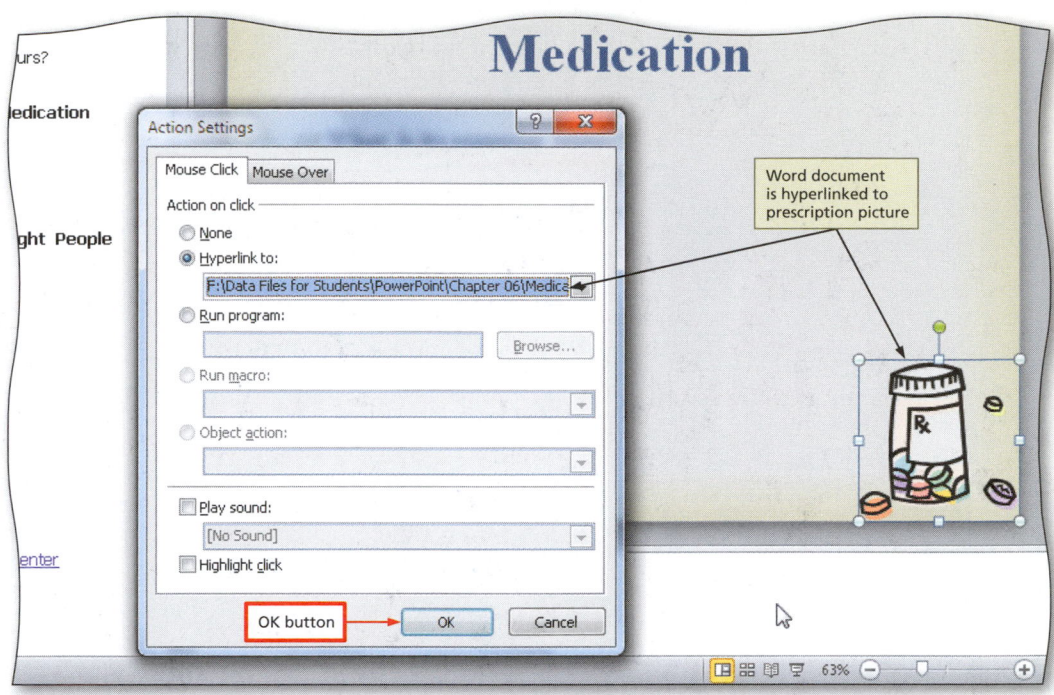

Figure 6−30

To Insert and Format Action Buttons on the Hyperlinked File

The action buttons on Slide 2 and Slide 3 hyperlink to slides in the Additional Health file. While running the presentation, if you click an action button that opens and then displays either Slide 1 or Slide 2, you may need to review this slide and then return to the previous slide displayed in the first presentation. The Return action button performs this function. The following steps open the Additional Health file and then insert and format the Return action button on both slides.

1 In the Backstage view, click the Open command to display the Open dialog box, click the File Type arrow to display the File Type list, and then click All PowerPoint Presentations to select this file type.

2 Open the Additional Health file located on the Data Files for Students.

3 With Slide 1 displaying, click the Shapes button (Insert tab | Illustrations group), and then click the Action Button: Return shape (seventh image).

4 Insert the action button in the lower-right corner of the slide.

5 Display the Action Settings dialog box and then hyperlink the action button to Slide 2 (Questions to Ask When Selecting a Doctor) in the Home Health presentation.

6 Size the action button so that it is approximately 0.5" × 0.5".

7 Change the action button fill color to Tan, Background 2, Lighter 40% (fourth color in third column).

8 Copy the action button to the same location on Slide 2 (Figure 6−31 on the next page). Display the Action Settings dialog box and then hyperlink this action button to Slide 4 (Increased Risks for Overweight People) in the Home Health presentation.

BTW

Showing a Range of Slides
If your presentation consists of many slides, you may want to show only a portion of them in your slide show. For example, if your 30-slide presentation is designed to accompany a 30-minute speech and you are given only 10 minutes to present, you may elect to display only the first 10 slides. Rather than have the show end abruptly after Slide 10, you can elect to show a range of slides. To specify this range, display the Slide Show tab, click the Set Up Slide Show button, and then specify the starting and ending slide numbers in the From and To boxes in the Show slides area (Set Up Show dialog box).

9 Save the file using the same file name.

10 Close the Additional Health file.

BODY FAT (%)		CLASSIFICATION
Male	Female	
2 - 4%	10 - 12%	Essential
6 - 13%	14 - 20%	Athletic
14 - 17%	21 - 24%	Fit
18 - 25%	25 - 31%	Acceptable
> 26%	> 32%	Obese

Return action button is hyperlinked to previous slide (Slide 4) and formatted

Figure 6–31

Break Point: If you wish to take a break, this is a good place to do so. Be sure to save the Home Health file again and then you can quit PowerPoint. To resume at a later time, start PowerPoint, open the file called Home Health, and continue following the steps from this location forward.

BTW

Measurement System
The vertical and horizontal rulers display the units of measurement in inches by default. This measurement system is determined by the settings in Microsoft Windows. You can change the measurement system to centimeters by customizing the numbers format in the Clock, Language, and Region area of Control Panel.

Positioning Slide Elements

At times you may desire to arrange slide elements in precise locations. PowerPoint provides useful tools to help you position shapes and objects on slides. **Drawing guides** are two straight dotted lines, one horizontal and one vertical. When an object is close to a guide, its corner or its center (whichever is closer) **snaps**, or aligns precisely on top of the guide. You can drag a guide to a new location to meet your alignment requirements. Another tool is the vertical or horizontal **ruler**, which can help you drag an object to a precise location on the slide. The center of a slide is 0.00 on both the vertical and the horizontal rulers.

Aligning and Distributing Objects

If you display multiple objects, PowerPoint can **align** them above and below each other (vertically) or side by side (horizontally). The objects, such as SmartArt graphics, clip art, shapes, text boxes, and WordArt, can be aligned relative to the slide so that they display along the top, left, right, or bottom borders or in the center or middle of the slide. They also can be aligned relative to each other, meaning that you position either the first or last object in the desired location and then command PowerPoint to move the remaining objects in the series above, below, or beside it. Depending on the alignment option that you click, objects will move straight up, down, left, or right, and might cover an object already located on the slide. Table 6–2 describes alignment options.

Table 6–2 Alignment Options

Alignment	Action
Left	Aligns the edges of the objects to the left
Center	Aligns the objects vertically through the centers of the objects
Right	Aligns the edges of the objects to the right
Top	Aligns the top edges of the objects
Middle	Aligns the objects horizontally through the middles of the objects
Bottom	Aligns the bottom edges of the objects
to Slide	Aligns one object to the slide

One object remains stationary when you align objects relative to each other by their edges. For example, Align Left aligns the left edges of all selected objects with the left edge of the leftmost object. The leftmost object remains stationary, and the other objects are aligned relative to it. Objects aligned to a SmartArt graphic are aligned to the leftmost edge of the SmartArt graphic, not to the leftmost shape in the SmartArt graphic. Objects aligned relative to each other by their middles or centers are aligned along a horizontal or vertical line that represents the average of their original positions. All of the objects might move.

Smart Guides appear automatically when two or more shapes are in spatial alignment with each other, even if the shapes vary in size. To evenly space multiple objects horizontally or vertically, you **distribute** them. PowerPoint determines the total length between either the outermost edges of the first and last selected object or the edges of the entire slide. It then inserts equal spacing among the items in the series. You also can distribute spacing by using the Size and Position dialog box, but the Distribute command automates this task.

To Display the Drawing Guides

Guides help you align objects on slides. When you point to a guide and then press and hold the mouse button, PowerPoint displays a box containing the exact position of the guide on the slide in inches. An arrow is displayed below the guide position to indicate the vertical guide either left or right of center. An arrow also is displayed to the right of the guide position to indicate the horizontal guide either above or below center. The following step displays the guides.

 1

- With the Home Health presentation displayed, click the View tab, and then click the Guides check box (View tab | Show group) to display the horizontal and vertical guides (Figure 6–32).

Other Ways

1. Right-click area of slide other than a placeholder or object, click Grid and Guides on shortcut menu, click 'Display drawing guides on screen' check box

2. Press ALT+F9

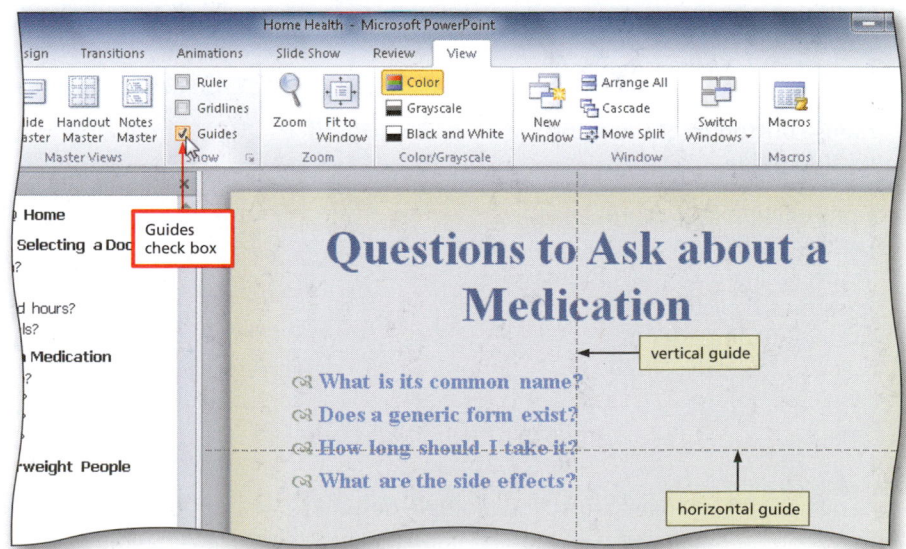

Figure 6–32

To Position a Picture Using Guides

The three pictures on Slides 2, 3, and 4 should be displayed in precisely the same location so they appear static as you transition from one slide to the next during the slide show. In addition, the top border of the three pictures on Slide 1 should align evenly. The following steps position the picture on Slide 3.

- Point to the horizontal guide anywhere except the text.

Q&A Why does 0.00 display when I hold down the mouse button?

The ScreenTip displays the horizontal guide's position. A 0.00 setting means that the guide is precisely in the middle of the slide and is not above or below the center.

- Click and then drag the horizontal guide to 1.50 inches below the center. Do not release the mouse button (Figure 6–33).

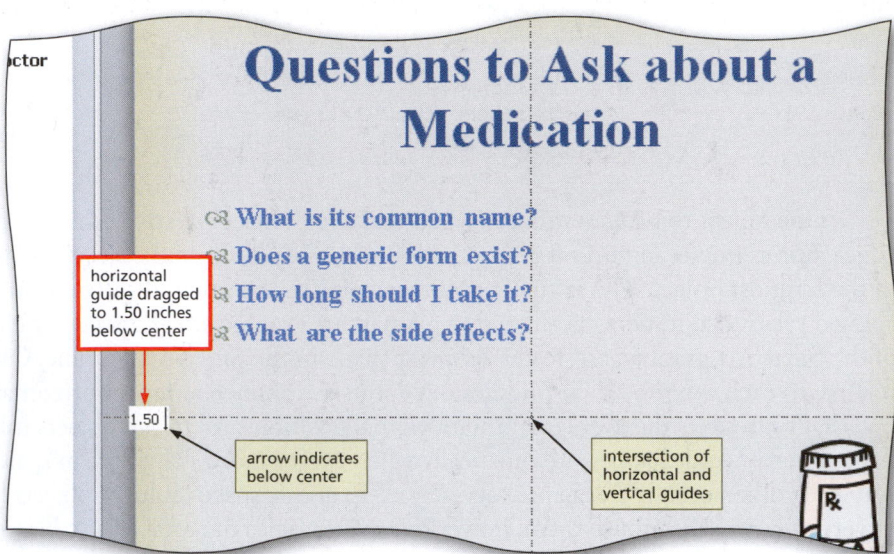

Figure 6–33

- Release the mouse button to position the horizontal guide at 1.50, which is the intended location of the picture's top border.

- Point to the vertical guide anywhere except the text in the content placeholder.

- Click and then drag the vertical guide to 2.50 inches right of the center and then release the mouse button to position the vertical guide.

- Drag the upper-left corner of the picture to the intersection of the vertical and horizontal guides to position the picture in the desired location (Figure 6–34).

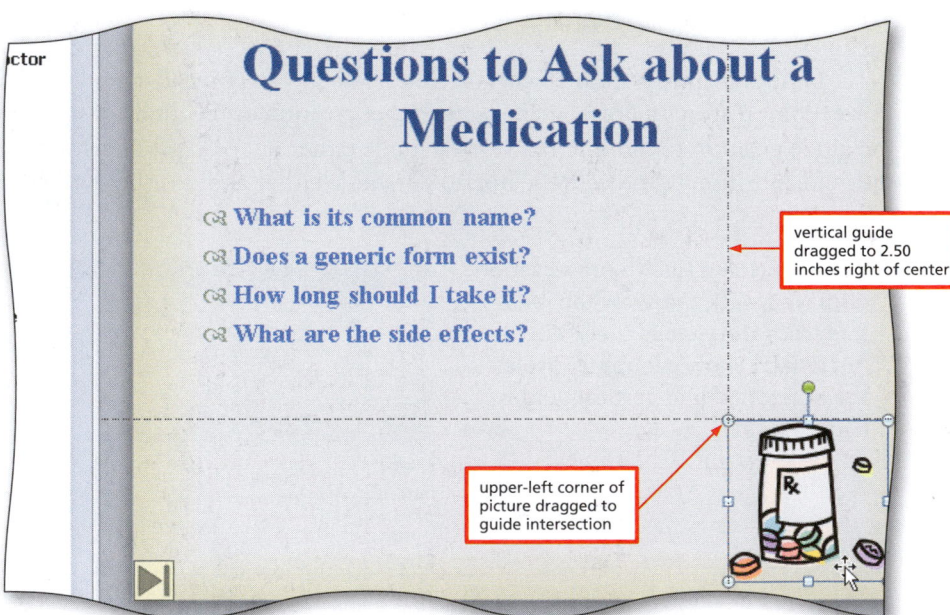

Figure 6–34

Q&A Can I add guides to help me align multiple objects?

Yes. Position the mouse pointer over one guide and then press the CTRL key. When you drag your mouse pointer, a second guide appears.

To Position the Slide 4 and Slide 2 Pictures

The pictures on Slide 4 and Slide 2 should be positioned in the same location as the Slide 3 picture. The guides will display in the same location as you display each slide, so you easily can align similar objects on multiple slides. The following steps position the pictures on Slide 4 and Slide 2.

1 Display Slide 4 and then drag the upper-left corner of the scale picture to the intersection of the guides.

2 Repeat Step 1 to position the stethoscope picture on Slide 2 (Figure 6–35).

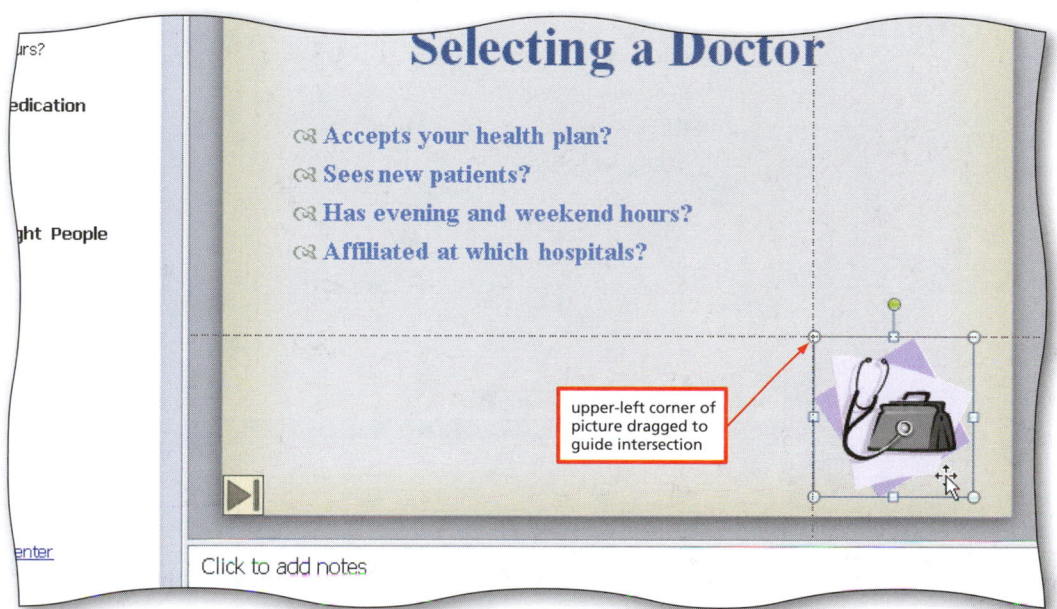

Figure 6–35

To Hide Guides

The three pictures on Slides 2, 3, and 4 are positioned in the desired locations, so the guides no longer are needed. The following step hides the guides.

1 If necessary, display the View tab and then click the Guides check box to remove the check mark.

Other Ways
1. Right-click area of slide other than a placeholder or object, click Grid and Guides on shortcut menu,   click 'Display drawing guides on screen' check box 2. Press ALT+F9

To Display the Rulers

To begin aligning the three Slide 1 objects, you need to position either the left or the right object. The vertical or horizontal **ruler** can help you drag an object to a precise location on the slide. The center of a slide is 0.00 on both the vertical and the horizontal rulers. The following step displays the rulers.

1
- If necessary, display the View tab and then click the Ruler check box (View tab | Show group) to display the vertical and horizontal rulers (Figure 6–36).

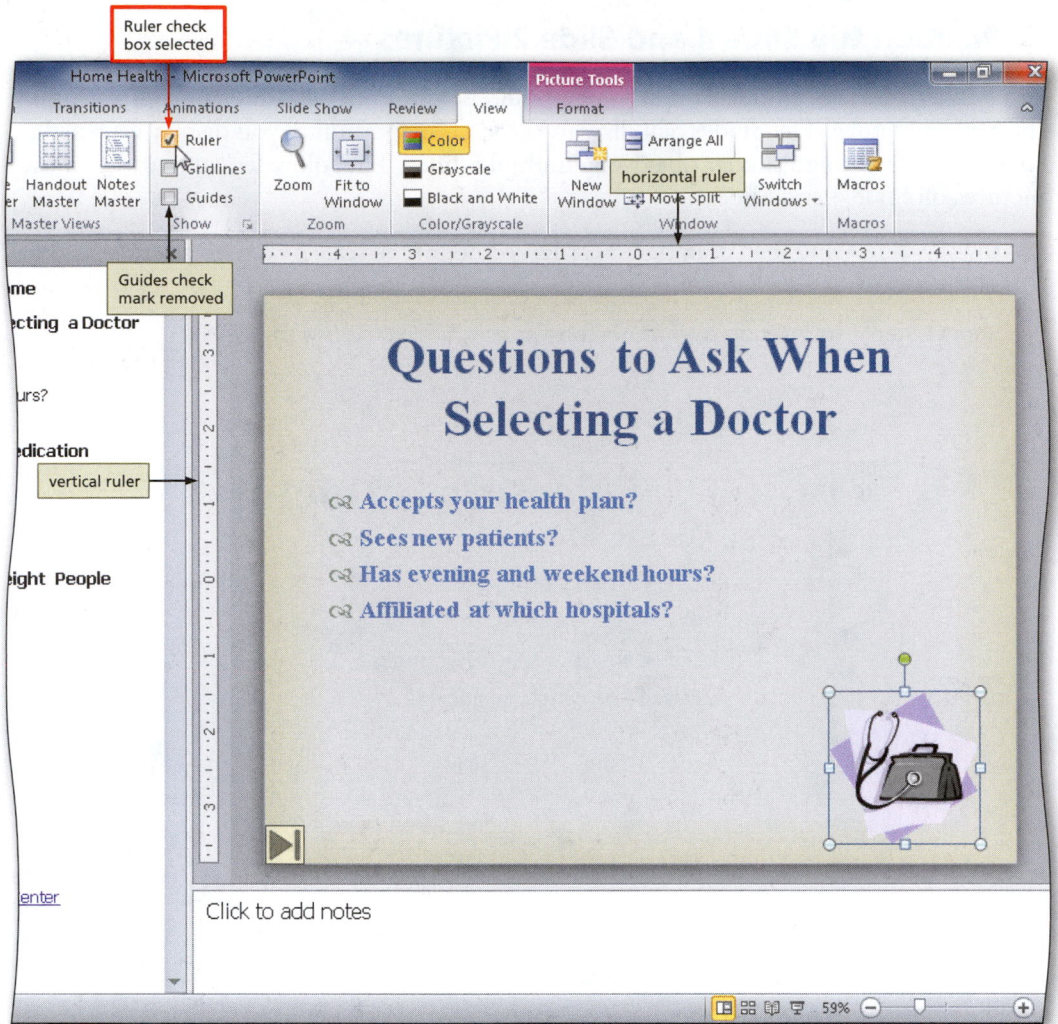

Figure 6–36

<table>
<tr><td>**Other Ways**</td></tr>
<tr><td>1. Right-click area of slide other than a placeholder or object, click Ruler</td></tr>
</table>

To Align Pictures

The three pictures on Slide 1 will look balanced if the bottom edges are aligned. One method of creating this orderly appearance is by dragging the borders to a guide. Another method that is useful when you have multiple objects is to use one of PowerPoint's align commands. On Slide 1, you will position the far left picture of the stethoscope and then align its bottom edge with those of the prescription and scale pictures. The following steps align the Slide 1 pictures.

1

- Display Slide 1 and then position the mouse pointer over the handle of the doctor's bag in the stethoscope picture.

- Drag the picture so that the bag handle is positioned 3 inches left of the center and 2½ inches below the center (Figure 6–37).

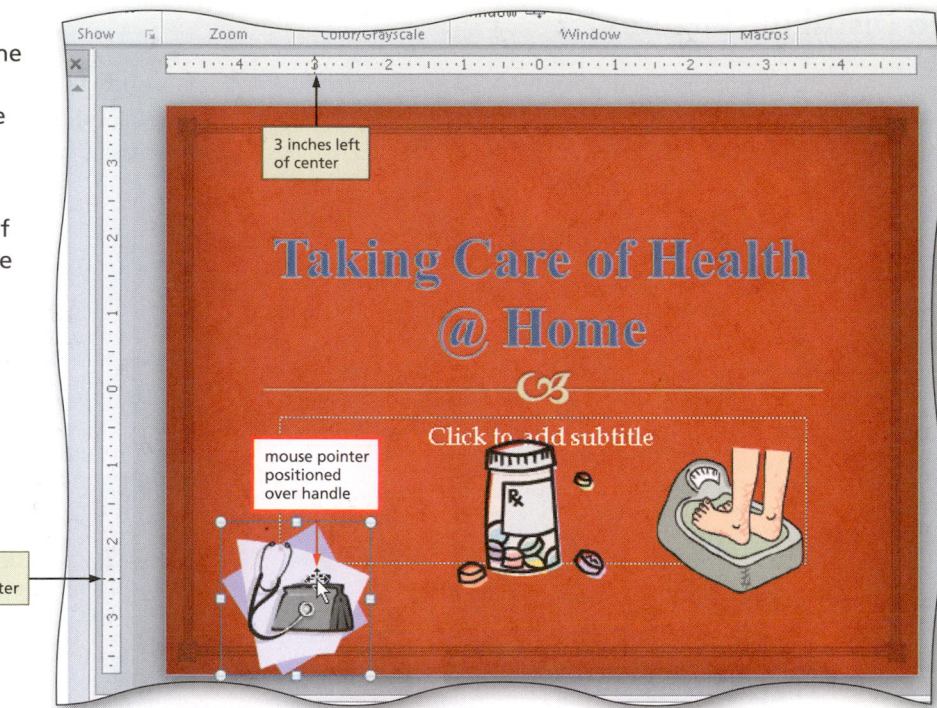

Figure 6–37

2

- Drag the prescription picture toward the bottom of the slide until the Smart Guide appears in the center of the stethoscope and prescription pictures (Figure 6–38).

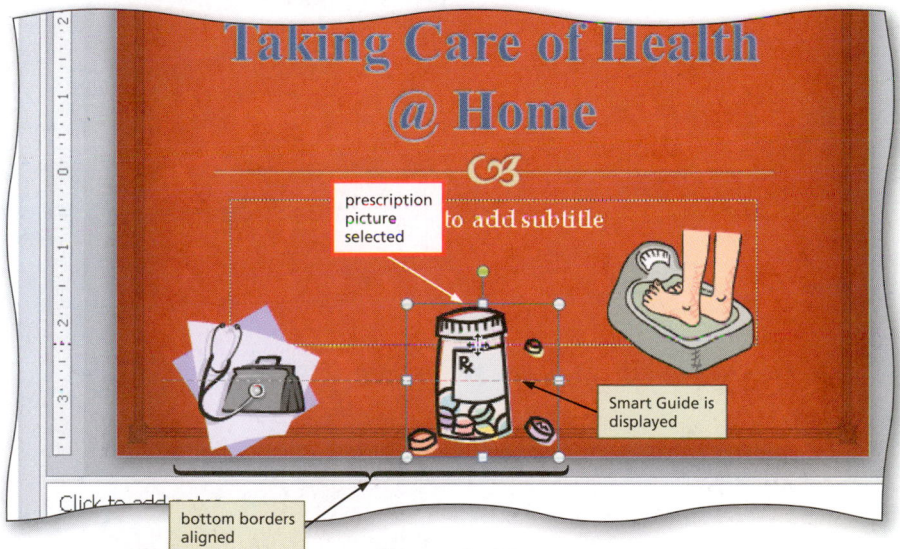

Figure 6–38

3

- Drag the scale picture toward the bottom of the slide until the Smart Guide appears in the center of all three pictures on the slide (Figure 6–39).

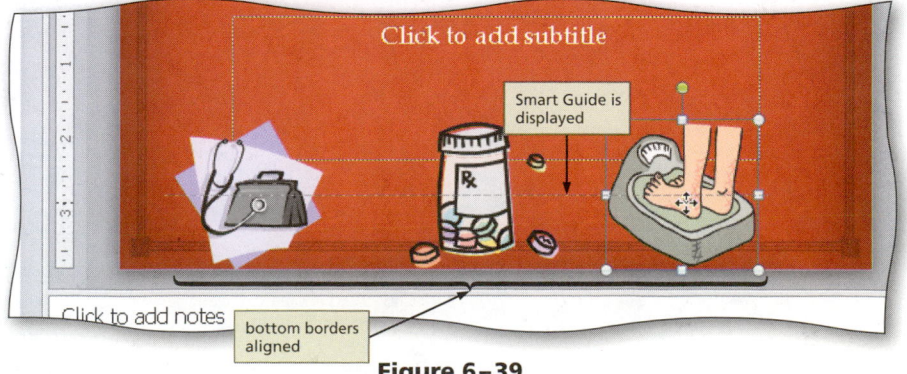

Figure 6–39

To Distribute Pictures

Now that the three Slide 1 pictures are aligned along their bottom edges, you can have PowerPoint place the same amount of space between the first and second pictures and the second and third pictures. You have two distribution options: Align to Slide spaces all the selected objects evenly across the entire width of the slide; Align Selected Objects spaces only the middle objects between the fixed right and left objects. The following steps use the Align to Slide option to horizontally distribute the Slide 1 pictures.

1

- Select the three Slide 1 pictures, display the Picture Tools Format tab, and then click the Align button (Picture Tools Format tab | Arrange group) to display the Align menu.

2

- If necessary, click Align to Slide so that PowerPoint will adjust the spacing of the pictures evenly between the slide edges and then click the Align button to display the Align menu again (Figure 6–40).

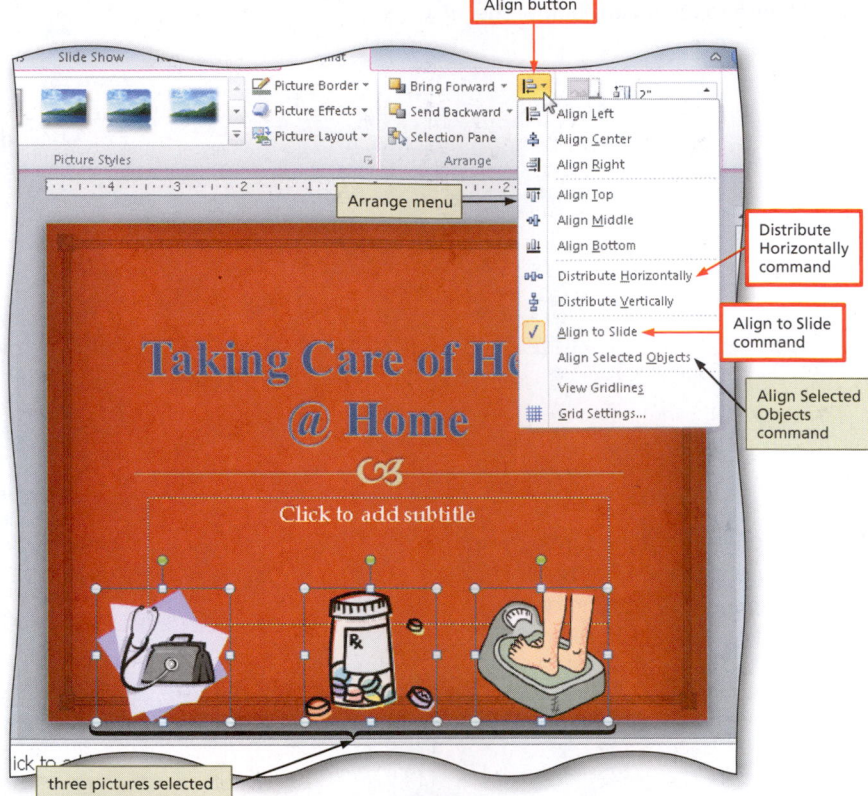

Figure 6–40

3

- Click Distribute Horizontally to adjust the spacing (Figure 6–41).

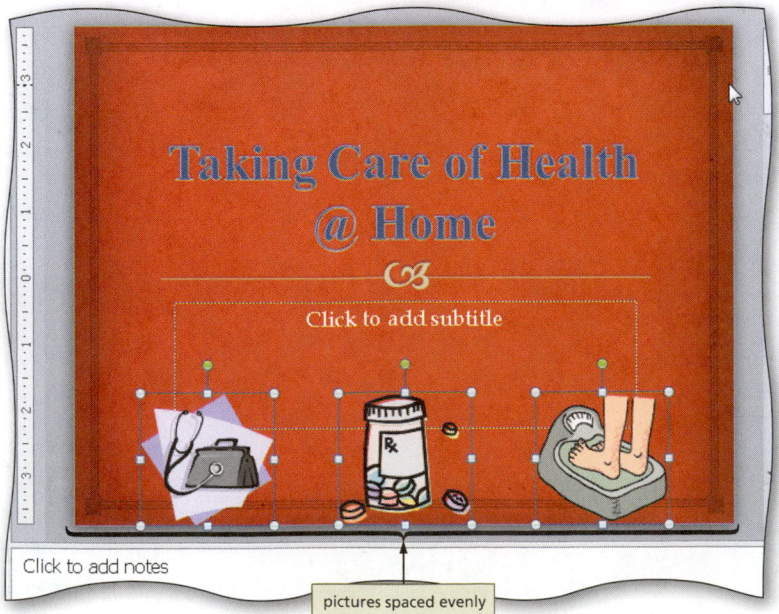

Figure 6–41

To Hide Rulers

The three pictures on Slide 1 are positioned in the desired locations, so the rulers no longer need to display. The following step hides the rulers.

1 Display the View tab and then click the Ruler check box to remove the check mark.

Hiding a Slide

Slides 2, 3, and 4 present a variety of health information with hyperlinks. Depending on the audience's needs and the time constraints, you may decide not to display one or more of these slides. If need be, you can use the **Hide Slide** command to hide a slide from the audience during the normal running of a slide show. When you want to display the hidden slide, press the H key. No visible indicator displays to show that a hidden slide exists. You must be aware of the content of the presentation to know where the supporting slide is located.

When you run your presentation, the hidden slide does not display unless you press the H key when the slide preceding the hidden slide is displaying. For example, Slide 4 does not display unless you press the H key when Slide 3 displays in Slide Show view. You continue your presentation by clicking the mouse or pressing any of the keys associated with running a slide show. You skip the hidden slide by clicking the mouse and advancing to the next slide.

To Hide a Slide

Slide 4 discusses health problems that overweight people face. If time permits, or if the audience requires information on this subject, you can display Slide 4. As the presenter, you decide whether to show Slide 4. You hide a slide in Slide Sorter view so you can see the slashed square surrounding the slide number, which indicates a slide is hidden. The following steps hide Slide 4.

1
- Click the Slide Sorter view button to display the slide thumbnails.

- Click Slide Show on the Ribbon to display the Slide Show tab and then click the Slide 4 thumbnail to select it (Figure 6–42).

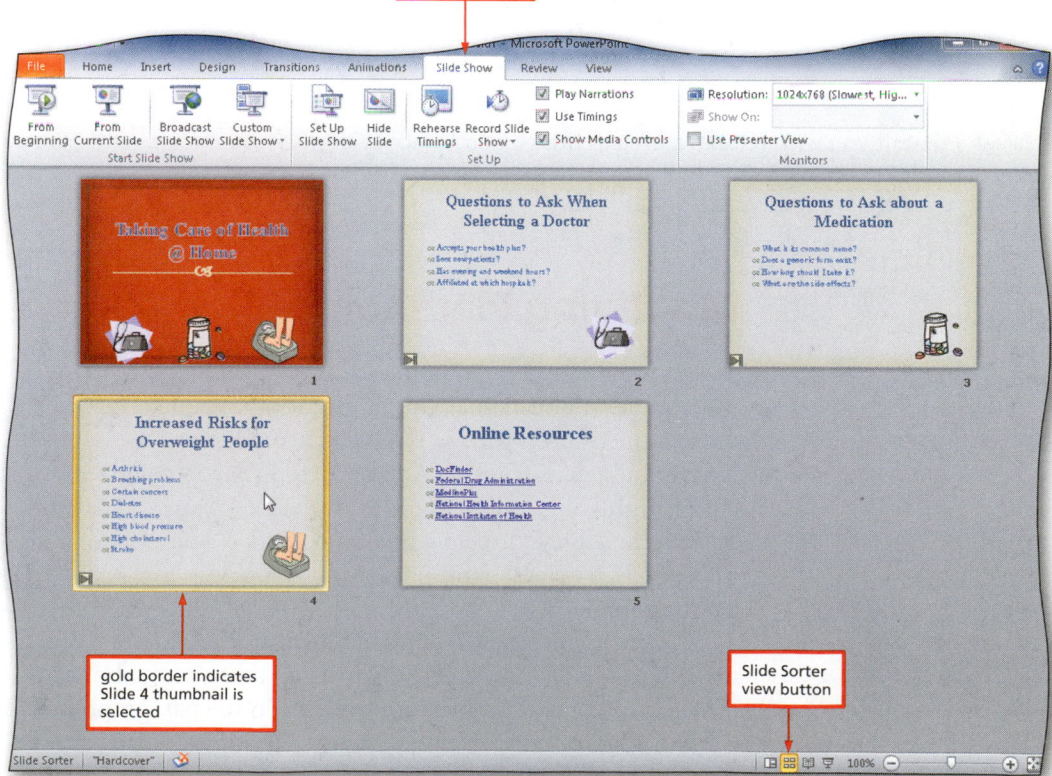

Figure 6–42

2
- Click the Hide Slide button (Slide Show tab | Set Up group) to hide Slide 4 (Figure 6–43).

Q&A How do I know that Slide 4 is hidden?

The rectangle with a slash surrounds the slide number to indicate Slide 4 is a hidden slide.

Q&A What if I decide I no longer want to hide a slide?

Repeat Steps 1 and 2. The Hide Slide button is a toggle; it either hides or displays a slide.

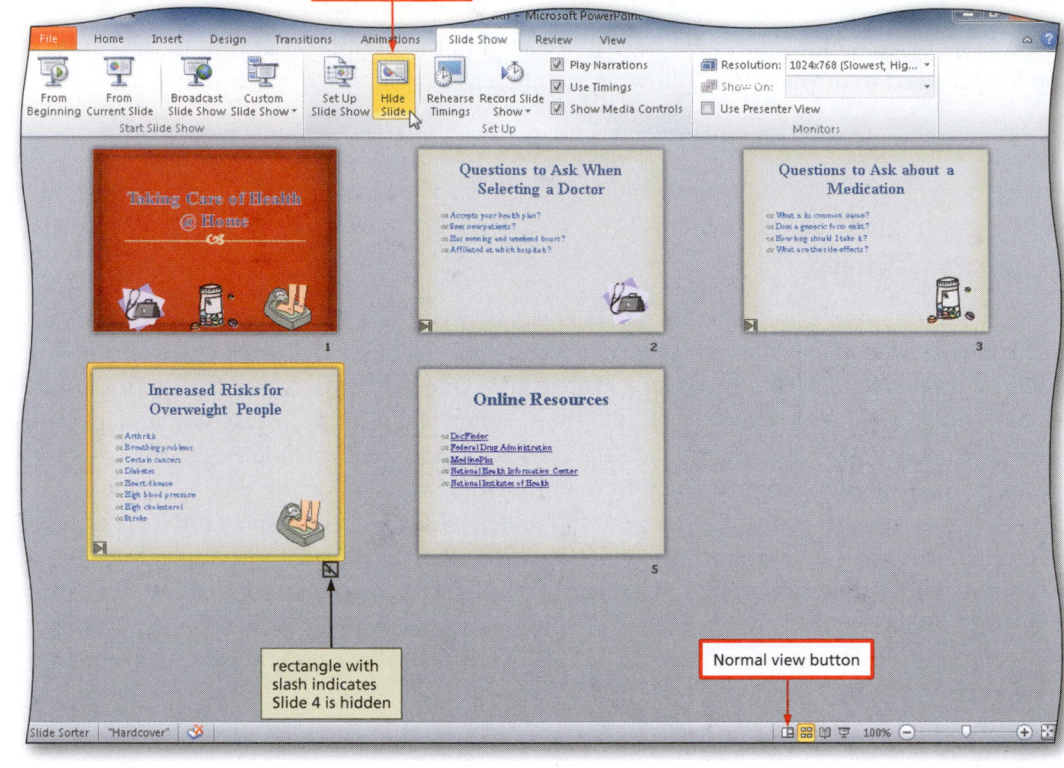

Figure 6–43

3
- Click the Normal view button to display Slide 4.

Other Ways
1. Change view to Slide Sorter, right-click desired slide, click Hide Slide on shortcut menu   2. Right-click slide thumbnail in Slides tab, click Hide Slide on shortcut menu

Break Point: If you wish to take a break, this is a good place to do so. Be sure to save the Home Health file again and then you can quit PowerPoint. To resume at a later time, start PowerPoint, open the file called Home Health, and continue following the steps from this location forward.

Modifying Placeholder Text Settings

The PowerPoint design themes specify default alignment of and spacing for text within a placeholder. For example, the text in most paragraphs is **left-aligned**, so the first character of each line is even with the first character above or below it. Text alignment also can be horizontally **centered** to position each line evenly between the left and right placeholder edges; **right-aligned**, so that the last character of each line is even with the last character of each line above or below it; and **justified**, where the first and last characters of each line are aligned and extra space is inserted between words to spread the characters evenly across the line.

When you begin typing text in most placeholders, the first paragraph is aligned at the top of the placeholder with any extra space at the bottom. You can change this default **paragraph alignment** location to position the paragraph lines centered vertically between the top and bottom placeholder edges, or you can place the last line at the bottom of the placeholder so that any extra space is at the top.

The design theme also determines the amount of spacing around the sides of the placeholder and between the lines of text. An internal **margin** provides a cushion of space between text and the top, bottom, left, and right sides of the placeholder. **Line spacing** is the amount of vertical space between the lines of text in a paragraph, and **paragraph spacing** is the amount of space above and below a paragraph. PowerPoint adjusts the line spacing and paragraph spacing automatically to accommodate various font sizes within the placeholder.

Long lists of items can be divided into several **columns** to fill the placeholder width and maximize the slide space. Once you have created columns, you can adjust the amount of space between the columns to enhance readability.

To Center Placeholder Text

By default, all placeholder text in the Hardcover document theme is left-aligned. For variety, you want the text to be centered, or placed with equal space horizontally between the left and right placeholder edges. The following steps center the text in the content placeholders on Slides 2, 3, 4, and 5.

1
- Display Slide 2 and then select the four paragraphs in the content placeholder (Figure 6–44).

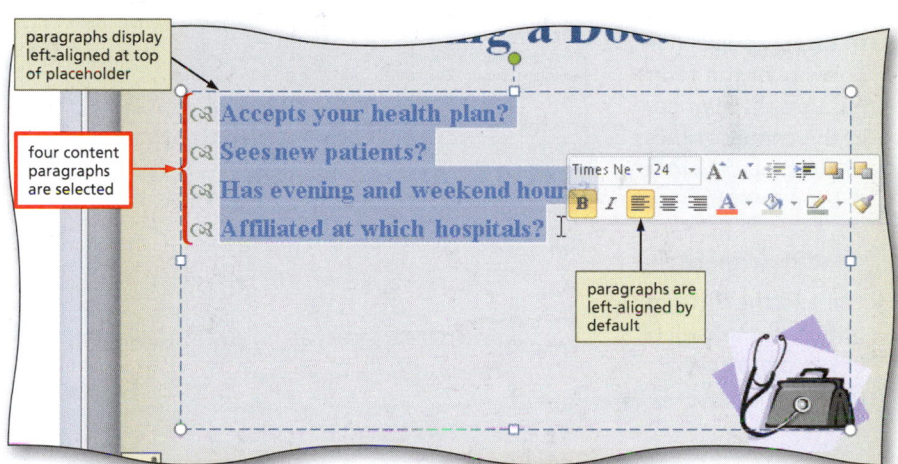

Figure 6–44

2
- Click the Center button on the Mini toolbar to center these paragraphs (Figure 6–45).

3
- Repeat Steps 1 and 2 to center the paragraph text in the content placeholders on Slides 3, 4, and 5.

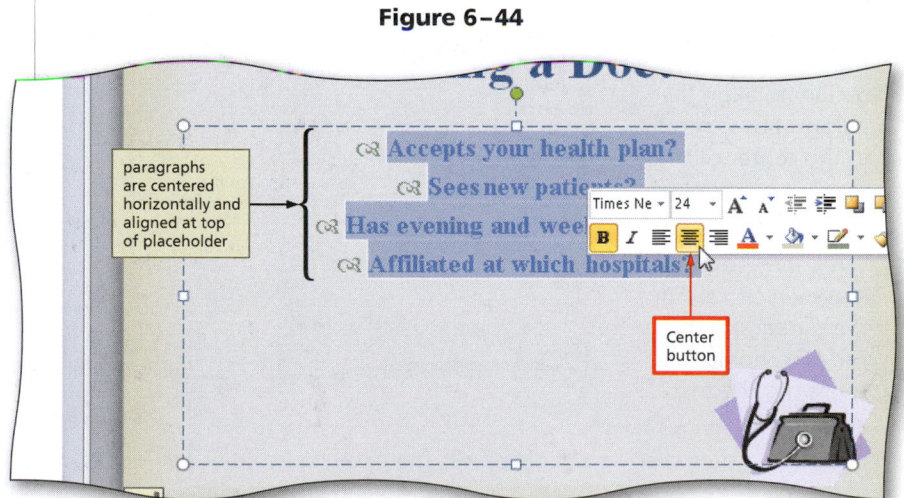

Figure 6–45

Other Ways		
1. Click Center button (Home tab | Font group) 2. Right-click selected text, click Paragraph on shortcut menu, click Alignment box	arrow (Paragraph dialog box), click Centered, click OK button 3. Click Paragraph Dialog Box Launcher (Home tab |	Paragraph group), click Alignment box arrow (Paragraph dialog box), click Centered, click OK button 4. Press CTRL+E

To Align Placeholder Text

The Hardcover document theme aligns the text paragraphs at the top of the content placeholders. This default setting can be changed easily so that the paragraphs either are centered or aligned at the bottom of the placeholder. The following steps align the paragraphs vertically in the center of the content placeholders on Slides 2, 3, 4, and 5.

1

- With the Slide 5 paragraphs still selected, display the Home tab and then click the Align Text button (Home tab | Paragraph group) to display the Align Text gallery.

- Point to Middle in the Align Text gallery to display a live preview of the four paragraphs aligned in the center of the content placeholder (Figure 6–46).

 **Experiment**

- Point to the Bottom option in the gallery to see a preview of that alignment.

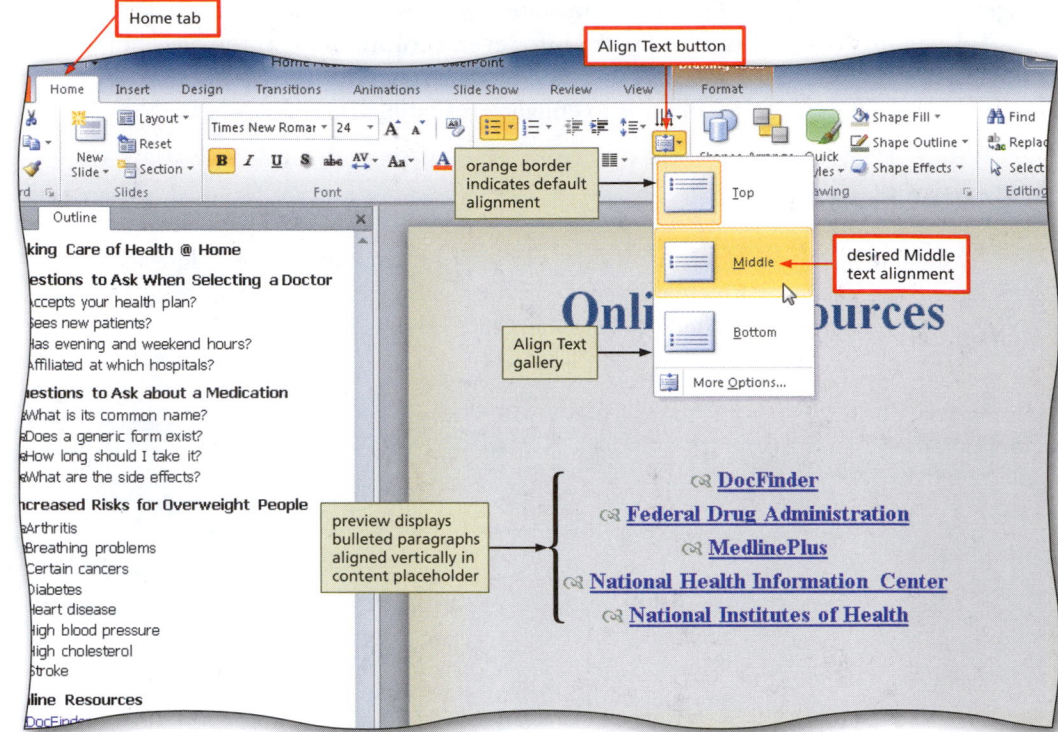

Figure 6–46

2

- Click Middle in the Align Text gallery to align the paragraphs vertically in the center of the content placeholder (Figure 6–47).

 What is the difference between centering the paragraphs in the placeholder and centering the text?

Clicking the Align Text button and then clicking Middle moves the paragraphs up or down so that the first and last paragraphs are equal distances from the top and bottom placeholder borders. The Center button, on the other hand, moves the paragraphs left or right so that the first and last words in each line are equal distances from the left and right text box borders.

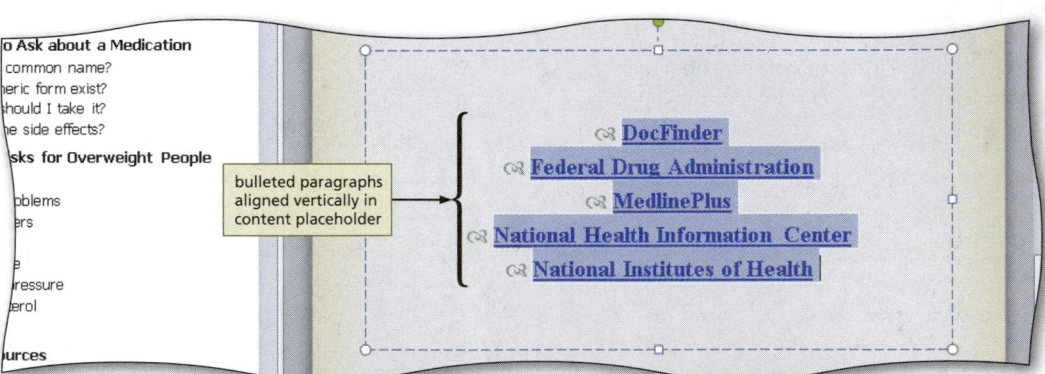

Figure 6–47

3

- Repeat Steps 1 and 2 to center the paragraph text in the middle of the content placeholders on Slides 2, 3, and 4.

To Change Paragraph Line Spacing

The vertical space between paragraphs is called **line spacing**. PowerPoint adjusts the amount of space based on font size. Default line spacing is 1.0, which is considered single spacing. Other preset options are 1.5, 2.0 (double spacing), 2.5, and 3.0 (triple spacing). You can specify precise line spacing intervals between, before, and after paragraphs in the Indents and Spacing tab of the Paragraph dialog box. The following steps increase the line spacing of the content paragraphs from single (1.0) to double (2.0) on Slides 2, 3, and 5.

1

- With the Home tab displayed, display Slide 2 and select the four content paragraphs.

- Click the Line Spacing button (Home tab | Paragraph group) to display the Line Spacing gallery.

- Point to 2.0 in the Line Spacing gallery to display a live preview of this line spacing (Figure 6–48).

🔍 **Experiment**

- Point to each of the line spacing options in the gallery to see a preview of that paragraph spacing.

2

- Click 2.0 in the Line Spacing gallery to change the paragraph line spacing to double.

3

- Repeat Steps 1 and 2 to change the line spacing for the paragraph text in the content placeholders on Slides 3 and 5. Do not change the line spacing on Slide 4.

Q&A Why is the line spacing not changing on Slide 4?

The content placeholder paragraphs will be changed into columns, so spacing is not a design concern at this time.

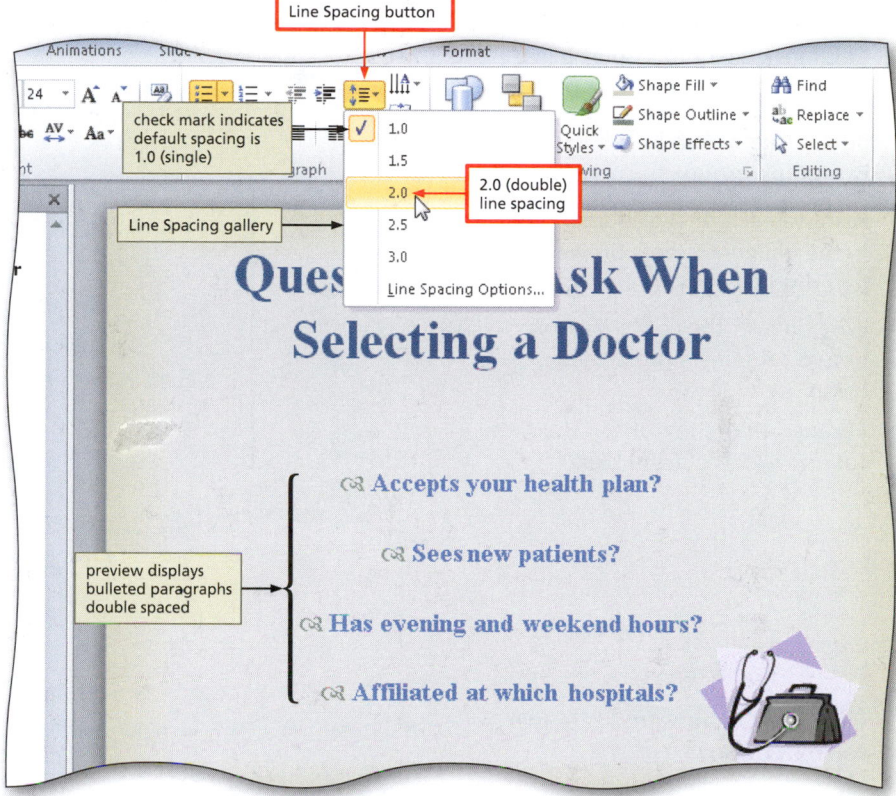

Figure 6–48

Other Ways

1. Right-click selected text, click Paragraph on shortcut menu, click Line Spacing box arrow (Paragraph dialog box), click Double, click OK button

2. Click Paragraph Dialog Box Launcher (Home tab | Paragraph group), click Line Spacing box arrow (Paragraph dialog box), click Double, click OK button

To Create Columns in a Placeholder

The list of health risks in the Slide 4 placeholder is lengthy and lacks visual appeal. You can change these items into two, three, or more columns and then adjust the column widths. The following steps change the placeholder elements into columns.

1

- Display Slide 4 and then click the content placeholder to select it.

- With the Home tab displayed, click the Columns button (Home tab | Paragraph group) to display the Columns gallery.

- Point to Two Columns in the Columns gallery to display a live preview of the text in the first column (Figure 6–49).

 Experiment

- Point to each of the column options in the gallery to see a preview of the text displaying in various columns.

Q&A Why doesn't the content display in two columns if I selected two columns?

Because all the text fits in the first column in the placeholder.

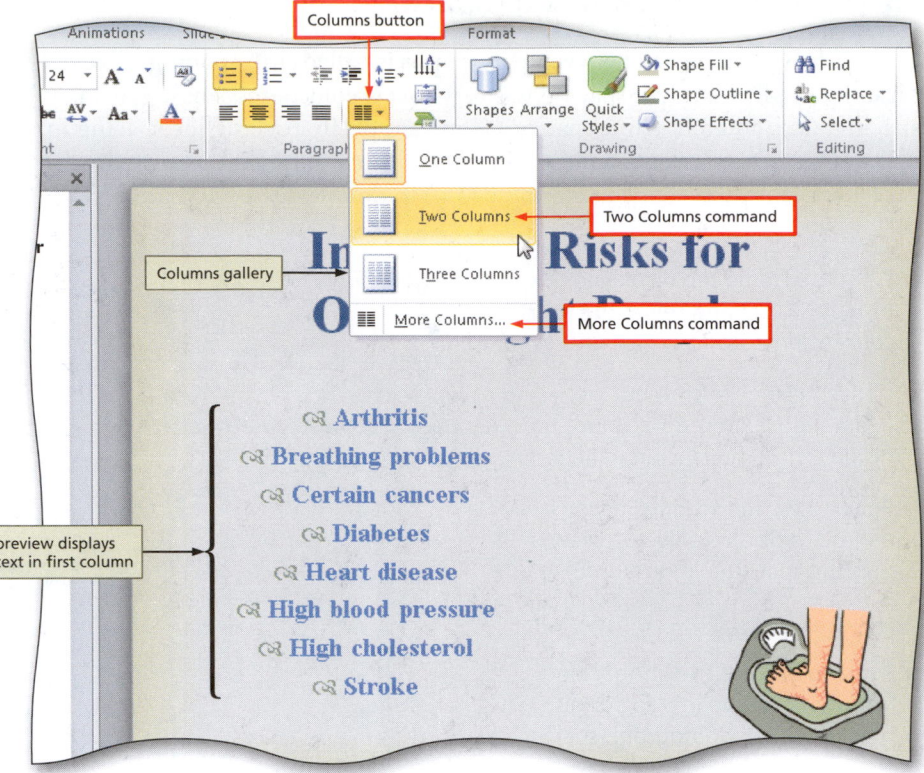

Figure 6–49

2

- Click Two Columns to create two columns of text.

- Drag the bottom sizing handle up to the location shown in Figure 6–50.

Q&A Why is the bottom sizing handle between the Diabetes and Heart Disease paragraphs?

Eight risks are listed in the content placeholder, so dividing the paragraphs in two groups of four will balance the layout.

3

- Release the mouse button to resize the content placeholder and create the two columns of text.

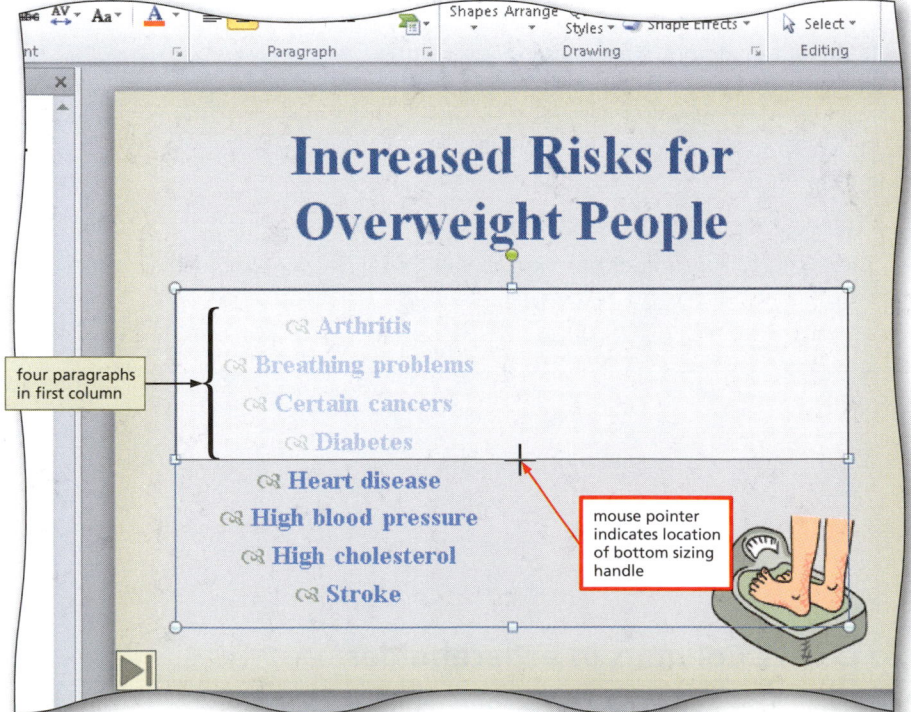

Figure 6–50

To Adjust Column Spacing

The space between the columns in the placeholder can be increased to make room for the scale picture in the lower-right corner. The following steps increase the spacing between the columns.

1
- With the placeholder selected, click the Columns button and then click More Columns.
- Click the Spacing box up arrow (Columns dialog box) until 1.5" is displayed (Figure 6–51).

Q&A Can I type a number in the text box instead of clicking the up arrow?

Yes. Double-click the text box and then type the desired measurement expressed in inches.

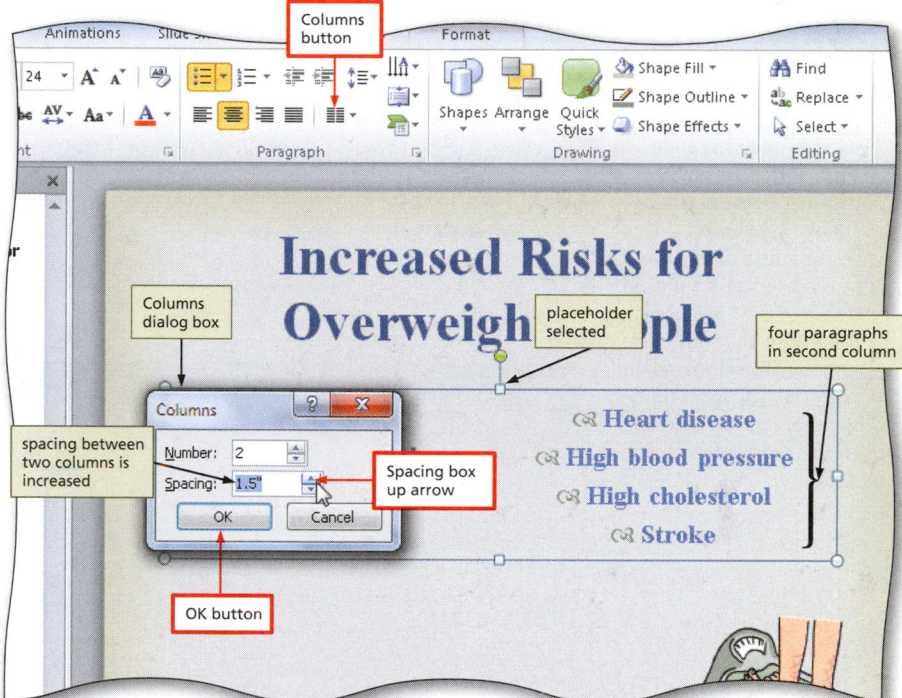

Figure 6–51

2
- Click the OK button to increase the spacing between the columns (Figure 6–52).

Q&A Can I change the paragraphs back to one column easily?

Yes. Click the Columns button and then click One Column.

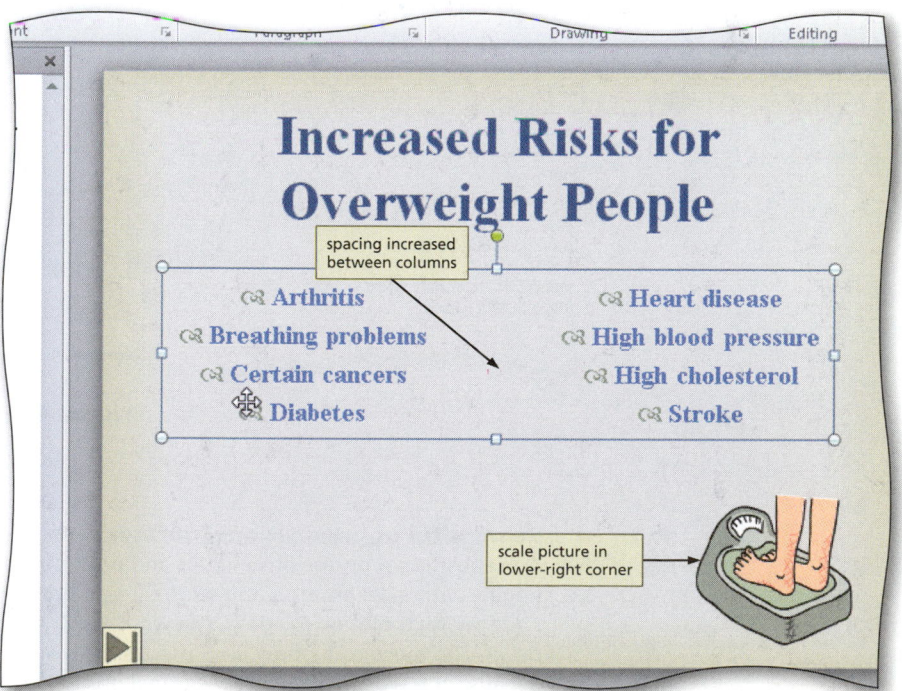

Figure 6–52

BTW

Displaying Slides
Slide 4 in this presentation has important information about potential health problems related to obesity. Your audience needs time to read and contemplate the risks listed in the content placeholder, so you must display the slide for a sufficient amount of time. Some public speaking experts recommend each slide in a presentation should display for at least one minute so that audience members can look at the material, focus on the speaker, and then refer to the slide again.

To Format the Content Placeholder

To add interest to the Slide 4 content placeholder, apply a Quick Style and then move the scale picture from the lower-right corner to the space between the columns. The following steps apply a green Subtle Effect style to the placeholder and then change the picture location.

1 With the placeholder selected, click the Quick Styles button (Home tab | Drawing group) to display the Quick Styles gallery.

2 Click Subtle Effect – Gray-50%, Accent 1 (second style in fourth row).

3 Move the scale clip from the lower-right corner to the area between the two columns (Figure 6–53).

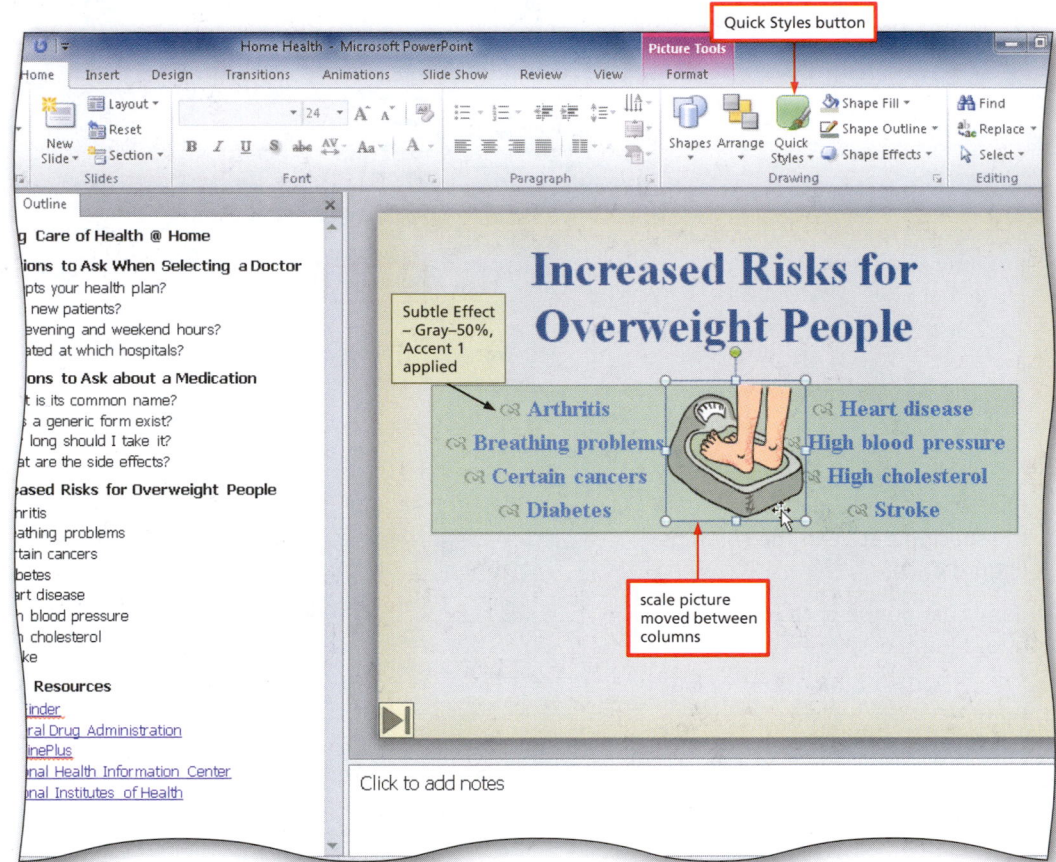

Figure 6–53

Plan Ahead

Be mindful of prepositional phrases.
A prepositional phrase links nouns and pronouns to the rest of a sentence. The phrase begins with a preposition and ends with a noun or pronoun. For example, in the sentence, I left my textbook on my desk, the word "on" is a preposition and the word "desk" is a noun. The more commonly used prepositions are at, by, for, from, in, of, on, to, and with. Because the words in the prepositional phrase work together as a unit, PowerPoint audience members often find it awkward when the entire prepositional phrase does not appear together in one line on the slide. It therefore is best to reword slide text or split multiple paragraph lines so that the prepositional phrase stays intact.

To Enter a Line Break

Slides 3 and 4 in your presentation have prepositional phrases in the title text placeholders. On Slide 3, the words, about a Medication, and on Slide 4 the words, for Overweight People, start on the first line and then continue to the second line. This break in the middle of the phrase can be disconcerting to your viewers who interpret each line as a separate thought. It is advisable to display all words in a prepositional phrase together on one line. If you press the ENTER key at the end of a line, PowerPoint automatically applies paragraph formatting, which could include indents and bullets. To prevent this formatting from occurring, you can press SHIFT+ENTER to place a **line break** at the end of the line, which moves the insertion point to the beginning of the next line. The following steps place a line break at the beginning of the prepositional phrases on Slide 3 and Slide 4.

- Display Slide 3 and then place the insertion point before the word, about (Figure 6–54).

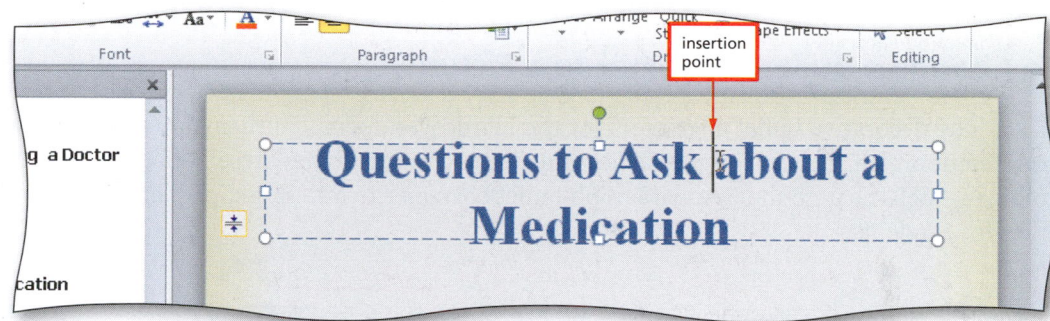

Figure 6–54

- Press SHIFT+ENTER to insert a line break character and move the word, about, to the second line in the placeholder.

- Display Slide 4, place the insertion point before the word, for, and then press SHIFT+ENTER to insert a line break character and move the word, for, to the second line (Figure 6–55).

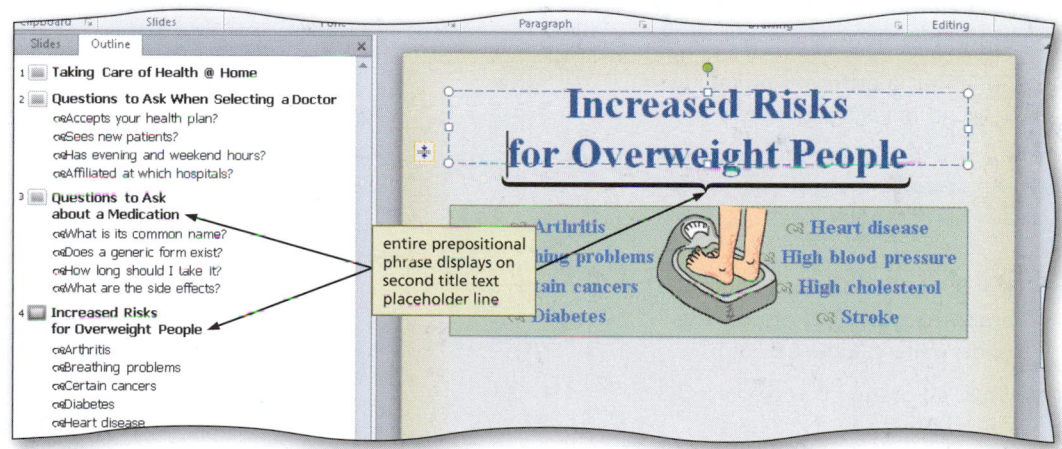

Figure 6–55

Modifying Bullets

PowerPoint allows you to change the default appearance of bullets in a slide show. The document themes determine the bullet character. A **bullet character** is a symbol, traditionally a closed circle, that sets off items in a list. It can be a predefined style, a variety of fonts and characters displayed in the Symbol gallery, or a picture from a file or the Clip Organizer. You may want to change a character to add visual interest and variety. Once you change the bullet character, you also can change its size and color.

If desired, you can change every bullet in a presentation to a unique character. If your presentation has many bulleted slides, however, you would want to have a consistent look on all slides by making the bullets a similar color and size.

To customize your presentation, you can change the default slide layout bullets to numbers by changing the bulleted list to a numbered list. PowerPoint provides a variety of numbering options, including Arabic and Roman numerals. These numbers can be sized and recolored, and the starting number can be something other than 1 or I. In addition, PowerPoint's numbering options include upper- and lowercase letters.

To Change a Bullet Character to a Picture

The decorative bullet characters for the Hardcover document theme do not fit the serious nature of a presentation with the topic of medicine. One method of modifying these bullets is to use a relevant picture. The following steps change the first paragraph bullet character to a stethoscope picture, which is located on the Data Files for Students.

- With the Home tab still displaying and your USB flash drive connected to one of the computer's USB ports, display Slide 2 and then select all four content placeholder paragraphs.

Q&A Can I insert a different bullet character in each paragraph?

Yes. Select only a paragraph and then perform the steps below for each paragraph:

- Click the Bullets arrow (Home tab | Paragraph group) to display the Bullets gallery (Figure 6–56).

Q&A Why is an orange box displayed around the three characters?

They are the default first-level bullet characters for the Hardcover document theme.

Experiment

- Point to each of the bullets displayed in the gallery to see a preview of the characters.

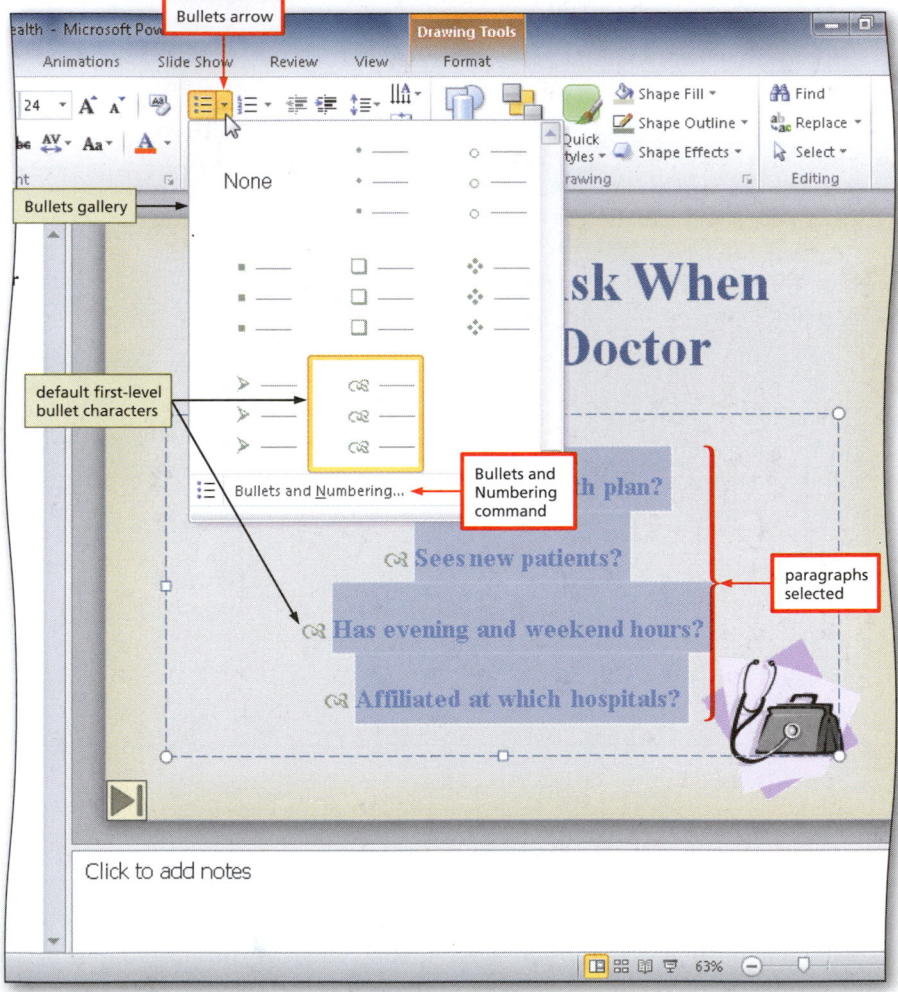

Figure 6–56

2

- Click Bullets and Numbering to display the Bullets and Numbering dialog box (Figure 6–57).

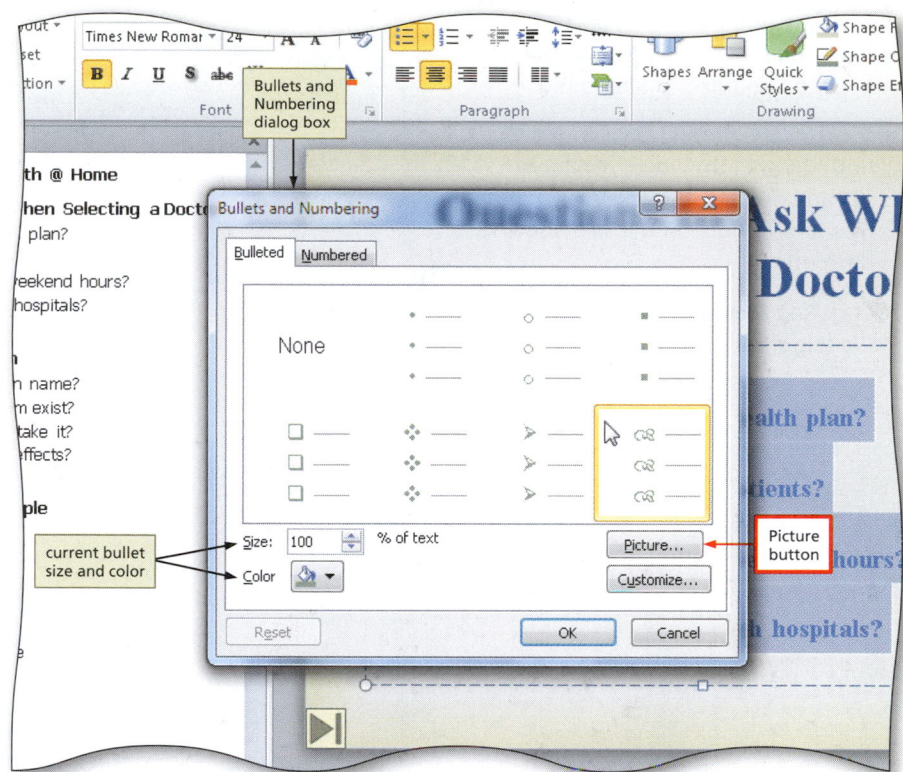

Figure 6–57

3

- Click the Picture button (Bullets and Numbering dialog box) to display the Picture Bullet dialog box (Figure 6–58).

Q&A

Why are my bullets different from those displayed in Figure 6–58?

The bullets most recently inserted are displayed as the first items in the dialog box.

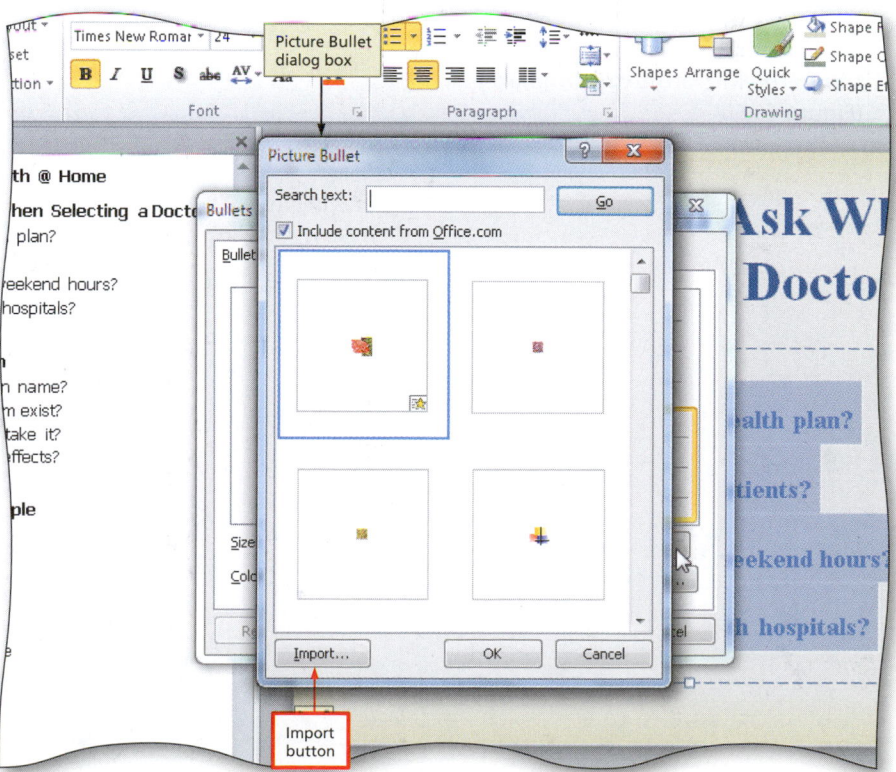

Figure 6–58

4

- Click the Import button (Picture Bullet dialog box) to display the Add Clips to Organizer dialog box.

- If necessary, double-click your USB flash drive in the list of available storage devices to display a list of files and folders on the selected USB flash drive.

- Click Red Stethoscope to select the file (Figure 6–59).

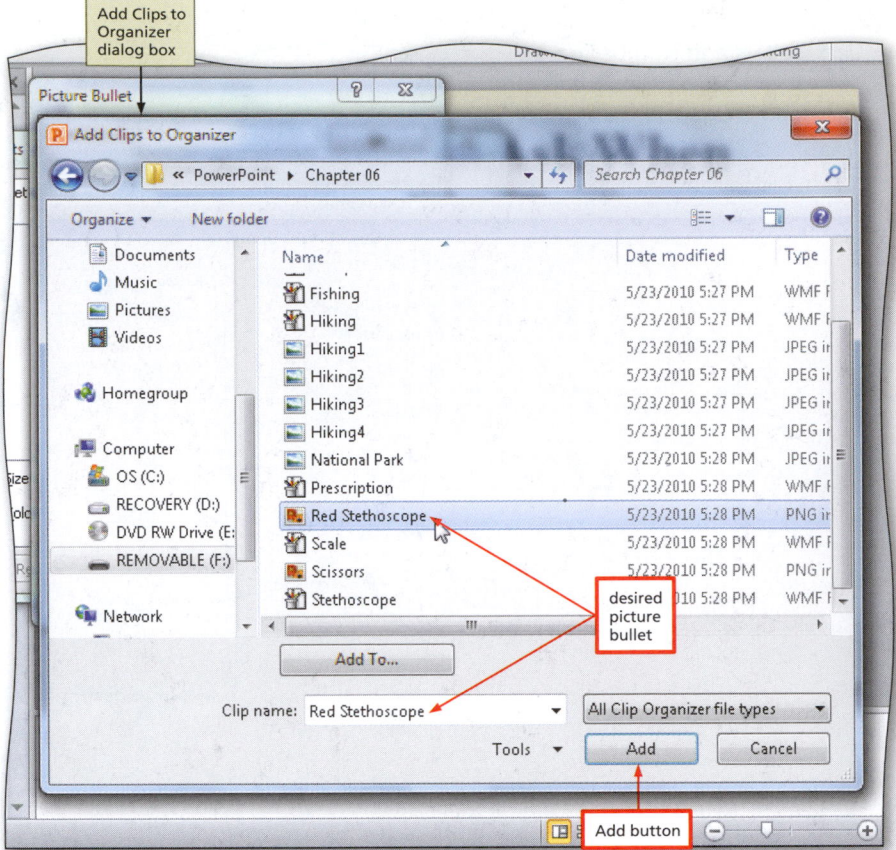

Figure 6–59

5

- Click the Add button (Add Clips to Organizer dialog box) to import the clip to the Microsoft Clip Organizer (Figure 6–60).

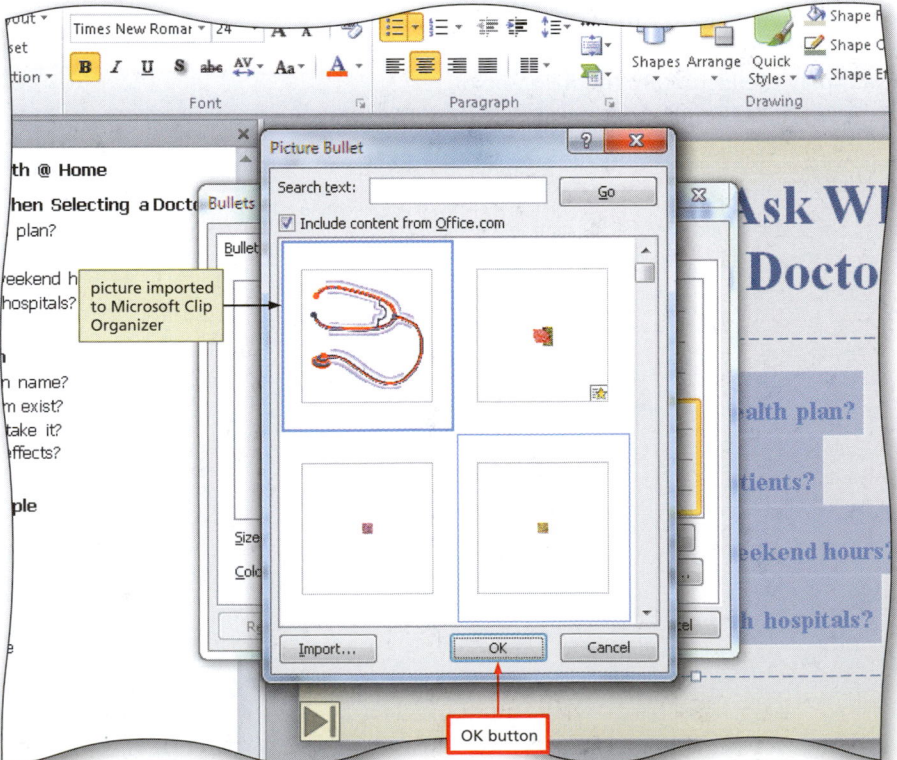

Figure 6–60

- Click the OK button (Picture Bullet dialog box) to insert the Red Stethoscope picture as the paragraph bullet character (Figure 6–61).

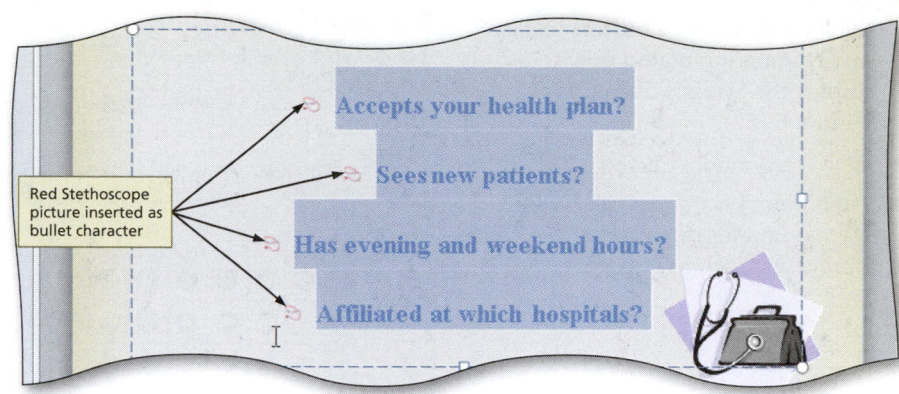

Figure 6–61

Other Ways

1. Right-click paragraph, point to Bullets on shortcut menu, click Bullets and Numbering

To Change a Bullet Character to a Symbol

Picture bullets add a unique quality to your presentations. Another bullet change you can make is to insert a symbol as the character. Symbols are found in several fonts, including Webdings, Wingdings, Wingdings 2, and Wingdings 3. The following steps change the bullet character on Slide 5 to a computer mouse symbol in the Wingdings font.

- Display Slide 5, select all five hyperlinked paragraphs, click the Bullets arrow, and then click Bullets and Numbering to display the Bullets and Numbering dialog box (Figure 6–62).

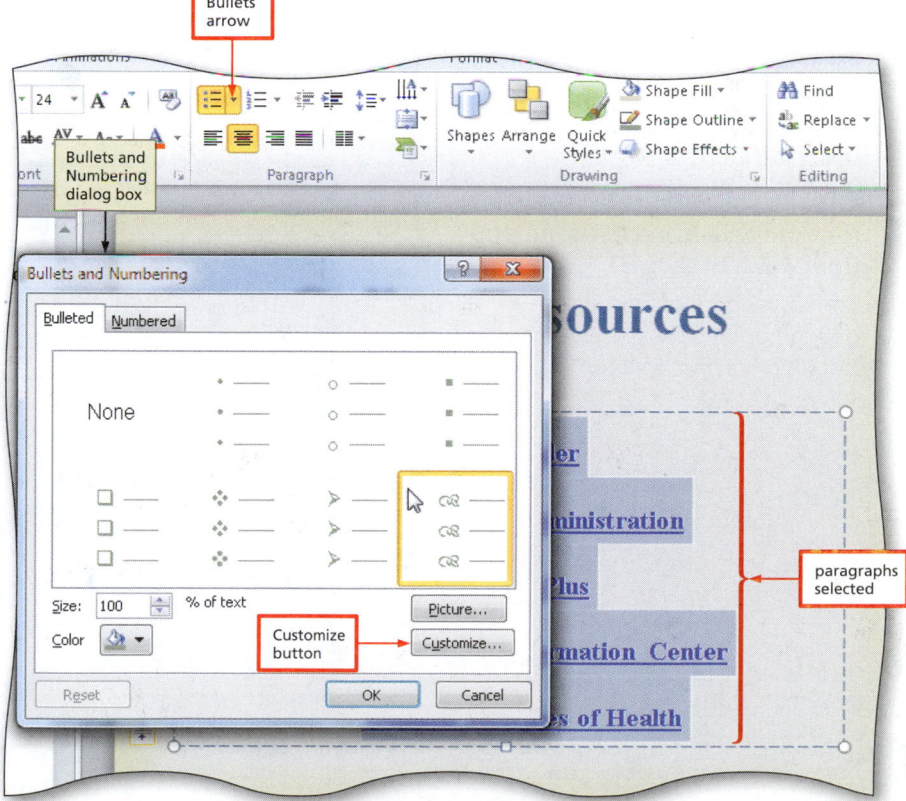

Figure 6–62

2

• Click the Customize button (Bullets and Numbering dialog box) to display the Symbol dialog box (Figure 6–63).

Q&A

Why is a symbol selected?

That symbol is the default bullet for the first-level paragraphs in the Hardcover document theme.

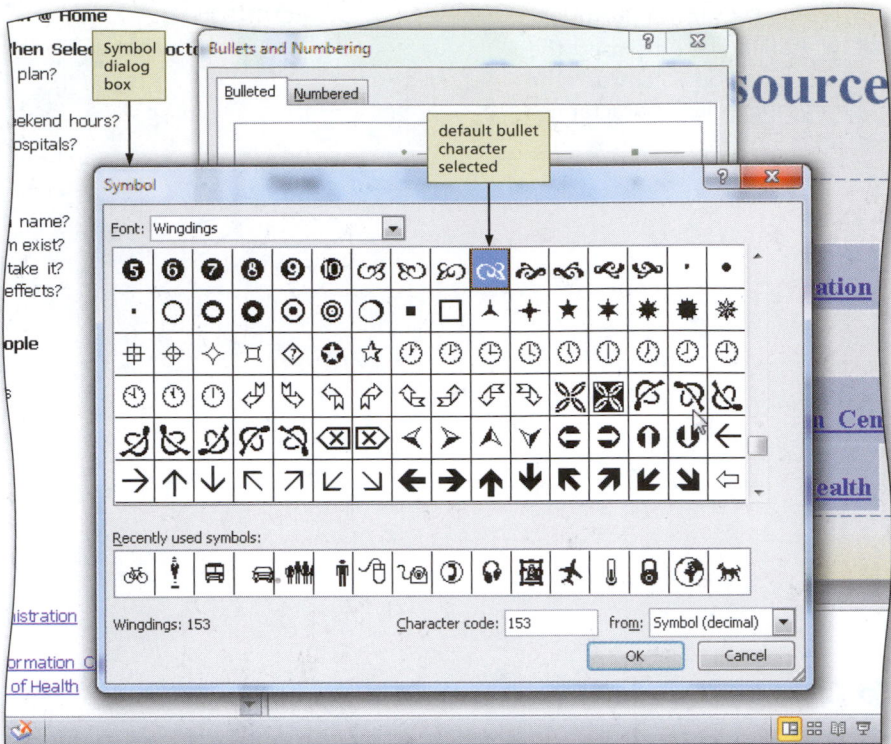

Figure 6–63

3

• Scroll up to locate the computer mouse symbol.

• Click the computer mouse symbol to select it (Figure 6–64).

Q&A

Why does my dialog box have more rows of symbols and different fonts from which to choose?

The rows and fonts displayed depend upon how PowerPoint was installed on your system.

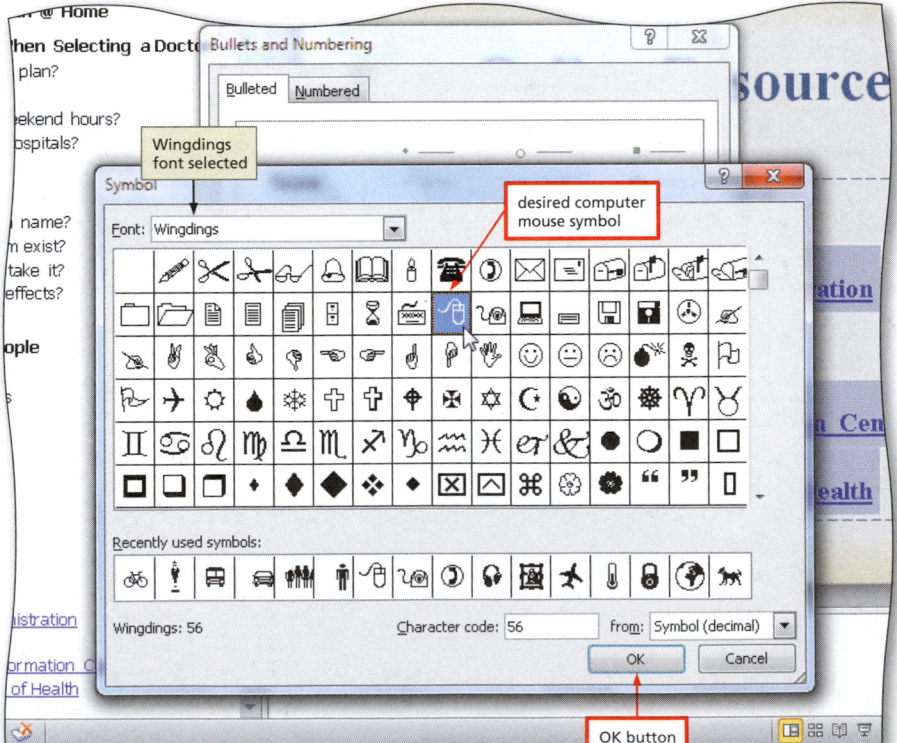

Figure 6–64

4

- Click the OK button (Symbol dialog box) to display the computer mouse bullet in the Bullets and Numbering dialog box (Figure 6–65).

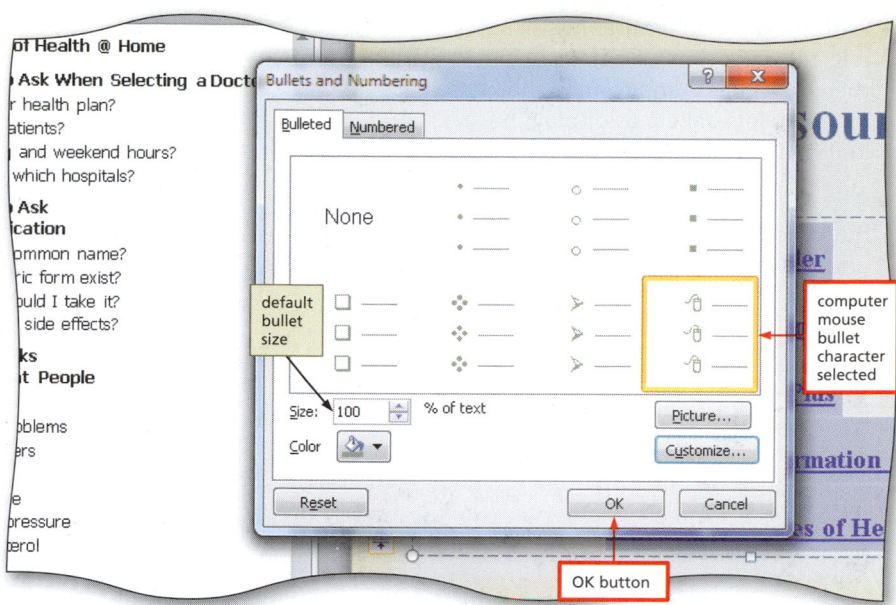

Figure 6–65

5

- Click the OK button (Bullets and Numbering dialog box) to insert the computer mouse symbol as the paragraph bullet (Figure 6–66).

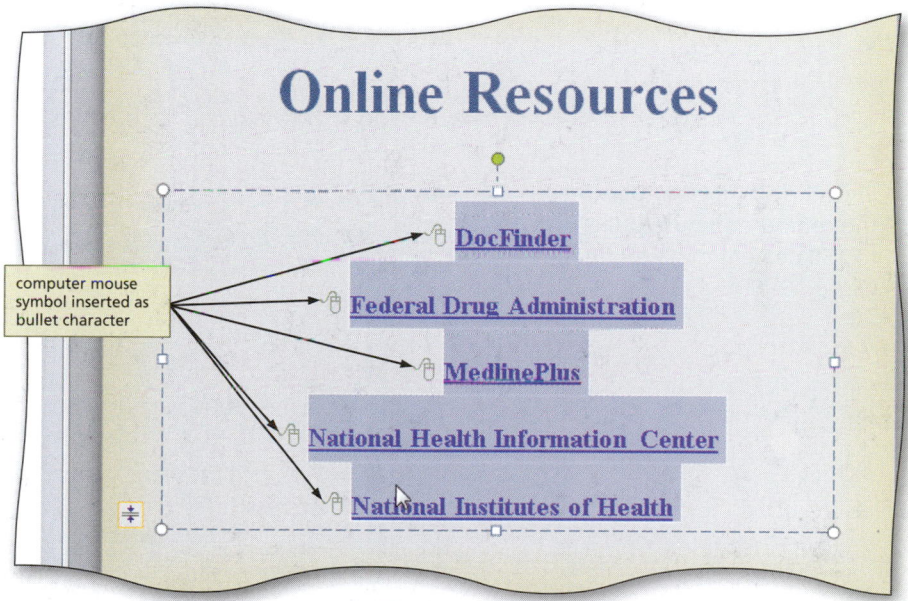

Figure 6–66

To Format a Bullet Size

Bullets have a default size determined by the document theme. **Bullet size** is measured as a percentage of the text size and can range from 25 to 400 percent. The following steps change the computer mouse character size.

1

- With the Slide 5 paragraphs still selected, click the Bullets arrow and then click Bullets and Numbering in the Bullets gallery to display the Bullets and Numbering dialog box.

- Click and hold down the mouse button on the Size box up arrow until 150 is displayed (Figure 6–67).

Q&A

Can I type a number in the text box instead of clicking the up arrow?

Yes. Double-click the text box and then type the desired percentage.

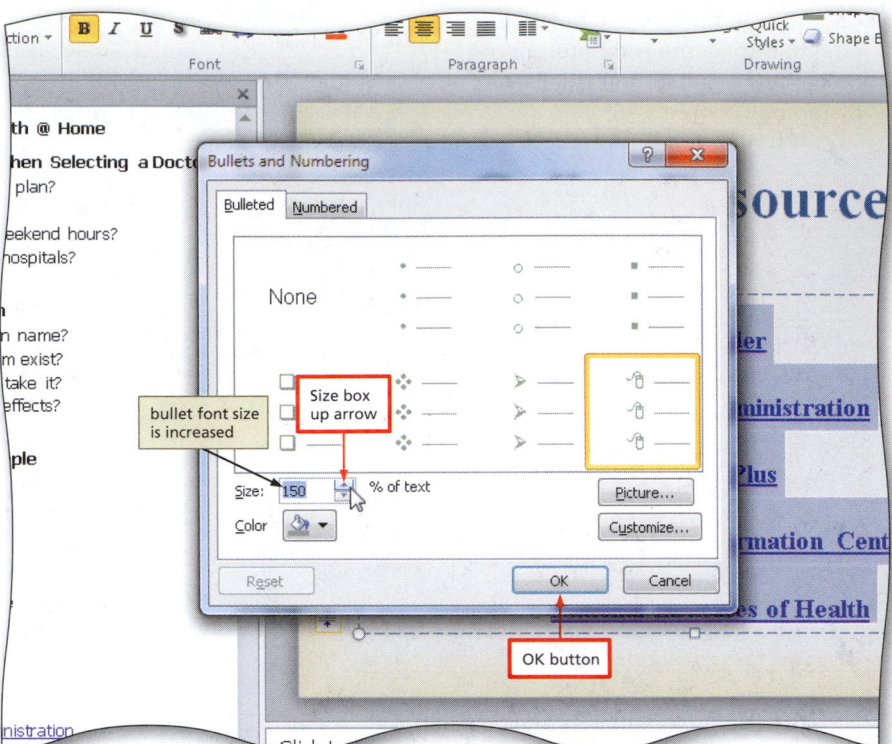

Figure 6–67

2

- Click the OK button to increase the computer mouse bullet size to 150 percent of its original size (Figure 6–68).

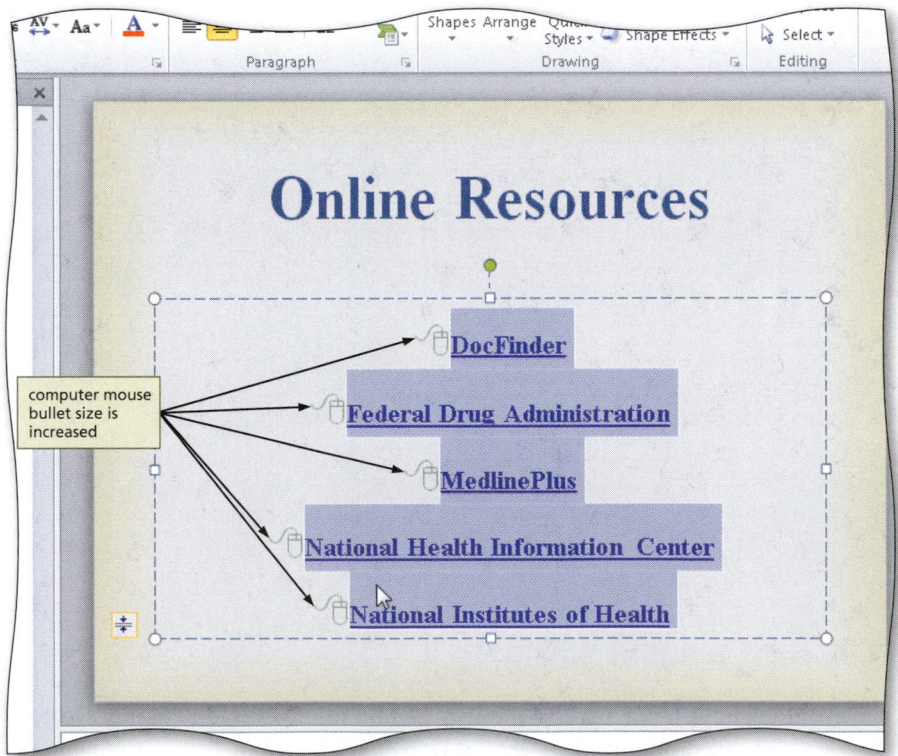

Figure 6–68

To Change the Size of Other Bullet Characters

For consistency, the bullet character on Slide 2 should have a similar size as that on Slide 5. The following steps change the size of the Red Stethoscope bullets.

1 Display Slide 2 and then select the four paragraphs in the content placeholder.

2 Display the Bullets and Numbering dialog box, increase the bullet size to 160% of text, and then click the OK button (Figure 6–69).

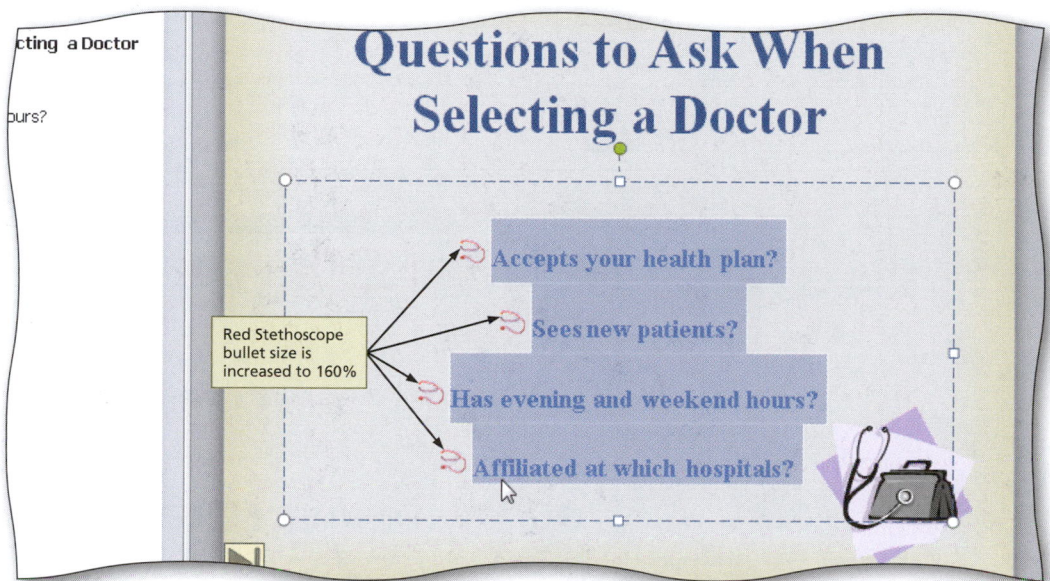

Figure 6–69

To Format a Bullet Color

A default **bullet color** is based on the eight colors in the design theme. Additional standard and custom colors also are available. The following steps change the computer mouse bullet color to Red.

- Display Slide 5, select the five hyperlinked paragraphs, display the Bullets and Numbering dialog box, and then click the Color button to display the Color gallery (Figure 6–70).

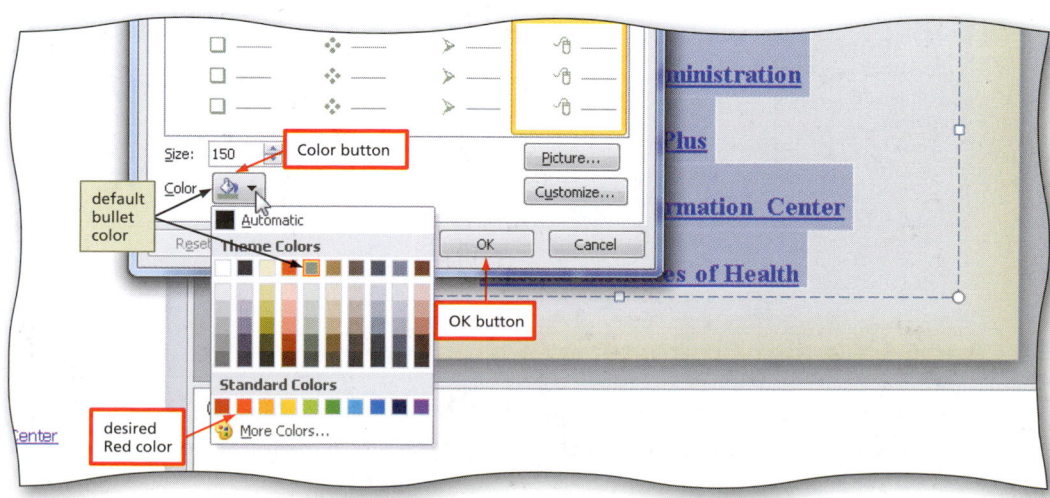

Figure 6–70

2

- Click the color Red in the Standard Colors area to change the bullet color to Red (second color in the Standard Colors area) (Figure 6–71).

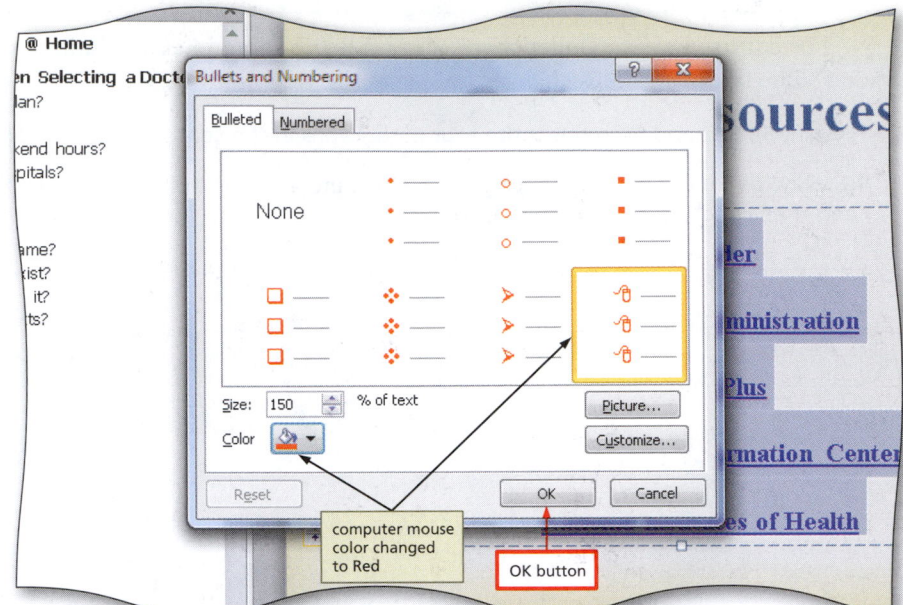

Figure 6–71

3

- Click the OK button to apply the color Red to the computer mouse bullet (Figure 6–72).

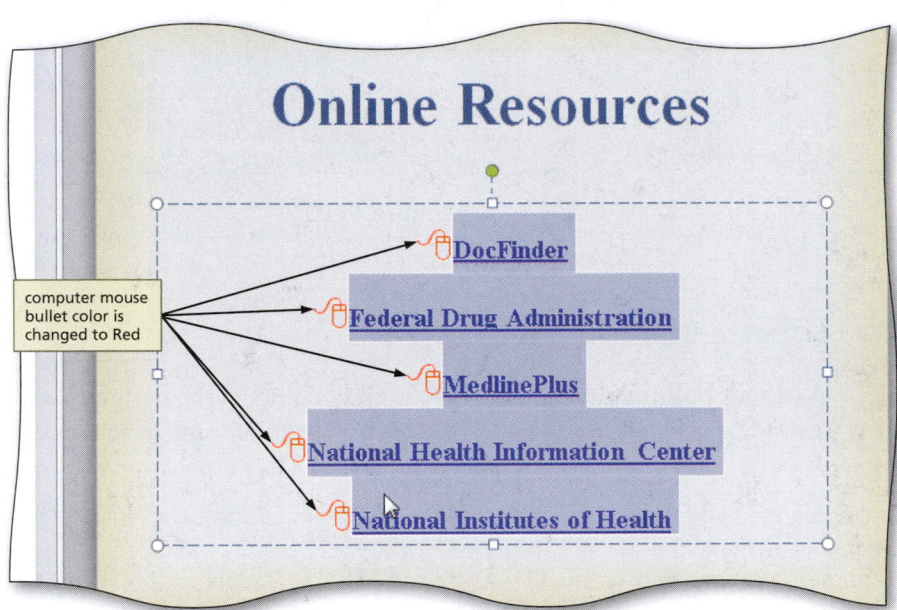

Figure 6–72

Other Ways
1. Right-click paragraph, point to Bullets on shortcut menu, click Bullets and Numbering, select color

To Change a Bullet Character to a Number

PowerPoint allows you to change the default bullets to numbers. The process of changing the bullet characters is similar to the process of changing bullets to symbols. The following steps change the first-level paragraph bullet characters on Slide 3 to numbers.

1

- Display Slide 3 and then select all four content paragraphs.

- With the Home tab still displaying, click the Numbering button arrow (Home tab | Paragraph group) to display the Numbering gallery.

- Point to the 1) 2) 3) numbering option in the Numbering gallery to display a live preview of these numbers (Figure 6–73).

🔍 **Experiment**

- Point to each of the numbers in the Numbering gallery to watch the numbers change on Slide 3.

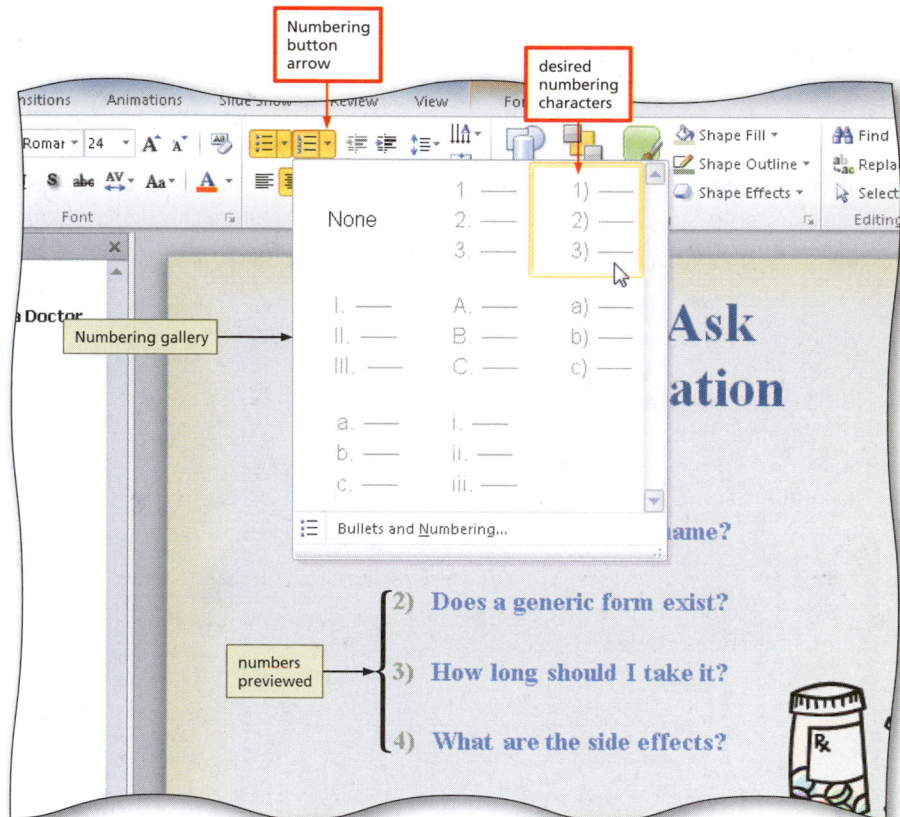

Figure 6–73

2

- Click the 1) 2) 3) numbering option to insert these numbers as the first-level paragraph characters (Figure 6–74).

Q&A

How do I change the first number in the list?

Click Bullets and Numbering at the bottom of the Numbering gallery and then click the up or down arrow in the Start at text box to change the number.

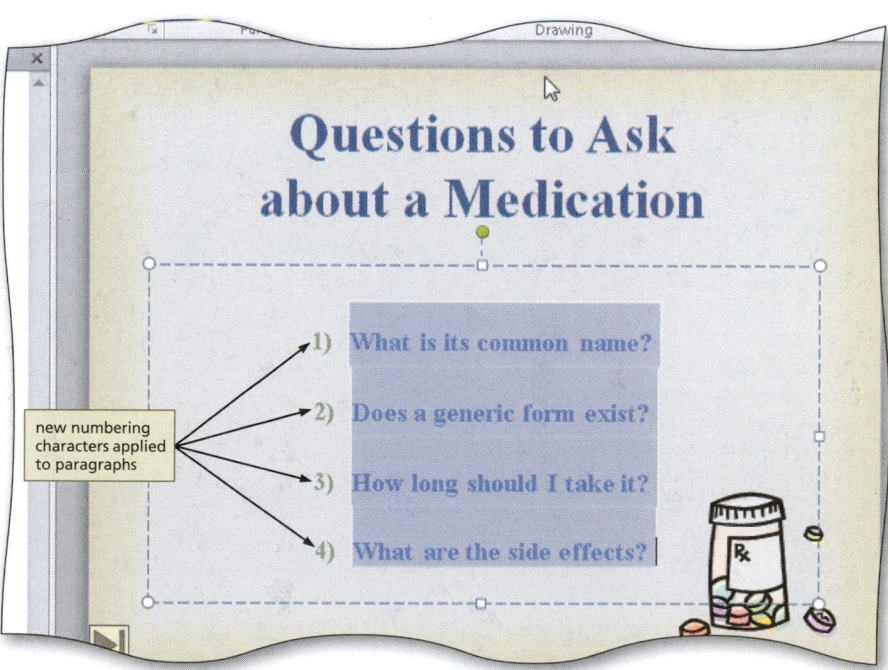

Figure 6–74

Other Ways

1. Right-click paragraph, point to Numbering on shortcut menu, select numbering characters

To Format a Numbered List

To add emphasis, you can increase the size of the new numbers inserted in Slide 3. As with bullets, these characters are measured as a percentage of the text size and can range from 25 to 400 percent. The color of these numbers also can change. The original color is based on the eight colors in the design theme. Additional standard and custom colors are available. The following steps change the size and colors of the numbers to 125 percent and Red, respectively.

- With the Slide 3 content paragraphs still selected, click the Numbering button arrow (Home tab | Paragraph group) to display the Numbering gallery and then click Bullets and Numbering to display the Bullets and Numbering dialog box.

- Click the Size box up arrow several times to change the size to 125%.

Q&A

Can I type a number in the text box instead of clicking the up arrow?

Yes. Double-click the text box and then type the desired percentage.

- Click the Color button to display the Color gallery and then click Red (second color in the Standard Colors area) to change the numbers' font color (Figure 6–75).

- Click the OK button to apply the new numbers' font size and color.

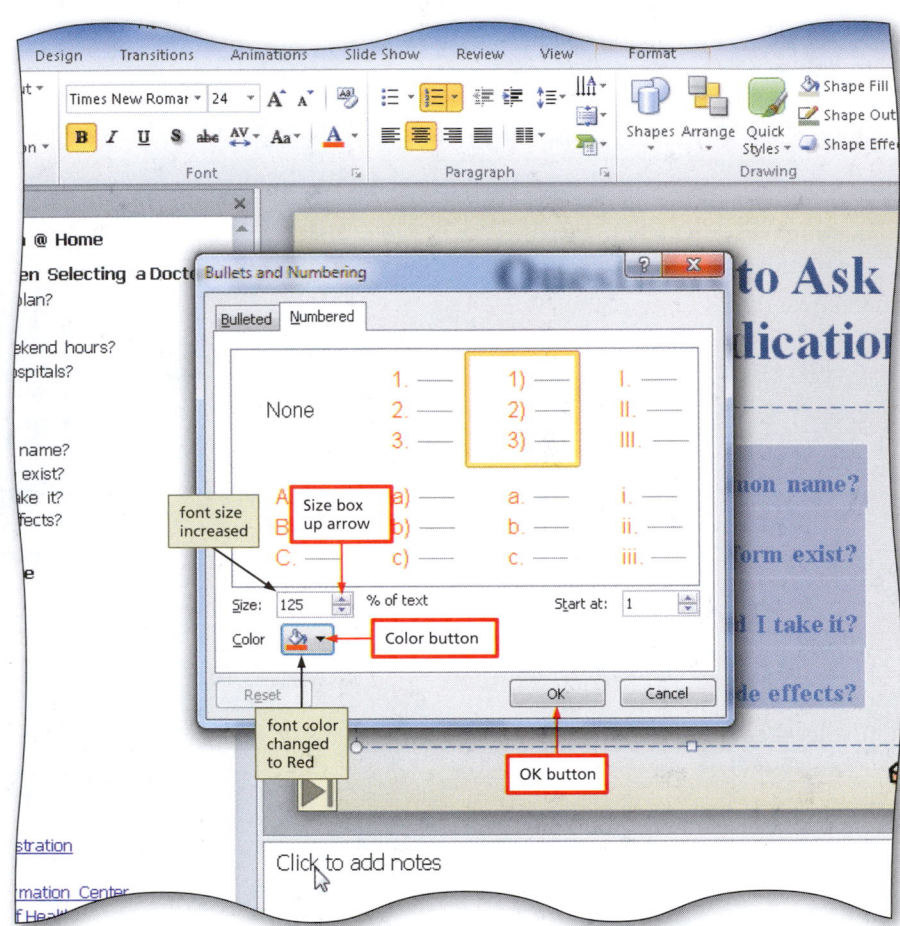

Figure 6–75

Other Ways	
1. Right-click paragraph, point to Numbering on shortcut menu, click Bullets and Numbering, click up or down Size	arrow until desired size is displayed, click Color button, select color, click OK button

To Remove Bullet Characters

The health risks listed in the two Slide 4 columns are preceded by an ornate bullet character. The slide may appear less cluttered if you remove the bullets. The following steps remove the bullet characters from the items in the two columns on Slide 4.

- Display Slide 4, select all the text in the two columns, and then click the Bullets button arrow.

- Point to the None option in the Bullets gallery to display a live preview of how the slide will appear without bullets (Figure 6–76).

- Click the None option to remove the bullet characters on Slide 4.

- If necessary, move the scale picture to center it between the two columns.

Q&A

Would I use the same technique to remove numbers from a list?

Yes. The None option also is available in the Numbering gallery.

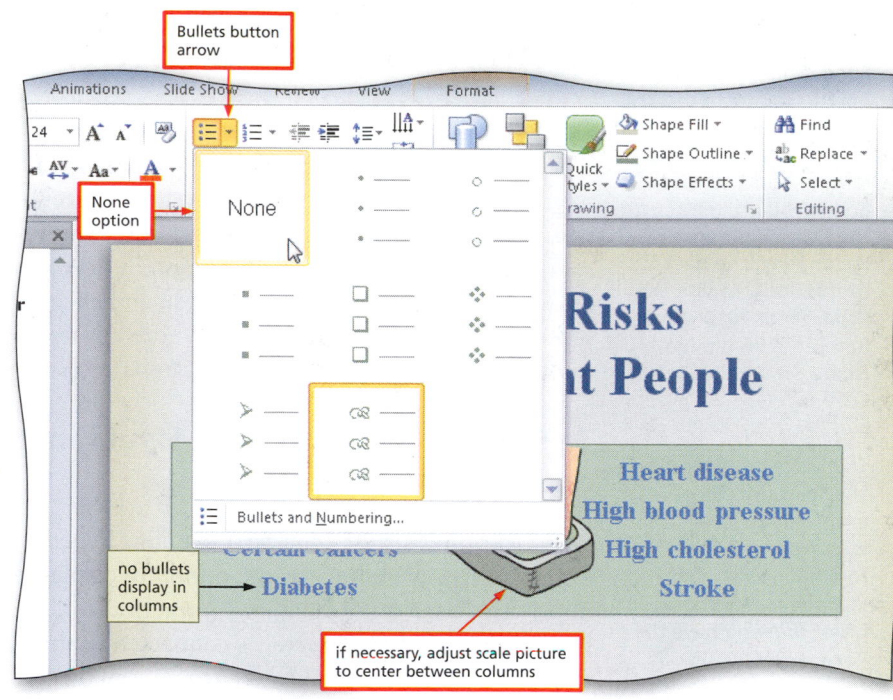

Figure 6–76

To Change Document Properties

Before saving the presentation again, you want to add your name, class name, and some keywords as document properties. The following steps use the Document Information Panel to change document properties.

1 Display the Document Information Panel and then type your name as the Author property.

2 Type your course and section in the Subject property.

3 Type `home health, medication record, doctor selection, overweight risks` as the Keywords property.

4 Close the Document Information Panel.

Consider the audience's interests.

Plan Ahead

As audience members start to view your presentation, they often think about their personal needs and wonder, "How will this presentation benefit me?" As you may have learned in your psychology classes, Maslow's hierarchy of needs drives much of your behavior, starting with basic sustenance and moving on to safety, belonging, ego-status, and self-actualization. Audience members cannot move to the next higher level of needs until their current level is satisfied. For example, an individual must first satisfy his needs of hunger and thirst before he can consider partaking in leisure time activities. Your presentations must meet the requirements of your audience members; otherwise, these people will not consider your talk as benefiting their needs. Having hyperlinks and action buttons can help you tailor a presentation to fulfill the audience's satisfaction level.

BTW

Quick Reference
For a table that lists how to complete the tasks covered in this book using the mouse, Ribbon, shortcut menu, and keyboard, see the Quick Reference Summary at the back of this book, or visit the PowerPoint 2010 Quick Reference Web page (scsite.com/ppt2010/qr).

BTW

Certification
The Microsoft Office Specialist (MOS) program provides an opportunity for you to obtain a valuable industry credential — proof that you have the PowerPoint 2010 skills required by employers. For more information, visit the PowerPoint 2010 Certification Web page (scsite.com/ ppt2010/cert).

BTW

Saving the Presentation as an Outline
You began this project by opening a Microsoft Word outline, and you can save the presentation as an outline to use in a word processor or another PowerPoint project. An outline is saved in Rich Text Format (.rtf) and contains only text. To save the presentation as an outline, open the Backstage view, click Save As, type a file name in the File name text box (Save As dialog box), click the 'Save as type' arrow and select Outline/RTF in the Save as type list, and then click the Save button.

Running a Slide Show with Hyperlinks and Action Buttons

The Home Health presentation contains a variety of useful features that provide value to an audience. The graphics should help viewers understand and recall the information being presented. The hyperlinks on Slide 5 show useful Web sites that give current medical information. In addition, the action button allows a presenter to jump to Slide 5 while Slides 2 or 3 are being displayed. If an audience member asks a question or if the presenter needs to answer specific questions regarding weight when Slide 3 is displaying, the information on the hidden Slide 4 can be accessed immediately by pressing the H key.

To Run a Slide Show with Hyperlinks, Action Buttons, and a Hidden Slide

Running a slide show that contains hyperlinks and action buttons is an interactive experience. A presenter has the option to display slides in a predetermined sequence or to improvise based on the audience's reaction and questions. When a presentation contains hyperlinks and the computer is connected to the Internet, the speaker can click the links to command the default browser to display the Web sites. The following steps run the Home Health presentation.

1 Click Slide 1 on the Outline tab. Click the Slide Show button to run the slide show and display Slide 1.

2 Click the stethoscope picture to display Slide 2.

3 On Slide 2, click the stethoscope picture to link to the first slide in the Additional Health presentation.

4 Click the Return action button on the first slide to return to Slide 2 in the Home Health presentation.

5 Press the ENTER key to display Slide 3. Click the prescription picture to start Microsoft Word and open the Medication Record file. View the information and then click the Close button on the title bar to quit Word and return to Slide 3.

6 Press the H key to display Slide 4. Click the scale picture to link to the second slide in the Additional Health presentation. Click the Return action button on the second slide to return to Slide 4 in the Home Health presentation.

7 Press the ENTER key to display Slide 5. Click the first hyperlink to start your browser and access the DocFinder online physician directory Web page. If necessary, maximize the Web page window when the page is displayed. Click the Close button on the Web page title bar to close the browser.

8 Continue using the hyperlinks and action buttons and then end the presentation.

To Save, Print, and Quit PowerPoint

The presentation now is complete. You should save the slides, print a handout, and then quit PowerPoint.

1 Save the Home Health presentation again with the same file name.

2 Print the presentation as a handout with two slides per page (Figure 6–77).

3 Quit PowerPoint, closing all open documents.

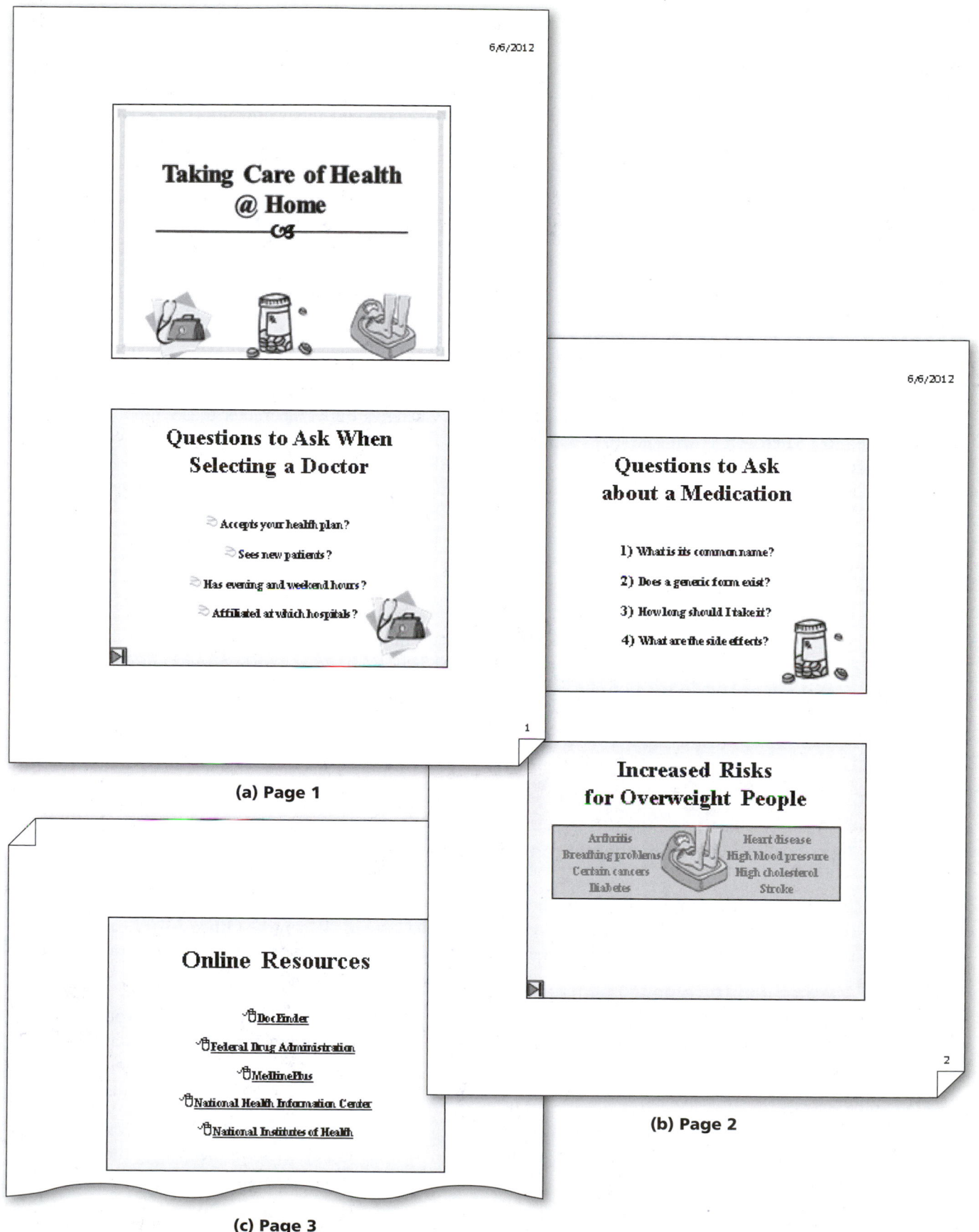

(a) Page 1

(b) Page 2

(c) Page 3

Figure 6–77

Chapter Summary

In this chapter you have learned how to open a Microsoft Word outline as a PowerPoint presentation, develop slides with hyperlinks and action buttons, position slide elements using the drawing guides and rulers, align and distribute pictures, center and align placeholder text, and create columns and then adjust the width. You then learned to change a bullet character to a picture or a symbol and then change its size and color. Finally, you ran the presentation using the action buttons and hyperlinks. The items listed below include all the new PowerPoint skills you have learned in this chapter.

1. Open a Microsoft Word Outline as a Presentation (PPT 335)
2. Add a Hyperlink to a Picture (PPT 339)
3. Add a Hyperlink to a Paragraph (PPT 341)
4. Insert an Action Button (PPT 344)
5. Change an Action Button Fill Color (PPT 346)
6. Copy an Action Button (PPT 348)
7. Edit an Action Button Action Setting (PPT 349)
8. Hyperlink to Another PowerPoint File (PPT 350)
9. Hyperlink to a Microsoft Word File (PPT 353)
10. Display the Drawing Guides (PPT 357)
11. Position a Picture Using Guides (PPT 358)
12. Display the Rulers (PPT 359)
13. Align Pictures (PPT 360)
14. Distribute Pictures (PPT 362)
15. Hide a Slide (PPT 363)
16. Center Placeholder Text (PPT 365)
17. Align Placeholder Text (PPT 366)
18. Change Paragraph Line Spacing (PPT 367)
19. Create Columns in a Placeholder (PPT 367)
20. Adjust Column Spacing (PPT 369)
21. Enter a Line Break (PPT 371)
22. Change a Bullet Character to a Picture (PPT 372)
23. Change a Bullet Character to a Symbol (PPT 375)
24. Format a Bullet Size (PPT 377)
25. Format a Bullet Color (PPT 379)
26. Change a Bullet Character to a Number (PPT 380)
27. Format a Numbered List (PPT 382)
28. Remove Bullet Characters (PPT 382)

 If you have a SAM 2010 user profile, your instructor may have assigned an autogradable version of this assignment. If so, log into the SAM 2010 Web site at www.cengage.com/sam2010 to download the instruction and start files.

Learn It Online

Test your knowledge of chapter content and key terms.

Instructions: To complete the Learn It Online exercises, start your browser, click the Address bar, and then enter the Web address `scsite.com/ppt2010/learn`. When the Office 2010 Learn It Online page is displayed, click the link for the exercise you want to complete and then read the instructions.

Chapter Reinforcement TF, MC, and SA
A series of true/false, multiple choice, and short answer questions that test your knowledge of the chapter content.

Flash Cards
An interactive learning environment where you identify chapter key terms associated with displayed definitions.

Practice Test
A series of multiple choice questions that test your knowledge of chapter content and key terms.

Who Wants To Be a Computer Genius?
An interactive game that challenges your knowledge of chapter content in the style of a television quiz show.

Wheel of Terms
An interactive game that challenges your knowledge of chapter key terms in the style of the television show *Wheel of Fortune*.

Crossword Puzzle Challenge
A crossword puzzle that challenges your knowledge of key terms presented in the chapter.

Apply Your Knowledge

Reinforce the skills and apply the concepts you learned in this chapter.

Revising a Presentation with Action Buttons, Bullet Styles, and Hidden Slides

Note: To complete this assignment, you will be required to use the Data Files for Students. See the inside back cover of this book for instructions on downloading the Data Files for Students, or contact your instructor for information about accessing the required files.

Instructions: Start PowerPoint. Open the presentation, Apply 6-1 Anatomy, located on the Data Files for Students.

The six slides in the presentation identify names seldom used for parts of the body. You plan to use the presentation as a study guide for your anatomy class. The document you open is an unformatted presentation. You are to add a style to the pictures; insert action buttons on Slide 1; hide Slides 2, 3, 4, and 5; and format the bullets on Slides 2 through 6 so the slides look like Figure 6–78 on the next page.

Perform the following tasks:

1. Change the document theme to Grid. Apply the WordArt style, Fill – Tan, Accent 2, Warm Matte Bevel, to the title text and add the Chevron Up text effect.

2. On Slide 1, apply the Rotated, White picture style to the upper-left picture, apply the Metal Frame picture style to the upper-right picture, apply the Metal Rounded Rectangle picture style to the lower-left picture, and apply the Bevel Perspective Left, White picture style to the lower-right picture, as shown in Figure 6–78a.

3. Hyperlink each picture to the corresponding slide. For example, the upper-left picture should hyperlink to Slide 2. The other three pictures should hyperlink to Slides 3, 4, and 5, respectively.

4. Center the subtitle text and then bold this text.

5. On Slide 2, insert a Home action button and hyperlink it to the first slide. Change the action button fill color to Yellow, and then change the transparency to 60%. Do not play a sound. Size the button so that it is approximately 0.75" × 0.75" and then move it to the location shown in Figure 6–78b. Copy this action button to Slides 3, 4, and 5.

6. On Slides 2 through 6, add Arrow Bullets to the content text paragraphs and then increase the size of the bullets to 135% of text. Change the color of the body part terms at the beginning of each paragraph to Tan, Accent 1 on all slides.

7. Hide Slides 2, 3, 4, and 5.

8. Change the Transition from Zoom to Split. Change the duration to 02.50.

9. Display the revised presentation in Slide Sorter view to check for consistency.

10. Change the document properties, as specified by your instructor. Save the presentation using the file name, Apply 6-1 Parts of the Body. Submit the revised document in the format specified by your instructor.

Continued >

Apply Your Knowledge *continued*

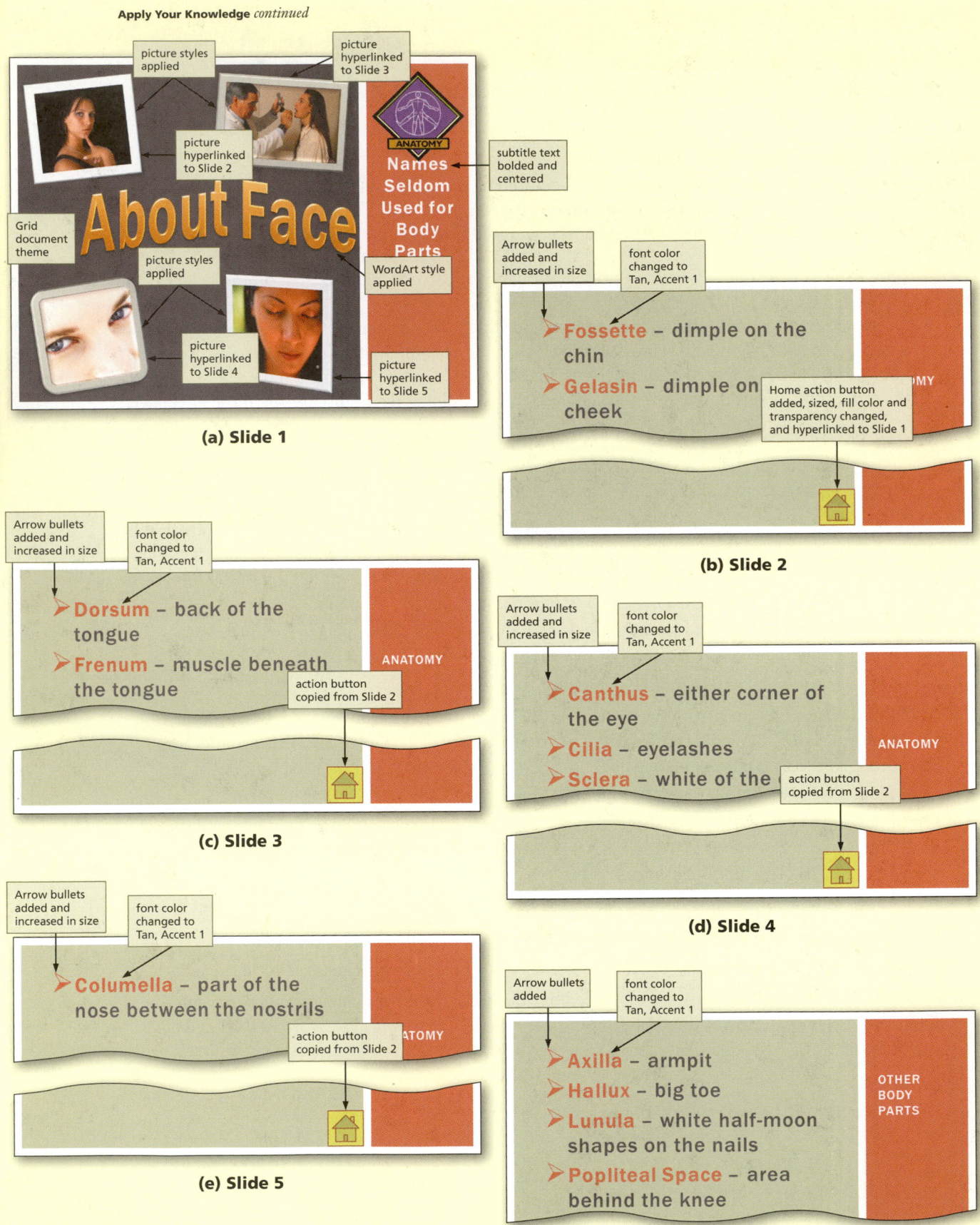

(a) Slide 1

(b) Slide 2

(c) Slide 3

(d) Slide 4

(e) Slide 5

(f) Slide 6

Figure 6–78

Extend Your Knowledge

Extend the skills you learned in this chapter and experiment with new skills. You may need to use Help to complete the assignment.

Inserting a Picture into an Action Button and Changing a Bullet Character to a Picture

Note: To complete this assignment, you will be required to use the Data Files for Students. See the inside back cover of this book for instructions on downloading the Data Files for Students, or contact your instructor for information about accessing the required files.

Instructions: Start PowerPoint. Open the presentation, Extend 6-1 Camp, located on the Data Files for Students.

You will insert hyperlinks on the title slide; enter the data from Table 6–3 on Slide 2; insert action buttons on Slides 2, 3, and 4; and change the bullet characters to pictures on Slides 5 and 6, as shown in Figure 6–79 on the next page.

Table 6–3 Adams Family Camp Trails		
Trail	**Length**	**Trail Head**
Mountainview	10.2 miles	Behind clubhouse
Lakeside	11.5 miles	Main dock
Upper Bend	12.8 miles	Behind clubhouse

Perform the following tasks:

1. On Slide 1, hyperlink each picture to the corresponding slide. For example, the top picture should hyperlink to Slide 2. The other two pictures should hyperlink to Slides 3 and 4, respectively. Use the Smart Guides to align the three pictures to the slide and then distribute these images vertically. Once the pictures are distributed vertically, use the Arrange list to align their centers as well.

2. On Slide 2, insert a Custom action button in the lower-left area of the slide and hyperlink it to the first slide. Format this shape by inserting the picture, Hiking, located on the Data Files for Students, as shown in Figure 6–79b.

3. Enter the data from Table 6–3 in the text box on Slide 2. Change the paragraph line spacing to 1.5 and center all text.

4. On Slide 3, insert a Custom action button in the lower-left corner of the slide and hyperlink it to the first slide. Format this shape by inserting the picture, Fishing, located on your Data Files for Students, as shown in Figure 6–79c.

5. On Slide 4, insert a Forward or Next action button in the lower-right corner of the slide.

6. On Slide 5, change the bullet character to the Scissors picture located on the Data Files for Students. Increase the size of the bullets to 150% of text.

7. On Slide 6, insert a picture bullet by importing the Camera picture located on the Data Files for Students, and then increase the size of the bullets to 150% of text.

8. Change the title text paragraph alignment on Slides 5 and 6 to Distributed by selecting the title text, displaying the Home tab, clicking the Paragraph Dialog Box Launcher button (Home tab | Paragraph group), clicking the Alignment box arrow, and then clicking Distributed.

9. Apply a transition to all slides.

10. Change the document properties, as specified by your instructor. Save the presentation using the file name, Extend 6-1 Family Summer Camp.

11. Submit the revised document in the format specified by your instructor.

Continued >

Extend Your Knowledge *continued*

(a) Slide 1

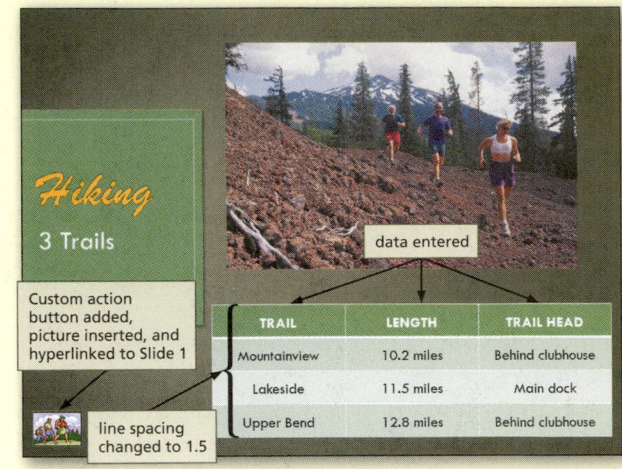

(b) Slide 2

(c) Slide 3

(d) Slide 4

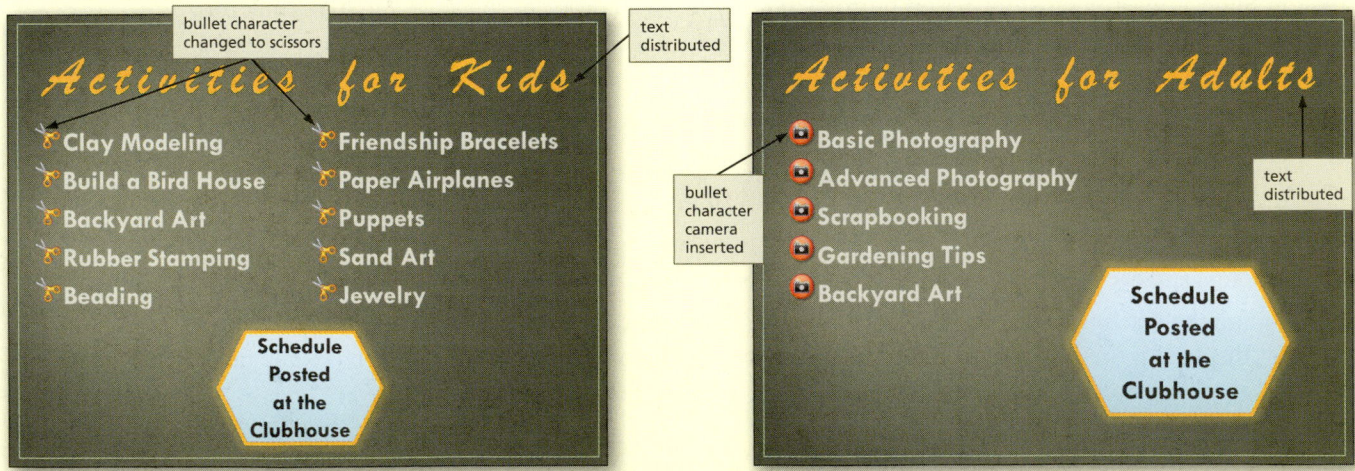

(e) Slide 5

(f) Slide 6

Figure 6–79

Make It Right

Analyze a presentation and correct all errors and/or improve the design.

Modifying Text and Line Spacing in a Placeholder

Note: To complete this assignment, you will be required to use the Data Files for Students. See the inside back cover of this book for instructions on downloading the Data Files for Students, or contact your instructor for information about accessing the required files.

Instructions: Start PowerPoint. Open the presentation, Make It Right 6-1 Golf, located on the Data Files for Students. Correct the formatting problems and errors in the presentation while keeping in mind the guidelines presented in this chapter.

Perform the following tasks:

1. On Slide 1, shown in Figure 6–80, select the four words, What's in Your Bag?, at the top of the slide and then decrease the font size to 28 point. Make sure that these four words show in the box. Change the title text font size to 40 point and then right-align this text. Center the text in both subtitle placeholders.

2. Remove the artistic effect from the picture and change the style to Rotated, White.

3. Increase the font size of the text in the right placeholder to 22 point.

4. Align the text in both placeholders vertically in the center.

5. Increase the size of the bullets to 200% of the text size.

6. Check the spelling and correct the misspellings.

7. Change the document properties, as specified by your instructor. Save the presentation using the file name, Make It Right 6-1 Golf Clubs.

8. Submit the revised document in the format specified by your instructor.

Figure 6–80

In the Lab

Design and/or create a presentation using the guidelines, concepts, and skills presented in this chapter. Labs 1, 2, and 3 are listed in order of increasing difficulty.

Lab 1: Aligning Text and Creating Columns in a Text Box, Moving a Placeholder, and Changing a Bullet Character to a Picture

Note: To complete this assignment, you will be required to use the Data Files for Students. See the inside back cover of this book for instructions on downloading the Data Files for Students, or contact your instructor for information about accessing the required files.

Problem: You belong to a garden club in the city and find that many members have limited yard space for planting a garden. The president of the club asked if you would modify an existing presentation that describes the basics of container gardening. You create the slides shown in Figure 6–81 using files located on the Data Files for Students.

Perform the following tasks:

1. Open the presentation, Lab 6-1 Vegetables, located on the Data Files for Students.

2. Change the presentation theme colors to Hardcover.

3. On Slide 1, change the title text placeholder vertical alignment to Top. Insert a line break after the dash in the first line and then delete the space before the word, No, in the second line. Change the font size to 54 point, and the font color to Light Green, and then bold this text. Change the subtitle text font to Vani and the font size to 36 point. Increase the size of the three clips, as shown in Figure 6–81a, and then use the Smart Guides to align the two flowerpots.

4. On Slide 2, add bullets and then change the bullet character to the Clay Pot picture located on the Data Files for Students. Increase the size of these bullets to 250% of text.

5. On Slide 3, change the four bullet characters to the 1) 2) 3) numbering format. Change the numbering color to Orange, Accent 2 and the size to 100% of text.

6. On Slide 4, create three columns in the text box, adjust the column spacing to 1", and then change the line spacing to 1.5. Move the two clips to the locations shown in Figure 6–81d.

7. Apply the Window transition and change the duration to 2.25 for all slides.

8. Change the document properties, as specified by your instructor. Save the presentation using the file name, Lab 6-1 Container Vegetable Garden.

9. Submit the revised document in the format specified by your instructor.

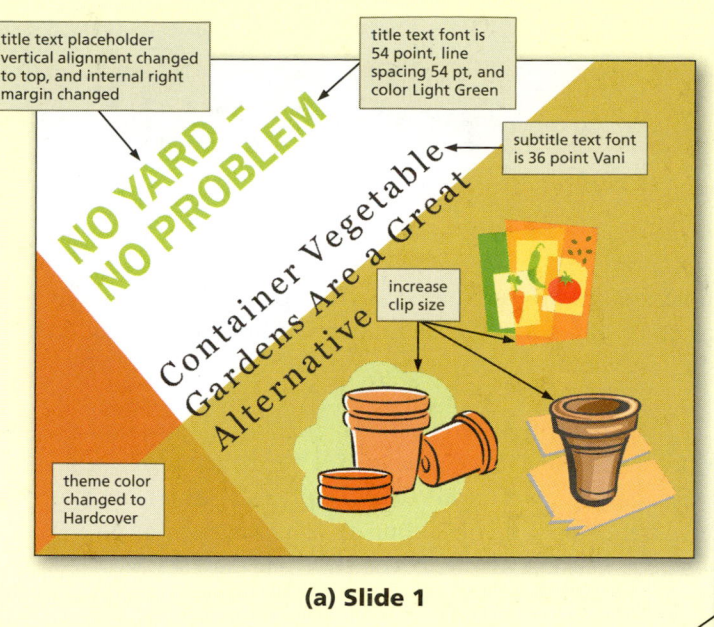

title text placeholder vertical alignment changed to top, and internal right margin changed

title text font is 54 point, line spacing 54 pt, and color Light Green

subtitle text font is 36 point Vani

increase clip size

theme color changed to Hardcover

NO YARD – NO PROBLEM

Container Vegetable Gardens Are a Great Alternative

(a) Slide 1

LOCATION

- Need sun
- Keep containers small enough to move
- Ensure proper drainage

bullet character changed to clay pot

(b) Slide 2

bullet characters changed and formatted

WATERING AND FEEDING

1) Must be well watered
2) Use mulch around top of container
3) May need additional fertilizer due to extra watering
4) Use a diluted water-soluble fertilizer

(c) Slide 3

VEGETABLES TO CONSIDER

Tomatoes	Cabbage	Cucumbers
Lettuce	Peas	Cauliflower
Beets	Beans	Broccoli
Carrots	Peppers	Herbs

three-column textbox

column spacing adjusted

clips moved

(d) Slide 4

Figure 6–81

In the Lab

Lab 2: Creating a Presentation from a Microsoft Word Outline, Inserting Hyperlinks to Other Office Documents, Hiding Slides, and Copying and Editing Action Buttons

Note: To complete this assignment, you will be required to use the Data Files for Students. See the inside back cover of this book for instructions on downloading the Data Files for Students, or contact your instructor for information about accessing the required files.

Problem: The members of your school's hiking club are planning an eight-day backpacking trip in a national park. As program chairman, you are working on the details of the trip. The president asks you to give a presentation at your next meeting to discuss some of the trip's details and gives you a Microsoft Word outline with points to cover during your speech. To supplement your talk, the treasurer gives you an Excel file that has the club's membership information, and you have created a Microsoft Word document that lists items everyone should pack and bring on the trip. You will use the outline as the basis for your presentation and create hyperlinks to the other documents to display during your presentation. You borrowed photos from your cousin, who took a trip to this park, and you will use those pictures in your presentation. The trip will include visits to Baer Woods, Ruff Summit, Pine Cone Valley, and Stoop Falls. You create the slides shown in Figure 6–82 using files located on the Data Files for Students.

Perform the following tasks:

1. Create a new presentation using the Office Theme. Import the outline, Lab 6-2 Backpacking Outline, shown in Figure 6–82a, located on the Data Files for Students. Change the new Slide 1 layout to Title Slide.

2. On Slide 1, create a background by inserting the picture called National Park located on the Data Files for Students. Change the transparency to 62%.

3. Increase the title text font size to 54 point. Create a hyperlink for all the title text to the Excel document, Tooterville Hiking Club (Figure 6–82i), located on the Data Files for Students. Bold the subtitle text.

4. On Slide 2, convert the bulleted list to SmartArt by applying the Continuous Picture List (List area). Change the colors to Colorful Range – Accent Colors 2 to 3 and then apply the Polished 3D style to the graphic. Insert the pictures, Hiking1, Hiking2, Hiking3, and Hiking4, from the Data Files for Students, as shown in Figure 6–82b.

5. On all slides except the title slide, change the background to Style 10.

6. On Slide 3 (Figure 6–82c), change the bullet character to the Compass picture located on the Data Files for Students. Increase the size of the bullets to 110% of the text. Insert the Return action button in the lower-right corner of this slide and then hyperlink the button to the Last Slide Viewed, which will be Slide 2 when you run the presentation.

7. Duplicate Slide 3 three times to add the new three slides to create new Slides 4, 5, and 6. The current Slide 4 becomes Slide 7.

8. On Slide 2, insert a hyperlink on each picture. Link the Baer Woods picture to Slide 3, the Ruff Summit picture to Slide 4, the Pine Cone Valley picture to Slide 5, and the Stoop Falls picture to Slide 6. Play the sound, Camera, for each hyperlink.

9. On Slides 3, 4, 5, and 6, change the font color of the bulleted paragraphs to match the corresponding SmartArt graphic color, as shown in Figures 6–82d through 6–82g. The Baer Woods color is Red, Accent 2; the Ruff Summit color is Orange, Accent 6; the Pine Cone Valley color is Orange; and the Stoop Falls color is Olive Green, Accent 3, Darker 50%. Bold each of the colored paragraphs.

10. Hide Slides 3, 4, 5, and 6.

11. On Slide 7 (Figure 6–82h), insert a hyperlink in the title text to the Word document, Packing List (Figure 6–82j), located on the Data Files for Students. Change the six bullet characters to the 1.2.3. numbering format, the color to Blue, and the size to 125% of the text. Bold all the numbered paragraphs on the slide.

12. Apply the Honeycomb transition and then change the duration to 3.25 for all slides.

13. Check the spelling and correct any errors.

14. Change the document properties, as specified by your instructor. Save the presentation using the file name, Lab 6-2 Backpacking Trip.

15. Submit the revised document in the format specified by your instructor.

(a) Backpacking Outline — Microsoft Word Document

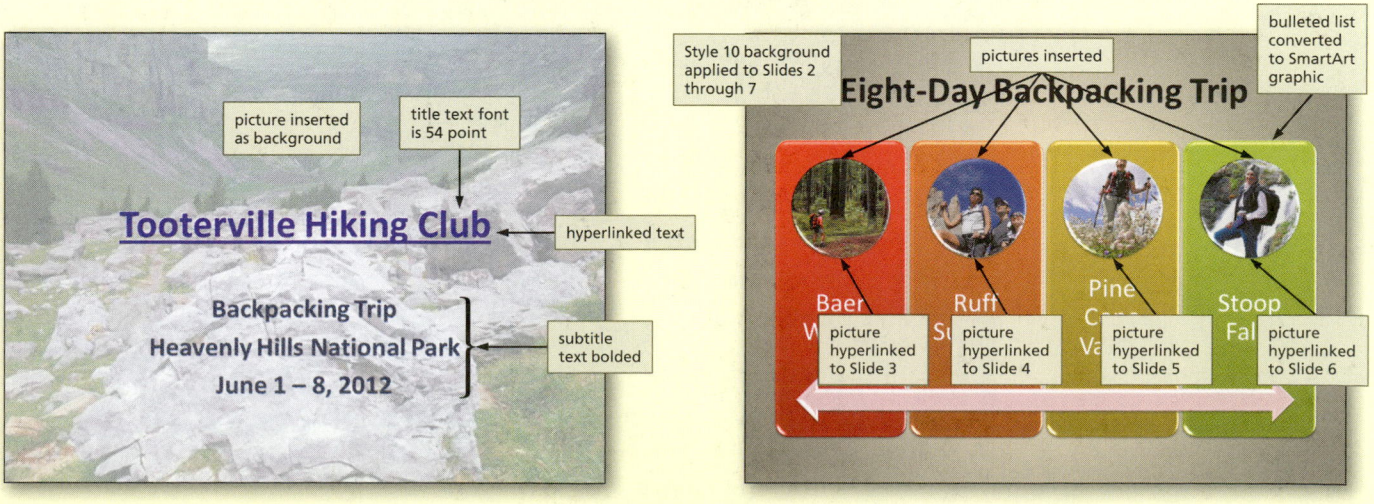

(b) Slide 1

(c) Slide 2

Figure 6–82

Continued >

STUDENT ASSIGNMENTS

In the Lab *continued*

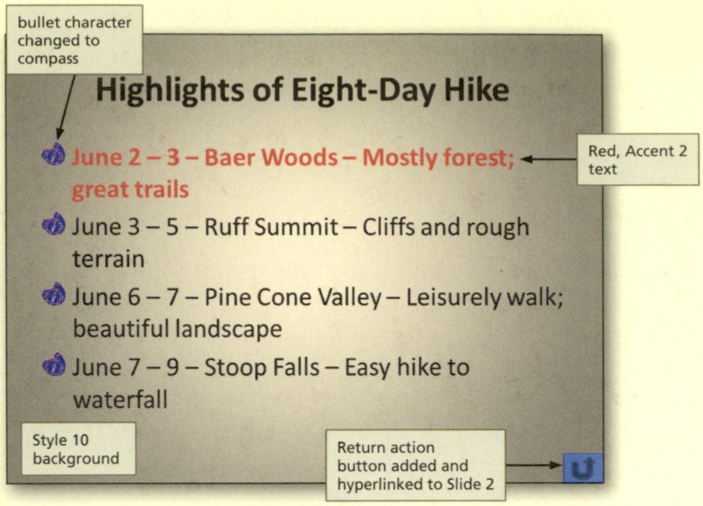

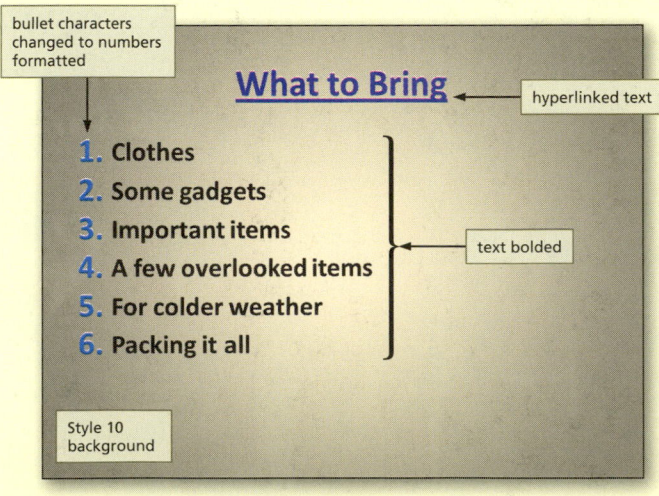

(d) Slide 3

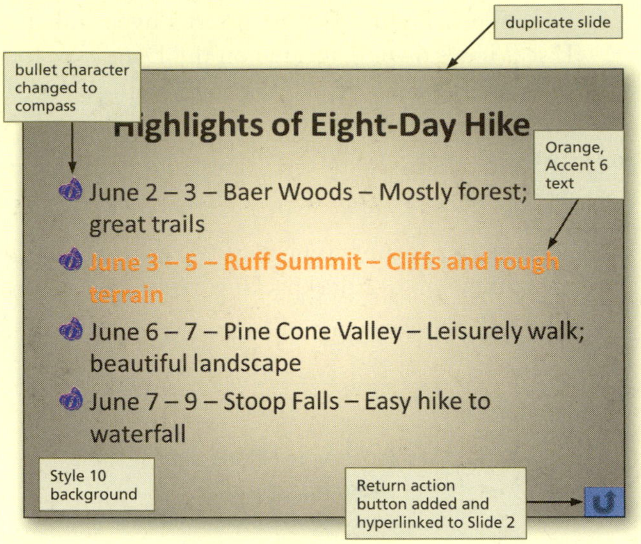

(e) Slide 4

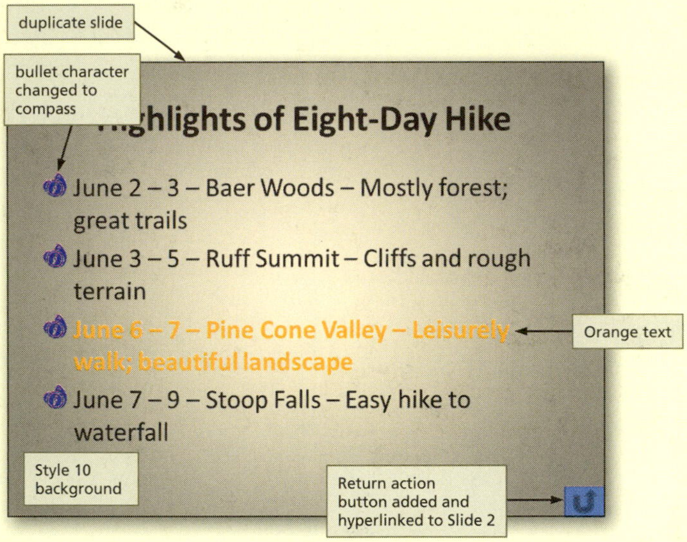

(f) Slide 5

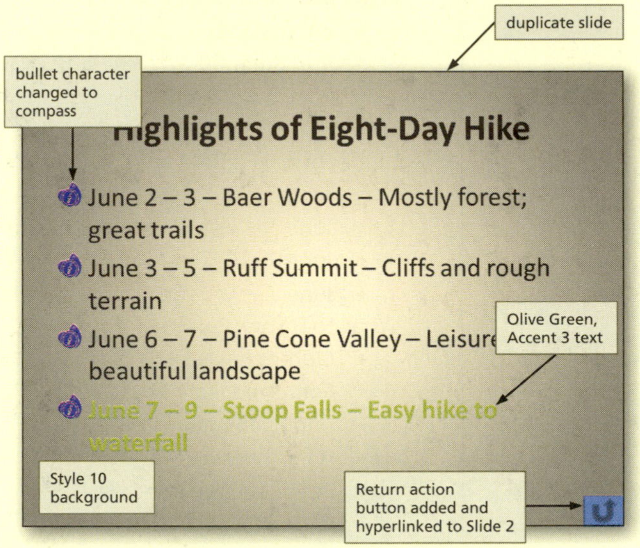

(g) Slide 6

(h) Slide 7

Figure 6–82 (Continued)

	A	B	C	D	E
1	**Tooterville Hiking Club - Membership Roster**				
2	**Name**		**Joined**	**Dues Paid**	**June 2012 Trip**
3	Abbot	Carol	2006	Yes	No
4	Anders	Robert	2009	Yes	Yes
5	Bolt	Abigail	2009	Yes	Yes
6	Conners	Jimmie	2008	Yes	No
7	Cranz	Nancy	2009	Yes	Yes
8	Cravin	Joe	2008	Yes	Yes
9	Davis	Sandy	2009	Yes	Yes
10	Dorm	Janie	2006	No	No
11	Evins	Erick	2006	Yes	Yes
12	Flap	Susan	2007	No	Yes
13	Foster	Chris	2006	Yes	No
14	Hope	Candy	2006	No	Yes
15	Jones	Felix	2006	Yes	No
16	Kwik	Joshua	2008	Yes	No
17	Morgan	Nicholas	2009	Yes	Yes
18	Mullin	Benjamin	2009	Yes	No
19	Nallon	Miriam	2007	No	No
20	Olson	Jack	2008	Yes	Yes
21	Platt	Calista	2009	Yes	Yes
22	Wyatt	Brian	2008	No	No
23	Yore	Suzie	2007	Yes	No
24	Yulepp	Kendra	2009	Yes	Yes
25	Zanders	Amy	2008	Yes	Yes

(i) Membership Roster — Microsoft Excel File

Clothes
- Shirts (long- and short-sleeved)
- Thin fleece jacket
- Socks and underwear
- Two pair of jeans
- Baseball hat, sun hat
- Swimming gear
- Hiking boots/shoes and sandals

Some gadgets
- Camera and spare battery
- Chargers and plug adaptor if needed
- Mini LED flashlight or head light
- Cell phone
- Calculator

Important Items
- ATM, credit card, and cash
- Sun glasses
- Glasses and contacts lenses and solutions
- First aid/medicine kit
- Shower kit
- Mosquito net and tape
- Documents: emergency numbers, insurance cards, flight details, etc.
- Guidebook

A few overlooked items
- Pen and notepad
- Packets of tissues
- Towel
- Sleeping sac
- Entertainment: book(s), magazine(s), cards, MP3 player, handheld games
- Umbrella or waterproof shell
- Earplugs, eye mask
- Snacks

For colder weather
- Heavy fleece jacket
- Thermal vest
- Gloves, knit hat, thick socks, an outer windproof shell, thermal leggings

Packing it all
- Money belt
- Mini padlock and cable lock
- Shoulder bag or fanny pack for day use
- Small plastic bags and containers for storage
- A bag/backpack to store everything

(j) Packing List — Microsoft Word File

Figure 6–82 (Continued)

In the Lab

Lab 3: Inserting Hyperlinks and Action Buttons, Hiding Slides, Using Guides, and Formatting Bullets

Note: To complete this assignment, you will be required to use the Data Files for Students. See the inside back cover of this book for instructions on downloading the Data Files for Students, or contact your instructor for information about accessing the required files.

Problem: Your public speaking instructor has assigned an informative speech, and you have decided to discuss landlocked countries. You create the presentation in Figure 6–83 that consists of six slides with hyperlinks, and you decide to hide four slides. Required files are located on the Data Files for Students.

Perform the following tasks:

1. Open the presentation, Lab 6-3 Landlocked, from the Data Files for Students. Change the document theme to Civic and then change the presentation theme colors to Adjacency.

2. On Slide 1, change the title text font to Algerian. Increase the font size of the first line of the title text to 48 point, and then decrease the second line's font size to 36 point. Convert the bulleted list to SmartArt by applying the Vertical Circle List (List area). Decrease the font size of the first line to 30 point and the countries' names to 24 point. Apply the Bevel Perspective picture style to the picture.

3. On Slides 2, 3, and 4, resize the globe and map pictures so that they are approximately 3.39" × 5.4" and then move them to the locations shown in Figure 6–83. Display the rulers, click to the left and below the center of the globe, and then move the graphic so that the mouse pointer is positioned at the center of both the vertical and horizontal rulers. Hide the rulers.

4. On Slides 2, 3, and 4, resize the country symbols in the lower-right corners so that they are approximately 0.75" × 1.67". Display the drawing guides. Set the horizontal guide to 2.33 below center and the vertical guide to 3.17 right of center. Move the country symbols so that their upper-left sizing handles align with the intersection of the guides. Hide the guides.

5. On Slide 5, change the color of the map to Tan, Accent color 5 Dark.

6. On Slide 6, center all six content text paragraphs and then align these paragraphs in the middle of the placeholder.

7. On Slide 1, insert a hyperlink for each country. Kazakhstan should be hyperlinked to Slide 2, Mongolia should be hyperlinked to Slide 3, and Hungary should be hyperlinked to Slide 4.

8. On Slides 2, 3, and 4, insert a hyperlink for each country symbol to Slide 1. Then insert a hyperlink for each country's name to the country's Web site shown in Slide 6.

9. On Slide 5, change the bullets to the Star Bullets, change the color to Orange, and then increase the size of the two first-level paragraph bullets to 130% of text and the four countries to 120% of text. Right-align all six bulleted paragraphs.

10. Hide Slides 2, 3, 4, and 6.

11. Apply the Flip transition to all slides and then change the duration to 2.50.

12. Click the Slide Sorter view button, view the slides for consistency, and then click the Normal view button.

13. Change the document properties, as specified by your instructor. Save the presentation using the file name, Lab 6-3 Landlocked Countries.

14. Submit the revised document in the format specified by your instructor.

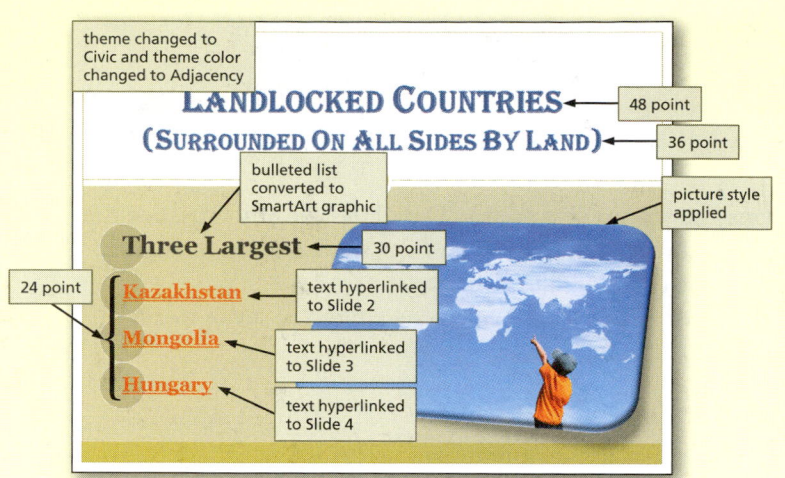

(a) Slide 1

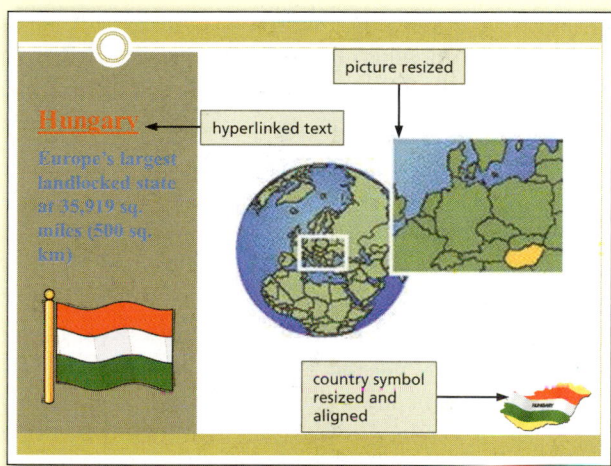

(b) Slide 2

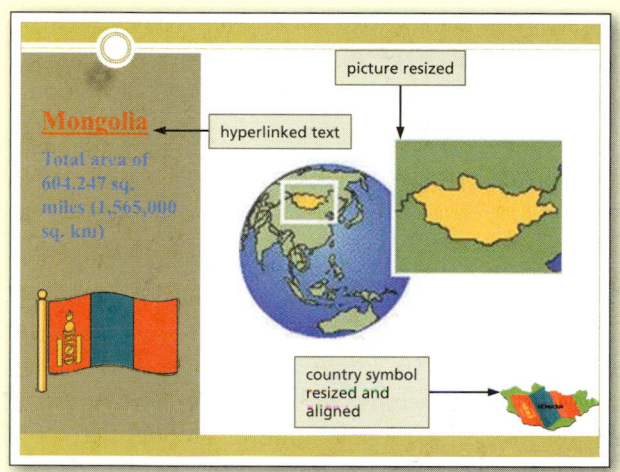

(c) Slide 3

(d) Slide 4

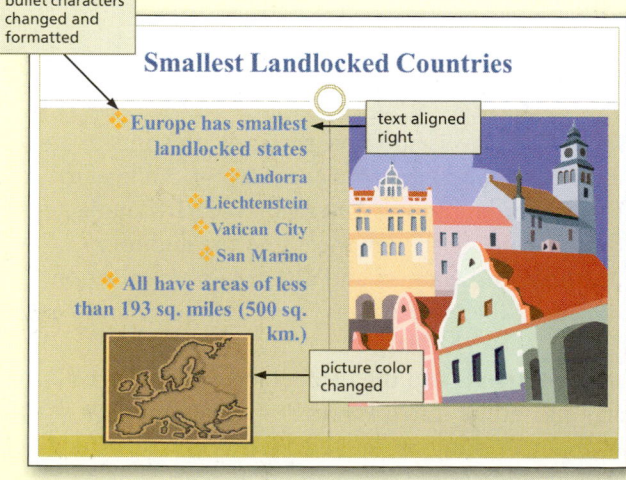

(e) Slide 5

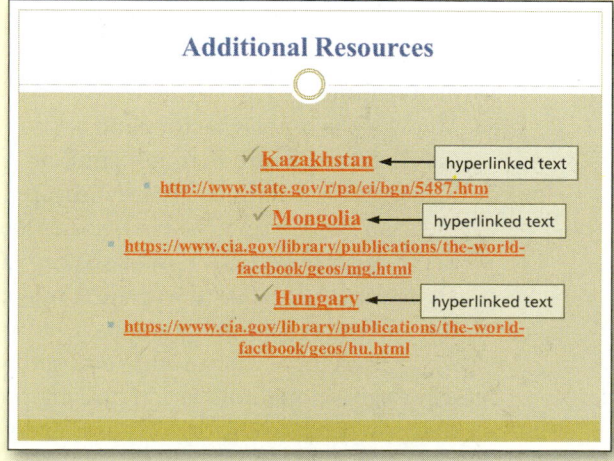

(f) Slide 6 (Hidden Slide)

Figure 6–83

Cases and Places

Apply your creative thinking and problem-solving skills to design and implement a solution.

Note: To complete these assignments, you may be required to use the Data Files for Students. See the inside back cover of this book for instructions on downloading the Data Files for Students, or contact your instructor for information about accessing the required files.

As you design the presentations, remember to use the 7 × 7 rule: a maximum of seven words on a line and a maximum of seven lines on one slide.

1: Designing and Creating a Presentation about Hurricane Names

Academic

You are studying tropical cyclones in your Earth Science class and learning about the names given to hurricanes worldwide. The World Meteorological Organization (WMO) manages the 10 lists of agreed-upon names for the storms throughout the world. The National Hurricane Center developed the original lists of names in 1953. Create a presentation for your class with columns of hurricane names for the Atlantic and North Pacific oceans. Also include the history of naming hurricanes, including when men's names were added to the rotation, when names are retired, and how often the lists are rotated. Apply at least three objectives found at the beginning of this chapter to develop the presentation. Hide at least one slide. Be sure to check spelling.

2: Designing and Creating a Presentation about First Aid Kits

Personal

To be prepared for emergencies, it is a good idea to have a first aid kit in your home and vehicle. You can purchase a kit at a local store or you can assemble one yourself. The Red Cross (www.redcross.org) and the Ready America (www.ready.gov) Web sites provide lists of recommended items to include in a first aid kit. Visit these Web sites and use the information regarding basic first aid kit supplies to create a presentation to share with your family, urging them to buy their own kits or check their current kits. Create a title slide introducing the topic, and create text slides containing columns of supplies that should be included in a first aid kit. Create another slide reminding your family to check the kit contents' expiration dates and flashlight batteries. Also include a hyperlink to your local Red Cross chapter for details on taking a class, donating blood, and volunteering. Use at least three objectives found at the beginning of this chapter to develop the presentation. Use bullets related to medical or emergency themes. Be sure to check spelling.

3: Designing and Creating a Presentation about Sound Levels

Professional

You work in a noisy factory and are concerned about the sound levels and how they are affecting your hearing. More than nine million workers are subjected to loud noises on the job that can lead to hearing loss. Sound levels are measured in decibels (dB). According to the American Speech-Language-Hearing Association (ASHA), noises louder than 80 dB can damage the inner ear and the auditory nerve. Visit the ASHA (www.asha.org) and National Institute on Deafness and Other Communication Disorders (NIDCD) (www.nidcd/nih.org) Web sites and read the information regarding noise levels in the workplace and the relationship to noise-induced hearing loss (NIHL).

Develop a Microsoft Word outline regarding specific sounds and the decibel levels, prolonged exposure to loud noises, and hearing protection. Insert this outline into a PowerPoint presentation that you can share with your boss and your coworkers about working around hazardous noise. Include a table showing the decibel levels of various sounds. Also include information about how employees can benefit physiologically and psychologically from reduced noise levels in the workplace and how they can protect their hearing. Include hyperlinks to the ASHA, NIDCD, and the National Institute for Occupational Safety and Health (www.cdc.gov/niosh) Web sites. Include action buttons and bullet characters that have been changed to pictures or symbols. Be certain to check spelling.

7 | Creating a Self-Running Presentation Containing Animation

Objectives

You will have mastered the material in this chapter when you can:

- Remove a picture background
- Crop and compress a picture
- Insert entrance, emphasis, and exit effects
- Add and adjust motion paths
- Reorder animation sequences
- Associate sounds with animations

- Control animation timing
- Animate SmartArt graphics and charts
- Insert and animate a text box
- Animate bulleted lists
- Rehearse timings
- Set slide show timings manually

7 | Creating a Self-Running Presentation Containing Animation

BTW

Animation Enhancements
Microsoft made many changes and enhancements to animation features in PowerPoint 2010. The Animation tab is reorganized and contains the Animation group to add effects to slide objects. The Timing group allows designers to change the order of elements and set the precise time when they appear on each slide. In addition, the transitions that appeared on the PowerPoint 2007 Animation tab are moved to their own tab.

Introduction

One method used for disseminating information is a **kiosk**. This freestanding, self-service structure is equipped with computer hardware and software and is used to provide information or reference materials to the public. Some have a touch screen or keyboard that serves as an input device and allows users to select various options so they can browse or find specific information. Advanced kiosks allow customers to place orders, make payments, and access the Internet. Many kiosks have multimedia devices for playing sound and video clips.

Various elements on PowerPoint slides can have movement to direct the audience's attention to the point being made. For example, each paragraph in a bulleted list can fade or disappear after being displayed for a set period of time. Each SmartArt graphic component can appear in sequence. A picture can grow, shrink, bounce, or spin, depending upon its relationship to other slide content. PowerPoint's myriad animation effects allow you to use your creativity to design imaginative and distinctive presentations.

Project — Presentation with Adjusted Pictures, Animated Content, and Slide Timings

BTW

Animation Effect Icon Colors
Animation effects allow you to control how objects enter, move on, and exit slides. Using a traffic signal analogy may help you remember the sequence of events. Green icons indicate when the animation effect starts on the slide. Yellow icons represent the object's motion; use them with caution so they do not distract from the message you are conveying to your audience. Red icons indicate when the object stops appearing on a slide.

Interest in the sport of snowboarding, which also is called boarding, has grown since its commercial start in the 1970s and its entry into the Olympics in 1998. Today, almost every North American ski resort allows snowboarders to perform their jumps and aerial feats. Downhill enthusiasts of all ages have experienced the sport, with the average age ranging between 18 and 24 years. Approximately 25 percent of the boarding population is women. The snowboarding project in this chapter (Figure 7–1) explores the sport and uses animation to give a feeling of the twists and turns the boarders experience while on the slopes. The title slide (Figure 7–1a) has animated title text and a snowboarder who performs a flip as she cruises down the mountain. The second slide (Figure 7–1b) shows a snowboarder clip that carves graceful turns during a gentle snowfall. The third slide (Figure 7–1c) uses animated SmartArt to explain how to find the correct snowboard length based on the boarder's height. The growth of the snowboarding industry is depicted in the animated chart on Slide 4 (Figure 7–1d). The last slide (Figure 7–1e) has two lists that describe the essential gear a snowboarder needs to have an enjoyable day on the slopes and an upward-rolling credit line to end the presentation.

(a) Slide 1 (Title Slide with Animated WordArt and Picture)

(b) Slide 2 (Animated Clip with Motion Path and Sound)

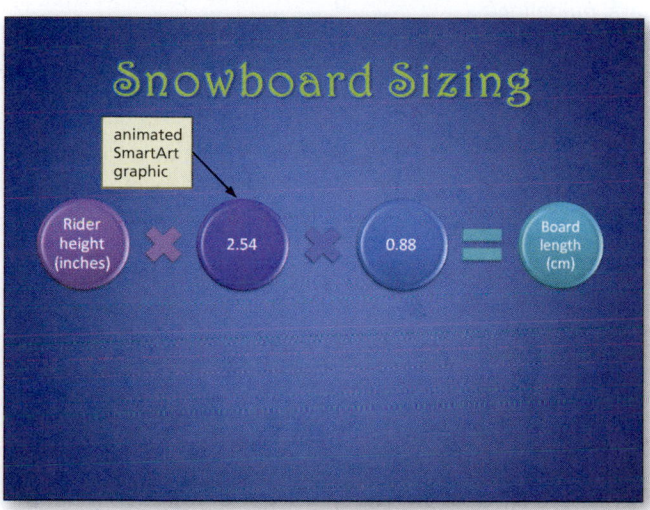

(c) Slide 3 (Animated SmartArt)

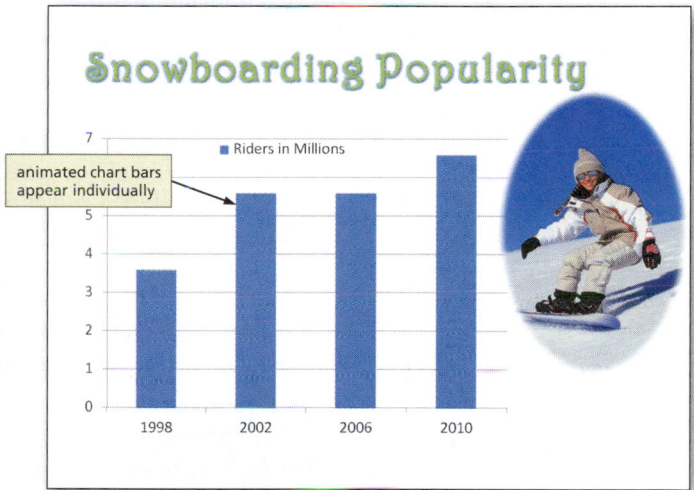

(d) Slide 4 (Animated Chart)

(e) Slide 5 (Animated Bulleted List and Credits)

Figure 7–1

BTW

The Ribbon and Screen Resolution
PowerPoint may change how the groups and buttons within the groups appear on the Ribbon, depending on the computer's screen resolution. Thus, your Ribbon may look different from the ones in this book if you are using a screen resolution other than 1024 × 768.

Overview

As you read through this chapter, you will learn how to create the presentation shown in Figure 7–1 by performing these general tasks:

- Remove picture backgrounds.
- Crop and compress pictures.
- Add entrance, emphasis, and exit animations.
- Create custom animations.
- Animate text boxes, SmartArt, and charts.
- Change transition effect options.
- Set slide show timings.

Plan Ahead

> **General Project Guidelines**
>
> When creating a PowerPoint presentation, the actions you perform and the decisions you make will affect the appearance and characteristics of the finished document. As you create a presentation with illustrations, such as the project shown in Figure 7–1 on the previous page, you should follow these general guidelines:
>
> 1. **Use animation sparingly.** Prior to using an animation effect, think about why you need it and how it will affect your presentation. Do not use animation merely for the sake of using animation.
>
> 2. **Select colors for dimming text.** Paragraphs of text can change color after they display on the slide. This effect, called dimming, can be used effectively to emphasize important points and draw the audience's attention to another area of the slide. Select dimming colors that suit the purpose of the presentation.
>
> 3. **Use quotations judiciously.** At times, the words of noted world leaders, writers, and prominent entertainers can create interest in your presentation and inspire audiences. If you choose to integrate their quotations into your slide show, give credit to the source and keep the original wording.
>
> 4. **Give your audience sufficient time to view your slides.** On average, an audience member will spend only eight seconds viewing a basic slide with a simple graphic or a few words. They need much more time to view charts, graphs, and SmartArt graphics. When you are setting slide timings, keep this length of time in mind, particularly when the presentation is viewed at a kiosk without a speaker's physical presence.
>
> When necessary, more specific details concerning the above guidelines are presented at appropriate points in the chapter. The chapter also will identify the actions performed and decisions made regarding these guidelines during the creation of the presentation shown in Figure 7–1.

To Start PowerPoint, Open a Presentation, and Rename the Presentation

To begin this presentation, you will open a file located on the Data Files for Students. See the inside back cover of this book for instructions on downloading the Data Files for Students, or contact your instructor for more information about accessing the required files. If you are using a computer to step through the project in this chapter and you want your screens to match the figures in this book, you should change your screen's resolution to 1024 × 768.

The following steps start PowerPoint, open a file, and then save it with a new file name.

1 Start PowerPoint. If necessary, maximize the PowerPoint window.

2 Open the presentation, Snowboarding, located on the Data Files for Students.

3 Save the presentation using the file name, Animated Snowboarding.

Adjusting and Cropping a Picture

At times you may desire to emphasize one section of a picture and eliminate distracting background content. PowerPoint includes picture formatting tools that allow you to edit pictures. The **Remove Background** command isolates the foreground from the background, and the **Crop** command removes content along the top, bottom, left, or right edges. Once you format the picture to include only the desired content, you can **compress** the image to reduce the file size.

To Remove a Background

The title slide in the Animated Snowboarding presentation has a picture of a snowboarder wearing tan and white clothes in the foreground. Snow is present in the background of this picture, and you want to eliminate it to direct the viewers' attention to the snowboarder. PowerPoint 2010's Background Removal feature makes it easy to eliminate extraneous aspects. When you click the Remove Background button, PowerPoint attempts to select the foreground of the picture and overlay a magenta marquee selection on this area. You then can adjust the marquee shape and size to contain all foreground picture components you want to keep. The following steps remove the background from the snowboarder picture.

1

• With the title slide displaying, double-click the snowboarder picture in the foreground to display the Picture Tools Format tab.

• Click the Remove Background button (Picture Tools Format tab | Adjust group) to display the Background Removal tab and a marquee selection area (Figure 7–2).

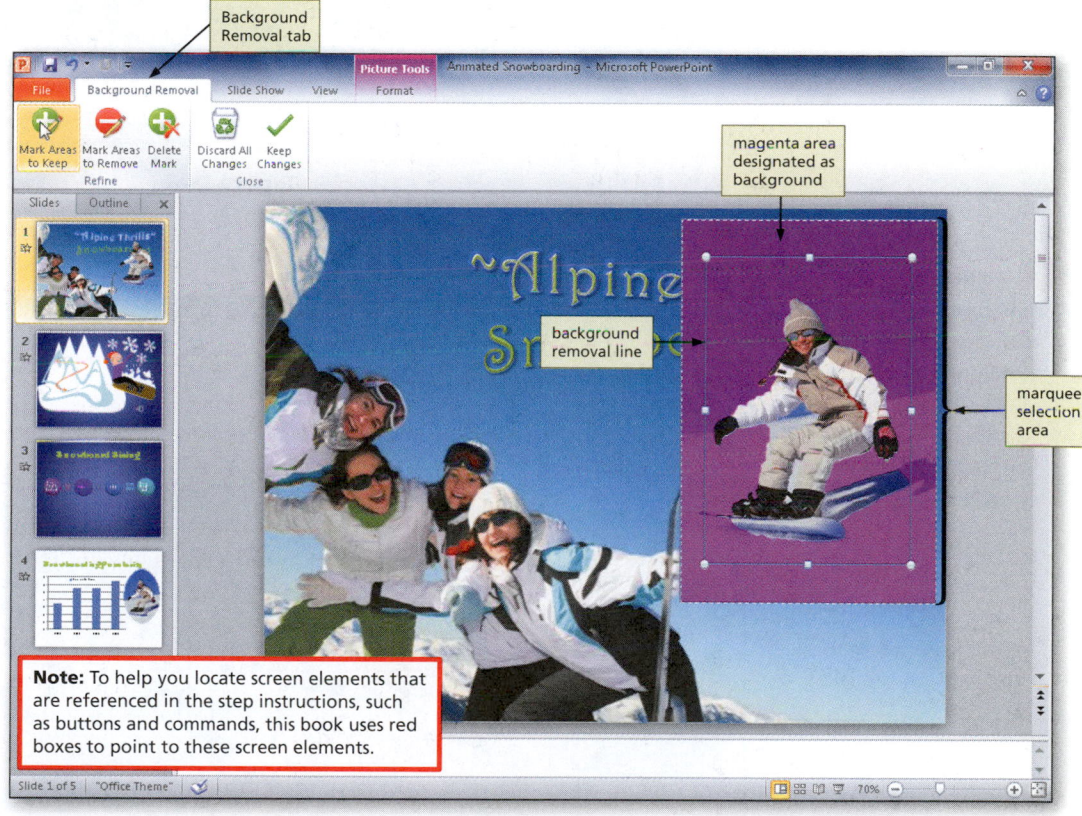

Figure 7–2

Note: To help you locate screen elements that are referenced in the step instructions, such as buttons and commands, this book uses red boxes to point to these screen elements.

Q&A How does PowerPoint determine the area to display within the marquee?
Microsoft Research software engineers developed the algorithms that determine the portions of the picture in the foreground.

• Click and drag the handles on the background removal lines so that the snowboarder and her snowboard are contained within the marquee (Figure 7–3).

Q&A

Why do some parts of the background, such as the area under her right arm and below her knees, still display?

The removal tool was not able to determine that those areas are part of the background. You will remove them in the next set of steps.

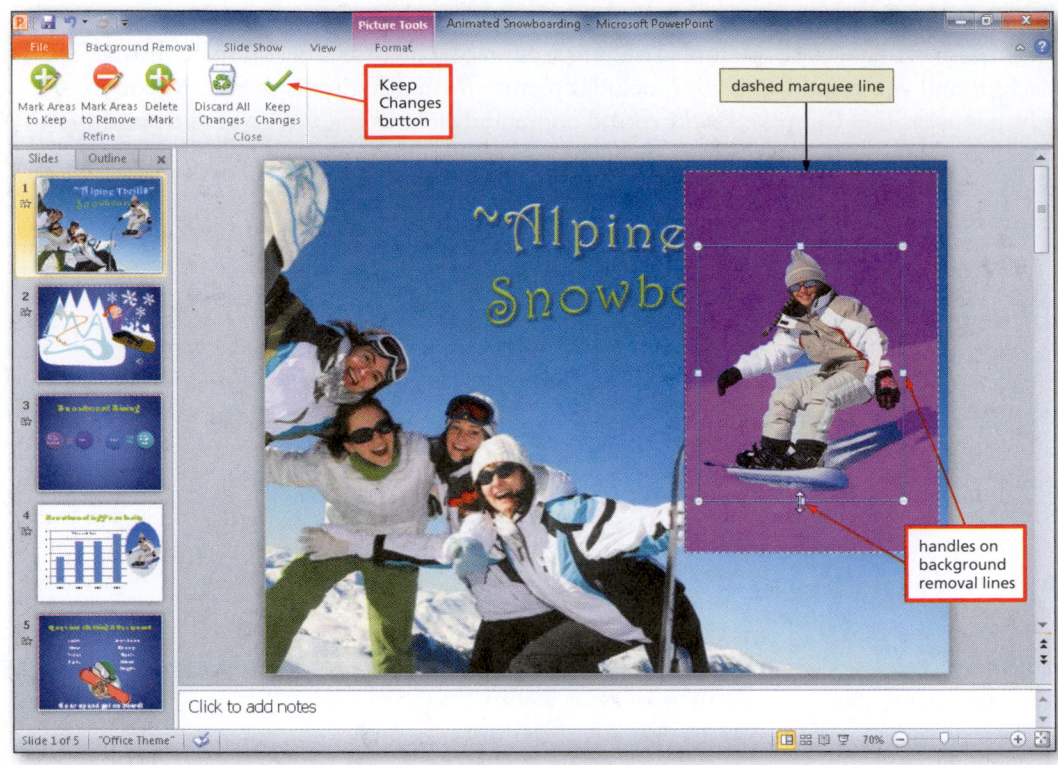

Figure 7–3

• Click the Keep Changes button (Background Removal tab | Close group) to discard the unwanted picture background (Figure 7–4).

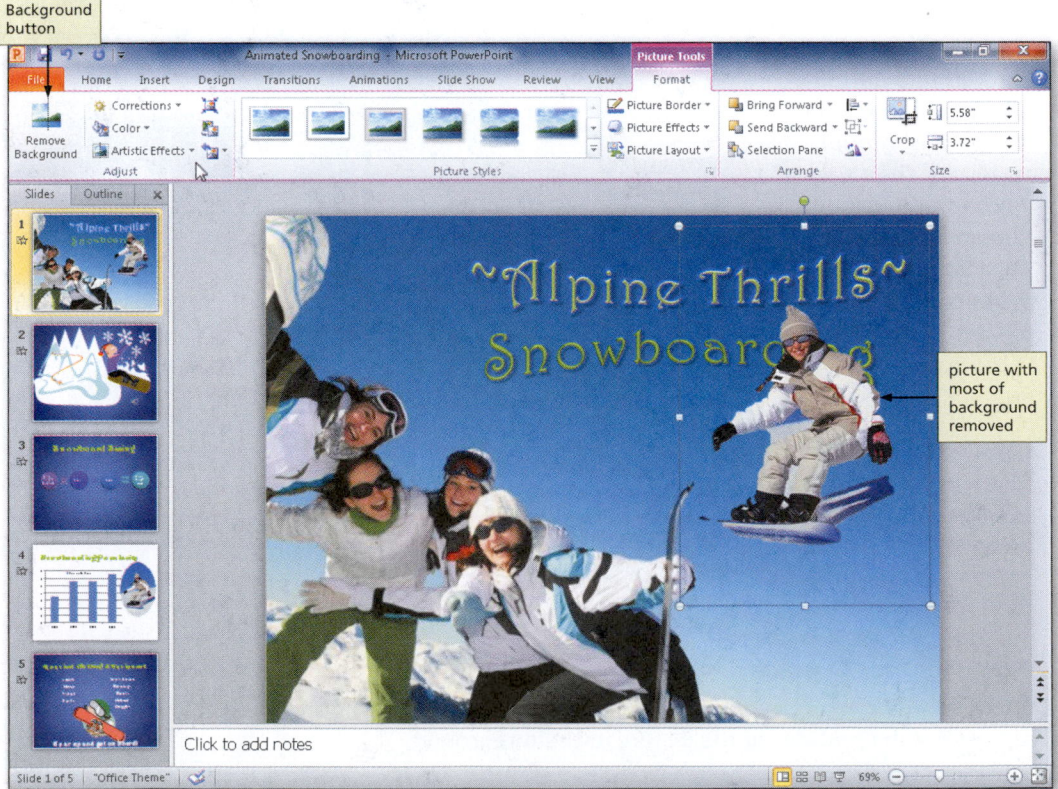

Figure 7–4

To Refine Background Removal

In many cases, the Remove Background command discards all the undesired picture components. Occasionally, however, some pieces remain when the background is integrated closely with the foreground picture. In the title slide snowboarding picture, for example, the algorithms could not distinguish the snow and sky between the boarder's right arm and torso, below her knees, and directly behind her. Tools on the Background Removal tab allow you to mark specific areas to remove. The following steps remove the unwanted background areas from around the snowboarder.

• Click the Remove Background button again to display the Background Removal tab and the marquee selection area.

• Click the Mark Areas to Remove button (Background Removal tab | Refine group) and then position the mouse pointer in the white area above the snowboarder's right knee (Figure 7–5).

Q&A Why did my mouse pointer change shape?

The mouse pointer changed to a pencil to indicate you are about to draw on a precise area of the picture.

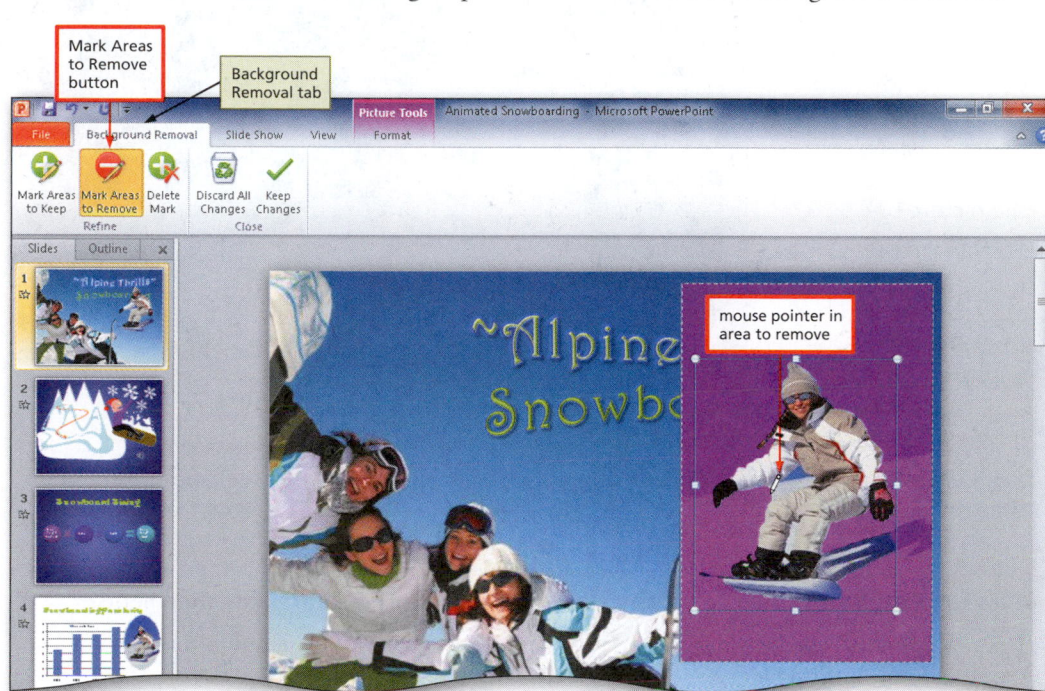

Figure 7–5

• Click and then drag the mouse pointer to the snowboarder's jacket to indicate the portion of the background to delete (Figure 7–6).

Q&A Why does a circle with a minus sign display on the dotted line?

That symbol indicates that you manually specified the deletion of a portion of the background.

Q&A Why does some of the background remain on my picture?

The location where you drew your line determines the area that PowerPoint deletes. You may need to make several passes to remove all of the unwanted background.

Figure 7–6

3

- Repeat Step 2 to delete the white area below her knees and the area to the right of her left boot (Figure 7–7).

Q&A

I mistakenly removed the snowboard when I tried to remove some of the background. How can I keep the snowboard in the picture?

You can mark the snowboard as an area to keep and then delete the background.

Figure 7–7

Q&A

If I marked an area with a line and now want to keep it, can I reverse my action?

Yes. Click the Delete Mark button (Background Removal tab | Refine area) and then click the line to remove it. You also can press CTRL+Z immediately after you draw the line.

4

- Click the Keep Changes button to review the results of your background refinements.

Q&A

The tail no longer is connected to the rest of the board, or my entire board is removed. Can I add this missing piece?

Yes. In the next step, you will instruct PowerPoint to keep any necessary area that was discarded.

5

- Click the Remove Background button again, click the Mark Areas to Keep button (Background Removal tab | Refine group), and then position the mouse pointer on the snow on the tail of the snowboard.

- Click and then drag the mouse pointer to the front of the snowboard (Figure 7–8).

6

- Click the Keep Changes button to review the results of your background refinement.

Figure 7–8

Q&A

If I want to see the original picture at a later time, can I display the components I deleted?

Yes. If you click the Discard All Changes button (Background Removal tab | Close area), all the deleted pieces will reappear.

To Crop a Picture

The Remove Background command deleted the snow and sky components of the picture from your view, but they still remain in the picture. Because you will not need to display the background in this presentation, you can remove the unnecessary edges of the picture. When you crop a picture, you trim the vertical or horizontal sides so that the most important area of the picture is displayed. Any picture file type except animated GIF can be cropped. The following steps crop the title slide snowboarder picture.

1
- With the snowboarder picture still selected, click the Crop button (Picture Tools Format tab | Size group) to display the cropping handles on the picture.

- Position the mouse pointer over the center cropping handle on the right side of the picture (Figure 7–9).

Q&A Why did my mouse pointer change shape?

The mouse pointer changed to indicate you are about to crop a picture.

Figure 7–9

2
- Drag the center cropping handle inward so that the right edge of the marquee is beside the snowboarder's glove on her left hand.

- Drag the center cropping handles on the left, upper, and lower edges of the background removal lines inward to frame the picture (Figure 7–10).

Q&A Does cropping actually cut the picture's edges?

No. Although you cannot see the cropped edges, they exist until you save the file.

3
- Click an area of the slide other than the picture to crop the edges.

Q&A Can I change the crop lines?

If you have not saved the file, you can undo your crops by clicking the Undo button on the Quick Access Toolbar, clicking the Reset Picture button (Picture Tools Format tab | Adjust group), or pressing CTRL+Z.

Figure 7–10

Other Ways
1. Enter dimensions in Left, Right, Top, and Bottom boxes in Crop position   area (Format Picture dialog box | Crop tab)

To Compress a Picture

Pictures inserted into slides greatly increase the total PowerPoint file size. PowerPoint automatically compresses picture files inserted into slides by eliminating details, generally with no visible loss of quality. You can increase the compression and, in turn, decrease the file size if you instruct PowerPoint to compress a picture you have cropped so you can save space on a storage medium such as a hard disk, USB flash drive, or optical disk. Although these storage devices generally have a large storage capacity, you might want to reduce the file size for e-mailing the file or reducing the download time from an FTP or Web site.

The snowboard picture on the title slide picture is cropped and displays only the female snowboarder. You will not need any of the invisible portions of the picture, so you can delete them permanently and reduce the picture file size. The following steps compress the title slide snowboarder picture.

1
- Double-click the snowboarder picture to display the Picture Tools Format tab. Click the Compress Pictures button (Picture Tools Format tab | Adjust group) to display the Compress Pictures dialog box (Figure 7–11).

Q&A Should I apply an artistic effect prior to or after compressing a picture?

Compress a picture and then apply the artistic effect.

2
- Click the OK button (Compress Pictures dialog box) to delete the cropped portions of this picture and compress the image.

Q&A Can I undo the compression?

Yes, as long as you have not closed the file.

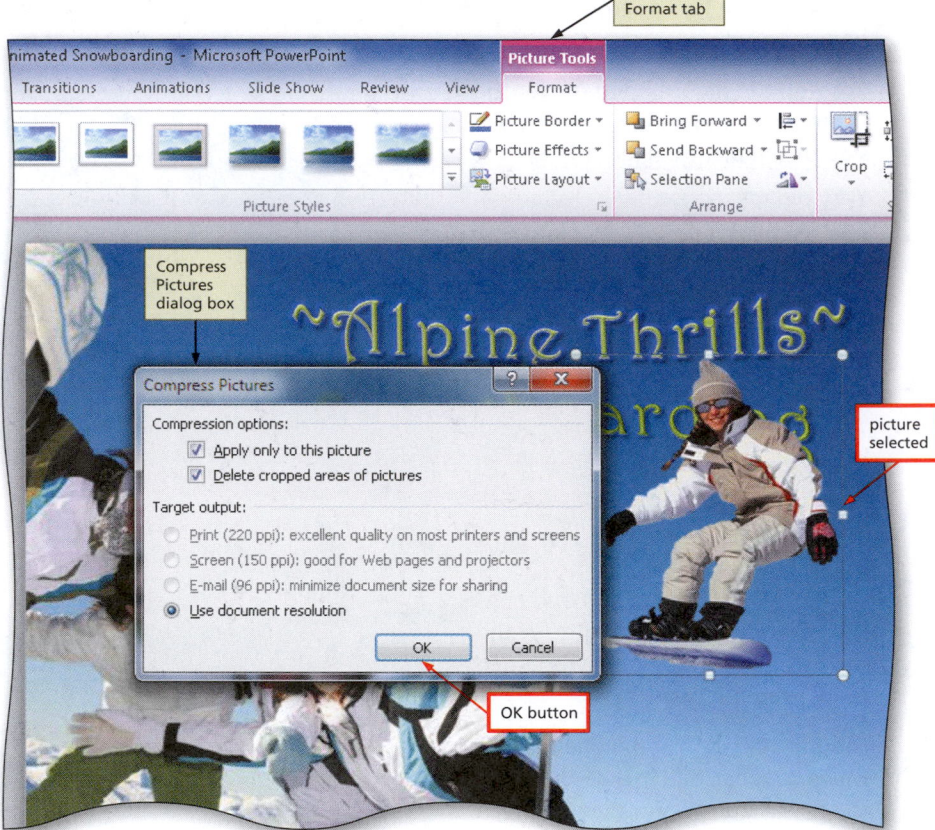

Figure 7–11

Animating Slide Content

Animation includes special visual and sound effects applied to text or other content. You already are familiar with one form of animation: transitions between slides. To add visual interest and clarity to a presentation, you can animate various parts of an individual slide, including clips, shapes, text, and other slide elements. For example, each paragraph on the slide can spin as it is displayed. Individual letters and shapes also can spin or move in a wide variety of motions. PowerPoint has a variety of built-in animations that will fade, wipe, or fly-in text and graphics.

Custom Animations

You can create your own **custom animations** to meet your unique needs. Custom animation effects are grouped in categories: entrance, exit, emphasis, and motion paths. **Entrance** effects, as the name implies, determine how slide elements first appear on a slide. **Exit** animations work in the opposite manner as entrance effects: They remove slide elements. **Emphasis** effects modify text and objects displayed on the screen. For example, letters may darken or increase in font size. The entrance, exit, and emphasis animations are grouped into categories: Basic, Subtle, Moderate, and Exciting. You can set the animation speed to Very Fast, Fast, Medium, Slow, or Very Slow.

The Slide 1 background picture shows skiing enthusiasts posing on a ski slope. When the presentation begins, the audience will view these skiers and then see a snowboarder enter from the upper-left corner, slide down the slope, perform an aerial trick as she reaches the center of the slide, and then continue down the slope toward the lower-right corner. To create this animation on the slide, you will use entrance, emphasis, and exit effects.

If you need to move objects on a slide once they are displayed, you can define a **motion path**. This predefined movement determines where an object will be displayed and then travel. Motion paths are grouped into the Basic, Lines & Curves, and Special categories. You can draw a **custom path** if none of the predefined paths meets your needs.

Plan Ahead

Use animation sparingly.
PowerPoint audience members usually take notice the first time an animation is displayed on the screen. When the same animation effect is applied throughout a presentation, the viewers generally become desensitized to the effect unless it is highly unusual or annoying. Resist the urge to use animation effects simply because PowerPoint provides the tools to do so. You have options to decide how text or a slide element enters and exits a slide and how it is displayed once it is present on the slide; your goal, however, is to use these options wisely. Audiences soon tire of a presentation riddled with animations, causing them to quickly lose their impact.

To Animate a Picture Using an Entrance Effect

The snowboarder you modified will not appear on Slide 1 when you begin the presentation. Instead, she will enter the slide from the uphill part of the slope, which is in the upper-left corner of the slide, to give the appearance she is snowboarding down the mountain. She will then continue downhill until she reaches the center of the slide. Entrance effects are colored green in the Animation gallery. The following steps apply an entrance effect to the snowboarder picture.

● With Slide 1 displaying, move the snowboarder picture to the center of the slide, as shown in Figure 7–12.

Q&A Why am I moving the picture to this location?

This area of the slide is where you want the picture to stop moving after she enters the slide in the upper-left corner.

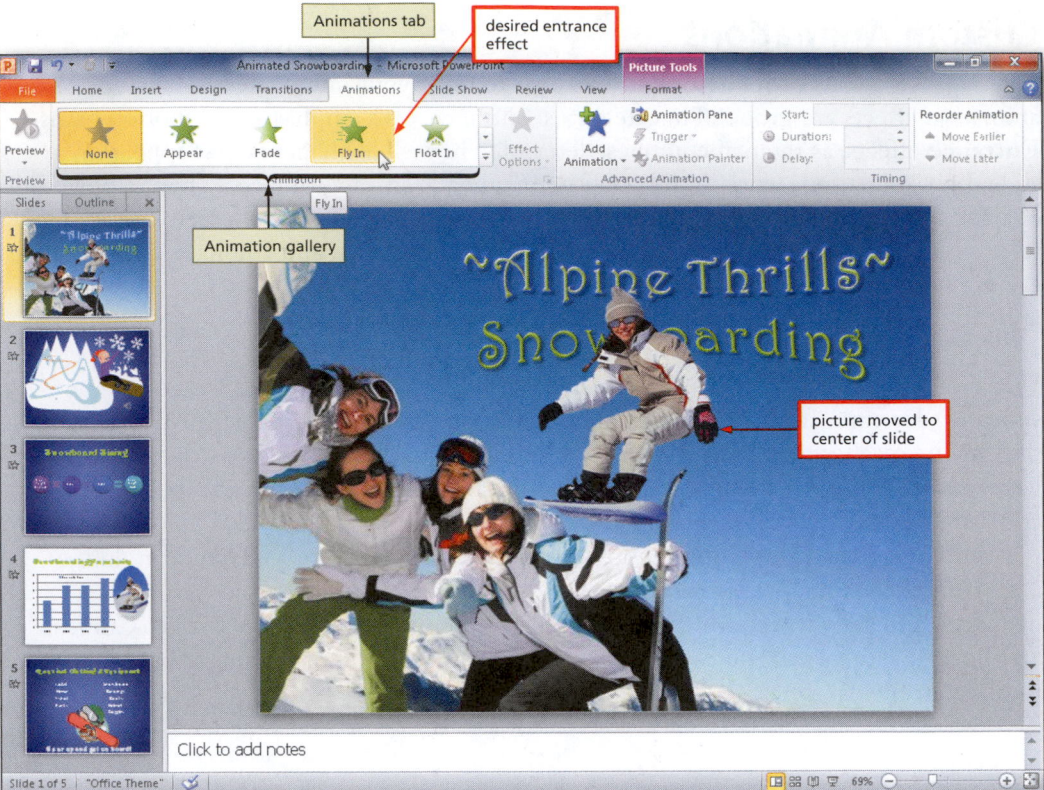

Figure 7–12

● Click the Animations tab on the Ribbon and then point to the Fly In animation in the Animation gallery (Animation group) to display a live preview of this animation (Figure 7–12).

🔍 **Experiment**

● Point to three other animations shown in the Animation gallery and watch the snowboarder enter the slide.

Q&A Are more entrance animations available?

Yes. Click the More button in the Animation gallery to see additional animations. You can select one of the 13 entrance animations that are displayed, or you can click the More Entrance Effects command to expand the selection.

● Click Fly In to apply this entrance animation to the snowboarder picture.

Q&A Why does the number 1 appear in a box on the left side of the picture?

The 1 is a sequence number and indicates Fly In is the first animation that will appear on the slide when you click the mouse.

To Change Animation Direction

By default, the picture appears on the slide by entering from the bottom edge. You can modify this direction and specify that it enters from another side or from a corner. The following steps change the snowboard picture entrance animation direction to the upper-left corner.

1

- Click the Effect Options button (Animations tab | Animation group) to display the Direction gallery (Figure 7–13).

Q&A Why does a gold box appear around the From Bottom arrow?

From Bottom is the default entrance direction applied to the animation.

- Point to From Top-Left in the Direction gallery to display a live preview of this animation effect.

🔍 **Experiment**

- Point to various arrows in the Direction gallery and watch the snowboarder enter the slide from different sides and corners.

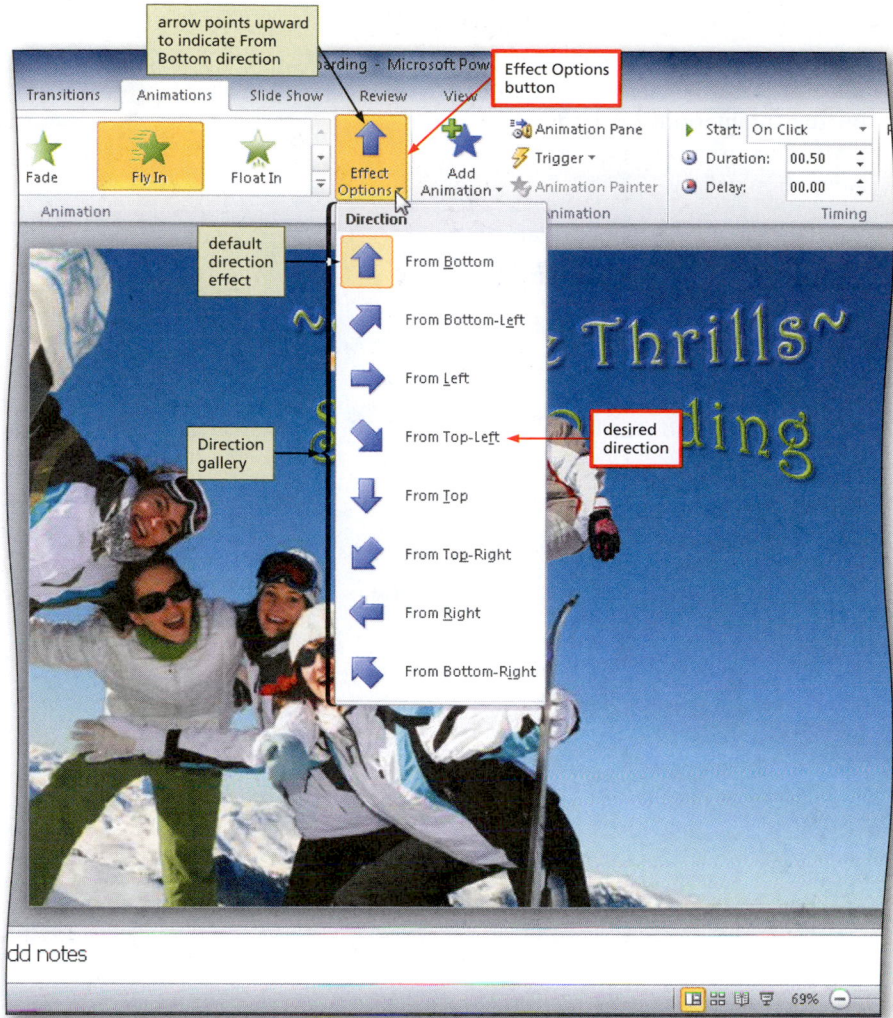

Figure 7–13

2

- Click the From Top-Left arrow to apply this direction to the entrance animation.

Q&A Can I change this entrance effect?

Yes. Repeat Step 1 to select another direction.

To Animate a Picture Using an Emphasis Effect

The snowboarder will enter the slide from the upper-left corner and stop in the center of the slide. You then want her to perform an acrobatic trick. PowerPoint provides several effects that you can apply to a picture once it appears on a slide. These movements are categorized as emphasis effects, and they are colored yellow in the Animation gallery. You already have applied an entrance effect to the snowboarder picture, so you want to add another animation to this picture. The following steps apply an emphasis effect to the snowboarder picture after the entrance effect.

- With the snowboarder picture still selected, click the Add Animation button (Animations tab | Advanced Animation group) to expand the Animation gallery.

- Point to Spin in the Emphasis area to display a live preview of this effect (Figure 7–14).

🔍 Experiment

- Point to various effects in the Emphasis area and watch the snowboarder.

Q&A Are more emphasis effects available in addition to those shown in the Animation gallery?

Yes. To see additional emphasis effects, click More Emphasis Effects in the lower portion of the Animation gallery. The effects are arranged in the Basic, Subtle, Moderate, and Exciting categories.

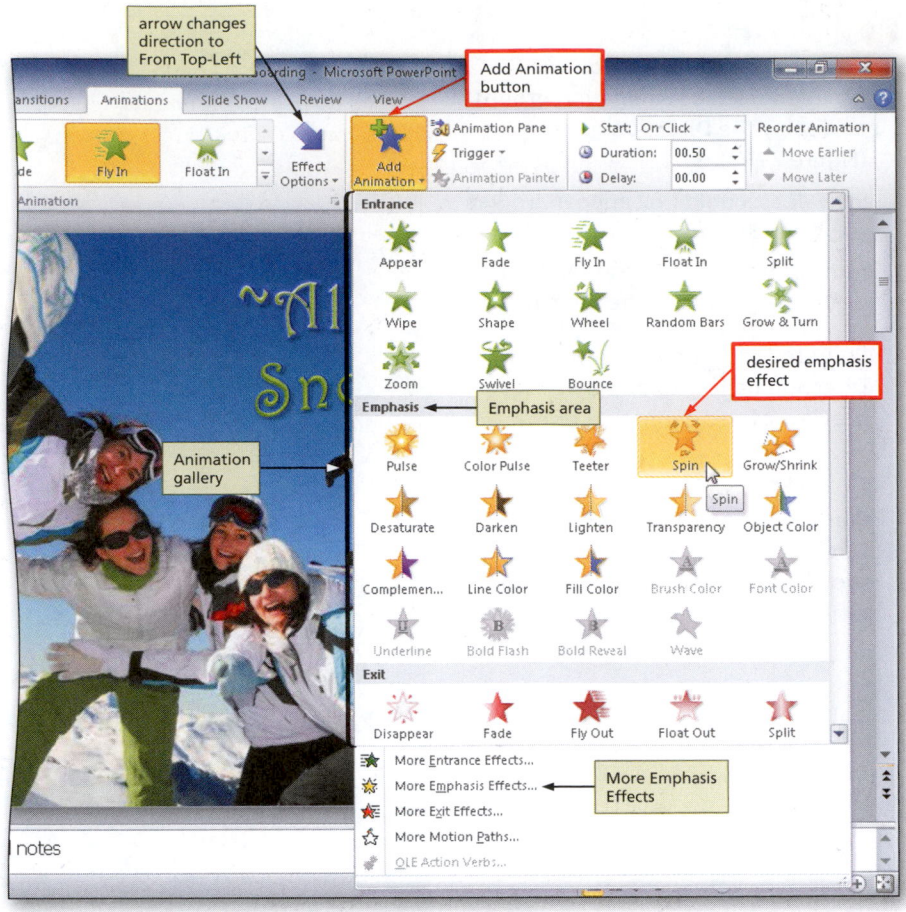

Figure 7–14

- Click Spin to apply this emphasis effect to the snowboarder picture.

Q&A Do I need to use both an entrance and an emphasis effect, or can I use only an emphasis effect?

You can use one or the other effect, or both effects.

Q&A Why does the number 2 appear in a box below the number 1 on the left side of the picture?

The 2 in the numbered tag indicates a second animation is applied in the animation sequence.

To Animate a Picture Using an Exit Effect

The animated snowboarder picture will enter the slide from the upper-left corner, stop in the center of the slide, and then perform a spin trick. She then will continue down the slope and snowboard off the slide in the lower-right corner. To continue this animation sequence, you first need to apply an exit effect. As with the entrance and emphasis effects, PowerPoint provides a wide variety of effects that you can apply to remove a picture from a slide. These exit effects are colored red in the Animation gallery. You already have applied the Fly In entrance effect, so the Fly Out exit effect would give continuity to the animation sequence. The following steps add this exit effect to the snowboarder picture after the emphasis effect.

1

● With the snowboarder picture still selected, click the Add Animation button again to expand the Animation gallery.

● Point to Fly Out in the Exit area to display a live preview of this effect (Figure 7–15).

Experiment

● Point to various effects in the Exit area and watch the snowboarder. You will not be able to view all the effects because they are hidden by the Animation gallery, but you can move the snowboarder clip to the left side of the slide to view the effects and then move her back to the middle of the slide.

Q&A | Are more exit effects available in addition to those shown in the Animation gallery?

Yes. To see additional exit effects, click More Exit Effects in the lower portion of the Animation gallery. The effects are arranged in the Basic, Subtle, Moderate, and Exciting categories.

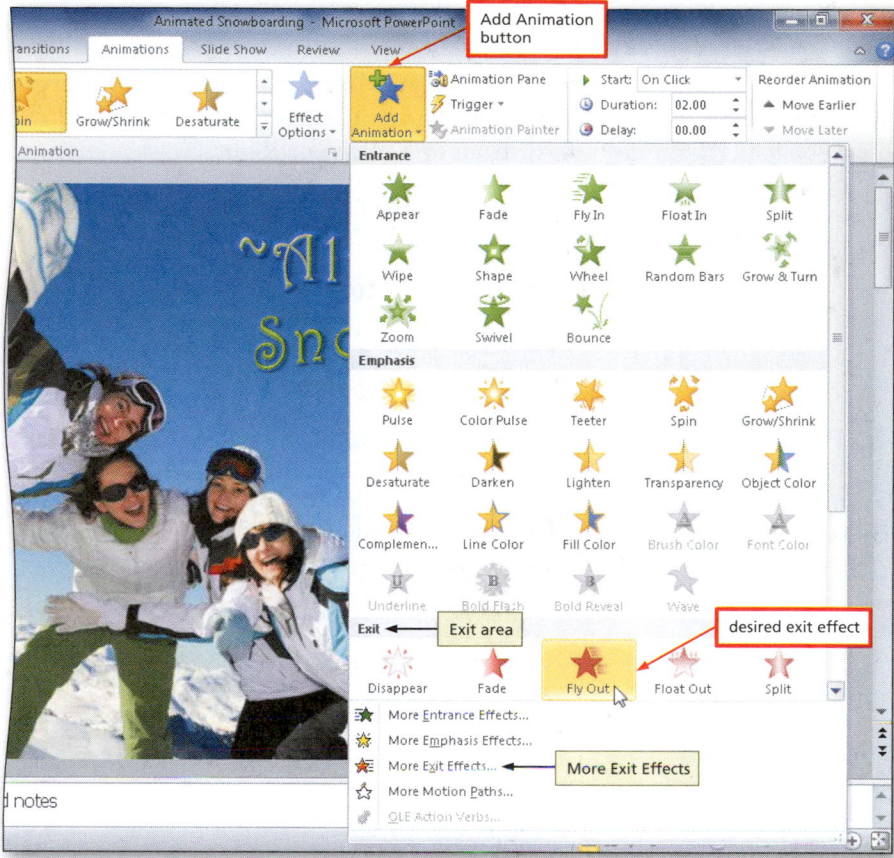

Figure 7–15

2

● Click Fly Out to add this exit effect to the sequence of snowboarder picture animations (Figure 7–16).

Q&A | How can I tell that this exit effect has been applied?

The Fly Out effect is displayed in the Animation gallery (Animations tab | Animation group), and the number 3 is displayed to the left of the snowboarder picture.

Figure 7–16

To Change Exit Animation Direction

The default direction for a picture to exit a slide is To Bottom. In this presentation, you want the snowboarder to exit in the lower-right corner to give the impression she is continuing down the slope. The following steps change the exit animation direction from To Bottom to To Bottom-Right.

1 Click the Effect Options button (Animations tab | Animation group) to display the Direction gallery.

2 Click the To Bottom-Right arrow to apply this direction to the exit animation effect.

To Preview an Animation Sequence

Although you have not completed developing the presentation, you should view the animation you have added. By default, the entrance, emphasis, and exit animations will be displayed when you run the presentation and click the mouse. The following step runs the presentation and displays the three animations.

1

- Click the Preview button (Animations tab | Preview group) to view all the Slide 1 animations (Figure 7–17).

Q&A | Why does a red square appear in the middle of the circle on the Preview button when I click that button?

The red square indicates the animation sequence is in progress. Ordinarily, a green arrow is displayed in the circle.

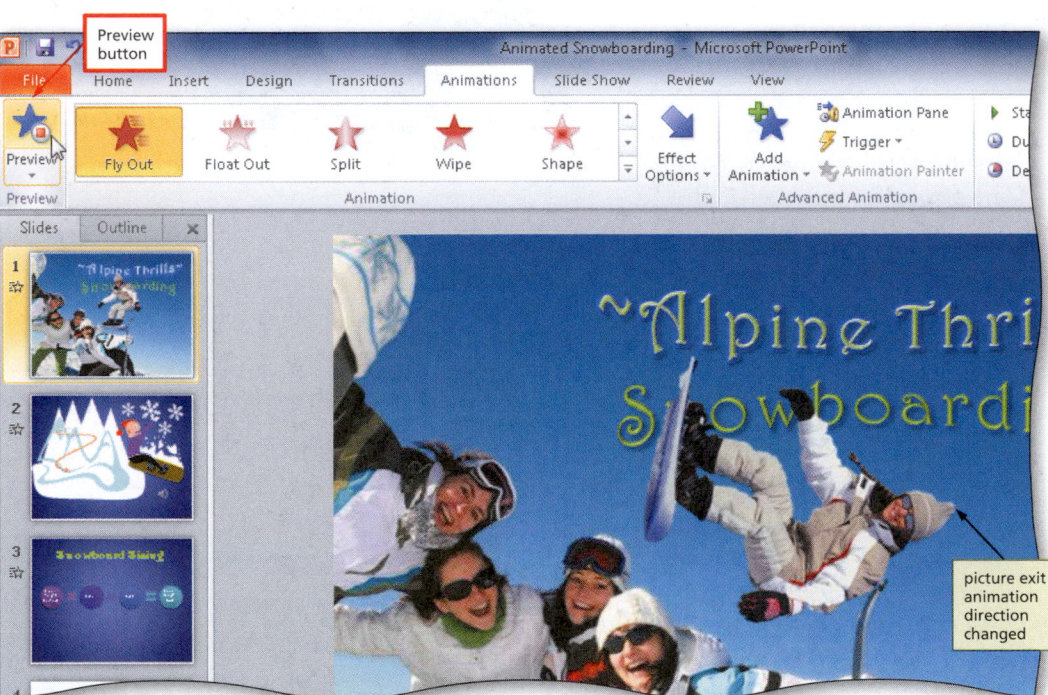

Figure 7–17

To Modify Entrance Animation Timing

The three animation effects are displayed quickly. To create a dramatic effect, you can change the timing so that the background picture displays and then, a few seconds later, the snowboarder starts to glide down the mountain slowly. The default setting is to start each animation with a mouse click, but you can change this setting so that the entrance effect is delayed until a specified number of seconds has passed. The following steps modify the start, delay, and duration settings for the entrance animation.

1
• Click the 1 numbered tag on the left side of the snowboarder picture and then click the Start Animation Timing button arrow (Animations tab | Timing group) to display the Start menu (Figure 7–18).

2
• Click After Previous to change the start timing setting.

Q&A Why did the numbered tags change from 1, 2, 3 to 0, 1, 2?

The first animation now occurs automatically without a mouse click. The first and second mouse clicks now will apply the emphasis and exit animations.

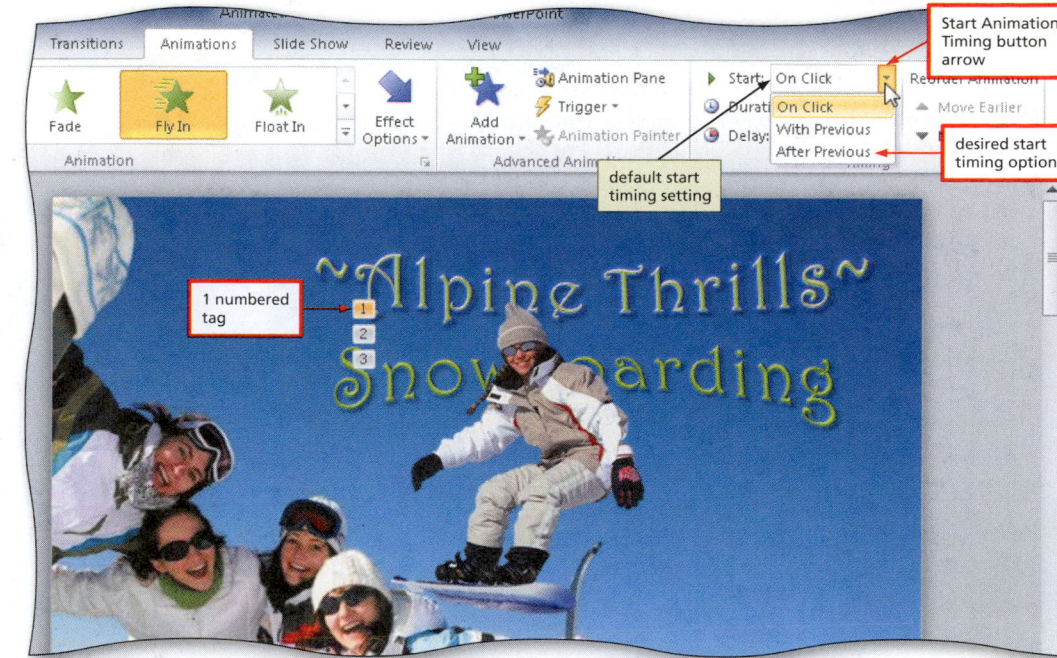

Figure 7–18

Q&A What is the difference between the With Previous and After Previous settings?

The With Previous setting starts the effect simultaneously with any prior animation; the After Previous setting starts the animation after a prior animation has ended. If the prior animation is fast or a short duration, it may be difficult for a viewer to discern the difference between these two settings.

3
• Click the Animation Duration up arrow (Animations tab | Timing group) several times to increase the time from 00.50 second to 05.00 seconds (Figure 7–19).

• Click the Preview button to view the animations.

Q&A What is the difference between the duration time and the delay time?

The duration time is the length of time in which the animation occurs; the delay time is the length of time that passes before the animation begins.

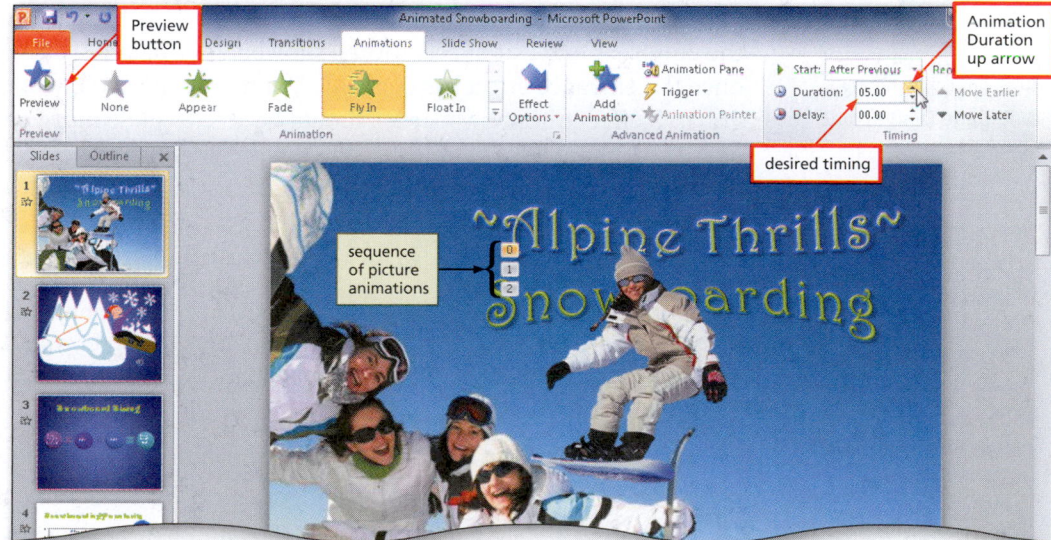

Figure 7–19

Q&A Can I type the speed in the Duration text box instead of clicking the arrow to adjust the speed?

Yes. Typing the numbers allows you to set a precise timing.

4

- Click the Animation Delay up arrow (Animations tab | Timing group) several times to increase the time from 00.00 seconds to 04.00 seconds (Figure 7–20).

- Click the Preview button to view the animations.

Q&A

Can I adjust the delay time I just set?

Yes. Click the Animation Delay up or down arrows and run the slide show to display Slide 1 until you find the time that best fits your presentation.

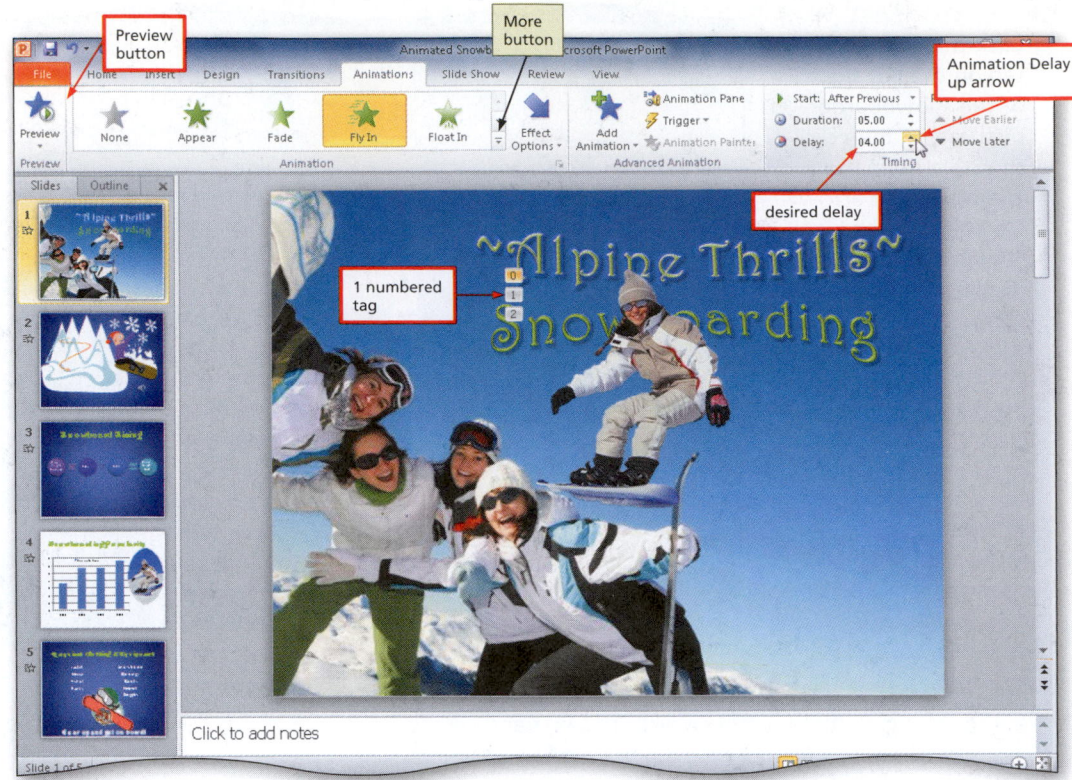

Figure 7–20

BTW

Q&As

For a complete list of the Q&As found in many of the step-by-step sequences in this book, visit the PowerPoint 2010 Q&A Web page (scsite.com/ppt2010/qa).

To Modify Emphasis and Exit Timings

Now that the entrance animation settings have been modified, you then can change the emphasis and exit effects for the snowboarder picture. The emphasis effect can occur once the entrance effect has concluded, and then the exit effect can commence. With gravity's effect, the snowboarder should be able to glide more quickly down the lower part of the mountain, so you will shorten the duration of her exit effect compared with the duration of the entrance effect. The animation sequence should flow without stopping, so you will not change the default delay timing of 00.00 seconds. The following steps modify the start and duration settings for the emphasis and exit animations.

1 Click the 1 sequence number, which represents the emphasis effect, on the left side of the snowboarder picture, click the Start Animation Timing button arrow (Animations tab | Timing group) to display the Start menu and then click After Previous to change the start timing option setting.

2 Click the Animation Duration up arrow (Animations tab | Timing group) several times to increase the time to 03.00 seconds.

3 Click the 1 sequence number, which now represents the exit effect, click the Start Animation Timing button arrow, and then click After Previous.

4 Click the Animation Duration up arrow several times to increase the time to 04.00 seconds.

5 Preview the Slide 1 animation.

To Animate Title Text Placeholder Paragraphs

The snowboarder picture on Slide 1 has one entrance, one emphasis, and one exit animation, and you can add similar animations to the two paragraphs in the Slide 1 title text placeholder. For a special effect, you can add several emphasis animations to one slide element. The following steps add one entrance and two emphasis animations to the title text paragraphs.

1

• Double-click the Slide 1 title text placeholder border so that it displays as a solid line.

• Click the More button (shown in Figure 7–20) in the Animation gallery (Animations tab | Animation group) to expand the Animation gallery (Figure 7–21).

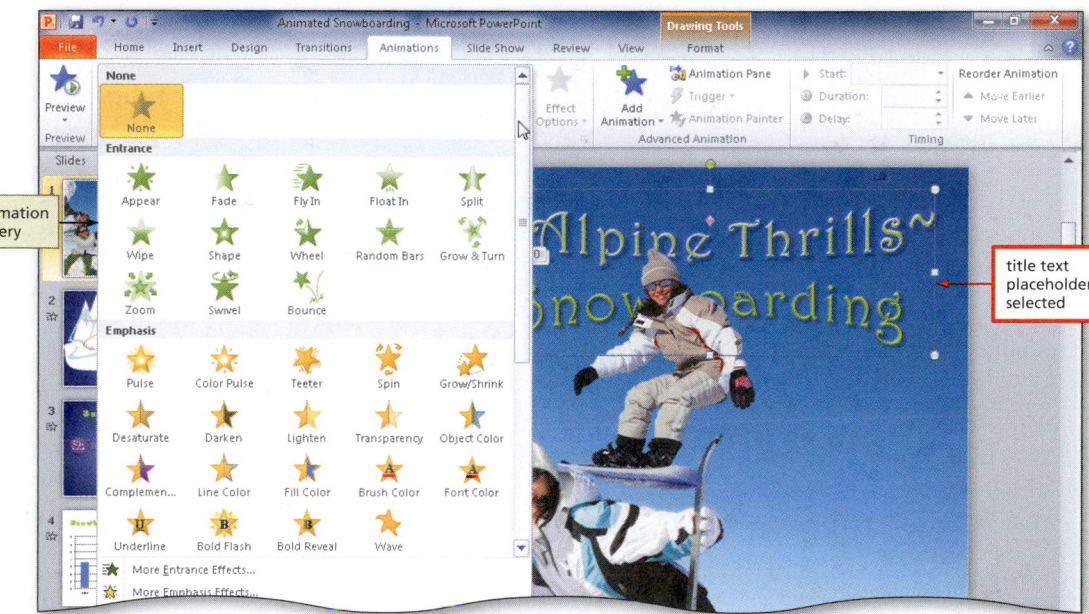

Figure 7–21

2

• Point to the Zoom entrance effect in the Animation gallery to display a live preview of this effect.

 Experiment

• Point to various effects in the Entrance area and watch the title text. You will not be able to view all the effects because they are hidden by the Animation gallery, but you can move the title text placeholder to the left side of the slide to view the effects and then move the placeholder back to its original position.

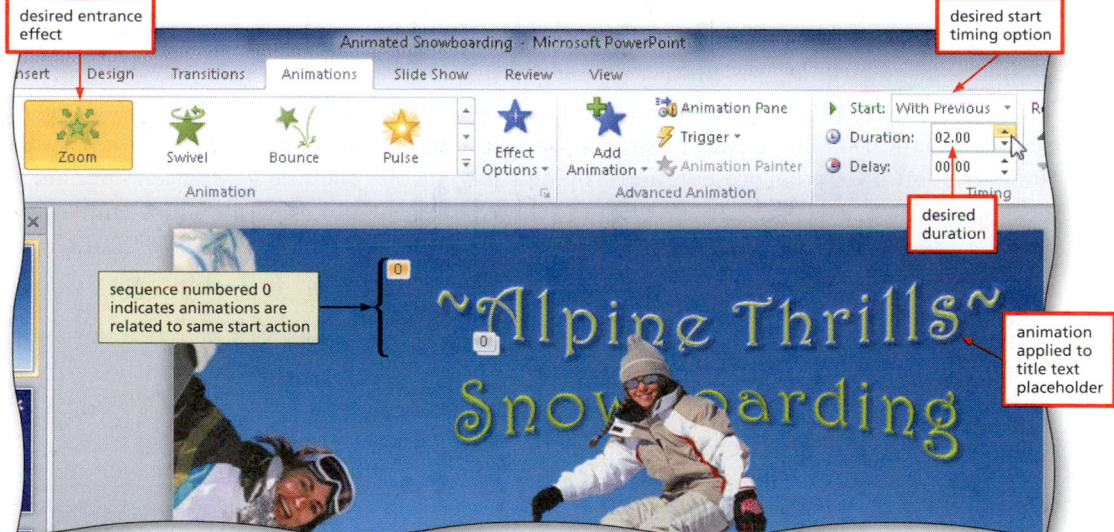

Figure 7–22

• Click the Zoom entrance effect in the Animation gallery to add this animation.

• Change the start timing option to With Previous.

• Change the duration time to 02.00 seconds (Figure 7–22).

Q&A | Do I need to change the delay time?

No. The title text placeholder can start appearing on the slide when the snowboarder exit effect is beginning.

3

- Click the Add Animation button and then click the Font Color emphasis animation effect.

- Change the start timing option to After Previous.

- Click the Add Animation button and then click the Underline emphasis animation effect.

- Change the start timing option to With Previous (Figure 7–23).

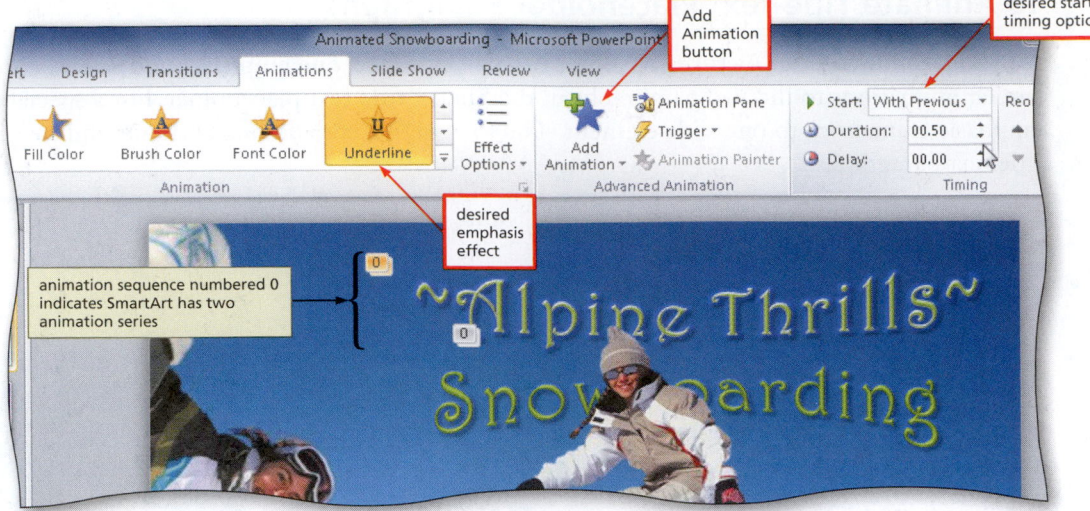

Figure 7–23

Q&A Why is a second set of animation numbered tags starting with 0 displaying on the left side of the title text placeholder?

They represent the three animations associated with the paragraphs in that placeholder.

To Change Animation Order

Two title slide elements have animations: the snowboarder picture and the title text placeholder. PowerPoint applies the animations in the order you created them, so on this slide the snowboarder picture animations will appear first and then the title text placeholder animation will follow. You can reorder animation elements if you decide one set of animation should appear before another set, and you also can reorder individual animation elements within an animation group. In this presentation, you decide to display the title text placeholder animation first, and then you decide that the Underline emphasis effect should appear before the Font Color emphasis effect. The following steps reorder the two animation groups on the slide and then reorder the Font Color and Underline emphasis effects.

1

- Double-click the Slide 1 title text placeholder border so that it displays as a solid line. Click the far-left orange sequence order tag to display the Animation Pane task pane (Figure 7–24).

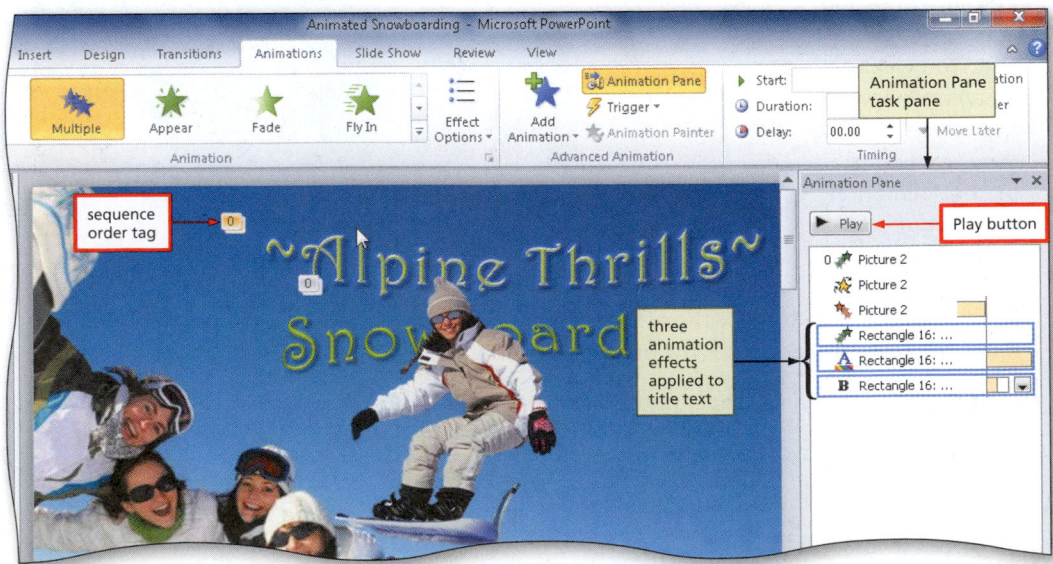

Figure 7–24

Q&A Why do blue lines appear around the three Rectangle effects?

The lines correspond to the three animation effects that you applied to the title text placeholder. The green star indicates the entrance effect, the A with the multicolor underline indicates the Font Color emphasis effect, and the black B indicates the Underline emphasis effect.

Q&A Why do I see a different number after the Rectangle label?

PowerPoint numbers slide elements consecutively, so you may see a different number if you have added and deleted pictures, text, and other graphics. You will rename these labels in a later set of steps.

 2

- Click the Move Earlier button (Animations tab | Timing group) three times to move the three Rectangle animations above the Picture animations (Figure 7–25).

- Click the Play button (Animation Pane task pane) to see the reordered animation.

Q&A Can I click the Re-Order up button at the bottom of the Animation Pane task pane instead of the Move Earlier button on the Ribbon?

Yes. Either button will change the animation order.

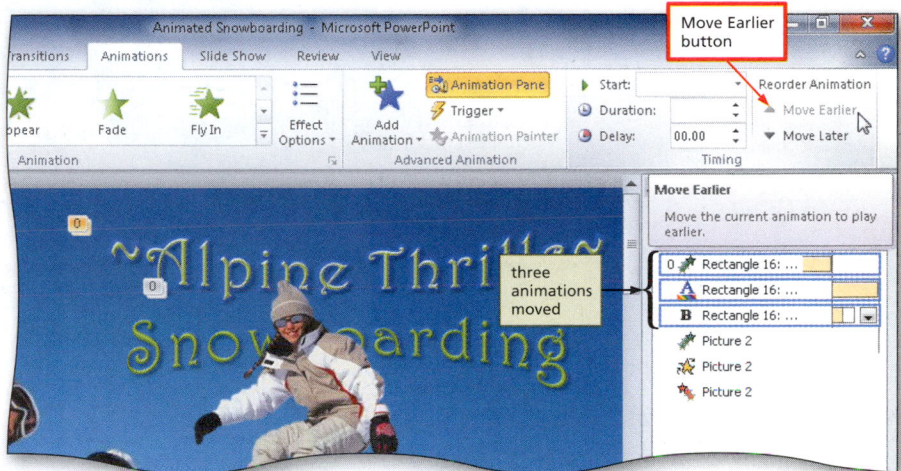

Figure 7–25

3

- In the Animation Pane task pane, click the second Rectangle label representing the Font Color animation to select it and then click the Move Later button (Animations tab | Timing group) to move this animation below the Rectangle label representing the Underline animation (Figure 7–26).

- Click the Play button (Animation Pane task pane) to see the reordered text placeholder animation.

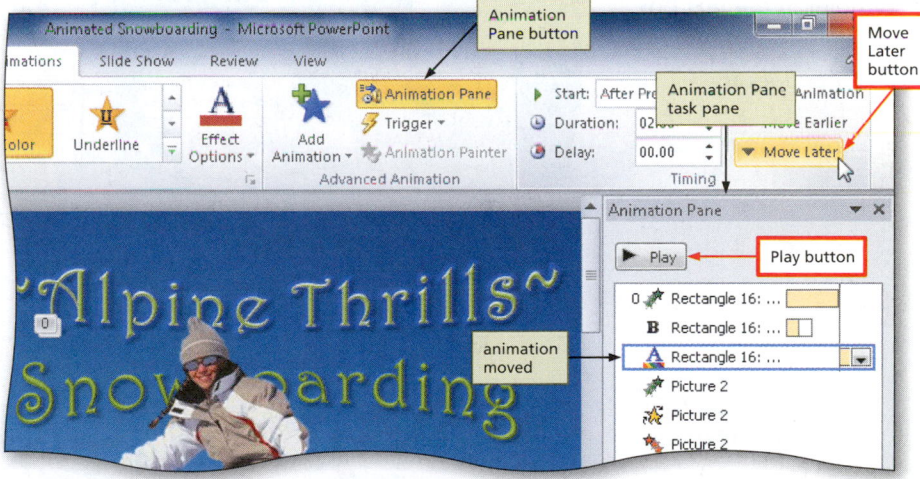

Figure 7–26

Q&A Can I view the Animation Pane task pane at any time when I am adding and adjusting animation effects?

Yes. Click the Animation Pane button (Animations tab | Advanced Animation group) to display the Animation Pane task pane.

To Rename Slide Objects

The two animated title slide elements are listed in the Animation Pane task pane as Rectangle and Picture. You can give these objects meaningful names so that you can identify them in the animation sequence. The following steps rename the animated Slide 1 objects.

- Display the Home tab and then click Select (Home tab | Editing group) to display the Select menu (Figure 7–27).

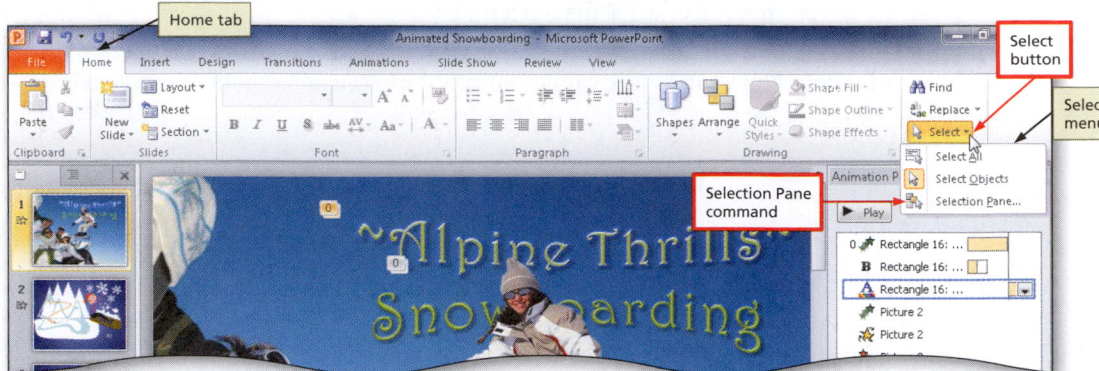

Figure 7–27

- Click Selection Pane in the Select menu to display the Selection and Visibility task pane.

- Click the Picture label in the Shapes on this Slide area and then click the label again to place the insertion point in the text box (Figure 7–28).

Q&A

What does the Picture label represent on three animations?

The green entry, yellow emphasis, and red exit animations are applied to the snowboarder picture.

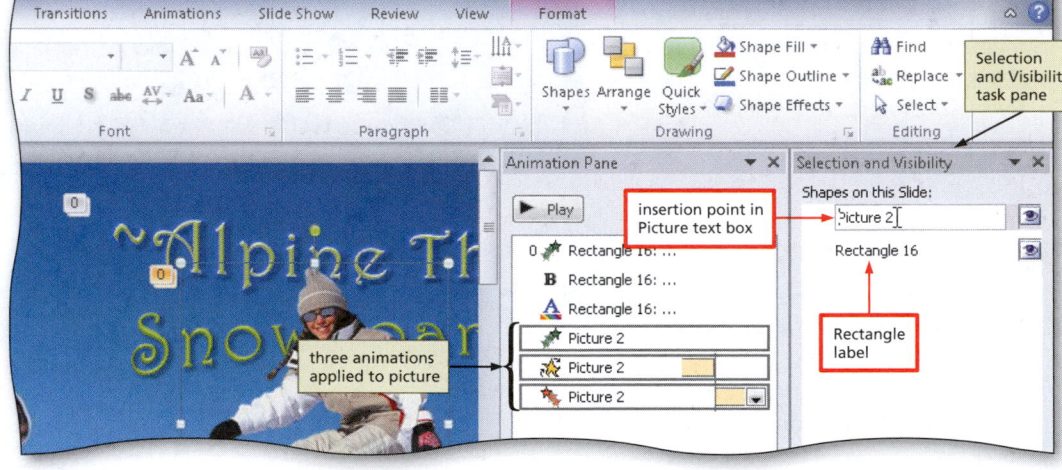

Figure 7–28

- Delete the text and then type **Snowboarder** in the Picture text box.

- Click the Rectangle label in the Shapes on this Slide area, click the label again, delete the text, and then type **Title Text** in the Rectangle text box (Figure 7–29).

Figure 7–29

Q&A

What does the Rectangle label represent on three animations?

The green entry and two emphasis animations are applied to the title text placeholder.

4
- Click the Close button on the Selection and Visibility task pane.

- Click the Close button on the Animation Pane task pane.

BTW

Selecting Text Animation Options
Multi-level bulleted list paragraphs can have animation effects that help direct the audience's attention. For example, you can animate the second-level paragraphs so they are displayed individually along with any associated third-level paragraphs. To specify a text animation option, display the Animation Pane, click an animation you want to manipulate in the list, click this animation's list arrow to display a menu, click Effect Options in the list, and then click the Text Animation tab. If desired, you can click the Group Text arrow and select a paragraph level, such as 2nd level, in the list. Click the Automatically after check box and enter a time if you want the next bulleted paragraph to appear after a specific number of seconds. In addition, click the 'In reverse order' check box to build the paragraphs from the bottom to the top of the slide.

Break Point: If you wish to take a break, this is a good place to do so. Be sure to save the Animated Snowboarding file again and then you can quit PowerPoint. To resume at a later time, start PowerPoint, open the file called Animated Snowboarding, and continue following the steps from this location forward.

To Insert a Text Box and Format Text

Slide 2 contains three elements that you will animate. First, you will add a text box, format and animate the text, and add a motion path and sound. Next, you will add an entrance effect and custom motion path to the snowboarder clip. Finally, you will animate one snowflake and copy the animation to the other snowflakes using the Animation Painter.

You can add the parts of the animation in any order and then change the sequence. You can save time, however, if you develop the animation using the sequence in which the elements will display on the slide. The first sequence will be a text box in the lower-left corner of the slide. The following steps add a text box to Slide 2.

1
- Display Slide 2 and then display the Insert tab.

- Click the Text Box button (Insert tab | Text group) and then position the mouse pointer in the blue area in the lower-left corner of the slide (Figure 7–30).

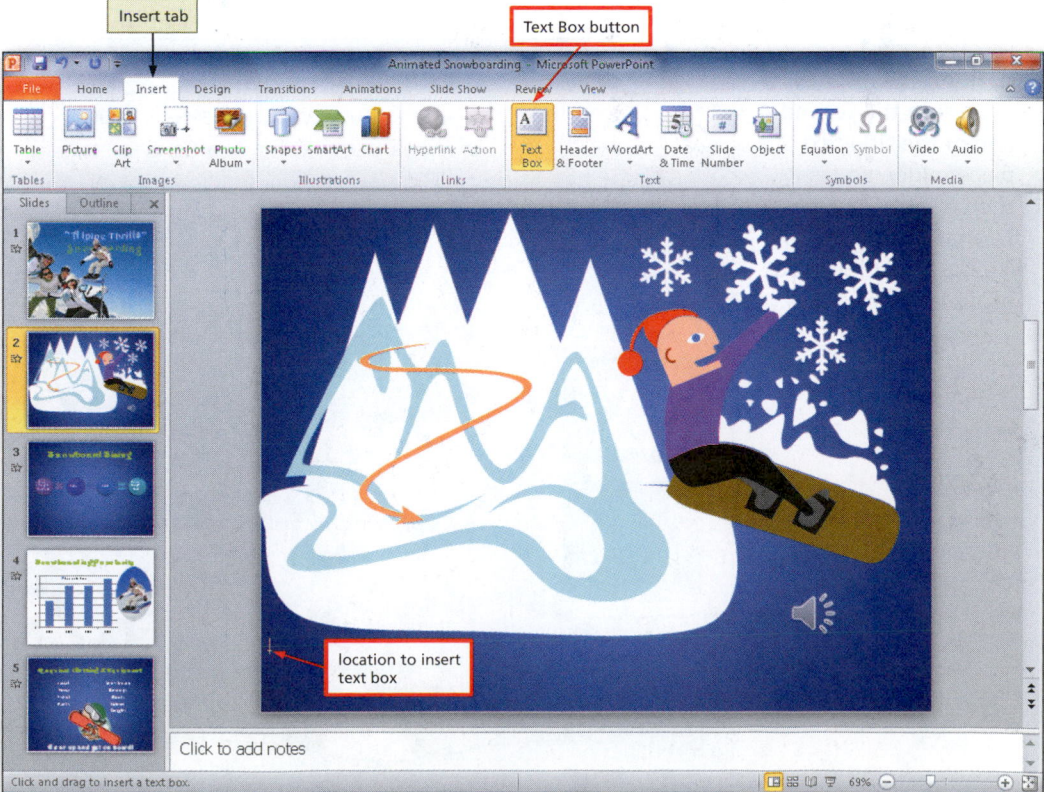

Figure 7–30

● Click the slide and then type `Carve Some Turns` in the text box (Figure 7–31).

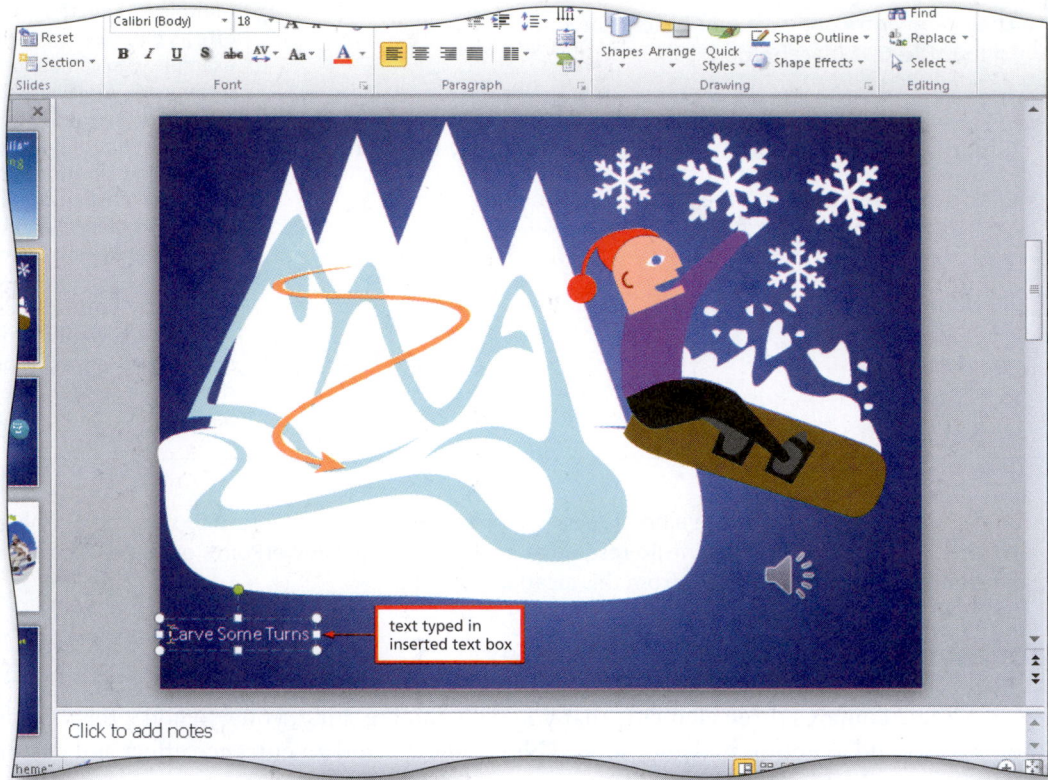

Figure 7–31

● Display Slide 1, position the mouse pointer in the second line of the title text placeholder, and then double-click the Format Painter button (Home tab | Clipboard group) (Figure 7–32).

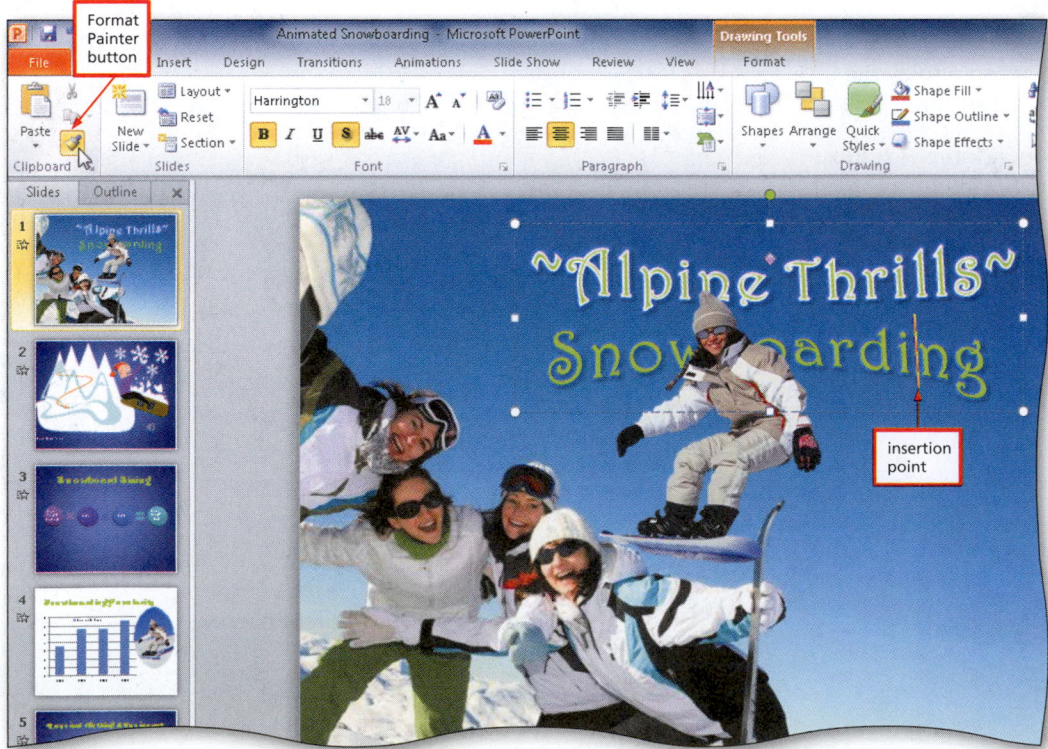

Figure 7–32

4

- Display Slide 2 and then triple-click the inserted text box to apply the Slide 1 title text format to the text in the text box.

- Press the ESC key to turn off the Format Painter feature.

- Display the Drawing Tools Format tab, click the Text Effects button (Drawing Tools Format tab | WordArt Styles group), and then apply the Wave 1 WordArt text effect (first effect in fifth row of the Warp area of the Transform gallery) to the words in the text box (Figure 7–33). If

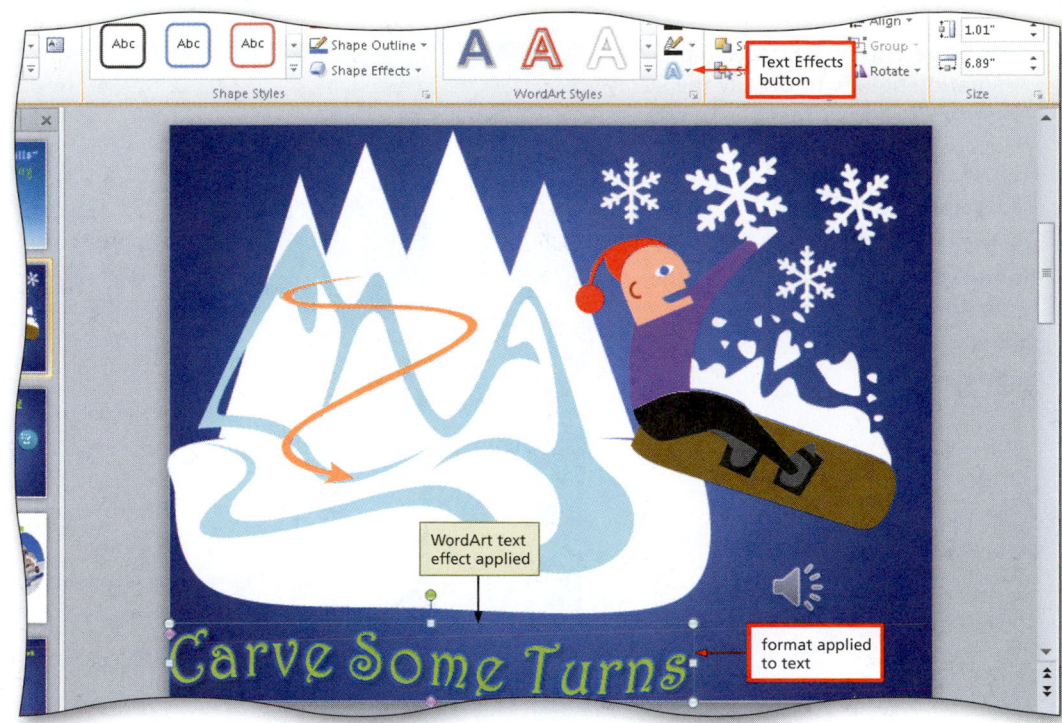

Figure 7–33

necessary, move the text box so that all the letters display on the slide.

To Animate a Text Box Using an Entrance Effect

Text boxes can have the same animation effects applied to pictures and placeholders. Entrance, emphasis, and exit animations can add interest to slides, and the default timings can be changed to synchronize with the slide content. The 13 effects shown in the Entrance area of the Animation gallery are some of the more popular choices; PowerPoint provides many more effects that are divided into the Basic, Subtle, Moderate, and Exciting categories. The following steps add an entrance effect to the text box.

1

- If necessary, click the text box to select it and then display the Animations tab.

- Click the More button in the Animation gallery (Animations tab | Animation group) to expand the Animation gallery (Figure 7–34).

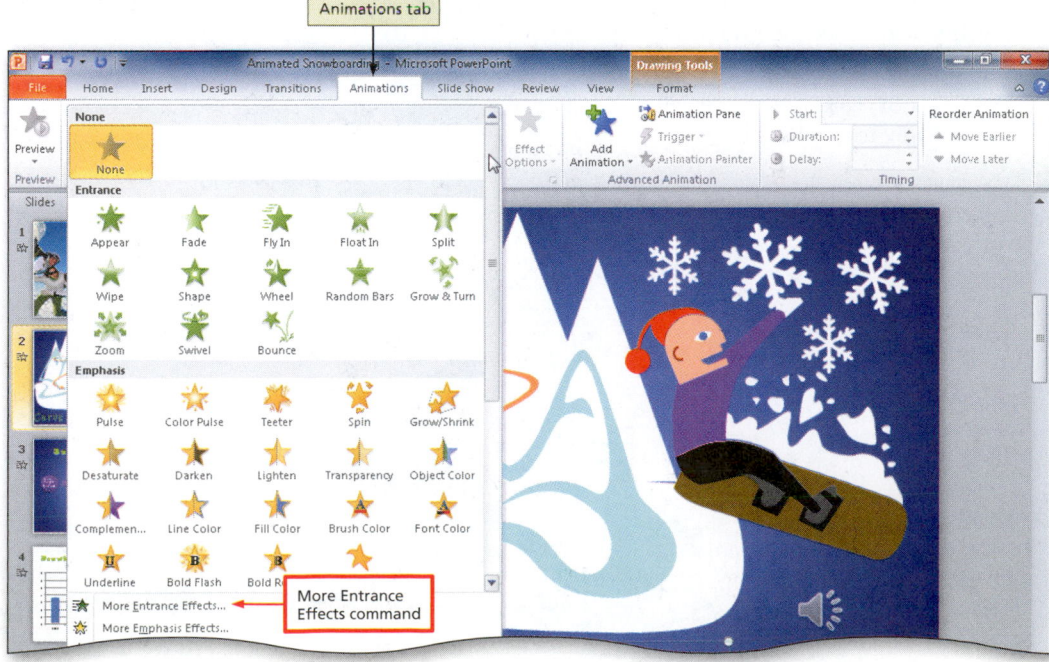

Figure 7–34

2

• Click More Entrance Effects in the Animation gallery to display the Change Entrance Effect dialog box (Figure 7–35).

🔍 **Experiment**

• Click some of the entrance effects in the various areas and watch the effect preview in the text box on Slide 2.

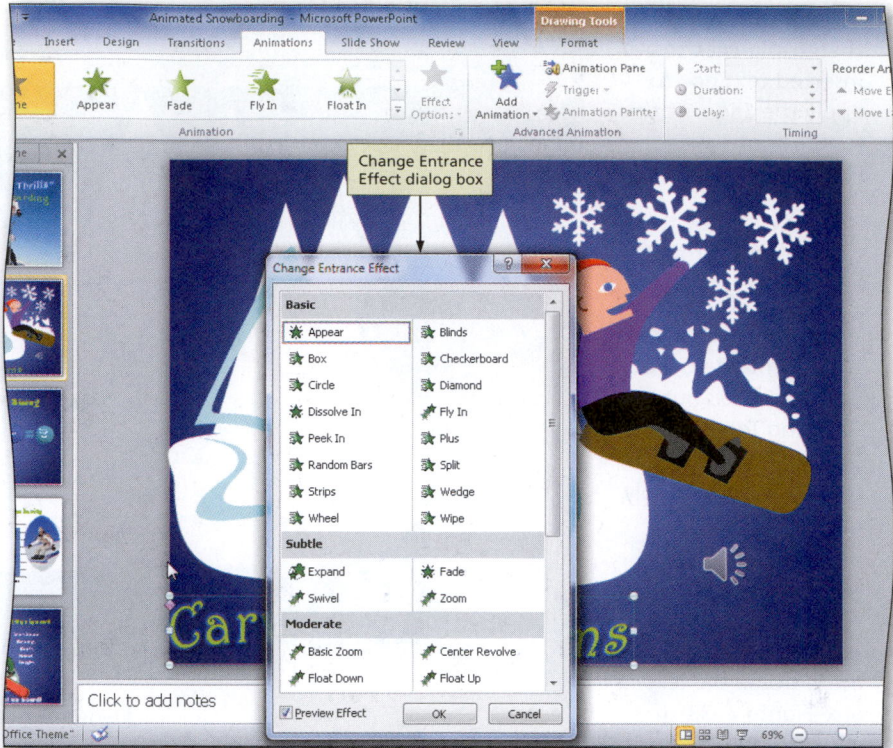

Figure 7–35

Q&A Can I move the dialog box so that I can see the effect preview?

Yes. Drag the dialog box title bar so that the dialog box does not cover the text box.

3

• Scroll down and then click Flip in the Exciting area (Figure 7–36).

Q&A Why do I see a preview of the effects when I click their names?

The Preview Effect box is selected. If you do not want to see previews, click the box to deselect it.

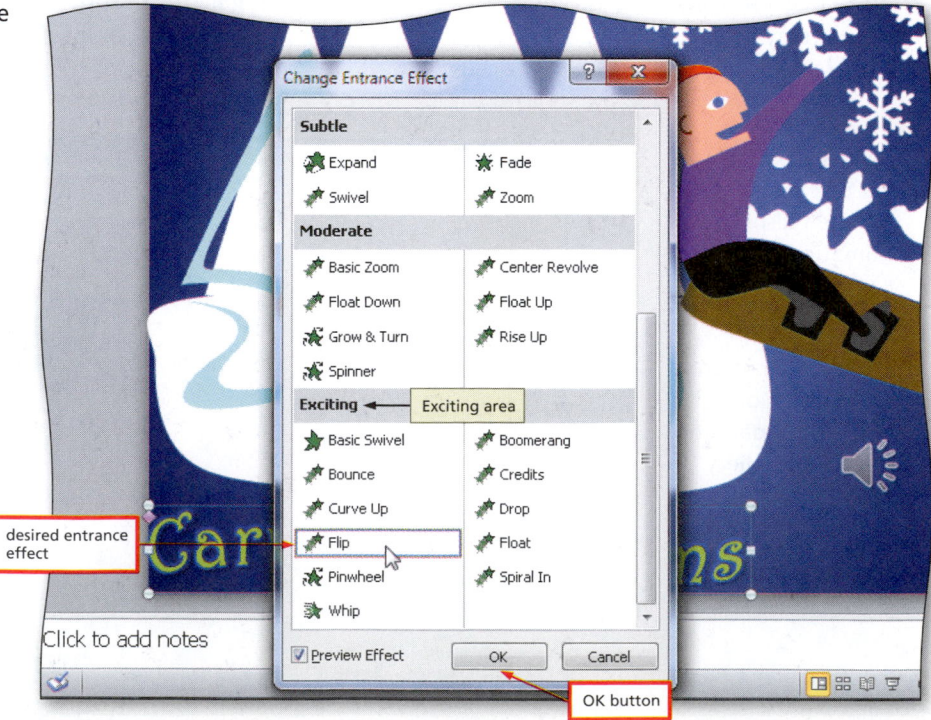

Figure 7–36

4

- Click the OK button to apply the Flip entrance effect to the text.

- Change the start timing option to With Previous.

- Change the duration to 02.00 seconds (Figure 7–37).

Q&A Can I remove an animation?

Yes. Click None (Animations tab | Animation group). You may need to click the More button to see None.

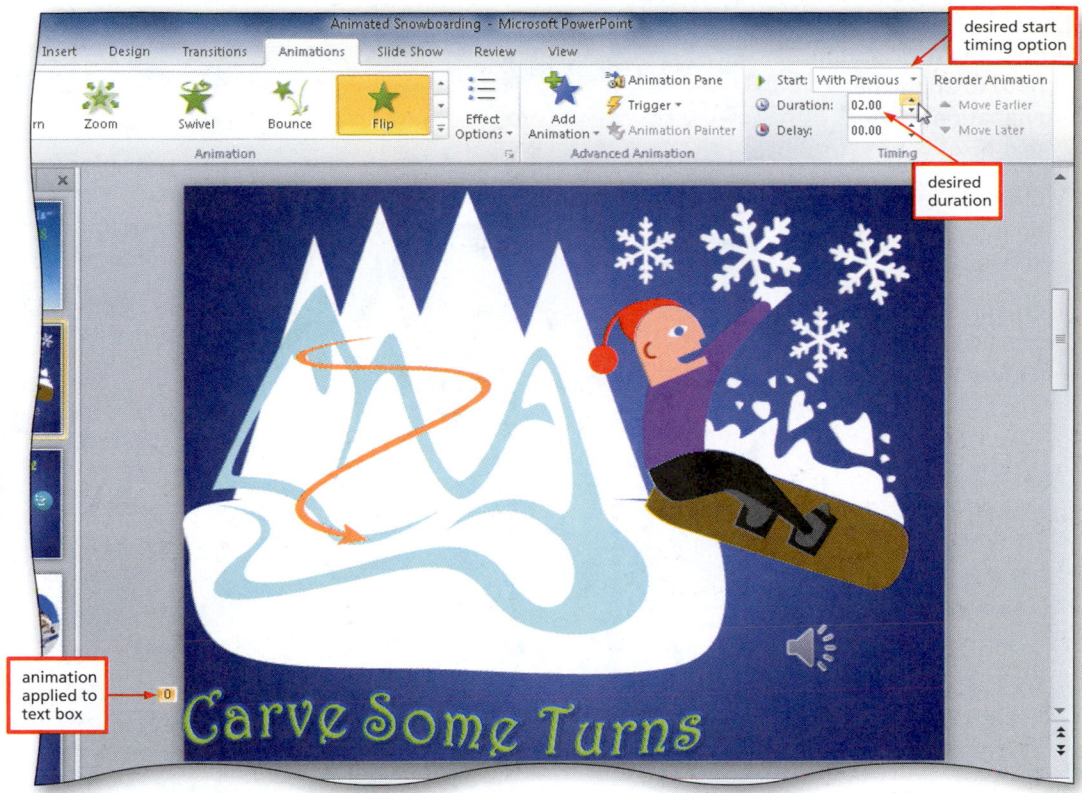

Figure 7–37

To Animate a Text Box by Applying a Motion Path

One of the more effective methods of animating slide objects is to use a motion path to predetermine the route the object will follow. In your presentation, the text box will move from the left side of the slide to the right side in a curving motion that simulates a snowboarder's sideslip ride across the slope. The following steps apply a motion path to the Slide 2 text box.

1

- Click the Add Animation button (Animations tab | Advanced Animation group) to expand the Animation gallery.

- Scroll down until the Motion Paths area is visible (Figure 7–38).

 Experiment

- Point to some of the motion paths and watch the animation preview in the text box.

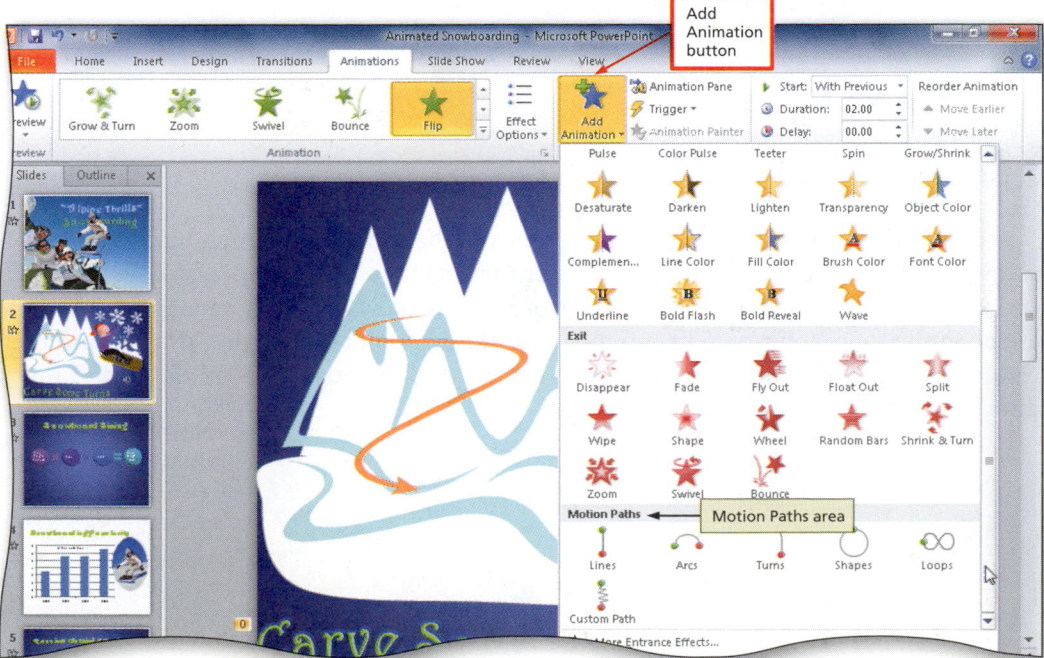

Figure 7–38

2

- Click the Arcs motion path to apply the animation to the text box.

- Change the start timing option to After Previous.

- Change the duration to 04.00 seconds (Figure 7–39).

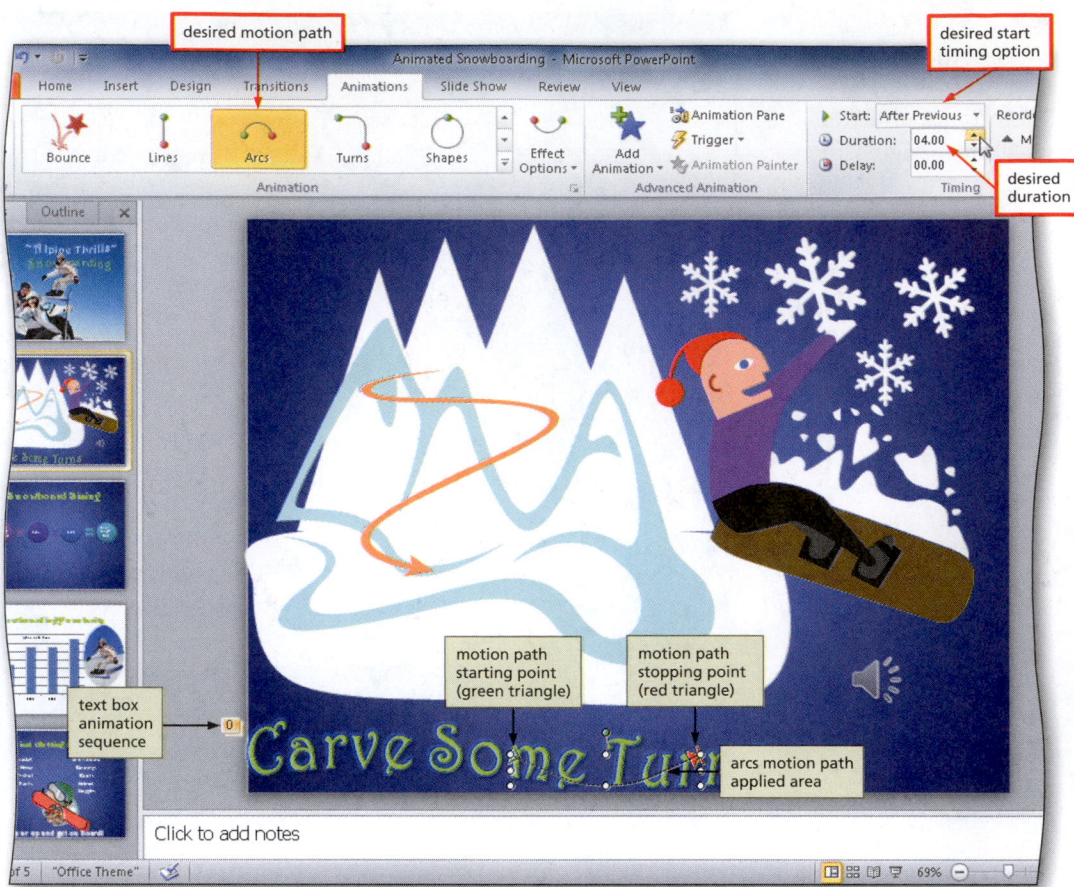

Figure 7–39

Are more motion paths available in addition to those shown in the Animation gallery?

Yes. To see additional motion paths, click More Motion Paths in the lower portion of the Animation gallery. The motion paths are arranged in the Basic, Lines & Curves, and Special categories.

To Adjust a Motion Path

The Arcs motion path moves the text box in the correct directions, but the path can be extended to move across the entire width of the slide. The green triangle in the middle of the word, Some, indicates the starting point, and the red triangle in the middle of the word, Turns, indicates the stopping point. For the maximum animation effect on the slide, you would like to move the starting point toward the left edge and the stopping point toward the right edge. The following steps move the starting and stopping points on the Slide 2 text box and then reverse the direction of the arc.

1

- With the motion path selected in the text box, click the red stopping point and position the cursor over the upper-right sizing handle so that your cursor is displayed as a two-headed arrow.

- Drag the red stopping point to the location shown in Figure 7–40.

 Q&A My entire motion path moved. How can I move only the red stopping point arrow?

Be certain your cursor is a two-headed arrow and not a four-headed arrow.

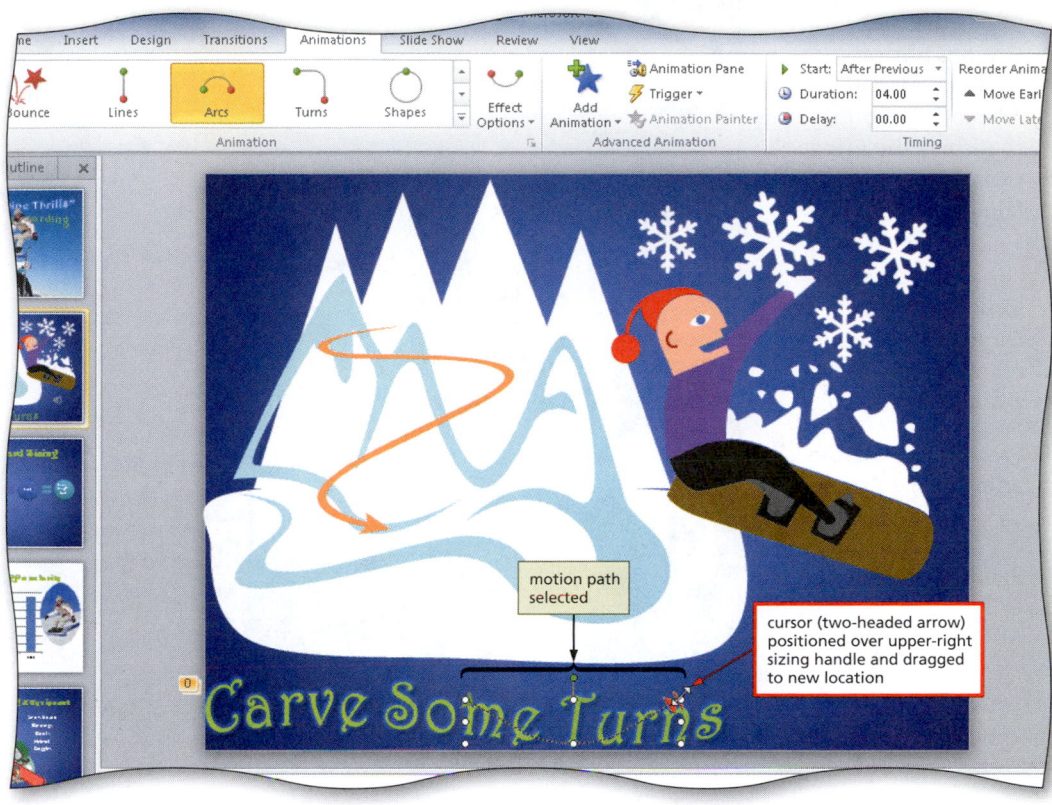

Figure 7–40

2

- Drag the green starting point to the location shown in Figure 7–41.

- Drag the upper-center sizing handle to the location shown in Figure 7–41.

- Preview the custom animation (Figure 7–41).

Q&A My animation is not exactly like the path shown in Figure 7–41. Can I change the path?

Yes. Continue adjusting the starting and stopping points and playing the animation until you are satisfied with the effect.

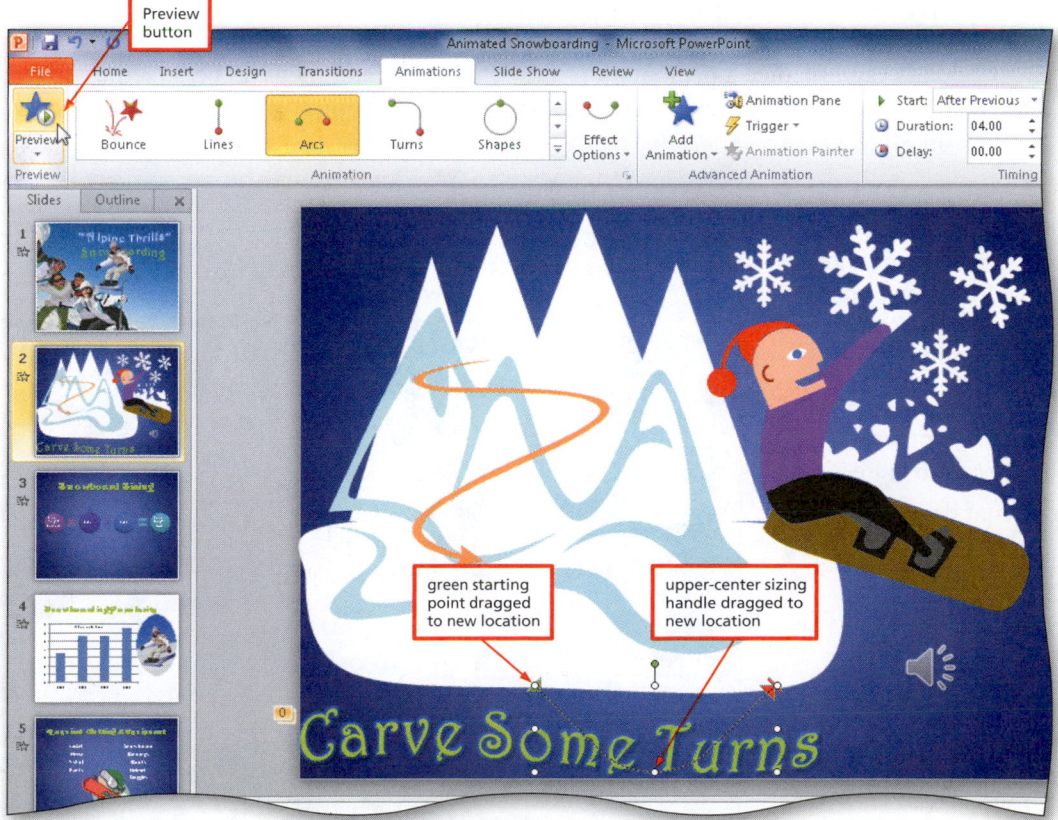

Figure 7–41

3
- Click the Effect Options button (Animations tab | Animation group) to display the Effect Options gallery (Figure 7–42).

4
- Click Up in the Direction area to reverse the direction from Down to Up.

- Preview the custom animation.

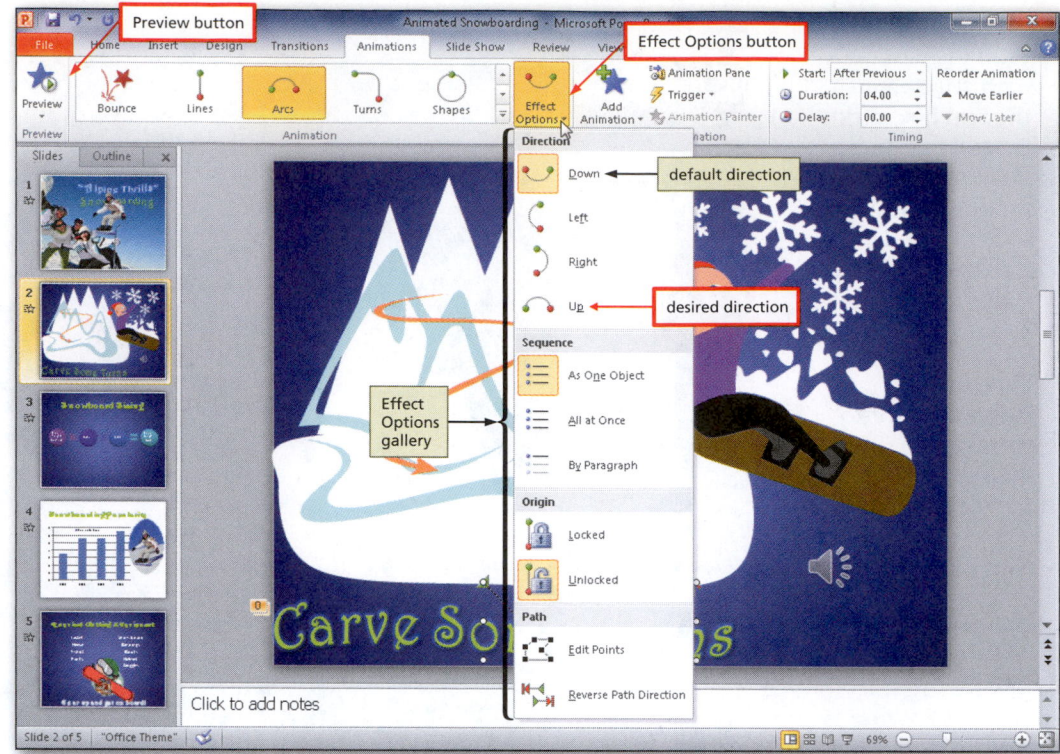

Figure 7–42

To Associate a Sound with an Animation

Sounds can enhance a presentation if used properly, and they can be linked to other animations on the slide. Slide 2 already has the inserted sound of a snowboarder carving turns. The following step associates a sound with the text box on Slide 2.

1
- Click the sound icon on Slide 2 and then click Play animation (Animations tab | Animation group).

- Change the start timing option to With Previous (Figure 7–43).

Q&A

What does the duration Auto setting control?

The sound will play automatically and will repeat as long as the text box is animated.

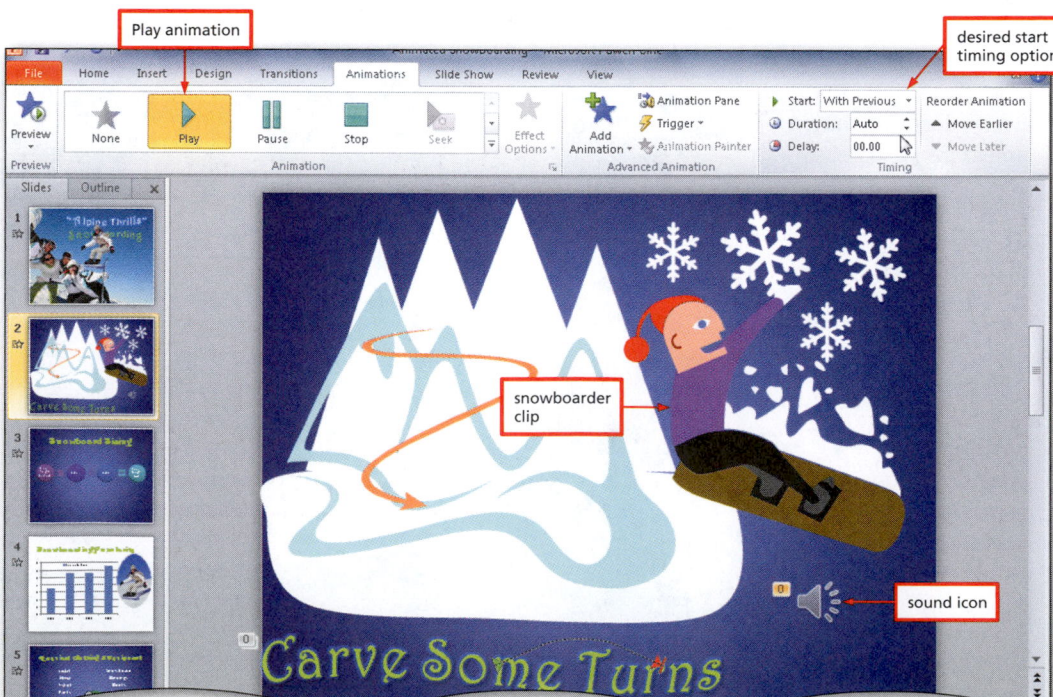

Figure 7–43

To Draw a Custom Motion Path

Although PowerPoint supplies a wide variety of motion paths, at times they may not fit the precise animations your presentation requires. In that situation, you can draw a custom path that specifies the unique movement your slide element should make. Slide 2 has a clip of a mountain and another clip of a snowboarder. The mountain has an orange curvy line running down the face of the slope, and you can animate the snowboarder to follow this line. No preset motion path presents the exact motion you want to display, so you will draw your own custom path.

Drawing a custom path requires some practice and patience. You click the mouse to begin drawing the line. If you want the line to change direction, such as to curve, you click again. When you have completed drawing the path, you double-click to end the line. The following steps draw a custom motion path.

1

• Select the snowboarder clip, apply the Fade entrance effect, and then change the start timing option to After Previous.

• Click the Add Animation button and then scroll down until the entire Motion Paths area is visible (Figure 7–44).

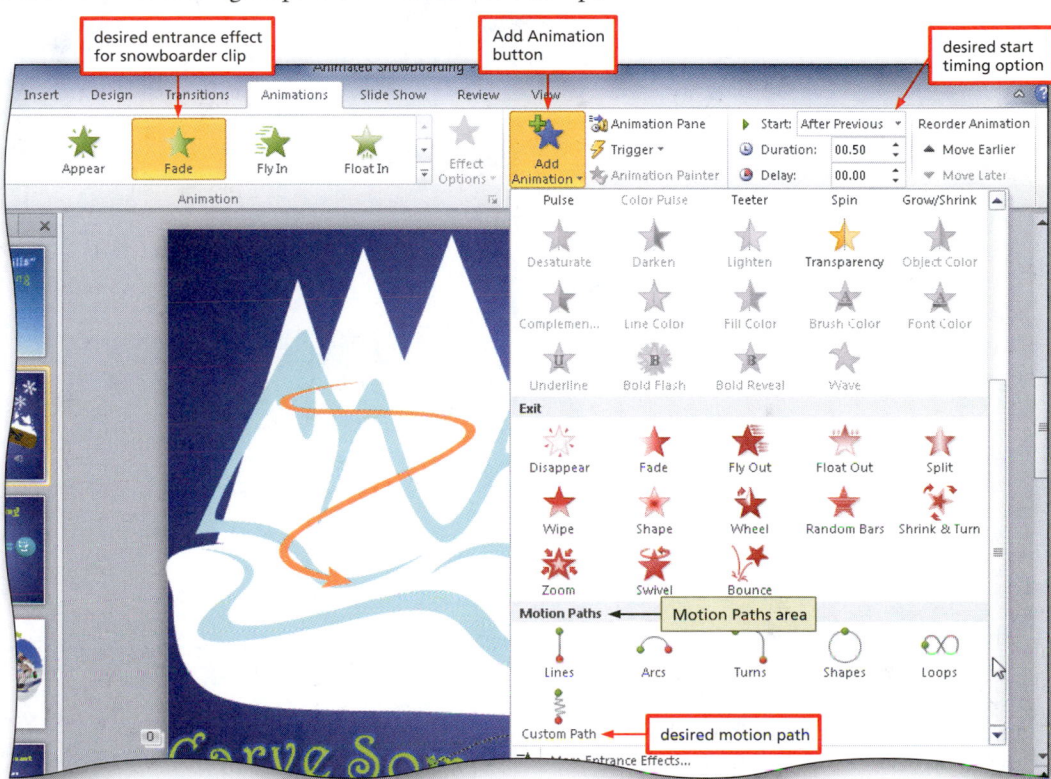

Figure 7–44

2

• Click Custom Path in the Motion Paths gallery to add this animation.

• Click the Effect Options button (Animations tab | Animation group) to display the Type gallery (Figure 7–45).

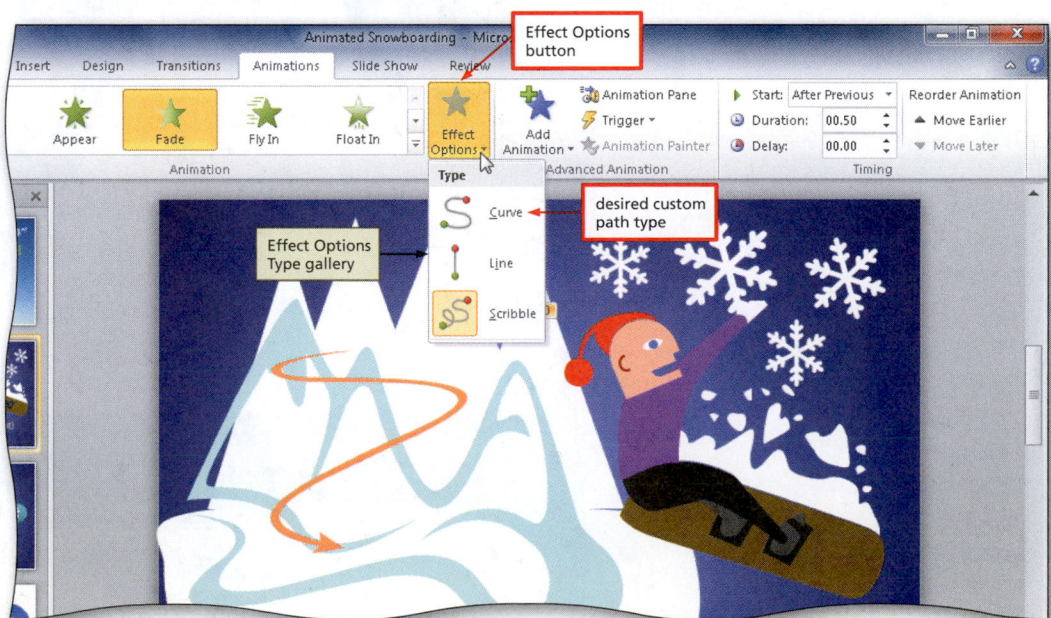

Figure 7–45

3

- Click Curve in the Type gallery and then position the mouse pointer at the beginning of the orange line at the top of the mountain.

Q&A

Why did I need to change the option from Scribble to Curve?

Your custom motion path will follow the orange curves on the mountain clip, and the Curve type will create rounded edges to connect the lines you draw. The Scribble option would draw only straight lines, so the snowboarder would not carve smooth turns as he comes downhill.

- Click the mouse to indicate where the curve will start and then move the mouse pointer to the location shown in Figure 7–46, which is where the curve will change direction.

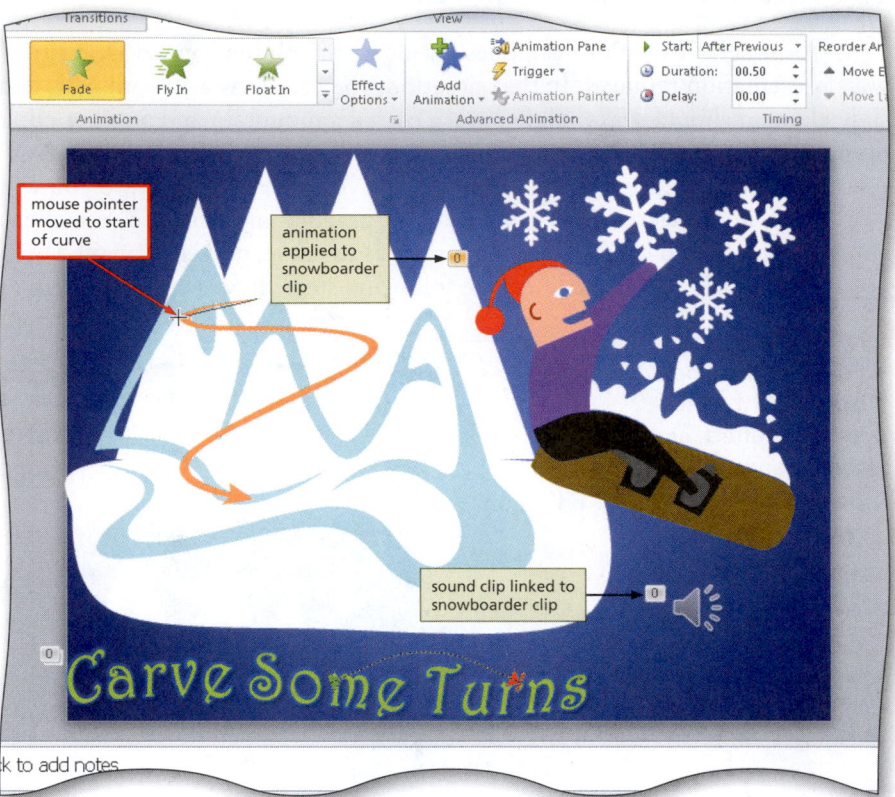

Figure 7–46

4

- Click the mouse, position the mouse pointer at the top of the far-right orange curve, and then click to indicate the end of this direction of travel.

- Position the mouse pointer at the top of the lower-left curve and then click to indicate the end of this curve (Figure 7–47).

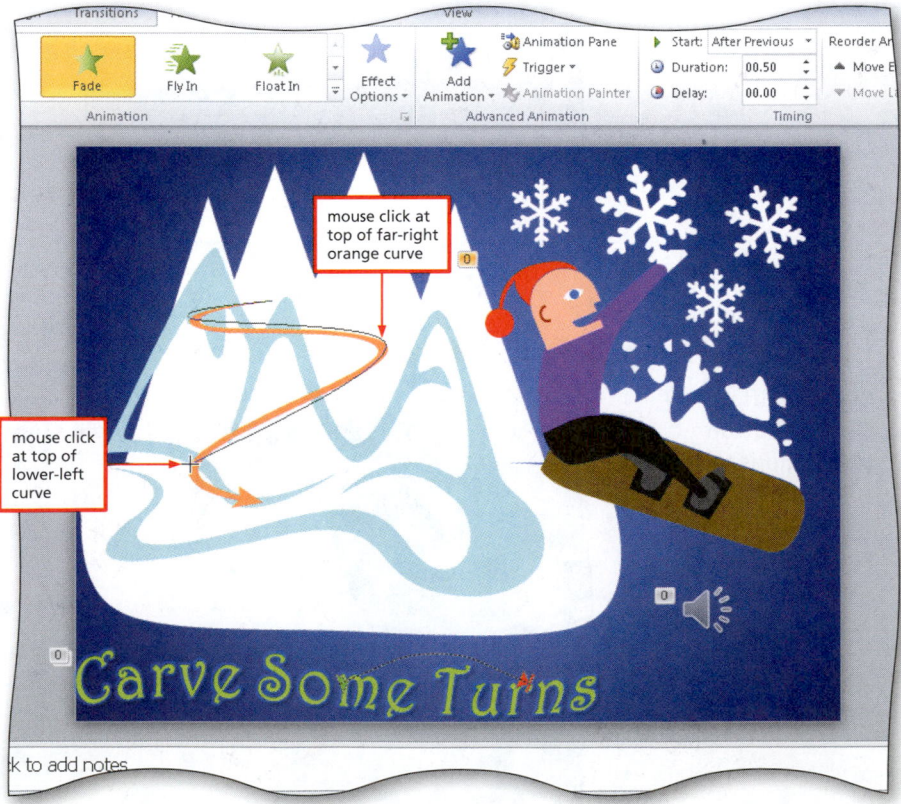

Figure 7–47

5
- Position the mouse pointer at the tip of the orange arrowhead and then double-click to indicate the end of the motion path and preview the animation (Figure 7–48).

- Change the start timing option to With Previous and the duration setting to 05.00 seconds.

Q&A If my curve is not correct, can I delete it?

Yes. Select the motion path, press the DELETE key, and then repeat the previous steps.

Figure 7–48

To Use the Animation Painter to Animate a Clip

At times, you may desire to apply the same animation effects to several objects on a slide. On Slide 2, for example, you want to animate the four snowflakes with identical entrance, emphasis, and exit effects. As with the Format Painter that is used to duplicate font and paragraph attributes, the Animation Painter copies animation effects. Using the Animation Painter can save time by duplicating numerous animations quickly and consistently. The following steps animate one snowflake and then use the Animation Painter to copy these effects to three other snowflakes.

1
- Select the snowflake in the upper-right corner of the slide and then apply the Fly In entrance effect.

- Click the Effect Options button and then change the direction to From Top.

- Change the start timing option to With Previous and the duration to 06.00 seconds (Figure 7–49).

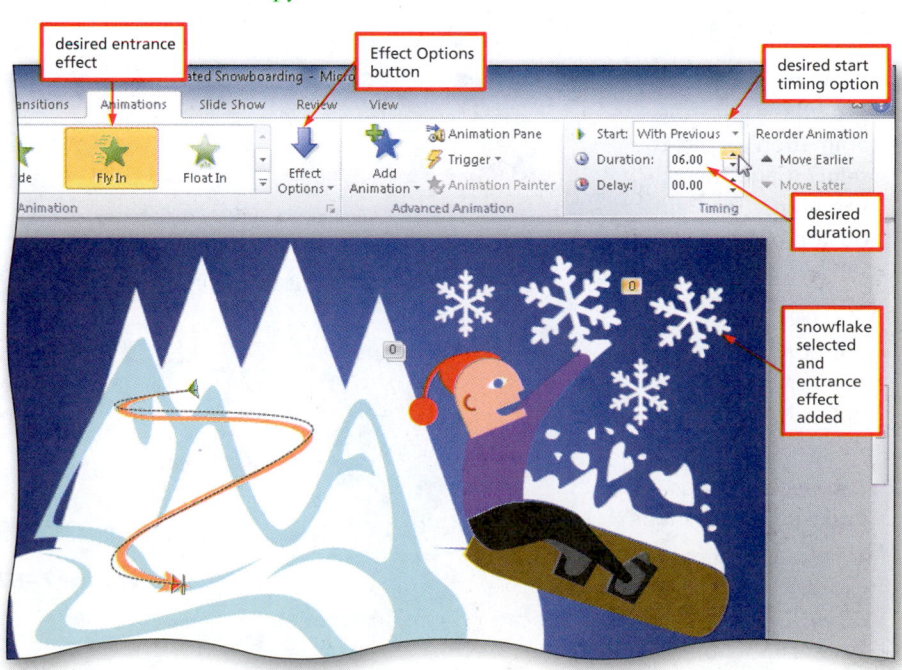

Figure 7–49

2

- With the snowflake still selected, add the Teeter emphasis effect, change the start timing option to After Previous, and then change the duration to 01.50 seconds (Figure 7–50).

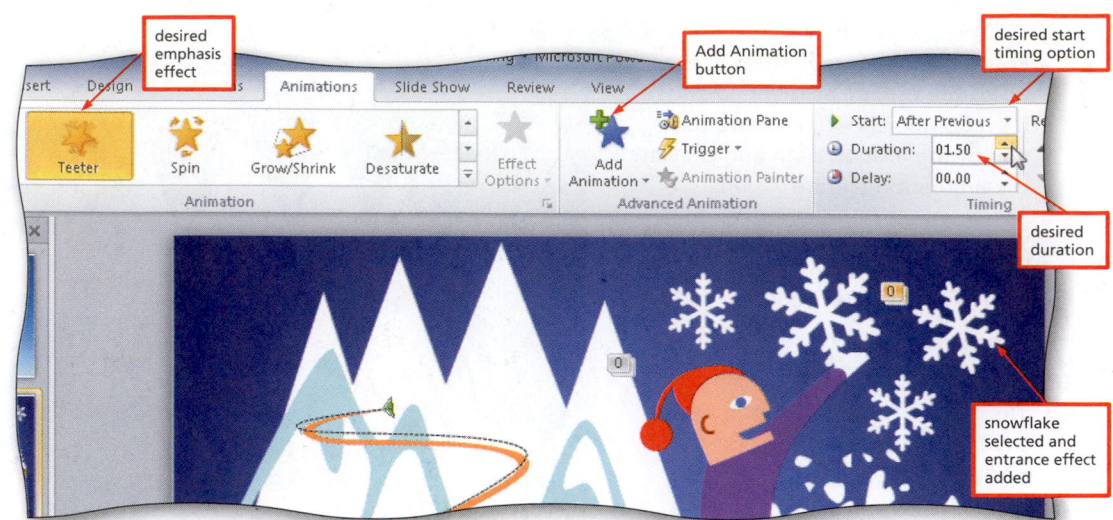

Figure 7–50

3

- Add the Fade exit effect, change the start timing option to After Previous, and then change the duration to 03.00 seconds (Figure 7–51).

 Can I copy the animation to an object on another slide?

Yes. Once you establish the desired animation effects, you can copy them to any object that can be animated on any slide.

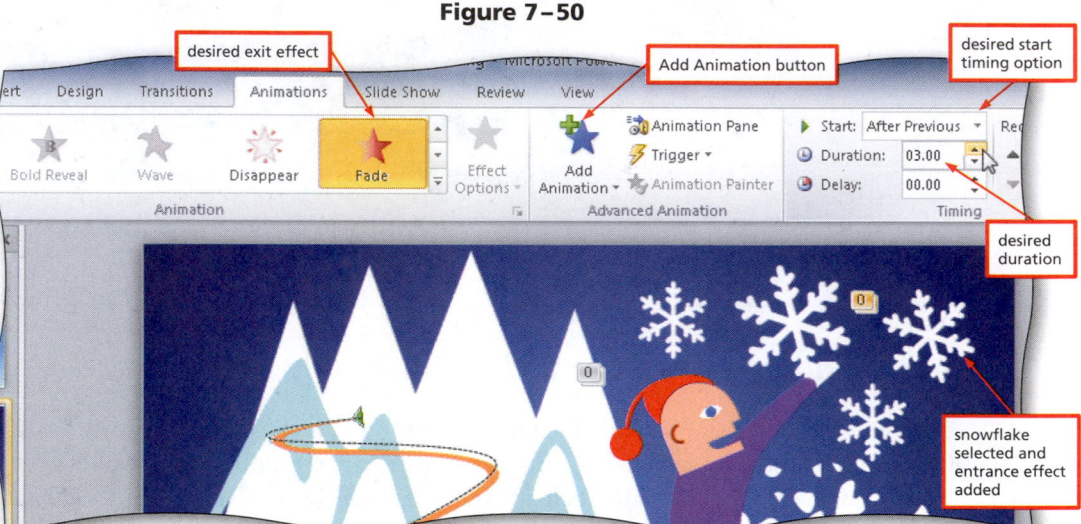

Figure 7–51

4

- Click the upper-right snowflake with the animation effects to select it and then click the Animation Painter button (Animations tab | Advanced Animation group).

- Position the mouse pointer over the upper-left snowflake (Figure 7–52).

Why did my mouse pointer change shape?

The mouse pointer changed shape by displaying a paintbrush to indicate that the Animation Painter function is active.

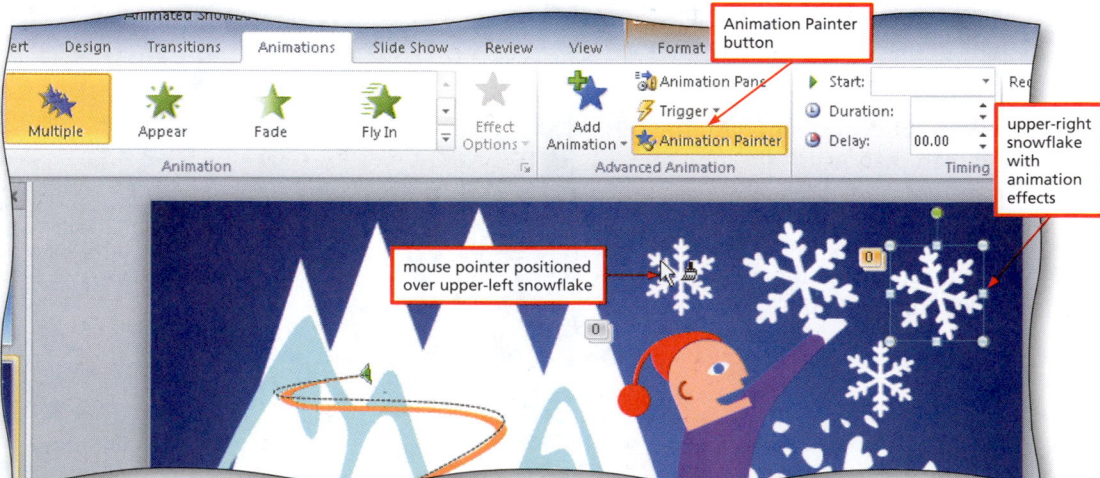

Figure 7–52

- Click the upper-left snowflake to apply the same entrance, emphasis, and exit animation effects as those added to the upper-right snowflake.

- Click the Animation Painter button and then click the center snowflake.

- Click the Animation Painter button again and then click the lower-right snowflake (Figure 7–53).

- Preview the animation effects.

Q&A

Can I copy the animation to more than one object simultaneously?

No. Unlike using the Format Painter, you must click the Animation Painter button each time you want to copy the animation to an object on the slide.

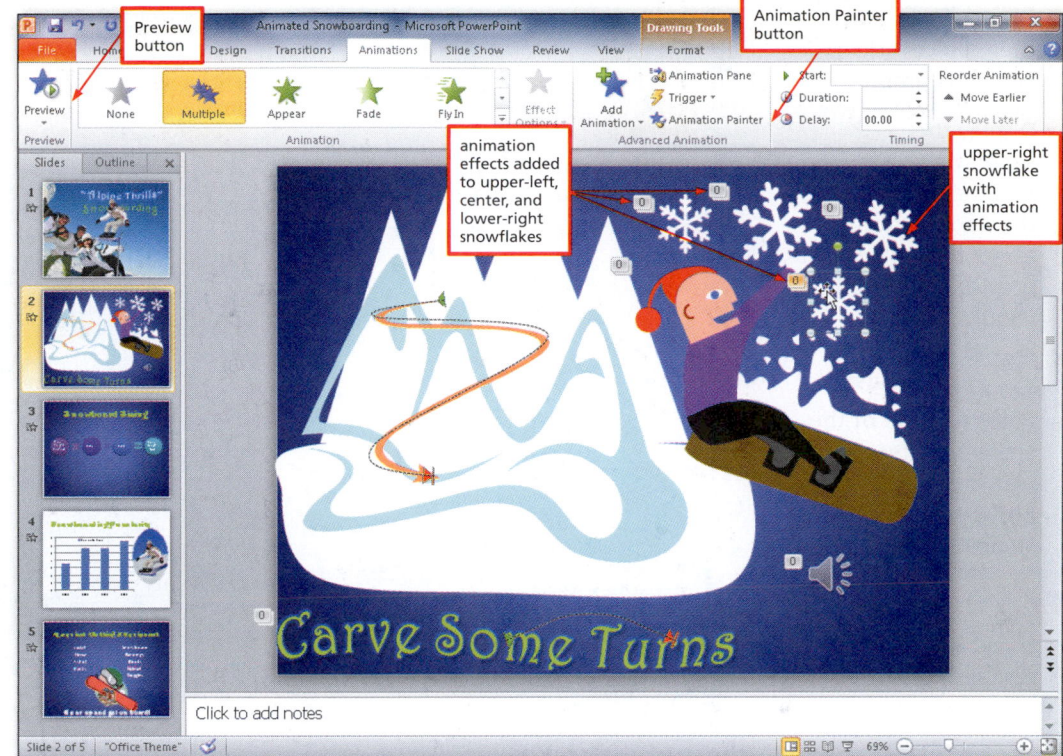

Figure 7–53

Break Point: If you wish to take a break, this is a good place to do so. Be sure to save the Animated Snowboarding file again and then you can quit PowerPoint. To resume at a later time, start PowerPoint, open the file called Animated Snowboarding, and continue following the steps from this location forward.

To Animate a SmartArt Graphic

The bulleted lists on the text slides are animated, and you can build on this effect by adding animation to the Slide 3 SmartArt graphic. You can add a custom animation to each shape in the cycle, but you also can use one of PowerPoint's built-in animations to simplify the animation procedure. The following steps apply an entrance animation effect to the Equation diagram.

1

• Display Slide 3 and then select the SmartArt graphic.

• Display the Animation gallery and then point to the Zoom entrance effect to display a live preview of this effect (Figure 7–54).

🔍 **Experiment**

• Point to some of the entrance effects and watch the animation preview in the SmartArt objects.

2

• Select the Zoom entrance effect.

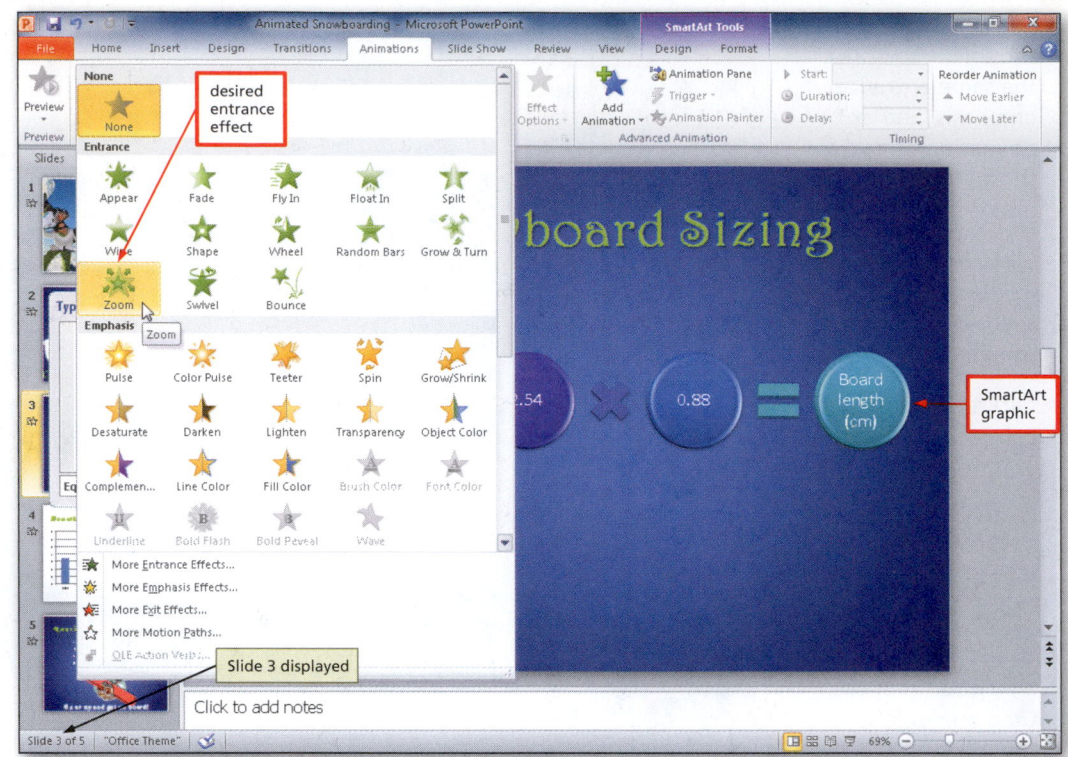

Figure 7–54

To Change a SmartArt Graphic Animation Sequence

By default, all SmartArt graphic components enter the slide simultaneously. You can modify this setting and change the entrance sequence so that each element enters one at a time and builds the mathematical sequence from left to right. The following steps change the sequence for the SmartArt animation to One by One.

1

• Click the Effect Options button to display the Effect Options gallery (Figure 7–55).

Q&A

Can I reverse the order of individual shapes in the SmartArt sequence?

No. You can reverse the order of the entire SmartArt graphic but not individual shapes within the sequence.

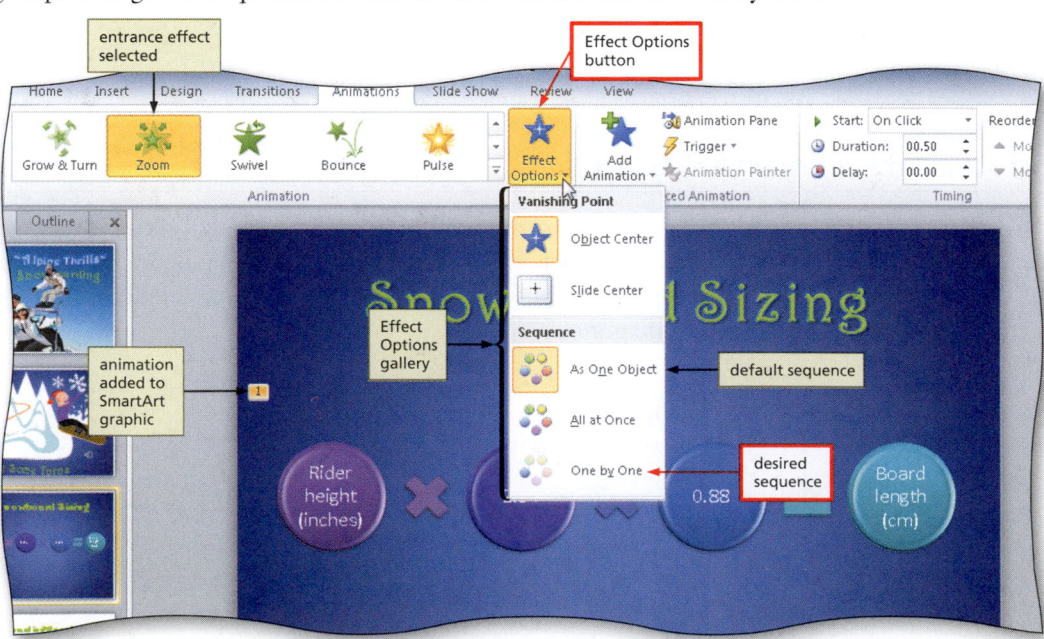

Figure 7–55

②
- Click One by One in the Sequence area to change the animation order.

- Change the start timing option to After Previous, the duration to 5.00 seconds, and the delay to 01.00 second (Figure 7–56).

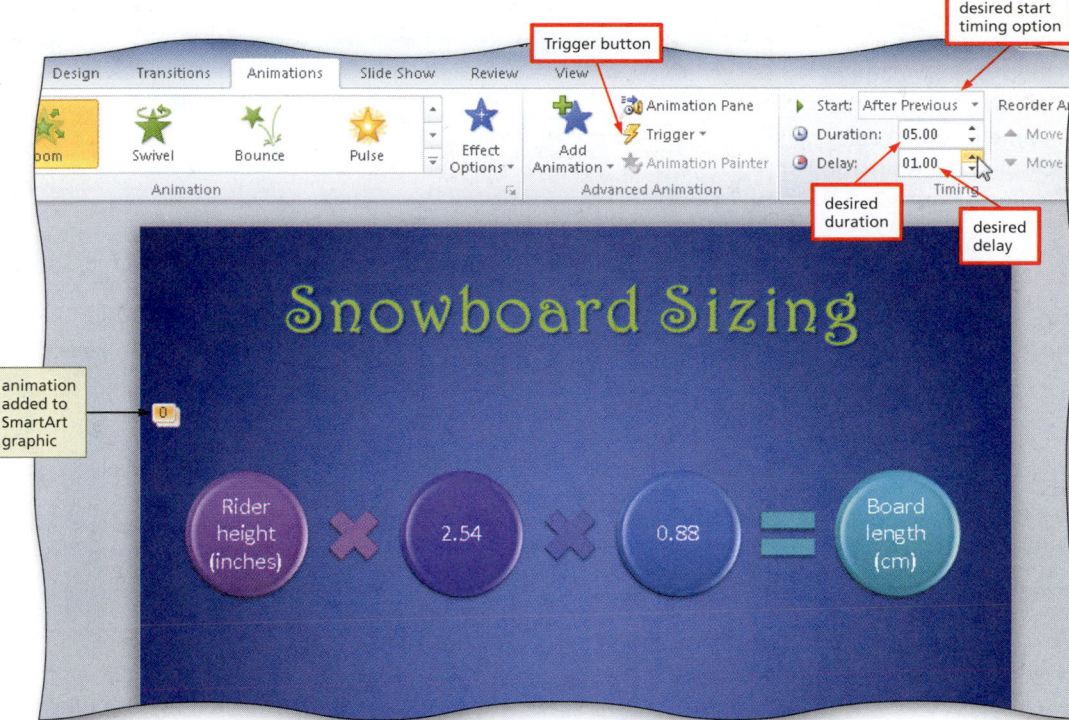

Figure 7–56

TO TRIGGER AN ANIMATION EFFECT

If you select the On Click start timing option and run the slide show, PowerPoint starts the animation when you click any part of the slide or press the SPACEBAR. You may, however, want the option to play an animation in a particular circumstance. For example, you may have an animated sequence ready to show if time permits or if you believe your audience needs time to understand a process and would understand the concept more readily if you revealed one part of a SmartArt graphic at a time. A **trigger** specifies when an animation or other action should occur. It is linked to a particular component of a slide so that the action occurs only when you click this slide element. If you click any other part of the slide, PowerPoint will display the next slide in the presentation. If you need to set a slide object as the trigger to start an animation, you would follow these steps.

1. Click the Trigger button (Animations tab | Advanced Animation group) to display the Trigger menu and then point to On Click Of to display the list of slide elements.

2. Click the desired slide element to set the trigger on the click of that object.

BTW

Displaying Equations
One of PowerPoint 2010's enhancements is the Equation Tools Design tab. This feature allows you to type mathematical symbols and insert structures, including functions, integrals, operators, and radicals.

To Animate a Chart

The chart on Slide 4 depicts the growth of the sport of snowboarding. In 10 years, the number of snowboarders practically has doubled. To emphasize this increase in popularity, you can animate the bars of the chart so that each one enters the slide individually. As with the SmartArt animation, PowerPoint gives you many options to animate the chart data. The following steps animate the Slide 4 chart bars.

1

• Display Slide 4 and then click an edge of the chart so that the frame is displayed. Display the Animation gallery (Figure 7–57).

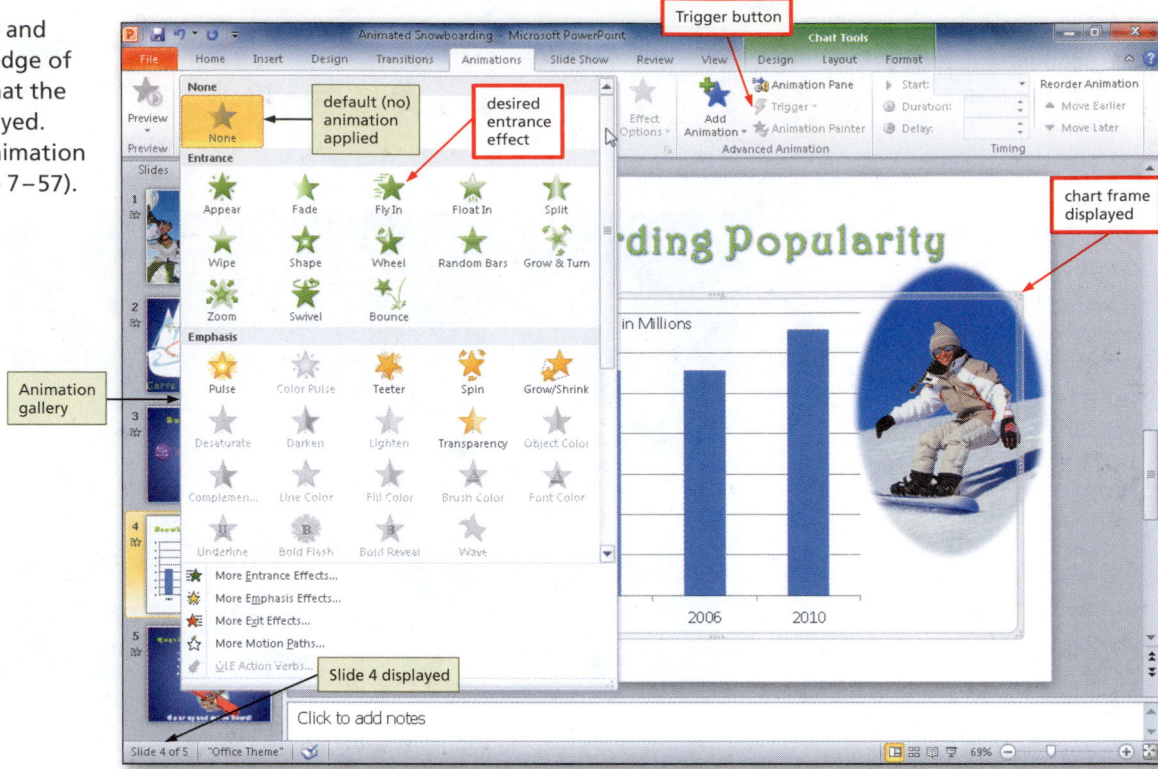

Figure 7–57

2

• Click the Fly In entrance effect, change the start timing option to After Previous, change the duration to 02.00 seconds, and change the delay to 02.50 seconds.

3

• Click the Effect Options button to display the Effect Options gallery (Figure 7–58).

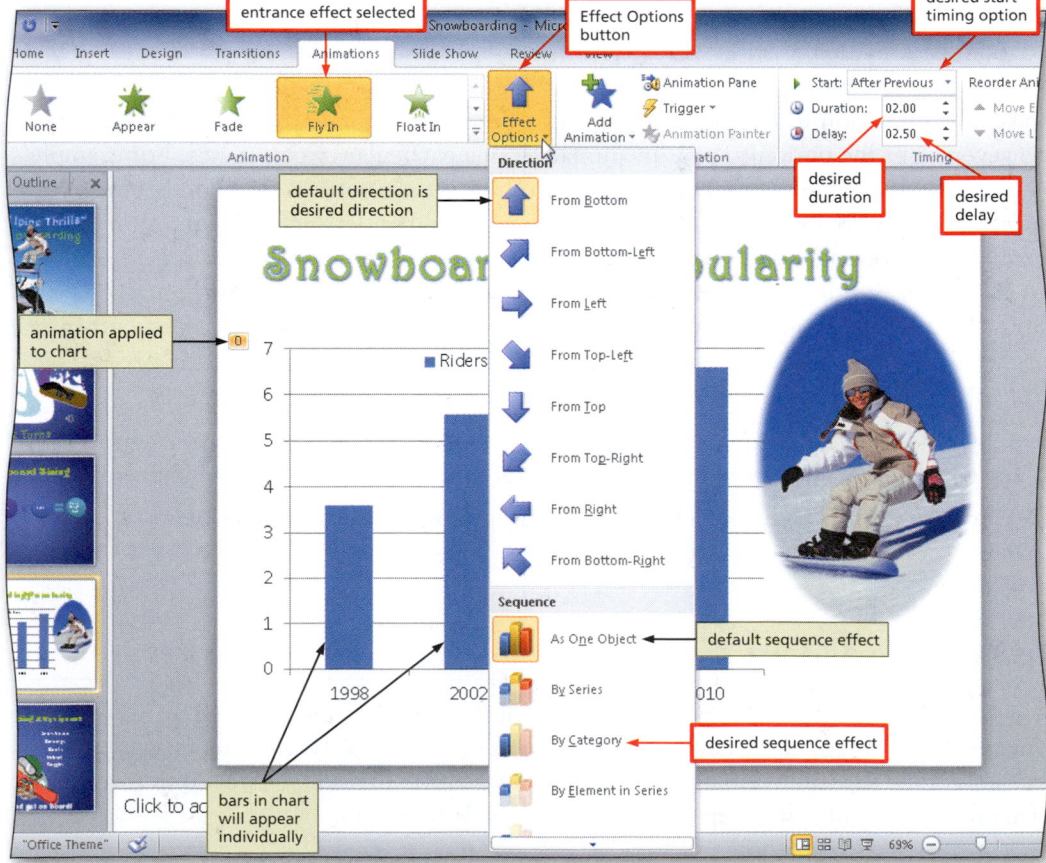

Figure 7–58

 **4**

- Point to By Category to preview the chart animation so that each bar for the first category, Number of Snowboarders in Millions, appears individually for each year.

Experiment

- Point to some of the animations in the various categories and watch the animations preview on Slide 4.

- Click By Category to change the chart animation for the first category.

- Change the start timing option to After Previous, change the duration to 03.00 seconds, and change the delay to 03.50 seconds.

To Animate a List

The two lists on Slide 5 give the minimum clothing and equipment required to snowboard warmly and safely. Each item in the placeholder is a separate paragraph. To add interest during a presentation, you can have each paragraph in the left list enter the slide individually. When the entire list has displayed, the list can disappear and then each paragraph in the right list can appear. The following steps animate the Slide 5 paragraph lists.

1

- Display Slide 5 and then select the four items in the left text placeholder.

- Apply the Shape entrance animation effect, change the start timing option to After Previous, change the duration to 03.00 seconds, and change the delay to 01.50 seconds (Figure 7–59).

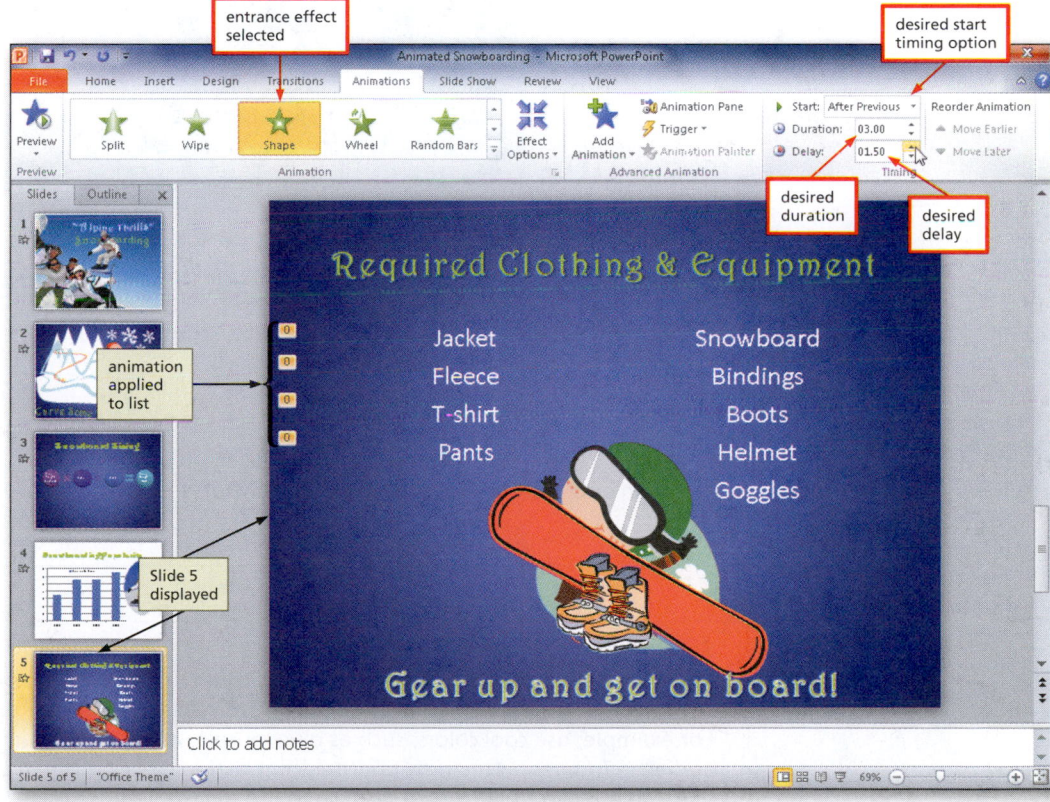

Figure 7–59

- Click the Effect Options button to display the Effect Options gallery (Figure 7–60).

Experiment

- Point to the Out direction and the Box, Diamond, and Plus Shapes and watch the animations preview on the Slide 5 left list paragraphs.

Figure 7–60

- Change the Shapes from Circle to Box.

- Click the Effect Options button again and then change the Direction to Out.

Plan Ahead

Select colors for dimming text.

After paragraphs of text are displayed, you can change the color, or dim the text, to direct the audience's attention to another area of the slide. Choose the dimming colors carefully. For example, use cool colors, such as blue, purple, and turquoise, as backgrounds so that the audience focuses on the next brighter, contrasting color on the slide. Avoid using light blue because it often is difficult to see, especially against a dark background. In addition, use a maximum of three colors unless you have a compelling need to present more variety.

To Dim Text after Animation

As each item in the list is displayed, you may desire to have the previous item removed from the screen or to have the font color change, or **dim**. PowerPoint provides several options for you to alter this text by specifying an After Animation effect. The following steps dim each item in the left placeholder list by changing the font color to Purple.

- Select the four paragraphs in the left placeholder and then click the Animation Pane button (Animations tab | Advanced Animation group) to display the Animation Pane task pane.

- Click the Pants Animation Order list arrow to display the Animation Order menu (Figure 7–61).

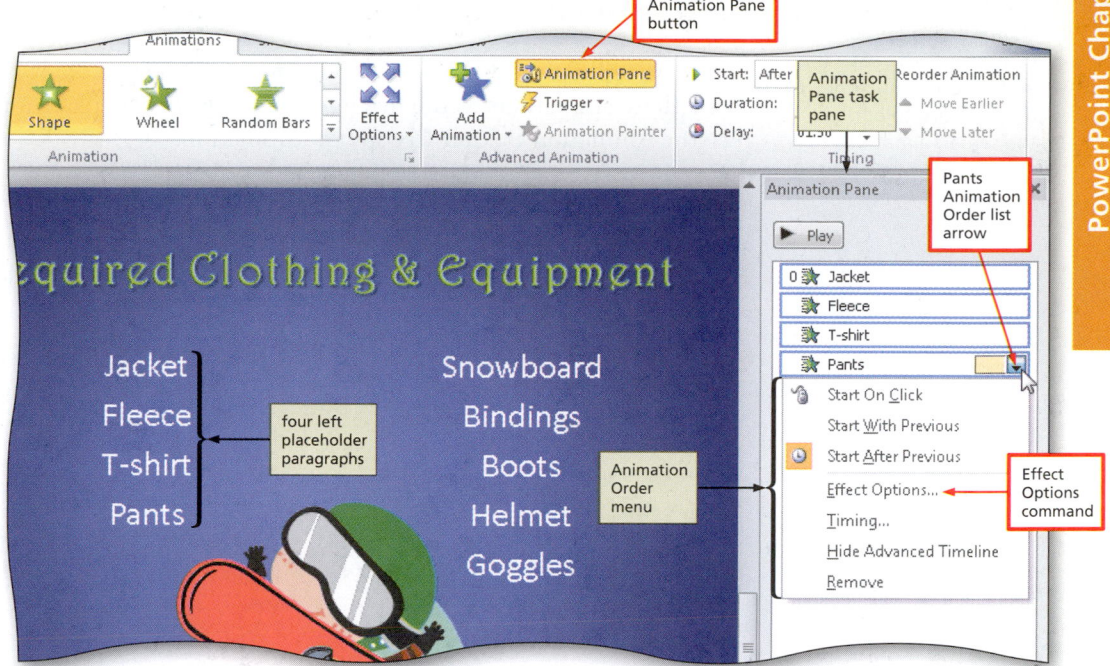

Figure 7–61

- Click Effect Options on the Animation Order list to display the Box dialog box.

- Click the After animation list arrow to display the After animation menu (Figure 7–62).

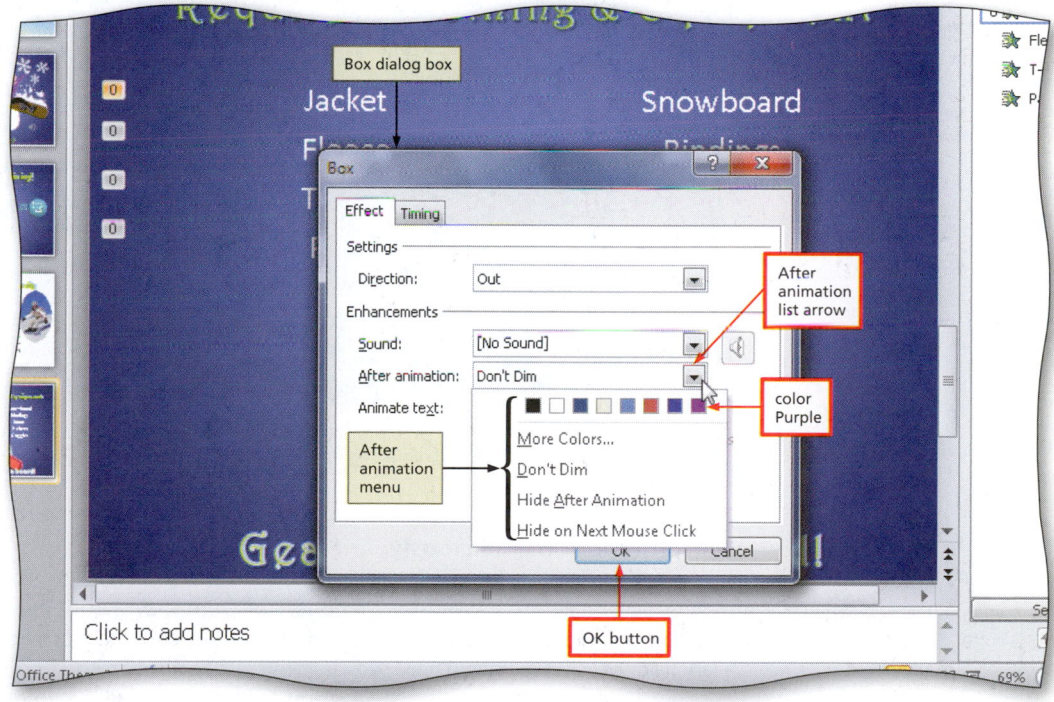

Figure 7–62

- Click the color Purple (last color in the row of colors) to select this color for the dim effect.

- Click the OK button (Box dialog box) to apply the dim effect to the four items in the left placeholder on Slide 5.

- Close the Animation Pane task pane.

BTW

Animation Painter
Using the Animation Painter helps to save time and ensure consistency if you desire to apply the same animations to multiple objects. This tool is a new PowerPoint 2010 element.

To Use the Animation Painter to Copy Animations

All animations have been applied to the left placeholder paragraphs. You now can copy these animations to the five items in the right text placeholder. The following steps use the Animation Painter to copy the animation.

1 Click one item in the list in the left text placeholder and then click the Animation Painter button.

2 Click the word, Snowboard, in the right list to copy the animations in the left list to the five words in the right list.

3 Select the five words in the list in the right placeholder and then change the start timing option to After Previous, the duration to 03.00 seconds, and the delay to 01.50 seconds (Figure 7–63).

Figure 7–63

Plan Ahead

Use quotations judiciously.
Quotations and sayings are available from a variety of print sources, such as *Quotable Quotes, The Merriam-Webster Dictionary of Quotations,* and *Bartlett's Familiar Quotations.* Web sites, including bartleby.com and quotations.com, also provide direct quotes organized into specific categories. These words often add insight to the beginning or the end of a slide show. If you use a quotation, give credit to the person who said or wrote the words. Also, do not change the wording unless it is offensive or biased.

To Create Credits

Many motion pictures use rolling credits at the end of the movie to acknowledge the people who were involved in the filmmaking process or to provide additional information about the actors or setting. You, too, can use a credit or closing statement at the end of your presentation to thank individuals or companies who helped you develop your slide show or to leave your audience with a final thought. The following steps display text as an ascending credit line on Slide 5.

1

- With Slide 5 displaying, click the text box with the words, Gear up and get on board!, at the bottom of the slide to select it.

- Display the Animation gallery and then click More Entrance Effects (Figure 7–64).

Figure 7–64

2

- Click the Credits entrance animation effect in the Exciting area and then click the OK button (Change Entrance Effect dialog box) to apply the effect.

3

- Change the start timing option to After Previous, the duration to 18.00 seconds, and the delay to 01.00 second (Figure 7–65).

- Preview the animation.

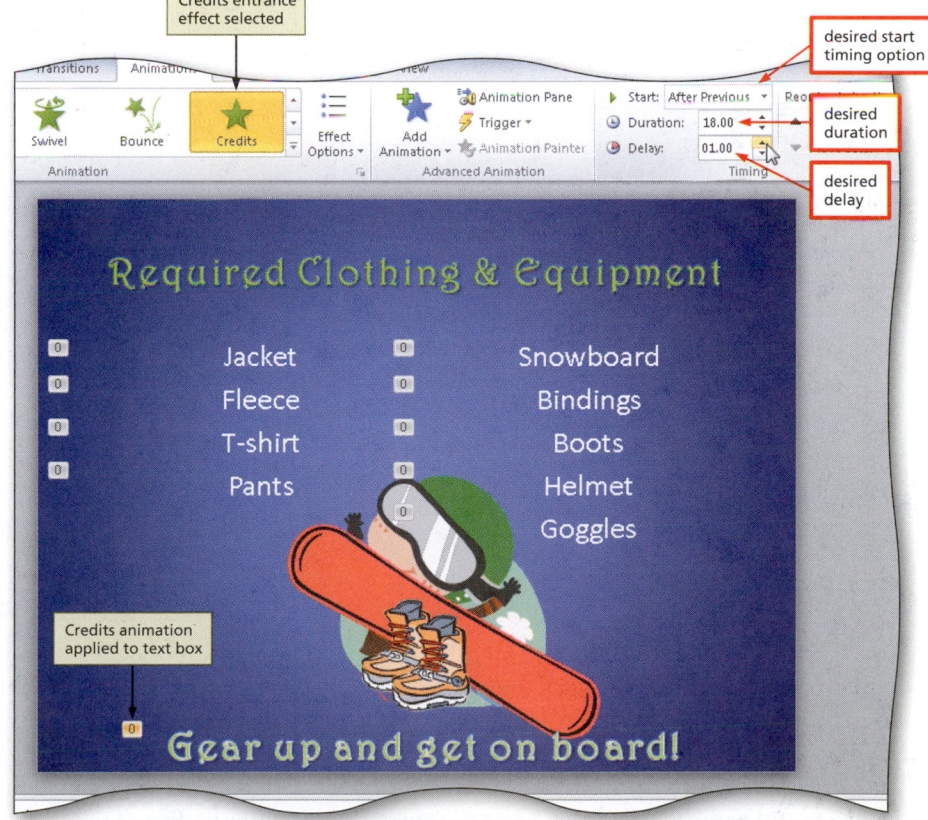

Figure 7–65

Preparing for a Self-Running Presentation

In previous slide shows, you clicked to advance from one slide to the next. Because all animations have been added to the slides in the presentation, you now can set the time each slide is displayed on the screen. You can set these times in one of two ways. The first method is to specify each slide's display time manually. The second method is to use PowerPoint's **rehearsal feature**, which allows you to advance through the slides at your own pace, and the amount of time you view each slide is recorded. You will use the second technique in this chapter and then adjust the last slide's timing manually.

When you begin rehearsing a presentation, the Rehearsal toolbar is displayed. The **Rehearsal toolbar** contains buttons that allow you to start, pause, and repeat viewing the slides in the slide show and to view the times for each slide as well as the elapsed time. Table 7–1 describes the buttons on the Rehearsal toolbar.

Table 7–1 Rehearsal Toolbar Buttons		
Button Name	**Image**	**Description**
Next	➡	Displays the next slide or next animated element on the slide.
Pause Recording	II	Stops the timer. Click the Next or Pause Recording button to resume timing.
Slide Time	0:00:00	Indicates the length of time a slide has been displayed. You can enter a slide time directly in the Slide Time box.
Repeat	↩	Clears the Slide Time box and resets the timer to 0:00:00.
Elapsed Time	0:00:00	Indicates slide show total time.

Plan Ahead

Give your audience sufficient time to view a slide.
The presentation in this chapter is designed to run continuously at a kiosk without a speaker's physical presence. Your audience, therefore, must read or view each slide and absorb the information without your help as a narrator. Be certain to give them time to read the slide and grasp the concept you are presenting. They will become frustrated if the slide changes before they have finished viewing and assimilating the material. As you set the slide timings, read each slide aloud and note the amount of time that elapses. Add a few seconds to this time and use this amount for the total time the slide is displayed.

To Rehearse Timings

You need to determine the length of time each slide should be displayed. Audience members need sufficient time to read the text and watch the animations. Table 7–2 indicates the desired timings for the five slides in the snowboarding presentation. Slide 1 is displayed and then the title text and animated snowboarder picture appear for 25 seconds. The Slide 2 title text, sound, and clip are displayed for 50 seconds. Slide 3 has the animated SmartArt, and it takes one minute for the elements to display. The bars on the Slide 4 chart can display in 40 seconds, and the two lists and rolling credits on Slide 5 display for one minute, five seconds.

Table 7–2 Slide Rehearsal Timings		
Slide Number	Display Time	Elapsed Time
1	0:00	0:25
2	0:50	1:15
3	1:00	2:15
4	0:40	2:55
5	1:05	4:00

The following steps add slide timings to the slide show.

1

• Display Slide 1 and then click Slide Show on the Ribbon to display the Slide Show tab (Figure 7–66).

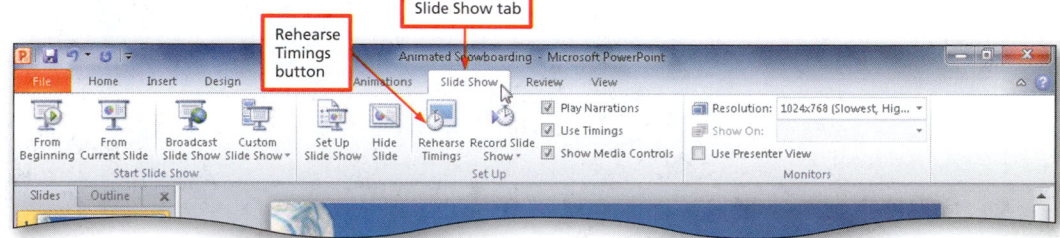

Figure 7–66

2

• Click the Rehearse Timings button (Slide Show tab | Set Up group) to start the slide show and the counter (Figure 7–67).

Figure 7–67

3

• When the Elapsed Time displays 0:25, click the Next button to display Slide 2.

• When the Elapsed Time displays 1:15, click the Next button to display Slide 3.

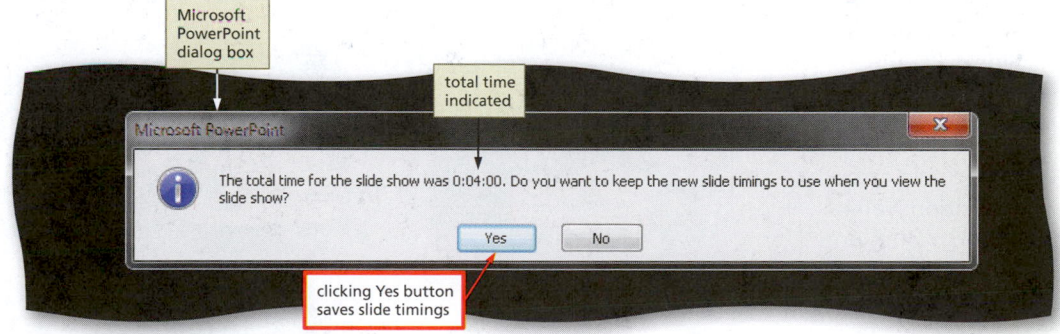

Figure 7–68

• When the Elapsed Time displays 2:15, click the Next button to display Slide 4.

• When the Elapsed Time displays 2:55, click the Next button to display Slide 5.

• When the Elapsed Time displays 4:00, click the Next button to display the black slide (Figure 7–68).

4

- Click the Yes button in the Microsoft Office PowerPoint dialog box to keep the new slide timings with an elapsed time of 4:00.

- Review each slide's timing displayed in the lower-left corner in Slide Sorter view (Figure 7–69).

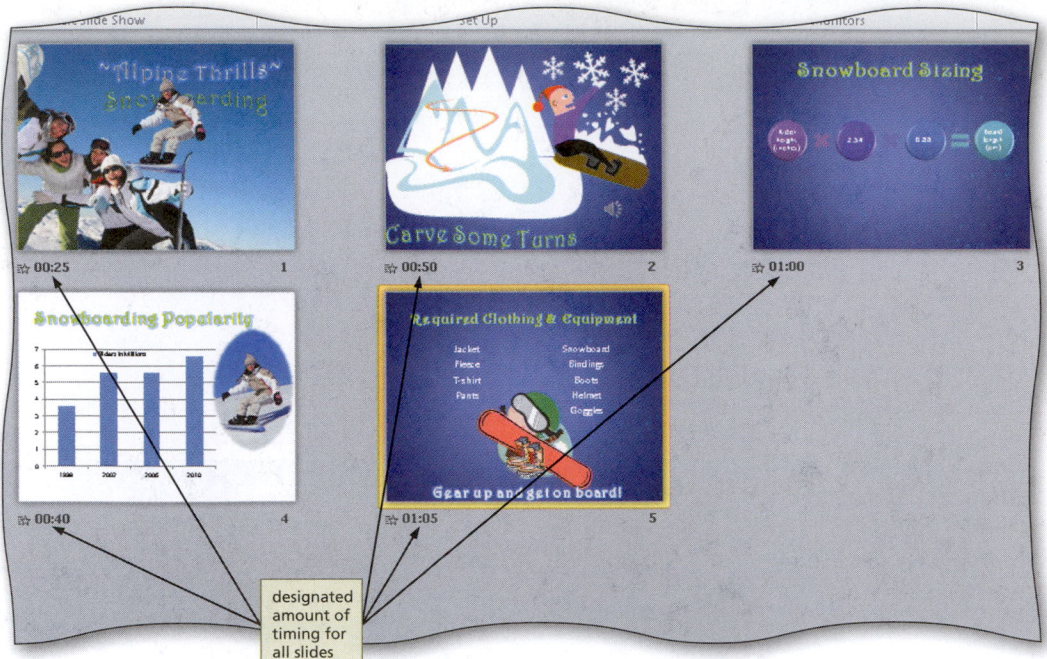

Figure 7–69

To Adjust Timings Manually

If the slide timings need adjustment, you manually can change the length of time each slide is displayed. In this presentation, you decide to display Slide 4 for 30 seconds instead of 40 seconds. The following step decreases the Slide 4 timing.

1

- In Slide Sorter view, display the Transitions tab and then select Slide 4.

- Click and hold down the Advance Slide After down arrow (Transitions tab | Timing group) until 00:30.00 is displayed (Figure 7–70).

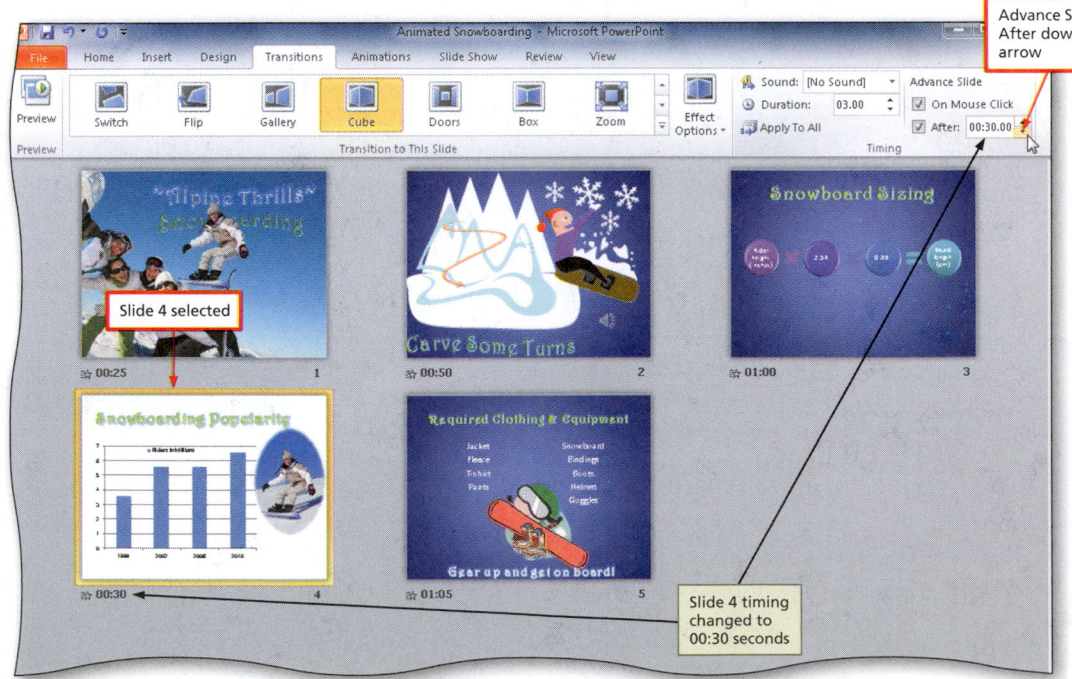

Figure 7–70

To Modify a Transition Effect

The Cube transition is applied to the five slides in this presentation. The default rotation is From Right, so the current slide turns to the left while the new slide appears from the right side of the screen. To keep the downhill theme of the presentation in mind, you can change the Cube rotation so that the current slide moves to the bottom of the screen and the new slide appears from the top. The following steps modify the Transition Effect for all slides in the presentation.

1

- With the Transitions tab still selected, click the Effect Options button (Transitions tab | Transition to This Slide group) to display the Effect Options gallery (Figure 7–71).

Are the same four effects available for all transitions?

No. The transition effects vary depending upon the particular transition selected.

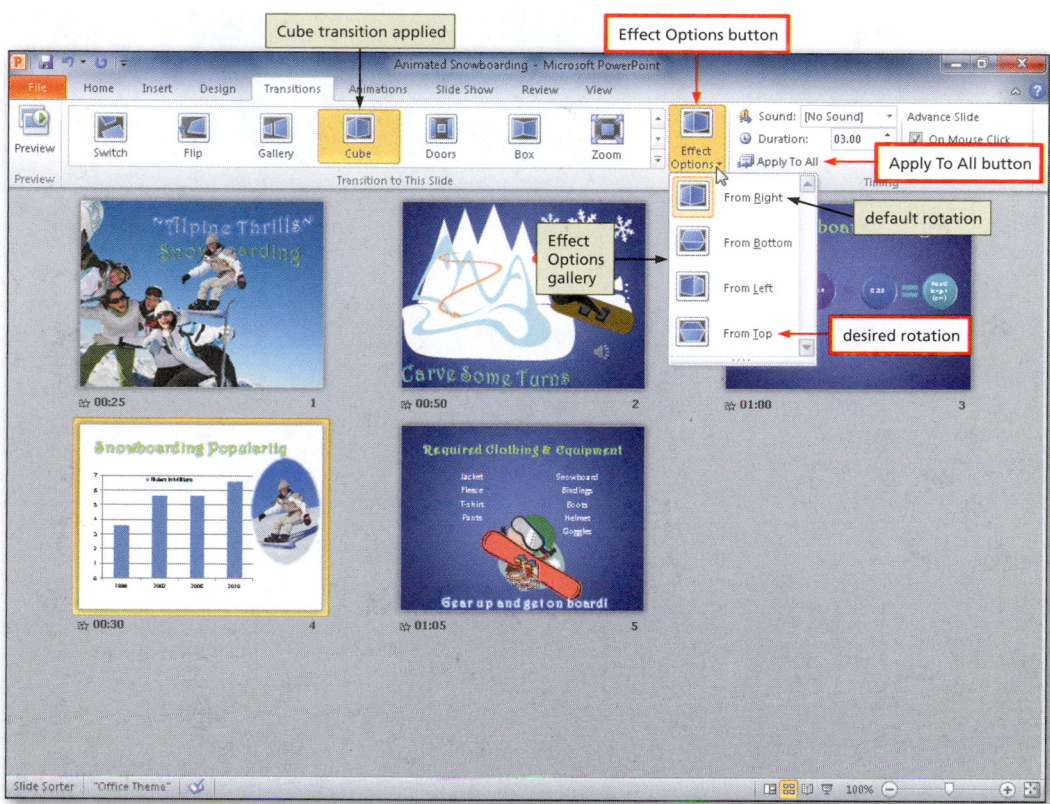

Figure 7–71

2

- Click the From Top effect to change the rotation.

- Click the Apply To All button (Transitions tab | Timing group) to set the From Top transition effect for all slides in the presentation.

To Create a Self-Running Presentation

The snowboarding presentation can accompany a speech, but it also can run unattended at sporting goods stores and ski resorts. When the last slide in the presentation is displayed, the slide show **loops**, or restarts, at Slide 1. PowerPoint has the option of running continuously until the user presses the ESC key. The following steps set the slide show to run in this manner.

1

• Display the Slide Show tab and then click the Set Up Slide Show button (Slide Show tab | Set Up group) to display the Set Up Show dialog box (Figure 7–72).

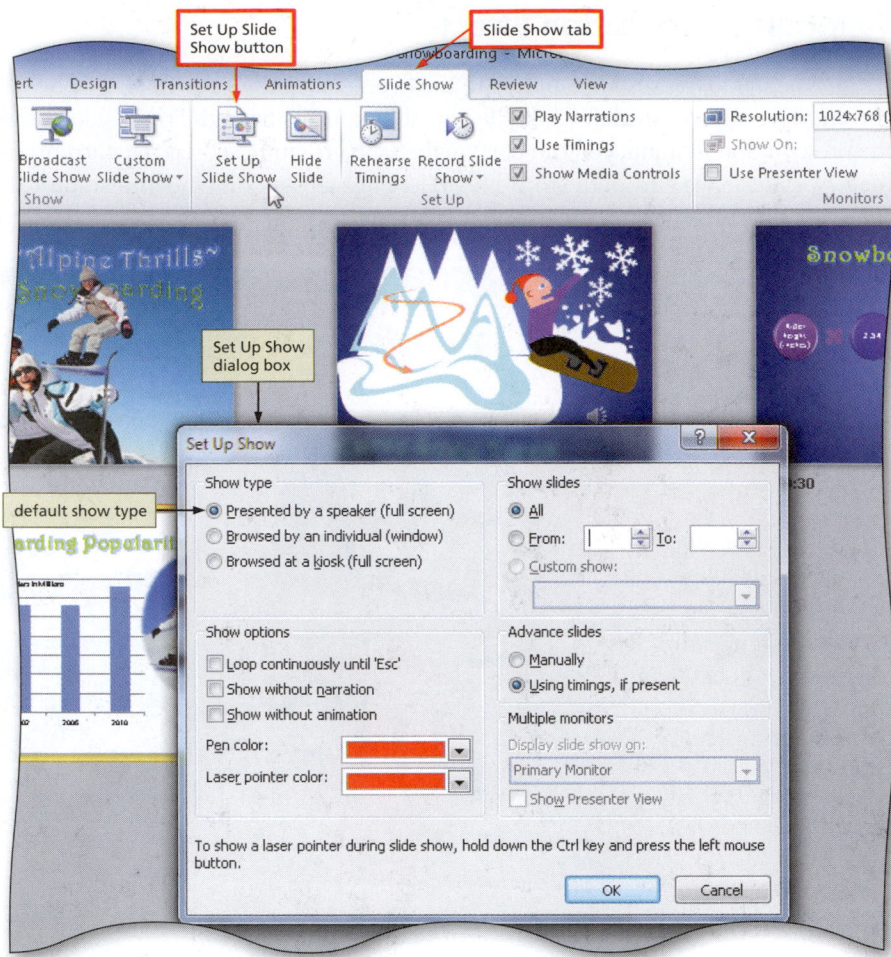

Figure 7–72

2

• Click 'Browsed at a kiosk (full screen)' in the Show type area (Figure 7–73).

3

• Click the OK button to apply this show type.

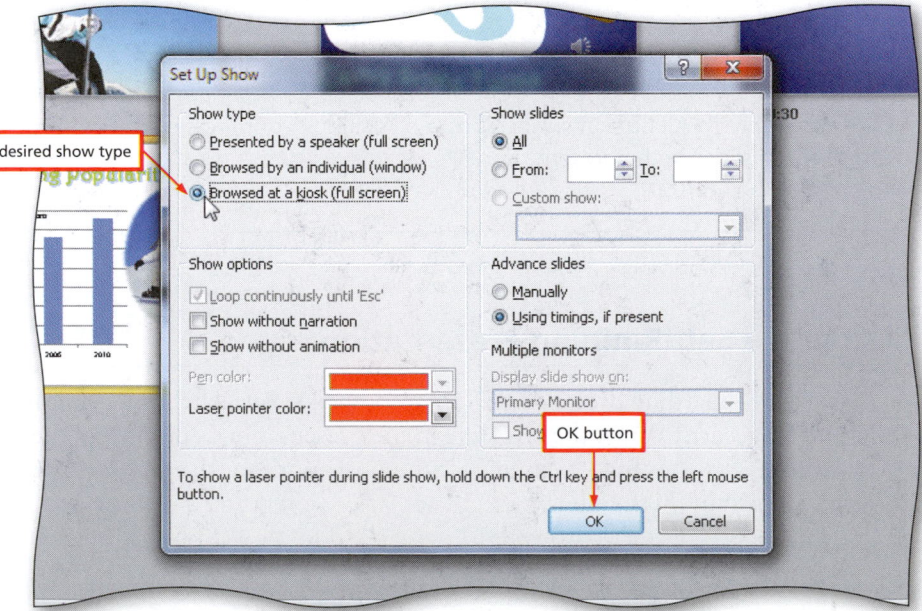

Figure 7–73

To Run an Animated Slide Show

All changes are complete. You now can view the Animated Snowboarding presentation. The following steps run the slide show.

1 Click the Normal View button, display the title slide, and then click the Slide Show button to start the presentation.

2 As each slide automatically is displayed, review the information.

3 When Slide 1 is displayed again, press the ESC key to stop the presentation.

To Change Document Properties

Before saving the presentation again, you want to add your name, class name, and some keywords as document properties. The following steps use the Document Information Panel to change document properties.

1 Display the Document Information Panel and then type your name as the Author property.

2 Type your course and section in the Subject property.

3 Type `snowboarding, snowboard size, popularity, clothing, equipment` as the Keywords property.

4 Close the Document Information Panel.

To Save, Print, and Quit PowerPoint

The presentation now is complete. You should save the slides, print a handout, and then quit PowerPoint.

1 Save the Animated Snowboarding presentation again with the same file name.

2 Print the presentation as a handout with two slides per page (Figure 7–74 on the next page).

3 Quit PowerPoint, closing all open documents.

BTW

Certification
The Microsoft Office Specialist (MOS) program provides an opportunity for you to obtain a valuable industry credential — proof that you have the PowerPoint 2010 skills required by employers. For more information, visit the PowerPoint 2010 Certification Web page (scsite.com/ppt2010/cert).

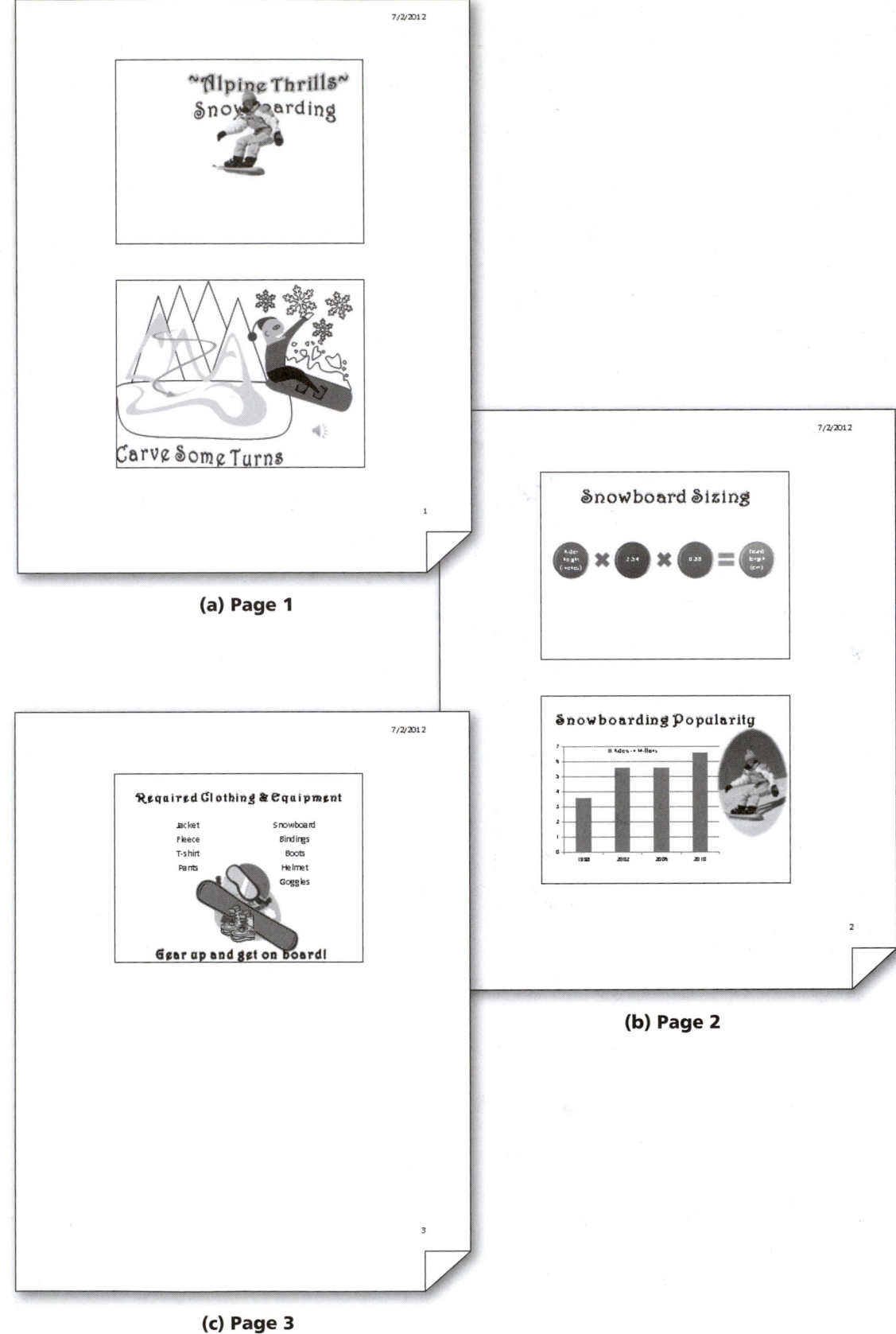

(a) Page 1

(b) Page 2

(c) Page 3

Figure 7–74

Chapter Summary

In this chapter you have learned how to remove a background from a picture and then crop and compress the image. You then applied entrance, emphasis, and exit effects to slide content and created a custom animation using a motion path. Also, you inserted and animated a text box and associated a sound with this text. You animated a SmartArt graphic, a chart, and two lists. Then, you set timing so that the slide show runs automatically. The items listed below include all the new PowerPoint skills you have learned in this chapter.

1. Remove a Background (PPT 405)
2. Refine Background Removal (PPT 407)
3. Crop a Picture (PPT 409)
4. Compress a Picture (PPT 410)
5. Animate a Picture Using an Entrance Effect (PPT 411)
6. Change Animation Direction (PPT 412)
7. Animate a Picture Using an Emphasis Effect (PPT 413)
8. Animate a Picture Using an Exit Effect (PPT 414)
9. Preview an Animation Sequence (PPT 416)
10. Modify Entrance Animation Timing (PPT 416)
11. Animate Title Text Placeholder Paragraphs (PPT 419)
12. Change Animation Order (PPT 420)
13. Rename Slide Objects (PPT 422)
14. Insert a Text Box and Format Text (PPT 423)
15. Animate a Text Box Using an Entrance Effect (PPT 425)
16. Animate a Text Box by Applying a Motion Path (PPT 427)
17. Adjust a Motion Path (PPT 428)
18. Associate a Sound with an Animation (PPT 430)
19. Draw a Custom Motion Path (PPT 431)
20. Use the Animation Painter to Animate a Clip (PPT 433)
21. Animate a SmartArt Graphic (PPT 435)
22. Change a SmartArt Graphic Animation Sequence (PPT 436)
23. Animate a Chart (PPT 437)
24. Animate a List (PPT 439)
25. Dim Text after Animation (PPT 440)
26. Create Credits (PPT 442)
27. Rehearse Timings (PPT 444)
28. Adjust Timings Manually (PPT 446)
29. Modify a Transition Effect (PPT 447)
30. Create a Self-Running Presentation (PPT 447)

 If you have a SAM 2010 user profile, your instructor may have assigned an autogradable version of this assignment. If so, log into the SAM 2010 Web site at www.cengage.com/sam2010 to download the instruction and start files.

Learn It Online

Test your knowledge of chapter content and key terms.

Instructions: To complete the Learn It Online exercises, start your browser, click the Address bar, and then enter the Web address `scsite.com/ppt2010/learn`. When the Office 2010 Learn It Online page is displayed, click the link for the exercise you want to complete and then read the instructions.

Chapter Reinforcement TF, MC, and SA
A series of true/false, multiple choice, and short answer questions that test your knowledge of the chapter content.

Flash Cards
An interactive learning environment where you identify chapter key terms associated with displayed definitions.

Practice Test
A series of multiple choice questions that test your knowledge of chapter content and key terms.

Who Wants To Be a Computer Genius?
An interactive game that challenges your knowledge of chapter content in the style of a television quiz show.

Wheel of Terms
An interactive game that challenges your knowledge of chapter key terms in the style of the television show *Wheel of Fortune*.

Crossword Puzzle Challenge
A crossword puzzle that challenges your knowledge of key terms presented in the chapter.

Apply Your Knowledge

Reinforce the skills and apply the concepts you learned in this chapter.

Applying Entrance Effects

Note: To complete this assignment, you will be required to use the Data Files for Students. See the inside back cover of this book for instructions on downloading the Data Files for Students or contact your instructor for information about accessing the required files.

Instructions: Start PowerPoint. Open the presentation, Apply 7-1 Losing Weight, located on the Data Files for Students.

The slide in this presentation gives a few suggestions on losing weight. The document you open is an unformatted presentation. You are to add an entrance effect to the title, convert the text to a SmartArt graphic, and then add an entrance effect to the SmartArt graphic so the slide looks like Figure 7–75.

Perform the following tasks:
1. Change the document theme to Angles and change the presentation theme colors to Clarity.
2. Apply the Brown, Accent 2 WordArt text fill and the Dark Red, Accent 6 WordArt text outline to the title text. Then change the text outline weight to 2¼ pt. Also apply the WordArt Transform text effect, Fade Right, in the Warp area, to this text. Increase the size of the WordArt to 1.27" × 8.23".
3. Click More Entrance Effects in the Animation gallery and then apply the Grow & Turn entrance effect in the Moderate category to the title text. Change the start timing setting to After Previous and the duration to 02.00 seconds.

4. Reduce the picture size to 3.62" × 2.42" and apply the Soft Edges, 10 Point effect. Move the picture to the lower-right corner of the slide, as shown in Figure 7–75. Then apply the Appear entrance effect and change the duration from Auto to 01.00 second. Change the start timing setting to After Previous.

5. Convert the bulleted text to the Basic Target layout (Relationship area) SmartArt graphic. Change the color to the Colorful Range - Accent Colors 5 to 6 in the Colorful area. Apply the Polished 3-D SmartArt Style and then resize this graphic to approximately 5.5" × 10".

6. Increase the font size of the SmartArt graphic to 22 point. Change the width of the first three text boxes in the SmartArt graphic to 3.5". Use the Ruler and Guides to align the first three text boxes with the fourth and fifth text boxes.

7. Apply the Zoom entrance effect to the SmartArt graphic. Add the One by One effect option. Change the duration to 02.50 seconds. Move the SmartArt graphic to the location shown in Figure 7–75.

8. Change the transition from Reveal to Shape and then change the duration to 03.50 seconds.

9. Change the document properties, as specified by your instructor. Save the presentation using the file name, Apply 7-1 Aim for Losing Weight. Submit the revised document in the format specified by your instructor.

Figure 7–75

Extend Your Knowledge

Extend the skills you learned in this chapter and experiment with new skills. You may need to use Help to complete the assignment.

Changing and Reordering Animations, Adding Sound to Animations, Inserting a Text Box, and Cropping a Picture to a Shape

Note: To complete this assignment, you will be required to use the Data Files for Students. See the inside back cover of this book for instructions on downloading the Data Files for Students or contact your instructor for information about accessing the required files.

Instructions: Start PowerPoint. Open the presentation, Extend 7-1 Blue Moon, located on the Data Files for Students. You will change the title text animations, animate a bulleted list, dim text after animation, add sound to animations, and insert a text box, as shown in Figure 7–76. You will need to show more entrance, emphasis, and exit effects to locate the required animations.

Perform the following tasks:

1. On the Slide 1 title, change the Bounce entrance effect to the Float In entrance effect. Change the start timing option from On Click to After Previous, the duration to 02.00 seconds, and the direction to Float Down. Add the Wave emphasis effect in the Advanced Animation area, change the start timing option to After Previous, and change the duration to 05.50 seconds. Have the Brass Wind Chime sound, which is next to the title text on the slide, play with the Wave emphasis effect, and hide the sound icon during the show.

2. Apply the Fly In from Bottom Left Entrance animation to the three bulleted paragraphs so that they enter one at a time on click and then change the duration to 03.75 seconds.

3. Apply the Fly In from Left entrance animation to the moon clip. Change the duration to 03.00 seconds. Change the start timing option to After Previous. Have the Drum Roll Loud sound, which is next to the moon clip, play with this clip, change the volume to High, and hide the sound icon during the show.

4. Change the font of the vertically rotated text, Next Blue Moon 2015, to Eras Bold ITC, the color of the text to Dark Blue, and the font size to 40 point. Center this text. Add the Dissolve In entrance effect to this text. Change the start timing option to After Previous and the duration to 02.50 seconds. Add the Grow With Color emphasis to the text. Click the Effect Options button and select the teal color (ninth color in Theme Colors row). Change the start timing option to After Previous and change the duration to 03.00 seconds.

5. Apply the Flash transition to Slide 1 and change the duration to 04.50 seconds.

6. On Slide 2, select the moon picture, and, while holding down the CTRL key, move the picture to the right to duplicate it. Remove the background from the duplicate picture, click the handles on the marquee, and then drag the lines so that the moon is centered in the picture. Change the color of this picture to Blue, Accent Color 1 Dark and then move this picture on top of the original picture until the blue moon is lined up directly on top of the white moon.

7. Apply the Shrink & Turn exit effect to the blue moon picture, change the start timing option to After Previous, and change the duration to 05.00 seconds. Change the name of the blue moon picture in the Animation pane from Picture 4 to Blue Moon.

8. On Slide 2, select the Wave shape and add the Float In entrance effect. Change the direction to Float Down. Change the start timing option to After Previous and the duration to 2.00. Resize the oval shape so that it is approximately 2.19" × 2.25", and also reduce the font size to fit into the shape. Add the Fly In entrance effect, change the direction to From Right, and then change the start timing option to After Previous and the duration to 02.50 seconds.

9. Insert the Moon picture located on the Data Files for Students. Crop the picture so that the moon is centered within the black background. Increase the size of the picture to 3.28" × 3.66" and then

crop the picture to fill the Moon shape. You may need to use Help to learn how to crop to a shape. Move the Moon picture to the location shown in the figure.

10. Apply the Orbit transition to Slide 2 and change the duration to 04.50 seconds.

11. Change the document properties, as specified by your instructor. Save the presentation using the file name, Extend 7-1 Once in a Blue Moon.

12. Submit the revised document in the format specified by your instructor.

(a) Slide 1

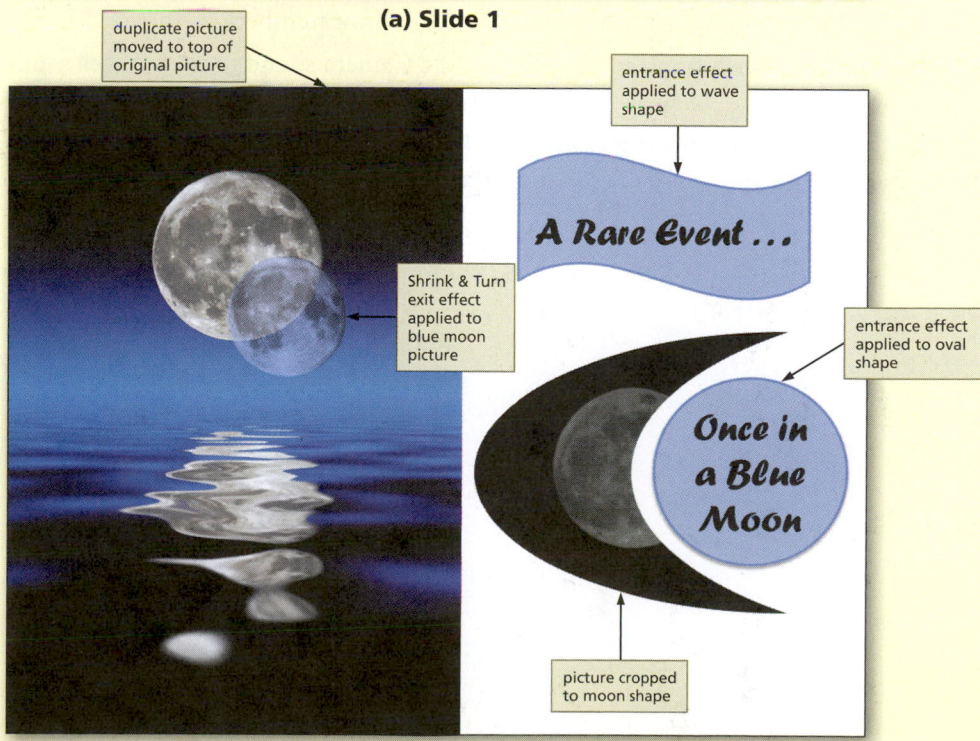

(b) Slide 2

Figure 7–76

Make It Right

Analyze a presentation and correct all errors and/or improve the design.

Removing and Changing Animation, and Copying Animation Using the Animation Painter

Note: To complete this assignment, you will be required to use the Data Files for Students. See the inside back cover of this book for instructions on downloading the Data Files for Students or contact your instructor for information about accessing the required files.

Instructions: Start PowerPoint. Open the presentation, Make It Right 7-1 Footprints, located on the Data Files for Students.

Correct the formatting problems and errors in the presentation while keeping in mind the guidelines presented in this chapter. This presentation was created as part of an interactive exhibit for children at the local nature center. The instructions for the matching game are as follows: First, select the green number 1; then, click on the animal's picture. The correct picture will display with a Grow & Turn animation and an orange border. Then click on green number 2. Continue selecting the green numbers to match all the animals with their tracks.

The footprints and pictures shown in Figure 7–77 are not in the correct order. You volunteer to modify the presentation so that the animals match their tracks.

Perform the following tasks:

1. Display the Animation tab, and remove the animation from all the footprints except number 1. Remove the animation from all the pictures except the skunk picture. Use the Animation Painter to copy the animation from the first footprint picture to the five remaining footprint pictures. Then copy the animation from the skunk picture to the five remaining animal pictures.

2. Reorder the animations so that the animal picture follows the footprint. Footprint number 1 is the skunk, footprint number 2 is the deer, footprint number 3 is the squirrel, footprint number 4 is the mink, footprint number 5 is the wolf, and footprint number 6 is the fox.

3. Change the Fade transition to Rotate, change the Camera sound to the Wolves sound, and then change the duration to 04.50 seconds.

4. Change the document properties, as specified by your instructor. Save the presentation using the file name, Make It Right 7-1 Animal Footprints.

5. Submit the revised document in the format specified by your instructor.

Figure 7–77

In the Lab

Design and/or create a presentation using the guidelines, concepts, and skills presented in this chapter. Labs 1, 2, and 3 are listed in order of increasing difficulty.

Lab 1: Creating a Presentation with an Animated Chart

Note: To complete this assignment, you will be required to use the Data Files for Students. See the inside back cover of this book for instructions on downloading the Data Files for Students or contact your instructor for information about accessing the required files.

Problem: In many countries around the world, people do not have clean drinking water. You belong to a science club, and your group has decided to develop a water project that can change salt water to fresh water. You decide to create a PowerPoint presentation to introduce the basic facts about water on Earth. You create the slides shown in Figure 7–78 on pages PPT 458 and PPT 459 using files located on the Data Files for Students. You will need to show more entrance and emphasis effects to locate the required animations.

Perform the following tasks:

1. Open the presentation, Lab 7-1 Water, located on the Data Files for Students.
2. On Slide 1, apply the Wedge entrance effect to the title text. Change the start timing option to With Previous and the duration to 03.50 seconds. Then add a Wave emphasis effect to the title text, change the start timing option to With Previous, and change the duration to 04.00 seconds.

Continued >

In the Lab *continued*

3. On Slide 2, apply the Wheel entrance effect to the title text. Change the start timing option to After Previous and change the duration to 03.50 seconds.

4. Apply the Random Bars entrance effect to the clip. Change the start timing option to After Previous and change the duration to 04.50 seconds.

5. Apply the Wipe entrance effect to the chart. Change the duration to 05.25 seconds.

6. Apply the Fly In From Left entrance effect to all paragraphs in the content placeholder. Change the duration to 02.50 seconds.

7. Dim the second bulleted paragraph (Ocean and seas), the third bulleted paragraph, and the three second-level paragraphs (Fresh water; Lakes, Rivers; Glaciers; Ground) after animation using a blue and a green color displayed in the pie chart. To select these colors, click the After animation arrow in the Enhancements area (Fly In dialog box), click More Colors in the After animation menu, and then click the colors that best match the chart colors.

8. Add the Style 5 background style to Slide 2. *Hint:* Right-click Style 5 and then click Apply to Selected Slides in the shortcut menu.

9. Apply the Ripple transition and change the duration to 03.00 seconds for all slides.

10. Change the document properties, as specified by your instructor. Save the presentation using the file name, Lab 7-1 Water on Earth.

11. Submit the revised document in the format specified by your instructor.

entrance and emphasis effects applied to title text

(a) Slide 1

Figure 7–78

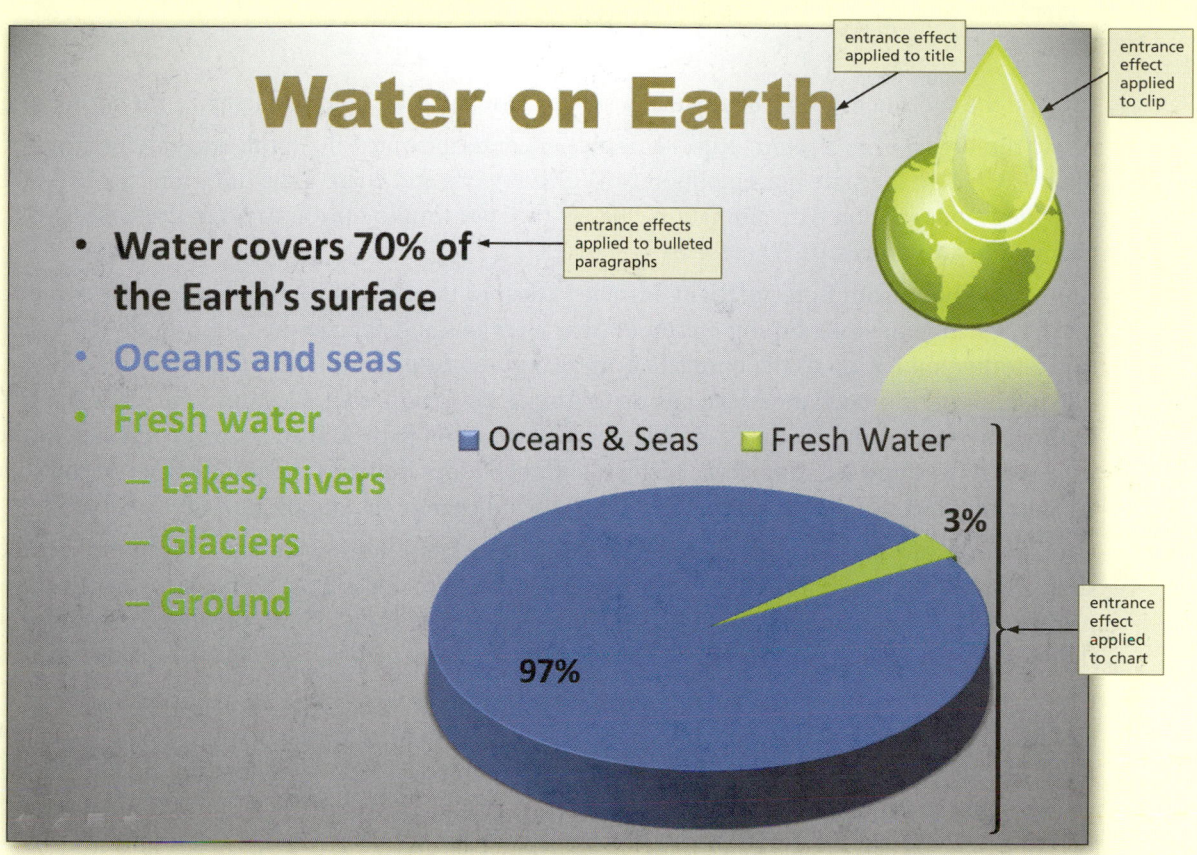

(b) Slide 2

Figure 7–78

In the Lab

Lab 2: Creating a Self-Running Presentation and Animating a Clip Using a Motion Path

Note: To complete this assignment, you will be required to use the Data Files for Students. See the inside back cover of this book for instructions on downloading the Data Files for Students or contact your instructor for information about accessing the required files.

Problem: You are studying botany and work part time at a local botanic garden. The garden's directors announced recently that a butterfly conservatory will be opening next year. In the interim, they are setting up a temporary exhibit. The master gardener, who is overseeing the planting of flowers and bushes that attract butterflies, has asked you to assist with the design of the conservatory. One of your assignments is to create a self-running PowerPoint presentation that will be viewed on a kiosk at the temporary exhibit. He asked you to gear your presentation to children because the botanic gardens are visited frequently by groups of children on field trips, and the butterfly conservatory will be designed with children in mind. You create the slides shown in Figure 7–79 on pages PPT 460 and PPT 461 using files located on the Data Files for Students.

Perform the following tasks:

1. Open the presentation, Lab 7-2 Butterfly, located on the Data Files for Students, and then add the Slipstream document theme.

2. On Slide 1, increase the size of the picture and add the Reflected Bevel, White picture style. Change the border to Turquoise, Accent 2.

3. Increase the title text font size to 54 point so that it is on two lines, as shown in Figure 7–79a.

Continued >

In the Lab *continued*

4. Change the subtitle font to Eurostyle or a similar font and then bold and italicize the author's name.

5. Apply the Fly In from Bottom-Right entrance effect to the butterfly in the upper-left corner of Slide 1. Change the start timing option to With Previous and change the duration to 02.50 seconds. Add the Loops motion path animation, change the start timing option to After Previous, and change the duration to 03.00 seconds.

6. Apply the Fly In from Bottom-Right entrance effect to the butterfly in the lower-right corner of Slide 1. Change the start timing option to After Previous and change the duration to 01.75 seconds. Add another animation to the butterfly by drawing a custom motion path. To draw the path, select the butterfly, click the More button in Animation group, click Custom Path, click the Effect Options button, and then click Scribble. Draw the motion path so it starts at the left side of the slide and moves upward toward the picture, and then loops down to the right corner of the slide. Change the start timing option to After Previous and change the duration to 02.75 seconds.

7. On Slide 2, insert the Butterfly picture located on the Data Files for Students. Crop the picture to show more of the butterfly and then resize the picture so that it is close to the size of the caterpillar picture (4.25" × 2.81"). Add the Beveled Oval Black picture style to both pictures and then move the pictures to the locations shown in Figure 7–79b.

8. Convert the bulleted text to the Block Cycle SmartArt graphic, change the color to Accent Colors 4 to 5, and apply the Sunset Scene style. Increase the size of the graphic to approximately 5.25" × 7.25" and move it to the location shown in Figure 7–79b. Apply the Fly In, One by One (in Sequence area), entrance effect to the SmartArt graphic. Change the start timing option to After Previous and change the duration to 02.75 seconds.

9. Apply the Honeycomb transition and then change the duration to 04.00 seconds for all slides.

10. Rehearse the presentation and then set the slide timings to 22 seconds for Slide 1 and 28 seconds for Slide 2.

11. Change the document properties, as specified by your instructor. Save the presentation using the file name, Lab 7-2 Butterfly Mystique.

12. Submit the revised document in the format specified by your instructor.

(a) Slide 1

Figure 7–79

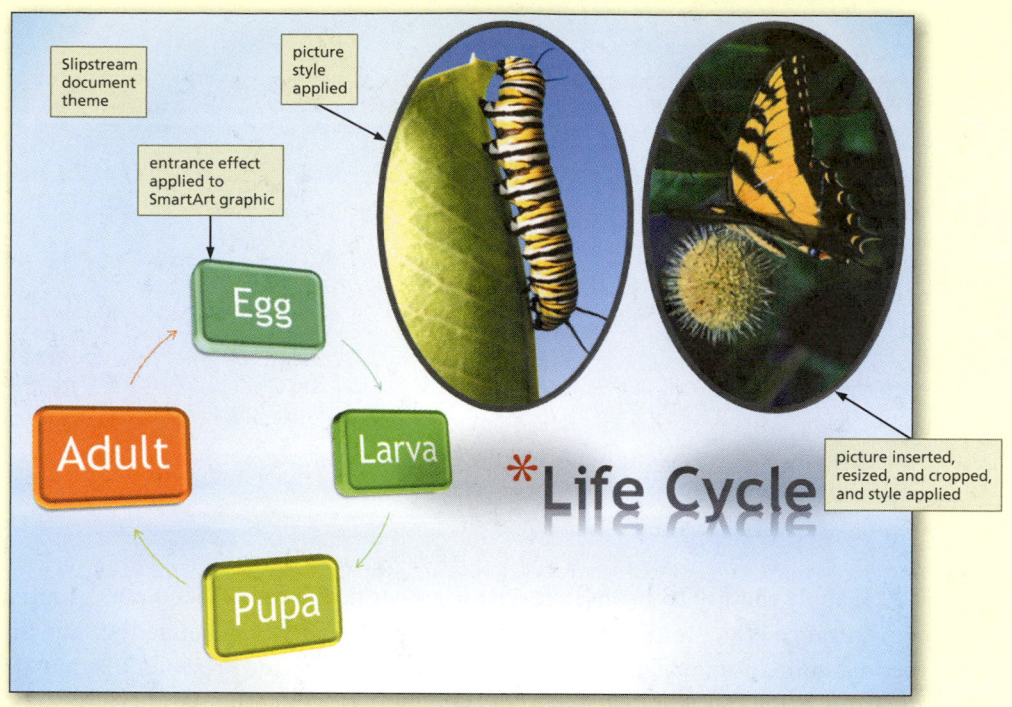

(b) Slide 2

Figure 7–79

In the Lab

Lab 3: Animating a Chart, Adding Credits, and Removing a Background from a Picture

Note: To complete this assignment, you will be required to use the Data Files for Students. See the inside back cover of this book for instructions on downloading the Data Files for Students or contact your instructor for information about accessing the required files.

Problem: You volunteer a few days each week at the local animal shelter, and the manager of the shelter asks if you would create a PowerPoint presentation to show to prospective dog owners. You create the presentation in Figure 7–80 on page PPT 463 consisting of three slides and a closing slide.

Perform the following tasks:

1. Open the presentation, Lab 7-3 Dog, located on the Data Files for Students, and change the document theme to Trek.

2. On Slide 1, add the Bounce entrance effect to the WordArt. Change the start timing option to After Previous and change the duration to 02.75 seconds.

3. Change the subtitle so that the text is on three lines, increase font size to 40 point, and then move the subtitle to the location shown in Figure 7–80a. Add the Fade entrance effect to the subtitle. Change the start timing option to After Previous and change the duration to 01.50 seconds. Add the Wipe From Top exit effect to this text, change the start timing option to After Previous, change the duration to 03.00 seconds, and change the delay to 02.25 seconds.

4. On Slide 2, remove the background from the German Shepherd picture and then increase the size of the picture to approximately 5.19" x 4.14", as shown in Figure 7–80b.

5. Apply the animation effects to the seven bulleted paragraphs and pictures using Table 7–3 as a guide.

Continued >

In the Lab *continued*

Table 7–3 Slide 2 Animation Effects

Text or Picture	Entrance Effect	Start	Duration	Delay
First bulleted paragraph	Appear	After Previous	3.00	2.00
Second bulleted paragraph	Fly In From Left	On Click	2.50	—
White dog picture	Float Down	With Previous	2.50	—
Third bulleted paragraph	Fly In From Left	On Click	2.50	—
Brown puppy picture	Float Down	With Previous	2.50	—
Fourth bulleted paragraph	Fly In From Left	On Click	2.50	—
German Shepherd picture	Fly In From Right	With Previous	2.50	—
Fifth, sixth, and seventh bulleted paragraphs	Fly In From Left	On Click	2.50	—

6. On Slide 3, apply the Fly In From Left – By Element in Category (Sequence group in Effect Options) entrance effect to the chart, as shown in Figure 7–80c. Change the start timing option for only the first animation, which is the chart background, to After Previous. Change the duration for all animations to 03.25 seconds.

7. Apply Background Style 6 to Slides 2 and 3.

8. Create a fourth slide for a closing slide and use the Title and Content layout. In the title text placeholder, type **Thank You for Your Support**. Change the font color to Orange, Accent 1 and then center and italicize this text, as shown in Figure 7–80d. Apply the Dissolve In entrance animation effect (Basic group) and then change the duration to 07.00 seconds.

9. Insert the Bulldog picture located in the Data Files for Students on Slide 4. Remove the background from the picture and then refine the background removal by keeping and removing areas around the bulldog. Crop the picture, resize it so that it is approximately 5" × 6.76", and then move it to the location shown in the figure. Compress this picture.

10. Insert a text box at the bottom of the slide and type **Clifford Mason, Manager** as the first paragraph and **Southtown Animal Shelter** as the second paragraph. Change the font color to Light Yellow, Text 2 and the font size to 32 point. Center this text. Bring this text box forward so that the text will be in front of the bulldog. Apply the Credits entrance animation, change the start timing option to With Previous, and change the duration to 13.00 seconds. Add the Applause sound to this text and change the volume to the highest level.

11. Apply Background Style 3 to Slide 4.

12. Add a trigger to display the Thank You for Your Support text box when the bulldog picture is clicked. Rename the trigger animation Bulldog Picture.

13. Change the document properties, as specified by your instructor. Save the presentation using the file name, Lab 7-3 Adopting a Dog.

14. Submit the revised document in the format specified by your instructor.

(a) Slide 1

(b) Slide 2

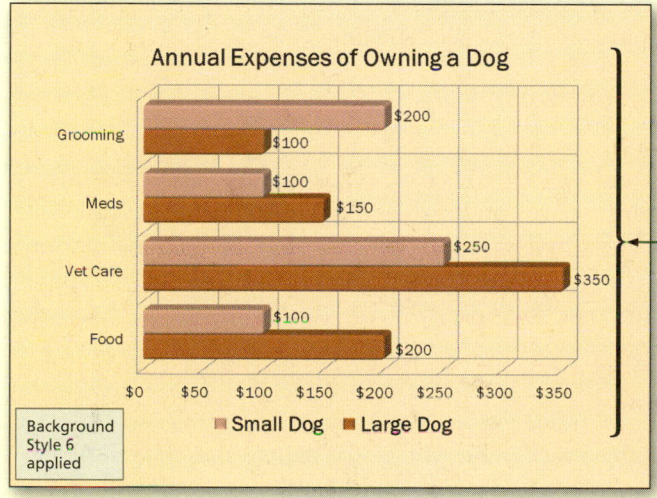

(c) Slide 3

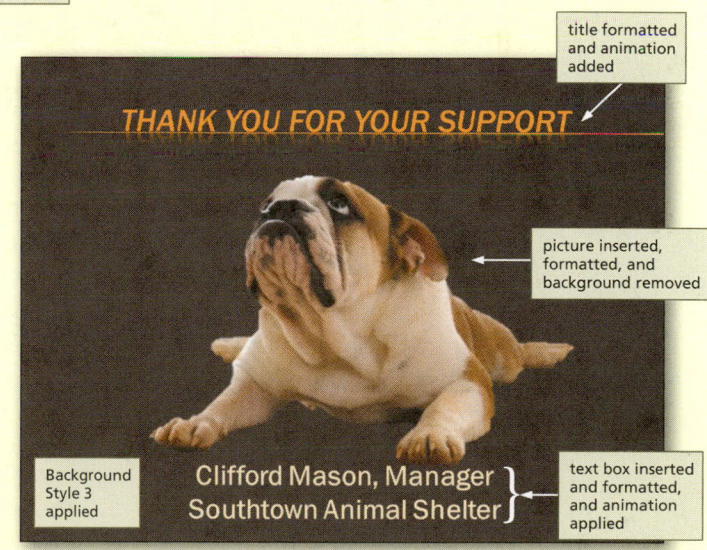

(d) Slide 4

Figure 7–80

Cases and Places

Apply your creative thinking and problem-solving skills to design and implement a solution.

Note: To complete these assignments, you may be required to use the Data Files for Students. See the inside back cover of this book for instructions on downloading the Data Files for Students, or contact your instructor for information about accessing the required files.

As you design the presentations, remember to use the 7 × 7 rule: a maximum of seven words on a line and a maximum of seven lines on one slide.

1: Designing and Creating a Presentation about the Dwarf Planet Pluto

Academic

The International Astronomical Union (IAU) determined, after changing the definition of what constitutes a planet, that Pluto is now considered a dwarf planet. Even though Pluto was once considered the ninth planet in our solar system, other planets have been discovered since that are larger than Pluto. In your Astronomy class, you are studying the planets in our solar system. You decide to create a PowerPoint presentation to explain why Pluto is now considered a dwarf planet. Include information about other dwarf planets. Apply at least three objectives found at the beginning of this chapter to develop the presentation, including a cropped picture and an animated picture or a SmartArt graphic. Use pictures and diagrams from Office.com if they are appropriate for this topic. Be sure to check spelling.

2: Designing and Creating a Presentation about Sailing

Personal

You always have wanted to learn how to sail. You and a few friends have registered for sailing lessons and want to learn some things in advance to better prepare you for the sailing lessons. Use at least three objectives found at the beginning of this chapter to develop the presentation, including a motion path and dimmed text. Use pictures from Office.com if they are appropriate for this topic or use your personal digital pictures. Be sure to check spelling.

3: Designing and Creating a Presentation about Planning a Retirement Community

Professional

You work for an architectural firm that is developing a retirement village for people ages 55 and older. The 30-acre village will have condominiums, townhomes, and a few single-family homes. It will offer a community clubhouse with an indoor-outdoor swimming pool, a fitness center, party rooms, a large banquet room, a small movie theater, and a game room. Your firm has assigned you the job of putting together a presentation listing all the amenities this retirement village will offer. There will also be a community garden for residents to plant vegetables and flowers; tennis courts; shuffleboard courts; and a small landscaped park that will feature a fountain, a pond, benches, and picnic tables. You will be showing your slide show at a town hall meeting for community residents and also plan to run the self-running presentation at a kiosk. Use pictures from Office.com if they are appropriate for this topic or use your personal digital pictures. Add credits on the last slide. Be certain to check spelling.

4 Financial Functions, Data Tables, and Amortization Schedules

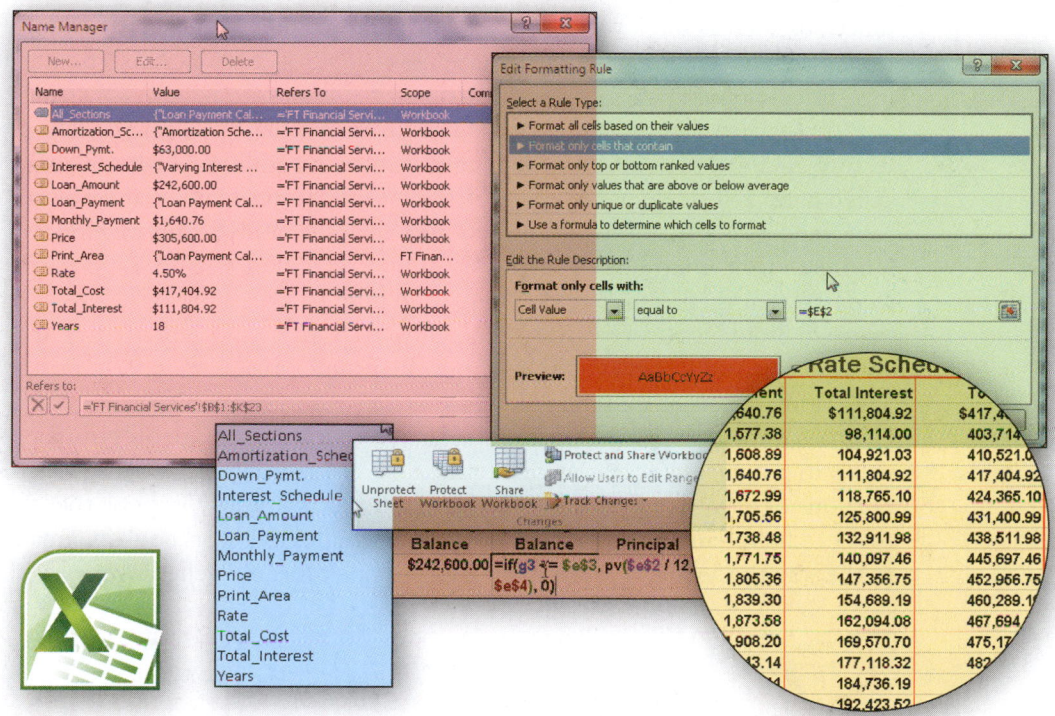

Objectives

You will have mastered the material in this chapter when you can:

- Control the color and thickness of outlines and borders
- Assign a name to a cell and refer to the cell in a formula using the assigned name
- Determine the monthly payment of a loan using the financial function PMT
- Use the financial functions PV (present value) and FV (future value)
- Create a data table to analyze data in a worksheet
- Add a pointer to a data table

- Create an amortization schedule
- Analyze worksheet data by changing values
- Use names and print sections of a worksheet
- Set print options
- Protect and unprotect cells in a worksheet
- Use the formula checking features of Excel
- Hide and unhide cell gridlines, rows, columns, sheets, and workbooks

4 Financial Functions, Data Tables, and Amortization Schedules

Introduction

Two of the more powerful aspects of Excel are its wide array of functions and its capability of organizing answers to what-if questions. In this chapter, you will learn about financial functions such as the PMT function, which allows you to determine a monthly payment for a loan, and the PV function, which allows you to determine the present value of an investment.

In earlier chapters, you learned how to analyze data by using Excel's recalculation feature and goal seeking. This chapter introduces an additional what-if analysis tool, called data tables. You use a **data table** to automate data analyses and organize the answers returned by Excel. Another important loan analysis tool is an amortization schedule. An **amortization schedule** shows the beginning and ending balances and the amount of payment that is applied to the principal and interest over a period.

In previous chapters, you learned how to print in a variety of ways. In this chapter, you will learn additional methods of printing using range names and a print area.

Finally, this chapter introduces you to cell protection; hiding and unhiding rows, columns, sheets, and workbooks; and formula checking. **Cell protection** ensures that users do not change values inadvertently that are critical to the worksheet. **Hiding** portions of a workbook lets you show only the parts of the workbook that the user needs to see. The **formula checker** examines the formulas in a workbook in a manner similar to the way the spell checker examines a workbook for misspelled words.

Project — Loan Payment Calculator with Data Table and Amortization Schedule

The project in the chapter follows proper design guidelines and uses Excel to create the worksheet shown in Figure 4–1. FT Financial Services provides loans for homes and other types of property. The company's chief financial officer has asked for a workbook that calculates loan payment information, displays an amortization schedule, and displays a table that shows loan payments for varying interest rates. To ensure that the loan officers do not delete the formulas in the worksheet, she has asked that cells in the worksheet be protected so that they cannot be changed accidentally.

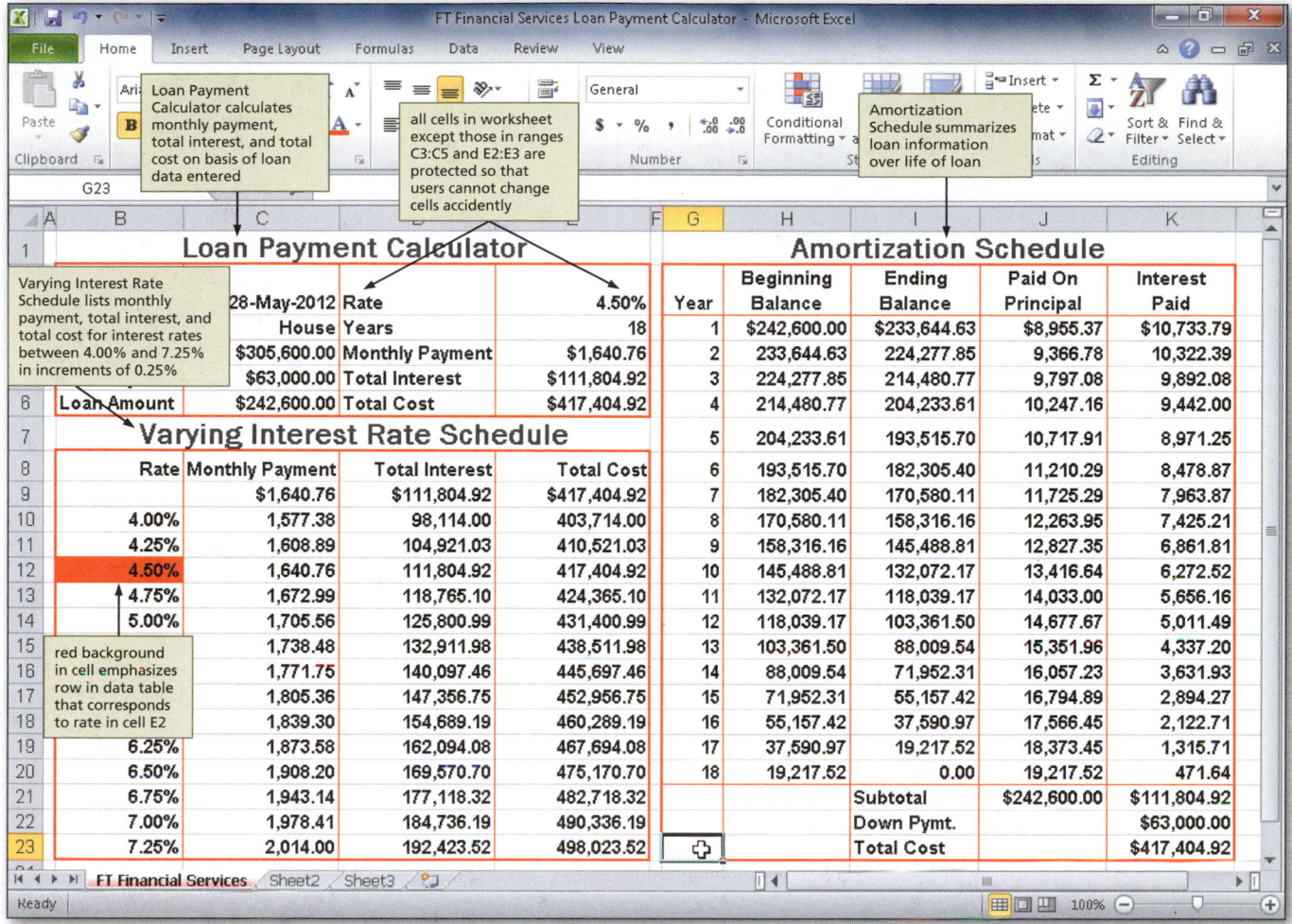

Figure 4–1

The requirements document for the FT Financial Services Loan Payment Calculator worksheet is shown in Figure 4–2 on the following page. It includes the needs, source of data, summary of calculations, special requirements, and other facts about its development.

REQUEST FOR NEW WORKBOOK

Date Submitted:	May 14, 2012
Submitted By:	Samuel Clewes, Jr.
Worksheet Title:	Loan Payment Calculator
Needs:	An easy-to-read worksheet (Figure 4-3 on page EX 230) that: 1. determines the monthly payment, total interest, and total cost for a loan; 2. shows a data table that answers what-if questions based on changing interest rates; 3. highlights the rate in the data table that matches the actual interest rate; 4. shows an amortization schedule that lists annual summaries.
Source of Data:	The data (item, price of the item, down payment, interest rate, and term of the loan in years) is determined by the loan officer and customer when they initially meet to review the loan. The Excel Data Table command creates the data table in the varying interest rate schedule.

Calculations:	1. The following calculations must be made for each loan:
	   a. Loan Amount = Price − Down Payment
	   b. Monthly Payment = PMT function
	   c. Total Interest = 12 × Years × Monthly Payment − Loan Amount
	   d. Total Cost = 12 × Years x Monthly Payment + Down Payment
	2. The amortization schedule involves the following calculations:
	   a. Beginning Balance = Loan Amount
	   b. Ending Balance = PV function or 0
	   c. Paid on Principal = Beginning Balance − Ending Balance
	   d. Interest Paid = 12 × Monthly Payment − Paid on Principal or 0
	   e. Paid on Principal Subtotal = SUM function
	   f. Interest Paid Subtotal = SUM function

Special Requirements	1. Assign names to the ranges of the three major sections of the worksheet and the worksheet itself, so that the names can be used to print each section separately. 2. Protect the worksheet in such a way that the loan officers cannot enter data into wrong cells mistakenly.

Approvals

Approval Status:	X	Approved
		Rejected
Approved By:		Donna Demers, Chief Information Officer
Date:		May 21, 2012
Assigned To:		J. Quasney, Spreadsheet Specialist

Figure 4–2

Overview

As you read this chapter, you will learn how to create the worksheet shown in Figure 4–1 on page EX 227 by performing these general tasks:

- Create and format the Loan Payment Calculator section and use the payment function.
- Create and format a data table that includes the varying interest rate schedule.
- Create and format the amortization schedule and use the present value and future value functions.
- Create and test print areas in the worksheet.
- Protect cells in the worksheet.
- Check the formulas in the worksheet.

BTW

Good Worksheet Design
Do not create worksheets as if you are going to use them only once. Carefully design worksheets as if they will be on display and evaluated by your fellow workers. Smart worksheet design starts with visualizing the results you need. A well-designed worksheet often is used for many years.

Plan Ahead

General Project Guidelines

While creating an Excel worksheet, the actions you perform and decisions you make will affect the appearance and characteristics of the finished worksheet. As you create the worksheet required to meet the requirements shown in Figure 4–2, you should follow these general guidelines:

1. **Create and format the data entry section of the worksheet.** A data entry section of a worksheet includes data items entered by a user of a worksheet. Place such data items in close proximity to each other on a worksheet so that the worksheet does not require the user to search for data items to enter. Format or delineate each section of a worksheet to make it distinct from the other sections of the worksheet. Cell borders help to set off sections of a worksheet.

2. **Create and format the data table section of the worksheet.** While Excel does not require that a data table have column or row headings, use them when possible in order to clarify the meaning of data in a data table. Cell borders or fill colors help to set off values computed in a data table.

3. **Create and format an amortization schedule in the worksheet.** Because an amortization schedule often includes complex formulas and functions, use descriptive column and row headings for the schedule. When possible, include subtotals and totals that allow a user of the worksheet quickly to find important results of what-if calculations.

4. **Specify and name print areas of the worksheet.** When users of the worksheet require the option to print the individual sections of the worksheet, name these sections and then print the sections by name. The ability of Excel to use range names to specify sections of a worksheet, such as a data table, makes printing easier for the user of the worksheet. Also, you quickly can modify range names when you add columns or rows to sections of the worksheet.

5. **Determine which cells to protect and unprotect in the worksheet.** When creating a workbook for use by others, the spreadsheet designer should consider which cells another user of the worksheet should be able to manipulate. Leave such cells unprotected. Protect all other cells in the worksheet from input by the user of the worksheet.

When necessary, more specific details concerning the above guidelines are presented at appropriate points in the chapter. The chapter also will identify the actions performed and decisions made regarding these guidelines during the creation of the worksheet shown in Figure 4–1 on page EX 227.

In addition, using a sketch of the worksheet can help you visualize its design. The sketch of the worksheet consists of titles, column and cell headings, the location of data values, and a general idea of the desired formatting (Figure 4–3).

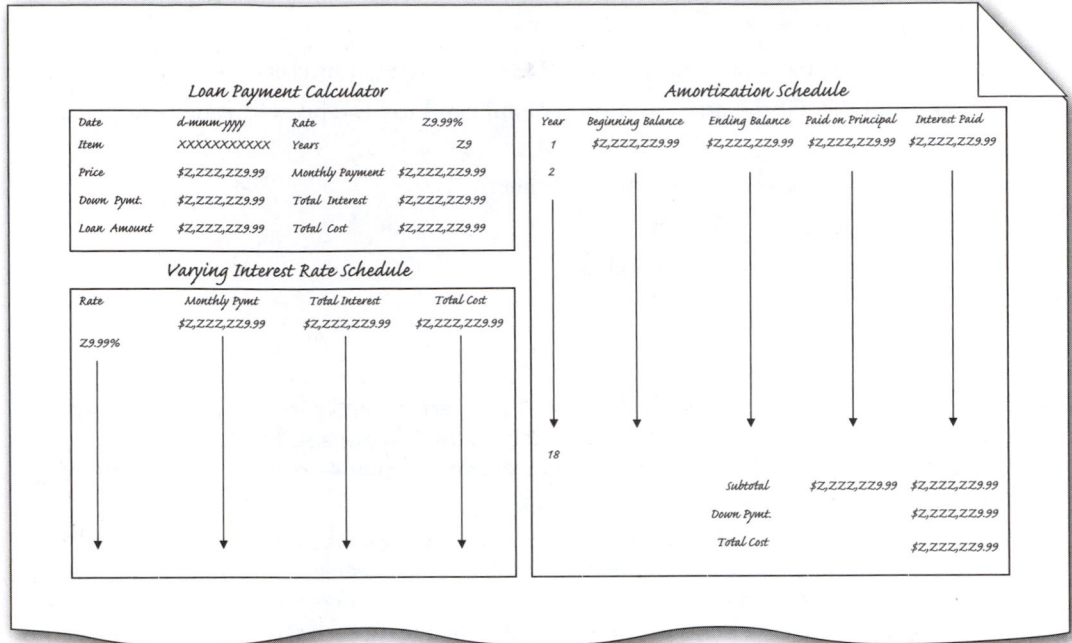

Figure 4–3

As shown in the worksheet sketch in Figure 4–3, the three basic sections of the worksheet are (1) the Loan Payment Calculator on the upper-left side, (2) the Varying Interest Rate Schedule data table on the lower-left side, and (3) the Amortization Schedule on the right side. The worksheet will be created in this order.

With a good understanding of the requirements document, an understanding of the necessary decisions, and a sketch of the worksheet, the next step is to use Excel to create the worksheet.

To Start Excel

If you are using a computer to step through the project in this chapter and you want your screens to match the figures in this book, you should change your screen's resolution to 1024 × 768. The following steps, which assume Windows 7 is running, start Excel based on a typical installation. You may need to ask your instructor how to start Excel for your computer.

1 Click the Start button on the Windows 7 taskbar to display the Start menu.

2 Type **Microsoft Excel** as the search text in the 'Search programs and files' text box, and watch the search results appear on the Start menu.

3 Click Microsoft Excel 2010 in the search results on the Start menu to start Excel and display a new blank workbook in the Excel window.

4 If the Excel window is not maximized, click the Maximize button next to the Close button on its title bar to maximize the window.

To Apply a Theme and Bold the Entire Worksheet

The following steps apply the Technic theme to the workbook and assign a bold format to the entire worksheet so that all entries will be emphasized.

1 Apply the Technic theme to the workbook.

2 Click the Select All button immediately above row heading 1 and to the left of column heading A to select the entire worksheet.

3 Click the Bold button (Home tab | Font group) to bold the entire worksheet.

Global Formatting
To assign formats to all the cells in all the worksheets in a workbook, click the Select All button, right-click a sheet tab, and click Select All Sheets on the shortcut menu. Next, assign the formats. To deselect the sheets, hold down the SHIFT key and click the Sheet1 tab. You also can select a cell or a range of cells and then select all sheets to assign formats to that cell or a range of cells on all sheets in a workbook.

To Enter the Section and Row Titles and System Date

The next step is to enter the Loan Payment Calculator section title, row titles, and system date. To make the worksheet easier to read, the width of column A will be decreased and used as a separator between the Loan Payment Calculator section and the row headings on the left. Using a column as a separator between sections on a worksheet is a common technique employed by spreadsheet specialists. The width of columns B through E will be increased so that the intended values fit. The height of row 1, which contains the title, will be increased so that it stands out. The Loan Payment Calculator section title also will be changed to the Title cell style and vertically middle-aligned.

The following steps enter the section title, row titles, and system date.

1 Select cell B1 and then type **Loan Payment Calculator** as the section title.

2 Select the range B1:E1 and then click the Merge & Center button (Home tab | Alignment group) to merge and center the section title in the selected range.

3 Click the Cell Styles button (Home tab | Styles group) and then click Title cell style in the Cell Styles gallery to apply the selected style to the active cell.

4 Click the Middle Align button (Home tab | Alignment group) to vertically center the text in the selected cell.

5 Position the mouse pointer on the bottom boundary of row heading 1 and then drag up until the ScreenTip indicates Height: 20.25 (27 pixels) to change the row height.

6 Position the mouse pointer on the bottom boundary of row heading 2 and then drag down until the ScreenTip indicates Height: 30.00 (40 pixels) to change the row height.

7 Select cell B2, Type **Date** as the row title, and then press the TAB key to complete the entry in the cell and select the cell to the right.

8 With cell C2 selected, type **=now()** and then click the Enter box to add a function to the cell that displays the system date.

9 Right–click cell C2 to open a shortcut menu and then click Format Cells on the shortcut menu to display the Format Cells dialog box. If necessary, click the Number tab to display the Number sheet, click Date in the Category list, scroll down in the Type list, and then click 14-Mar–2001 to select a date format.

10 Click the OK button (Format Cells dialog box) to close the Format Cells dialog box.

BTW

The Ribbon and Screen Resolution
Excel may change how the groups and buttons within the groups appear on the Ribbon, depending on the computer's screen resolution. Thus, your Ribbon may look different from the ones in this book if you are using a screen resolution other than 1024 x 768.

11 Enter the following text in the indicated cells:

Cell	text	Cell	text
		D2	Rate
B3	Item	D3	Years
B4	Price	D4	Monthly Payment
B5	Down Pymt.	D5	Total Interest
B6	Loan Amount	D6	Total Cost

12 Position the mouse pointer on the right boundary of column heading A and then drag to the left until the ScreenTip indicates Width: .77 (10 pixels) to change the column width.

13 Position the mouse pointer on the right boundary of column heading B and then drag to the right until the ScreenTip indicates Width: 12.13 (102 pixels) to change the column width.

BTW

BTWs
For a complete list of the BTWs found in the margins of this book, visit the Excel 2010 BTW Web page (scsite.com/ex2010/btw).

14 Click column heading C to select it and then drag through column headings D and E to select multiple columns. Position the mouse pointer on the right boundary of column heading C and then drag until the ScreenTip indicates Width: 15.00 (125 pixels) to change multiple column widths (Figure 4–4).

15 Click cell B2 to deselect the selected columns.

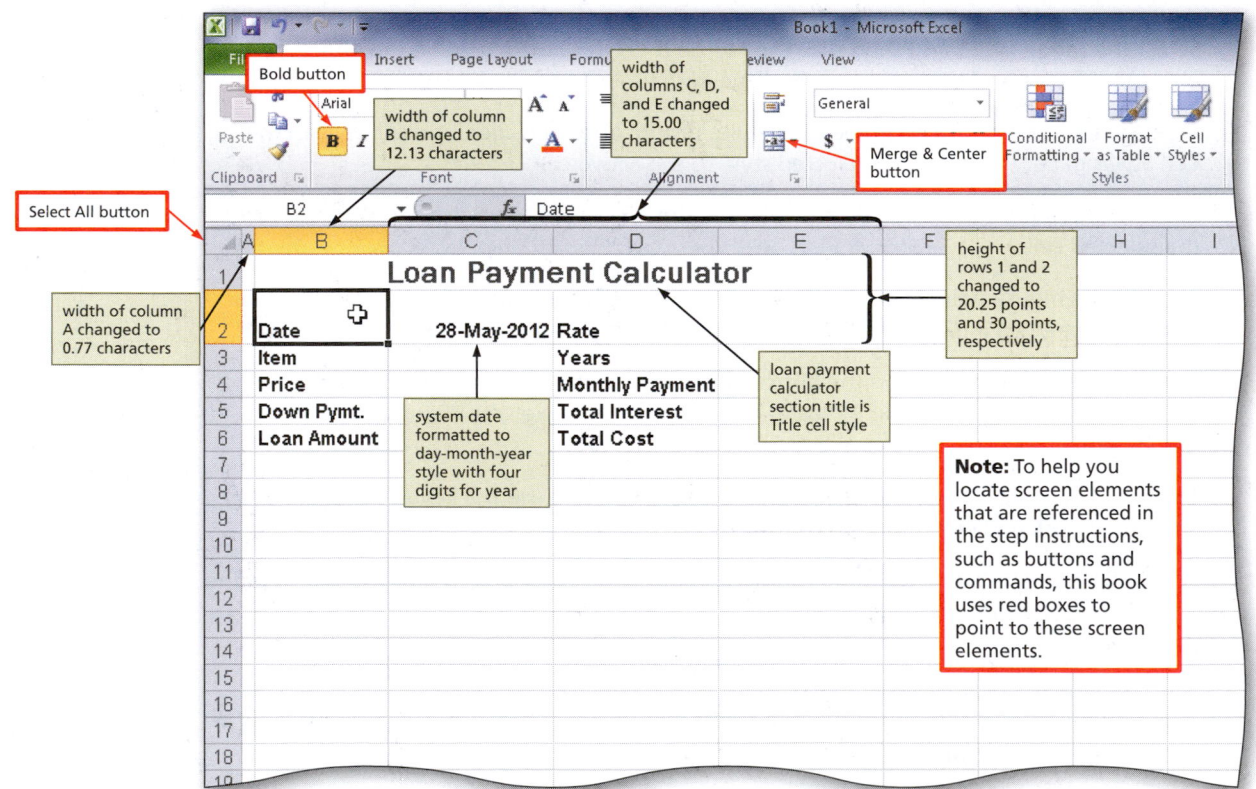

Figure 4–4

To Change the Sheet Name, Enter Document Properties, and Save the Workbook

The following steps change the Sheet1 name to a meaningful name, enter document properties, and then save the workbook.

1 Double-click the Sheet1 tab and then enter `FT Financial Services` as the sheet name.

2 Right-click the tab to display a shortcut menu and then point to Tab Color on the shortcut menu. Click Red (column 2, row 1) in the Standard Colors area to change the sheet tab color (Figure 4–5).

3 Change the document properties as specified by your instructor.

4 With a USB flash drive connected to one of the computer's USB ports, click the Save button on the Quick Access Toolbar to display the Save As dialog box.

5 Type `FT Financial Services Loan Payment Calculator` in the File name text box to change the file name. Do not press the ENTER key after typing the file name because you do not want to close the dialog box at this time.

6 Navigate to the desired save location (in this case, the Excel folder in the CIS 101 folder [or your class folder] on the USB flash drive).

7 Click the Save button (Save As dialog box) to save the document in the selected folder on the selected drive with the entered file name.

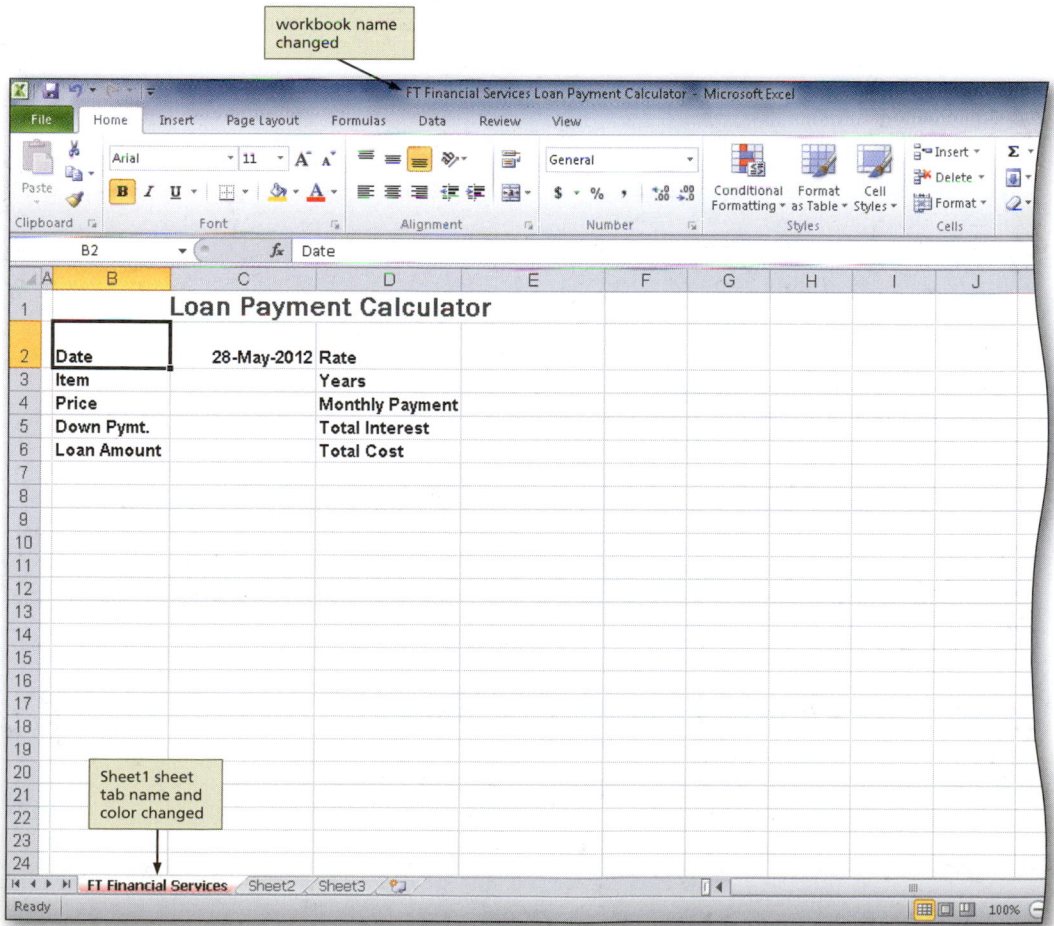

Figure 4–5

BTW

Cell References in Formulas

Are you tired of writing formulas that make no sense when you read them because of cell references? The Name Manager can help add clarity to your formulas by allowing you to assign names to cells. You then can use the names, such as Rate, rather than the cell reference, such as D2, in the formulas you create. To access the Name Manager, click the Name Manager button (Formulas tab | Defined Names).

Adding Custom Borders to a Range and Creating Cell Names

Previous chapters introduced you to outlining a range using cell borders or cell background colors to differentiate portions of a worksheet. The Borders button (Home tab | Font group), however, offers only a limited selection of border thicknesses. To control the color and thickness, Excel requires that you use the Border sheet in the Format Cells dialog box.

Worksheets often have column titles at the top of each column and row titles to the left of each row that describe the data within the worksheet. You can use these titles within formulas when you want to refer to the related data by name. A cell **name** often is created from column and row titles. You also can define descriptive names that are not column titles or row titles to represent cells, ranges of cells, formulas, or constants.

To Add Custom Borders to a Range

The following steps add a thick red border to the Loan Payment Calculator section. To subdivide the row titles and numbers further, light borders also are added within the section, as shown in Figure 4–1 on page EX 227.

1

- Select the range B2:E6 and then right–click to display a shortcut menu and Mini toolbar (Figure 4–6).

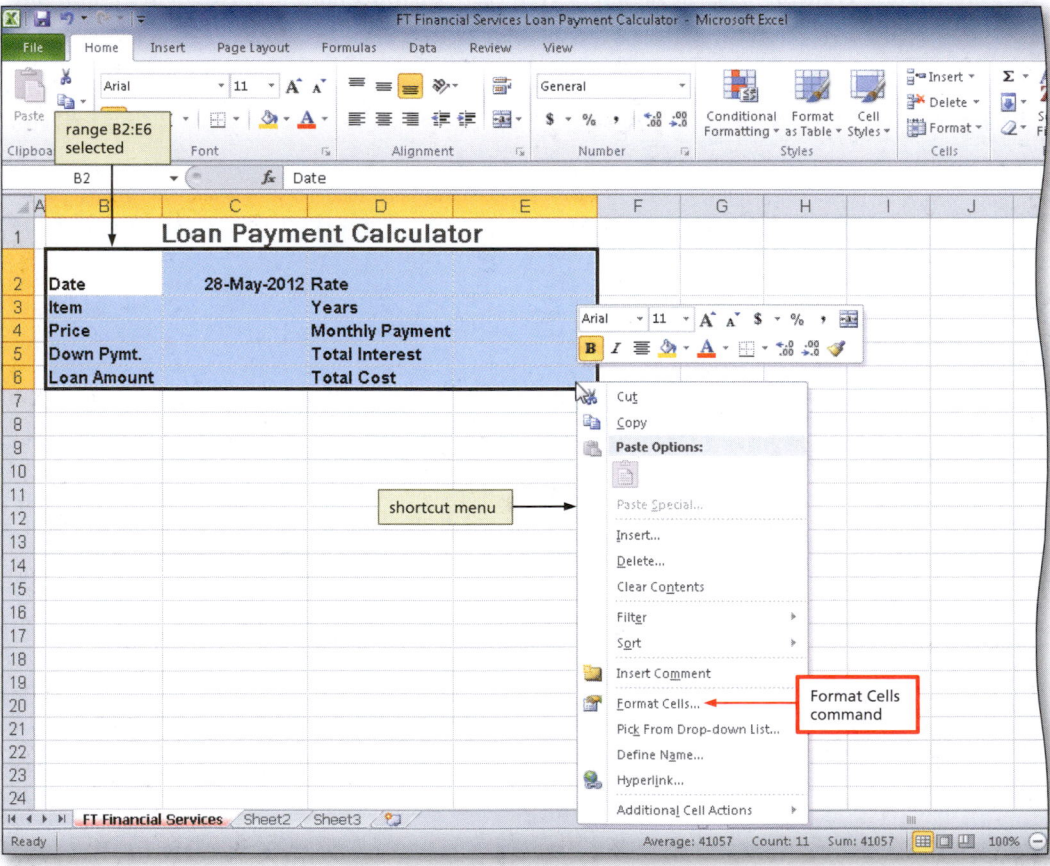

Figure 4–6

2

- Click Format Cells on the shortcut menu to display the Format Cells dialog box.

- Display the Border tab (Format Cells dialog box).

- Click the Color box arrow to display the Colors palette and then select the red color in the Standard Colors area.

- Click the medium border in the Style area (column 2, row 5) (Format Cells dialog box) to select the line style for the border.

- Click the Outline button in the Presets area (Format Cells dialog box) to display a preview of the outline border in the Border area (Figure 4–7).

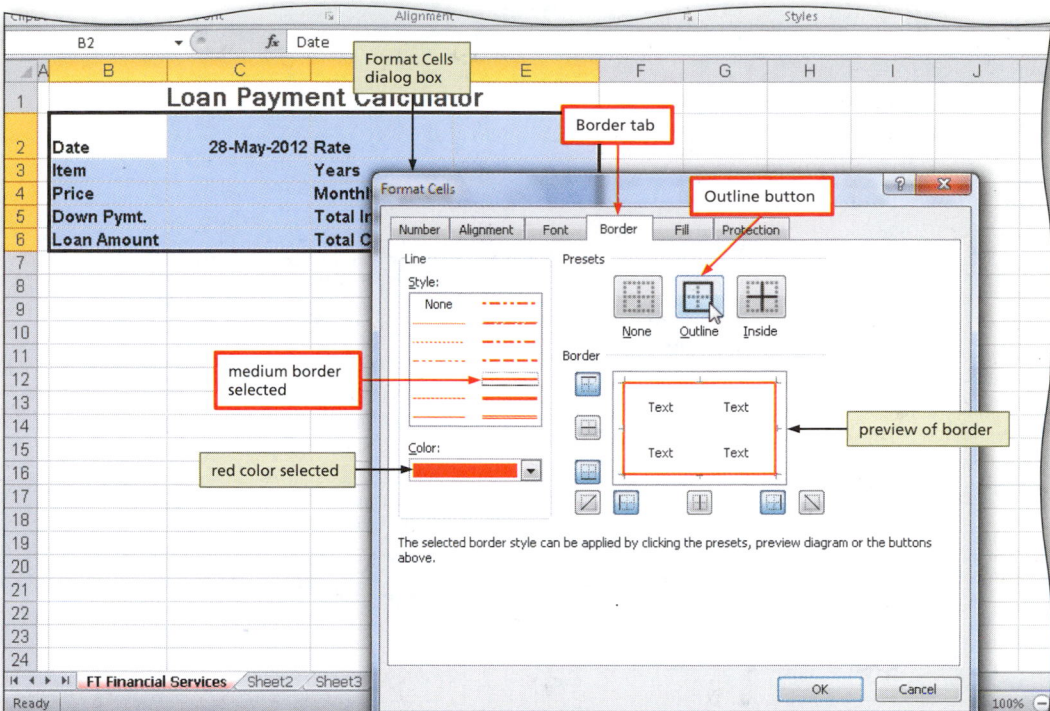

Figure 4–7

3

- Click the light border in the Style area (column 1, row 7) (Format Cells dialog box) and then click the Vertical Line button in the Border area to preview the red vertical border in the Border area (Figure 4–8).

Q&A

How should I create my desired border?

As shown in Figure 4–8, you can add a variety of borders with different colors to a cell or range of cells to improve its appearance. It is important that you select border characteristics in the order specified in the steps; that is, (1) choose the border color, (2) choose the border line style, and (3) choose the border type. If you attempt to do these steps in any other order, you may not end up with the desired borders.

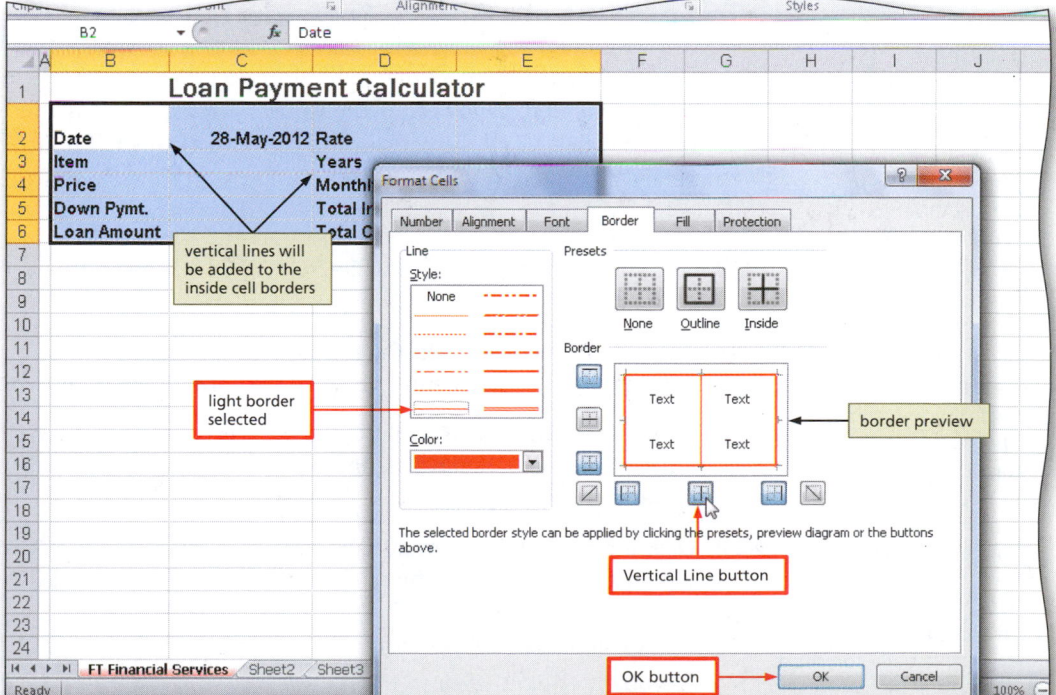

Figure 4–8

4

- Click the OK button (Format Cells dialog box) to add a red outline with vertical borders to the right side of each column in the selected range, B2:E6 in this case (Figure 4–9).

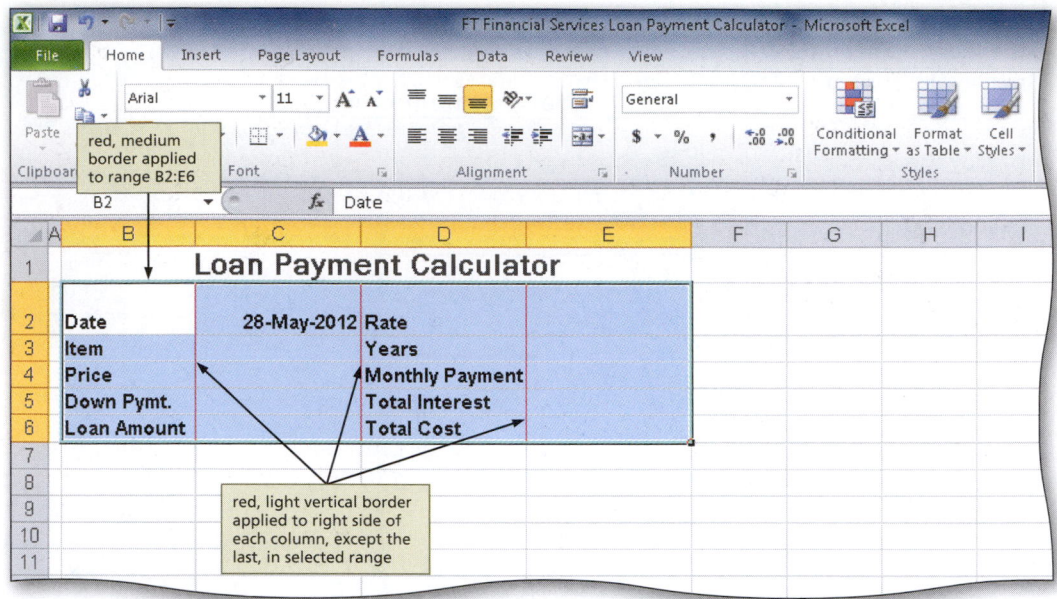

Figure 4–9

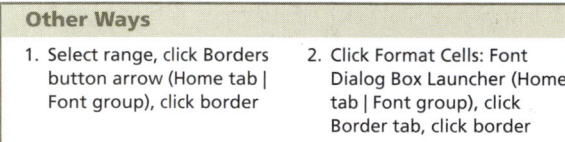

Other Ways
1. Select range, click Borders button arrow (Home tab | Font group), click border	2. Click Format Cells: Font Dialog Box Launcher (Home tab | Font group), click Border tab, click border

To Format Cells Before Entering Values

While usually you format cells after you enter values in cells, Excel also allows you to format cells before you enter the values. For example, at the beginning of this chapter, bold was applied to all the cells in the blank worksheet. The following steps assign the Currency style format with a floating dollar sign to the ranges C4:C6 and E4:E6 before the values are entered.

1 Select the range C4:C6 and, while holding down the CTRL key, select the nonadjacent range E4:E6.

2 Right-click one of the selected ranges to display a shortcut menu and then click Format Cells on the shortcut menu to display the Format Cells dialog box.

3 Click the Number tab (Format Cells dialog box) to display the Number sheet, select Currency in the Category list, and then select the second format, $1,234.10, in the Negative numbers list.

4 Click the OK button (Format Cells dialog box) to assign the Currency style format with a floating dollar sign to the selected ranges, C4:C6 and E4:E6 in this case.

Q&A What will happen when I enter values in the cells that were formatted in these steps?

As you enter numbers into these cells, Excel will display the numbers using the Currency style format. You also could have selected the range B4:E6 rather than the nonadjacent ranges and assigned the Currency style format to this range, which includes text. The Currency style format has no impact on text in a cell.

BTW

Q&As
For a complete list of the Q&As found in many of the step-by-step sequences in this book, visit the Excel 2010 Q&A Web page (scsite.com/ex2010/qa)

BTW

When to Format
Excel lets you format (1) before you enter data; (2) when you enter data, through the use of format symbols; (3) incrementally after entering sections of data; and (4) after you enter all the data. Spreadsheet specialists usually format a worksheet in increments as they build the worksheet, but occasions do exist where it makes sense to format cells before you enter any data.

To Enter the Loan Data

As shown in the Source of Data section of the Request for New Workbook document in Figure 4–2 on page EX 228, five items make up the loan data in the worksheet: the item to be purchased, the price of the item, the down payment, the interest rate, and the number of years until the loan is paid back (also called the term of the loan). These items are entered into cells C3 through C5 and cells E2 and E3. The steps below enter the following loan data: Item — House; Price — $305,600.00; Down Pymt. — $63,000.00; Interest Rate — 4.50%; and Years — 18.

1 Select cell C3. Type `House` and then click the Enter box in the formula bar to enter text in the selected cell.

2 With cell C3 still active, click the Align Text Right button (Home tab | Alignment group) to right-align the text in the selected cell.

3 Select cell C4 and then enter `305600` for the price of the house.

4 Select cell C5 and then enter `63000` for the down payment.

5 Select cell E2 and then enter `4.50%` for the interest rate.

6 Select cell E3 and then enter `18` for the number of years.

7 Click the Enter box in the formula bar to complete the entry of data in the worksheet (Figure 4–10).

Q&A Why are the entered values already formatted?

The values in cells C4 and C5 in Figure 4–10 are formatted using the Currency style with two decimal places, because this format was assigned to the cells prior to entering the values. Excel also automatically formats the interest rate in cell E2 to the Percent style with two decimal places, because the percent sign (%) was appended to 4.50 when it was entered.

Q&A Do lenders provide 18-year loans?

While not as popular as 30-year, 20-year, or 15-year mortgages, many lending institutions offer 18-year loans. The reasons for choosing a particular length for a loan depend on several factors, including the goals of the recipient of the loan. A person who is wavering between a 15-year and 20-year loan may choose an 18-year loan as a preferable solution.

BTW

Entering Percents
When you format a cell to display percentages, Excel assumes that whatever you enter into that cell in the future will be a percentage. Thus, if you enter the number .5, Excel translates the value as 50%. A potential problem arises, however, when you start to enter numbers greater than or equal to one. For instance, if you enter the number 25, do you mean 25% or 2500%? If you want Excel to treat the number 25 as 25% instead of 2500% and Excel interprets the number 25 as 2500%, then click the Options in the Backstage View. When the Excel Options dialog box appears, click Advanced in the left pane, and make sure the 'Enable automatic percent entry' check box in the right pane is selected.

BTW

Entering Interest Rates
An alternative to requiring the user to enter an interest rate in percent form, such as 4.50%, is to allow the user to enter the interest rate as a number without an appended percent sign (4.50) and then divide the interest rate by 1200, rather than 12.

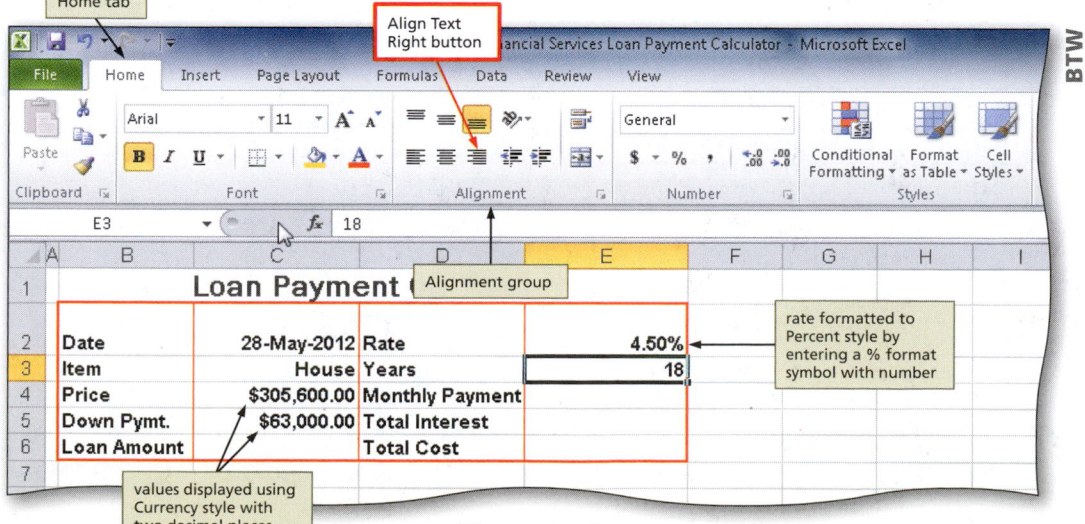

Figure 4–10

To Create Names Based on Row Titles

Naming a cell that you plan to reference in a formula helps make the formula easier to read and remember. For example, the loan amount in cell C6 is equal to the price in cell C4 minus the down payment in cell C5. According to what you learned in earlier projects, you can enter the loan amount formula in cell C6 as =C4 – C5. By naming cells C4 and C5 using the corresponding row titles in cells B4 and B5, however, you can enter the loan amount formula as =Price – Down_Pymt., which is clearer and easier to understand than =C4 – C5.

The following steps assign the row titles in the range B4:B6 to their adjacent cell in column C and assign the row titles in the range D2:D6 to their adjacent cell in column E.

1
- Select the range B4:C6.
- Display the Formulas tab (Figure 4–11).

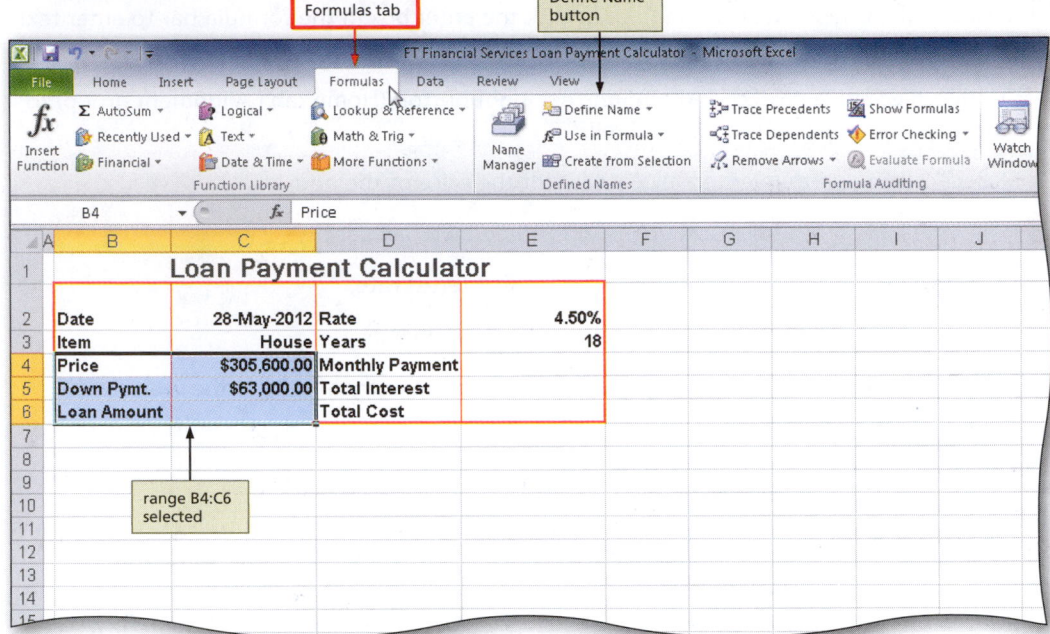

Figure 4–11

2
- Click the Create from Selection button (Formulas tab | Defined Names group) to display the Create Names from Selection dialog box (Figure 4–12).

How does Excel determine which option to select automatically in the Create Names from Selection dialog box?

Excel automatically selects the Left column check box in the 'Create names from values in the' area because the left column of the cells selected in Step 1 contains text.

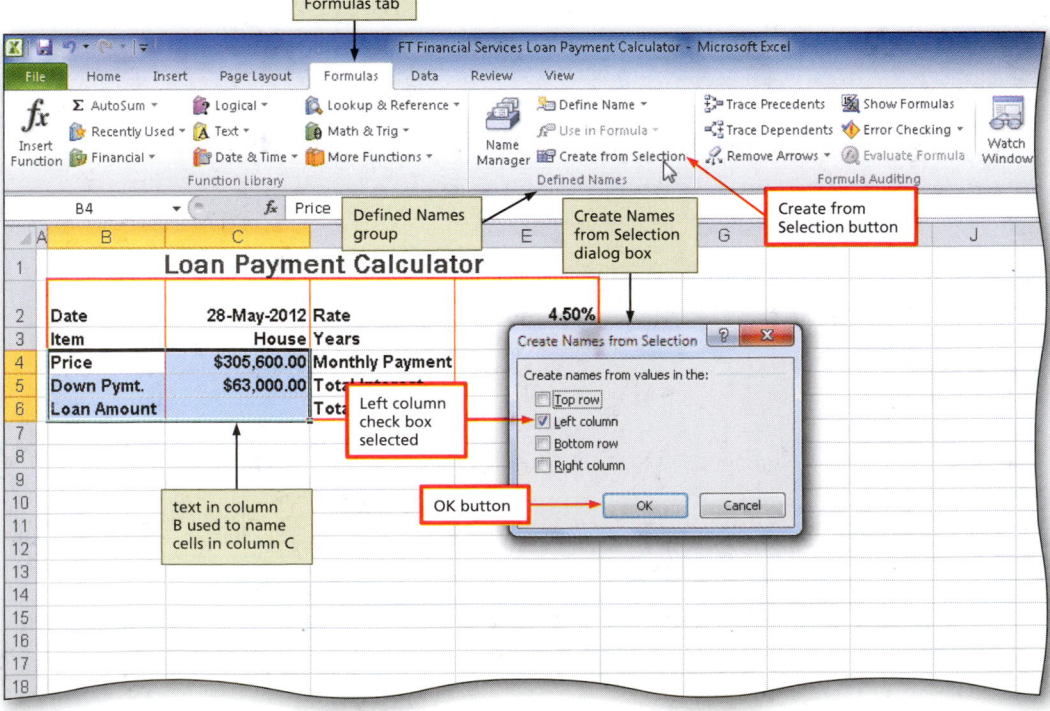

Figure 4–12

3

- Click the OK button (Create Names from Selection dialog box) to name the cells selected in the right column of the selection, C4:C6 in this case.

- Select the range D2:E6 and then click the Create from Selection button (Formulas tab | Defined Names group) to display the Create Names from Selection dialog box.

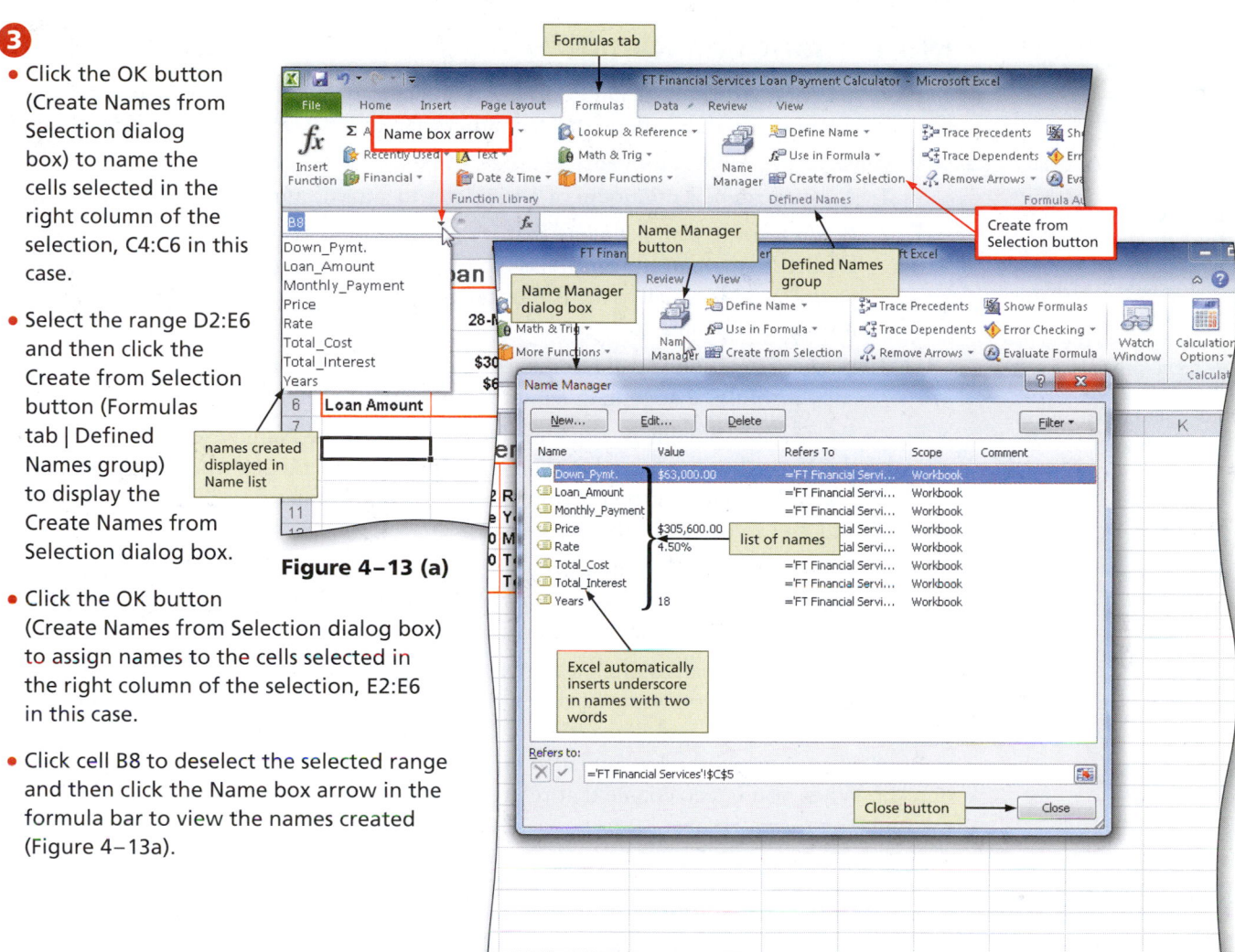

Figure 4–13 (a)

- Click the OK button (Create Names from Selection dialog box) to assign names to the cells selected in the right column of the selection, E2:E6 in this case.

- Click cell B8 to deselect the selected range and then click the Name box arrow in the formula bar to view the names created (Figure 4–13a).

Figure 4–13 (b)

Q&A How can the cell names be used?

You now can use the assigned names in formulas to reference cells in the ranges C4:C6 or E2:E6. Excel is not case sensitive with respect to names of cells. You, therefore, can enter the names of cells in formulas in uppercase or lowercase letters. To use a name that consists of two or more words in a formula, you should replace any space with the underscore character (_), as this is a commonly used standard for creating cell names. For example, the name, Down Pymt, is written as down_pymt. or Down_Pymt. when you want to reference the adjacent cell C5. The Name Manager dialog box appears when you click the Name Manager button (Figure 4–13b).

Q&A Is the period at the end of the Down_Pymt. cell name valid?

Yes. Periods and underscore characters are allowed in cell names. A cell name may not, however, begin with a period or an underscore.

Other Ways

1. Select cell or range, type name in Name box, press ENTER key

2. Select cell or range, click Define Name button (Formulas tab | Defined Names group), [type name], click OK button (New Name dialog box)

3. Select cell or range, click Name Manager button (Formulas tab | Defined Names group), click New (Name Manager dialog box), [type name], click OK button (New Name dialog box), click Close button (Name Manager dialog box)

BTW

Selecting Cells
If you double-click the
top of the heavy black
border surrounding an
active cell, Excel will make
the first nonblank cell
in the column the active
cell. If you double-click
the left side of the heavy
black border surrounding
the active cell, Excel will
make the first nonblank
cell in the row the active
cell. This procedure works
in the same fashion for
the right border and the
bottom border of the
active cell.

More about Cell Names

If you enter a formula using Point mode and click a cell that has an assigned name, then Excel will insert the name of the cell rather than the cell reference. Consider these additional points regarding the assignment of names to cells:

1. A name can be a minimum of 1 character to a maximum of 255 characters.

2. If you want to assign a name that is not a text item in an adjacent cell, use the Define Name button (Formulas tab | Defined Names group) (Figure 4–11 on page EX 238) or select the cell or range and then type the name in the Name box in the formula bar.

3. Names are absolute cell references. This is important to remember if you plan to copy formulas that contain names rather than cell references.

4. Excel displays the names in alphabetical order in the Name list when you click the Name box arrow and in the Name Manager dialog box when you click the Name Manager button (Formulas tab | Defined Names group) (Figures 4–13a and 4–13b on the previous page).

5. Names are **global** to the workbook. That is, a name assigned to a cell or cell range on one worksheet in a workbook can be used on other sheets in the same workbook to reference the named cell or range.

Spreadsheet specialists often assign names to a cell or range of cells so that they can select them quickly. If you want to select a cell or range of cells using the assigned name, you can click the Name box arrow (Figure 4–13a) and then click the name of the cell you want to select. This method is similar to using the F5 key to select a cell, but it is much quicker. When you select a name that references a range in the Name list, Excel highlights the range on the worksheet.

To Enter the Loan Amount Formula Using Names

To determine the loan amount in cell C6, subtract the down payment in cell C5 from the price in cell C4. As indicated earlier, this can be done by entering the formula =C4 – C5 or by entering the formula =Price – Down_Pymt. in cell C6. The following steps enter the formula using Point mode.

• Select cell C6.

• Type = (equal sign), click cell C4, type – (minus sign), and then click cell C5 to display the formula in the selected cell, C6 in this case, and in the formula bar using the names of the cells rather than the cell references (Figure 4–14).

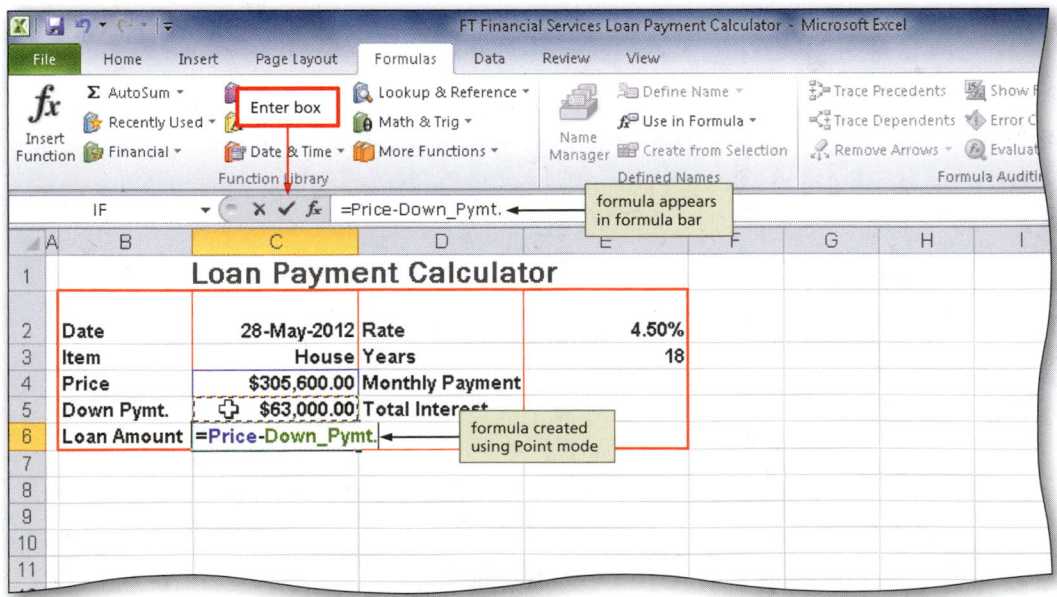

Figure 4–14

2

● Click the Enter box to assign the formula to the selected cell, =Price − Down_Pymt. to cell C6 in this case (Figure 4−15).

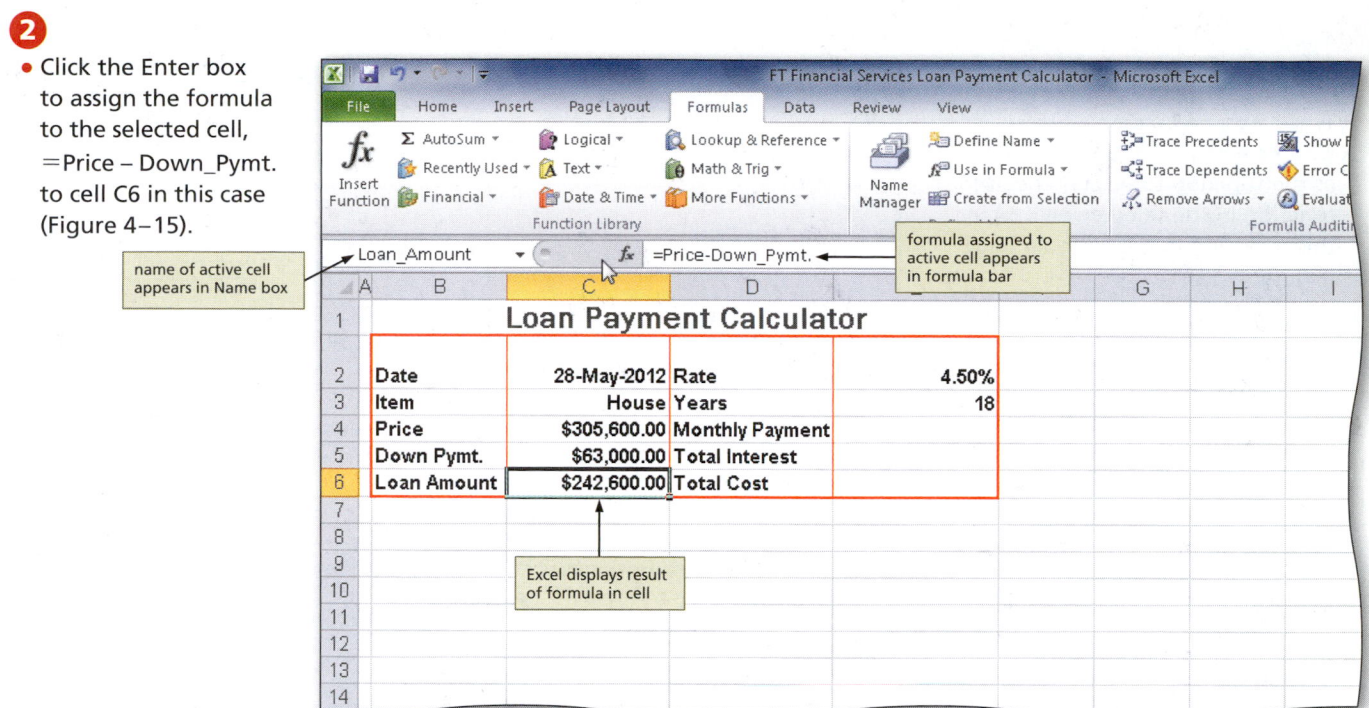

Figure 4−15

To Enter the PMT Function

The next step is to determine the monthly payment for the loan in cell E4. You can use Excel's PMT function to determine the monthly payment. The **PMT function** has three arguments: rate, payment, and loan amount. Its general form is as follows:

=PMT(rate, periods, loan amount)

where rate is the interest rate per payment period, periods is the number of payments, and loan amount is the amount of the loan.

In the worksheet shown in Figure 4−15, Excel displays the annual interest rate in cell E2. Financial institutions, however, calculate interest on a monthly basis. The rate value in the PMT function is, therefore, Rate / 12 (cell E2 divided by 12), rather than just Rate (cell E2). The periods (or number of payments) in the PMT function is 12 * Years (12 times cell E3) because each year includes 12 months, or 12 payments, per year.

Excel considers the value returned by the PMT function to be a debit and, therefore, returns a negative number as the monthly payment. To display the monthly payment as a positive number, begin the function with a negative sign instead of an equal sign. The PMT function for cell E4 is:

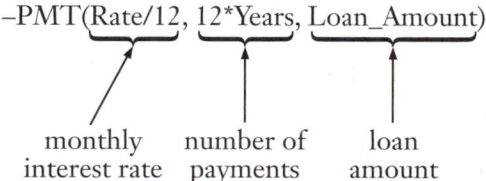

−PMT(Rate/12, 12*Years, Loan_Amount)

monthly interest rate   number of payments   loan amount

The steps on the following page use the keyboard, rather than Point mode or the Insert Function dialog box, to enter the PMT function to determine the monthly payment in cell E4.

1

- Select cell E4.

- Type **-pmt(Rate/12, 12*Years, Loan_Amount** as the function to display the PMT function in the selected cell, E4 in this case, and in the formula bar (Figure 4–16).

Q&A

What happens as I enter the function?

The ScreenTip shows the general form of the PMT function. The arguments in brackets in the ScreenTip are optional and not required for the computation required in this project. The Formula AutoComplete list shows functions and cell names that match the letters that you type on the keyboard. You can type the complete cell name, such as Loan_Amount, or select the cell name from the list. Excel will add the closing parenthesis to the function automatically. Excel also may scroll the worksheet to the right in order to accommodate the display of the ScreenTip.

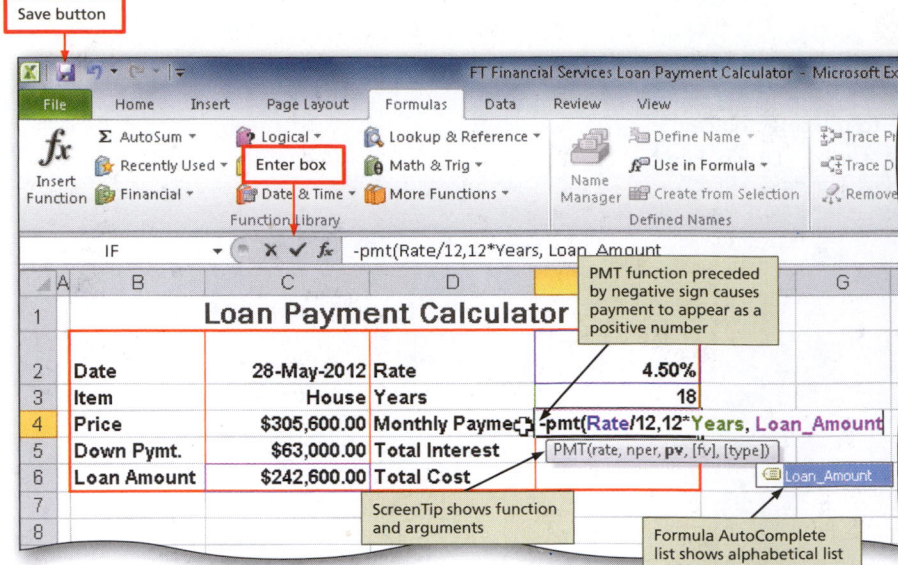

Figure 4–16

2

- If necessary, scroll the worksheet to the far left using the horizontal scroll bar to display column A.

- Click the Enter box in the formula bar to complete the function (Figure 4–17).

Q&A

What does Excel display after I click the Enter box?

Excel displays the monthly payment $1,640.76 in cell E4, based on a loan amount of $305,600.00 (cell C4) with an annual interest rate of 4.50% (cell E2) for a term of 18 years (cell E3), as shown in Figure 4–17.

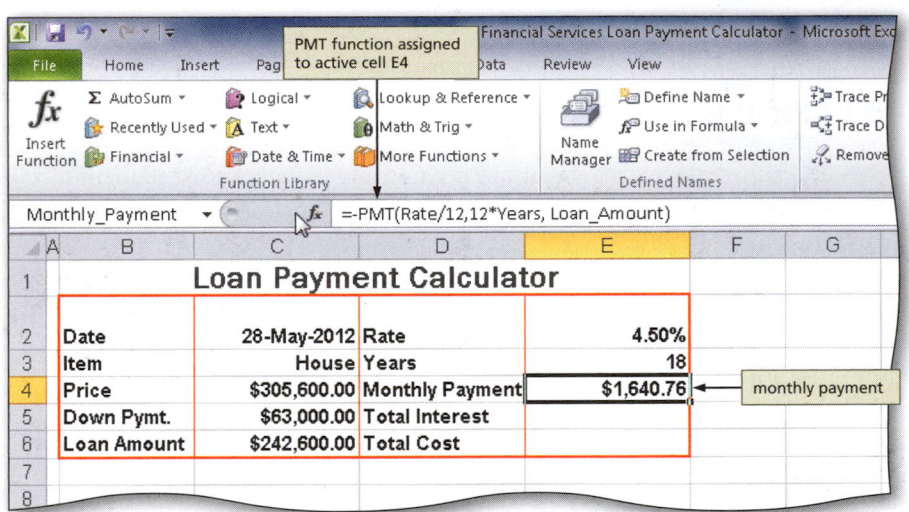

Figure 4–17

Other Ways

1. Click Financial button (Formulas tab | Function Library group), select PMT function, enter arguments, click OK button

2. Click Insert Function button in formula bar, select Financial category, select PMT function, click OK button, enter arguments, click OK button (Function Arguments dialog box)

Other Financial Functions

In addition to the PMT function, Excel provides more than 50 financial functions to help you solve the most complex finance problems. These functions save you from entering long, complicated formulas to obtain needed results. Table 4–1 summarizes three of the more frequently used financial functions.

Table 4–1 Frequently Used Financial Functions

Function	Description
FV (rate, periods, payment)	Returns the future value of an investment based on periodic, constant payments, and a constant interest rate.
PMT (rate, periods, loan amount)	Calculates the payment for a loan based on the loan amount, constant payments, and a constant interest rate.
PV (rate, periods, payment)	Returns the present value of an investment. The present value is the total amount that a series of future payments now is worth.

To Determine the Total Interest and Total Cost

The next step is to determine the total interest the borrower will pay on the loan (the lending institution's gross profit on the loan) and the total cost the borrower will pay for the item being purchased. The total interest (cell E5) is equal to the number of payments times the monthly payment, less the loan amount:

=12 * Years * Monthly_Payment – Loan_Amount

The total cost of the item to be purchased (cell E6) is equal to the price plus the total interest:

=Price + Total_Interest

The following steps enter formulas to determine the total interest and total cost using names.

1 Select cell E5 and then use Point mode and the keyboard to enter the formula `=12 * years * monthly_payment - loan_amount` to determine the total interest.

2 Select cell E6 and then use Point mode and the keyboard to enter the formula `=price + total_interest` to determine the total cost.

3 Select cell B8 (Figure 4–18).

4 Click the Save button on the Quick Access Toolbar to save the workbook using the file name, FT Financial Services Loan Payment Calculator.

Q&A

What are the new values displayed by Excel?

Excel displays a total interest (the lending institution's gross profit) of $111,804.92 in cell E5 and a total cost of $417,404.92 in cell E6, which is the total cost of the home to the borrower (Figure 4–18).

BTW

Range Finder
Remember to check all formulas carefully. You can double-click a cell with a formula and Excel will use Range Finder to highlight the cells that provide data for the formula. While Range Finder is active, you can drag the outlines from one cell to another to change the cells referenced in the formula, provided the cells have not been named.

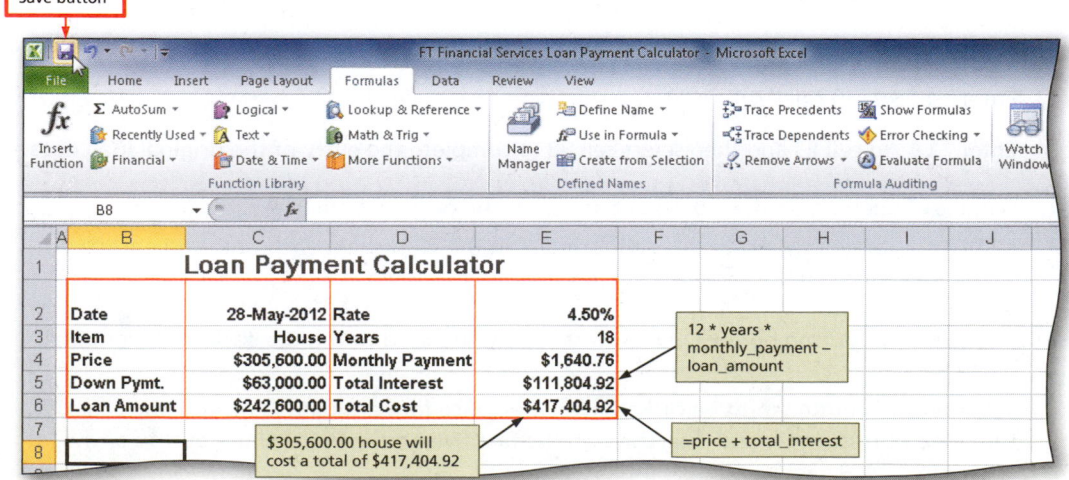

Figure 4–18

To Enter New Loan Data

Assume you want to purchase a condominium for $125,500.00. You have $32,000 for a down payment and you want the loan for a term of 10 years. FT Financial Services currently is charging 5.15% interest for a 10–year loan. The following steps enter the new loan data.

1 Enter `Condominium` in cell C3.

2 Enter `125500` in cell C4.

3 Enter `32000` in cell C5.

4 Enter `5.15%` in cell E2.

5 Enter `10` in cell E3 and then select cell B8 to recalculate the loan information in cells C6, E4, E5, and E6 (Figure 4–19).

Q&A What do the results of the new calculation mean?

As you can see from Figure 4–19, the monthly payment for the condominium is $998.58. By paying for the condominium over a 10–year period at an interest rate of 5.15%, you will pay total interest of $26,329.85 on the loan and pay a total cost of $151,829.85 for a $125,500.00 condominium.

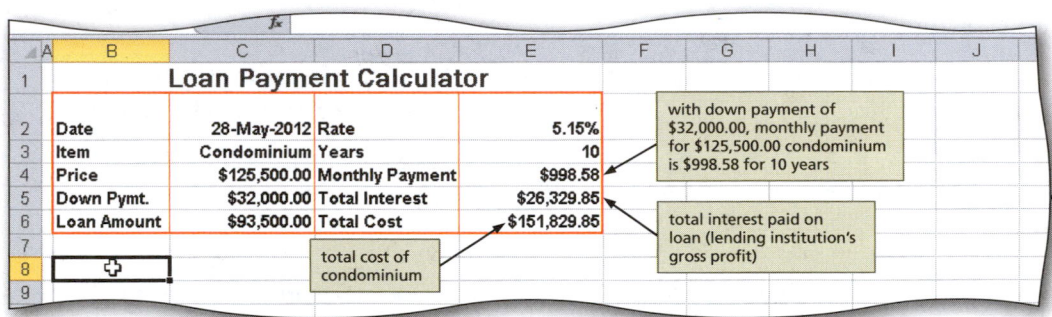

Figure 4–19

To Enter the Original Loan Data

The following steps reenter the original loan data.

1 Enter `House` in cell C3.

2 Enter `305600` in cell C4.

3 Enter `63000` in cell C5.

4 Enter `4.50` in cell E2.

5 Enter `18` in cell E3 and then select cell B8 to complete the entry of the original loan data.

Q&A What is happening on the worksheet as I enter the original data?

Excel instantaneously recalculates all formulas in the worksheet each time you enter a value. Excel displays the original loan information as shown in Figure 4–18.

Q&A Can the Undo button on the Quick Access Toolbar be used to change back to the original data?

Yes. The Undo button must be clicked five times, once for each data item. You also can click the Undo button arrow and drag through the first five entries in the Undo button arrow list.

Using a Data Table to Analyze Worksheet Data

You already have seen that if you change a value in a cell, Excel immediately recalculates and displays the new results of any formulas that reference the cell directly or indirectly. But what if you want to compare the results of the formula for several different values? Writing down or trying to remember all the answers to the what-if questions would be unwieldy. If you use a data table, however, Excel will organize the answers in the worksheet for you automatically.

A data table is a range of cells that shows the answers generated by formulas in which different values have been substituted. Data tables must be built in an unused area of the worksheet (in this case, the range B7:E23). Figure 4–20a illustrates the makeup of a one-input data table. With a **one-input data table**, you can vary the value in one cell (in this worksheet, cell E2, the interest rate). Excel then calculates the results of one or more formulas and fills the data table with the results.

An alternative to a one–input table is a two-input data table. A **two-input data table** allows you to vary the values in two cells, but you can apply a two-input data table to only one formula. A two-input data table example is illustrated in the Extend Your Knowledge exercise on page EX 283.

The interest rates that will be used to analyze the loan formulas in this project range from 4.00% to 7.25%, increasing in increments of 0.25%. The one–input data table shown in Figure 4–20b illustrates the impact of varying the interest rate on three formulas: the monthly payment (cell E4), total interest paid (cell E5), and the total cost of the item to be purchased (cell E6). The series of interest rates in column B are called **input values**.

BTW

Expanding Data Tables
The data table created in this chapter is relatively small. You can continue the series of percents to the bottom of the worksheet and insert additional formulas in columns to create as large a data table as you want.

BTW

Data Tables
Data tables have one purpose: to organize the answers to what-if questions. You can create two kinds of data tables. The first type involves changing one input value to see the resulting effect on one or more formulas. The second type involves changing two input values to see the resulting effect on one formula.

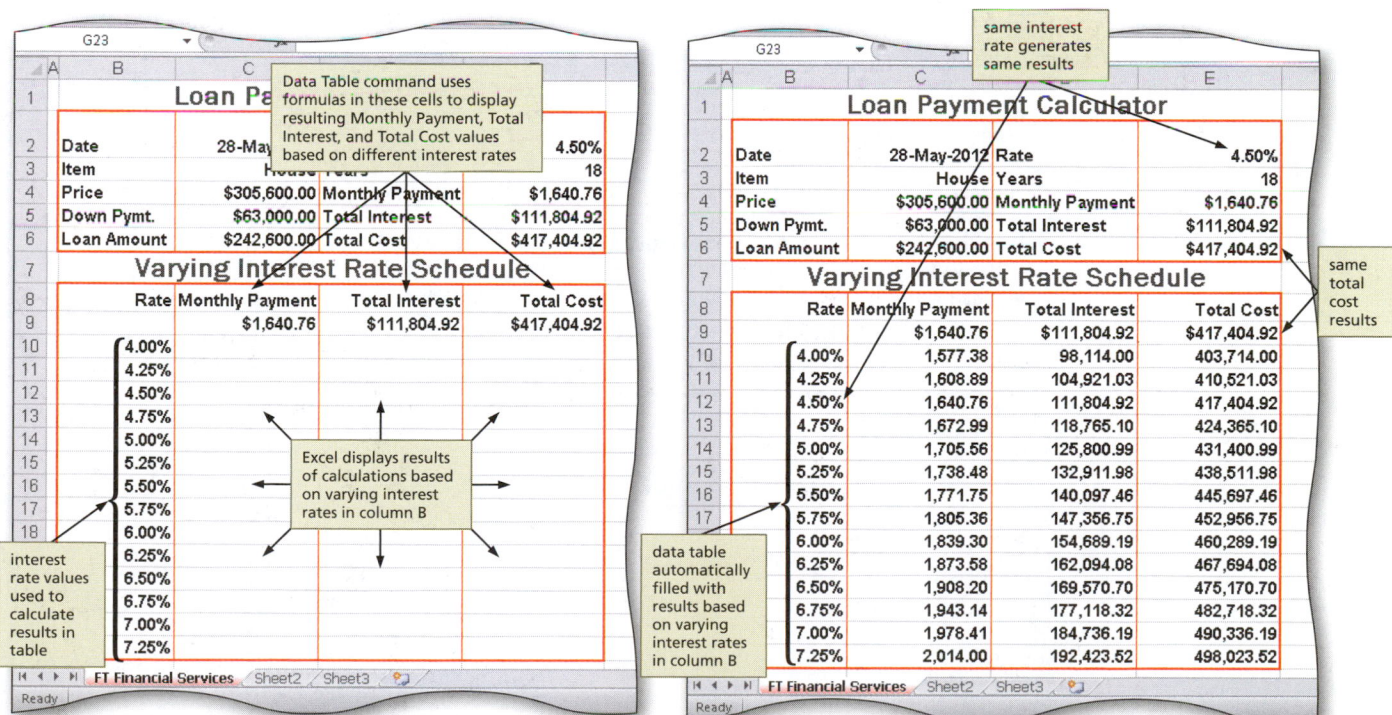

Figure 4–20 (a)   Figure 4–20 (b)

To Enter the Data Table Title and Column Titles

The first step in constructing the data table shown in Figure 4–20b is to enter the data table section title and column titles in the range B7:E8 and adjust the heights of rows 7 and 8.

1 Select cell B7 and then type `Varying Interest Rate Schedule` as the data table section title.

2 Select cell B1 and then click the Format Painter button (Home tab | Clipboard group) to copy the format of the cell. Click cell B7 to apply the copied format to the cell.

3 Enter the column titles in the range B8:E8, as shown in Figure 4–21, to create headers for the data table. Select the range B8:E8 and then click the Align Text Right button (Home tab | Alignment group) to right-align the column titles.

4 Position the mouse pointer on the bottom boundary of row heading 7 and then drag up until the ScreenTip indicates Height: 20.25 (27 pixels).

5 Position the mouse pointer on the bottom boundary of row heading 8 and then drag down until the ScreenTip indicates Height: 18.00 (24 pixels).

6 Click cell B10 to deselect the range B8:E8 (Figure 4–21).

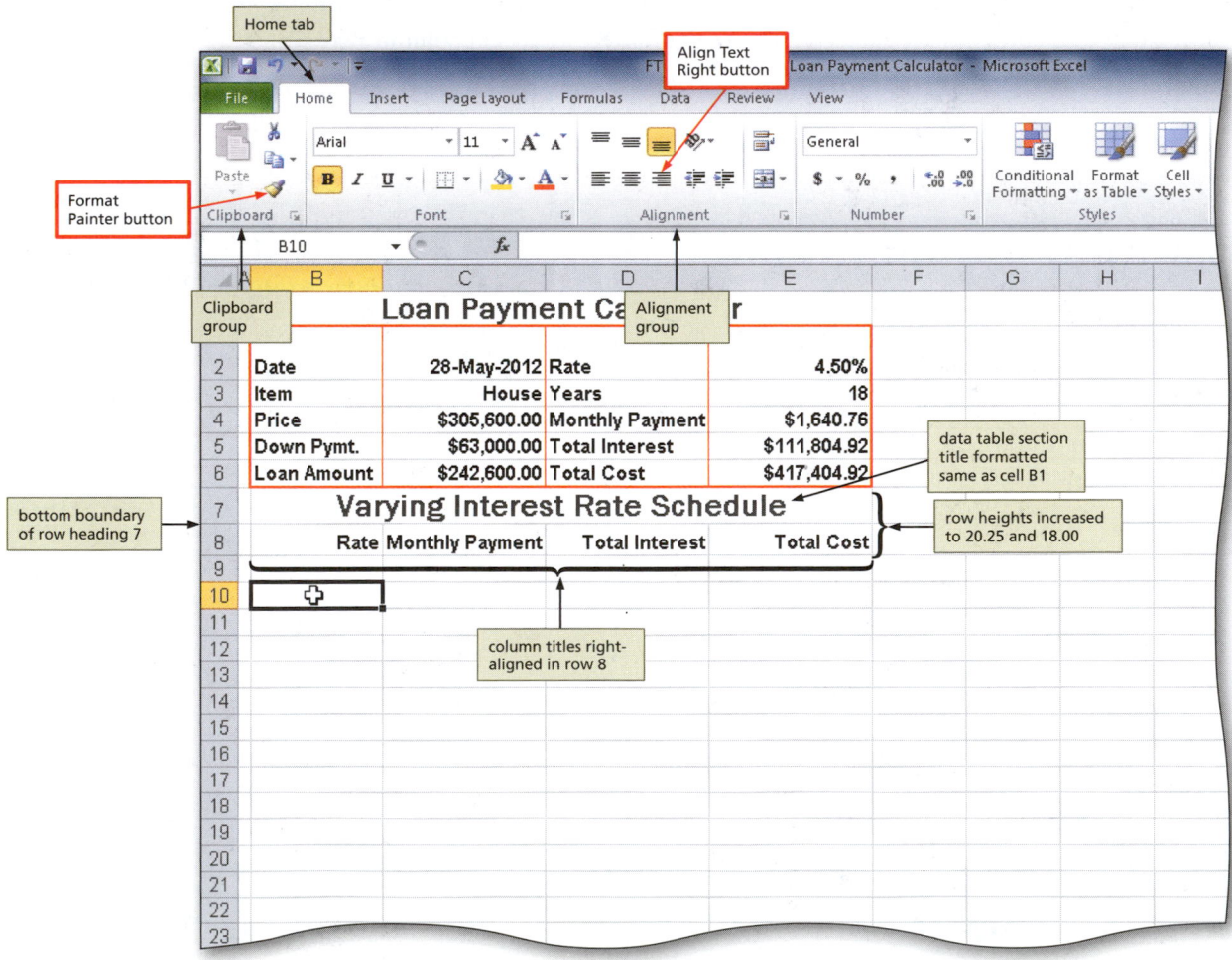

Figure 4–21

To Create a Percent Series Using the Fill Handle

The next step is to create the percent series in column B using the fill handle. These percent figures will serve as the input data for the data table.

1

- With cell B10 selected, type **4.00%** as the first number in the series.

- Select cell B11 and then type **4.25%** as the second number in the series.

- Select the range B10:B11.

- Drag the fill handle through cell B23 to create the border of the fill area as indicated by the shaded border (Figure 4–22). Do not release the mouse button.

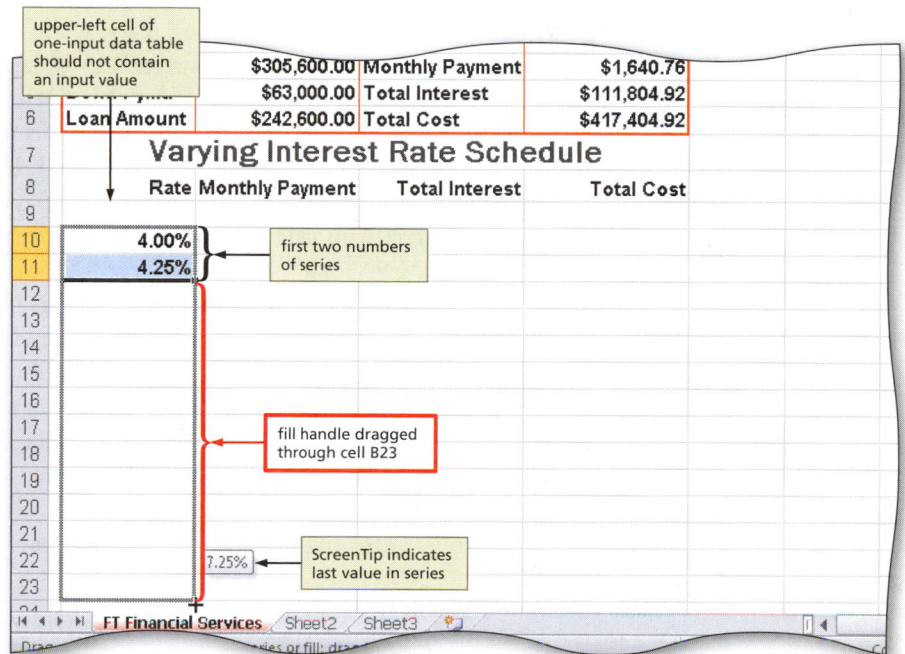

Figure 4–22

2

- Release the mouse button to generate the percent series, in this case from 4.00% to 7.25%, and display the Auto Fill Options button.

- Click cell C9 to deselect the selected range, B10:B23 in this case (Figure 4–23).

Q&A

What is the purpose of the percent figures in column B?

Excel will use the percent figures in column B to calculate the formulas to be evaluated and entered at the top of the data table in row 9. This series begins in cell B10, not cell B9, because the cell immediately to the upper-left of the formulas in a one-input data table should not include an input value.

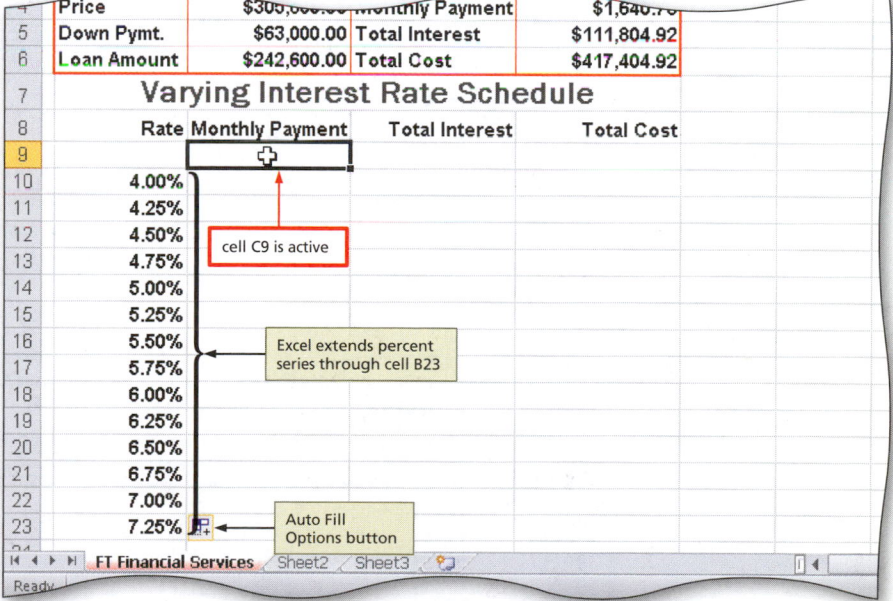

Figure 4–23

BTW

Formulas in Data Tables
Any experienced Excel user will tell you that to enter the formulas at the top of the data table, you should enter the cell reference or name of the cell preceded by an equal sign (Figure 4-24). This ensures that if you change the original formula in the worksheet, Excel automatically will change the corresponding formula in the data table. If you use a cell reference, Excel also copies the format to the cell. If you use a name, Excel does not copy the format to the cell.

To Enter the Formulas in the Data Table

The next step in creating the data table is to enter the three formulas at the top of the table in cells C9, D9, and E9. The three formulas are the same as the monthly payment formula in cell E4, the total interest formula in cell E5, and the total cost formula in cell E6. The number of formulas you place at the top of a one-input data table depends on the application. Some one-input data tables will have only one formula, while others might have several. In this case, three formulas are affected when the interest rate changes.

Excel provides four ways to enter these formulas in the data table: (1) retype the formulas in cells C9, D9, and E9; (2) copy cells E4, E5, and E6 to cells C9, D9, and E9, respectively; (3) enter the formulas =monthly_payment in cell C9, =total_interest in cell D9, and =total_cost in cell E9; or (4) enter the formulas =e4 in cell C9, =e5 in cell D9, and =e6 in cell E9.

The best alternative to define the formulas in the data table is the fourth alternative, which involves using the cell references preceded by an equal sign. This method is best because: (1) it is easier to enter the cell references; (2) if you change any of the formulas in the range E4:E6, the formulas at the top of the data table are updated automatically; and (3) Excel automatically assigns the format of the cell reference (Currency style format) to the cell. Using the third alternative, which involves using cell names, is nearly as good an alternative, but if you use cell names, Excel will not assign the format to the cells. The following steps enter the formulas of the data table in row 9.

1 With cell C9 active, type =e4 and then press the RIGHT ARROW key to enter the first parameter of the function to be used in the data table.

2 Type =e5 in cell D9 and then press the RIGHT ARROW key to enter the second parameter of the function to be used in the data table.

3 Type =e6 in cell E9 and then click the Enter box to complete the assignment of the formulas and Currency style format to the selected range, C9:E9 in this case (Figure 4–24).

Q&A

Why are these cells assigned the values of cells in the Loan Payment Calculator area of the worksheet?

It is important to understand that the entries in the top row of the data table (row 9) refer to the formulas that the company wants to evaluate using the series of percentages in column B. Furthermore, recall that when you assign a formula to a cell, Excel applies the format of the first cell reference in the formula to the cell. Thus, Excel applies the Currency style format to cells C9, D9, and E9 because that is the format of cells E4, E5, and E6.

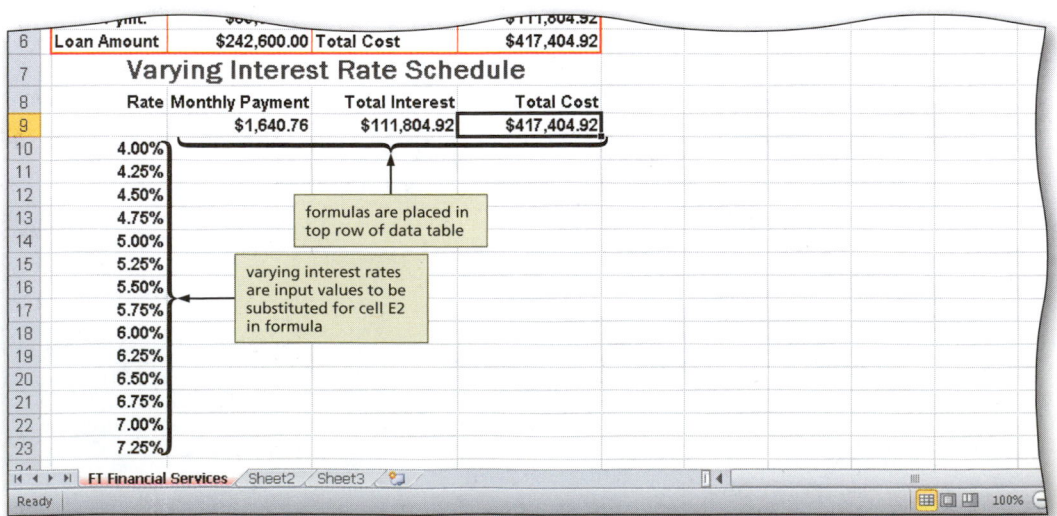

Figure 4–24

To Define a Range as a Data Table

After creating the interest rate series in column B and entering the formulas in row 9, the next step is to define the range B9:E23 as a data table. Cell E2 is the input cell for the data table, which means cell E2 is the cell in which values from column B in the data table are substituted in the formulas in row 9.

1

- Select the range B9:E23 as the range in which to create the data table.

- Display the Data tab and then click the What-If Analysis button (Data tab | Data tools) to display the What-IfAnalysis menu (Figure 4–25).

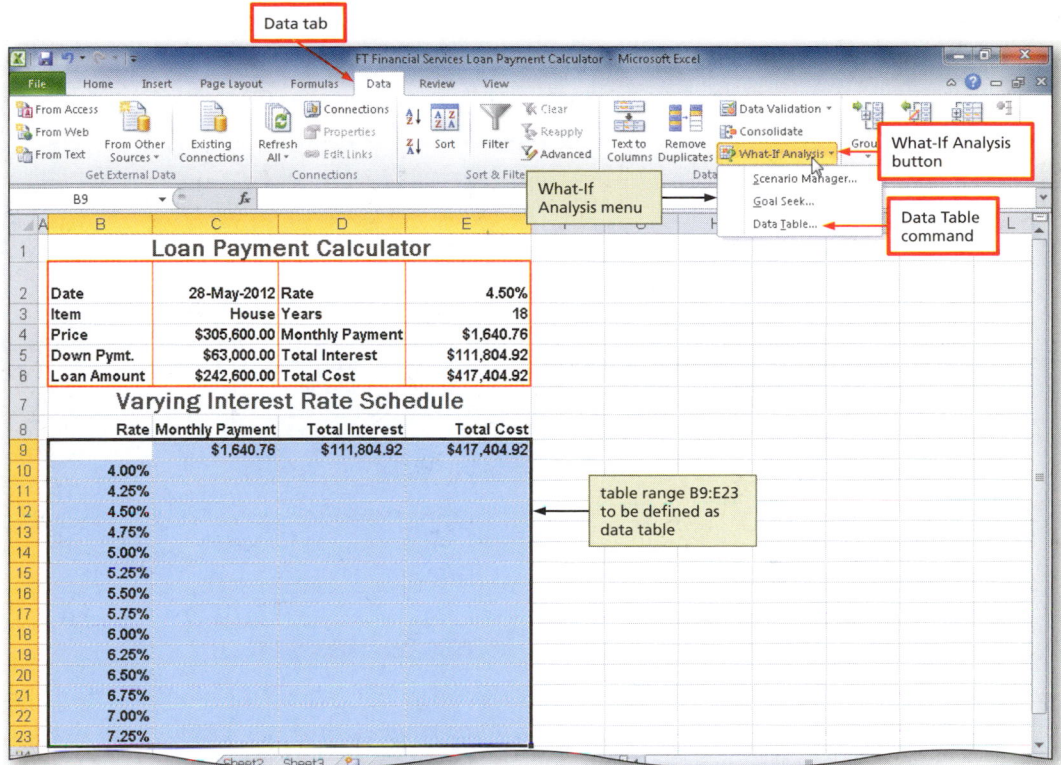

Figure 4–25

2

- Click Data Table on the What-If Analysis menu to display the Data Table dialog box.

- Click the 'Column input cell' box (Data Table dialog box) and then click cell E2 in the Loan Payment Calculator section of the spreadsheet to select the input cell for the data table (Figure 4–26).

Q&A

What is the purpose of clicking cell E2?

The purpose of clicking cell E2 is to select it for the Column input cell. A marquee surrounds the selected cell E2, indicating it will be the input cell in which values from column B in the data table are substituted in the formulas in row 9. $E$2 now appears in the Column input cell box in the Data Table dialog box.

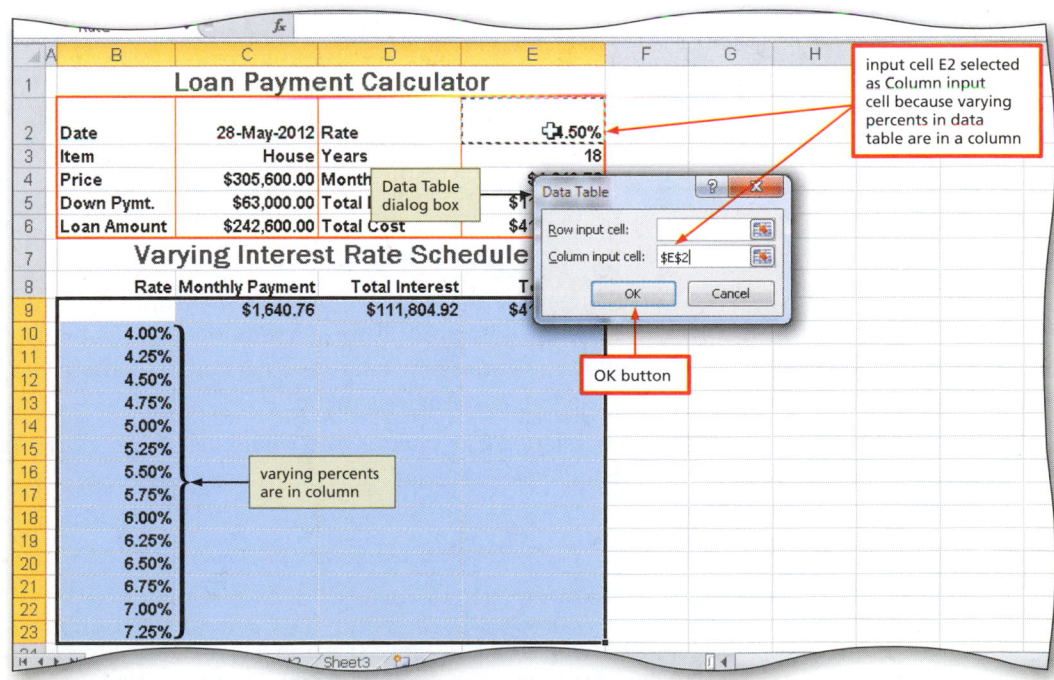

Figure 4–26

3

- Click the OK button (Data Table dialog box) to create the data table (Figure 4–27).

Q&A

How does Excel create the data table?

Excel calculates the results of the three formulas in row 9 for each interest rate in column B and immediately fills columns C, D, and E of the data table. The resulting values for each interest rate are displayed in the corresponding rows.

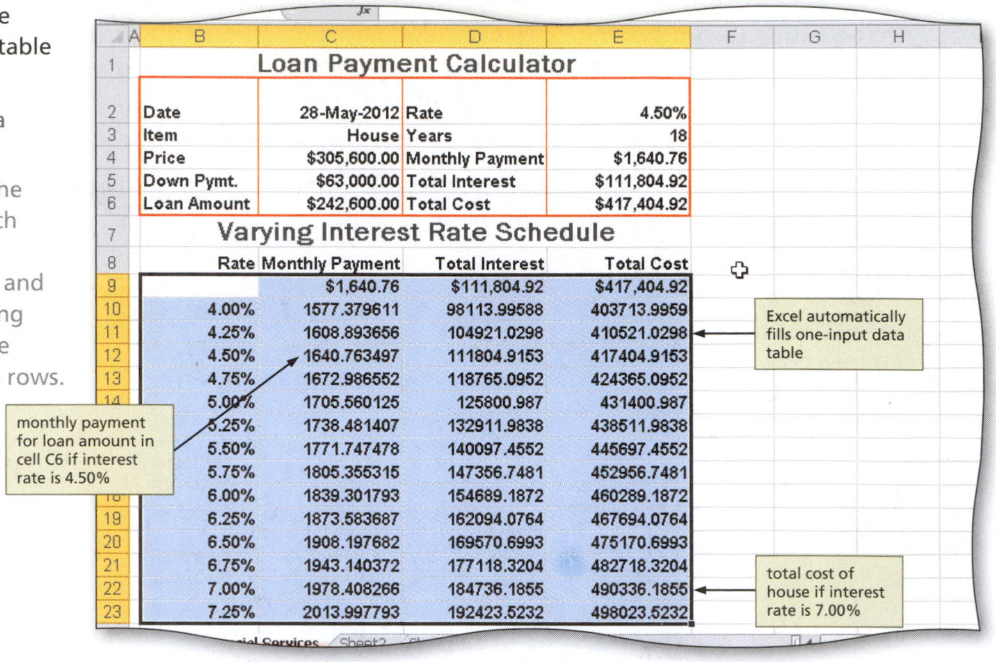

Figure 4–27

More about Data Tables

In Figure 4–27, the data table shows the monthly payment, total interest, and total cost for the interest rates in the range B10:B23. For example, if the interest rate is 4.50% (cell E2), the monthly payment is $1,640.76 (cell E4). If the interest rate is 7.00% (cell B22), however, the monthly payment is $1,978.41 rounded to the nearest cent (cell C22). If the interest rate is 5.75% (cell B17), then the total cost of the house is $452,956.75 rounded to the nearest cent (cell E17), rather than $417,404.92 (cell E6). Thus, a 1.25% increase from the interest rate of 4.50% to 5.75% results in a $35,551.83 increase in the total cost of the house.

The following list details important points you should know about data tables:

1. The formula(s) you are analyzing must include a cell reference to the input cell.

2. You can have as many active data tables in a worksheet as you want.

3. While only one value can vary in a one–input data table, the data table can analyze as many formulas as you want.

4. To include additional formulas in a one-input data table, enter them in adjacent cells in the same row as the current formulas (row 9 in Figure 4–27) and then define the entire new range as a data table by using the Data Table command on the What-If Analysis menu.

5. You delete a data table as you would delete any other item on a worksheet. That is, select the data table and then press the DELETE key.

To Format the Data Table

The following steps format the data table to improve its readability.

1 Select the range B8:E23. Right-click the selected range to display a shortcut menu and then click Format Cells on the shortcut menu to display the Format Cells dialog box.

2 Click the Border tab (Format Cells dialog box) to display the Border sheet. Click the Color box arrow to display the Colors palette and then click Red (column 2, row 1) in the Standard Colors area to change the border color.

3 Click the medium border in the Style area (column 2, row 5) to select the line style of the border. Click the Outline button in the Presets area to preview the border in the Border area.

4 Click the light border in the Style area (column 1, row 7) and then click the Vertical Line button in the Border area to preview the border in the Border area.

5 Click the OK button (Format Cells dialog box) to apply custom borders to the selected range.

6 Select the range C10:E23, right-click the selected range to display a shortcut menu, and then click Format Cells on the shortcut menu to display the Format Cells dialog box.

7 Click the Number tab (Format Cells dialog box) to display the Number sheet.

8 Click Currency in the Category list (Format Cells dialog box) to select a currency format and then click the Symbol box arrow to display the Symbol list. Click None to choose no currency symbol, and then click the second format, 1,234.10, in the Negative numbers list to assign a currency format to the selected range.

9 Click the OK button (Format Cells dialog box) to apply a currency format to the selected range and then select cell G23 to display the worksheet, as shown in Figure 4–28.

10 Click the Save button on the Quick Access Toolbar to save the workbook using the file name, FT Financial Services Loan Payment Calculator.

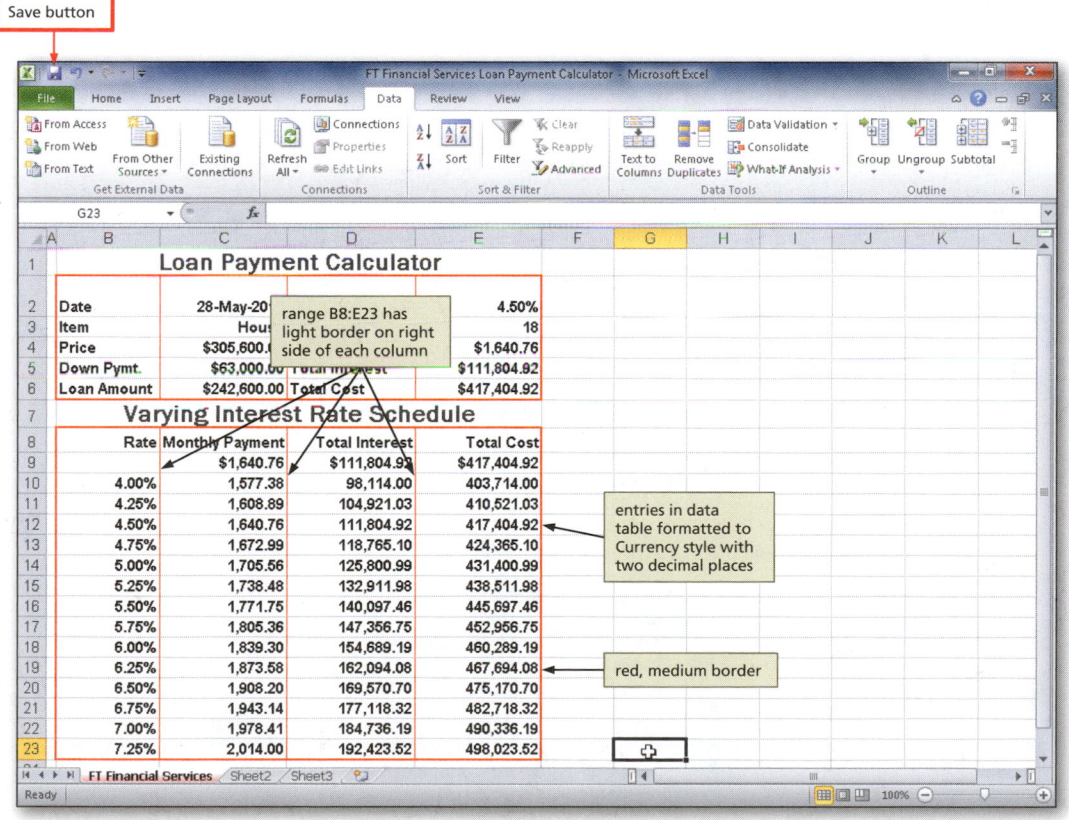

Figure 4–28

Break Point: If you wish to take a break, this is a good place to do so. You can quit Excel now. To resume at a later time, start Excel, open the file called FT Financial Services Loan Payment Calculator, and continue following the steps from this location forward.

BTW

Conditional Formatting
You can add as many conditional formats to a range as you like. After adding the first condition, click the Conditional Formatting button (Home tab | Styles group) and then click New Rule to add more conditions. If more than one condition is true for a cell, then Excel applies the formats of each condition, beginning with the first.

Adding a Pointer to the Data Table Using Conditional Formatting

If the interest rate in cell E2 is between 4.00% and 7.25% and its decimal portion is a multiple of 0.25 (such as 4.50%), then one of the rows in the data table agrees exactly with the monthly payment, interest paid, and total cost in the range E4:E6. For example, in Figure 4–28 on the previous page, row 15 (4.50%) in the data table agrees with the results in the range E4:E6, because the interest rate in cell B12 is the same as the interest rate in cell E2. Analysts often look for the row in the data table that agrees with the input cell results.

To Add a Pointer to the Data Table

To make the row stand out, you can add formatting that serves as a pointer to a row. To add a pointer, you can use conditional formatting to make the cell in column B that agrees with the input cell (cell E2) stand out. The following steps apply conditional formatting to column B in the data table.

1
- Select the range B10:B23 and then click the Conditional Formatting button (Home tab | Styles group) to display the Conditional Formatting list (Figure 4–29).

2
- Click New Rule on the Conditional Formatting list to display the New Formatting Rule dialog box.

- Click 'Format only cells that contain' in the Select a Rule Type box (New Formatting Rule dialog box) to select the type of rule to create.

- Select equal to in the second box from the left.

- Type =$E$2 in the right box to complete the condition for the rule based on a cell value.

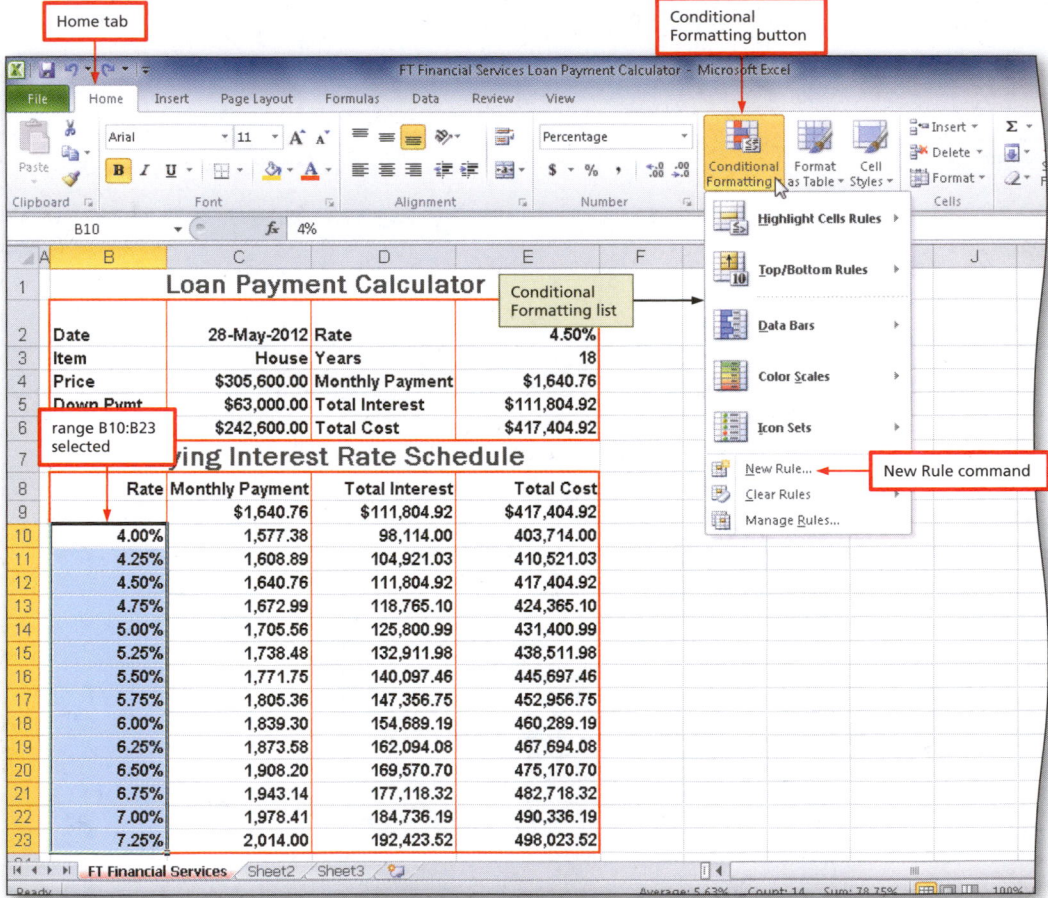

Figure 4–29

3

- Click the Format button (New Formatting Rule dialog box), click the Fill tab to display the Fill sheet, and then click Red (column 2, row 7) in the Background Color area to select a background color for the conditional format.

- Click the OK button (Format Cells dialog box) to display the New Formatting Rule dialog box with a preview of the conditional format (Figure 4–30).

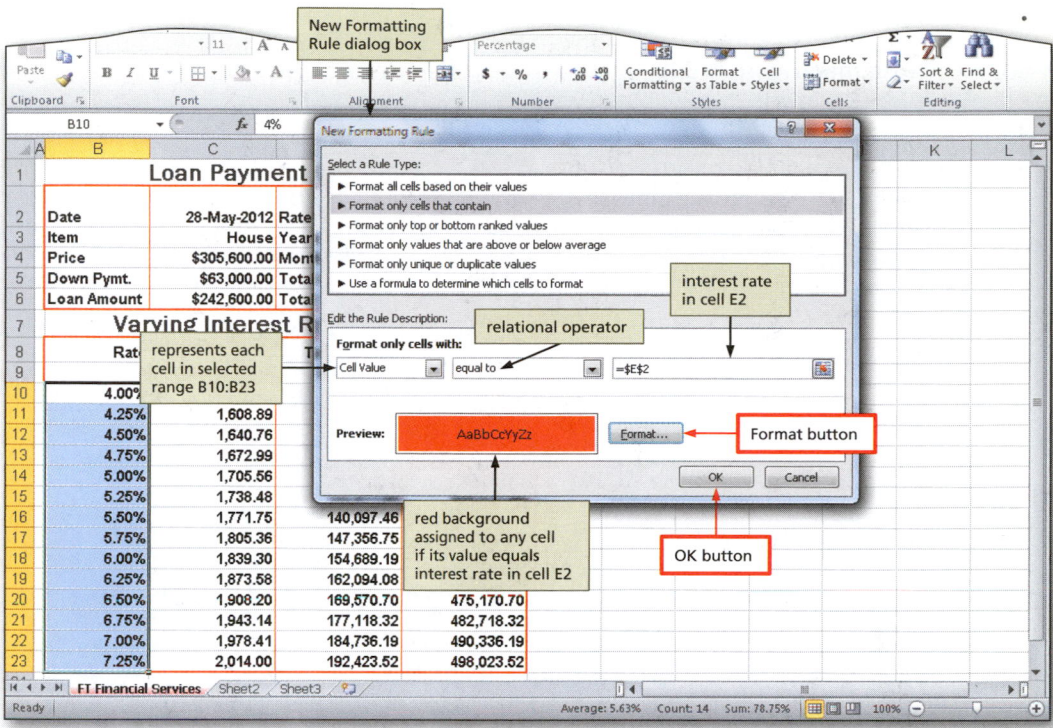

Figure 4–30

4

- Click the OK button (New Formatting Rule dialog box) to apply the conditional formatting rule.

- Click cell G23 to deselect the selected range, B10:B23 in this case (Figure 4–31).

Q&A

How does Excel apply the conditional formatting?

Cell B12 in the data table, which contains the value, 4.50%, appears with a red background, because the value 4.50% is the same as the interest rate value in cell E2.

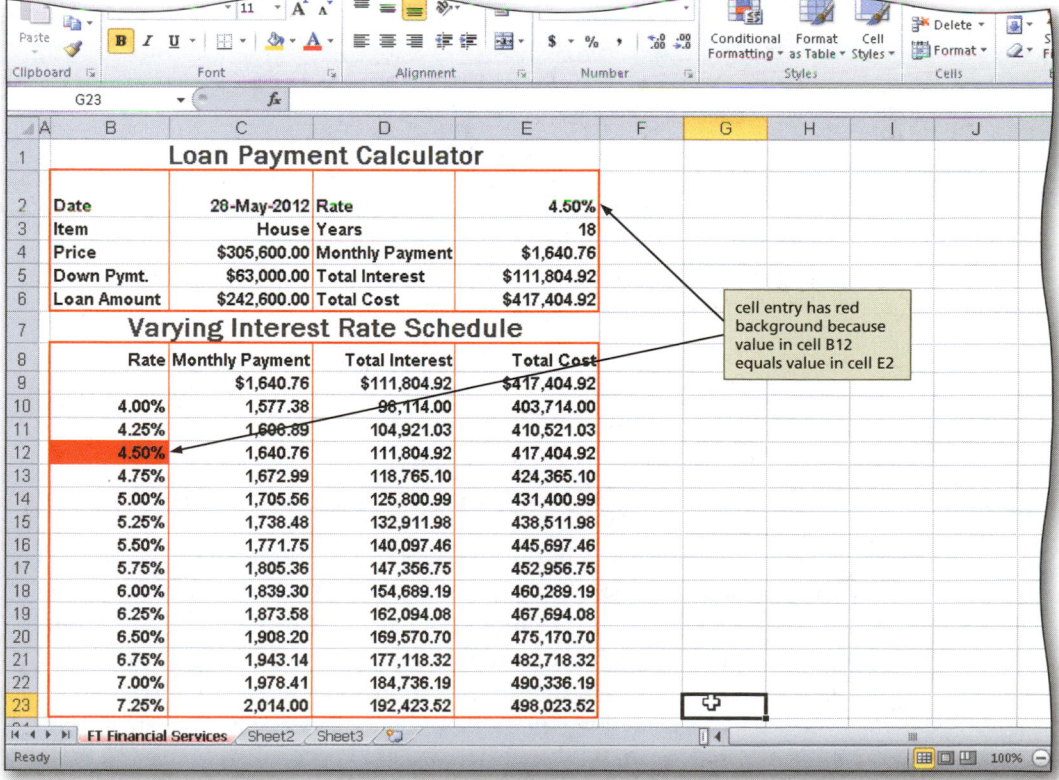

Figure 4–31

5

• Select cell E2 and then enter 7.25 as the interest rate (Figure 4–32).

6

• Enter 4.50 in cell E2 to return the Loan Payment Calculator section and Varying Interest Rate Schedule section to their original states, as shown in Figure 4–31.

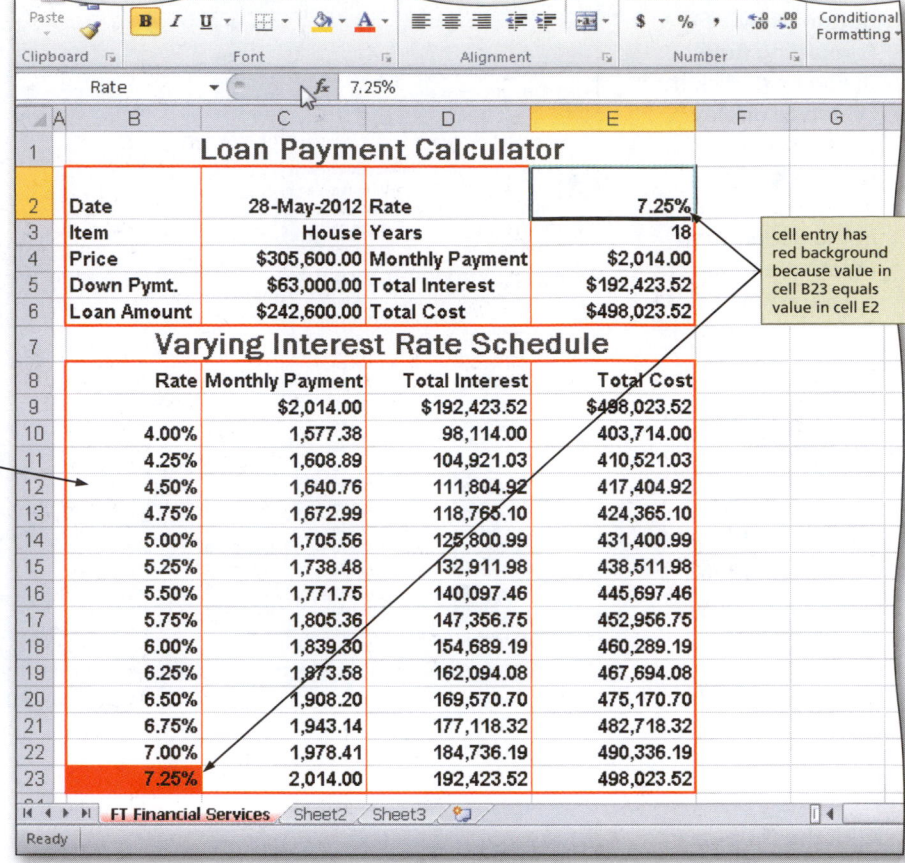

Figure 4–32

Q&A

What happens if I change the interest rate from 4.50% to something else?

Excel immediately displays the cell containing the new rate with a red background and displays cell B12 with a white background (Figure 4–32). Thus, the red background serves as a pointer in the data table to indicate the row that agrees with the input cell (cell E2). When the loan officer using this worksheet enters a different percent in cell E2, the pointer will move or disappear. It will disappear whenever the interest rate in cell E2 is outside the range of the data table or its decimal portion is not a multiple of 0.25, such as when the interest rate is 9.71% or 4.90%.

BTW

Amortization Schedules
Hundreds of Web sites offer amortization schedules. To find these Web sites, use a search engine, such as Google, and search using the keywords, amortization schedule.

Creating an Amortization Schedule

The next step in this project is to create the Amortization Schedule section on the right side of Figure 4–33. An amortization schedule shows the beginning and ending balances of a loan and the amount of payment that applies to the principal and interest for each year over the life of the loan. For example, if a customer wanted to pay off the loan after six years, the Amortization Schedule section would tell the loan officer what the payoff would be (cell I8 in Figure 4–33). The Amortization Schedule section shown in Figure 4–33 will work only for loans of up to 18 years. You, however, could extend the table to any number of years. The Amortization Schedule section also contains summaries in rows 21, 22, and 23. These summaries should agree exactly with the corresponding amounts in the Loan Payment Calculator section in the range B1:E6.

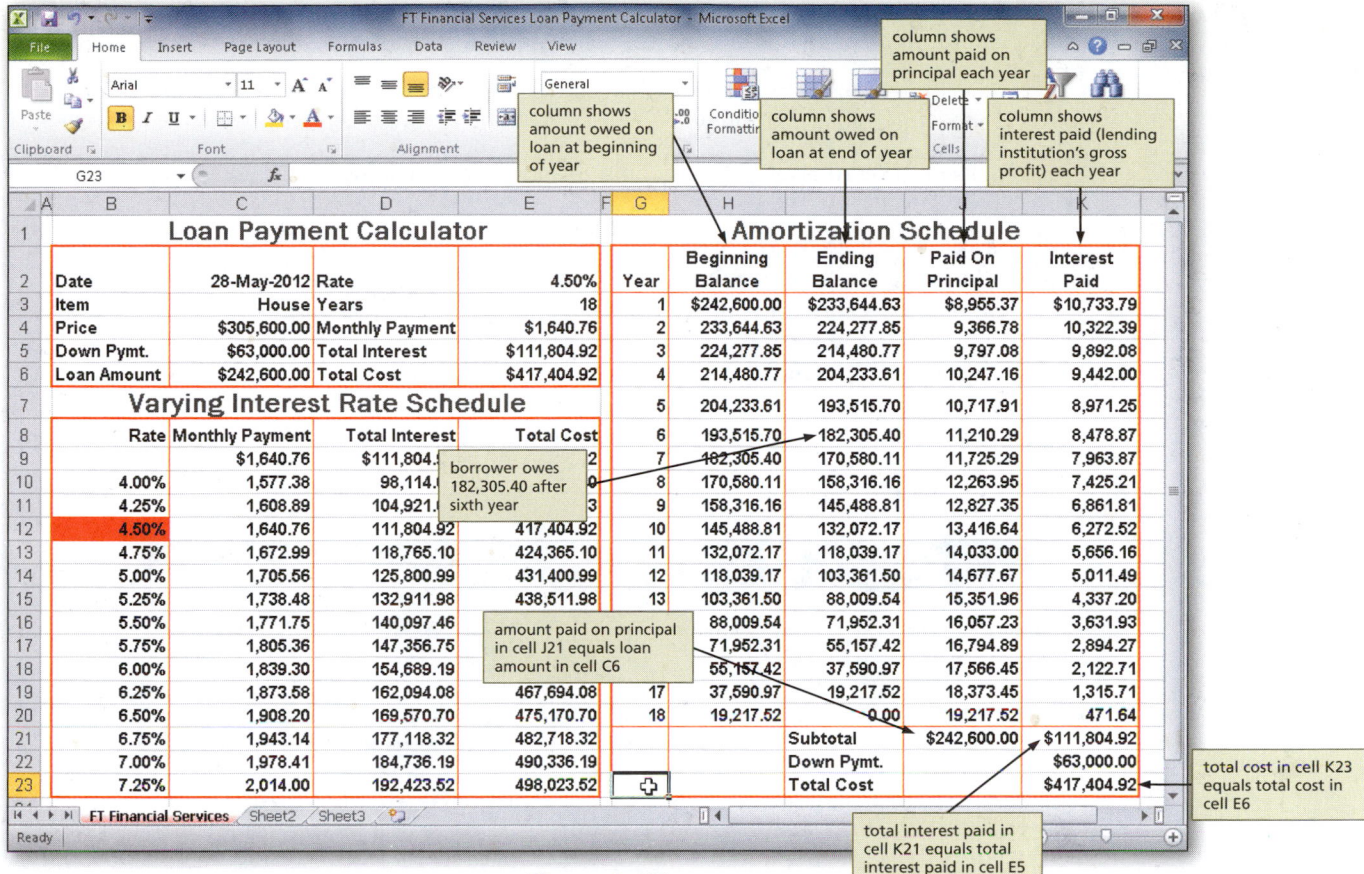

Figure 4–33

To Change Column Widths and Enter Titles

The first step in creating the Amortization Schedule section is to adjust the column widths and enter the Amortization Schedule section title and column titles. The following steps adjust column widths and enter column titles for the Amortization Schedule.

1 Position the mouse pointer on the right boundary of column heading F and then drag to the left until the ScreenTip shows Width: .77 (10 pixels) to change the column width.

2 Position the mouse pointer on the right boundary of column heading G and then drag to the left until the ScreenTip shows Width: 5.63 (50 pixels) to change the column width.

3 Drag through column headings H through K to select them. Position the mouse pointer on the right boundary of column heading K and then drag to the right until the ScreenTip shows Width: 12.13 (102 pixels) to change the column widths.

4 Select cell G1. Type **Amortization Schedule** and then press the ENTER key to enter the section title.

5 Select cell B1 and then click the Format Painter button (Home tab | Clipboard group) to start the format painter. Click cell G1 to copy the format of the selected cell, cell B1 in this case.

6 Click the Merge & Center button (Home tab | Alignment group) to split the selected cell, cell G1 in this case. Select the range G1:K1 and then click the Merge & Center button (Home tab | Alignment group) to merge and center the section title over the selected range.

BTW

Column Borders
In this chapter, columns A and F are used as column borders to divide sections of the worksheet from one another, as well as from the row headings. A column border is an unused column with a significantly reduced width. You also can use row borders to separate sections of a worksheet.

7 Enter the column headings in the range G2:K2, as shown in Figure 4–34. Where appropriate, press ALT+ENTER to enter the headings on two lines.

8 Select the range G2:K2 and then click the Center button (Home tab | Alignment group) to center the column headings.

9 Select cell G3 to display the section title and column headings, as shown in Figure 4–34.

Q&A Why was cell G1 split in step 6?

After using the format painter, Excel attempted to apply to merge and center the text in cell G1 because the source of the format, cell B1, is merged and centered across four columns. The Amortization Schedule section, however, includes five columns. Splitting cell G1, therefore, changed cell G1 from including four columns to include one column. Next, the section heading was merged and centered across five rows as required by the design of the worksheet (Figure 4–3 on page EX 230).

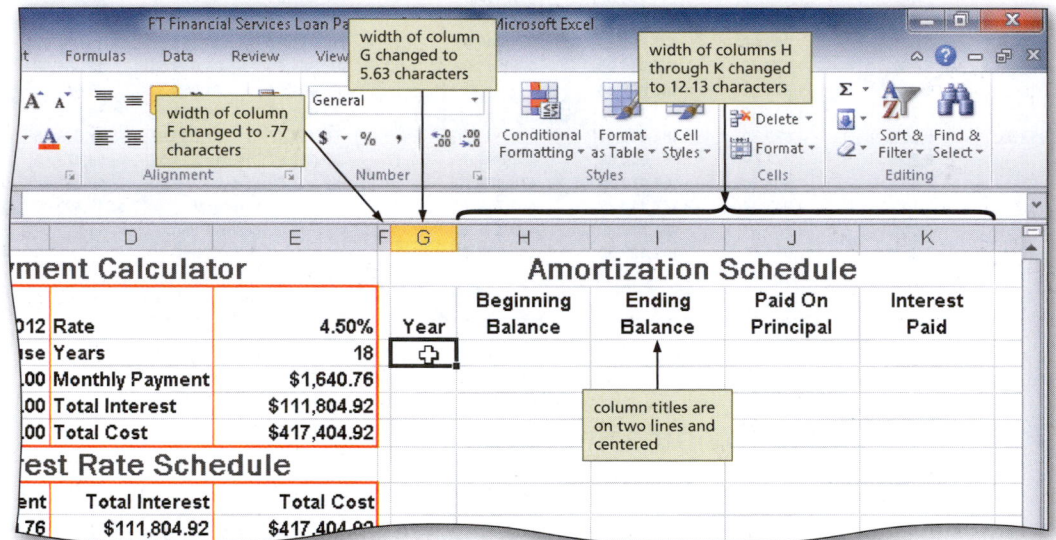

Figure 4–34

To Create a Series of Integers Using the Fill Handle

The next step is to create a series of numbers, using the fill handle, that represent the years during the life of the loan. The series begins with 1 (year 1) and ends with 18 (year 18). The following steps create a series of years in the range G3:G20.

1 With cell G3 active, type 1 as the initial year. Select cell G4 and then type 2 to represent the next year.

2 Select the range G3:G4 and then drag the fill handle through cell G20 to complete the creation of a series of integers, 1 through 18 in the range G3:G20 in this case (Figure 4–35).

Q&A Why is year 5 of the amortization schedule larger than the other rows in the amortization schedule?

The design of the worksheet (Figure 4–3 on page EX 230) called for a large font size for the varying interest rate schedule section of the worksheet, which is in row 7 of the worksheet. To accommodate the larger font size, the height of row 7 was increased. Year 5 of the worksheet is in the taller row 7 and, therefore, is taller than the other years in the amortization schedule.

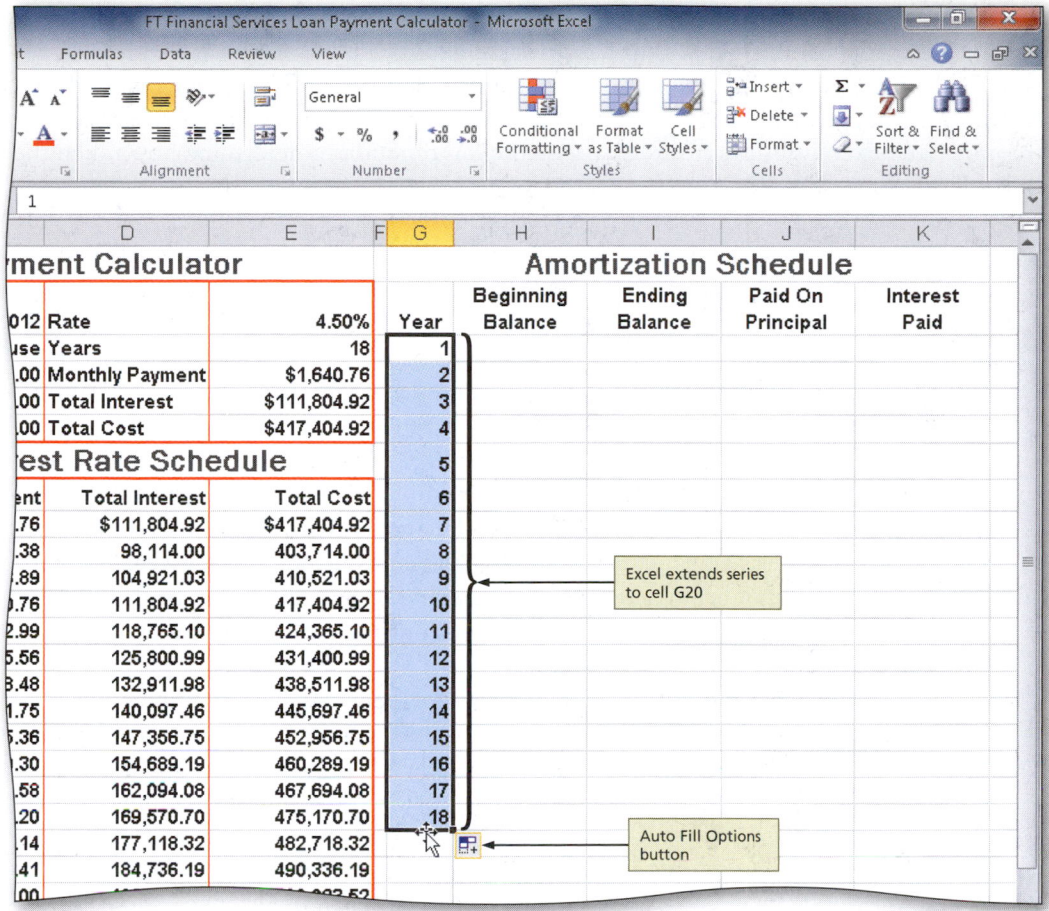

Figure 4–35

To Enter the Formulas in the Amortization Schedule

The next step is to enter the four formulas that form the basis of the amortization schedule in row 3. Later, these formulas will be copied through row 20. The formulas are summarized in Table 4–2.

Cell	Column heading	Formula	Example
Table 4–2 Formulas for the Amortization Schedule			
H3	Beginning Balance	=C6	The beginning balance (the balance at the end of a year) is the initial loan amount in cell C6.
I3	Ending Balance	=IF(G3<=$E$3, PV($E$2/12, 12*($E$3–G3), –$E$4), 0)	The ending balance (the balance at the end of a year) is equal to the present value of the payments paid over the remaining life of the loan.
J3	Paid on Principal	=H3–I3	The amount paid on the principal at the end of the year is equal to the beginning balance (cell H3) less the ending balance (cell I3).
K3	Interest Paid	=IF(H3>0, 12*$E$4–J3, 0)	The interest paid during the year is equal to 12 times the monthly payment (cell E4) less the amount paid on the principal (cell J3).

Of the four formulas in Table 4–2 on the previous page, perhaps the most difficult to understand is the PV function that will be assigned to cell I3. The **PV function** returns the present value of an annuity. An **annuity** is a series of fixed payments (such as the monthly payment in cell E4) made at the end of each of a fixed number of periods (months) at a fixed interest rate. You can use the PV function to determine how much the borrower of the loan still owes at the end of each year.

The PV function is used to determine the ending balance after the first year (cell I3) by using a term equal to the number of months for which the borrower still must make payments. For example, if the loan is for 18 years (216 months), then the borrower still owes 204 payments after the first year (216 months – 12 months). The number of payments outstanding can be determined from the formula 12 * (E3–G3) or 12*(18–1), which equals 204. Recall that column G contains integers that represent the years of the loan. After the second year, the number of payments remaining is 192, and so on.

If you assign the PV function as shown in Table 4–2 to cell I3 and then copy it to the range I4:I20, the ending balances for each year will be displayed properly. If the loan is for less than 18 years, however, then the ending balances displayed for the years beyond the time the loan is due are invalid. For example, if a loan is taken out for 5 years, then the rows representing years 6 through 18 in the amortization schedule should be 0. The PV function, however, will display negative numbers even though the loan already has been paid off.

To avoid the display of negative ending balances the worksheet should include a formula that assigns the PV function to the range I3:I20 as long as the corresponding year in column G is less than or equal to the number of years in cell E3. If the corresponding year in column G is greater than the number of years in cell E3, then the ending balance for that year and the remaining years should be 0. The following IF function causes the value of the PV function or 0 to be displayed in cell I3, depending on whether the corresponding value in column G is less than or equal to the number of years in cell E3. Recall that the dollar signs within the cell references indicate the cell references are absolute and, therefore, will not change as you copy the function downward.

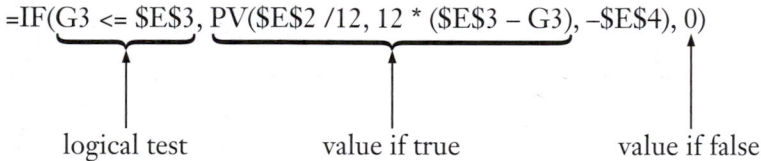

=IF(G3 <= $E$3, PV($E$2 /12, 12 * ($E$3 – G3), –$E$4), 0)

logical test   value if true   value if false

In the preceding formula, the logical test determines if the year in column G is less than or equal to the term of the loan in cell E3. If the logical test is true, then the IF function assigns the PV function to the cell. If the logical test is false, then the IF function assigns zero (0) to the cell. You also could use two double-quote symbols (" ") to indicate to Excel to leave the cell blank if the logical test is false.

The PV function in the IF function includes absolute cell references (cell references with dollar signs) to ensure that the references to cells in column E do not change when the IF function later is copied down the column.

The following steps enter the four formulas shown in Table 4–2 into row 3. Row 3 represents year 1 of the loan.

1

- Select cell H3 and then enter `=c6` as the beginning balance of the loan.

- Select cell I3 and then type `=if(g3 <= $e$3, pv($e$2 / 12, 12 * ($e$3 – g3), –$e$4), 0)` as the entry (Figure 4–36).

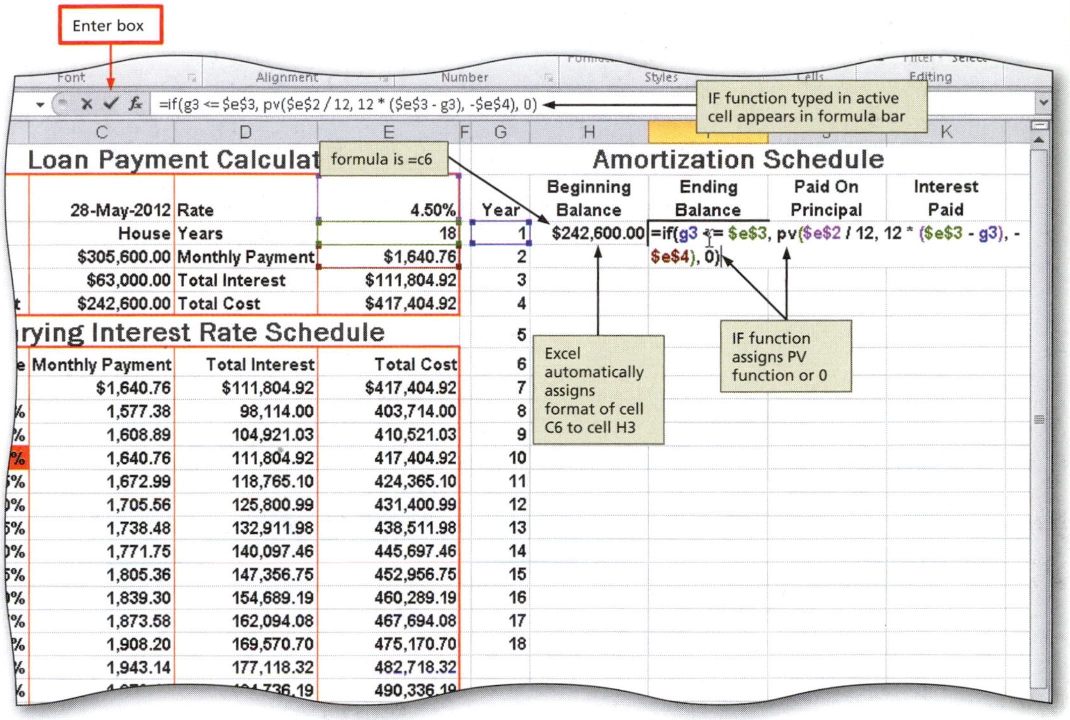

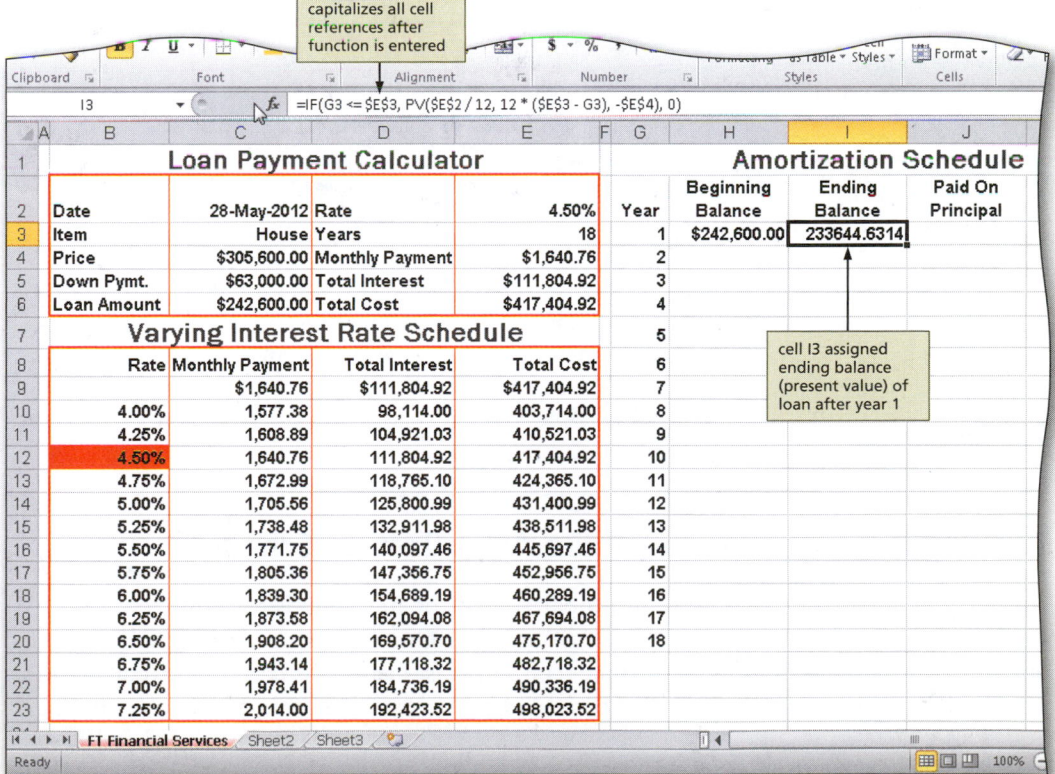

Figure 4–36

2

- Click the Enter box in the formula bar to insert the formula in the selected cell (Figure 4–37).

Q&A

What happens when the Enter box is clicked?

Excel evaluates the IF function in cell I3 and displays the result of the PV function (233644.6314) because the value in cell G3 (1) is less than or equal to the term of the loan in cell E3 (18). With cell I3 active, Excel also displays the formula in the formula bar. If the borrower wanted to pay off the loan after one year, the cost would be $233,644.63.

Figure 4–37

3

- Select cell J3. Enter the formula
  =h3 - i3 and then press the
  RIGHT ARROW key to complete the
  entry.

- Select cell K3. Enter the formula
  =if(h3 > 0, 12 * e4 -
  j3, 0) (Figure 4–38).

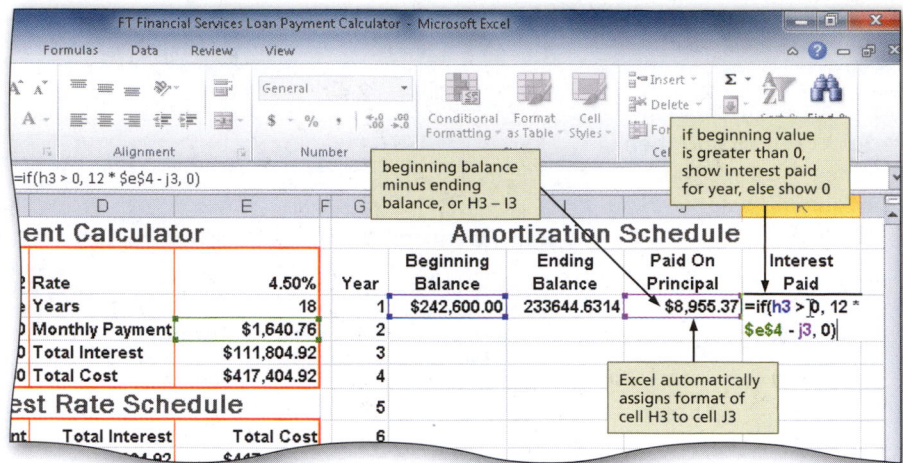

Figure 4–38

4

- Click the Enter box in the formula
  bar to complete the entry of the
  formula (Figure 4–39).

Q&A What happens when the Enter box
is clicked?

Excel displays the interest paid after
1 year (10733.79339) in cell K3.
Thus, the lending company's gross
profit for the first year of the loan is
$10,733.79.

Q&A Why are some of the cells in the
range H3:K3 formatted?

When you enter a formula in a
cell, Excel assigns the cell the same
format as the first cell reference in
the formula. For example, when you
enter =c6 in cell H3, Excel assigns the
format in cell C6 to cell H3. The same applies to cell J3. Although this method of formatting
also works for most functions, it does not work for the IF function. Thus, the results of the IF
functions in cells I3 and K3 are displayed using the General style format, which is the format
of all cells when you open a new workbook.

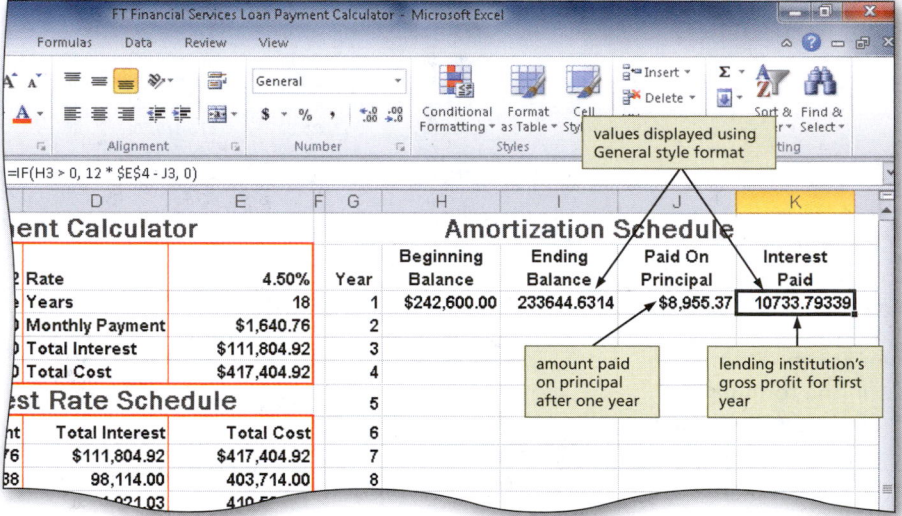

Figure 4–39

To Copy the Formulas to Fill the Amortization Schedule

With the formulas entered into the first row, the next step is to copy them to the remaining rows in the
amortization schedule. The required copying is straightforward, except for the beginning balance column. To
obtain the next year's beginning balance (cell H4), last year's ending balance (cell I3) must be used. After cell I3
(last year's ending balance) is copied to cell H4 (next year's beginning balance), then H4 can be copied to the
range H5:H20. The following steps copy the formulas in the range I3:K3 and cell H4 through to the remainder
of the amortization schedule.

1

- Select the range I3:K3 and then drag the fill handle down through row 20 to copy the formulas through the amortization schedule, I4:K20 in this case (Figure 4–40).

Q&A

Why do some of the numbers seem incorrect?

Many of the numbers displayed are incorrect because the cells in column H — except for cell H3 — do not yet contain beginning balances.

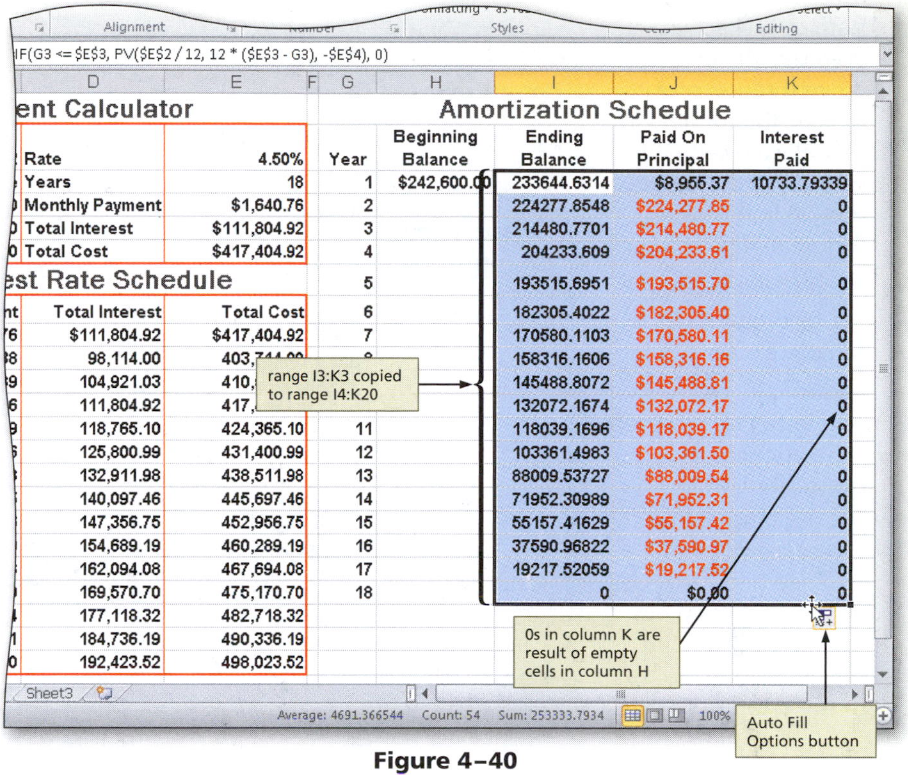

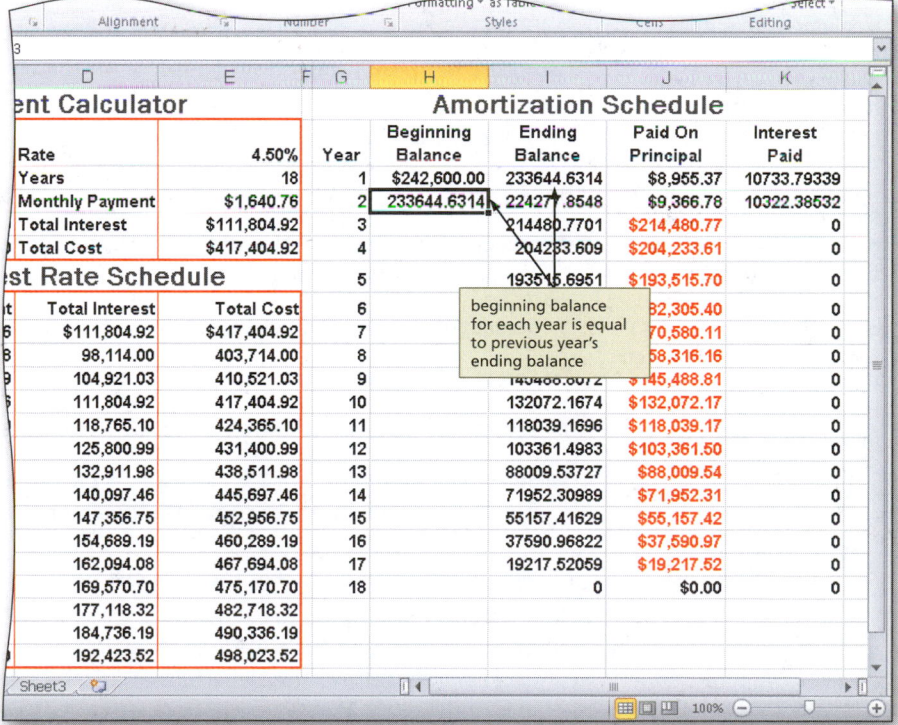

Figure 4–40

2

- Select cell H4, type `=i3` as the cell entry, and then click the Enter box in the formula bar to display the ending balance (233644.6314) for year 1 as the beginning balance for year 2 (Figure 4–41).

Figure 4–41

3

- With cell H4 active, drag the fill handle down through row 20 to copy the formula in the selected cell, cell H4 (=I3) to the range H5:H20 in this case (Figure 4–42).

Q&A

What happens after the fill operation is complete?

Because the cell reference I3 is relative, Excel adjusts the row portion of the cell reference as it is copied downward. Thus, each new beginning balance in column H is equal to the ending balance of the previous year.

fx =I3

Loan Payment Calc

	C	D	
	28-May-2012	Rate	
	House	Years	
	$305,600.00	Monthly Payment	$1,640.76
	$63,000.00	Total Interest	$111,804.92
	$242,600.00	Total Cost	$417,404.92

rying Interest Rate Schedule

	Monthly Payment	Total Interest	Total Cost
	$1,640.76	$111,804.92	$417,404.92
%	1,577.38	98,1	14.00
%	1,608.89	104,9	21.03
%	1,640.76	111,804.92	417,404.92
%	1,672.99	118,765.10	424,365.10
%	1,705.56	125,800.99	431,400.99
%	1,738.48	132,911.98	438,511.98
%	1,771.75	140,097.46	445,697.46
%	1,805.36	147,356.75	452,956.75
%	1,839.30	154,689.19	460,289.19
%	1,873.58	162,094.08	467,694.08
%	1,908.20	169,570.70	475,170.70
%	1,943.14	177,118.32	482,718.32
%	1,978.41	184,736.19	490,336.19
%	2,014.00	192,423.52	498,023.52

with beginning balances for each year calculated, remaining values in amortization schedule now are correct

cell H4 copied to range H5:H20

Amortization Schedule

Year	Beginning Balance	Ending Balance	Paid On Principal	Interest Paid
1	$242,600.00	233644.6314	$8,955.37	10733.79339
2	233644.6314	224277.8548	$9,366.78	10322.38532
3	224277.8548	214480.7701	$9,797.08	9892.077244
4	214480.7701	204233.609	$10,247.16	9442.000886
5	204233.609	193515.6951	$10,717.91	8971.248099
6	193515.6951	182305.4022	$11,210.29	8478.869012
7	182305.4022	170580.1103	$11,725.29	7963.870115
8	170580.1103	158316.1606	$12,263.95	7425.212259
9	158316.1606	145488.8072	$12,827.35	6861.808555
10	145488.8072	132072.1674	$13,416.64	6272.522184
11	132072.1674	118039.1696	$14,033.00	5656.1641
12	118039.1696	103361.4983	$14,677.67	5011.490633
13	103361.4983	88009.53727	$15,351.96	4337.20098
14	88009.53727	71952.30989	$16,057.23	3631.934579
15	71952.30989	55157.41629	$16,794.89	2894.268362
16	55157.41629	37590.96822	$17,566.45	2122.713889
17	37590.96822	19217.52059	$18,373.45	1315.714338
18	19217.52059	0	$19,217.52	471.6413684

ending balance for year 18 is 0

Auto Fill Options button

al Services / Sheet2 / Sheet3

Average: 138367.2723   628   100%

Figure 4–42

BTW

The Magical Fill Handle If a worksheet contains a column with entries adjacent to the range you plan to drag the fill handle down through, then you can double-click the fill handle instead of dragging. For example, in Step 3 above, you could have double-clicked the fill handle instead of dragging the fill handle down through column 20 to copy the formula in cell H4 to the range H5:H20, because of the numbers in column G. This feature also applies to copying a range using the fill handle.

To Enter the Total Formulas in the Amortization Schedule

The next step is to determine the amortization schedule totals in rows 21 through 23. These totals should agree with the corresponding totals in the Loan Payment Calculator section (range B1:E6). The following steps enter the total formulas in the amortization schedule.

1 Select cell I21 and then enter **Subtotal** as the row title.

2 Select the range J21:K21 and then click the Sum button (Home tab | Editing group) to sum the selected range.

3 Select cell I22 and then enter **Down Pymt.** as the row title.

4 Select cell K22 and then enter **=c5** to copy the down payment to the selected cell.

5 Select cell I23 and then enter **Total Cost** as the row title.

6 Select cell K23, type **=j21 + k21 + k22** as the total cost, and then click the Enter box in the formula bar to complete the amortization schedule totals (Figure 4–43).

Q&A

What was accomplished in the previous steps?

The formula assigned to cell K23 (=j21 + k21 + k22) sums the total amount paid on the principal (cell J21), the total interest paid (cell K21), and the down payment (cell K22). Excel assigns cell J21 the same format as cell J3, because cell J3 is the first cell reference in =SUM(J3:J20). Furthermore, because cell J21 was selected first when the range J21:K21 was selected to determine the sum, Excel assigned cell K21 the same format it assigned to cell J21. Finally, cell K22 was assigned the Currency style format, because cell K22 was assigned the formula =c5, and cell C5 has a Currency style format. For the same reason, the value in cell K23 appears in Currency style format.

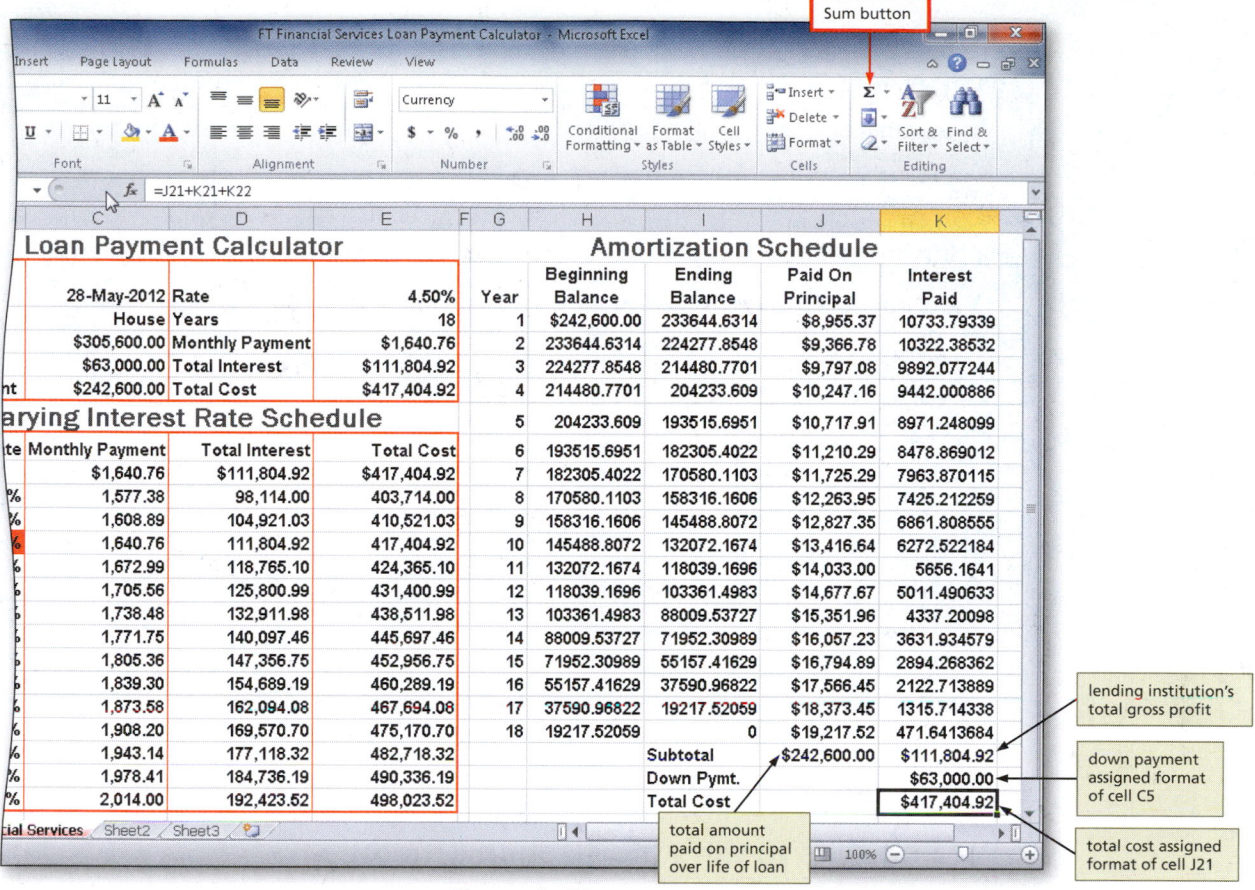

Figure 4–43

To Format the Numbers in the Amortization Schedule

The final step in creating the amortization schedule is to format it so that it is easier to read. The formatting is divided into two parts: (1) formatting the numbers and (2) adding borders.

When the beginning balance formula (=c6) was entered earlier into cell H3, Excel automatically copied the Currency style format along with the value from cell C6 to cell H3. The following steps copy the Currency style format from cell H3 to the range I3:K3. The Comma style then will be assigned to the range H4:K20.

1 Select cell H3 and then click the Format Painter button (Home tab | Clipboard group) to start the format painter. Drag through the range I3:K3 to assign the Currency style format to the cells.

2 Select the range H4:K20 and then right-click the selected range to display a shortcut menu. Click Format Cells on the shortcut menu to display the Format Cells dialog box and then, if necessary, click the Number tab (Format Cells dialog box) to display the Number sheet.

3 Click Currency in the Category list to select a currency format and then click the Symbol box arrow to display the Symbol list. Click None to choose no currency symbol, and then click the second format, 1,234.10, in the Negative numbers list to create a currency format.

4 Click the OK button (Format Cells dialog box) to apply the currency format to the selected range.

5 Select cell H21 to deselect the range H4:K20 and display the numbers in the amortization schedule, as shown in Figure 4–44 on the following page.

BTW

Round-Off Errors
If you manually add the numbers in column K (range K3:K20) and compare it to the sum in cell K21, you will notice that the total interest paid is $0.02 off. This round-off error is due to the fact that some of the numbers involved in the computations have additional decimal places that do not appear in the cells. You can use the ROUND function on the formula entered into cell K3 to ensure the total is exactly correct. For information on the ROUND function, click the Insert Function button in the formula bar, click Math & Trig in the 'Or select a category' list, scroll down in the 'Select a function' list, and then click ROUND.

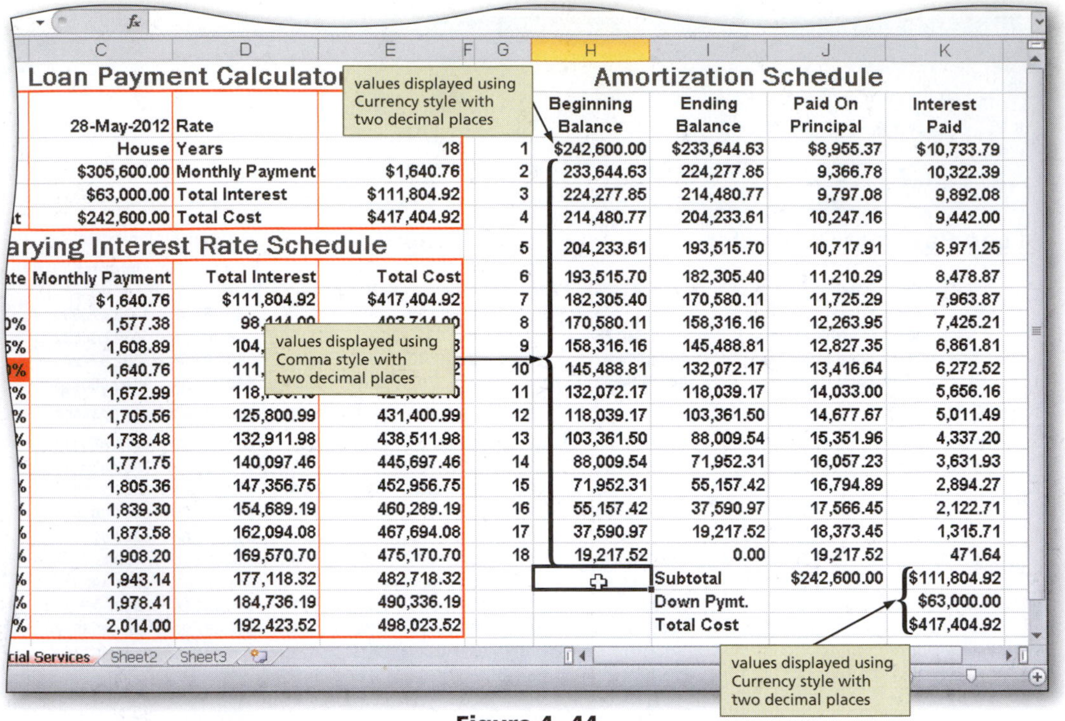

Figure 4–44

To Add Borders to the Amortization Schedule

The following steps add the borders to the amortization schedule.

1 Select the range G2:K23. Right-click the selected range to display a shortcut menu and then click Format Cells on the shortcut menu to display the Format Cells dialog box.

2 Click the Border tab (Format Cells dialog box) to display the Border sheet. Click the Color box arrow to display the Colors palette and then click Red (column 2, row 1) in the Standard Colors area to change the border color.

3 Click the medium border in the Style area (column 2, row 5). Click the Outline button in the Presets area to preview the border in the Border area.

4 Click the light border in the Style area (column 1, row 7). Click the Vertical Line button in the Border area to preview the border in the Border area.

5 Click the OK button (Format Cells dialog box) to apply custom borders to the selected range.

6 Select the range G2:K2 and then use the Format Cells dialog box to apply a red, light bottom border to the selected range.

7 Select the range G20:K20 and then use the Format Cells dialog box to apply a red, light bottom border to the selected range.

8 Select cell H22 to display the worksheet, as shown in Figure 4–45.

9 Click the Save button on the Quick Access Toolbar to save the workbook using the file name, FT Financial Services Loan Payment Calculator.

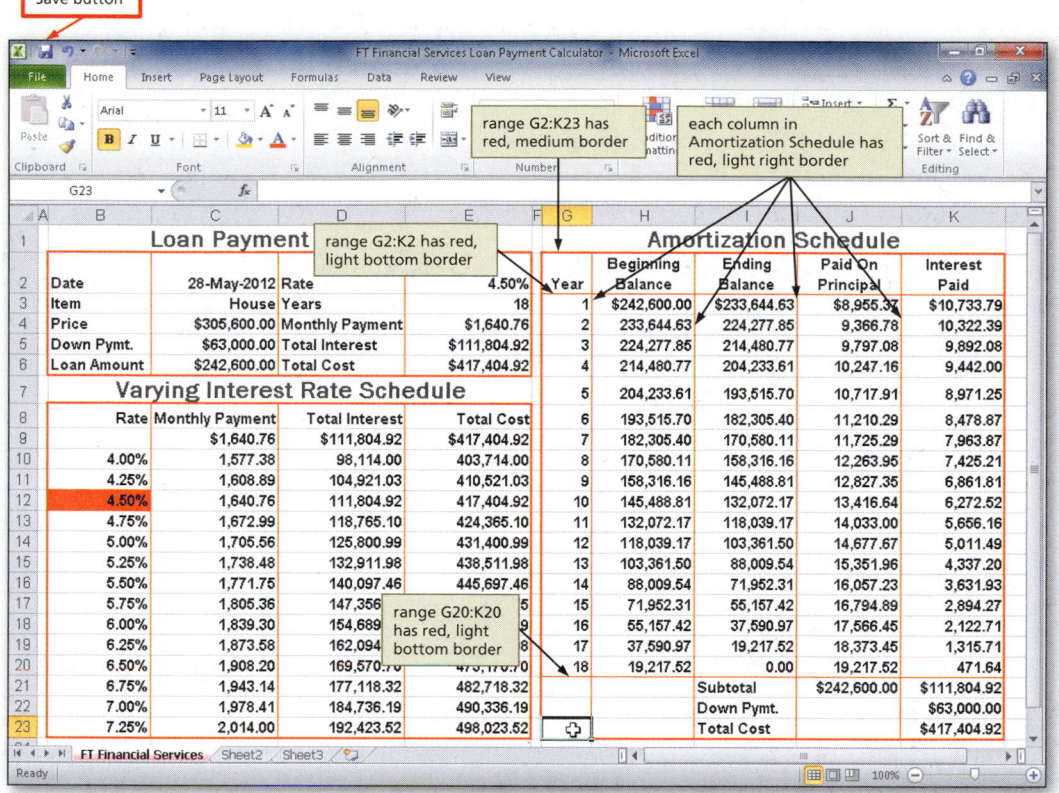

Figure 4–45

To Enter New Loan Data

With the Loan Payment Calculator, Varying Interest Rate Schedule, and Amortization Schedule sections of the worksheet complete, you can use them to generate new loan information. For example, assume you want to purchase land for $62,500.00. You have $9,000.00 for a down payment and want the loan for only 7 years. FT Financial Services currently is charging 7.25% interest for a 7–year loan on land. The following steps enter the new loan data.

1 Enter **Land** in cell C3.

2 Enter **62500** in cell C4.

3 Enter **9000** in cell C5.

4 Enter **7.25%** in cell E2.

5 Enter **7** in cell E3 and then press the DOWN ARROW key to calculate the loan data.

6 Select cell H22 to display the worksheet, as shown in Figure 4–46 on the following page.

Q&A

What happens on the worksheet when the new data is entered?

As shown in Figure 4–46, the monthly payment for the land is $814.01 (cell E4). The total interest is $14,877.04 (cell E5) and the total cost for the land is $77,377.04 (cell E6). Because the term of the loan is for 7 years, the rows for years 8 through 18 in the Amortization Schedule section display 0.00.

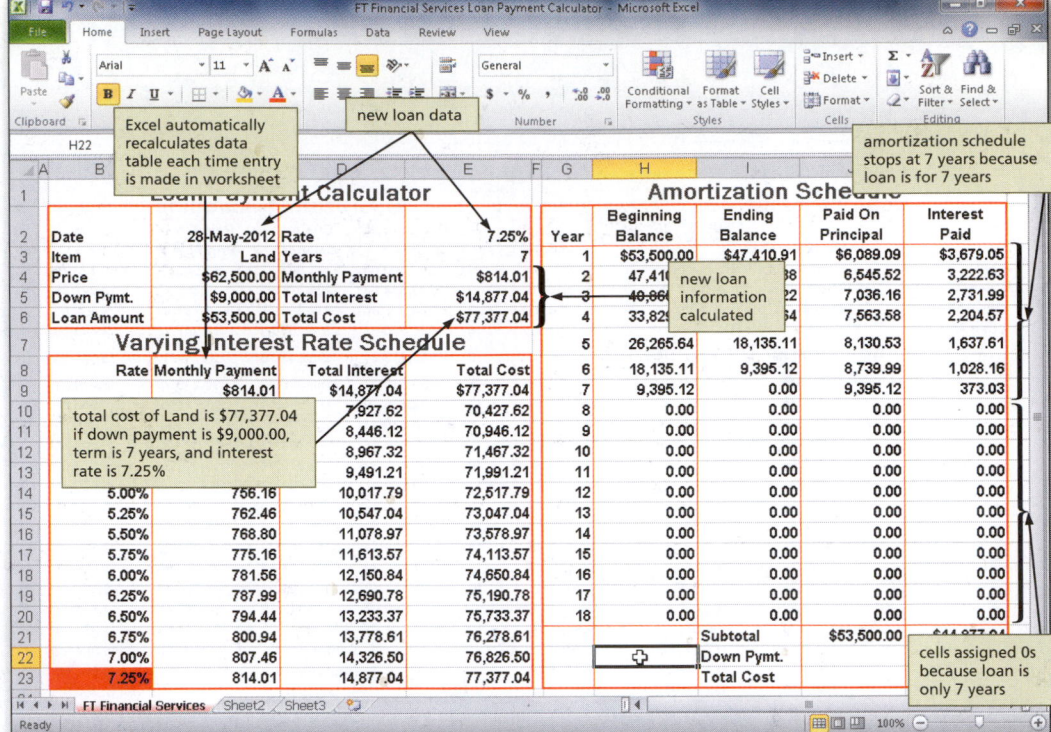

Figure 4–46

To Enter the Original Loan Data

The following steps reenter the original loan data.

1 Enter `House` in cell C3.

2 Enter `305600` in cell C4.

3 Enter `63000` in cell C5.

4 Enter `4.50` in cell E2.

5 Enter `18` in cell E3 and then select cell H22.

Conserving Ink and Toner

If you want to conserve ink or toner, you can instruct Excel to print draft quality documents by clicking File on the Ribbon to open the Backstage view, clicking Options in the Backstage view to display the Excel Options dialog box, clicking Advanced in the left pane (Excel Options dialog box), scrolling to the Print area in the right pane, make sure that the 'High quality mode for graphics' button is unchecked and then clicking the OK button. Then, use the Backstage view to print the document as usual.

Printing Sections of the Worksheet

In Chapter 2, you learned to print a section of a worksheet by selecting it and using the Selection option in the Print dialog box. If you find yourself continually selecting the same range in a worksheet to print, you can set a specific range to print each time you print the worksheet. When you set a range to print, Excel will continue to print only that range until you clear it.

To Set Up a Worksheet to Print

This section describes print options available in the Sheet tab in the Page Setup dialog box (Figure 4–47). These print options pertain to the way the worksheet will appear in the printed copy or when previewed. One important print option is the capability of printing in black and white, even when your printer is a color printer. Printing in black and white not only speeds up the printing process but also saves ink. The following steps ensure any printed copy fits on one page and prints in black and white.

1

- Display the Page Layout tab and then click the Page Setup Dialog Box Launcher (Page Layout tab | Page Setup group) to display the Page Setup dialog box.

- If necessary, click the Page tab (Page Setup dialog box) to display the Page sheet and then click Fit to in the Scaling area to set the worksheet to print on one page (Figure 4–47).

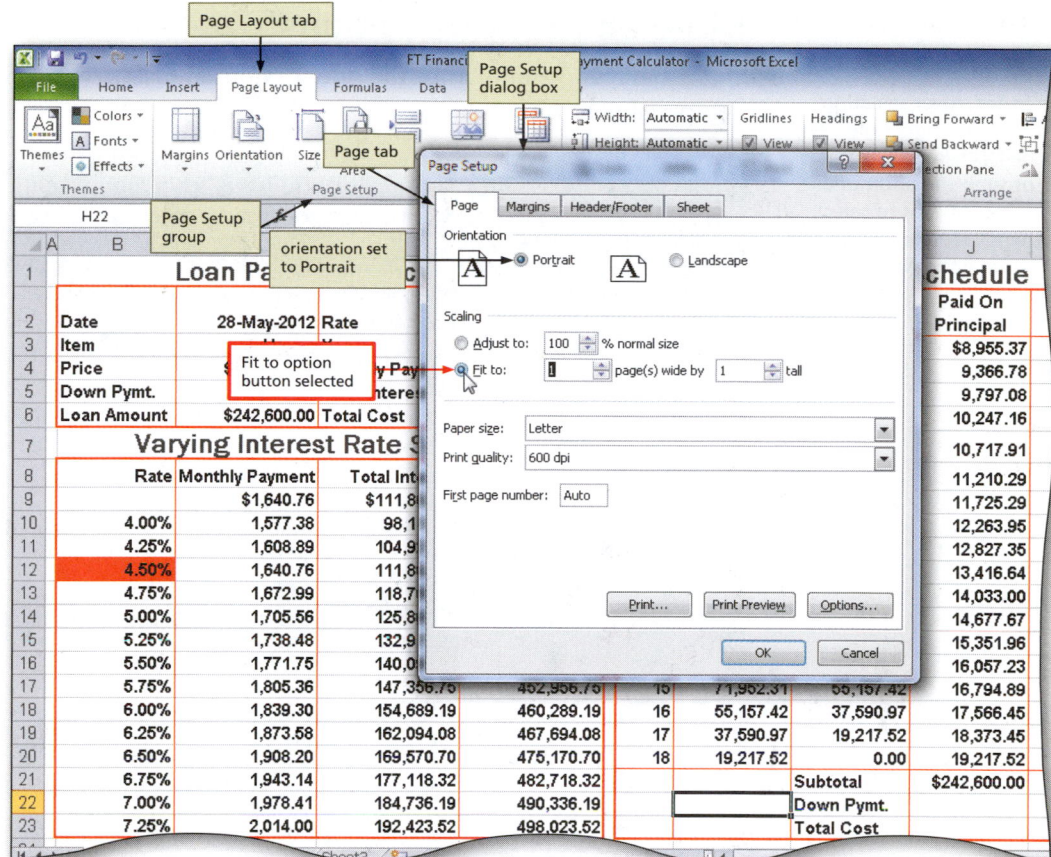

Figure 4–47

2

- Click the Sheet tab (Page Setup dialog box) to display the tab and then click 'Black and white' in the Print area to select the check box (Figure 4–48).

3

- Click the OK button (Page Setup dialog box) to close the Page Setup dialog box.

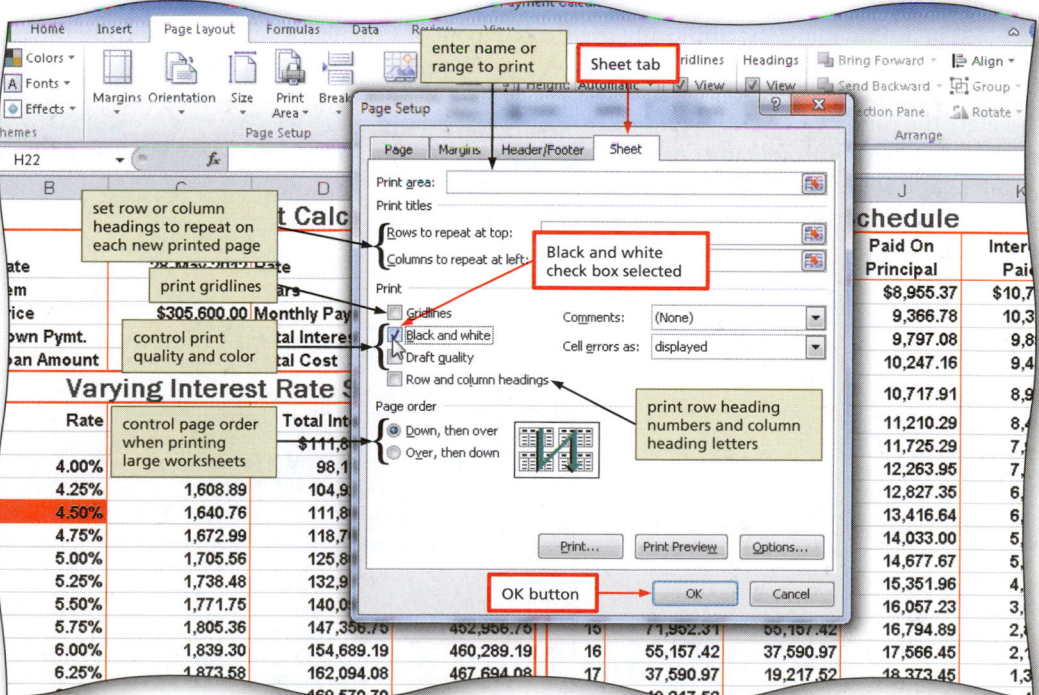

Figure 4–48

Naming Ranges
A name can be assigned to two or more nonadjacent ranges. After selecting the first range, hold down the CTRL key and drag through the additional ranges of cells to select them before entering the name in the Name box.

More about Print Options

Table 4–3 summarizes the print options available on the Sheet tab in the Page Setup dialog box.

Table 4–3 Print Options Available Using the Sheet Tab in the Page Setup Dialog Box

Print Option	Description
Print area box	Excel prints from cell A1 to the last occupied cell in a worksheet unless you instruct it to print a selected area. You can select a range to print with the mouse, or you can enter a range or name of a range in the Print area box. Nonadjacent ranges will print on a separate page.
Print titles area	This area is used to instruct Excel to print row titles and column titles on each printed page of a worksheet. You must specify a range, even if you are designating one column (e.g., 1:4 means the first four rows).
Gridlines check box	A check mark in this check box instructs Excel to print gridlines.
Black and white check box	A check mark in this check box speeds up printing and saves colored ink if you have colors in a worksheet and a color printer.
Draft quality check box	A check mark in this check box speeds up printing by ignoring formatting and not printing most graphics.
Row and column headings check box	A check mark in this check box instructs Excel to include the column heading letters (A, B, C, etc.) and row heading numbers (1, 2, 3, etc.) in the printout.
Comments box	Indicates where comments are to be displayed on the printout.
Cell errors as box	Indicates how errors in cells should be displayed on the printout.
Page order area	Determines the order in which multipage worksheets will print.

To Set the Print Area

The following steps print only the Loan Payment Calculator section by setting the print area to the range B1:E6.

1
• Select the range B1:E6 and then click the Print Area button (Page Layout tab | Page Setup group) to display the Print Area menu (Figure 4–49).

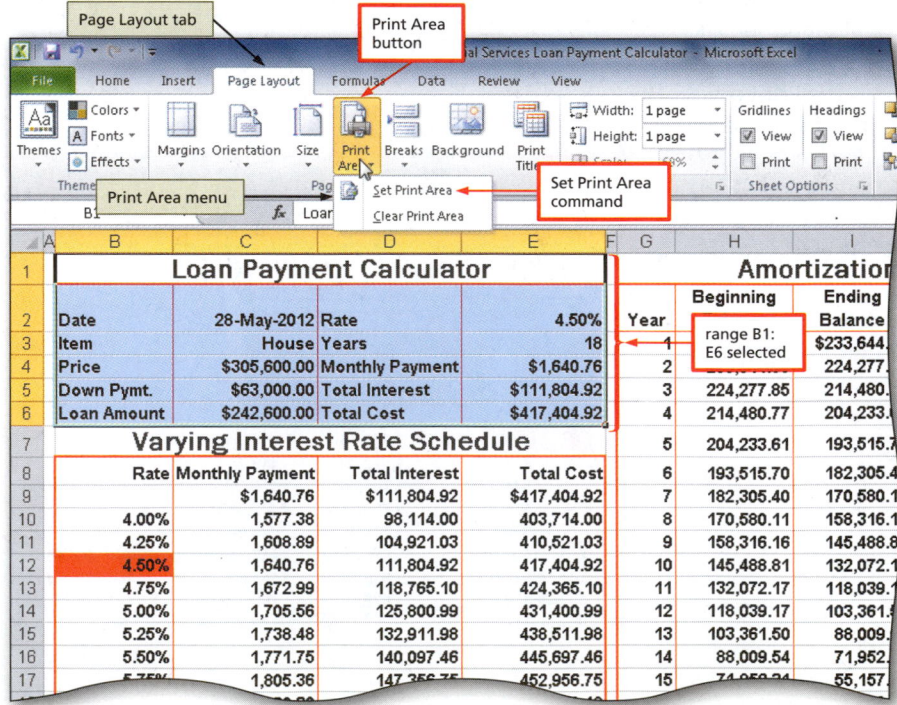

Figure 4–49

2

- Click Set Print Area on the Print Area menu to set the range of the worksheet which Excel should print.

- Click File on the Ribbon to open the Backstage view and then click the Print tab in the Backstage view to display the Print gallery.

- Click the Print button in the Print gallery to print the selected area (Figure 4–50).

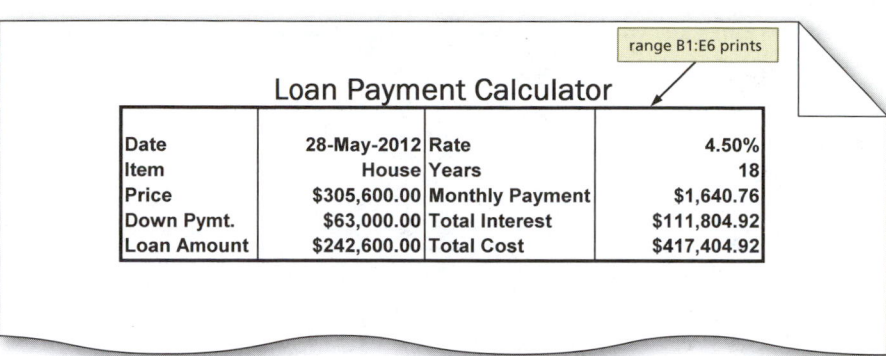

Figure 4–50

3

- Display the Page Layout tab.

- Click the Print Area button (Page Layout tab | Page Setup group) to display the Print Area list and then click the Clear Print Area command on the Print Area list to reset the print area to the entire worksheet.

Q&A   What happens when I set a print area?

Once you set a print area, Excel will continue to print the specified range, rather than the entire worksheet. If you save the workbook with the print area set, then Excel will remember the settings the next time you open the workbook and print only the specified range. To remove the print area so that the entire worksheet prints, click Clear Print Area on the Print Area menu as described in Step 3.

To Name and Print Sections of a Worksheet

With some spreadsheet applications, you will want to print several different areas of a worksheet, depending on the request. Rather than using the Set Print Area command or manually selecting the range each time you want to print, you can name the ranges using the Name box in the formula bar. You then can use one of the names to select an area before using the Set Print Area command or Selection option button. The following steps name the Loan Payment Calculator section, the Varying Interest Rate Schedule section, the Amortization Schedule section, and the entire worksheet, and then print each section.

1

- Click the Page Setup Dialog Box Launcher (Page Layout tab | Page Setup group) to display the Page Setup dialog box, click the Sheet tab to display the Sheet page, and, if necessary, click 'Black and white' to deselect the check box and ensure that Excel prints in color to color printers.

- Click the OK button (Page Setup dialog box) to close the Page Setup dialog box.

- If necessary, select the range B1:E6, click the Name box, and then type **Loan_Payment** as the name of the range to create a range name (Figure 4–51).

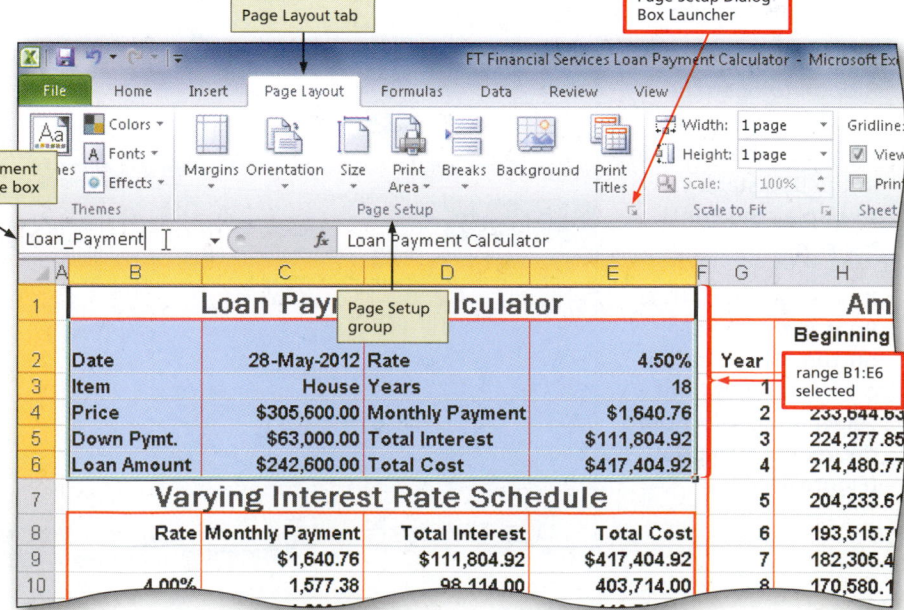

Figure 4–51

2

- Press the ENTER key to create a range name.

- Select the range B7:E23, click the Name box, type **Interest_Schedule** as the name of the range, and then press the ENTER key to create a range name.

- Select the range G1:K23, click the Name box, type **Amortization_Schedule** as the name of the range, and then press the ENTER key to create a range name.

- Select the range B1:K23, click the Name box, type **All_Sections** as the name of the range, and then press the ENTER key to create a range name.

- Select cell H22 and then click the Name box arrow in the formula bar to display the Name list with the new range names (Figure 4–52).

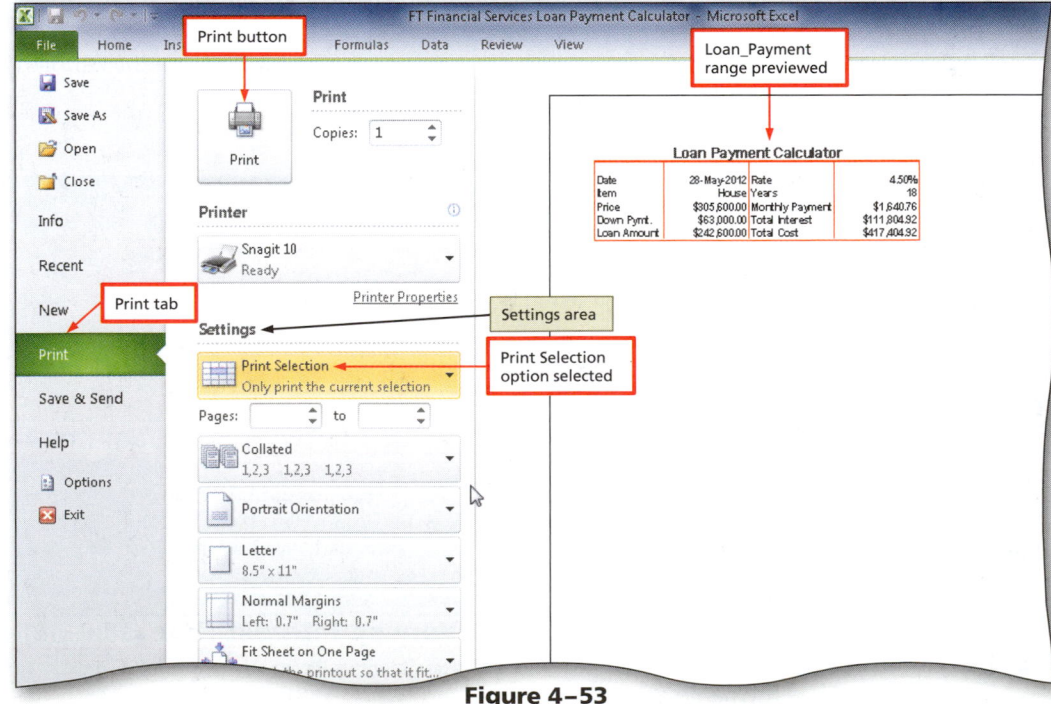

Figure 4–52

3

- Click Loan_Payment in the Name list to select the range associated with the name, B1:E6 in this case.

- Click File on the Ribbon to open the Backstage view and then click the Print tab in the Backstage view to display the Print gallery.

- If necessary, click the Print Active Sheets button in the Settings area and select Print Selection to select the desired item to print (Figure 4–53).

Figure 4–53

4

- Click the Print button in the Print gallery to print the selected named range, Loan_Payment in this case.

- One at a time, use the Name box to select the names Interest_Schedule, Amortization_ Schedule, and All_Sections, and then print them following the instructions in Step 3 to print the remaining named ranges (Figure 4–54).

5

- Click the Save button on the Quick Access Toolbar to save the workbook using the file name, FT Financial Services Loan Payment Calculator.

Q&A

Why does the All_Sections range print on one page?

Recall that the Fit to option was selected earlier (Figure 4–47 on page EX 267). This selection ensures that each of the printouts fits across the page in portrait orientation.

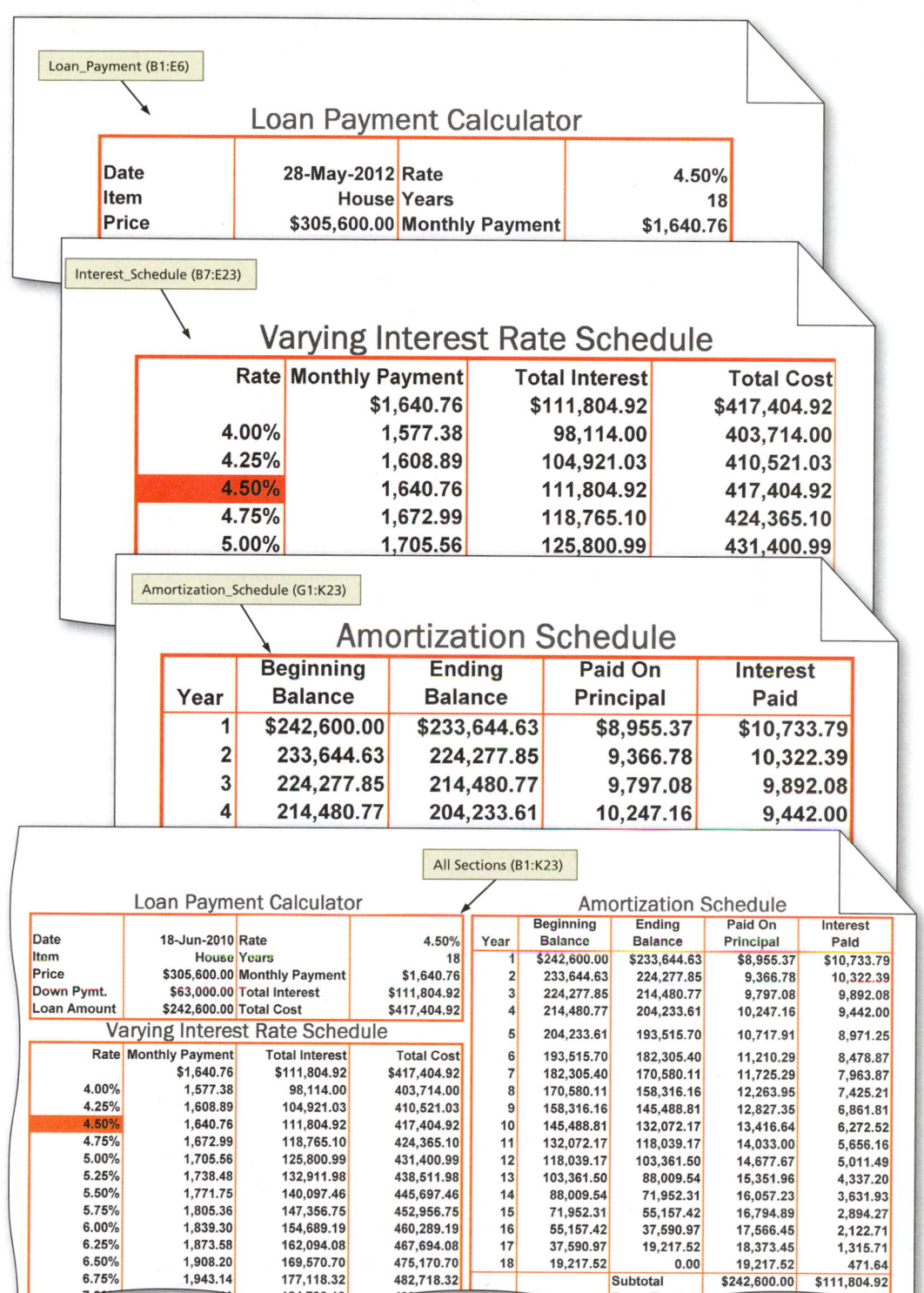

Figure 4–54

Other Ways

1. Select cell or range, click Define Name button (Formulas tab | Defined Names group), [type name], click OK button

2. Select cell or range, click Name Manager button (Formulas tab | Defined Names group), click New, [type name], click OK button, click Close button

Break Point: If you wish to take a break, this is a good place to do so. You can quit Excel now. To resume at a later time, start Excel, open the file called FT Financial Services Loan Payment Calculator, and continue following the steps from this location forward.

BTW

Hiding Worksheets
When sharing workbooks with others, you may not want them to see some of your worksheets. Hiding worksheets obscures the sheets from casual inspection; however, it is not only for hiding worksheets from others' eyes. Sometimes, you have several worksheets that include data that you rarely require or that you use only as a reference. To clean up the list of sheet tabs, you can hide worksheets that you usually do not need.

Protecting and Hiding Worksheets and Workbooks

When building a worksheet for novice users, you should protect the cells in the worksheet that you do not want changed, such as cells that contain text or formulas. Doing so prevents users from making ill-advised changes to text and formulas in cells.

When you create a new worksheet, all the cells are assigned a locked status, but the lock is not engaged, which leaves cells unprotected. **Unprotected cells** are cells whose values you can change at any time. **Protected cells** are cells that you cannot change.

Plan Ahead

> **Determine which cells to protect and unprotect in the worksheet.**
> In general, all cells should be protected except those that require an entry by the user of the worksheet. Any cells containing formulas should be protected so that a user of the worksheet cannot modify the formulas. You should protect cells only after the worksheet has been tested fully and the correct results appear. Protecting a worksheet is a two-step process:
>
> **1.** Select the cells you want to leave unprotected and then change their cell protection settings to an unlocked status.
>
> **2.** Protect the entire worksheet.
>
> At first glance, these steps may appear to be backwards. Once you protect the entire worksheet, however, you cannot change anything, including the locked status of individual cells.

To Protect a Worksheet

In the Loan Payment Calculator worksheet, the user should be able to make changes to only five cells: the item in cell C3, the price in cell C4, the down payment in cell C5, the interest rate in cell E2, and the years in cell E3 (Figure 4–55). These cells must remain unprotected so that users can enter the correct data. The remaining cells in the worksheet should be protected so that the user cannot change them.

The following steps protect the Loan Payment Calculator worksheet.

1

- Select the range C3:C5 and then, while holding down the CTRL key, select the nonadjacent range E2:E3 to select the ranges to unprotect.

- Right-click one of the selected ranges to display a shortcut menu and Mini toolbar (Figure 4–55).

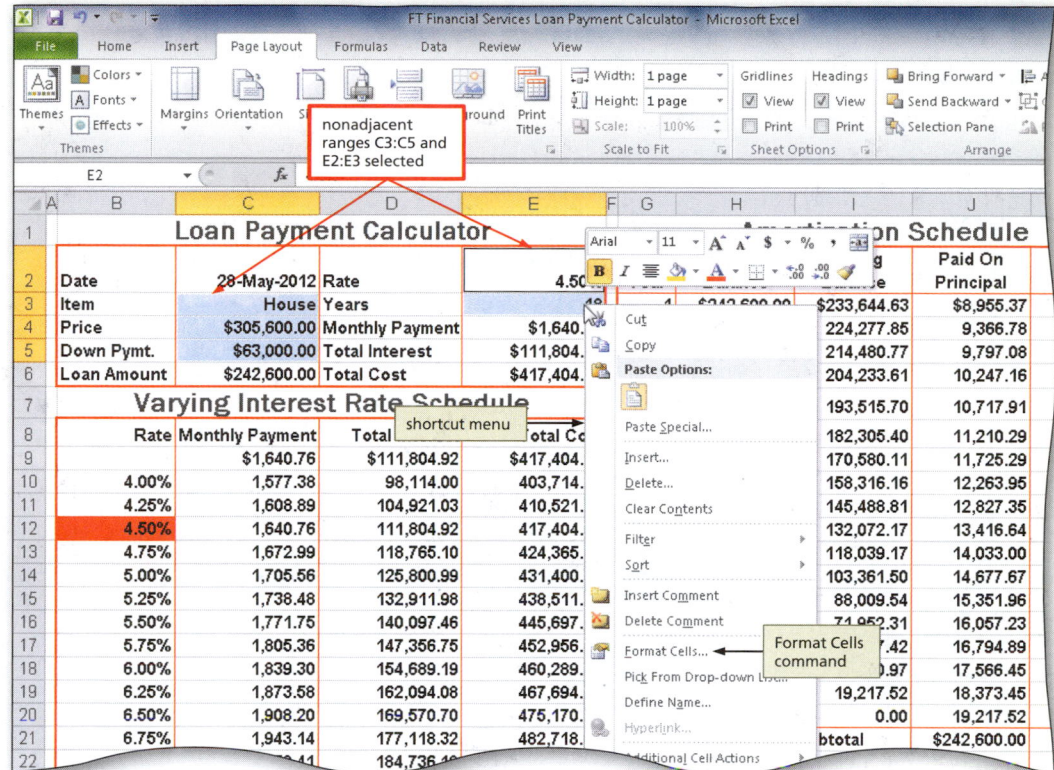

Figure 4–55

2

- Click Format Cells on the shortcut menu to display the Format Cells dialog box.

- Click the Protection tab (Format Cells dialog box) and then click Locked to remove the check mark (Figure 4–56).

Q&A

What is the meaning of the Locked check box?

Excel displays the Protection sheet in the Format Cells dialog box with the check mark removed from the Locked check box (Figure 4–56). This means the selected cells (C3:C5 and E2:E3) will not be protected when the Protect command is invoked later.

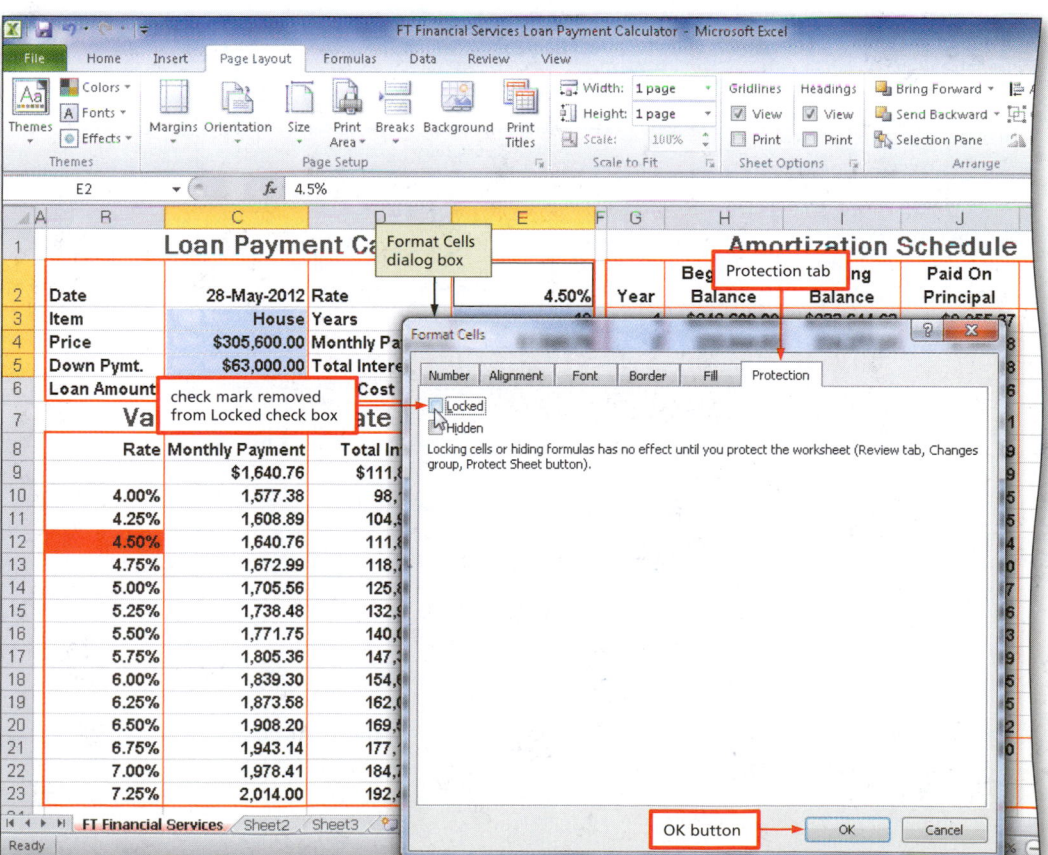

Figure 4–56

3

- Click the OK button to close the Format Cells dialog box.

- Select cell H22 to deselect the ranges, C3:C5 and E2:E3 in this case.

- Display the Review tab (Figure 4–57).

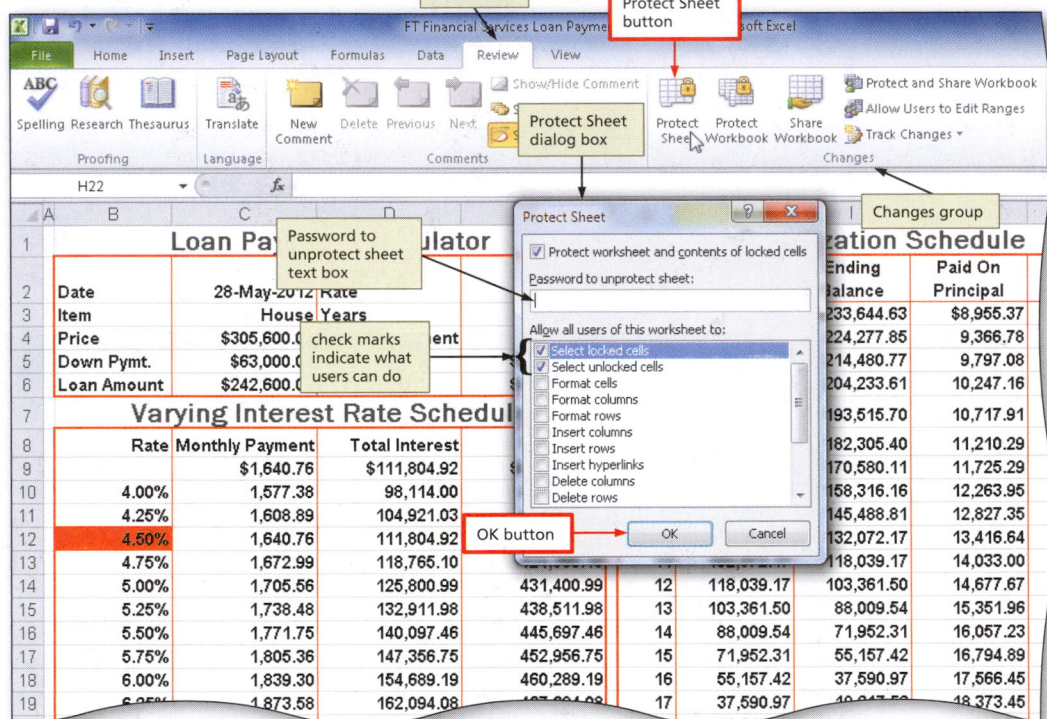

Figure 4–57

4

- Click the Protect Sheet button (Review tab | Changes group) to display the Protect Sheet dialog box.

- When Excel displays the Protect Sheet dialog box, ensure that the 'Protect worksheet and contents of locked cells' check box at the top of the dialog box and the first two check boxes in the list contain check marks so that the user of the worksheet can select both locked and unlocked cells (Figure 4–58).

Q&A

What do the three checked check boxes mean?

With all three check boxes selected, the worksheet (except for the cells left unlocked) is protected from changes to contents. The two check boxes in the list allow the user to select any cell on the worksheet, but the user can change only unlocked cells.

Figure 4–58

5

- Click the OK button (Protect Sheet dialog box) to close the Protect Sheet dialog box.

- Click the Save button on the Quick Access Toolbar to save the workbook.

Other Ways

1. Click Format Cells Dialog Box Launcher (Home tab | Font, Alignment, or Number group), click

Protection tab, remove check mark from Locked check box, click OK button

More about Worksheet Protection

All the cells in the worksheet, except for the ranges C3:C5 and E2:E3, are protected, The Protect Sheet dialog box in Figure 4–58 enables you to enter a password that can be used to unprotect the sheet. You should create a **password** when you want to keep others from changing the worksheet from protected to unprotected. The check boxes in the list in the Protect Sheet dialog box also give you the option to modify the protection so that the user can make certain changes, such as formatting cells or inserting hyperlinks.

If you want to protect more than one sheet in a workbook, select each sheet before you begin the protection process or click the Protect Workbook button (Review tab | Changes group), instead of clicking the Protect Sheet button (Review tab | Changes group) (Figure 4–57). If you want to unlock cells for specific users, you can use the Allow Users to Edit Ranges button (Review tab | Changes group).

When this workbook is made available to users, they will be able to enter data in only the unprotected cells. If they try to change any protected cell, such as the monthly payment in cell E4, Excel displays a dialog box with an error message, as shown in Figure 4–59. An alternative to displaying this dialog box is to remove the check mark from the 'Select unlocked cells' check box in the Protect Sheet dialog box (Figure 4–58). With the check mark removed, the users cannot select a locked cell.

BTW

Using Protected Worksheets
You can move from one unprotected cell to another unprotected cell in a worksheet by using the TAB and SHIFT+TAB keys. This is especially useful when the cells are not adjacent to one another.

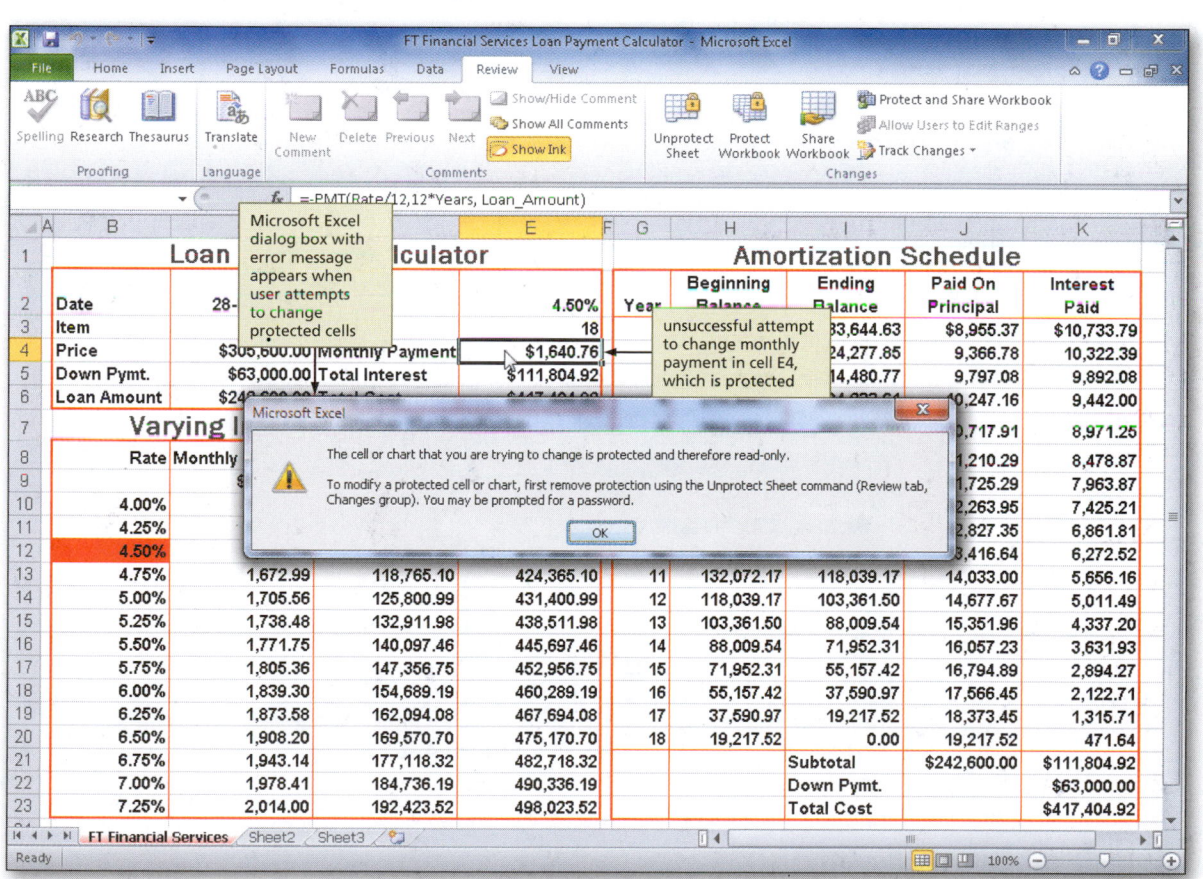

Figure 4–59

To unprotect the worksheet so that you can change all cells in the worksheet, unprotect the document by clicking the Unprotect Sheet button (Review tab | Changes group).

To Hide and Unhide a Sheet

You can hide rows, columns, and sheets that contain sensitive data. When you again need to access hidden rows, columns, and sheets, you can unhide them. You can use the mouse and keyboard to hide and unhide rows and columns by setting their heights and widths to zero. The following steps hide and then unhide a sheet.

1

- Right-click the FT Financial Services sheet tab to display a shortcut menu (Figure 4–60).

Q&A Why is the Unhide command on the shortcut menu dimmed?

Excel dims the Unhide command when no sheets are hidden.

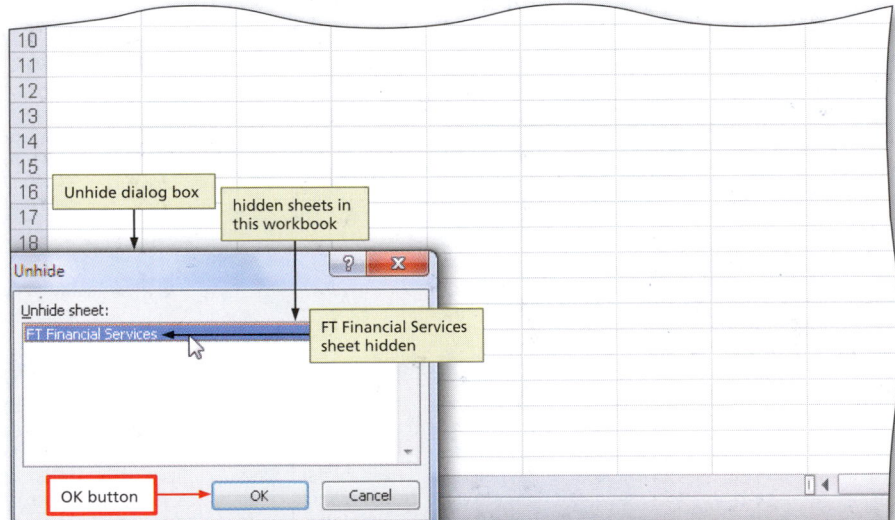

Figure 4–60

2

- Click Hide on the shortcut menu to hide the FT Financial Services sheet.

- Right-click any sheet tab to display a shortcut menu.

- Click Unhide on the shortcut menu to open the Unhide dialog box.

- When Excel displays the Unhide dialog box, if necessary, click FT Financial Services in the Unhide sheet list to select the sheet to unhide (Figure 4–61).

Q&A When should I hide a sheet?

Hiding sheets in a workbook is common when working with complex workbooks that have one sheet with the results the user needs to see and one or more sheets with essential data that, while important to the functionality of the workbook, is unimportant to the user of the workbook and, thus, hidden from view. The data and formulas on the hidden sheets remain available for use on other sheets in the workbook. This same logic applies to hidden rows and columns.

Figure 4–61

3

- Click the OK button (Unhide dialog box) to unhide the hidden sheet.

To Hide and Unhide a Workbook

In addition to hiding worksheets, you also can hide an entire workbook. Some users apply this feature when they leave a workbook open on an unattended computer and do not want others to be able to see the workbook. This feature is also useful when you have several workbooks open simultaneously and want the user to be able to view only one of them. The following steps hide and unhide a workbook.

1
- Display the View tab (Figure 4–62).

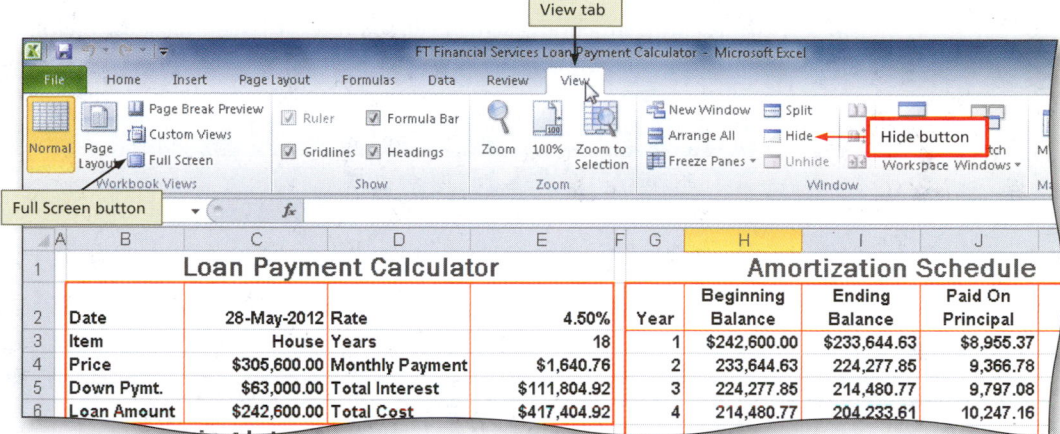

Figure 4–62

2
- Click the Hide button (View tab | Window group) to hide the FT Financial Services Loan Payment Calculator workbook.

- Click the Unhide button (View tab | Window group) to display the Unhide dialog box.

- If necessary, click FT Financial Services Loan Payment Calculator in the Unhide workbook list to select a workbook to unhide (Figure 4–63).

Q&A

What else can I hide?

You can hide most window elements in order to display more rows of worksheet data. These window elements include the Ribbon, formula bar, and status bar. The Excel window elements can be hidden by using the Full Screen button (View tab | Workbook Views group) (Figure 4–62). These elements remain hidden only as long as the workbook is open. They are redisplayed when you close the workbook and open it again.

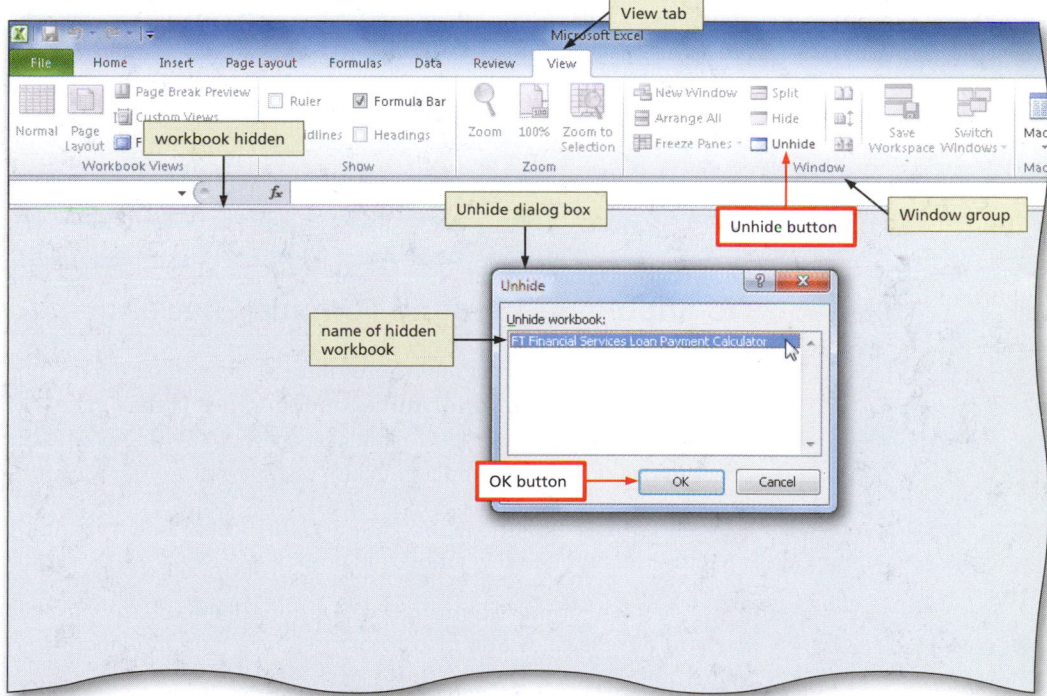

Figure 4–63

3
- Click the OK button (Unhide dialog box) to unhide the selected hidden workbook and display the workbook in the same state as it was in when it was hidden.

Formula Checking

Similar to the spell checker, Excel has a **formula checker** that checks formulas in a worksheet for rule violations. You invoke the formula checker by clicking the Error Checking button (Formulas tab | Formula Auditing group). Each time Excel encounters a cell with a formula that violates one of its rules, it displays a dialog box containing information about the formula and a suggestion about how to fix the formula. Table 4–4 lists Excel's error checking rules. You can choose which rules you want Excel to use by enabling and disabling them in the Formulas area in the Excel Options dialog box shown in Figure 4–64.

Table 4–4 Error Checking Rules		
Rule	**Name of Rule**	**Description**
1	Cells containing formulas that result in an error	The cell contains a formula that does not use the expected syntax, arguments, or data types.
2	Inconsistent calculated column formula in tables	The cell contains formulas or values that are inconsistent with the column formula or tables.
3	Cells containing years represented as 2 digits	The cell contains a text date with a two-digit year that can be misinterpreted as the wrong century.
4	Numbers formatted as text or preceded by an apostrophe	The cell contains numbers stored as text.
5	Formulas inconsistent with other formulas in the region	The cell contains a formula that does not match the pattern of the formulas around it.
6	Formulas which omit cells in a region	The cell contains a formula that does not include a correct cell or range reference.
7	Unlocked cells containing formulas	The cell with a formula is unlocked in a protected worksheet.
8	Formulas referring to empty cells	The cells referenced in a formula are empty.
9	Data entered in a table is invalid	The cell has a data validation error.

To Enable Background Formula Checking

Through the Excel Options dialog box, you can enable background formula checking. **Background formula checking** means that Excel continually will review the workbook for errors in formulas as you create or manipulate it. The following steps enable background formula checking.

1 Click the File on the Ribbon to open the Backstage view and then click the Options button to display the Excel Options dialog box.

2 Click the Formulas button (Excel Options dialog box) to display the Excel options related to formula calculation, performance, and error handling.

3 If necessary, click 'Enable background error checking' in the Error Checking area to select it.

4 Click any check box in the 'Error checking rules' area that does not contain a check mark to enable all error checking rules (Figure 4–64).

5 Click the OK button (Excel Options dialog box) to close the Excel Options dialog box.

Q&A How can I decide which rules to have the background formula checker check?

You can decide which rules you want the background formula checker to highlight by adding and removing check marks from the check boxes in the 'Error checking rules' area (Figure 4–64). If you add or remove check marks, then you should click the Reset Ignored Errors button to reset error checking.

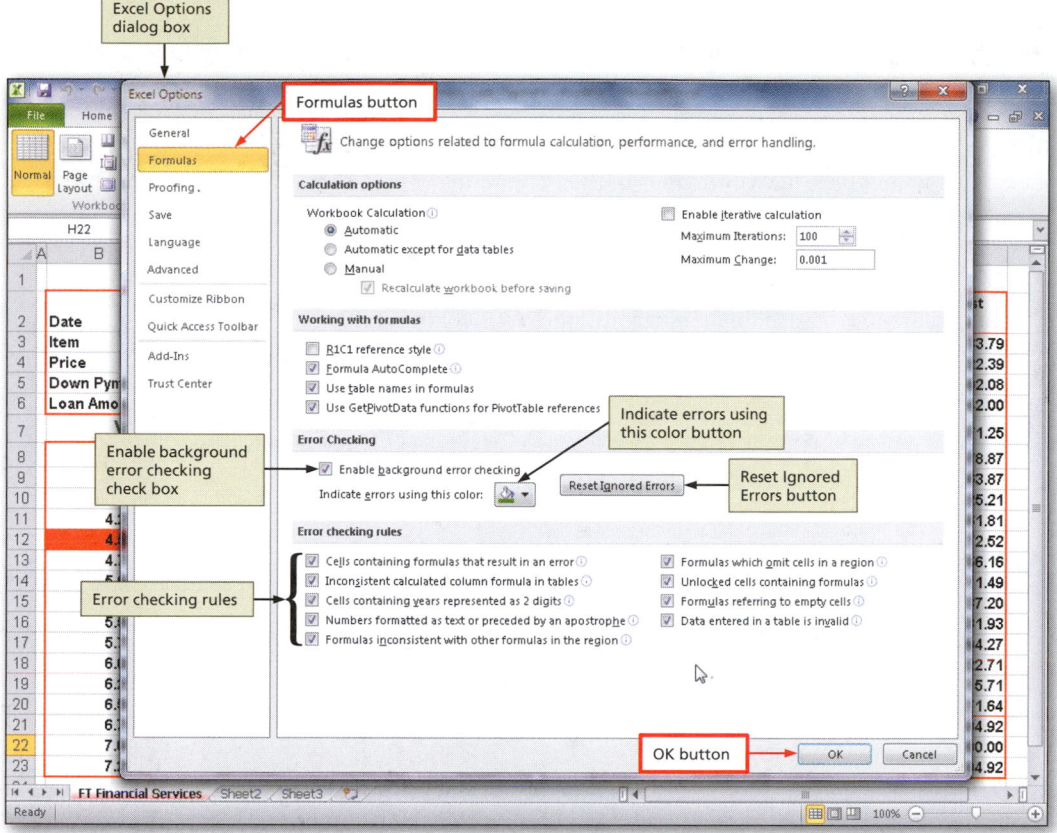

Figure 4–64

More about Background Formula Checking

When a formula fails to pass one of the rules and background formula checking is enabled, then Excel displays a small green triangle in the upper-left corner of the cell assigned the formula in question.

Assume, for example, that background formula checking is enabled and that cell E4, which contains the PMT function in the FT Financial Services Loan Payment Calculator workbook, is unlocked. Because rule 7 in Table 4–4 stipulates that a cell containing a formula must be locked, Excel displays a green triangle in the upper-left corner of cell E4.

When you select the cell with the green triangle, a Trace Error button appears next to the cell. If you click the Trace Error button, Excel displays the Trace Error menu (Figure 4–65). The first item in the menu identifies the error (Unprotected Formula). The remainder of the menu lists commands from which you can choose. The first

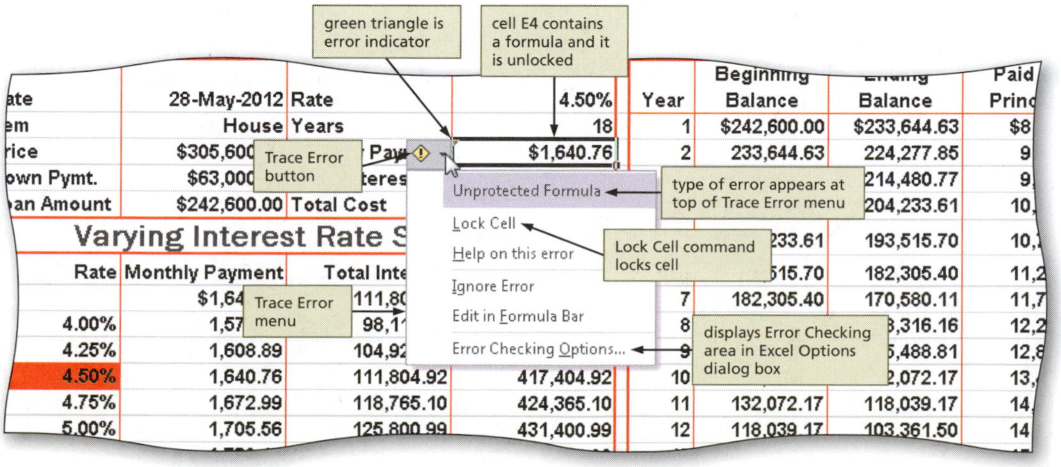

Figure 4–65

Certification
The Microsoft Office Specialist (MOS) program provides an opportunity for you to obtain a valuable industry credential — proof that you have the Excel 2010 skills required by employers. For more information, visit the Excel 2010 Certification Web page (scsite.com/ex2010/cert).

Quick Reference
For a table that lists how to complete the tasks covered in this book using the mouse, Ribbon, shortcut menu, and keyboard, see the Quick Reference Summary at the back of this book, or visit the Excel 2010 Quick Reference Web page (scsite.com/ex2010/qr).

command locks the cell. Invoking the Lock Cell command fixes the problem so that the formula no longer violates the rule. The Error Checking Options command instructs Excel to display the Excel Options dialog box with the Formulas area active, as shown in Figure 4–65 on the previous page.

The background formula checker can become annoying when you are creating certain types of worksheets that may violate the formula rules until referenced cells contain data. You often may end up with green triangles in cells throughout your worksheet. If this is the case, then disable background formula checking by removing the check mark from the 'Enable background error checking' check box (Figure 4–64) and use the Error Checking button (Formulas tab | Formula Auditing group) to check your worksheet once you have finished creating it.

Use the background formula checking or the Error Checking button (Formulas tab | Formula Auditing group) during the testing phase to ensure the formulas in your workbook do not violate the rules listed in Table 4–4 on page EX 278.

To Quit Excel

With the workbook complete, the following steps quit Excel.

1 Click the Close button on the upper-right corner of the title bar.

2 If the Microsoft Excel dialog box is displayed, click the Don't Save button (Microsoft Excel dialog box).

Chapter Summary

In this chapter, you learned how to use names, rather than cell references, to enter formulas, use financial functions, such as the PMT and PV functions, analyze data by creating a data table and amortization schedule, set print options and print sections of a worksheet using names and the Set Print Area command, protect a worksheet or workbook, and hide and unhide rows, columns, sheets, and workbooks. The items listed below include all the new Excel skills you have learned in this chapter.

1. Add Custom Borders to a Range (EX 234)
2. Create Names Based on Row Titles (EX 238)
3. Enter the Loan Amount Formula Using Names (EX 240)
4. Enter the PMT Function (EX 241)
5. Create a Percent Series Using the Fill Handle (EX 247)
6. Define a Range as a Data Table (EX 249)
7. Add a Pointer to the Data Table (EX 252)
8. Enter the Formulas in the Amortization Schedule (EX 257)
9. Copy the Formulas to Fill the Amortization Schedule (EX 260)
10. Set Up a Worksheet to Print (EX 266)
11. Set the Print Area (EX 268)
12. Name and Print Sections of a Worksheet (EX 269)
13. Protect a Worksheet (EX 272)
14. Hide and Unhide a Sheet (EX 276)
15. Hide and Unhide a Workbook (EX 277)
16. Enable Background Formula Checking (EX 278)

Learn It Online

Test your knowledge of chapter content and key terms.

Instructions: To complete the Learn It Online exercises, start your browser, click the Address bar, and then enter the Web address `scsite.com/ex2010/learn`. When the Excel 2010 Learn It Online page is displayed, click the link for the exercise you want to complete and then read the instructions.

Chapter Reinforcement TF, MC, and SA
A series of true/false, multiple choice, and short answer questions that test your knowledge of the chapter content.

Flash Cards
An interactive learning environment where you identify chapter key terms associated with displayed definitions.

Practice Test
A series of multiple choice questions that test your knowledge of chapter content and key terms.

Who Wants To Be a Computer Genius?
An interactive game that challenges your knowledge of chapter content in the style of a television quiz show.

Wheel of Terms
An interactive game that challenges your knowledge of chapter key terms in the style of the television show *Wheel of Fortune*.

Crossword Puzzle Challenge
A crossword puzzle that challenges your knowledge of key terms presented in the chapter.

Apply Your Knowledge

Reinforce the skills and apply the concepts you learned in this chapter.

Loan Payment Calculator
Purpose: In this exercise, you will name cells, determine the monthly payment on a loan, create a data table, and protect a worksheet.

Instructions: Start Excel. Open the workbook Apply 4-1 Loan Payment Calculator from the Data Files for Students. See the inside back cover of this book for instructions for downloading the Data Files for Students or see your instructor for information on accessing the files required in this book.

Perform the following tasks:
1. Select the range B4:C9. Use the Create from Selection button (Formulas tab | Defined Names group) to create names for cells in the range C4:C9 using the row titles in the range B4:B9.
2. Enter the formulas shown in Table 4–5.

Table 4–5 Loan Payment Calculator and Interest Rate Schedule Formulas	
Cell	**Formula**
C8	= -PMT(Interest_Rate/12, 12 * Years, Loan_Amount)
C9	=Price – Down_Payment
F4	=C8
G4	=H4-C4
H4	=12 * C6 * C8 + C4

Continued >

Apply Your Knowledge *continued*

3. Change the document properties as specified by your instructor. Change the worksheet header with your name, course number, and other information as specified by your instructor. Save the workbook using the file name, Apply 4-1 Loan Payment Calculator Complete.

4. Use the Data Table button in the What-If Analysis gallery (Data tab | Data Tools group) to define the range E4:H19 as a one-input data table. Use cell C7 (interest rate) as the column input cell. Format the data table so that it appears as shown in Figure 4–66.

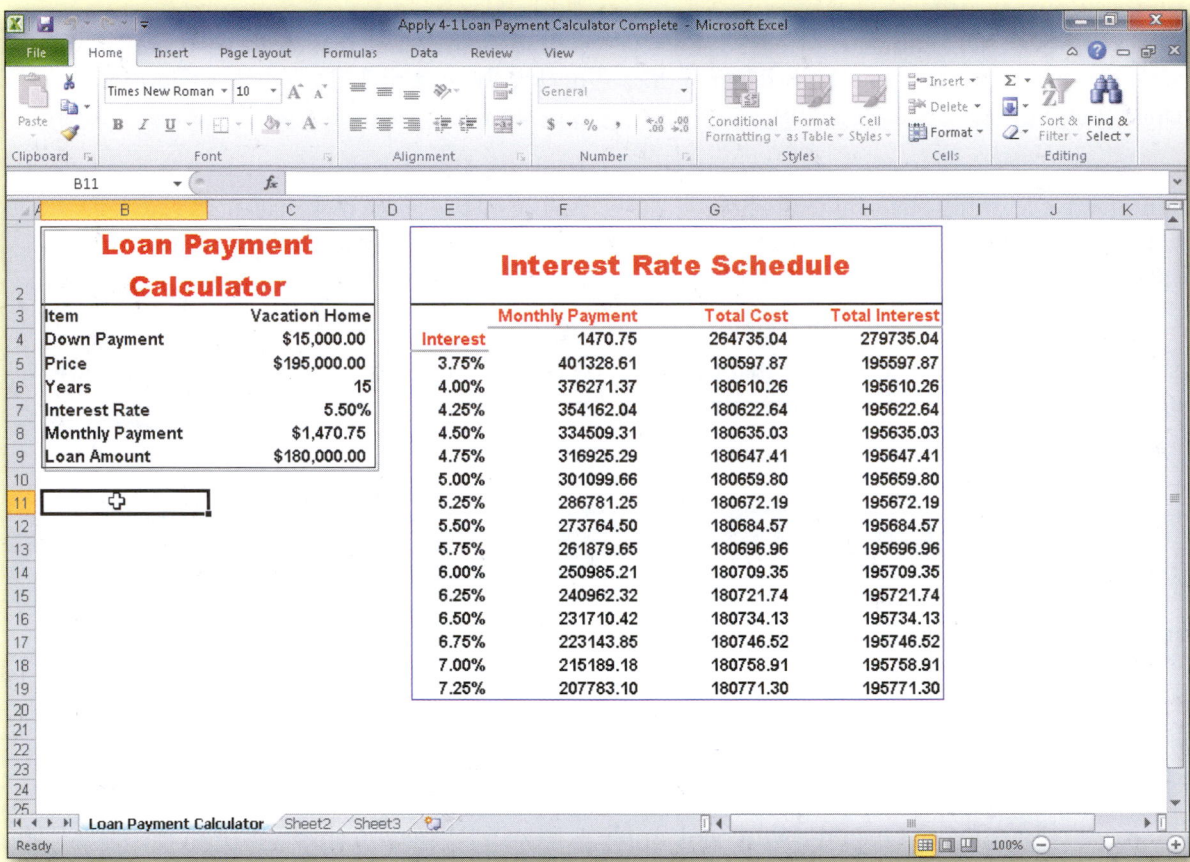

Figure 4–66

5. Use the Page Setup dialog box to select the Fit to and Black and white options. Select the range B2:C9 and then use the Set Print Area command to set a print area. Use the Print button in the Print gallery in the Backstage view to print the worksheet. Use the Clear Print Area command to clear the print area. Name the following ranges: B2:C9 – Calculator; E2:H19 – Rate_Schedule; and B2:H19 – All_Sections. Print each range by selecting the name in the Name box and using the Print Selection option on the Print tab in the Backstage view.

6. Unlock the range C3:C7. Protect the worksheet so that the user can select only unlocked cells.

7. Press CTRL+` and print the formulas version in landscape orientation. Press CTRL+` to display the values version.

8. Hide and then unhide the Loan Payment Calculator sheet. Hide and then unhide the workbook. Unprotect the worksheet and then hide columns E through H. Print the worksheet. Select columns D and I and unhide the hidden columns. Hide rows 11 through 19. Print the worksheet. Select rows 10 and 20 and unhide rows 11 through 19. Protect the worksheet.

9. Save the changes you have made to the workbook.

10. Determine the monthly payment and print the worksheet for each data set: (a) Item = Race Horse; Down Payment = $12,000.00; Price = $59,500.00; Years = 13; Interest Rate = 6.25%; (b) Item = Hybrid Car; Down Payment = $3,000.00; Price = $35,000.00; Years = 6; Interest Rate = 7.25%. You should get the following monthly payment results: (a) $445.50; (b) $549.42.

11. Submit the assignment as specified by your instructor.

Extend Your Knowledge

Extend the skills you learned in this chapter and experiment with new skills. You may need to use Help to complete the assignment.

Two-Input Data Table

Purpose: In this exercise you will use data from a 529C education savings account planning sheet (Figure 4–67a on the following page) to create a two-input data table (Figure 4–67b on the following page).

Instructions: Start Excel. Open the workbook Extend 4-1 529C Planning Sheet from the Data Files for Students. See the inside back cover of this book for instructions for downloading the Data Files for Students or see your instructor for information on accessing the files required in this book.

Perform the following tasks:

1. Enter the data table title and subtitle as shown in cells I1 and I3 in Figure 4–67b.

2. Change the document properties as specified by your instructor. Change the worksheet header with your name, course number, and other information as specified by your instructor. Save the workbook using the file name, Extend 4-1 529C Planning Sheet Complete.

3. Change the width of column H to 0.50 characters. Merge and center the titles over columns I through S. Format the titles as shown using the Title cell style for both the title and subtitle, a font size of 20 for the title, and a font size of 16 for the subtitle. Change the column widths of columns I through S to 11.71 characters.

4. For a two-input data table, the formula you are analyzing must be assigned to the upper-left cell in the range of the data table. Cell C14 contains the future value formula to be analyzed, therefore, enter `=C14` in cell I4.

5. Use the fill handle to create two lists of percents: (a) 2.00% through 6.50% in increments of 0.25% in the range I5:I23; and (b) 2.00% through 11.00% in increments of 1.00% in the range J4:S4.

6. Select the range I4:S23. Click the What-If Analysis button (Data tab | Data Tools group). Click the Data Table command on the What-If Analysis menu. When Excel displays the Data Table dialog box, enter C8 (expected annual return) in the Row input cell box and C5 (employee percent invested) in the Column input cell box. Click the OK button to populate the table.

7. Format the two-input data table as shown in Figure 4–67b.

8. Use conditional formatting to change the format of the cell in the two-input data table that is equal to the future value in cell C14 to blue underlined font on a Purple, Accent 4, Lighter 80% background.

9. Protect the worksheet so that the user can select only unlocked cells (C3:C6 and C8:C9).

10. Change the print orientation to landscape. Print the worksheet using the Fit to option. Print the formulas version of the worksheet.

Continued >

Extend Your Knowledge *continued*

11. Save your changes to the workbook.

12. Submit the assignment as requested by your instructor.

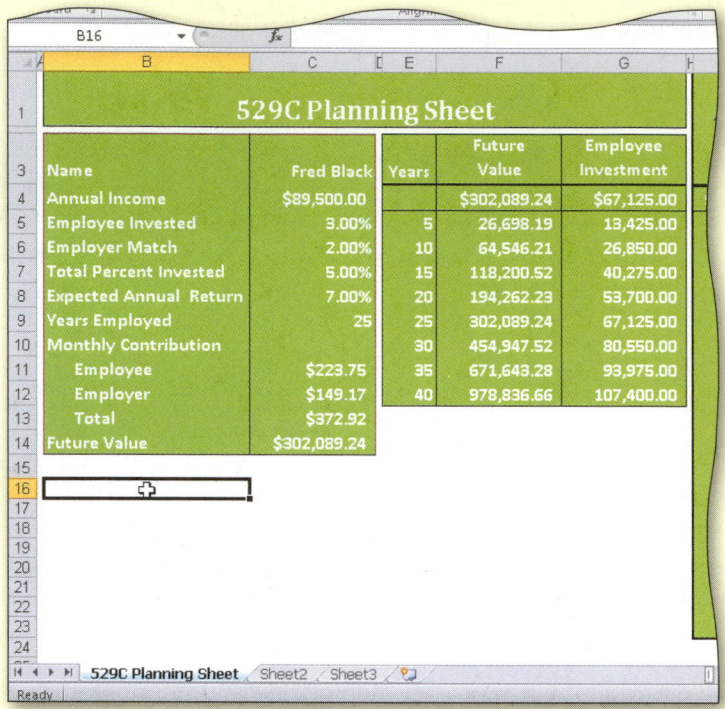

Figure 4–67 (a)

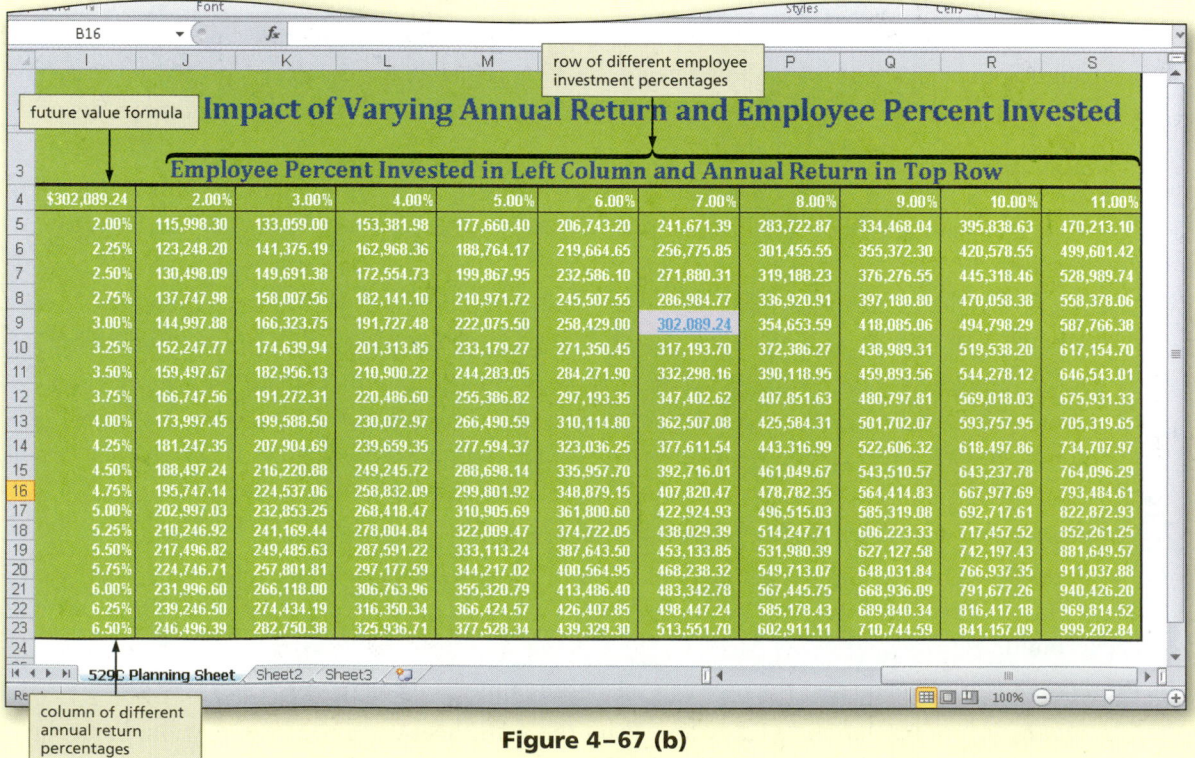

Figure 4–67 (b)

Make It Right

Analyze a workbook and correct all errors and/or improve the design.

Functions, Custom Borders, Cell Names, What-If Analysis, and Protection

Purpose: In this exercise, you will correct design and formula problems, complete what-if analysis, name cells, and protect the worksheet.

Instructions: Start Excel. Open the workbook Make It Right 4-1 Financial Calculator. See the inside back cover of this book for instructions for downloading the Data Files for Students, or see your instructor for information on accessing the files required for this book.

Perform the following tasks:

1. The worksheet is protected with no unprotected cells. Unprotect the worksheet so that the worksheet can be edited by clicking Unprotect Sheet (Review tab | Changes group).

2. Change the thick box border surrounding the range B2:C9 to a Dark Blue, Text 2 thick box border. Change the thick border separating columns B and C in the range B2:C9 to a Dark Blue, Text 2 light border.

3. Correct the Monthly Payment formula in cell C7 and the Total Interest formula in cell C8. The monthly payment should equal $2,050.00 and the total interest should equal $437,491.16. Use Goal Seek to change the down payment in cell C3 so that the monthly payment is $2,050.00, as shown in Figure 4–68.

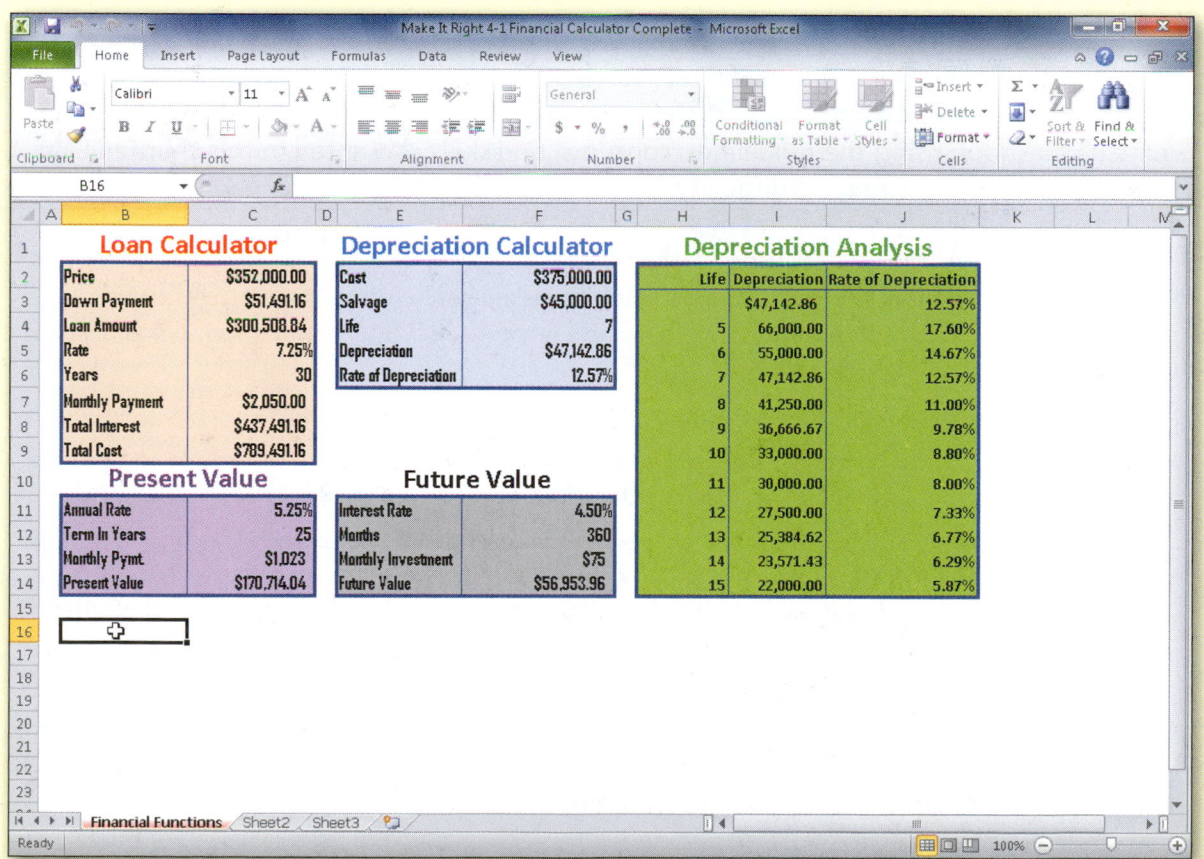

Figure 4–68

Continued >

Make It Right *continued*

4. Assign the name Loan_Calculator to the range B1:C9.

5. Assign the names in column E to the adjacent cells in column F for both the Depreciation Calculator and the Future Value. Edit the formulas in cells F5 and F6 and change the cell references to their corresponding names.

6. Correct the second argument in the Future Value function in cell F14 so that the number of months is not multiplied by 12. Correct the third argument in the Future Value function in cell F14. Display the future value as a positive number.

7. Correct the second and third arguments in the Present Value function in cell C14 so that the present value is displayed correctly as a positive number.

8. Complete the one–input data table in the range H3:J14 that determines the depreciation and rate of depreciation for varying years of life (cell F4). Format the numbers in the data table so that they appear as shown in Figure 4–68 on the previous page.

9. Change the document properties as specified by your instructor. Change the worksheet header so that it contains your name, course number, and other information as specified by your instructor.

10. Unlock the cells containing data (C2:C3, C5:C6, F2:F4, C11:C13, and F11:F13). Protect the worksheet so that the user can select only cells with data.

11. Save the workbook using the file name, Make It Right 4-1 Financial Calculator Complete.

12. Submit the revised workbook as requested by your instructor.

In the Lab

Create a workbook using the guidelines, concepts, and skills presented in this chapter. Labs are listed in order of increasing difficulty.

Lab 1: Mortgage Analysis and Amortization Schedule

Problem: The president of WeSavU National Bank has asked you to create a mortgage analysis worksheet including an amortization schedule as shown in Figure 4–69. He also wants you to demonstrate the goal seeking capabilities of Excel.

Instructions:

1. Start Excel. Apply the Foundry theme to a new worksheet. Bold the entire worksheet and change all the columns to a width of 17.00. Change the width of column A to .85.

2. Save the workbook using the file name Lab 4-1 WeSavU National Bank Loan Calculator.

3. Enter the worksheet title, WeSavU National Bank, in cell B1, apply the Title cell style, and change its font size to 28-point. Enter the worksheet subtitle, Subprime Loans for Everyone, in cell B2, and apply the Title cell style. One at a time, merge and center cells B1 and B2 across columns B through F.

4. Enter the row titles for the ranges B3:B5 and E3:E5 as shown in Figure 4–69. Use the Create from Selection button (Formulas tab | Defined Names group) to assign the row titles in the ranges B3:B5 and E3:E5 to the adjacent cells in ranges C3:C5 and F3:F5, respectively.

5. Enter 430000 (price) in cell C3, 110000 (down payment) in cell C4, 7.75% (interest rate) in cell F3, and 25 (years) in cell F4. Determine the loan amount by entering the formula =Price - Down_Payment in cell C5. Determine the monthly payment by entering the PMT function —PMT(Rate / 12, 12 * Years, Loan_Amount) in cell F5.

6. Create the amortization schedule in the range B6:F36 by assigning the first five formulas and functions in Table 4–6 to the cells indicated. Center the column headings. The years in column B starting at cell B7 should extend from 1 to 25 years centered. Use the fill handle to copy columns C, D, E and F of the amortization schedule down to the 25th year.

7. Enter the total titles in the range C32:E34 as shown in Figure 4–69. Enter the last four formulas in Table 4–6 on the following page.

8. Format the numbers in the amortization schedule as shown in Figure 4–69.

9. Change the colors and draw the borders as shown in Figure 4–69. Change the sheet tab name and color as shown in Figure 4–69.

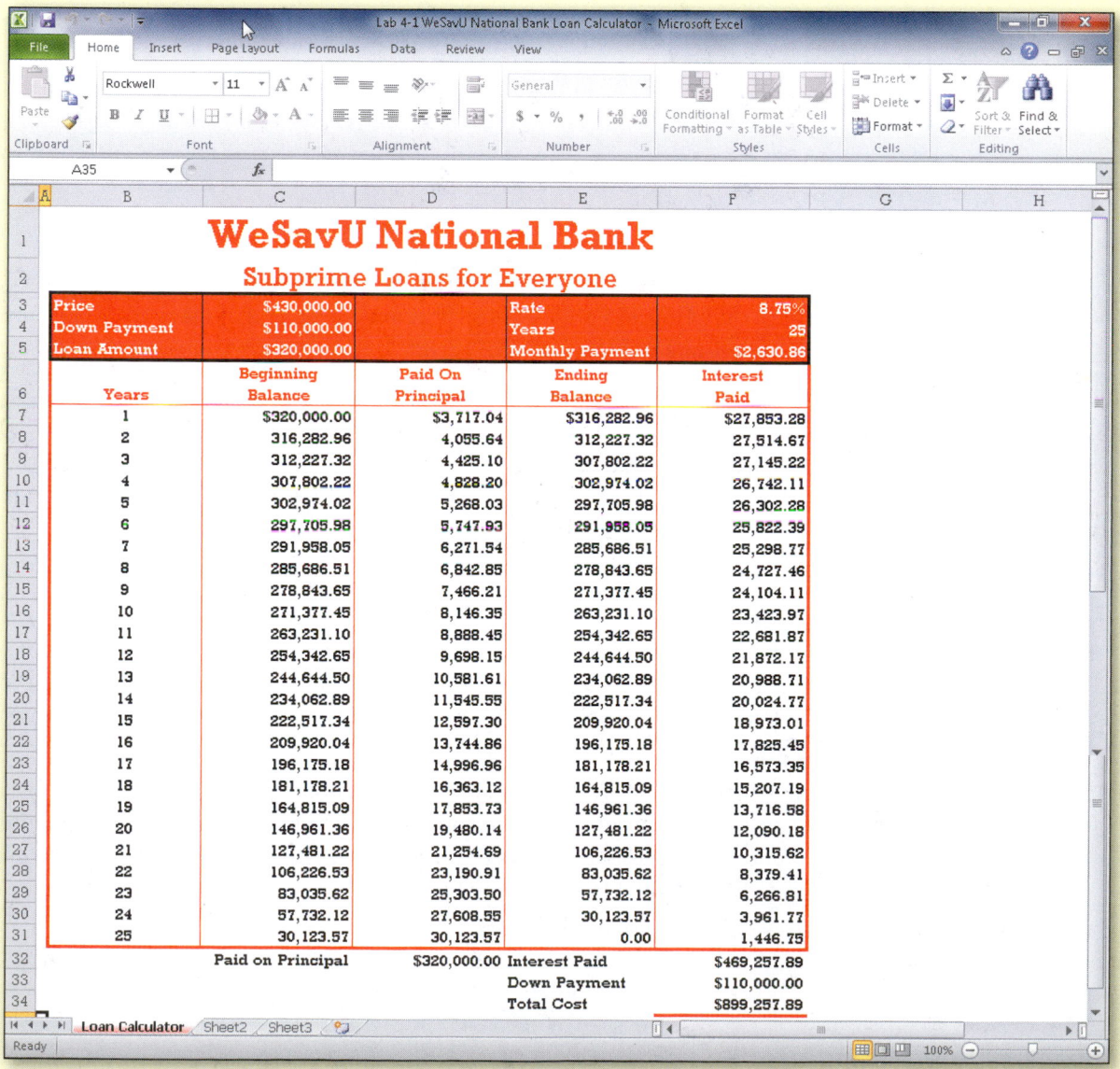

Figure 4–69

Continued >

In the Lab *continued*

10. Change the document properties as specified by your instructor. Change the worksheet header so that it contains your name, course number, and other information as specified by your instructor.

11. Spell check and formula check the worksheet. Use Range Finder (double–click cell) to check all formulas listed in Table 4–6.

Table 4–6 Cell Assignments	
Cell	**Formula or Function**
C7	=C5
D7	=C7–E7
E7	=IF(B7<= $F$4, PV($F$3/12, 12*($F$4–B7), –$F$5),0)
F7	=IF(C7>0, 12*$F$5–D7, 0)
C8	=E7
D32	=SUM(D7:D31)
F32	=SUM(F7:F31)
F33	=C4
F34	=D32+F32+F33

12. Use the Page Setup dialog box to select the Fit to and 'Black and white' options.

13. Unlock the cells in the ranges C3:C4 and F3:F4. Protect the worksheet so that users can select any cell in the worksheet, but can change only the unlocked cells.

14. Remove gridlines by clicking View (Page Layout tab | Sheet Options group).

15. WeSavU determined that a credit agency reduced the customer's credit score. WeSavU has decided, therefore, to raise the interest rate by 1% for the customer. Change the interest rate in F4 to 8.75%. The Monthly Payment should change to $2,630.86, and the Interest Paid should change to $469, 257.89.

16. Save your changes to the workbook.

17. Print the worksheet on one page. Print the formulas version of the worksheet.

18. Use Excel's goal seeking capabilities to determine the down payment required for the loan data if the monthly payment is set to $1,000.00. The down payment that results for a monthly payment of $1,000.00 is $308,336.75. Print the worksheet with the new monthly payment of $1,000.00. Close the workbook without saving changes.

19. Hide and then unhide the Loan Payment Calculator sheet. Hide and then unhide the workbook. Unprotect the worksheet and then hide columns D through F. Print the worksheet. Select columns C and G and unhide the hidden columns. Hide rows 6 through 34. Print the worksheet. Select rows 5 and 35 and unhide rows 6 through 39. Do not save the workbook.

20. Submit the assignment as requested by your instructor.

In the Lab

Lab 2: Analyzing Retirement Savings

Problem: You have been asked by the Employee Relations and Resource department to develop a retirement planning worksheet that will allow each current and prospective employee to see the effect (dollar accumulation) of investing a percent of his or her monthly salary over a period of years (Figure 4–70). The plan calls for the company to match an employee's investment, dollar for dollar, up to 2.50%. Thus, if an employee invests 5.00% of his or her annual salary, then the company matches the first 2.50%. If an employee invests only 1.75% of his or her annual salary, then the company matches the entire 1.75%. The Employee Relations and Resource department wants a one-input data table to show the future value of the investment for different years.

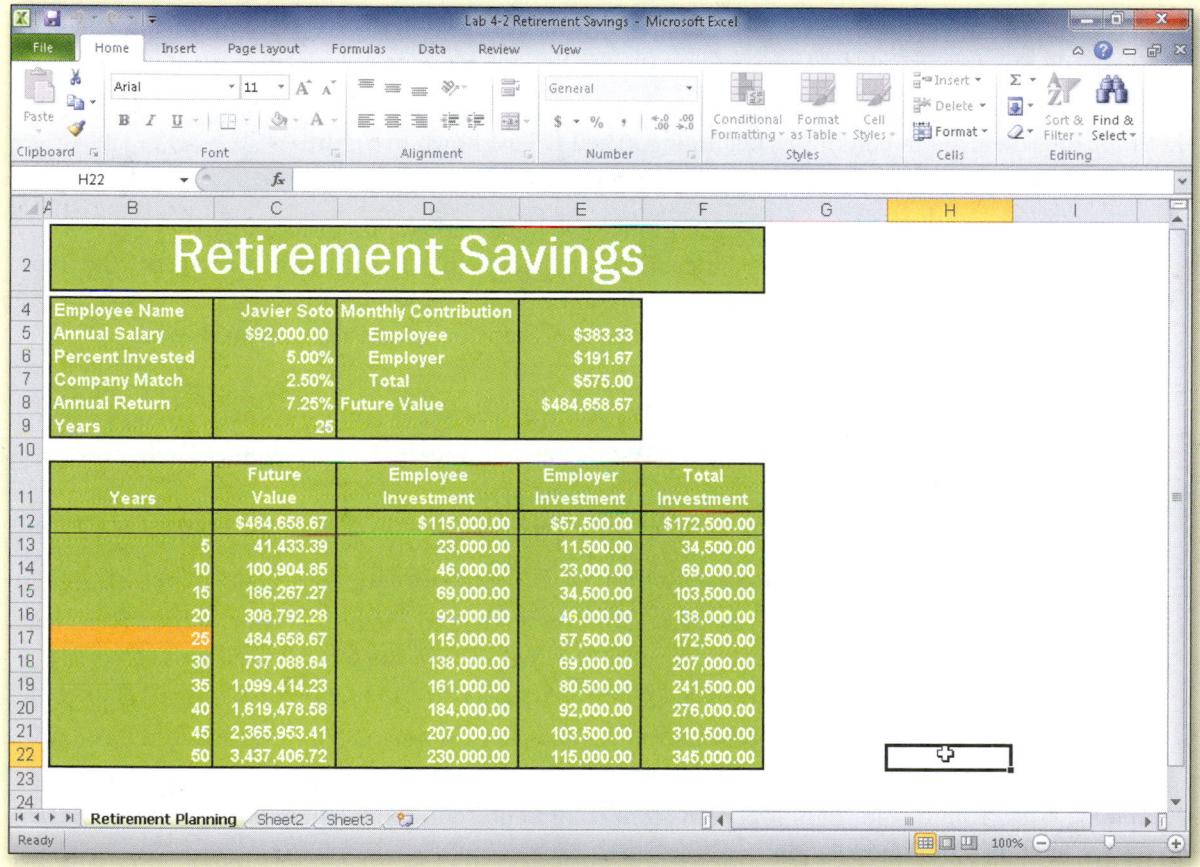

Figure 4–70

Instructions:

1. Start Excel. Apply the Technic theme to the worksheet and change the font of the entire worksheet to bold. Change the column widths to the following: A and D = 0.54; B = 17.00; C and F = 12.75. Change the heights of rows 1 and 3 to 4.50.

2. In cell B2, enter Retirement Savings as the worksheet title. Merge and center cell B2 across columns B through F. Apply the Title cell style to cell B2, and change the font size to 36 point. Change the background color of B2 to light green and change its font color to white. Draw a medium black border around cell B2.

Continued >

In the Lab *continued*

Table 4–7 Retirement Savings Employee Data	
Row Title	**Data**
Employee Name	Javier Soto
Annual Salary	$92,000.00
Percent Invested	5.00%
Company Match	2.50%
Annual Return	7.25%
Years	25

3. Enter the row titles in column B, beginning in cell B4 as shown in Figure 4–70 on the previous page. Add the data in Table 4–7 to column C. Use the dollar and percent signs format symbols to format the numbers in the range C5:C8.

4. Enter the row titles in column D, beginning in cell D4 as shown in Figure 4–70.

5. Save the workbook using the file name Lab 4-2 Retirement Savings.

6. Use the Create from Selection button (Formulas tab | Defined Names group) to assign the row titles in column B (range B4:B9) as cell names for the adjacent cells in column C and the row titles in column D (D5:D8) as cell names for the adjacent cells in column E5:E8. Use these newly created names to assign formulas to cells in the range E5:E8. Step 6e formats the displayed results of the formulas.

   a. Employee Monthly Contribution (cell E5) = Annual_Salary * Percent_Invested / 12

   b. Employer Monthly Contribution (cell E6) = IF(Percent_Invested < Company_Match, Percent_Invested * Annual_Salary / 12, Company_Match * Annual_Salary / 12)

   c. Total Monthly Contribution (cell E7) = SUM(E5:E6)

   d. Future Value (cell E8) = –FV(Annual_Return/12, 12 * Years, Total)

   The Future Value function (FV) in Step 6d returns to the cell the future value of the investment. The future value of an investment is its value at some point in the future based on a series of payments of equal amounts made over a number of periods earning a constant rate of return.

   e. If necessary, use the Format Painter button (Home tab | Clipboard group) to assign the Currency style format in cell C5 to the range E5:E8.

7. Add the background color light green, the font color white, and the medium borders to the range B4:E9, as shown in Figure 4–70.

8. Use the concepts and techniques developed in this chapter to add the data table in Figure 4–70 to the range B11:F22 as follows.

   a. Enter and format the table column titles in row 11.

   b. Use the fill handle to create the series of years beginning with 5 and ending with 50 in increments of 5 in column B, beginning in cell B13.

   c. In cell C12, enter `=E8` as the formula. In cell D12, enter `=12 * E5 * C9` as the formula (recall that using cell references in the formulas means Excel will copy the formats). In E12, enter `=12 * E6 * C9` as the formula. In F12, enter `=12 * E7 * C9` as the formula.

d. Use the Data Table command on the What-If Analysis gallery (Data tab | Data tools group) to define the range B12:F22 as a one-input data table. Use cell C9 as the column input cell.

e. Format the numbers in the range C13:F22 using the Comma style format. Underline rows 11 and 12 as shown in Figure 4–70 on page EX 289. Change the background color of the data table to light green and change its font color to white. Add borders to the range B11:F22, as shown in Figure 4–70.

9. Use the Conditional Formatting button (Home tab | Styles group) to add an orange pointer that shows the row that equates to the years in cell C9 to the Years column in the data table. Change the sheet tab name and color to light green as shown in Figure 4–70.

10. Remove gridlines by clicking View (Page Layout tab | Sheet Options group).

11. Change the document properties as specified by your instructor. Change the worksheet header with your name, course number, and other information as specified by your instructor.

12. Spell check and formula check the worksheet. Use Range Finder (double-click cell) to check all formulas.

13. Print the worksheet in landscape orientation. Print the formulas version of the worksheet.

14. Unlock the cells in the range C4:C9. Protect the worksheet. Allow users to select only unlocked cells.

15. Save your changes to the workbook.

16. Hide and then unhide the Retirement Planning Sheet worksheet. Hide and then unhide the workbook. Unprotect the worksheet and then hide rows 11 through 22. Print the worksheet. Select rows 10 and 23 and unhide the hidden rows. Hide rows 1 and 2. Print the worksheet. Click the Select All button and unhide rows 1 and 2.

17. Close the workbook without saving the changes.

18. Open the workbook Lab 4-2 Retirement Savings. Determine the future value for the data in Table 4–8. Print the worksheet for each data set. The following Future Value results should be displayed in cell E8: Data Set 1 = $395,756.16; Data Set 2 = $693,470.35; and Data Set 3 = $1,069,822.41. Quit Excel without saving the workbook.

Table 4–8 Future Value What-If Analysis Data			
	Data Set 1	**Data Set 2**	**Data Set 3**
Employee Name	John Roe	Dante Dacy	Janek Madhu
Annual Salary	$119,500.00	$65,000.00	$39,000.00
Percent Invested	2.50%	5.00%	6.00%
Company Match	2.50%	3.00%	2.00%
Annual Return	4.75%	6.50%	7.25%
Years	30	35	45

19. Submit the assignment as requested by your instructor.

In the Lab

Lab 3: Annual Income Statement and Break-Even Analysis

Problem: You are a summer intern at Telemobile, a company that sells the popular jPhone. Your area of expertise is cost-volume-profit or CVP (also called break-even analysis), which investigates the relationship among a product's expenses (cost), its volume (units sold), and the operating income (gross profit). Any money a company earns above the break-even point is called operating income, or gross profit (row 22 in the Break-Even Analysis table in Figure 4–71). You have been asked to prepare an annual income statement and a data table that shows revenue, expenses, and income for units sold between 140,000 and 220,000 in increments of 5,000.

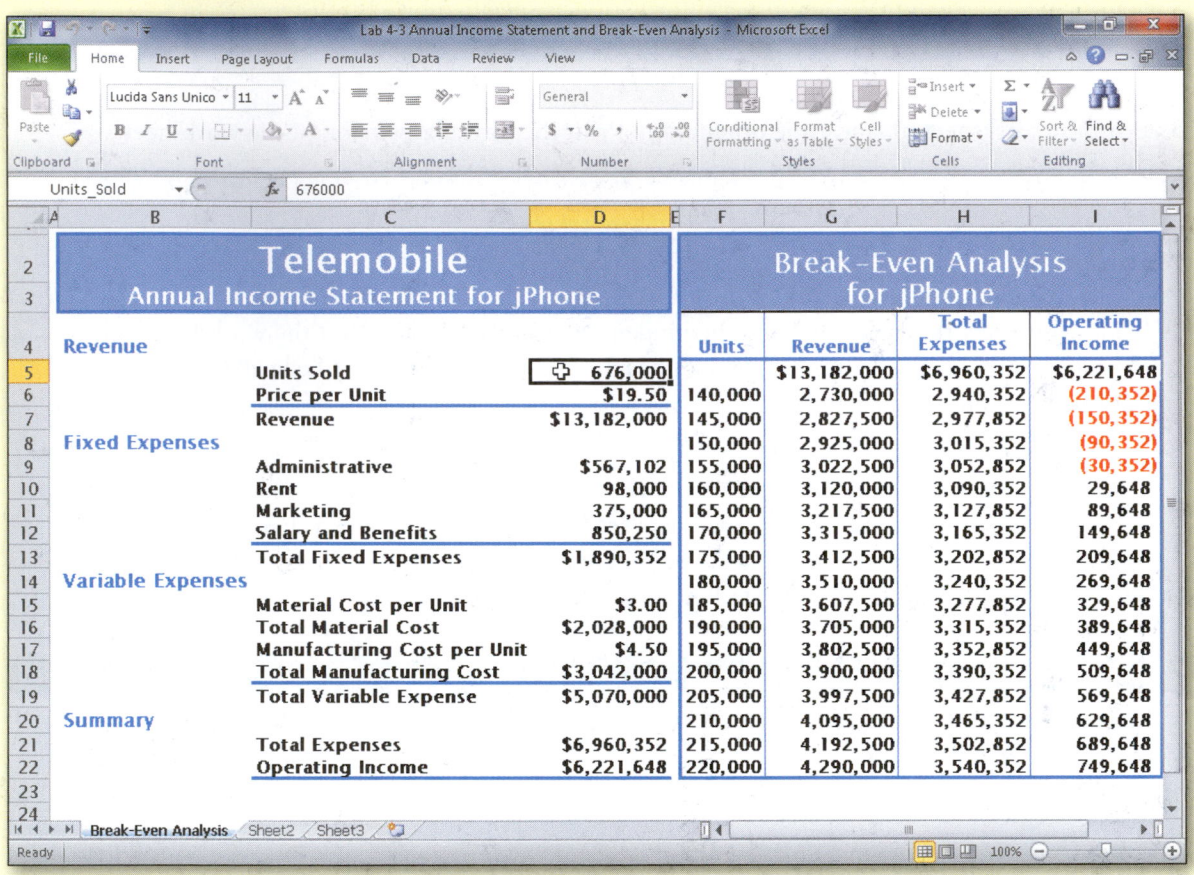

Figure 4–71

Instructions:

1. Start Excel. Apply the Concourse theme to the worksheet. Change the font of the entire worksheet to bold. Change the column widths to the following: A = 0.50; B = 18.00; C = 26.00; D = 12.78; E= 0.50; F = 7.44; and G through I = 12.00. Change the heights of rows 1 to 4.50; 2 to 30.75; and 3 to 19.50, respectively. Name the sheet tab Break–Even Analysis and color the tab blue.

2. Enter the worksheet titles: Telemobile in cell B2 and Annual Income Statement for jPhone in cell B3. Apply the Title cell style to both cells. Change the font sizes in cells B2 and B3 to 24 and 16, respectively. One at a time, merge and center cells B2 and B3 across columns B through D. Change the background color of cells B2 and B3 to Blue, Accent 4, Lighter 40%. Change the font color to white. Add a thick blue border to the range B2:B3.

3. Save the workbook using the file name, Lab 4-3 Annual Income Statement and Break-Even Analysis.

4. Enter the row titles in columns B and C as shown in Figure 4–71. Change the font size of the row titles in column B to 12–point and change the font color to blue. Add the data shown in Table 4–9 in column D. Format the numbers in column D as shown in Figure 4–71.

Table 4–9 Annual Income Statement Data		
Title	**Column D Cell**	**Column D Data**
Units Sold	D5	676000
Price per Unit	D6	19.50
Administrative	D9	567102
Rent	D10	98000
Marketing	D11	375000
Salary and Benefits	D12	850250
Material Cost per Unit	D15	3.00
Manufacturing Cost per Unit	D17	4.50

5. Assign the row titles in column C in the range C5:C22 to the adjacent cells in column D. Use these names to enter the following formulas in column C:

   a. Revenue (cell D7) = Units Sold * Price per Unit (or =D5 * D6)

   b. Fixed Expenses (cell D13) = SUM(D9:D12)

   c. Material Cost (cell D16) = Units Sold * Material Cost per Unit (or =D5 * D15)

   d. Total Manufacturing Cost (cell D18) = Units Sold * Manufacturing Cost per Unit (or =D5 * D17)

   e. Total Variable Expenses (cell D19) = Total Material Cost + Total Manufacturing Cost (or =D16 + D18)

   f. Total Expenses (cell D21) = Total Fixed Expenses + Total Variable Expense (or =D13 + D19)

   g. Operating Income (cell D22) = Revenue – Total Expenses (or =D7 – D21)

6. Assign the Currency style format in cell D9 to the unformatted dollar amounts in column D.

7. Add a thick blue bottom border to the ranges C6:D6, C12:D12, C18:D18, and C22:D22, as shown in Figure 4–71.

8. Use the concepts and techniques presented in this chapter to add the data table to the range F2:I22 as follows:

   a. Add the data table titles and format them as shown in Figure 4–71.

   b. Create the series in column F from 140,000 to 220,000 in increments of 5,000, beginning in cell F6.

   c. Enter the formula =D7 in cell G5. Enter the formula =D21 in cell H5. Enter the formula =D22 in cell I5. If necessary, adjust the column widths.

   d. Define the range F5:I22 as a one-input data table. Use cell C4 (Units Sold) as the column input cell.

   e. Format the range F6:I22 to the Comma style format with no decimal places and negative numbers in red with parentheses. Add a medium outline border and light vertical borders to the range F2:I22.

9. Remove gridlines by clicking View (Page Layout tab | Sheet Options group).

10. Change the document properties as specified by your instructor. Change the worksheet header so that it contains your name, course number, and other information as specified by your instructor.

11. Spell check and formula check the worksheet. Use Range Finder to check all formulas.

Continued >

In the Lab *continued*

12. Select Landscape, the Fit to, and 'Black and white' printing options. Print the worksheet. Print the formulas version of the worksheet.

13. Unlock the following cells: D5, D6, D15, and D17. Protect the workbook.

14. Save your changes to the workbook.

15. Hide and then unhide the Break-Even Analysis sheet. Hide and then unhide the workbook. Unprotect the worksheet and then hide columns E through I. Print the worksheet. Select columns D and J and unhide the hidden columns. Hide rows 8 through 22. Print the worksheet. Select rows 7 and 23 and unhide rows 8 through 22. Close the workbook without saving the changes.

16. Open the workbook Lab 4-3 Annual Income Statement and Break-Even Analysis. Determine the operating income for the data sets in Table 4–10. Print the worksheet for each data set. You should get the following Income results in cell D22: Data Set 1 = $3,191,648; Data Set 2 = ($265,852); and Data Set 3 = $218,648. Quit Excel without saving the workbook.

Table 4–10 Operating Income Data

Title	Cell	Data Set 1	Data Set 2	Data Set 3
Units Sold	D5	484000	342000	228000
Price per Unit	D6	18.50	12.00	28.00
Material Cost per Unit	D15	5.50	2.75	11.00
Manufacturing Cost per Unit	D17	2.50	4.50	7.75

17. Submit the assignment as requested by your instructor.

Cases and Places

Apply your creative thinking and problem solving skills to design and implement a solution.

1: Future Value of a 529 College Savings Plan

Academic

Jacob and Sophia's dream for their recently born daughter, Emily, is that one day she will attend their alma mater, Purdue University. For the next 18 years, they plan to make monthly payment deposits to a 529 College Savings Plan at a local bank. The account pays 5.25% annual interest, compounded monthly. Create a worksheet for Jacob and Sophia that uses a financial function to show the future value (FV) of their investment and a formula to determine the percentage of the college's tuition saved. Jacob and Sophia have supplied the following information:

Out of State Annual Tuition = $52,000; Rate (per month) = 5.25% / 12; Nper (number of monthly payments) = years * 12; Pmt (monthly payment) = $425; and percentage of Tuition Saved = FV / Tuition for Four Years.

Jacob and Sophia are not sure how much they will be able to save each month. Use the concepts and techniques presented in this chapter to create a data table that shows the future value and percentage of tuition saved for monthly payments from $175 to $775, in $50 increments. Unlock the rate, monthly payment, and years. Protect the workbook so that the user can select only unlocked cells. Submit the workbook as requested by your instructor.

2: Saving for a Down Payment on Your First Car

Personal

Find a new car in your area that you would like to someday purchase. Based on the estimated current price of the car, determine how much money you need to save each month so that in three years, you have enough to make a down payment of 20% of the current estimated value. Assume that you can save the money in an account that is getting a 4.50% return. Create a worksheet that determines how much you have to save each month so that in three years the value of the account is 20% of the current estimated value. (*Hint:* Use the FV function with a monthly savings of $300.) Then use the Goal Seek command to determine the monthly savings amount needed for the car of your choice. Unlock cells that include data. Protect the worksheet. Submit the workbook as requested by your instructor.

3: Determining the Break-Even Point

Professional

You have been hired by Julio Quatorze, owner of Shrub and Trees Landscape Inc., to create a data table that analyzes the break-even point for a new shrub for prices between $3.00 and $9.25 in increments of $0.25. You can calculate the number of units you must sell to break even (break-even point) if you know the fixed expenses, the price per unit, and the expense (cost) per unit. The following formula determines the break-even point:

Break-Even Point = Fixed Expenses / (Price per Unit – Expense per Unit)

Assume Fixed Expenses = $300,000; Price per Unit = $7.50; and Expense per Unit = $2.10. Use the concepts and techniques presented in this chapter to determine the break-even point and then create the data table. Use the Price per Unit as the input cell and the break-even value as the result. For a price per unit of $8.00, the data table should show a break-even point of 50,847 units. Protect the worksheet so that only cells with data can be selected. Submit the workbook as requested by your instructor.

5 Creating, Sorting, and Querying a Table

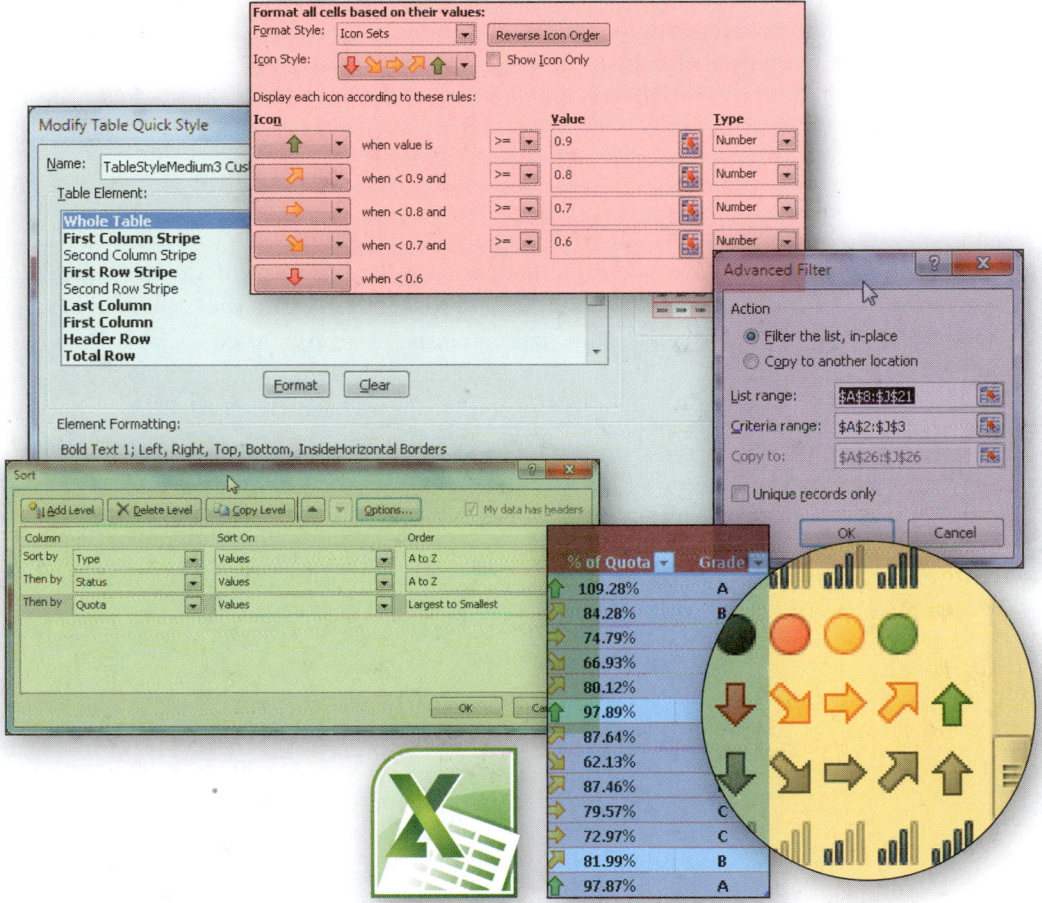

Objectives

You will have mastered the material in this chapter when you can:

- Create and manipulate a table
- Delete sheets in a workbook
- Add calculated columns to a table
- Use icon sets with conditional formatting
- Use the VLOOKUP function to look up a value in a table
- Print a table
- Add and delete records and change field values in a table

- Sort a table on one field or multiple fields
- Query a table
- Apply database functions, the SUMIF function, and the COUNTIF function
- Use the MATCH and INDEX functions to look up a value in a table
- Display automatic subtotals
- Use Group and Outline features to hide and unhide data

5 | Creating, Sorting, and Querying a Table

Introduction

A **table**, also called a **database**, is an organized collection of data. For example, a list of friends, a list of students registered for a class, a club membership roster, and an instructor's grade book all can be arranged as tables in a worksheet. In these cases, the data related to each person is called a record, and the individual data items that make up a record are called **fields**. For example, in a table of fundraisers, each fundraiser would have a separate record; each record might include several fields, such as name, experience, hire date, region, and fundraising quota.

A record in a table also can include fields (columns) that contain formulas and functions. A field, or column, that contains formulas or functions is called a **calculated column**. A calculated column displays results based on other columns in the table.

A worksheet's row-and-column structure can be used to organize and store a table. Each row of a worksheet can store a record, and each column can store one field for each record. Additionally, a row of column headings at the top of the worksheet can store field names that identify each field.

After you enter a table onto a worksheet, you can use Excel to (1) add and delete records; (2) change the values of fields in records; (3) sort the records so that Excel displays them in a different order; (4) determine subtotals for numeric fields; (5) display records that meet comparison criteria; and (6) analyze data using database functions. This chapter illustrates all six of these table capabilities.

Project — Kenson College Scholarship Fundraiser Table

The project in the chapter follows proper design guidelines and uses Excel to create the worksheet shown in Figures 5–1a and 5–1b. Kenson College raises funds for its scholarship program in several regions in the United States. The college's development director has asked for a workbook that summarizes key information about fundraisers and their performance. The data in the workbook should be easy to summarize, sort, edit, and query.

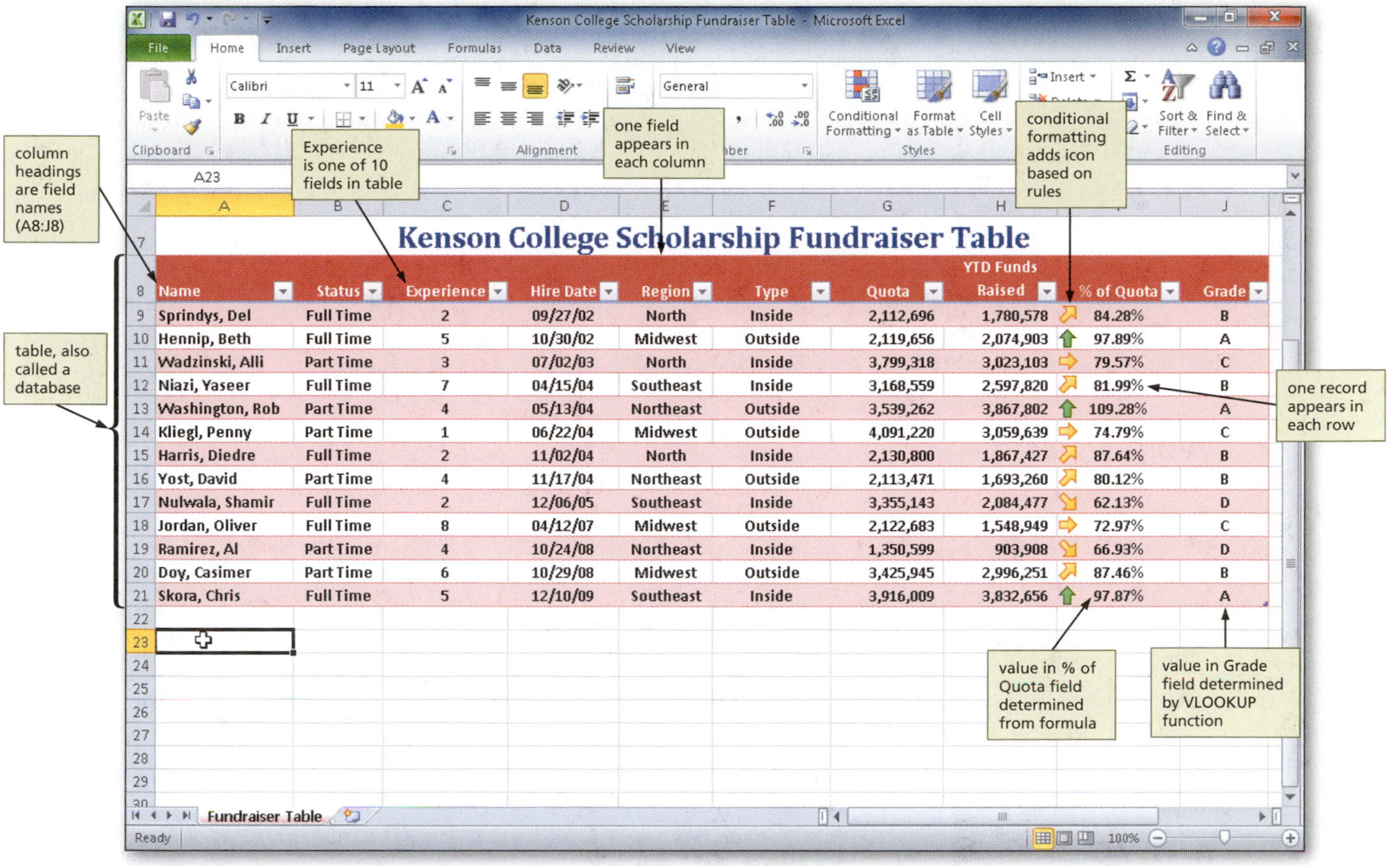

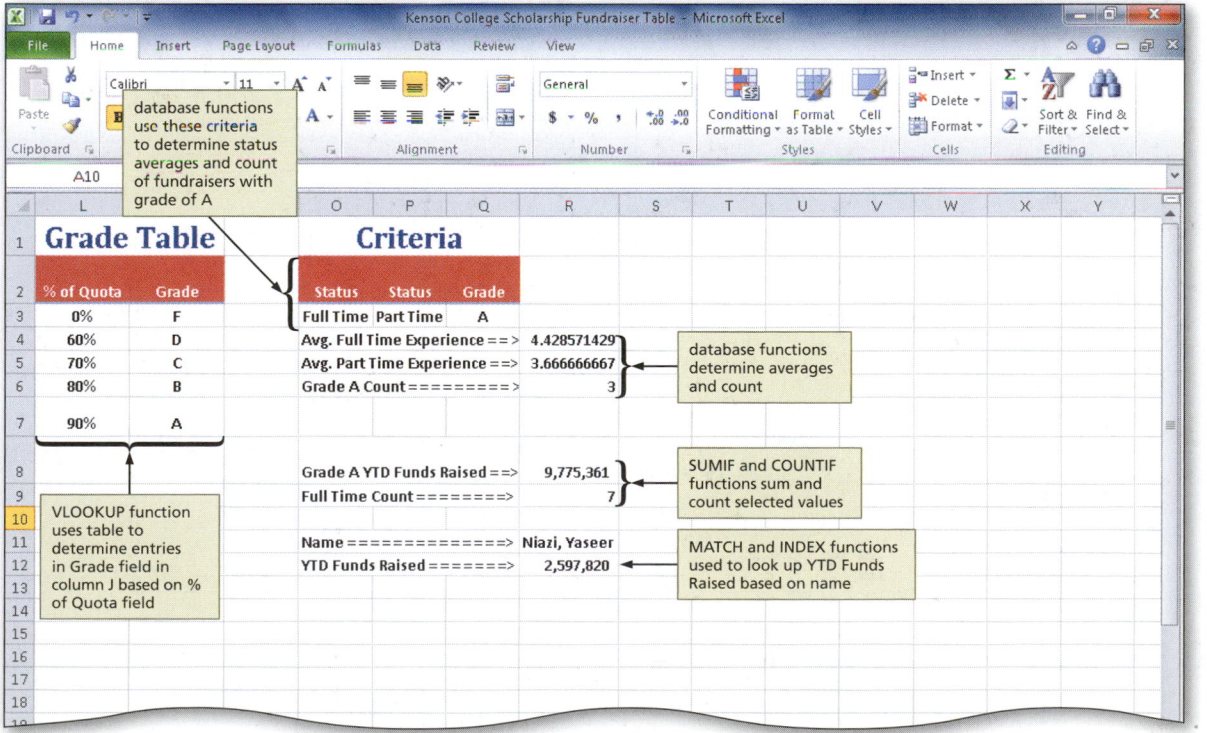

Figure 5–1 (a) Table

Figure 5–1 (b) Grade Table, Criteria, Statistics, and Look Up

The requirements document for the Kenson College Scholarship Fundraiser table is shown in Figure 5–2. It includes the needs, source of data, calculations, special requirements, and other facts about its development.

Table 5–1 describes the field names, columns, types of data, and column widths to use when creating the table.

REQUEST FOR NEW WORKBOOK

Date Submitted:	June 4, 2012
Submitted By:	Larry Chao
Worksheet Title:	Kenson College Scholarship Fundraiser Table
Needs:	Create a fundraiser table (Figure 5-3a on page EX 302) that can be sorted, queried, maintained, and printed to obtain meaningful information. Using the data in the table, compute statistics that include the average experience of full-time fundraisers, average experience of part-time fundraisers, grade A count, sum of YTD Funds Raised for those with grade A, and the count of the full-time fundraisers, as shown in Figure 5-3b on page EX 302. The table field names, columns, types of data, and column widths are described in Table 5-1. Because Larry will use the table online as he travels among the offices, it is important that it be readable and visible on the screen. Some of the column widths listed in Table 5-1, therefore, are set based on the number of characters in the field names and not the maximum length of the data. The last two fields (located in columns I and J) use a formula and function to determine values based on data within each fundraiser record.
Source of Data:	Larry will supply the fundraiser data required for the table.
Calculations:	Include the following calculations and look up: 1. % of Quota field in table = YTD Funds Raised / Quota 2. Grade field in table = VLOOKUP function that uses the Grade table in Figure 5-3b 3. Average Full-Time Experience = AVERAGE function that uses the Criteria table in Figure 5-3b 4. Average Part-Time Experience = AVERAGE function that uses the Criteria table in Figure 5-3b 5. Grade A Count = DCOUNT function that uses the Criteria table in Figure 5-3b 6. Grade A YTD Funds Raised Sum = SUMIF function 7. Full-Time Count = COUNTIF function 8. Look up YTD Funds Raised given the name of a fundraiser
Special Requirements:	1. Delete unused sheets. 2. A Criteria area will be created above the table, in rows 1 through 6, to store criteria for use in a query. An Extract area will be created below the table, beginnning in row 25, to receive records that meet a criteria.

Approvals

Approval Status:	X	Approved
		Rejected
Approved By:	Terrell Knox	
Date:	June 18, 2012	
Assigned To:	J. Quasney, Spreadsheet Specialist	

Figure 5–2

Column Headings (Field Names)	Column in Worksheet	Type of Data	Column Width	Description As It Pertains to a Fundraiser
Table 5–1 Column Information for Kenson College Scholarship Fundraiser Table				
Name	A	Text	16.43	Last name and first name
Status	B	Text	10.29	Full-time or part-time
Experience	C	Numeric	14.71	Fundraising experience in years
Hire Date	D	Date	13.14	Date hired
Region	E	Text	11.00	Fundraising territory
Type	F	Text	14.00	Inside or outside fundraising
Quota	G	Numeric	13.29	Annual fundraising quota
YTD Funds Raised	H	Numeric	13.29	Year-to-date funds raised
% of Quota	I	Numeric calculation (YTD Funds Raised / Quota)	14.57	Percent of annual quota met
Grade	J	Text calculation (VLOOKUP function)	10.29	Grade that indicates how much of quota has been met

Overview

As you read this chapter, you will learn how to create the worksheet shown in Figure 5–1 on page EX 299 by performing these general tasks:

- Create and format the fundraiser table.
- Sort the fundraiser table.
- Obtain answers to questions about the fundraisers using a variety of methods to query the fundraiser table.
- Extract records from the table based on given criteria.
- Display subtotals by grouping the fundraisers.

Plan Ahead

General Project Decisions

While creating an Excel worksheet, you need to make decisions that will determine the appearance and characteristics of the finished worksheet. As you create the worksheet required to meet the requirements shown in Figure 5–2, you should follow these general guidelines:

1. **Create and format the table.** A table should be formatted so that the records are easily distinguished. The data in the worksheet should start several rows from the top in order to leave room for the criteria area. Using banded rows (background colors varying between rows) to format the table provides greater readability. Some columns require calculations that can be created by using the table column headings within formulas. In some cases, calculated columns in tables require looking up values outside of the table. Excel's special lookup functions can be used in such cases. Totals also can be added to the table for averages, sums, and other types of calculations.

2. **Sort the table.** The user of the worksheet should be able to sort the table in a variety of manners and sort using multiple fields at the same time. Excel includes simple and advanced methods for sorting tables.

3. **Obtain answers to questions about the data in the table using a variety of methods to query the table.** A query can include filters, the use of which results in the table displaying only those records that meet certain criteria. Or, a query can include a calculation based on data in the table that then is displayed outside of the table but within the same worksheet.

4. **Extract records from the table based on given criteria.** A criteria area and extract area can be created on the worksheet. The **criteria area** can be used to enter rules regarding which records to extract, such as all full-time fundraisers with a grade of A. The **extract**

(continued)

(continued)

area can be used to store the records that meet the criteria. The column headings from the table should be used as column headings in both the criteria and extract areas of the worksheet, as this is required by Excel when working with criteria and extract areas.

5. **Display subtotals by grouping data in the table.** The user of the worksheet should be able to create subtotals of groups of records after sorting the table. Excel's grouping features provide for subtotaling.

When necessary, more specific details concerning the above guidelines are presented at appropriate points in the chapter. The chapter also will identify the actions you perform and decisions made regarding these guidelines during the creation of the worksheet shown in Figure 5–1 on page EX 299.

The fundraiser table should include the data provided in Table 5–1 on the previous page. Using a sketch of the worksheet can help you visualize its design. The sketch of the worksheet consists of the title, column headings, location of data values, and an idea of the desired formatting (Figure 5–3a). The sketch does not show the criteria area above the table and the extract area below the table, which are included as requirements in the requirements document (Figure 5–2 on page EX 300). The general layout of the grade table, criteria area, and required statistics and query are shown in Figure 5–3b.

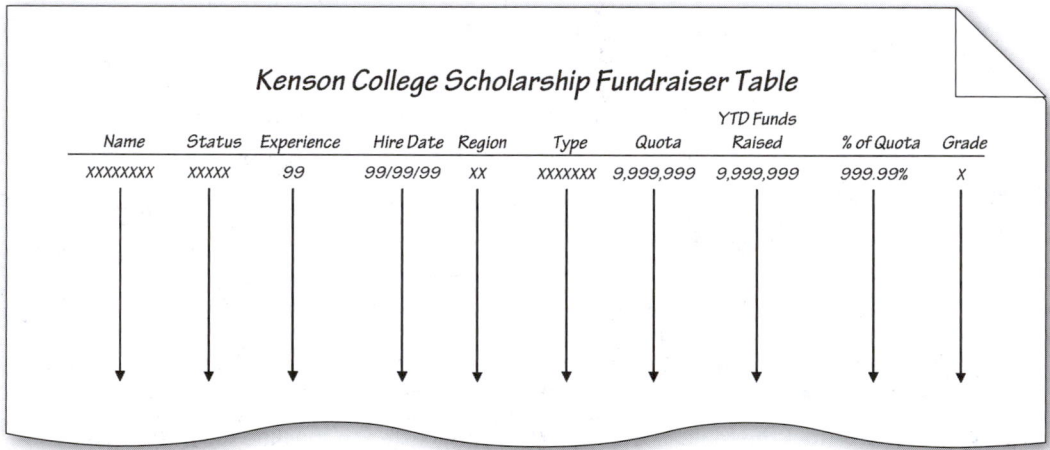

Kenson College Scholarship Fundraiser Table

Name	Status	Experience	Hire Date	Region	Type	Quota	YTD Funds Raised	% of Quota	Grade
XXXXXXX	XXXXX	99	99/99/99	XX	XXXXXXX	9,999,999	9,999,999	999.99%	X

Figure 5–3 (a) Table

Grade Table			Criteria			
% of Quota	Grade		Status	Status	Grade	
0%	F		Full Time	Part Time	A	
60%	D		Aug. Full Time Experience ======➜			99.99
70%	C		Aug. Part Time Experience ======➜			99.99
80%	B		Grade A Count ============➜			99
90%	A					
			Grade A YTD Funds Raised =====➜			99,999,999
			Full Time Count ============➜			99
			Name =================➜			XXXXXXX
			YTD Funds Raised ==========➜			99,999,999

Figure 5–3 (b) Grade Table, Criteria, and Statistics

With a good understanding of the requirements document, an understanding of the necessary decisions, and a sketch of the worksheet, the next step is to use Excel to create the worksheet.

To Start Excel

If you are using a computer to step through the project in this chapter and you want your screens to match the figures in this book, you should change your screen's resolution to 1024 × 768. The following steps, which assume Windows 7 is running, start Excel based on a typical installation. You may need to ask your instructor how to start Excel for your computer.

1 Click the Start button on the Windows 7 taskbar to display the Start menu.

2 Type `Microsoft Excel` as the search text in the 'Search programs and files' text box, and watch the search results appear on the Start menu.

3 Click Microsoft Excel 2010 in the search results on the Start menu to start Excel and display a new blank workbook in the Excel window.

4 If the Excel window is not maximized, click the Maximize button next to the Close button on its title bar to maximize the window.

BTW

Starting Excel
If you plan to open an existing workbook, you can start Excel and open the workbook at the same time by double-clicking the workbook file name in Windows Explorer.

> **Create and format the table.**
> One way to create a table in Excel is to follow these four steps: (1) Enter the column headings (field names); (2) Define a range as a table using the Format as Table button (Home tab | Styles group); (3) Format the row immediately below the column headings; and (4) Enter records into the table.
>
> Although Excel does not require a table title to be entered, it is a good practice to include one on the worksheet to show where the table begins. With Excel, you usually enter the table several rows below the first row in the worksheet. These blank rows later can be used as a criteria area to store criteria for use in a query.

Plan Ahead

When you create a table in Excel, you should follow some basic guidelines, as listed in Table 5–2.

Table 5–2 Guidelines for Creating a Table in Excel

Table Size and Workbook Location

1. Do not enter more than one table per worksheet.
2. Maintain at least one blank row between a table and other worksheet entries.
3. A table can have a maximum of 16,384 fields and 1,048,576 records on a worksheet.

Column Headings (Field Names)

1. Place column headings (field names) in the first row of the table.
2. Do not use blank rows or rows with repeating characters, such as dashes or underscores, to separate the column headings (field names) from the data.
3. Apply a different format to the column headings than to the data. For example, bold the column headings and format the data below the column headings using a regular style. Most quick table styles follow these guidelines.
4. Column headings (field names) can be up to 32,767 characters in length. The column headings should be meaningful.

Contents of Table

1. Each cell in any given column should have similar data. For example, Hire Date should be in the same column for all fundraisers.
2. Format the data to improve readability, but do not vary the format of the data within the cells of a column.

BTW

Setting Up a Table
When creating a table, leave several rows empty above the table on the worksheet to set up a criteria area for querying the table. Some spreadsheet specialists also leave several columns empty to the left of the table, beginning with column A, for additional worksheet activities. A range of blank rows or columns on the side of a table is called a moat of cells.

To Enter the Column Headings for a Table

The following steps change the column widths to those specified in Table 5–1, enter the table title, and enter and format the column headings. These steps also change the name of Sheet1 to Fundraiser Table, delete the unused sheets in the workbook, and save the workbook using the file name, Kenson College Scholarship Fundraiser Table.

Note: The majority of tasks involved in entering and formatting the table title and column headings of a list are similar to what you have done in previous chapters. Thus, if you plan to complete this chapter on your computer and want to skip the set of steps below, open the workbook Kenson College Scholarship Fundraiser Table from the Data Files for Students.

BTW

Merging and Centering Across a Selection
You merge and center across a selection when you want to treat the range of cells over which you center as a single cell. You center (but do not merge) across a selection when you want the selected range of cells to be independent of one another. With most workbooks, it makes little difference whether you center using one technique or the other. Thus, most spreadsheet specialists use the merge and center technique because the procedure easily is available by using the Merge & Center button (Home tab | Alignment group).

1 Use the mouse to change the column widths as follows: A = 16.43, B = 10.29, C = 14.71, D = 13.14, E = 11.00, F = 14.00, G = 13.29, H = 13.29, I = 14.57, and J = 10.29.

2 Enter `Kenson College Scholarship Fundraiser Table` as the table title in cell A7.

3 Select the range A7:H7. Right-click the selected range and then click Format Cells on a shortcut menu to display the Format Cells dialog box.

4 If necessary, click the Alignment tab (Format Cells dialog box) and then click the Horizontal box arrow in the Text alignment area to display a list of horizontal alignments.

5 Click Center Across Selection in the Horizontal list (Format Cells dialog box) to select the option to center the title through the selection, and then click the OK button (Format Cells dialog box) to close the Format Cells dialog box.

6 Apply the Title style to cell A7 and then change the font size to 20.

7 Enter the column headings in row 8 as shown in Figure 5–4. Center the column headings in the range B8:H8.

8 Apply the Heading 3 cell style to the range A8:H8 and then select cell A10.

9 Enter `Fundraiser Table` as the sheet name and then apply the Red, Accent 2 (column 6, row 1) color to the sheet tab.

10 Click the Sheet2 tab, hold down the CTRL key, and then click the Sheet3 tab to select both tabs.

11 Right-click the selected sheet tabs and then click Delete on a shortcut menu to delete the selected sheets from the workbook.

12 Update the document properties with your name and any other relevant information as specified by your instructor. Change the worksheet header by adding your name, course number, and other information as specified by your instructor.

13 With a USB flash drive connected to one of the computer's USB ports, click the Save button on the Quick Access Toolbar. Save the workbook using the file name, Kenson College Scholarship Fundraiser Table, on the USB flash drive (Figure 5–4).

Q&A

What is the difference between the Center Across Selection alignment and the Merge & Center button (Home tab | Alignment group)?

In Step 5, the Center Across Selection horizontal alignment was used to center the table title in row 7 horizontally across the range A7:H7. In earlier chapters, the Merge & Center button (Home tab | Alignment group) was used to center text across a range. The major difference between the Center Across Selection horizontal alignment and the Merge & Center button is that, unlike the Merge & Center button, the Center Across Selection horizontal alignment does not merge the selected cell range into one cell.

BTW

Q&As
For a complete list of the Q&As found in many of the step-by-step sequences in this book, visit the Excel 2010 Q&A Web page (scsite.com/ex2010/qa).

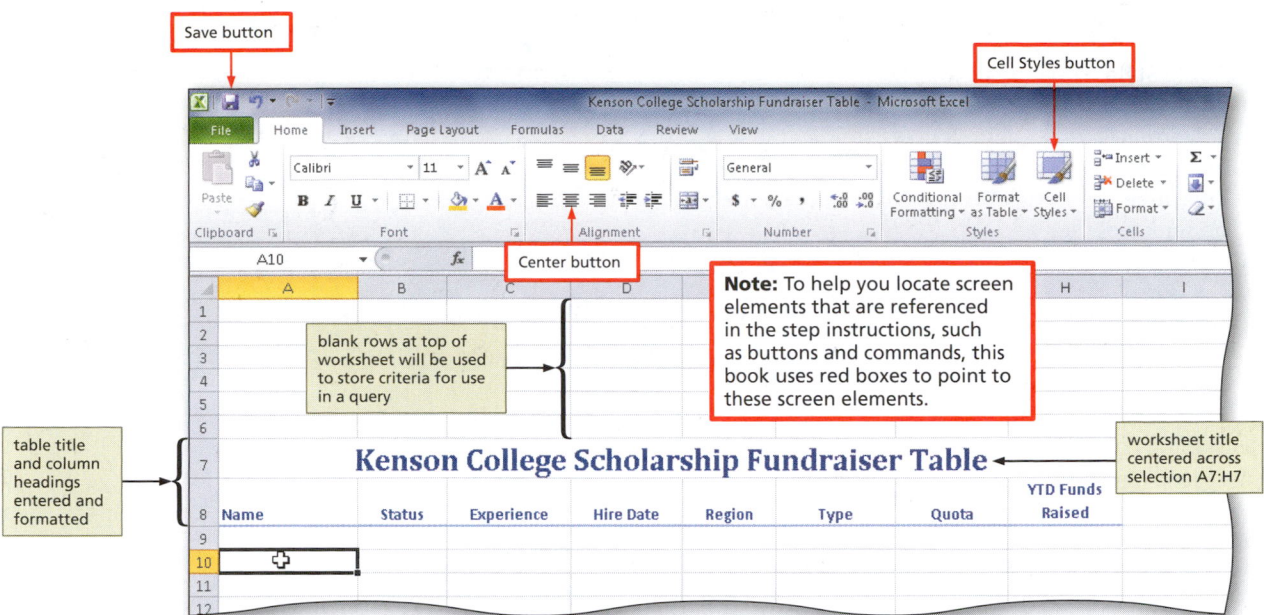

Figure 5–4

To Format a Range as a Table

The following steps define the range A8:H8 as a table by applying a table quick style to the range. Excel allows you to enter data in a range either before defining it as a table or after defining it as a table.

1

- Select the range A8:H8.

- Click the Format as Table button (Home tab | Styles group) to display the Format as Table gallery (Figure 5–5).

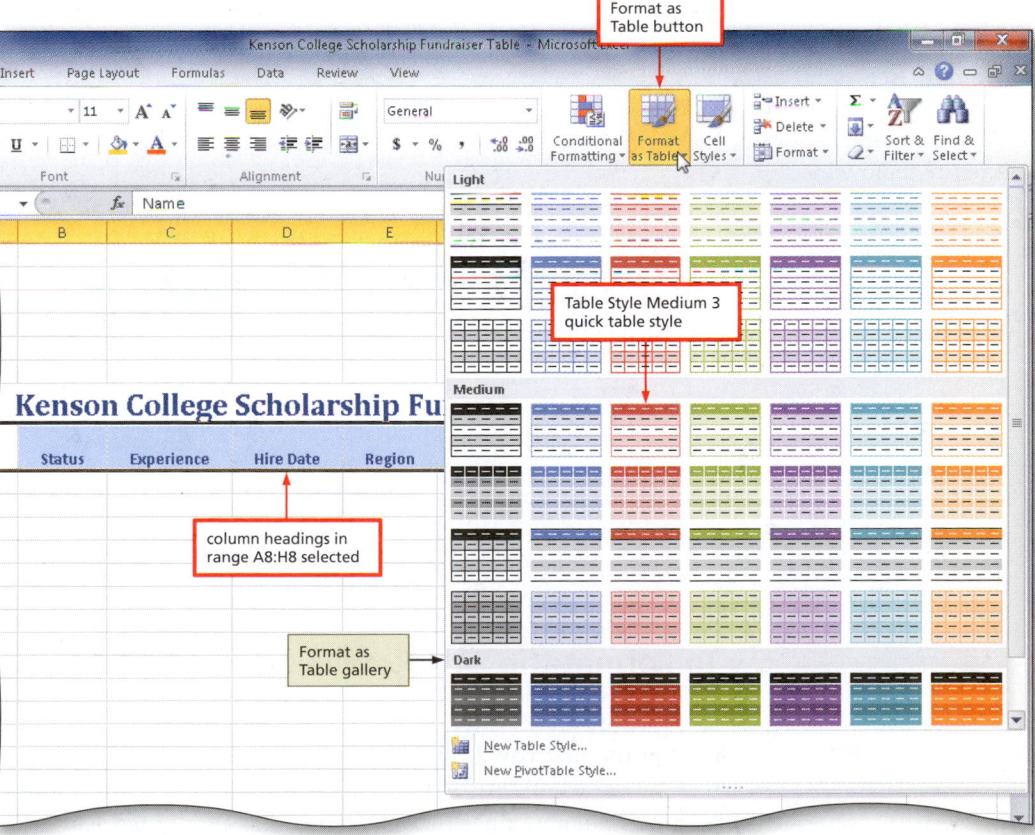

Figure 5–5

2

- Click the Table Style Medium 3 quick table style in the Format as Table gallery to display a marquee around the selected range and display the Format As Table dialog box.

- If necessary, click the 'My table has headers' check box to select the option to format the table with headers (Figure 5–6).

Experiment

- Point to a number of table quick styles in the Format as Table gallery to preview them on the worksheet.

Q&A Why is the range A8:H8 already selected in the Format As Table dialog box?

Because the range A8:H8 was selected before clicking the Format as Table button, Excel automatically selects this range for the 'Where is the data for your table?' box.

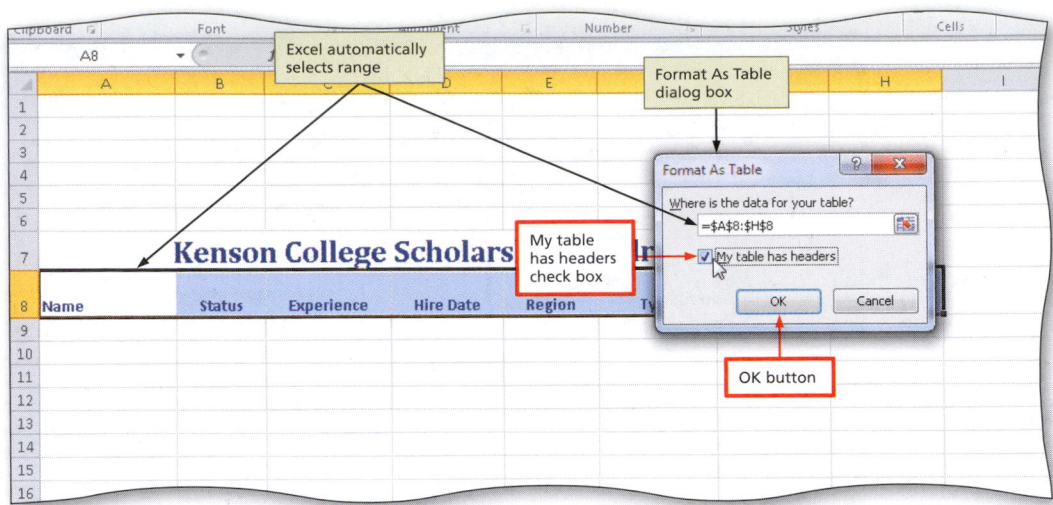

Figure 5–6

3

- Click the OK button to create a table from the selected column headings and corresponding cells in the row below it.

- Scroll down until row 7 is at the top of the worksheet window (Figure 5–7).

Q&A Why does Excel indicate that the cells in row 9 are in the table?

Excel automatically creates an empty row in the table so that you are ready to enter the first record in the table.

Figure 5–7

Other Ways

1. Select range, click Table (Insert tab | Tables group), click OK button

To Format the First Row in an Empty Table

If the table contains no data, as in Figure 5–7, then Excel sets the format of the cells in the first row to the default associated with the table quick style chosen when the table was created. Further, if you create an empty table and require that the records be formatted in a manner that is different from the manner associated with the selected table quick style, format the first row after you create the table, not before. Otherwise, the formatting will disappear when you create the table. The following steps format the first row of the table.

1 Select the range B9:H9 and then click the Center button (Home tab | Alignment group) to apply a center format to the range.

2 Right-click cell D9 to display a shortcut menu. Click Format Cells on the shortcut menu to display the Format Cells dialog box.

3 Click the Number tab (Format Cells dialog box), click Date in the Category list, click 03/14/01 in the Type list, and then click the OK button to apply a MM/DD/YY date format to the selected cell.

4 Apply the comma style to the range G9:H9. Click the Decrease Decimal button (Home tab | Number group) twice so that data in the selected columns is displayed as whole numbers.

BTW

The Ribbon and Screen Resolution
Excel may change how the groups and buttons within the groups appear on the Ribbon, depending on the computer's screen resolution. Thus, your Ribbon may look different from the ones in this book if you are using a screen resolution other than 1024 × 768.

Q&A Why are no changes apparent on the worksheet?

No visible changes appear on the worksheet because the table contains no records. As you enter records into the table, Excel applies the assigned formats to subsequent rows, even as you add more rows to the table.

To Modify a Table Quick Style

Before entering records in the table, the quick style used to create the table should be modified to make the table more readable. A bold font style with a black font color for the table's entries makes them more readable. The following steps create a new table quick style by copying the Table Style Medium 3 quick style and then modifying it so that a bold font style and black font color are applied to the entire table.

1
- If necessary, click cell A9 to activate the table.

- Click the Format as Table button (Home tab | Styles group) to display the Format as Table gallery and then right-click the Table Style Medium 3 quick table style to display a shortcut menu (Figure 5–8).

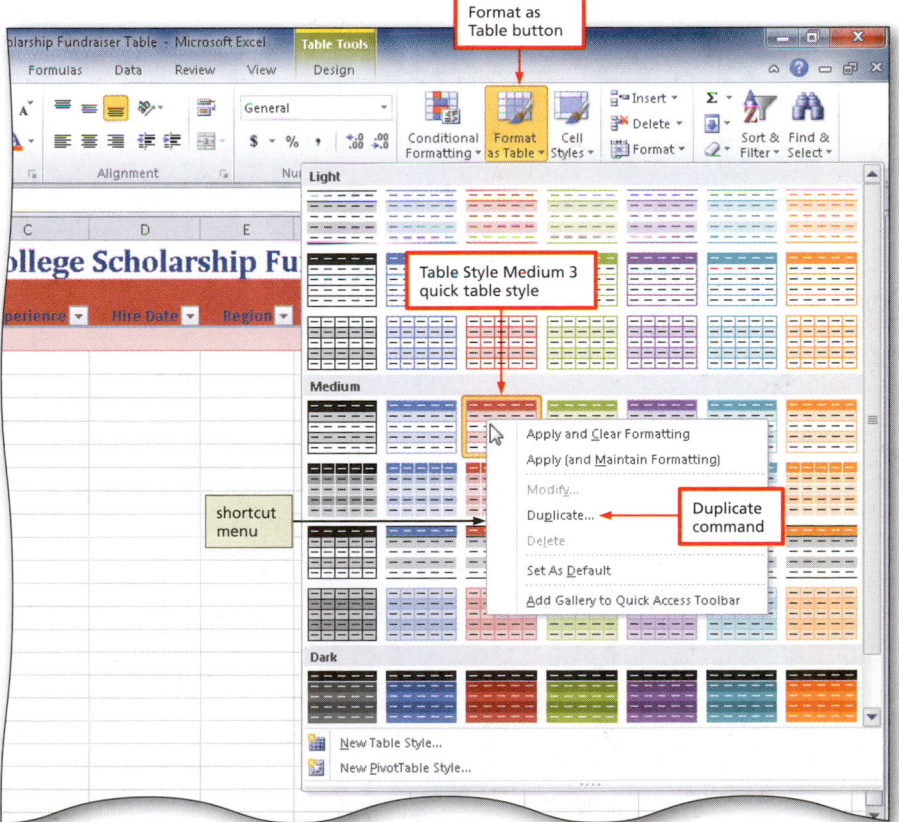

Figure 5–8

2

- Click Duplicate on the shortcut menu to display the Modify Table Quick Style dialog box.

- Type **TableStyleMedium3 – Custom** in the Name text box (Modify Table Quick Style dialog box) to name the new style (Figure 5–9).

Q&A

What elements of a table can I customize?

The Table Element list in the Modify Table Quick Style dialog box allows you to choose almost any aspect of a table to modify. You can change the formatting for each element listed in the Table Element list by clicking the element and then clicking the Format button to display the Format Cells dialog box.

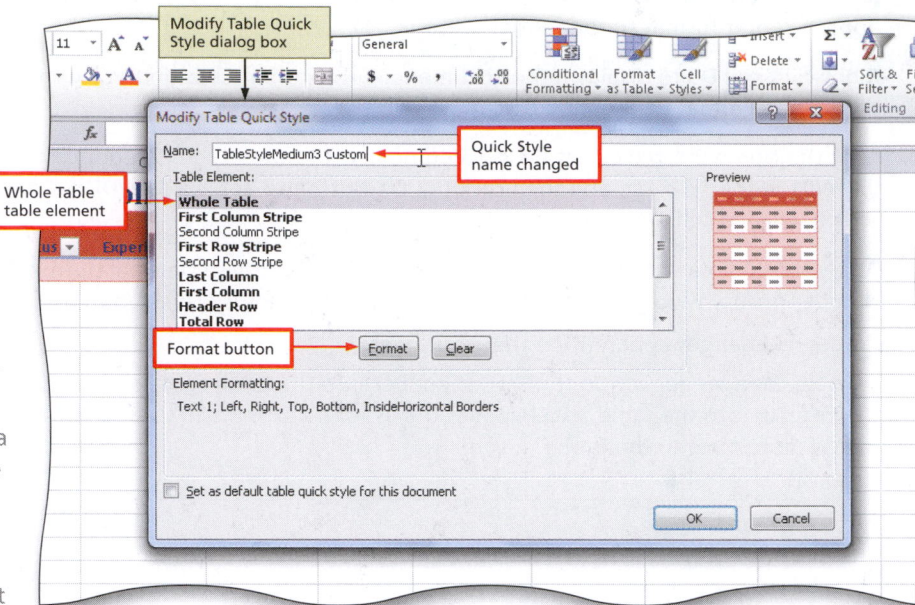

Figure 5–9

3

- With Whole Table selected in the Table Element list, click the Format button to display the Format Cells dialog box.

- If necessary, display the Font tab and then click Bold in the Font style list.

- Click the Color box arrow and then click the Black, Text 1 color (column 2, row 1) to select a font color for the new style (Figure 5–10).

4

- Click the OK button (Format Cells dialog box) to close the Format Cells dialog box.

- Click the OK button (Modify Table Quick Style dialog box) to close the Modify Table Quick Style dialog box.

- Apply the TableStyleMedium3 – Custom table style to the table.

- Select the range A8:H8 and then apply the White, Background 1 (column 1, row 1) font color to the range.

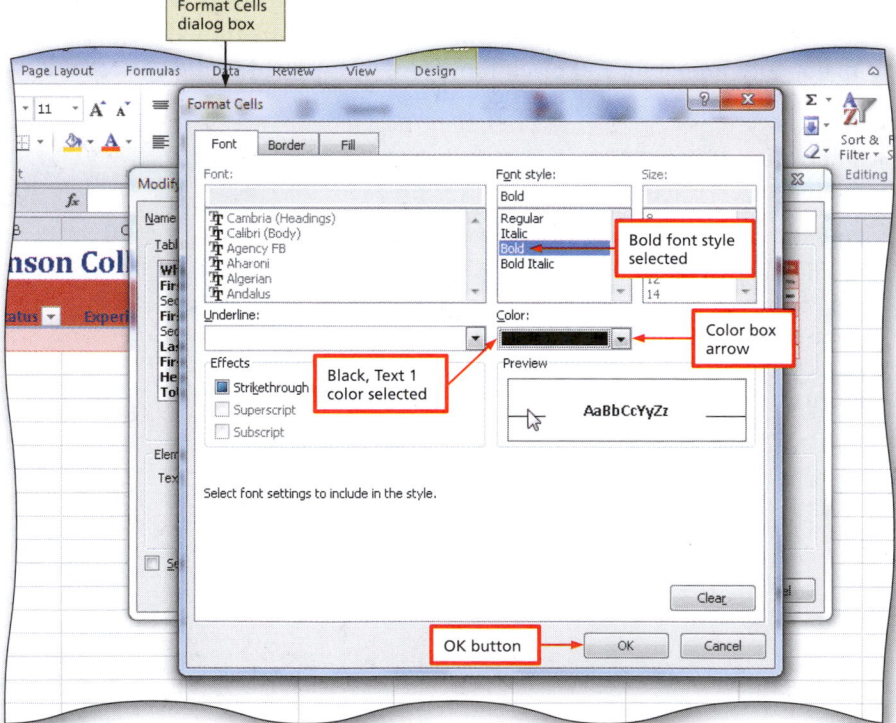

Figure 5–10

Q&A

Why should the font color of the header row be changed to white?

The white font color allows the text in the header rows to stand out against the background color of the header row.

To Enter Records into a Table

The next step is to enter the fundraisers' records into the table. As indicated earlier, the computational fields in columns I and J will be added after the data is in the table. The following steps enter records into the table.

1

- If necessary, click cell A9 to activate the table.

- Type the fundraiser information for row 9, as shown in Figure 5–11. After typing the data for a field, press the RIGHT ARROW key to move to the next field. After you type the YTD Funds Raised, press the TAB key to start a new record.

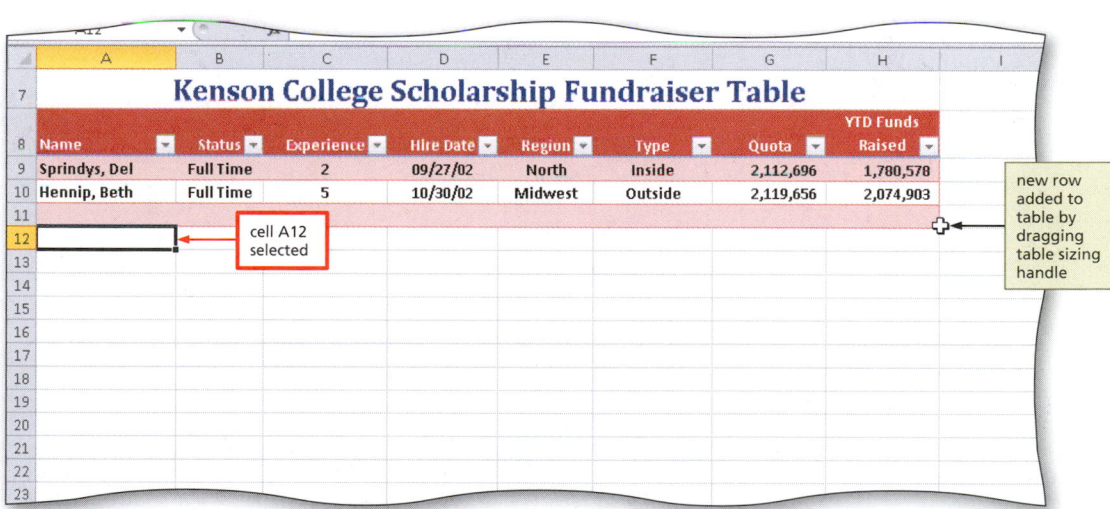

Figure 5–11

- Type the fundraiser information for row 10, as shown in Figure 5–11. After typing the data for a field, press the RIGHT ARROW key to move to the next field. After you type the YTD Funds Raised, click cell A12 to select it (Figure 5–11).

Q&A   Is row 10 now part of the table?

Yes. Pressing the TAB key when a cell in the last column in a table is selected adds the next row below the table to the table. Row 10 now is part of the fundraiser table.

2

- Drag the table sizing handle to the top of cell H12 to add another row to the table (Figure 5–12).

Figure 5–12

Q&A   Why does row 11 have a different background color than row 10?

The quick style used to create the table includes a type of formatting called row banding. **Row banding** causes adjacent rows to have different formatting so that each row in the table is distinguished from surrounding rows.

3

- Enter the fundraiser record for the third fundraiser, as shown in Figure 5–13, and then select cell A12.

- Drag the table sizing handle to cell H21 to add 10 new rows to the table (Figure 5–13).

Q&A

Why were all of the rows not added to the table in Step 1?

Steps 1 through 3 demonstrate three different methods of adding rows to a table. The first method can be used when you are adding a number of rows to the table and do not know how many rows you are going to add. Use the second method when you need to add one additional row to a table that you previously created. The third method can be used when you know exactly how many rows you need in a table.

Q&A

Why was cell A12 selected?

Cell A12 was selected after the first part of Step 3. A selected cell displays the fill handle instead of the table sizing handle. A different cell must be selected in order to display the table sizing handle in cell H11.

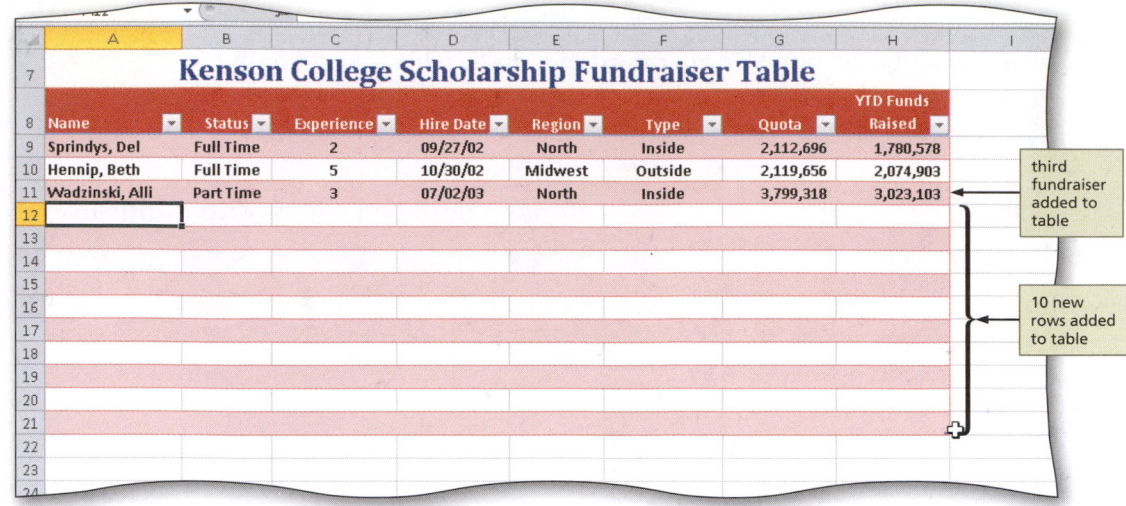

Figure 5–13

4

- Enter the remaining fundraisers' records as shown in Figure 5–14.

- Click cell A23 to deselect the table.

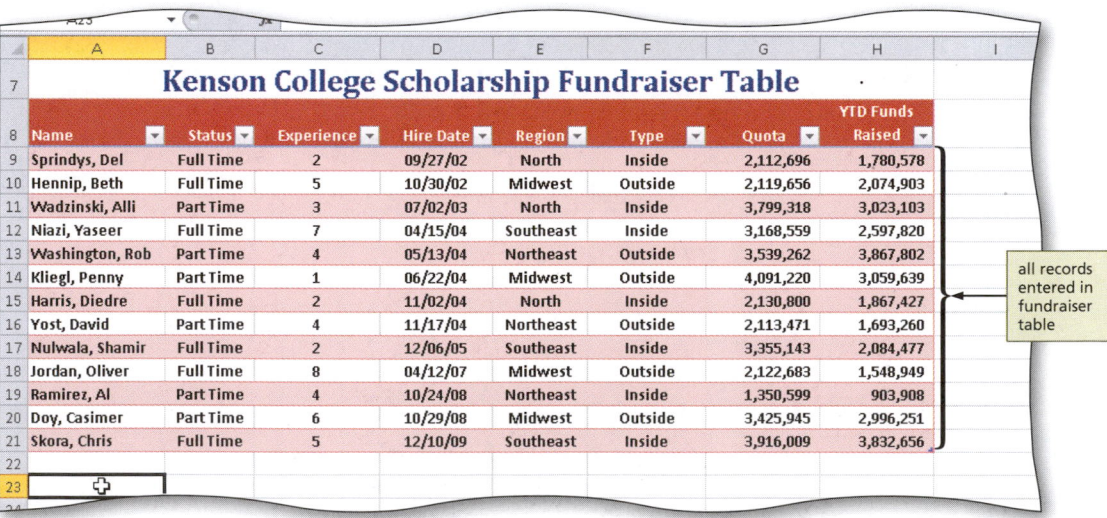

Figure 5–14

Break Point: If you wish to take a break, this is a good place to do so. Be sure to save the file again and then you can quit Excel. To resume at a later time, start Excel, open the file called Kenson College Scholarship Fundraiser Table, and continue following the steps from this location forward.

Adding Computational Fields to the Table

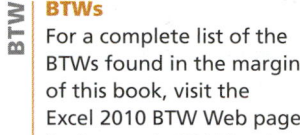

BTWs
For a complete list of the BTWs found in the margins of this book, visit the Excel 2010 BTW Web page (scsite.com/ex2010/btw).

The next step is to add the computational fields '% of Quota' in column I and Grade in column J. The first computational field involves dividing the YTD Funds Raised in column H by the Quota in column G. The second computational field involves a table lookup to determine a grade based upon the '% of Quota' in column I.

To Add New Fields to a Table

Adding new fields to a table in a worksheet illustrates another of Excel's powerful table capabilities. As shown in the following steps, if you add a new column heading in a column adjacent to the current column headings in the table, Excel automatically adds the adjacent column to the table's range and copies the format of the existing table heading to the new column heading. Adding a new row to a table works in a similar manner.

The first step in adding the two new fields is to enter the two column headings, or field names, in cells I8 and J8, enter the first '% of Quota' formula in cell I9, and then reformat the two cells immediately below the new column headings. The formula for the '% of Quota' in cell I9 is YTD FundsRaised / Quota. Rather than using cell references in the formula, Excel allows you to refer to the column headings in formulas by placing the column heading in brackets and adding the at symbol, or @, to the beginning of the column name. For example, the formula for cell I9 is =[@[YTD FundsRaised]] / [@Quota]. The column heading YTD Funds Raised must be between an open square bracket and a closed square bracket because the column heading includes spaces. Using this notation makes formulas easier to read, and the same formula could be used for all records in the table.

After you enter the formula in cell I9, Excel automatically copies the formula to the range I10:I21. When you enter a formula in the first row of a field, Excel creates a calculated column. A **calculated column** is a column in a table in which each row uses a common formula that references other fields in the table.

1

- Select cell I8 and type **% of Quota** as the new column heading.

- Select cell J8 and type **Grade** as the new column heading.

- Select cell I9, enter **=[@[YTD FundsRaised]] / [@Quota]** as the formula and then click the Enter box on the formula bar to create a calculated column (Figure 5–15).

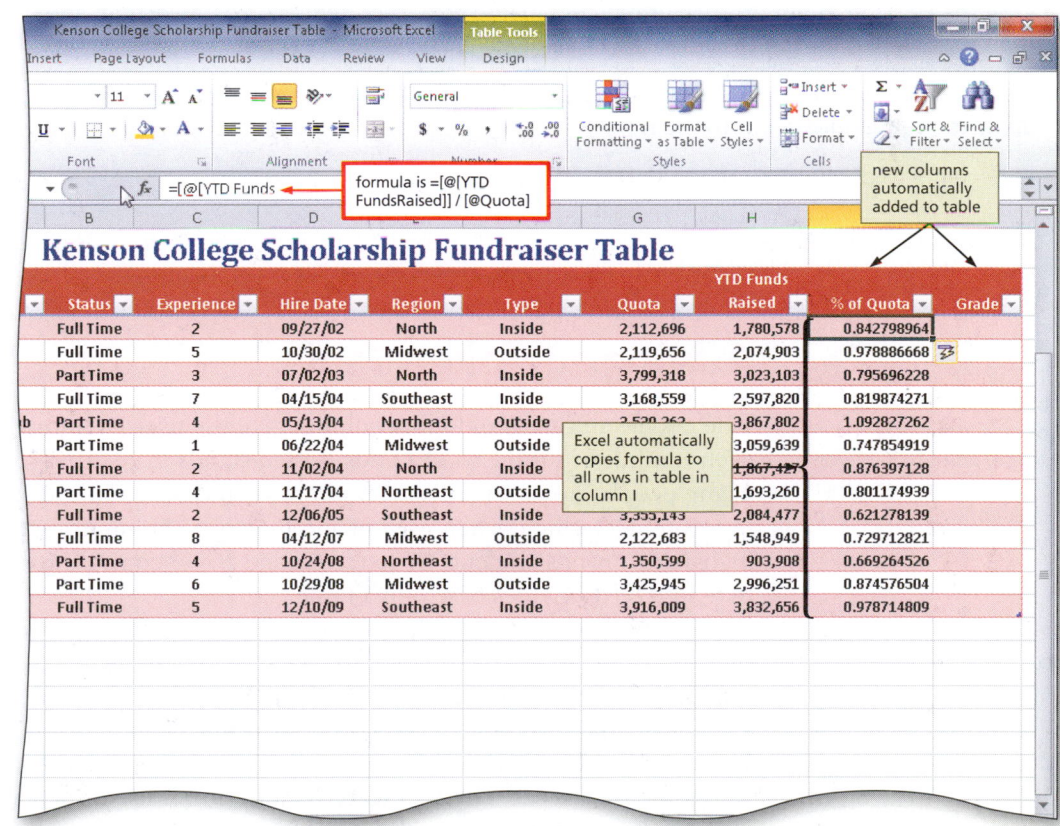

Figure 5–15

2

- Select the range I9:I21 and then click the Percent Style button (Home tab | Number group) to apply the percent style to the range.

- Click the Increase Decimal button (Home tab | Alignment group) twice to force numbers in the selected range to display two decimal places.

- Click the Center button (Home tab | Alignment group) to center the selected range (Figure 5–16).

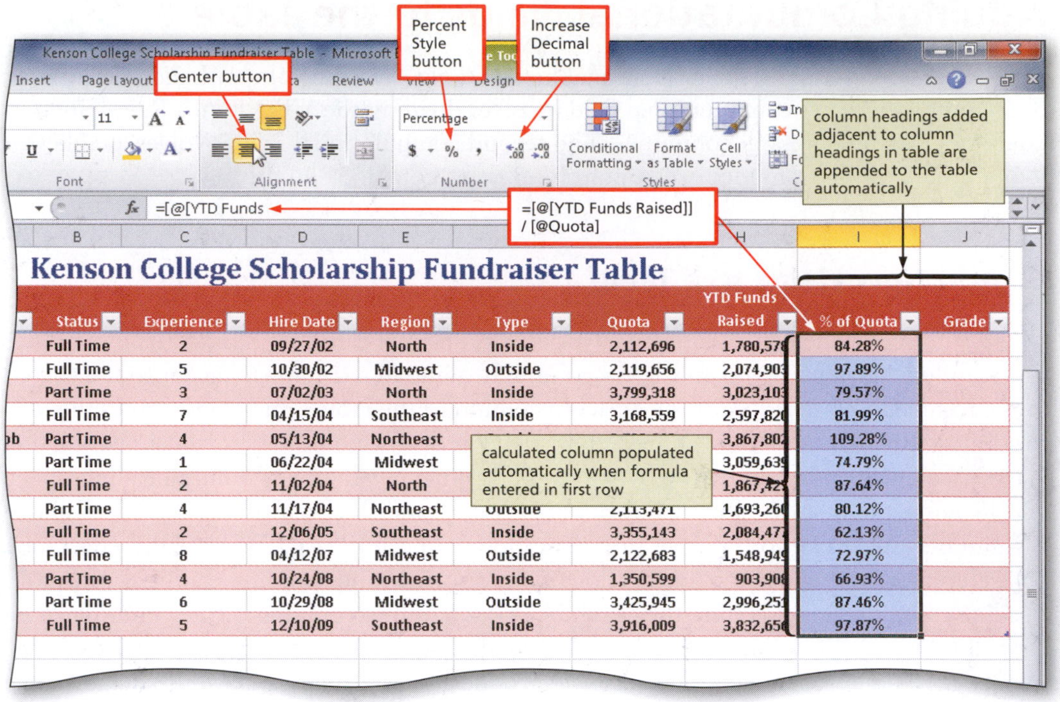

Figure 5–16

3

- Select the range A7:J7, right-click the selected range, click Format Cells on a shortcut menu, and then click the Alignment tab (Format Cells dialog box) to display the Alignment tab in the Format Cells dialog box.

- Click the Horizontal box arrow (Format Cells dialog box), click Center Across Selection, and then click the OK button to center the table heading and close the Format Cells dialog box.

- Select the range J9:J21 and then click the Center button (Home tab | Alignment group) to apply the center alignment to the range.

- Click cell J9 to deselect the range J9:J21.

BTW

Tables
To change an active table back to a normal range of cells, right-click the range, point to Table on a shortcut menu, and then click Convert to Range on the Table submenu.

Adding a Lookup Table

The entries in the % of Quota column give the user an immediate evaluation of where each fundraiser's total YTD Funds Raised stands in relation to his or her annual quota. Many people, however, dislike numbers as an evaluation tool. Most prefer simple letter grades, which, when used properly, group the fundraisers in the same way an instructor groups students by letter grades. Excel contains functions that allow you to assign letter grades based on a table.

Excel has several lookup functions that are useful for looking up values in tables such as tax tables, discount tables, parts tables, and grade tables. The two most widely used lookup functions are the HLOOKUP and VLOOKUP. Both functions look up a value in a table and return a corresponding value from the table to the cell containing the function. The **HLOOKUP function** is used when the table direction is horizontal, or across the worksheet. The **VLOOKUP function** is used when a table direction is vertical, or down the worksheet. The VLOOKUP function is by far the most often used because most tables are vertical, as is the table in this chapter.

To Create a Lookup Table

The grading scale in this chapter (Table 5–3) resembles the one that an instructor might use to determine your letter grade. As shown in Table 5–3, any score greater than or equal to 90% equates to a letter grade of A. Excel assigns scores greater than or equal to 80 and less than or equal to 89 a letter grade of B, and so on.

The VLOOKUP function requires that the table indicate only the lowest score for a letter grade. Furthermore, the table entries must be in sequence from lowest score to highest score. Thus, the entries in Table 5–3 must be resequenced for use with the VLOOKUP function so that they appear as shown in Table 5–4.

The general form of the VLOOKUP function is:

=VLOOKUP(lookup_value, table_array, col_index_num)

BTW

Lookup Functions
Lookup functions are powerful, useful, and interesting in the way they work. For additional information on lookup functions, enter vlookup in the Search box in the Excel Help window.

Table 5–3 Typical Grade Table

% of Quota	Grade
90% and higher	A
80% to 89%	B
70% to 79%	C
60% to 69%	D
0 to 59%	F

Table 5–4 Typical Grade Table Modified for the VLOOKUP Function

% of Quota	Grade
0	F
60%	D
70%	C
80%	B
90%	A

The VLOOKUP function searches the far-left column of the **table array**. The far-left column of the table_array contains what are called the **table arguments**. In this example, the table arguments include percentages (see Table 5–4). The VLOOKUP function uses the % of Quota value (called the lookup_value) in the record of a fundraiser to search the far-left column of the table array for a particular value. It then returns the corresponding **table value** from the column indicated by the col_index_num value. In this example, the grades are in the second, or far-right, column.

For the VLOOKUP function to work correctly, the table arguments must be in ascending sequence, because the VLOOKUP function will return a table value based on the lookup_value being less than or equal to the table arguments. Thus, if the % of Quota value is 77.61% (fifth record in Kenson College Scholarship Fundraiser table), then the VLOOKUP function returns a grade of C, because 77.61% is less than or equal to 79.

BTW

The VLOOKUP Function
A value being looked up outside the range of the table causes the VLOOKUP function to return an error message (#N/A) to the cell. For example, any % of Quota score less than zero in column I of the table in this chapter would result in the error message #N/A being assigned to the corresponding cell.

BTW

Sensitive Information in a Table

If you have a table with one or more columns of sensitive information, such as salary information, you can hide the columns by selecting them and then pressing CTRL + 0. Next, password protect the worksheet. To view the hidden columns, unprotect the worksheet, select the columns adjacent to the hidden columns, and then press CTRL + SHIFT + RIGHT PARENTHESIS.

The following steps create the grade table in the range L1:M7.

1 Change the width of columns L and M to 11.00 (82 pixels).

2 Select cell L1 and then enter `Grade Table` as the table title.

3 If necessary, scroll the worksheet to the left and click cell A7 to select it. Scroll the worksheet to the right so that cell L1 is visible.

4 Click the Format Painter button (Home tab | Clipboard group) and then click cell L1 to copy the format of the selected cell to another cell.

5 Drag through cell M1 and then click the Merge & Center button (Home tab | Alignment group) to merge and center the data in the selected cell.

6 Select the range I8:J8. While holding down the CTRL key, point to the border of the range I8:J8 and drag to the range L2:M2 to copy the column headings in the selected range. Make sure that the source cells in the marquee are directly over the destination range before releasing the mouse button.

7 Enter the table entries in Table 5–4 on the previous page in the range L3:M7. Select the range L3:M7 and then click the Bold button (Home tab | Font group) to bold the entries in the selected range.

8 Click the Center button (Home tab | Alignment group) to center the values in the selected range.

9 Format the range L3:L7 with the percent style format. Click cell J9 to deselect the range L3:M7 (Figure 5–17).

BTW

Using HLOOKUP

HLOOKUP uses the same arguments as VLOOKUP, but it searches rows of information instead of columns. HLOOKUP also uses the row_index_num argument instead of the col_index_num argument, as shown in Figure 5–18. When using HLOOKUP, be sure to sort the values in the first row of the table_array in ascending order to find an approximate match. Otherwise, specify FALSE as the range_lookup argument to find an exact match.

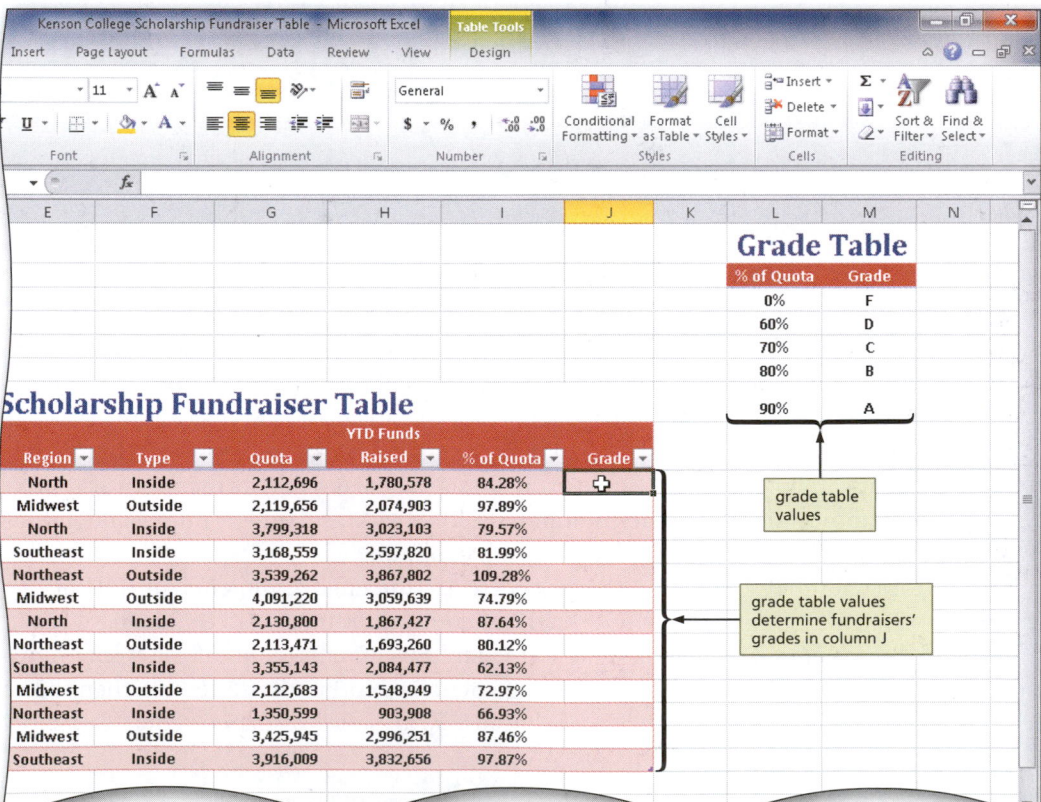

Grade Table

% of Quota	Grade
0%	F
60%	D
70%	C
80%	B
90%	A

Scholarship Fundraiser Table

Region	Type	Quota	YTD Funds Raised	% of Quota	Grade
North	Inside	2,112,696	1,780,578	84.28%	
Midwest	Outside	2,119,656	2,074,903	97.89%	
North	Inside	3,799,318	3,023,103	79.57%	
Southeast	Inside	3,168,559	2,597,820	81.99%	
Northeast	Outside	3,539,262	3,867,802	109.28%	
Midwest	Outside	4,091,220	3,059,639	74.79%	
North	Inside	2,130,800	1,867,427	87.64%	
Northeast	Outside	2,113,471	1,693,260	80.12%	
Southeast	Inside	3,355,143	2,084,477	62.13%	
Midwest	Outside	2,122,683	1,548,949	72.97%	
Northeast	Inside	1,350,599	903,708	66.93%	
Midwest	Outside	3,425,945	2,996,251	87.46%	
Southeast	Inside	3,916,009	3,832,656	97.87%	

grade table values

grade table values determine fundraisers' grades in column J

Figure 5–17

To Use the VLOOKUP Function to Determine Letter Grades

The following steps use the VLOOKUP function and the grade table to determine the letter grade for each fundraiser based on the fundraiser's % of Quota value. In this case, cell I9 is the lookup_value, $L$3:$M$7 is the table_array, and 2 is the col_index_num in the table_array.

1

- With cell J9 selected, type `=vlookup(i9, $l$3:$m$7, 2` as the cell entry (Figure 5–18).

Q&A Why are absolute cell references used in the function?

You need to use absolute cell references ($) for the table_array ($l$3:$m$7) in the VLOOKUP function so that Excel will not adjust the cell references when it creates the calculated column in the next step of this step sequence. If Excel adjusts the cell references, you will see unexpected results in column J.

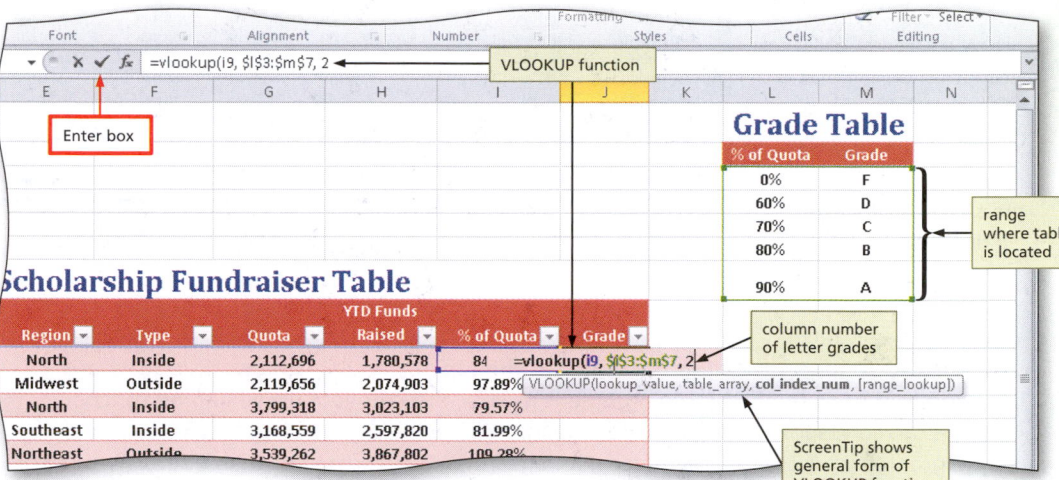

Figure 5–18

2

- Click the Enter box to create a calculated column for the selected field, the Grade field in this case (Figure 5–19).

Q&A What happens when the Enter box is clicked?

Because cell I9 is the first record in a table, Excel creates a calculated column in column I by copying the VLOOKUP function through row 21. As shown in Figure 5–19, any % of Quota value below 60 in column I returns a grade of F in column J. The seventh record (Harris in row 15) receives a grade of B because its % of Quota value is 87.64%. A % of Quota value of 90% is required to move up to the next letter grade. The ninth record (Nulwala) receives a grade of D because his % of Quota value is 62.13%, which is less than 70% but greater than 60%.

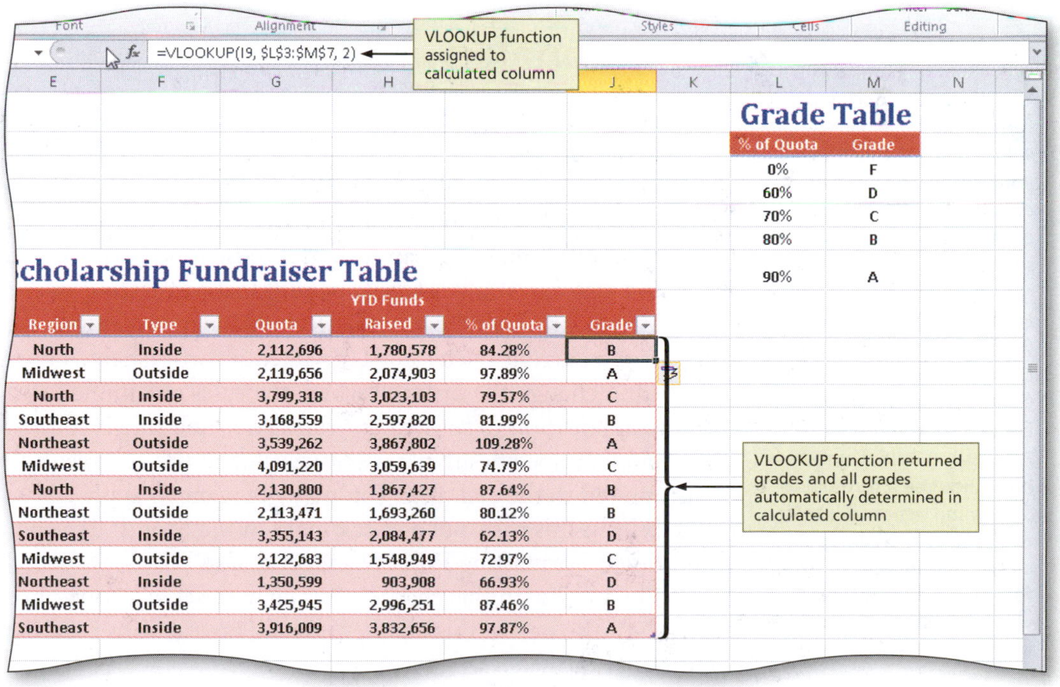

Figure 5–19

3

- Scroll the worksheet so that row 7 is the top row and then click cell A23 to show the completed table (Figure 5–20).

Q&A

How is the VLOOKUP function determining the grades?

From column J, you can see that the VLOOKUP function is not searching for a table argument that matches the lookup_value exactly.

Name	Status	Experience	Hire Date	Region	Type	Quota	YTD Funds Raised	% of Quota	Grade
Sprindys, Del	Full Time	2	09/27/02	North	Inside	2,112,696	1,780,578	84.28%	B
Hennip, Beth	Full Time	5	10/30/02	Midwest	Outside	2,119,656	2,074,903	97.89%	A
Wadzinski, Alli	Part Time	3	07/02/03	North	Inside	3,799,318	3,023,103	79.57%	C
Niazi, Yaseer	Full Time	7	04/15/04	Southeast	Inside	3,168,559	2,597,820	81.99%	B
Washington, Rob	Part Time	4	05/13/04	Northeast	Outside	3,539,262	3,867,802	109.28%	A
Kliegl, Penny	Part Time	1	06/22/04	Midwest	Outside	4,091,220	3,059,639	74.79%	C
Harris, Diedre	Full Time	2	11/02/04	North	Inside	2,130,800	1,867,427	87.64%	B
Yost, David	Part Time	4	11/17/04	Northeast	Outside	2,113,471	1,693,260	80.12%	B
Nulwala, Shamir	Full Time	2	12/06/05	Southeast	Inside	3,355,143	2,084,477	62.13%	D
Jordan, Oliver	Full Time	8	04/12/07	Midwest	Outside	2,122,683	1,548,949	72.97%	C
Ramirez, Al	Part Time	4	10/24/08	Northeast	Inside	1,350,599	903,908	66.93%	D
Doy, Casimer	Part Time	6	10/29/08	Midwest	Outside	3,425,945	2,996,251	87.46%	B
Skora, Chris	Full Time	5	12/10/09	Southeast	Inside	3,916,009	3,832,656	97.87%	A

table is complete

Figure 5–20

The VLOOKUP function begins the search at the top of the table and works downward. As soon as it finds the first table argument greater than the lookup_value, the function returns the corresponding value from column M. The letter grade of F is returned for any value greater than or equal to 0 (zero) and less than 60. A score less than 0 returns an error message (#N/A) to the cell assigned the VLOOKUP function.

Other Ways

1. Click Insert Function box in formula bar, click 'Or select a category' box arrow, click Lookup & Reference, click VLOOKUP in 'Select a function' list

2. Click Lookup & Reference button (Formulas tab | Function Library group), click VLOOKUP

BTW

Conditional Formatting with the IF Function

You can apply conditional formatting based on the value of any IF function you specify. To create a conditional format based on a function or formula, select a range and then click the Conditional Formatting button (Home tab | Styles group). Click New Rule in the Conditional Formatting list to display the New Formatting Rule dialog box. Click Use a formula to determine which cells to format and then enter the desired IF function, or other formula, in the 'Format values where the formula is true' box.

Conditional Formatting

Conditional formatting allows you to create rules that change the formatting of a cell or range of cells based on the value of a particular cell. Excel includes five types of conditional formats: highlight, top and bottom rules, data bars, color scales, and icon sets. Excel allows you to combine different types of formats on any cell or range. For example, based on a cell's value, you can format it to include both an icon and a specific background color. You also can apply multiple conditional formatting rules to a cell or range.

The Conditional Formatting Rules Manager dialog box allows you to view all of the rules for the current selection or for an entire worksheet. The dialog box also allows you to view and change the order in which the rules are applied to a cell or range. You also can stop the application of subsequent rules after one rule is found to be true. For example, if the first rule specifies that a negative value in the cell results in a red background color being applied to the cell, then you may not want to apply any other conditional formats to the cell. In this case, put a check mark in the Stop If True column for the rule in the Conditional Formatting Rules Manager dialog box.

The project in this chapter uses an icon set as a type of conditional format. The exercises at the end of this chapter include instructions regarding the use of other types of conditional formats.

To Add a Conditional Formatting Rule with an Icon Set

The Grade field was added to the table in order to provide succinct information to the user of the worksheet regarding each fundraiser's performance. Another method to succinctly present information regarding each fundraiser's performance is to display an icon next to the % of Quota percentage for each fundraiser. Conditional formatting provides a number of icons, including icons with the appearance of traffic signals, flags, bars, and arrows. Icon sets include sets of three, four, or five icons. You use an icon set depending on how many ways you need to group your data. For example, in the case of grades for the fundraisers, there are five different grades and, therefore, an icon set that includes five icons should be used. You define rules for the conditions under which each icon of the five is displayed in a cell. The following steps add a conditional format to the % of Quota field in the Fundraiser table.

1

- Select the range I9:I21 and then click the Conditional Formatting button (Home tab | Styles group) to display the Conditional Formatting list.

- Click New Rule in the Conditional Formatting list to display the New Formatting Rule dialog box.

- Click the Format Style box arrow (New Formatting Rule dialog box) to display the Format Style list (Figure 5–21).

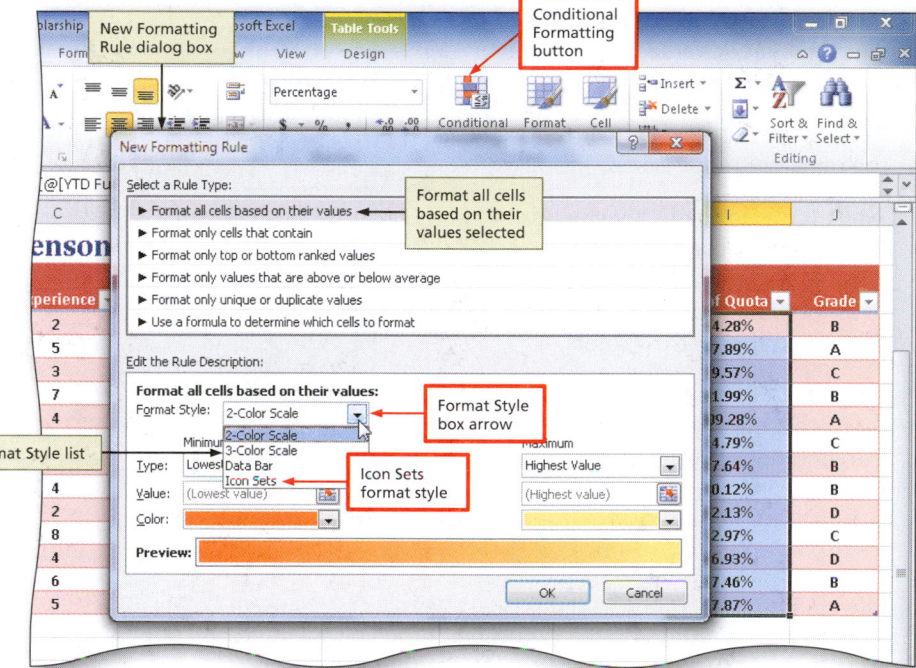

Figure 5–21

2

- Click Icon Sets in the Format Style list (New Formatting Rule dialog box) to display the Icon area in the Edit the Rule Description area.

- Click the Icon Style box arrow to display the Icon Style list and then scroll until 5 Arrows (Colored) appears in the list (Figure 5–22).

🔍 **Experiment**

- Click a variety of icon styles in the Icon Styles list to view the options in the Edit the Rule Description area for each option.

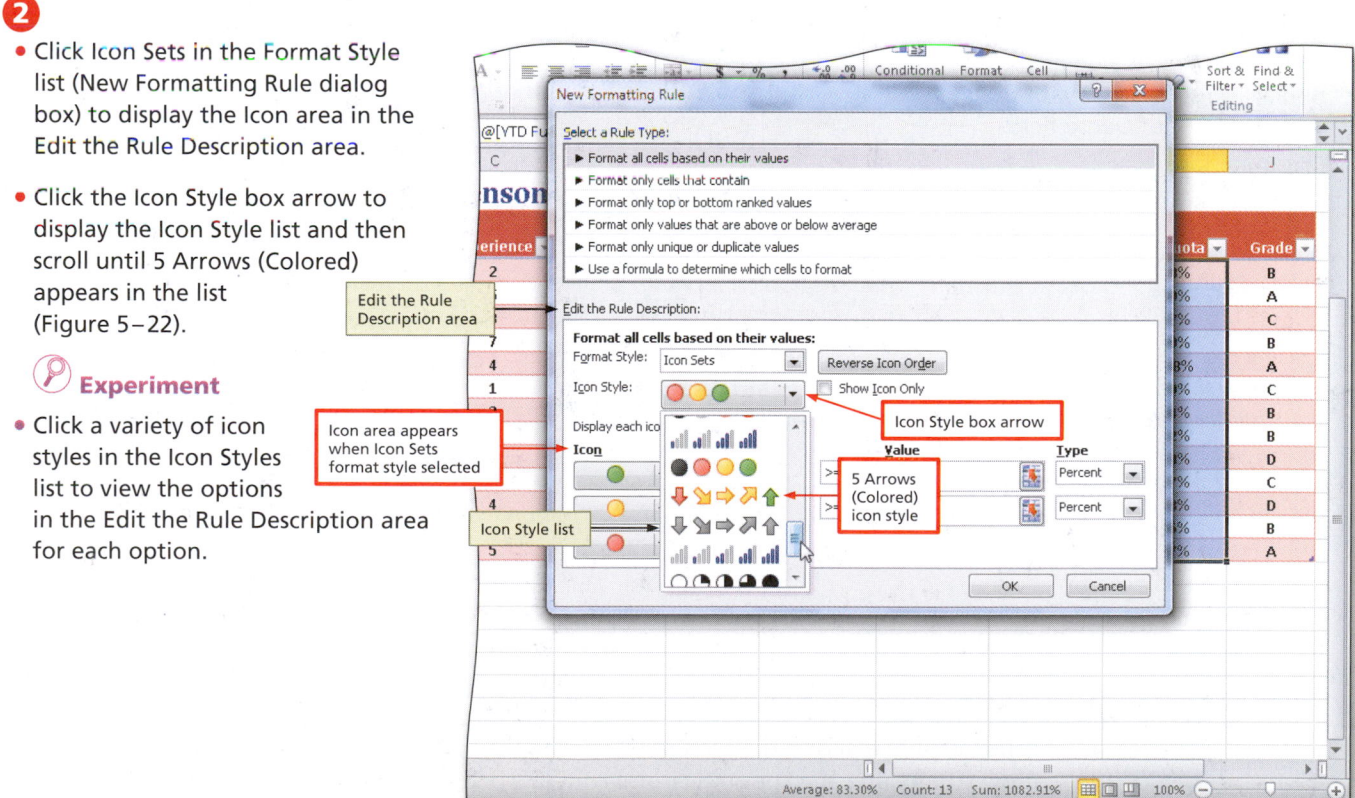

Figure 5–22

❸

- Click 5 Arrows (Colored) in the Icon Style list (New Formatting Rule dialog box) to select an icon style that includes five different colored arrows.

- Click the top Type box arrow and then click Number in the list to select a numeric value for the Type rather than a percent value.

- Change the Type to Number for the remaining Type boxes.

- Type **0.9** in the first Value box, **0.8** in the second Value box, and **0.7** in the third Value box to assign ranges of values to each of the first three arrow colors.

- Type **0.6** in the final Value box and then press the TAB key to complete the conditions (Figure 5–23).

Q&A Why do the numbers next to each icon change as I type?

The area below the word Icon models the current conditional formatting rule. Excel automatically updates this area as you change the conditions on the right side of the Edit the Rule Description area. Use this area as an easy-to-read status of the conditions that you are creating.

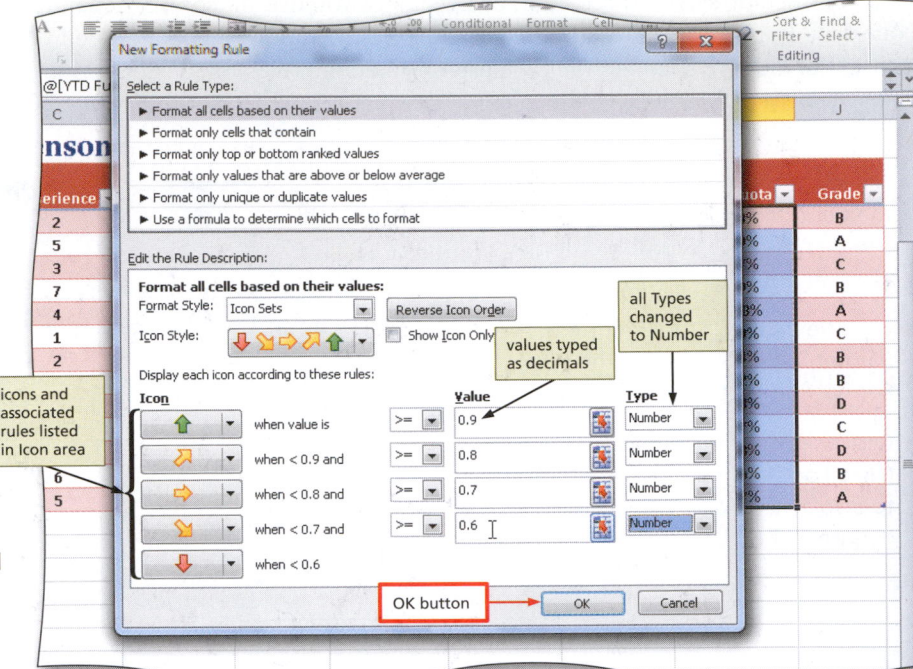

Figure 5–23

❹

- Click the OK button (New Formatting Rule dialog box) to display icons in each row of the table in the % of Quota field.

- Click cell A23 to deselect the table (Figure 5–24).

Q&A What do the icons represent?

In addition to the Grade field, the conditional formatting icons provide a visual representation of the fundraisers' progress on attaining their fundraising quotas. The green arrow and its direction represent a grade of A, the red arrow and its direction a grade of F, and the three different yellow arrows and their directions represent the B, C, and D levels. None of the fundraisers received a grade of F.

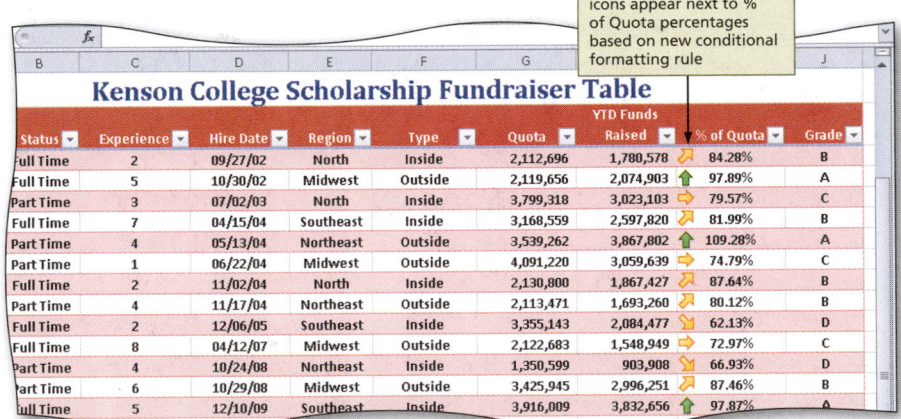

Figure 5–24

Working with Tables in Excel

When a table is active, the Design tab on the Ribbon provides powerful commands that allow you to alter the appearance and contents of a table quickly. For example, you quickly can add and remove header and total rows in a table. This section describes the use of these commands.

To Use the Total Row Check Box

The Total Row check box on the Design tab allows you to insert a **total row** at the bottom of the table. The total row sums the values that are in the far-right column of the table, if the values are numeric. If the values in the far-right column of the table are textual, then Excel counts the number of records and puts the number in the total row. For example, in Figure 5–26, the 13 in cell J22 on the right side of the total row is a count of the number of fundraiser records. Excel provides additional computations for the total row, as shown in the following steps.

1

- Click cell A9 to make the table active and then display the Table Tools Design tab (Figure 5–25).

 Experiment

- Select a variety of combinations of check boxes in the Table Style Options group on the Table Tools Design tab. When finished, make sure that the check boxes are set as shown in Figure 5–25.

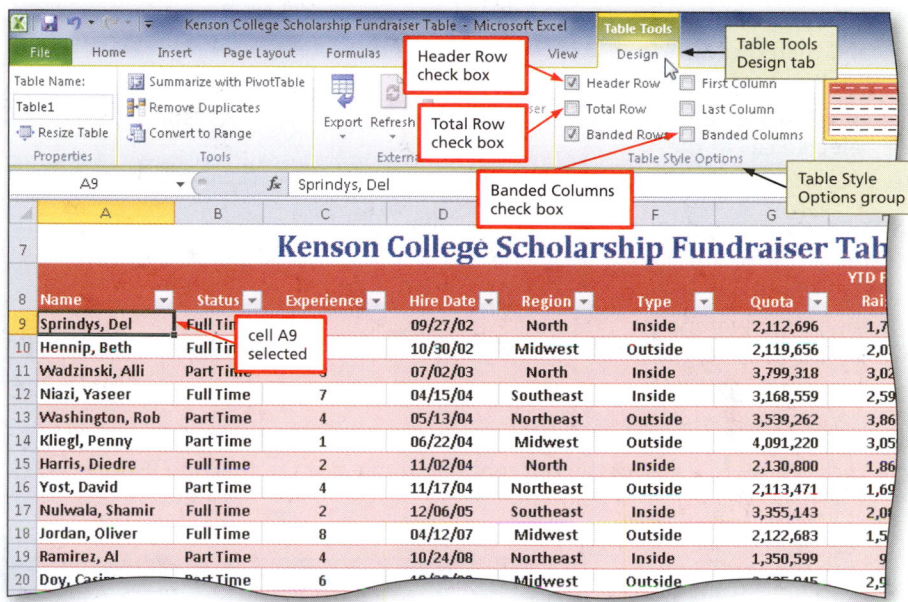

Figure 5–25

2

- Click the Total Row check box (Table Tools Design tab | Table Style Options group) to add the total row and display the record count in the far-right column of the table, cell J22 in this case.

- Select cell H22.

- Click the arrow on the right side of the cell to display a list of available statistical functions (Figure 5–26).

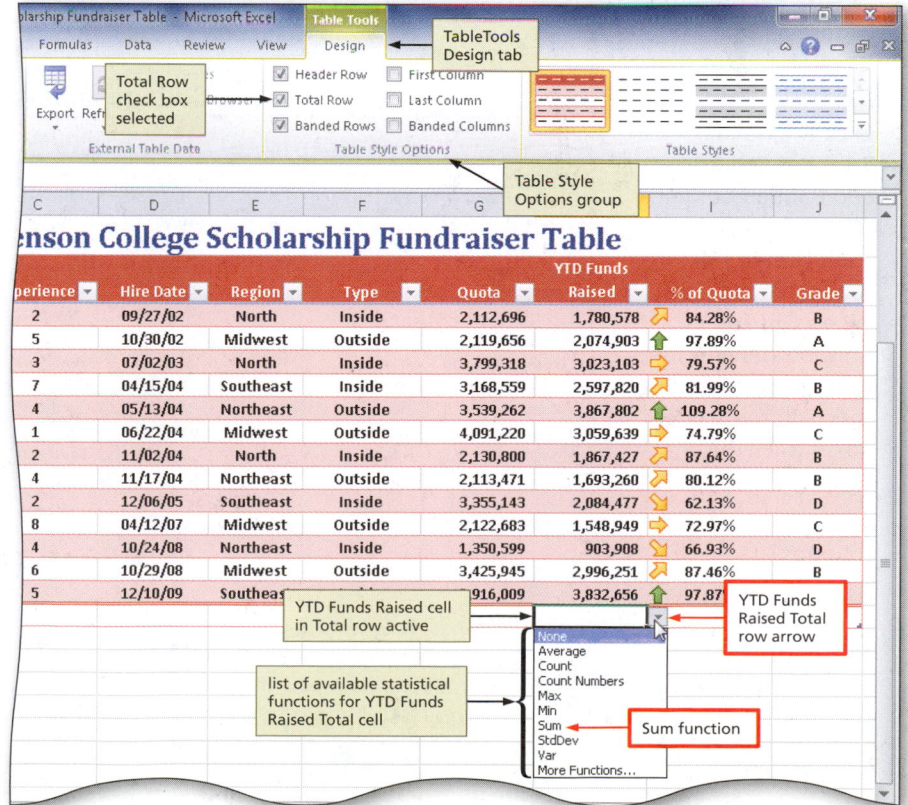

Figure 5–26

3

- Click Sum in the list to select the Sum function for the selected cell in the total row.

- Select cell G22, click the arrow on the right side of the cell, and then click Sum in the list to select the Sum function for the selected cell in the total row.

- Select cell C22, click the arrow on the right side of the cell, and then click Average in the list to select the Average function for the selected cell in the total row.

- Click cell A9 to deselect the cell containing the average function (Figure 5–27).

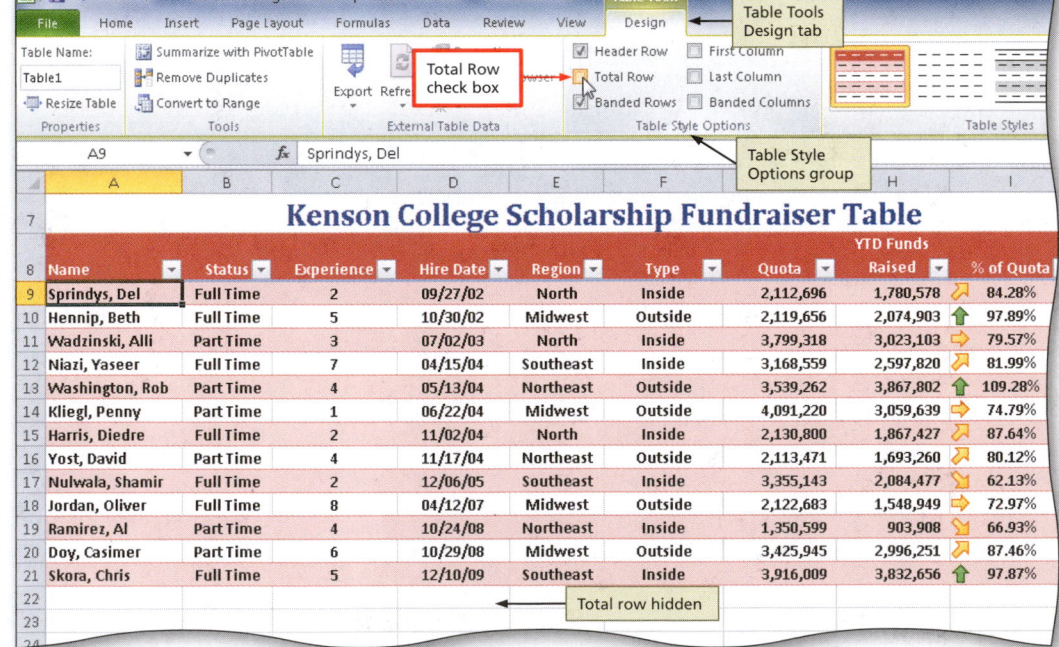

Figure 5–27

4

- Click the Total Row check box (Table Tools Design tab | Table Style Options group) to hide the total row (Figure 5–28).

🔍 **Experiment**

- Click the Header Row, Banded Rows, and Banded Columns check boxes (Table Tools Design tab | Table Style Options). When you are finished viewing the formatting caused by checking these check boxes, click the check boxes.

Q&A

What are banded columns?

As you have learned, banded rows include alternating colors every other row. Similarly, banded columns provide alternating colors every other column. You also can include a different color for the first and/or last column in a table. The quick style that you choose for a table must have these colors defined in the quick style. The quick style used in this chapter does not include special formatting for the first and last columns.

To Print the Table

When a table is selected and you display the Print tab in the Backstage view, an option in the Settings area allows you to print the contents of just the active table. The following steps print the table in landscape orientation using the Fit Sheet on One Page option.

- If necessary, click cell A9 to make the table active and then click File on the Ribbon to open the Backstage view.

- Click the Print tab to display the Print gallery.

- Click the Print Active Sheets in the Settings area to display a list of parts of the workbook to print.

- Select Print Selected Table to choose to print only the selected table.

- In the Settings area, select the options to print the table in landscape orientation using the Fit Sheet on One Page option (Figure 5–29).

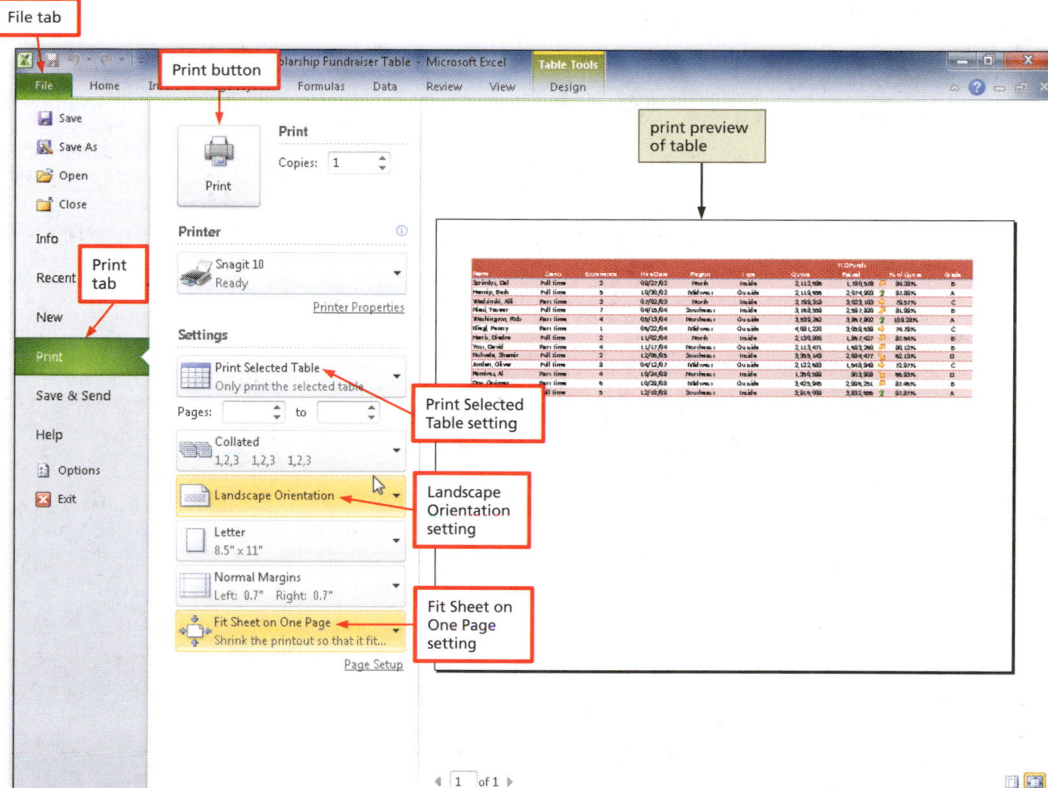

Figure 5–29

- Click the Print button to print the table (Figure 5–30).

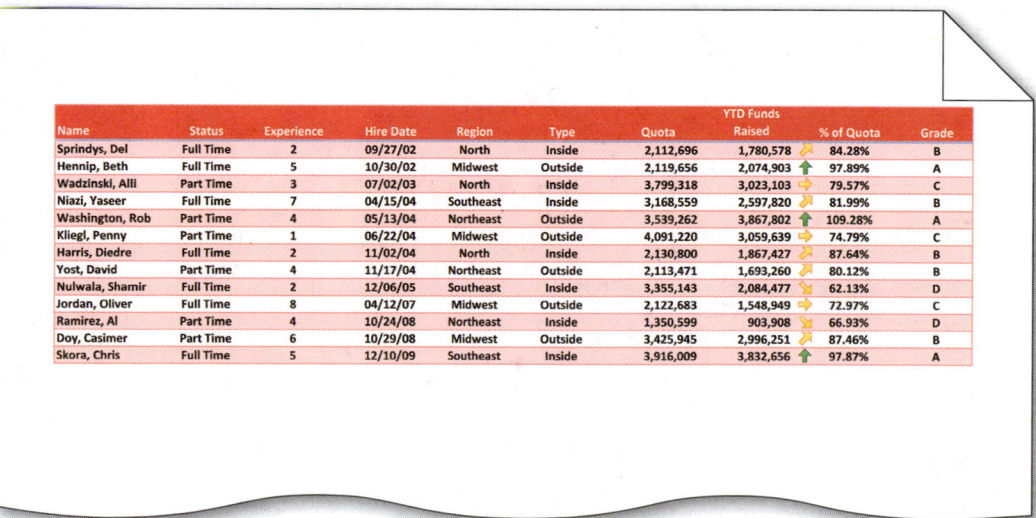

Name	Status	Experience	Hire Date	Region	Type	Quota	YTD Funds Raised	% of Quota	Grade
Sprindys, Del	Full Time	2	09/27/02	North	Inside	2,112,696	1,780,578	84.28%	B
Hennip, Beth	Full Time	5	10/30/02	Midwest	Outside	2,119,656	2,074,903	97.89%	A
Wadzinski, Alli	Part Time	3	07/02/03	North	Inside	3,799,318	3,023,103	79.57%	C
Niazi, Yaseer	Full Time	7	04/15/04	Southeast	Inside	3,168,559	2,597,820	81.99%	B
Washington, Rob	Part Time	4	05/13/04	Northeast	Outside	3,539,262	3,867,802	109.28%	A
Kliegl, Penny	Part Time	1	06/22/04	Midwest	Outside	4,091,220	3,059,639	74.79%	C
Harris, Diedre	Full Time	2	11/02/04	North	Inside	2,130,800	1,867,427	87.64%	B
Yost, David	Part Time	4	11/17/04	Northeast	Outside	2,113,471	1,693,260	80.12%	B
Nulwala, Shamir	Full Time	2	12/06/05	Southeast	Inside	3,355,148	2,084,477	62.13%	D
Jordan, Oliver	Full Time	8	04/12/07	Midwest	Outside	2,122,683	1,548,949	72.97%	C
Ramirez, Al	Part Time	4	10/24/08	Northeast	Inside	1,350,599	903,908	66.93%	D
Doy, Casimer	Part Time	6	10/29/08	Midwest	Outside	3,425,945	2,996,251	87.46%	B
Skora, Chris	Full Time	5	12/10/09	Southeast	Inside	3,916,009	3,832,656	97.87%	A

Figure 5–30

Sorting a Table

The data in a table is easier to work with and more meaningful if the records are arranged sequentially based on one or more fields. Arranging records in a specific sequence is called **sorting**. Data is in **ascending sequence** if it is in order from lowest to highest, earliest to most recent, or alphabetically from A to Z. Data is in **descending sequence** if it is sorted from highest to lowest, most recent to earliest, or alphabetically from Z to A. The field or fields you select to sort the records are called **sort keys**.

You can sort data in a table by using one of the following techniques:

1. Select a cell in the field on which to sort, click the Sort & Filter button (Home tab | Editing group), and then click one of the sorting options on the Sort & Filter menu.
2. With the table active, click the column heading arrow in the column on which to sort and then click one of the sorting options in the table.
3. Use the Sort button (Data tab | Sort & Filter group).
4. Right-click anywhere in a table and then point to Sort on a shortcut menu to display the Sort submenu.

To Sort a Table in Ascending Sequence by Name Using the Sort & Filter Button

The following steps sort the table in ascending sequence by the Name field using the Sort & Filter button (Home tab | Editing group).

1

- If necessary, display the Home tab.

- Click cell A9, if necessary, and then click the Sort & Filter button (Home tab | Editing group) to display the Sort & Filter menu (Figure 5–31).

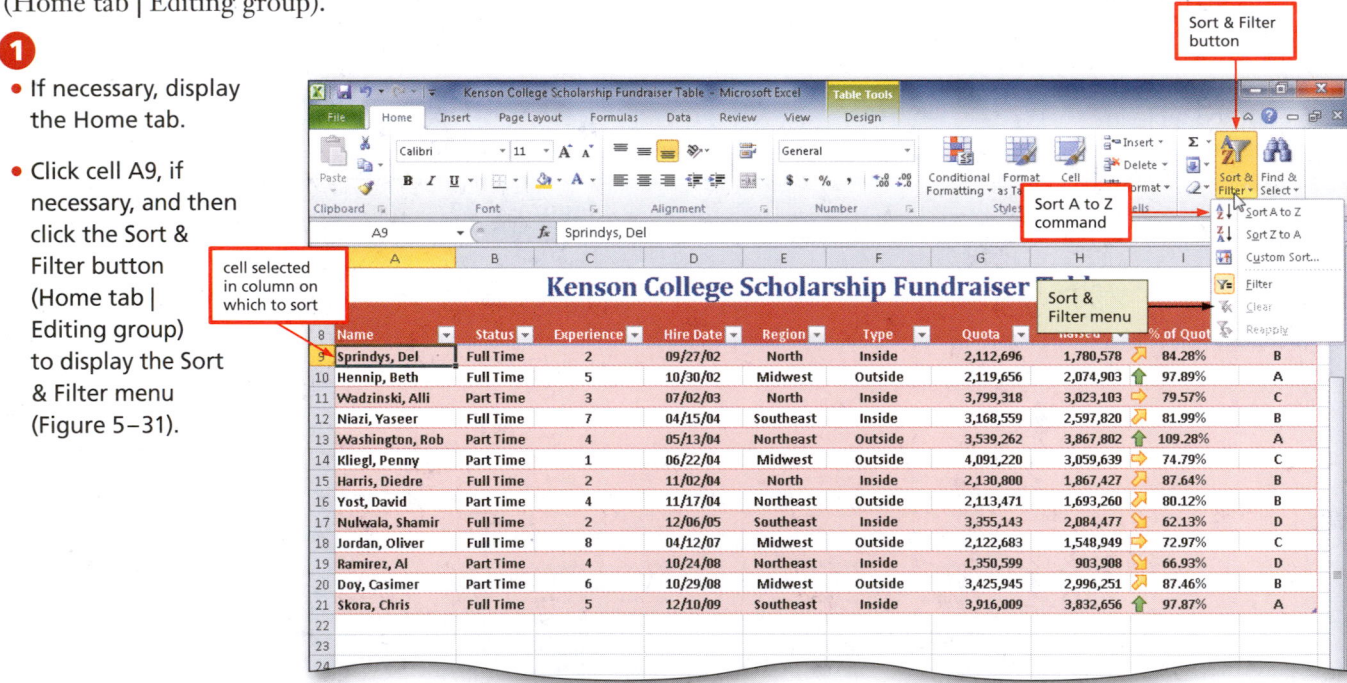

Figure 5–31

What if the column I choose includes numeric or date data?

If the column you choose includes numeric data, then the Sort & Filter menu would show the Sort Smallest to Largest and Sort Largest to Smallest commands instead of the Sort A to Z and Sort Z to A commands. If the column you choose includes date data, then the Sort & Filter menu would show the Sort Oldest to Newest and Sort Newest to Oldest commands instead of the Sort A to Z and Sort Z to A commands.

2

- Click the Sort A to Z command to sort the table in ascending sequence by the selected field, Name in this case (Figure 5–32).

🔍 **Experiment**

- Select other fields in the table and use the same procedure to sort on the fields you choose. When you are finished, remove any sorting, select cell A9, and repeat the two steps above.

records sorted in ascending sequence by name

Name	Status	Experience	Hire Date	Region	Type	Quota	YTD Fu... Raise...
Doy, Casimer	Part Time	6	10/29/08	Midwest	Outside	3,425,945	2,99
Harris, Diedre	Full Time	2	11/02/04	North	Inside	2,130,800	1,86
Hennip, Beth	Full Time	5	10/30/02	Midwest	Outside	2,119,656	2,07
Jordan, Oliver	Full Time	8	04/12/07	Midwest	Outside	2,122,683	1,5
Kliegl, Penny	Part Time	1	06/22/04	Midwest	Outside	4,091,220	3,0
Niazi, Yaseer	Full Time	7	04/15/04	Southeast	Inside	3,168,559	2,5
Nulwala, Shamir	Full Time	2	12/06/05	Southeast	Inside	3,355,143	2,0
Ramirez, Al	Part Time	4	10/24/08	Northeast	Inside	1,350,599	9
Skora, Chris	Full Time	5	12/10/09	Southeast	Inside	3,916,009	3,8
Sprindys, Del	Full Time	2	09/27/02	North	Inside	2,112,696	1,7
Wadzinski, Alli	Part Time	3	07/02/03	North	Inside	3,799,318	3,0
Washington, Rob	Part Time	4	05/13/04	Northeast	Outside	3,539,262	3,86
Yost, David	Part Time	4	11/17/04	Northeast	Outside	2,113,471	1,69

Figure 5–32

Other Ways

1. Select field in table, click Sort A to Z button (Data tab | Sort & Filter group)
2. Click column heading arrow of field on which to sort, click Sort A to Z
3. Right-click column to sort, point to Sort on shortcut menu, click Sort A to Z

To Sort a Table in Descending Sequence by Name Using the Sort Z to A Button on the Data Tab

The following steps sort the records in descending sequence by name.

1 If necessary, click cell A9 to select the table.

2 Display the Data tab.

3 Click the Sort Z to A button (Data tab | Sort & Filter group) to sort the table in descending sequence by the selected field, Name in this case (Figure 5–33).

BTW

Sorting
Some spreadsheet specialists use the fill handle to create a series in an additional field in the table that is used only to reorder the records into their original sequence.

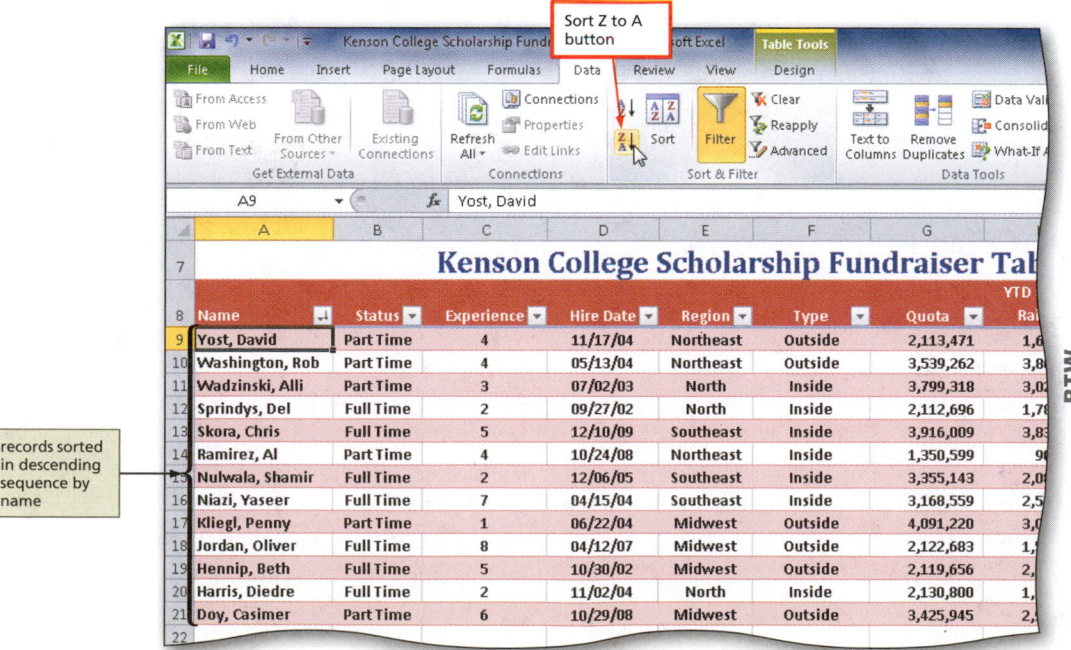

records sorted in descending sequence by name

Figure 5–33

BTW

Sort Order
Excel uses the following order of priority: numbers from smallest to largest positive, (space), special characters, text, (blanks). For example, the sort order is: 0 1 2 3 4 5 6 7 8 9 (space) ! " # $ % & ( ) * , . / : ; ? @ [\ ] ^ _ ` { | } ~ + < = > A B C D E F G H I J K L M N O P Q R S T U V W X Y Z (blanks).

To Sort a Table Using the Sort Command on an AutoFilter Menu

The following step sorts the table by Hire Date using the Sort Ascending command on an AutoFilter menu.

- Display the Home tab.

- Click the Hire Date AutoFilter arrow to display the AutoFilter menu for the selected field, Hire Date in this case (Figure 5–34).

- Click Sort Oldest to Newest in the Hire Date AutoFilter menu to sort the table in ascending sequence by the selected field.

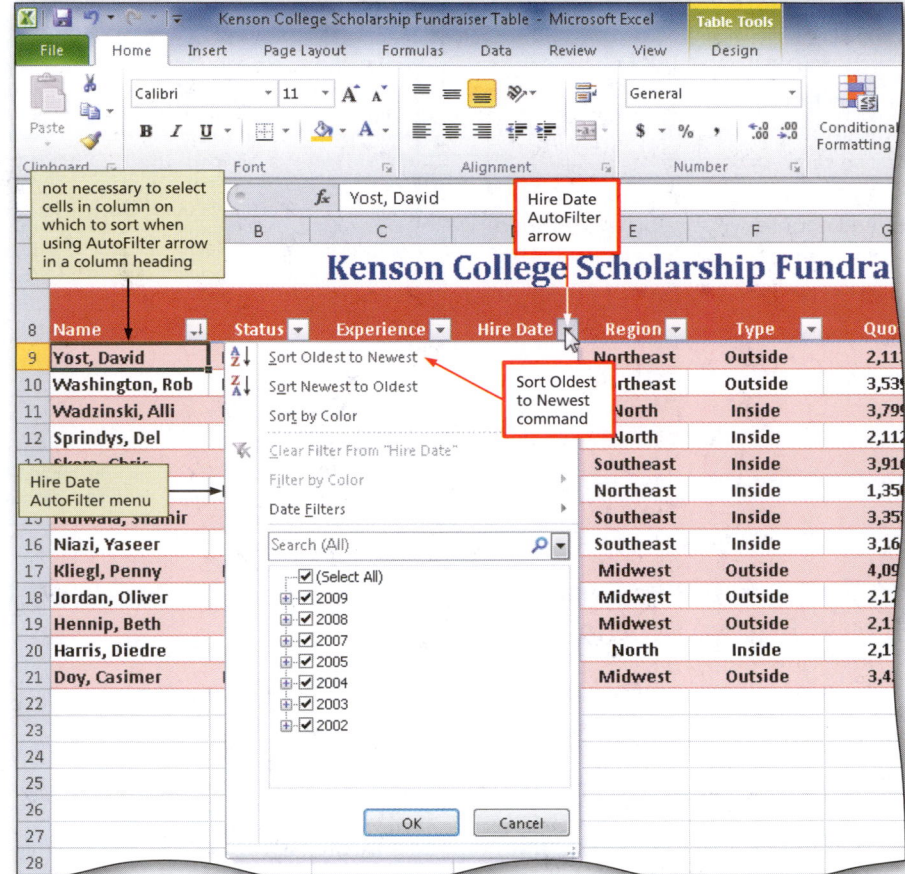

Figure 5–34

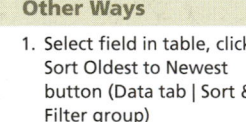

Other Ways

1. Select field in table, click Sort Oldest to Newest button (Data tab | Sort & Filter group)

2. Right-click column to sort, point to Sort on shortcut menu, click Sort Oldest to Newest

To Sort a Table on Multiple Fields Using the Custom Sort Command

Excel allows you to sort on a maximum of 256 fields in a single sort operation. For instance, the sort example in this part of the chapter uses the Custom Sort command on the Sort & Filter menu to sort the Kenson College Scholarship Fundraiser table by quota (column G) within status (column B) within type (column F). The Type and Status fields will be sorted in ascending sequence; the Quota field will be sorted in descending sequence.

The phrase, sort by quota within status within type, means that the records in the table first are arranged in ascending sequence by Type (Inside and Outside). Within Type, the records are arranged in ascending sequence by Status (Full Time or Part Time). Within Status, the records are arranged in descending sequence by the fundraiser's Quota. In this case, Type is the **major sort key** (Sort by field), Status is the **intermediate sort key** (first Then by field), and Quota is the **minor sort key** (second Then by field). The following steps sort the fundraiser table on multiple fields using the Custom Sort command.

1
• With a cell in the table active, click the Sort & Filter button (Home tab | Editing group) to display the Sort & Filter menu (Figure 5–35).

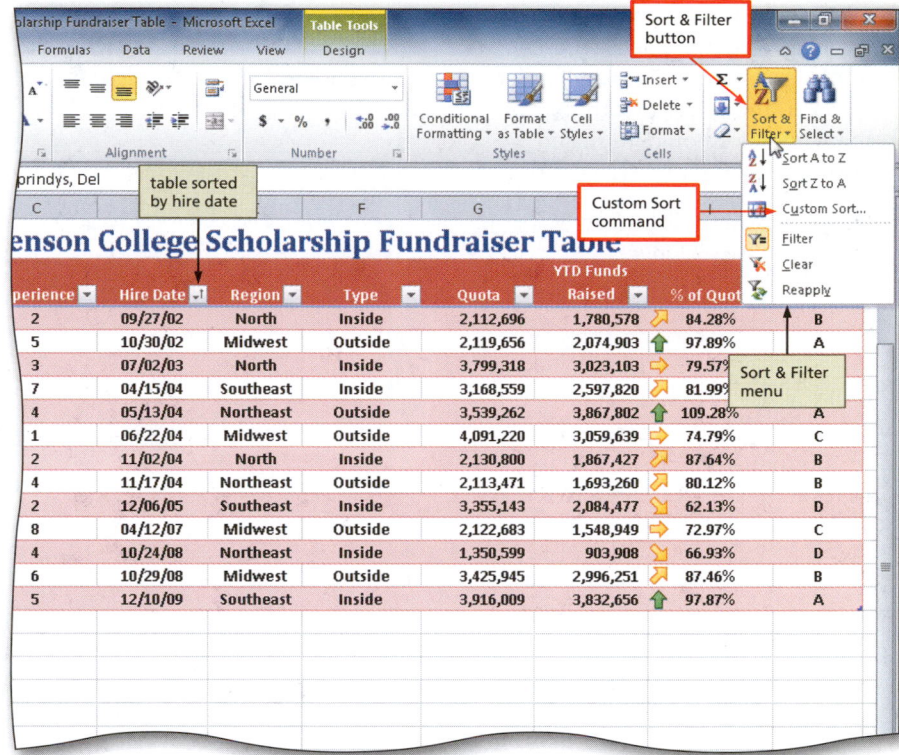

Figure 5–35

2
• Click Custom Sort on the Sort & Filter menu to display the Sort dialog box.

• Click the Sort by box arrow (Sort dialog box) to display the field names in the table (Figure 5–36).

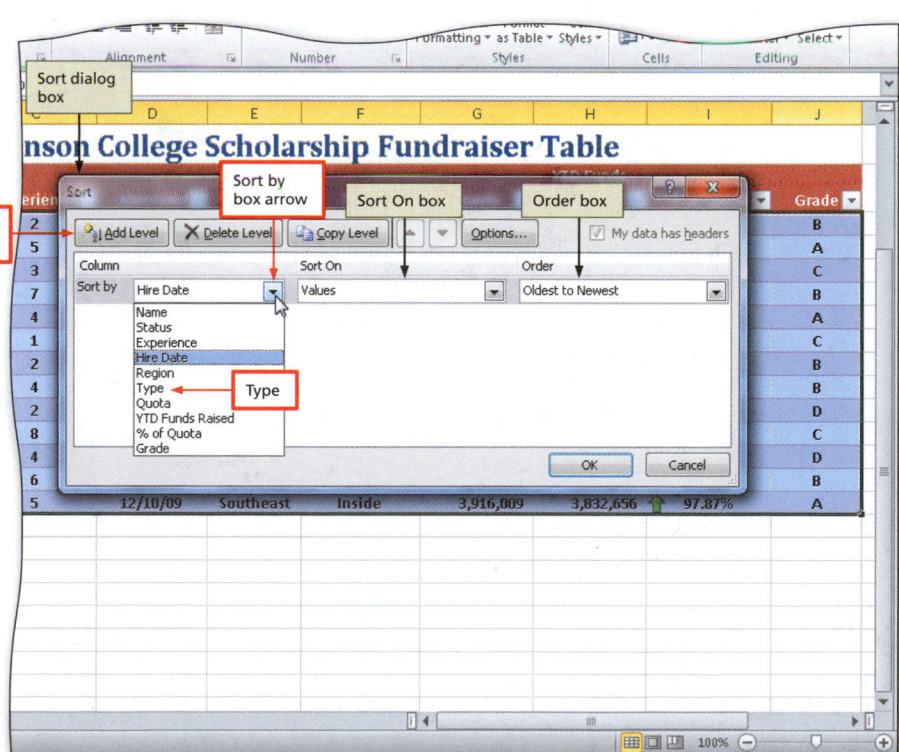

Figure 5–36

3

- Click Type to select the first sort level. If necessary, select Values in the Sort On box. If necessary, select A to Z in the Order box to specify that the field should be sorted alphabetically.

- Click the Add Level button to add a new sort level.

- Click the Then by box arrow and then click Status in the Then by list to select a second sort level. If necessary, select Values in the Sort On box and, if necessary, select A to Z in the Order box to specify that the field should be sorted alphabetically.

- Click the Add Level button to add a new sort level.

- Click the second Then by box arrow and then click Quota in the Then by list to select a third sort level. If necessary, select Values in the Sort On box. Select Largest to Smallest in the Order box to specify that the field should be sorted in reverse order (Figure 5–37).

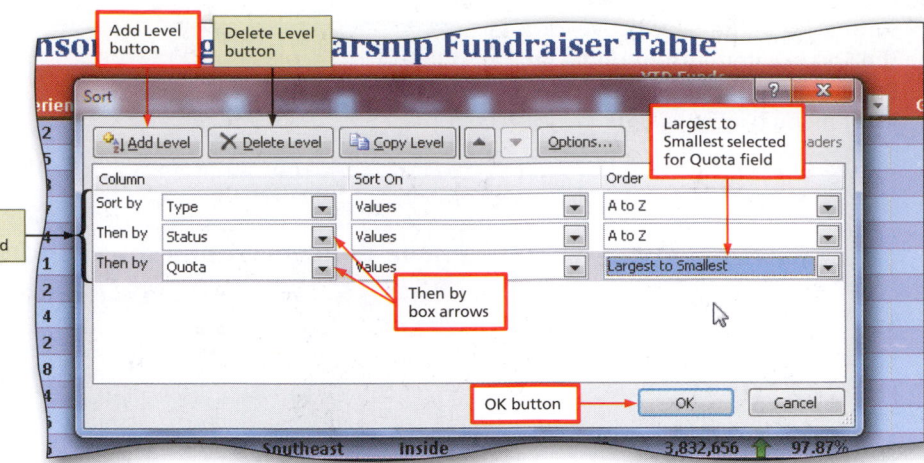

Figure 5–37

4

- Click the OK button to sort the table, in this case by quota within status within type (Figure 5–38).

Q&A

How are the records sorted?

As shown in Figure 5–38, Excel sorts the records in ascending sequence by type in column F. Within each type, the records are sorted in ascending sequence by status in column B. Finally, within status, the records are sorted in descending sequence by the quotas in column G. Remember, if you make a mistake in a sort operation, you can return the records to their original order by clicking the Undo button on the Quick Access Toolbar or by sorting the table by hire date, which is the order in which the data was entered.

Name	Status	Experience	Hire Date	Region	Type	Quota	
Skora, Chris	Full Time	5	12/10/09	Southeast	Inside	3,916,009	3,8
Nulwala, Shamir	Full Time	2	12/06/05	Southeast	Inside	3,355,143	2,0
Niazi, Yaseer	Full Time	7	04/15/04	Southeast	Inside	3,168,559	2,5
Harris, Diedre	Full Time	2	11/02/04	North	Inside	2,130,800	1,86
Sprindys, Del	Full Time	2	09/27/02	North	Inside	2,112,696	1,78
Wadzinski, Alli	Part Time	3	07/02/03	North	Inside	3,799,318	3,02
Ramirez, Al	Part Time	4	10/24/08	Northeast	Inside	1,350,599	90
Jordan, Oliver	Full Time	8	04/12/07	Midwest	Outside	2,122,683	1,54
Hennip, Beth	Full Time	5	10/30/02	Midwest	Outside	2,119,656	2,07
Kliegl, Penny	Part Time	1	06/22/04	Midwest	Outside	4,091,220	3,05
Washington, Rob	Part Time	4	05/13/04	Northeast	Outside	3,539,262	3,86
Doy, Casimer	Part Time	6	10/29/08	Midwest	Outside	3,425,945	2,9
Yost, David	Part Time	4	11/17/04	Northeast	Outside	2,113,471	1,6

Figure 5–38

Other Ways

1. Click minor field column heading arrow, click Sort Z to A button (Data tab | Sort & Filter group), click intermediate field column heading arrow, click Sort A to Z button (Data tab | Sort & Filter group), click major field column heading arrow, click Sort A to Z button (Data tab | Sort & Filter group)

Break Point: If you wish to take a break, this is a good place to do so. Be sure to save the file again and then you can quit Excel. To resume at a later time, start Excel, open the file called Kenson College Scholarship Fundraiser Table, and continue following the steps from this location forward.

Querying a Table Using AutoFilter

When you first create a table, Excel automatically enables AutoFilter; the column heading arrows thus appear to the right of the column headings. You can hide the arrows so that they do not show by toggling the Filter button (Data tab | Sort & Filter group) or the Filter command on the Sort & Filter menu (Home tab | Editing group). Clicking an arrow reveals the AutoFilter menu for the column heading. The query technique that uses the column heading arrows is called **AutoFilter**.

AutoFilter displays all records that meet the criteria as a subset of the table by hiding records that do not pass the test. Clicking a column heading arrow causes Excel to display commands and a list of all the items in the field (column) in an AutoFilter menu, which are all preselected. If you deselect an item from the AutoFilter menu, Excel immediately hides records that contain the item. The item you deselect from the AutoFilter menu is called the **filter criterion**. If you select a filter criterion from a second column heading while the first is still active, then Excel displays a subset of the first subset. The AutoFilter menu allows you to search for items in the column by typing in a Search box that appears above the list of items. The process of filtering activity based on one or more filter criteria is called a **query**.

To Sort a Table Using an AutoFilter Menu

The following steps sort the Kenson College Scholarship Fundraiser table into its previous sort order, sorted in ascending sequence by hire date.

1 Click cell A9 (or any cell in the table) to make the table active.

2 Click the Hire Date arrow and then click Sort Oldest to Newest in the Hire Date AutoFilter menu to sort the table in ascending sequence, in this case by hire date.

To Query a Table Using AutoFilter

The following steps query the Kenson College Scholarship Fundraiser table using AutoFilter, so that the table displays only those records that pass the following test:

Status = Full time AND Type = Inside

1

• Click the Status arrow in cell B8 to display the AutoFilter menu for the selected column (Figure 5–39).

What is displayed below the Text Filters command on the AutoFilter menu?

The list below the Text Filters command is a list of all of the values that occur in the selected column. The check mark in the top item, (Select All), indicates that all values for this field currently are displayed in the table.

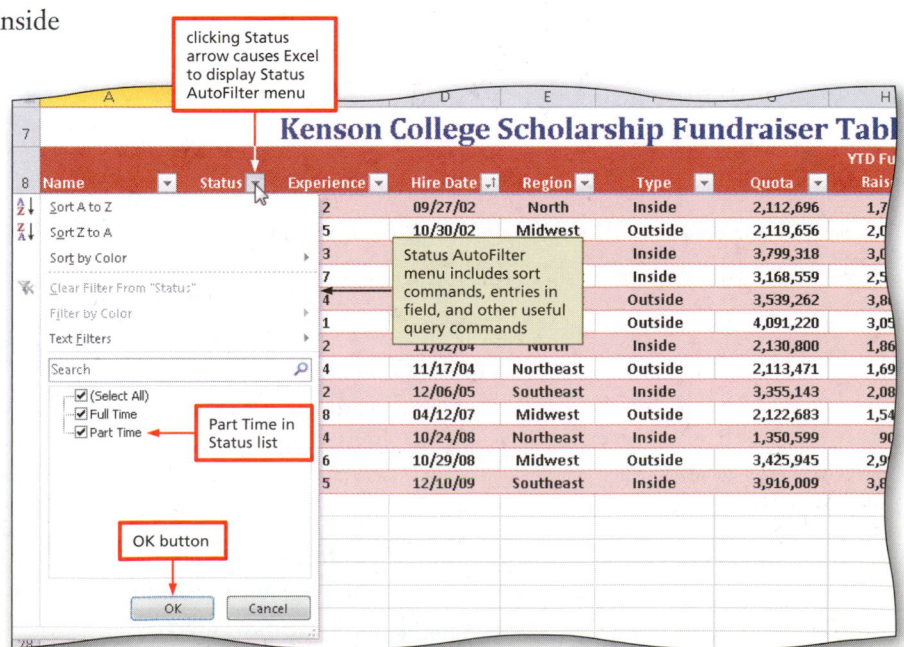

Figure 5–39

2

- Click Part Time in the Status list to remove the check mark and cause Excel to hide all records representing part-time fundraisers, so that only records representing full-time fundraisers appear.

- Click the OK button to apply the AutoFilter criterion.

- Click the Type arrow in row 8 to display the AutoFilter menu for the selected column (Figure 5–40).

3

- Click Outside in the Type list to remove the check mark and hide all records that do not match the AutoFilter criterion, in this case those that represent part-time fundraisers who are not inside fundraisers.

4

- Click the OK button to apply the AutoFilter criterion (Figure 5–41).

Why are the row headings of some rows displayed in blue?

Excel displays row headings in blue to indicate that these rows are the result of a filtering process.

Are both filters now applied to the table?

Yes. When you select a second filter criterion, Excel adds it to the first. Hence, in the previous steps, each record must pass two tests to appear as part of the final subset of the table.

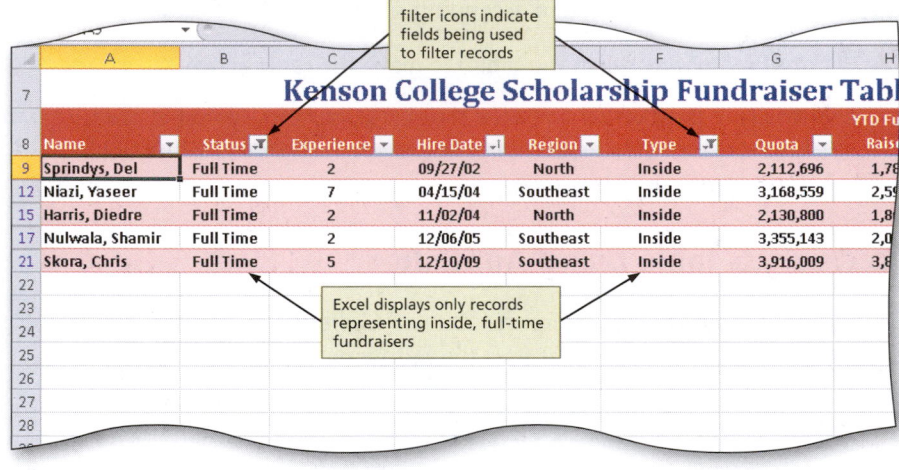

Figure 5–40

Figure 5–41

Other Ways

1. Click column heading AutoFilter arrow, type in Search box in AutoFilter menu, click OK button

More about AutoFilter

Other important points regarding AutoFilter include the following:

1. When you enable AutoFilter and records are hidden, Excel displays a filter icon in the table column heading arrows used to establish the filter. Excel also displays the row headings of the selected records in blue.

2. If the column heading arrows do not show, then you must manually enable AutoFilter by clicking the Filter command on the Sort & Filter menu (Home tab | Editing group). The Filter button also is on the Data tab.

3. To remove a filter criterion for a single field, select the Select All option from the column heading AutoFilter menu for that field.

4. When you create a formula in the total row of a table, the formula automatically recalculates the values even when you filter the list. For example, the results shown

in the total row in Figure 5–27 on page EX 320 are updated automatically if you apply a filter to the table.

5. You can filter and sort a column by color or conditional formatting using the Sort by Color and Filter by Color commands on the AutoFilter menu (Figure 5–39 on page EX 327).

To Show All Records in a Table

The following steps show all records in the table after a query hid some of the records.

• Display the Data tab.

• Click the Filter button (Data tab | Sort & Filter group) to display all of the records in the table (Figure 5–42).

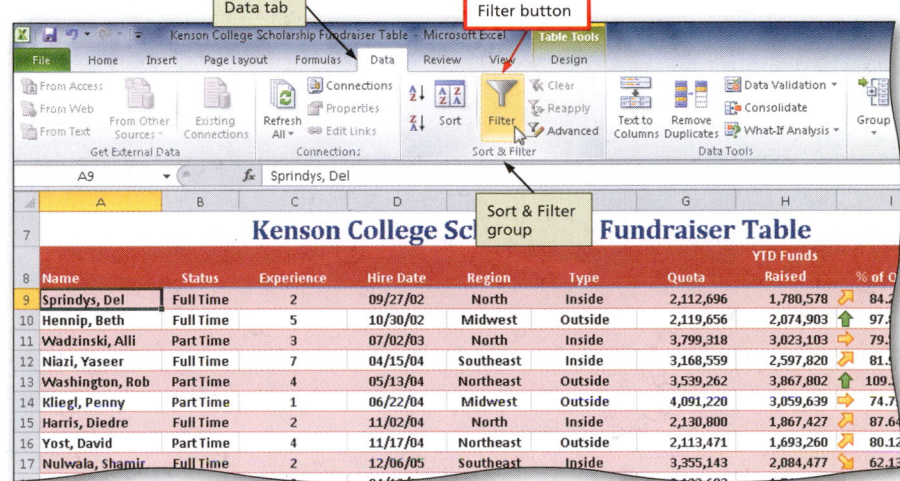

Figure 5–42

Other Ways

1. Click column heading AutoFilter arrow, click (Select All) in AutoFilter menu

To Enter Custom Criteria Using AutoFilter

One of the commands available in all AutoFilter menus is Custom Filter. The Custom Filter command allows you to enter custom criteria, such as multiple options or ranges of numbers. The following steps enter custom criteria to show records in the table that represent fundraisers whose experience is between 3 and 5 years, inclusive; that is, their experience is greater than or equal to 3 and less than or equal to 5 ($3 \leq$ Experience ≤ 5).

• Click the Filter button (Data tab | Sort & Filter group) to display the AutoFilter arrows in the table.

• With the table active, click the Experience arrow in cell C8 to display the AutoFilter menu for the selected column.

• Point to Number Filters to display the Number Filters submenu (Figure 5–43).

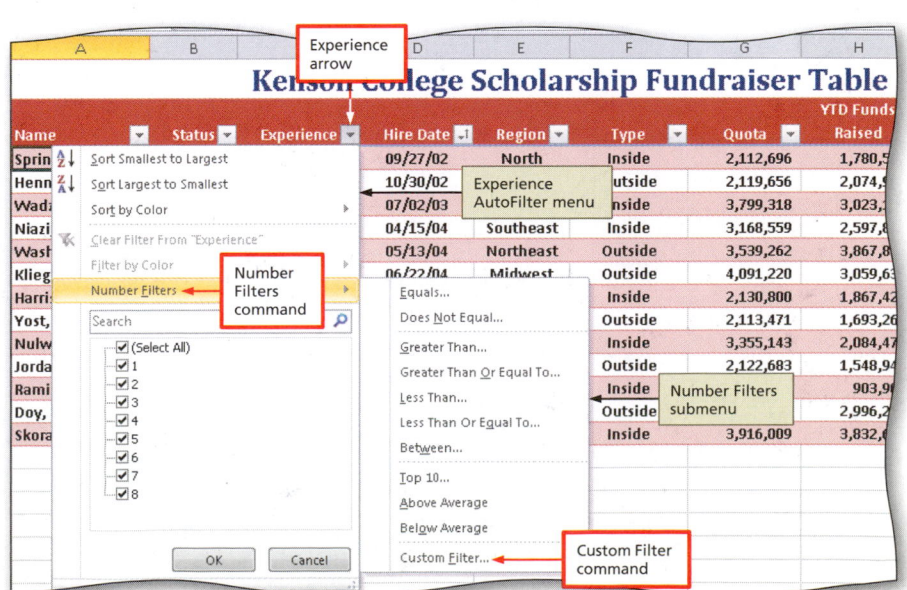

Figure 5–43

2

- Click Custom Filter to display the Custom AutoFilter dialog box.

- Click the top-left box arrow (Custom AutoFilter dialog box), click 'is greater than or equal to' in the list, and then type 3 in the top-right box.

- Click the bottom-left box arrow, click 'is less than or equal to' in the list, and then type 5 in the bottom-right box (Figure 5–44).

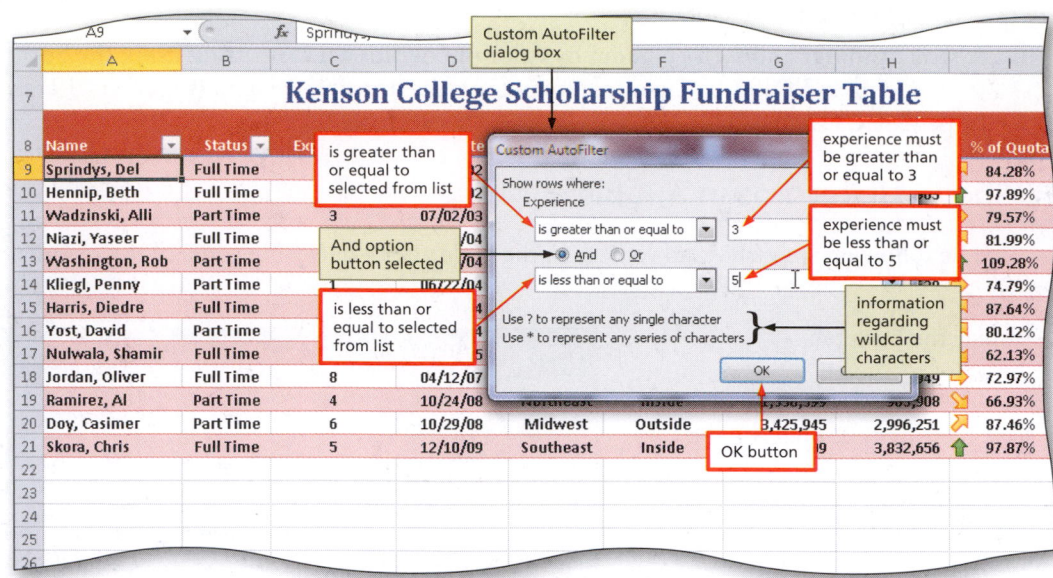

Figure 5–44

3

- Click the OK button (Custom AutoFilter dialog box) to display records in the table that match the customer AutoFilter criteria, in this case, fundraisers whose experience is between 3 and 5 inclusive (Figure 5–45).

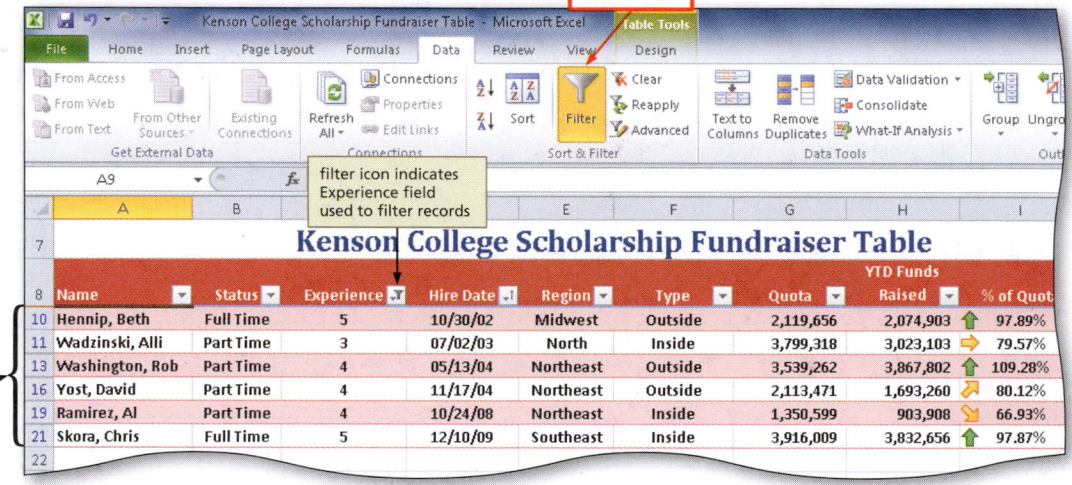

records representing fundraisers whose experience is greater than or equal to 3 AND less than or equal to 5

Figure 5–45

4

- After viewing the records that meet the custom criteria, click the Filter button (Data tab | Sort & Filter group) to remove the custom filter from the table.

 **Experiment**

- Create filters on other fields in the table, such as Type and Region. When you are finished, click the Filter button and then repeat the steps above so that the worksheet appears as it does in Figure 5–45.

Q&A

How are the And and Or option buttons used?

You can click the And option button or the Or option button to select the AND operator or the OR operator. The AND operator indicates that both parts of the criteria must be true; the OR operator indicates that only one of the two must be true. Use the AND operator when the custom criteria is continuous over a range of values, such as ($3 \leq$ Experience ≤ 5). Use the OR operator when the custom criteria is not continuous, such as Experience less than or equal to 3 OR greater than or equal to 5 ($3 \leq$ Experience ≥ 5).

Using a Criteria Range on the Worksheet

BTW

The AND and OR Operators
AND means each and every one of the comparison criteria must be true. OR means only one of the comparison criteria must be true.

You can set up a **criteria range** on the worksheet and use it to manipulate records that pass the comparison criteria. Using a criteria range on the worksheet involves two steps:

1. Create the criteria range and name it Criteria.
2. Use the Advanced button on the Data tab.

To Create a Criteria Range on the Worksheet

To set up a criteria range, first copy the column headings in the table to another area of the worksheet. If possible, copy the column headings to rows above the table. You should do this in case the table is expanded downward or to the right in the future; such an expansion can cause problems with references to contents of the table in formulas in the worksheet. Next, enter the comparison criteria in the row immediately below the field names you just copied to the criteria range. Then use the Name box in the formula bar to name the criteria range, Criteria.

The following step creates a criteria range in the range A2:J3 to find records that pass the test:

Status = Part Time AND Experience > 3 AND Grade > B

A grade greater than B alphabetically means that only fundraisers with grades of C, D, and F pass the test.

1

- Display the Home tab.

- Select the range A7:J8 and then click the Copy button (Home tab | Clipboard group).

- Select cell A1 and then press the ENTER key to paste the contents on the Office Clipboard to the destination area A1:J2.

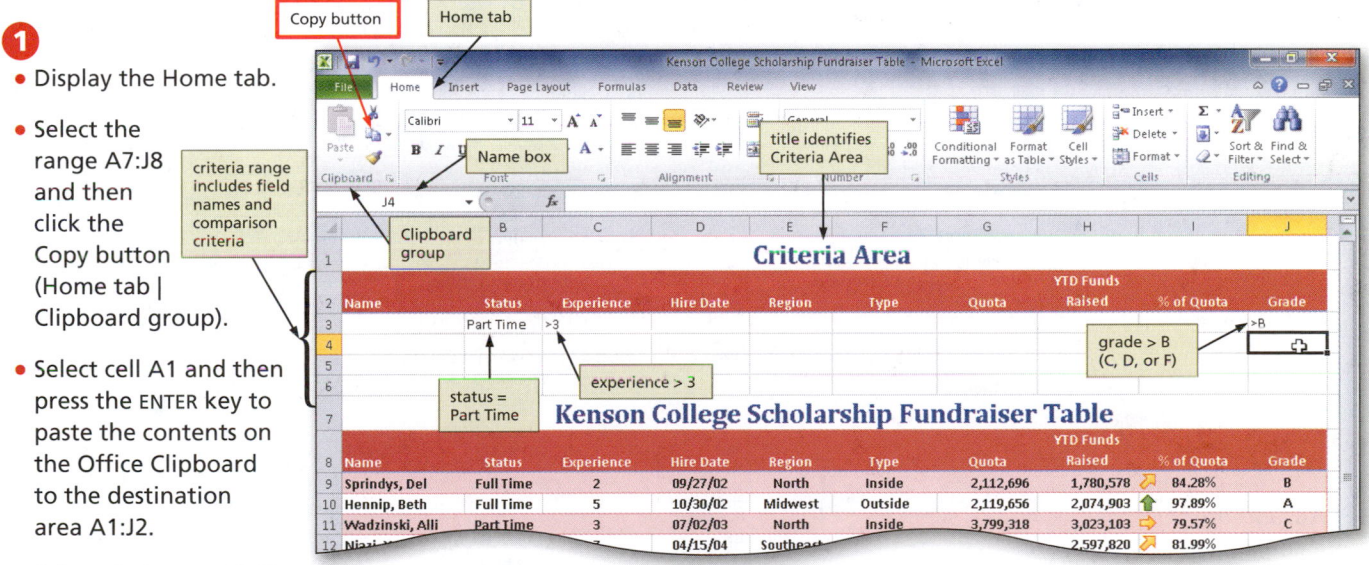

Figure 5–46

- Select the range A2:J2 and apply the Red Accent 2 Fill color to the range so that the text is displayed in the range.

- Change the title to `Criteria Area` in cell A1, enter `Part Time` in cell B3, enter `>3` in cell C3, and then enter `>B` in cell J3.

- Select the range A2:J3, click the Name box in the formula bar, type `Criteria` as the range name, press the ENTER key, and then select cell J4 (Figure 5–46).

Q&A

Must the text in the column headings in the criteria range match those in the table exactly?

Yes. To ensure the column headings in the criteria range are spelled exactly the same as the column headings in the table, copy and paste the column headings in the table to the criteria range as shown in the previous set of steps.

To Query a Table Using the Advanced Filter Dialog Box

Using the Advanced Filter dialog box is similar to using the AutoFilter query technique, except that it does not filter records based on comparison criteria you select from a table. Instead, this technique uses the comparison criteria set up in a criteria range (A2:J3) on the worksheet.

The following steps use the Advanced Filter dialog box to query a table and show only the records that pass the test established in the criteria range in Figure 5–46 on the previous page (Status = Part Time AND Experience > 3 AND Grade > B).

1

• Click cell A9 to activate the table.

• Display the Data tab and then click the Advanced button (Data tab | Sort & Filter group) to display the Advanced Filter dialog box (Figure 5–47).

Q&A

What is displayed already in the Advanced Filter dialog box?

In the Action area, the 'Filter the list, in-place' option button is selected automatically. Excel automatically selects the table (range $A$8:$J$21) in the List range box. Excel also automatically selects the criteria range ($A$2:$J$3) in the Criteria range box, because the name Criteria was assigned to the range A2:J3 earlier.

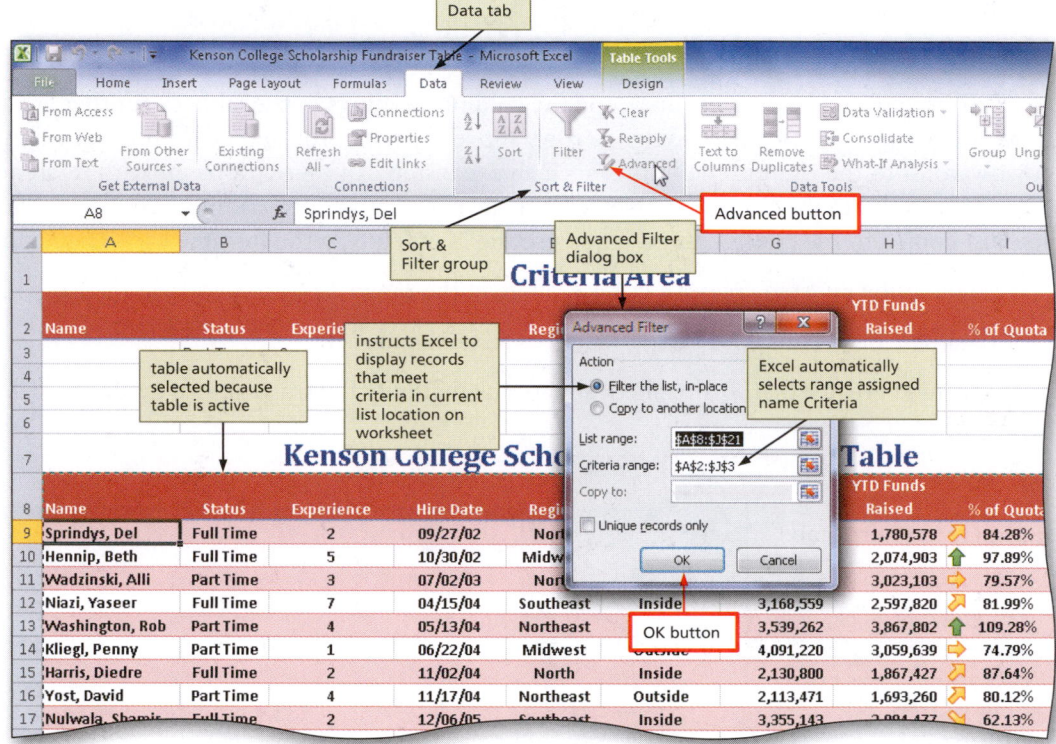

Figure 5–47

2

• Click the OK button (Advanced Filter dialog box) to hide all records that do not meet the comparison criteria (Figure 5–48).

Q&A

What is the main difference between using the AutoFilter query technique and using the Advanced Filter dialog box?

Like the AutoFilter

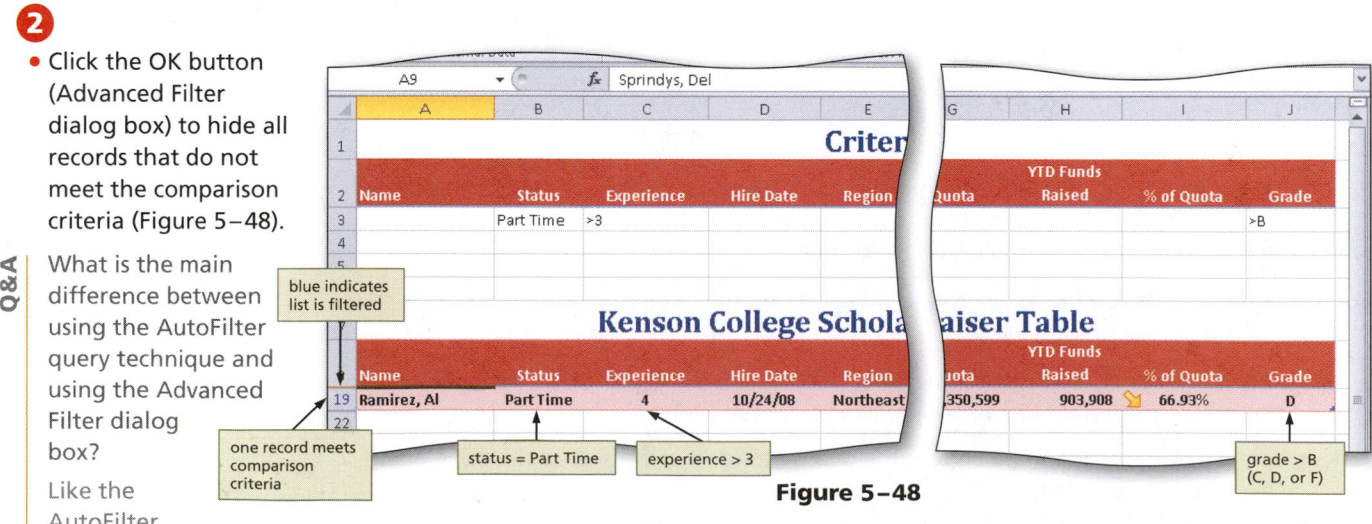

Figure 5–48

query technique, the Advanced Filter command displays a subset of the table. The primary difference between the two is that the Advanced Filter command allows you to create more complex comparison criteria, because the criteria range can be as many rows long as necessary, allowing for many sets of comparison criteria.

To Show All Records in a Table

The following step shows all records in the table.

1 Click the Filter button (Data tab | Sort & Filter group).

Q&A Why was AutoFilter turned off?

When the Advanced Filter command is invoked, Excel disables the AutoFilter command, thus hiding the column heading arrows in the active table, as shown in Figure 5–48.

BTW

Setting Up the Extract Range
When setting up the extract range, all of the column headings do not have to be copied in the table to the proposed extract range. Instead, copy only those column headings you want, in any order. You also can type the column headings rather than copy them, although this method is not recommended because it increases the likelihood of misspellings or other typographical errors.

Extracting Records

If you select the 'Copy to another location' option button in the Action area of the Advanced Filter dialog box (Figure 5–48), Excel copies the records that meet the comparison criteria in the criteria range to another part of the worksheet, rather than displaying them as a subset of the table. The location to where the records are copied is called the **extract range**.

Plan Ahead

> **Extract records from the table based on given criteria.**
> Extracting records allows you to pull data from a table so that you can analyze or manipulate the data further. For example, you may want to know which customers are delinquent on their payments. Extracting records that meet this criterion allows you to then use the records to create a mailing to such customers.
>
> Creating an extract range requires steps similar to those used to create a criteria range earlier in this chapter. Once the records that meet the comparison criteria in the criteria range are extracted (copied to the extract range), you can create a new table or manipulate the extracted records. To create an extract range, copy the field names of the table and then paste them to an area on the worksheet, preferably well below the table range. Next, name the pasted range Extract by using the Name box in the formula bar. Finally, use the Advanced Filter dialog box to extract the records.

To Create an Extract Range and Extract Records

The following steps create an extract range below the Kenson College Scholarship Fundraiser table and then extract records that meet the following criteria, as entered earlier in the Criteria range:

Status = Part Time AND Experience > 3 AND Grade > B

1

- Display the Home tab.

- Select range A7:J8, click the Copy button (Home tab | Clipboard group), select cell A25, and then press the ENTER key to paste the contents of the Office Clipboard to the destination area, A25:J26 in this case.

- Select the range A26:J26 and apply the Red Accent 2 Fill color to the range so that the text displays in the range with a red fill color.

- Click cell A25 and then enter **Extract Area** to title the extract area.

- Select the range A26:J26, enter the name **Extract** in the Name box in the formula bar, and then press the ENTER key to name the extract range.

2

- Click cell A9 to activate the table and then display the Data tab.

- Click the Advanced button (Data tab | Sort & Filter group) to display the Advanced Filter dialog box.

- Click 'Copy to another location' in the Action area (Advanced Filter dialog box) to cause the records that meet the criteria to be copied to a different location on the worksheet (Figure 5–49).

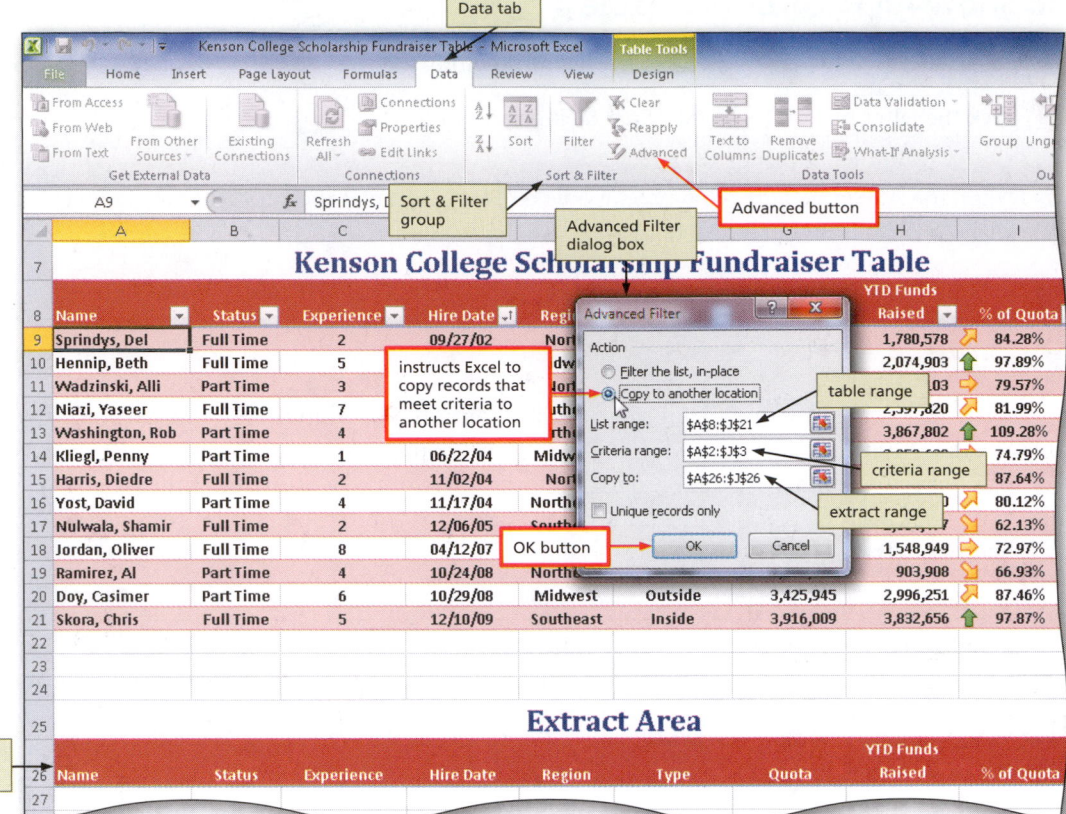

Figure 5–49

3

- Click the OK button to copy any records that meet the comparison criteria in the criteria range from the table to the extract range (Figure 5–50).

Q&A

What happens to the rows in the extract range if I perform another advanced filter operation?

Each time the Advanced Filter dialog box is used and the 'Copy to another location' option button is selected, Excel clears cells below the field names in the extract range. Hence, if you change the comparison criteria in the criteria range and then use the Advanced Filter dialog box a second time, Excel clears the previously extracted records before it copies a new set of records that pass the new test.

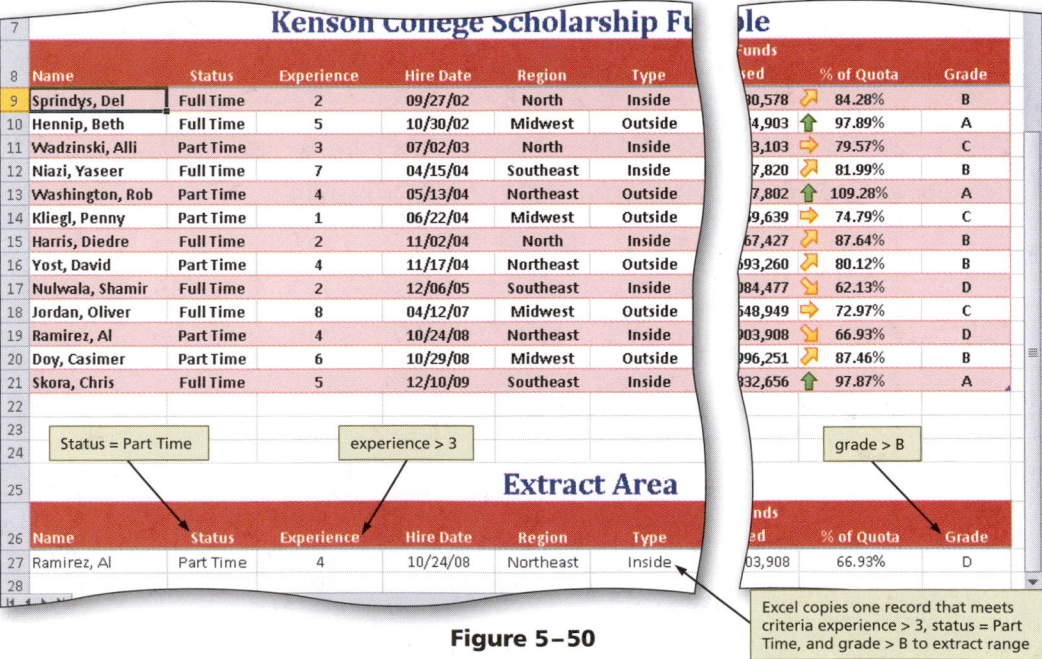

Figure 5–50

To Enable AutoFilter

As indicated earlier, when the Advanced Filter dialog box is used, Excel disables AutoFilter, thus hiding the column heading arrows in an active table. The following steps enable AutoFilter.

1 Click the Filter button (Data tab | Sort & Filter group) to display the column heading arrows in the table.

2 Display the Home tab.

More about the Criteria Range

The comparison criteria in the criteria range determine the records that will pass the test when the Advanced Filter dialog box is used. This section describes examples of different comparison criteria.

A Blank Row in the Criteria Range

If the criteria range contains a blank row, it means that no comparison criteria have been defined. Thus, all records in the table pass the test. For example, the blank row in the criteria range shown in Figure 5–51 means that all records will pass the test.

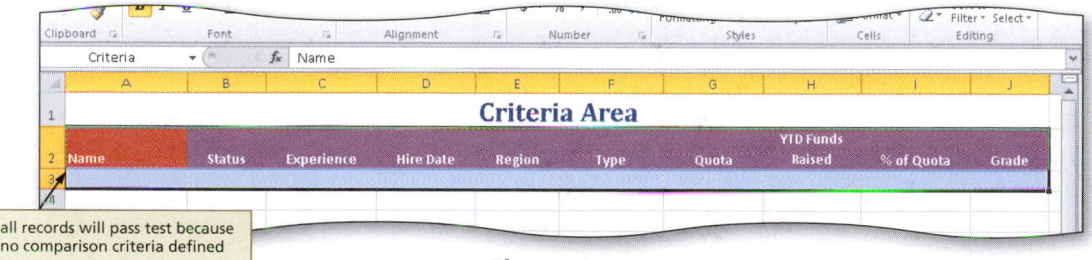

Figure 5–51

BTW

Criteria Area
When you add items in multiple rows to a criteria area, you must redefine the range with the name Criteria before you use it. To redefine the name Criteria, click the Name Manager button (Formulas tab | Defined Names group). When Excel displays the Name Manager dialog box, select Criteria in the table and then click the Delete button. Next, select the new Criteria area and name it Criteria using the Name box.

Using Multiple Comparison Criteria with the Same Field

If the criteria range contains two or more entries below the same field name, then records that pass either comparison criterion pass the test. For example, based on the criteria range shown in Figure 5–52, all records that represent fundraisers with a Region value of North or Midwest will pass the test.

If an AND operator applies to the same field name (Experience > 3 AND Experience < 5), then you must duplicate the field name (Experience) in the criteria range. That is, add the field name Experience in cell K2 to the right of Grade and then adjust the range assigned to the name Criteria by using the Define Name command (Formulas tab | Defined Name group).

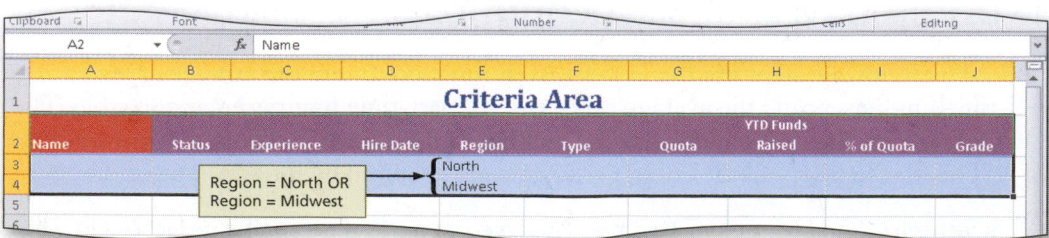

Figure 5–52

Comparison Criteria in Different Rows and Below Different Fields

When the comparison criteria below different field names are in the same row, then records pass the test only if they pass all the comparison criteria. If the comparison criteria for the field names are in different rows, then the records must pass only one of the tests. For example, in the criteria range shown in Figure 5–53, Full Time fundraisers OR Outside fundraisers pass the test.

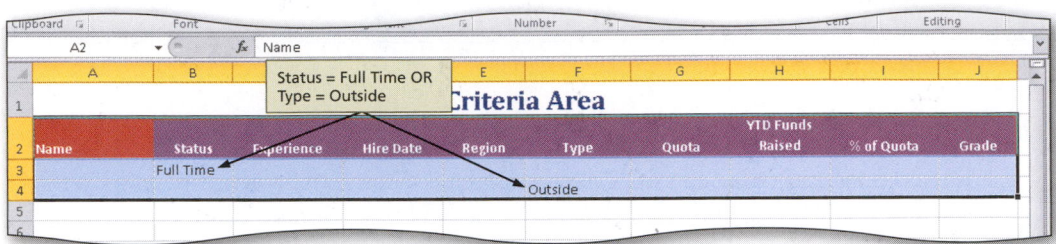

Figure 5–53

BTW

Database Functions
Database functions are useful when working with tables, such as the one in this chapter. Remembering the function arguments and their order within parentheses is not easy, however. Thus, it is recommended that you use the Insert Function button in the formula bar to assign a database function to your worksheet.

Using Database Functions

Excel includes 12 **database functions** that allow you to evaluate numeric data in a table. One of the functions is called the DAVERAGE function. As the name implies, the **DAVERAGE function** is used to find the average of numbers in a table field that pass a test. This function serves as an alternative to finding an average using the Subtotal button (Data tab | Outline group), which is described later in this chapter. The general form of the DAVERAGE function is:

=DAVERAGE(table range, "field name", criteria range)

where table range is the range of the table, field name is the name of the field in the table, and criteria range is the comparison criteria or test to pass.

Another often-used table function is the DCOUNT function. The **DCOUNT function** will count the number of numeric entries in a table field that pass a test. The general form of the DCOUNT function is:

=DCOUNT(table range, "field name", criteria range)

where table range is the range of the table, field name is the name of the field in the table, and criteria range is the comparison criteria or test to pass.

To Use the DAVERAGE and DCOUNT Database Functions

The following steps use the DAVERAGE function to find the average experience of full-time fundraisers and the average experience of part-time fundraisers in the table. The DCOUNT function is used to count the number of fundraisers' records that have a grade of A. The first step sets up the criteria areas that are required by these two functions.

1 Select cell O1 and then type **Criteria** to enter a criteria area title. Select cell L1, click the Format Painter button (Home tab | Clipboard group), and then click cell O1 to copy the format of one cell to another. Center the title, Criteria, across the range O1:Q1.

2 Select cell O2 and then type `Status` to enter a field name. Select cell P2 and, again, type `Status` to enter a field name. Select cell Q2 and then type `Grade` to enter a field name.

3 Select cell L2. Click the Format Painter button (Home tab | Clipboard group) and then drag through the range O2:Q2 to copy the format of a cell to a range.

4 Enter `Full Time` in cell O3 as the Type code for full-time fundraisers. Enter `Part Time` in cell P3 as the Type code for part-time fundraisers.

5 Enter `A` in cell Q3 as the Grade value. Select M3, click the Format Painter button (Home tab | Clipboard group), and then drag through the range O3:Q3 to copy the format of a cell to a range.

6 Enter `Avg. Full Time Experience = = >` in cell O4. Enter `Avg. Part Time Experience = =>` in cell O5. Enter `Grade A Count = = = = = = = = = > ` in cell O6. If necessary, increase the width of column O so that the text does not extend into column R.

7 Select cell R4 and then type `=daverage(a8:j21, "Experience", o2:o3)` to enter a database function.

8 Select cell R5 and then type `=daverage(a8:j21, "Experience", p2:p3)` to enter a database function.

9 Click cell R6 and then type `=dcount(a8:j21, "Experience", q2:q3)` to enter a database function.

10 Apply the bold style to the range O4:R6 and then select cell O8 (Figure 5–54).

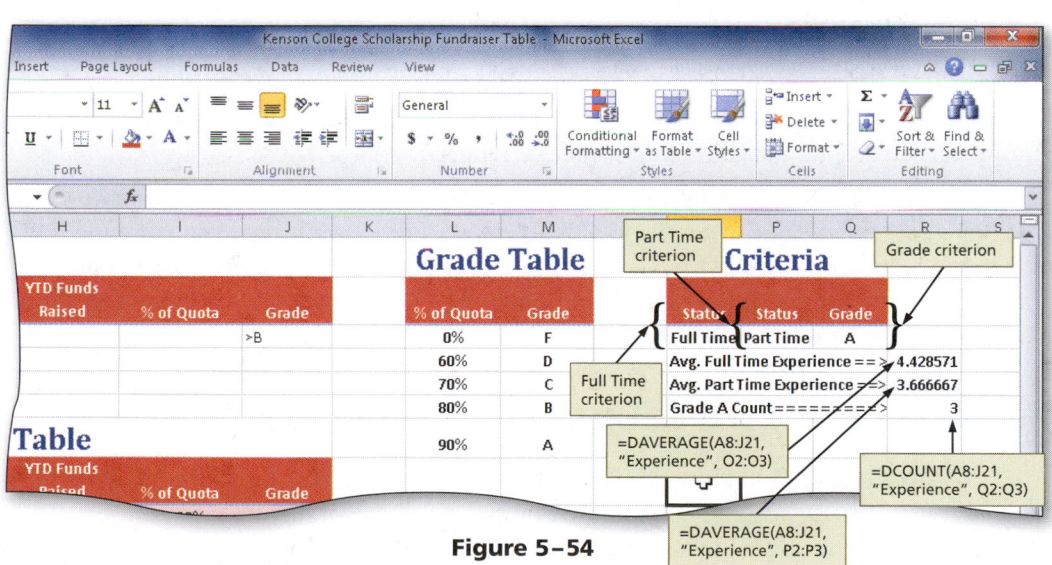

Figure 5–54

More about Using Database Functions

In Figure 5–54, the first value in the DCOUNT function, A8:J21, refers to the table range defined earlier in this chapter (range A8:J21). Instead of using the cell range, you can name the table using the Name box in the formula bar and then use the table name as the first argument in the database functions. Database is the name most often assigned to a table. If the table were named Database, then the DCOUNT function would be entered as:

=DCOUNT(Database, "Experience", Q2:Q3)

Excel uses the criteria range Q2:Q3 to select the records in the range Database where the Grade is A; it then counts the numeric Experience field in these records to determine the number of records that pass the criteria. Excel requires that you surround the field name Experience with quotation marks unless the field has been assigned a name through the Name box in the formula bar.

The third value, Q2:Q3, is the criteria range for the grade count. In the case of the DCOUNT function, you must select a numeric field to count even though the value of the numeric field itself is not used.

Other Database Functions

Other database functions that are similar to the functions described in previous chapters include the DMAX, DMIN, and DSUM functions. For a complete list of the database functions available for use with a table, click the Insert Function box in the formula bar. When Excel displays the Insert Function dialog box, select Database in the 'Or select a category' list. The 'Select a function' box displays the database functions. If you click a database function name, Excel displays a description of the function above the OK button in the Insert Function dialog box.

BTW

Quick Reference
For a table that lists how to complete the tasks covered in this book using the mouse, Ribbon, shortcut menu, and keyboard, see the Quick Reference Summary at the back of this book, or visit the Excel 2010 Quick Reference Web page (scsite.com/ex2010/qr).

Using the SUMIF, COUNTIF, MATCH, and INDEX Functions

The following list describes the reasons to use the SUMIF, COUNTIF, MATCH, and INDEX functions.

- The SUMIF and COUNTIF functions are useful when you want to sum values in a range or count values in a range only if they meet a criteria.
- Excel's MATCH function tells you the relative position of an item in a range or table that matches a specified value in a specified order.
- The INDEX function returns the value or reference of the cell at the intersection of a particular row and column in a table or range.

When used together, the MATCH and INDEX function provide the ability to look up a particular value in a table for some criteria. For example, you can combine the functions to look up the YTD funds raised based on the name of the fundraiser. The range for any of these functions need not be a table. The following sections use these four functions with the Kenson College Scholarship Fundraiser table.

To Use the SUMIF and COUNTIF Functions

Assume you want to know the sum of the YTD funds raised for the fundraisers that have a grade of A. Or, assume you want to know the number of full-time fundraisers. The first query can be answered by using the SUMIF function as follows:

=SUMIF(J9:J21, "A",H9:H21)

where the first argument J9:J21 is the range containing the numbers to add, the second argument "A" is the criteria, and the third argument H9:H21 is the range containing the cells with which to compare the criteria.

The second query can be answered by using the COUNTIF function as follows:

=COUNTIF(B9:B21,"Full Time")

where the first argument B9:B21 is the range containing the cells with which to compare the criteria.

The following steps enter identifiers and these two functions in the range O8:R9.

1 Enter `Grade A YTD Funds Raised = =>` in cell O8.

2 Enter `Full Time Count = = = = = = = =>` in cell O9.

3 Select cell R8 and then type `=SUMIF(j9:j21,"A",h9:h21)` to enter a function.

4 Select cell R9 and then type `=COUNTIF(b9:b21,"Full Time")` to enter a function.

5 Apply the bold style to the range O8:R9.

6 Apply the comma style to cell R8 and then click the Decrease Decimal button (Home tab | Number group) twice to decrease the number of decimal places to zero in the selected cell.

7 Double-click the right border of column heading R to change the width of column R to best fit (Figure 5–55).

Q&A Are there any differences when using these functions on a range?

Yes. The COUNTIF, SUMIF, and database functions will work on any range. The difference between using these functions on a range and table is that if the function references a table, then Excel automatically adjusts the first argument as a table grows or shrinks. The same cannot be said if the function's first argument is a range reference that is not defined as a table.

BTW

Using SUMIFS, COUNTIFS, and AVERAGEIFS Functions
SUMIF is designed to work with a single criterion, but the SUMIFS function lets you add two or more ranges and criteria. For example, =SUMIF(C1:C6,"<10") adds the values in C1:C6 that are less than 10. The formula =SUMIFS(C1:C6, D1:D6, "<10", D1:D6, ">5") sums the values in C1:C6 where the amounts in D1:D6 are between 5 and 10. COUNTIFS and AVERAGEIFS work the same way in relation to COUNTIF and AVERAGEIF respectively.

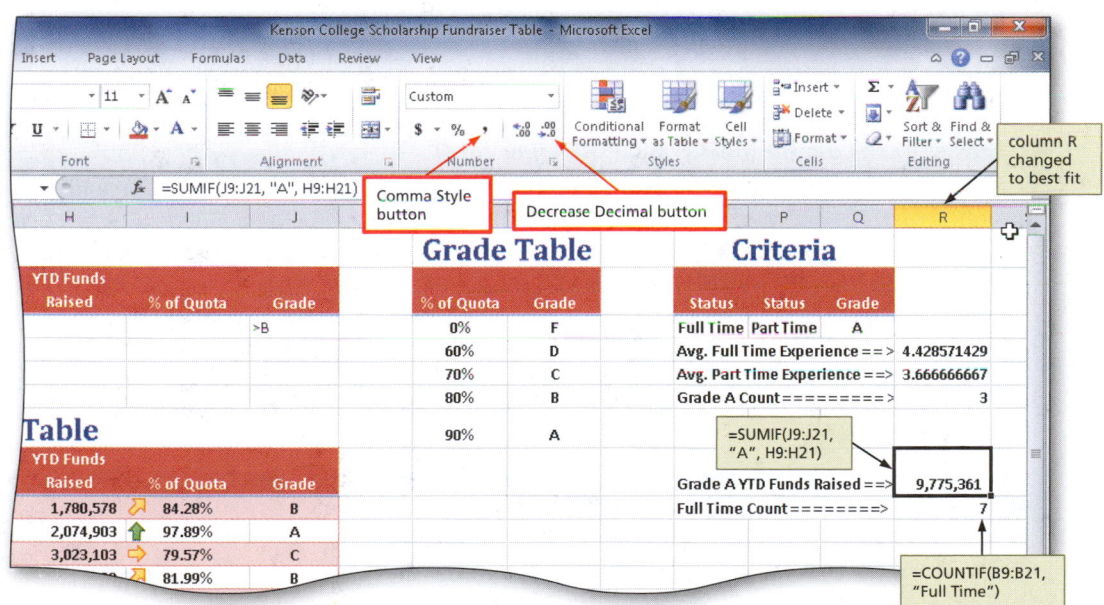

Figure 5–55

To Use the MATCH and INDEX Functions

Assume you want to look up the YTD funds raised for any fundraisers by name. The MATCH and INDEX functions can be placed in a formula together. The MATCH function can be used to find the row number given a name as follows:

=MATCH(R11, A9:A21, 0)

where the first argument R11 is the cell containing the name to look up, the second argument A9:A21 is the range in which the MATCH function should look for the name, and the third argument 0 informs the MATCH function to match a value exactly as given in the first argument.

Finding the Last Entry in a Range
Suppose you had a large range with many rows of data. You might want to find the last entry in the range that contains data in a particular column. For example, if a worksheet includes millions of order numbers in column A, you might like to find the last order number in column A so that you can add the next order. You can use the MATCH function to search column A by asking the function to search for the first million rows for the last entry by using the function =MATCH ("*", A1:A1000000, "−1").

The result of the MATCH function can be placed in the INDEX function to tell the INDEX function the row number of the table in which to look. The INDEX function returns a value in a table given a row and column. The INDEX function can be used to find the YTD funds raised for a given fundraiser's name as follows:

=INDEX(A9:J21, MATCH(R11, A9:A21, 0), 8)

range in which to look   MATCH function   column in which to look

where the first argument A9:J21 is the range in which the INDEX function looks. The second argument is the row of the table, in this case the result of the MATCH function, and the third argument is the column of the table in which the MATCH function should look. The following steps enter identifiers, the lookup value, and formula containing the MATCH and INDEX functions in the range O11:R12.

1 Enter `Name = = = = = = = = = = = = = => ` in cell O11.

2 Enter `YTD Funds Raised = = = = = = => ` in cell O12.

3 Select cell R11 and then type `Niazi, Yaseer` to enter a lookup value.

4 Select cell R12 and then type `=INDEX(A9:J21, MATCH(R11, A9:A21, 0), 8)` to enter a function.

5 Apply the bold style to the range O11:R12.

6 Apply the comma style to cell R12 and then click the Decrease Decimal button (Home tab | Number group) twice to decrease the number of decimal places to zero in the selected cell.

7 Double-click the right border of column heading R to change the width of column R to best fit and then select cell O14 (Figure 5–56).

The INDEX Function
The Index function can search for values in multiple ranges at the same time. To use the Index function to search noncontiguous ranges at the same time, enclose each range in parentheses in the first argument of the INDEX function.

Q&A

How else can I use the MATCH and INDEX functions?

The MATCH and INDEX functions provide greater flexibility than with the VLOOKUP and HLOOKUP functions. While the MATCH and INDEX functions can be used independently of each other, they are most productive when used together. As noted above, providing the third argument to the MATCH function with a value of zero resulted in an exact lookup of a name. This value also can be 1 or -1. A value of 1 matches the largest value that is less than or equal to the lookup value. A value of -1 finds the smallest value that is greater than or equal to the lookup value. In the first case, the values in the range must be sorted in ascending order. In the second case, the values in the range must be sorted in descending order.

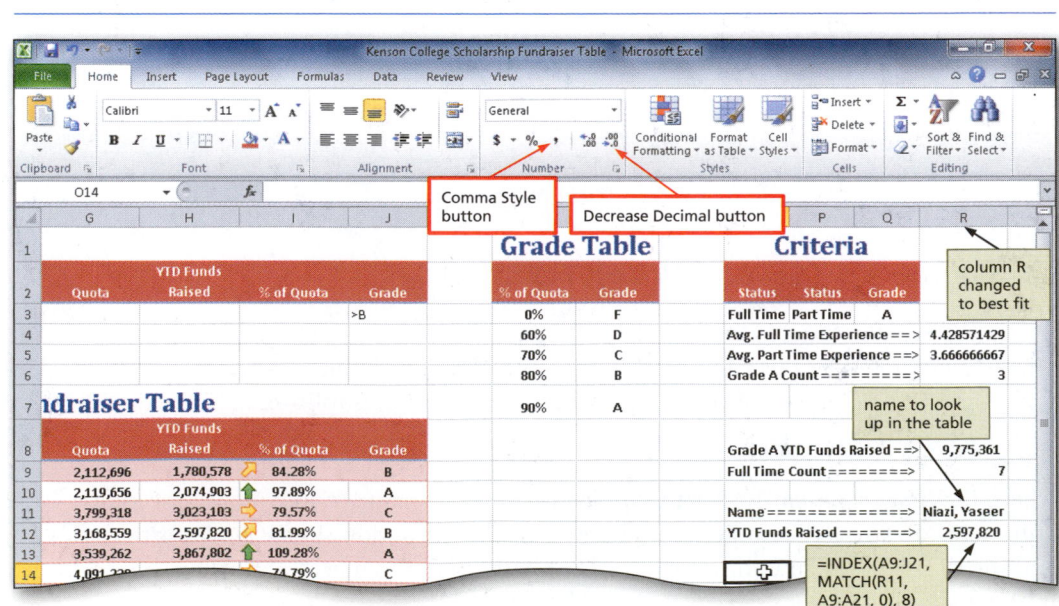

Figure 5–56

To Print the Worksheet and Save the Workbook

The following steps print the worksheet on one page and save the workbook.

1 Ready the printer.

2 Click File on the Ribbon to open the Backstage view.

3 Click the Print tab in the Backstage view to display the Print gallery.

4 If necessary, click the Portrait Orientation button in the Settings area and then select Landscape Orientation to select the desired orientation.

5 If necessary, click the No Scaling button in the Settings area and then select 'Fit Sheet on One Page' to cause the workbook to print on one page.

6 If necessary, click the Printer Status button in the Print gallery to display a list of available printer options and then click the desired printer to change the currently selected printer.

7 Click the Print button in the Print gallery to print the worksheet in landscape orientation on the currently selected printer.

8 When the printer stops, retrieve the printed worksheet (Figure 5–57).

9 Save the workbook.

BTW

Printing Document Properties
To print document properties, click the File on the Ribbon to open the Backstage view, click the Print tab in the Backstage view to display the Print gallery, click the first button in the Settings area to display a list of options specifying what you can print, click Document Properties in the list to specify you want to print the document properties instead of the actual document, and then click the Print button in the Print gallery to print the document properties on the currently selected printer.

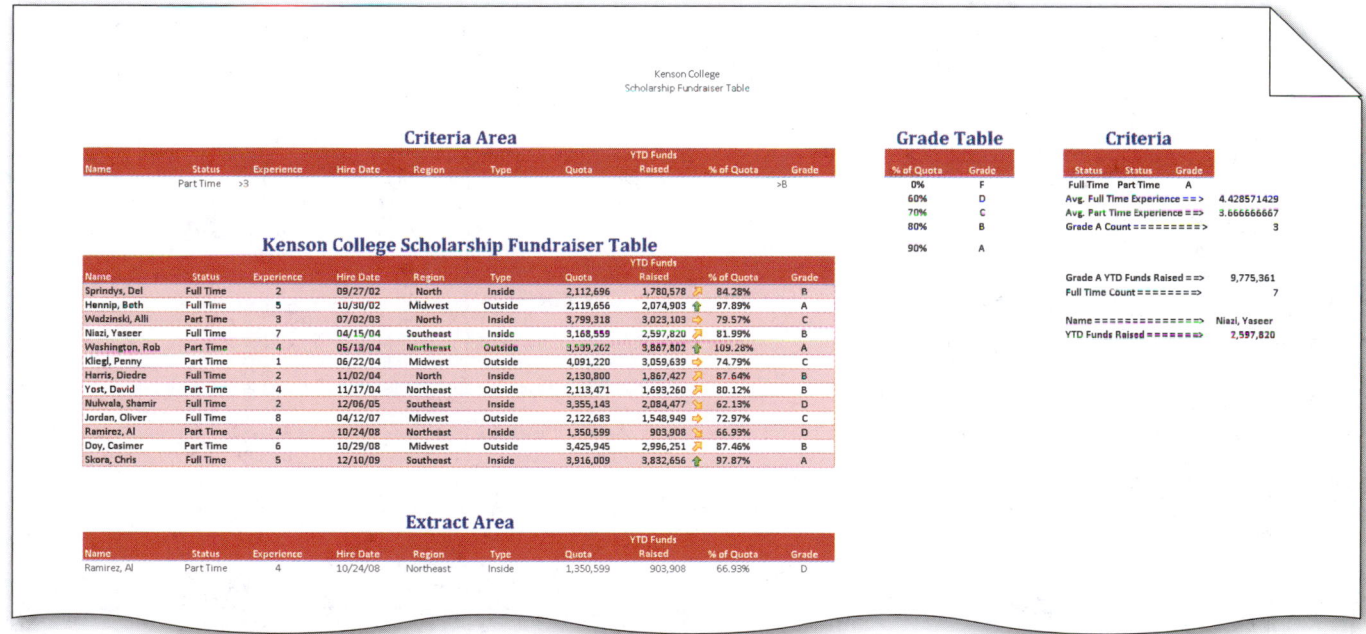

Figure 5–57

Displaying Automatic Subtotals in a Table

Displaying **automatic subtotals** is a powerful tool for summarizing data in a table. To display automatic subtotals, Excel requires that you sort the table on the field on which the subtotals will be based, convert the table to a range, and then use the Subtotal button (Data tab | Outline group).

The field on which you sort prior to clicking the Subtotal button is called the **control field**. When the control field changes, Excel displays a subtotal for the numeric fields selected in the Subtotal dialog box. For example, if you sort on the Region field and

BTW

Printing
To print individual sections of the worksheet, click the Name box in the formula bar, click the name of the section (Criteria or Extract) you want to print, and then click Print on the Office Button menu. When Excel displays the Print dialog box, click Selection in the Print what area and then click the OK button.

request subtotals for the Quota and YTD Funds Raised fields, then Excel recalculates the subtotal and grand total each time the Region field changes. The most common subtotal used with the Subtotals command is the SUM function, which causes Excel to display a sum each time the control field changes.

Plan Ahead

BTW

Certification
The Microsoft Office Specialist (MOS) program provides an opportunity for you to obtain a valuable industry credential – proof that you have the Excel 2010 skills required by employers. For more information, visit the Excel 2010 Certification Web page (scsite.com/ex2010/cert).

> **Display subtotals by grouping data in the table.**
> In general, the process for grouping data in a table involves four steps:
>
> 1. Convert the table back to a range.
> 2. Determine which field you will use as a control field and then sort the data using this field
> 3. Determine which fields will include calculations when the control field changes
> 4. Decide on the calculations that you want to perform on the fields that include calculations
>
>   When possible, create a sketch of your plan for grouping data before beginning your work in Excel.

To Display Automatic Subtotals in a Table

The following steps display subtotals for the Quota field and YTD Funds Raised field by region.

 1

- If necessary, display the Home tab and then scroll the worksheet so that column A is displayed and row 7 is the top row displayed.

- If necessary, select cell A9 and then enable AutoFilter. Click the Region arrow in cell E8 and then click Sort A to Z in the Region AutoFilter menu to sort the table in ascending order by the selected column, in this case Region.

- With cell A9 active, right-click anywhere in the table and then point to the Table command on the shortcut menu to display the Table submenu (Figure 5–58).

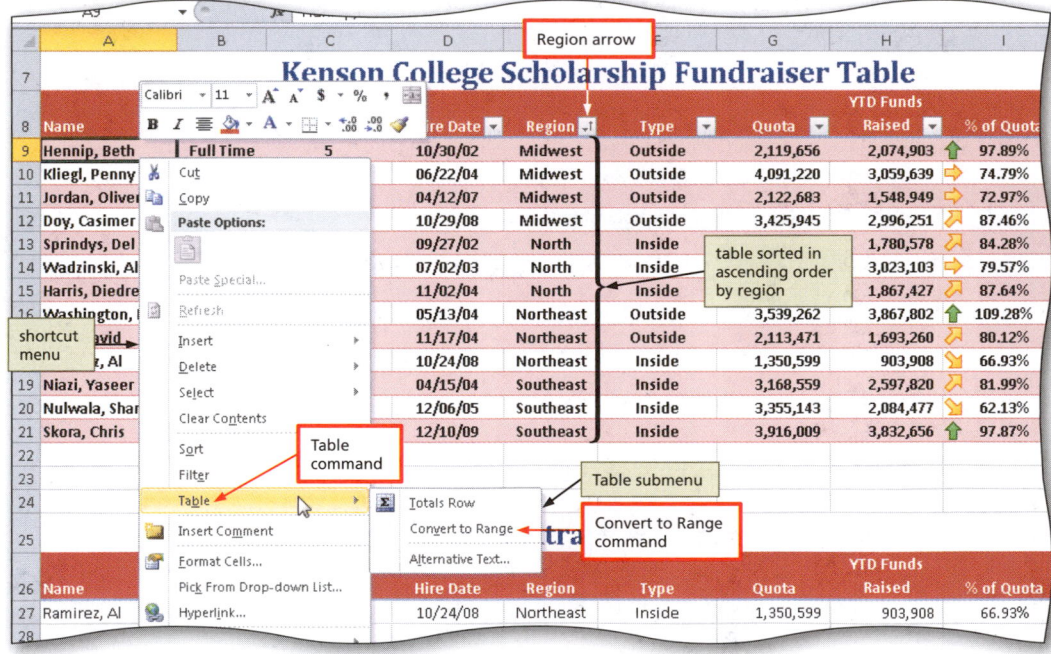

Figure 5–58

command on the shortcut menu to display the Table submenu (Figure 5–58).

Q&A Why does the table need to be converted to a range?

It is most important that you convert the table to a range before attempting to click the Subtotal button. If the table is not converted to a range, then the Subtotal button (Data tab | Outline group) is dimmed (not available).

Q&A Why are the rows no longer banded?

When performing some sort operations, Excel may lose the row banding formatting. If you want to see the row banding, change the table style to a different style, and then reapply the desired table style.

2

- Click Convert to Range on the Table submenu to display a Microsoft Excel dialog box.

- Click the Yes button (Microsoft Excel dialog box) to convert a table to a range.

- Display the Data tab and then click the Subtotal button (Data tab | Outline group) to display the Subtotal dialog box.

- Click the 'At each change in' box arrow (Subtotal dialog box) and then click Region to select a column heading on which to create subtotals.

- If necessary, select Sum in the Use function list.

- In the 'Add subtotal to' list (Subtotal dialog box), click Grade to clear it and then click Quota and YTD FundsRaised to select values to subtotal (Figure 5–59).

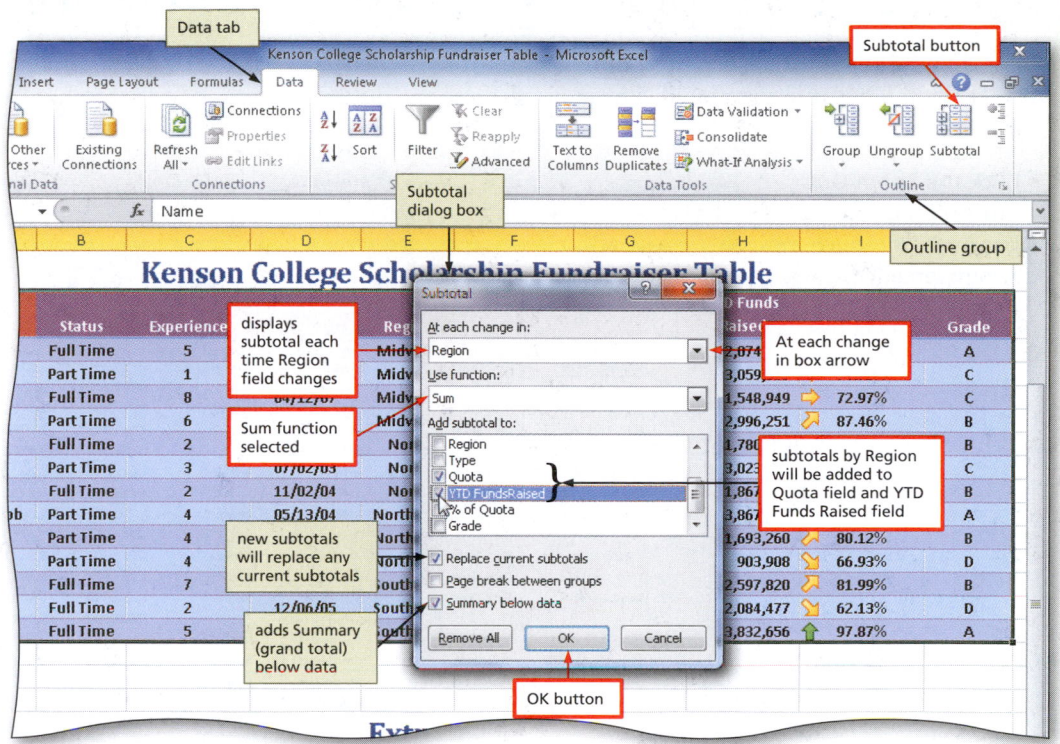

Figure 5–59

3

- Click the OK button to add subtotals to the range (Figure 5–60).

Q&A

What changes does Excel make to the worksheet?

As shown in Figure 5–60, Excel adds four subtotal rows and one grand total row to the table, including one subtotal for each different region and one grand total row for the entire table. The names for each subtotal row are derived from the region names and appear in bold. Thus, the text, Midwest Total, in cell E13 identifies the subtotal row that contains Quota and YTD Funds Raised totals for the Midwest.

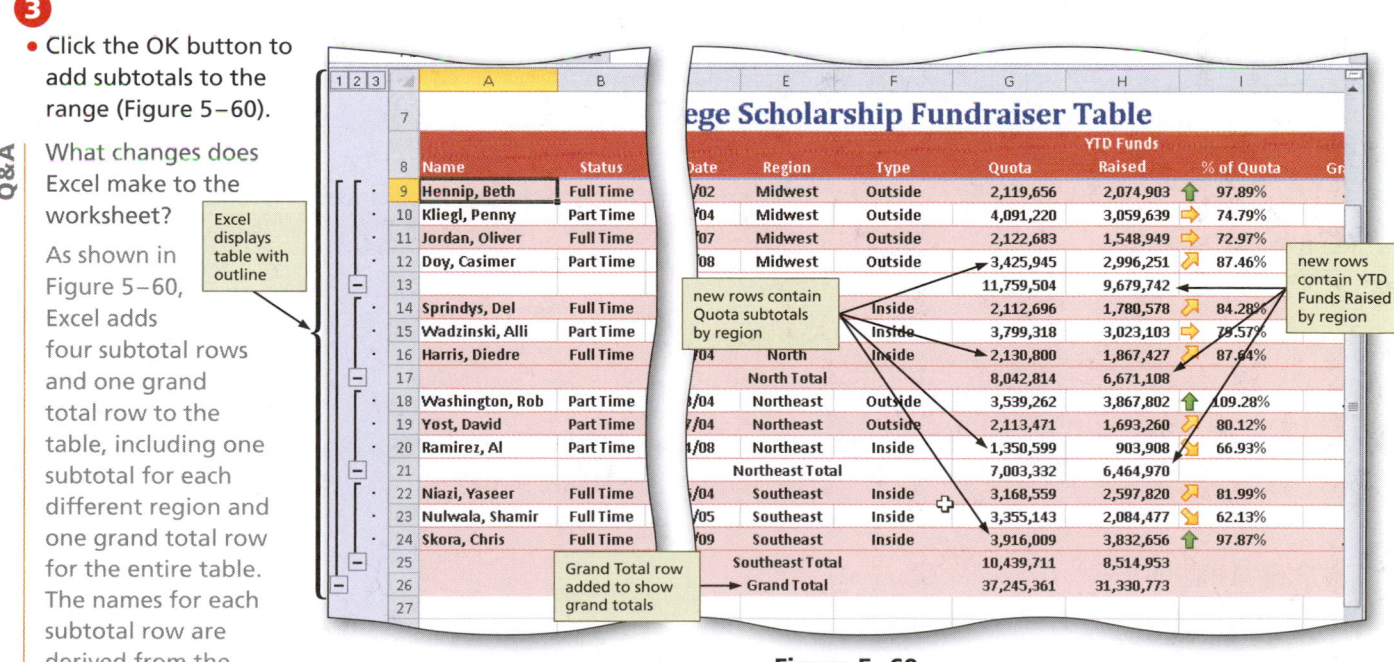

Figure 5–60

To Zoom Out on a Subtotaled Table and Use the Outline Feature

The following steps use the Zoom Out button on the status bar to reduce the magnification of the worksheet so that the table is more readable. The steps also use the outline features of Excel to hide and unhide data and totals.

• Click the Zoom Out button on the status bar once to reduce the zoom percent to 90% (Figure 5–61).

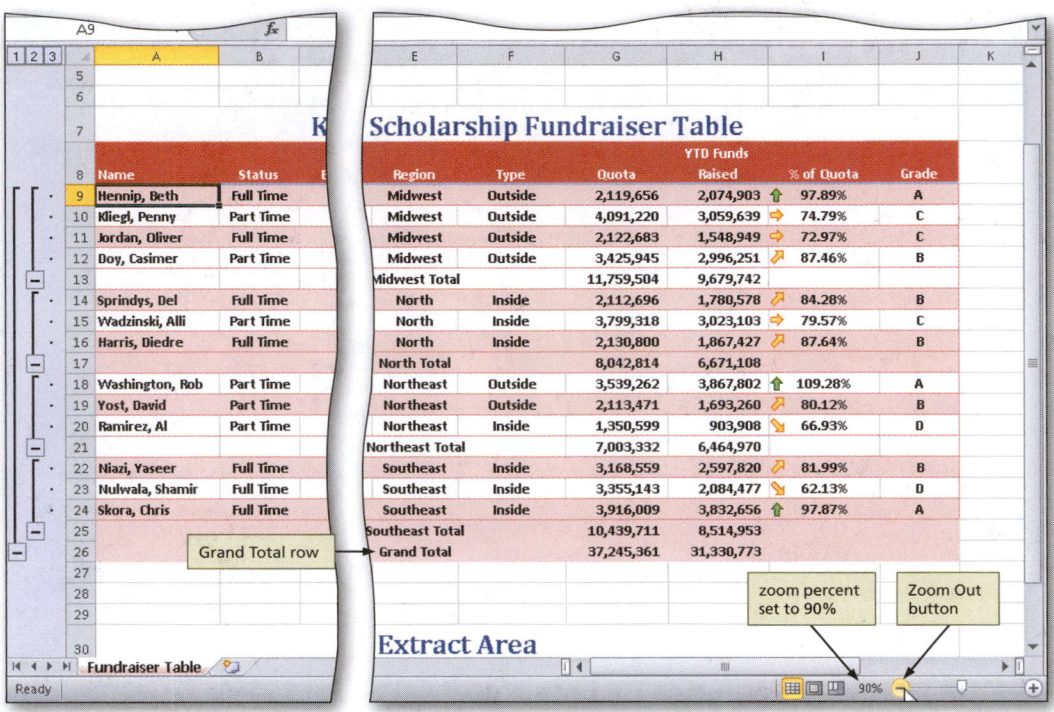

Figure 5–61

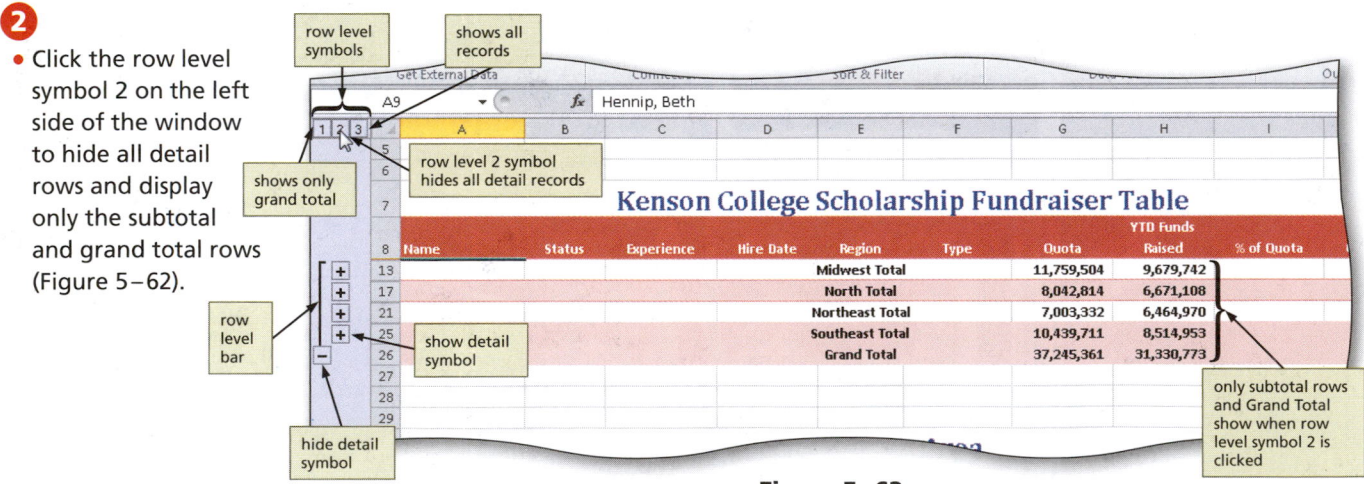

• Click the row level symbol 2 on the left side of the window to hide all detail rows and display only the subtotal and grand total rows (Figure 5–62).

Figure 5–62

Q&A

How can I use the outlining features?

By utilizing the **outlining features** of Excel, you quickly can hide and show detail rows. You can click the **row level symbols** to expand or collapse rows in the worksheet. Row level symbol 1, immediately below the Name box, hides all rows except the Grand Total row. Row level symbol 2 hides the detail records so the subtotal rows and Grand Total row appear as shown in Figure 5–62. Row level symbol 3 shows all rows.

3

• Click each of the lower two show detail symbols (+) on the left side of the window to display detail records, in this case for the Northeast and Southeast regions, and change the show detail symbols to hide detail symbols (Figure 5–63).

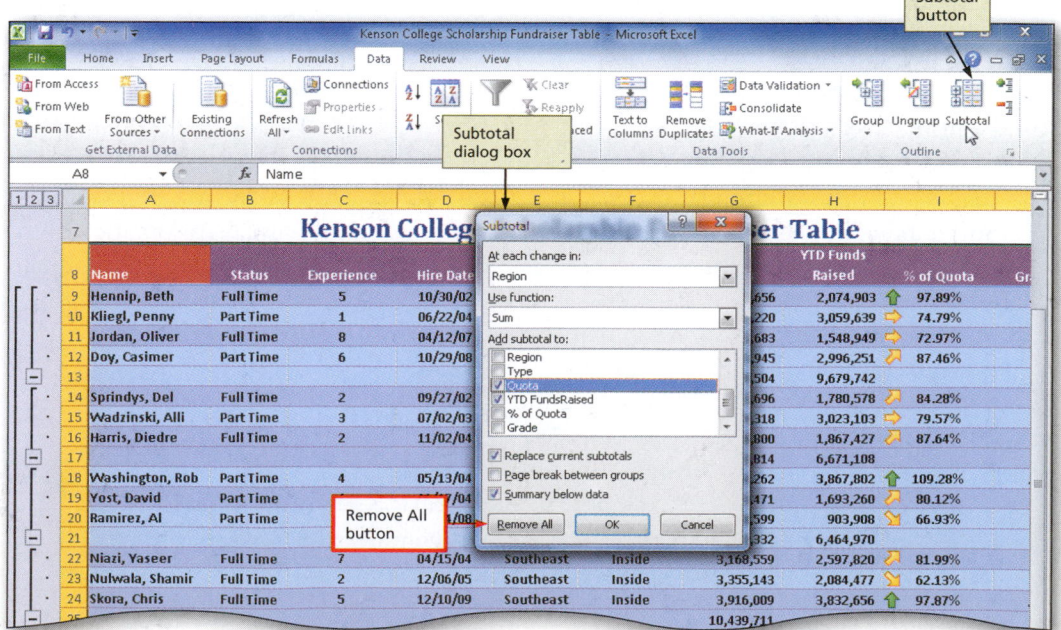

Figure 5–63

4

• Click the row level symbol 3 on the left side of the window to show all detail rows.

• Click the Zoom In button on the status bar once to change the zoom percent back to 100%.

Q&A

Can I group and outline without subtotals?

Yes. You do not have to use the Subtotals button to outline a worksheet. You can outline a worksheet by using the Group button (Data tab | Outline group). Usually, however, the Group button is useful only when you already have total lines in a worksheet.

Other Ways

1. To group and outline, click Group button (Data tab | Outline group), click Group (Group dialog box)

2. To zoom, hold CTRL key while scrolling mouse wheel towards you

3. To zoom, click Zoom button (View tab | Zoom group), select magnification

---

To Remove Automatic Subtotals from a Table

The following steps remove the subtotals and convert the range back to a table.

 1

• Click the Subtotal button (Data tab | Outline group) to display the Subtotal dialog box (Figure 5–64).

2

• Click the Remove All button (Subtotal dialog box) to remove all subtotals and close the Subtotal dialog box.

Figure 5–64

- Select the range A8:J21 and then display the Home tab.

- Click the Format as Table button (Home tab | Styles group) and then click the Custom quick style in the Format as Table gallery to apply the quick style to the selected range.

- When Excel displays the Format As Table dialog box, click the OK button to close the Format As Table dialog box.

4

- Save the workbook.

To Quit Excel

The following steps quit Excel.

1 Click the Close button on the right side of the title bar.

2 If the Microsoft Office Excel dialog box is displayed, click the Don't Save button.

Chapter Summary

In this chapter, you learned how to create, sort, and filter a table (also called a database); create subtotals; and use database functions such as SUMIF, COUNTIF, MATCH, and INDEX. The items listed below include all the new Excel skills you have learned in this chapter.

1. Format a Range as a Table (EX 305)
2. Modify a Table Quick Style (EX 307)
3. Enter Records in a Table (EX 309)
4. Add New Fields to a Table (EX 311)
5. Create a Lookup Table (EX 313)
6. Use the VLOOKUP Function to Determine Letter Grades (EX 315)
7. Add a Conditional Formatting Rule with an Icon Set (EX 316)
8. Use the Total Row Check Box (EX 319)
9. Print the Table (EX 321)
10. Sort a Table in Ascending Sequence by Name Using the Sort & Filter Button (EX 322)
11. Sort a Table in Descending Sequence by Name Using the Sort Z to A Button on the Data Tab (EX 323)
12. Sort a Table Using the Sort Command on an AutoFilter Menu (EX 324)
13. Sort a Table on Multiple Fields Using the Custom Sort Command (EX 324)
14. Query a Table Using AutoFilter (EX 327)
15. Show All Records in a Table (EX 329)
16. Enter Custom Criteria Using AutoFilter (EX 329)
17. Create a Criteria Range on the Worksheet (EX 331)
18. Query a Table Using the Advanced Filter Dialog Box (EX 332)
19. Create an Extract Range and Extract Records (EX 333)
20. Use the DAVERAGE and DCOUNT Database Functions (EX 336)
21. Use the SUMIF and COUNTIF Functions (EX 338)
22. Use the MATCH and INDEX Functions (EX 339)
23. Display Automatic Subtotals in a Table (EX 342)
24. Zoom Out on a Subtotaled Table and Use the Outline Feature (EX 344)
25. Remove Automatic Subtotals from a Table (EX 345)

If you have a SAM 2010 user profile, your instructor may have assigned an autogradable version of this assignment. If so, log into the SAM 2010 Web site at www.cengage.com/sam2010 to download the instruction and start files.

Learn It Online

Test your knowledge of chapter content and key terms.

Instructions: To complete the Learn It Online exercises, start your browser, click the Address bar, and then enter the Web address `scsite.com/ex2010/learn`. When the Excel 2010 Learn It Online page is displayed, click the link for the exercise you want to complete and then read the instructions.

Chapter Reinforcement TF, MC, and SA
A series of true/false, multiple choice, and short answer questions that test your knowledge of the chapter content.

Flash Cards
An interactive learning environment where you identify chapter key terms associated with displayed definitions.

Practice Test
A series of multiple choice questions that test your knowledge of chapter content and key terms.

Who Wants To Be a Computer Genius?
An interactive game that challenges your knowledge of chapter content in the style of a television quiz show.

Wheel of Terms
An interactive game that challenges your knowledge of chapter key terms in the style of the television show *Wheel of Fortune*.

Crossword Puzzle Challenge
A crossword puzzle that challenges your knowledge of key terms presented in the chapter.

Apply Your Knowledge

Reinforce the skills and apply the concepts you learned in this chapter.

Querying a List

Instructions: Assume that the figures that accompany each of the following six problems make up the criteria range for the College Textbook Sales Representative List shown in Figure 5–65. Fill in the comparison criteria to select records from the list to solve each of these six problems. So that you understand better what is required for this assignment, the answer is given for the first problem. You can open the workbook Apply 5-1 College Textbook Sales Representative List from the Data Files for Students and use the Filter button to verify your answers. See the inside back cover of this book for instructions for downloading the Data Files for Students or see your instructor for information on accessing the files required in this book.

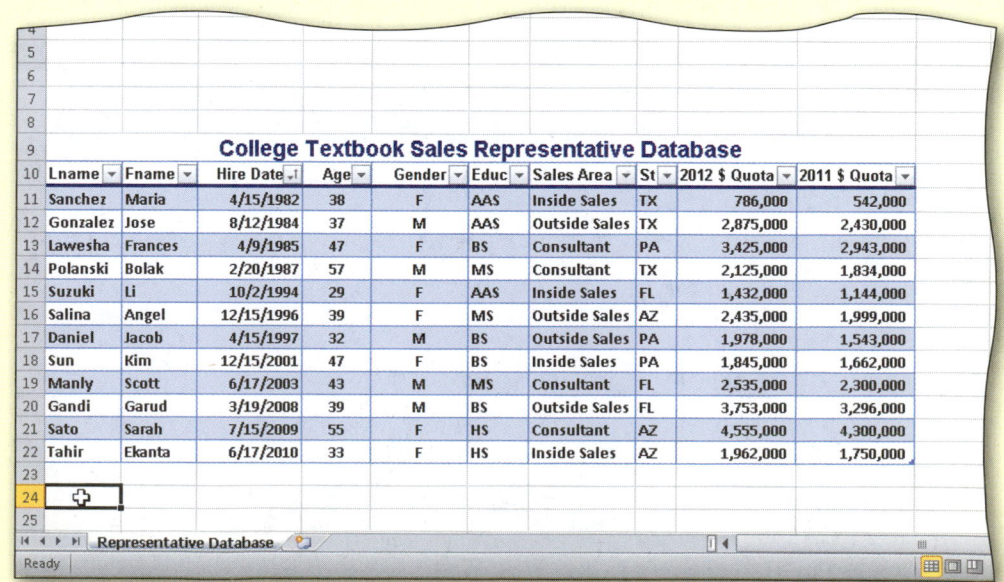

Lname	Fname	Hire Date	Age	Gender	Educ	Sales Area	St	2012 $ Quota	2011 $ Quota
Sanchez	Maria	4/15/1982	38	F	AAS	Inside Sales	TX	786,000	542,000
Gonzalez	Jose	8/12/1984	37	M	AAS	Outside Sales	TX	2,875,000	2,430,000
Lawesha	Frances	4/9/1985	47	F	BS	Consultant	PA	3,425,000	2,943,000
Polanski	Bolak	2/20/1987	57	M	MS	Consultant	TX	2,125,000	1,834,000
Suzuki	Li	10/2/1994	29	F	AAS	Inside Sales	FL	1,432,000	1,144,000
Salina	Angel	12/15/1996	39	F	MS	Outside Sales	AZ	2,435,000	1,999,000
Daniel	Jacob	4/15/1997	32	M	BS	Outside Sales	PA	1,978,000	1,543,000
Sun	Kim	12/15/2001	47	F	BS	Inside Sales	PA	1,845,000	1,662,000
Manly	Scott	6/17/2003	43	M	MS	Consultant	FL	2,535,000	2,300,000
Gandi	Garud	3/19/2008	39	M	BS	Outside Sales	FL	3,753,000	3,296,000
Sato	Sarah	7/15/2009	55	F	HS	Consultant	AZ	4,555,000	4,300,000
Tahir	Ekanta	6/17/2010	33	F	HS	Inside Sales	AZ	1,962,000	1,750,000

College Textbook Sales Representative Database

Figure 5–65

Continued >

1. Select records that represent sales representatives who are less than 40 years old and hold an AAS degree.

Lname	Fname	Hire Date	Age	Gender	Educ	Sales Area	St	2012 $ Quota	2011 $ Quota
			<40		=AAS				

2. Select records that represent sales representatives who cover the states of TX or AZ.

Lname	Fname	Hire Date	Age	Gender	Educ	Sales Area	St	2012 $ Quota	2011 $ Quota

3. Select records that represent females whose last names begin with the letter S and who are greater than 35 years old.

Lname	Fname	Hire Date	Age	Gender	Educ	Sales Area	St	2012 $ Quota	2011 $ Quota

4. Select records that represent males who are at least 40 years old and have an MS degree.

Lname	Fname	Hire Date	Age	Gender	Educ	Sales Area	St	2012 $ Quota	2011 $ Quota

5. Select records that represent females whose hire date was after 1995 or work Inside Sales.

Lname	Fname	Hire Date	Age	Gender	Educ	Sales Area	St	2012 $ Quota	2011 $ Quota

6. Select records that represent sales representatives who are less than 35 years old or greater than 50 years old.

Lname	Fname	Hire Date	Age	Gender	Educ	Sales Area	St	2012 $ Quota	2011 $ Quota

Extend Your Knowledge

Extend the skills you learned in this chapter and experiment with new skills. You may need to use Help to complete the assignment.

More Conditional Formatting

Instructions: Start Excel. Open the workbook Extend 5-1 Rommel's Auto Parts Six-Year Financial Projection from the Data Files for Students. See the inside back cover of this book for instructions for downloading the Data Files for Students or see your instructor for information on accessing the files required in this book. You have been asked to add conditional formatting to highlight the lowest and highest total expenses, to add conditional formatting to show data bars for income taxes that are greater than zero, and add conditional formatting to show a three-icon set for net income (Figure 5–66). Complete the following tasks to add and manage conditional formatting rules in the worksheet.

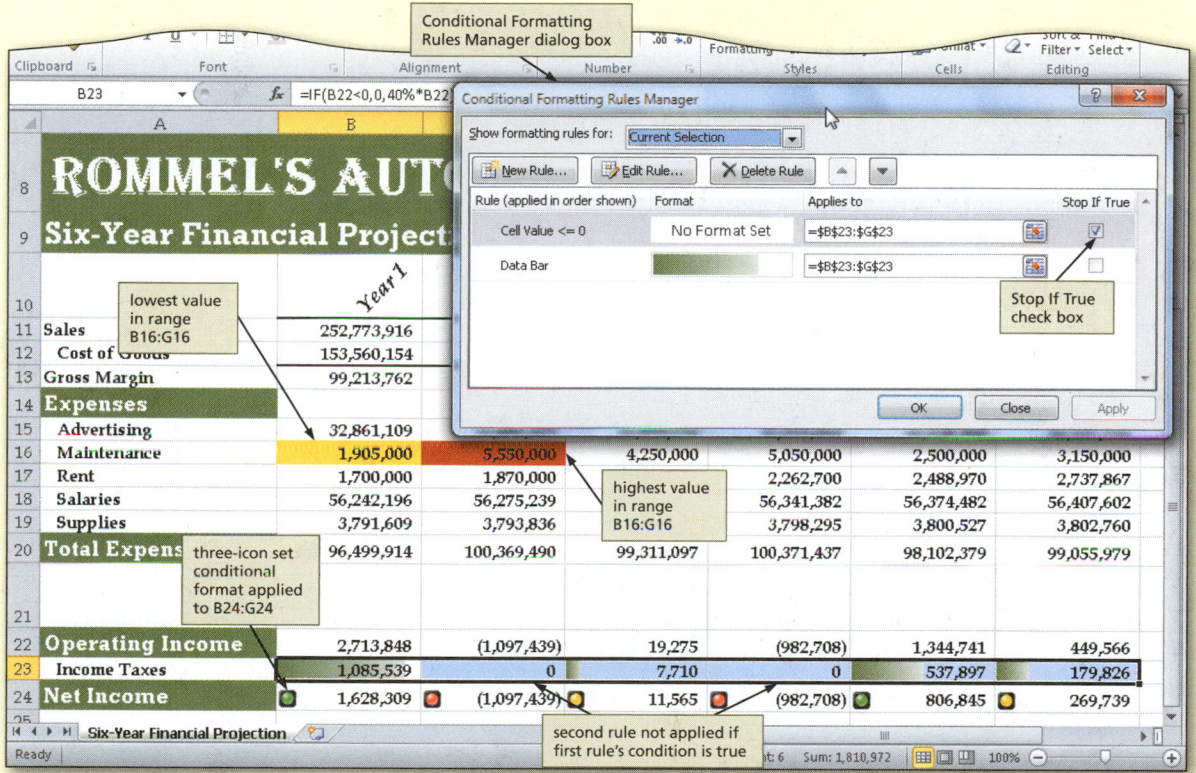

Figure 5–66

1. Save the workbook using the file name, Extend 5-1 Rommel's Auto Parts Six-Year Financial Projection Complete.

2. Select the range B16:G16. Click the Conditional Formatting button (Home tab | Styles group) and then click New Rule. When Excel displays the New Formatting Rule dialog box, select 'Format only top or bottom ranked values' in the Select a Rule Type list. In the 'Format values that rank in the' area, type 1 in the center text box. Click the Format button in the Preview area. When Excel displays the Format Cells dialog box, click the Fill tab, click the dark red color (column 1, row 7) in the Background Color area, and then click the OK button. Click the OK button in the New Formatting Rule dialog box.

Continued >

Extend Your Knowledge *continued*

3. With the range B16:G16 selected, add a second rule to the range following the procedure from Step 2. When creating the new rule, select Bottom in the 'Format values that rank in the' list and type 1 in the center text box. Click the Format button and then select the yellow color (column 4, row 7) in the Background Color area. Click the OK button in the Format Cells dialog box and then click the OK button in the New Formatting Rule dialog box.

4. With the range B16:G16 selected, click the Conditional Formatting button (Home tab | Styles group) and then click Manage Rules to view the rules for the range. Click the Close button in the Conditional Formatting Rules Manager dialog box.

5. Select the range B23:G23. Add a new conditional formatting rule to format all cells based on their values. Select the Data Bar format style. Select Olive Green, Accent 2, Darker 25% (column 6, row 5) in the Bar Color palette. Select Gradient Fill as the Bar Appearance Fill and then close the New Formatting Rule dialog box.

6. With range B23:G23 selected, add a new conditional formatting rule. Select 'Format only cells that contain' as the rule type. Format only cells with a cell value less than or equal to zero. Do not select a format using the Format button. Make sure that the Preview area indicates that no format is set and then click the OK button to add the rule.

7. With the range B23:G23 selected, click the Conditional Formatting button (Home tab | Styles group) and then click Manage Rules to view the rules for the range. Click the Stop If True check box for the first rule in the dialog box to ensure that the second rule is not applied to negative values in the range (Figure 5–66 on the previous page). Click the OK button to close the Conditional Formatting Rules Manager dialog box.

8. With the range B24:G24 selected, add a new conditional formatting rule to format all cells based on their values. Select the Icon Sets format style. Select 3 Traffic Lights (Rimmed) in the Icon Styles and then close the New Formatting Rule dialog box.

9. Change the document properties as specified by your instructor. Change the worksheet header with your name, course number, and other information as specified by your instructor. Print the worksheet in landscape orientation using the 'Fit Sheet on One Page' option. Save the workbook.

10. Select the range B15:G19. Click the Conditional Formatting button (Home tab | Styles group), point to Color Scales on the Conditional Formatting menu, and then click Green – Yellow – Red Color Scale in the Color Scales gallery. Print the worksheet in landscape orientation using the 'Fit Sheet on One Page' option. Do not save the workbook.

11. Submit the assignment as requested by your instructor.

Make It Right

Analyze a workbook and correct all errors and/or improve the design.

Tables, Conditional Formatting, and Database Functions

Instructions: Start Excel. Open the workbook Make It Right 5-1 Kenson College Scholarship Fundraiser Table and then save the file using the file name, Make It Right 5-1 Kenson College Scholarship Fundraiser Table Complete. See the inside back cover of this book for instructions for downloading the Data Files for Students, or see your instructor for information on accessing the files required for this book. Correct the following table, conditional formatting, and database function problems so that the worksheet appears as shown in Figure 5–67.

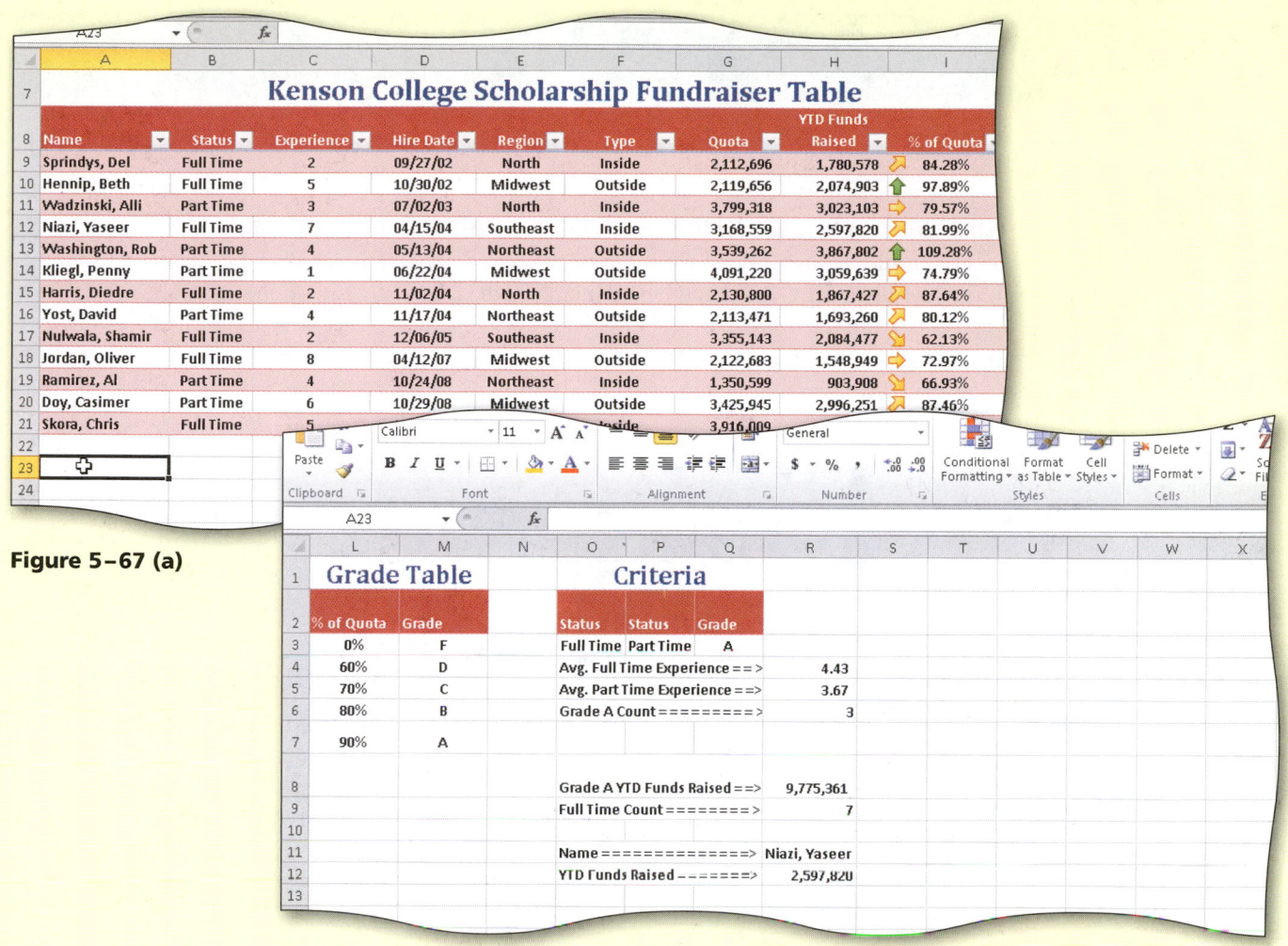

Figure 5–67 (a)

Figure 5–67 (b)

1. Use the Table Style Options group on the Design tab to make certain that the table in the worksheet includes banded rows.

2. The table does not show all of the records because the Experience field is filtered. Ensure that all records in the table are displayed.

3. The conditional formatting for the % of Quota field uses only four icons in the rule instead of five. Change the icon style of the rule to use 5 Arrows (Colored).

4. The values used by the conditional formatting rule to choose each arrow style are incorrect and should be based on the values listed in the grade table. Edit the conditional formatting rule so that the values in the grade table are reflected in the rules.

5. Correct the third argument in the DAVERAGE function used to calculate the average part-time experience.

6. Correct the second and third arguments in the SUMIF function used to calculate the grade A YTD Funds sum.

7. Change the formula for % of Quota to use [@Column_title] for YTD Funds Raised and Quota.

8. Change the document properties as specified by your instructor. Change the worksheet header with your name, course number, and other information as specified by your instructor.

9. Save the workbook and submit the revised workbook as requested by your instructor.

In the Lab

Create a workbook using the guidelines, concepts, and skills presented in this chapter. Labs are listed in order of increasing difficulty.

Lab 1: Creating, Filtering, and Sorting a Table and Determining Subtotals

Problem: You are employed by Anderson Scholastic, a company that markets books for several school types. The employees are assigned to each department and have varying sales and commissions by Dept. The three departments are K-12, Higher Ed, and Trade. The director of the Human Resources department has asked you to create an employee table (Figure 5–68), run queries against the table, generate various sorted reports, and generate subtotal information.

Anderson Scholastic Employees

Dept	Lname	Fname	Age	Gender	Sales	Commission
K-12	Day	Janice	32	F	▽ 1,075,800	80,685
Higher Ed	Angston	Lee	27	M	— 5,500,400	412,530
K-12	Wyler	Deshanet	56	F	▽ 1,589,000	119,175
Trade	Cole	Arlene	30	F	▲ 11,500,000	977,500
K-12	Ruiz	Jorge	39	M	— 5,347,500	401,063
Higher Ed	Grazier	Kim	25	F	▽ 3,005,000	225,375
K-12	Lipes	Jim	57	M	▽ 2,300,500	172,538
K-12	Steinberg	Josh	28	M	▽ 2,500,000	187,500
K-12	Beam	Saul	34	M	— 5,500,000	412,500
Trade	Yenkle	Lisa	33	F	▽ 3,200,000	272,000
Trade	Wyler	Len	38	M	▲ 10,900,000	926,500
Higher Ed	Stavish	Napoleon	47	M	— 5,890,000	441,750
Higher Ed	Goldberg	Joan	62	F	▽ 3,000,000	225,000
Total			39.07692308	13	61,308,200	4,854,115

Dept	Rate
K-12	6.50%
Higher Ed	7.50%
Trade	8.50%

Anderson Scholastic Employees

Figure 5–68

Instructions Part 1: Create the table shown in Figure 5–68 using the techniques learned in this chapter and following the instructions below.

1. Bold the entire worksheet.

2. Enter the table title in row 6 and apply the Title cell style. Enter and format the field names in row 7.

3. Use the Format as Table button (Home tab | Styles group) to create a table using data from the range A7:G7. Use Table Style Medium 7 to format the table. Format the first row below the field names and then enter the rows of data shown in rows 8 through 20 of Figure 5–68. Change the Sheet1 tab name to Anderson Scholastic Employees and delete Sheet2 and Sheet3. Enter the column data except for the commission column.

4. Copy the formatting from cell A7 to the range A25:B25. Enter the data shown in Figure 5–68 in A26:B28.

5. Enter a formula for commission that calculates the commission based upon multiplying Sales times the appropriate commission from the data in A26:B28. Use [@Column_title] referencing and the INDEX and MATCH functions for looking up data in the A26:B28 cell range.

6. With a cell in the employee table active, display the Design tab and then click the Total Row check box in the Table Style Options group. Show the record count in the Gender column, the average age in the Age column, and sums in the Sales and Commission columns, as shown in Figure 5–68.

7. Add the icon set 3 triangles using conditional formatting to the Sales column (F8:F20): Sales >=70; 70>Sales>=40; Sales<40, as shown in Figure 5–68. To add the conditional formatting, select the range F8:F20, click the Conditional Formatting button (Home tab | Styles group), and click the New Rule command. When Excel displays the New Formatting Rule dialog box, click the Icon Style box arrow, scroll up and click 3 Triangles. Click the Value box and enter the Sales limits described earlier.

8. Change the document properties as specified by your instructor. Change the worksheet header with your name, course number, and other information as specified by your instructor.

9. Print the worksheet in landscape orientation using the 'Fit Sheet on One Page' option. Save the workbook using the file name, Lab 5-1 Anderson Scholastic Employees. Submit the assignment as requested by your instructor.

Instructions Part 2: Open the workbook Lab 5-1 Anderson Scholastic Employees created in Part 1. Do not save the workbook in this part. Step through each query exercise in Table 5–5 and print (or write down for submission to your instructor) the results for each. To complete a filter exercise, use the AutoFilter technique. If the arrows are not showing to the right of the column headings when the table is active, then click the Filter button (Data tab | Sort & Filter group). Select the appropriate arrow(s) to the right of the field names and option(s) on the corresponding menus. Use the Custom Filter option on the Number Filters list for field names that do not contain appropriate selections. For the filters that require it, use the Search box on the AutoFilter menu to query the table. Following each query, print the worksheet and then click the Filter button (Data tab | Sort & Filter group) twice to clear the query and reactivate the arrows in the field names. You should end up with the following number of records for Filters 1 through 12: 1 = 3; 2 = 4; 3 = 2; 4 = 1; 5 = 4; 6 = 5; 7 = 2; 8 = 3; 9 = 2; 10 = 2; 11 = 1; and 12 = 13. When you are finished querying the table, close the workbook without saving changes. Submit the assignment as requested by your instructor.

Table 5–5 Anderson Scholastic Employees Filter Criteria

Filter	Dept	Lname	Fname	Age	Gender	Sales	Commission
1	Trade						
2	K-12				M		
3					F		> 250000
4	Higher Ed			M		589000	
5				<40	F		
6				>30 and <40			
7		Wyler				>1500000	
8	Higher Ed					>3000000	
9						<=2500000	<150000
10			Begins with L				<600000
11	K-12			>50	F		
12	All	All	All	All	All	All	All

Instructions Part 3: Open the workbook Lab 5-1 Anderson Scholastic Employees created in Part 1. Do not save the workbook in this part. Sort the table according to the following six sort problems. Print the table for each sort in landscape orientation using the 'Fit Sheet on One Page' option (or write down the last name in the first record for submission to your instructor). Begin problems 2 through 6 by sorting the Dept. field in descending sequence to sort the table back into its original order.

Continued >

In the Lab *continued*

1. Sort the table in descending sequence by Dept.

2. Sort the table by first name within last name within department. All three sort keys are to be in ascending sequence.

3. Sort the table by gender within dept. Both sort keys are to be in ascending sequence.

4. Sort the table by first name within last name within age within department. All four sort keys are to be in descending sequence.

5. Sort the table in ascending sequence by commission.

6. Sort the table by commission within sales within department. All three sort keys are to be in descending sequence.

7. Hide columns F and G by selecting them and pressing CTRL+0 (zero). Print the table. Press CTRL+A to select the entire table. In the Cells group on the Home tab, click the Format button. Point to Hide & Unhide and then click Unhide Columns. Close the Lab 5-1 Anderson Scholastic Employees workbook without saving changes. Submit the assignment as requested by your instructor.

Instructions Part 4: Open the Lab 5-1 Anderson Scholastic Employees workbook created in Part 1 and complete the following tasks. Do not save the workbook in this part.

1. Click a cell in the table to activate the table. Display the Design tab and then click the Total Row check box to remove the total row. Sort the table by sales within department. Select ascending sequence for both sort keys.

2. Select cell A8. Right-click anywhere in the table, point to the Table command on the shortcut menu, and then click the Convert to Range command on the Table submenu. When Excel displays the Microsoft Office Excel dialog box, click the Yes button to convert the table to a range. Display the Data tab and then click the Subtotal button (Data tab | Outline group). When Excel displays the Subtotal dialog box, click the 'At each change in' box arrow and then click Dept. If necessary, select Sum in the Use function list. In the 'Add subtotal to' list, click Sales and Commission to select them and then click the OK button. Print the table. Click row level symbol 1 and print the table. Click row level symbol 2 and print the table. Click the Subtotal button (Data tab | Outline group) and then click the Remove All button in the Subtotal dialog box to remove all subtotals. Close the workbook without saving changes. Submit the assignment as requested by your instructor.

In the Lab

Lab 2: Sorting, Finding, and Advanced Filtering

Problem: Cornelli's Inc. has many stores across the nation. Depending on the store classification, there are different departments available at the location; however, they do not have to have all the same departments. The company uses a table (Figure 5–69) that shows what departments are at each location as well as the store classification.

The CEO, Juniper Alvarez, has asked you to sort, query, and determine some statistics from the table. Carefully label each required printout by using the part number and step. If a step results in multiple printouts, label them a, b, c, and so on.

Instructions Part 1: Start Excel and perform the following tasks.

1. Open the workbook Lab 5-2 Cornelli's Department Availability Table from the Data Files for Students. See the inside back cover of this book for instructions for downloading the Data Files for Students or see your instructor for information on accessing the files required in this book. Do not save the workbook in this part.

	Location	Classification	Auto	Bath	Clothing	Electronics	Furniture	Grocery	Jewelry	Kitchen	Home	Pharmacy	Count
9					Cornelli's Department Availability Table								
11	Orlando, FL	Superstore	Y	Y	Y	Y	Y	Y	Y	Y	Y	Y	10
12	Little Rock, AR	Home Store	N	Y	N	Y	Y	N	N	Y	Y	N	5
13	San Antonio, TX	Home Store	N	Y	N	Y	Y	N	N	Y	Y	N	5
14	Philadelphia, PA	Department	Y	Y	Y	Y	N	N	Y	Y	Y	N	7
15	Jacksonville, FL	Automotive	Y	N	N	N	N	N	N	N	N	N	1
16	Los Angeles, CA	Automotive	Y	N	N	N	N	N	N	N	N	N	1
17	New York, NY	Superstore	Y	Y	Y	Y	Y	Y	Y	Y	Y	Y	10
18	Austin, TX	Drugstore	N	N	N	N	N	Y	Y	N	N	Y	4
19	Memphis, TN	Wholesale	N	Y	Y	Y	Y	Y	N	Y	N	Y	7
20	Baltimore, MD	MiniMart	Y	Y	N	N	N	Y	N	N	N	N	3
21	San Francisco, CA	Automotive	Y	N	N	N	N	N	N	N	N	N	1
22	Columbus, OH	Department	Y	Y	Y	Y	N	N	Y	Y	Y	N	7
23	San Jose, CA	Automotive	Y	N	N	N	N	N	N	N	N	N	1
24	Dallas, TX	Wholesale	Y	Y	N	Y	Y	Y	Y	Y	Y	N	8
25	Denver, CO	MiniMart	Y	Y	N	N	N	Y	N	N	N	N	3
26	Nashville, TN	Department	N	Y	Y	Y	N	N	Y	Y	Y	N	6
27	Boston, MA	Superstore	N	Y	Y	Y	Y	Y	Y	Y	Y	Y	9
28	El Paso, TX	MiniMart	Y	Y	N	N	N	Y	N	N	N	N	3
29	Fort Smith, AR	Drugstore	N	N	N	Y	N	Y	Y	N	N	Y	4
30	Seattle, WA	Wholesale	Y	N	Y	Y	Y	Y	Y	Y	N	N	7

Figure 5–69

2. Complete the following tasks:

   a. Sort the records in the table into ascending sequence by location. Austin, TX should appear first in the table. Seattle, WA should appear last. Print the table. Undo the sort.

   b. Sort the records in the table by Classification within Location. Select descending sequence for the Classification and ascending sequence for Location. Austin, TX should be the first record. Print the table. Undo the sort.

   c. Sort the table by Home within Furniture within Bath within Auto. Apply sort descending for all four fields. Sort the table first on Home, then Furniture, then Bath, and finally Auto. Those locations with all four departments will rise to the top of the table. Orlando, FL should be the first record. Print the table. Close the workbook without saving it. Submit the assignment as requested by your instructor.

Instructions Part 2:   Open the workbook Lab 5-2 Cornelli's Department Availability Table from the Data Files for Students. Do not save the workbook in this part. Select a cell within the table. If the column heading arrows do not appear, then click the Filter button (Data tab | Sort & Filter group). Use the column heading arrows to find the records that meet the criteria in items 1 through 4 below. Use the Show All command on the Filter submenu before starting items 2, 3, and 4. Print the table for each query. You should end up with the following number of records for items 1 through 4: item 1 should have 7; item 2 should have 3; item 3 should have 4; and item 4 should have 1. Close the workbook without saving the changes. Submit the assignment as requested by your instructor.

1. Find all records that have a pharmacy and a grocery department.

2. Find all records that represent locations with more than 7 departments that have a pharmacy and a clothing department.

3. Find all records that have a location in TX using search.

4. Find all records that have a location in CA using search and that are drugstores.

Instructions Part 3:   Open the workbook Lab 5-2 Cornelli's Department Availability Table from the Data Files for Students and then save the workbook using the file name, Lab 5-2 Cornelli's Department Availability Table Final. Perform the following tasks:

1. Add a criteria range by copying the table title and field names (range A9:M10) to the range A2:M3 (Figure 5–70 on the following page). Change cell A2 to Criteria Area and then color the title area as shown in Figure 5–70. Use the Name box in the formula bar to name the criteria range (A3:M4) Criteria.

Continued >

In the Lab *continued*

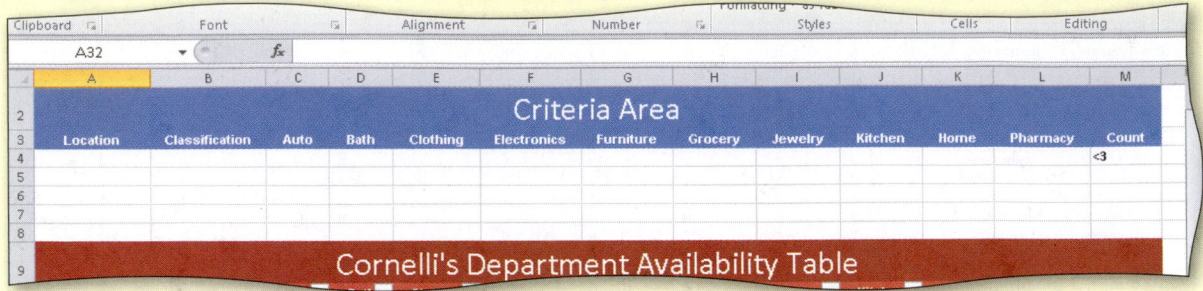

Figure 5–70

2. Add an extract range by copying the table title and field names (range A9:M10) to the range A34:M35 (Figure 5–71). Change cell A34 to Extract Area and then color the title area as shown in Figure 5–71. Use the Name box in the formula bar to name the extract range (range A35:M35) Extract.

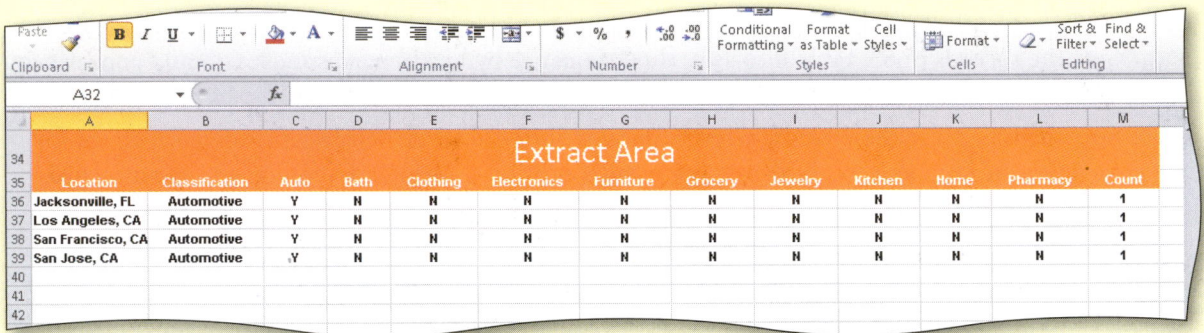

Figure 5–71

3. With the table active, use the Advanced button (Data tab | Sort & Filter group) to extract records that pass the tests listed below in a through d. Print the worksheet in landscape orientation using the 'Fit Sheet on One Page' option for each extract.

   a. Extract the records that represent locations that have all of the departments. You should extract two records.

   b. Extract the records that represent superstores that have a pharmacy but not an auto department. You should extract one record.

   c. Extract the records that represent locations that have an auto department and have less than 7 departments total. The field Count in column M uses the COUNTIF function to count the number of Ys in a record. A count of 4 means the record represents a location with four departments. You should extract seven records.

   d. Extract the records that represent locations with less than three departments. You should extract 4 records.

4. Change the document properties as specified by your instructor. Change the worksheet header with your name, course number, and other information as specified by your instructor. Save the workbook using the current file name. Close the workbook. Submit the assignment as requested by your instructor.

Instructions Part 4: Open the workbook Lab 5-2 Cornelli's Department Availability Table Final created in Part 3. If you did not complete Part 3, then open Lab 5-2 Cornelli's Department Availability Table from the Data Files for Students. Perform the following tasks:

1. Scroll to the right to display cell H1 in the upper-left corner of the window. Enter the criteria in the range O2:Q4 as shown in Figure 5–72. Enter the row titles in cells O7:O12 as shown in Figure 5–72.

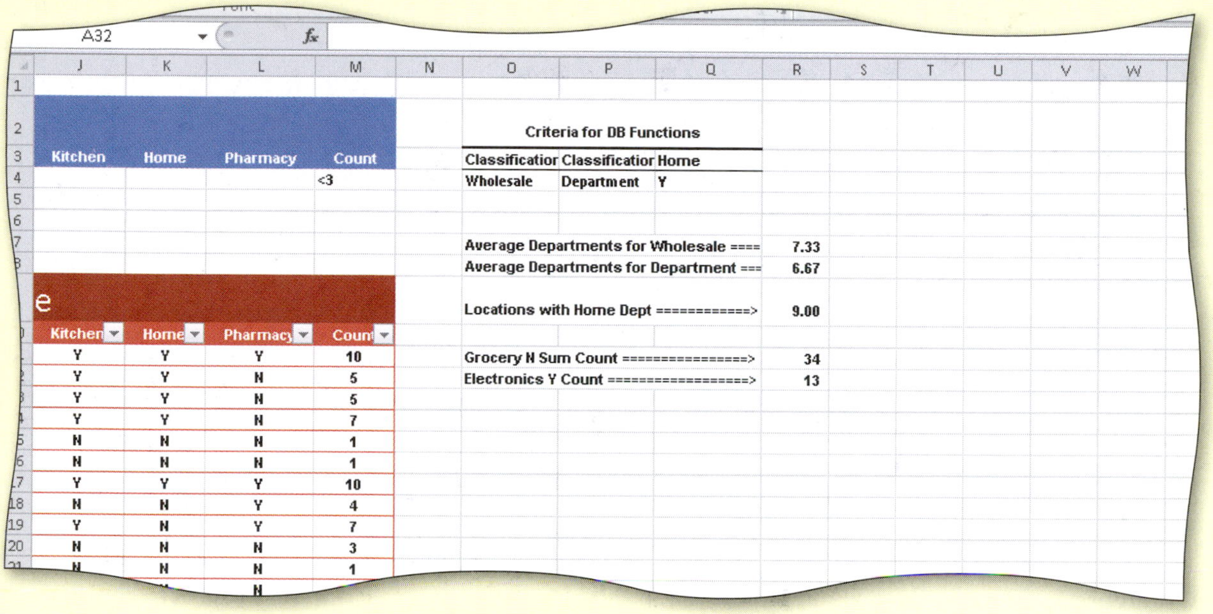

Figure 5–72

2. Use the database function DAVERAGE and the appropriate criteria in the range O3:Q4 to determine the average number of departments of the Wholesale and Department stores in the range. Use the table function DCOUNT and the appropriate criteria in the range O3:Q4 to determine the record count of those locations that have a Home department. The DCOUNT function requires that you choose a numeric field in the table to count, such as Count.

3. Use the SUMIF function to determine the Grocery N Sum Count in cell R11. That is, sum the Count field for all records containing an N in the Grocery column. Use the COUNTIF function to determine the Electronics Y Count in cell R12.

4. Print the worksheet in landscape orientation using the 'Fit Sheet on One Page' option. Save the workbook using the file name, Lab 5-2 Cornelli's Department Availability Table Final. Submit the assignment as requested by your instructor.

In the Lab

Lab 3: Creating a Table with a Lookup Function

Problem: You are a member of the Mega SaveMart, a grocery store chain in the Midwest. The produce manager wants you to create a table to help him manage the shelf life of his produce (Figure 5–73 on the following page). You decide it is a great opportunity to show your Excel skills. In addition to including the number of days of shelf life left for the product, the manager also would like a grade assigned to each based on the days left. Produce with a grade lower than C is ready to be rotated off the shelf.

Continued >

In the Lab *continued*

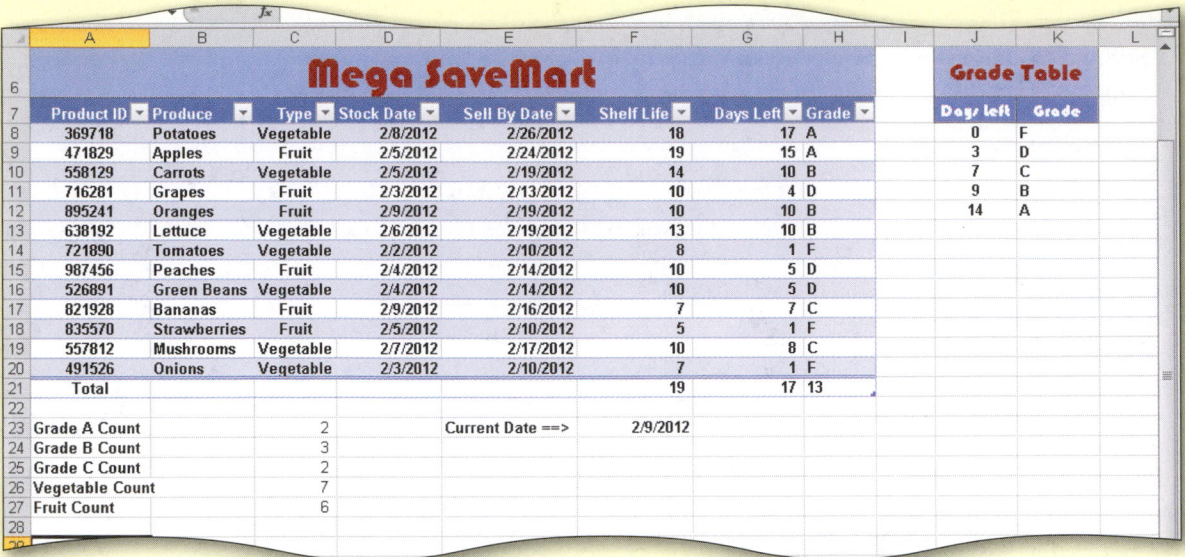

Figure 5–73

Instructions Part 1:   Perform the following tasks to create the table shown in the range A7:20 in Figure 5–73.

1. Create a new workbook and then bold the entire Sheet1 worksheet. Create the table shown in Figure 5–73 using the techniques learned in this chapter. Assign appropriate formats to row 8, the row immediately below the field names. Rename the Sheet1 tab and delete Sheet2 and Sheet3.

2. Enter the data shown in the range A8:A20 and in E23:F23.

3. Calculate the Shelf Life in F8 by subtracting the Stock Date from the Sell By Date. Copy the function in cell F8 to range F9:F20.

4. Calculate the Days Left in G8 by subtracting the Current Date (F23) from the Sell By Date. Copy the function in cell G8 to range G9:G20.

5. Enter the Grade table in the range J6:K12. In cell H8, enter the function `=vlookup(G8, $J$8:$K$12, 2)` to determine the letter grade that corresponds to the Days Left in cell G8. Copy the function in cell H8 to the range H9:H20.

6. Select the Total Row option on the Design tab to determine the maximum shelf life, the maximum days left, and the record count in the Grade column in row 21.

7. Enter the total row headings in the range A23:A27. Use the COUNTIF functions to determine the totals in the range C23:C27.

8. Change the document properties as specified by your instructor. Change the worksheet header so that it contains your name, course number, and other information as specified by your instructor.

9. Save the workbook using the file name, Lab 5-3 Mega SaveMart Table. Print the worksheet in landscape orientation using the 'Fit Sheet on One Page' option. At the bottom of the printout, explain why the dollar signs ($) are necessary in the VLOOKUP function in Step 3. Submit the assignment as requested by your instructor.

Instructions Part 2:   Open the workbook Lab 5-3 Mega SaveMart Table. Do not save the workbook in this part. Sort the table as follows. Print the table after each sort. After completing the third sort, close the workbook without saving the changes.

1. Sort the table in ascending sequence by the Stock Date.

2. Sort the table by Shelf Life within Type. Use ascending sequence for both fields.

3. Sort the table by Days Left within Type. Use descending sequence for both fields.

Instructions Part 3:   Open the workbook Lab 5-3 Mega SaveMart Table. Use the concepts and techniques presented in this chapter to search the table using the AutoFilter search box. After completing each search, print the worksheet. After the last search, close the workbook without saving the changes.

1. Search for produce that was stocked on the 5th (three records).
2. Days left of 1 (three records).
3. Vegetables with shelf life of 10 (two records).
4. Fruit with grade of F (one record).
5. Submit the assignment as requested by your instructor.

Cases and Places

Apply your creative thinking and problem solving skills to design and implement a solution.

1: Inventory Level Priority

Academic

Create an Intro to Biology grade table from the data in Table 5–6. Also include a Final % field and a Grade field. Both are calculated columns. Final % is calculated with each quiz being worth 10% and each test being worth 35%. Create a Grade table in the range J6:K20 using the data shown in Table 5–7. Use the VLOOKUP function to determine the grade to assign to each record. Add the total row to the table. Show the averages of each quiz and test. In cell range A19:B19 show Mark Kennedy's grade using the MATCH and INDEX functions. Print the worksheet in landscape orientation using the 'Fit Sheet on One Page' option. Save the workbook.

Table 5–6 Intro to Biology Grades					
Name	**Quiz 1**	**Quiz 2**	**Quiz 3**	**Test 1**	**Test 2**
Cyrus, Hannah	85	88	78	90	87
Settle, Lee	58	49	43	50	49
Barnett, Betty	93	80	82	81	72
Kennedy, Mark	82	48	59	68	64
Francisco, Steven	60	58	64	57	56
Frye, Janice	73	84	88	87	89
Savage, Hector	79	75	72	72	70
Kidinger, Robert	97	100	85	85	100

Table 5–7 Grade Table			
Final %	**Grade**	**Final %**	**Grade**
0%	F	70%	B-
50%	D-	74%	B
54%	D	77%	B+
57%	D+	80%	A-
60%	C-	85%	A
64%	C	90%	A+
67%	C+		

Continued >

Cases and Places *continued*

2: Conditional Formatting and Sorting a Table

Personal

You want to create an expense log to show your expenses for the past six months (Jan–Jun). You have compiled your data together (as shown in Table 5–8). Create a household expense log using the data in Table 5–8. Name your table Database. Use the database functions you learned in this chapter to determine the minimum and maximum payments for food, cell phone, and travel. Indicate how much was spent for clothing in March. Finally, display a count of the total number of months in the expense log.

Table 5–8 Household Expense Log

Month	Rent	Food	Utilities	Cell Phone	Car Payments	Insurance	Clothing	Internet	Travel
Jan	680.00	601.89	225.00	75.00	275.41	149.50	350.89	81.99	190.00
Feb	680.00	582.89	210.00	80.00	275.41	149.50	101.55	81.99	120.00
Mar	680.00	451.88	175.00	75.00	275.41	149.50	55.75	81.99	150.00
April	680.00	515.45	165.00	95.00	275.41	149.50	75.69	95.85	450.00
May	680.00	632.85	120.00	75.00	275.41	149.50	259.86	81.99	120.00
Jun	680.00	650.11	135.00	75.00	275.41	149.50	180.00	87.00	180.00

3: Creating a Table of Companies

Professional

You have gathered information about companies at which you may want to work in your next job. Create a company info table using the data in Table 5–9. The information includes company name, state, city, miles from your current residence, and a rating for each company between 1 and 4, with 4 being the most preferred. Save the file as Case 5-3 Company Info Table. Complete the following sorts, print each sorted version of the table, and then undo the sorts in preparation for the next sort: (a) alphabetically (A to Z) by state, and (b) descending (smallest to largest) by miles from home. Filter the list for records with a rating greater than 2. Print the table and then show all of the records. Use the search filter to show which records are from Texas. Print the table and then show all of the records. Group the records by state, using the Average function in the Use function list in the Subtotal dialog box. Print the worksheet.

Table 5–9 Company Info

Company Name	State	City	Distance	Rating
GameTech	Florida	Orlando	960	4
CompIT Inc.	Arkansas	Little Rock	730	1
InfoSolutions	Pennsylvania	Philadelphia	480	3
Cyber Intelligence	New York	New York	560	3
Games InDesign	Texas	El Paso	590	4
Web Kings, Inc.	Maryland	Baltimore	430	2
BeachBiz IT Design	California	San Francisco	2430	4
HighTech Masters	Texas	Dallas	1050	2
Mountain Lightning IT	Colorado	Denver	1240	3
ALTSolutions	Washington	Seattle	2350	1

6 Working with Multiple Worksheets and Workbooks

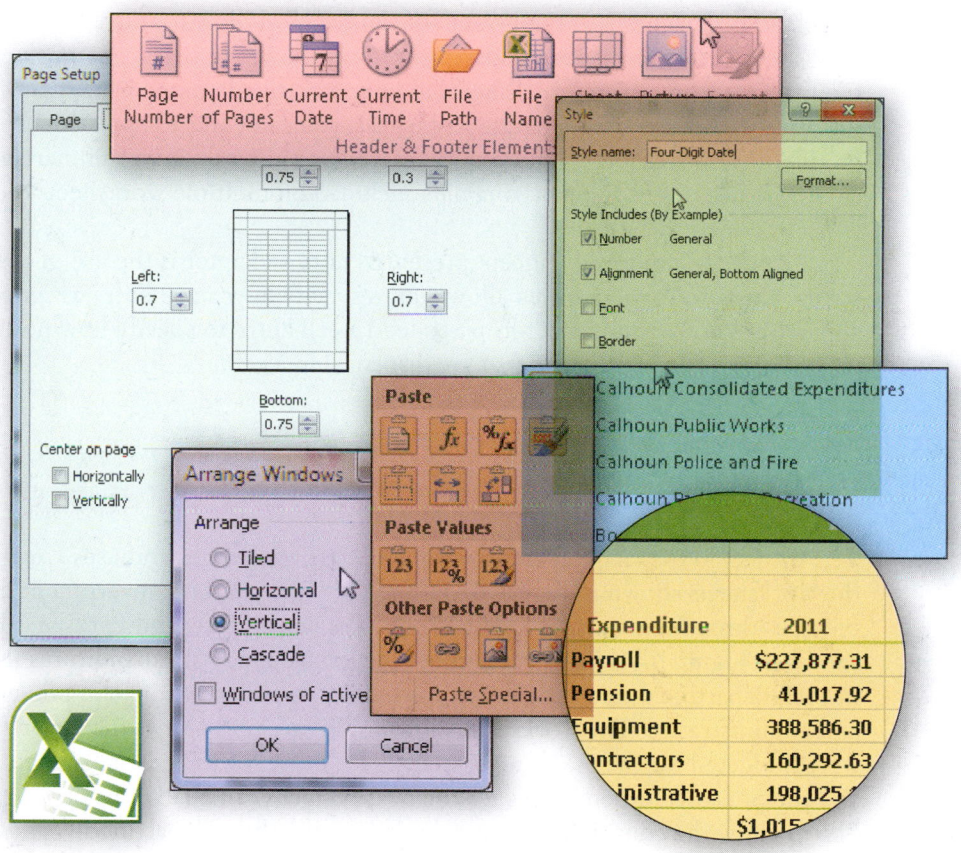

Objectives

You will have mastered the material in this chapter when you can:

- Use the ROUND function
- Use custom format codes
- Define, apply, and remove a style
- Add a worksheet to a workbook
- Create formulas that use 3-D cell references
- Add data to multiple worksheets at the same time

- Add a header or footer and change margins
- Insert and move a page break
- Save a workbook as a PDF or XPS file
- Create a workspace file
- Consolidate data by linking workbooks

6 | Working with Multiple Worksheets and Workbooks

Introduction

An organization may keep data from various departments or regions in different worksheets. If you enter each department's data on a worksheet in a workbook, you can click the sheet tabs at the bottom of the Excel window to move from worksheet to worksheet, or department to department. Note, however, that many business applications require data from several worksheets to be summarized on one worksheet. To facilitate this summarization, on a separate worksheet, you can enter formulas that reference cells on the other worksheets. This type of referencing allows you to summarize workbook data. The process of summarizing data included on multiple worksheets on one worksheet is called **consolidation**.

Another important concept presented in this chapter is the use of custom format codes. **Custom format codes** allow you to specify how a cell entry assigned a format will appear. You can customize a format code in a cell entry to specify how positive numbers, negative numbers, zeros, and text are displayed in a cell.

Project — Consolidated Expenditures Worksheet

The project in the chapter follows proper design guidelines and uses Excel to create the worksheets shown in Figure 6–1. The City of Calhoun's government organization includes three departments, Public Works, Police and Fire, and Parks and Recreation, as shown in Figure 6–1. Each department incurs five types of expenditures that are common to each department in a budget year, including payroll, pension, equipment, contractors, and administrative. The worksheet shown in Figure 6–1 shows the expenditures that were budgeted for the past budget year, 2011; those for the current budget year, 2012; and the proposed expenditures for the next budget year, 2013. The city manager would like to know the consolidated expenditures for the three departments. She also would like to see the individual department expenditures on separate worksheets. Additionally, she would like to see the consolidated and individual percent increases or decreases for each expenditure.

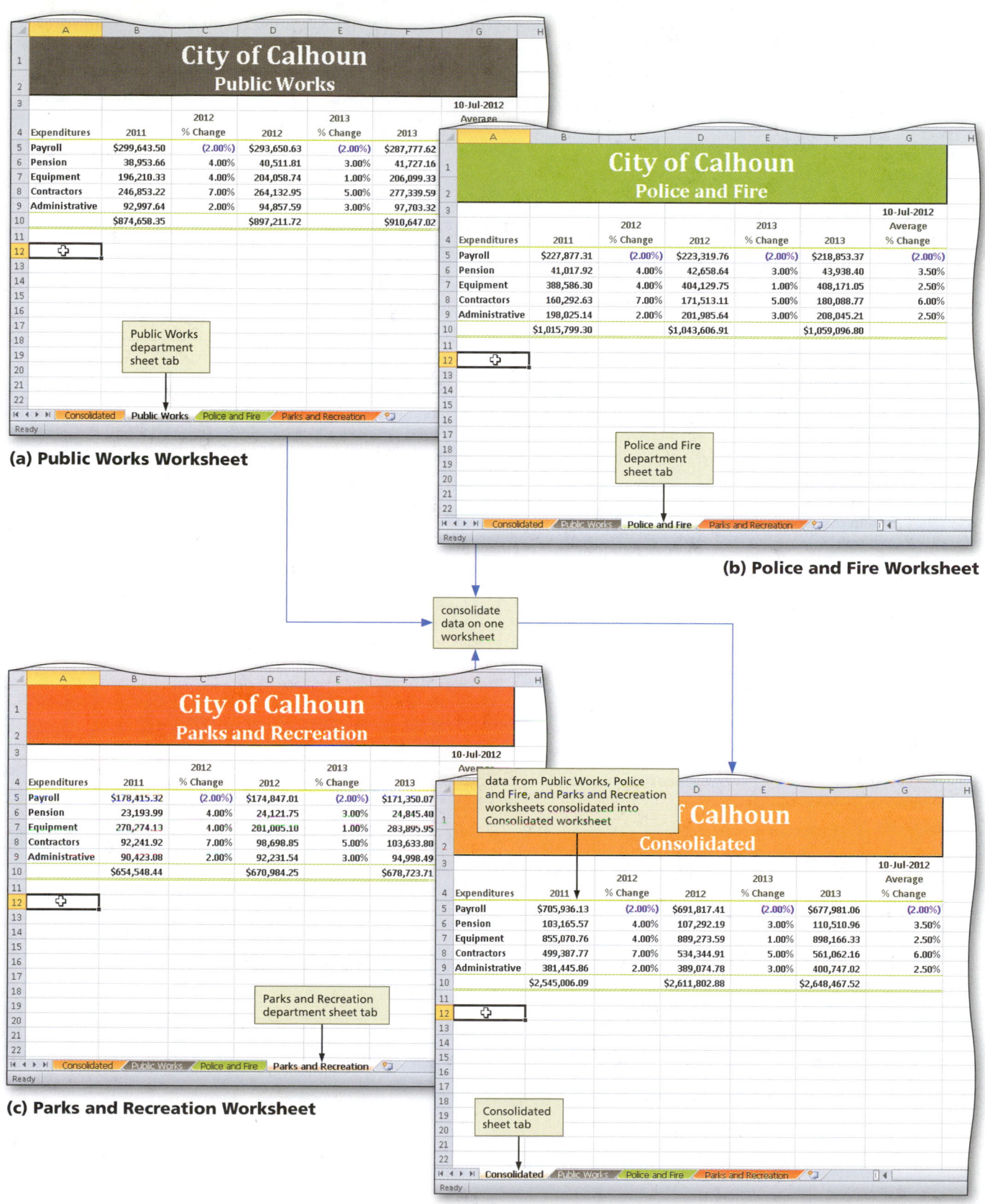

(a) Public Works Worksheet

(b) Police and Fire Worksheet

(c) Parks and Recreation Worksheet

(d) Consolidated Worksheet

Figure 6–1

The requirements document for the City of Calhoun Consolidated Expenditures workbook is shown in Figure 6–2. It includes the needs, source of data, summary of calculations, special requirements, and other facts about its development.

REQUEST FOR NEW WORKBOOK

Date Submitted:	July 3, 2012
Submitted By:	Dana Gatz
Worksheet Title:	City of Calhoun Consolidated Expenditures
Needs:	The needs are as follows: 1. A workbook containing three worksheets for the three major city departments and one worksheet to consolidate the city expenditure data. 2. Each worksheet should be identical in structure and allow for display of the previous, current, and next year's expenditures. 3. The worksheets should print with a common header and footer and meet the city's standards for worksheet printouts.
Source of Data:	The data will be collected and organized by the city manager, Dana Gatz.
Calculations:	Include the following formulas in each worksheet: 1. 2012 Expenditure = 2011 Expenditure + 2011 Expenditure × 2012 % Change in Expenditure 2. 2013 Expenditure = 2012 Expenditure + 2012 Expenditure × 2013 % Change in Expenditure 3. Average % Change in Expenditure = (2012 % Change in Expenditure + Expected 2013 % Change in Expenditure) / 2 4. Use the SUM function to determine totals. **Note:** Use dummy data in the consolidated worksheet to verify the formulas. Round the Average % Change to the nearest one-tenth of a percent.
Special Requirements:	Investigate a way the city can consolidate data from multiple workbooks into another workbook.

Approvals

Approval Status:	X	Approved
		Rejected
Approved By:	Brandon Stevens	
Date:	July 10, 2012	
Assigned To:	J. Quasney, Spreadsheet Specialist	

Figure 6–2

Overview

As you read this chapter, you will learn how to create the worksheets shown in Figure 6–1 by performing these general tasks:

- Add a worksheet to the workbook.
- Create and apply a custom format.
- Reference data on other worksheets.
- Add data to multiple worksheets at the same time.
- Print the worksheets with proper headers, footers, margins, and page breaks.
- Create a workspace and consolidate data by linking workbooks.

Plan Ahead

General Project Decisions

While creating an Excel worksheet, you need to make several decisions that will determine the appearance and characteristics of the finished worksheet. As you create the worksheets to meet the requirements shown in Figure 6–2, you should follow these general guidelines:

1. **Design the consolidated worksheet and plan the formatting.** When a workbook contains multiple worksheets with the same layout, spreadsheet specialists often create **sample data**—that is, sample data used in place of actual data to verify the formulas in the worksheet—and formatting on one worksheet and then copy that worksheet to additional worksheets. This practice avoids the need to format multiple worksheets separately.

2. **Identify additional worksheets needed in the workbook.** After the initial worksheet is created using sample data and the required formulas and then saved, it should be copied to the other worksheets. Actual data for the three other worksheets will replace the copied sample data. The data from the additional worksheets then can be consolidated onto the initial worksheet.

3. **Plan the layout and location of the required custom format codes.** Some organizations require that certain types of data be formatted in a specific manner. If the specific type of format is not included in Excel's list of formats, such as Currency or Accounting, then you must create a custom format code that meets the requirement and then apply the custom format code to the necessary cells.

4. **Examine the options, including headers, margins, and page breaks, that you have for printing worksheets.** When working with multiple worksheets, using properly formatted page headers and footers is important. Excel allows you to print page numbers and the sheet name of each sheet. In addition, margins and page breaks also can be adjusted to provide professional-looking printed worksheets.

5. **Identify workbooks to be consolidated into a workspace and then linked to create a consolidated workbook of the initial workbooks.** The special requirement for the project listed in the requirements document asks that methods to combine workbooks be investigated (Figure 6–2). Excel allows you to work with separate workbooks in a workspace and then link the workbooks to provide a consolidated view of the data in the workbooks.

When necessary, more specific details concerning the above guidelines are presented at appropriate points in the chapter. The chapter also will identify the actions you perform and decisions made regarding these guidelines during the creation of the worksheets shown in Figure 6–1 on page EX 363.

In addition, using a sketch of the worksheet can help you visualize its design. The sketch of the consolidated worksheet consists of titles, column and row headings, the location of data values, and a general idea of the desired formatting (Figure 6–3 on the following page).

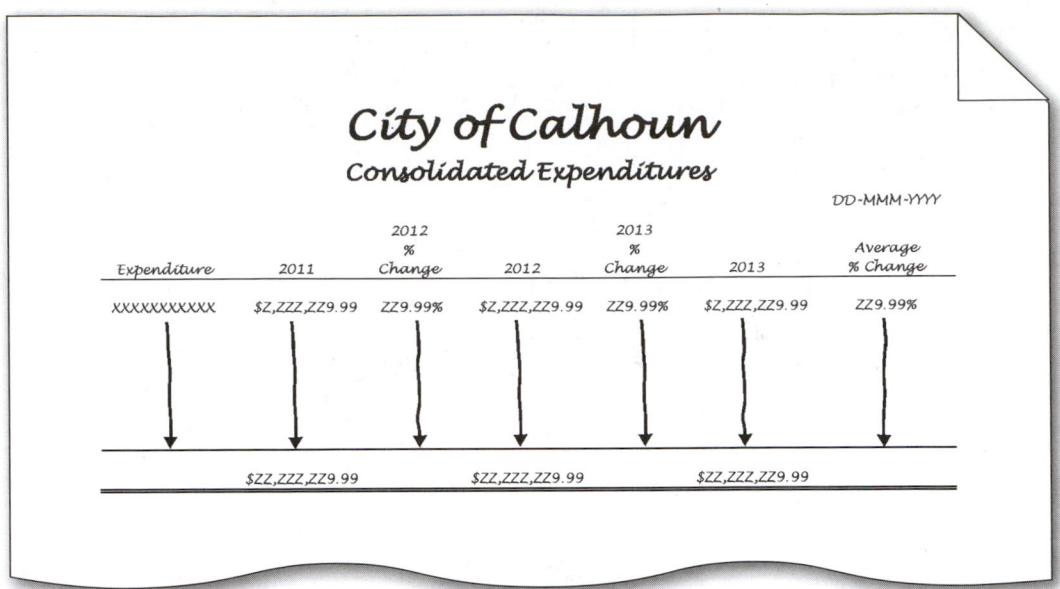

Figure 6-3

With a solid understanding of the requirements document, an understanding of the necessary decisions, and a sketch of the consolidated worksheet, the next step is to use Excel to create the consolidated worksheet.

To Start Excel

If you are using a computer to step through the project in this chapter and you want your screens to match the figures in this book, you should change your screen's resolution to 1024 × 768. The following steps start Excel.

① Start Excel.

② If the Excel window is not maximized, click the Maximize button next to the Close button on its title bar to maximize the window.

Creating the Consolidated Worksheet

The first step in building the workbook is to create and save a workbook that includes the consolidated worksheet that contains the titles, column and row headings, formulas, and formats used on each of the departments' sheets.

Plan Ahead

> **Design the consolidated worksheet and plan the formatting.**
> The consolidated worksheet will be used to create a number of other worksheets. Thus, it is important to consider the layout, cell formatting, and contents of the worksheet.
>
> • **Set row heights and column widths.** Row heights and column widths should be set to sizes large enough to accommodate future needs.
>
> • **Use placeholders for data when possible.** Placeholders often are used when creating an initial consolidated worksheet to guide users of the worksheet regarding what type of data to enter in cells. For example, the word Department could be used in a subtitle to indicate to a user of the worksheet to place the department name in the subtitle.
>
> *(continued)*

(continued)

Plan Ahead

- **Use sample data to verify formulas.** When an initial consolidated worksheet is created, sample data should be used in place of actual data to verify the formulas in the worksheet. Selecting simple numbers such as 1, 2, and 3 allows you to check quickly to see if the formulas are generating the proper results. In consolidated worksheets with more complex formulas, you may want to use numbers that test the extreme boundaries of valid data.

- **Format cells in the worksheet.** Formatting that can be modified for each worksheet should be applied to titles and subtitles to provide cues to users of the worksheets. For example, by using a fill color for the title and subtitle, the fill color for additional worksheets can be changed after the consolidated worksheet is copied to subsequent worksheets. All numeric cell entry placeholders—sample data—should be formatted properly for unit numbers and currency amounts.

The first step in creating the workbook is to create the consolidated expenditures worksheet, shown in Figure 6–4. The consolidated worksheet then will be copied to three other worksheets. Each worksheet will contain expenditures for one of three departments.

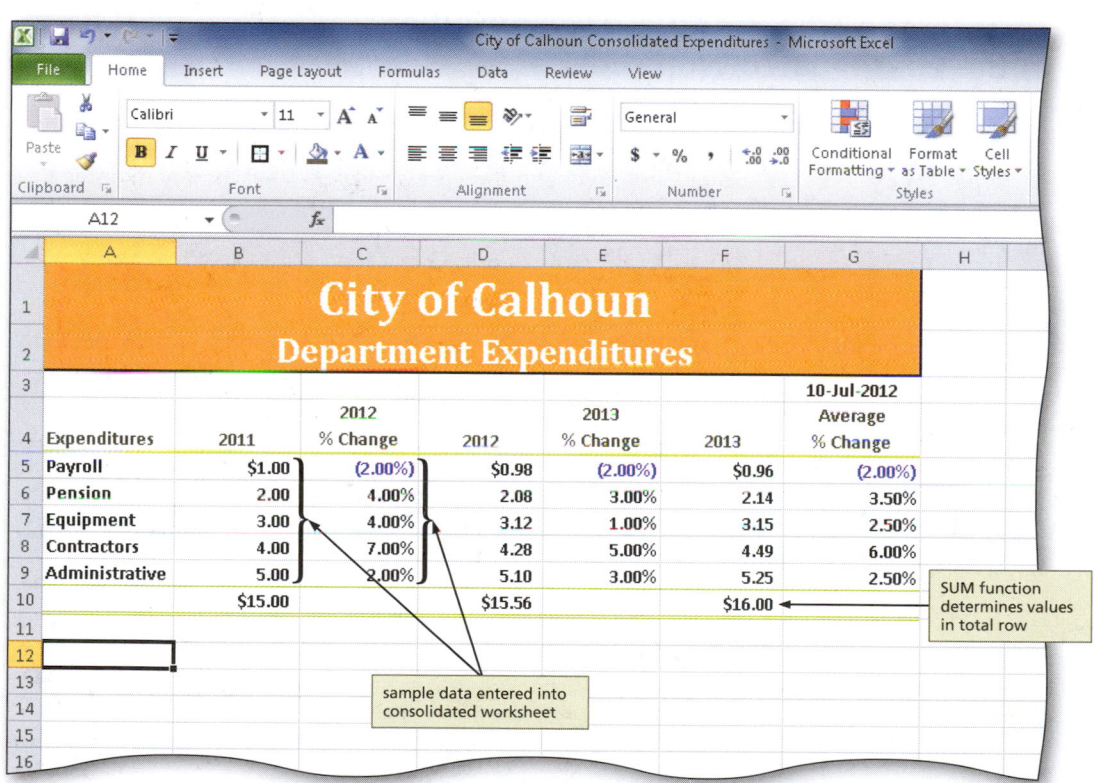

Figure 6–4

To Change the Font Style to Bold and Adjust the Row Heights and Column Widths of the Consolidated Worksheet

The first step in creating the consolidated worksheet with sample data is to change the font style to bold and adjust the height of row 4 to 30.75 points and column widths of column A to 13.57 characters; B, D, and F to 12.86 characters; C and E to 12.14 characters; and G to 14.14 characters. The row heights and column widths need to be changed to accommodate the data in the worksheet. The following steps change the font style to bold and adjust the row heights and column widths of the consolidated worksheet.

BTW

Selecting a Range of Cells
You can select any range of cells with entries surrounded by blank cells by clicking a cell in the range and pressing CTRL+SHIFT+ASTERISK (*).

BTW

Q&As
For a complete list of the Q&As found in many of the step-by-step sequences in this book, visit the Excel 2010 Q&A Web page (scsite.com/ex2010/qa).

1 Click the Select All button immediately above row heading 1 and to the left of column heading A and then click the Bold button (Home tab | Font group) to bold the entire work-sheet. Select cell A1 to deselect the worksheet.

2 Drag the bottom boundary of row heading 4 down until the row height is 30.75 (41 pixels) to change the row height.

3 Drag the right boundary of column heading A to the right until the column width is 13.57 (100 pixels) to change the column width.

4 Select columns B, D, and F, and then drag the right boundary of column heading F right until the column width is 12.86 (95 pixels) to change several column widths at the same time.

5 Select columns C and E, and then drag the right boundary of column heading E right until the column width is 12.14 (90 pixels) to change several column widths at the same time.

6 Select column G, and then drag the right boundary of the column heading right until the column width is 14.14 (104 pixels) to change the column width. Select cell A1 to deselect column G.

BTW

Displaying Future Dates
You can display a future date, such as tomorrow's date, in a cell by adding a number to the NOW or TODAY function. For example, =NOW()+1 displays tomorrow's date in a cell and =NOW()+14 displays a date two weeks in the future. The function =NOW()−1 displays yesterday's date.

To Enter the Title, Subtitle, and Row Titles in the Consolidated Worksheet

The following steps enter the titles in cells A1 and A2 and the row titles in column A.

1 Type `City of Calhoun` in cell A1 and then press the DOWN ARROW key to enter a worksheet title.

2 Type `Department Expenditures` in cell A2 and then press the DOWN ARROW key twice to make cell A4 active and to enter a worksheet subtitle.

3 Type `Expenditures` and then press the DOWN ARROW key to enter a column heading.

4 With cell A5 active, enter the remaining row titles in column A, as shown in Figure 6–5.

To Enter Column Titles and the System Date in the Consolidated Worksheet

The next step is to enter the column titles in row 4 and the system date in cell G3. The following steps enter column titles and the system date in the consolidated worksheet.

BTW

Manipulating Dates
You can use the DATE function to change a year, month, and day to a serial number that automatically is formatted to mm/dd/yyyy. For example, if cell A1 equals the year 2012, cell A2 equals the month 2, cell A3 equals day 10, and cell A4 is assigned the function =DATE (A1, A2, A3), then 2/10/2012 appears in cell A4. The DATE function is most useful in formulas where year, month, and day are formulas, not constants.

1 Select cell B4. Type `2011` and then press the RIGHT ARROW key to enter a column heading.

2 Type `2012` and then press ALT+ENTER to begin a new line of text in the selected cell. Type `% Change` and then press the RIGHT ARROW key to enter a column heading.

3 With cell D4 active, enter the remaining column titles in row 4 as shown in Figure 6–5.

4 Select cell G3. Type `=now()` and then press the ENTER key to enter the system date.

5 Right-click cell G3 to display a shortcut menu and then click Format Cells on the shortcut menu.

6 When Excel displays the Format Cells dialog box, click Date in the Category list and then click 3/14/01 13:30 in the Type list to format a date with a 2-digit year and a time.

7 Click the OK button (Format Cells dialog box) to close the dialog box.

8 Select cell A12 to deselect cell G3.

Q&A

Why was the date not formatted as it appears in Figure 6–4?

The format assigned to the system date in cell G3 is temporary. For now, it ensures that the system date will appear properly, rather than as a series of number signs (#). The system date will be assigned a permanent format later in this chapter. The date might be displayed as a series of number signs if the date, as initially formatted by Excel, does not fit in the width of the cell.

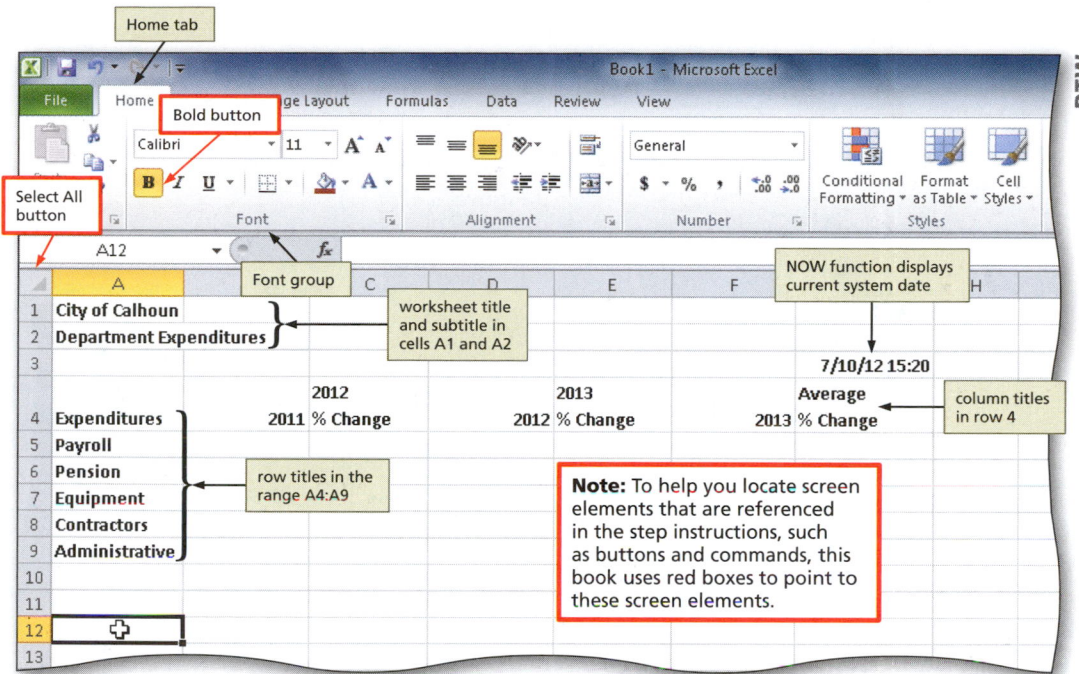

Figure 6–5

BTW

Sample Data
As you develop more sophisticated workbooks, it will become increasingly important that you create good test data to ensure your workbooks are free of errors. The more you test a workbook, the more confident you will be in the results generated. Always take the time to select test data that tests the limits of the formulas.

To Enter Sample Data in the Consolidated Worksheet Using the Fill Handle

While creating the consolidated worksheet in this chapter, sample data is used for the 2011 expenditure values in the range B5:B9 and the 2012 % Change values in the range C5:C9. The sample data is entered by using the fill handle to create a series of numbers in columns B and C. The series in column B begins with 1 and increments by 1; the series in column C begins with 2 and increments by 2. Recall that you must enter the first two numbers in a series so that Excel can determine the increment amount. If the cell to the right of the start value is empty and you want to increment by 1, however, you can create a series by entering only one number. The following steps enter sample data in the consolidated worksheet using the fill handle.

• Select cell B5.

• Type 1 and then press the ENTER key to enter the first value in the series.

• Select the range B5:C5.

• Drag the fill handle through cells B9 and C9 to begin a fill series operation. Do not release the mouse button (Figure 6–6).

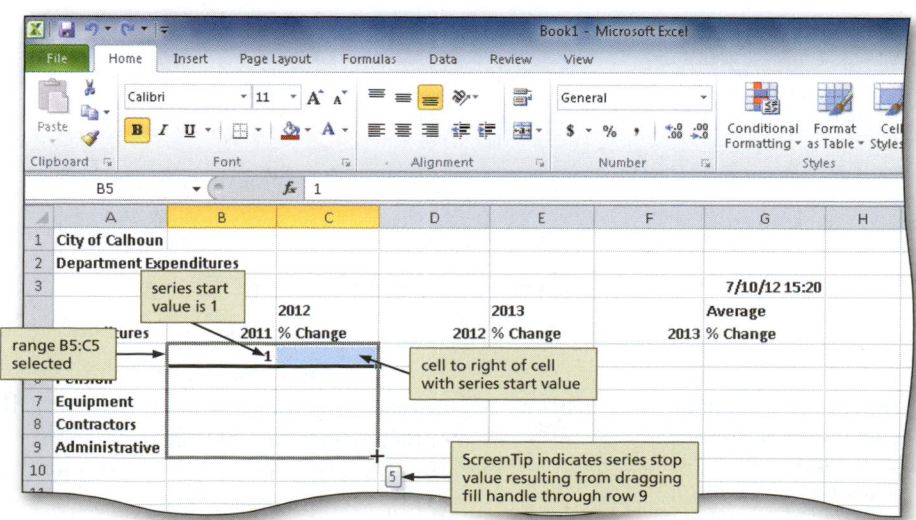

Figure 6–6

2

- Release the mouse button to create the series, 1 through 5 in this case, in increments of 1 in the first column of the selected range (Figure 6–7).

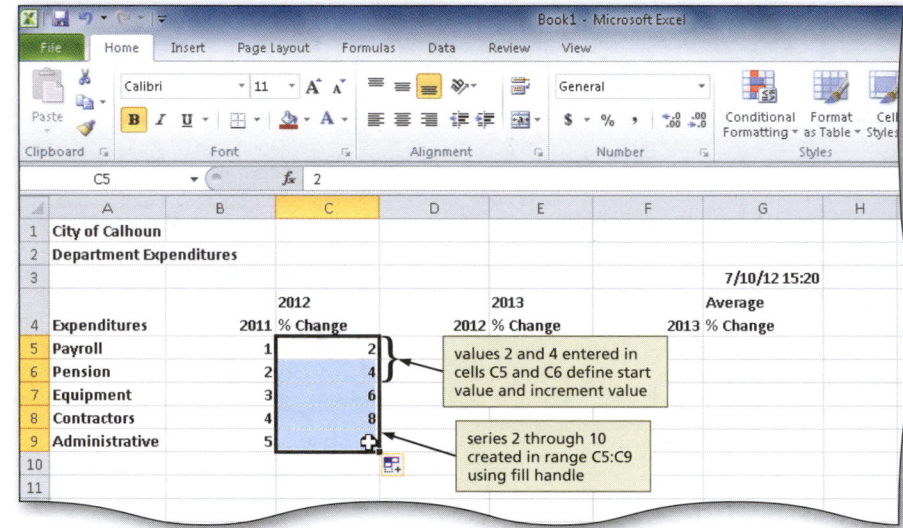

Figure 6–7

3

- Enter 2 in cell C5.

- Enter 4 in cell C6.

- Select the range C5:C6. Drag the fill handle through cell C9 to create a series in increments of 2 in the selected range, C5:C9 in this case (Figure 6–8).

Q&A

What other types of series can I create?

Excel allows you to create many types of series, including a **date series** (Jan, Feb, Mar, etc.), an **auto fill series** (1, 1, 1, etc.), and a **linear series** (1, 2, 3, etc. or 2, 4, 6, etc.), which was created in the previous steps. A fourth type of series is a growth series. A **growth series** multiplies values by a constant factor. You can create a growth series by entering an initial value in the first cell, selecting the range to fill, clicking the Fill button (Home tab | Editing group), clicking Series, clicking Growth in the type area, and then entering a constant factor in the Step value box.

Figure 6–8

4

- Repeat Step 3 to create a series in increments of 2 starting at 2 in the range E5:E9.

Other Ways		
1. Enter first number; click fill handle; while holding down CTRL key, drag through range	2. Enter start value, select range, click Fill button (Home tab | Editing group), click Series, enter	parameters (Series dialog box), click OK button

The ROUND Function and Entering Formulas in the Template

BTW

Accuracy
The result of an arithmetic operation, such as multiplication or division, is accurate to the factor with the least number of decimal places.

The next step is to enter the three formulas for the first expenditure, Payroll, in cells D5, F5, and G5. When you multiply or divide decimal numbers that result in an answer with more decimal places than the format allows, you run the risk of the column totals being off by a penny or so because, for example, resulting values of calculations could include fractions of a penny beyond the two decimal places that currency formats usually display. For example, as shown in the worksheet sketch in Figure 6–3 on page EX 366, columns B and D use the Currency and Comma style formats with two decimal places. And yet, the formulas used to calculate values for these columns result in several additional decimal places that Excel maintains for computation purposes. For this reason, it is recommended that you use the **ROUND function** on formulas that potentially can result in more decimal places than the applied format displays in a given cell. The general form of the ROUND function is

=ROUND (number, number of digits)

where the number argument can be a number, a cell reference that contains a number, or a formula that results in a number; and the number of digits argument can be any positive or negative number used to determine the number of places to which the number will be rounded.

The following is true about the ROUND function:

1. If the number of digits argument is greater than 0 (zero), then the number is rounded to the specified number of digits to the right of the decimal point.
2. If the number of digits argument is equal to 0 (zero), then the number is rounded to the nearest integer.
3. If the number of digits argument is less than 0 (zero), then the number is rounded to the specified number of digits to the left of the decimal point.

BTW

Fractions
The forward slash (/) has multiple uses. For example, dates often are entered using the slash. In formulas, the slash represents division. What about fractions? To enter a fraction, such as ½, type .5 or 0 1/2 (i.e., type zero, followed by a space, followed by the number 1, followed by a slash, followed by the number 2). If you type 1/2 without the preceding zero, Excel will store the value in the cell as the date January 2.

To Enter Formulas and Determine Totals in the Consolidated Worksheet

Table 6–1 shows the three formulas to enter in the consolidated worksheet in cells D5, F5, and G5. The ROUND function is used to round the values resulting from the formulas assigned to the cells to two decimal places.

Table 6–1 Formulas Used to Determine Expenditures and an Average			
Cell	**Description**	**Formula**	**Entry**
D5	2012	ROUND(2011 Expenditure + 2011 Expenditure × 2012 % Change, 4)	= ROUND(B5 + B5 * C5, 4)
F5	2013	ROUND(2012 Expenditure + 2012 Expenditure × 2013 % Change, 4)	= ROUND(D5 + D5 * E5, 4)
G5	Average % Change	ROUND((2012 % Change + 2013 % Change) / 2, 4)	= ROUND((C5 + E5) / 2, 4)

The following steps enter the three formulas in Table 6–1 in cells D5, F5, and G5. After the formulas are entered for Payroll in row 5, the formulas will be copied for the remaining four expenditures. The Sum button then is used to determine the totals in row 10. The following steps enter formulas and determine totals in the consolidated worksheet.

- Select cell D5. Type
  `=round(b5+b5*c5,4)` and then click the Enter box in the formula bar to display the formula in the formula bar and the resulting value in the select cell, in this case 3 in cell D5 (Figure 6–9).

Q&A

Why does the formula result in a value of 3 rather than a percent change from cell A5?

Because the values in column C have not been entered or formatted as percentages, the values are treated as whole numbers in the calculation. Once the values in column C are entered and formatted as percentages, the resulting values in column D will display as expected, which is a percent change from column A.

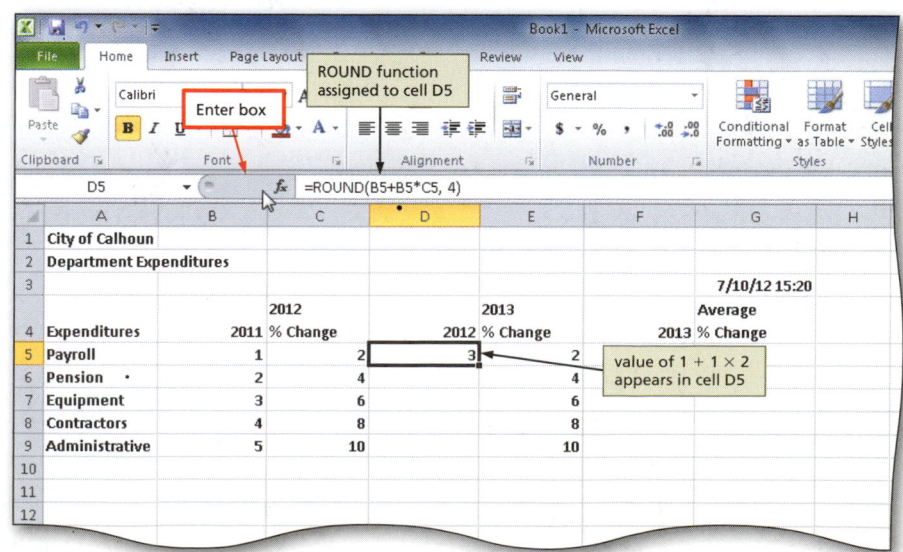

Figure 6–9

2

• Select cell F5. Type
`=round(d5+d5*e5,4)` and
then click the Enter box in the
formula bar to display the formula
in the formula bar and the resulting
value in the select cell, in this case 9
in cell F5 (Figure 6–10).

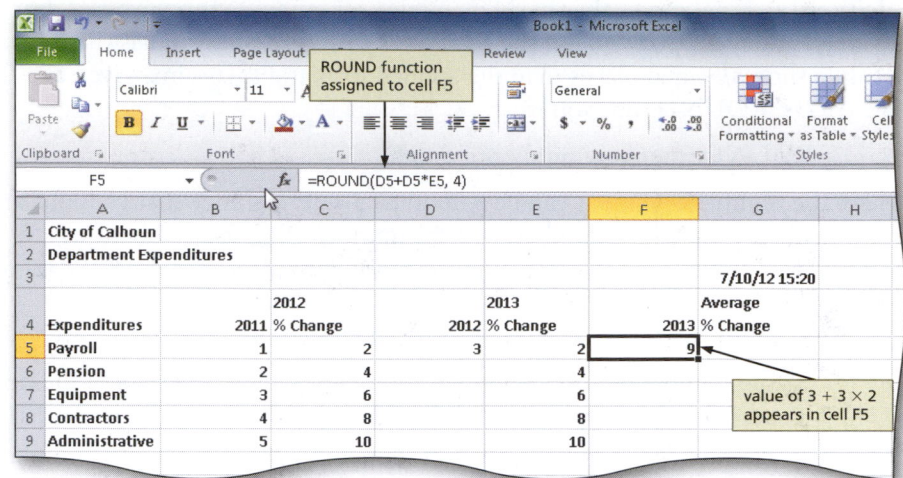

Figure 6–10

3

• Select cell G5. Type
`=round((c5+e5)/2,4)` and
then click the Enter box in the
formula bar to display the formula
in the formula bar and the resulting
value in the select cell, in this case 2
in cell G5 (Figure 6–11).

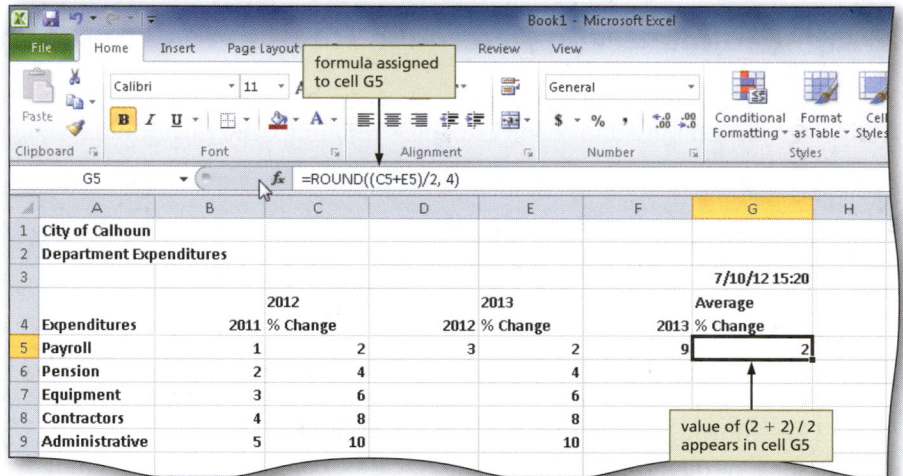

Figure 6–11

4

• Select cell D5, point to the fill
handle, and then drag down
through cell D9 to copy the formula
in the selected cell through the
selected range, D6:D9 in this case.

• Select the range F5:G5 and then
point to the fill handle to begin
a fill operation (Figure 6–12).

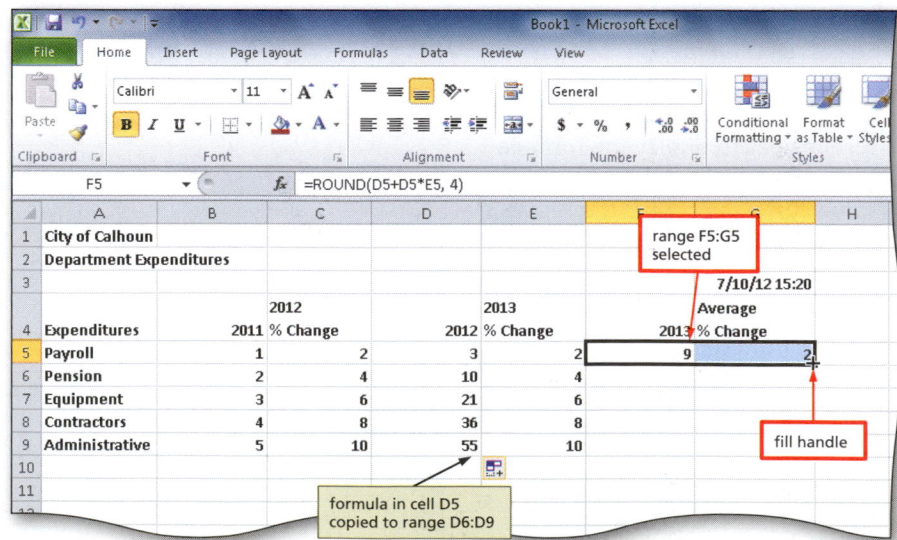

Figure 6–12

5
- Drag down through the range F6:G9 to copy the formulas in the selected range, F5:G5 in this case, to the selected range, F6:G9 in this case (Figure 6–13).

6
- Select cell B10 and then click the Sum button (Home tab | Editing group), select the range B5:B9, and then press the ENTER key to add a SUM function to the selected cell.

- If the Trace Error button is displayed, click it and then click Ignore Error on the Trace Error menu to ignore an error that Excel mistakenly reported.

- Select cell D10, click the Sum button (Home tab | Editing group), select the range D5:D9, and then press the ENTER key to add a SUM function to the selected cell.

- Select cell F10, click the Sum button (Home tab | Editing group), select the range F5:F9, and then press the ENTER key to add a SUM function to the selected cell.

- Select cell A12 to deselect the selected cell and display the values based on the sample data entered earlier (Figure 6–14).

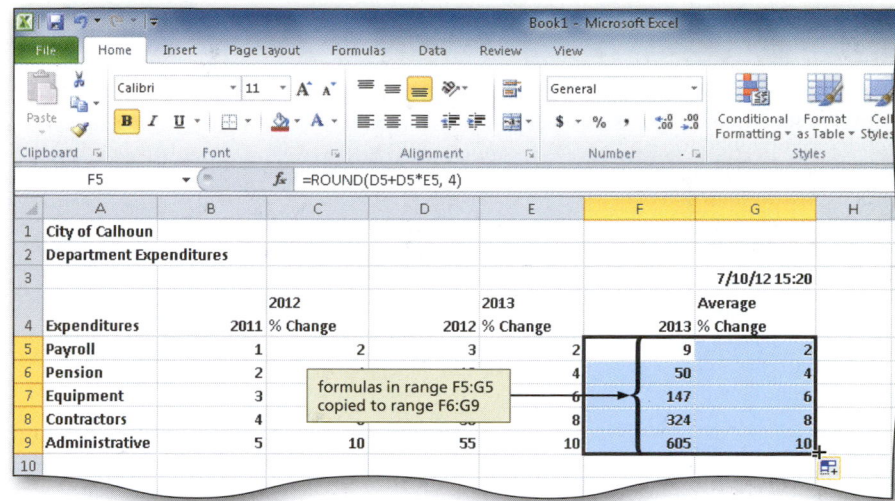

Figure 6–13

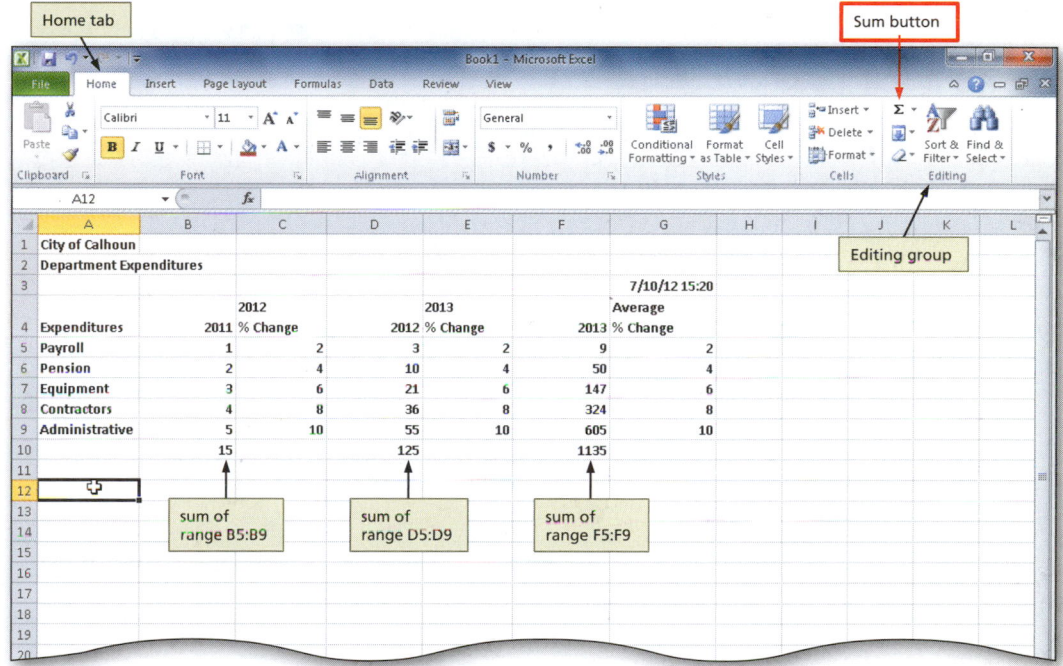

Figure 6–14

To Save the Worksheet

The following steps save the consolidated worksheet on a USB drive in drive E using the file name, City of Calhoun Consolidated Expenditures.

1 Update the document properties with your name and any other relevant information as specified by your instructor.

2 With a USB flash drive connected to one of the computer's USB ports, click the Save button on the Quick Access Toolbar. Save the workbook using the file name, City of Calhoun Consolidated Expenditures, on the USB flash drive.

Note: If you wish to take a break, this is a good place to do so. You can quit Excel now. To resume at a later time, start Excel, open the file called City of Calhoun Consolidated Expenditures, and continue following the steps from this location forward.

Formatting the Consolidated Worksheet

The next step is to format the consolidated worksheet so that it appears as shown in Figure 6–15. The following list summarizes the steps required to format the consolidated worksheet.

1. Format the titles in cells A1 and A2.
2. Format the column titles and total rows.
3. Assign the Currency style format with a floating dollar sign to cells B5, D5, F5, B10, D10, and F10.
4. Assign a Custom style format to the ranges C5:C9, E5:E9, and G5:G9.
5. Assign a Comma style format to the range B6:B9, D6:D9, and F6:F9.
6. Create a format style and assign it to the date in cell G3.

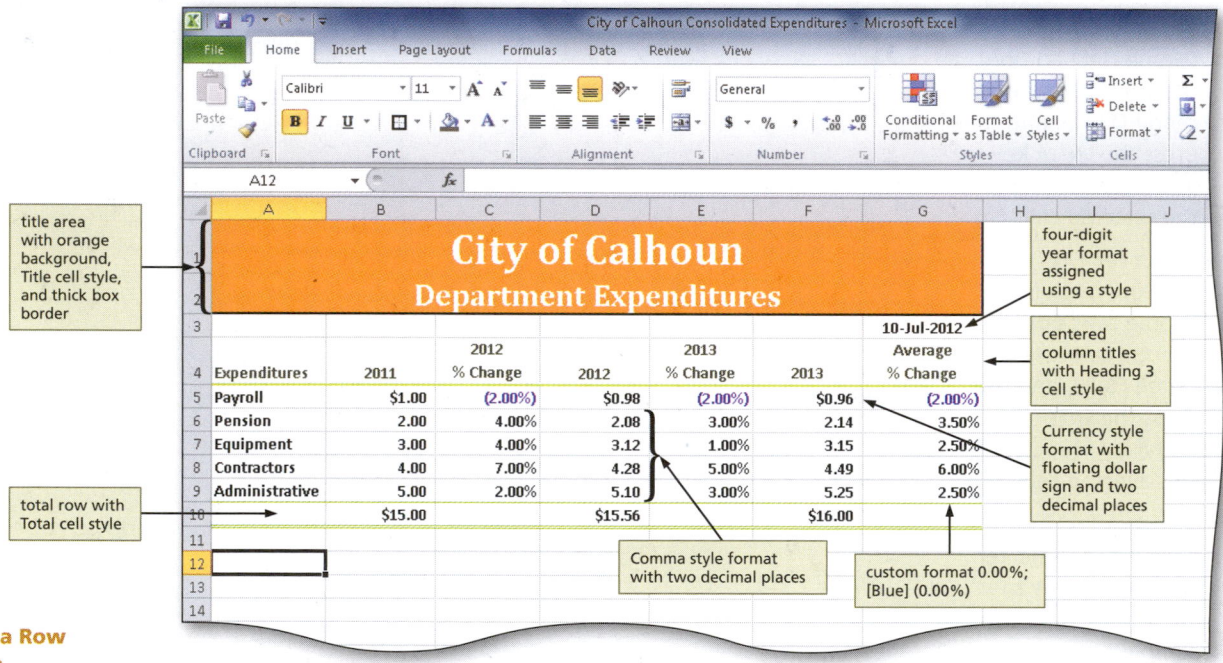

Figure 6–15

To Format the Consolidated Worksheet's Title and Subtitle

The steps used to format the consolidated worksheet's title and subtitle include changing cell A1 to 28-point with the Title cell style, changing cell A2 to 20-point with the Title cell style, centering both titles across columns A through G, changing the title background color to orange and the title font to white, and drawing a thick box border around the title area. The color scheme associated with the default Office template also will be changed to a new color scheme. One reason to change the color scheme is to add variety to the look of the worksheet that you create. The following steps format the title and subtitle.

 Display the Page Layout tab. Click the Colors button (Page Layout tab | Themes group) to display the Colors gallery and then click Austin in the Colors gallery to apply a new color scheme to the workbook.

2 Select the range A1:A2. Display the Home tab and apply the Title cell style to the range. Change the font size of cell A1 to 28.

3 Select the range A1:G1. Click the Merge & Center button (Home tab | Alignment group) to merge and center the text in the selected range.

4 Change the font size of cell A2 to 20. Select the range A2:G2.

5 Click the Merge & Center button (Home tab | Alignment group) to merge and center the text in the selected range.

6 Select the range A1:A2, click the Fill Color button arrow (Home tab | Font group) to display the Fill Color gallery, and then click Orange, Accent 6 (column 10, row 1) on the Fill Color gallery to change the fill color of the cells in the selected range.

7 Click the Font Color button arrow (Home tab | Font group) to display the Font Color gallery and then click White, Background 1 (column 1, row 1) on the Font Color gallery to change the font color of the cells in the selected range.

8 Click the Borders button arrow (Home tab | Font group) to display the Borders menu and then click Thick Box Border in the Borders list to apply a border to the selected range.

9 Select cell A12 to deselect the range A1:A2.

BTW

Copying
To copy the contents of a cell to the cell directly below it, click in the target cell and press CTRL+D.

To Format the Column Titles and Total Row

The following steps center and underline the column titles and draw a top and double bottom border on the total row in row 10.

1 Select the range B4:G4 and then click the Center button (Home tab | Alignment group) to center the text in the cells of the selected range.

2 Hold down the CTRL key, click cell A4 to add it to the selection, and then apply the Heading 3 cell style to the range.

3 Select the range A10:G10, assign the Total cell style to the range, and then select cell A12 (Figure 6–16).

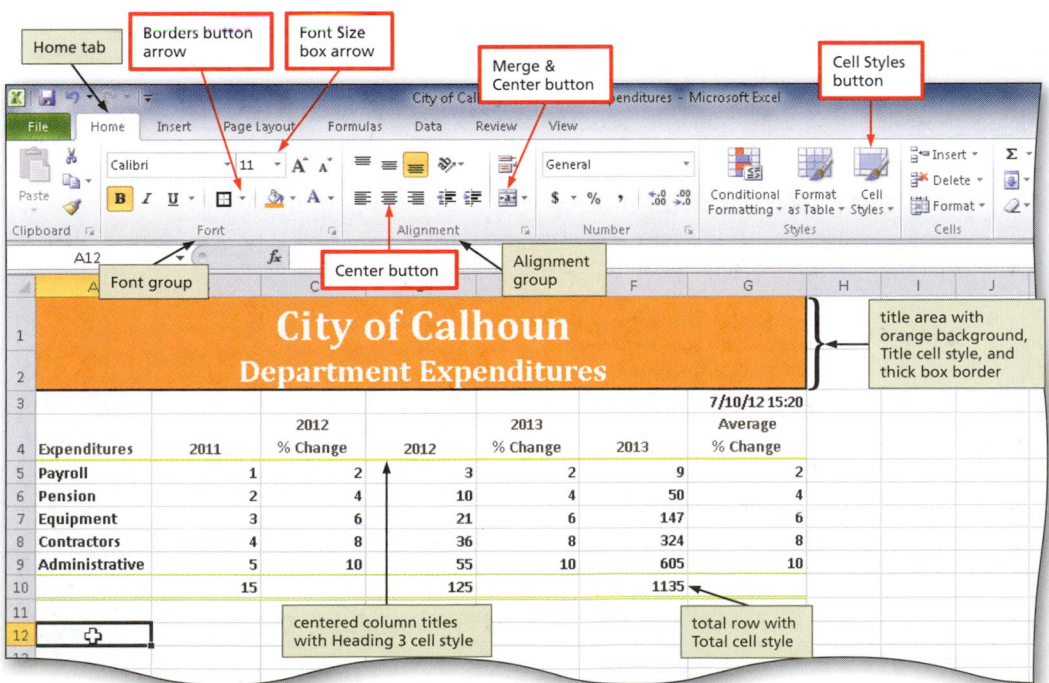

Figure 6–16

To Assign a Currency Style Using the Format Cells Dialog Box

As shown in Figure 6–15 on page EX 374, the consolidated worksheet for this chapter follows the **standard accounting format** for a table of numbers; that is, it contains floating dollar signs in the first row of numbers (row 5) and the totals row (row 10). Recall that while a fixed dollar sign always appears in the same position in a cell (regardless of the number of significant digits), a floating dollar sign always appears immediately to the left of the first significant digit in the cell. To assign a fixed dollar sign to rows 5 and 10, select the range and then click the Accounting Number Format button (Home tab | Number group). Assigning a floating dollar sign, by contrast, requires you to select the desired format in the Format Cells dialog box.

The following steps use the Format Cells dialog box to assign a Currency style with a floating dollar sign and two decimal places to cells B5, D5, F5, B10, D10, and F10.

- Select cell B5.

- While holding down the CTRL key, select the nonadjacent cells D5, F5, B10, D10, and F10 and then right-click any selected cell to highlight the nonadjacent ranges and display a shortcut menu and a Mini toolbar (Figure 6–17).

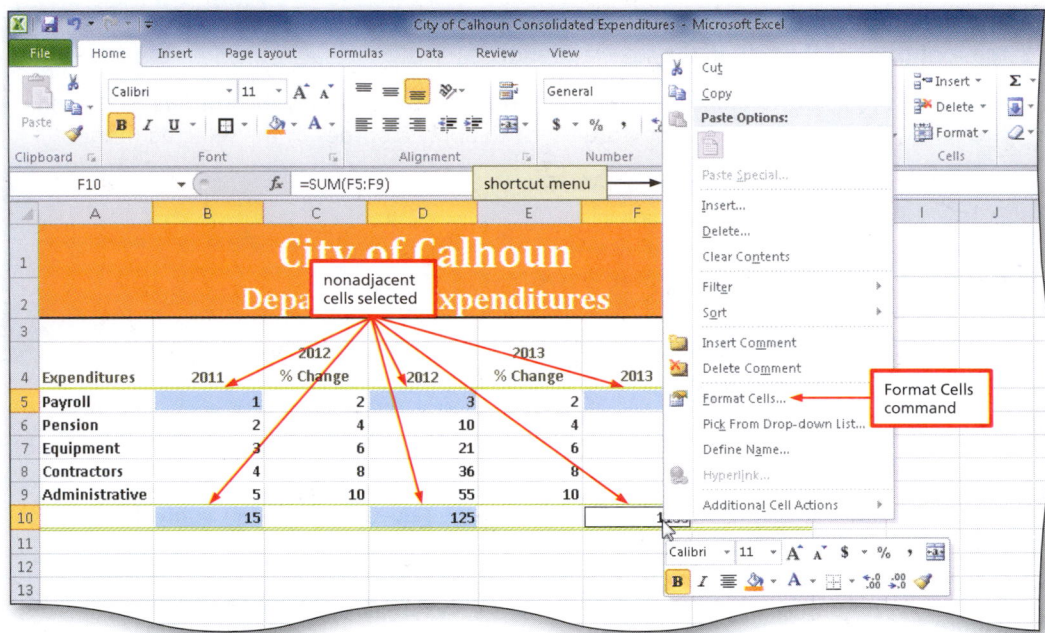

Figure 6–17

- Click Format Cells on the shortcut menu to display the Format Cells dialog box.

- If necessary, click the Number tab (Format Cells dialog box) to display the Number tab, click Currency in the Category list to select the type of format to apply, and then click the red ($1,234.10) in the Negative numbers list to select a currency format that displays negative numbers in red with parentheses (Figure 6–18).

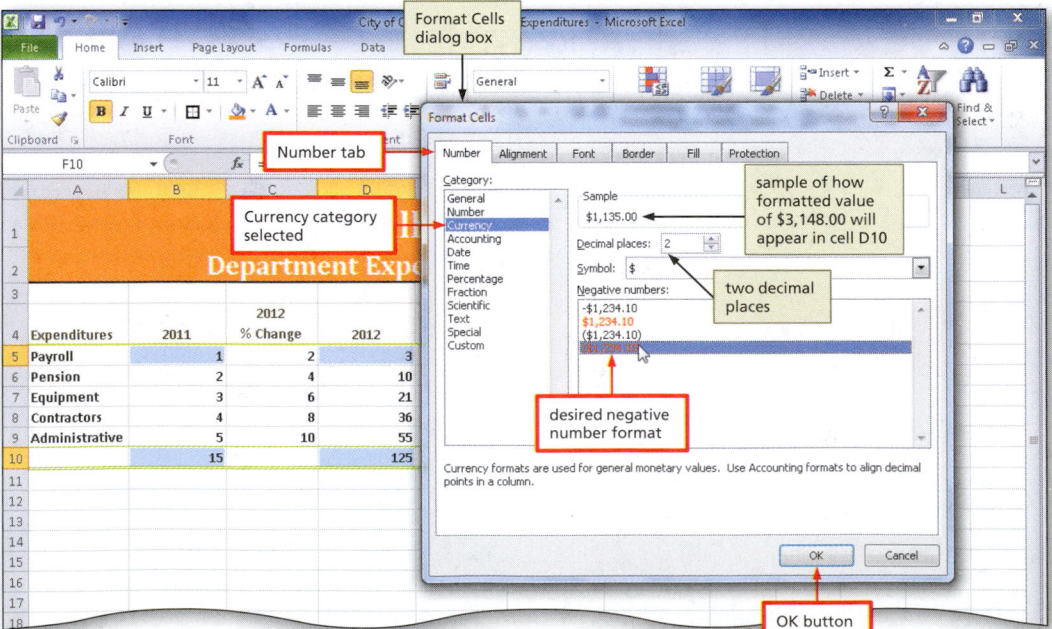

Figure 6–18

3

- Click the OK button (Format Cells dialog box) to assign the Currency style with a floating dollar sign and two decimal places to the selected cells. Select cell A12 to deselect the nonadjacent cells (Figure 6–19).

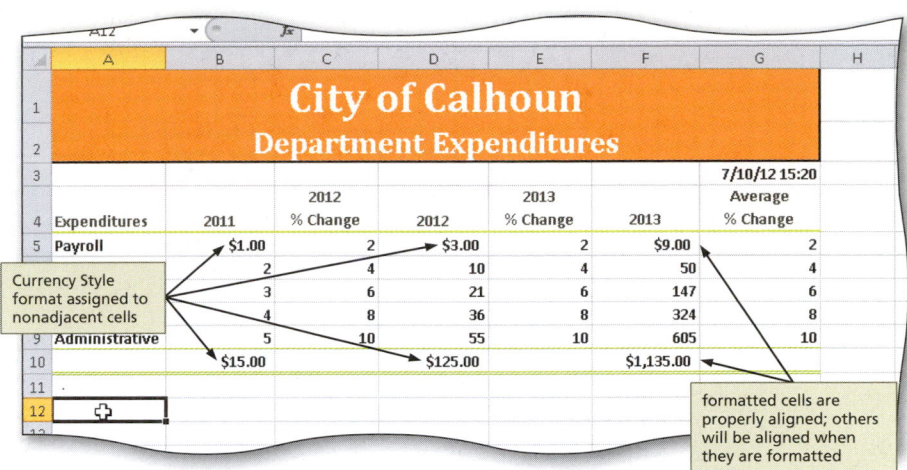

Figure 6–19

Other Ways

1. Press CTRL+1, click Number tab (Format Cells dialog box), select format, click OK button

Format Codes

Excel assigns a format code to every format style listed in the Category list in the Number sheet in the Format Cells dialog box. As shown in Table 6–2, a **format code** is a series of format symbols that defines how a cell entry assigned a format will appear. To view the entire list of format codes that come with Excel, select Custom in the Category list (Figure 6–18).

BTW

Creating Customized Formats
Each format symbol within the format code has special meaning. Table 6–2 summarizes the more frequently used format symbols and their meanings.

Table 6–2 Format Symbols in Format Codes		
Format Symbol	**Example of Symbol in Code**	**Description**
# (number sign)	###.##	Serves as a digit placeholder. If the value in a cell has more digits to the right of the decimal point than number signs in the format, Excel rounds the number. Extra digits to the left of the decimal point are displayed.
0 (zero)	0.00	Works like a number sign (#), except that if the number is less than 1, Excel displays a 0 in the one's place.
. (period)	#0.00	Ensures Excel will display a decimal point in the number. The placement of period symbols determines how many digits appear to the left and right of the decimal point.
% (percent)	0.00%	Displays numbers as percentages of 100. Excel multiplies the value of the cell by 100 and displays a percent sign after the number.
, (comma)	#,##0.00	Displays a comma as a thousand's separator.
( )	#0.00;(#0.00)	Displays parentheses around negative numbers.
$ or + or −	$#,##0.00; ($#,##0.00)	Displays a floating sign ($, +, or −).
* (asterisk)	$*##0.00	Displays a fixed sign ($, +, or −) to the left, followed by spaces until the first significant digit.
[color]	#.##;[Red]#.##	Displays the characters in the cell in the designated color. In the example, positive numbers appear in the default color, and negative numbers appear in red.
" " (quotation marks)	$0.00 "Surplus"; $-0.00 "Shortage"	Displays text along with numbers entered in a cell.
_ (underscore)	(#,##0.00_)	Skips the width of the character that follows the underscore.

Before creating custom format codes or modifying an existing custom format code, you should understand their makeup. As shown below, a format code can have up to four sections: positive numbers, negative numbers, zeros, and text. Each section is divided by a semicolon.

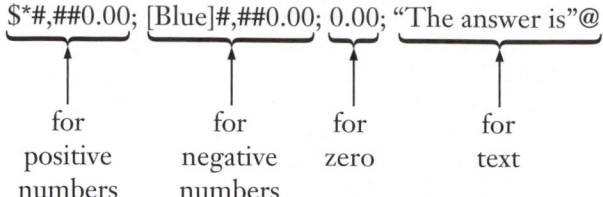

$*#,##0.00; [Blue]#,##0.00; 0.00; "The answer is"@

| for positive numbers | for negative numbers | for zero | for text |

A format code need not have all four sections. For most applications, a format code will have only a positive section and possibly a negative section.

To Create and Assign a Custom Format Code and a Comma Style Format

The next step is to create and assign a custom format code to the ranges that contain percentages: C5:C9, E5:E9, and G5:G9. The format code will display percentages with two decimal places to the right of the decimal point and also display negative percent values in blue with parentheses. The following steps create and assign a custom format code to percent values and then apply a comma style format to unformatted currency values.

1

- Select the ranges C5:C9, E5:E9, and G5:G9, right-click any of the selected ranges to display a shortcut menu, and then click Format Cells on the shortcut menu to display the Format Cells dialog box.

- If necessary, click the Number tab (Format Cells dialog box) to display the Number tab and then click Custom in the Category list to begin creating a custom format code.

- Delete the word General in the Type box (Format Cells dialog box) and then type `0.00%;[Blue] (0.00%)` to enter a custom format code (Figure 6–20).

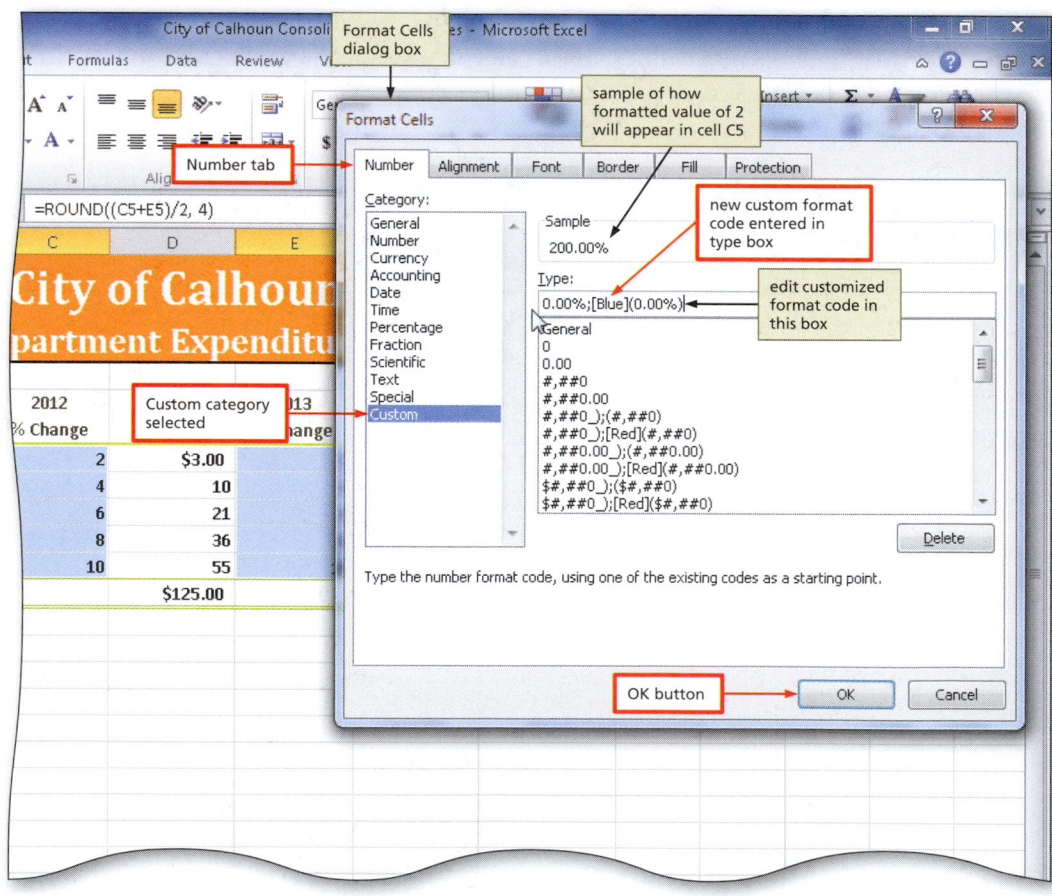

Figure 6–20

Q&A What does the custom format mean?

The custom format has been modified to show percent values with two decimal places and to show negative percent values in blue with parentheses. In the Sample area, Excel displays a sample of the custom format assigned to the first number in the selected ranges.

2

- Click the OK button (Format Cells dialog box) to display the numbers in the ranges C5:C9, E5:E9, and G5:G9 using the custom format code created in Step 1.

- Select the ranges B6:B9, D6:D9, and F6:F9.

- Click the Comma Style button (Home tab | Number group) to display the numbers in the selected ranges using the Comma style format (Figure 6–21).

- Select cell A12.

Q&A Can I reuse the custom format code?

Yes. When you create a new custom format code, Excel adds it to the bottom of the Type list in the Number sheet in the Format Cells dialog box to make it available for future use.

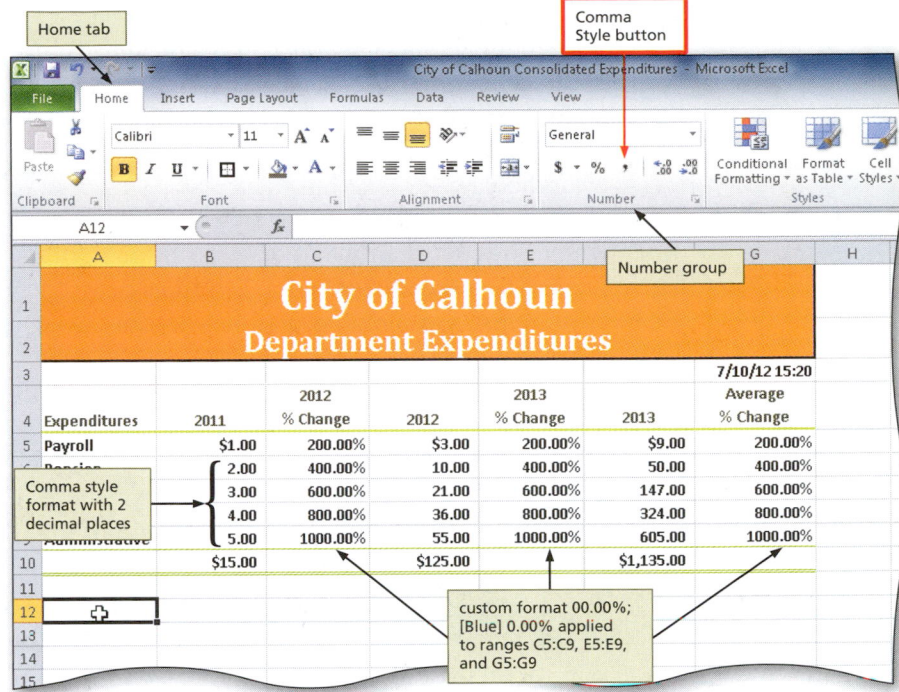

Figure 6–21

Q&A Why is the Comma style format used for numbers that are not large enough to display commas?

The Comma style allows the values in the cells to align properly with the values in rows 5 and 10, which are formatted with the Currency style with floating dollar signs and parentheses for negative numbers.

Cell Styles

A **style** is a group of format specifications that are assigned to a style name. Most of the cell styles in the Cell Styles gallery that are displayed when you click the Cell Styles button (Home tab | Styles group) include formatting only of visual characteristics, such as font name, font size, font color, and fill color. A cell style, however, also can contain information regarding nonvisual characteristics, such as cell protection.

Excel makes several general styles available with all workbooks and themes, as described in Table 6–3. You can apply these existing styles to a cell or cells in a worksheet, modify an existing style, or create an entirely new style.

BTW

Normal Style
The Normal style is the format style that Excel initially assigns to all cells in a workbook. If you change the Normal style, Excel applies the new format specifications to all cells that are not assigned another style.

Table 6–3 Styles Available with All Workbooks via the Cell Styles Button on the Home Tab	
Style Name	**Description**
Normal	Number = General; Alignment = General, Bottom Aligned; Font = Arial 10; Border = No Borders; Patterns = No Shading; Protection = Locked
Comma	Number = (*#,##0.00)_;_(*(#,##0.00);_(*"-"_);_(@_)
Comma(0)	Number = (*#,##0_);_(*(#,##0);_(*"-"_);_(@_)
Currency	Number = ($#,##0.00_);_($*(#,##0.00);_($*"-"??_);_(@_)
Currency(0)	Number = ($#,##0_);_($*(#,##0);_($*"-"_);_(@_)
Percent	Number = 0%

You can create and then assign a style to a cell, a range of cells, a worksheet, or a workbook in the same way you assign a format using the buttons on the Home tab on the Ribbon. In fact, the Comma Style button, Currency Style button, and Percent Style button assign the Comma, Currency, and Percent styles in Table 6–3, respectively. Excel automatically assigns the Normal style in Table 6–3 to all cells when you open a new workbook.

By right-clicking styles in the Cell Styles gallery, you also can delete, modify, and duplicate styles. The Merge Styles button in the Cell Styles gallery allows you to merge styles from other workbooks. You add a new style to a workbook or merge styles when you plan to use a group of format specifications over and over.

To Create a New Style

The following steps create a new style called Four-Digit Year by modifying the existing Normal style and assigning the style to cell G3, which contains the system date. The new style will include the following formats: Number = 14-Mar-2001 and Alignment = Horizontal Center and Bottom Aligned.

1

- Click the Cell Styles button (Home tab | Styles group) to display the Cell Styles gallery (Figure 6–22).

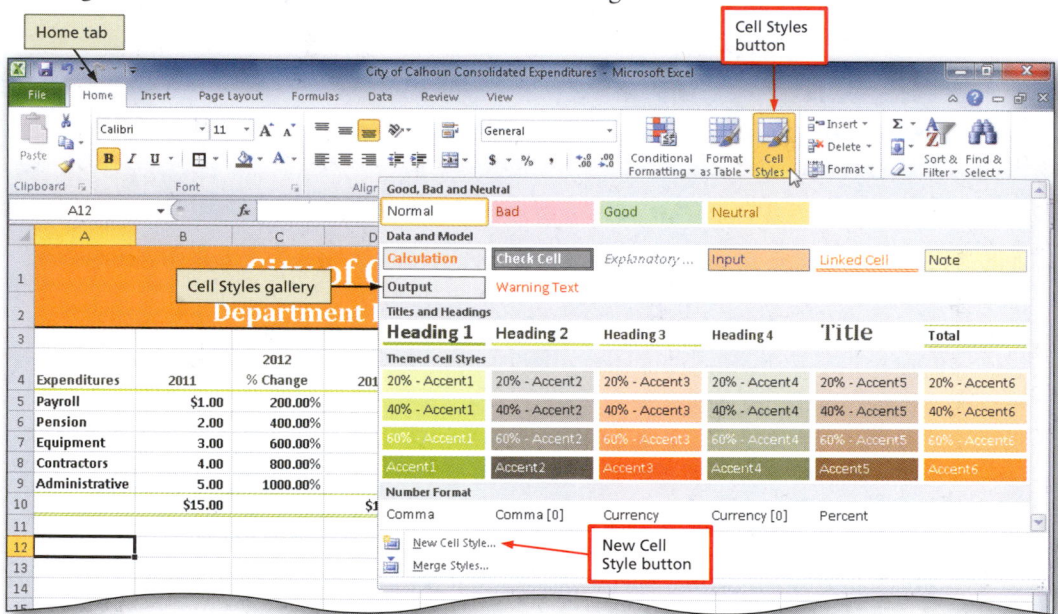

Figure 6–22

2

- Click the New Cell Style button in the Cell Styles gallery to display the Style dialog box.

- Type **Four-Digit Year** to name a new style (Figure 6–23).

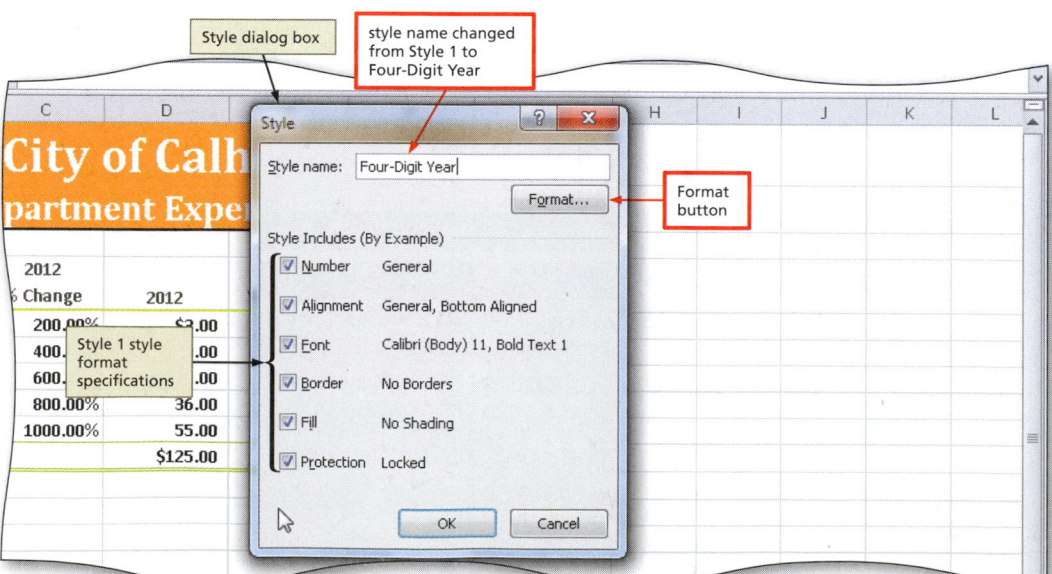

Figure 6–23

3
- Click the Format button (Style dialog box) to display the Format Cells dialog box.

- If necessary, click the Number tab (Format Cells dialog box) to display the Number tab, click Date in the Category list to display the list of date formats, and then click 14-Mar-2001 in the Type list to define the new style as a date style (Figure 6–24).

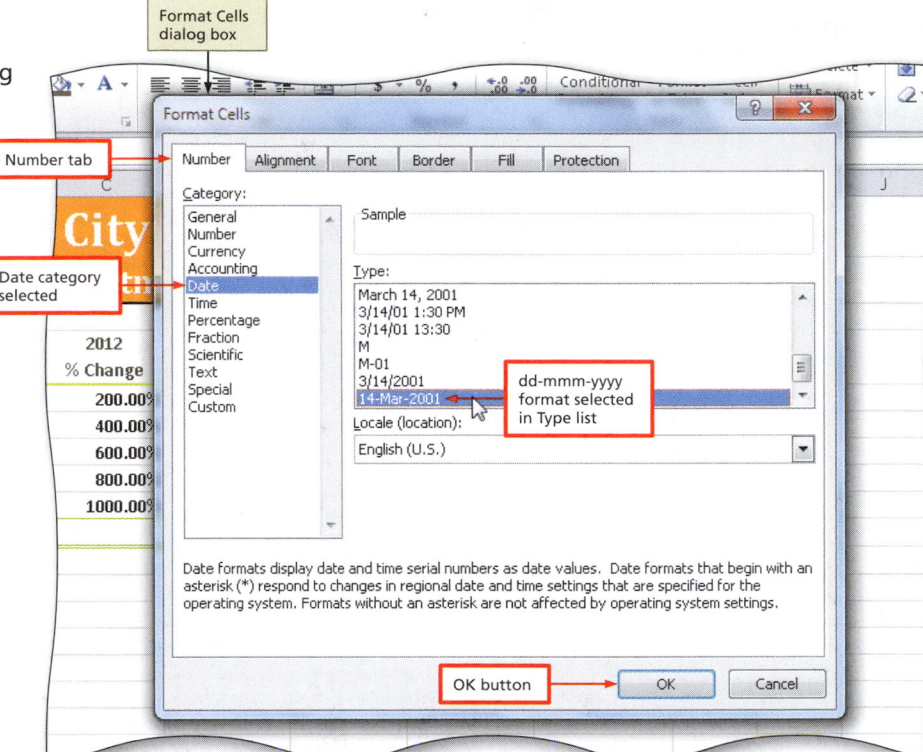

Figure 6–24

4
- Click the Alignment tab (Format Cells dialog box) to display the Alignment tab, click the Horizontal box arrow to display the Horizontal list, and then click Center in the Horizontal list to define the alignment of a new style.

- Click the OK button (Format Cells dialog box) to close the Format Cells dialog box.

- When the Style dialog box becomes active, click Font, Border, Fill, and Protection to clear the check boxes, indicating that the new style does not use these characteristics (Figure 6–25).

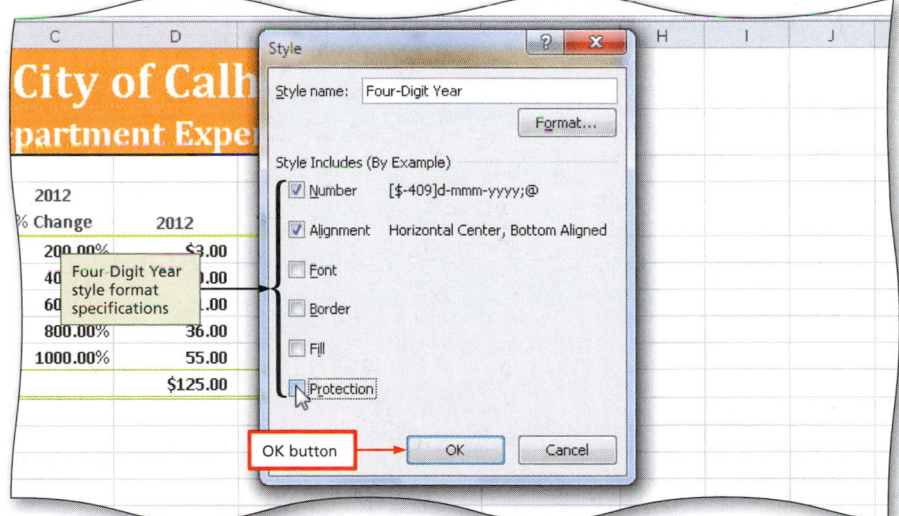

Figure 6–25

Q&A

What is the purpose of the Font, Border, Fill, and Protection settings?

When one of these settings is selected, the cell style will include that setting's formatting attributes. When not selected, as with the cell style created in this set of steps, the cell style does not include any information about these formatting attributes. When the cell style is applied, therefore, no information about the font, borders, fill color, or protection is applied to the cell or range.

5
- Click the OK button (Style dialog box) to add the new style, Four-Digit Year style in this case, to the list of styles available with the current workbook in the Cell Styles gallery.

To Apply a New Style

In earlier steps, cell G3 was assigned the system date using the NOW() function. The following steps assign cell G3 the Four-Digit Year style, which centers the content of the cell and assigns it the date format dd-mmm-yyyy.

1

• Select cell G3 and then click the Cell Styles button (Home tab | Styles group) to display the Cell Styles gallery (Figure 6–26).

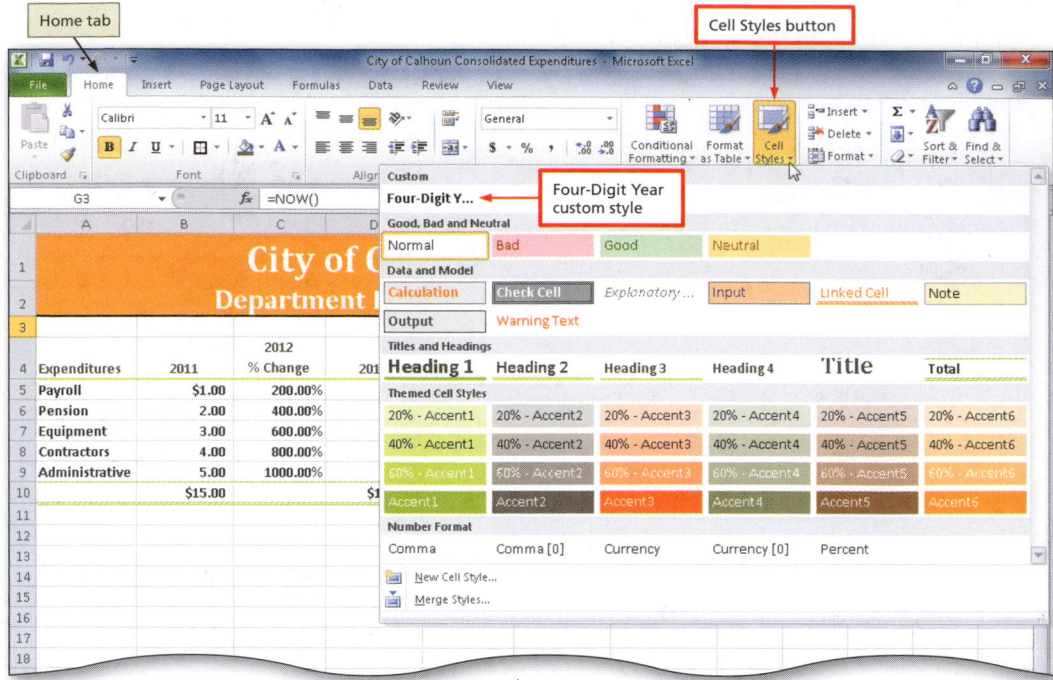

Figure 6–26

2

• Click the Four-Digit Year style to assign the style to the selected cell, cell G3 in this case (Figure 6–27).

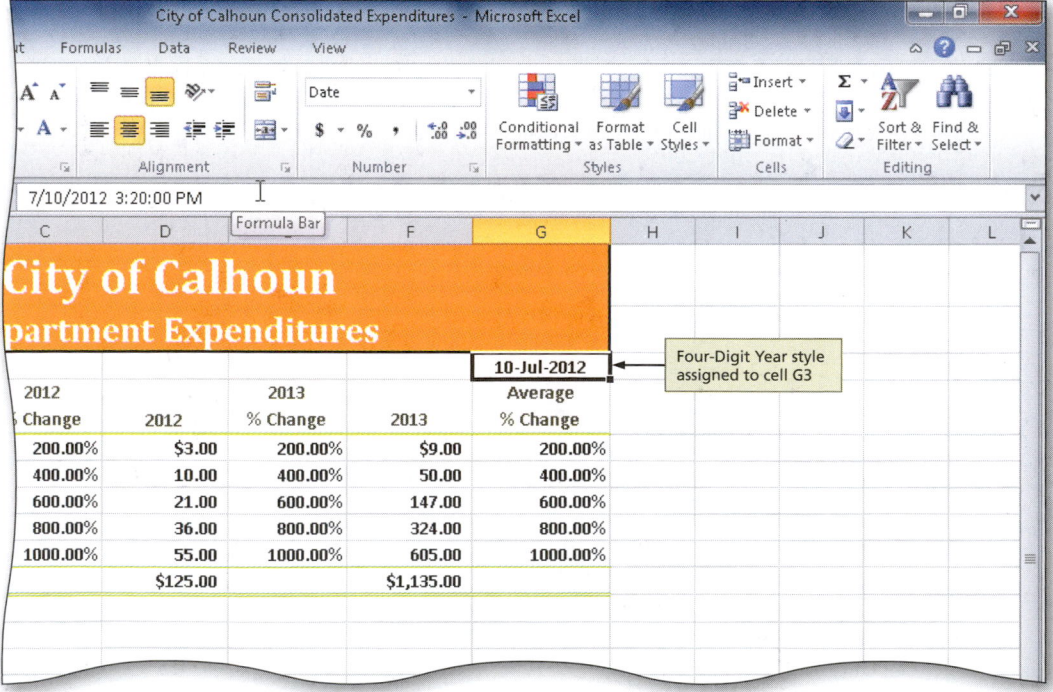

Figure 6–27

More About Using Styles

Keep in mind the following additional points concerning styles:

1. A style affects the format of a cell or range of cells only if the corresponding check box is selected in the Style Includes area in the Style dialog box (Figure 6–25 on page EX 381). For example, if the Font check box is not selected in the Style dialog box, then the cell assigned the style maintains the font format it had before the style was assigned.

2. If you assign two different styles to a range of cells, Excel adds the second style to the first, rather than replacing it. If the two cell styles include different settings for an attribute, such as fill color, then Excel applies the setting for the second style.

3. You can merge styles from another workbook into the active workbook by using the Merge Styles button in the Cell Styles gallery. You must, however, open the workbook that contains the desired styles before you use the Merge Styles button.

4. The six check boxes in the Style dialog box are identical to the six tabs in the Format Cells dialog box (Figure 6–24 on page EX 381).

BTW

Opening a Workbook at Startup
You can instruct Windows to open a workbook (or template) automatically when you turn on your computer by adding the workbook (or template) to the Startup folder. Use Windows Explorer to copy the file to the Startup folder. The Startup folder is in the All Programs list.

To Spell Check, Save, and Print the Consolidated Worksheet

With the formatting complete, the next step is to spell check the worksheet, save it, and then print it.

1 Select cell A1. Click the Review tab, and then click the Spelling button (Review tab | Proofing group) to spell check the workbook. Correct any misspelled words.

2 Click the Save button on the Quick Access Toolbar to save the workbook.

3 Print the workbook.

Note: If you wish to take a break, this is a good place to do so. You can quit Excel now. To resume at a later time, start Excel, open the file called City of Calhoun Consolidated Expenditures, and continue following the steps from this location forward.

Working with Multiple Worksheets

A workbook contains three worksheets by default. Excel limits the number of worksheets you can have in a workbook based upon the amount of memory in your computer. When working with multiple worksheets, you should name and color the sheet tabs so that you easily can identify them. With the consolidated worksheet complete, the next steps in completing the project are to add a worksheet to the workbook, copy the data in the consolidated worksheet to the department worksheets, and adjust the formatting and values in the department worksheets.

Identify additional worksheets needed in the workbook.
Excel provides three basic choices when you consider how to use Excel to organize data. Use a single worksheet when the data is tightly related. In this case you may want to analyze the data in a table and use a column, such as Department, Region, or Quarter, to identify groups of data. Use multiple worksheets when data is related but can stand alone on its own. For example, each region, department, or quarter may contain enough detailed information that you may want to analyze the data in separate worksheets. Use multiple workbooks when data is loosely coupled, or when workbooks come from multiple sources or must be gathered from multiple sources.

Plan Ahead

To Add a Worksheet to a Workbook

The City of Calhoun Consolidated Expenditures workbook requires four worksheets—one for each of the three departments and one for the consolidated totals. Thus, a worksheet must be added to the workbook. When you add a worksheet, Excel places the new sheet tab to the left of the active tab. To keep the worksheet with the sample data shown in Figure 6–27 on page EX 382 on top—that is, to keep its tab (Sheet1) to the far left—spreadsheet specialists often add a new worksheet between Sheet1 and Sheet2, rather than to the left of Sheet1. The following steps select Sheet2 before adding a worksheet to the workbook.

1

- Click the Sheet2 tab at the bottom of the window and then click the Insert Cells button arrow (Home tab | Cells group) to display the Insert Cells menu (Figure 6–28).

Q&A

Can I start a new workbook with more sheets?

Yes. An alternative to adding worksheets is to change the default number of worksheets before you open a new workbook. To change the default number of worksheets in a blank workbook, click the Excel Options button in the Backstage view, and then change the number in the 'Include this many sheets' box in the 'When creating new workbooks' area of the Excel Options dialog box. Recall from Chapter 4 that you can delete a worksheet by right-clicking the sheet tab of the worksheet you want to delete and then clicking Delete on the shortcut menu.

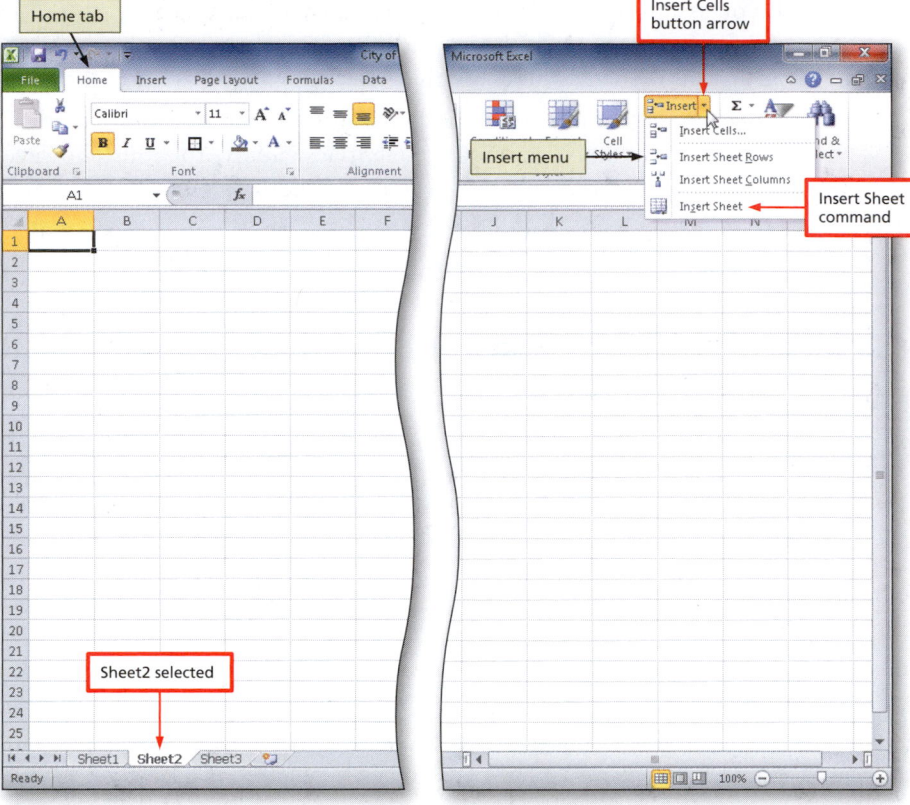

Figure 6–28

2

- Click Insert Sheet on the Insert Cells menu to add a new worksheet to a workbook, in this case a sheet named Sheet 4 between Sheet 1 and Sheet 2 (Figure 6–29).

Q&A

Can I insert more than one worksheet at a time?

Yes. You can insert as many worksheets at once as there are tabs in the current workbook. To insert multiple worksheets, select multiple tabs corresponding to the number of sheets you want to insert, and then select Insert Sheet on the Insert Cells menu.

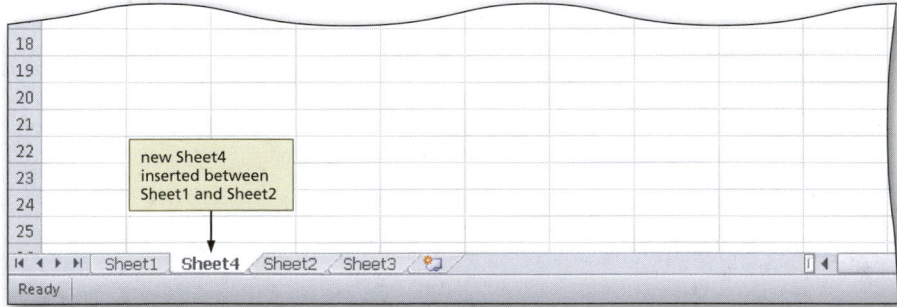

Figure 6–29

Other Ways

1. Right-click tab, click Insert on shortcut menu

To Copy the Contents of a Worksheet to Other Worksheets in a Workbook

With four worksheets in the workbook, the next step is to copy the contents of Sheet1 to Sheet4, Sheet2, and Sheet3. Sheet1 eventually will be used as the Consolidated worksheet with the consolidated data. Sheet4, Sheet2, and Sheet3 will be used for the three department worksheets.

1

- Click the Sheet1 tab to display the worksheet on the sheet tab.

- Click the Select All button to select the entire worksheet and then click the Copy button (Home tab | Clipboard group) to copy the contents of the worksheet (Figure 6–30).

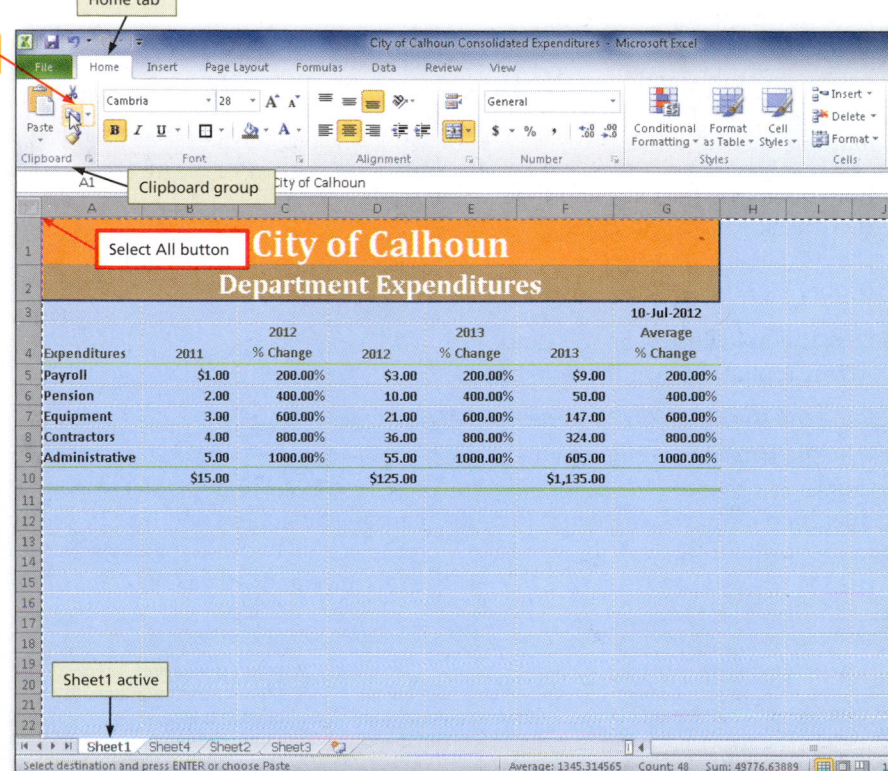

Figure 6–30

2

- Click the Sheet4 tab to display the worksheet on the sheet tab.

- While holding down the SHIFT key, click the Sheet3 tab to select all three blank worksheets in the workbook.

- Click the Paste button (Home tab | Clipboard group) to copy the data on the Office Clipboard to all of the selected sheets (Figure 6–31).

Q&A

Why does the word Group appear on the title bar?

The term [Group] following the workbook name on the title bar indicates that multiple worksheets are selected.

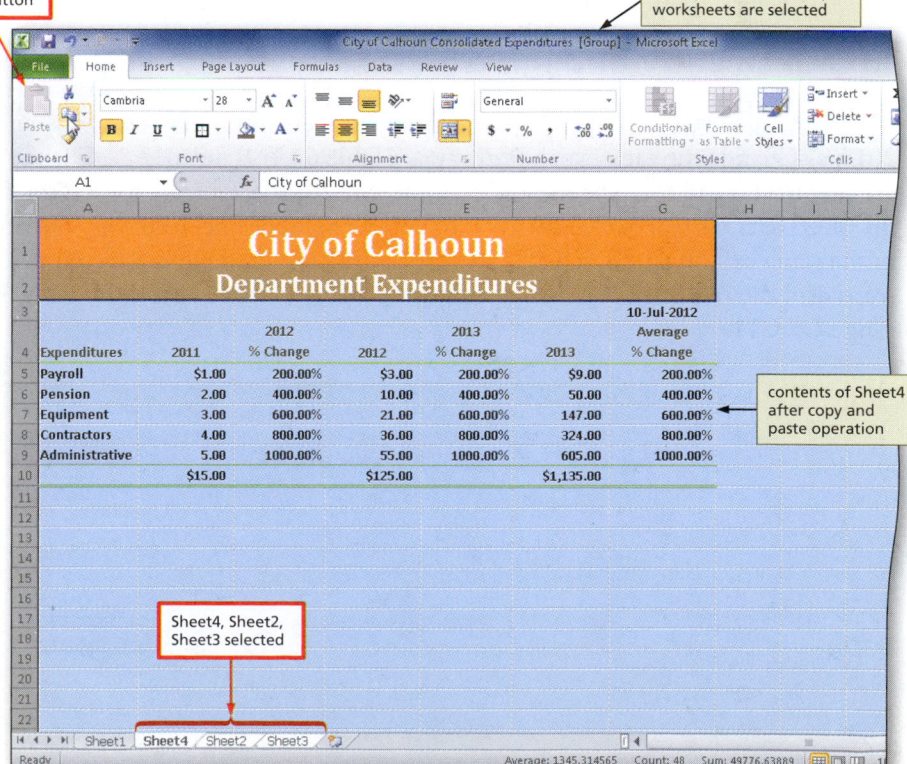

Figure 6–31

3

- Click the Sheet1 tab to display the worksheet on the sheet tab and then press the ESC key to remove the marquee surrounding the selection.

- Hold down the SHIFT key, click the Sheet3 tab to display the worksheet on the sheet tab, and then select cell A12 to select the same cell in multiple sheets.

- Hold down the SHIFT key and then click the Sheet1 tab to deselect Sheet4, Sheet2, and Sheet3 (Figure 6–32).

- Click the Save button on the Quick Access Toolbar to save the workbook.

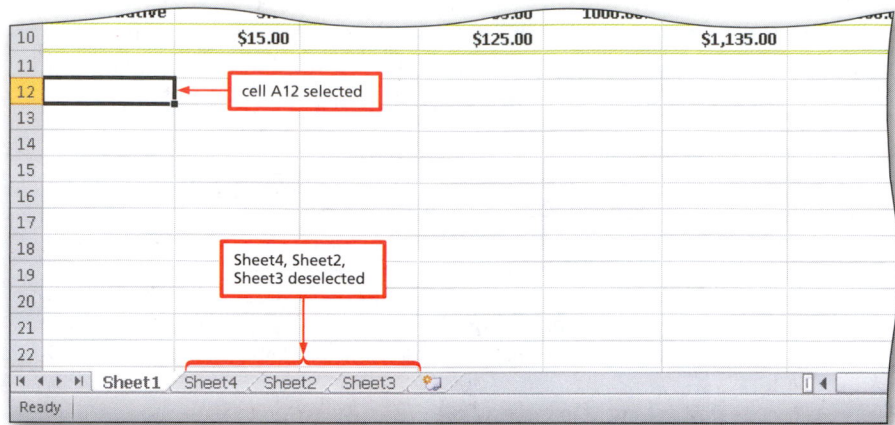

Figure 6–32

Q&A

Can I use the ENTER key to paste the data?

Yes. The ENTER key could have been used rather than the Paste button (Home tab | Clipboard group) to complete the paste operation in Step 2. Recall that if you complete a paste operation using the ENTER key, then the marquee disappears and the Office Clipboard no longer contains the copied data following the action. Because the Paste button was used, the ESC key was used in Step 3 to clear the marquee and Office Clipboard of the copied data.

Other Ways

1. Select source area, click Copy button (Home tab | Editing group), select worksheets, click Paste button (Home tab | Editing group)
2. Right-click source area, click Copy on shortcut menu, select worksheets, click Paste on shortcut menu
3. Select source area, press CTRL+C, select worksheets, press CTRL+V

To Drill an Entry through Worksheets

The next step is to replace the sample numbers in the ranges C5:C9 and E5:E9 with the 2012 % Change and 2013 % Change for each expenditure type (Table 6–4). The 2012 % Change and 2013 % Change for expenditures are identical on all four sheets. For example, the 2012 % Change for Payroll in cell C5 is -2.00% on all four sheets. To speed data entry, Excel allows you to enter a number once and copy it through worksheets so that it is entered in the same cell on all the selected worksheets. This technique is referred to as **drilling an entry**. The following steps drill the five 2012 % Change and five 2013 % Change entries in Table 6–4 through all four worksheets in the range C5:C11.

Table 6–4 2012 % Change and 2013 % Change Values			
Cell	**2012 % Change**	**Cell**	**2013 % Change**
C5	–2.00	E5	–2.00
C6	4.00	E6	3.00
C7	4.00	E7	1.00
C8	7.00	E8	5.00
C9	2.00	E9	3.00

1

- With Sheet1 active, hold down the SHIFT key and then click the Sheet3 tab to select all four tabs at the bottom of the window.

- Select cell C5. Type −2.00 and then press the DOWN ARROW key to change sample data in the selected cell to a proper value.

- Enter the nine remaining 2012 % Change and 2013 % Change values in Table 6−4 in the ranges C6:C9 and E5:E9 to display the proper values.

- Select cell A12 to select the same cell in all of the selected worksheets (Figure 6−33).

Figure 6−33

2

- Hold down the SHIFT key and then click the Sheet1 tab to deselect multiple sheets.

- One at a time, click the Sheet4 tab, the Sheet2 tab, and the Sheet3 tab to verify that all four sheets are identical (Figure 6−34).

Q&A

What is the benefit of drilling data through worksheets?

In the previous set of steps, seven new numbers were entered on one worksheet. As shown in Figure 6−34, by drilling the entries through the four other worksheets, 28 new numbers now appear, seven on each of the four worksheets. Excel's capability of drilling data through worksheets is an efficient way to enter data that is common among worksheets.

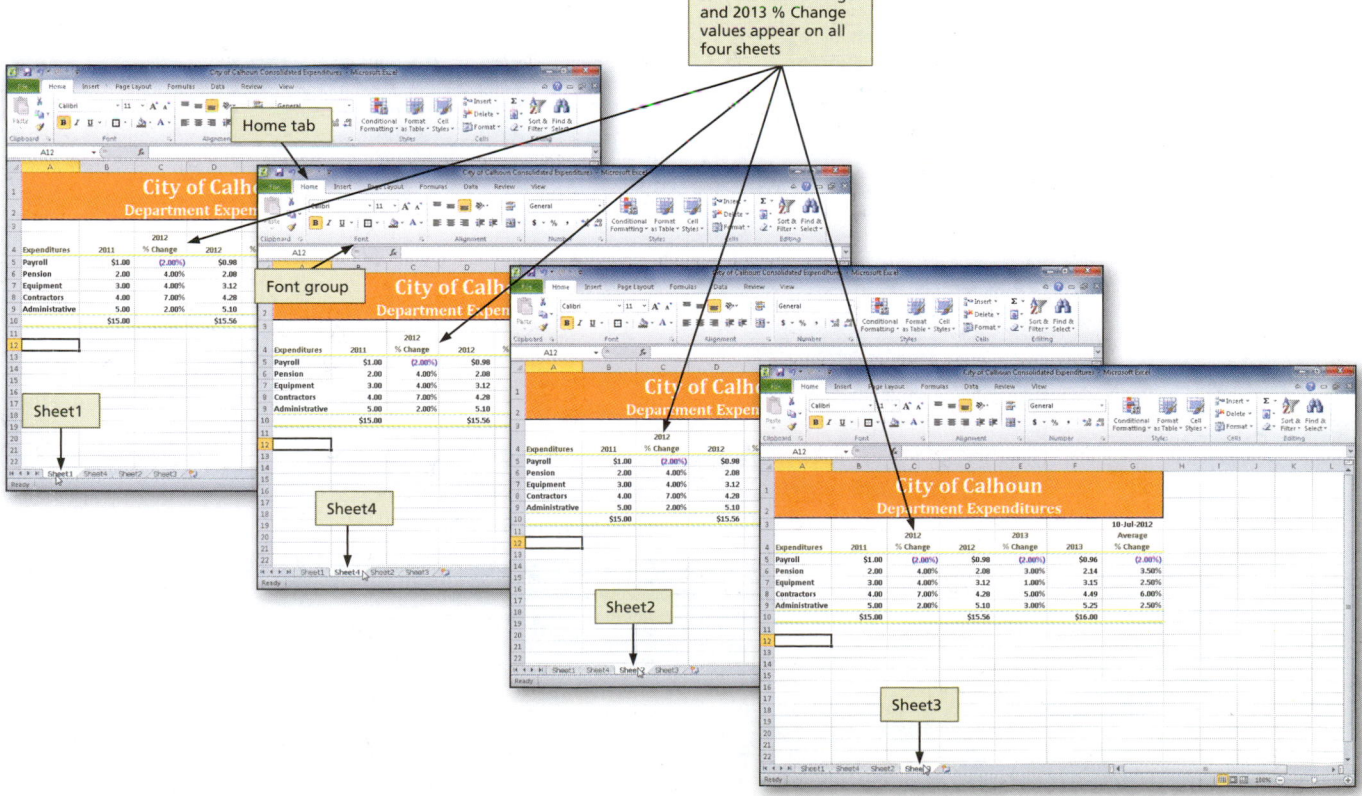

Figure 6−34

BTW

Drilling an Entry
Besides drilling a
number down through
a workbook, you can drill
a format, a function, or a
formula down through
a workbook.

To Modify the Public Works Sheet

With the outline of the City of Calhoun Consolidated Expenditures workbook created, the next step is to modify the individual sheets. The following steps modify the Public Works sheet (Sheet 4) by changing the sheet name, tab color, and worksheet subtitle; changing the color of the title area; and entering the 2011 expenditures in column B.

1 Double-click the Sheet4 tab to begin editing the sheet name. Type **Public Works** and then press the ENTER key to change the sheet name.

2 Right-click the Public Works tab to display a shortcut menu, point to Tab Color on the shortcut menu, and then click Brown, Accent 2 (column 6, row 1 in the Theme Colors area) on the Color palette to change the tab color.

3 Double-click cell A2 to begin editing text in a cell, drag through the words Department Expenditures to select the text, and then type **Public Works** to change the worksheet subtitle.

4 Select the range A1:A2, click the Fill Color button arrow (Home tab | Font group) to display the Fill Color gallery, and then click Brown, Accent 2 (column 6, row 1 in the Standard Colors area) on the Fill Color gallery to change the fill color of the selected range.

5 Enter the data listed in Table 6–5 in the range B5:B9 (Figure 6–35).

6 Select cell A12 and then click the Save button on the Quick Access Toolbar to save the workbook.

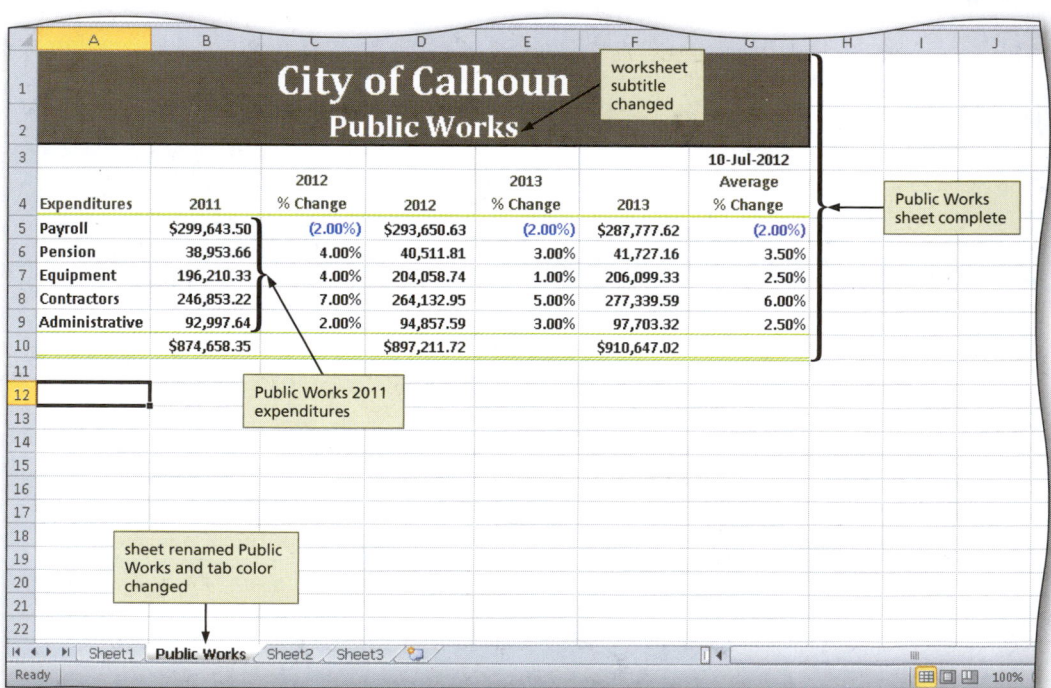

Figure 6–35

Table 6–5 Public Works 2011 Expenditures	
Cell	**2011 Expenditures**
B5	299643.50
B6	38953.66
B7	196210.33
B8	246853.22
B9	92997.64

To Modify the Police and Fire Sheet

The following steps modify the Police and Fire sheet (Sheet2).

1 Double-click the Sheet2 tab. Type **Police and Fire** and then press the ENTER key to change the sheet name.

2 Right-click the Police and Fire tab, point to Tab Color on the shortcut menu, and then click Green, Accent 1 (column 5, row 1 in the Theme Colors area) on the Color palette to change the tab color.

3 Double-click cell A2, drag through the word, Department Expenditures, and then type **Police and Fire** to change the worksheet subtitle.

4 Select the range A1:A2, click the Fill Color button arrow on the Ribbon, and then click Green, Accent 1 (column 5, row 1 in the Theme Colors area) in the Fill Color gallery.

5 Enter the data listed in Table 6–6 in the range B5:B9 (Figure 6–36).

6 Select cell A12 and then click the Save button on the Quick Access Toolbar.

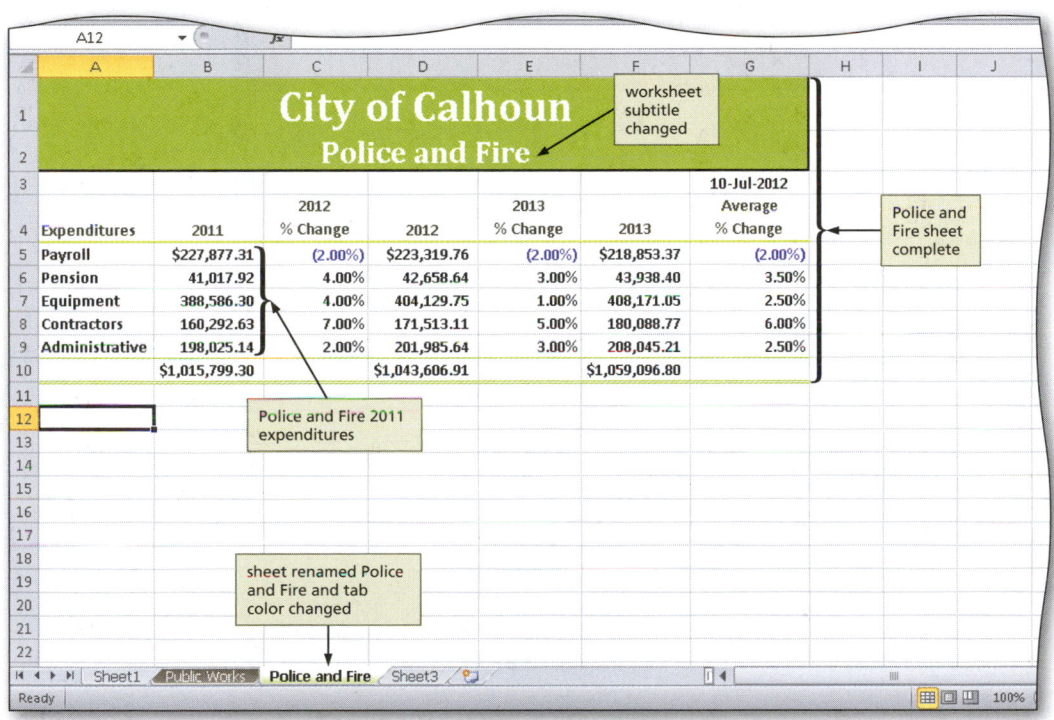

Figure 6–36

Table 6–6 Police and Fire 2011 Expenditures	
Cell	**2011 Expenditures**
B5	227877.31
B6	41017.92
B7	388586.30
B8	160292.63
B9	198025.14

To Modify the Parks and Recreation Sheet

As with the Public Works and Police and Fire sheets, the sheet name, tab color, worksheet subtitle, data, and background colors must be changed on the Parks and Recreation sheet. The following steps modify the Parks and Recreation sheet.

BTW

Importing Data

Expenditures, such as those entered into the range B5:B9, often are maintained in another workbook, a file, or a database. If the expenditures are maintained elsewhere, ways exist to link to a workbook or import data from a file or database into a workbook. Linking to a workbook is discussed later in this chapter. For information on importing data, see the From Other Sources button (Data tab | Get External Data group).

1 Double-click the Sheet3 tab. Type `Parks and Recreation` and then press the ENTER key to change the sheet name.

2 Right-click the Parks and Recreation tab, point to Tab Color on the shortcut menu, and then click Orange, Accent 3 (column 7, row 1 in the Standard Colors area) on the Color palette to change the tab color.

3 Double-click cell A2, drag through the word, Department, and then type `Parks and Recreation` to change the worksheet subtitle.

4 Select the range A1:A2, click the Fill Color button arrow on the Ribbon, and then click Orange, Accent 3 (column 7, row 1 in the Standard Colors area) on the Fill Color gallery to change the fill color of the selected cell.

5 Enter the data listed in Table 6–7 in the range B5:B9 (Figure 6–37).

6 Select cell A12 and then click the Save button on the Quick Access Toolbar.

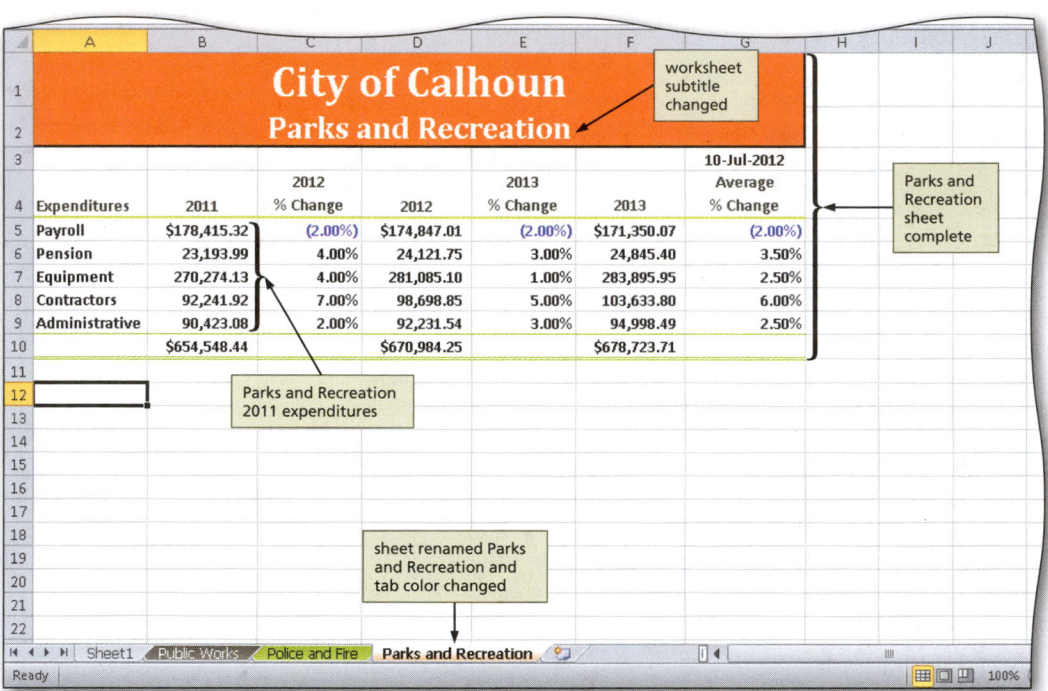

Figure 6–37

Table 6–7 Parks and Recreation 2011 Expenditures	
Cell	**2011 Expenditures**
B5	178415.32
B6	23193.99
B7	270274.13
B8	92241.92
B9	90423.08

Referencing Cells in Other Sheets in a Workbook

With the three region sheets complete, the next step is to modify Sheet1, which will serve as the consolidation worksheet containing totals of the data on the Public Works, Police and Fire, and Parks and Recreation sheets. Because this sheet contains totals of the data, you need to understand how to reference cells in other sheets in a workbook before modifying Sheet1.

To reference cells in other sheets in a workbook, you use the sheet name, which serves as the **sheet reference**, and the cell reference. For example, you refer to cell B5 on the Public Works sheet as shown below. The sheet name must be included in single quotation marks when the sheet name contains a space character.

='Public Works'!B5

Using this method, you can sum cell B5 from each of the three department sheets by selecting cell B5 on the Sheet1 sheet and then entering:

='Public Works'!B5 + 'Police and Fire'!B5 + 'Parks and Recreation'!B5

A much quicker way to total the three cells is to use the SUM function as follows:

=SUM('Public Works:Parks and Recreation'!B5)

The SUM argument ('Public Works':'Parks and Recreation'!B5) instructs Excel to sum cell B5 on each of the three sheets (Public Works, Police and Fire, and Parks and Recreation). The colon (:) between the first sheet name and the last sheet name instructs Excel to include these sheets and all sheets in between, just as it does with a range of cells on a sheet. A range that spans two or more sheets in a workbook, such as 'Public Works':'Parks and Recreation'!B5, is called a **3-D range**. The reference to this range is a **3-D reference**.

A sheet reference such as 'Public Works'! always is absolute. Thus, the sheet reference remains constant when you copy formulas.

BTW

Circular References
A circular reference is a formula that depends on its own value. The most common type is a formula that contains a reference to the same cell in which the formula resides.

To Modify the Consolidated Sheet

This section modifies the Consolidated sheet by changing the sheet name, tab color, and subtitle and then entering the SUM function in cells B5, D5, and F5. The SUM functions will determine the total expenditures for each year, by expenditure type. Cell B5 on the Consolidated sheet, for instance, will contain the sum of the Payroll expenditures, which are located in Public Works!B5, Police and Fire!B5, and Parks and Recreation!B5. Before determining the totals, the following steps change the sheet name from Sheet1 to Consolidated, color the tab, and change the subtitle to Consolidated Expenditures.

1 Double-click the Sheet1 sheet tab to display the worksheet. Type `Consolidated` and then press the ENTER key to rename the sheet.

2 Right-click the Consolidated tab to display the worksheet, point to Tab Color on the shortcut menu, and then click Orange, Accent 6 (column 10, row 1 in the Standard Colors area) on the Color palette to change the tab color.

3 Double-click cell A2 to begin editing a cell, drag through the words Department Expenditures to select the words in the cell, and then type `Consolidated` as the worksheet subtitle. Press the ENTER key to complete the change of the subtitle.

BTW

3-D References
If you are summing numbers on noncontiguous sheets, hold down the CTRL key rather than the SHIFT key when selecting the sheets.

To Enter and Copy 3-D References Using the Paste Gallery

You can enter a sheet reference in a cell by typing the sheet reference or by clicking the appropriate sheet tab while in Point mode. When you click the sheet tab, Excel activates the sheet and automatically adds the sheet name and an exclamation point after the insertion point in the formula bar. Next, select or drag through the cells you want to reference on the sheet.

If the range of cells to be referenced is located on several worksheets (as when selecting a 3-D range), click the first sheet tab and then select the cell or drag through the range of cells. Next, while holding down the SHIFT key, click the sheet tab of the last sheet you want to reference. Excel will include the cell(s) on the first sheet, the last sheet, and any sheets in between.

The following steps enter the 3-D references used to determine the total 2011 expenditures for each of the five types of expenditures. In these steps, the Formulas button on the Paste gallery is used to complete the paste operation. When the Formulas button is used, the paste operation pastes only the formulas, leaving the formats of the destination area unchanged.

1

- Select cell B5 and then click the Sum button (Home tab | Editing group) to display the SUM function and ScreenTip (Figure 6–38).

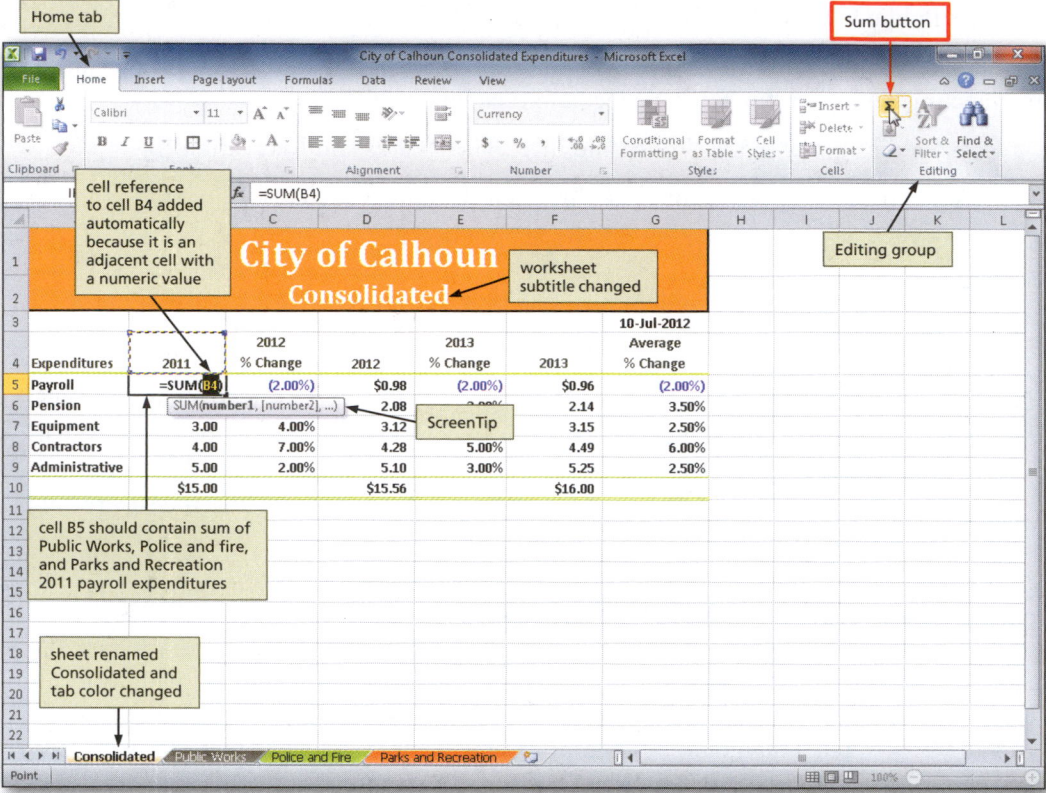

Figure 6–38

2

- Click the Public Works tab to display the worksheet and then click cell B5 to select the first portion of the argument for the SUM function.

- While holding down the SHIFT key, click the Parks and Recreations tab to select the ending range of the argument for the SUM function (Figure 6–39).

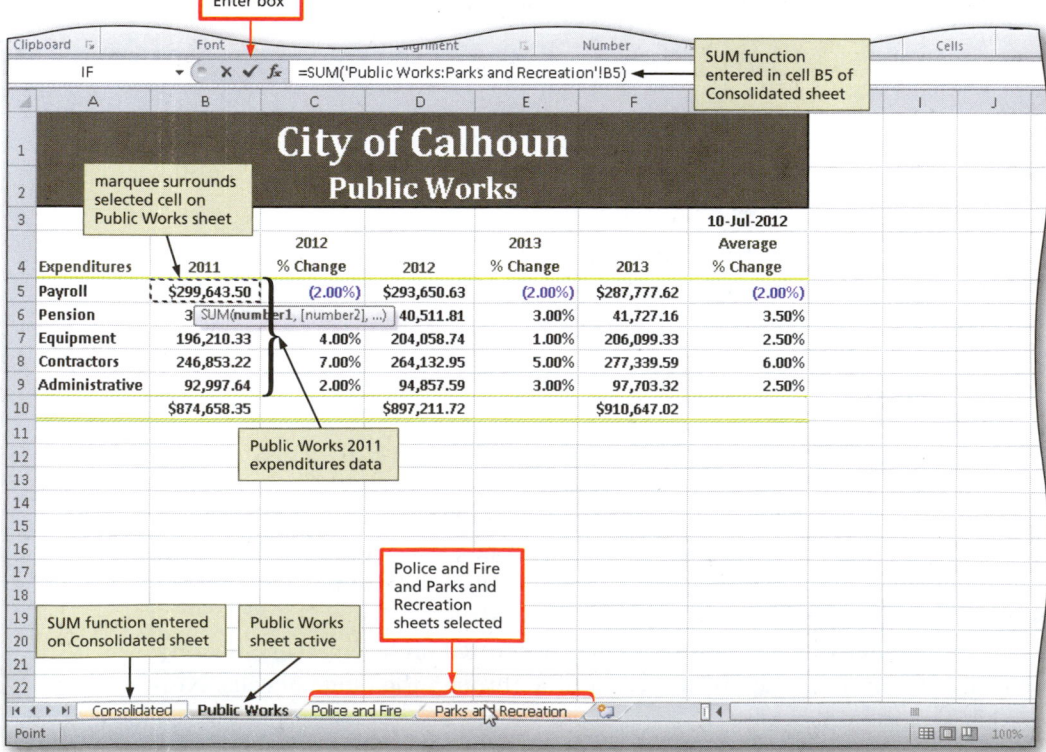

Figure 6–39

3

• Click the Enter box in the formula bar to enter the SUM function with the 3-D references in the selected cell, in this case Consolidated!B5 (Figure 6–40).

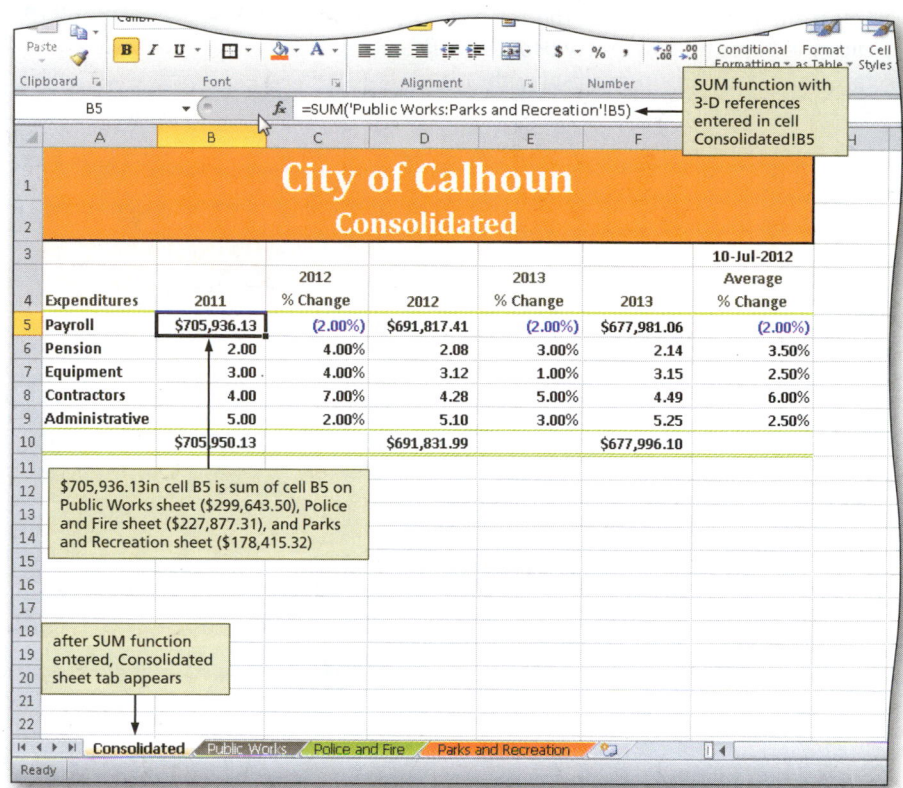

Figure 6–40

4

• With cell B5 active, click the Copy button (Home tab | Clipboard group) to copy the SUM function and the formats assigned to the selected cell to the Office Clipboard (Figure 6–41).

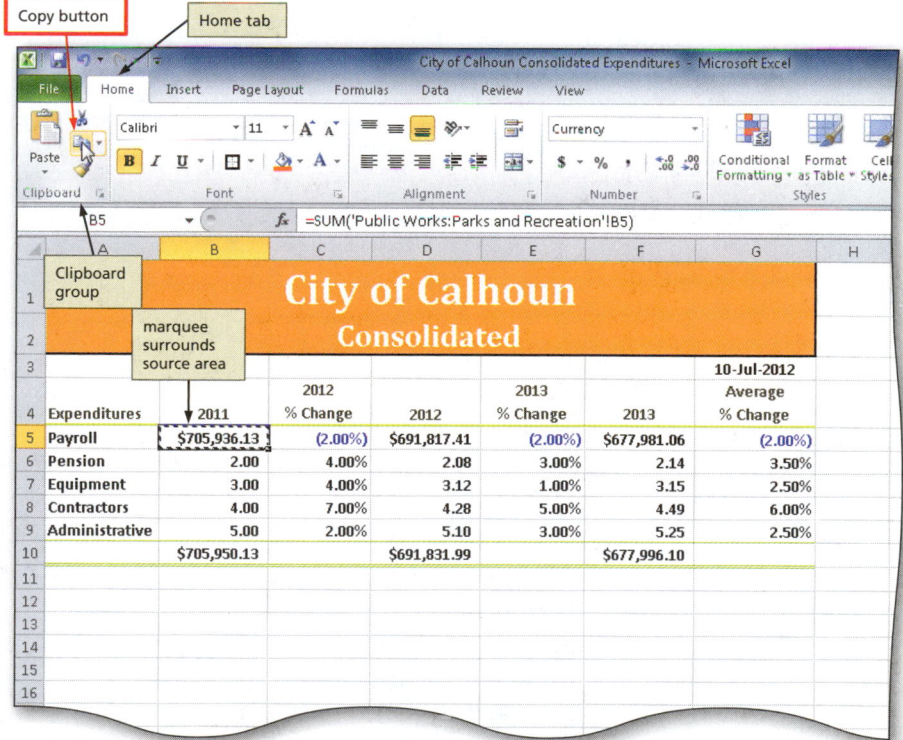

Figure 6–41

5

- Select the range B6:B9 and then click the Paste button arrow (Home tab | Clipboard group) to display the Paste gallery (Figure 6–42).

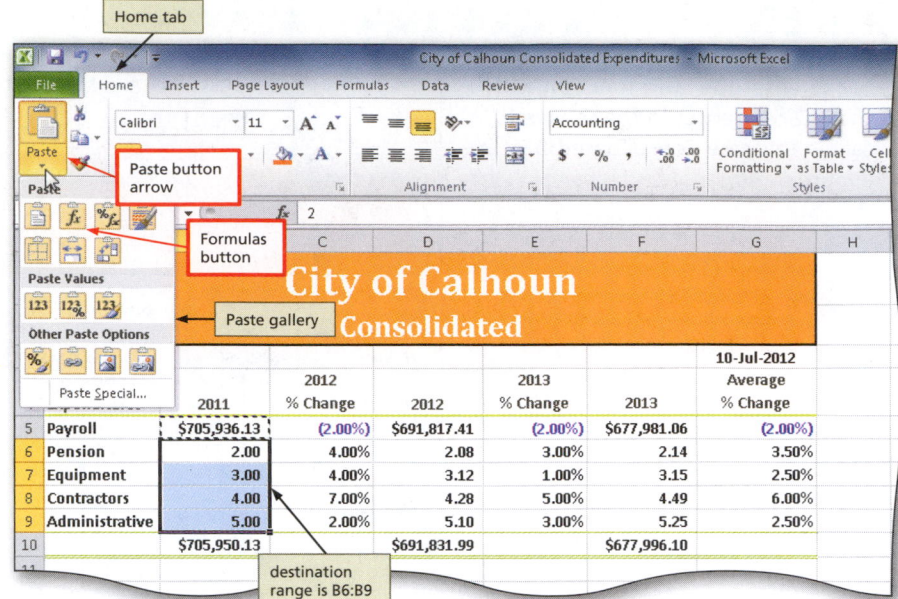

Figure 6–42

6

- Click the Formulas button on the Paste gallery to copy the SUM function in cell B5 to the range B6:B9 and automatically adjust the cell references in the SUM function to reference the corresponding cells on the three sheets in the workbook.

- Press the ESC key to clear the marquee surrounding the source cell, B5 in this case, and then select cell A12 to deselect the destination range, B6:B9 in this case.

- Click the Save button on the Quick Access Toolbar to save the workbook (Figure 6–43).

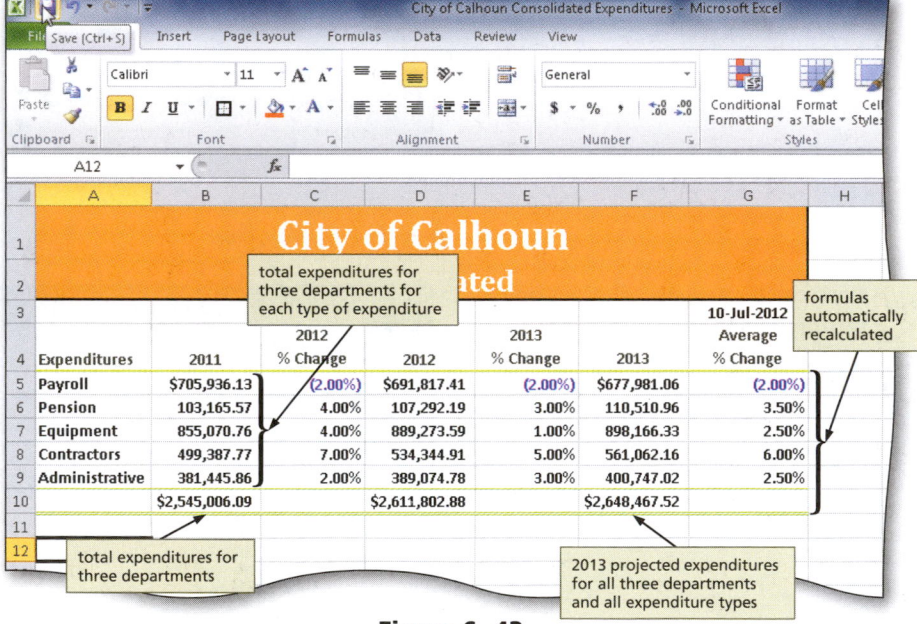

Figure 6–43

More About Pasting

If you click the Paste button (Home tab | Clipboard group) to complete the paste operation, rather than using the Formulas button as shown in Figure 6–42, any formats assigned to cell B5 also will be copied to the range B6:B9. Completing the paste operation by using the fill handle or by pressing the ENTER key also will copy any formats from the source area to the destination area. Oftentimes, as in the steps shown above, the formats of the source area and destination area differ; when you use the Formulas button on the Paste gallery, Excel copies the SUM function, but not the format, assigned to the source area. The Paste gallery, thus, is a useful option to complete the copy and paste operation without copying the formatting of the source area. Table 6–8 summarizes the commands available on the Paste gallery, as shown in Figure 6–42 on the next page.

Table 6–8 Paste Gallery Commands

Paste Option Icon	Paste Option	Shortcut Key	Description
	Paste	CTRL+P	Copy contents and format of source area. This option is the default.
	Formulas	CTRL+F	Copy formulas from the source area, but not the contents and format.
	Formulas & Number Formatting	CTRL+O	Copy formulas and format for numbers and formulas of source area, but not the contents.
	Keep Source Formatting	CTRL+K	Copy contents, format, and styles of source area.
	No Borders	CTRL+B	Copy contents and format of source area, but not any borders.
	Keep Source Column Widths	CTRL+W	Copy contents and format of source area. Change destination column widths to source column widths.
	Transpose	CTRL+T	Copy the contents and format of the source area, but transpose, or swap, the rows and columns.
	Values	CTRL+V	Copy contents of source area but not the formatting for formulas.
	Values & Number Formatting	CTRL+A	Copy contents and format of source area for numbers or formulas, but use format of destination area for text.
	Values & Source Formatting	CTRL+E	Copy contents and formatting of source area but not the formula.
	Formatting	CTRL+R	Copy format of source area but not the contents.
	Paste Link	CTRL+N	Copy contents and format and link cells so that a change to the cells in source area updates the corresponding cells in destination area.
	Picture	CTRL+U	Copy an image of the source area as a picture.
	Linked Picture	CTRL+I	Copy an image of the source area as a picture so that a change to the cells in source area updates the picture in destination area.

Note: If you wish to take a break, this is a good place to do so. You can quit Excel now. To resume at a later time, start Excel, open the file called City of Calhoun Consolidated Expenditures, and continue following the steps from this location forward.

Adding a Header and Footer, Changing the Margins, and Printing the Workbook

Before printing a workbook, consider the **page setup**, which defines the appearance and format of a printed worksheet. You can add a **header**, which appears at the top of every printed page, and a **footer**, which appears at the bottom of every printed page. You also can change the **margins** to increase or decrease the white space surrounding the printed worksheet or chart.

<table>
<tr><td>**Plan Ahead**</td><td>**Examine the options, including headers, margins, and page breaks, that you have for printing worksheets.**

If you plan to distribute printed copies of worksheets, decide whether to select page setup options before printing.

- **Add headers and footers.** By default, both the header and footer are blank. You can change either so that information, such as the workbook author, date, page number, or tab name, prints at the top or bottom of each page. The headers and footers for chart sheets must be assigned separately.

- **Change the margins.** The default margins in Excel for both portrait and landscape orientation are set to the following: Top = .75 inch; Bottom = .75 inch; Left = .7 inch; Right = .7 inch. The header and footer are set at .3 inches from the top and bottom, respectively. Change these settings to provide more or less white space on the printed page.

- **Apply other page setup options.** Display the Page Layout tab to specify page setup options, such as setting the location of page breaks or centering a printout horizontally and vertically. Be sure to select all the sheets you want to modify before you change page setup options.</td></tr>
</table>

To Change Margins and Center the Printout Horizontally

As you modify the page setup, remember that Excel does not copy page setup characteristics when one sheet is copied to another. Thus, even if you assigned page setup characteristics to the consolidated worksheet before copying it to each department's worksheet, the page setup characteristics would not be copied to the new sheet. The following steps use the Page Setup dialog box to change the margins and center the printout of each department's worksheet horizontally.

- With the Consolidated sheet active, if necessary, scroll to the top of the worksheet.

- While holding down the SHIFT key, click the Parks and Recreation sheet tab to select the four worksheet tabs.

- Display the Page Layout tab (Figure 6–44).

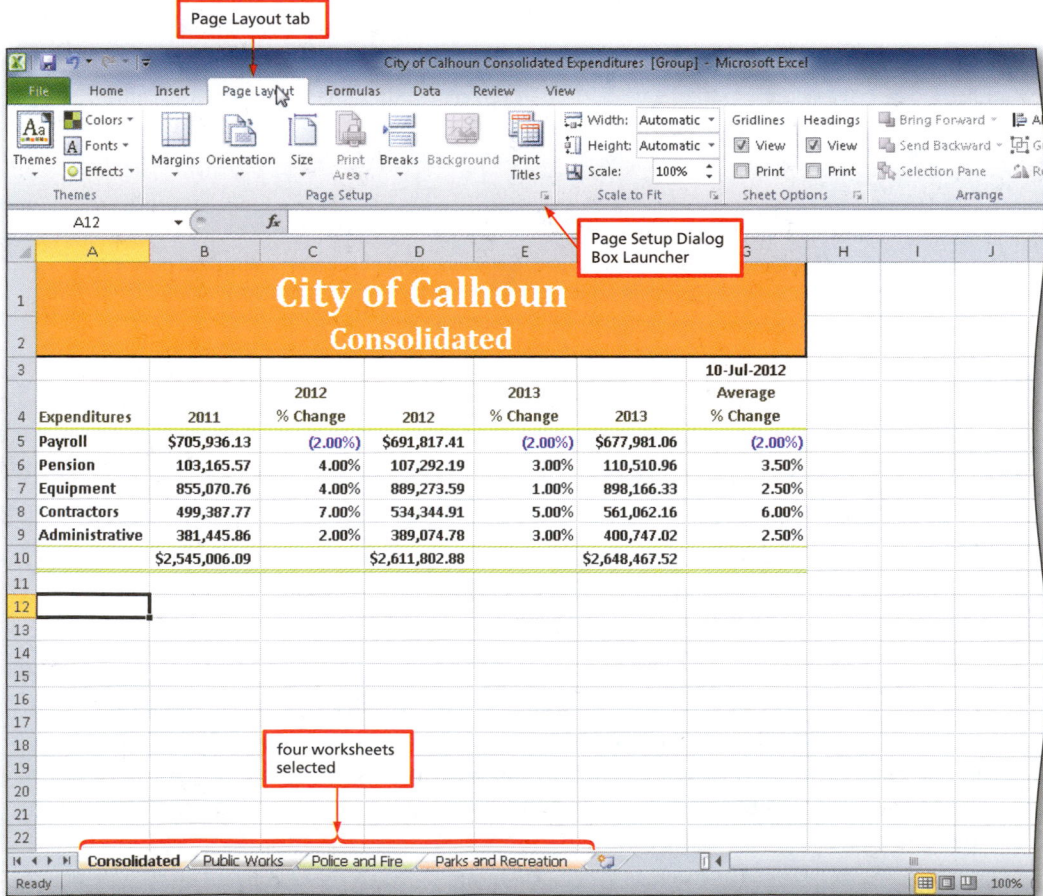

Figure 6–44

- Click the Page Setup Dialog Box Launcher (Page Layout tab | Page Setup group) to display the Page Setup dialog box.

- When Excel displays the Page Setup dialog box, if necessary, click the Margins tab.

- Double-click the Top box and then type **1.5** to change the top margin.

- Enter **.5** in both the Left box and Right box to change the left and right margins.

- Click the Horizontally check box in the 'Center on page' area to center the worksheet on the printed page horizontally (Figure 6–45).

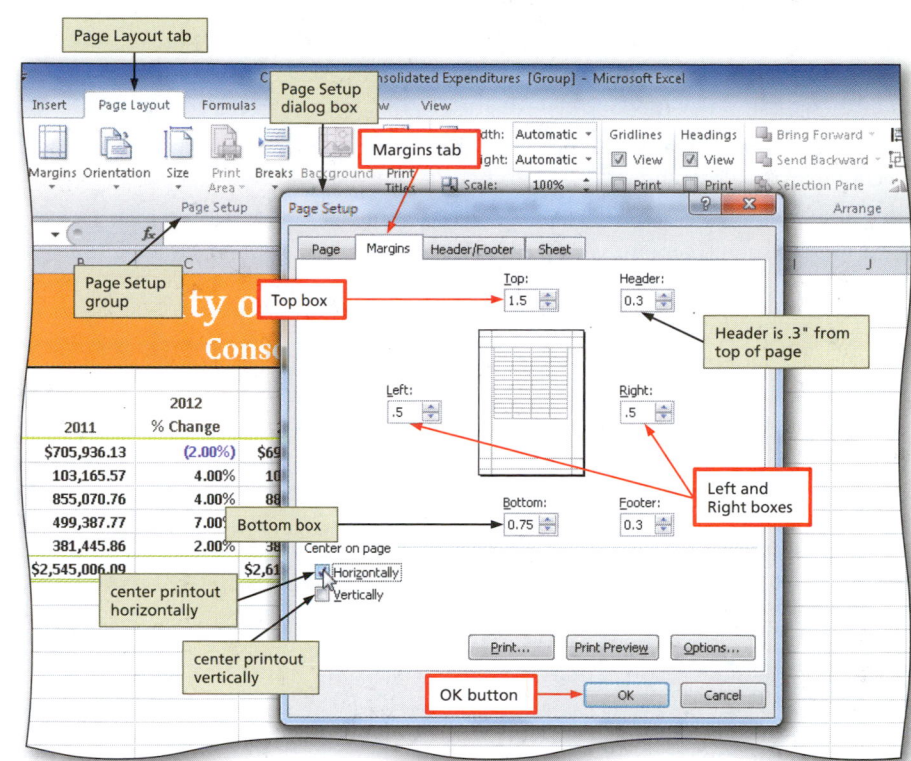

3

- Click the OK button (Page Setup dialog box) to close the Page Setup dialog box.

Figure 6–45

Other Ways

1. In Backstage view, click Normal Margins button (Print tab | Settings area), click Custom Margins

To Add a Header and Footer

The following steps use Page Layout view to change the headers and footers of the worksheets.

- Click the Page Layout button on the status bar to display the worksheet in Page Layout view (Figure 6–46).

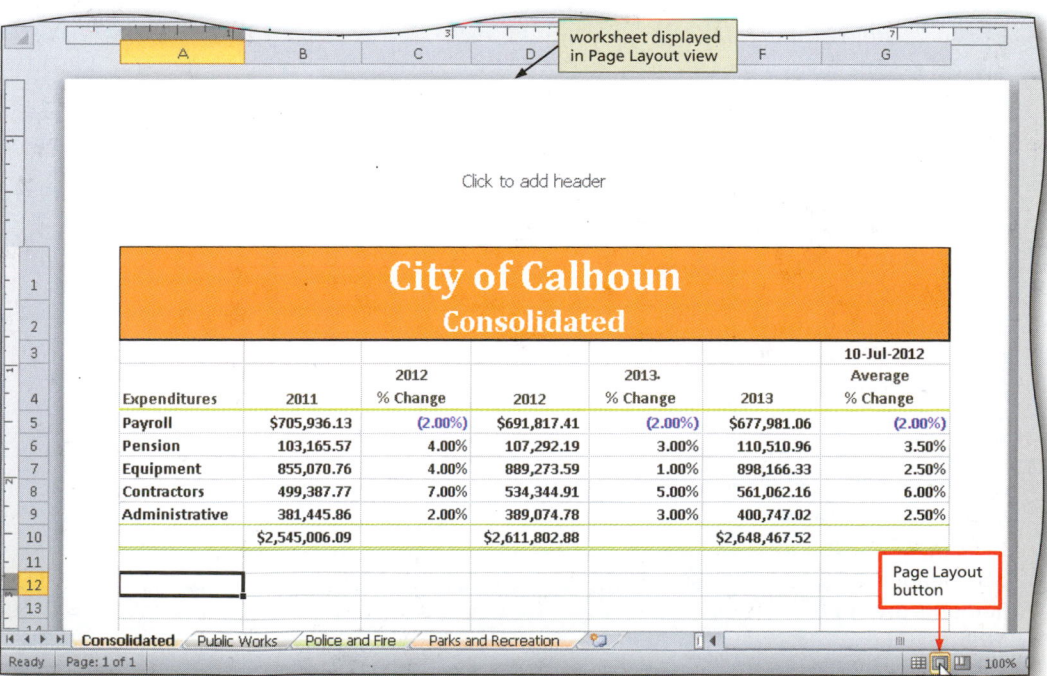

Figure 6–46

2

- If necessary, scroll the worksheet up until the Header area is displayed. Click the left Header box to select the left Header box as the area for a header and type `Shelly Cashman` (or your name) to enter a page header in the left Header box.

- Click the center Header box to select the center Header box as the area for a header and then type `City of Calhoun`. Press the ENTER key to begin a new line.

- Click the Sheet Name button (Header & Footer Tools Design tab | Header & Footer Elements group) to instruct Excel to insert the sheet name that appears on the sheet tab as part of the header.

- Click the right Header box to select the right Header box as the area for a header, click the Current Date button (Header & Footer Tools Design tab | Header & Footer Elements group) to insert the current date.

- Press the COMMA key and, then click the Current Time button (Header & Footer Tools Design tab | Header & Footer Elements group) to insert the date and time in the Header (Figure 6–47).

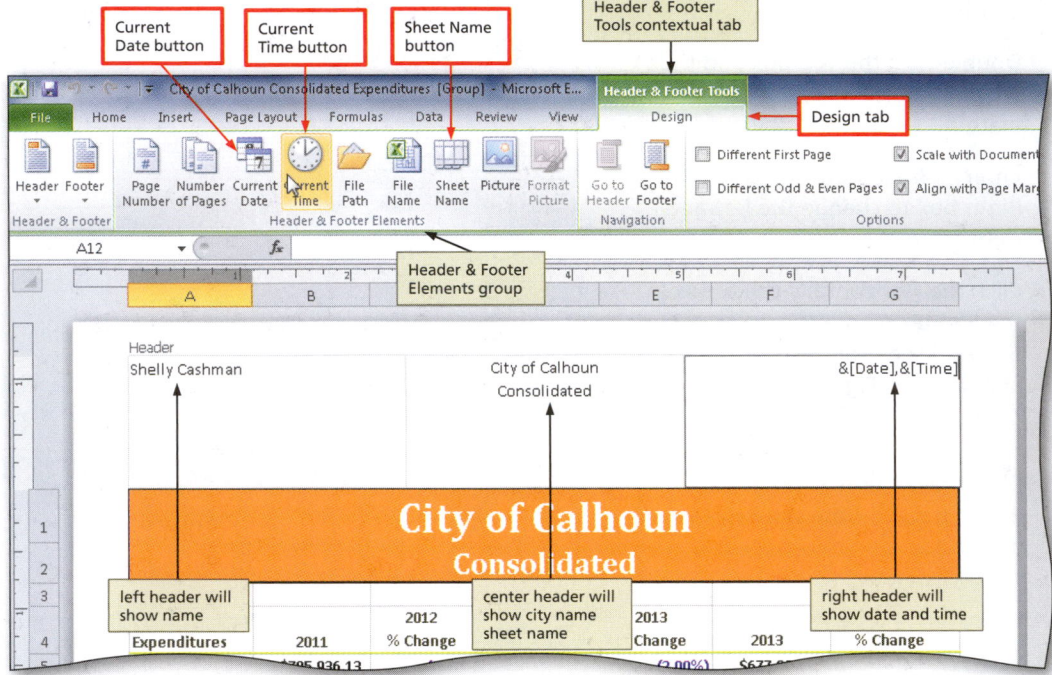

Figure 6–47

3

- Scroll the workbook down to view the Footer area.

- Click the middle Footer box to select the middle section box as the area for a footer and then type `Page`. Press the SPACEBAR, click the Page Number button (Header & Footer Tools Design tab | Header & Footer Elements group) to insert the page number, press the SPACEBAR, and then type `of` followed by the SPACEBAR.

- Click the Number of Pages button (Header & Footer Tools Design tab | Header & Footer Elements group) to add the number of pages to the footer (Figure 6–48).

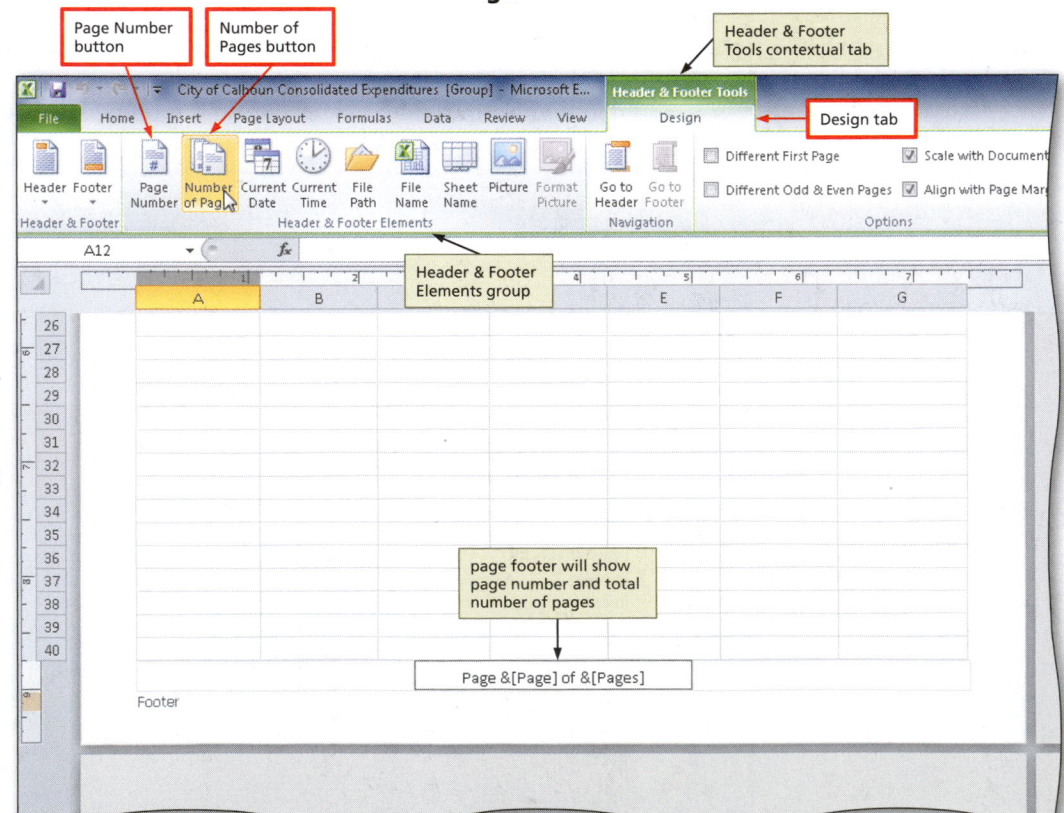

Figure 6–48

Experiment

- Click the left Footer box, and then click other buttons in the Header & Footer Elements group on the Header & Footer Tools Design tab.

- Click the right Footer box to display the results, and then delete the contents of the left Footer box.

Q&A

What does Excel insert when I click a button in the Header & Footer Tools group on the Ribbon?

Excel enters a code (similar to a format code) into the active header or footer section. A code such as &[Page] instructs Excel to insert the page number.

4

- Click anywhere on the worksheet to deselect the page footer.

- Click the Normal view button on the status bar to return to Normal view and then select cell A12.

- Display the Page Layout tab and then click the Page Setup Dialog Box Launcher (Page Layout tab | Page Setup group) to display the Page Setup dialog box.

- Click the Print Preview button (Page Setup dialog box) to preview the current sheet in the Backstage view (Figure 6–49).

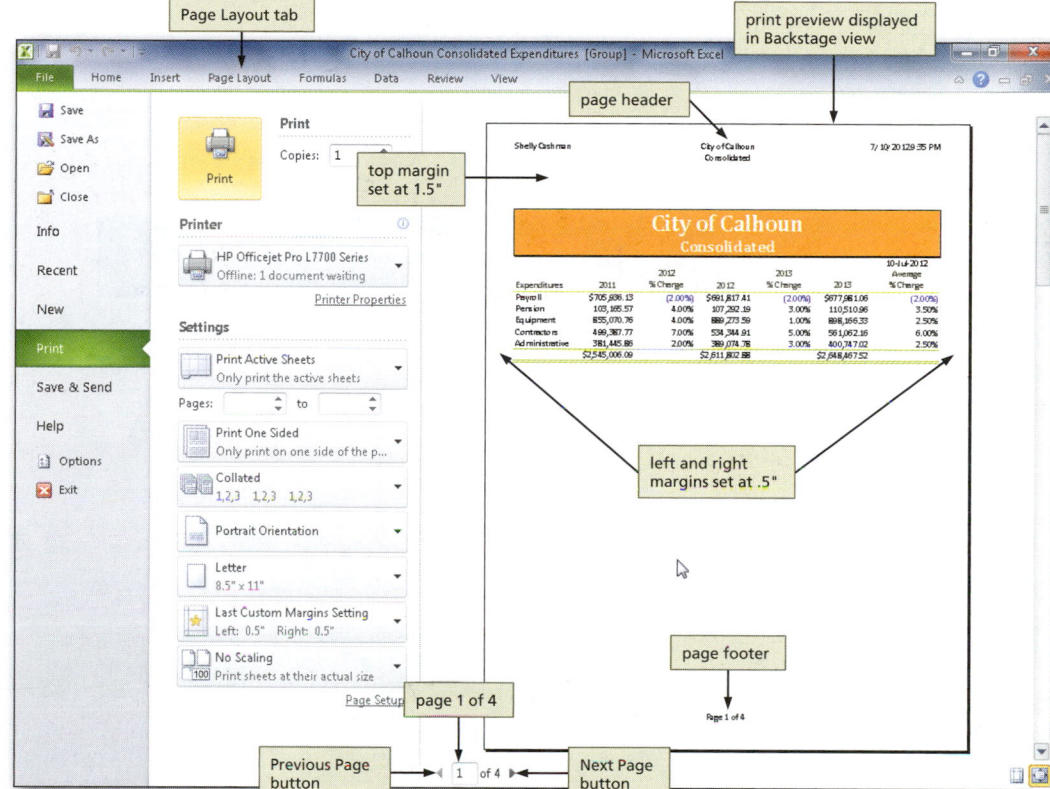

Figure 6–49

5

- Click the Next Page button and Previous Page buttons below the preview to preview the other pages.

- After previewing the printout, display the Home tab.

To Print All Worksheets in a Workbook

The following steps print all four sheets in the workbook.

1 Ready the printer.

2 Open the Backstage view, click the Print tab in the Backstage view to display the Print gallery, and then click the Print button to print the workbook as shown in Figure 6–50.

3 Hold down the SHIFT key and then click the Consolidated sheet tab to deselect all sheets but the Consolidated sheet.

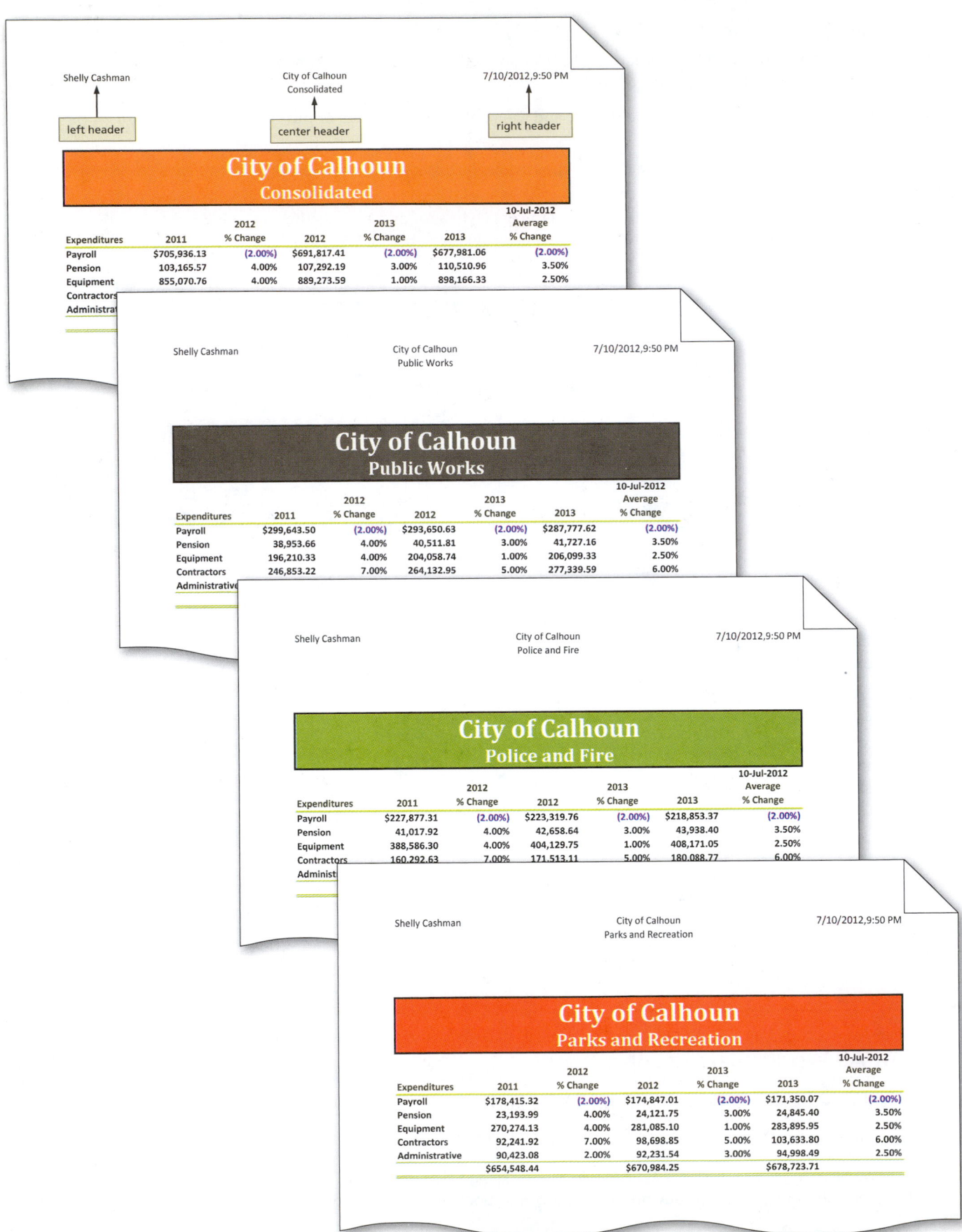

Figure 6–50

To Print Nonadjacent Sheets in a Workbook

In some situations, nonadjacent sheets in a workbook may need to be printed. To select nonadjacent sheets, select the first sheet and then hold down the CTRL key and click the nonadjacent sheets. The following steps print the nonadjacent Consolidated and Parks and Recreation sheets.

1 With the Consolidated sheet active, hold down the CTRL key, and then click the Parks and Recreation sheet tab.

2 Open the Backstage view, click the Print tab in the Backstage view to display the Print gallery, and then click the Print button to print the nonadjacent worksheets.

3 Hold down the SHIFT key and click the Consolidated sheet tab to deselect the Parks and Recreation sheet.

Selecting and Deselecting Sheets

Beginning Excel users sometimes have difficulty trying to select and deselect sheets. Table 6–9 summarizes how to select and deselect sheets.

Table 6–9 Summary of How to Select and Deselect Sheets	
Task	**How to Carry Out the Task**
Select adjacent sheets	Select the first sheet by clicking its tab and then hold down the SHIFT key and click the sheet tab at the other end of the list of adjacent sheet tabs.
Select nonadjacent sheets	Select the first sheet by clicking its tab and then hold down the CTRL key and click the sheet tabs of the remaining sheets you want to select.
Multiple sheets are selected and you want to select a sheet that is selected, but not active (sheet tab name not in bold)	Click the sheet tab you want to select.
Multiple sheets are selected and you want to select the active sheet (sheet tab name in bold)	Hold down the SHIFT key and then click the sheet tab of the active sheet.

To Insert and Remove a Page Break

When you print a worksheet or use the Page Setup dialog box, Excel inserts **page breaks** that show the boundaries of what will print on each page. These page breaks are based upon the margins selected in the Margins sheet in the Page Setup dialog box and the type of printer you are using. If the Page breaks option is selected, Excel displays dotted lines on the worksheet to show the boundaries of each page. For example, the dotted line in Figure 6–52 shows the right boundary of the first page. If the dotted line does not show on your screen, then click the Options button in the Backstage view. When Excel displays the Excel Options dialog box, click the Advanced command to display Advanced Excel options. Scroll the window until the 'Display options for this worksheet' area appears. Click the Show page breaks check box (Figure 6–53 on page EX 403).

You can insert both horizontal and vertical page breaks in a worksheet. Manual page breaks are useful if you have a worksheet that is several pages long and you want certain parts of the worksheet to print on separate pages. For example, say you had a worksheet that comprised ten departments in sequence and each department had many rows of information. If you wanted each department to begin on a new page, then inserting page breaks would satisfy the requirement.

The following steps insert both a horizontal and vertical page break.

1
- With the Consolidated sheet active, select cell B10 and then display the Page Layout tab.

- Click the Breaks button (Page Layout tab | Page Setup group) to display the Breaks menu and then click Insert Page Break on the Breaks menu to insert a page break (Figure 6–51).

Q&A

What appears on the worksheet?
Excel inserts a dotted line above row 10 indicating a horizontal page break and inserts a dotted line to the left of column B indicating a vertical page break (Figure 6–51). Excel displays a dotted line between pages.

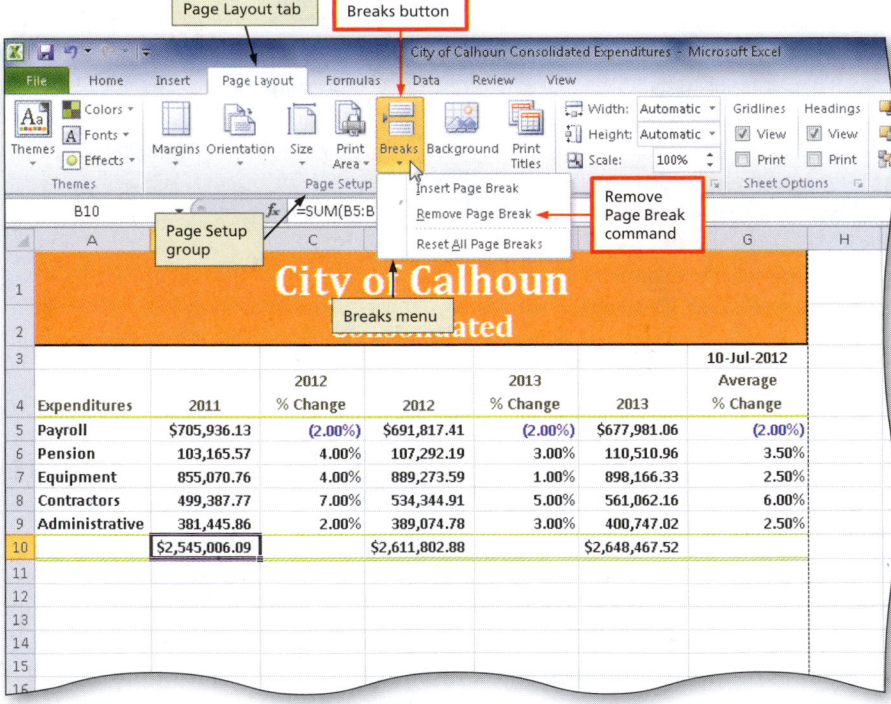

Figure 6–51

2
- With cell B10 active, click the Breaks button (Page Layout tab | Page Setup group) to display the Breaks menu (Figure 6–52).

3
- Click Remove Page Break on the Breaks menu to remove the page breaks.

Q&A

Is there a way to move page breaks?
Yes. An alternative to using the Breaks button on the Page Layout tab to insert page breaks is to click the Page Break Preview button on the status bar. When the Page Break preview appears, you can drag the blue boundaries, which represent page breaks, to new locations.

Figure 6–52

Other Ways

1. Click Page Break Preview button on status bar, click OK button (Welcome to Page Break Preview dialog box), drag page breaks

To Hide Page Breaks

When working with a workbook, page breaks can be an unnecessary distraction, especially to users who have no interest in where pages break. The following steps hide the dotted lines that represent page breaks.

- Open the Backstage view.

- Click the Options button in the Backstage view to display the Excel Options dialog box.

- Click the Advanced button (Excel Options dialog box) to display Advanced Excel options.

- Scroll the window until the 'Display options for this worksheet' area appears.

- Click the 'Show page breaks' check box to clear the check box (Figure 6–53).

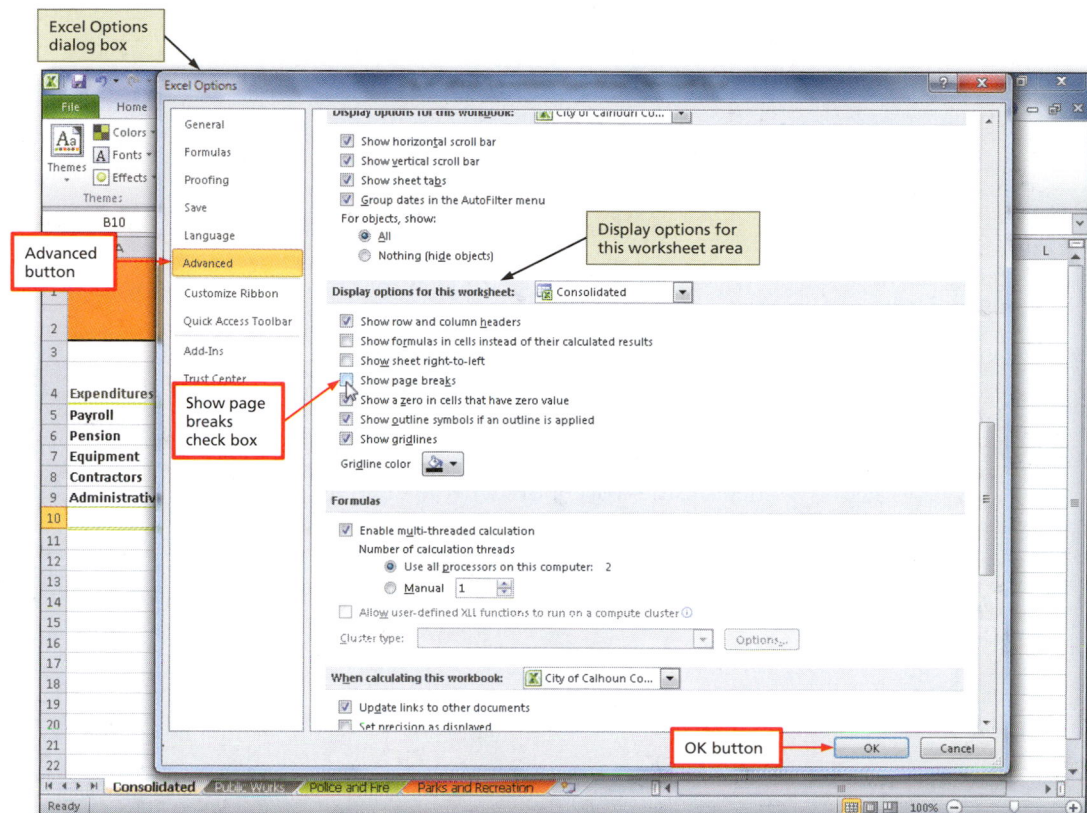

Figure 6–53

- Click the OK button to close the Excel Options dialog box and hide the page breaks (Figure 6–54).

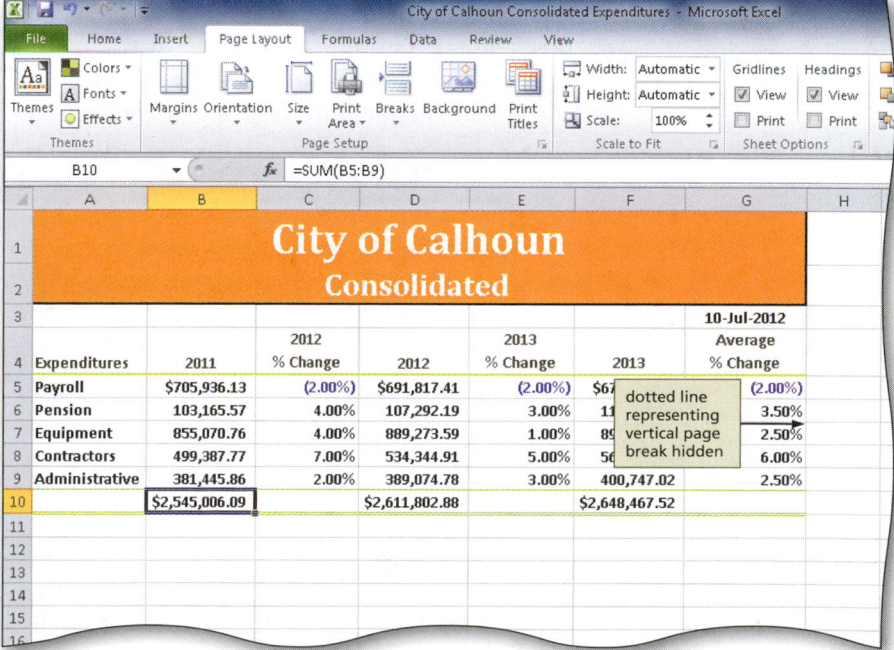

Figure 6–54

To Quit Excel

With the workbook complete, the following steps quit Excel.

1 Click the Close button on the upper-right corner of the title bar.

2 If the Microsoft Excel dialog box is displayed, click the Don't Save button so that any changes made to the workbook are not saved (Microsoft Excel dialog box).

BTW

Consolidation
You also can consolidate data across different workbooks using the Consolidate button (Data tab | Data Tools group), rather than by entering formulas. For more information on the Consolidate button, type consolidate in the Search box in the Excel Help dialog box, and then click the 'Consolidate data in multiple worksheets' link in the Results list.

Consolidating Data by Linking Workbooks

Earlier in this chapter, the data from three worksheets was consolidated into a fourth worksheet in the same workbook using 3-D references. An alternative to this method is to consolidate data from worksheets that are in other workbooks. Consolidating data from other workbooks also is referred to as linking. A **link** is a reference to a cell or range of cells in another workbook. In the case below, the 3-D reference also includes a workbook name. For example, the following 3-D reference pertains to cell B5 on the Public Works sheet in the workbook City of Calhoun Consolidated Expenditures located on drive E.

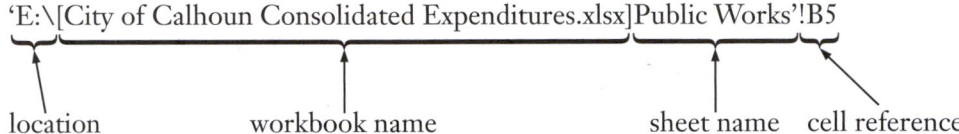

'E:\[City of Calhoun Consolidated Expenditures.xlsx]Public Works'!B5

location   workbook name   sheet name   cell reference

The single quotation marks surrounding the location, workbook name, and sheet name are required if any of the three names contain spaces. If the workbook to which you are referring is in the same folder as the active workbook, the location (in this case, E:\) is not necessary. The brackets surrounding the workbook name are required.

To illustrate linking cells between workbooks, the Consolidated, Public Works, Police and Fire, and Parks and Recreation worksheets from the workbook created earlier in this chapter are on the Data Files for Students in separate workbooks as described in Table 6–10. The department workbooks contain the department data, but the Calhoun Consolidated Expenditures workbook does not include any consolidated data. The consolidation of data from the three department workbooks into the Calhoun Consolidated Expenditures workbook will be completed later in this section.

BTW

Quick Reference
For a table that lists how to complete the tasks covered in this book using the mouse, Ribbon, shortcut menu, and keyboard, see the Quick Reference Summary at the back of this book, or visit the Excel 2010 Quick Reference Web page (scsite.com/ex2010/qr).

Table 6–10 Workbook Names	
Worksheet in Calhoun Consolidated Expenditures Workbook Using the Workbook Name	**Saved on the Data Files for Students As**
Consolidated	Calhoun Consolidated Expenditures
Public Works	Calhoun Public Works Expenditures
Police and Fire	Calhoun Police and Fire Expenditures
Parks and Recreation	Calhoun Parks and Recreation Expenditures

The remaining sections of this chapter demonstrate how to search for the four workbooks in Table 6–10 on a USB flash drive, how to create a workspace from the four workbooks, and finally how to link the three department workbooks to consolidate the data into the Calhoun Consolidated Expenditures workbook.

To Search for and Open Workbooks

Excel has a powerful search tool that you can use to locate workbooks (or any file) stored on disk. You search for files using the Search text box in the Open dialog box. If you view files on the Data Files for Students, then you will see the four workbooks listed in the right column of Table 6–10. The following steps, however, search for workbooks and often are used when you cannot remember exactly the name of the file or its location. In this example, the search text Calhoun will be used to locate the workbooks. The located workbooks then are opened and **arranged** so that each one appears in its own window.

- Start Excel.

- Open the Backstage view.

- Click the Open button to display the Open dialog box and then select the drive for your USB port, Removable (E:) in this case, in the Address bar to select a drive to search.

- Type **Calhoun** in the Search box as the search text (Figure 6–55).

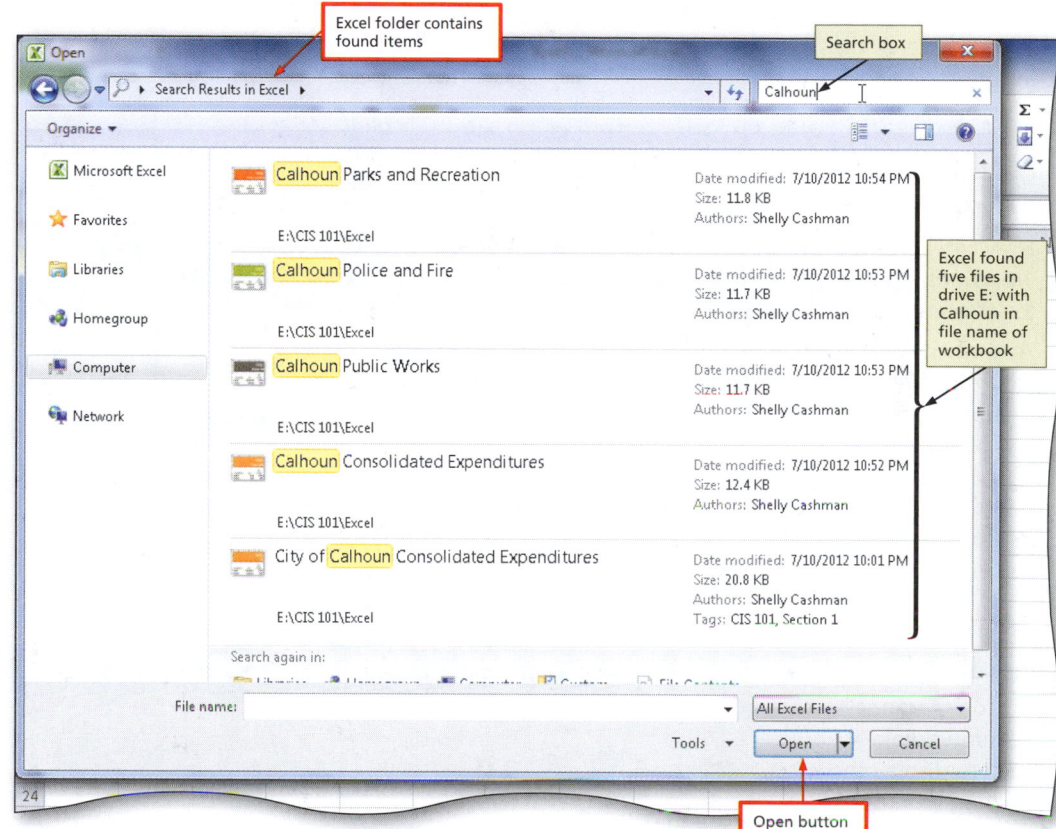

Figure 6–55

- In the File list, while holding down the CTRL key, click each of the three department workbook names one at a time and then click the Calhoun Consolidated Expenditures workbook name to select several workbooks to open.

- Click the Open button (Open dialog box) to open the selected workbooks.

- Display the View tab and then click the Switch Windows button (View tab | Window group) to display the names of the workbooks with a check mark to the left of the active workbook (Figure 6–56).

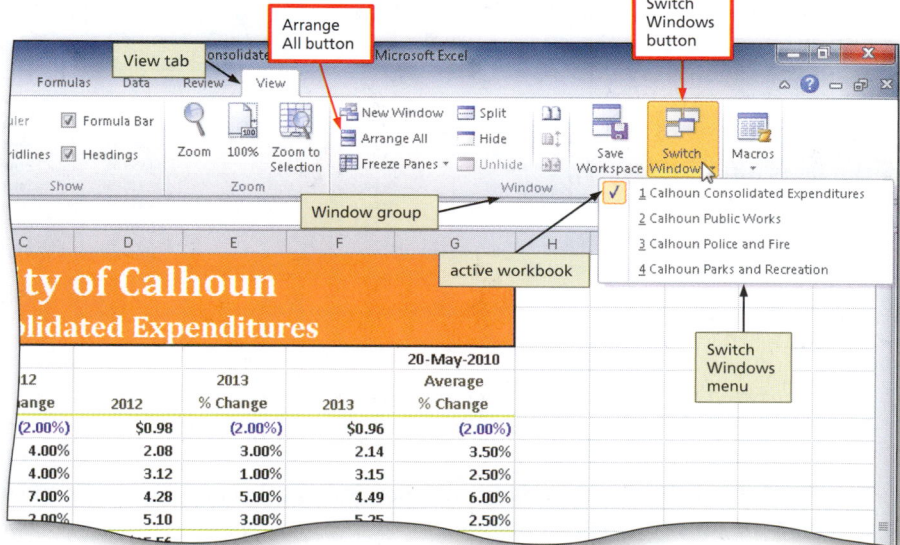

Figure 6–56

3

- Click the Arrange All button (View tab | Window group) to display the Arrange Windows dialog box.

- Click Vertical (Arrange Windows dialog box) to arrange the windows vertically, and then, if necessary, click the 'Windows of active workbook' check box to clear it (Figure 6–57).

Q&A

How can I arrange workbooks in the Excel window?

As shown in Figure 6–57, multiple opened workbooks can be arranged in four ways. The option name in the Arrange Windows dialog box identifies the resulting window's configuration. You can modify any of the arranged workbooks by clicking within its window to activate it. To return to showing one workbook, double-click its title bar as described in Step 5.

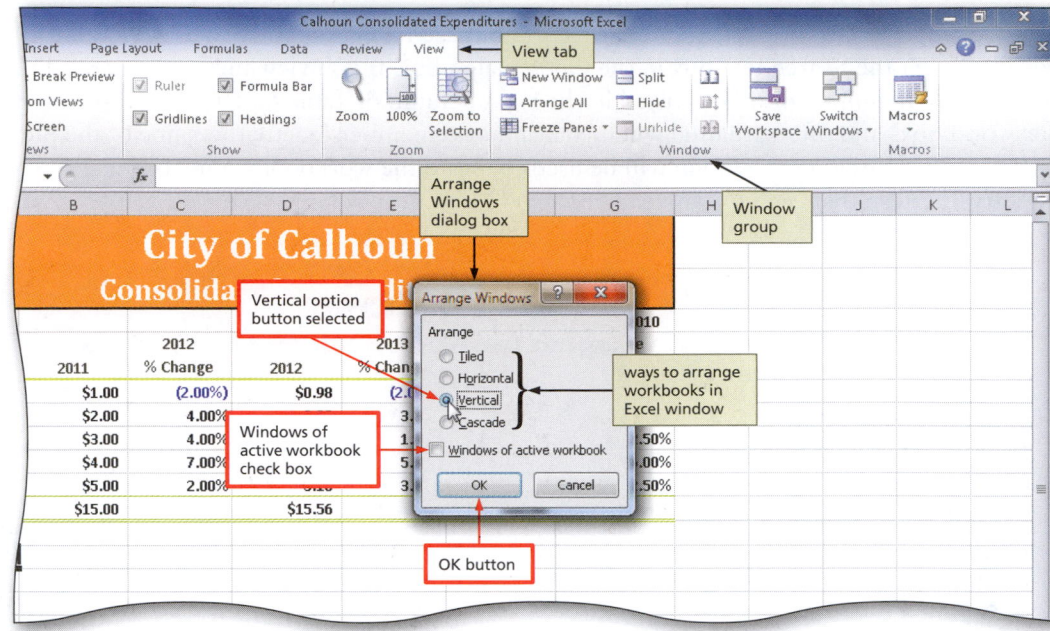

Figure 6–57

4

- Click the OK button (Arrange Windows dialog box) to display the opened workbooks arranged vertically (Figure 6–58).

Q&A

Why do the windows display horizontally across the screen, yet the screens were tiled vertically?

The tiling effect determines the change on an individual window, not the group of windows. When tiling windows vertically, therefore, each individual window appears vertically as tall as possible. When tiling windows horizontally, the windows appear as wide as possible.

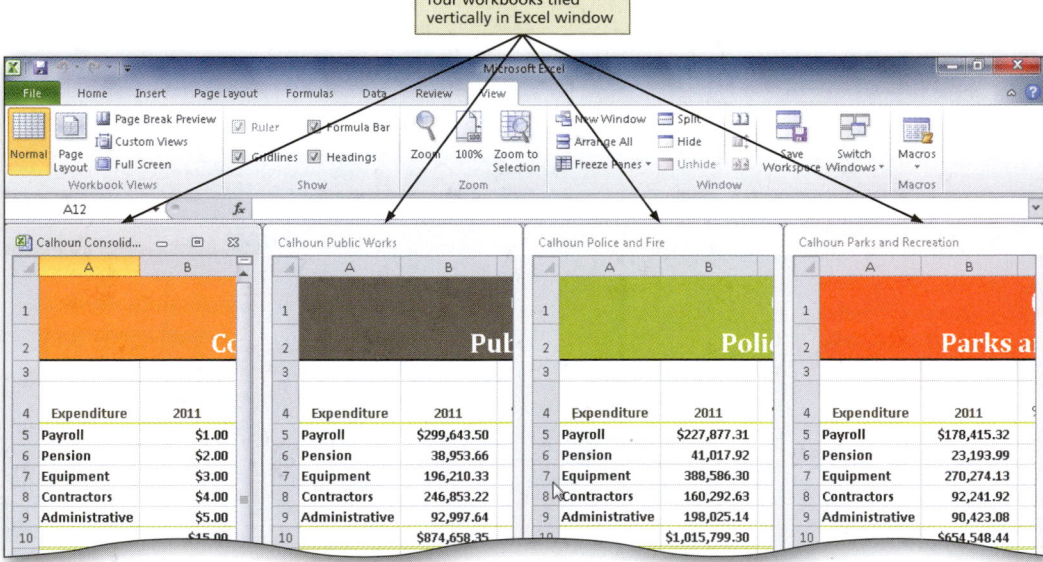

Figure 6–58

5

- Double-click the Calhoun Consolidated Expenditures title bar to maximize the window and hide the other opened workbooks.

To Create a Workspace File

If you plan to consolidate data from other workbooks, it is recommended that you first bind the workbooks together using a workspace file. A **workspace file** saves information about all the workbooks that are open. The workspace file does not contain the actual workbooks; rather, it stores information required to open the files associated with the workspace file, including file names, which file was active at the time of the save, and other display settings. After you create and save a workspace file, you can open all of the associated files by opening the workspace. The following steps create a workspace file from the files opened in the previous set of steps.

1

- With the four workbooks opened and the Calhoun Consolidated Expenditures workbook active, if necessary, display the View tab (Figure 6–59).

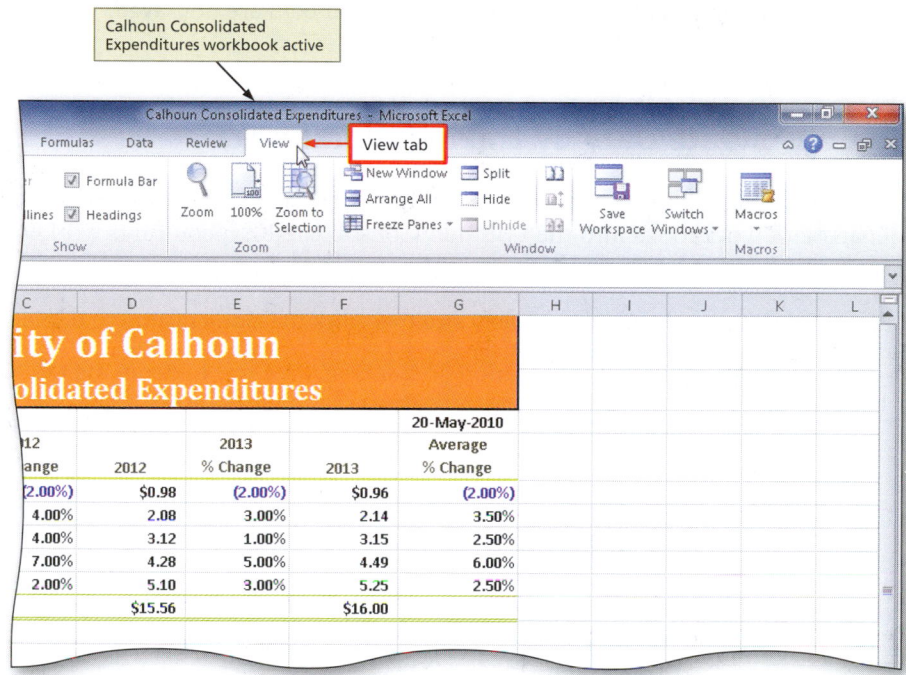

Figure 6–59

2

- Click the Save Workspace button (View tab | Window group) to display the Save Workspace dialog box.

- Select the drive for your USB port, Removable (E:) in this case, in the Address bar (Save Workspace dialog box).

- Navigate to the desired save location (in this case, the Excel folder in the CIS 101 folder [or your class folder] on the USB flash drive).

- Type **Calhoun Workspace** in the File name box to enter a name of a workspace to save (Figure 6–60).

Q&A

Can I still open the workbooks separately or must I always open the workspace?

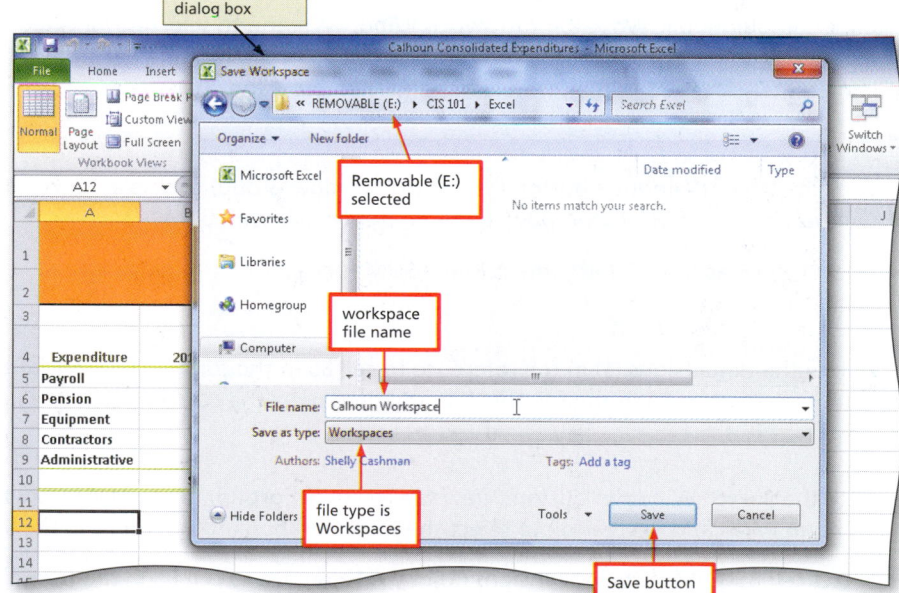

Figure 6–60

After the workspace is saved to disk, you can open the workbooks one at a time as you did in the past, or you can open all of the associated workbooks by opening the workspace. When you invoke the Open command, workspace file names appear in the Open dialog box, the same as any workbook file name.

- Click the Save button (Save Workspace dialog box) to save the file names of the workbooks open, of the workbooks displaying, and other display settings.

- If the Microsoft Excel dialog box is displayed for any of the workbooks, click the Don't Save button to ensure that any changes inadvertently made to the workbooks do not get saved.

- Open the Backstage view and then click the Exit button to quit Excel.

- If the Microsoft Excel dialog box is displayed for any workbooks that remain open, click the Don't Save button to ensure that any changes inadvertently made to the workbooks are not saved.

To Consolidate Data by Linking Workbooks

The following steps open the workspace file Calhoun Workspace and consolidate the data from the three department workbooks into the Calhoun Consolidated Expenditures workbook.

- Start Excel. Open the Backstage view and then click the Open button to display the Open dialog box.

- Navigate to the desired open location (in this case, the Excel folder in the CIS 101 folder [or your class folder] on the USB flash drive).

- Double-click Calhoun Workspace to open the four workbooks saved in the workspace.

- Make Calhoun Consolidated Expenditures the active worksheet. If necessary, double-click the Calhoun Consolidated Expenditures window title bar to maximize it.

2

- Select cell B5 and then click the Sum button (Home tab | Editing group) to begin a SUM function entry.

- Display the View tab and then click the Switch Windows button (View tab | Window group) to display the Switch Windows menu.

- Click Calhoun Public Works on the Switch Windows menu to select a worksheet to reference. Click cell B5 and then delete the dollar signs ($) in the reference to cell B5 in the formula bar so that the reference is not absolute. Click immediately after B5 in the formula bar and then press the COMMA key.

3

- Click the Switch Windows button (View tab | Window group) to display the Switch Windows menu and then click Calhoun Police and Fire workbook name to display the workbook.

- Select cell B5 as the next argument in the SUM function.

4

- Delete the dollar signs ($) in the reference to cell B5 in the formula bar so that the reference is not absolute. Click immediately after B5 in the formula bar and then press the COMMA key.

5

- Click the Switch Windows button (View tab | Window group) to display the Switch Windows menu and then click Calhoun Parks and Recreation to select the final workbook to reference in the SUM function.

- Select cell B5. Delete the dollar signs ($) in the reference to cell B5 in the formula bar so that the reference is not absolute.

- Click the Enter box to complete the SUM function.

Q&A

Why did the formulas need to be edited for each workbook?

As you link workbooks, remember that the cell reference inserted by Excel each time you click a cell in a workbook is an absolute cell reference ($B$5). You must edit the formula and change these to relative cell references because the SUM function later is copied to the range B6:B9. If the cell references are left as absolute, then the copied function always would refer to cell B5 in the three workbooks no matter where you copy the SUM function.

6

• With cell B5 active in the Calhoun Consolidated Expenditures workbook, drag the cell's fill handle through cell B9, and then select cell B5 (Figure 6–61).

7

• Click the Save button on the Quick Access Toolbar to save the workbook. If Excel displays a dialog box, select Overwrite changes.

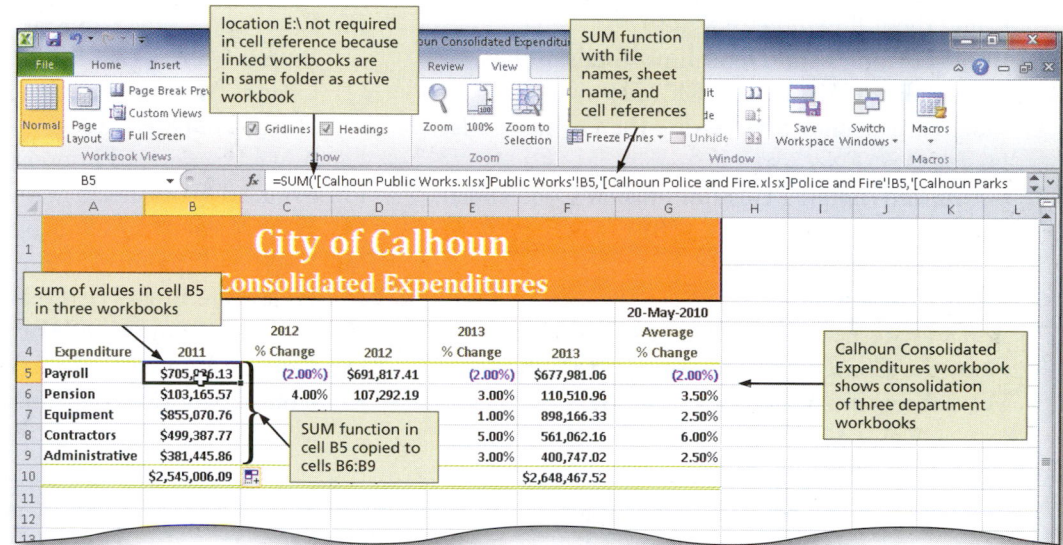

Figure 6–61

• If necessary, click the OK button (Microsoft Excel dialog box) to save the workbook.

• Print the worksheet.

Updating Links

Later, if you open the Calhoun Consolidated Expenditures workbook by itself, also called the **dependent workbook**, and if the linked workbooks are open, Excel automatically reads the data in the linked workbooks and recalculates formulas in the dependent workbook. The linked workbooks are called the **source workbooks**.

If the linked workbooks are not open, then Excel displays a security warning in a pane below the Ribbon. If you click the Enable Content button in the warning pane, Excel reads the data in the source workbooks and recalculates the formulas in the dependent workbook, but it does not open the source workbooks. If the three source workbooks are open along with the dependent workbook, as in the previous set of steps, Excel automatically updates the links (recalculates) in the Calhoun Consolidated Expenditures workbook when a value changes in any one of the source workbooks.

To Close All Workbooks at One Time and Quit Excel

To close all four workbooks at one time and quit Excel, complete the following steps.

1 Open the Backstage view and then click the Exit button to quit Excel.

2 If Excel displays the Microsoft Excel dialog box, click the Don't Save button.

BTW

Workspace Files
A workspace file saves display information about open workbooks, such as window sizes, print areas, screen magnification, and display settings. Workspace files do not contain the workbooks themselves.

BTW

Certification
The Microsoft Office Specialist (MOS) program provides an opportunity for you to obtain a valuable industry credential — proof that you have the Excel 2010 skills required by employers. For more information, visit the Excel 2010 Certification Web page (scsite.com/ex2010/cert).

Chapter Summary

In this chapter, you learned how to create and use a consolidated worksheet, customize formats, create styles, use 3-D reference to reference cells in other sheets and workbooks, add, remove, and change pages breaks, and create a workspace file. The items listed below include all the new Excel skills you have learned in this chapter.

1. Enter Sample Data in the Consolidated Worksheet Using the Fill Handle (EX 369)
2. Enter Formulas and Determine Totals in the Consolidated Worksheet (EX 371)
3. Assign a Currency Style Using the Format Cells Dialog Box (EX 376)
4. Create and Assign a Custom Format Code and a Comma Style Format (EX 378)
5. Create a New Style (EX 380)
6. Apply a New Style (EX 382)
7. Add a Worksheet to a Workbook (EX 384)
8. Copy the Contents of a Worksheet to Other Worksheets in a Workbook (EX 385)
9. Drill an Entry through Worksheets (EX 386)
10. Enter and Copy 3-D References Using the Paste Button Gallery (EX 391)
11. Change Margins and Center the Printout Horizontally (EX 396)
12. Add a Header and Footer (EX 397)
13. Print All Worksheets in a Workbook (EX 399)
14. Print Nonadjacent Sheets in a Workbook (EX 401)
15. Insert and Remove a Page Break (EX 401)
16. Hide Page Breaks (EX 403)
17. Search for and Open Workbooks (EX 405)
18. Create a Workspace File (EX 407)
19. Consolidate Data by Linking Workbooks (EX 408)

If you have a SAM 2010 user profile, your instructor may have assigned an autogradable version of this assignment. If so, log into the SAM 2010 Web site at www.cengage.com/sam2010 to download the instruction and start files.

Learn It Online

Test your knowledge of chapter content and key terms.

Instructions: To complete the Learn It Online exercises, start your browser, click the Address bar, and then enter the Web address `scsite.com/ex2010/learn`. When the Excel 2010 Learn It Online page is displayed, click the link for the exercise you want to complete and then read the instructions.

Chapter Reinforcement TF, MC, and SA
A series of true/false, multiple choice, and short answer questions that test your knowledge of the chapter content.

Flash Cards
An interactive learning environment where you identify chapter key terms associated with displayed definitions.

Practice Test
A series of multiple choice questions that test your knowledge of chapter content and key terms.

Who Wants To Be a Computer Genius?
An interactive game that challenges your knowledge of chapter content in the style of a television quiz show.

Wheel of Terms
An interactive game that challenges your knowledge of chapter key terms in the style of the television show *Wheel of Fortune*.

Crossword Puzzle Challenge
A crossword puzzle that challenges your knowledge of key terms presented in the chapter.

Apply Your Knowledge

Reinforce the skills and apply the concepts you learned in this chapter.

Consolidating Data in a Workbook

Note: To complete this assignment, you will be required to use the Data Files for Students. See the inside back cover of this book for instructions on downloading the Data Files for Students, or contact your instructor for information about accessing the required files.

Instructions: Follow the steps below to consolidate the four quarterly mileage cost sheets on the Yearly Costs sheet in the workbook Apply 6-1 Yearly Mileage Costs (Figure 6–62). At the conclusion of the instructions, the Yearly Mileage Costs sheet be should displayed as shown in the lower screen in Figure 6–62.

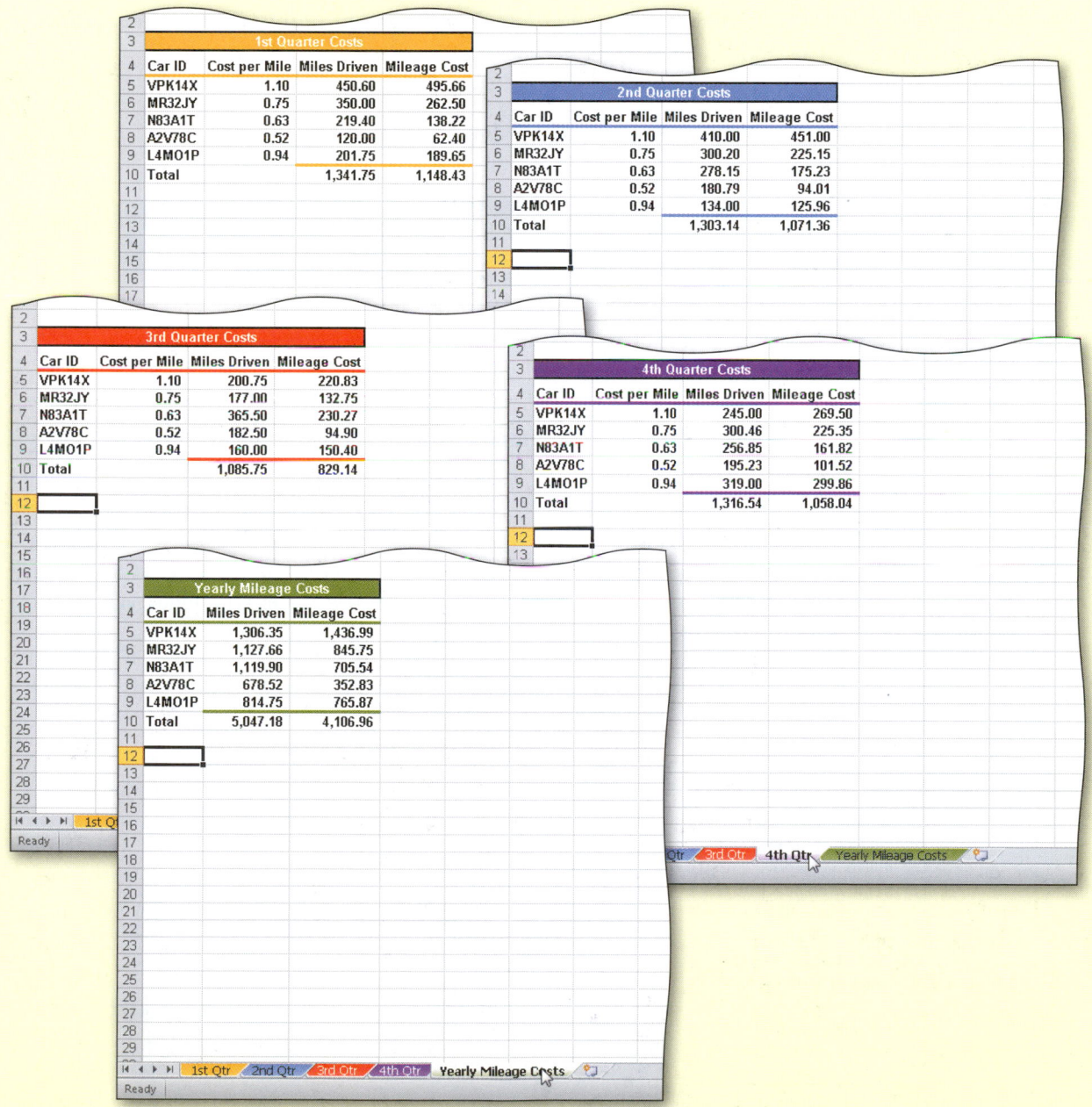

Figure 6–62

Continued >

Apply Your Knowledge *continued*

Perform the following tasks:

1. Start Excel. Open the workbook Apply 6-1 Yearly Mileage Costs from the Data Files for Students and then save the workbook as Apply 6-1 Yearly Mileage Costs Complete. One by one, click the first four tabs and review the quarterly payroll totals. Click the Yearly Mileage Costs sheet tab.

2. Determine the miles driven totals on the Yearly Mileage Costs sheet by using the SUM function and 3-D references to sum the hours worked on the four quarterly sheets in cell B5. Do the same to determine the yearly mileage cost in cell C5. Copy the range B5:C5 to the range B6:C9 by using the Copy button (Home tab | Clipboard group) and the Formulas command on the Paste gallery (Home tab | Clipboard group).

3. Change the document properties as specified by your instructor. Select all five worksheets. Add a worksheet header with your name, course number, and other information as specified by your instructor. Add the page number and total number of pages to the footer. Center all worksheets horizontally on the page and print without gridlines. Preview and print the five worksheets. Click the Yearly Mileage Costs sheet tab to select the sheet.

4. Save the workbook with the new page setup. Close the workbook.

5. Submit the assignment as requested by your instructor.

Extend Your Knowledge

Extend the skills you learned in this chapter and experiment with new skills. You may need to use Help to complete the assignment.

Creating Custom Format Codes

Note: To complete this assignment, you will be required to use the Data Files for Students. See the inside back cover of this book for instructions on downloading the Data Files for Students, or contact your instructor for information about accessing the required files.

Instructions: Complete the following tasks.

1. Start Excel. Open the workbook Extend 6-1 Custom Format Codes from the Data Files for Students and then save the workbook as Extend 6-1 Custom Format Codes Complete. When completed, the Custom Formats sheet should appear as shown in Figure 6-63.

	A	B	C	D	E	F
1	Custom Format Codes					
2						
3						
4	10-digit phone number	(321) 787-4955				
5	6-digit number with text	PID 025831				
6	dollars and cents	110 dollars and .95 cents				
7	negative number with text	150.00 loss				
8	4-digit year with text	The year is 2012				
9	day followed by date	Thursday - 8/9/2012				
10	day and month with text	Day 4 of June				
11	negative % with parenthesis	(-80%)				
12	% and text	75% of work completed				
13	hours and minutes	11 hours and 30 minutes				
14	military time with text	1700 hours				
15						
16						

Figure 6-63

2. Select cell B4. Right-click the selected cell and click Format Cells on the shortcut menu to display the Format Cells dialog box. Click Custom in the Category list. Enter the format code for cell B4 as shown in Table 6–11.

Table 6–11 Format Codes	
Cell	**Format Code**
B4	(000) 000–0000
B5	"PID" 000000
B6	0 "dollars and" .00 "cents"
B7	#,##0.00; #,##0.00 "loss"
B8	"The year is " yyyy
B9	dddd "-" m/d/yyyy
B10	"Day " d "of" mmmm
B11	0%;(–0%)
B12	0% " of work completed"
B13	h "hours and " mm "minutes"
B14	hhmm "hours"

3. Using Table 6–11, select each cell in range B5:B14 and create the corresponding custom format code for each cell using the Format Cells dialog box.

4. Change the document properties as specified by your instructor. Change the worksheet header with your name, course number, and other information as specified by your instructor. Print the worksheet. Save the workbook.

5. Submit the assignment as requested by your instructor.

Make It Right

Analyze a workbook and correct all errors and/or improve the design.

Using Custom Formats, Rounding Totals, and Correcting 3-D Cell References

Note: To complete this assignment, you will be required to use the Data Files for Students. See the inside back cover of this book for instructions on downloading the Data Files for Students, or contact your instructor for information about accessing the required files.

Instructions: Start Excel. Open the workbook Make It Right 6-1 Maxwell Books and then save the workbook as Make It Right 6-1 Maxwell Books Complete. Correct the following design and formula problems so that the Sales Totals sheet appears as shown in Figure 6–64 on the following page.

Continued >

Make It Right *continued*

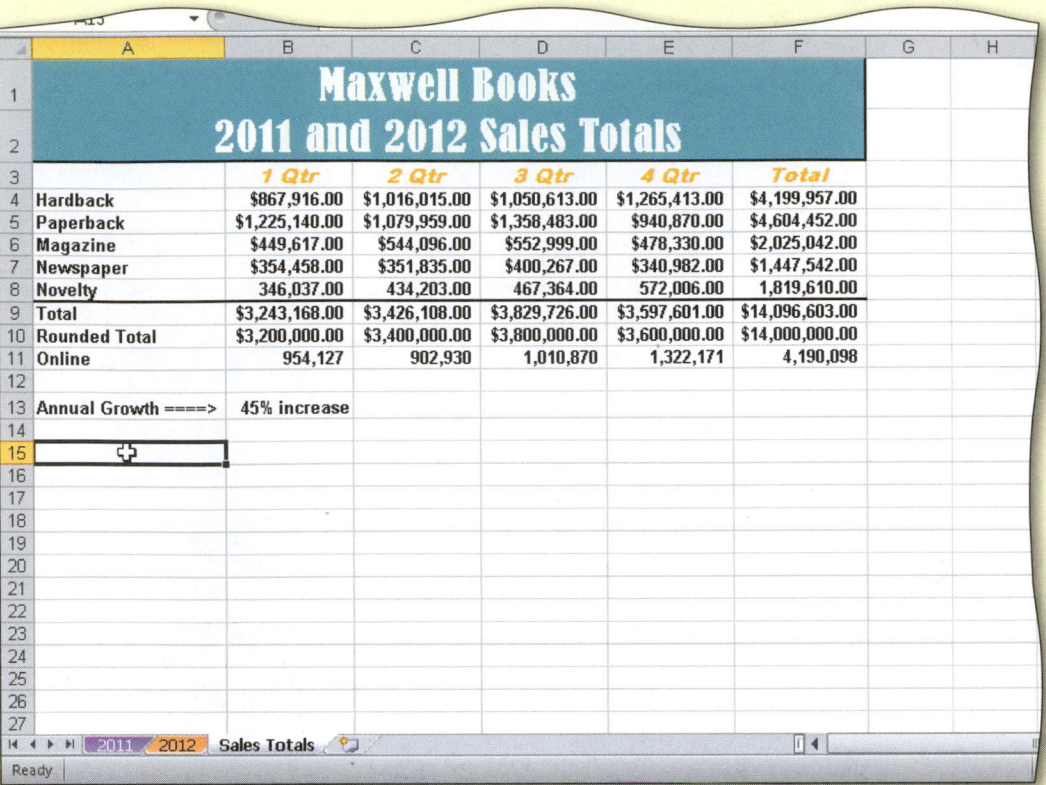

Figure 6–64

Perform the following tasks:

1. Edit the header for the worksheet and change the fixed date to the current date using the Current Date header element.

2. Select the cell range B3:E3. Change the custom format code by using the Format Cells Dialog box to change the format to show a number followed by the text "Qtr".

3. Select cell B4, the supposed sum of cell B4 on the 2011 and 2012 sheets. Note that the SUM function is not referencing cell B4 on the 2011 sheet. Reenter the SUM function and select the appropriate range to sum. Do the same for cells B5, B6, B7, and B8. Copy the range B4:B8 to the range C4:E8.

4. Select cell B11, the supposed sum of cell B10 on the 2011 and 2012 sheets. Note that the SUM function is not referencing cell B10 on the 2011 and 2012 sheet. Reenter the SUM function and select the appropriate range to sum. Copy the bell B11 to the range C11:E11.

5. Select Cell B10, the supposed rounded value of B9 to the nearest 100,000 value. Note that the value is rounding to the nearest 100 value. Reenter the ROUND function to round to the nearest 100,000 value. Copy the cell B10 to the range C10:E10.

6. Select cell B13. Change the custom format code by using the Format Cells Dialog box to change the format to show the percent followed by the text "increase".

7. Change the document properties as specified by your instructor. Change the three worksheet headers to include your name, course number, and other information as specified by your instructor.

8. Save the workbook, and submit the revised workbook as requested by your instructor.

In the Lab

Create a workbook using the guidelines, concepts, and skills presented in this chapter. Labs are listed in order of increasing difficulty.

Lab 1: Using a Master Sheet to Create a Multiple-Sheet Workbook

Note: To complete this assignment, you will be required to use the Data Files for Students. See the inside back cover of this book for instructions on downloading the Data Files for Students, or contact your instructor for information about accessing the required files.

Problem: AtHome Blu-Ray is a company that specializes in home Blu-Ray players. The company has three stores in Chicago, New York, and Seattle. Their corporate office is in Los Angeles. The corporate officers in Los Angeles use a master sheet to create a profit potential analysis workbook. The workbook contains four sheets, one for each of the three stores and one sheet to consolidate data and determine the company totals. The Consolidated sheet appears as shown in Figure 6–65.

AtHome Blu-Ray
Company Profit Potential

Company	Units On Hand	Store Discount	Average Cost	Total Cost	Average Unit Price	Total Value	May 20 Profit Potential
Memorex	371	$40.00	$98.75	$36,636.25	$105.22	$39,036.62	$2,400.37
Phillips	355	10.00	127.45	45,244.75	177.43	62,987.65	17,742.90
Pioneer	633	26.67	118.75	75,168.75	147.96	93,660.79	18,492.04
Samsung	485	15.00	101.48	49,217.80	134.24	65,106.40	15,888.60
Sony	555	28.33	135.27	75,074.85	170.60	94,681.15	19,606.30
Sylvania	679	30.00	165.80	112,578.20	213.82	145,183.78	32,605.58
Vizio	605	55.00	110.25	75,521.25	107.13	73,384.05	(2,137.20)
	3,763 Units			$469,441.85		$574,040.44	$104,598.59

Sheet tabs: **Consolidated** | Chicago | New York | Seattle

Ready

Figure 6–65

The master sheet used to create the profit potential analysis workbook is part of the Data Files for Students. Alice Stewart, the company's accountant, has asked you to use the master sheet to create the profit potential analysis workbook.

Instructions Part 1: *Perform the following tasks.*

1. Open the workbook Lab 6-1 AtHome Blu-Ray Master from the Data Files for Students. Save the workbook as a workbook using the file name, Lab 6-1 AtHome Blu-Ray Profit Potential Analysis.

2. Add a worksheet to the workbook between Sheet1 and Sheet2 and then paste the contents of Sheet1 to the three empty sheets.

Continued >

In the Lab *continued*

3. From left to right, rename the sheet tabs Consolidated, Chicago, New York, and Seattle. Color the tabs as shown in Figure 6–65. (The Consolidated tab uses the Tan, Accent 1 color.) On each of the three store sheets, change the subtitle in cell A2 to match the sheet tab name. Change the title style for each title area in the range A1:F1 to match the sheet tab color. Enter the data in Table 6–12 into the three store sheets.

Table 6–12 AtHome Blu-Ray Units on Hand and Store Discounts			
		Units on Hand	Store Discounts
Chicago	Memorex	100	$35.00
	Phillips	119	0.00
	Pioneer	135	15.00
	Samsung	180	35.00
	Sony	255	60.00
	Sylvania	179	10.00
	Vizio	201	50.00
New York	Memorex	75	$35.00
	Phillips	135	15.00
	Pioneer	200	30.00
	Samsung	146	10.00
	Sony	90	0.00
	Sylvania	175	25.00
	Vizio	225	60.00
Seattle	Memorex	196	$50.00
	Phillips	101	15.00
	Pioneer	298	35.00
	Samsung	159	0.00
	Sony	210	25.00
	Sylvania	325	55.00
	Vizio	259	55.00

4. On the Consolidated worksheet, use the SUM and AVERAGE functions, 3-D references, and copy and paste capabilities of Excel to total the corresponding cells on the three store sheets. First, compute the sum in cell B4 and then compute the average in cell C5. Copy the range B4:C5 to the range B5:C11. The Consolidated sheet should resemble Figure 6–65.

5. Change the document properties as specified by your instructor. Select all four sheets. Add a worksheet header with your name, course number, and other information as specified by your instructor. Add the page number and total number of pages to the footer. Change the left and right margins to .5.

6. With the four sheets selected, preview and then print the workbook in landscape orientation and use the Black and white option.

7. Save the workbook with the new page setup characteristics. Close the workbook.

8. Submit the assignment as requested by your instructor.

Instructions Part 2: Complete the following tasks.

1. Start Excel. Open the workbook Lab 6-1 AtHome Blu-Ray Profit Potential Analysis.

2. Select the range D6:H11 on the Consolidated worksheet. Select all the worksheets.

3. Use the Format Cells dialog box to apply a custom format of #,##0.00; [Green](#,##0.00).

4. Select the cell B12 on the Consolidated worksheet. Select all the worksheets.

5. Use the Format Cells dialog box to apply a custom format of #,##0 "Units". Widen Column B so that contents of cell B12 are visible.

6. Save the workbook and then close the workbook.

7. Submit the assignment as requested by your instructor.

Instructions Part 3: Complete the following tasks.

1. Start Excel. Open the workbook Lab 6-1 AtHome Blu-Ray Profit Potential Analysis.

2. Use the Cell Styles button (Home tab | Styles group) to create the following new cell styles:

   a. Name this style Month and Day. Use the Format button in the Cell Styles gallery to create a format using the Format Cells dialog box. Use the Number tab (Format Cells dialog box) to create a custom format using the format code mmmm d. Check only the Number and Alignment check boxes in the Style dialog box.

   b. Name this style My Title. Use the Format button to create a format using the Format Cells dialog box. Use the Font tab (Format Cells dialog box) to select the Broadway font. Check only the Alignment and Font check boxes in the Style dialog box.

   c. Name this style Grand Totals. Use the Format button in the Cell Styles gallery to create a format using the Format Cells dialog box. Use the Number tab (Format Cells dialog box) to create a custom currency style that colors negative numbers blue. Check only the Number and Alignment check boxes in the Style dialog box.

3. Select the cell H3 on the Consolidated worksheet. Select all the worksheets. Apply the Month and Day style to the cell.

4. Select the cell A1 on the Consolidated worksheet. Select all the worksheets. Apply the My Title style to the cell.

5. Select the cells E12, G12, and H12 on the Consolidated worksheet. Select all the worksheets. Apply the Grand Totals style to the cells.

6. Save the workbook and then close the workbook.

7. Submit the assignment as requested by your instructor.

In the Lab

Lab 2: Consolidating Data and Linking to a Workbook

Note: To complete this assignment, you will be required to use the Data Files for Students. See the inside back cover of this book for instructions on downloading the Data Files for Students, or contact your instructor for information about accessing the required files.

Problem: SciMat Containment is a company that manages three radioactive isotope containment facilities in the Western, Central, and Southern regions. Some agency watchdogs are concerned about containment costs while the material still is radioactive. The agency director has asked your group to prepare a workbook showing the amount of radioactive material remaining, containment costs, estimated agency appropriations, and the percentage of appropriations that will be spent on

Continued >

In the Lab *continued*

containment every year for the next decade. You have been given a master sheet to use to create your workbook as well as a workbook with the containment assumptions. The workbook you create will contain four sheets, one for each of the three regions and one sheet to consolidate data and determine the agency totals. The consolidated sheet, named Overall Costs, appears as shown in Figure 6–66.

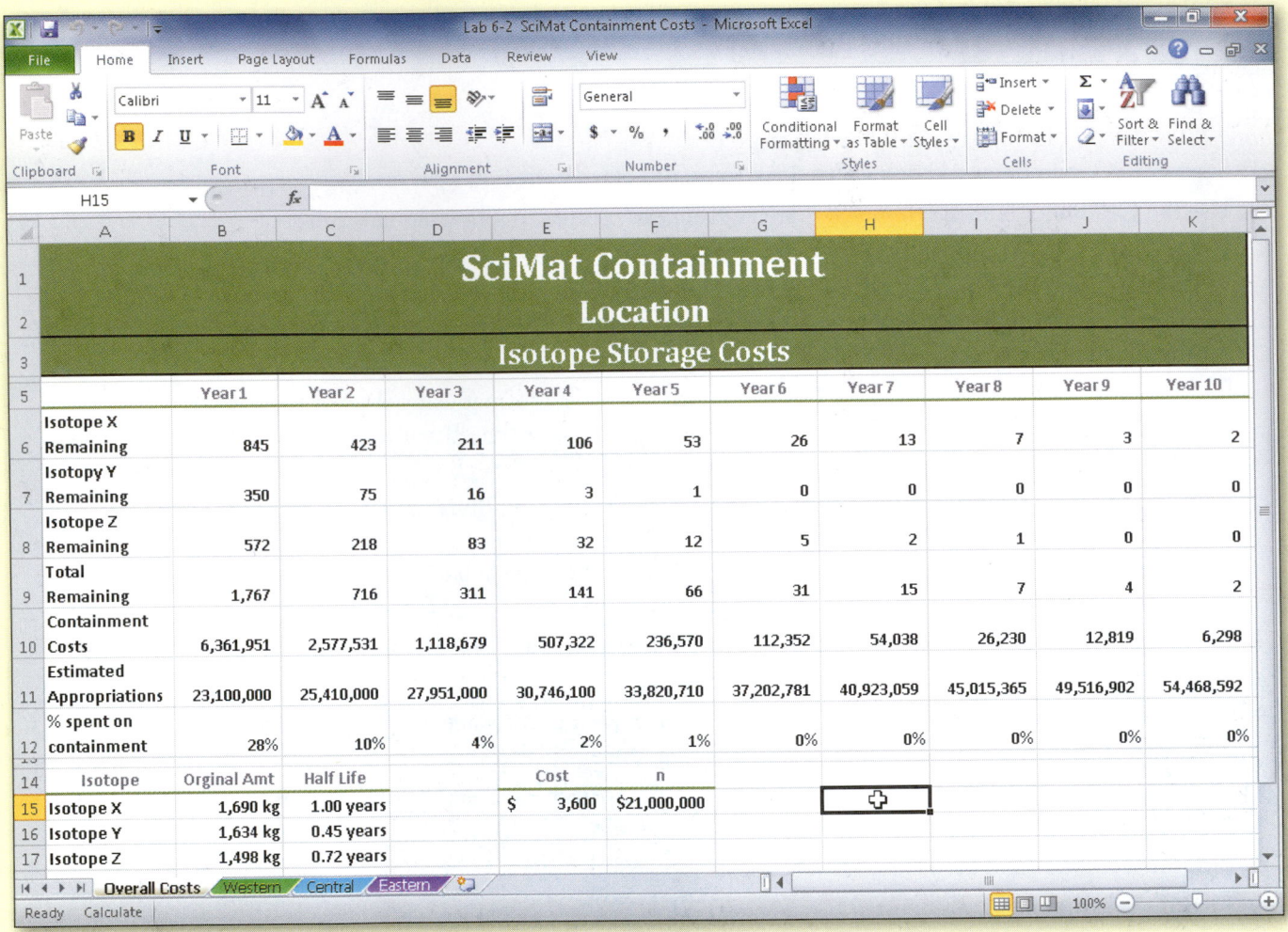

Figure 6–66

The master sheet and containment assumptions used to create the containment analysis workbook are part of the Data Files for Students.

Instructions Part 1: Perform the following tasks.

1. Open the workbook Lab 6-2 Containment Assumptions from the Data Files for Students.

2. Open the workbook Lab 6-2 SciMat Containment Master from the Data Files for Students. Save the workbook as a workbook using the file name, Lab 6-2 SciMat Containment Costs.

3. Add a worksheet to the workbook between Sheet1 and Sheet2 and then paste the contents of Sheet1 to the three empty sheets.

4. From left to right, rename the sheet tabs Overall Costs, Western, Central, and Eastern. Color the tabs as shown in Figure 6–66. (The Overall Costs tab uses the Tan, Accent 1, Darker 50% color.) On each of the three region sheets, change the subtitle in cell A2 to match the tab name.

Change the title style for each title area in the range A1:F1 to match the tab color. Enter the data in Table 6–13 into the three region sheets.

Table 6–13 SciMat Containment Isotope Starting Amounts		
		Original AMT
Western	Isotope X	300
	Isotope Y	750
	Isotope Z	500
Central	Isotope X	580
	Isotope Y	425
	Isotope Z	600
Eastern	Isotope X	810
	Isotope Y	459
	Isotope Z	398

5. On the Western worksheet, select cell E15 and select all worksheets except the Overall Costs sheet. Type '='. Click the Switch Windows button (View tab | Window group), and then click Lab 6-2 Containment Assumptions and then select cell B7 and press ENTER.

6. On the Western worksheet, select cell F15, select all worksheets except the Overall Costs sheet. Type '='. Click the Switch Windows button (View tab | Window group), and then click Lab 6-2 Containment Assumptions and then select cell B8 and press ENTER.

7. On the Overall Costs worksheet, select cell C15 and select all worksheets. Type '='. Click the Switch Windows button (View tab | Window group), and then click Lab 6-2 Containment Assumptions and then select cell B4 and press ENTER.

8. On the Overall Costs worksheet, select cell C16 and select all worksheets. Type '='. Click the Switch Windows button (View tab | Window group), and then click Lab 6-2 Containment Assumptions and then select cell B5 and press ENTER.

9. On the Overall Costs worksheet, select cell C17, select all worksheets. Type '='. Click the Switch Windows button (View tab | Window group), and then click Lab 6-2 Containment Assumptions and then select cell B6 and press ENTER.

10. On the Overall Costs worksheet, use the SUM function, 3-D references, and copy and paste capabilities of Excel to total the corresponding cells on the three region sheets. First, compute the sum in cell B15. Copy the cell B15 to the range B16:B17. Next, compute the sum in cell E15, and finally, compute the sum in cell F15. The Overall Costs sheet should resemble the one shown in Figure 6–66.

11. Change the document properties as specified by your instructor. Select all four sheets. Add a worksheet header with your name, course number, and other information as specified by your instructor. Add the page number and total number of pages to the footer. Change the left and right margins to .5.

12. With the four sheets selected, preview and then print the workbook in landscape orientation and use the Black and white option.

13. Save the workbook with the new page setup characteristics. Close the open workbooks.

14. Submit the assignment as requested by your instructor.

Continued >

In the Lab *continued*

Instructions Part 2:   Complete the following tasks.

1. Start Excel. Open the workbook Lab 6-2 SciMat Containment Costs.
2. Select the range B5:K5 on the Overall Costs worksheet. Select all the worksheets.
3. Use the Format Cells dialog box to apply a custom format of "Year" 0.
4. Select the range B15:B17 on the Overall Costs worksheet. Select all the worksheets.
5. Use the Format Cells dialog box to apply a custom format of #,##0 "kg".
6. Select the range C15:C17 on the Overall Costs worksheet. Select all the worksheets.
7. Use the Format Cells dialog box to apply a custom format of 0.00 "years".
8. Save the workbook and then close the workbook.
9. Submit the assignment as requested by your instructor.

In the Lab

Lab 3: Consolidating Data by Linking Workbooks

Note: To complete this assignment, you will be required to use the Data Files for Students. See the inside back cover of this book for instructions on downloading the Data Files for Students, or contact your instructor for information about accessing the required files.

Problem: The Apply Your Knowledge exercise in this chapter calls for consolidating the Miles Driven and Mileage Cost from four worksheets on a fifth worksheet in the same workbook (see Figure 6–62 on page EX 411). This exercise takes the same data stored in four separate workbooks and consolidates the Qty on Hand and Total Value by linking to a fifth workbook.

Instructions Part 1:   Perform the following tasks.

1. Start Excel. Open the following five files from the Data Files for Students. You can open them one at a time or you can open them all at one time by selecting the five files and then clicking the Open button.
   - Lab 6-3 Audio Ace Annual Inventory Totals
   - Lab 6-3 Audio Ace Quarter 1 Inventory Totals
   - Lab 6-3 Audio Ace Quarter 2 Inventory Totals
   - Lab 6-3 Audio Ace Quarter 3 Inventory Totals
   - Lab 6-3 Audio Ace Quarter 4 Inventory Totals

2. Click the Switch Windows button (View tab | Window group) and then click Lab 6-3 Audio Ace Annual Inventory Totals.

3. Click the Save Workspace button (View tab | Window group). When the Save Workspace dialog box is displayed, save the workspace using the file name, Lab 6-3 Audio Ace Inventory Workspace.

4. Close all the open workbooks. Open the workspace Lab 6-3 Audio Ace Inventory Workspace. When the Lab 6-3 Audio Ace Annual Inventory Totals window is displayed, click the Maximize button in the upper-right corner to maximize the window. Save the workbook using the file name, Lab 6-3 Part 1 Audio Ace Annual Inventory Totals.

5. Consolidate the data in the four quarterly inventory workbooks into the range B11:C14 in the workbook Lab 6-3 Part 1 Audio Ace Annual Inventory Totals by doing the following:
   a. Click cell B11. Display the Home tab and then click Sum button (Home tab | Editing group).
   b. Click the Switch Windows button (View tab | Window group) and then click Lab 6-3 Audio Ace Quarter 1 Inventory Totals. When the workbook is displayed, click cell C11, click the Switch Windows button (View tab | Window group), and then click Lab 6-3 Part 1 Audio Ace Annual Inventory Totals. Change the absolute cell reference $C$11 in the formula bar to the relative cell reference C11 by deleting the dollar signs. Click immediately after C11 in the formula bar and then press the COMMA key.

c. Click the Switch Windows button (View tab | Window group) and then click Lab 6-3 Audio Ace Quarter 2 Inventory Totals. When the workbook is displayed, click cell C11, click the Switch Windows button (View tab | Window group), and then click Lab 6-3 Part 1 Audio Ace Annual Inventory Totals. Change the absolute cell reference $C$11 in the formula bar to the relative cell reference C11 by deleting the dollar signs. Click immediately after C11 in the formula bar and then press the COMMA key.

d. Click the Switch Windows button (View tab | Window group) and then click Lab 6-3 Audio Ace Quarter 3 Inventory Totals. When the workbook is displayed, click cell C11, click the Switch Windows button (View tab | Window group), and then click Lab 6-3 Part 1 Audio Ace Annual Inventory Totals. Change the absolute cell reference $C$11 in the formula bar to the relative cell reference C11 by deleting the dollar signs. Click immediately after C11 in the formula bar and then press the COMMA key.

e. Click the Switch Windows button (View tab | Window group) and then click Lab 6-3 Audio Ace Quarter 4 Inventory Totals. When the workbook is displayed, click cell C11, click the Switch Windows button (View tab | Window group), and then click Lab 6-3 Part 1 Audio Ace Annual Inventory Totals. Change the absolute cell reference $C$11 in the formula bar to the relative cell reference C11 by deleting the dollar signs. Press the ENTER key to sum the four quarter hours worked. You should end up with an annual total of 777 quantity on hand in cell B11.

f. With the workbook Lab 6-3 Part 1 Audio Ace Annual Inventory Totals window active, select cell B11. Drag the fill handle through cell C11 to display the annual total value in cell C11. Select the range B11:C11. Drag the fill handle down to cell C14. When the Auto Fill Options button is displayed next to cell C14, click the Auto Fill Options button and then click the Fill Without Formatting option.

6. Change the document properties as specified by your instructor. Change the worksheet header with your name, course number, and other information as specified by your instructor. Preview and print the annual inventory totals. Save the workbook using the file name, Lab 6-3 Part 1 Audio Ace Annual Inventory Totals. Close all workbooks. Submit the assignment as requested by your instructor.

Instructions Part 2: Perform the following tasks to update the hours worked for Quarter 2 and Quarter 4.

1. Start Excel. Open Lab 6-3 Audio Ace Quarter 1 Inventory Totals from the Data Files for Students. Change the quantity on hand for item no. TZ3919 in row 12 from 145 to 219. Save the workbook using the file name, Lab 6-3 Audio Ace Quarter 1 Inventory Totals. Close the workbook.

2. Open Lab 6-3 Audio Ace Quarter 3 Inventory Totals. Change the quantity on hand for item no. LG6527 in row 14 from 160 to 145. Save the workbook using the file name, Lab 6-3 Audio Ace Quarter 3 Inventory Totals. Close the workbook.

3. Open Lab 6-3 Part 1 Audio Ace Annual Inventory Totals workbook saved earlier in Part 1 of this exercise. Save the workbook using the file name, Lab 6-3 Part 2 Audio Ace Annual Inventory Totals. Display the Data tab. Click the Edit Links button (Data tab | Connections group). Select each file in the Edit Links dialog box and then click the Update Values button to instruct Excel to apply the current values in the four source workbooks to the consolidated workbook (Figure 6–67).

4. Insert a page break on Row 8. Preview and print the consolidated workbook. Remove the page break Save the workbook. Submit the assignment as requested by your instructor.

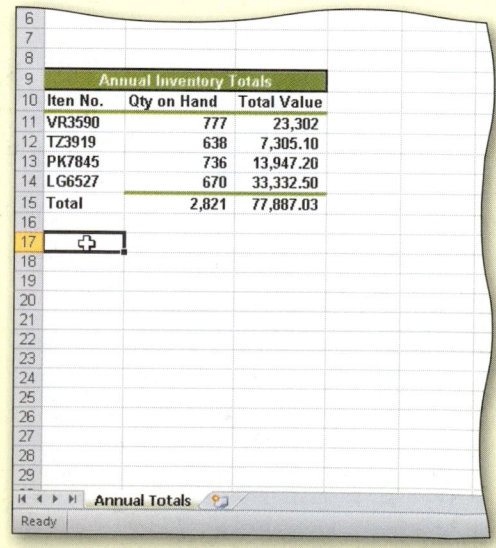

Figure 6–67

Cases and Places

Apply your creative thinking and problem solving skills to design and implement a solution.

1: Analyzing Annual College Expenses and Resources

Academic

College expenses are skyrocketing and your resources are limited. To plan for the upcoming year, you have decided to organize your anticipated expenses and resources in a workbook. The data required to prepare the workbook is shown in Table 6–14.

Create a workbook and add a worksheet for the consolidated data called Academic Year with the data for the first semester in Table 6–14 in mind. Sum both the expenses and resources for the semester. Copy the worksheet to create three more worksheets for each of the three semesters. Enter the data from Table 6–14 in each of the semester worksheets. Use 3-D cell references to consolidate the data on the Academic Year worksheet in the workbook. Use the concepts and techniques described in this chapter to format the workbook.

Table 6–14 Next Year's Anticipated College Expenses and Resources			
Expenses	**1st Semester**	**2nd Semester**	**Summer**
Rent	6,350.00	5,750.00	2,612.00
Car	1,500.00	1,500.00	900.00
Tuition	11,420.00	11,420.00	3,806.00
Books	1,350.00	1,450.00	230.00
Clothing	475.00	350.00	150.00
Personal Expenses	600.00	500.00	200.00
Miscellaneous	359.00	350.00	175.00
Resources	**1st Semester**	**2nd Semester**	**Summer**
Savings	3,500.00	3,500.00	600.00
Parents	5,300.00	8,200.00	2,120.00
Part-time job	1,540.00	1,295.00	785.00
Student Loan	8,000.00	8,000.00	4,205.00
Scholarship	2,500.00	2,500.00	500.00

2: Consolidating a Yearly Personal Budget

Personal

You want to create a workbook to help you analyze your personal budget. You have budgeted amounts and calculations of what you actually will pay for each month. You will include these in columns as well as a column to calculate the difference between the budgeted amounts and what you actually paid each month. Table 6–15 shows the data for the first four months.

Table 6–15 First 4 Months of Yearly Personal Expenses

		Budgeted Amount	Actual Amount
Jan	Rent	680.00	680.00
	Food	450.00	450.00
	Utilities	225.00	225.00
	Cell Phone	75.00	90.00
	Car Payments	275.41	275.41
	Insurance	149.50	149.50
	Clothing	250.00	100.00
	Internet	69.99	69.90
	Travel	110.00	250.00
Feb	Rent	680.00	680.00
	Food	450.00	450.00
	Utilities	225.00	225.00
	Cell Phone	75.00	90.00
	Car Payments	275.41	275.41
	Insurance	149.50	149.50
	Clothing	250.00	100.00
	Internet	69.99	69.90
	Travel	110.00	250.00
Mar	Rent	680.00	680.00
	Food	450.00	500.00
	Utilities	225.00	215.00
	Cell Phone	75.00	75.00
	Car Payments	275.41	275.41
	Insurance	149.50	149.50
	Clothing	250.00	230.00
	Internet	69.99	75.00
	Travel	110.00	100.00
Apr	Rent	680.00	680.00
	Food	450.00	450.00
	Utilities	225.00	225.00
	Cell Phone	75.00	90.00
	Car Payments	275.41	275.41
	Insurance	149.50	149.50
	Clothing	250.00	100.00
	Internet	69.99	69.90
	Travel	110.00	250.00

Continued >

Cases and Places *continued*

Create an annual worksheet based on the first month's personal expenses. Be sure to include a difference column that calculates the difference between the budgeted and actual amounts. Also include a total for the difference column. Using the annual worksheet, create worksheets for the 12 months. Enter the data for the first four months from Table 6–15. The rest of the 12 months follow the same pattern so you can use the data in Table 6–15 to fill in the remaining months.

Consolidate the budgeted and actual amounts on the annual worksheet using 3-D references. Using the techniques from the book, format the worksheet and add a custom format to the difference column so that it shows negative numbers as blue.

3: Analyzing Company Profits by Category

Professional

Starling Electronics sells various electronic devices and support materials ranging from HD TVs to wall mounts for the TVs. Merchandise is divided into six categories based on profit margin: TV & video (25%), cameras & camcorders (15%), audio (11%), game systems (20%), gadgets (9%), and support hardware (20%). Last year's sales data has been collected for the Philadelphia and Cincinnati Stores as shown in Table 6–16.

Develop a worksheet that can be used to determine marketing strategies for next year. Include sales, profit margins, profits (sales × profit margin), total sales, total profits, and functions to determine the most and least sales, profit margins, and profits. Create a custom style for the title of your worksheet.

Use the worksheet to create a workbook for each store and a consolidated workbook. Consolidate the data from the two stores into the consolidated workbook by applying techniques from the chapter regarding linking workbooks.

Table 6–16 Last Year's Sales for Philadelphia and Cincinnati Stores		
	Philadelphia	**Cincinnatti**
TV & Video	345,215.00	822,156.00
Cameras & Camcorders	140,135.00	255,812.00
Audio	75,912.00	72,345.00
Game Systems	46,125.00	58,012.00
Gadgets	8,532.00	12,589.00
Support Hardware	15,235.00	34,921.00

7 Creating Templates, Importing Data, and Working with SmartArt, Images, and Screen Shots

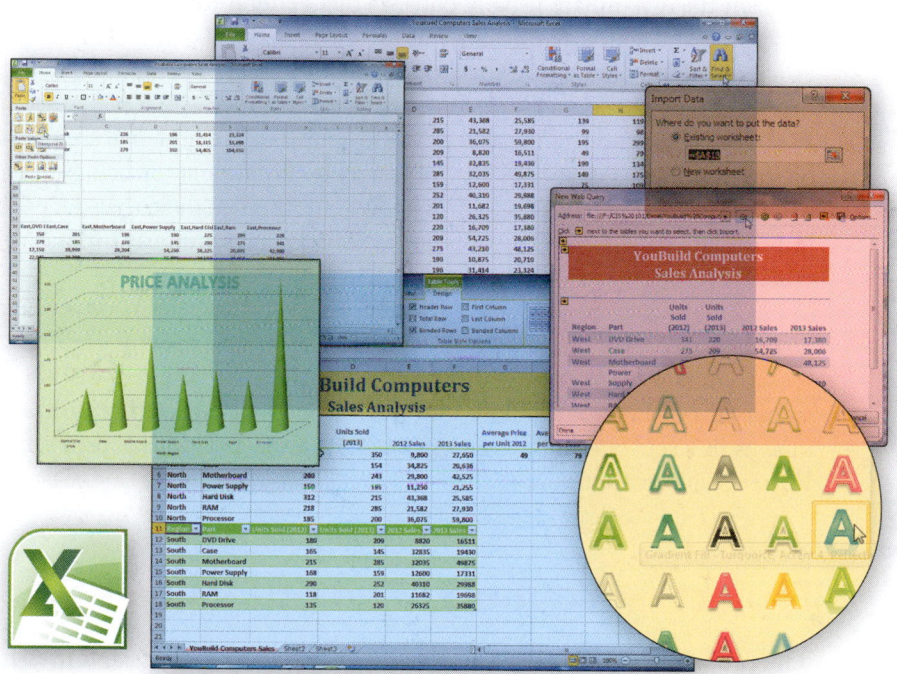

Objectives

You will have mastered the material in this chapter when you can:

- Create and use a template

- Import data from a text file, an Access database, a Web page, and a Word document

- Transpose data while pasting it

- Convert text to columns

- Use Find and Replace commands

- Draw a Clustered Cone chart

- Use WordArt to create a title and to create and modify shapes

- Insert and modify an image

- Insert and modify a SmartArt graphic

- Insert a screen shot

7 | Creating Templates, Importing Data, and Working with SmartArt, Images, and Screen Shots

BTW

XML

XML can describe any type of data. Banks use it to transfer financial information among various systems, and graphic artists use it to share multimedia data. The versatility of XML is matched by its simplicity. XML also is being used to make queries over the Web using a common set of rules available to any user. For example, a user can send an XML query to a travel Web site and receive the current information for a specific flight in XML format.

BTW

BTWs

For a complete list of the BTWs found in the margins of this book, visit the Excel 2010 BTW Web page (scsite.com/ex2010/btw).

Introduction

In today's business environment, you often find that you need to create multiple worksheets or workbooks that follow the same basic format. A **template** is a special workbook you can create and then use as a pattern to create new, similar workbooks or worksheets. A template usually consists of a general format (worksheet title, column and row titles, and numeric format) and formulas that are common to all the worksheets. One efficient way to create the workbook is first to create a template, save the template, and then copy the template to a workbook as many times as necessary.

Another important concept is the ability to use and analyze data from a wide variety of sources. In this chapter, you will learn how to import, or bring in, data from various external sources into an Excel worksheet and then analyze that data. Excel allows you to import data from a number of types of sources, including text files, Web pages, database tables, data stored in Word documents, and XML files.

Finally, a chart, a graphic, image, or screen shot often conveys information or an idea better than words or numbers. You insert and modify graphics, images, and screen shots in order to enhance the visual appeal of an Excel workbook and illustrate its contents. Many of the skills you learn when working with graphics, screen shots, and images in Excel will be similar when working in other Office programs, such as Word, PowerPoint, or Outlook.

Project — YouBuild Computers Sales Analysis

The project in the chapter follows proper design guidelines and uses Excel to create the workbook shown in Figure 7–1. YouBuild Computers provides computer parts to local businesses to sell for those who want to build their own computers. The company provides parts in four regions. The company owner has requested that the sales results for the last two years be compared among the four regions. One of the regions provides the requested data in text format (Figure 7–1a) rather than in an Excel workbook. To make use of that data in Excel, the data must be imported before it can be formatted and manipulated. The same is true of other formats in which the offices in various regions store data, such as Microsoft Access tables (Figure 7–1b), Web pages (Figure 7–1c), or Word documents (Figure 7–1d). Excel provides the tools necessary to import and manipulate the data from these sources into a worksheet (Figure 7–1e and Figure 7–1f). Using the data from the worksheet, you can create the Clustered Cone chart (Figure 7–1g).

You then can add SmartArt graphics to create the SmartArt, (Figure 7–1h) along with images. Finally, you can add a screen shot to support your work (Figure 7–1i).

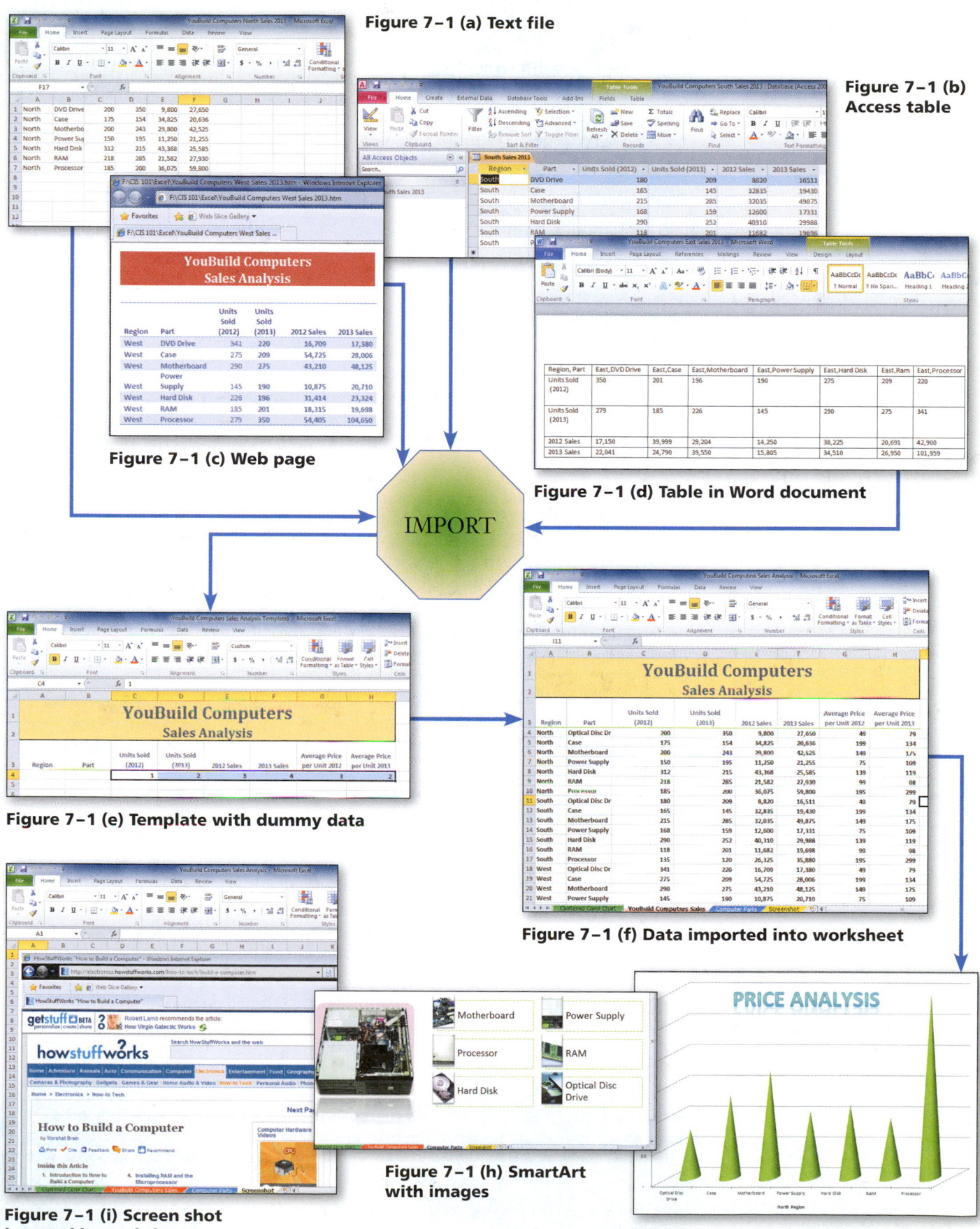

Figure 7–1 (a) Text file

Figure 7–1 (b) Access table

Figure 7–1 (c) Web page

Figure 7–1 (d) Table in Word document

IMPORT

Figure 7–1 (e) Template with dummy data

Figure 7–1 (f) Data imported into worksheet

Figure 7–1 (i) Screen shot inserted in worksheet

Figure 7–1 (h) SmartArt with images

Figure 7–1 (g) Clustered Cone chart

Overview

As you read this chapter, you will learn how to create the workbook shown in Figure 7–1 on the previous page by performing these general tasks:

- Create a template.
- Import data to an Excel worksheet from a text file, an Access database, a Web page, and a Word document.
- Insert WordArt on a chart.
- Insert and modify a SmartArt graphic.
- Add effects to a SmartArt graphic.
- Insert and modify an image.
- Add a screen shot to a worksheet.

Plan Ahead

General Project Guidelines

When creating templates, importing data, customizing charts, and modifying graphics, images, and screen shots, such as those shown in Figure 7–1, you should follow these general guidelines:

1. **Design the template and plan the formatting.** Templates help speed and simplify work because Excel users often work with the same types of problems repeatedly. Using a template allows you to begin your work with a preformatted worksheet. In the case of YouBuild Computers, the template saves the work of formatting the sales analysis worksheet. The formatting is done once in the template, and then that formatting is carried over to the new worksheet automatically.

2. **Analyze the existing workbook and the formats of the data to be imported.** You should have a good understanding of the layout of the data you want to import and how each data element will be arranged in the worksheet.

3. **Determine whether data you import needs to be standardized.** When you import data from multiple sources into a single workbook, the terminology used in each source might vary slightly. To make the terminology consistent, it may be necessary to find and replace text.

4. **Plan the layout and location of the required chart.** The chart may require additional artwork, including WordArt and, therefore, would be more suited for placement on a new worksheet. A Clustered Cone chart type is a proper choice for the YouBuild Computers chart because data from a few sales regions is compared. The tapering of the cones allows space for additional elements without any overlapping.

5. **Choose the type of SmartArt graphics to add.** Consider what you want to convey in your SmartArt. For example, for the components used in building a computer, the Picture Strips works best for displaying the different components and their names.

6. **Obtain the images to be used in the worksheet.** The images to be used are included with the Data Files for Students. Once the images are inserted on the worksheet, the image files no longer are needed because copies of the images become part of the worksheet. When obtaining an image, you must use only those images for which you have permission. Several sources provide royalty-free images, meaning that you do not have to pay to use them.

When necessary, more specific details concerning the above guidelines are presented at appropriate points in the chapter. The chapter also will identify the actions performed and decisions made regarding these guidelines during the creation of the workbook shown in Figure 7–1.

Figure 7–2 illustrates the requirements document for the YouBuild Computers Sales Analysis worksheet. It includes the needs, source of data, calculations, and other facts about the worksheet's development.

REQUEST FOR NEW WORKBOOK

Date Submitted:	January 1, 2013
Submitted By:	Carla Francis
Worksheet Title:	YouBuild Computers Sales Analysis
Needs:	The needs are as follows: 1. A template (Figure 7-1e) that can be used to create similar worksheets. 2. A workbook made from the template containing a worksheet (Figure 7-1f) that combines data imported from the four sales regions (Figures 7-1a, 7-1b, 7-1c, 7-1d). 3. A chart (Figure 7-1g) that compares the unit prices for the different computer parts in inventory for the North region. The chart should be placed on a separate sheet.
Source of Data:	The four sales managers for YouBuild Computers will submit data from their respective regions via a text file (North), an Access database (South), a Web page (West), and a Word document (East).
Calculations:	Include the following formulas in the template for each item: 1. Avg . Price per Unit 2012 = IF(Units Sold (2012) > 0, 2012 Sales / Units Sold (2012), 0) 2. Avg . Price per Unit 2013 = IF(Units Sold (2013) > 0, 2013 Sales / Units Sold (2013), 0)
Chart Requirements:	Create a Clustered Cone chart to compare the average price per unit for the North region. Use WordArt to create a title for the chart to enhance its appearance.

Approvals

Approval Status:	X	Approved
		Rejected
Approved By:	Juan Gutierrez	
Date:	January 10, 2013	
Assigned To:	S. Freund, Spreadsheet Specialist	

Figure 7–2

BTW

Workbook Survival
For workbooks to be successful and survive their expected life cycle in a business environment, they must be well documented and easy to understand. You document a workbook by adding comments to cells that contain complex formulas or to cells containing content that may not be understood easily. The documentation also should serve those who will maintain the workbook. You create easy-to-understand workbooks by reviewing alternative designs prior to creating the workbook. The more time you spend documenting and designing a workbook, the easier it will be for users and spreadsheet maintenance specialists to understand.

To Start Excel

If you are using a computer to step through the project in this chapter and you want your screens to match the figures in this book, you should change your screen's resolution to 1024 × 768. The following steps start Excel.

1 Start Excel.

2 If the Excel window is not maximized, click the Maximize button next to the Close button on its title bar to maximize the window.

Creating Templates

The first step in building the workbook is to create and save a template that contains the titles, column and row headings, formulas, and formats used on each of the worksheets.

Plan Ahead

> **Design the template and plan the formatting.**
>
> As mentioned earlier, a template is workbook that you use to create other similar workbooks. A template usually contains data and formatting that appears in every workbook created from that template. On Microsoft Office Online, Microsoft provides templates you can download and use as the basis for workbooks. You also can develop custom templates by creating a workbook and then saving it as a template. Because the template will be used to create a number of other worksheets, make sure you consider the layout, cell formatting, and contents of the workbook as you design the template.
>
> - **Set row heights and column widths.** Row heights and column widths should be set to sizes large enough to accommodate future needs.
>
> - **Use placeholders for data when possible.** Placeholders can guide users of the template regarding what type of data to enter in cells. For example, the words Sales Analysis should be used in the subtitle to indicate to a user of the template that the worksheet is included for sales analysis.
>
> - **Use dummy data to verify formulas.** When a template is created, **dummy data** — that is, sample data used in place of actual data to verify the formulas in the template — should be used in place of actual data to verify the formulas in the template. Selecting simple numbers such as 1, 2, and 3 allows you to check quickly to see if the formulas are generating the proper results. In templates with more complex formulas, you may want to use numbers that test the extreme boundaries of valid data.
>
> - **Format cells in the template.** Formatting should be applied to titles and subtitles that can be changed to provide cues to worksheet users. For example, using a fill color for the title and subtitle makes the text more noticeable. All numeric cell entry placeholders — dummy data — should be properly formatted for unit numbers and currency amounts.

BTW

Templates
Templates are most helpful when you need to create several similar or identical workbooks. They help reduce work and ensure consistency. Templates can contain: (1) text and graphics, such as a company name and logo; (2) formats and page layouts; and (3) formulas or macros.

After the template is saved, it can be used every time a similar workbook is developed. Because templates help speed and simplify their work, many Excel users create a template for each project on which they work. Templates can be simple — possibly using a special font or worksheet title, or they can be more complex — perhaps using specific formulas and format styles, such as the template for the YouBuild Computers Sales Analysis workbook.

Creating a template, such as the one shown in Figure 7–3, follows the same basic steps used to create a workbook. The only difference between developing a workbook and a template is the file type used to save the template.

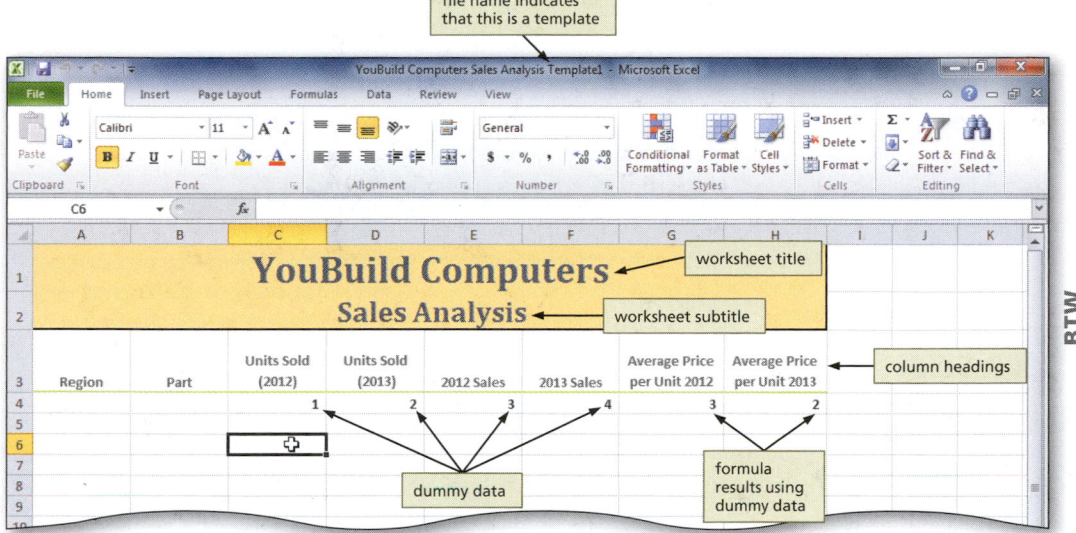

Figure 7–3

BTW

Dummy Numbers
As you develop more sophisticated workbooks, you need to create good test data to ensure your workbooks are free of errors. The more you test a workbook, the more confident you will be in the results it generates. Always take the time to select dummy data that tests the limits of the formulas.

BTW

The Ribbon and Screen Resolution
Excel may change how the groups and buttons within the groups appear on the Ribbon, depending on the computer's screen resolution. Thus, your Ribbon may look different from the ones in this book if you are using a screen resolution other than 1024 × 768.

To Bold the Font and Adjust the Row Heights and Column Widths of the Template

The first step in creating the template is to format the cells. The following steps change the font style to bold and adjust the height of row 3 to 45.75 points, the column widths of columns A through F to 13.00 characters, and the column widths of columns G and H to 14.00 characters.

1 Click the Select All button immediately above row heading 1 and to the left of column heading A and then click the Bold button (Home tab | Font group) to bold the cells. Select cell A1 to deselect the worksheet.

2 Drag the bottom boundary of row heading 3 down until the ScreenTip, Height 45.75 (61 pixels), appears, to change the height of the row.

3 Click column heading A, drag through to column heading F, and then drag the right boundary of column heading F right until the ScreenTip, Width: 13.00 (96 pixels), appears, to change the width of the selected columns.

4 Click column heading G, drag through to column heading H, and then drag the right boundary of column heading H right until the ScreenTip, Width: 14.00 (103 pixels), appears, to change the width of the selected columns. Select cell A1 to deselect columns G through H.

To Enter the Title and Subtitle in the Template

The following steps enter the titles in cells A1 and A2.

1 Type `YouBuild Computers` in cell A1 and then press the DOWN ARROW key to enter the worksheet title.

2 Type `Sales Analysis` in cell A2 and then press the DOWN ARROW key to enter the worksheet subtitle.

To Enter Column Titles in the Template

The following steps enter the column titles in row 3.

1 In cell A3, type `Region` and then press the RIGHT ARROW key to enter the title for column A.

2 In cell B3, type `Part` and then press the RIGHT ARROW key to enter the title for column B.

3 In cell C3, type `Units Sold` and then press ALT+ENTER. Type `(2012)` and then press the RIGHT ARROW key to enter the title for column C on two lines.

4 With cell D3 active, enter the remaining column titles in row 3 (shown in Figure 7–4).

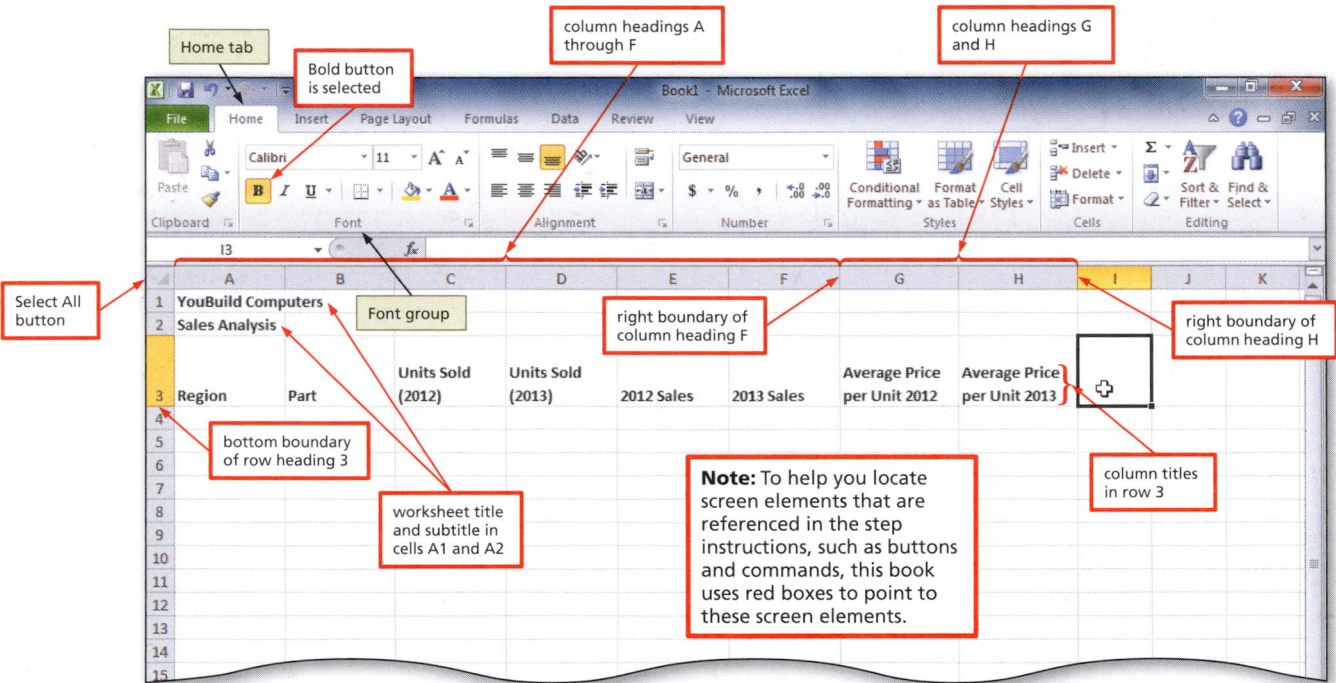

Figure 7–4

To Enter Sample Data in the Template Using the Fill Handle

While creating the YouBuild Computers template in this chapter, sample data is used for the Region, Part, Units Sold (2012), Units Sold (2013), 2012 Sales, and 2013 Sales (range A4:F4). The sample data is entered by using the fill handle to create a series of numbers in columns A through F for row 4. The series in row 4 begins with 1 and increments by 1. Recall that you must enter the first two numbers in a series so that Excel can determine the increment amount as illustrated in the following steps.

1 Select cell C4. Type `1` and then press the RIGHT ARROW key to enter the first number in the series.

2 Type `2` and then press the ENTER key to enter the second number in the series.

3 Select the range C4:D4. Drag the fill handle through cell F4 to create the series 1 through 4 in increments of 1 in the range C4:F4 (Figure 7–5).

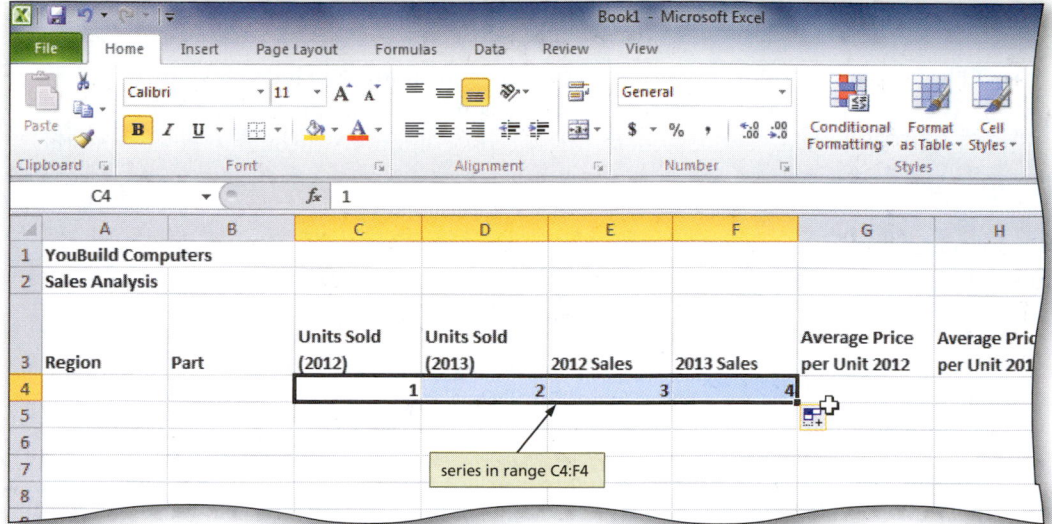

Figure 7–5

To Enter an IF Function

The following steps use the IF function to enter formulas to calculate the average price per unit for 2012 and 2013.

1 Select cell G4. Type `=IF(C4>0, E4/C4, 0)` as the formula for calculating the average price per unit for 2012, and then press the RIGHT ARROW key to select cell H4.

2 Type `=IF(D4>0, F4/D4, 0)` and then press the ENTER key to enter the formula for calculating the average price per unit for 2013 in cell H4 (Figure 7–6).

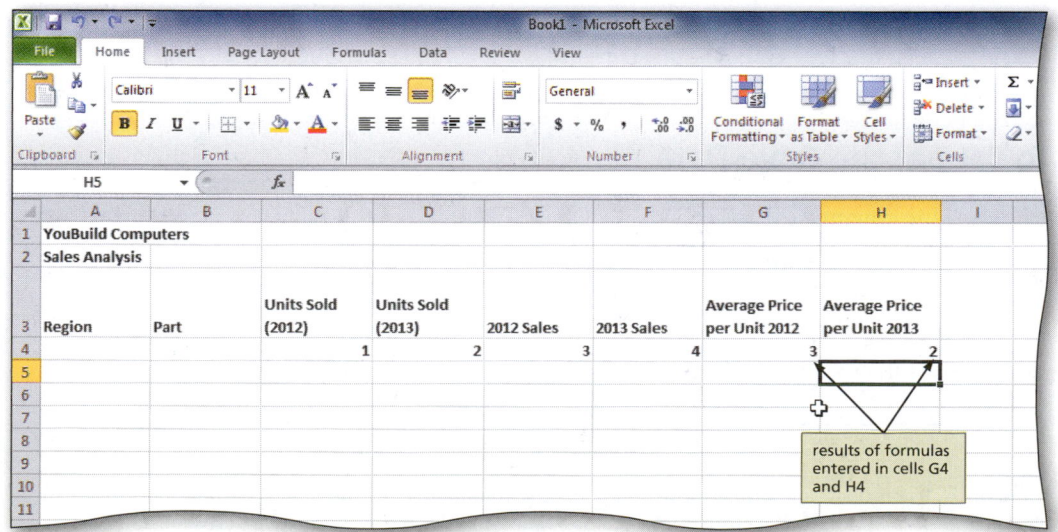

Figure 7–6

To Format the Template Title and Subtitle

The steps used to format the template title and subtitle include changing the text in cell A1 to 28-point with the Title cell style; changing the text in cell A2 to 22-point with the Title cell style; centering both titles across columns A through G; changing the title background color to light blue, and the title font color to white; and drawing a thick box border around the title area (cells A1 and A2). The color scheme associated with the default Office template also will be changed to a new color scheme. One reason to change the color scheme is to add variety to the look of the worksheet that you create. The following steps format the title and subtitle.

1 Click Page Layout on the Ribbon to display the Page Layout tab. Click the Colors button (Page Layout tab | Themes group) and then click Metro in the Colors gallery to apply the Metro colors to the worksheet.

2 Select the range A1:A2. Display the Home tab, and then apply the Title cell style to the range. Select cell A1. Click the Font Size box arrow (Home tab | Font group) and then click 28 in the Font Size list to change the font size of cell A1. Select the range A1:H1. Click the Merge & Center button (Home tab | Alignment group) to merge and center the selected cells.

3 Select cell A2, click the Font Size box arrow (Home tab | Font group), and then click 22 in the Font Size list to change the font size of cell A2. Select the range A2:H2. Click the Merge & Center button (Home tab | Alignment group) to merge and center the selected cells.

4 Select the range A1:A2, click the Fill Color button arrow (Home tab | Font group), and then click Gold, Accent 3, Lighter 60% (column 7, row 3) on the Fill Color palette to set the fill color for the range.

5 Click the Borders button arrow (Home tab | Font group), and then click Thick Box Border in the Borders gallery to apply a border to the range.

6 Select cell A3 to deselect the range A1:A2.

To Format the Column Titles

The following steps format the column titles in row 3.

1 Select the range A3:H3, click the Center button (Home tab | Alignment group), and then apply the Heading 3 cell style to the range.

To Format the Table Data

The following steps format the cells in row 4 to use the Comma style.

1 Select the range C4:H4.

2 Apply the Comma style to the range.

3 Decrease the decimal of C4:H4 twice to not show any decimal places (Figure 7–7).

BTW

Summing a Row or Column
You can reference an entire column or row in a function argument by listing only the column or only the row. For example, =SUM(a:a) sums all the values in all the cells in column A, and =SUM(1:1) sums all the values in all the cells in row 1. You can verify this by entering =SUM(a:a) in cell C1 and then begin entering numbers in a few of the cells in column A. Excel will respond by showing the sum of the numbers in cell C1.

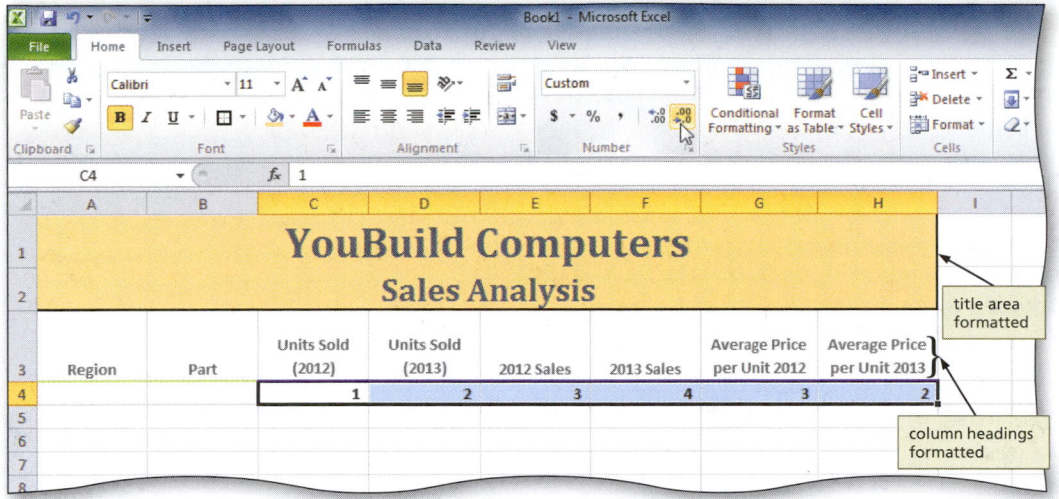

Figure 7–7

To Save the Template

Saving a template is similar to saving a workbook, except that the file type, Excel Template, is selected in the 'Save as type' box in the Save As dialog box. The following steps save the template on a USB flash drive in drive F using the file name, YouBuild Computers Sales Analysis Template.

1

• Update the document properties with your name and any other relevant information as specified by your instructor to identify your workbook.

• Change the sheet name to YouBuild Computers Sales to provide a descriptive name for the worksheet.

• Change the tab color to red to format the tab.

• Click the Save button on the Quick Access Toolbar to display the Save As dialog box (Figure 7–8).

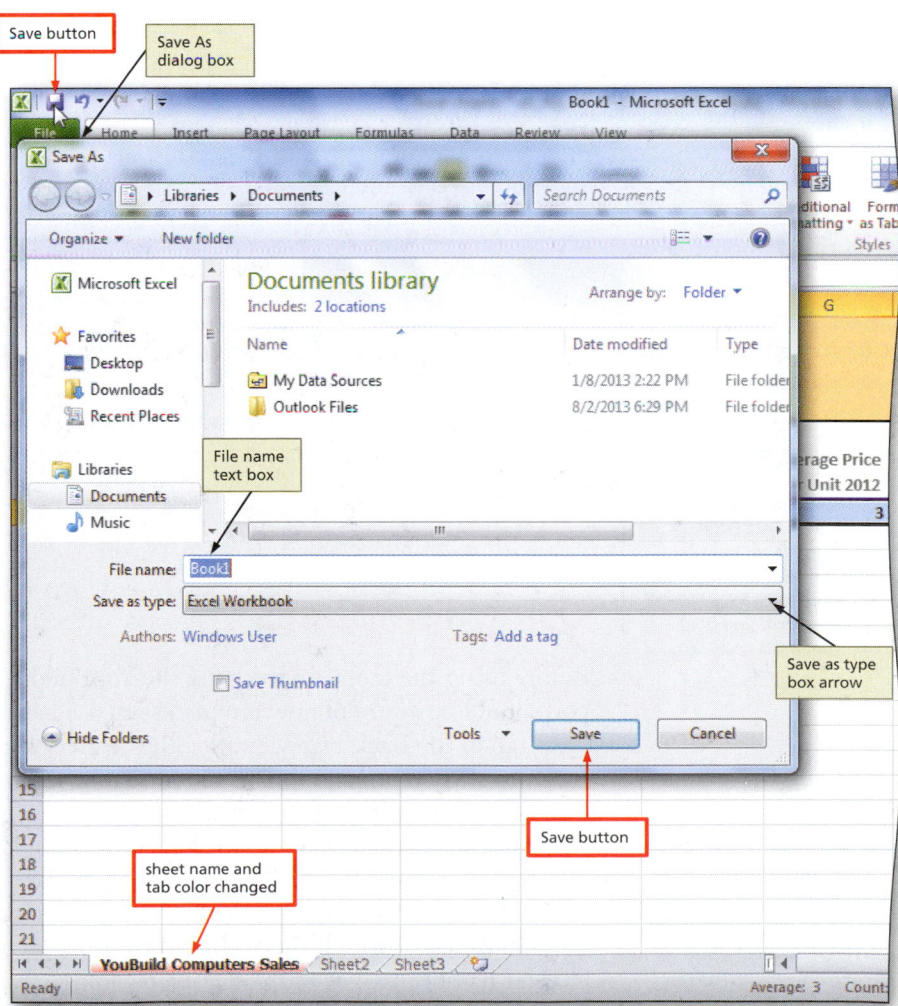

Figure 7–8

2

- Type **YouBuild Computers Sales Analysis Template** in the File name text box to enter a name for the file.

- Click the 'Save as type' box arrow and then click Excel Template in the list to specify that this workbook is saved as a template.

- Navigate to the location of the file to be saved (in this case, the Excel folder in the CIS 101 folder [or your class folder] on the USB flash drive).

- Click the Save button (Save As dialog box) to save the template on the USB flash drive and display the file name, YouBuild Computers Sales Analysis Template, on the title bar (Figure 7–9).

Q&A

Why does Excel change the folder name when the Excel Template file type is chosen?

When the Excel Template file type is chosen in the 'Save as type' box, Excel automatically changes the contents of the Save in box to the Templates folder created when Office 2010 was installed. In a production environment — that is, when you are creating a template for a business, school, or personal application — the template typically would be saved in the Templates folder, not on the USB flash drive.

new file name on title bar

Close Window button

Figure 7–9

3

- Click the Close Window button on the right side of the worksheet window to close the workbook and leave Excel open.

Other Ways

1. Press CTRL+S, type file name, select Excel Template in 'Save as type' box, select drive or folder, click Save button (Save As dialog box)

Using Templates

Before using the template to create the YouBuild Computers Sales Analysis workbook, you should be aware of how templates are used and their importance. If you click the New tab in the Backstage view, the New gallery appears (Figure 7–10). The New gallery includes a My templates link in the Available Templates list, which you can click to view a list of Excel templates that you have saved on your computer.

Recall that Excel automatically chose Templates as the Save in folder when the template in this chapter initially was saved (Figure 7–8 on the previous page). Saving templates in the Templates folder rather than another folder is the standard procedure in the business world. If the YouBuild Computers Sales Analysis Template created in this chapter had been saved in the Templates folder, then the template would appear in the New dialog box after clicking My templates in the Available Templates list. The template then could have been selected to create a new workbook.

When you select a template from the New gallery or New dialog box to create a new workbook, Excel names the new workbook using the template name with an appended digit 1 (for example, Template1). This is similar to what Excel does when you first start Excel and it assigns the name Book1 to the workbook.

Excel provides additional workbook templates, which you can access by clicking the links in the Templates list shown in Figure 7–10. Additional workbook templates also are available on the Web. To access the templates on the Web, click the links in the Office.com Templates list.

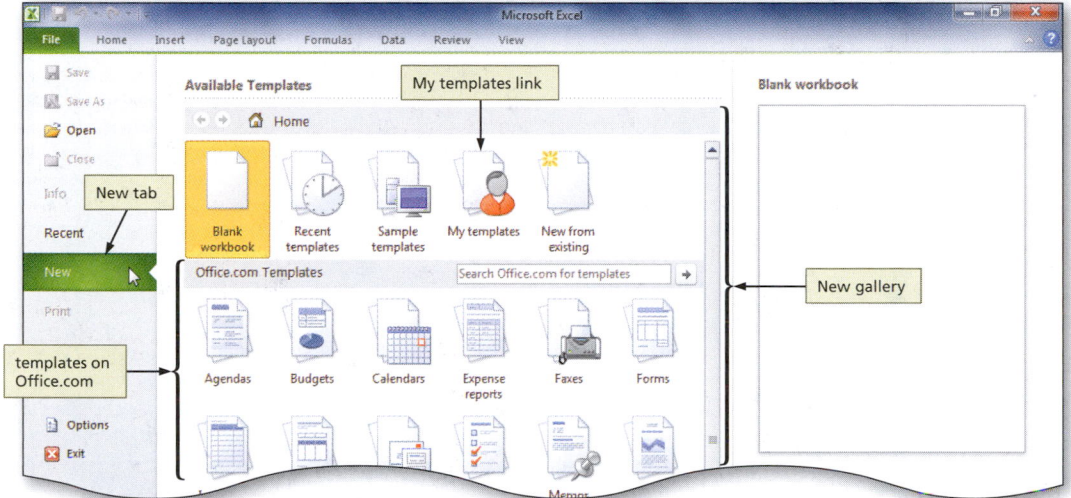

Figure 7–10

To Open a Template and Save It as a Workbook

The following steps open the YouBuild Computers Sales Analysis template and save it as a workbook.

1
- With Excel active, click File on the Ribbon to open the Backstage view.
- Click the Open command to display the Open dialog box.
- Navigate to the location of the file to be opened (in this case, the Excel folder on the USB flash drive).
- Click the YouBuild Computers Sales Analysis Template file to select it (Figure 7–11).

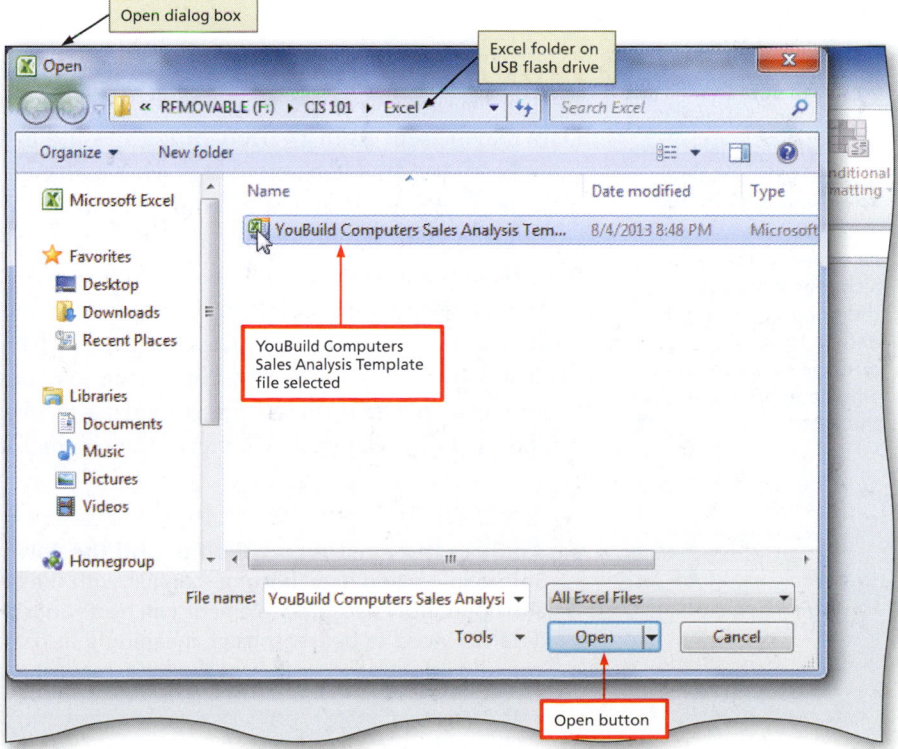

Figure 7–11

2

- Click the Open button (Open dialog box) to open the selected file.

- Click File on the Ribbon to open the Backstage view, and then click the Save As command to display the Save As dialog box.

- Type **YouBuild Computers Sales Analysis** in the File name box.

- Click the 'Save as type' box arrow and then click Excel Workbook to save the file as a workbook (Figure 7–12).

3

- Click the Save button (Save As dialog box) to save the workbook.

Q&A

How does Excel automatically select the file type and file name?

In a production environment in which templates are saved to the Templates folder, Excel automatically selects Excel Workbook as the file type when you attempt to save a template as a workbook. Excel also appends the digit 1 to the workbook name as described earlier.

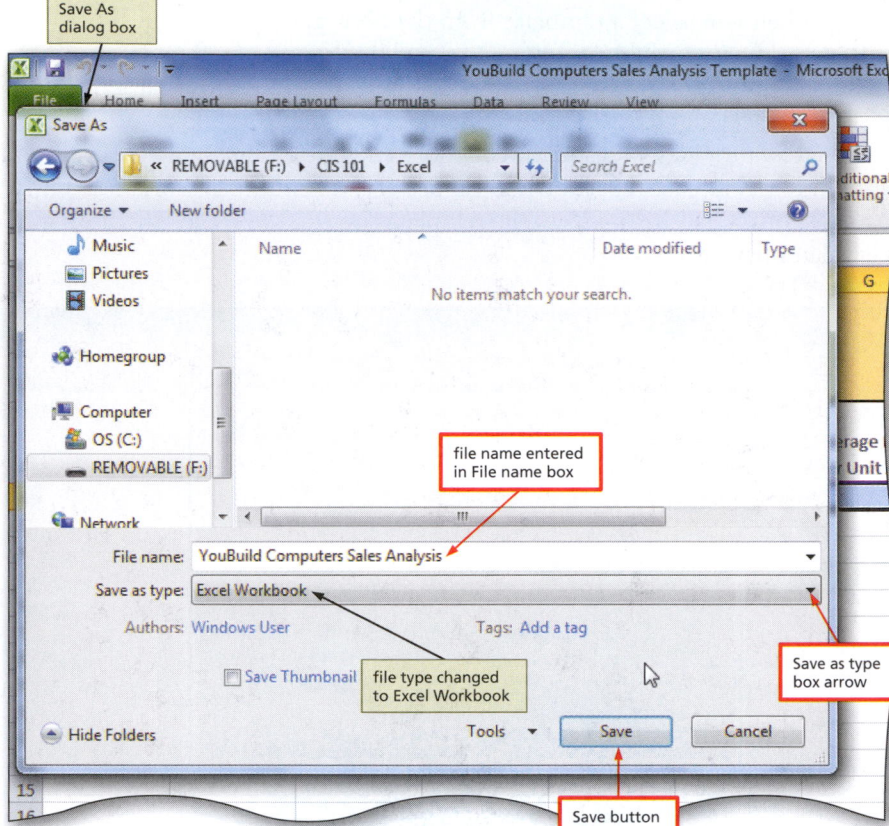

Figure 7–12

External Data

Imported data that maintains a refreshable link to its external source is called external data. When you use external data, your worksheet will be updated whenever a change is made to the original file and the data in the worksheet is refreshed. You can choose when and how to refresh the data.

Importing Data

Data may be sent from a variety of sources and in a range of formats. Even though many users keep data in databases such as Microsoft Access, it is common to receive text files with fields of data separated by commas, especially from mainframe computer users. In addition, with the popularity of the World Wide Web, more companies are creating HTML files and posting data on the Web as a Web page. Word documents, especially those including tables of data, often are used in business as a source of data for workbooks. XML also is a very popular format for data exchange. Excel allows you to import data made available in many formats, including text files, Access tables, Web pages, Word documents, and XML files. Importing data into Excel can create a refreshable link that can be used to update data whenever the original file changes.

Plan Ahead

Analyze the existing workbook and the formats of the data to be imported.
Before importing data, become familiar with the layout of the data, so that you can anticipate how each data element will be arranged in the worksheet. In some cases, the data will need to be transposed, meaning that the rows and columns need to be switched. You also might need to format the data, move it, or convert it from or into a table.

Importing Text Files

A **text file** contains data with little or no formatting. Many programs, including Excel, offer an option to import data from a text file, also called an ASCII text file. **ASCII** stands for the American Standard Code for Information Interchange.

In text files, commas, tabs, or other characters often separate the fields. Alternately, the text file may have fields of equal length in columnar format. Each record usually exists on a separate line. A **delimited file** contains data fields separated by a selected character, such as a comma. Such a file is called a comma-delimited text file. A **fixed width file** contains data fields of equal length with spaces between the fields. In the case of a fixed width file, a special character need not separate the data fields. During the import process, Excel provides a preview to help identify the type of text file being imported.

BTW

Dragging and Dropping a Text File
You also can import a text file by dragging a text file from a folder window to a blank worksheet. You then can format the data easily using the Text to Columns button on the Data tab on the Ribbon. The data does not maintain a refreshable link to the text file.

To Import Data from a Text File into a Worksheet

The following steps import a comma-delimited text file into the YouBuild Computers Sales Analysis workbook using the Text Import Wizard. The text file on the Data Files for Students contains data about sales for the North region for 2012 and 2013 (Figure 7–1a on page EX 427).

1

- With the YouBuild Computers Sales Analysis worksheet active, if necessary, select cell A4.

- Click Data on the Ribbon to display the Data tab (Figure 7–13).

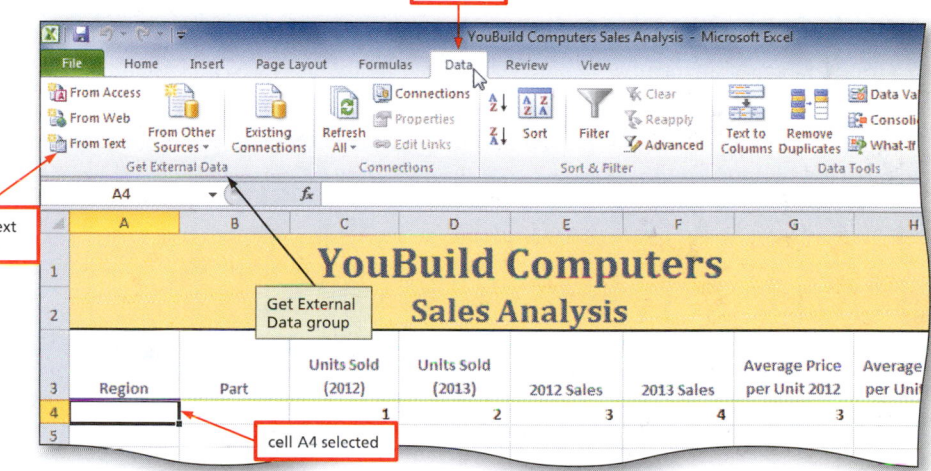

Figure 7–13

2

- Click the From Text button (Data tab | Get External Data group) to display the Import Text File dialog box.

- If necessary, navigate to the location of the file containing text to insert (in this case, the Excel folder on the USB flash drive) to display the Data Files (Figure 7–14).

Q&A

Why can I not find the From Text button?

If you have more than one Excel add-in installed, such as Solver, the From Text button may appear on a submenu that is displayed when you click the Get External Data button. The Get External Data group on the Ribbon may be collapsed to a single Get External Data button.

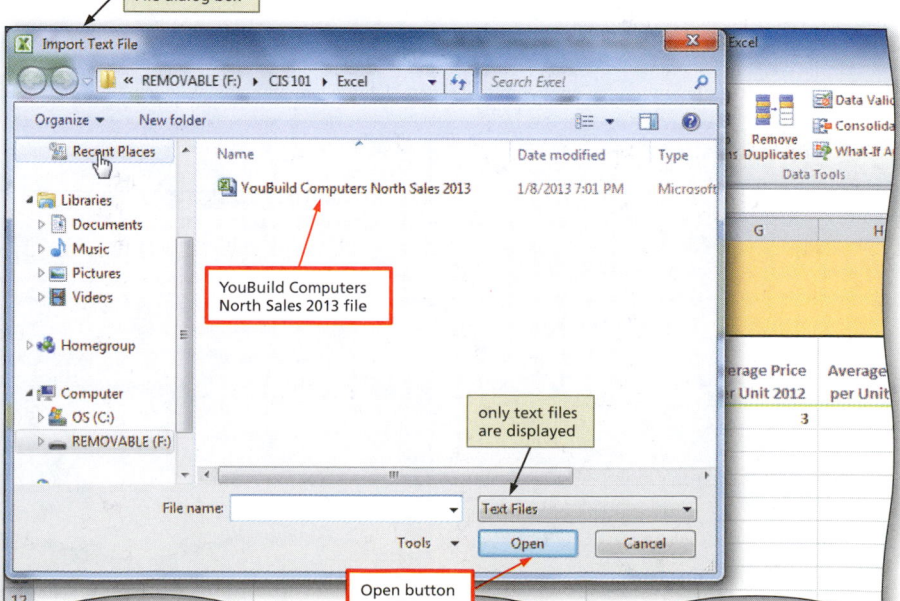

Figure 7–14

3

- Click the file name, YouBuild Computers North Sales 2013, to select it.

- Click the Import button (Import Text File dialog box) to start the Text Import Wizard and display the Text Import Wizard – Step 1 of 3 dialog box (Figure 7–15).

Q&A What is the purpose of the Text Import Wizard?

The Text Import Wizard provides step-by-step instructions for importing data from a text file into an Excel worksheet. The Preview box shows that the text file contains one record per line and the fields are separated by commas. The Delimited option button is selected in the 'Original data type' area.

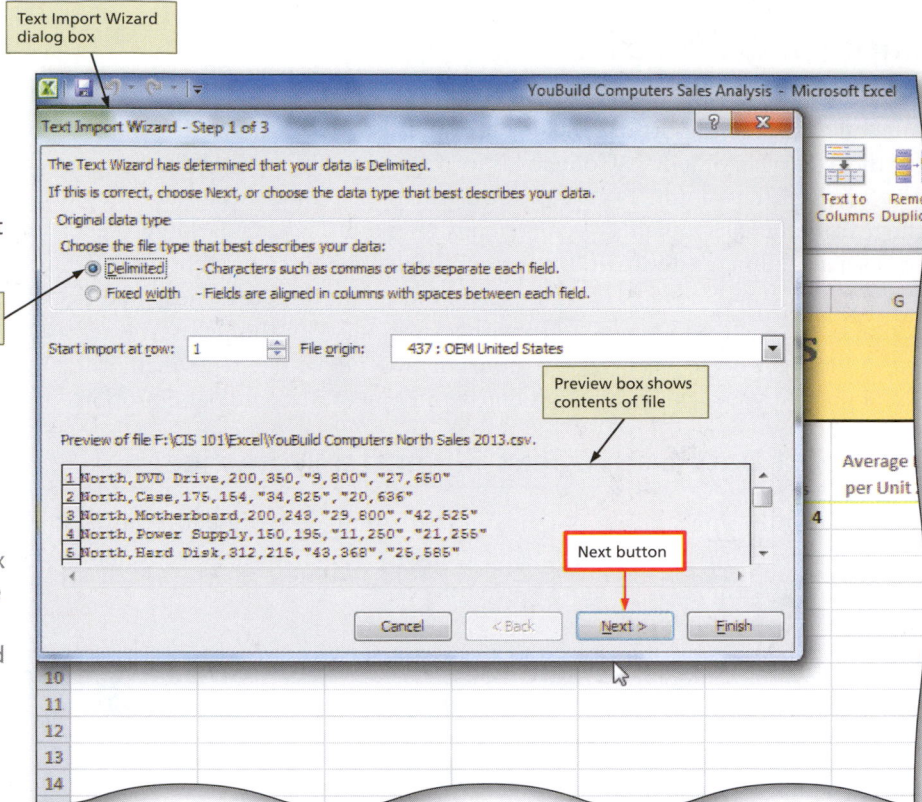

Figure 7–15

4

- Click the Next button (Text Import Wizard – Step 1 of 3 dialog box) to display the Text Import Wizard – Step 2 of 3 dialog box (Figure 7–16).

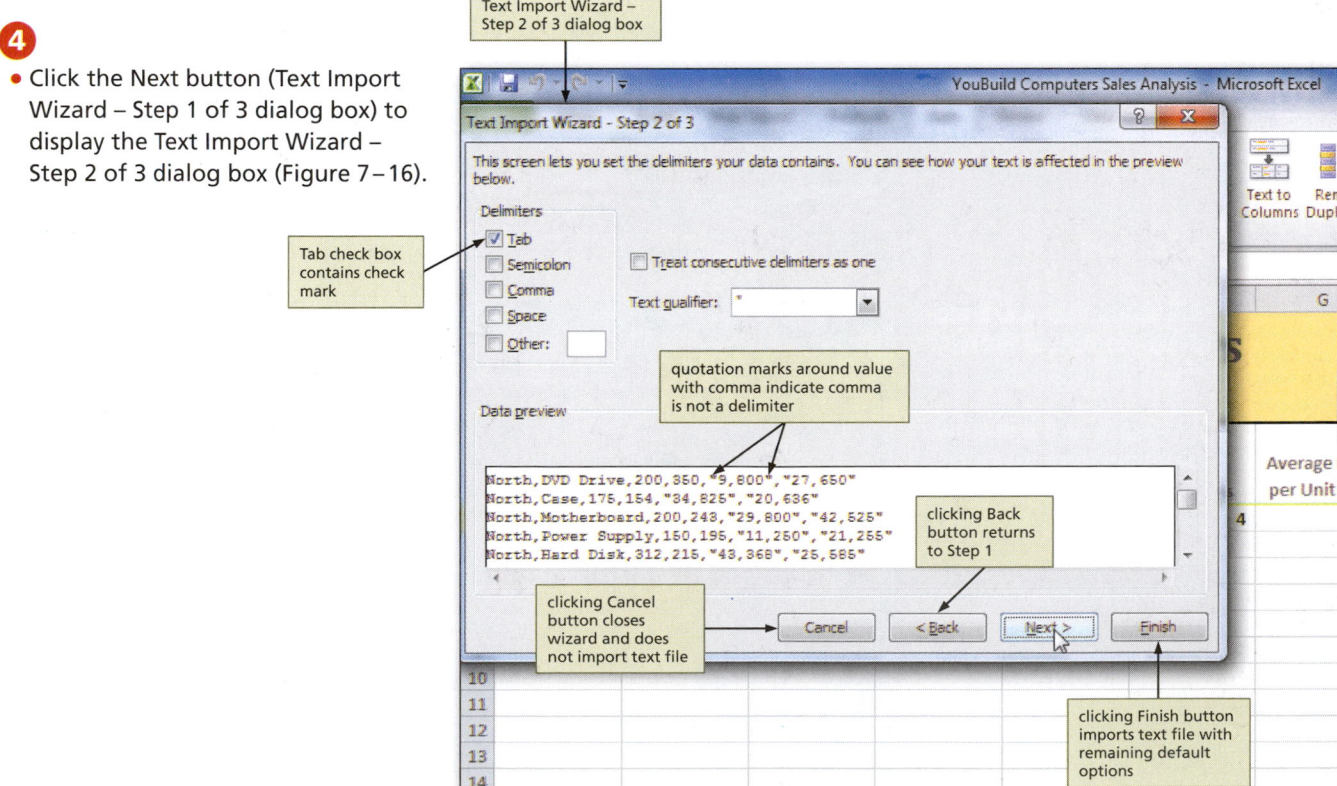

Figure 7–16

5

- Click Comma to place a check mark in the Comma check box and to display the data fields correctly in the Data preview area.

- Click Tab to remove the check mark from the Tab check box (Figure 7–17).

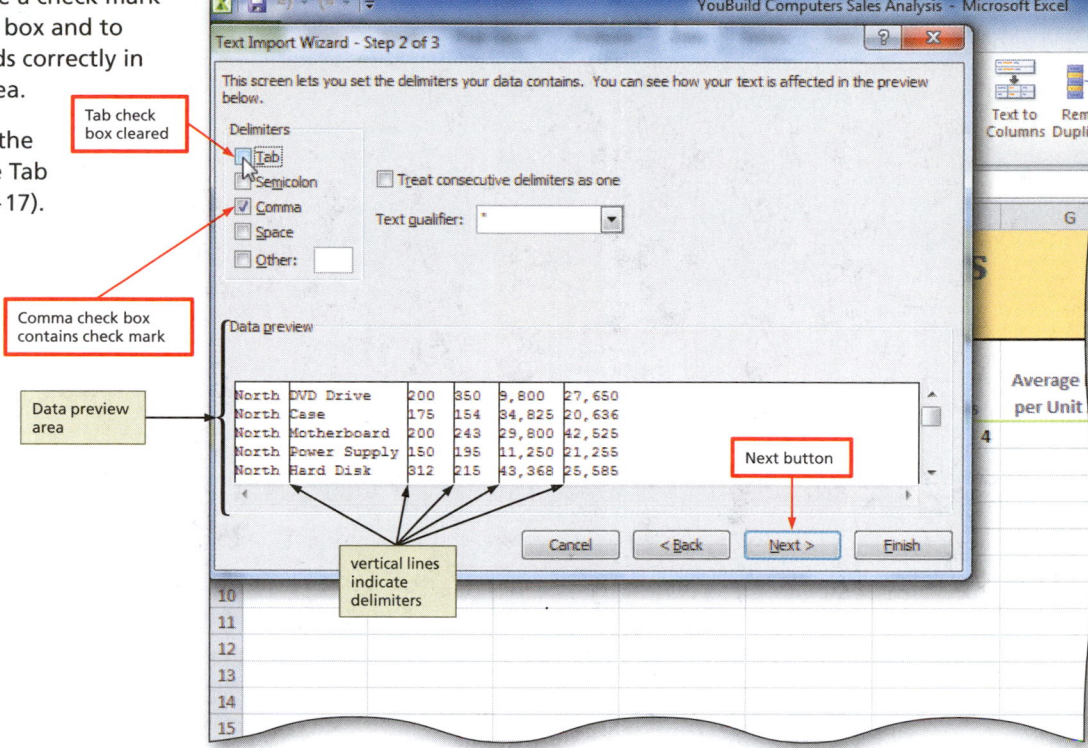

Figure 7–17

6

- Click the Next button (Text Import Wizard – Step 2 of 3 dialog box) to display the Text Import Wizard – Step 3 of 3 dialog box (Figure 7–18).

Q&A

What is shown in the Text Import Wizard – Step 3 of 3 dialog box?

Step 3 allows the format of each column of data to be selected. General is the default selection. The Data preview area shows the data separated based on the comma delimiter. The commas in the last two columns of numbers in the Data preview area (Figure 7–18) are not considered to be delimiters because each of these data values was surrounded by quotation marks in the text file.

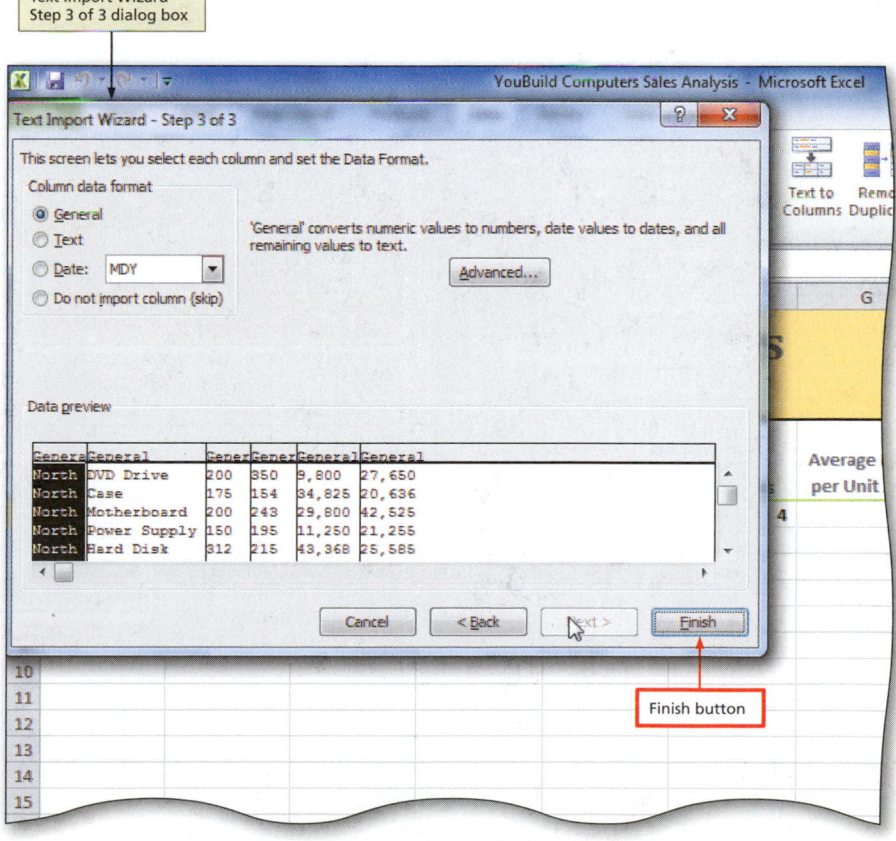

Figure 7–18

7

- Click the Finish button (Text Import Wizard – Step 3 of 3 dialog box) to finish importing the selected text file and display the Import Data dialog box.

Q&A

What is shown in the Import Data dialog box when importing text?

The Import Data dialog box allows you to choose in which cell to import the text and to specify properties of the imported text.

- Click the Properties button (Import Data dialog box) to display the External Data Range Properties dialog box.

- Click 'Adjust column width' to remove the check mark from the 'Adjust column width' check box.

- Click the 'Overwrite existing cells with new data, clear unused cells' option button to select the option button (Figure 7–19).

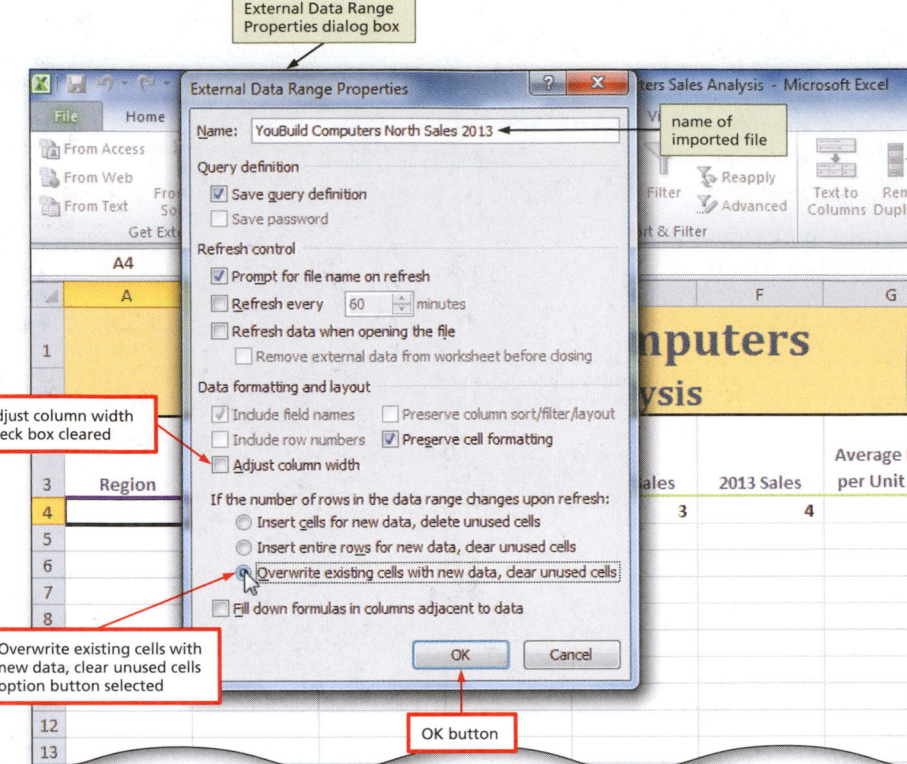

Figure 7–19

8

- Click the OK button (External Data Range Properties dialog box) to accept the settings and display the Import Data dialog box again.

- Click the OK button (Import Data dialog box) to import the data from the text file into the worksheet beginning at cell A4.

- Display the Home tab.

- Select the range C4:F4 to prepare for copying its formatting.

- Click the Format Painter button (Home tab | Clipboard group) and then drag though the range C5:F10 to copy the formatting to the range C5:F10 (Figure 7–20).

Q&A

What if the data in the text file is changed?

After the text file is imported, Excel can refresh, or update, the data whenever the original text file changes using the Refresh All button (Data tab | Connections group).

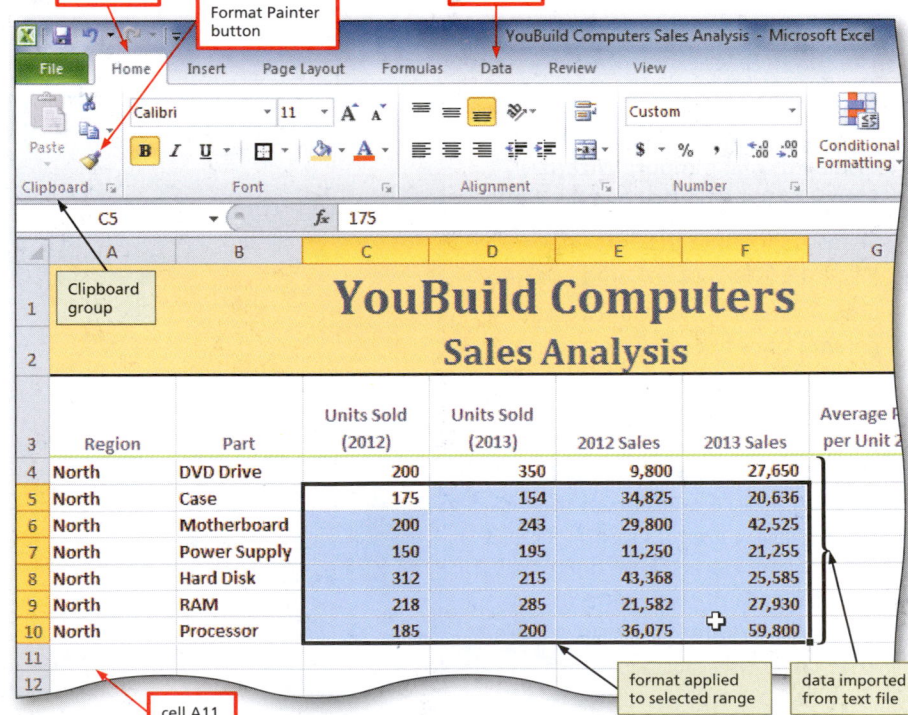

Figure 7–20

Other Ways

1. Select text, right-click selection, click Format Painter button on Mini toolbar

Importing Data from a Database

To import data from an Access database, the first step is to make a query of the data. A **query** is a way to qualify the data to import by specifying a matching condition or asking a question of a database. For example, a query can identify only those records that pass a certain test, such as records containing numeric fields greater than a specific amount or records containing text fields matching a specific value. When Excel imports a database table, the data is placed in a table. A table format is not desirable for the YouBuild Computers Sales Analysis worksheet, so the table must be converted to a range and the cells and should be reformatted after Excel imports the data.

BTW

Dragging and Dropping an Access File
If you have both Excel and Access open on your desktop, you can drag and drop an entire table or query from Access to Excel. In the Access window, select the table or query you want to transfer, and then drag it to the desired location in the worksheet.

To Import Data from an Access Table into a Worksheet

The following steps import an entire table from an Access database into an Excel table and then reformat the data to match the existing worksheet. The table in the Access database on the Data Files for Students contains data about sales revenue in the South region for 2012 and 2013 (Figure 7–1b on page EX 427).

1

• Select cell A11 so that the Access table is imported starting in cell A11.

• Click Data on the Ribbon to display the Data tab.

• Click the From Access button (Data tab | Get External Data group) to display the Select Data Source dialog box.

• Navigate to the location of the Access database file containing the table to insert (in this case, the Excel folder on the USB flash drive) (Figure 7–21).

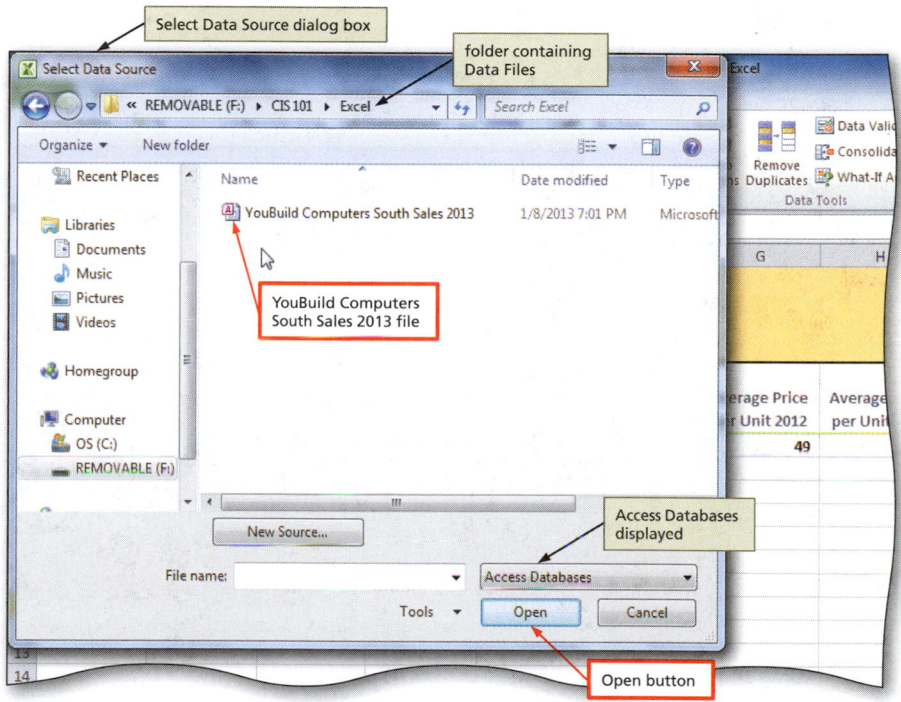

Figure 7–21

2

• Click the file name, YouBuild Computers South Sales 2013, in the Name list to select the file.

• Click the Open button (Select Data Source dialog box) to display the Import Data dialog box (Figure 7–22).

Q&A

What if the database contains more than one table?

If more than one table is in the database, then Excel allows you to choose which table to import.

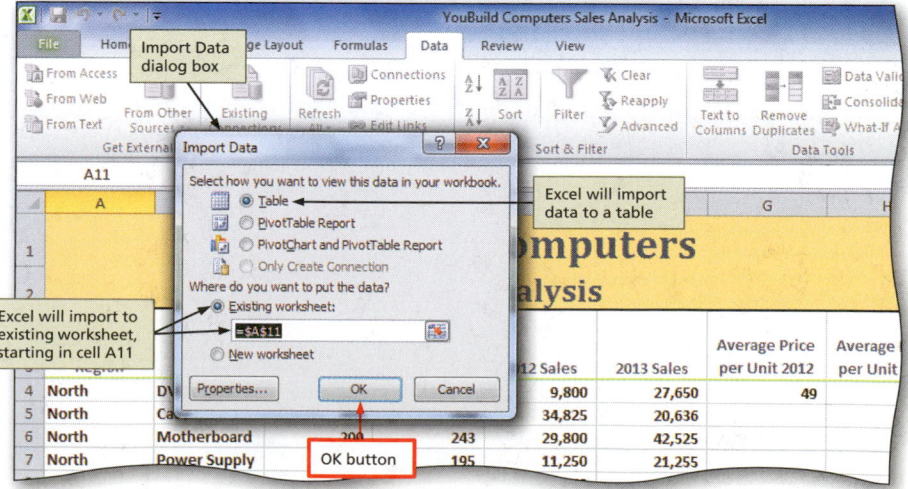

Figure 7–22

3

• Click the OK button (Import Data dialog box) to import the data in the database to a table in the range A11:F18 (Figure 7–23).

Q&A

What is shown in the Import Data dialog box when importing from an Access database?

The Import Data dialog box allows you to choose whether to import the data into a table, a PivotTable Report, or a PivotChart and associated PivotTable Report. You also can choose to import the data to an existing worksheet or a new worksheet.

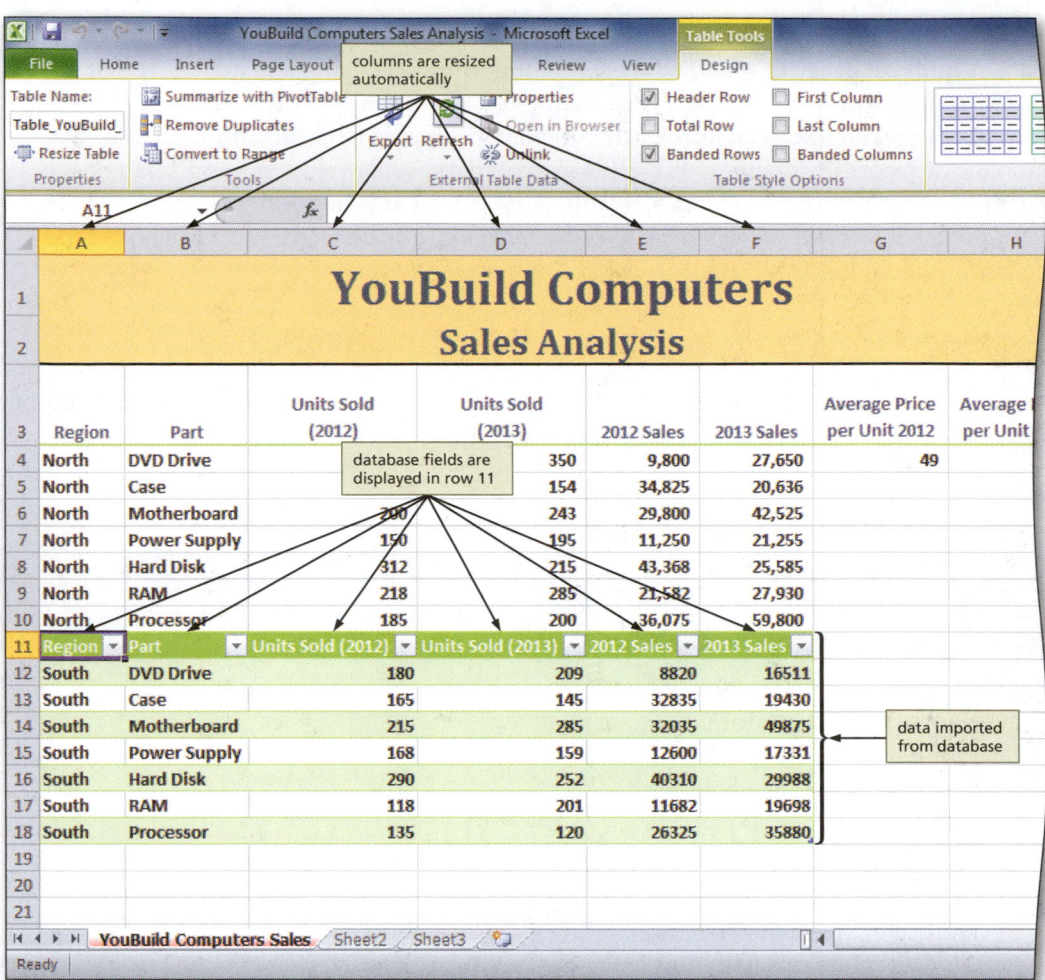

Figure 7–23

Q&A

What happened to the layout of the worksheet when Excel imported the data?

Excel created a table using the data in the only table in the database. The names of the fields in the Access database appear in row 11. The table is formatted with the default table style for the worksheet's theme. Excel also changed the widths of the columns in the worksheet.

Q&A

How should I format the worksheet now?

The table in the range A11:F18 must be converted to a range. When the table is converted to a range, the cells in each column in the converted range should be formatted to match the data in the cells that were imported for the North region. The table headers in row 11 should be deleted by deleting the entire row.

4

- Right-click cell A11, point to Table on the shortcut menu, and then click Convert to Range to display the Microsoft Excel dialog box, which asks whether Excel should convert the table to a normal range.

- Click the OK button (Microsoft Excel dialog box) to convert the table to a range (Figure 7–24).

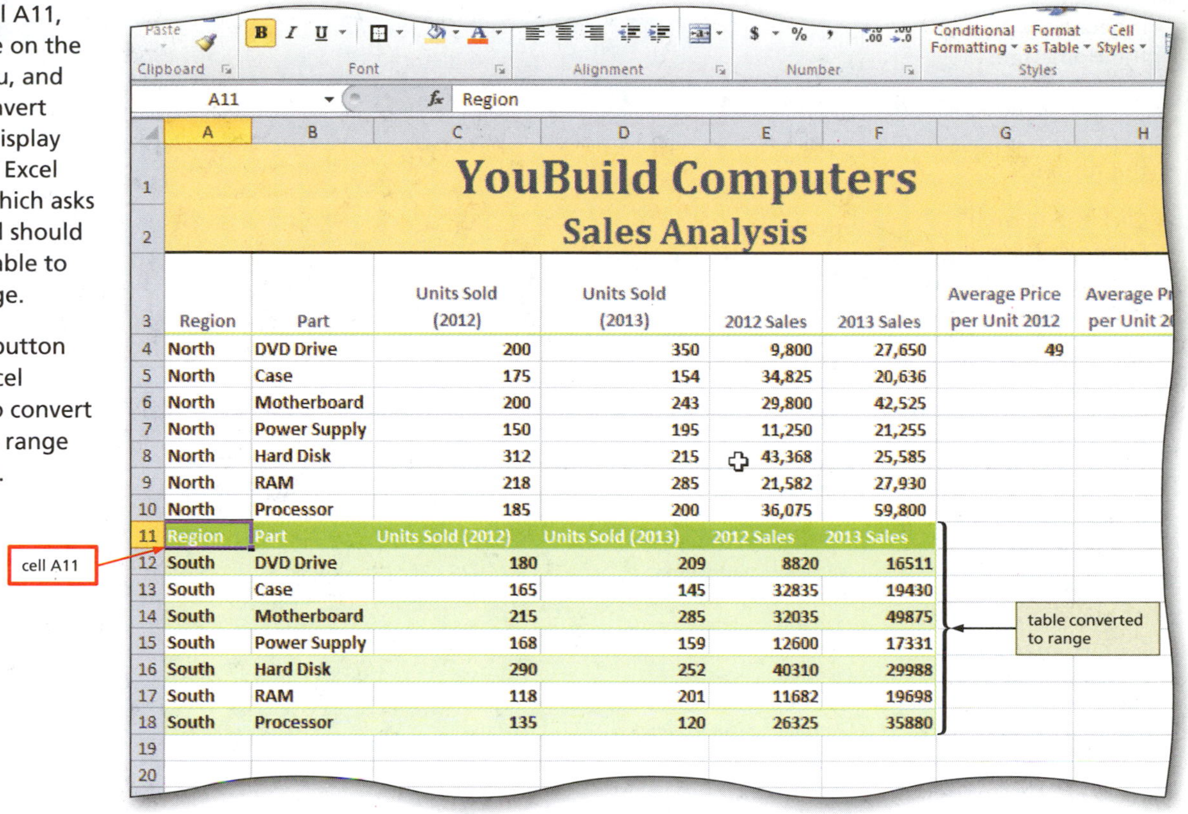

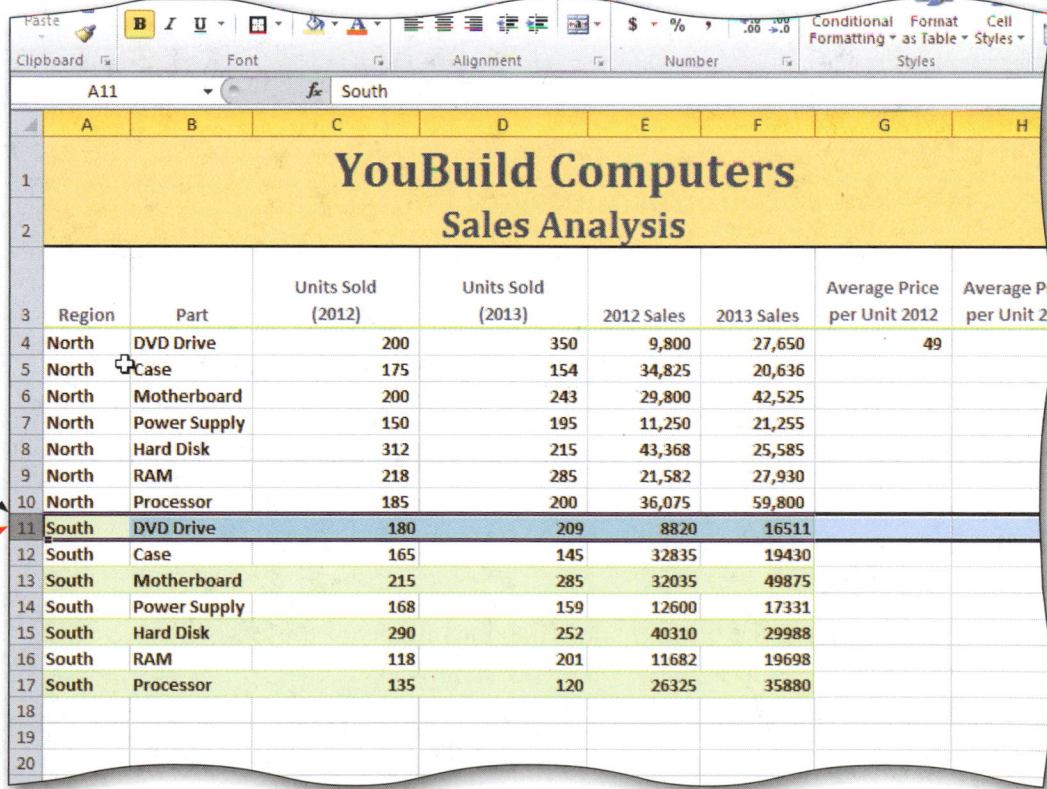

Figure 7–24

5

- Right-click the row heading for row 11 to display the shortcut menu.

- Click Delete on the shortcut menu to delete row 11 (Figure 7–25).

Figure 7–25

6

- If necessary, display the Home tab.

- Select the range A7:F7 to prepare for copying the formatting.

- Click the Format Painter button (Home tab | Clipboard group), and then drag though the range A11:F17 to copy the formats of the selected range to the range A11:F17.

- Click cell A18 to deselect the range and prepare for importing other data (Figure 7–26).

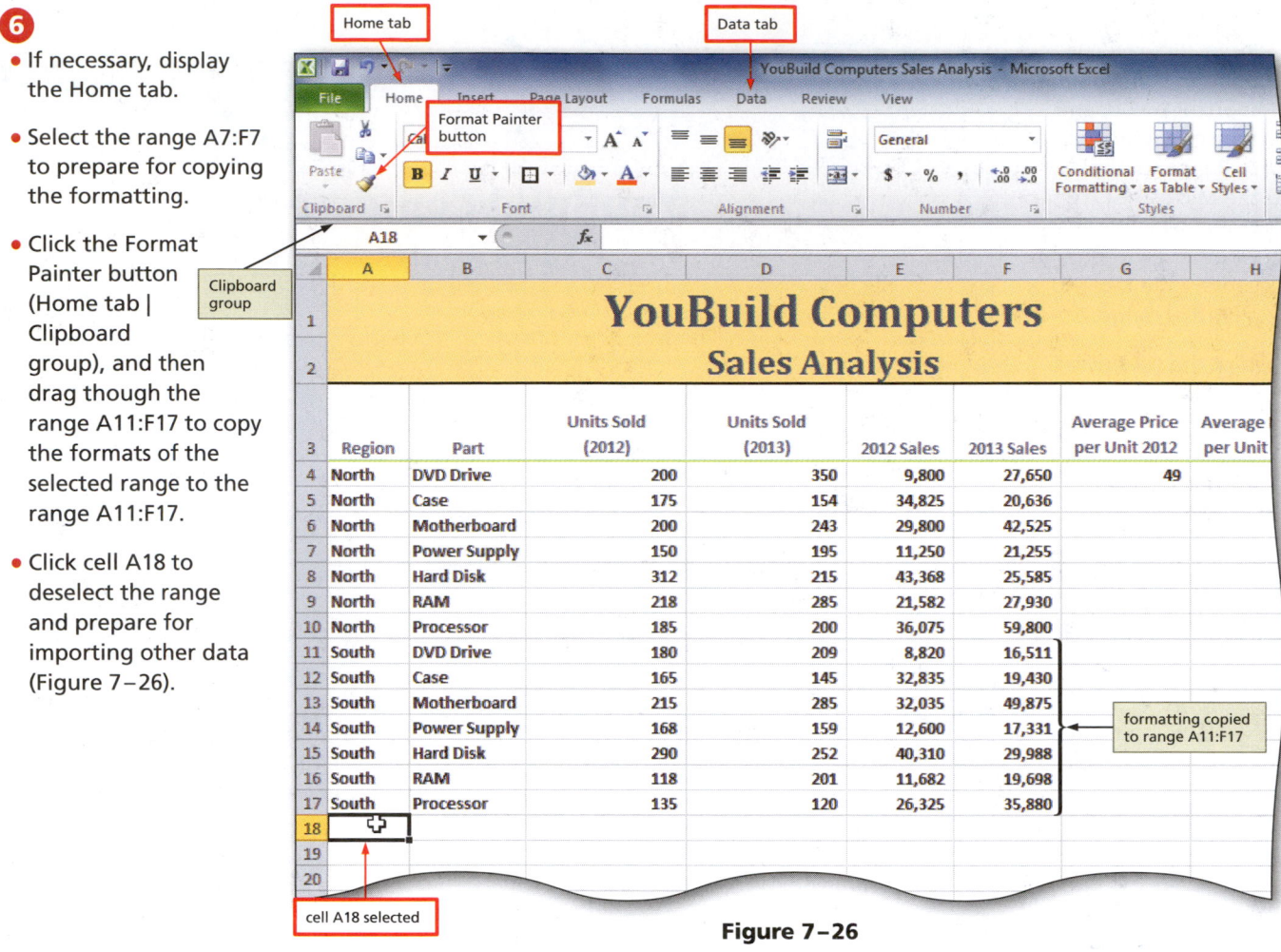

Figure 7–26

Other Ways

1. Select text, right-click selection, click Format Painter button on Mini toolbar

Importing Web Page Data

Web pages use a file format called HTML. HTML stands for Hypertext Markup Language, which is a language that Web browsers can interpret. Excel can import data from a Web page into preformatted areas of the worksheet using a Web query. A **Web query** selects data from the Internet to add to the Excel worksheet. The Web Query dialog box includes options to specify which parts of the Web page to import and how much of the HTML formatting to keep.

To Import Data from a Web Page into a Worksheet

The following steps create a new Web query and import data from a Web page into a worksheet. Performing these steps does not require being connected to the Internet, because the Web page (Figure 7–1c on page EX 427) is available with the Data Files for Students.

1

- With cell A18 selected, display the Data tab.

- Click the From Web button (Data tab | Get External Data group) to display the New Web Query dialog box.

- Type **F:\CIS 101\Excel\ YouBuild Computers West Sales 2013.htm** in the Address bar and then click the Go button (New Web Query dialog box) to display the Web page in the preview area (Figure 7–27).

Q&A Why does file:/// appear at the beginning of the address in the Address bar?

Excel appends file:/// to the beginning of the address to indicate that the address points to a file saved on disk.

Q&A What should I do if my Data Files on are on a different drive?

Substitute the name of your drive (such as E:) for F: in the address.

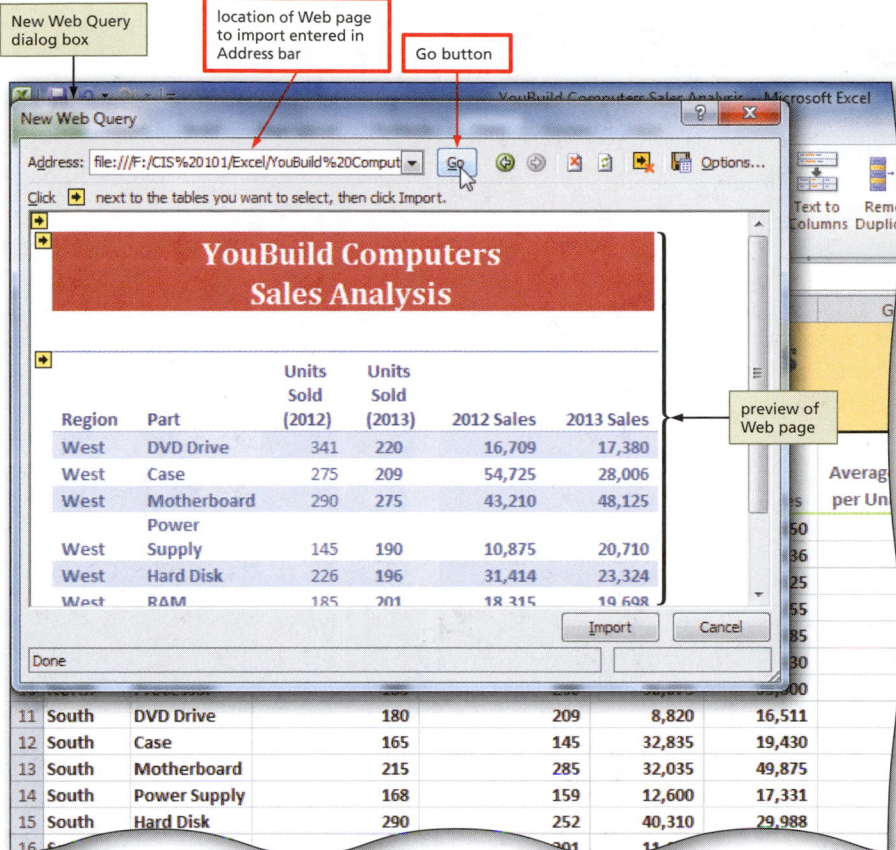

Figure 7–27

2

- Click the second 'Click to select this table' arrow to select the HTML table containing the West region sales report (Figure 7–28).

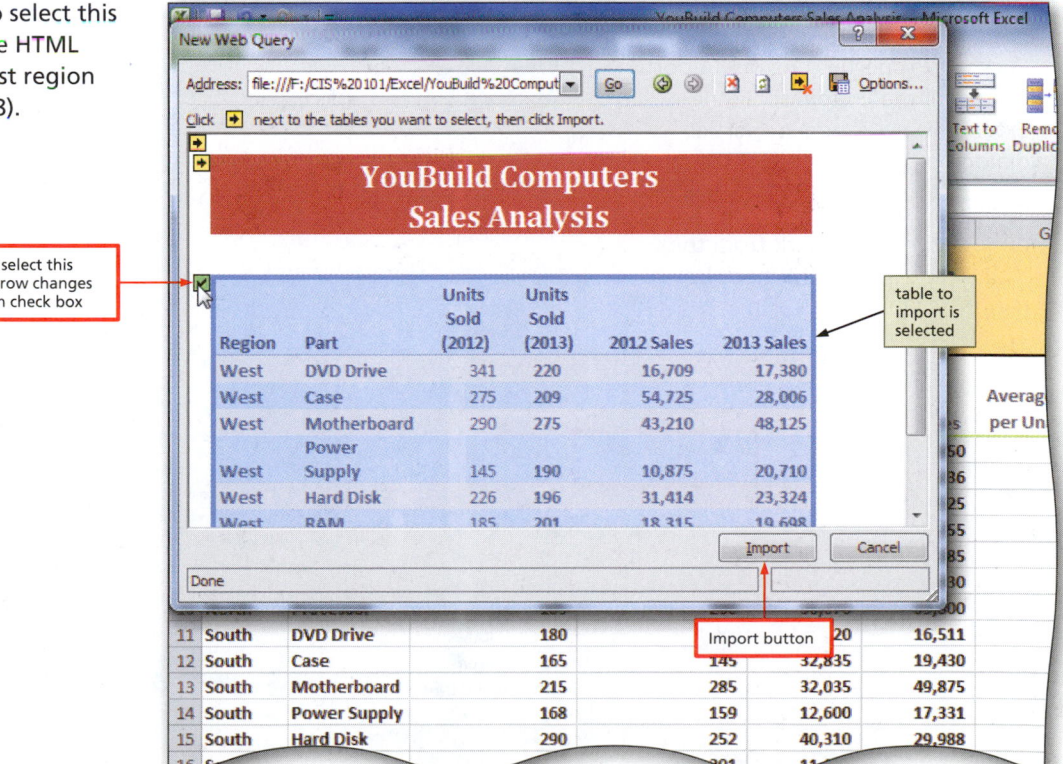

Figure 7–28

3

- Click the Import button (New Web Query dialog box) to display the Import Data dialog box and a marquee around cell A18 (Figure 7–29).

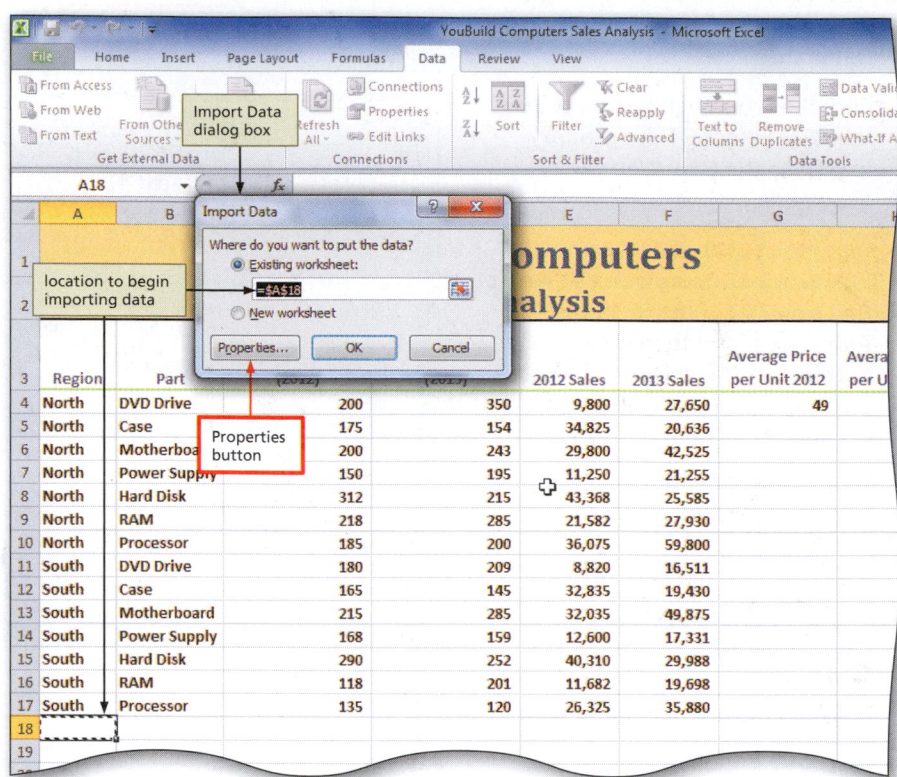

Figure 7–29

4

- Click the Properties button (Import Data dialog box) to display the External Data Range Properties dialog box.

- Click 'Adjust column width' to remove the check mark from the 'Adjust column width' check box (Figure 7–30).

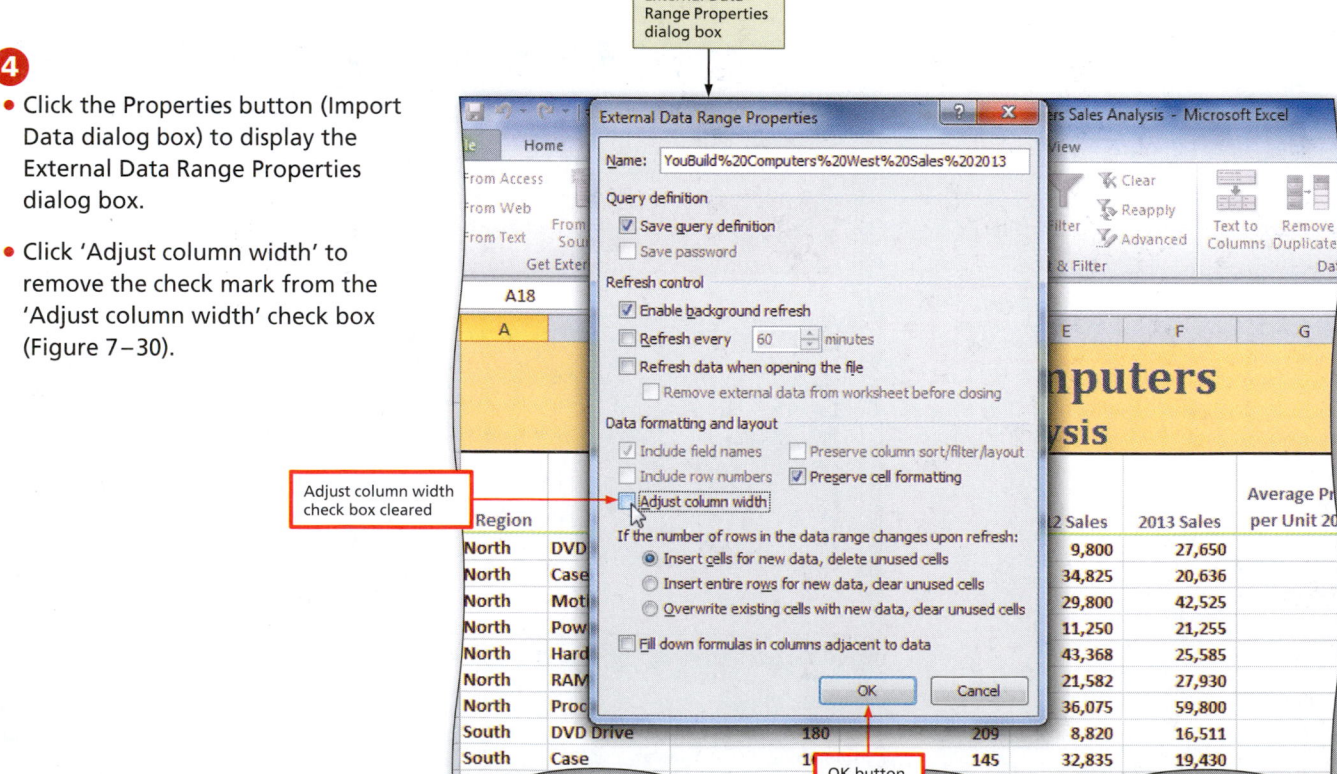

Figure 7–30

5

• Click the OK button (External Data Range Properties dialog box) to close the dialog box, instruct Excel not to adjust the column widths when the data is imported, and display the Import Data dialog box again.

• Click the OK button (Import Data dialog box) to import the data from the Web page into the worksheet beginning at cell A18 (Figure 7–31).

Q&A

Why is the data imported starting in cell A18?

By default, the cell that is active when the Web query is performed will become the upper-left cell of the imported range. To import the data to a different location, change the location in the Import Data dialog box.

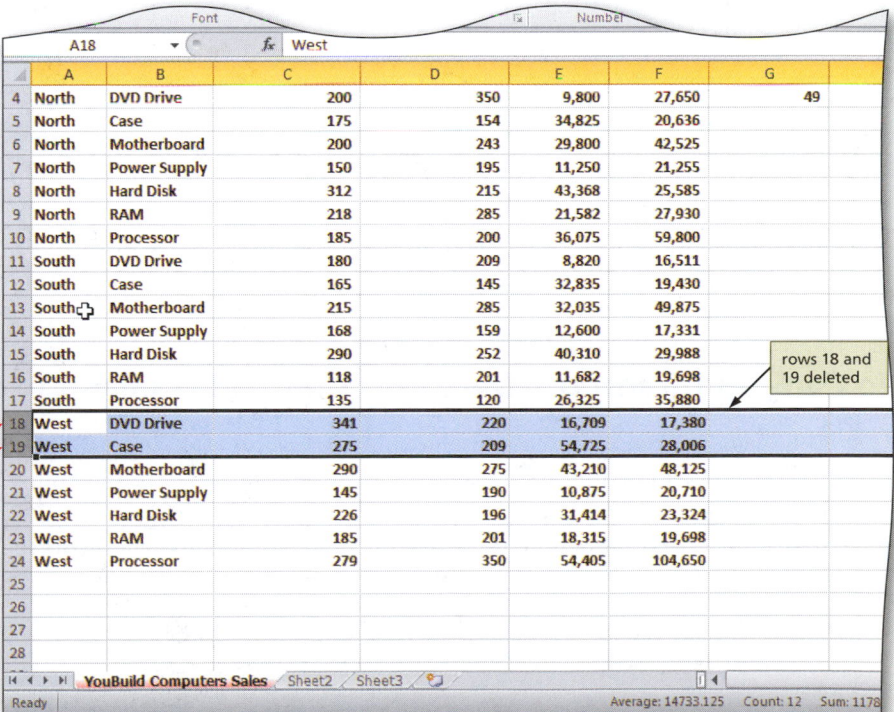

Figure 7–31

6

• Drag through the row headings in rows 18 and 19 to select the rows.

• Right-click the selected rows, and then click Delete on the shortcut menu to delete rows 18 and 19, which contained the column headings from the Web page (Figure 7–32).

Q&A

Why are the column headings repeated in row 18?

Because the column headings appeared in the Web page, they are imported with the other data and are displayed in rows 18 and 19. The extra column headings must be deleted from the imported Web page table.

Figure 7–32

7

- Display the Home tab.

- Select the range A17:F17 to prepare for copying its formatting.

- Click the Format Painter button (Home tab | Clipboard group), and then drag though the range A18:F24 to copy the formats of the selected range to the range A18:F24.

- Select cell A34 to deselect the range and prepare for importing other data (Figure 7–33).

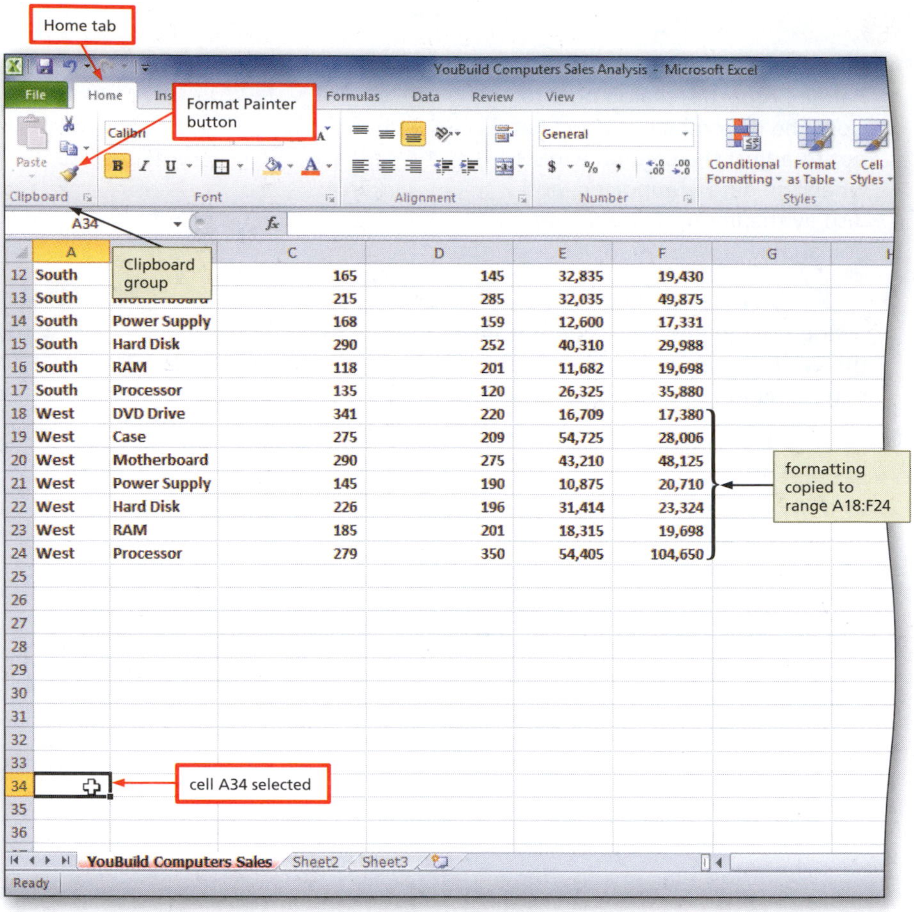

Q&A

Why should I use a Web query instead of copying and pasting from a Web page?

Using a Web query has advantages over other methods of importing data from a Web page. For example, copying data from Web pages to the Office Clipboard and then pasting it into Excel does not maintain all of the Web page formatting. In addition, copying only the desired data from a Web page can be tedious. Finally, copying and pasting does not create a link to the Web page for future updating.

Figure 7–33

Other Ways

1. Select text, right-click selection, click Format Painter button on Mini toolbar

BTW

Copying
To copy the contents of a cell to the cell directly below it, click in the target cell and press CTRL+D.

Importing Word Data

A Word document often contains data stored in a table. You can use the Office Clipboard and Copy and Paste commands to copy the data in the table to an Excel worksheet. On some occasions, imported data requires a great deal of manipulation once you import it into Excel. For example, the imported data may be easier to work with if the rows and columns were switched, or **transposed**. In other situations, you may find that an imported column of data should be split into two columns.

To Copy and Transpose Data from a Word Document to a Worksheet

The Word document that contains the East region's sales data (Figure 7–1d on page EX 427) includes a table in which the rows and columns are switched when compared with the YouBuild Computers Sales worksheet. The first column of data also includes data for both the region and the part type. The following steps copy and transpose the data from the Word document to the YouBuild Computers Sales worksheet.

1

- With cell A34 selected, start Word and then open the Word document named, YouBuild Computers East Sales 2013, from the Data Files for Students.

- In Word, if necessary, display the Home tab.

- Drag through all of the cells in the second through last columns in the table in the Word document to select the table cells.

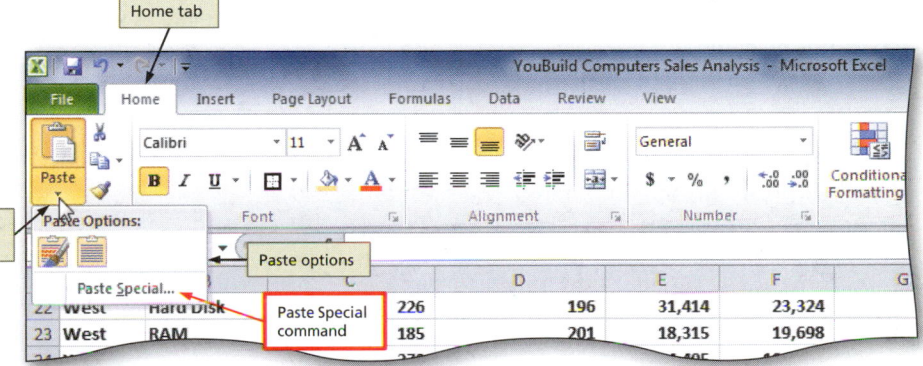

Region, Part	East,DVD Drive	East,Case	East,Motherboard	East,Power Supply	East,Hard Disk	East,Ram	East,Processor
Units Sold (2012)	350	201	196	190	275	209	220
Units Sold (2013)	279	185	226	145	290	275	341
2012 Sales	17,150	39,999	29,204	14,250	38,225	20,691	42,900
2013 Sales	22,041	24,790	39,550	15,805	34,510	26,950	101,959

Figure 7–34

- Click the Copy button (Home tab | Clipboard group) to copy the contents of the table to the Office Clipboard (Figure 7–34).

2

- Quit Word and, if necessary, click the YouBuild Computers Sales Analysis workbook taskbar button to make Excel the active window.

- Click the Paste button arrow (Home tab | Clipboard group) to display the Paste options (Figure 7–35).

Figure 7–35

3

- Click Paste Special on the Paste menu to display the Paste Special dialog box.

- Click Text in the As list (Figure 7–36).

Q&A Why do I select Text in the As list?

If a different format is selected, then formatting and other information may be pasted with the data. Importing the data as text provides greater flexibility for manipulating and formatting the data in Excel.

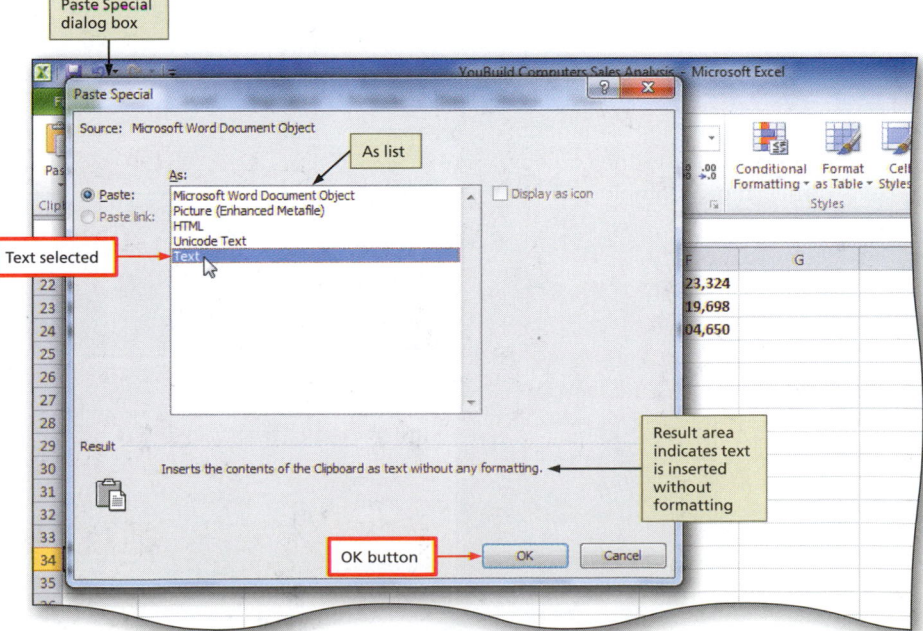

Figure 7–36

4

- Click the OK button (Paste Special dialog box) to paste the contents of the Office Clipboard to the range A34:G38 (Figure 7–37).

Q&A
Why is the data pasted to the range A34:G38?

Excel's Transpose command requires that the source of the transposed data be different from the destination. In this case, the source is the range A34:G38 and the destination will be the range A25:E31.

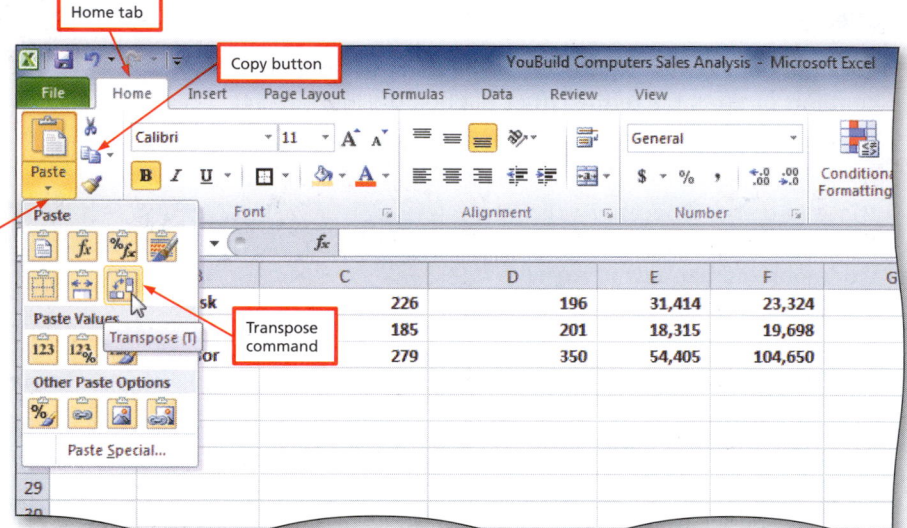

Figure 7–37

5

- Click the Copy button (Home tab | Clipboard group) to copy the range A34:G38 to the Office Clipboard.

- Select cell A25 to prepare for pasting the copied data to the range beginning with cell A25.

- Click the Paste button arrow (Home tab | Clipboard group) and then point to Transpose on the Paste menu (Figure 7–38).

Figure 7–38

6

- Click Transpose on the Paste menu to transpose and paste the copied cells to the range beginning with cell A25 (Figure 7–39).

Q&A
What happens when the range is copied and transposed?

When the range is transposed, the first row of the selected range becomes the first column of the destination range, and so on. For example, row 34 (A34:G38) in the source range becomes column A (A25:E31) in the destination range.

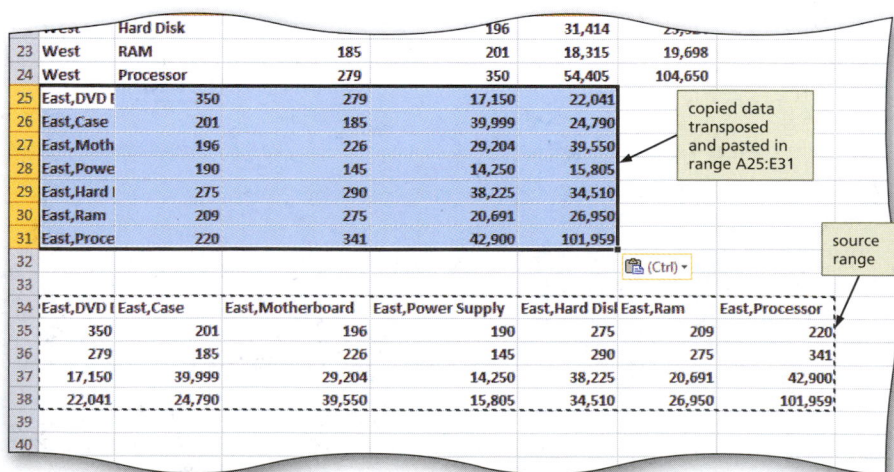

Figure 7–39

To Convert Text to Columns

As stated earlier and shown in Figure 7–33 on page EX 450, column A of the imported East data includes both the region and part data. The data must be separated using Excel's Convert Text to Columns command so that the shop type information is in column B. Before doing so, the source range for the data (A34:G38) should be deleted because it no longer is needed. Also, the cells in the range B25:E31 must be shifted one column to the right to accommodate the part data.

The following steps clear the range A34:G38, move the range B25:E31 one column to the right, and move the part data in column A to column B.

1

- If necessary, display the Home tab.

- Select the range A34:G38 and then press the DELETE key to delete the range.

- Select the range B25:E31 and then click the Cut button (Home tab | Clipboard group) to delete the range from the worksheet and copy it to the Office Clipboard (Figure 7–40).

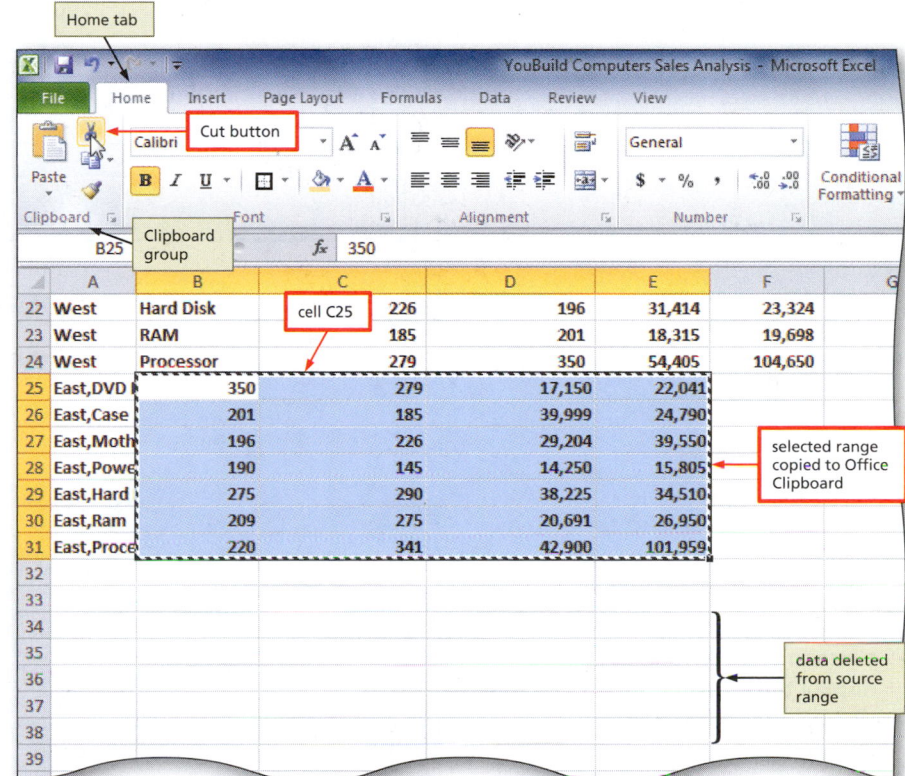

Figure 7–40

2

- Select cell C25 and then click the Paste button (Home tab | Clipboard group) to paste the source data beginning in cell C25 (Figure 7–41).

Q&A

Why does the range B25:E31 need to be cut and pasted to the new range?

The data in the range B25:E31 contains the part information that needs to be placed in the range C25:F31. Moving the range B25:E31 one column to the right will accommodate the part information.

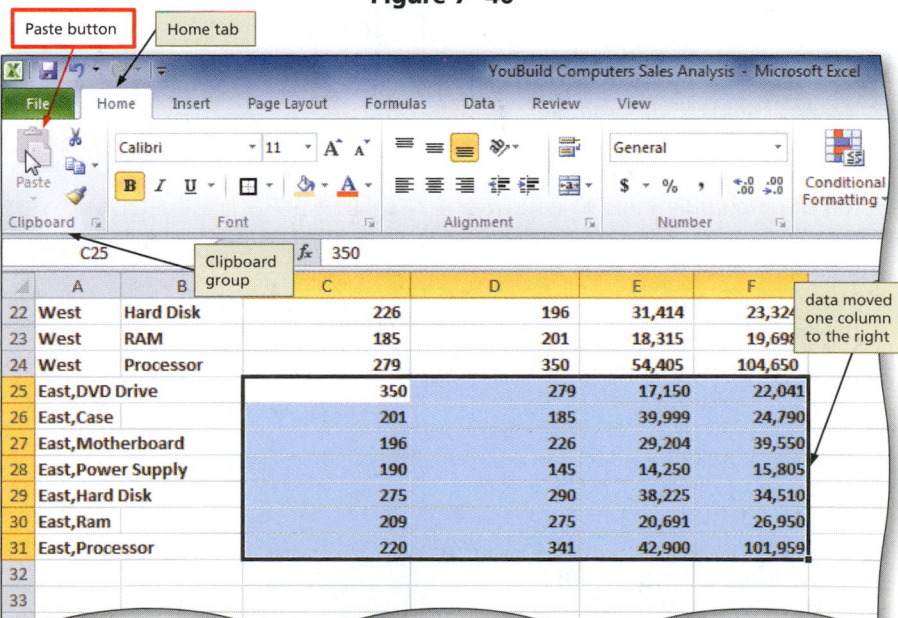

Figure 7–41

- Select the range A23:F23 and then click the Format Painter button (Home tab | Clipboard group) to copy the formatting of the selected cells.

- Select the range A25:F31 to copy the formats from range A23:F23 to the range A25:F31 (Figure 7–42).

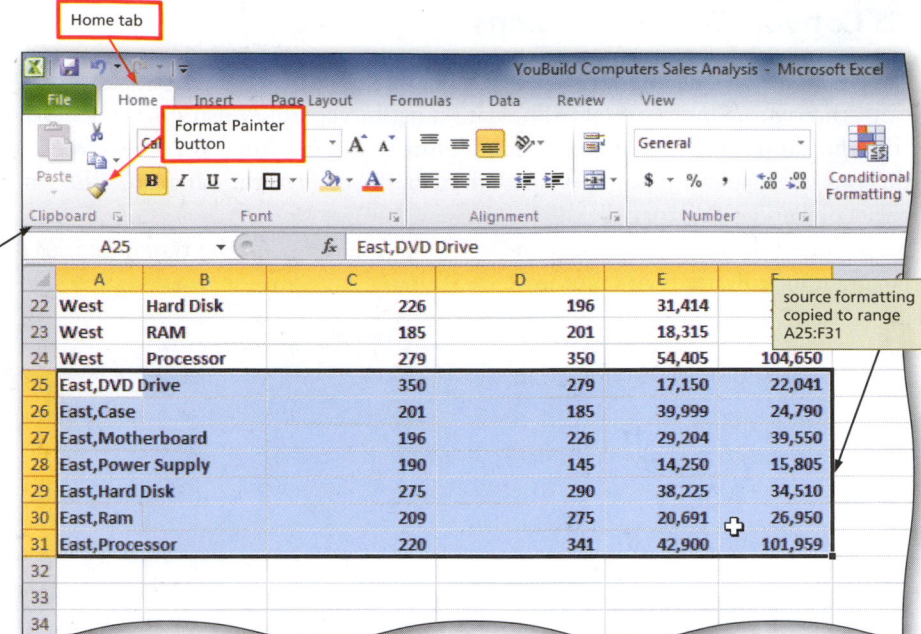

Figure 7–42

- Select the range A25:A31 to prepare for converting the text to columns.

- Display the Data tab.

- Click the Text to Columns button (Data tab | Data Tools group) to display the Convert Text to Columns Wizard – Step 1 of 3 dialog box (Figure 7–43).

Q&A

What other tasks can be accomplished using the Convert Text to Columns Wizard?

The wizard can be used only when a range that includes a single column is selected. The Convert Text to Columns Wizard is a powerful tool for manipulating text data in columns, such as splitting first and last names into separate columns. Most often, however, you will use the wizard to manipulate imported data. For example, survey data may be imported in one column as a series of Y and N characters, indicating answers to questions on the survey (e.g., YNNYYN). You can split the answers into separate columns by specifying fixed width fields of one character each.

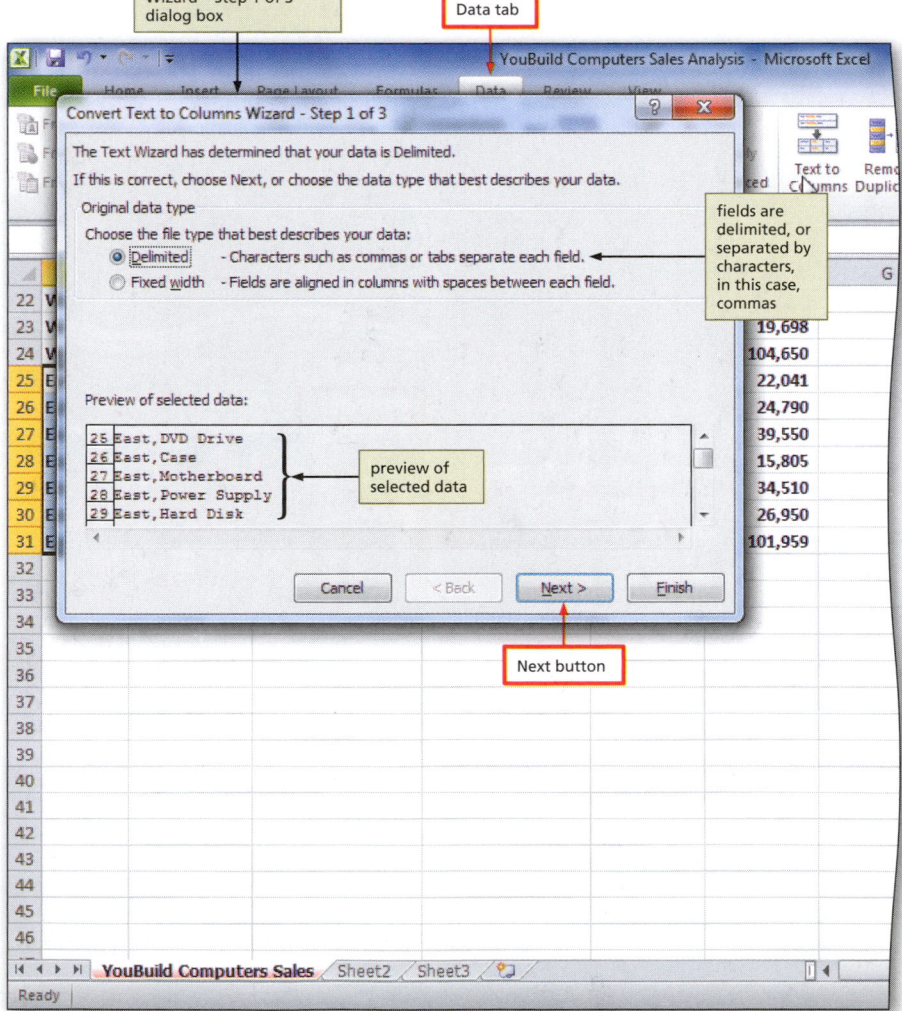

Figure 7–43

5
- Click the Next button (Convert Text to Columns Wizard – Step 1 of 3 dialog box) to accept Delimited as the file type of the data and to display the Convert Text to Columns Wizard – Step 2 of 3 dialog box.

- Click Comma to insert a check mark in the Comma check box and to display the data fields correctly in the Data preview area.

- Click Tab to remove the check mark from the Tab check box (Figure 7–44).

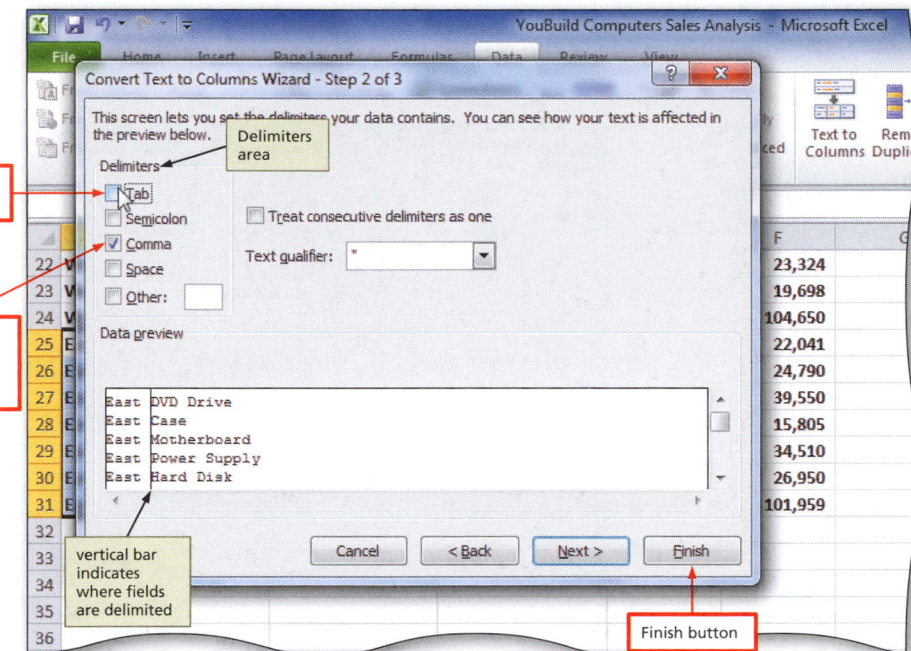

Figure 7–44

6
- Click the Finish button (Convert Text to Columns Wizard – Step 2 of 3 dialog box) to close the dialog box and separate the data in column A into two columns.

- Display the Home tab to prepare for the next task (Figure 7–45).

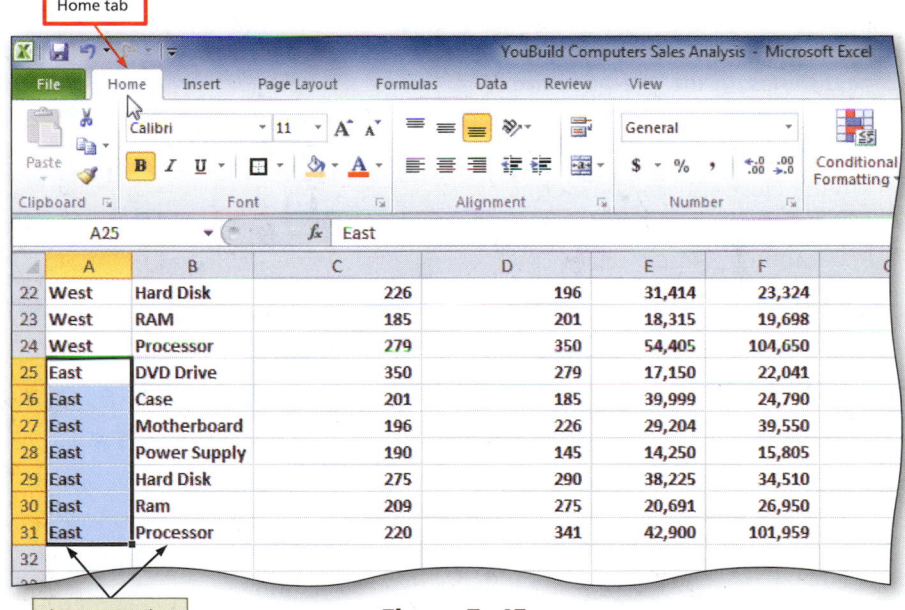

Figure 7–45

Replicating Formulas after Importing

The workbook opened at the beginning of this project contained a worksheet title, headings for each column, and formulas in cells G4 and H4 to calculate the average price per unit for 2012 and 2013. The formulas must be copied, or replicated, through row 31 to complete the calculations for the remaining rows in the worksheet. Some spreadsheet specialists refer to copying formulas as **replication**. You often replicate formulas after completing an import because the total number of records to be imported usually is unknown.

BTW

Selecting a Range of Cells
You can select any range of cells with entries surrounded by blank cells by clicking a cell in the range and pressing CTRL+SHIFT+ASTERISK (*).

To Replicate Formulas

The following steps use the fill handle to replicate the formulas.

1
- Select the range G4:H4 to prepare for copying the formulas in the range (Figure 7–46).

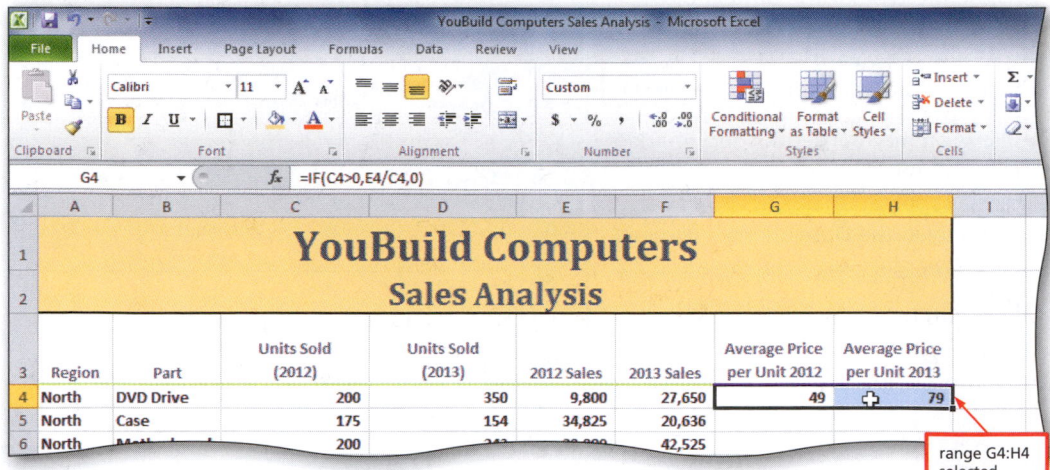

Figure 7–46

2
- Drag the fill handle down through row 31 to copy the two formulas to the range G5:H31 and display the new values for the Average Price per Unit 2012 and Average Price per Unit 2013 columns (Figure 7–47).

What if I just want to copy formulas rather than replicate them?

Replicating a formula causes Excel to adjust the cell references so that the new formulas contain references corresponding to the new locations. Excel then performs calculations using the appropriate values. To create an exact copy without replication, hold down the CTRL key while dragging the fill handle. Holding down the SHIFT key while dragging the fill handle inserts new cells, rather than overwriting existing data.

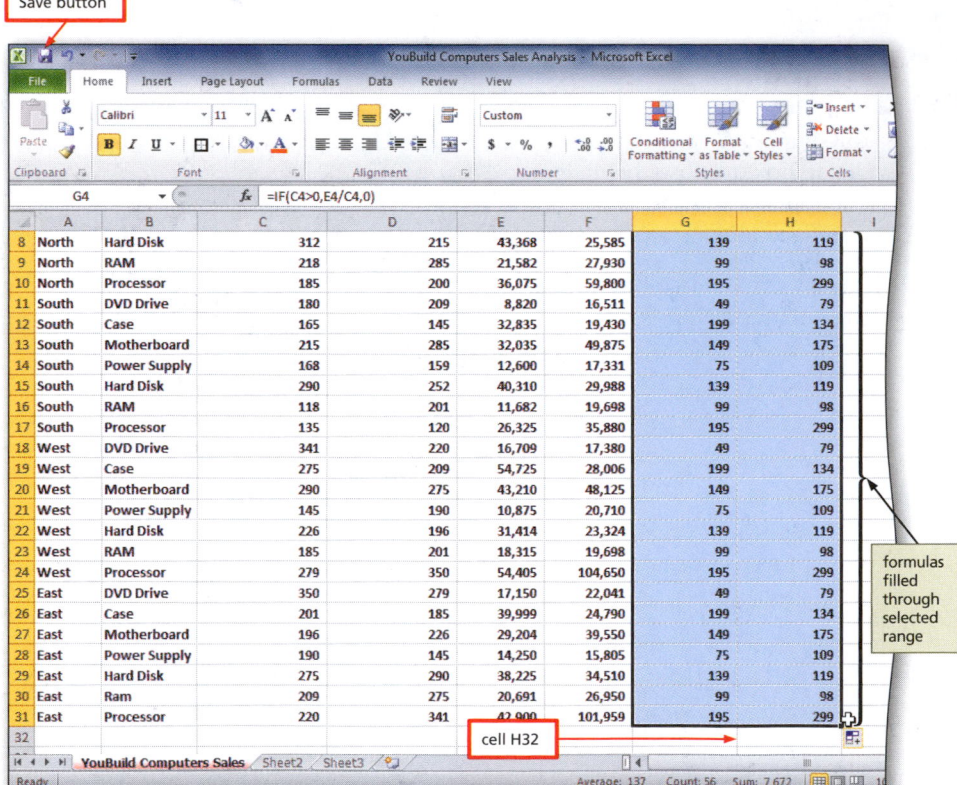

Figure 7–47

3
- Click Cell H32 to deselect the range G5:H31.

- Click the Save button on the Quick Access Toolbar to save the workbook using the same file name, YouBuild Computers Sales Analysis.

Other Ways

1. Click Copy button on Quick Access Toolbar, click Paste button on Quick Access Toolbar

2. Press CTRL+C, press CTRL+V

3. Click Copy on shortcut menu, click Paste on shortcut menu

Break Point: If you wish to take a break, this is a good place to do so. You can quit Excel now. To resume at a later time, start Excel, open the file called YouBuild Computers Sales Analysis, and continue following the steps from this location forward.

Using the Find and Replace Commands

A **string** can be a single character, a word, or a phrase in a cell on a worksheet. To locate a string in a worksheet, you can use the Find command on the Find & Select menu. Display the Find & Select menu by clicking the Find & Select button on the Home tab. To locate one string and then replace it with another string, use the Replace command on the Find & Select menu. The Find and Replace commands are not available for a chart sheet.

Selecting the Find or Replace command displays the Find and Replace dialog box. The Find and Replace dialog box has two variations. One version displays minimal options, while the other version displays all of the available options. When you select the Find or Replace command, Excel displays the dialog box variation that was used the last time either command was selected.

BTW

The Find Command
If you want to search only a specified range of a worksheet, select the range before using the Find command. The range can consist of adjacent cells or nonadjacent cells.

Determine whether data you import needs to be standardized.
Before importing files from various sources, examine the data to determine whether it fits in with the other data. For example, the author of one source might refer to a DVD drive, while the author of another source might refer to the same item as an optical disc drive. Determine which terminology you want to use in your spreadsheet, and use the appropriate commands to standardize all wording.

Plan Ahead

To Find a String

The following steps show how to locate the string, Motherboard. The Find and Replace dialog box that displays all the options will be used to customize the search by using the Match case and 'Match entire cell contents' options. Match case means that the search is case sensitive and the cell contents must match the word exactly the way it is typed. 'Match entire cell contents' means that the string cannot be part of another word or phrase and must be unique in the cell. If you have a cell range selected, the Find and Replace commands search only the range; otherwise, the Find and Replace commands begin at cell A1, regardless of the location of the active cell.

1
- Click the Find & Select button (Home tab | Editing group) to display the Find & Select menu (Figure 7–48).

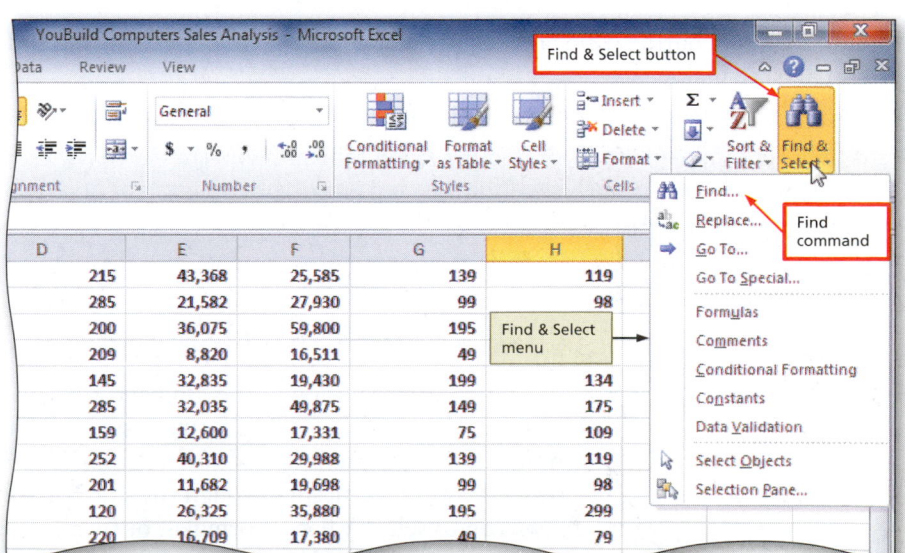

Figure 7–48

2

- Click Find to display the Find and Replace dialog box.

- Click the Options button (Find and Replace dialog box) to expand the dialog box so that it appears as shown in Figure 7–49.

- Type **Motherboard** in the Find what box to enter the search text.

- Click Match case and then click 'Match entire cell contents' to insert check marks in those check boxes (Figure 7–49).

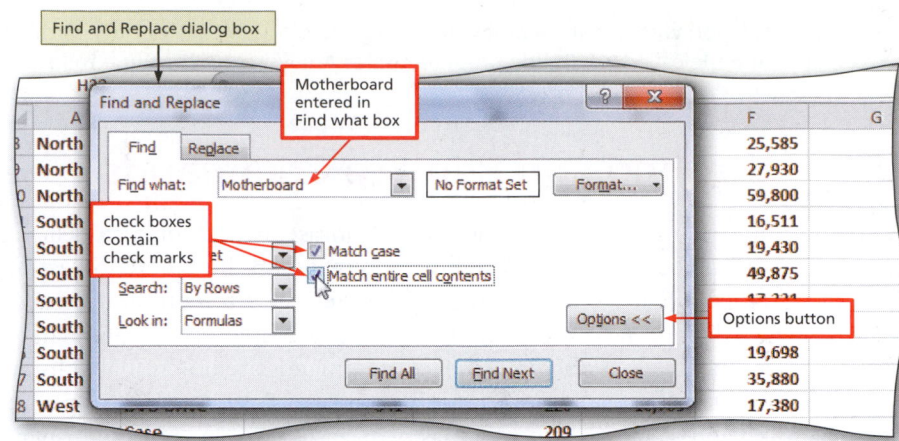

Figure 7–49

Q&A

Why does the appearance of the Options button change?

The two less than signs pointing to the left on the Options button indicate that the more comprehensive Find and Replace dialog box is active.

3

- Click the Find Next button (Find and Replace dialog box) to cause Excel to begin the search at cell A1 on the YouBuild Computers Sales worksheet and make cell B6 the active cell (Figure 7–50).

Q&A

Why is cell B6 the active cell after completing Step 3?

Cell B6 is the first cell to match the search string.

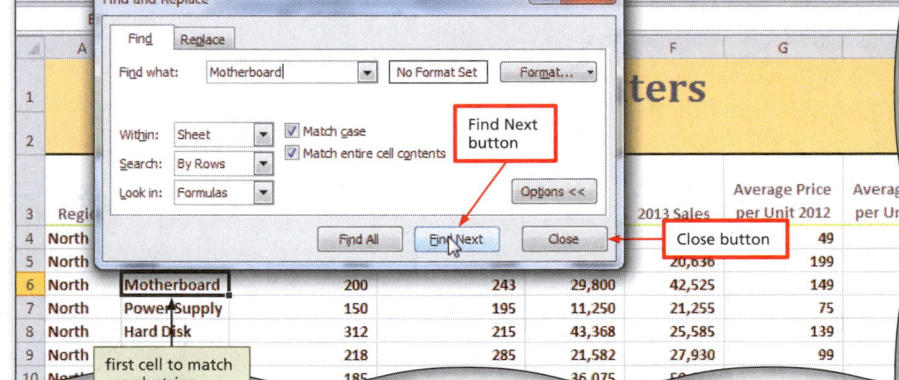

Figure 7–50

4

- Continue clicking the Find Next button (Find and Replace dialog box) to find the string, Motherboard, in three other cells on the worksheet.

- Click the Close button (Find and Replace dialog box) to stop searching and close the Find and Replace dialog box.

Q&A

What if Excel does not find the search string?

If the Find command does not find the string for which you are searching, Excel displays a dialog box indicating it searched the selected worksheets and cannot find the search string.

Other Ways
1. Press CTRL+F

Working with the Find and Replace Dialog Box

The Format button in the Find and Replace dialog box in Figure 7–50 allows you to fine-tune the search by adding formats, such as bold, font style, and font size, to the string. The Within box options include Sheet and Workbook. The Search box indicates whether Excel will search vertically through rows or horizontally across columns. The Look in box allows you to select Values, Formulas, or Comments. If you select Values, Excel will look for the search string only in cells that do not have formulas. If you select Formulas, Excel will look in all cells. If you select Comments, Excel will look only in comments. If you select the Match case check box, Excel will locate only cells in which the string is in the same case. For example, ram is not the same as RAM. If you select the 'Match entire cell contents' check box, Excel will locate only the cells that contain the string and no other characters. For example, Excel will find a cell entry of RAM, but not DVD RAM.

To Replace a String with Another String

Use the Replace command to replace the found search string with a new string. You can use the Find Next and Replace buttons to find and replace a string one occurrence at a time, or you can use the Replace All button to replace the string in all locations at once. The following steps show how to use the Replace All button to replace the string, DVD Drive, with the string, Optical Disc Drive.

1
- Click the Find & Select button (Home tab | Editing group) to display the Find & Select menu.

- Click Replace on the Find & Select menu to display the Find and Replace dialog box.

- Type **DVD Drive** in the Find what box and **Optical Disc Drive** in the Replace with box to specify the text to find and to replace.

- If necessary, click Match case and then click 'Match entire cell contents' to insert check marks in those check boxes (Figure 7–51).

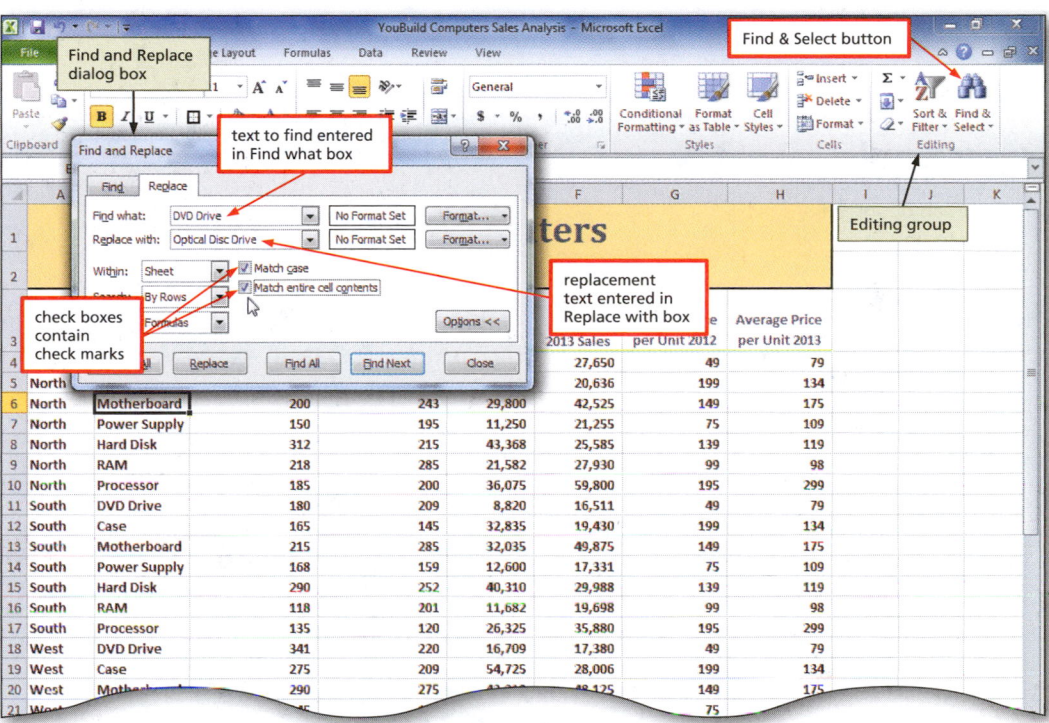

Figure 7–51

2
- Click the Replace All button (Find and Replace dialog box) to replace the string (Figure 7–52).

3
- Click the OK button (Microsoft Office Excel dialog box).

- Click the Close button (Find and Replace dialog box).

Q&A What happens when Excel replaces the string?

Excel replaces the string, DVD Drive, with the replacement string, Optical Disc Drive, throughout the entire worksheet. If other worksheets contain matching cells, Excel replaces those cells as well. Excel displays the Microsoft Excel dialog box indicating four replacements were made.

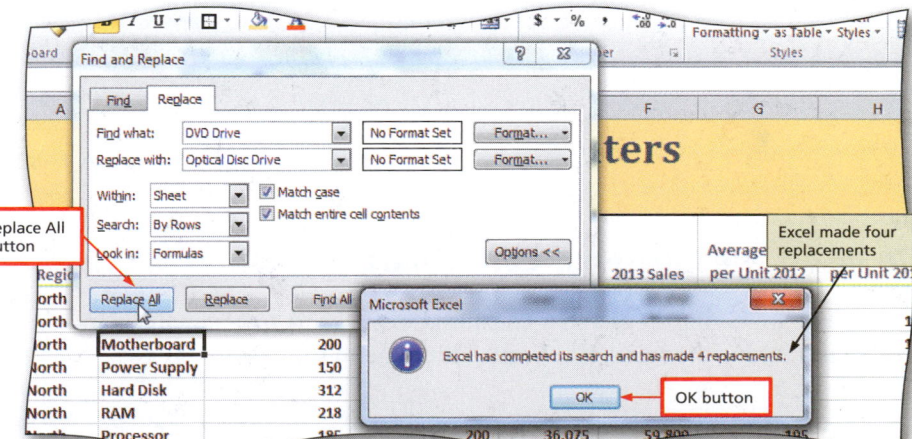

Figure 7–52

Other Ways
1. Press CTRL+H

Inserting a Clustered Cone Chart

The requirements document shown in Figure 7–2 on page EX 429 specifies that the workbook should include a Clustered Cone chart. The Clustered Cone chart is similar to a 3-D Bar chart in that it can show trends or illustrate comparisons among items.

Plan Ahead

Plan the layout and location of the required chart.
The Clustered Cone chart in Figure 7–53, for example, compares the average price per unit for 2013 of the different parts for the North region. The chart should be placed on a separate worksheet. WordArt is used to draw the reflected chart title, Price Analysis, in an eye-catching and professional format.

BTW

Certification
The Microsoft Office Specialist (MOS) program provides an opportunity for you to obtain a valuable industry credential — proof that you have the Excel 2010 skills required by employers. For more information, visit the Excel 2010 Certification Web page (scsite.com/ex2010/cert).

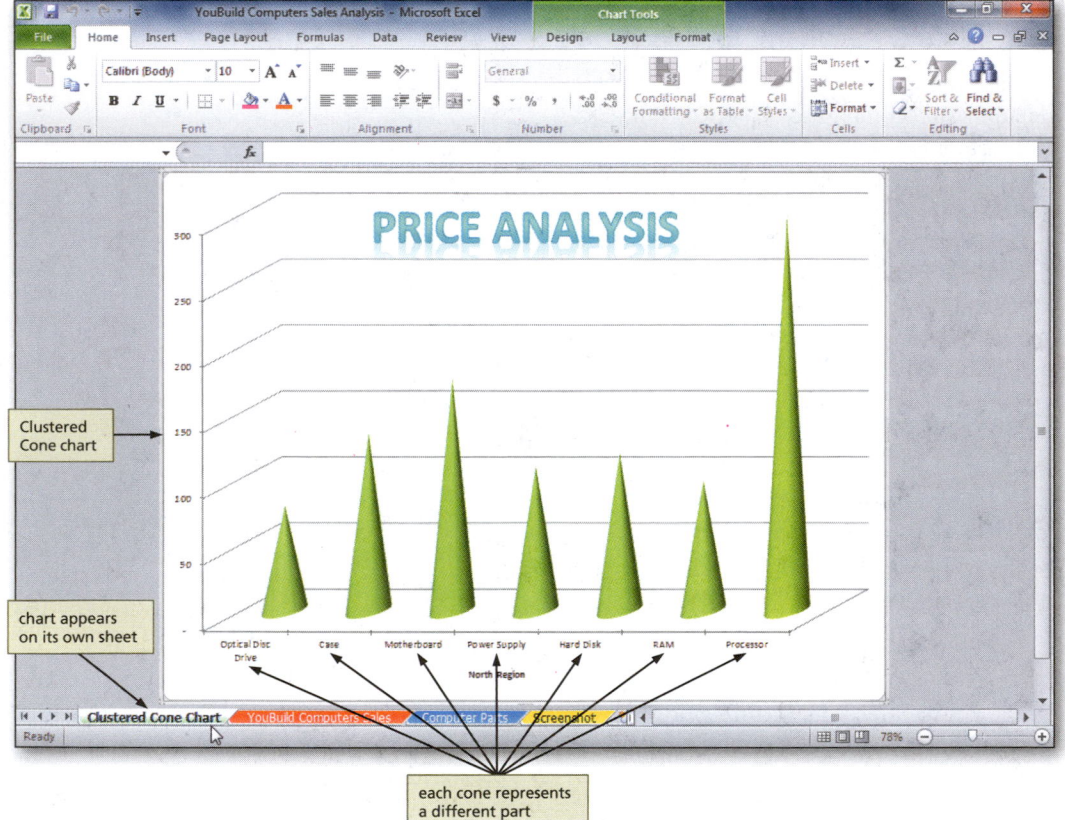

Figure 7–53

To Insert the Clustered Cone Chart

The following steps add a Clustered Cone chart to a new sheet and then change the layout of the chart to rotate it, remove the series label, and add a title to the horizontal axis.

1

- Select the range B4:B10 to select the first set of data to include in the chart.

- Hold down the CTRL key and then select the range H4:H10 to select the second set of data for the chart.

- Click Insert on the Ribbon to display the Insert tab.

- Click the Column button (Insert tab | Charts group) and then click Clustered Cone (column 1, row 4) in the Column gallery to insert a Clustered Cone chart (Figure 7–54).

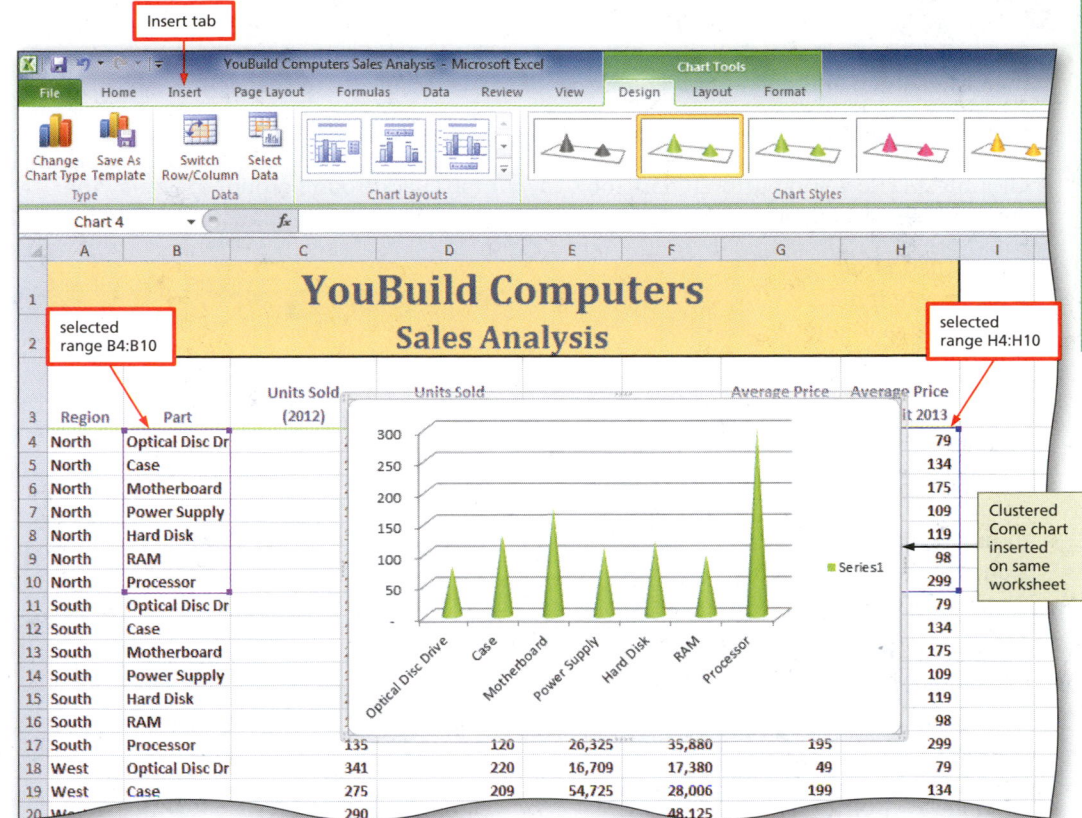

Figure 7–54

2

- Click the Move Chart button (Chart Tools Design tab | Location group) to display the Move Chart dialog box.

- Click the New sheet option button and then type `Clustered Cone Chart` as the sheet name in the New sheet text box.

- Click the OK button (Move Chart dialog box) to move the chart to the new sheet (Figure 7–55).

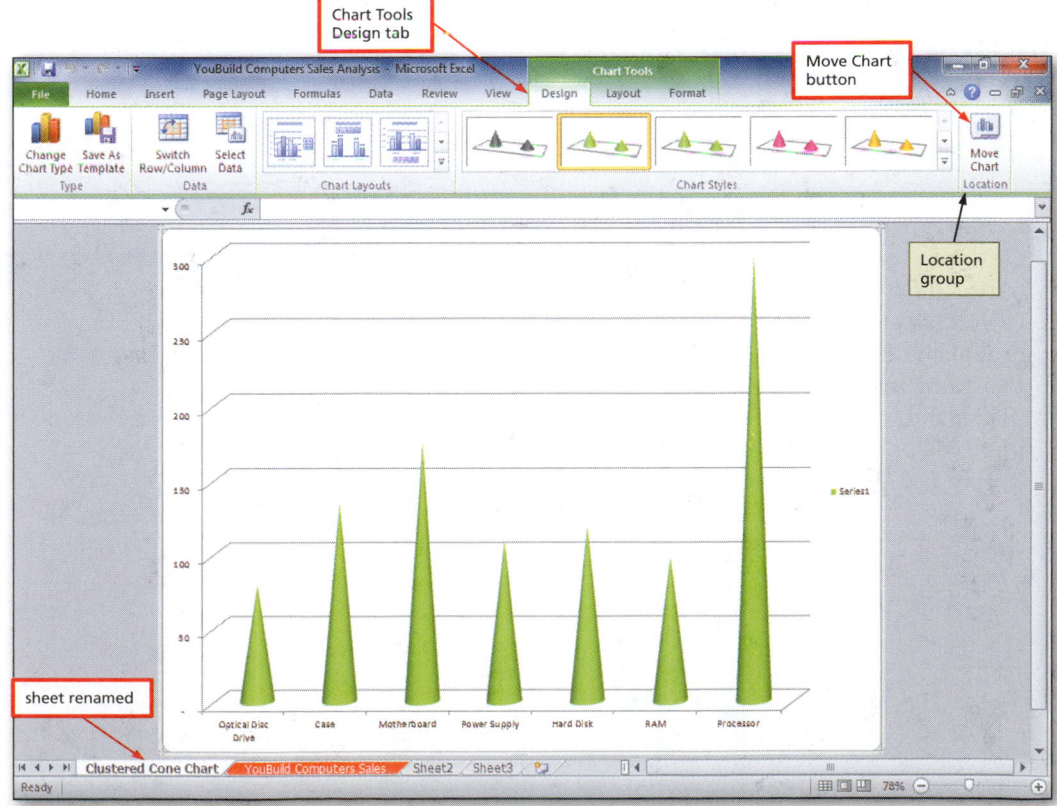

Figure 7–55

3

- Right-click the Clustered Cone Chart sheet tab, point to Tab Color on the shortcut menu, and then click Green in the Standard Colors row of the Color palette to change the tab color.

- Click Layout on the Ribbon to display the Chart Tools Layout tab.

- Click the 3-D Rotation button (Chart Tools Layout tab | Background group) to display the Format Chart Area dialog box.

- Type 7 0 in the X text box in the Rotation area to rotate the chart 70 degrees along the x-axis.

- Type 3 0 in the Y text box in the Rotation area to rotate the chart 30 degrees along the y-axis.

- Click the Close button (Format Chart Area dialog box) to finish formatting the chart (Figure 7–56).

 Experiment

- Try entering different values in the X and Y text boxes to see how changing the values affects the rotation of the chart. When you are finished, return the values to those specified in Step 3.

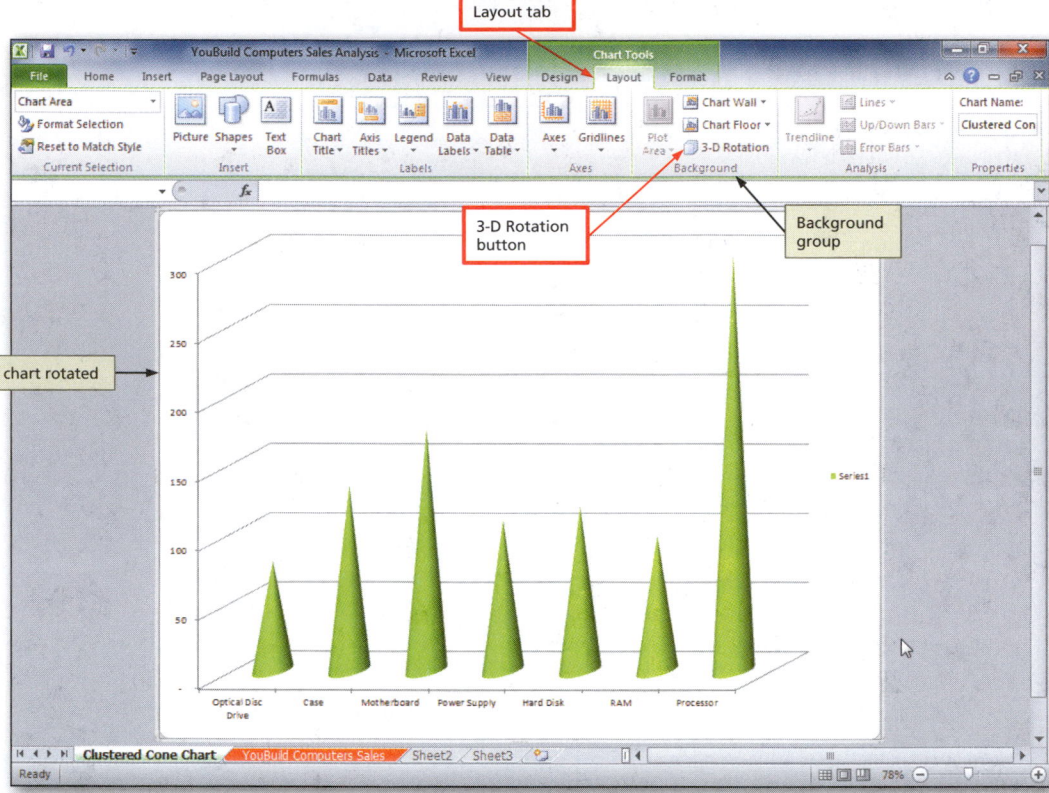

Figure 7–56

4

- Click the Legend button (Chart Tools Layout tab | Labels group) and then click None to remove the legend from the right side of the chart (Figure 7–57).

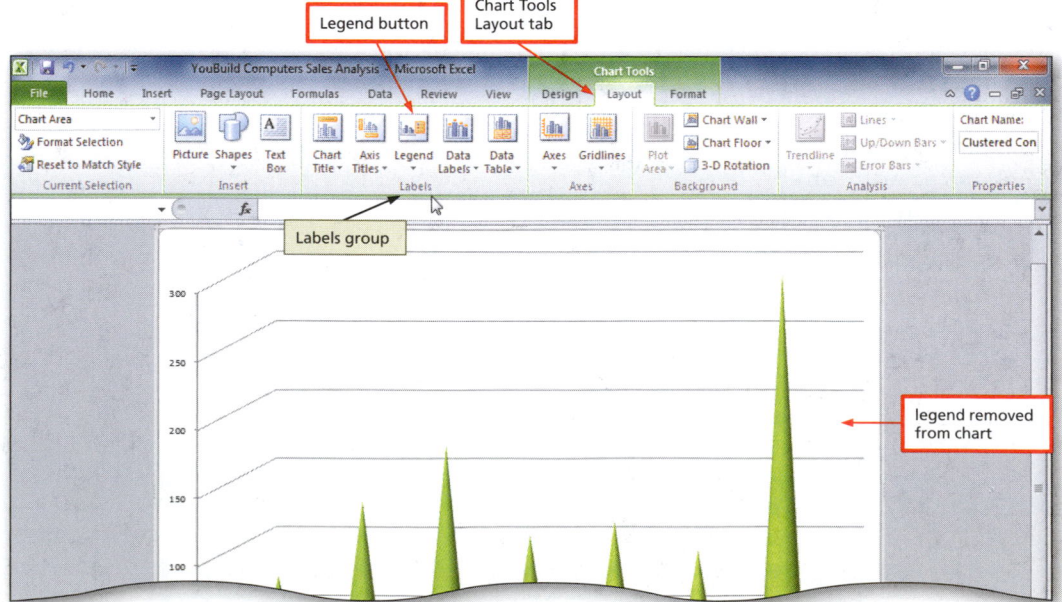

Figure 7–57

5
- Click the Axis Titles button (Chart Tools Layout tab | Labels group) to display the Axis Titles menu.

- Point to Primary Horizontal Axis Title on the Axis Titles menu and then click Title Below Axis in the Primary Horizontal Axis Title gallery to add a title to the horizontal axis.

- Select the Axis Title text and then type **North Region** as the new title (Figure 7–58).

Q&A

What does the chart show?

The Clustered Cone chart compares the prices of the seven different computer parts. You can see from the chart that, of the parts sold, the processor is the most expensive, and the optical disc drive is the least expensive.

Other Ways

1. Select range, click chart type button (Insert tab | Charts group), click chart type in gallery

2. Select range, press F11

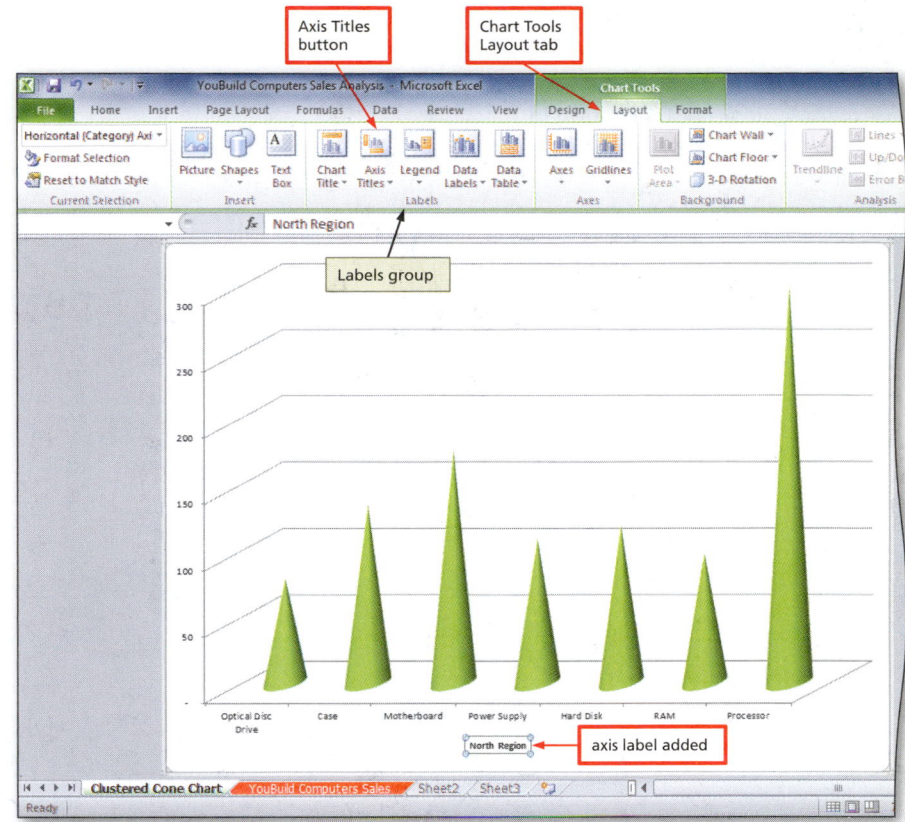

Figure 7–58

To Add a Chart Title Using the WordArt Tool

Earlier, you learned how to add a chart title by using the Chart Title button on the Chart Tools Layout tab, and how to format it using the Home tab. You also can create a chart title using the WordArt tool. The WordArt tool allows you to create shadowed, skewed, rotated, and stretched text on a chart sheet or worksheet and apply other special text formatting effects. The WordArt text added to a worksheet is called an object. The following steps show how to add a chart title using the WordArt tool.

1
- With the Clustered Cone Chart sheet active, click anywhere on the chart.

- Display the Insert tab.

- Click the WordArt button (Insert tab | Text group) to display the WordArt gallery.

- Point to the Gradient Fill – Turquoise, Accent 4, Reflection (column 5, row 4) selection in the WordArt gallery to highlight that color and effect (Figure 7–59).

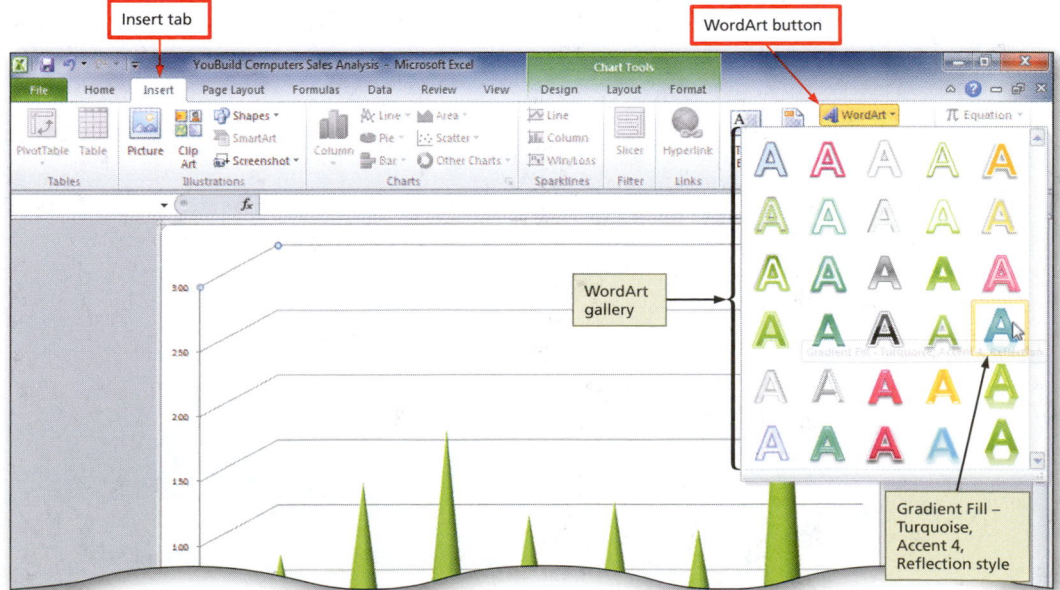

Figure 7–59

2

- Click the Gradient Fill – Turquoise, Accent 4, Reflection selection in the WordArt gallery to insert a new WordArt object.

- Type **Price Analysis** as the title of the Clustered Cone chart (Figure 7–60).

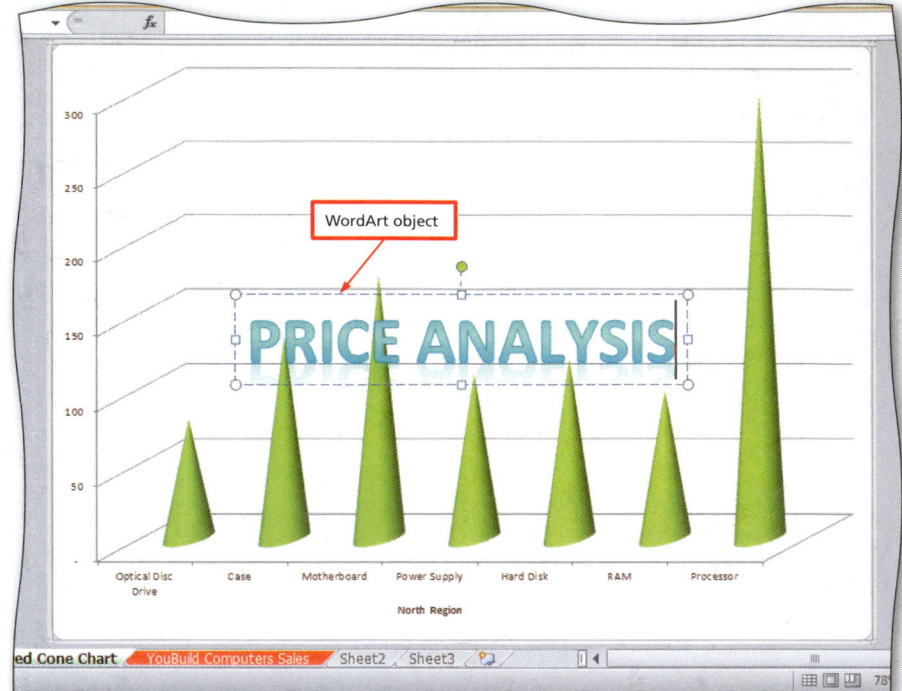

Figure 7–60

3

- Select the text in the WordArt object to display the Mini toolbar (Figure 7–61).

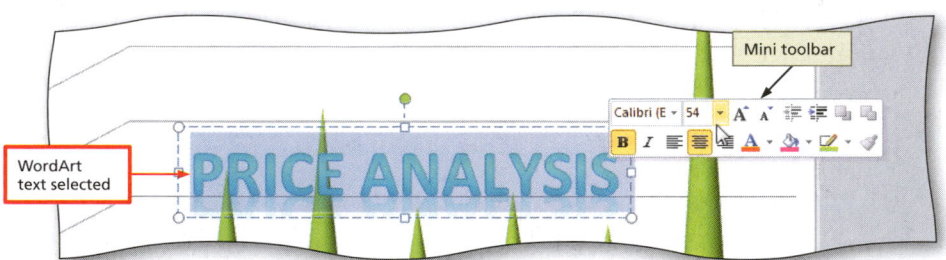

Figure 7–61

4

- Click the Font Size box arrow on the Mini toolbar and then click 44 in the Font Size list to change the font size of the WordArt object to 44 points (Figure 7–62).

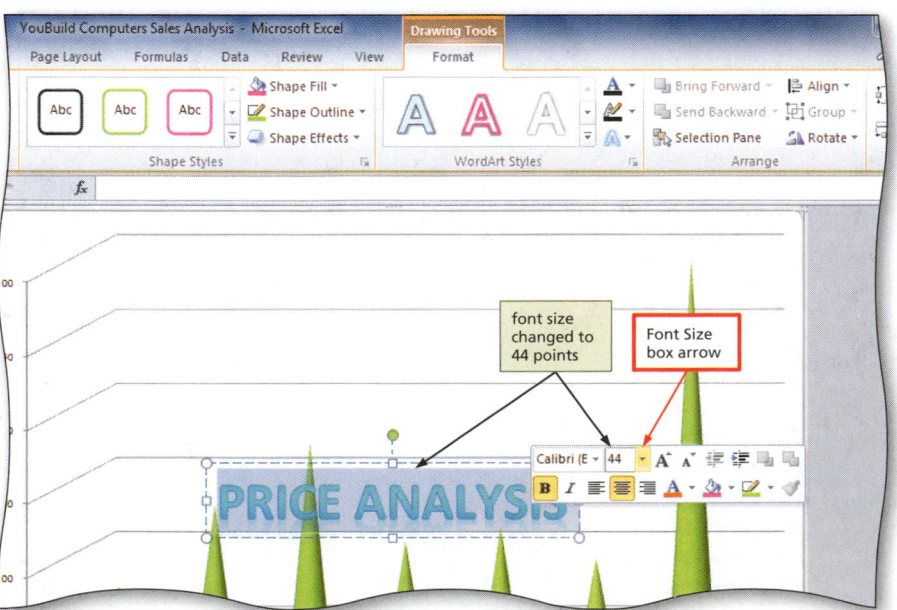

Figure 7–62

5
- Drag the top edge of the WordArt object so that the object is positioned in the upper-middle part of the chart (as shown in Figure 7–63).

Figure 7–63

6
- Click outside the chart area to deselect the WordArt object (Figure 7–64).

7
- Click the Save button on the Quick Access Toolbar to save the workbook using the file name, YouBuild Computers Sales Analysis.

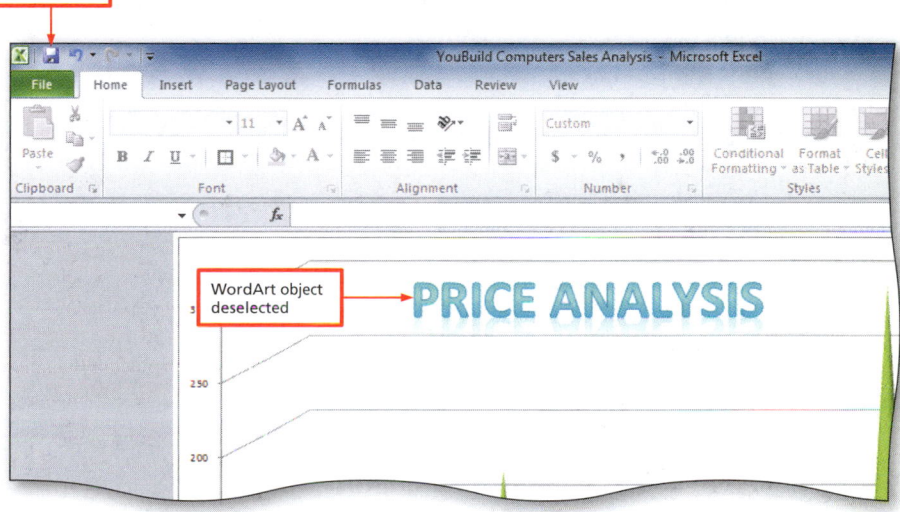

Figure 7–64

Working with SmartArt Graphics

A SmartArt graphic is a customizable diagram that you use to pictorially present lists, processes, and relationships. For example, you can use a SmartArt graphic to illustrate the manufacturing process to produce an item. Excel includes nine types of SmartArt graphics: List, Process, Cycle, Hierarchy, Relationship, Matrix, Pyramid, Picture, and Office.com. Each type of graphic includes several layouts, or templates, from which to choose. After selecting a SmartArt graphic type and layout, you customize the graphic to meet your needs and present your information and ideas in a compelling manner.

Choose the type of SmartArt graphics to add.
Consider what you want to illustrate in the SmartArt graphic. For example, if you are showing nonsequential or grouped blocks of information, select a SmartArt graphic in the List category. To show progression or sequential steps in a process or task, select a Process diagram. After inserting a SmartArt graphic, increase its visual appeal by formatting the graphic, for example, with 3-D effects and coordinated colors.

Plan Ahead

To Insert a Picture Strips SmartArt Graphic

Excel allows you to insert SmartArt graphics that can contain pictures. To illustrate the type of computer parts YouBuild Computers sells, you decide to use a Picture Strips SmartArt graphic. The following steps insert a Picture Strips SmartArt graphic.

1

- Click the Sheet2 tab to make Sheet2 the active worksheet.

- Rename the worksheet **Computer Parts** to provide a descriptive name for the worksheet.

- Change the color of the tab to blue to distinguish it from other sheets.

- Click View on the Ribbon to display the View tab.

- Click the Gridlines check box (View tab | Show group) to turn off gridlines on the worksheet (Figure 7–65).

Q&A

Why should I turn off gridlines?

Although useful during the process of creating a worksheet, many spreadsheet specialists remove the gridlines to reduce the clutter on the screen. This is especially true when working with graphics and images on a worksheet.

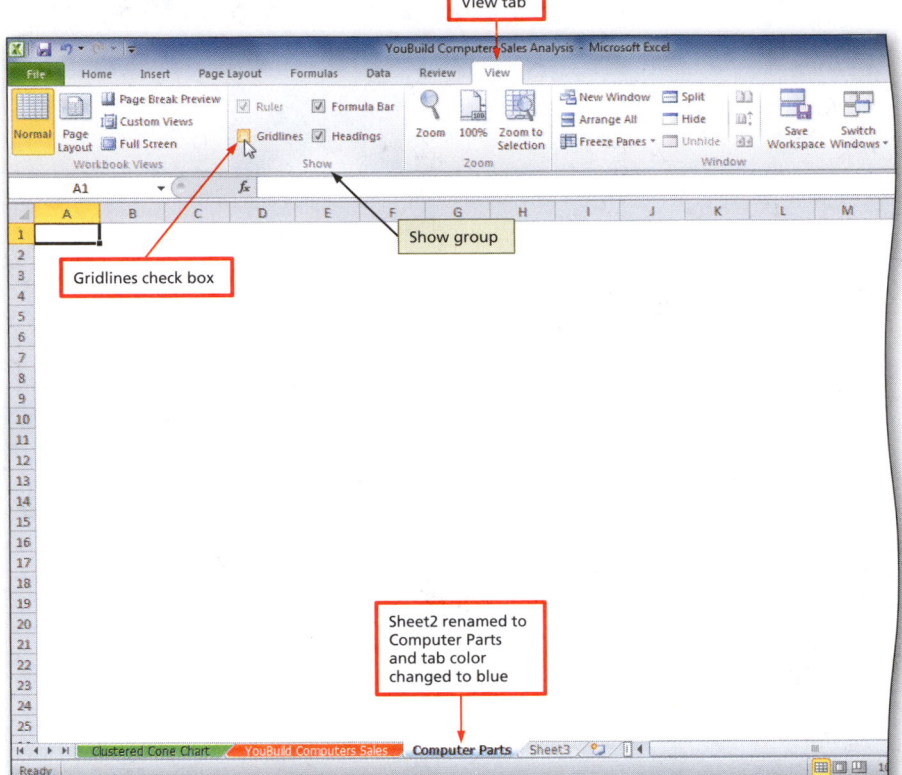

Figure 7–65

2

- Display the Insert tab.

- Click the SmartArt button (Insert tab | Illustrations group) to display the Choose a SmartArt Graphic dialog box (Figure 7–66).

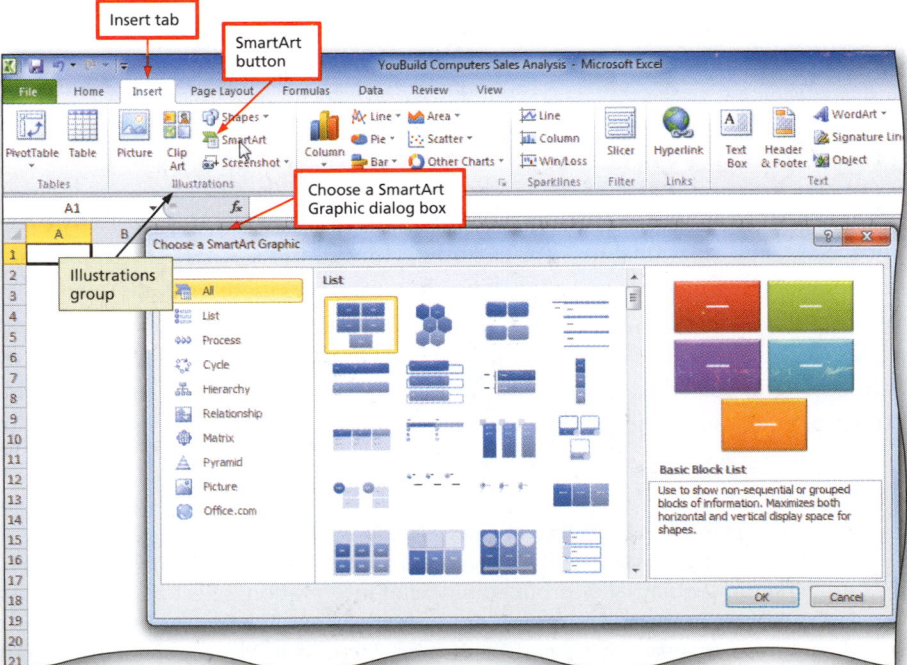

Figure 7–66

3

- Click Picture in the Type list in the left pane of the Choose a SmartArt Graphic dialog box.

Q&A

What do the middle and right panes of the dialog box display?

The middle pane of the dialog box (the layout list) displays a gallery of picture charts, and the right pane (the preview area) displays a preview of the selected SmartArt graphic.

- Click Picture Strips (column 2, row 4) in the layout list to see a preview of the chart in the preview area (Figure 7–67).

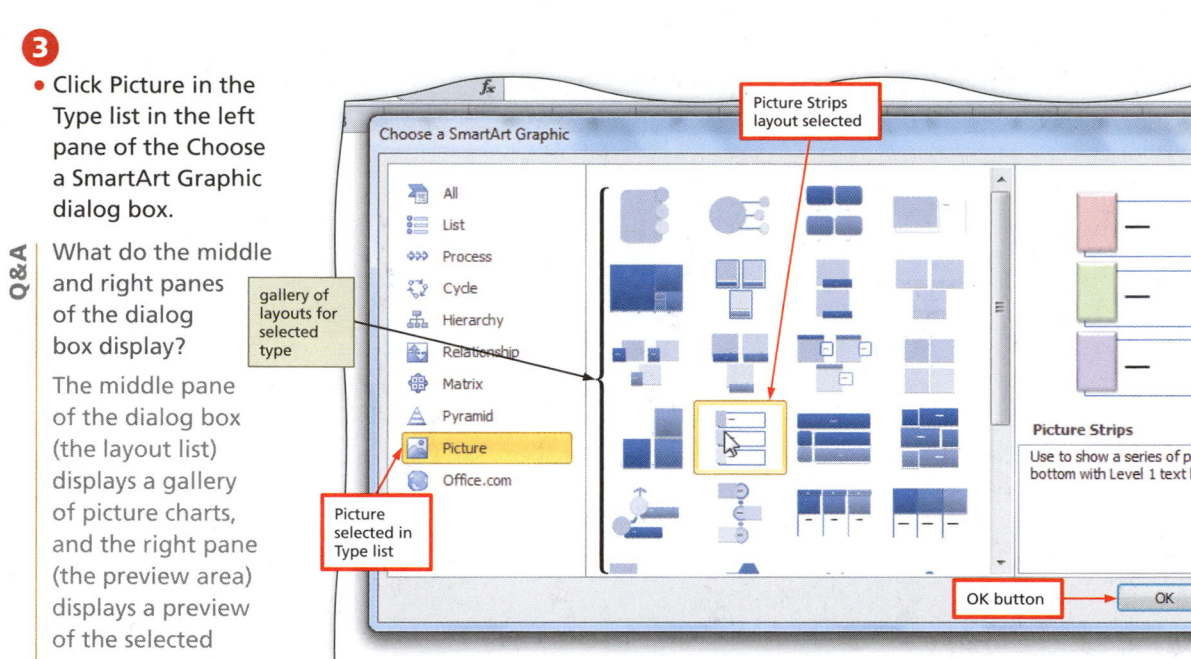

Figure 7–67

 Experiment

- Click the various SmartArt graphics to see a preview of each in the preview area. When you are finished, click Picture Strips in the layout list.

4

- Click the OK button (Choose a SmartArt Graphic dialog box) to insert a Picture Strips SmartArt graphic in the worksheet.

- If necessary, click the Text Pane button (SmartArt Tools Design tab | Create Graphic group) to display the Text pane (Figure 7–68).

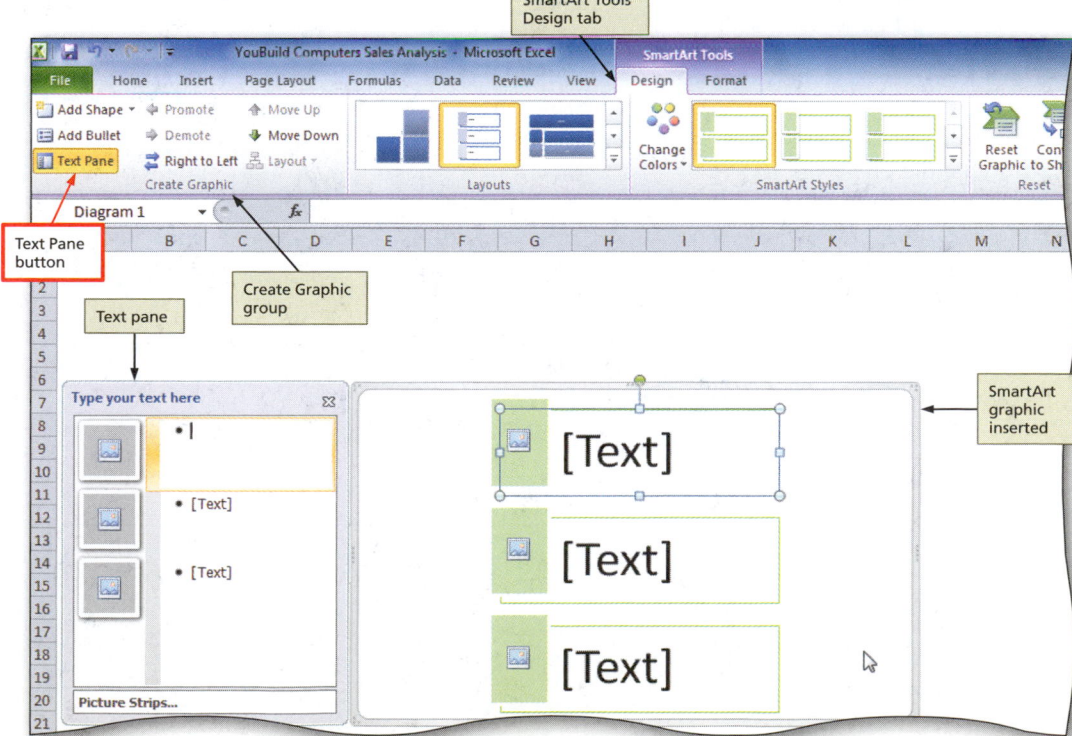

Figure 7–68

5

- While holding down the ALT key, click and drag the top of the SmartArt graphic so that the upper-left corner is over cell G1 (Figure 7–69).

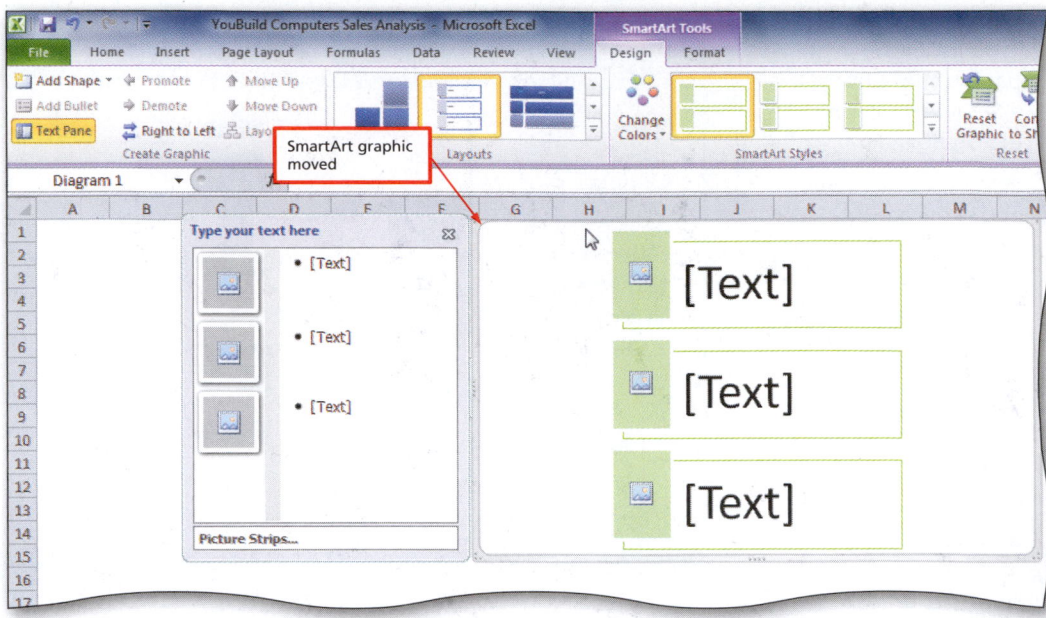

Figure 7–69

6

- Click the middle sizing handle on the right edge of the SmartArt graphic, hold down the ALT key, and then drag the sizing handle until the right edge of the SmartArt graphic is aligned with the right edge of column O.

- Release the ALT key, point to the middle sizing handle on the bottom edge of the chart, hold down the ALT key, and then drag the sizing handle until the bottom edge of the chart is aligned with the bottom edge of row 25 (Figure 7–70).

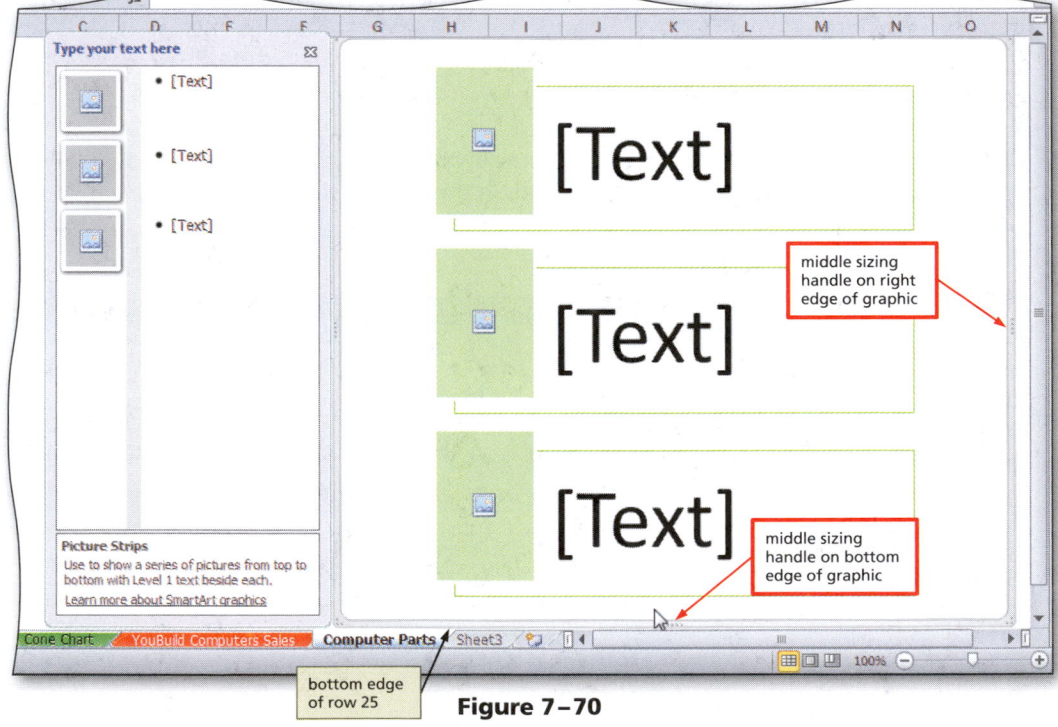

Figure 7–70

Other Ways

1. To display or hide Text pane, right-click SmartArt, click Show Text Pane or Hide Text Pane

2. To display Text pane, click expand button on SmartArt tab

To Add Shapes in the Picture Strips SmartArt Graphic

The default Picture Strips SmartArt graphic layout includes three shapes. You need six shapes to show the six computer parts that must be installed in a computer's case when building a computer. The following steps add three new shapes to the Picture Strips SmartArt graphic.

1

- Right-click the top shape in the Picture Strips SmartArt graphic to display the shortcut menu.

- Point to Add Shape on the shortcut menu to display the Add Shape submenu (Figure 7–71).

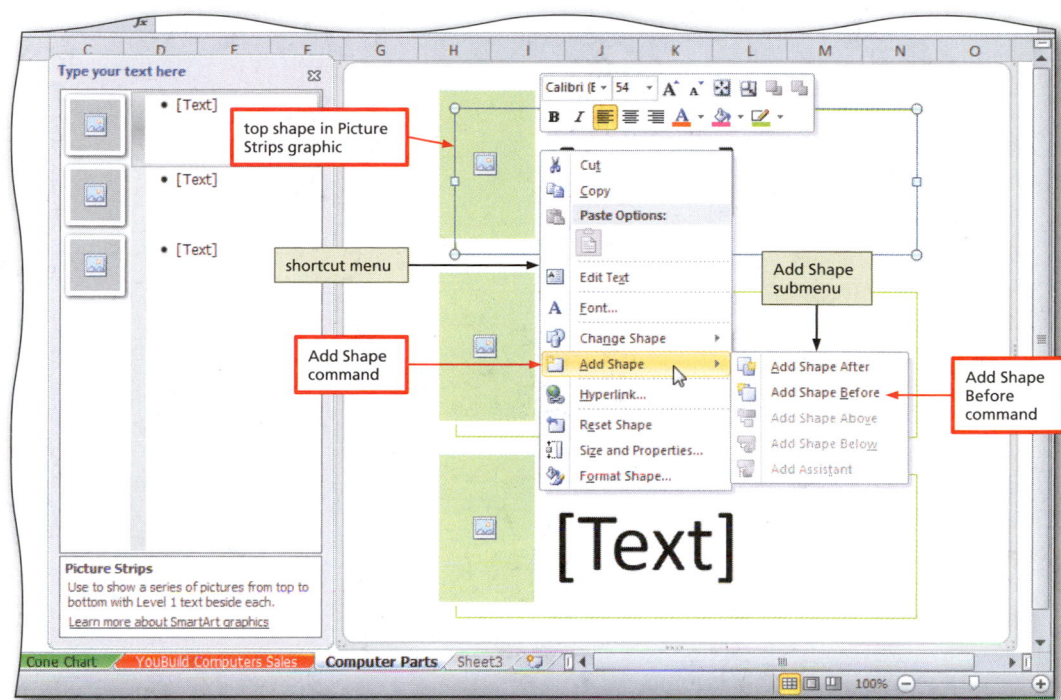

Figure 7–71

2

- Click Add Shape Before to add a new shape to the Picture Strips SmartArt graphic (Figure 7–72).

Q&A

Why does Excel change the layout of the chart?

When you add a new shape to a SmartArt graphic, Excel rearranges the shapes in the graphic to fit in the same area. As shown in Figure 7–72, Excel reduces the size of each shape and the font size of the text to accommodate the added shape.

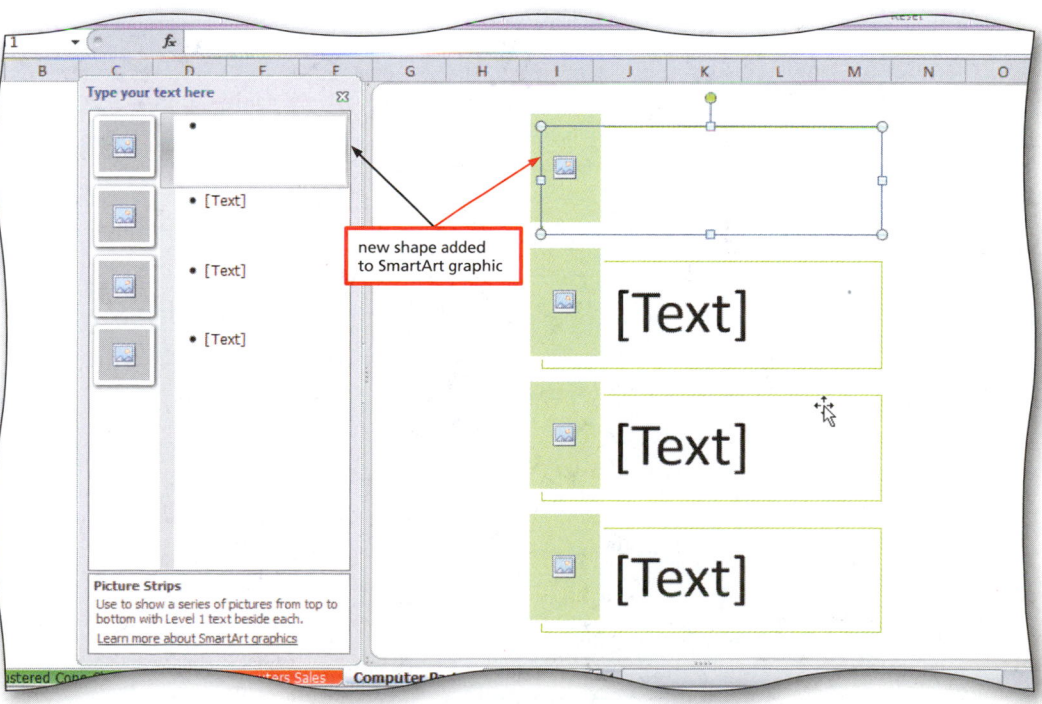

Figure 7–72

3

- If necessary, click the first shape of the chart to select it.

- If necessary, display the SmartArt Tools Design tab.

- Click the Add Shape button arrow (SmartArt Tools Design tab | Create Graphic group) to display the Add Shape menu.

- Click Add Shape After on the Add Shape menu to add a new shape below the first shape.

- Repeat these steps to insert a third additional shape to the Picture Strips SmartArt graphic (Figure 7–73).

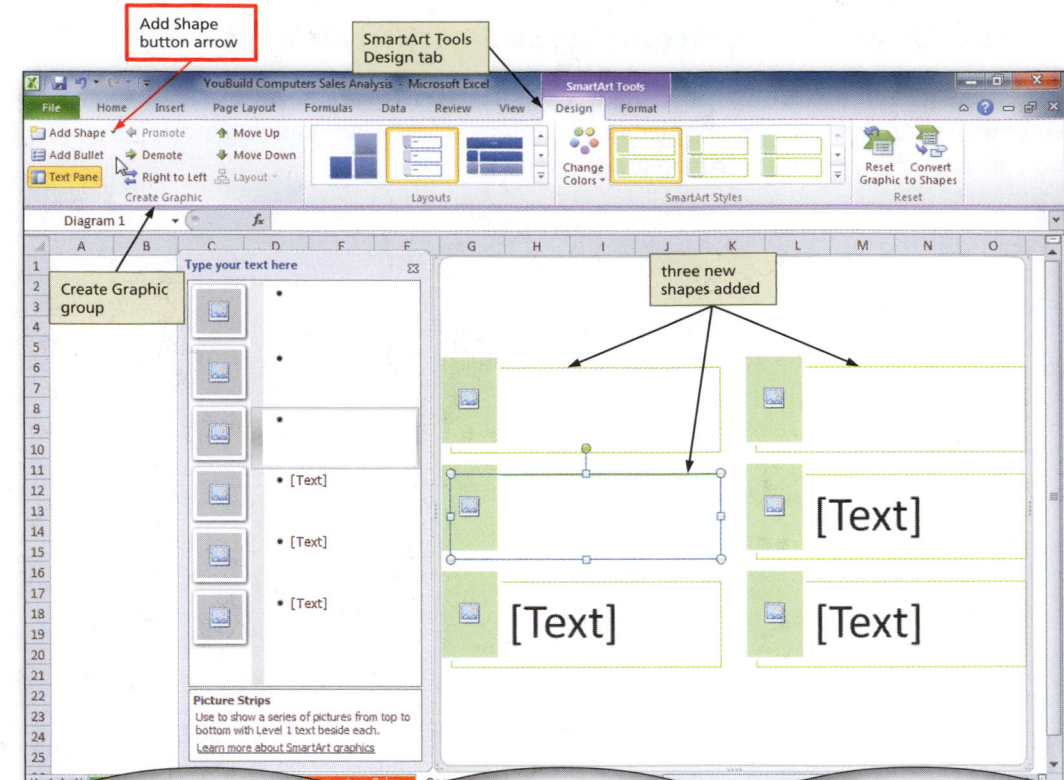

Figure 7–73

Other Ways

1. Select shape, click Add Shape (SmartArt Tools	Design tab	Create Graphic group)	2. Select shape, press CTRL+C, press CTRL+V

To Add Text to Shapes in the Picture Strips SmartArt Graphic

The following steps add text to the Picture Strips SmartArt graphic.

1

- Click the first shape's text box and then type **Motherboard** to add text to the shape (Figure 7–74).

Q&A

Why does Excel add the same text to the Text pane?

As you change the text in the chart, the Text pane reflects those changes in an outline. You can type text in the shapes or type text in the Text pane, as shown in the following step.

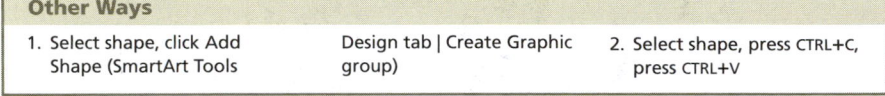

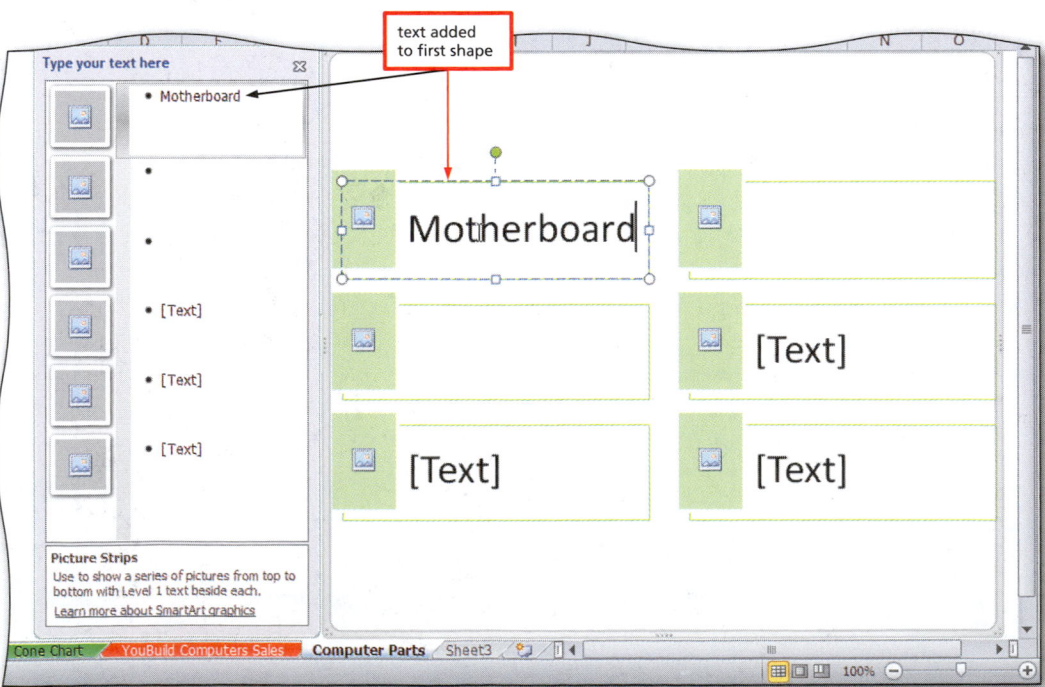

Figure 7–74

• Click the entry under Motherboard in the Text pane to select it.

• Type **Power Supply** in the second line of the Text pane to change the text in the second shape (Figure 7–75).

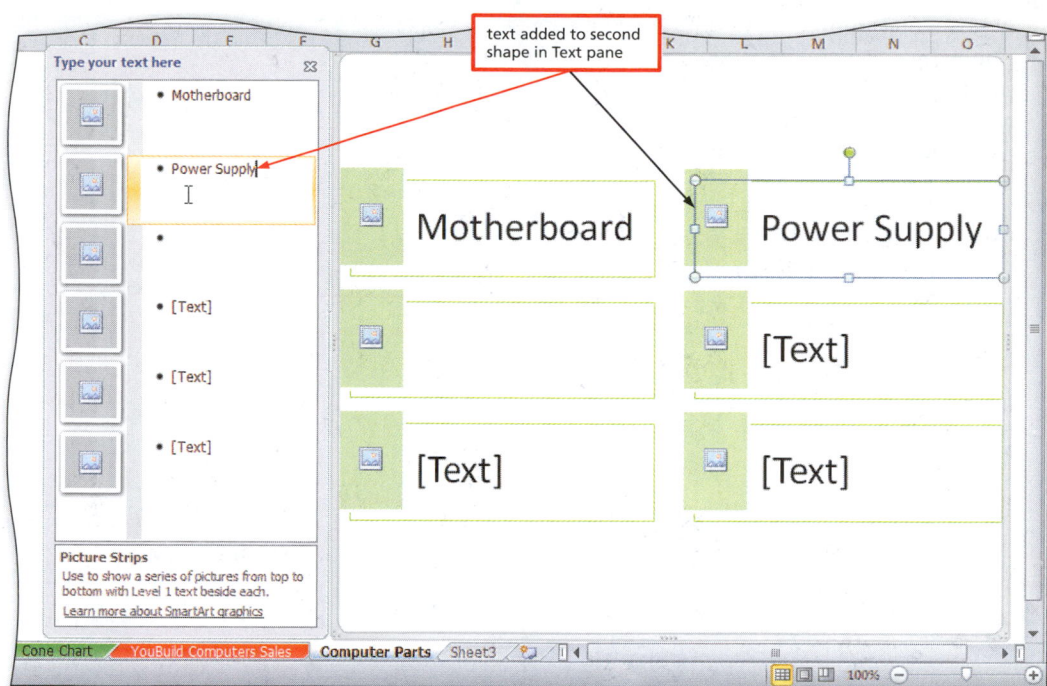

Figure 7–75

• Repeat Step 2 for each of the remaining shapes in the Picture Strips SmartArt graphic and enter text in each shape as shown in Figure 7–76.

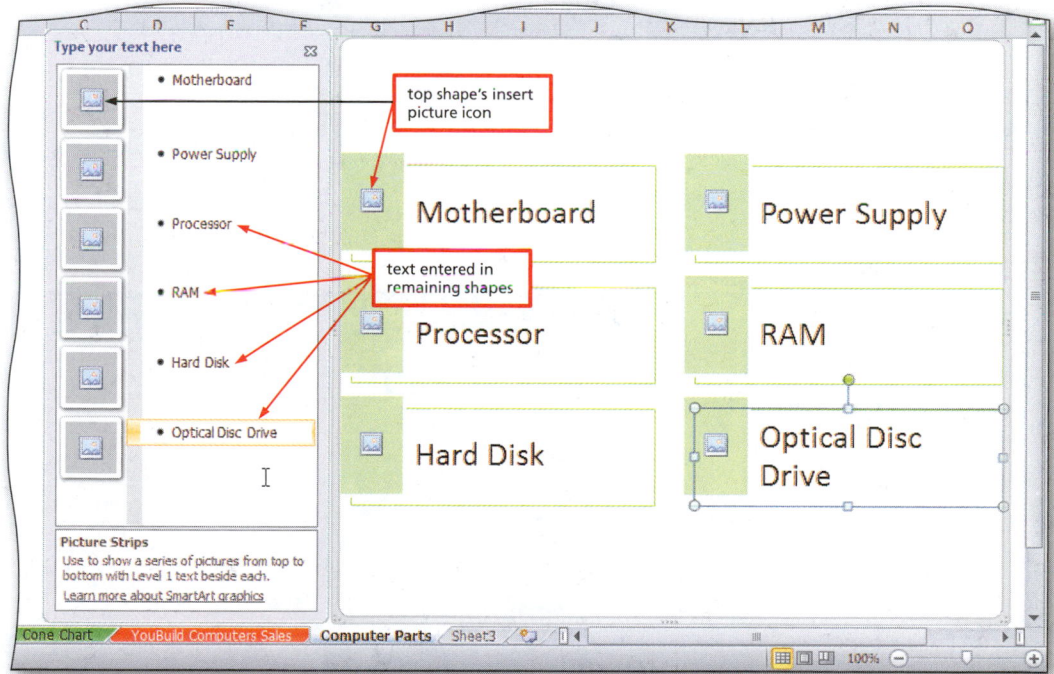

Figure 7–76

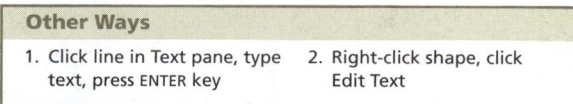

Other Ways	
1. Click line in Text pane, type text, press ENTER key	2. Right-click shape, click Edit Text

To Add Pictures to Shapes in the Picture Strips SmartArt Graphic

The following steps add pictures to the Picture Strips SmartArt graphic. The pictures to add are provided with the Data Files for Students and each has the same name as the computer part it displays.

1

- Click the upper-left shape's Insert Picture icon to display the Insert Picture dialog box.

- Navigate to the location of the picture to insert (in this case, the Excel folder on the USB flash drive) and click the Motherboard file to select the picture (Figure 7–77).

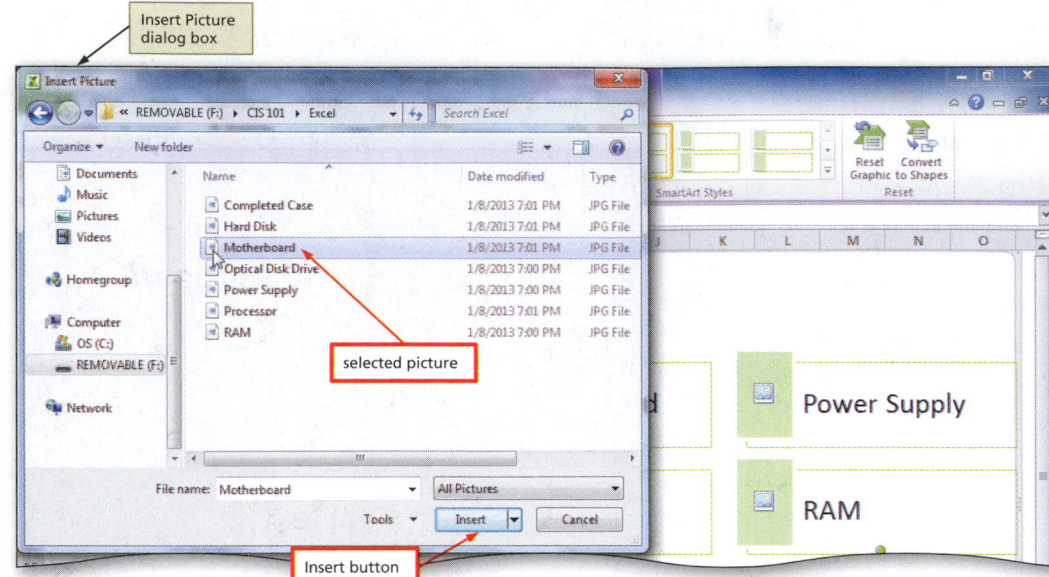

Figure 7–77

2

- Click the Insert button (Insert Picture dialog box) to insert the picture in the first shape (Figure 7–78).

Q&A

Could I also use the Insert Picture icon in the Text pane?

Yes, as with the text, you can add a picture from either the Text pane or the shape itself.

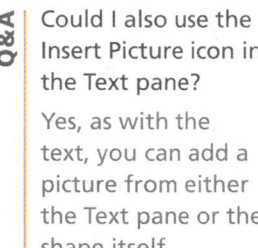

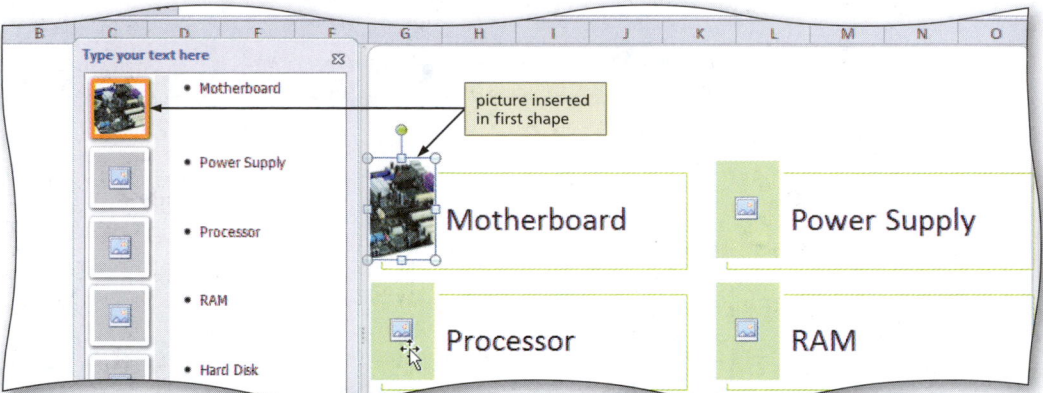

Figure 7–78

3

- Repeat Steps 1 and 2 for each of the remaining shapes in the picture strips and enter the picture in each shape (as shown in Figure 7–79).

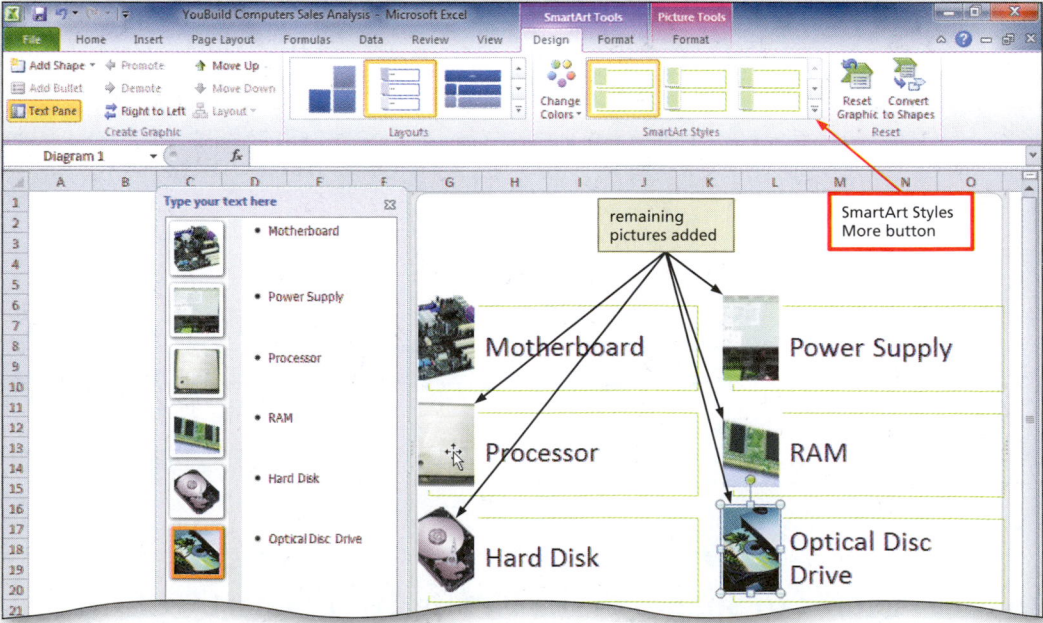

Figure 7–79

To Add an Effect to the Picture Strips SmartArt Graphic

Excel allows you to change the style of your SmartArt graphic to create different effects. The following steps change the style of the Picture Strips SmartArt graphic for added emphasis.

 1

- If necessary, display the SmartArt Tools Design tab.

- Click the SmartArt Styles More button (SmartArt Tools Design tab | SmartArt Styles group) to display the SmartArt Styles gallery.

- Point to the Intense Effect SmartArt style (column 2, row 2) in the Best Match for Document section to display a preview of the style in the worksheet (Figure 7–80).

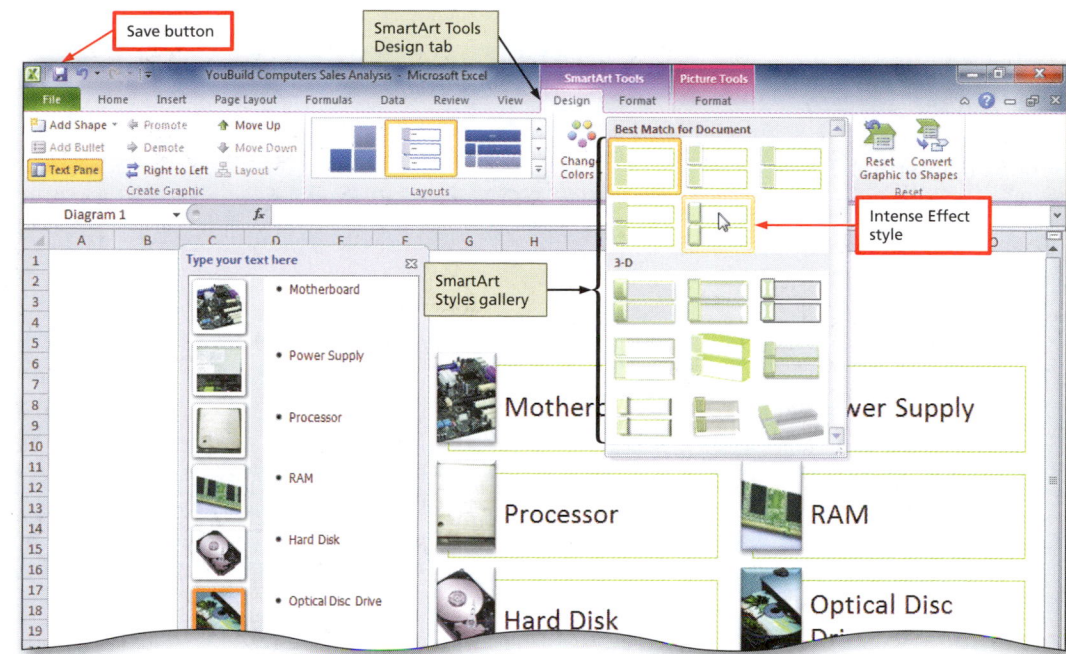

Figure 7–80

 2

- Click the Intense Effect SmartArt style to apply the style to the SmartArt graphic.

- Click cell A1 to deselect the Picture Strips SmartArt graphic.

- Click the Save button on the Quick Access Toolbar to save your work.

Using Images on a Worksheet

Besides adding images to SmartArt, Excel allows you to insert images on a worksheet and then modify the image by changing its shape and size or adding borders and effects. You can enhance a worksheet by including an image such as a corporate logo, photograph, diagram, or map. To use an image, the image must be stored digitally in a file.

BTW

Quick Reference
For a table that lists how to complete the tasks covered in this book using the mouse, Ribbon, shortcut menu, and keyboard, see the Quick Reference Summary at the back of this book, or visit the Excel 2010 Quick Reference Web page (scsite.com/ex2010/qr).

Plan Ahead

Obtain the images to be used in the worksheet.
Before inserting an image in a workbook, make sure you have permission to use the image. Although you might not need to pay for images available on Web sites, you most likely still need to request and receive permission to duplicate and use the images according to copyright law. Only images that are in the public domain are free for anyone to use without permission, although you still should credit the source of the image, even if the image creator is not specifically named. For example, include a credit line such as "Courtesy of NPS" if you use a public-domain photo from the National Park Service.

To Insert and Modify an Image in the Worksheet

The following steps insert an image of a computer case with all the parts installed, position and resize the image, and add an effect to the image.

1
- Display the Insert tab.

- Click the Insert Picture from File button (Insert tab | Illustrations group) to display the Insert Picture dialog box.

- Navigate to the location of the picture to insert (in this case, the Excel folder on the USB flash drive) and then click the Completed Case file to select the picture (Figure 7–81).

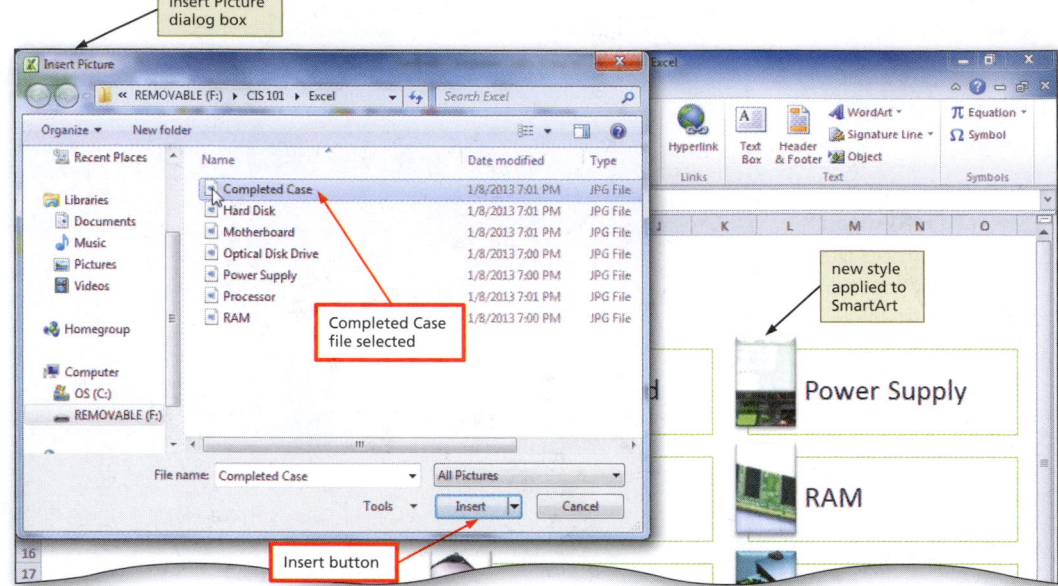

Figure 7–81

2
- Click the Insert button (Insert Picture dialog box) to insert the picture in the worksheet (Figure 7–82).

Q&A
How does Excel determine where to insert the image?

Excel inserts the image so that the upper-left corner of the image is located at the upper-left corner of the selected cell, which is cell A1 in this case.

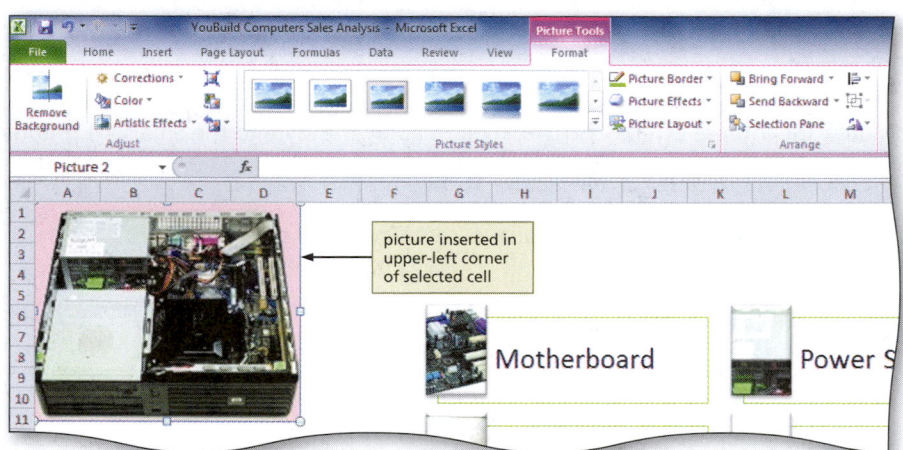

Figure 7–82

3
- Click anywhere in the image, hold down the ALT key, drag the image so that the upper-left corner is aligned with the upper-left corner of cell B7, and then release the ALT key.

- Drag the lower-right sizing handle of the image to the lower-right corner of cell E19 (Figure 7–83).

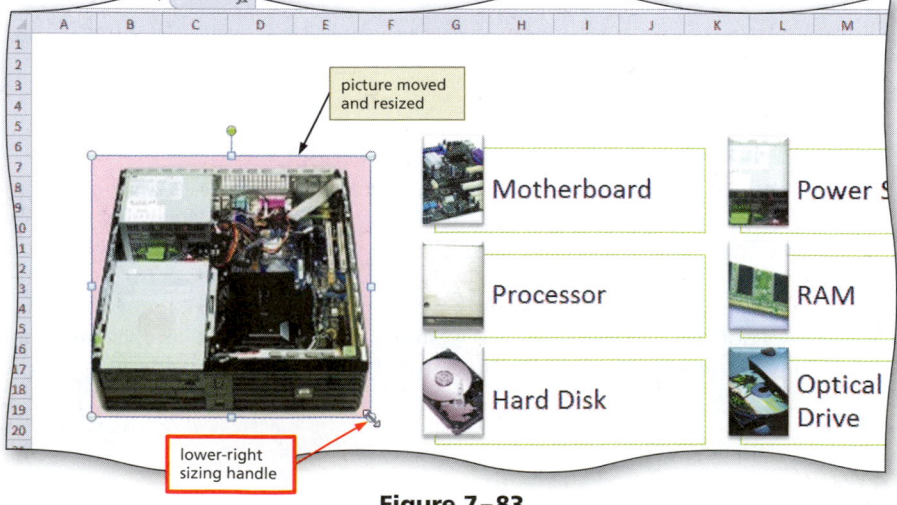

Figure 7–83

4

- If necessary, click Format on the Ribbon to display the Picture Tools Format tab.

- Click the Picture Styles More button (Format tab | Picture Styles group) to display the Picture Styles gallery.

- Point to the Reflected Rounded Rectangle picture style (column 5, row 1) to see a preview of the style in the worksheet (Figure 7–84).

Experiment

- Point to the various picture styles to see a preview of each style in the worksheet.

 5

- Click the Reflected Rounded Rectangle picture style to apply the style to the image.

- Click the Save button on the Quick Access Toolbar to save the workbook.

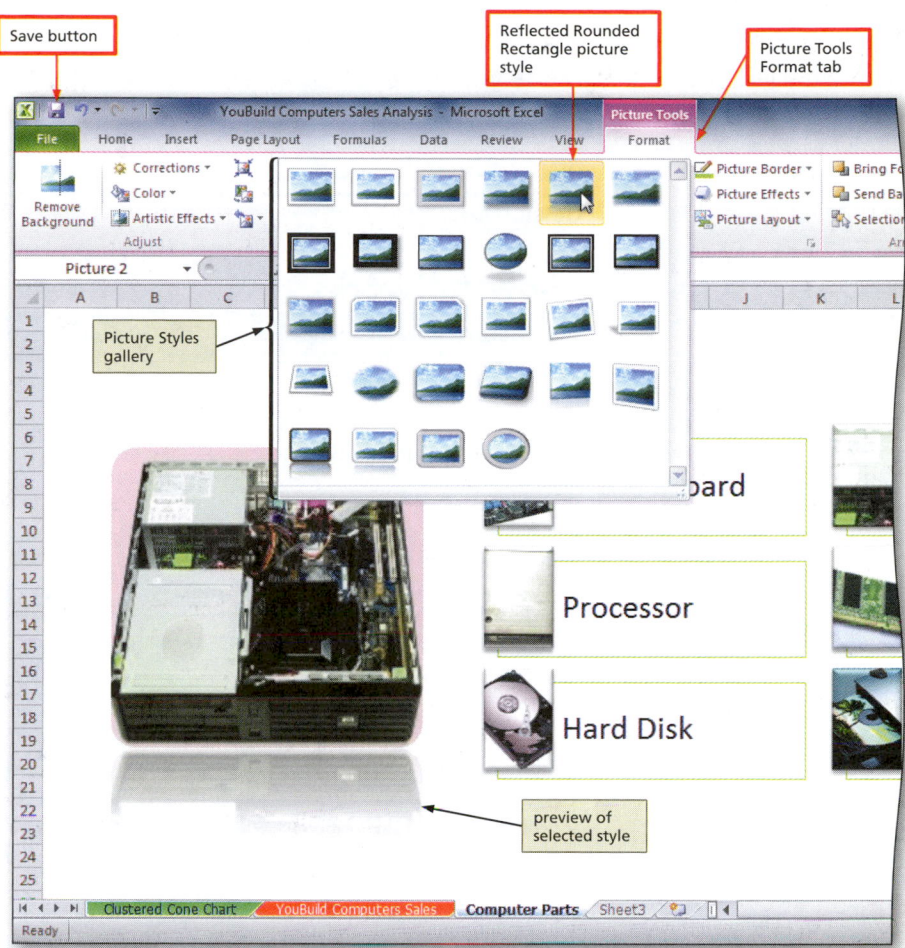

Figure 7–84

Using Screen Shots on a Worksheet

Excel allows you to take a screen shot of any open window and add it to a workbook. Using the screen shot feature, you can capture whole windows or only part of a window. For example, if your company has a Web page, you can take a screen shot of the page and insert it into a workbook before presenting the workbook at a meeting. In addition, you can capture a screen clipping to include in your Excel workbook. A **screen clipping** is a portion, usually of one object or section of a window, of the screen.

To Insert a Screen Shot on a Worksheet

The staff at YouBuild Computers often share helpful sites that contain instructions about building computers. In anticipation of an upcoming meeting where the sales analysis will be reviewed, the CEO requests a screen shot of a popular Web site that provides instructions about building a computer. The steps on the next pages add a screen shot to a worksheet.

BTW

Rotating Illustrations
To rotate pictures in Excel, select the image to be rotated, click the Rotate button (Picture Tools Format tab | Arrange group). You can select 90 degree left and right rotations from the menu, or select More Rotation Options from the menu and then specify the degree of rotation desired in the Format Picture dialog box.

- Click the Internet Explorer button on the taskbar to start Internet Explorer.

- Type `http://electronics.howstuffworks.com/how-to-tech/build-a-computer.htm` in the Address bar and press the ENTER key to display the Web page (Figure 7–85).

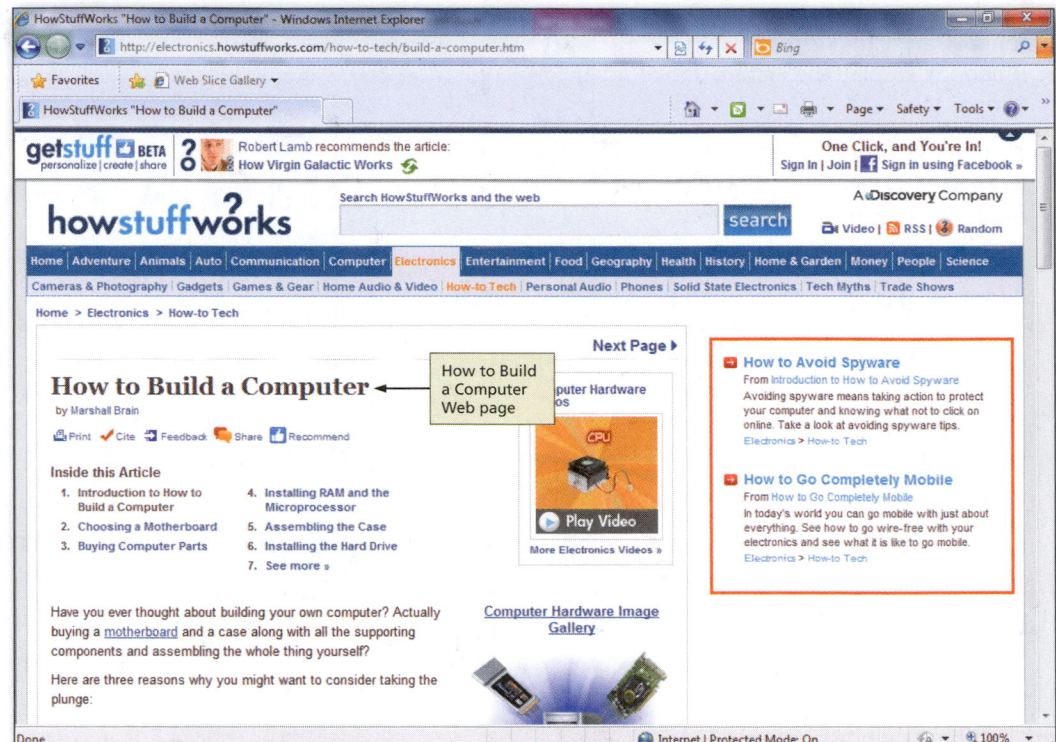

Figure 7–85

- Make the Excel window the active window.

- Click the Sheet3 tab to make it the active worksheet.

- Rename the worksheet to `Screenshot` and color the tab yellow to distinguish it from other worksheets.

- Display the View tab.

- Click the Gridlines check box (View tab | Show group) to turn off gridlines on the worksheet.

- If necessary, click cell A1 to make it the active cell (Figure 7–86).

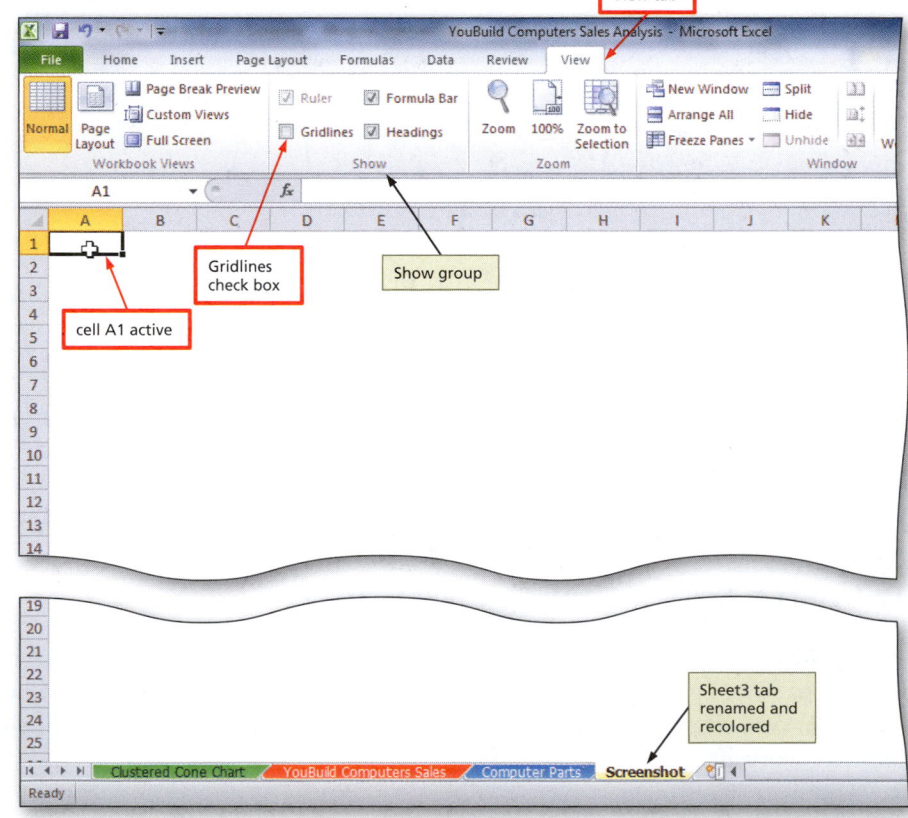

Figure 7–86

3

- Display the Insert tab.

- Click the Screenshot button (Insert tab | Illustrations group) to display the Screenshot menu (Figure 7–87).

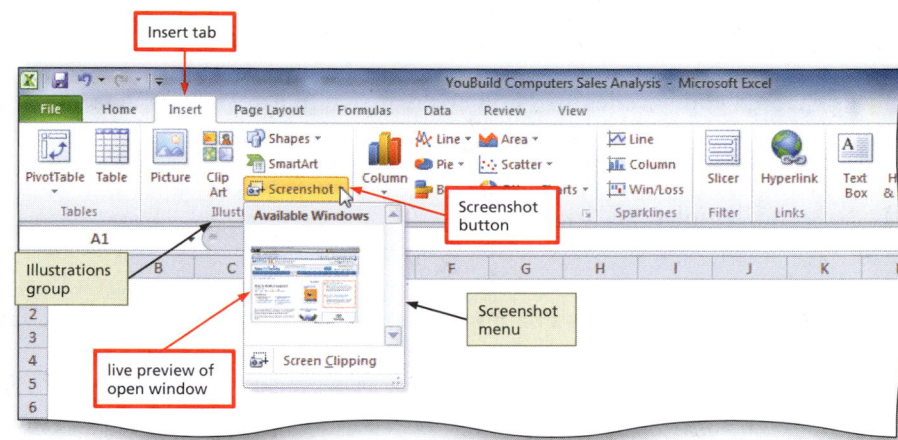

Figure 7–87

4

- Click the 'HowStuffWorks "How to Build a Computer" – Windows Internet Explorer' live preview to insert a screen shot of the 'HowStuffWorks "How to Build a Computer" – Windows Internet Explorer' window (Figure 7–88).

- Click the Save button on the Quick Access Toolbar to save your work.

- Close Internet Explorer.

Q&A

How do you insert a screen clipping?

To insert a screen clipping instead of a screen shot, click the Screenshots button (Insert tab | Illustrations group) to display the Screenshots gallery, click Screen Clipping, and then draw a rectangle over the portion of the screen you want to insert into the Excel workbook.

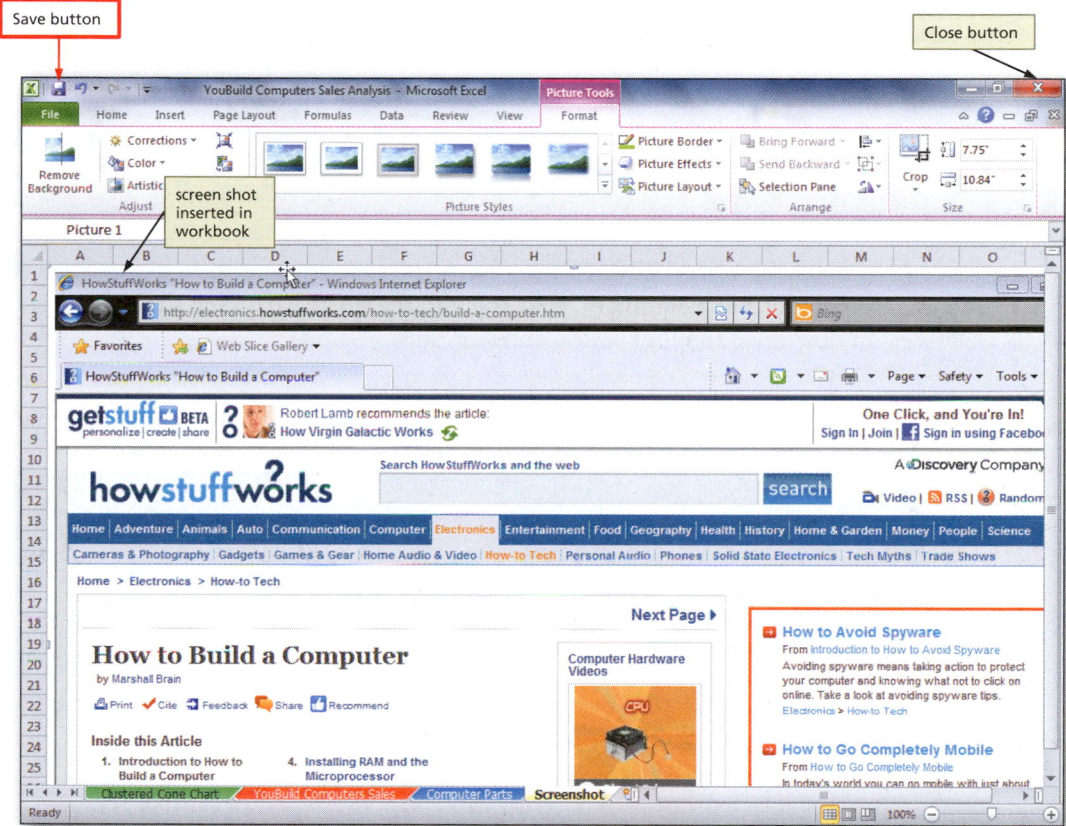

Figure 7–88

To Quit Excel

The project is complete. Thus, the following step quits Excel.

1 Click the Close button on the right side of the title bar to quit Excel.

Chapter Summary

In this chapter, you have learned how to create a template, import data, insert WordArt on a chart, insert SmartArt, insert images, and add a screen shot on a worksheet. The items listed below include all the new Excel skills you have learned in this chapter.

1. Save the Template (EX 435)
2. Open a Template and Save It as a Workbook (EX 437)
3. Import Data from a Text File into a Worksheet (EX 439)
4. Import Data from an Access Table into a Worksheet (EX 443)
5. Import Data from a Web Page into a Worksheet (EX 446)
6. Copy and Transpose Data from a Word Document to a Worksheet (EX 450)
7. Convert Text to Columns (EX 453)
8. Replicate Formulas (EX 456)
9. Find a String (EX 457)
10. Replace a String with Another String (EX 459)
11. Insert the Clustered Cone Chart (EX 460)
12. Add a Chart Title Using the WordArt Tool (EX 463)
13. Insert a Picture Strips SmartArt Graphic (EX 466)
14. Add Shapes in the Picture Strips SmartArt Graphic (EX 469)
15. Add Text to Shapes in the Picture Strips SmartArt Graphic (EX 470)
16. Add Pictures to Shapes in the Picture Strips SmartArt Graphic (EX 471)
17. Add an Effect to the Picture Strips SmartArt Graphic (EX 473)
18. Insert and Modify an Image on the Worksheet (EX 474)
19. Insert a Screen Shot on a Worksheet (EX 475)

 If you have a SAM 2010 user profile, your instructor may have assigned an autogradable version of this assignment. If so, log into the SAM 2010 Web site at www.cengage.com/sam2010 to download the instruction and start files.

Learn It Online

Test your knowledge of chapter content and key terms.

Instructions: To complete the Learn It Online exercises, start your browser, click the Address bar, and then enter the Web address `scsite.com/ex2010/learn`. When the Excel 2010 Learn It Online page is displayed, click the link for the exercise you want to complete and then read the instructions.

Chapter Reinforcement TF, MC, and SA
A series of true/false, multiple choice, and short answer questions that test your knowledge of the chapter content.

Flash Cards
An interactive learning environment where you identify chapter key terms associated with displayed definitions.

Practice Test
A series of multiple choice questions that test your knowledge of chapter content and key terms.

Who Wants To Be a Computer Genius?
An interactive game that challenges your knowledge of chapter content in the style of a television quiz show.

Wheel of Terms
An interactive game that challenges your knowledge of chapter key terms in the style of the television show *Wheel of Fortune*.

Crossword Puzzle Challenge
A crossword puzzle that challenges your knowledge of key terms presented in the chapter.

Apply Your Knowledge

Reinforce the skills and apply the concepts you learned in this chapter.

Importing Data into an Excel Worksheet

Note: To complete this assignment, you will be required to use the Data Files for Students. See the inside back cover of this book for instructions on downloading the Data Files for Students, or contact your instructor for information about accessing the required files.

Instructions: Start Excel. Open the workbook Apply 7-1 Hinkley's Bazaar from the Data Files for Students, and then save the workbook as Apply 7-1 Hinkley's Bazaar Complete. In this workbook, you are to consolidate information about quarterly sales from four sources. Figure 7–89 shows the completed Quarterly Sales worksheet.

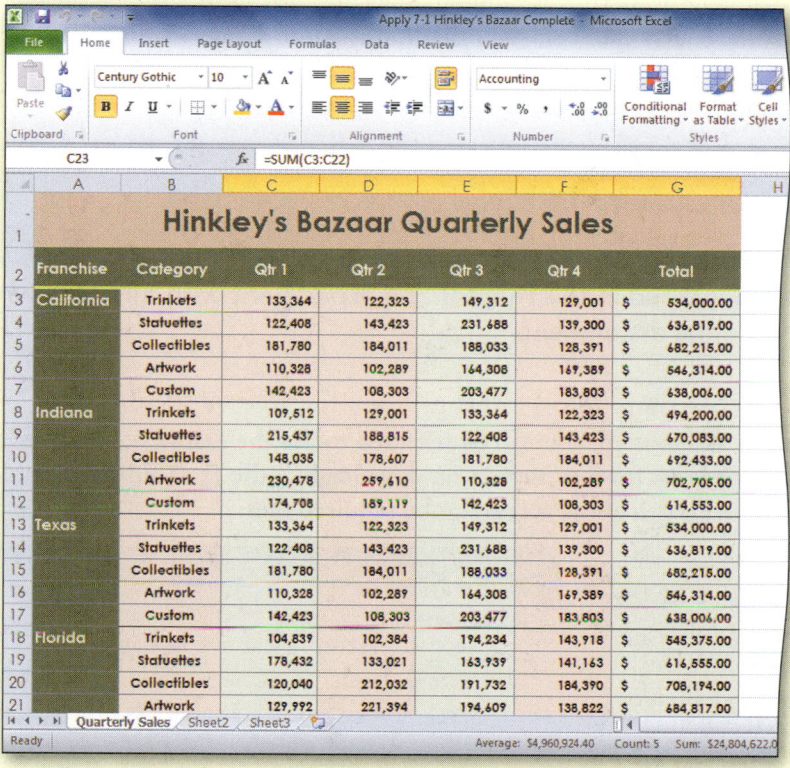

Figure 7–89

Perform the following tasks:

1. Select cell A3, and then enter the text **California**. Select cell A9, and then enter the text **Indiana**. Select cell A14, and then enter the text **Texas**. Select cell A20 and then enter the text **Florida**.

2. Select cell B3. Import the comma-delimited text file, Apply 7-1 California, from the Data Files for Students. In the Text Import Wizard - Step 2 of 3 dialog box, use Comma delimiters, not Tab delimiters; otherwise accept the default settings. In the Import Data dialog box, click the Properties button. In the External Data Range Properties dialog box, do not adjust the column width. Import the text data to cell B3 of the worksheet.

3. Select cell B8. Import the Access database file, Apply 7-1 Indiana, from the Data Files for Students. Choose to view the data as a table, and insert the data starting in cell B8 in the existing workbook. Accept all of the default settings to import the data. Right-click any cell in the table, point to Table, and then click Convert to Range. Click the OK button to permanently remove the connection to the query. Delete row 8.

Continued >

STUDENT ASSIGNMENTS

Apply Your Knowledge *continued*

4. Start Microsoft Word, and then open the Word file, Apply 7-1 Texas, from the Data Files for Students. Copy all of the data in the table except for the first row. Switch to Excel. Select cell B13, and then use the Paste Special command to paste the data as text into the Quarterly Sales worksheet. Close Word without saving any changes. Adjust the column widths as necessary to display all of the data.

5. Select cell B18. Import the Web page, Apply 7-1 Florida.htm, from the Data Files for Students. Select the HTML table containing the Florida sales data. In the Import Data dialog box, click the Properties button. In the External Data Range Properties dialog box, do not adjust the column width. Import the text data to cell B18 of the existing worksheet. Delete row 18.

6. Select cell G3 and then total the row. Copy the formula to cells G4:G23.

7. Select cell C23 and then total the column. Copy the formula to cells D23:F23.

8. Format the range C3:F22 in the Comma style with no decimal places. Format the ranges G3:G23 and C23:F23 in the Accounting Number format with two decimal places. Adjust the column widths as necessary to display all of the data.

9. Change the document properties as requested by your instructor. Change the worksheet header to include your name, course number, and other information as specified by your instructor.

10. Print the worksheet, and then save the workbook.

11. Submit the assignment as requested by your instructor.

Extend Your Knowledge

Extend the skills you learned in this chapter and experiment with new skills. You may need to use Help to complete the assignment.

Inserting a SmartArt Organization Chart and Image on a Worksheet

Note: To complete this assignment, you will be required to use the Data Files for Students. See the inside back cover of this book for instructions on downloading the Data Files for Students, or contact your instructor for information about accessing the required files.

Instructions: Start Excel. Open the workbook Extend 7-1 BCIA Medical from the Data Files for Students and then save the workbook as Extend 7-1 BCIA Medical Complete. You will add a SmartArt graphic and an image to the workbook and then format both graphics as shown in Figure 7–90.

Perform the following tasks:

1. In cell A12, insert a SmartArt graphic using the Hierarchy type and the Organization Chart layout (column 1, row 1).

2. Using the Add Shape shortcut menu, add an Assistant shape to the first shape.

3. Using the Add Shape shortcut menu, add a shape after the last shape in the third row.

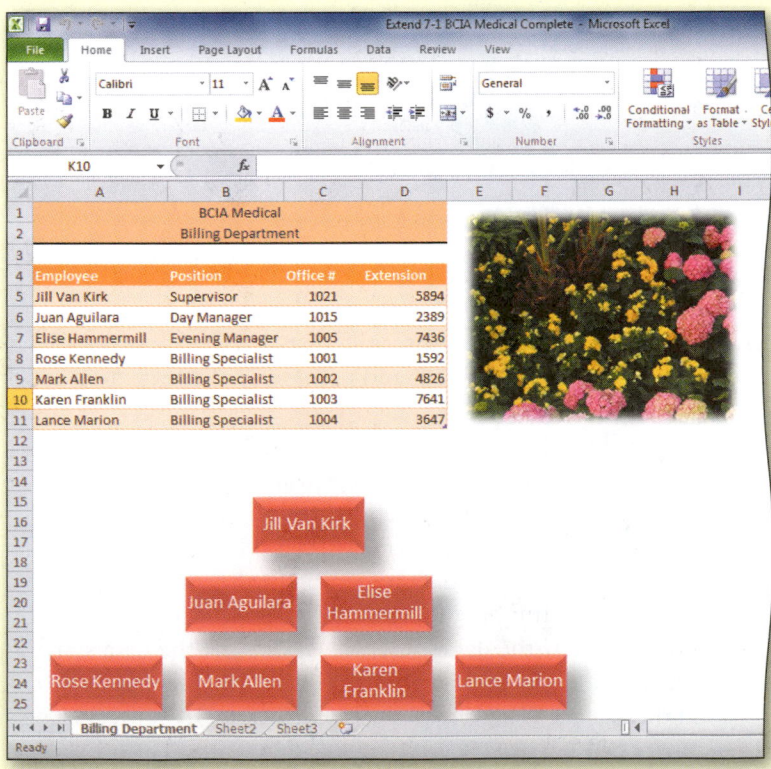

Figure 7–90

4. Change the text in the first shape to read Jill Van Kirk. Change the text in the middle row to read Juan Aguilara in the left shape and Elise Hammermill in the right shape. Change the text in the third row to read, from left to right, Rose Kennedy, Mark Allen, Karen Franklin, and Lance Marion.

5. Change the color scheme of the hierarchy chart to Colored Fill – Accent 2 (column 2, row 4) in the Change Colors gallery.

6. Change the font size of the text in the shapes to 14 points.

7. Use the Shape Effect gallery to change the effects on the SmartArt shapes to Preset 4 in the Preset gallery.

8. Close the Text pane, if necessary, and then move the SmartArt graphic so the upper-left corner of the graphic is in the upper-left corner of cell A12.

9. In cell E1, insert the Extend 7-1 LobbyFlowers image file from the Data Files for Students on the worksheet.

10. Move and resize the image so that the upper-left corner of the image is aligned with the upper-left corner of cell E1 and the lower-right corner of the image is in cell I11.

11. Format the image to use the Soft Edge Rectangle style (column 6, row 1) in the Picture Styles Gallery.

12. Change the document properties as specified by your instructor. Change the worksheet header so that it contains your name, course number, and other information as specified by your instructor. Save the workbook. Submit the assignment as requested by your instructor.

Make It Right

Analyze a workbook and correct all errors and/or improve the design.

Manipulating SmartArt and Using Find & Replace

Note: To complete this assignment, you will be required to use the Data Files for Students. See the inside back cover of this book for instructions on downloading the Data Files for Students, or contact your instructor for information about accessing the required files.

Instructions: Start Excel. Open the workbook Make It Right 7-1 GreenFirst Services and then save the workbook as Make It Right 7-1 GreenFirst Services Complete. The Site List worksheet contains design flaws and other errors. Correct the problems so that the Site List sheet appears as shown in Figure 7–91.

Perform the following tasks:

1. Edit the shape on the left of the cycle chart so that it says Reduce.

2. Add a new shape after the Recycle shape. Insert the text Reuse in the new shape.

3. Find all occurrences of Kenway Rd and replace them with Charles Ave (without any punctuation).

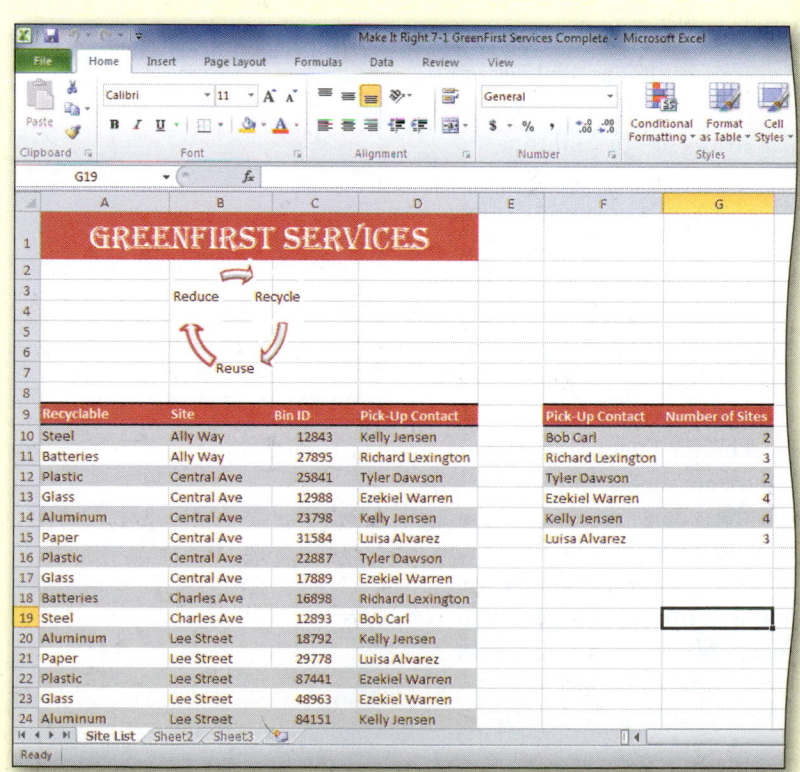

Figure 7–91

Continued >

Make It Right *continued*

4. Find all occurrences of Kelly Montag and replace them with Kelly Jensen (without any punctuation).

5. Use the Find All button in the Find and Replace dialog box to find and list all occurrences of Bob Carl in the range A9:D27. Be sure not to include the range F9:G15 in the search. Enter the number of the occurrences in G10.

6. Use the same technique to find and list all occurrences of the text and enter the number of occurrences as shown in Table 7–1.

7. Change the document properties as specified by your instructor. Change the worksheet headers to include your name, course number, and other information as specified by your instructor.

8. Save the workbook, and submit the revised workbook as requested by your instructor.

Table 7–1 Text to Find and Count	
Find All Occurrences of:	**Enter Number of Occurrences in Cell:**
Richard Lexington	G11
Tyler Dawson	G12
Ezekiel Warren	G13
Kelly Jensen	G14
Luisa Alvarez	G15

In the Lab

Create or modify workbooks using the guidelines, concepts, and skills presented in this chapter. Labs are listed in order of increasing difficulty.

Lab 1: Using a Template to Create a Multiple-Sheet Workbook

Note: To complete this assignment, you will be required to use the Data Files for Students. See the inside back cover of this book for instructions on downloading the Data Files for Students, or contact your instructor for information about accessing the required files.

Problem: Natalee's Organic is a company that specializes in all organic products. The company has stores in Washington, Tampa, Cincinnati, Boston, and Atlanta, and a corporate office in Orlando. All of the five stores sell their products online, in the store, and through mail order. Every year, the corporate officers in Orlando use a template to create a year-end sales analysis workbook. The workbook contains four sheets, one for each of the three sales types, or channels (online, in-store, and mail), and one sheet to consolidate data and determine the company totals. Figure 7–92 shows the Consolidated sheet.

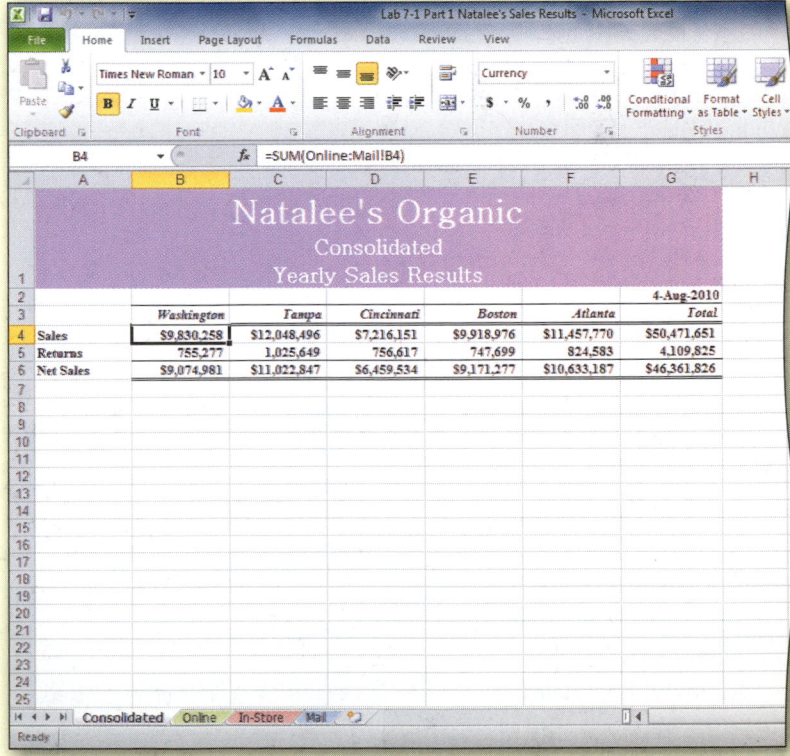

Figure 7–92

The template you need to create the sales analysis workbook is part of the Data Files for Students. Alice Stewart, the company's accountant, has asked you to use the template to create the sales analysis workbook.

Instructions Part 1:   Perform the following tasks:

1. Open the template Lab 7-1 Natalee's Organic Template from the Data Files for Students. Save the template as a workbook using the file name, Lab 7-1 Part 1 Natalee's Sales Results. Make sure Excel Workbook is selected in the 'Save as type' list when you save the workbook.

2. Add a worksheet to the workbook between Sheet1 and Sheet2, copy the contents of Sheet1, and then paste it to the three empty sheets.

3. From left to right, rename the sheet tabs Consolidated, Online, In-Store, and Mail. Color the tabs from left to right as purple, green, red, and blue. On each of the three sales channel sheets, double-click cell A1 and change the "Location" subtitle to match the tab name. Use the title, Consolidated, in cell A1 of the Consolidated worksheet. Change the fill color for each title area in the range A1:G1 to match its tab color. Enter the data in Table 7–2 into the three sales channel sheets.

Table 7–2 Natalee's Organic Yearly Sales Data by Store and Sales Channel		Online	In-Store	Mail
Washington	Sales	4589123	1950125	3291010
	Returns	275375	451002	28900
Tampa	Sales	5789632	2101054	4157810
	Returns	500250	62198	463201
Cincinnati	Sales	3698741	1258473	2258937
	Returns	352677	105520	298420
Boston	Sales	2587471	3100500	4231005
	Returns	250500	435001	62198
Atlanta	Sales	6541280	1975200	2941290
	Returns	137980	612453	74150

4. On the Consolidated worksheet, use the SUM function, 3-D references, and copy-and-paste capabilities of Excel to total the corresponding cells on the three sales channel sheets. First, compute the sum in cell B4 and then compute the sum in cell B5. Copy the range B4:B5 to the range C4:F5. The Consolidated sheet should resemble Figure 7–92.

5. Change the document properties as specified by your instructor. Select all four sheets. Add a worksheet header with your name, course number, and other information as specified by your instructor. Add the page number and total number of pages to the footer. Change the left and right margins to 0.5.

6. With the four sheets selected, preview and then print the workbook in landscape orientation and use the Black and white option.

7. Save the workbook with the new page setup characteristics. Close the workbook.

8. Submit the assignment as requested by your instructor.

Instructions Part 2:   Perform the following tasks:

1. Start Excel. Open the workbook Lab 7-1 Part 1 Natalee's Sales Results and then save the workbook using the file name, Lab 7-1 Part 2 Natalee's Sales Results.

2. Create an embedded Clustered Cylinder chart in the range A8:H25 on the Consolidated worksheet by charting the range A3:F5.

3. Move the chart to a separate sheet using the Move Chart button on the Design tab. Name the sheet Chart and color the sheet tab yellow. Drag the Chart sheet tab to the far right.

Continued >

In the Lab *continued*

4. Increase the font size of the labels on both axes to 12-point bold. Increase the font size of the legends on the right side of the chart to 16 points.

5. Change the chart style to Style 8 using the Chart Styles gallery on the Chart Tools Design tab.

6. Use the WordArt button on the Insert tab to add the chart title Annual Sales and Returns. Select Fill – Orange, Accent 6, Gradient Outline – Accent 6 (column 2, row 3) from the WordArt gallery. Figure 7–93 shows the completed chart.

7. Preview and print all five sheets at one time. Save the workbook and then close the workbook.

8. Submit the assignment as requested by your instructor.

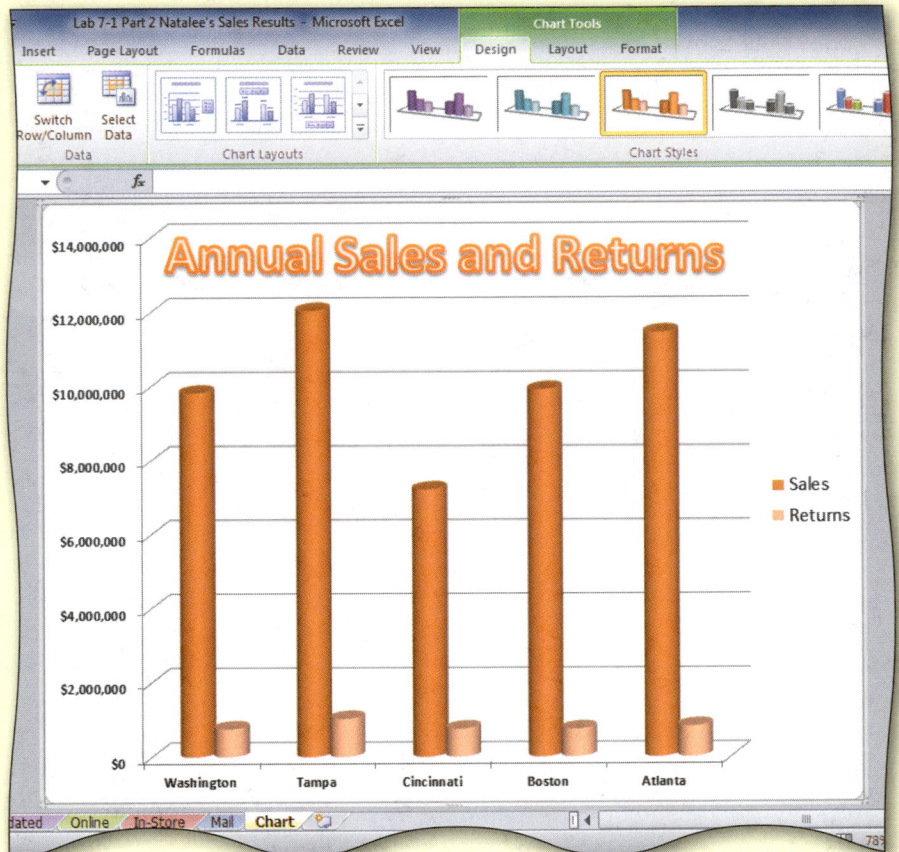

Figure 7–93

Instructions Part 3: Perform the following tasks:

1. Start Excel. Open the workbook Lab 7-1 Part 2 Natalee's Sales Results. Do not save the workbook with a different name in this part of the exercise.

2. Select cell A1 on the Consolidated worksheet. Select all the worksheets except for the Chart sheet.

3. Use the Find & Select button on the Home tab to list all occurrences of the word, Sales, in the workbook. Use the Find All button in the Find and Replace dialog box. Write down the number of occurrences and the cell locations of the word Sales.

4. Repeat Step 3, but find only cells that exactly match the word Sales. If necessary, click the Options button to display the desired check box. Use the Find & Select button to find all occurrences of the word Sales. Write down the number of occurrences and the cell locations that exactly match the word Sales.

5. Use the Find & Select button to find all occurrences of the word, Sales, in bold white font. For this find operation, clear the check mark from the Match entire cell contents check box.

6. Use the Replace command to replace the word, Sales, with the word, Revenue, on all four sheets. Print the four sheets. Close the workbook without saving changes.

7. Submit the assignment as requested by your instructor.

In the Lab

Lab 2: Inserting a Balance Chart and Image on a Worksheet

Note: To complete this assignment, you will be required to use the Data Files for Students. See the inside back cover of this book for instructions on downloading the Data Files for Students, or contact your instructor for information about accessing the required files.

Problem: Pattierson Artist, your company, is considering having a mural painted on the side of their building. You have been asked to create a worksheet with a high-level overview of the pros and cons regarding the mural. The finished worksheet should look like Figure 7–94.

Figure 7–94

Perform the following tasks:

1. Open the workbook Lab 7-2 Pattierson Artists from the Data Files for Students. Save it as Lab 7-2 Pattierson Artists Complete.
2. Insert the Pattierson Mural image file from the Data Files for Students on the worksheet.
3. Move and resize the image so that its upper-left corner is aligned with the upper-left corner of cell A4 and the lower-right corner of the image is aligned with the lower-right corner of cell F19.
4. Select the image. On the Picture Tools Format tab, click the Picture Effects button, point to Shadow in the Picture Effects gallery, and then select Perspective Diagonal Upper Right (column 2, row 8).
5. Click the Picture Effects button, point to Bevel in the Picture Effects gallery, and then select Art Deco (column 4, row 4) in the Bevel gallery.
6. Deselect the image, and then insert a SmartArt graphic using the Relationship type and the Balance layout (column 1, row 1).
7. Move and resize the SmartArt graphic so that its upper-left corner is aligned with the upper-left corner of H4 and the lower-right corner of the graphic is aligned with the lower-right corner of cell M19.

Continued >

In the Lab *continued*

8. Use the Text pane to enter the text for the balance chart as shown in Table 7–3, making certain that the Pros column appears on the left of the chart. Be sure to delete the unused shape on the right side of the balance chart by right-clicking the shape and then clicking Cut on the shortcut menu. The upper-left shape in the chart should read Pros, and the upper-right shape in the chart should read Cons. Note that the direction of the tilt of the balance changes when more pros than cons are entered in the chart.

Table 7–3 Pros and Cons	
Pros	**Cons**
Shows Off Talent	Costly
Promotes Marketing	Difficult to Replace
Beautifies Neighborhood	

9. Change the color scheme of the Balance chart to Colored Fill – Accent 3 (column 2, row 5) in the Change Colors gallery.
10. Apply the Subtle Effect SmartArt style (column 3, row 1) to the Balance chart.
11. Change the document properties as specified by your instructor. Add a worksheet header with your name, course number, and other information as specified by your instructor. Save the workbook. Submit the assignment as requested by your instructor.

In the Lab

Lab 3: Using a Template and Importing Data

Note: To complete this assignment, you will be required to use the Data Files for Students. See the inside back cover of this book for instructions on downloading the Data Files for Students, or contact your instructor for information about accessing the required files.

Problem: You work as a teacher at a private school. You teach every subject to the four students in your gifted class except for art, computers, and physical education. To help you in determining a student's grade for a semester, you ask the art, computers, and physical education instructors to send you grades for your four students, although each data set is in a different format. The art teacher sends you a Web page from the school's Web system. The computer teacher, who uses an Access database to maintain data, queried the database to create a table for you. The physical education teacher typed all the information in a Word table. At the conclusion of the instructions, the Grades Summary worksheet should appear as shown in Figure 7–95.

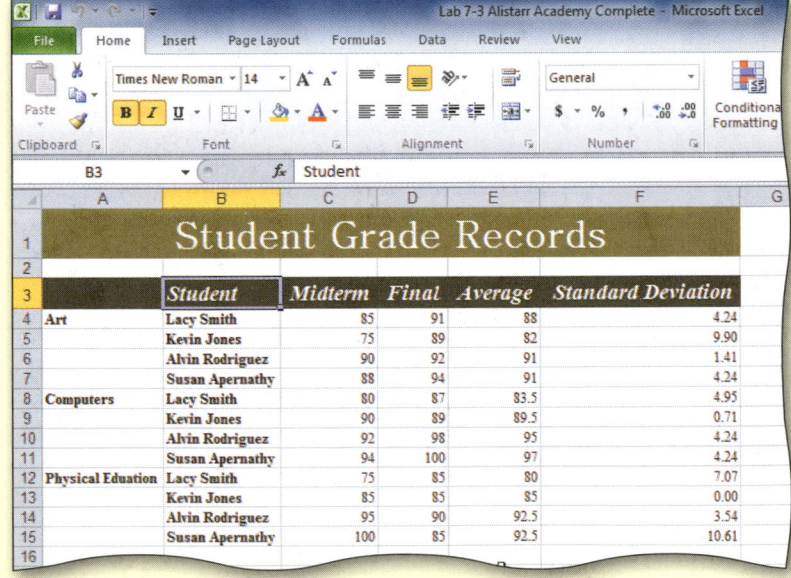

Figure 7–95

Perform the following tasks:

1. Open the template Lab 7-3 Alistarr Academy Template from the Data Files for Students. Save the template as a workbook using the file name, Lab 7-3 Alistarr Academy Complete. Make sure Excel Workbook is selected in the 'Save as type' list when you save the workbook.
2. Select cell B4. Import the Web page, Lab 7-3 Art.htm, from the Data Files for Students. Select the HTML table containing the art grades. In the Import Data dialog box, click the Properties button. In the External Data Range Properties dialog box, do not adjust the column width. Import the text data to cell B4 of the existing worksheet. Delete row 4.

3. Select cell B8. Import the Access database file, Lab 7-3 Computer, from the Data Files for Students. Choose to view the data as a table, and insert the data starting in cell B8 in the existing workbook. Accept all of the default settings to import the data. Right-click any cell in the table, point to Table, and then click Convert to Range. Click the OK button to permanently remove the connection to the query. Delete row 8. Copy the format from B7:D7 to B8:D11.

4. Start Microsoft Word, and then open the Word file, Lab 7-3 Physical Education, from the Data Files for Students. Copy all except the first column of data in the table. Switch to Excel. Select cell B18, and then use the Paste Special command to paste only the text into the Grades Summary worksheet. Close Word without saving any changes. Copy the range B18:E20. Select cell B12, and then use the Paste Special command to paste and transpose the data. Adjust the column widths as necessary to display all of the data.

5. Delete the range B18:E20, and then delete row 16. Copy the formatting of cells C11:D11 and apply the formatting to the range C12:D15. Copy the formula in cell E11 to the range E12:E15.

6. Change the document properties as requested by your instructor. Change the worksheet header to include your name, course number, and other information as specified by your instructor.

7. Print the worksheet, and then save the workbook.

8. Submit the assignment as requested by your instructor.

Cases and Places

Apply your creative thinking and problem solving skills to design and implement a solution.

Note: To complete these assignments, you may be required to use the Data Files for Students. See the inside back cover of this book for instructions on downloading the Data Files for Students, or contact your instructor for information about accessing the required files.

1: Create a Cover Sheet

Academic

You are competing to design a cover sheet for your school's department to include in their workbooks when they send out school statistics. Open your Web browser and view the Web page for a department at your school. Create a workbook and turn off the viewing of gridlines for the first sheet. Insert a screen shot of the department Web page and size it appropriately. Insert a SmartArt bulleted list to highlight three or four of the best qualities of your department. Below the bulleted list, add a screen clipping of the school's logo. Finally, next to the logo add your name and format it so that it appears as a title. Below your name, in a smaller font, insert the course name.

2: Create a SmartArt Graphic with Photos

Personal

You decide to create a workbook with pictures to chronicle your favorite activity, such as skiing or cooking. Find five digital photos that convey your experience in your favorite activity. Create an Excel workbook. Insert a Titled Picture Blocks SmartArt in a worksheet. Add your five photos and enter a title for each one as well as a caption that describes the photo.

3: Import and Analyze Sales Data

Professional

Open the template Case 7-3 SecurityEnablers Template. Save the template as a workbook named Case 7-3 SecurityEnablers. Import the data from the Sales table in the Case 7-3 SecurityEnablers database to a table starting in cell A4. Import the data from the text file Case 7-3 Security Enablers Text starting in cell A16. Replace all instances of NorthCentral with Central. If necessary, copy the formula in cell F4 to the range F5:F23, and format the data appropriately. Update the totals in the range C24:F24.

4 | Creating Reports and Forms

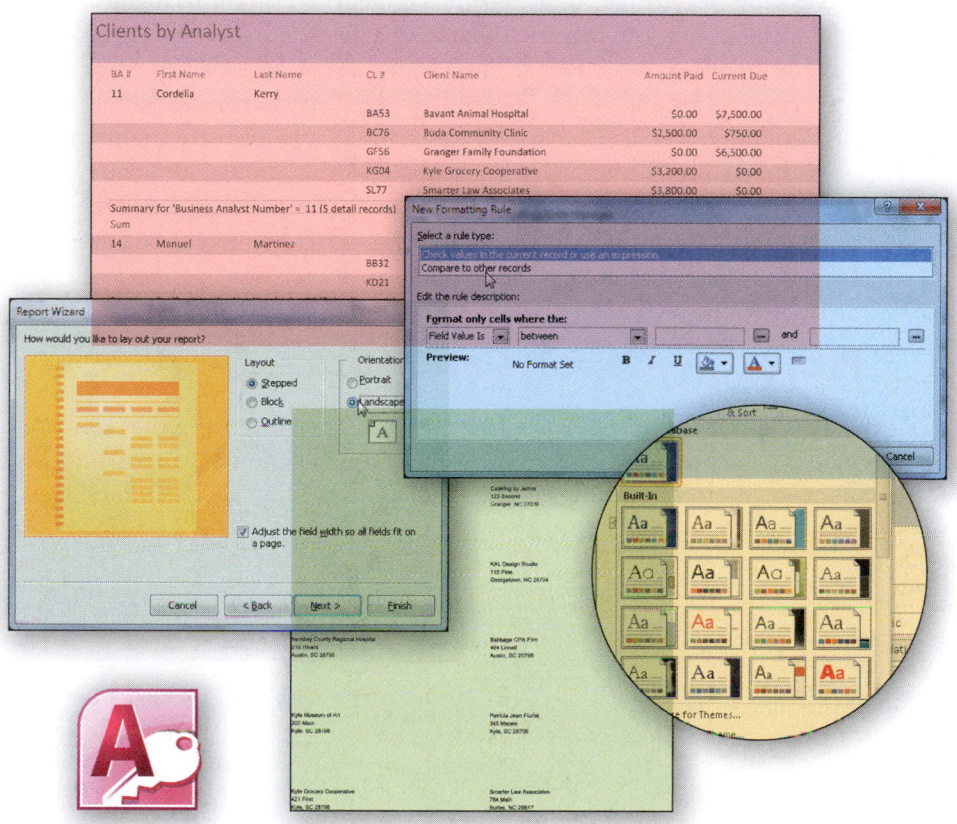

Objectives

You will have mastered the material in this chapter when you can:

- Create reports and forms using wizards
- Modify reports and forms in Layout view
- Group and sort in a report
- Add totals and subtotals to a report
- Conditionally format controls
- Resize columns
- Filter records in reports and forms

- Print reports and forms
- Apply themes
- Add a field to a report or form
- Include gridlines
- Add a date
- Change the format of a control
- Move controls
- Create and print mailing labels

4 | Creating Reports and Forms

BTW

Q&As
For a complete list of the Q&As found in many of the step-by-step sequences in this book, visit the Access 2010 Q&A Web page (scsite.com/ac2010/qa).

Introduction

One of the advantages to maintaining data in a database is the ability to present the data in attractive reports and forms that highlight certain information. Reports present specific data in an organized format that is usually printed. The data can come from one or more tables. You usually view forms on the screen, although you can print them. You often use forms to view specific data. You may use them to update data. Like reports, the data in the form can come from one or more tables. This chapter shows how to create reports and forms by creating two reports and a form. There are several ways to create both reports and forms. The most common is to use the Report or Form Wizard to create an initial report or form. If the layout created by the wizard is satisfactory, you are done. If not, you can use either Layout view or Design view to customize the report or form. In this chapter, you will use Layout view for this purpose. In later chapters, you will learn how to use Design view. You also will use the Label Wizard to produce mailing labels.

Project — Reports and Forms

Camashaly Design has realized several benefits from using the database of clients and analysts. Camashaly hopes to realize additional benefits using two custom reports that meet their specific needs. Figure 4–1 shows the first report, which is a modified version

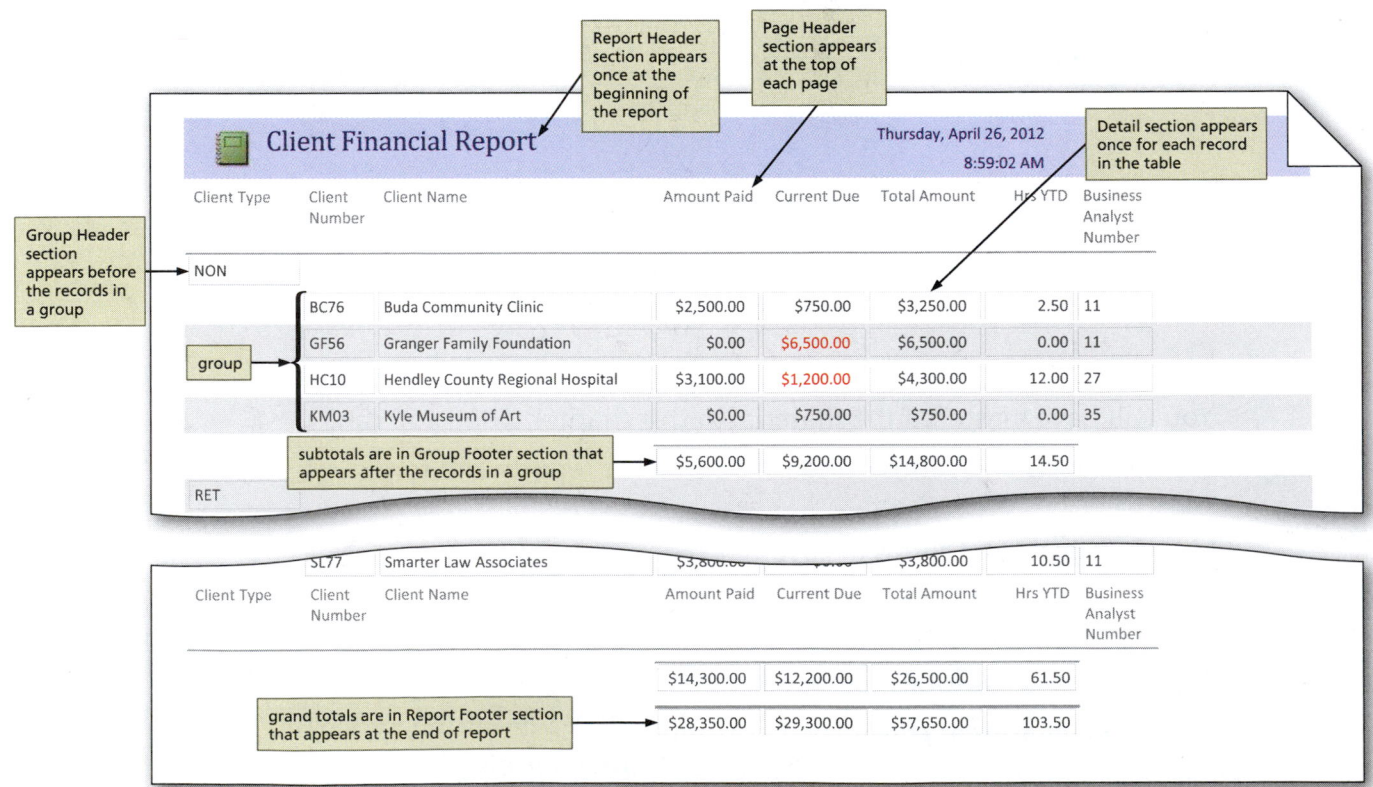

Figure 4–1

of an existing report. The report features grouping. The report shown in Figure 4–1 groups records by client types. There are three separate groups, one each for the three possible client types: NON, RET, and SER. The appropriate type appears before each group. The totals of the Amount Paid, Current Due, Total Amount, and Hrs YTD fields for the clients in the group (called a **subtotal**) appear after the group. At the end of the report are grand totals of the same fields.

Figure 4–2 shows the first page of the second report. This report encompasses data from both the Business Analyst Table and the Client table. Like the report in Figure 4–1, the data is grouped, although this time it is grouped by analyst number. Not only does the analyst number appear before each group, but the first name and last name of the analyst appear as well. Like the first report, this report contains subtotals.

Clients by Analyst

BA #	First Name	Last Name	CL #	Client Name	Amount Paid	Current Due
11	Cordelia	Kerry				
			BA53	Bavant Animal Hospital	$0.00	$7,500.00
			BC76	Buda Community Clinic	$2,500.00	$750.00
			GF56	Granger Family Foundation	$0.00	$6,500.00
			KG04	Kyle Grocery Cooperative	$3,200.00	$0.00
			SL77	Smarter Law Associates	$3,800.00	$0.00
Summary for 'Business Analyst Number' = 11 (5 detail records)						
Sum					$9,500.00	$14,750.00
14	Manuel	Martinez				
			BB32	Babbage CPA Firm	$1,500.00	$500.00
			KD21	KAL Design Studio	$6,000.00	$3,200.00
Summary for 'Business Analyst Number' = 14 (2 detail records)						
Sum					$7,500.00	$3,700.00
27	Jan	Liu				
			CJ29	Catering by Jenna	$3,000.00	$1,000.00
			HC10	Hendley County Regional Hospital	$3,100.00	$1,200.00
			ME14	Mike's Electronic Stop	$2,500.00	$1,500.00
			PJ34	Patricia Jean Florist	$0.00	$5,200.00
			TB17	The Bikeshop	$2,750.00	$1,200.00
Summary for 'Business Analyst Number' = 27 (5 detail records)						
Sum					$11,350.00	$10,100.00
35	Jeff	Scott				
			KM03	Kyle Museum of Art	$0.00	$750.00
BA #	First Name	Last Name	CL #	Client Name	Amount Paid	Current Due
Summary for 'Business Analyst Number' = 35 (1 detail record)						
Sum					$0.00	$750.00
Grand Total					$28,350.00	$29,300.00

Figure 4–2

Camashaly also wants to improve the data entry process by using a custom form, as shown in Figure 4–3. The form has a title and a date. It does not contain all the fields in the Client table, and the fields are in a different order than in the table. For this form, Camashaly likes the appearance of including the fields in a grid.

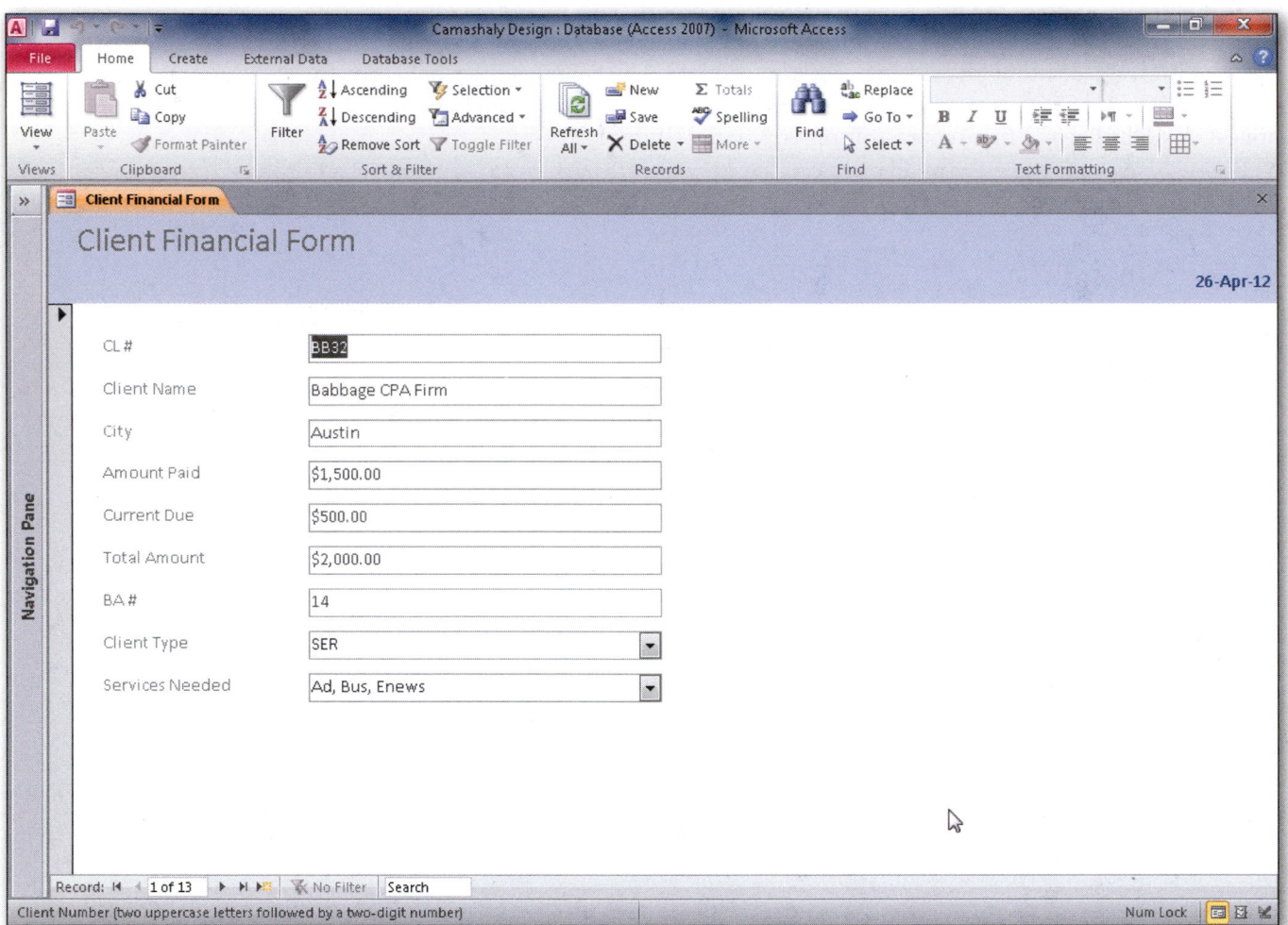

Figure 4–3

BTWs

For a complete list of the BTWs found in the margins of this book, visit the Access 2010 BTW Web page (scsite.com/ac2010/btw).

Camashaly also wants to be able to produce mailing labels for its clients. These labels must align correctly with the particular labels Camashaly uses and must be sorted by postal code (Figure 4–4).

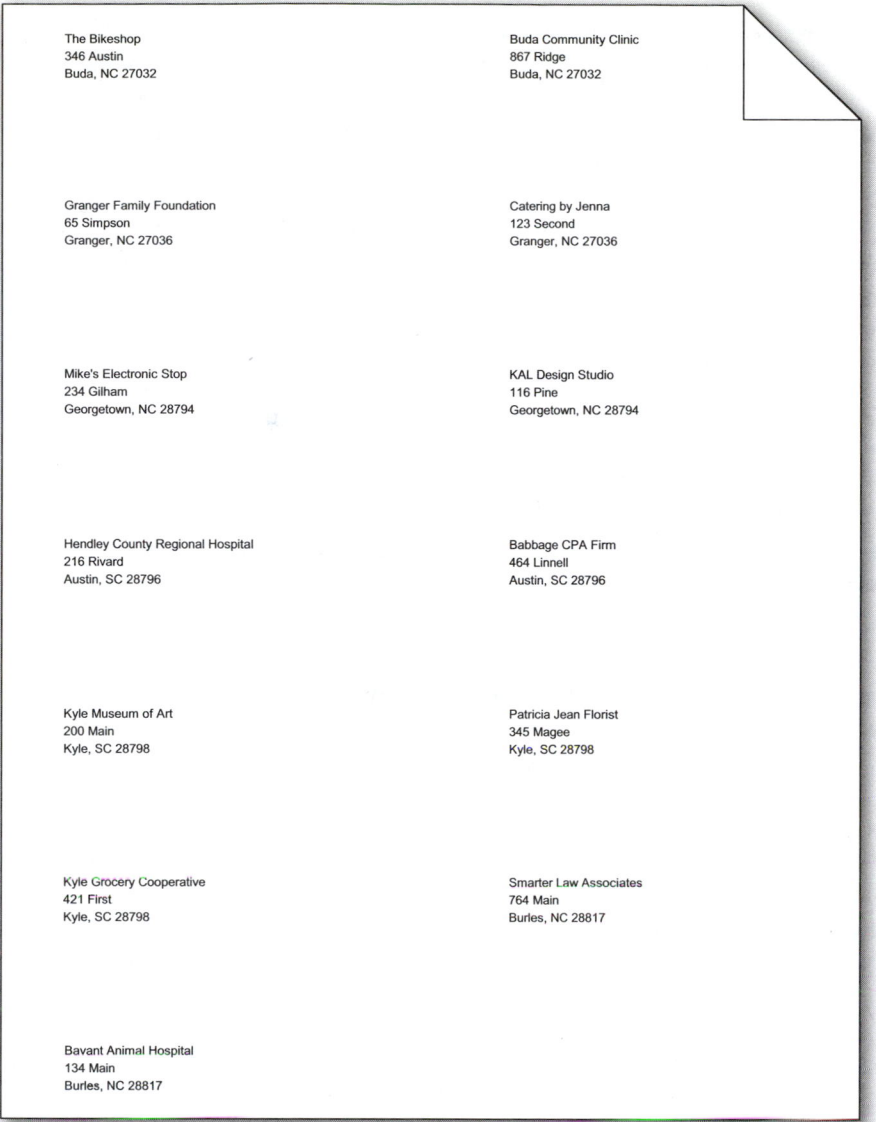

The Bikeshop
346 Austin
Buda, NC 27032

Buda Community Clinic
867 Ridge
Buda, NC 27032

Granger Family Foundation
65 Simpson
Granger, NC 27036

Catering by Jenna
123 Second
Granger, NC 27036

Mike's Electronic Stop
234 Gilham
Georgetown, NC 28794

KAL Design Studio
116 Pine
Georgetown, NC 28794

Hendley County Regional Hospital
216 Rivard
Austin, SC 28796

Babbage CPA Firm
464 Linnell
Austin, SC 28796

Kyle Museum of Art
200 Main
Kyle, SC 28798

Patricia Jean Florist
345 Magee
Kyle, SC 28798

Kyle Grocery Cooperative
421 First
Kyle, SC 28798

Smarter Law Associates
764 Main
Burles, NC 28817

Bavant Animal Hospital
134 Main
Burles, NC 28817

Figure 4–4

Overview

As you read this chapter, you will learn how to create reports and forms by performing these general tasks:

- Use Layout view to modify an existing report.
- Group and sort the report in Layout view.
- Add totals and subtotals to the report.
- Conditionally format a control.
- Filter records in the report.
- Use the Report Wizard to create a report on the Business Analyst and Client tables.
- Add a field to the report and include totals.
- Use the Form Wizard to create a form on the Client table.
- Include gridlines and a date in the form.
- Add a field to the form.
- Filter and sort records in the form.
- Create mailing labels.

Plan Ahead

Consider Your Audience
Always design reports and forms with your audience in mind. Make your reports and forms accessible to individuals who may have problems with color blindness or reduced vision.

Report and Form Design Guidelines

When creating reports and forms, you must identify the intended usage, audience, content, and formatting. To design reports and forms, you should follow these general guidelines:

1. **Determine whether the data should be presented in a report or a form.** Do you intend to print the data? If so, a report would be the appropriate choice. Do you intend to view the data on the screen? If so, a form would be the appropriate choice. Is the user going to update data? If so, a form would be the appropriate choice.

2. **Determine the intended audience for the report or form.** Who will use the report or form? Will the report or form be used by individuals external to the organization? For example, many government agencies require reports from organizations. If so, government regulations will dictate the report requirements. If the report is for internal use, the user will have specific requirements based on the intended use. The data required for a report or form depends on its use. Adding unnecessary data to a report or form can make the form or report unreadable. Include only data necessary for the intended use. What level of detail do they need? Reports used in day-to-day operations need more detail than weekly or monthly reports requested by management.

3. **Determine the tables that contain the data needed for the report or form.** Is all the data found in a single table, or does it come from multiple related tables?

4. **Determine the fields that should appear on the report or form.** What data items does the user of the report or form need?

5. **Determine the organization of the report or form.** In what order should the fields appear? How should they be arranged? Should the records in a report be grouped in some way?

6. **Determine the format of the report or form.** What should be in the report or form header? Do you want a title and date, for example? Do you want a logo? What should be in the body of the report and form? What should the style be? In other words, determine the visual characteristics that the various portions of the report or form should have.

7. **Review the report or form after it has been in operation to determine whether any changes are necessary.** Is the order of the fields still appropriate? Are any additional fields required?

8. **For mailing labels, determine the contents, order, and type of label.** What fields should appear on the label? How should they be arranged? Is there a certain order (for example, by postal code) in which the labels should be printed? Who is the manufacturer of the labels and what is the style number for the labels? What are the dimensions for each label? How many labels print across a page?

When necessary, more specific details concerning the above decisions and/or actions are presented at appropriate points in the chapter. The chapter also will identify the actions performed and decisions made regarding these guidelines in the design of the reports, forms, and labels such as those shown in Figures 4–1, 4–2, 4–3, and 4–4.

To Start Access

The following steps, which assume Windows 7 is running, start Access based on a typical installation. You may need to ask your instructor how to start Access for your computer.

1 Click the Start button on the Windows 7 taskbar to display the Start menu.

2 Type `Microsoft Access` as the search text in the 'Search programs and files' text box and watch the search results appear on the Start menu.

3 Click Microsoft Access 2010 in the search results on the Start menu to start Access.

4 If the Access window is not maximized, click the Maximize button next to the Close button on its title bar to maximize the window.

To Open a Database from Access

The following steps open the Camashaly database from the Access folder in the CIS 101 folder on the USB flash drive.

1 With your USB flash drive connected to one of the computer's USB ports, click File on the Ribbon to open the Backstage view.

2 Click Open in the Backstage view to display the Open dialog box.

3 Navigate to the location of the file to be opened (in this case, the USB flash drive, then to the CIS 101 folder [or your class folder], and then to the Access folder).

4 Click Camashaly Design to select the file to be opened.

5 Click the Open button (Open dialog box) to open the selected file and display the opened database in the Access window.

6 If a Security Warning appears, click the Enable Content button.

BTW

The Ribbon and Screen Resolution
Access may change how the groups and buttons within the groups appear on the Ribbon, depending on the computer's screen resolution. Thus, your Ribbon may look different from the ones in this book if you are using a screen resolution other than 1024 × 768.

Report Creation

Unless you want a report that simply lists all the fields and all the records in a table, the simplest way to create a report design is to use the Report Wizard. In some cases, the Report Wizard can produce exactly the desired report. Other times, however, you first must use the Report Wizard to produce a report that is as close as possible to the desired report. Then, use Layout view to modify the report and transform it into the correct report. In either case, once you have created and saved the report, you can print it whenever you need to. Access will use the current data in the database for the report, formatting and arranging it in exactly the way you specified when you created the report.

Determine the tables and fields that contain the data needed for the report.
If you determine that data should be presented as a report, you then need to determine what tables and fields contain the data for the report. The following guidelines apply to this decision.

- **Examine the requirements for the report in general to determine the tables.** Do the requirements only relate to data in a single table, or does the data come from multiple tables? What is the relationship between the tables?

- **Examine the specific requirements for the report to determine the fields necessary.** Look for all the data items specified for the report. Each should correspond to a field in a table or be able to be computed from fields in a table. This information gives you the list of fields to include.

- **Determine the order of the fields.** Examine the requirements to determine the order in which the fields should appear. Be logical and consistent in your ordering. For example, in an address, the city should come before the state and the state should come before the postal code, unless there is some compelling reason for another order.

Plan Ahead

Using Layout View in a Report

When working with a report in Access, there are four different ways to view the report: Report view, Print Preview, Layout view, and Design view. Report view shows the report on the screen. Print Preview shows the report as it will appear when printed. Layout view is similar to Report view in that it shows the report on the screen, but it also allows you to make changes to the report. It is usually the easiest way to make such changes. Design view also allows you to make changes, but it does not show you the actual report. It is most useful when the changes you need to make are especially complex. In this chapter, you will use Layout view to modify the report.

Understanding Report Sections

Report Design Considerations
The purpose of any report is to present specific information. Make sure that the meaning of the row and column headings is clear. You can use different fonts and sizes by changing the appropriate properties, but do not overuse them. Finally, be consistent when creating reports. Once you decide on a general report style or theme, stick with it throughout your database.

A report is divided into various sections to help clarify the presentation of data. In Design view, which you will use in later chapters, the sections are labeled on the screen. Even though they are not labeled in Layout view, it is still useful to understand the purpose of the various sections. A typical report consists of a Report Header section, Page Header section, Detail section, Page Footer section, and Report Footer section (see Figure 4–1).

The contents of the Report Header section print once at the beginning of the report. In the Client Financial Report, the title is in the Report Header section. The contents of the Report Footer section print once at the end of the report. In the Client Financial Report, the Report Footer section contains the grand totals of Amount Paid, Current Due, Total Amount, and Hrs YTD. The contents of the Page Header section print once at the top of each page and typically contain the column headers. The contents of the Page Footer section print once at the bottom of each page and often contain a date and a page number. The contents of the Detail section print once for each record in the table; for example, once for Buda Community Clinic, once for Granger Family Foundation, and so on. In this report, they contain the client number, client name, amount paid, current due, total amount, hrs YTD, and business analyst number.

When the data in a report is grouped, there are two additional sections. The contents of the Group Header section are printed before the records in a particular group, and the contents of the Group Footer section are printed after the group. In the Client Financial Report, the Group Header section contains the Client Type, and the Group Footer section contains subtotals of Amount Paid, Current Due, Total Amount, and Hrs YTD.

Plan Ahead

> **Determine the organization of the report or form.**
> Determine various details concerning how the data in your report or form is to be organized.
>
> - **Determine sort order.** Is there a special order in which the records should appear?
>
> - **Determine grouping.** Should the records be grouped in some fashion? If so, what should appear before the records in a group? If, for example, clients are grouped by city, the name of the city should probably appear before the group. What should appear after the group? For example, are there some fields for which subtotals should be calculated? If so, the subtotals would come after the group. Determine whether you need multiple levels of grouping.

To Group and Sort in a Report

Camashaly has determined that the records in the report should be grouped by client type. That is, all the clients of a given type should appear together immediately after the type. Within the clients in a given type, the clients are to be ordered by client number. In Layout view of the report, you can specify both grouping and sorting by using the Group & Sort button on the Design tab. The following steps open the Client Financial Report in Layout view and then specify both grouping and sorting in the report.

1
- Right-click the Client Financial Report in the Navigation Pane to produce a shortcut menu.

- Click Layout View on the shortcut menu to open the report in Layout view.

- Close the Navigation Pane.

- If a field list appears, close the field list by clicking the Add Existing Fields button (Report Layout Tools Design tab | Tools group).

- Click the Group & Sort button (Report Layout Tools Design tab | Grouping & Totals group) to display the Group, Sort, and Total pane (Figure 4–5).

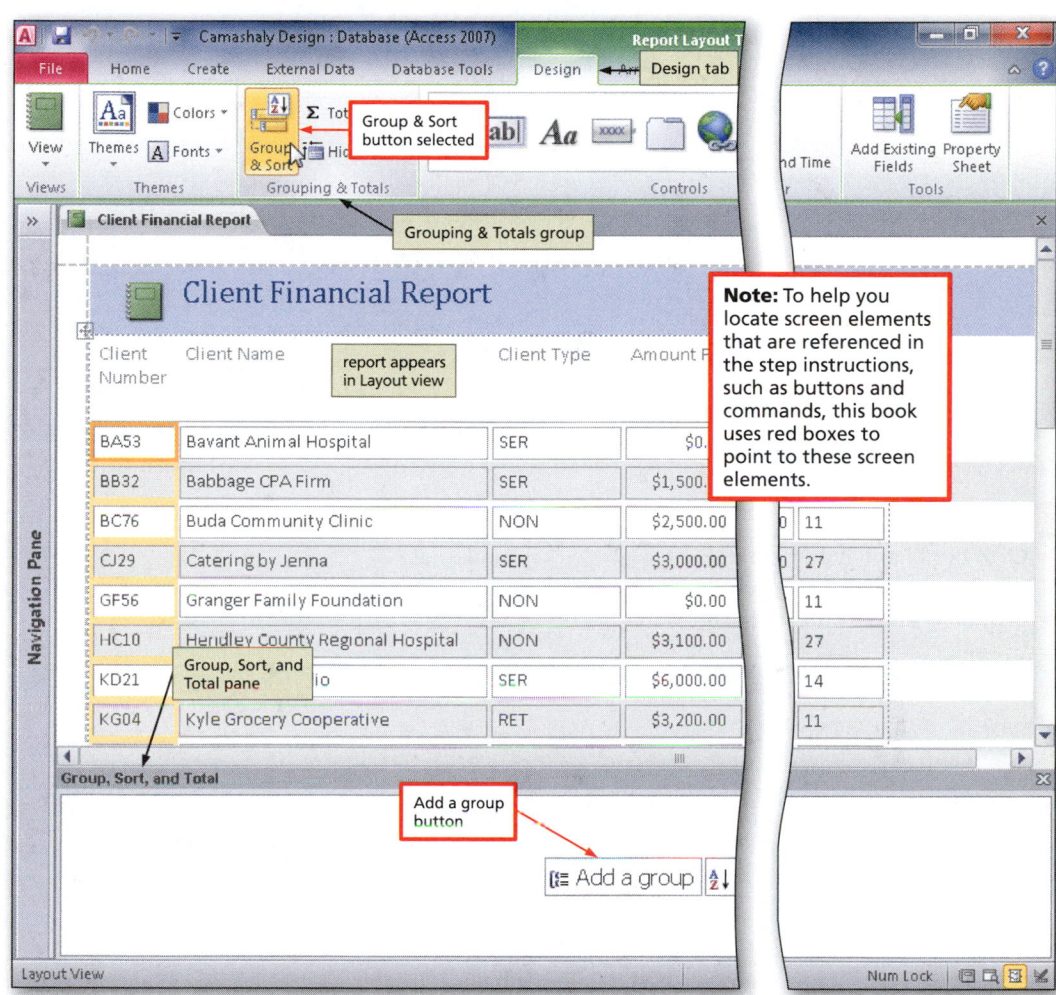

Figure 4–5

2

- Click the 'Add a group' button to add a group (Figure 4–6).

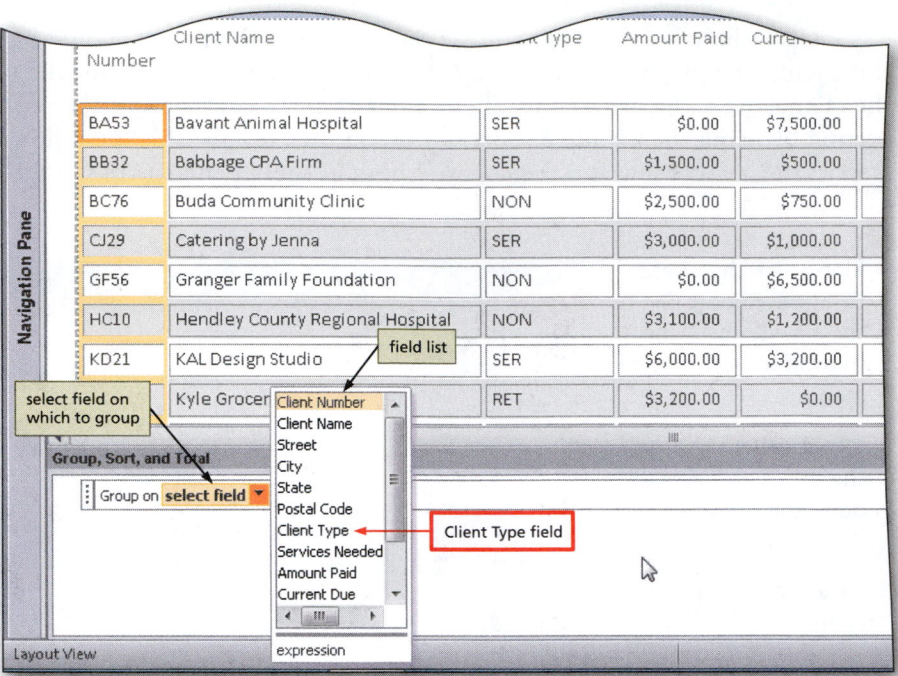

Figure 4–6

3

- Click the Client Type field in the field list to select a field for grouping and group the records on the selected field (Figure 4–7).

Q&A

Does the field on which I group have to be the first field?

No. If you select a field other than the first field, Access will move the field you select into the first position.

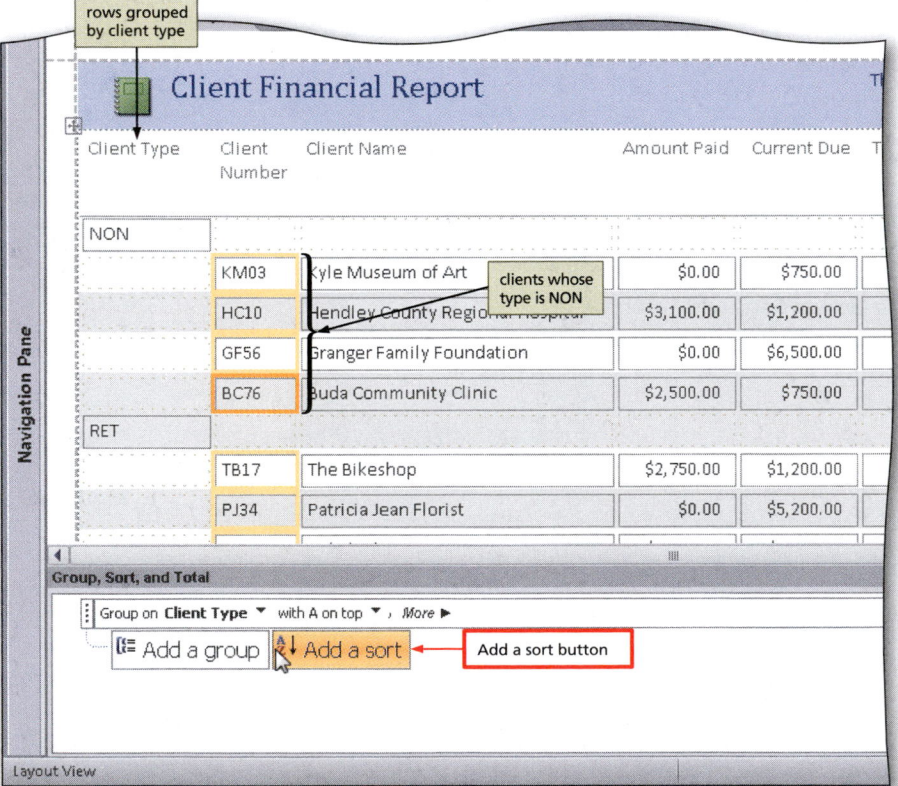

Figure 4–7

4
- Click the 'Add a sort' button to add a sort (Figure 4–8).

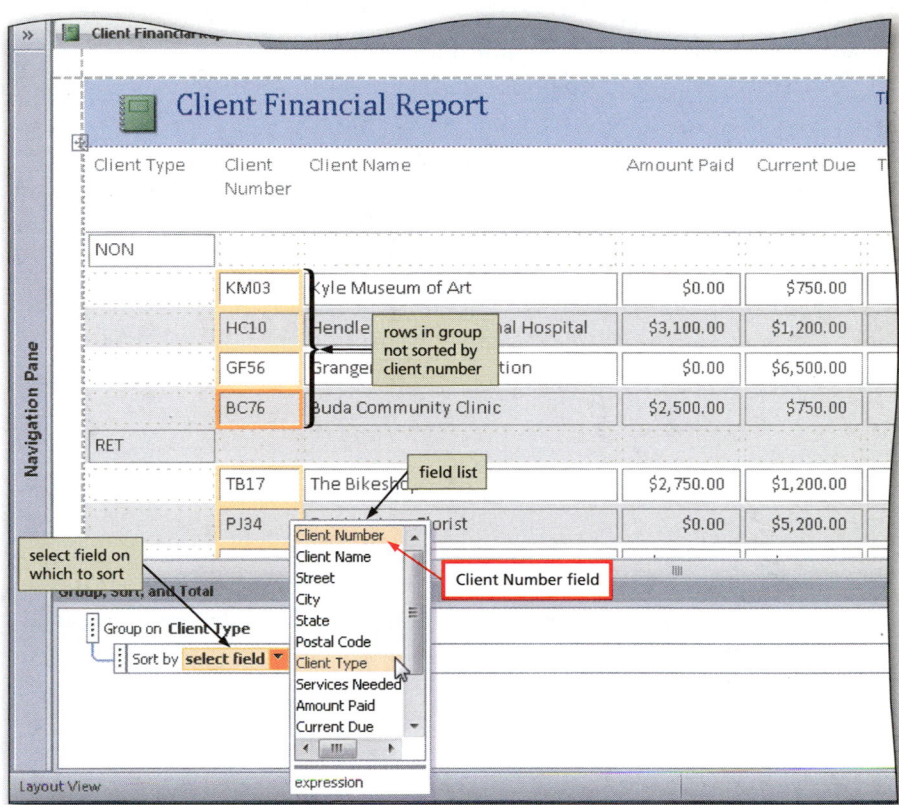

Figure 4–8

5
- Click the Client Number field in the field list to specify the field on which the records in each group will be sorted (Figure 4–9).

Q&A

I thought the report would be sorted by Client Type, because I chose to group on that field. What is the effect of choosing to sort by Client Number?

This sort takes place within groups. You are specifying that within the list of clients of the same type, the clients will be ordered by client number.

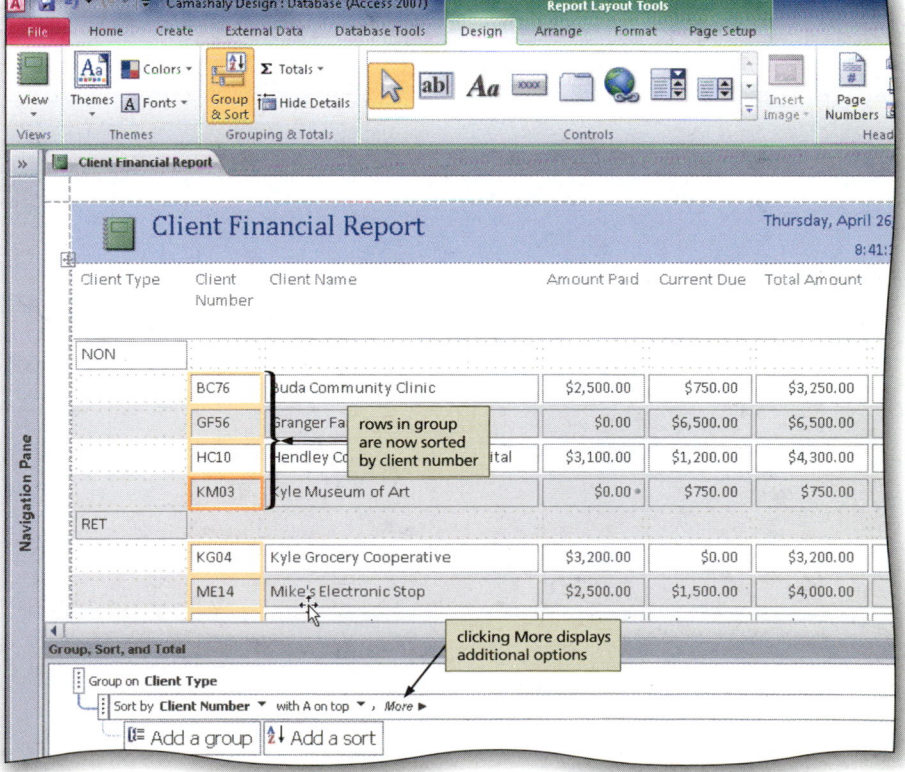

Figure 4–9

Grouping and Sorting Options

For both grouping and sorting, you can click the More button to specify additional options (see Figure 4–10). The options you then could select are:

- Value. You can choose the amount of the value on which to group. Typically, you would group by the entire value, for example, the entire city name. You could choose, however, to only group on the first character, in which case all clients in cities that begin with the same letter would be considered a group. You also could group by the first two characters or by a custom number of characters.

- Totals. You can choose the values to be totaled. You can specify whether the totals are to appear in the group header or in the group footer and whether there is to be a grand total. You can also choose whether to show group totals as a percentage of the grand total.

- Title. You can customize the group title.

- Header section. You can include or omit a header section for the group.

- Footer section. You can include or omit a footer section for the group.

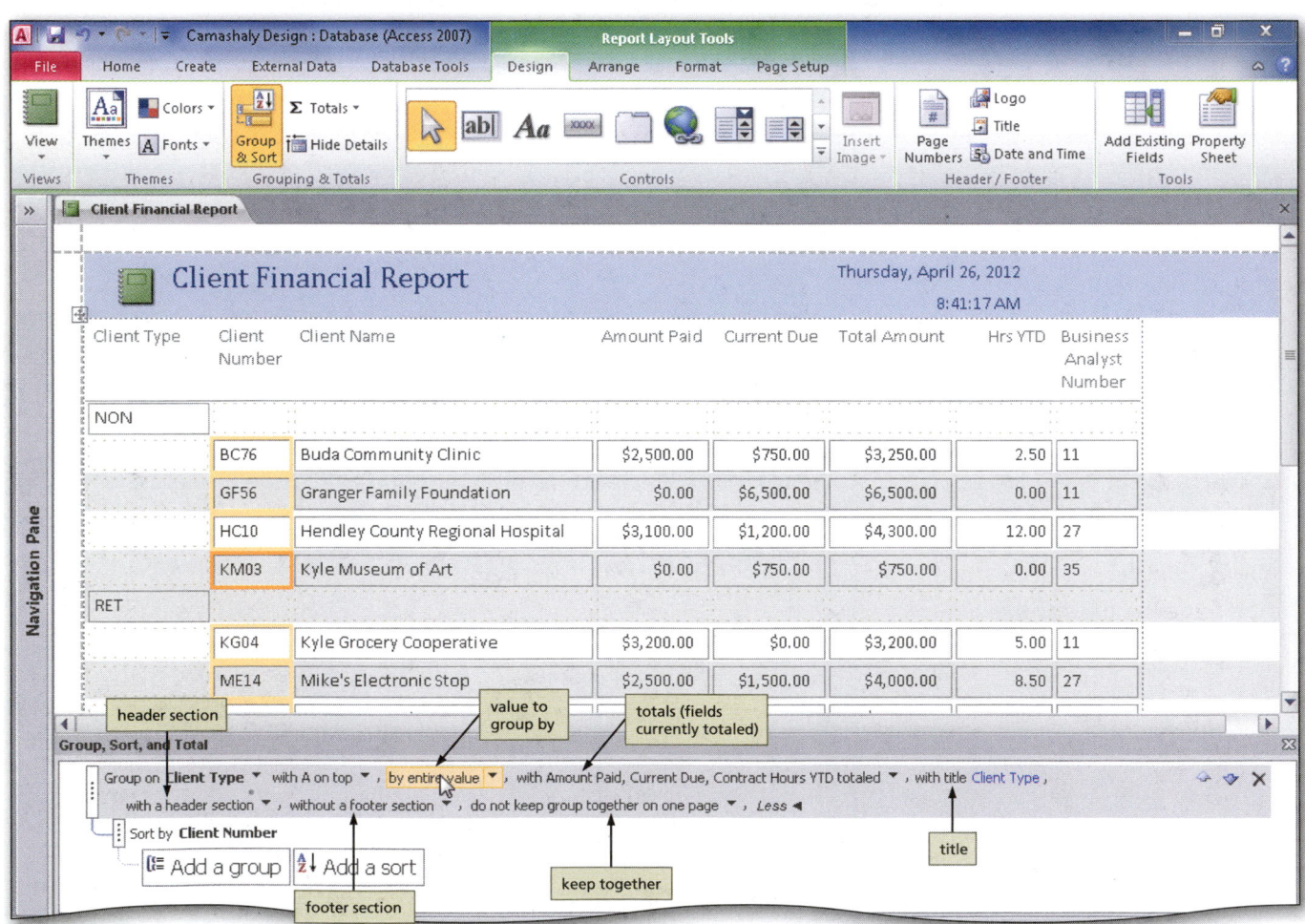

Figure 4–10

• Keep together. You can indicate whether Access is to attempt to keep portions of a group together on the same page. The default setting does not keep portions of a group together, but you can specify that Access should attempt to keep a whole group together on one page. If the group will not fit on the remainder of the page, Access will move the group header and the records in a group to the next page. Finally, you can choose to have Access keep the header and the first record together on one page. If the header would fit at the bottom of a page, but there would not be room for the first record, Access will move the header to the next page.

Understanding Report Controls

The various objects on a report are called **controls**. The report title, column headers, contents of various fields, subtotals, and so on are all contained in controls. When working in Layout view, as you will do in this chapter, Access handles details concerning these controls for you automatically. When working in Design view, you will see and manipulate the controls. Even when working in Layout view, however, it is useful to understand the concepts of controls.

The report has a control containing the title, Client Financial Report. Also included is a control containing each column header (Client Type, Client Number, Client Name, Amount Paid, Current Due, Total Amount, Hrs YTD, and Business Analyst Number). A control in the Group Header section displays the client type. There are four controls in the Group Footer section: One control displays the subtotal of Amount Paid, a second displays the subtotal of Current Due, a third displays the subtotal of Total Amount, and the fourth displays the subtotal of Hrs YTD. The Detail section has controls containing the client number, client name, amount paid, current due, total amount, hrs YTD, and business analyst number.

There are three types of controls: bound controls, unbound controls, and calculated controls. **Bound controls** are used to display data that comes from the database, such as the client number and name. **Unbound controls** are not associated with data from the database and are used to display such things as the report's title. Finally, **calculated controls** are used to display data that is calculated from other data, such as a total.

To Add Totals and Subtotals

Along with determining to group data in this report, Camashaly also determines that subtotals of the Amount Paid, Current Due, Total Amount, and Hrs YTD fields should be included. To add totals or other statistics, use the Totals button on the Design tab. You then select from a menu of aggregate functions, which are functions that perform some mathematical function against a group of records. The available aggregate functions, or calculations, are Sum (total), Average, Count Records, Count Values, Max (largest value), Min (smallest value), Standard Deviation, and Variance. The following steps add totals of the Amount Paid, Current Due, Total Amount, and Hrs YTD fields. Because the report is grouped, each group will have a subtotal, that is, a total for just the records in the group. At the end of the report, there will be a grand total, that is, a total for all records.

The following steps specify totals for the desired fields. Even though you previously specified totals for the Amount Paid, Current Due, and Hrs YTD fields, you need to do so again because of the grouping.

1

● Click the Amount Paid column header to select the field.

Q&A Does it have to be the column header?

No, you could click the Amount Paid field on any record.

● Click the Totals button (Report Layout Tools Design tab | Grouping & Totals group) to display the list of available calculations (Figure 4–11).

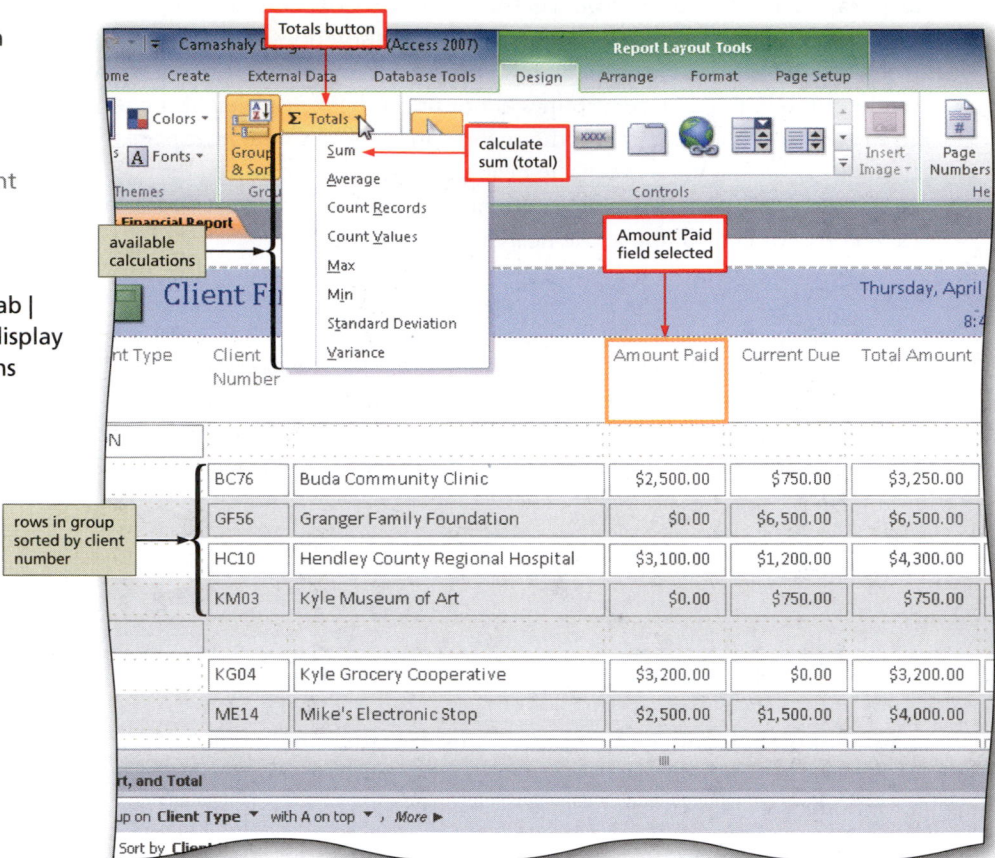

Figure 4–11

2

● Click Sum to calculate the sum of amount paid values.

Q&A Is Sum the same as Total?

Yes.

● If the total does not appear completely, drag the bottom of the control for the subtotal to the approximate position shown in Figure 4–12.

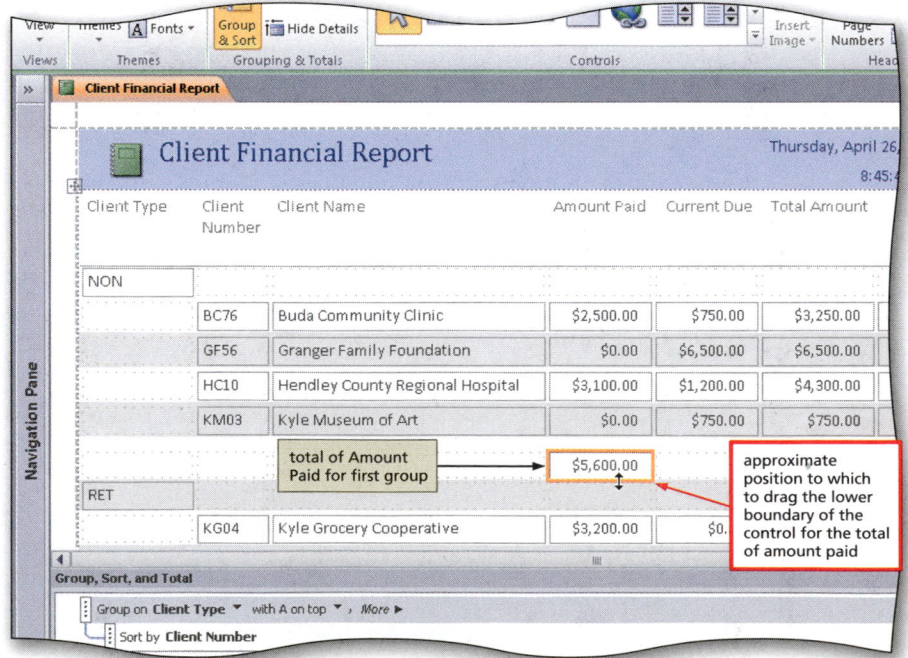

Figure 4–12

3
- Using the same technique as in Steps 1 and 2, add totals for the Current Due, Total Amount, and Hrs YTD fields (Figure 4–13).

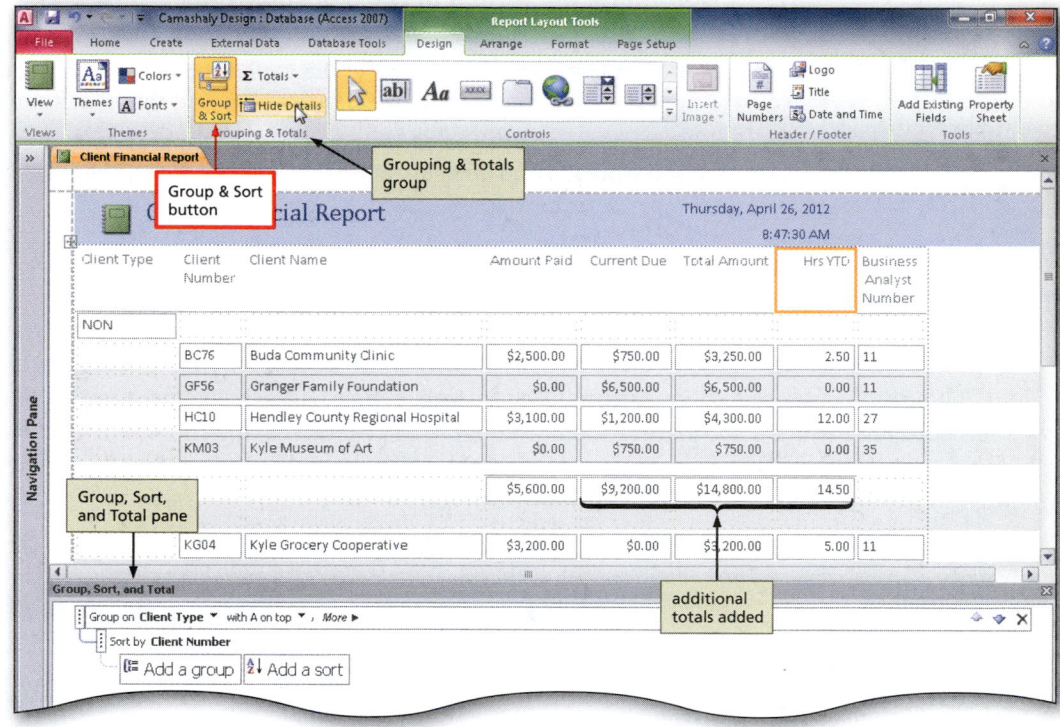

Figure 4–13

To Remove the Group, Sort, and Total Pane

You have specified the grouping and sorting that you need for the report, so you no longer need the Group, Sort, and Total pane. The following step removes the Group, Sort, and Total pane from the screen.

1
- Click the Group & Sort button (Report Layout Tools Design tab | Grouping & Totals group) to remove the Group, Sort, and Total pane (Figure 4–14).

Q&A
Do I need to remove the Group, Sort, and Total pane?

Technically not. It gives more room on the screen for the report, however. You can easily display the pane whenever you need it by clicking the Group & Sort button again.

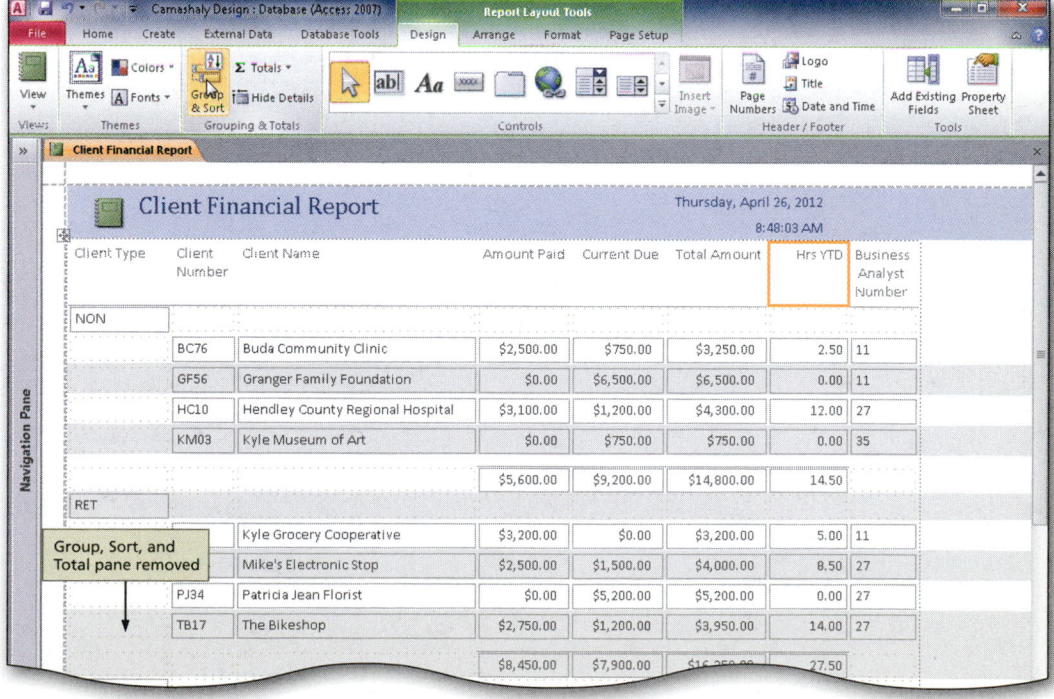

Figure 4–14

Plan
Ahead

Determine the format of the report or form.
Determine details concerning the appearance of the report.

- **Determine the font or colors for the various sections of the reports.** Which combination of colors and fonts convey the best look for your report or form?

- **Determine whether conditional formatting is appropriate.** Are there any fields in which you would like to emphasize certain values by giving them a different appearance?

To Conditionally Format Controls

You can emphasize values in a column that satisfy some criterion by formatting them differently from other values. This emphasis is called **conditional formatting**. Camashaly management would like to emphasize values in the Current Due field that are greater than or equal to $1,000 by making them red. The following steps conditionally format the Current Due field by specifying a **rule** that states that if the values in the field are greater than or equal to $1,000, such values will be formatted in red.

1

- Click Format on the Ribbon to display the Format tab.

- Click the Current Due field on the first record to select the field (Figure 4–15).

Q&A

Does it have to be the first record?

No. You could click the field on any record.

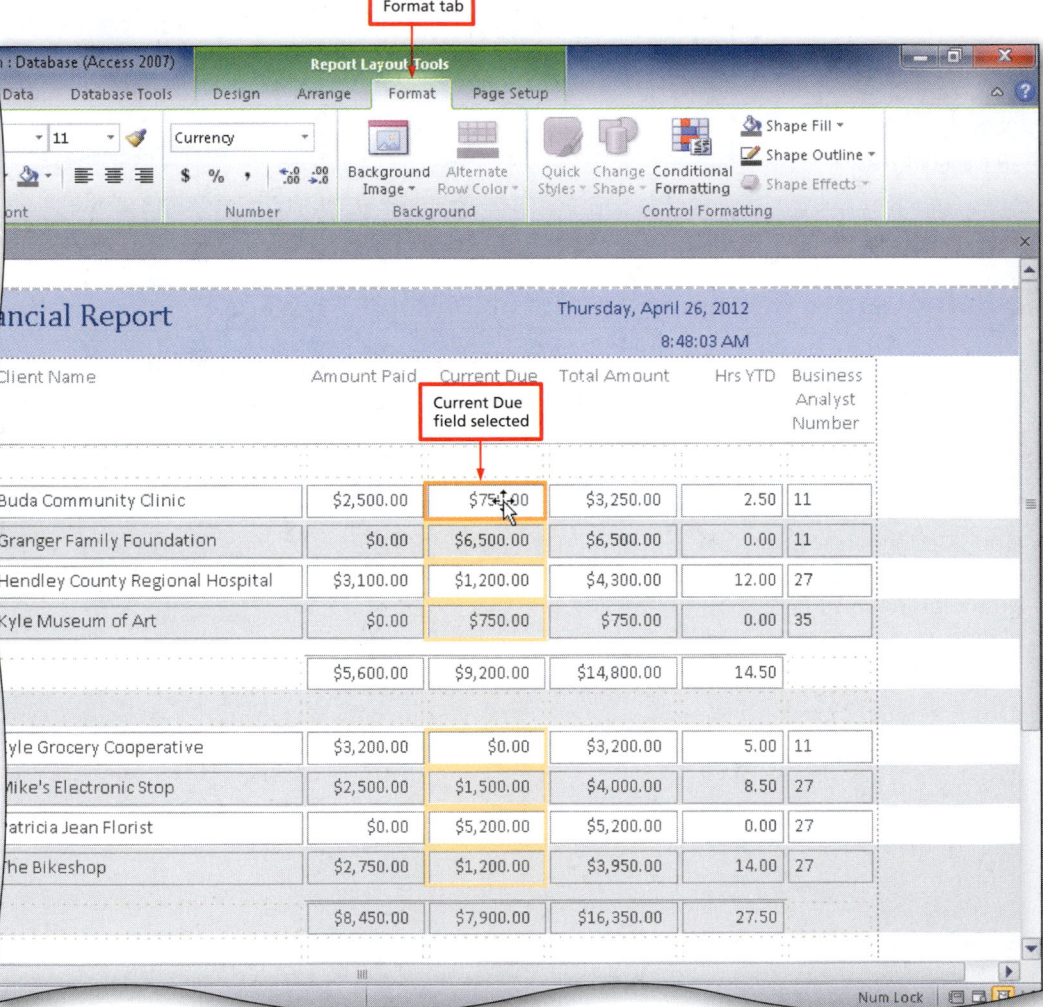

Figure 4–15

2
- Click the Conditional Formatting button (Report Layout Tools Format tab | Control Formatting group) to display the Conditional Formatting Rules Manager dialog box (Figure 4–16).

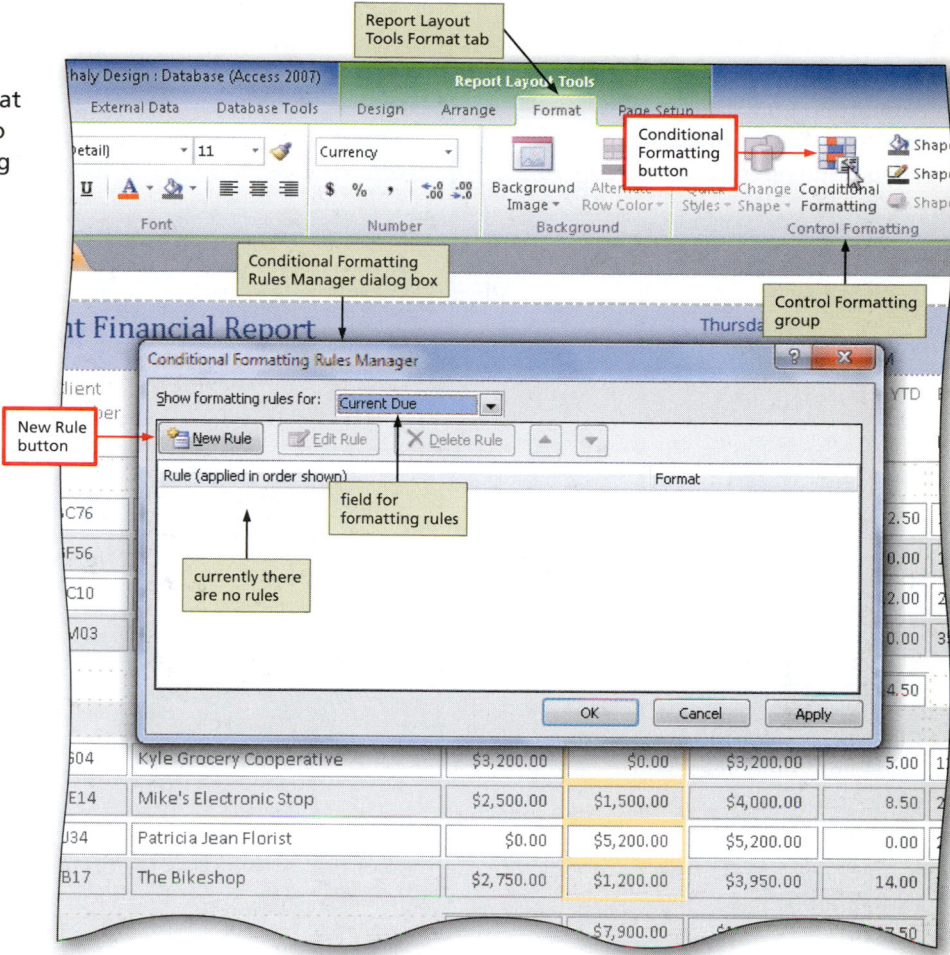

Figure 4–16

3
- Click the New Rule button (Conditional Formatting Rules Manager dialog box) to display the New Formatting Rule dialog box (Figure 4–17).

Q&A

I see that there are two boxes to enter numbers. I only have one number to enter, 1000. Am I on the right screen?

Yes. You will next change the comparison operator from between to 'greater than or equal to.' Once you have done so, Access will only display one box for entering a number.

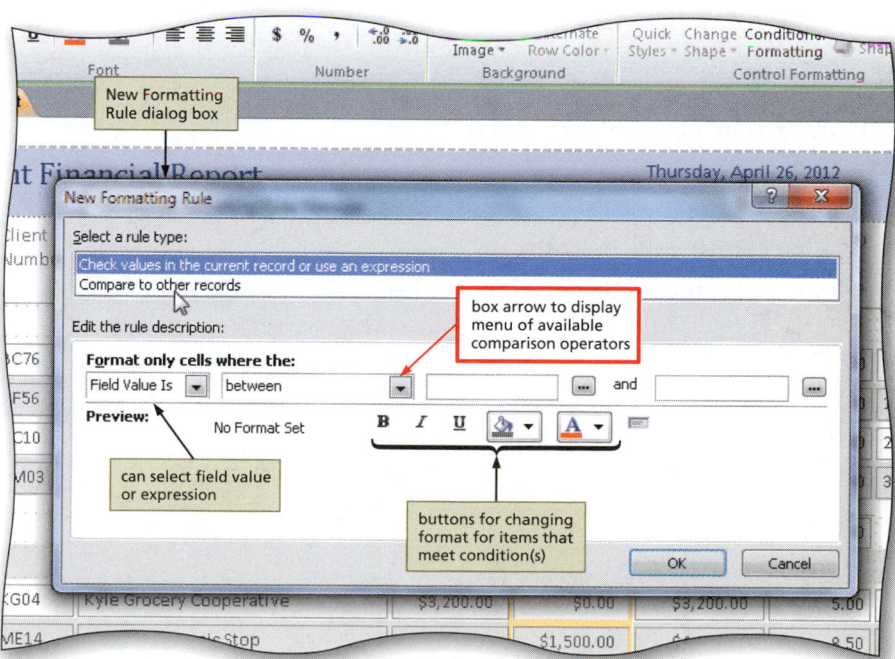

Figure 4–17

4

- Click the box arrow (New Formatting Rule dialog box) to display the list of available comparison operators (Figure 4–18).

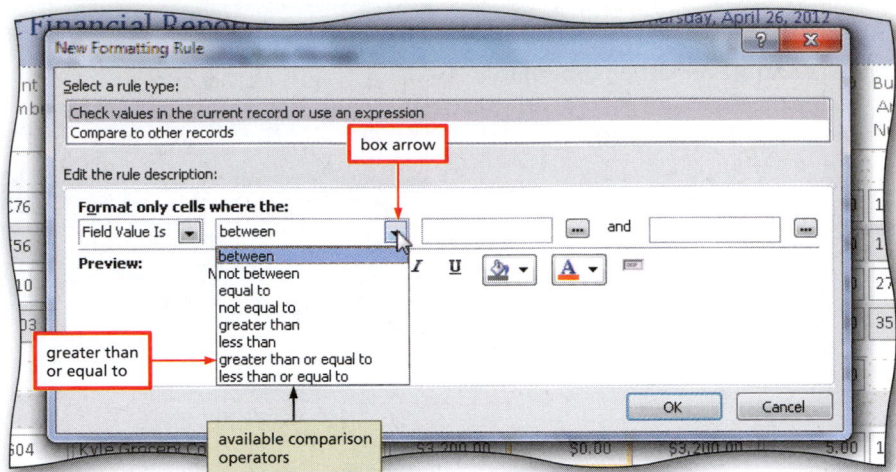

Figure 4–18

5

- Click 'greater than or equal to' to select the comparison operator.

- Click the box for the comparison value and then type 1000 as the comparison value.

Q&A

What is the effect of selecting this comparison operator and entering this number?

Values in the field that are greater than or equal to 1000 satisfy this rule. Any formatting that you now specify will apply to those values and no others.

- Click the Font Color button arrow (New Formatting Rule dialog box) to display a color palette (Figure 4–19).

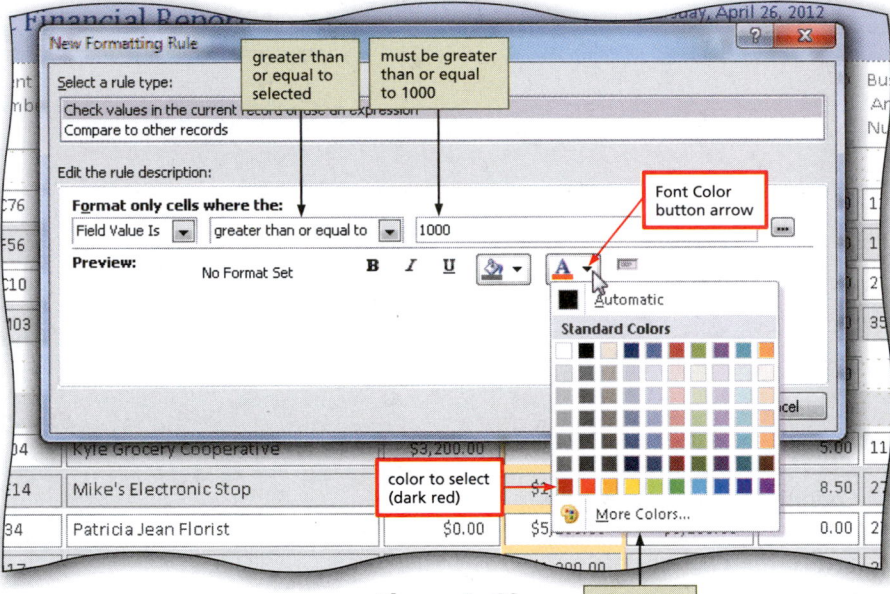

Figure 4–19

6

- Click the dark red color in the lower-left corner of the color palette to select the color (Figure 4–20).

Q&A

What other changes could I specify for those values that satisfy the rule?

You could specify that the value is bold, italic, and/or underlined. You could also specify a background color.

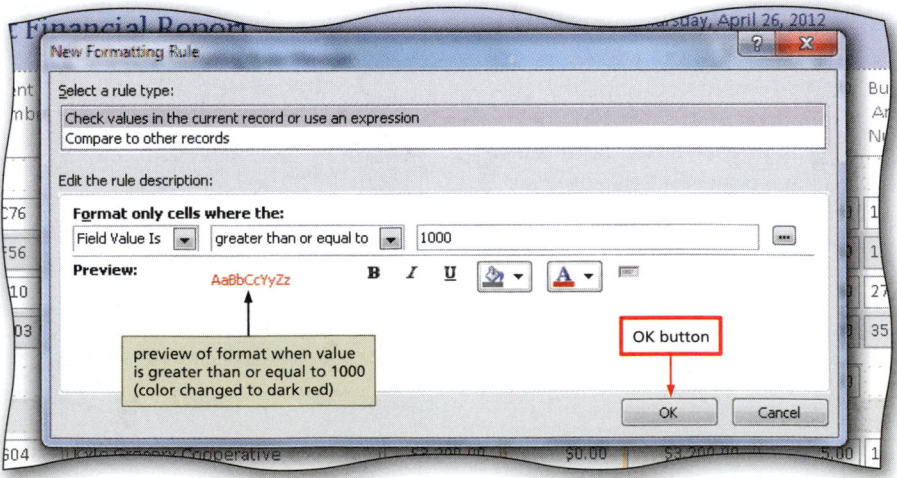

Figure 4–20

7

- Click the OK button (New Formatting Rule dialog box) to enter the rule (Figure 4–21).

Q&A

What if I have more than one rule?

The rules are applied in order. If a value satisfies the first rule, the specified formatting will apply, and no further rules will be tested. If not, the value will be tested against the second rule. If it satisfies the rule, the formatting for the second rule would apply. If not, the value would be tested against the third rule, and so on.

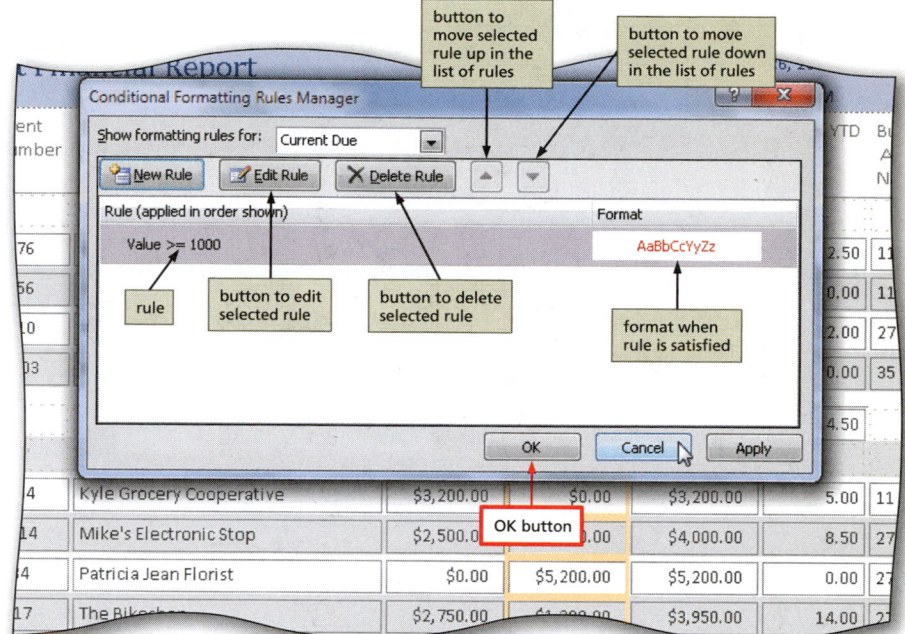

Figure 4–21

Q&A

Can I change this conditional formatting later?

Yes. Select the field for which you had applied conditional formatting on any record, click the Conditional Formatting button (Report Layout Tools Format tab | Control Formatting group), click the rule you want to change, click the Edit Rule button, and then make the necessary changes. You also can delete the selected rule by clicking the Delete Rule button or move the selected rule by clicking the up or down arrows.

8

- Click the OK button (Conditional Formatting Rules Manager dialog box) to complete the entry of the conditional formatting rules and apply the rule (Figure 4–22).

9

- Save your changes by clicking the Save button on the Quick Access Toolbar.

Experiment

- After saving your changes, experiment with different rules. Add a second rule that changes the format for any current due amount that is greater than or equal to $500 to a different color to see the effect of multiple rules. Change the order of rules to see the effect of a different order. When you have finished, delete any additional rules you have added so that the report contains only the one rule that you created earlier.

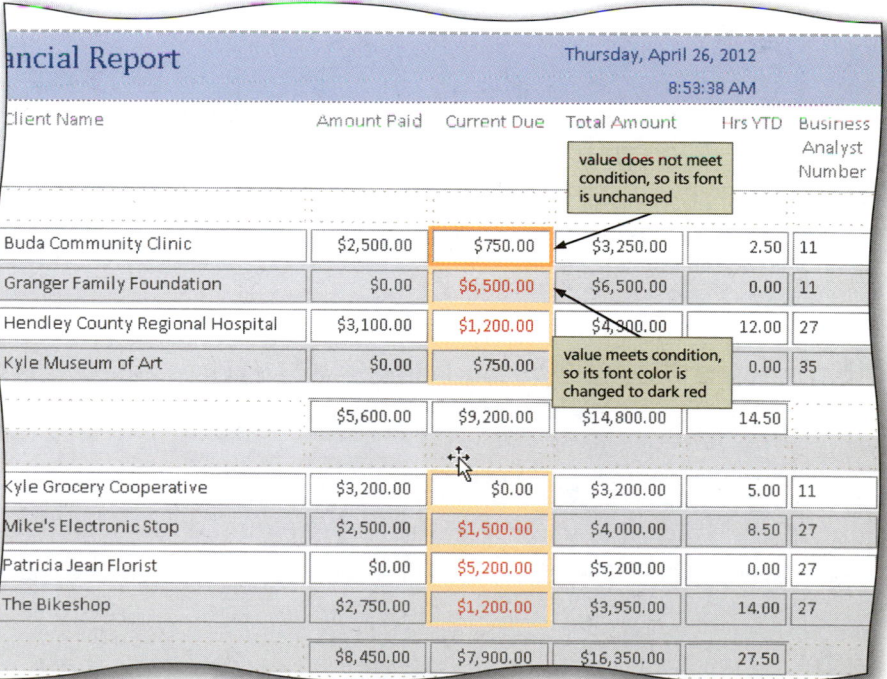

Figure 4–22

To Filter Records in a Report

You can filter records in a report. You can use the filter buttons in the Sort & Filter group on the Home tab in exactly the same way you did on a datasheet on page AC 148. If the filter involves only one field, however, right-clicking the field provides a simple way to filter. The following steps filter the records in the report to include only those records on which the amount paid is not $0.00.

1
- Right-click the Amount Paid field on the second record to display the shortcut menu (Figure 4–23).

Q&A Did I have to pick the second record?

No. You could pick any record on which the Amount Paid is $0.00.

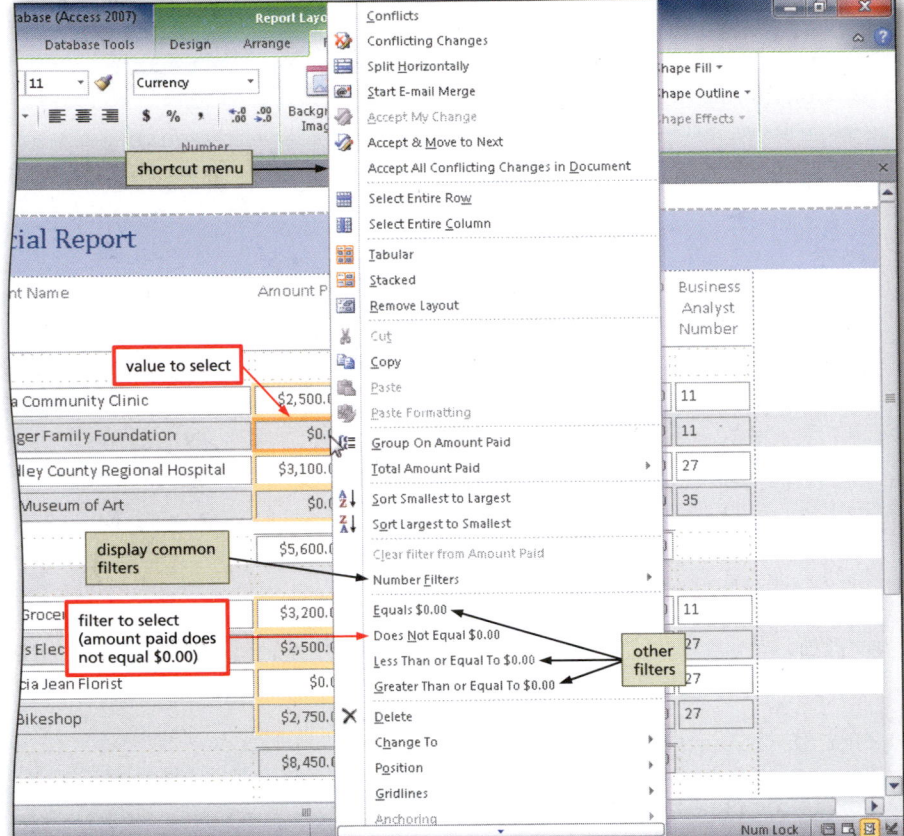

Figure 4–23

2
- Click 'Does Not Equal $0.00' on the shortcut menu to restrict the records to those on which the Amount Paid is not $0.00 (Figure 4–24).

Q&A When would you use Number Filters?

You would use Number Filters if you need filters that are not on the main shortcut menu or if you need the ability to enter specific values other than the ones shown on the shortcut menu. If those filters are insufficient for your needs, you can use Advanced Filter/Sort, which is accessible through the Advanced button (Home tab | Sort & Filter group).

Other Ways

1. Click Selection button (Home tab | Sort & Filter group)

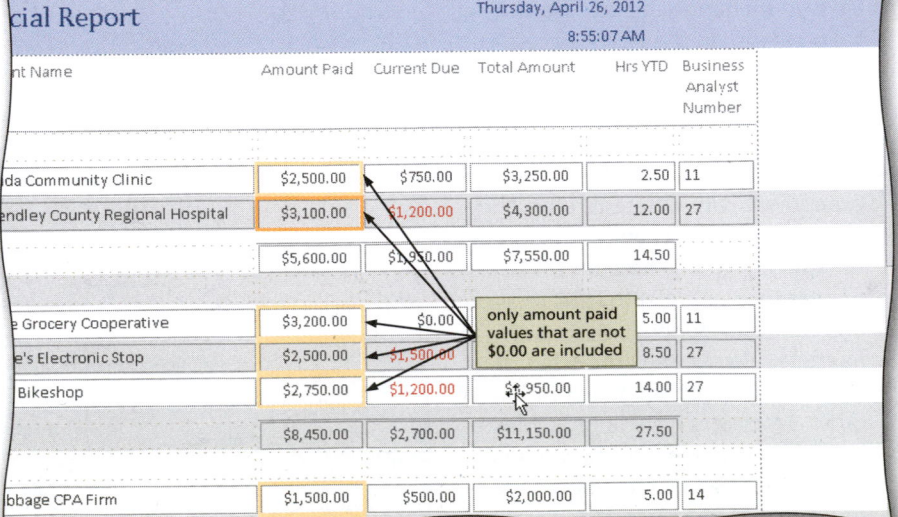

Figure 4–24

To Clear a Report Filter

When you no longer want the records to be filtered, you clear the filter. The following steps clear the filter on the Amount Paid field.

1

- Right-click the Amount Paid field on the second record to display the shortcut menu (Figure 4–25).

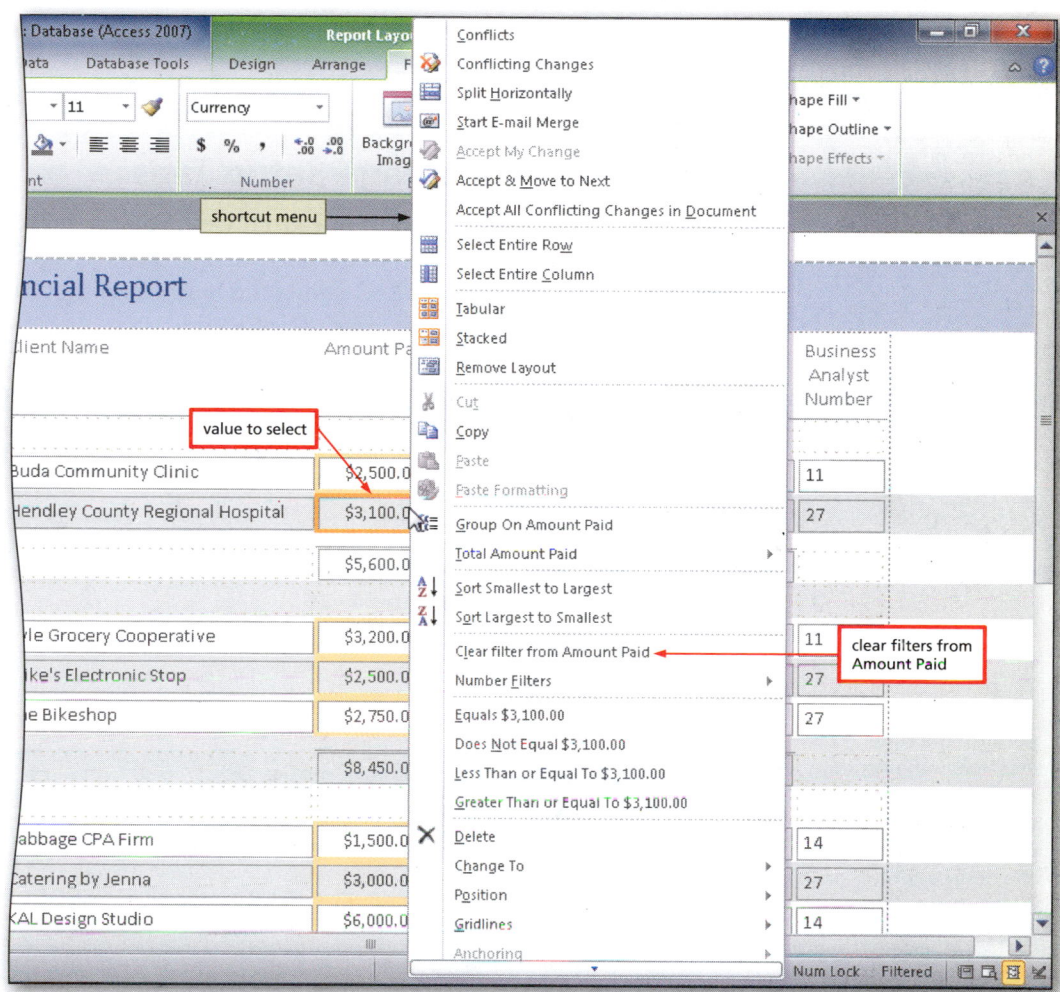

Figure 4–25

Did I have to pick the second record?

No. You could pick the Amount Paid field on any record.

2

- Click 'Clear filter from Amount Paid' on the shortcut menu to clear the filter and redisplay all records.

 **Experiment**

- Try other filters on the shortcut menu for the Amount Paid to see their effect. When done with each, clear the filter.

Other Ways
1. Click Advanced button (Home tab | Sort & Filter group), click Clear All Filters on Advanced menu

BTW

Conditional Formatting
Conditional formatting is available for forms as well as reports. To conditionally format controls on a form, open the Form in Layout view or Design view, select the control to format, click the Conditional Formatting button (Format tab | Control Formatting group), and then follow the steps on pages AC 225 through AC 227.

To Save and Close a Report

Now that you have completed your work on your report, you should save the report and close it. The following steps first save your work on the report and then close the report.

1 Click the Save button on the Quick Access Toolbar to save your work.

2 Close the Client Financial Report.

The Arrange and Page Setup Tabs

When working on a report in Layout view, you can make additional layout changes by using the Report Layout Tools Arrange and/or Page Setup tabs. The Arrange tab is shown in Figure 4–26. Table 4–1 shows the buttons on the Arrange tab along with the Enhanced ScreenTips that describe their function.

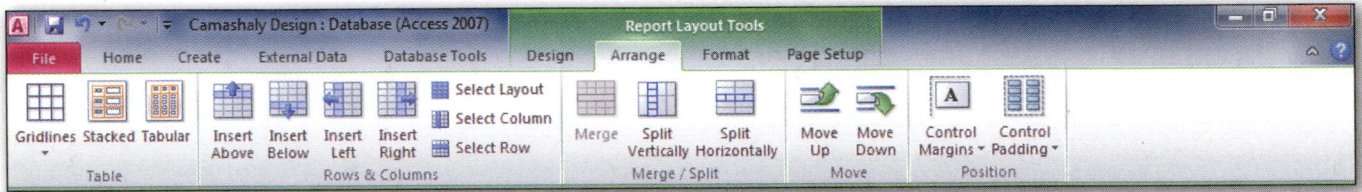

Figure 4–26

BTW

Using the Arrange tab
Because the commands located on the Arrange tab are actions associated with previously selected controls, be sure to select the desired control or controls first.

Table 4–1 Arrange Tab

Button	Enhanced ScreenTip
Gridlines	Gridlines
Stacked	Create a layout similar to a paper form, with labels to the left of each field.
Tabular	Create a layout similar to a spreadsheet, with labels across the top and data in columns below the labels.
Insert Above	Insert Above
Insert Below	Insert Below
Insert Left	Insert Left
Insert Right	Insert Right
Select Layout	Select Layout
Select Column	Select Column
Select Row	Select Row
Merge	Merge Cells
Split Vertically	Split the selected control into two rows.
Split Horizontally	Split the selected control into two columns.
Move Up	Move Up
Move Down	Move Down
Control Margins	Control Margins
Control Padding	Control Padding

The Report Layout Tools Page Setup tab is shown in Figure 4–27. Table 4–2 shows the buttons on the Page Setup tab along with the Enhanced ScreenTips that describe their function.

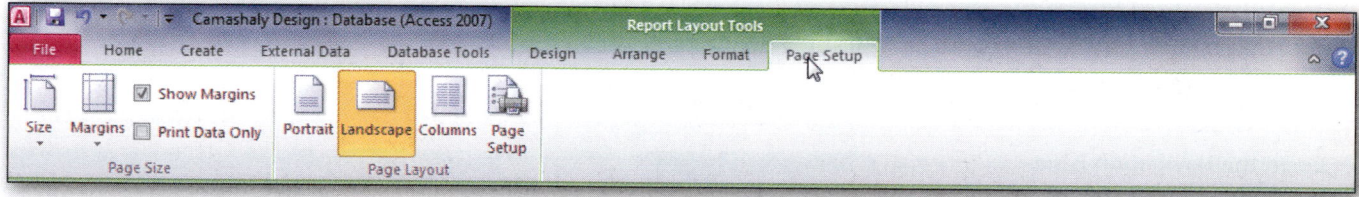

Figure 4–27

Table 4–2 Page Setup Tab	
Button	**Enhanced ScreenTip**
Size	Choose a paper size for the current section.
Margins	Select the margin sizes for the entire document or the current section.
Show Margins	Show Margins
Print Data Only	Print Data Only
Portrait	Change to portrait orientation.
Landscape	Change to landscape orientation.
Columns	Columns
Page Setup	Show the Page Setup dialog box.

To Print a Report

The following steps print the report.

1. If necessary, open the Navigation Pane.

2. With the Client Financial Report selected in the Navigation Pane, click File on the Ribbon to open the Backstage view.

3. Click the Print tab in the Backstage view to display the Print gallery.

4. Click the Quick Print button to print the report.

Q&A How can I print multiple copies of my report?

Click File on the Ribbon to open the Backstage view. Click the Print tab, click Print in the Print gallery to display the Print dialog box, increase the number in the Number of Copies box, and then click the OK button (Print dialog box).

Q&A How can I print a range of pages rather than printing the whole report?

Click File on the Ribbon to open the Backstage view. Click the Print tab, click Print in the Print gallery to display the Print dialog box, click the Pages option button in the Print Range area, enter the desired page range, and then click the OK button (Print dialog box).

Multitable Reports

You may determine that the data required for a report comes from more than one table. You can use the Report Wizard to create a report on multiple tables just as you can use it to create reports on single tables or queries.

To Create a Report that Involves Multiple Tables

Camashaly needs a report that includes the Business Analyst Number, First Name, and Last Name fields from the Business Analyst Table. In addition, for each client of the analyst, they need the Client Number, Client Name, Amount Paid, and Current Due fields from the Client table. The following steps use the Report Wizard to create a report that includes fields from both the Business Analyst and Client tables.

1

- Open the Navigation Pane if it is currently closed.

- Click the Business Analyst Table in the Navigation Pane to select it.

- Click Create on the Ribbon to display the Create tab.

- Click the Report Wizard button (Create tab | Reports group) to start the Report Wizard (Figure 4–28).

Q&A

My Navigation Pane does not look like the one in this screen. Is that a problem? How do I change it?

No, it is not a problem, but you should change it so it matches the screens in this chapter. To do so, click the Navigation Pane arrow and then click Object Type.

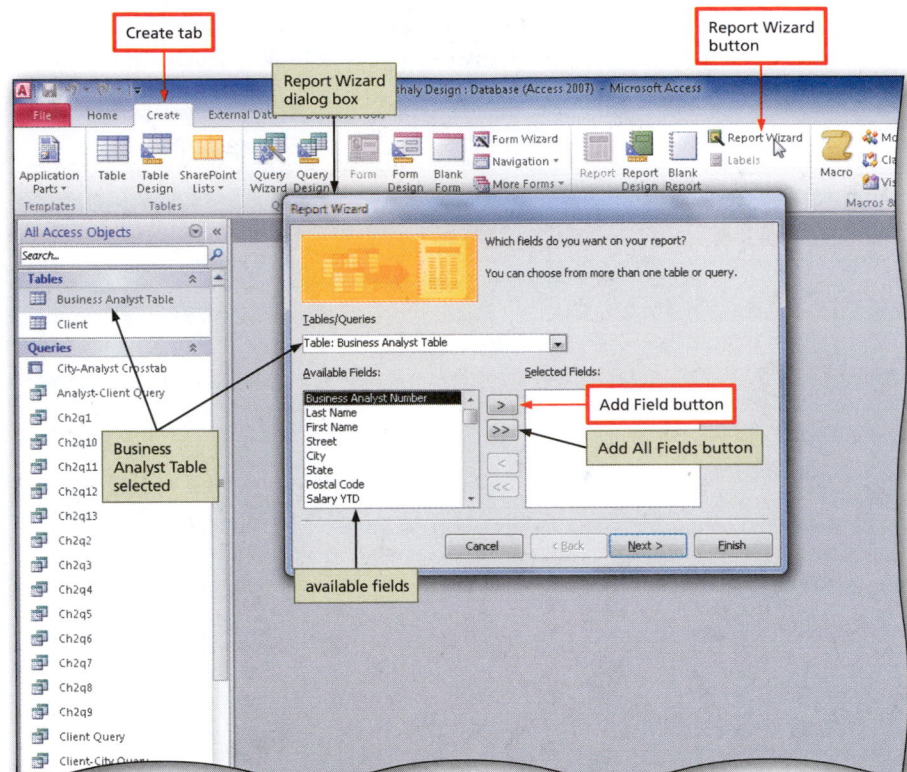

Figure 4–28

2

- Click the Add Field button to add the Business Analyst Number field to the report.

- Add the First Name field by clicking it and then clicking the Add Field button.

- Add the Last Name field in the same manner.

- Click the Tables/Queries arrow, and then click Table: Client in the Tables/Queries list box (Figure 4–29).

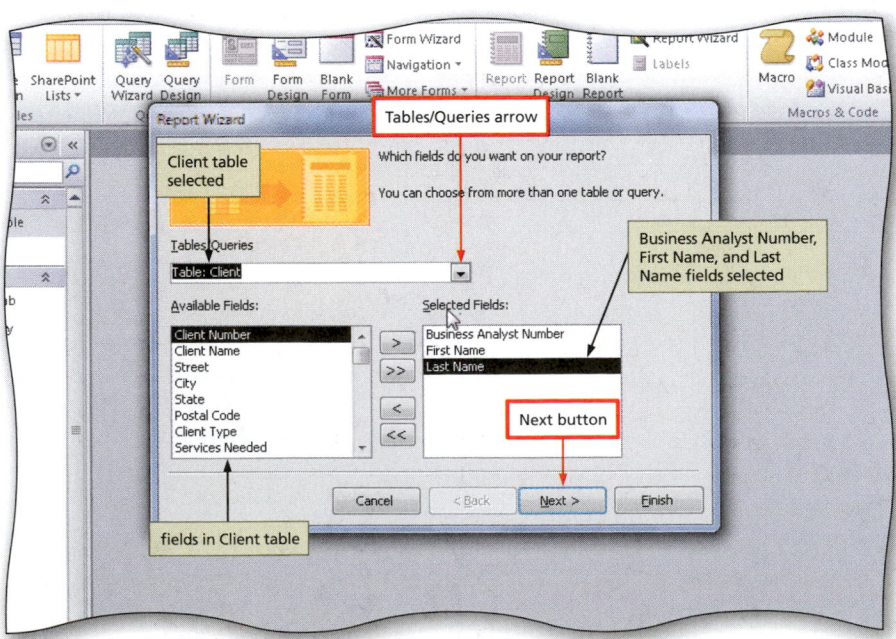

Figure 4–29

3
- Add the Client Number, Client Name, Amount Paid, and Current Due fields by clicking the field and then clicking the Add Field button.

- Click the Next button (Figure 4–30).

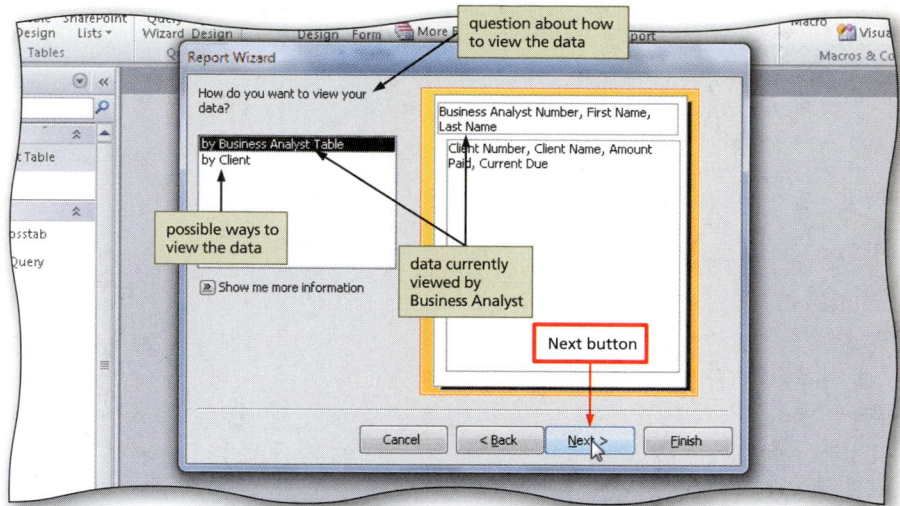

Figure 4–30

4
- Because the report is to be viewed by Business Analyst Table, and by Business Analyst Table already is selected, click the Next button (Figure 4–31).

Q&A I did not get this screen. Instead, I got an error message that said something about the tables not being related.

In Chapter 3, you create a relationship between the tables (page AC 188). That relationship must exist for the Report Wizard to be able to create the report. You will need to create the relationship and then begin these steps again.

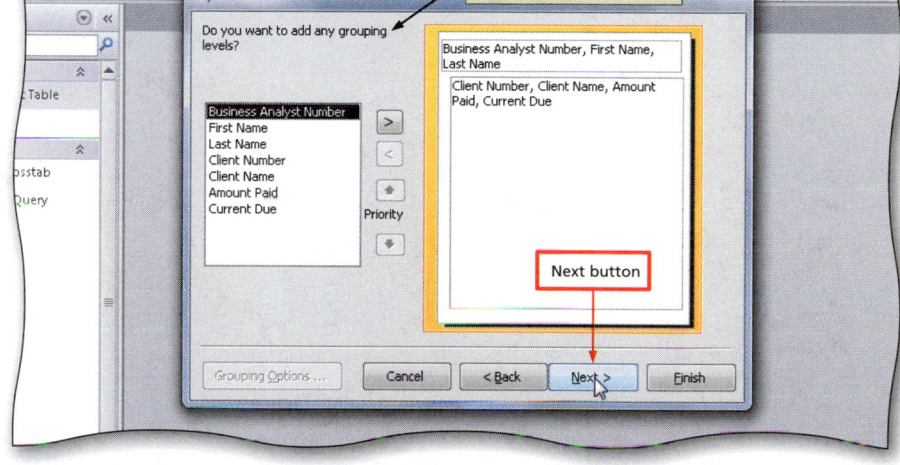

Figure 4–31

5
- Click the Next button to move to the next Report Wizard screen.

- Click the box arrow in the text box labeled 1 and then click the Client Number field in the list to select the sort order (Figure 4–32).

Q&A When would I use the Summary Options button?

You would use the Summary Options button if you want to specify subtotals or other calculations within the wizard. You also can use it to produce a summary report by selecting Summary Only, which will omit all detail records from the report.

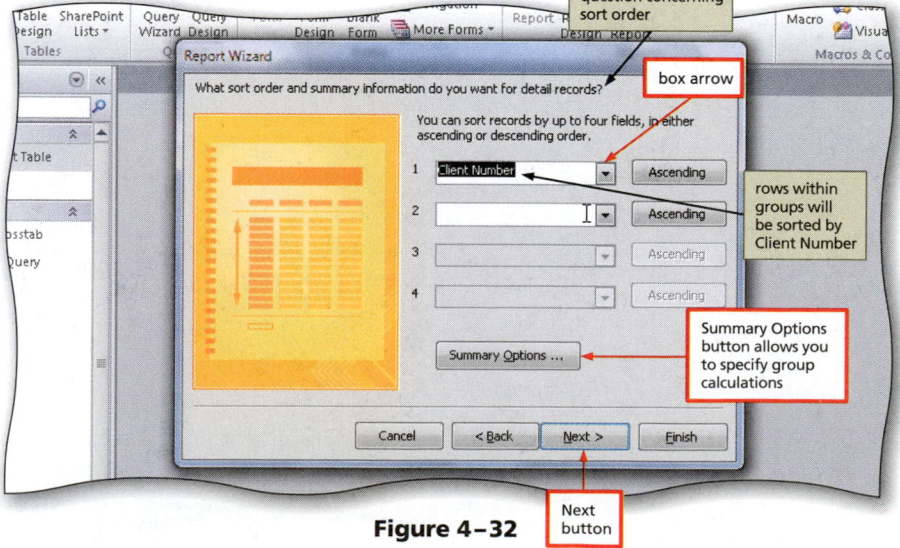

Figure 4–32

6

- Click the Summary Options button to display the Summary Options dialog box.

- Click the check boxes to calculate the sum of Amount Paid and the sum of Current Due (Figure 4–33).

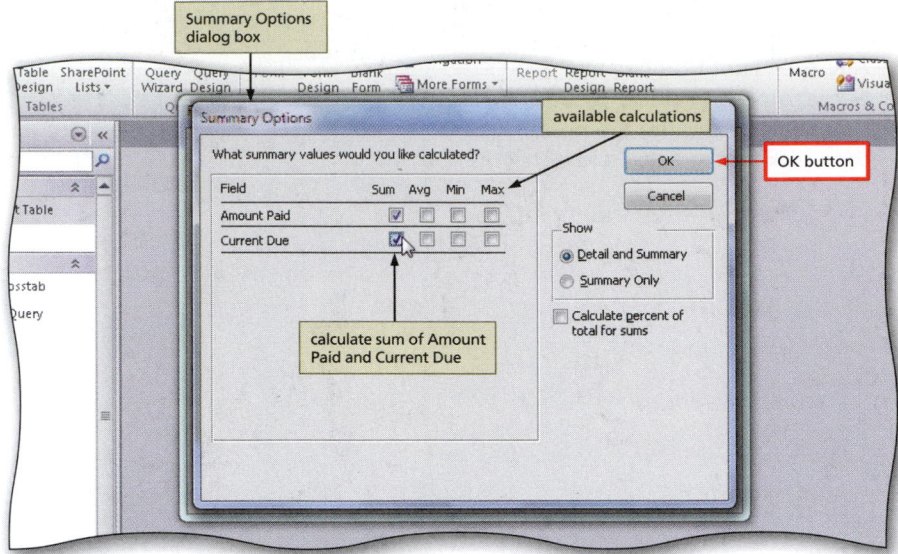

Figure 4–33

7

- Click the OK button (Summary Options dialog box).

- Click the Next button, be sure the Stepped layout is selected, and then click the Landscape option button to select the orientation (Figure 4–34).

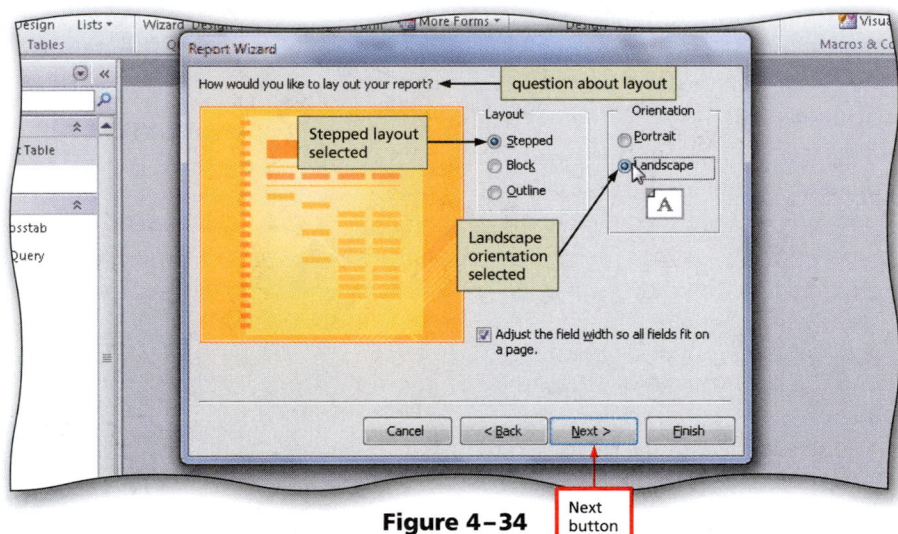

Figure 4–34

8

- Click the Next button to move to the next Report Wizard screen, and then type `Clients by Analyst` as the report title (Figure 4–35).

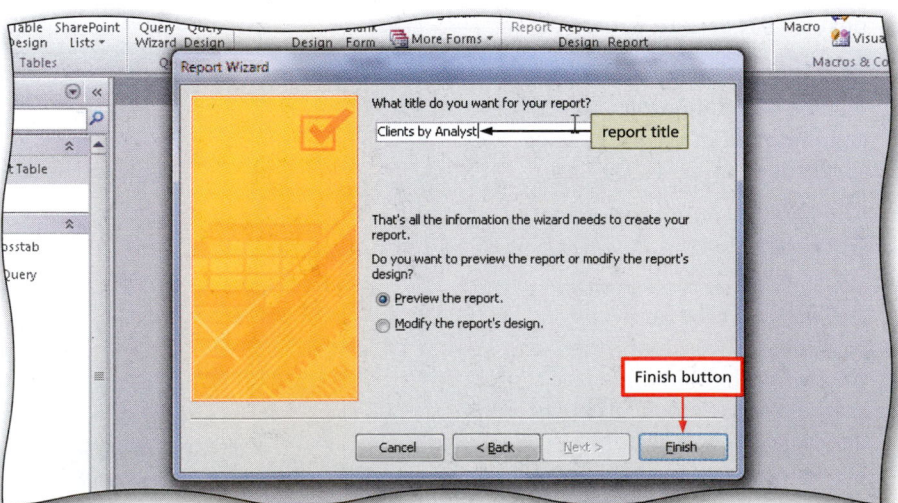

Figure 4–35

9
- Click the Finish button to produce the report (Figure 4–36).

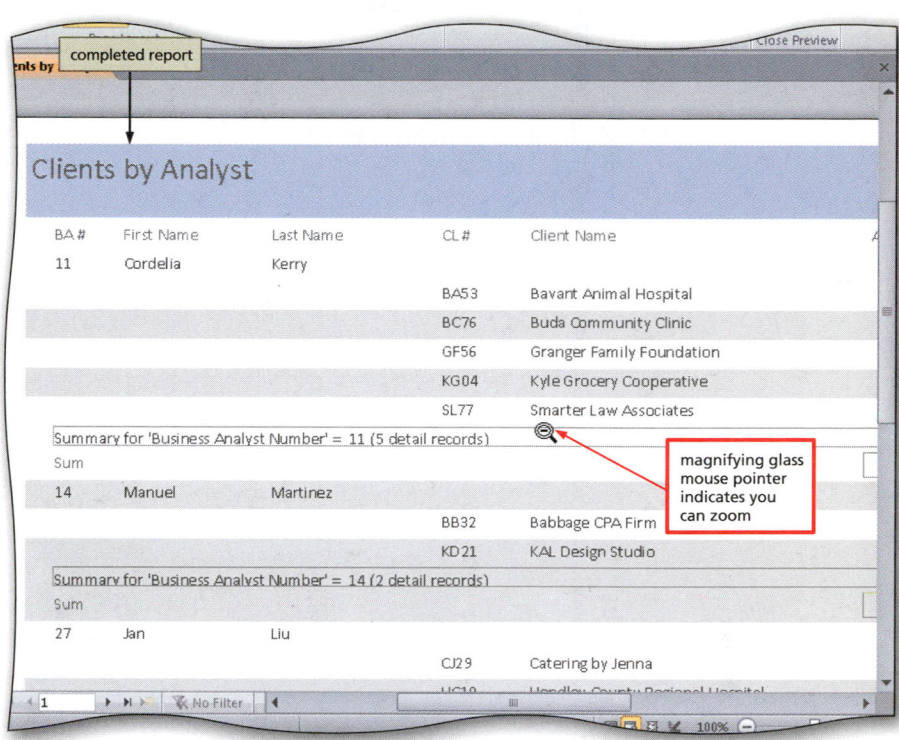

Figure 4–36

10
- Click the magnifying glass mouse pointer somewhere within the report to view more of the report (Figure 4–37).

 **Experiment**

- Zoom in on various positions within the report. When finished, view a complete page of the report.

11
- Click the Save button on the Quick Access Toolbar to save your work.
- Click the Close button for the report to close the report and remove it from the screen.

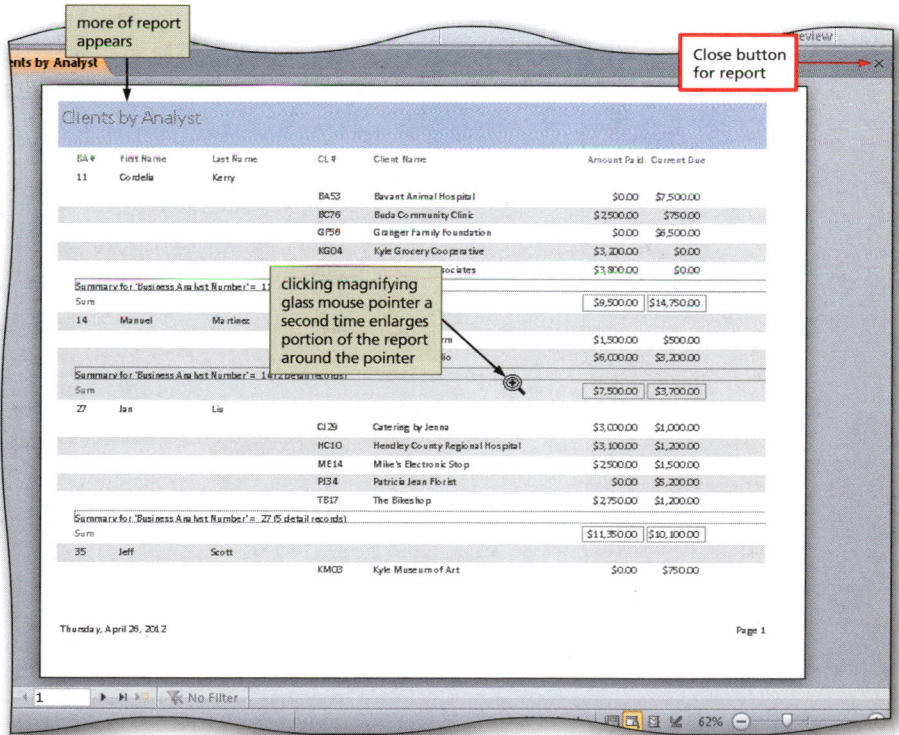

Figure 4–37

To Print a Report

The following steps print the Clients by Analyst report.

1 Open the Navigation Pane, select the Clients by Analyst report, and then click File on the Ribbon to open the Backstage view.

2 Click the Print tab in the Backstage view to display the Print gallery.

3 Click the Quick Print button to print the report.

Creating a Report in Layout View

You can use Layout view to create single- and multiple-table reports. To do so, you would first create a blank report and display a field list for the table containing the first fields you want to include on the report (Figure 4–38).

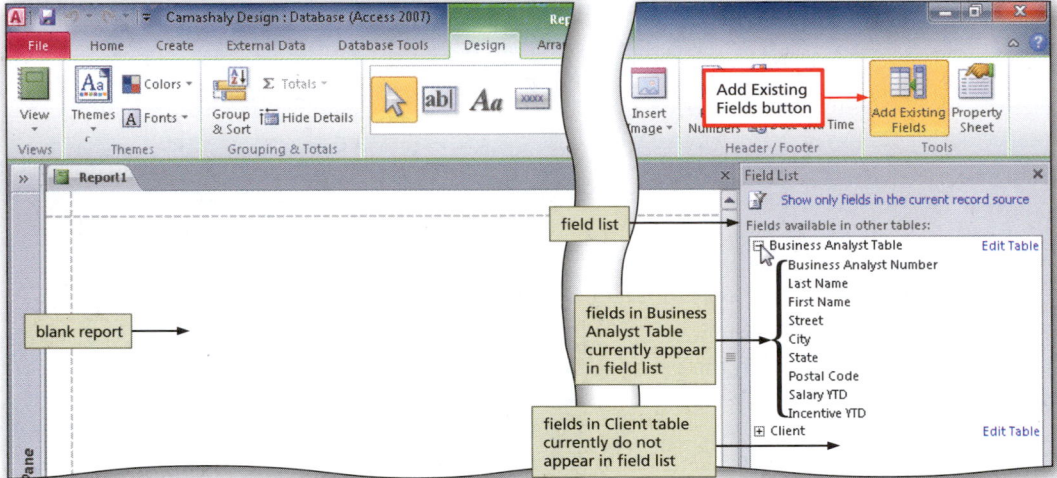

Figure 4–38

You would then drag any fields you want from the table onto the report in the order you want them to appear (Figure 4–39).

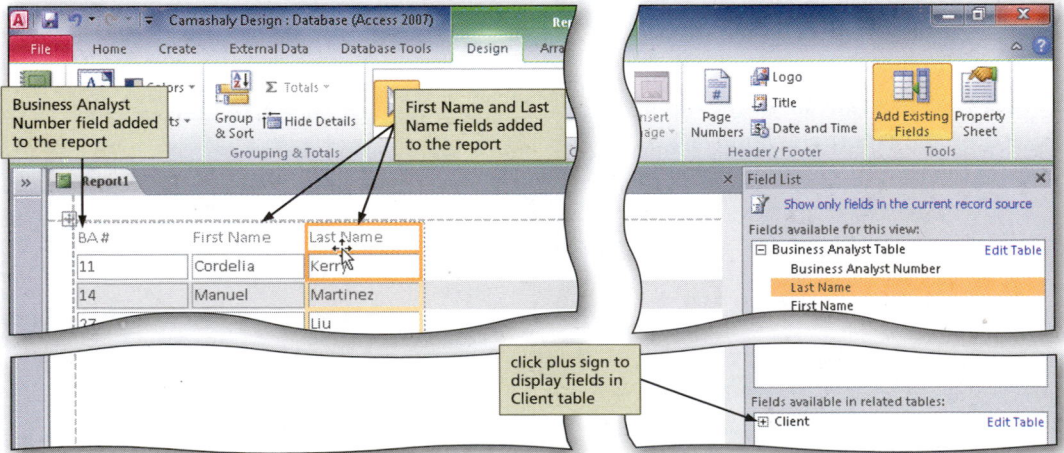

Figure 4–39

If there is a second table involved in the report, you would be sure a field list for the second table appears and then drag the fields from the second table onto the report in the desired order (Figure 4–40).

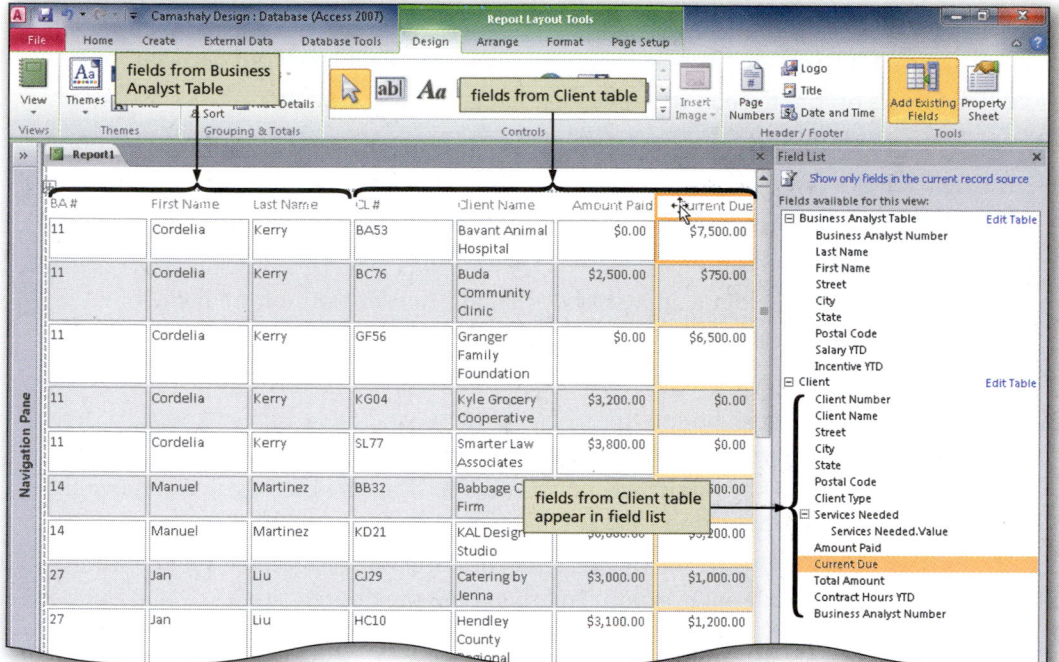

Figure 4–40

When you create a report in Layout view, the report does not automatically contain a title, but you can add one by clicking the Title button (Report Layout Tools Design tab | Header/Footer group) (Figure 4–41).

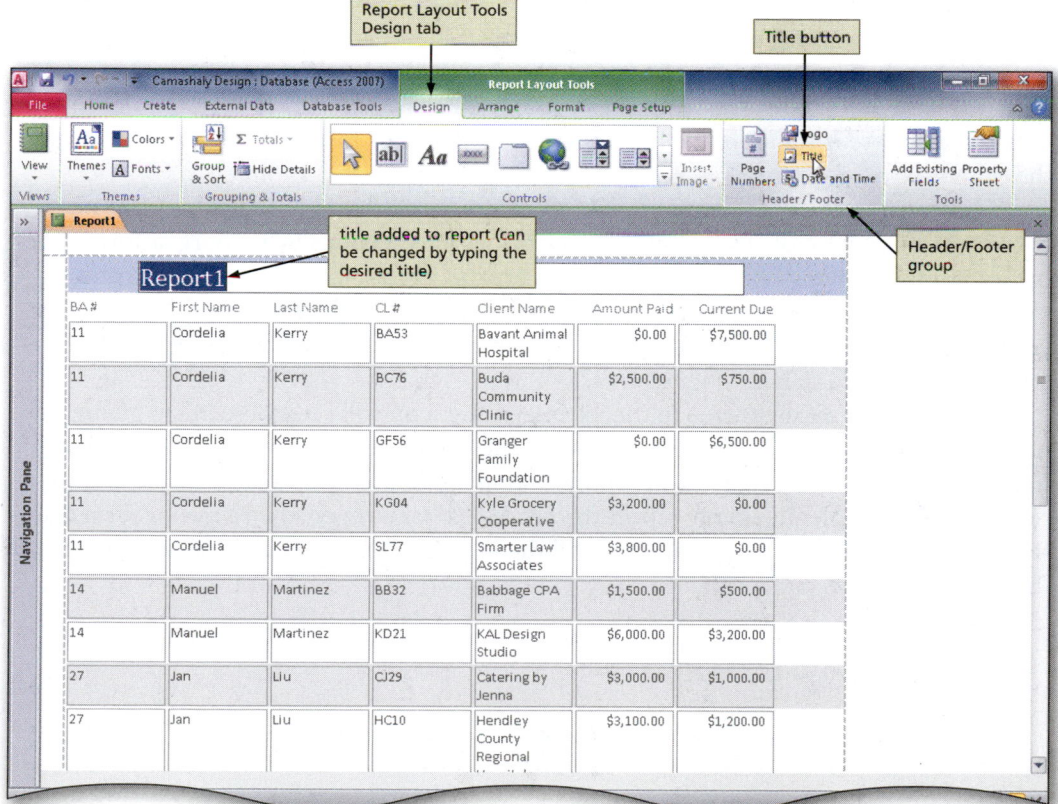

Figure 4–41

Once you have added the title, you can type whatever title you want for the report.

BTW

Multicolumn Reports
There are times when you may want to create a report that has multiple columns. For example, a telephone list with employee name and phone number could print in multiple columns. To do so, create the report using Layout view or Design view and then click the Page Setup button (Page Setup tab | Page Layout group), click the Columns tab, enter the number of columns, select the desired column layout, and then click the OK button (Page Setup dialog box).

To Create a Report in Layout View

If you want to create a report in Layout view, you would use the following steps.

1. Click Create on the Ribbon to display the Create tab.
2. Click the Blank Report button (Create tab | Reports group) to create a blank report.
3. If a field list does not appear, display a field list by clicking the Add Existing Fields button (Report Layout Tools Design tab | Tools group).
4. If the tables do not appear in the field list, click Show All Tables.
5. If the fields in a table do not appear, click the plus sign in front of the name of the table.
6. Drag the fields from the field list onto the report in the desired order.
7. If there is a second table, be sure the fields in the second table appear, and then drag the fields from the second table onto the report in the desired order. (If the field list covers the portion of the report where you want to drag the fields, you can move the field list to a different position by dragging its title bar.)
8. If you want to add a title to the report, click the Title button (Report Layout Tools Design tab | Header / Footer group) and then type the desired title.

BTW

Themes
Themes are standardized across all Office applications. You can download themes and share themes with others via Office Online or e-mail.

Using Themes

The most important characteristic of a report or form is that it contains the desired data arranged in an appropriate fashion. Another important characteristic, however, is the general appearance of the form. The colors and fonts that you use in the various sections of a report or form contribute to this look. There are two important goals to keep in mind when assigning colors and fonts. First, the various colors and fonts should complement each other. A clash of colors or two fonts that do not go well together can produce a report that looks unprofessional. Second, the choice of colors and fonts should be consistent. That is, all the reports and forms within a database should use the same colors and fonts unless there is some compelling reason for a report or form to look different from the others.

Fortunately, Access themes provide an easy way to achieve both goals. A **theme** consists of a selection of colors and fonts for the various sections in a report or form. The colors and fonts in any of the built-in themes are designed to complement each other. When you assign a theme, the theme immediately applies to all reports and forms, unless you specifically indicate otherwise. To assign a theme, you use the Theme picker, which is a menu of available themes (Figure 4–42).

If you point to any theme in the Theme picker, you will see a ScreenTip giving the name of the theme. When you select a theme, the colors and fonts represented by that theme will immediately apply to all reports and forms. If you later decide that you would prefer a different theme, simply repeat the process. That is, open any report or form and select a new theme. Its colors and fonts will then replace the colors and fonts of the old theme in all reports and forms.

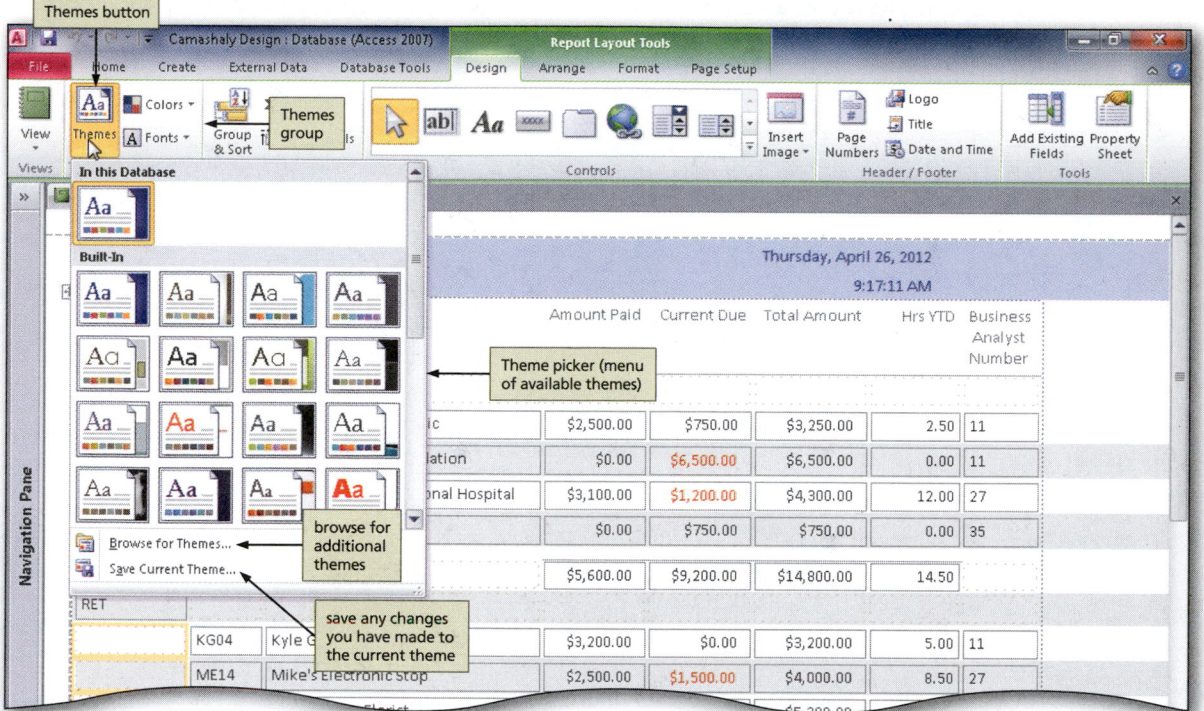

Figure 4–42

You can also use the Browse for Themes command to browse for themes that are not listed but are available for download. If you have specified a combination of fonts and colors that you like but that is not already on the list of themes, you can use the Save Current Theme command to save your combination. If, after selecting a theme using the Themes button, you do not like the colors in the current theme, you can change the theme's colors. Click the Colors button (Report Layout Tools Design tab | Themes group) (Figure 4–43), and then select an alternative color scheme.

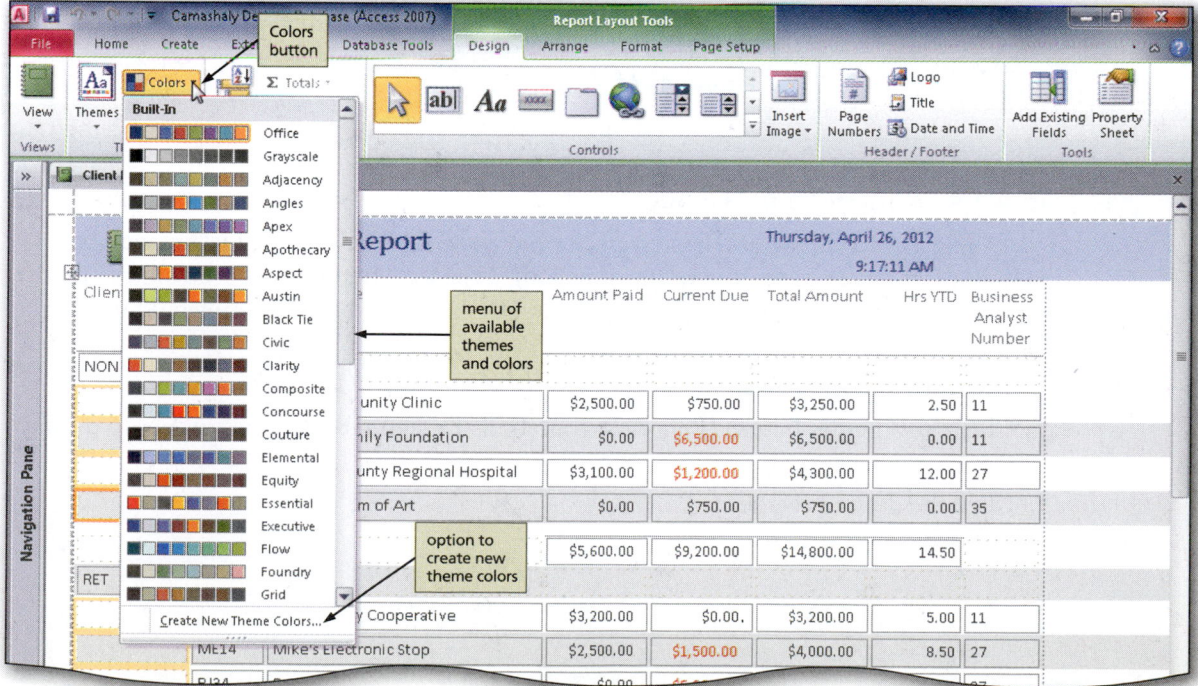

Figure 4–43

Similarly, if you do not like the fonts in the current theme, you can click the Fonts button (Report Layout Tools Design tab | Themes group) (Figure 4–44). You then can select an alternative font.

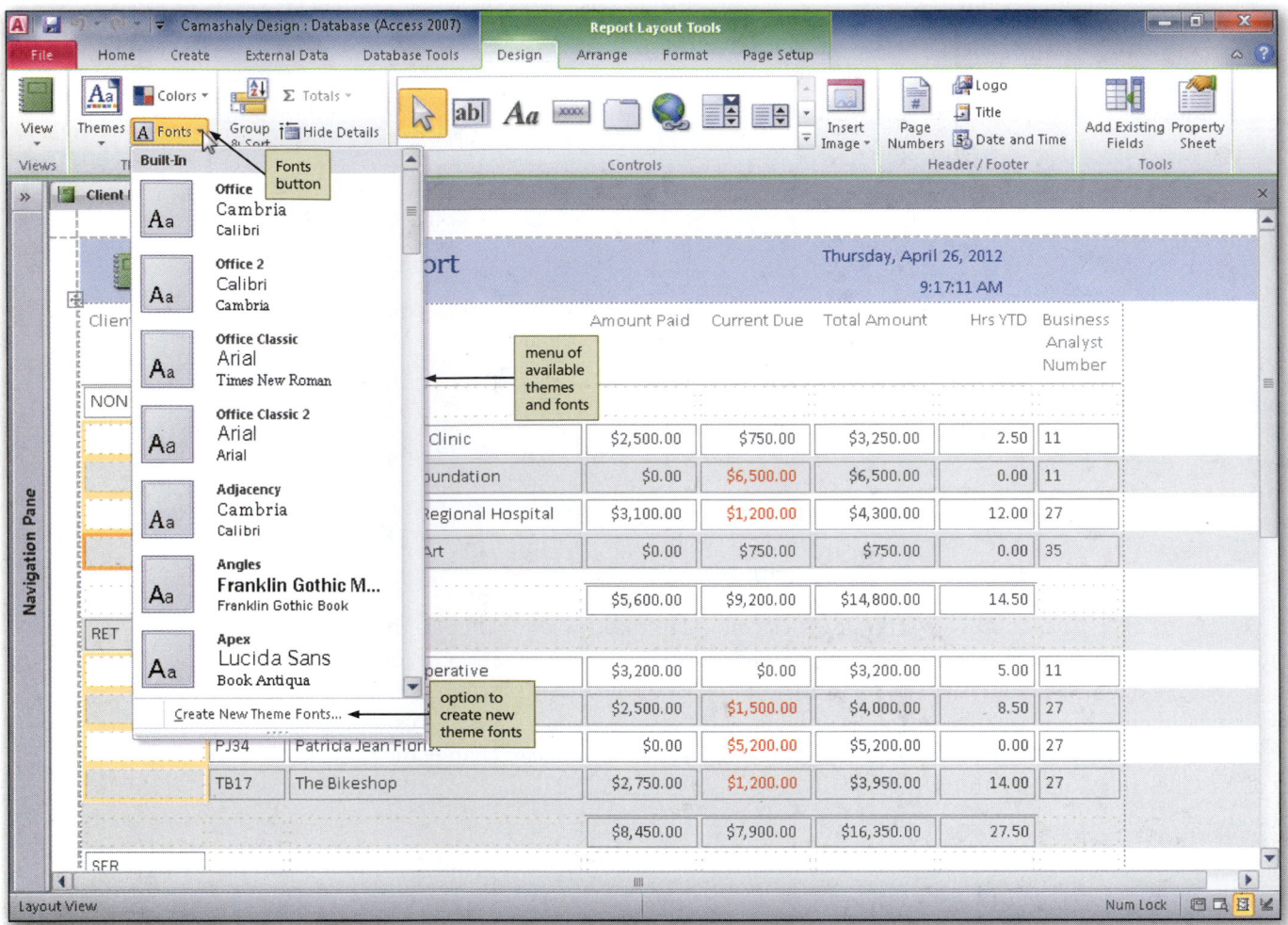

Figure 4–44

TO ASSIGN A THEME TO ALL OBJECTS

To assign a theme, it is easiest to use Layout view. You can use Design view as well, but it is easier to see the result of picking a theme when you are viewing the report or form in Layout view. To assign a theme to all reports and forms, you would use the following steps.

1. Open any report or form in Layout view.

2. Click the Themes button (Report Layout Tools Design tab | Themes group) to display the Theme picker.

3. Click the desired theme.

TO ASSIGN A THEME TO A SINGLE OBJECT

In some cases, you might only want to apply a theme to the current report or form, while all other reports and forms would retain the characteristics from the original theme. To assign a theme to a single object, you would use the following steps.

1. Open the specific report or form to which you want to assign a theme in Layout view.
2. Click the Themes button (Report Layout Tools Design tab | Themes group) to display the Theme picker.
3. Right-click the desired theme to produce a shortcut menu.
4. Click the Apply Theme to This Object Only command on the shortcut menu to apply the theme to the single object on which you are working.

Live Preview for Themes

When selecting themes, Access furnishes a **live preview** of what the report or form will look like with the theme before you actually select the theme. The report or form will appear as it would in the theme to which you are currently pointing (Figure 4–45). If you like that theme, you then can select the theme by clicking the left mouse button.

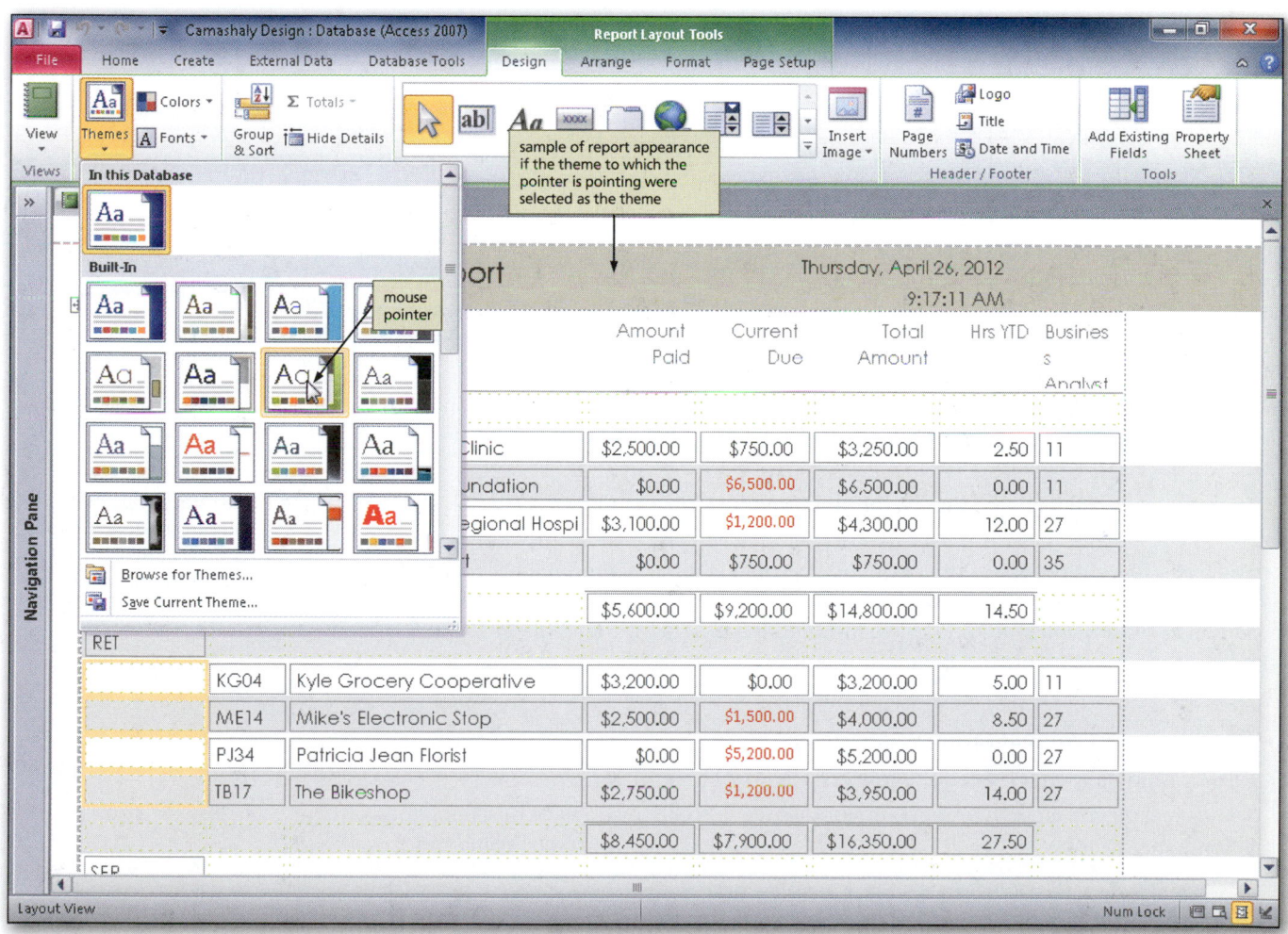

Figure 4–45

To Create a Summary Report

You may determine that a report should be organized so that it only shows the overall group calculations, but not all the records. A report that includes the group calculations such as subtotals, but does not include the individual detail lines, is called a **summary report**. The following steps hide the detail lines in the Client Financial Report, thus creating a summary report.

1

● Open the Client Financial Report in Layout view and close the Navigation Pane.

2

● Click the Hide Details button (Report Layout Tools Design tab | Grouping & Totals group) to hide the details in the report (Figure 4–46).

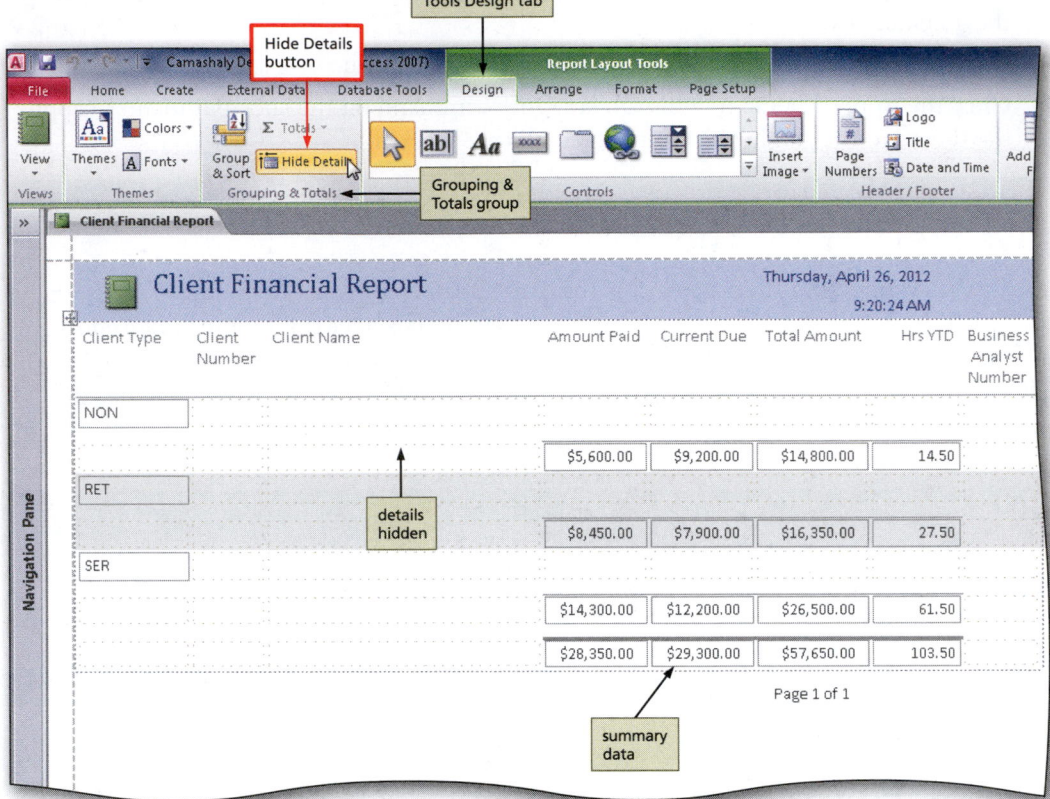

Figure 4–46

Q&A How can I see the details once I have hidden them?

Click the Hide Details button a second time.

Q&A There seems to be a lot of space before the Amount Paid and Current Due fields. Is that a problem?

The extra space is the space that would be occupied by the client number and name if you had not hidden the details. It is not a problem. If you wanted a report that was strictly a summary report, you would not have included those fields. If the fields were not included, hiding the details would not have produced this space.

BTW

Summary Reports
You can create a summary report in either Layout view or Design view.

3

● Close the report without saving your changes.

Q&A What would happen if I saved the report?

The next time you view the report, the details would still be hidden. If that happened and you wanted to show all the details, just click the Hide Details button a second time.

Break Point: If you wish to take a break, this a good place to do so. You can quit Access now. To resume at a later time, start Access, open the database called Camashaly Design, and continue following the steps from this location forward.

Form Creation

As with reports, it is usually simplest to begin creating a form by using the wizard. Once you have used the Form Wizard to create a form, you can modify that form in either Layout view or Design view.

To Use the Form Wizard to Create a Form

The following steps use the Form Wizard to create an initial version of the Client Financial Form. This initial version will contain the Client Number, Client Name, Client Type, Services Needed, Amount Paid, Current Due, Total Amount, and Business Analyst Number fields.

1

- Open the Navigation Pane and select the Client table.

- Click Create on the Ribbon to display the Create tab.

- Click the Form Wizard button (Create tab | Forms group) to start the Form Wizard (Figure 4–47).

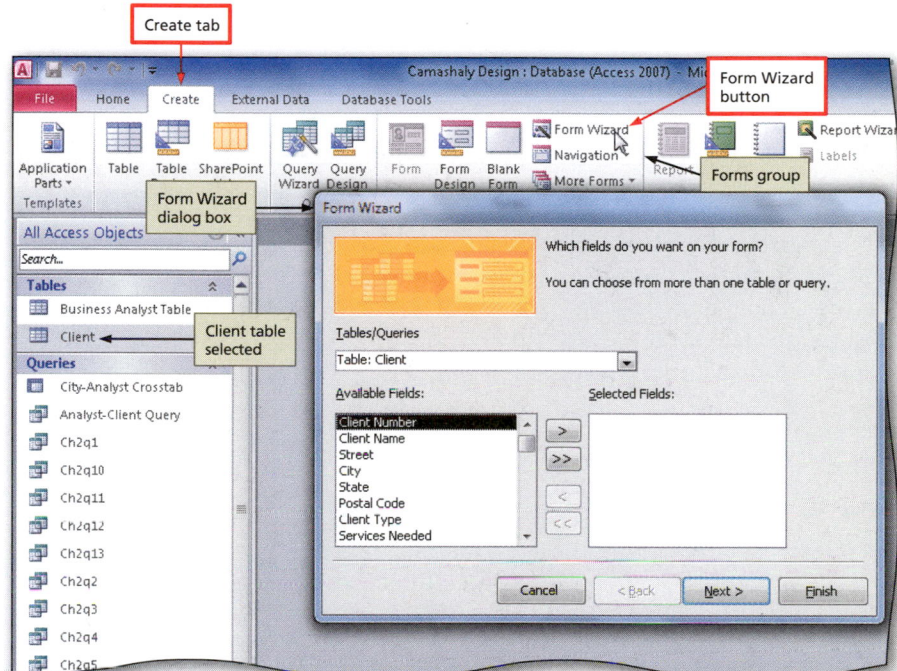

Figure 4–47

2

- Add the Client Number, Client Name, Client Type, Services Needed, Amount Paid, Current Due, Total Amount, and Business Analyst Number fields to the form (Figure 4–48).

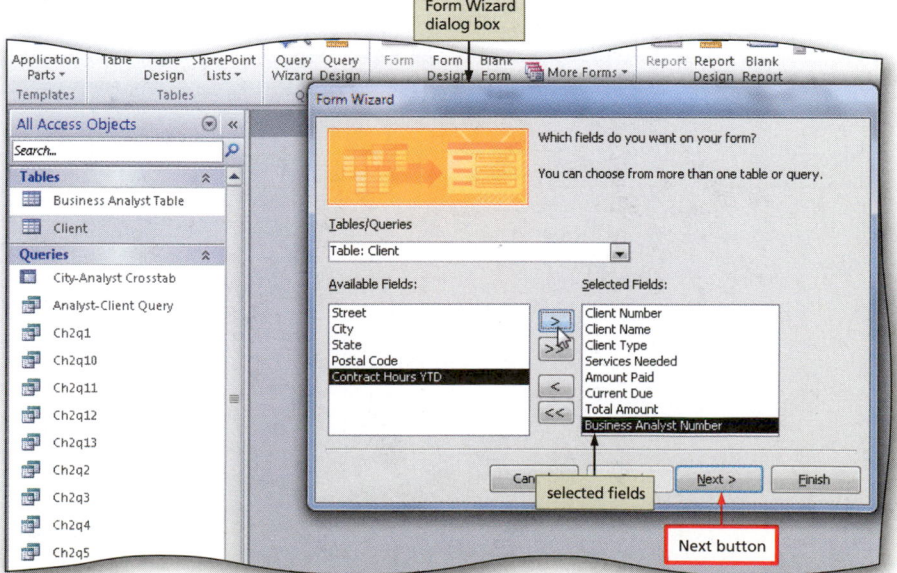

Figure 4–48

- Click the Next button to display the next Form Wizard screen (Figure 4–49).

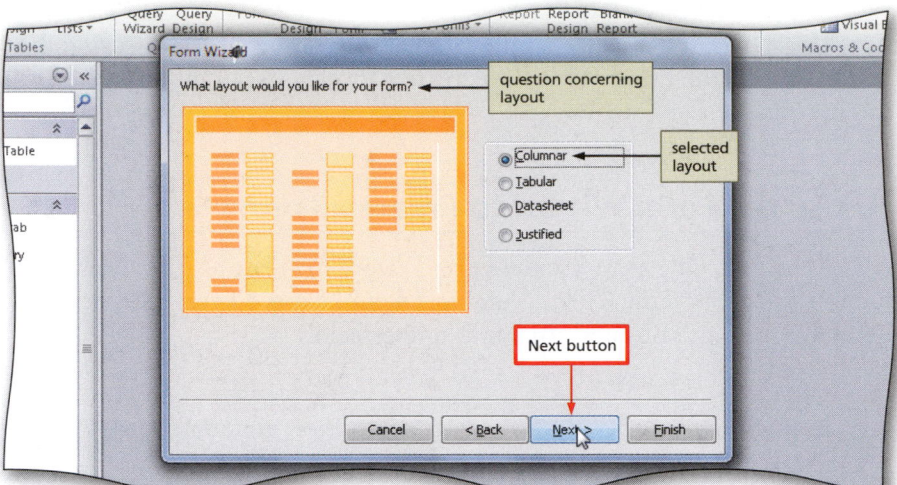

Figure 4–49

- Be sure the Columnar layout is selected, click the Next button to display the next Form Wizard screen, and then type **Client Financial Form** as the title for the form (Figure 4–50).

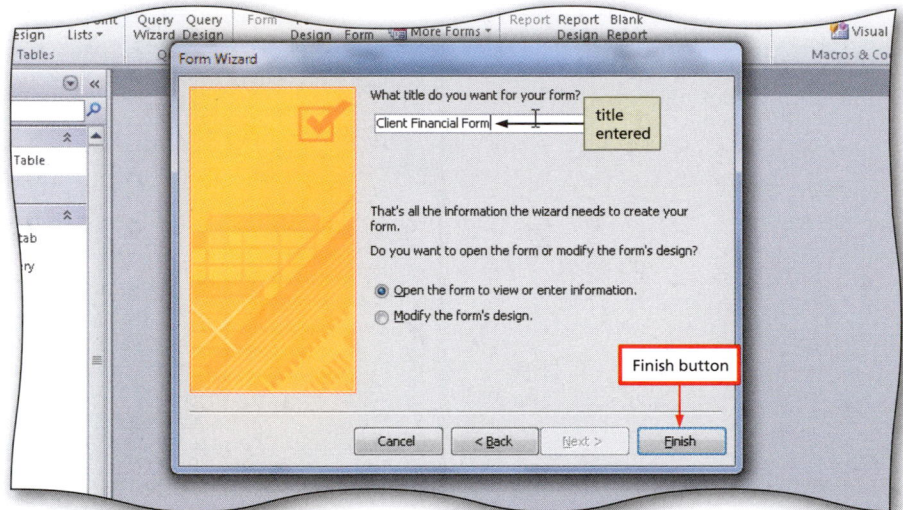

Figure 4–50

- Click the Finish button to complete and display the form (Figure 4–51).

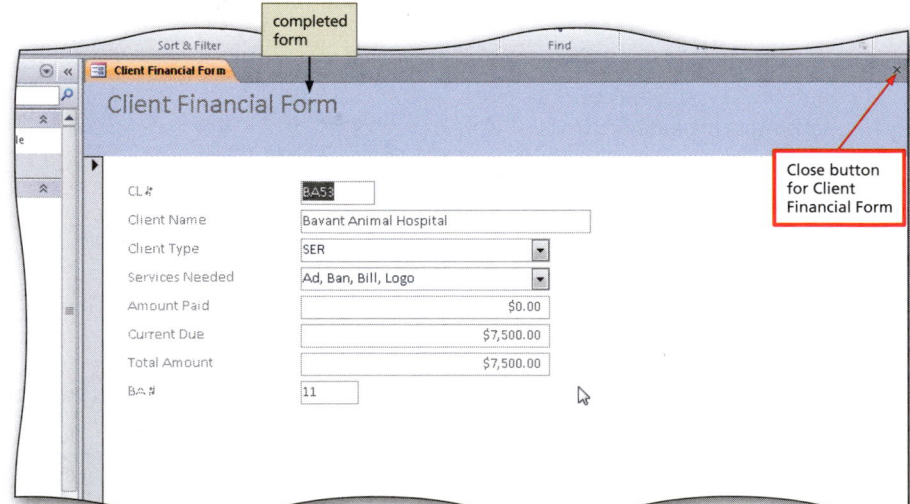

- Click the Close button for the Client Financial Form to close the form.

Figure 4–51

Understanding Form Sections

A form typically has only three sections. The Form Header section appears at the top of the form and usually contains the form title. It also may contain a logo and/or a date. The body of the form is in the Detail section. The Form Footer section appears at the bottom of the form and is often empty.

Understanding Form Controls

Just as with reports, the various items on a form are called controls. Forms include the same three types of controls: bound controls, unbound controls, and calculated controls. Bound controls have attached labels that typically display the name of the field that supplies the data for the control. The **attached label** for the Client Number field, for example, is the portion of the screen immediately to the left of the field. It contains the words, Client Number.

Using Layout View in a Form

When working with a form in Access, there are three different ways to view the form. They are Form view, Layout view, and Design view. Form view shows the form on the screen and allows you to use the form to update data. Layout view is similar to Form view in that it shows the form on the screen. In Layout view, you cannot update the data, but you can make changes to the layout of the form, and it is the usually the easiest way to make such changes. Design view also allows you to make changes, but it does not show you the actual form. It is most useful when the changes you need to make are especially complex. In this chapter, you will use Layout view to modify the form.

> **BTW**
>
> **Form Design Considerations**
> Forms should be appealing visually and present data logically and clearly. Properly designed forms improve both the speed and accuracy of data entry. Forms that are too cluttered or contain too many different effects can be hard on the eyes. Some colors are more difficult than others for individuals to see. Be consistent when creating forms. Once you decide on a general style or theme for forms, stick with it throughout your database.

To Place Controls in a Control Layout

To use Layout view with a form, the controls must be placed in a control layout, which is a set of controls grouped together so that they can be manipulated as a single unit. The following steps place the controls and their attached labels in a control layout.

①

- Open the Client Financial Form in Layout view and close the Navigation Pane.

- Click Arrange on the Ribbon to display the Form Layout Tools Arrange tab.

- Click the attached label for the Business Analyst Number control to select the control.

- While holding the SHIFT key down, click the remaining attached labels and all the controls (Figure 4–52).

Q&A

Did I have to select the attached labels and controls in that order?

No. As long as you select all of them, the order in which you selected them does not matter.

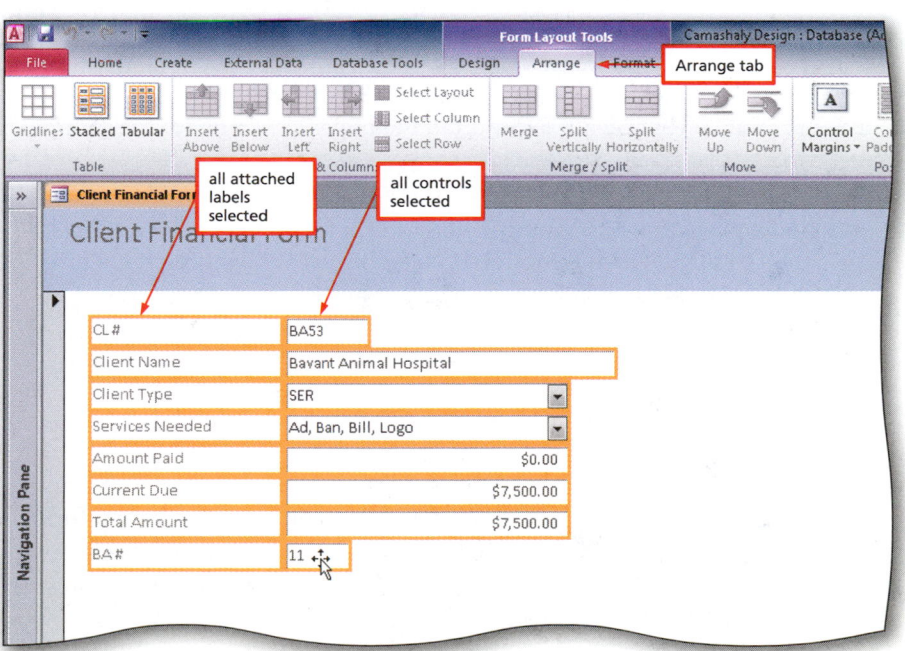

Figure 4–52

Q&A When I clicked some of the controls, they moved so they are no longer aligned as well as they are in the figure. What should I do?

You do not have to worry about it. Once you complete the next step, they will once again be aligned properly.

2

• Click the Stacked button (Form Layout Tools Arrange tab | Table group) to place the controls in a stacked layout (Figure 4–53).

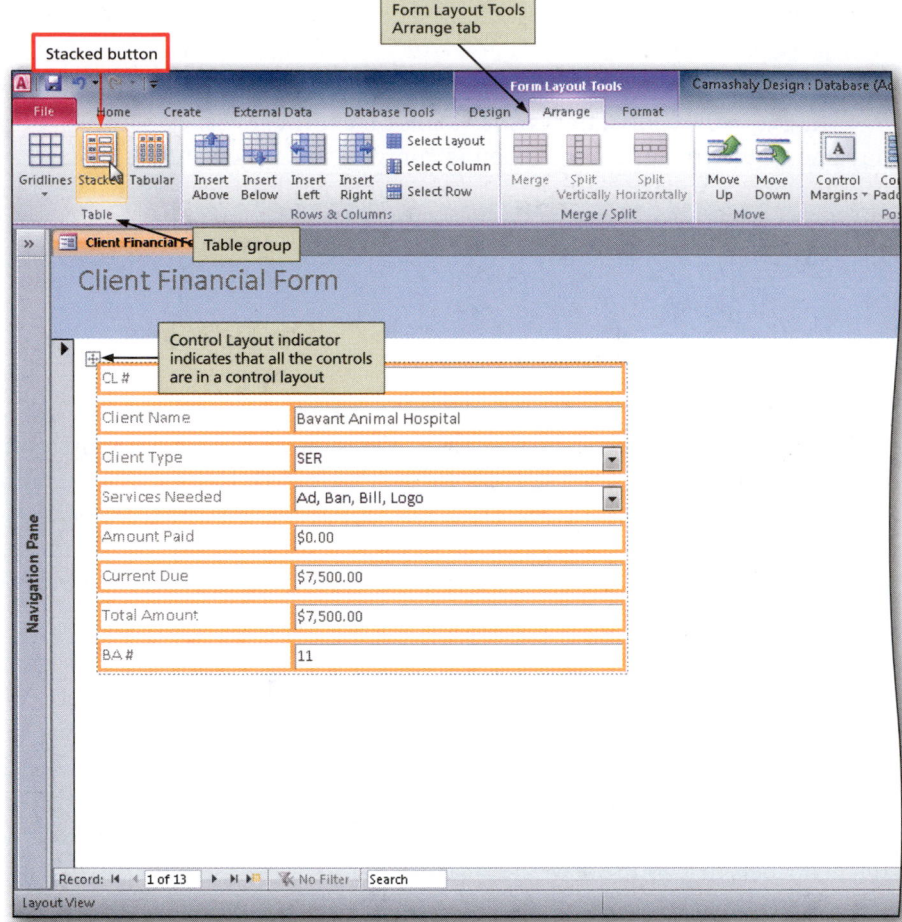

Figure 4–53

Q&A How can I tell whether the controls are in a control layout?

Look for the Control Layout indicator in the upper-left corner of the control layout.

Q&A What is the difference between stacked layout and tabular layout?

In a stacked layout, which is more often used in forms, the controls are placed vertically with the labels to the left of the controls. In a tabular layout, which is more often used in reports, the controls are placed horizontally with the labels above the controls.

To Add a Date

You can add special items, such as a logo or title, to reports and forms. You can also add the date and/or the time. In the case of reports, you can add a page number as well. To add any of these items, you use the appropriate button in the Header/Footer group of the Design tab. The following steps use the Date and Time button to add a date to the Client Financial Form.

1

- Click Design on the Ribbon to display the Design tab.

- Click the Date and Time button (Form Layout Tools Design tab | Header/Footer group) to display the Date and Time dialog box (Figure 4–54).

Q&A What is the relationship between the various check boxes and option buttons?

If the Include Date check box is checked, you must pick a date format from the three option buttons underneath the check box. If it is not checked, the option buttons will be dimmed. If the Include Time check box is checked, you must pick a time format from the three option buttons underneath the check box. If it is not checked, the option buttons will be dimmed.

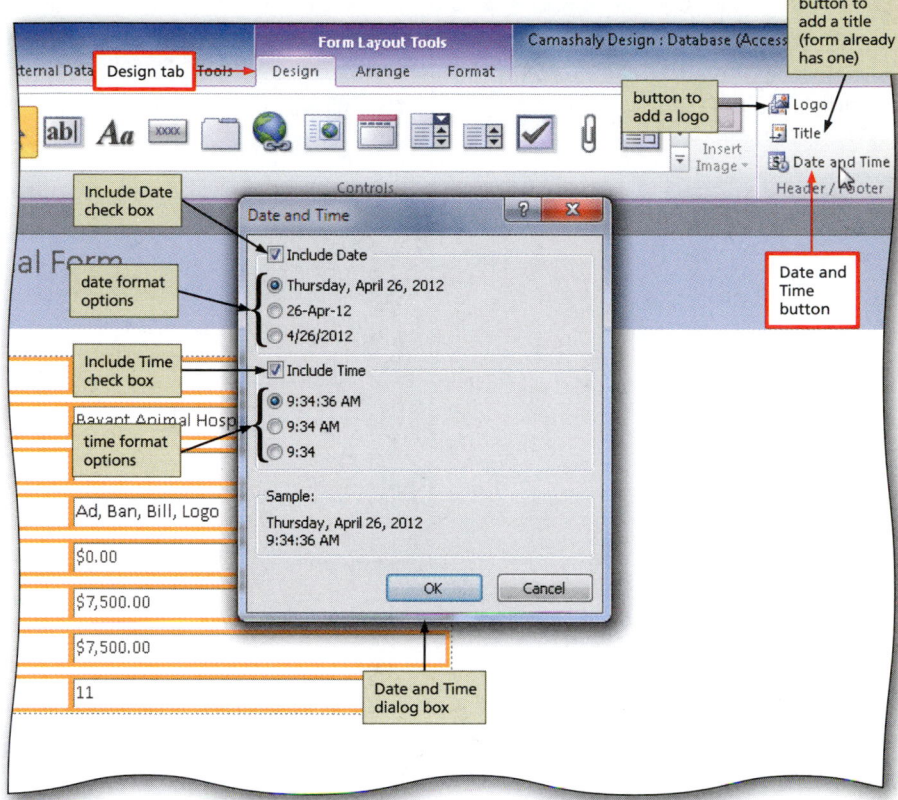

Figure 4–54

2

- Click the option button for the second date format to select the format that shows the day of the month, followed by the abbreviation for the month, followed by the year.

- Click the Include Time check box to remove the check mark (Figure 4–55).

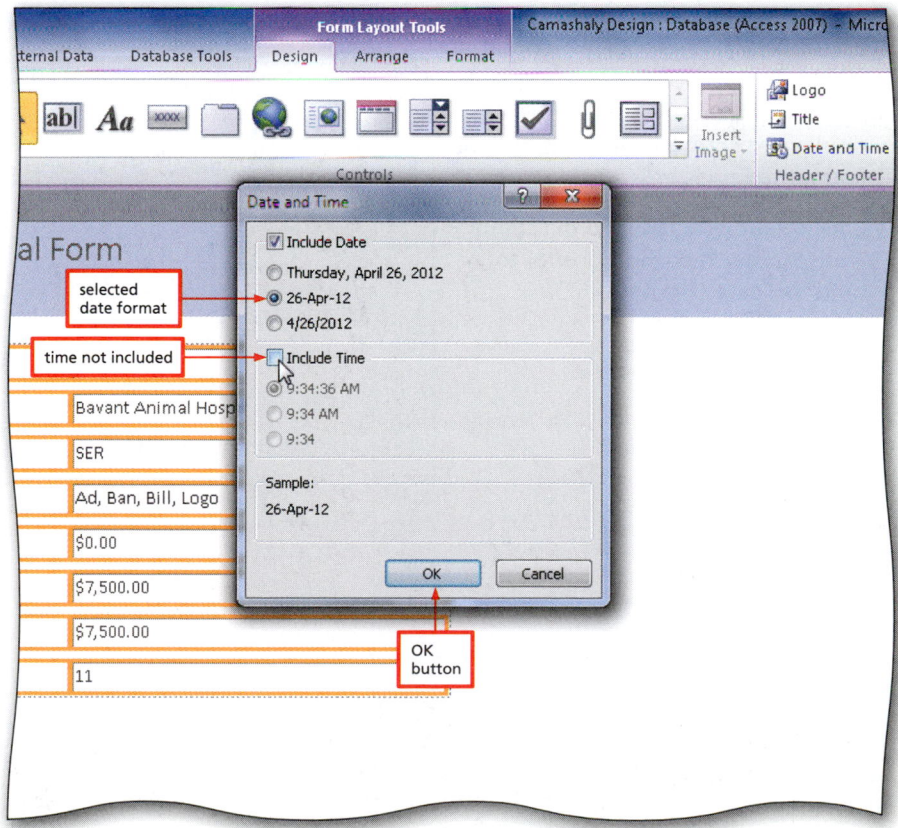

Figure 4–55

- Click the OK button (Date and Time dialog box) to add the date to the form (Figure 4–56).

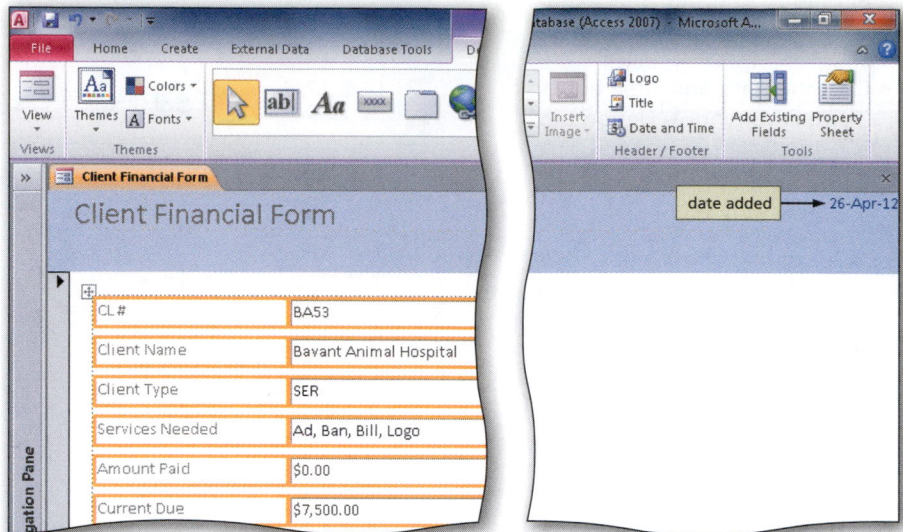

Figure 4–56

To Change the Format of a Control

You can change the format of a control by clicking the control and then clicking the appropriate button on the Format tab. The following step uses this technique to bold the date.

- Click the Date control to select it.

- Click Format on the Ribbon to display the Form Layout Tools Format tab.

- Click the Bold button (Form Layout Tools Format tab | Font group) to bold the date (Figure 4–57).

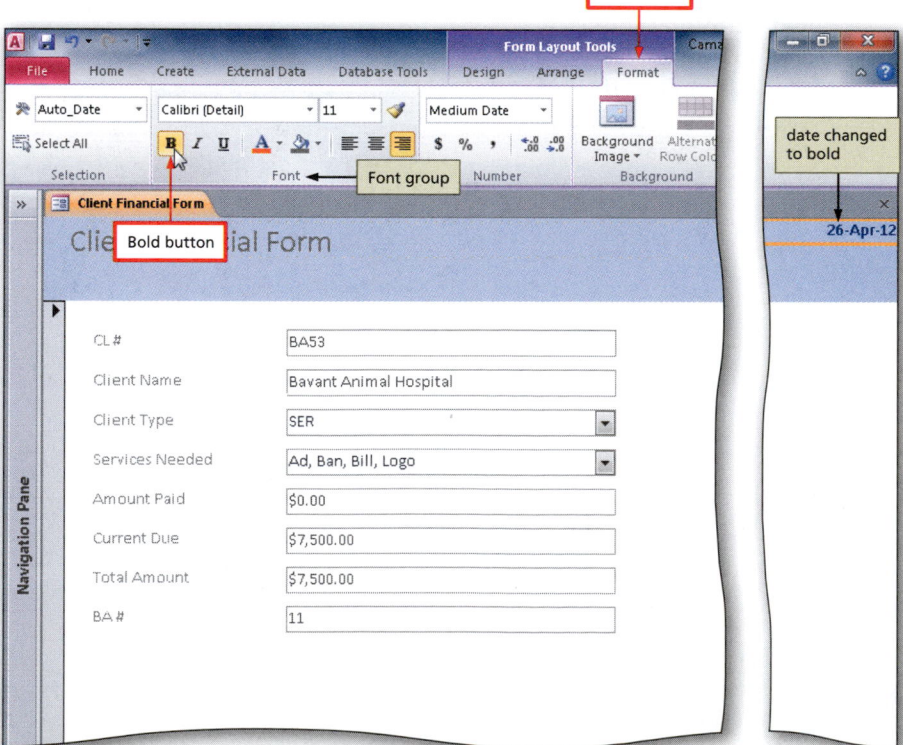

Figure 4–57

To Move a Control

You can move a control by dragging the control. The following step moves the Date control to the lower edge of the form header.

1

- Point to the Date control so that the mouse pointer changes to a four-headed arrow and then drag the Date control to the lower boundary of the form header (Figure 4–58).

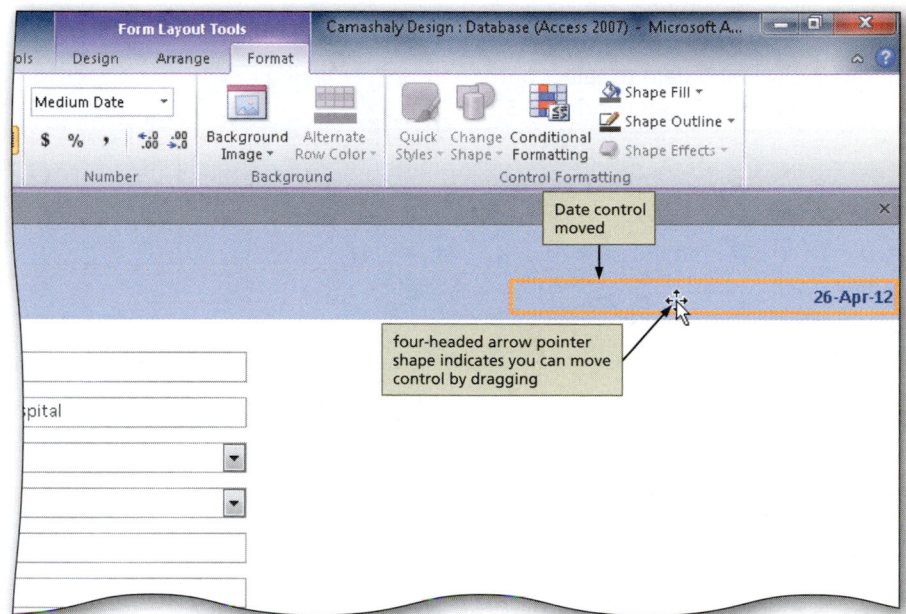

Figure 4–58

Q&A
I moved my pointer a little bit and it became a two-headed arrow. Can I still drag the pointer?

If you drag when the pointer is a two-headed arrow, you will resize the control. To move the control, it must be a four-headed arrow.

Q&A
Could I drag other objects as well? For example, could I drag the title to the center of the form header?

Yes. Just be sure you are pointing at the object and the pointer is a four-headed arrow. You can then drag the object to the desired location.

To Move Controls in a Control Layout

The controls for the fields are arranged in control layouts. A **control layout** is a guide that aligns the controls to give the form a uniform appearance. There are two types of control layouts. A **stacked layout** arranges the controls vertically with labels to the left of the control. A **tabular layout** arranges the controls horizontally with the labels across the top, typically in the Form Header section. The Client Financial Form contains a stacked layout.

Just as you moved the Date control in the previous section, you can move a control within a control layout by dragging the control to the location you want. As you move it, a line will indicate the position where the control will be placed when you release the left mouse button. You can move more than one control in the same operation by selecting both controls prior to moving them.

The following steps move the Client Type and Services Needed fields so that they follow the Business Analyst Number field.

1

- Click the label for the Client Type field to select it.

- Hold the SHIFT key down and click the control for the Client Type field, then click the label for the Services Needed field and the control for the Services Needed field to select both fields and their labels (Figure 4–59).

Q&A

Why did I have to hold the SHIFT key down when I clicked the remaining controls?

If you did not hold the SHIFT key down, you would only select the control for the Services Needed field (the last control selected). The other controls would no longer be selected.

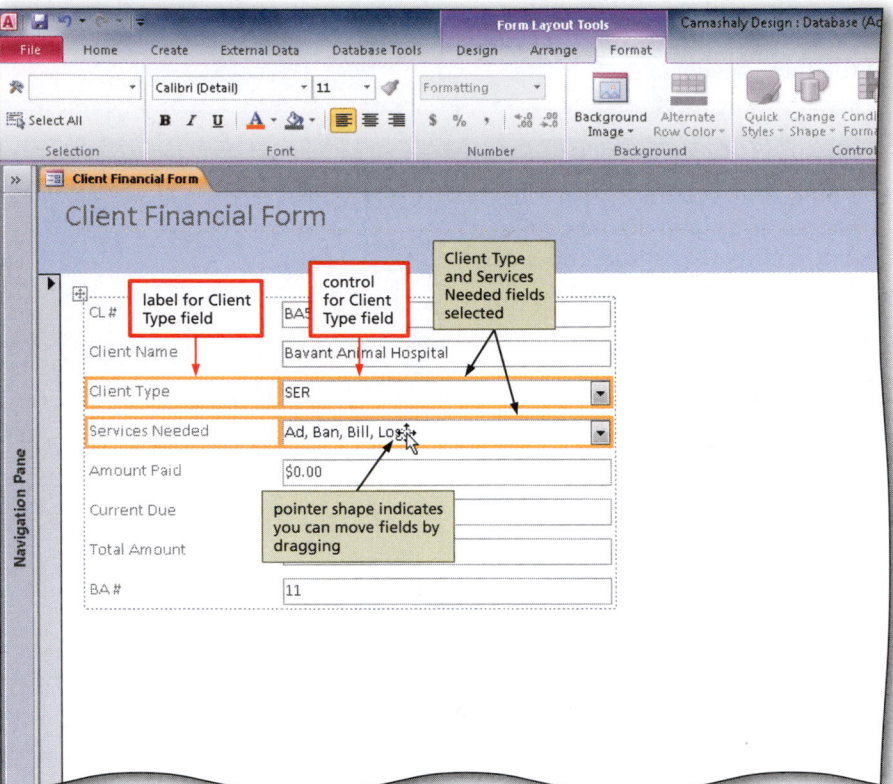

Figure 4–59

2

- Press the left mouse button and then drag the fields straight down to the position shown in Figure 4–60, making sure that the line by the mouse pointer is under the data.

Q&A

What is the purpose of the line by the mouse pointer?

It shows you where the fields will be positioned.

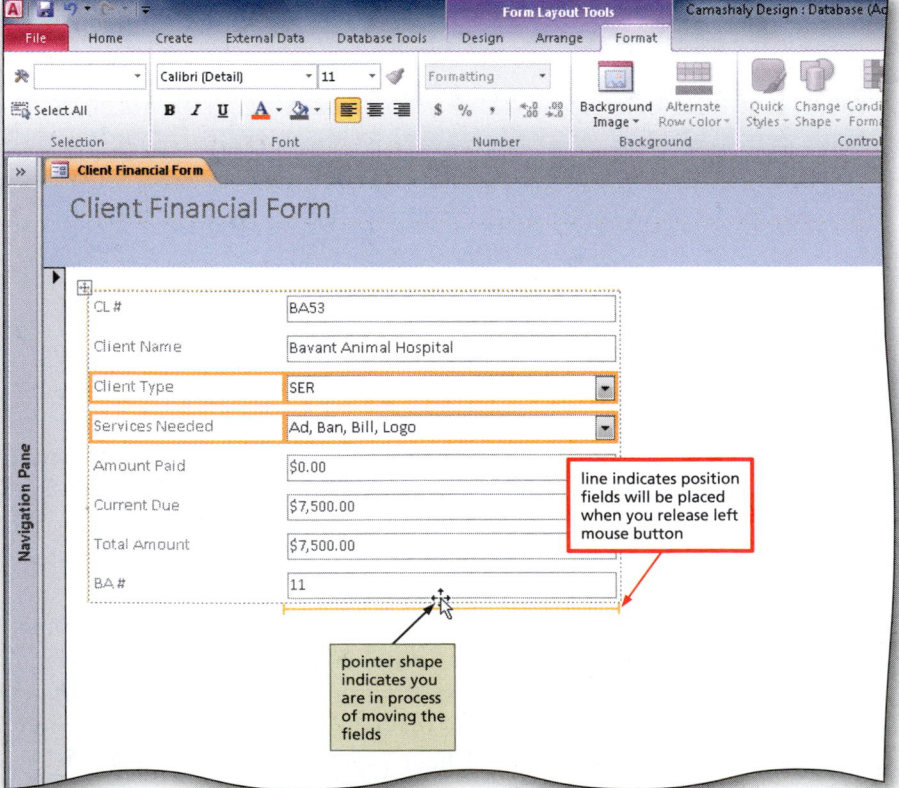

Figure 4–60

3

- Release the left mouse button to complete the movement of the fields (Figure 4–61).

Q&A I inadvertently had the line under the label rather than the data when I released the mouse button. The data that I moved is now under the field names. How do I fix this?

You can try to move it back where it was, but that can be tricky. The easiest way is to click the Undo button on the Quick Access Toolbar to undo your change.

Q&A I inadvertently moved my pointer so that the line became vertical and was located between a label and the corresponding data when I released the mouse button. It seemed to split the form. The data I moved appears right where the line was. It is between a label and the corresponding data. How do I fix this?

Just as in the previous answer, the easiest way is to click the Undo button on the Quick Access Toolbar to undo your change.

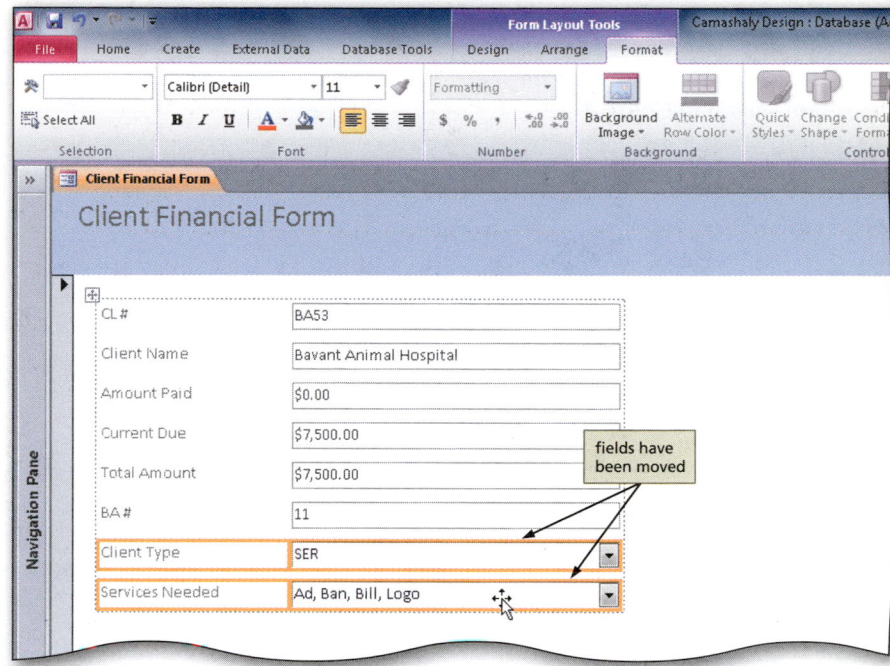

Figure 4–61

To Add a Field

Just as with a report, once you have created an initial form, you may decide that the form should contain an additional field. The following steps use a field list to add the City field to the Client Financial Form.

1

- Click Design on the Ribbon to display the Form Layout Tools Design tab.

- Click the Add Existing Fields button (Form Layout Tools Design tab | Tools group) to display a field list (Figure 4–62).

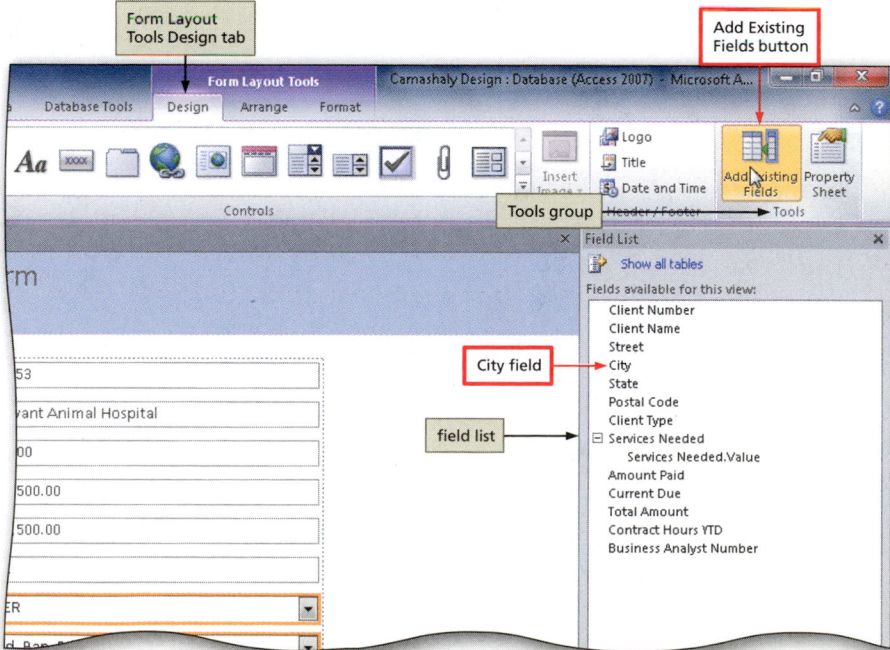

Figure 4–62

2

- Point to the City field in the field list, press the left mouse button, and then drag the pointer to the position shown in Figure 4–63.

Q&A Does it have to be exact?

The exact pointer position is not critical as long as the line is in the position shown in the figure.

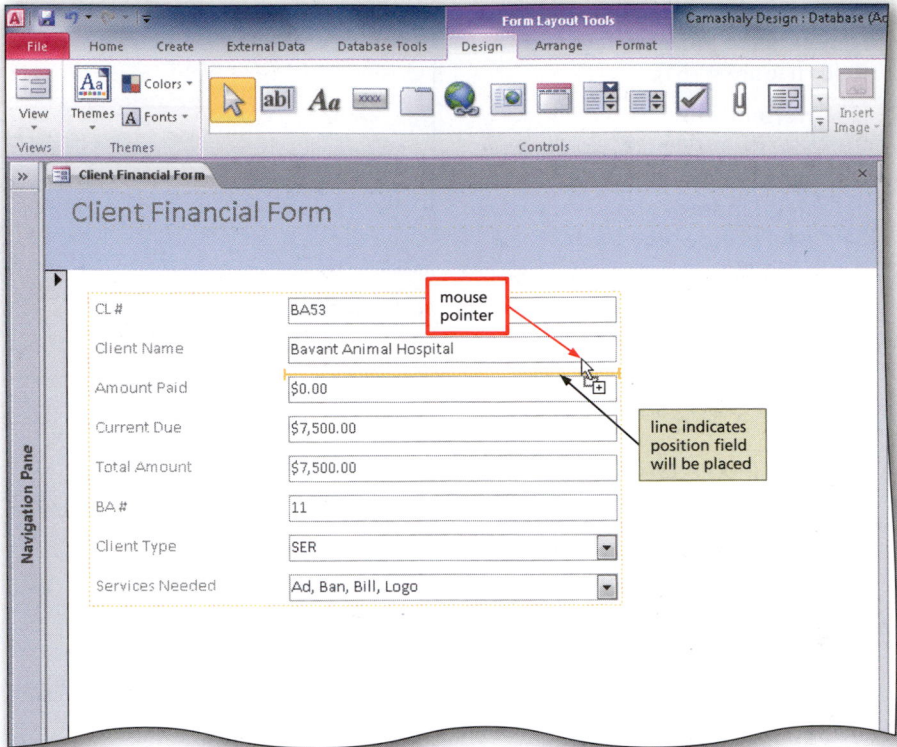

Figure 4–63

3

- Release the left mouse button to place the field (Figure 4–64).

Q&A What if I make a mistake?

Just as when you are modifying a report, you can delete the field by clicking the field and then pressing the DELETE key. You can move the field by dragging it to the correct position.

4

- Click the Add Existing Fields button (Form Layout Tools Design tab | Tools group) to remove the field list.

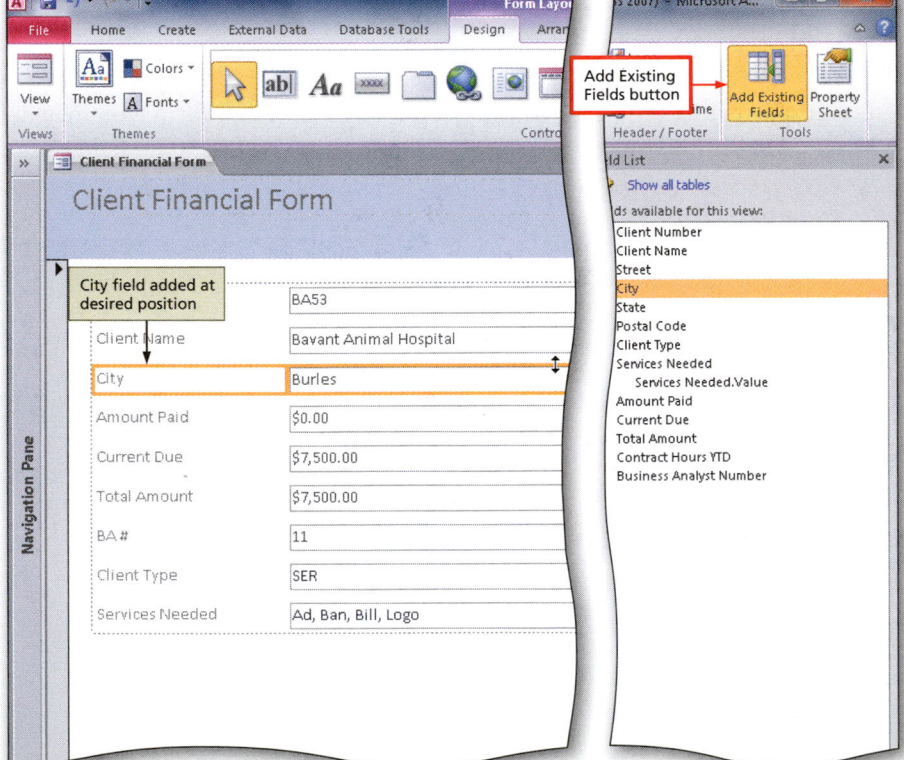

Figure 4–64

To Filter and Sort Using a Form

Just as in a datasheet, you can filter and sort using Advanced Filter/Sort, which is a command on the Advanced menu. The following steps use Advanced Filter/Sort to filter the records to those records whose city begins with the letters, Gr. They also sort the records by client name. The effect of this filter and sort is that as you use the form to move through clients, you will only encounter those clients whose cities begin with Gr. In addition, you will encounter those clients in client name order.

1
- Click Home on the Ribbon to display the Home tab.

- Click the Advanced button (Home tab | Sort & Filter group) to display the Advanced menu (Figure 4–65).

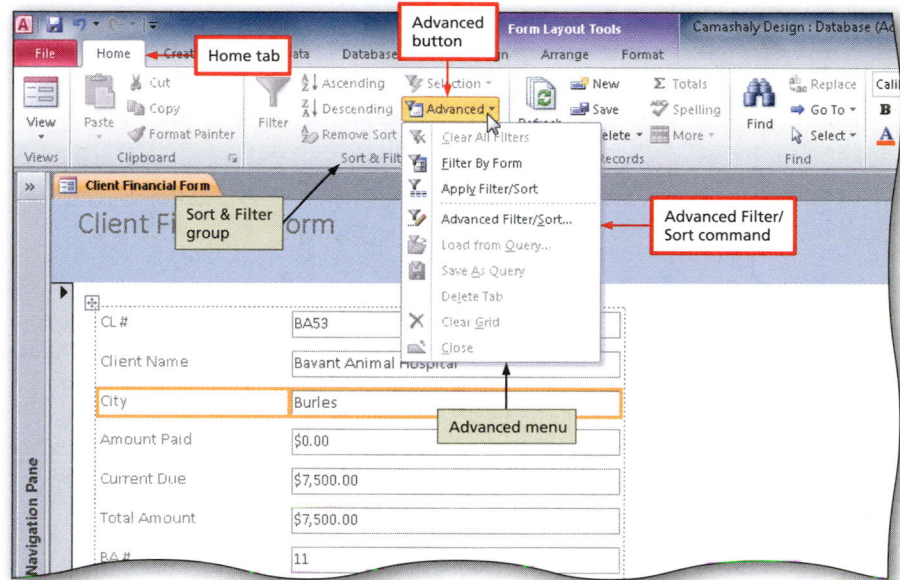

Figure 4–65

2
- Click Advanced Filter/Sort on the Advanced menu.

- Resize the field list so that all the fields appear.

- Add the Client Name field to the design grid and select Ascending sort order.

- Add the City field and type `Gr*` as the criterion for the City field (Figure 4–66).

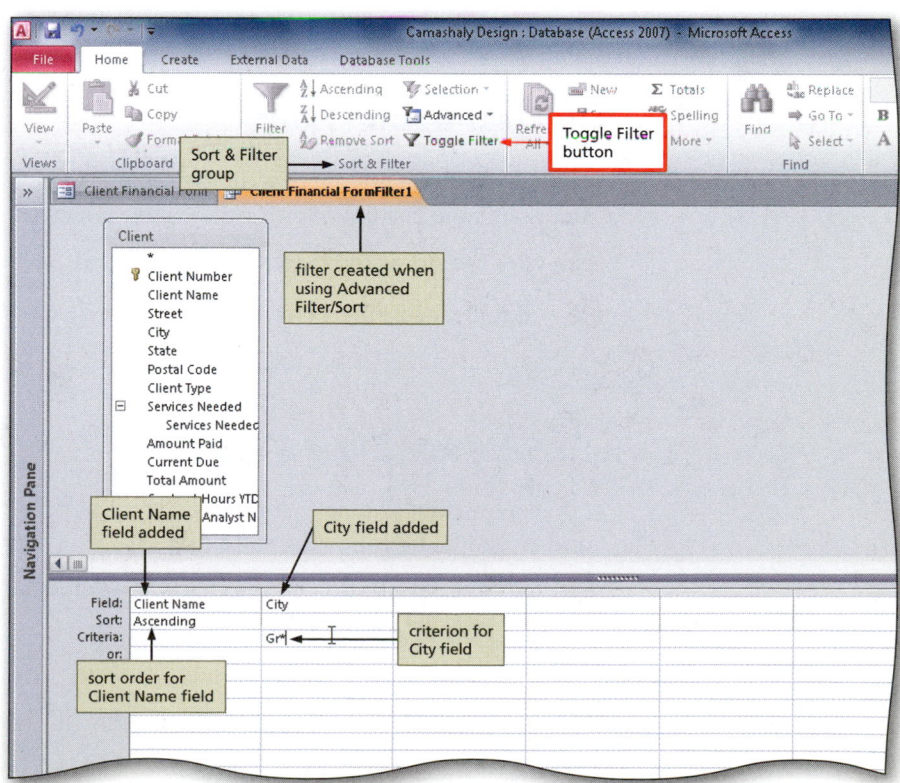

Figure 4–66

3

- Click the Toggle Filter button (Home tab | Sort & Filter group) to filter the records (Figure 4–67).

Q&A

I can only see one record at a time in the form. How can I see which records are included?

You would have to scroll through the records. For example, you could repeatedly click the Next Record button.

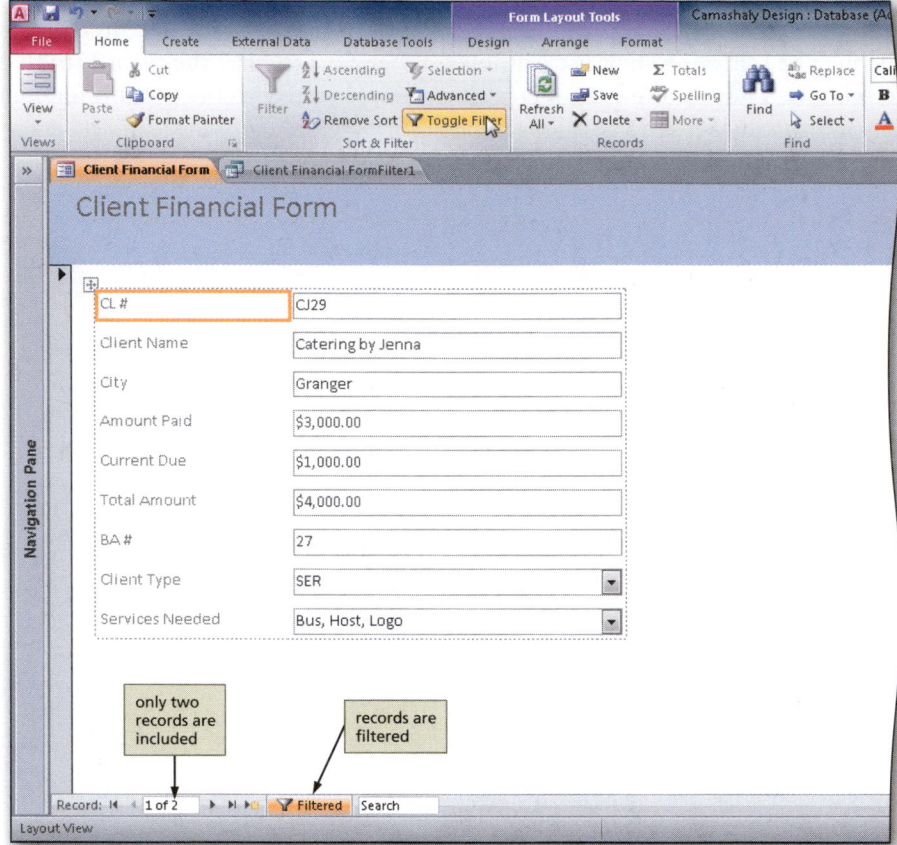

Figure 4–67

To Clear a Form Filter

When you no longer want the records to be filtered, you clear the filter. The following steps clear the current filter for the Client Financial Form.

1 Click the Advanced button (Home tab | Sort & Filter group) to display the Advanced menu.

2 Click Clear All Filters on the Advanced menu to clear the filter.

To Save and Close a Form

Now that you have completed your work on your form, you should save the form and close it. The following steps first save your work on the form and then close the form.

1 Click the Save button on the Quick Access Toolbar to save your work.

2 Close the Client Financial Form.

To Print a Form

You can print all records, a range of records, or a selected record of a form by selecting the appropriate print range. To print the selected record, the form must be open. To print all records or a range of records, the form can simply be highlighted in the Navigation Pane. The following steps open the Client Financial Form and then print the first record in the form, which is the selected record.

1 Open the Navigation Pane, and then, if necessary, select the Client Financial Form.

2 Right-click the Client Financial Form and click Open on the shortcut menu.

3 Click File on the Ribbon to open the Backstage view.

4 Click the Print tab in the Backstage view to display the Print gallery.

5 Click the Print button to display the Print dialog box.

6 Click the Selected Record(s) option button in the Page Range box, and then click the OK button.

BTW

Certification
The Microsoft Office Specialist (MOS) program provides an opportunity for you to obtain a valuable industry credential – proof that you have the Access 2010 skills required by employers. For more information, visit the Access 2010 Certification Web page (scsite.com/ac2010/cert).

The Arrange Tab

Forms, like reports, have an Arrange tab that you can use to modify the form's layout. However, the Page Setup tab is not available for forms. The buttons on the Arrange tab and the functions of those buttons are just like the ones described in Table 4–1 on page AC 230, with one exception. When working with a form, there is an extra button, the Anchoring button. The function of this button is to tie a control to a section or another control so that it moves or resizes in conjunction with the movement or resizing of its parent.

BTW

Customizing Mailing Labels
Once you create mailing labels, you can customize them just as you can customize other reports. In Design view, you can add a picture to the label, change the font size, adjust the spacing between controls, or make any other desired changes.

Mailing Labels

Organizations need to send invoices and other correspondence to clients on a regular basis. Using preprinted mailing labels eliminates much of the manual labor involved in preparing mailings. In Access, mailing labels are a special type of report. When this report prints, the data appears on the mailing labels aligned correctly and in the order you specify.

To Create Labels

You create labels just as you create reports. The Label Wizard assists you in the process. Using the wizard, you can specify the type and dimensions of the label, the font used for the label, and the content of the label. The following steps create the labels.

1

- If necessary, open the Navigation Pane and select the Client table.

- Click Create on the Ribbon to display the Create tab.

- Click the Labels button (Create tab | Reports group) to display the Label Wizard dialog box.

- Ensure that English is selected as the Unit of Measure and that Avery is selected in the 'Filter by manufacturer' box.

- Scroll through the label types until C2163 appears and then click C2163 in the Product number list to select the specific type of labels (Figure 4–68).

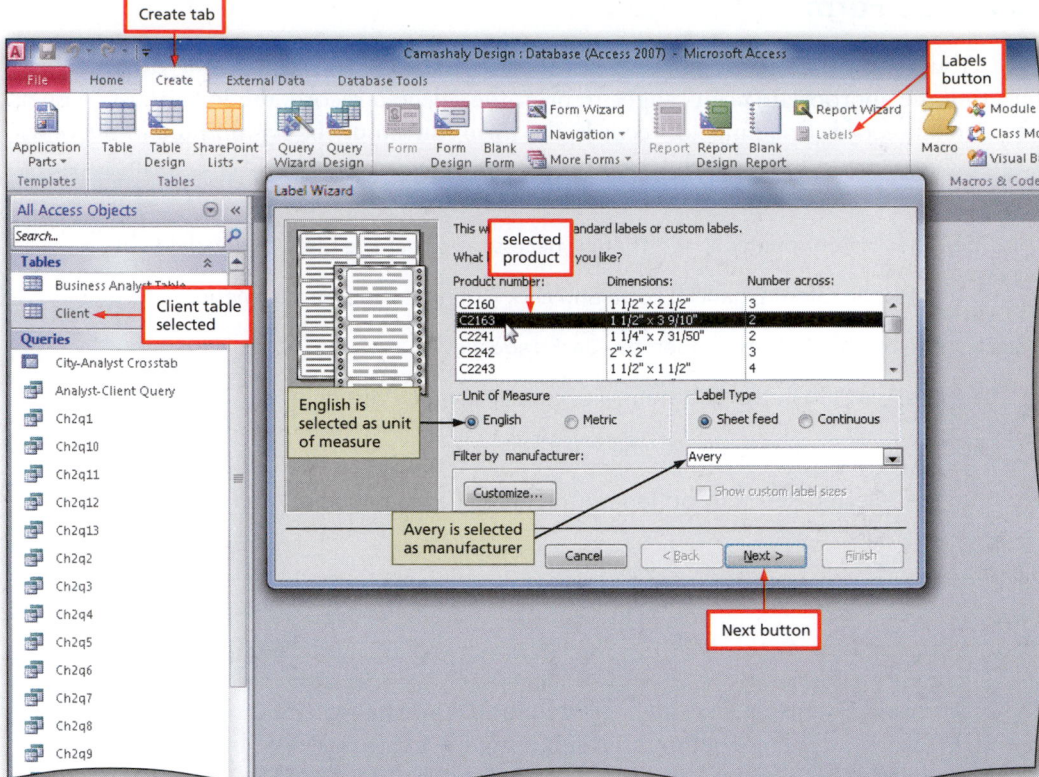

Figure 4–68

2

- Click the Next button (Figure 4–69).

Q&A

What font characteristics could I change with this screen?

You could change the font, the font size, the font weight, and/or the font color. You could also specify italic or underlining.

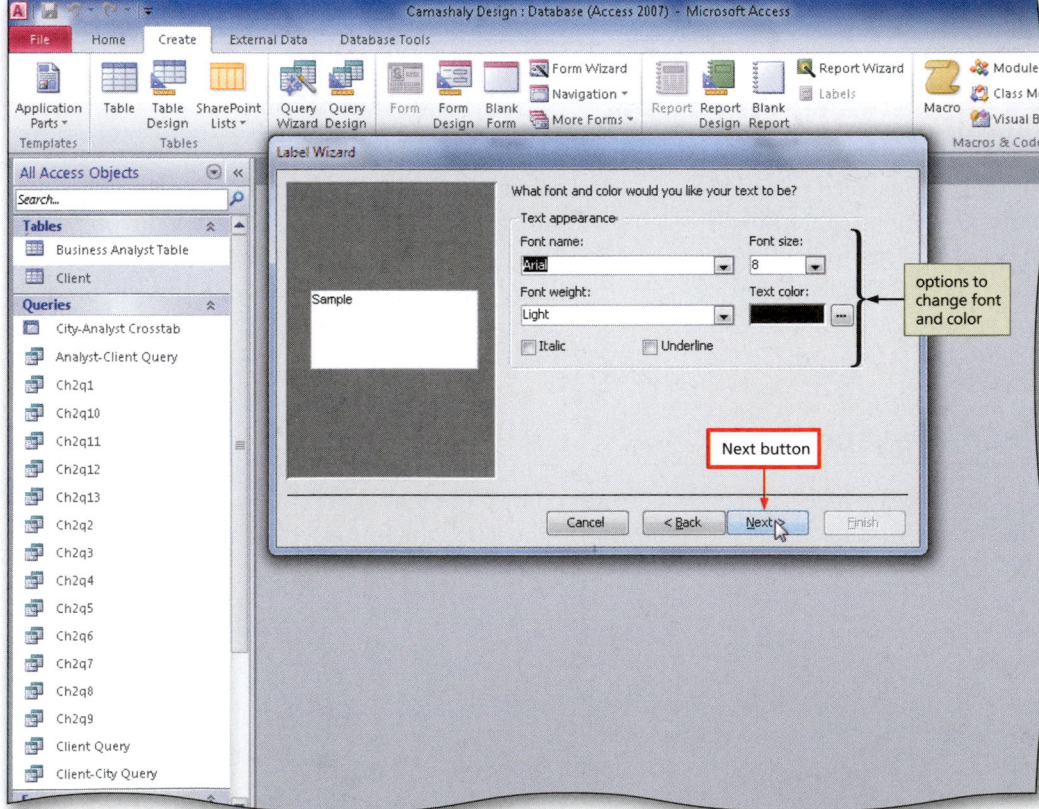

Figure 4–69

3
- Click the Next button to accept the default font and color settings.

- Click the Client Name field and then click the Add Field button (Figure 4–70).

Q&A

What if I make a mistake?

You can erase the contents of any line in the label by clicking in the line to produce an insertion point and then using the DELETE or BACKSPACE keys to erase the current contents. You can then add the correct field by clicking the field and then clicking the Add Field button.

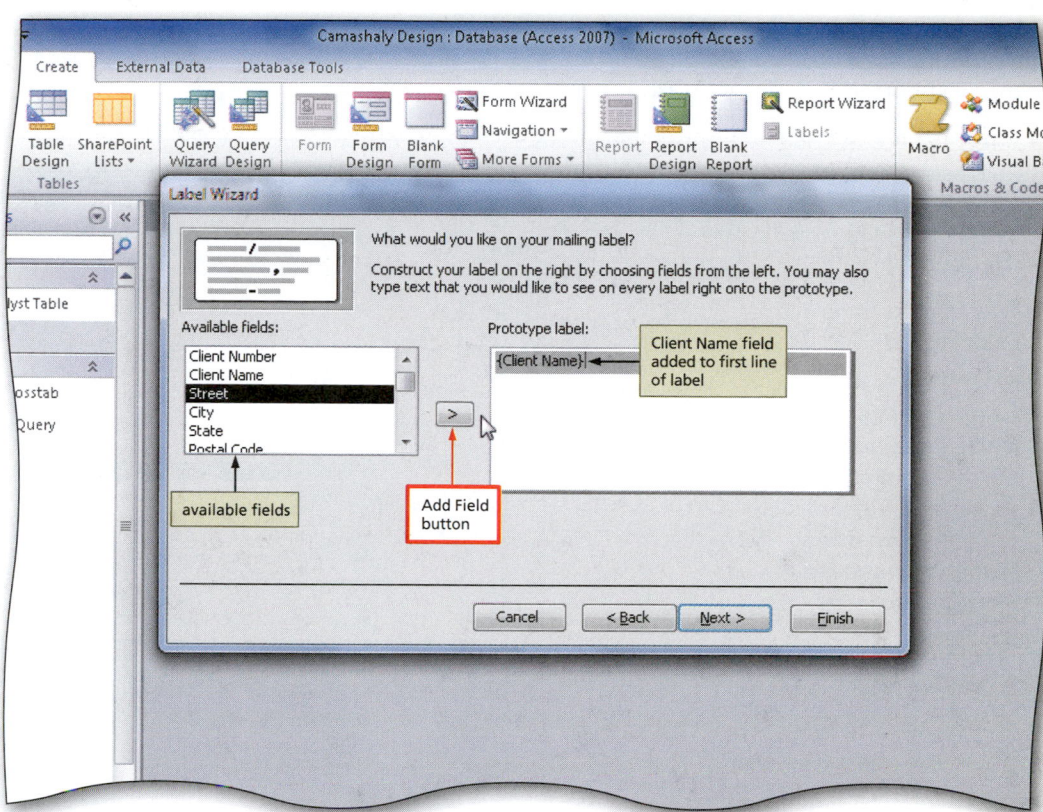

Figure 4–70

4
- Click the second line in the label, and then add the Street field.

- Click the third line of the label.

- Add the City field, type , (a comma), press the SPACEBAR, add the State field, press the SPACEBAR, and then add the Postal Code field (Figure 4–71).

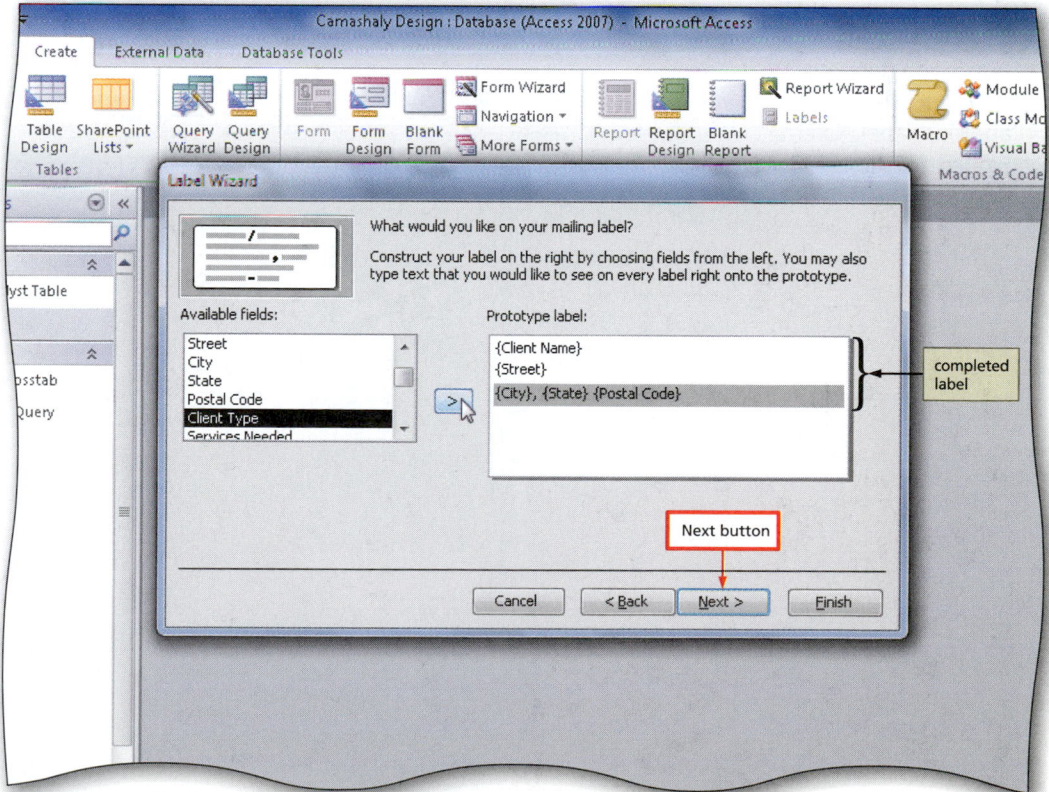

Figure 4–71

5

- Because the label is now complete, click the Next button.

- Select the Postal Code field as the field to sort by, and then click the Add Field button (Figure 4–72).

Q&A

Why am I sorting by postal code?

When you need to do a bulk mailing, that is, mail a large number of items using a special mail rate, mail organizations often require that the mail be sorted in postal code order.

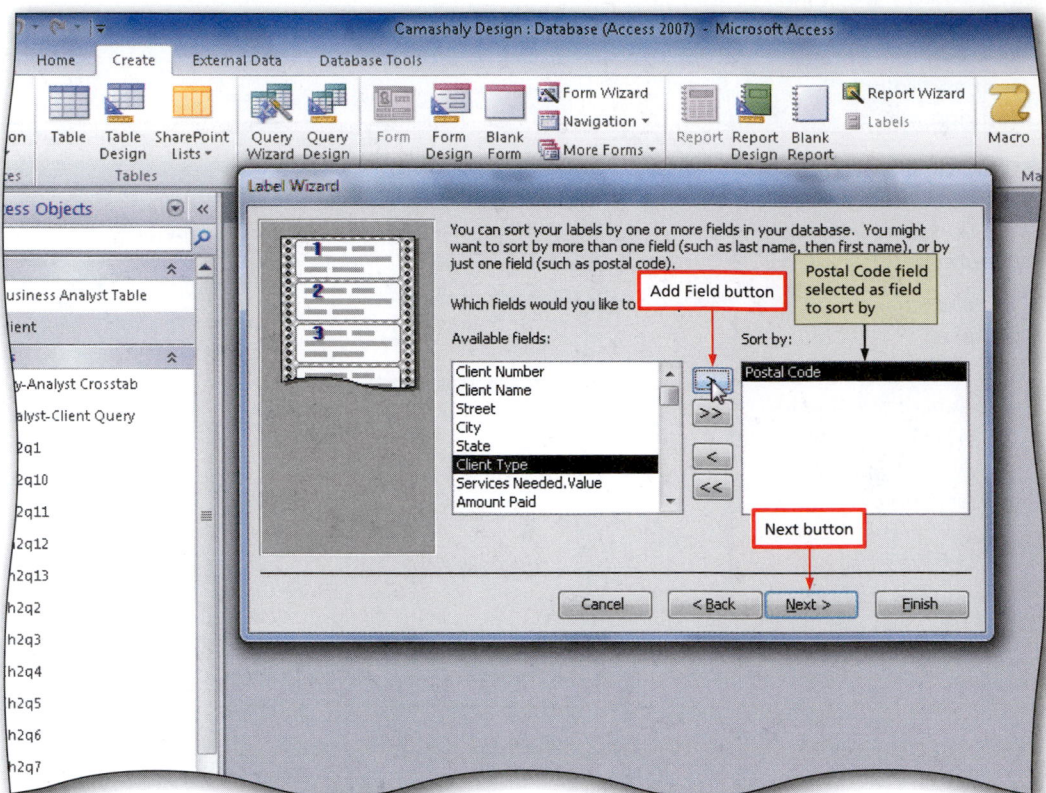

Figure 4–72

6

- Click the Next button.

- Ensure the name for the report (that is, the labels) is Labels Client (Figure 4–73).

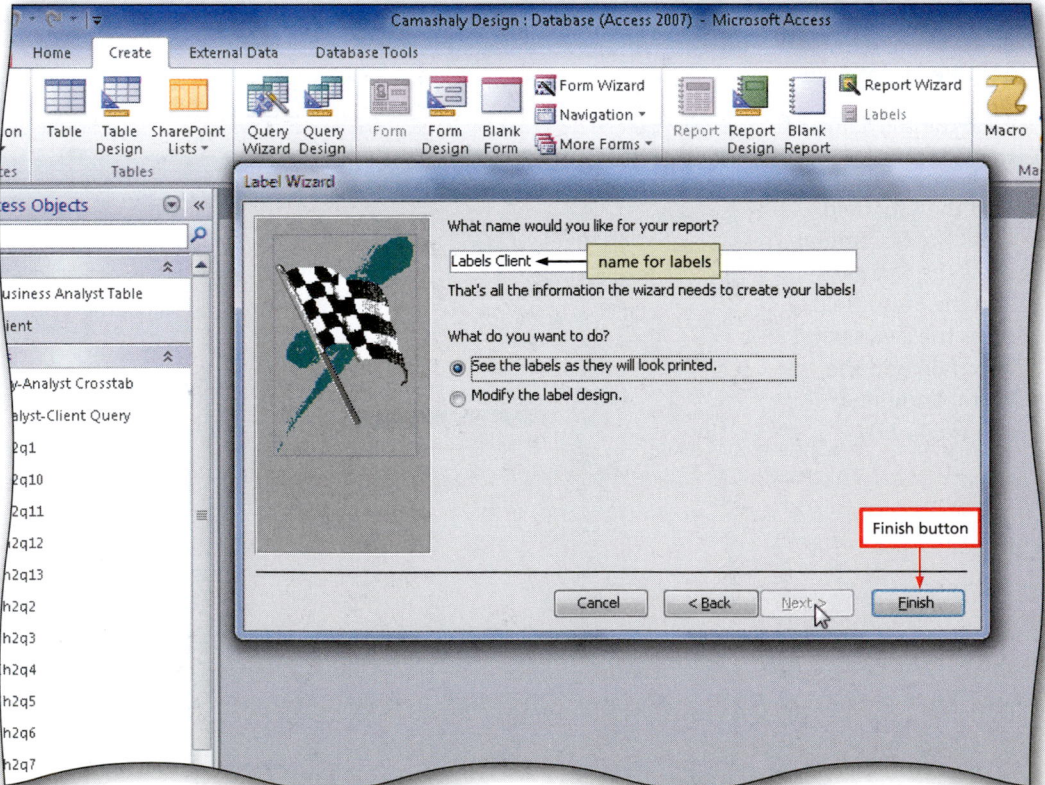

Figure 4–73

7
- Click the Finish button to complete the labels (Figure 4–74).

8
- Close the Labels Client report.

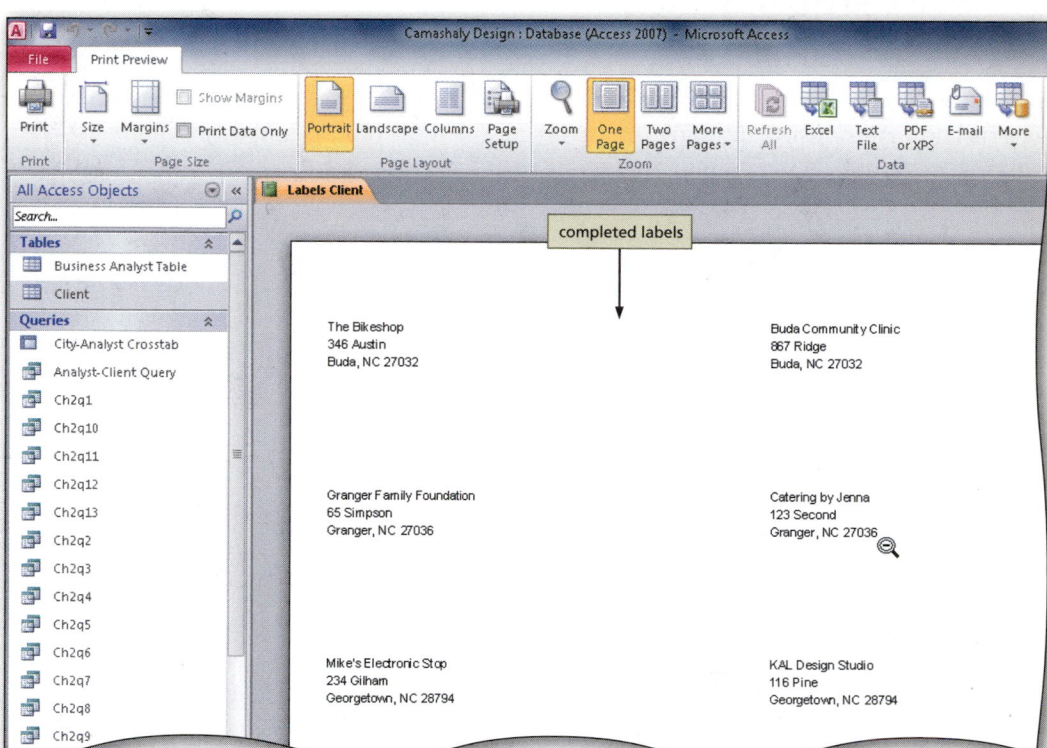

Figure 4–74

To Print Labels

You print labels just as you print a report. The only difference is that you must load the labels in the printer before printing. The following steps print the labels once you have loaded labels in your printer.

1 With the Labels Client report selected in the Navigation Pane, click File on the Ribbon to open the Backstage view.

2 Click the Print tab in the Backstage view to display the Print gallery.

3 Click the Quick Print button to print the labels.

Q&A
I want to load the correct number of labels. How do I know how many pages of labels will print?

If you are unsure how many pages of labels will print, open the label report in Print Preview first. Use the Navigation buttons in the status bar of the Print Preview window to determine how many pages of labels will print.

To Quit Access

The following steps quit Access.

1 Click the Close button on the right side of the title bar to quit Access.

2 If a Microsoft Access dialog box appears, click the Save button to save any changes made to the object since the last save.

BTW

Quick Reference
For a table that lists how to complete the tasks covered in this book using the mouse, Ribbon, shortcut menu, and keyboard, see the Quick Reference Summary at the back of this book, or visit the Access 2010 Quick Reference Web page (scsite.com/ac2010/qr).

Chapter Summary

In this chapter you have learned to use wizards to create reports and forms, modify the layout of reports and forms using Layout view, group and sort in a report, add totals to a report, conditionally format controls, filter records in reports and forms, resize and move controls, add fields to reports and forms, include gridlines, add a date, move controls in a control layout, apply themes, and create mailing labels. The items listed below include all the new Access skills you have learned in this chapter.

1. Group and Sort in a Report (AC 217)
2. Add Totals and Subtotals (AC 221)
3. Remove the Group, Sort, and Total Pane (AC 223)
4. Conditionally Format Controls (AC 224)
5. Filter Records in a Report (AC 228)
6. Clear a Report Filter (AC 229)
7. Create a Report that Involves Multiple Tables (AC 232)
8. Create a Report in Layout View (AC 238)
9. Assign a Theme to All Objects (AC 240)
10. Assign a Theme to a Single Object (AC 241)
11. Create a Summary Report (AC 242)
12. Use the Form Wizard to Create a Form (AC 243)
13. Place Controls in a Control Layout (AC 245)
14. Add a Date (AC 246)
15. Change the Format of a Control (AC 248)
16. Move a Control (AC 249)
17. Move Controls in a Control Layout (AC 249)
18. Add a Field (AC 251)
19. Filter and Sort Using a Form (AC 253)
20. Create Labels (AC 255)

 If you have a SAM 2010 user profile, your instructor may have assigned an autogradable version of this assignment. If so, log into the SAM 2010 Web site at www.cengage.com/sam2010 to download the instruction and start files.

Learn It Online

Test your knowledge of chapter content and key terms.

Instructions: To complete the Learn It Online exercises, start your browser, click the Address bar, and then enter the Web address `scsite.com/ac2010/learn`. When the Access 2010 Learn It Online page is displayed, click the link for the exercise you want to complete and then read the instructions.

Chapter Reinforcement TF, MC, and SA
A series of true/false, multiple choice, and short answer questions that test your knowledge of the chapter content.

Flash Cards
An interactive learning environment where you identify chapter key terms associated with displayed definitions.

Practice Test
A series of multiple choice questions that test your knowledge of chapter content and key terms.

Who Wants To Be a Computer Genius?
An interactive game that challenges your knowledge of chapter content in the style of a television quiz show.

Wheel of Terms
An interactive game that challenges your knowledge of chapter key terms in the style of the television show *Wheel of Fortune*.

Crossword Puzzle Challenge
A crossword puzzle that challenges your knowledge of key terms presented in the chapter.

Apply Your Knowledge

Reinforce the skills and apply the concepts you learned in this chapter.

Creating a Report and a Form

Instructions: Start Access. If you are using the Microsoft Access 2010 Complete or the Microsoft Access 2010 Comprehensive text, open the Babbage CPA Firm database that you used in Chapter 3. Otherwise, see your instructor for information on accessing the files required in this book.

Perform the following tasks:

1. Create the Clients by Bookkeeper report shown in Figure 4–75. The report is grouped by bookkeeper number and sorted by client number within bookkeeper number. Include totals for the Amount Paid and Balance Due fields. Change the orientation to landscape.

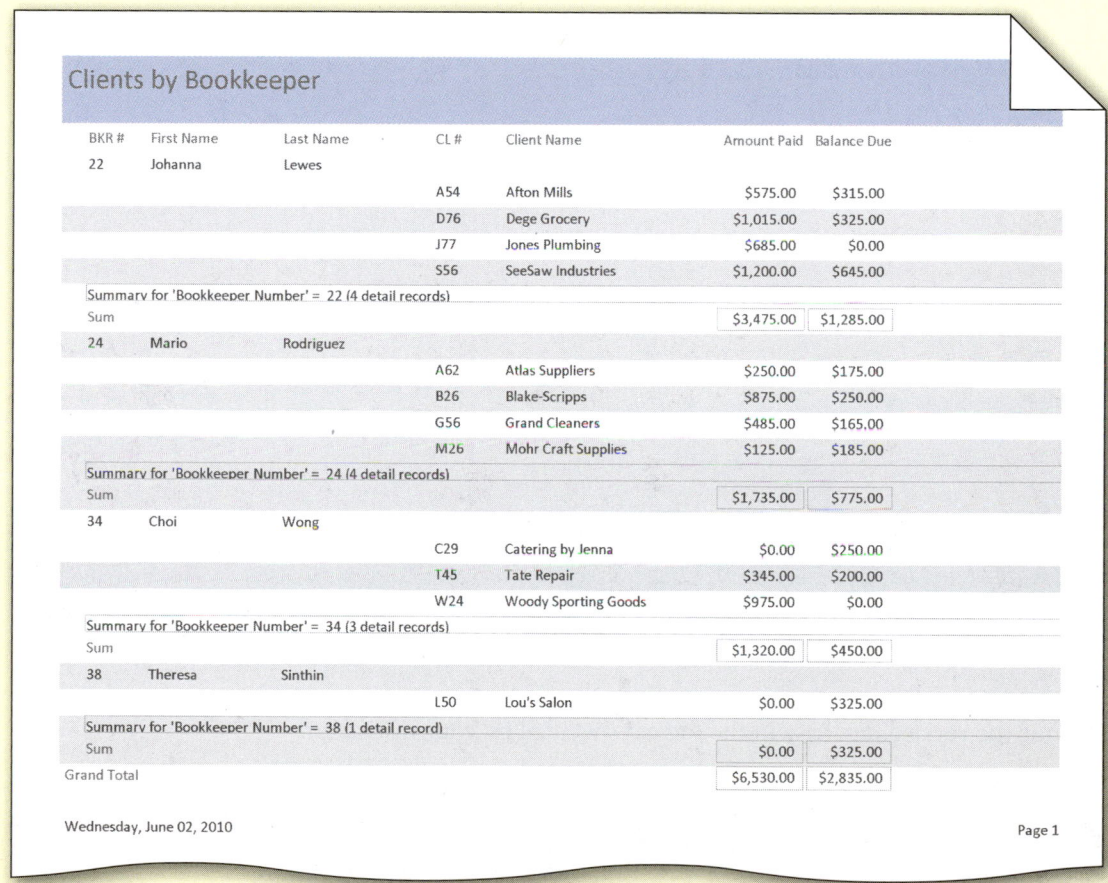

Clients by Bookkeeper

BKR #	First Name	Last Name	CL #	Client Name	Amount Paid	Balance Due
22	Johanna	Lewes				
			A54	Afton Mills	$575.00	$315.00
			D76	Dege Grocery	$1,015.00	$325.00
			J77	Jones Plumbing	$685.00	$0.00
			S56	SeeSaw Industries	$1,200.00	$645.00
Summary for 'Bookkeeper Number' = 22 (4 detail records)						
Sum					$3,475.00	$1,285.00
24	Mario	Rodriguez				
			A62	Atlas Suppliers	$250.00	$175.00
			B26	Blake-Scripps	$875.00	$250.00
			G56	Grand Cleaners	$485.00	$165.00
			M26	Mohr Craft Supplies	$125.00	$185.00
Summary for 'Bookkeeper Number' = 24 (4 detail records)						
Sum					$1,735.00	$775.00
34	Choi	Wong				
			C29	Catering by Jenna	$0.00	$250.00
			T45	Tate Repair	$345.00	$200.00
			W24	Woody Sporting Goods	$975.00	$0.00
Summary for 'Bookkeeper Number' = 34 (3 detail records)						
Sum					$1,320.00	$450.00
38	Theresa	Sinthin				
			L50	Lou's Salon	$0.00	$325.00
Summary for 'Bookkeeper Number' = 38 (1 detail record)						
Sum					$0.00	$325.00
Grand Total					$6,530.00	$2,835.00

Wednesday, June 02, 2010

Page 1

Figure 4–75

Continued >

Apply Your Knowledge *continued*

2. Create the Client Financial Form shown in Figure 4–76 for the Client table. The form includes the current date and is similar in style to that shown in Figure 4–3 on page AC 212.

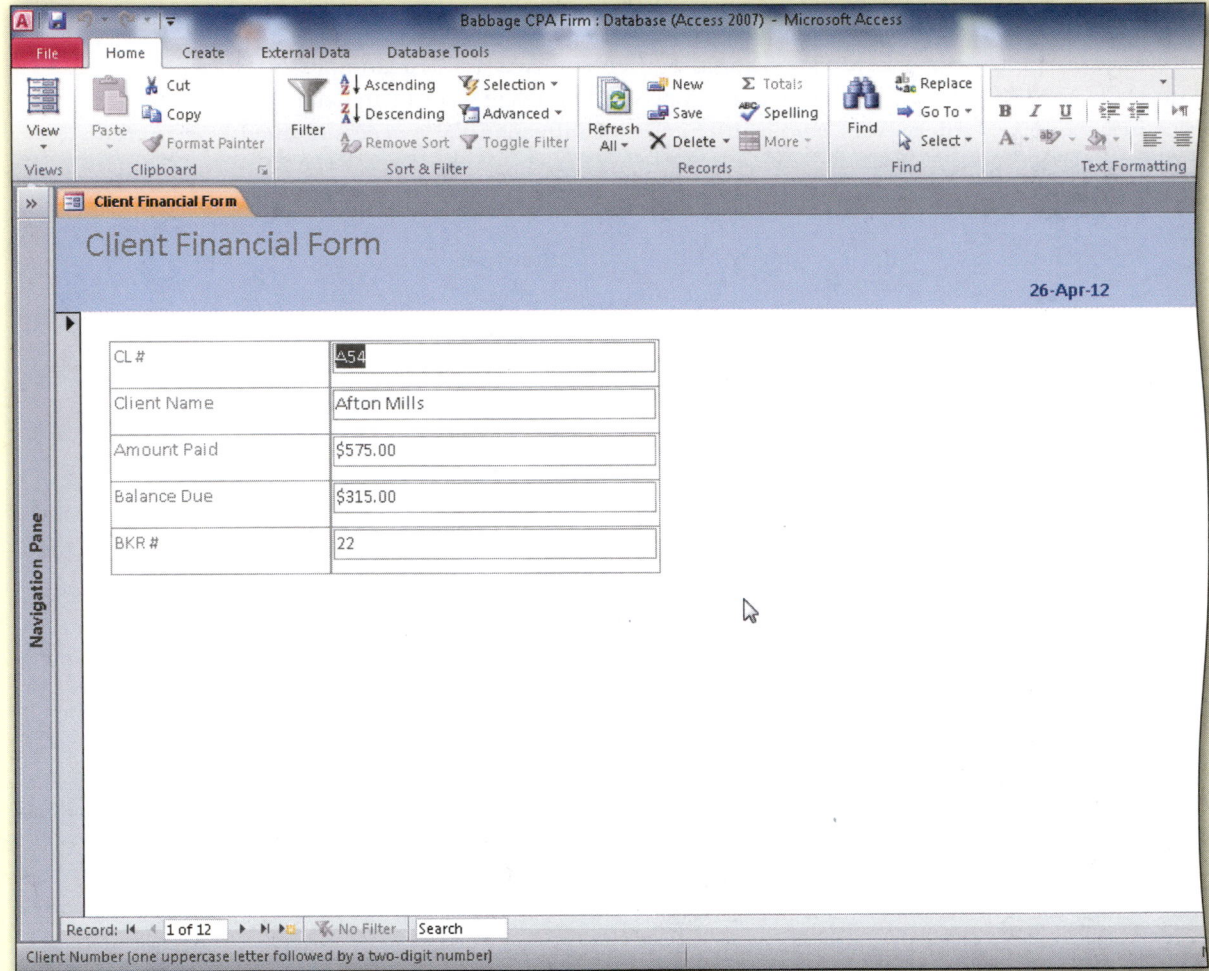

Figure 4–76

3. Submit the revised database in the format specified by your instructor.

Extend Your Knowledge

Extend the skills you learned in this chapter and experiment with new skills. You may need to use Help to complete the assignment.

Creating a Summary Report and Assigning a Theme to a Form

Instructions: See the inside back cover of this book for instructions for downloading the Data Files for Students, or see your instructor for information on accessing the required files.

The College Helpers database contains data for a group of college students who perform miscellaneous jobs for homeowners to earn tuition money. You will create the summary report shown in Figure 4–77. You also will create the form shown in Figure 4–78.

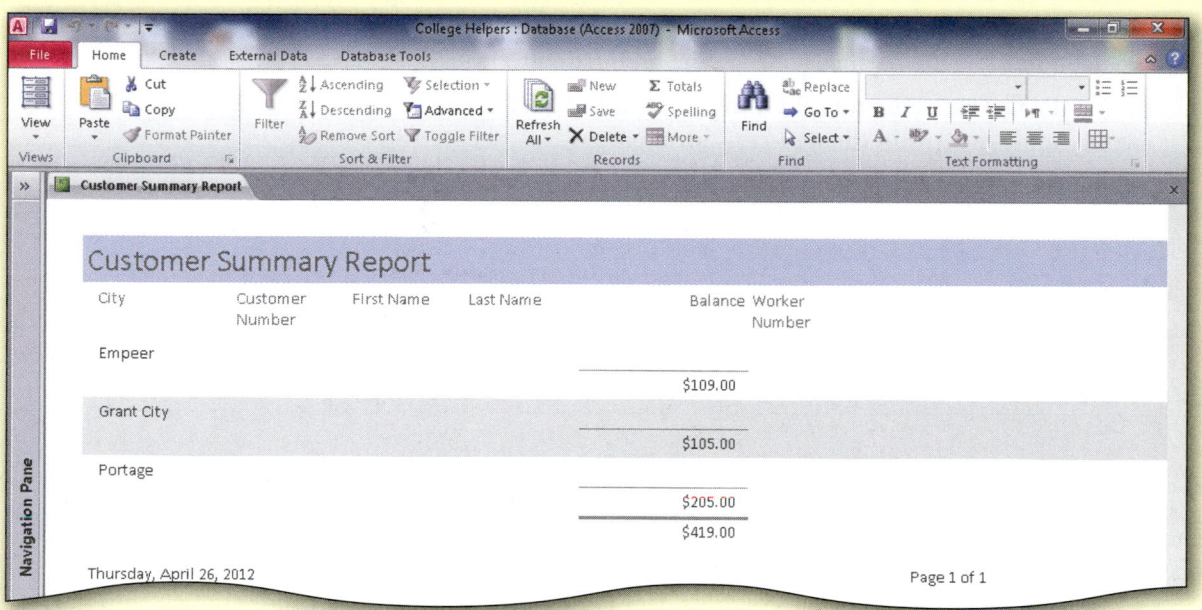

Figure 4–77

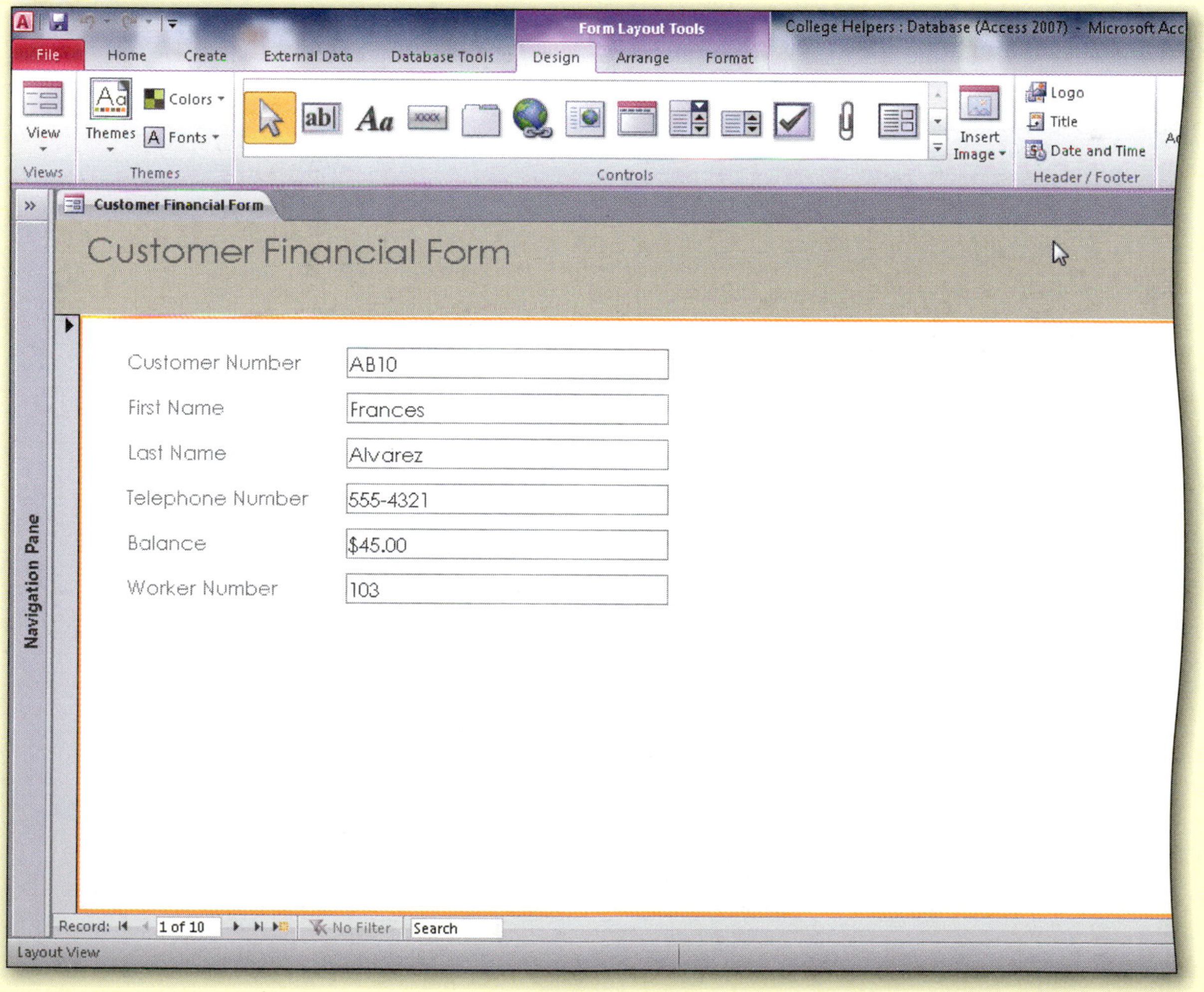

Figure 4–78

Continued >

Extend Your Knowledge *continued*

Perform the following tasks:

1. Use the Report Wizard to create the summary report shown in Figure 4–77. Name the report Customer Summary Report. Group the report by city and sort by customer number within city. Include totals for the balance. Change the orientation to landscape.

2. Create the Customer Financial Form shown in Figure 4–78. The form has a stacked control layout. Apply the Austin theme to this form only.

3. Submit the revised database in the format specified by your instructor.

Make It Right

Analyze a database and correct all errors and/or improve the design.

Correcting Report and Form Design Errors

Instructions: Start Access. Open the WeClean4You database. See the inside back cover of this book for instructions for downloading the Data Files for Students, or see your instructor for information on accessing the required files.

The WeClean4You database contains data for a company that does residential cleaning. The owner of the company has created the report shown in Figure 4–79 using the Report Wizard, but she forgot to sort the report by customer number. She does not know how to total the Balance and Amount Paid fields. She would like to differentiate customers whose amount paid value is $0.00 by making the amount appear in a bold red font. *Hint:* Use Layout view to make the corrections.

Customers by Worker

Worker Number	Worker First Name	Worker Last Name	Customer Number	Customer First Name	Customer Last Name	Balance	Amount Paid
303	Joe	Levin					
			KL12	Cynthia	Klinger	$60.00	$104.00
			HJ07	Bill	Heijer	$29.00	$135.00
			AB10	Frances	Alvarez	$45.00	$305.00
305	Brad	Rogers					
			TR35	Gerry	Trent	$40.00	$223.00
			PR80	Martin	Prestz	$95.00	$168.00
			GM52	Frank	Gammort	$70.00	$0.00
			BR16	Alex	Breaton	$80.00	$280.00
307	Maria	Rodriguez					
			SA23	Maria	Santoro	$0.00	$0.00
			MA34	Lisa	Manston	$0.00	$145.00
			FE45	Jean	Ferdon	$0.00	$370.00

Figure 4–79

She also created the form shown in Figure 4–80 for the Customer table, but she forgot to add the Telephone Number field. The Telephone Number field should appear before the Balance field. She would like the customer first name to appear before the customer last name and she would like to add the date to the form header.

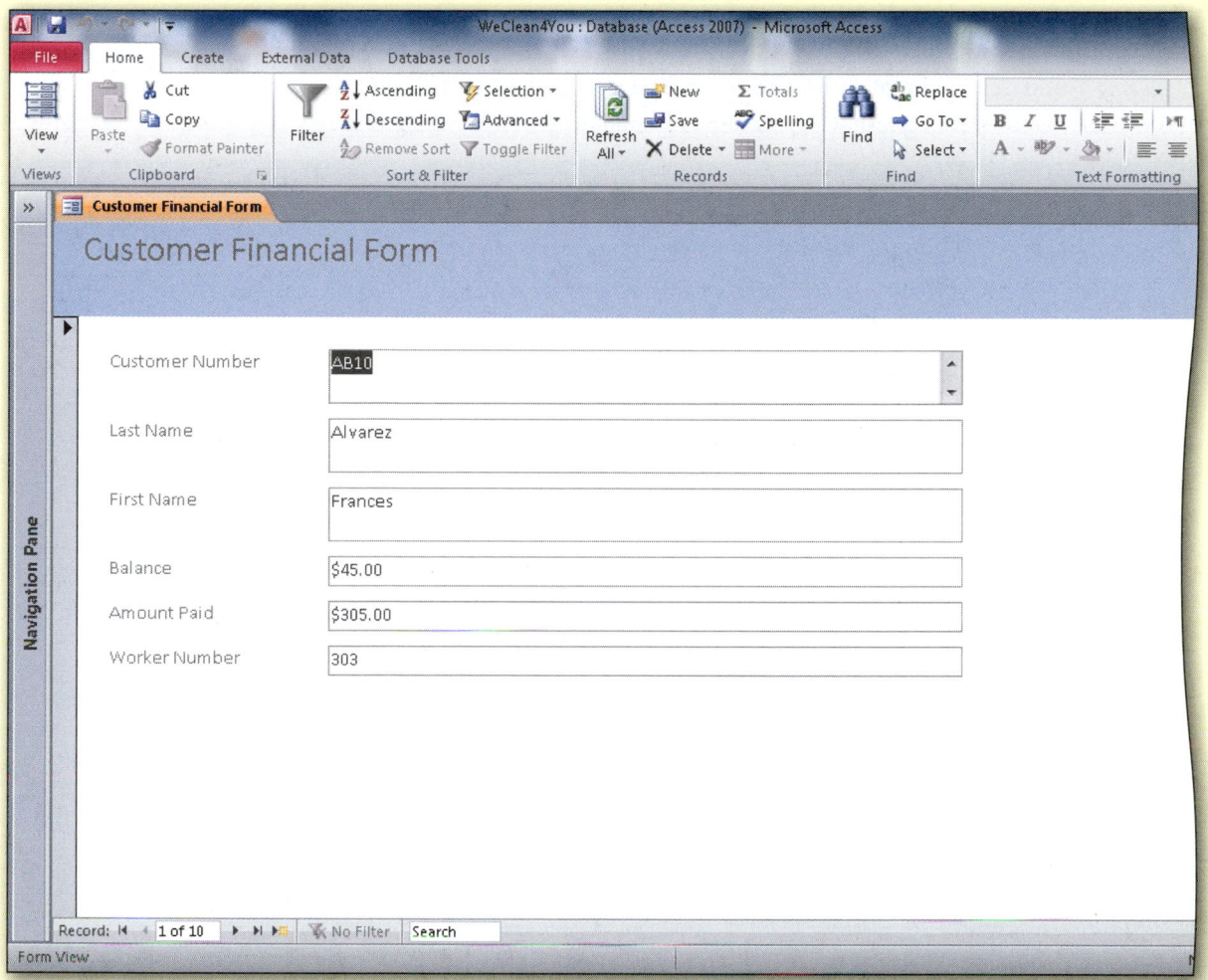

Figure 4–80

Submit the revised database in the format specified by your instructor.

In the Lab

Design, create, modify, and/or use a database following the guidelines, concepts, and skills presented in this chapter. Labs 1, 2, and 3 are listed in order of increasing difficulty.

Lab 1: Presenting Data in the ECO Clothesline Database

Problem: The management of ECO Clothesline already has realized the benefits from the database of customers and sales reps that you created. The management now would like to prepare reports and forms for the database.

Instructions: If you are using the Microsoft Access 2010 Complete or the Microsoft Access 2010 Comprehensive text, open the ECO Clothesline database that you used in Chapter 3. Otherwise, see your instructor for information on accessing the files required in this book.

Perform the following tasks:
1. Open in Layout view the Customer Balance Report you created in Chapter 1 and revised in Chapter 3. Modify the report to create the report shown in Figure 4–81. Group the report by Customer Type and sort by Customer Number within Customer Type. Add the Amount Paid field to the report and include totals for the Balance and Amount Paid fields.

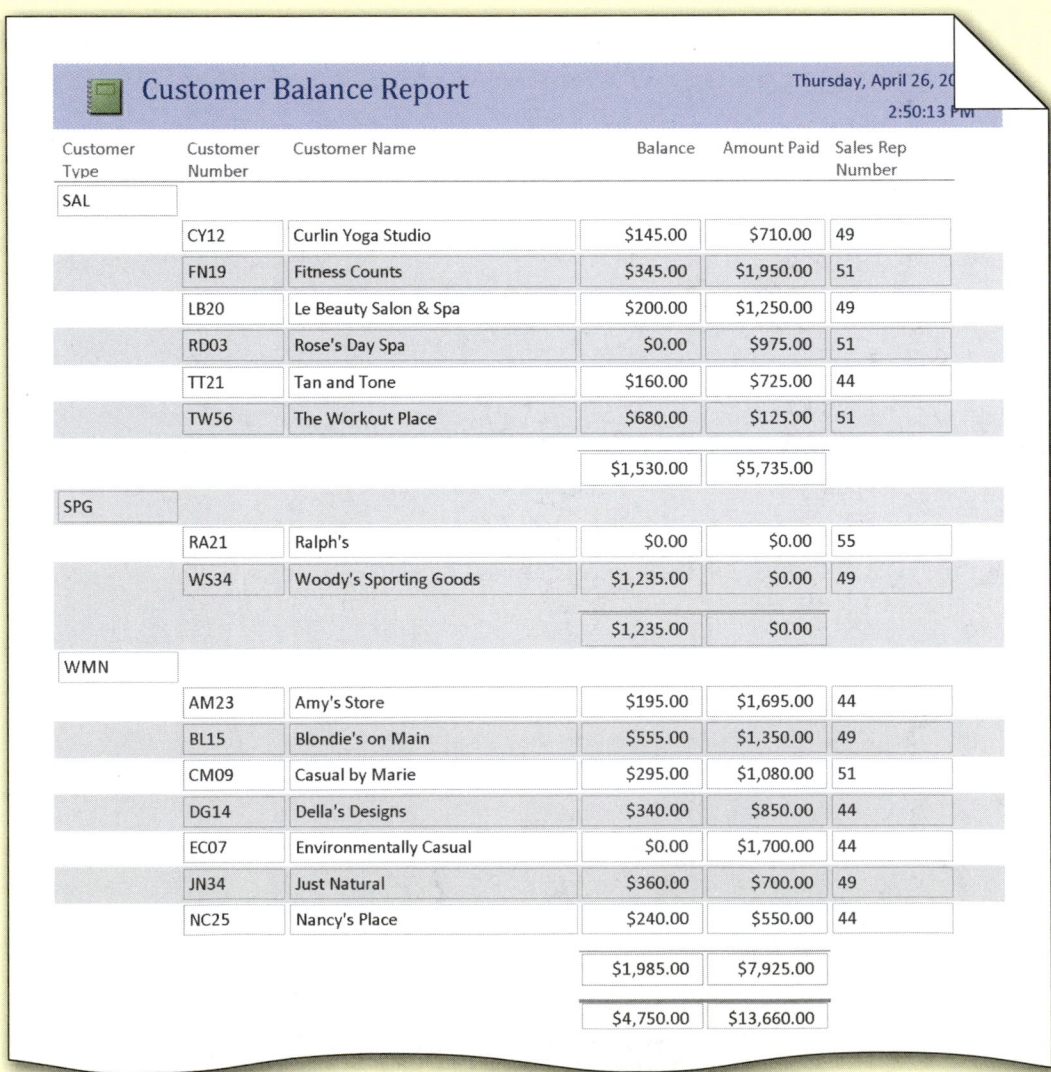

Customer Type	Customer Number	Customer Name	Balance	Amount Paid	Sales Rep Number
SAL					
	CY12	Curlin Yoga Studio	$145.00	$710.00	49
	FN19	Fitness Counts	$345.00	$1,950.00	51
	LB20	Le Beauty Salon & Spa	$200.00	$1,250.00	49
	RD03	Rose's Day Spa	$0.00	$975.00	51
	TT21	Tan and Tone	$160.00	$725.00	44
	TW56	The Workout Place	$680.00	$125.00	51
			$1,530.00	$5,735.00	
SPG					
	RA21	Ralph's	$0.00	$0.00	55
	WS34	Woody's Sporting Goods	$1,235.00	$0.00	49
			$1,235.00	$0.00	
WMN					
	AM23	Amy's Store	$195.00	$1,695.00	44
	BL15	Blondie's on Main	$555.00	$1,350.00	49
	CM09	Casual by Marie	$295.00	$1,080.00	51
	DG14	Della's Designs	$340.00	$850.00	44
	EC07	Environmentally Casual	$0.00	$1,700.00	44
	JN34	Just Natural	$360.00	$700.00	49
	NC25	Nancy's Place	$240.00	$550.00	44
			$1,985.00	$7,925.00	
			$4,750.00	$13,660.00	

Customer Balance Report — Thursday, April 26, 20__ 2:50:13 PM

Figure 4–81

2. Create the Customers by Sales Rep report shown in Figure 4–82. Include a total for the Balance field. Change the orientation to landscape. Make sure the total control displays completely. (*Hint:* Use Layout view to make this adjustment.)

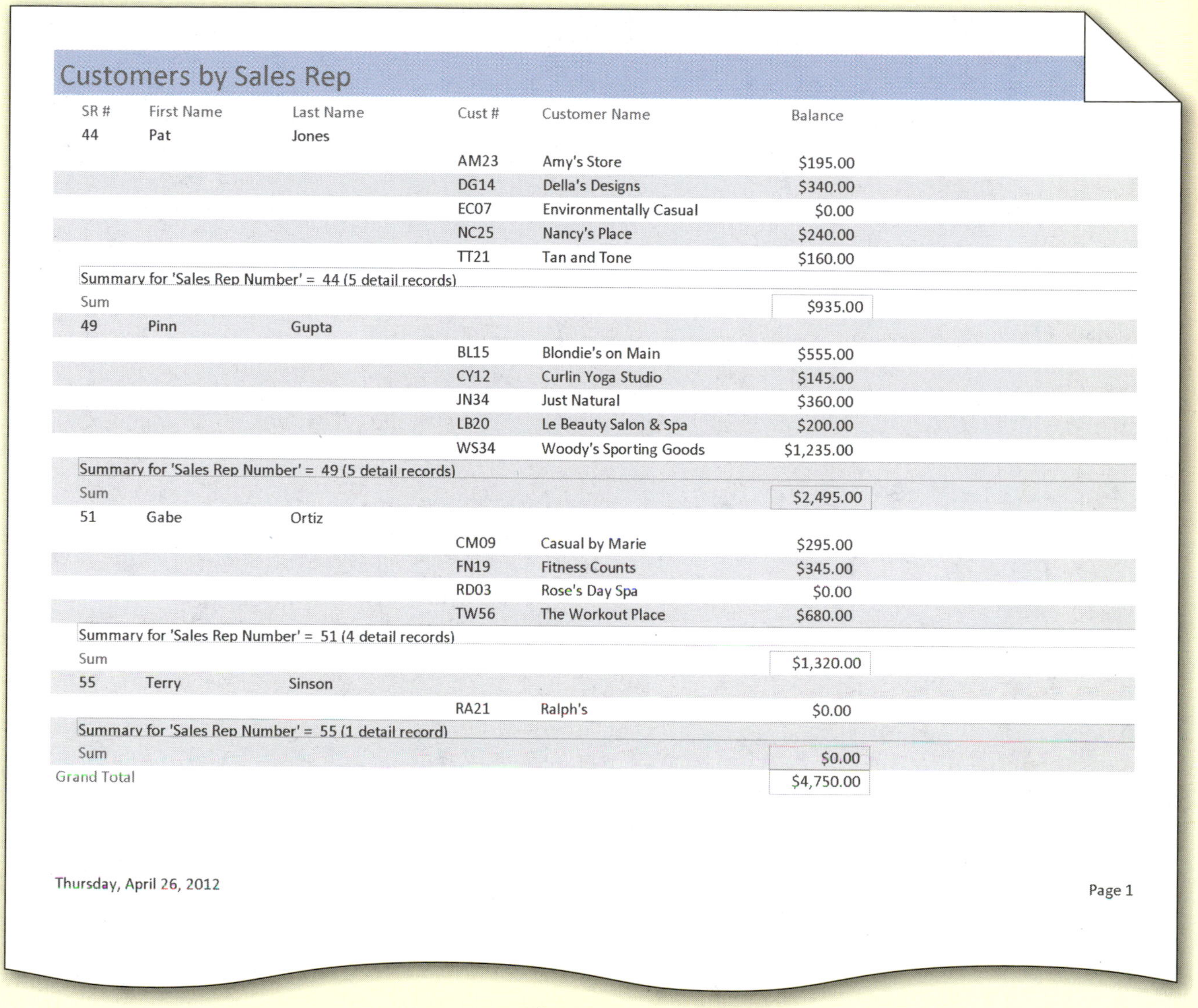

Customers by Sales Rep

SR #	First Name	Last Name	Cust #	Customer Name	Balance
44	Pat	Jones			
			AM23	Amy's Store	$195.00
			DG14	Della's Designs	$340.00
			EC07	Environmentally Casual	$0.00
			NC25	Nancy's Place	$240.00
			TT21	Tan and Tone	$160.00

Summary for 'Sales Rep Number' = 44 (5 detail records)

Sum					$935.00
49	Pinn	Gupta			
			BL15	Blondie's on Main	$555.00
			CY12	Curlin Yoga Studio	$145.00
			JN34	Just Natural	$360.00
			LB20	Le Beauty Salon & Spa	$200.00
			WS34	Woody's Sporting Goods	$1,235.00

Summary for 'Sales Rep Number' = 49 (5 detail records)

Sum					$2,495.00
51	Gabe	Ortiz			
			CM09	Casual by Marie	$295.00
			FN19	Fitness Counts	$345.00
			RD03	Rose's Day Spa	$0.00
			TW56	The Workout Place	$680.00

Summary for 'Sales Rep Number' = 51 (4 detail records)

Sum					$1,320.00
55	Terry	Sinson			
			RA21	Ralph's	$0.00

Summary for 'Sales Rep Number' = 55 (1 detail record)

Sum					$0.00
Grand Total					$4,750.00

Thursday, April 26, 2012

Page 1

Figure 4–82

Continued >

In the Lab *continued*

3. Create the Customer Financial Form shown in Figure 4–83. The form includes the date.

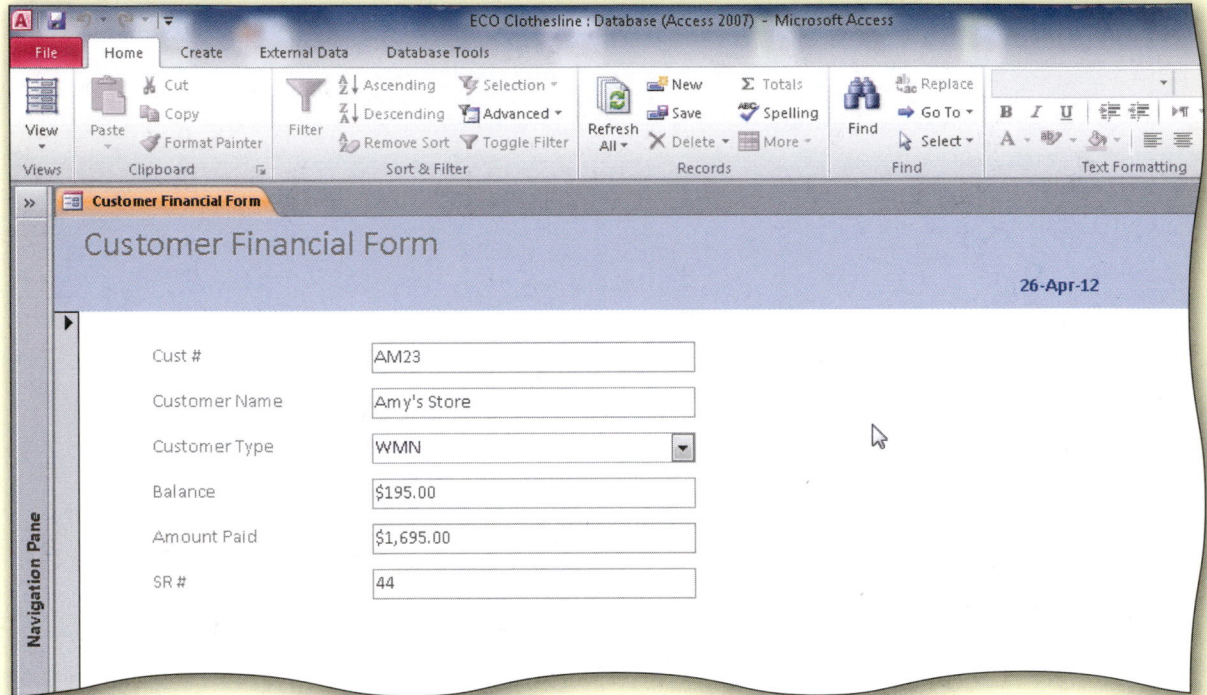

Figure 4–83

4. Create mailing labels for the Customer table. Use Avery labels C2163 and format the labels with customer name on the first line, street on the second line, and city, state, and postal code on the third line. Include a comma and a space after city and a space between state and postal code. Sort the labels by postal code.

5. Submit the revised database in the format specified by your instructor.

In the Lab

Lab 2: Presenting Data in the Walburg Energy Alternatives Database

Problem: The management of Walburg Energy Alternatives already has realized the benefits from the database of items and vendors that you created. The management now would like to prepare reports and forms for the database.

Instructions: If you are using the Microsoft Access 2010 Complete or the Microsoft Access 2010 Comprehensive text, open the Walburg Energy Alternatives database that you used in Chapter 3. Otherwise, see your instructor for information on accessing the files required in this book.

Perform the following tasks:

1. Open in Layout view the Inventory Status Report that you created in Chapter 1. Add a total for the Inventory Value field. Be sure the total is completely displayed. Display the average cost. If there are fewer than 10 items on hand, the value should appear in a red bold font. Filter the report for all items where the number on hand is 5 or less. Save the filtered report as Filtered Inventory Status Report.

2. Create the Items by Vendor report shown in Figure 4–84.

Items by Vendor

Vendor Code	Vendor Name	Item Number	Description	On Hand	Cost
AS	Asterman Industries				
		2216	Child Safety Caps	15	$2.89
		3663	Air Deflector	8	$5.45
		4553	Energy Saving Kit	7	$42.75
		6234	Programmable Thermostat	3	$34.25
		8136	Smoke Detector	10	$6.10
		9458	Windows Insulator Kit	10	$4.95
Summary for 'Vendor Code' = AS (6 detail records)					
Avg					$16.07
JM	JMZ Technologies				
		1234	Adhesive Door Sweep	5	$3.45
		2234	Clothes Dryer Heat Saver	4	$8.99
		3673	Energy Booklet	25	$2.70
		4583	Fluorescent Light Bulb	18	$4.50
		6185	Luminescent Night Light	12	$3.75
		7123	Retractable Clothesline	10	$13.25
		8590	Water Conservation Kit	8	$13.45
Summary for 'Vendor Code' = JM (7 detail records)					
Avg					$7.16
SD	Scryps Distributors				
		2310	Drip Counter	10	$1.79
		2789	Hot Water Gauge	6	$2.75
		4573	Faucet Aerator	20	$0.89
		5923	Low Flow Shower Head	11	$8.75
Vendor Code	Vendor Name	Item Number	Description	On Hand	Cost
		6345	Rain Gauge	16	$2.89
		7934	Shower Timer	15	$2.45
		8344	Toilet Tank Water Saver	18	$3.35
Summary for 'Vendor Code' = SD (7 detail records)					
Avg					$3.27

Figure 4–84

Continued >

In the Lab *continued*

3. Create the form shown in Figure 4–85. If there are fewer than 10 items on hand, the value should appear in a red bold font. Save the form as Item Update Form.

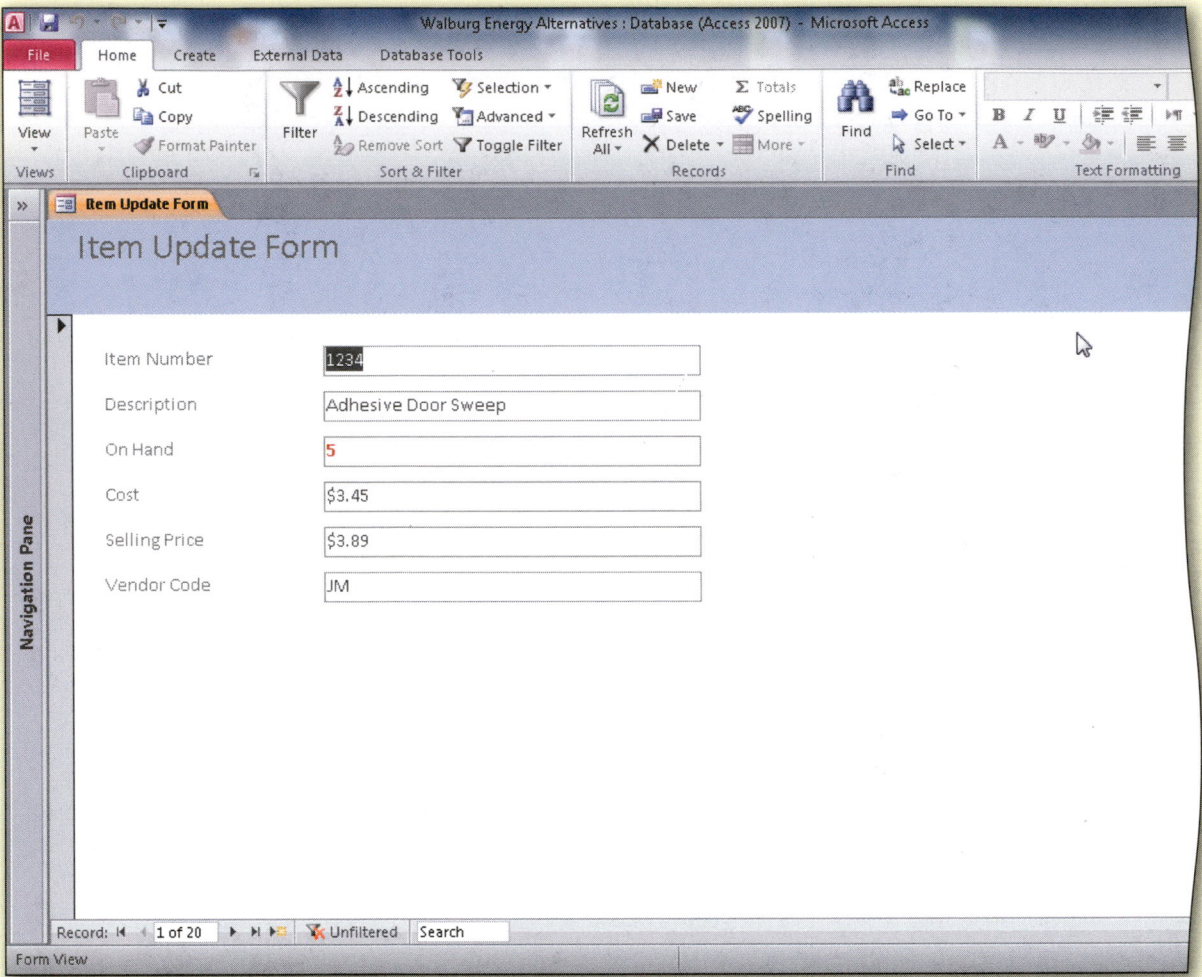

Figure 4–85

4. Filter the Item Update Form for all items where the cost is less than $3.00 and sort the results in descending order by cost. Save the form as Filtered Item Update Form.

5. Submit the revised database in the format specified by your instructor.

In the Lab

Lab 3: Presenting Data in the Philamar Training Database

Problem: The management of Philamar Training already has realized the benefits from the database you created. The management now would like to prepare reports and forms for the database.

Instructions: If you are using the Microsoft Access 2010 Complete or the Microsoft Access 2010 Comprehensive text, open the Philamar Training database that you used in Chapter 3. Otherwise, see your instructor for information on accessing the files required in this book. Submit the revised database in the format specified by your instructor.

Instructions Part 1: Modify the Client Status Report created in Chapter 1. Add the Client Type field to the report and group records by client type. Include totals for the Amount Paid and Current Due fields. If the amount due on any record is $0.00, the value should appear in a red bold font. The report should be similar to the Client Financial Report shown in Figure 4–1 on page AC 210.

Instructions Part 2: Create a Clients by Trainer report for Philamar Training. The report should be similar to the Clients by Analyst report shown in Figure 4–2 on page AC 211 with the records grouped by trainer number. Include the Trainer Number, First Name, and Last Name fields from the Trainer table. Include the Client Number, Client Name, Amount Paid, and Current Due fields from the Client table. Provide subtotals and a grand total for the Amount Paid and Current Due fields. Change the page layout to landscape.

Instructions Part 3: Create a Client Financial Form for Philamar Training that is similar to the form shown in Figure 4–3 on page AC 212. The form should include the Client Number, Client Name, Amount Paid, Current Due, Trainer Number, Client Type, and Training Needed fields.

Cases and Places

Apply your creative thinking and problem solving skills to design and implement a solution.

See the inside back cover of this book for instructions for downloading the Data Files for Students, or see your instructor for information on accessing the required files.

1: Presenting Data in the Chamber of Commerce Database

Academic

If you are using the Microsoft Access 2010 Complete or the Microsoft Access 2010 Comprehensive text, open the Chamber of Commerce database that you used in Chapter 3. Otherwise, see your instructor for information on accessing the files required in this book. Use the concepts and techniques presented in this chapter to perform each of the following tasks:

a. Create a report that groups advertisers by advertiser type. Include the Advertiser Type, Advertiser Number, Advertiser Name, Balance, Amount Paid, and Ad Rep Number fields in the report. Include totals for the two currency fields. Use conditional formatting to emphasize any values in the Balance field that are greater than $200.

b. Create a report that includes data from both the Ad Rep table and the Advertiser table. Include the Ad Rep Number, First Name, and Last Name fields from the Ad Rep table. Include the Advertiser Number, Advertiser Name, Balance, and Amount Paid fields from the Advertiser table. Group the report by ad rep number. Include totals for the two currency fields. Change the orientation to landscape.

Continued >

Cases and Places *continued*

c. Create a form for the Advertiser table. Include the Advertiser Number, Advertiser Name, Balance, Amount Paid, Advertiser Type, and Ad Rep Number fields on the form.

Submit the revised database in the format specified by your instructor.

2: Presenting Data in the Consignment Database

Personal

If you are using the Microsoft Access 2010 Complete or the Microsoft Access 2010 Comprehensive text, open the Consignment database that you used in Chapter 3. Otherwise, see your instructor for information on accessing the files required in this book. Use the concepts and techniques presented in this chapter to perform each of the following tasks:

a. Modify the Available Items Report you created in Chapter 1. Group the report by the condition of the item and sort by description. Include the average price.

b. Create a report that includes data from both the Seller and the Items table. Include the Seller Code, First Name, and Last Name fields from the Seller table. Include all fields except Seller Code from the Items table. Group the report by seller code and sort by description within group. Do not include any totals.

c. Create labels for the Items table. These labels will be used to tag items in the store. Include the seller code on the first line, the item number and description on the second line, the price on the third line, and the date posted on the fourth line. Use a font size and weight that will make it easy for individuals to read the label.

Submit the revised database in the format specified by your instructor.

3: Presenting Data in the Senior Care Database

Professional

If you are using the Microsoft Access 2010 Complete or the Microsoft Access 2010 Comprehensive text, open the Senior Care database that you used in Chapter 3. Otherwise, see your instructor for information on accessing the files required in this book. Use the concepts and techniques presented in this chapter to perform each of the following tasks:

a. Create a report that includes data from both the Helper table and the Client table. Include the Helper Number, First Name, and Last Name fields from the Helper table. Include the Client Number, First Name, Last Name, and Services Needed fields from the Client table. Group the report by helper number, and sort the report by client number. Change the page layout to Landscape.

b. Create a form for the Client table. Include the Client Number, First Name, Last Name, Amount Paid, Balance, Helper Number, and Services Needed fields.

Submit the revised database in the format specified by your instructor.

5 | Multitable Forms

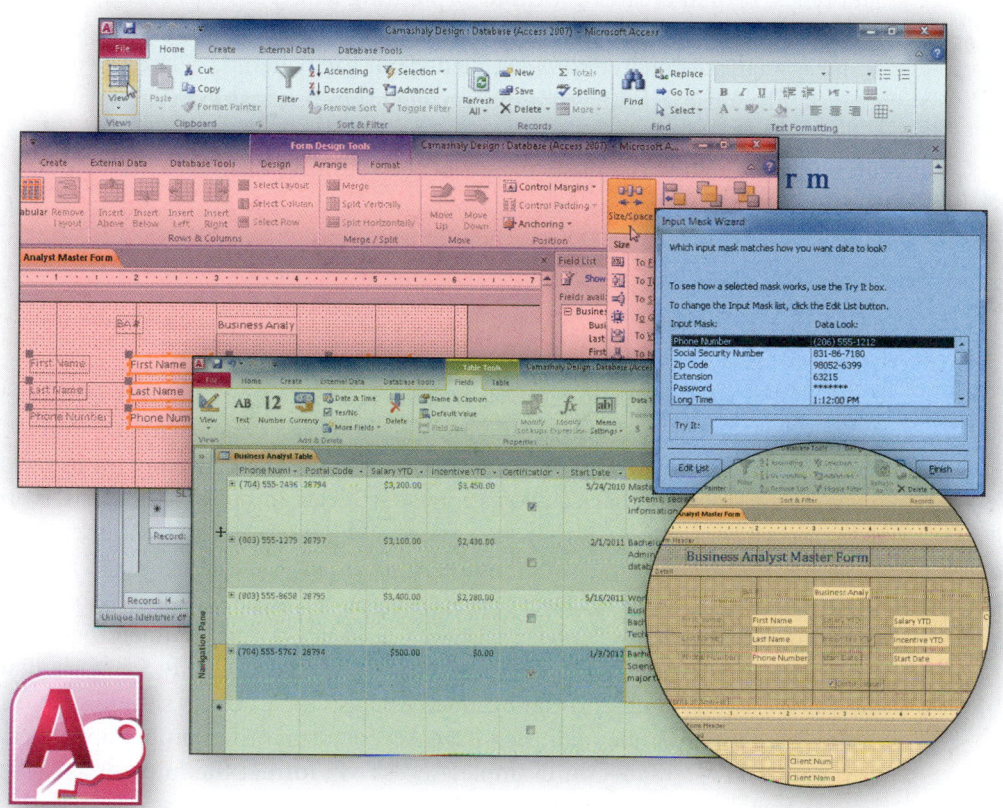

Objectives

You will have mastered the material in this project when you can:

- Add Yes/No, Date/Time, Memo, OLE Object, and Attachment fields

- Use the Input Mask Wizard

- Update fields and enter data

- Change row and column size

- Create a form with a subform in Design view

- Modify a subform and form design

- Enhance the form title

- Change tab stops and tab order

- Use the form to view data and attachments

- View object dependencies

- Use Date/Time, Memo, and Yes/No fields in a query

- Create a form with a datasheet

5 | Multitable Forms

Introduction

This chapter adds several additional fields to the Camashaly database that require special data types. It then creates a form incorporating data from two tables. The two tables, Business Analyst and Client, are related in a one-to-many relationship. That is, one business analyst is related to *many* clients, but each client is related to only *one* business analyst. The Business Analyst Table is called the "one" table in the relationship and the Client table is called the "many" table. The form will show one business analyst at a time, but also will include the many clients of that business analyst. This chapter also creates queries that use the added fields.

Project — Multitable Forms

Camashaly Design uses its database to keep records about clients and business analysts. After using the database for several months, however, Camashaly has found that it needs to maintain additional data on its business analysts. The company wants to identify those business analysts who have a professional certificate in business analysis, store the start date of each business analyst in the database, and include notes about each business analyst as well as the business analyst's picture. Additionally, business analysts now maintain files about potential contacts. These files are separate from the database; some are maintained in Word and others in Excel. Camashaly would like a way to attach these files to the corresponding business analyst's record in the database. Finally, Camashaly wants to add the Phone Number field to the Business Analyst Table. Users should type only the digits in the telephone number and then have Access format the number appropriately. If the user enters 7195558364, for example, Access will format the number as (719) 555-8364.

After the proposed fields have been added to the database, Camashaly wants users to be able to use a form that incorporates the Client and Business Analyst tables and that includes the newly added fields as well as some of the existing fields. The form also should include the client number, name, amount paid, and current due amount for the clients of each business analyst. Camashaly would like to see multiple clients on the screen at the same time (Figure 5–1). The database should allow users to scroll through all the clients of a business analyst and to open any of the attachments concerning the business analyst's Client Notes. Finally, Camashaly requires queries that use the Certification, Start Date, and Comment fields.

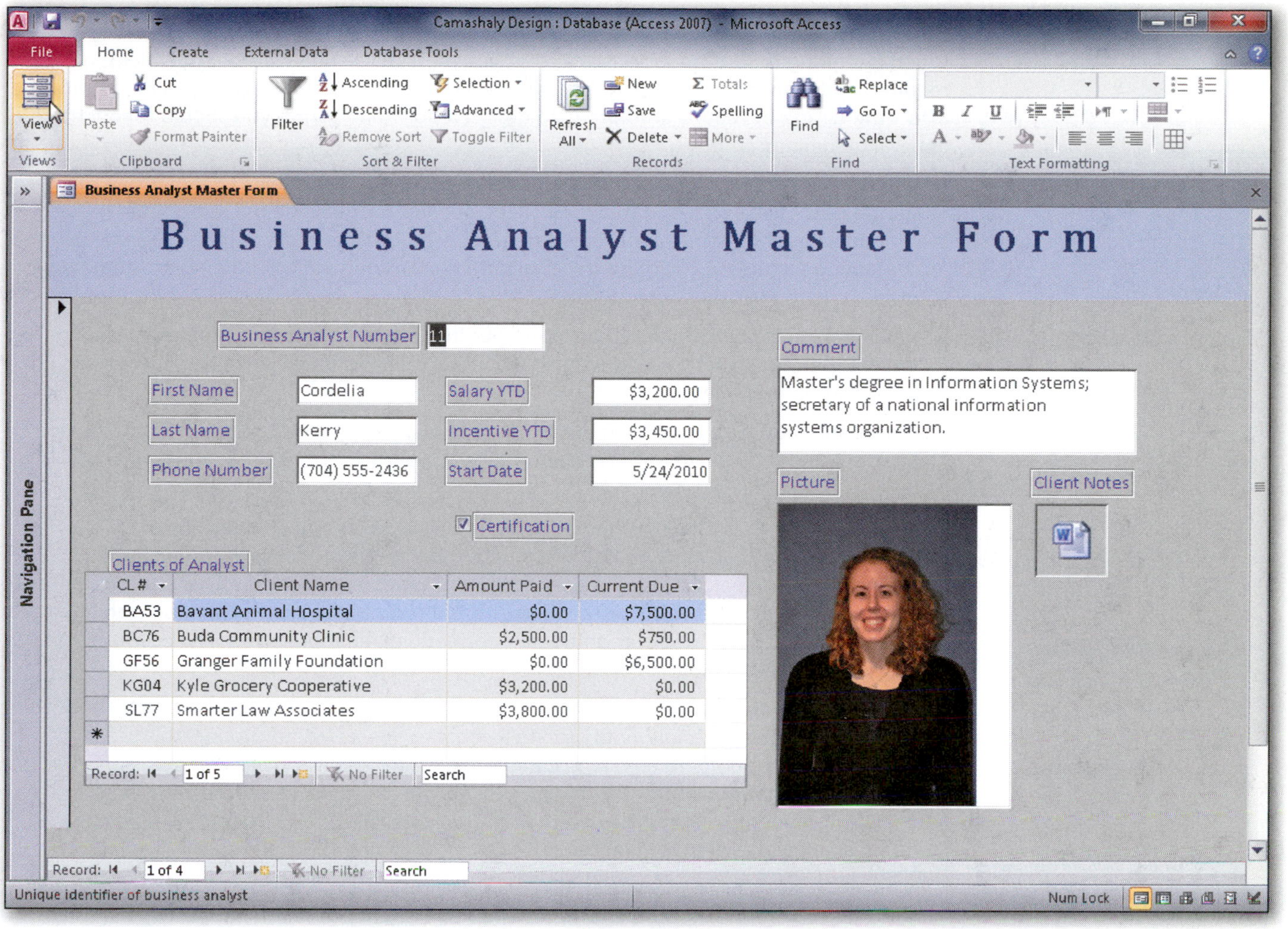

Figure 5–1

Overview

As you read through this chapter, you will learn how to create forms by performing these general tasks:

- Add the Certification, Start Date, Comment, Picture, and Client Notes fields to the Business Analyst Table and assign each field the appropriate data type.
- Add the Phone Number to the Business Analyst Table and create an appropriate input mask to automatically format the number.
- Create the Business Analyst Master Form and add the fields from the Business Analyst Table at the appropriate positions.
- Add a subform containing the Client Number, Client Name, Amount Paid, and Current Due fields from the Client table.
- Enhance the form by applying colors and various special effects.
- Create and run queries that involve the Certification, Start Date, and Comment fields.

Plan Ahead

Report and Form Design Guidelines

When designing reports and forms in Access, you must determine whether new fields are required and identify the source (table or tables) of the data. The decisions you make will affect the design of reports and forms. To design reports and forms, you should follow these general guidelines:

1. **When new fields are needed, determine the purpose of those fields to see if they need special data types.** Special data types will be needed for those fields that contain dates, contain values of Yes or No, or record an extended description of something. Fields containing pictures also require a special data type, as do fields containing attachments of files created in other applications.

2. **When a form is required, determine whether the form requires data from more than one table.** Determine whether all the data is found in a single table or whether it comes from multiple related tables.

3. **If the form requires data from more than one table, determine the relationship between the tables.** Identify one-to-many relationships. For each relationship, identify the "one" table and the "many" table.

4. **If the form requires data from more than one table, determine on which of the tables the form is to be based.** Which table contains data that is the focus of the form? For example, determine whether it is a form about business analysts that happens to require some client data to be effective or whether it is a form about clients that also includes some business analyst data as additional information. The table on which the form is based is the main table.

5. **Determine the fields from each table that need to be on the form.** Decide exactly how the form will be used and identify the fields that are necessary to support this use. Determine whether there are any additional fields that, while not strictly necessary, would make the form more functional. For example, if a user is entering a business analyst number on a form based on clients, it may be helpful to also see the name of the business analyst with that number.

When necessary, more specific details concerning the above decisions and/or actions are presented at appropriate points within the chapter. The chapter also will identify the use of these guidelines in the design of forms such as the one shown in Figure 5–1.

To Start Access

The Ribbon and Screen Resolution
Access may change how the groups and buttons within the groups appear on the Ribbon, depending on the computer's screen resolution. Thus, your Ribbon may look different from the ones in this book if you are using a screen resolution other than 1024 × 768.

The following steps, which assume Windows 7 is running, start Access based on a typical installation. You may need to ask your instructor how to start Access for your computer.

1 Click the Start button on the Windows 7 taskbar to display the Start menu.

2 Type `Microsoft Access` as the search text in the 'Search programs and files' text box and watch the search results appear on the Start menu.

3 Click Microsoft Access 2010 in the search results on the Start menu to start Access.

4 If the Access window is not maximized, click the Maximize button next to the Close button on its title bar to maximize the window.

To Open a Database from Access

The following steps open the Camashaly Design database from the Access folder in the CIS 101 folder on the USB flash drive.

1 With your USB flash drive connected to one of the computer's USB ports, click File on the Ribbon to open the Backstage view.

2 Click Open in the Backstage view to display the Open dialog box.

3 Navigate to the location of the file to be opened (in this case, the USB flash drive, then to the CIS 101 folder [or your class folder], and then to the Access folder).

4 Click Camashaly Design to select the file to be opened.

5 Click the Open button (Open dialog box) to open the selected file and display the opened database in the Access window.

6 If a Security Warning appears, click the Enable Content button.

Adding Special Fields

Having analyzed its requirements, the management of Camashaly has identified a need for some new fields for the Business Analyst Table. They need a Phone Number field and they want to assist users in entering the correct format for a phone number, so the field will use an input mask. An **input mask** specifies how data is to be entered and how it will appear. Camashaly also needs a Certification field, which uses a value of Yes or No to indicate whether an analyst is certified; this field's data type will be Yes/No. They need a Start Date field, which will be a Date/Time field, that is, a field whose data type is Date/Time. They need a Comment field, which will be a Memo field. Because no special text formatting, such as bold or italic, is required in the Comment field, the value of the Text Format property will remain Plain Text rather than Rich Text. The Client Notes field, which must be able to contain multiple attachments for each business analyst, will be an Attachment field. The Picture field is the only field whose data type is uncertain — it could be either OLE Object, which can contain objects created by a variety of applications, or Attachment.

Certainly OLE Object is an appropriate data type for a picture, because when you store an image as an OLE object, the image stays with the database. On the other hand, if an Attachment field contains a picture, the field will display the picture. For other types of attachments, such as Word documents and Excel spreadsheets, however, the Attachment field displays an icon representing the attachment. Camashaly Design has decided to use OLE Object as the Picture field data type for two reasons. First, the form shown in Figure 5–1 contains another field that must be an Attachment field, the Client Notes field. In Datasheet view, an Attachment field appears as a paper clip rather than the field name. Thus, if the Picture field were also an Attachment field, the form would display two paper clips, leading to potential confusion. A second potential problem with using an Attachment field for pictures occurs when you have multiple attachments to a record. Only the first attachment routinely appears in the field on either a datasheet or form. Thus, if the picture were not the first attachment, it would not appear.

BTW

Memo Fields
If you need to keep a historical record of changes to a memo field, set the value for the Append Only property to yes.

**Plan
Ahead**

Determine the purpose of new fields to see if they need special data types.
If you determine that you need new fields in a table, you then need to determine data types for these fields. Special data types include Yes/No, Date/Time, Memo, OLE Object, Attachment, and Hyperlink. To standardize the appearance of data, you can create an input mask, which applies common formatting to date, phone number, and other types of information.

- **Determine whether an input mask is appropriate.** Sometimes the data in the field should be displayed in a special way, for example, with parentheses and a hyphen like a phone number, or separated into three groups of digits like a Social Security number. If so, should Access assist the user in entering the data in the right format? For example, by including an input mask in a field, Access can automatically insert the parentheses and a hyphen when a user enters a phone number.

- **Determine whether the Yes/No data type is appropriate.** A field is a good candidate for the Yes/No data type if the only possible field values are Yes or No, True or False, or On or Off.

- **Determine whether the Date/Time data type is appropriate.** If a field contains a date, assigning it the Date/Time data type accomplishes several things. First, Access will ensure that the only values entered in the field are legitimate dates. Second, you can perform date arithmetic. For example, you can subtract one date from another to find the number of days between the two dates. Finally, you can sort the field and the dates will sort chronologically.

- **Determine whether the Memo data type is appropriate.** A field that contains text that is variable in length and potentially very lengthy is an appropriate use of the Memo data type. If you want to use special text effects, such as bold and italic, you can assign the field the Memo data type and change the value of the field's Text Format property from Plain Text to Rich Text. You can also collect history on the changes to a Memo field by changing the value of the field's Append Only property from No to Yes. If you do so, when you right-click the field and click Show Column History on the shortcut menu, you will see a record of all changes made to the field.

- **Determine whether the OLE Object data type is appropriate.** Does the field contain objects created by other applications that support **OLE (Object Linking and Embedding)** as a server? OLE is a feature of Microsoft Windows that creates a special relationship between Microsoft Access and the application that created the object. When you edit the object, Microsoft Access returns automatically to the application that created the object.

- **Determine whether the Attachment data type is appropriate.** Will the field contain one or more attachments that were created in other applications? If so, the Attachment data type is appropriate. It allows you to store multiple attachments on each record. You can view and manipulate these attachments in their original application.

- **Determine whether the Hyperlink data type is appropriate.** Will the field contain links to other Office documents or to Web pages? If so, Hyperlink is appropriate.

To Add Fields with New Data Types to a Table

You add the new fields to the Business Analyst Table by modifying the design of the table and inserting the fields at the appropriate position in the table structure. The following steps add the Certification, Start Date, Comment, Picture, and Client Notes fields to the Business Analyst Table.

1

- If necessary, open the Navigation Pane.

- Right-click the Business Analyst Table to display a shortcut menu (Figure 5–2).

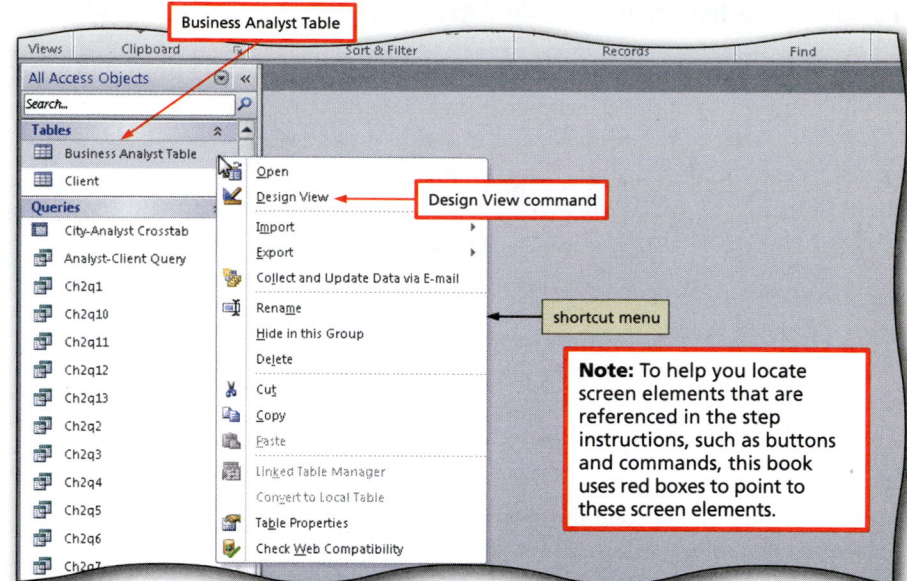

Figure 5–2

2

- Click Design View on the shortcut menu to open the table in Design view (Figure 5–3).

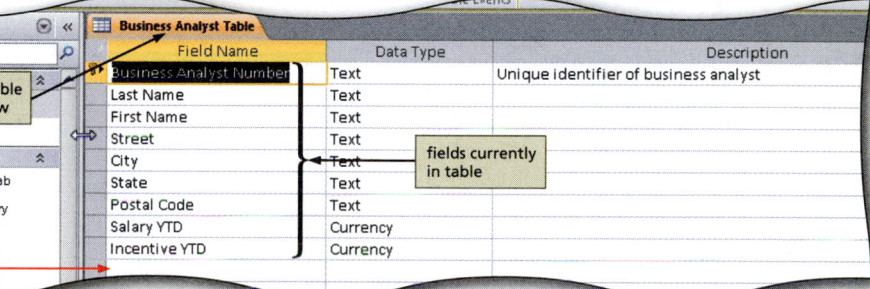

Figure 5–3

3

- Click the first open field to select the position for the first additional field.

- Type **Certification** as the field name, press the TAB key, select Yes/No as the data type, and then press the TAB key twice to move to the next field.

- In a similar fashion, add a field with **Start Date** as the field name and Date/Time as the data type, a field with **Comment** as the field name and Memo as the data type, a field with **Picture** as the field name and OLE Object as the data type, and a field with **Client Notes** as the field name and Attachment as the data type (Figure 5–4).

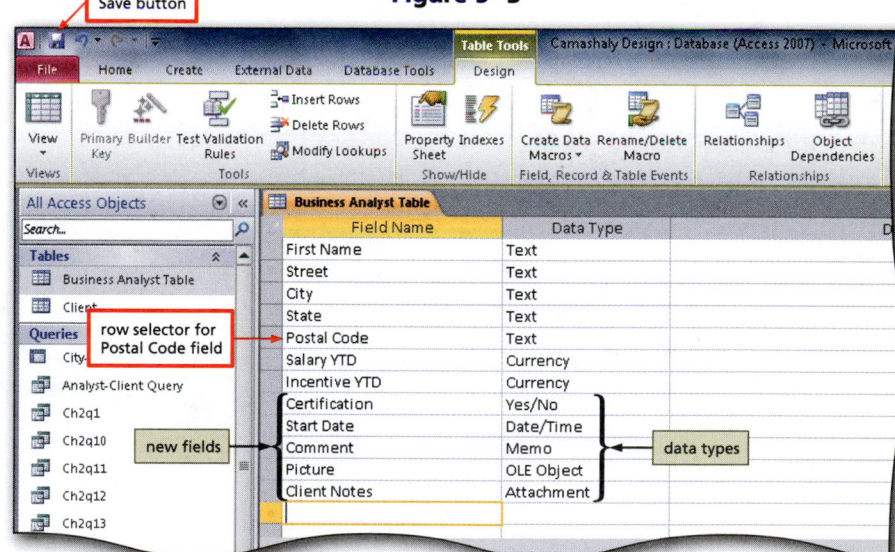

Figure 5–4

Q&A

Why use Date/Time as a data type for date fields rather than Text?

If you use Date/Time, the computer will ensure that only legitimate dates are entered in the field. In addition, you can perform appropriate arithmetic with dates. You also can sort by date.

4

- Click the Save button on the Quick Access Toolbar to save your changes.

To Use the Input Mask Wizard

An **input mask** specifies how data is to be entered and how it will appear. You can enter an input mask directly or you can use the Input Mask Wizard. The wizard assists you in the creation of the input mask by allowing you to select from a list of the most frequently used input masks.

To use the Input Mask Wizard, select the Input Mask property in the field's property sheet and then select the Build button. The following steps add the Phone Number field and then specify how the telephone number is to appear by using the Input Mask Wizard.

- Click the row selector for the Postal Code field (shown in Figure 5–4), and then press the INSERT key to insert a blank row above Postal Code.

- Click the Field Name column for the new field.

- Type **Phone Number** as the field name and then press the TAB key to enter the field.

- Click the Input Mask property box (Figure 5–5).

Q&A

Do I need to change the data type?

No. Text is the appropriate data type for the Phone Number field.

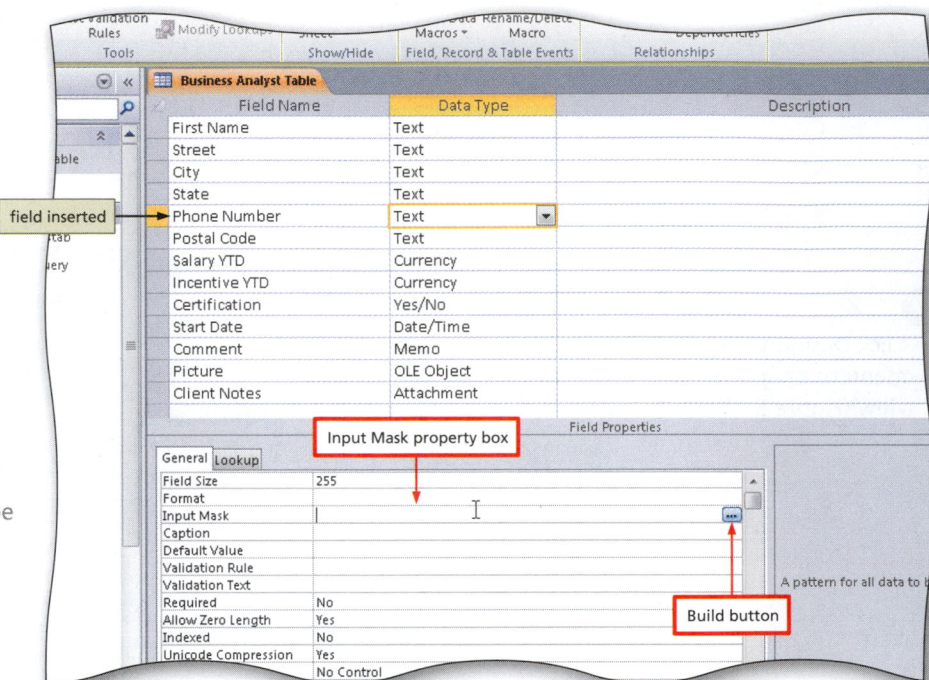

Figure 5–5

2

- Click the Build button to use a wizard to enter the input mask.

- If a dialog box appears asking you to save the table, click the Yes button. (If a dialog box displays a message that the Input Mask Wizard is not installed, check with your instructor before proceeding with the following steps.)

- Ensure that Phone Number is selected (Figure 5–6).

 **Experiment**

- Click different input masks and enter data in the Try It text box to see the effect of the input mask. When done, click the Phone Number input mask.

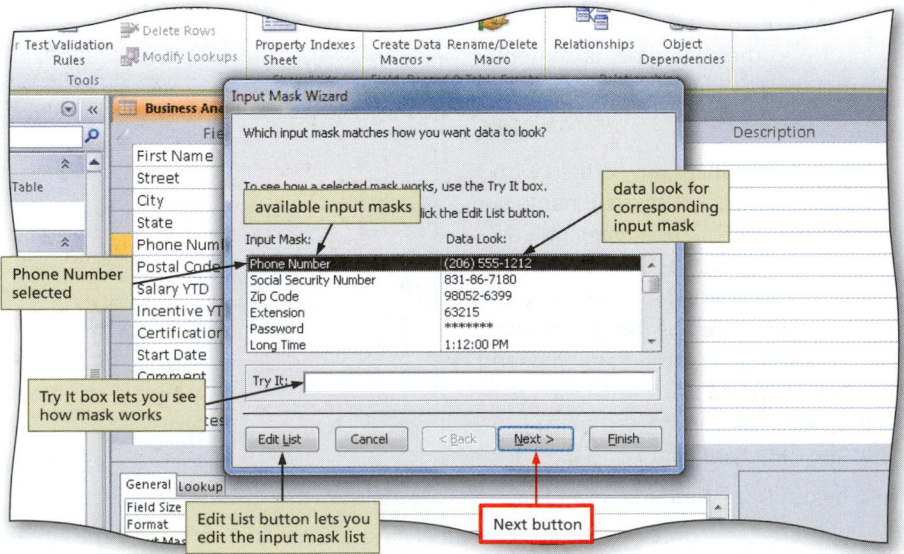

Figure 5–6

3

- Click the Next button to move to the next Input Mask Wizard screen, where you then are given the opportunity to change the input mask.

- Because you do not need to change the mask, click the Next button a second time (Figure 5–7).

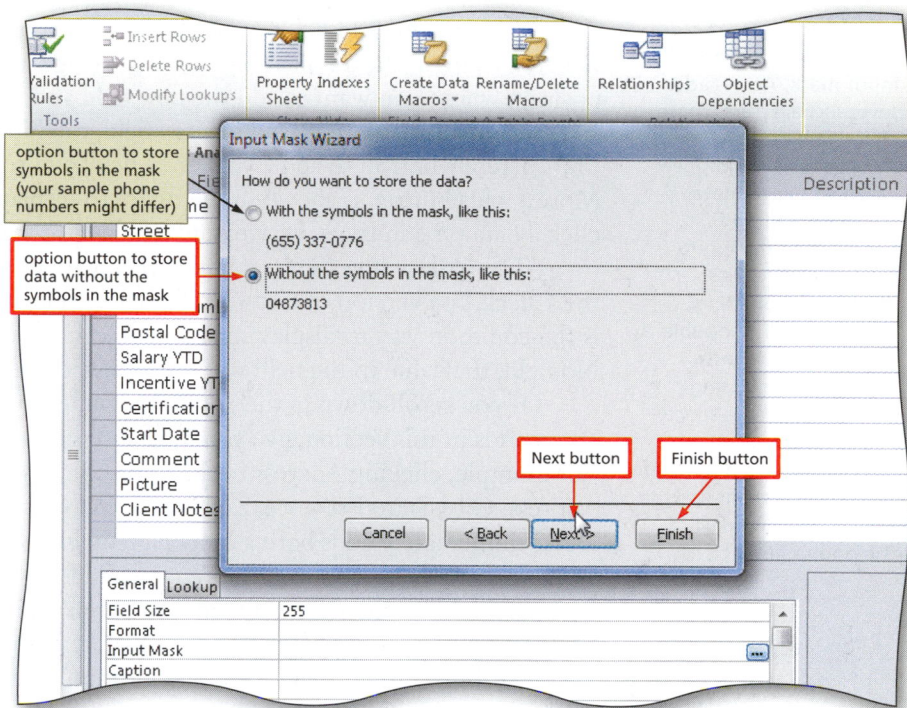

Figure 5–7

4

- Be sure the 'Without the symbols in the mask, like this' option button is selected, click the Next button to move to the next Input Mask Wizard screen, and then click the Finish button (Figure 5–8).

Q&A Why does the data type not change to Input Mask?

The data type of the Phone Number field is still Text. The only thing that changed is one of the field properties, the Input Mask property.

Q&A Could I have typed the value in the Input Mask property myself, rather than using the wizard?

Yes. Input masks can be complex, however, so it is usually easier and safer to use the wizard.

5

- Click the Save button on the Quick Access Toolbar to save your changes.

- Close the Business Analyst Table.

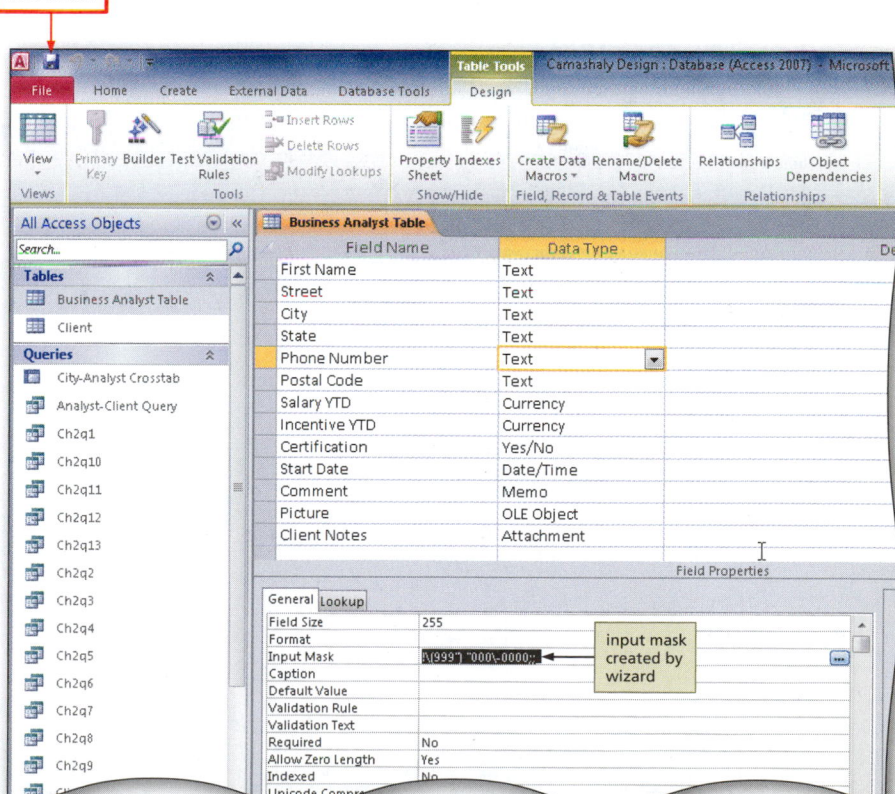

Figure 5–8

Adding Fields in Datasheet View

Input Mask Characters
When you create an input mask, Access adds several characters. These characters control the literal values that appear when you enter data. For example, the first backslash in the input mask in Figure 5–8 displays the opening parenthesis. The double quotes force Access to display the closing parenthesis and a space. The second backslash forces Access to display the hyphen that separates the first and second part of the phone number.

You can also add fields in Datasheet view. One way to do so is to use the Add & Delete group on the Table Tools Fields tab (Figure 5–9). Select the field that precedes the position where you want to add the new field and then click the appropriate button. You can click the Text button to add a Text field, the Number button to add a Number field, the Currency button to add a Currency field, and so on. Alternatively, you can click the More Fields button as shown in the figure to display the Data Type gallery. You then can click a data type in the gallery to add a field with that type.

The gallery gives some additional control on the data type. For example, if you click the Check Box version of a Yes/No field, the field will be displayed as a check box, which is the common way to display such a field. If instead you click the Yes/No version of a Yes/No field, the value in the field will be displayed as either the word, Yes, or the word, No.

If you scroll down in the Data Type gallery, you will find a Quick Start section. The commands in this section give you quick ways of adding some common types of fields. For example, clicking Address in the Quick Start section immediately adds several fields: Address, City, State Province, Zip Postal, and Country Region. Clicking Start and End Dates immediately adds both a Start Date field and an End Date field.

In Datasheet view, you can rename fields by right-clicking the field name, clicking Rename Field on the shortcut menu, and then typing the new name. Delete a field by clicking the field and then clicking the Delete button (Table Tools Fields tab | Add & Delete group). Move a field from one location to another by dragging the field.

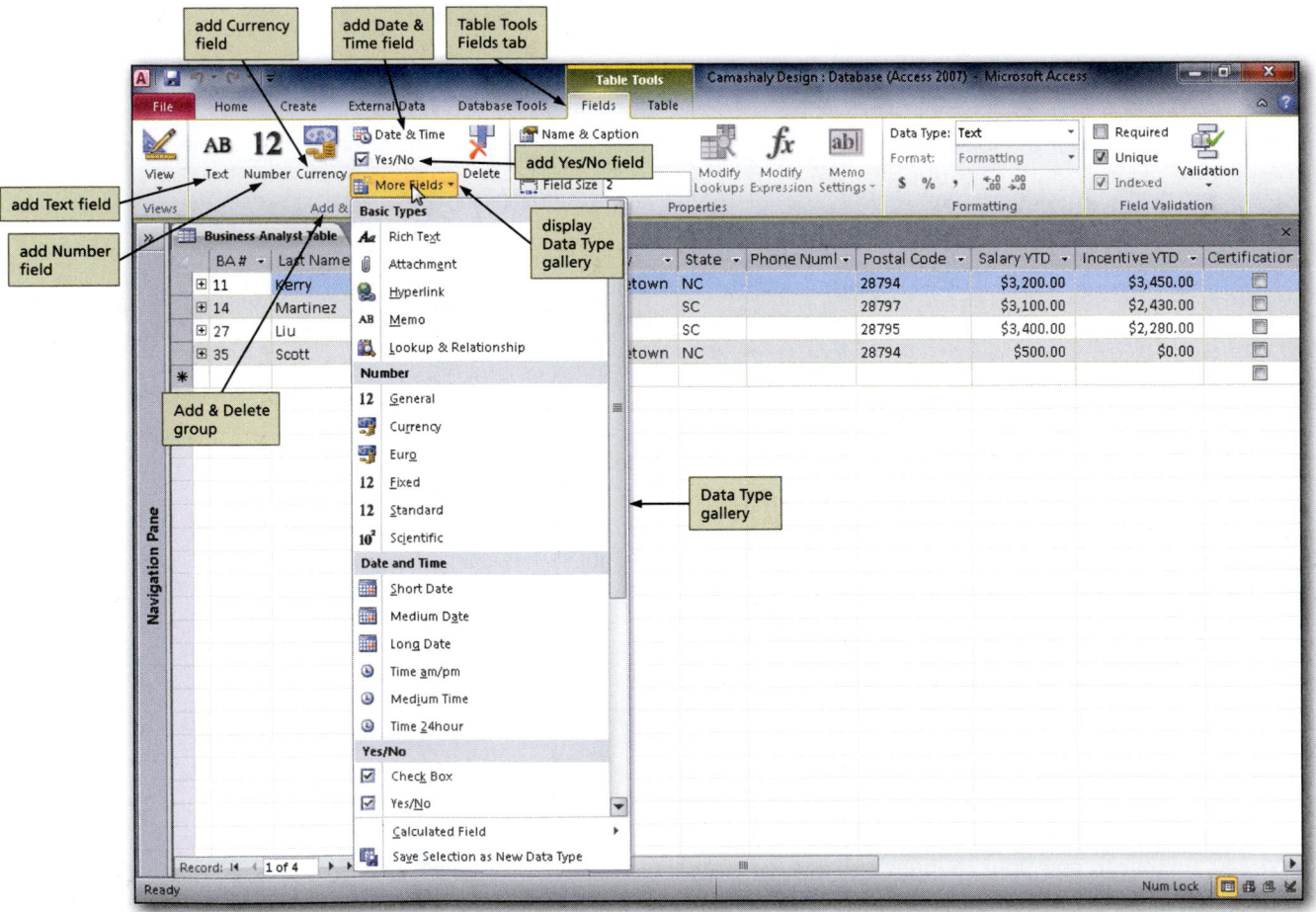

Figure 5–9

Updating the New Fields

After adding the new fields to the table, the next task is to enter data into the fields. The data type determines the manner in which this is accomplished. The following sections cover the methods for updating fields with an input mask, Yes/No fields, Date/Time fields, Memo fields, OLE fields, and Attachment fields. They also show how you would enter data in Hyperlink fields.

To Enter Data Using an Input Mask

When you are entering data in a field that has an input mask, Access will insert the appropriate special characters in the proper positions. This means Access automatically will insert the parentheses around the area code, the space following the second parenthesis, and the hyphen in the Phone Number field. The following steps use the input mask to add the telephone numbers.

1
- Open the Business Analyst Table and close the Navigation Pane.

- Click at the beginning of the Phone Number field on the first record to display an insertion point in the field (Figure 5–10).

Q&A
Q&A I do not see the parentheses and hyphen as shown in the figure. Did I do something wrong?

It depends on exactly where you click as to whether you will see the symbols. In any case, as soon as you start typing in the field, the symbols should appear.

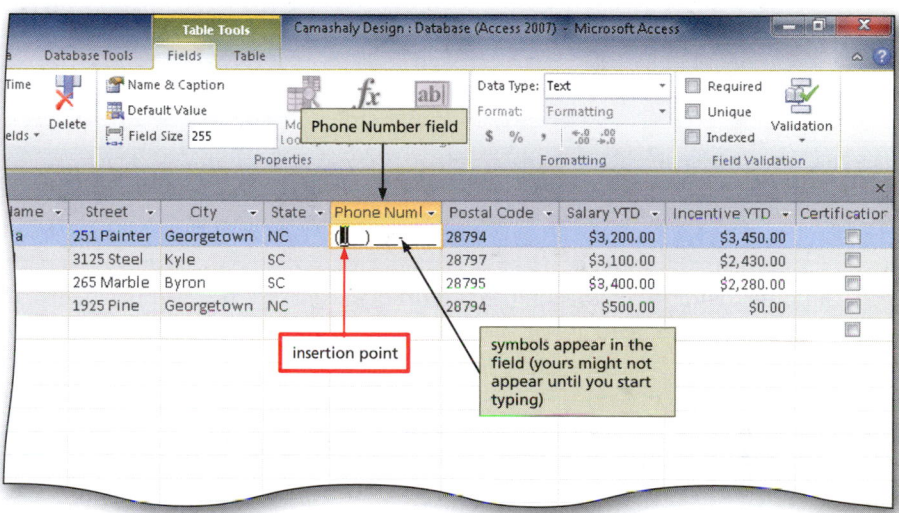

Figure 5–10

2
- Type 7045552436 as the telephone number (Figure 5–11).

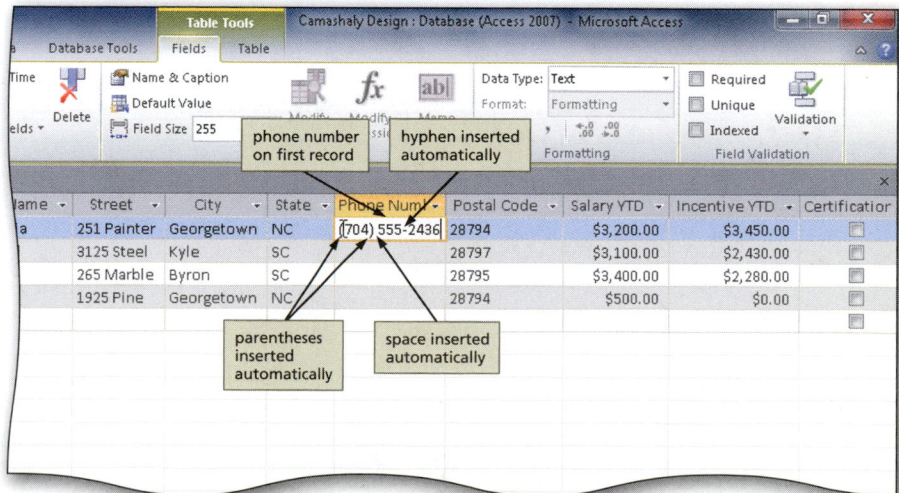

Figure 5–11

3

- Use the same technique to enter the remaining telephone numbers, as shown in Figure 5–12.

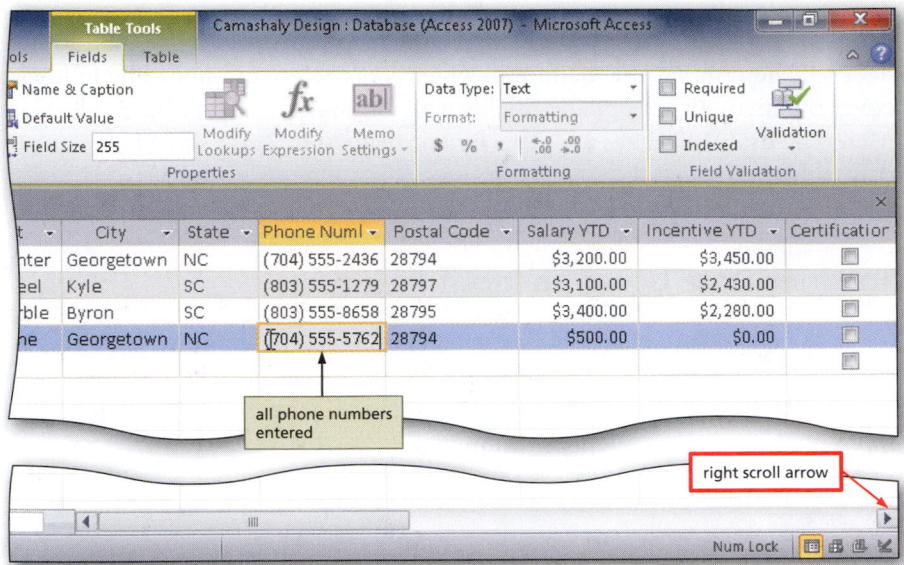

Figure 5–12

To Enter Data in Yes/No Fields

Fields that are Yes/No fields contain check boxes. To set the value to Yes, place a check mark in the check box. To set a value to No, leave the check box blank. The following steps set the value of the Certification field, a Yes/No field, to Yes for the first and fourth records.

1

- Repeatedly click the right scroll arrow (shown in Figure 5–12) until the new fields appear.

- Click the check box in the Certification field on the first record to place a check mark in the box (Figure 5–13).

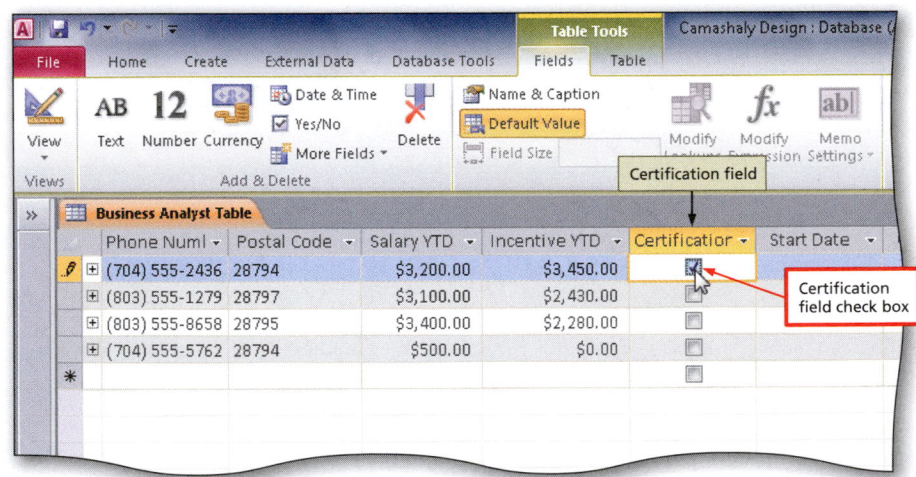

Figure 5–13

Q&A

What is the meaning of the check mark?

A check mark indicates the value in the Certification field is Yes. If there is no check mark, the value is No.

2

- Click the check box in the Certification field on the fourth record to place a check mark in the box.

To Enter Data in Date/Time Fields

To enter data in Date/Time fields, you can simply type the dates and include slashes (/). As an alternative, you can click the field, click the Date Picker that will appear next to the field, and then use the calendar to select the date. The following step adds the start dates for the business analysts.

- Click the Start Date field on the first record, type `5/24/2010` as the date on the first record, and then press the DOWN ARROW key.

- Type `2/1/2011` as the start date on the second record, and then press the DOWN ARROW key.

- Type `5/16/2011` as the start date on the third record, and then press the DOWN ARROW key.

- Type `1/9/2012` as the start date on the fourth record (Figure 5–14).

Q&A

How do I use the Date Picker?

Click the Date Picker to display a calendar. Scroll to the month and year you want and then click the desired day of the month.

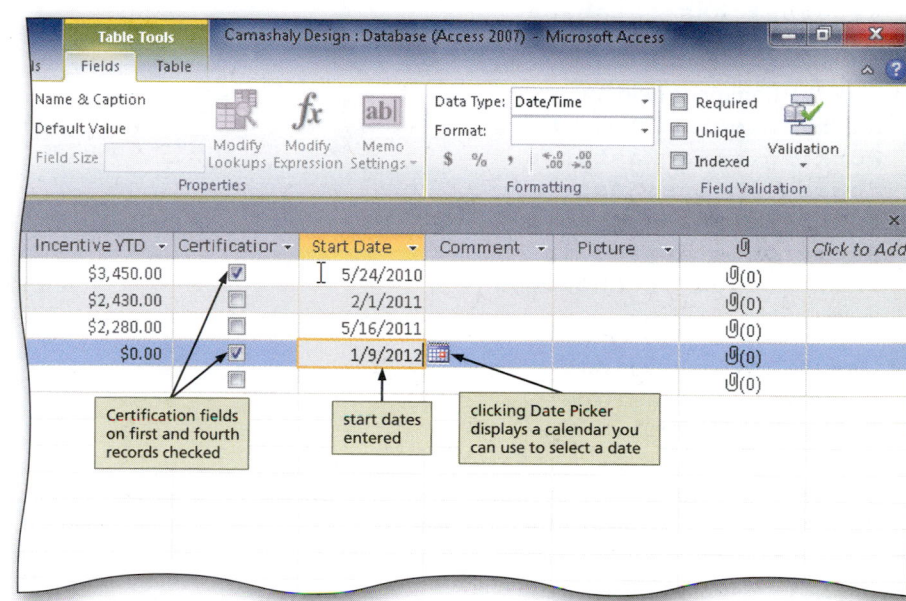

Figure 5–14

Experiment

- Click the Date Picker on the last record and use it to assign a date. When finished, change the date to 1/9/2012.

BTW

Memo Fields
You also can enter data in a memo field using the Zoom dialog box. To do so, click the memo field and then press SHIFT+F2 to open the Zoom dialog box.

To Enter Data in Memo Fields

To update a memo field, simply type the data in the field. With the current row and column spacing on the screen, only a small portion of the memo will appear. To correct this problem, you will change the spacing later to allow more room for the memo. The following steps enter each business analyst's comment.

- If necessary, click the right scroll arrow (shown in Figure 5–12) so the Comment field appears.

- Click the Comment field on the first record, and then type `Master's degree in Information Systems; secretary of a national information systems organization.` as the entry (Figure 5–15).

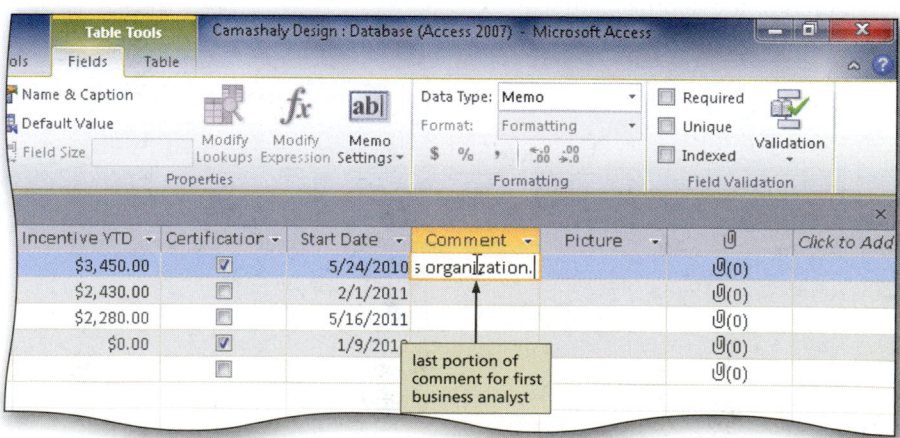

Figure 5–15

2

- Click the Comment field on the second record, and then type `Bachelor's degree in Business Administration; veteran; has database experience.` as the entry.

- Click the Comment field on the third record, and then type `Working on a Master's degree in Business Administration; has a Bachelor's degree in Information Technology.` as the entry.

- Click the Comment field on the fourth record, and then type `Bachelor's degree in Computer Science; active in promoting CS as a major to young adults.` as the entry (Figure 5–16).

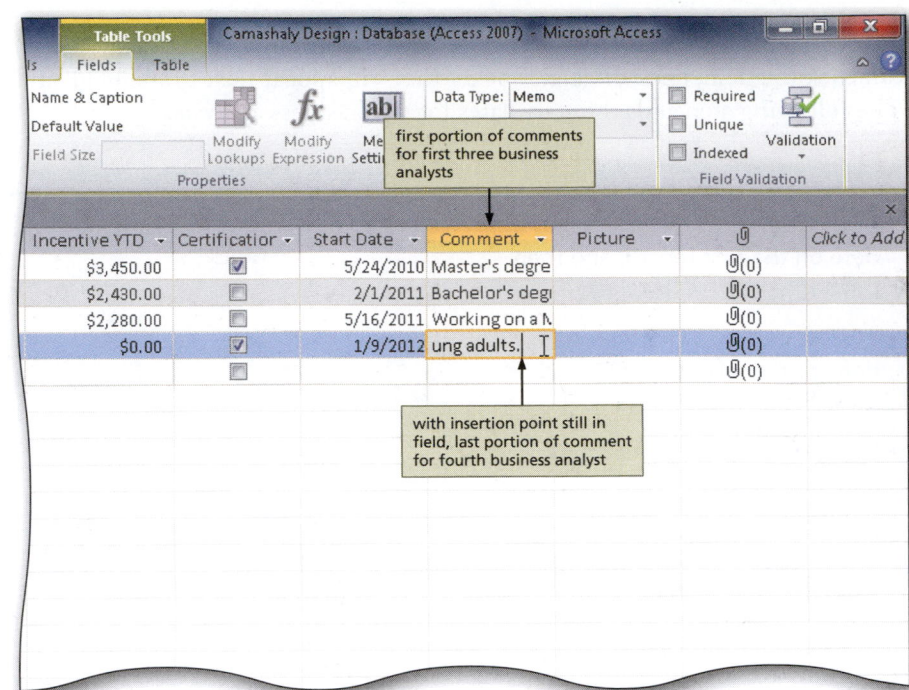

Figure 5–16

To Change the Row and Column Size

Only a small portion of the comments appears in the datasheet. To allow more of the information to appear, you can expand the size of the rows and the columns. You can change the size of a column by using the field selector. The **field selector** is the bar containing the field name. To change the size of a row, you use a record's **record selector**, which is the small box at the beginning of each record.

The following steps resize the column containing the Comment field and the rows of the table so a larger portion of the Comment field text will appear.

1

- Drag the right edge of the field selector for the Comment field to the right to resize the Comment column to the approximate size shown in Figure 5–17.

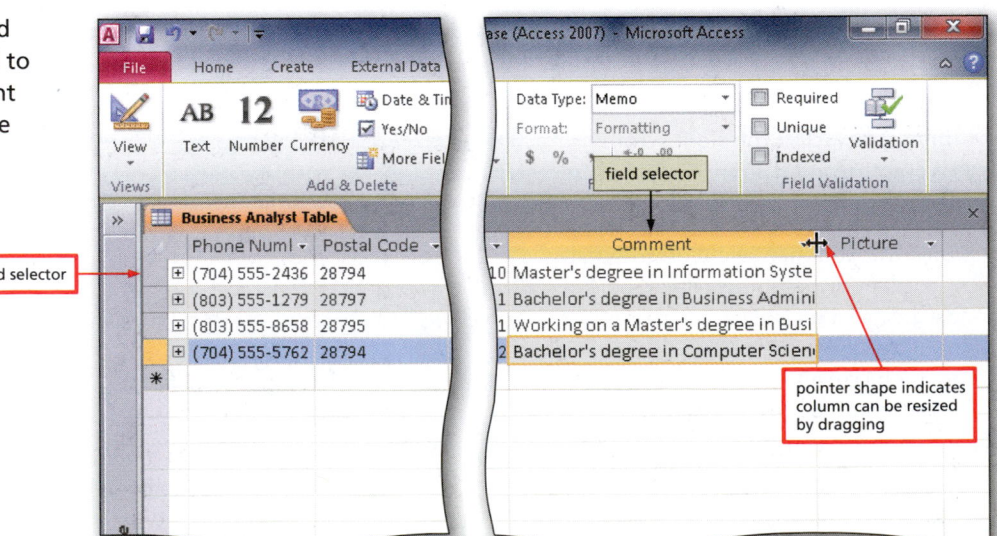

Figure 5–17

2

- Drag the lower edge of the record selector to approximately the position shown in Figure 5–18.

Q&A Can rows be different sizes?

No. All rows must be the same size.

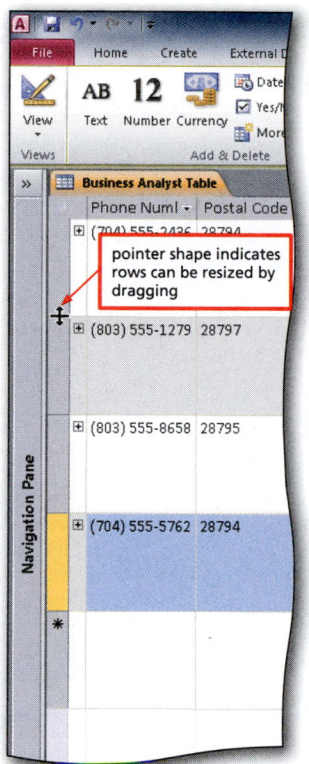
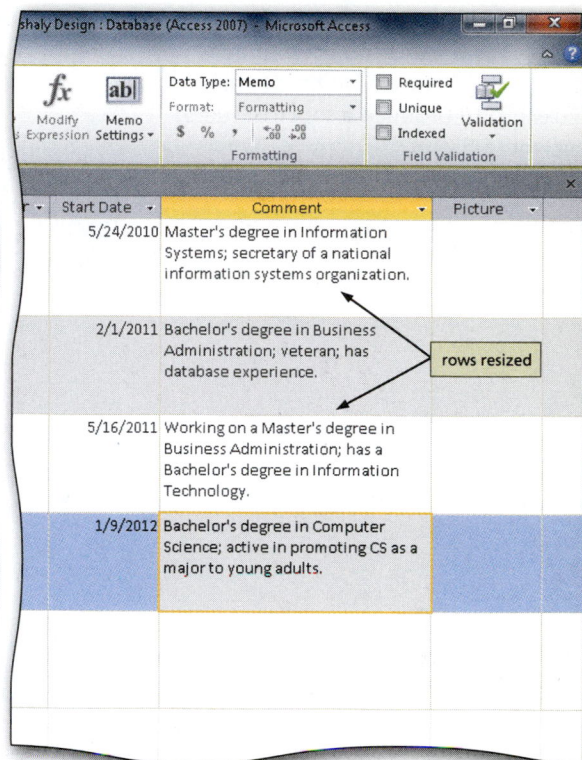

Figure 5–18

Other Ways	
1. Right-click record selector, click Row Height to change row spacing	2. Right-click field selector, click Field Width to change column size

Undoing Changes to Row Height and Column Width

If you later find that the changes you made to the row height or the column width are no longer appropriate, you can undo them. To undo changes to the row height, right-click the row selector, click Row Height on the shortcut menu, and then click the Standard Height check box in the Row Height dialog box. To undo changes to the column width, right-click the field selector, click Field Width on the shortcut menu, and then click the Standard Width check box in the Column Width dialog box.

To Enter Data in OLE Object Fields

To insert data into an OLE Object field, you use the Insert Object command on the OLE field's shortcut menu. The Insert Object command presents a list of the various types of objects that can be inserted. Access then opens the corresponding application to create the object; for example, Microsoft Excel Chart. If the object already is created and stored in a file, as is the case in this project, you simply insert it directly from the file.

The following steps insert pictures into the Picture field. The pictures will be visible as photographs in the form; however, the table will display the text, Bitmap Image, in the Picture field. The steps assume that the pictures are located in a folder called AccessData on your USB drive. If your pictures are located elsewhere, you will need to make the appropriate changes.

1

- Ensure the Picture field appears on your screen, and then right-click the Picture field on the first record to produce a shortcut menu (Figure 5–19).

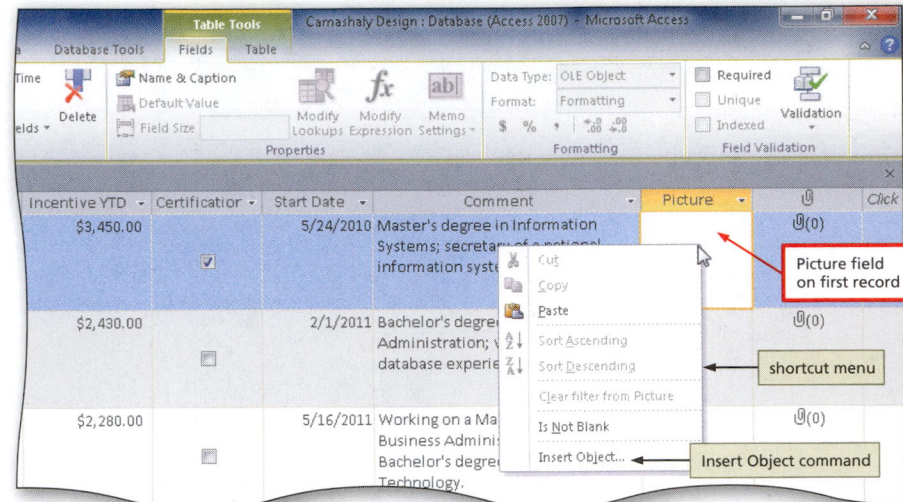

Figure 5–19

2

- Click Insert Object on the shortcut menu to display the Microsoft Access dialog box (Figure 5–20).

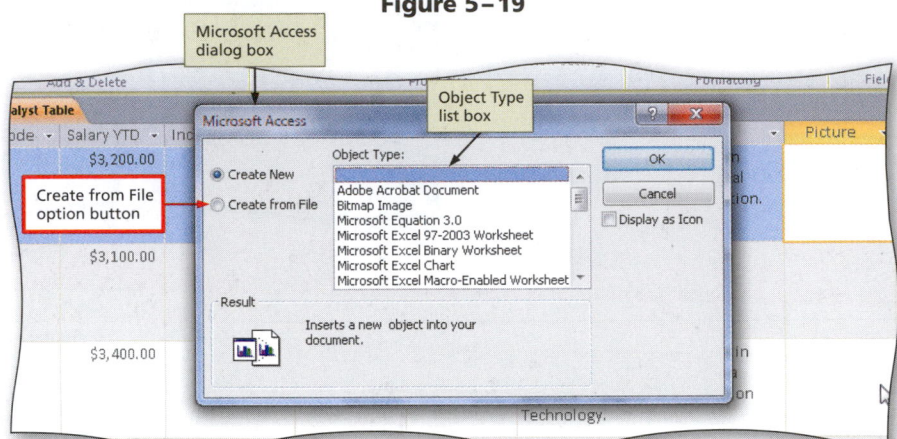

Figure 5–20

3

- Click the 'Create from File' option button, and then click the Browse button to display the Browse dialog box.

- Navigate to the AccessData folder on your USB drive in the Browse dialog box. (If your pictures are located elsewhere, navigate to the folder where they are located instead of the AccessData folder.)

- Click Pict1 and then click the OK button (Browse dialog box) to select the appropriate picture (Figure 5–21).

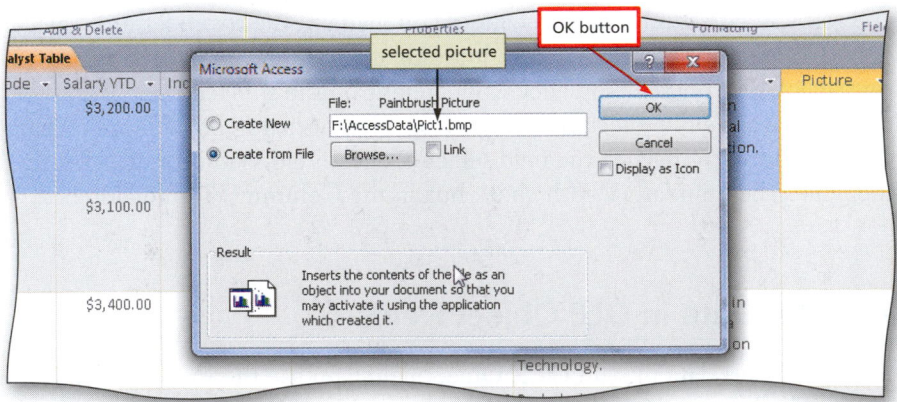

Figure 5–21

4

- Click the OK button to insert the picture into the table.

Q&A

I do not see the picture. I just see the words, Bitmap Image. Is that correct?

Yes. You will see the actual picture when you use this field in a form.

Bitmap Image

The entries in the Picture field all should be the words, Bitmap Image. You will not see the actual picture of the business analyst. The entries may initially be something other than the words, Bitmap Image, but, if so, they should change to the words, Bitmap Image, after you move to another record. They also should change after you close and reopen the table.

To Change Picture Field Entries to Bitmap Image

If the entries do not change to the words, Bitmap Image, there is a problem either with the graphics filters that are installed or with the file associations for BMP files. You would use a slightly different technique to add the pictures, as in the following steps:

1. Right-click the Picture field, click Insert Object, *and then* select the Bitmap Image object type from the Object Type list.
2. Click the OK button to open the Paint application. If necessary, maximize the Paint window.
3. Click the Paste button arrow (Home tab | Clipboard group), and then click the Paste from command.
4. Navigate to the location for the desired BMP file, select the file, and then click the Open button.
5. Click the Paint button, which is just to the left of the Home tab, and then click the 'Exit and return to document' command to return to the table.

BTW

OLE Fields
OLE fields can occupy a great deal of space. To save space in your database, you can convert a picture from Bitmap Image to Picture (Device Independent Bitmap). To make the conversion, right-click the field, click Bitmap Image Object, click Convert, and then select Picture (Device Independent Bitmap) in the Convert dialog box.

To Enter the Remaining Pictures

The following step adds the remaining pictures. If you have the problem indicated in the previous section, you should use the suggested technique to add the pictures.

1 Insert the pictures into the second, third, and fourth records using the techniques illustrated in the previous set of steps. For the second record, select the picture named Pict2. For the third record, select the picture named Pict3. For the fourth record, select Pict4.

To Enter Data in Attachment Fields

To insert data into an Attachment field, you use the Manage Attachments command on the Attachment field's shortcut menu. The Manage Attachments command displays the Attachments dialog box, which you can use to attach as many files as necessary to the field. The following steps attach two files to the first business analyst and one file to the fourth business analyst. The second and third business analysts currently have no attachments.

1

- Ensure the Client Notes field, which has a paper clip in the field selector, appears on your screen, and then right-click the Client Notes field on the first record to produce a shortcut menu (Figure 5–22).

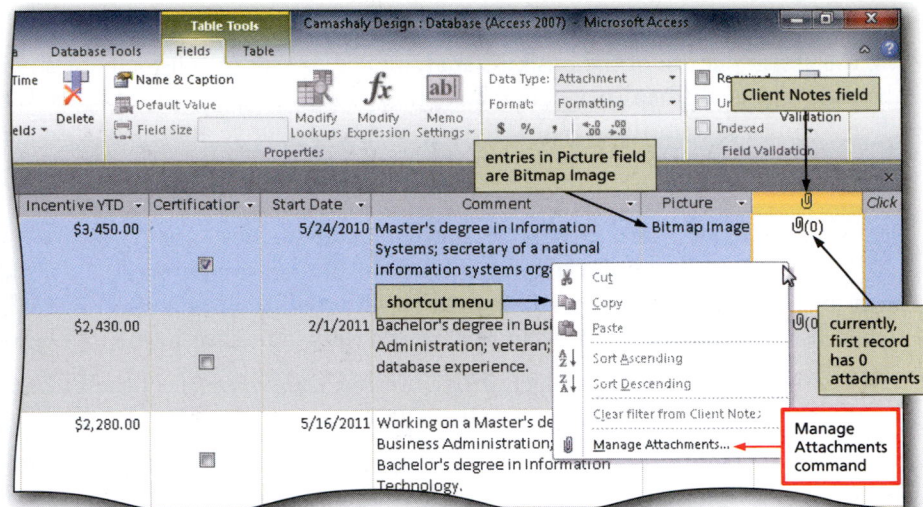

Figure 5–22

2

- Click Manage Attachments on the shortcut menu to display the Attachments dialog box (Figure 5–23).

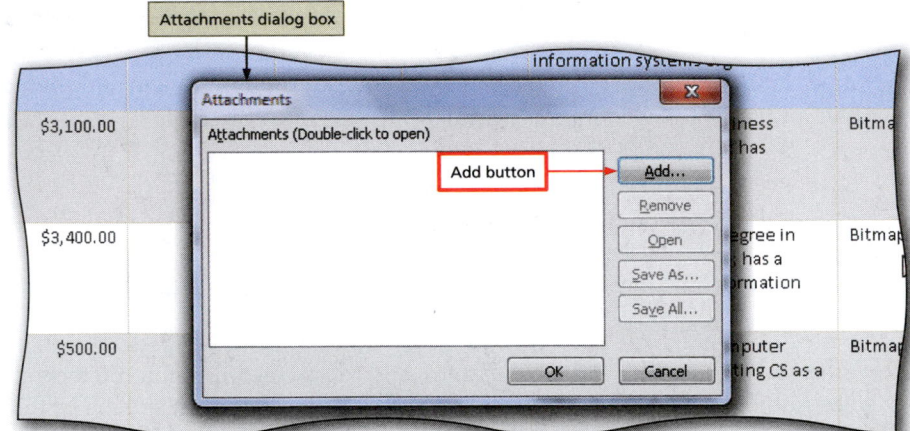

Figure 5–23

3

- Click the Add button (Attachments dialog box) to add an attachment.

- Navigate to the AccessData folder on your USB drive in the Choose File dialog box. (If your files are located elsewhere, navigate to the folder where they are located instead of the AccessData folder.)

- Click Cordelia Kerry Clients, a Word file, and then click the Open button (Choose File dialog box) to attach the file.

- Click the Add button (Attachments dialog box).

- Click the Cordelia Kerry Potential Clients, an Excel file, and then click the Open button to attach the file (Figure 5–24).

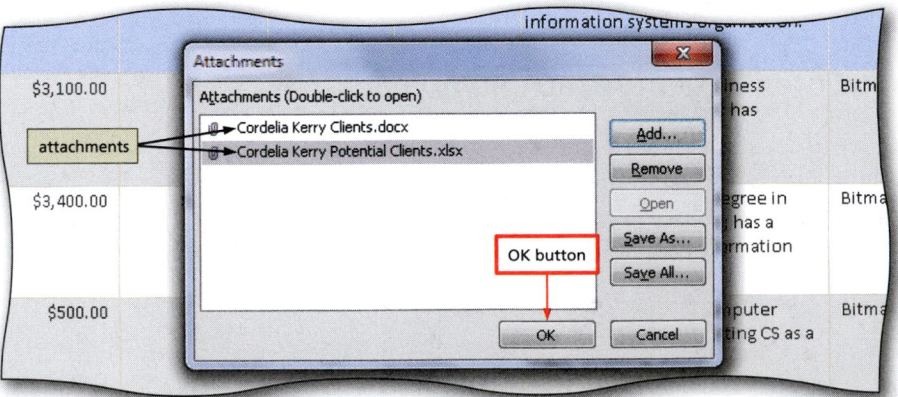

Figure 5–24

4

- Click the OK button (Attachments dialog box) to close the Attachments dialog box.

- Using the same technique, attach the Jeff Scott Potential Clients file to the fourth record (Figure 5–25). (The second and third records have no attachments.)

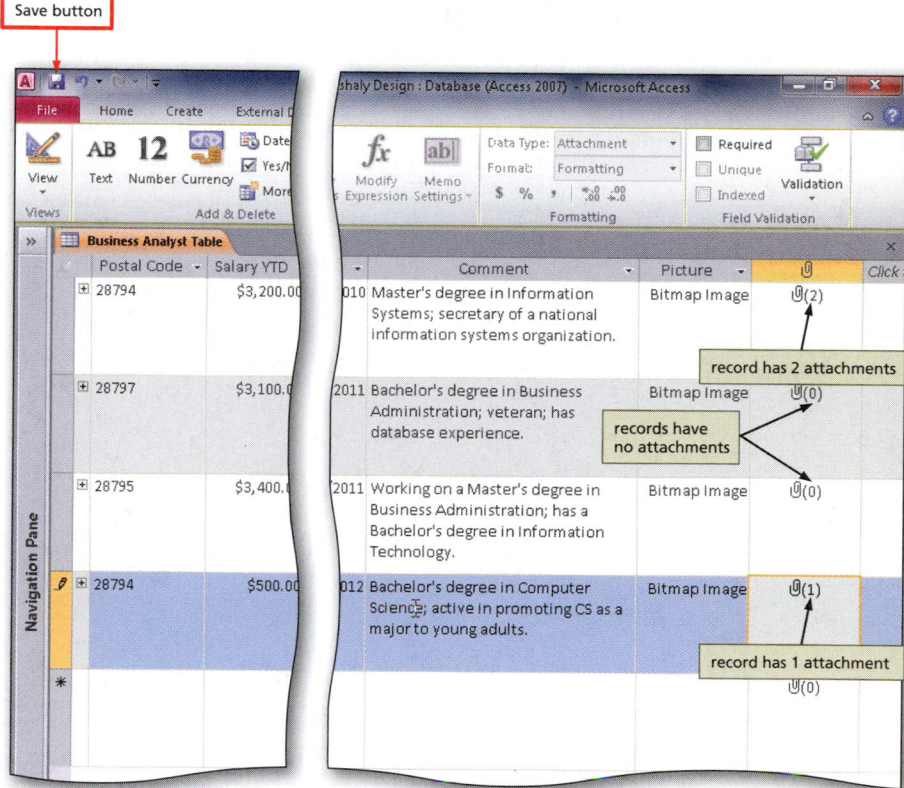

Figure 5–25

TO ENTER DATA IN HYPERLINK FIELDS

If you had a Hyperlink field, you would insert data by using the following steps.

1. Right-click the Hyperlink field in which you want to enter data to display a shortcut menu.

2. Click Hyperlink on the shortcut menu to display the Hyperlink submenu.

3. Click Edit Hyperlink on the Hyperlink submenu to display the Insert Hyperlink dialog box.

4. Type the desired Web address in the Address text box.

5. Click the OK button (Insert Hyperlink dialog box).

To Save the Properties and Close the Table

The row and column spacing are table properties. When changing any table properties, the changes apply only as long as the table is active *unless they are saved*. Once you have saved them, they will apply every time you open the table.

The following steps first save the properties and then close the table.

1 Click the Save button on the Quick Access Toolbar to save the changes to the table properties.

2 Close the table.

Break Point: If you wish to stop working through the chapter at this point, you can resume the project at a later time by starting Access, opening the database called Camashaly Design, and continuing to follow the steps from this location forward.

Viewing Pictures and Attachments in Datasheet View

Although the pictures do not appear on the screen, you can view them within the table. To view the picture of a particular business analyst, right-click the Picture field for the business analyst. Click Bitmap Image Object on the shortcut menu, and then click Open. The picture will appear. Once you have finished viewing the picture, close the window containing the picture by clicking its Close button.

You can view the attachments in the Client Notes field by right-clicking the field and then clicking Manage Attachments on the shortcut menu. The attachments then appear in the Attachments dialog box. To view an attachment, click the attachment and then click the Open button (Attachments dialog box). The attachment will appear in its original application. After you have finished viewing the attachment, close the original application and close the dialog box.

Multitable Form Techniques

With the additional fields in place, Camashaly Design management is ready to incorporate data from both the Business Analyst and Client tables in a single form. The form will display data concerning one business analyst. It also will display data concerning the many clients assigned to the business analyst. The relationship between business analysts and clients is a one-to-many relationship in which the Business Analyst Table is the "one" table and the Client table is the "many" table.

To include the data for the many clients of a business analyst on the form, the client data will appear in a **subform**, which is a form that is contained within another form. The form in which the subform is contained is called the main form. Thus, the **main form** will contain business analyst data, and the subform will contain client data.

Plan Ahead

> **Determine on which of the tables the form is to be based.**
> Once you determine that you need data from more than one table, you need to determine the main table and its relationship to any other table.
>
> - **Determine the main table the form is intended to view and/or update.** You need to identify the purpose of the form and the table it is really intended to show, which is the main table. If the database contains a table that could be omitted and still have the form make sense, that is *not* the main table.
>
> - **Determine how the additional table should fit into the form.** If the additional table is the "many" part of the relationship, the data should probably be in a subform or datasheet. If the additional table is the "one" part of the relationship, the data should probably appear simply as fields on the form.

Plan Ahead

> **Determine the fields from each table that need to be on the form.**
> After you decide on which tables the form is based, you need to decide which fields to include.
>
> - **Determine the fields from the main table that should be included on the form.** Identify the fields that users want on the form and determine whether a particular order for the fields would be most useful.
>
> - **Determine the fields from the additional table that should be included on the form.** Identify the fields from the additional table that would be helpful in updating or viewing the fields from the main table and determine whether users should be able to change these fields using the form. (Often they should not be able to change the fields.)

To Create a Form in Design View

You can create a form in Design view, which gives you the most flexibility in laying out the form using a blank design on which you place objects. The following steps create a form in Design view.

1

- If necessary, open the Navigation Pane and be sure the Business Analyst Table is selected.

- Click Create on the Ribbon to display the Create tab (Figure 5–26).

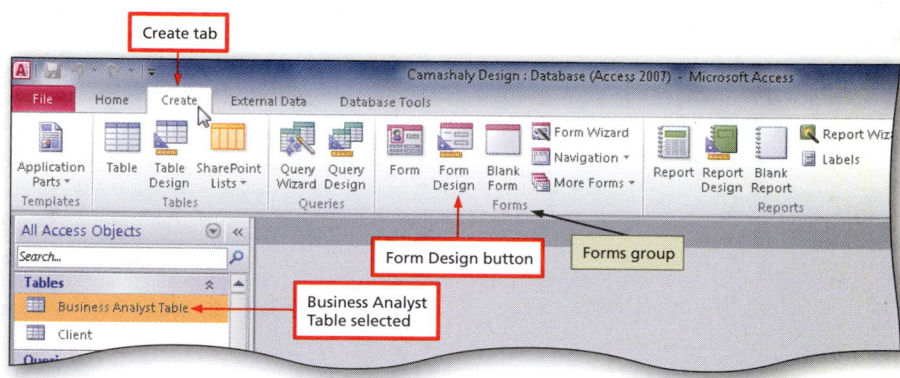

Figure 5–26

2

- Click the Form Design button (Create tab | Forms group) to create a new form in Design view.

- Close the Navigation Pane.

- If a field list does not appear, click the Add Existing Fields button (Form Design Tools Design tab | Tools group) to display a field list (Figure 5–27). If you do not see the tables listed, click Show all tables. (Your list might show all fields in the Client table.)

How do I display the fields in the Business Analyst Table?

Click the expand indicator (+) in front of the Business Analyst Table to display the fields.

Figure 5–27

To Add a Control for a Field to the Form Design

To place a control for a field on a form, drag the field from the field list to the desired position. The following steps place the Business Analyst Number field on the form.

1

- If necessary, click the expand indicator for the Business Analyst Table to display the fields in the table. Point to the Business Analyst Number field in the field list for the Business Analyst Table, press the left mouse button, and then drag the field to the approximate position shown in Figure 5–28.

Do I have to be exact?

No. Just be sure you are in the same general location.

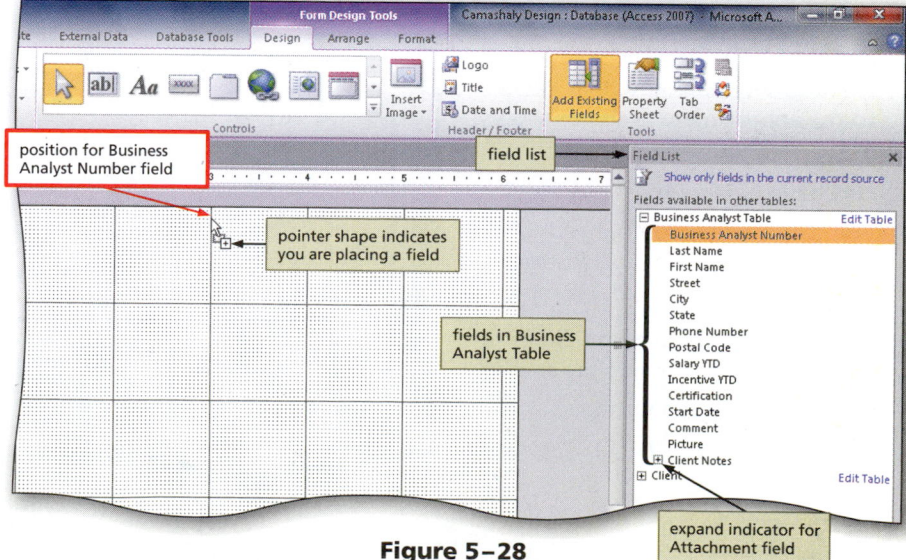

Figure 5–28

2
- Release the left mouse button to place a control for the field (Figure 5–29).

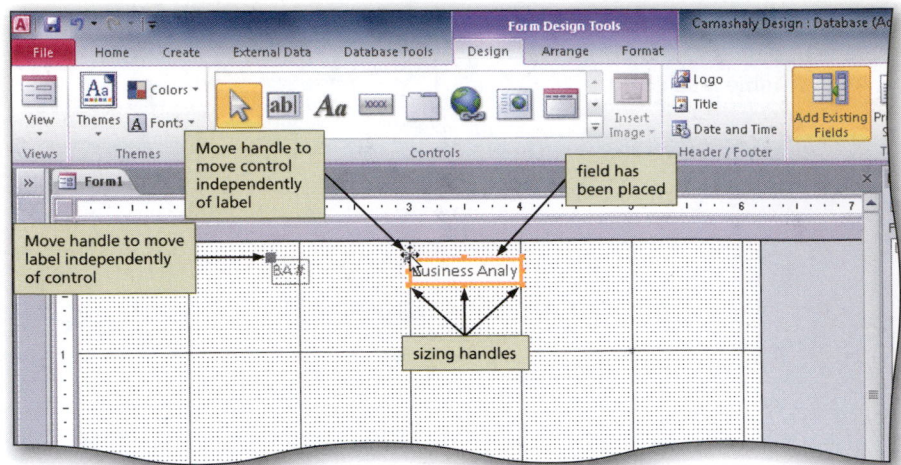

Figure 5–29

To Save the Form

Before continuing with the form creation, it is a good idea to save the form. The following steps save the form and assign it the name Business Analyst Master Form.

1 Click the Save button on the Quick Access Toolbar.

2 Type `Business Analyst Master Form` as the name of the form.

3 Click the OK button to save the form.

To Add Controls for Additional Fields

The following step places controls for the First Name, Last Name, Phone Number, Salary YTD, Incentive YTD, Start Date, and Certification fields on the form by dragging the fields from the field list.

1
- Drag the First Name, Last Name, Phone Number, Salary YTD, Incentive YTD, Start Date, and Certification fields and their labels to the approximate positions shown in Figure 5–30.

Q&A Do I have to align them precisely?

You can, but you do not need to. In the next steps, you will instruct Access to align the fields properly.

Q&A What if I drag the wrong field from the field list? Can I undo my action?

Yes. Click the Undo button.

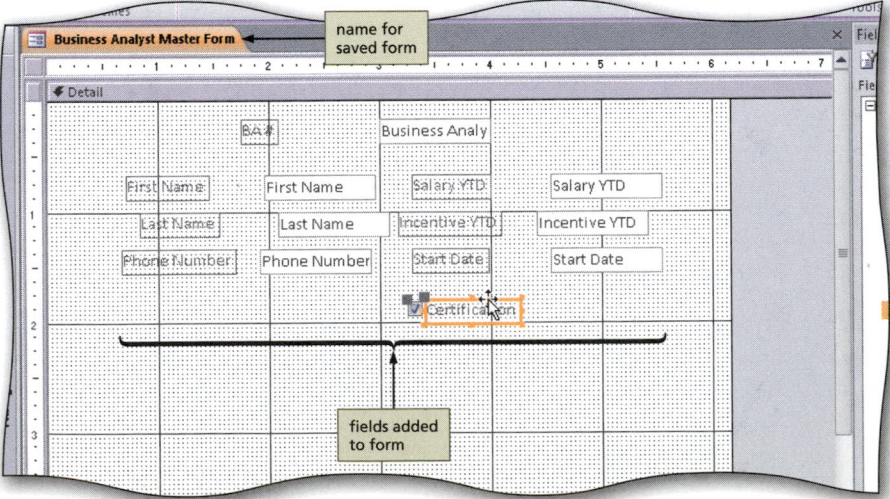

Figure 5–30

To Align Controls on the Left

Often, you will want form controls to be aligned in some fashion. For example, the controls may be aligned so their right edges are even with each other. In another case, controls may be aligned so their top edges are even. To ensure that a collection of controls is aligned properly with each other, select all of the affected controls, and then use the appropriate alignment button on the Arrange tab.

There are two ways to select multiple controls. One way is to use a ruler. If you click a position on the horizontal ruler, you will select all the controls for which a portion of the control is under that position on the ruler. Similarly, if you click a position on the vertical ruler, you will select all the controls for which a portion of the control is to the right of that position on the ruler.

The second way to select multiple controls is to select the first control by clicking it. Then, select all the other controls by holding down the SHIFT key while clicking the control.

The following steps select the First Name, Last Name, and Phone Number controls and then align them so their left edges line up.

1

- Click the First Name control (the white space, not the label) to select the control.

- Hold the SHIFT key down and click the Last Name control to select an additional control.

- Hold the SHIFT key down, click the Phone Number control to select a third control, and then release the SHIFT key.

Q&A

I selected the wrong collection of fields. How can I start over?

Simply begin the process again, making sure you do not hold the SHIFT key down when you select the first field.

- Click Arrange on the Ribbon to display the Form Design Tools Arrange tab.

- Click the Align button (Form Design Tools Arrange tab | Sizing & Ordering group) to display the Align menu (Figure 5–31).

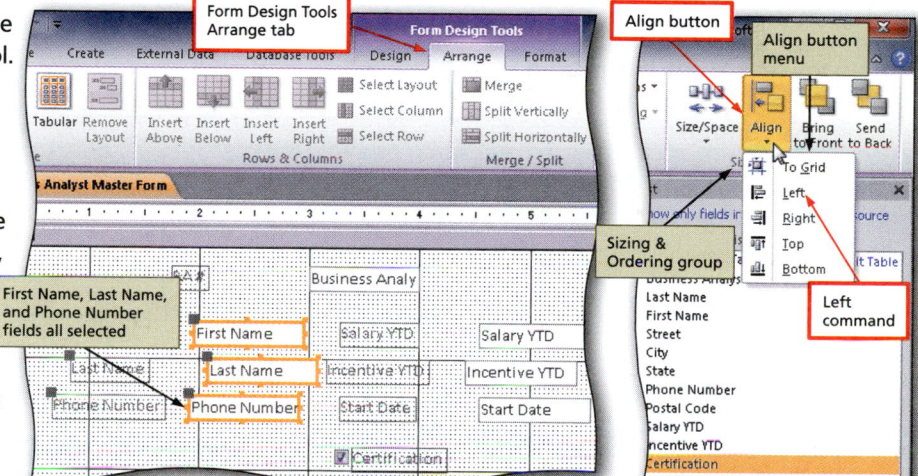

Figure 5–31

2

- Click the Left command on the Align menu to align the controls on the left (Figure 5–32).

3

- Click outside any of the selected controls to deselect the controls.

- Using the same technique, align the labels for the First Name, Last Name, and Phone Number fields on the left.

- Using the same technique, align the Salary YTD, Incentive YTD, and Start Date fields on the left.

- If necessary, align the labels for the Salary YTD, Incentive YTD, and Start Date fields on the left.

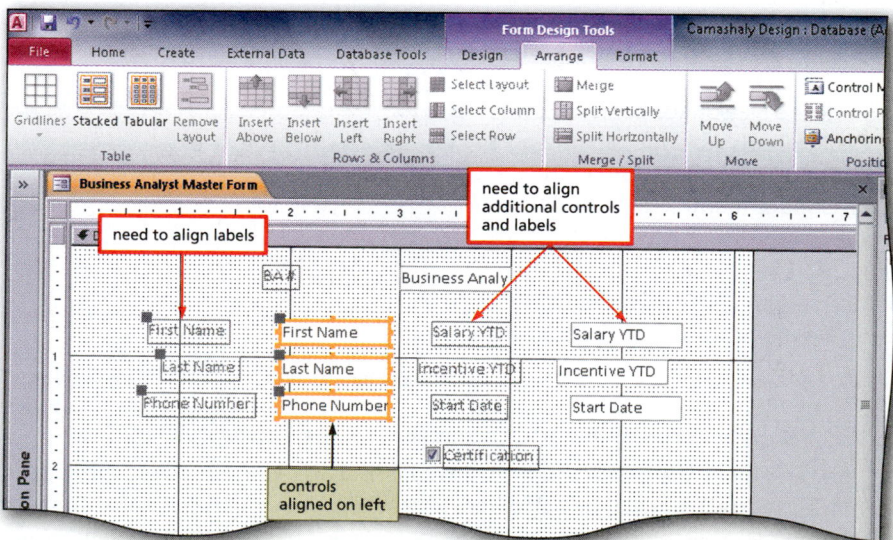

Figure 5–32

Other Ways

1. Right-click selected controls, click Align

To Align Controls on the Top and Adjust Vertical Spacing

You also can align controls so that their top edges line up. In addition, you can adjust spacing so that the vertical spacing between controls is the same. The following steps align the First Name and Salary YTD controls so that they are aligned on the top. Once these controls are aligned, you adjust the vertical spacing so that same amount of space separates each row of controls.

- Click the label for the First Name control to select the control.

- Hold the SHIFT key down and click the First Name control to select the additional control.

- Hold the SHIFT key down and click the label for the Salary YTD control to select the label as well.

- Hold the SHIFT key down and click the Salary YTD control to select an additional control.

- Click the Align button (Form Design Tools Arrange tab | Sizing & Ordering group) to display the Align menu (Figure 5–33).

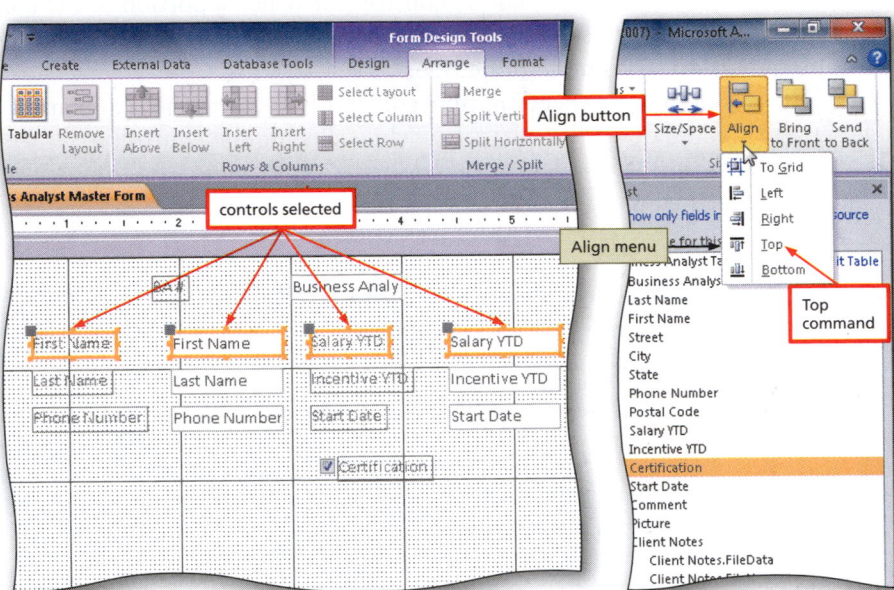

Figure 5–33

- Click the Top command on the Align menu to align the controls on the top.

- Click outside any of the selected controls to deselect the controls.

- Select the First Name, Last Name, Phone Number, Salary YTD, Incentive YTD, and Start Date fields.

- Click the Size/Space button (Form Design Tools Arrange tab | Sizing & Ordering group) to display the Size/Space menu (Figure 5–34).

3

- Click Equal Vertical on the Size/Space menu to specify the spacing.

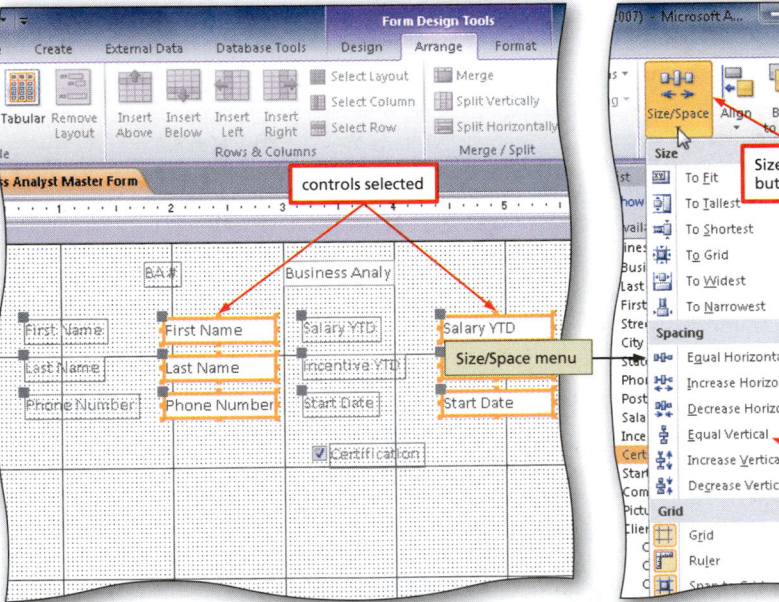

Figure 5–34

Q&A

What is the purpose of the other commands on the Size/Space menu?

You can adjust the spacing to fit the available space. You can adjust the space to match the tallest, shortest, widest, or narrowest section. You can adjust the space to match the closest grid points. You can specify equal horizontal spacing. Finally, you can increase or decrease either the vertical or the horizontal spacing.

To Move the Field List

Sometimes Access will obscure part of the form with the field list, making it difficult to place fields in the desired locations. To solve this problem, you can move the field list to a different location. The following step moves the field list in preparation for placing controls in the area it currently occupies.

• Move the field list to the approximate position shown in Figure 5–35 by dragging its title bar.

Q&A My field list changed size when I moved it. How can I return it to its original size?

Point to the border of the field list so that the mouse pointer changes to a double-headed arrow. You then can drag to adjust the size.

Q&A Can I make the field list smaller so I can see more of the screen?

Yes, you can adjust the size to whatever is most comfortable for you.

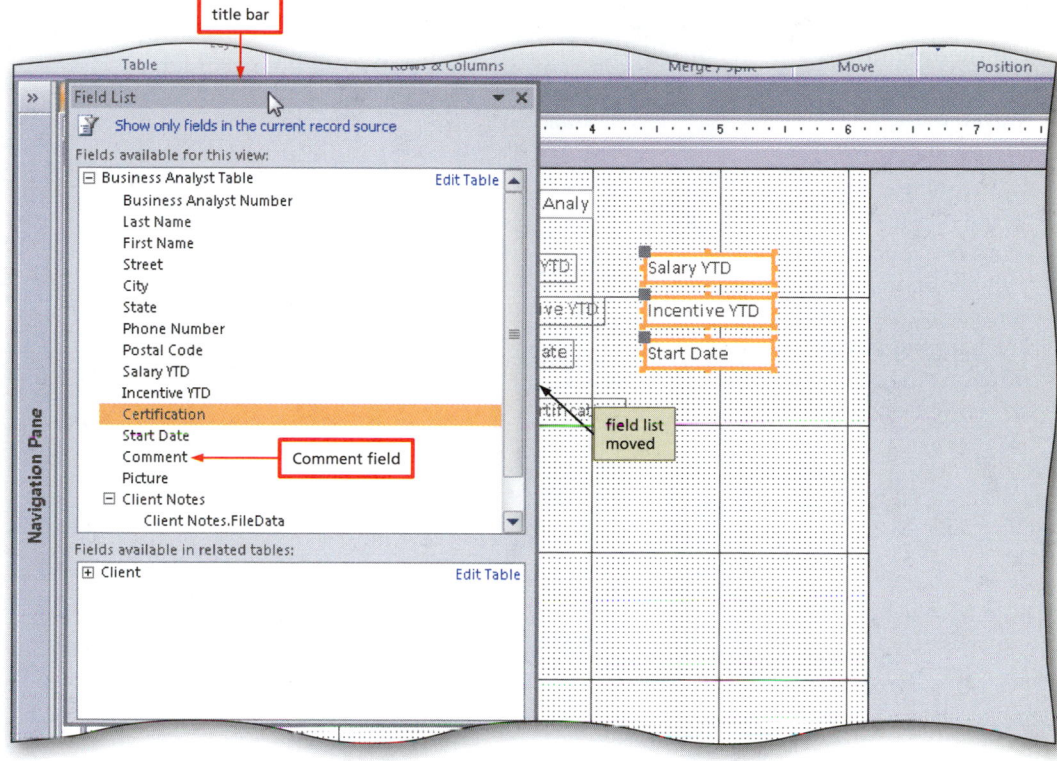

Figure 5–35

To Add Controls for the Remaining Fields

The following steps place controls for the Comment, Picture, and Client Notes fields and also move their attached labels to the desired position.

• Drag the control for the Comment field from the field list to the approximate position shown in Figure 5–36.

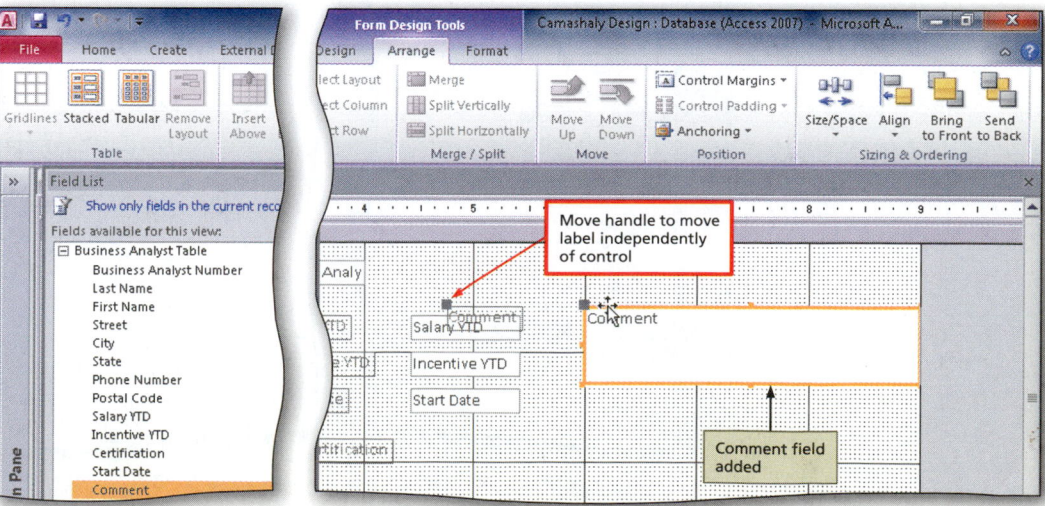

Figure 5–36

2

• Move the label for the Comment field to the position shown in Figure 5–37 by dragging its Move handle.

Q&A

I started to move the label and the control moved along with it. What did I do wrong?

You were not pointing at the handle to move the label independently of the control. Make sure you are pointing to the little box in the upper-left corner of the label.

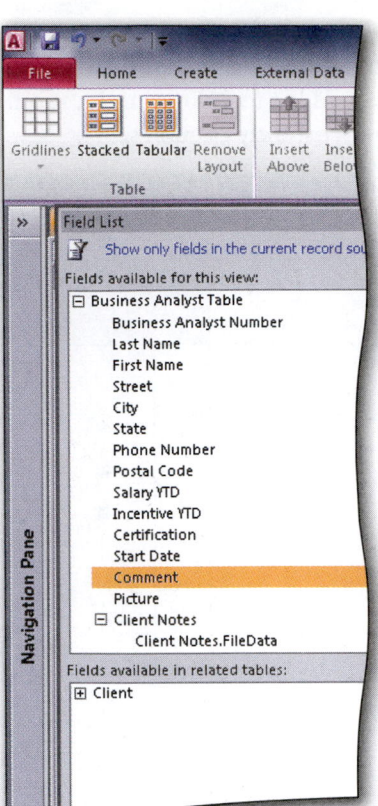

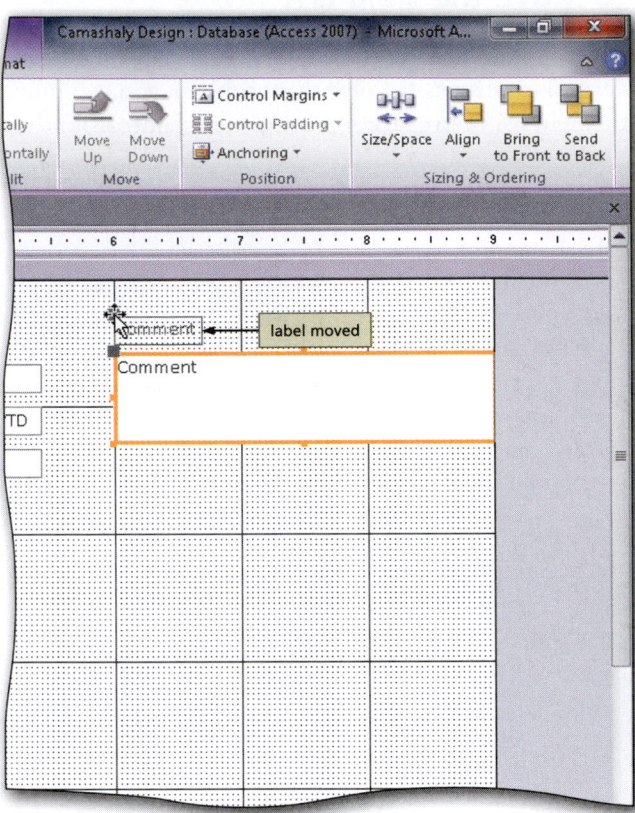

Figure 5–37

3

• Using the same techniques, move the control for the Picture field to the approximate position shown in Figure 5–38 and move its label to the position shown in the figure.

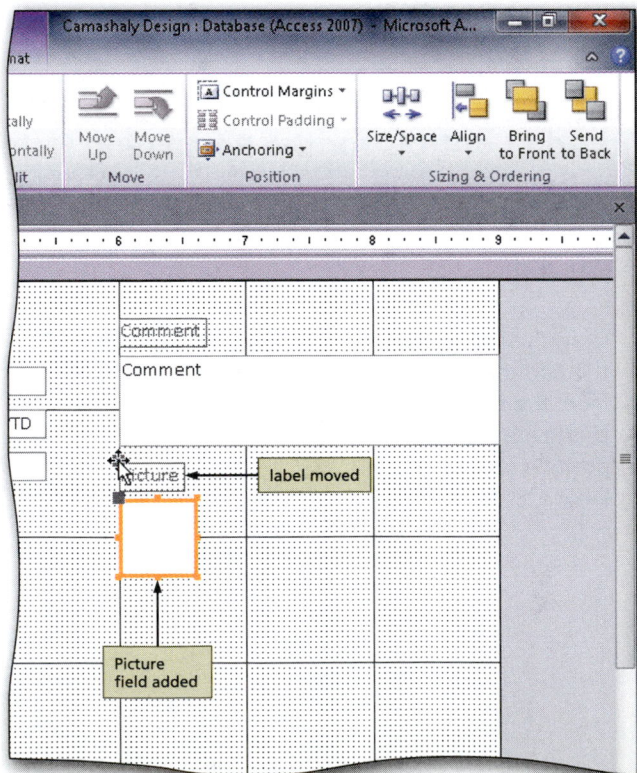

Figure 5–38

4
- Click the control for the Picture field and drag the lower-right corner to the approximate position shown in Figure 5–39 to resize the control.

- Add the control for the Client Notes field in the position shown in the figure and move its attached label to the position shown in the figure.

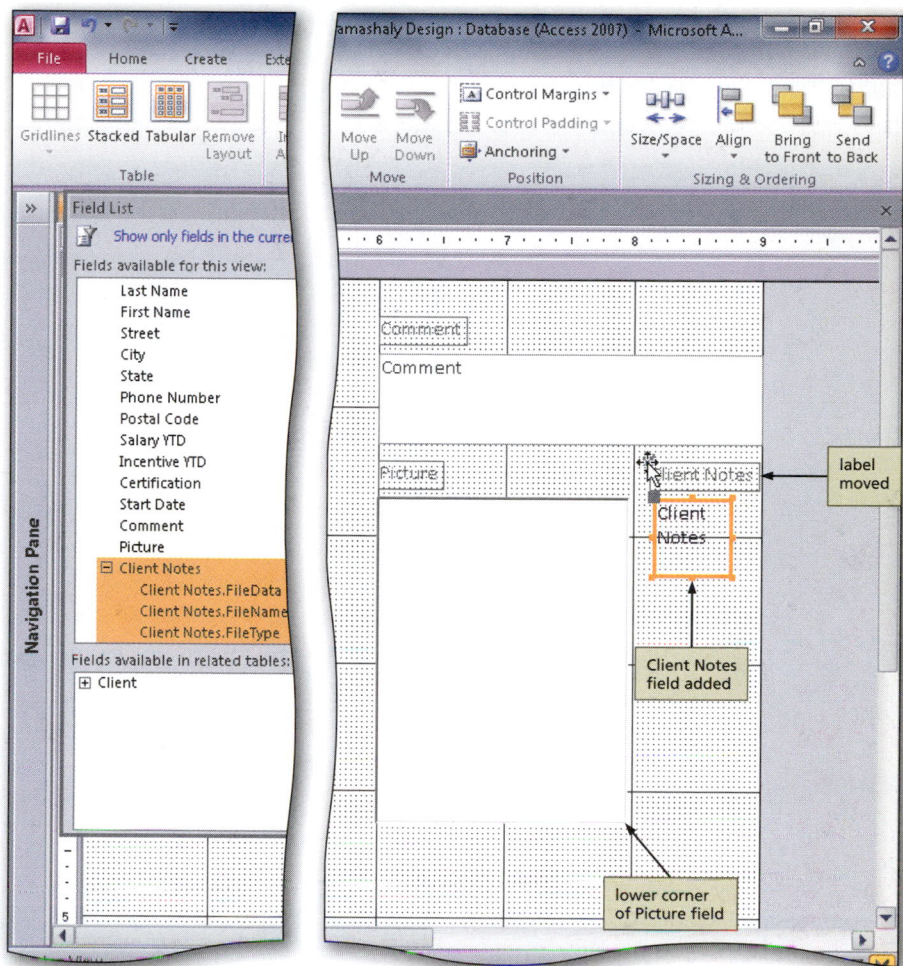

Figure 5–39

 Q&A
When would I need to click the expand indicator for the Client Notes field?

By clicking the expand indicator, you have access to three special properties of the field: FileData, FileName, and FileType. If you drag one of these onto the form, you will only get the corresponding information in the control. For example, if you drag Client Notes.FileName, the control will display the file name for the attachment. Most of the time, you want the field itself, so you would not use any of these properties.

5
- Close the field list by displaying the Design tab and then clicking the Add Existing Fields button (Form Design Tools Design tab | Tools group), which is shown in Figure 5–27.

Q&A
Where will the field list be positioned the next time I display it?

Usually it will be in the position it was when you closed it. If that is the case and you want it in its typical position, move it there by dragging its title bar.

Other Ways
1. Click Close button for field list

To Use a Shortcut Menu to Change the Fill/Back Color

You can use the Background Color button on the Form Design Tools Format tab to change the background color of a form. In some cases, you also can use a shortcut menu. The following steps use a shortcut menu to change the background color of the form to gray.

1

- Right-click in the approximate position shown in Figure 5–40 to produce a shortcut menu.

Q&A

Does it matter where I right-click?

You can right-click anywhere on the form as long as you are outside of all the controls.

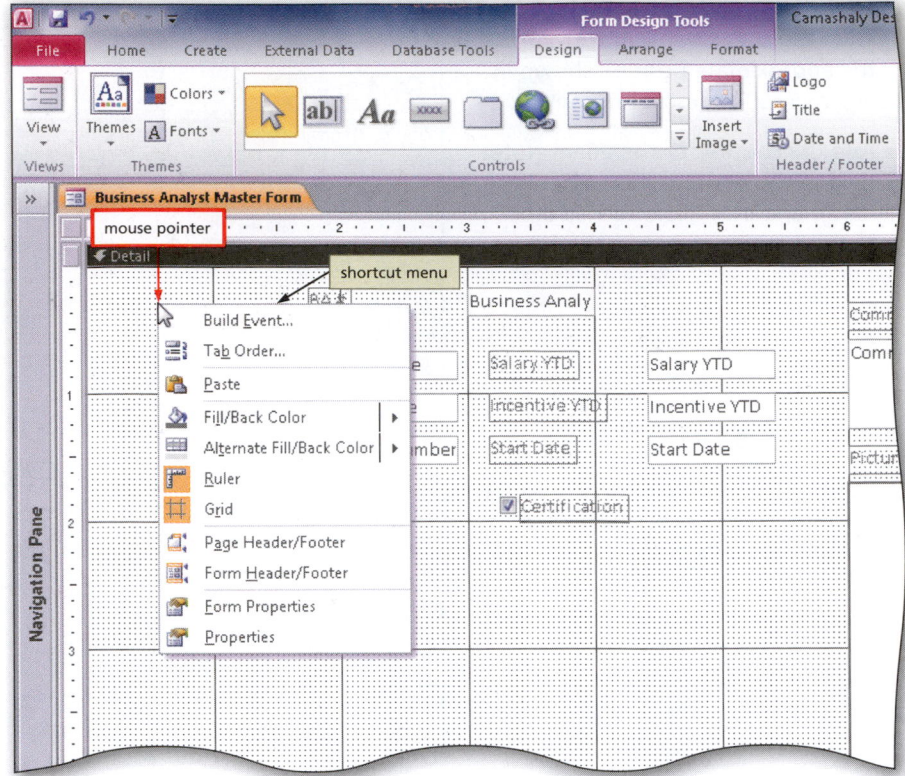

Figure 5–40

2

- Point to the Fill/Back Color command arrow on the shortcut menu to display a color palette (Figure 5–41).

3

- Click the gray color shown in Figure 5–41 to change the fill/back color to gray.

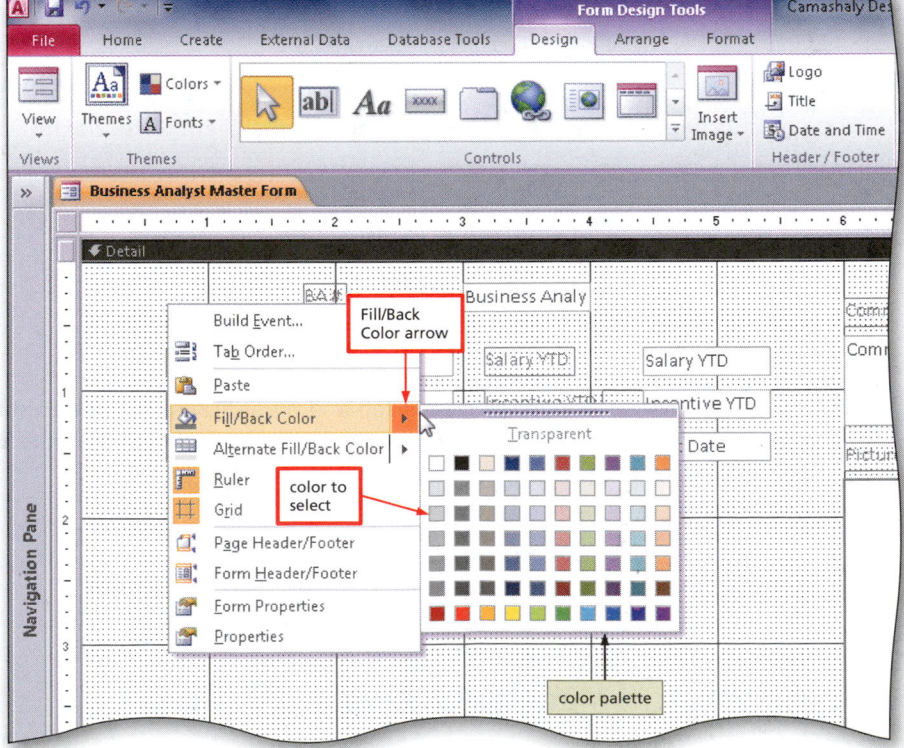

Figure 5–41

To Add a Title

A form should have a descriptive title. The following step adds a title to the form.

- Be sure the Design tab is selected.

- Click the Title button (Form Design Tools Design tab | Header/Footer group) to add a title to the form (Figure 5–42).

Q&A Why is there a new section?

The form title belongs in the Form Header section. When you clicked the Title button, Access added the Form Header section automatically and placed the title in it.

Q&A Could I add a Form Header section without having to click the Title button?

Yes. Right-click anywhere on the form background and click Form Header/Footer on the shortcut menu.

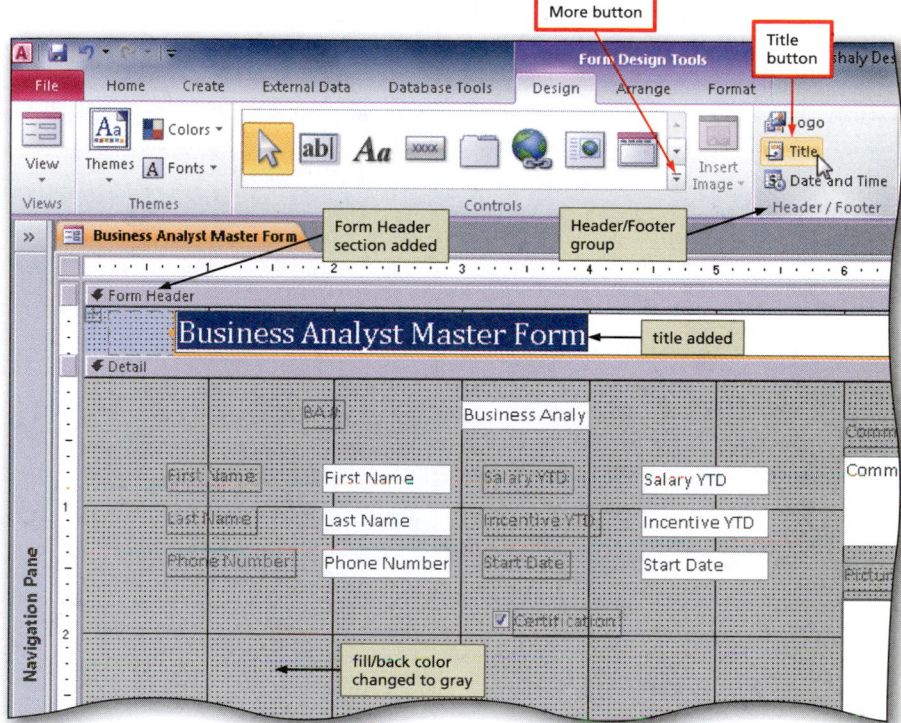

Figure 5–42

To Place a Subform

The Controls group on the Form Design Tools Design tab contains buttons called tools that you use to place a variety of types of controls on a form. To place a subform on a form, you use the Subform/Subreport tool. If the Use Control Wizards button is selected, a wizard will guide you through the process of adding the subform. The following steps use the Subform Wizard to place a subform.

- Click the More button (Form Design Tools Design tab | Controls group) to display a gallery of available tools (Figure 5–43).

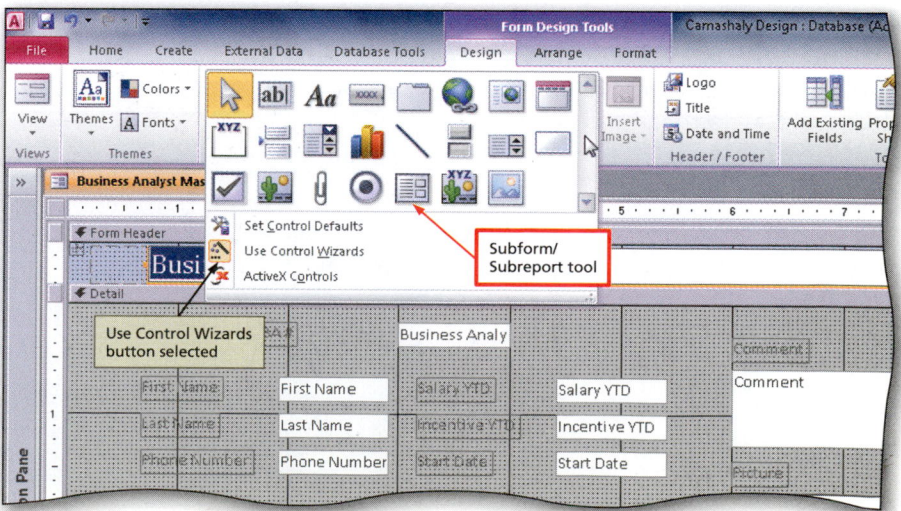

Figure 5–43

2

● Be sure the Use Control Wizards button is selected, click the Subform/Subreport tool on the Form Design Tools Design tab, and then move the mouse pointer to the approximate position shown in Figure 5–44.

Q&A
How can I tell whether the Use Control Wizards button is selected?

The icon for the Use Control Wizards button will be highlighted, as shown in Figure 5–43. If it is not, click the Use Control Wizards button to highlight it, and then click the Subform/Subreport tool.

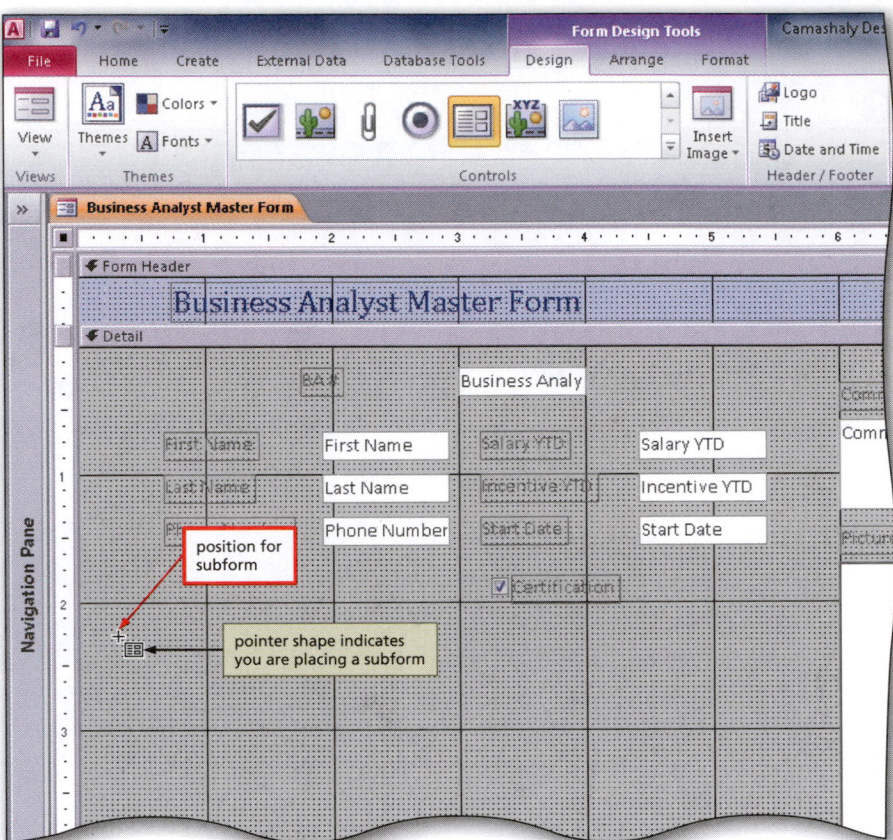

Figure 5–44

3

● Click the position shown in Figure 5–44 and then ensure the 'Use existing Tables and Queries' option button is selected (SubForm Wizard dialog box) (Figure 5–45).

Q&A
My control is placed on the screen, but no wizard appeared. What should I do?

Press the DELETE key to delete the control you placed. Ensure that the Use Control Wizards button is selected, as described previously.

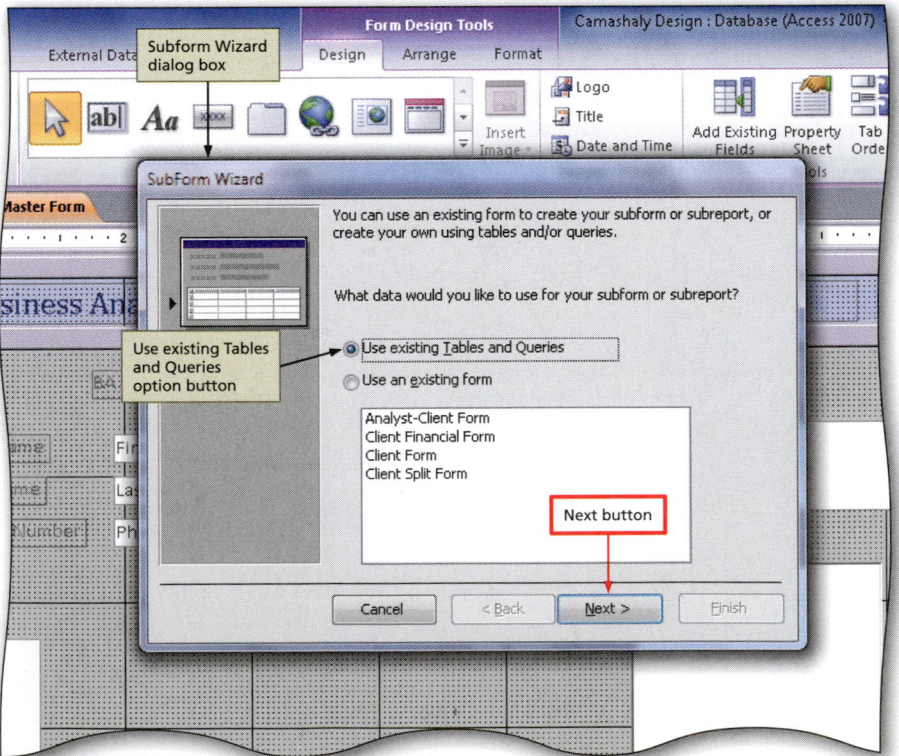

Figure 5–45

4

• Click the Next button.

• Click the Tables/Queries box arrow and then click the Client table to select the table that contains the fields for the subform.

• Add the Client Number, Client Name, Amount Paid, and Current Due fields by clicking the field and then clicking the Add Field button (SubForm Wizard dialog box) (Figure 5–46).

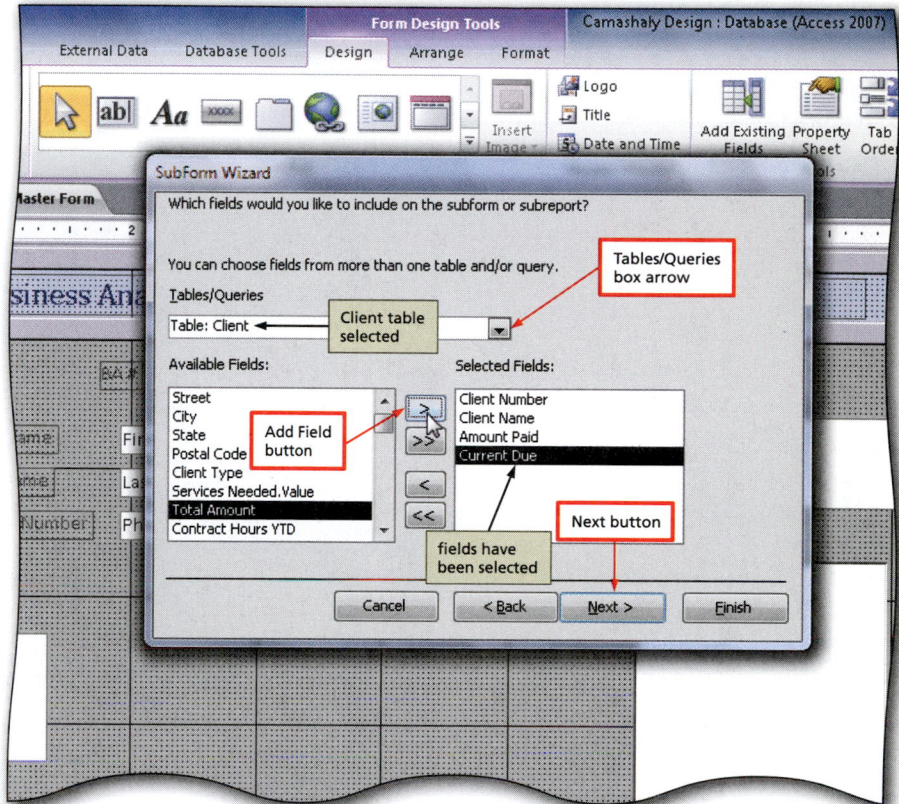

Figure 5–46

5

• Click the Next button to move to the next SubForm Wizard dialog box.

• Be sure the 'Choose from a list' option button is selected (Figure 5–47).

Why do I use this option?

Most of the time, Access will have determined the appropriate fields to link the subform and the main form and placed an entry specifying those fields in the list. By choosing from the list, you can take advantage of the information that Access has created for you. The other option is to define your own, in which case you would need to specify the appropriate fields.

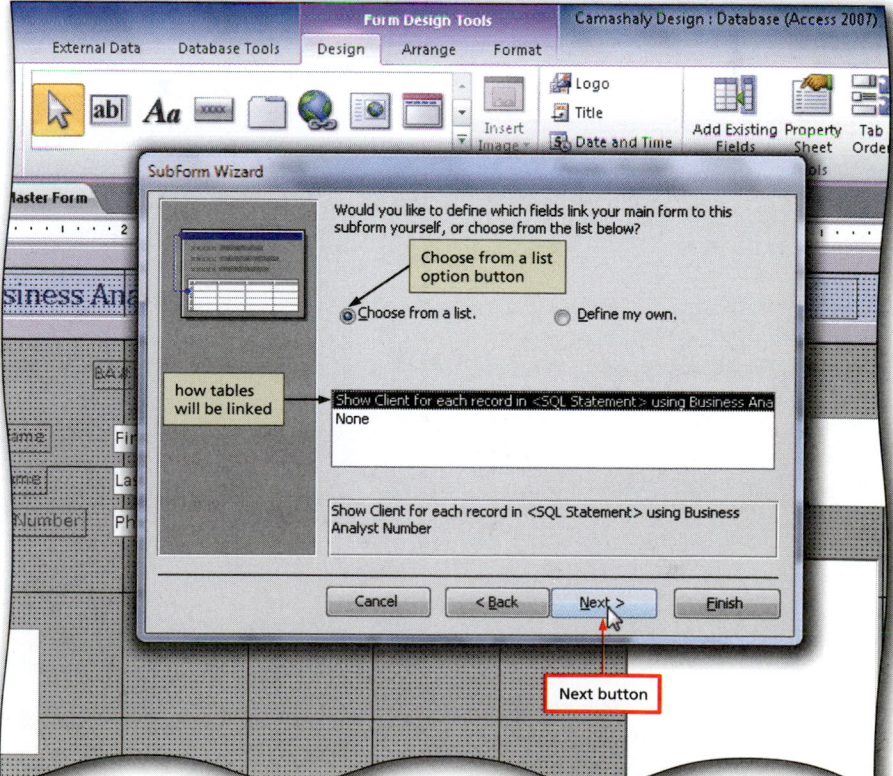

Figure 5–47

6

- Click the Next button.

- Type **Clients of Analyst** as the name of the subform (Figure 5–48).

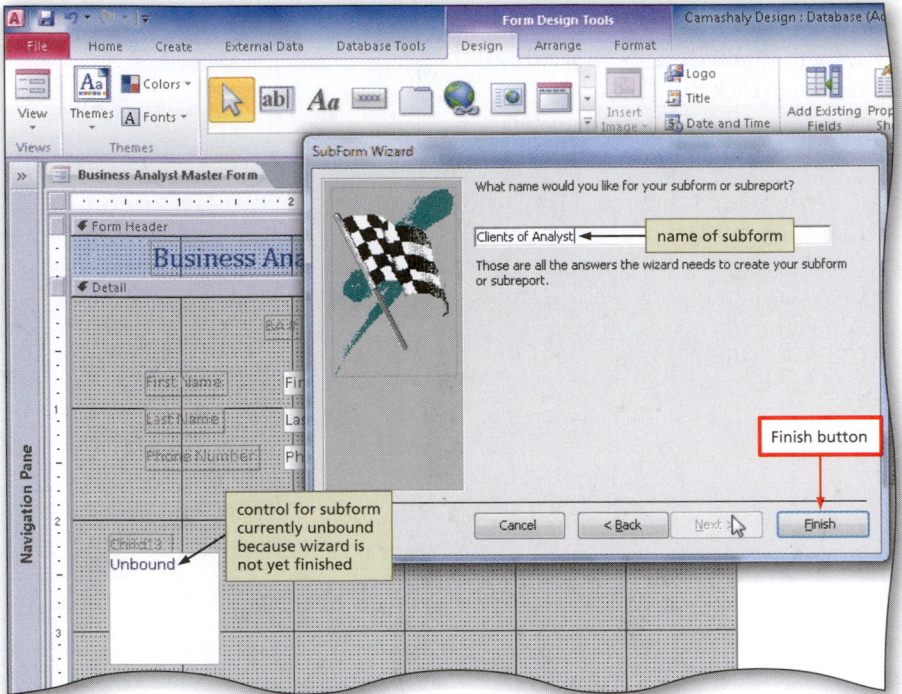

Figure 5–48

7

- Click the Finish button to place the subform (Figure 5–49).

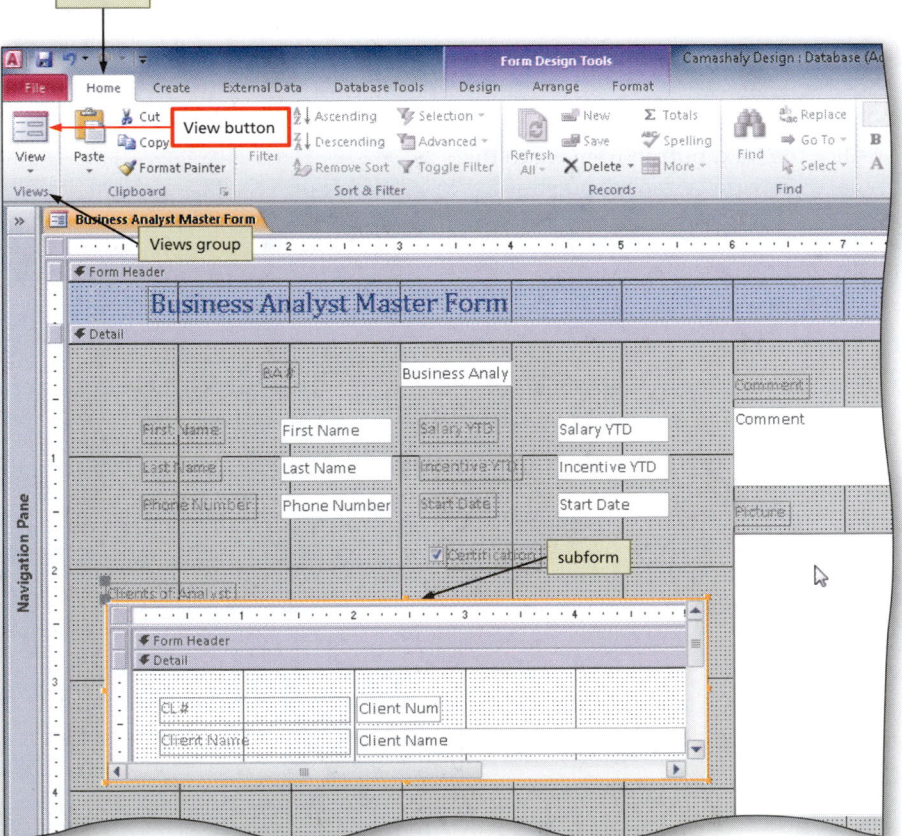

Figure 5–49

To View the Form

When working with a form in Design view, you can see the effect of the changes you have made by viewing the form in Form view. The following step views the form in Form view.

1
- Click the View button (Home tab | Views group) to view the form in Form view (Figure 5–50).

Q&A

Everything looks good except the subform. I do not see all the fields I should see. What should I do?

You need to modify the subform, which you will do in the upcoming steps.

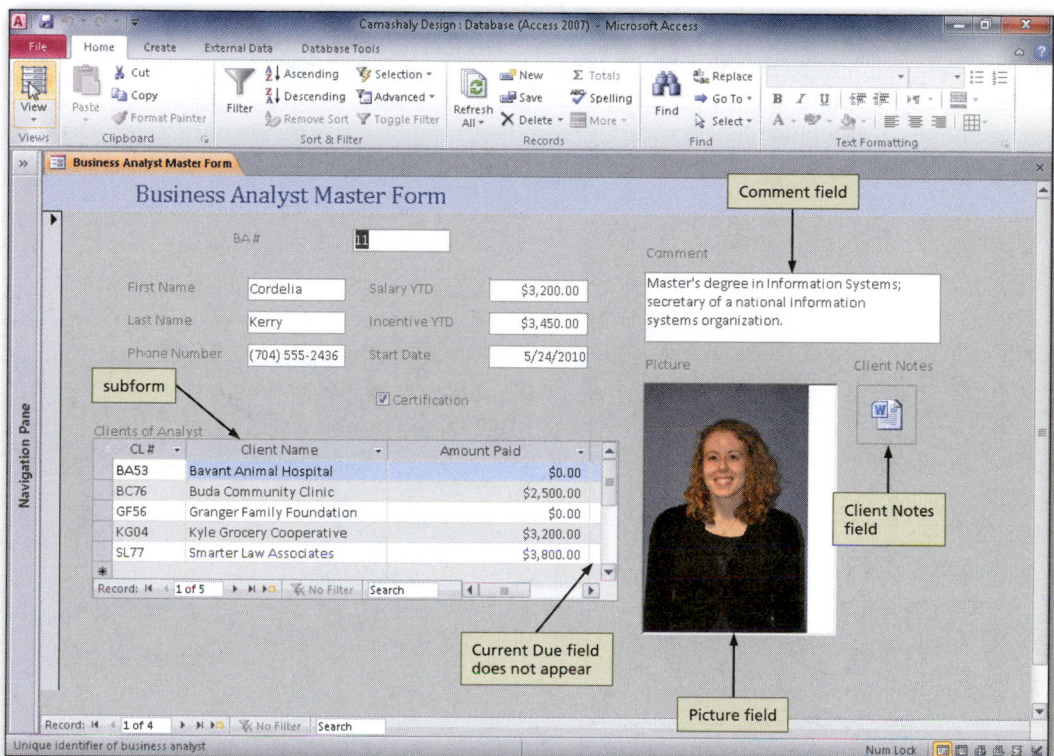

Figure 5–50

To Close and Save a Form

The following steps first save and then close the Business Analyst Master Form.

1 Click the Save button on the Quick Access Toolbar to save the form.

2 Close the Business Analyst Master Form by clicking the Close button for the form.

Break Point: If you wish to stop working through the chapter at this point, you can resume the project at a later time by starting Access, opening the database called Camashaly Design, and continuing to follow the steps from this location forward.

To Modify a Subform

The next task is to resize the columns in the subform, which appears on the form in Datasheet view. The subform exists as a separate object in the database; it is stored independently of the main form. The following steps open the subform and then resize the columns. They then center the data in the Client Number column.

1

- Open the Navigation Pane.

- Right-click the Clients of Analyst form to produce a shortcut menu.

- Click Open on the shortcut menu to open the form.

- Resize the columns to best fit the data by double-clicking the right boundaries of the field selectors (Figure 5–51).

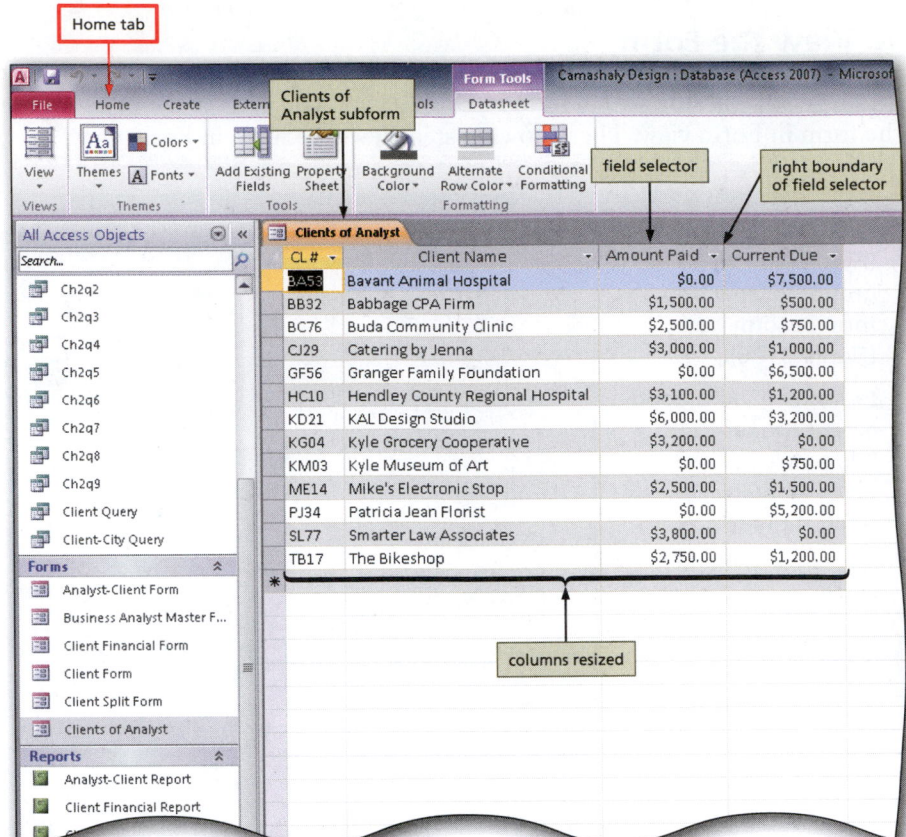

Figure 5–51

2

- Click Home on the Ribbon to display the Home tab.

- Click the Client Number field on the first record.

Q&A Did it have to be the first record?

No. The whole column will be aligned at once no matter which record you pick.

- Click the Center button (Home tab | Text Formatting group) to center the data in the column (Figure 5–52).

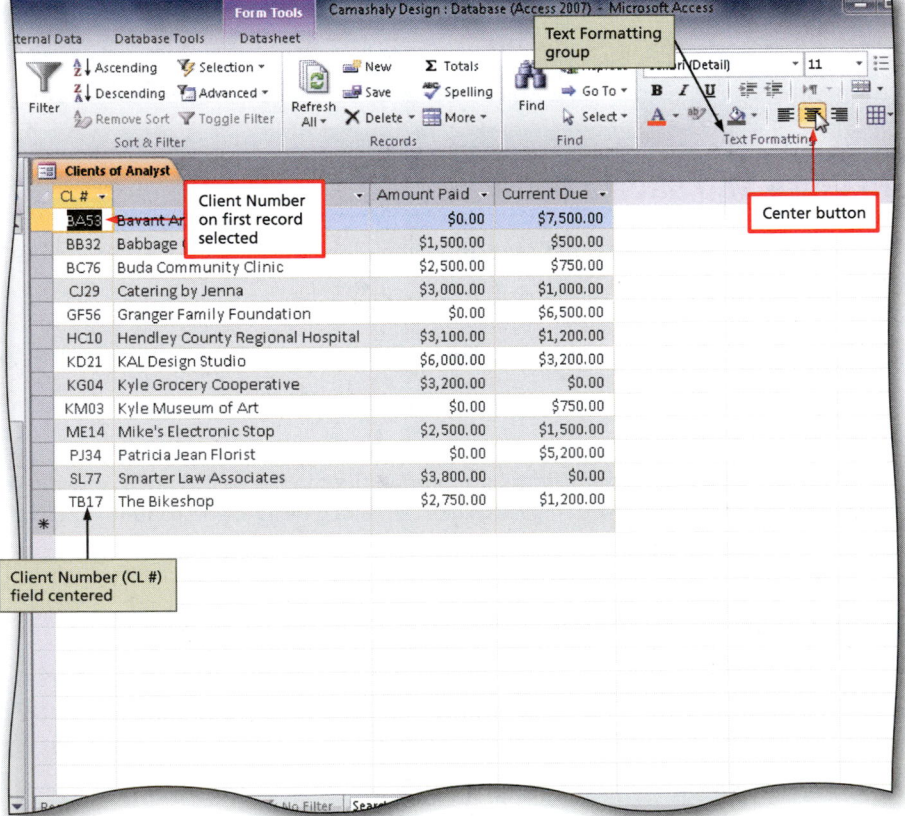

Figure 5–52

3

- Save your changes and then close the subform.

- Open the Business Analyst Master Form in Design view and then close the Navigation Pane.

- Click the boundary of the subform to select it.

- Adjust the approximate size and position of the subform to match the one shown in Figure 5–53.

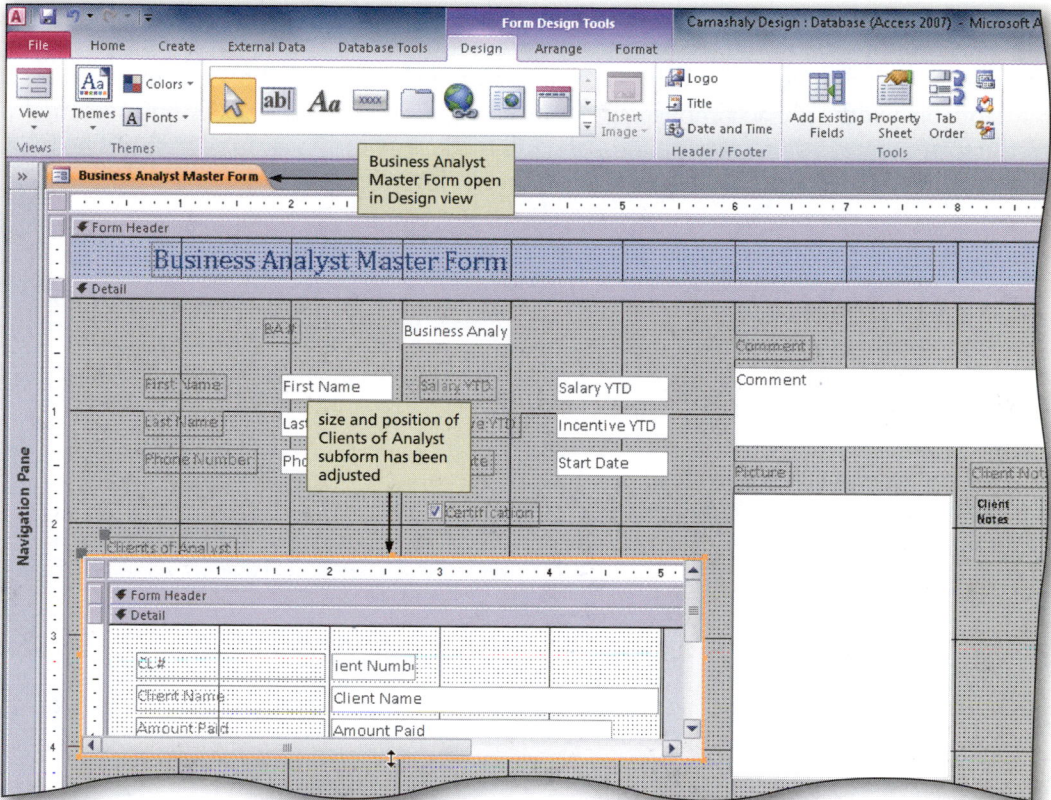

Figure 5–53

4

- Click the View button (Form Design Tools Design tab | Views group) to view the form in Form view (Figure 5–54).

Q&A Could I have clicked the View button arrow and then clicked Form View?

Yes. You always can use the arrow. If the icon for the view you want appears on the face of the View button, however, you also can just click the button.

Q&A Could I have clicked the Form View button in the lower-right corner of the screen to move to Form view?

Yes. Those buttons are always an option. Use whichever approach you find most convenient.

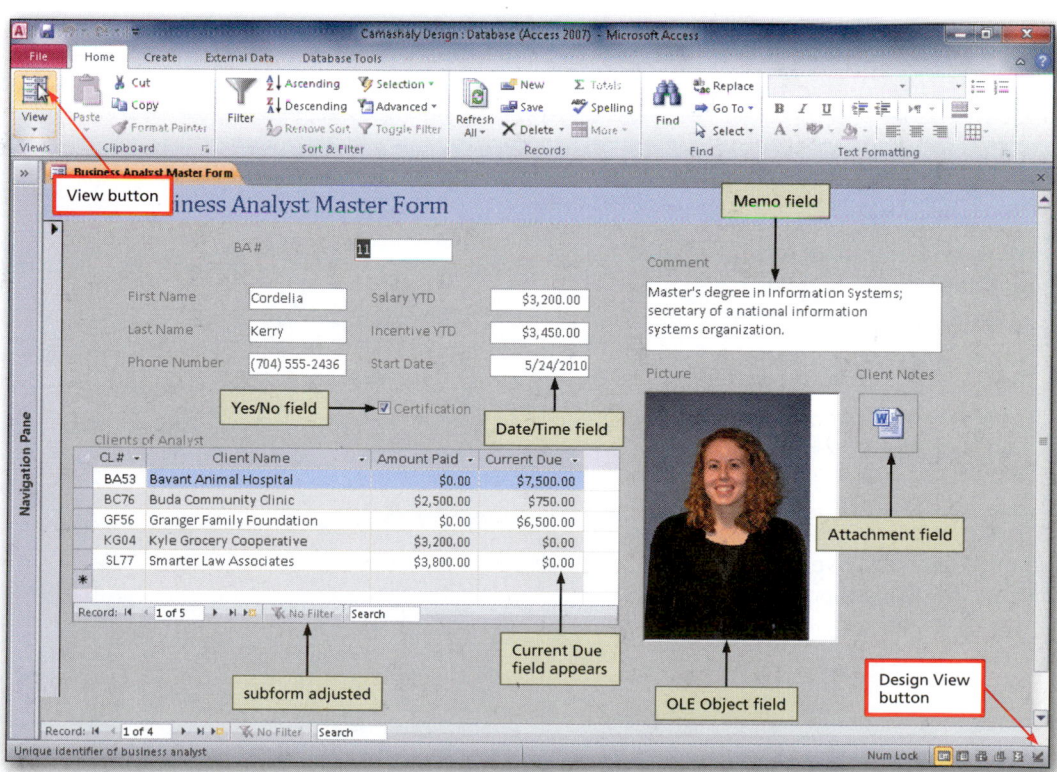

Figure 5–54

To Change a Label

In Datasheet view, shortening the heading for the Business Analyst Number column to BA # made sense. With business analyst numbers only being two characters long, having a short column heading enabled the column to have a reasonable width. You accomplished that by changing the caption for the Business Analyst Number field to BA #. In the form, there is plenty of room for the full field name to appear in the label. The following steps change the contents of the label from BA # to Business Analyst Number.

1

- Return to Design view, and then click the label for the Business Analyst Number to select the label.

- Click the label a second time to produce an insertion point.

- Erase the current label (BA #) and then type **Business Analyst Number** as the new label (Figure 5–55).

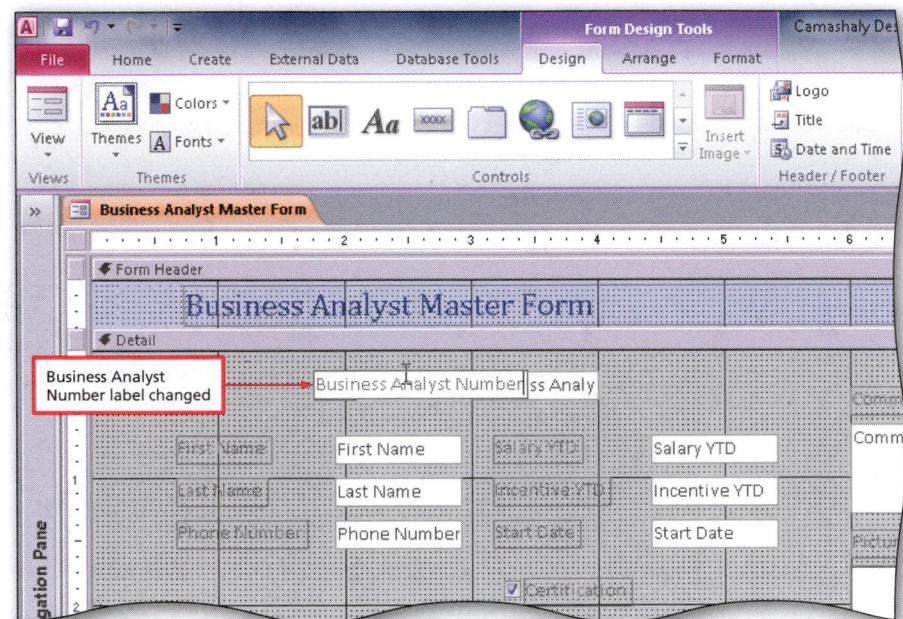

Figure 5–55

2

- Click outside the label to deselect it.

- Click the label to select it.

Q&A

Why did I need to deselect the label and then select it again?

With the insertion point appearing in the label, you could not move the label. By deselecting it and then selecting it again, the label will be selected, but there will be no insertion point.

- Drag the Move handle in the upper-left corner to move the label to the approximate position shown in Figure 5–56.

3

- Save your changes.

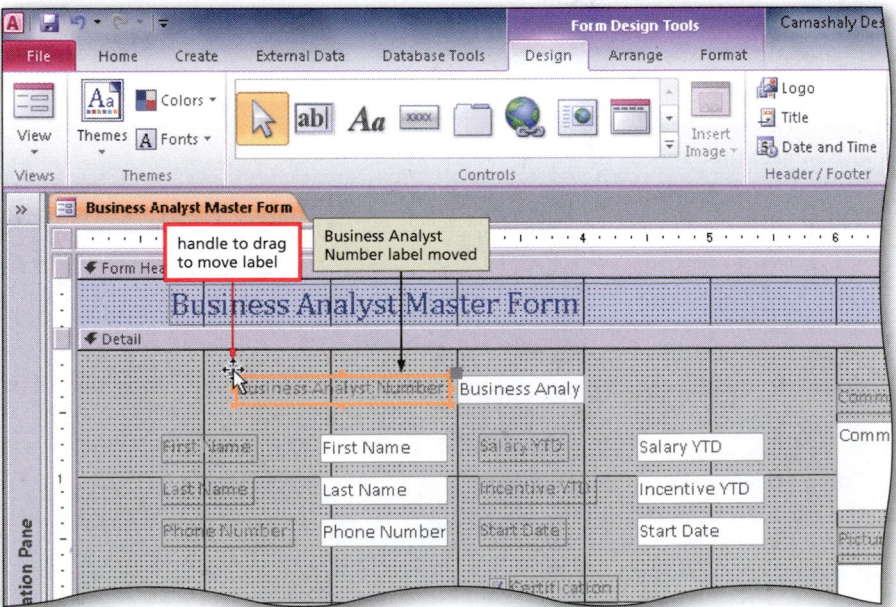

Figure 5–56

Size Mode for Pictures

The portion of a picture that appears as well as the way it appears is determined by the property called **size mode**. The possible size modes are as follows:

1. Clip — This size mode displays only the portion of the picture that will fit in the space allocated to it.

2. Stretch — This size mode expands or shrinks the picture to fit the precise space allocated on the screen. For photographs, usually this is not a good choice because fitting a photograph to the allocated space can distort the image, giving it a stretched appearance.

3. Zoom — This size mode does the best job of fitting the picture to the allocated space without changing the look of the picture. The entire picture will appear and be proportioned correctly. Some white space may be visible either above or to the right of the picture, however.

TO CHANGE THE SIZE MODE

Currently, the size mode should be Zoom, which is appropriate. If it were not and you wanted to change it, you would use the following steps.

1. Click the control containing the picture, and then click the Property Sheet button (Form Design Tools Design tab | Tools group) to display the control's property sheet.

2. Click the Size Mode property, and then click the Size Mode property box arrow.

3. Click Zoom and then close the property sheet by clicking its Close button.

To Change Special Effects and Colors

Access allows you to change many of the characteristics of the labels in the form. You can change the border style and color, the background color, the font, and the font size. You also can apply special label effects, such as raised or sunken. The following steps change the font color and add special effects of the labels.

1

- Click the Business Analyst Number label to select it.

- Select each of the remaining labels by holding down the SHIFT key while clicking the label. Be sure to include the label for the subform (Figure 5–57).

Q&A

Does the order in which I select the labels make a difference?

No. The only thing that is important is that they are all selected when you are done.

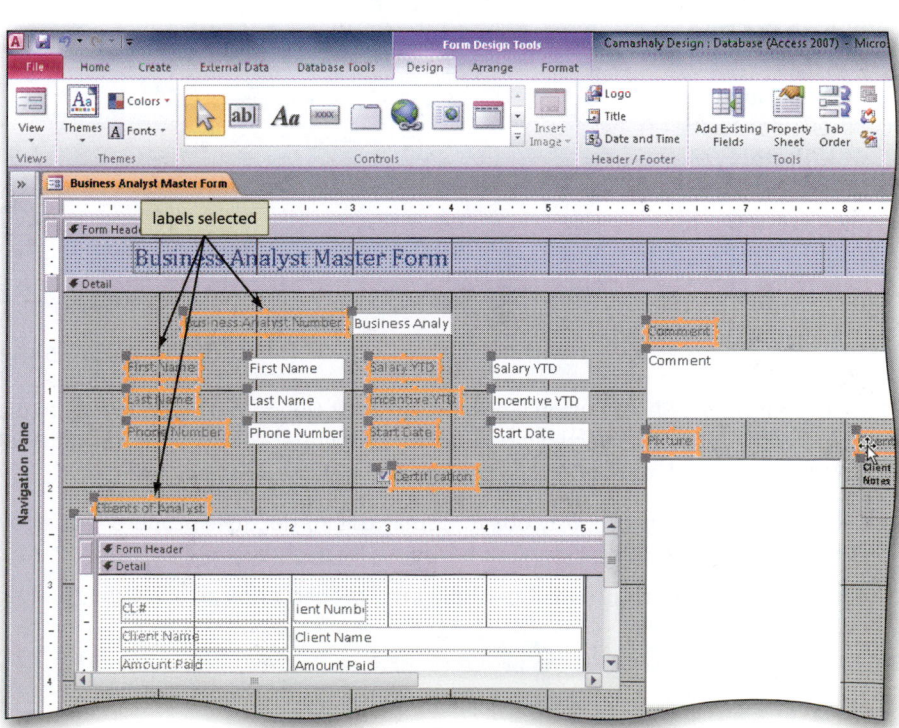

Figure 5–57

2

- Display the Format tab.

- Click the Font Color arrow (Form Design Tools Format tab | Font group) to display a color palette (Figure 5–58).

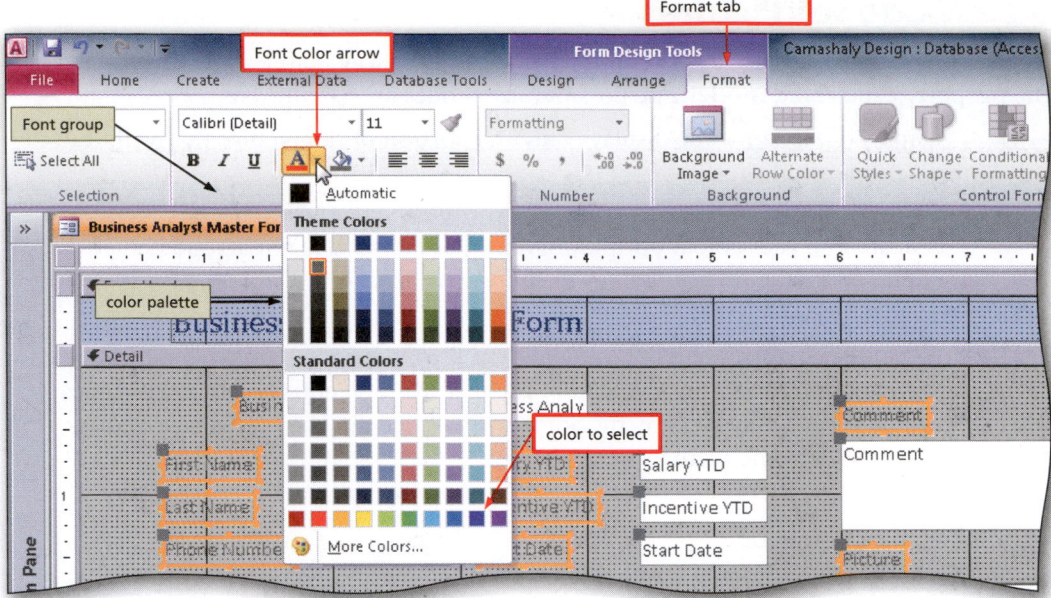

Figure 5–58

3

- Click the blue color in the second position from the right in the bottom row of Standard Colors to change the font color for the labels.

 **Experiment**

- Try other colors by clicking the Font Color arrow and then clicking the other color to see which colors you think would be good choices for the font. When done, select the blue color.

- Display the Design tab.

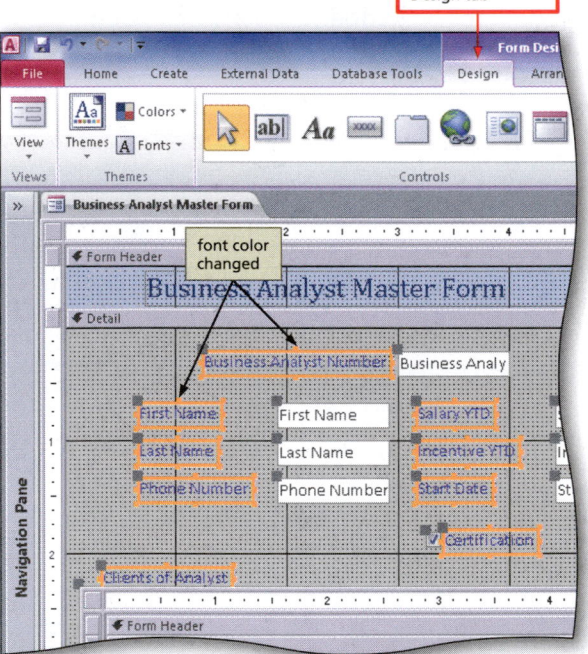

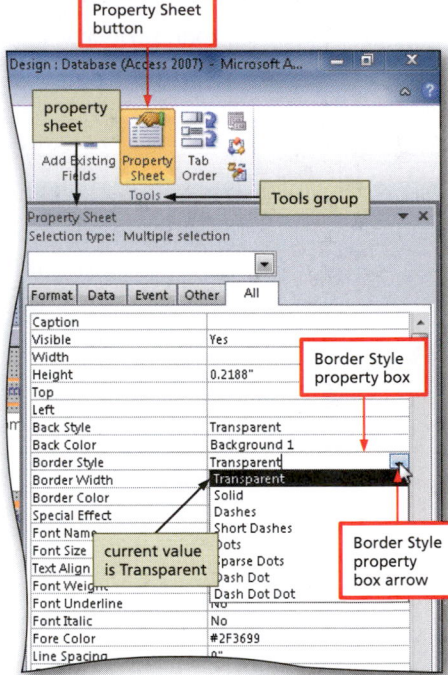

Figure 5–59

- Click the Property Sheet button (Form Design Tools Design tab | Tools group) to produce the property sheet for the selected labels. If your property sheet still appears on the left side of the screen, drag it back to the right. Make sure the All tab is selected.

- Click the Border Style property box to display the Border Style property box arrow, and then click the arrow to display a menu of border styles (Figure 5–59).

Q&A

The property sheet is too small to display the property box arrow. Can I change the size of the property sheet?

Yes. Point to the border of the property sheet so that the mouse pointer changes to a two-headed arrow. You then can drag to adjust the size.

4

- Click Solid in the menu of border styles to select a border style.

- Click the Border Width property box to display the Border Width property box arrow, and then click the arrow to display a menu of border widths.

- Click 3 pt to change the border width to 3 pt.

- Click the Special Effect property box to display the Special Effect property box arrow, and then click the arrow to display a menu of special effects (Figure 5–60).

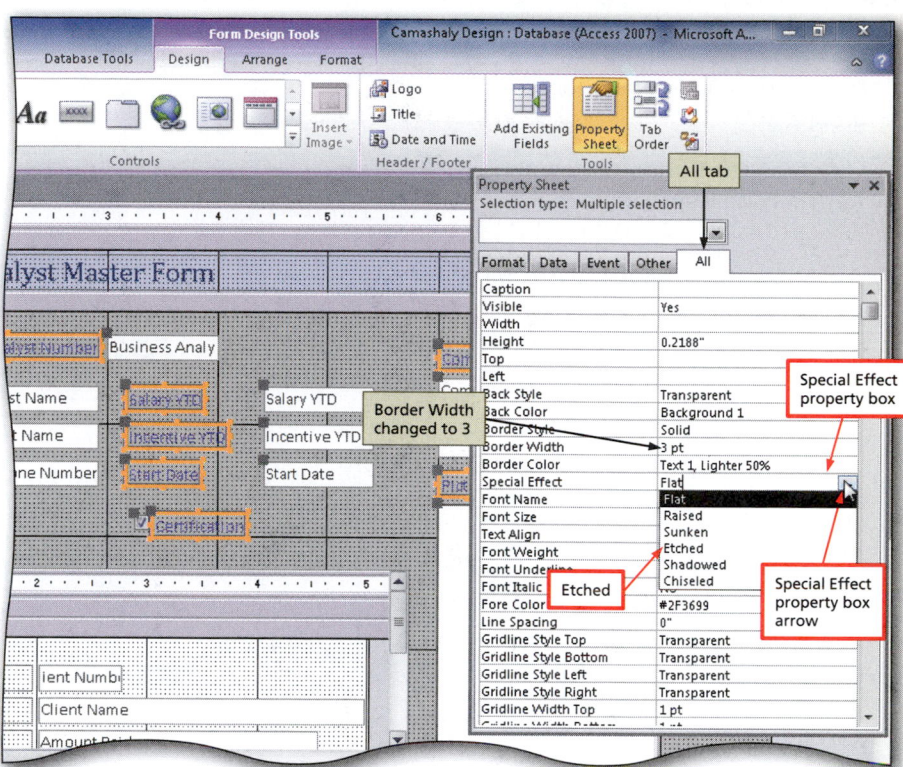

Figure 5–60

5

- Click Etched in the menu of special effects to select a special effect.

Experiment

- Try other special effects. In each case, view the form to see the special effect you selected and then return to Design view. When done, select Etched.

- Close the property sheet.

- Click the Business Analyst Number control (the white space, not the label) to select it.

- Select each of the remaining controls by holding down the SHIFT key while clicking the control. Do not include the subform.

- Display the property sheet.

- Select Sunken for the special effect (Figure 5–61).

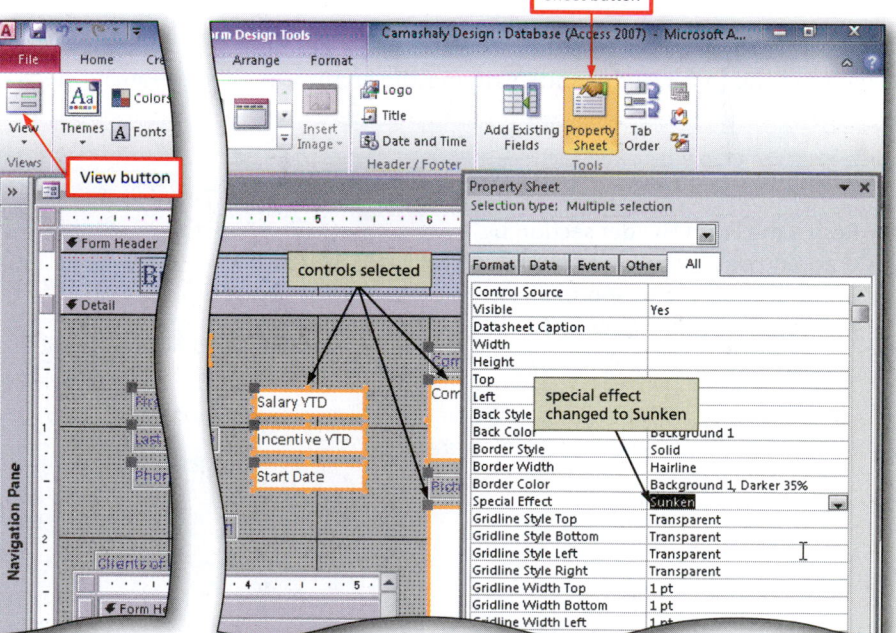

Figure 5–61

6
- Close the property sheet by clicking the Property Sheet button (Form Design Tools Design tab | Tools group).

- Click the View button to view the form in Form view (Figure 5–62).

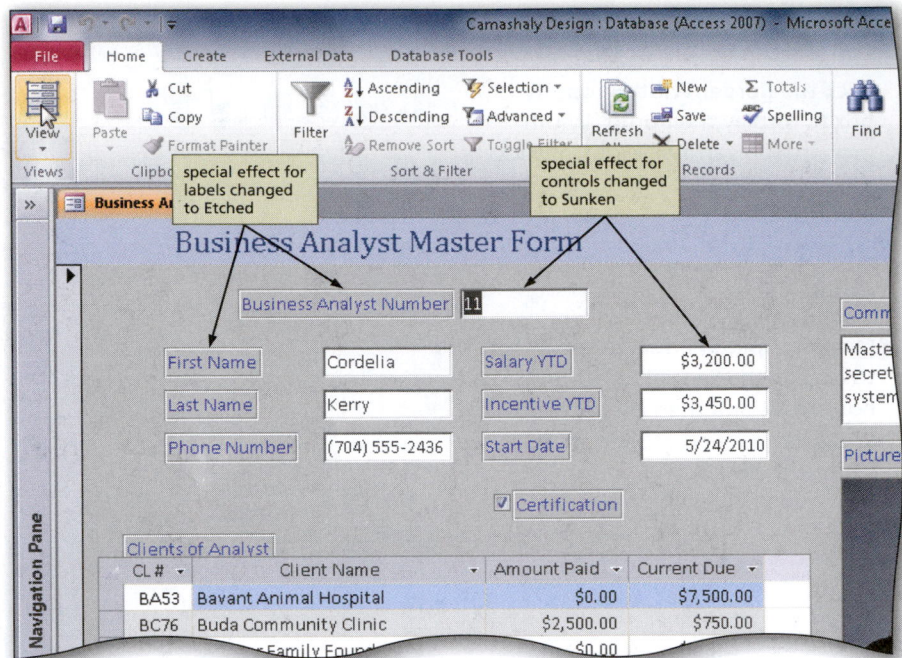

Figure 5–62

To Modify the Appearance of a Form Title

You can enhance the title in a variety of ways. These include moving it, resizing it, changing the font size, changing the font weight, and changing the alignment. The following steps enhance the form title.

1
- Return to Design view.

- Resize the Form Header section by dragging down the lower boundary of the section to the approximate position shown in Figure 5–63.

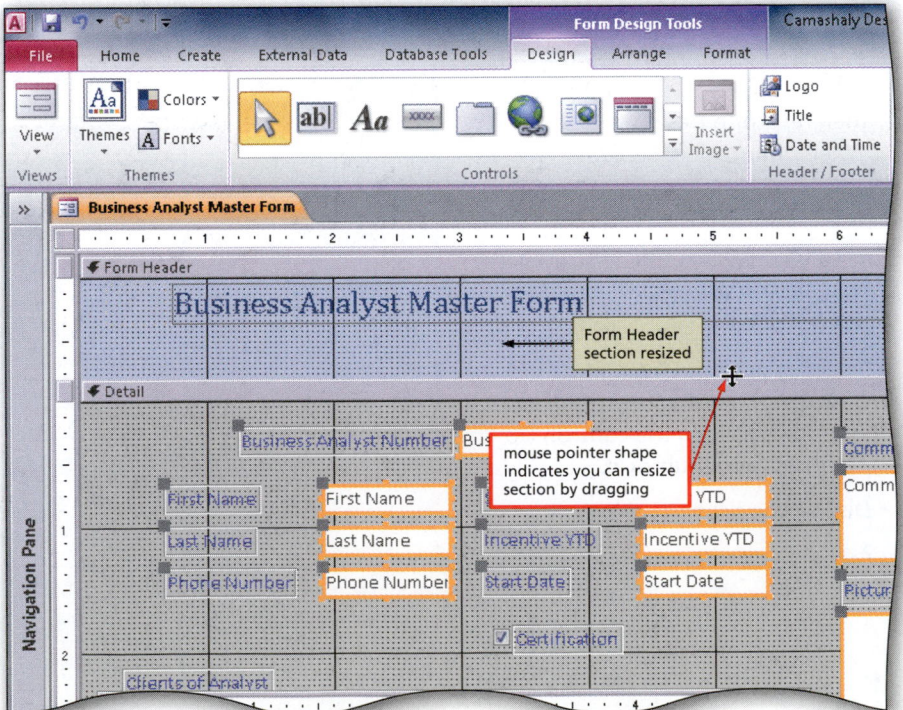

Figure 5–63

2
- Click the control containing the form title to select the control.
- Drag the lower-right sizing handle to resize the control to the approximate size shown in Figure 5–64.

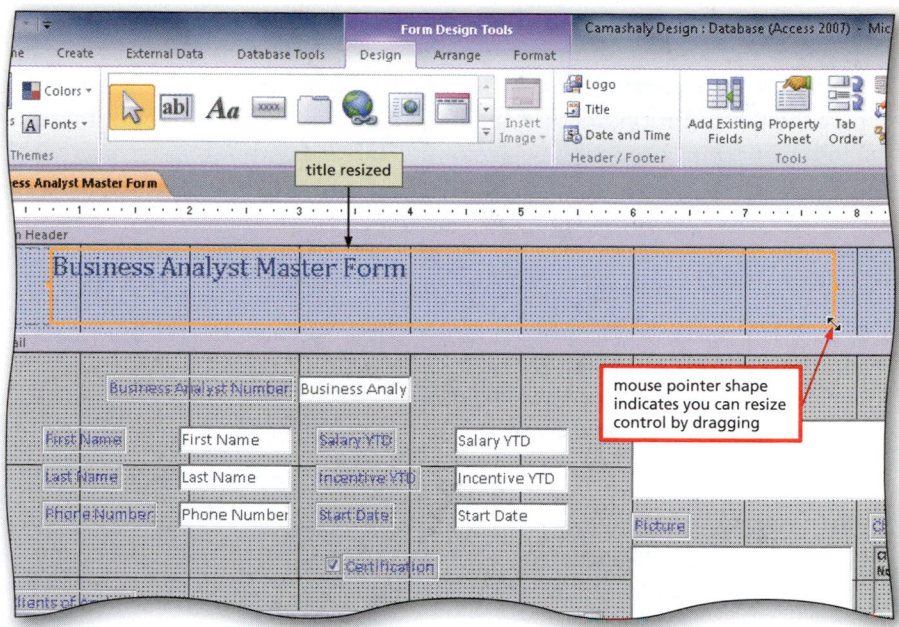

Figure 5–64

3
- Click the Property Sheet button (Form Design Tools Design tab | Tools group) to display the control's property sheet.
- Click the Font Size property box, click the Font Size property box arrow, and then click 26 to change the font size.
- In a similar fashion, change the Text Align property value to Distribute and the Font Weight property value to Semi-bold (Figure 5–65).

4
- Close the property sheet by clicking the Property Sheet button (Form Design Tools Design tab | Tools group).

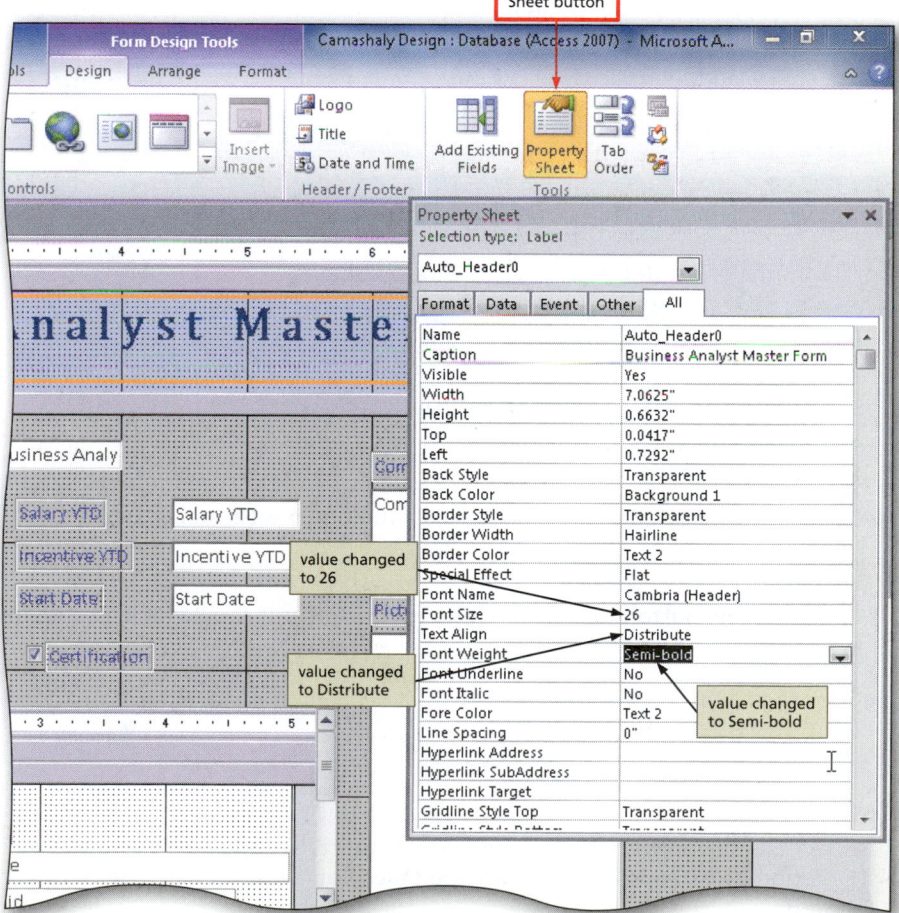

Figure 5–65

To Change a Tab Stop

Users may repeatedly press the TAB key to move through the controls on the form; however, they should bypass the Certification, Picture, and Client Notes controls. To omit these controls from the tab stop sequence, the following steps change the value of the Tab Stop property for the controls from Yes to No.

- Click the Certification control to select it.

- In addition, select the Picture control and the Client Notes control by holding down the SHIFT key while clicking each control (Figure 5–66).

- Click the Property Sheet button (Form Design Tools Design tab | Tools group) to display the property sheet.

- Make sure the All tab (Property Sheet) is selected, click the down scroll arrow until the Tab Stop property appears, click the Tab Stop property, click the Tab Stop property box arrow, and then click No.

- Close the property sheet.

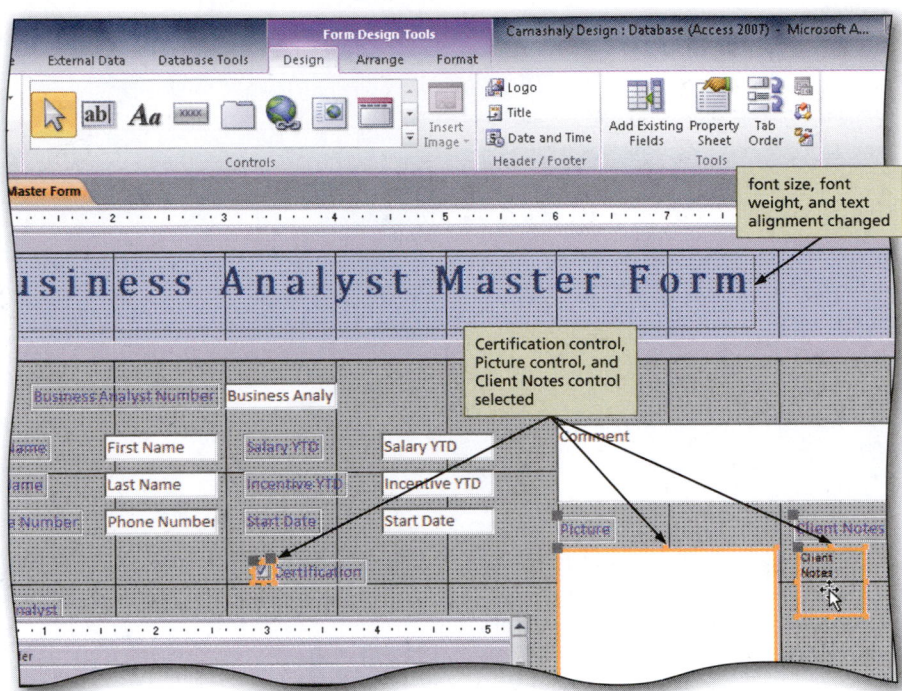

Figure 5–66

Q&A What is the effect of this change?

When a user tabs through the controls, he or she will bypass the Certification control, the Picture control, and the Client Notes control.

Q&A I do not see the Tab Stop property. What did I do wrong?

You clicked the labels for the controls, not the controls.

- Click the Save button on the Quick Access Toolbar to save your changes.

- Click the View button to view the form in Form view. It should look like the form shown in Figure 5–1.

- Close the form.

Break Point: If you wish to stop working through the chapter at this point, you can resume the project at a later time by starting Access, opening the database called Camashaly Design, and continuing to follow the steps from this location forward.

Changing the Tab Order

Users can repeatedly press the TAB key to move through the fields on a form. Access determines the order in which the fields are encountered in this process. If you prefer a different order, you can change the order by clicking the Tab Order button (Form Design Tools Design tab | Tools group). You can then use the Tab Order dialog box (Figure 5–67) to change the order by dragging rows to their desired position as indicated in the dialog box.

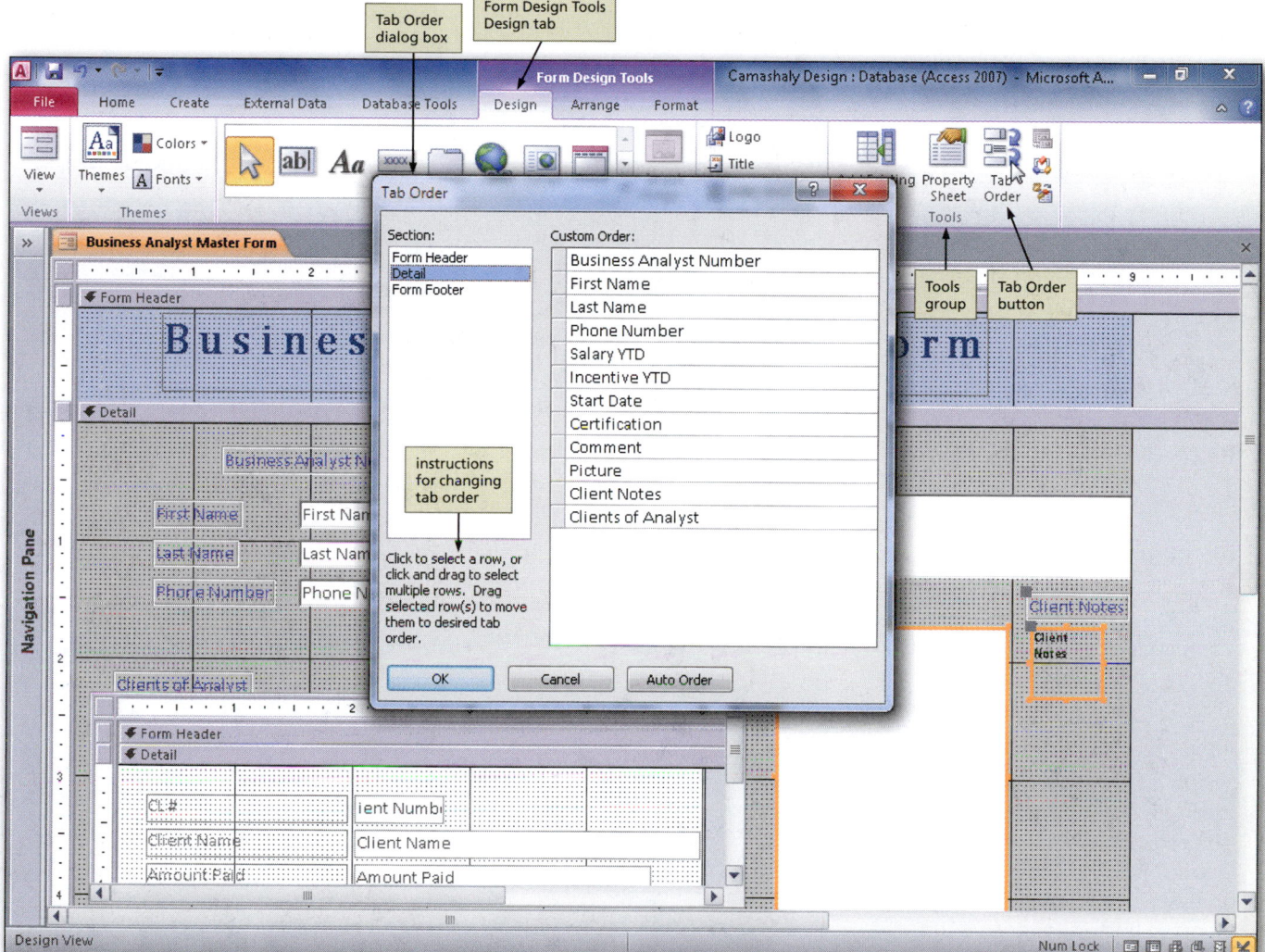

Figure 5–67

To Use the Form

To use a form to view data, right-click the form in the Navigation Pane, and then click Open on the shortcut menu that appears. You then can use the Navigation buttons at the bottom of the screen to move among business analysts. You can use the Navigation buttons in the subform to move among the clients of the business analyst currently shown on the screen. The following steps use the form to display desired data.

1

- Open the Navigation Pane if it is currently closed.

- Right-click the Business Analyst Master Form and then click Open on the shortcut menu.

- Close the Navigation Pane.

- Right-click the Client Notes field to display a shortcut menu (Figure 5–68).

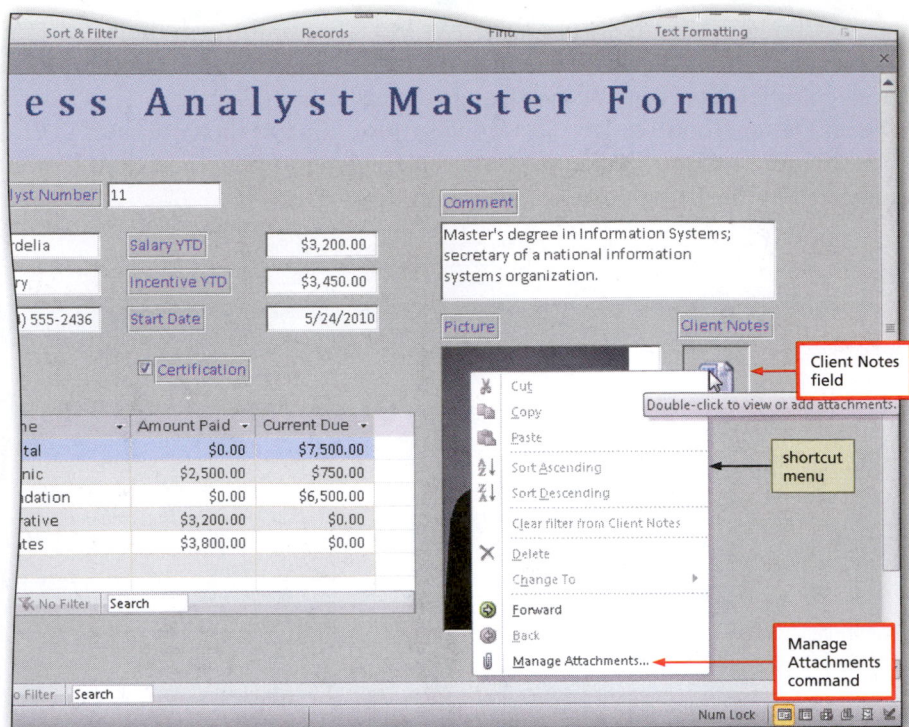

Figure 5–68

2

- Click the Manage Attachments command on the shortcut menu to display the Attachments dialog box (Figure 5–69).

Q&A How do I use this dialog box?

Select an attachment and click the Open button to view the attachment in its original application. Click the Add button to add a new attachment or the Remove button to remove the selected attachment. By clicking the Save button, you can save the selected attachment as a file in whatever location you specify. You can save all attachments at once by clicking the Save All button.

🔍 **Experiment**

- Open both attachments to see how they look in the original applications. When finished, close each original application.

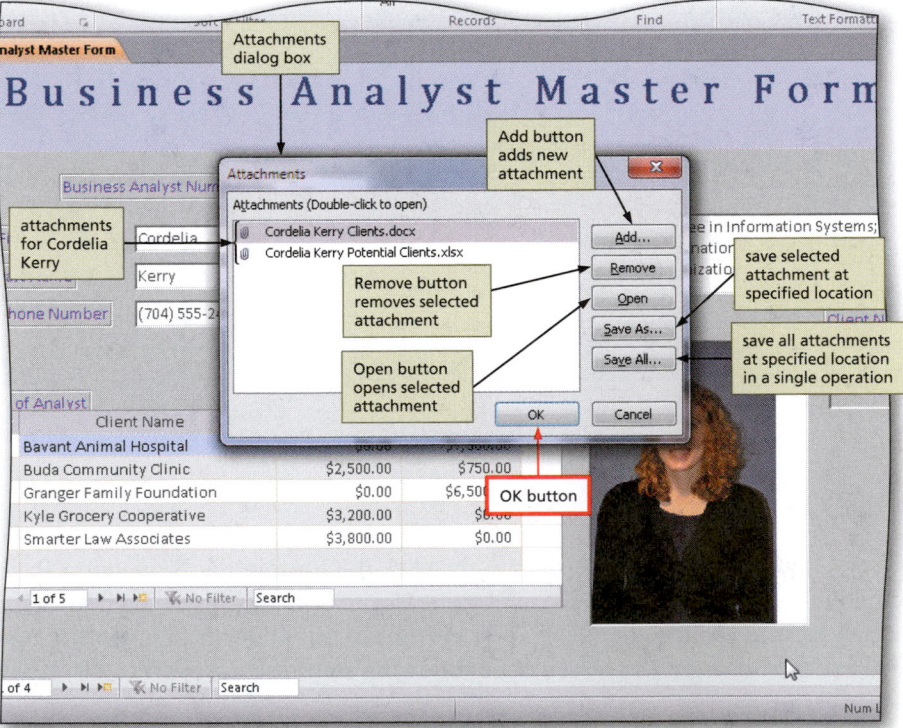

Figure 5–69

3
- Click the OK button to close the Attachments dialog box.
- Click the form's Next record button twice to display the data for business analyst 27 (Figure 5–70).

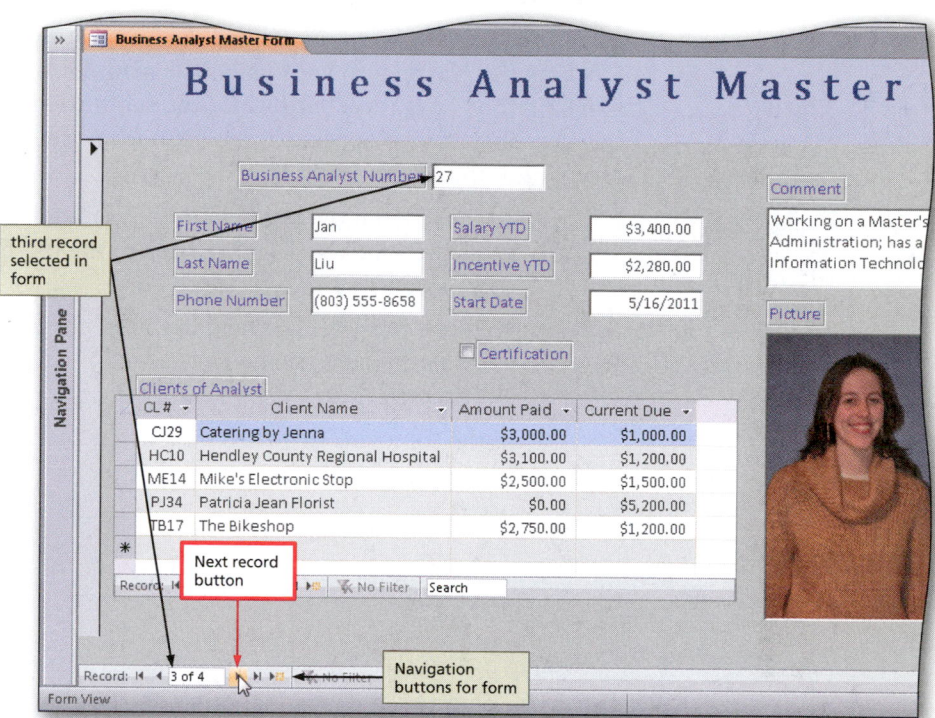

Figure 5–70

4
- Click the subform's Next record button twice to highlight the third client of business analyst 27 (Figure 5–71).

5
- Close the form.

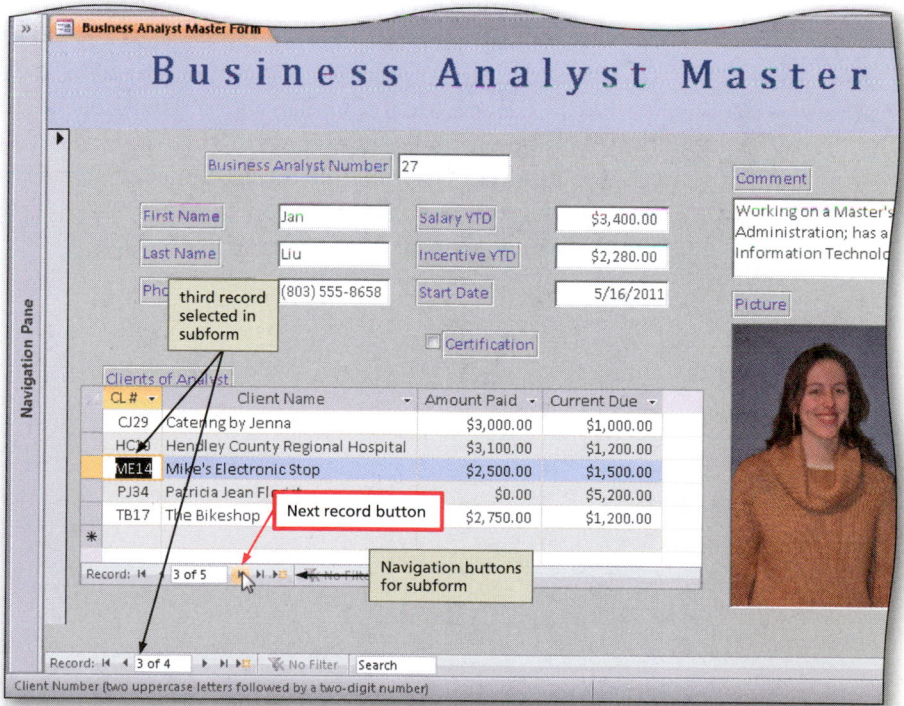

Figure 5–71

Other Ways
1. Double-click Attachments control

Navigation in the Form

The previous steps illustrated the way you work with a main form and subform. Clicking the Navigation buttons for the main form moves to a different business analyst. Clicking the Navigation buttons for the subform moves to a different client of the business analyst who appears in the main form. The following are other actions you can take within the form:

1. To move from the last field in the main form to the first field in the subform, press the TAB key. To move back to the last field in the main form, press CTRL+SHIFT+TAB.

2. To move from the last field in the subform to the first field in the next record's main form, press CTRL+TAB.

3. To switch from the main form to the subform using the mouse, click anywhere in the subform. To switch back to the main form, click any control in the main form. Clicking the background of the main form will not cause the switch to occur.

Object Dependencies

In Access, objects can depend on other objects. For example, a report depends on the table or query on which it is based. A change to the structure of the table or query could affect the report. You can view information on dependencies between database objects. Viewing a list of objects that use a specific object helps in the maintenance of a database and avoids errors when changes are made to the objects involved in the dependency. For example, many items, such as queries and forms, use data from the Client table and thus depend on the Client table. By clicking the Object Dependencies button, you can see what items are based on the object. You also can see the items on which the object depends.

If you are unfamiliar with a database, viewing object dependencies can help you better understand the structure of the database. Viewing object dependencies is especially useful after you have made changes to the structure of tables. An understanding of which reports, forms, and queries depend on a table can assist in making any necessary changes.

To View Object Dependencies

The following steps view the objects that depend on the Client table.

- Open the Navigation Pane and click the Client table.

- Display the Database Tools tab.

- Click the Object Dependencies button (Database Tools tab | Relationships group) to display the Object Dependencies pane.

- If necessary, click the 'Objects that depend on me' option button to select it (Figure 5–72).

 **Experiment**

- Click the 'Objects that I depend on' option button to see the objects on which the Client table depends. Then try both options for other objects in the database.

- Close the Object Dependencies pane by clicking the Object Dependencies button (Database Tools tab | Relationships group) a second time.

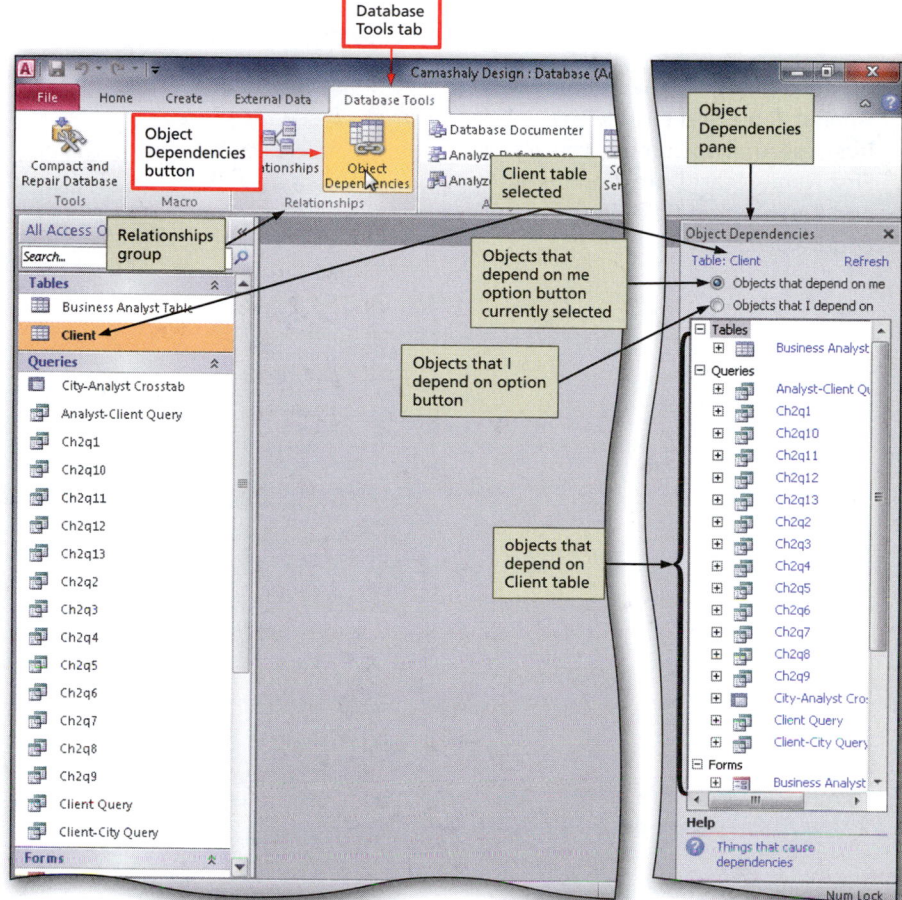

Figure 5–72

Date/Time, Memo, and Yes/No Fields in Queries

By specifying business analyst start dates using Date/Time fields, Camashaly Design can run queries to find business analysts hired before or after a certain date. Other uses of the date field might include calculating an analyst's length of service by subtracting the start date from the current date. Similarly, management can search for business analysts with specific qualifications by adding memos and Yes/No fields.

To use Date/Time fields in queries, you simply type the dates, including the slashes. To search for records with a specific date, you must type the date. You also can use comparison operators. To find all the business analysts whose start date is prior to January 1, 2011, for example, you type <1/1/2011 as the criterion.

You also can use Memo fields in queries. Typically, you will want to find all the records on which the Memo field contains a specific word or phrase. To do so, you use wildcards. For example, to find all the business analysts who have the word, Information, somewhere in the Comment field, you type *Information* as the criterion. The asterisk at the beginning indicates that any characters can appear before the word, Information. The asterisk at the end indicates that any characters can appear after the word, Information.

To use Yes/No fields in queries, type the word, Yes, or the word, No, as the criterion. The following steps create and run queries that use Date/Time, Memo, and Yes/No fields.

BTW

Searching Memo Fields
When you search memo fields, consider alternative spellings and phrases. For example, Computer Science also can be referenced as CS.

To Use Date/Time, Memo, and Yes/No Fields in a Query

The following steps use Date/Time, Memo, and Yes/No fields in queries to search for business analysts who meet specific criteria.

● Create a query for the Business Analyst Table and include the Business Analyst Number, Last Name, First Name, Start Date, Comment, and Certification fields in the query (Figure 5–73).

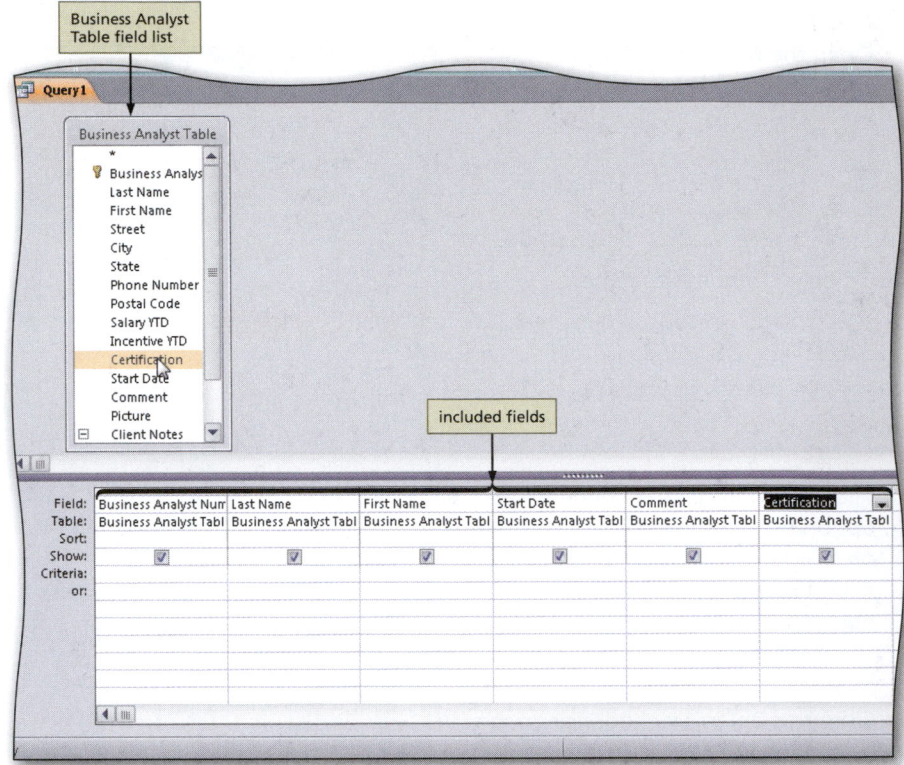

Figure 5–73

● Click the Criteria row under the Comment field and then type ***Information*** as the criterion.

● Click the Criteria row under the Start Date field, and then type **<1/1/2011** as the criterion (Figure 5–74).

Q&A

What happened to the criteria for the Comment field?

Access automatically reformatted it appropriately by adding the word, like, and placing quotation marks around the criterion.

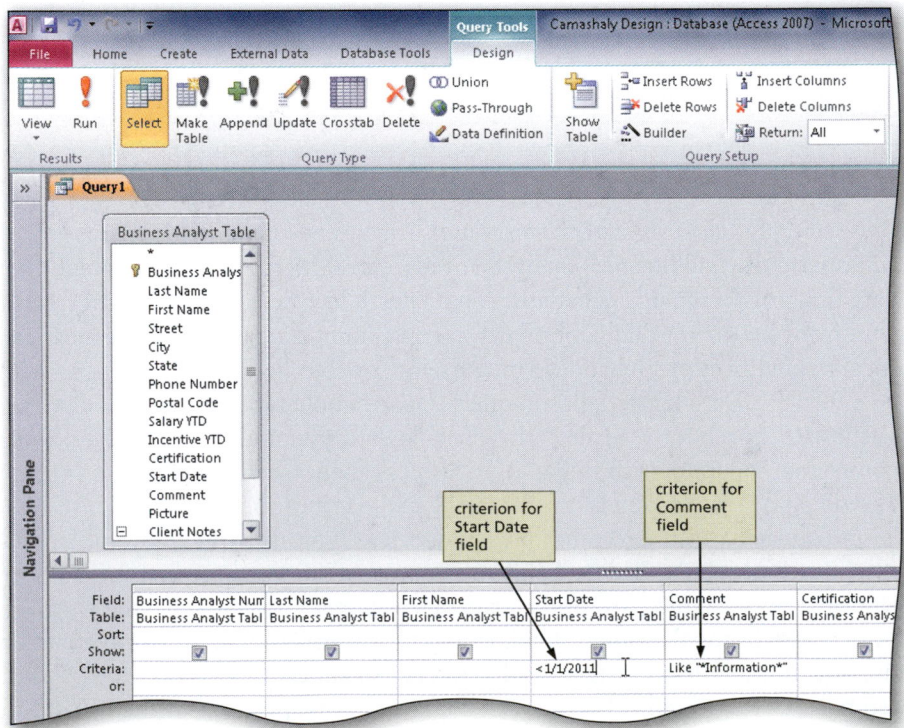

Figure 5–74

3

- Click the View button to view the results (Figure 5–75).

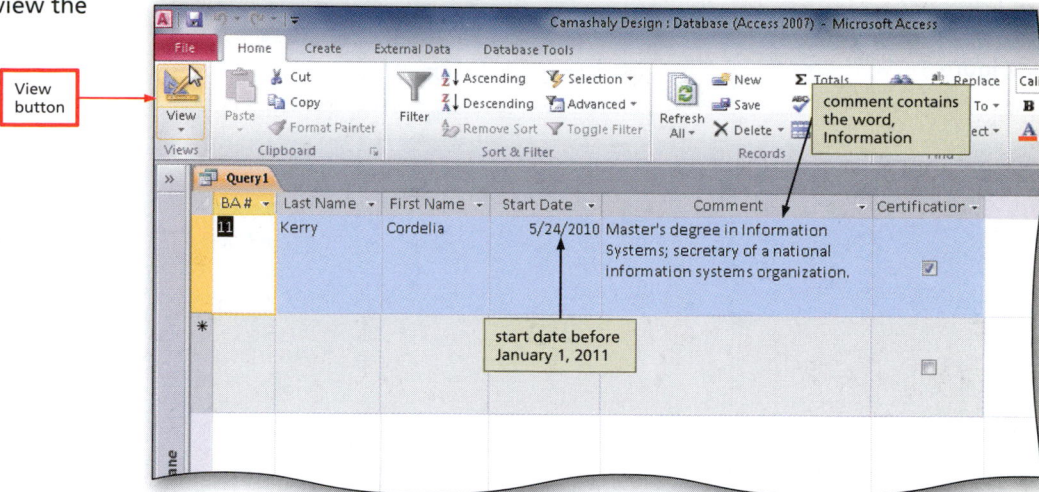

Figure 5–75

4

- Click the View button to return to Design view (Figure 5–76).

Q&A

Why does the date have number signs (#) around it?

This is the date format in Access. You usually do not have to enter the number signs because Access will insert them automatically.

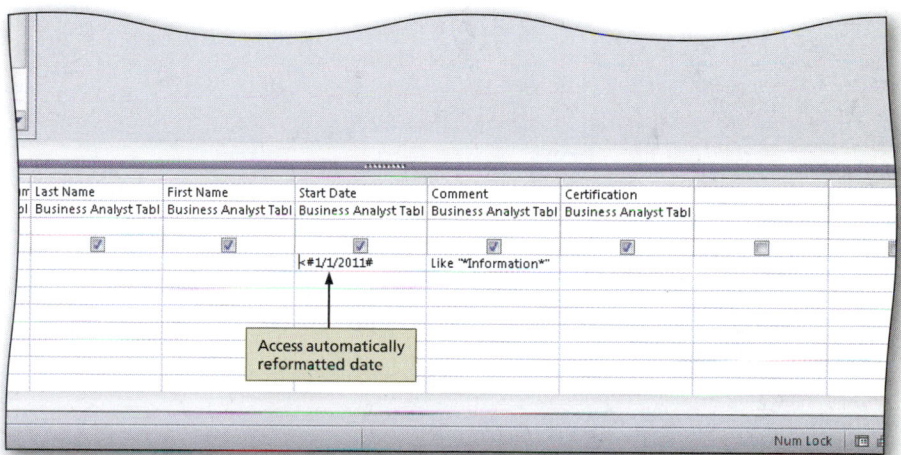

Figure 5–76

5

- Erase the criteria in the Start Date and Comment fields.

- Click the Criteria row under the Certification field and then type **Yes** as the criterion (Figure 5–77).

Q&A

Do I have to type Yes?

You also could type True.

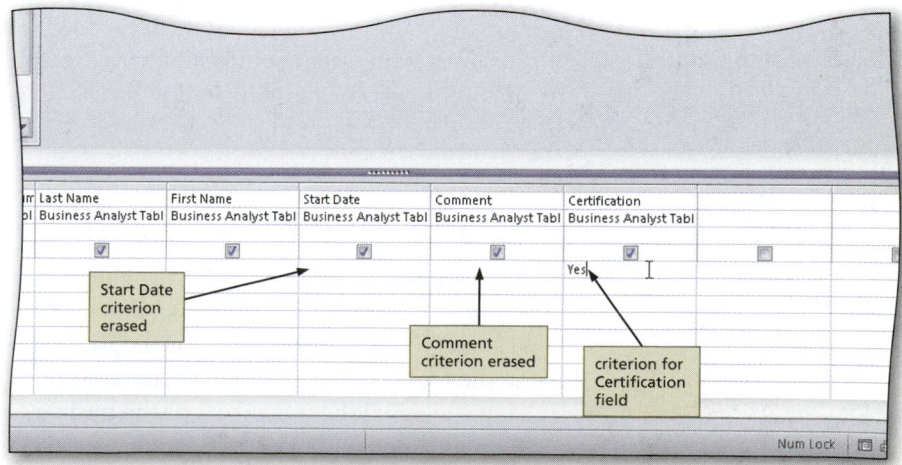

Figure 5–77

6
- Click the View button to view the results (Figure 5–78).

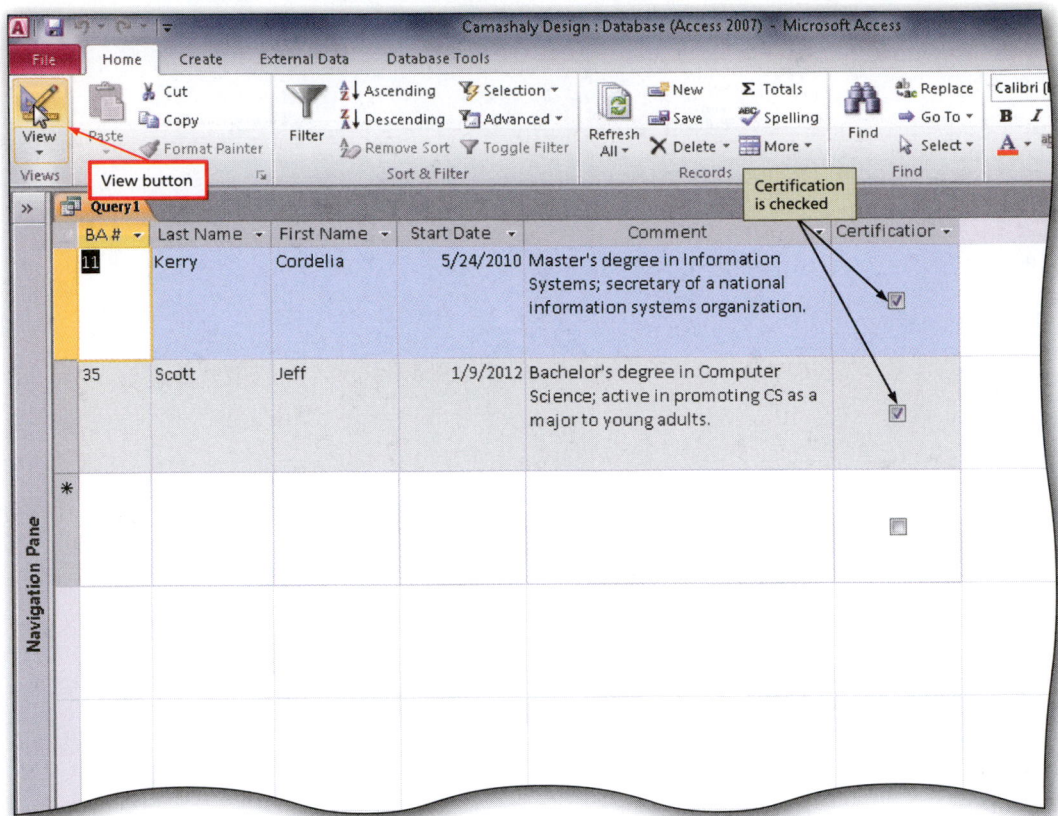

Figure 5–78

 **Experiment**
- Try other combinations of values in the Start Date field, the Comment field, and/or the Certification field. In each case, view the results.

7
- Close the query without saving the results.

Date Fields in Queries
To test for the current date in a query, type Date() in the Criteria row of the appropriate column. Typing <Date() in the Criteria row for the Start Date, for example, finds those business analysts who started anytime before the date on which you run the query.

Datasheets in Forms

In forms created in Layout view, subforms are not available, but you can achieve similar functionality to subforms by including datasheets. Like subforms, the datasheets contain data for the "many" table in the relationship.

Creating a Simple Form with a Datasheet

If you create a simple form for a table that is the "one" table in a one-to-many relationship, Access automatically includes the "many" table in a datasheet within the form. If you create a simple form for the Business Analyst Table, for example, Access will include the Client table in a datasheet within the form, as in Figure 5–79. The clients in the datasheet will be the clients of the business analyst currently on the screen, in this case, Cordelia Kerry.

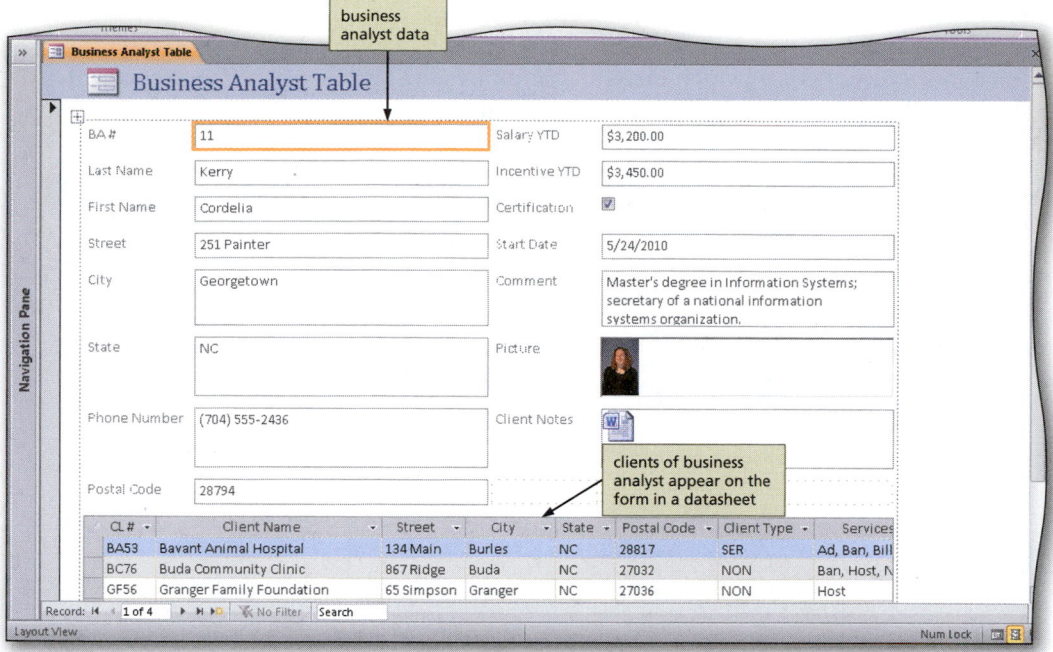

Figure 5-79

TO CREATE A SIMPLE FORM WITH A DATASHEET

To create a simple form with a datasheet, you would use the following steps.

1. Select the table in the Navigation Pane that is the "one" part of a one-to-many relationship.

2. Display the Create tab.

3. Click the Form button (Create tab | Forms group).

Creating a Form with a Datasheet in Layout View

You can create a form with a datasheet in Layout view. To do so, you would first use the field list to add any fields from the "one" table, as shown in Figure 5–80, in which fields from the Business Analyst Table have been added to the form.

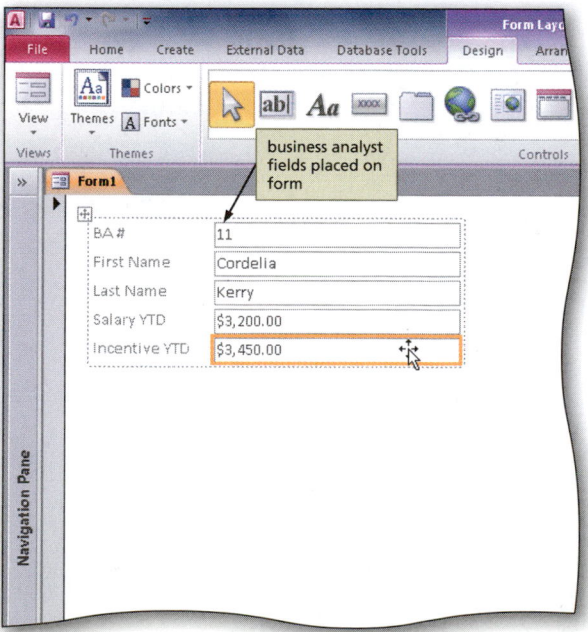
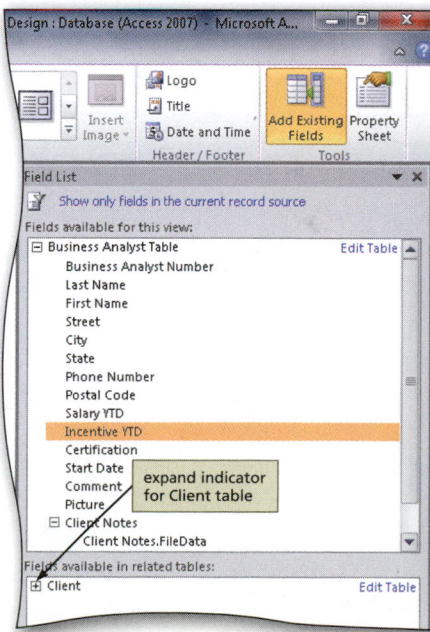

Figure 5-80

Next, you would use the field list to add a single field from the "many" table, as shown in Figure 5–81, in which the Client Number field has been added. Access will automatically create a datasheet containing this field.

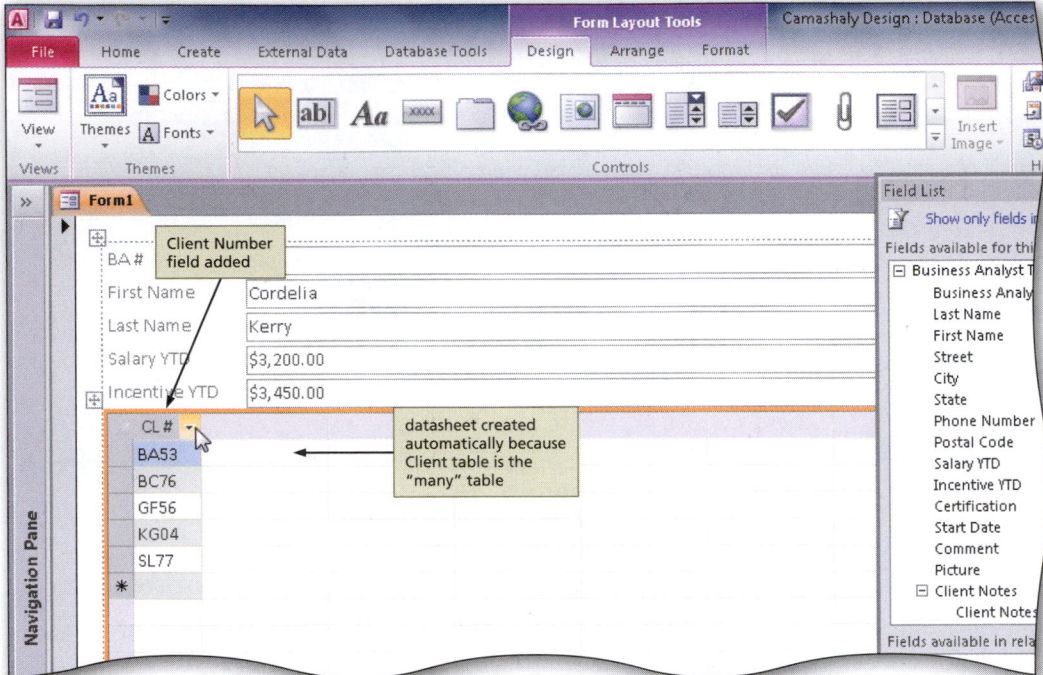

Figure 5–81

Finally, you would click the datasheet to select it and then use the field list to add the other fields from the "many" table that you want to be included in the form, as shown in Figure 5–82.

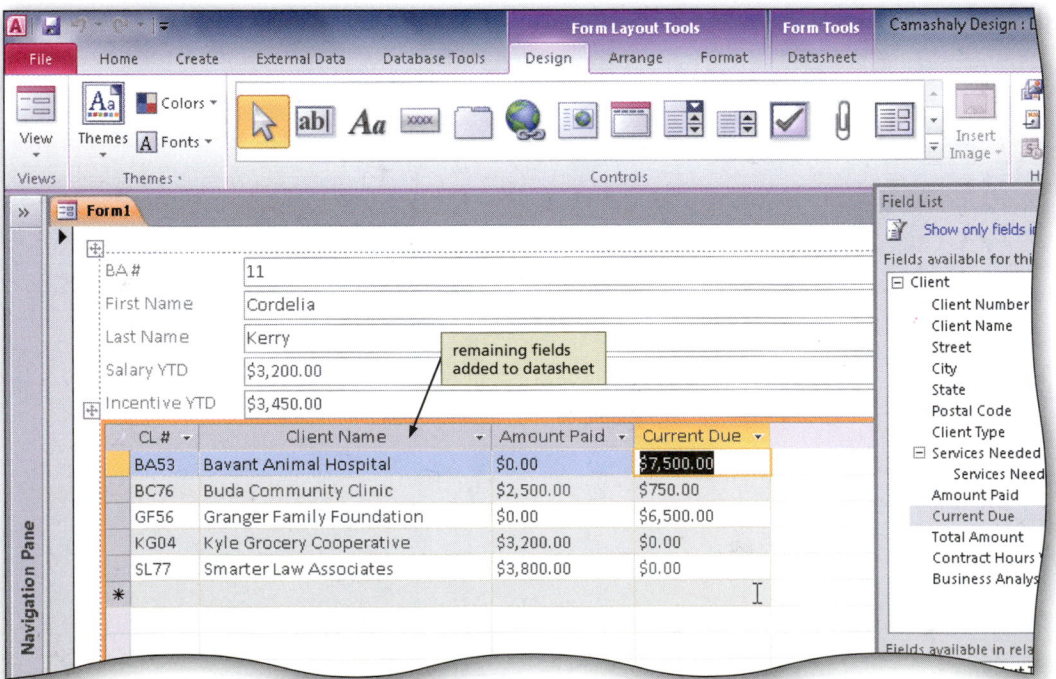

Figure 5–82

To Create a Form with a Datasheet in Layout View

Specifically, to create a form with a datasheet in Layout view, you would use the following steps.

1. Display the Create tab.

2. Click the Blank Form button (Create tab | Forms group) to create a form in Layout view.

3. If a field list does not appear, click the Add Existing Fields button (Form Design Tools Design tab | Tools group) to display a field list.

4. If necessary, click Show all tables to display the available tables.

5. Click the expand indicator (the plus sign) for the "one" table to display the fields in the table and then drag the fields to the desired positions.

6. Click the expand indicator for the "many" table and drag the first field for the datasheet onto the form to create the datasheet.

7. Select the datasheet and drag the remaining fields for the datasheet from the field list to the desired locations in the datasheet.

Creating a Multitable Form Based on the Many Table

All the forms discussed so far in this chapter were based on the "one" table, in this case, the Business Analyst Table. The records from the "one" table were included in a subform. You can also create a multitable form based on the "many" table, in this case, the Client table. Such a form is shown in Figure 5–83.

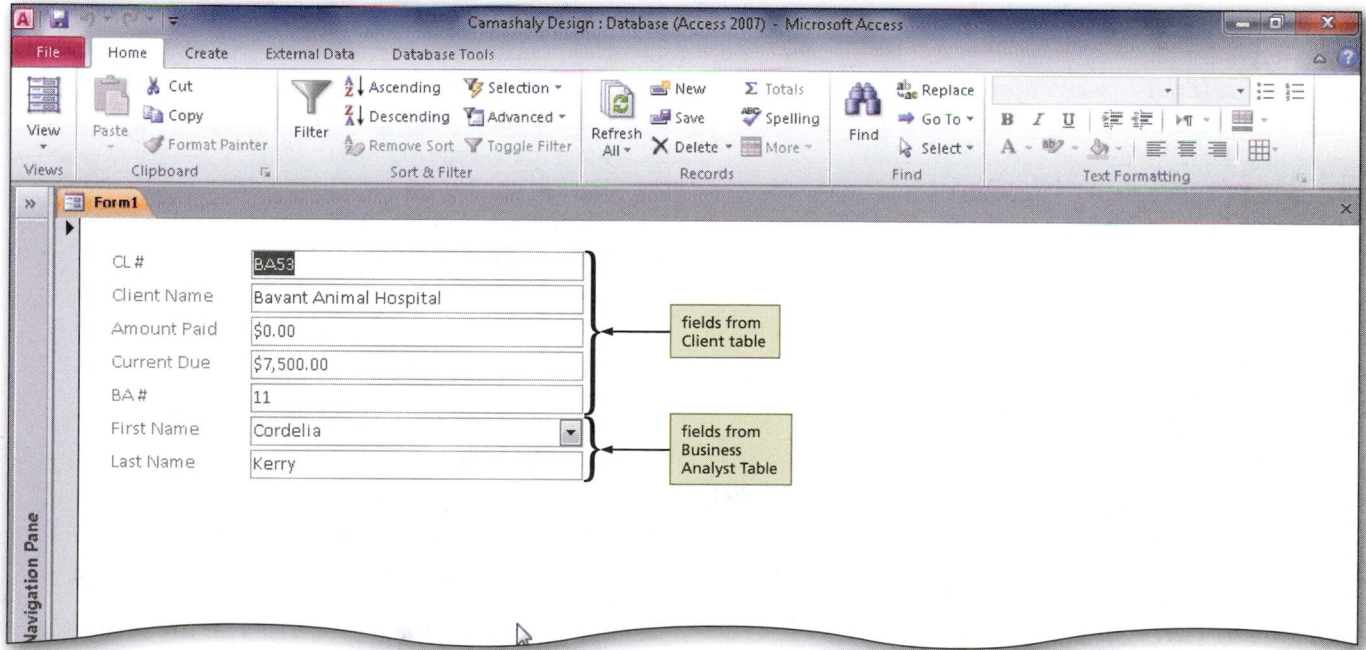

Figure 5–83

In this form, the Client Number, Client Name, Amount Paid, Current Due, and Business Analyst Number fields are in the Client table. The First Name and Last Name fields are found in the Business Analyst Table and are included in the form to help to identify the business analyst whose number appears in the Business Analyst Number field.

TO CREATE A MULTITABLE FORM BASED ON THE MANY TABLE

To create a multitable form based on the "many" table, you would use the following steps.

1. Click the Blank Form button (Create tab | Forms group) to create a form in Layout view.
2. If a field list does not appear, click the Add Existing Fields button on the Design tab to display a field list.
3. Drag the fields for the "many" table to the desired positions.
4. Drag the fields for the "one" table to the desired positions.

To Quit Access

The following steps quit Access.

1 Click the Close button on the right side of the title bar to quit Access.

2 If a Microsoft Access dialog box appears, click the Save button to save any changes made to the object since the last save.

Chapter Summary

In this chapter you have learned to use Yes/No, Date/Time, Memo, OLE Object, and Attachment data types; create and use an input mask; create a form and add a subform; enhance the look of the controls on a form; use a form with a subform; create queries involving Yes/No, Date/Time, and Memo fields; view object dependencies; and create forms containing datasheets in Layout view. The items listed below include all the new Access skills you have learned in this chapter.

1. Add Fields with New Data Types to a Table (AC 278)
2. Use the Input Mask Wizard (AC 280)
3. Enter Data Using an Input Mask (AC 283)
4. Enter Data in Yes/No Fields (AC 284)
5. Enter Data in Date/Time Fields (AC 285)
6. Enter Data in Memo Fields (AC 285)
7. Change the Row and Column Size (AC 286)
8. Enter Data in OLE Object Fields (AC 287)
9. Change Picture Field Entries to Bitmap Images (AC 289)
10. Enter Data in Attachment Fields (AC 289)
11. Enter Data in Hyperlink Fields (AC 291)
12. Create a Form in Design View (AC 292)
13. Add a Control for a Field to the Form Design (AC 293)
14. Add Controls for Additional Fields (AC 294)
15. Align Controls on the Left (AC 295)
16. Align Controls on the Top and Adjust Vertical Spacing (AC 296)
17. Move the Field List (AC 297)
18. Add Controls for the Remaining Fields (AC 297)
19. Use a Shortcut Menu to Change the Fill/Back Color (AC 299)
20. Add a Title (AC 301)
21. Place a Subform (AC 301)
22. View the Form (AC 305)
23. Modify a Subform (AC 305)
24. Change a Label (AC 308)
25. Change the Size Mode (AC 309)
26. Change Special Effects and Colors (AC 309)
27. Modify the Appearance of a Form Title (AC 312)
28. Change a Tab Stop (AC 314)
29. Use the Form (AC 315)
30. View Object Dependencies (AC 319)
31. Use Date/Time, Memo, and Yes/No Fields in a Query (AC 320)
32. Create a Simple Form with a Datasheet (AC 323)
33. Create a Form with a Datasheet in Layout View (AC 325)
34. Create a Multitable Form Based on the Many Table (AC 326)

If you have a SAM 2010 user profile, your instructor may have assigned an autogradable version of this assignment. If so, log into the SAM 2010 Web site at www.cengage.com/sam2010 to download the instruction and start files.

Learn It Online

Test your knowledge of chapter content and key terms.

Instructions: To complete the Learn It Online exercises, start your browser, click the Address bar, and then enter the Web address `scsite.com/ac2010/learn`. When the Access 2010 Learn It Online page is displayed, click the link for the exercise you want to complete and then read the instructions.

Chapter Reinforcement TF, MC, and SA
A series of true/false, multiple choice, and short answer questions that test your knowledge of the chapter content.

Flash Cards
An interactive learning environment where you identify chapter key terms associated with displayed definitions.

Practice Test
A series of multiple choice questions that test your knowledge of chapter content and key terms.

Who Wants To Be a Computer Genius?
An interactive game that challenges your knowledge of chapter content in the style of a television quiz show.

Wheel of Terms
An interactive game that challenges your knowledge of chapter key terms in the style of the television show *Wheel of Fortune*.

Crossword Puzzle Challenge
A crossword puzzle that challenges your knowledge of key terms presented in the chapter.

Apply Your Knowledge

Reinforce the skills and apply the concepts you learned in this chapter.

Adding Date/Time and OLE Fields, Using an Input Mask Wizard, and Querying Date/Time Fields

Instructions: Start Access. If you are using the Microsoft Access 2010 Complete or the Microsoft Access 2010 Comprehensive text, open the Babbage CPA Firm database that you used in Chapter 4. Otherwise, see your instructor for information on accessing the files required in this book.

Perform the following tasks:

1. Add the Start Date and Picture fields to the Bookkeeper table structure, as shown in Figure 5–84. Create an input mask for the Start Date field. Use the Short Date input mask type.

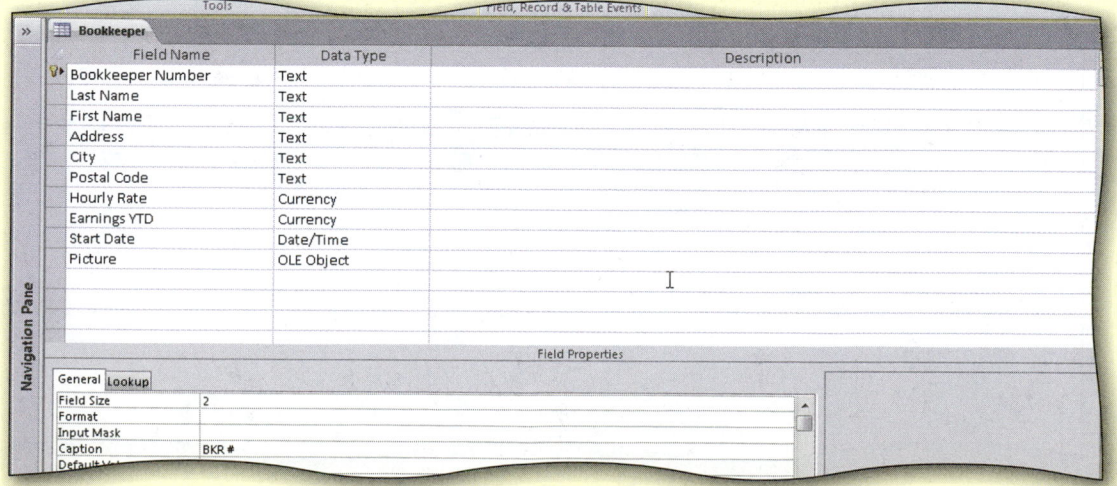

Figure 5–84

Continued >

Apply Your Knowledge *continued*

2. Add the data shown in Table 5–1 to the Bookkeeper table.

Table 5–1 Data for Bookkeeper Table		
Bookkeeper Number	**Start Date**	**Picture**
22	03/07/2011	Pict1.bmp
24	06/07/2010	Pict2.bmp
34	05/09/2011	Pict3.bmp
38	02/06/2012	Pict4.bmp

3. Query the Bookkeeper table to find all bookkeepers who started after January 1, 2012. Include the Bookkeeper Number, First Name, Last Name, Hourly Rate, and Earnings YTD in the query results. Save the query as Start Date Query.

4. Submit the revised database in the format specified by your instructor.

Extend Your Knowledge

Extend the skills you learned in this chapter and experiment with new skills. You may need to use Help to complete the assignment.

Adding Hyperlink Fields and Creating Multitable Forms Using Layout View

Instructions: Start Access. Open the Any School District database. See the inside back cover of this book for instructions on downloading the Data Files for Students, or contact your instructor for more information about accessing the required files.

The Human Resources director at Any School District has several job openings for the two high schools in the district. To keep track of teacher candidates, she created a database. She would like a Hyperlink field added to this database. You will add this field. You also will create the form shown in Figure 5–85.

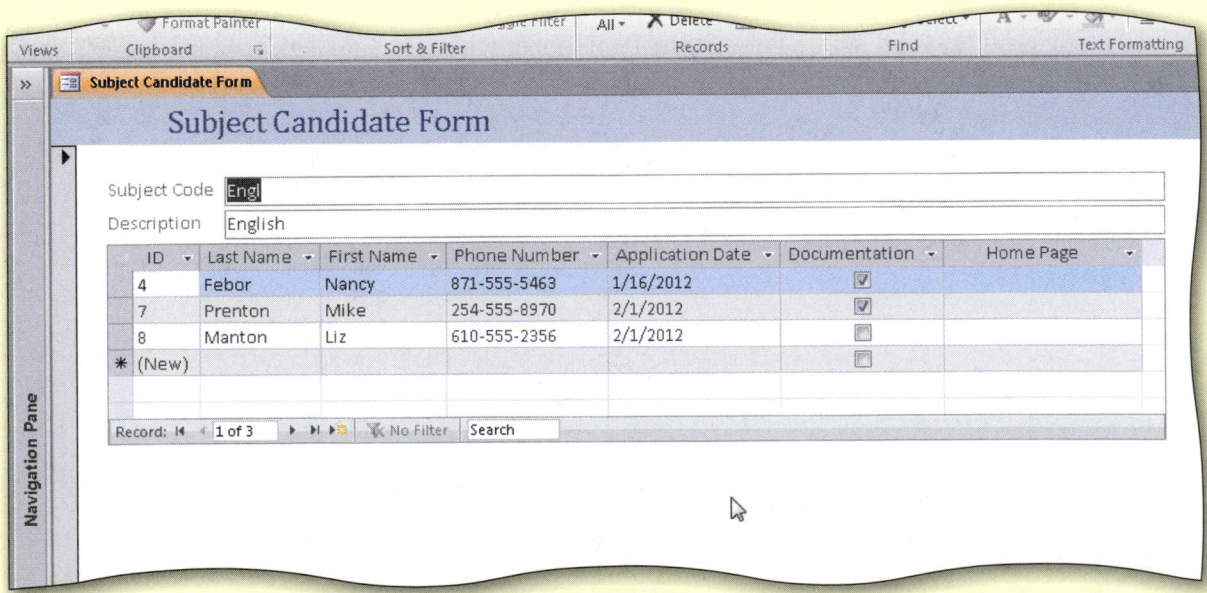

Figure 5–85

Perform the following tasks:

1. Open the Candidate table in Design view and add a Hyperlink field. Insert the field after the Documentation field. Use Home Page as the name of the field.

2. Open the Candidate table in Datasheet view and add data for the Hyperlink field to the first record. If the teachers at your school have individual Web pages, link to one of those pages. Otherwise, use your school home page as the URL. Resize the column to ensure that the complete URL is visible in the datasheet.

3. Use Layout view to create the multitable form shown in Figure 5–85. The Candidate table appears as a subform in the form. Use Subject Candidate Form as the title and save the form with the same name. Decrease the size of the subform.

4. Create a query for the Candidate table to find all candidates who have not submitted documentation. Include the ID, first name, last name, and phone number in the query results. Save the query as Documentation Query.

5. Submit the revised database in the format specified by your instructor.

Make It Right

Analyze a database and correct all errors and/or improve the design.

Correcting Form Design Errors

Instructions: Start Access. Open the LawnAndGarden database. See the inside back cover of this book for instructions on downloading the Data Files for Students, or contact your instructor for more information about accessing the required files.

The LawnAndGarden database contains data for a company that provides lawn and gardening services. The owner of the company has created the form shown in Figure 5–86 but he has encountered some problems with modifying the form.

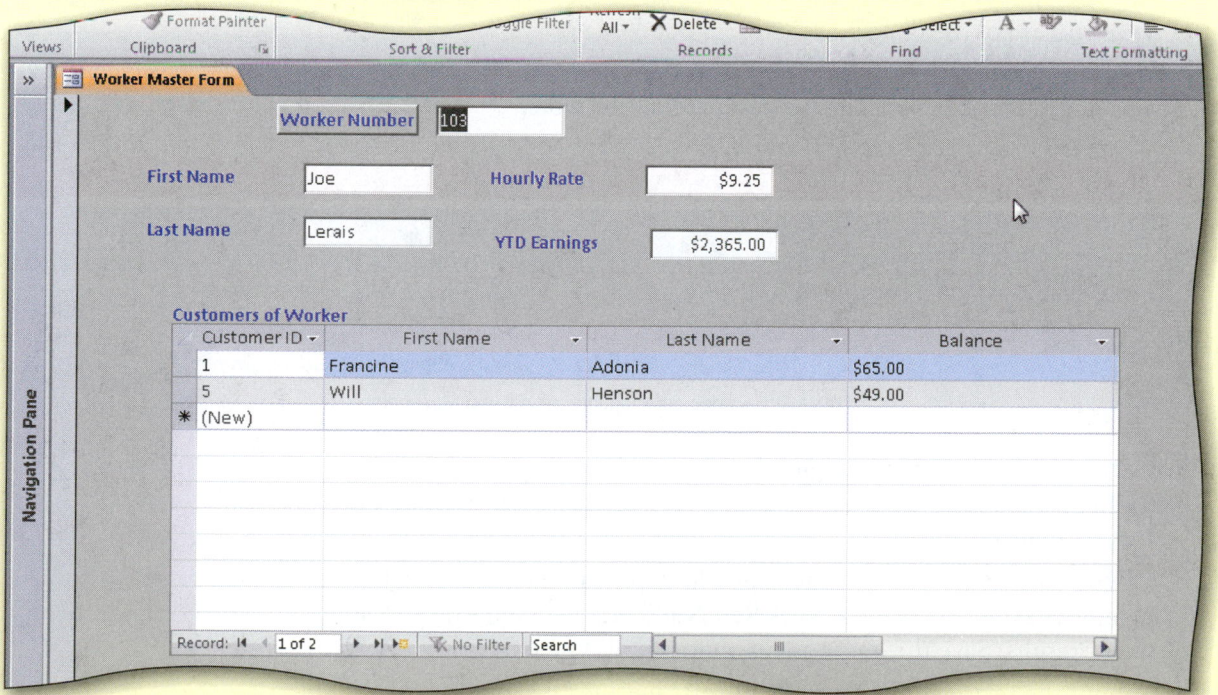

Figure 5–86

Continued >

Make It Right *continued*

The Worker Master Form currently has the Raised special effect for the Worker Number label. All labels should have a raised special effect. The Worker Number control has a Sunken special effect. All other controls except the subform also should have the sunken special effect property. The subform is too big and needs to be resized. The Balance and Amount Paid fields should be right-aligned. The Last Name and YTD Earnings controls should be aligned to the top. The Hourly Rate and YTD Earnings labels should be aligned to the left. Finally, the form needs a title. The owner would like the title, Worker Master Form. The title should have a raised appearance, a text alignment of Distribute with a font size of 24, and a font weight of bold.

Submit the revised database in the format specified by your instructor.

In the Lab

Design, create, modify, and/or use a database following the guidelines, concepts, and skills presented in this chapter. Labs are listed in order of increasing difficulty.

Lab 1: Adding Fields and Creating Multitable Forms for the ECO Clothesline Database

Problem: ECO Clothesline needs to maintain additional data on each sales rep. The company needs to add the date each rep started as well as notes concerning the sales rep and a picture of the sales rep. The company wants a form that displays sales rep information and the customers for whom they are responsible.

Instructions: If you are using the Microsoft Access 2010 Complete or the Microsoft Access 2010 Comprehensive text, open the ECO Clothesline database that you used in Chapter 4. Otherwise, see the inside back cover of this book for instructions on downloading the Data Files for Students, or contact your instructor for more information about accessing the required files.

Perform the following tasks:

1. Add the Start Date, Notes, and Picture fields to the end of the Sales Rep table. Save the changes to the structure of the table.

2. Add the data shown in Table 5–2 to the Sales Rep table. Adjust the row and column spacing to best fit the data. Save the changes to the layout of the table.

Table 5–2 Data for Sales Rep Table

Sales Rep Number	Start Date	Notes	Picture
44	5/10/2010	Excellent computer skills. Helps to train new employees.	Pict1.bmp
49	6/14/2010	Has a BBA in Marketing. Working on an MBA in Management.	Pict4.bmp
51	5/23/2011	Certified Personal Trainer. Enjoys working with health and fitness centers.	Pict2.bmp
55	1/16/2012	Has an AA degree. Working on a BBA in Management.	Pict3.bmp

3. Create the form shown in Figure 5–87. Use Sales Rep Master Form as the name of the form and Customers of Sales Rep as the name of the subform. Users should not be able to tab through the Picture control. The title is centered with a font size of 24 and a font weight of bold.

4. Query the Sales Rep table to find all sales reps who started before January 1, 2012, and who have computer skills. Include the Sales Rep Number, First Name, Last Name, and Notes fields in the query results. Save the query as Computer Skills Query.

5. Submit the revised database in the format specified by your instructor.

Figure 5–87

In the Lab

Lab 2: Adding Fields and Creating Multitable Forms for the Walburg Energy Alternatives Database

Problem: The management of Walburg Energy Alternatives has found that they need to maintain additional data on suppliers. Management needs to keep track of the last date an order was placed, whether the vendor accepts returns, and whether the vendor allows online ordering. Management also would like to attach to each vendor's record Excel files that contain historical cost data. Walburg Energy Alternatives requires a form that displays information about the vendor as well as the items that are purchased from vendors.

Instructions: If you are using the Microsoft Access 2010 Complete or the Microsoft Access 2010 Comprehensive text, open the Walburg Energy Alternatives database that you used in Chapter 4. Otherwise, see the inside back cover of this book for instructions on downloading the Data Files for Students, or contact your instructor for more information about accessing the required files.

Perform the following tasks:
1. Add the fields Last Order Date, Returns, Online Ordering, and Cost History to the end of the Vendor table structure. Last Order Date is a Date/Time field, Returns and Online Ordering are Yes/No fields, and Cost History is an Attachment field. Create an input mask for the Last Order Date that uses the Short Date input mask.

Continued >

In the Lab *continued*

2. Add the data shown in Table 5–3 to the Vendor table.

Table 5–3 Data for Vendor Table				
Vendor Code	**Last Order Date**	**Returns**	**Online Ordering**	**Cost History**
AS	3/30/2012	Yes	No	AS_History.xlsx
JM	3/26/2012	No	Yes	JM_History.xlsx
SD	4/4/2012	Yes	Yes	SD_History.xlsx

3. Create the form shown in Figure 5–88. Use Vendor Master Form as the name of the form and Items of Vendor as the name of the subform. The title is raised, semi-bold, and distributed with a font size of 24. The labels are blue, bold, and etched with a transparent border style. The fields have a sunken special effect.

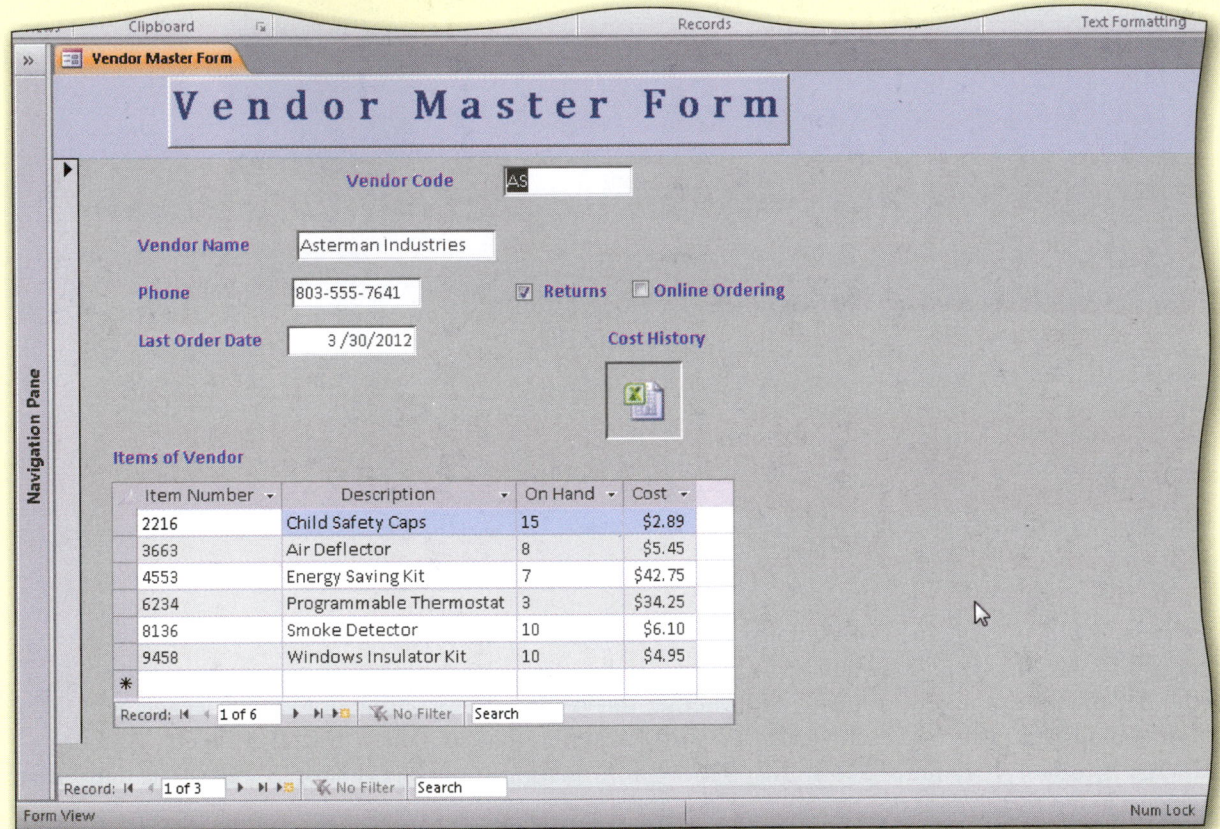

Figure 5–88

4. Open the Vendor Master Form and then open the cost history for Asterman Industries. Change the previous cost for item 4553 to $40.95. Save the change to the workbook.

5. Query the Vendor table to find all vendors that accept returns and allow online ordering. Include the Vendor Code and Name in the query results. Save the query as Returns-Online Query.

6. Submit the revised database in the format specified by your instructor.

In the Lab

Lab 3: Adding Fields and Creating Multitable Forms for the Philamar Training Database

Problem: The management of Philamar Training needs to maintain additional data on trainers. Management needs to store the date the trainer started, comments about each trainer, whether the trainer has MOS certification, and a picture of the trainer. Management wants a form that displays trainer information and the clients they represent.

Instructions: If you are using the Microsoft Access 2010 Complete or the Microsoft Access 2010 Comprehensive text, open the Philamar Training database that you used in Chapter 4. Otherwise, see the inside back cover of this book for instructions on downloading the Data Files for Students, or contact your instructor for more information about accessing the required files. Submit the revised database in the format specified by your instructor.

Instructions Part 1: Add the Start Date, Notes, MOS Certification, and Picture fields to the Trainer table and then add the data shown in Table 5–4 to the Trainer table. Be sure the datasheet displays the entire comment.

Table 5–4 Data for Trainer Table

Trainer Number	Start Date	Notes	Mos Certification	Picture
42	5/10/2010	Has done corporate training for 5 years.	Yes	Pict1.bmp
48	10/11/2010	Specialist in database design and development.	No	Pict2.bmp
53	4/25/2011	Teaches computing courses at the community college.	Yes	Pict4.bmp
67	1/4/2012	Previous elementary school teacher.	No	Pict3.bmp

Instructions Part 2: Create a form for the Trainer table that is similar in design to the form shown in Figure 5–1 on page AC 275. Include all fields from the Trainer table except Address, City, State, and Postal Code. Include the Client Number, Client Name, Amount Paid, and Current Due fields from the Client table in the Clients of Trainer subform. Users should not be able to tab to the Picture field and should tab to the Notes field before the MOS Certification field. Save the form as Trainer Master Form.

Instructions Part 3: Find all trainers that have MOS certification and started before January 1, 2011. Include the Trainer Number, First Name, and Last Name fields in the query result. Save the query as Certification Query.

Cases and Places

Apply your creative thinking and problem solving skills to design and implement a solution.

See the inside back cover of this book for instructions for downloading the Data Files for Students, or see your instructor for information on accessing the required files.

1: Adding Fields and Creating Multitable Forms for the Chamber of Commerce Database

Academic

If you are using the Microsoft Access 2010 Complete or the Microsoft Access 2010 Comprehensive text, open the Chamber of Commerce database that you used in Chapter 4. Otherwise, see your instructor for more information about accessing the required files.

Continued >

Cases and Places *continued*

As part of your internship with the Chamber of Commerce, you worked temporarily as an ad rep when one of the reps was on vacation. This provided an opportunity to learn more about the marketing strategies of some of the advertisers. Now the Chamber has asked you to do some additional database work. Use the concepts and techniques presented in this chapter to perform each of the following tasks:

a. Add the Phone Number, Start Date, and Comment fields to the Ad Rep table. Place the Phone Number field after the Postal Code field and use an input mask of your choosing for both the Phone Number and the Start Date fields. Place the Start Date and Comment fields at the end of the table. Add the data shown in Table 5–5 to the Ad Rep table. Be sure the datasheet displays the entire comment.

Table 5–5 Data for Ad Rep Table

Ad Rep Number	Phone Number	Start Date	Comment
22	215-555-1234	10/4/2010	Excellent copy editor.
29	610-555-2345	3/11/2011	Records radio advertisements for chamber.
32	215-555-8976	9/12/2011	Also works as a freelance journalist.
35	610-555-6578	3/15/2012	Semi-retired with extensive sales experience.

b. Create an Ad Rep Master Form for the Ad Rep table that is similar in design to the form shown in Figure 5–1 on page AC 275. Include all fields from Ad Rep table except Address, City, and Postal Code. Include an Advertisers of Ad Rep subform that includes the advertiser number, advertiser name, advertiser type, balance, and amount paid.

c. Create an Advertiser Update form for the Advertiser table. Include the advertiser number, advertiser name, balance, amount paid, advertiser type, and ad rep number. Include the first name and last name from the Ad Rep table. Users should not be able to change the ad rep name data.

Submit the revised database in the format specified by your instructor.

2: Creating Multitable Forms for the Consignment Database

Personal

If you are using the Microsoft Access 2010 Complete or the Microsoft Access 2010 Comprehensive text, open the Consignment database that you used in Chapter 4. Otherwise, see your instructor for more information about accessing the required files. Because many individuals volunteer at the consignment shop, you have been asked to simplify the task of entering data on sellers. Use the concepts and techniques presented in this chapter to perform each of the following tasks:

a. Create a Seller Master Form for the Seller table that is similar in design to the form shown in Figure 5–1 on page AC 275. Include all fields in the Seller table on the form. The Items of Seller subform should display all fields in the Items table except Seller Code. Customize the form by adding special effects to controls and labels as well as changing the background color of the form. Add the current date to the form header.

b. Create a query for the Items table to find all items posted during the month of March. Include the Item Number, Description, and Date Posted fields in the query results. Save the query as March Items Query.

Submit the revised database in the format specified by your instructor.

3: Adding Fields and Creating Multitable Forms for the Senior Care Database

Professional

If you are using the Microsoft Access 2010 Complete or the Microsoft Access 2010 Comprehensive text, open the Senior Care database that you used in Chapter 4. Otherwise, see your instructor for more information about accessing the required files. You and your co-owner have decided that you need

to add some additional data to the Helper table. Use the concepts and techniques presented in this chapter to perform each of the following tasks:

a. Add a Phone Number and a Comment field to the Helper table. Add the Phone Number field after the First Name field. Create an input mask of your choosing for the Phone Number field. Add the Comment field to the end of the table. Change the Text Format property for the Comment field to Rich Text and the Append Only property to Yes.

b. Add the data shown in Table 5–6 to the Helper table. Make sure all data appears in the datasheet.

Table 5–6 Data for Helper Table		
Helper Number	**Phone Number**	**Comment**
203	803-555-3456	Has previous nursing home experience.
205	704-555-9876	Speaks Spanish. Has an AA degree.
207	704-555-2341	Excellent organizational skills.
209	803-555-4554	Has a chauffer's license.

c. Create a Helper Master Form for the Helper table. Include all fields from the Helper table. Include a Clients of Helper subform that includes the client number, client first name and last name, amount paid, and balance. Use your own design specifications for the form.

d. Open the Helper Master Form and bold the word Spanish in the Comment field for helper 205. Add the following sentence to the Comment field for helper 207: Working on an AA degree. Be sure the complete comment for helper 207 displays in the datasheet.

e. Create a query that finds all clients who need hygiene services and have a helper who speaks Spanish. Include the client number, client first and last names, helper number, and helper last name in the query results. Save the query as Hygiene-Spanish Query.

Submit the revised database in the format specified by your instructor.

6 | Advanced Report Techniques

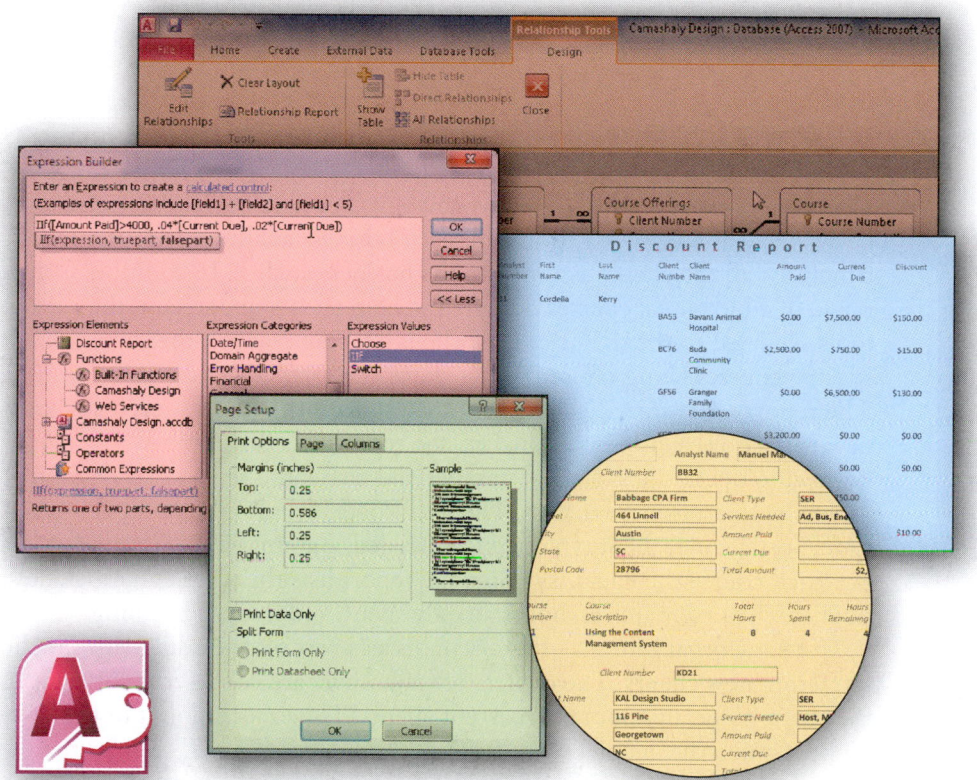

Objectives

You will have mastered the material in this project when you can:

- Create and relate additional tables
- Create queries for reports
- Create reports in Design view
- Add fields and text boxes to a report
- Format report controls
- Group and ungroup report controls
- Update multiple report controls

- Add and modify a subreport
- Modify section properties
- Add a title, page number, and date
- Preview, print, and publish a report
- Add totals and subtotals
- Include a conditional value in a report

6 | Advanced Report Techniques

Introduction

Q&As

For a complete list of the Q&As found in many of the step-by-step sequences in this book, visit the Access 2010 Q&A Web page (scsite.com/ac2010/qa).

In this chapter, you will create two reports in Design view. Both reports feature grouping and sorting. The first report contains a subreport, which is a report that is contained within another report. The subreport contains data from a query and is related to data in the main report. The second report uses aggregate functions to calculate subtotals and grand totals. It also uses a function to calculate a value where the calculation will vary from record to record depending on whether a given criterion is true.

Project — Advanced Report Techniques

BTWs

For a complete list of the BTWs found in the margins of this book, visit the Access 2010 BTW Web page (scsite.com/ac2010/btw).

The owners of Camashaly Design want a master list of business analysts. This list should be available as an Access report. For each business analyst, the report is to include full details for all the clients assigned to the business analyst. In addition, Camashaly offers a range of educational courses designed to help clients understand the various marketing tools available to them. For clients who are taking courses, the report should list the specific courses being offered to the client. The actual report is shown in Figure 6–1a. The report is organized by business analyst, with the data for each analyst beginning on a new page. For each business analyst, the report lists the number, first name, and last name. Following the business analyst number and name, the report lists data for each client served by that business analyst. The client data includes the number, name, street, city, state, postal code, client type, services needed, amount paid, current due, and total amount. For each course the client is taking, the report lists the course number, description, total hours the course requires, hours already spent, and hours remaining.

Many organizations offer discounts as a way of rewarding current clients and attracting new clients. The owners of Camashaly are considering offering a discount on the current due amount to its current clients. The exact amount of the discount depends on how much the client already has paid. If the amount paid is more than $4,000, the discount will be 4% of the current due amount. If the amount paid is $4,000 or less, then the discount will be 2% of the current due amount. To assist in determining the discount, Camashaly needs a report like the one shown in Figure 6–1b on page AC 340. The report groups clients by business analyst. It includes subtotals of both the Amount Paid and Current Due fields. Also, although not visible in the figure, it includes grand totals of both fields at the end of the report. Finally, it shows the discount amount, which is calculated by multiplying the current due amount by .04 (4%) for those clients for whom the amount paid is more than $4,000 and by .02 (2%) for all others.

The Ribbon and Screen Resolution

Access may change how the groups and buttons within the groups appear on the Ribbon, depending on the computer's screen resolution. Thus, your Ribbon may look different from the ones in this book if you are using a screen resolution other than 1024 × 768.

Overview

As you read through this chapter, you will learn how to create the reports by performing these general tasks:

- Create and relate additional tables.
- Create queries for a report.
- Create a report, specify grouping and sorting, and add fields and text boxes to the report.
- Add a subreport to the report.
- Add a title, page number, and date to the report.
- Print and publish a report.
- Create a second report, specify grouping and sorting, and add fields and text boxes to the report.
- Add totals and subtotals to the report, and add a text box that uses a function.

(a) Business Analyst Master List – Page 4

Figure 6–1

D i s c o u n t   R e p o r t

Analyst Number	First Name	Last Name	Client Numbe	Client Name	Amount Paid	Current Due	Discount
11	Cordelia	Kerry					
			BA53	Bavant Animal Hospital	$0.00	$7,500.00	$150.00
			BC76	Buda Community Clinic	$2,500.00	$750.00	$15.00
			GF56	Granger Family Foundation	$0.00	$6,500.00	$130.00
			KG04	Kyle Grocery Cooperative	$3,200.00	$0.00	$0.00
			SL77	Smarter Law Associates	$3,800.00	$0.00	$0.00
				Subtotals	$9,500.00	$14,750.00	
14	Manuel	Martinez					
			BB32	Babbage CPA Firm	$1,500.00	$500.00	$10.00
			KD21	KAL Design Studio	$6,000.00	$3,200.00	$128.00
				Subtotals	$7,500.00	$3,700.00	
27	Jan	Liu					
			CJ29	Catering by Jenna	$3,000.00	$1,000.00	$20.00
			HC10	Hendley County Regional Hospital	$3,100.00	$1,200.00	$24.00
			ME14	Mike's Electronic Stop	$2,500.00	$1,500.00	$30.00
			PJ34	Patricia Jean Florist	$0.00	$5,200.00	$104.00
			TB17	The Bikeshop	$2,750.00	$1,200.00	$24.00

(b) Discount Report

Figure 6 – 1

Plan
Ahead

Report Design Guidelines

When designing a report, the requirements of the users and the decisions you make will affect the appearance of the report. As you create reports and subreports, such as the ones shown in Figure 6–1, you should follow these general guidelines:

1. **Determine the intended audience and purpose of the report.** Identify the user or users of the report and determine how they will use it. Specify the necessary data and level of detail to include in the report.

2. **Determine the source of data for the report.** Determine whether all the data is in a single table or whether it comes from multiple related tables. The data may be found in a query. You might need to create multiple reports for a query where the criterion for a field changes, in which case, you would use a parameter query and enter the criterion when you run the report. If the data comes from multiple related tables, you might want to create a query and use the query as a source of data.

3. **Determine the fields that belong on the report.** Identify the data items that are needed by the user of the report.

4. **Determine the organization of the report.** The report may be enhanced by displaying the fields in a particular order and arranged in a certain way. Should the records in the report be grouped in some way? Should the report contain any subreports?

5. **Determine any calculations required for the report.** Should the report contain totals or subtotals? Are there any special calculations? If so, you may need to include functions to handle calculations. For example, the Business Analyst Master List contains a Total Amount field that is calculated by adding the contents of the Amount Paid field and the Current Due field. The Discount Report contains a Discount field, which is calculated by multiplying the amount in the Current Due field by 4% if the amount in the Amount Paid field is greater than $4,000 and by 2% otherwise.

6. **Determine the format and style of the report.** What information should be in the report heading? Do you want a title and date, for example? Do you want a logo? What should be in the body of the report? What should the style be? In other words, what visual characteristics should the various portions of the report have? Does the organization have specific style requirements for reports?

When necessary, more specific details concerning the above decisions and/or actions are presented at appropriate points in the chapter. The chapter also will identify the use of these guidelines in the design of the reports such as the ones shown in Figure 6–1.

To Start Access

The following steps, which assume Windows 7 is running, start Access based on a typical installation. You may need to ask your instructor how to start Access for your computer.

1 Click the Start button on the Windows 7 taskbar to display the Start menu.

2 Type `Microsoft Access` as the search text in the 'Search programs and files' text box and watch the search results appear on the Start menu.

3 Click Microsoft Access 2010 in the search results on the Start menu to start Access.

4 If the Access window is not maximized, click the Maximize button next to the Close button on its title bar to maximize the window.

To Open a Database from Access

The following steps open the Camashaly Design database from the Access folder in the CIS 101 folder on the USB flash drive.

1 With your USB flash drive connected to one of the computer's USB ports, click File on the Ribbon to open the Backstage view.

2 Click Open in the Backstage view to display the Open dialog box.

3 Navigate to the location of the file to be opened (in this case, the USB flash drive, then to the CIS 101 folder [or your class folder], and then to the Access folder).

4 Click Camashaly Design to select the file to be opened.

5 Click the Open button (Open dialog box) to open the selected file and display the opened database in the Access window.

6 If a Security Warning appears, click the Enable Content button.

Additional Tables

Because the business analysts at Camashaly work collaboratively with clients, they are frequently asked to present courses on various Internet and Web development topics. Camashaly would like to incorporate this data in the Camashaly Design database.

Before creating the reports, you need to create two additional tables for the Camashaly Design database. The first table, Course, is shown in Tables 6–1a and 6–1b. As described in Table 6–1a, each course has a number and a description. The table also includes the total hours for which the course usually is offered and its increments; that is, the standard time blocks in which the course usually is offered. Table 6–1b contains the specific courses that the business analysts at Camashaly Design offer to their clients. The first row, for example, indicates that course C01 is called Using the Content Management System. It typically is offered in two-hour increments for a total of eight hours.

Table 6–1a Structure of Course Table

Field Name	Data Type	Field Size	Comments
Course Number	Text	3	Primary Key
Course Description	Text	40	
Hours	Number	Integer	
Increments	Number	Integer	

Table 6–1b Course Table

Course Number	Course Description	Hours	Increments
C01	Using the Content Management System	8	2
C02	HTML Basics	4	1
C03	Digital Image Management	6	3
C04	JavaScript Basics	12	3
C05	Understanding Social Networks	2	2
C06	Using Shopping Carts	4	2
C07	Understanding Cascading Style Sheets	8	2
C08	Podcasting	6	3

The second table is Table 6–2a, Course Offerings, which contains a client number, a course number, the total number of hours that the course is scheduled for the client, and the number of hours already spent in the course. The primary key of the Course Offerings table is a combination of the Client Number and Course Number fields.

Table 6–2b gives the data for the Course Offerings table. For example, the first record shows that client number BA53 currently has scheduled course C05 (Understanding Social Networks). The course is scheduled for 2 hours, and they have not yet spent any hours in class.

If you examine the data in Table 6–2b, you see that the Client Number field cannot be the primary key for the Course Offerings table. The fourth and fifth records, for example, both have a client number of HC10. The Course Number field also cannot be the primary key. The first and fifth records, for example, both have course number C05. Rather, the primary key is the combination of both Client Number and Course Number.

Table 6–2a Structure of Course Offerings Table

Field Name	Data Type	Field Size	Description
Client Number	Text	4	Part of Primary Key
Course Number	Text	3	Part of Primary Key
Total Hours	Number	Integer	
Hours Spent	Number	Integer	

Table 6–2b Course Offerings Table

Client Number	Course Number	Total Hours	Hours Spent
BA53	C05	2	0
BB32	C01	8	4
CJ29	C03	6	3
HC10	C04	12	6
HC10	C05	2	1
KD21	C03	6	0
KD21	C07	8	4
KG04	C01	8	6
KG04	C05	2	0
KG04	C08	6	4
ME14	C06	4	2
PJ34	C06	4	2
SL77	C04	12	9
SL77	C08	6	2
TB17	C02	4	2

BTW

AutoNumber Field as Primary Key
When you create a table in Datasheet view, Access automatically creates an ID field with the AutoNumber data type as the primary key field. As you add records to the table, Access increments the ID field so that each record will have a unique value in the field. AutoNumber fields are useful when there is no data field in a table that is a suitable primary key.

To Create the New Tables

You can create new Access tables in either Datasheet view or Design view. In Design view, you define the structure of the tables. The steps to create the new tables are similar to the steps you used previously to add fields to an existing table and to define primary keys. The only difference is the way you specify a primary key consisting of more than one field. First, you select both fields that make up the primary key by clicking the row selector for the first field, and then hold down the SHIFT key while clicking the row selector for the second field. Once the fields are selected, you can use the Primary Key button to indicate that the primary key consists of both fields.

The following steps create the tables in Design view.

1
- If necessary, close the Navigation Pane.
- Display the Create tab (Figure 6–2).

2
- Click the Table Design button (Create tab | Tables group) to create a table in Design view.
- Enter the information for the fields in the Course table as indicated in Table 6–1a on page AC 342, selecting Course Number as the primary key.
- Save the table using the name `Course` and close the table.

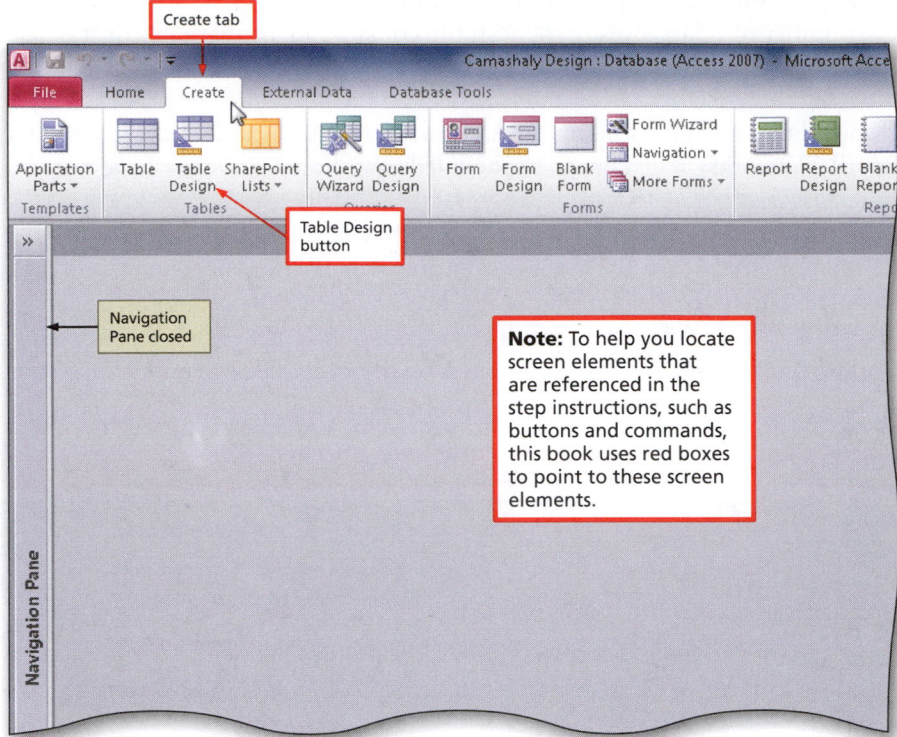

Figure 6–2

3
- Display the Create tab and then click the Table Design button (Create tab | Tables group) to create a second table in Design view.
- Enter the information for the fields in the Course Offerings table as indicated in Table 6–2a on page AC 343.
- Click the row selector for the Client Number field.
- Hold down the SHIFT key and then click the row selector for the Course Number field so both fields are selected.
- Click the Primary Key button (Table Tools Design tab | Tools group) to select the combination of the two fields as the primary key (Figure 6–3).

4
- Save the table using the name `Course Offerings` and close the table.

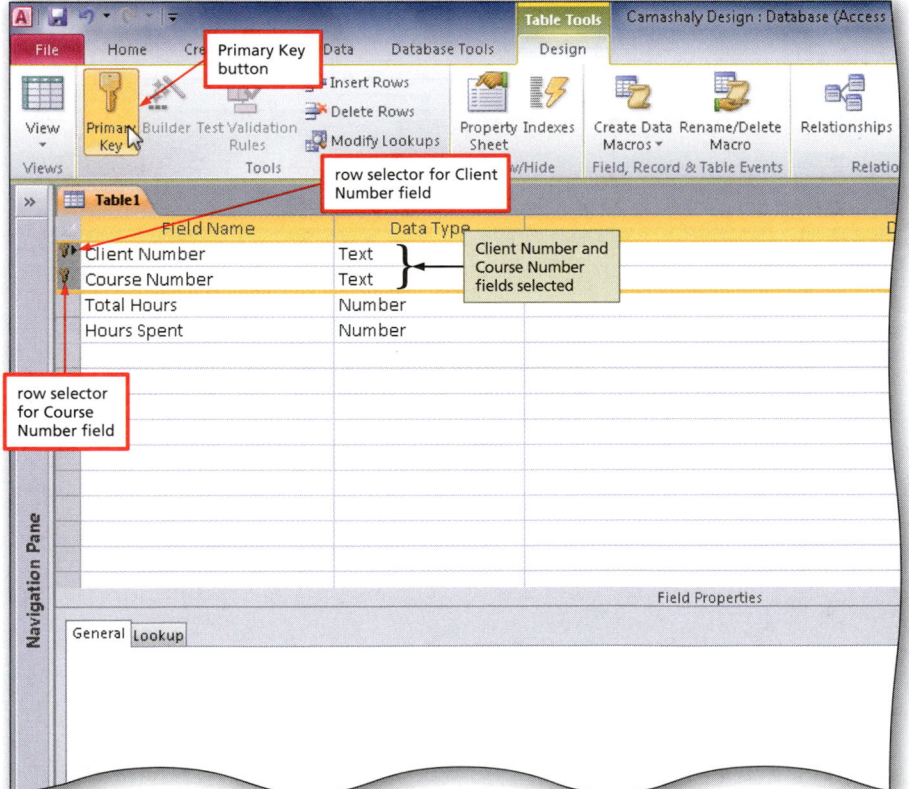

Figure 6–3

To Import the Data

Now that the tables have been created, you need to add data to them. You could enter the data manually, or if the data is already in electronic form, you could import the data. The data for the Course and Course Offerings tables is included in the Data Files for Students. The files are text files formatted as delimited files. The Course data is in a tab-delimited text (.txt) file, and the Course Offerings data is in a comma-separated values (.csv) file. The following steps import the data.

1 With the Camashaly Design database open, display the External Data tab and then click the Text File button (External Data tab | Import & Link group) to display the Get External Data – Text File dialog box.

2 Click the Browse button (Get External Data – Text File dialog box) and select the location of the file to be imported (for example, the folder called AccessData on drive F:). Select the Course file and click the Open button.

3 Select the 'Append a copy of records to the table' option button, select the Course table from the drop-down list, and then click the OK button. With the Delimited option button selected, click the Next button.

4 With the Tab option button selected, click the 'First Row Contains Field Names' check box, click the Next button, and then click the Finish button.

5 Click the Close button to close the Get External Data – Text Box dialog box without saving the import steps.

6 Use the technique shown in Steps 1 through 5 to import the Course Offerings.csv file into the Course Offerings table. Be sure the Comma option button is selected and there is a check mark in the 'First Row Contains Field Names' check box.

Q&A I got an error message after I clicked the Finish button that indicated there were errors. The data was not imported. What should I do?

First, click the Cancel button to terminate the process. Then, review the structure of the table in Design view to ensure that the field names are all spelled correctly and that the data types are correct. Correct any errors you find, save your work, and then redo the steps to import the data.

Linking versus Importing

When an external table or worksheet is imported, or converted, into an Access database, a copy of the data is placed in a table in the database. The original data still exists, just as it did before, but no further connection exists between it and the data in the database. Changes to the original data do not affect the data in the database. Likewise, changes in the database do not affect the original data.

It also is possible to link data stored in a variety of formats to Access databases. To do so, you would select the 'Link to the data source by creating a linked table' option button when importing data, rather than the 'Import the source data into a new table in the current database' or 'Append a copy of the records to the table' option buttons. With linking, the connection is maintained; changes made to the data in the external table or worksheet affect the Access table.

To identify that a table is linked to other data, Access displays an arrow in front of the table in the Navigation Pane. In addition, an icon is displayed in front of the name that indicates the type of file to which the data is linked. For example, an Excel icon in front of the name indicates that the table is linked to an Excel worksheet.

BTW

Importing and Linking Files
You can import and link Excel workbooks, Access databases, ODBC databases such as SQL Server, text files, SharePoint lists, HTML documents, Outlook folders, and dBASE files. You can import but not link XML files.

BTW

Importing
You do not need to create a table before you import data. Instead, you can have Access automatically create a table to contain the imported data. To import an Excel workbook to an Access database without first creating the table, click the External Data tab on the Ribbon and then click the Excel button (External Data tab | Import & Link group) to display the Get External Data – Excel Spreadsheet dialog box. Click the Browse button (Get External Data – Excel Spreadsheet dialog box), select the file to be imported, and click the Open button. Select the 'Import the source data into a new table in the current database' option button, and then click the OK button. Follow the directions in the dialog box to finish importing the file.

BTW

Linking
Two of the primary reasons to link data from another program to Access are to use the query and report features of Access. When you link an Access database to data in another program, all changes to the data must be made in the source program. For example, if you link an Excel workbook to an Access database, you cannot edit the linked table in Access. You must make all changes to the data in Excel.

The Linked Table Manager

After you link tables between a worksheet and a database or between two databases, you can modify many of the linked table's features. For example, you can rename the linked table, set view properties, and set links between tables in queries. If you move, rename, or modify linked tables, you can use the Linked Table Manager within the Database Tools tab to update the links.

To Relate Several Tables

The new tables need to be related to the existing tables in the Camashaly Design database. The Client and Course Offerings tables are related through the Client Number fields in both. The Course and Course Offerings tables are related through the Course Number fields in both. The following steps illustrate the process of relating the tables.

1

- If necessary, close any open datasheet on the screen by clicking its Close button, and then display the Database Tools tab.

- Click the Relationships button (Database Tools tab | Relationships group) to open the Relationships window (Figure 6–4).

Q&A

I only see one table, did I do something wrong?

Click the All Relationships button to display all tables in relationships.

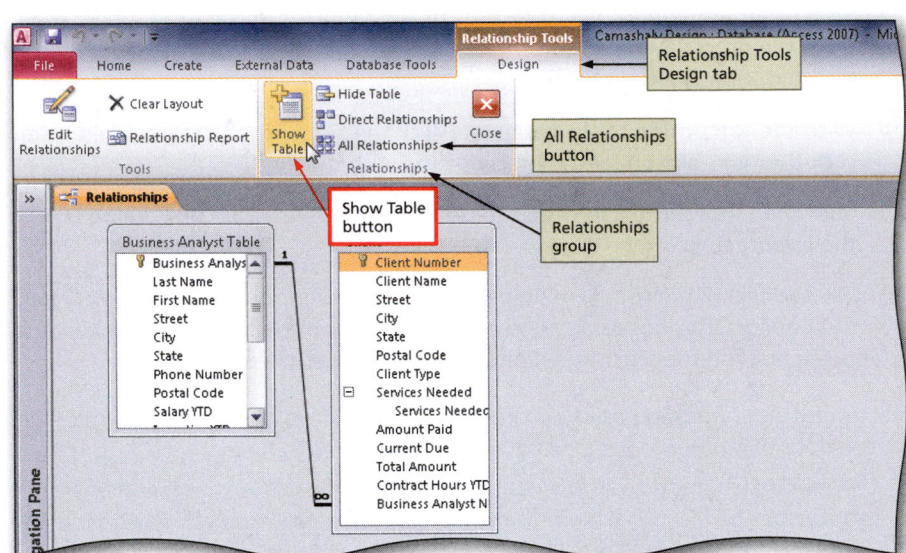

Figure 6–4

2

- Click the Show Table button (Relationship Tools Design tab | Relationships group) to display the Show Table dialog box (Figure 6–5).

3

- Click the Course Offerings table, click the Add button (Show Table dialog box), click the Course table, click the Add button again, and then click the Close button.

Q&A

I cannot see the Course Offerings table. Should I repeat the step?

If you can't see the table, it is behind the dialog box. You do not need to repeat the step.

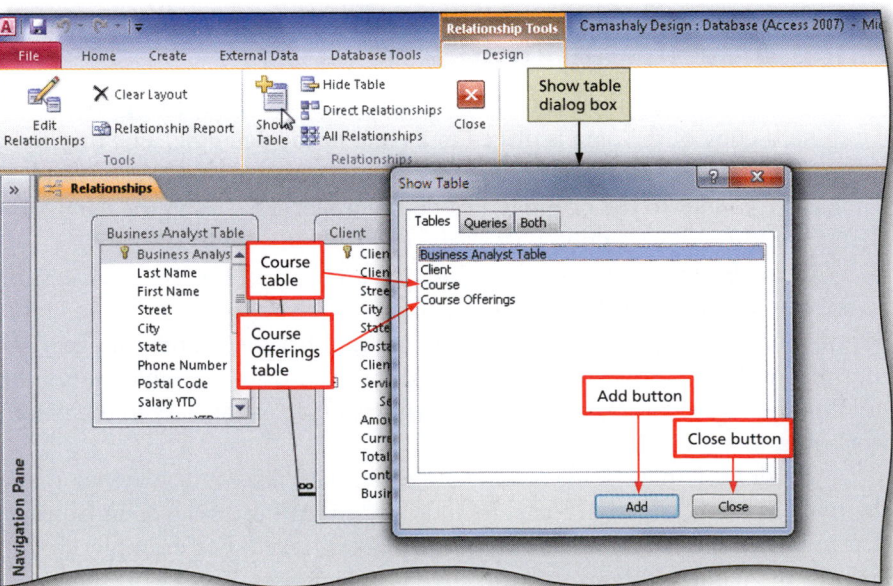

Figure 6–5

- Point to the Client Number field in the Client table, press the left mouse button, drag to the Client Number field in the Course Offerings table, and then release the left mouse button to display the Edit Relationships dialog box. Click the Enforce Referential Integrity check box (Edit Relationships dialog box) and then click the Create button to create the relationship.

- Drag the Course Number field from the Course table to the Course Number field in the Course Offerings table. Click the Enforce Referential Integrity check box (Edit Relationships dialog box) and then click the Create button to create the relationship (Figure 6–6).

 4

- Click the Save button to save the changes and then click the Close button (Relationship Tools Design tab | Relationships group).

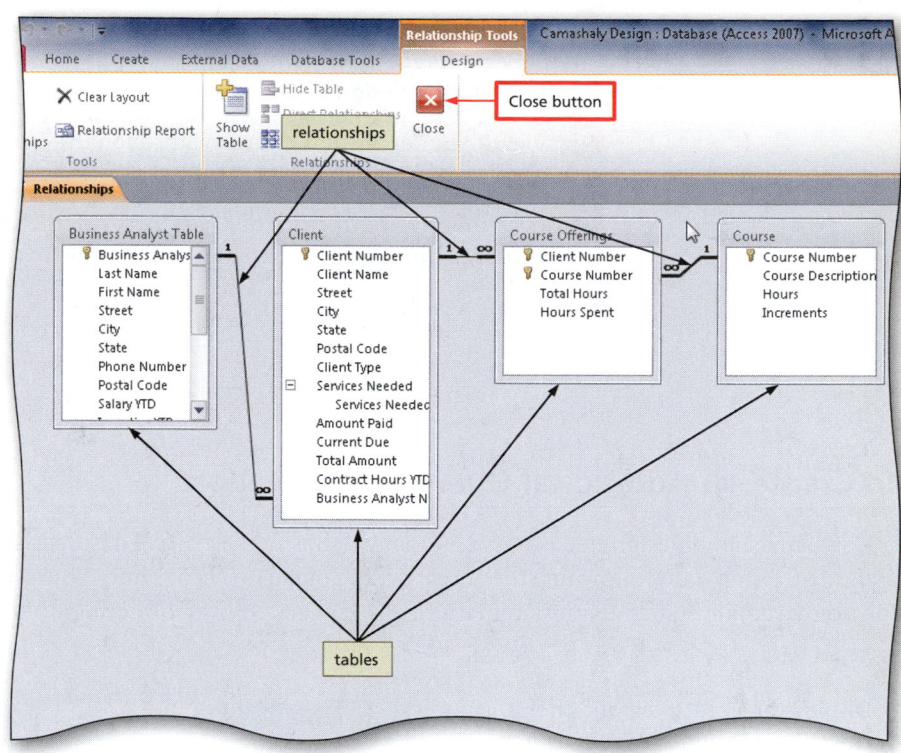

Figure 6–6

Creating Reports in Design View

Previously, you have used both Layout view and the Report Wizard to create reports. However, you simply can create the report in Design view. You also can use Design view to modify a report created by the wizard. If you do not use the wizard before moving to Design view, the design will be empty. It is then up to you to place all the fields in the desired locations. It is also up to you to specify any sorting or grouping that is required.

Whether you use the wizard or simply use Design view, you must determine on which table or query to base the report. If the report is to be based on a query, you first must create the query, unless, of course, it already exists.

To Create a Query for the Report

Camashaly's requirements for the reports specify that it would be convenient to use two queries for the report. These queries do not yet exist. You will need to create the two queries. The first query relates business analysts and clients, and the second query relates courses and course offerings. The following steps create the Business Analysts and Clients query.

1 If necessary, close the Navigation Pane, display the Create tab, and then click the Query Design button (Create tab | Queries group) to create a new query.

2 If necessary click the Business Analyst Table, click the Add button (Show Table dialog box), click the Client table, click the Add button, close the Show Table dialog box by clicking its Close button, and then resize the field lists to display as many fields as possible.

3 Double-click the Business Analyst Number, First Name, and Last Name fields from the Business Analyst Table to display them in the design grid.

BTW

Modify Composite Primary Keys
To change part of a composite primary key, open the table in Design view, click any field that participates in the primary key, and click the Primary Key button to remove the primary key. If the fields are adjacent to each other, click the row selector for the first field, hold down the SHIFT key and click the row selector for the second field. Then click the Primary Key button.

4 Double-click the Client Number, Client Name, Street, City, State, Postal Code, Client Type, Services Needed, Amount Paid, and Current Due fields from the Client table to add the fields to the design grid.

5 View the query results and scroll through the fields to make sure you have included all the necessary fields. If you have omitted a field, return to Design view and add it.

6 Click the Save button on the Quick Access Toolbar to save the query, type `Business Analysts and Clients` as the name of the query, and then click the OK button.

7 Close the query.

To Create an Additional Query for the Report

Camashaly Design needs to include in the Business Analyst Master List the number of hours that remain in a course offering. The following steps create the Course Offerings and Courses query that includes a calculated field for hours remaining. The hours remaining are calculated by subtracting hours spent from total number of hours.

1

- Display the Create tab and then click the Query Design button (Create tab | Queries group) to create a new query.

- Click the Course table, click the Add button (Show Table dialog box), click the Course Offerings table, click the Add button, and then click the Close button to close the Show Table dialog box.

- Double-click the Client Number and Course Number fields from the Course Offerings table to add the fields to the design grid.

- Double-click the Course Description field from the Course table.

- Double-click the Total Hours and Hours Spent fields from the Course Offerings table to add the fields to the design grid.

- Click the first open column in the design grid to select it.

- Click the Builder button (Query Tools Design tab | Query Setup group) to display the Expression Builder dialog box (Figure 6–7).

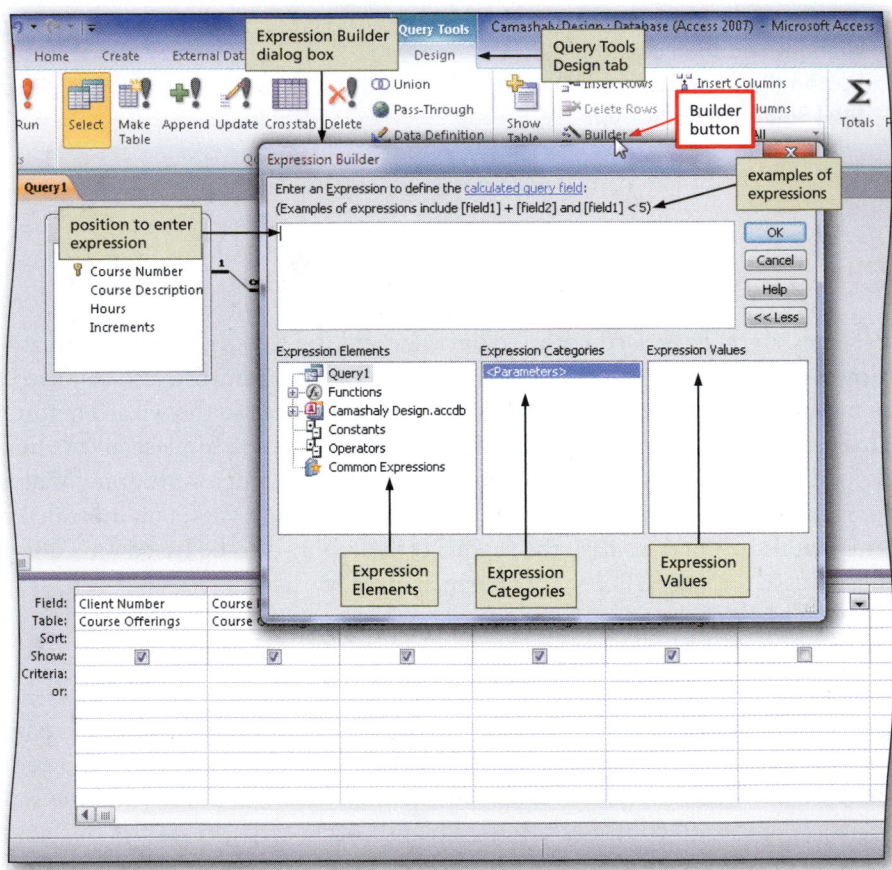

Figure 6–7

2

- Double-click Camashaly Design in the Expression Elements section to display the categories of objects within the Camashaly Design database, and then double-click Tables to display a list of tables.

- Click the Course Offerings table to select it.

- Double-click the Total Hours field to add it to the expression.

- Type a minus sign (–) to add it to the expression.

- Double-click the Hours Spent field to add it to the expression (Figure 6–8).

Q&A Why are the fields preceded by a table name and an exclamation point?

This notation qualifies the field; that is, it indicates to which table the field belongs.

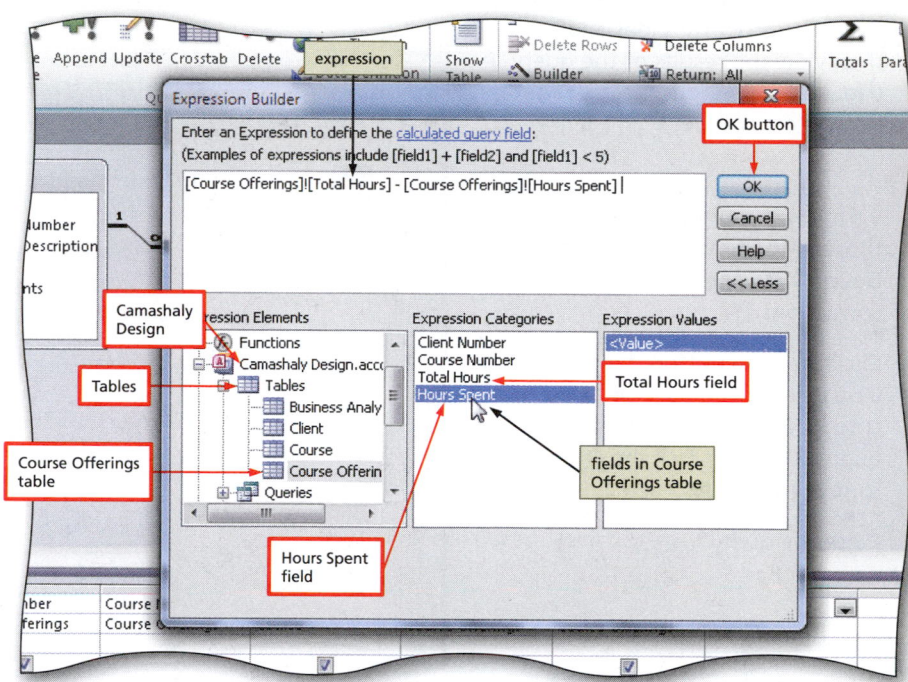

Figure 6–8

Q&A Could I type the expression instead of using the Expression Builder?

Yes. You could type it directly into the design grid. You could also right-click the column and click Zoom to allow you to type the expression in the Zoom dialog box. Finally, you could use the Expression Builder, but simply type the expression rather than clicking any buttons. Use whichever method you find most convenient.

3

- Click the OK button (Expression Builder dialog box).

- With the field in the grid where you entered the expression selected, click the Property Sheet button (Query Tools Design tab | Show/Hide group) to display the property sheet for the new field.

Q&A The wrong property sheet appeared. What went wrong? What should I do?

You either did not click in the right location, or you have not yet completed entering the expression. The easiest way to ensure you have done both is to click any other column in the grid and then click the column with the expression.

- Click the Caption property box and type **Hours Remaining** as the caption (Figure 6–9).

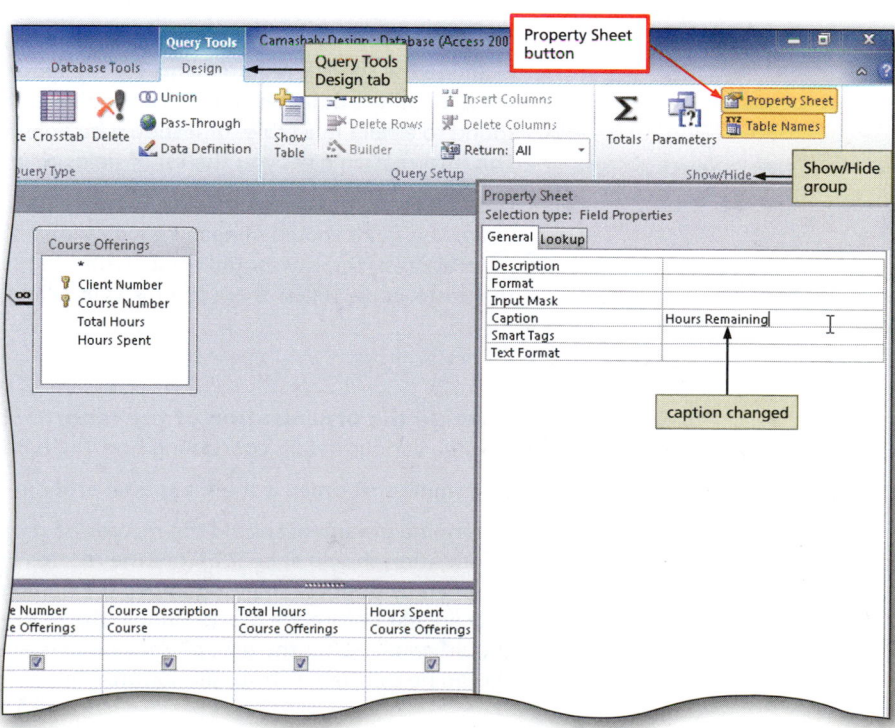

Figure 6–9

4

• Close the property sheet and then view the results of the query (Figure 6–10). (Your results might be in a different order.)

5

• Verify that your query results match those in the figure. If not, return to Design view and make the necessary corrections.

• Click the Save button, type **Course Offerings and Courses** as the name of the query, and then click the OK button to save the query.

• Close the query.

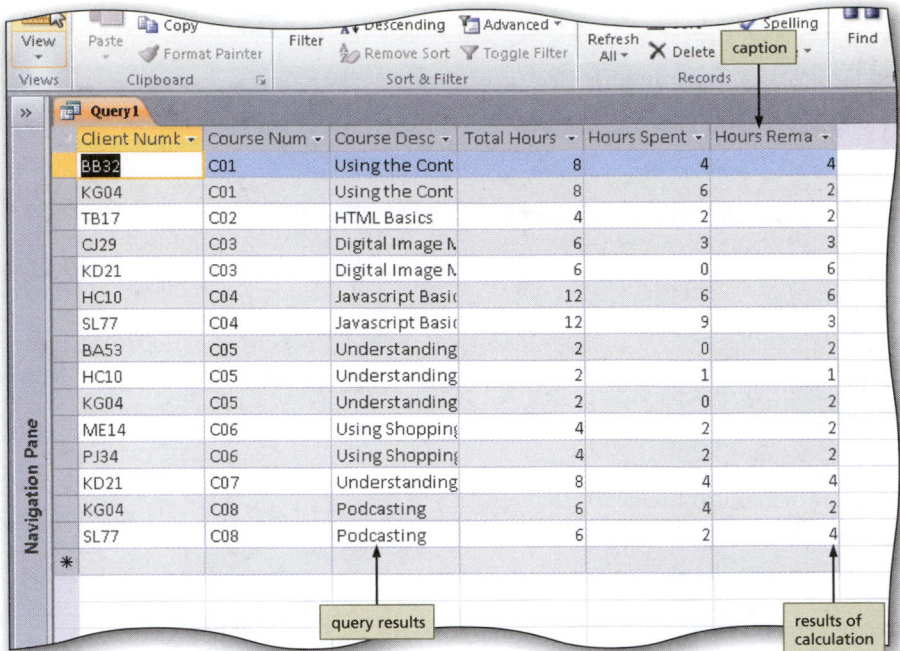

Figure 6–10

Plan
Ahead

Determine the fields that belong on the report.
If you determine that data should be presented as a report, you then need to determine what tables and fields contain the data for the report.

• **Examine the requirements for the report in general to determine the tables.** Do the requirements only relate to data in a single table, or does the data come from multiple tables? Is the data in a query, or could you create a query that contains some or all of the fields necessary for the report?

• **Examine the specific requirements for the report to determine the fields necessary.** Look for all the data items that are specified for the report. Each item should correspond to a field in a table, or it should be able to be computed from a field in a table. This information gives you the list of fields to include in the query.

• **Determine the order of the fields.** Examine the requirements to determine the order in which the fields should appear. Be logical and consistent in your ordering. For example, in an address, the city should come before the state, and the state should come before the postal code, unless there is some compelling reason for another order.

Plan
Ahead

Determine the organization of the report.
Determine various details concerning how the data in your report is to be organized.

• **Determine sort order.** Is there a special order in which the records should appear?

• **Determine grouping.** Should the records be grouped in some fashion? If so, what information should appear before the records in a group? If, for example, clients are grouped by business analyst number, the number of the business analyst should probably appear before the group. Should the business analyst name also appear? What should appear after the group? For example, are there some fields for which subtotals should be calculated? If so, the subtotals would come after the group.

(continued)

(continued)

Plan Ahead

- **Determine whether to include a subreport.** Rather than use grouping, you may choose to include a subreport, as shown in the Business Analyst Master List on page AC 339. The data concerning course offerings for the client could have been presented by grouping the course offerings' data by client number. The headings currently in the subreport would have appeared in the group header. Instead, it is presented in a subreport. Subreports, which are reports in their own right, offer more flexibility in formatting than group headers and footers. More important, in the Business Analyst Master List, some clients do not have any course offerings. If this information were presented using grouping, the group header will still appear for these clients. With a subreport, clients who have no course offerings do not appear.

To Create an Initial Report in Design View

Creating the report shown in Figure 6–1a on page AC 339 from scratch involves creating the initial report in Design view, adding the subreport, modifying the subreport separately from the main report, and then making the final modifications to the main report.

When you want to create a report from scratch, you use Design view rather than the Report Wizard. The Report Wizard is suitable for simple, customized reports. With Report Design, you can make advanced design changes, such as adding subreports. The following steps create the initial version of the Business Analyst Master List and select the **record source** for the report; that is, the table or query that will furnish the data for the report. The steps then specify sorting and grouping for the report.

1

- Display the Create tab.

- Click the Report Design button (Create tab | Reports group) to create a report in Design view.

- Ensure the selector for the entire report, the box in the upper-left corner of the report, is selected.

- Click the Property Sheet button (Report Design Tools Design tab | Tools group) to display a property sheet.

- With the All tab (Property Sheet) selected, click the Record Source property box arrow to display the list of available tables and queries (Figure 6–11).

Q&A Can I make the property sheet box wider so I can see more of the items in the Record Source list?

Yes, you can make the property sheet wider by dragging its right border.

Q&A The right side of the property sheet is cut off. Can I move the property sheet?

Yes, you can move the property sheet by dragging its title bar.

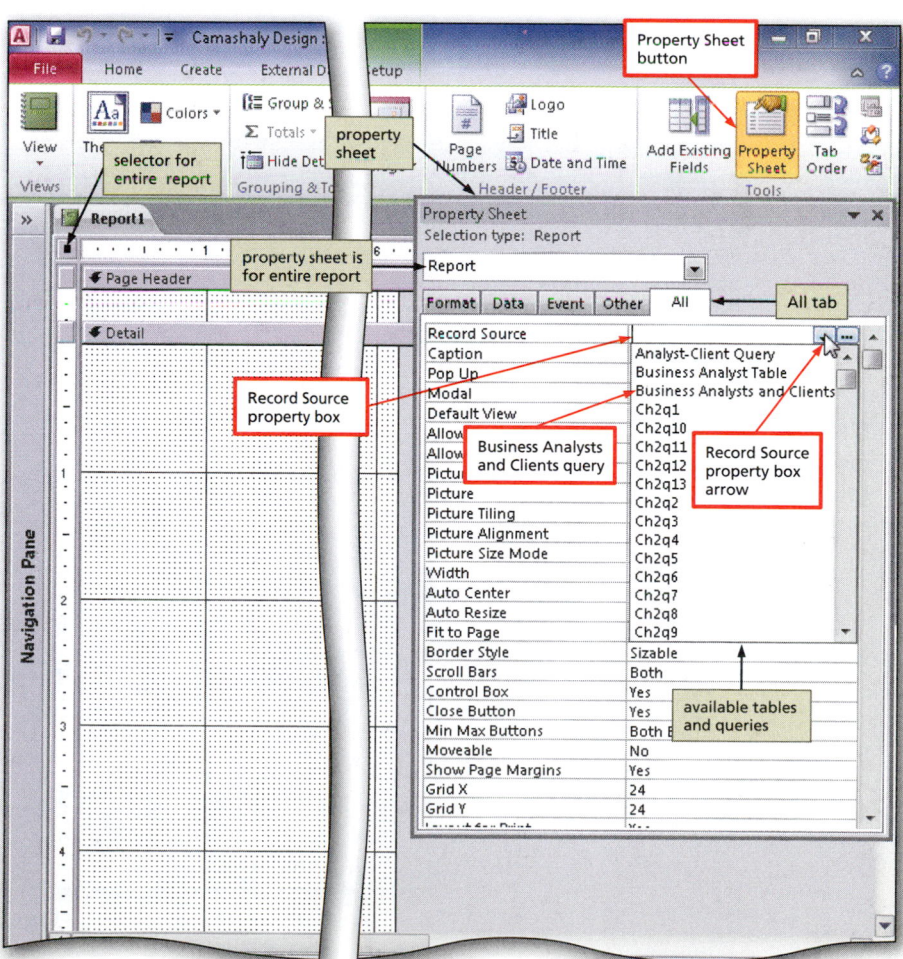

Figure 6–11

2

- Click the Business Analysts and Clients query to select the query as the record source for the report.

- Close the property sheet by clicking the Property Sheet button (Report Design Tools Design tab | Tools group).

- Click the Group & Sort button (Report Design Tools Design tab | Grouping & Totals group) to display the Group, Sort, and Total pane (Figure 6–12).

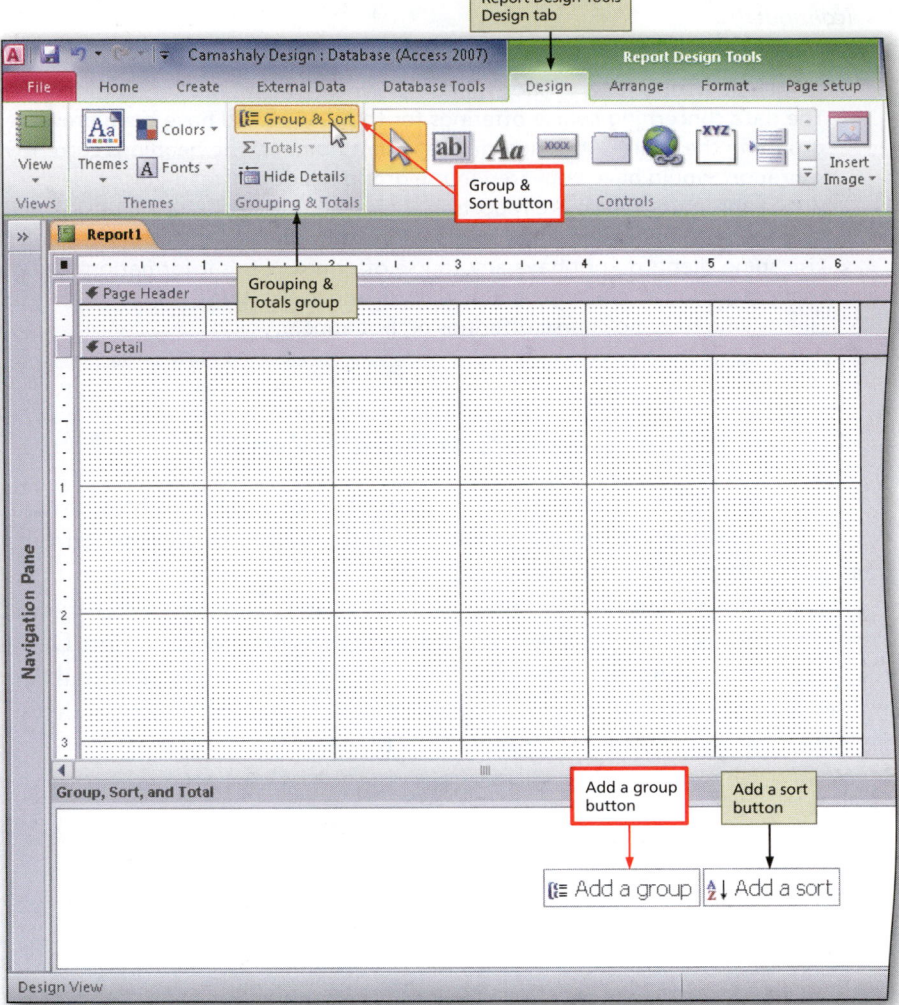

Figure 6–12

3

- Click the 'Add a group' button to display the list of available fields for grouping (Figure 6–13).

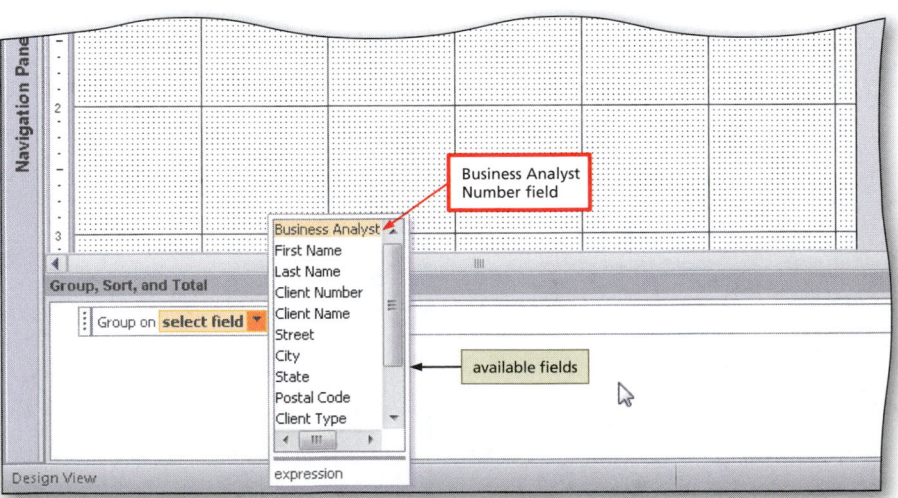

Figure 6–13

4

● Click the Business Analyst Number field to group by business analyst number (Figure 6–14).

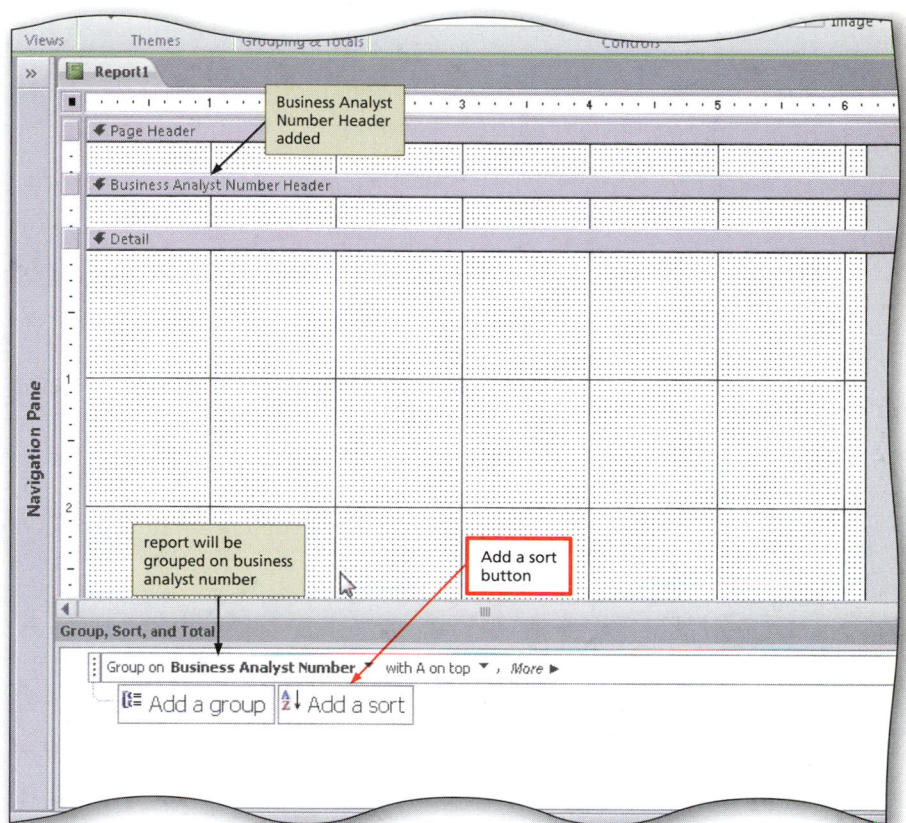

Figure 6– 14

5

● Click the 'Add a sort' button to display the list of available fields for sorting (Figure 6–15).

6

● Click the Client Number field to sort by client number.

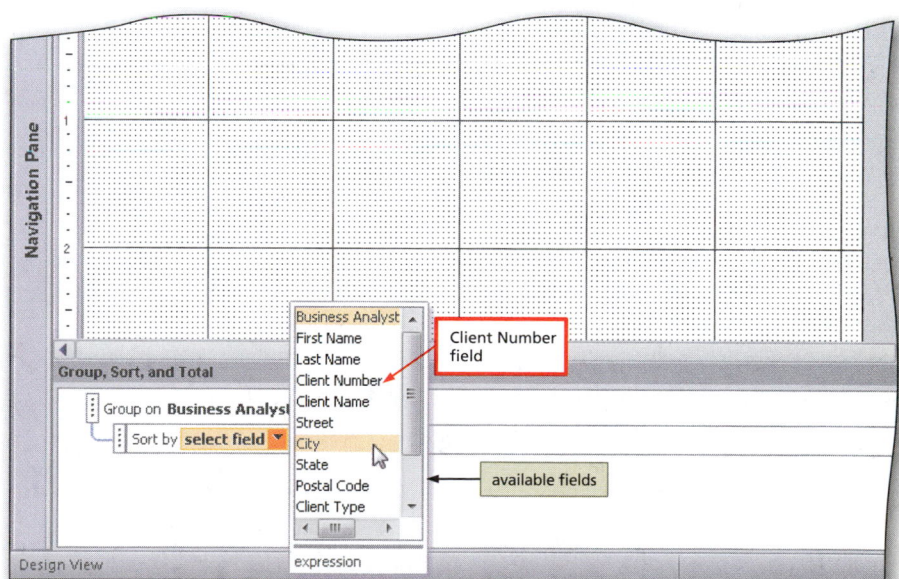

Figure 6– 15

To Save the Report

Before proceeding with the next steps in the modification of the report, it is a good idea to save your work. The following steps save the report as Business Analyst Master List.

1 Click the Save button on the Quick Access Toolbar.

2 Type **Business Analyst Master List** as the report name.

3 Click the OK button.

BTW

Expression Builder
The Expression Builder provides easy access to built-in functions, table names, and field names. In Access 2010, the Expression Builder was enhanced to include IntelliSense that shows you options as you type. It also displays help for the currently selected expression value.

Recall from Chapter 4 that a report contains three types of controls: bound controls, unbound controls, and calculated controls. As you learned previously, reports contain standard sections, including the Report Header, Report Footer, Page Header, Page Footer, and Detail sections. When the data in a report is grouped, there are two additional possible sections. The contents of the **Group Header section** are printed before the records in a particular group, and the contents of the **Group Footer section** are printed after the group. In the Discount Report (Figure 6–1b), for example, which is grouped by business analyst number, the Group Header section contains the business analyst number and name, and the Group Footer section contains subtotals of the Amount Paid and Current Due fields.

To Add Fields to the Report in Design View

When you have determined the fields that are necessary for the report, you need to add them. You can add the fields to the report by dragging them from the field list to the appropriate position on the report. The following steps add the fields to the report.

1

- Remove the Group, Sort, and Total pane by clicking the Group & Sort button (Report Design Tools Design tab | Grouping & Totals group).

- Click the Add Existing Fields button (Report Design Tools Design tab | Tools group) to display a field list.

- Drag the Business Analyst Number field to the approximate position shown in Figure 6–16.

Q&A

My field list does not look like the one in the figure. It has several tables listed, and at the top it has Show only fields in the current record source. Yours has Show all tables. What should I do?

Click the 'Show only field in the current record source' link. Your field list should then match the one in the figure.

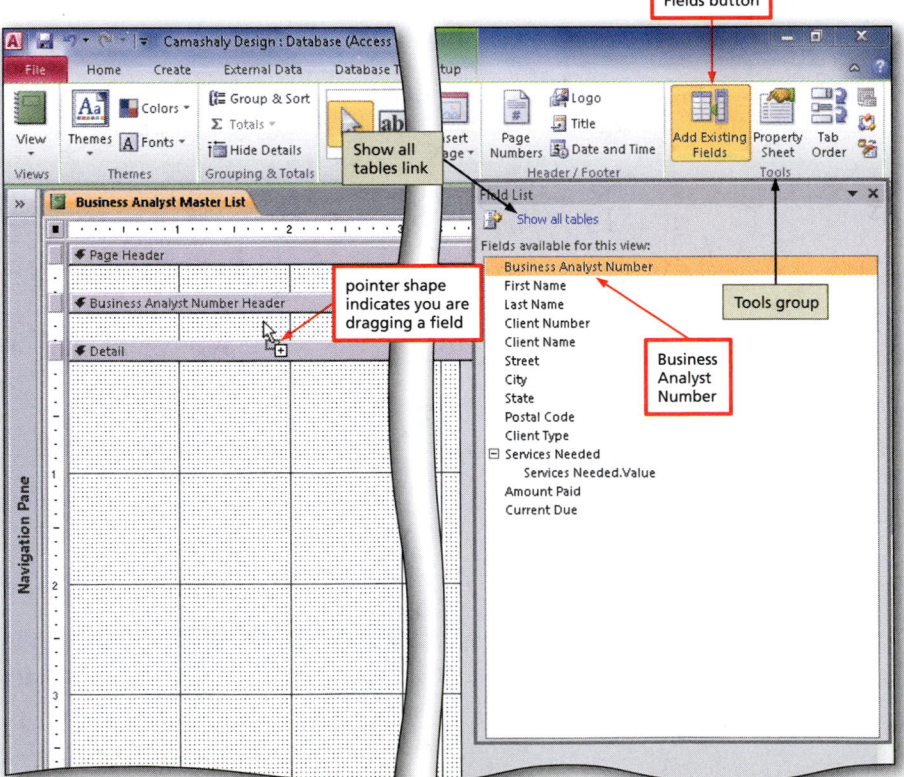

Figure 6–16

2

- Release the left mouse button to place the field (Figure 6–17).

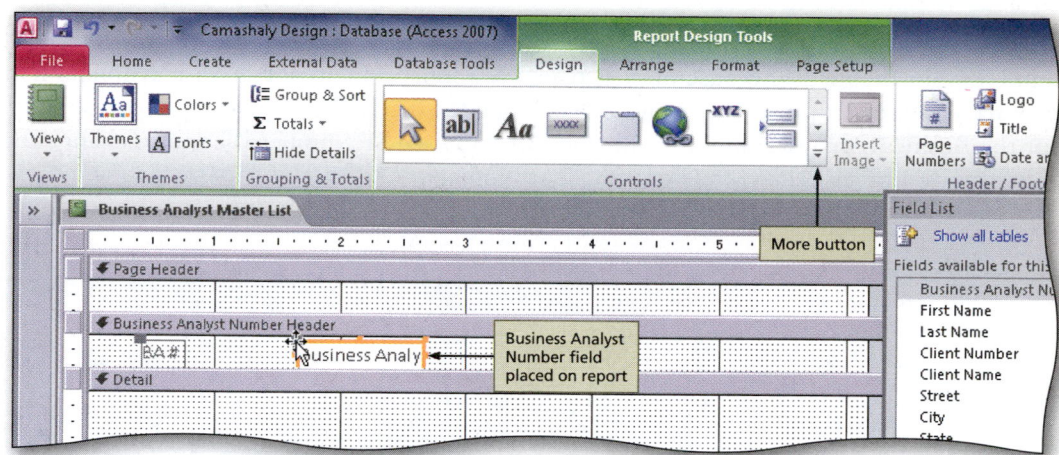

Figure 6–17

3

- Place the remaining fields in the positions shown in Figure 6–18.

- Display the Arrange tab.

- Adjust the positions of the labels to those shown in the figure. If any field is not in the correct position, drag it to its correct location. To move the control or the attached label separately, drag the large handle in the upper-left corner of the control or label. You can align controls using the Align button (Report Design Tools Arrange tab | Sizing & Ordering group) or adjust spacing by using the Size/Space button (Report Design Tools Arrange tab | Sizing & Ordering group).

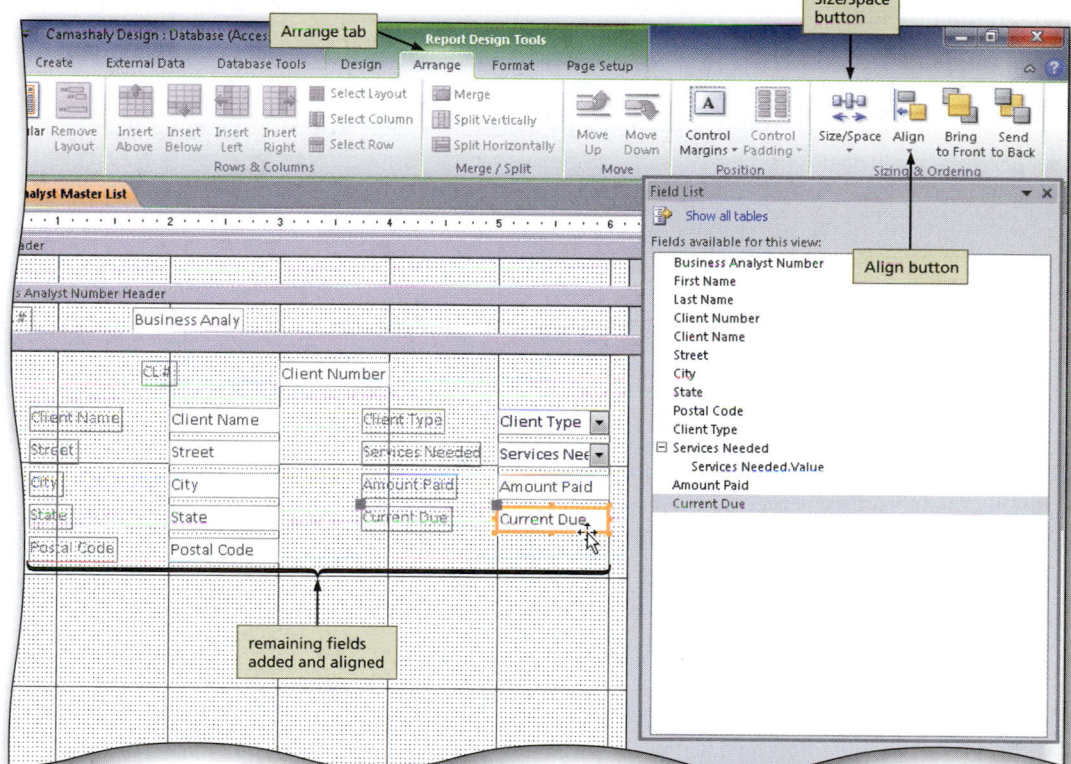

Figure 6–18

Experiment

- Select more than one control and then experiment with the Size/Space and the Align buttons (Report Design Tools Arrange tab | Sizing & Ordering group) to see their effects. After trying each one, click the Undo button to undo the change.

4

- Display the Design tab.

- Remove the field list by clicking the Add Existing Fields button (Report Design Tools Design tab | Tools group), which is shown in Figure 6–16.

To Change Labels

The labels for the Business Analyst Number and Client Number fields currently contain the captions BA # and CL # for the fields. Because there is plenty of room on the report to display longer names for both fields, you can make the report more descriptive by changing the labels. The following step changes the contents of the label for the Business Analyst Number field from BA # to Analyst Number. They also change the contents of the label for the Client Number field from CL # to Client Number.

- • Click the label for the Business Analyst Number field twice, once to select it and the second time to produce an insertion point.

- • Use the BACKSPACE or DELETE key to erase the current entry in the label and then type **Analyst Number** as the new entry.

- • Click the label for the Client Number field twice to produce an insertion point.

- • Use the BACKSPACE or DELETE key to erase the current entry in the label and then type **Client Number** as the new entry (Figure 6–19).

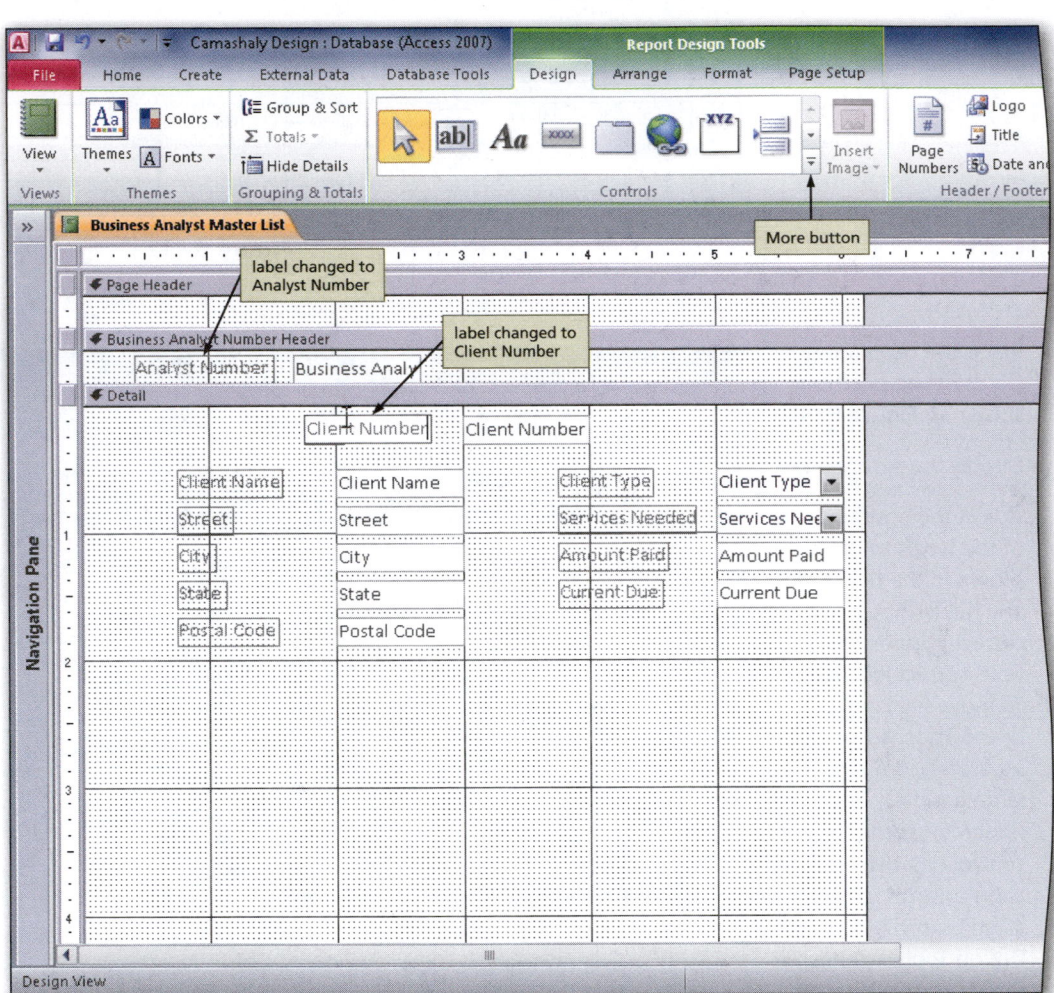

Figure 6–19

Control Tools
You also can scroll the list of tools in the Control group by clicking the arrows at the right side of the group. The More button (shown in Figure 6–19) displays all the controls at once.

Using Other Tools in the Controls Group

Previously, you used the Subform/Subreport tool within the Controls group on the Design tab to place special controls on a form. The Controls group has additional tools available that can be used with forms and reports. A description of the additional tools appears in Table 6–3.

Table 6–3 Additional Tools in the Controls Group

Tool	Description	Button
Select	Enables sizing, moving, or editing of existing controls. If you click another tool and then want to cancel the effect of the tool before using it, you can click the Select tool.	
Text Box	Creates a text box for entering, editing, and displaying data. You can also bind the text box to a field in the underlying table or query.	
Label	Creates a label, a box containing identifying text that is independent of other controls, such as a title.	
Button	Creates a command button.	
Tab Control	Creates a tab control, which contains a series of tabbed pages. Each tabbed page can contain its own controls.	
Hyperlink	Inserts a hyperlink to an existing file, Web page, database object, or e-mail address.	
Option Group	Creates an option group, a rectangle containing a collection of option buttons. To select an option, you simply click the corresponding option button.	
Insert or Remove Page Break	Inserts or removes a physical page break (typically in a report).	
Combo box	Creates a combo box, which is a combination of a text box and a list box.	
Chart	Creates a chart.	
Line	Draws a line on a form or report.	
Toggle Button	Adds a toggle button. With a toggle button, a user can make a Yes/No selection by clicking the button. The button either appears to be pressed (for Yes) or not pressed (for No).	
List Box	Creates a list box, a box that allows the user to select from a list of options.	
Rectangle	Creates a rectangle.	
Check Box	Inserts a check box. With a check box, a user can make multiple Yes/No selections.	
Unbound Object Frame	Inserts an OLE object (for example, a graph, picture, sound file, or video) that is not contained in a field in a table within the database.	
Attachment	Inserts an Attachment field.	
Option Button	Inserts an option button. With an option button, a user can make a single Yes/No selection from among a collection of at least two choices.	
Subform/ Subreport	Creates a subform (a form contained within another form) or a subreport (a report contained within another report).	
Bound Object Frame	Inserts an OLE object (for example, a graph, picture, sound file, or video) that is contained in a field in a table within the database.	
Image	Inserts a frame into which you can insert a graphic. The graphic will be the same for all records.	

BTW

Use Control Wizards Button

Many of the tools shown in Table 6-3 have a wizard associated with them to assist you in specifying options and values for the control. To use the wizard, make sure the Use Control Wizards button is selected before you add a control to a form or report.

BTW

Hyperlink Controls

You can add a hyperlink to tables, forms, and reports. To add a hyperlink, which provides single-click access to Web pages, to a report, click the Hyperlink tool (Report Design Tools Design tab | Controls group), enter the hyperlink in the Address text box (Insert Hyperlink dialog box) and click the OK button. If necessary, move the hyperlink control to the desired location on the report.

BTW

Drop Down Controls

Drop down boxes can be combo boxes or list boxes. To add a combo box to a report, click the Combo Box tool (Report Design Tools Design tab | Controls group), move the mouse pointer to the desired location, and click the position to place the combo box. Follow the directions in the Combo Box Wizard dialog box to specify the options and values for the combo box. To add a list box to a report, click the List Box tool (Report Design Tools Design tab | Controls group) and follow the steps listed above for a combo box.

BTW

Graphs

You can add graphs (charts) to a report using the Chart tool. To add a graph (chart) to a report, click the Chart tool (Report Design Tools Design tab | Controls group), move the mouse pointer to the desired location, and click the position to place the graph. Follow the directions in the Chart Wizard dialog box to specify the data source for the chart, the values for the chart, and the chart type.

To Add Text Boxes

You can place a text box on a report or form by using the Text Box tool in the Controls group on the Design tab. The text box consists of a control that is initially unbound and an attached label. When you enter an expression in the text box, it becomes a calculated control. If the expression is just a single field (for example, =[Amount Paid]), it would be a bound control. Expressions also can be arithmetic operations; for example, calculating the sum of amount paid and current due. Many times, you need to **concatenate**, or combine, two or more text data items into a single expression; the process is called **concatenation**. To concatenate strings, you use the **ampersand (&)** operator. The process of converting an unbound control to a bound control is called **binding**.

The following steps add text boxes and create calculated controls.

1
- Click the Text Box tool (Report Design Tools Design tab | Controls group) and move the pointer to the approximate position shown in Figure 6–20.

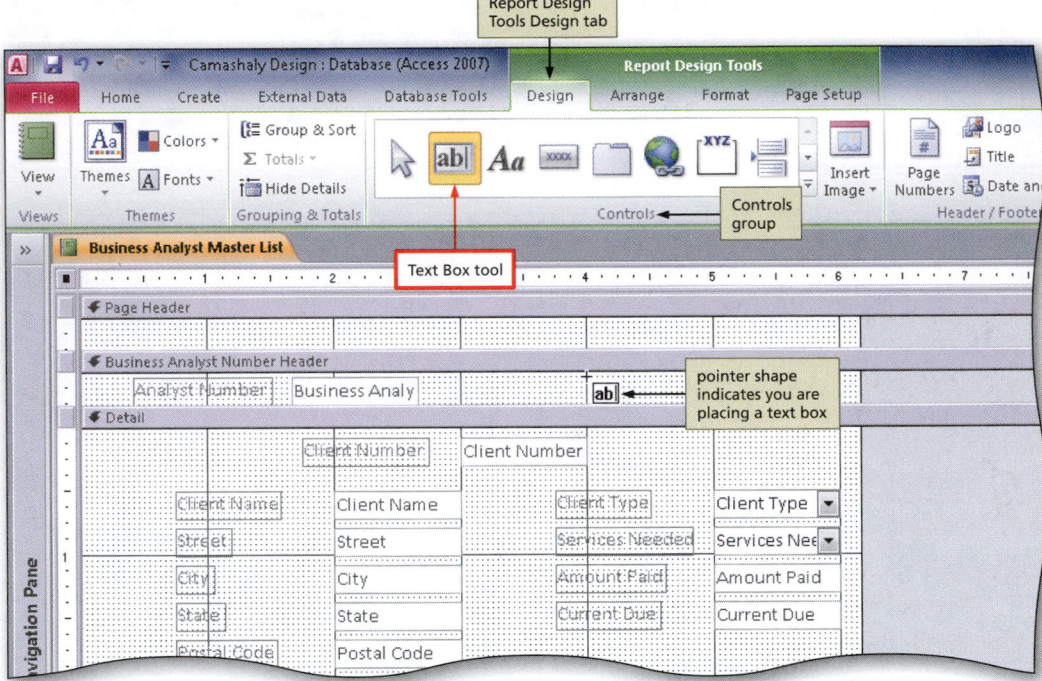

Figure 6–20

2
- Click the position shown in Figure 6–20 to place a text box on the report (Figure 6–21).

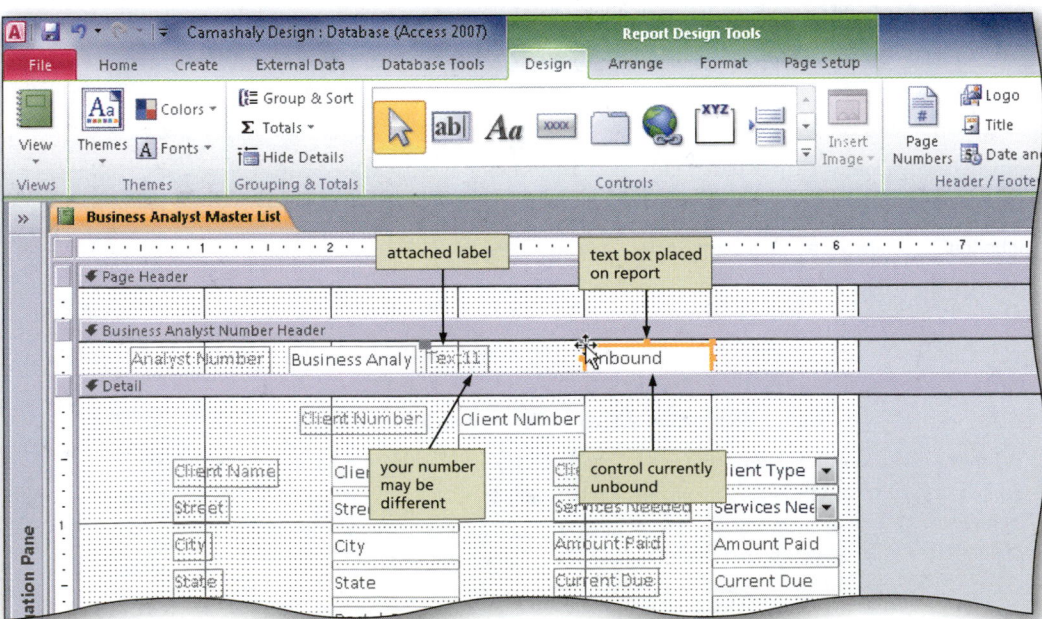

Figure 6–21

3

● Click in the text box to produce an insertion point (Figure 6–22).

Q&A I inadvertently clicked somewhere else, so the text box was no longer selected. When I clicked the text box a second time, it was selected, but there was no insertion point. What should I do?

Simply click another time.

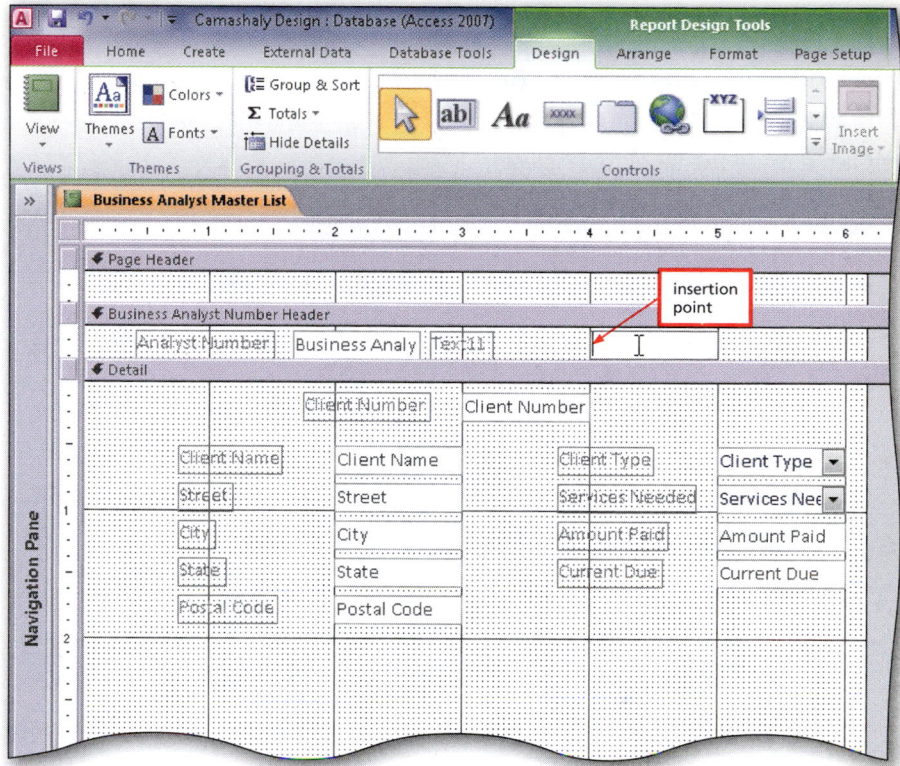

Figure 6–22

4

● In the text box, type
`=[First Name]&' '&[Last Name]` as the entry.

Q&A What is the result of the expression I just entered?

The expression will display the first name of the business analyst, followed by a space, and then the last name of the business analyst. Any extra spaces at the end of the first name will be removed.

Q&A Could I use the Expression Builder instead of typing the expression?

Yes. Click the Property Sheet button and then click the Build button, which contains three dots, next to the Control Source property.

Q&A Do I need to use single quotes (')?

No. You also could use double quotes (").

● Click in the text box label to select the label and then click the label a second time to produce an insertion point (Figure 6–23).

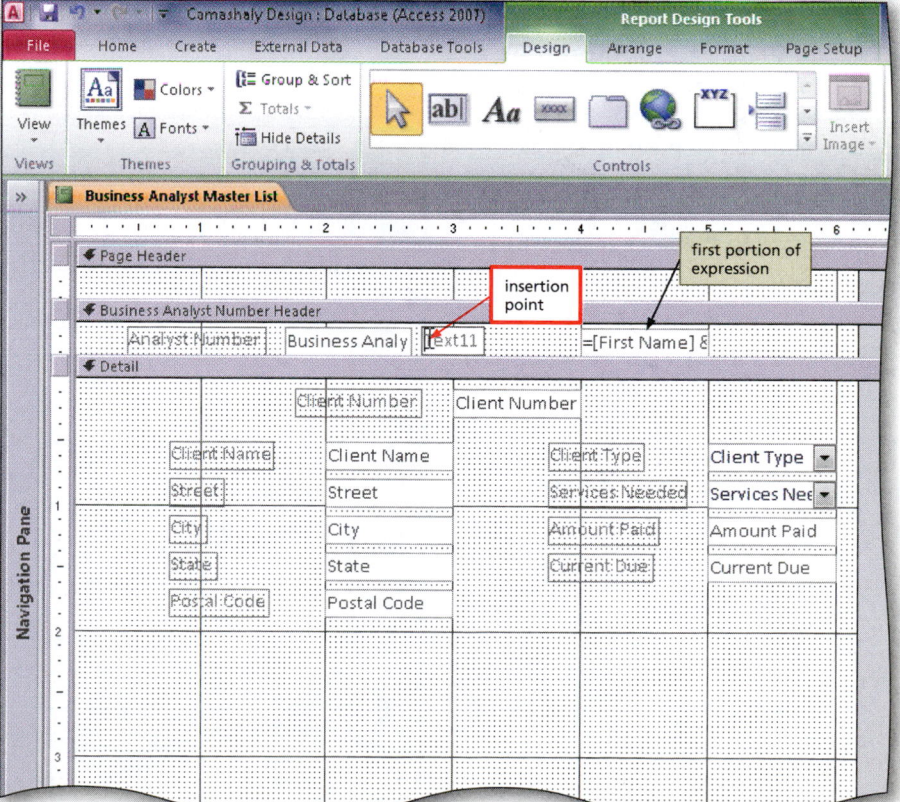

Figure 6–23

5

- Use the BACKSPACE or DELETE key to erase the current entry in the label and then type `Analyst Name` as the new entry.

- Click outside the label to deselect it and then drag the label to the position shown in the figure by dragging the Move handle in the upper-left corner of the label (Figure 6–24).

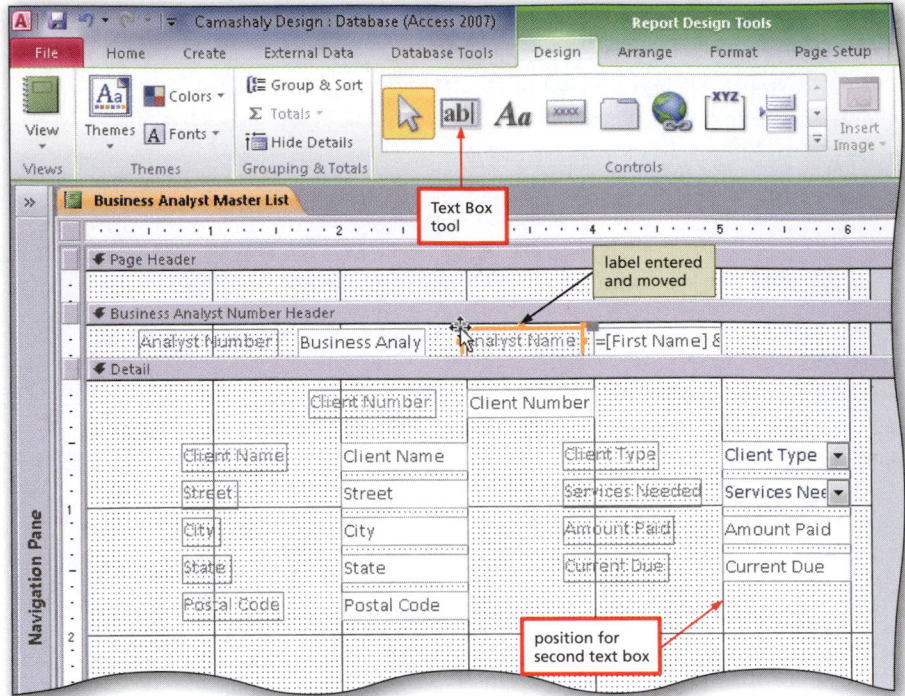

Figure 6–24

6

- Use the techniques in Steps 1 to 5 to place a second text box in the position indicated in Figure 6–24. Type `=[Amount Paid]+[Current Due]` as the expression in the text box, drag the label to the position shown in the figure, erase the contents of the label, and type `Total Amount` in the label (Figure 6–25).

Q&A My label is not in the correct position. What should I do?

Click outside the label to deselect it, click the label, and then drag it to the desired position.

Q&A Total Amount already is a calculated field in the Client table. Why am I adding it to the report?

Access 2007 does not recognize calculated fields. If you want to share this report with individuals who use Access 2007, you will need to add the calculated control to the report.

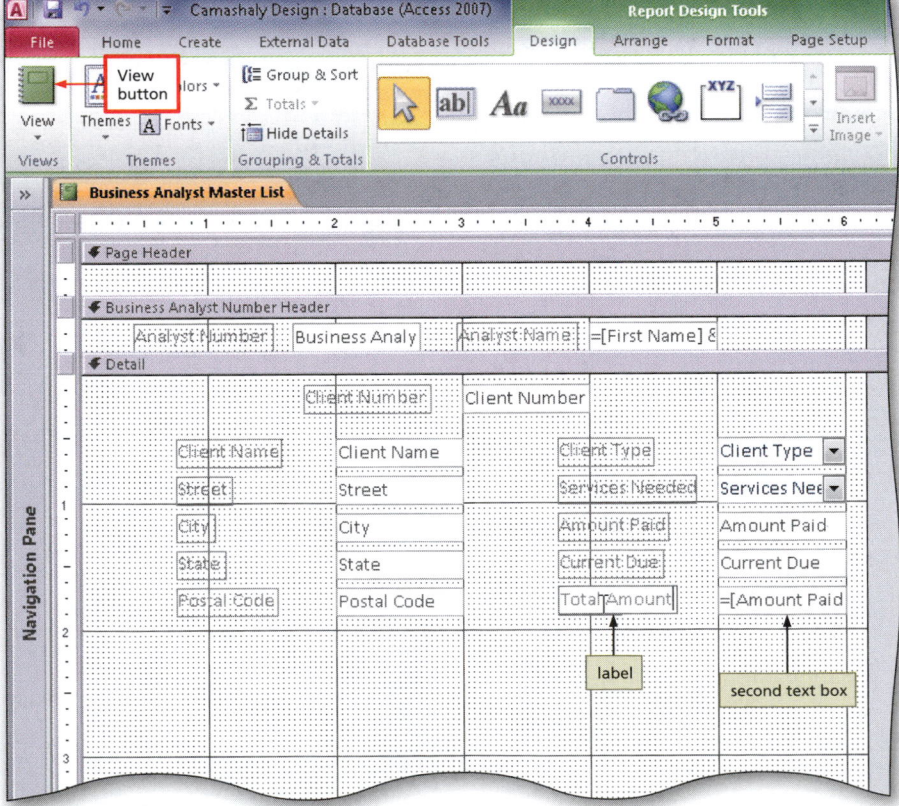

Figure 6–25

To View the Report in Print Preview

As you are working on a report in Design view, it is useful to periodically view the report to gauge how it will look containing data. One way to do so is to use Print Preview. The following steps view the report in Print Preview.

1
- Click the View button arrow (Report Design Tools Design tab | Views group) to produce the View button menu.

- Click Print Preview on the View button menu to view the report in Print Preview (Figure 6–26).

Q&A What would happen if I clicked the View button instead of the View button arrow?

The icon on the View button is the icon for Report View, so you would view the results in Report view. This is another useful way to view a report, but compared with Print Preview, Report View does not give as accurate a picture of how the final printed report will look.

Q&A The total amount does not appear as currency, and the Services Needed field does not display all the values. How can I fix these issues?

You will see how to fix these issues in the next sections.

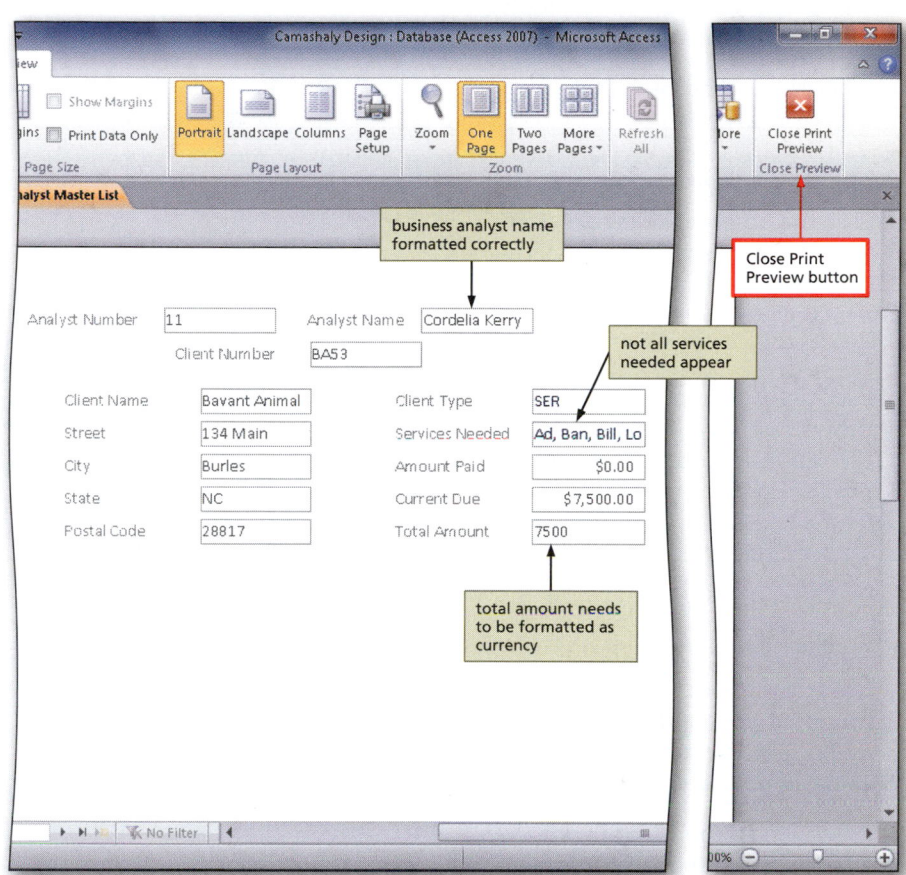

Figure 6–26

2
- Click the Close Print Preview button on the Print Preview tab to return to Design view.

Other Ways
1. Click Print Preview button on status bar

To Format a Control

When you add a calculated control to a report, you often need to format the control. You can use a control's property sheet to change the value in the appropriate property. If a property does not appear on the screen, you have two choices. You can click the tab on which the property is located. For example, if it were a control related to data, you would click the Data tab to only show data-related properties. Many people, however, prefer to click the All tab, which shows all properties, and then simply scroll through the properties, if necessary, until locating the appropriate property. The following steps change the format of the Total Amount control to Currency by changing the value of the Format property and the Decimal Places property.

1

- Click the control containing the expression for Total Amount to select it and then click the Property Sheet button (Report Design Tools Design tab | Tools group) to display the property sheet.

- If necessary, click the All tab (Figure 6–27).

 Experiment

- Click the other tabs in the property sheet to see the types of properties on each tab. When finished, once again click the All tab.

2

- Click the Format property box, click the arrow that appears, and then click Currency to select Currency as the format.

- Click the Decimal Places property box, click the arrow that appears, and then click 2 to select two decimal places.

- Remove the property sheet by clicking the Property Sheet button (Report Design Tools Design tab | Tools group) a second time.

- Preview the report using Print Preview to see the effect of the property changes.

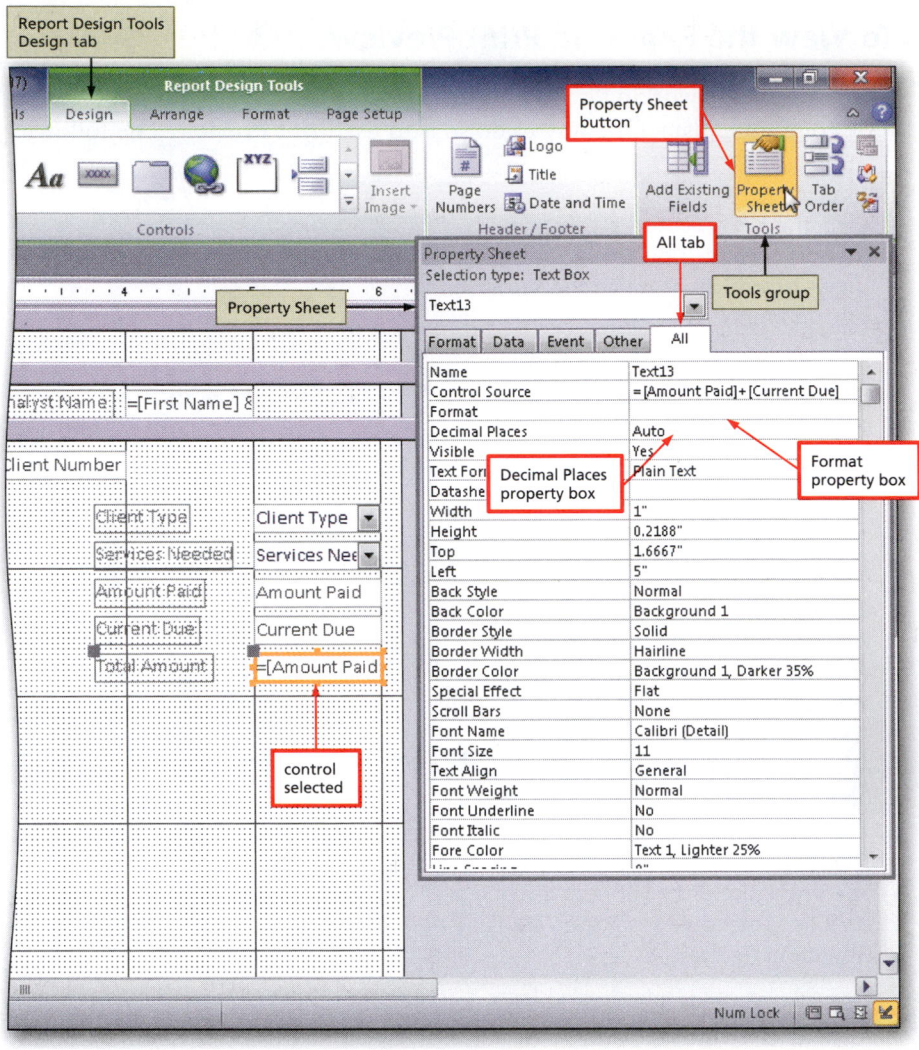

Figure 6–27

Other Ways

1. Right-click control, click Properties

To Group Controls

If your report contains a collection of controls that you frequently will want to modify in the same way, you can simplify the process of selecting all the controls by grouping them. Once they are grouped, selecting any control in the group automatically selects all of the controls in the group. You then can apply the desired change to all the controls.

The following steps group the controls within the Detail section.

1

• Click the Client Number control to select it.

Q&A Do I click the white space or the label?

The white space.

• While holding the SHIFT key down, click all the other controls in the Detail section to select them.

Q&A Does it matter in which order I select the other controls?

No. It is only important that you ultimately select all the controls.

• Release the SHIFT key.

• Display the Arrange tab.

• Click the Size/Space button (Report Design Tools Arrange tab | Sizing & Ordering group) to display the Size/ Space button menu (Figure 6–28).

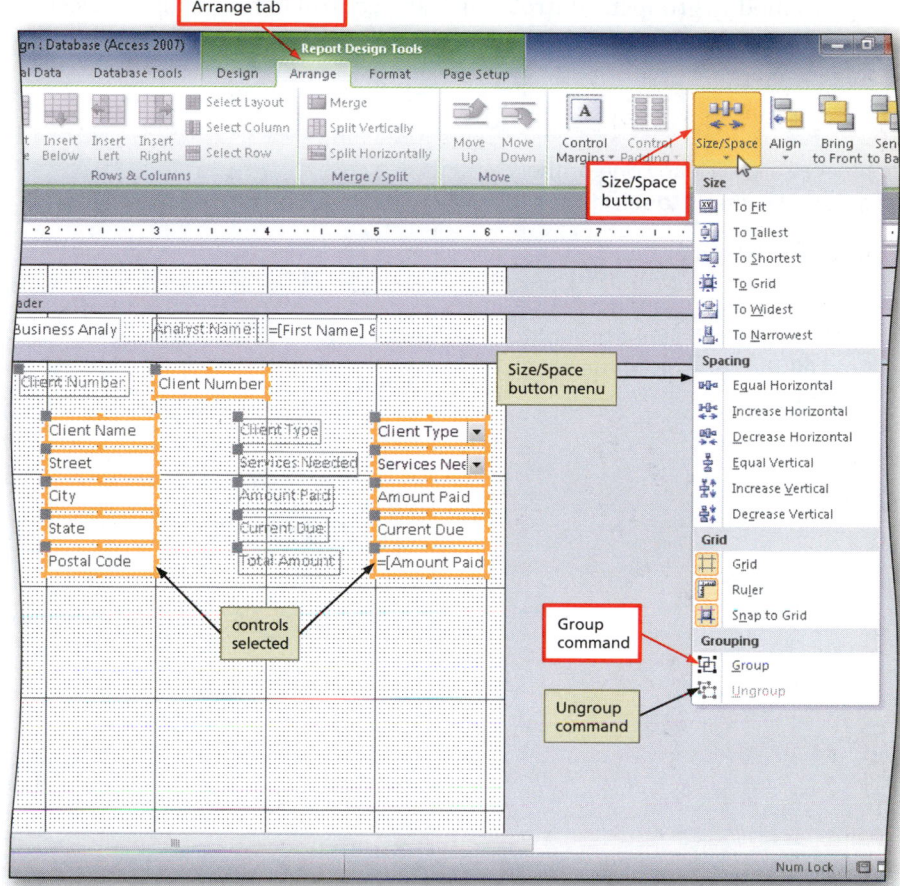

Figure 6–28

2

• Click Group on the Size/Space button menu to group the controls.

Q&A What if I make a mistake and group the wrong collection of controls?

Ungroup the controls using the steps shown in the next section, and then group the correct collection of controls.

TO UNGROUP CONTROLS

If you no longer need to simultaneously modify all the controls you have placed in a group, you can ungroup the controls. To do so, you would use the following steps.

1. Click any of the controls in a group to select the entire group.

2. Display the Arrange tab.

3. Click the Size/Space button (Report Design Tools Arrange tab | Sizing & Ordering group) to display the Size/Space button menu.

4. Click the Ungroup button on the Size/Space button menu to ungroup the controls.

To Modify Grouped Controls

To modify grouped controls, click any control in the group to select the entire group. Any change you then make affects all controls in the group. The following steps bold the controls in the group, resize them, and then change the border style.

1
- If necessary, click any one of the grouped controls to select the group.
- Display the Format tab.
- Click the Bold button (Report Design Tools Format tab | Font group) to bold all the controls in the group (Figure 6–29).

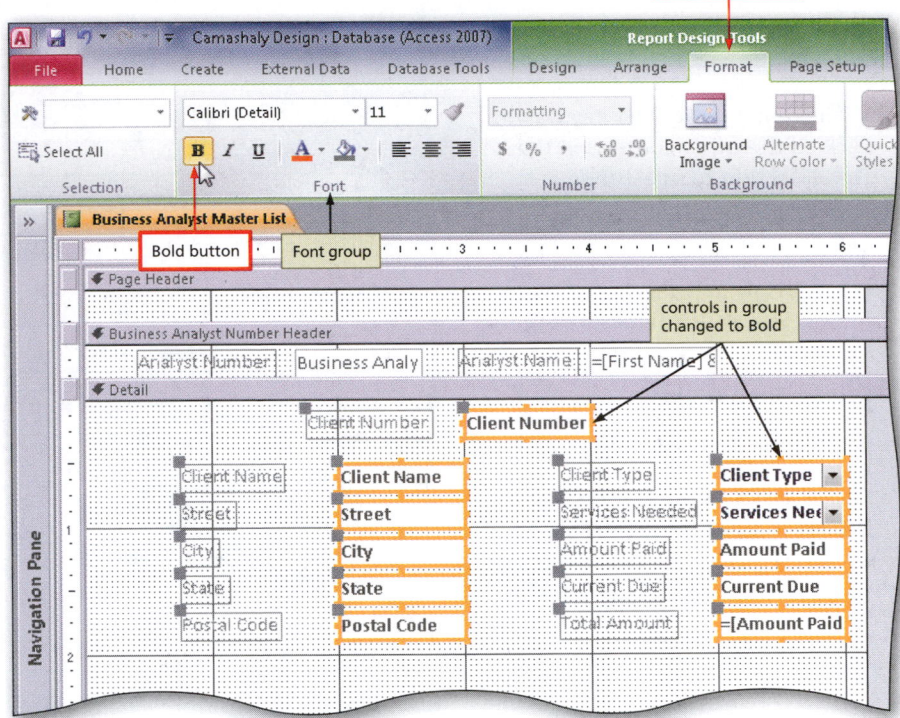

Figure 6–29

2
- Display the Design tab.
- Drag the right sizing handle of the Services Needed field to the approximate position shown in Figure 6–30 to resize all the controls in the group.

Q&A How do I change only one control in the group?

Double-click the control to select just the one control and not the entire group. You then can make any change you want to that control.

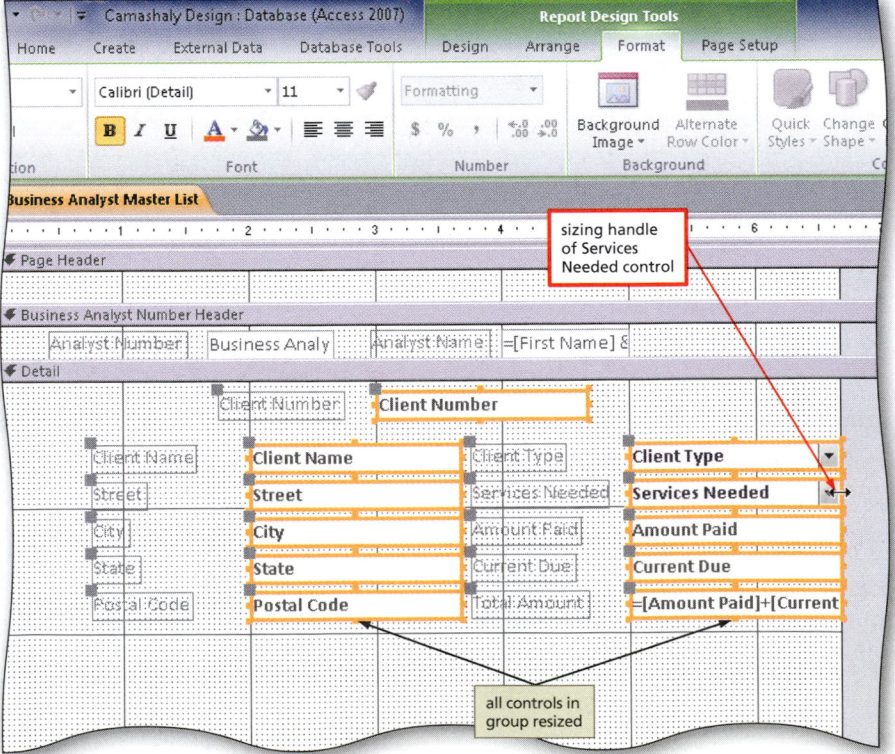

Figure 6–30

3

- Click the Property Sheet button (Report Design Tools Design tab | Tools group) to display the property sheet for the grouped controls.

- With the All tab (Property Sheet) selected, ensure the Border Style property is set to Solid. If it is not, click the Border Style property box to display an arrow, click the arrow to display the list of available border styles, and click Solid.

- Click the Border Width property box to display an arrow and then click the arrow to display the list of available border widths (Figure 6–31).

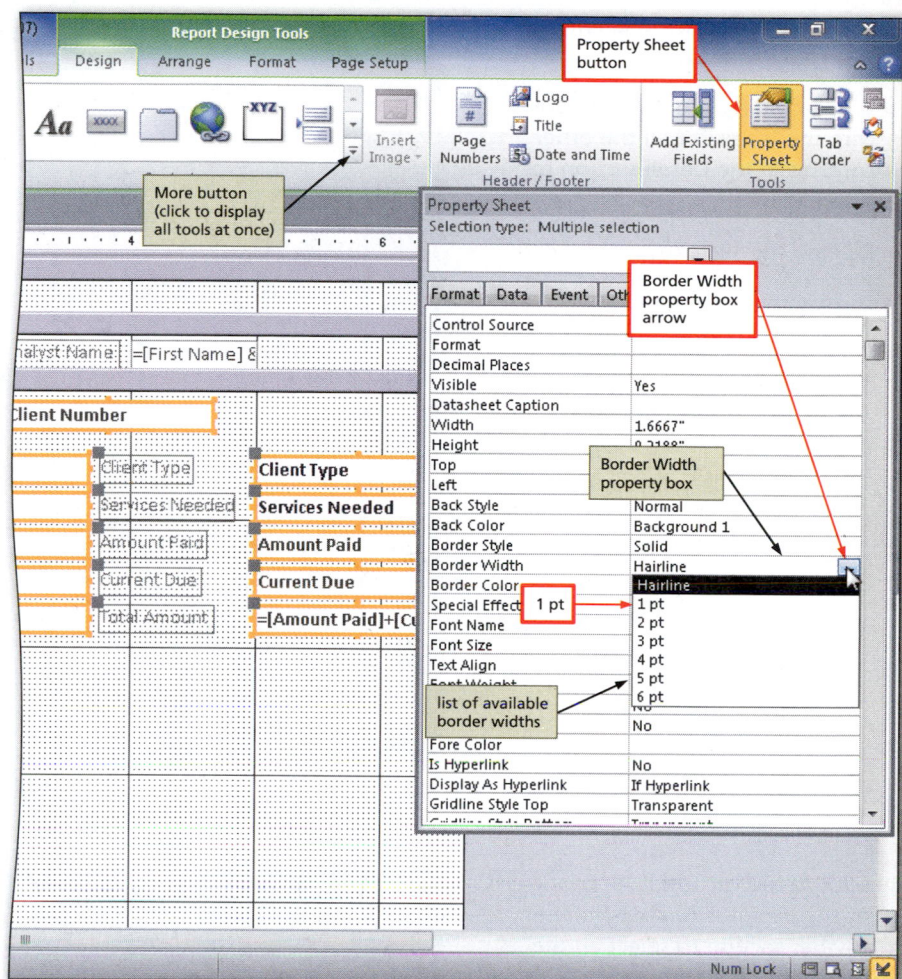

Figure 6–31

4

- Click 1 pt to select the border width.

Experiment

- Try the other border styles and widths to see their effects. In each case, view the report and then return to Design view. When finished, once again select Solid as the border style and 1 pt as the border width.

- Close the property sheet.

To Modify Multiple Controls That Are Not Grouped

To modify multiple controls that are not grouped together, you must simultaneously select all the controls you want to modify. To do so, click one of the controls and then hold the SHIFT key down while selecting the others. The following steps italicize all the labels in the Detail section and then bold all the controls and labels in the Business Analyst Number Header section. Finally, the steps increase the size of the Business Analyst Name control so that the entire name will be visible.

1

- Click the label for the Client Number control to select it.

- While holding the SHIFT key down, click the labels for all the other controls in the Detail section to select them.

- Release the SHIFT key.

- Display the Format tab.

- Click the Italic button (Report Design Tools Format tab | Font group) to italicize the labels (Figure 6–32).

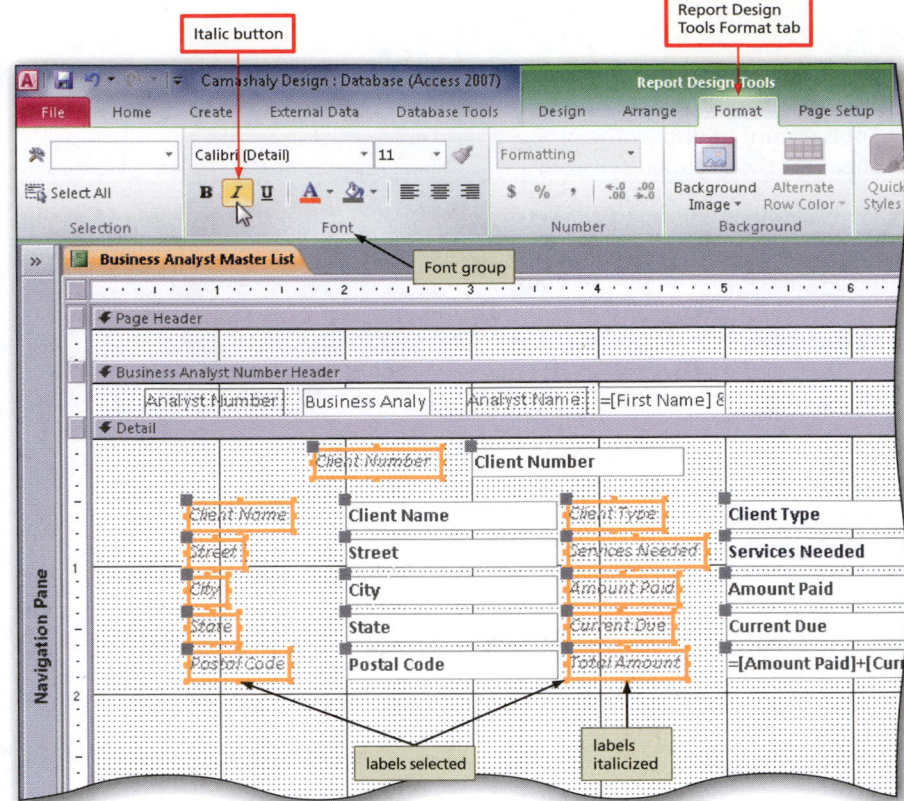

Figure 6–32

2

- Click in the vertical ruler to the left of the Business Analyst Number Header section to select all the controls in the section.

Q&A

What exactly is selected when I click in the vertical ruler?

If you picture a horizontal line through the point you clicked, any control that intersects that horizontal line would be selected.

- Click the Bold button (Report Design Tools Format tab | Font group) to bold all the selected controls (Figure 6–33).

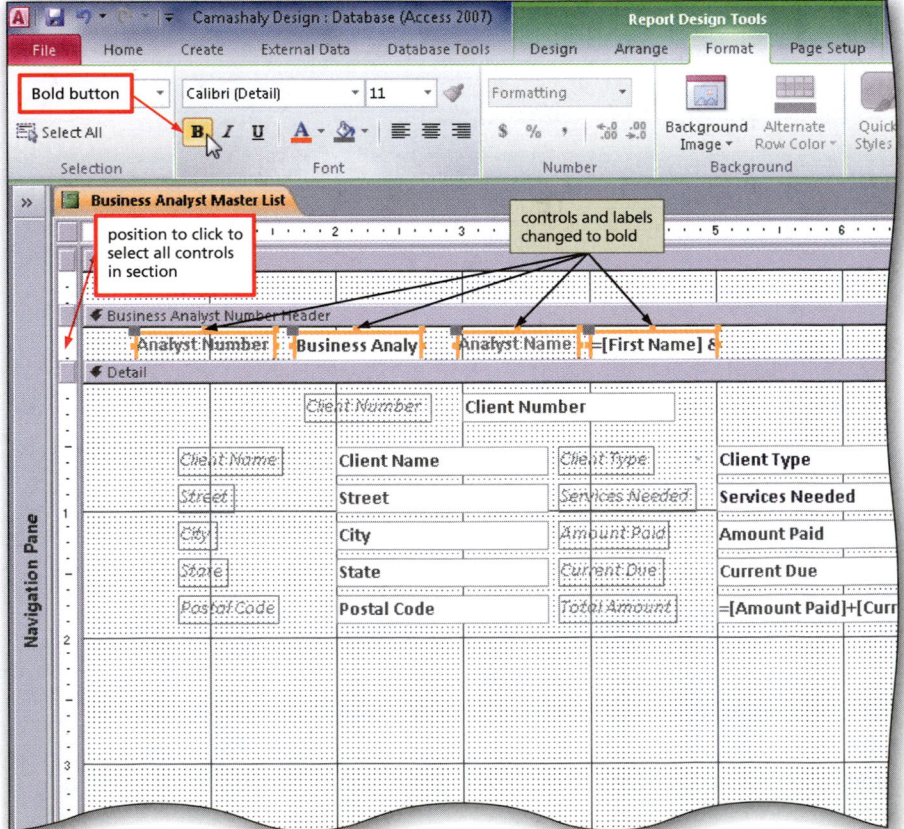

Figure 6–33

3

- Click outside the selected controls to deselect them. Click the control containing the expression for the business analyst's name to select it.

Q&A

Why do I have to deselect the controls and then select one of them a second time?

If you do not do so, any action you take would apply to all the selected controls rather than just the one you want.

- Drag the right sizing handle of the selected control to the approximate position shown in Figure 6–34.

- View the report and then make any necessary adjustments.

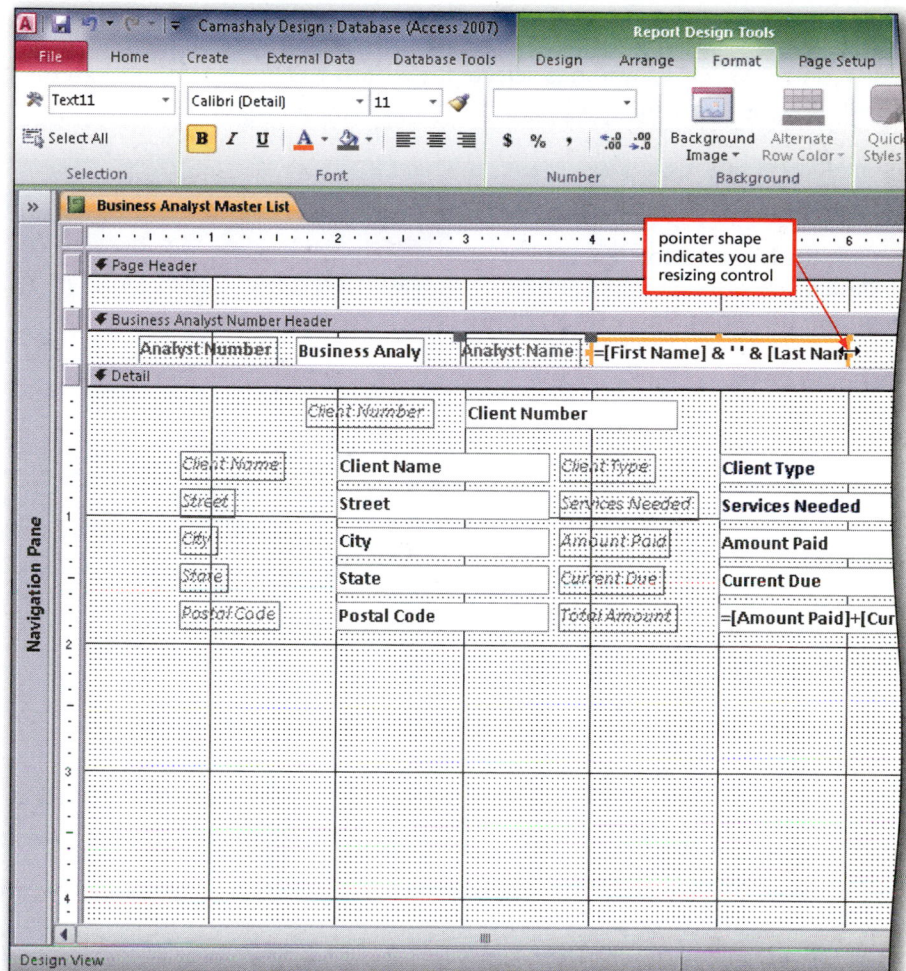

Figure 6–34

Undoing and Saving

Remember that if you make a mistake, you often can correct it by clicking the Undo button on the Quick Access Toolbar. Clicking the Undo button will reverse your most recent change. You also can click the Undo button more than once to reverse multiple changes.

You should save your work frequently. That way, if you have problems that the Undo button will not fix, you can close the report without saving it and open it again. The report will be in exactly the state it was in at the time you saved it.

To Add a Subreport

To add a subreport to a report, you use the Subform/Subreport tool on the Design tab. Provided the Use Control Wizards button is selected, a wizard will guide you through the process of adding the subreport. The following steps add a subreport to display the course data.

1

- Display the Design tab.

- Click the More button (Report Design Tools Design tab | Controls group) (shown in Figure 6–31) to display a menu of available tools (Figure 6–35).

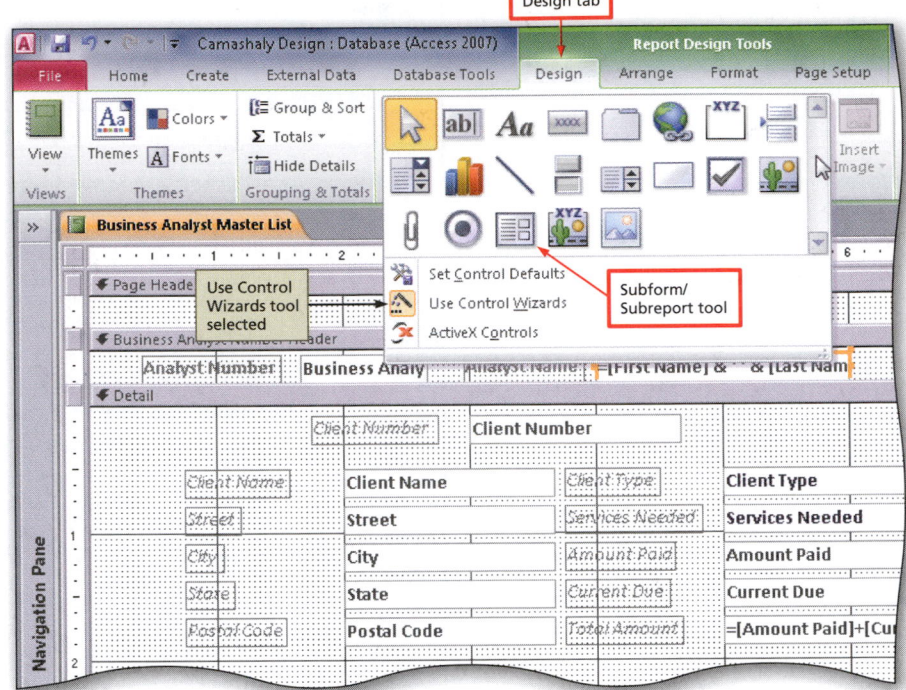

Figure 6–35

2

- Be sure the Use Control Wizards button is selected, click the Subform/Subreport tool, and then move the mouse pointer, which has changed to a plus sign with a subreport, to the approximate position shown in Figure 6–36.

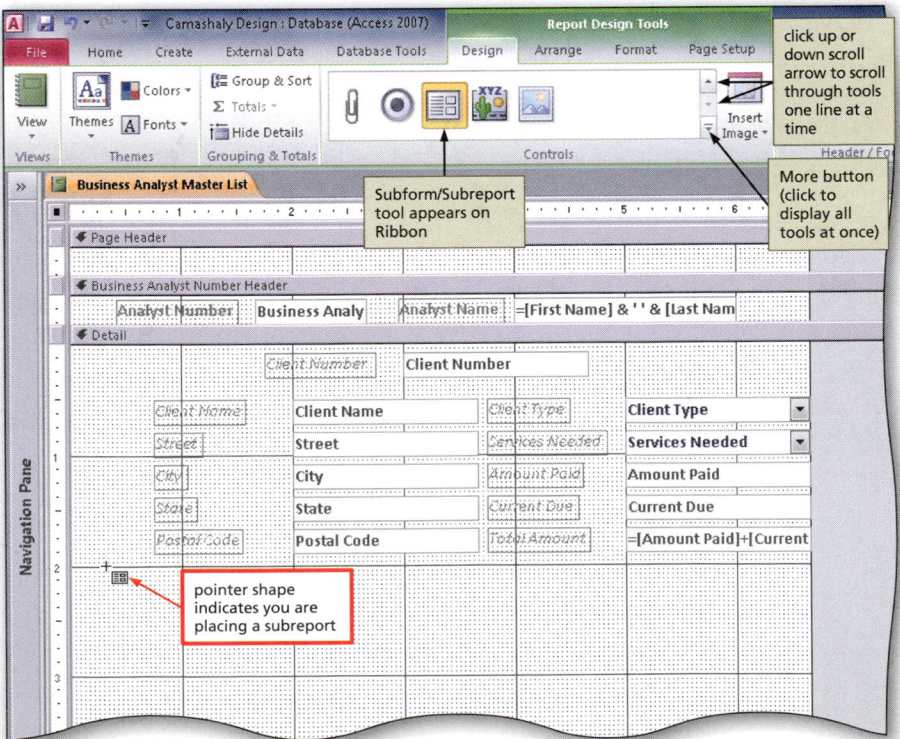

Figure 6–36

3

- Click the position shown in Figure 6–36 to place the subreport and display the SubReport Wizard dialog box. Be sure the 'Use existing Tables and Queries' option button is selected (Figure 6–37).

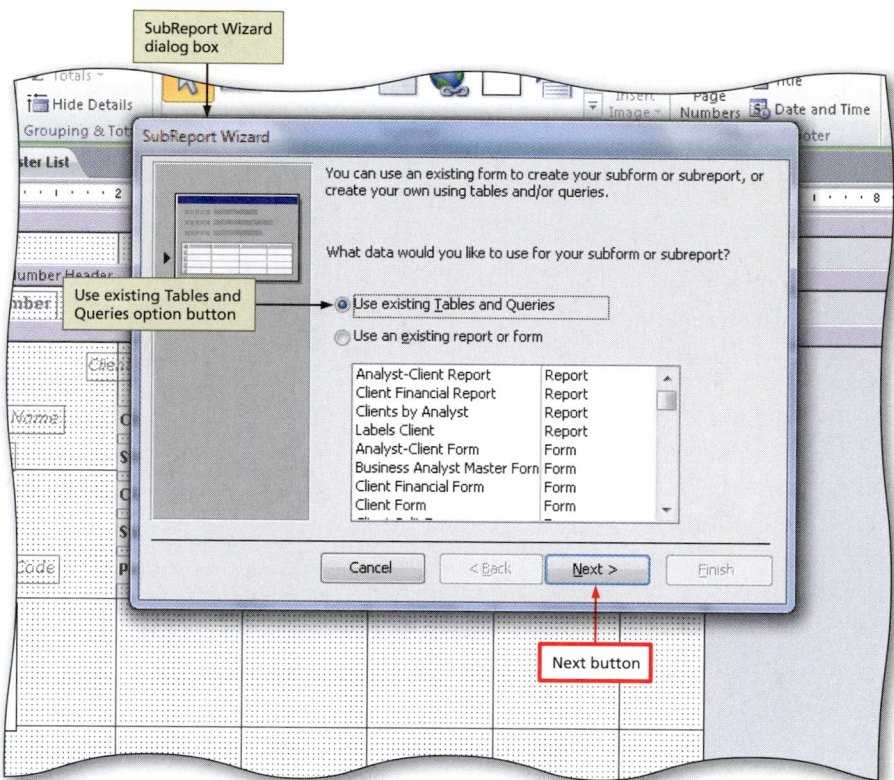

Figure 6–37

4

- Click the Next button.

- Click the Tables/Queries box arrow.

- Scroll down until Query: Course Offerings and Courses is visible, click Query: Course Offerings and Courses, and then click the Add All Fields button to select all the fields in the query (Figure 6–38).

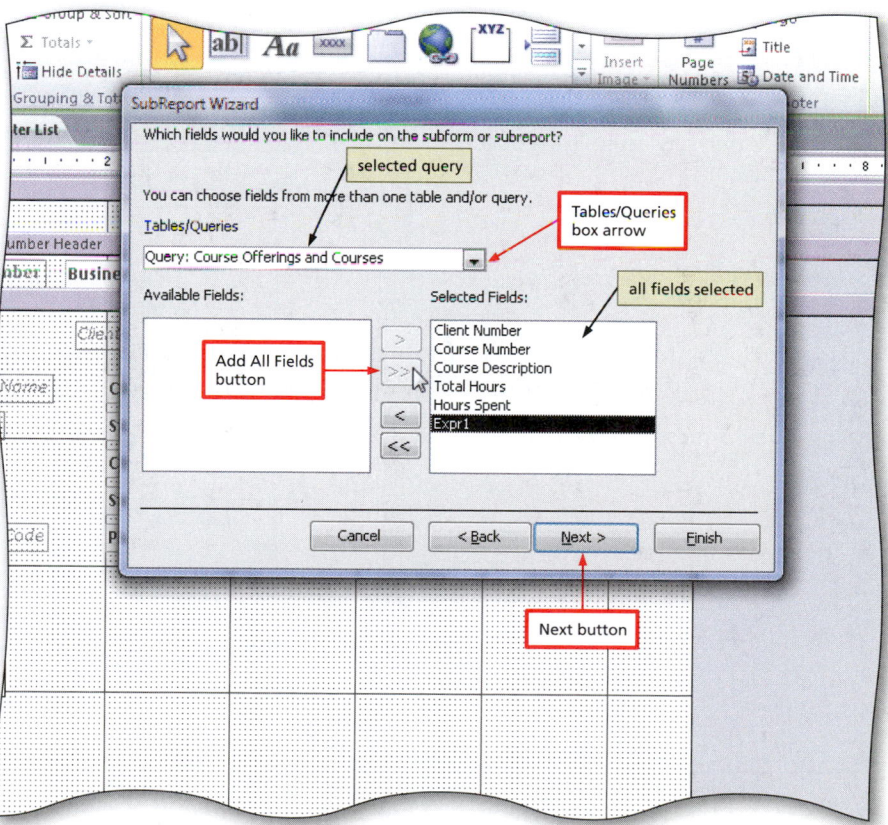

Figure 6–38

5
- Click the Next button and then ensure the 'Choose from a list' option button is selected (Figure 6–39).

Q&A

What is the purpose of this dialog box?

You use this dialog box to indicate the fields that link the main report (referred to as "form") to the subreport (referred to as "subform"). If the fields have the same name, as they often will, you can simply select Choose from a list and then accept the selection Access already has made.

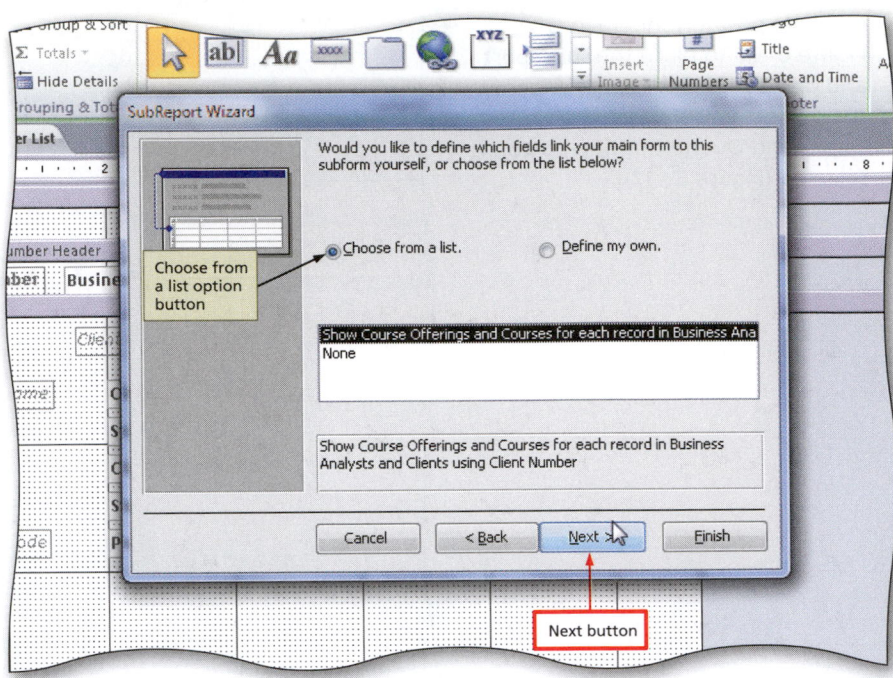

Figure 6–39

6
- Click the Next button, type **Course Offerings by Client** as the name of the subreport, and then click the Finish button to add the subreport to the Business Analyst Master List report (Figure 6–40).

7
- Click outside the subreport to deselect the subreport.

- Click the Save button on the Quick Access Toolbar to save your changes.

- Close the Business Analyst Master List report.

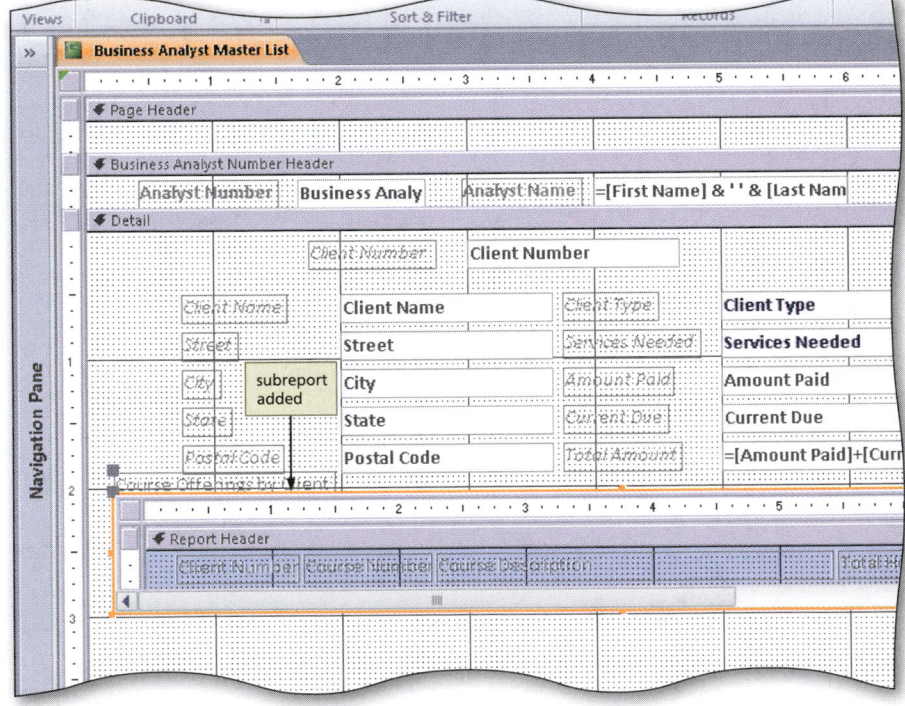

Figure 6–40

Break Point: If you wish to stop working through the chapter at this point, you can resume the project at a later time by starting Access, opening the database called Camashaly Design, and continuing to follow the steps from this location forward.

To Open the Subreport in Design View

The subreport appears as a separate report in the Navigation Pane. It can be modified just like any other report. The following step opens the subreport in Design view.

1

- Open the Navigation Pane, scroll down so that the Course Offerings by Client report appears, and then right-click the Course Offerings by Client report to produce a shortcut menu.

- Click Design View on the shortcut menu to open the subreport in Design view.

- Close the Navigation Pane (Figure 6–41).

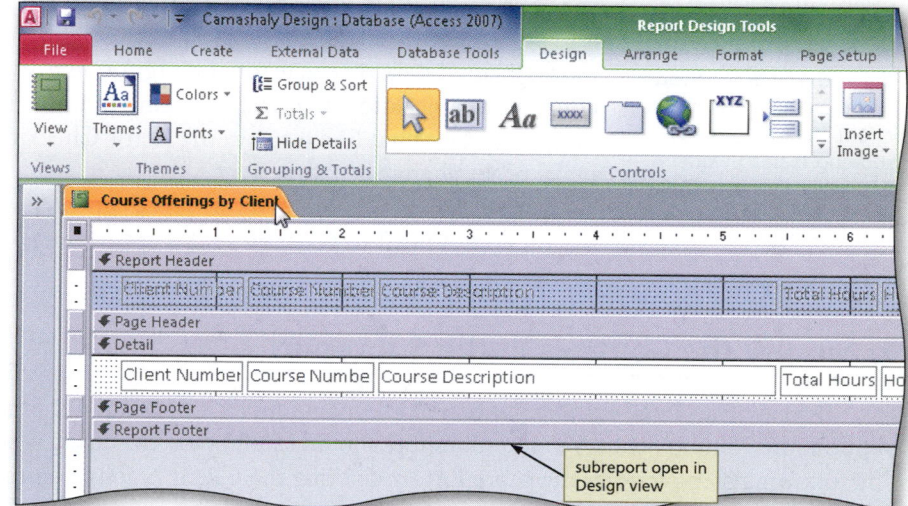

Figure 6–41

Print Layout Issues

If there is a problem with your report, for example, a report that is too wide for the printed page, you will get a green triangular symbol in the upper-left corner of the report. The green triangle is called an error indicator. Clicking it displays an Error Checking Options button. Clicking the Error Checking Options button produces the Error Checking Options menu, as shown in Figure 6–42.

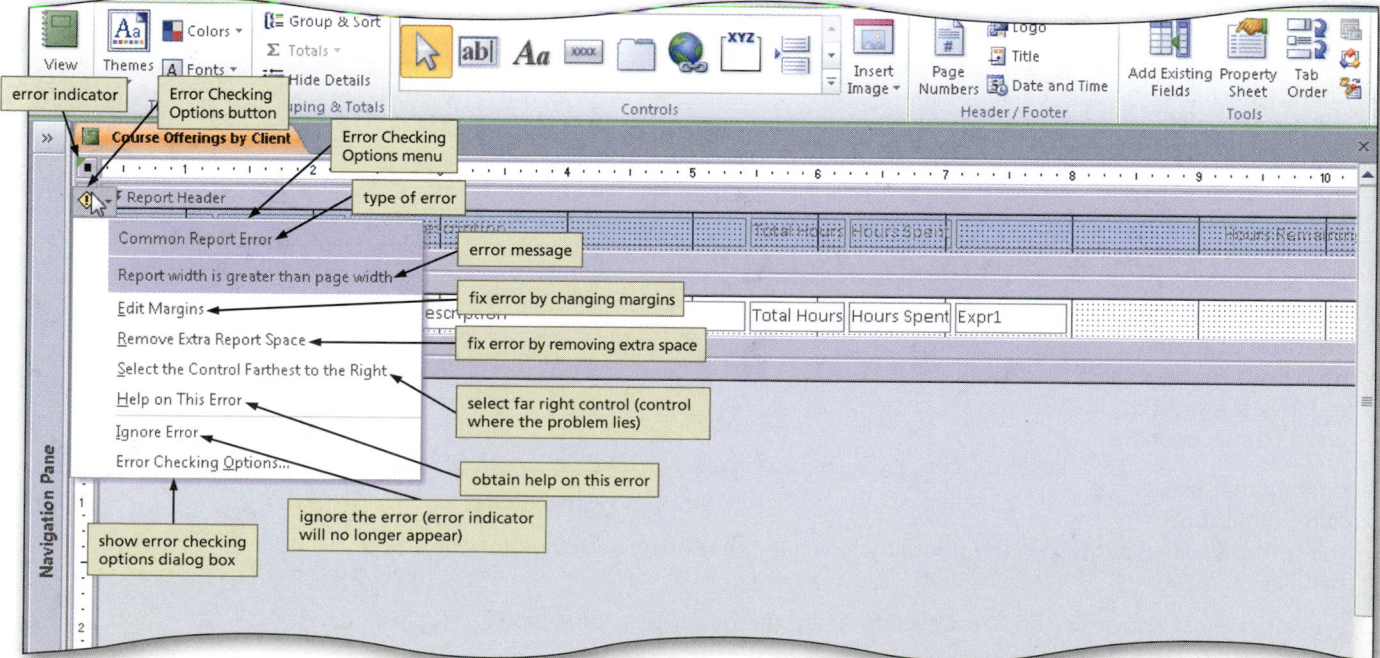

Figure 6–42

Subreports

Subreports provide more control in presenting data effectively than multiple levels of grouping can. Because grouping places headers in columns, it often can be difficult to determine the relationship between the group header and the detail. Also, you might want to present subreports side by side. You cannot do that with grouping.

The first line in the menu is simply a statement of the type of error that occurred. The second is a description of the specific error; in this case, the fact that the report width is greater than the page width. This situation could lead to data not appearing where you expect it to, as well as the printing of some blank pages.

The next three lines provide alternatives for addressing the error. You could change the margins to allow more space for the report. You could remove some extra space. You could select the control farthest to the right and move it. The fourth line gives more detailed help on the error. The Ignore Error command instructs Access to not consider this situation an error. Selecting Ignore Error would cause the error indicator to disappear. The final line displays the Error Checking Options dialog box, where you can make other changes.

Later in this chapter, you will fix the problem by changing the width of the report, so you do not need to take any action at this time.

To Modify the Controls in the Subreport

Because the client number appears in the main report, it does not need to be duplicated in the subreport. In addition, the column headers in the subreport should extend over two lines, as shown in Figure 6–1a on page AC 339. The following step modifies the subreport by deleting the Client Number control and revising the column headings.

1
- Click the Client Number control in the Detail section to select the control. Hold the SHIFT key down and click the Client Number control in the Report Header section to select both controls.

- With both controls selected, press the DELETE key to delete the controls.

- Change the labels in the Report Header section to match those shown in Figure 6–43. To extend a heading over two lines, click in front of the second word to produce an insertion point and then press SHIFT+ENTER to move the second word to a second line.

- Change the sizes and positions of the controls to match those in the figure by selecting the controls and dragging the sizing handles.

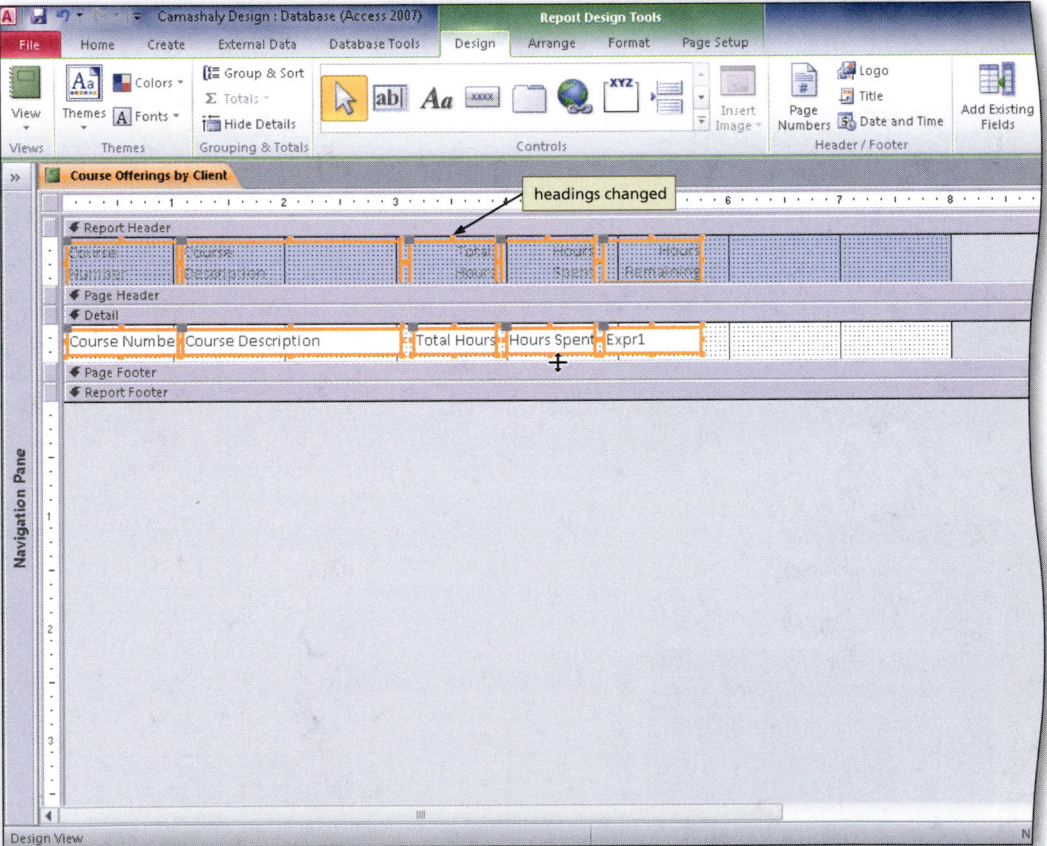

Figure 6–43

Q&A

Why does Expr1 appear in the Detail section under the Hours Remaining label?

Expr1 indicates that Hours Remaining is a calculated control.

🔍 **Experiment**

- There is currently a space between the two names in the Report Header labels. To delete the space, click immediately after the first word to produce an insertion point and then press the DELETE key. Try the various alignments (left, right, and center) before removing the space. Remove the space and try the various alignments again to see if the removal of the space makes any difference. When finished, make sure your labels look like the one in the figure.

To Change the Can Grow Property

If you preview the report, you will see that some of the course descriptions are too long to fit in the available space. This problem can be addressed in several ways.

1. Move the controls to allow more space in between controls. Then, drag the appropriate handles on the controls that need to be expanded to enlarge them.

2. Use the Font Size property to select a smaller font size. This will allow more data to fit in the same space.

3. Use the Can Grow property. By changing the value of this property from No to Yes, the data can be spread over two lines, thus allowing all the data to print. Access will split data at natural break points, such as commas, spaces, and hyphens.

The third approach is the easiest to use and also produces a very readable report. The following steps change the Can Grow property for the Course Description field. First, you preview the report to verify that there are some course descriptions that are too long for the available space and then make the necessary corrections.

1

- Click the View button arrow and then click Print Preview to preview the report (Figure 6–44).

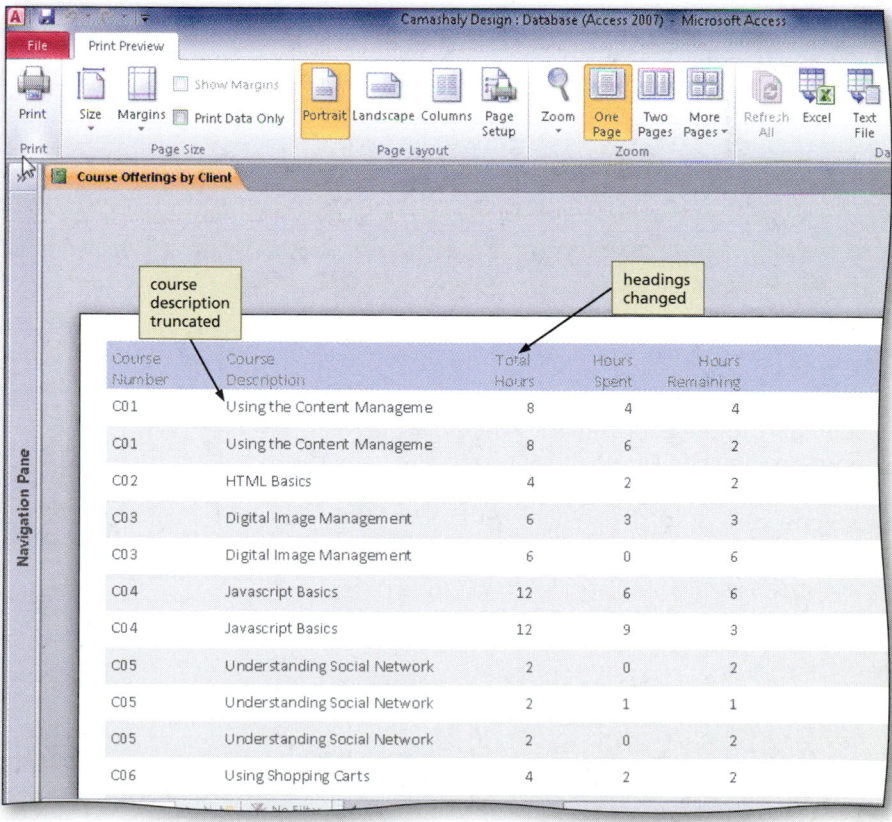

Figure 6–44

2

- Click the Close Print Preview button to return to Design view.

- Click the Course Description control to select it.

- Click the Property Sheet button (Report Design Tools Design tab | Tools group) to display the property sheet.

- With the All tab selected, scroll down until the Can Grow property appears, and then click the Can Grow property box arrow to display the list of possible values for the Can Grow property (Figure 6–45).

What is the effect of the Can Shrink property?

If the value of the Can Shrink property is set to Yes, Access will remove blank lines that occur when the field is empty.

3

- Click Yes in the list to allow the Course Description control to grow as needed.

- Close the property sheet.

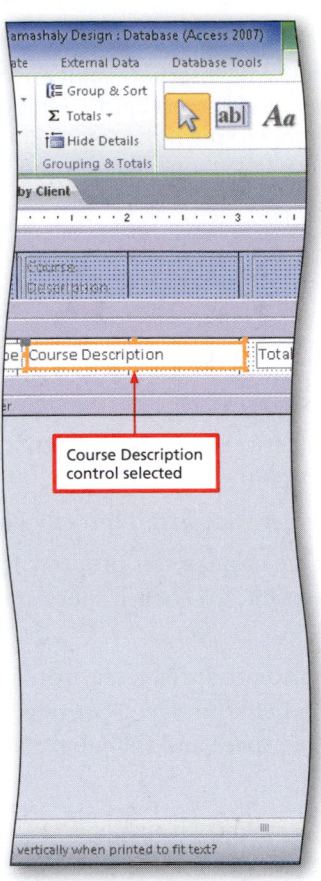
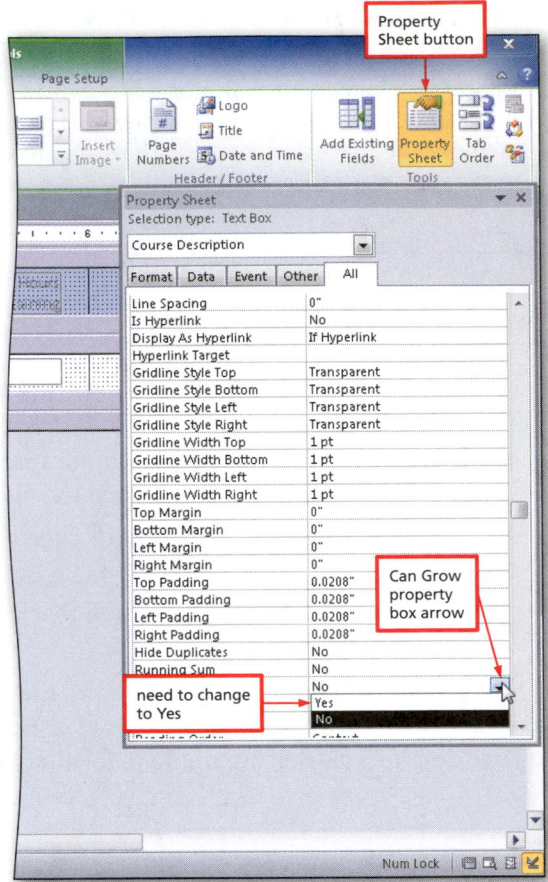

Figure 6–45

To Change the Appearance of the Controls in the Subreport

The following steps change the controls in the Detail section to Bold and the controls in the Report Header section to italic. They also change the background color in the Report Header section to white.

1

- Drag the right boundary of the subreport to the approximate position shown in Figure 6–46.

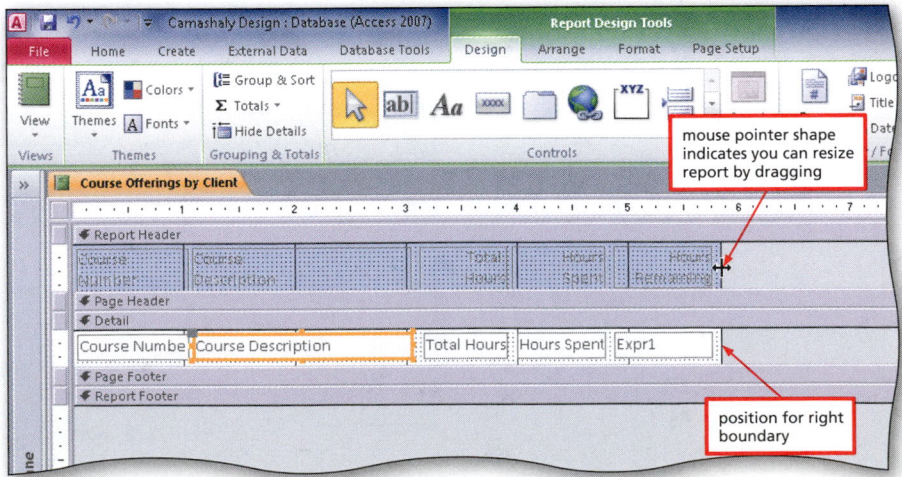

Figure 6–46

2

- Display the Format tab.

- Click the ruler to the left of the controls in the Detail section to select the controls, and then click the Bold button (Report Design Tools Format tab | Font group) to bold the controls.

- Click the ruler to the left of the controls in the Report Header section to select the controls, and then click the Italic button (Report Design Tools Format tab | Font group) to italicize the controls.

- Click the title bar for the Report Header to select the header without selecting any of the controls in the header.

- Click the Background Color button arrow (Report Design Tools Format tab | Font group) to display a color palette (Figure 6–47).

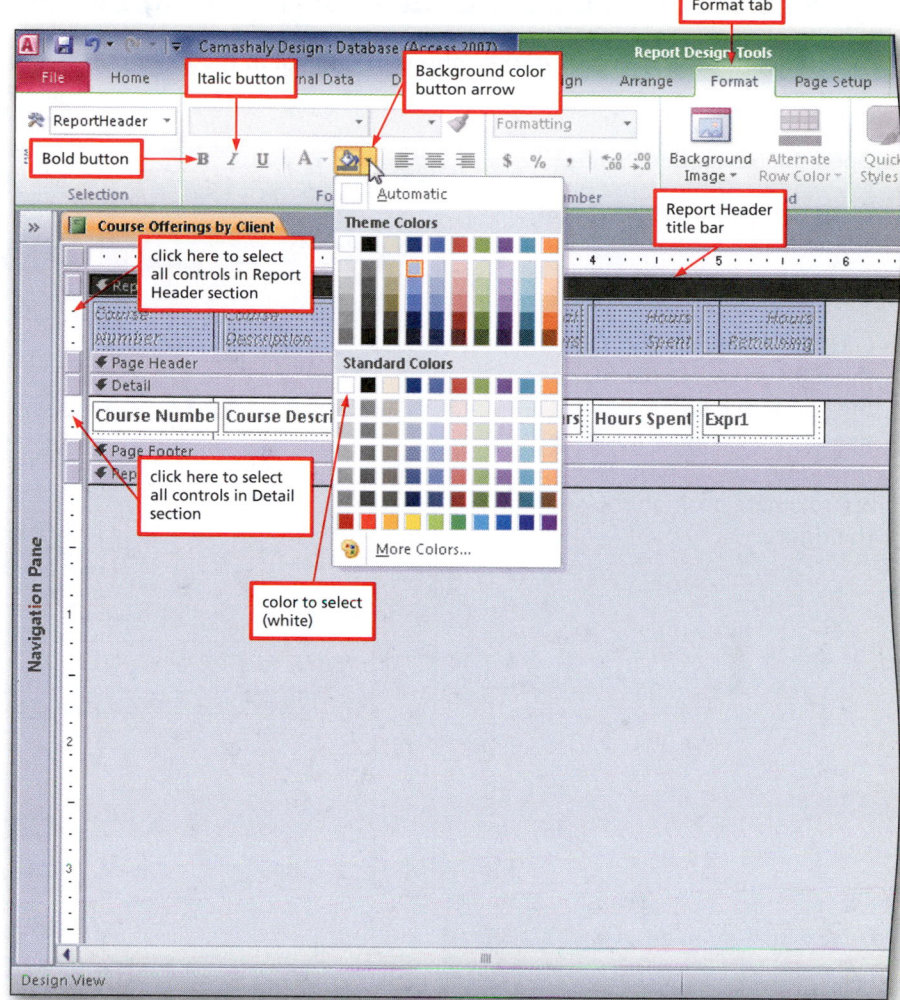

Figure 6–47

3

- Click White in the first row, first column of the Standard Colors to change the background color to white.

Q&A

What is the difference between clicking a color in the Theme colors and clicking a color in the Standard Colors?

The theme colors are specific to the currently selected theme. The first column, for example, represents "background 1," one of the selected background colors in the theme. The various entries in the column represent different intensities of the color at the top of the column. The colors would be different if a different theme were selected. If you select one of the theme colors and a different theme is selected in the future, the color you selected would change to the color in the same location. On the other hand, if you select a standard color, a change of theme would have no effect on the color.

- Click the Save button on the Quick Access Toolbar to save the changes.

- Close the Course Offerings by Client subreport.

To Resize the Subreport and the Report in Design View

The following steps resize the subreport control in the main report and then resize the main report.

- Open the Navigation Pane.

- Open the Business Analyst Master List in Design view.

- Close the Navigation Pane.

- Click the subreport and then drag the right sizing handle to change the size to the approximate size shown in Figure 6–48, and then drag the subreport to the approximate position shown in the figure.

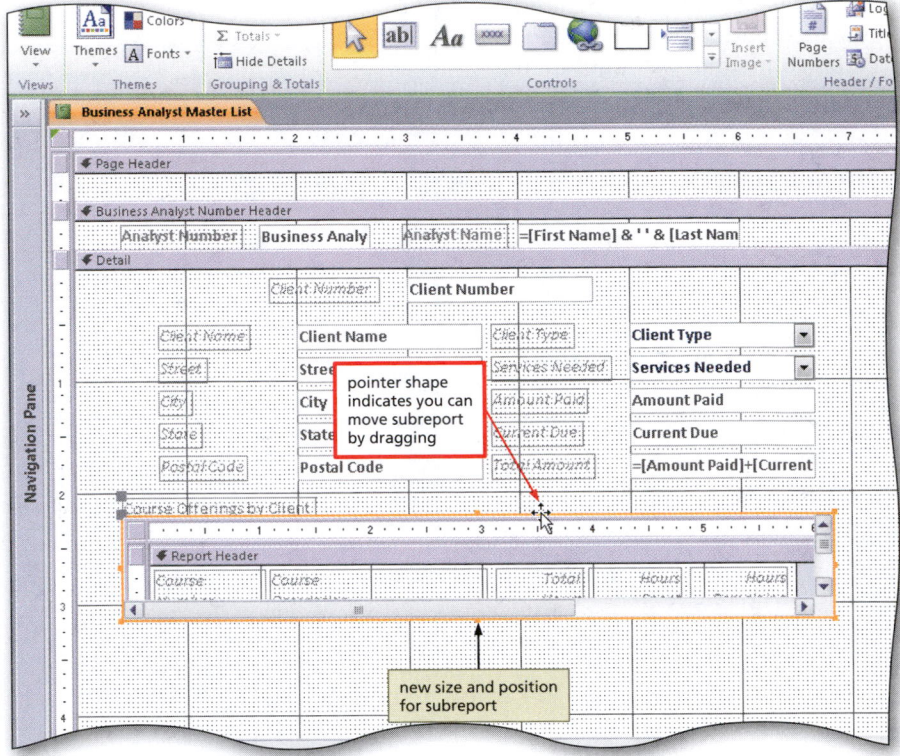

Figure 6–48

- Scroll down in the main report so that the lower boundary of the Detail section appears, and then drag the lower boundary of the section so that there is approximately the same amount of space below the subreport as that shown in Figure 6–49.

Q&A

I scrolled down to see the lower boundary of the Detail section and the controls are no longer on the screen. What is the easiest way to drag the boundary when the position to which I want to drag it is not visible?

You do not need to see the location to drag to it. As you get close to the top of the visible portion of the screen, Access will automatically scroll. You might find it easier, however, to drag the boundary near the top of the visible portion of the report, use the scroll bar to scroll up, and then drag some more. You might have to scroll a couple of times.

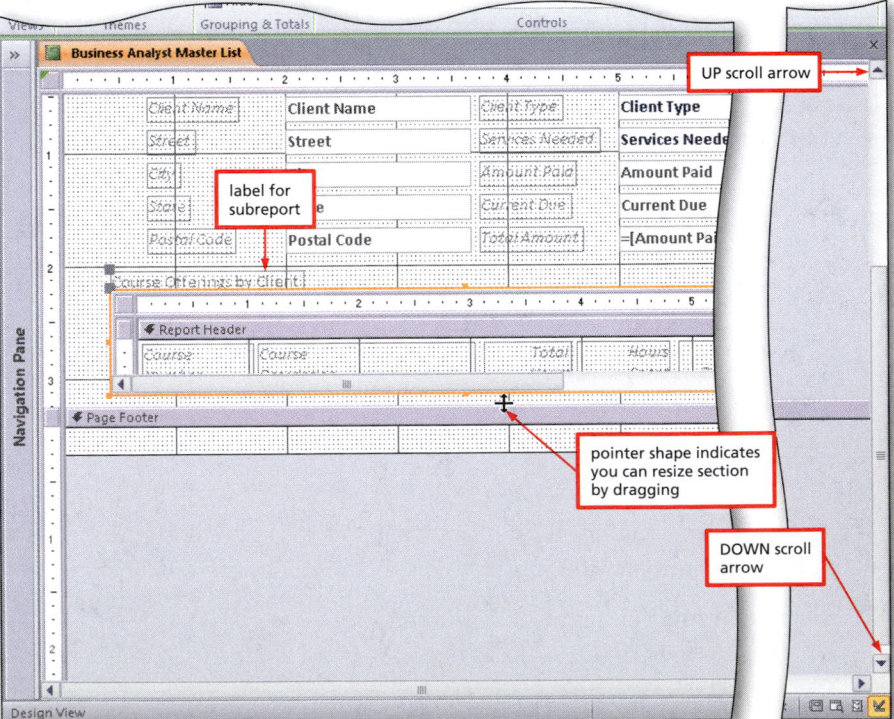

Figure 6–49

To Modify Section Properties

The following step first deletes the label for the subreport and then makes two modifications to the Business Analyst Number Header section. The first modification, which causes the contents of the Group Header section to appear at the top of each page, changes the Repeat Section property to Yes. Without this change, the business analyst number and name would only appear at the beginning of the group of clients of that business analyst. If the list of clients occupies more than one page, it would not be apparent on subsequent pages which business analyst is associated with those clients. The second modification changes the Force New Page property to Before Section, causing each section to begin at the top of a page.

1

- If necessary, scroll back up to the top of the report, and then click the label for the subreport (the label that reads Course Offerings by Client), and then press the DELETE key to delete the label.

- Click the Business Analyst Number Header bar to select the header, and then click the Property Sheet button (Report Design Tools Design tab | Tools group) to display the property sheet.

- With the All tab selected, click the Repeat Section property box, click the arrow that appears, and then click Yes to cause the contents of the group header to appear at the top of each page of the report.

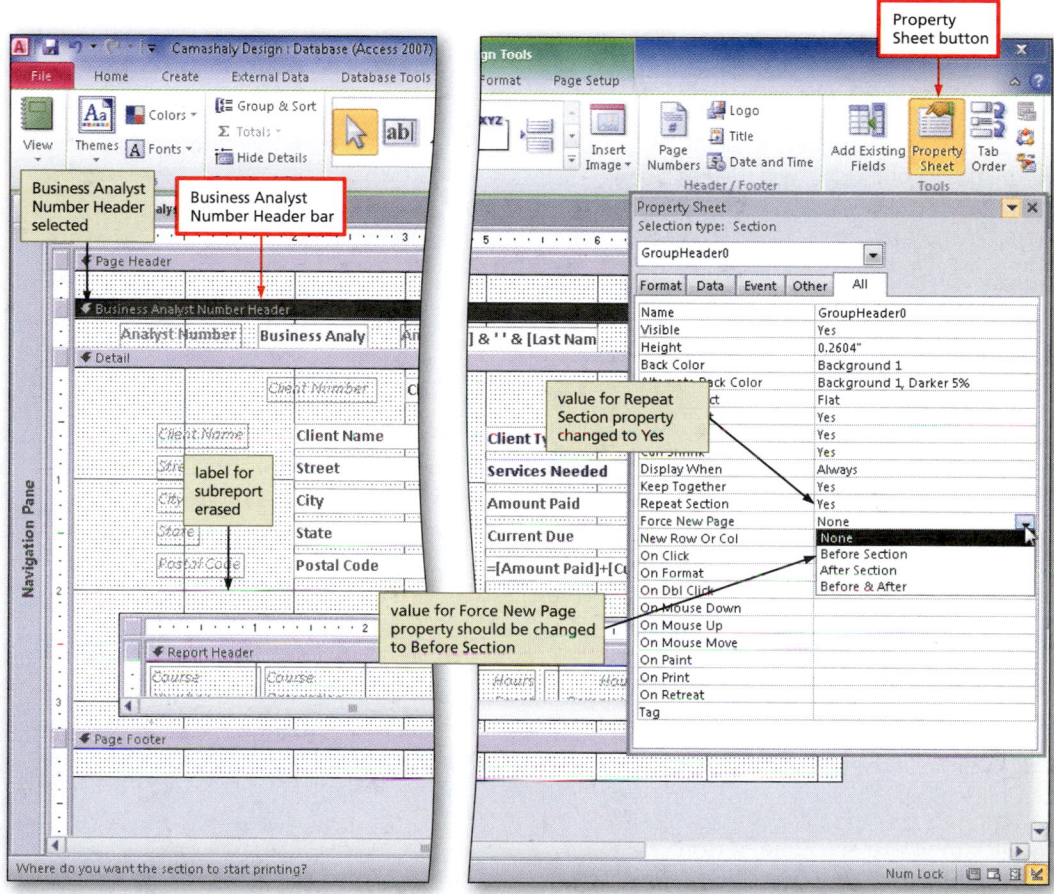

Figure 6–50

- Click the Force New Page property box, and then click the arrow that appears to display the menu of possible values (Figure 6–50).

2

- Click Before Section to cause a new group to begin at the top of the next page.

- Close the property sheet.

To Add a Title, Page Number, and Date

You can add a title, a page number, and a date to a report or apply other formatting using buttons on the Design tab. The following steps add a title, page number, and date to the Business Analyst Master List report. The date is automatically added to the report header. The steps move the date to the page header by first cutting the date from its original position and then pasting it into the page header.

1
- Display the Design tab, and then click the Title button (Report Design Tools Design tab | Header/Footer group) to add a title.

Q&A

The title is the same as the name of the report object. Can I change the report title without changing the name of the report object in the database?

Yes. The report title is a label, and you can change it using any of the techniques that you used for changing column headings and other labels.

- Click the Page Numbers button (Report Design Tools Design tab | Header/Footer group) to display the Page Numbers dialog box.

- Be sure the Page N and Top of Page [Header] option buttons are selected.

- If necessary, click the Alignment arrow and select Left (Figure 6–51).

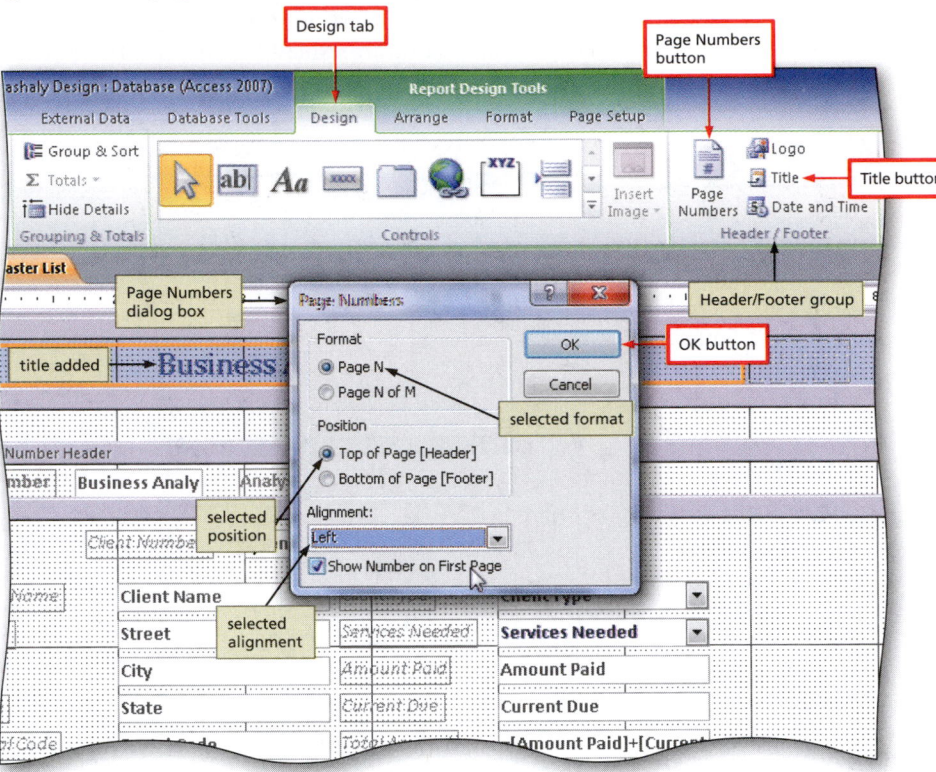

Figure 6–51

2
- Click the OK button (Page Numbers dialog box) to add the page number.

- Click the Date and Time button (Report Design Tools Design tab | Header/Footer group) to display the Date and Time dialog box.

- Click the option button for the third date format and click the Include Time check box to remove the check mark (Figure 6–52).

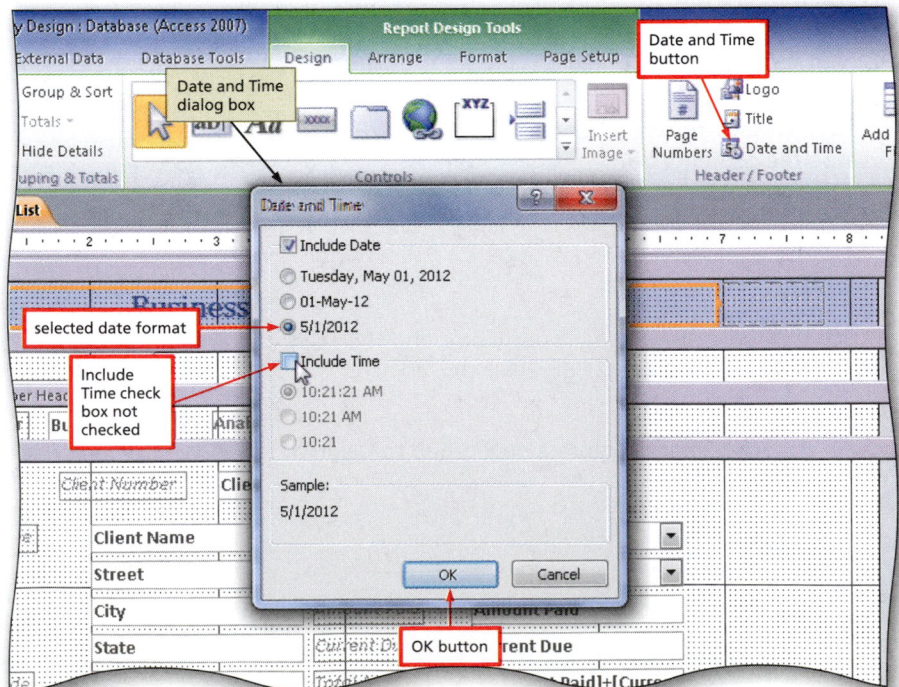

Figure 6–52

3

- Click the OK button (Date and Time dialog box) to add the date to the Report Header and display the Home tab (Figure 6–53).

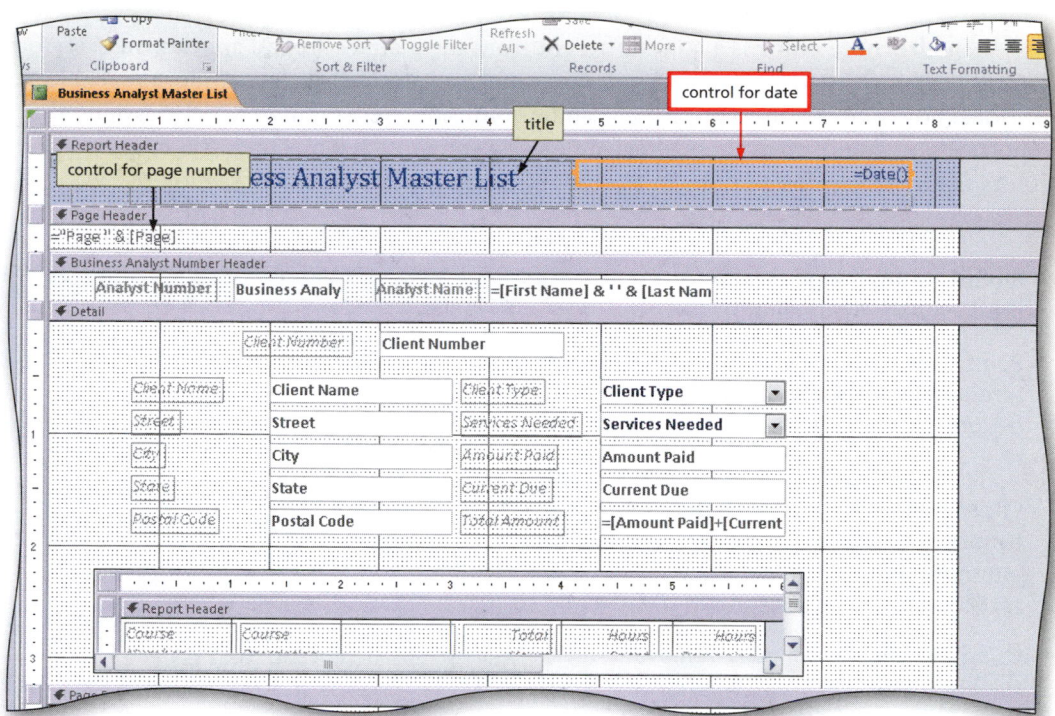

Figure 6–53

4

- With the control containing the date selected, click the Cut button (Home tab | Clipboard group) to cut the date, click the title bar for the page header to select the page header, and then click the Paste button (Home tab | Clipboard group) to paste the Date control at the beginning of the page header.

- Drag the Date control, which is currently sitting on top of the Page Number control, to the position shown in Figure 6–54.

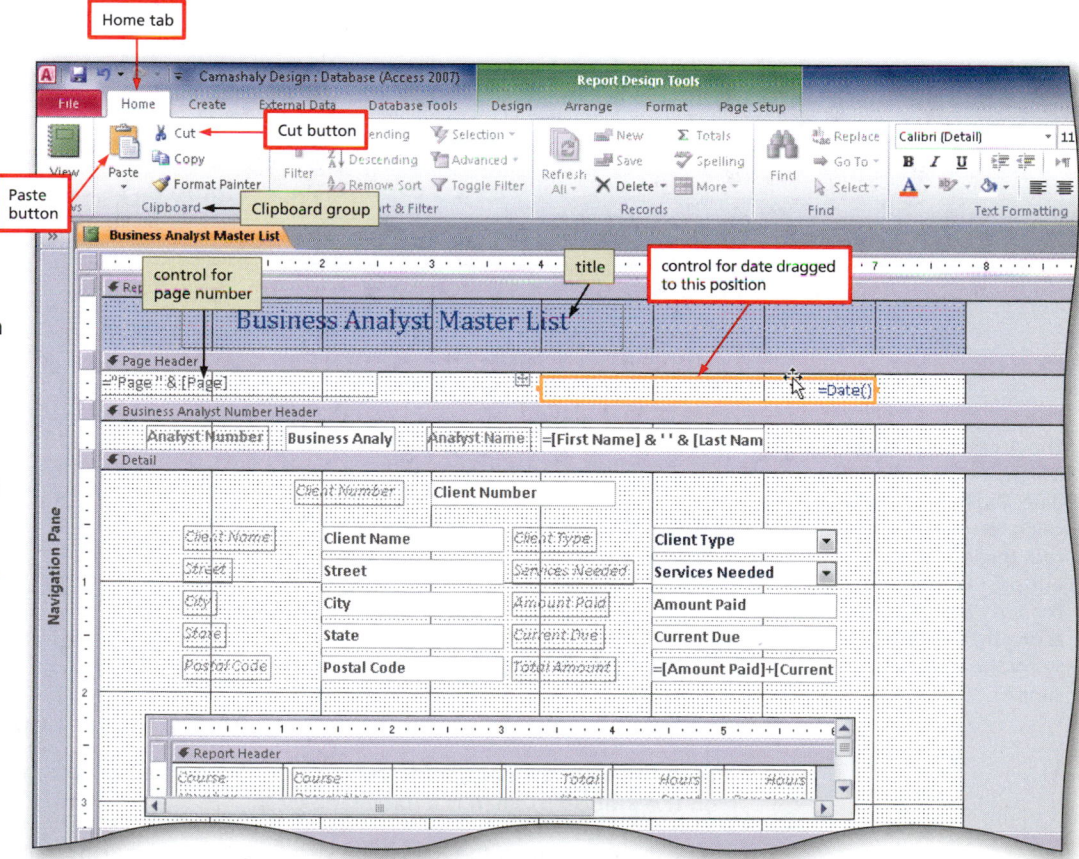

Figure 6–54

To Remove the Alternate Color

An **alternate color** is a color different from the main color and appears on every other line in a datasheet or report. Using alternate colors can sometimes make a datasheet or report more readable. In reports with multiple sections, however, the alternate colors can be confusing. Access automatically assigns alternate colors within the report. If you do not want these alternate colors, you must remove them. The following steps remove the alternate colors from the various sections in the report, starting with the Detail section.

- Right-click the Detail section to produce a shortcut menu.

- Point to the Alternate Fill/Back Color arrow to produce a color palette (Figure 6–55).

- Click None on the color palette to specify that there is to be no alternate color for the selected section.

- Using the same techniques, remove the alternate color from all other sections, including the subreport. (For some sections, the command may be dimmed.)

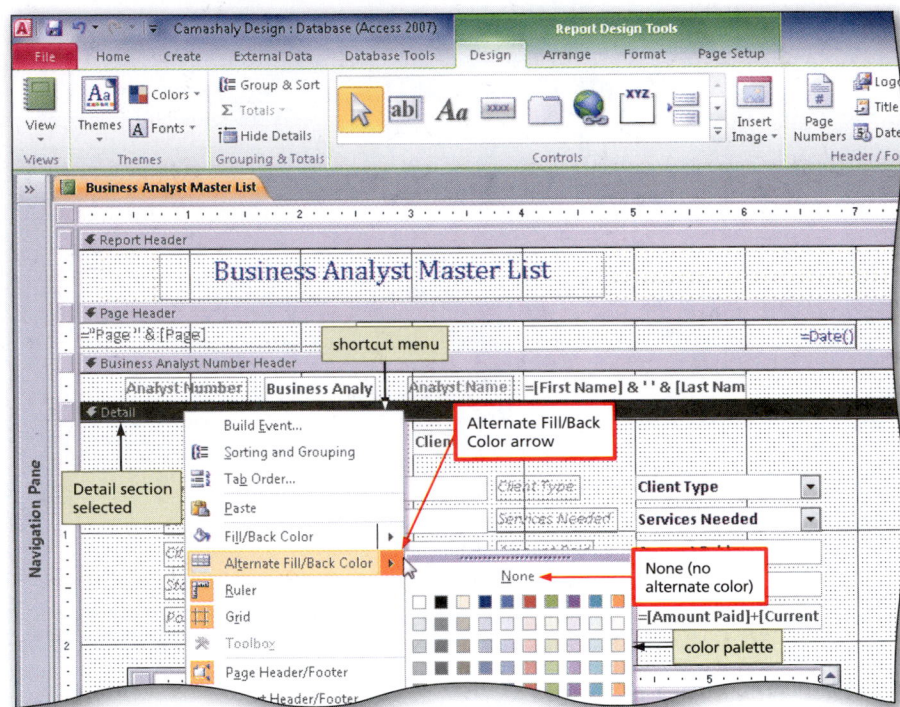

Figure 6–55

To Save and Close the Report

BTW

Dates
The Access default theme assigns a blue color to the date. To change the date color, select the control and click the Property Sheet button. Click the Fore Color property box, click the arrow that appears and select the color of your choice.

The following steps save the final report and then close the report.

1 Click the Save button on the Quick Access Toolbar to save the report.

2 Close the report by clicking the Close 'Business Analyst Master List' button.

To Print the Report

The following steps print the Business Analyst Master List report.

1 With the Business Analyst Master List selected in the Navigation Pane, click File on the Ribbon to open the Backstage view.

2 Click the Print tab in the Backstage view to display the Print gallery.

3 Click the Quick Print button to print the report.

To Publish a Report

You can make a report available through e-mail by publishing the report as either a PDF or XPS file. If you wanted to do so, you would use the following steps.

1. Select the report to be published in the Navigation Pane.
2. Display the External Data tab.
3. Click the PDF or XPS button (External Data tab | Export group) to display the Publish as PDF or XPS dialog box.
4. Select the appropriate Save as type (either PDF or XPS).
5. Select either 'Standard (publishing online and printing)' or 'Minimum size (publishing online).'
6. If you want to publish only a range of pages, click the Options button and select the desired range.
7. Click the Publish button to publish the report in the desired format.
8. If you want to save the export steps, click the Save button and then click the 'Save export steps' check box. If not, click the Close button.

BTW

Page Breaks
You can force a page break to occur at a particular position in a report by adding a page break to the report. To do so, click the Insert Page Break tool (Report Design Tools Design tab | Controls group), move the mouse pointer to the desired position, and click the position to place the page break.

Break Point: If you wish to stop working through the chapter at this point, you can resume the project at a later time by starting Access, opening the database called Camashaly Design, and continuing to follow the steps from this location forward.

To Create a Second Report

Camashaly Design also would like a report that groups clients by business analyst. The report should include subtotals and grand totals. Finally, it should show the discount amount for each client. The discount amount is based on the current due amount. Clients who owe more than $4,000 will receive a 4% discount, and clients who owe $4,000 or less will receive a 2% discount. The following steps create the Discount Report, select the record source, and specify grouping and sorting options.

1 Close the Navigation Pane.

2 Display the Create tab and then click the Report Design button (Create tab | Reports group) to create a report in Design view.

3 Ensure the selector for the entire report, which is the box in the upper-left corner of the report, is selected, and then click the Property Sheet button (Report Design Tools Design tab | Tools group) to display a property sheet.

4 With the All tab selected, click the Record Source property box arrow, and then click the Business Analysts and Clients query to select the query as the record source for the report.

5 Close the property sheet.

6 Click the Group & Sort button (Report Design Tools Design tab | Grouping & Totals group) to display the Group, Sort, and Total pane.

7 Click the 'Add a group' button to display the list of available fields for grouping, and then click the Business Analyst Number field to group by business analyst number.

8 Click the 'Add a sort' button to display the list of available fields for sorting, and then click the Client Number field to sort by client number.

9 Remove the Group, Sort, and Total pane by clicking the Group & Sort button (Report Design Tools Design tab | Grouping & Totals group).

10 Click the Save button on the Quick Access Toolbar, type `Discount Report` as the report name, and click the OK button to save the report.

Q&A

Why save it at this point?

You do not have to save it at this point. It is a good idea to save it often, however. Doing so will give you a convenient point from which to restart if you have problems. If you have problems, you could close the report without saving it. When you reopen the report, it will be in the state it was in when you last saved it.

To Add and Move Fields in a Report

As with the previous report, you can add a field to the report by dragging the field from the field list. You can drag an attached label separately from the control to which it is attached by dragging the Move handle in its upper-left corner. This technique does not work, however, if you want to drag the attached label to a different section from the control's section. If you want the label to be in a different section, you must select the label, cut the label, select the section to which you want to move the label, and then paste the label. You then can move the label to the desired location.

The following steps add the Business Analyst Number field to the Business Analyst Number Header section and then move the label to the Page Header section.

1

• Click the Add Existing Fields button (Report Design Tools Design tab | Tools group) to display a field list. (Figure 6–56).

Q&A

My field list displays Show only fields in the current record source, not Show all tables, as in the figure. What should I do?

Click the 'Show only fields in the current record source' link at the top of the field list to display only those fields in the Business Analysts and Clients query.

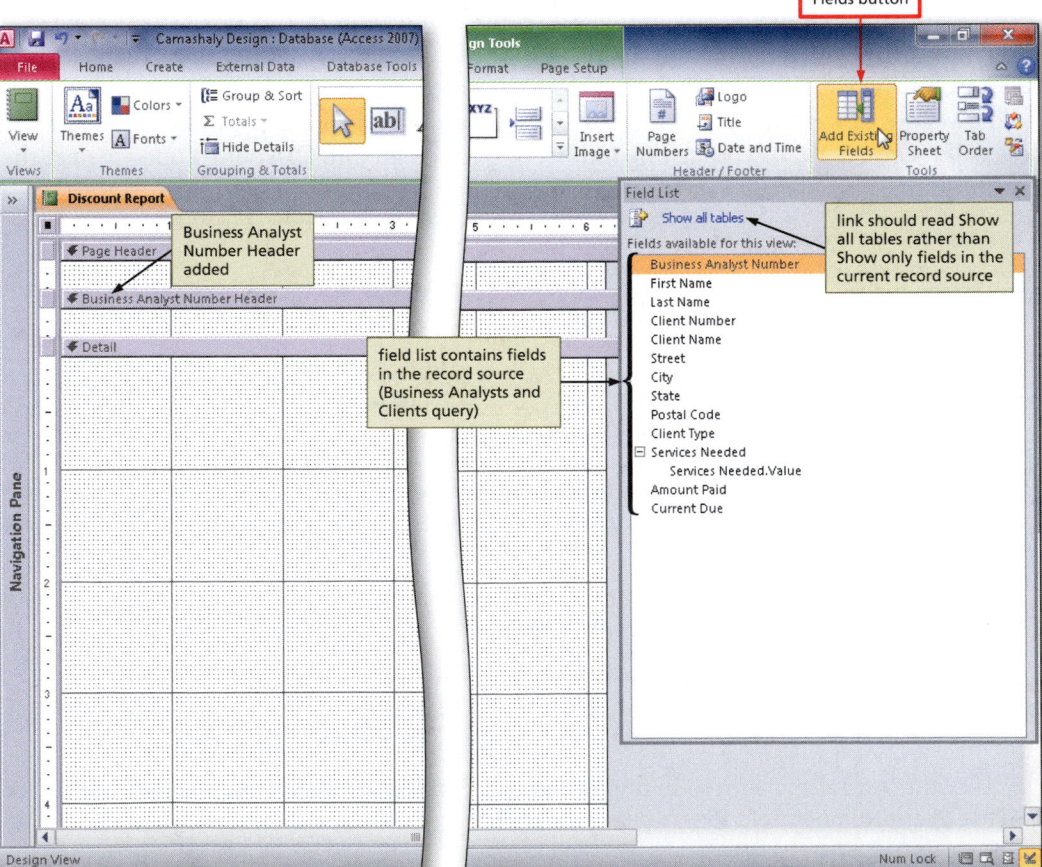

Figure 6–56

2
• Drag the Business
Analyst Number field
to the approximate
position shown in
Figure 6–57.

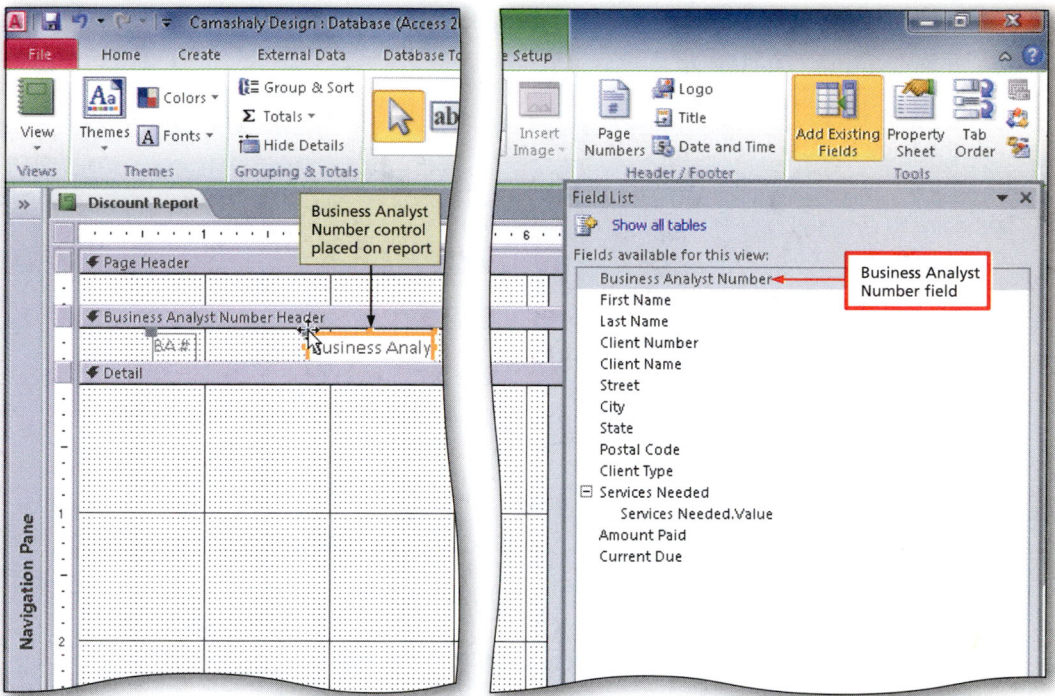

Figure 6–57

3
• Click the label for
the Business Analyst
Number control to
select it (Figure 6–58).

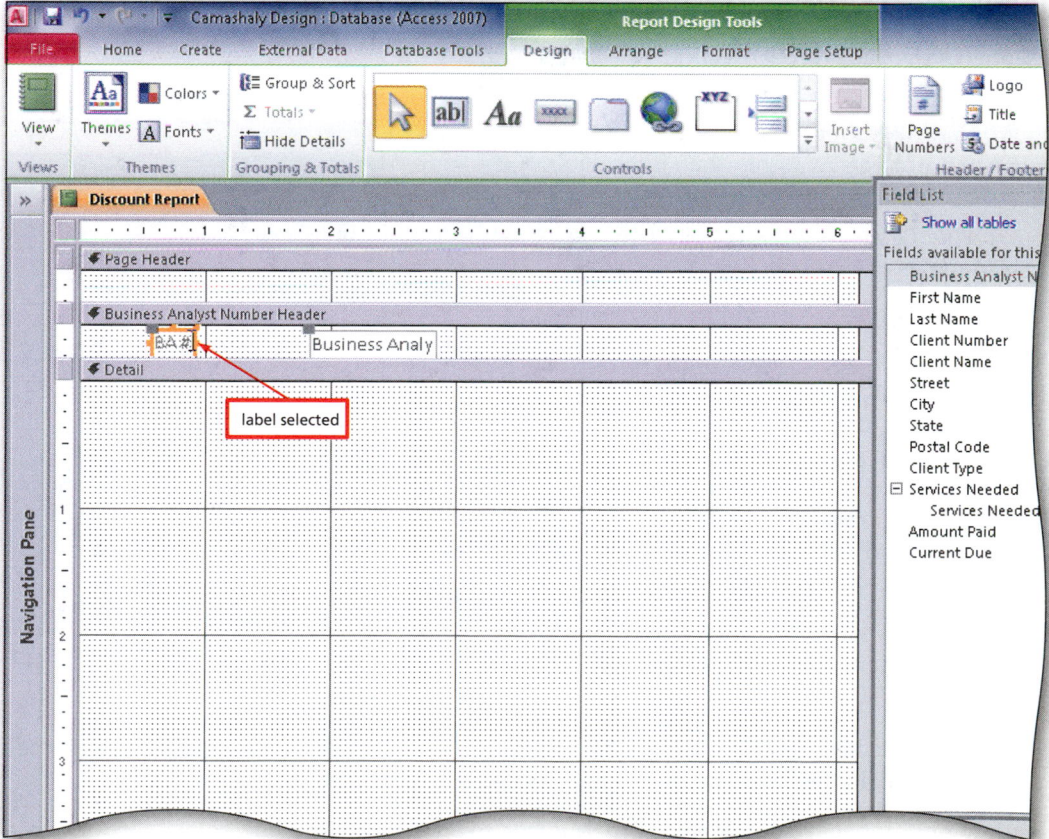

Figure 6–58

4

- Display the Home tab.

- Click the Cut button (Home tab | Clipboard group) to cut the label.

- Click the Page Header bar to select the page header (Figure 6–59).

Q&A

Do I have to click the bar, or could I click somewhere else within the section?

You also could click within the section. Clicking the bar is usually safer, however. If you click in a section intending to select the section, but click within one of the controls in the section, you will select the control rather than the section. Clicking the bar always selects the section.

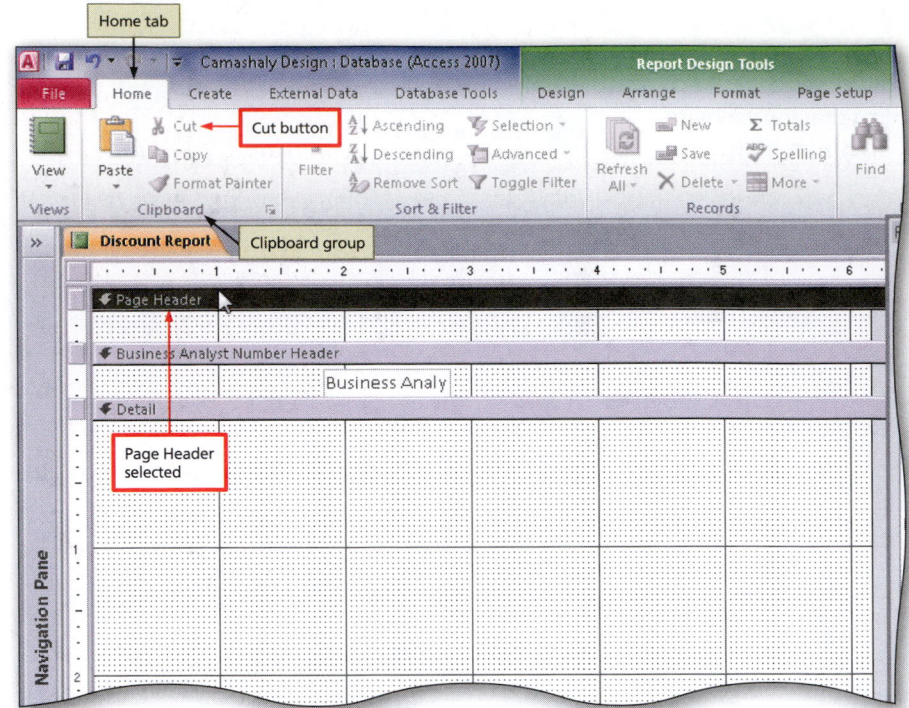

Figure 6–59

5

- Click the Paste button (Home tab | Clipboard group) to paste the label in the Page Header section (Figure 6–60).

Q&A

When would I want to click the Paste button arrow rather than just the button?

Clicking the arrow displays the Paste button menu, which includes the Paste command and two additional commands. Paste Special allows you to paste data into different formats. Paste Append, which is available if you have cut or copied a record, allows you to paste the record to a table with a similar structure. If you want the simple Paste command, you can just click the button.

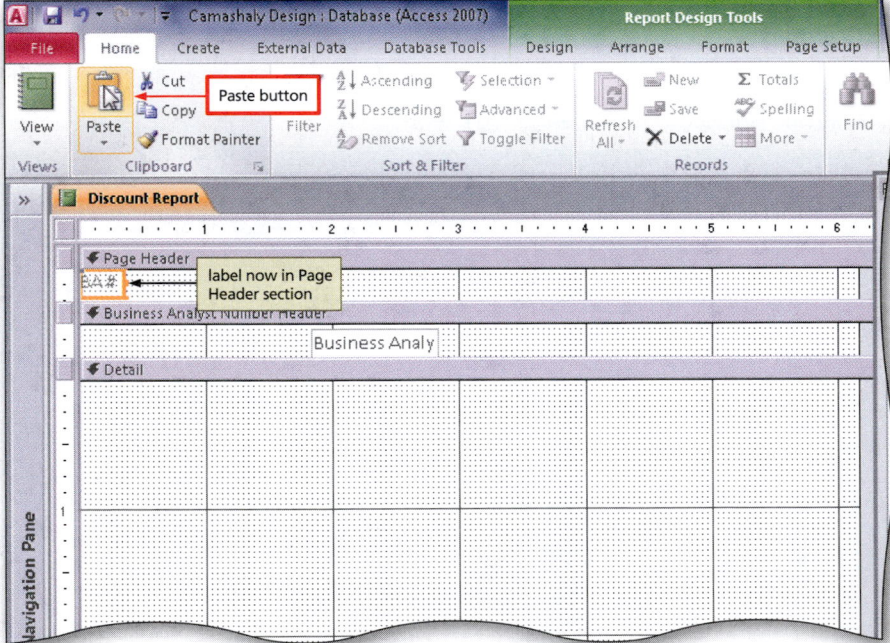

Figure 6–60

6

- Click in the label to produce an insertion point, use the BACKSPACE or DELETE key to erase the current entry in the label, and then type **Analyst Number** as the new entry.

- Click in the label in front of the word, Number, to produce an insertion point.

- Press SHIFT+ENTER to move the word, Number, to a second line.

To Add the Remaining Fields

The following steps add the remaining fields by dragging them into the Detail section. They next save the report, move the labels into the Page Header section, and move the controls containing the fields to the appropriate locations.

1

- Resize and move the Business Analyst Number control to the approximate size and position shown in Figure 6–61.

- Resize the Business Analyst Number label to the size shown in the figure.

- Drag the First Name, Last Name, Client Number, Client Name, Amount Paid, and Current Due fields into the Detail section, as shown in the figure.

Q&A

Why drag them to the positions shown in the figure? That is not where they appear on the report. Could I drag them all at once?

Dragging them gets them onto the report, where you can now move the controls and labels individually to the desired locations. You can drag multiple fields by selecting the first field, holding down the SHIFT key, and then selecting other adjacent fields. To select fields that are not adjacent to each other, use the CTRL key. How you choose to select fields and drag them onto the report is a matter of personal preference.

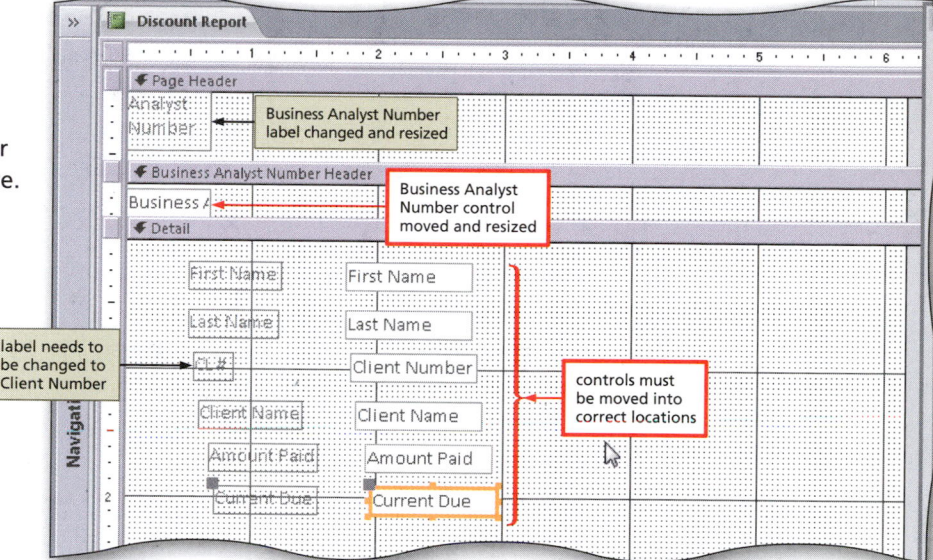

Figure 6– 61

2

- Close the field list.

- One at a time, cut each of the labels, paste the label into the Page Header section, and then resize, reformat, and move the labels to the approximate positions shown in Figure 6–62.

Q&A

When I paste the label, it always places it at the left edge, superimposing the Business Analyst Number control. Can I change where Access places it?

Unfortunately, when you paste to a different section, Access places the control at the left edge. You will need to drag each control to its proper location after pasting it into the Page Header section.

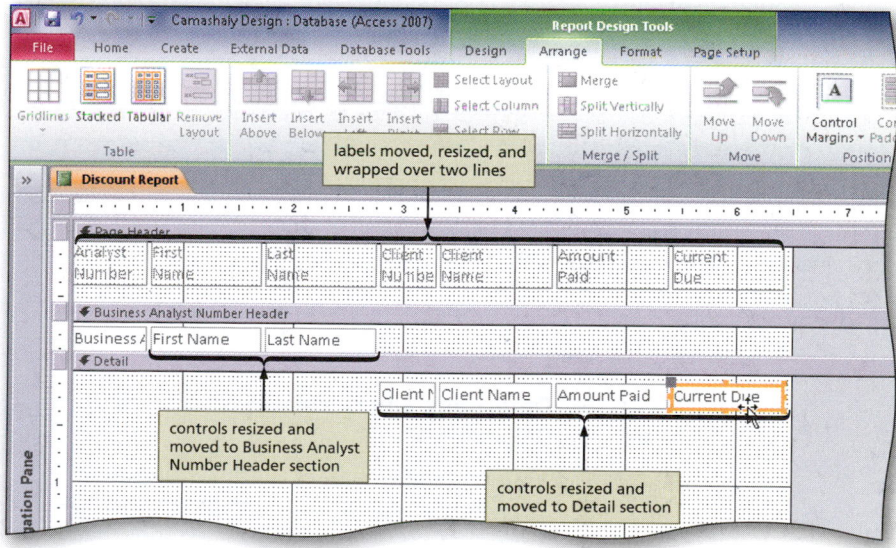

Figure 6– 62

- One at a time, resize and move the First Name and Last Name controls to the approximate positions in the Business Analyst Number Header section shown in the figure.

- One at a time, resize and move the Client Number, Client Name, Amount Paid, and Current Due controls to the approximate positions in the Detail section shown in the figure.

- Display the Arrange tab.

- Use the Align button (Report Design Tools Arrange tab | Sizing & Ordering group) as necessary to align all the controls as shown in Figure 6–62 on the previous page.

To Change the Can Grow Property

The following steps change the Can Grow property for the Client Name control so that names that are too long to fit in the available space will extend to additional lines.

1 Select the Client Name control.

2 Display the property sheet and scroll down until the Can Grow property appears.

3 Click the Can Grow property box and then click the Can Grow property box arrow to display the menu of available values for the Can Grow property.

4 Click Yes to change the value for the Can Grow property.

5 Close the property sheet.

To Resize the Detail Section

The following step resizes the Detail section of the Discount Report to remove most of the extra space below the controls in the section.

- Scroll down so that the lower boundary of the Detail section appears, and then drag the lower boundary of the section to a position just slightly below the controls in the section.

Q&A

I scrolled down to see the lower boundary of the Detail section, and the controls are no longer on the screen. What is the easiest way to drag the boundary when the position to which I want to drag it is not visible?

You do not need to see the location to drag to it. As you get close to the top of the visible portion of the screen, Access will automatically scroll. You might find it easier, however, to drag it near the top of the visible portion of the report, use the scroll bar to scroll up, and then drag some more. You might have to scroll a couple of times.

Plan Ahead

Determine any calculations required for the report.
Determine details concerning any calculations required for the report.

- **Determine whether to include calculations in the group and report footers.** The group footers or report footers might require calculated data such as subtotals or grand totals. Determine whether the report needs other statistics that must be calculated (for example, average).

- **Determine whether any additional calculations are required.** Are there any special calculations? If so, determine the fields that are involved and how they are to be combined. Determine whether any of the calculations depend on whether a criterion is true or false, in which case the calculations are conditional.

Totals and Subtotals

To add totals or other statistics to a footer, add a text box control. You can use any of the aggregate functions: COUNT, SUM, AVG (average), MAX (largest value), MIN (smallest value), STDEV (standard deviation), VAR (variance), FIRST, and LAST. To use a function, type an equal (=) sign, followed by the function name. You then include a set of parentheses containing the item for which you want to perform the calculation. If the item name contains spaces, such as Amount Paid, you must enclose it in square brackets. For example, to calculate the sum of the amount paid values, the expression would be =SUM([Amount Paid]).

Access will perform the calculation for the appropriate collection of records. If you enter this expression in the Business Analyst Number Footer section, Access only will calculate the total for clients with the given business analyst; that is, it will calculate the appropriate subtotal. If you enter the expression in the Report Footer section, Access will calculate the total for all clients.

To Add Totals and Subtotals

An analysis of requirements at Camashaly indicated that the Discount Report should contain subtotals and grand totals of amounts paid and current due. The following steps first display the Business Analyst Number Footer section and then add the total of amount paid and current due to both the Business Analyst Number Footer section and the Report Footer section. The steps label the totals in the Business Analyst Number Footer section as subtotals and the totals in the Report Footer section as grand totals. The steps change the format of the new controls to currency and the number of decimal places to 2.

1

- If necessary, display the Design tab.

- Click the Group & Sort button (Report Design Tools Design tab | Grouping & Totals group) to display the Group, Sort, and Total pane.

- Click Group on Business Analyst Number (Figure 6–63).

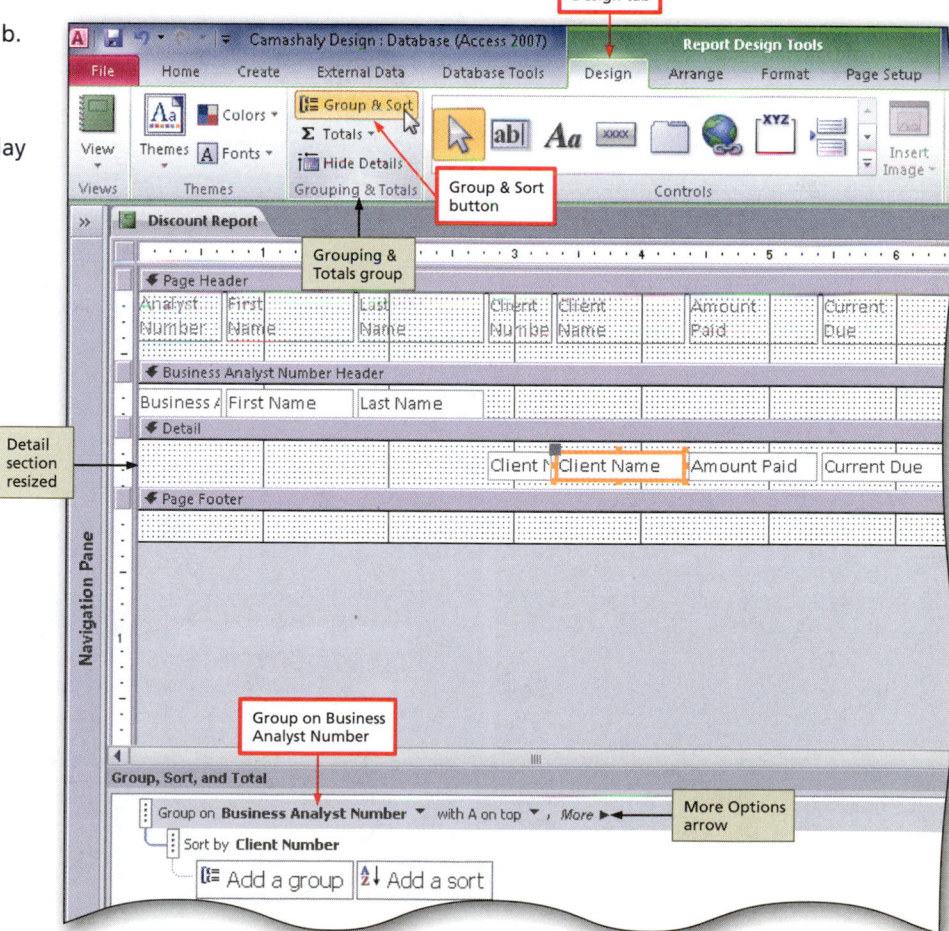

Figure 6–63

2

- Click the More arrow to display additional options for grouping.

- Click the 'without a footer section' arrow to display the available options (Figure 6–64).

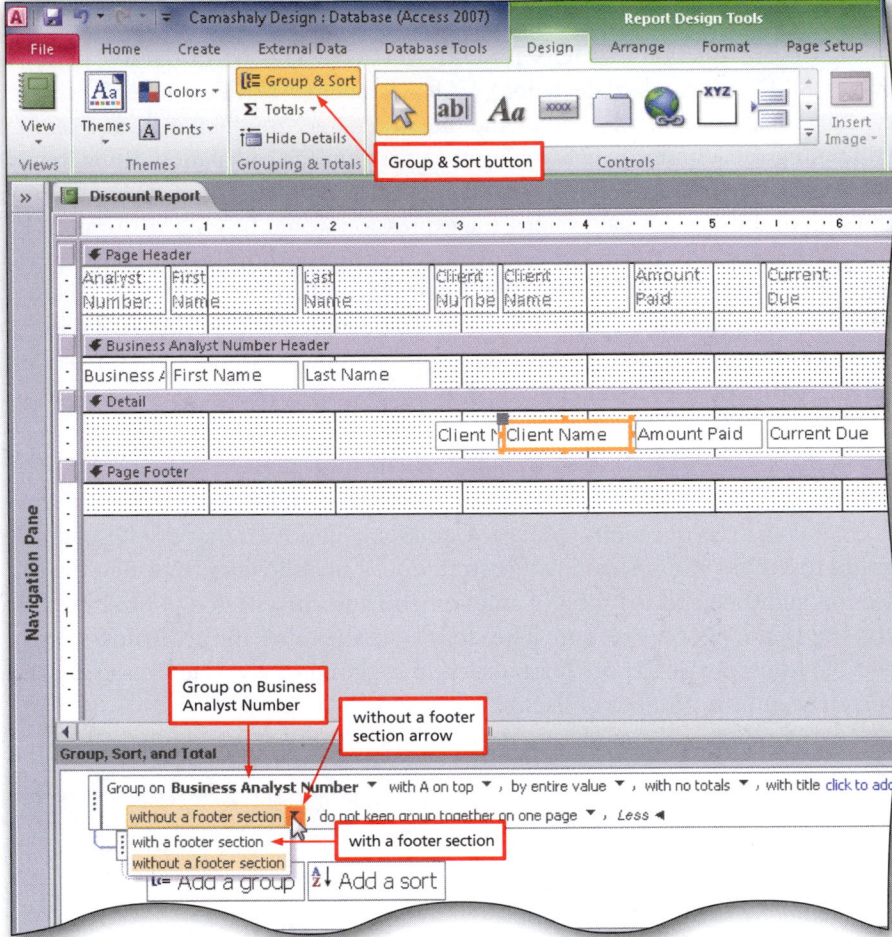

Figure 6–64

3

- Click 'with a footer section' to add a footer.

- Close the Group, Sort, and Total pane by clicking the Group & Sort button (Report Design Tools Design tab | Grouping & Totals group).

- Click the Text Box tool (Report Design Tools Design tab | Controls group), and then point to the position shown in Figure 6–65.

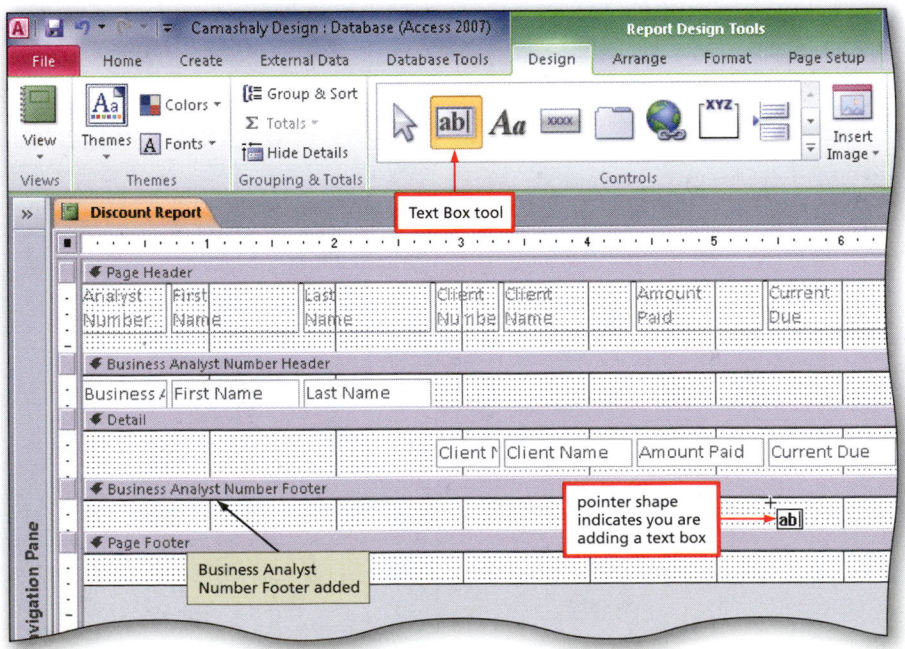

Figure 6–65

4

- Click the position shown in Figure 6–65 to place a text box (Figure 6–66).

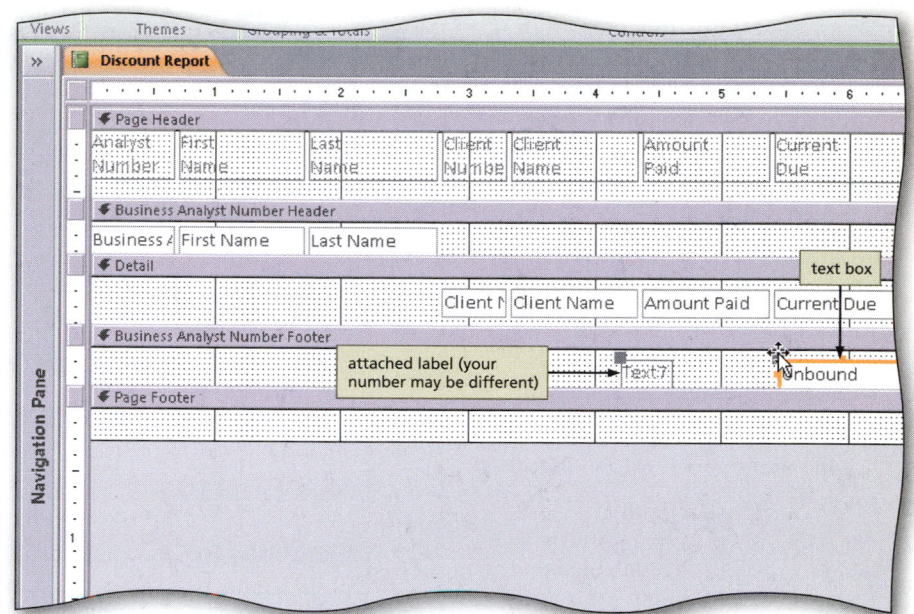

Figure 6–66

5

- Click the text box to produce an insertion point.

- Type `=Sum([Current Due])` in the control to enter the expression calculation, and then press the ENTER key.

- Click the text box label to select it.

- Click the label a second time to produce an insertion point.

- Use the DELETE or BACKSPACE key to delete the Text7 (your number might be different).

- Type `Subtotals` as the label.

- Click outside the label to deselect it.

- Resize and align the Current Due controls in the Detail section and the Business Analyst Number Footer section as shown in Figure 6–67.

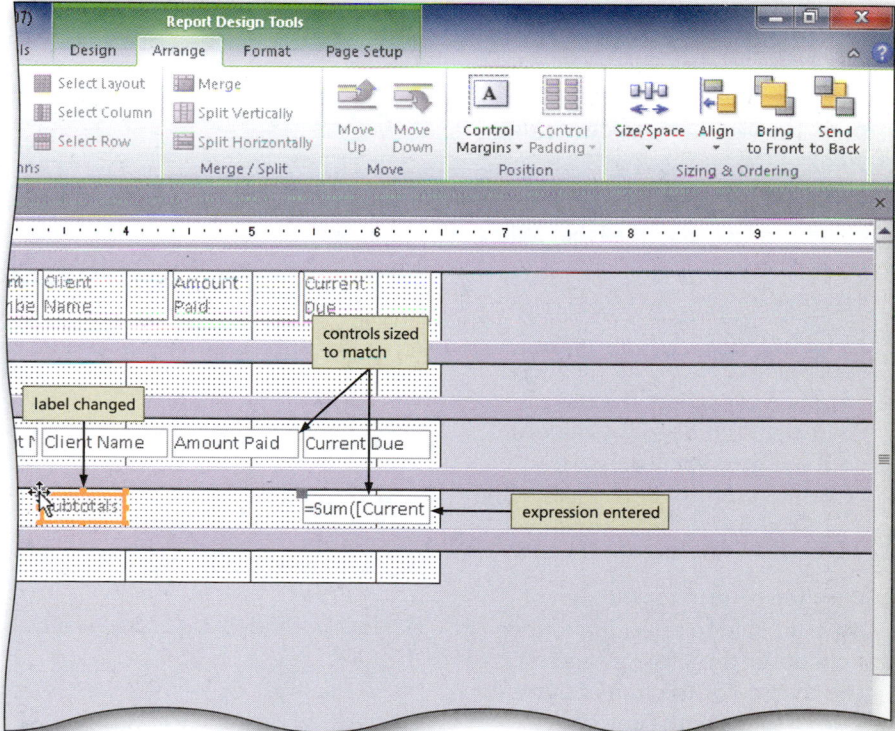

Figure 6–67

6

- Click the Text Box tool (Report Design Tools Design tab | Controls group), and then click in the Business Analyst Number Footer section just to the left of the control for the sum of Current Due to place another text box.

- Click the text box to produce an insertion point, type `=Sum([Amount Paid])` in the control, and then press the ENTER key to enter the expression (Figure 6–68).

Could I add the controls in the other order?

Yes. The only problem is that the label of the second control overlaps the first control. Adding the controls in the order shown in the steps reduces the overlap. It is not a major difference, however.

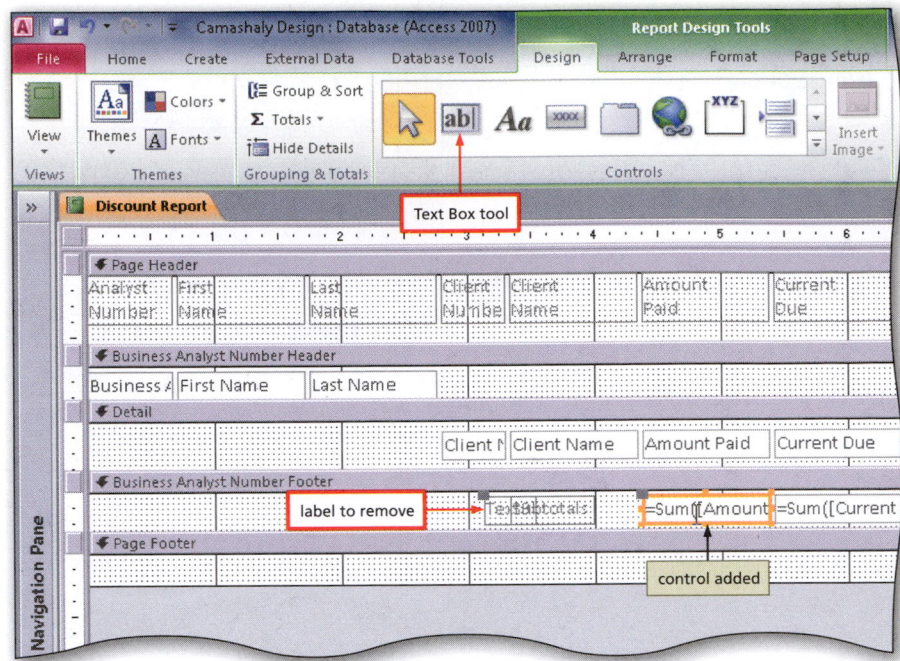

Figure 6–68

7

- Click the label to select it, and then press the DELETE key to delete the label.

I inadvertently deleted the other control rather than the label. What should I do?

The first thing to try is to click the Undo button on the Quick Access Toolbar to reverse your deletion. You then can delete the correct control. If that does not work for you, you can simply delete the remaining control or controls in the section and start these steps over.

- Click the control for the sum of Amount Paid to select it and then hold down the SHIFT key and click the control for the sum of Current Due to select both controls.

- Click the Property Sheet button (Report Design Tools Design tab | Tools group) to display the property sheet.

- Change the format to Currency and the number of decimal places to 2 (Figure 6–69).

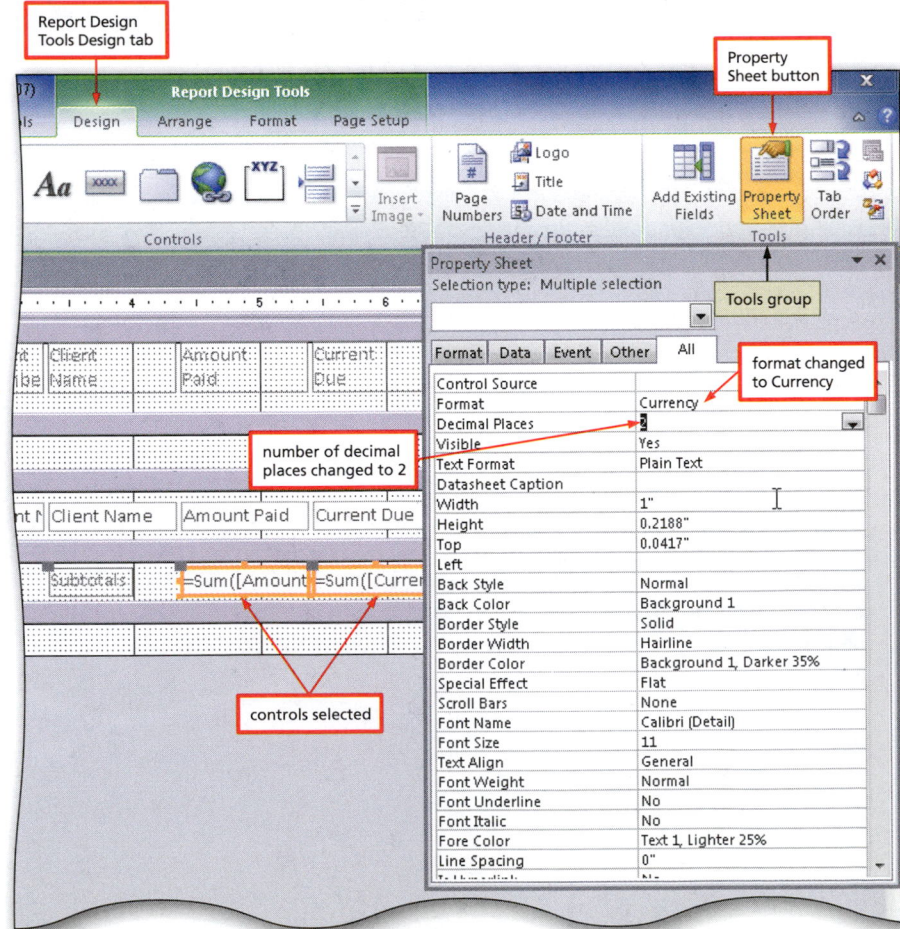

Figure 6–69

8
- Close the property sheet.
- Right-click any open area of the report to display a shortcut menu (Figure 6–70).

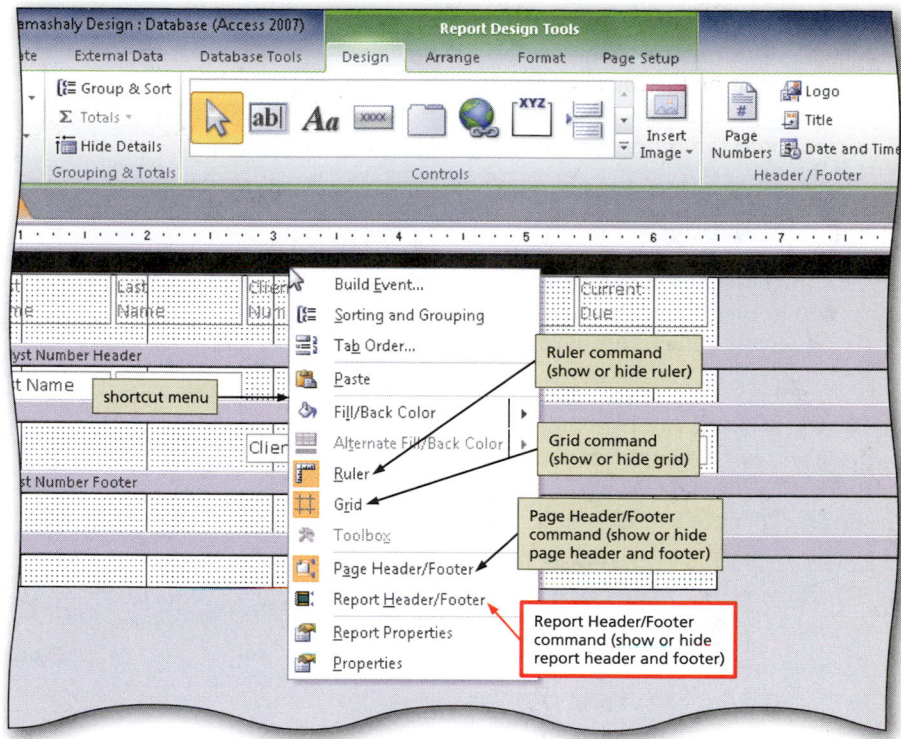

Figure 6–70

9
- Click Report Header/Footer to display the Report Header and Footer sections.
- Click the ruler in the Business Analyst Number Footer to the left of the controls in the section to select the controls.
- Display the Home tab.
- Click the Copy button (Home tab | Clipboard group) to copy the selected controls to the Clipboard (Figure 6–71).

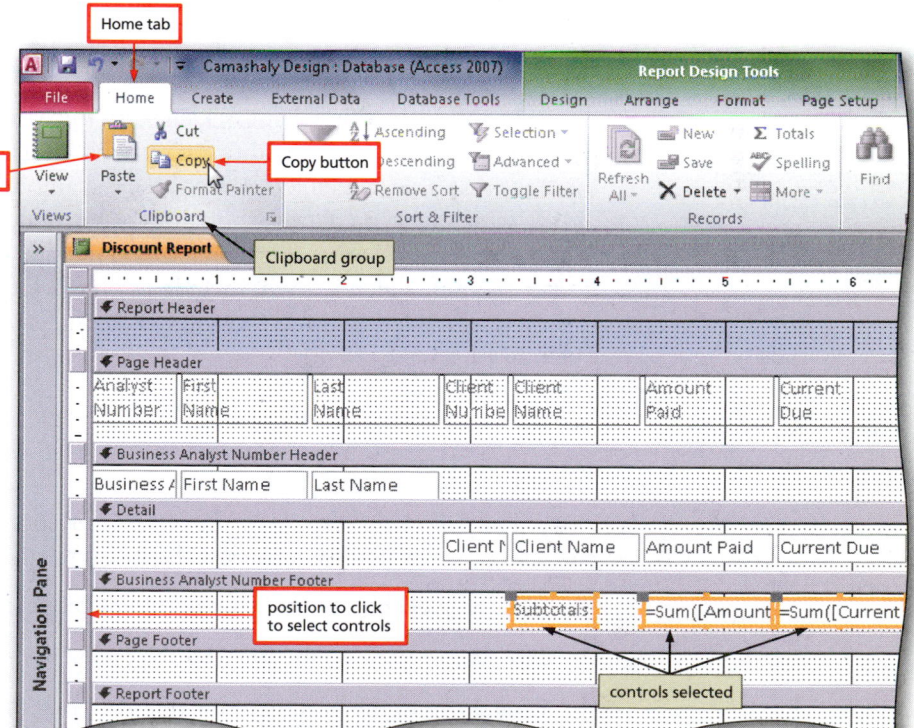

Figure 6–71

10

- Click the Report Footer bar to select the footer and then click the Paste button (Home tab | Clipboard group) to paste a copy of the controls into the report footer.

- Move the controls to the positions shown in Figure 6–72.

- Click the label in the Report Footer section to select the label and then click a second time to produce an insertion point.

- Use the BACKSPACE or DELETE key to erase the current contents, and then type **Grand totals** to change the label (Figure 6–72).

Q&A

Could I enter the controls just as I did earlier rather than copying and pasting?

Yes. Copying and pasting is a little simpler, but it is a matter of personal preference.

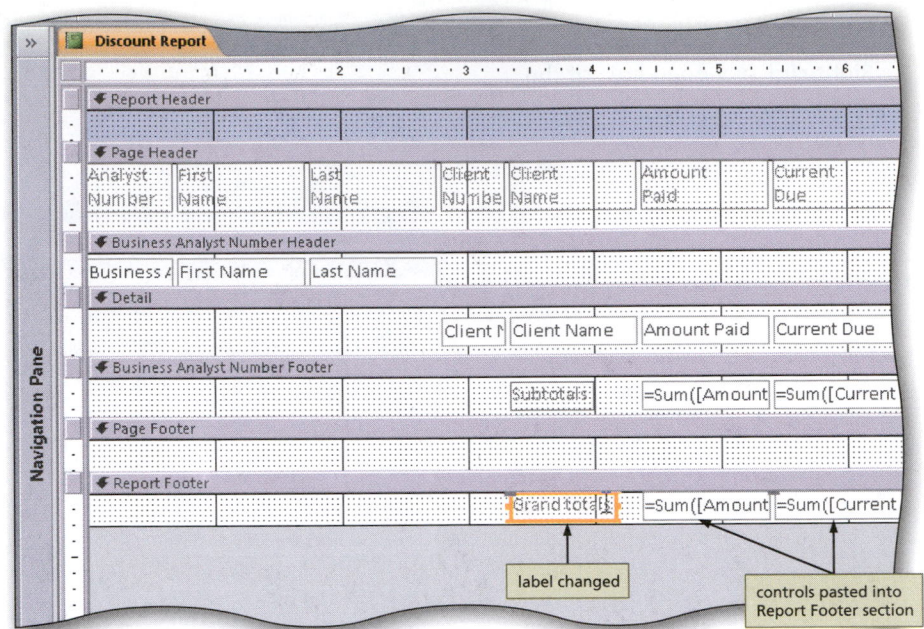

Figure 6–72

Grouping and Sorting Options

As you learned in Chapter 4, clicking the More button in the Group, Sort, and Total pane allows you to specify additional options for grouping and sorting. The additional options are: Value, which lets you choose the amount of the value on which to group; Totals, which lets you choose the values to be totaled; Title, which lets you customize the group title; Header section, which lets you include or omit a header section for the group; Footer section, which lets you include or omit a footer section for the group; and Keep together, which lets you specify whether Access is to attempt to keep portions of a group together on a page.

To View the Report

The following steps view the report in Report view, which is sometimes more convenient when you want to view the lower portion of the report.

1 Click the View button arrow on the Home tab to display the View button menu.

2 Click Report View on the View button menu to view the report in Report view.

3 Scroll down to the bottom of the report so that the grand totals appear on the screen (Figure 6–73).

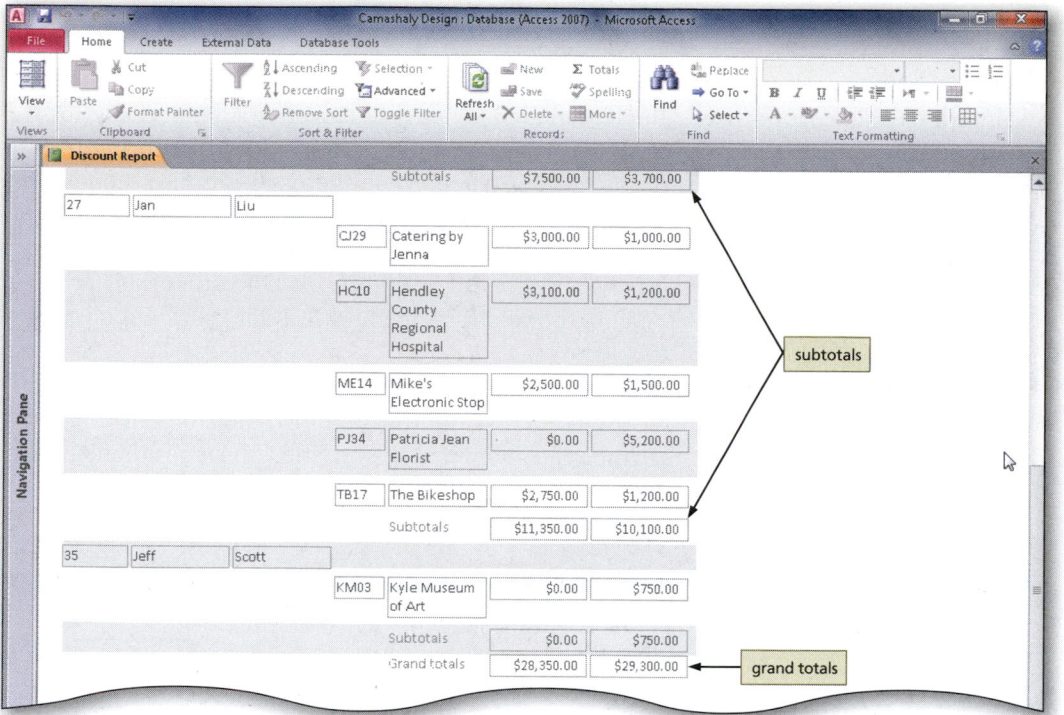

Figure 6–73

To Remove the Color from the Report Header

The following steps remove the color from the Report Header section by changing the background color for the header to white.

- Click the View button arrow and then click Design View to return to Design view.

- Right-click the report header to produce a shortcut menu.

- Point to the Fill/Back Color arrow on the shortcut menu to display a color palette (Figure 6–74).

2

- Click White in the first row, first column to change the background color to white.

Q&A Why do I not see standard colors and theme colors like I did when I changed the background color in the other report?

When you use the Background Color button on the Ribbon, you see both standard colors and theme colors. When you use the shortcut menu, you only see the standard colors.

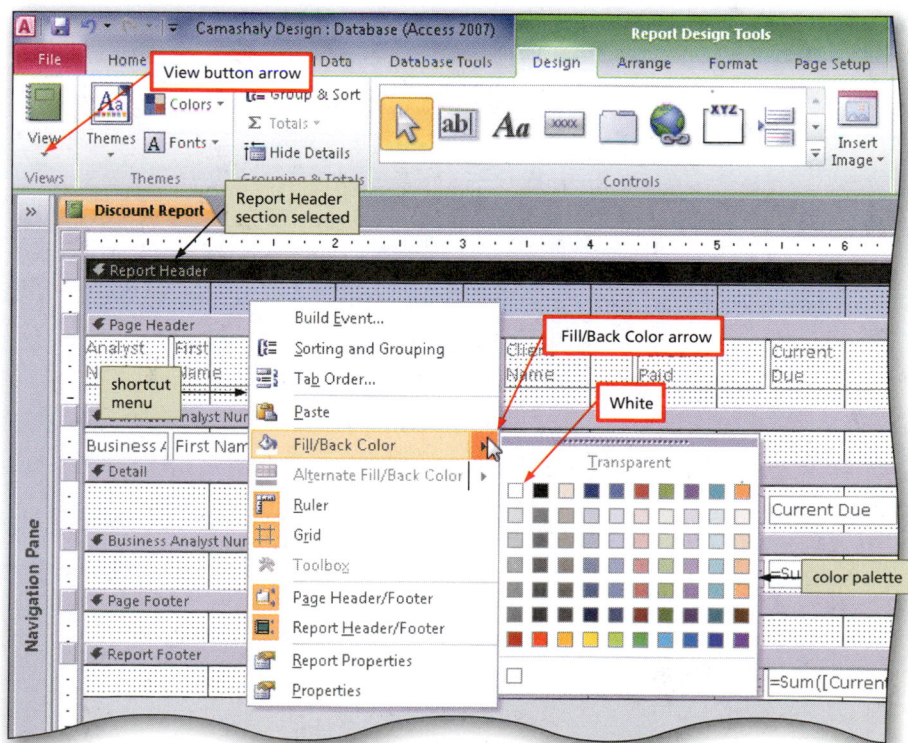

Figure 6–74

To Assign a Conditional Value

The Camashaly requirements for this report also involved a conditional value related to the amount of a client's discount. To assign a conditional value, you will use the IIf function. The IIf function consists of the letters IIf followed by three items, called **arguments**, in parentheses. The first argument is a criterion; the second and third arguments are expressions. If the criterion is true, the function assigns the value of the expression in the second argument. If the criterion is false, the function assigns the value of the expression in the third argument. The IIf function you will use is IIf([Amount Paid]>4000, .04*[Current Due], .02*[Current Due]). This function applies the following rules: If the amount paid is greater than $4,000, the value assigned is .04*[Current Due], that is, 4% of the current due amount. If the amount paid is not greater than $4,000, the value assigned is .02*[Current Due], that is, 2% of the current due amount.

The following steps add a text box and then use the Expression Builder to enter the appropriate IIf function in the text box. The steps then change the format of the text box. The steps modify and move the label for the text box. They also add a title, page number, and date, and then change the alignment of the title. The steps then change the size of the report.

1

- If necessary, display the Design tab.

- Click the Text Box tool (Report Design Tools Design tab | Controls group) and point to the approximate position shown in Figure 6–75.

Q&A How can I place the control accurately when there are no grid lines?

When you click the position for the control, Access automatically will expand the grid. You then can adjust the control using the grid.

Q&A Can I automatically cause controls to be aligned to the grid?

Yes. Click the Size/Space button (Report Design Tools Arrange tab | Sizing & Ordering group) and then click Snap to Grid on the Size/Space menu. From that point on, any controls you add will be automatically aligned to the grid.

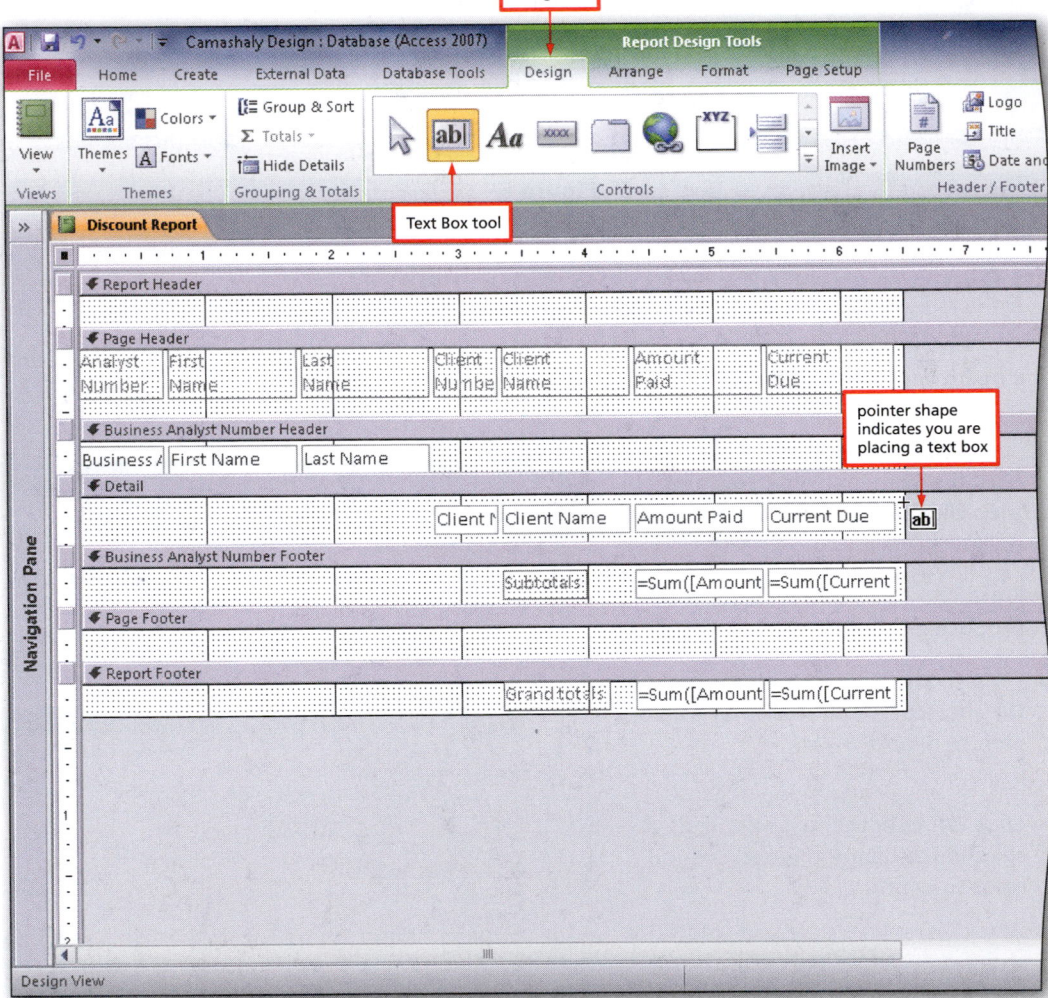

Figure 6–75

2

- Click the position shown in Figure 6–75 to place a text box.

- Click the attached label to select it and then press the DELETE key to delete the attached label.

- Click the text box to select it, and then click the Property Sheet button (Report Design Tools Design tab | Tools group) to display a property sheet.

- Click the Control Source property to select it (Figure 6–76).

Why did I choose Control Source, not Record Source?

You use Record Source to select the source of the records in a report, usually a table or a query. You use the Control Source property to specify the source of data for the control. This allows you to bind an expression or field to a control.

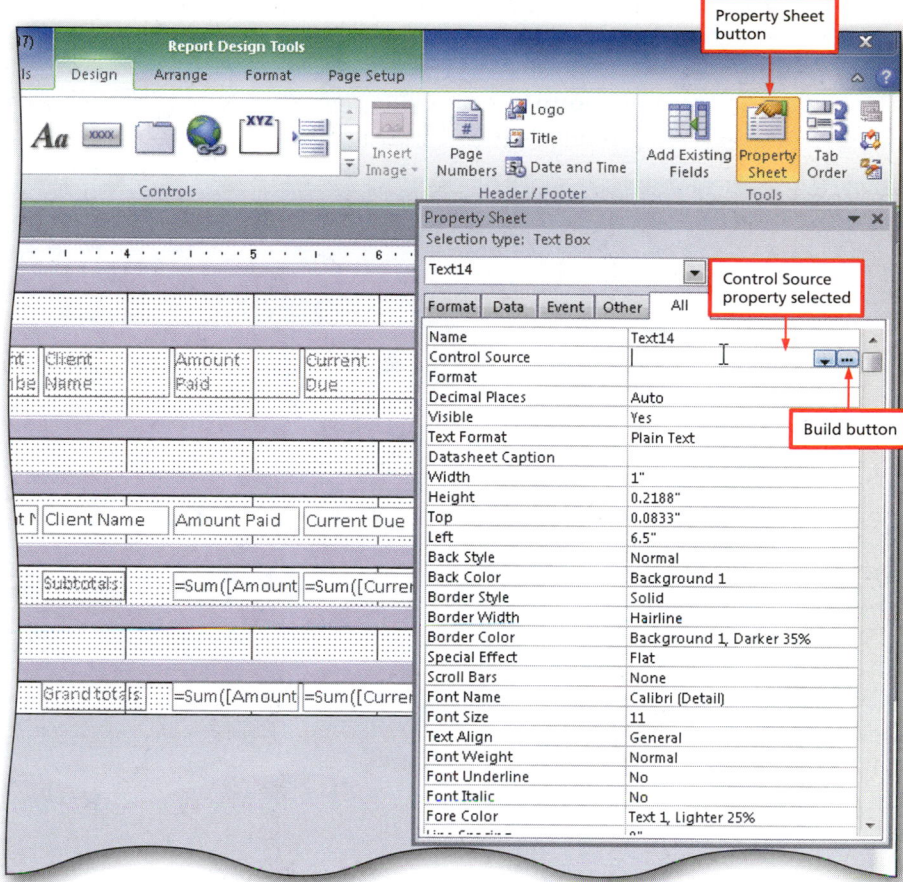

Figure 6–76

3

- Click the Build button to display the Expression Builder dialog box.

- Double-click Functions in the first column to display the function subfolders.

- Click Built-In Functions in the first column to display the various function categories in the second column.

- Scroll down in the second column so that Program Flow appears, and then click Program Flow to display the available program flow functions in the third column.

- Double-click IIf in the third column to select the IIf function (Figure 6–77).

Do I have to select Program Flow? Could I not just scroll down to IIf?

You do not have to select Program Flow. You could indeed scroll down to IIf. You will have to scroll through a large number of functions in order to get to IIf, however.

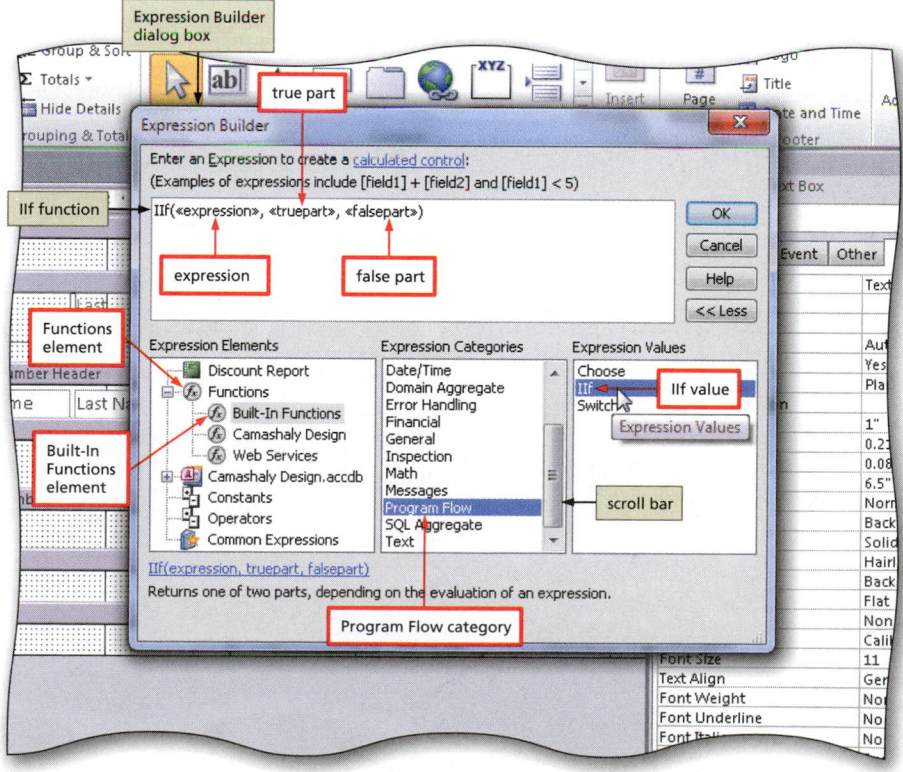

Figure 6–77

4

- Click the <expression> argument to select it and type **[Amount Paid]>4000** as the expression.

- Click the <truepart> argument to select it and type **.04*[Current Due]** as the true part.

- Click the <falsepart> argument to select it and type **.02*[Current Due]** as the false part (Figure 6–78).

Q&A

Are there other ways I could enter the expression?

Yes. You could just type the whole expression. On the other hand, you could select the function just as in these steps, and, when entering each argument, you could select the fields from the list of fields and click the desired operators.

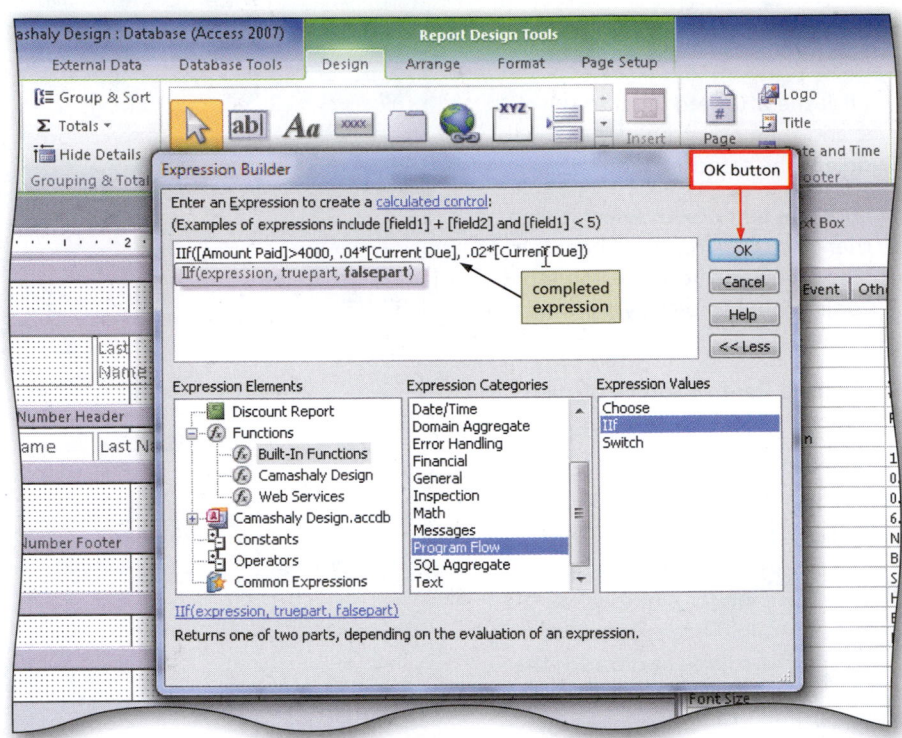

Figure 6–78

5

- Click the OK button (Expression Builder dialog box) to specify the expression as the control source for the text box.

Q&A

My property sheet is covering my OK button. What should I do?

Click in the Expression Builder dialog box to bring the entire dialog box in front of the property sheet.

- Change the Format to Currency.

- Change the number of decimal places to 2.

- Close the property sheet by clicking the Property Sheet button.

- Click the Label tool on the Design tab and point to the approximate position shown in Figure 6–79.

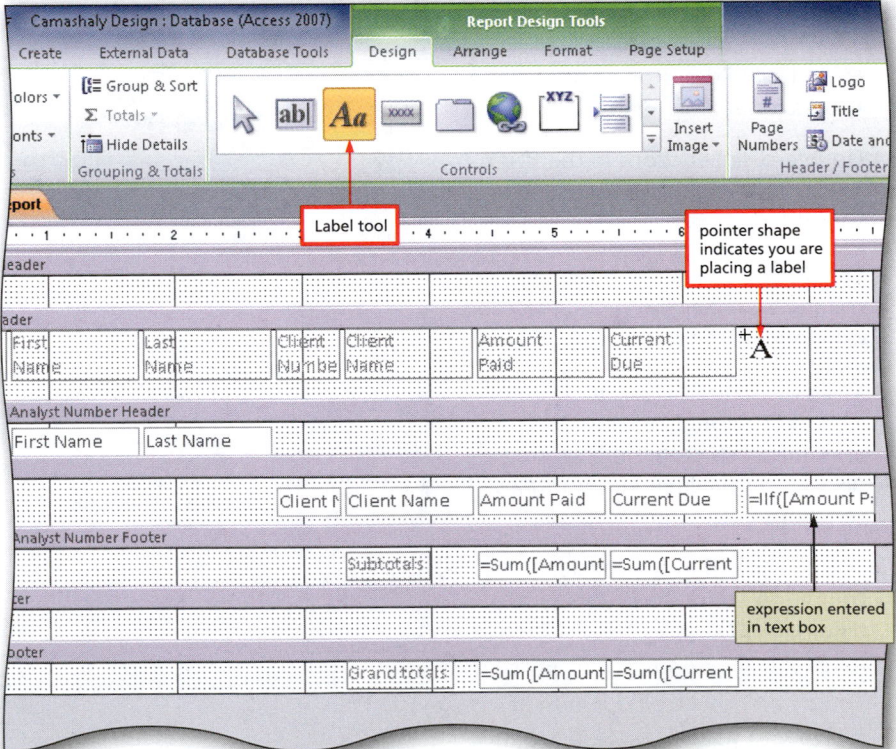

Figure 6–79

6

• Press and hold the left mouse button, drag the pointer to the approximate position as the lower-right corner of the label shown in Figure 6–80, and then release the left mouse button to place the label.

Q&A I made the label the wrong size. What should I do?

With the label selected, drag the sizing handles to resize the label as needed. Drag the control in a position away from the sizing handles if you need to move the label.

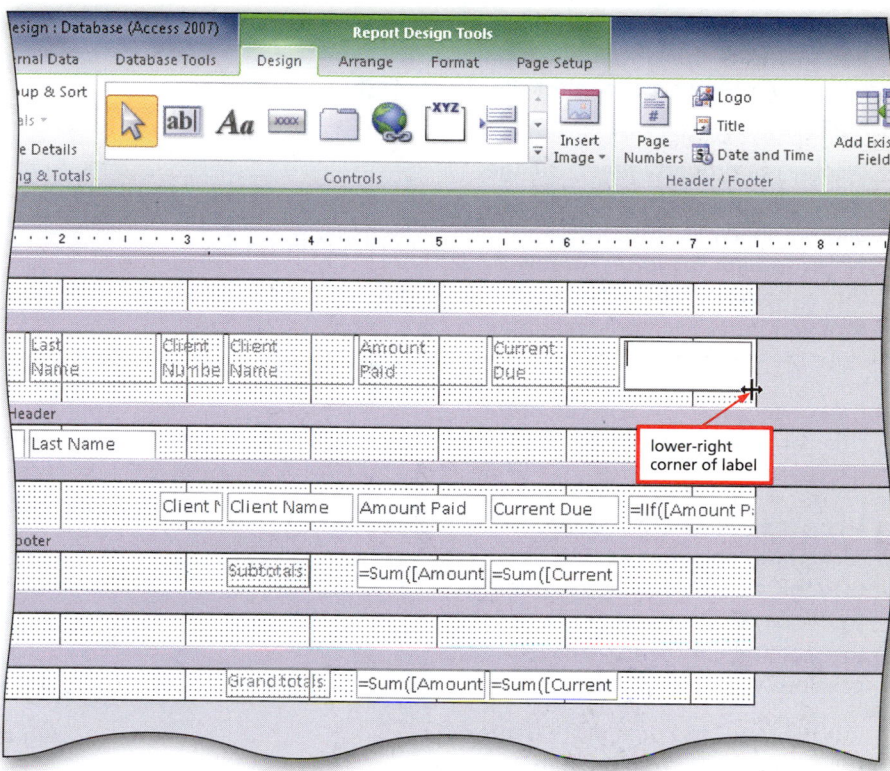

Figure 6–80

7

• Type **Discount** to enter the name of the label.

• Click outside the label to deselect the label and then select the Amount Paid, Current Due, and Discount labels.

• With the labels selected, display the Format tab and then click the Align Text Right button (Report Design Tools Format tab | Font group) to right-align the text within the labels.

• Move or resize the Discount label as necessary so that it aligns with the new text box and with the other controls in the Page Header section.

• Expand the Report Header section to the approximate size shown in Figure 6–81, place a label in the approximate position shown in the figure, and then type **Discount Report** in the label.

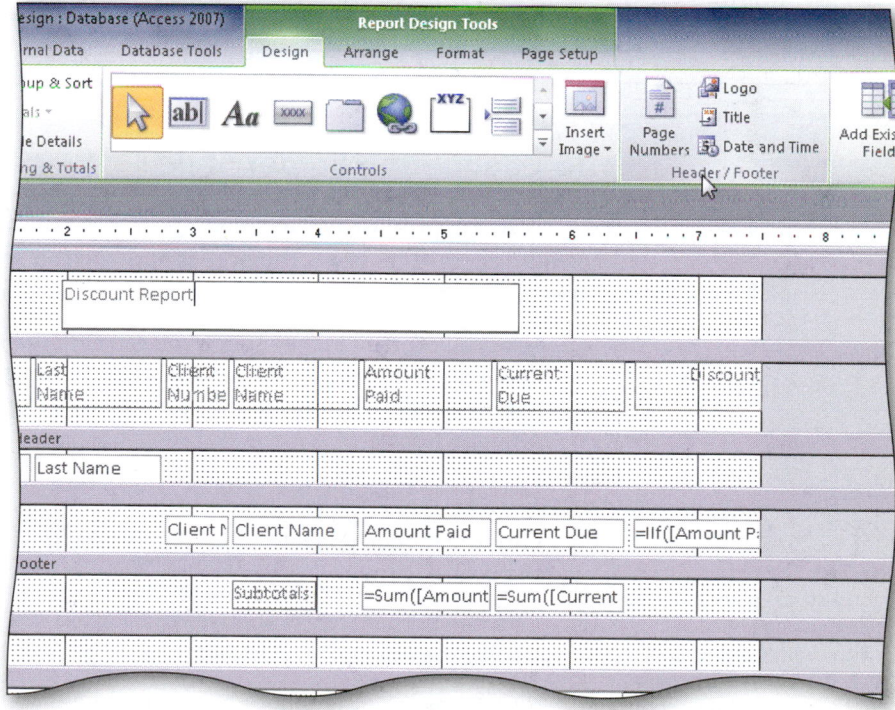

Figure 6–81

8

- Click outside the label to deselect it and then click the label in the report header a second time to select the entire label.

- Display the property sheet, change the font size to 20 and the text align property to Distribute, which spreads the letters evenly throughout the label. Change the font weight to Semi-bold, and then close the property sheet.

- If necessary, increase the size of the title control so that the entire title is displayed.

- Using the Design tab and the techniques on pages AC 378 through AC 379, add a page number to the page footer, and add a date (use the same format you have used previously in this chapter).

- Cut the date, and then paste it into the page footer. Drag the date so that the date is positioned in the approximate position shown in Figure 6–82.

- Drag the right boundary of the report to the position shown in the figure to reduce the width of the report.

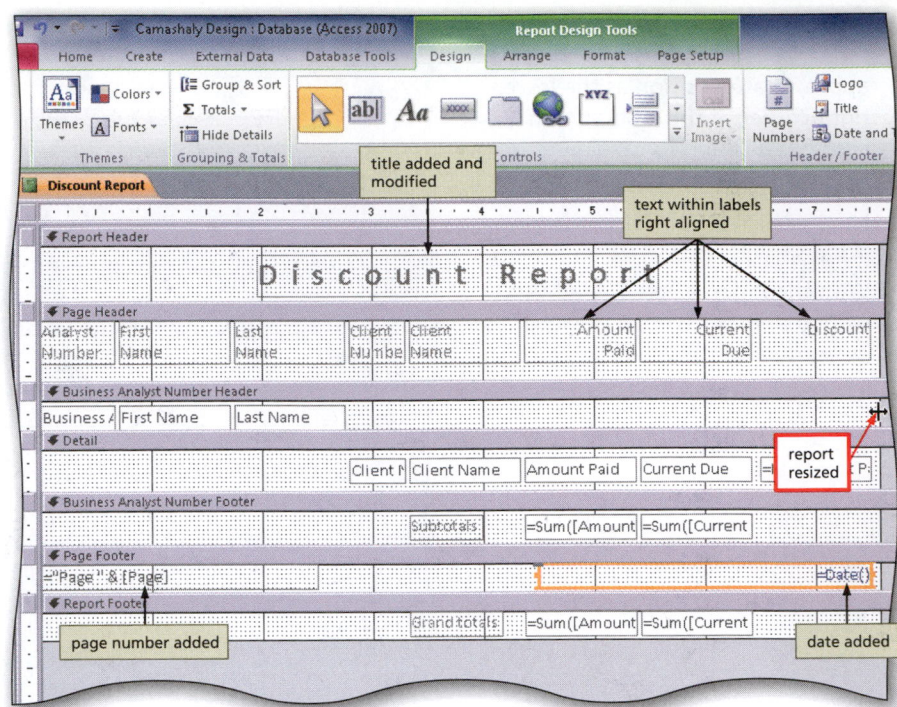

Figure 6–82

To Change the Border Style

If you print or preview the report, you will notice that all the controls have boxes around them. The box is the border and you can select the border style. The following steps remove the boxes around the controls by changing the border style to transparent.

1 Select all controls in the report. You can click the first one, and then hold the SHIFT key down while clicking all the others. Alternatively, you can click in the ruler to the left of the Report Header section and then hold the SHIFT key down while clicking to the left of all the other sections.

2 Display the Design tab.

3 Click the Property Sheet button (Report Design Tools Design tab | Tools group) to display the property sheet.

4 Click the Border Style property box and then click the Border Style property box arrow to display the menu of available border styles.

5 Click Transparent to change the border style.

To Remove the Alternate Color

Just as with the Business Analyst Master List, the Discount Report also has alternate colors that need to be removed. The following steps remove the alternate colors from the various sections in the report, starting with the Detail section.

1 Right-click the Detail section to produce a shortcut menu.

2 Point to the Alternate Fill/Back Color arrow to produce a color palette.

3 Click None on the color palette to specify that there is to be no alternate color for the selected section.

4 Using the same techniques, remove the alternate color from all other sections. (For some sections, the command may be dimmed.)

Obtaining Help on Functions

There are many functions available in Access for a variety of purposes. To see the list of functions, use the Expression Builder. Double-click Functions in the first column and then click Built-In Functions. You then can scroll through the entire list of functions in the third column. Alternatively, you can click a function category in the second column, in which case the third column only will contain the functions in that category. To obtain detailed help on a function, highlight the function in the third column and click the Help button. The Help presented will show the syntax of the function, that is, the specific rule for how you must type the function and any arguments. It will give you general comments on the function as well as examples illustrating the use of the function.

BTW

Arguments
An argument is a piece of data on which a function operates. For example, in the expression =SUM ([Amount Paid]), Amount Paid is the argument because the SUM function will calculate the total of Amount Paid.

Page Setup Tab

You can use the buttons on the Page Setup tab to change margins, orientation, and other page setup characteristics of the report (Figure 6–83a). If you click the Margins button, you can choose from among some predefined margins or set your own custom margins (Figure 6–83b). If you click the Columns button, you will see the Page Setup dialog box with the Columns tab selected (Figure 6–83c). You can use this tab to specify multiple columns in a report as well as the column spacing. If you click the Page Setup button, you will see the Page Setup dialog box with the Print Options tab selected (Figure 6–83d). You can use this tab to specify custom margins. You can specify orientation by clicking the Page tab (Figure 6–83e). You also can select paper size, paper source, and printer using this tab.

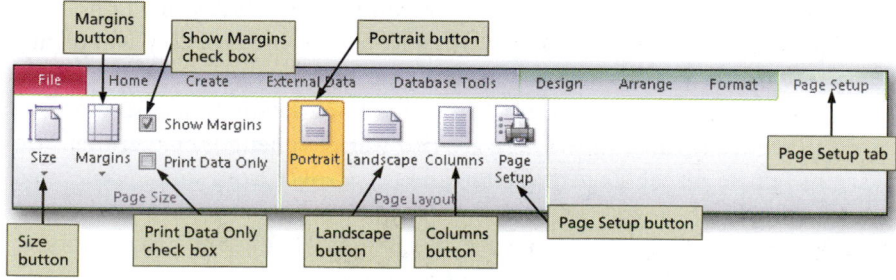

(a) Page Setup tab
Figure 6–83

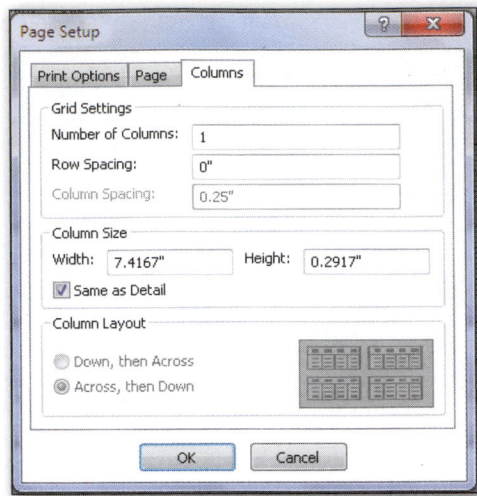

(b) Margins button menu

(c) Columns tab

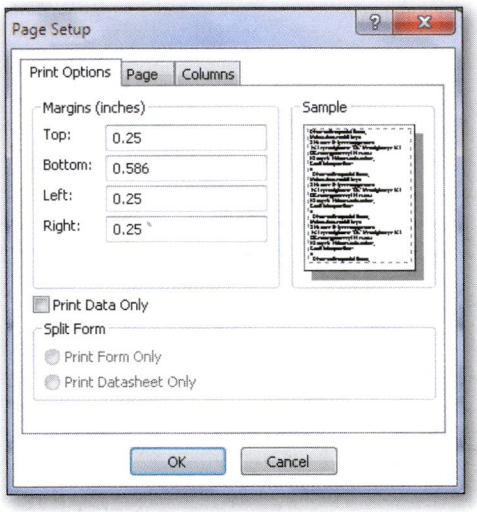

(d) Print Options tab

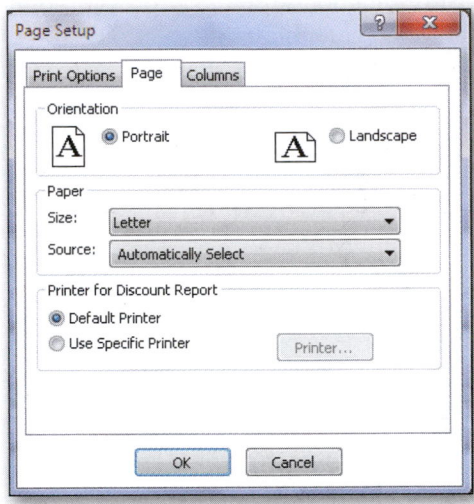

(e) Page tab

Figure 6−83

Default Names for Controls

Because each control has properties associated with it, Access assigns a default name to each new control. The default name includes a control identifier and a number. For example, if you create a text box on a report, the default name may be Text32. You should change the default name to something meaningful to make it easier to remember the purpose of the control.

To Change the Report Margins

If you look at the horizontal ruler in Figure 6–82 on page AC 398, you will notice that the report width is slightly over seven inches. Because the report probably will print on standard 8½" × 11" paper, a seven-inch report with one-inch margins on the left and right, which would result in a nine-inch width, will not fit. To allow the report to fit on the page, you need to reduce the margins. There are two ways to change the margins. You can click the Margins button on the Page Setup tab and then select from some predefined options. If you want more control, you can click the Page Setup button to display the Page Setup dialog box. You then can specify your own margins, change the orientation, and also specify multiple columns if you want a multicolumn report.

The following steps use the Margins button to select Narrow margins.

1 Display the Page Setup tab.

2 Click the Margins button (Report Design Tools Page Setup tab | Page Size group).

3 If necessary, click Narrow to specify the Narrow margin option.

Fine-Tuning a Report

When you have finished a report, you should review several of its pages in Print Preview to make sure the layout is precisely what you want. You may find that you need to increase the size of a control, which you can do by selecting the control and dragging the appropriate sizing handle. You may realize you need an additional control, which you could add by using the appropriate tool in the Controls group or by dragging a field from the field list.

In both cases, you have a potential problem. You may not have the room to increase the size or to add an additional control. If the control is part of a control layout that you had when you modified earlier reports in Layout view, you can resize controls or add new fields, and the remaining fields automatically adjust for the change. In Design view with individual controls, you must make any necessary adjustments manually.

TO MAKE ROOM FOR RESIZING OR ADDITIONAL CONTROLS

To make room for resizing a control or for adding additional controls, you would use the following steps.

1. Select all controls to the right of the control you want to resize or the position where you want to add another control.

2. Drag any of the selected controls to the right to make room for the change.

To Save and Close a Report

Now that you have completed your work on your report, you should save the report and close it. The following steps first save your work on the report and then close the report.

1 Click the Save button on the Quick Access Toolbar to save your work.

2 Close the Discount Report.

To Print a Report

The following steps print the report.

1 With the Discount Report selected in the Navigation Pane, click File on the Ribbon to open the Backstage view.

2 Click the Print tab in the Backstage view to display the Print gallery.

3 Click the Quick Print button to print the report and compare your results to Figure 6–1b on page AC 340.

BTW

Certification
The Microsoft Office Specialist (MOS) program provides an opportunity for you to obtain a valuable industry credential — proof that you have the Access 2010 skills required by employers. For more information, visit the Access 2010 Certification Web page (scsite.com/ac2010/cert).

BTW

Quick Reference
For a table that lists how to complete the tasks covered in this book using the mouse, Ribbon, shortcut menu, and keyboard, see the Quick Reference Summary at the back of this book, or visit the Access 2010 Quick Reference Web page (scsite.com/ac2010/qr).

To Quit Access

The following steps quit Access.

1 Click the Close button on the right side of the title bar to quit Access.

2 If a Microsoft Access dialog box appears, click the Save button to save any changes made to the object since the last save.

Chapter Summary

In this chapter you have learned to create and relate additional tables; create queries for a report; create reports in Design view; add fields and text boxes to a report; format controls; group and ungroup controls; modify multiple controls; add and modify a subreport; modify section properties; add a title, page number, and date; add totals and subtotals; use a function in a text box; and publish a report. The items listed below include all the new Access skills you have learned in this chapter.

1. Create the New Tables (AC 343)
2. Relate Several Tables (AC 346)
3. Create an Additional Query for the Report (AC 348)
4. Create an Initial Report in Design View (AC 351)
5. Add Fields to the Report in Design View (AC 354)
6. Change Labels (AC 356)
7. Add Text Boxes (AC 358)
8. View the Report in Print Preview (AC 361)
9. Format a Control (AC 361)
10. Group Controls (AC 362)
11. Ungroup Controls (AC 363)
12. Modify Grouped Controls (AC 364)
13. Modify Multiple Controls That Are Not Grouped (AC 365)
14. Add a Subreport (AC 368)
15. Open the Subreport in Design View (AC 371)
16. Modify the Controls in the Subreport (AC 372)
17. Change the Can Grow Property (AC 373)
18. Change the Appearance of the Controls in the Subreport (AC 374)
19. Resize the Subreport and the Report in Design View (AC 376)
20. Modify Section Properties (AC 377)
21. Add a Title, Page Number, and Date (AC 378)
22. Remove the Alternate Color (AC 380)
23. Publish a Report (AC 381)
24. Add and Move Fields in a Report (AC 382)
25. Add the Remaining Fields (AC 385)
26. Resize the Detail Section (AC 386)
27. Add Totals and Subtotals (AC 387)
28. Remove the Color from the Report Header (AC 393)
29. Assign a Conditional Value (AC 394)
30. Make Room for Resizing or Additional Controls (AC 401)

If you have a SAM 2010 user profile, your instructor may have assigned an autogradable version of this assignment. If so, log into the SAM 2010 Web site at www.cengage.com/sam2010 to download the instruction and start files.

Learn It Online

Test your knowledge of chapter content and key terms.

Instructions: To complete the Learn It Online exercises, start your browser, click the Address bar, and then enter the Web address **scsite.com/ac2010/learn**. When the Access 2010 Learn It Online page is displayed, click the link for the exercise you want to complete and then read the instructions.

Chapter Reinforcement TF, MC, and SA
A series of true/false, multiple choice, and short answer questions that test your knowledge of the chapter content.

Flash Cards
An interactive learning environment where you identify chapter key terms associated with displayed definitions.

Practice Test
A series of multiple choice questions that test your knowledge of chapter content and key terms.

Who Wants To Be a Computer Genius?
An interactive game that challenges your knowledge of chapter content in the style of a television quiz show.

Wheel of Terms
An interactive game that challenges your knowledge of chapter key terms in the style of the television show *Wheel of Fortune*.

Crossword Puzzle Challenge
A crossword puzzle that challenges your knowledge of key terms presented in the chapter.

Apply Your Knowledge

Reinforce the skills and apply the concepts you learned in this chapter.

Adding a Table and Creating a Report with a Subreport
Instructions: Start Access. If you are using the Microsoft Access 2010 Complete or the Microsoft Access 2010 Comprehensive text, open the Babbage CPA Firm database that you used in Chapter 5. Otherwise, see your instructor for information on accessing the files required in this book.

Perform the following tasks:
1. Create a table in which to store data about bookkeeping services performed for clients. Use Accounts as the name of the table. The Accounts table has the structure shown in Table 6–4.

Table 6–4 Structure of Accounts Table

Field Name	Data Type	Field Size	Description
Client Number	Text	3	Part of Primary Key
Service Date	Date/Time (Change Format property to Short Date)		Part of Primary Key
Hours Worked	Number (Change Format property to Fixed and Decimal Places to 2)	Single	

2. Import the Accounts.xlsx workbook to the Accounts table.
3. Create a one-to-many relationship between the Client table and the Accounts table.
4. Create a query that joins the Bookkeeper and Client tables. Include the Bookkeeper Number, First Name, and Last Name fields from the Bookkeeper table. Include all fields except the bookkeeper number from the Client table. Save the query as Bookkeepers and Clients.

Continued >

Apply Your Knowledge *continued*

5. Create the report shown in Figure 6–84. The report uses the query that you created in Step 4 and the Accounts table. Use the name Bookkeeper Master List for the report. The report is in the same style as the Business Analyst Master List shown in Figure 6–1a on page AC 339.

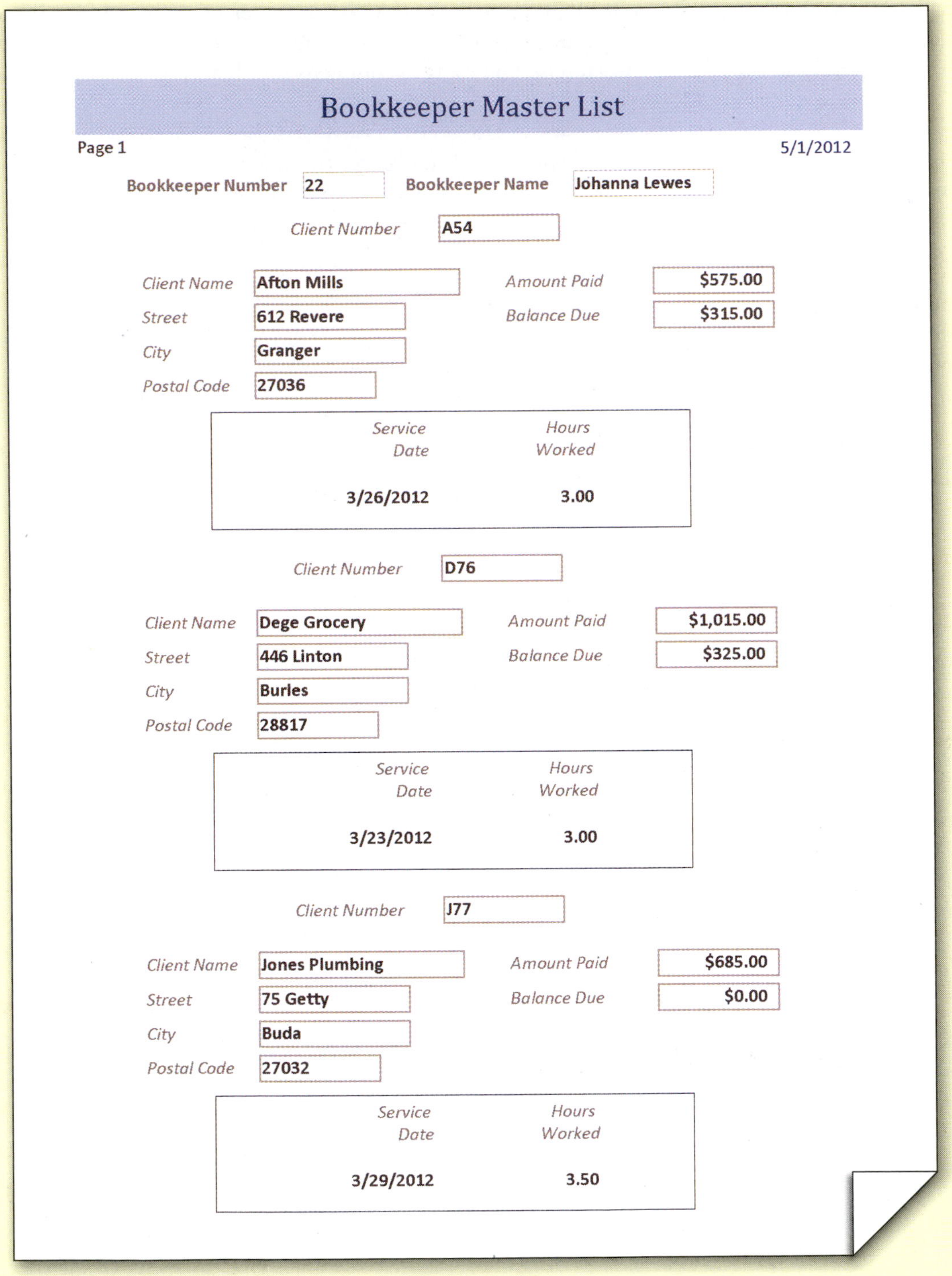

Bookkeeper Master List

Page 1   5/1/2012

Bookkeeper Number 22   **Bookkeeper Name** Johanna Lewes

Client Number   A54

Client Name	Afton Mills	*Amount Paid*	$575.00
Street	612 Revere	*Balance Due*	$315.00
City	Granger		
Postal Code	27036		

Service Date	*Hours Worked*
3/26/2012	3.00

Client Number   D76

Client Name	Dege Grocery	*Amount Paid*	$1,015.00
Street	446 Linton	*Balance Due*	$325.00
City	Burles		
Postal Code	28817		

Service Date	*Hours Worked*
3/23/2012	3.00

Client Number   J77

Client Name	Jones Plumbing	*Amount Paid*	$685.00
Street	75 Getty	*Balance Due*	$0.00
City	Buda		
Postal Code	27032		

Service Date	*Hours Worked*
3/29/2012	3.50

Figure 6–84

6. Submit the revised database in the format specified by your instructor.

Extend Your Knowledge

Extend the skills you learned in this chapter and experiment with new skills. You may need to use Help to complete the assignment.

Modifying Reports

Instructions: Copy the Camashaly Design database and rename the database to Chapter 6 Camashaly Design. Start Access and open the database that you copied and renamed.

Perform the following tasks:

1. Open the Business Analyst Master List in Design view. Add your name to the report footer. Your name should appear on the left.

2. Change the report title from Business Analyst Master List to Business Analyst/Course Master List. Change the font color to red and underline the title. Change the report header background to white. Change the date format to Long Date. Change the border width for the subreport control to 4 pt.

3. Open the Discount Report in Design view. Calculate the average aggregate statistics for both the Amount Paid and Current Due columns. Place these statistics in the report footer only. Include an appropriate label for the statistics. Use conditional formatting to format the discount value in a bold red font for all records where the value is equal to or greater than $100.

4. Submit the revised database in the format specified by your instructor.

Make It Right

Analyze a database and correct all errors and/or improve the design.

Correcting Report Design Errors

Instructions: Start Access. Open the Condo Rentals database. See the inside back cover of this book for instructions on downloading the Data Files for Students, or contact your instructor for more information about accessing the required files.

The Condo Rentals database contains data about a company that rents condos in a popular resort community. The owner of the company has created the report shown in Design view in Figure 6–85, but there are a few problems. She really wanted to concatenate the first and last name of the owner with the label, Name. Bold the control and the label. The title of the report should be centered across the report and should appear in the report header, not in the page header. The page number and the date should appear in the page header, not the page footer. Finally, she would like to add a label to the report footer. The label should contain the text, End of Report, to indicate the end of the report. Bold the end-of-report label.

Continued >

Make It Right *continued*

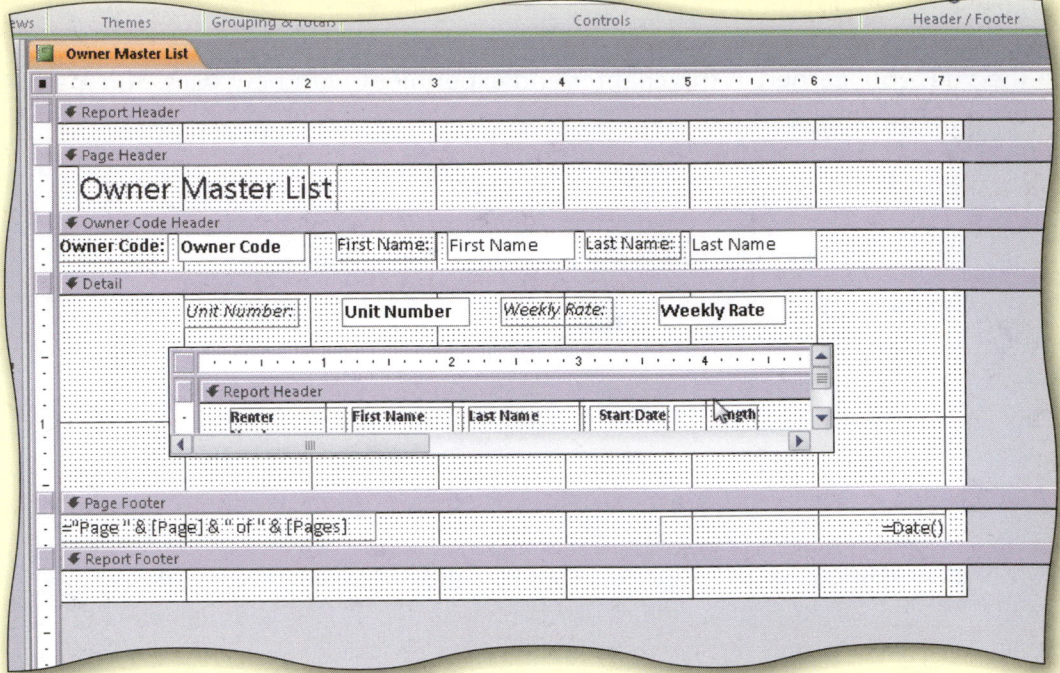

Figure 6–85

Correct these errors and submit the revised database in the format specified by your instructor.

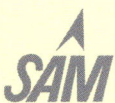

In the Lab

Design, create, modify, and/or use a database following the guidelines, concepts, and skills presented in this chapter. Labs are listed in order of increasing difficulty.

Lab 1: Adding Tables and Creating Reports for the ECO Clothesline Database

Problem: ECO Clothesline needs to maintain data on a weekly basis on the open orders for its customers. These are orders that have not yet been delivered. To track this information requires a new table, an Open Orders table. The company also needs a report that displays sales rep information as well as information about customers and any open orders that the customer has. The company would like to show its appreciation to current customers by discounting the amount customers currently owe.

Instructions: If you are using the Microsoft Access 2010 Complete or the Microsoft Access 2010 Comprehensive text, open the ECO Clothesline database that you used in Chapter 5. Otherwise, see the inside back cover of this book for instructions on downloading the Data Files for Students, or contact your instructor for more information about accessing the required files.

Perform the following tasks:

1. Create the Open Orders table using the structure shown in Table 6–5.

Table 6–5 Structure of Open Orders Table			
Field Name	**Data Type**	**Field Size**	**Description**
Order Number	Text	4	Primary Key: Yes
Amount	Currency		
Customer Number	Text	4	Foreign Key: matches primary key of Customer table

2. Import the Open Orders.txt file into the Open Orders table.

3. Create a one-to-many relationship between the Customer table and the Open Orders table.

4. Create a query that joins the Sales Rep and the Customer tables. Include the Sales Rep Number, Last Name, and First Name fields from the Sales Rep table. Include all fields except the Sales Rep Number field from the Customer table. Save the query as Sales Reps and Customers.

5. Create the report shown in Figure 6–86. The report uses the Sales Reps and Customers query as the basis for the main report and the Open Orders table as the basis for the subreport. Use the name Sales Rep Master List for the report. The report title has a Text Align property value of Distribute. The Border Width property is hairline and the subreport label is Open Orders. The report is similar in style to the Business Analyst Master List shown in Figure 6–1a on page AC 339.

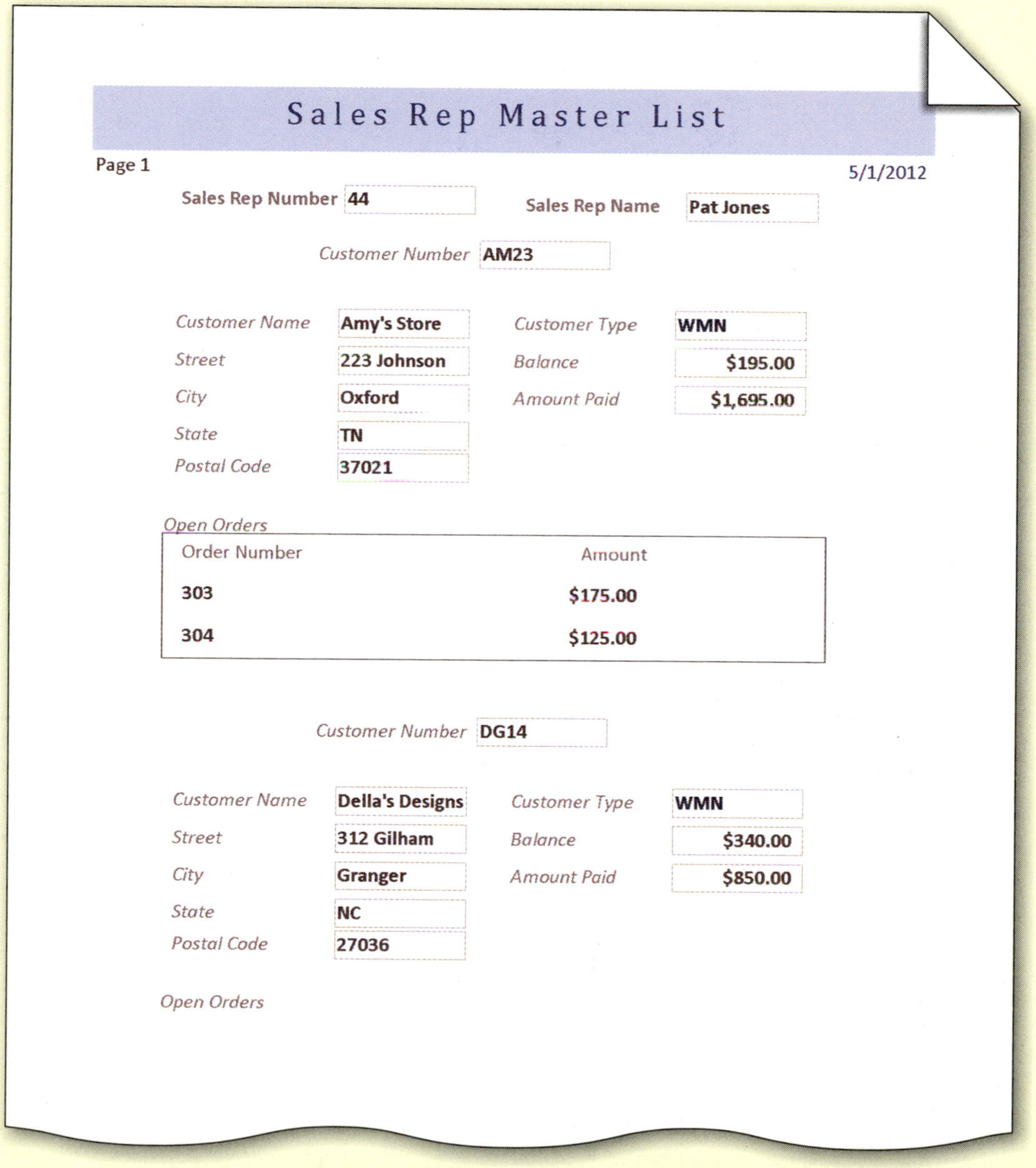

Figure 6–86

Continued >

In the Lab *continued*

6. Create the Customer Discount Report shown in Figure 6–87. The report uses the Sales Reps and Customers query. Customers who have paid $500 or more will receive a 3% discount on the remaining balance, and customers who have paid less than $500 will receive a 1% discount on the remaining balance. The report includes subtotals and grand totals for the Balance and Amount Paid fields. The report is similar in style to the Discount Report shown in Figure 6–1b on page AC 340.

7. Submit the revised database in the format specified by your instructor.

Customer Discount Report

Sales Rep Number	First Name	Last Name	Customer Number	Customer Name	Balance	Amount Paid	Discount
44	Pat	Jones					
			AM23	Amy's Store	$195.00	$1,695.00	$5.85
			DG14	Della's Designs	$340.00	$850.00	$10.20
			EC07	Environmentally Casual	$0.00	$1,700.00	$0.00
			NC25	Nancy's Place	$240.00	$550.00	$7.20
			TT21	Tan and Tone	$160.00	$725.00	$4.80
				Subtotals	$935.00	$5,520.00	
49	Pinn	Gupta					
			BL15	Blondie's on Main	$555.00	$1,350.00	$16.65
			CY12	Curlin Yoga Studio	$145.00	$710.00	$4.35
			JN34	Just Natural	$360.00	$700.00	$10.80
			LB20	Le Beauty Salon & Spa	$200.00	$1,250.00	$6.00
			WS34	Woody's Sporting Goods	$1,235.00	$0.00	$12.35
				Subtotals	$2,495.00	$4,010.00	
51	Gabe	Ortiz					
			CM09	Casual by Marie	$295.00	$1,080.00	$8.85
			FN19	Fitness Counts	$345.00	$1,950.00	$10.35
			RD03	Rose's Day Spa	$0.00	$975.00	$0.00

Figure 6–87

In the Lab

Lab 2: Adding Tables and Creating Reports for the Walburg Energy Alternatives Database

Problem: The manager of the Walburg Energy Alternatives store needs to track items that are being reordered from vendors. The manager must know when an item was ordered and how many were ordered. He also needs a report that displays vendor information as well as information about items and the order status of items. Walburg is considering an in-store sale and would like a report that shows the regular selling price as well as the sale price of all items.

Instructions: If you are using the Microsoft Access 2010 Complete or the Microsoft Access 2010 Comprehensive text, open the Walburg Energy Alternatives database that you used in Chapter 5. Otherwise, see the inside back cover of this book for instructions on downloading the Data Files for Students, or contact your instructor for more information about accessing the required files.

Perform the following tasks:

1. Create a table in which to store the item reorder information using the structure shown in Table 6–6. Use Reorder as the name of the table. Import the data from the Reorder.xlsx workbook.

Table 6–6 Structure of Reorder Table

Field Name	Data Type	Field Size	Description
Item Number	Text	4	Part of Primary Key
Date Ordered	Date/Time (Use Short Date format)		Part of Primary Key
Number Ordered	Number	Integer	

2. Add the Reorder table to the Relationships window and establish a one-to-many relationship between the Item table and the Reorder table.

3. Create the report shown in Figure 6–88. The report uses the Vendor-Item Query that was previously created as the basis for the main report and the Reorder table as the basis for the subreport. Use the name Vendor Master Report for the report. The report is the same style as that demonstrated in the project. Use conditional formatting to display the on hand value in bold red font color for all items with fewer than 10 items on hand. Change the Border Style property to Transparent. Change the Text Align property for the title to Distribute.

Continued >

In the Lab *continued*

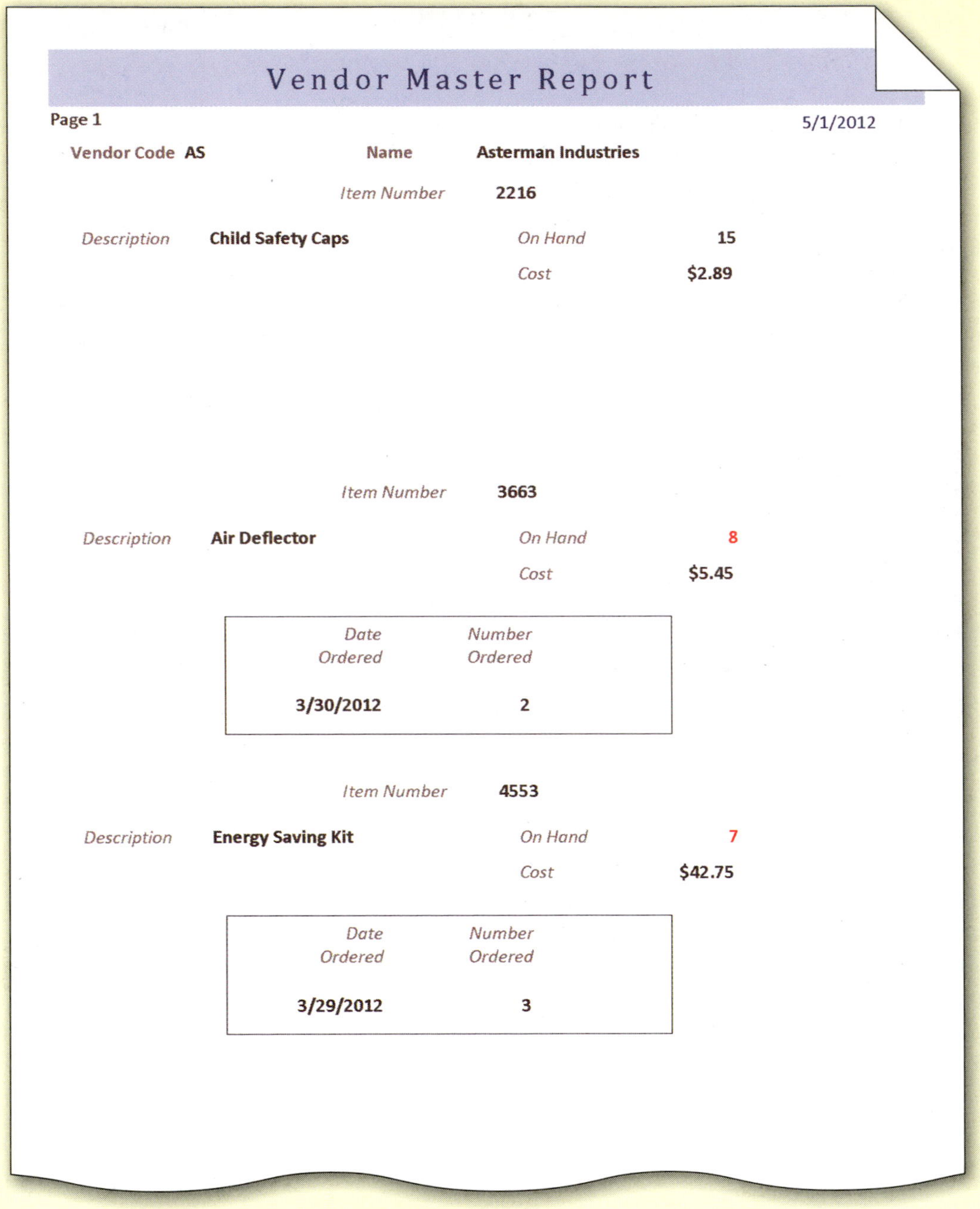

Vendor Master Report

Page 1   5/1/2012

| Vendor Code | AS | Name | Asterman Industries |

Item Number | **2216**

Description | **Child Safety Caps** | On Hand | **15**
| | Cost | **$2.89**

Item Number | **3663**

Description | **Air Deflector** | On Hand | **8**
| | Cost | **$5.45**

Date Ordered	Number Ordered
3/30/2012	**2**

Item Number | **4553**

Description | **Energy Saving Kit** | On Hand | **7**
| | Cost | **$42.75**

Date Ordered	Number Ordered
3/29/2012	**3**

Figure 6–88

4. Open the Vendor-Item Query in Design view and add the Selling Price field to the query. Save the query.

5. Create the Item Discount Report shown in Figure 6–89. The report uses the Vendor-Item Query and calculates the sale amount for each item. Items with a selling price of $10.00 or more have a 6% discount and 3% otherwise. Note that the report shows the sale price, not the discount. The report is similar to the Discount Report shown in Figure 6–1b on page AC 340. However, there are no group subtotals or report grand totals. The page number and the current date appear in the page footer. Change the Can Grow property for the Description field to Yes.

Item Discount Report

Vendor Code	Vendor Name	Item Number	Description	On Hand	Cost	Selling Price	Sale Price
AS	Asterman Industries						
		2216	Child Safety Caps	15	$2.89	$3.25	$3.15
		3663	Air Deflector	8	$5.45	$5.99	$5.81
		4553	Energy Saving Kit	7	$42.75	$43.25	$40.66
		6234	Programmable Thermostat	3	$34.25	$36.99	$34.77
		8136	Smoke Detector	10	$6.10	$6.50	$6.31
		9458	Windows Insulator Kit	10	$4.95	$5.25	$5.09
JM	JMZ Technologies						
		1234	Adhesive Door Sweep	5	$3.45	$3.89	$3.77
		2234	Clothes Dryer Heat Saver	4	$8.99	$9.19	$8.91
		3673	Energy Booklet	25	$2.70	$2.99	$2.90
		4583	Fluorescent Light Bulb	18	$4.50	$4.75	$4.61
		6185	Luminescent Night Light	12	$3.75	$4.50	$4.37
		7123	Retractable Clothesline	10	$13.25	$13.99	$13.15
		8590	Water Conservation Kit	8	$13.45	$13.99	$13.15
SD	Scryps Distributors						
		2310	Drip Counter	10	$1.79	$1.99	$1.93
		2789	Hot Water Gauge	6	$2.75	$2.99	$2.90
		4573	Faucet Aerator	20	$0.89	$0.99	$0.96
		5923	Low Flow Shower Head	11	$8.75	$8.99	$8.72
		6345	Rain Gauge	16	$2.89	$3.15	$3.06
		7934	Shower Timer	15	$2.45	$2.99	$2.90
		8344	Toilet Tank Water Saver	18	$3.35	$3.50	$3.40

Page 1   5/1/2012

Figure 6–89

6. Submit the revised database in the format specified by your instructor.

In the Lab

Lab 3: Adding Tables and Creating a Report for the Philamar Training Database

Problem: Philamar Training needs to track the classes its trainers offer to clients. The company also needs a report that displays trainer information as well as information about clients and class offerings.

Instructions: If you are using the Microsoft Access 2010 Complete or the Microsoft Access 2010 Comprehensive text, open the Philamar Training database that you used in Chapter 5. Otherwise, see the inside back cover of this book for instructions on downloading the Data Files for Students, or contact your instructor for more information about accessing the required files.

Instructions Part 1:   Create two tables in which to store the data concerning classes and class offerings. The Class table contains data about the classes that Philamar offers. The Class Offerings table contains data about classes currently being offered by the trainers. The structure of the Class table is shown in Table 6–7, and the structure of the Class Offerings table is shown in Table 6–8.

Table 6–7 Structure of Class Table

Field Name	Data Type	Field Size	Description
Class Code	Text	3	Primary Key
Class Description	Text	40	
Hours	Number	Integer	
Increments	Number	Integer	

Table 6–8 Structure of Class Offerings Table

Field Name	Data Type	Field Size	Description
Client Number	Text	4	Part of Primary Key
Class Code	Text	3	Part of Primary Key
Total Hours	Number	Integer	
Hours Spent	Number	Integer	

The data for the Class table is in the Class.txt file, and the data for the Class Offerings table is in the Class Offerings.csv file. Add the data to the two tables and then update the relationships for the Philamar Training database.

Instructions Part 2:   Create a query that joins the Trainer and Client tables. Include the trainer number, first name, and last name from the Trainer table. Include all fields except trainer number from the Client table. Save the query as Trainers and Clients. Create a query that joins the Class and Class Offerings table. Include the Client Number and Class Code fields from the Class Offerings table. Then, include the Class Description, Total Hours, and Hours Spent fields. Add a calculated field, Hours Remaining, that contains the difference between Total Hours and Hours Spent. Save the query as Class Offerings and Classes. The query should be similar to the Course and Course Offerings query created in the chapter.

Instructions Part 3: Create the report shown in Figure 6–90. The report is based on the two queries created in Part 2. The Date control uses the Long Date format, the title uses Distribute as the Text Align property, and there are no borders. The report is similar in style to the Business Analyst Master List shown in Figure 6–1a on page AC 339.

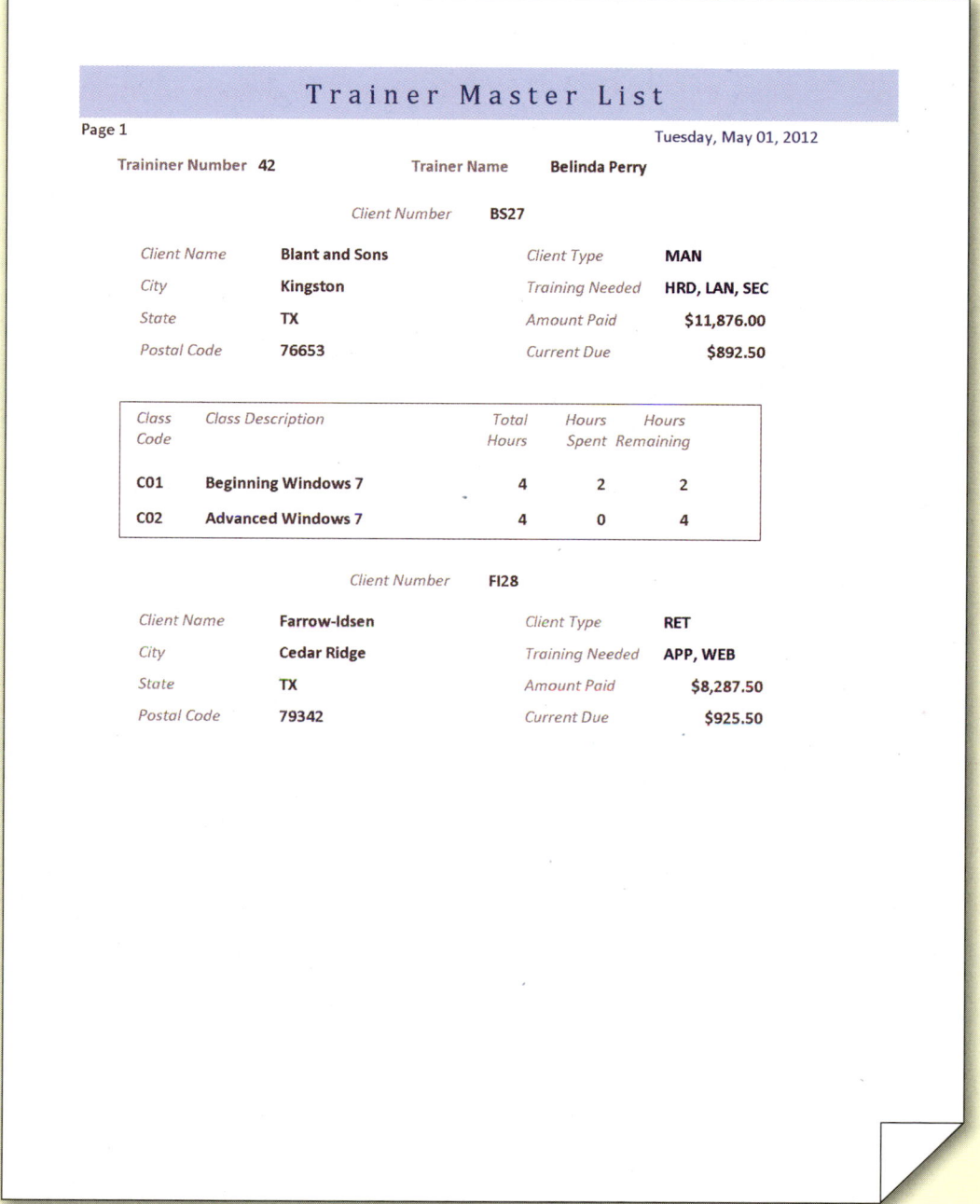

Figure 6–90

Cases and Places

Apply your creative thinking and problem solving skills to design and implement a solution.

See the inside back cover of this book for instructions for downloading the Data Files for Students, or see your instructor for information on accessing the required files.

1: Adding Tables and Creating a Report for the Chamber of Commerce Database

Academic

If you are using the Microsoft Access 2010 Complete or the Microsoft Access 2010 Comprehensive text, open the Chamber of Commerce database that you used in Chapter 5. Otherwise, see your instructor for more information about accessing the required files.

Your internship with the Chamber of Commerce has taught you the value of a good advertising strategy. Now the Chamber would like you to help them track active advertising accounts. Advertisers contract with the chamber to advertise for one month. The same ad may run for several months or be replaced monthly with an ad of a different size or design. The Chamber must track the active accounts for the current year. They also need a report grouped by ad rep that includes client and active account information. Use the concepts and techniques presented in this chapter to perform each of the following tasks:

a. Create the two tables necessary to track active accounts. The structure for the Ad Categories table is shown in Table 6–9, and the structure for the Active Accounts table is shown in Table 6–10. Import the Active Accounts text file into the Active Accounts table and the Ad Categories text file into the Ad Categories table. Then, update the relationships for the Chamber of Commerce database.

Table 6–9 Structure of Ad Categories Table

Field Name	Data Type	Field Size	Description
Category Code	Text	2	Primary Key
Category Description	Text	40	

Table 6–10 Structure of Active Accounts Table

Field Name	Data Type	Field Size	Description
Advertiser Number	Text	4	Part of Primary Key
Ad Month	Text	3	Part of Primary Key
Category Code	Text	3	Foreign Key: matches primary key of Ad Categories table

b. Create a query to join the Ad Rep table and the Advertiser table. Include the Ad Rep Number, First Name, and Last Name fields from the Ad Rep table. Include all fields from the Advertiser table except the Ad Rep Number fields. Save the query as Ad Reps and Advertisers. Create a query to join the Active Accounts and the Ad Categories table. Include the Advertiser Number, Ad Month, Category Code, and Category Description fields. Save the query as Ad Categories and Active Accounts.

c. Create an Ad Rep Master Report that uses the Ad Reps and Advertisers query as the basis for the main report and the Ad Categories and Active Accounts query as the basis for the subreport. The report should be similar to the report shown in Figure 6–1a on page AC 339. Concatenate the ad rep first and last names. Place the page number in the page footer.

Submit the revised database in the format specified by your instructor.

2: Adding Tables and Creating a Report for the Consignment Database

Personal

If you are using the Microsoft Access 2010 Complete or the Microsoft Access 2010 Comprehensive text, open the Consignment database that you used in Chapter 5. Otherwise, see your instructor for more information about accessing the required files. The volunteer group that manages the consignment shop would like you to prepare two reports for them. Both reports group data by seller code. They also would like to link to the database an Excel workbook that lists suggested prices for used items. Use the concepts and techniques presented in this chapter to perform each of the following tasks:

a. Create a query that joins the Seller table and Items table. Include the Seller Code, First Name, and Last Name fields from the Seller table. Include the Item Number, Description, Price, and Date Posted fields from the Items table. Save the query as Sellers and Items Query.

b. Create a report that is similar in style to the Discount Report shown in Figure 6–1b on page AC 340. Group the report by seller code and include the seller's first name and last name. The Detail section should include the item number, description, date posted, and price. Create a calculated control, Sale Price, that displays the sale price (not the discount) for all items. Items that have a price of $20.00 or more will have a 4% discount. Items that have a price of less than $20.00 will have a 2% discount. Do not include any subtotals or grand totals. Name the report Item Sale Report. Select your own fonts for the report.

c. Create a report that is similar in style to the Discount Report shown in Figure 6–1b on page AC 340. Group the report by seller code and include the seller's first name and last name. The Detail section should include the item number, description, date posted, and price. Create a calculated control, Reduced Price, that displays the Reduced Price (not the discount) for all items. Items that have a date posted earlier than March 4, 2012, will have a 5% discount. Items that have a date posted of March 4, 2012, or later will have a 3% discount. Do not include any subtotals or grand totals. Name the report Reduced Price Report. Select your own fonts for the report.

d. Link the Prices worksheet to the database. Rename the linked Prices table as Suggested Prices. Then, use the Linked Table Manager to update the link between the Excel worksheet and the Access table.

Submit the revised database in the format specified by your instructor.

3: Adding Tables and Creating a Report for the Senior Care Database

Professional

If you are using the Microsoft Access 2010 Complete or the Microsoft Access 2010 Comprehensive text, open the Senior Care database that you used in Chapter 5. Otherwise, see your instructor for more information about accessing the required files. You and your co-owner have decided that you need to better track the number of hours that helpers work. You also need a report that will list helpers as well as the clients they serve. Use the concepts and techniques presented in this chapter to perform each of the following tasks:

a. Create a table in which to store data about the services offered to clients. The table has the same structure as the Accounts table shown in Table 6–4, except that the field size for the Client Number field should be 4. (*Hint:* See the BTW on copying the structure of a table.) Name the table Services and import the Services.xlsx workbook. Update the relationships for the Senior Care database.

b. Create a query that joins the Helper and the Client tables. Include the Helper Number, First Name, and Last Name fields from the Helper table. Include all fields from the Client table except the Helper Number field. Save the query as Helpers and Clients.

c. Create a Helper Master Report that uses the Helpers and Clients query as the basis for the main report and the Services table as the basis for the subreport. The report should be similar to the report shown in Figure 6–1a on page AC 339. Add a Total Amount field to the main report that is the sum of Amount Paid and Balance. (*Hint:* This calculation is for each client record.) Concatenate the helper first and last names. (*Hint:* Because the fields First Name and Last Name are in both tables, you must qualify the field names in the concatenation formula.) Be sure to change the labels for client first name and client last name so that the table name is not included on the report.

Submit the revised database in the format specified by your instructor.

7 | Using SQL

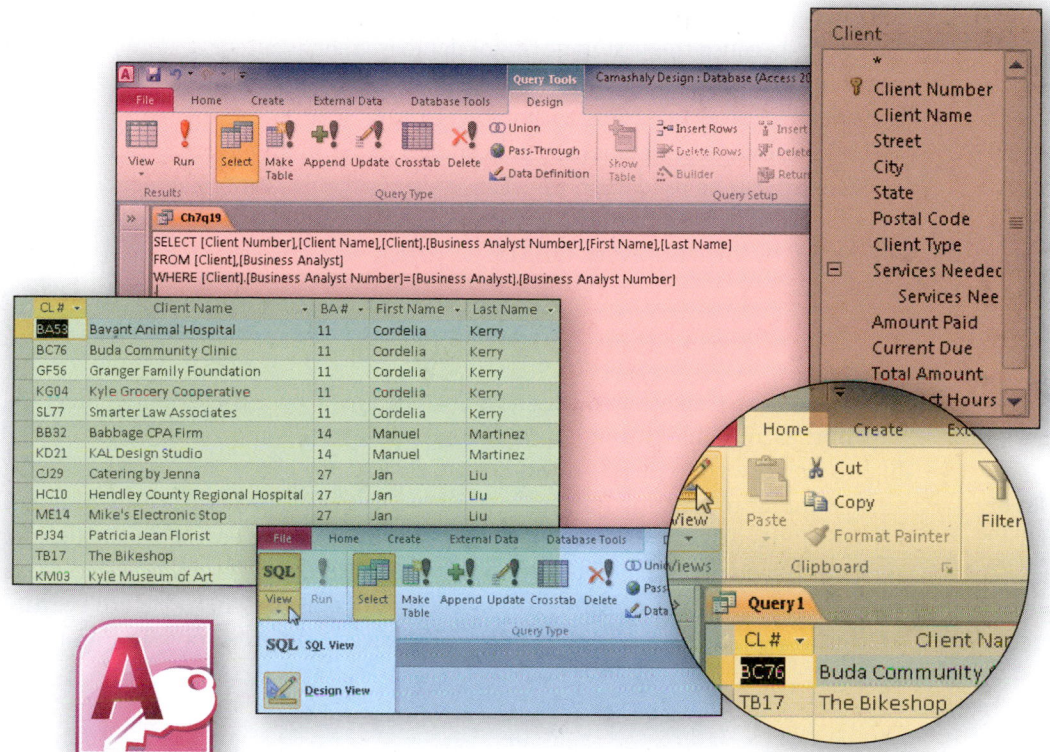

Objectives

You will have mastered the material in this project when you can:

- Change the font or font size for SQL queries
- Create SQL queries
- Include fields in SQL queries
- Include simple and compound criteria in SQL queries
- Use computed fields and built-in functions in SQL queries
- Sort the results in SQL queries

- Use aggregate functions in SQL queries
- Group the results in SQL queries
- Join tables in SQL queries
- Use subqueries
- Compare SQL queries with Access-generated SQL
- Use INSERT, UPDATE, and DELETE queries to update a database

7 | Using SQL

Introduction

Q&A

Q&As
For a complete list of the Q&As found in many of the step-by-step sequences in this book, visit the Access 2010 Q&A Web page (scsite.com/ac2010/qa).

The language called **SQL (Structured Query Language)** is a very important language for querying and updating databases. It is the closest thing to a universal database language, because the vast majority of database management systems, including Access, use it in some fashion. Although some users will be able to do all their queries through the query features of Access without ever using SQL, those in charge of administering and maintaining the database system should be familiar with this important language. Access also can be used as an interface to other database management systems, such as SQL Server. To use or interface with SQL Server requires knowledge of SQL. SQL is supported by virtually every DBMS.

Project — Using SQL

The owners of Camashaly Design want to be able to use the extended data management capabilities available through SQL. In becoming familiar with SQL, Camashaly would like to create a wide variety of SQL queries.

BTW

BTWs
For a complete list of the BTWs found in the margins of this book, visit the Access 2010 BTW Web page (scsite.com/ac2010/btw).

Similar to creating queries in Design view, SQL provides a way of querying relational databases. In SQL, however, instead of making entries in the design grid, you type commands into SQL view to obtain the desired results, as shown in Figure 7–1a. You then can click the View button to view the results just as when you are creating queries in Design view. The results for the query in Figure 7–1a are shown in Figure 7–1b.

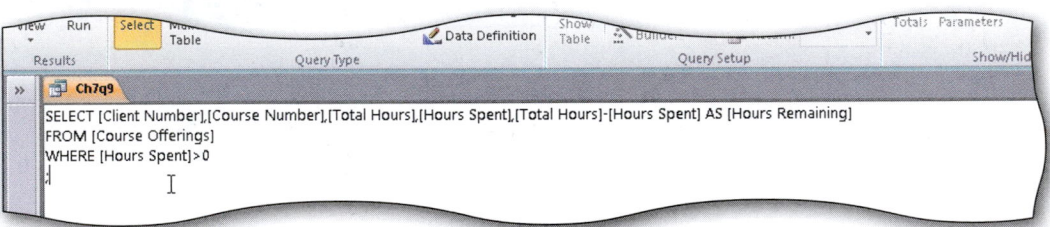

(a) Query in SQL

```
SELECT [Client Number],[Course Number],[Total Hours],[Hours Spent],[Total Hours]-[Hours Spent] AS [Hours Remaining]
FROM [Course Offerings]
WHERE [Hours Spent]>0
;
```

CL #	Course Num	Total Hours	Hours Spent	Hours Rema
BB32	C01	8	4	4
CJ29	C03	6	3	3
HC10	C04	12	6	6
HC10	C05	2	1	1
KD21	C07	8	4	4
KG04	C01	8	6	2
KG04	C08	6	4	2
ME14	C06	4	2	2
PJ34	C06	4	2	2
SL77	C04	12	9	3
SL77	C08	6	2	4
TB17	C02	4	2	2

(b) Results

Figure 7–1

Overview

As you read through this chapter, you will learn how to create SQL queries by performing these general tasks:

- Create queries involving criteria.
- Sort the results of a query.
- Group records in a query and perform group calculations.
- Join tables in queries.
- Create a query that involves a subquery.
- Update data using the INSERT, UPDATE, and DELETE commands.

Plan Ahead

SQL Query Guidelines.
When querying a database using SQL, you must design queries appropriately, identifying the required fields, tables, criteria, sorting, grouping, and operations to use. Querying in SQL also requires proper expression of queries using SQL clauses and formatting.

1. **Select the fields for the query.** Examine the requirements for the query you are constructing to determine which fields are to be included.

2. **Determine which table or tables contain these fields.** For each field, determine the table in which it is located.

3. **Determine criteria.** Determine any criteria that data must satisfy to be included in the results. If there are more than two tables in the query, determine the criteria to be used to ensure the data matches correctly.

4. **Determine sort order.** Is the data to be sorted in some way? If so, by what field or fields is it to be sorted?

5. **Determine grouping.** Is the data to be grouped in some way? If so, by what field is it to be grouped? Identify any calculations to be made for the group.

6. **Determine any update operations to be performed.** Determine whether rows need to be inserted, changed, or deleted. Determine the tables involved.

When necessary, more specific details concerning the above decisions and/or actions are presented at appropriate points in the chapter. The chapter also will identify the use of these guidelines in creating SQL queries such as the one shown in Figure 7–1.

To Start Access

The following steps, which assume Windows 7 is running, start Access based on a typical installation. You may need to ask your instructor how to start Access for your computer.

1 Click the Start button on the Windows 7 taskbar to display the Start menu.

2 Type **Microsoft Access** as the search text in the 'Search programs and files' text box and watch the search results appear on the Start menu.

3 Click Microsoft Access 2010 in the search results on the Start menu to start Access.

4 If the Access window is not maximized, click the Maximize button next to the Close button on its title bar to maximize the window.

BTW

The Ribbon and Screen Resolution
Access may change how the groups and buttons within the groups appear on the Ribbon, depending on the computer's screen resolution. Thus, your Ribbon may look different from the ones in this book if you are using a screen resolution other than 1024 × 768.

To Open a Database from Access

The following steps open the Camashaly Design database from the USB flash drive.

1 With your USB flash drive connected to one of the computer's USB ports, click File on the Ribbon to open the Backstage view.

2 Click Open in the Backstage view to display the Open dialog box.

3 Navigate to the location of the file to be opened (in this case, the USB flash drive, then to the CIS 101 folder [or your class folder], and then to the Access folder).

4 Click Camashaly Design to select the file to be opened.

5 Click the Open button (Open dialog box) to open the selected file and display the opened database in the Access window.

6 If a Security Warning appears, click the Enable Content button.

SQL Background

In this chapter, you query and update a database using the language called **SQL** (**Structured Query Language**). Similar to using the design grid in the Access Query window, SQL provides users with the capability of querying a relational database. Because SQL is a language, however, you must enter **commands** to obtain the desired results, rather than completing entries in the design grid. SQL uses commands to update tables and to retrieve data from tables. The commands that are used to retrieve data are usually called **queries**.

SQL was developed under the name SEQUEL at the IBM San Jose research facilities as the data manipulation language for IBM's prototype relational model DBMS, System R, in the mid-1970s. In 1980, it was renamed SQL to avoid confusion with an unrelated hardware product called SEQUEL. It is used as the data manipulation language for IBM's current production offerings in the relational DBMS arena — SQL/DS and DB2. Most relational DBMSs, including Microsoft Access and Microsoft SQL Server, use a version of SQL as a data manipulation language.

Some people pronounce SQL by pronouncing the three letters, that is, "ess-que-ell." It is very common, however to pronounce it as the name under which it was developed originally, that is, "sequel."

To Change the Font Size

You can change the font and/or the font size for queries using the Options button in the Backstage view and then Object Designers in the list of options in the Access Options dialog box. There usually is not a compelling reason to change the font, unless there is a strong preference for some other font. It often is worthwhile to change the font size, however. With the default size of 8, the queries can be hard to read. Increasing the font size to 10 can make a big difference. The following steps change the font size for queries to 10.

1

- Click File on the Ribbon to open the Backstage view.

- Click Options to display the Access Options dialog box.

- Click Object Designers to display the Object Designer options.

- In the Query design area, click the Size box arrow, and then click 10 in the list to change the size to 10 (Figure 7–2).

2

- Click the OK button to close the Access Options dialog box.

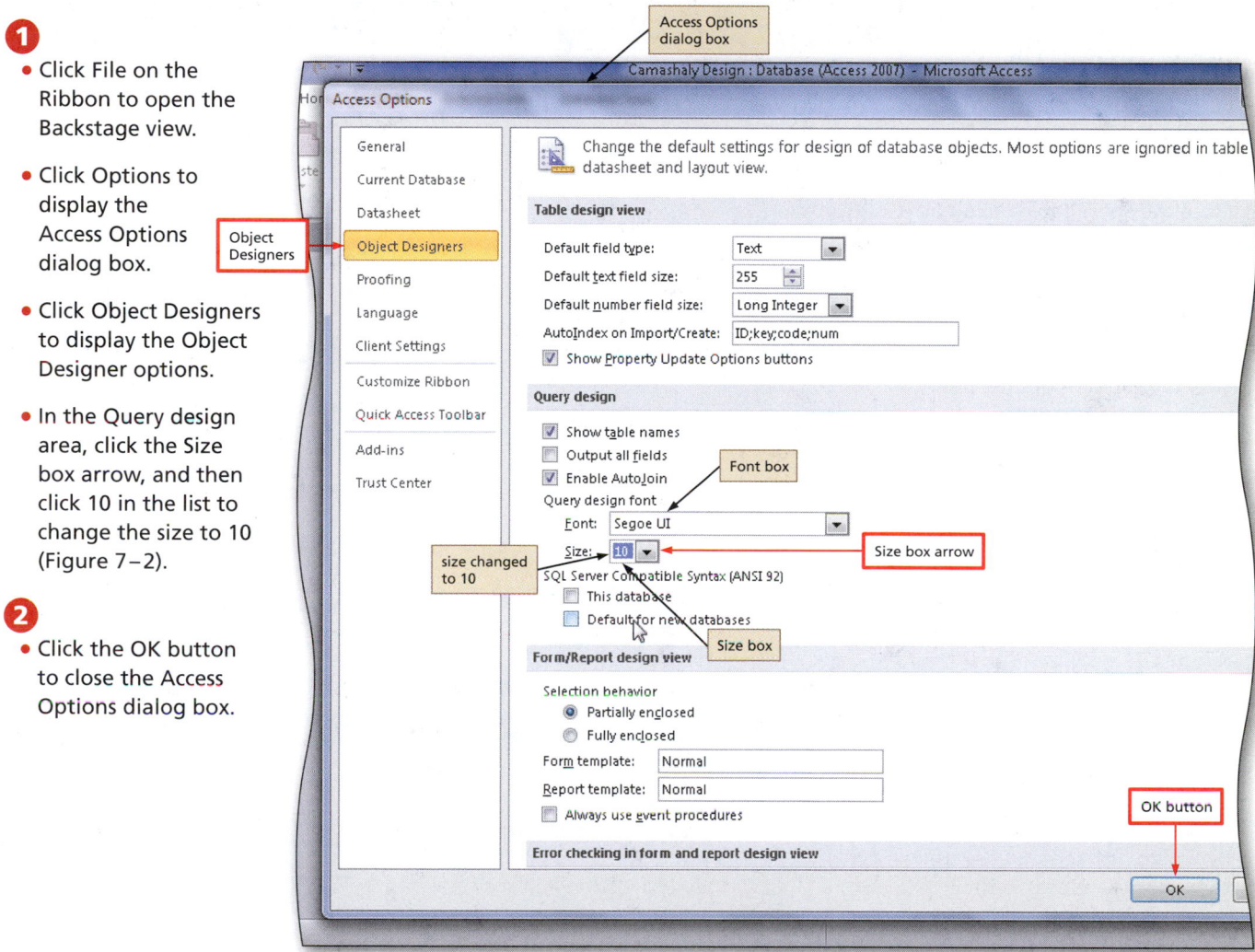

Figure 7–2

SQL Queries

When you query a database using SQL, you type commands in a blank window rather than filling in the design grid. When the command is complete, you can view your results just as you do with queries you create using the design grid.

To Create a New SQL Query

You begin the creation of a new **SQL query**, which is a query expressed using the SQL language, just as you begin the creation of any other query in Access. The only difference is that you will use SQL view instead of Design view. The following steps create a new SQL query.

- Close the Navigation Pane.

- Display the Create tab.

- Click the Query Design button (Create tab | Queries group) to create a query.

- Close the Show Table dialog box without adding any tables.

- Click the View button arrow (Query Tools Design tab | Results group) to display the View menu (Figure 7–3).

Q&A Why did the icon on the View button change to SQL, and why are there only two items on the menu instead of the usual five?

Without any tables selected, you cannot view any results. You only can use the normal Design view or SQL view.

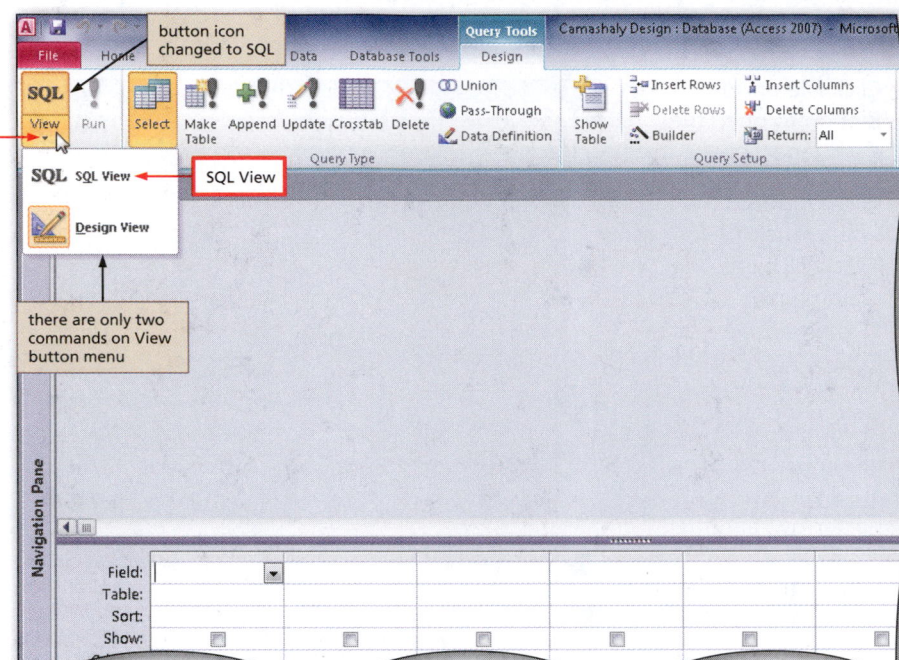

Figure 7–3

- Click SQL View to view the query in SQL view (Figure 7–4).

Q&A What happened to the design grid?

In SQL view, you specify the queries by typing SQL commands rather than making entries in the design grid.

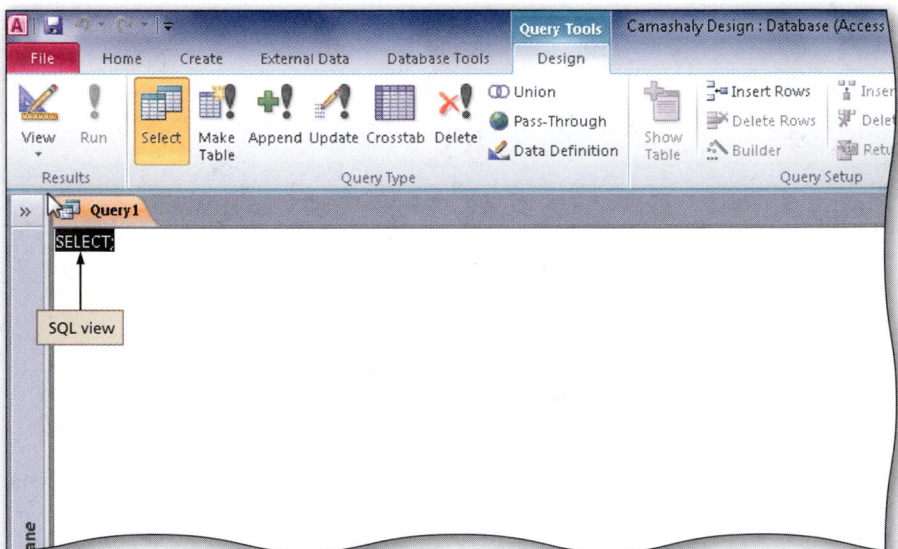

Figure 7–4

SQL Commands

The basic form of SQL expressions is quite simple: SELECT-FROM-WHERE. The command begins with a **SELECT clause**, which consists of the word, SELECT, followed by a list of those fields you want to include. The fields will appear in the results in the order in which they are listed in the expression. Next, the command contains a **FROM clause**, which consists of the word, FROM, followed by a list of the table or tables involved in the query. Finally, there is an optional **WHERE clause**, which consists of the word, WHERE, followed by any criteria that the data you want to retrieve must satisfy. The command ends with a semicolon (;), which in this text will appear on a separate line.

SQL has no special format rules for placement of terms, capitalization, and so on. The style used by this text is to place the word FROM on a new line, and then place the word WHERE, when it is used, on the next line. This makes the commands easier to read. This text also shows words that are part of the SQL language in uppercase and others in a combination of uppercase and lowercase. Because it is a common convention, and necessary in some versions of SQL, place a semicolon (;) at the end of each command.

Microsoft Access has its own version of SQL that, unlike some other versions of SQL, allows spaces within field names and table names. There is a restriction, however, to the way such names are used in SQL queries. When a name containing a space appears in SQL, it must be enclosed in square brackets. For example, Client Number must appear as [Client Number] because the name includes a space. On the other hand, City does not need to be enclosed in square brackets because its name does not include a space. For consistency, all names in this text are enclosed in square brackets. Thus, the City field would appear as [City] even though the brackets technically are not required by SQL.

To Include Only Certain Fields

To include only certain fields in a query, list them after the word, SELECT. If you want to list all rows in the table, you do not need to include the word, WHERE. The following steps create a query for Camashaly Design that will list the number, name, amount paid, and current due amount of all clients.

BTW

SQL Standards
The International Organization for Standardization (ISO) and the American National Standards Institute (ANSI) recognize SQL as a standardized language. Different relational database management systems may support the entire set of standardized SQL commands or only a subset.

BTW

Context-Sensitive Help in SQL
When you are working in SQL view, you can obtain context-sensitive help on any of the keywords in your query. To do so, click anywhere in the word about which you want to obtain help and press F1.

1

- Type `SELECT [Client Number],[Client Name],[Amount Paid],[Current Due]` as the first line of the command, and then press the ENTER key.

- Type `FROM [Client]` as the second line, press the ENTER key, and then type a semicolon (;) on the third line.

- Click the View button (Query Tools Design tab | Results group) to view the results (Figure 7–5).

Q&A My screen displays a dialog box that asks me to enter a parameter value. What did I do wrong?

You typed a field name incorrectly. Click Cancel to close the dialog box and then correct your SQL statement.

Q&A Why does CL # appear as the column heading for the Client Number field?

This is the caption for the field. If the field has a special caption defined, Access will use the caption rather than the field name. You will learn how to change this later in this chapter.

Q&A Can I save the query if I want to use it again?

You certainly can. Click the Save button on the Quick Access Toolbar and assign a name in the Save As dialog box.

2

- Click the Save button on the Quick Access Toolbar, type `Ch7q1` as the name in the Save As dialog box, and click the OK button to save the query as Ch7q1.

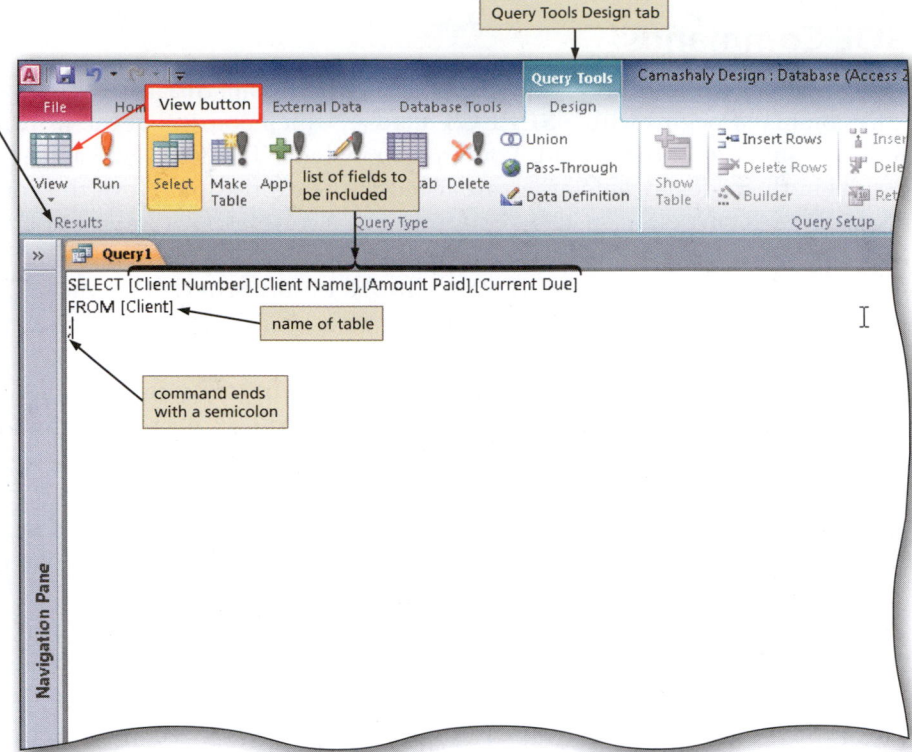

(a) Query

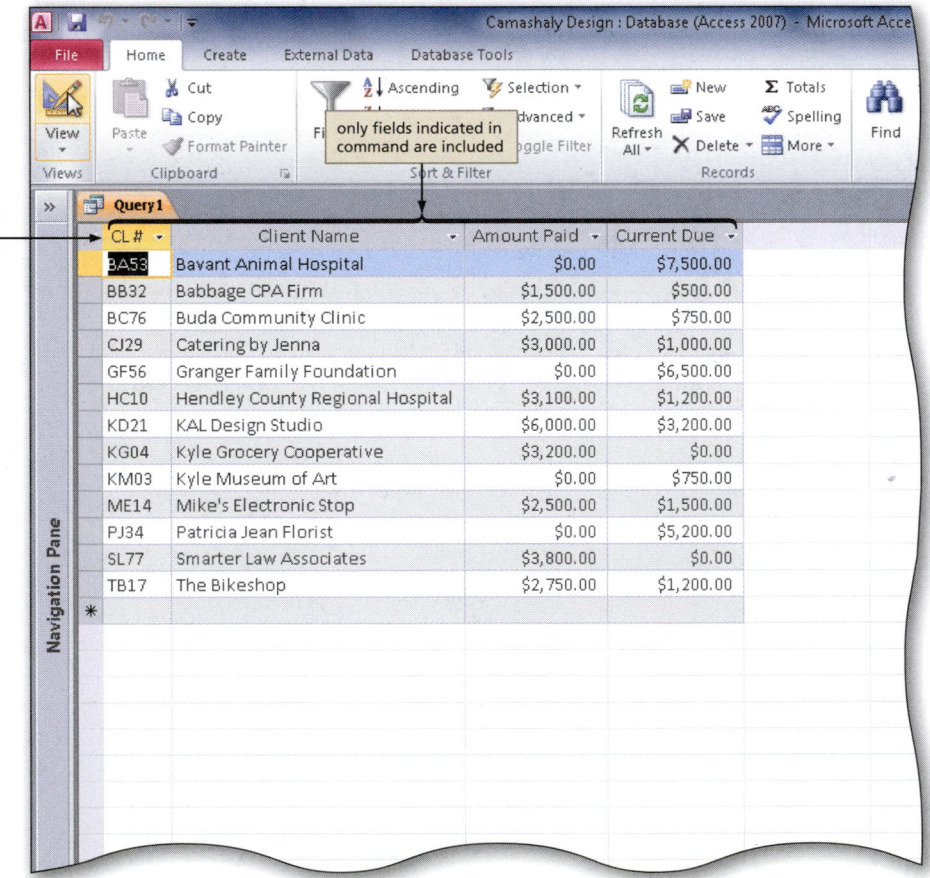

(b) Results

Figure 7–5

To Prepare to Enter a New SQL Query

To enter a new SQL query, you could close the window, click the No button when asked if you want to save your changes, and then begin the process from scratch. A quicker alternative is to use the View menu and then select SQL View. You then will be returned to SQL view with the current command appearing. At that point, you could erase the current command and then enter a new one. (If the next command is similar to the previous one, it might be simpler to modify the current command instead of erasing it and starting over.) The following steps show how to prepare to enter a new SQL query.

1
- Click the View button arrow (Home tab | Views group) to display the View button menu (Figure 7–6).

2
- Click SQL View to return to SQL view.

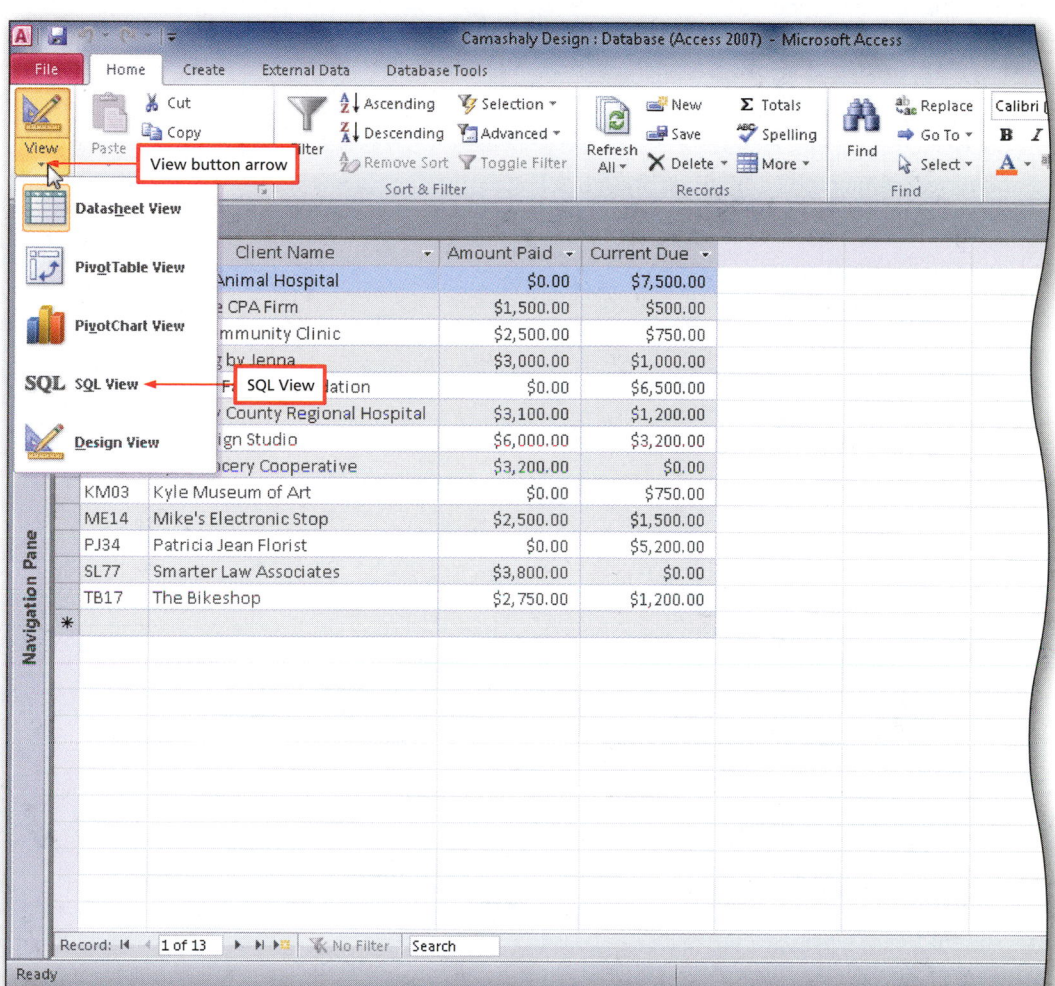

Figure 7–6

Could I just click the View button, or do I have to click the arrow?

Because the icon on the button is not the icon for SQL view, you must click the arrow.

To Include All Fields

To include all fields, you could use the same approach as in the previous steps, that is, list each field in the Client table after the word, SELECT. There is a shortcut, however. Instead of listing all the field names after SELECT, you can use the asterisk (*) symbol. This indicates that you want all fields listed in the order in which you described them to the system during data definition. The following steps list all fields and all records in the Client table.

- Press the DELETE key to delete the current command, type **SELECT *** as the first line of the command, and then press the ENTER key.

- Type **FROM [Client]** as the second line, press the ENTER key, and type a semicolon (**;**) on the third line.

- View the results (Figure 7–7).

Q&A Can I use copy and paste commands when I enter SQL commands?

Yes, you can use copy and paste as well as other editing techniques, such as replacing text.

- Click File on the Ribbon to open the Backstage view, click Save Object As to display the Save As dialog box, type **Ch7q2** as the name for the saved query, and click the OK button to save the query as Ch7q2. Click File on the Ribbon to close the Backstage view and return to the query.

Q&A Why can I not just click the Save button on the Quick Access Toolbar as I did when I saved the previous query?

If you did, you would replace the previous query with the version you just created. Because you want to save both the previous query and the new one, you need to save the new version with a different name. To do so, you must use Save Object As, which is available through the Backstage view.

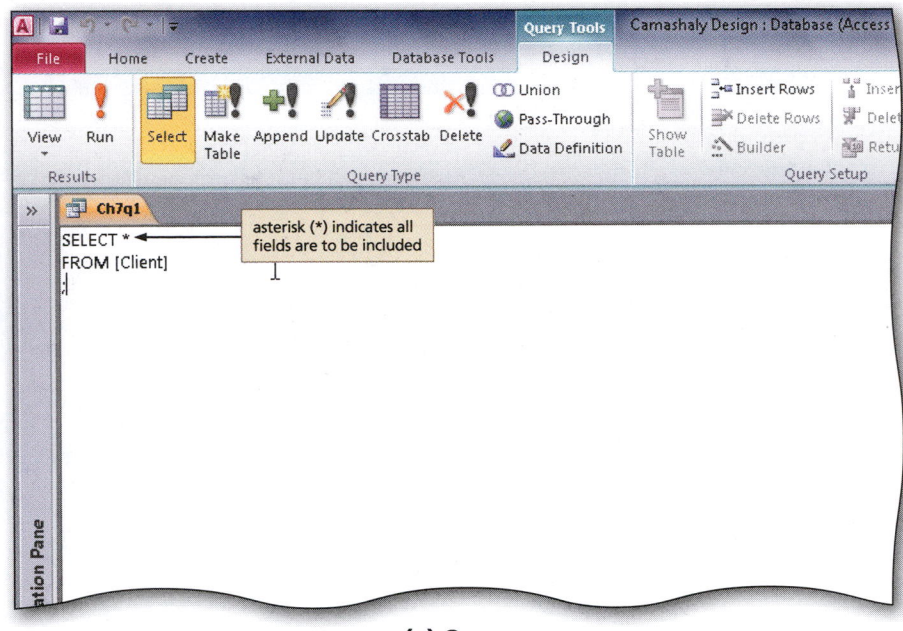

(a) Query

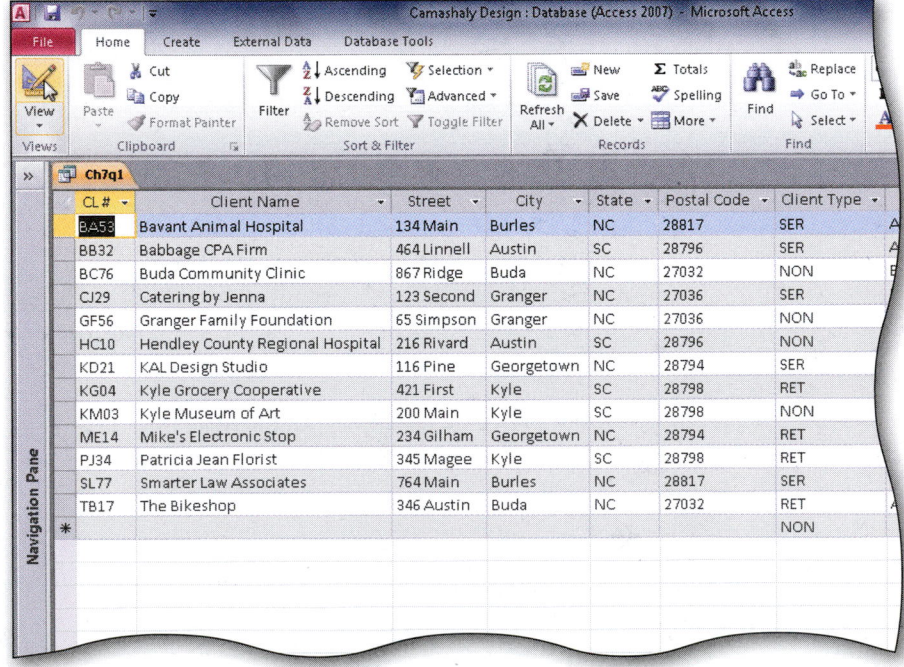

(b) Results

Figure 7–7

To Use a Criterion Involving a Numeric Field

To restrict the records to be displayed, include the word WHERE followed by a criterion as part of the command. If the field involved is a numeric field, you simply type the value. In typing the number, you do not type commas or dollar signs. The following steps create a query to list the client number and name of all clients whose current due amount is $0.00.

- Click the View button arrow, click SQL View to return to SQL view, and then delete the current command.

- Type **SELECT [Client Number],[Client Name]** as the first line of the command.

- Type **FROM [Client]** as the second line.

- Type **WHERE [Current Due]=0** as the third line, and then type a semicolon (**;**) on the fourth line.

- View the results (Figure 7–8).

Q&A

On my screen, the clients are listed in a different order. Did I do something wrong?

No. The order in which records display in a query result is random unless you specifically order the records. You will see how to order records later in this chapter.

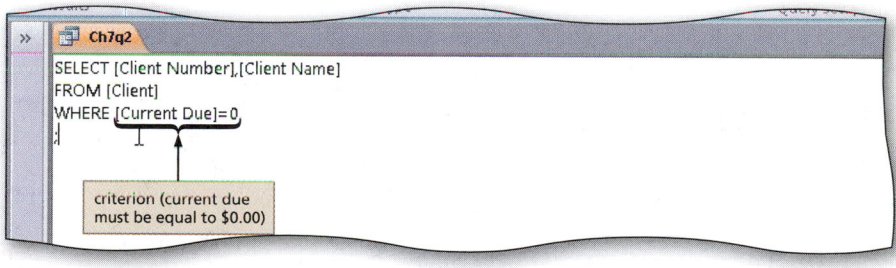

(a) Query

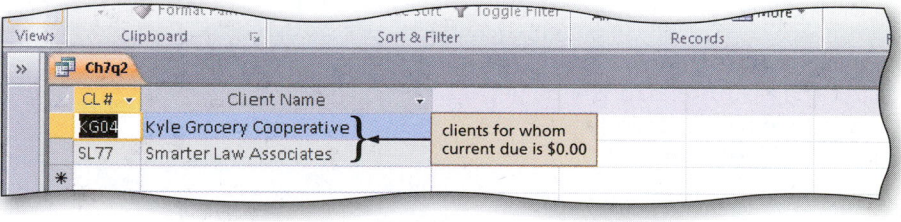

(b) Results

Figure 7–8

- Save the query as Ch7q3. Return to the query.

Simple Criteria

The criterion following the word WHERE in the preceding query is called a simple criterion. A **simple criterion** has the form: field name, comparison operator, then either another field name or a value. The possible comparison operators are shown in Table 7–1. Note that there are two different versions for "not equal to" (<> and !=). You must use the one that is right for your particular implementation of SQL. If you use the wrong one, your system will let you know instantly. Simply use the other.

Table 7–1 Comparison Operators	
Comparison Operator	**Meaning**
=	equal to
<	less than
>	greater than
<=	less than or equal to
>=	greater than or equal to
<> or !=	not equal to

To Use a Comparison Operator

In the following steps, Camashaly Design uses a comparison operator to list the client number, client name, amount paid, and current due for all clients whose amount paid is greater than $3,000.

- Click the View button arrow, click SQL View to return to SQL view, and then delete the current command.

- Type **SELECT [Client Number],[Client Name],[Amount Paid],[Current Due]** as the first line of the command.

- Type **FROM [Client]** as the second line.

- Type **WHERE [Amount Paid] >3000** as the third line, and then type a semicolon (;) on the fourth line.

- View the results (Figure 7–9).

- Save the query as Ch7q4. Return to the query.

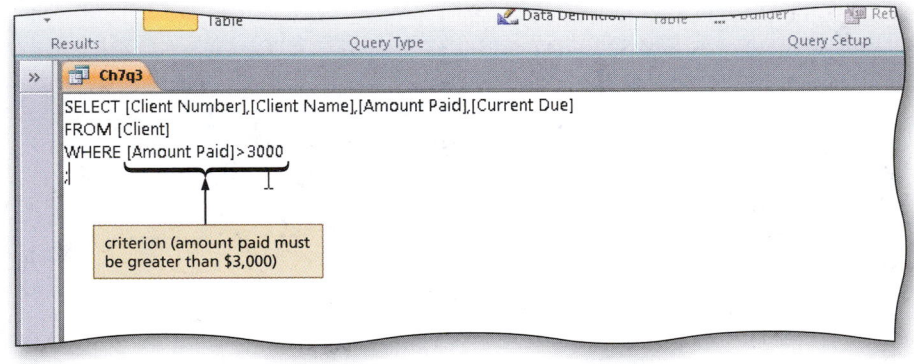

(a) Query

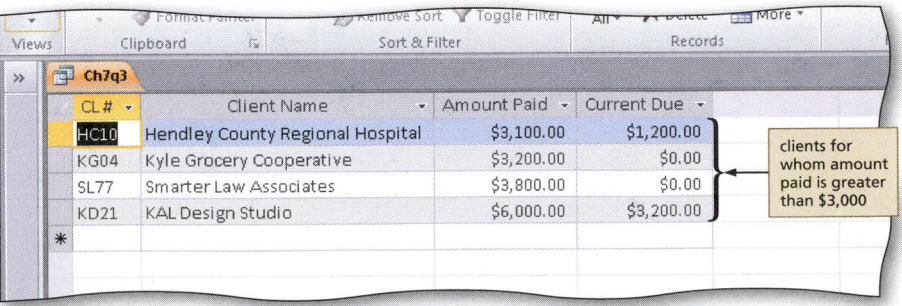

(b) Results

Figure 7–9

To Use a Criterion Involving a Text Field

If the criterion involves a text field, the value must be enclosed in single quotation marks. The following example lists the client number and name of all of Camashaly Design's clients located in Buda, that is, all clients for whom the value in the City field is Buda.

- Return to SQL view, delete the previous query, and type **SELECT [Client Number],[Client Name]** as the first line of the command.

- Type **FROM [Client]** as the second line.

- Type **WHERE [City]='Buda'** as the third line and type a semicolon (**;**) on the fourth line.

- View the results (Figure 7–10).

Q&A Could I enclose the text field value in double quotation marks instead of single quotation marks?

Yes. It is usually easier, however, to use single quotes when entering SQL commands.

- Save the query as Ch7q5. Return to the query.

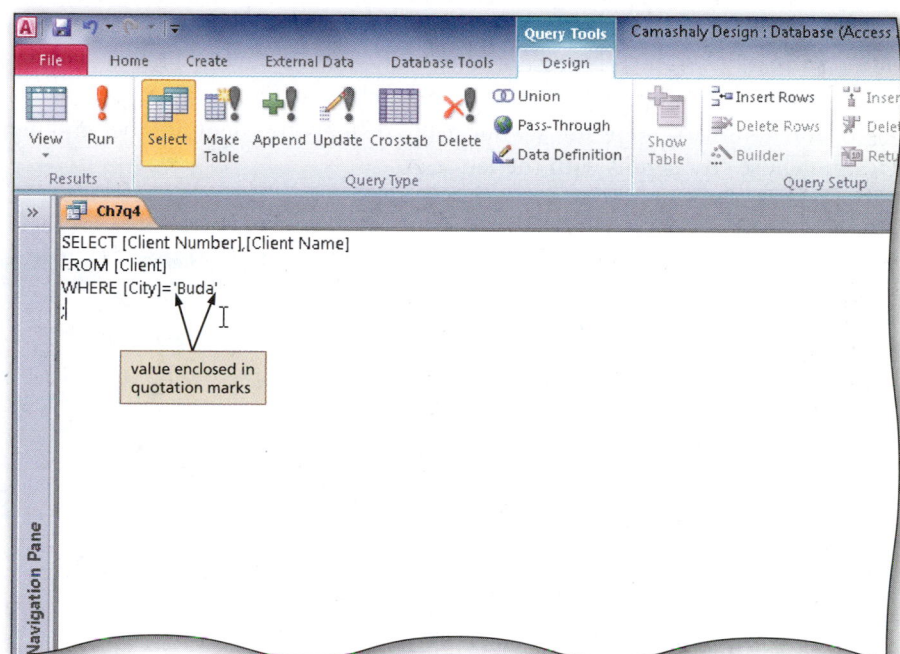

(a) Query

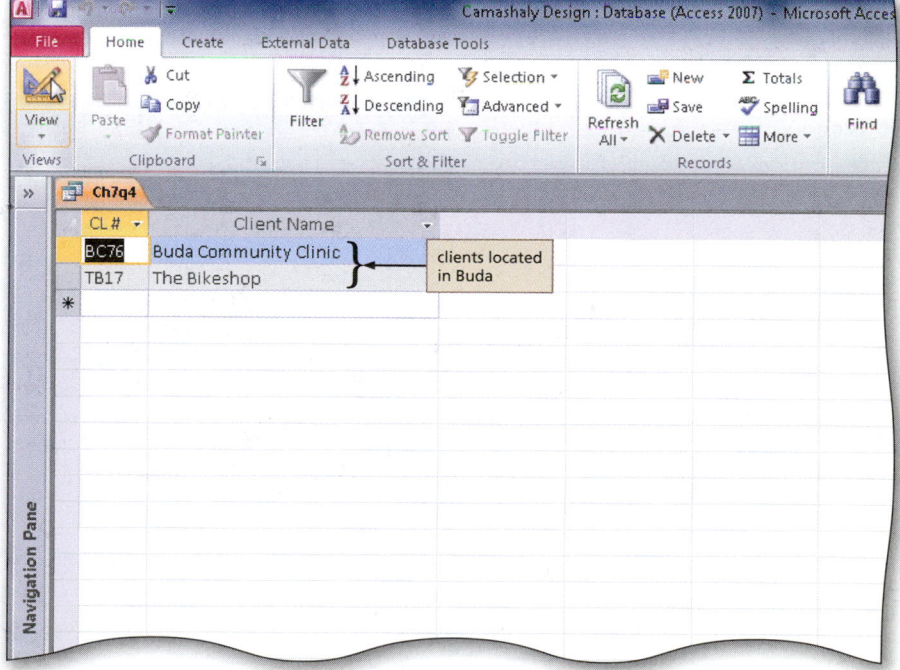

(b) Results

Figure 7–10

To Use a Wildcard

In most cases, the conditions in WHERE clauses involve exact matches, such as retrieving rows for each customer located in the city of Buda. In some cases, however, exact matches do not work. For example, you might know that the desired value contains only a certain collection of characters. In such cases, you use the LIKE operator with a wildcard symbol. Rather than testing for equality, the LIKE operator uses one or more wildcard characters to test for a pattern match. One common wildcard in Access, the **asterisk** (*), represents any collection of characters. Thus, B* represents the letter, B, followed by any string of characters. Another wildcard symbol is the question mark (?), which represents any individual character. Thus T?m represents the letter, T, followed by any single character, followed by the letter, m, such as in Tim or Tom.

The following steps use a wildcard to display the client number and name for every client of Camashaly Design whose city begins with the letter, B.

1

- Return to SQL view, delete the previous query, and type `SELECT [Client Number],[Client Name]` as the first line of the command.

- Type `FROM [Client]` as the second line.

- Type `WHERE [City] LIKE 'B*'` as the third line and type a semicolon (;) on the fourth line.

- View the results (Figure 7–11).

2

- Save the query as Ch7q6. Return to the query.

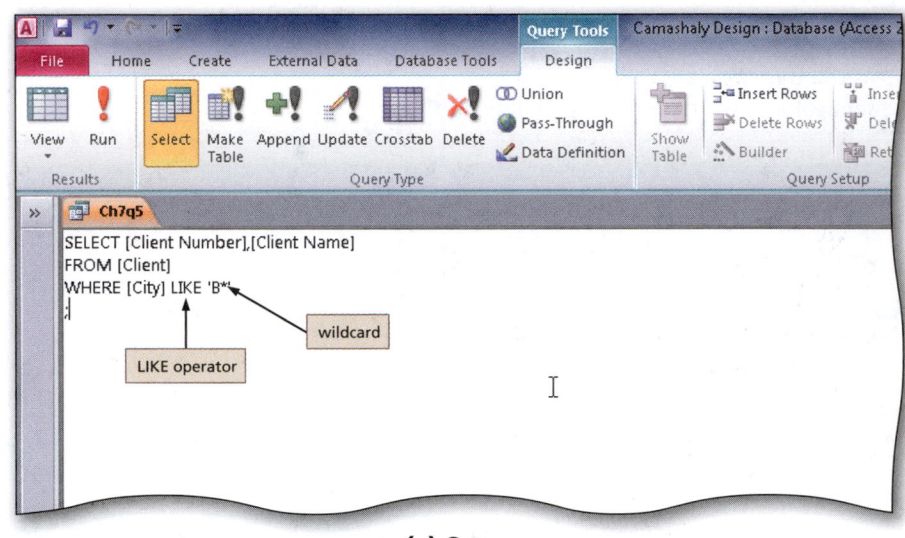

(a) Query

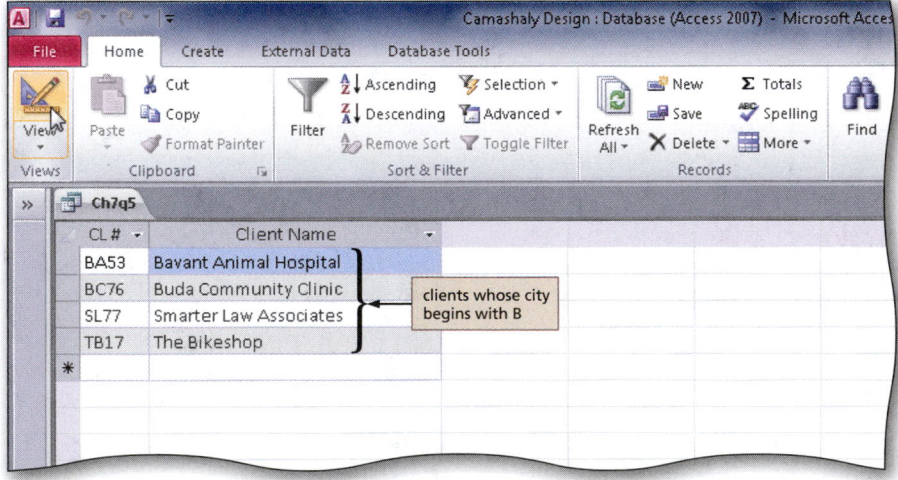

(b) Results

Figure 7–11

Break Point: If you wish to stop working through the chapter at this point, you can close Access now. You can resume the project at a later time by starting Access, opening the database called Camashaly Design, creating a new query in SQL view, and continuing to follow the steps from this location forward.

Compound Criteria

You are not limited to simple criteria. You also can use compound criteria. **Compound criteria** are formed by connecting two or more simple criteria using AND, OR, and NOT. When simple criteria are connected by the word AND, all the simple criteria must be true in order for the compound criterion to be true. When simple criteria are connected by the word OR, the compound criterion will be true whenever any of the simple criteria are true. Preceding a criterion by the word NOT reverses the truth or falsity of the original criterion. That is, if the original criterion is true, the new criterion will be false; if the original criterion is false, the new one will be true.

BTW

Wildcards
Other implementations of SQL do not use the asterisk (*) and question mark (?) wildcards. In SQL for Oracle and for SQL Server, the percent sign (%) is used as a wildcard to represent any collection of characters. In Oracle and SQL Server, the WHERE clause shown in Figure 7–11 on page AC 430 would be WHERE [City] LIKE 'B%'.

To Use a Compound Criterion Involving AND

The following steps use a compound criterion to allow Camashaly Design to impose two conditions. In particular, the steps display the number and name of those clients located in Buda who have a current due amount greater than $1,000.

- Return to SQL view, delete the previous query, and type **SELECT [Client Number],[Client Name]** as the first line of the command.

- Type **FROM [Client]** as the second line.

- Type **WHERE [City]='Buda'** as the third line.

- Type **AND [Current Due]>1000** as the fourth line and type a semicolon (**;**) on the fifth line.

- View the results (Figure 7–12).

- Save the query as Ch7q7. Return to the query.

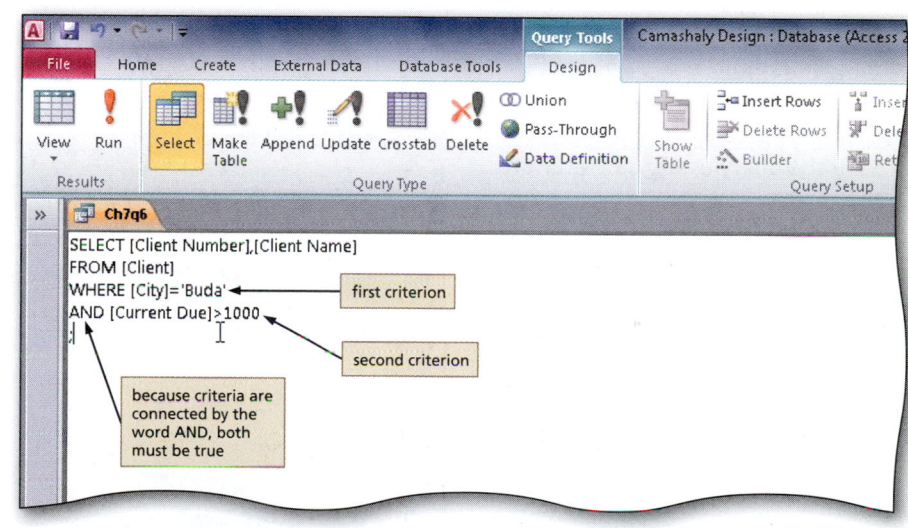

(a) Query

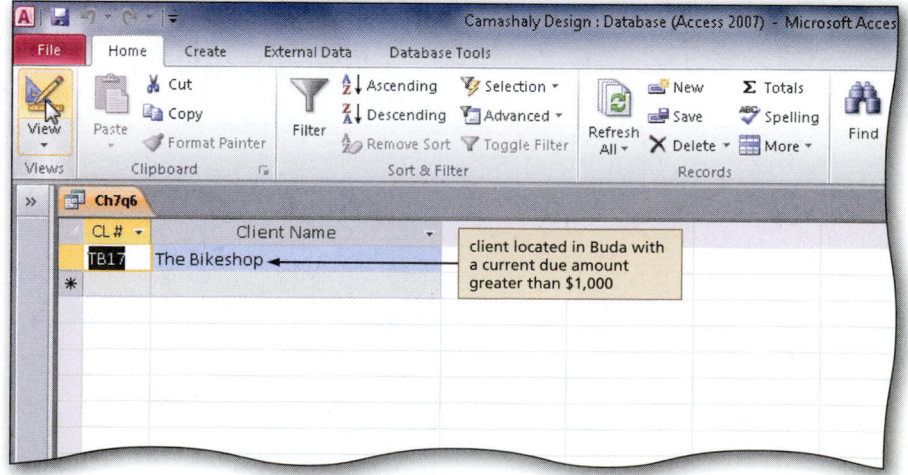

(b) Results

Figure 7–12

To Use a Compound Criterion Involving OR

The following steps use a compound criterion to enable Camashaly Design to display the client number and name of those clients located in Buda or for whom the current due amount is greater than $1,000.

1

- Return to SQL view, delete the previous query, and type **SELECT [Client Number],[Client Name],[City]** as the first line of the command.

- Type **FROM [Client]** as the second line.

- Type **WHERE [City]='Buda'** as the third line.

- Type **OR [Current Due]>1000** as the fourth line and type a semicolon (**;**) on the fifth line.

- View the results (Figure 7–13).

2

- Save the query as Ch7q8. Return to the query.

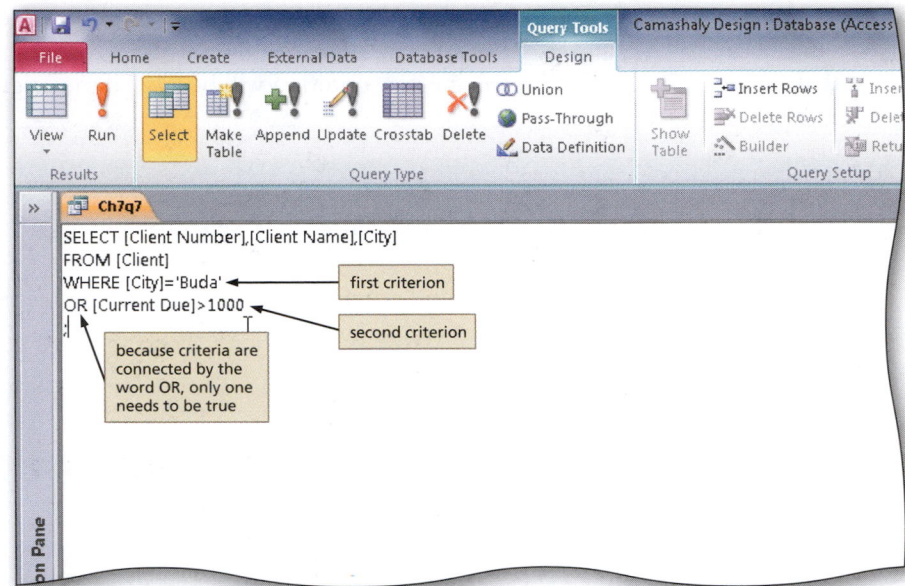

(a) Query

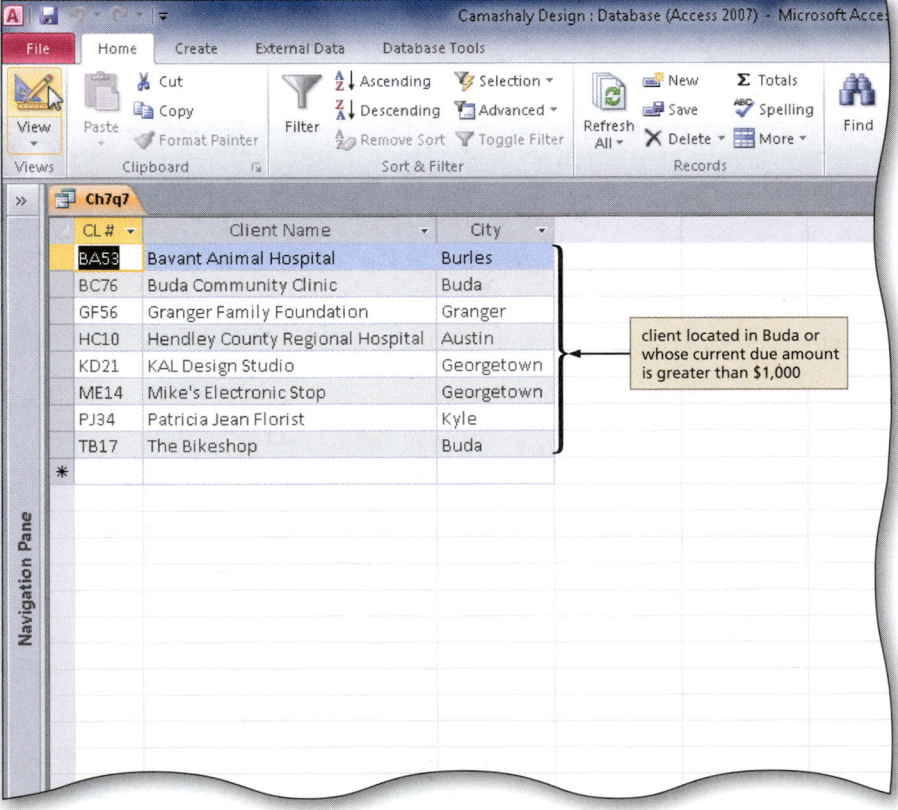

(b) Results

Figure 7–13

To Use NOT in a Criterion

To use the word NOT in a criterion, precede the criterion with the word NOT. The following steps list the numbers and names of the clients of Camashaly Design not located in Buda.

 1
- Return to SQL view and delete the previous query.

- Type **SELECT [Client Number],[Client Name],[City]** as the first line of the command.

- Type **FROM [Client]** as the second line.

- Type **WHERE NOT [City]= 'Buda'** as the third line and type a semicolon (**;**) on the fourth line.

- View the results (Figure 7–14).

 2
- Save the query as Ch7q9. Return to the query.

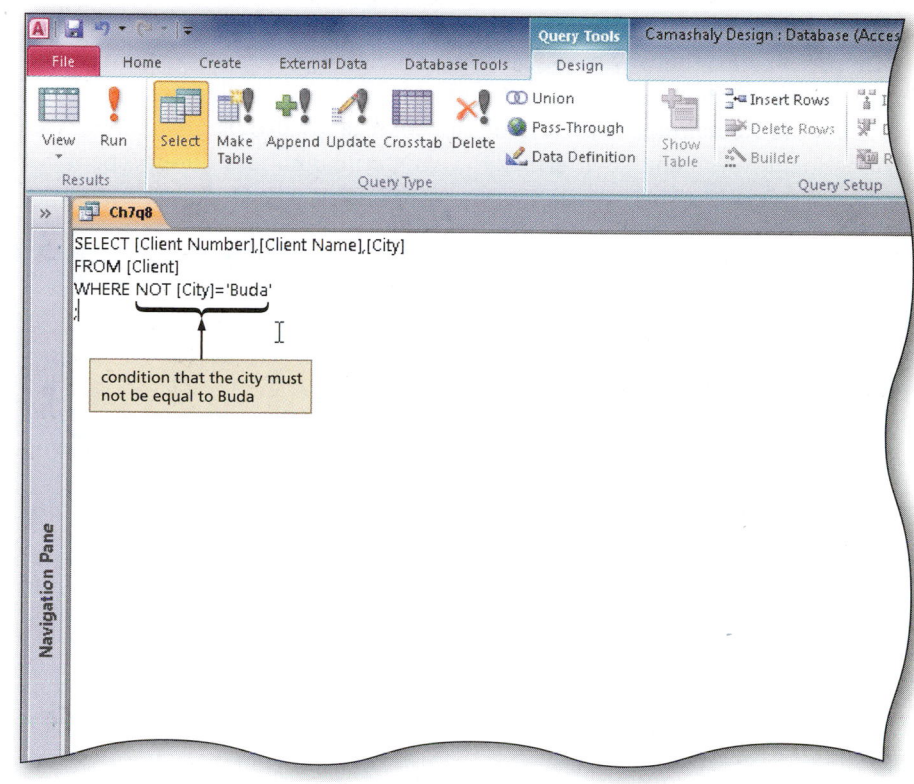

(a) Query

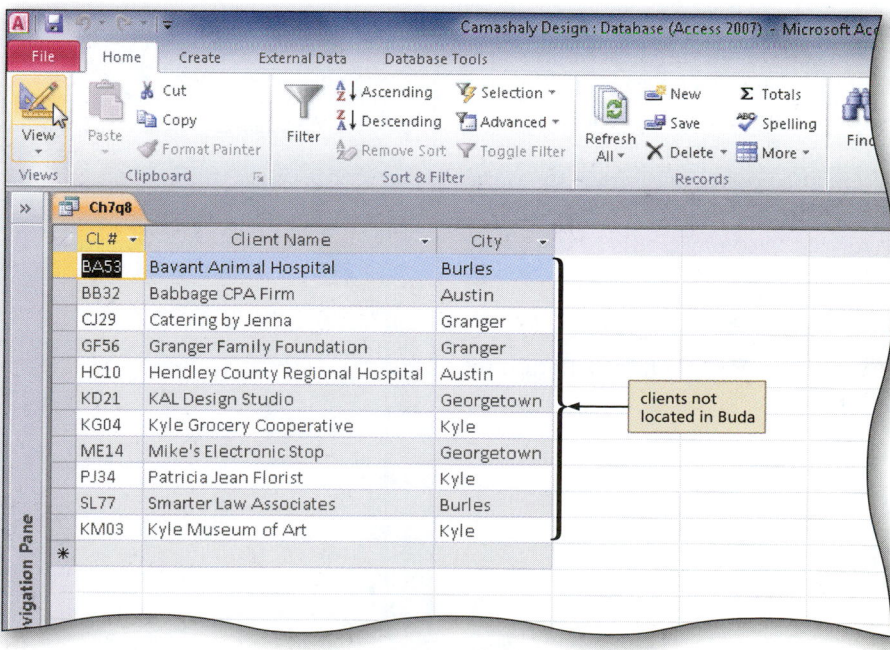

(b) Results

Figure 7–14

To Use a Computed Field

Just as with queries created in Design view, you can include fields in queries that are not in the database, but that can be computed from fields that are in the database. Such a field is called a computed or calculated field. Such computations can involve addition (+), subtraction (–), multiplication (*), or division (/). The query in the following steps computes the hours remaining, which is equal to the total hours minus the hours spent.

To indicate the contents of the new field (the computed field), you can name the field by following the computation with the word, AS, and then the name you want to assign the field. The following steps calculate the hours remaining for each course offered by subtracting the hours spent from the total hours and then assigning the name Hours Remaining to the calculation. The steps also list the Client Number, Course Number, Total Hours, and Hours Spent for all course offerings for which the number of hours spent is greater than 0.

- Return to SQL view and delete the previous query.

- Type **SELECT [Client Number],[Course Number], [Total Hours],[Hours Spent],[Total Hours]- [Hours Spent] AS [Hours Remaining]** as the first line of the command.

- Type **FROM [Course Offerings]** as the second line.

- Type **WHERE [Hours Spent]>0** as the third line and type a semicolon on the fourth line.

- View the results (Figure 7–15).

Q&A

The new name, Hours Remaining, is partially hidden. What should I do to see the entire name?

You could drag the right boundary of the field selector (the box containing Hours Remaining) to enlarge the field to the desired size. You also could double-click the right boundary of the field selector to resize the column so that it best fits the data.

2

- Save the query as Ch7q10. Return to the query.

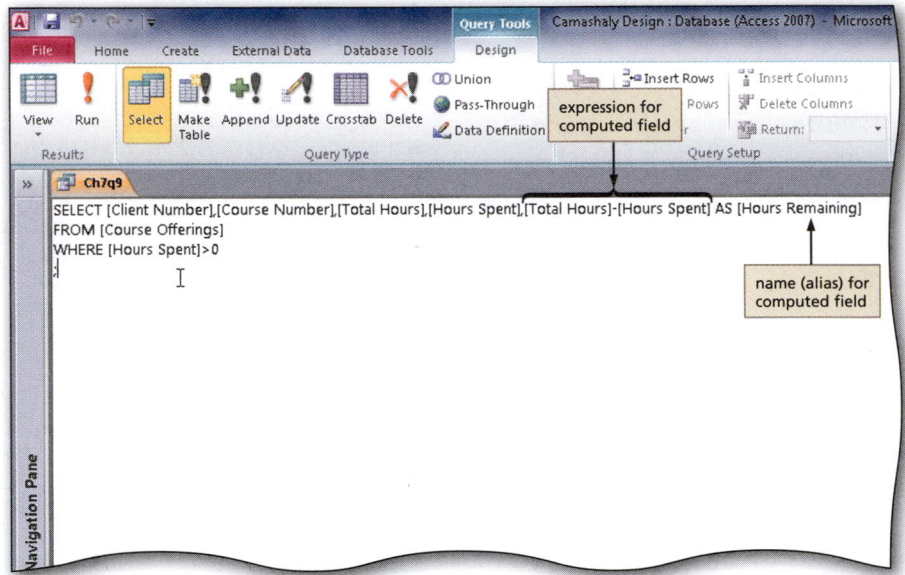

(a) Query

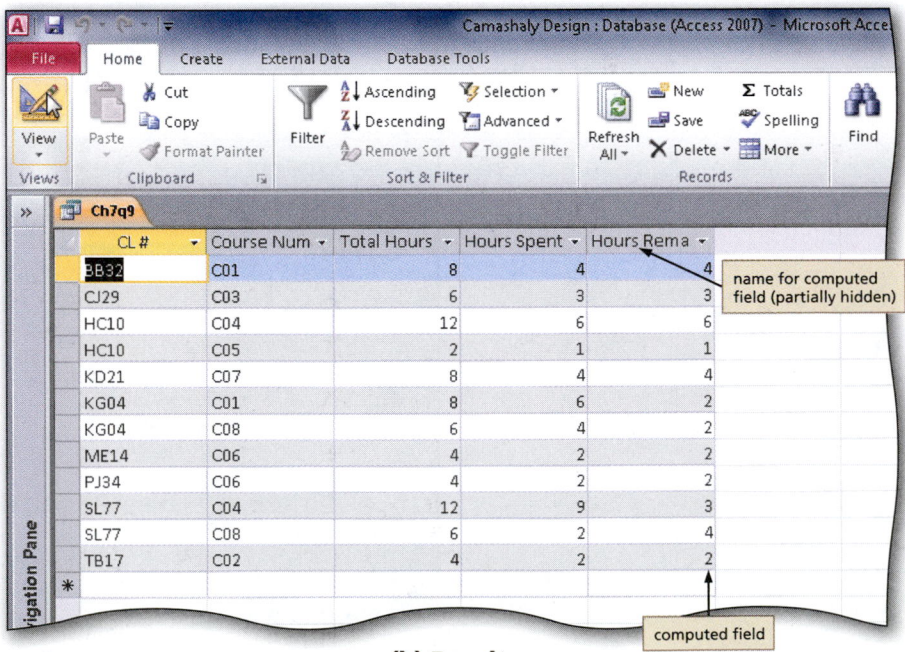

(b) Results

Figure 7–15

Sorting

Sorting in SQL follows the same principles as when using Design view to specify sorted query results, employing a sort key as the field on which data is to be sorted. SQL uses major and minor sort keys when sorting on multiple fields. By following a sort key with the word DESC with no comma in between, you can specify descending sort order. If you do not specify DESC, the data will be sorted in ascending order.

To sort the output, you include an **ORDER BY clause**, which consists of the words ORDER BY followed by the sort key. If there are two sort keys, the major sort key is listed first. Queries that you construct in Design view require that the major sort key is to the left of the minor sort key in the list of fields to be included. In SQL, there is no such restriction. The fields to be included in the query are in the SELECT clause, and the fields to be used for sorting are in the ORDER BY clause. The two clauses are totally independent.

Determine sort order.

Examine the query or request to see if it contains words such as order or sort that would imply that the order of the query results is important. If so, you need to sort the query.

- **Determine whether data is to be sorted.** Examine the requirements for the query looking for words like sorted by, ordered by, arranged by, and so on.

- **Determine sort keys.** Look for the fields that follow sorted by, ordered by, or any other words that signify sorting. If the requirements for the query include the phrase, ordered by client name, then Client Name is a sort key.

- **If there is more than one sort key, determine which one will be the major sort key and which will be the minor sort key.** Look for words that indicate which field is more important. For example, if the requirements indicate that the results are to be ordered by amount paid within analyst number, Business Analyst Number is the more important sort key.

Plan Ahead

To Sort the Results on a Single Field

The following steps list the client number, name, amount paid, current due, and analyst number for all clients. Camashaly Design wants this data to be sorted by client name.

1

- Return to SQL view and delete the previous query.

- Type `SELECT [Client Number],[Client Name], [Amount Paid],[Current Due],[Business Analyst Number]` as the first line of the command.

- Type `FROM [Client]` as the second line.

- Type `ORDER BY [Client Name]` as the third line and type a semicolon (`;`) on the fourth line.

- View the results (Figure 7–16).

2

- Save the query as Ch7q11. Return to the query.

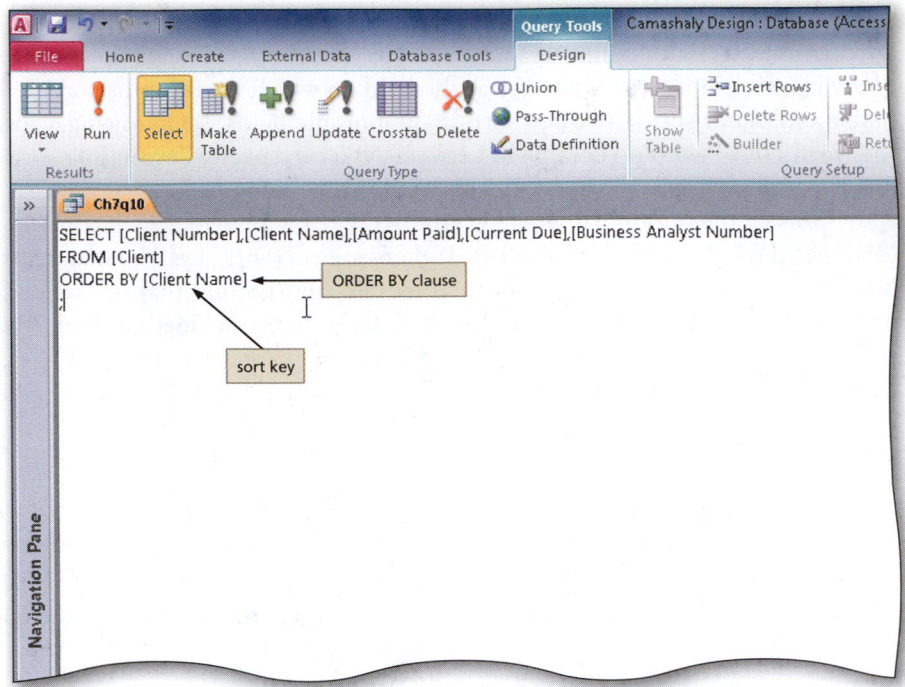

(a) Query

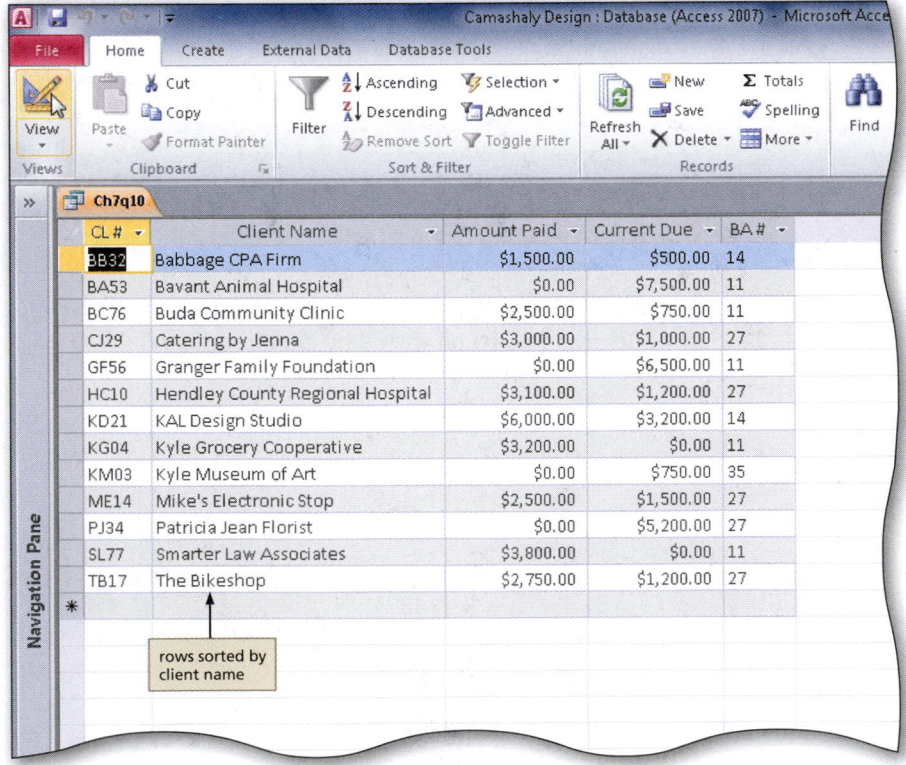

(b) Results

Figure 7–16

To Sort the Results on Multiple Fields

The following steps list the client number, name, amount paid, current due, and analyst number for all clients. This time, Camashaly wants the data to be sorted by amount paid within analyst number. That is, the data is to be sorted by analyst number. In addition, within the group of clients that have the same analyst number, the data is to be sorted further by amount paid. This means that the Business Analyst Number field is the major (primary) sort key and the Amount Paid field is the minor (secondary) sort key.

1

- Return to SQL view and delete the previous query.

- Type `SELECT [Client Number],[Client Name],[Amount Paid],[Current Due],[Business Analyst Number]` as the first line of the command.

- Type `FROM [Client]` as the second line.

- Type `ORDER BY [Business Analyst Number],[Amount Paid]` as the third line and type a semicolon (;) on the fourth line.

- View the results (Figure 7–17).

Experiment

- Try reversing the order of the sort keys to see the effect. Also, try to specify descending order for one or both of the sort keys. In each case, view the results to see the effect of your choice. When finished, return to the original sorting order for both fields.

2

- Save the query as Ch7q12. Return to the query.

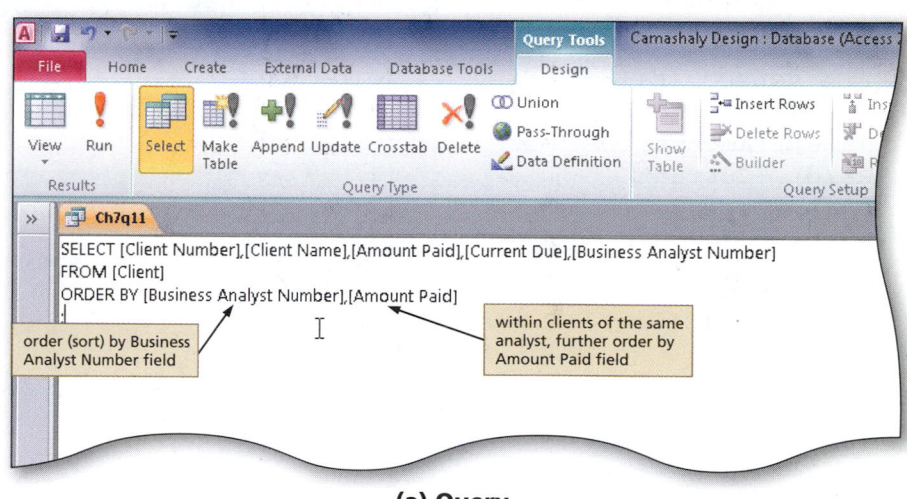

(a) Query

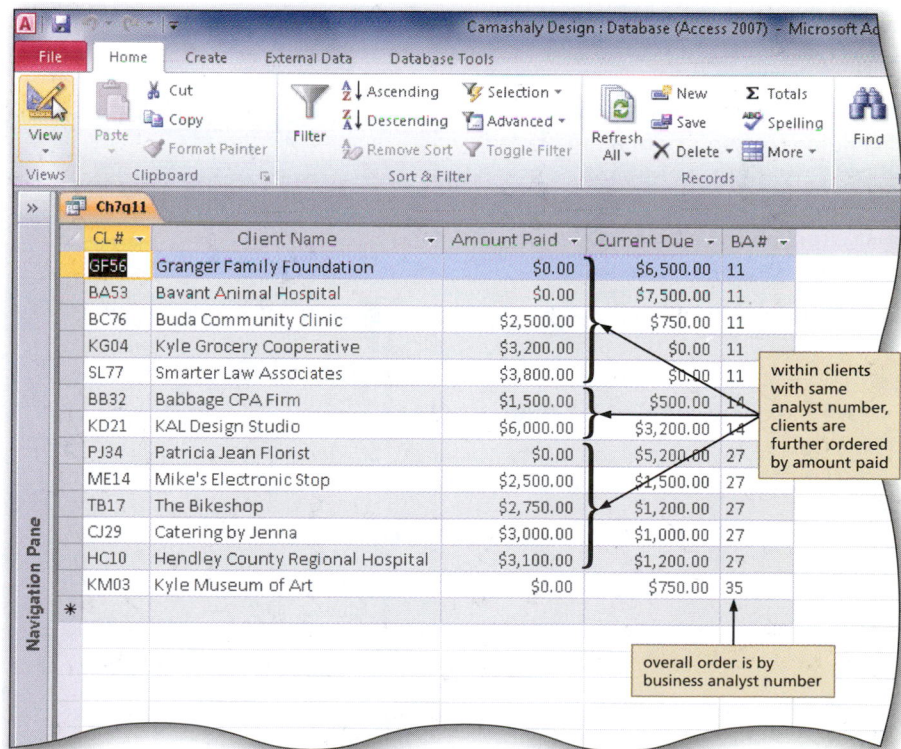

(b) Results

Figure 7–17

To Sort the Results in Descending Order

To sort in descending order, you follow the name of the sort key with the DESC operator. The following steps list the client number, name, amount paid, current due, and analyst number for all clients. Camashaly wants the data to be sorted by descending current due within analyst number. That is, within the clients having the same analyst number, the data is to be sorted further by current due in descending order.

1

- Return to SQL view and delete the previous query.

- Type **SELECT [Client Number],[Client Name],[Amount Paid],[Current Due],[Business Analyst Number]** as the first line of the command.

- Type **FROM [Client]** as the second line.

- Type **ORDER BY [Business Analyst Number],[Current Due] DESC** as the third line and type a semicolon (**;**) on the fourth line.

Q&A

Do I need a comma between [Current Due] and DESC?

No. In fact, you must not use a comma. If you did, SQL would assume that you want a field called DESC. Without the comma, SQL knows that the DESC indicates that the sort on the [Current Due] field is to be in descending order.

- View the results (Figure 7–18).

2

- Save the query as Ch7q13. Return to the query.

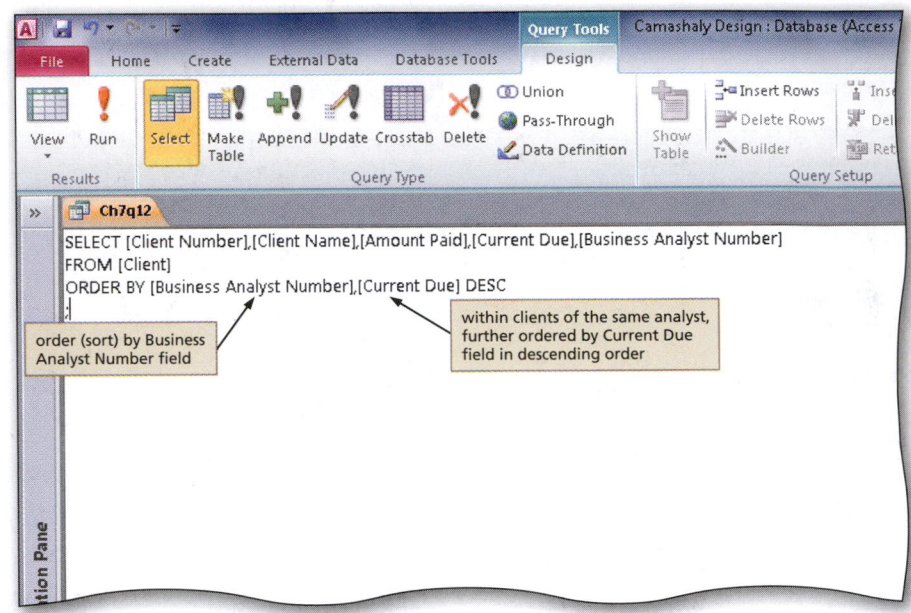

(a) Query

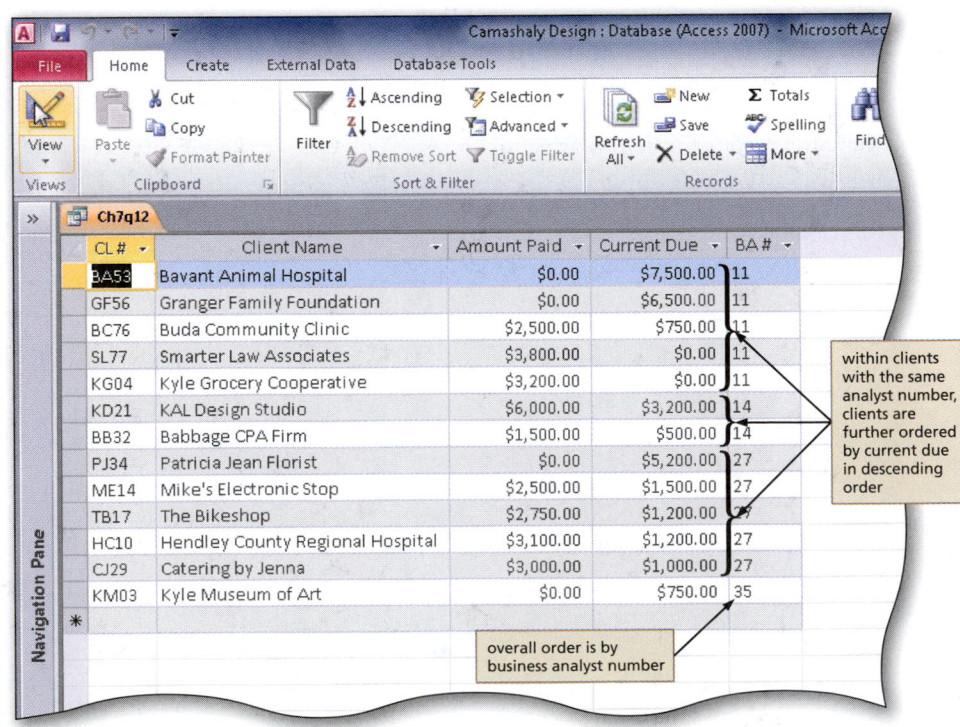

(b) Results

Figure 7–18

To Omit Duplicates When Sorting

When you sort data, duplicates normally are included. The query in Figure 7–19 sorts the client numbers in the Course Offerings table. Because any client can be offered many courses at a time, client numbers can be included more than once. Camashaly does not find this useful and would like to eliminate these duplicate client numbers.

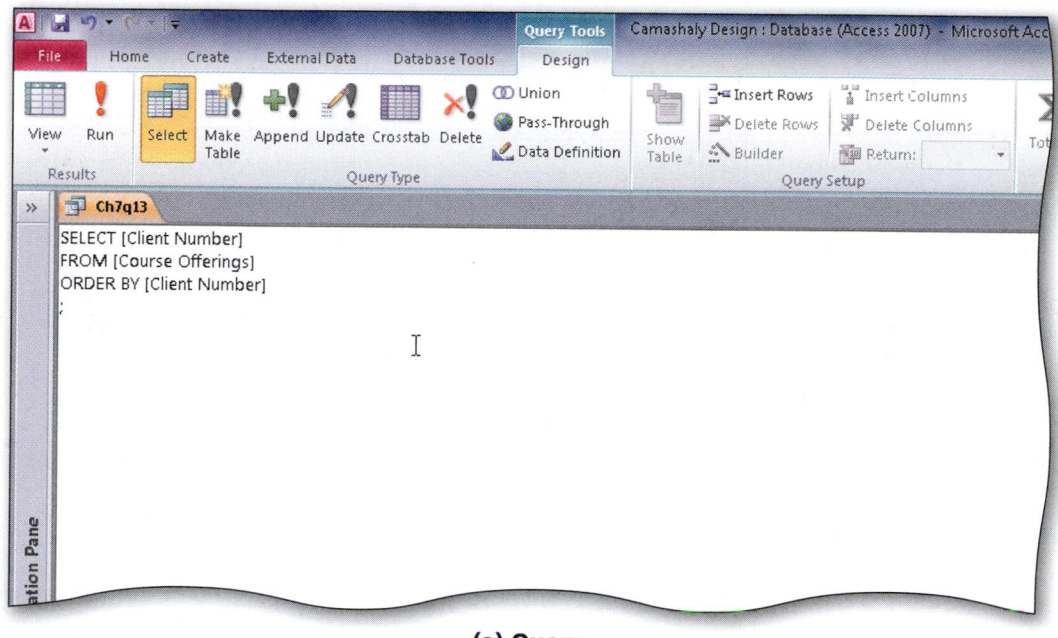

(a) Query

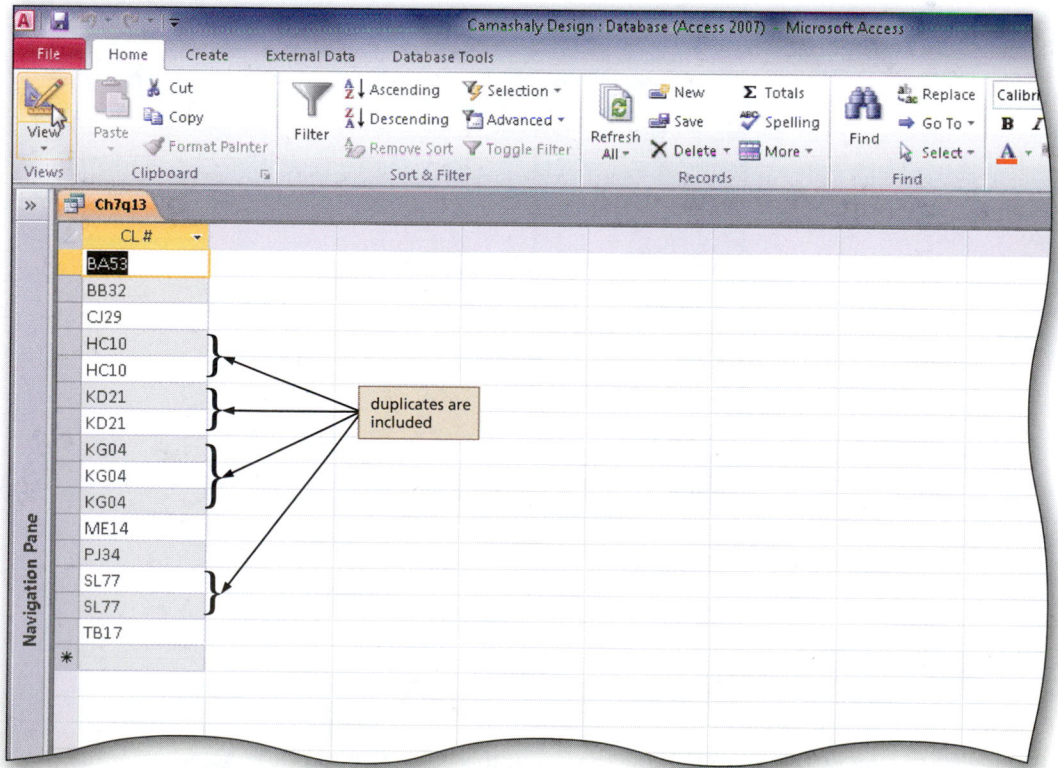

(b) Results

Figure 7–19

The **DISTINCT operator** eliminates duplicate values in the results of a query. To use the operator, you follow the word DISTINCT with the field name in parentheses. The following steps display the client numbers in the Course Offerings table in client number order, but with any duplicates removed.

1

- Return to SQL view and delete the previous query.

- Type **SELECT DISTINCT ([Client Number])** as the first line of the command.

- Type **FROM [Course Offerings]** as the second line.

- Type **ORDER BY [Client Number]** as the third line and type a semicolon (**;**) on the fourth line.

- View the results (Figure 7–20).

2

- Save the query as Ch7q14. Return to the query.

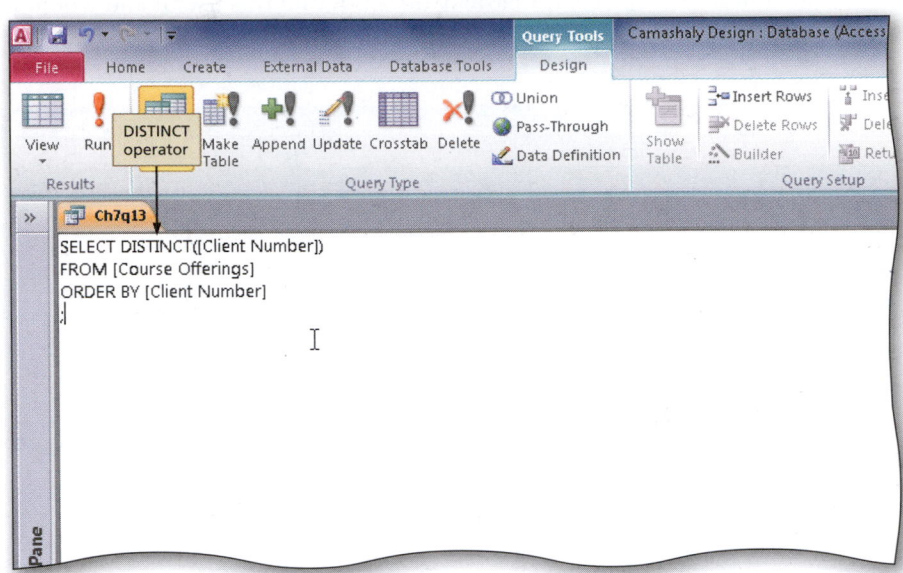

(a) Query

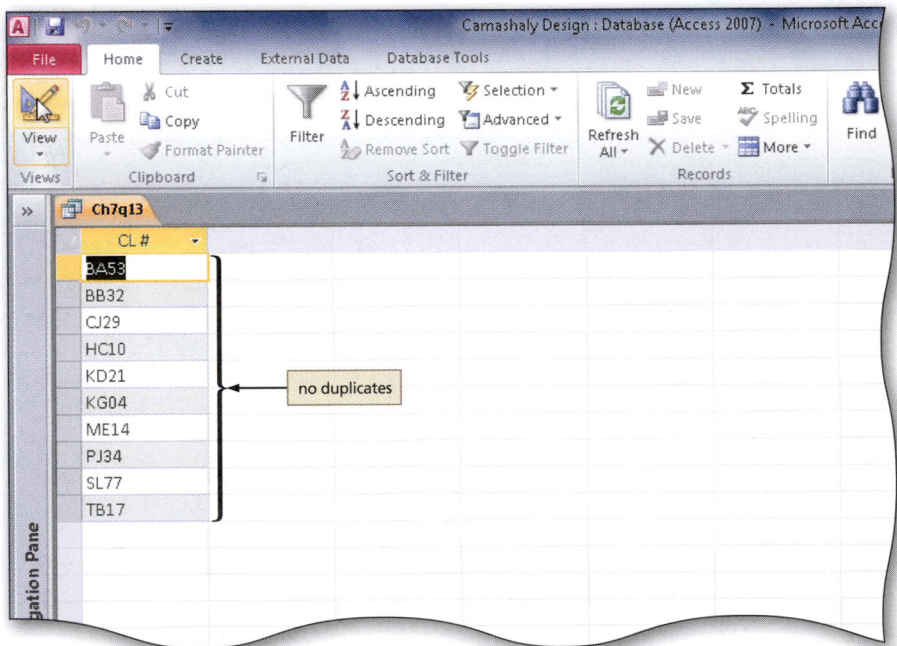

(b) Results

Figure 7–20

Break Point: If you wish to stop working through the chapter at this point, you can close Access now. You can resume the project at a later time by starting Access, opening the database called Camashaly Design, creating a new query in SQL view, and continuing to follow the steps from this location forward.

To Use a Built-In Function

SQL has built-in functions, also called aggregate functions, to perform various calculations. Similar to the functions you learned about in Chapter 2, these functions in SQL are called COUNT, SUM, AVG, MAX, and MIN, respectively.

Camashaly uses the following steps to determine the number of clients assigned to analyst number 11 by using the COUNT function with an asterisk (*).

1

- Return to SQL view and delete the previous query.

- Type **SELECT COUNT(*)** as the first line of the command.

- Type **FROM [Client]** as the second line.

- Type **WHERE [Business Analyst Number]='11'** as the third line and type a semicolon (;) on the fourth line.

- View the results (Figure 7–21).

Q&A

Why does Expr1000 appear in the column heading of the results?

Because the column is a computed column, it does not have a name. Access assigns a generic expression name. You can add a name for the column by including the AS clause in the query, and it is good practice to do so.

2

- Save the query as Ch7q15. Return to the query.

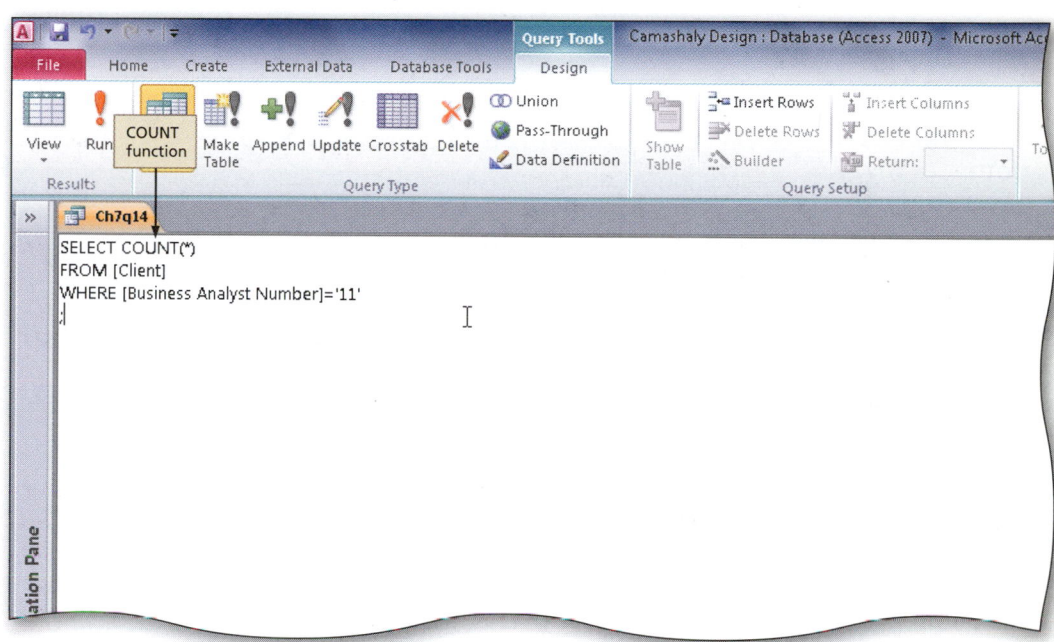

(a) Query

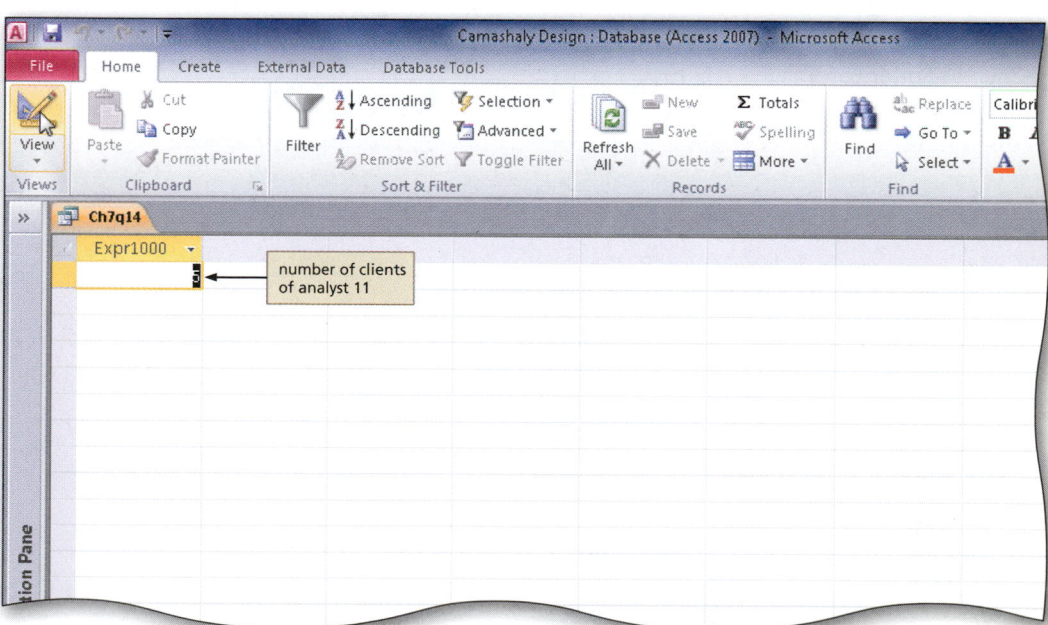

(b) Results

Figure 7–21

To Assign a Name to the Results of a Function

Camashaly Design would prefer to have a more meaningful name than Expr1000 for the results of counting client numbers. Fortunately, just as you can assign a name to a calculation that includes two fields, you can assign a name to the results of a function. To do so, follow the expression for the function with the word AS and then the name to be assigned to the result. The following steps assign the name, Client Count, to the expression in the previous query.

- Return to SQL view and delete the previous query.

- Type **SELECT COUNT(*) AS [Client Count]** as the first line of the command.

- Type **FROM [Client]** as the second line.

- Type **WHERE [Business Analyst Number]='11'** as the third line and type a semicolon (;) on the fourth line.

- View the results (Figure 7–22).

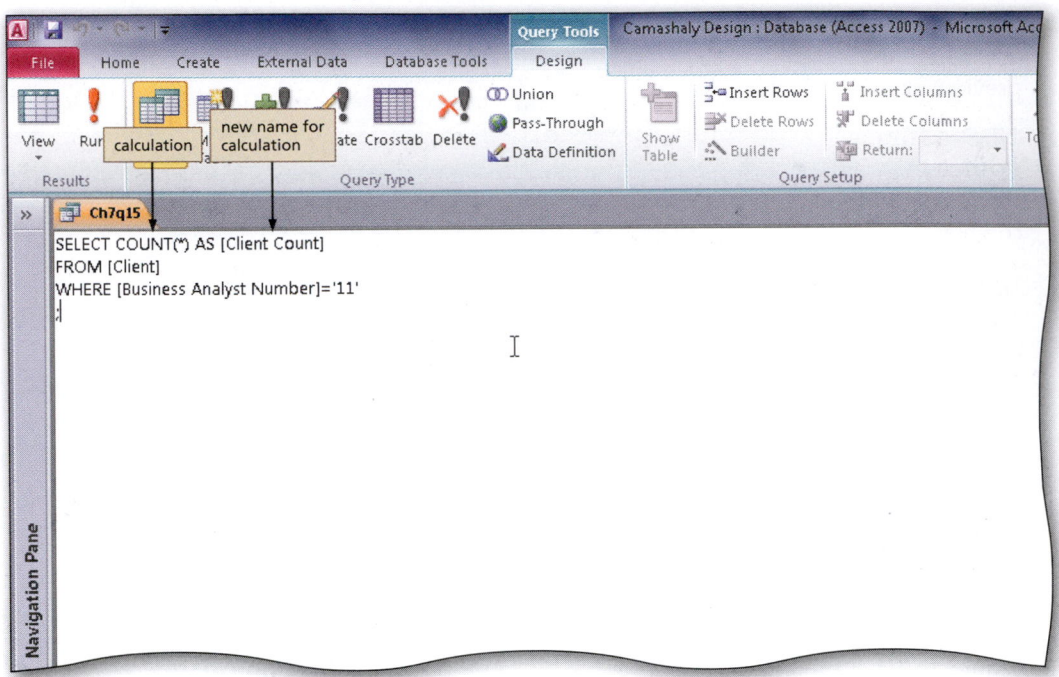

(a) Query

- Save the query as Ch7q16. Return to the query.

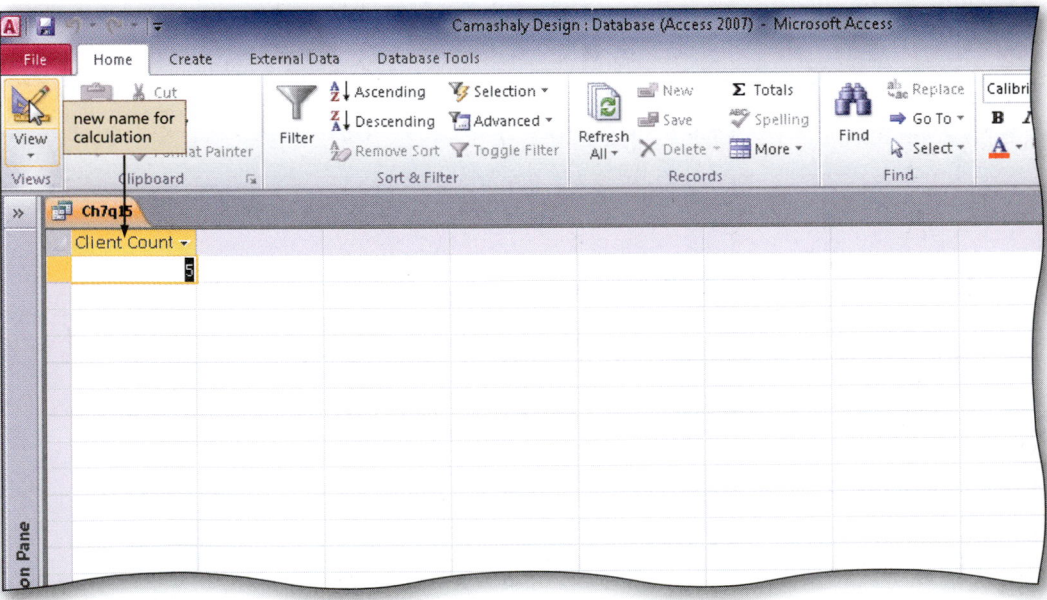

(b) Results

Figure 7–22

To Use Multiple Functions in the Same Command

There are only two differences between COUNT and SUM, other than the obvious fact that they are computing different statistics. First, in the case of SUM, you must specify the field for which you want a total, instead of an asterisk (*); second, the field must be numeric. You could not calculate a sum of names or addresses, for example. The following steps use both the COUNT and SUM functions to count the number of clients and calculate the sum, or total, of their amount paid amounts.

- Return to SQL view and delete the previous query.

- Type **SELECT COUNT(*) AS [Client Count], SUM([Amount Paid]) AS [Sum Paid]** as the first line of the command.

- Type **FROM [Client]** as the second line and type a semicolon (**;**) on the third line.

- View the results (Figure 7–23).

🔍 Experiment

- Try using the other functions in place of SUM. In each case, view the results to see the effect of your choice. When finished, once again select SUM.

2

- Save the query as Ch7q17. Return to the query.

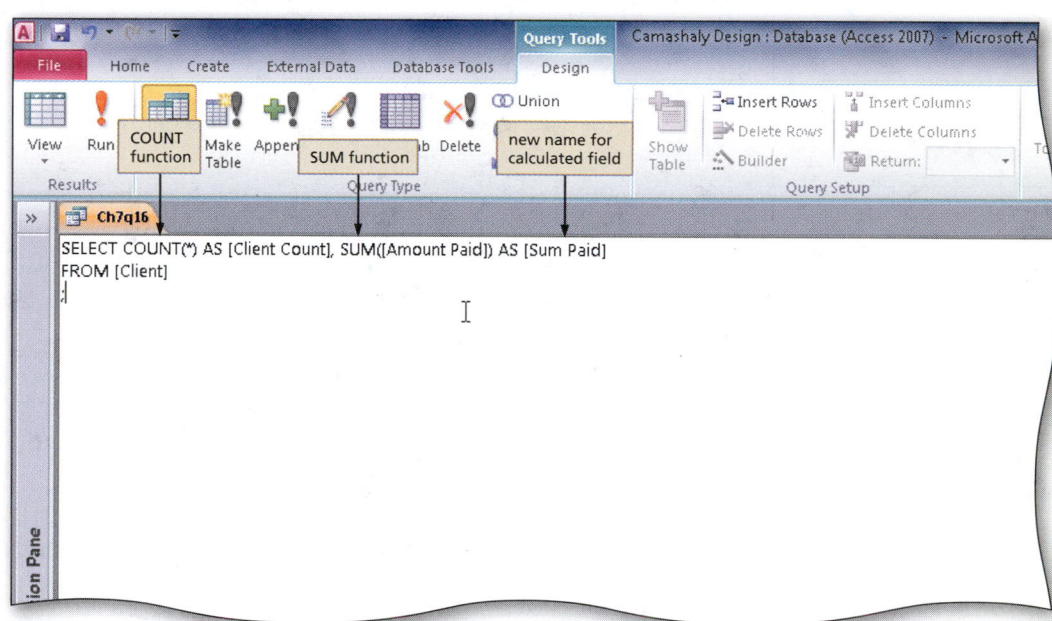

(a) Query

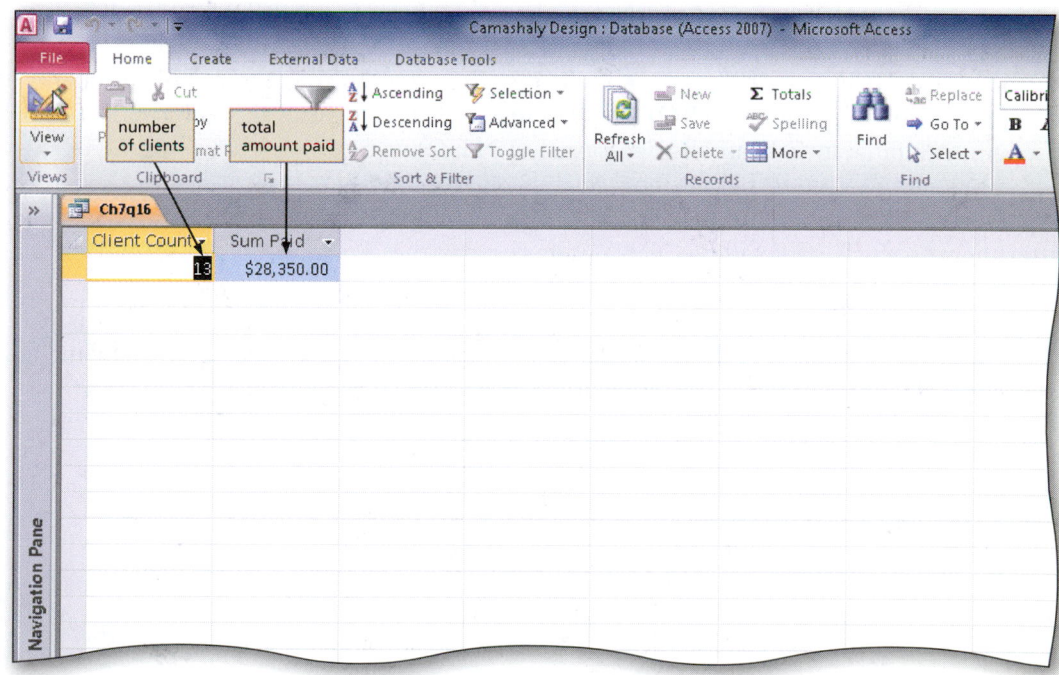

(b) Results

Figure 7–23

The use of AVG, MAX, and MIN is similar to SUM. The only difference is that a different statistic is calculated.

Grouping

Recall that grouping means creating groups of records that share some common characteristic. When you group rows, any calculations indicated in the SELECT command are performed for the entire group.

Plan Ahead

Determine grouping.
Examine the query or request to determine whether records should be organized by some common characteristic.

- **Determine whether data is to be grouped in some fashion.** Examine the requirements for the query to see if they contain individual rows or information about groups of rows.

- **Determine the field or fields on which grouping is to take place.** By which field is the data to be grouped? Look to see if the requirements indicate a field along with several group calculations.

- **Determine which fields or calculations are appropriate to display.** When rows are grouped, one line of output is produced for each group. The only output that can appear are statistics that are calculated for the group or fields whose values are the same for all rows in a group. For example, it would make sense to display the analyst number, because all the clients in the group have the same analyst number. It would not make sense to display the client number, because the client number will vary from one row in a group to another. SQL could not determine which client number to display for the group.

To Use Grouping

Camashaly Design wants to calculate the totals of the Amount Paid field, called Total Paid, and the Current Due field, called Total Due, for the clients of each analyst. To calculate the totals, the command will include the calculations, SUM([Amount Paid]) and SUM([Current Due]). To get totals for the clients of each analyst, the command also will include a **GROUP BY clause**, which consists of the words, GROUP BY, followed by the field used for grouping, in this case, Business Analyst Number.

Including GROUP BY Business Analyst Number will cause the clients for each analyst to be grouped together; that is, all clients with the same analyst number will form a group. Any statistics, such as totals, appearing after the word SELECT will be calculated for each of these groups. Using GROUP BY does not mean that the information will be sorted.

The following steps use the GROUP BY clause to produce the results Camashaly wants. The steps also rename the total amount paid as Sum Paid and the total current due as Sum Due by including appropriate AS clauses; finally, the steps sort the records by business analyst number.

1
- Return to SQL view and delete the previous query.

- Type `SELECT [Business Analyst Number], SUM([Amount Paid]) AS [Sum Paid], SUM([Current Due]) AS [Sum Due]` as the first line of the command.

- Type `FROM [Client]` as the second line.

- Type `GROUP BY [Business Analyst Number]` as the third line.

- Type `ORDER BY [Business Analyst Number]` as the fourth line and type a semicolon (;) on the fifth line.

- View the results (Figure 7–24).

2
- Save the query as Ch7q18. Return to the query.

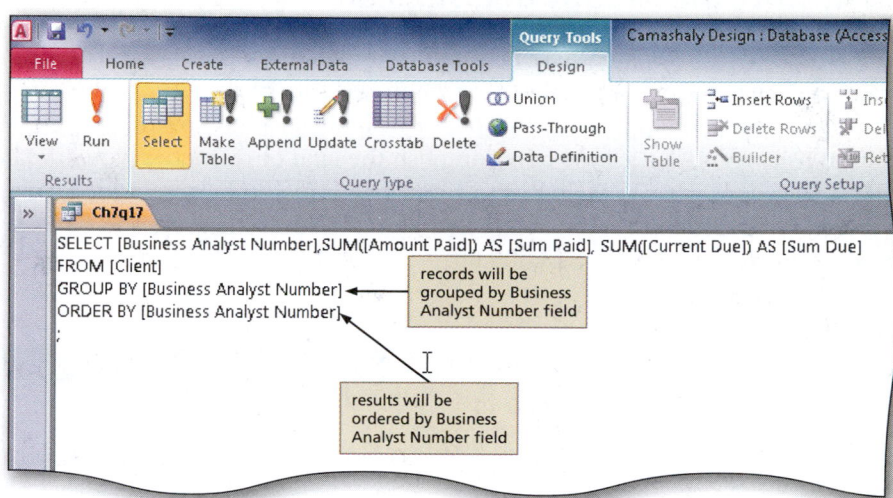

(a) Query

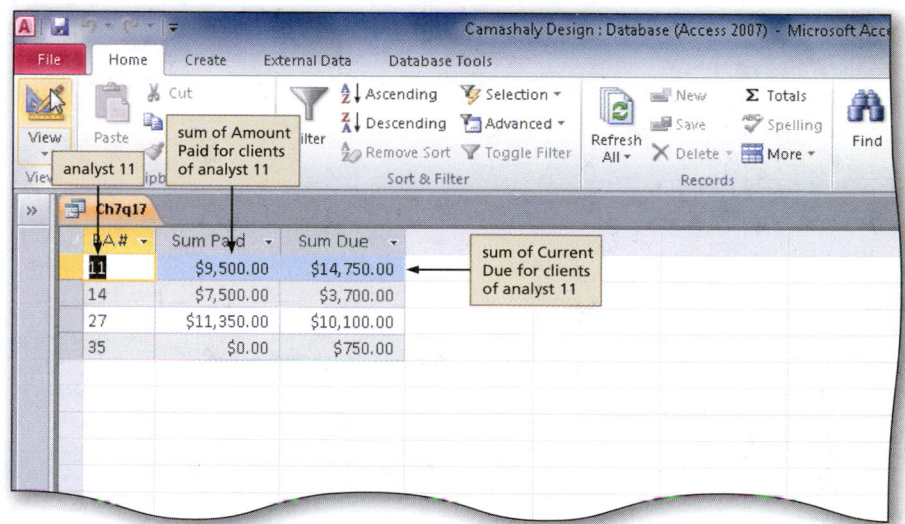

(b) Results

Figure 7–24

Grouping Requirements

When rows are grouped, one line of output is produced for each group. The only output that can be displayed are statistics that are calculated for the group or columns whose values are the same for all rows in a group. When rows are grouped by business analyst number, it is appropriate to display the business analyst number, because the number in one row in a group must be the same as the number in any other row in the group. It is appropriate to display the sum of the Amount Paid and Current Due fields because they are statistics calculated for the group. It would not be appropriate to display a client number, however, because the client number varies on the rows in a group; the analyst is associated with many clients. SQL would not be able to determine which client number to display for the group. SQL will display an error message if you attempt to display a field that is not appropriate, such as the client number.

To Restrict the Groups that Appear

In some cases, Camashaly Design may only want to display certain groups. For example, management may want to display only those analysts for whom the sum of the current due amounts are greater than $10,000. This restriction does not apply to individual rows, but instead to groups. Because WHERE applies only to rows, you cannot use a WHERE clause to accomplish the kind of restriction you have here. Fortunately, SQL provides a clause that is to groups what WHERE is to rows. The HAVING clause, which consists of the word HAVING followed by a criterion, is used in the following steps, which restrict the groups to be included to those on which the sum of the current due is greater than $10,000.00.

1

- Return to SQL view.

- Click the beginning of the fourth line (ORDER BY [Business Analyst Number]) and press the ENTER key to insert a new blank line.

- Click the beginning of the new blank line, and then type **HAVING SUM([Current Due])>10000** as the new fourth line.

- View the results (Figure 7–25).

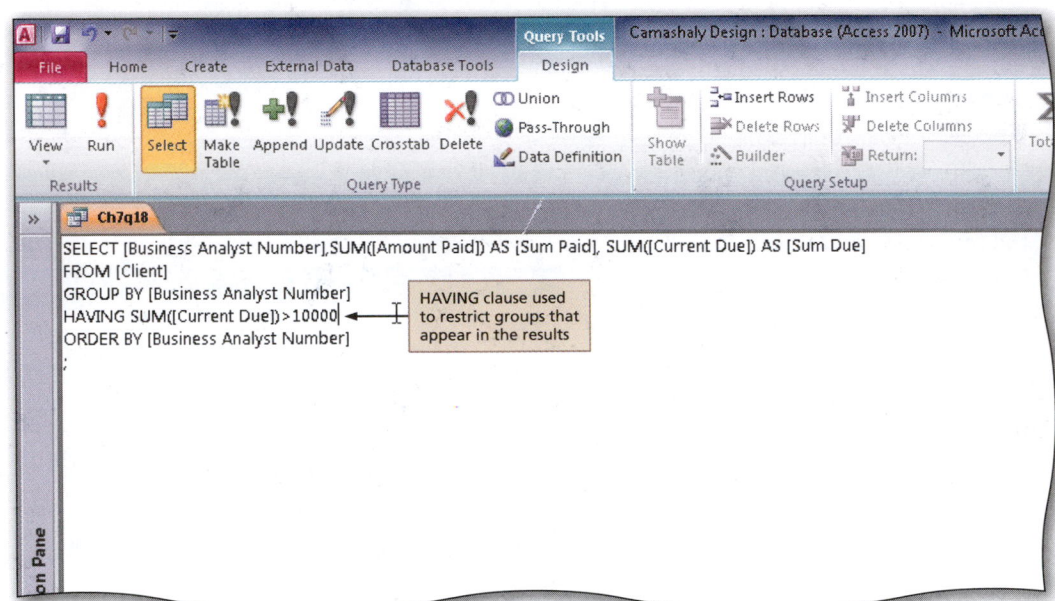

(a) Query

2

- Save the query as Ch7q19. Return to the query.

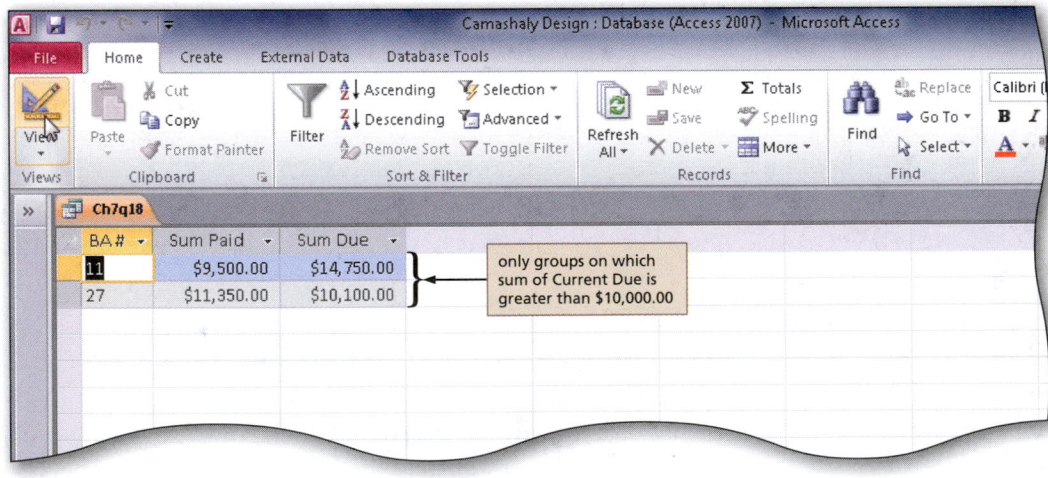

(b) Results

Figure 7–25

Break Point: If you wish to stop working through the chapter at this point, you can close Access now. You can resume the project at a later time by starting Access, opening the database called Camashaly Design, creating a new query in SQL view, and continuing to follow the steps from this location forward.

Joining Tables

Many queries require data from more than one table. Just as with creating queries in Design view, SQL should provide a way to **join** tables, that is, to find rows in two tables that have identical values in matching fields. In SQL, this is accomplished through appropriate criteria following the word WHERE.

If you want to list the client number, name, analyst number, first name of the analyst, and last name of the analyst for all clients, you need data from both the Client and Business Analyst tables. The Business Analyst Number field is in both tables, the Client Number field is only in the Client table, and the First Name and Last Name fields are only in the Business Analyst Table. You need to access both tables in your SQL query, as follows:

1. In the SELECT clause, you indicate all fields you want to appear.
2. In the FROM clause, you list all tables involved in the query.
3. In the WHERE clause, you give the criterion that will restrict the data to be retrieved to only those rows included in both of the two tables, that is, to the rows that have common values in matching fields.

BTW

Inner Joins
A join that compares the tables in the FROM clause and lists only those rows that satisfy the condition in the WHERE clause is called an inner join. SQL has an INNER JOIN clause. You could replace the FROM and WHERE clauses in the query shown in Figure 7–26a on page AC 448 with FROM Client INNER JOIN [Business Analyst] ON [Client].[Business Analyst Number]=[Business Analyst]. [Business Analyst Number] to get the same results as shown in Figure 7–26b.

Qualifying Fields

There is a problem in indicating the matching fields. The matching fields are both called Business Analyst Number. There is a field in the Client table called Business Analyst Number, as well as a field in the Business Analyst Table called Business Analyst Number. In this case, if you only enter Business Analyst Number, it will not be clear which table you mean. It is necessary to **qualify** Business Analyst Number, that is, to specify to which field in which table you are referring. You do this by preceding the name of the field with the name of the table, followed by a period. The Business Analyst Number field in the Client table, for example, is [Client].[Business Analyst Number].

Whenever there is potential ambiguity, you must qualify the fields involved. It is permissible to qualify other fields as well, even if there is no confusion. For example, instead of [Client Name], you could have typed [Client].[Client Name] to indicate the Client Name field in the Client table. Some people prefer to qualify all fields, and this is not a bad approach. In this text, you only will qualify fields when it is necessary to do so.

To Rename a Table

In Chapter 1, you assigned the name Business Analyst Table to the Business Analyst table. In this chapter, you will change the name to Business Analyst to make it easier to enter SQL commands. The following steps change the name.

1 Open the Navigation Pane and right-click the Business Analyst Table.

2 Click Rename on the shortcut menu.

3 Delete the current entry, type **Business Analyst** as the new table name, and press the ENTER key.

4 Close the Navigation Pane.

To Join Tables

Camashaly Design wants to list the client number, client name, analyst number, first name of the analyst, and last name of the analyst for all clients. Because the data comes from two tables, the following steps create a query to join the tables.

1

- Return to SQL view and delete the previous query.

- Type **SELECT [Client Number],[Client Name],[Client].[Business Analyst Number],[First Name],[Last Name]** as the first line of the command.

- Type **FROM [Client], [Business Analyst]** as the second line.

- Type **WHERE [Client]. [Business Analyst Number]=[Business Analyst].[Business Analyst Number]** as the third line and type a semicolon (**;**) on the fourth line.

Q&A What is the purpose of the WHERE clause?

The WHERE clause specifies that only rows on which the analyst numbers match are to be included. In this case, the analyst number in the Client table ([Client].[Business Analyst Number]) must be equal to the analyst number in the Business Analyst table ([Business Analyst]. [Business Analyst Number]).

- View the results (Figure 7–26).

2

- Save the query as Ch7q20. Return to the query.

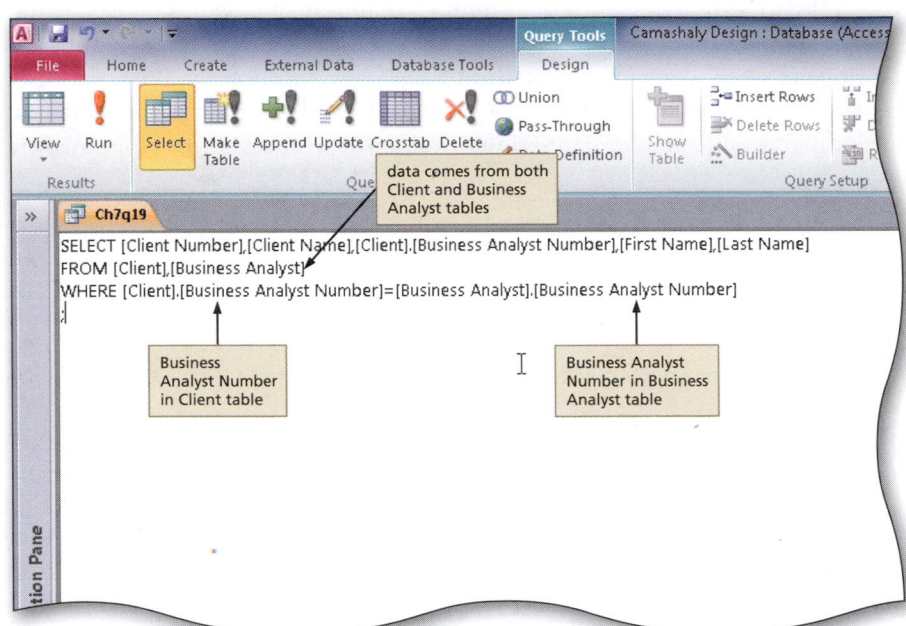

(a) Query

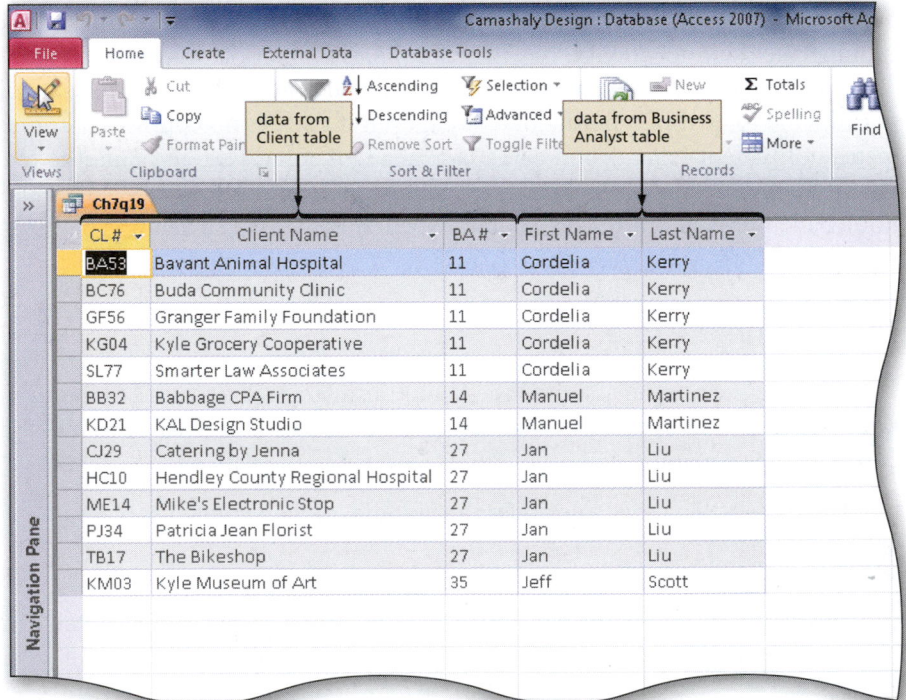

(b) Results

Figure 7–26

To Restrict the Records in a Join

You can restrict the records to be included in a join by creating a compound criterion. The criterion will include the criterion necessary to join the tables along with a criterion to restrict the records. The criteria will be connected with AND.

Camashaly would like to modify the previous query so that only analysts whose start date is prior to May 1, 2011, are included. The following steps modify the previous query appropriately. The date is enclosed between number signs (#).

1

- Return to SQL view.

- Click immediately prior to the semicolon on the last line.

- Type `AND [Start Date] <#5/1/2011#` and press the ENTER key.

Q&A Could I use other formats for the date in the criterion?

Yes. You could type #May 1, 2011# or #1-May-2011#.

- View the results (Figure 7–27).

2

- Save the query as Ch7q21. Return to the query.

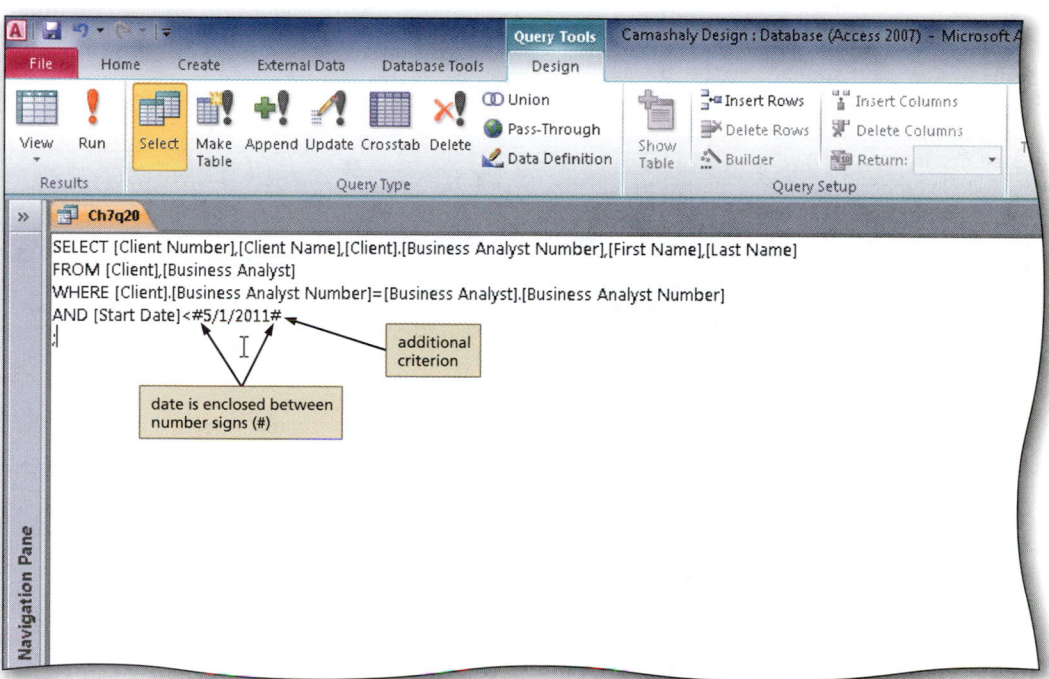

(a) Query

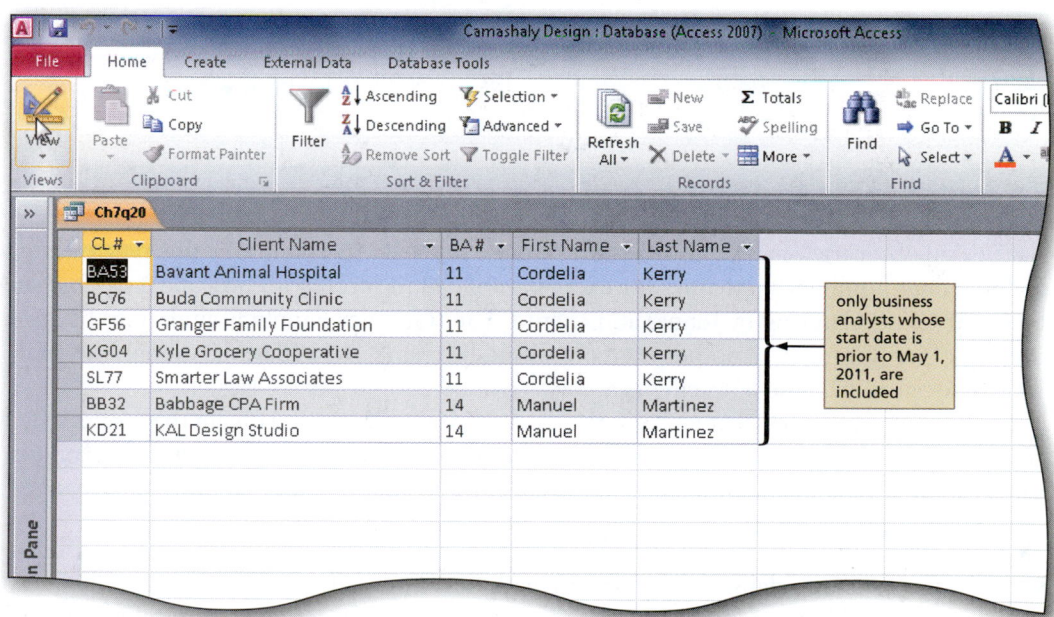

(b) Results

Figure 7–27

BTW

Outer Joins

Sometimes you need to list all the rows from one of the tables in a join, regardless of whether they match any rows in the other table. For example, you can perform a join on the Client and Course Offerings table but display all clients — even the ones without course offerings. This type of join is called an outer join. In a left outer join, all rows from the table on the left (the table listed first in the query) will be included regardless of whether they match rows from the table on the right (the table listed second in the query). Rows from the right will be included only if they match. In a right outer join, all rows from the table on the right will be included regardless of whether they match rows from the table on the left. The SQL clause for a left outer join is LEFT JOIN and the SQL clause for a right outer join is RIGHT JOIN.

Aliases

When tables appear in the FROM clause, you can give each table an **alias**, or an alternative name, that you can use in the rest of the statement. You create an alias by typing the name of the table, pressing the SPACEBAR, and then typing the name of the alias. No commas or periods are necessary to separate the two names.

You can use an alias for two basic reasons: for simplicity or to join a table to itself. Figure 7–28 shows the same query as in Figure 7–27, but with the Client table assigned the letter, C, as an alias and the Business Analyst table assigned the letter, B. The query in Figure 7–28 is less complex. Whenever you need to qualify a field name, you can use the alias. Thus, you only need to type B.[Business Analyst Number] rather than [Business Analyst].[Business Analyst Number].

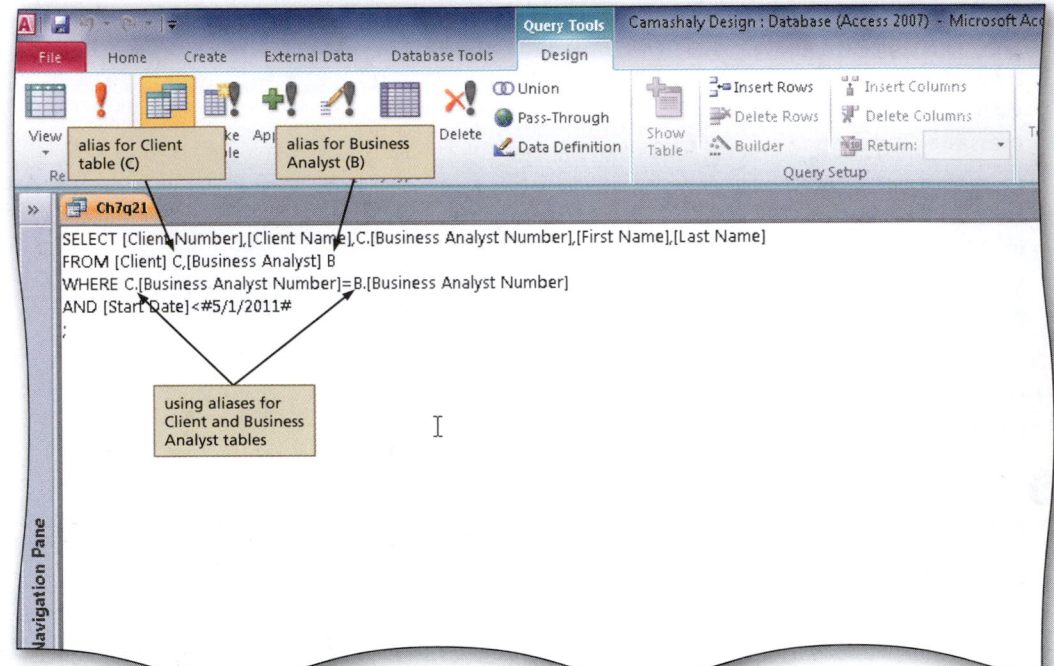

Figure 7–28

To Join a Table to Itself

The other use of aliases is in joining a table to itself. An example of this type of join would enable Camashaly to find client numbers and names for every pair of clients located in the same city. One such pair, for example, would be client CJ29 (Catering by Jenna) and client GF56 (Granger Family Foundation) because both clients are located in the same city (Granger). Another example would be client BA53 (Bavant Animal Hospital) and client SL77 (Smarter Law Associates) because both clients are located in the same city (Burles).

If there were two Client tables in the database, Camashaly could obtain the results they want by simply joining the two Client tables looking for rows where the cities were the same. Even though there is only one Client table, you actually can treat the Client table as two tables in the query by creating two aliases. You would change the FROM clause to:

```
FROM CLIENT F, CLIENT S
```

SQL treats this clause as a query of two tables. The clause assigns the first Client table the letter, F, as an alias. It also assigns the letter, S, as an alias for the Client table. The fact that both tables are really the single Client table is not a problem. The following steps assign two aliases (F and S) to the Client table and list the client number and client name of both clients as well as the city in which both are located.

1

- Return to SQL view and delete the previous query.

- Type **SELECT F.[Client Number],F. [Client Name],S.[Client Number],S. [Client Name],F. [City]** as the first line of the command.

- Type **FROM [Client] F,[Client] S** as the second line.

- Type **WHERE F.[City]=S. [City]** as the third line.

- Type **AND F.[Client Number]<S. [Client Number]** as the fourth line and type a semicolon (**;**) on the fifth line.

- View the results (Figure 7–29).

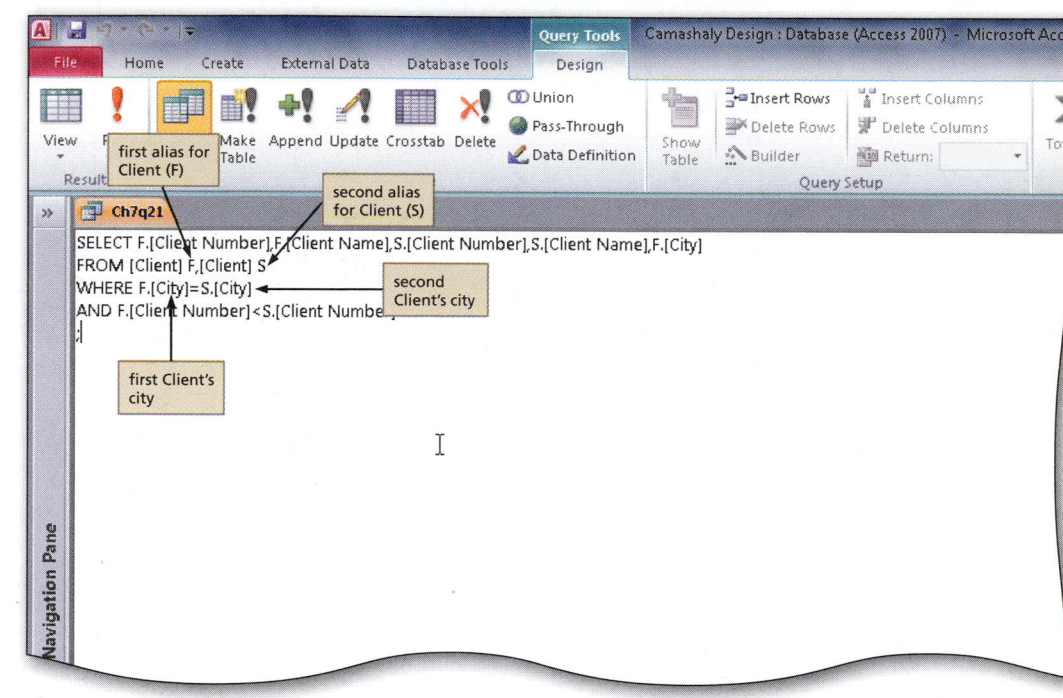

(a) Query

Q&A

Why is the criterion F.[Client Number] < S.[Client Number] included in the query?

If you did not include this criterion, the query would contain four times as many results. On the first row in the results, for example, the first client number is CJ29 and the second is GF56. Without this criterion, there would be a row on which both the first and second client numbers are CJ29, a row on which both are GF56, and a row on which the first is GF56 and the second is CJ29. This criterion only selects the one row on which the first client number (CJ29) is less than the second client number (GF56).

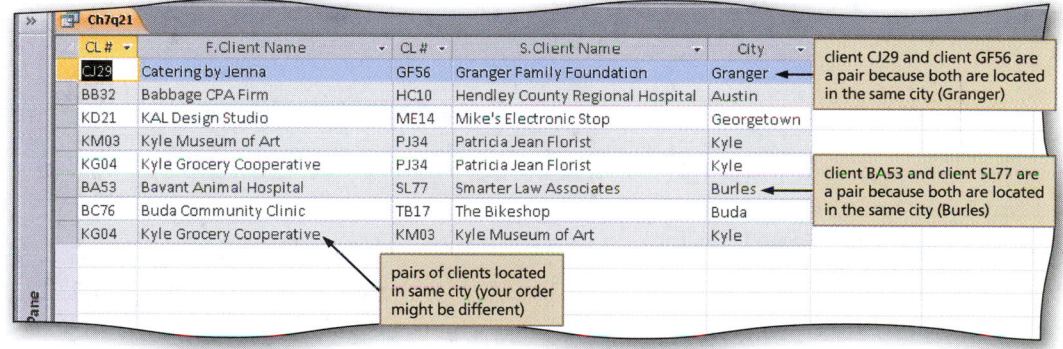

(b) Results

Figure 7–29

2

- Save the query as Ch7q22. Return to the query.

Subqueries

It is possible to place one query inside another. Figure 7–30, on the following page, illustrates a **subquery**, which is an inner query, contained within parentheses, that is evaluated first. Then the outer query can use the results of the subquery to find its results. In some cases, using a subquery can be the simplest way to produce the desired results, as illustrated in the following query.

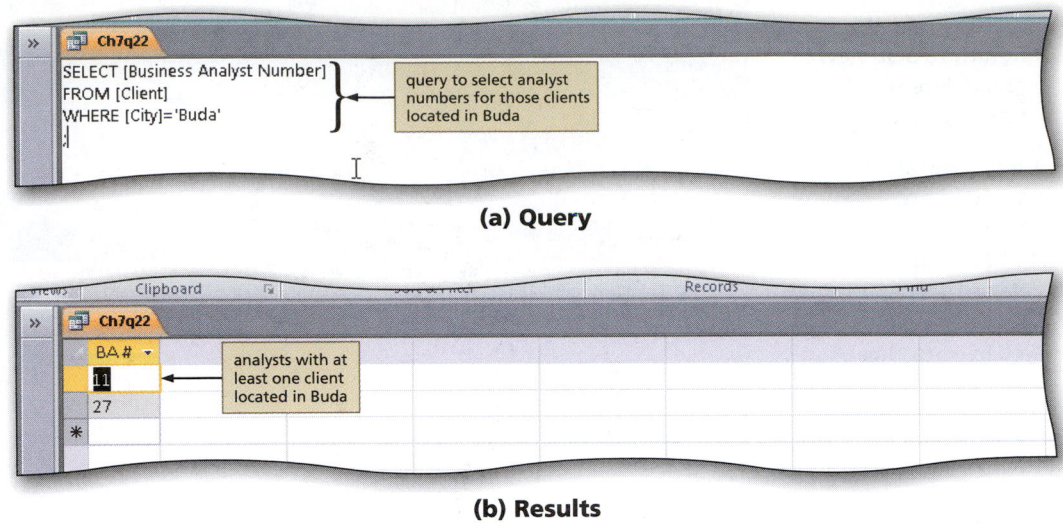

(a) Query

(b) Results

Figure 7–30

To Use a Subquery

The following steps use the query shown in Figure 7–30 as a subquery. This query selects analyst numbers from those records in the Client table on which the City is Buda. In other words, Camashaly Design can use this query to select analyst numbers for those analysts who have at least one client located in Buda.

After the subquery is evaluated, the outer query will select the analyst number, first name, and last name for those analysts whose analyst number is in the list produced by the subquery.

- Return to SQL view and delete the previous query.

- Type **SELECT [Business Analyst Number],[First Name],[Last Name]** as the first line of the command.

- Type **FROM [Business Analyst]** as the second line.

- Type **WHERE [Business Analyst Number] IN** as the third line.

- Type **(SELECT [Business Analyst Number]** as the fourth line.

- Type **FROM [Client]** as the fifth line.

- Type **WHERE [City]= 'Buda')** as the sixth line and type a semicolon (**;**) on the seventh line.

- View the results (Figure 7–31).

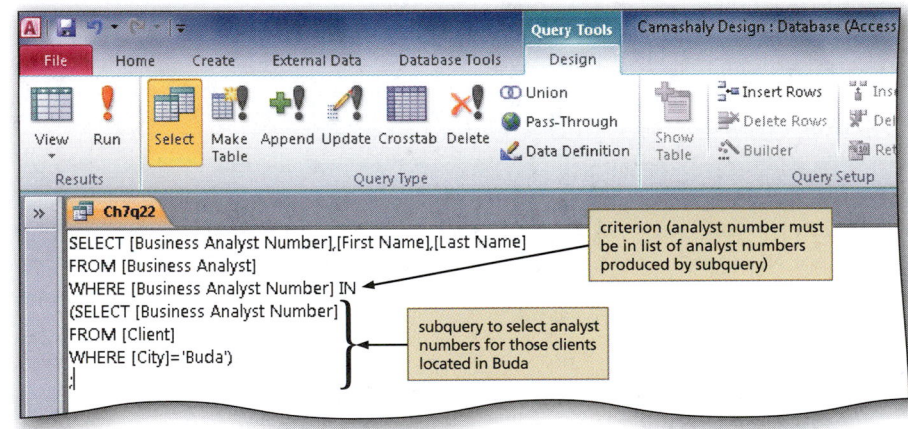

(a) Query

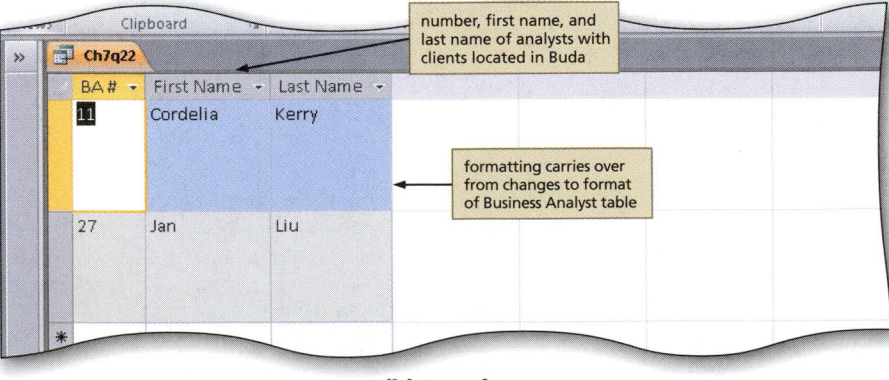

(b) Results

Figure 7–31

2

- Save the query as Ch7q23. Return to the query.

Using an IN Clause

The query in Figure 7–31 uses an IN clause with a subquery. You can also use an IN clause with a list as an alternative to an OR criterion when the OR criterion involves a single field. For example, to find clients whose city is Buda, Georgetown, or Granger, the criterion using IN would be City IN ('Buda','Georgetown','Granger'). The corresponding OR criterion would be City='Buda' OR City='Georgetown' OR City='Granger'. The choice of which one to use is a matter of personal preference.

You also can use this type of IN clause when creating queries in Design view. To use the criterion in the previous paragraph, for example, include the City field in the design grid and enter the criterion in the Criteria row.

BTW

BETWEEN Operator
The BETWEEN operator allows you to search for a range of values in one field. For example, to find all clients whose amount paid amount is between $20,000 and $30,000, the WHERE clause would be WHERE Amount Paid BETWEEN 20000 AND 30000.

Comparison with Access-Generated SQL

When you create a query in Design view, Access automatically creates a corresponding SQL query that is similar to the queries you have created in this chapter. The Access query shown in Figure 7–32, for example, was created in Design view and includes the Client Number and Client Name fields. The City field has a criterion (Buda), but the City field will not appear in the results.

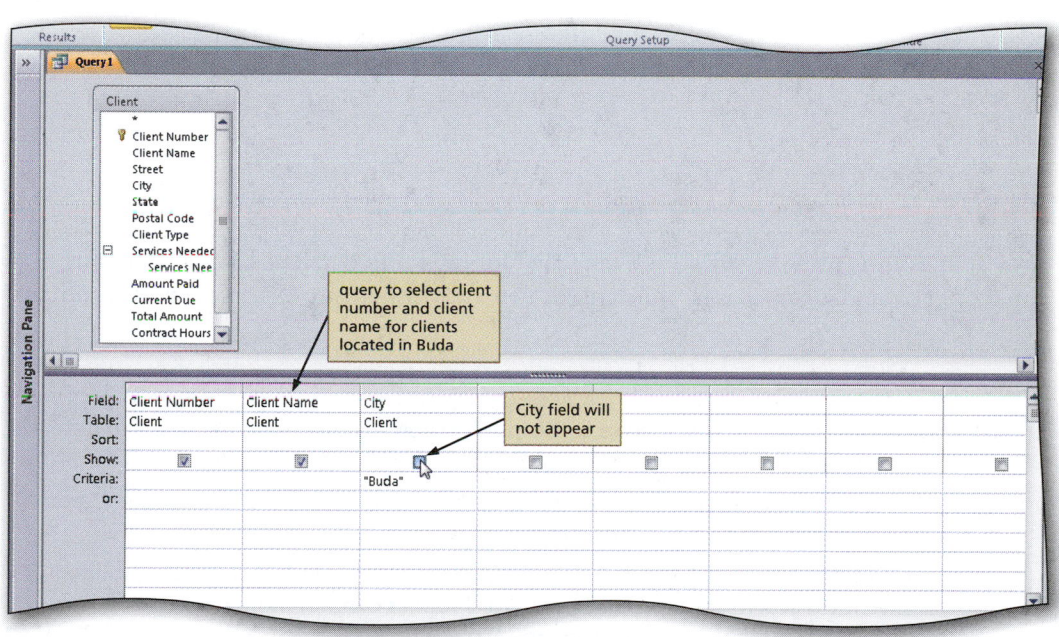

(a) Query

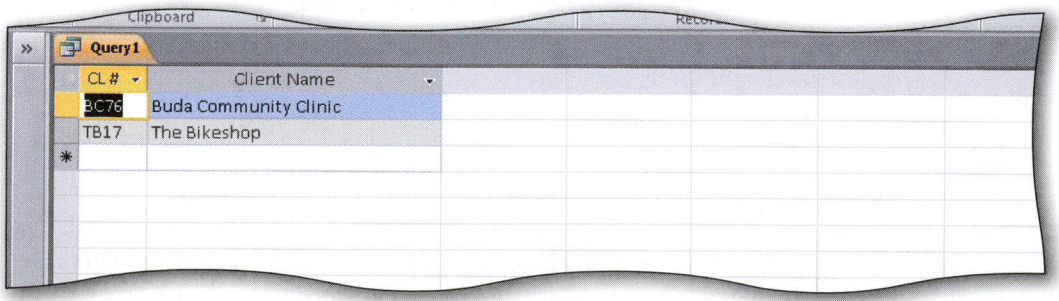

(b) Results

Figure 7–32

Union, Pass-Through, and Data Definition Queries
There are three queries that can only be created in SQL view. The Union query combines fields from more than one table into one query result set. The Pass-Through query enables you to send SQL commands directly to ODBC (Open Database Connectivity) databases using the ODBC database's SQL syntax. The Data Definition query allows you to create or alter database tables or create indexes in Access directly.

The SQL query that Access generates in correspondence to the Design view query is shown in Figure 7–33. The query is very similar to the queries you have entered, but there are three slight differences. First, the fields are qualified (Client.[Client Number] and Client.[Client Name]), even though they do not need to be; only one table is involved in the query, so no qualification is necessary. Second, the City field is not enclosed in square brackets. The field legitimately is not enclosed in square brackets because there are no spaces or other special characters in the field name. Finally, there are extra parentheses in the criteria.

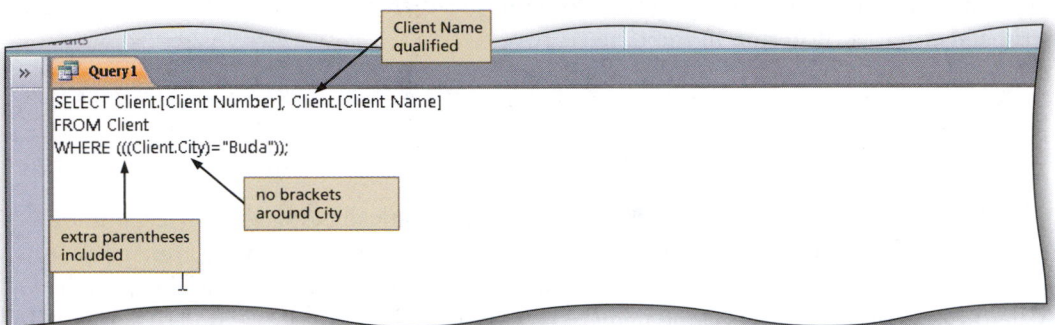

Figure 7–33

Both the style used by Access and the style you have been using are legitimate. The choice of style is a personal preference.

Updating Data through SQL

Although SQL is often regarded as a language for querying databases, it also contains commands to update databases. You can add new records, update existing records, and delete records.

Plan Ahead

Determine any update operations to be performed. Examine the database to determine if records must be added, updated, and/or deleted.

- **Determine INSERT operations.** Determine whether new records need to be added. Determine to which table they should be added.

- **Determine UPDATE operations.** Determine changes that need to be made to existing records. Which fields need to be changed? Which tables contain these fields? What criteria identify the rows that need to be changed?

- **Determine DELETE operations.** Determine which tables contain records that are to be deleted. What criteria identify the rows that need to be deleted?

To Use an INSERT Command

You can add records to a table using the SQL INSERT command. The command consists of the words INSERT INTO followed by the name of the table into which the record is to be inserted. Next is the word VALUE followed by the values for the fields in the record. Values for Text fields must be enclosed within quotation marks. The following steps add a record that Camashaly Design wants to add to the Course Offerings table. The record is for client BA53 and Course C06, and indicates that the course will be offered for a total of 4 hours, of which 0 hours already have been spent.

1

- If necessary, return to SQL view and delete the existing query.

- Type `INSERT INTO [Course Offerings]` as the first line of the command.

- Type `VALUES` as the second line.

- Type `('BA53','C06',4,0)` as the third line and type a semicolon (`;`) on the fourth line (Figure 7–34).

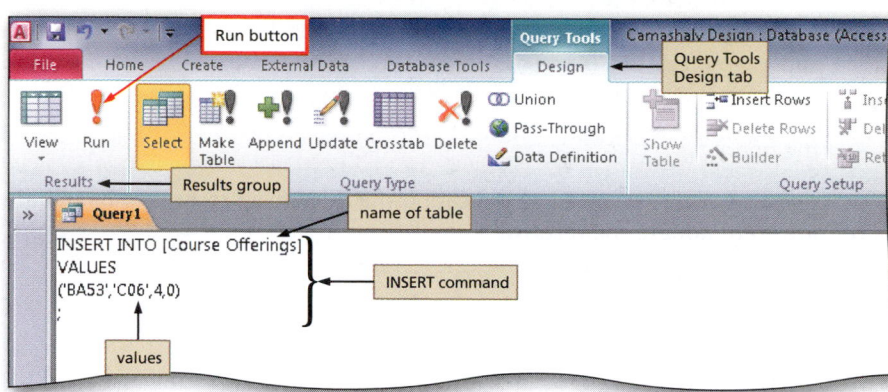

Figure 7–34

2

- Run the query by clicking the Run button (Query Tools Design tab | Results group).

- When Access displays a message indicating the number of records to be inserted (appended), click the Yes button to insert the records.

Q&A I clicked the View button and did not get the message. Do I need to click the Run button?

Yes. You are making a change to the database, so you must click the Run button, or the change will not be made.

Q&A How can I see if the record was actually inserted?

Use a SELECT query to view the records in the Course Offerings table.

3

- Save the query as Ch7q24. Return to the query.

To Use an UPDATE Command

You can update records in SQL by using the UPDATE command. The command consists of UPDATE, followed by the name of the table in which records are to be updated. Next, the command contains one or more SET clauses, which consist of the word SET, followed by a field to be updated, an equal sign, and the new value. The SET clause indicates the change to be made. Finally, the query includes a WHERE clause. When you execute the command, all records in the indicated table that satisfy the criterion will be updated. The following steps use the SQL UPDATE command to perform an update requested by Camashaly Design. Specifically, they change the Hours Spent to 2 on all records in the Course Offerings table on which the client number is BA53 and the course number is C06. Because the combination of the Client Number and Course Number fields is the primary key, only one record will be updated.

1

- Delete the existing query.

- Type `UPDATE [Course Offerings]` as the first line of the command.

- Type `SET [Hours Spent]=2` as the second line.

- Type `WHERE [Client Number]='BA53'` as the third line.

- Type `AND [Course Number]='C06'` as the fourth line and type a semicolon (`;`) on the fifth line (Figure 7–35).

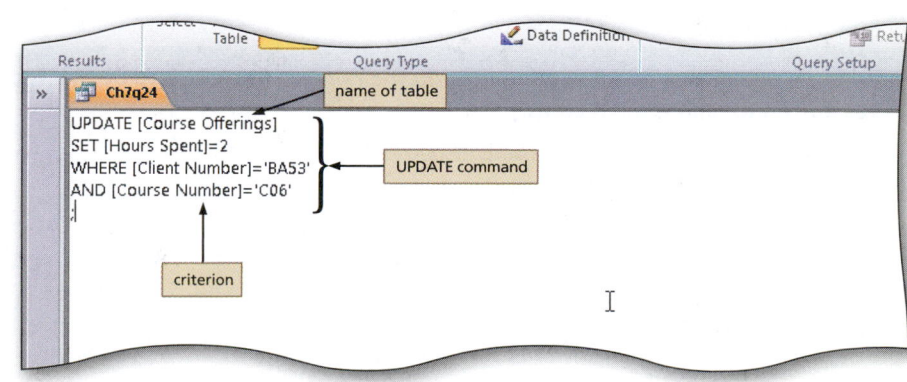

Figure 7–35

Q&A Do I need to change a field to a specific value like 2?

No. You could use an expression. For example, to add $100 to the Current Due amount, the SET clause would be SET [Current Due]=[Current Due]+100.

2

- Run the query.

- When Access displays a message indicating the number of records to be updated, click the Yes button to update the records.

Q&A How can I see if the update actually occurred?

Use a SELECT query to view the records in the Course Offerings table.

3

- Save the query as Ch7q25. Return to the query.

To Use a DELETE Command

You can delete records in SQL using the DELETE command. The command consists of DELETE FROM, followed by the name of the table from which records are to be deleted. Finally, you include a WHERE clause to specify the criteria. When you execute the command, all records in the indicated table that satisfy the criterion will be deleted. The following steps use the SQL DELETE command to delete all records in the Course Offerings table on which the client number is BA53 and the Course number is C06, as Camashaly Design has requested. Because the combination of the Client Number and Course Number fields is the primary key, only one record will be deleted.

1

- Delete the existing query.

- Type **DELETE FROM [Course Offerings]** as the first line of the command.

- Type **WHERE [Client Number]='BA53'** as the second line.

- Type **AND [Course Number]='C06'** as the third line and type a semicolon (;) on the fourth line (Figure 7–36).

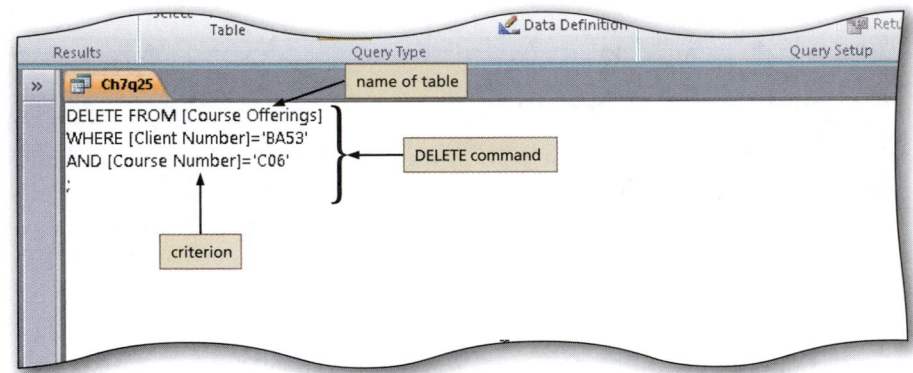

Figure 7–36

2

- Run the query.

- When Access displays a message indicating the number of records to be deleted, click the Yes button to delete the records.

Q&A How can I see if the deletion actually occurred?

Use a SELECT query to view the records in the Course Offerings table.

3

- Save the query as Ch7q26. Return to the query.

- Close the query.

To Restore the Font Size

Earlier you changed the font size from its default setting of 8 to 10 so the SQL queries would be easier to read. Unless you prefer to retain this new setting, you should change the setting back to the default. The following steps restore the font size to its default setting.

1 Click File on the Ribbon to open the Backstage view.

2 Click Options to display the Access Options dialog box.

3 Click Object Designers to display the Object Designer options.

4 In the Query design area, click the Size box arrow, and then click 8 in the list that appears to change the size back to 8.

5 Click the OK button to close the Access Options dialog box.

BTW

Quick Reference
For a table that lists how to complete the tasks covered in this book using the mouse, Ribbon, shortcut menu, and keyboard, see the Quick Reference Summary at the back of this book, or visit the Access 2010 Quick Reference Web page (scsite.com/ac2010/qr).

To Quit Access

The following steps quit Access.

1 Click the Close button on the right side of the title bar to quit Access.

2 If a Microsoft Access dialog box appears, click the Save button to save any changes made to the object since the last save.

Chapter Summary

In this chapter you have learned to create SQL queries; include fields in a query; use criteria involving both numeric and text fields as well as use compound criteria; use computed fields and rename the computation; sort the results of a query; use the built-in functions; group records in a query and also restrict the groups that appear in the results; join tables and restrict the records in a join; use subqueries; and use the INSERT, UPDATE, and DELETE commands to update data. Finally, you looked at the SQL that is generated automatically by Access. The items listed below include all the new Access skills you have learned in this chapter.

1. Change the Font Size (AC 421)
2. Create a New SQL Query (AC 422)
3. Include Only Certain Fields (AC 423)
4. Prepare to Enter a New SQL Query (AC 425)
5. Include All Fields (AC 426)
6. Use a Criterion Involving a Numeric Field (AC 427)
7. Use a Comparison Operator (AC 428)
8. Use a Criterion Involving a Text Field (AC 429)
9. Use a Wildcard (AC 430)
10. Use a Compound Criterion Involving AND (AC 431)
11. Use a Compound Criterion Involving OR (AC 432)
12. Use NOT in a Criterion (AC 433)
13. Use a Computed Field (AC 434)
14. Sort the Results on a Single Field (AC 435)
15. Sort the Results on Multiple Fields (AC 437)
16. Sort the Results in Descending Order (AC 438)
17. Omit Duplicates When Sorting (AC 439)
18. Use a Built-In Function (AC 441)
19. Assign a Name to the Results of a Function (AC 442)
20. Use Multiple Functions in the Same Command (AC 443)
21. Use Grouping (AC 444)
22. Restrict the Groups that Appear (AC 446)
23. Join Tables (AC 448)
24. Restrict the Records in a Join (AC 449)
25. Join a Table to Itself (AC 450)
26. Use a Subquery (AC 452)
27. Use an INSERT Command (AC 454)
28. Use an UPDATE Command (AC 455)
29. Use a DELETE Command (AC 456)

Learn It Online

Test your knowledge of chapter content and key terms.

Instructions: To complete the Learn It Online exercises, start your browser, click the Address bar, and then enter the Web address **scsite.com/ac2010/learn**. When the Access 2010 Learn It Online page is displayed, click the link for the exercise you want to complete and then read the instructions.

Chapter Reinforcement TF, MC, and SA

A series of true/false, multiple choice, and short answer questions that test your knowledge of the chapter content.

Flash Cards

An interactive learning environment where you identify chapter key terms associated with displayed definitions.

Practice Test

A series of multiple choice questions that test your knowledge of chapter content and key terms.

Who Wants To Be a Computer Genius?

An interactive game that challenges your knowledge of chapter content in the style of a television quiz show.

Wheel of Terms

An interactive game that challenges your knowledge of chapter key terms in the style of the television show *Wheel of Fortune*.

Crossword Puzzle Challenge

A crossword puzzle that challenges your knowledge of key terms presented in the chapter.

Apply Your Knowledge

Reinforce the skills and apply the concepts you learned in this chapter.

Using Criteria, Joining Tables, and Sorting in SQL Queries

Instructions: Start Access. If you are using the Microsoft Access 2010 Complete or the Microsoft Access 2010 Comprehensive text, open the Babbage CPA Firm database that you used in Chapter 6. Otherwise, see your instructor for information on accessing the files required in this book.

Perform the following tasks using SQL:

1. Find all clients whose amount paid amount is greater than $1,000. Display all fields in the query result. Save the query as Apply 7 Step 1 Query.

2. Find all clients whose amount paid amount or balance due amount is $0.00. Display the Client Number, Client Name, Amount Paid, and Balance Due fields in the query result. Save the query as Apply 7 Step 2 Query.

3. Find all records in the Client table where the postal code is not 27036. Display the Client Number, Client Name, and City in the query result. Save the query as Apply 7 Step 3 Query.

4. Display the Client Number, Client Name, Bookkeeper Number, First Name, and Last Name for all clients. Sort the records in ascending order by bookkeeper number and client number. Save the query as Apply 7 Step 4 Query.

5. Submit the revised database in the format specified by your instructor.

Extend Your Knowledge

Extend the skills you learned in this chapter and experiment with new skills. You may need to use Help to complete the assignment.

Instructions: Start Access. Open the LawnYard Maintenance database. See the inside back cover of this book for instructions for downloading the Data Files for Students, or see your instructor for information on accessing the files required in this book.

LawnYard Maintenance is a small landscaping and maintenance company. The owners have created an Access database in which to store information about the customers they serve and the workers they employ. You will create SQL queries using the LIKE, IN, and BETWEEN operators. You also will create a query that uses a subquery.

Perform the following tasks:

1. Find all customers where the customer's first name is either Frances or Francis. Display the Customer Number, Last Name, First Name, and City fields in the result. Save the query as Extend 7 Step 1 Query.

2. Find all customers who live in Kingston or Anderson. Use the IN operator. Display the Customer Number, Last Name, First Name, and City fields in the result. Save the query as Extend 7 Step 2 Query.

3. Find all customers whose amount paid amount is greater than or equal to $200 and less than or equal to $300. Use the BETWEEN operator. (*Hint*: Use Help to solve this problem.) Display the Customer Number, Last Name, First Name, and Amount Paid fields in the result. Save the query as Extend 7 Step 3 Query.

4. Use a subquery to find all workers whose customers are located in Anderson. Display the worker number, first name, and last name. Save the query as Extend 7 Step 4 Query.

5. Submit the revised database and in the format specified by your instructor.

Make It Right

Analyze a database, correct all errors, and/or improve the design.

Correcting Errors in the Query Design

Instructions: Start Access. Open the College Pet Sitters database. See the inside back cover of this book for instructions for downloading the Data Files for Students, or see your instructor for information on accessing the files required in this book.

College Pet Sitters is a database maintained by a small pet-sitting business owned by college students. The queries shown in Figure 7–37 contain a number of errors that need to be corrected before the queries run properly. The query shown in Figure 7–37a displays the Enter Parameter Value dialog box, but this is not a parameter query. Also, the owners wanted to assign the name, Total Amount, to the Balance + Paid calculation. Save the query with your changes.

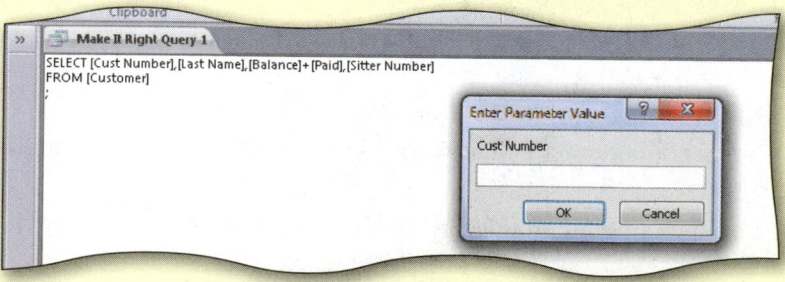

(a) Incorrect Field Name Query

Figure 7–37

Continued >

Make It Right *continued*

When you view the results for the query shown in Figure 7–37b, you get 30 records. You know this is wrong. Also, the query did not sort correctly. The query results should be sorted first by sitter number and then by descending balance. Correct the errors and save the query with your changes.

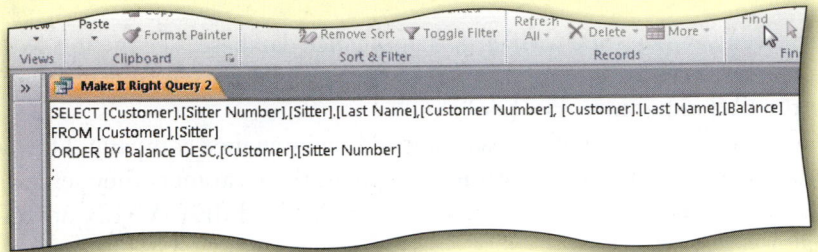

```
SELECT [Customer].[Sitter Number],[Sitter].[Last Name],[Customer Number], [Customer].[Last Name],[Balance]
FROM [Customer],[Sitter]
ORDER BY Balance DESC,[Customer].[Sitter Number]
;
```

(b) Incorrect Join and Sort Query

Figure 7–37

Change the database properties, as specified by your instructor. Submit the revised database in the format specified by your instructor.

In the Lab

Design, create, modify, and/or use a database following the guidelines, concepts, and skills presented in this chapter. The assignments are listed in order of increasing difficulty.

Lab 1: Querying the ECO Clothesline Database Using SQL

Problem: The management of ECO Clothesline wants to learn more about SQL and has determined a number of questions it wants SQL to answer. You must obtain answers to the questions posed by management.

Instructions: If you are using the Microsoft Access 2010 Complete or the Microsoft Access 2010 Comprehensive text, open the ECO Clothesline database that you used in Chapter 6. Otherwise, see your instructor for information on accessing the files required in this book.

Perform the following tasks:

1. Find all customers where the customer type is SAL. Include the Customer Number, Customer Name, and Sales Rep Number fields in the result. Save the query as Lab 7-1 Step 1 Query.

2. Find all customers located in Tennessee (TN) with a paid amount greater than $1,500.00. Include the Customer Number, Customer Name, and Amount Paid fields in the result. Save the query as Lab 7-1 Step 2 Query.

3. Find all customers whose names begin with the letter, C. Include the Customer Number, Customer Name, and City fields in the result. Save the query as Lab 7-1 Step 3 Query.

4. List all cities in descending order. Each city should appear only once. Save the query as Lab 7-1 Step 4 Query.

5. Display the customer number, name, sales rep number, first name, and last name for all customers. Sort the results in ascending order by sales rep number and customer number. Save the query as Lab 7-1 Step 5 Query.

6. List the average balance amount grouped by sales rep number. Name the average balance as Average Billed. Save the query as Lab 7-1 Step 6 Query.

7. Find the customer number and name for every pair of customers who are located in the same city. Save the query as Lab 7-1 Step 7 Query.

8. Find the customer numbers, names, and sales rep numbers for all customers that have open orders. Use the alias O for the Open Orders table and C for the Customer table. Each customer should appear only once. Save the query as Lab 7-1 Step 8 Query.

9. Use a subquery to find all sales reps whose customers are located in Pineville. Save the query as Lab 7-1 Step 9 Query.

10. Find the average balance amount for sales rep 44. Save the query as Lab 7-1 Step 10 Query.

11. Submit the revised database in the format specified by your instructor.

In the Lab

Lab 2: Querying the Walburg Energy Alternatives Database Using SQL

Problem: The manager of the Walburg Energy Alternatives store would like to learn more about SQL and has determined a number of questions he wants SQL to answer. You must obtain answers to the questions posed by the manager.

Instructions: If you are using the Microsoft Access 2010 Complete or the Microsoft Access 2010 Comprehensive text, open the Walburg Energy Alternatives database that you used in Chapter 6. Otherwise, see your instructor for information on accessing the files required in this book.

Perform the following tasks:

1. Find all records in the Item table where the difference between the cost of the item and the selling price of the item is less than $0.25 (25 cents). Display the item number, description, cost, and selling price in the query result. Save the query as Lab 7-2 Step 1 Query.

2. Display the item number, description, and profit (selling price – cost) for all items. Name the computed field Profit. Save the query as Lab 7-2 Step 2 Query.

3. Find all items where the description begins with the letter, W. Include the item number and description in the result. Save the query as Lab 7-2 Step 3 Query.

4. Display the vendor name, item number, description, and cost for all items where the number on hand is less than 10. Sort the results in ascending order by vendor name and description. Save the query as Lab 7-2 Step 4 Query.

5. Find the average cost by vendor. Name the computed field Average Cost. Save the query as Lab 7-2 Step 5 Query.

6. Find the total number of reordered items for each item in the Reorder table. Name the computed field Total Ordered. Include the item number in the result. Save the query as Lab 7-2 Step 6 Query.

7. Add the following record to the Reorder table.

Item Number	Date Ordered	Number Ordered
8590	4/12/2012	3

Save the steps to add the record as Lab 7-2 Step 7 Query.

8. Update the Number Ordered field to 5 for those records where the Item Number is 8590 and the date ordered is 4/12/2012. Save the steps to update the record as Lab 7-2 Step 8 Query.

9. Delete all records where the Item Number is 8590 and the date ordered is 4/12/2012. Save the steps to delete the record as Lab 7-2 Step 9 Query.

10. Submit the revised database in the format specified by your instructor.

In the Lab

Lab 3: Querying the Philamar Training Database Using SQL

Problem: The management team of Philamar Training would like to learn more about SQL and has determined a number of questions it wants SQL to answer. You must obtain answers to the questions posed by management.

Instructions: If you are using the Microsoft Access 2010 Complete or the Microsoft Access 2010 Comprehensive text, open the Philamar Training database that you used in Chapter 6. Otherwise, see your instructor for information on accessing the files required in this book. Save each query using a format similar to the following: Lab 7-3 Part 1a Query, Lab 7-3 Part 2a Query, and so on. Submit the revised database in the format specified by your instructor.

Instructions Part 1: For all the queries in Part 1, include the Client Number, Client Name, Amount Paid, and Current Due fields in the query results. Create SQL queries that answer the following questions: (a) Which clients are located in cities that start with the letter, C? (b) Which clients have a client type other than MAN? (c) Which clients have a current due amount of $0.00 and an amount paid amount of $0.00? (d) Which clients have an amount paid amount between $3,000.00 and $6,000.00? (e) For each client, what is the total of the current due and amount paid? Display the total in the result as Total Amount.

Instructions Part 2: (a) Create a SQL query that includes the Trainer Number, First Name, Last Name, Client Number, Client Name, and Amount Paid fields. Sort the records in ascending order by trainer number and client number. (b) Restrict the records retrieved in part (a) to only those clients whose client type is MAN. (c) Find the client numbers and names for every pair of clients located in the same city. (d) In which cities does Philamar have clients? List each city only once.

Instructions Part 3: Create queries to calculate the following statistics: (a) How many clients does Philamar have, and what is the total of their amount paid amounts? Assign Client Count and Sum Paid as the names for the calculations. (b) What is the total current due amount and total amount paid amount for all clients grouped by trainer? Assign Sum Paid and Sum Due as the names for the calculations. (c) Restrict the records retrieved in (b) to those on which the sum of the current due is greater than $1,000.

Cases and Places

Apply your creative thinking and problem solving skills to design and implement a solution.

See the inside back cover of this book for instructions on downloading the Data Files for Students, or contact your instructor for information about accessing the required files.

1: Querying the Chamber of Commerce Database

Academic

If you are using the Microsoft Access 2010 Complete or the Microsoft Access 2010 Comprehensive text, open the Chamber of Commerce database that you used in Chapter 6. Otherwise, see your instructor for more information about accessing the required files. One of your courses at school requires that you learn to use SQL. The Chamber has agreed that you can use the database and create

SQL queries. Use the concepts and techniques presented in this chapter to create SQL queries for the following:

a. Find the advertiser names and addresses of all advertisers located on Berton Street.

b. Find the advertiser number, advertiser name, balance, and amount paid for all advertisers whose balance is less than $100 and whose amount paid is $0.00.

c. Find the total of the balance and amount paid amounts for each advertiser. Show the advertiser number, advertiser name, and total amount.

d. Use a subquery to find all ad reps whose advertisers have an advertiser type of RET. Display the ad rep number, first name, and last name.

e. Find the ad rep for each advertiser. List the ad rep number, first name, last name, advertiser number, advertiser name, and balance. Restrict retrieval to only those records where the balance is greater than $200. Sort the results in ascending order by ad rep number and advertiser number.

f. Add a record to the Active Accounts table for advertiser number G346. The advertiser would like to place a quarter-page ad for the month of Jun.

g. Change the category code to 3 for all records in the Active Accounts table where the advertiser number is G346 and the ad month is Jun.

h. Delete all records in the Active Accounts table where the advertiser number is G346 and the ad month is Jun.

Submit the revised database in the format specified by your instructor.

2: Querying the Consignment Database

Personal

If you are using the Microsoft Access 2010 Complete or the Microsoft Access 2010 Comprehensive text, open the Consignment database that you used in Chapter 6. Otherwise, see your instructor for more information about accessing the required files. You recently attended a seminar on the use of Access databases by nonprofit organizations. Now you would like to learn SQL to enhance your understanding of databases. Use the concepts and techniques presented in this chapter to create SQL queries for the following:

a. Find the item number and description of all items that contain the word, Kitchen.

b. Find the item number, description, condition, and date of all items with a date posted prior to March 1, 2012.

c. Find the total price (price * quantity) of each item available for sale. Show the item number, item description, and total price.

d. Find the seller of each item. Show the seller's first name and last name as well as the item number, item description, price, quantity, and date posted. Sort the results by item description within seller last name.

e. Modify the query you created in Step d to restrict retrieval to those items with a price less than $10.00.

f. Find all items in good or excellent condition. Use the IN operator and display all fields in the query result.

g. Find all items posted between March 4, 2012, and March 7, 2012. The user should see all fields in the query result.

Submit the revised database in the format specified by your instructor.

Continued >

Cases and Places *continued*

3: Querying the Senior Care Database

Professional

If you are using the Microsoft Access 2010 Complete or the Microsoft Access 2010 Comprehensive text, open the Senior Care database that you used in Chapter 6. Otherwise, see your instructor for more information about accessing the required files. You and your co-owner are interested in learning SQL. Use the concepts and techniques presented in this chapter to create SQL queries for the following:

a. Find the first names, last names, and addresses of all clients whose first name begins with the letters, Fr.

b. Find the total of the balance and amount paid amounts for each client. Show the client number, client first name, client last name, and total amount.

c. Restrict the records retrieved in Step b to only those records where the total amount is greater than $1,000.

d. Find the helper for each client. List the helper number, helper last name, helper first name, client number, client last name, and client first name. Assign aliases to the Client and Helper tables. Sort the results in ascending order by helper number and client number.

e. Restrict the records retrieved in Step d to only those helpers who speak Spanish.

f. Find the average balance amount grouped by helper number.

g. Restrict the records retrieved in Step f to only those groups where the average balance amount is greater than $125.

Submit the revised database in the format specified by your instructor.

3 | Managing Contacts and Personal Contact Information with Outlook

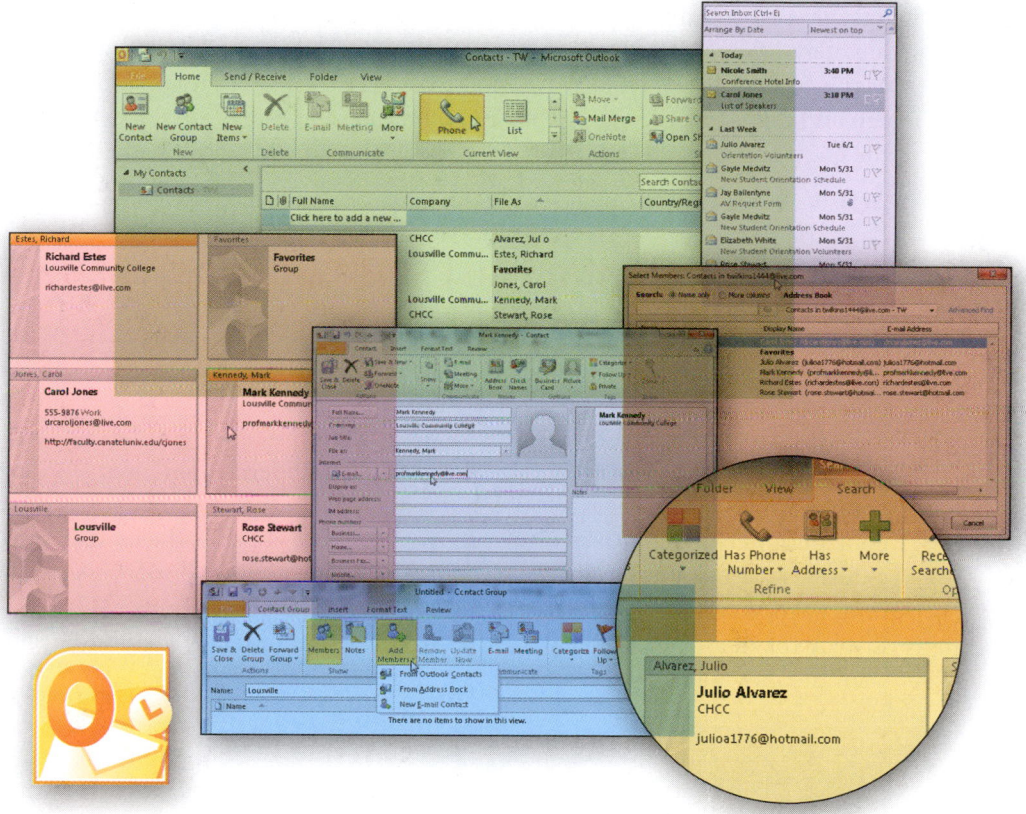

Objectives

You will have mastered the material in this chapter when you can:

- Create a new contact
- Create a contact from an e-mail message
- Modify a contact
- Manipulate attachments to contacts
- Display your contacts in different views
- Find contacts using complete or partial information

- Find contacts from any Outlook folder
- Create a contact group
- Modify a contact group
- Add and remove names in a contact group
- Preview a contact list
- Print a contact list

3 | Managing Contacts and Personal Contact Information with Outlook

Introduction

To keep track of your friends, business partners, family, and others with whom you communicate, you can use Outlook to create contact lists and contact groups. A **contact list** lets you record information about people, such as their e-mail address, phone number, birthday, and physical address. Each person's information is recorded in a contact record in the contact list. If you have several colleagues at work that you e-mail frequently, you can add them to a contact group. You then can send e-mail messages to the group using the contact group rather than having to select each contact individually.

Project — Contact List with Groups

People and businesses create contact lists to keep track of people that are important to them or their business. A contact list may contain groups so that several contacts can be using the group name rather than each individual contact. Managing your contacts using a contact list can increase productivity greatly.

The project in this chapter follows general guidelines and uses Outlook to create the contact list shown in Figure 3–1. This contact list in the TW mailbox includes individual contacts and contact groups displayed in a view that presents the contact information in a business card layout. In this layout, the individual contacts display essential information only, such as the name, affiliation, and e-mail address of the contact. The contact groups display the name of the group, have a Group label, and include a different border graphic than the individual contacts.

Overview

As you read this chapter, you will learn how to create the contact list shown in Figure 3–1 by performing these general tasks:

- Create a new contact.
- Edit a contact.
- Change the view of the contact folder.
- Find a contact.
- Create a contact group.
- Print the contact list.

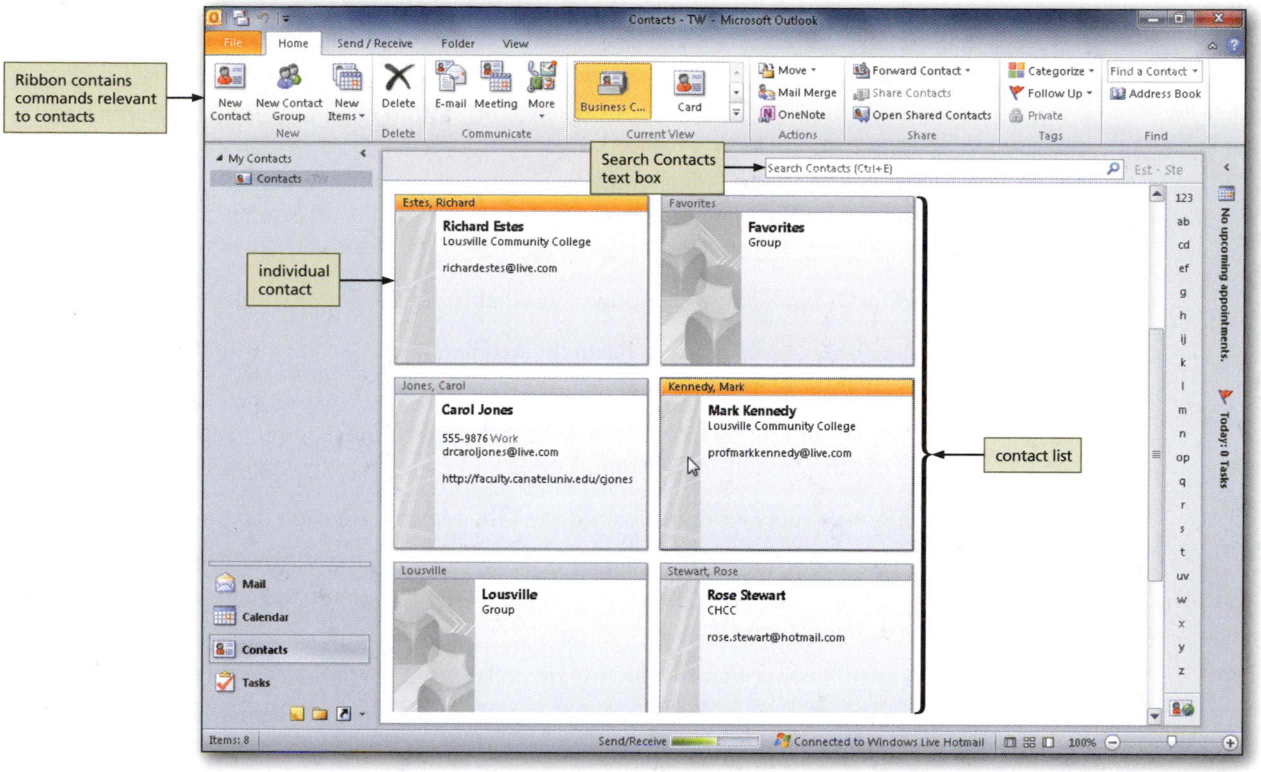

Figure 3–1

General Project Guidelines

When creating and organizing contacts, the actions you perform and decisions you make will affect the appearance and characteristics of your contact list. As you create and group your contacts, such as those shown in Figure 3–1, you should follow these general guidelines:

1. **Determine whom you want to have as contacts.** People use contacts to keep track of the people with whom they interact the most. For example, students may add study partners as contacts and business professionals may add customer and colleagues as contacts. It also is common for people to add their family and friends as contacts.

2. **Determine the information you want to store for a contact.** For any contact, you can use many contact fields for tracking contact information. In addition to name and e-mail address, you can record information such as phone numbers, Web page addresses, and mailing addresses. You also can attach files such as Word documents to a contact record.

3. **Determine how you would like to view your contacts.** Select a view to display contact information you refer to often, such as phone numbers or business names.

4. **Determine what groups you may need.** Adding contacts to a group allows you to e-mail and work with the group as a whole. For example, you can send advertisements and event information to a group containing clients. Students might create a class project group to communicate with other students working with them on a project.

5. **Determine the best method for distributing a contact list.** Consider whether you need to share a contact with others. If you do, you can share contacts electronically in Outlook or print a contact list and distribute printed copies.

When necessary, more specific details concerning the above guidelines are presented at appropriate points in the chapter. The chapter also will identify the actions performed and decisions made regarding these guidelines during the creation of the contact list shown in Figure 3–1.

Plan Ahead

To Start Outlook

BTW

BTWs
For a complete list of the BTWs found in the margins of this book, visit the Outlook 2010 BTW Web page (scsite.com/out2010/btw).

BTW

Q&As
For a complete list of the Q&As found in many of the step-by-step sequences in this book, visit the Outlook 2010 Q&A Web page (scsite.com/out2010/qa).

If you are using a computer to step through the project in this chapter and you want your screens to match the figures in this book, you should change your screen's resolution to 1024 × 768.

The following steps, which assume Windows 7 is running, start Outlook based on a typical installation. You may need to ask your instructor how to start Outlook for your computer.

1 Click the Start button on the Windows 7 taskbar to display the Start menu.

2 Type `Microsoft Outlook` as the search text in the 'Search programs and files' text box and watch the search results appear on the Start menu.

3 Click Microsoft Outlook 2010 in the search results on the Start menu to start Outlook with your Inbox as the default Mail folder.

4 If the Outlook window is not maximized, click the Maximize button next to the Close button on its title bar to maximize the window.

5 Click the Contacts button in the Navigation Pane to display the Contacts – TW – Microsoft Outlook window (Figure 3–2).

Q&A Why does my title bar not match the title bar in Figure 3–2?

The title bar always displays the name of the Outlook data file, which may include your name or initials instead of "TW."

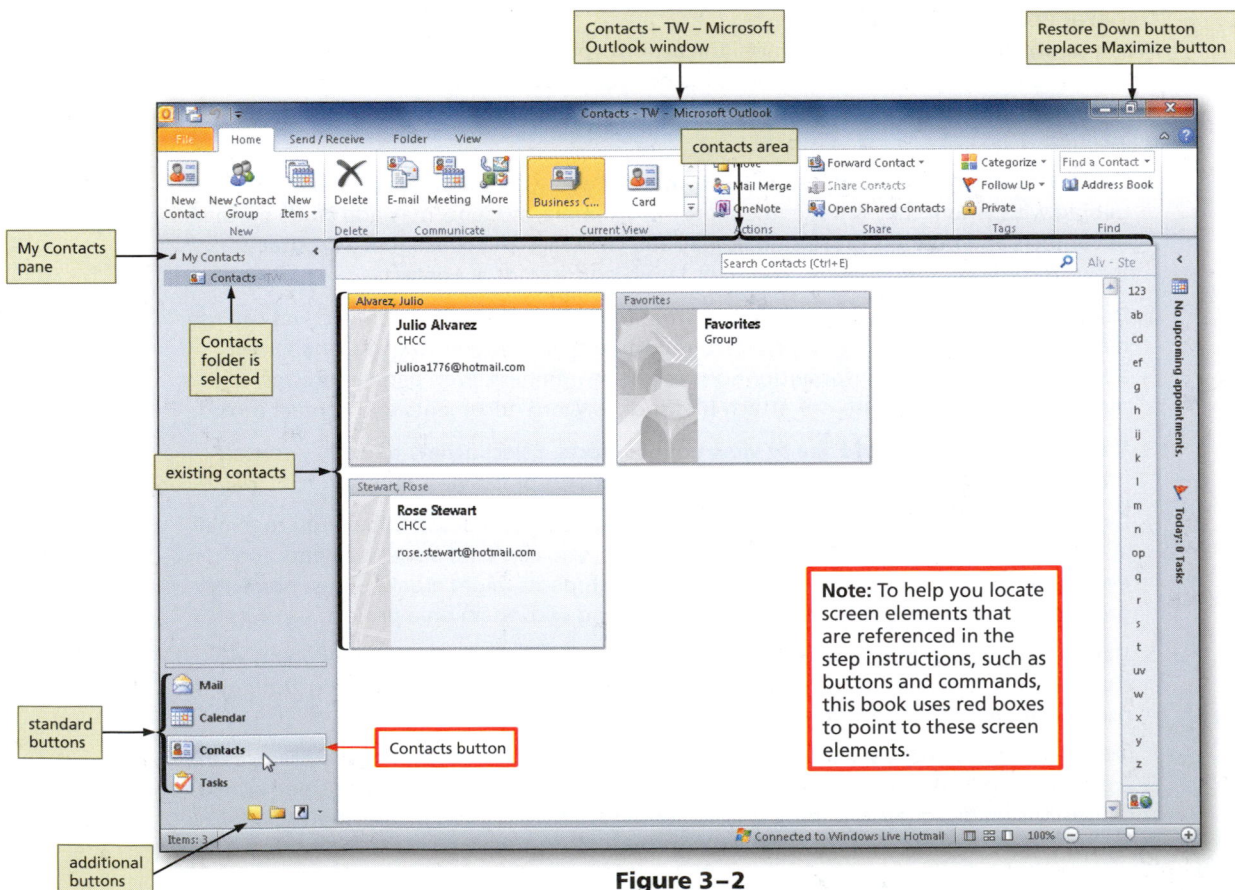

Figure 3–2

Contacts Window

The Contacts – TW – Microsoft Outlook window shown in Figure 3–2 includes a variety of features to help you work efficiently. It contains many elements similar to the windows in other Office programs, as well as some that are unique to Outlook. The main elements of the Contacts window are the Navigation Pane, the contacts area, and the To-Do bar.

The Navigation Pane includes two sets of buttons (standard and additional) and the My Contacts pane. The **My Contacts pane** displays the available contact lists, each of which is stored in its own folder. The standard buttons represent shortcuts to the standard items that are part of Microsoft Outlook mailbox: Mail, Calendar, Contacts, and Tasks. Additional buttons are displayed below the standard buttons and represent shortcuts to other Outlook functions, such as Notes, Folder List shortcuts, and Configure buttons, which allow you to specify which folders to display.

Creating a Contact List

The first step in creating a contact list is to select a folder for storing your contacts. By default, Outlooks stores contacts in the Contacts folder, but you also can create a personal folder to store your contacts using the technique presented in Chapter 2. In this chapter, you will create contacts and groups in the Contacts folder.

> **Determine who you want to have as contacts.**
> You can make contacts for nearly everyone you know or who has sent you an e-mail message. However, not everyone should be added to your contacts. Only create contacts for those people with whom you plan to interact on a regular basis, such as your friends, family, and co-workers. Adding too many contacts can make it difficult to manage your contact list.
>
> **Determine the information you want to store for a contact.**
> In addition to name and e-mail address, you can record information such as phone numbers, Web page addresses, and mailing addresses. Attach one or more files to a contact to store documents, tables, pictures, or clip art, for example, along with contact information.

Plan Ahead

To Create a New Contact

To create the contact list in this chapter, you will start by adding the first contact, Mark Kennedy. He is coming to a lecture series that you will be holding, so you want to create a contact record for him to make sure he receives updates and relevant information. The steps on the next pages create a new contact for Mark Kennedy.

BTW

Contacts Window
By default, clicking the Contacts button in the Navigation Pane displays the contacts in the Microsoft Outlook window. To display the contacts in a new window, right-click the Contacts button in the Navigation Pane, and then click Open in New Window on the shortcut menu.

BTW

The Ribbon and Screen Resolution
Outlook may change how the groups and buttons within the groups appear on the Ribbon, depending on the computer's screen resolution. Thus, your Ribbon may look different from the ones in this book if you are using a screen resolution other than 1024 × 768.

1

- If the Home tab is not the active tab, click Home on the Ribbon to display the Home tab.

- Click the New Contact button (Home tab | New group) to display the Untitled – Contact window (Figure 3–3).

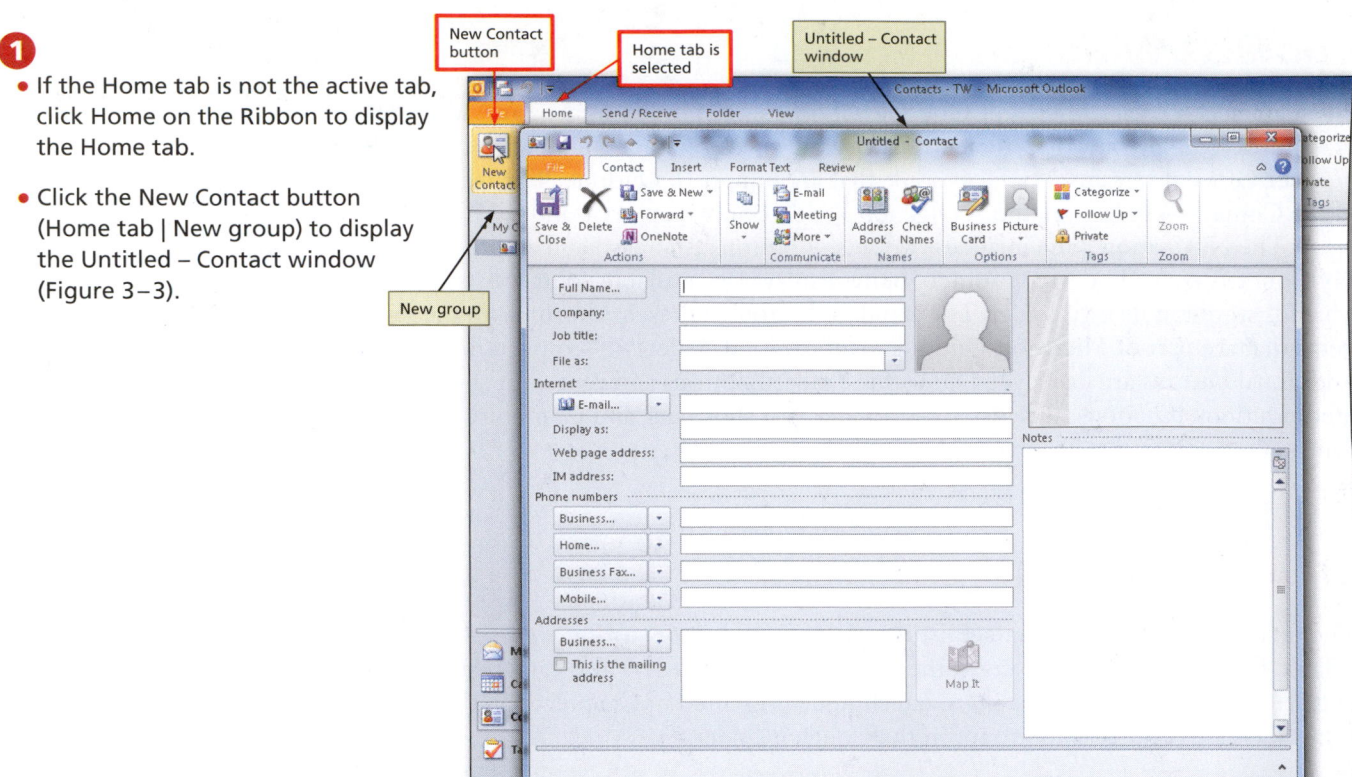

Figure 3–3

2

- Type **Mark Kennedy** in the Full Name text box to enter a name for the contact.

- Type **Lousville Community College** in the Company text box to enter a company for the contact.

- Type **profmarkkennedy@ live.com** in the E-mail text box to enter an e-mail address for the contact (Figure 3–4).

Q&A Why did the title of the Contact window change after I entered the name?

As soon as you enter the name, Outlook updates the Contact window title to reflect the information you have entered. Outlook also displays the name in the File as text box. The contact is not saved, however; only the window title and File as text boxes are updated.

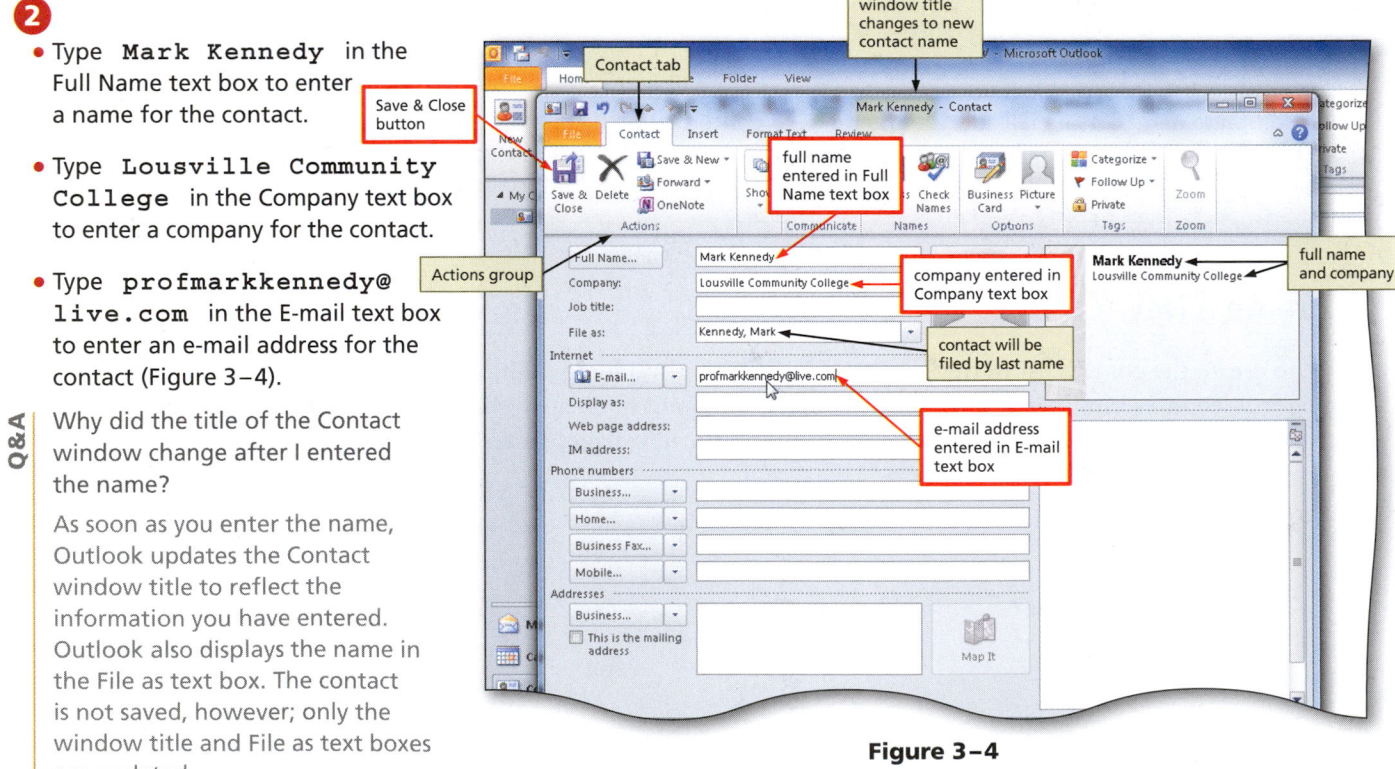

Figure 3–4

Q&A Can I add information to other fields for a contact?

Certainly. As long as you have the information, you can fill out the fields accordingly. You even can add fields besides those listed.

3

- Click the Save & Close button (Contact tab | Actions group) to save the contact and close the Contact window (Figure 3–5).

Q&A Can I send contact information to someone else?

Yes. To forward a contact, select the contact, click Forward Contact (Home tab | Share group), and then click the method you want to use to forward the contact.

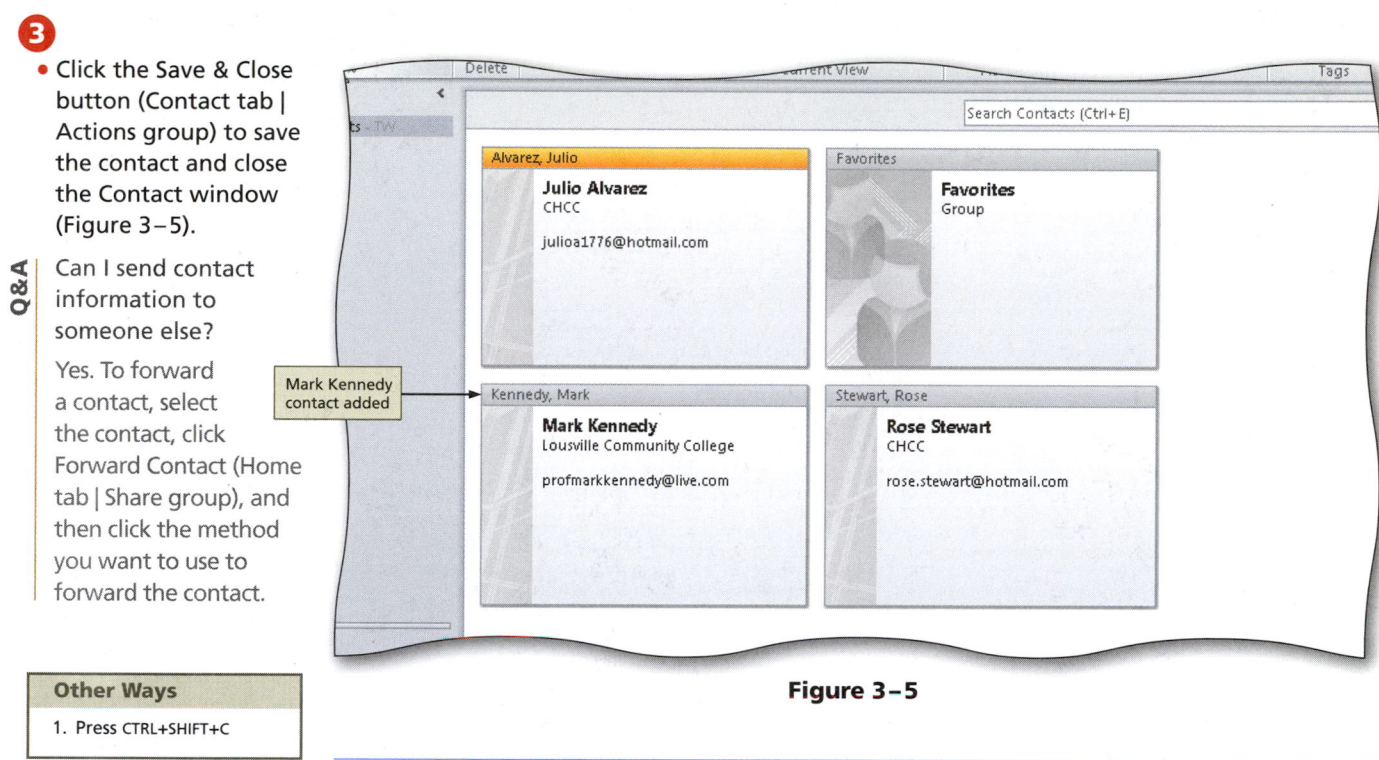

Figure 3–5

Other Ways

1. Press CTRL+SHIFT+C

To Create a Contact from an E-Mail Message

Carol Jones frequently e-mails you about your work. You want to add her to your contact list to better keep track of her information. Outlook can create a contact based on the information located in the e-mail message. The following steps create a contact from an e-mail message from Carol Jones.

1

- Click the Mail button in the Navigation Pane to display your mailbox.

- Click the Carol Jones message header to preview the e-mail message in the Reading Pane (Figure 3–6).

Q&A What if I do not have an e-mail message from Carol Jones?

If you did not import the data file for this chapter, you might not have an e-mail message from Carol Jones. In that case, perform these steps using another e-mail message in your mailbox.

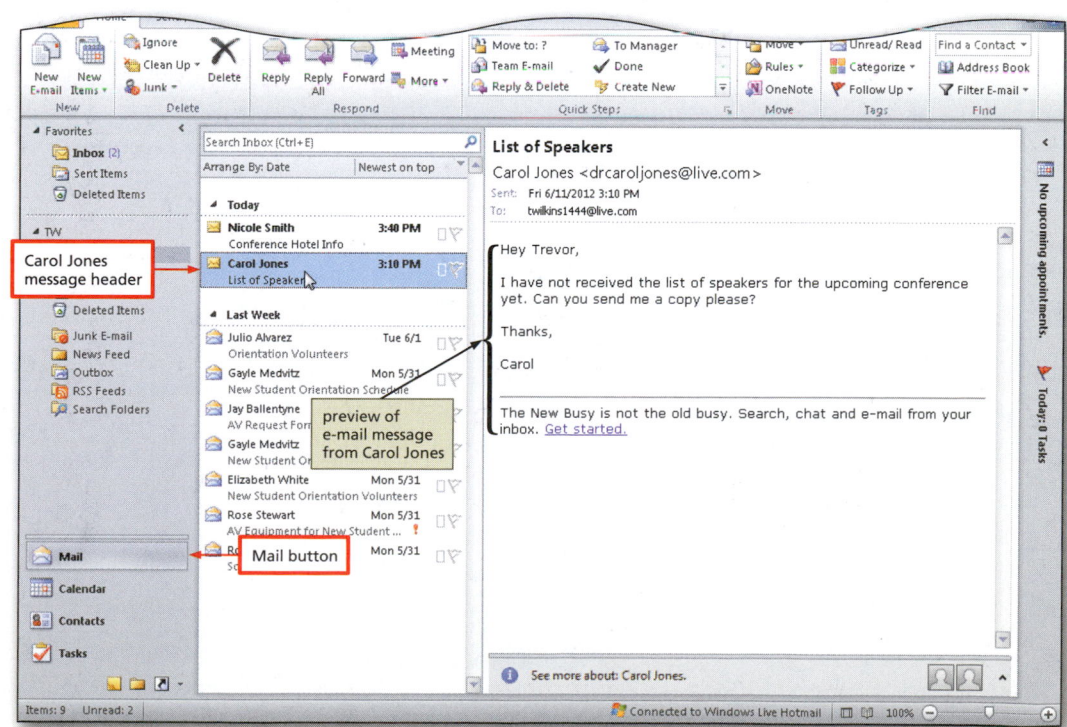

Figure 3–6

2

- Right-click Carol Jones's e-mail address to display a shortcut menu (Figure 3–7).

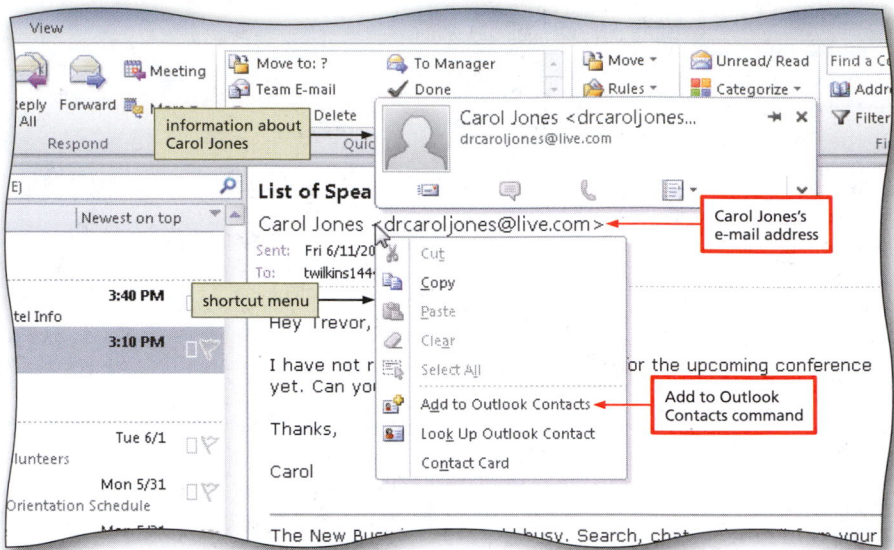

Figure 3–7

3

- Click Add to Outlook Contacts to display the Carol Jones – Contact window (Figure 3–8).

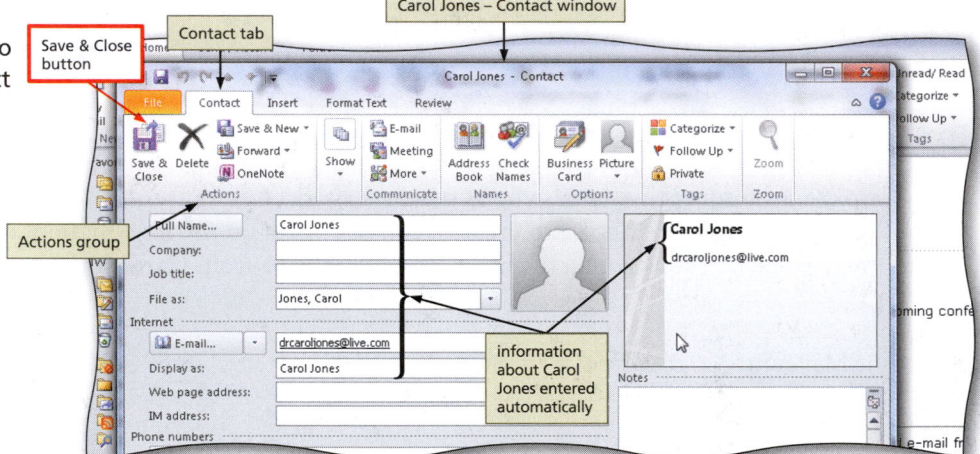

Figure 3–8

4

- Click the Save & Close button (Contact tab | Actions group) to save the contact and close the Contact window.

- Click the Contacts button in the Navigation Pane to display your contacts, including the new contact for Carol Jones (Figure 3–9).

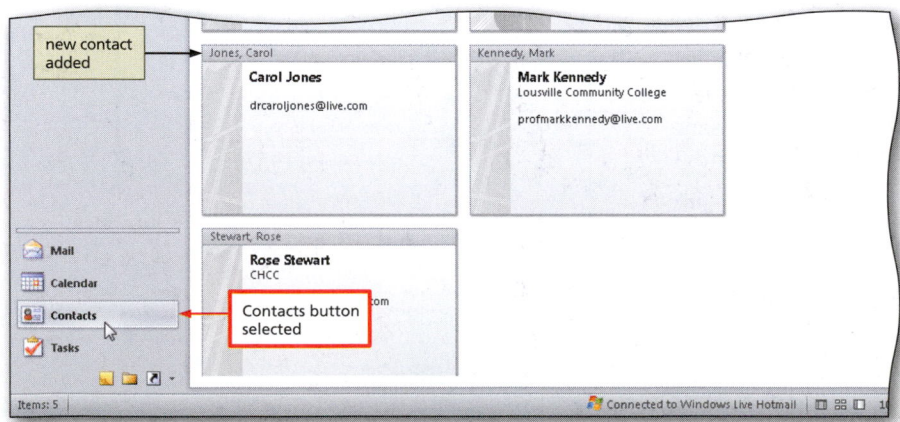

Figure 3–9

To Create a Contact from an Existing Contact

Mark asked his colleague, Richard Estes, to accompany him to the upcoming lecture series. You want to add Richard Estes as a new contact. When a new contact shares information with an existing contact, you can create a new contact from the existing contact, and then edit only the information unique to the new contact. The following steps copy the Mark Kennedy contact to create a contact for Richard Estes.

1

- Click the Mark Kennedy contact to select it (Figure 3–10).

Q&A Why is the top bar of the Mark Kennedy contact orange?

The orange bar indicates that the contact is selected.

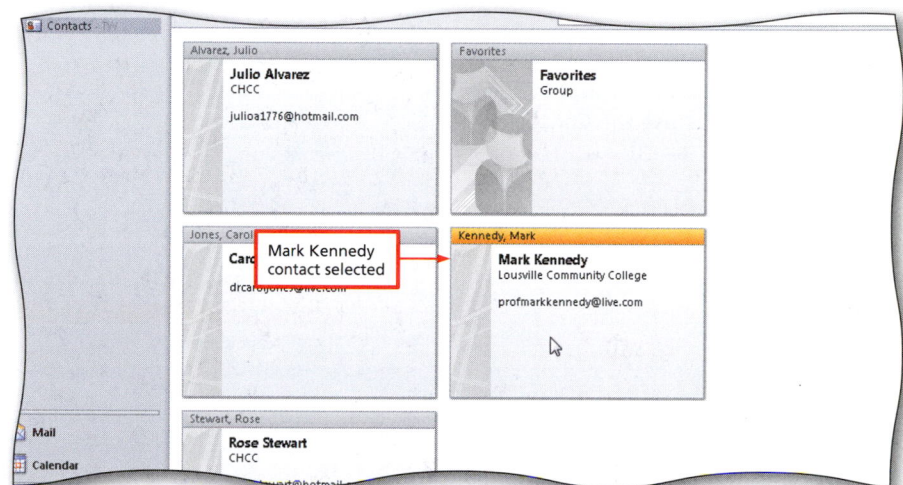

Figure 3–10

2

- Click the New Items button (Home tab | New group) to display the New Items menu (Figure 3–11).

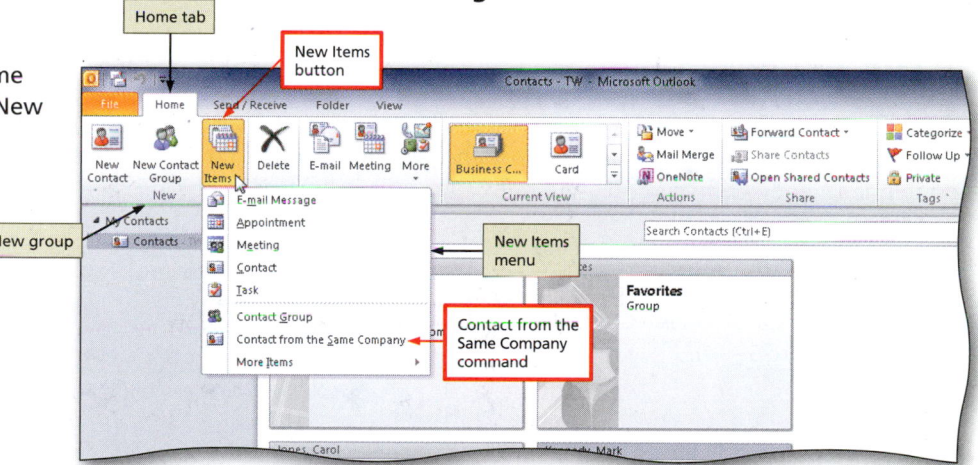

Figure 3–11

3

- Click Contact from the Same Company to display a new Contact window with selected information from the previously selected contact, in this case, Mark Kennedy (Figure 3–12).

Q&A Why does the title of the Contact window show the company name?

Until you enter a name for the contact, Outlook uses the company name as the title of the window. When you enter the contact's name, Outlook changes the title of the window accordingly.

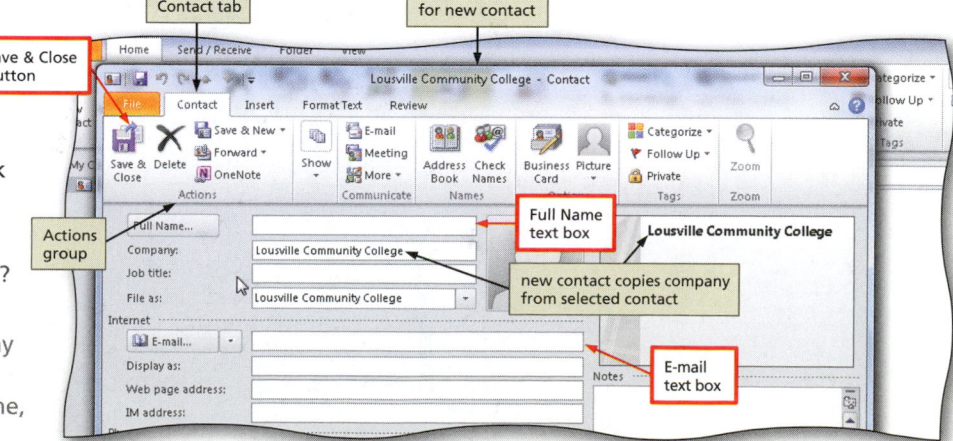

Figure 3–12

4

- Type `Richard Estes` in the Full Name text box to enter a name for the contact.

- Type `richardestes@live.com` in the E-mail text box to enter an e-mail address for the contact.

- Click the Save & Close button (Contact tab | Actions group) to save the contact and close the Contact window (Figure 3–13).

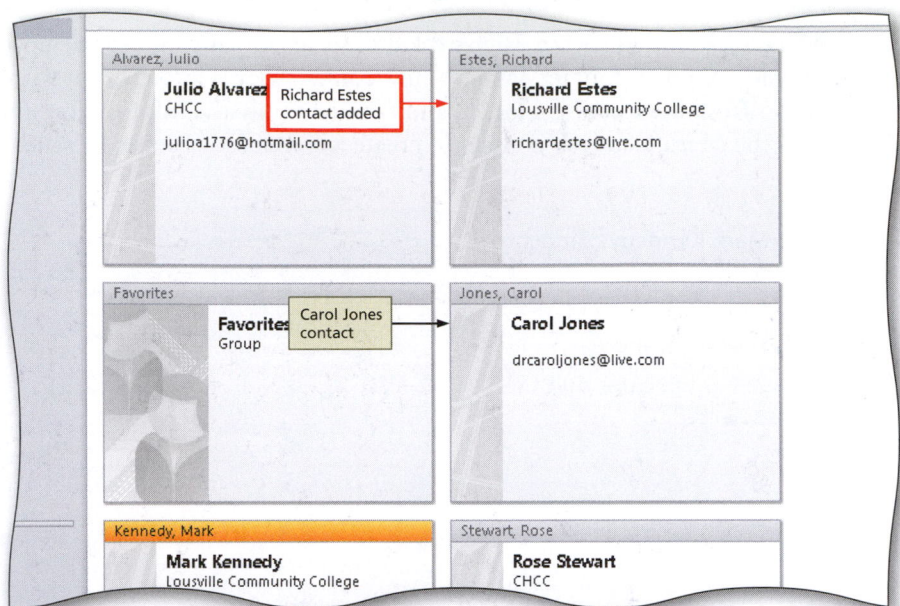

Figure 3–13

To Edit a Contact

When you created a contact record for Carol Jones, it did not include her work phone number and e-mail address. She now has given you her work phone number and e-mail address, and you want to edit her contact record to include the new information. The following steps edit the Carol Jones contact.

1

- Double-click the Carol Jones contact to display the Carol Jones – Contact window (Figure 3–14).

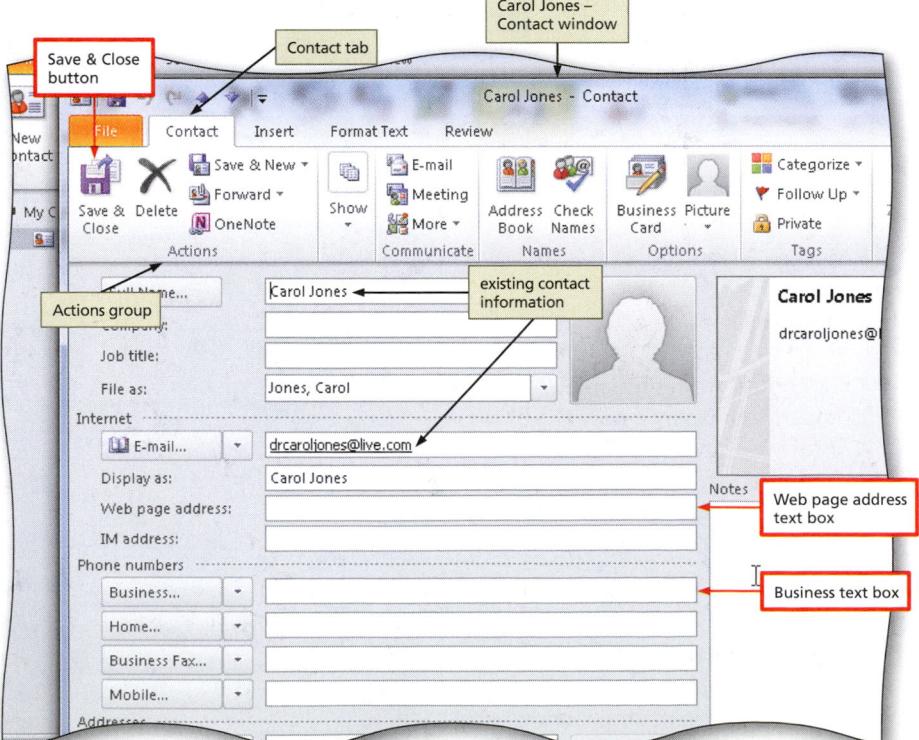

Figure 3–14

- Type `http://faculty .canateluniv.edu/cjones` in the 'Web page address' text box to enter a Web page address for the contact.

- Type `555-9876` in the Business text box to enter a business phone number for the contact.

- Click the Save & Close button (Contact tab | Actions group) to save the contact and close the Contact window (Figure 3–15).

Q&A Why did the title of the contact icon change?

When you edit the contact, the contact icon updates to display the new information.

Q&A Why did the area code appear after entering the business phone number?

Depending on the configuration of your computer and its programs, Outlook might insert the local area code automatically.

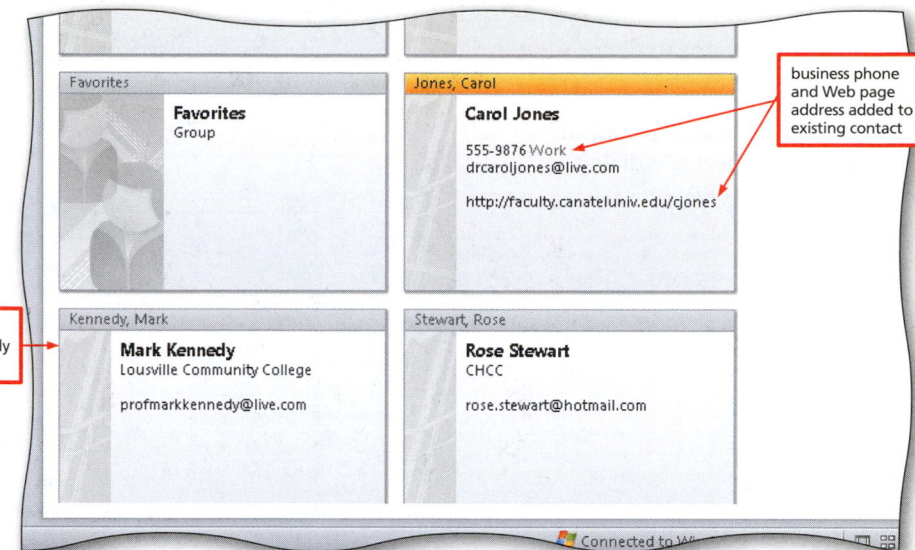

Figure 3–15

To Add an Attachment to a Contact

Mark Kennedy has sent you a document listing the hours he will be available in the tutoring center. You decide to include this document as part of his contact record so that you can find this schedule easily. Any files you attach to a contact are displayed in the Notes section of the Contact window. You also can insert items such as tables, pictures, and clip art to the Notes section. The following steps add Mark's tutoring hours to his contact information.

- Double-click the Mark Kennedy contact to display the Mark Kennedy – Contact window (Figure 3–16).

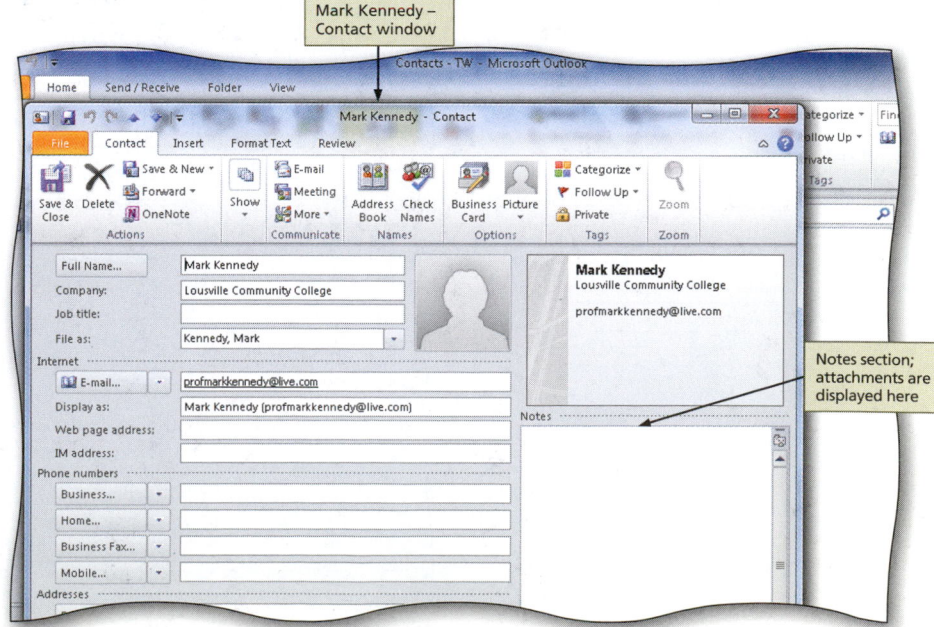

Figure 3–16

2

• Click Insert on the Ribbon to display the Insert tab.

• Click the Attach File button (Insert tab | Include group) to display the Insert File dialog box (Figure 3–17).

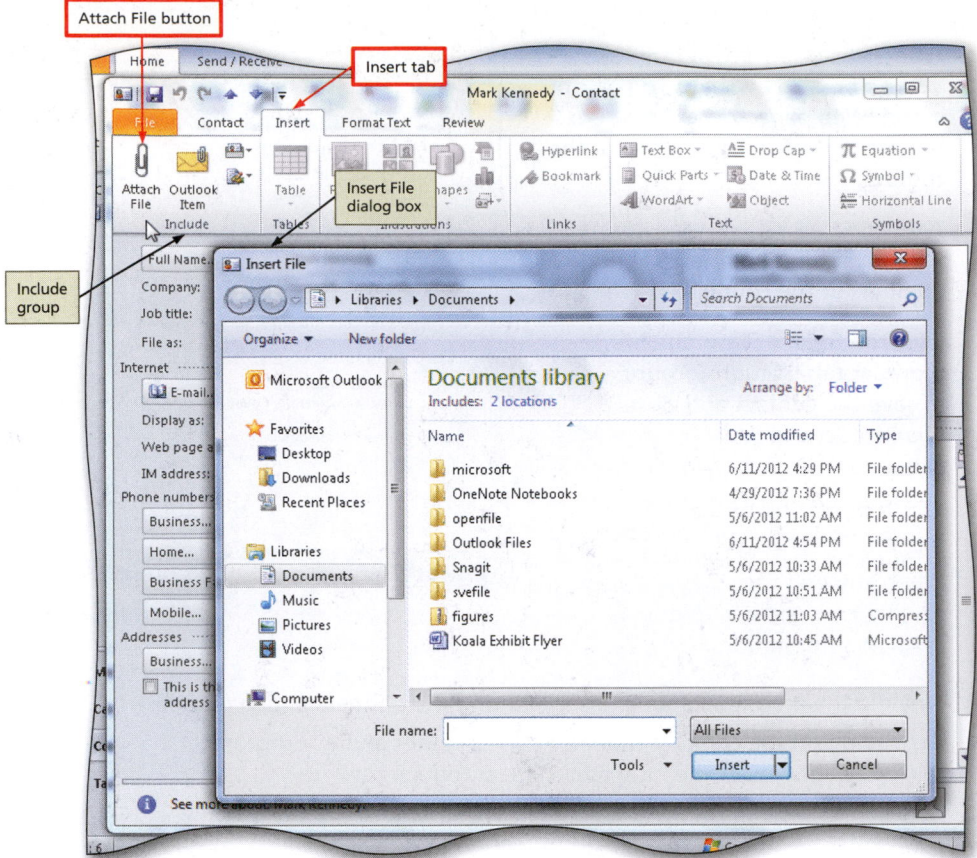

Figure 3–17

3

• Navigate to the file location (in this case, the Chapter 03 folder in the Outlook folder in the Data Files for Students folder on a USB flash drive).

• Click the Tutoring Schedule document to select it (Figure 3–18).

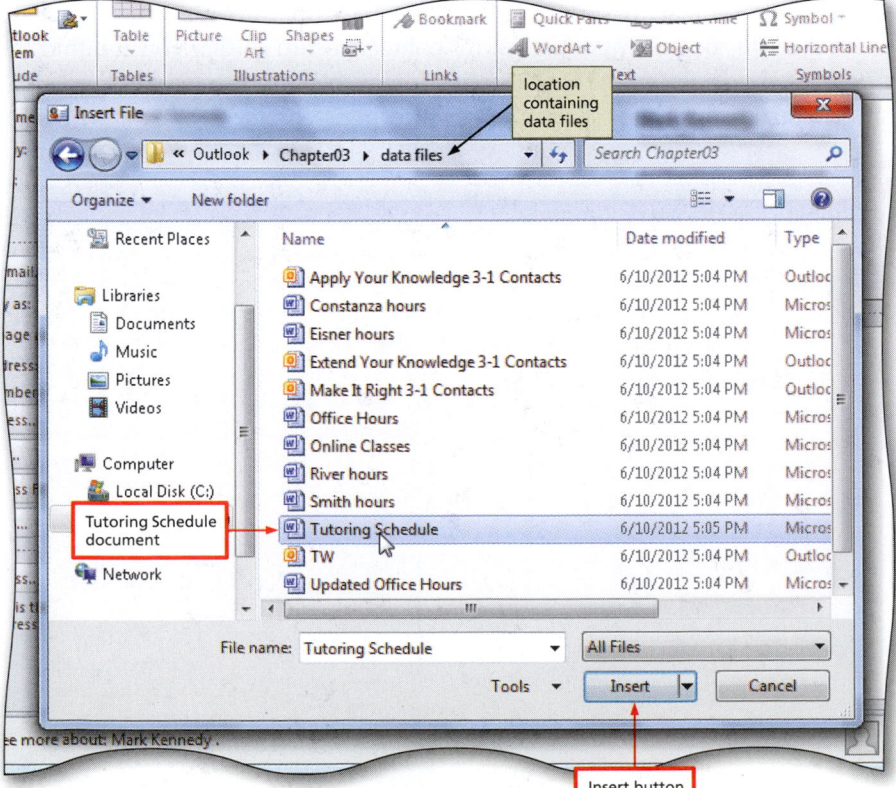

Figure 3–18

4

• Click the Insert button (Insert File dialog box) to attach the document to the contact (Figure 3–19).

Q&A Can I add more than one attachment?

Yes; you can add as many attachments as you want.

Q&A How do I view an attachment after I have added it?

Open the contact and then double-click the attachment to open it.

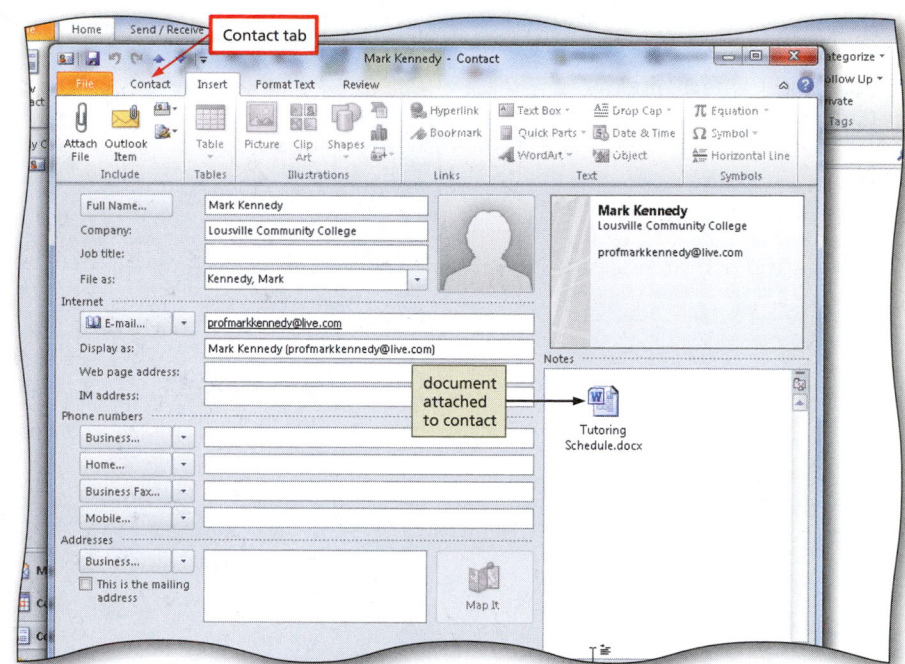

Figure 3–19

5

• Click Contact on the Ribbon to display the Contact tab.

• Click the Save & Close button (Contact tab | Actions group) to save the contact and close the Contact window (Figure 3–20).

Q&A Can I send a meeting request to a contact?

Yes. To send a meeting request to a contact, click the contact to select it, click Meeting (Home tab | Communicate group), enter the details of the meeting in the Untitled – Meeting window, and then click the Send button.

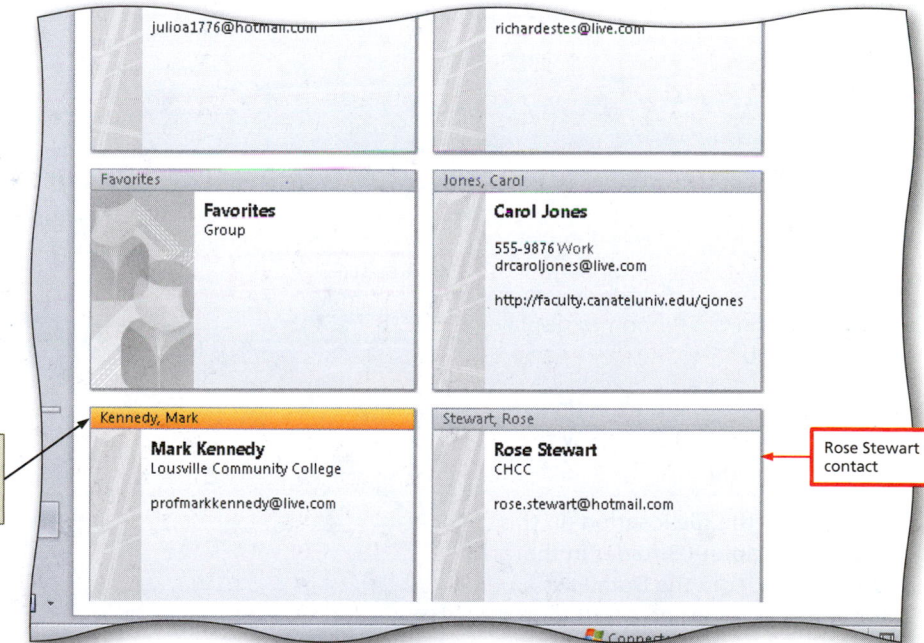

Figure 3–20

To Change an Attachment to a Contact

Rose Stewart has sent you updated office hour information. You need to replace the attachment in her contact with the document containing the updated office hours. The steps on the next pages change the attachment for the Rose Stewart contact.

1

• Double-click the Rose Stewart contact to display the Rose Stewart – Contact window (Figure 3–21).

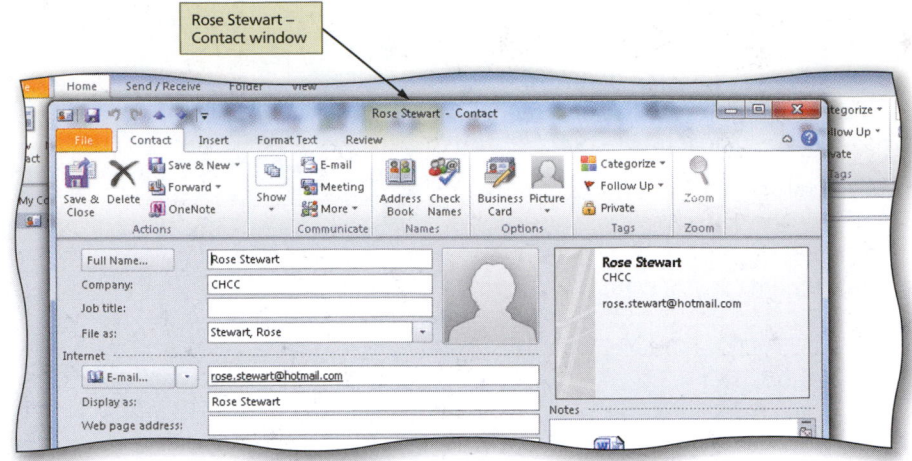

Figure 3–21

2

• Click the Office Hours document to select it (Figure 3–22).

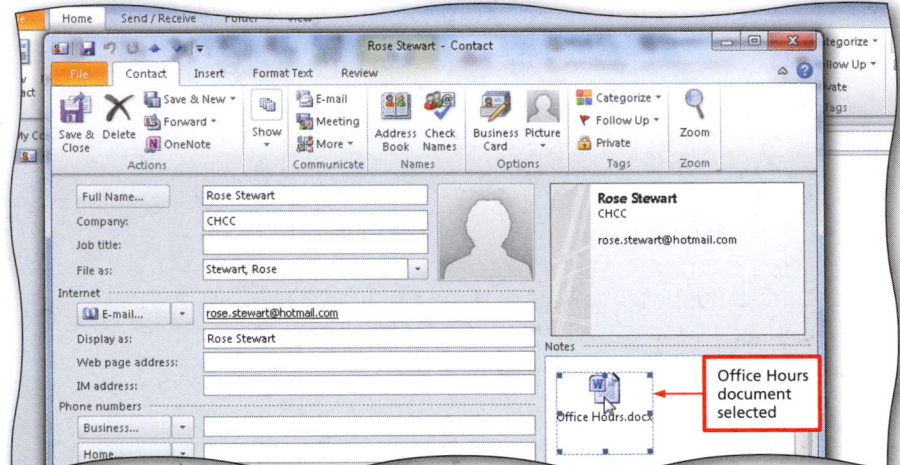

Figure 3–22

3

• Click Insert on the Ribbon to display the Insert tab.

• Click the Attach File button (Insert tab | Include group) to display the Insert File dialog box.

• Navigate to the file location (in this case, the Chapter 03 folder in the Outlook folder in the Data Files for Students folder on a USB flash drive).

• Click the Updated Office Hours document to select it.

• Click the Insert button (Insert File dialog box) to change the attachment for the contact (Figure 3–23).

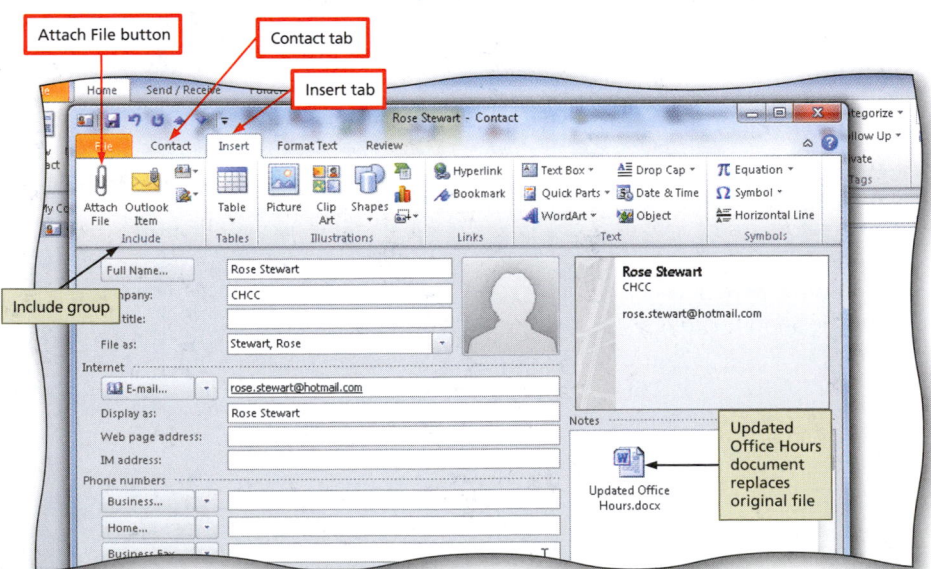

Figure 3–23

Why did the new file replace the original file?

Because the original file was selected before attaching the new file, the new file replaced the original file. If the original file were not selected, Outlook would add the new file while keeping the original file.

4

- Click Contact on the Ribbon to display the Contact tab.

- Click the Save & Close button (Contact tab | Actions group) to save the contact and close the Contact window (Figure 3–24).

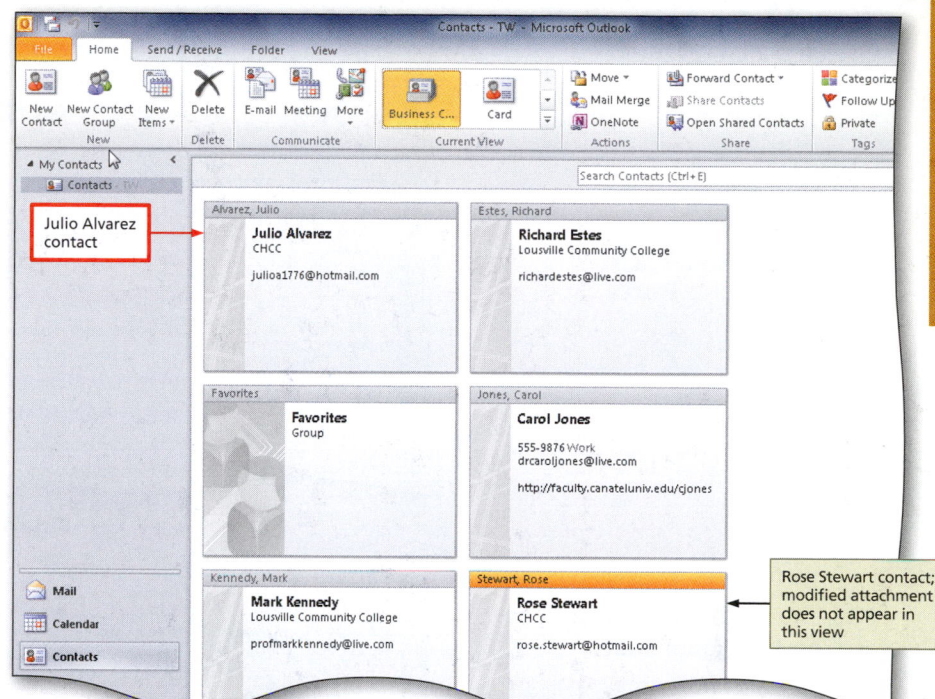

Figure 3–24

To Remove an Attachment to a Contact

Sometimes you need to remove attachments that you have added to a contact. Julio Alvarez was teaching online classes for the previous semester but now is not teaching any online classes. You need to remove the list of online classes from his contact. The following steps remove the attachment from the Julio Alvarez contact.

1

- Double-click the Julio Alvarez contact to display the Julio Alvarez – Contact window (Figure 3–25).

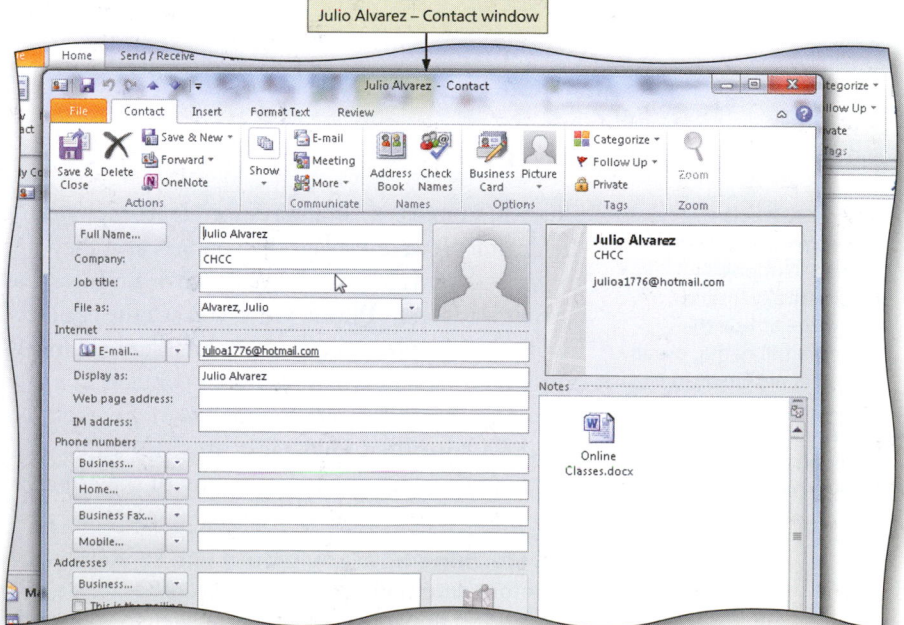

Figure 3–25

2

• Click the Online Classes document to select it (Figure 3–26).

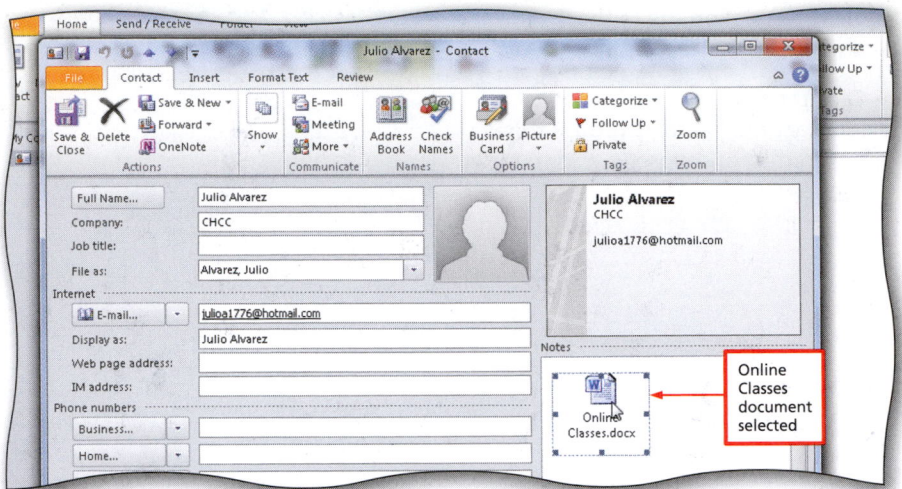

Figure 3–26

3

• Press the DELETE key to remove the attachment (Figure 3–27).

4

• Click the Save & Close button (Contact tab | Actions group) to save the contact and close the Contact window.

Figure 3–27

Viewing and Sorting Your Contact List

Filing Contacts
When creating a new contact, Outlook automatically inserts in the File as box the contact's full name, usually in LastName, FirstName format. Outlook sorts contacts on the value stored in the File as box for each contact.

Outlook supports several ways for you to view your contact list. **Business Card view** is the default view; it displays the contacts as if they were business cards. **Card view** shows the contacts as cards but much smaller than Business Card view, with most information being only partially visible. In **Phone view**, you see the contacts in a list displaying phone information. Finally, in **List view**, the contacts are arranged in a list according to businesses. You also can create custom views to display your contacts in a way that suits a particular purpose.

When working with contacts in any view, you can sort the contacts to display them in a different order. Each view provides different sort options. For example, in Phone view, you can sort the list using any of the column heading buttons that are displayed.

Plan Ahead

Determine how you would like to view your contacts.
Before determining a view or sort order to use for your contacts, consider what you are trying to find in your contacts, as well as your preferred way to view information. This can help you quickly find the information for which you are looking.

To Change the Current View

While Business Card view provides useful information, you want to explore the other views. Phone view, for example, is very helpful when you are looking for a contact's phone number in a long list. Changing the view sometimes can help you find a contact's information more quickly. The following steps change the current view to Phone view and then back to the default Business Card view.

1
● Click the Phone button (Home tab | Current View group) to switch to Phone view (Figure 3–28).

Q&A What if the Phone button is not displayed in the Current View group?

Click the More button or Change View button (Home tab | Current View group) to display a list of available views, and then click Phone.

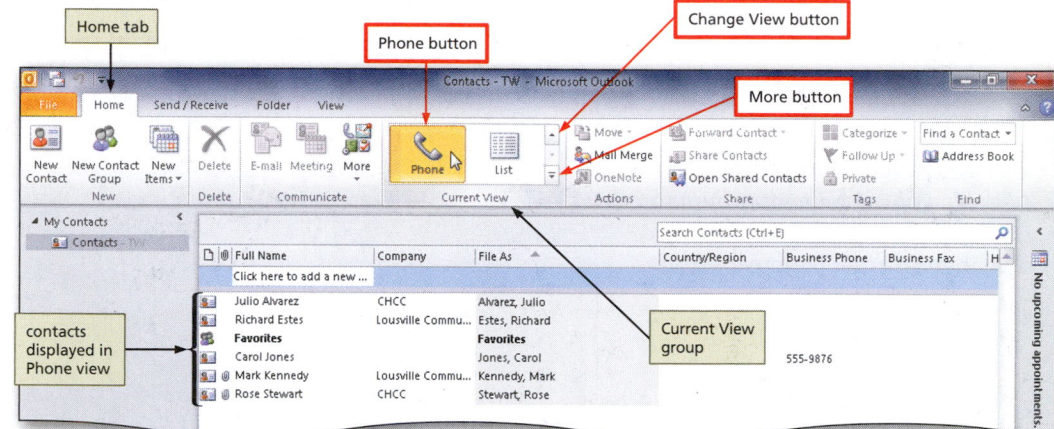

Figure 3–28

2
● Click the More button (Home tab | Current View group), and then click Business Card to switch to Business Card view (Figure 3–29).

Q&A What if the More button is not displayed in the Current View group?

You likely are using a higher resolution than 1024 × 768, so the Ribbon can display additional buttons. Click the Business Card button in the Current View group to switch to Business Card view.

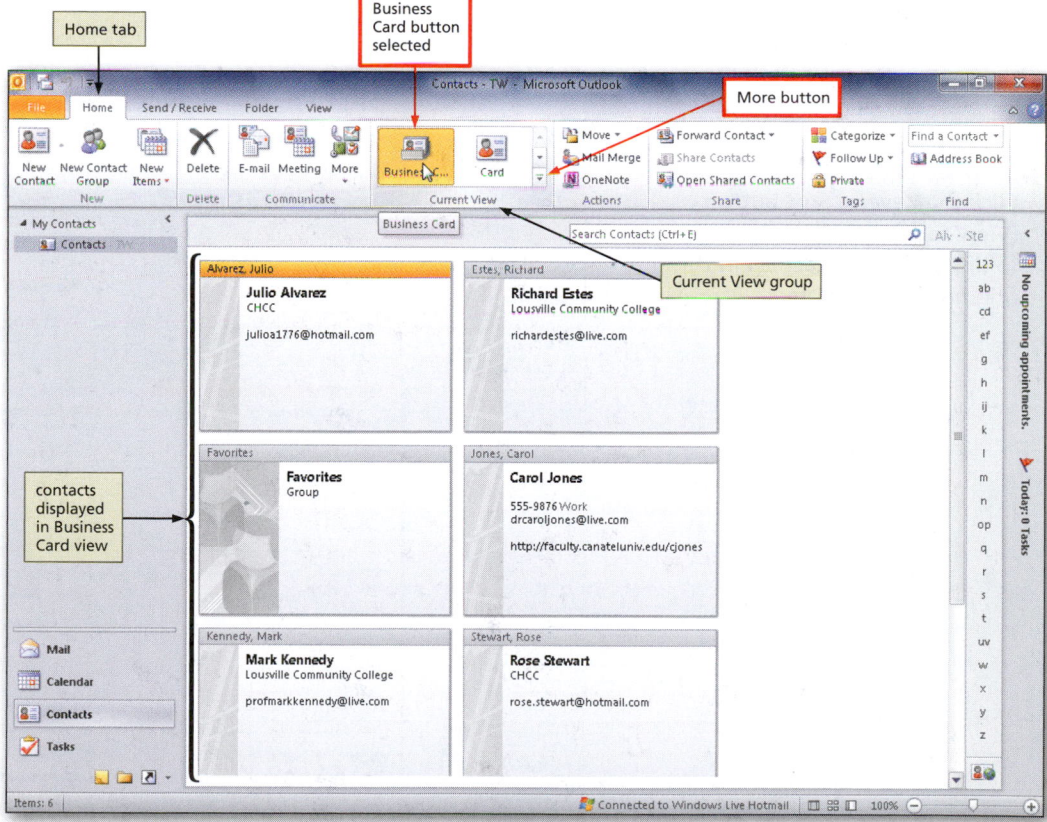

Figure 3–29

Experiment

● Click the other views in the Current View group to view the contacts in other arrangements. When you are finished, click Business Card to return to Business Card view.

To Sort Contacts

Business Card view displays the contacts in alphabetical order by default; however, you can sort them to view the contacts in reverse order, which is especially helpful if you want to quickly open a record for a contact at the end of a long contact list. The following steps sort the contact list in reverse order, and then switch back to alphabetical order.

1
- Click View on the Ribbon to display the View tab.

- Click the Reverse Sort button (View tab | Arrangement group) to display the contact list in reverse alphabetical order (Figure 3–30).

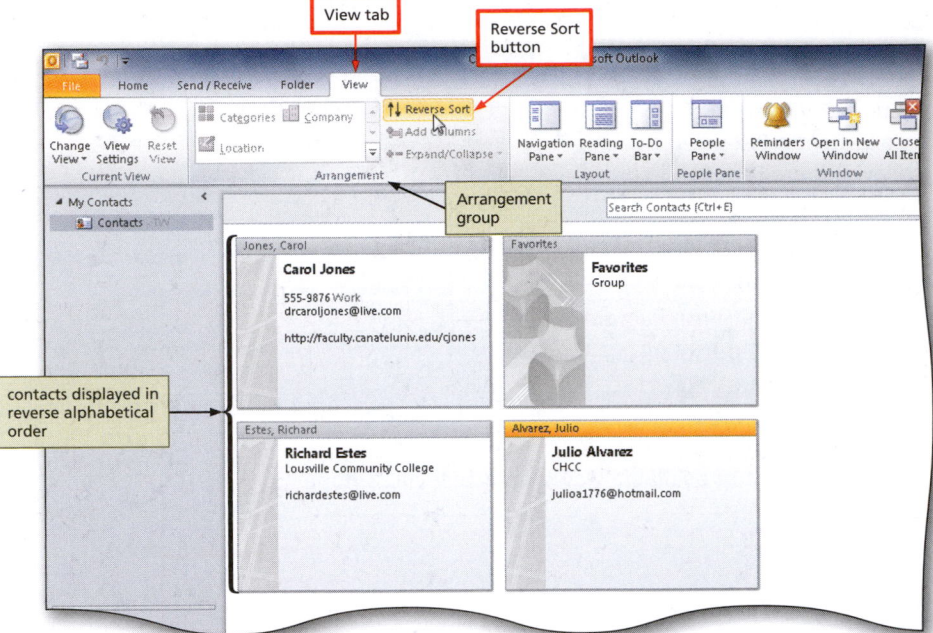

Figure 3–30

2
- Click the Reverse Sort button (View tab | Arrangement group) to display the contact list in the original order (Figure 3–31).

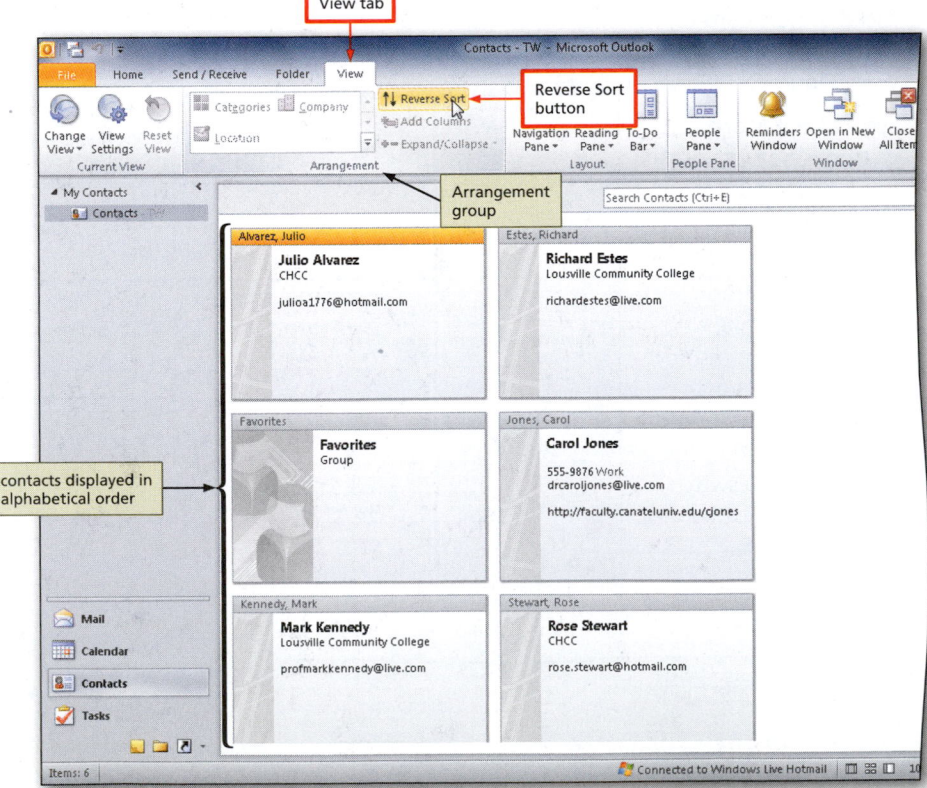

Figure 3–31

Break Point: If you wish to take a break, this is a good place to do so. To resume at a later time, start Outlook and continue following the steps from this location forward.

Using Search to Find a Contact

Over time, contact lists can grow quite large, making them difficult to navigate. In addition, you sometimes may not remember details about a contact you want to find. For example, you may remember that someone works for a particular company, but not their name. Alternatively, you may remember a phone number but nothing else. If this happens, you can use the Search Contacts text box to search your contact list.

You also can find contacts using the Find a Contact search box in the Find group on the Home tab. This works no matter which folder you are using (such as Mail, Calendar, Contacts, or Tasks). This means that anytime you need to find your contacts, you quickly can look them up.

You can maximize your search efforts if you create a list of keywords that you can assign to contacts. The more general the keyword, the more results you will find. Using more specific keywords will reduce the number of results.

BTW

Start Menu Search Box
In addition to using the search features in Outlook to locate a contact, you also can search for a contact using the Search box on the Start menu.

To Find a Contact by Searching for an E-Mail Address

If you only know partial information such as the area code in a phone number, the first word in a school name, or the domain name in an e-mail address, you can use it to find matching contacts. Note that you might find many contacts that contain the text for which you are searching. The text you are using as the search term could be part of an e-mail address or a name, for example. Therefore, you may have to examine the results further. The following steps find all contacts that contain the text, hotmail.

1

- Click the Search Contacts text box to display the Search Tools Search tab (Figure 3–32).

Q&A

Why is the Search Tools Search tab displayed when I click the Search Contacts text box?

The Search Tools Search tab is a tool tab that contains buttons and commands that can help you search contacts.

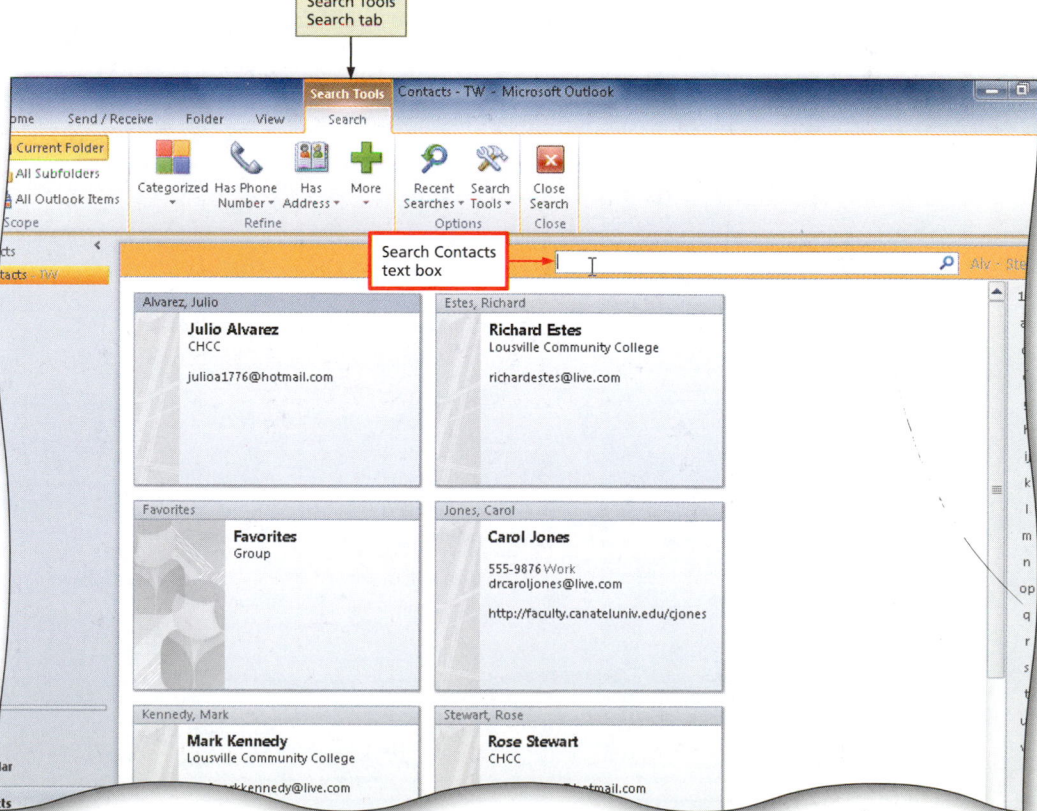

Figure 3–32

2

• Type **hotmail** in the Search Contacts text box to search for all contacts containing the text, hotmail (Figure 3–33).

Q&A

Can I modify a search further after getting the initial results?

Certainly. You can use the Search Tools Search tab to refine your search by specifying a phone number or address, for example. You also can expand the search to include all of the Outlook folders.

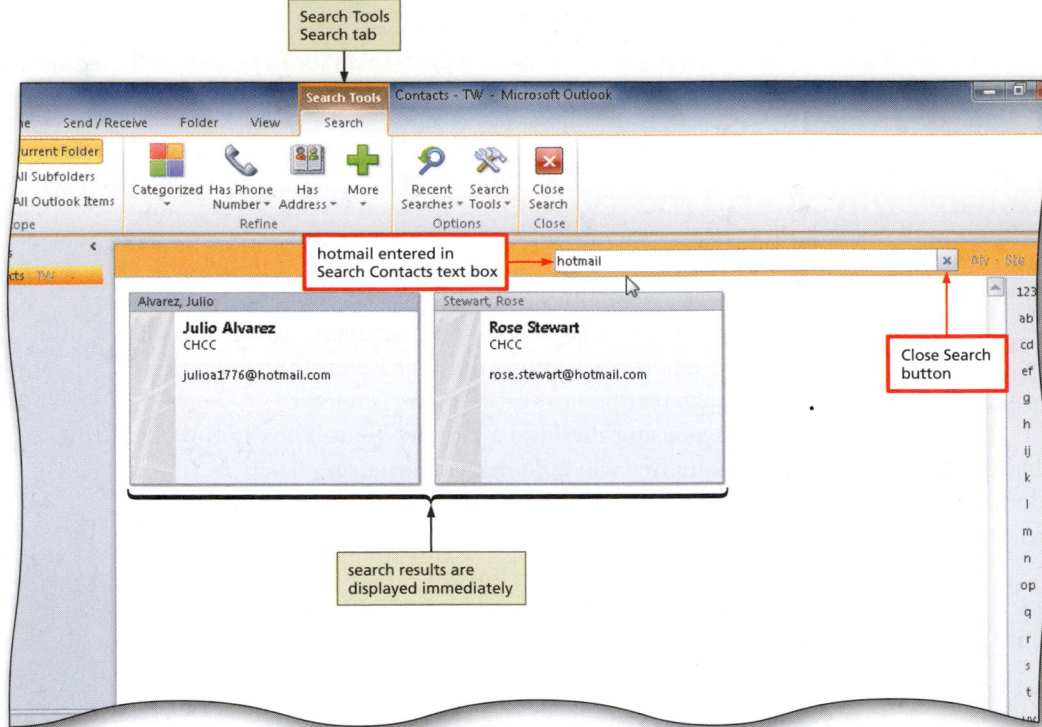

Figure 3–33

3

• Click the Close Search button in the Search Contacts text box to close the search and return to the Contact folder (Figure 3–34).

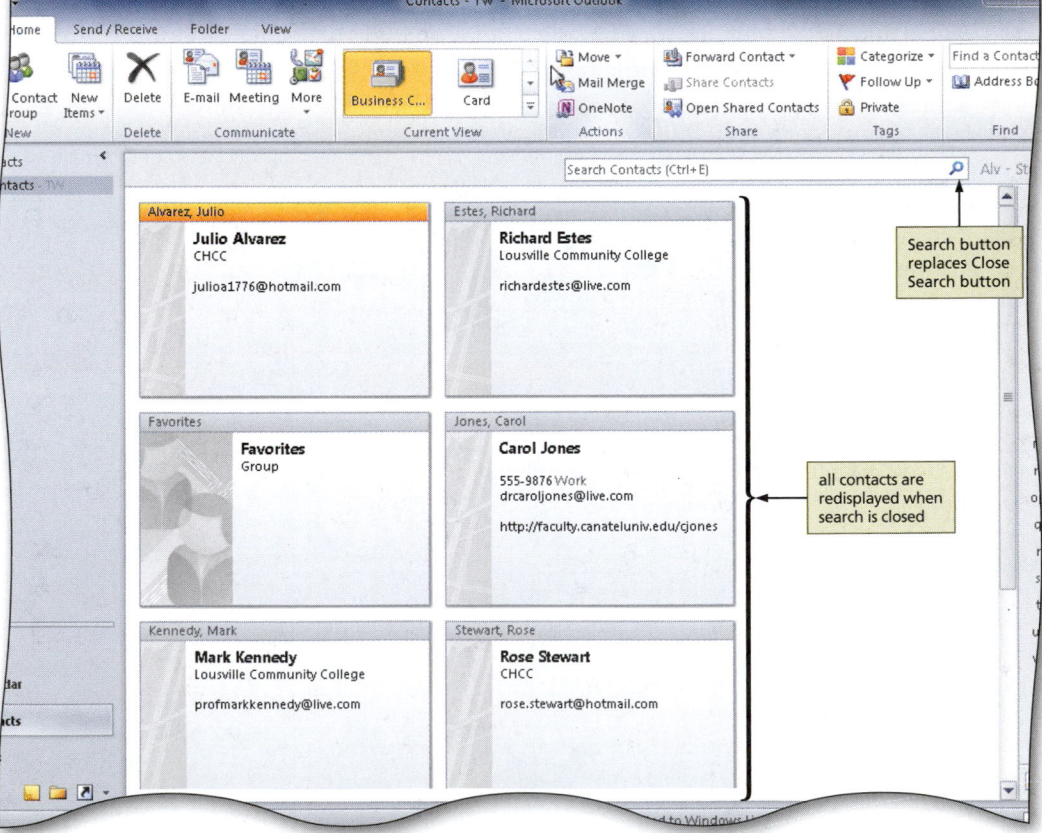

Figure 3–34

To Refine a Search

If you type a full name or e-mail address in the Search Contacts text box, you will find your contact, but the information need not be in only the Full Name field or the E-mail field. The results might contain contacts where the name or e-mail address is part of the Notes field, for example. Instead, you can find a contact by searching only a particular field. The results will contain only contacts that contain the search term in the specified field. No contacts will appear that contain the search term in a different field.

You want to update the Richard Estes contact record by searching only the Full Name field. The following steps search for the Richard Estes contact.

1
- Click the Search Contacts text box to display the Search Tools Search tab.

- Click the More button (Search Tools Search tab | Refine group) to display a list of common properties for refining a search (Figure 3–35).

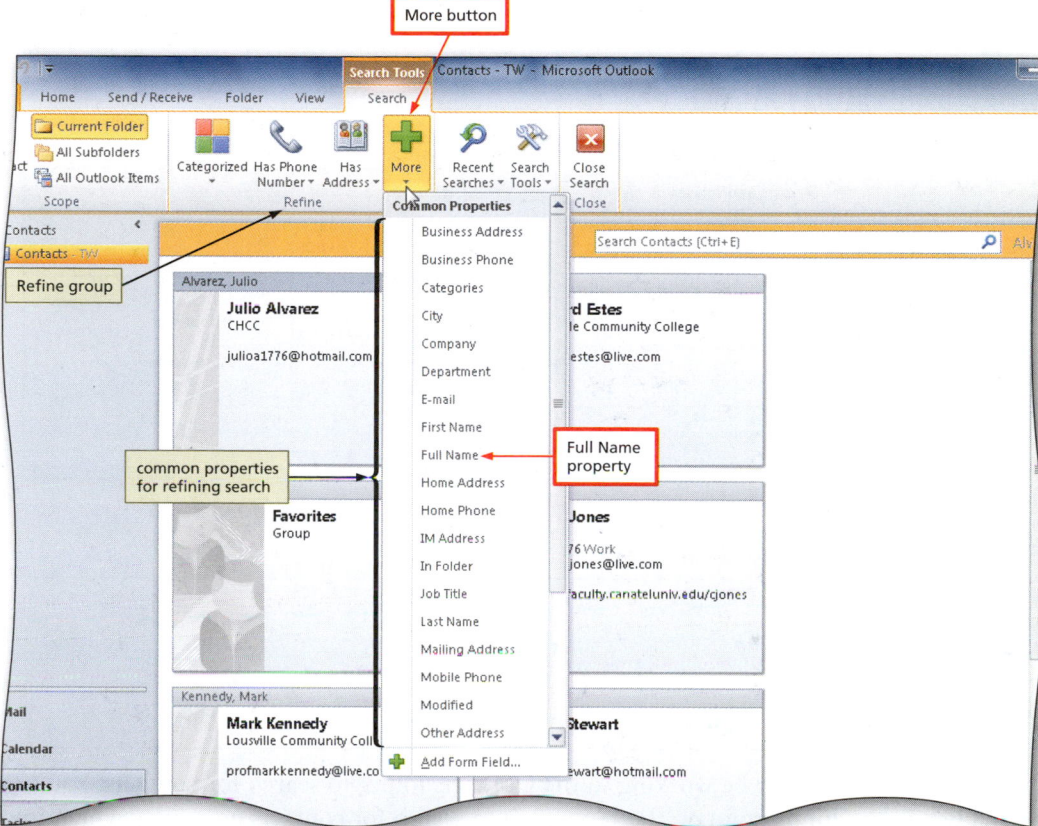

Figure 3–35

2
- Click Full Name to display the Full Name text box.

- Type **Richard Estes** in the Full Name text box to search for the Richard Estes contact (Figure 3–36).

Q&A Why might Outlook display search results that do not appear to contain the search text?

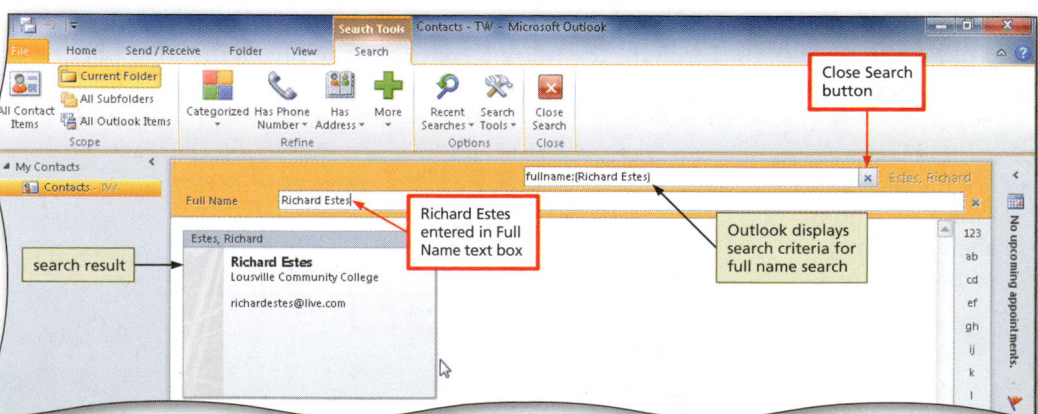

Figure 3–36

When you perform a search, Outlook searches all specified fields for a match. However, the matching fields might not be displayed in the list of search results, although the contact record does contain the search text.

3

- Double-click the Richard Estes contact to open it.

- Type **Manages Seminar Blog** in the Notes field to update the contact.

- Click the Save & Close button (Contact tab | Actions group) to save the contact and close the Contact window.

- Click the Close Search button in the Search Contacts text box to close the search and return to the Contact folder (Figure 3–37).

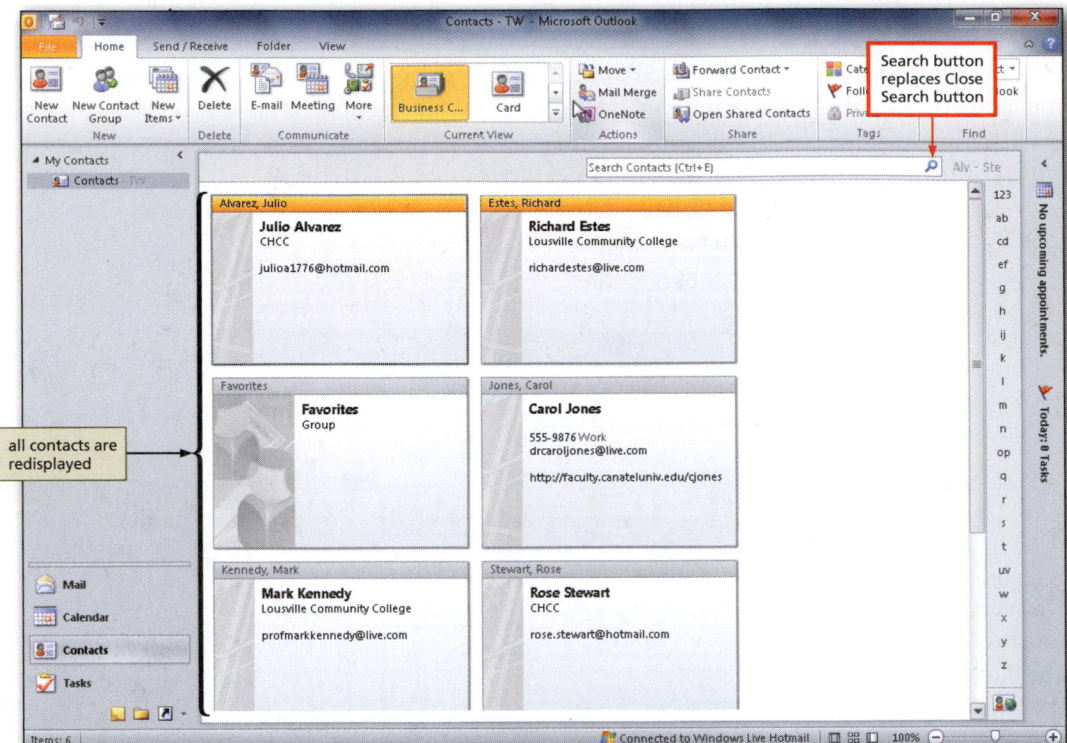

Figure 3–37

Other Ways

1. Press CTRL+E, type search criteria

To Find a Contact from any Outlook Folder

You do not have to be working in the Contacts folder to search for contacts. You can use the Find a Contact search box in the Find group on the Home tab to search for contacts no matter which folder you are viewing. If what you type in the search box matches a single contact, that entry will be displayed in a contact window. If what you type matches more than one entry, you will be asked to select the contact that you want to view. For example, if you search for a contact using part of the company name, more than one contact may appear in the search results. You then can select a single contact from the results.

The following steps search for the Mark Kennedy contact from the Mail folder using only part of the company name, Lousville.

1

- Click the Mail button in the Navigation Pane to display your mailbox (Figure 3–38).

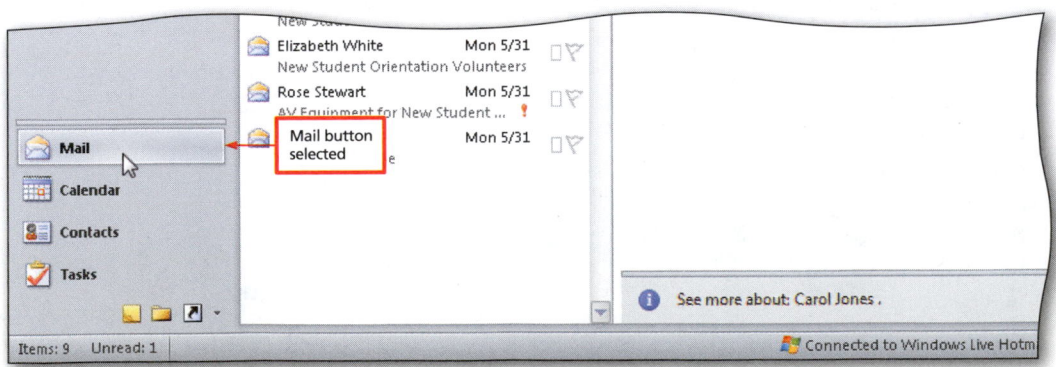

Figure 3–38

2

- Type **Lousville** in the Find a Contact search box (Home tab | Find group) to search for contacts containing the search text (Figure 3–39).

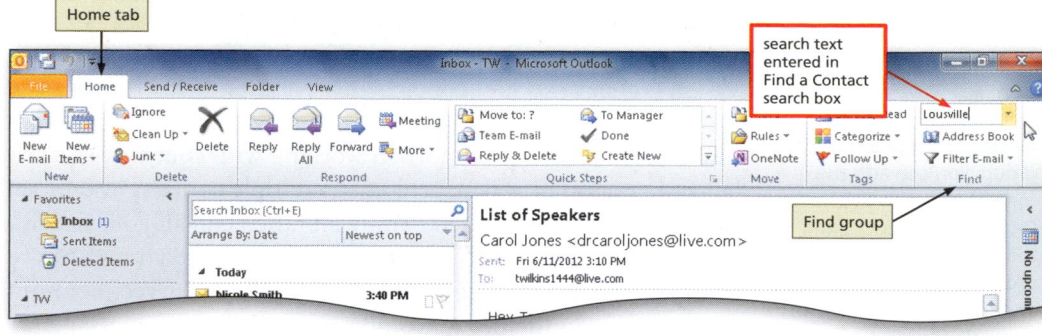

Figure 3–39

3

- Press ENTER to display the Choose Contact dialog box (Figure 3–40).

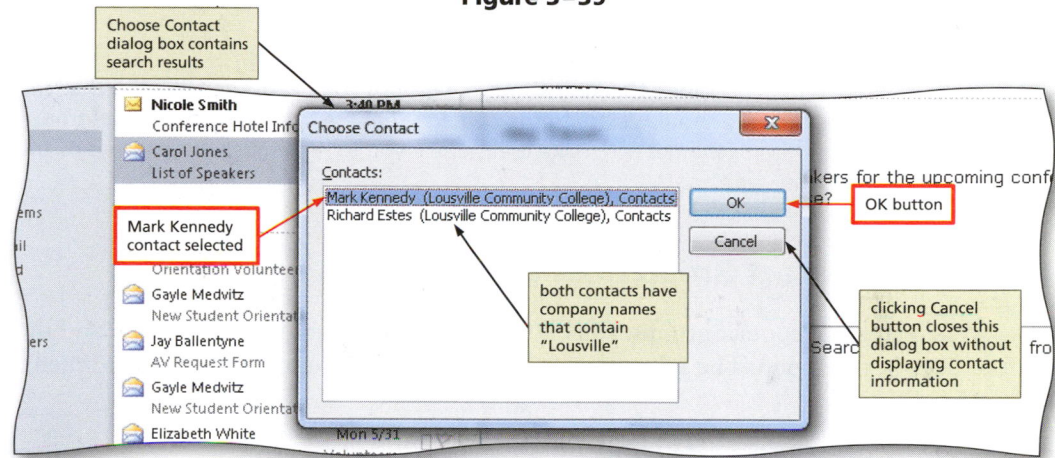

Figure 3–40

4

- If necessary, click Mark Kennedy to select the contact.

- Click the OK button (Choose Contact dialog box) to display the contact record (Figure 3–41).

Figure 3–41

5

- Click the Close button to close the window.

- Click the Contacts button in the Navigation Pane to return to the Contacts folder (Figure 3–42).

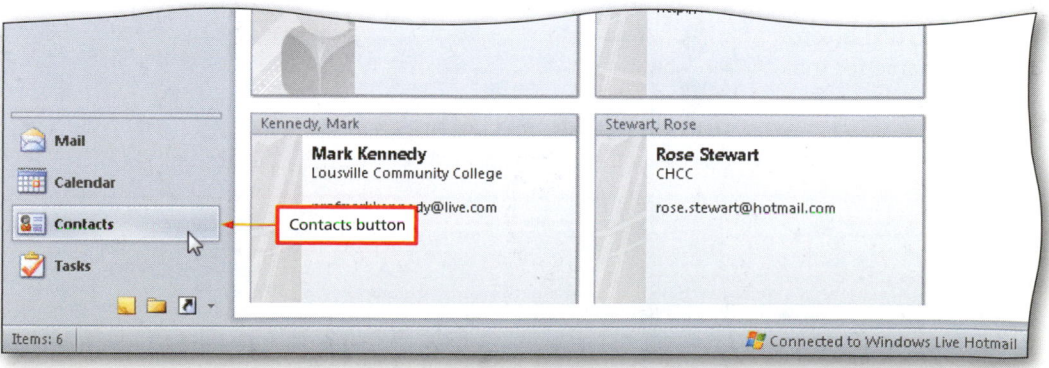

Figure 3–42

Create and Edit a Contact Group

When you have several contacts that you frequently e-mail or work with as a group, you can create a contact group and add the contacts to it. A **contact group** provides a single name for you to use when working with contacts. You are not creating subfolders, but rather another way to reference multiple contacts at one time. For example, you could create a group called Family and then add all your family members to the group. Whenever you want to send an e-mail message to your entire family at one time, you could enter the contact group name, Family, as the recipient of the e-mail message and every contact in the group would receive the e-mail message.

Plan Ahead

> **Determine what groups you may need.**
> When thinking about the groups you need, keep in mind that the names of the groups should relate to the contacts that are organized under the group name. Choosing good names will make it easier for you to remember the purpose of the group.

To Create a Contact Group from Existing Contacts

When creating contact groups, you choose the name for your contact group and then add the contacts you want to have in the group. The following steps create a Lousville contact group and then add the Lousville-related contacts to the group.

- Click the New Contact Group button (Home tab | New group) to display the Untitled – Contact Group window (Figure 3–43).

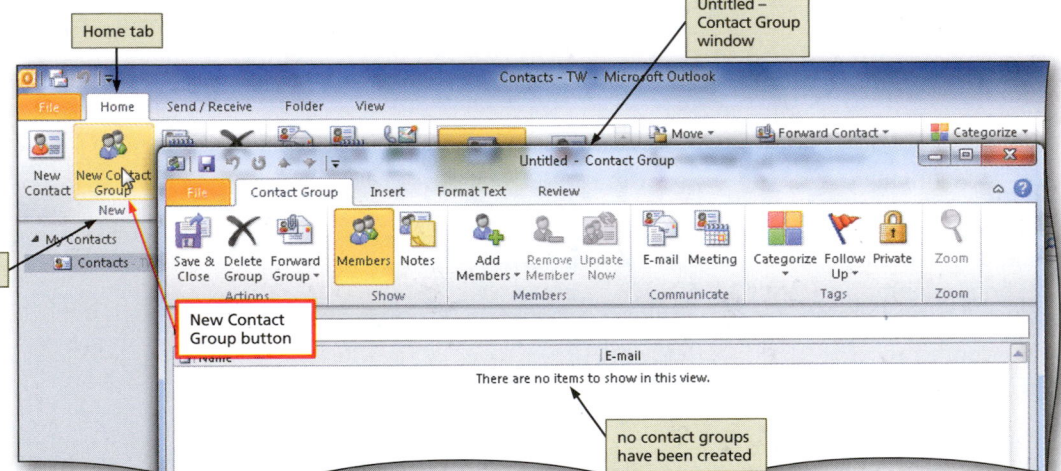

Figure 3–43

- Type **Lousville** in the Name text box to enter a name for the group (Figure 3–44).

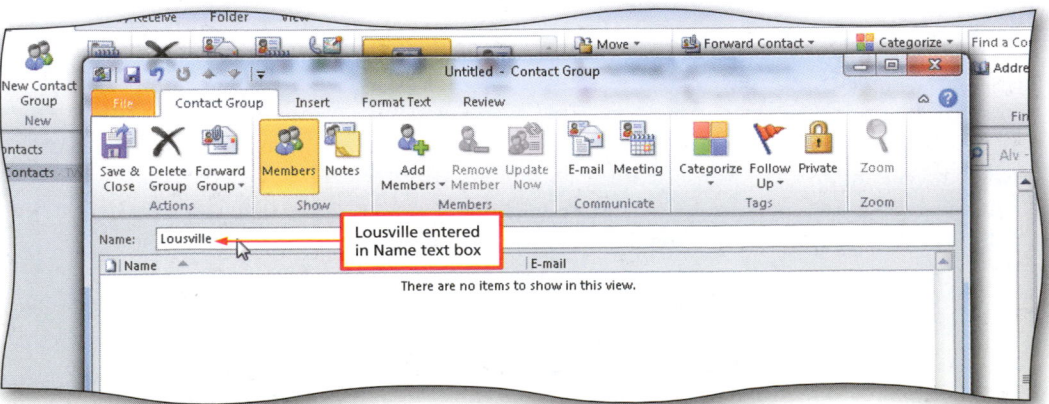

Figure 3–44

3

- Click the Add Members button (Contact Group tab | Members group) to display the Add Members menu (Figure 3–45).

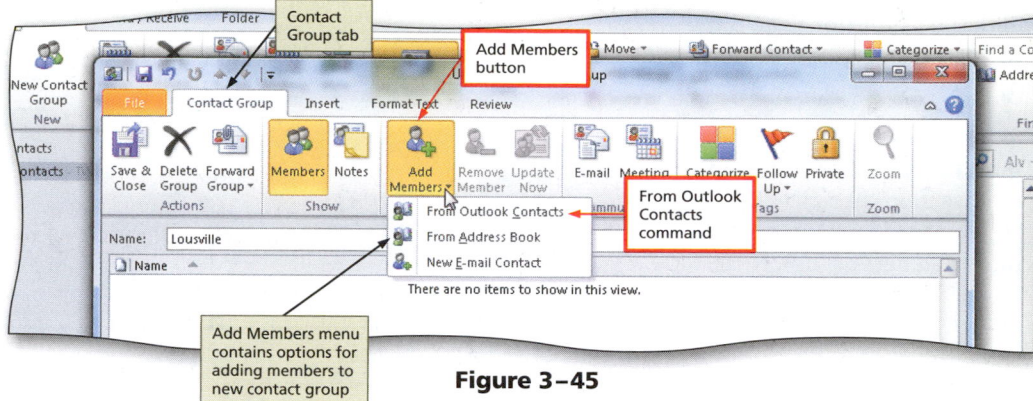

Figure 3–45

4

- Click From Outlook Contacts to display the Select Members dialog box (Figure 3–46).

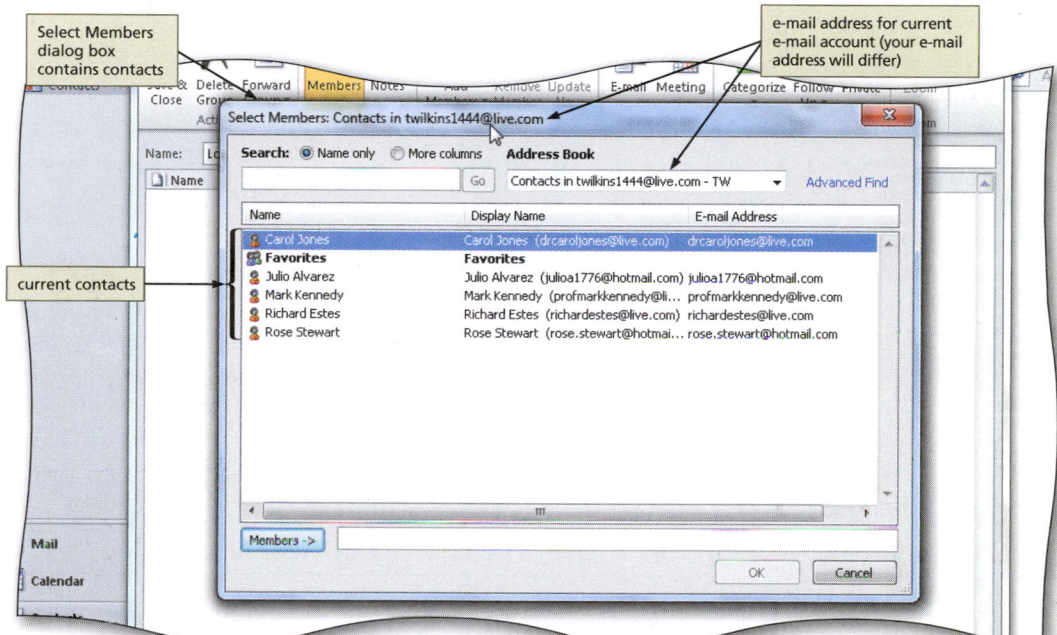

Figure 3–46

5

- Click the Mark Kennedy contact to select it, press and hold the CTRL key, and then click the Richard Estes contact to select both contacts.

- Click the Members button (Select Members dialog box) to move the information to the Members text box (Figure 3–47).

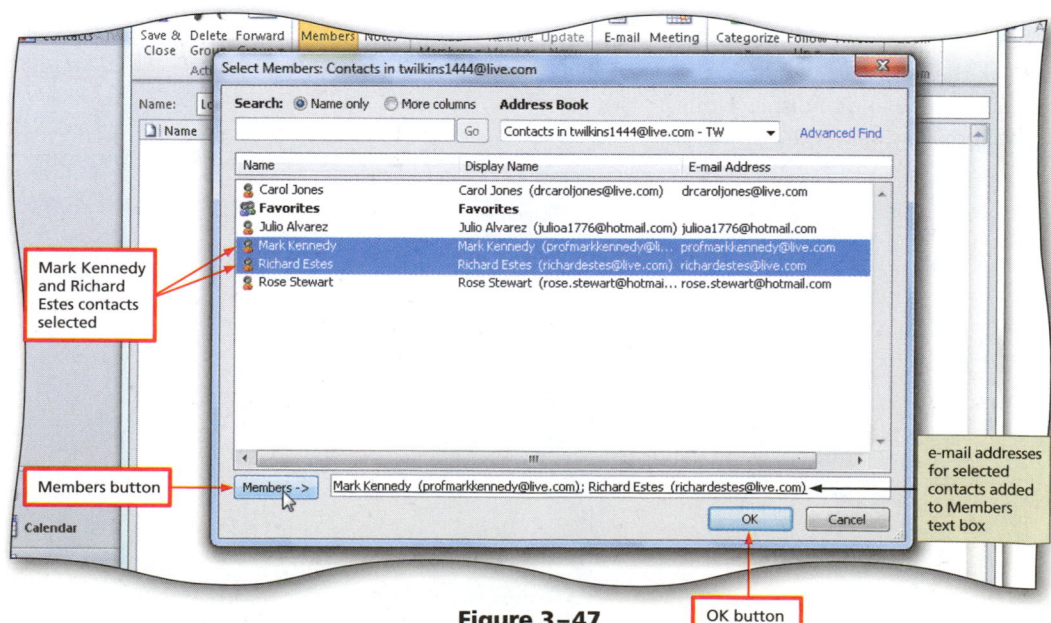

Figure 3–47

6
- Click the OK button to add the contacts to the group (Figure 3–48).

Q&A What if I add the wrong member(s)?

In the Contact Group window, select the member you want to remove, and then click the Remove Member button (Contact Group tab | Members group). Next, repeat Steps 3 – 6 to add any missing members.

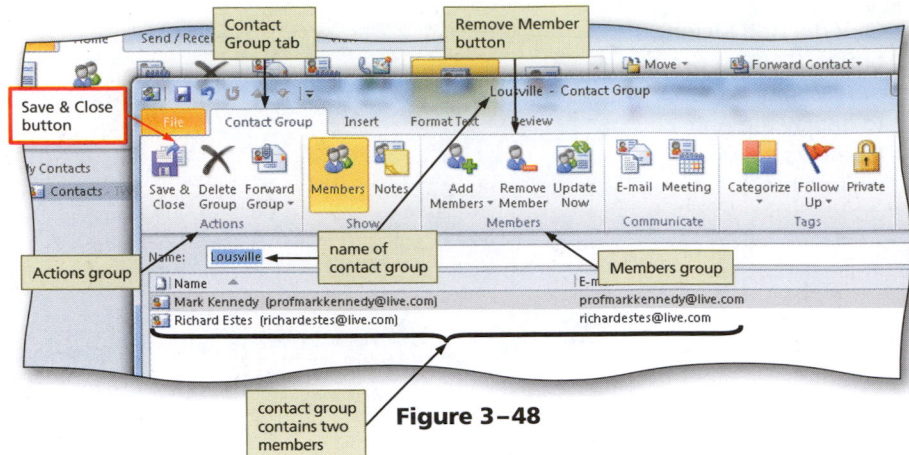

Figure 3–48

7
- Click the Save & Close button (Contact Group tab | Actions group) to save the contact group and close the window (Figure 3–49).

Q&A Why are the contacts and the group displayed in the Contacts window?

You use a contact group to send e-mail messages to a set of contacts using the group name; it does not replace or move the existing contacts.

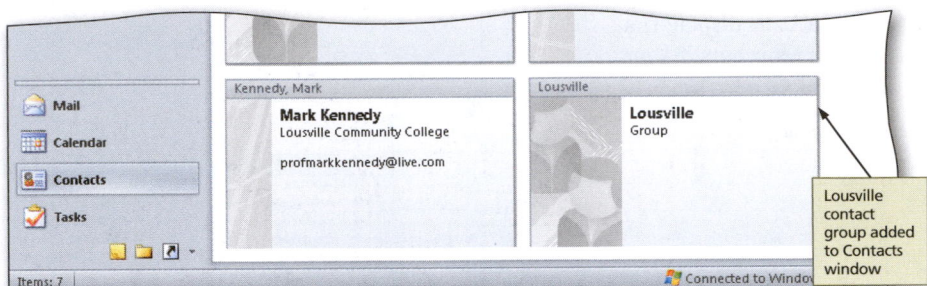

Figure 3–49

To Create a Contact Group from an Existing E-Mail Message

Outlook allows you to create a group for individuals who are not in your contact list yet, but who have sent you an e-mail message. To do this, you copy a name from an e-mail message and then paste the name in the Select Members dialog box when creating the group. The following steps create a contact group named Conference and then add a member by using information in an e-mail message from Nicole Smith.

1
- Click the Mail button in the Navigation Pane to display your mailbox (Figure 3–50).

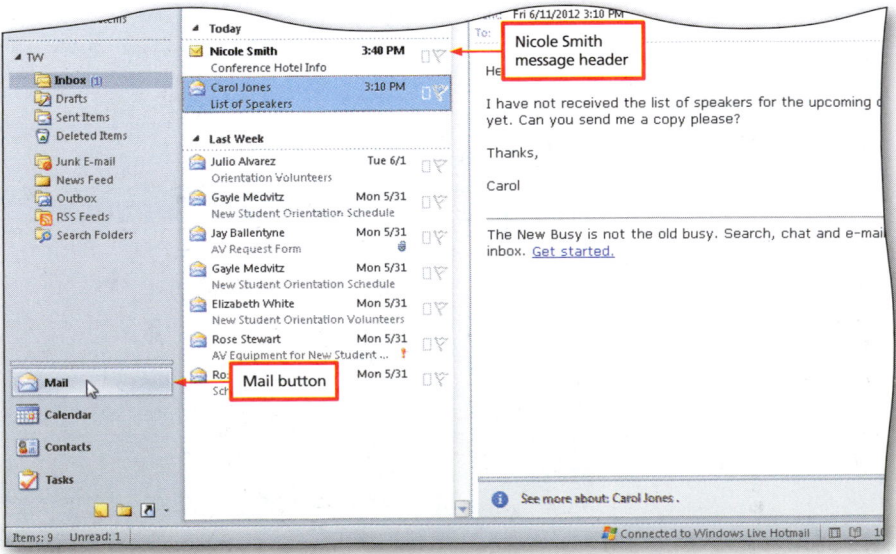

Figure 3–50

2

- Click the Nicole Smith message header to preview the e-mail message in the Reading Pane.

- In the Reading Pane, right-click the e-mail address to display a shortcut menu (Figure 3–51).

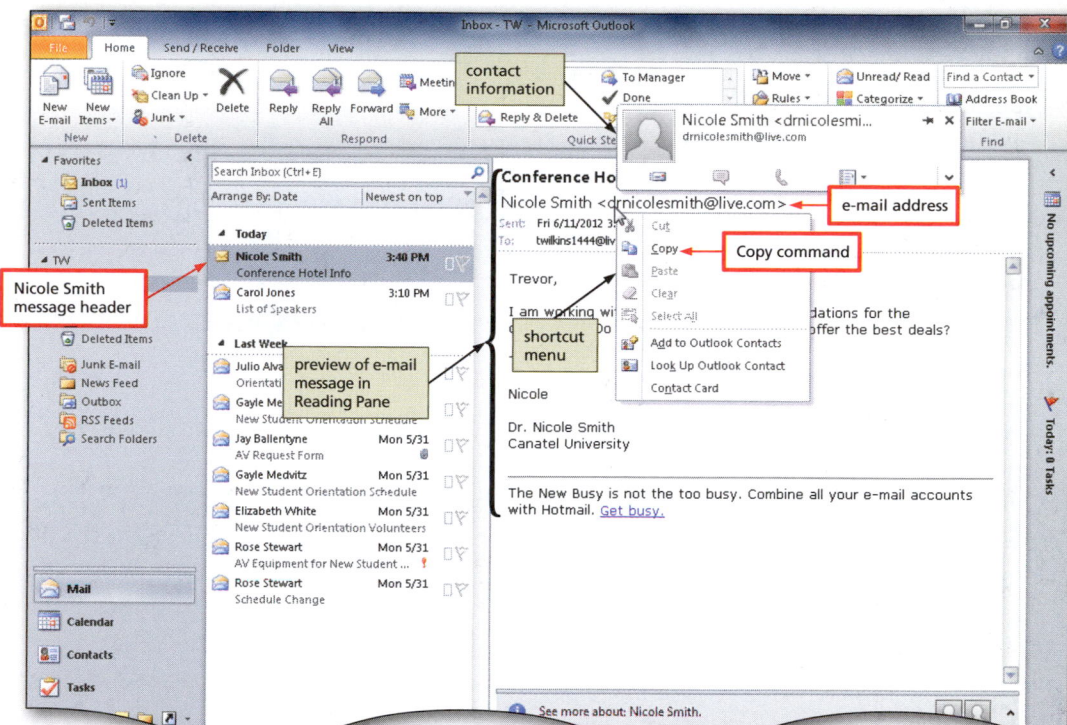

Figure 3–51

3

- Click Copy to copy the name and e-mail address.

- Click the New Items button (Home tab | New group) to display the New Items menu.

- Click More Items to display the More Items submenu (Figure 3–52).

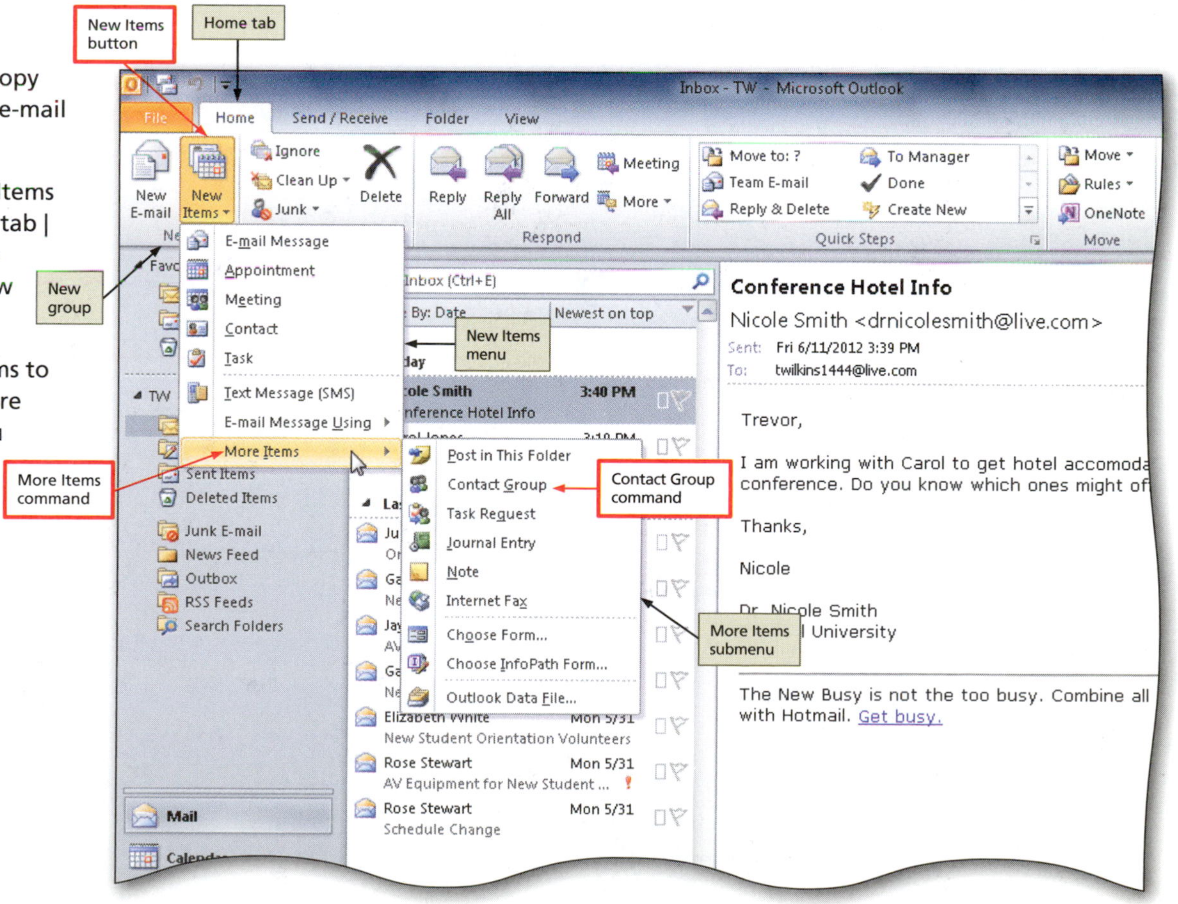

Figure 3–52

4

- Click Contact Group to display the Untitled – Contact Group window.

- Type **Conference** in the Name text box to enter a name for the group.

- Click the Add Members button (Contact Group tab | Add Members group) to display the Add Members menu.

- Click From Outlook Contacts to display the Select Members dialog box (Figure 3–53).

Q&A

Why did I click From Outlook Contacts?

You need to display the Select Members dialog box, and the From Outlook Contacts menu option opens it. You also could have clicked From Address Book to display the dialog box.

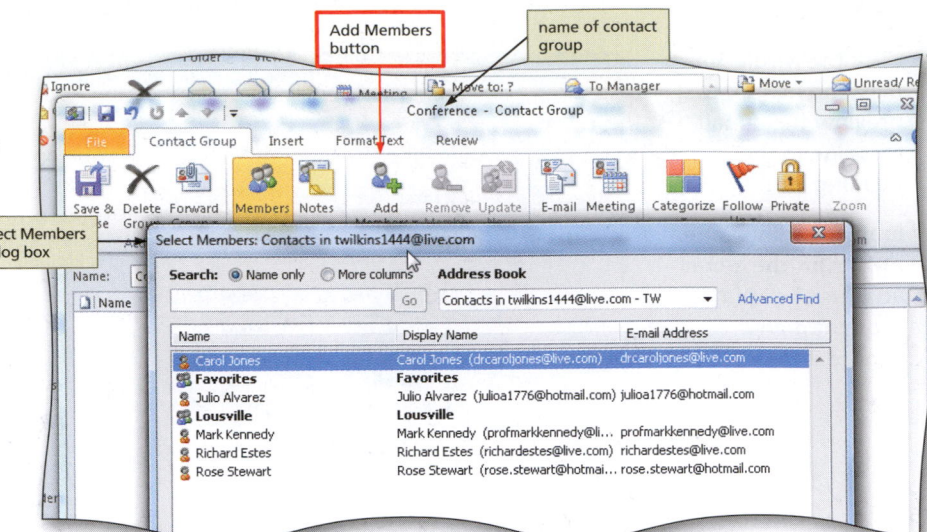

Figure 3–53

5

- Right-click the Members text box to display a shortcut menu.

- Click Paste to paste the copied name and e-mail address (Figure 3–54).

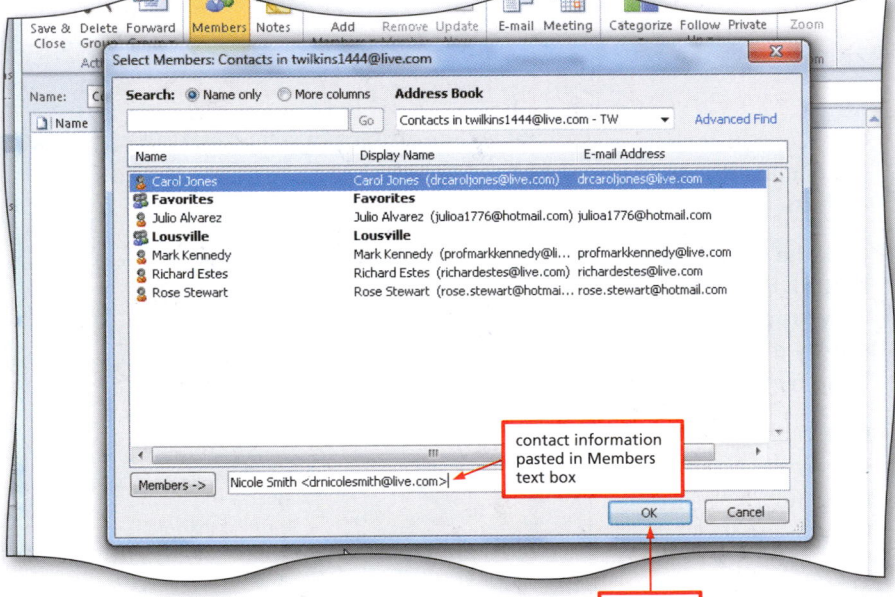

Figure 3–54

6

- Click the OK button (Select Members dialog box) to add the contact to the group (Figure 3–55).

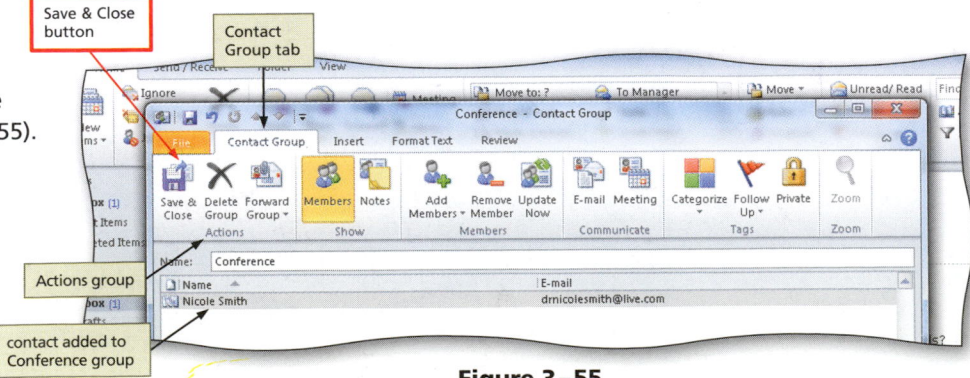

Figure 3–55

7

- Click the Save & Close button (Contact Group tab | Actions group) to save the contact and close the window.

- Click the Contacts button in the Navigation Pane to display your contacts (Figure 3–56).

Q&A

Can I forward a contact group to someone else?

Yes. You can forward a contact group by selecting the contact group, clicking Forward Contact (Home tab | Share group), and then selecting the option you want to use to forward the contact group.

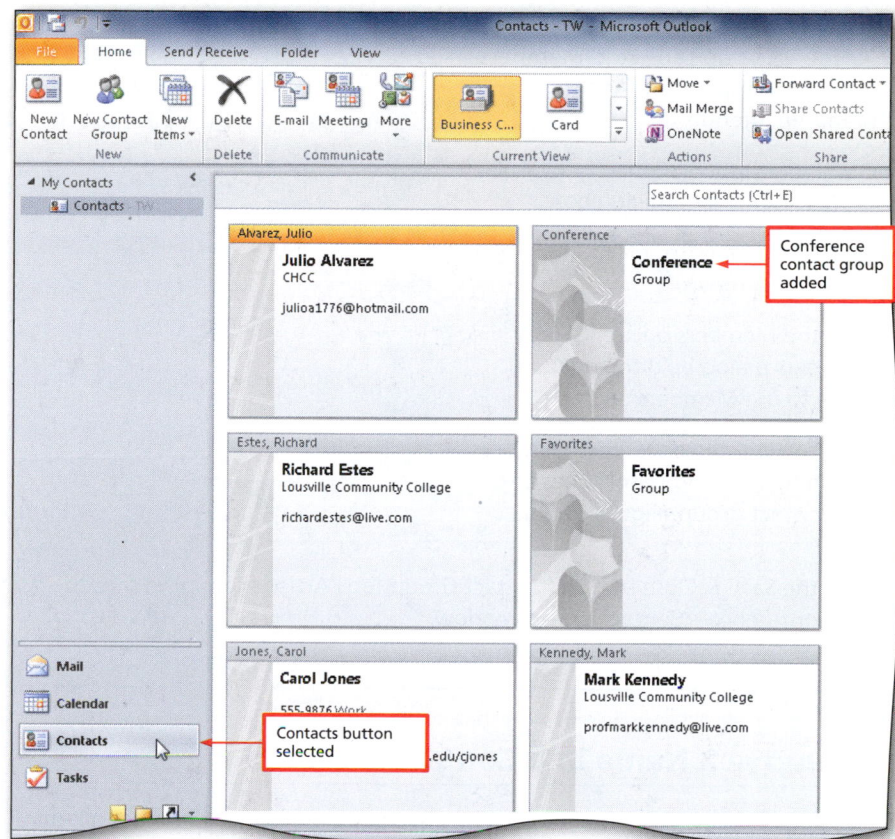

Figure 3–56

To Add a Name to a Contact Group

As you meet and work with people, you can add them to one or more contact groups. Carol Jones indicated that she will be attending the upcoming conference, and you want to add her to the Conference contact group so that she receives e-mail messages regarding the conference. The following steps add Carol Jones to the Conference contact group.

1

- Double-click the Conference contact group to display the Conference – Contact Group window (Figure 3–57).

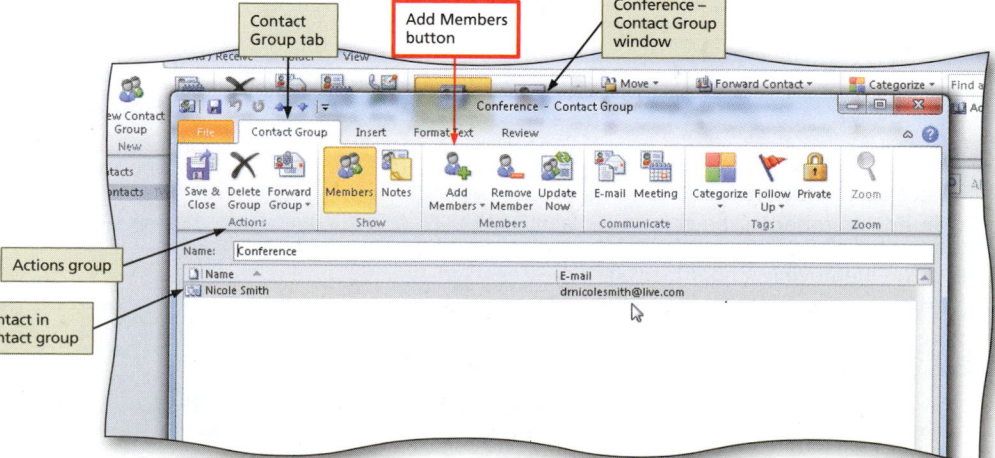

Figure 3–57

2

- Click the Add Members button (Contact Group tab | Add Members group) to display the Add Members menu.

- Click From Outlook Contacts to display the Select Members dialog box.

- Click Carol Jones to select her contact record.

- Click the Members button (Select Members dialog box) to add Carol Jones to the Members text box.

- Click the OK button (Select Members dialog box) to add Carol Jones to the contact group (Figure 3–58).

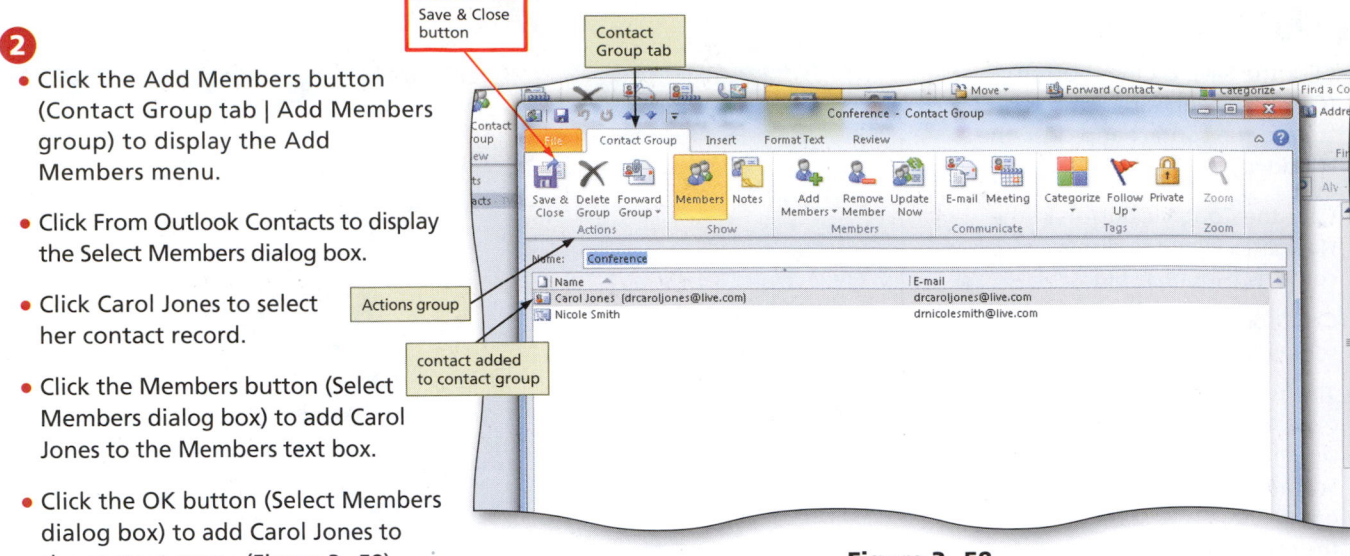

Figure 3–58

3

- Click the Save & Close button (Contact Group tab | Actions group) to save the contact and close the Conference – Contact Group window.

To Remove a Name in a Contact Group

Periodically, you may need to remove someone from a contact group. For example, contacts may switch jobs or ask to be removed from your list as they no longer are working on a particular project. Mark Kennedy is going on a sabbatical for one year and you have decided to remove him from the Lousville contact group so that he will not receive e-mail messages sent to the group. The following steps remove Mark Kennedy from the Lousville group.

1

- If necessary, scroll in the Contacts window until the Lousville contact group is visible.

- Double-click the Lousville contact group to display the Lousville – Contact Group window (Figure 3–59).

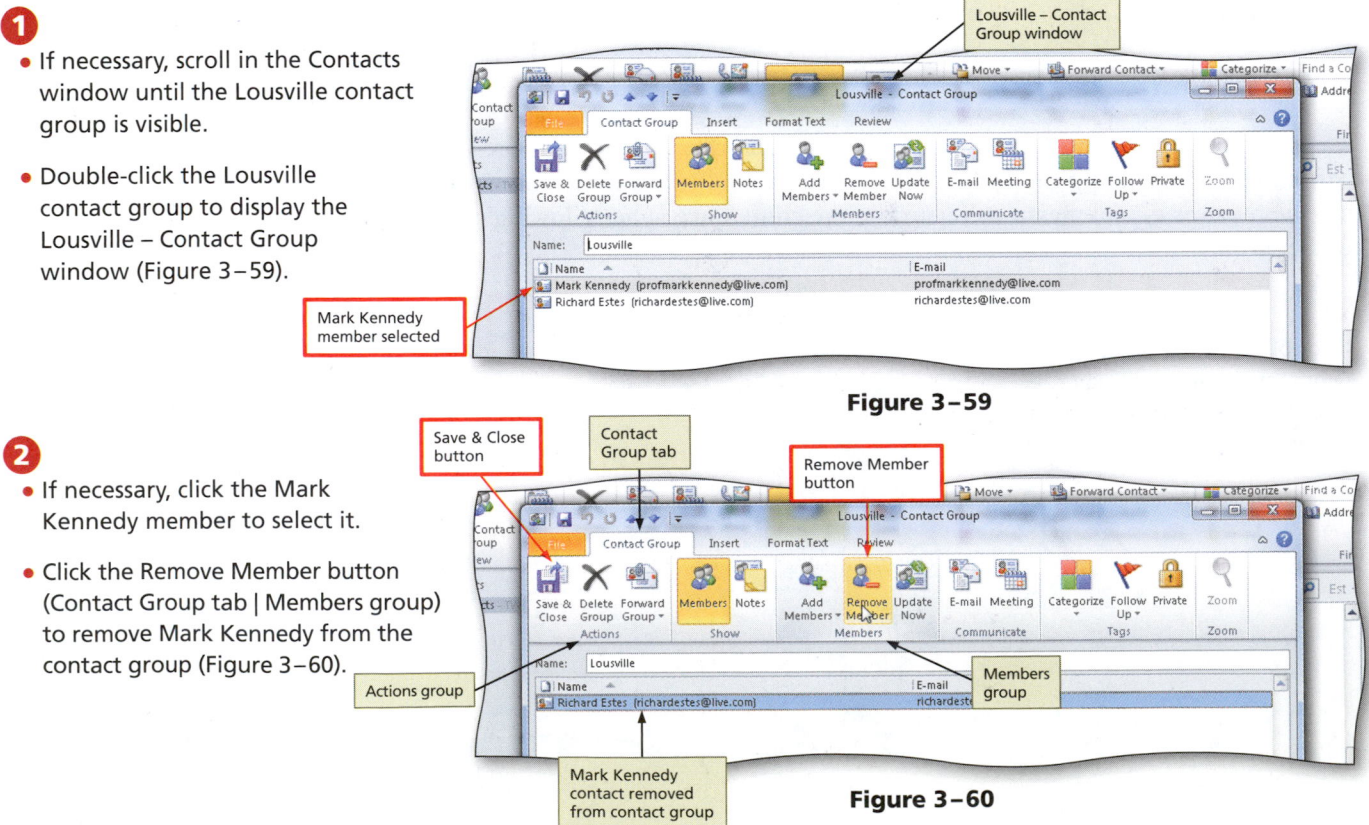

Figure 3–59

2

- If necessary, click the Mark Kennedy member to select it.

- Click the Remove Member button (Contact Group tab | Members group) to remove Mark Kennedy from the contact group (Figure 3–60).

Figure 3–60

3

- Click the Save & Close button (Contact Group tab | Actions group) to save the changes to the contact group and close the window (Figure 3–61).

Q&A When you remove a contact from a contact group, does it also remove the contact from Outlook?

No. The contact remains in Outlook, even after removing it from a contact group.

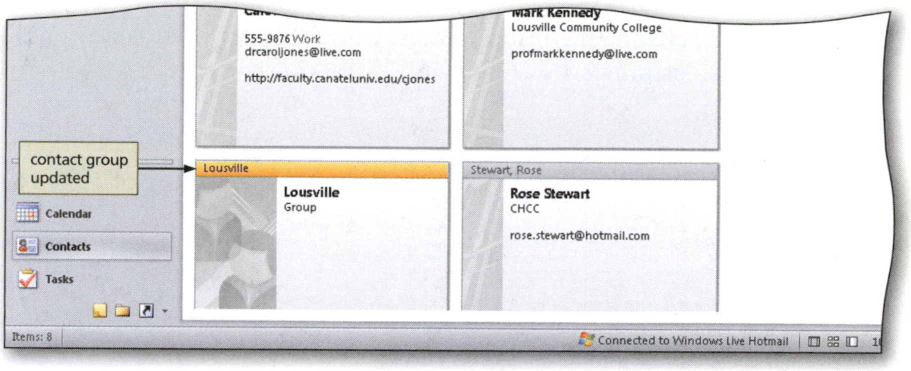

Q&A How can I delete a contact group?

To delete a contact group, select the contact group to delete, and then click Delete (Home tab | Delete group).

Figure 3–61

Printing Your Contacts

All or part of your contacts can be printed in a number of different views, or **print styles**. You can distribute a printed contact or contact list to others in a form that can be read or viewed, but cannot be edited. You can choose to print only one contact or the entire list. To print only part of your contacts, select one or more contacts and then change the print options so that you print your selection. This section previews the entire contact list and then prints the selected contacts in Card style. Table 3–1 lists the print styles available for printing your contacts from Contact view.

Table 3–1 Print Styles for Contact View

Print Style	Description
Card	Prints a list of contacts separated by alphabet dividers and with a sheet for adding more contact information
Small Booklet	Prints a list of contacts similar to Card style but designed so that it can be folded into a small booklet
Medium Booklet	Prints a list of contacts similar to Card style but designed so that it can be folded into a medium-sized booklet
Memo	Prints a page for each contact, each page formatted to look like a memo
Phone Directory	Prints a list of contacts showing phone numbers only

BTW

Conserving Ink and Toner
If you want to conserve ink or toner, you can instruct Outlook to print draft quality documents by clicking File on the Ribbon to open the Backstage view, clicking the Print tab in the Backstage view to display the Print gallery, clicking the Print Options button, and then clicking the Properties button (Print dialog box). The Properties dialog box will vary depending on the type of printer you are using, but look for and select fast, economical options for the print quality. Then, use the Backstage view to print the document as usual.

Determine the best method for distributing a contact list.
The traditional method of distributing a contact list uses a printer to produce a hard copy. A **hard copy** or **printout** is information that exists on a physical medium such as paper. Hard copies can serve as reference material if your storage medium is lost or becomes corrupted and you need to re-create the contact list.

Plan Ahead

BTW Certification
The Microsoft Office Specialist program provides an opportunity for you to obtain a valuable industry credential — proof that you have the Outlook 2010 skills required by employers. For more information, visit the Outlook 2010 Certification Web page (scsite.com/out2010/cert).

BTW Quick Reference
For a table that lists how to complete the tasks covered in this book using the mouse, Ribbon, shortcut menu, and keyboard, see the Quick Reference Summary at the back of this book, or visit the Outlook 2010 Quick Reference Web page (scsite.com/out2010/qr).

To Preview a Contact List

Unless you change the print options, you will see all your contacts when you preview the list before printing. The following steps preview the contact list in various print styles.

1
- In the Contacts window, select the Richard Estes and Mark Kennedy contacts (Figure 3–62).

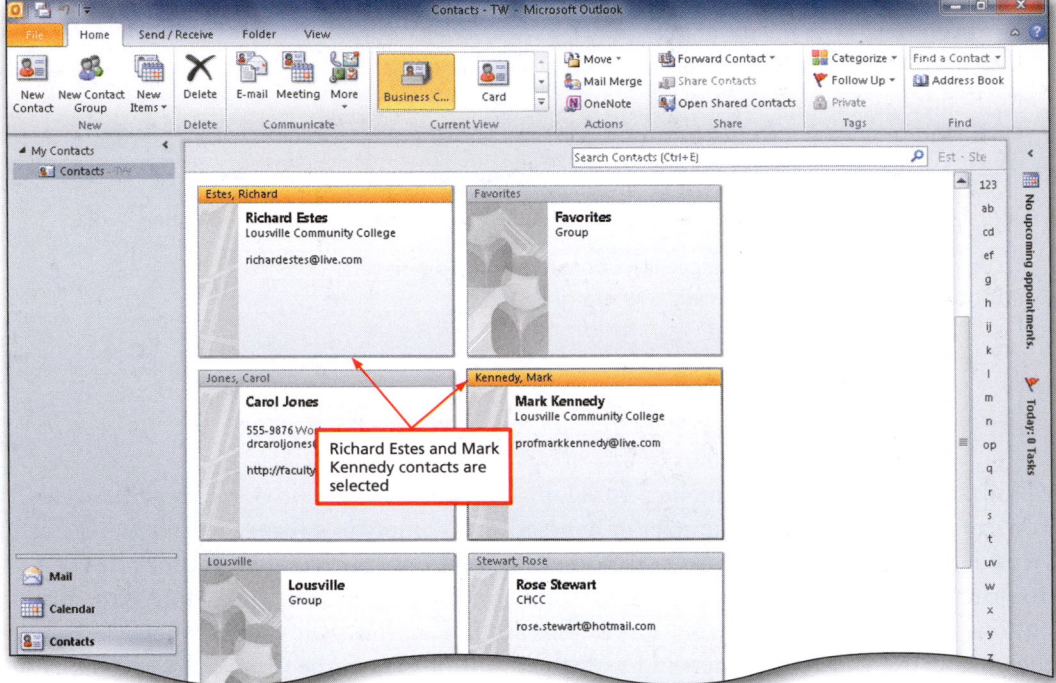

Figure 3–62

2
- Click File on the Ribbon to open the Backstage view.

- Click the Print tab in the Backstage view to display the Print gallery (Figure 3–63).

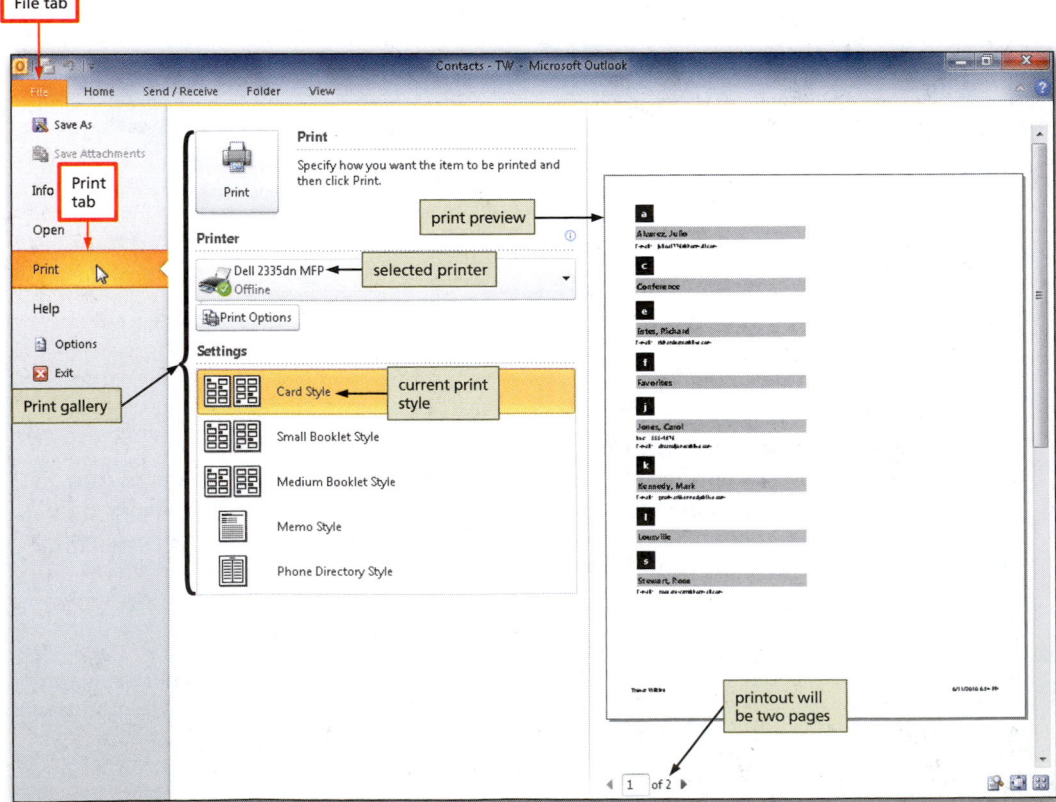

Figure 3–63

3
- Click Medium Booklet Style in the Settings area to change the print style (Figure 3–64).

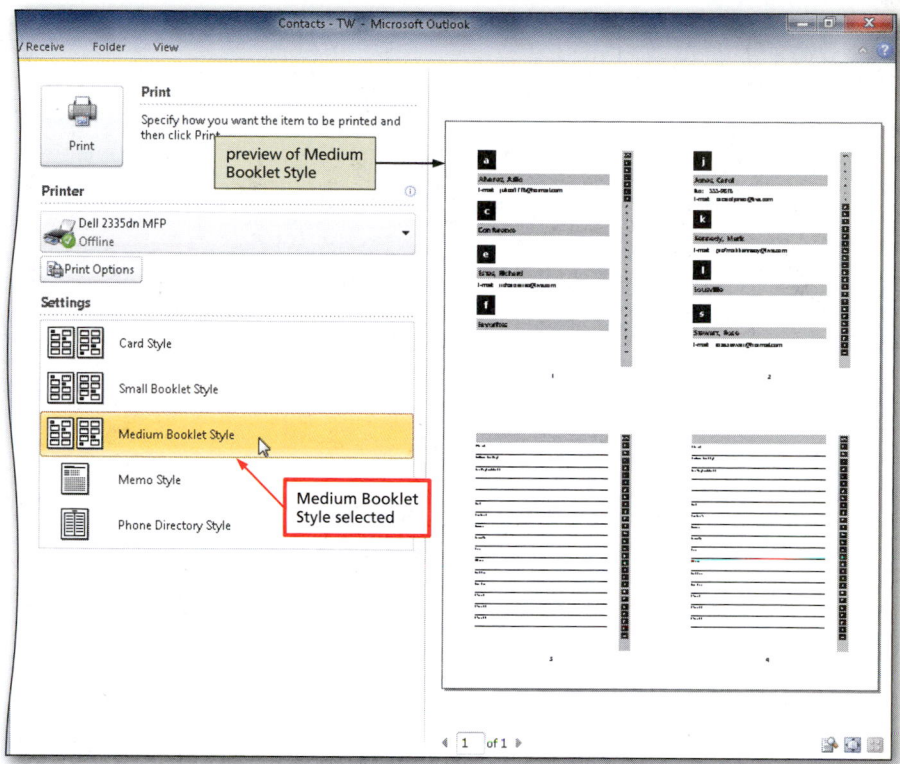

Figure 3–64

4
- Click Phone Directory Style in the Settings area to change to Phone Directory Style (Figure 3–65).

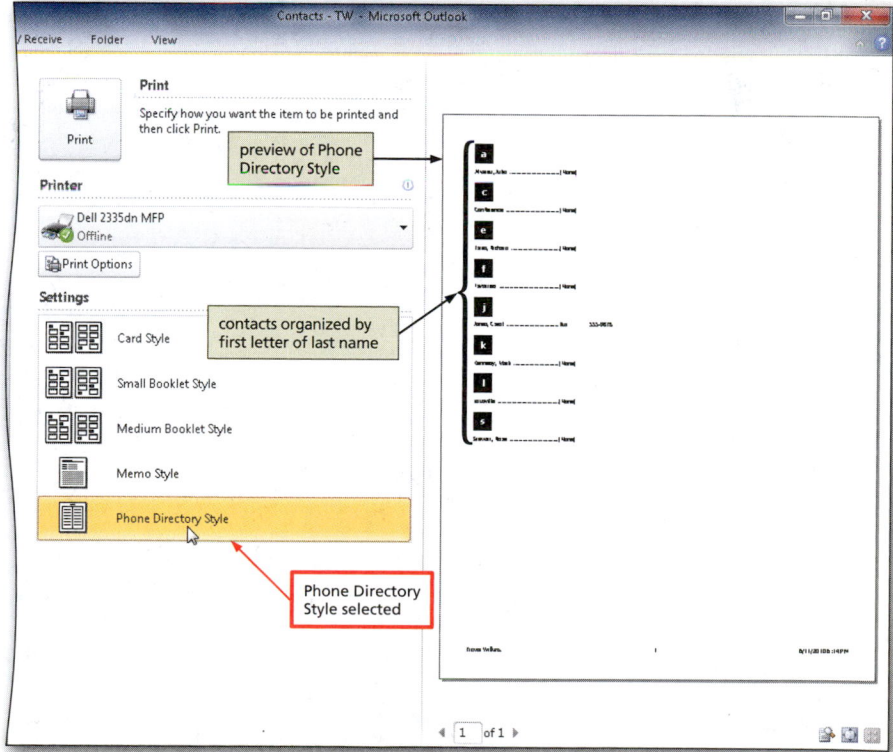

Figure 3–65

5

• Click Card Style in the Settings area to change to Card Style (Figure 3–66).

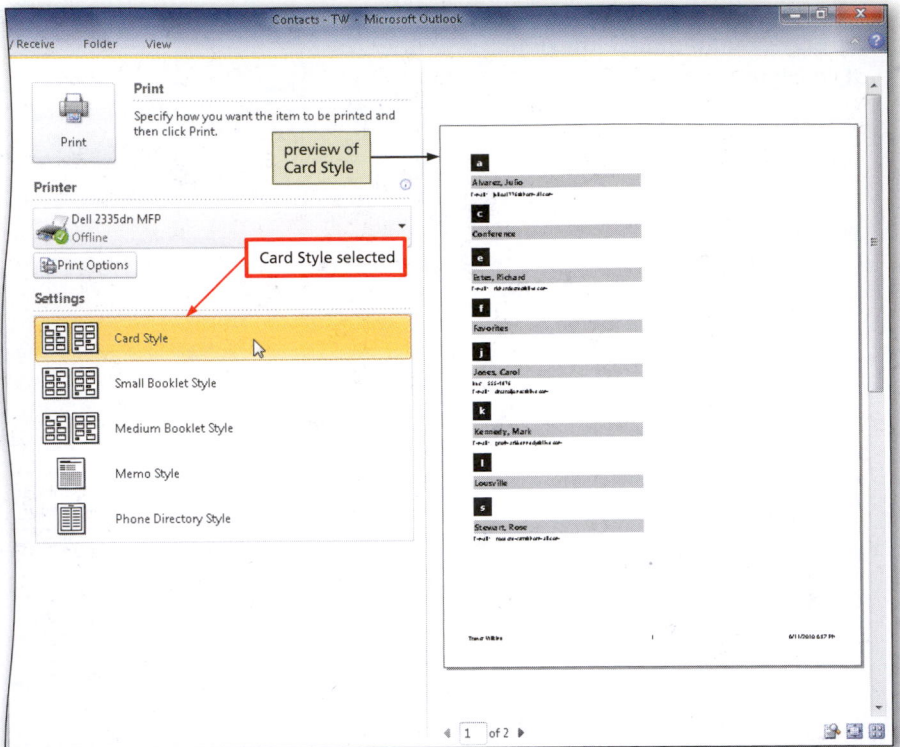

Figure 3–66

6

• Click the Print Options button to display the Print dialog box (Figure 3–67).

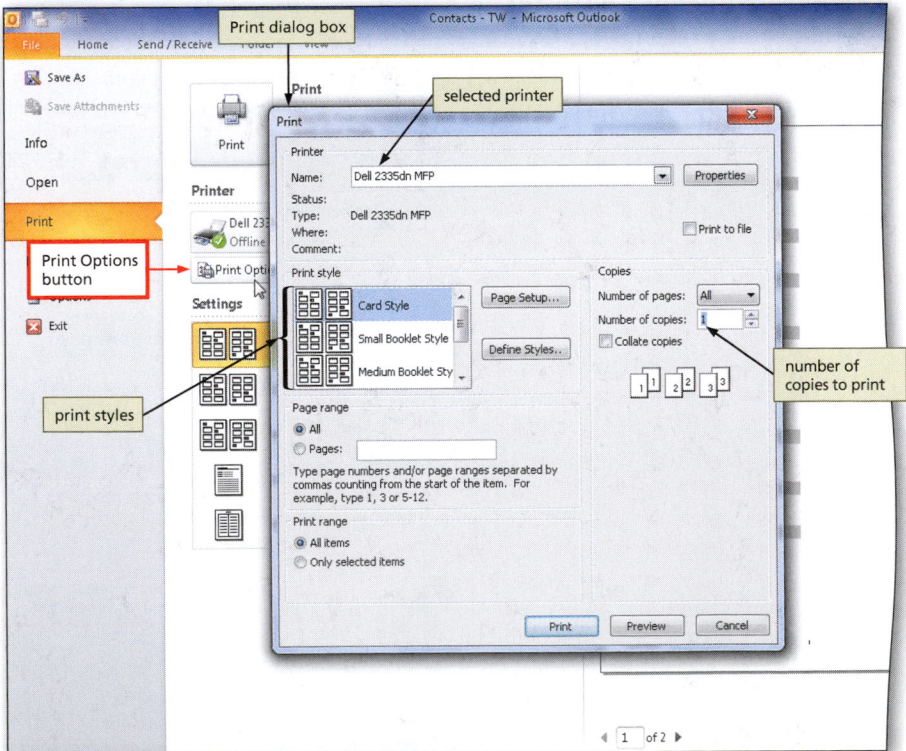

Figure 3–67

7
- Click the 'Only selected items' option button (Print dialog box) to preview only the selected contacts (Figure 3–68).

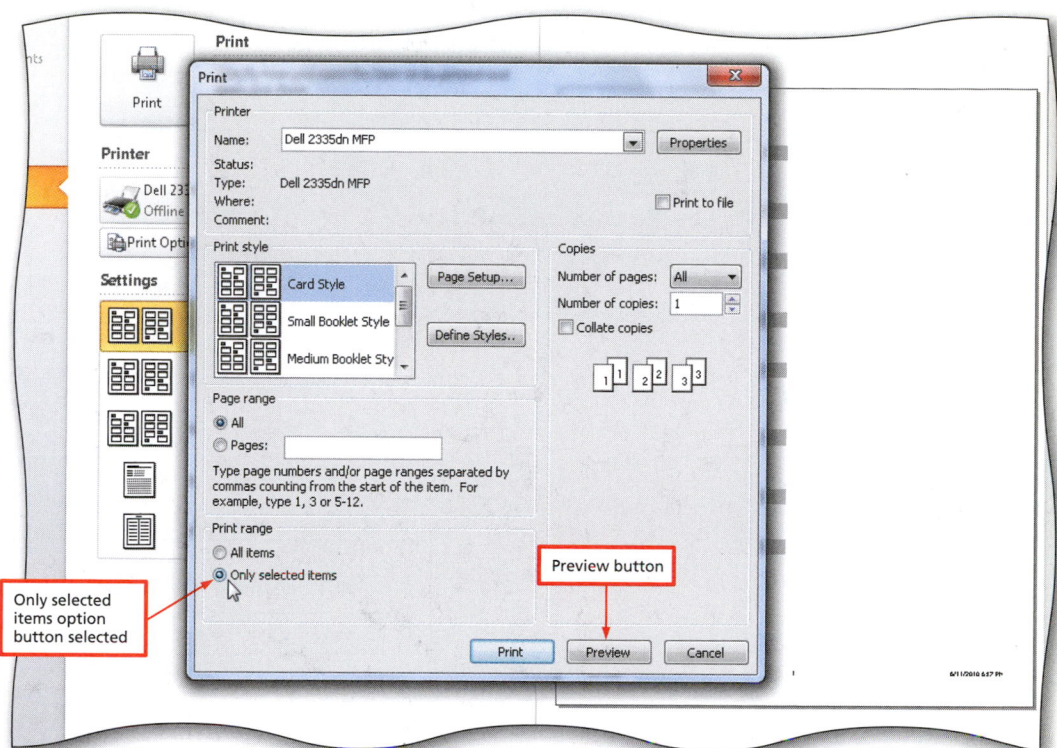

Figure 3–68

8
- Click the Preview button (Print dialog box) to close the dialog box and preview only the selected contacts (Figure 3–69).

Q&A

If I click the other styles, will they only show selected contacts?

No. If you change the style, the preview returns to showing all contacts. To see the selected contacts in a particular style, you select the style and then change the print options.

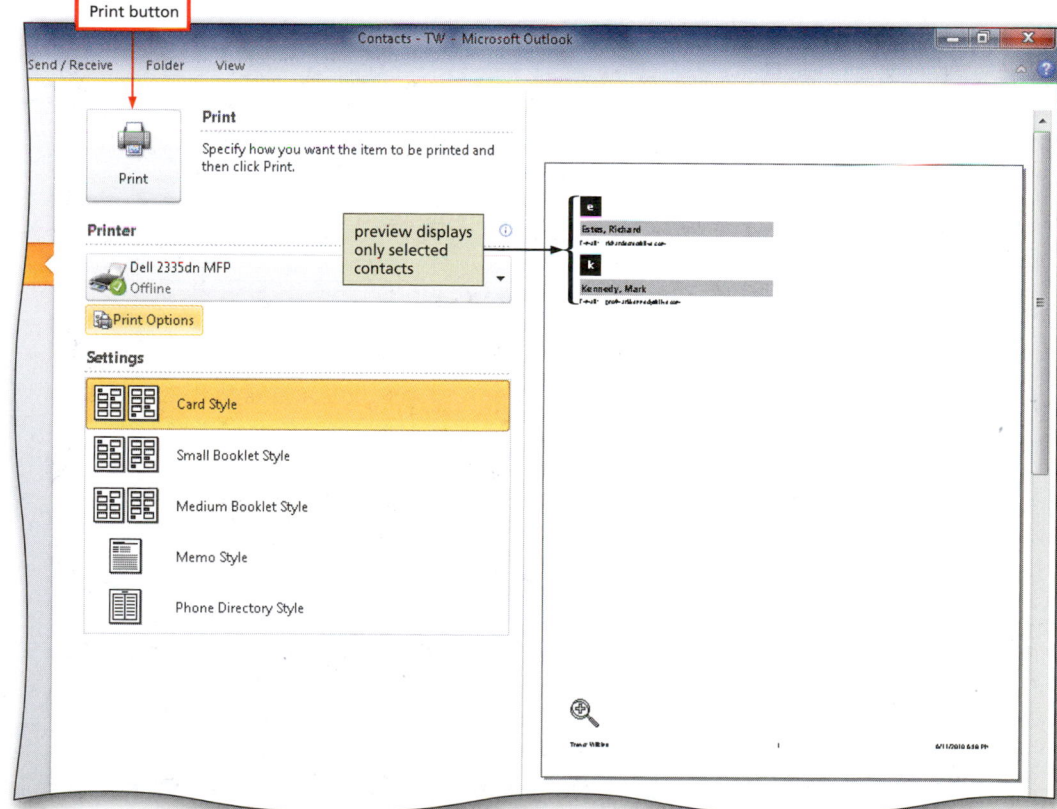

Figure 3–69

To Print the Contact List

The following step prints the selected contacts in Card style.

● Click the Print button to print the selected contacts (Figure 3–70).

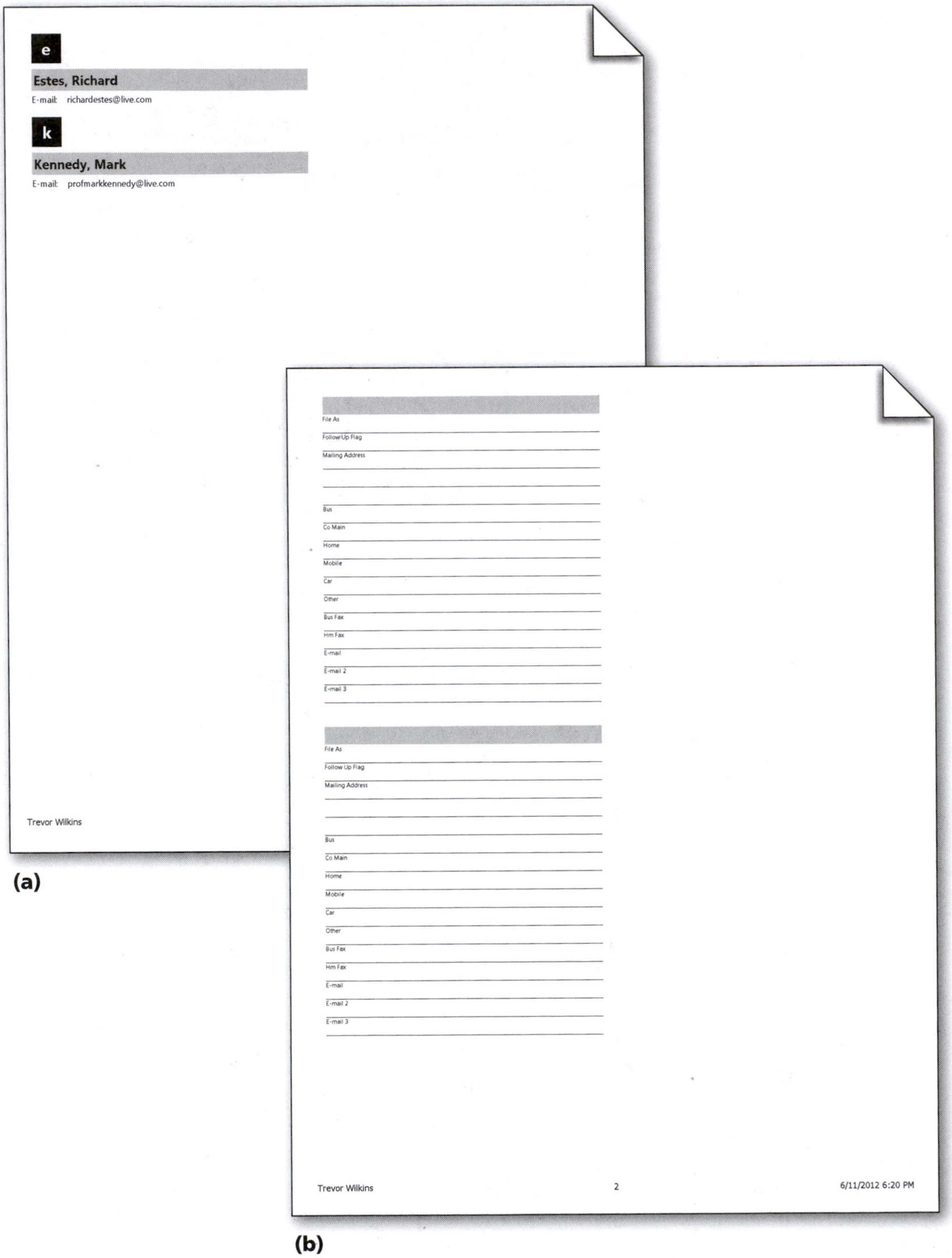

e

Estes, Richard
E-mail: richardestes@live.com

k

Kennedy, Mark
E-mail: profmarkkennedy@live.com

Trevor Wilkins

(a)

File As
FollowUp Flag
Mailing Address

Bus
Co Main
Home
Mobile
Car
Other
Bus Fax
Hm Fax
E-mail
E-mail 2
E-mail 3

File As
Follow Up Flag
Mailing Address

Bus
Co Main
Home
Mobile
Car
Other
Bus Fax
Hm Fax
E-mail
E-mail 2
E-mail 3

Trevor Wilkins   2   6/11/2012 6:20 PM

(b)

Figure 3–70

To Quit Outlook

The project is complete. Thus, the following step quits Outlook.

 1 Click the Close button on the right side of the title bar to quit Outlook.

Chapter Summary

In this chapter, you have learned how to create a contact list, view and sort contacts, search for contacts, create and edit a contact group, and print contacts. The items listed below include all the new Outlook skills you have learned in this chapter.

1. Create a New Contact (OUT 125)
2. Create a Contact from an E-Mail Message (OUT 127)
3. Create a Contact from an Existing Contact (OUT 129)
4. Edit a Contact (OUT 130)
5. Add an Attachment to a Contact (OUT 131)
6. Change an Attachment to a Contact (OUT 133)
7. Remove an Attachment to a Contact (OUT 135)
8. Change the Current View (OUT 137)
9. Sort Contacts (OUT 138)
10. Find a Contact by Searching for an E-Mail Address (OUT 139)
11. Refine a Search (OUT 141)
12. Find a Contact from any Outlook Folder (OUT 142)
13. Create a Contact Group from Existing Contacts (OUT 144)
14. Create a Contact Group from an Existing E-Mail Message (OUT 146)
15. Add a Name to a Contact Group (OUT 149)
16. Remove a Name in a Contact Group (OUT 150)
17. Preview a Contact List (OUT 152)
18. Print the Contact List (OUT 156)

 If you have a SAM 2010 user profile, your instructor may have assigned an autogradable version of this assignment. If so, log into the SAM 2010 Web site at www.cengage.com/sam2010 to download the instruction and start files.

Learn It Online

Test your knowledge of chapter content and key terms.

Instructions: To complete the Learn It Online exercises, start your browser, click the Address bar, and then enter the Web address **scsite.com/out2010/learn**. When the Outlook 2010 Learn It Online page is displayed, click the link for the exercise you want to complete and then read the instructions.

Chapter Reinforcement TF, MC, and SA

A series of true/false, multiple choice, and short answer questions that test your knowledge of the chapter content.

Flash Cards

An interactive learning environment where you identify chapter key terms associated with displayed definitions.

Practice Test

A series of multiple choice questions that test your knowledge of chapter content and key terms.

Who Wants To Be a Computer Genius?

An interactive game that challenges your knowledge of chapter content in the style of a television quiz show.

Wheel of Terms

An interactive game that challenges your knowledge of chapter key terms in the style of the television show *Wheel of Fortune.*

Crossword Puzzle Challenge

A crossword puzzle that challenges your knowledge of key terms presented in the chapter.

Apply Your Knowledge

Reinforce the skills and apply the concepts you learned in this chapter.

Editing a Contact List

Note: To complete this assignment, you will be required to use the Data Files for Students. See the inside back cover of this book for instructions on downloading the Data Files for Students, or contact your instructor for information about accessing the required files.

Instructions: Start Outlook. Edit the contact list provided in the file called Apply Your Knowledge 3-1 Contacts, located on the Data Files for Students. The Apply Your Knowledge 3-1 Contacts is a contacts folder containing the contacts of Dr. Carol Jones. Many of the contacts have changed and some are incomplete. You now need to revise these contacts and print them in Card view (Figure 3–71).

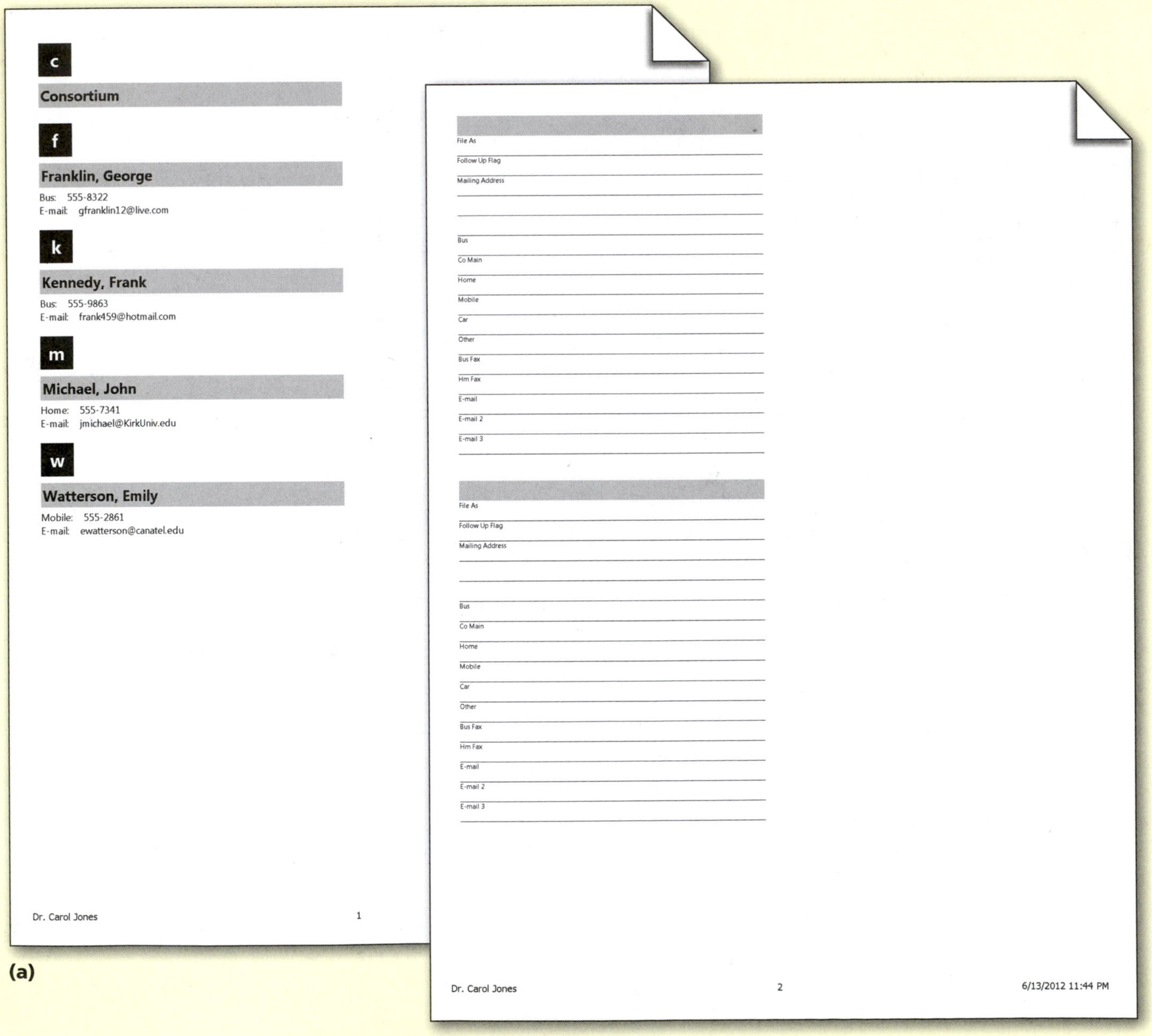

(a)

(b)

Figure 3–71

Perform the following tasks:

1. Import the Apply Your Knowledge 3-1 Contacts folder.

2. Change Frank Kennedy's company to Smyrna CC. Move the Home phone number to the Business phone number text box. Add the Job title of Professor.

3. Change George Franklin's Job title to adjunct. Add the company name, CHCC, to the contact. Type `gfranklin12@live.com` as the e-mail address. The Business phone should be 555-8322.

4. Change John Michael's e-mail address to jmichael@KirkUniv.edu. Change the Web page address to http://www.KirkUniv.edu/jmichael. Add a Home phone of 555-7341.

5. Enter the company name, Canatel University, for Emily Watterson. Type `ewatterson@canatel.edu` for the e-mail address. Enter a mobile phone number of 555-2861.

6. Change the Consort contact group name to Consortium. Add all the contacts to the contact group.

7. Print the final contact list in Card view, as shown in Figure 3–71, and then submit the printout to your instructor.

8. Export the Apply Your Knowledge 3-1 Contacts folder to a USB flash drive and then delete the folder from the hard disk.

Extend Your Knowledge

Extend the skills you learned in this chapter and experiment with new skills. You may need to use Help to complete the assignment.

Creating a Contact Folder

Note: To complete this assignment, you will be required to use the Data Files for Students. See the inside back cover of this book for instructions on downloading the Data Files for Students, or contact your instructor for information about accessing the required files.

Instructions: Start Outlook. Edit the contact list provided in the file called Extend Your Knowledge 3-1 Contacts, located on the Data Files for Students. The Extend Your Knowledge 3-1 Contacts folder has no contacts. You will create a new contacts folder, add contacts to the new contacts folder, and print the contact list. You also will share the contact folder with others.

Perform the following tasks:

1. Use Help to learn about creating a contacts folder and sharing a contact list.

2. Start Outlook and create a new contacts folder named Marketing Department.

3. Create the contacts displayed in Table 3–2.

Table 3–2 Marketing Department Information				
Full Name	**Company**	**Job Title**	**E-Mail Address**	**Work Phone**
Bob McCornly	Music Oddities	Advertising	mccornly@musicoddities.com	555-1278
Max Vindo	Music Oddities	Research	vindo@musicoddities.com	555-1290
Susie Wells	Music Oddities	Planning	wells@musicoddities.com	555-1358
Tammi Townsend	Music Oddities	Purchasing	townsend@musicoddities.com	555-2751
Vicki Wickers	Music Oddities	Research	wickers@musicoddities.com	555-2776
Al Sanders	Music Oddities	Research	sanders@musicoddities.com	555-2689

Continued >

Extend Your Knowledge *continued*

4. Create a contact group called Everyone. Add all of the contacts to this group.

5. Create a contact group called Research Group. Add all the employees with Research as their job title to this group.

6. Print the contact list in Phone Directory view, as shown in Figure 3–72, and then submit the printout to your instructor.

7. Use the Share Contacts button (Home tab | Share group) to e-mail the contact list to your instructor.

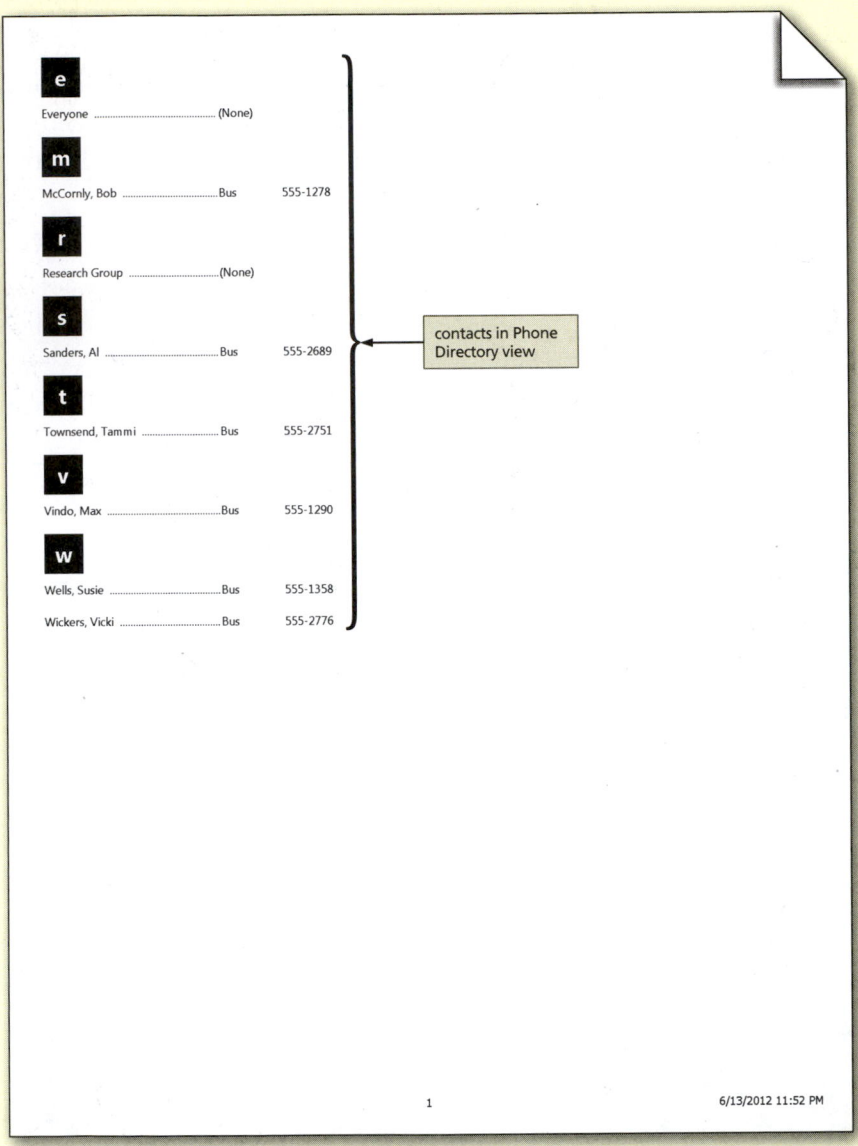

Figure 3–72

Make It Right

Analyze contacts and correct all errors and/or improve the design.

Correcting Contacts and Contact Groups

Note: To complete this assignment, you will be required to use the Data Files for Students. See the inside back cover of this book for instructions on downloading the Data Files for Students, or contact your instructor for information about accessing the required files.

Instructions: Start Outlook. Import the Make It Right 3-1 Contacts folder in the Data Files for Students folder into Outlook. While reviewing your Outlook contacts, you realize that you created several contacts incorrectly, failed to add a contact, and incorrectly added contacts to your contact group. You will identify and open the incorrect contacts, edit them so that they reflect the correct information, add the missing contact, edit the contact group, and then save all changes. You will also print the contacts in Small Booklet style (Figure 3–73).

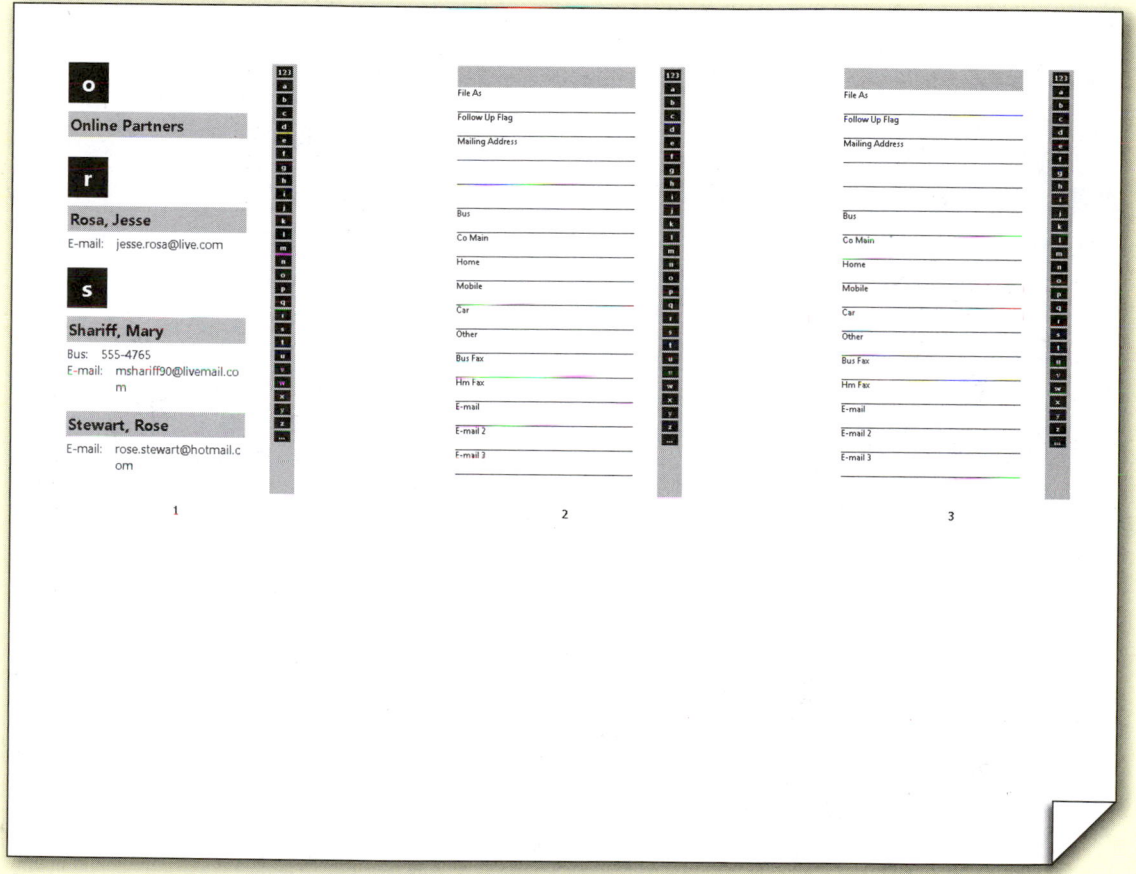

Figure 3–73

Continued >

Make It Right *continued*

Perform the following tasks:

1. Display only the Make It Right 3-1 Contacts folder in the Outlook Contacts window.

2. While adding the Jesse Rosa contact, you inadvertently recorded the e-mail address as jesse.rosa@com.live.edu. Change the e-mail address to jesse.rosa@live.com. If necessary, press the F5 key to update the change.

3. Mary Shariff works for Alentawn Bakery with a work phone of 555-4765. Edit the contact to show the correct information.

4. You were supposed to add Rose Stewart, who had sent you an e-mail message, to your contacts. Add her now as a contact, using the e-mail message she sent you.

5. Your online partners only include Jesse Rosa and Rose Stewart; however, your Online Partners contact group includes Mary Shariff instead of Rose Stewart. Edit the group to include the correct members.

6. Print the contacts using the Small Booklet style (Figure 3 – 73).

7. Export the Make It Right 3-1 Contacts folder to your USB flash drive and then delete the folder from the hard disk.

8. Submit the Contacts folder in a format specified by your instructor.

In the Lab

Design, create, modify, and/or use a document using the guidelines, concepts, and skills presented in this chapter. Labs are listed in order of increasing difficulty.

Lab 1: Creating Departmental Contacts

Problem: You are a graduate assistant for the provost at South Landis Community College (SLCC) and have been asked to create a contact list of the departmental offices on campus. Each department now has an e-mail address, so that e-mail messages can be sent there and then forwarded by the dean of each department as necessary. Table 3 – 3 lists each department's contact information. Enter the contacts into the contacts list. The contact list you create will look like that in Figure 3 – 74.

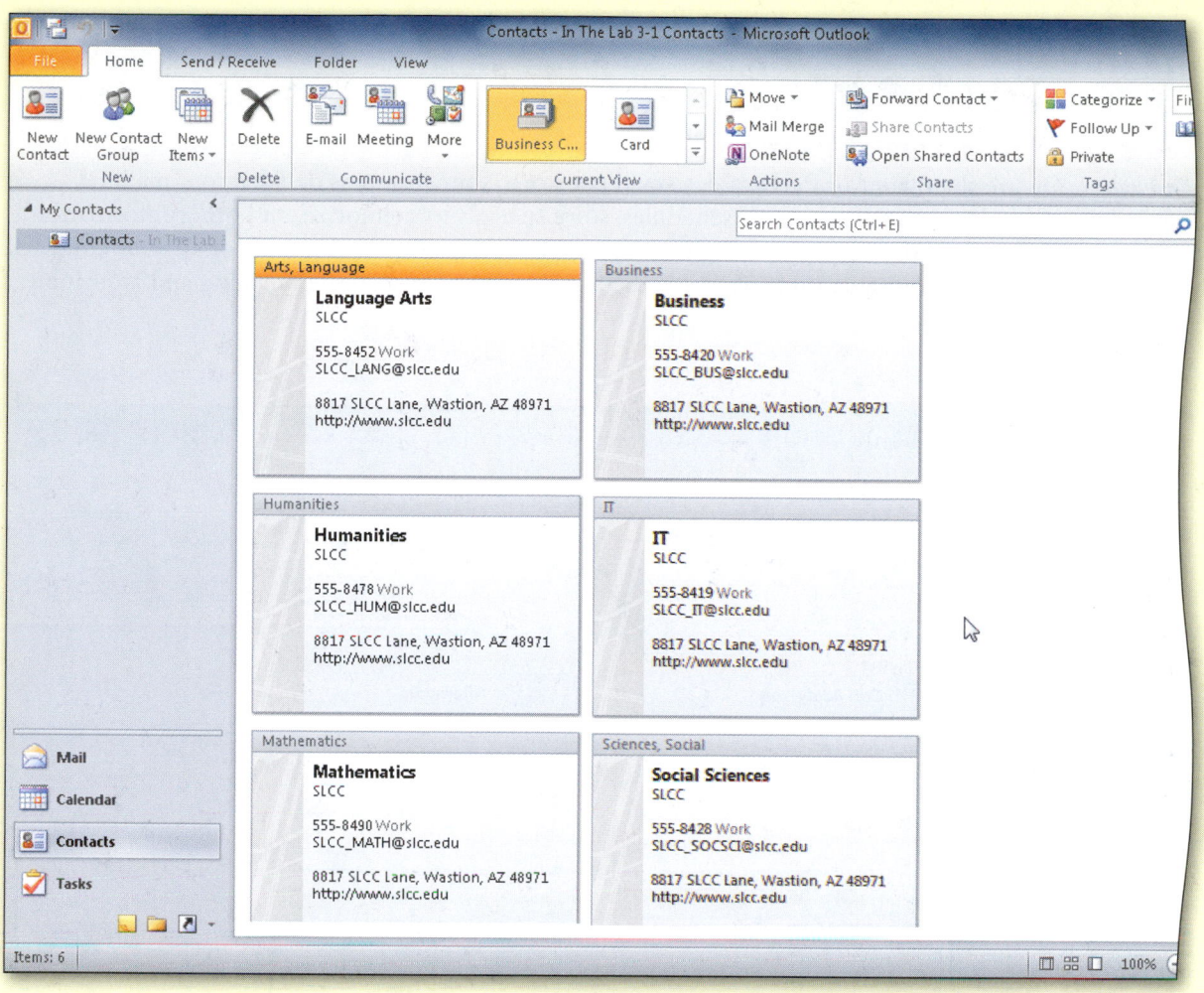

Figure 3–74

Perform the following tasks:

1. Create the contacts in the Contacts folder, using the information listed in Table 3–3.

Table 3–3 Departmental Information			
Department	**E-Mail Address**	**Phone**	**Fax**
IT	SLCC_IT@slcc.edu	555-8419	555-8513
Social Sciences	SLCC_SOCSCI@slcc.edu	555-8428	555-8529
Humanities	SLCC_HUM@slcc.edu	555-8478	555-8578
Business	SLCC_BUS@slcc.edu	555-8420	555-8525
Language Arts	SLCC_LANG@slcc.edu	555-8452	555-8554
Mathematics	SLCC_MATH@slcc.edu	555-8490	555-8593

2. For each contact, list the full name using the department name.

3. For each contact, list the company as SLCC.

4. For each contact, list the Web page address as http://www.slcc.edu.

5. For each contact, list the business address as 8817 SLCC Lane, Wastion, AZ 48971.

6. Print the contacts list using Memo style, and submit it in a format specified by your instructor.

In the Lab

Lab 2: Creating an Employee Contact List

Problem: You are the owner of PetExotic, a small pet store. Your store has decided to e-mail reminders to employees such as weekly schedules, store specials to memorize, and other information. You have two shifts in your store, morning and afternoon. You need to create a list of all your contacts, and also add contact groups, so that you send specific information just to the morning and afternoon employees (Figure 3–75).

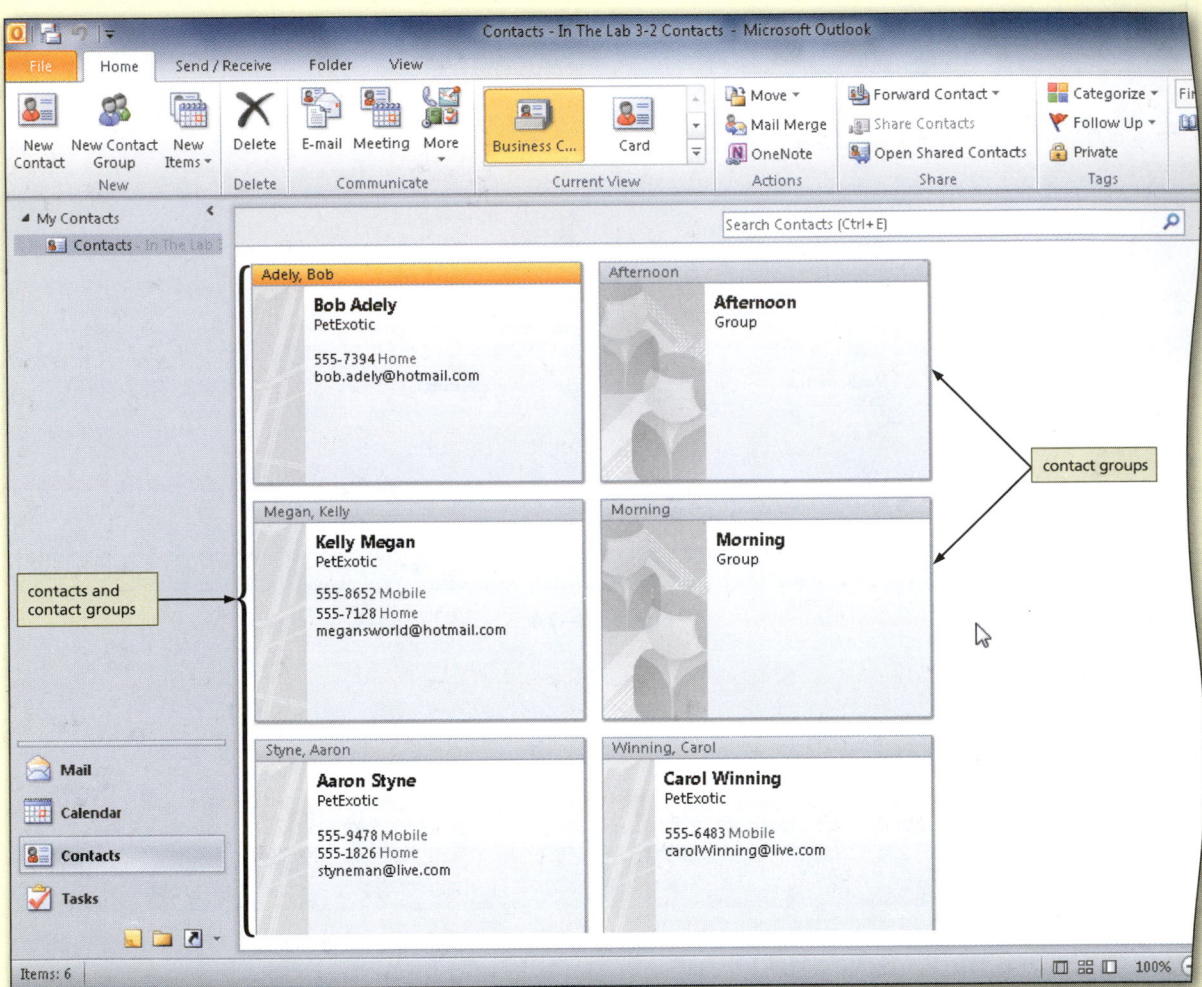

Figure 3–75

Perform the following tasks:

1. Create two contact groups called Morning and Afternoon.
2. Enter the contacts in the Contacts folder, using the information listed in Table 3–4. Do not add the shift information to the contacts. Use the shift information to determine in which contact group you should place the contacts. Add the contacts to the appropriate contact group.

Table 3–4 PetExotic Store Employee Information

Full Name	E-Mail Address	Home Phone	Mobile Phone	Shift
Bob Adely	bob.adely@hotmail.com	555-7394		Morning
Aaron Styne	styneman@live.com	555-1826	555-9478	Morning
Carol Winning	carolwinning@live.com		555-6483	Afternoon
Kelly Megan	megansworld@hotmail.com	555-7128	555-8652	Afternoon

3. Print the contacts list in Small Booklet style, and then submit it in the format specified by your instructor.

In the Lab

Lab 3: Creating Contacts with Attachments

Note: To complete this assignment, you will be required to use the Data Files for Students. See the inside back cover of this book for instructions on downloading the Data Files for Students, or contact your instructor for information about accessing the required files.

Problem: Start Outlook. You are to create a contact list for Lattel's Hardware Store using Table 3–5. The contact list you create is shown in Figure 3–76. Each employee will have an attachment of the hours they work weekly, which you will add to their contact information.

You will need the documents from the Data Files for Students folder to attach to the contacts.

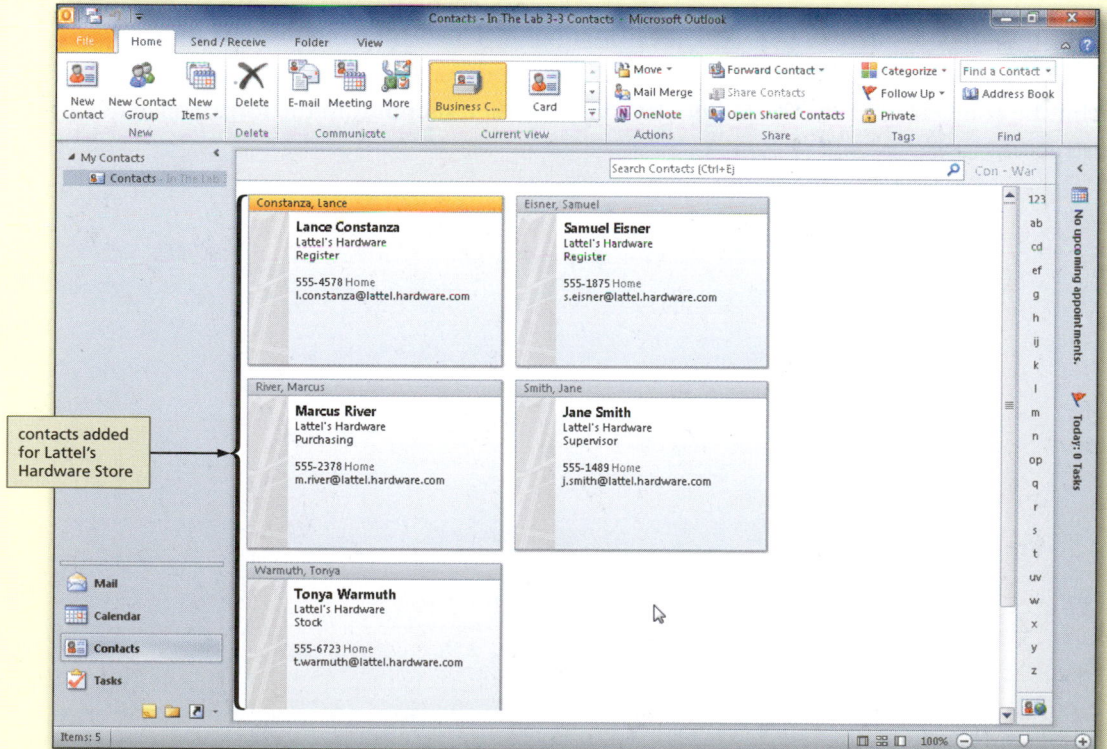

Figure 3–76

Continued >

In the Lab *continued*

Perform the following tasks:

1. Create contacts for each employee using the information in Table 3–5. Create the first contact including the company name, and then create the rest from that contact.

Table 3–5 Lattel's Hardware Information			
Employee	**Position**	**E-Mail Address**	**Home**
Jane Smith	Supervisor	j.smith@lattel.hardware.com	555-1489
Marcus River	Purchasing	m.river@lattel.hardware.com	555-2378
Tonya Warmuth	Stock	t.warmuth@lattel.hardware.com	555-6723
Lance Constanza	Register	l.constanza@lattel.hardware.com	555-4578
Samuel Eisner	Register	s.eisner@lattel.hardware.com	555-1875

2. Edit the Jane Smith contact. Add the Smith hours document from the data files as an attachment to the contact.

3. Edit the Marcus River contact. Add the River hours document from the data files as an attachment to the contact.

4. Edit the Tonya Warmuth contact. Add the Warmuth hours document from the data files as an attachment to the contact.

5. Edit the Lance Constanza contact. Add the Constanza hours document from the data files as an attachment to the contact.

6. Edit the Samuel Eisner contact. Add the Eisner hours document from the data files as an attachment to the contact.

7. Print the contacts list in Medium Booklet style, and then submit it in the format specified by your instructor.

STUDENT ASSIGNMENTS

Cases and Places

Apply your creative thinking and problem solving skills to design and implement a solution.

Note: To complete these assignments, you may be required to use the Data Files for Students. See the inside back cover of this book for instructions on downloading the Data Files for Students, or contact your instructor for information about accessing the required files.

1: Create a Study Group List

Academic

Create contacts for a study group at Canatel University using the information in Table 3–6. Use Canatel University as the company name. You should create the first contact and then create the rest as contacts from the same company. Print the list in Card style and in Phone Directory style. Submit it in the format specified by your instructor.

Table 3–6 Study Group Members			
Full Name	**E-Mail Address**	**Home Phone**	**Mobile Phone**
Marge Jones	mjones@live.com	555-7812	
Juan Escobar	gocanatel@hotmail.com	555-8772	555-9871
April Kent	April.Kent@live.com		555-2145
Addison Hu	addison9871@live.com		555-8912
Larry Honda	SuperHonda@hotmail.com	555-7728	555-3476
Kim Young	Kim.Young@live.com	555-5874	

2: Create a Team List

Professional

At Hank's Handheld Mobile, you are in charge of scheduling your team of employees. The business is located at 9821 South End Dr, Tarnnel, IN 33389. Whenever you create a schedule, you need to e-mail it to your entire team. You also use e-mail to send your team important information they should know. Create contacts for each member of your team using the information in Table 3–7. Create a contact group called Team and add the contacts to the group. Print the contact list in Card style and submit it in the format specified by your instructor.

Table 3–7 Hank's Handheld Mobile Information		
Full Name	**E-Mail Address**	**Home Phone**
Carla Angel	angel@hankshandheld.com	555-1278
Angel Esposita	esposita@hankshandheld.com	555-8221
Abigail Shin	shin@hankshandheld.com	555-9856
Nina Montgomery	montgomery@hankshandheld.com	555-3846
Stan Applebaum	applebaum@hankshandheld.com	555-2877
Josiah Bell	bell@hankshandheld.com	555-8745

Continued >

Cases and Places *continued*

3: Create a Family List

Personal

Create a list of family contacts. Use Table 3–8 to add these items to your contacts. After you have made the contacts, your sister Emily sends you an e-mail message and reminds you that she has recently gotten married to Benjamin Genius and has moved to 1789 Willow Lane, Soonerville, OH 44218. The home phone has changed to 555-8319 and Ben's mobile phone number is 555-7811. He does not have an e-mail address yet. She asks if you could update the information since you often print and mail the contact list to the rest of the family. Edit the entry and print the contacts list in Medium Booklet style.

Table 3–8 Marion Family Information				
Name	**Address**	**E-Mail Address**	**Home Phone**	**Mobile Phone**
Emily Marion	1289 Oak Ave Soonerville, OH 44218	EmilyBlogs@live.com	555-8744	555-7412
Susan Marion	8871 South Dr. Soonerville, OH 44218		555-2977	
Peter Marion	8871 South Dr. Soonerville, OH 44218	MarionFamily@hotmail.com	555-2977	
Lance Marion	89201 Central Ave. Soonerville, OH 44218	lmarion@hotmail.com	555-8863	555-1799
Katelyn Marion	2821 Oak Ave Soonerville, OH 44218	katelynmarion@canateluniv.edu		555-2859

NOTES

NOTES

NOTES

NOTES

Appendix A

Project Planning Guidelines

Using Project Planning Guidelines

The process of communicating specific information to others is a learned, rational skill. Computers and software, especially Microsoft Office 2010, can help you develop ideas and present detailed information to a particular audience.

Using Microsoft Office 2010, you can create projects such as Word documents, PowerPoint presentations, Excel spreadsheets, and Access databases. Productivity software such as Microsoft Office 2010 minimizes much of the laborious work of drafting and revising projects. Some communicators handwrite ideas in notebooks, others compose directly on the computer, and others have developed unique strategies that work for their own particular thinking and writing styles.

No matter what method you use to plan a project, follow specific guidelines to arrive at a final product that presents information correctly and effectively (Figure A–1). Use some aspects of these guidelines every time you undertake a project, and others as needed in specific instances. For example, in determining content for a project, you may decide that a chart communicates trends more effectively than a paragraph of text. If so, you would create this graphical element and insert it in an Excel spreadsheet, a Word document, or a PowerPoint slide.

Determine the Project's Purpose

Begin by clearly defining why you are undertaking this assignment. For example, you may want to track monetary donations collected for your club's fund-raising drive. Alternatively, you may be urging students to vote for a particular candidate in the next election. Once you clearly understand the purpose of your task, begin to draft ideas of how best to communicate this information.

Analyze Your Audience

Learn about the people who will read, analyze, or view your work. Where are they employed? What are their educational backgrounds? What are their expectations? What questions do they have?

PROJECT PLANNING GUIDELINES

1. DETERMINE THE PROJECT'S PURPOSE
Why are you undertaking the project?

2. ANALYZE YOUR AUDIENCE
Who are the people who will use your work?

3. GATHER POSSIBLE CONTENT
What information exists, and in what forms?

4. DETERMINE WHAT CONTENT TO PRESENT TO YOUR AUDIENCE
What information will best communicate the project's purpose to your audience?

Figure A–1

Design experts suggest drawing a mental picture of these people or finding photos of people who fit this profile so that you can develop a project with the audience in mind.

By knowing your audience members, you can tailor a project to meet their interests and needs. You will not present them with information they already possess, and you will not omit the information they need to know.

Example: Your assignment is to raise the profile of your college's nursing program in the community. How much do they know about your college and the nursing curriculum? What are the admission requirements? How many of the applicants admitted complete the program? What percent pass the state board exams?

Gather Possible Content

Rarely are you in a position to develop all the material for a project. Typically, you would begin by gathering existing information that may reside in spreadsheets or databases. Web sites, pamphlets, magazine and newspaper articles, and books could provide insights of how others have approached your topic. Personal interviews often provide perspectives not available by any other means. Consider video and audio clips as potential sources for material that might complement or support the factual data you uncover.

Determine What Content to Present to Your Audience

Experienced designers recommend writing three or four major ideas you want an audience member to remember after reading or viewing your project. It also is helpful to envision your project's endpoint, the key fact you wish to emphasize. All project elements should lead to this ending point.

As you make content decisions, you also need to think about other factors. Presentation of the project content is an important consideration. For example, will your brochure be printed on thick, colored paper or posted on the Web? Will your PowerPoint presentation be viewed in a classroom with excellent lighting and a bright projector, or will it be viewed on a notebook computer monitor? Determine relevant time factors, such as the length of time to develop the project, how long readers will spend reviewing your project, or the amount of time allocated for your speaking engagement. Your project will need to accommodate all of these constraints.

Decide whether a graph, photo, or artistic element can express or emphasize a particular concept. The right hemisphere of the brain processes images by attaching an emotion to them, so audience members are more apt to recall these graphics long term rather than just reading text.

As you select content, be mindful of the order in which you plan to present information. Readers and audience members generally remember the first and last pieces of information they see and hear, so you should place the most important information at the top or bottom of the page.

Summary

When creating a project, it is beneficial to follow some basic guidelines from the outset. By taking some time at the beginning of the process to determine the project's purpose, analyze the audience, gather possible content, and determine what content to present to the audience, you can produce a project that is informative, relevant, and effective.

Appendix B

Publishing Office 2010 Web Pages Online

With Office 2010 programs, you use the Save As command in the Backstage view to save a Web page to a Web site, network location, or FTP site. **File Transfer Protocol** (**FTP**) is an Internet standard that allows computers to exchange files with other computers on the Internet.

You should contact your network system administrator or technical support staff at your Internet access provider to determine if their Web server supports Web folders, FTP, or both, and to obtain necessary permissions to access the Web server.

Using an Office Program to Publish Office 2010 Web Pages

When publishing online, someone first must assign the necessary permissions for you to publish the Web page. If you are granted access to publish online, you must obtain the Web address of the Web server, a user name, and possibly a password that allows you to connect to the Web server. The steps in this appendix assume that you have access to an online location to which you can publish a Web page.

TO CONNECT TO AN ONLINE LOCATION

To publish a Web page online, you first must connect to the online location. To connect to an online location using Windows 7, you would perform the following steps.

1. Click the Start button on the Windows 7 taskbar to display the Start menu.
2. Click Computer in the right pane of the Start menu to open the Computer window.
3. Click the 'Map network drive' button on the toolbar to display the Map Network Drive dialog box. (If the 'Map network drive' button is not visible on the toolbar, click the 'Display additional commands' button on the toolbar and then click 'Map network drive' in the list to display the Map Network Drive dialog box.)
4. Click the 'Connect to a Web site that you can use to store your documents and pictures' link (Map Network Drive dialog box) to start the Add Network Location wizard.
5. Click the Next button (Add Network Location dialog box).
6. Click 'Choose a custom network location' and then click the Next button.
7. Type the Internet or network address specified by your network or system administrator in the text box and then click the Next button.
8. Click 'Log on anonymously' to deselect the check box, type your user name in the User name text box, and then click the Next button.
9. If necessary, enter the name you want to assign to this online location and then click the Next button.
10. Click to deselect the Open this network location when I click Finish check box, and then click the Finish button.

11. Click the Cancel button to close the Map Network Drive dialog box.

12. Close the Computer window.

TO SAVE A WEB PAGE TO AN ONLINE LOCATION

The online location now can be accessed easily from Windows programs, including Microsoft Office programs. After creating a Microsoft Office file you wish to save as a Web page, you must save the file to the online location to which you connected in the previous steps. To save a Microsoft Word document as a Web page, for example, and publish it to the online location, you would perform the following steps.

1. Click File on the Ribbon to display the Backstage view and then click Save As in the Backstage view to display the Save As dialog box.

2. Type the Web page file name in the File name text box (Save As dialog box). Do not press the ENTER key because you do not want to close the dialog box at this time.

3. Click the 'Save as type' box arrow and then click Web Page to select the Web Page format.

4. If necessary, scroll to display the name of the online location in the navigation pane.

5. Double-click the online location name in the navigation pane to select that location as the new save location and display its contents in the right pane.

6. If a dialog box appears prompting you for a user name and password, type the user name and password in the respective text boxes and then click the Log On button.

7. Click the Save button (Save As dialog box).

The Web page now has been published online. To view the Web page using a Web browser, contact your network or system administrator for the Web address you should use to connect to the Web page.

Appendix C

Saving to the Web Using Windows Live SkyDrive

Introduction

Windows Live SkyDrive, also referred to as **SkyDrive**, is a free service that allows users to save files to the Web, such as documents, presentations, spreadsheets, databases, videos, and photos. Using SkyDrive, you also can save files in folders, providing for greater organization. You then can retrieve those files from any computer connected to the Internet. Some Office 2010 programs including Word, PowerPoint, and Excel can save files directly to an Internet location such as SkyDrive. SkyDrive also facilitates collaboration by allowing users to share files with other SkyDrive users (Figure C–1).

Figure C–1

Note: An Internet connection is required to perform the steps in this appendix.

To Save a File to Windows Live SkyDrive

You can save files directly to SkyDrive from within Word, PowerPoint, and Excel using the Backstage view. The following steps save an open Word document (Koala Exhibit Flyer, in this case) to SkyDrive. These steps require you to have a Windows Live account. Contact your instructor if you do not have a Windows Live account.

1

- Start Word and then open a document you want to save to the Web (in this case, the Koala Exhibit Flyer).

- Click File on the Ribbon to display the Backstage view (Figure C–2).

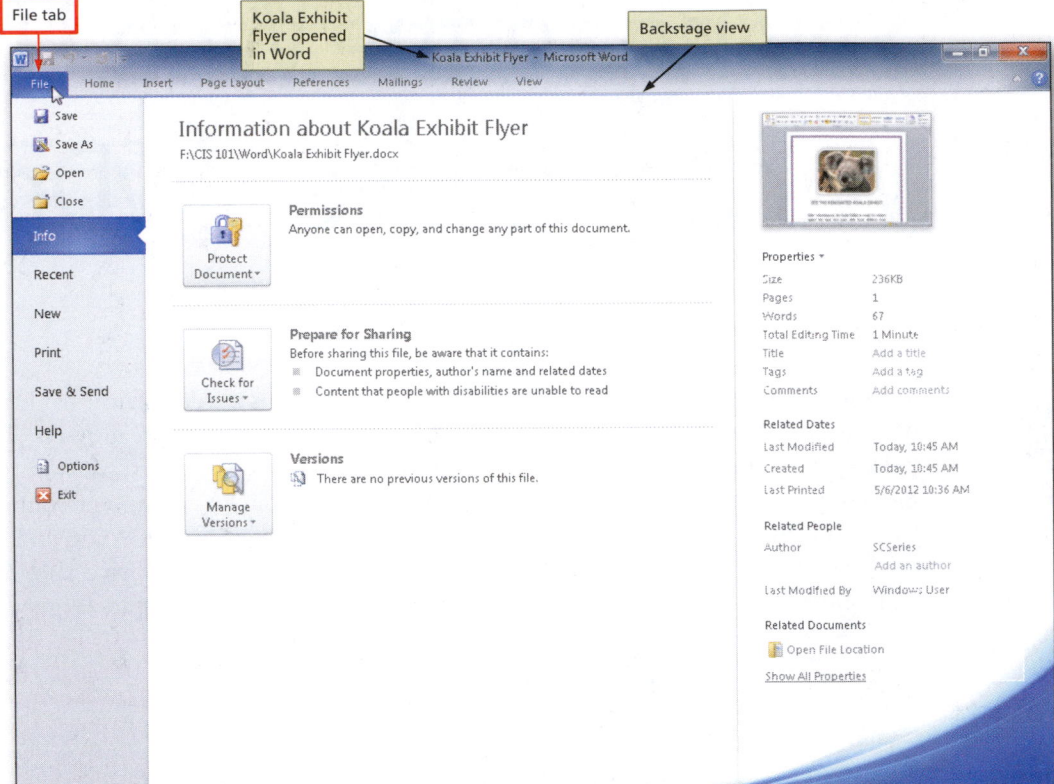

Figure C–2

2

- Click the Save & Send tab to display the Save & Send gallery (Figure C–3).

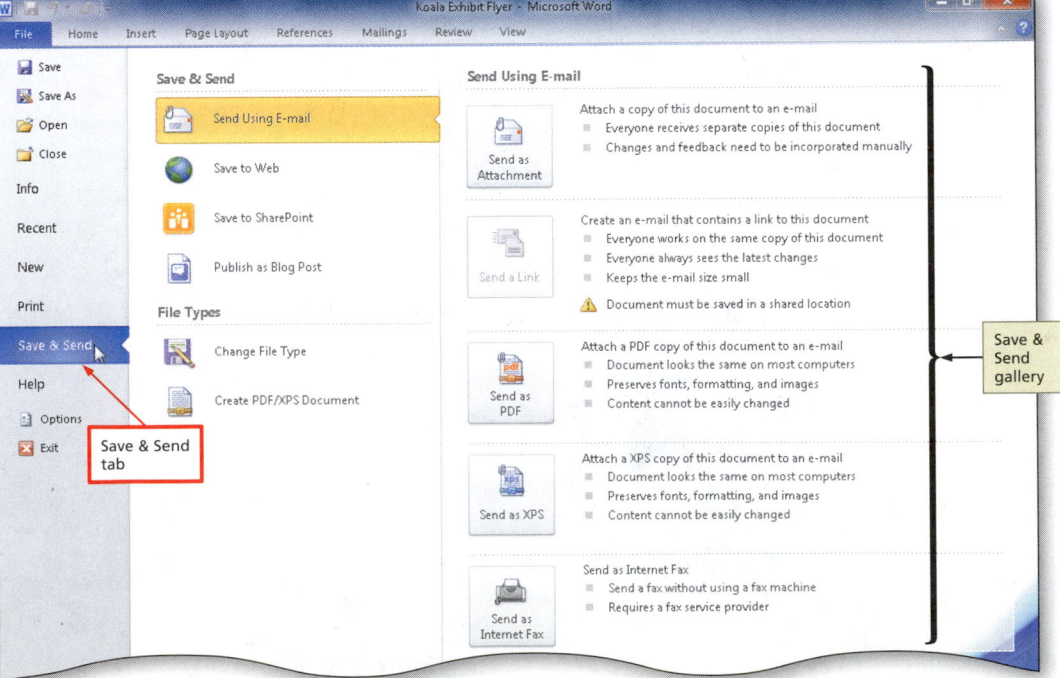

Figure C–3

3
- Click Save to Web in the Save & Send gallery to display information about saving a file to the Web (Figure C–4).

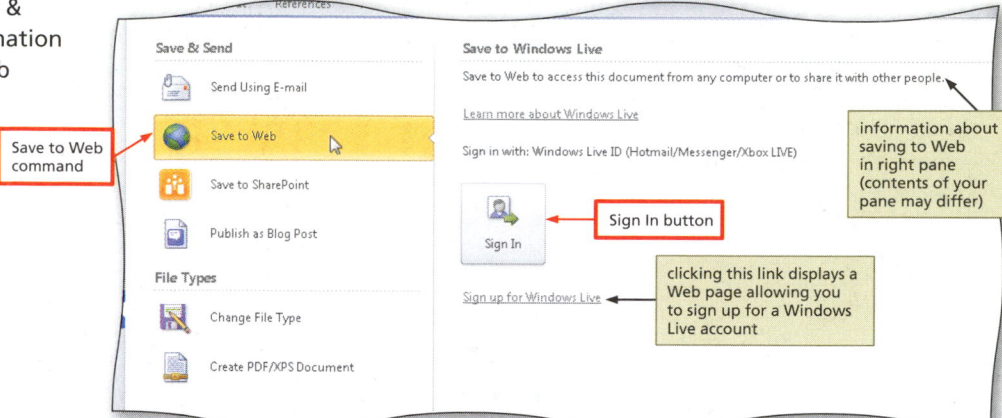

Figure C–4

4
- Click the Sign In button to display a Windows Live login dialog box that requests your e-mail address and password (Figure C–5).

Q&A What if the Sign In button does not appear?

If you already are signed into Windows Live, the Sign In button will not be displayed. Instead, the contents of your Windows Live SkyDrive will be displayed. If you already are signed into Windows Live, proceed to Step 6.

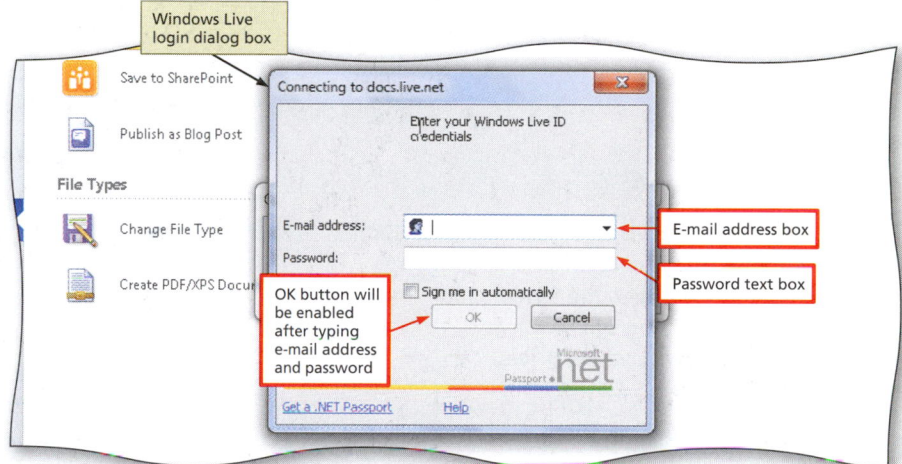

Figure C–5

5
- Enter your Windows Live e-mail address in the E-mail address box (Windows Live login dialog box).
- Enter your Windows Live password in the Password text box.
- Click the OK button to sign into Windows Live and display the contents of your Windows Live SkyDrive in the right pane of the Save & Send gallery.
- If necessary, click the My Documents folder to set the save location for the document (Figure C–6).

Q&A What if the My Documents folder does not exist?

Click another folder to select it as the save location. Record the name of this folder so that you can locate and retrieve the file later in this appendix.

Q&A My SkyDrive shows personal and shared folders. What is the difference?

Personal folders are private and are not shared with anyone. Shared folders can be viewed by SkyDrive users to whom you have assigned the necessary permissions.

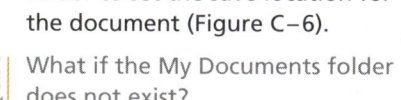
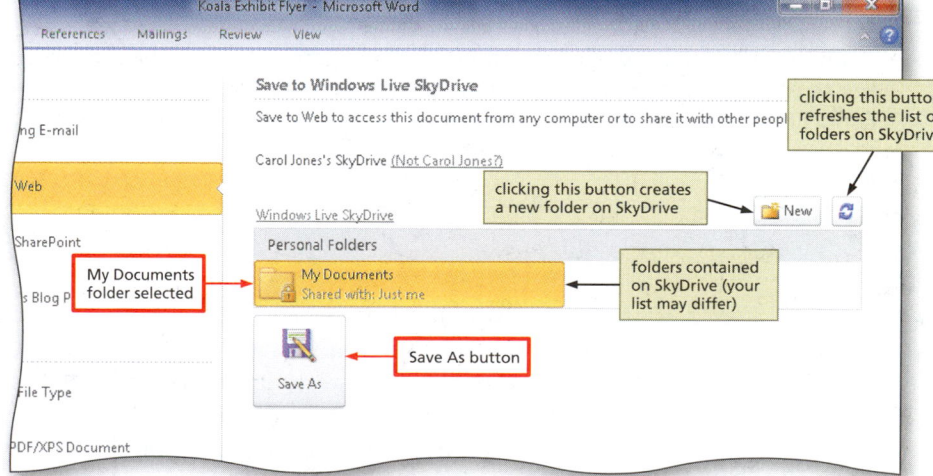

Figure C–6

6

- Click the Save As button in the right pane of the Save & Send gallery to contact the SkyDrive server (which may take some time, depending on the speed of your Internet connection) and then display the Save As dialog box (Figure C–7).

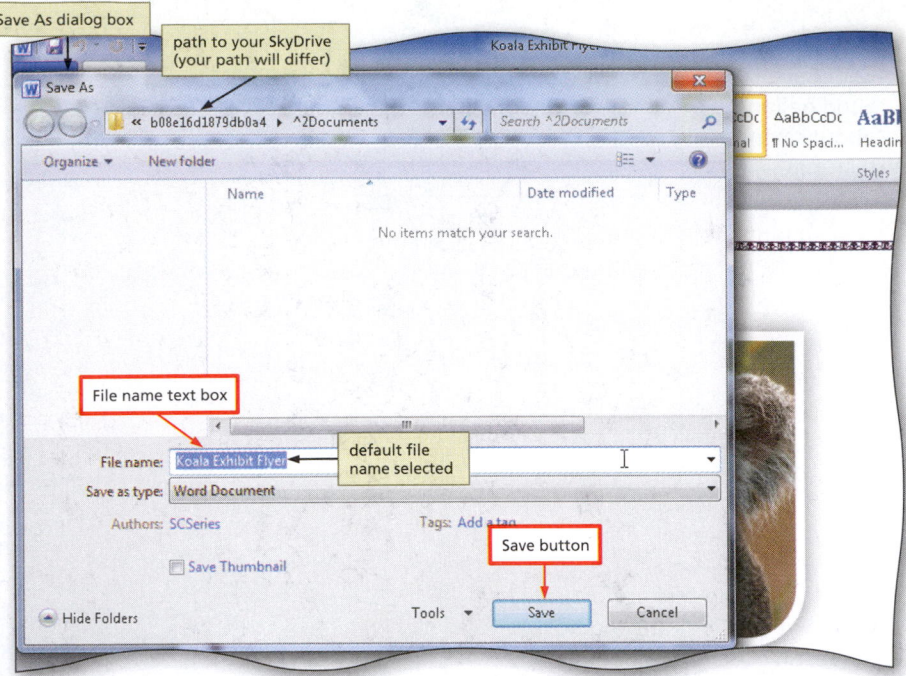

Figure C–7

7

- Type **Koala Exhibit Web** in the File name text box to enter the file name and then click the Save button (Save As dialog box) to save the file to Windows Live SkyDrive (Figure C–8).

Is it necessary to rename the file?

It is good practice to rename the file. If you download the file from SkyDrive to your computer, having a different file name will preserve the original file.

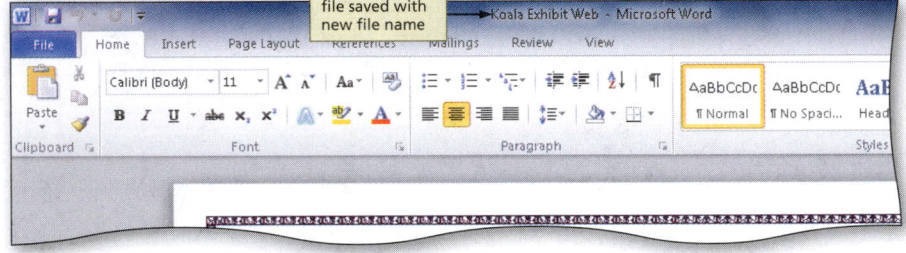

Figure C–8

8

- If you have one Word document open, click the Close button on the right side of the title bar to close the document and quit Word; or if you have multiple Word documents open, click File on the Ribbon to open the Backstage view and then click Exit in the Backstage view to close all open documents and quit Word.

Web Apps

Microsoft has created a scaled-down, Web-based version of its Microsoft Office suite, called **Microsoft Office Web Apps,** or **Web Apps**. Web Apps contains Web-based versions of Word, PowerPoint, Excel, and OneNote that can be used to view and edit files that are saved to SkyDrive. Web Apps allows users to continue working with their files even while they are not using a computer with Microsoft Office installed. In addition to working with files located on SkyDrive, Web Apps also enables users to create new Word documents, PowerPoint presentations, Excel spreadsheets, and OneNote notebooks. After returning to a computer with the Microsoft Office suite, some users choose to download files from SkyDrive and edit them using the associated Microsoft Office program.

Note: As with all Web applications, SkyDrive and Office Web Apps are subject to change. Consequently, the steps required to perform the actions in this appendix might be different from those shown.

To Download a File from Windows Live SkyDrive

Files saved to SkyDrive can be downloaded from a Web browser using any computer with an Internet connection. The following steps download the Koala Exhibit Web file using a Web browser.

1

- Click the Internet Explorer program button pinned on the Windows 7 taskbar to start Internet Explorer.

- Type `skydrive.live.com` in the Address bar and then press the ENTER key to display a SkyDrive Web page requesting you sign in to your Windows Live account (Figure C–9). (If the contents of your SkyDrive are displayed instead, you already are signed in and can proceed to Step 3 on the next page.)

Q&A Why does the Web address change after I enter it in the Address bar?

The Web address changes because you are being redirected to sign into Windows Live before you can access SkyDrive.

Q&A Can I open the file from Microsoft Word instead of using the Web browser?

If you are opening the file on the same computer from which you saved it to the SkyDrive, click File on the Ribbon to open the Backstage view. Click the Recent tab and then click the desired file name (Koala Exhibit Web, in this case) in the Recent Documents list, or click Open and then navigate to the location of the saved file (for a detailed example of this procedure, refer to the Office 2010 and Windows 7 chapter at the beginning of this book).

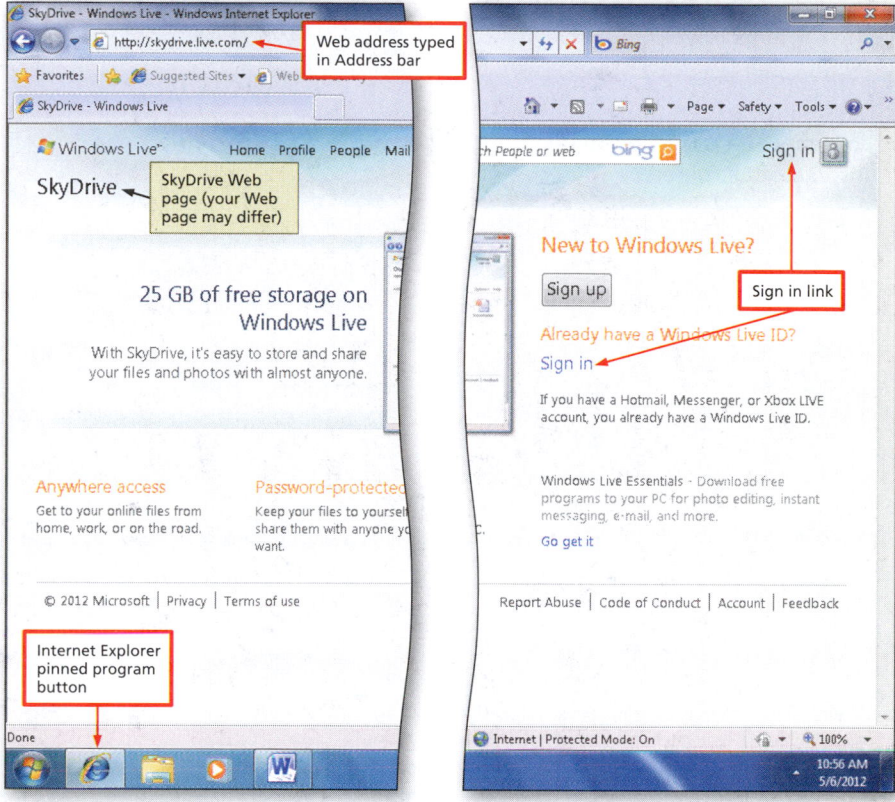

Figure C–9

2

- Click the Sign in link to display the Windows Live ID and Password text boxes (Figure C–10).

Q&A Why can I not locate the Sign in link?

If your computer remembers your Windows Live sign in credentials from a previous session, your e-mail address already may be displayed on the SkyDrive Web page. In this case, point to your e-mail address to display the Sign in button, click the Sign in button, and then proceed to Step 3. If you cannot locate your e-mail address or Sign in link, click the Sign in with a different Windows Live ID link and then proceed to Step 3.

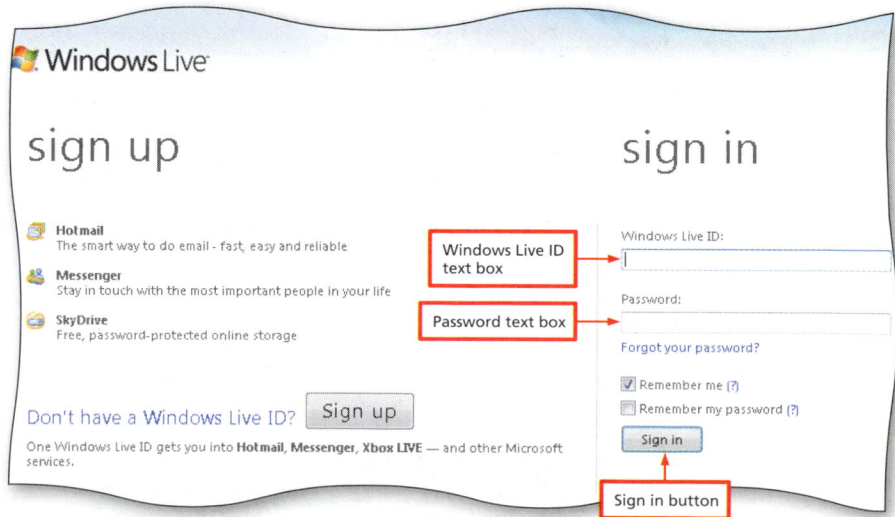

Figure C–10

3

- If necessary, enter your Windows Live ID and password in the appropriate text boxes and then click the Sign in button to sign into Windows Live and display the contents of your SkyDrive (Figure C–11).

Q&A What if my screen shows the contents of a particular folder, instead of all folders?

To display all folders on your SkyDrive, point to Windows Live in the upper-left corner of the window and then click SkyDrive on the Windows Live menu.

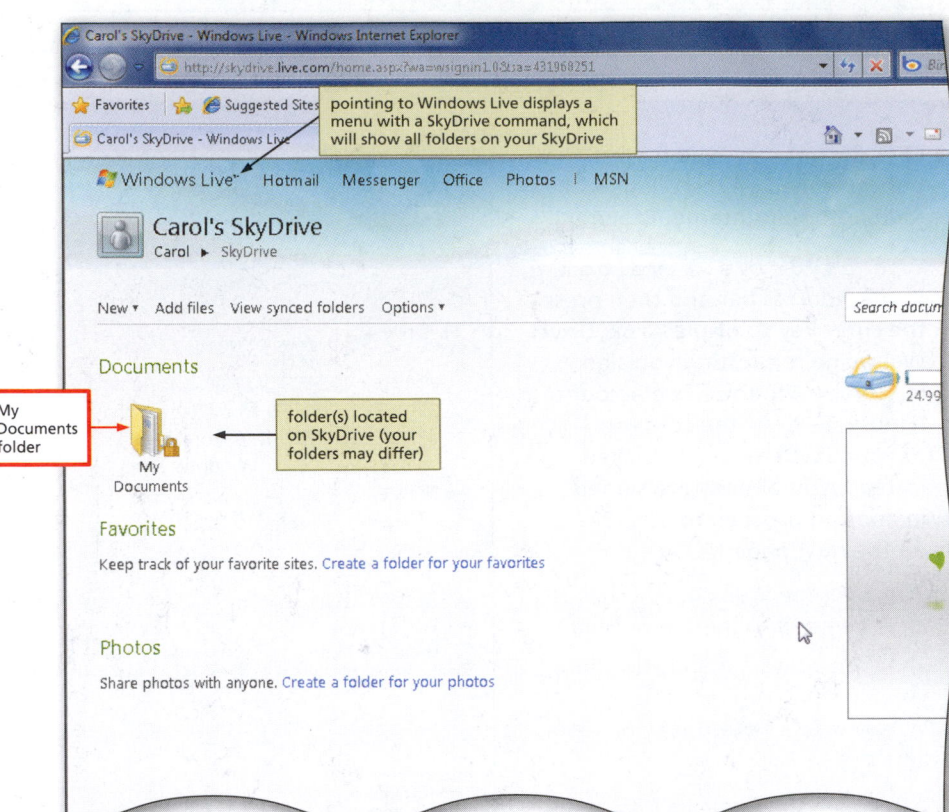

Figure C–11

4

- Click the My Documents folder, or the link corresponding to the folder containing the file you wish to open, to select the folder and display its contents (Figure C–12).

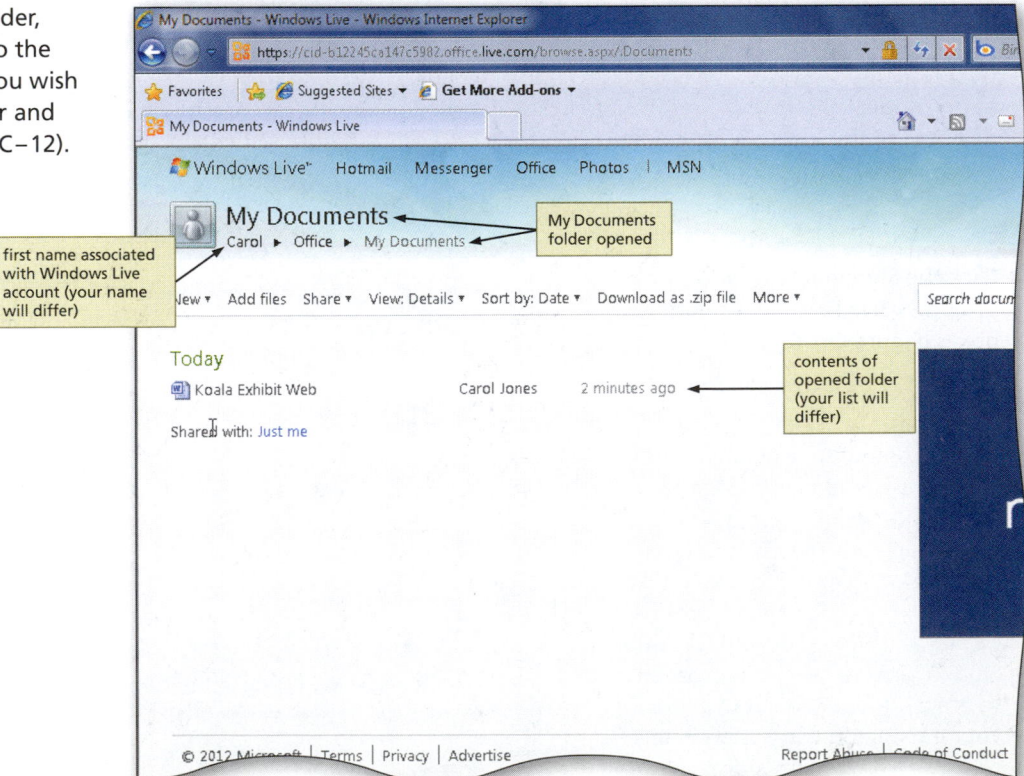

Figure C–12

5
- Point to the Koala Exhibit Web file to select the file and display commands associated with the file.
- Click the More link to display the More menu (Figure C–13).

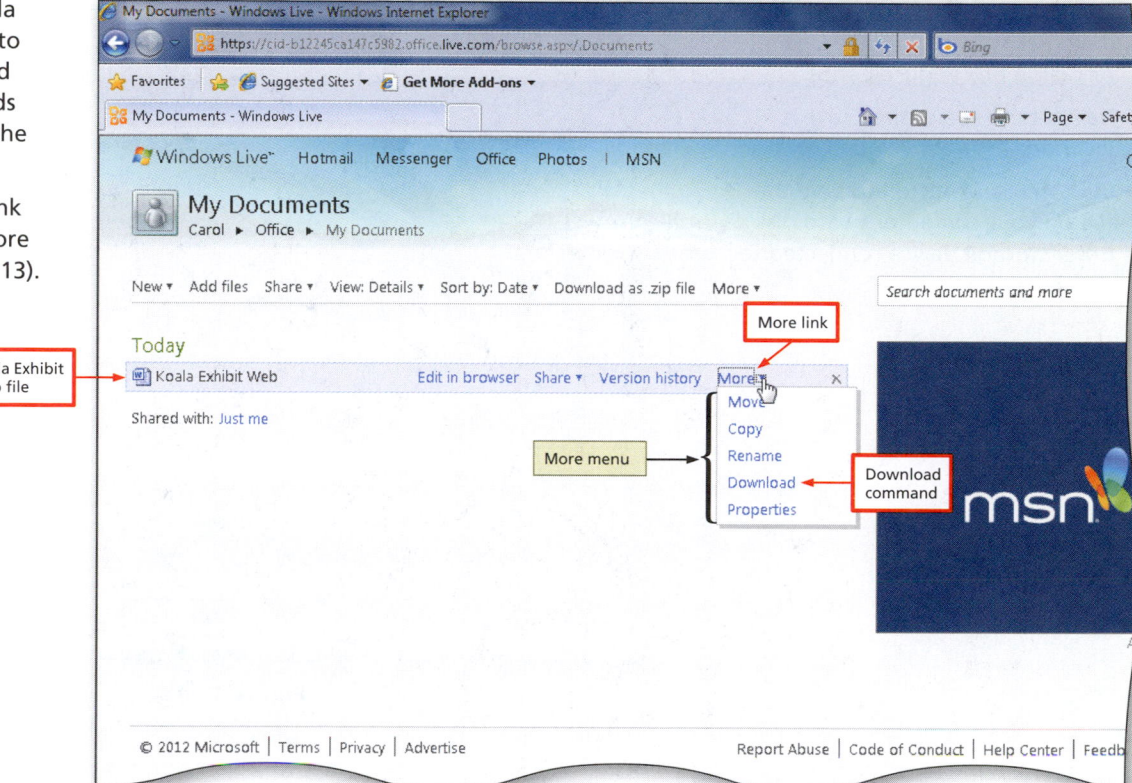

Figure C–13

6
- Click Download on the More menu to display the File Download dialog box (Figure C–14).

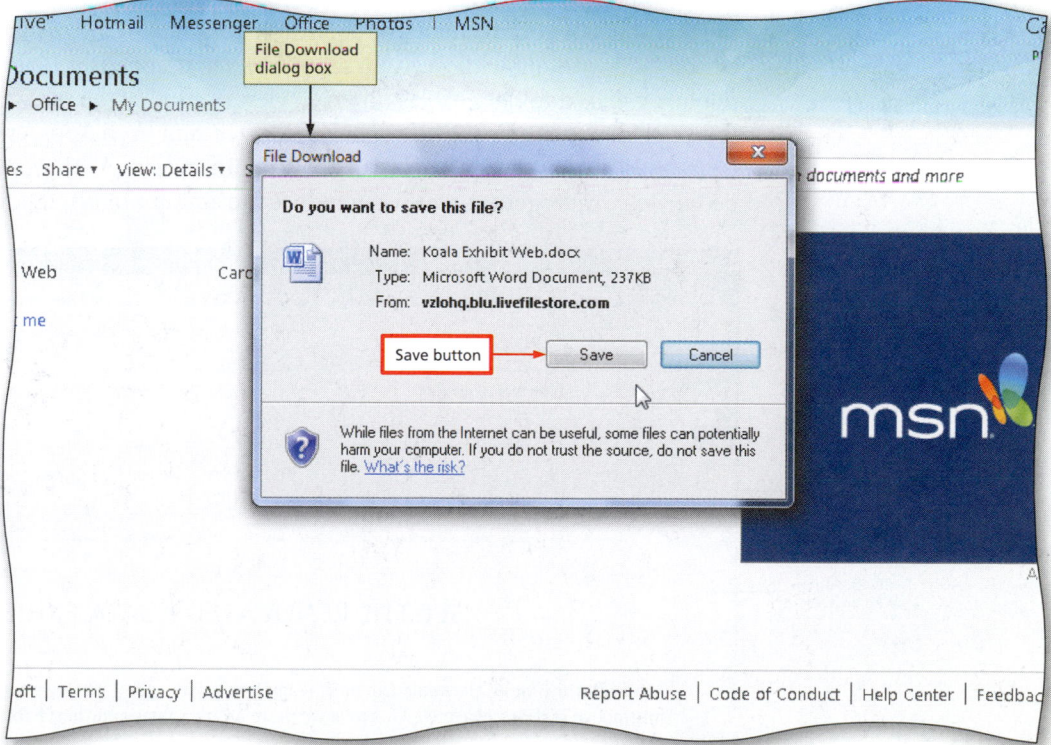

Figure C–14

7

- Click the Save button (File Download dialog box) to display the Save As dialog box (Figure C–15).

- Navigate to the desired save location.

- Click the Save button to save the file on your computer's hard disk or other storage device connected to the computer.

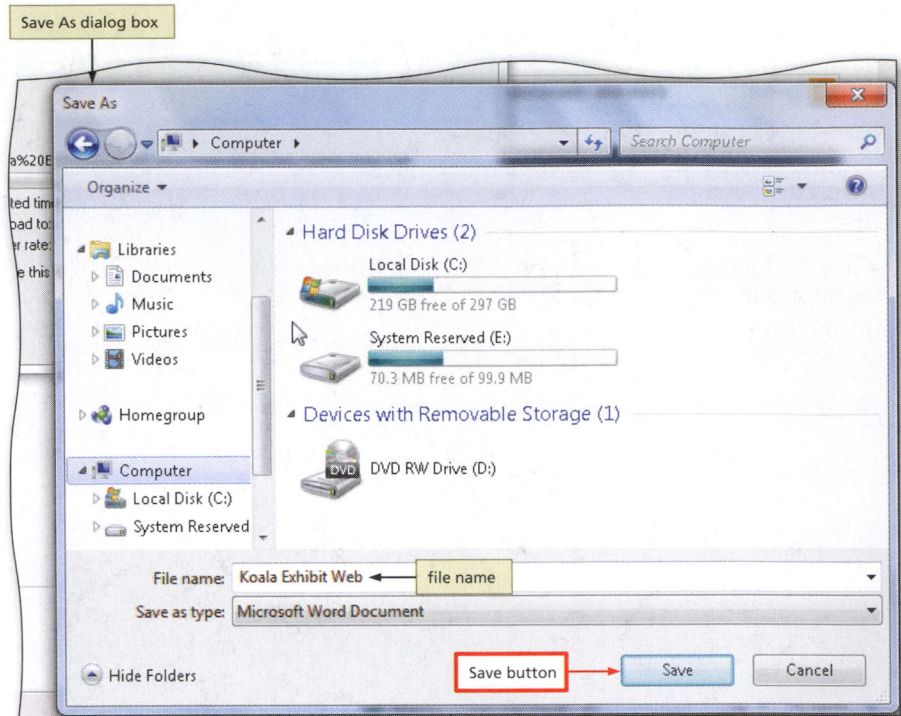

Figure C–15

Collaboration

In today's workplace, it is common to work with others on projects. Collaborating with the members of your team often requires sharing files. It also can involve multiple people editing and working with a certain set of files simultaneously. Placing files on SkyDrive in a public or shared folder enables others to view or modify the files. The members of the team then can view and edit the files simultaneously using Web Apps, enabling the team to work from one set of files (Figure C–16). Collaboration using Web Apps not only enables multiple people to work together, it also can reduce the amount of time required to complete a project.

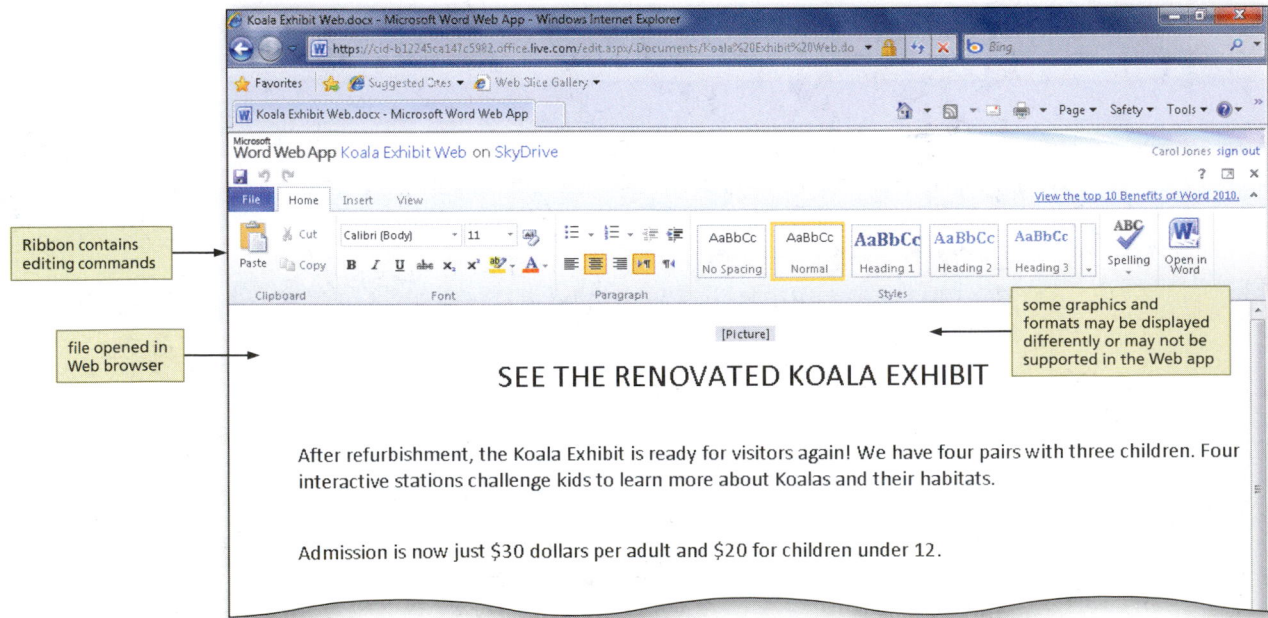

Figure C–16

Capstone Project

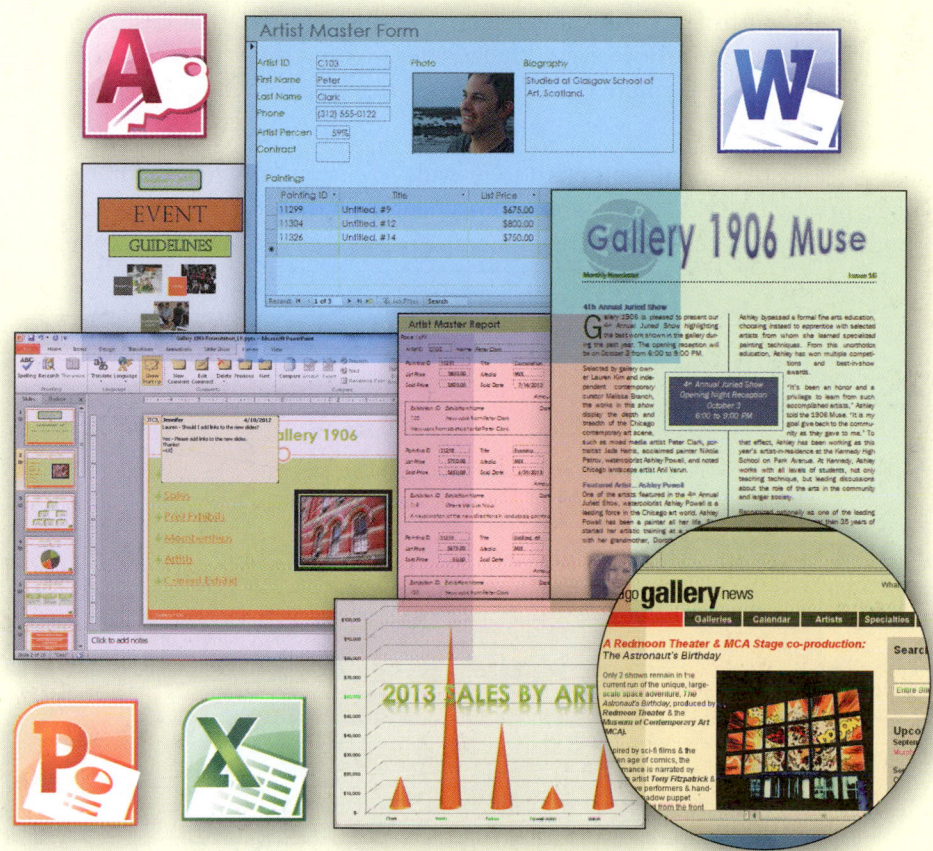

Word Advanced Capstone Project

Note: To complete this assignment, you will be required to use the Data Files for Students. See the inside back cover of this book for instructions on downloading the Data Files for Students, or contact your instructor for information about accessing the required files.

Problem: Gallery 1906 is a successful art gallery located in Chicago. The gallery owner, Lauren Kim, wants to take advantage of your computer skills and have you create documents for the gallery that she can reuse in upcoming months. These documents include a sales proposal for customers who would like to use the gallery's space for private events and a letter inviting the gallery's patrons to a special reception. Lauren also would like you to create a monthly newsletter to highlight upcoming exhibitions and other events at Gallery 1906.

Instructions Part 1:   You create a sales proposal to provide to customers who are interested in using the gallery space for a private event. In a new document, change the theme to Civic and then change the theme colors and theme fonts to Austin. Create the title page similar to the one shown in Figure 1–1.

Insert Gallery_logo.jpg picture file from Data Files for Students

72-point Perpetua Titling MT font; bold; color: Brown Accent 5, Darker 50%; shadow: Inside Center

border: 6-pt Black, Text 1, Lighter 25%; fill: Orange, Accent 6, Darker 25%

48-point Perpetua Titling MT font; color: White, Background 1; outline: 2.25-pt Green, Accent 1, Darker 50%; paragraph indent 0.5"

border: 3-pt Black Text 1, Lighter 25%; fill: Light Green, Background 2, Darker 25%

SmartArt graphic type – Picture; layout; Bending Picture Block; color: Colorful – Accent Colors; style: Moderate Effect

28-point Copperplate Gothic Light font; color: Brown, Accent 5, Darker 25%

Figure 1–1

Indent the left and right edges of the Guidelines paragraph by 0.5 inches. Insert the SmartArt graphic, as shown in the figure. Three picture files are available on the Data Files for Students: Wedding.jpg, Party.jpg, and Corporate.jpg. Resize the pictures as necessary. Insert a next page section break at the end of the title page.

Insert the draft body of the proposal below the title page. The draft is named CAP Event Proposal Draft in the Data Files for Students. Insert a header using the Alphabet style on the first page of the body of the draft. Insert a footer with the page number located in the bottom right and then change the starting page number to 1.

Format the headings as Heading 1 style. Format the list below the Restrictions heading as a bulleted list, using the picture bullet style of your choice, and then sort the bulleted list. Format the word, not, in the Restrictions section and the word, all, in the first paragraph of the Catering section using the Intense Reference style. Format the questions in the Frequently Asked Questions section using the Intense Emphasis style. Modify the first page of the body of the proposal so that it looks like Figure 1–2 by creating the multilevel list and the table as shown. Check the spelling. Save the document with the file name, CAP Gallery 1906 Event Proposal.

Continued >

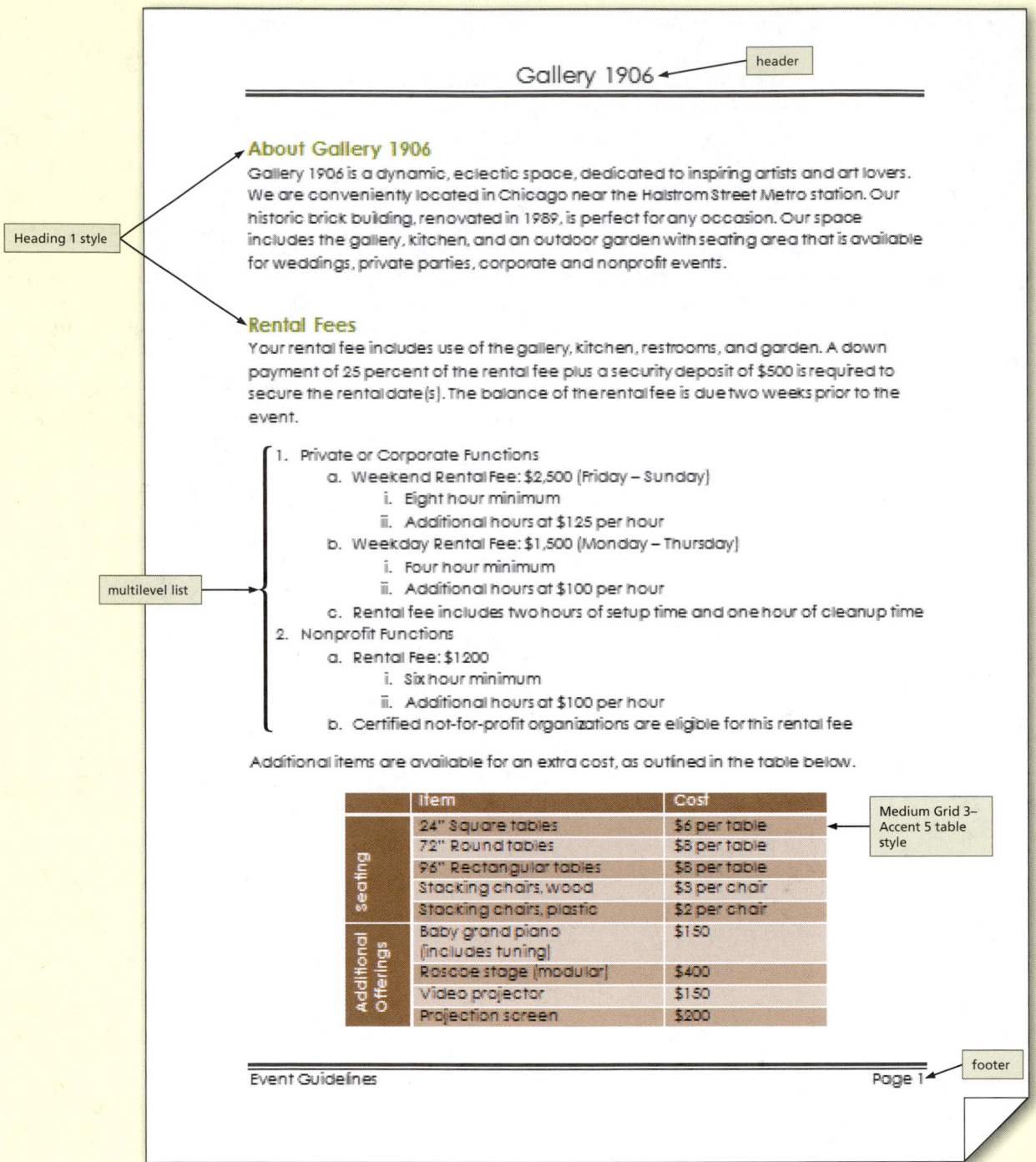

Figure 1–2

Instructions Part 2:   Create a letter to be mailed to previous buyers of artwork at Gallery 1906 inviting them to a special reception for the 4th Annual Juried Show. Use the Equity Merge Letter template to create the letter. Change the document theme to Austin. Change the margins to Moderate. Change the Normal style font size to 12 point. Save the letter with the file name, CAP Gallery 1906 Letter. Insert today's date. Add the gallery's name and address. Delete the name content control (and the accompanying blank line) that appears above the gallery's name. Format the gallery name with an 18-point font size and a font color of Green, Accent 1, Darker 50% as shown in Figure 1–3. Create a Quick Style called Name using this format.

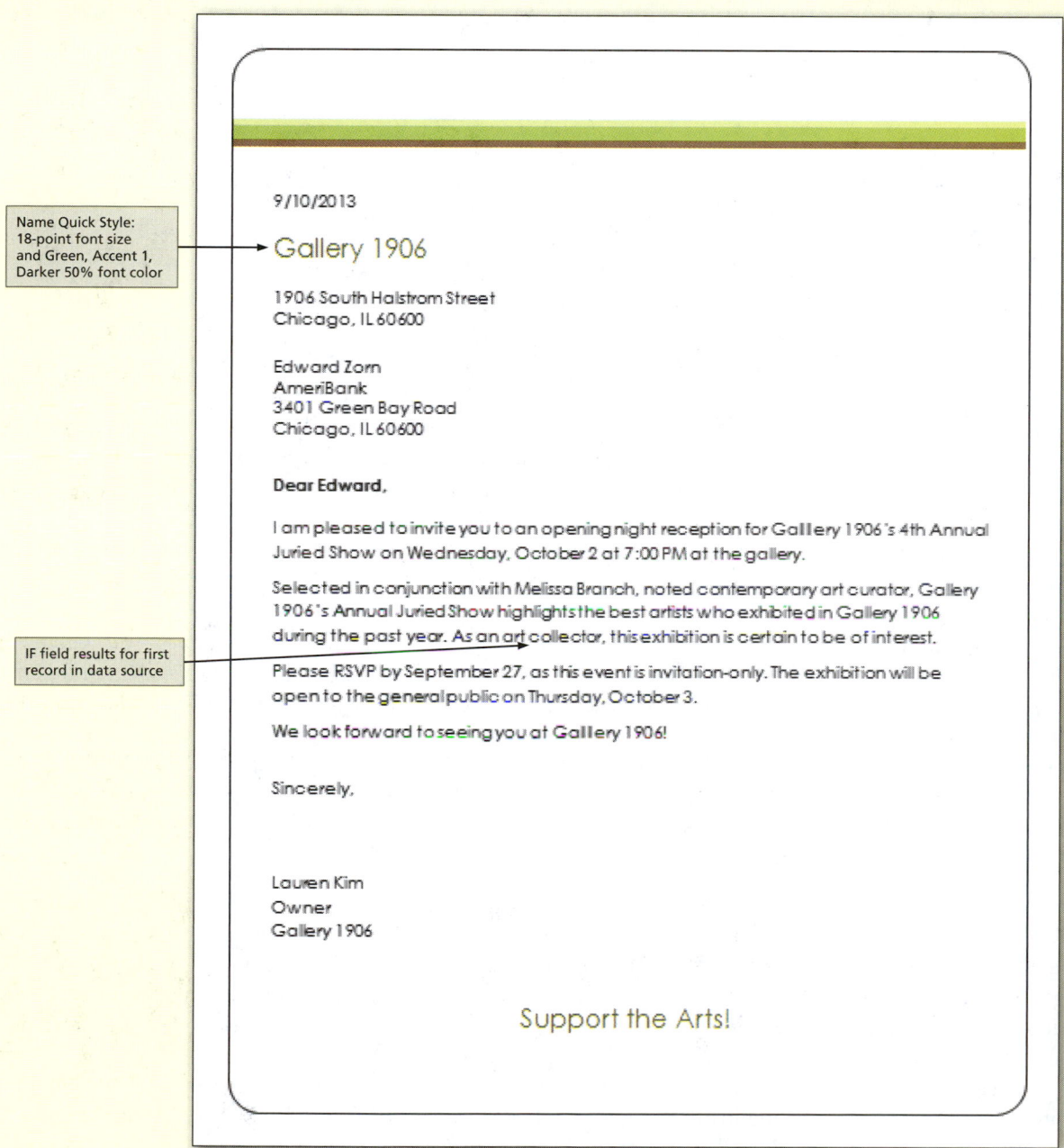

Name Quick Style: 18-point font size and Green, Accent 1, Darker 50% font color

IF field results for first record in data source

Figure 1–3

Continued >

Create a new data source in Word containing seven records, using the data shown in Table 1–1. Delete field names not used. Note that some of the buyers are individuals and some represent corporations or organizations. Save the data source with the file name, CAP Gallery 1906 Mailing List.

Table 1–1

Title	First Name	Last Name	Organization Name	Address	City	State	ZIP Code	Buyer
Mr.	Edward	Zorn	AmeriBank, Inc.	3401 Green Bay Road	Chicago	IL	60600	Y
Ms.	Isabella	Swan	Swan Investment Partners	1259 Grand Avenue #201	Chicago	IL	60600	N
Mr.	Alfredo	Selim		970 S. Highland Avenue	Chicago	IL	60642	Y
Mrs.	Rose	Weaver		27 Lake Street	Evanston	IL	60210	Y
Ms.	Jennifer	Kowalski	New Art Museum	300 Midway Park	Oak Park	IL	60648	Y
Mr.	Jacob	Cohen		324 W. Lyndale Street	Chicago	IL	60635	N
Dr.	Rashika	Mathews	Demeter Healthcare	850 N. Washington Street	Naperville	IL	60562	Y

Enter the body of the letter as shown in Figure 1–3. Insert an IF field in the last sentence of the second paragraph, following the phrase, As an art. The IF field tests if the Buyer merge field is Y (Yes); if it is, then print the text, collector; otherwise print the text, enthusiast. Below the letter body, enter the complimentary close and signature block in the appropriate content controls as shown in the figure. Insert a footer, Support the Arts! Center the footer text and apply the Name Quick Style. Merge the form letters to a new document with the file name, CAP Gallery 1906 Merged Letters.

Address envelopes in ZIP code order using the same data source you created for the letters. Exclude Jennifer Kolwaski's record. Save the envelopes with the file name, CAP Gallery 1906 Envelopes.

Because Lauren would like to keep a record of the buyers, merge the data source to a directory, selecting only those records where the Buyer merge field is Y. Convert the directory to a Word table sorted by last name. Apply the Light List – Accent 3 table style, with banded rows and a header row. Change the theme font to Austin. Apply the Confidential 2 watermark. Change the page orientation to landscape and adjust the width of the columns as needed. Save the directory as a PDF or XPS document with the file name CAP Gallery 1906 Buyer Directory. Send the PDF or XPS document via e-mail to your instructor, if permitted. If you have access to a Web server, FTP site, or Windows SkyDrive, save the directory to the server, FTP site, or online storage location.

Instructions Part 3: Create a newsletter of the upcoming exhibitions and events at the gallery. Change the margins to .75 inches. Apply the Executive theme colors and the Angles theme fonts. Create the nameplate using the formats identified in Figure 1–4. Create the title using WordArt. Set a right-aligned custom tab stop at the right margin. Use the Clip Art pane to locate the image shown, using the search term, palette. Resize the clip art and recolor it to Indigo, Accent color 1 Light. Format the clip art as Behind Text, rotate it, and then position it as shown.

Create a continuous section break below the nameplate. Format section 2 as two columns. Enter the text in section 2 using justified paragraph formatting. Change the Normal style font size to 12 point. Insert the picture, Powell.bmp, supplied with your Data Files. Format the picture as indicated in the figure. Position the picture in the bottom left with square text wrapping. Insert the table shown in the bottom of the right column and format it as indicated.

Insert a Pinstripes Quote text box for the pull quote, and enter the text shown in the pull quote in the figure. Change the fill of the text box to Indigo, Accent 1, Darker 25%, and resize and reposition the text box so that it is similar to the figure. Make any additional formatting as necessary, and save the newsletter as CAP Gallery 1906 Newsletter.

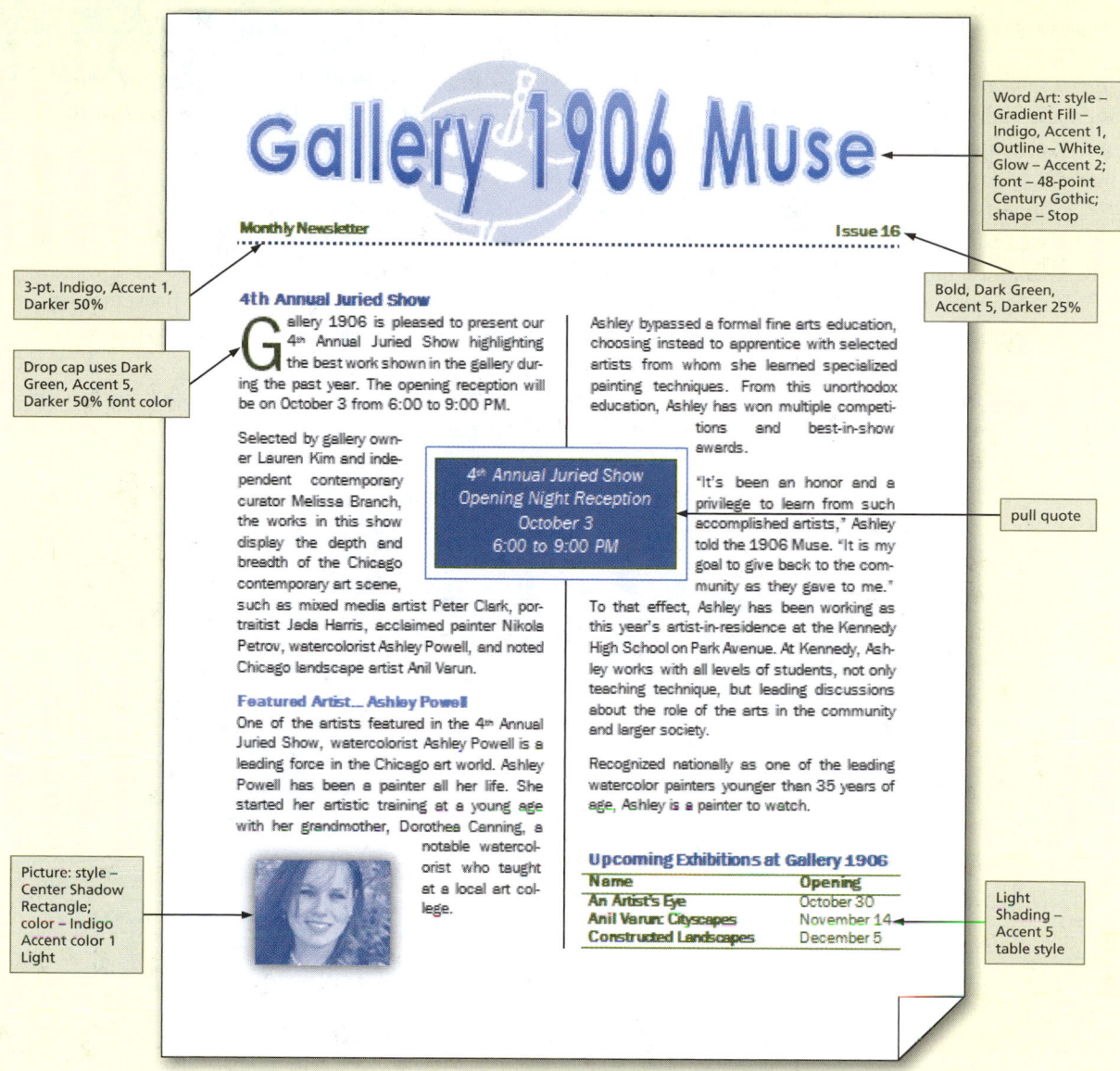

Figure 1–4

Callout labels in Figure 1–4:

- Word Art: style – Gradient Fill – Indigo, Accent 1, Outline – White, Glow – Accent 2; font – 48-point Century Gothic; shape – Stop
- 3-pt. Indigo, Accent 1, Darker 50%
- Bold, Dark Green, Accent 5, Darker 25%
- Drop cap uses Dark Green, Accent 5, Darker 50% font color
- pull quote
- Picture: style – Center Shadow Rectangle; color – Indigo Accent color 1 Light
- Light Shading – Accent 5 table style

Gallery 1906 Muse

Monthly Newsletter   Issue 16

4th Annual Juried Show

Gallery 1906 is pleased to present our 4th Annual Juried Show highlighting the best work shown in the gallery during the past year. The opening reception will be on October 3 from 6:00 to 9:00 PM.

Selected by gallery owner Lauren Kim and independent contemporary curator Melissa Branch, the works in this show display the depth and breadth of the Chicago contemporary art scene, such as mixed media artist Peter Clark, portraitist Jada Harris, acclaimed painter Nikola Petrov, watercolorist Ashley Powell, and noted Chicago landscape artist Anil Varun.

Featured Artist… Ashley Powell

One of the artists featured in the 4th Annual Juried Show, watercolorist Ashley Powell is a leading force in the Chicago art world. Ashley Powell has been a painter all her life. She started her artistic training at a young age with her grandmother, Dorothea Canning, a notable watercolorist who taught at a local art college.

> 4th Annual Juried Show
> Opening Night Reception
> October 3
> 6:00 to 9:00 PM

Ashley bypassed a formal fine arts education, choosing instead to apprentice with selected artists from whom she learned specialized painting techniques. From this unorthodox education, Ashley has won multiple competitions and best-in-show awards.

"It's been an honor and a privilege to learn from such accomplished artists," Ashley told the 1906 Muse. "It is my goal to give back to the community as they gave to me." To that effect, Ashley has been working as this year's artist-in-residence at the Kennedy High School on Park Avenue. At Kennedy, Ashley works with all levels of students, not only teaching technique, but leading discussions about the role of the arts in the community and larger society.

Recognized nationally as one of the leading watercolor painters younger than 35 years of age, Ashley is a painter to watch.

Upcoming Exhibitions at Gallery 1906

Name	Opening
An Artist's Eye	October 30
Anil Varun: Cityscapes	November 14
Constructed Landscapes	December 5

PowerPoint Advanced Capstone Project

Creating a Presentation for Investors

Note: To complete this assignment, you will be required to use the Data Files for Students. See the inside back cover of this book for instructions on downloading the Data Files for Students, or contact your instructor for information about accessing the required files.

Problem: Gallery 1906 is looking for potential investors. Your boss, Lauren Kim, has asked you to create a presentation that can be used to show investors the past successes and future plans for the gallery. You will use a Word outline and slides from an existing PowerPoint presentation as the basis, and then add graphics, SmartArt, a chart, and a table to present data. Lauren will collaborate with you to make edits and notes on the presentation. You will add hyperlinks and animations to the presentation and insert action buttons. Lastly, you will prepare the presentation for delivery and add protection settings.

Continued >

PowerPoint Advanced Capstone Project *continued*

Instructions Part 1: Open the outline file Gallery 1906 Outline.rtf in PowerPoint. Apply the Civic theme and change the color and font themes to Austin. Refer to Figure 1–5 to make changes to the slides. Change the slide title formatting. On Slide 1, insert the Gallery 1906 logo and remove its background. Add and format text and symbols to Slide 1.

Convert the bulleted text on Slides 4 and 5 to SmartArt objects. Insert a slide footer to all but the first slide. Add a table to Slide 6. Enter text and images, and change the formatting. On Slide 3, create and format a chart. Create and format a SmartArt graphic on Slide 2.

Insert a new slide after Slide 1. On the new Slide 2, add hyperlinks to slides in your presentation using a bulleted list with custom bullets, and 1.5 line spacing. Add and format the gallery_building.jpg file to the new Slide 2.

Add the Previous action button to Slide 3. Change the hyperlink on the action button to return to the last slide viewed. Copy and paste the action button to the other slides. On Slide 8, display the guides and use them to position a newly inserted image. Add effects, motion paths, and animations as shown in Table 1–2.

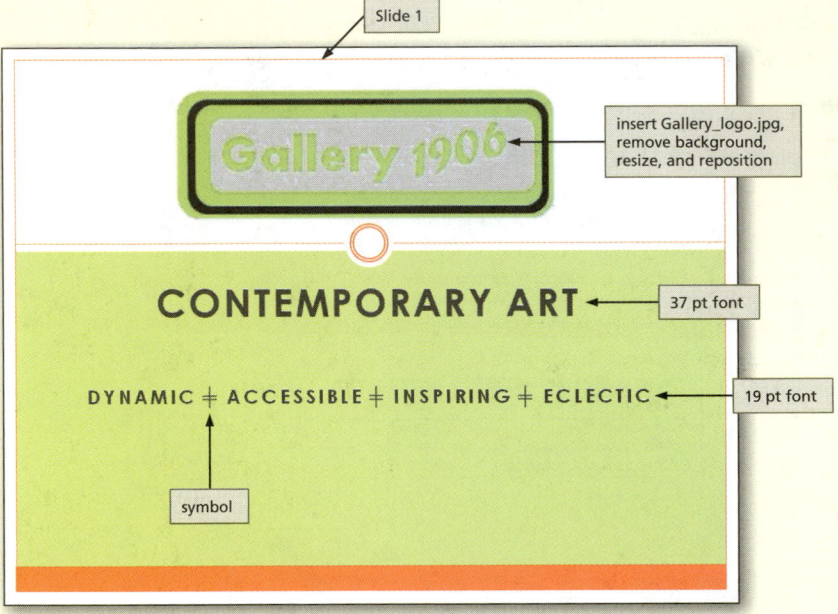

Slide 1

insert Gallery_logo.jpg, remove background, resize, and reposition

CONTEMPORARY ART ← 37 pt font

DYNAMIC ⊹ ACCESSIBLE ⊹ INSPIRING ⊹ ECLECTIC ← 19 pt font

symbol

(a) Slide 1

About Gallery 1906

format slide titles with bold, Green, Accent 1, 42 pt font

custom bullets

apply 1.5 line spacing

⊹ Employees
⊹ Sales
⊹ Past Exhibits
⊹ Memberships
⊹ Artists
⊹ Current Exhibit

hyperlinks to all slides in presentation

apply Civic theme, and Austin fonts and colors

gallery_building.jpg with Double Frame, Black picture style and Pastels Smooth artistic effect

new Slide 2

Gallery 1906 — add footer to all but first slide

(b) Slide 2

Figure 1–5

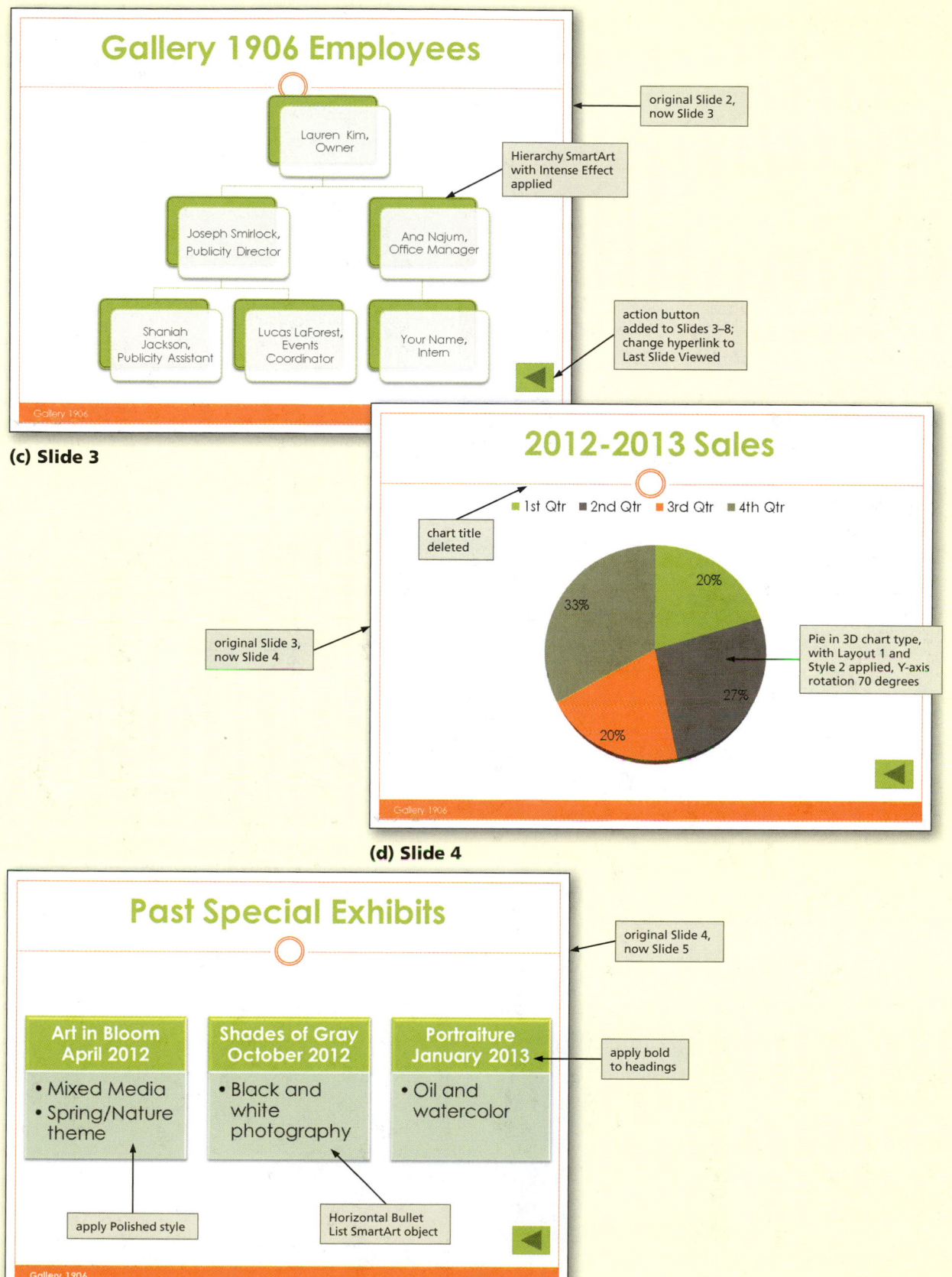

(c) Slide 3

(d) Slide 4

(e) Slide 5

Figure 1–5 (Continued)

Continued >

PowerPoint Advanced Capstone Project *continued*

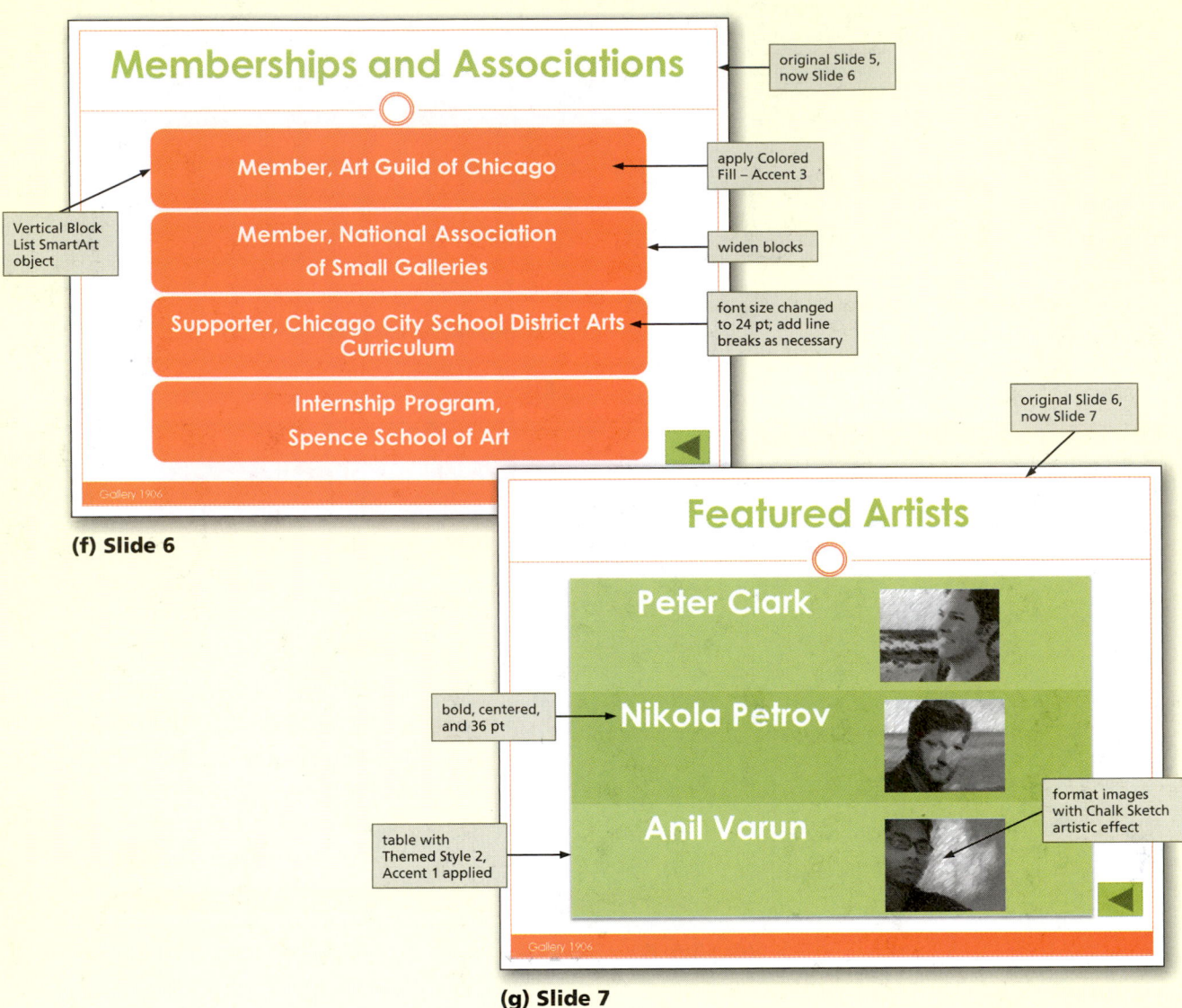

Memberships and Associations

original Slide 5, now Slide 6

Member, Art Guild of Chicago

apply Colored Fill – Accent 3

Vertical Block List SmartArt object

Member, National Association of Small Galleries

widen blocks

Supporter, Chicago City School District Arts Curriculum

font size changed to 24 pt; add line breaks as necessary

Internship Program, Spence School of Art

Gallery 1906

(f) Slide 6

original Slide 6, now Slide 7

Featured Artists

Peter Clark

bold, centered, and 36 pt

Nikola Petrov

format images with Chalk Sketch artistic effect

table with Themed Style 2, Accent 1 applied

Anil Varun

Gallery 1906

(g) Slide 7

original Slide 7, now Slide 8

Current Exhibit

- Artist David Kim
- Watercolor portraits
- *Ball Pit, 2008*

format image with Thick Matte, Black style

use guides to position image as shown

Gallery 1906

(h) Slide 8

Figure 1–5 (Continued)

Table 1-2 Slide and Object Effects	
Slide Number	**Effect**
All	Apply Split transition, 1.00 duration to all slides
3	Apply Wheel entrance effect to SmartArt graphic
4	Apply Fly In entrance effect to chart
7	Apply Shapes motion path to table
8	Apply Shape entrance effect to image

Instructions Part 2: Compress all images. Reuse slides from the 2013 Revenue Plan presentation and insert them at the end of the slide show. Make formatting changes as necessary to match Figure 1–6.

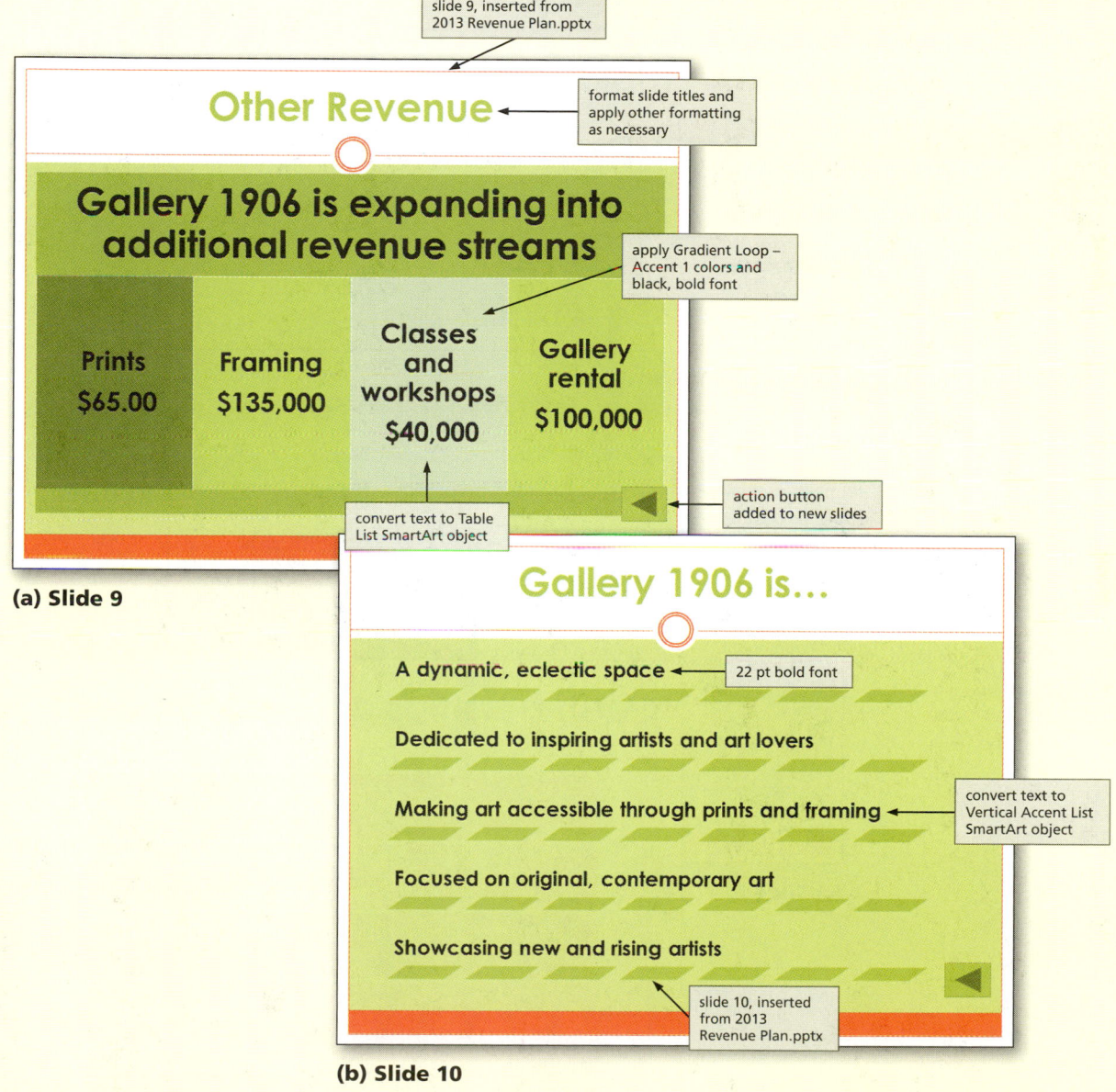

(a) Slide 9

(b) Slide 10

Figure 1–6

Instructions Part 3: Make edits and add comments as shown in Figure 1–7. Combine Lauren's edits by merging the Gallery 1906_LK presentation, using the password, Gallery, if necessary. Accept all edits make the changes suggested by Lauren, then save the file as **Gallery 1906 Presentation_Final.pptx**. Set the following slide timings: Slides 1 and 2: 3 seconds; Slides 3–9: 8 seconds; Slide 10: 10 seconds. Test the slide timings, and then disable them.

Continued >

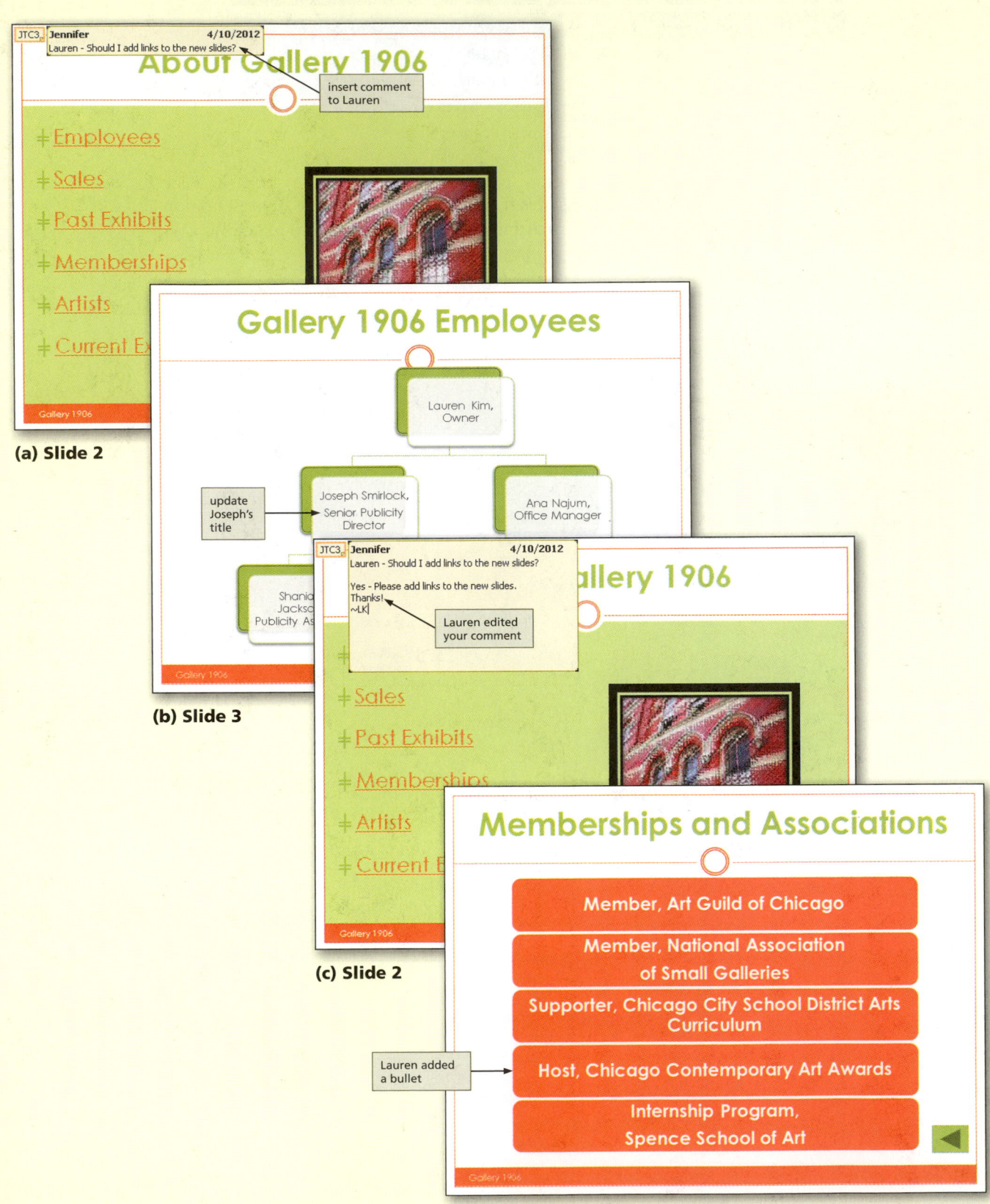

(a) Slide 2

(b) Slide 3

(c) Slide 2

(d) Slide 6

Figure 1–7

Instructions Part 4: Use the Document Inspector to remove the remaining comments. Add the password Gallery to the presentation. Run the presentation, and add annotations as shown in Figure 1–8. Save the annotations, and then save the file. Save the presentation as a PowerPoint show. Make sure the presentation (not the show) is open, then package the presentation for storage on a compact disc. Save the presentation as a PowerPoint 2003 file.

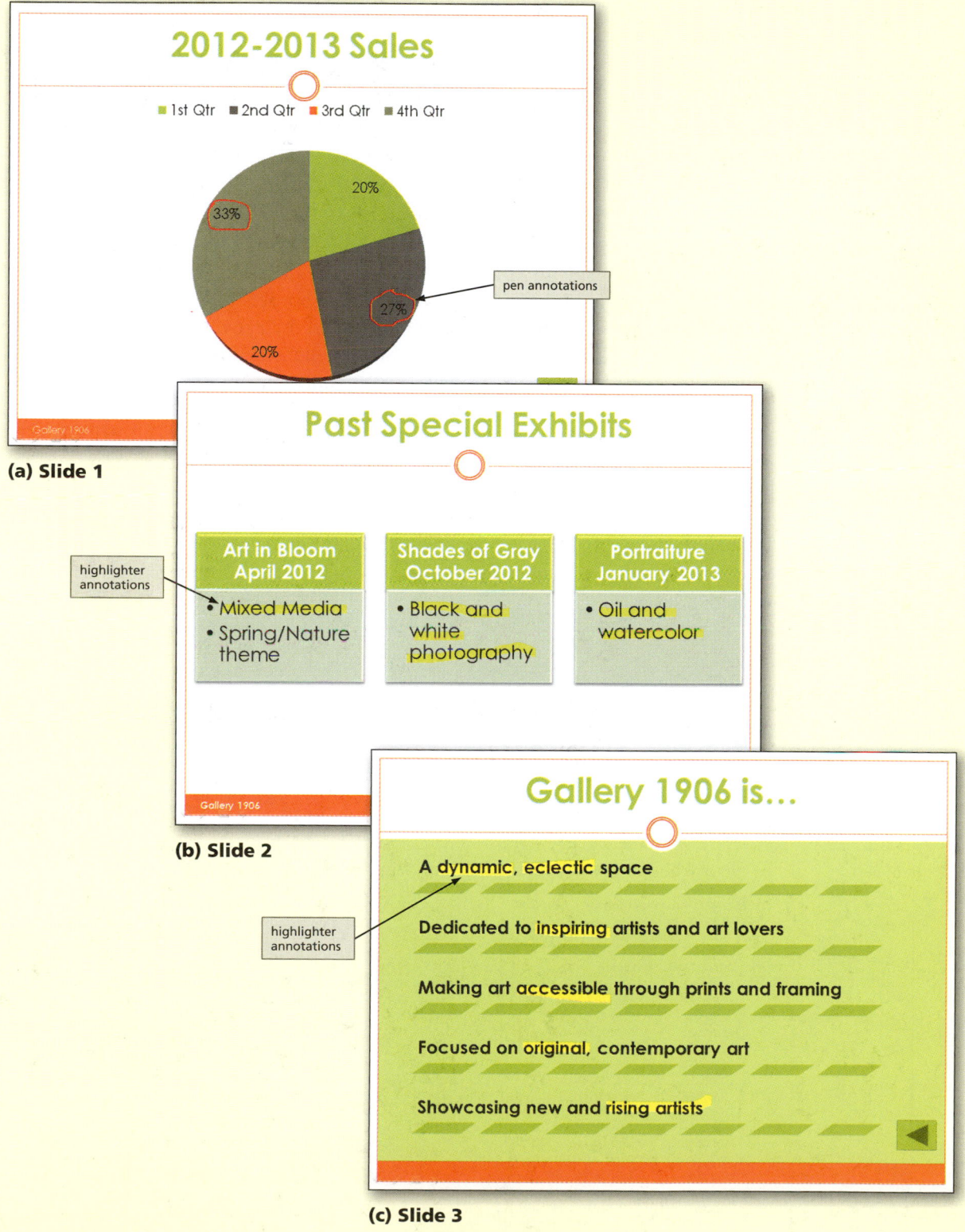

(a) Slide 1

(b) Slide 2

(c) Slide 3

Figure 1–8

Excel Advanced Capstone Project

Creating Worksheets for Analysis

Note: To complete this assignment, you will be required to use the Data Files for Students. See the inside back cover of this book for instructions on downloading the Data Files for Students, or contact your instructor for information about accessing the required files.

Problem: Gallery 1906 is going through transitions, including the possible purchase of the building the gallery now rents. Lauren Kim, your boss, asked you to create workbooks that she can use to analyze the finances and make decisions. She requested that you create the following workbooks: analyze a building loan; consolidate information about the income from artists the gallery currently represents; the gallery's monthly expenditures. She also requested that you create a template that can be used to analyze sales and then use the template to create a new workbook.

Instructions Part 1: Create a new workbook called Mortgage with the Austin theme, and change the font size to 10 pt. Change the Sheet1 name to Mortgage. To create the Loan Payment Calculator, enter the text labels, and add data to the ranges C2:C5, E2: E3. Add custom borders to the range B2:E6. Assign names to each cell within the ranges B4:B6 and E2:E6 based on their row titles. Use the names to enter the loan amount in cell C6. Calculate the Loan Amount in cell C6 and then use the PMT function in cell E4 to calculate the monthly payment. Use cell names to enter the interest and cost formulas.

Create a new data table in the range B9:E23 by entering the column headings in the range B7:E8. Enter data in the range B10:B11 and then use the Fill handle to complete the data for cells B12:B23. Use a What-If Analysis to create the data table. Format the data table. Add a pointer to the data table that indicates the cell which contains the current rate.

Create an amortization schedule by entering the column heads in cells G1:K2. Enter integers 1–15 in row G using the Fill handle. Enter the data and formulas shown in Figure 1–9 into the amortization schedule, and then copy them down the columns through row 17. Create the subtotals, down payment, and total costs in the range I18:K20.

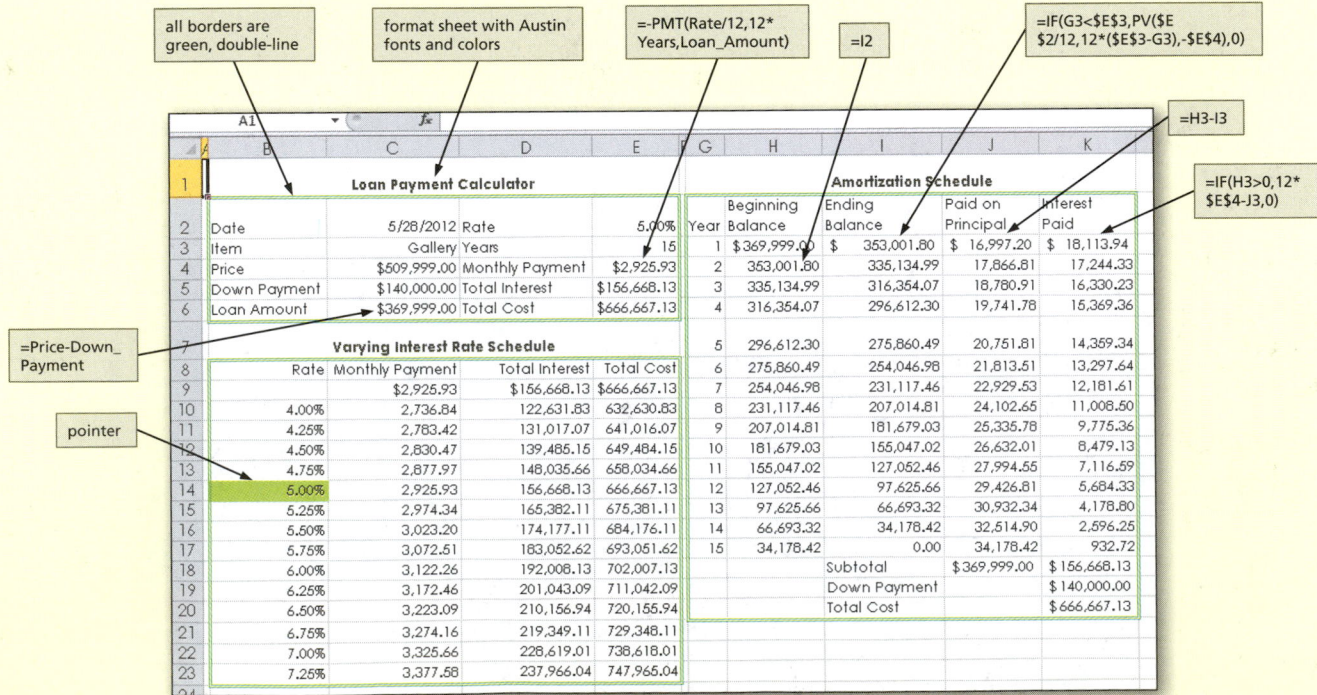

Figure 1–9

Set up the worksheet to print in black and white and change the orientation to Landscape. Set the print area to the range B1:E6. Assign names to the Loan_Payment, Interest_Schedule, and Amortization_Schedule worksheet areas and print each section. Protect the worksheet so that only cells C3:C5 and E2:E3 are unprotected. Check the formulas for errors.

Instructions Part 2: To create the September Sales workbook, import data from the September Sales table from the Gallery 1906 Sales Access database. Apply the Austin colors and fonts. Insert a new column H, and convert the data in column G to two columns. Apply the Table Quick Style as shown in Figure 1–10, apply the Currency format to columns E and F, and then adjust column widths as necessary. Add a new column G with the column header of % of List Price and enter and copy down a formula.

Delete column C. Create a VLOOKUP table in columns L and M. Use the table to determine the type of sale in column J. Add a conditional formatting rule with an icon set to the % of List Price column. Sort the table by Last Name. Query the table for Artist_ID using AutoFilter, and then remove the filter.

Create an extract range and extract the Artist_ID P161. Create a criteria range in cells A1:J3 and use functions as shown in Figure 1–10. Display automatic subtotals and use the outline feature, and then remove the subtotals and convert the range back to a table.

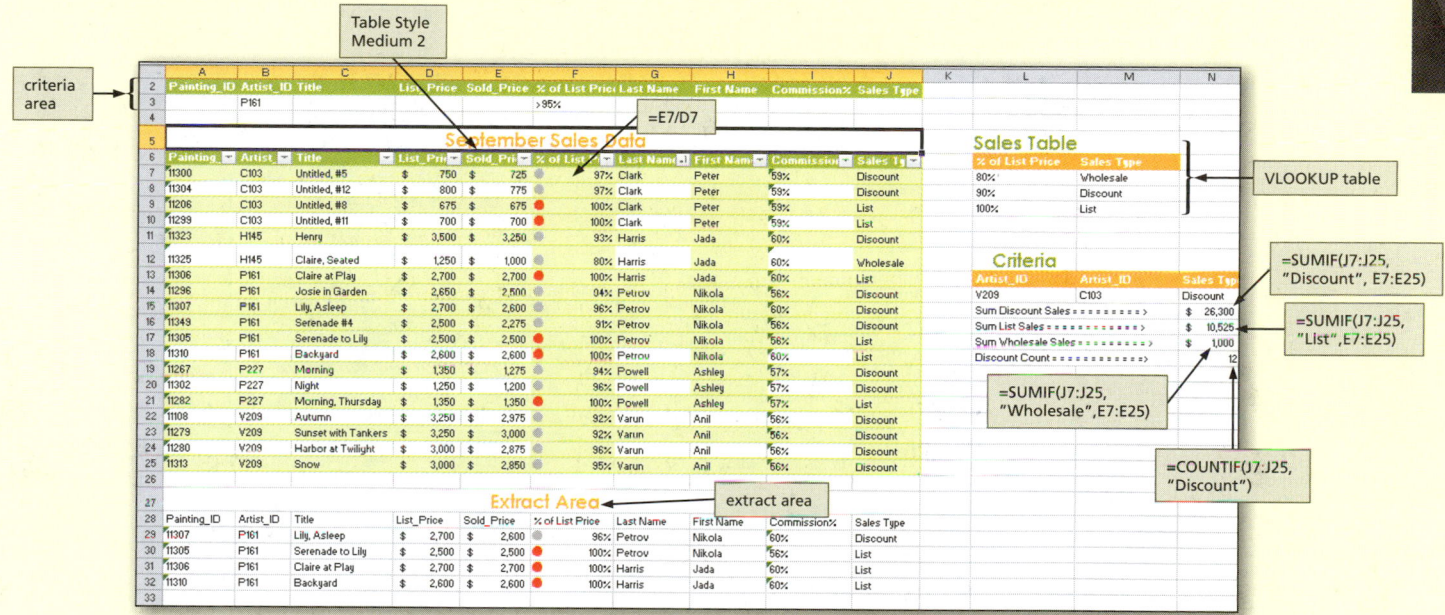

Figure 1–10

Instructions Part 3: Create a new Expenses workbook with the Austin colors and fonts applied. Create a new worksheet (Sheet 4). Copy and paste the data from the Gallery Expenses Word document to the new sheet, copy the data on the new sheet, then use Paste Special to transpose the rows and columns. Copy the transposed data and paste it into Sheet 1, starting in cell A3. Delete Sheet 4 and rename Sheet 1 as Expenses – Management.

Enter the sample data, functions, formatting, and custom format codes shown in Figure 1–11. Add the headings shown in Figure 1–11 to rows 1–3, and add the total to row 9. Copy the data from the Expenses – Management worksheet to Sheet 2 and Sheet 3. Name the new worksheets Expenses – Publicity and Expenses – Maintenance. Drill the data shown in the ranges C5:C8 and E5:E8 in Figure 1–11(b) through all three Expenses worksheets.

Continued >

Excel Advanced Capstone Project *continued*

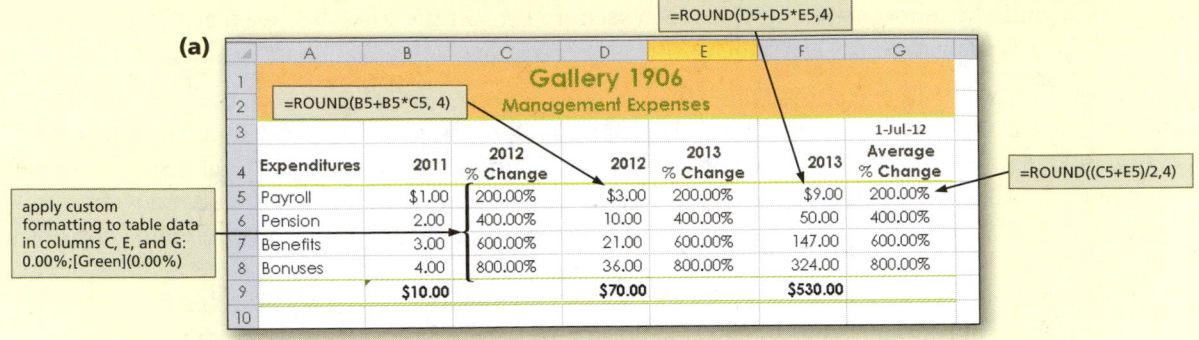

(a)

=ROUND(D5+D5*E5,4)

=ROUND(B5+B5*C5, 4)

Expenditures	2011	2012 % Change	2012	2013 % Change	2013	Average % Change
						1-Jul-12
Payroll	$1.00	200.00%	$3.00	200.00%	$9.00	200.00%
Pension	2.00	400.00%	10.00	400.00%	50.00	400.00%
Benefits	3.00	600.00%	21.00	600.00%	147.00	600.00%
Bonuses	4.00	800.00%	36.00	800.00%	324.00	800.00%
	$10.00		$70.00		$530.00	

Gallery 1906 — Management Expenses

apply custom formatting to table data in columns C, E, and G: 0.00%;[Green](0.00%)

=ROUND((C5+E5)/2,4)

(b)

Gallery 1906 — Management Expenses

Management worksheet

drill table data in columns C and E across 3 worksheets

Expenditures	2011	2012 % Change	2012	2013 % Change	2013	Average % Change
						10-Jul-12
Payroll	$135,089.00	(1.00%)	$133,738.11	(1.00%)	$132,400.73	(1.00%)
Pension	3,508.67	5.00%	3,684.10	3.00%	3,794.63	4.00%
Benefits	16,931.00	3.80%	17,574.38	(8.00%)	16,168.43	(2.10%)
Bonuses	10,000.00	(5.00%)	9,500.00	0.00%	9,500.00	(2.50%)
	$165,528.67		$164,496.59		$161,863.78	

(c)

Gallery 1906 — Publicity Expenses

Publicity worksheet

Expenditures	2011	2012 % Change	2012	2013 % Change	2013	Average % Change
						10-Jul-12
Payroll	$87,334.67	(1.00%)	$86,461.32	(1.00%)	$85,596.71	(1.00%)
Pension	1,566.09	5.00%	1,644.39	3.00%	1,693.73	4.00%
Benefits	13,099.70	3.80%	13,597.49	(8.00%)	12,509.69	(2.10%)
Bonuses	5,000.00	(5.00%)	4,750.00	0.00%	4,750.00	(2.50%)
	$107,000.46		$106,453.21		$104,550.13	

(d)

Gallery 1906 — Maintenance Expenses

Maintenance worksheet

Expenditures	2011	2012 % Change	2012	2013 % Change	2013	Average % Change
						10-Jul-12
Payroll	$49,823.90	(1.00%)	$49,325.66	(1.00%)	$48,832.40	(1.00%)
Pension	907.00	5.00%	952.35	3.00%	980.92	4.00%
Benefits	7,089.44	3.80%	7,358.84	(8.00%)	6,770.13	(2.10%)
Bonuses	2,000.00	(5.00%)	1,900.00	0.00%	1,900.00	(2.50%)
	$59,820.34		$59,536.85		$58,483.46	

(e)

Gallery 1906 — Total Expenses

Total Expenses worksheet

Expenditures	2011	2012 % Change	2012	2013 % Change	2013	Average % Change
						10-Jul-12
Payroll	$272,247.57	(1.00%)	$269,525.09	(1.00%)	$266,829.84	(1.00%)
Pension	5,981.76	5.00%	6,280.85	3.00%	6,469.27	4.00%
Benefits	37,120.14	3.80%	38,530.71	(8.00%)	35,448.25	(2.10%)
Bonuses	17,000.00	(5.00%)	16,150.00	0.00%	16,150.00	(2.50%)
	$332,349.47		$330,486.65		$324,897.37	

Figure 1–11

Add a new sheet called Total Expenses, and copy the data from one of the Expenses worksheets starting in cell A1. Use 3-D references in cell B5 to calculate the sum of the payroll expenses from the other three worksheets, and then copy the formula to the range B6:B9.

Add a header to the worksheets and change the margins to 1" top and bottom and .5" left and right. Save the workbook using the PDF file format. Create a workspace file using the worksheet layout shown in Figure 1–12.

Instructions Part 4: Create a template called Sales Analysis as shown in Figure 1–13 with the Austin colors and fonts applied and then save and close the template. Open the template and save it as a new workbook named Sales Analysis. Import data from the 2012–2013 Sales Data text file to replace the sample data (don't forget to delete the values from columns C through F, first). Find the string, Powell, and replace it with Powell-Arkin, and then compare your worksheet to Figure 1–14.

Make any necessary formatting changes. Insert a clustered cone chart on a new worksheet, remove the legend, and add a WordArt title as shown in Figure 1–15. On Sheet 2, insert and format a SmartArt graphic with images as shown in Figure 1–16. On Sheet 3, insert a screenshot from the www. chicagogallerynews.com Web site on Sheet 3 as shown in Figure 1–17. Rename sheet tabs as shown in Figure 1–17.

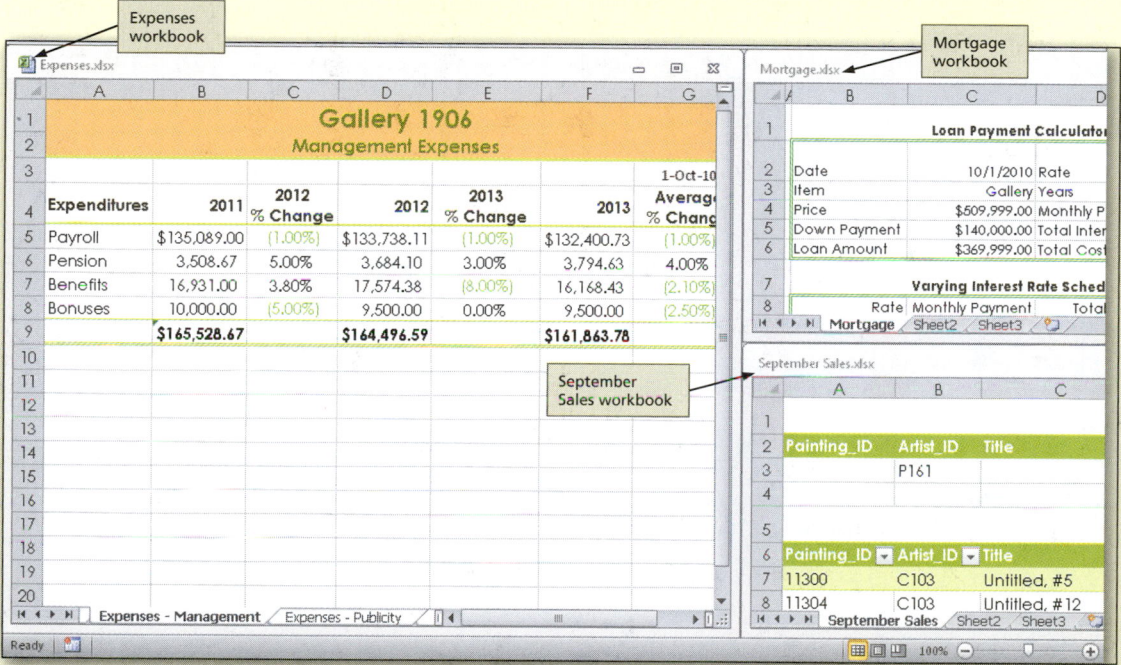

Figure 1–12

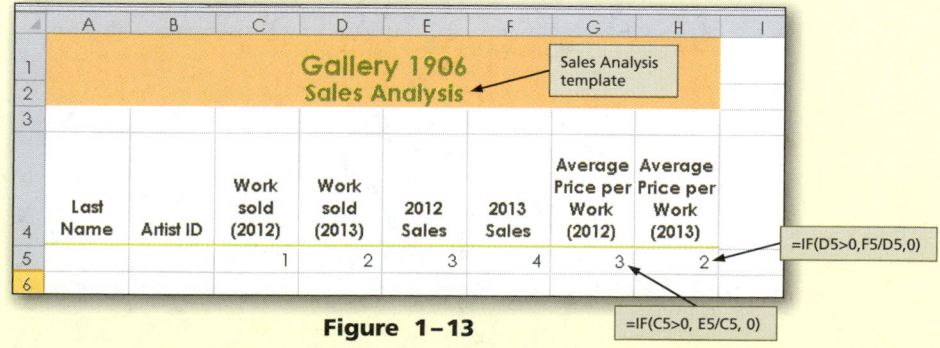

Figure 1–13

Continued >

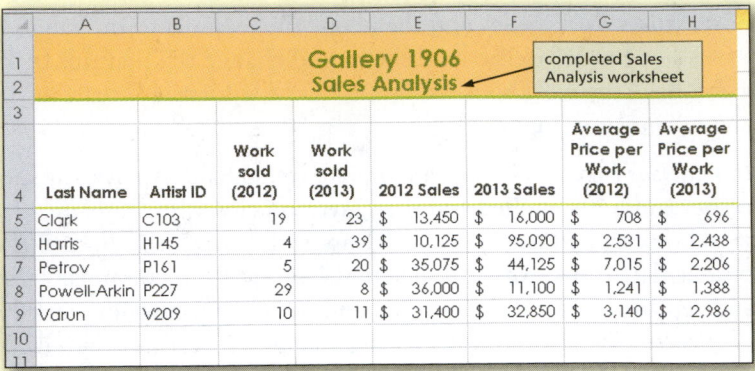

Figure 1–14

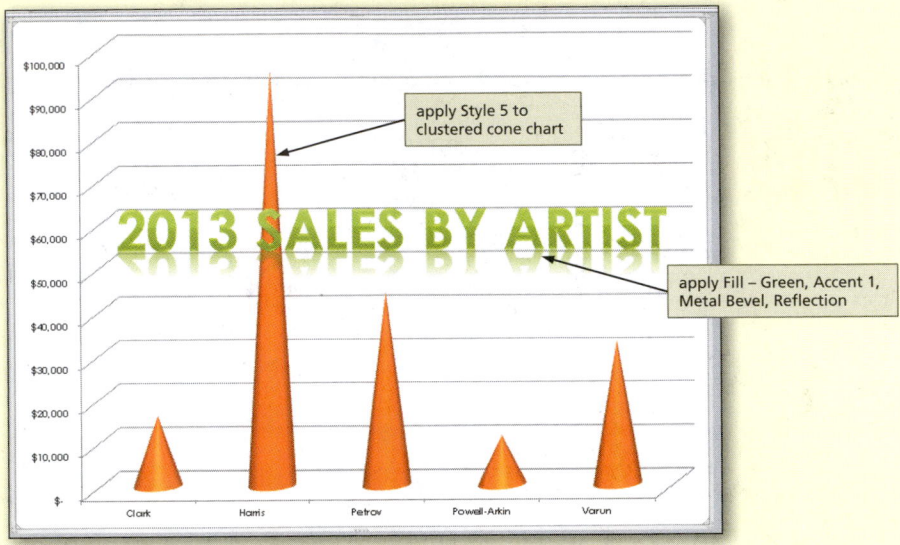

Figure 1–15

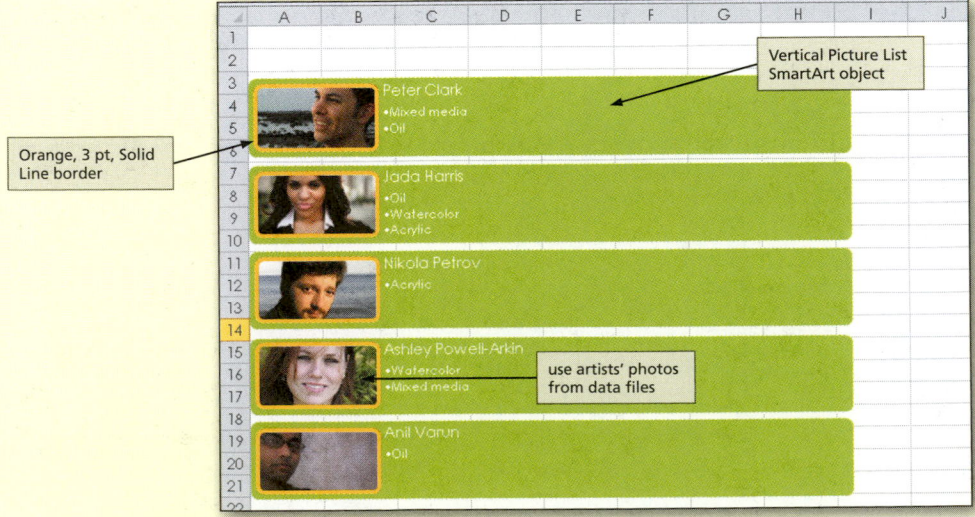

Figure 1–16

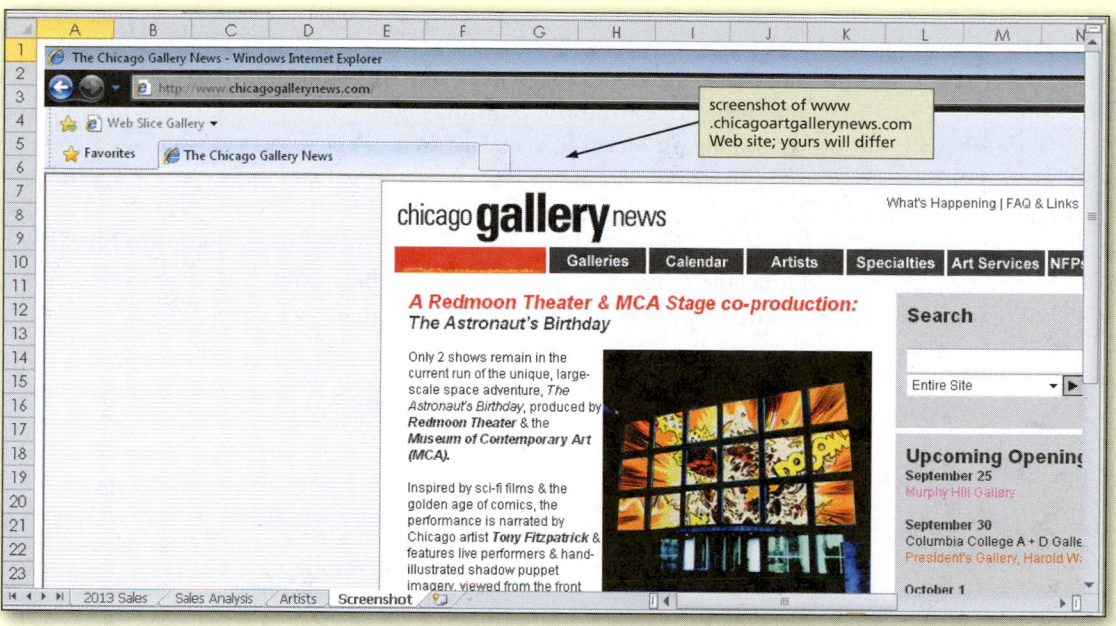

screenshot of www
.chicagoartgallerynews.com
Web site; yours will differ

Figure 1–17

Access Advanced Capstone Project

Note: To complete this assignment, you will be required to use the Data Files for Students. See the inside back cover of this book for instructions on downloading the Data Files for Students, or contact your instructor for information about accessing the required files.

Problem: Gallery 1906 is a successful art gallery located in Chicago. You are working for the owner, Lauren Kim, as an intern. The gallery is doing so well that it needs to move to a larger space. As part of the transition to a larger space, Lauren also wants to take advantage of your computer skills to computerize her records. Because paintings are all originals, not prints, and appear more often in exhibitions, you are going to begin by focusing on the paintings.

Instructions Part 1: Open the Gallery1906 database supplied with your Data Files. Modify the existing Paintings report to create the report shown in Figure 1–18. Add the Media field to the report and then group records by media type. Sort the report by Painting ID. Include totals for List Price and Sold Price fields. If the sold price is greater than $0.00 on any record, the value should appear in a green bold font.

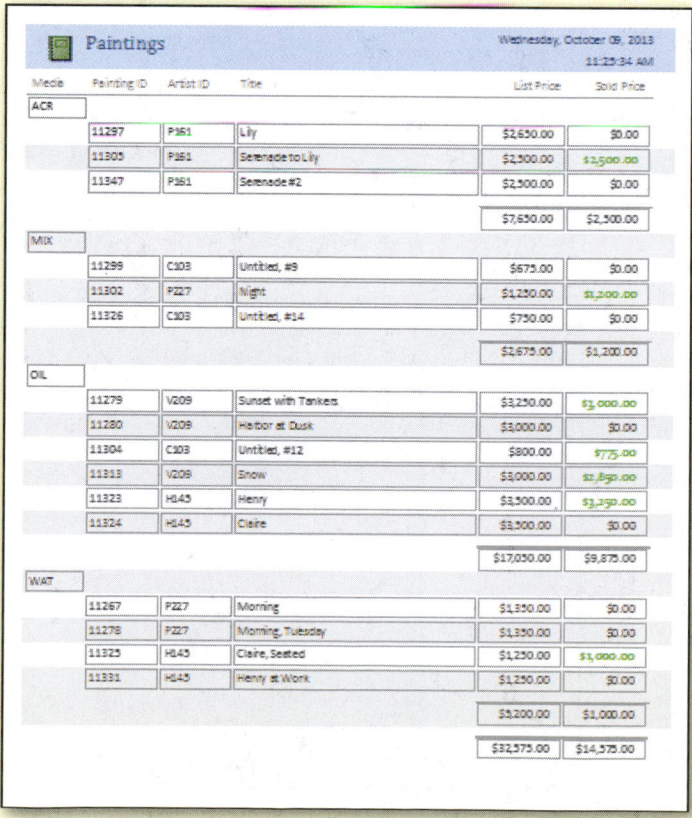

Figure 1–18

Continued >

Create a Paintings by Artist report for the gallery, shown in Figure 1–19. The records should be grouped by Artist ID, and include the Artist ID and Last Name fields from the Artists table. Include the Painting ID, Title, List Price, and Sold Price from the Paintings table. Sort the paintings in alphabetical order by Title. Provide subtotals and a grand total for the List Price and Sold Price fields. Change the page layout to landscape and apply the Paper theme to this object only. If necessary, use Layout view to adjust the column placement and width in order to display the data.

Create a Paintings Entry form, as shown in Figure 1–20, that includes the Painting Number, Title, List Price, Sold Price, Media, and Artist ID. Create mailing labels using the Artists table. Use the Avery C2242 label size, sort the labels by postal code, and save the labels as Labels Artists.

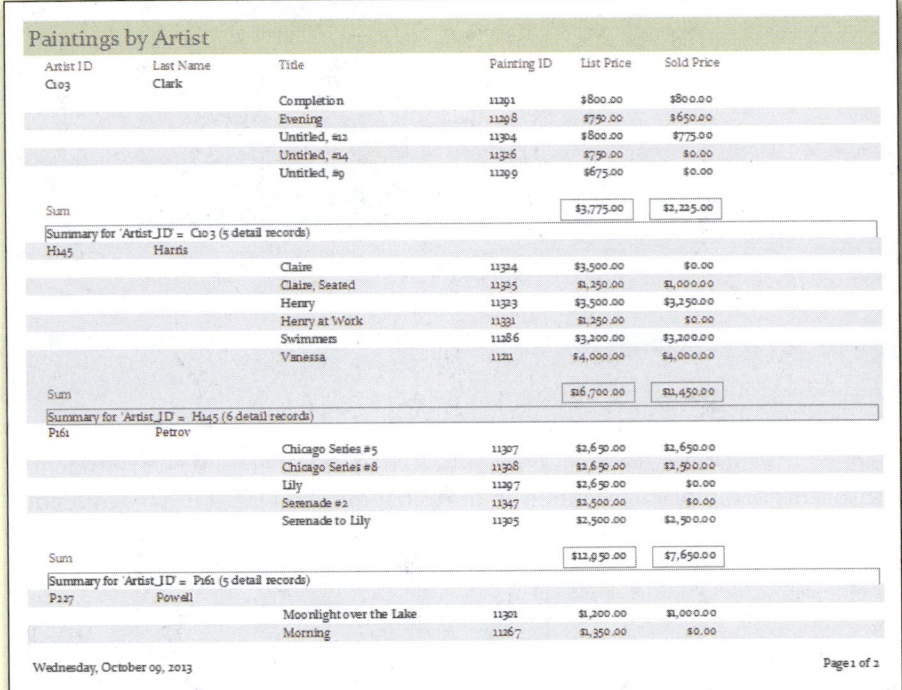

Figure 1–19

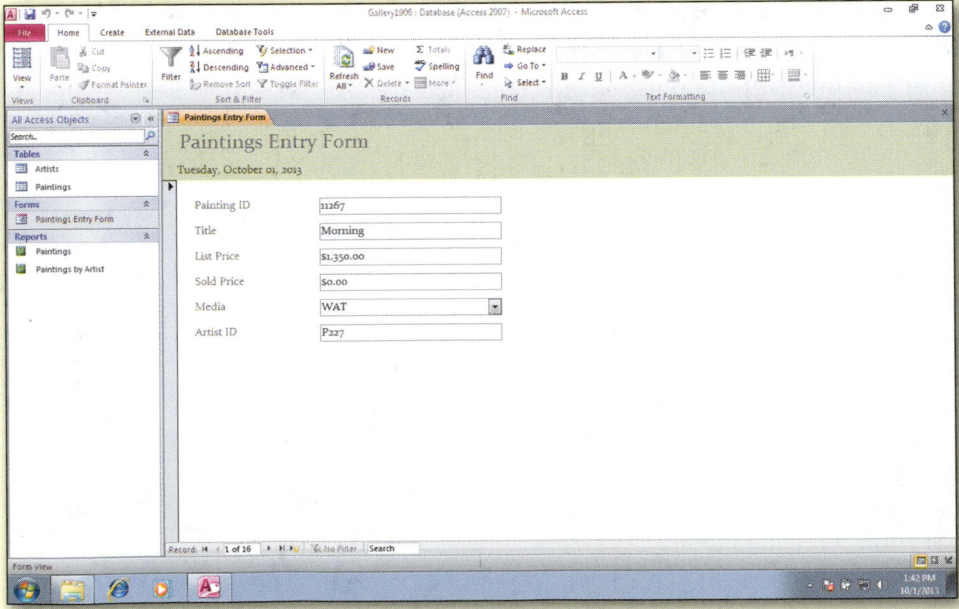

Figure 1–20

Instructions Part 2: Add the following fields to the Paintings table: Sold check box (Yes/No) and Sold Date. Create an update query that finds all records where the Sold Price is greater than 0, and change the Sold Yes/No field to Yes and the Sold Date field to 10/3/2013. Save the Query as Update Query. (*Hint:* Use 1 in the Update to field to add a check mark to the check box.)

Add the Phone Number, Photo, Biography, and Contract fields to the Artists table and add the data as shown in Table 1–3. Add the Phone Number field following the Postal Code field. Add the caption Phone, and use an input mask. Use the OLE Object data type for the Photo field. Use the Memo data type for the Biography field. Be sure the datasheet displays the entire biography. Use the Attachment data type for the Contract field.

Table 1–3				
Artist ID	**Phone Number**	**Artist Photo**	**Biography**	**Contract**
C103	(312) 555-0122	Photo1.bmp	Studied at Glasgow School of Art, Scotland.	none
H145	(312) 555-0103	Photo2.bmp	Certificate from the School of the Art Institute of Chicago.	none
P161	(312) 555-0187	Photo3.bmp	Works as adjunct Art faculty for local college.	PetrovContract.doc
P227	(312) 555-0156	Photo4.bmp	2011 Best in Show at the Illinois Annual Open Juried Exhibition.	none
V209	(312) 555-0145	Photo5.bmp	Painting in collection of the Museum of Contemporary Art.	none

Create a form for the Artists table, as shown in Figure 1–21. Include all fields from the Artists table except for Address, City, State, and Postal Code. Include the Painting ID, Title, List Price, Sold Price, and Sold Date from the Paintings table in the Paintings by Artist subform. You should not be able to tab to the Photo or the Contract. Change the Theme to Civic, and the Color and Font to Austin for this object only. For the label color, choose Green, Accent 1, Darker 50%. For the form title, change the font size to 22 and the font weight to semi-bold. Save the form as Artist Master Form.

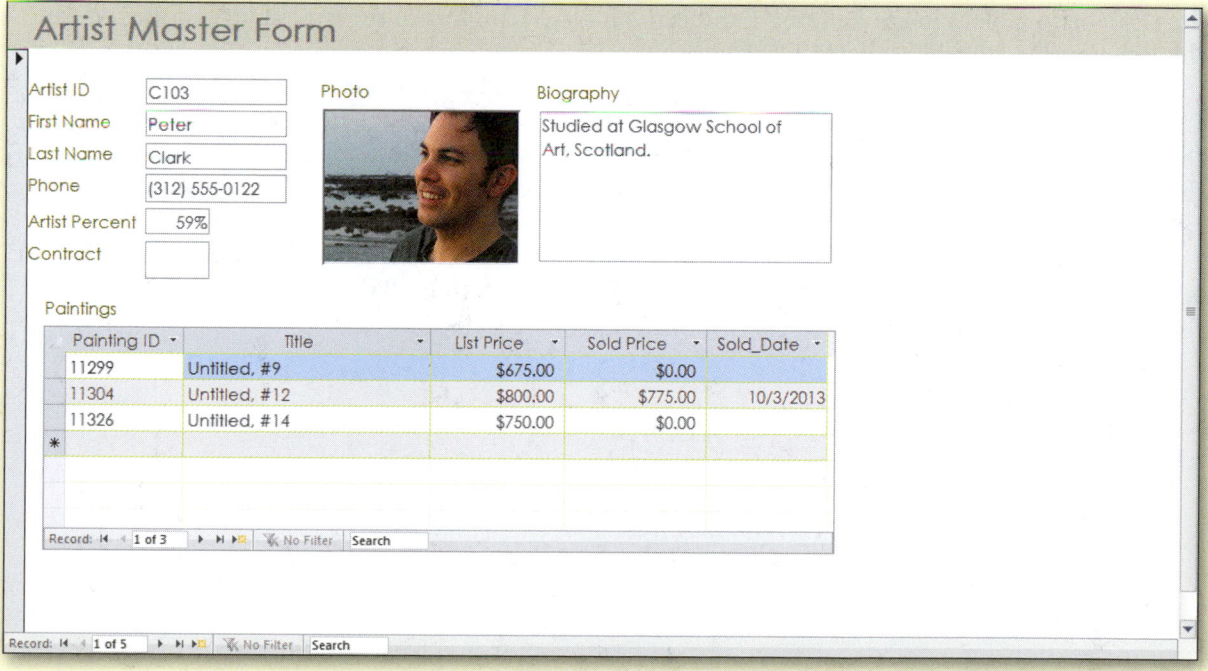

Figure 1–21

Continued >

Create a query for the Paintings table that finds all records where the Sold field contains a check mark. (*Hint:* The value of the sold field is true.) Save the query as Paintings Sold Query.

Instructions Part 3: Lauren has given you a list of additional paintings that have sold in the last few months. Import the SoldPaintings.csv, found in your Data Files, into the Paintings table.

Create two tables in which to store the data concerning exhibitions held at the gallery. The Exhibitions table contains data about recent and upcoming exhibitions. The Paintings Exhibited table contains data about which paintings appeared (or will appear) in any given exhibitions. The structure of the Exhibitions table is shown in Table 1–4, and the structure of the Paintings Exhibited table is shown in Table 1–5. Add captions where necessary to make field names easy to read.

Table 1–4

Field Name	Data Type	Field Size	Description
Exhibition_ID	Text	3	Primary Key
Exhibition_Name	Text	50	
Date_Opened	Date		
Date_Closed	Date		
Description	Memo		

Table 1–5

Field Name	Data Type	Field Size	Description
Exhibition_ID	Text	3	Part of Primary Key
Painting_ID	Text	5	Part of Primary Key

The data for the Exhibitions table is in the ExhbitionSchedule.txt file, and the data for the Paintings Exhibited table is in the PaintingsExhibit.xlxs file. Add the data to the two tables and then update the Relationships for the Gallery1906 database.

Create a query that joins the Artists and the Paintings tables. Include the Artist ID, First Name, Last Name, and Artist Percent fields from the Artists table. Include all the fields except Artist ID from the Paintings table. Add a calculated field, Amount Owed Artist, that multiplies the Artist Percent by the Sold Price. In the Property Sheet, add a caption and change the format to Currency for the calculated field. Save the query as Artists and Paintings.

Create a query that joins the Paintings Exhibited and Exhibitions tables. Include the Painting ID and Exhibition ID fields from the Paintings Exhibited table. Include all the fields except Exhibition ID from the Exhibition table. Save the query as Paintings and Exhibitions.

Create the report, Artist Master Report, shown in Figure 1–22. The report is based on the two queries created in the previous step. Apply the Civic theme, and change the color and font to Austin for this report and subreport only. The title background uses Light Green, Background 2, the Date control uses the Long Date format, and the border style is dots.

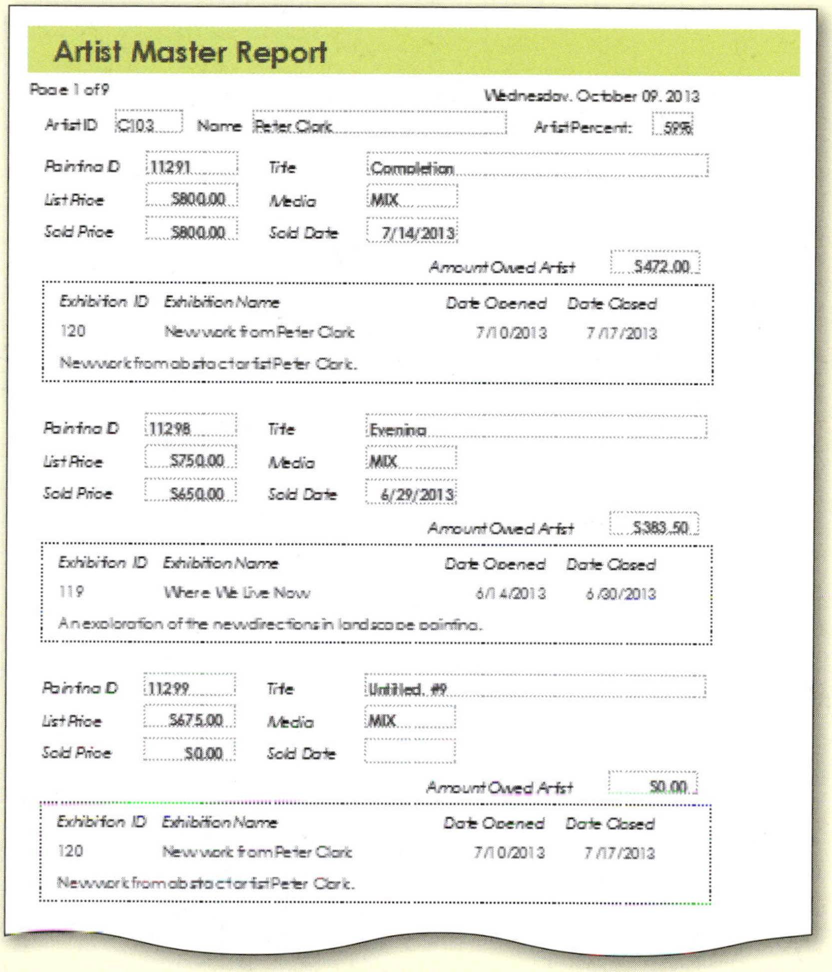

Figure 1–22

Create the report, Discount Report, shown in Figure 1–23. Include the Artist ID and Last Name from the Artists table, and the Painting ID, List Price, and Sold Price from the Paintings table. Create a calculated control, Discount, that displays the discounted List Price (not the discount) for all paintings. Paintings where the Sold Price equals zero will have a 10% discount. Paintings that have a Sold Price of greater than zero will display the Sold Price.

Continued >

Access Advanced Capstone Project *continued*

Discount Report

Artist ID	Last Name	Painting ID	List Price	Sold Price	Discount
C103	Clark				
		11298	$750.00	$650.00	$650.00
		11299	$675.00	$0.00	$607.50
		11304	$800.00	$775.00	$775.00
		11328	$750.00	$0.00	$675.00
		11291	$800.00	$800.00	$800.00
H145	Harris				
		11211	$4,000.00	$4,000.00	$4,000.00
		11286	$3,200.00	$3,200.00	$3,200.00
		11323	$3,500.00	$3,250.00	$3,250.00
		11324	$3,500.00	$0.00	$3,150.00
		11325	$1,250.00	$1,000.00	$1,000.00
		11331	$1,250.00	$0.00	$1,125.00
P161	Petrov				
		11307	$2,650.00	$2,650.00	$2,650.00
		11305	$2,500.00	$2,500.00	$2,500.00
		11308	$2,650.00	$2,500.00	$2,500.00
		11347	$2,500.00	$0.00	$2,250.00
		11297	$2,650.00	$0.00	$2,385.00
P227	Powell				
		11265	$1,000.00	$1,000.00	$1,000.00
		11267	$1,350.00	$0.00	$1,215.00
		11278	$1,350.00	$0.00	$1,215.00
		11301	$1,200.00	$1,000.00	$1,000.00
		11302	$1,250.00	$1,200.00	$1,200.00
V209	Varun				
		11313	$3,000.00	$2,850.00	$2,850.00
		11279	$3,250.00	$3,000.00	$3,000.00
		11280	$3,000.00	$0.00	$2,700.00
		11282	$3,000.00	$2,975.00	$2,975.00
		11292	$2,500.00	$2,500.00	$2,500.00

Wednesday, October 09, 2013 Page 1 of 1

Figure 1–23

Instructions Part 4: Create SQL queries to answer the following questions, using the Painting ID, Title, Media, List Price, and Sold Price: (a) Which paintings' titles begin with the letter, M? (b) Which paintings have a media type other than OIL? (c) Which paintings have a list price greater than $1000 or have the media type MIX? (d) Which paintings have a sold price between $2000 and $3000? (e) For each painting, what is the difference between the list price and the sold price? (Do not include paintings that have not sold.) Display the total in the result as Difference.

Create a SQL query that joins the Artists and Paintings tables, including Artist ID, First Name, Last Name, Painting ID, Title, Media, and Sold Price: (f) Group the records in ascending order by artist ID, and descending order by sold price. (g) Restrict the records retrieved in Part (f) to only those paintings with a sold price greater than zero.

Create a SQL query that joins the Artists and Paintings tables to answer the following question: (h) In which media type(s) does each painter work?

Create SQL queries to calculate the following statistics: (i) How many paintings has Gallery 1906 represented, and what is the total of their sale price? Assign Painting Count and Sum Sold as the names for the calculations. (j) What is the total list price and sale price for all paintings grouped by artist? Assign Sum List and Sum Sold as the names for the calculations. (k) Restrict those records retrieved in Part (j) to those in which the sum sold is greater than $5000.

Index

Quick Reference Summary

Table 1: Microsoft Word 2010 Quick Reference Summary

Task	Page Number	Mouse	Ribbon	Shortcut Menu	Keyboard Shortcut
AddressBlock Merge Field, Add	WD 349		Address Block button (Mailings tab | Write & Insert Fields group) or Address block link in Mail Merge task pane		
AddressBlock Merge Field, Edit	WD 349			Edit Address Block	
Arrange All Open Word Documents on Screen	WD 439		Arrange All button (View tab | Window group)		
Background Color, Add	WD 316		Page Color button (Page Layout tab | Page Background group)		
Border Paragraph	WD 206, WD 415		Border button arrow (Home tab | Paragraph group) or Page Borders button (Page Layout tab | Page Background group), Borders tab (Borders and Shading dialog box)		
Building Block, Insert	WD 291		Quick Parts button (Insert tab | Text group		F3
Bullets, Customize	WD 235		Bullets button arrow (Home tab | Paragraph group), Define New Bullet in Bullets gallery		
Character Spacing, Modify	WD 216		Font Dialog Box Launcher (Home tab | Font group), Advanced tab (Font dialog box)	Font, Advanced tab (Font dialog box)	
Column Break, Insert	WD 434		Insert Page and Section Breaks button (Page Layout tab | Page Setup group)		CTRL+SHIFT+ ENTER
Column, Increase Width	WD 429	Double-click space between columns on ruler or drag column boundaries on ruler	Columns button (Page Layout tab | Page Setup group), More Columns, Width box up arrow (Columns dialog box)		

Table 1: Microsoft Word 2010 Quick Reference Summary *(continued)*

Task	Page Number	Mouse	Ribbon	Shortcut Menu	Keyboard Shortcut
Columns, Balance	WD 447		Insert Page and Section Breaks button (Page Layout tab | Page Setup group), Continuous in Insert Page and Section Breaks gallery		
Columns, Change Number of	WD 426		Columns button (Page Layout tab | Page Setup group)		
Columns, Insert Vertical Rule between	WD 429		Columns button (Page Layout tab | Page Setup group), More Columns, Line between check box (Columns dialog box) or Borders button (Home tab | Paragraph group)		
Compatibility Checker	WD 305		Check for Issues button (File tab | Info tab), Check Compatibility		
Content Control, Delete	WD 285		Cut button (Home tab | Clipboard group)	Remove Content Control	CTRL+X, DELETE, or BACKSPACE
Content Control, Format	WD 283	Select content control, apply formats			
Content Control, Modify Text	WD 283	Select content control, type new text			
Convert Text to a Table	WD 382		Table button (Insert tab | Tables group), Convert Text to Table in Table gallery		
Copy	WD 439, WD 453		Copy button (Home tab | Clipboard group)	Copy	CTRL+C
Data Source, Create	WD 340		'Type a new list' in Select recipients area in Mail Merge task pane, Create link in 'Type new list' area, Customize Columns button (New Address List dialog box) or Select Recipients button (Mailings tab | Start Mail Merge group), Type New List		
Data Source, Find and Display Data	WD 370		Find Recipient button (Mailings tab | Preview Results group), enter search text, Find Next button (Find Entry dialog box)		
Data Source, Save	WD 345		Enter file name in File name text box (Save Address List dialog box)		
Data Source, Sort Records	WD 368		Edit Recipient List button (Mailings tab | Start Mail Merge group), button arrow to right of field on which to sort		

Table 1: Microsoft Word 2010 Quick Reference Summary *(continued)*

Task	Page Number	Mouse	Ribbon	Shortcut Menu	Keyboard Shortcut
Date, Insert Current	WD 348		Insert Date and Time button (Insert tab | Text group)		Click content control box arrow, click desired date or type date in content control
Document Inspector	WD 311		Check for Issues button (File tab | Info tab), Inspect Document		
Document Theme, Change	WD 279		Themes button (Page Layout tab | Themes group)		
Document, Create New	WD 279		Blank document (File tab | New tab), Create button		CTRL+N
Document, Create from Template	WD 277		File tab | New tab		
Drop Cap	WD 431		Drop Cap button (Insert tab | Text group)		
E-Mail Attachments, Customize How Word Opens	WD 311		Options (File tab), General (Word Options dialog box)		
E-Mail, Send Document as	WD 310		Send Using E-Mail (File tab | Save & Send tab), Send as Attachment		
Field Code, Display	WD 358			Toggle Field Codes	SHIFT+F9
Field Codes, Print	WD 359		Options (File tab), Advanced (Word Options dialog box), Print area		
Fill Effect, Add to Background	WD 316		Page Color button (Page Layout tab | Page Background group), Fill Effects in Page Color gallery		
Folder, Create while Saving	WD 338		Save button on Quick Access Toolbar, navigate to new location (Save As dialog box), New folder button		CTRL+F12
Font Settings, Modify Default	WD 225		Font Dialog Box Launcher (Home tab | Font group), Font tab (Font dialog box), Set As Default button		
Format Characters	WD 216		Font Dialog Box Launcher (Home tab | Font group), Font tab (Font dialog box)	Font, Font tab (Font dialog box)	
Format Painter	WD 233		Format Painter button (Home tab | Clipboard group)		
Graphic, Crop	WD 418		Crop button (Picture Tools Format tab | Size group)		
Graphic, Rotate	WD 421	Drag graphic's rotate handle			
GreetingLine Merge Field, Add	WD 349		Greeting Line button (Mailings tab | Write & Insert Fields group) or Greeting line link in Mail Merge task pane		

Table 1: Microsoft Word 2010 Quick Reference Summary *(continued)*

Task	Page Number	Mouse	Ribbon	Shortcut Menu	Keyboard Shortcut
GreetingLine Merge Field, Edit	WD 351			Edit Greeting Line	
Header, Different from Previous	WD 229		Deselect Link to Previous button (Header & Footer Tools Design tab | Navigation group)		
Hyperlink, Edit	WD 315		Insert Hyperlink button (Insert tab | Links group)	Edit Hyperlink	CTRL+K
Hyperlink, Format Text as	WD 314		Insert Hyperlink button (Insert tab | Links group)	Hyperlink	CTRL+K
Hyphenate	WD 430		Hyphenation button (Page Layout tab | Page Setup group)		
If Field, Insert	WD 355		Rules button (Mailings tab | Write & Insert Fields group)		
Indent Paragraph	WD 210, WD 290	Drag Left Indent and Right Indent markers on ruler	Indent Left or Indent Right box arrow (Page Layout tab | Paragraph group) or Paragraph Dialog Box Launcher (Home tab | Paragraph group), Indents and Spacing tab (Paragraph dialog box)	Paragraph, Indents and Spacing tab (Paragraph dialog box)	
Indent, Decrease	WD 290	Drag Left Indent Indent marker on horizontal ruler	Decrease Indent button (Home tab | Paragraph group)	Paragraph, Indents and Spacing tab (Paragraph dialog box)	CTRL+SHIFT+M
Indent, Increase	WD 290	Drag Left Indent marker on horizontal ruler	Increase Indent button (Home tab | Paragraph group) or Paragraph Dialog Box Launcher (Home tab | Paragraph group), Indents and Spacing tab (Paragraph dialog box)	Paragraph, Indents and Spacing tab (Paragraph dialog box)	CTRL+M
Insert Word Document in Existing Document	WD 222, WD 428		Insert Object button arrow (Insert tab | Text group), Text from File		
Justify Paragraph	WD 427		Justify button (Home tab | Paragraph group) or Paragraph Dialog Box Launcher (Home tab or Page Layout tab | Paragraph group), Indents and Spacing tab (Paragraph dialog box)	Paragraph, Indents and Spacing tab (Paragraph dialog box)	CTRL+J
Line Break, Insert	WD 289				SHIFT+ENTER
Mail Merge, Envelopes	WD 377		Create button (File tab | New tab), Start Mail Merge button (Mailings tab | Start Mail Merge group)		
Mail Merge, Labels	WD 371		Create button (File tab | New tab), Start Mail Merge button (Mailings tab | Start Mail Merge group)		

Table 1: Microsoft Word 2010 Quick Reference Summary *(continued)*

Task	Page Number	Mouse	Ribbon	Shortcut Menu	Keyboard Shortcut
Main Document, Identify for Form Letter	WD 333		Start Mail Merge button (Mailings tab | Start Mail Merge group)		
Margin Settings, Change	WD 405	Drag margin boundary on ruler	Margins button (Page Layout tab | Page Setup group)		
Merge Condition, Remove	WD 368		Edit Recipient List button (Mailings tab | Start Mail Merge group), Filter link (Mail Merge Recipients dialog box), Clear All button (Filter and Sort dialog box)		
Merge Errors, Check for	WD 362		Auto Check for Errors button (Mailings tab | Preview Results group)		
Merge Field, Insert	WD 353		Insert Merge Field button arrow (Mailings tab | Write & Insert Fields group)		
Merge Fields, Highlight	WD 358		Highlight Merge Fields button (Mailings tab | Write & Insert Fields group)		
Merge Form Letters to New Document	WD 361		Finish & Merge button (Mailings tab | Finish group), Edit Individual Documents, All (Merge to New Document dialog box)		
Merge Form Letters to Printer	WD 364		Finish & Merge button (Mailings tab | Finish group), Print Documents, or Print link in Mail Merge task pane		
Merge to a Directory	WD 379		Start Mail Merge button (Mailings tab | Start Mail Merge group), Select Recipients button (Mailings tab | Start Mail Merge group), select merge fields		
Merge, Select Records	WD 364		Edit Recipient List button (Mailings tab | Start Mail Merge group)		
Merged Data, View in Main Document	WD 349		Preview Results button (Mailings tab | Preview Results group)		
Multilevel Numbered List	WD 236		Numbering button (Home tab | Paragraph group)	Numbering	Type 1., SPACEBAR
Page Border, Add	WD 458		Page Borders button (Page Layout tab | Page Background group)		
Page Numbers, Start at Different	WD 230		Insert Page Number button (Header & Footer Tools Design tab | Header & Footer group) or (Insert tab | Header & Footer group), Format Page Numbers, Start at option button (Page Number Format dialog box)		

Table 1: Microsoft Word 2010 Quick Reference Summary *(continued)*

Task	Page Number	Mouse	Ribbon	Shortcut Menu	Keyboard Shortcut
Page Orientation, Change	WD 379		Page Orientation button (Page Layout tab | Page Setup group)		
Paste	WD 439, WD 455		Paste button (Home tab | Clipboard group) or Clipboard Dialog Box Launcher (Home tab | Clipboard group)	Paste	CTRL+V
PDF Document, Create	WD 301		Create PDF/XPS Document (File tab | Save & Send tab)		
Placeholder Text, Replace	WD 284	Select placeholder text, type new text			
Print Specific Pages	WD 223		Print tab | File tab, type desired page numbers in Pages text box		CTRL+P
Quick Style, Create	WD 296		More button in the Quick Styles gallery (Home tab | Styles group), Save Selection as a New Quick Style in Quick Styles gallery	Save Selection as a New Quick Style	
Reveal Formatting	WD 298				SHIFT+F1
Save Location, Set Default	WD 314		Options (File tab), Save (Word Options dialog box)		
Save Word 2010 Document in Earlier Format	WD 306		Change File Type (File tab | Save & Send tab), Word 97-2003 Document		F12
Save Word Document as Different File Type	WD 308		Change File Type (File tab | Save & Send tab)		
Save Word Document as Web Page	WD 312		Change File Type (File tab | Save & Send tab)		F12
Section Break, Continuous	WD 425		Insert Page and Section Breaks button (Page Layout tab | Page Setup group), Continuous		
Section Break, Delete	WD 221			Cut	BACKSPACE or DELETE
Section Break, Next Page	WD 220, WD 433		Insert Page and Section Breaks button (Page Layout tab | Page Setup group), Next Page		
Select Nonadjacent Items	WD 244	Select first item, hold down CTRL key while selecting item(s)			
Selection Pane	WD 421		Selection Pane button (Drawing Tools Format tab or Picture Tools Format tab | Arrange group)		
Small Caps	WD 216		Font Dialog Box Launcher (Home tab | Font group), Font tab (Font dialog box)		CTRL+SHIFT+K
SmartArt Graphic, Add Shape	WD 216		Add Shape button (SmartArt Tools Design tab | Create Graphic group)		

Table 1: Microsoft Word 2010 Quick Reference Summary *(continued)*

Task	Page Number	Mouse	Ribbon	Shortcut Menu	Keyboard Shortcut
SmartArt Graphic, Add Text	WD 214, WD 451	Select shape, enter text, or click Text Pane control, enter text in Text Pane	Text Pane button (SmartArt Tools Design tab | Create Graphic group), enter text in Text Pane		
SmartArt Graphic, Adjust Shape Size	WD 452		Smaller button or Larger button (SmartArt Tools Format tab | Shapes group)		
SmartArt Graphic, Apply Style	WD 216		More button in SmartArt Styles gallery (SmartArt Tools Design tab | SmartArt Styles group)		
SmartArt Graphic, Change Color	WD 215		Change Colors button (SmartArt Tools Design tab | SmartArt Styles group)		
SmartArt Graphic, Change Layout	WD 449		Layouts gallery (SmartArt Tools Design tab | Layouts group)		
SmartArt Graphic, Delete Shape	WD 214				Select shape, DELETE
SmartArt Graphic, Insert	WD 213		Insert SmartArt Graphic button (Insert tab | Illustrations group)		
SmartArt Graphic, Layer in Front of Text	WD 456		Arrange button (SmartArt Tools Format tab | Arrange group), Bring Forward button arrow		
Sort Paragraphs	WD 232		Sort button (Home tab | Paragraph group)		
Split Window	WD 438	Double-click resize pointer	Split button (View tab | Window group)		ALT+CTRL+S, ENTER
Style, Modify	WD 299		Styles Dialog Box Launcher (Home tab | Styles group), click [style name], Modify	Modify	
Switch from One Open Document to Another	WD 454	Click live preview on Windows taskbar	Switch Windows button (View tab | Window group)		ALT+TAB
Tab Stops, Set Custom	WD 413	Click desired tab stop on ruler	Paragraph Dialog Box Launcher (Home tab or Page Layout tab | Paragraph group), Tabs button (Paragraph dialog box)		
Table Cell, Shade	WD 243		Shading button arrow (Table Tools Design tab | Table Styles group)		
Table Column Width, Change	WD 240	Drag Move Table Column marker on horizontal ruler or double-click column boundary	Table Column Width box (Table Tools Layout tab	Cell Size group or Table Properties button (Table Tools Layout tab | Table group)		
Table Gridlines, Show/Hide	WD 239		View Table Gridlines button (Table Tools Layout tab | Table group)		

Table 1: Microsoft Word 2010 Quick Reference Summary *(continued)*

Task	Page Number	Mouse	Ribbon	Shortcut Menu	Keyboard Shortcut
Table Item, Copy and Paste	WD 293		Copy button (Home tab | Clipboard group), then Paste button (Home tab | Clipboard group)	Copy, then Paste	CTRL+C, then CTRL+V
Table, Border	WD 254		Borders button arrow (Table Tools Design tab | Table Styles group)		
Table, Change Cell Spacing	WD 246		Cell Margins button (Table Tools Layout tab | Alignment group) or Table Properties button (Table Tools Layout tab | Table group)	Table Properties	
Table, Change Row Height	WD 241	Drag row boundary or Adjust Table Row marker on vertical ruler	Table Row Height box up or down arrows (Table Tools Layout tab | Cell Size group) or Table Properties button (Table Tools Layout tab | Table group)	Table Properties	
Table, Delete Row or Column	WD 247		Delete button (Table Tools Layout tab | Rows & Columns group)	Select row/column, Delete Rows or Delete Columns	
Table, Display Text Vertically in Cell	WD 252		Text Direction button (Table Tools Layout tab | Alignment group)		
Table, Distribute Columns	WD 250		Distribute Columns button (Table Tools Layout tab | Cell Size group)		
Table, Distribute Rows	WD 251		Distribute Rows button (Table Tools Layout tab | Cell Size group)		
Table, Move Cell Boundary	WD 250	Drag cell boundary or Move Table Column marker on horizontal ruler			
Table, Move Rows	WD 286	Drag selected rows	Cut button (Home tab | Clipboard group); Paste button (Home tab | Clipboard group)	Cut; Keep Source Formatting	CTRL+X; CTRL+V
Table, Repeat Header Rows	WD 384		Repeat Header Rows button (Table Tools Layout tab | Data group)		
Table, Sort	WD 248		Sort button (Table Tools Layout tab | Data group)		
Table, Sort by Multiple Columns	WD 385		Sort button (Table Tools Layout tab | Data group), Sort by box arrow (Sort dialog box), Then by box arrow (Sort dialog box)		
Table, Split Cells	WD 249		Split Cells button (Table Tools Layout tab | Merge group)	Split Cells	
Table, Sum Columns	WD 254		Formula button (Table Tools Layout tab | Data group)		
Text Box, Insert	WD 437		Text Box button (Insert tab | Text group)		

Table 1: Microsoft Word 2010 Quick Reference Summary *(continued)*

Task	Page Number	Mouse	Ribbon	Shortcut Menu	Keyboard Shortcut
Text Box, Position	WD 442	Drag to new location			
Theme Effects, Modify	WD 453		Theme Effects button (Page Layout tab | Themes group)		
Theme Fonts, Change	WD 226		Change Styles button (Home tab | Styles group) or Theme Fonts button (Page Layout tab | Themes group)		
Theme Fonts, Customize	WD 295		Change Styles button (Home tab | Styles group), Fonts, Create New Theme Fonts in Fonts gallery or Theme Fonts button (Page Layout tab | Themes group), Create New Theme Fonts in Fonts gallery		
Themes, Save Customized	WD 453		Themes button (Page Layout tab | Themes group), Save Current Theme in Themes gallery		
User Name and Initials, Change	WD 335		Options (File tab), General (Word Options dialog box)		
Watermark, Create	WD 258		Watermark button (Page Layout tab | Page Background group)		
White Space, Hide/Show	WD 241	Double-click space between pages	Options (File tab), Display (Word Options dialog box), Page display options		
WordArt, Change Fill Color	WD 410		Text Fill button arrow (Drawing Tools Format tab | WordArt Styles group)		
WordArt, Change Shape	WD 413		Text Effects button (Drawing Tools Format tab | WordArt Styles group), Transform in Text Effects gallery		
WordArt, Insert	WD 407		WordArt button (Insert tab | Text group)		
XPS Document, Create	WD 303		Create PDF/XPS Document (File tab | Save & Send tab)		

Table 2: Microsoft PowerPoint 2010 Quick Reference Summary

Task	Page Number	Mouse	Ribbon	Shortcut Menu	Keyboard Shortcut
Action Button, Copy	PPT 348		Copy button (Home tab | Clipboard group)	Copy	CTRL+C
Action Button, Edit Setting	PPT 349		Action button (Insert tab | Links group)		
Action Button, Insert	PPT 344		Shapes button (Insert tab | Illustrations group), Action Buttons area		
Animation, Add after Existing Effect	PPT 413, 414		Add Animation button (Animations tab | Advanced Animation group)		

Table 2: Microsoft PowerPoint 2010 Quick Reference Summary (continued)

Task	Page Number	Mouse	Ribbon	Shortcut Menu	Keyboard Shortcut
Animation, Associate Sound with	PPT 430		Add sound to slide, click sound icon, Play button (Animations tab | Animation group), With Previous		
Animation, Change Direction	PPT 412		Effect Options button (Animations tab | Animation group)		
Animation, Change Order	PPT 420		Animation Pane button (Animations tab | Advanced Animation group)		
Animation, Dim Text After	PPT 440		Animation Pane button (Animations tab | Advanced Animation group), Animation Order list arrow, Effect Options, After animation list arrow		
Animation, Modify Timing	PPT 416		Start Animation Timing button arrow (Animations tab | Timing group)		
Animation, Preview Sequence	PPT 416		Preview button (Animations tab | Preview group)		
Animation Painter, Use to Copy Animations	PPT 433		Animation Painter button (Animations tab | Advanced Animation group)		
Bullet, Format Color	PPT 379		Bullets button arrow (Home tab | Paragraph group), Bullets and Numbering, Color button	Bullets, Bullets and Numbering	
Bullet, Format Size	PPT 377		Bullets button arrow (Home tab | Paragraph group), Bullets and Numbering, Size box	Bullets, Bullets and Numbering	
Bullet Character, Change to Number	PPT 380		Numbering button arrow (Home tab | Paragraph group)	Bullets, Bullets and Numbering	
Bullet Character, Change to Picture	PPT 372		Bullets button arrow (Home tab | Paragraph group), Bullets and Numbering, Picture button (Bullets and Numbering dialog box)		
Bullet Character, Change to Symbol	PPT 375		Bullets button arrow (Home tab | Paragraph group), Bullets and Numbering, Customize button (Bullets and Numbering dialog box)		
Bullet Characters, Remove	PPT 382		Bullets button arrow (Home tab | Paragraph group), None	Bullets, None	
Chart, Animate	PPT 437		More button (Animations tab | Animation group)		
Chart, Apply Style	PPT 223		More button (Chart Tools Design tab | Chart Styles group)		
Chart, Change Layout	PPT 226		More button (Chart Tools Design tab | Chart Layouts group)		

Table 2: Microsoft PowerPoint 2010 Quick Reference Summary (continued)

Task	Page Number	Mouse	Ribbon	Shortcut Menu	Keyboard Shortcut
Chart, Insert	PPT 220	Insert Chart button in content placeholder	Chart button (Insert tab | Illustrations group)		
Chart, Resize	PPT 228	Drag sizing handle to desired location			
Chart, Rotate	PPT 230		Format Selection button (Chart Tools Format tab | Current Selection group)		
Chart, Separate a Pie Slice	PPT 229	Select slice and drag			
Chart Shape, Change Outline Color	PPT 226		Shape Outline button arrow (Chart Tools Format tab | Shape Styles group)		
Chart Shape, Change Outline Weight	PPT 224		Shape Outline button arrow (Chart Tools Format tab | Shape Styles group), Weight		
Columns, Adjust Spacing	PPT 369		Columns button (Home tab | Paragraph group), More Columns, Spacing box		
Columns, Create in a Placeholder	PPT 367		Columns button (Home tab | Paragraph group)		
Comment, Delete	PPT 274		Delete Comment button (Review tab | Comments group)		
Comment, Edit	PPT 282		Edit Comment button (Review tab | Comments group)		
Comment, Insert	PPT 281		New Comment button (Review tab | Comments group)		
Comments, Print	PPT 271		Page Layout button (File tab | Print tab), check 'Print Comments and Ink Markup' box		CTRL+P
Copy	PPT 348		Copy button (Home tab | Clipboard group)	Copy	CTRL+C
Credits, Create	PPT 442		More button (Animations tab | Animation group), More Entrance Effects, Credits		
Digital Signature, Create and Add	PPT 309		Protect Presentation button (File tab | Info tab), Add a Digital Signature		
Document Inspector, Start	PPT 303		Check for Issues button (File tab | Info tab), Inspect Document		
Footer, Add	PPT 289		Header & Footer button (Insert tab | Text group)		
Guides, Display	PPT 357		Guides check box (View tab | Show group)	Grid and Guides, Display drawing guides on screen check box	ALT+F9
Header, Add	PPT 289		Header & Footer button (Insert tab | Text group)		
Hyperlink, Add	PPT 339, 341		Hyperlink button (Insert tab | Links group)	Hyperlink	CTRL+K

Table 2: Microsoft PowerPoint 2010 Quick Reference Summary *(continued)*

Task	Page Number	Mouse	Ribbon	Shortcut Menu	Keyboard Shortcut
Hyperlink to Another PowerPoint File	PPT 350		Action button (Insert tab | Links group), Hyperlink to list arrow, Other PowerPoint Presentation		
Hyperlink to a Word File	PPT 353		Action button (Insert tab | Links group), Hyperlink to list arrow, Other File		
Line Break, Enter	PPT 371				SHIFT+ENTER
Line Spacing, Change	PPT 367		Line Spacing button (Home tab | Paragraph group)	Paragraph	
List, Animate	PPT 439		More button (Animations tab | Animation group)		
Merge a Presentation	PPT 270		Compare button (Review tab | Compare group)		
Numbered List, Format	PPT 382		Numbering button arrow (Home tab | Paragraph group), Bullets and Numbering	Numbering, Bullets and Numbering	
Outline, Open as Presentation	PPT 335		Open (File tab), File Type arrow, All Outlines, select Word file, Open button		
Password, Set	PPT 305		Protect Presentation button (File tab | Info tab), Encrypt with Password		
Picture, Animate	PPT 411, 414, 415, 425		Select picture, choose animation in Animation gallery (Animations tab | Animation group)		
Picture, Clear Formatting	PPT 291		Reset Picture button (Picture Tools Format tab | Adjust group)		
Picture, Compress	PPT 410		Compress Pictures button (Picture Tools Format tab | Adjust group)		
Picture, Crop	PPT 409		Crop button (Picture Tools Format tab | Size group), drag cropping handles		
Picture, Remove Background	PPT 405, 407		Remove Background button (Picture Tools Format tab | Adjust group)		
Pictures, Align	PPT 360, 362		Align button (Picture Tools Format tab | Arrange group)		
Presentation, Check for Compatibility	PPT 301		Check for Issues button, (File tab | Info tab), Check Compatibility		
Presentation, Create Self-Running	PPT 447		Set Up Slide Show button (Slide Show tab | Set Up group), 'Browsed at a kiosk (full screen)' option		
Presentation, Mark as Final	PPT 308		Protect Presentation button, (File tab | Info tab), Mark as Final		

Table 2: Microsoft PowerPoint 2010 Quick Reference Summary *(continued)*

Task	Page Number	Mouse	Ribbon	Shortcut Menu	Keyboard Shortcut
Presentation, Package for CD or DVD	PPT 297		Package Presentation for CD (File tab | Send & Save tab), Package Presentation for CD button		
Presentation Change, Accept	PPT 276		Accept Change button (Review tab | Compare group)		
Presentation Change, Reject	PPT 278, 280		Reject Change button (Review tab | Compare group)		
Presentation Changes, End Review	PPT 283		End Review button (Review tab | Compare group)		
Presentation Changes, Review	PPT 273		Reviewing Pane button (Review tab | Compare group)		
Presentation, Print	PPT 271		Print button (File tab | Print tab)		CTRL+P
Rulers, Display	PPT 359		Ruler check box (View tab | Show group)	Ruler	
Save a Presentation	PPT 295, 297, 300	Save button on Quick Access Toolbar	Save or Save As (File tab)		CTRL+S or F12
Save a Slide as an Image	PPT 296		Save As button, JPEG File Interchange Format (File tab, Save & Send tab, Change File Type tab)		
Save as a PowerPoint Show	PPT 295		Change File Type (File tab | Save & Send tab), Save As button		
Save in a Previous Format	PPT 300		Change File Type (File tab | Save & Send tab), PowerPoint 97-2003 Presentation		
Screen Clipping, Use	PPT 288		Screenshot button (Insert tab | Images group), Screen Clipping command		
Shape, Change Fill Color	PPT 347		Shape Fill button arrow (Drawing Tools Format tab | Shape Styles group)		
Slide, Hide	PPT 363		Hide Slide button (Slide Show tab | Set Up group) (must be in Slide Sorter view)	Hide Slide (Slide Sorter view or thumbnail on Slides tab)	
Slide, Reuse from an Existing Presentation	PPT 285		New Slide button arrow (Home tab | Slides group), Reuse Slides command		
Slide, Set Size	PPT 292		Page Setup button (Design tab | Page Setup group), 'Slides sized for' box arrow		
Slide Objects, Rename	PPT 422		Select button (Home tab | Editing group), Selection Pane		
Slide Show, Adjust Timings Manually	PPT 446		In Slide Sorter view, select slide and set timing (Transitions tab | Timing group)		

Table 2: Microsoft PowerPoint 2010 Quick Reference Summary *(continued)*

Task	Page Number	Mouse	Ribbon	Shortcut Menu	Keyboard Shortcut
Slide Show, Draw on Slides During Show	PPT 313		Pointer button, Pen (Slide Show toolbar), drag mouse to draw		
Slide Show, Highlight Items During Show	PPT 312		Pointer button, Highlighter (Slide Show toolbar), drag mouse to highlight		
Slide Show, Rehearse Timings	PPT 444		Rehearse Timings button (Slide Show tab | Set Up group)		
Slide Show, Set Resolution	PPT 294		Resolution box arrow (Slide Show tab | Monitors group)		
SmartArt Graphic, Add Text	PPT 208		Text Pane button (SmartArt Tools Design tab | Create Graphic group)		See Table 4–2, PPT 207
SmartArt Graphic, Animate	PPT 435, 436		More button (Animations tab | Animation group)		
SmartArt Graphic, Apply Style	PPT 210		More button (SmartArt Tools Design tab | SmartArt Styles group)		
SmartArt Graphic, Change Color	PPT 211		Change Colors button (SmartArt Tools Design tab | SmartArt Styles group)		
SmartArt Graphic, Insert	PPT 206		SmartArt button (Insert tab | Illustrations group)		
SmartArt Graphic, Insert Picture	PPT 209	Insert Picture from File button in picture placeholder			
SmartArt Graphic, Resize	PPT 212	Drag sizing handle to desired location			
Symbol, Insert	PPT 233		Symbol button (Insert tab | Symbols group)		
Table, Add Borders	PPT 238		Border button arrow (Table Tools Design tab | Table Styles group)		
Table, Add Effect	PPT 238		Effects button (Table Tools Design tab | Table Styles group)		
Table, Apply Style	PPT 236		More button (Table Tools Design tab | Table Styles group)		
Table, Insert	PPT 232	Insert Table button in content placeholder	Table button (Insert tab | Tables group)		
Table, Merge Cells	PPT 242		Merge Cells button (Table Tools Layout tab | Merge group)	Merge Cells	
Table, Resize	PPT 240	Drag sizing handle to desired location			
Table Cell, Add Image	PPT 241			Format Shape, Picture or texture fill	
Table Cell, Center Text Vertically	PPT 245		Center Vertically button (Table Tools Layout tab | Alignment group)	Format Shape, Text Box, Vertical alignment arrow	

Table 2: Microsoft PowerPoint 2010 Quick Reference Summary *(continued)*

Task	Page Number	Mouse	Ribbon	Shortcut Menu	Keyboard Shortcut
Table Cell, Change Text Direction	PPT 244		Text Direction button (Table Tools Layout tab | Alignment group)	Format Shape, Text Box, Text direction arrow	
Text, Align Vertically	PPT 366		Align Text button (Home tab | Paragraph group), Top, Middle, or Bottom		
Text, Animate	PPT 425, 427		More button in Animation gallery (Animations tab | Animation group)		
Text, Convert to SmartArt Graphic	PPT 213		Convert to SmartArt Graphic button (Home tab | Paragraph group)	Convert to SmartArt	
Text Box, Animate	PPT 425, 427		More button (Animations tab | Animation group)		
Text Box, Insert	PPT 423		Text Box button (Insert tab | Text group)		
Transition Effect, Modify	PPT 447		Effect Options button (Transitions tab | Transition to This Slide group)		

Table 3: Microsoft Excel 2010 Quick Reference Summary

Task	Page Number	Mouse	Ribbon	Shortcut Menu	Keyboard Shortcut
3-D Chart, Rotate	EX 462		3-D Rotation button (Chart Tools Layout tab | Background group), change rotation (Format Chart Area dialog box)		
3-D Reference, Enter	EX 392	Start entering formula, click sheet tab, click cell			
Access Data, Import	EX 443		From Access button (Data tab | Get External Data group), double-click file (Select Data Source dialog box)		
Add Worksheet to Workbook	EX 384	Click Insert Worksheet tab	Insert Cells button arrow (Home tab | Cells group), Insert Sheet	Insert	SHIFT+F11
Advanced Filter, Apply	EX 332		Advanced button (Data tab | Sort & Filter group)		
Arrange Multiple Workbooks	EX 406		Arrange All button (View tab | Window group), click Arrange option (Arrange Windows dialog box)		
AutoFilter Data in Table	EX 324	Click AutoFilter button arrow, click filter option *or* click AutoFilter button arrow, type in Search box, click OK			
Borders, Add Custom	EX 234		Borders button arrow (Home tab | Font group), Borders & Shading	Format Cells, Border tab (Format Cells dialog box)	

Table 3: Microsoft Excel 2010 Quick Reference Summary *(continued)*

Task	Page Number	Mouse	Ribbon	Shortcut Menu	Keyboard Shortcut
Cell Names, Create Based on Row Titles	EX 238		Create from Selection button (Formulas tab | Defined Names group)		
Cell Names, Enter	EX 238	Click Name box, type name	Define Name button (Formulas tab | Defined Names group)		
Cell Style, Apply	EX 382		Cell Styles button (Home tab | Styles group), click style		
Cell Style, Create	EX 380		Cell Styles button (Home tab | Styles group), New Cell Style		
Change Margins	EX 397	In the Backstage view, click Normal Margins button	Page Setup Dialog Box Launcher (Page Layout tab | Page Setup group), Margins tab (Page Setup dialog box)		
Chart, Move	EX 461		Move Chart button (Chart Tools Design tab | Location group), select option (Move Chart dialog box)		
Chart, Remove Legend	EX 462		Legend button (Chart Tools Layout tab | Labels group), None		
Color Tab	EX 233			Tab Color	
Comma-Delimited Text File, Import	EX 439		From Text button (Data tab | Get External Data group), double-click file (Import File dialog box), complete wizard		
Conditional Formatting Rule, Add with Icon Set	EX 317		Conditional Formatting button (Home tab | Styles group), New Rule, Format Style box arrow (New Formatting Rule dialog box), Icon Sets, enter condition		
Convert Table to Range	EX 312			Table, Convert to Range	
Copy Data to Multiple Worksheets	EX 386		Copy button (Home tab | Clipboard group), select worksheets, Paste button (Home tab | Clipboard group)	Copy, select worksheets, Paste	CTRL+C, select worksheets, CTRL+V
Create Cell Style	EX 380		Cell Styles button (Home tab | Styles group), New Cell Style		
Create Workspace File	EX 407		Save Workspace (View tab | Window group)		
Custom Filter, Apply to Numeric Data	EX 329	Click AutoFilter arrow, point to Number Filters, click Custom Filter			
Custom Format, Create	EX 378			Format Cells, Number tab (Format Cells dialog box), Custom category	

Table 3: Microsoft Excel 2010 Quick Reference Summary *(continued)*

Task	Page Number	Mouse	Ribbon	Shortcut Menu	Keyboard Shortcut
Custom Sort, Apply to Table	EX 325		Sort & Filter button (Home tab | Editing group), click Custom Sort	Sort, click Custom Sort	
Data, Copy to Multiple Worksheets	EX 386		Copy button (Home tab | Clipboard group), select worksheets, Paste button (Home tab | Clipboard group)	Copy, select worksheets, Paste	CTRL+C, select worksheets, CTRL+V
Data, Enter on Multiple Worksheets at the Same Time	EX 387	Select worksheets, enter data			
Define Range as Data Table	EX 249		What-If Analysis button (Data tab | Data Tools group), Data Table		
Display Hidden Workbook	EX 277		Unhide button (View tab | Window group), click workbook name (Unhide dialog box)		
Display Hidden Worksheet	EX 276			Unhide, click worksheet name (Unhide dialog box)	
Drill Data through Worksheets	EX 387	Select worksheets, enter data			
Fill Handle, Create Series with	EX 247	Select range, drag fill handle	Fill button (Home tab | Editing group), click option	Right-drag fill handle, click Fill Series	
Find and Replace Text	EX 459		Find & Select button (Home tab | Editing group), Replace		CTRL+H
Find Text	EX 457		Find & Select button (Home tab | Editing group), Find		CTRL+F
Footer, Add	EX 398	Click Page Layout button in status bar, click Footer box			
Footer, Insert Page Number in	EX 398	In Page Layout view, click Footer box, type & [Page]	Page Number button (Header & Footer Tools Design tab | Header & Footer Elements group)		
Format Range as Table	EX 305		Format as Table button (Home tab | Styles group), click table style		
Gridlines, Show or Hide	EX 466		Gridlines check box (View tab | Show group)		
Header, Add	EX 397	Click Page Layout button in status bar, click Header box			
Header, Insert Current Date in	EX 398	In Page Layout view, click Header box, type & [Date]	Current Date button (Header & Footer Tools Design tab | Header & Footer Elements group)		
Header, Insert Current Time in	EX 398	In Page Layout view, click Header box, type & [Time]	Current Time button (Header & Footer Tools Design tab | Header & Footer Elements group)		
Hide Workbook	EX 277		Hide button (View tab | Window group)		

Table 3: Microsoft Excel 2010 Quick Reference Summary *(continued)*

Task	Page Number	Mouse	Ribbon	Shortcut Menu	Keyboard Shortcut
Hide Worksheet	EX 276			Hide	
Icon Set, Use in Conditional Formatting Rule	EX 317		Conditional Formatting button (Home tab | Styles group), New Rule, Format Style box arrow (New Formatting Rule dialog box), Icon Sets, enter condition		
Image, Add to Worksheet	EX 474		Insert Picture from File button (Insert tab | Illustrations group), double-click file		
Image, Apply style to	EX 475		Picture Styles More button (Format tab | Picture Styles group), click style		
Import Access Data	EX 443		From Access button (Data tab | Get External Data group), double-click file (Select Data Source dialog box)		
Import Comma-Delimited Text File	EX 439		From Text button (Data tab | Get External Data group), double-click file (Import File dialog box), complete wizard		
Import Web Page Data	EX 447		From Web button (Data tab | Get External Data group), enter address (New Web Query dialog box), select table, click Import		
Insert Page Break	EX 402		Breaks button (Page Layout tab | Page Setup group), Insert Page Break		
Legend, Remove from Chart	EX 462		Legend button (Chart Tools Layout tab | Labels group), None		
Modify Table Quick Style	EX 307		Format as Table button (Home tab | Styles group), right-click table style, click Duplicate, type style name, set formatting options		
Move Chart	EX 461		Move Chart button (Chart Tools Design tab | Location group), select option (Move Chart dialog box)		
Multiple Workbooks, Arrange	EX 406		Arrange All button (View tab | Window group), click Arrange option (Arrange Windows dialog box)		
Name Cells	EX 238	Click Name box, type name	Define Name button (Formulas tab | Defined Names group)		
Outline Worksheet	EX 345		Group button (Data tab | Outline group)		

Table 3: Microsoft Excel 2010 Quick Reference Summary (continued)

Task	Page Number	Mouse	Ribbon	Shortcut Menu	Keyboard Shortcut
Page Break, Hide	EX 403		File tab, Options button, Advanced button (Excel Options dialog box), 'Show page breaks' check box		
Page Break, Insert	EX 402		Breaks button (Page Layout tab | Page Setup group), Insert Page Break		
Page Break, Remove	EX 402		Breaks button (Page Layout tab | Page Setup group), Remove Page Break		
Percent Series, Create with Fill Handle	EX 247	Select range, drag fill handle	Fill button (Home tab | Editing group), click option	Right-drag fill handle, click Fill Series	
Print Area, Set	EX 268		Page Area button (Page Layout tab | Page Setup group), Set Print Area		
Protect Worksheet	EX 274		Protect Sheet button (Review tab | Changes group)		
Range, Format as Table	EX 305		Format as Table button (Home tab | Styles group), click table style		
Remove Page Break	EX 402		Breaks button (Page Layout tab | Page Setup group), Remove Page Break		
Rotate 3-D Chart	EX 462		3-D Rotation button (Chart Tools Layout tab | Background group), change rotation (Format Chart Area dialog box)		
Row, Add to Table	EX 309	Drag table sizing handle	Insert button arrow (Home tab | Cells group), Insert Table Rows Above or Insert Table Row Below	Insert, Table Rows Above or Table Row Below	TAB (in last cell)
Screen Shot, Add to Worksheet	EX 477		Screenshot button (Insert tab | Illustrations group), click screen image		
Set Print Area	EX 268		Print Area button (Page Layout tab | Page Setup group), Set Print Area		
Set Up Worksheet to Print	EX 267		Page Setup Dialog Box Launcher (Page Layout tab | Page Setup group)		
SmartArt, Add Effect to	EX 473		SmartArt Styles More button (SmartArt Tools Design tab | SmartArt Styles group), click style		
SmartArt, Add Picture to	EX 472	Click Insert Picture icon, double-click file			
SmartArt, Add Shape to	EX 469			Add Shape, add shape option	

Table 3: Microsoft Excel 2010 Quick Reference Summary (continued)

Task	Page Number	Mouse	Ribbon	Shortcut Menu	Keyboard Shortcut
SmartArt, Add to Worksheet	EX 466		SmartArt button (Insert tab | Illustrations group), click type (Choose a SmartArt Graphic dialog box), click layout		
Sort Table	EX 322		Sort & Filter button (Home tab | Editing group), click sort option	Sort, click sort option	
Subtotals, Display in Table	EX 342		Convert table to range, click Subtotal button (Data tab | Outline group)	Table, Convert to Range, click Yes (Microsoft Excel dialog box), click Subtotal button (Data tab | Outline group)	
Subtotals, Remove	EX 345		Subtotal button (Data tab | Outline group), Remove All button (Subtotal dialog box)		
Switch to Other Open Workbook	EX 405		Switch Windows button (View tab | Window group), click open workbook		
Table Quick Style, Modify	EX 307		Format as Table button (Home tab | Styles group), right-click table style, click Duplicate, type style name, set formatting options		
Table, Add Row to	EX 309	Drag table sizing handle	Insert button arrow (Home tab | Cells group), Insert Table Rows Above *or* Insert Table Row Below	Insert, Table Rows Above *or* Table Row Below	TAB (in last cell)
Table, Add Total Row to	EX 319		Total Row check box (Table Tools Design tab | Table Style Options group)	Table, Totals Row	
Table, Apply Custom Sort	EX 325		Sort & Filter button (Home tab | Editing group), click Custom Sort	Sort, click Custom Sort	
Table, Convert to Range	EX 312			Table, Convert to Range	
Table, Sort	EX 322		Sort & Filter button (Home tab | Editing group), click sort option	Sort, click sort option	
Template, Create from Workbook	EX 435	Click Save button, click 'Save as type' box arrow, click Excel Template			CTRL+S, 'Save as type' box arrow, Excel Template
Template, Save as Workbook	EX 438		File tab, Save As, 'Save as type' box arrow, Excel Workbook		
Text, Convert to Columns	EX 454		Text to Columns button (Data tab | Data Tools group), complete wizard		
Total Row, Add to Table	EX 319		Total Row check box (Table Tools Design tab | Table Style Options group)	Table, Totals Row	

Table 3: Microsoft Excel 2010 Quick Reference Summary (continued)

Task	Page Number	Mouse	Ribbon	Shortcut Menu	Keyboard Shortcut
Transpose Copied Word Data	EX 451		Paste button arrow (Home tab | Clipboard group), Transpose		
Unlock Cells	EX 273			Format Cells, Protection tab (Format Cells dialog box), Locked check box	
Unprotect Worksheet	EX 275		Unprotect Sheet button (Review tab | Changes group)		
Web Page Data, Import	EX 447		From Web button (Data tab | Get External Data group), enter address (New Web Query dialog box), select table, click Import		
Word Data, Transpose When Pasted	EX 451		Paste button arrow (Home tab | Clipboard group), Transpose		
WordArt, Add to Worksheet	EX 463		WordArt button (Insert tab | Text group), click WordArt		
Workbook, Display Hidden	EX 277		Unhide button (View tab | Window group), click workbook name (Unhide dialog box)		
Workbook, Hide	EX 277		Hide button (View tab | Window group)		
Workbook, Save as Template	EX 436	Click Save button, click 'Save as type' box arrow, click Excel Template			CTRL+S, 'Save as type' box arrow, Excel Template
Workbook, Switch to Other Open	EX 405		Switch Windows button (View tab | Window group), click open workbook		
Worksheet, Add to Workbook	EX 384	Click Insert Worksheet tab	Insert Cells button arrow (Home tab | Cells group), Insert Sheet	Insert	SHIFT+F11
Worksheet, Display Hidden	EX 276			Unhide, click worksheet name (Unhide dialog box)	
Worksheet, Hide	EX 276			Hide	
Worksheet, Outline	EX 345		Group button (Data tab | Outline group)		
Worksheet, Prepare to Print	EX 267		Page Setup Dialog Box Launcher (Page Layout tab | Page Setup group)		
Worksheet, Protect	EX 274		Protect Sheet button (Review tab | Changes group)		
Worksheet, Unprotect	EX 275		Unprotect Sheet button (Review tab | Changes group)		
Workspace File, Create	EX 407		Save Workspace button (View tab | Window group)		

Table 4: Microsoft Access 2010 Quick Reference Summary

Task	Page Number	Mouse	Ribbon	Shortcut Menu	Keyboard Shortcut
Border Style, Change	AC 398		Select controls, Property Sheet button (Report Design Tools Design tab | Tools group), click Border Style property box, select style	Select controls, right-click a control, click Properties, click Border Style property box, select style	
Calculated Field in Query, Create Using Expression Builder	AC 348		Builder button (Query Tools Design tab | Query Setup group)	Right-click field row, Build	
Can Grow Property, Change	AC 373, AC 386		Select control, Property Sheet button (Report Design Tools Design tab | Tools group), change Can Grow property to Yes	Right-click control, click Properties, change Can Grow property to Yes	
Conditional Value, Assign	AC 394		Text Box tool (Report Design Tools Design tab | Controls group), select text box, click Property Sheet button (Report Design Tools Design tab | Tools group), click Control Source property, click Build button, assign condition using Expression Builder dialog box		
Control, Change Format	AC 248		Select control, Form Layout Tools Format tab, select formatting option from Font group		
Control for a Field, Add to Form Design	AC 293	Drag field from field list to form			
Control, Move	AC 249	Point to control, drag with four-headed mouse pointer			
Controls, Align	AC 295	Click+SHIFT to select controls, Align button (Form Design Tools Arrange tab | Sizing & Ordering group), select alignment style			
Controls, Conditionally Format	AC 224		Conditional Formatting button (Report Layout Tools Format tab | Control Formatting group), New Formatting Rule dialog box, specify rule		
Controls, Move in Control Layout	AC 249	Select labels and controls for fields, drag to desired location			
Data, Enter in Attachment Field	AC 289			Right-click field for attachment, Manage Attachments command, Add button	
Data, Enter in Date Fields	AC 285	In Datasheet view, click field, type date			

Table 4: Microsoft Access 2010 Quick Reference Summary (continued)

Task	Page Number	Mouse	Ribbon	Shortcut Menu	Keyboard Shortcut
Data, Enter in Hyperlink Field	AC 291			Right-click hyperlink field, Hyperlink command, enter Web address	
Data, Enter in Memo Fields	AC 285	In Datsheet view, click field, type data			
Data, Enter in OLE Object Field	AC 287			Right-click object field, Insert Object command, navigate to file to insert	
Data, Enter in Yes/No Fields	AC 284	In Datasheet view, click check box to indicate Yes value			
Data, Enter Using an Input Mask	AC 283	In Datasheet view, type data into field			
Data, Import	AC 345		Button for imported data format (External Data tab | Import & Link group)	Right-click object, click selected format on Import menu	
Date, Add	AC 246		In form, click Date and Time button (Form Layout Tools Design tab | Header/Footer group), select format, OK button		
Field, Add to Form	AC 251		Add Existing Fields button (Form Layout Tools Design tab | Tools group), drag fields from field list to form		
Field List, Move	AC 297	Drag field list title bar			
Filter and Sort Using Form	AC 253		Advanced button (Home tab | Sort & Filter group), add field names to design grid, select sort order and specify criteria in design grid, Toggle Filters button		
Form, Create in Design View	AC 292		Select table, Form Design button (Create tab | Forms group)		
Form, Create Using Form Wizard	AC 243		Select table, Form Wizard button (Create tab | Forms group)		
Form Fill/Back Color, Change	AC 299			Right-click form, Fill/Back Color command, select color	
Form Label, Change	AC 308	In Design View, click twice to produce insertion point, edit text			
Form Title, Modify Appearance	AC 312	In Design view, select control, Property Sheet button (Form Design Tools Design tab | Tools group)		Right-click control, click Properties	

Table 4: Microsoft Access 2010 Quick Reference Summary *(continued)*

Task	Page Number	Mouse	Ribbon	Shortcut Menu	Keyboard Shortcut
Form, Use	AC 315	Open Form in Form view, view records using navigation buttons, manipulate data using form fields			
Form, View in Form View	AC 305		View button (Home tab | Views group)		
Form with a Datasheet, Create in Layout View	AC 325		Blank Form button (Create tab | Forms group), display field list, click Show all tables, expand "one" table and drag fields to desired locations, expand "many" table and drag first field onto form, drag remaining fields		
Group and Sort in Report	AC 217		Open report in Layout view, Group & Sort button (Report Layout Tools Design tab | Grouping & Totals group), Add a group or Add a sort button		
Group, Sort and Total Pane, Remove	AC 223	Close Grouping Dialog Box button	Group & Sort button (Design tab | Grouping & Totals group)		
Input Mask Wizard, Use	AC 280	In Design view, click Input Mask property box in Field Properties pane, Build button, select desired mask			
Labels, Create	AC 255		Labels button (Create tab | Reports group)		
Multitable Form Based on Many Table, Create	AC 326		Blank Form button (Create tab | Forms group), Add Existing Fields button		
Multitable Report, Create	AC 232		Select table, Report Wizard button (Create tab | Reports group), add fields for first table in Report Wizard, select second table, add fields for second table		
Object Dependencies, View	AC 319		Select table, Object Dependencies button (Database Tools tab | Relationships group), 'Objects that depend on me' option button		
Place Controls in a Control Layout	AC 245		Open form in Layout view, Form Layout Tools Arrange tab, select form controls, select control style from Table group		
Query, Create in Design View	AC 347		Query Design button (Create tab | Queries group)		
Records, Filter in Report	AC 228		Selection button (Home tab | Sort & Filter group)	Right-click field, select filter	

Table 4: Microsoft Access 2010 Quick Reference Summary *(continued)*

Task	Page Number	Mouse	Ribbon	Shortcut Menu	Keyboard Shortcut
Referential Integrity, Specify	AC 346		Relationships button (Database Tools tab | Relationships group)		
Report, Add a Date	AC 378		Date and Time button (Report Design Tools Design tab | Header/Footer group)		
Report, Add a Group	AC 352		Group & Sort button (Report Design Tools Design tab | Grouping & Totals group)		
Report, Add a Page Number	AC 378		Page Numbers button (Report Design Tools Design tab | Header/Footer group)		
Report, Add a Sort	AC 353		Group & Sort button (Report Design Tools Design tab | Grouping & Totals group)		
Report, Add a Subreport	AC 368		More button (Report Design Tools Design tab | Controls group), click Subform/Subreport tool		
Report, Add a Text Box	AC 358		Text Box tool (Report Design Tools Design tab | Controls group)		
Report, Add a Title	AC 378		Title button (Report Design Tools Design tab | Header/Footer group)		
Report, Add Additional Fields	AC 385	Drag field from field list to report			
Report, Add Fields	AC 354, AC 382, AC 385		Add Existing Fields button (Report Design Tools Design tab | Tools group)		
Report, Add Totals and Subtotals	AC 387		Group & Sort button (Report Design Tools Design tab | Grouping & Totals group)		
Report, Create in Design View	AC 351		Report Design button (Create tab | Reports group)		
Report, Create in Layout View	AC 236		Blank Report button (Create tab | Reports group)		
Report Filter, Clear	AC 229			Right-click field, clear filter from menu option	
Report, Group Controls	AC 362		Select controls, Size/Space button (Report Design Tools Arrange tab | Sizing & Ordering group), click Group		
Report Margins, Change	AC 400		Margins button (Report Design Tools Page Setup tab | Page Size group)		
Report, Publish	AC 381		PDF or XPS button (External Data tab | Export group)	Right-click report, click PDF or XPS on Export menu	

Table 4: Microsoft Access 2010 Quick Reference Summary *(continued)*

Task	Page Number	Mouse	Ribbon	Shortcut Menu	Keyboard Shortcut
Row and Column Size, Change	AC 286	In Datasheet view, drag field selector edge for column and drag row selector edge for row			
Simple Form with a Datasheet, Create	AC 323	Select "one" table, Form button (Create tab | Forms group)			
Size Mode, Change	AC 309	Click control, Property Sheet button (Form Design Tools Design tab | Tools group), Size Mode property			
Subform, Place on a Form	AC 301		More button (Form Design Tools Design tab | Controls group), Subform/Subreport tool, click in form to launch SubForm Wizard		
Summary Report, Create	AC 242		Open report in Layout view, Hide Details button (Report Layout Tools Design tab | Grouping & Totals group)		
Tab Stop, Change	AC 314		In Design view, select control, Property Sheet button (Form Design Tools Design tab | Tools group), All tab, change Tab Stop property to No		
Table, Create in Design View	AC 343		Table Design button (Create tab | Tables group)		
Theme, Assign to a Single Object	AC 241		Open object in Layout view, Themes button (Design tab | Themes group), right-click theme in Theme picker, click the Apply Theme to This Object Only command		
Theme, Assign to All Objects	AC 240		Open object in Layout view, Themes button (Design tab | Themes group), select theme from Theme picker		
Title, Add to a Form	AC 301		Title button (Form Design Tools Design tab | Header/Footer group)		
Totals and Subtotals, Add	AC 221		Select field, Totals button (Report Layout Tools Design tab | Grouping & Totals group), Sum command		Right-click column header, click Total

Table 5: Microsoft Outlook 2010 Quick Reference Summary

Task	Page Number	Mouse	Ribbon	Shortcut Menu	Keyboard Shortcut
Add Attachment to Contact	OUT 131		Attach File button (Insert tab | Include group), select file, click Insert		
Add Name to Contact Group	OUT 149		Add Members button (Contact Group tab | Add Members group)		
Attachment to Contact, Change	OUT 134	Double-click contact, click attachment, click Attach File button (Insert tab | Include group), select file, click Insert	Attach File button (Insert tab | Include group), select file, click Insert		
Attachment to Contact, Remove	OUT 135	Double-click contact, click attachment, press DELETE			DELETE
Attachment, Add to Contact	OUT 131		Attach File button (Insert tab | Include group), select file, click Insert		
Change Attachment to Contact	OUT 134	Double-click contact, click attachment, click Attach File button (Insert tab | Include group), select file, click Insert	Attach File button (Insert tab | Include group), select file, click Insert		
Contact Group, Create from E-Mail Message	OUT 146		New Items button (Home tab | New group), click More Items, click Contact Group, enter name, click Add Members button (Contact Group tab | Members group), click Members text box, enter e-mail address		
Contact Group, Create from Existing Contacts	OUT 144		New Contact Group button (Home tab | New group), enter name, click Add Members button (Contact Group tab | Members group)		
Contact List, Preview	OUT 152		File tab | Print tab		
Contact List, Print	OUT 156		File button (File tab | Print tab)		
Contact List, Print Only Selected Items	OUT 154		Print Options button (File tab | Print tab), Only selected items option button, Print		
Contact List, Select Style	OUT 153		File tab | Print tab		
Contact View, Change	OUT 137		More button (Home tab | Current View group), click view		
Contact, Create	OUT 126		New Contact button (Home tab | New group)		CTRL+SHIFT+C
Contact, Create from E-Mail Message	OUT 127			Right-click e-mail message, click Add to Outlook Contacts	
Contact, Create from Existing Contact	OUT 129		New Items button (Home tab | New group), click Contact from the Same Company		

Table 5: Microsoft Outlook 2010 Quick Reference Summary *(continued)*

Task	Page Number	Mouse	Ribbon	Shortcut Menu	Keyboard Shortcut
Contact, Edit	OUT 130	Double-click contact			
Contact, Find by Searching for E-Mail Address	OUT 139	Click Search All Contact Items text box, type search text			CTRL+E
Contact, Find from Any Outlook Folder	OUT 142	Click folder in Navigation Pane, type search text in Find a Contact search box (Home tab | Find group)			
Contacts, Sort	OUT 138		Reverse Sort button (View tab | Arrangement group)		
Create contact	OUT 126		New Contact button (Home tab | New group)		CTRL+SHIFT+C
Create Contact from E-Mail Message	OUT 127			Right-click e-mail message, click Add to Outlook Contacts	
Create Contact from Existing Contact	OUT 129		New Items button (Home tab | New group), click Contact from the Same Company		
Create Contact Group Create from E-Mail Message	OUT 146		Copy e-mail address, click New Items button (Home tab | New group), click More Items, click Contact Group, enter name, click Add Members button (Contact Group tab | Members group), click Members text box, paste e-mail address		
Create Contact Group from Existing Contacts	OUT 144		New Contact Group button (Home tab | New group), enter name, click Add Members button (Contact Group tab | Members group)		
Current View, Change for Contacts	OUT 137		More button (Home tab | Current View group), click view		
Edit Contact	OUT 130	Double-click contact			
File Attached to Contact, Remove	OUT 135	Double-click contact, click attachment, press DELETE			DELETE
File, Attach to Contact	OUT 131		Attach File button (Insert tab | Include group), select file, click Insert		
Find Contact by Searching for E-Mail Address	OUT 139	Click Search All Contact Items text box, type search text			CTRL+E
Find Contact from Any Outlook Folder	OUT 142	Click folder in Navigation Pane, type search text in Find a Contact search box (Home tab | Find group)			
Member, Add to Contact Group	OUT 149		Add Members button (Contact Group tab | Members group)		

Table 5: Microsoft Outlook 2010 Quick Reference Summary *(continued)*

Task	Page Number	Mouse	Ribbon	Shortcut Menu	Keyboard Shortcut
Name, Add to Contact Group	OUT 149		Add Members button (Contact Group tab | Members group)		
Name, Remove from Contact Group	OUT 150		Remove Member button (Contact Group tab | Members group)		
Refine Search	OUT 141		Click Search Contacts text box, click More button (Search Tools Search tab | Refine group), click property		CTRL+E
Remove Attachment to Contact	OUT 135	Double-click contact, click attachment, press DELETE			DELETE
Remove Name from Contact Group	OUT 150		Remove Member button (Contact Group tab | Members group)		
Search, Refine	OUT 141		Click Search All Contact Items text box, click More button (Search Tools Search tab | Refine group), click property		CTRL+E
Select Style for Contact List	OUT 152		File tab | Print tab		
Sort Contacts	OUT 138		Reverse Sort button (View tab | Arrangement group)		

Credits